NATIONAL GEOGRAPHIC

COLLEGIATE ATLAS OF THE WORLD

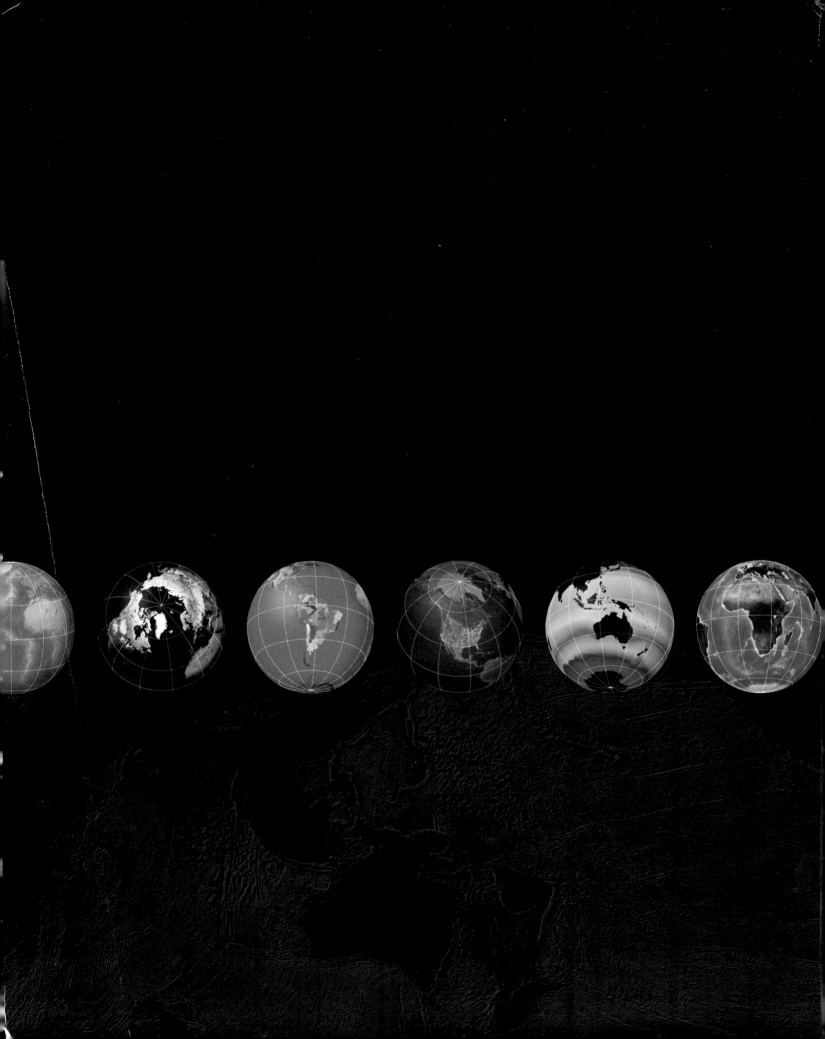

NATIONAL GEOGRAPHIC

COLLEGIATE ATLAS OF THE WORLD

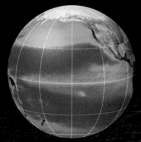
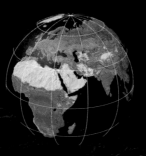
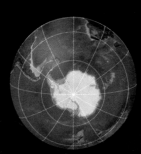
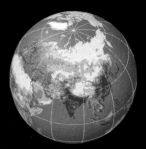

NATIONAL GEOGRAPHIC, WASHINGTON, D.C.

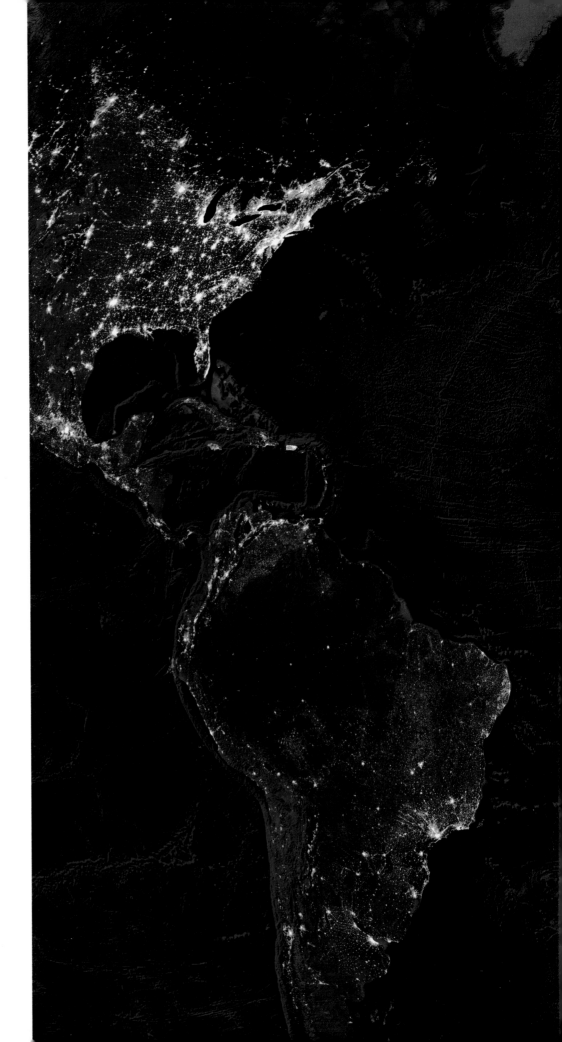

NATIONAL GEOGRAPHIC

COLLEGIATE ATLAS
OF THE WORLD

Founded in 1888, the National Geographic Society is one of the largest nonprofit scientific and educational organizations in the world. It reaches more than 285 million people worldwide each month through its official journal, NATIONAL GEOGRAPHIC, and its four other magazines; the National Geographic Channel; television documentaries; radio programs; films; books; videos and DVDs; maps; and interactive media. National Geographic has funded more than 8,000 scientific research projects and supports an education program combating geographic illiteracy.

For more information, please call
1-800-NGS LINE (647-5463)
or write to the following address:
National Geographic Society
1145 17th Street N.W.
Washington, D.C. 20036-4688 U.S.A.

Log on to nationalgeographic.com;
AOL Keyword: NatGeo.

For information about special discounts
for bulk purchases, please contact
National Geographic Books Special Sales:
ngspecsales@ngs.org

PREFACE

This atlas was created digitally by cartographers working on two continents. The mapmakers performed their work on networked computers using Geographic Information Systems (GIS) software. They communicated instantaneously via email and trans-Atlantic conference calls and swapped digital files via the Internet. They used desktop graphics programs to refine map designs and tapped other software to help position thousands of place-names on political maps. For thematic maps, they utilized imagery captured by satellites, manipulated elevation data gathered by radar instruments carried into orbit by astronauts, and tapped Earth data gathered by thousands of sensors scattered across the face of the planet.

The tools used to make this book—that we cartographers take for granted as standard methods of the trade—would have been considered almost miraculous by the gentlemen who founded the National Geographic Society in 1888 on a late winter evening in Washington, D.C. Among their ranks were Alexander Graham Bell, inventor of the telephone, and John Wesley Powell, leader of the first expedition through the rapids of the Grand Canyon.

The mission the founders articulated for the fledgling Society was "the increase and diffusion of geographic knowledge." They sensed, perhaps, that the Age of Exploration was drawing to a close and that scientific inquiry would replace discovery and conquest. They likely surmised that a globe whose limits were finite would require conservation and stewardship. They no doubt recognized that new mass communication technologies, including telephony and photography, could be used to spread knowledge.

They would have been visionaries indeed if they could have foreseen how the next century's new information technologies would transform geography itself. The cumulative revolution wrought by computers, satellite and aerial photography, global positioning systems satellites, GIS, and the Internet turned geographers from the relatively passive pursuits of observing and documenting the planet to the active endeavors of analysis, synthesis, prediction, and decision making. Geography can now assimilate and present—in its unique expression, cartography—a vast array of high-quality information, giving us an incomparable basis for understanding our world and taking action in it. Bell and Powell would be thrilled.

Today, scientists, businesspeople, soldiers, policy makers, and informed citizens of every country on Earth tap geographic knowledge via their computers, laptops, handheld devices—and modern atlases. The book in your hands is a conduit to a complex and nuanced view of the world you are entering. In time, you will take the world itself into your hands—to preserve, improve, and make safer and more properous.

Allen Carroll

Chief Cartographer
National Geographic Society

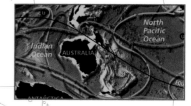

Explore the exclusive COLLEGIATE ATLAS OF THE WORLD online
resource component at www.nationalgeographic.com/collegiateatlas
User Name: collegiate Password: 360worldview

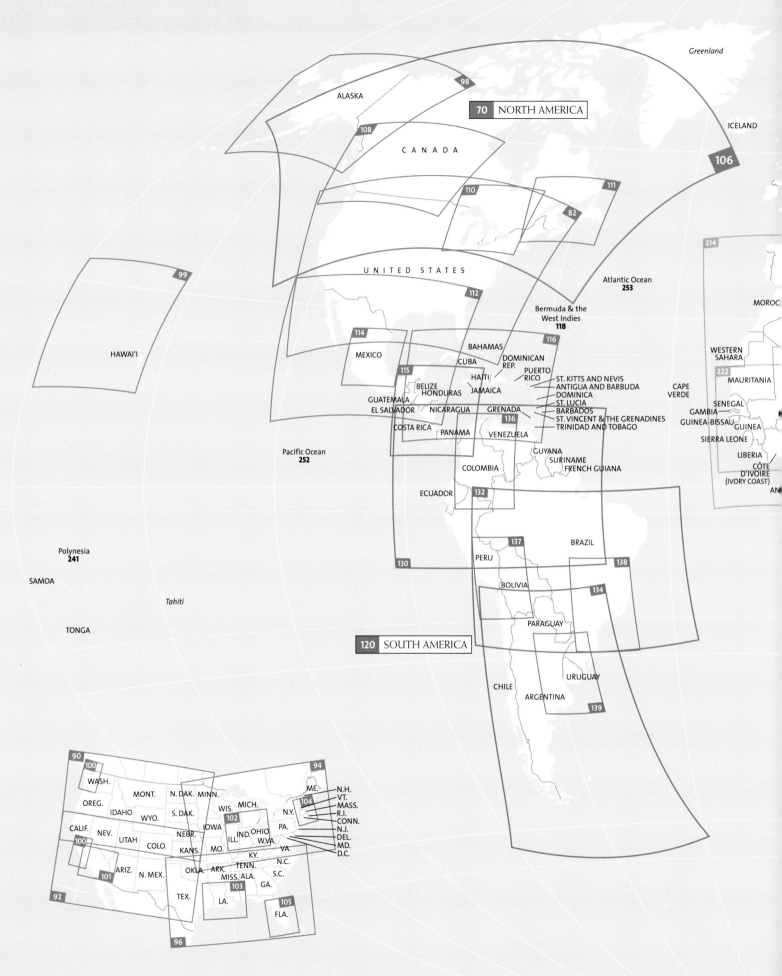

NORTH AMERICA **70**

SOUTH AMERICA **120**

Greenland

ICELAND

98

ALASKA

CANADA

108

106

110

111

82

UNITED STATES

99

112

Atlantic Ocean
253

214

HAWAI'I

Bermuda & the
West Indies
118

116

MOROC

114

BAHAMAS

WESTERN
SAHARA

MEXICO

CUBA

DOMINICAN
REP.

222

MAURITANIA

115

HAITI

PUERTO
RICO

ST. KITTS AND NEVIS
ANTIGUA AND BARBUDA

CAPE
VERDE

BELIZE

JAMAICA

DOMINICA

SENEGAL

GAMBIA

GUATEMALA

HONDURAS

ST. LUCIA

GUINEA-BISSAU

GUINEA

EL SALVADOR

NICARAGUA

GRENADA

BARBADOS
ST. VINCENT & THE GRENADINES

SIERRA LEONE

COSTA RICA

136

TRINIDAD AND TOBAGO

LIBERIA

PANAMA

VENEZUELA

CÔTE
D'IVOIRE
(IVORY COAST)

Pacific Ocean
252

COLOMBIA

GUYANA
SURINAME
FRENCH GUIANA

AN

ECUADOR

132

Polynesia
241

137

BRAZIL

130

PERU

138

SAMOA

BOLIVIA

134

Tahiti

PARAGUAY

TONGA

URUGUAY

CHILE

ARGENTINA

139

90

100

94

WASH.

ME.

N.H.

OREG.

MONT.

N. DAK.

MINN.

104

VT.
MASS.

IDAHO

WYO.

S. DAK.

WIS.

MICH.

N.Y.

R.I.
CONN.

CALIF.

NEV.

UTAH

COLO.

NEBR.

IOWA

102

ILL.

IND.

OHIO

PA.

W.VA.

N.J.
DEL.
MD.
D.C.

100

KANS.

MO.

KY.

VA.

ARIZ.

N. MEX.

OKLA.

ARK.

TENN.

N.C.

101

MISS.

ALA.

S.C.

92

TEX.

103

GA.

LA.

105

96

FLA.

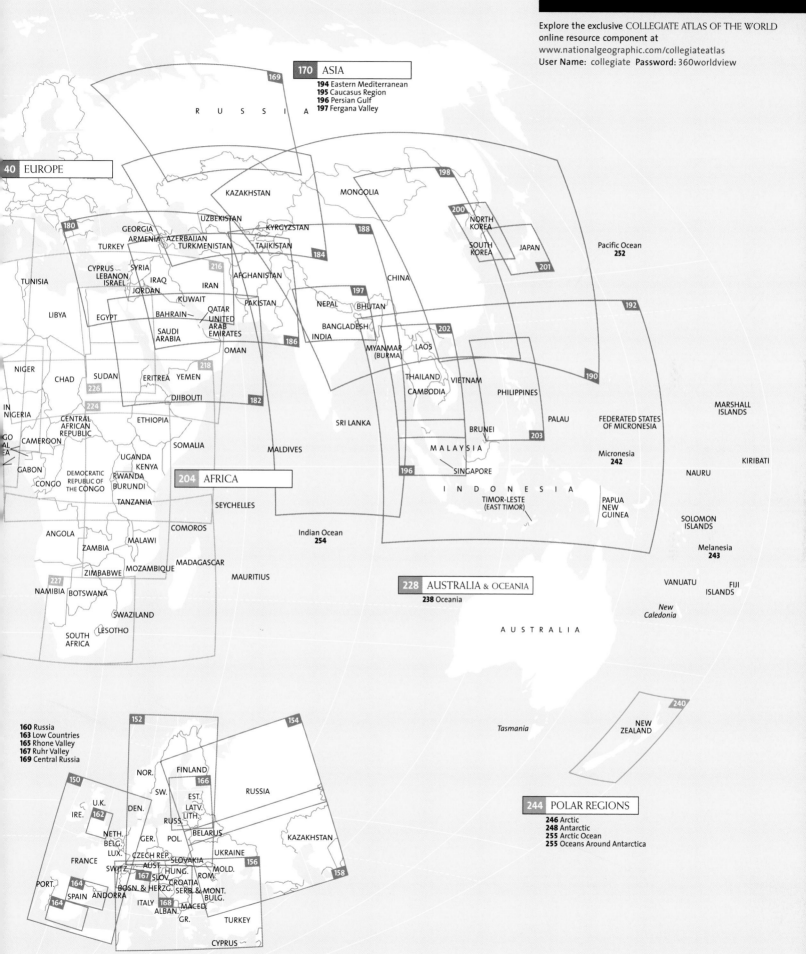

Explore the exclusive COLLEGIATE ATLAS OF THE WORLD
online resource component at
www.nationalgeographic.com/collegiateatlas
User Name: collegiate Password: 360worldview

169

170 ASIA
194 Eastern Mediterranean
195 Caucasus Region
196 Persian Gulf
197 Fergana Valley

R U S S I A

40 EUROPE

KAZAKHSTAN

MONGOLIA

198

180

UZBEKISTAN

KYRGYZSTAN

188

200 NORTH KOREA

GEORGIA
ARMENIA AZERBAIJAN
TURKEY TURKMENISTAN TAJIKISTAN **184**

SOUTH KOREA JAPAN

Pacific Ocean
252

201

CYPRUS
LEBANON SYRIA
ISRAEL IRAQ **216** AFGHANISTAN
JORDAN

IRAN

CHINA

197

TUNISIA

192

LIBYA

KUWAIT
BAHRAIN QATAR
UNITED ARAB EMIRATES
EGYPT
SAUDI ARABIA

PAKISTAN

NEPAL BHUTAN

186

BANGLADESH
INDIA

OMAN

MYANMAR (BURMA) LAOS

202

190

NIGER CHAD SUDAN **218** ERITREA YEMEN

THAILAND VIETNAM
CAMBODIA

MARSHALL ISLANDS

226

DJIBOUTI

182

PHILIPPINES

PALAU

FEDERATED STATES OF MICRONESIA

224

IN NIGERIA

CENTRAL AFRICAN REPUBLIC ETHIOPIA

SOMALIA

SRI LANKA

BRUNEI

203

KIRIBATI

GO CAMEROON
AL
EA

MALDIVES

M A L A Y S I A

Micronesia
242

NAURU

GABON
CONGO

DEMOCRATIC REPUBLIC OF THE CONGO

UGANDA
KENYA
RWANDA
BURUNDI

204 AFRICA

196 SINGAPORE

I N D O N E S I A

TANZANIA

SEYCHELLES

TIMOR-LESTE (EAST TIMOR)

PAPUA NEW GUINEA

SOLOMON ISLANDS

ANGOLA

COMOROS

MALAWI
ZAMBIA

Indian Ocean
254

Melanesia
243

227

ZIMBABWE

MOZAMBIQUE MADAGASCAR

MAURITIUS

228 AUSTRALIA & OCEANIA
238 Oceania

VANUATU FIJI ISLANDS

NAMIBIA BOTSWANA

SWAZILAND

New Caledonia

AUSTRALIA

SOUTH AFRICA

LESOTHO

152

154

Tasmania

240

NEW ZEALAND

NOR. FINLAND **166**

RUSSIA

150

SW. EST. LATV. LITH.

244 POLAR REGIONS

U.K. DEN.

IRE. **162**

RUSS.

BELARUS

NETH.
BELG. GER. POL.
LUX.

KAZAKHSTAN

FRANCE

UKRAINE

CZECH REP. SLOVAKIA
SWITZ. **167** AUST. HUNG. MOLD.
SLOV. ROM.

156

158

164

BOSN. & HERZG. CROATIA
SERB. & MONT.
BULG.

PORT.

ANDORRA

164 SPAIN

ITALY **168** MACED.
ALBAN.
GR.

TURKEY

CYPRUS

POLITICAL MAP SYMBOLS

BOUNDARIES

	Defined
	Disputed or undefined
	Offshore line of separation

CITIES

⊛⊛⊛ Capitals

••• Towns

TRANSPORTATION

UNDER CONSTRUCTION	Passenger railroad High-speed
UNDER CONSTRUCTION	Main line
	Tunnel
	Railroad ferry
UNDER CONSTRUCTION	Superhighway
UNDER CONSTRUCTION	Road
	Auto ferry
	Highway tunnel
INTERSTATE 75 FEDERAL 17 STATE 21 OTHER 10	Highway numbers
	Trail
✈	Scheduled air service
⌁	Spaceport

WATER FEATURES

	Drainage
	Intermittent drainage
	Intermittent lake
	Dry salt lake
	Swamp
	Channel
	Water hole or well
	Limit of drift ice
	Bank or shoal
	Coral reef
302 200 84	Depth curves and soundings in meters
	Falls or rapids

PHYSICAL FEATURES

	Tundra
	Relief
⊛	Crater
	Lava and volcanic debris
+8850 (29035 ft)	Elevation in meters
⤬	Pass
	Sand
	Below sea level
	Ice shelf
	Glacier

CULTURAL FEATURES

	Dam
	Wall
	Park
⌑	Site
∴	Ruin
✕	Battle
	Oil field
UNDER CONSTRUCTION	Oil pipeline
	Canal

BOUNDARIES AND POLITICAL DIVISIONS

Red dots:
Claimed boundary; India claims the entire region of Kashmir—including areas now controlled by Pakistan and China

Broken boundary dots:
Disputed boundary; the line of control, a cease-fire line dating back to 1972, separates Indian and Pakistani forces

Single color band:
Internal country boundary

Double color band:
International boundary

Internal region type:
In this case, Punjab, a state of India

Most political boundaries depicted in this *Atlas* are stable and uncontested. Those that are disputed receive special treatment. Disputed areas are shown in a gray color, including the Palestinian territories (West Bank and Gaza Strip) and separatist states still claimed by other countries.

CITIES AND TOWNS

Star with ring:
Administrative capital for internal regions, such as provinces, states, and territories in Australia, Canada, Mexico, United Kingdom, and the United States

Small type and town spot:
City or town with fewer than 100,000 people

Bull's-eye:
Administrative capital for internal regions in most countries and for dependent territories

Star with double ring:
National capital; larger type size shows Dublin as a city between 100,000 and one million people

The regional political maps that form the bulk of this *Atlas* depict four categories of cities or towns. The largest cities, over five million, are shown in capital letters (for example, **LONDON**).

▼ WORLD THEMATIC MAPS

Thematic maps show the spatial distribution of physical or cultural phenomena in a way that is graphically illuminating and useful. This thematic map on language was created by National Geographic Maps, using a combination of data on subjects such as cultures, linguistics, and migrations, as well as consultation with experts. Thematic maps also use quantitative sources in the presentation of topics such as economics or health.

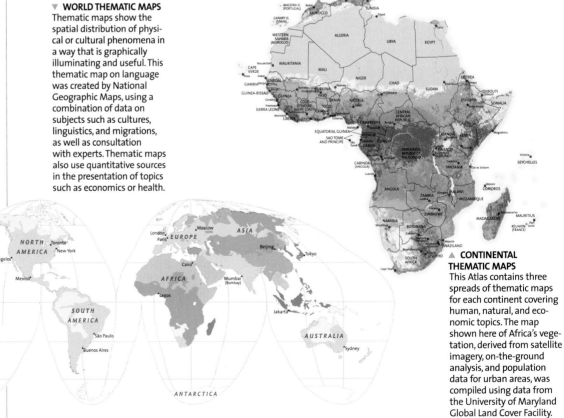

Major language families today

- Afro-Asiatic
- Altaic
- Austro-Asiatic
- Austronesian
- Dravidian
- Indo-European
- Japanese/Korean
- Kam-Tai
- Niger-Congo
- Nilo-Saharan
- Sino-Tibetan
- Uralic
- Other

▲ CONTINENTAL THEMATIC MAPS

This *Atlas* contains three spreads of thematic maps for each continent covering human, natural, and economic topics. The map shown here of Africa's vegetation, derived from satellite imagery, on-the-ground analysis, and population data for urban areas, was compiled using data from the University of Maryland Global Land Cover Facility.

TRANSPORTATION

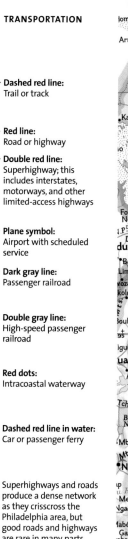

Dashed red line:
Trail or track

Red line:
Road or highway

Double red line:
Superhighway; this includes interstates, motorways, and other limited-access highways

Plane symbol:
Airport with scheduled service

Dark gray line:
Passenger railroad

Double gray line:
High-speed passenger railroad

Red dots:
Intracoastal waterway

Dashed red line in water:
Car or passenger ferry

Superhighways and roads produce a dense network as they crisscross the Philadelphia area, but good roads and highways are rare in many parts of the world.

OTHER FEATURES

Brown dot pattern:
Sand

Blue circle:
Well or water hole

Dashed blue line:
Outlines intermittent lakes or dry salt lakes; here it marks the former shoreline of Lake Chad

Blue dot pattern:
Dry salt lake bed; often arid salt flats or pans that become ephemeral lakes after rainstorms

Blue line:
River

Blue swamp pattern:
Swamp, marsh, or other wetland

Blue line and dots:
Intermittent drainage; usually flows due to seasonal rains

Blue area with blue outline:
Perennial lake

Cross:
Mountain summit; elevation in meters— also in feet for highest elevations

Ironically, water features web this largely semiarid region of central Africa. Water is key to life on Earth. Lack of water can lead to desertification and human migration.

"When people at a party ask me where I'm from and I say Morocco, the conversation often comes to a complete halt. Even if they know nothing about my country, people could ask where it is. Then they might ask me about its languages or religions or its physical appearance."

Twenty-four year-old Amine Elouazzani, who recently graduated from an American college, could be describing how to use the *National Geographic Collegiate Atlas of the World*. A well-educated person should know how to ask good questions and be able to read, understand, and appreciate maps. Use the political and thematic maps in this Atlas to orient yourself to the world at present and to inform your direction for the future.

The maps in the political, or reference, section of this Atlas show international boundaries, cities, national parks, road networks, and other features. They are organized by continent, and each section begins with an overview of the continent's physical and human geography. In the index, most entries are keyed to place-names on the political maps, citing the page number, followed by their geographic coordinates. The thematic maps at the front of the Atlas explore topics in depth, revealing the rich patchwork and infinite interrelatedness of our changing planet. In selecting from the vast storehouse of knowledge about the Earth, the Atlas editors relied upon proven data sources, such as the World Health Organization, United Nations, World Wildlife Fund, Bureau of the Census, and U.S. Department of Commerce.

Maps inform us, feed our curiosity, and help us shape our inquiry in spatial and temporal terms. They enable us to move beyond our boundaries and engage in conversation with each other.

GRAPHS, CHARTS, AND TABLES

Conveying relationships, facts, and trends quickly and efficiently is the work of these types of displays. They are diagrams that compare information in visual form. Three common types are the bar graph, the line graph, and the circle (or pie) chart. This Atlas uses all three conventions. The bar graph below, from the Health & Literacy thematic spread, compares male and female literacy rates for a range of countries and in relation to world averages. The viewer gains immediate insight not only into the level of literacy in a society but also into the relative value and status accorded to women. These graphic presentations summarize complex data and are most valuable when they generate deep and penetrating inquiry.

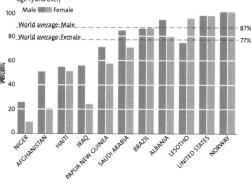

Male and female literacy rates, 2005 estimate
(as a percentage of total population age 15 and over)

GeoBytes

UNIQUE SPECIES
Madagascar and the Indian Ocean islands are home to many species found nowhere else. Of the region's 13,000 plant species, more than 89% are endemic, meaning that is the only place on Earth they live.

FRAGILE POPULATIONS
Nearly half of the world's tortoises and freshwater turtles are threatened.

HUMAN HEALTH
Medicines derived from plants and animals are the primary source of health care for 80% of the world's population.

ECONOMIC VALUE
Scientists estimate that ecosystems worldwide provide goods and services, such as nutrient recycling and waste treatment, valued at more than $20 trillion a year.

EXTINCTION RISK
One in every eight birds and one in every four mammals face a high risk of extinction in the near future.

BEETLEMANIA
Beetles are the most diverse life-form on Earth. More than a thousand different kinds can live on a single tree in the forests of South America.

TEXT AND GEOBYTES
A blue box on each spread is headed GeoBytes—short, striking facts chosen on a need-to-know or fun-to-know basis. Each thematic spread is introduced with a text block that discusses the theme and alludes to the graphic presentations. Each map or graphic is anchored by explanatory text for a complete and coherent unit.

OTHER UNIQUE FEATURES
The Atlas employs a variety of images and mapping techniques to express data. A cartogram, for instance, depicts the size of an object, such as a country, in relation to an attribute, not geographic space. Grounded in research by the Population Reference Bureau, this cartogram represents countries by unit of population, with only a suggestive nod to geographical location. An economic cartogram shows the relative prosperity of the countries of the world. In both cases, editors chose cartograms as the most visually striking way to convey the information. On a map showing the distribution of human population, LandScan global population databases were used, as the most reliable and visually striking tool. While this Atlas is distinguished by its thematic maps, individual thematic maps are, in turn, distinguished by the number of variables analyzed. For example, a thematic map on economy shows Gross Domestic Product by agriculture, manufacturing, and services. Another on land cover parses out pasture, cropland, and forest.

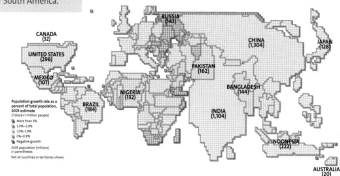

Population growth rate as a percent of total population, 2005 estimate

MAP SCALE RELATIONSHIPS IN THIS ATLAS

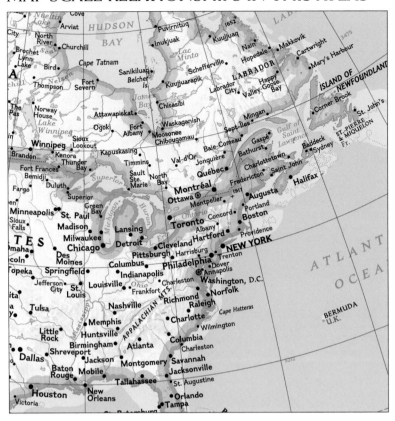

MAP PROJECTIONS

▲ **LAMBERT AZIMUTHAL EQUAL-AREA**
Distortion away from the center makes this projection a poor choice for world maps but useful for fairly circular regions. It is used on the Trade & Globalization spread, pages 56-57, in the Income Group, 2005, map.

▼ **ORTHOGRAPHIC**
Designed to show Earth as seen from a distant point in space, the orthographic is usually used to portray hemispheres. Distortion at the edges, however, compresses landmasses.

▲ **ALBERS CONIC EQUAL-AREA**
The Albers is a good format for mapping mid-latitude regions that are larger east to west than north to south. Most maps of the United States in the Atlas appear on this projection.

▲ **AZIMUTHAL EQUIDISTANT**
Mapmakers can choose any center point, from which directions and distances are true, but in outer areas shapes and sizes are distorted. On this projection, Antarctica, the Arctic Ocean, and several continents appear.

▲ **MOLLWEIDE**
In 1805, Carl B. Mollweide, a German mathematician, devised this elliptical equal-area projection that represents relative sizes accurately but distorts shapes at the edges. Many thematic maps in the Atlas use the Mollweide.

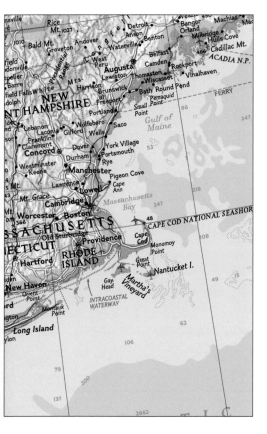

Map scale describes the relationship between distance on a map and distance on the ground. It is usually presented as a ratio or fraction in any of three ways. Verbal scale is a written description of scale, such as "one centimeter equals 100 kilometers," meaning one centimeter on the map is equal to 100 kilometers on the ground. A graphic scale is a bar or line with tick marks showing units such as kilometers or miles that graphically represent scale. A representative fraction (RF) or ratio scale indicates how much the size of a physical area was reduced to fit on the map by showing the relationship between one unit on the map and one unit of the same length on the ground. For example, if the scale is in centimeters and reads 1:10,000,000 (or 1/10,000,000), then each centimeter on the map represents 100 kilometers on the ground.

Political maps in this Atlas were created in a range of scales from global cartographic databases that merged data from maps NGS created in the past. These "seamless" databases give NGS the ability to map anywhere in the world at an appropriate scale.

From left to right, these four maps illustrate the relationship between the scale of a map and the area shown. The area shown decreases as scale increases, while the level of detail shown increases. Smaller scale maps such as the U.S. map on the far left (1:36,000,000) show more area but only the largest features are visible. Large scale maps, such as the map of Cape Cod (1:1,750,000), show a small area but in greater detail.

▲ **WINKEL TRIPEL**
First developed by Oswald Winkel in 1921, this "tripel" projection avoids the congestion and compression of polar areas that are common to many projections. The shapes of countries and islands closely resemble their true shapes as one would see on a globe.

▼ **INTERRUPTED GOODE HOMOLOSINE**
To minimize distortion of shape and preserve horizontal scale, this projection interrupts the globe. Its equal-area quality makes it suitable for mapping distributions of various kinds of information.

▶ **BUCKMINSTER FULLER**
Also known as the "Dymaxion map," this projection created by Richard Buckminster Fuller in the mid-20th century mostly retains the relative size of each part of the globe. Because the continents are not split, one can better see the interconnectedness of the Earth's landmasses.

◀ **MERCATOR**
Named for Gerardus Mercator, the Flemish geographer who invented it in 1569, this most famous of all map projections was intended for navigation. Useful for showing constant bearings as straight lines, the Mercator greatly exaggerates areas at higher latitudes.

◀ **ECKERT EQUAL-AREA**
Produced by German educator Max Eckert, this projection represents the Poles by a line one-half the length of the Equator. Polar regions are less compressed than on elliptical projections; low-latitude landmasses are elongated.

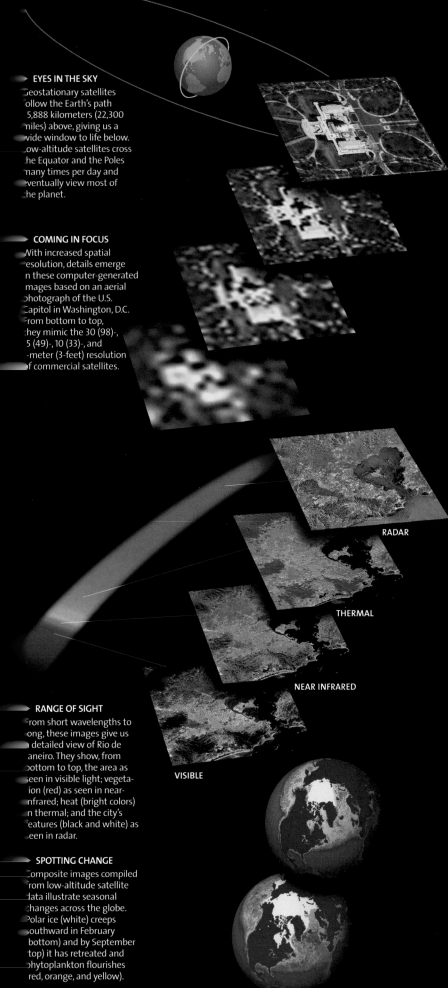

EYES IN THE SKY
Geostationary satellites follow the Earth's path 35,888 kilometers (22,300 miles) above, giving us a wide window to life below. Low-altitude satellites cross the Equator and the Poles many times per day and eventually view most of the planet.

COMING IN FOCUS
With increased spatial resolution, details emerge in these computer-generated images based on an aerial photograph of the U.S. Capitol in Washington, D.C. From bottom to top, they mimic the 30 (98)-, 15 (49)-, 10 (33)-, and 1-meter (3-feet) resolution of commercial satellites.

RADAR

THERMAL

NEAR INFRARED

VISIBLE

RANGE OF SIGHT
From short wavelengths to long, these images give us a detailed view of Rio de Janeiro. They show, from bottom to top, the area as seen in visible light; vegetation (red) as seen in near-infrared; heat (bright colors) in thermal; and the city's features (black and white) as seen in radar.

SPOTTING CHANGE
Composite images compiled from low-altitude satellite data illustrate seasonal changes across the globe. Polar ice (white) creeps southward in February (bottom) and by September (top) it has retreated and phytoplankton flourishes (red, orange, and yellow).

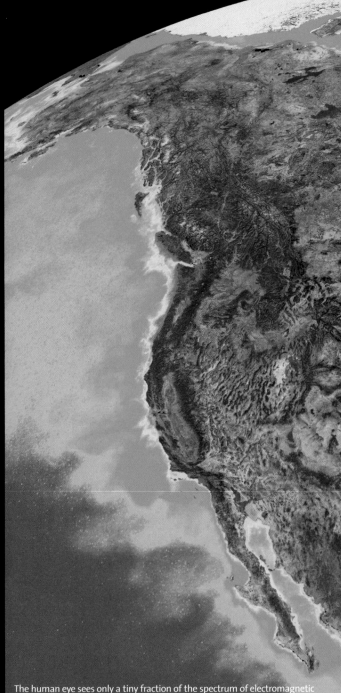

The human eye sees only a tiny fraction of the spectrum of electromagnetic radiation that illuminates the world, a narrow band known as "visible" radiation. With the aid of remote sensing, we are able to view a wider range of that spectrum, including infrared, thermal, and microwave bands. From space, we are also able to view large expanses of the Earth, as well as small areas, in great detail. From an altitude of 730 kilometers (454 miles), Landsat 7 can view features as small as 15 meters (49 feet) across. Scientists use remote-sensing satellite data to understand global processes on the Earth's surface, in the oceans, and in the lower atmosphere.

This mosaic image of North America illustrates some of the types of remotely sensed data that scientists have access to today. The eastern third of the continent shows clusters of light on the Earth's surface visible from space at night, helping us better understand urbanization and population density. False-color is used in the middle of the continent to show surface-feature classes. Reds and purples represent different classes or types of vegetation; blues show arid land. Images like this are useful for environmental monitoring. The westernmost part of the continent is in true color. The greener areas are more densely vegetated and less populated. Vibrant colors of the oceans represent sea-surface temperature. Areas in red are the warmest; the blues are the coolest.

To create this image, data were extracted from a number of datasets—the Advanced Very High Resolution Radiometer (AVHRR), the Moderate Resolution Imaging Spectroradiometer (MODIS), and versions 4, 5, and 7 of the Landsat Enhanced Thematic Mapper (ETM). The base of the image was enhanced with shaded relief produced from Shuttle Radar Topography Mission (SRTM) digital elevation model (DEM) data.

A century ago balloonists recorded bird's-eye views of the landscape below on film. Today satellites take increasingly detailed pictures of Earth, penetrating darkness and clouds to create composite images of the land and seafloor and to map once-elusive features such as the ozone hole. Remote sensing—the examination of the Earth from a distance—has widespread applications, from military surveillance to archeological exposure. And, by layering different sets of remotely sensed data, scientists can study relationships between phenomena such as shrinking polar ice and rising global temperatures.

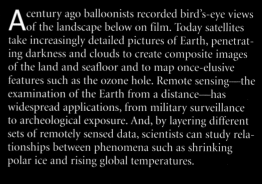

Satellite images from 1973 to 1999 were used to measure change along Canada's Beaufort Sea coastline, an area highly sensitive to erosion. This image illustrates areas of rapid erosion (red), moderate erosion (orange), no detectable erosion (green), and accretion (blue).

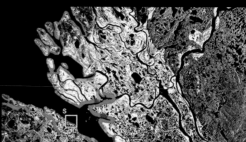

This image shows the widespread flooding that occurred throughout North Carolina in late September 1999 after the region was hit by Hurricanes Dennis and Floyd. Flooded areas are shown in light blue, rivers in dark blue, roads in red, and the coastline in green.

Nearly 4,450 hectares (11,000 acres) burned in the February 2006 Sierra fire in Orange County, California. Deep red tones in the center of this Landsat image show the burned areas on February 12th, the day the fire was contained.

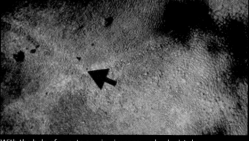

With the help of remote-sensing imagery, archeologists have identified ancient footpaths in the Arenal Region of Costa Rica. These 2,500-year-old footpaths are being used to study the prehistoric religious, economic, political, and social organization of the region.

UNDERSTANDING OUR WORLD THROUGH GIS

Geographic Information Systems (GIS) is a digitally organized collection of computer hardware, software, methodology, and data assemblage and storage. GIS supports the capture, manipulation, and analysis of place-based information. A highly adaptable tool, GIS provides the means to store and display geographic data and to analyze and describe patterns, distributions, and phenomena. Because so many human and environmental issues can be usefully considered in geographic terms, GIS is becoming increasingly common across a range of enterprises. Foresters use GIS data to inventory trees. Epidemiologists model and predict the spread of disease. Policy makers, environmentalists, and city planners employ GIS technologies to analyze issues and provide dramatic visualizations for matters ranging from wildfire management in the western United States to the rates of suburban sprawl in India's burgeoning cities. The attraction of GIS comes from the magnitude of its analytical capabilities that, in turn, derive from once-unimaginable powers of manipulation of spatial data to suit specific needs. For example, a table with latitude/longitude coordinates of car crashes can be overlaid with a road network to route emergency service vehicles and estimate their arrival time. Combine the crash incident database with other geospatial data, such as terrain, weather, transportation infrastructure, or socioeconomic characteristics, and traffic planners can determine contributing factors to accidents and recommend preventative action. More and more, GIS is the analytical tool for understanding patterns and processes that affect our lives.

◀ **GEOGRAPHIC DATA LAYERS**

GIS enables the layering of data. Vector data represents precise location in terms of a point (a city or airport, for example), a line (roadways, rivers, boundaries), or a polygon (an enclosed area such as a body of water or a protected area category). Raster data presents continuous data (such as elevation) or classes of data (for example, population densities) that cover the area in pixels, the discrete elements that make up an image. Vector and raster data are geographically referenced, allowing for overlay.

Vector data (point)

Vector data (line)

Vector data (polygon)

Raster data (relief)

Raster data (population density classes)

Vector and raster data combined (physical)

Vector and raster data combined (political)

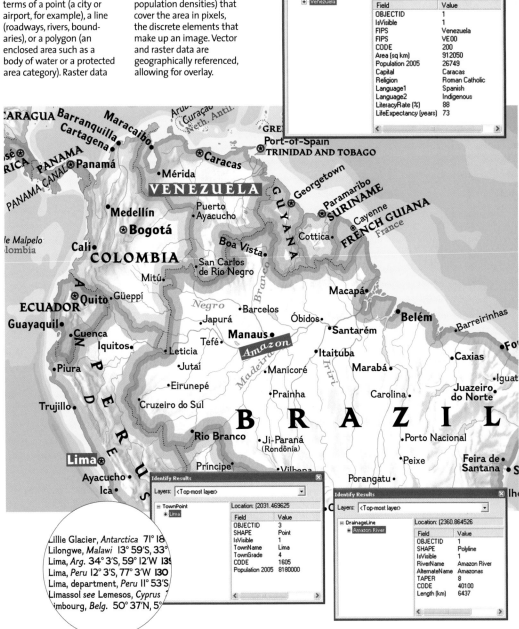

▲ **GIS DATA STRUCTURE**

GIS data have both spatial and attribute components. Spatial components are mapped features, such as the cities and rivers on this map of South America. Attribute components consist of stored data, as shown in the windows above. Attribute components might include, for example, socioeconomic characteristics of a city. GIS correlates spatial and attribute data, creating overlays that reveal geospatial relationships. Another use of GIS is digital indexing, which constituted a major advance over laborious and error-prone manual compilation. This Atlas used customized GIS software to coordinate place-names with latitude and longitude (bubble).

URBAN PLANNING

GIS can be used to inventory and visualize urban land use patterns. The strict code of zoning laws and classifications common to cities and towns requires an accurate database management system. GIS can not only manage the zoning database but can also portray the data in a map. Such visualization can help clarify development issues, plan resource allocations, or identify park and open space needs. Maps with specific GIS overlays can provide common ground for discussion in public forums that may address questions of, for example, school zones, land ownership, or sprawl.

TRANSPORTATION

Many applications of GIS exist within the transportation sector and work particularly well when coupled with the pinpoint accuracy of Global Positioning System (GPS) technology. Freight shipping companies frequently turn to GIS to estimate arrival times of their trucks, using real-time traffic information, digital representations of nationwide transportation infrastructure, and GPS information. Individual drivers have become accustomed to using GIS and GPS for finding directions and avoiding traffic jams.

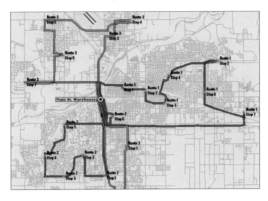

At the dawn of the Age of Exploration, the problem facing mapmakers was a dearth of information. With geospatial data flowing from satellite imagery, aerial photography, on-the-ground surveying, quantitative data, and archival records, the challenge for cartographers became how to manage a wealth of information. Geographic Information Systems (GIS), a sophisticated and versatile digital tool set with a wide range of applications, provides a solution. The data management capabilities of this digital technology make geospatial information readily available for analysis, modeling, and mapping. Scientists use GIS to inventory plant and animal species in their native habitats. Disaster relief managers identify at-risk areas and evacuation routes. The 2004 U.S. presidential election marked the first time that GIS software was used to collate and present near-real-time voting tallies. While GIS allows the layering of information, on-board and handheld Global Positioning System (GPS) devices pinpoint location. Today, geospatial concepts permeate ordinary life to an extraordinary degree.

EMERGENCY MANAGEMENT

In emergency management, GIS can be used to model potential disasters, track real-time weather, plan and adjust evacuation routes, define disaster areas, and inventory damage. Predicting and tracking wildfire helps fire management crews plan and allocate resources. GIS can show the before-and-after appearance of the land affected by a disaster, which can help recovery and show how to plan ahead for next time.

DEMOGRAPHICS & CENSUS

The U.S. Census Bureau stores demographic and socioeconomic data at numerous levels, even at the county, tract, or city-block level. Applying spatial analysis techniques to such archival data can reveal patterns, trends, and distributions. The findings can be put to various uses, including encouraging economic development or indicating the results of elections.

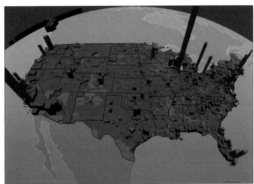

HEALTH

During the 2002-03 SARS outbreak in China, an Internet GIS server allowed for the rapid collection and dissemination of data to health officials and the public. This application tracked the spread of the disease, detected patterns, and distributed accurate information. GIS is currently being used to monitor the H5N1 strain of avian flu around the world, combining outbreaks with pertinent data such as wildfowl migration routes and locations of poultry farms.

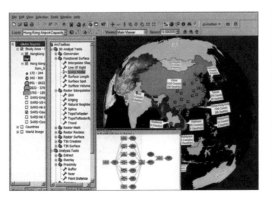

CONSERVATION

Mapping the effects of human population growth and deforestation on Asian elephant habitat highlights the versatility of GIS. Satellite images, demographic data, and elephant locations derived from radio tracking and GPS yielded a comprehensive database and visualization of elephant viability in Myanmar (formerly Burma). The study demonstrated that the rate of deforestation caused by human population growth was lower here than in most countries of Southeast Asia and that as a result elephant populations were less affected.

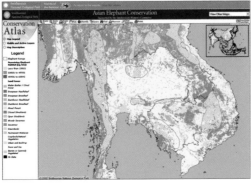

Earth was born of an agglomeration of dust and rock, gravity sucking
ever more fragments into its mass as the young planet wobbled in its
orbital path. Early on, an infant planet about the size of Mars struck
Earth. With the aggregation of solid particles from the impact, the
Moon took shape. Earth stabilized in its orbit around the Sun. A
bombardment of comets and asteroids pocked the Moon; Earth
absorbed meteor hits with little visible impact. Continents drifted and
collided, oceans filled the basins. Another great agent of change, life in
the form of massive colonies of photosynthesizing cyanobacteria
pumped oxygen into the atmosphere. Oxygen-breathing organisms
evolved on land. Now humans—all six billion and more—have become
a major force. Our burning of fossil fuels pumps carbon dioxide, a
major greenhouse gas, into the atmosphere and heats the planet.
Industrial and agricultural chemicals, human effluent, and rubbish
pollute land, air, and water. Travel, more common and speedier than
ever before, spreads ideas, commerce, culture, alien plant and animal
species, and diseases at an unprecedented rate. Resources of food and
fuel are unevenly distributed. Ideologies clash; turmoil and wars
devastate societies. Yet good will, learning, and ingenuity may be
marshaled to mitigate adverse consequences. Earth goes forward on
its own course and in its own time. The adventure continues, and
geography helps to write the record.

The human footprint
on planet Earth

Most impacted

Least impacted

PHYSICAL REGIONS
This artist-rendered relief map depicts Earth's land-forms above and below the surface of the ocean. Major mountain systems are shaded to emphasize their elevation. The Himalaya tower over India's Ganges plain; the Andes and Rocky Mountains reign over the Americas. All are dwarfed by the Mid-Atlantic Ridge, a submarine mountain range that stretches from Iceland to near Antarctica.

WESTERN HEMISPHERE

WINKEL TRIPEL PROJECTION, CENTRAL MERIDIAN 0°
SCALE 1:96,338,000
1 centimeter = 963 kilometers; 1 inch = 1520 miles at the equator

0   500 1000 1500 2000 2500
KILOMETERS

0   500   1000   1500   2000   2500
STATUTE MILES

EASTERN HEMISPHERE

POLITICAL BOUNDARIES

The world is divided into 192 independent countries, with colors on the map showing the extents of national sovereignty. International boundaries only occasionally mark true cultural boundaries; they are more often a complex artifact of colonialism, conquest, religious conversion, and conflict. The political map is a useful but all-too-neat construct for a bewilderingly complicated world.

ARCTIC REGION

0   600 km
0   600 mi
Azimuthal Equidistant Projection

WINKEL TRIPEL PROJECTION, CENTRAL MERIDIAN 0°
SCALE 1:96,338,000
1 centimeter = 963 kilometers; 1 inch = 1520 miles at the equator

0   500 1000 1500 2000 2500
KILOMETERS

0   500 1000 1500 2000 2500
STATUTE MILES

ANTARCTIC REGION

0   600 km
0   600 mi
Azimuthal Equidistant Projection
• Research station

HISTORICAL EARTH AND TECTONICS

Cataclysms such as volcanoes and earthquakes, which occur most often along plate boundaries, capture attention, but the tectonic movement that underlies them is imperceptibly slow. How slow? The Mid-Atlantic Ridge, for example, which is being built up by magma oozing between the North American and African plates, grows at about the speed of a human fingernail.

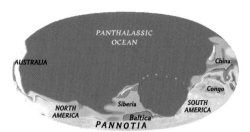

◀ 600 MILLION YEARS AGO
A supercontinent, known as Rodina, split apart, and oceans filled the basins. Fragments collided, thrusting up mountain ranges. Glaciers spread, twice covering the Equator. A new polar supercontinent, Pannotia, formed.

◀ 500 MILLION YEARS AGO
A breakaway chunk of Pannotia drifted north, splitting into three masses—Laurentia (North America), Baltica (northern Europe), and Siberia. In shallow waters, the first multicellular animals with exoskeletons appeared, and the Cambrian explosion of life took off.

◀ 300 MILLION YEARS AGO
Laurentia collided with Baltica and later with Avalonia (Britain and New England). The Appalachian mountains arose along the edge of the supercontinent, Pangaea, as a new ice age ensued.

◀ 200 MILLION YEARS AGO
Dinosaurs roamed the Pangaean land mass, which stretched nearly from Pole to Pole and almost encircled Tethys, the oceanic ancestor of the Mediterranean Sea. The Pacific's predecessor, the immense Panthalassic Ocean, surrounded the supercontinent.

◀ 100 MILLION YEARS AGO
Pangaea broke apart. The Atlantic poured in between Africa and the Americas. India split away from Africa, and Antarctica and Australia were stranded near the South Pole.

◀ 50 MILLION YEARS AGO
A meteorite wiped out the dinosaurs. Drifting continental fragments collided—Africa into Eurasia, pushing up the Alps; India into Asia, raising the Himalaya. Birds and once-tiny mammals began to fill the ecological niche vacated by dinosaurs.

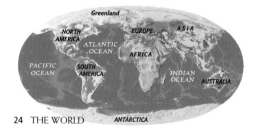

◀ PRESENT DAY
Formation of the Isthmus of Panama and the split of Australia from Antarctica changed ocean currents, cooling the air. Ice sheets gouged out the Great Lakes just 20,000 years ago. Since then, warmer temperatures have melted ice, and sea levels have risen.

1. SEAFLOOR SPREADING
Adjacent oceanic plates slowly diverge, at the rate of a few centimeters a year. Along such boundaries—the Mid-Atlantic Ridge and the East Pacific Rise—molten rock (magma) pours forth to form new crust (lithosphere).

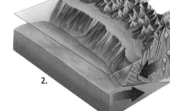
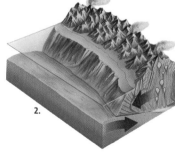

2. SUBDUCTION
When two massive plates collide, the older, colder, denser one—usually the oceanic plate meeting a continental plate—takes a dive. Pushed into the interior of the Earth, it is transformed into molten material that may rise again in volcanic eruption. Subduction also causes earthquakes, raises coastal mountains, and creates island arcs such as the Aleutians and the Lesser Antilles.

Tectonic feature
Plate boundary
- ⌒ Divergent
- ▲▲ Convergent
- ═ Transform zone

Plate motion
- ← Divergent (arrow length proportional to plate motion speed)
- ← Convergent
- ○ Hot spot

Major tectonic event in the last 100 years
Earthquake
- ○ Ten deadliest
- △ Ten costliest
- · Other

Volcanic eruption
- △ Notable
- Known during the past 10,000 years

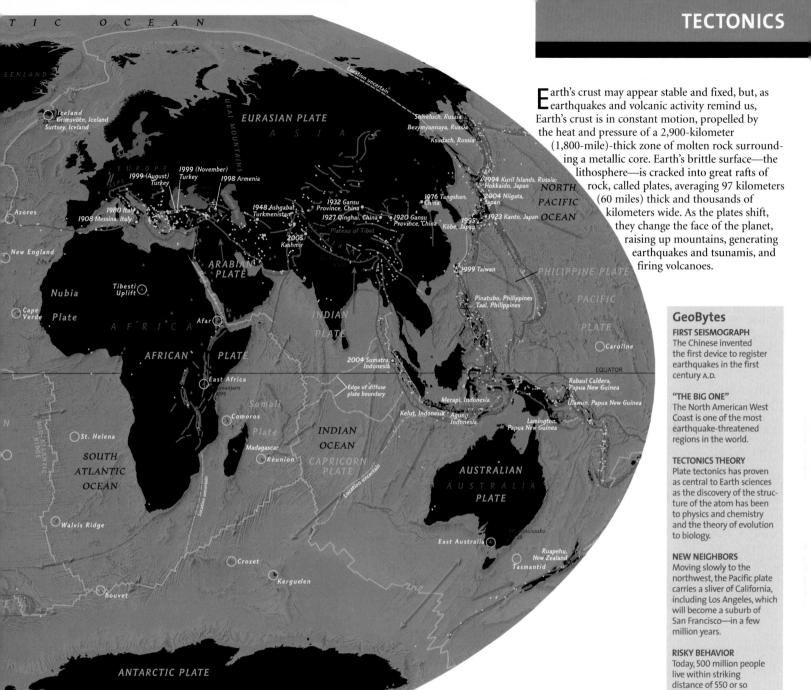

T I C   O C E A N

EENLAND

Iceland
Grímsvötn, Iceland
Surtsey, Iceland

EUROPE

ALPS

Azores

New England

Cape Verde

Nubia Plate

Tibesti Uplift

A F R I C A

AFRICAN PLATE

ARABIAN PLATE

Afar

EURASIAN PLATE

A S I A

URAL MOUNTAINS

1999 (August) Turkey
1999 (November) Turkey
1998 Armenia
1980 Italy
1908 Messina, Italy

1948 Ashgabat Turkmenistan
1932 Gansu Province, China
1927 Qinghai, China

2005 Kashmir

Plateau of Tibet

INDIAN PLATE

Shiveluch, Russia
Bezymyannaya, Russia
Ksudach, Russia

1994 Kuril Islands, Russia; Hokkaido, Japan
1976 Tangshan, China
2004 Niigata, Japan
1920 Gansu Province, China
1995 Kōbe, Japan
1923 Kanto, Japan

NORTH PACIFIC OCEAN

1999 Taiwan

PHILIPPINE PLATE

Pinatubo, Philippines
Taal, Philippines

PACIFIC PLATE

Caroline

EQUATOR

2004 Sumatra, Indonesia

Edge of diffuse plate boundary

East Africa
Kilimanjaro 1895

Comoros

Somali Plate

St. Helena

SOUTH ATLANTIC OCEAN

Madagascar
Réunion

Walvis Ridge

MID-ATLANTIC RIDGE

INDIAN OCEAN

CAPRICORN PLATE

Location uncertain

Crozet

Kerguelen

Bouvet

Merapi, Indonesia
Kelut, Indonesia
Agung, Indonesia

Rabaul Caldera, Papua New Guinea
Ulawun, Papua New Guinea
Lamington, Papua New Guinea

AUSTRALIAN PLATE

A U S T R A L I A

Mt. Kosciuszko

East Australia

Tasmantid

Ruapehu, New Zealand

ANTARCTIC PLATE

A N T A R C T I C A

Location uncertain

E arth's crust may appear stable and fixed, but, as earthquakes and volcanic activity remind us, Earth's crust is in constant motion, propelled by the heat and pressure of a 2,900-kilometer (1,800-mile)-thick zone of molten rock surrounding a metallic core. Earth's brittle surface—the lithosphere—is cracked into great rafts of rock, called plates, averaging 97 kilometers (60 miles) thick and thousands of kilometers wide. As the plates shift, they change the face of the planet, raising up mountains, generating earthquakes and tsunamis, and firing volcanoes.

GeoBytes

FIRST SEISMOGRAPH
The Chinese invented the first device to register earthquakes in the first century A.D.

"THE BIG ONE"
The North American West Coast is one of the most earthquake-threatened regions in the world.

TECTONICS THEORY
Plate tectonics has proven as central to Earth sciences as the discovery of the structure of the atom has been to physics and chemistry and the theory of evolution to biology.

NEW NEIGHBORS
Moving slowly to the northwest, the Pacific plate carries a sliver of California, including Los Angeles, which will become a suburb of San Francisco—in a few million years.

RISKY BEHAVIOR
Today, 500 million people live within striking distance of 550 or so active volcanoes.

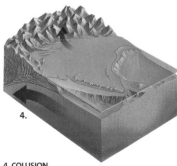

3. ACCRETION
As ocean plates advance on continental edges or island arcs and slide under them, seamounts on the ocean floor are skimmed off and pile up in submarine trenches. The buildup can fuse with continental plates, as most geologists agree was the case with Alaska and much of western North America.

4. COLLISION
When continental plates meet, the resulting forces can build impressive mountain ranges. Earth's highest landforms—the Himalaya and adjacent Tibetan Plateau—were born when the Indian plate rammed into the Eurasian plate 50 million years ago.

5. FAULTING
Boundaries at which plates slip alongside each other are called transform faults. An example is California's San Andreas fault, which accommodates the stresses between the North American and Pacific plates. Large and sudden displacements—strike-slip movements—can create high-magnitude earthquakes.

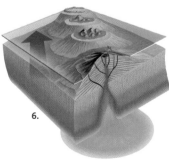

6. HOT SPOTS
A column of magma rising from deep in the mantle, a hot spot is a thermal plume that literally burns a hole in Earth's rocky crust. The result? Volcanoes, geysers, and new islands. Eruptions occur at plate boundaries, such as in Iceland and the Galápagos, as well as within plates, such as the volcanoes of Hawai'i and the geysers of Yellowstone.

EOLIAN LANDFORMS
Sand dunes

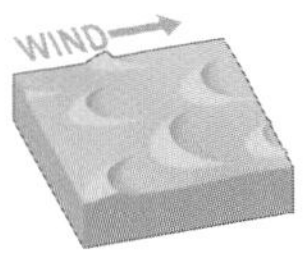
WIND

BARCHAN
The most common type of sand dune, the points of these crescent-shaped dunes lie downwind.

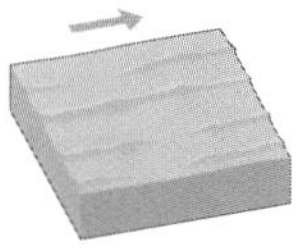

LONGITUDINAL
These are narrow, lengthy sand ridges that lie parallel to the prevailing wind direction.

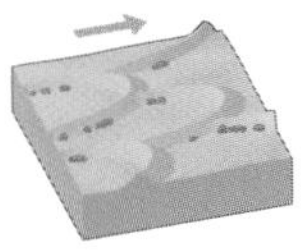

PARABOLIC
Similar in shape to barchans, the points of these crescent-shaped dunes lie upwind.

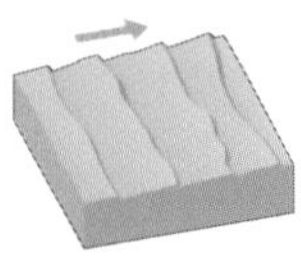

TRANSVERSE
Looking like sandy sea waves, these dunes form perpendicular to the prevailing wind.

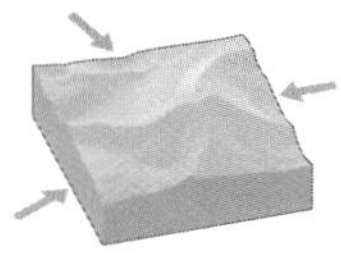

STAR
Formed by winds blowing from many directions, these pyramidal sand mounds grow upward.

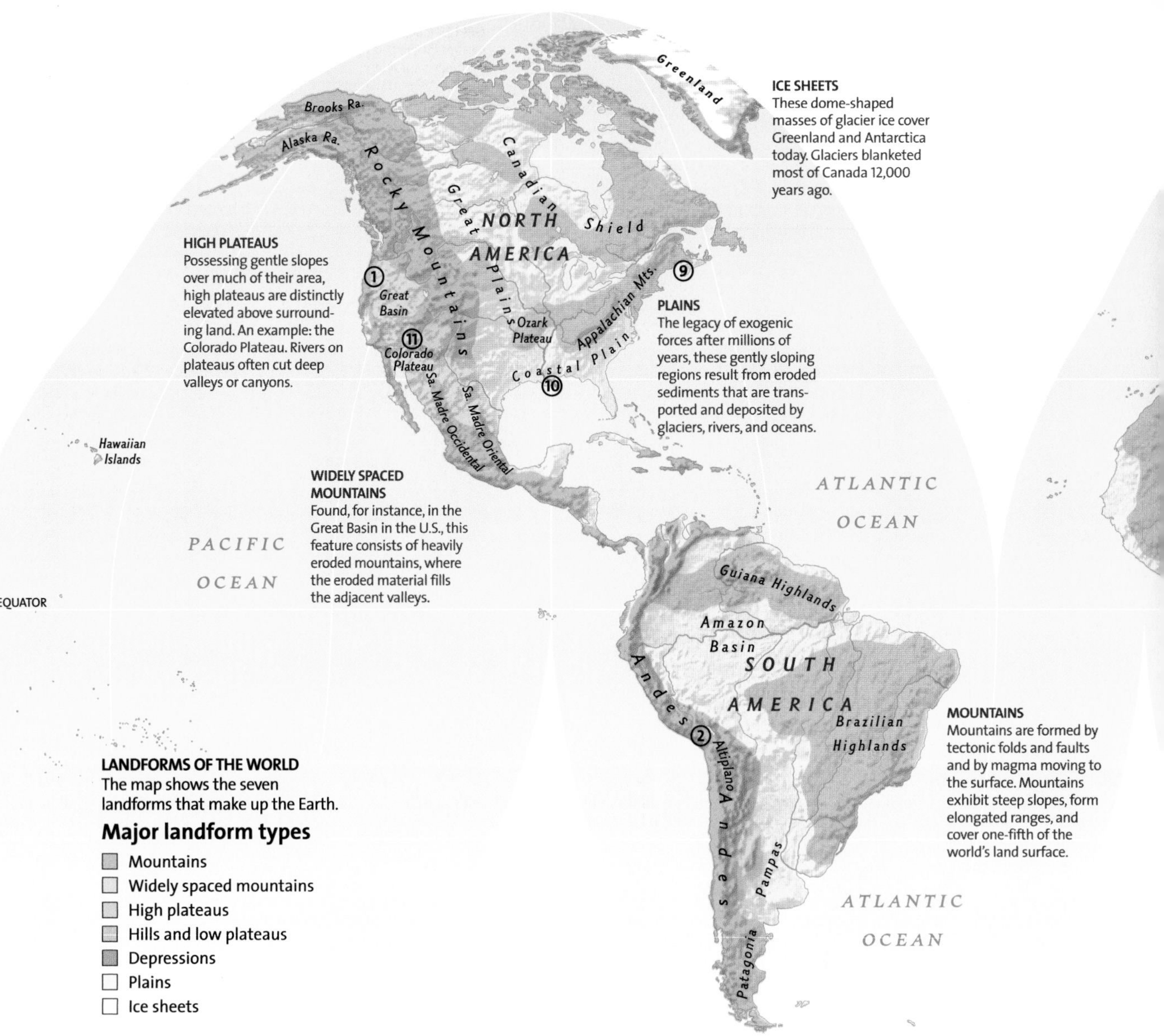
Greenland
Brooks Ra.
Alaska Ra.
Rocky Mountains
Canadian Shield
Great Plains
NORTH AMERICA
Great Basin
Colorado Plateau
Ozark Plateau
Appalachian Mts.
Coastal Plain
Sa. Madre Occidental
Sa. Madre Oriental
Hawaiian Islands
PACIFIC OCEAN
ATLANTIC OCEAN
EQUATOR
Guiana Highlands
Amazon Basin
SOUTH AMERICA
Andes
Altiplano
Brazilian Highlands
Pampas
Patagonia
ATLANTIC OCEAN
1
2
9
10
11

ICE SHEETS
These dome-shaped masses of glacier ice cover Greenland and Antarctica today. Glaciers blanketed most of Canada 12,000 years ago.

HIGH PLATEAUS
Possessing gentle slopes over much of their area, high plateaus are distinctly elevated above surrounding land. An example: the Colorado Plateau. Rivers on plateaus often cut deep valleys or canyons.

PLAINS
The legacy of exogenic forces after millions of years, these gently sloping regions result from eroded sediments that are transported and deposited by glaciers, rivers, and oceans.

WIDELY SPACED MOUNTAINS
Found, for instance, in the Great Basin in the U.S., this feature consists of heavily eroded mountains, where the eroded material fills the adjacent valleys.

MOUNTAINS
Mountains are formed by tectonic folds and faults and by magma moving to the surface. Mountains exhibit steep slopes, form elongated ranges, and cover one-fifth of the world's land surface.

LANDFORMS OF THE WORLD
The map shows the seven landforms that make up the Earth.

Major landform types
- Mountains
- Widely spaced mountains
- High plateaus
- Hills and low plateaus
- Depressions
- Plains
- Ice sheets

GeoBytes

LOESS PLATEAU, CHINA
The thickest known loess (windblown silt) deposits are 335 meters (1,100 feet) deep. The plateau possesses fertile soil and high cliffs.

GANGES RIVER DELTA
The world's largest delta is formed by the Ganges and Brahmaputra Rivers. Its area is about the size of Ireland.

PERU–BOLIVIA ALTIPLANO
Second only to Tibet's plateau in elevation and extent, the Altiplano is a basin 4,000 meters (13,000 feet) high.

LAKE BAIKAL, RUSSIA
This lake lies in the planet's deepest fault-generated trough, a rift about 9 kilometers (5.6 miles) deep.

LANDFORMS

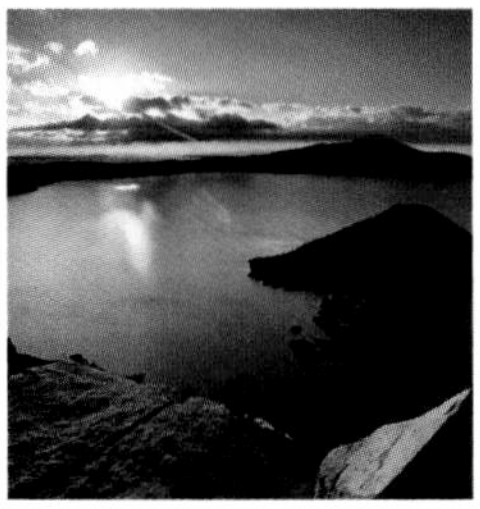

VOLCANIC
1. Crater Lake, Oregon
The caldera, now filled by Crater Lake, was produced by an eruption some 7,000 years ago.

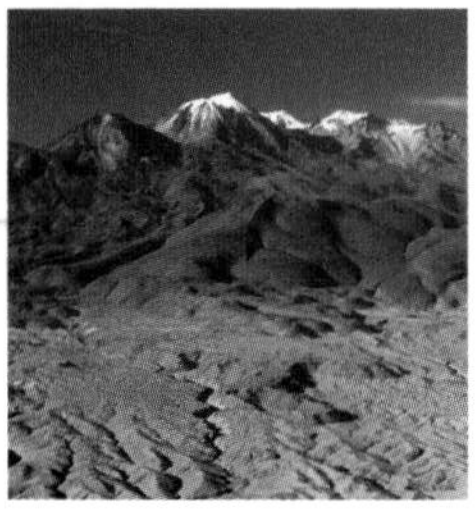

VOLCANIC
2. Misti Volcano, Peru
A stratovolcano, or composite volcano, it is composed of hardened lava and volcanic ash.

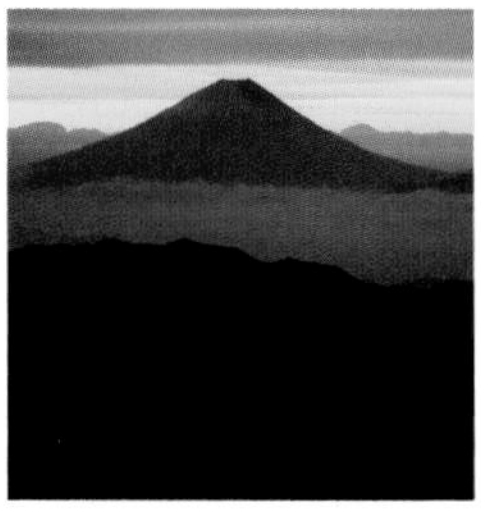

VOLCANIC
3. Mount Fuji, Japan
Japan's highest peak at 3,776 meters (12,388 feet), Mt. Fuji is made up of three superimposed volcanoes.

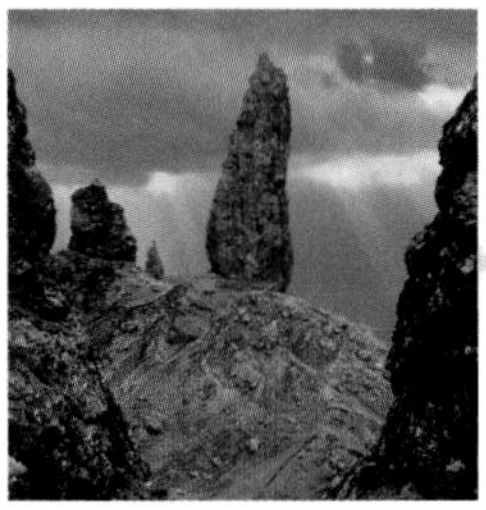

EXOGENIC
4. Isle of Skye, Scotland
A pinnacle of basalt lava, known as the Old Man of Storr, resulted from millions of years of erosion.

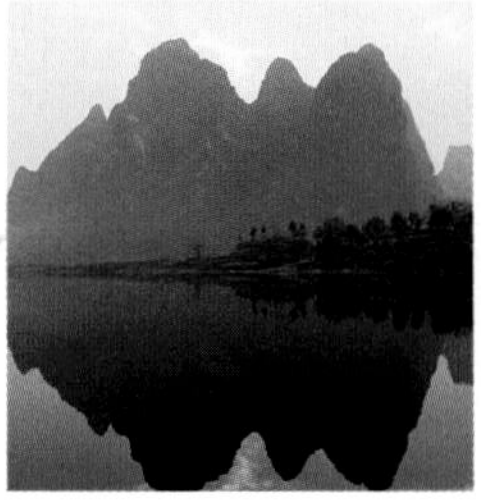

KARST
5. Southern China
Steep-sided hills, or tower karst, dominate a karst landscape,where rainfall erodes limestone rock.

FLUVIAL LANDFORMS

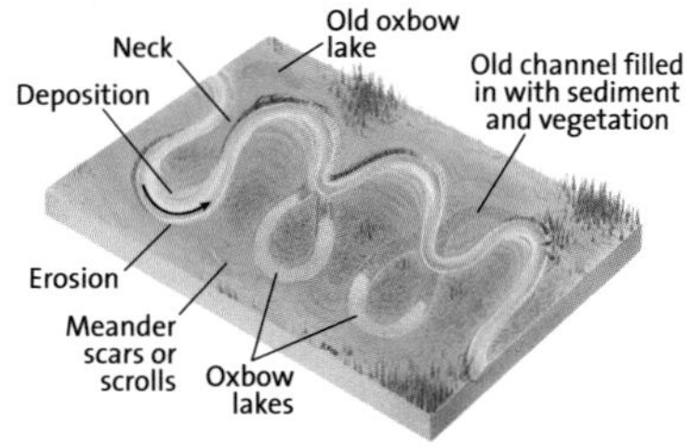
Neck
Old oxbow lake
Old channel filled in with sediment and vegetation
Deposition
Erosion
Meander scars or scrolls
Oxbow lakes

▲ **MEANDERS**
Meanders are the smooth, rounded bends of rivers that increase in size as a floodplain widens. Meanders form as faster currents erode the river's outer banks while adding sediment to the inner banks. Erosion eventually cuts off the meander, creating an oxbow lake. Floods can suddenly change a river's course.

GLACIAL LANDFORMS

▼ **GLACIAL**
Glaciers fill river valleys and bury them in ice. Ice sheets, including the ones that covered parts of North America and Europe, can be hundreds of meters thick. Migrating glacial ice transforms preglacial topography as it grinds away rock in its path. Debris, carried by the ice, is deposited when the glacier stops advancing—further changing the terrain.

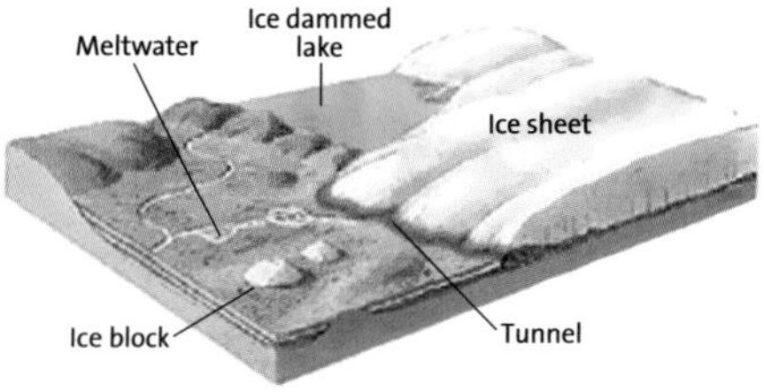
Meltwater
Ice dammed lake
Ice sheet
Ice block
Tunnel

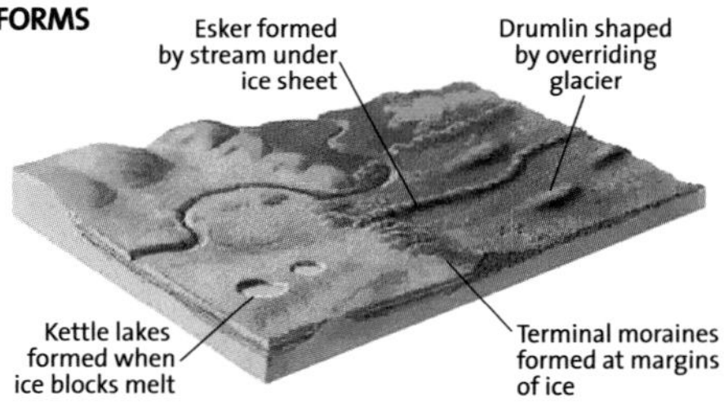
Esker formed by stream under ice sheet
Drumlin shaped by overriding glacier
Kettle lakes formed when ice blocks melt
Terminal moraines formed at margins of ice

▲ **POSTGLACIAL**
Mountain glaciers leave behind sharp-edged ridges and steep-sided valleys—causing waterfalls to plunge down sheer slopes. Areas that were covered with ice sheets, such as the Canadian Shield, exhibit stony soils, lowlands dotted with lakes, and grooved bedrock surfaces.

EUROPE
Alps

Northern European Plain

Ural Mts.

West Siberian Plain

Central Siberian Plateau

ASIA

Kazakh Uplands

Lake Baikal

Caucasus Mts.

Turan Lowland

Mongolian Plateau

Manchurian Plain

Zagros Mts.

Tian Shan

Tarim Basin

Hindu Kush

Kunlun Mts.

Plateau of Tibet

Loess Plateau

Sichuan Basin

Himalaya

Ahaggar Mts.

AFRICA

Ethiopian Highlands

Deccan Plateau

Ganges River Delta

Western Ghats

Annam Cord.

Congo Basin

Central Range

Bié Plateau

Ankarana

INDIAN OCEAN

Drakensberg

④

③

⑤

⑥

⑦

DEPRESSIONS
Oceans fill the greatest depressions, but land features often result from downward folds or faults in the crust. China's Tarim Basin is an example.

HILLS AND LOW PLATEAUS
These low-relief landforms, usually less than 300 meters (1,000 feet), are created by the erosion of higher features or by the deposition of sediments from wind or glaciers.

EQUATOR

Owen Stanley Ra.

AUSTRALIA

Great Dividing Range

⑧

What are the many forces that mold the land-forms on Earth's surface? Geomorphology is the science that studies the various relief features and the forces that form them. Endogenic forces (internal processes within the planet) produce folding, faulting, and magma movement in the Earth's crust. Subsidence in the crust causes depressions, and uplift builds mountains and plateaus. Exogenic (external) forces hold sway on the surface of the planet. In a process known as weathering, ice, water, and organisms like plant roots break down rock. Weathered rock material is carried great distances by rivers, glaciers, and other erosional agents. These forces of nature are usually gradual, often taking millions of years, but heavy rains and high winds can transform a landscape in a matter of hours. Human activities such as deforestation and poor farming practices, however, can rapidly accelerate soil erosion.

EOLIAN
6. Namibia, Africa
Arid conditions and windstorms combine to build some of the tallest sand dunes in Africa.

FLUVIAL
7. Blyde River Canyon, Africa
South Africa's Blyde River carved a steep, colorful canyon some 800 meters (2,600 ft) deep.

COASTAL
8. Victoria, Australia
Ocean waves erode coastal cliffs, leaving behind sea stacks made of more resistant rock.

POSTGLACIAL
9. Kejimkujik, Nova Scotia
Drumlins, shaped by overriding glaciers, are elliptical mounds paralleling past glacial movement.

FLUVIAL
10. Mississippi River Delta
Deltas result from the deposition of river sediments and vary in shape and size depending on discharge, currents, and waves.

OTHER LANDFORMS
11. Meteor Crater, Arizona
Some 150 visible impact craters exist on Earth; others may have eroded away or been covered.

NORTH AMERICA EUROPE ASIA
Gobi
Sahara
AFRICA
SOUTH AMERICA
Kalahari Desert
AUSTRALIA
☐ Desert
☐ Loess deposit
ANTARCTICA

▲ **EOLIAN LANDFORMS**
Eolian (from Aeolus, the Greek god of the winds) describes landforms shaped by the wind, and it works best as a geomorphic agent when wind velocity is high—and moisture and vegetation are low.

Desert dunes are the most common eolian landform. During the last glaciation, however, strong winds carried vast clouds of silt that were deposited as loess (a fine-grained, fertile soil).

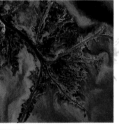

Yenisey-Angara
Ob-Irtysh
Amur
Mississippi-Missouri
Nile
Niger
Amazon
Lake Chad Congo
Paraná
Major watersheds
☐ Ten largest
☐ Other

▲ **WATERSHEDS**
The map above shows the watersheds, or drainage basins, of Earth's largest river systems. Rivers rise in mountains or plateaus, eroding and depositing sediments along their entire

length. Erosional landforms created by rivers include mesas and canyons; depositional (aggradational) landforms include levees and deltas.

NORTH AMERICA EUROPE ASIA
AFRICA
SOUTH AMERICA
AUSTRALIA
☐ Greatest extent of ice during last ice age
ANTARCTICA

▲ **ICE AGES**
A glacier is a mass of ice moving slowly down a slope or valley. Glacial ice that spreads over vast non-mountainous areas is known as an ice sheet. For millions of years ice sheets have gone

through cycles of advancing over continents—and then melting back. The most recent glacial period ended some 10,000 years ago.

□ Maximum glaciation 20,000 years ago

Present-day

□ Projected sea level rise: 13m (43ft)

▲ SEA LEVEL CHANGES

Earth's hydrologic cycle shows that oceans expand as ice sheets melt and that oceans contract as glaciers grow. Global sea level 20,000 years ago was about 125 meters (410 feet) lower than today—when ice sheets covered much of North America, and the continental shelf was above water. We currently live in an interglacial period (a time of relatively warmer global temperatures). In recent geologic history, global sea level was up to 6 meters (20 feet) higher than today's levels. A future 13-meter (43-foot) rise in sea level, caused primarily by ice sheet melting, would flood areas in the United States affecting about a quarter of the population, mainly in the Gulf and East Coast states.

▶ A SLICE OF EARTH

A cross-section shows that the oceanic crust includes plains, volcanoes, and ridges. The abyssal plains, deepest parts of the the oceanic floor, can reach greater than 3,000 meters (9,840 feet) beneath the surface of the ocean. Underwater volcanoes are called seamounts if they rise more than 1,000 meters (3,300 feet) above the seafloor. The Mid-Atlantic Ridge is a vast submarine mountain range beneath the Atlantic Ocean. Surrounding most continents is an underwater extension of the landmass known as a continental shelf—a shallow, submerged plain. Continental slopes connect the continental shelf with the oceanic crust in the form of giant escarpments that can descend some 2,000 meters (6,600 feet).

▼ EARTH'S HIGHS AND LOWS

This computer-generated image of the Earth is a digital elevation model—color-coded to show elevation differences. The image was derived from satellite altimetry and shipboard echo-sounding measurements. The deepest point, Challenger Deep at 10,920 meters (35,827 feet) below sea level, is dark blue , while the highest point, Mount Everest at 8,850 meters (29,035 feet) above sea level, is brown. Antarctica, the world's highest continent thanks to its thick ice sheet, shows up in shades of red, with a 2,300 meters (7,546 feet) average elevation. Also red is Greenland's ice sheet, about one-eighth the size of Antarctica's. Green expanses highlight lowland areas, and the adjacent aqua-hued regions reveal underwater continental shelves.

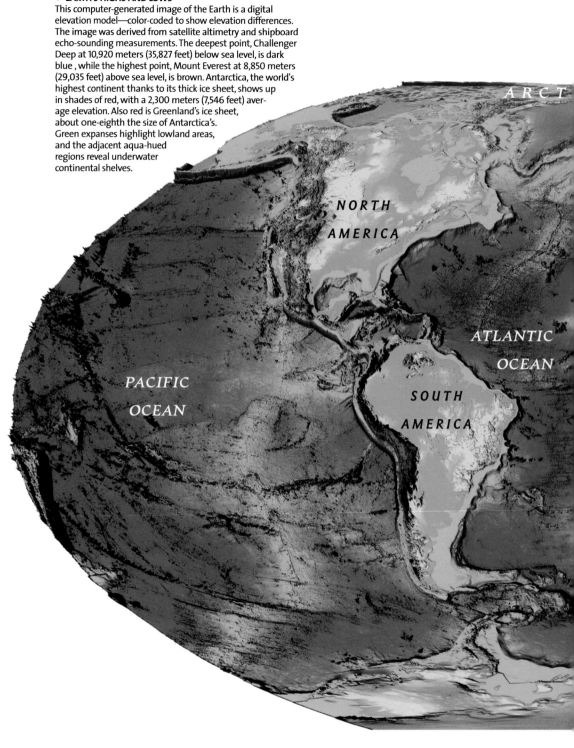

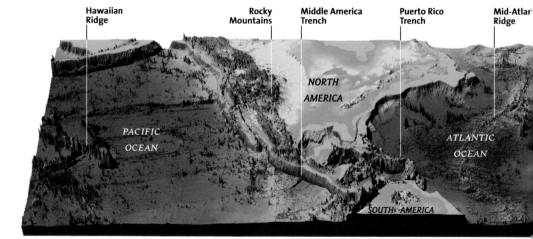

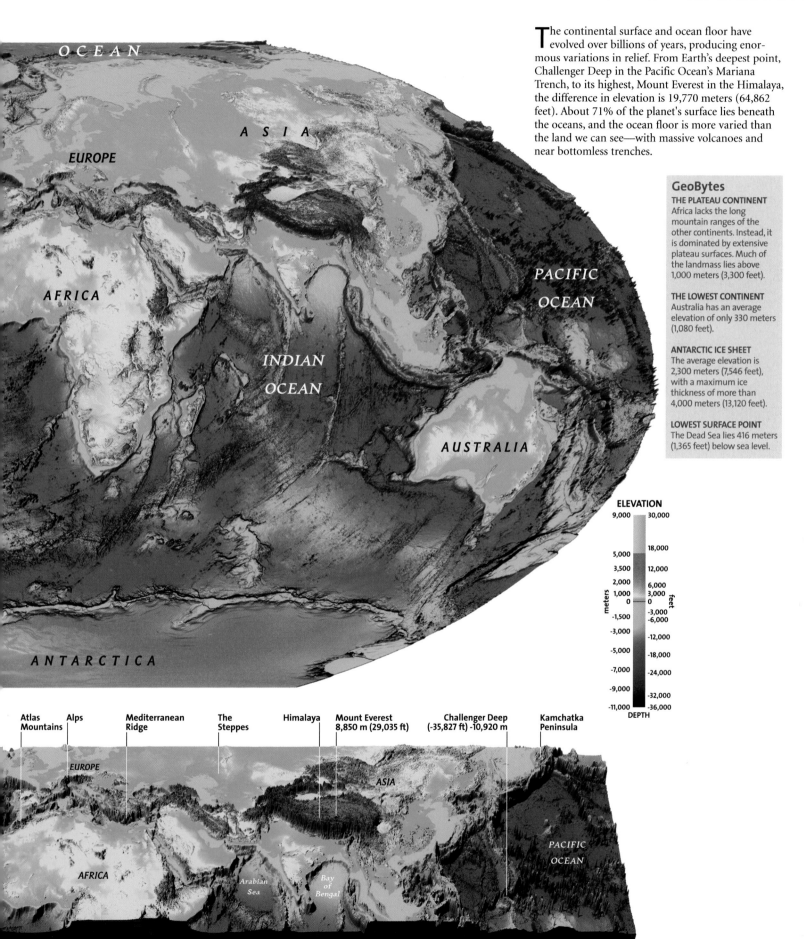

The continental surface and ocean floor have evolved over billions of years, producing enormous variations in relief. From Earth's deepest point, Challenger Deep in the Pacific Ocean's Mariana Trench, to its highest, Mount Everest in the Himalaya, the difference in elevation is 19,770 meters (64,862 feet). About 71% of the planet's surface lies beneath the oceans, and the ocean floor is more varied than the land we can see—with massive volcanoes and near bottomless trenches.

GeoBytes

THE PLATEAU CONTINENT
Africa lacks the long mountain ranges of the other continents. Instead, it is dominated by extensive plateau surfaces. Much of the landmass lies above 1,000 meters (3,300 feet).

THE LOWEST CONTINENT
Australia has an average elevation of only 330 meters (1,080 feet).

ANTARCTIC ICE SHEET
The average elevation is 2,300 meters (7,546 feet), with a maximum ice thickness of more than 4,000 meters (13,120 feet).

LOWEST SURFACE POINT
The Dead Sea lies 416 meters (1,365 feet) below sea level.

OCEAN

ASIA

EUROPE

AFRICA

PACIFIC OCEAN

INDIAN OCEAN

AUSTRALIA

ANTARCTICA

ELEVATION

meters	feet
9,000	30,000
5,000	18,000
3,500	12,000
2,000	6,000
1,000	3,000
0	0
-1,500	-3,000 / -6,000
-3,000	-12,000
-5,000	-18,000
-7,000	-24,000
-9,000	-32,000
-11,000	-36,000

DEPTH

Atlas Mountains | Alps | Mediterranean Ridge | The Steppes | Himalaya | Mount Everest 8,850 m (29,035 ft) | Challenger Deep (-35,827 ft) -10,920 m | Kamchatka Peninsula

EUROPE

ASIA

AFRICA

Arabian Sea

Bay of Bengal

PACIFIC OCEAN

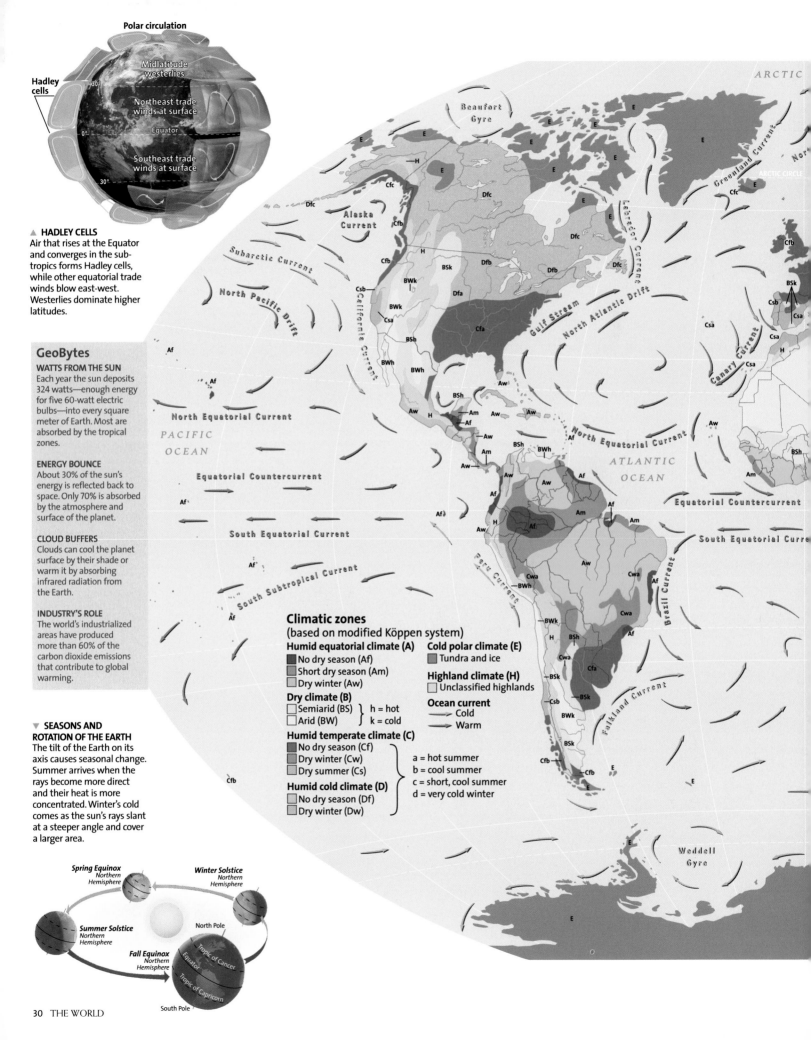

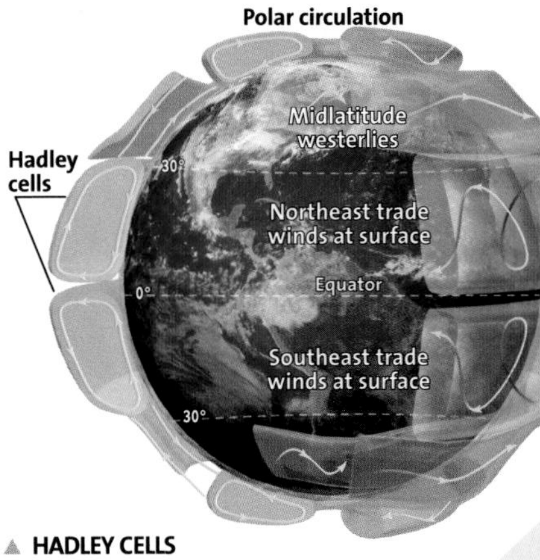
Polar circulation
Hadley cells
Midlatitude westerlies
30°
Northeast trade winds at surface
Equator
0°
Southeast trade winds at surface
30°

▲ **HADLEY CELLS**
Air that rises at the Equator and converges in the subtropics forms Hadley cells, while other equatorial trade winds blow east-west. Westerlies dominate higher latitudes.

GeoBytes

WATTS FROM THE SUN
Each year the sun deposits 324 watts—enough energy for five 60-watt electric bulbs—into every square meter of Earth. Most are absorbed by the tropical zones.

ENERGY BOUNCE
About 30% of the sun's energy is reflected back to space. Only 70% is absorbed by the atmosphere and surface of the planet.

CLOUD BUFFERS
Clouds can cool the planet surface by their shade or warm it by absorbing infrared radiation from the Earth.

INDUSTRY'S ROLE
The world's industrialized areas have produced more than 60% of the carbon dioxide emissions that contribute to global warming.

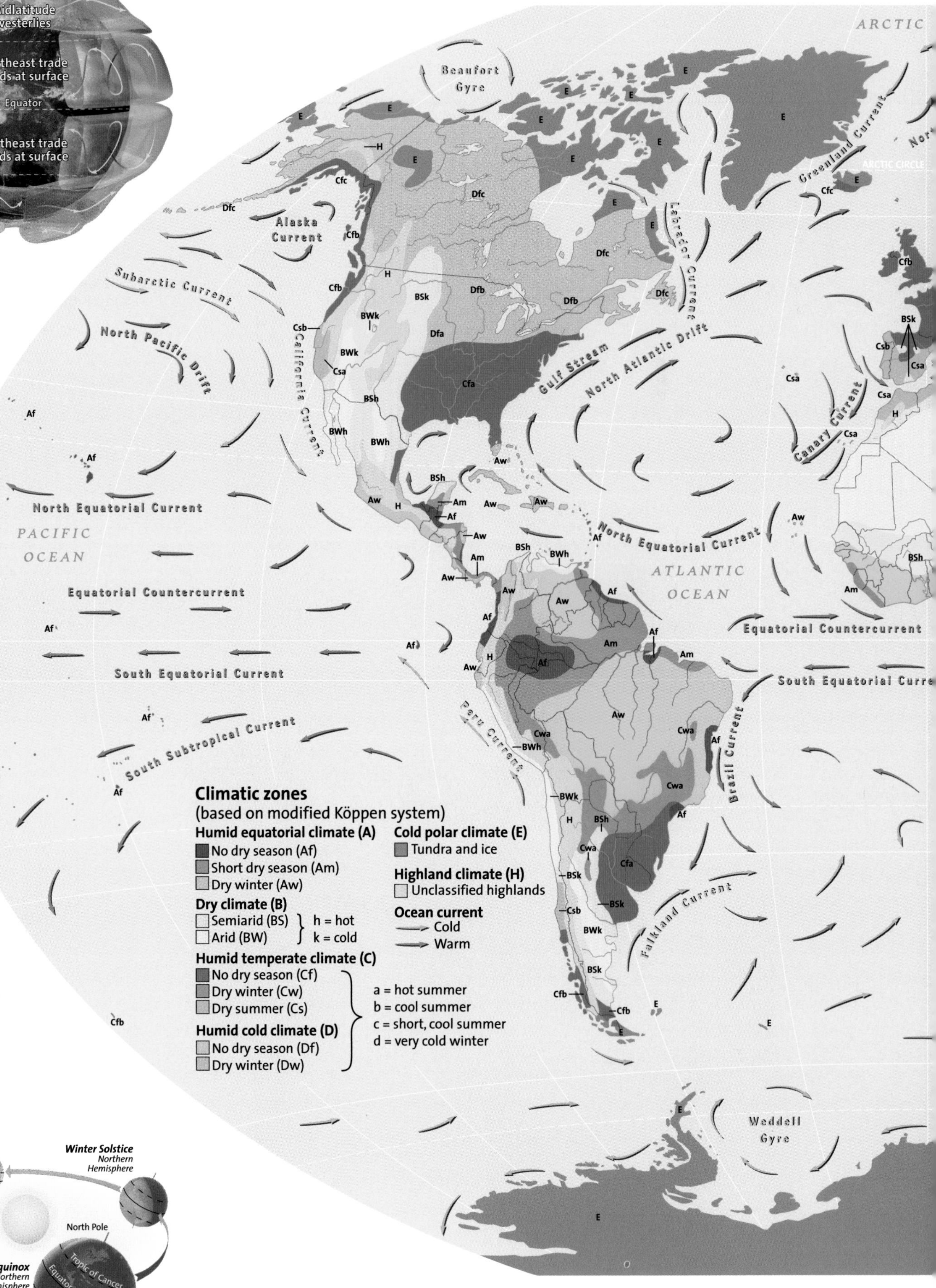
ARCTIC
ARCTIC CIRCLE
Beaufort Gyre
Greenland Current
Alaska Current
Subarctic Current
North Pacific Drift
California Current
Labrador Current
Gulf Stream
North Atlantic Drift
Canary Current
North Equatorial Current
PACIFIC OCEAN
ATLANTIC OCEAN
Equatorial Countercurrent
South Equatorial Current
South Subtropical Current
Peru Current
Brazil Current
Falkland Current
Weddell Gyre
Climatic zones
(based on modified Köppen system)
Humid equatorial climate (A)
No dry season (Af)
Short dry season (Am)
Dry winter (Aw)
Dry climate (B)
Semiarid (BS)
Arid (BW)
h = hot
k = cold
Humid temperate climate (C)
No dry season (Cf)
Dry winter (Cw)
Dry summer (Cs)
Humid cold climate (D)
No dry season (Df)
Dry winter (Dw)
a = hot summer
b = cool summer
c = short, cool summer
d = very cold winter
Cold polar climate (E)
Tundra and ice
Highland climate (H)
Unclassified highlands
Ocean current
Cold
Warm

▼ **SEASONS AND ROTATION OF THE EARTH**
The tilt of the Earth on its axis causes seasonal change. Summer arrives when the rays become more direct and their heat is more concentrated. Winter's cold comes as the sun's rays slant at a steeper angle and cover a larger area.

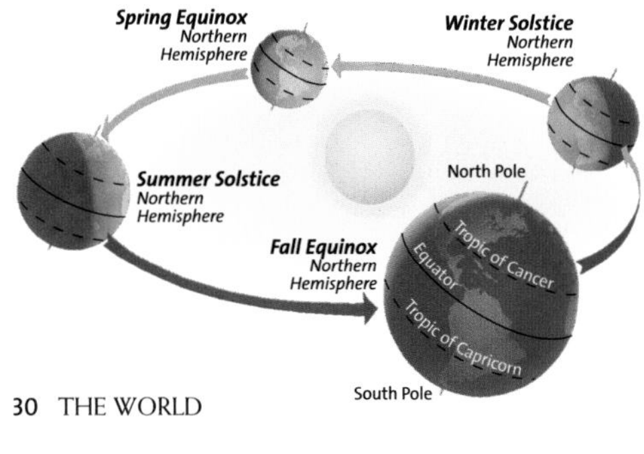
Spring Equinox
Northern Hemisphere
Winter Solstice
Northern Hemisphere
Summer Solstice
Northern Hemisphere
North Pole
Fall Equinox
Northern Hemisphere
Tropic of Cancer
Equator
Tropic of Capricorn
South Pole

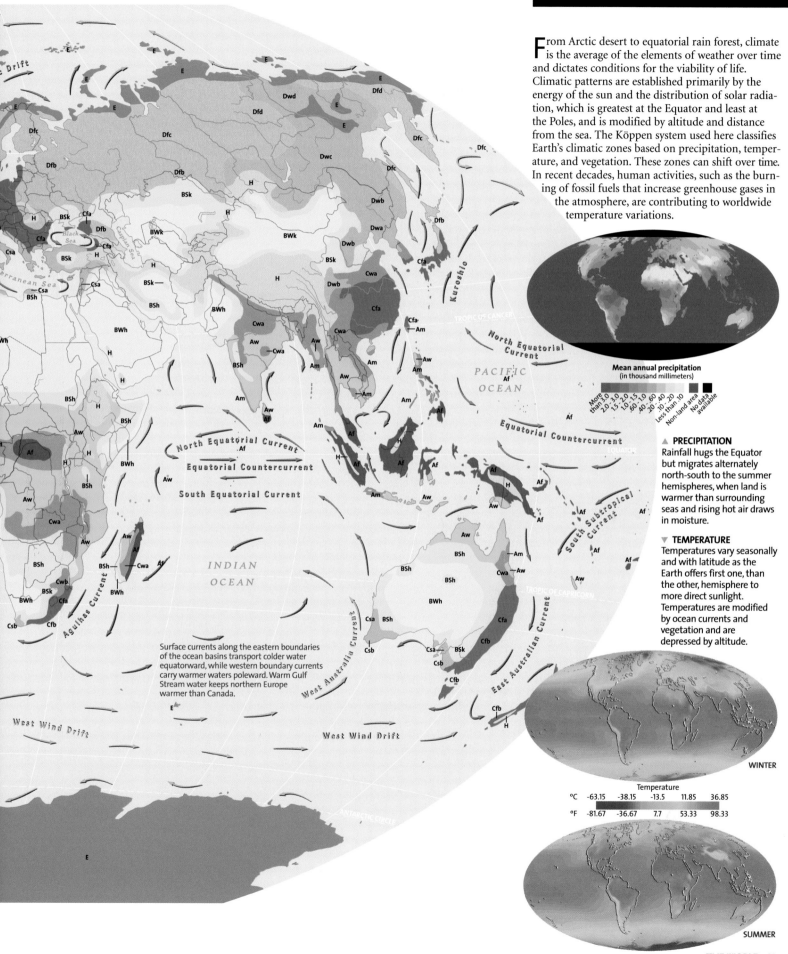

From Arctic desert to equatorial rain forest, climate is the average of the elements of weather over time and dictates conditions for the viability of life. Climatic patterns are established primarily by the energy of the sun and the distribution of solar radiation, which is greatest at the Equator and least at the Poles, and is modified by altitude and distance from the sea. The Köppen system used here classifies Earth's climatic zones based on precipitation, temperature, and vegetation. These zones can shift over time. In recent decades, human activities, such as the burning of fossil fuels that increase greenhouse gases in the atmosphere, are contributing to worldwide temperature variations.

Mean annual precipitation
(in thousand millimeters)

More than 3.0 · 2.0 - 3.0 · 1.5 - 2.0 · 1.0 - 1.5 · .60 - 1.0 · .40 - .60 · .20 - .40 · .10 - .20 · Less than .10 · Non-land area · No data available

▲ **PRECIPITATION**
Rainfall hugs the Equator but migrates alternately north-south to the summer hemispheres, when land is warmer than surrounding seas and rising hot air draws in moisture.

▼ **TEMPERATURE**
Temperatures vary seasonally and with latitude as the Earth offers first one, than the other, hemisphere to more direct sunlight. Temperatures are modified by ocean currents and vegetation and are depressed by altitude.

WINTER

Temperature

| °C | -63.15 | -38.15 | -13.5 | 11.85 | 36.85 |
| °F | -81.67 | -36.67 | 7.7 | 53.33 | 98.33 |

SUMMER

Surface currents along the eastern boundaries of the ocean basins transport colder water equatorward, while western boundary currents carry warmer waters poleward. Warm Gulf Stream water keeps northern Europe warmer than Canada.

TRACKING WEATHER PATTERNS

▼ **PRESSURE AND PREDOMINANT WINDS**

The sun's direct rays shift from south of the Equator in January to north in July, creating large temperature differences over the globe.

These, in turn, lead to air density differences and the creation of high and low pressure areas. Winds result from air attempting to

equalize these pressure differences, but the influence of the rotating planet deflects them from a straight line path.

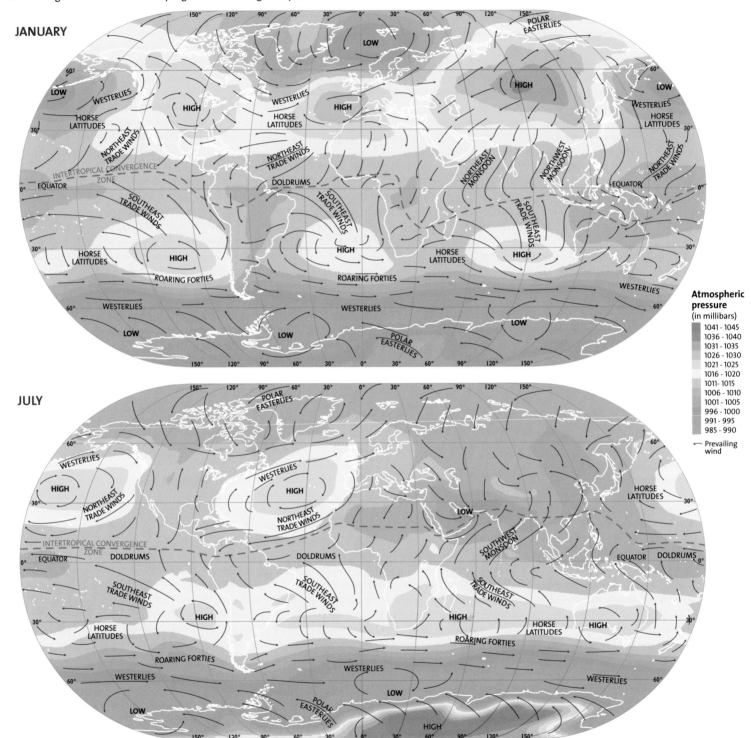

JANUARY

JULY

Atmospheric pressure
(in millibars)

1041 - 1045
1036 - 1040
1031 - 1035
1026 - 1030
1021 - 1025
1016 - 1020
1011 - 1015
1006 - 1010
1001 - 1005
996 - 1000
991 - 995
985 - 990

← Prevailing wind

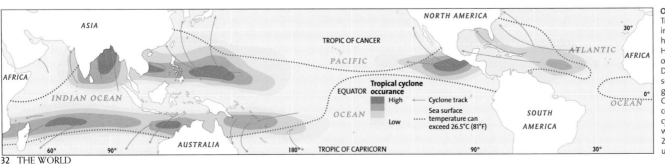

Tropical cyclone occurance

High
Low

— Cyclone track
···· Sea surface temperature can exceed 26.5°C (81°F)

OCEANS AND CYCLONES

Tropical cyclones (called typhoons in the Eastern Hemisphere and hurricanes in the Western Hemisphere) are most likely to occur in areas of greatest heating. Dotted lines show where the sea surface temperature can be greater than 26.5°C (81°F). Cyclones last until they move over cooler water or hit land. When a cyclone encounters warmer waters, as Hurricane Katrina did in 2005 in the Gulf of Mexico, it picks up energy and strength.

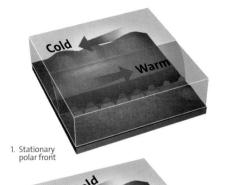

1. Stationary polar front

2. Cyclogenesis

3. Low pressure cell—undeveloped

4. Low pressure cell—developed

5. Occlusion

GeoBytes

CHRISTMAS GIFTS
El Niño, the baby, is named for the Christ Child, because the oceanic temperature rise traditionally comes around Christmas.

MONSIEUR CORIOLIS
The Coriolis Effect, the apparent force exerted on winds and ocean currents by the rotation of the earth, was first described by Gastave-Gaspard Coriolis, a French mathematician, in 1835.

SUPER STORMS
One hurricane during its life cycle can expend as much energy as 10,000 nuclear bombs.

BIG STORMS
Frontal systems are the most common weather feature in the mid-latitudes and give precipitation to large, populated areas of the globe. Most occluded fronts have a life of 3 to 6 days.

Weather is the state of the atmosphere—as indicated by temperature, moisture, wind speed and direction, and barometric pressure—at a specific time and place. Although still frustratingly difficult to predict, weather acts in some known patterns. Variations in ocean temperatures off the South American coast influence storm formation and rainfall around the globe. Jet streams that speed around the planet can usher in winter storms. And the right combination of warm water, wind, and energy from heated water vapor can cook up lethal hurricanes and typhoons that can overwhelm shorelines and cities.

Solar Radiation

Earth's Rotation

MIDLATITUDE CYCLONE

COLD AIR

Polar Jet Stream

Subtropical Jet Stream

TROPICAL CYCLONE

EQUATOR

Pacific Ocean

WARM AIR

Gulf of Mexico

Atlantic Ocean

▲ FORMATION OF A MID-LATITUDE CYCLONE

Mid-latitude cyclones are found between 35° and 70° of latitude in the zone of the westerly winds. Most are occluded fronts. (1) Characterized by intense, heavy precipitation, cold polar air—with a boundary known as a front—meets warm tropical air. (2) A wave develops along the frontal boundary as the opposing air masses interact. Cyclogenesis (the birth of a cyclone) begins. (3) The faster-moving cold air forces the warm air to lift above the cold. (4) Full rotation develops, counterclockwise in the Northern Hemisphere and clockwise in the Southern Hemisphere. (5) Complete occlusion occurs as the warm air, fully caught-up by the cold air, has been lifted away from the surface. Because the warm air is completely separated from the surface, the characteristics of the cold air are felt on the ground in the form of unsteady, windy, and wet weather.

Sea surface height anomaly

cm	-12	-8	-4	0	4	8	12
in	-5	-3	-2	0	2	3	5

◀ EL NIÑO AND LA NIÑA

El Niño, an anomoly of sea-surface height or "relief" of the sea, brings warm water to South America's west coast, leading to severe short-term changes in world weather. La Niña, a cooling of those waters, has opposite effects.

▲ HOW WEATHER HAPPENS

Weather is ultimately the atmospheric response to unequal inputs of solar energy over the globe, as a surplus of heat in low latitudes is transferred to higher latitudes by air motion and by mid-latitude storms. Part of that dynamic are jet streams—rivers of westerly winds speeding as fast as 400 kph (250 mph) in the upper atmosphere, which are also instrumental in the genesis of storms: The Polar Front Jet, which snakes along the front between Arctic and warmer continental air, is instrumental in the formation and direction of cyclonic North Pacific winter storms; the Subtropical Jet blows along the boundary of tropical circulation cells and can also abet storm formation, bringing warm, moist air and precipitation into the continent. Weather patterns are also influenced by the different properties of oceans and continents to absorb or reflect heat, which creates pressure differences that give rise to moving air masses.

◄ **OUR LAYERED OCEAN**
With depth, the ocean's five layers get colder, darker, saltier, denser, and more devoid of life.

200 meters (660 feet)
The epipelagic is the sunlit zone where photosynthesis by plants can take place and where the vast majority of all marine animals live.

1,000 meters (3,300 feet)
Only some light penetrates the mesopelagic, or twilight zone. Thus no plants grow, but large fish and whales hunt and bioluminescent fish first appear.

3,960 meters (13,000 feet)
No light reaches the midnight zone, or bathypelagic, but sperm whales and rays are known to hunt here for food.

6,100 meters (20,000 feet)
Pressure is crushing in the abyssopelagic, or abyss zone, home to bizarre angler fish and invertebrates such as sponges and sea cucumbers.

10,060 meters (33,000 feet)
The hadalpelagic zone penetrates into the deepest ocean trenches yet is home to small crustaceans called isopods.

Marine Sediments
The vast majority of the Earth's biologically fixed carbon lies in marine sediments trapped at the bottom of the seas. Carbon deposits from past eras are seen in current landforms upthrust from the oceans, such as the white cliffs of Dover.

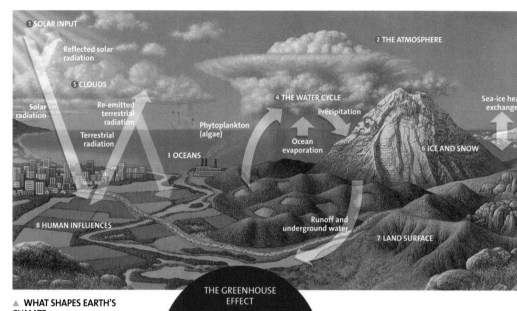

1 SOLAR INPUT
Reflected solar radiation
5 CLOUDS
2 THE ATMOSPHERE
Solar radiation
Re-emitted terrestrial radiation
4 THE WATER CYCLE
Precipitation
Sea-ice heat exchange
Terrestrial radiation
Phytoplankton (algae)
Ocean evaporation
6 ICE AND SNOW
3 OCEANS
8 HUMAN INFLUENCES
Runoff and underground water
7 LAND SURFACE

▲ **WHAT SHAPES EARTH'S CLIMATE**
Much of the sun's heat (1) is held in the atmosphere (2) by greenhouses gases as well as in the top layer of oceans. Oceans (3) distribute heat; evaporation lifts moisture (4). Clouds (5) reflect heat and cool Earth; they also warm it by trapping heat. Ice and snow (6) reflect sunlight, cooling Earth. Land (7) can influence the formation of clouds, and human use (8) can alter natural processes.

▲ **GREENHOUSE HEAT TRAP**
The atmosphere acts like a greenhouse, allowing sunlight to filter through. Gases such as carbon dioxide, methane, ozone, and nitrous oxide help the atmosphere hold heat. This heating is key in Earth's ability to stay warm and sustain life.

THE GREENHOUSE EFFECT
Greenhouse gases
Solar radiation
Trapped heat

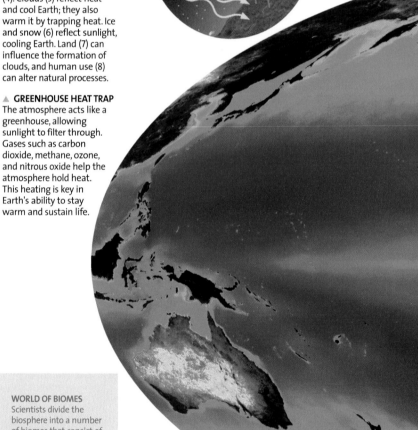

GeoBytes

BIOGENESIS
The evolution of the biosphere is thought to have begun some 3.5 billion years ago.

A NEW SCIENCE
In 1926 a Soviet scientist, Vladimir I. Vernadsky, argued that human reason is capable of ensuring the sustainability of the biosphere.

BOTTOM BIOMASS
The microbes that live deep beneath the Earth's surface could exceed all animal and plant life on the surface by biomass.

WORLD OF BIOMES
Scientists divide the biosphere into a number of biomes that consist of broadly similar flora and fauna. Terrestrial biomes include deserts, forests, and grasslands; oceanic ones are coral reefs, estuaries, oceans, and the deep abyssal zone.

BIRDS SOAR ABOVE
High-flying birds, such as the Ruppell's vulture and the bar-headed geese, are found at altitudes greater than Mt. Everest's nearly 9,140 meters (30,000 feet).

▶ **EARTH'S GREEN BIOMASS**
Earth's vegetative biomass, the foundation of most life on the planet, is measured by chlorophyll-producing plants. Both land and sea process an equal amount of carbon—50 to 60 billion metric tonnes per year. Photoplankton provides the basis of measurement in the oceans; green-leaf mass on land.

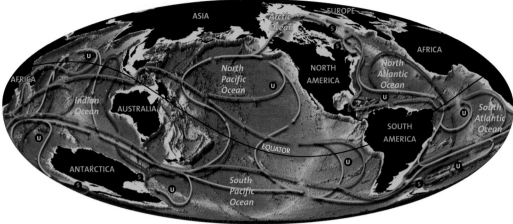

OCEAN CIRCULATION
Ocean circulation, driven by wind, density, and Earth's rotation, conveys heat energy around the globe. Tropical surface waters move toward the Poles, cool, sink, and loop around to upwell near the Equator. The Gulf Stream, for example, warms northern Europe. Other, density-driven currents flow vertically to replenish deeper waters.

Ocean circulation
- Warmer than 3.5°C (38.3°F)
- 1°C – 3.5°C
- Cooler than 1°C (33.8°F)

S Sinking
U Upwelling

The biosphere is Earth's thin layer of life. Containing all known life in the solar system, the biosphere, if viewed from miles above the planet, would be at a scale no thicker than this page. Although the biosphere is 19 kilometers (12 miles) from top to bottom, the bulk of it ocean depths, most living things occupy a three-kilometer-wide (two-mile-wide) band extending from the sunlit ocean layer to the snowline of high mountains. The biosphere—and its communities of plants and animals—interacts with the other key spheres of physical geography: the lithosphere, Earth's solid outer crust; the atmosphere, the layer of air above; and the hydrosphere, the oceans and all water on and within Earth. The ecosystems of the biosphere are in constant flux as the planet turns, as weather and climate shift, and as the human impacts of forestry, agriculture, and urbanization affect the fundamental components of the biosphere—carbon dioxide and other gases, water, and the photosynthesis of plants.

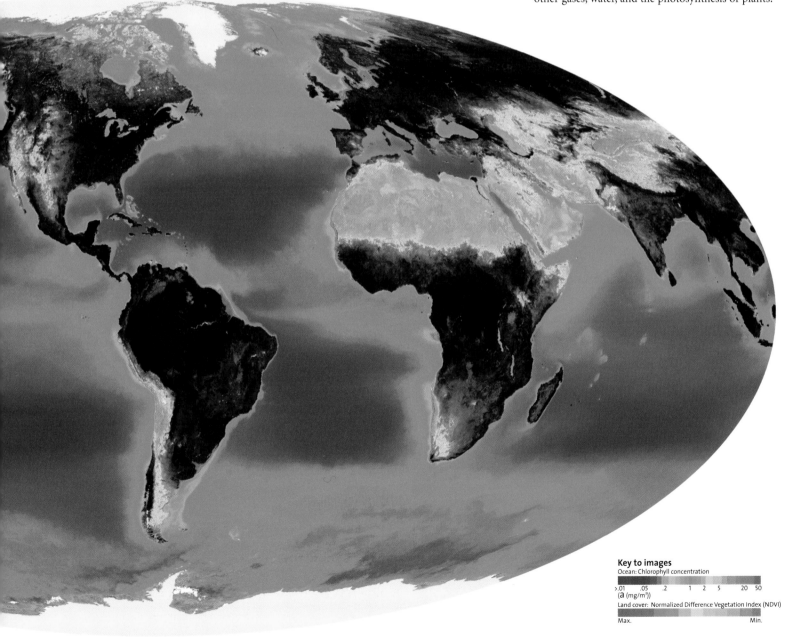

Key to images
Ocean: Chlorophyll concentration

>.01 .05 .2 1 2 5 20 50
(a (mg/m³))
Land cover: Normalized Difference Vegetation Index (NDVI)

Max. Min.

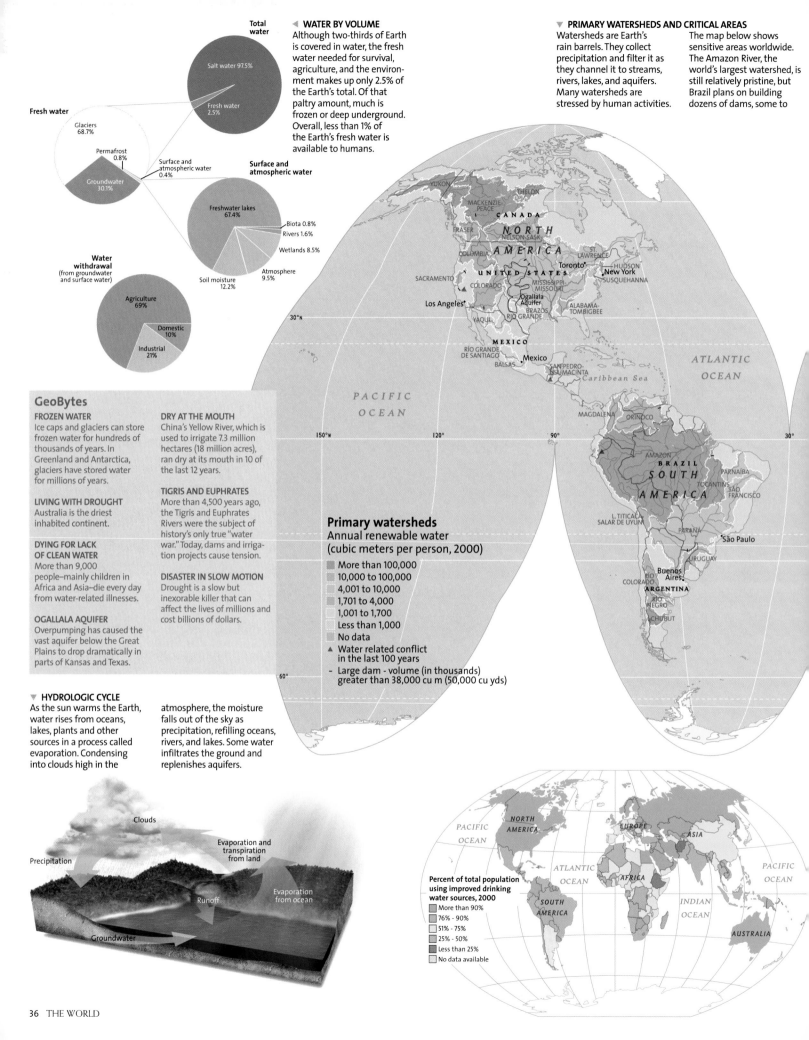

WATER BY VOLUME

Although two-thirds of Earth is covered in water, the fresh water needed for survival, agriculture, and the environment makes up only 2.5% of the Earth's total. Of that paltry amount, much is frozen or deep underground. Overall, less than 1% of the Earth's fresh water is available to humans.

Total water
Salt water 97.5%
Fresh water 2.5%

Fresh water
Glaciers 68.7%
Permafrost 0.8%
Groundwater 30.1%
Surface and atmospheric water 0.4%

Surface and atmospheric water
Freshwater lakes 67.4%
Biota 0.8%
Rivers 1.6%
Wetlands 8.5%
Atmosphere 9.5%
Soil moisture 12.2%

Water withdrawal
(from groundwater and surface water)
Agriculture 69%
Domestic 10%
Industrial 21%

PRIMARY WATERSHEDS AND CRITICAL AREAS

Watersheds are Earth's rain barrels. They collect precipitation and filter it as they channel it to streams, rivers, lakes, and aquifers. Many watersheds are stressed by human activities.

The map below shows sensitive areas worldwide. The Amazon River, the world's largest watershed, is still relatively pristine, but Brazil plans on building dozens of dams, some to

GeoBytes

FROZEN WATER
Ice caps and glaciers can store frozen water for hundreds of thousands of years. In Greenland and Antarctica, glaciers have stored water for millions of years.

LIVING WITH DROUGHT
Australia is the driest inhabited continent.

DYING FOR LACK OF CLEAN WATER
More than 9,000 people–mainly children in Africa and Asia–die every day from water-related illnesses.

OGALLALA AQUIFER
Overpumping has caused the vast aquifer below the Great Plains to drop dramatically in parts of Kansas and Texas.

DRY AT THE MOUTH
China's Yellow River, which is used to irrigate 7.3 million hectares (18 million acres), ran dry at its mouth in 10 of the last 12 years.

TIGRIS AND EUPHRATES
More than 4,500 years ago, the Tigris and Euphrates Rivers were the subject of history's only true "water war." Today, dams and irrigation projects cause tension.

DISASTER IN SLOW MOTION
Drought is a slow but inexorable killer that can affect the lives of millions and cost billions of dollars.

Primary watersheds
Annual renewable water
(cubic meters per person, 2000)

- More than 100,000
- 10,000 to 100,000
- 4,001 to 10,000
- 1,701 to 4,000
- 1,001 to 1,700
- Less than 1,000
- No data
- ▲ Water related conflict in the last 100 years
- – Large dam - volume (in thousands) greater than 38,000 cu m (50,000 cu yds)

HYDROLOGIC CYCLE

As the sun warms the Earth, water rises from oceans, lakes, plants and other sources in a process called evaporation. Condensing into clouds high in the atmosphere, the moisture falls out of the sky as precipitation, refilling oceans, rivers, and lakes. Some water infiltrates the ground and replenishes aquifers.

Clouds
Precipitation
Evaporation and transpiration from land
Runoff
Evaporation from ocean
Groundwater

Percent of total population using improved drinking water sources, 2000
- More than 90%
- 76% - 90%
- 51% - 75%
- 25% - 50%
- Less than 25%
- No data available

power aluminum smelters. In Africa and Asia, lack of access to water and water-related diseases are the main problems. In Europe and the Middle East, overuse, pollution, and disagreement over diverting water are the major challenges. Hope rests in better planning and community-scale projects.

I t's as vital to life as air. Yet fresh water is one of the rarest resources on Earth. Only 2.5% of Earth's water is fresh, and of that the usable portion for humans is less than 1% of all fresh water, or 0.01% of all water on Earth. Water is constantly recycling through Earth's hydrologic cycle. But population growth and pollution are combining to make less and less available per person per year, while global climate change adds new uncertainty.

Efficiency, conservation, and technology can help ensure that the water you absorb today will still be usable and clean hundreds of years from now.

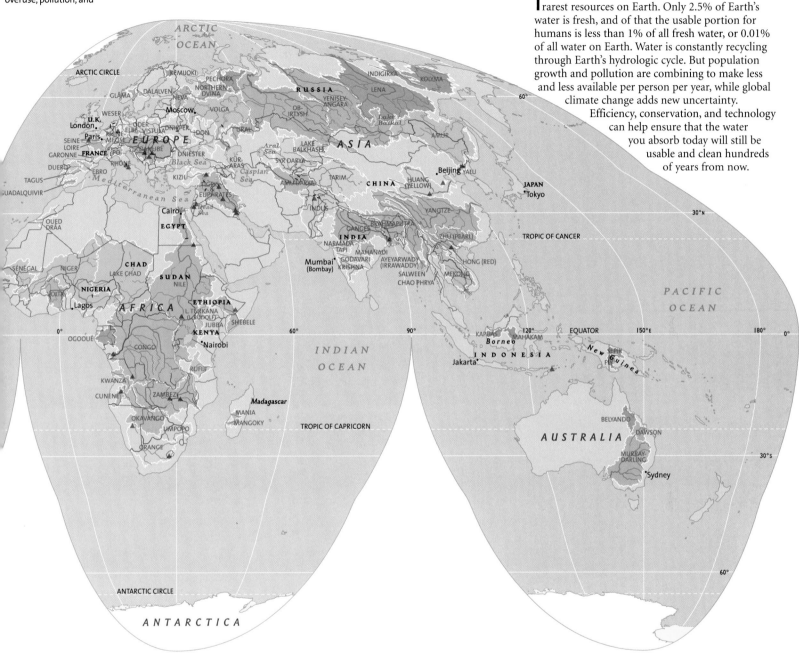

◀ ACCESS TO FRESH WATER
Access to clean fresh water is critical for human health. Yet, in many regions, potable water is becoming scarce because of heavy demands and pollution. Especially worrisome is the poisoning of aquifers—a primary source of water for nearly a third of the world—by sewage, pesticides, and heavy metals.

▼ GLOBAL IRRIGATED AREAS AND WATER WITHDRAWALS
Since 1970, global water withdrawals have correlated with the rise in irrigated area. Some 70% of withdrawals are for agriculture, mostly for irrigation that helps produce 40% of the world's food.

Freshwater withdrawal as a percentage of total water utilization, 2000

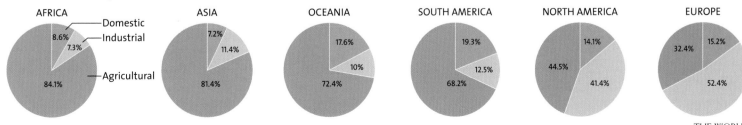

AFRICA
Domestic 8.6%
Industrial 7.3%
Agricultural 84.1%

ASIA
7.2%
11.4%
81.4%

OCEANIA
17.6%
10%
72.4%

SOUTH AMERICA
19.3%
12.5%
68.2%

NORTH AMERICA
14.1%
44.5%
41.4%

EUROPE
15.2%
32.4%
52.4%

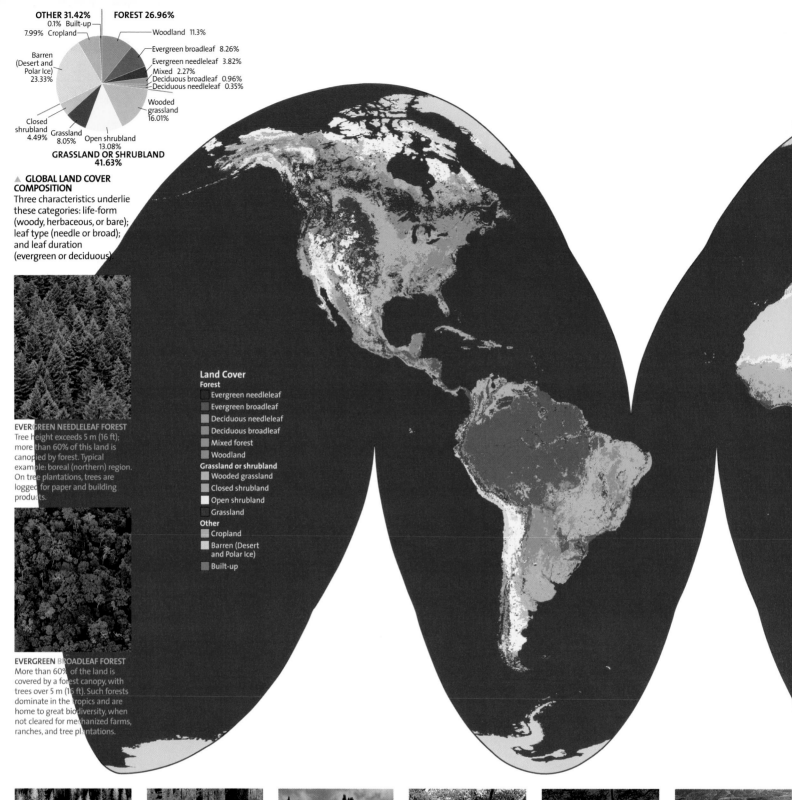

OTHER 31.42%
- 0.1% Built-up
- 7.99% Cropland
- Barren (Desert and Polar Ice) 23.33%
- Closed shrubland 4.49%
- Grassland 8.05%
- Open shrubland 13.08%

FOREST 26.96%
- Woodland 11.3%
- Evergreen broadleaf 8.26%
- Evergreen needleleaf 3.82%
- Mixed 2.27%
- Deciduous broadleaf 0.96%
- Deciduous needleleaf 0.35%
- Wooded grassland 16.01%

GRASSLAND OR SHRUBLAND 41.63%

▲ **GLOBAL LAND COVER COMPOSITION**
Three characteristics underlie these categories: life-form (woody, herbaceous, or bare); leaf type (needle or broad); and leaf duration (evergreen or deciduous).

Land Cover

Forest
- Evergreen needleleaf
- Evergreen broadleaf
- Deciduous needleleaf
- Deciduous broadleaf
- Mixed forest
- Woodland

Grassland or shrubland
- Wooded grassland
- Closed shrubland
- Open shrubland
- Grassland

Other
- Cropland
- Barren (Desert and Polar Ice)
- Built-up

EVERGREEN NEEDLELEAF FOREST
Tree height exceeds 5 m (16 ft); more than 60% of this land is canopied by forest. Typical example: boreal (northern) region. On tree plantations, trees are logged for paper and building products.

EVERGREEN BROADLEAF FOREST
More than 60% of the land is covered by a forest canopy, with trees over 5 m (16 ft). Such forests dominate in the tropics and are home to great biodiversity, when not cleared for mechanized farms, ranches, and tree plantations.

DECIDUOUS NEEDLELEAF FOREST
A forest canopy covers more than 60% of the land; tree height exceeds 5 m (16 ft). This class is dominant only in Siberia, taking the form of larch forests.

DECIDUOUS BROADLEAF FOREST
More than 60% of the land is covered by a forest canopy; tree height exceeds 5 m (16 ft). In temperate regions, much of this forest has been converted to cropland.

MIXED FOREST
Both needle and deciduous types of trees appear. This type is largely found between temperate deciduous and boreal evergreen forests.

WOODLAND
Land has herbaceous or woody understory; trees exceed 5 m (16 ft) and may be deciduous or evergreen. Highly degraded in long-settled human environments, such as in West Africa.

WOODED GRASSLAND
Woody or herbaceous understories are punctuated by trees. Examples are African savannah as well as open boreal borderland between trees and tundra.

CLOSED SHRUBLAND
Found where prolonged cold or dry seasons limit plant growth, this cover is dominated by bushes or shrubs not exceeding 5 m (16 ft). Tree canopy is less than 10%.

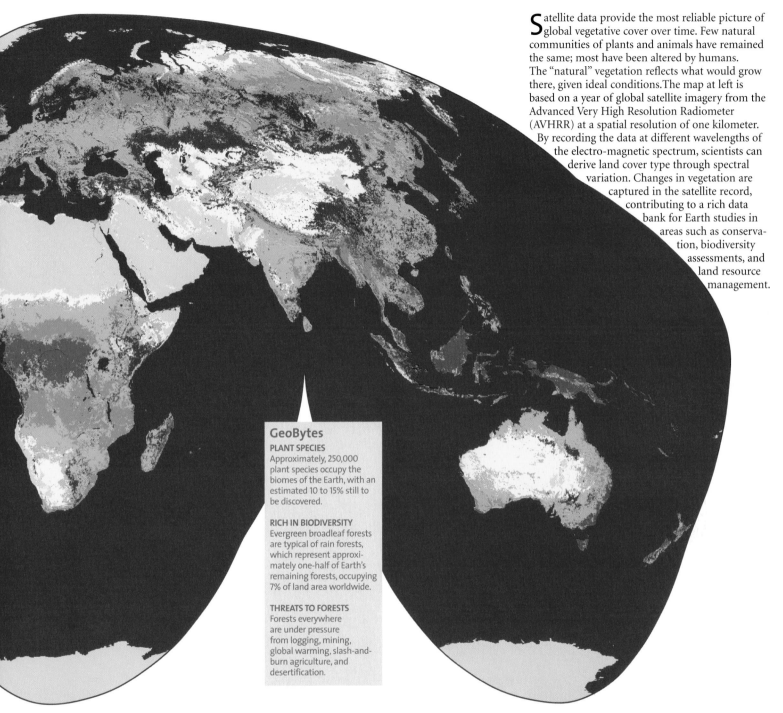

Satellite data provide the most reliable picture of global vegetative cover over time. Few natural communities of plants and animals have remained the same; most have been altered by humans. The "natural" vegetation reflects what would grow there, given ideal conditions. The map at left is based on a year of global satellite imagery from the Advanced Very High Resolution Radiometer (AVHRR) at a spatial resolution of one kilometer. By recording the data at different wavelengths of the electro-magnetic spectrum, scientists can derive land cover type through spectral variation. Changes in vegetation are captured in the satellite record, contributing to a rich data bank for Earth studies in areas such as conservation, biodiversity assessments, and land resource management.

GeoBytes

PLANT SPECIES
Approximately, 250,000 plant species occupy the biomes of the Earth, with an estimated 10 to 15% still to be discovered.

RICH IN BIODIVERSITY
Evergreen broadleaf forests are typical of rain forests, which represent approximately one-half of Earth's remaining forests, occupying 7% of land area worldwide.

THREATS TO FORESTS
Forests everywhere are under pressure from logging, mining, global warming, slash-and-burn agriculture, and desertification.

OPEN SHRUBLAND
Shrubs are dominant, not exceeding 2 m (6.5 ft) in height. They can be evergreen or deciduous. This type occurs in semiarid or severely cold areas.

GRASSLAND
Occurring in a wide range of habitats, this landscape has continuous herbaceous cover. The American Plains and central Russia are the premier examples.

CROPLAND
Crop-producing fields constitute over 80% of the land. Temperate regions are home to large areas of mechanized farming; in the developing world, plots are small.

BARREN (DESERT)
The land never has more than 10% vegetated cover. True deserts, such as the Sahara, as well as areas succumbing to desertification, are examples.

BUILT-UP
This class was mapped using the populated places layer that is part of the "Digital Chart of the World" (Danko, 1992). It represents the most densely inhabited areas.

BARREN (POLAR ICE)
Permanent snow cover characterizes this class, the greatest expanses of which are in the polar regions, as well as on high elevations in Alaska and the Himalaya.

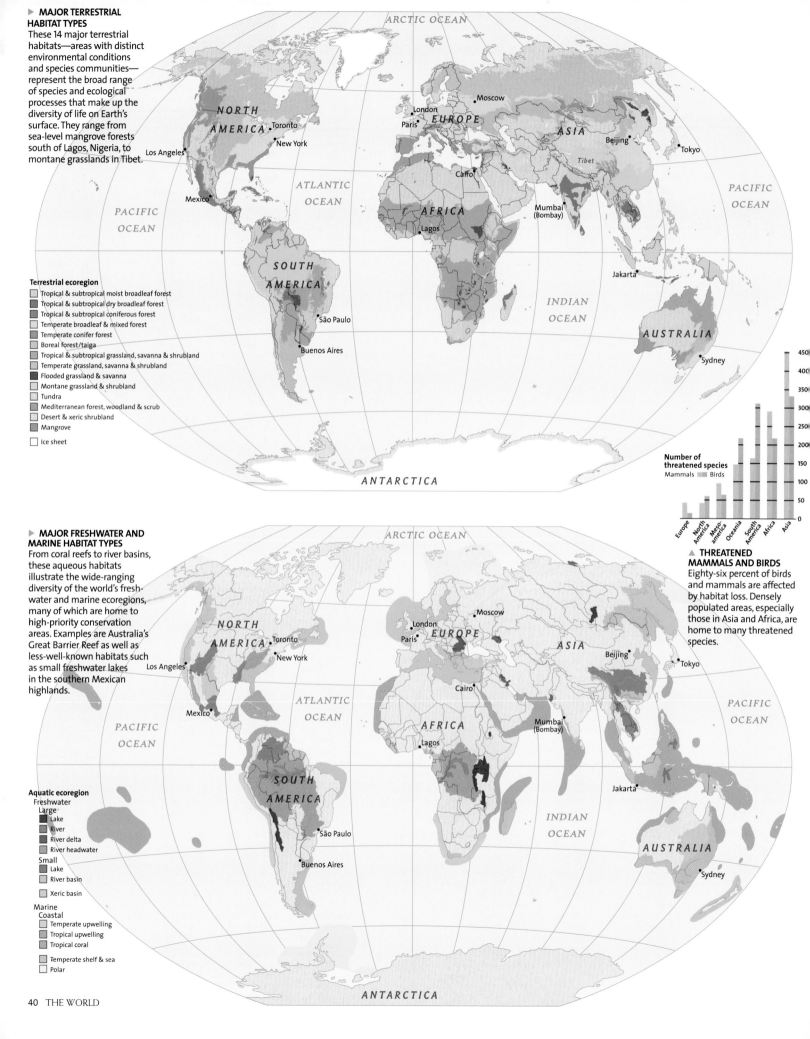

▶ MAJOR TERRESTRIAL HABITAT TYPES

These 14 major terrestrial habitats—areas with distinct environmental conditions and species communities—represent the broad range of species and ecological processes that make up the diversity of life on Earth's surface. They range from sea-level mangrove forests south of Lagos, Nigeria, to montane grasslands in Tibet.

Terrestrial ecoregion
- Tropical & subtropical moist broadleaf forest
- Tropical & subtropical dry broadleaf forest
- Tropical & subtropical coniferous forest
- Temperate broadleaf & mixed forest
- Temperate conifer forest
- Boreal forest/taiga
- Tropical & subtropical grassland, savanna & shrubland
- Temperate grassland, savanna & shrubland
- Flooded grassland & savanna
- Montane grassland & shrubland
- Tundra
- Mediterranean forest, woodland & scrub
- Desert & xeric shrubland
- Mangrove

- Ice sheet

▲ THREATENED MAMMALS AND BIRDS

Eighty-six percent of birds and mammals are affected by habitat loss. Densely populated areas, especially those in Asia and Africa, are home to many threatened species.

Number of threatened species
Mammals | Birds

▶ MAJOR FRESHWATER AND MARINE HABITAT TYPES

From coral reefs to river basins, these aqueous habitats illustrate the wide-ranging diversity of the world's freshwater and marine ecoregions, many of which are home to high-priority conservation areas. Examples are Australia's Great Barrier Reef as well as less-well-known habitats such as small freshwater lakes in the southern Mexican highlands.

Aquatic ecoregion
Freshwater
Large
- Lake
- River
- River delta
- River headwater
Small
- Lake
- River basin

- Xeric basin

Marine
Coastal
- Temperate upwelling
- Tropical upwelling
- Tropical coral

- Temperate shelf & sea
- Polar

Biodiversity refers to the rich variety of life among the world's living organisms and the ecological communities they are part of. It includes the number of different species, the genetic diversity within species, and the ecosystems in which species live. Some areas, such as coral reefs, are replete with diversity; others, like the polar regions, are noted for their lack of diversity. The biodiversity of any given place is shaped by biogeographic conditions including local and regional climate, latitude, range of habitats, evolutionary history, and biological productivity—a place's capacity to generate and support life. Out of the estimated 5 to 30 million species that exist, only 1.9 million species have been named. Experts estimate that species are becoming extinct at a rate of 100 to 1,000 times higher than might be expected from natural extinction, akin to a mass extinction. Humans rely on the world's diverse assets for survival—food, medicine, clean air, drinkable water, habitable climates—yet it is our activities that pose the greatest threat to the world's biodiversity.

▲ BIODIVERSITY HOTSPOTS
What areas are vital for conserving biodiversity? Conservation International identified 34 "hotspots," defined as habitat holding at least 1,500 endemic plant species and having lost 70% of its original extent.

▼ THREATS TO BIODIVERSITY
The greatest threats to biodiversity—habitat loss and fragmentation, invasion of non-native species, pollution, and unsustainable exploitation—are all caused by human economic activity and population growth.

Projected status of biodiversity, 1998–2018
- ☐ Critical and endangered
- ☐ Threatened
- ☐ Relatively stable/intact

GeoBytes

UNIQUE SPECIES
Madagascar and the Indian Ocean islands are home to many species found nowhere else. Of the region's 13,000 plant species, more than 89% are endemic, meaning that is the only place on Earth they live.

FRAGILE POPULATIONS
Nearly half of the world's tortoises and freshwater turtles are threatened.

HUMAN HEALTH
Medicines derived from plants and animals are the primary source of health care for 80% of the world's population.

ECONOMIC VALUE
Scientists estimate that ecosystems worldwide provide goods and services, such as nutrient recycling and waste treatment, valued at more than $20 trillion a year.

EXTINCTION RISK
One in every eight birds and one in every four mammals face a high risk of extinction in the near future.

BEETLEMANIA
Beetles are the most diverse life-form on Earth. More than a thousand different kinds can live on a single tree in the forests of South America.

1. THE BERING SEA
The Bering Sea, separating Alaska and Russia, is one of the world's most diverse marine environments. Polar bears, seals, sea lions, walruses, whales, enormous populations of seabirds, and more than 400 species of fish, crustaceans, and mollusks live in this ecoregion. It is also home to one of the world's largest salmon runs. Global warming, pollution, overfishing, and mining are major threats to this region's biodiversity.

2. SOUTHEASTERN U.S. RIVERS AND STREAMS
From Appalachian streams to saltwater marshes along the Atlantic and Gulf coasts, this ecoregion harbors hundreds of species of fish, snails, crayfish, and mussels. A single river in the region, the Cahaba River in Alabama, has more fish species per mile than any other river in North America. Population growth and increasing streamside development, dams, and water diversion for irrigation are long-term threats.

3. THE AMAZON RIVER AND FLOODED FORESTS
More than 3,000 species of freshwater fish and many mammals, including the pink river dolphin, inhabit this ecoregion. The Amazon Basin is Earth's largest watershed and is noted for having the world's largest expanse of seasonally flooded forests, habitat for a wide array of migratory species. Selective logging and the conversion of floodplains for ranching and agricultural use are threats to the region.

4. RIFT VALLEY LAKES
This cluster of freshwater and alkaline lakes spread across East Africa's Great Lakes region. It is home to nearly 800 species of cichlid fishes, all derived from a common ancestor, a process called species radiation. These radiations are an extraordinary example of evolutionary adaptation. The lakes also provide important bird habitat—half of the world's flamingo population lives here. Threats to the region include deforestation, pollution, and the spread of non-native species.

5. EASTERN HIMALAYAN BROADLEAF AND CONIFER FORESTS
Snaking across the lowlands and foothills of the Himalaya, this ecoregion supports a remarkable diversity of plants and animals, including endangered mammals such as the clouded leopard, Himalayan black bear, and the golden langur. These sub-alpine forests are also a significant endemic bird area. Because forests are slow to regenerate, conversion to cropland and timber extraction are serious threats to this region's biodiversity.

6. SULU-SULAWESI SEAS
Extensive coral reefs, mangroves, and seagrass beds make this one of the richest habitats for reef animals and plants in the world. More than 450 species of coral, six of the world's eight species of marine turtles, and numerous species of fish, sharks, and whales live in this marine ecoregion between Indonesia, Malaysia, and the Philippines. These reefs continue to be threatened by coastal erosion, pollution, and overfishing.

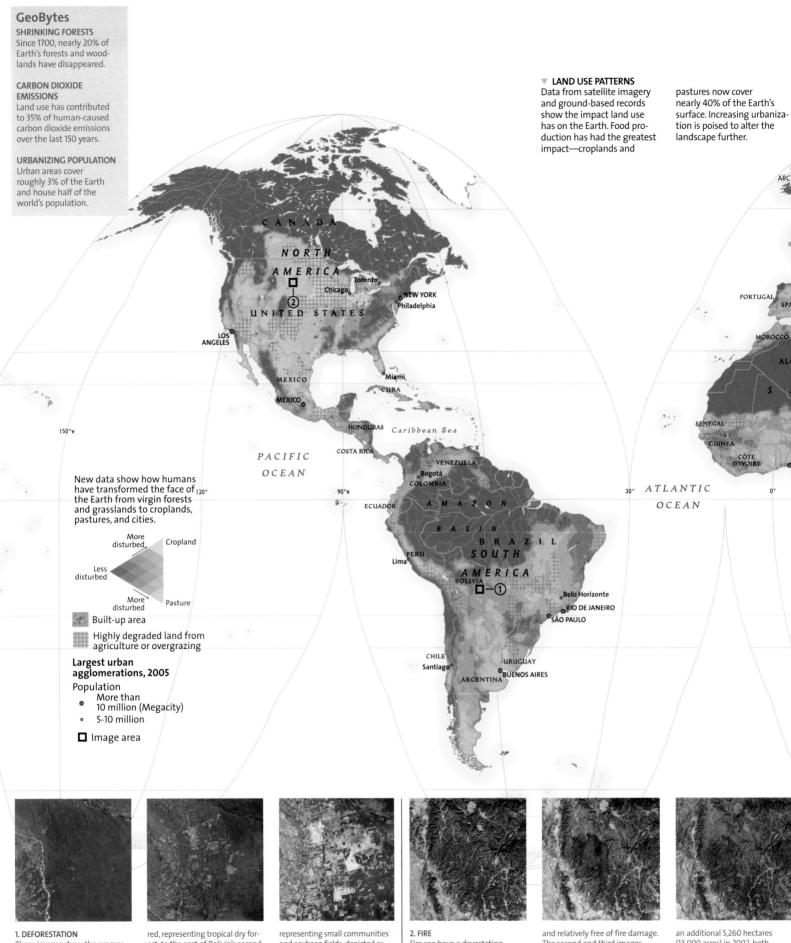

▼ **LAND USE PATTERNS**
Data from satellite imagery and ground-based records show the impact land use has on the Earth. Food production has had the greatest impact—croplands and pastures now cover nearly 40% of the Earth's surface. Increasing urbanization is poised to alter the landscape further.

New data show how humans have transformed the face of the Earth from virgin forests and grasslands to croplands, pastures, and cities.

Cropland
More disturbed
Less disturbed
More disturbed
Pasture

Built-up area

Highly degraded land from agriculture or overgrazing

Largest urban agglomerations, 2005
Population
- More than 10 million (Megacity)
- 5-10 million

□ Image area

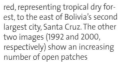

1. DEFORESTATION
These images show the progression of deforestation and increasing agricultural development in Bolivia. The first image (1975) shows a large expanse of solid red, representing tropical dry forest, to the east of Bolivia's second largest city, Santa Cruz. The other two images (1992 and 2000, respectively) show an increasing number of open patches representing small communities and soybean fields, depicted as light-colored rectangles, in areas that were once forested.

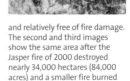

2. FIRE
Fire can have a devastating and immediate impact on the landscape. In 1999, the Black Hills of South Dakota were covered with vegetation, shown in green, and relatively free of fire damage. The second and third images show the same area after the Jasper fire of 2000 destroyed nearly 34,000 hectares (84,000 acres) and a smaller fire burned an additional 5,260 hectares (13,000 acres) in 2002, both shown in red. It will take decades for the area to recover.

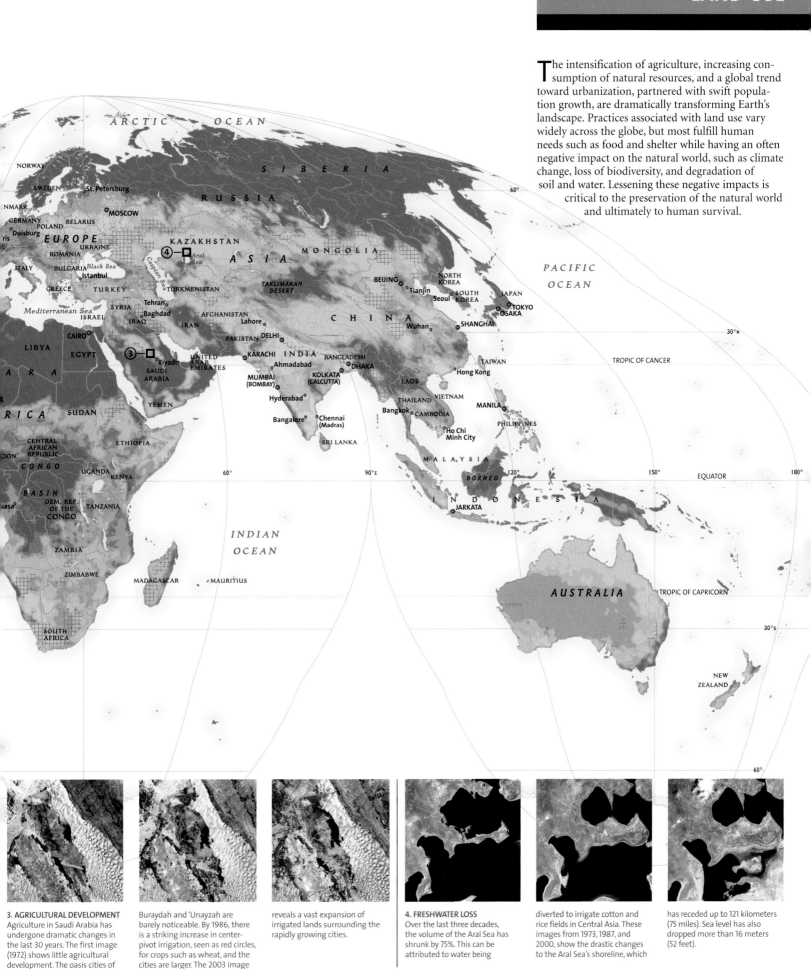

LAND USE

The intensification of agriculture, increasing consumption of natural resources, and a global trend toward urbanization, partnered with swift population growth, are dramatically transforming Earth's landscape. Practices associated with land use vary widely across the globe, but most fulfill human needs such as food and shelter while having an often negative impact on the natural world, such as climate change, loss of biodiversity, and degradation of soil and water. Lessening these negative impacts is critical to the preservation of the natural world and ultimately to human survival.

3. AGRICULTURAL DEVELOPMENT
Agriculture in Saudi Arabia has undergone dramatic changes in the last 30 years. The first image (1972) shows little agricultural development. The oasis cities of Buraydah and 'Unayzah are barely noticeable. By 1986, there is a striking increase in center-pivot irrigation, seen as red circles, for crops such as wheat, and the cities are larger. The 2003 image reveals a vast expansion of irrigated lands surrounding the rapidly growing cities.

4. FRESHWATER LOSS
Over the last three decades, the volume of the Aral Sea has shrunk by 75%. This can be attributed to water being diverted to irrigate cotton and rice fields in Central Asia. These images from 1973, 1987, and 2000, show the drastic changes to the Aral Sea's shoreline, which has receded up to 121 kilometers (75 miles). Sea level has also dropped more than 16 meters (52 feet).

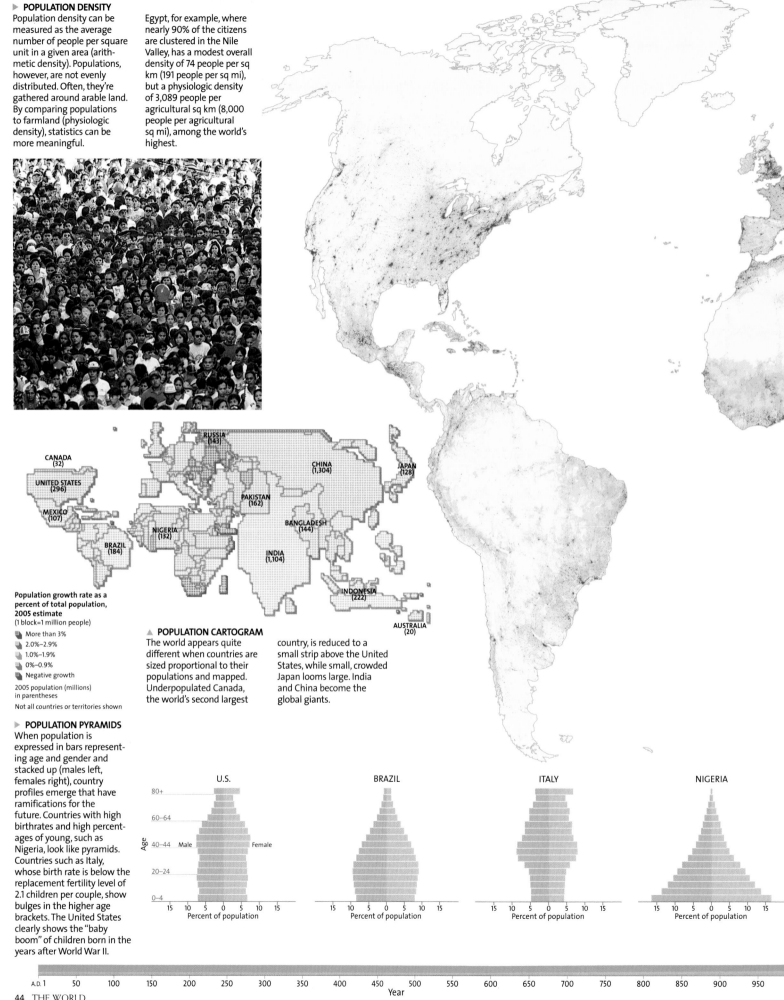

▶ POPULATION DENSITY

Population density can be measured as the average number of people per square unit in a given area (arithmetic density). Populations, however, are not evenly distributed. Often, they're gathered around arable land. By comparing populations to farmland (physiologic density), statistics can be more meaningful.

Egypt, for example, where nearly 90% of the citizens are clustered in the Nile Valley, has a modest overall density of 74 people per sq km (191 people per sq mi), but a physiologic density of 3,089 people per agricultural sq km (8,000 people per agricultural sq mi), among the world's highest.

Population growth rate as a percent of total population, 2005 estimate
(1 block=1 million people)

- More than 3%
- 2.0%–2.9%
- 1.0%–1.9%
- 0%–0.9%
- Negative growth

2005 population (millions) in parentheses

Not all countries or territories shown

CANADA (32)
UNITED STATES (296)
MEXICO (107)
BRAZIL (184)
RUSSIA (143)
CHINA (1,304)
JAPAN (128)
PAKISTAN (162)
NIGERIA (132)
BANGLADESH (144)
INDIA (1,104)
INDONESIA (222)
AUSTRALIA (20)

▲ POPULATION CARTOGRAM

The world appears quite different when countries are sized proportional to their populations and mapped. Underpopulated Canada, the world's second largest country, is reduced to a small strip above the United States, while small, crowded Japan looms large. India and China become the global giants.

▶ POPULATION PYRAMIDS

When population is expressed in bars representing age and gender and stacked up (males left, females right), country profiles emerge that have ramifications for the future. Countries with high birthrates and high percentages of young, such as Nigeria, look like pyramids. Countries such as Italy, whose birth rate is below the replacement fertility level of 2.1 children per couple, show bulges in the higher age brackets. The United States clearly shows the "baby boom" of children born in the years after World War II.

U.S.
Male | Female
Age: 80+, 60–64, 40–44, 20–24, 0–4
Percent of population: 15 10 5 0 5 10 15

BRAZIL
Percent of population: 15 10 5 0 5 10 15

ITALY
Percent of population: 15 10 5 0 5 10 15

NIGERIA
Percent of population: 15 10 5 0 5 10 15

A.D. 1 50 100 150 200 250 300 350 400 450 500 550 600 650 700 750 800 850 900 950 10
Year

Geographers approach the study of human populations, or demography, from a spatial perspective, asking why density, distribution, resources, births, deaths, and migrations vary from place to place. Earth's population, now at 6.5 billion, grows by 80 million a year, or 1.2% annually. The bulk of the increase occurs in developing countries in Asia, Africa, and Latin America. Physiologic density—the number of people per unit of agricultural land—shows concentrations in Asia, in particular in China and India; in Europe, from Britain into Russia; along the eastern seaboard of the United States; and in West Africa in Nigeria and along the Nile Valley.

GeoBytes

COUNTING HEADS
Most governments conduct a population census every ten years, although the process is expensive and accuracy is difficult to attain for most.

PACKED NEIGHBORHOODS
The most densely populated place in the world is Macau, a Chinese Special Administrative Region, with 18,960 people per sq km (47,400 people per sq mi). The least dense is Greenland.

IOWA VS. BANGLADESH
Bangladesh's rural population density is up to 12,950 per sq km (5,000 per sq mi) in an area the size of Iowa. In Iowa, the figure is fewer than 145 per sq km (55 per sq mi).

SHEER NUMBERS
The most populated country is the People's Republic of China, with 1.3 billion. The least populated jurisdiction is Pitcairn Island in the Pacific, with 46 people.

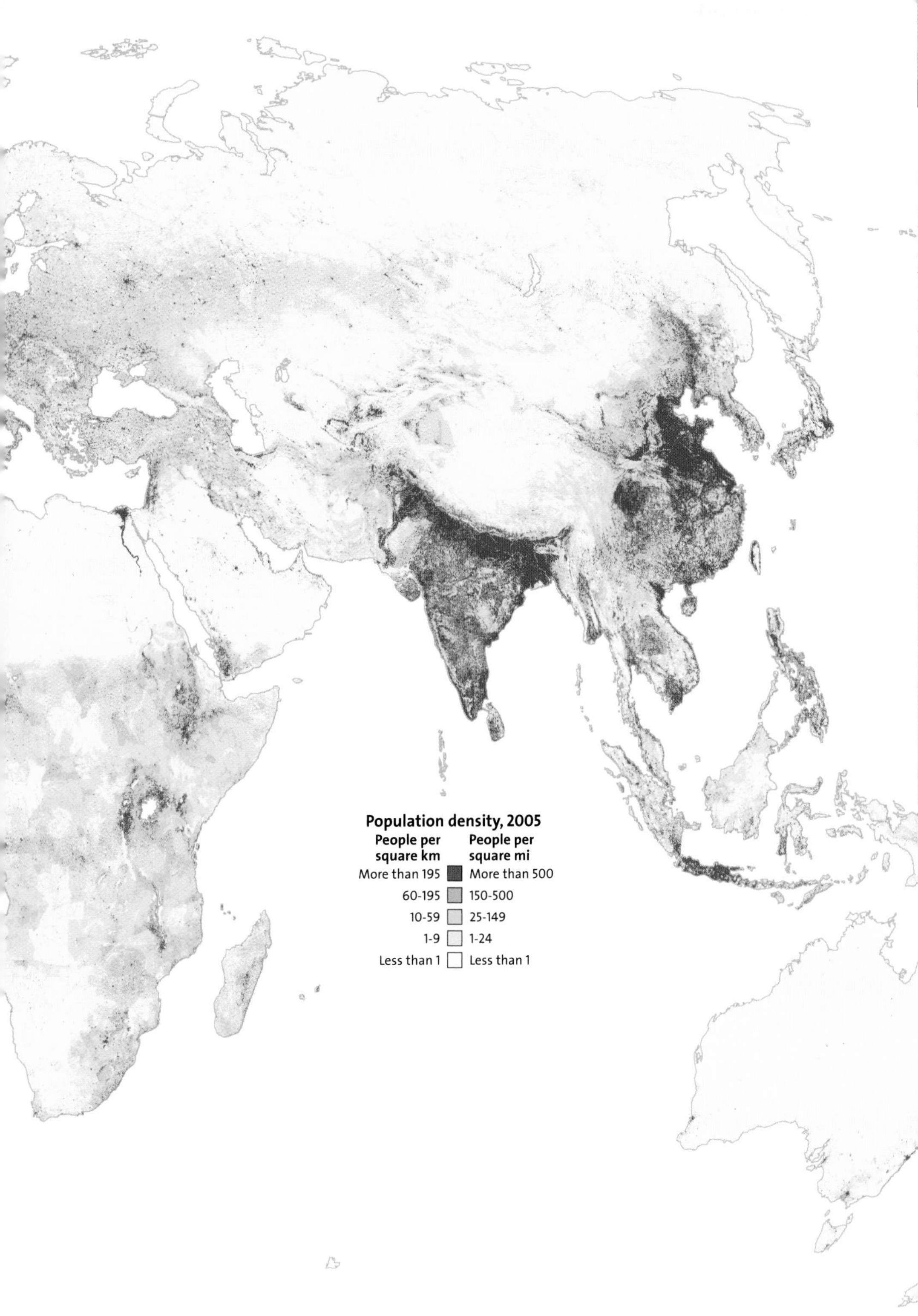

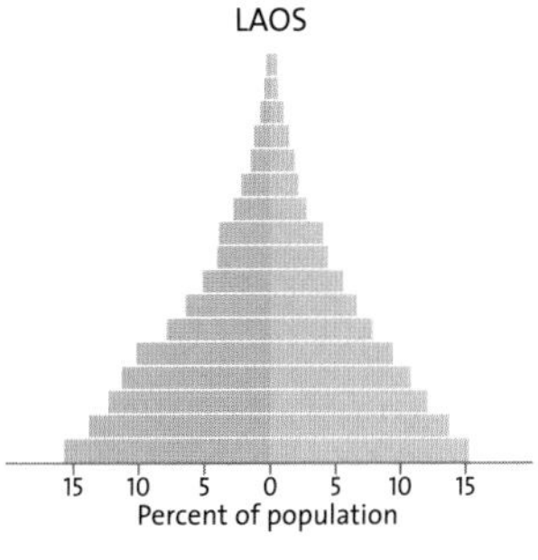

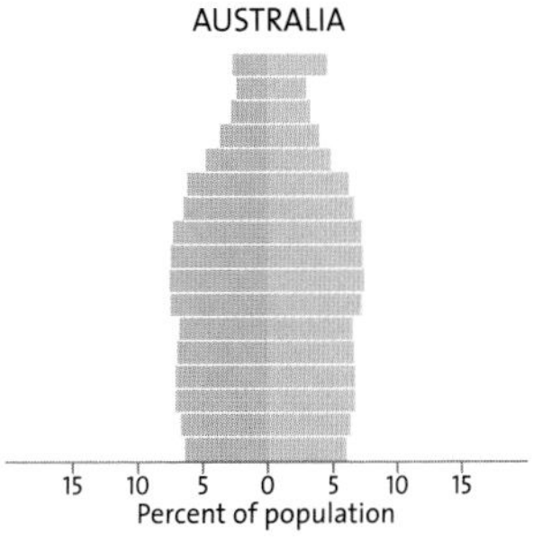

Population density, 2005

People per square km	People per square mi
More than 195	More than 500
60-195	150-500
10-59	25-149
1-9	1-24
Less than 1	Less than 1

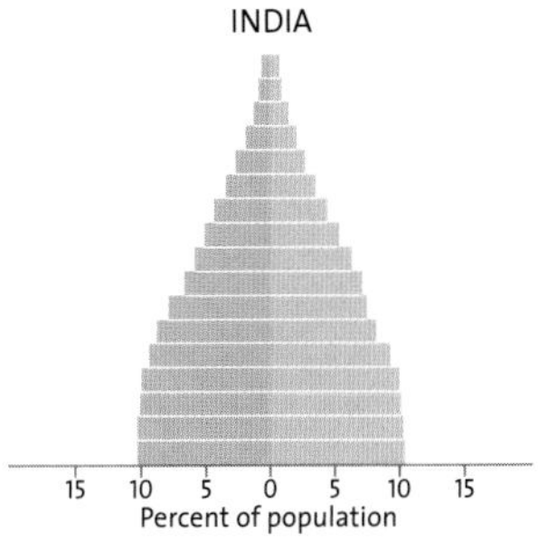

INDIA
Percent of population

LAOS
Percent of population

AUSTRALIA
Percent of population

REGIONAL POPULATION GROWTH
Earth's population has burgeoned since 1800, from approximately one billion to today's 6.5 billion. Africa is sustaining high fertility rates (average number of children per woman) and is projected to contain 21% of the world's population by 2050.

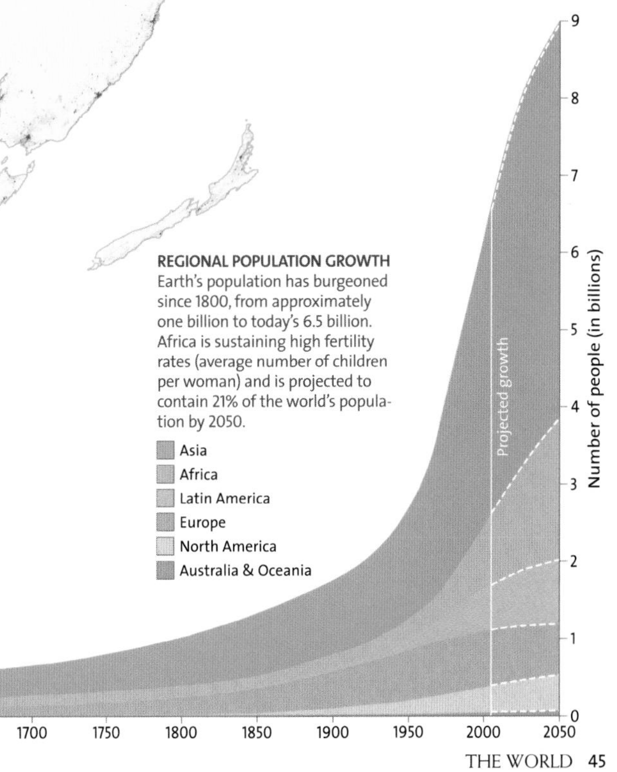

- Asia
- Africa
- Latin America
- Europe
- North America
- Australia & Oceania

Year

Number of people (in billions)

Projected growth

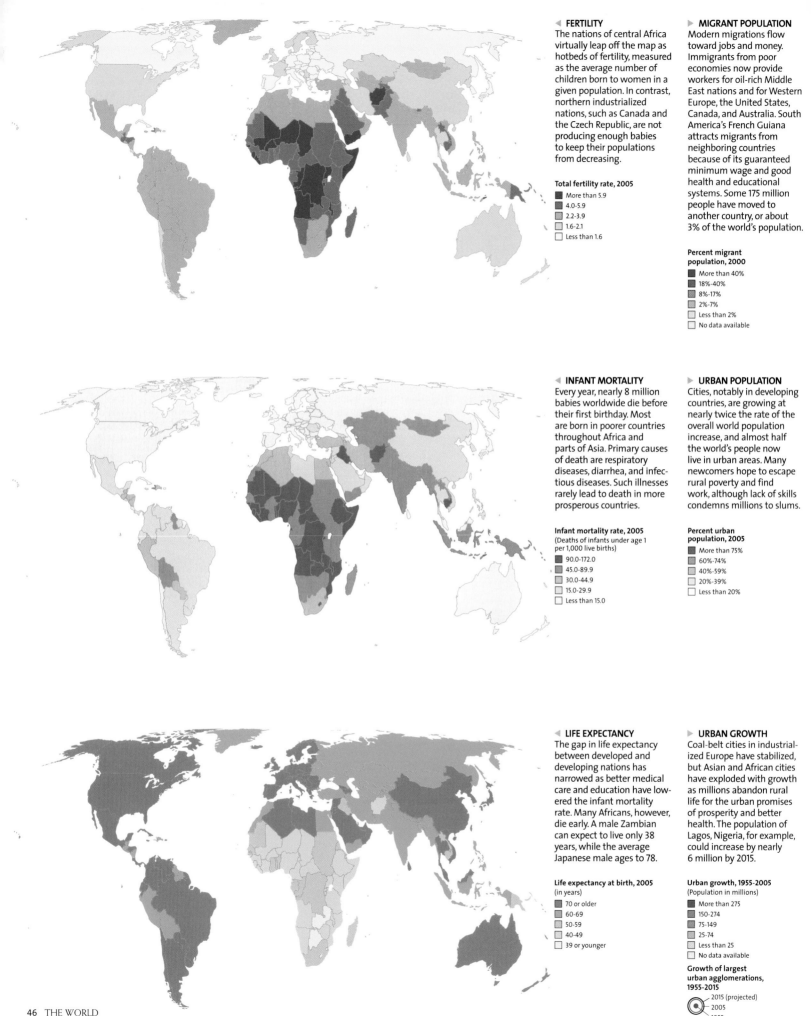

FERTILITY

The nations of central Africa virtually leap off the map as hotbeds of fertility, measured as the average number of children born to women in a given population. In contrast, northern industrialized nations, such as Canada and the Czech Republic, are not producing enough babies to keep their populations from decreasing.

Total fertility rate, 2005
- More than 5.9
- 4.0-5.9
- 2.2-3.9
- 1.6-2.1
- Less than 1.6

MIGRANT POPULATION

Modern migrations flow toward jobs and money. Immigrants from poor economies now provide workers for oil-rich Middle East nations and for Western Europe, the United States, Canada, and Australia. South America's French Guiana attracts migrants from neighboring countries because of its guaranteed minimum wage and good health and educational systems. Some 175 million people have moved to another country, or about 3% of the world's population.

Percent migrant population, 2000
- More than 40%
- 18%-40%
- 8%-17%
- 2%-7%
- Less than 2%
- No data available

INFANT MORTALITY

Every year, nearly 8 million babies worldwide die before their first birthday. Most are born in poorer countries throughout Africa and parts of Asia. Primary causes of death are respiratory diseases, diarrhea, and infectious diseases. Such illnesses rarely lead to death in more prosperous countries.

Infant mortality rate, 2005
(Deaths of infants under age 1 per 1,000 live births)
- 90.0-172.0
- 45.0-89.9
- 30.0-44.9
- 15.0-29.9
- Less than 15.0

URBAN POPULATION

Cities, notably in developing countries, are growing at nearly twice the rate of the overall world population increase, and almost half the world's people now live in urban areas. Many newcomers hope to escape rural poverty and find work, although lack of skills condemns millions to slums.

Percent urban population, 2005
- More than 75%
- 60%-74%
- 40%-59%
- 20%-39%
- Less than 20%

LIFE EXPECTANCY

The gap in life expectancy between developed and developing nations has narrowed as better medical care and education have lowered the infant mortality rate. Many Africans, however, die early. A male Zambian can expect to live only 38 years, while the average Japanese male ages to 78.

Life expectancy at birth, 2005
(in years)
- 70 or older
- 60-69
- 50-59
- 40-49
- 39 or younger

URBAN GROWTH

Coal-belt cities in industrialized Europe have stabilized, but Asian and African cities have exploded with growth as millions abandon rural life for the urban promises of prosperity and better health. The population of Lagos, Nigeria, for example, could increase by nearly 6 million by 2015.

Urban growth, 1955-2005
(Population in millions)
- More than 275
- 150-274
- 75-149
- 25-74
- Less than 25
- No data available

Growth of largest urban agglomerations, 1955-2015
- 2015 (projected)
- 2005
- 1955

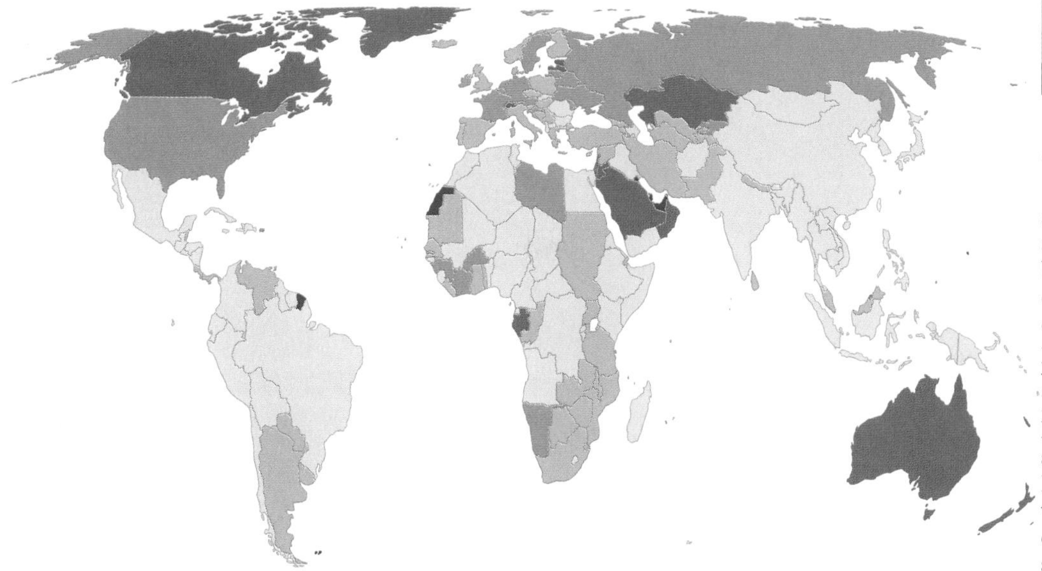

The 21st century will witness substantial world population growth, even as the rate of growth slows, total fertility rates decline, and populations age. Sheer numbers will increase simply because the base population is so great; the benchmark figure of 6 billion was reached in October 1999. By mid-century, up to 10 billion humans may be sharing the planet. Of the 80 million people being added each year, some 90% are born into developing countries. In some African and Muslim countries, one key to limiting growth is improving the status of women and their access to education and contraception. By 2050, the elderly could constitute 22% of the world's population, affecting economies, savings, employment, and health care. The toll of AIDS in sub-Saharan Africa and adult male mortality in some Eastern European countries are disturbing trends. In the future, cities will grow, and more people will cross international boundaries in search of employment and security.

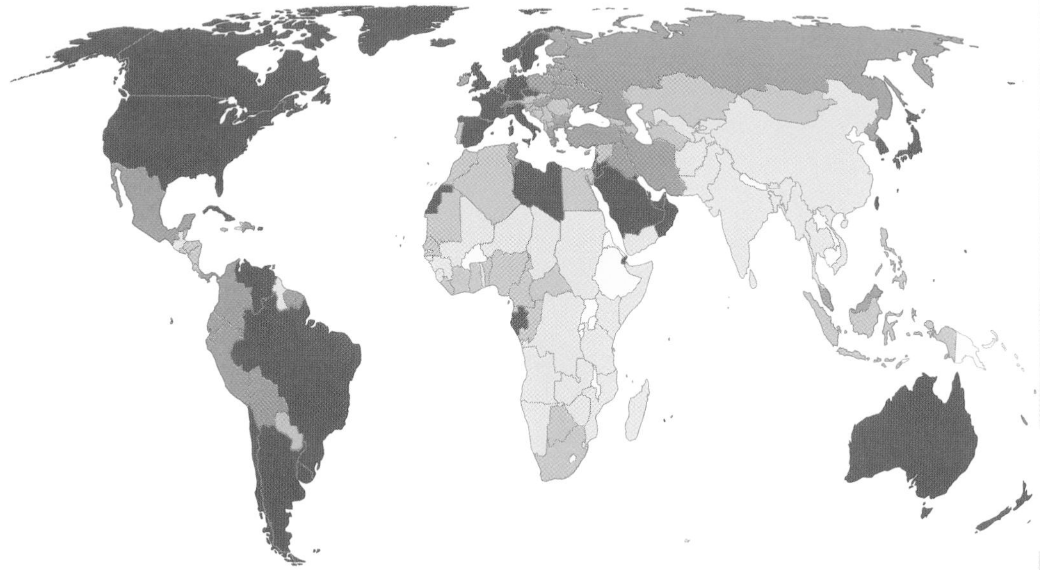

GeoBytes

PEOPLE THROUGH TIME
The total number of humans born since 50,000 B.C. is 106 billion.

FAST FORWARD
Today the world gains one billion people every 11 years. With current growth rates, world population could reach 10 billion by 2050.

SIX BILLION STRONG
At the beginning of the 21st century, world population stood at 6.4 billion people, or an estimated 6% of the total who have ever lived.

SMALL CITIES
Pre-Industrial Age cities were comparatively small. Rome, the largest city of antiquity, had only 350,000 people.

NATIVITY DISCREPANCY
The death rate of mothers during childbirth in developing countries is 22 times higher than that of women in the developed world.

MOST CHILDREN
In 2005, the the highest fertility rate in the world was in Niger, where women averaged eight children.

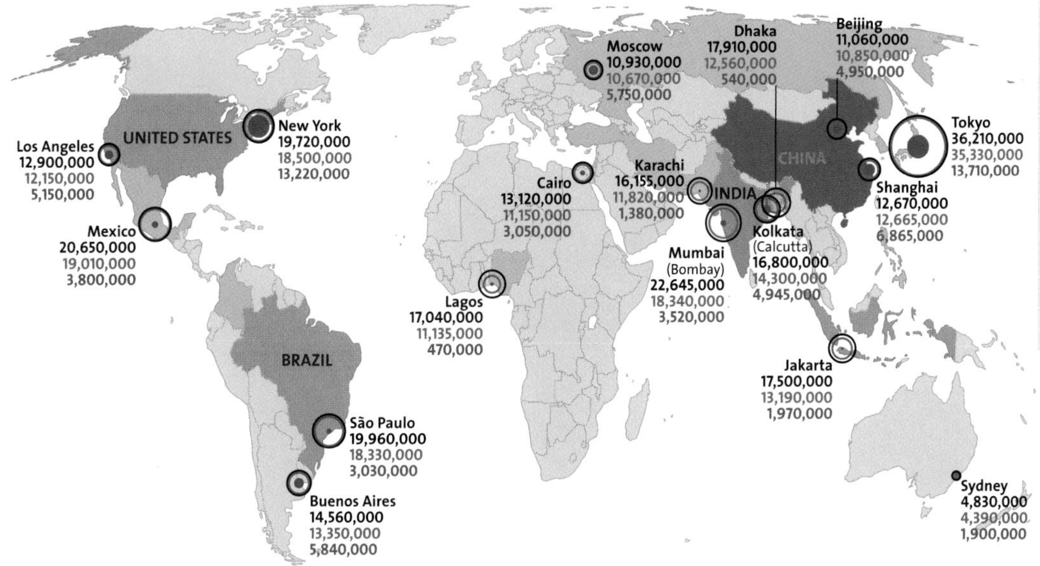

MOST POPULOUS COUNTRIES, Mid-2005

1	China	1,303,701,000	6	Pakistan	162,420,000
2	India	1,103,596,000	7	Bangladesh	144,233,000
3	United States	296,483,000	8	Russia	143,025,000
4	Indonesia	221,932,000	9	Nigeria	131,530,000
5	Brazil	184,184,000	10	Japan	127,728,000

MOST DENSELY POPULATED PLACES, Mid-2005

		Population density per sq km	(sq mi)
1	Macau	18,960	(47,400)
2	Monaco	16,500	(33,000)
3	Singapore	6,509	(16,847)
4	Hong Kong	6,338	(16,400)
5	Gibraltar	4,143	(9,667)
6	Vatican City	1,995	(3,990)
7	Malta	1,282	(3,320)
8	Bermuda	1,170	(2,952)
9	Bahrain	1,020	(2,639)
10	Maldives	987	(2,557)

Moscow
10,930,000
10,670,000
5,750,000

Dhaka
17,910,000
12,560,000
540,000

Beijing
11,060,000
10,850,000
4,950,000

Tokyo
36,210,000
35,330,000
13,710,000

Los Angeles
12,900,000
12,150,000
5,150,000

UNITED STATES

New York
19,720,000
18,500,000
13,220,000

Cairo
13,120,000
11,150,000
3,050,000

Karachi
16,155,000
11,820,000
1,380,000

INDIA

CHINA

Shanghai
12,670,000
12,665,000
6,865,000

Mexico
20,650,000
19,010,000
3,800,000

Kolkata
(Calcutta)
16,800,000
14,300,000
4,945,000

Mumbai
(Bombay)
22,645,000
18,340,000
3,520,000

Lagos
17,040,000
11,135,000
470,000

BRAZIL

Jakarta
17,500,000
13,190,000
1,970,000

São Paulo
19,960,000
18,330,000
3,030,000

Buenos Aires
14,560,000
13,350,000
5,840,000

Sydney
4,830,000
4,390,000
1,900,000

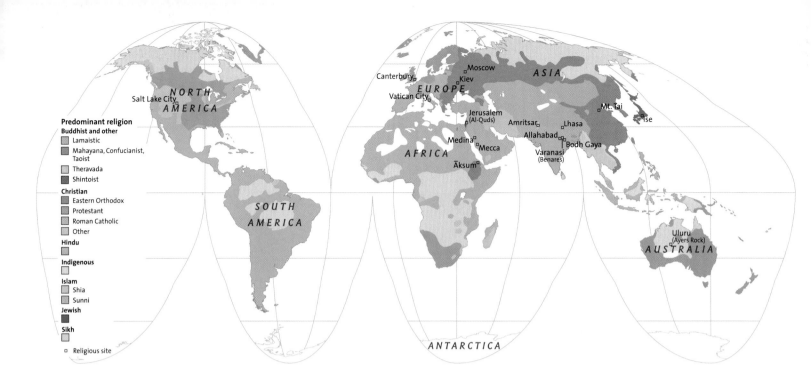

Predominant religion

Buddhist and other
- Lamaistic
- Mahayana, Confucianist, Taoist
- Theravada
- Shintoist

Christian
- Eastern Orthodox
- Protestant
- Roman Catholic
- Other

Hindu

Indigenous

Islam
- Shia
- Sunni

Jewish

Sikh

□ Religious site

NORTH AMERICA

Salt Lake City

SOUTH AMERICA

Canterbury
Vatican City
EUROPE
Moscow
Kiev
ASIA
Jerusalem (Al-Quds)
Medina
Mecca
Āksum
AFRICA
Amritsar
Allahabad
Lhasa
Bodh Gaya
Varanasi (Benares)
Mt. Tai
Ise

Uluru (Ayers Rock)
AUSTRALIA

ANTARCTICA

▼ WORLD LANGUAGES

Indo-European languages dominate the West, and English has become the language of aviation and technology. But a global language is not yet at hand. More people speak Mandarin Chinese than speak English, Spanish, German, and French combined. Half of the 6,000 languages in the world today are spoken by fewer than 10,000 people; a quarter by fewer than a thousand. Only a score are on the tongues of millions. After Mandarin Chinese and English, Hindi ranks third.

POPULATION vs LANGUAGE

Even as population increases, languages decline. Some 90% of languages today face extinction, leaving only about 600 languages worldwide.

Estimated number of languages (in thousands)

Population (in billions)

10,000 B.C.   A.D. 1   1500   1990   2100

▲ MAJOR RELIGIONS

Christianity, spread mostly by European conquest, has the most adherents of the five major religions, but a resurgent Islam has blossomed on the African-Asian axis. Hinduism and Buddhism today maintain wide blocs of the faithful in Asia, while the homeland of Judaism in Israel is a beleaguered bastion.

World religions (adherents in millions)

Christianity | Islam | Hinduism | Buddhism | Judaism

Asia 2,453.1
Africa 755.1 — Hinduism - 2.6, Buddhism - .15, Judaism - .22
Europe 592.1 — Hinduism - 1.5, Buddhism - 1.6, Judaism - 2.0
Latin America and the Caribbean 574.5 — Islam - 1.7, Hinduism - .77, Buddhism - .70, Judaism - 1.2
U.S. and Canada 289.7 — Islam - 5.1, Hinduism - 1.4, Buddhism - 3.1, Judaism - 6.2
Australia and Oceania 27.6 — Islam - .41, Hinduism - .42, Buddhism - .50, Judaism - .10

Total adherents in italics

REGIONAL RELIGION ADHERENCE

A high birth rate in Africa and Asia makes Islam the world's fastest growing religion; Christianity holds sway on the other continents.

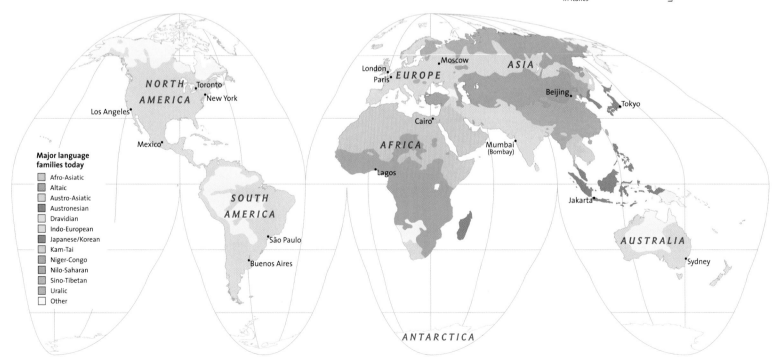

Major language families today

- Afro-Asiatic
- Altaic
- Austro-Asiatic
- Austronesian
- Dravidian
- Indo-European
- Japanese/Korean
- Kam-Tai
- Niger-Congo
- Nilo-Saharan
- Sino-Tibetan
- Uralic
- Other

NORTH AMERICA

Los Angeles
Toronto
New York
Mexico

SOUTH AMERICA

São Paulo
Buenos Aires

London
Paris
EUROPE
Moscow
ASIA
Beijing
Tokyo
Cairo
AFRICA
Mumbai (Bombay)
Lagos
Jakarta

AUSTRALIA
Sydney

ANTARCTICA

Religious adherence

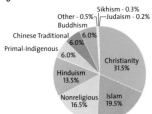

- Sikhism - 0.3%
- Judaism - 0.2%
- Other - 0.5%
- Buddhism
- Chinese Traditional 6.0%
- Primal-Indigenous 6.0%
- 6.0%
- Christianity 31.5%
- Hinduism 13.5%
- Nonreligious 16.5%
- Islam 19.5%

GeoBytes

FIRST URBANITES
The Sumerians developed the first city on the broad alluvial plain of the Tigris and Euphrates Rivers.

ACROSS THE STRAIT
Walking dry-shod across a land bridge, ancestors of Native Americans crossed into present-day Alaska from Siberia more than 14,000 years ago.

A TROVE OF LANGUAGES
Papua New Guinea is home to more than 800 languages.

CHINA KEPT OUTSIDERS OUT
The rulers of ancient China were so fearful of external influences that they shut off their kingdom for centuries. The quarantine led to technological stagnation.

STONE TOOLS IN AN AGE OF EXPLORATION
In Australia, Africa, South America, and India's Andaman and Nicobar Islands, European explorers found indigenous people living with Stone Age technology.

From the food we eat to the values we cherish, culture is at the heart of how we live and understand our human world. Not just a collection of customs, rituals, or artifacts, culture is a complex building up of ideas, innovation, and ideologies. Distinct cultures emerged in river valleys, along coastlines, on islands, and across land masses, as humans spread to every continent but Antarctica. Conquest and trade helped dominant cultures to expand. Today, electronic communication, transportation networks, and economic globalization bring major cultures closer. Cultural perceptions can play a part in misunderstanding and conflict. Yet cultures arose in the first place in response to a human need for stability and progress.

RELIGIOUS ADHERENCE
The classification of religion and adherents has changed over time. In Western thought and early "world-religion" writing, three religions were recognized: Judaism, Christianity, and Paganism. As Eastern history was more understood, other faiths were added to the list of world religions. Around 1800, the "big five" religions were classified as Judaism, Christianity, Islam, Hinduism, and Buddhism. Most recently, nonreligious has been added as an important segment.

SATELLITE IMAGES OF HOLY SITES
The Old City of Jerusalem surrounds Al' Aqsa Mosque and the Dome of the Rock (left). Al' Aqsa is the second oldest mosque in Islam after the Kaaba in Mecca and is third in holiness after the mosques in Mecca and Medina. It holds up to 400,000 worshippers at one time. The shrine of the Dome of the Rock, built in A.D. 692, commemorates the Prophet Muhammad's ascension to heaven. Also visible is the Western (Wailing) Wall of the Jews, the holiest site in the Jewish world. Part of the retaining wall supporting the Temple of Jerusalem built by Herod in 20 B.C., it is visited by Jews from all over the world. Here, too, is the Via Dolorosa, the traditional route of Christ's crucifixion. Christians pray along the route. The streets of Mecca huddle around the Kaaba (center), Islam's holiest shrine. At Allahabad, the Ganges and Yamuna Rivers (right) draw over 30 million Hindus to bathe in their waters during the Maha Kumbh Mela, the largest gathering of human beings ever recorded.

OLD CITY OF JERUSALEM, ISRAEL

MECCA, SAUDI ARABIA

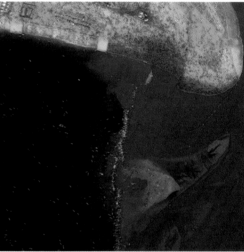

ALLAHABAD, INDIA

Indigenous languages
- Existing, marked in region of origin
- Nearly extinct

▲ STRUGGLING CULTURES
Almost by definition, the world's 5,000 indigenous cultures are struggling. They are the remnants of agricultural and hunter-gatherer societies that existed before modern nation-states. The world has passed them by. Yet, as ethnobiologist Wade Davis has written, "Each language is an old-growth forest of the mind, a watershed of thought, an ecosystem of spiritual possibilities."

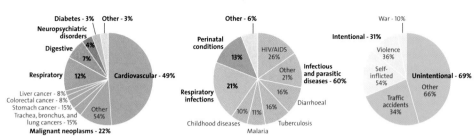

Causes of deaths as a percentage of world totals, 2002 estimates

Noncommunicable diseases – 59%
- Diabetes – 3%
- Other – 3%
- Neuropsychiatric disorders 4%
- Digestive 7%
- Respiratory 12%
- Cardiovascular – 49%
- Other 54%
- Malignant neoplasms – 22%
  - Liver cancer – 8%
  - Colorectal cancer – 8%
  - Stomach cancer – 15%
  - Trachea, bronchus, and lung cancers – 15%

Communicable diseases – 32%
- Other – 6%
- Perinatal conditions 13%
- HIV/AIDS 26%
- Other 21%
- Respiratory infections 21%
- Infectious and parasitic diseases – 60%
- Diarrhoeal 16%
- Childhood diseases 10%
- Malaria 11%
- Tuberculosis 16%

Injuries – 9%
- War – 10%
- Intentional – 31%
- Violence 36%
- Self-inflicted 54%
- Unintentional – 69%
- Other 66%
- Traffic accidents 34%

▲ HOW DO PEOPLE DIE?

Nearly one-third of those who die each year succumb to communicable diseases such as tuberculosis and HIV/AIDS, especially in developing nations where treatment is lacking. In deaths from injuries, suicide accounts for as many as war and violence combined. The aging populations of more developed nations more often die from noncommunicable, chronic conditions such as cardiovascular diseases and cancers.

▼ CARDIOVASCULAR DISEASE

Cardiovascular diseases—heart diseases and stroke—seem to be by-products of the more affluent lifestyle that afflicts the developed world, especially in Russia and Eastern Europe. Stress, alcohol abuse, smoking, inactivity, and diets lacking in fruits and vegetables and rich in cholesterol and saturated fats are risk factors that exacerbate the diseases that kill some 17 million people a year, nearly one-third of all deaths.

▼ HIV/AIDS

Acquired Immunodeficiency Syndrome (AIDS) came to the world's attention in the 1980s. Since then, more than 25 million people have died of the disease, which is carried by the Human Immunodeficiency Virus (HIV). Although HIV/AIDS symptoms can be stabilized by modern drugs, 40 million people remain infected at the end of 2005. Many of these live in countries where poverty, denial, lack of health-delivery systems, and drug production and patent problems limit access to prevention and treatment strategies.

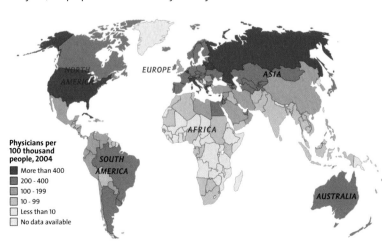

Cardiovascular deaths per 100 thousand people, 2002
- More than 400
- 300 to 400
- 200 to 299
- 100 to 199
- Less than 100
- No data

Percentage of adults (ages 15-49) living with HIV/AIDS, 2003
- 20.0% - 38.0%
- 10.0% - 19.9%
- 5.0% - 9.9%
- 2.0% - 4.9%
- 0.1% - 1.9%
- No data available

▼ DOCTORS WITHIN BORDERS

A shortage of physicians is critical in sub-Saharan African countries. Liberia and Eritrea, for example, had only three doctors for every 100,000 people in 2004. In contrast, Italy had 606, and Cuba, where health care is centralized, had 590. Now the gap between haves and have-nots is widening as many formerly socialist countries decentralize health care and physicians emigrate from poor societies to wealthier.

▼ MALARIA RAVAGES TROPICS

Malaria is a mostly tropical, parasitic disease transmitted from human to human by mosquito bites. Worldwide, over 500 million people suffer from illness caused by the malaria parasite. In sub-Saharan Africa exposure to malaria-infected mosquitoes is so intense that over a million people die each year. Use of insecticide-treated mosquito nets and new drugs to alleviate the disease will continue to make a difference while scientists work to develop an effective vaccine.

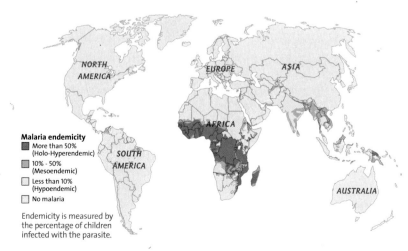

Physicians per 100 thousand people, 2004
- More than 400
- 200 - 400
- 100 - 199
- 10 - 99
- Less than 10
- No data available

Malaria endemicity
- More than 50% (Holo-Hyperendemic)
- 10% - 50% (Mesoendemic)
- Less than 10% (Hypoendemic)
- No malaria

Endemicity is measured by the percentage of children infected with the parasite.

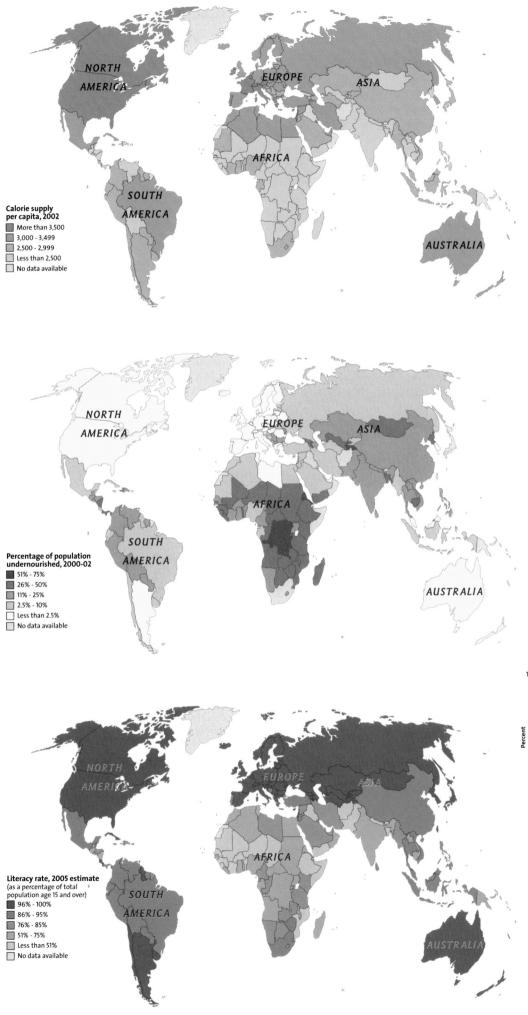

Calorie supply per capita, 2002
- More than 3,500
- 3,000 - 3,499
- 2,500 - 2,999
- Less than 2,500
- No data available

Percentage of population undernourished, 2000-02
- 51% - 75%
- 26% - 50%
- 11% - 25%
- 2.5% - 10%
- Less than 2.5%
- No data available

Literacy rate, 2005 estimate
(as a percentage of total population age 15 and over)
- 96% - 100%
- 86% - 95%
- 76% - 85%
- 51% - 75%
- Less than 51%
- No data available

Developed and developing nations show major differences in the rates and causes of death, with AIDS the most significant difference. Cardiovascular disease, the major cause of death in the developed world, is an increasing contributor to mortality in developing nations. Closely tied to health measurements are literacy rates—the percentage of a population who can read—mainly because literacy is an indicator of the reach and effectiveness of a nation's educational system. Educating girls and women improves health indices not only for females but for families. Girls' education makes a difference—in lowered infant mortality and overall mortality rates and in increased rates at which health care is sought.

◀ CALORIE CONSUMPTION

How many calories do people need to stay healthy? At least 2,500 a day. But Afghans consume a paltry 1,523 a day, and one-third of sub-Saharan African children are undernourished. In wealthy countries, such as the United States, high calorie intake means a high rate of obesity—a risk factor for heart disease, diabetes, and cancer. Middle-income countries, such as Mexico and Brazil, are beginning to confront their own epidemics of obesity.

◀ HUNGER

Although the world produces 20% more food than its population can consume, nearly a billion people suffer from chronic hunger, a condition provoked by drought, war, social conflicts, and inept public policy. Some five million children under age five die each year from lack of food. In sub-Saharan Africa, where desertification has overtaken agricultural lands and there is little irrigation, drought precedes famine.

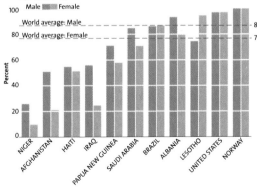

Male and female literacy rates, 2005 estimate
(as a percentage of total population age 15 and over)

Male / Female

World average: Male — 87%
World average: Female — 77%

NIGER, AFGHANISTAN, HAITI, IRAQ, PAPUA NEW GUINEA, SAUDI ARABIA, BRAZIL, ALBANIA, LESOTHO, UNITED STATES, NORWAY

◀ LITERACY

A nation's success depends on an educated population; thus illiteracy remains strongly tied to poverty. In some regions of Asia, Africa, and the Middle East, women suffer much higher rates of illiteracy than men, a reflection of a systematic social bias against them and a denial or discouragment of women's access to education.

▶ CURRENT GDP POPULATION DATA

Cartograms are value-by-area maps. As a graphic representation that depicts the size of an object (such as a country) in relation to an attribute (such as Gross Domestic Product or GDP per capita), cartograms do not delineate geographic space but rather express a thematic relationship. In the cartogram at right, each block represents one hundred U.S. dollars. With some geographical facsimile, countries are associated with neighboring countries and land masses, but the size of an individual country is related to its Gross Domestic Product per capita, that is, the value of final goods and services produced within a country in a year, divided by population. Luxembourg, a tiny inland area, is the giant among the nations of the world in terms of GDP per capita, at $58,900. The United States is next, at $40,100. Russia ranks a middling 82, at $9,800, in GDP per capita. Ranked 231 and 232 are Malawi and Timor-Leste (East Timor), at $600 and $400, respectively.

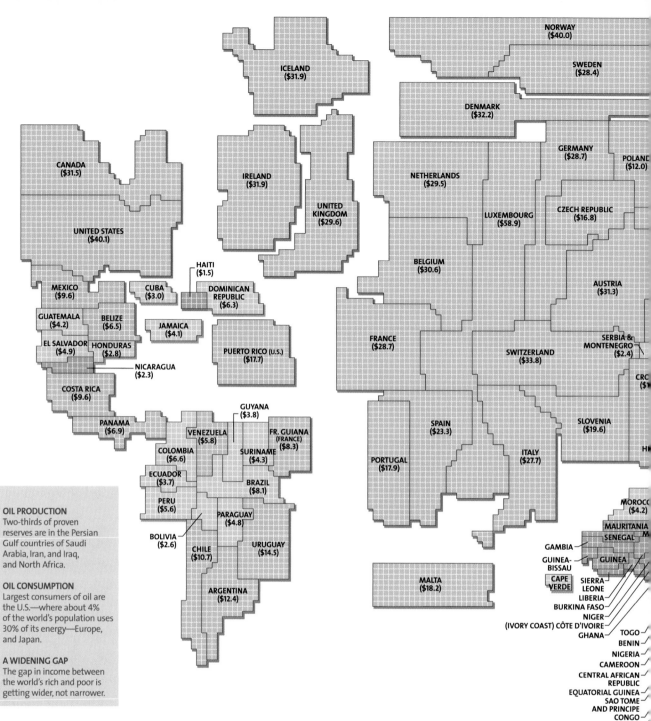

NORWAY ($40.0)

ICELAND ($31.9)

SWEDEN ($28.4)

DENMARK ($32.2)

GERMANY ($28.7)

POLAND ($12.0)

CANADA ($31.5)

IRELAND ($31.9)

NETHERLANDS ($29.5)

CZECH REPUBLIC ($16.8)

UNITED KINGDOM ($29.6)

LUXEMBOURG ($58.9)

UNITED STATES ($40.1)

BELGIUM ($30.6)

AUSTRIA ($31.3)

HAITI ($1.5)

MEXICO ($9.6)

CUBA ($3.0)

DOMINICAN REPUBLIC ($6.3)

SERBIA & MONTENEGRO ($2.4)

GUATEMALA ($4.2)

BELIZE ($6.5)

JAMAICA ($4.1)

FRANCE ($28.7)

SWITZERLAND ($33.8)

EL SALVADOR ($4.9)

HONDURAS ($2.8)

NICARAGUA ($2.3)

PUERTO RICO (U.S.) ($17.7)

CRO ($1

COSTA RICA ($9.6)

GUYANA ($3.8)

SPAIN ($23.3)

SLOVENIA ($19.6)

PANAMA ($6.9)

VENEZUELA ($5.8)

FR. GUIANA (FRANCE) ($8.3)

ITALY ($27.7)

H

COLOMBIA ($6.6)

SURINAME ($4.3)

PORTUGAL ($17.9)

ECUADOR ($3.7)

BRAZIL ($8.1)

MOROCCO ($4.2)

PERU ($5.6)

PARAGUAY ($4.8)

MAURITANIA

BOLIVIA ($2.6)

CHILE ($10.7)

URUGUAY ($14.5)

SENEGAL M

GAMBIA

GUINEA-BISSAU

GUINEA

MALTA ($18.2)

CAPE VERDE

SIERRA LEONE

ARGENTINA ($12.4)

LIBERIA

BURKINA FASO

NIGER

(IVORY COAST) CÔTE D'IVOIRE

GHANA

TOGO

BENIN

NIGERIA

CAMEROON

CENTRAL AFRICAN REPUBLIC

EQUATORIAL GUINEA

SAO TOME AND PRINCIPE

CONGO

DEM. REP. OF THE CONGO

GeoBytes

HUNTING AND GATHERING
This mode of production supported people for more than 95% of the time humans have lived on Earth.

NEOLITHIC REVOLUTION
Around 10,000 B.C., agriculture ushered in settled societies and increasing populations.

FIVE COUNTRIES
The largest deposits of strategic minerals, essential to industry, are concentrated in Canada, the U.S., Russia, South Africa, and Australia.

OIL PRODUCTION
Two-thirds of proven reserves are in the Persian Gulf countries of Saudi Arabia, Iran, and Iraq, and North Africa.

OIL CONSUMPTION
Largest consumers of oil are the U.S.—where about 4% of the world's population uses 30% of its energy—Europe, and Japan.

A WIDENING GAP
The gap in income between the world's rich and poor is getting wider, not narrower.

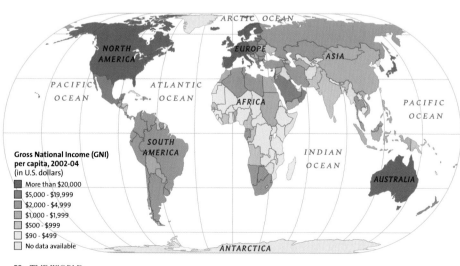

ARCTIC OCEAN

NORTH AMERICA

EUROPE

ASIA

PACIFIC OCEAN

ATLANTIC OCEAN

AFRICA

PACIFIC OCEAN

SOUTH AMERICA

INDIAN OCEAN

Gross National Income (GNI) per capita, 2002-04
(in U.S. dollars)
- More than $20,000
- $5,000 - $19,999
- $2,000 - $4,999
- $1,000 - $1,999
- $500 - $999
- $90 - $499
- No data available

AUSTRALIA

ANTARCTICA

◀ GROSS NATIONAL INCOME

Broad terms such as First or Third World, or the global North-South divide, conceal as much as they reveal. Yet the division between the haves and the have-nots is real. One measurement is Gross National Income at Purchasing Power Parity (GNI PPP), which measures a currency's buying power based on U.S. dollars. In 2004, GNI PPP ranged from Norway's high of $36,690 to a low of $500 in Sierra Leone.

NORTH AMERICA

(from ASIA)

ATLANTIC OCEAN

PACIFIC OCEAN

(to Japan)

SOUTH AMERICA

Gross Domestic Product (GDP) at Purchasing Power Parity (PPP), 2001-04 estimates
(in billions of U.S. dollars)
- $9,001 - $11,750
- $2,001 - $9,000
- $401 - $2,000
- $15 - $400
- Less than $15
- No data available
- Labor force migration

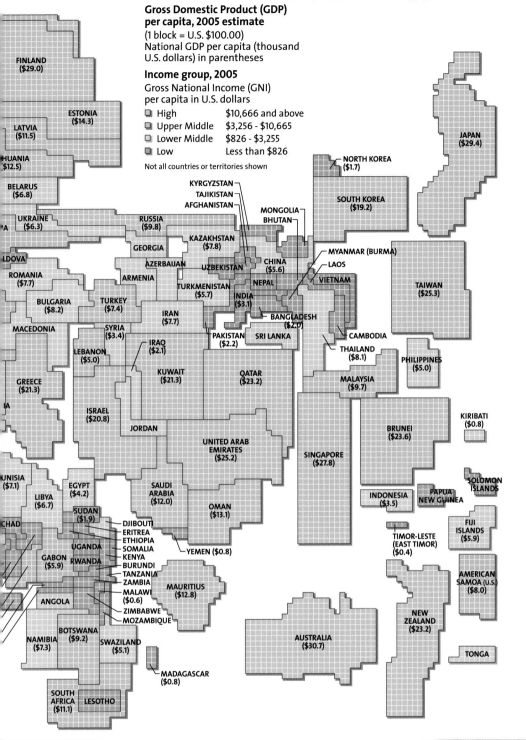

Gross Domestic Product (GDP) per capita, 2005 estimate
(1 block = U.S. $100.00)
National GDP per capita (thousand U.S. dollars) in parentheses

Income group, 2005
Gross National Income (GNI) per capita in U.S. dollars

High	$10,666 and above
Upper Middle	$3,256 - $10,665
Lower Middle	$826 - $3,255
Low	Less than $826

Not all countries or territories shown

FINLAND ($29.0)
ESTONIA ($14.3)
LATVIA ($11.5)
HUANIA ($12.5)
BELARUS ($6.8)
UKRAINE ($6.3)
A
LDOVA
ROMANIA ($7.7)
BULGARIA ($8.2)
MACEDONIA
GREECE ($21.3)
IA
UNISIA ($7.1)
LIBYA ($6.7)
CHAD
GABON ($5.9)
ANGOLA
NAMIBIA ($7.3)
BOTSWANA ($9.2)
SOUTH AFRICA ($11.1)
LESOTHO
SWAZILAND ($5.1)
MADAGASCAR ($0.8)
MAURITIUS ($12.8)
EGYPT ($4.2)
SUDAN ($1.9)
UGANDA
RWANDA
DJIBOUTI
ERITREA
ETHIOPIA
SOMALIA
KENYA
BURUNDI
TANZANIA
ZAMBIA
MALAWI ($0.6)
ZIMBABWE
MOZAMBIQUE
YEMEN ($0.8)
SAUDI ARABIA ($12.0)
OMAN ($13.1)
UNITED ARAB EMIRATES ($25.2)
QATAR ($23.2)
KUWAIT ($21.3)
ISRAEL ($20.8)
JORDAN
LEBANON ($5.0)
IRAQ ($2.1)
IRAN ($7.7)
SYRIA ($3.4)
TURKEY ($7.4)
PAKISTAN ($2.2)
AFGHANISTAN
TAJIKISTAN
KYRGYZSTAN
RUSSIA ($9.8)
KAZAKHSTAN ($7.8)
GEORGIA
AZERBAIJAN
ARMENIA
TURKMENISTAN ($5.7)
UZBEKISTAN
NEPAL
INDIA ($3.1)
BANGLADESH ($2.0)
SRI LANKA
MONGOLIA
BHUTAN
CHINA ($5.6)
MYANMAR (BURMA)
LAOS
VIETNAM
THAILAND ($8.1)
CAMBODIA
NORTH KOREA ($1.7)
SOUTH KOREA ($19.2)
JAPAN ($29.4)
TAIWAN ($25.3)
PHILIPPINES ($5.0)
MALAYSIA ($9.7)
SINGAPORE ($27.8)
BRUNEI ($23.6)
INDONESIA ($3.5)
PAPUA NEW GUINEA
KIRIBATI ($0.8)
SOLOMON ISLANDS
TIMOR-LESTE (EAST TIMOR) ($0.4)
FIJI ISLANDS ($5.9)
AMERICAN SAMOA (U.S.) ($8.0)
NEW ZEALAND ($23.2)
AUSTRALIA ($30.7)
TONGA

The world's economies are increasingly interrelated. The exchange of farm products, natural resources, manufactured goods, and services benefits trading partners by allowing them to sell what they best produce at home and buy what is economical for them to purchase from overseas. Regional trade is on the rise, as agreements among countries offer each other preferential access to markets, improving the economy of neighboring blocs of countries and the general standard of living. Nevertheless, the stark difference between high- and low-income countries is apparent in a cartogram, which depicts quantitative data not dependent on scale or area. Dominant economies generally occupy the Northern Hemisphere. Oil-rich countries in the Middle East hold their own. The burden of poverty falls mainly on countries in sub-Saharan Africa and in Asia.

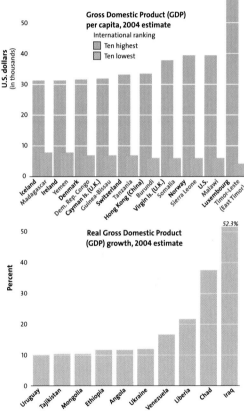

Gross Domestic Product (GDP) per capita, 2004 estimate
International ranking
- Ten highest
- Ten lowest

$58.9

U.S. dollars (in thousands)

Iceland, Madagascar, Ireland, Yemen, Denmark, Dem. Rep. Congo, Cayman Is. (U.K.), Guinea-Bissau, Switzerland, Tanzania, Hong Kong (China), Burundi, Virgin Is. (U.K.), Somalia, Norway, Sierra Leone, U.S., Malawi, Luxembourg, Timor-Leste (East Timor)

Real Gross Domestic Product (GDP) growth, 2004 estimate

52.3%

Percent

Uruguay, Tajikistan, Mongolia, Ethiopia, Angola, Ukraine, Venezuela, Liberia, Chad, Iraq

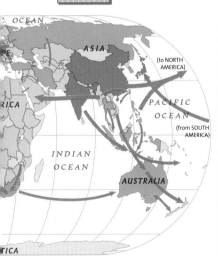

LABOR MIGRATION
Globalization has made migration from low GDP countries to high GDP counties easier, but integrating this new labor force into the social fabric of destination countries has become a major public policy issue.

(to NORTH AMERICA)
(from SOUTH AMERICA)

OCEAN
ASIA
PACIFIC OCEAN
INDIAN OCEAN
AUSTRALIA
RICA
TICA

WORLD EMPLOYMENT
Manufacturing–the production of goods from raw materials–long powered industrialized societies such as the U.S., Europe, and Japan, now more service oriented. Manufacturing is increasingly important in developing economies.

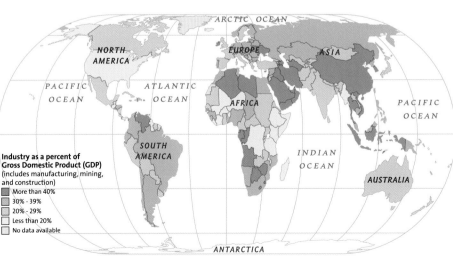

Industry as a percent of Gross Domestic Product (GDP) (includes manufacturing, mining, and construction)
- More than 40%
- 30% - 39%
- 20% - 29%
- Less than 20%
- No data available

ARCTIC OCEAN
NORTH AMERICA
EUROPE
ASIA
PACIFIC OCEAN
ATLANTIC OCEAN
AFRICA
PACIFIC OCEAN
SOUTH AMERICA
INDIAN OCEAN
AUSTRALIA
ANTARCTICA

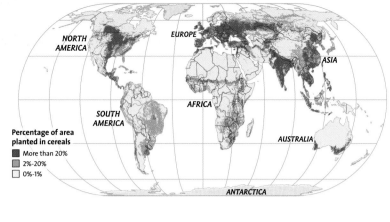

Percentage of area
planted in cereals
- More than 20%
- 2%-20%
- 0%-1%

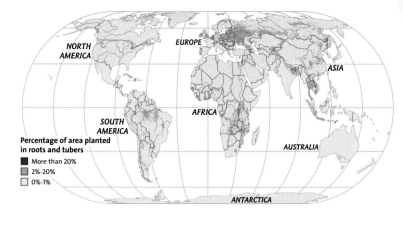

Percentage of area planted
in roots and tubers
- More than 20%
- 2%-20%
- 0%-1%

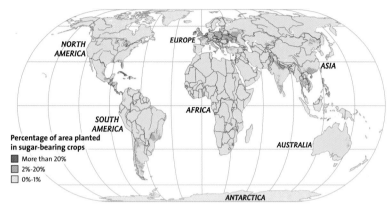

Percentage of area planted
in sugar-bearing crops
- More than 20%
- 2%-20%
- 0%-1%

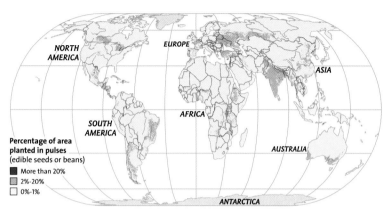

Percentage of area
planted in pulses
(edible seeds or beans)
- More than 20%
- 2%-20%
- 0%-1%

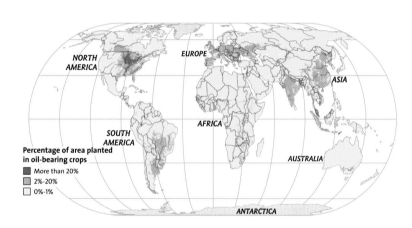

Percentage of area planted
in oil-bearing crops
- More than 20%
- 2%-20%
- 0%-1%

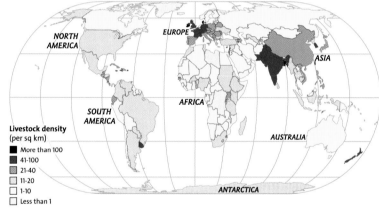

Livestock density
(per sq km)
- More than 100
- 41-100
- 21-40
- 11-20
- 1-10
- Less than 1

▲ CEREALS
Cereal grains, including barley, maize, millet, rice, rye, sorghum, and wheat, are agricultural staples across the globe. They cover 61% of the world's cultivated land and contribute more calories and protein to the human diet than any other food group.

▲ SUGAR-BEARING CROPS
Our taste for sweetness is met by two sugar-bearing crops: sugarcane and sugar beets. Sugarcane is grown in the subtropics, mostly in the Caribbean and Florida. Sugar beets thrive in the temperate latitudes of the Northern Hemisphere, primarily in Europe.

▲ OIL-BEARING CROPS
Major oil-bearing crops—soybeans, groundnuts, rapeseed, sunflower, and oil palm fruit—account for 10% of the total calories available for human consumption. Asia and the Americas are the largest producers of these crops, with soybeans contributing the greatest share.

▲ ROOTS AND TUBERS
Although cultivation of tubers such as cassava, potatoes, sweet potatoes, taro, and manioc makes up less than 5% of the world's harvested area, these foods are staples across the globe and are critical to subsistence farming in Africa, Asia, and Latin America.

▲ PULSES
Pulses—the edible seeds of legumes such as dry beans, chick-peas, and lentils—have two to three times as much protein as most cereals. They are cultivated broadly, but nearly 90% of the world's crop is consumed in developing countries.

▲ ANIMAL PRODUCTS
Consumption of meat, milk, and eggs, all high-protein foods, is unequal across the globe. Wealthier industrialized nations consume 30% more meat than developing nations. With population growth, rising incomes, and urbanization, worldwide demand for animal products is increasing.

◄ MAIZE
Corn, or maize, was domesticated 6,000 years ago in Mexico. It is now intensively grown in the United States, China, along Africa's Rift Valley, and throughout Eastern Europe. Although it remains a staple food, more than 70% of the world's harvest is for animal feed.

◄ WHEAT
Wheat—the most widely grown cereal—is cultivated across the globe. Most of it is grown, however, in the temperate latitudes of the Northern Hemisphere. Wheat, mainly in baked goods, is a major source of calories for more than half of the world's population.

◄ RICE
Rice plays a dominant role in the agriculture and diet of Asia. Nearly 90% of the world's rice is consumed and produced in Asia, mostly on small family farms. Larger scale commercial cultivation of rice takes place in the southern United States, southern Australia, and the Amazon Basin.

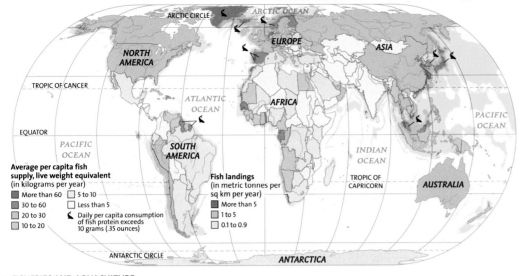

▲ FISHERIES AND AQUACULTURE

Fish is a vital source of protein for much of the world. Yet the world's primary fisheries are under stress from overfishing and environmental degradation. The tonnage of fish caught in the wild has remained relatively stable over the past five years, while tonnage of fish produced by aquaculture has increased markedly. Aquaculture, primarily in freshwater environments, now accounts for more than 30% of total fish production. China leads in aquaculture production, growing more than two-thirds of all farm-raised fish.

More than 850 million people worldwide do not have access to adequate food. Hunger, found across the globe and even in the richest countries, is chronic in rural areas of the developing world, places not always well suited for agriculture or managed for sustainable yield. Other countries with climates and soils better suited to agriculture, such as the United States, grow and consume far more food than is required to meet the needs of their populations. We are faced with closing this gap between the hungry and the overfed at a time when the world's population, mostly in developing countries, is expected to grow by three billion over the next 50 years. Lack of space for cropland expansion, climate change, and environmental stresses such as deforestation, desertification, and erosion add to the challenge of agricultural management and productivity.

World diets, 2003
(as a percentage of daily calorie consumption)

Cereals* - excluding beer
Fruits* - excluding wine
Milk* - excluding butter

NORTH AMERICA

EUROPE

AUSTRALIA & OCEANIA

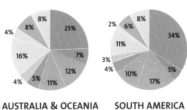
SOUTH AMERICA

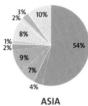
ASIA

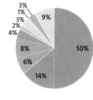
AFRICA

▲ WHAT THE WORLD EATS

The foods people eat vary widely and are chosen on the basis of availability, income, and cultural preference. Cereals, arguably the most significant food source worldwide, make up a large percentage of diets in Africa and Asia. High caloric foods—sugars, meats, and oils—make up a significant portion of diets in Oceania, the Americas, and Europe.

▼ GENETICALLY MODIFIED AGRICULTURE

Planting of genetically modified (GM) or "biotech" crops, mainly soybeans, corn, cotton, and canola, is still conservative but on the rise despite continued debate over ecological impacts and human health hazards. GM crops first became an industry in 1996. Some 75% of GM planting today is in countries such as the United States, Argentina, Canada, and Brazil. Some developing nations are beginning to grow GM crops in hopes of increasing output in areas where traditional crops do not meet the needs of the population.

▶ DISTRIBUTION OF CROPS

The distribution of the world's staple crops varies across the globe. Wheat, maize, and barley thrive in the temperate climates of the United States, Europe, and Australia, whereas sugarcane is better suited to the tropical climate of the Caribbean. Rice thrives in high rainfall areas of Asia, and drought-resistant crops such as millet and sorghum are staples of drier places, such as the Sahel on the southern fringe of the Sahara Desert in Africa.

PERCENTAGE OF WORLD CROP PRODUCTION BY REGION

Highest producers		Lowest producers	
Conterminous U.S.	87%	Caribbean	60%
Maize	28%	Sugarcane	36%
Wheat	26%	Maize	8%
Soybean	24%	Pulses*	6%
Cotton	5%	Rice	6%
Sorghum	4%	Cassava	4%
Central Asia	87%	Eastern Africa	59%
Wheat	51%	Maize	27%
Barley	23%	Pulses*	10%
Cotton	9%	Sorghum	9%
Millet	2%	Cassava	8%
Rye	2%	Rice	5%
Australia & New Zealand	85%	East Asia	57%
Wheat	51%	Rice	20%
Barley	18%	Wheat	17%
Pulses*	11%	Maize	12%
Sorghum	3%	Soybean	5%
Sugarcane	2%	Rapeseed	3%
Southern Africa	84%	Southern Europe	51%
Maize	54%	Wheat	21%
Wheat	15%	Barley	16%
Sunflower	6%	Maize	6%
Sorghum	5%	Sunflower	6%
Sugarcane	4%	Pulses*	2%

*Pulses-edible seeds or beans

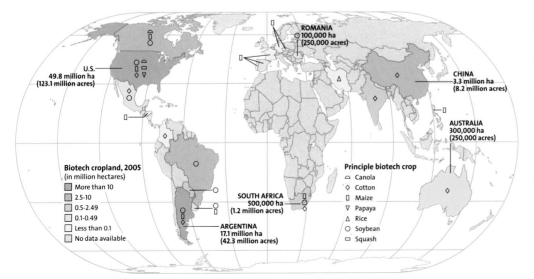

GeoBytes

AGRICULTURAL HEARTLANDS
The world's largest agricultural areas are in China, Australia, the United States, Kazakhstan, the Russian Federation, Brazil, Argentina, India, and Saudi Arabia.

GM CROPS
Nearly 30% of the world's total area of soybeans, maize, cotton, and canola is planted with genetically modified (GM) varieties.

UNEQUAL CONSUMPTION
On average, people in North America and Europe consume more than 3,000 calories per day, whereas people in some African countries consume barely half that. In countries such as Eritrea, the Democratic Republic of the Congo, and Burundi, up to 70% of the population is undernourished.

Common interests encourage neighboring countries to form trade blocs to benefit from increased trade and growth. Trade blocs steer a course between protectionism and unbridled capitalism. Such agreements fall into two classes: free trade zones, such as NAFTA (North American Free Trade Agreement), which removes internal tariffs but allows participants to set external tariffs; and customs unions, such as the EU (European Union), in which all agree to common outside tariffs.

NORTH AMERICA
EUROPE ASIA
AFRICA
SOUTH AMERICA
AUSTRALIA

Most active regional trade blocs, 2005

- Agadir Agreement
- Andean Community
- APEC - Asia-Pacific Economic Cooperation
- ASEAN - Association of Southeast Asian Nations
- CACM - Central American Common Market
- CARICOM - Caribbean Community and Common Market
- CEMAC - Economic and Monetary Community of Central Africa
- COMESA - Common Market for Eastern and Southern Africa
- EAC - East African Community
- Not an active bloc member
- ECOWAS - Economic Community of West African States
- EU - European Union
- EurAsEC - Eurasian Economic Community
- GCC - Gulf Cooperation Council
- MERCOSUR - Southern Common Market
- NAFTA - North American Free Trade Agreement
- PARTA - Pacific Regional Trade Agreement
- SAARC - South Asian Association for Regional Cooperation
- SACU - Southern African Customs Union

GeoBytes

LARGEST TRADE BLOC
The European Union (EU) member states account for nearly one-third of the global economy, making the EU the largest economic body in the world.

LARGEST ECONOMY
The country with the largest economy is the United States, with an income of more than $12 trillion.

LARGEST ASIAN ECONOMY
Japan has the world's second largest economy at $4.7 trillion—the biggest in Asia.

LARGEST EUROPEAN ECONOMY
Germany maintains the largest economy in Europe, with a national income of more than $2.4 trillion.

LARGEST SOUTH AMERICAN ECONOMY
The Brazilian economy, which exceeds $550 billion, dominates South America.

▶ **WORLD DEBT**
Debt hinders many developing countries. The World Bank classifies countries by debt level. A country with debt at or above 80% of its gross national income (GNI) is classified as severely indebted and in danger of defaulting on loans.

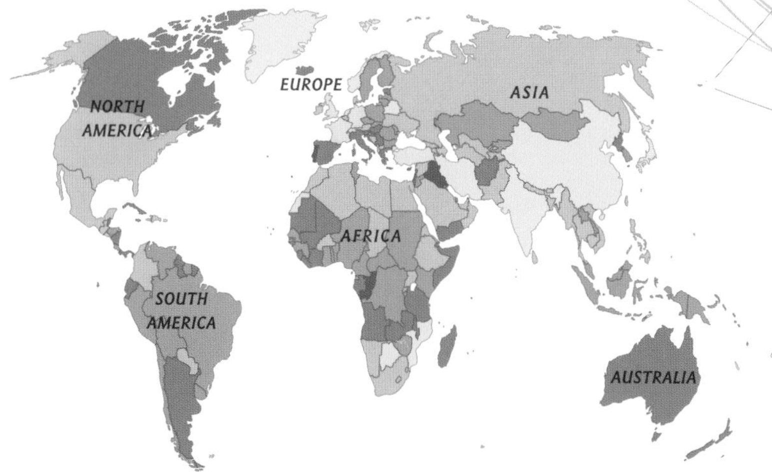

Estimated external debt as a percentage of Gross Domestic Product (GDP) at Purchasing Power Parity, 2002-04 estimates
(GDP PPP based upon U.S. dollars)

- More than 100%
- 30% - 100%
- 15% - 29%
- 5% - 14%
- Less than 5%
- No data available

NIUE (NEW ZEALAND)
AMERICAN SAMOA (U.S.)

NORTH AMERICA
GUATEMALA
BELIZE
NICARAGUA
CUBA
Latin America
DOMINICAN REPUBLIC
ST. VINCENT AND THE GRENADINES
VENEZUELA
ANTIGUA AND BARBUDA
ST. LUCIA
ARGENTINA
TRINIDAD AND TOBAGO
SURINAME
SOUTH AMERICA
GREENLAND (DENMARK)
ICELAND
FAROE ISLANDS (DENMARK)
URUGUAY
WESTERN SAHARA (MOROCCO)
GAMBIA
B. FA BEN
GUINEA-BISSAU
E
CÔTE D'IVOIRE (IVORY COAS

NORTH AMERICA
EUROPE ASIA
AFRICA
SOUTH AMERICA
AUSTRALIA

▲ **TRADE FLOW**
International trade of goods is a major avenue of globalization. The arrows above show the value of trade between major regions of the world. More than half of world trade occurs between high-income areas such as Japan, the United States, and Western Europe. Trade is increasing, however, between these high-income countries and developing countries in Asia, South America, and Africa. Lowered trade barriers offer opportunities for low-income countries, although still limited. Labor-intensive merchandise, such as textiles, can be produced and exported at a low cost from developing

To multinational corporations, globalization means that products can be produced in multiple locations and distributed worldwide. To consumers, globalization means lower prices. To governments, globalization can mean job losses, multinational mergers, and price-fixing cartels. While the benefits of globalization have not been universally shared, it has been a force in bringing economic growth. The World Trade Organization (WTO) works with governments and international organizations to regulate trade and reduce economic inequality among countries. Global integration increases the flow of trade, capital, information, and people across borders by reducing or eliminating trade restrictions and customs barriers. Globalization presents both challenges and opportunities—for new markets, jobs, and export-led growth.

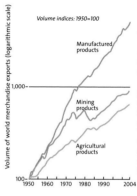

GROWTH OF TRADE
Since World War II, manufactured exports have grown faster than other products. Transnational corporations are the primary leaders of the growth and globalization of trade. These companies locate factories and sell products outside their country of origin. For example, Toyota has 12 plants in Japan, with 53 manufacturing companies in 27 other countries, and it sells vehicles in more than 170 countries.

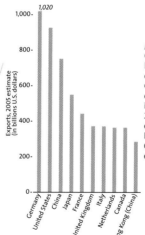

MERCHANDISE EXPORTS
China has risen quickly to become the third-largest exporter of merchandise after Germany. China's growth rate exceeds that of any large industrial country. From 2000 to 2004, the value of merchandise exports grew by 24% annually, largely due to the undervalued Chinese currency that makes exports cheap.

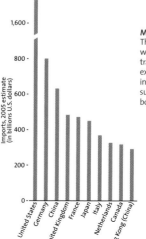

MERCHANDISE IMPORTS
The United States is by far the world's largest importer—the U.S. trade deficit (more imports than exports) approached $725 billion in 2005. China's growing trade surplus is fueling an economic boom in that country.

nations. Trade in agricultural commodities is a key issue between developing and high-income countries. Two billion families in the world make a living from farming. About 60 countries are dependent on commodities for more than 40% of their export income—in some African countries the figure is 80%. Stormy meetings of the World Trade Organization (WTO) focus on making the European Union (EU) and the United States end subsidies to their farmers to increase trade opportunities for developing nations.

Income Group, 2005
Gross National Income (GNI) per capita in U.S. dollars

High	$10,066 and above
Upper middle	$3,256 - $10,065
Lower middle	$826 - $3,255
Low	Less than $826
No data available	

Interregional merchandise trade
(in billions of U.S. dollars)

- $240 and above
- $120 - $240
- $60 - $119
- $30 - $59
- $5 - $29
- Less than $5

● Stock exchange (World Federation of Exchanges member)

Single-commodity-dependent economy
(commodity comprising more than 40 percent of total exports)

- ☐ Agriculture
- ◇ Cotton
- ⊖ Crude oil and petroleum products
- ✺ Fishing
- ✕ Gems, metals, and minerals
- △ Machinery and equipment
- ▣ Textiles and apparel

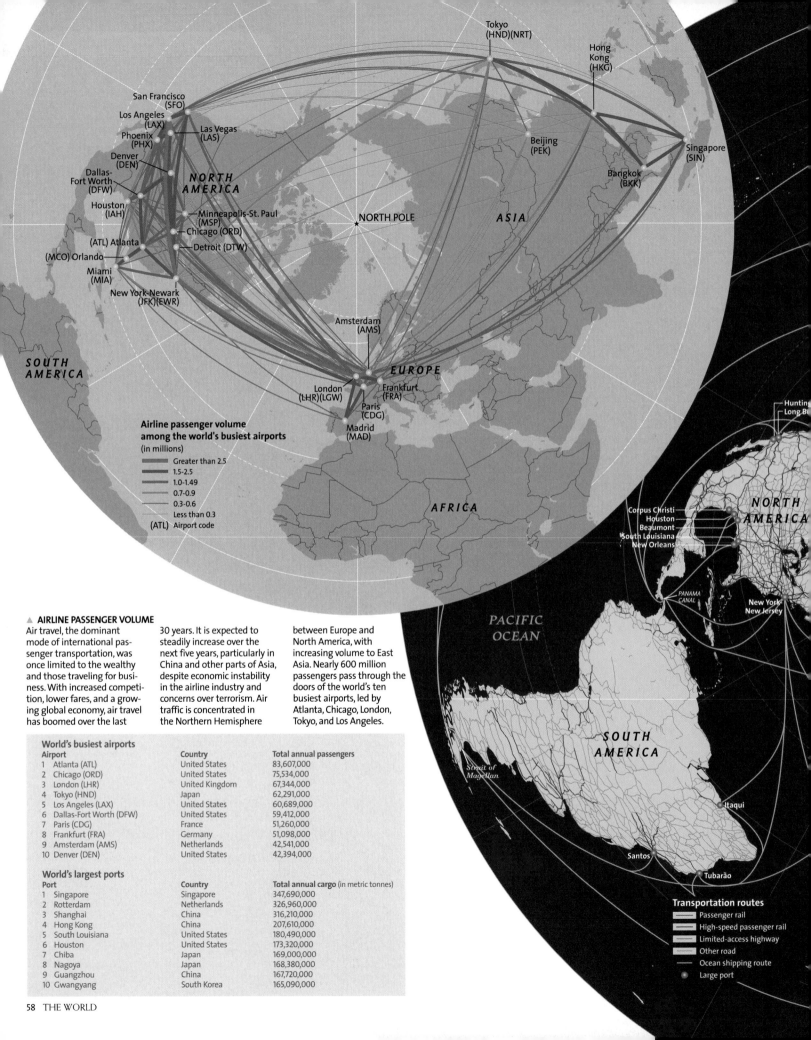

Airline passenger volume among the world's busiest airports

(in millions)

▬▬▬	Greater than 2.5
▬▬▬	1.5-2.5
▬▬▬	1.0-1.49
────	0.7-0.9
────	0.3-0.6
────	Less than 0.3
(ATL)	Airport code

▲ AIRLINE PASSENGER VOLUME

Air travel, the dominant mode of international passenger transportation, was once limited to the wealthy and those traveling for business. With increased competition, lower fares, and a growing global economy, air travel has boomed over the last 30 years. It is expected to steadily increase over the next five years, particularly in China and other parts of Asia, despite economic instability in the airline industry and concerns over terrorism. Air traffic is concentrated in the Northern Hemisphere between Europe and North America, with increasing volume to East Asia. Nearly 600 million passengers pass through the doors of the world's ten busiest airports, led by Atlanta, Chicago, London, Tokyo, and Los Angeles.

World's busiest airports

	Airport	Country	Total annual passengers
1	Atlanta (ATL)	United States	83,607,000
2	Chicago (ORD)	United States	75,534,000
3	London (LHR)	United Kingdom	67,344,000
4	Tokyo (HND)	Japan	62,291,000
5	Los Angeles (LAX)	United States	60,689,000
6	Dallas-Fort Worth (DFW)	United States	59,412,000
7	Paris (CDG)	France	51,260,000
8	Frankfurt (FRA)	Germany	51,098,000
9	Amsterdam (AMS)	Netherlands	42,541,000
10	Denver (DEN)	United States	42,394,000

World's largest ports

	Port	Country	Total annual cargo (in metric tonnes)
1	Singapore	Singapore	347,690,000
2	Rotterdam	Netherlands	326,960,000
3	Shanghai	China	316,210,000
4	Hong Kong	China	207,610,000
5	South Louisiana	United States	180,490,000
6	Houston	United States	173,320,000
7	Chiba	Japan	169,000,000
8	Nagoya	Japan	168,380,000
9	Guangzhou	China	167,720,000
10	Gwangyang	South Korea	165,090,000

Transportation routes

▬▬▬	Passenger rail
▬▬▬	High-speed passenger rail
▬▬▬	Limited-access highway
▬▬▬	Other road
────	Ocean shipping route
●	Large port

Throughout history, the movement of goods and people linked places and their economies. Early transport was undertaken on foot or by animals such as horses and camels. Long distances were traveled over water by pole and current-propelled boats, then by oar and later by sail. With the introduction of mechanical means of transport—steamboats, railroad locomotives, and eventually automobiles and airplanes—movement from place to place accelerated rapidly. Speed, efficiency, and safety are some of the metrics of modern transportation systems. Today, people and goods move quickly about the world via a web of land, sea, and air networks that together keep the global economy humming.

GeoBytes

SAVING TIME BY CANAL
With the opening of the Suez Canal in 1869, the journey from London to Mumbai (Bombay) shrunk from nearly six months to about two months.

SAVING TIME BY TRAIN
First launched in Japan in 1964, high-speed trains can carry passengers at speeds exceeding 300 kph (186 mph). Europe, East Asia, and the U.S. have adopted fast trains to provide national, inter-urban transport.

◀ **TRANSPORTATION ROUTES**
Nearly all of the world's freight headed for international destinations is transported via ships in standardized containers. These sealed metal containers have dramatically altered the face of international freight transport. They are designed to be easily transferred from one mode of transport to another, for instance, from a ship to a train, thereby increasing efficiency and reducing cost. As with passenger airline traffic, maritime freight traffic is concentrated. The largest 15 ports, led by Singapore, Rotterdam, Shanghai, Hong Kong, and South Louisiana, handle more than 50% of global freight traffic.

PACIFIC OCEAN

AUSTRALIA

Newcastle
Gladstone
Hay Point

Tokyo
Chiba
Yokohama
Nagoya
Kobe
Osaka
Kitakyushu
Busan
Ulsan
Gwangyang
Incheon
Shanghai
Ningbo

Port
Headland
Dampier

Kaohsiung
Guangzhou
Shenzhen
Hong Kong

Qingdao
Dalian
Qinhuangdao
Tianjin

Singapore
Port Kelang

Strait of
Malacca

ARCTIC OCEAN

NORTH POLE

ASIA

INDIAN OCEAN

Vancouver

Strait of
Hormuz

Hamburg
Grimsby & Immingham
Amsterdam
Rotterdam
Antwerp
Le Harve

EUROPE

Bosporus

Dubai

Marseille

SUEZ CANAL

Algeciras
Strait of
Gibraltar

ATLANTIC OCEAN

AFRICA

Richards Bay

COMMUNICATIONS SATELLITES

Although satellites do not have the voice and data carrying capacity of fiber-optic cables, they remain a vital component of global communication services. They serve large geographic areas, making them well-suited to television and radio broadcasting, maritime and aeronautical communications, emergency services, and fleet management. In areas underserved by landlines, including much of Asia and Africa, they provide mobile phone service and Internet connectivity.

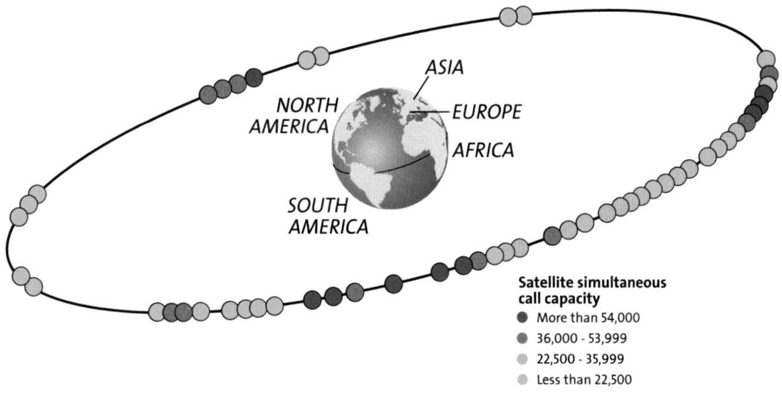

ASIA
NORTH AMERICA
EUROPE
AFRICA
SOUTH AMERICA

Satellite simultaneous call capacity
- More than 54,000
- 36,000 - 53,999
- 22,500 - 35,999
- Less than 22,500

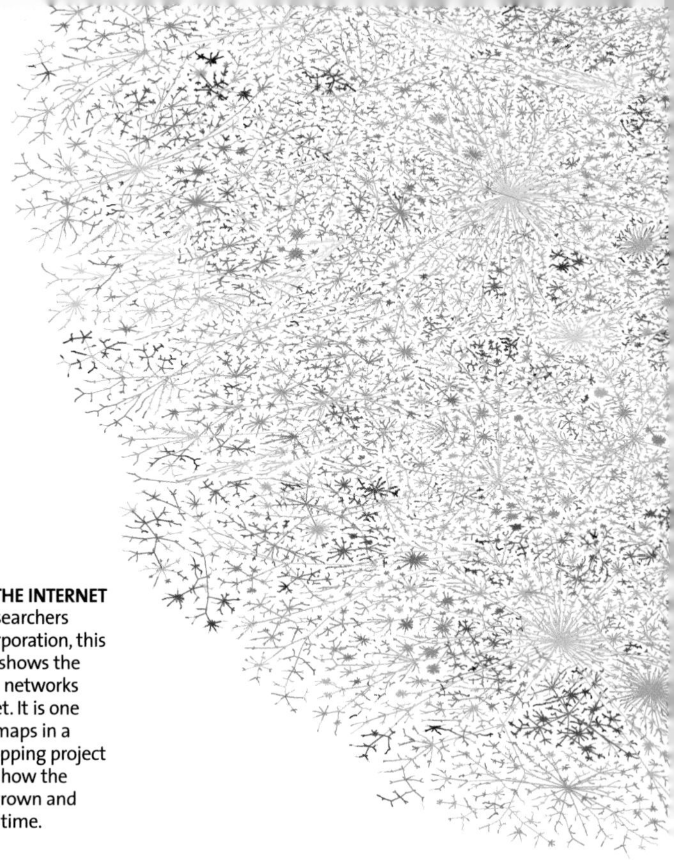

MAPPING THE INTERNET

Created by researchers at Lumeta Corporation, this tree-like map shows the paths of most networks on the Internet. It is one of a series of maps in a long-term mapping project documenting how the Internet has grown and changed over time.

INTERNET EXPLOSION

With more than one billion users worldwide, the Internet is a powerful, if unequally distributed, form of global communication. The U.S. leads in Internet usage, with about one-fifth of all users. In 2005, China displaced Japan for the second-highest number of users, but the 100 million Chinese users represent fewer than 10% of the county's population.

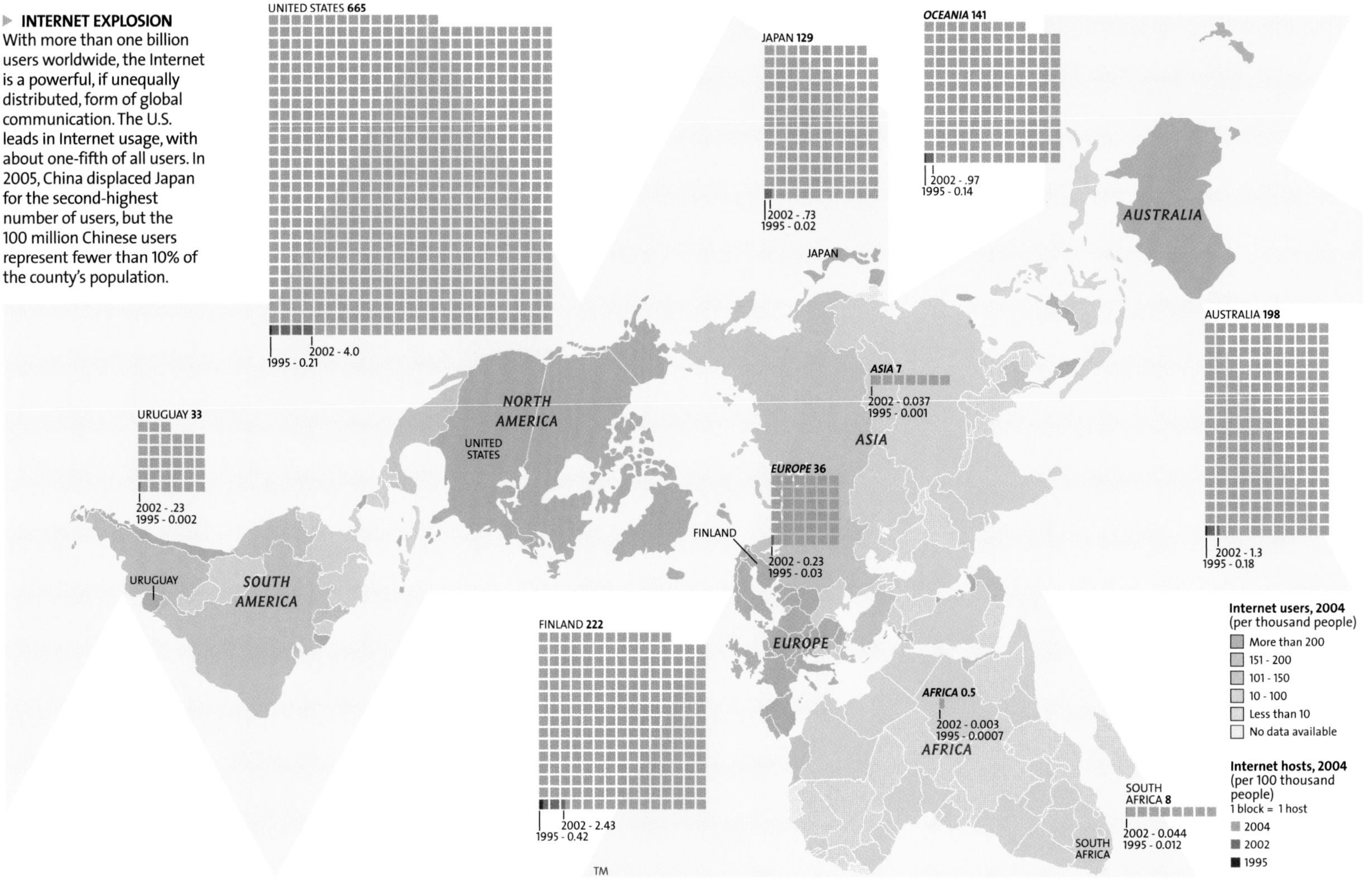

UNITED STATES **665**
2002 - 4.0
1995 - 0.21

JAPAN **129**
2002 - .73
1995 - 0.02

OCEANIA **141**
2002 - .97
1995 - 0.14

AUSTRALIA **198**
2002 - 1.3
1995 - 0.18

URUGUAY **33**
2002 - .23
1995 - 0.002

ASIA **7**
2002 - 0.037
1995 - 0.001

EUROPE **36**
2002 - 0.23
1995 - 0.03

FINLAND **222**
2002 - 2.43
1995 - 0.42

AFRICA **0.5**
2002 - 0.003
1995 - 0.0007

SOUTH AFRICA **8**
2002 - 0.044
1995 - 0.012

NORTH AMERICA
UNITED STATES
URUGUAY
SOUTH AMERICA
FINLAND
EUROPE
ASIA
AUSTRALIA
JAPAN
AFRICA
SOUTH AFRICA

Internet users, 2004
(per thousand people)
- More than 200
- 151 - 200
- 101 - 150
- 10 - 100
- Less than 10
- No data available

Internet hosts, 2004
(per 100 thousand people)
1 block = 1 host
- 2004
- 2002
- 1995

TM

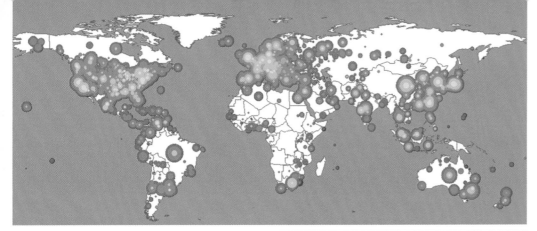

▲ **SPREAD OF A COMPUTER VIRUS**
This map shows the spread of the CodeRed worm on July 19, 2001, which disproportionately affected small businesses and home users. Some 360,000 computers were infected, spreading in early (yellow), middle (orange), and late (red) zones. Clearly, not all software programs are benign. Programs designed to intentionally disrupt, damage, or interfere with computer functions, files, and data are commonly referred to as computer viruses. Much like human-spread viruses, they range in complexity, severity and speed of transmission. One particularly fast-spreading type of virus is called worms. They spread themselves automatically by controlling other software programs such as email.

GeoBytes

EXPLOSIVE GROWTH
In 1981, the Internet had barely more than 200 host computers. Today there are more than 400 million, with millions more being added every month.

MOBILE WORLD
More than 75% of the world's population lives within range of a mobile phone network, whereas only 50% have access to a fixed-line telephone.

TV AND RADIO
In the last thirty years, television viewers in the developing world have multiplied 55 fold. The number of radios per 1,000 habitants has more than doubled.

U.S. OWNS THE SKIES
The United States owns more than half of the world's satellites, with Russia a distant second. Other satellite holders include Japan and China. Satellites serve a mix of civilian, commercial, and military uses.

Advances in and widespread use of communication technologies have quickly changed the face of international communication. Enormous amounts of data can be shared nearly instantaneously, and voice communication is now possible across much of the globe. Neither would have been possible a few decades ago when nearly all telecommunication services were carried over copper wire. The Internet has fostered entrepreneurship, helped open new markets, created new industries and jobs, and provided accessibility to and sharing of vast amounts of information. Cellular phones have made voice communication a reality for many who previously had no access to land-line phone service. And without the widespread network of fiber-optic cables, the rapid transmission of volumes of data and crystal-clear voice communication—hallmarks of international communication today—would not be possible. Although these technologies have helped foster communication and economic activity across the globe, they are not truly global. Many areas, both in the developed and developing world, do not have access to these technologies, creating a divide between the digital haves and have-nots.

▶ **CONNECTING THE PLANET**
The world is increasingly connected by underground and undersea fiber-optic cables and cellular networks. Fiber-optic cables allow for lightening-fast transmission of email, data, and voice calls, whereas cellular technology has extended phone service to parts of the world previously without any land-line service, including rural regions in Asia and Africa.

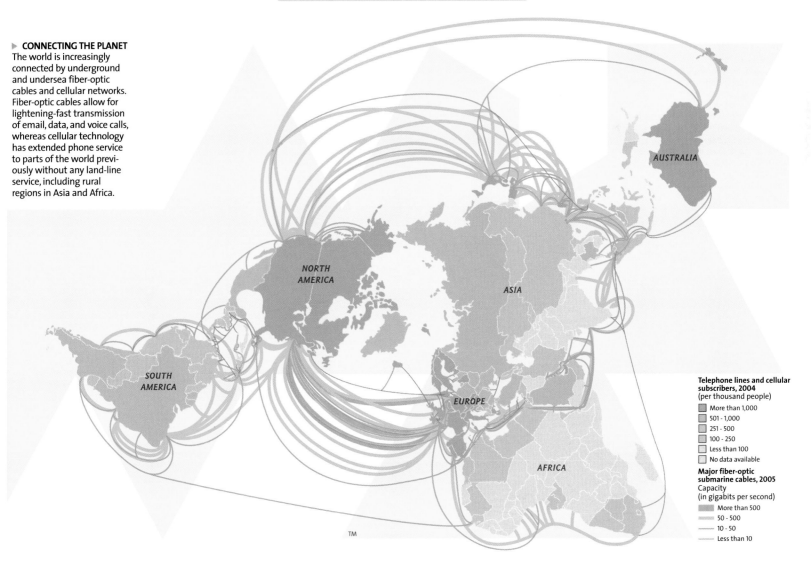

Telephone lines and cellular subscribers, 2004
(per thousand people)
- More than 1,000
- 501 - 1,000
- 251 - 500
- 100 - 250
- Less than 100
- No data available

Major fiber-optic submarine cables, 2005
Capacity
(in gigabits per second)
- More than 500
- 50 - 500
- 10 - 50
- Less than 10

► ENERGY CONSUMPTION

The use and availability of primary energy resources are unequally distributed across the globe. More than 86% of energy consumed globally is from nonrenewable fossil fuels—coal, oil, and natural gas. Consumption of these fuels is greatest in industrialized nations, with the U.S. using up nearly one-quarter. Developing countries, especially those in sub-Saharan Africa, rely on more traditional sources of energy, such as firewood and dung.

HYDROPOWER

NUCLEAR

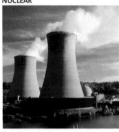

SOLAR

WIND

GEOTHERMAL

ALTERNATIVE ENERGIES

Hydropower provides nearly 18% of the world's electricity, but it is limited to countries with adequate water resources, and it poses threats to local watersheds. **Nuclear energy** makes up 17% of the Earth's electricity, but few countries have adopted it because of potential environmental risks and waste disposal issues. **Solar** and **wind energy** are inexhaustible and are the focus of new energy technologies and research. **Geothermal energy** is efficient but limited to countries with ready sources of hot ground water, such as Iceland.

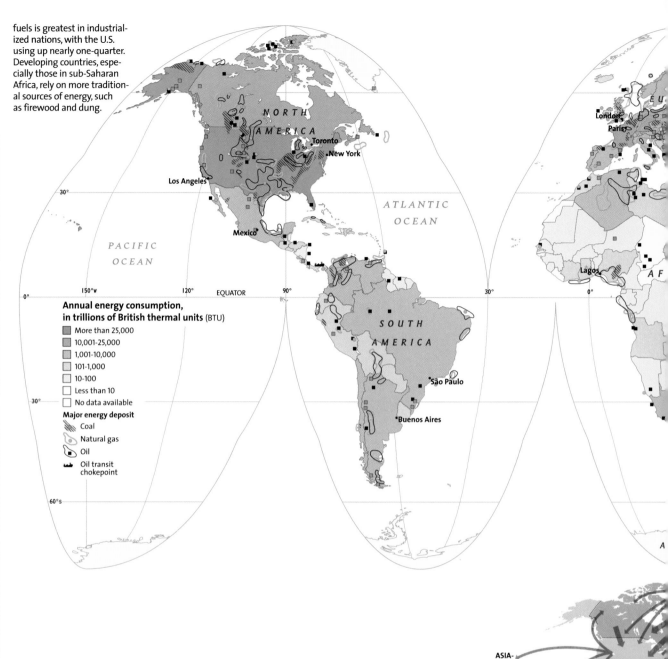

Annual energy consumption, in trillions of British thermal units (BTU)

- More than 25,000
- 10,001-25,000
- 1,001-10,000
- 101-1,000
- 10-100
- Less than 10
- No data available

Major energy deposit
- Coal
- Natural gas
- Oil
- Oil transit chokepoint

▼ RENEWABLE ENERGY

Renewable sources of energy—geothermal, solar, and wind—make up a small percentage of the world's energy supply. They have a significant impact, however, on local and regional energy supplies, especially for electricity, in places such as the U.S., Japan, and Germany. These sources of energy can be regenerated or renewed in a relatively short time, whereas fossil fuels form over geologic time spans.

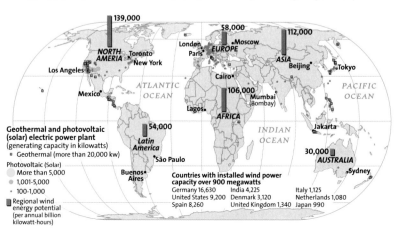

Geothermal and photovoltaic (solar) electric power plant
(generating capacity in kilowatts)
- Geothermal (more than 20,000 kw)

Photovoltaic (Solar)
- More than 5,000
- 1,001-5,000
- 100-1,000

Regional wind energy potential (per annual billion kilowatt-hours)

Countries with installed wind power capacity over 900 megawatts

Germany 16,630	India 4,225	Italy 1,125
United States 9,200	Denmark 3,120	Netherlands 1,080
Spain 8,260	United Kingdom 1,340	Japan 990

► FLOW OF OIL WORLDWIDE

Major oil reserves are clustered in a handful of countries, more than half of which are in the Middle East, whereas the greatest demand for oil is in the United States, Europe, Japan, and China. Other major oil exporters include the Russian Federation, Norway, Venezuela, and Mexico.

Oil imports, 2004
(in million metric tonnes)
- More than 250
- 175-250
- 75-174
- Less than 75

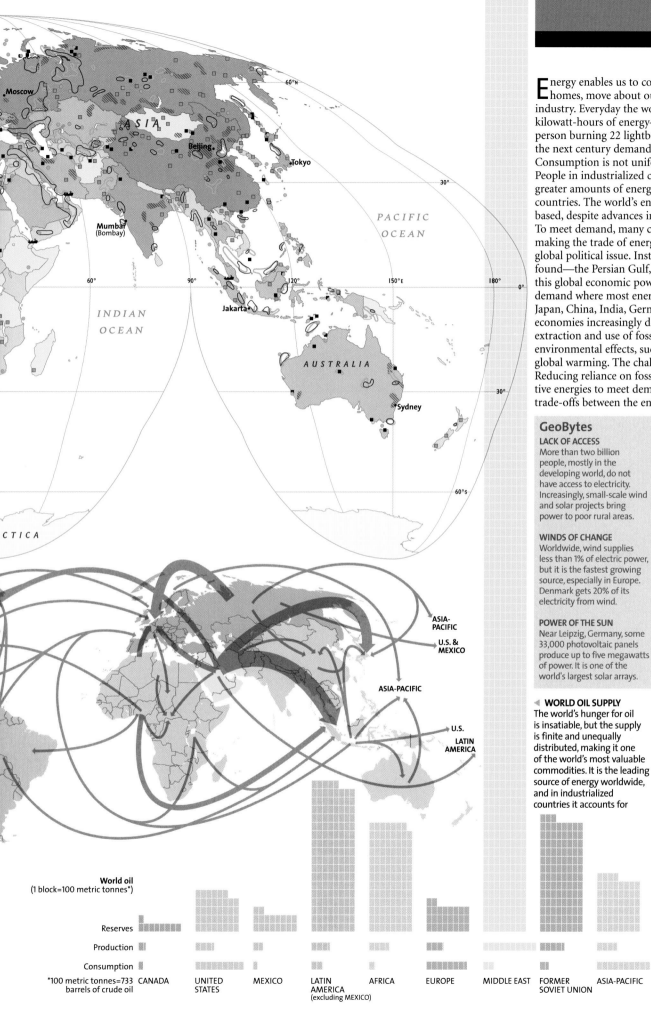

ENERGY

Energy enables us to cook our food, heat our homes, move about our planet, and run industry. Everyday the world uses some 320 billion kilowatt-hours of energy—equivalent to each person burning 22 lightbulbs nonstop, and over the next century demand may increase threefold. Consumption is not uniform across the globe. People in industrialized countries consume far greater amounts of energy than those in developing countries. The world's energy supply is still fossil-fuel based, despite advances in alternative energy sources. To meet demand, many countries must import fuels, making the trade of energy a critical, often volatile global political issue. Instability where most oil is found—the Persian Gulf, Nigeria, Venezuela—make this global economic powerline fragile. Insatiable demand where most energy is consumed—the U.S., Japan, China, India, Germany—makes national economies increasingly dependent. Furthermore, extraction and use of fossil fuel have serious environmental effects, such as air pollution and global warming. The challenge for the future? Reducing reliance on fossil fuels, developing alternative energies to meet demand, and mediating the trade-offs between the environment and energy.

GeoBytes

LACK OF ACCESS
More than two billion people, mostly in the developing world, do not have access to electricity. Increasingly, small-scale wind and solar projects bring power to poor rural areas.

WINDS OF CHANGE
Worldwide, wind supplies less than 1% of electric power, but it is the fastest growing source, especially in Europe. Denmark gets 20% of its electricity from wind.

POWER OF THE SUN
Near Leipzig, Germany, some 33,000 photovoltaic panels produce up to five megawatts of power. It is one of the world's largest solar arrays.

GOING NUCLEAR
France gets 78% of its electricity from nuclear power. Developing nations, such as China and India, are building new reactors to reduce pollution and meet soaring energy demands.

GROWING PAINS
China is fueling its economic growth with huge quantities of coal, and it suffers from energy-related environmental problems. China is second only to the United States in greenhouse gas emissions that contribute to global warming.

◄ **WORLD OIL SUPPLY**
The world's hunger for oil is insatiable, but the supply is finite and unequally distributed, making it one of the world's most valuable commodities. It is the leading source of energy worldwide, and in industrialized countries it accounts for more than one-third of all energy consumed. Pressure on the world's oil supply continues to mount as both industrialized and developing countries grow more dependent on it to meet increasing energy needs.

World oil
(1 block=100 metric tonnes*)

Reserves

Production

Consumption

*100 metric tonnes=733 barrels of crude oil

CANADA   UNITED STATES   MEXICO   LATIN AMERICA (excluding MEXICO)   AFRICA   EUROPE   MIDDLE EAST   FORMER SOVIET UNION   ASIA-PACIFIC

ASIA-PACIFIC

U.S. & MEXICO

ASIA-PACIFIC

U.S.

LATIN AMERICA

FLIGHT FROM CONFLICT

By the end of 2004, the number of refugees worldwide reached an estimated 9.2 million, and the flows of people uprooted from their homes because of war, violence, and oppression showed no sign of abating in 2005. The bar graph below indicates the scale of refugee displacement and sanctuary. In Colombia, decades of conflict have led to a vast number of internal displaced persons (IDPs), shown by the brown bar. The blue bar shows the number of Colombians who have fled their homes. Large numbers of Afghans are displaced internally (brown bar) and have left the country. Pakistan has given residence to many (brown bar). Germany and the United States shelter refugees from around the world (brown bars).

United Nations High Commission for Refugees trucks evacuate people from Srebrenica during the Bosnian conflict in 1993.

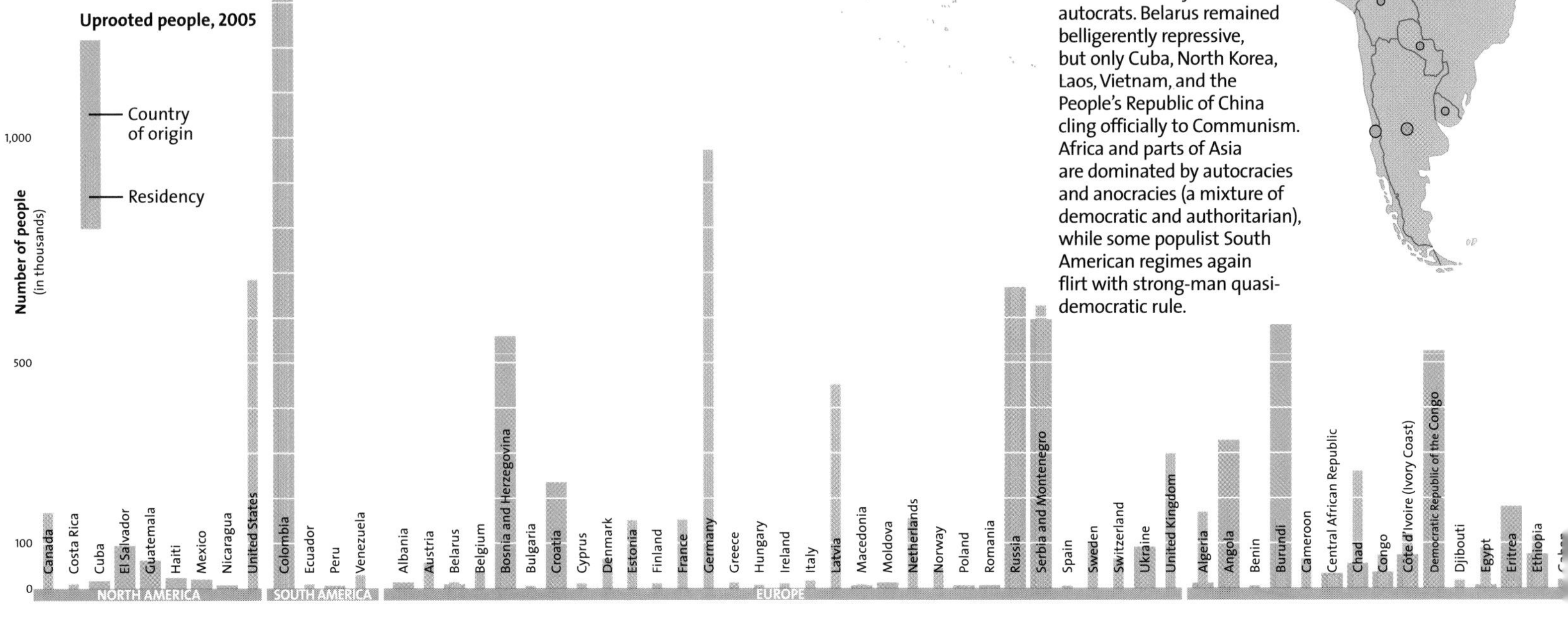

Uprooted people, 2005

— Country of origin

— Residency

Number of people (in thousands)

1,000

500

100

0

NORTH AMERICA: Canada, Costa Rica, Cuba, El Salvador, Guatemala, Haiti, Mexico, Nicaragua, United States

SOUTH AMERICA: Colombia, Ecuador, Peru, Venezuela

EUROPE: Albania, Austria, Belarus, Belgium, Bosnia and Herzegovina, Bulgaria, Croatia, Cyprus, Denmark, Estonia, Finland, France, Germany, Greece, Hungary, Ireland, Italy, Latvia, Macedonia, Moldova, Netherlands, Norway, Poland, Romania, Russia, Serbia and Montenegro, Spain, Sweden, Switzerland, Ukraine, United Kingdom

Algeria, Angola, Benin, Burundi, Cameroon, Central African Republic, Chad, Congo, Côte d'Ivoire (Ivory Coast), Democratic Republic of the Congo, Djibouti, Egypt, Eritrea, Ethiopia

▶ MEASURING DEMOCRACY

Democracy surged in the 1990s as Eastern and Central European states emerged from the Soviet Union, while Latin Americans tossed out many of their autocrats. Belarus remained belligerently repressive, but only Cuba, North Korea, Laos, Vietnam, and the People's Republic of China cling officially to Communism. Africa and parts of Asia are dominated by autocracies and anocracies (a mixture of democratic and authoritarian), while some populist South American regimes again flirt with strong-man quasi-democratic rule.

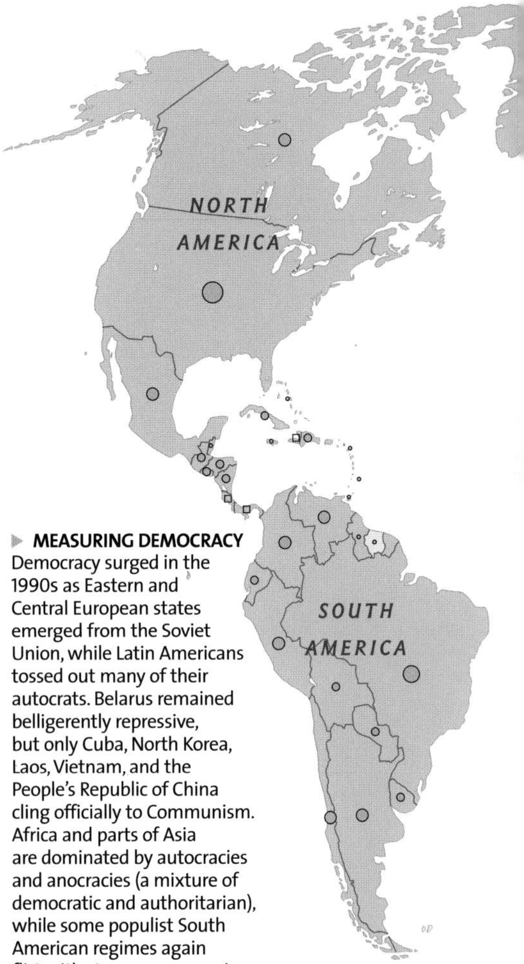

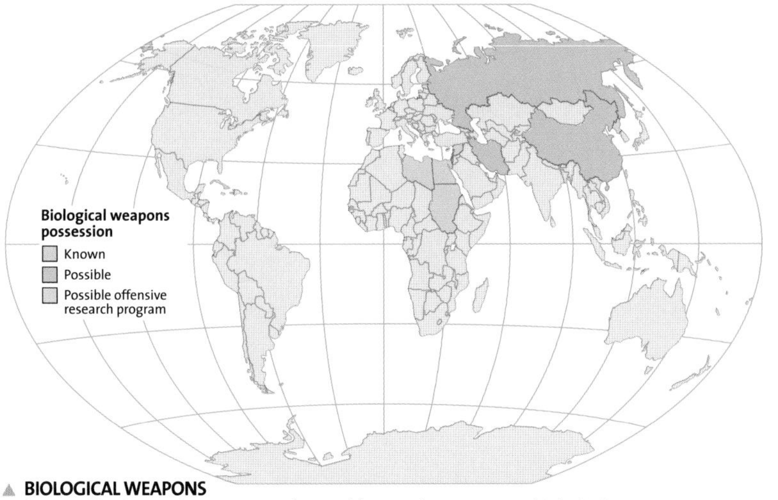

NORTH AMERICA

SOUTH AMERICA

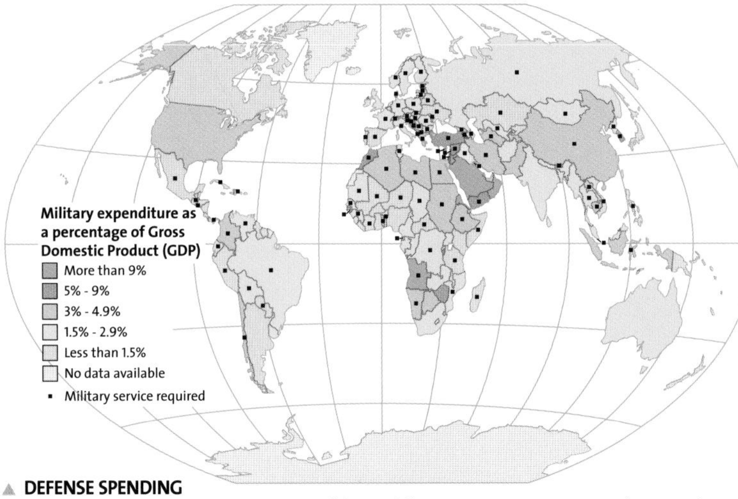

▲ DEFENSE SPENDING

Military spending soaks up a large percentage of GDP (Gross Domestic Product) in many countries that can ill afford it. Angola, whose 26-year-old civil war ended in 2002, is awash in arms. The states of the Middle East, some with weak economies and beset by popular insurrections, continue to maintain large defense forces. A resurgent China flexes new military muscle. The United States spends as much on defense as the rest of the world combined. More than 80 nations, headed by both democracies and totalitarian governments, require military service of their youth.

Military expenditure as a percentage of Gross Domestic Product (GDP)
- More than 9%
- 5% - 9%
- 3% - 4.9%
- 1.5% - 2.9%
- Less than 1.5%
- No data available
- ▪ Military service required

▲ BIOLOGICAL WEAPONS

Only a small volume of a toxic biological agent, if properly dispersed, could cause massive casualties in a densely populated area. Moreover, its manufacture could be virtually undetectable, as only a small facility is needed, and much of the material and equipment has legitimate medical and agricultural use. Although only about 8 countries have offensive biological weapons programs, that number is expected to grow with the increased international flow of technology, goods, and information.

Biological weapons possession
- Known
- Possible
- Possible offensive research program

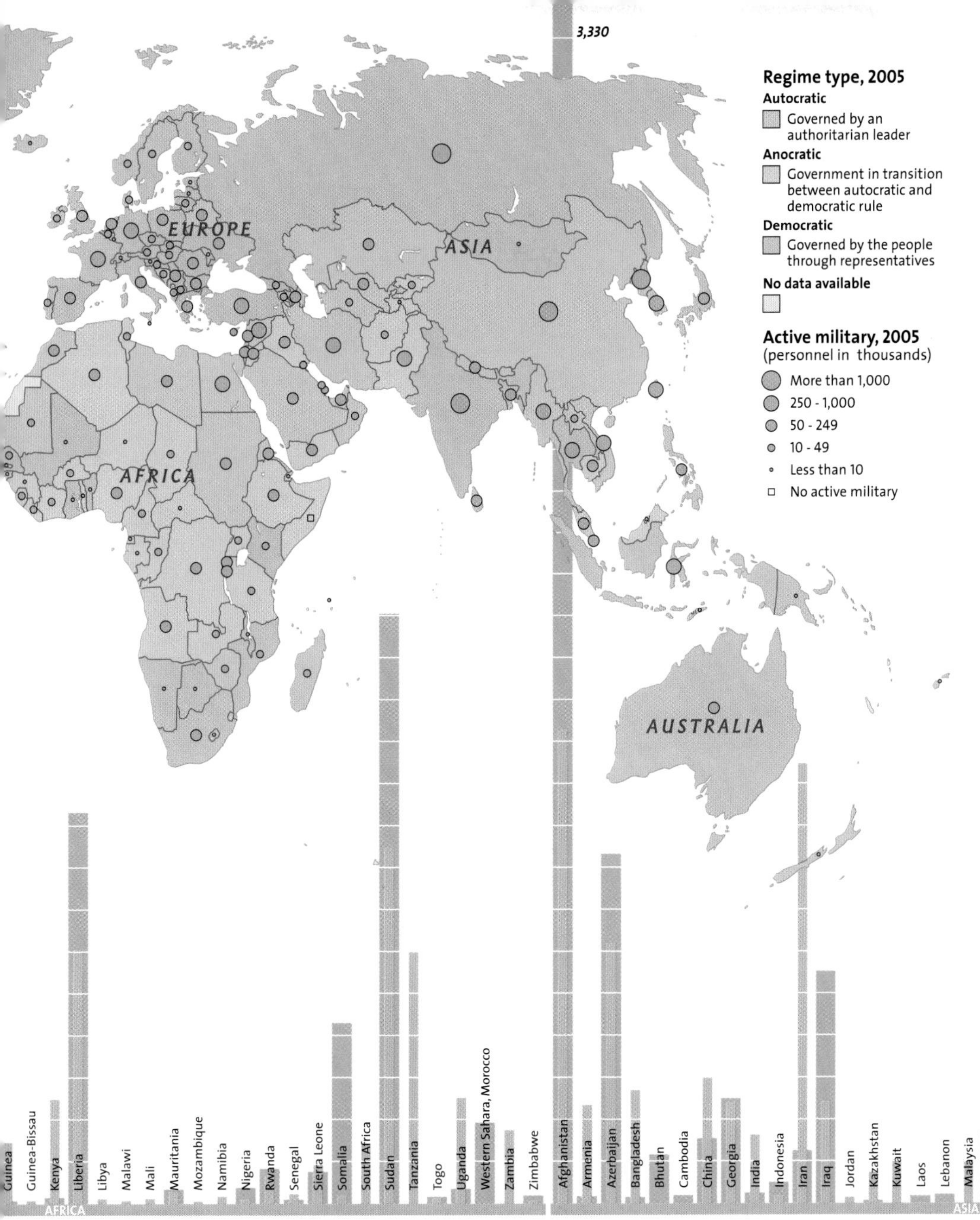

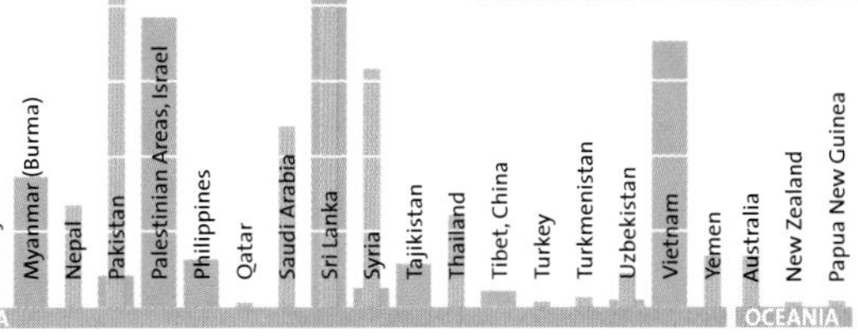

Regime type, 2005

Autocratic
Governed by an authoritarian leader

Anocratic
Government in transition between autocratic and democratic rule

Democratic
Governed by the people through representatives

No data available

Active military, 2005
(personnel in thousands)

- More than 1,000
- 250 - 1,000
- 50 - 249
- 10 - 49
- Less than 10
- No active military

EUROPE

ASIA

AFRICA

AUSTRALIA

3,330

In the 21st century, the threat of war between sovereign nations has largely given way to war within states—conflicts between aggrieved religious, tribal, or ethnic groups. Even more sinister threats involve forces unattached to sovereign states—globally dispersed ideological cadres, loyal to no government, whose use of new communication technologies makes them elusive. Not since Iraq rolled into Kuwait in 1991 has one nation tried to forcibly incorporate another, although the United States and its coalition of allies, in response to the September 11, 2001, attacks by the radical Islamists of al Qaeda, have invaded both Afghanistan and Iraq. The shock waves have dispersed millions of refugees into Pakistan, Iran, and Western Europe. Even as the Cold War superpowers disarm, nuclear proliferation by unstable governments remains alarmingly possible.

GeoBytes

NEVER AGAIN?
Atomic weapons have been used only in World War II—in 1945 by the United States against Japan.

BIO-WEAPON SCARE
Envelopes containing the biological agent anthrax were mailed only months after 9/11, killing five.

CHECHNYA IN RUINS
Two protracted wars by Russia against its recalcitrant territory of Chechnya have created another platform for Muslim extremists.

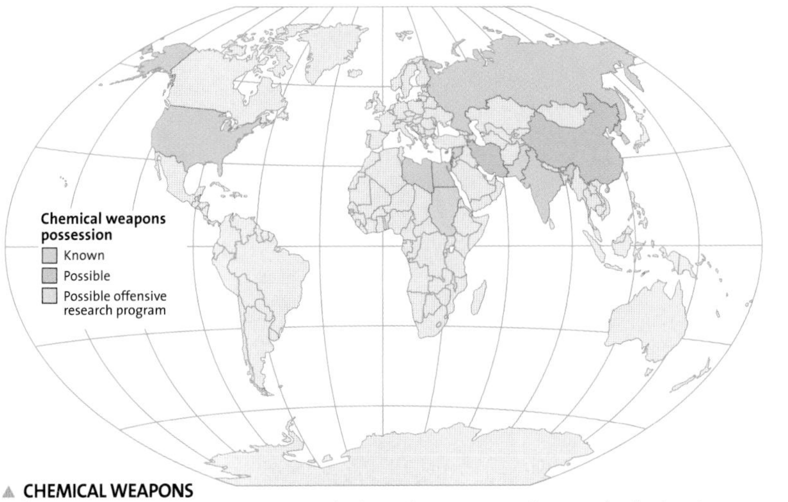

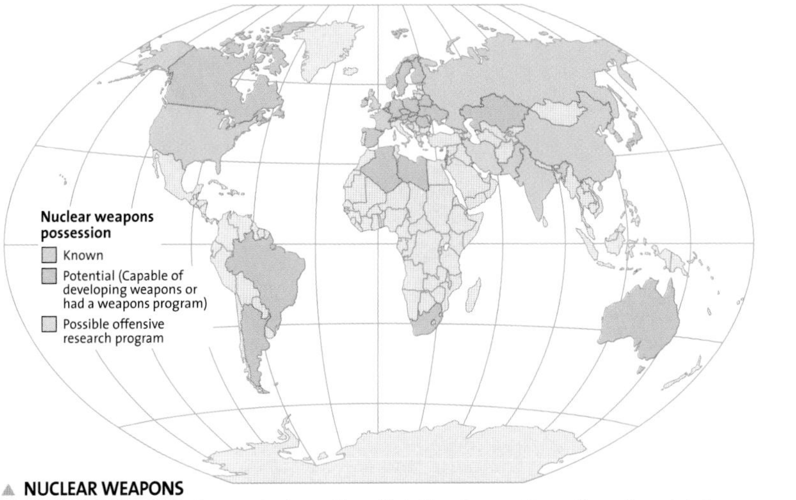

AFRICA: Guinea, Guinea-Bissau, Kenya, Liberia, Libya, Malawi, Mali, Mauritania, Mozambique, Namibia, Nigeria, Rwanda, Senegal, Sierra Leone, Somalia, South Africa, Sudan, Tanzania, Togo, Uganda, Western Sahara, Morocco, Zambia, Zimbabwe

ASIA: Afghanistan, Armenia, Azerbaijan, Bangladesh, Bhutan, Cambodia, China, Georgia, India, Indonesia, Iran, Iraq, Jordan, Kazakhstan, Kuwait, Laos, Lebanon, Malaysia, Myanmar (Burma), Nepal, Pakistan, Palestinian Areas, Israel, Philippines, Qatar, Saudi Arabia, Sri Lanka, Syria, Tajikistan, Thailand, Tibet, China, Turkey, Turkmenistan, Uzbekistan, Vietnam, Yemen

OCEANIA: Australia, New Zealand, Papua New Guinea

Chemical weapons possession

- Known
- Possible
- Possible offensive research program

Nuclear weapons possession

- Known
- Potential (Capable of developing weapons or had a weapons program)
- Possible offensive research program

▲ **CHEMICAL WEAPONS**
Only 9 sovereign nations, including the United States, Russia, South Korea, and India, acknowledge chemical weapon stockpiles, but little doubt remains that additional countries and subnational groups also have them. Under the Chemical Weapons Convention (CWC), member countries are scheduled to destroy stockpiles by 2007, although Russia and the United States have received extensions. Terror groups seldom acknowledge international treaties, and materials for chemical weapons are readily available to those who would have them.

▲ **NUCLEAR WEAPONS**
The United States, United Kingdom, China, France, and Russia remain the world's only declared nuclear weapon states under the Nuclear Non-Proliferation Treaty, but Pakistan and India have conducted nuclear tests, and Israel is believed also to possess arsenals. Libya recently gave up its nuclear program, and Belarus, Kazakhstan, and Ukraine all relinquished Soviet nuclear weapons on their territories. But North Korea, thwarting global non-proliferation attempts, has gathered materials for several weapons, and Iran may be operating a clandestine nuclear-weapons program along with power production.

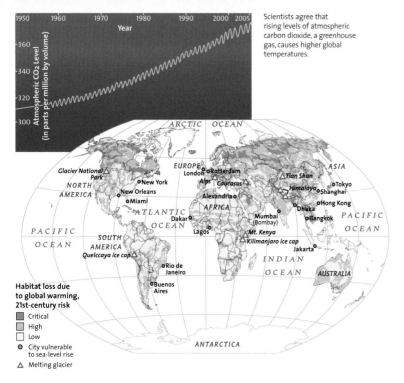

Scientists agree that rising levels of atmospheric carbon dioxide, a greenhouse gas, causes higher global temperatures.

Clear-cutting large tracts of timber, without sustainable replanting, contributes to deforestation, erosion, and loss of habitat.

Habitat loss due to global warming, 21st-century risk
- Critical
- High
- Low
- ◎ City vulnerable to sea-level rise
- △ Melting glacier

Vanishing forest
- ■ Frontier forest (large, mostly virgin forest)
- ■ Degraded forest
- □ Frontier forest 8,000 years ago

▲ GLOBAL WARMING

Temperatures across the world are increasing at a rate not seen at any other time in the last 10,000 years. Although climate variation is a natural phenomenon, human activities that release carbon dioxide and other greenhouse gases into the atmosphere—industrial processes, fossil fuel consumption, deforestation, and land use change—are contributing to this warming trend. Scientists predict that if this trend continues, one-third of plant and animal habitats will be dramatically altered and more than one million species will be threatened with extinction in the next 50 years. And even small increases in global temperatures can melt glaciers and polar ice sheets, raising sea levels and flooding coastal cities and towns.

▲ DEFORESTATION

Of the 13 million hectares (32 million acres) of forest lost each year, mostly to make room for agriculture, more than half are in South America and Africa, where many of the world's tropical rain forests and terrestrial plant and animal species can be found. Loss of habitat in such species-rich areas takes a toll on the world's biodiversity. Deforested areas also release, instead of absorb, carbon dioxide into the atmosphere, contributing to global climate change. Deforestation can also affect local climates by reducing evaporative cooling, leading to decreased rainfall and higher temperatures.

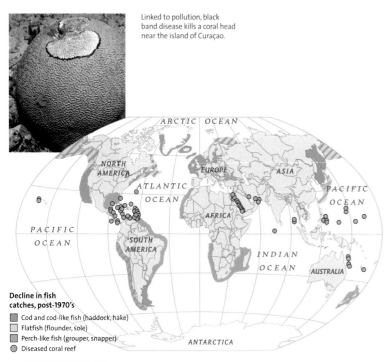

Linked to pollution, black band disease kills a coral head near the island of Curaçao.

In China's Tengger Desert, sand threatens to engulf nearby railroad lines despite a grid of straw meant to help stabilize the drifts.

Decline in fish catches, post-1970's
- ■ Cod and cod-like fish (haddock, hake)
- □ Flatfish (flounder, sole)
- ■ Perch-like fish (grouper, snapper)
- ◎ Diseased coral reef

Risk of desertification
- ■ Very high
- ■ High
- □ Moderate
- □ Low

▲ THREATENED OCEANS

Oceans cover more than two-thirds of the Earth's surface and are home to at least half of the world's biodiversity, yet they are the least understood ecosystems. The combined stresses of overfishing, pollution, increased carbon dioxide emissions, global climate change, and coastal development are having a serious impact on the health of oceans and ocean species. Over 70% of the world's fish species are depleted or nearing depletion, and 50% of coral reefs worldwide are threatened by human activities.

▲ DESERTIFICATION

Climate variability and human activities, such as grazing and conversion of natural areas to agricultural use, are leading causes of desertification, the degradation of land in arid, semiarid, and dry subhumid areas. The environmental consequences of desertification are great— loss of topsoil, increased soil salinity, damaged vegetation, regional climate change, and a decline in biodiversity. Equally critical are the social consequences—more than 2 billion people live in and make a living off these dryland areas, covering about 41% of Earth's surface.

POLAR ICE CAP

Over the last 50 years, the extent of polar sea ice has noticeably decreased. Since 1970 alone, an area larger than Norway, Sweden, and Denmark combined has melted. This trend is predicted to accelerate as temperatures rise in the Arctic and across the globe.

ASIA

Projected minimum area of sea ice, 2050

North Pole

2000

1950

NORTH AMERICA

EUROPE

GeoBytes

ACIDIFYING OCEANS
Oceans are absorbing an unprecedented 20 to 25 million tonnes (22 to 28 millions tons) of carbon dioxide each day, increasing the water's acidity.

ENDANGERED REEFS
Some 95% of coral reefs in Southeast Asia have been destroyed or are threatened.

RECORD TEMPERATURES
The 1990s were the warmest decade on record in the last century.

WARMING ARCTIC
While the world as a whole has warmed nearly 0.6°C (1°F) over the last hundred years, parts of the Arctic have warmed 4 to 5 times as much in only the last 50 years.

DISAPPEARING RAIN FORESTS
Scientists predict that the world's rain forests will disappear within the next one hundred years if the current rate of deforestation continues.

OIL POLLUTION
Nearly 1.3 million tonnes (1.4 million tons) of oil seep into the world's oceans each year from the combined sources of natural seepage, extraction, transportation, and consumption.

ACCIDENTAL DROWNINGS
Entanglement in fishing gear is one of the greatest threats to marine mammals.

A FAREWELL TO FROGS?
Worldwide, almost half of the 5,700 named amphibian species are in decline.

With the growth of scientific record keeping, observation, modeling, and analysis, our understanding of Earth's environment is improving. Yet even as we deepen our insight into environmental processes, we are changing what we are studying. At no other time in history have humans altered their environment with such speed and force. Nothing occurs in isolation, and stress in one area has impacts elsewhere. Our agricultural and fishing practices, industrial processes, extraction of resources, and transportation methods are leading to extinctions, destroying habitats, devastating fish stocks, disturbing the soil, and polluting the oceans and the air. As a result, biodiversity is declining, global temperatures are rising, polar ice is shrinking, and the ozone layer continues to thin.

POLLUTION

No corner of the earth is immune to pollution, be it in the air, soil, or water. Concentrations of pollution can be found in the industrial centers of North America, Europe, and, increasingly, Asia—and areas downwind or downstream from them. Shipping routes are sources of pollution, from oil spills to garbage dumpings.

Environmental stress factor

Accident
* Industrial
* Oil rig explosion
— Oil spill
⟳ Acid rain

Deforestation
☐ Temperate forest
☐ Tropical forest
☐ Desertification
⟳ Pollution from shipping

NORTH AMERICA — Los Angeles, Toronto, New York, Mexico
ATLANTIC OCEAN
PACIFIC OCEAN
EUROPE — London, Paris, Moscow
ASIA — Beijing, Tokyo
AFRICA — Cairo, Lagos, Mumbai (Bombay)
SOUTH AMERICA — São Paulo, Buenos Aires
INDIAN OCEAN
Jakarta
PACIFIC OCEAN
AUSTRALIA — Sydney
ANTARCTICA

OZONE DEPLETION

First noted in the mid-1980s, the springtime "ozone hole" over the Antarctic continues to grow. With sustained efforts to restrict chlorofluorocarbons (CFCs) and other ozone-depleting chemicals, scientists have begun to see what they hope is a leveling off in the rate of depletion. Stratospheric ozone shields the Earth from the sun's ultraviolet radiation. Thinning of this protective layer puts people at risk for skin cancer and cataracts. It can also have devastating effects on the Earth's biological functions.

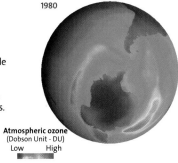
1980

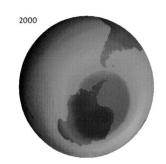
2000

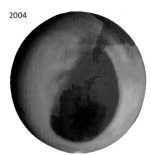
2004

Atmospheric ozone
(Dobson Unit - DU)
Low   High

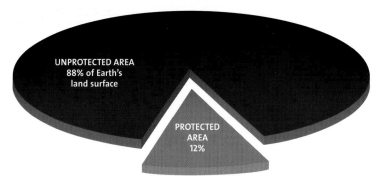

UNPROTECTED AREA
88% of Earth's land surface

PROTECTED AREA 12%

GeoBytes

LARGEST NATIONAL PARK
North East Greenland National Park, Greenland, 972,000 sq km (375,000 sq mi)

LARGEST MARINE PARK
Great Barrier Reef Marine Park, Australia, a World Heritage site 347,800 sq km (134,286 sq mi)

LARGEST TROPICAL FOREST PARK
Tumucumaque National Park in the Brazilian Amazon 24,135 sq km (9,319 sq mi)

BIODIVERSITY HOTSPOTS
Conservation International identifies world regions suffering from a severe loss of biodiversity.

WORLD HERITAGE SITES
The United Nations Educational, Scientific, and Cultural Organization (UNESCO) recognizes natural and cultural sites of "universal value."

HAWAI'I VOLCANOES NATIONAL PARK, HAWAI'I
The park includes two of the world's most active volcanoes, Kilauea and Mauna Loa. The landscape shows the results of 70 million years of volcanism, including calderas, lava flows, and black sand beaches. Lava spreads out to build the island, and seawater vaporizes as lava hits the ocean at 1,149°C (2,100° F). The national park, created in 1916, covers 10% of the island of Hawai'i and is a refuge for endangered species, like the hawksbill turtle and Hawaiian goose. It was made a World Heritage site in 1987.

GALÁPAGOS NATIONAL PARK, ECUADOR
Galápago means tortoise in Spanish, and at one time 250,000 giant tortoises roamed the islands. Today about 15,000 remain, and three of the original 14 subspecies are extinct—and the Pinta Island tortoise may be extinct soon. In 1959, Ecuador made the volcanic Galápagos Islands a national park, protecting the giant tortoises and other endemic species. The archipelago became a World Heritage site in 1978, and a marine reserve surrounding the islands was added in 2001.

WESTERN UNITED STATES
An intricate public lands pattern—including national forests, wilderness areas, wildlife refuges, and national parks such as Arches (above)—embraces nearly half the surface area of 11 western states. Ten out of 19 World Heritage sites in the United States are found here. It was in the West that the modern national park movement was born in the 19th century with the establishment of Yellowstone and Yosemite National Parks.

MADIDI NATIONAL PARK, BOLIVIA
Macaws may outnumber humans in Madidi, Bolivia's second largest national park, established in 1995. A complex community of plants, animals, and native Indian groups share this 18,900-sq-km (7,300-sq-mi) reserve, part of the tropical Andes biodiversity hotspot. Indigenous communities benefit from ecotourism.

AMAZON BASIN, BRAZIL
Indigenous peoples help manage reserves in Brazil that are linked with Jaú National Park. The park and reserves are part of the Central Amazon Conservation Complex, a World Heritage site covering more than 60,000 sq km (23,000 sq mi). It is the largest protected area in the Amazon Basin and one of the most biologically rich regions on the planet.

ARCTIC REGIONS
Polar bears find safe havens in Canadian parks, such as on Ellesmere Island, and in Greenland's huge protected area—Earth's largest—that preserves the island's frigid northeast. In 1996 countries with Arctic lands adopted the Circumpolar Protected Areas Network Strategy and Action Plan to help conserve ecosystems. Today 15% of Arctic land area is protected.

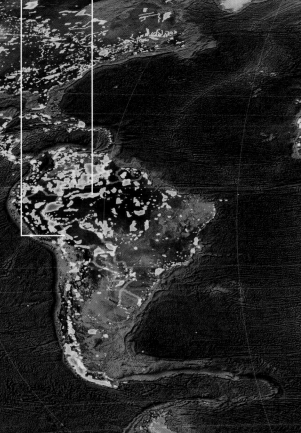

PROTECTED AREAS WORLDWIDE
What are protected areas? Most people agree that such territories are dedicated to protecting and maintaining biodiversity and are often managed through legal means. Yellowstone National Park, established in 1872, is often cited as the start of the modern era of protected areas. From a mere handful in 1900, the number of protected areas worldwide now exceeds 104,790, covering more than 20 million sq km (7.7 million sq mi). North America claims the most protected land of any region, amounting to almost 18% of its territory. South Asia, at about 7%, has the least amount of land under some form of protection. Not all protected areas are created or managed equally, and management categories developed by IUCN range from strict nature reserve to areas for sustainable use. Management effectiveness varies widely and can be affected by such factors as conservation budgets, and political stability. Throughout the world—but especially in tropical areas—protected areas are threatened by illegal hunting, overfishing, pollution, and the removal of native vegetation. Countries and international organizations no longer choose between conservation and development; rather the goal for societies is to balance the two for equitable and sustainable resource use.

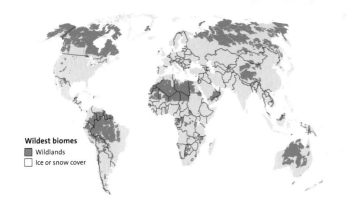

◄ **WILDEST AREAS**

Although generally far from cities, the world's remaining wild places play a vital role in a healthy global ecosystem. The boreal (northern) forests of Canada and Russia, for instance, help cleanse the air we breathe by absorbing carbon dioxide and providing oxygen. With the human population increasing by an estimated one billion over the next 15 years, many wild places could fall within reach of the plow or under a cloud of smog.

For millennia, lands have been set aside as sacred ground or as hunting reserves for the powerful. Today, great swaths are protected for recreation, habitat conservation, biodiversity preservation, and resource management. Some groups may oppose protected spaces because they want access to resources now. Yet local inhabitants and governments are beginning to see the benefits of conservation efforts and sustainable use for human health and future generations.

SAREKS NATIONAL PARK, SWEDEN

This remote 1,970-sq-km (760-sq-mi) park, established in 1909 to protect the alpine landscape, is a favorite of backcountry hikers. It boasts some 200 mountains more than 1,800 m (5,900 ft) high, narrow valleys, and about 100 glaciers. Sareks forms part of the Laponian Area World Heritage site and has been a home to the Saami (or Lapp) people since prehistoric times.

AFRICAN RESERVES

Some 120,000 elephants roam Chobe National Park in northern Botswana. Africa has more than 7,500 national parks, wildlife reserves, and other protected areas, covering about 9% of the continent. Protected areas are under enormous pressure from expanding populations, civil unrest and war, and environmental disasters.

WOLONG NATURE RESERVE, CHINA

Giant pandas freely chomp bamboo in this 2,000-sq-km (772-sq-mi) reserve in Sichuan Province, near the city of Chengdu. Misty bamboo forests host a number of endangered species, but the critically endangered giant panda—among the rarest mammals in the world—is the most famous resident. Only about 1,600 giant pandas exist in the wild.

KAMCHATKA, RUSSIA

Crater lakes, ash-capped cones, and diverse plant and animal species mark the Kamchatka Peninsula—a World Heritage site—located between the icy Bering Sea and Sea of Okhotsk. The active volcanoes and glaciers form a dynamic landscape of great beauty, known as "The Land of Fire and Ice." Kamchatka's remoteness and rugged landscape help fauna flourish, producing record numbers of salmon species and half of the Steller's sea-eagles on Earth.

GUNUNG PALUNG NATIONAL PARK, INDONESIA

A tree frog's perch could be precarious in this 900-sq-km (347-sq-mi) park on the island of Borneo, in the heart of the Sundaland biodiversity hotspot. The biggest threat to trees and animals in the park and region is illegal logging. Gunung Palung contains a wider range of habitats than any other protected area on Borneo, from mangroves to lowland and cloud forests. A number of endangered species, such as orangutans and sun bears, depend on the dense forests.

AUSTRALIA & NEW ZEALAND

Uluru, a red sandstone monolith (formerly known as Ayers Rock), and the vast Great Barrier Reef, largest marine park in the world, are outstanding examples of Australia's protected areas—which make up more than 10% of the country's area and conserve a diverse range of unique ecosystems. About a third of New Zealand is protected, and it is a biodiversity hotspot because of threats to flightless native birds, such as the kakapo and kiwi. Cats, stoats, and other predators, introduced to New Zealand by settlers, kill thousands of birds each year.

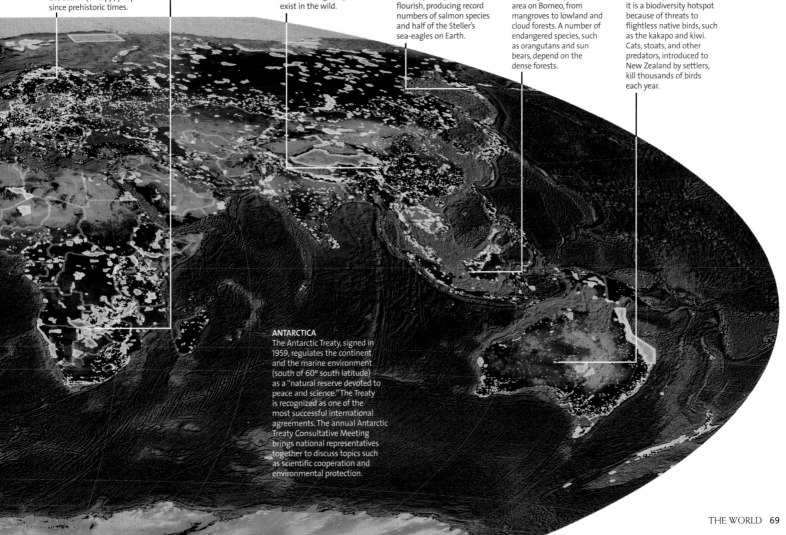

ANTARCTICA

The Antarctic Treaty, signed in 1959, regulates the continent and the marine environment (south of 60° south latitude) as a "natural reserve devoted to peace and science." The Treaty is recognized as one of the most successful international agreements. The annual Antarctic Treaty Consultative Meeting brings national representatives together to discuss topics such as scientific cooperation and environmental protection.

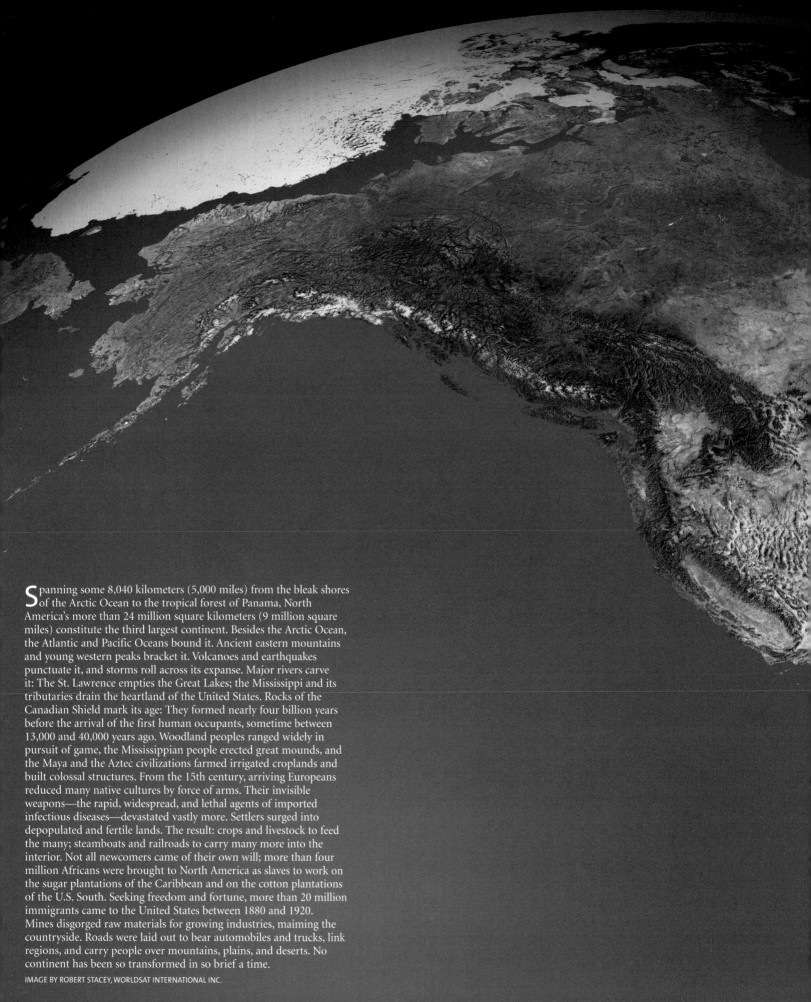

Spanning some 8,040 kilometers (5,000 miles) from the bleak shores of the Arctic Ocean to the tropical forest of Panama, North America's more than 24 million square kilometers (9 million square miles) constitute the third largest continent. Besides the Arctic Ocean, the Atlantic and Pacific Oceans bound it. Ancient eastern mountains and young western peaks bracket it. Volcanoes and earthquakes punctuate it, and storms roll across its expanse. Major rivers carve it: The St. Lawrence empties the Great Lakes; the Mississippi and its tributaries drain the heartland of the United States. Rocks of the Canadian Shield mark its age: They formed nearly four billion years before the arrival of the first human occupants, sometime between 13,000 and 40,000 years ago. Woodland peoples ranged widely in pursuit of game, the Mississippian people erected great mounds, and the Maya and the Aztec civilizations farmed irrigated croplands and built colossal structures. From the 15th century, arriving Europeans reduced many native cultures by force of arms. Their invisible weapons—the rapid, widespread, and lethal agents of imported infectious diseases—devastated vastly more. Settlers surged into depopulated and fertile lands. The result: crops and livestock to feed the many; steamboats and railroads to carry many more into the interior. Not all newcomers came of their own will; more than four million Africans were brought to North America as slaves to work on the sugar plantations of the Caribbean and on the cotton plantations of the U.S. South. Seeking freedom and fortune, more than 20 million immigrants came to the United States between 1880 and 1920. Mines disgorged raw materials for growing industries, maiming the countryside. Roads were laid out to bear automobiles and trucks, link regions, and carry people over mountains, plains, and deserts. No continent has been so transformed in so brief a time.

IMAGE BY ROBERT STACEY, WORLDSAT INTERNATIONAL INC.

Date Line

North Pole

ARCTIC OCEAN

Siberia
RUSSIA

CHUKCHI
SEA

North Magnetic Pole ✳

Lincoln Sea
Wandel
Sea

KONG
FREDERIK
VIII LAND

GREENLAND SEA

BERING SEA

Pribilof
Is.

Point Barrow

ARCTIC CIRCLE

NORTH SLOPE

BEAUFORT SEA

Cape Prince Alfred

QUEEN

Sverdrup
Is.

Lands End

ELIZABETH

Parry
Islands

ISLANDS

KONG
CHRISTIAN
X Land

GREENLAND

Kong
Christian
IX Land

Kong Frederik VI Coast

ICELAND

Reykjavik ⊕

Faröe Is.
(Føroyar)
Shetland
Is.

Orkney Is.

Hebrides

North
Sea

NOR.

Norton
Sound

Seward
Peninsula

Yukon

ALASKA

Brooks Range

Highest point in
North America
Mt. McKinley

Kenai
Pen.

Anchorage

Alaska Range

YUKON
PLATEAU

Mackenzie Mts.

Cape Kellett

Banks
Island

Viscount Melville
Sound

Victoria
Island

Brodeur
Peninsula

Boothia
Peninsula

Ellesmere
Island

Kane
Basin

BAFFIN
BAY

Qeqertarsuaq
(Disko)

DAVIS
STRAIT

Nuuk
(Godthåb)

Dennmark Strait

Bristol
Bay

Aleutian Range

Gulf of
Alaska

Juneau

Keele
Peak

Mt. Logan

Source of the
Yukon

Queen
Maud
Gulf

Melville
Peninsula

North Geomagnetic
Pole

Cumberland
Peninsula

Baffin Island

Nunap Isua
(Kap Farvel)

Queen Charlotte
Islands

Alexander
Archipelago

Mt. Roosevelt

ROCKY

Source of the
Mackenzie

Great
Bear Lake

Thelon

Kazan

Southampton
Island

Foxe
Peninsula

Foxe
Basin

Hall
Peninsula

LABRADOR SEA

Vancouver

Mt. Robson

Hay

Great
Slave Lake

Nueltin
Lake

HUDSON

Ungava
Peninsula

Mount Caubvick
(Mont D'Iberville)

Hecate Str.

COAST MTS

Athabasca

Lake
Athabasca

Reindeer
Lake

Seal

BAY

Lac
Minto

LABRADOR

Edmonton

Peace

CANADA

Churchill

Nelson

Cape Tatnam

Belcher
Islands

James
Bay

Smallwood
Reservoir

Seattle

Mt. St. Helens

Mt. Rainier

Saskatchewan

Lake
Winnipeg

ISLAND OF NEWFOUNDLAND

Avalon
Peninsula

Cape Mendocino

Columbia Plateau

Lake
Manitoba

Winnipeg

Lake
Nipigon

Gaspe
Pen.

Gulf of
Saint
Lawrence

Cape Breton
Island

Mt. Katahdin

COAST RANGES

Borah
Peak

Snake

Source of the
Missouri-Red Rock

Source of the
Mississippi

Lake Superior

St. Lawrence

Montréal

Ottawa ⊛

Lake
Huron

NOVA SCOTIA

Great
Salt
Lake

Salt Lake City

Sierra Nevada

UNITED STATES

Chicago

Lake
Michigan

Toronto

Lake
Ontario

Boston
Cape Cod

Los Angeles

Death
Valley

Lowest point in
North America

Grand
Canyon

Denver

Pikes Peak

Missouri

Ohio

APPALACHIAN MOUNTAINS

Lake
Erie

New York

Philadelphia

Washington ⊛

San Diego

Phoenix

Ozark Plateau

Atlanta

Cape Hatteras

Dallas

Mississippi

COASTAL

AZIMUTHAL EQUIDISTANT PROJECTION
SCALE 1:36,000,000

TROPIC OF CANCER

Punta Eugenia

Rio Grande

Houston

New Orleans

Cape Canaveral
(Cape Kennedy)

0 KILOMETERS   600 800 1000

0 MILES 200   400   600   800   1000

Gulf of California

BAJA CALIFORNIA

SIERRA MADRE ORIENTAL

SIERRA MADRE OCCIDENTAL

Lake
Okeechobee

Florida

Miami

Nassau

Bahama Islands

ATLANTIC
OCEAN

Cabo San Lucas

Islas
Marías

GULF OF MEXICO

BAHAMAS

Turks and
Caicos Is.

Islas
Revillagigedo

Guadalajara

MEXICO

La Habana
(Havana)

CUBA

Hispaniola

WEST INDIES

Virgin Is.

Mexico

Pico de Orizaba

Yucatán
Peninsula

Cayman Is.

Greater
Antilles

HAITI

DOM.
REP.

Santo
Domingo

San Juan

Puerto
Rico

Lesser Antilles

PACIFIC
OCEAN

Sierra Madre del Sur

Istmo de
Tehuantepec

BELIZE
Belmopan

Kingston

JAMAICA

Port-au-
Prince

CARIBBEAN SEA

Lesser Antilles

TRINIDAD &
TOBAGO
Port-
of-Spain

Golfo de
Tehuantepec

Guatemala

GUATEMALA

San Salvador
EL SALVADOR

HONDURAS

Tegucigalpa

Managua

NICARAGUA

Lago de
Maracaibo

Caracas

Georgetown

GUYANA

Mt.
Roraima

COSTA
RICA

San José

Volcán Irazú

Panamá

Istmo de Panamá

PANAMA

Golfo de
Panamá

ANDES

COLOMBIA

Bogotá

VENEZUELA

BRAZIL

Longitude West 100° of Greenwich

RUSSIA

Monday
Sunday
Date Line

North Pole

ARCTIC OCEAN

North Magnetic Pole *

QUEEN
ELIZABETH
ISLANDS

GREENLAND
(KALAALLIT NUNAAT)
Denmark

GREENLAND SEA

ARCTIC CIRCLE

BEAUFORT SEA

CHUKCHI SEA

BERING SEA

ALASKA

Anchorage

Fairbanks

Mt. McKinley
(Denali)

Juneau

Alexander
Archipelago

Queen
Charlotte Is.

Victoria
Island

BAFFIN
BAY

Baffin
Island

GULF OF ALASKA

PACIFIC OCEAN

CANADA

Great Bear
Lake

Great Slave
Lake

Yellowknife

Edmonton

Calgary

Vancouver

Vancouver I.
Victoria

Seattle
Mt. Rainier

Olympia
Portland
Salem

HUDSON
BAY

LABRADOR SEA

ICELAND
Reykjavík

UNITED KINGDOM

LABRADOR

ISLAND OF
NEWFOUNDLAND

Winnipeg

Regina

UNITED STATES

Salt Lake City

San Francisco
San Jose

Los Angeles
Long Beach
San Diego

Tijuana

Phoenix
Tucson

MEXICO

Denver

Minneapolis
St. Paul

Chicago

Milwaukee

Detroit

ATLANTIC
OCEAN

Montréal
Ottawa
Toronto

Boston

NEW YORK
Philadelphia
Washington, D.C.

BERMUDA
U.K.

Dallas

Houston

San
Antonio

Monterrey

GULF OF MEXICO

Miami

Nassau

BAHAMAS

TROPIC OF CANCER

Guadalajara
León

MÉXICO
Puebla
Veracruz

Acapulco

La Habana
(Havana)

CUBA

HAITI
Port-au-Prince

DOM.
REP.
Santo
Domingo

PUERTO
RICO
U.S.

JAMAICA
Kingston

CARIBBEAN SEA

BELIZE
Belmopan

GUATEMALA
Guatemala
EL SALVADOR
San Salvador

HONDURAS
Tegucigalpa

NICARAGUA
Managua

COSTA RICA
San José

PANAMA
Panama

PACIFIC
OCEAN

Barranquilla

Maracaibo
Caracas

VENEZUELA

COLOMBIA
BOGOTÁ

Medellín

GUYANA
Georgetown

TRINIDAD
AND
TOBAGO

BRAZIL
Boa Vista

AZIMUTHAL EQUIDISTANT PROJECTION
SCALE 1:36,000,000

0 KILOMETERS   600 800 1000

0 MILES   200   400   600   800   1000

Longitude West 100° of Greenwich

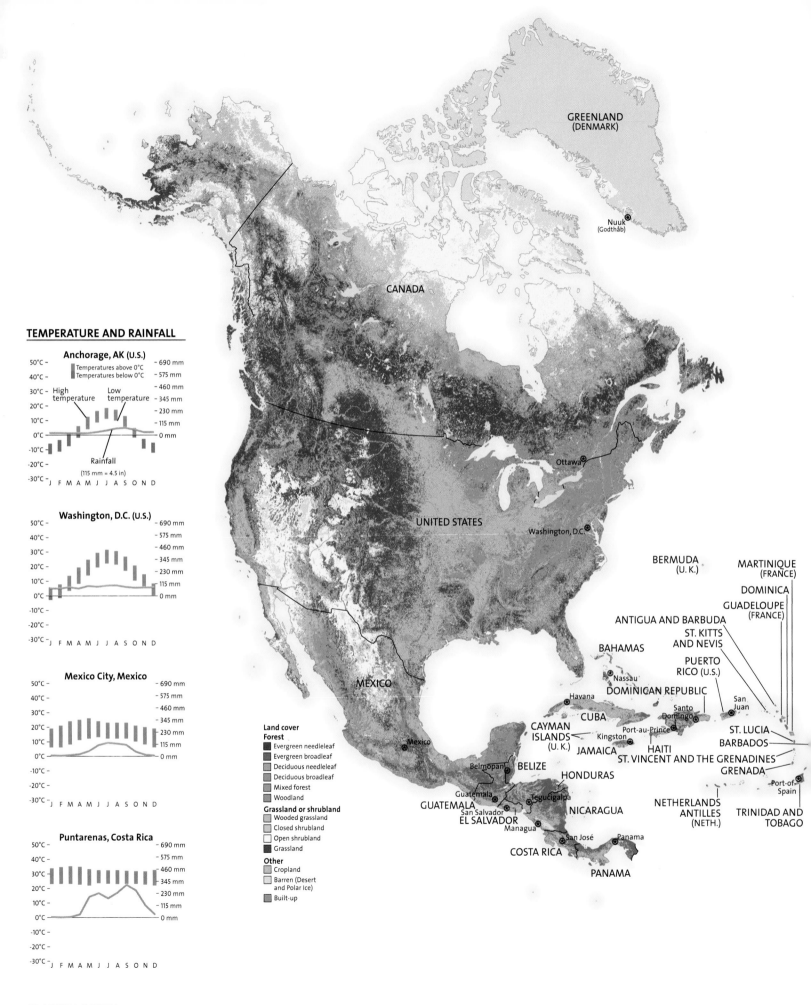

TEMPERATURE AND RAINFALL

Anchorage, AK (U.S.)

- Temperatures above 0°C
- Temperatures below 0°C

High temperature
Low temperature
Rainfall
(115 mm = 4.5 in)

Washington, D.C. (U.S.)

Mexico City, Mexico

Puntarenas, Costa Rica

GREENLAND
(DENMARK)

Nuuk
(Godthåb)

CANADA

Ottawa

UNITED STATES

Washington, D.C.

MEXICO

Mexico

BERMUDA
(U. K.)

MARTINIQUE
(FRANCE)

DOMINICA

GUADELOUPE
(FRANCE)

ANTIGUA AND BARBUDA

ST. KITTS
AND NEVIS

BAHAMAS

PUERTO
RICO (U.S.)

Nassau

DOMINICAN REPUBLIC

Havana

San
Juan

CUBA

Santo
Domingo

CAYMAN
ISLANDS
(U. K.)

Port-au-Prince

ST. LUCIA

Kingston

BARBADOS

JAMAICA

HAITI

ST. VINCENT AND THE GRENADINES

Belmopan

BELIZE

GRENADA

Guatemala

HONDURAS

Port-of-
Spain

Tegucigalpa

GUATEMALA

NETHERLANDS
ANTILLES
(NETH.)

San Salvador

NICARAGUA

TRINIDAD AND
TOBAGO

EL SALVADOR

Managua

San José

Panama

COSTA RICA

PANAMA

Land cover

Forest
- Evergreen needleleaf
- Evergreen broadleaf
- Deciduous needleleaf
- Deciduous broadleaf
- Mixed forest
- Woodland

Grassland or shrubland
- Wooded grassland
- Closed shrubland
- Open shrubland
- Grassland

Other
- Cropland
- Barren (Desert and Polar Ice)
- Built-up

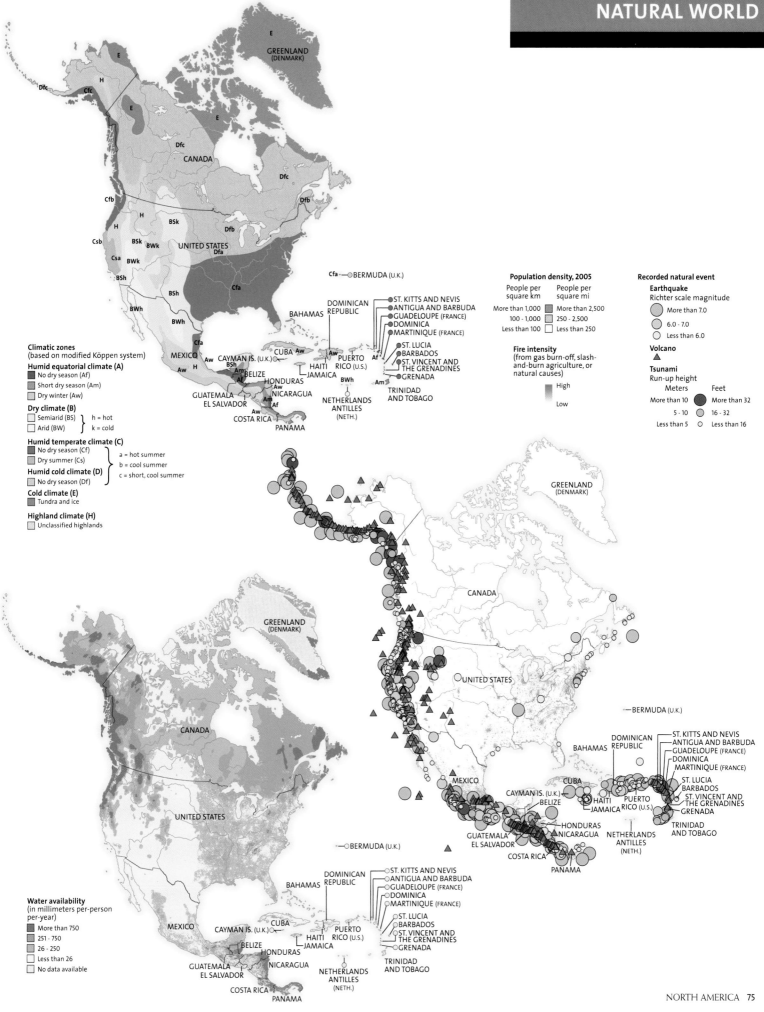

Climatic zones
(based on modified Köppen system)

Humid equatorial climate (A)
- No dry season (Af)
- Short dry season (Am)
- Dry winter (Aw)

Dry climate (B)
- Semiarid (BS) } h = hot
- Arid (BW) } k = cold

Humid temperate climate (C)
- No dry season (Cf)
- Dry summer (Cs) } a = hot summer
  } b = cool summer
Humid cold climate (D) } c = short, cool summer
- No dry season (Df)

Cold climate (E)
- Tundra and ice

Highland climate (H)
- Unclassified highlands

Population density, 2005

People per square km	People per square mi
More than 1,000	More than 2,500
100 - 1,000	250 - 2,500
Less than 100	Less than 250

Fire intensity
(from gas burn-off, slash-and-burn agriculture, or natural causes)

High

Low

Recorded natural event

Earthquake
Richter scale magnitude
- More than 7.0
- 6.0 - 7.0
- Less than 6.0

Volcano

Tsunami
Run-up height

Meters	Feet
More than 10	More than 32
5 - 10	16 - 32
Less than 5	Less than 16

Water availability
(in millimeters per-person per-year)
- More than 750
- 251 - 750
- 26 - 250
- Less than 26
- No data available

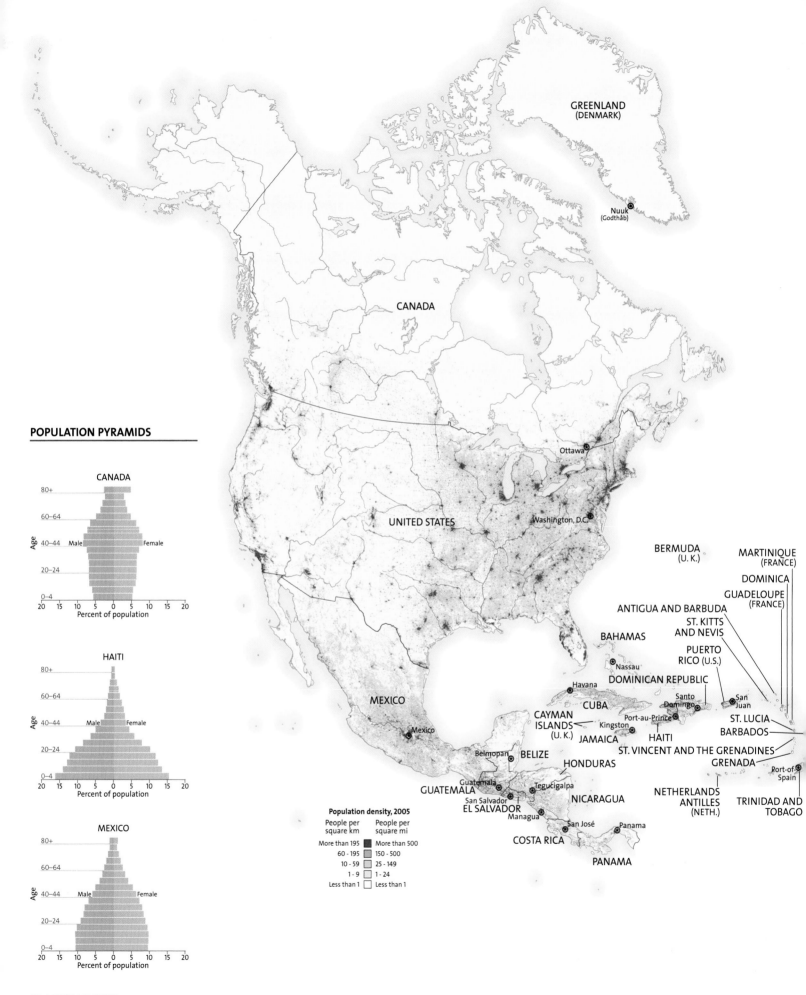

POPULATION PYRAMIDS

CANADA

Age | Male | Female
Percent of population
20 15 10 5 0 5 10 15 20

HAITI

Age | Male | Female
Percent of population
20 15 10 5 0 5 10 15 20

MEXICO

Age | Male | Female
Percent of population
20 15 10 5 0 5 10 15 20

GREENLAND
(DENMARK)

Nuuk
(Godthåb)

CANADA

Ottawa

UNITED STATES

Washington, D.C.

BERMUDA
(U. K.)

MARTINIQUE
(FRANCE)

DOMINICA

GUADELOUPE
(FRANCE)

ANTIGUA AND BARBUDA

ST. KITTS
AND NEVIS

BAHAMAS

PUERTO
RICO (U.S.)

Nassau

DOMINICAN REPUBLIC

Havana

Santo
Domingo

San
Juan

MEXICO

CUBA

CAYMAN
ISLANDS
(U. K.)

Kingston

Port-au-Prince

ST. LUCIA

BARBADOS

Mexico

JAMAICA

HAITI

ST. VINCENT AND THE GRENADINES

Belmopan

BELIZE

HONDURAS

GRENADA

Port-of
Spain

Guatemala

Tegucigalpa

GUATEMALA

San Salvador

NICARAGUA

NETHERLANDS
ANTILLES
(NETH.)

TRINIDAD AND
TOBAGO

EL SALVADOR

Managua

San José

Panama

COSTA RICA

PANAMA

Population density, 2005

People per square km	People per square mi
More than 195	More than 500
60 - 195	150 - 500
10 - 59	25 - 149
1 - 9	1 - 24
Less than 1	Less than 1

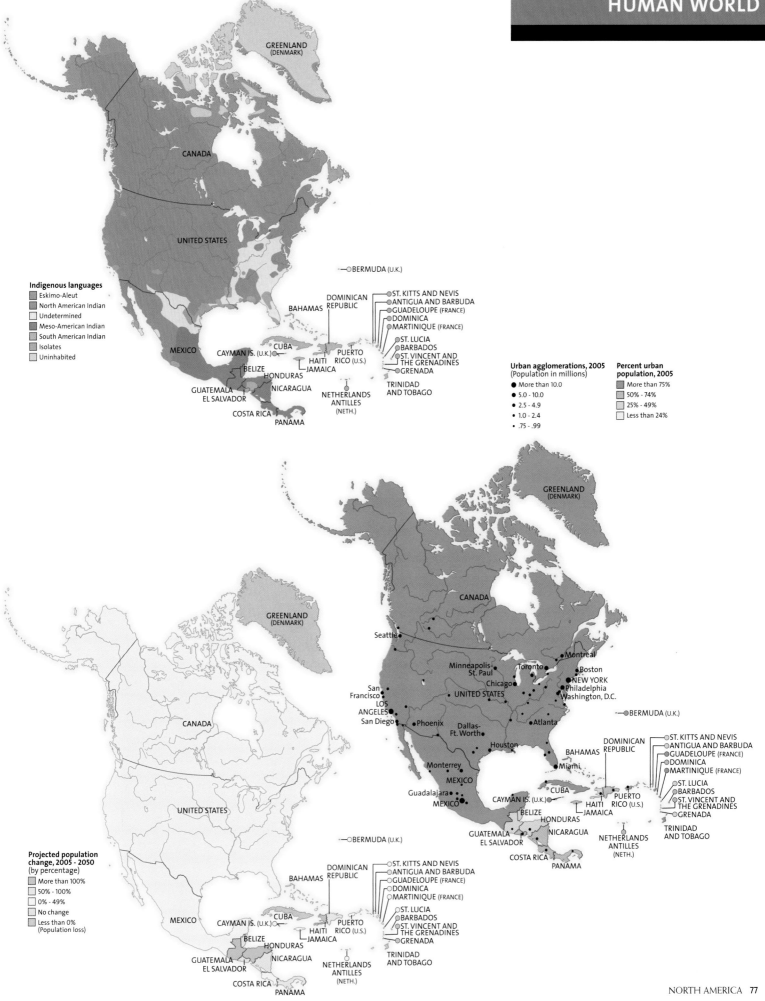

GREENLAND
(DENMARK)

CANADA

UNITED STATES

BERMUDA (U.K.)

Indigenous languages

- Eskimo-Aleut
- North American Indian
- Undetermined
- Meso-American Indian
- South American Indian
- Isolates
- Uninhabited

BAHAMAS

DOMINICAN
REPUBLIC

ST. KITTS AND NEVIS
ANTIGUA AND BARBUDA
GUADELOUPE (FRANCE)
DOMINICA
MARTINIQUE (FRANCE)

CUBA

CAYMAN IS. (U.K.)

MEXICO

HAITI
JAMAICA

PUERTO
RICO (U.S.)

ST. LUCIA
BARBADOS
ST. VINCENT AND
THE GRENADINES
GRENADA

BELIZE
HONDURAS
GUATEMALA
EL SALVADOR
NICARAGUA

COSTA RICA
PANAMA

NETHERLANDS
ANTILLES
(NETH.)

TRINIDAD
AND TOBAGO

Urban agglomerations, 2005
(Population in millions)

- ● More than 10.0
- ● 5.0 - 10.0
- ● 2.5 - 4.9
- · 1.0 - 2.4
- · .75 - .99

**Percent urban
population, 2005**

- More than 75%
- 50% - 74%
- 25% - 49%
- Less than 24%

GREENLAND
(DENMARK)

CANADA

Seattle

Montreal

Minneapolis-
St. Paul

Toronto
Boston

Chicago
NEW YORK
Philadelphia
Washington, D.C.

San
Francisco
LOS
ANGELES

UNITED STATES

San Diego
Phoenix
Dallas-
Ft. Worth
Atlanta

BERMUDA (U.K.)

Houston

Monterrey
Miami

MEXICO
BAHAMAS

DOMINICAN
REPUBLIC

ST. KITTS AND NEVIS
ANTIGUA AND BARBUDA
GUADELOUPE (FRANCE)
DOMINICA
MARTINIQUE (FRANCE)

Guadalajara

MEXICO
CAYMAN IS. (U.K.)

CUBA
PUERTO
RICO (U.S.)

ST. LUCIA
BARBADOS
ST. VINCENT AND
THE GRENADINES

BELIZE
HAITI
JAMAICA

HONDURAS
GRENADA

GUATEMALA
EL SALVADOR
NICARAGUA

COSTA RICA
PANAMA

NETHERLANDS
ANTILLES
(NETH.)

TRINIDAD
AND TOBAGO

GREENLAND
(DENMARK)

CANADA

UNITED STATES

**Projected population
change, 2005 - 2050**
(by percentage)

- More than 100%
- 50% - 100%
- 0% - 49%
- No change
- Less than 0%
  (Population loss)

MEXICO

CAYMAN IS. (U.K.)

CUBA

BERMUDA (U.K.)

BAHAMAS

DOMINICAN
REPUBLIC

ST. KITTS AND NEVIS
ANTIGUA AND BARBUDA
GUADELOUPE (FRANCE)
DOMINICA
MARTINIQUE (FRANCE)

HAITI
JAMAICA

PUERTO
RICO (U.S.)

ST. LUCIA
BARBADOS
ST. VINCENT AND
THE GRENADINES
GRENADA

BELIZE
HONDURAS
GUATEMALA
EL SALVADOR
NICARAGUA

COSTA RICA
PANAMA

NETHERLANDS
ANTILLES
(NETH.)

TRINIDAD
AND TOBAGO

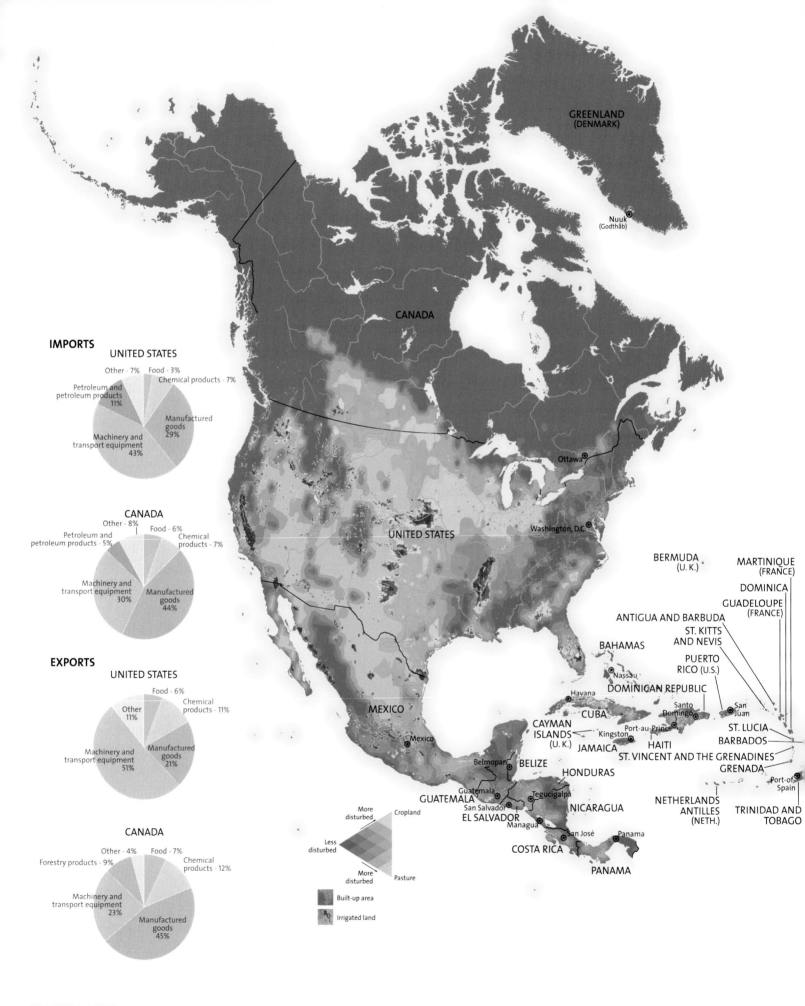

IMPORTS

UNITED STATES

Other - 7%
Food - 3%
Chemical products - 7%
Petroleum and petroleum products 11%
Manufactured goods 29%
Machinery and transport equipment 43%

CANADA

Other - 8%
Food - 6%
Petroleum and petroleum products - 5%
Chemical products - 7%
Machinery and transport equipment 30%
Manufactured goods 44%

EXPORTS

UNITED STATES

Food - 6%
Other 11%
Chemical products - 11%
Machinery and transport equipment 51%
Manufactured goods 21%

CANADA

Other - 4%
Food - 7%
Forestry products - 9%
Chemical products - 12%
Machinery and transport equipment 23%
Manufactured goods 45%

GREENLAND (DENMARK)

Nuuk (Godthåb)

CANADA

Ottawa

UNITED STATES

Washington, D.C.

BERMUDA (U. K.)

MARTINIQUE (FRANCE)

DOMINICA

GUADELOUPE (FRANCE)

ANTIGUA AND BARBUDA

ST. KITTS AND NEVIS

BAHAMAS

PUERTO RICO (U.S.)

DOMINICAN REPUBLIC

Nassau

Havana

Santo Domingo

San Juan

CUBA

CAYMAN ISLANDS (U. K.)

Kingston

Port-au-Prince

ST. LUCIA

BARBADOS

HAITI

JAMAICA

ST. VINCENT AND THE GRENADINES

MEXICO

Mexico

GRENADA

Port-of-Spain

Belmopan

BELIZE

NETHERLANDS ANTILLES (NETH.)

TRINIDAD AND TOBAGO

Guatemala

HONDURAS

GUATEMALA

Tegucigalpa

San Salvador

NICARAGUA

EL SALVADOR

Managua

San José

Panama

COSTA RICA

PANAMA

More disturbed
Cropland
Less disturbed
More disturbed
Pasture

Built-up area

Irrigated land

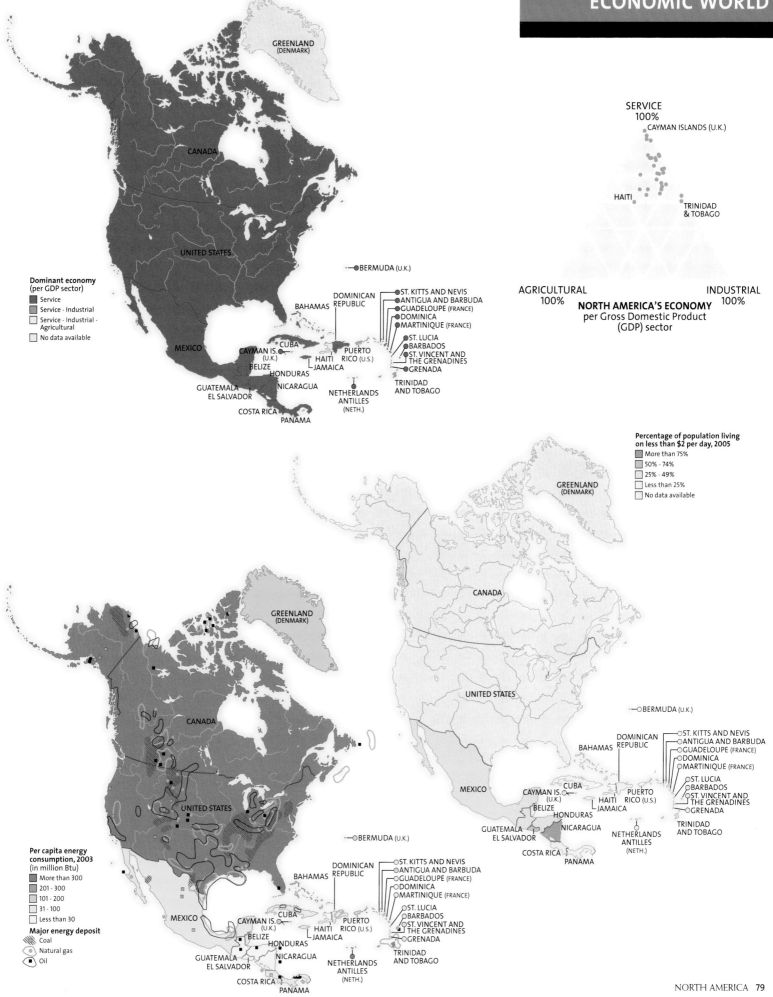

SERVICE
100%

CAYMAN ISLANDS (U.K.)

HAITI

TRINIDAD
& TOBAGO

AGRICULTURAL
100%

NORTH AMERICA'S ECONOMY
per Gross Domestic Product
(GDP) sector

INDUSTRIAL
100%

GREENLAND
(DENMARK)

CANADA

UNITED STATES

BERMUDA (U.K.)

ST. KITTS AND NEVIS
ANTIGUA AND BARBUDA
GUADELOUPE (FRANCE)
DOMINICA
MARTINIQUE (FRANCE)

DOMINICAN
REPUBLIC

BAHAMAS

CUBA
CAYMAN IS.
(U.K.)
BELIZE
HONDURAS
GUATEMALA
EL SALVADOR
NICARAGUA
COSTA RICA
PANAMA

HAITI
JAMAICA

PUERTO
RICO (U.S.)

ST. LUCIA
BARBADOS
ST. VINCENT AND
THE GRENADINES
GRENADA

NETHERLANDS
ANTILLES
(NETH.)

TRINIDAD
AND TOBAGO

MEXICO

Dominant economy
(per GDP sector)
- Service
- Service - Industrial
- Service - Industrial - Agricultural
- No data available

Percentage of population living on less than $2 per day, 2005
- More than 75%
- 50% - 74%
- 25% - 49%
- Less than 25%
- No data available

GREENLAND
(DENMARK)

CANADA

UNITED STATES

BERMUDA (U.K.)

ST. KITTS AND NEVIS
ANTIGUA AND BARBUDA
GUADELOUPE (FRANCE)
DOMINICA
MARTINIQUE (FRANCE)

DOMINICAN
REPUBLIC

BAHAMAS

CUBA
CAYMAN IS.
(U.K.)
BELIZE
HONDURAS
GUATEMALA
EL SALVADOR
NICARAGUA
COSTA RICA
PANAMA

HAITI
JAMAICA

PUERTO
RICO (U.S.)

ST. LUCIA
BARBADOS
ST. VINCENT AND
THE GRENADINES
GRENADA

NETHERLANDS
ANTILLES
(NETH.)

TRINIDAD
AND TOBAGO

MEXICO

GREENLAND
(DENMARK)

CANADA

UNITED STATES

Per capita energy consumption, 2003
(in million Btu)
- More than 300
- 201 - 300
- 101 - 200
- 31 - 100
- Less than 30

Major energy deposit
- Coal
- Natural gas
- Oil

BERMUDA (U.K.)

ST. KITTS AND NEVIS
ANTIGUA AND BARBUDA
GUADELOUPE (FRANCE)
DOMINICA
MARTINIQUE (FRANCE)

DOMINICAN
REPUBLIC

BAHAMAS

CUBA
CAYMAN IS.
(U.K.)
BELIZE
HONDURAS
GUATEMALA
EL SALVADOR
NICARAGUA
COSTA RICA
PANAMA

HAITI
JAMAICA

PUERTO
RICO (U.S.)

ST. LUCIA
BARBADOS
ST. VINCENT AND
THE GRENADINES
GRENADA

NETHERLANDS
ANTILLES
(NETH.)

TRINIDAD
AND TOBAGO

MEXICO

PACIFIC

OCEAN

D A

Lower Red L.
Mesabi Ra.
Eagle 701 Mt.
Isle Royale
Keweenaw Peninsula
Lake Superior
Leech Lake
Mille Lacs L.
MNNESOTA
Wolf
Menominee
Upper Peninsula
Georgian Bay
Mt. Katahdin 1606
Moosehead Lake
MAINE
Saint Paul
Timms Hill 595
WISCONSIN
Strs. of Mackinac
MICHIGAN
Lake Huron
St. Lawrence
Lake Champlain
Adirondack Mountains
Mt. Mansfield Mt. 1339
Mt. Marcy
Montpelier Mt. 1917 White Mts.
Washington N.H.
Augusta
Mt. Desert I.
nnesota
Mississippi
Wisconsin
Madison
Lake Winnebago
Lake Michigan
Lower Peninsula
Muskegon
Saginaw Bay
Grand Lansing
St. Clair
Lake Ontario
Niagara Falls
Finger Lakes
NEW YORK
Catskill Mountains
Albany
Hartford
Concord
Boston
Providence R.I.
Cape Cod
MASS.
Nantucket I.
Martha's Vineyard
Gulf of Maine
IOWA
Des Moines
Cedar
Iowa
Charles Mound 376
Rock
Lake Erie
Maumee
Campbell Hill 472
OHIO
Columbus
Allegheny
PENNSYLVANIA
Harrisburg
Susquehanna
Delaware
Trenton
New York
Long Island
Long Island Sd.
CONN.
Hudson
NEW JERSEY
Des Moines
C E N T R A L   L O W L A N D
ILLINOIS
Springfield
Indianapolis
INDIANA
Wabash
Gt. Miami
Scioto
Ohio
Mt. Davis 1024
MARYLAND
Washington D.C.
Annapolis
Dover
DEL.
Delaware Bay
Pine Barrens
Illinois
Kaskaskia
Kentucky
Frankfort
WEST VIRGINIA
Charleston
Allegheny Mountains
VIRGINIA
James
Richmond
Potomac
Chesapeake Bay
Chincoteague Bay
Cape Charles
Jefferson City
Missouri
Osage
Harry S. Truman Res.
Lake of the Ozarks
MISSOURI
540
Taum Sauk Mt.
Ozark Plateau
Kentucky
Lake Barkley
Lake Cumberland
Cumberland
Nashville
KENTUCKY
Ohio
Black Mt. 1265
Clinch
Cumberland Plateau
Great Smoky Mts. 2037
Clingmans Dome 2024
Mt. Mitchell 2037
Tar
Roanoke
NORTH CAROLINA
Raleigh
Neuse
Great Dismal Swamp
Albemarle Sound
Pamlico Sound
Cape Hatteras
Cape Lookout
Boston Mountains
Magazine 839 Mt.
White
Black
St. Francis
Little Rock
Woodall Mountain
Tennessee
TENNESSEE
Blue Ridge
Cape Fear
SOUTH CAROLINA
Columbia
Pee Dee
Santee
Cape Fear
ARKANSAS
Lake Ouachita
Ouachita Mountains
Saline
Ouachita
Black
Tombigbee
Cheaha Mt. 734
Coosa
Atlanta
GEORGIA
Oconee
Oostanaula
Savannah
ATLANTIC OCEAN
Driskill Mt. 163
ALABAMA
Montgomery
Alabama
Flint
Chattahoochee
Altamaha
Sea Islands
MISSISSIPPI
Jackson
Pearl
Yazoo
Mississippi
Red
Sabine
ayburn Res.
LOUISIANA
Baton Rouge
Lake Pontchartrain
Mississippi River Delta
Pensacola
Mobile Bay
Cape San Blas
Apalachee Bay
L. Seminole
Okefenokee Swamp
Tallahassee
Suwannee
FLORIDA
Cape Canaveral
Galveston Bay
Marsh I.
Timbalier Bay
Breton Sound
io Bay
Gulf of Mexico
Tampa Bay
Peace
Kissimmee
Lake Okeechobee
Charlotte Harbor
Cape Romano
The Everglades
Biscayne Bay
BAHAMAS
TROPIC OF CANCER
Cape Sable
Dry Tortugas
Marquesas Keys
Florida Keys
Straits of Florida

LAMBERT CONFORMAL CONIC PROJECTION
SCALE 1:12,000,000
0 KILOMETERS 200 300
0 MILES 100 200 300

LAMBERT CONFORMAL CONIC PROJECTION
SCALE 1:12,000,000

0 KILOMETERS   200   300

0 MILES   100   200   300

ATLANTIC
OCEAN

Gulf of
Mexico

BAHAMAS

TROPIC OF CANCER

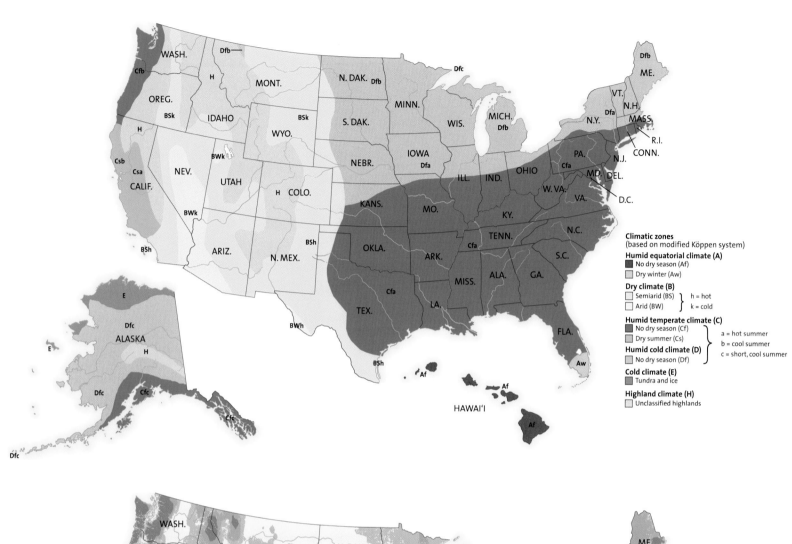

Climatic zones
(based on modified Köppen system)

Humid equatorial climate (A)
- No dry season (Af)
- Dry winter (Aw)

Dry climate (B)
- Semiarid (BS)   h = hot
- Arid (BW)   k = cold

Humid temperate climate (C)
- No dry season (Cf)   a = hot summer
- Dry summer (Cs)   b = cool summer

Humid cold climate (D)   c = short, cool summer
- No dry season (Df)

Cold climate (E)
- Tundra and ice

Highland climate (H)
- Unclassified highlands

Water availability
(in millimeters per-person per-year)
- More than 750
- 251 - 750
- 26 - 250
- Less than 26
- No data available

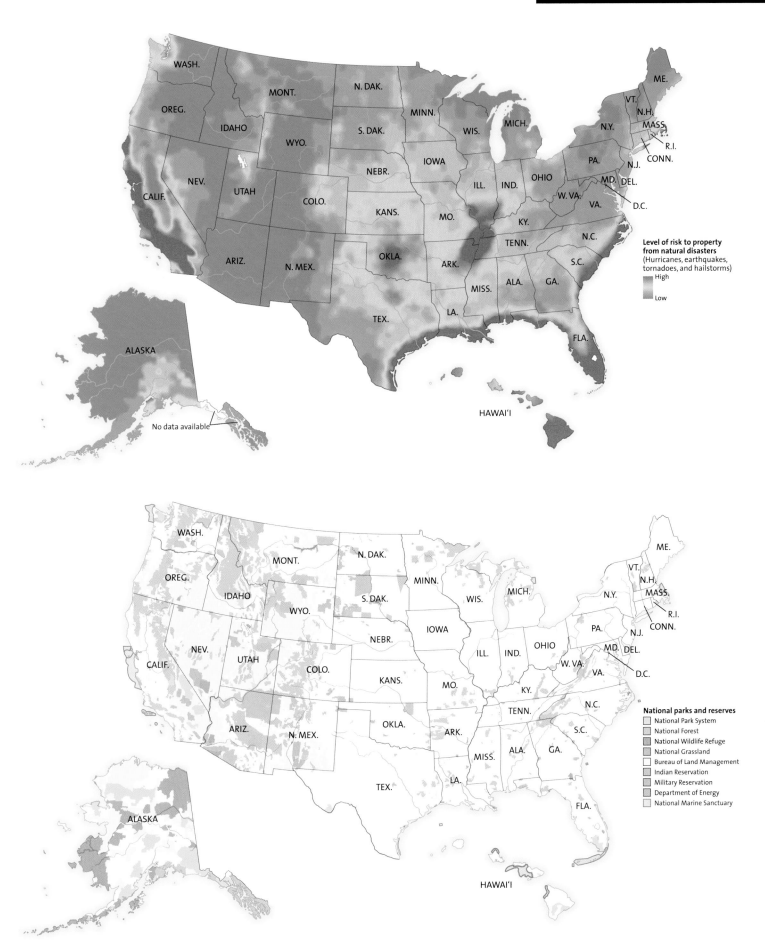

Level of risk to property from natural disasters
(Hurricanes, earthquakes, tornadoes, and hailstorms)

High

Low

No data available

National parks and reserves

- National Park System
- National Forest
- National Wildlife Refuge
- National Grassland
- Bureau of Land Management
- Indian Reservation
- Military Reservation
- Department of Energy
- National Marine Sanctuary

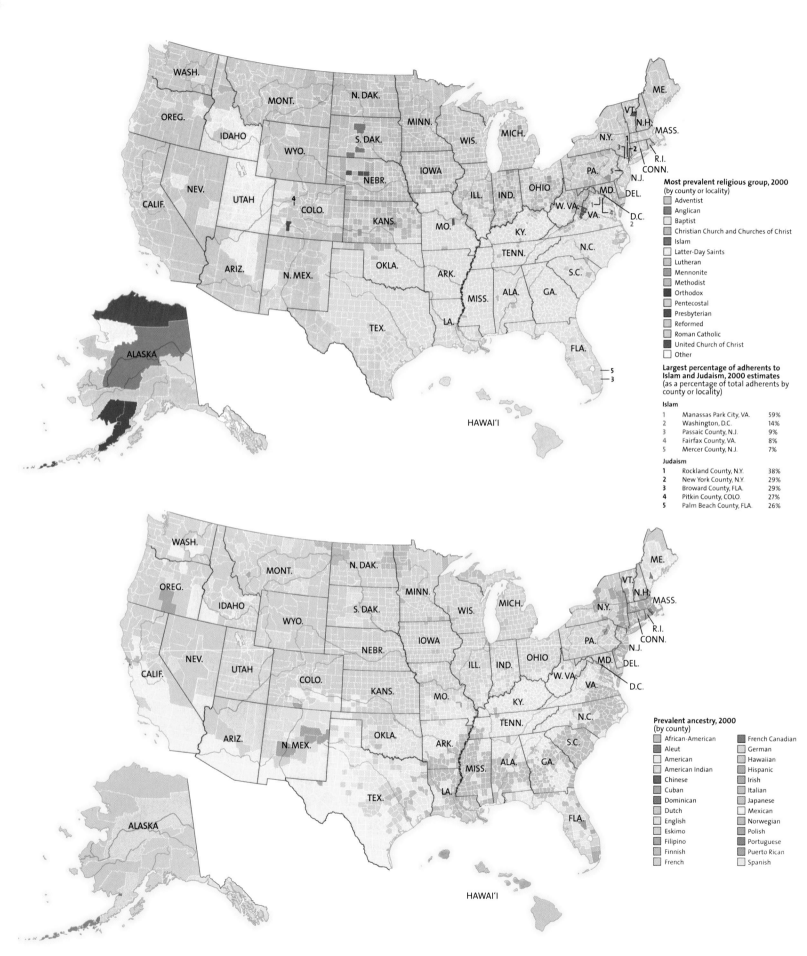

Most prevalent religious group, 2000
(by county or locality)

- Adventist
- Anglican
- Baptist
- Christian Church and Churches of Christ
- Islam
- Latter-Day Saints
- Lutheran
- Mennonite
- Methodist
- Orthodox
- Pentecostal
- Presbyterian
- Reformed
- Roman Catholic
- United Church of Christ
- Other

Largest percentage of adherents to Islam and Judaism, 2000 estimates
(as a percentage of total adherents by county or locality)

Islam

1	Manassas Park City, VA.	59%
2	Washington, D.C.	14%
3	Passaic County, N.J.	9%
4	Fairfax County, VA.	8%
5	Mercer County, N.J.	7%

Judaism

1	Rockland County, N.Y.	38%
2	New York County, N.Y.	29%
3	Broward County, FLA.	29%
4	Pitkin County, COLO.	27%
5	Palm Beach County, FLA.	26%

Prevalent ancestry, 2000
(by county)

- African-American
- Aleut
- American
- American Indian
- Chinese
- Cuban
- Dominican
- Dutch
- English
- Eskimo
- Filipino
- Finnish
- French
- French Canadian
- German
- Hawaiian
- Hispanic
- Irish
- Italian
- Japanese
- Mexican
- Norwegian
- Polish
- Portuguese
- Puerto Rican
- Spanish

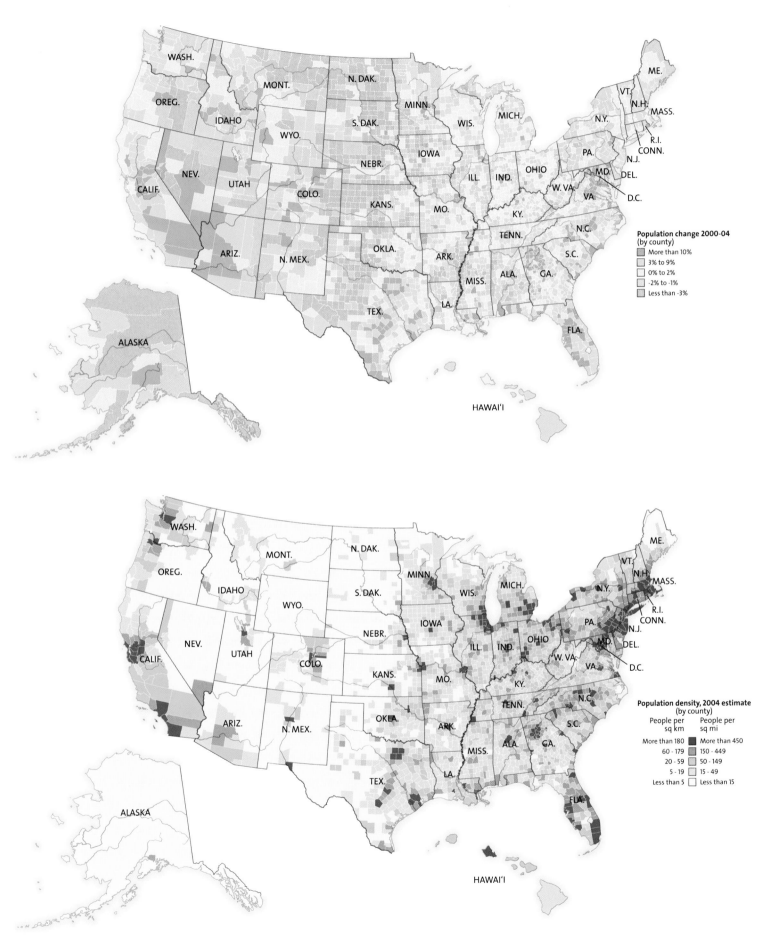

Population change 2000-04
(by county)
- More than 10%
- 3% to 9%
- 0% to 2%
- -2% to -1%
- Less than -3%

Population density, 2004 estimate
(by county)

People per sq km	People per sq mi
More than 180	More than 450
60 - 179	150 - 449
20 - 59	50 - 149
5 - 19	15 - 49
Less than 5	Less than 15

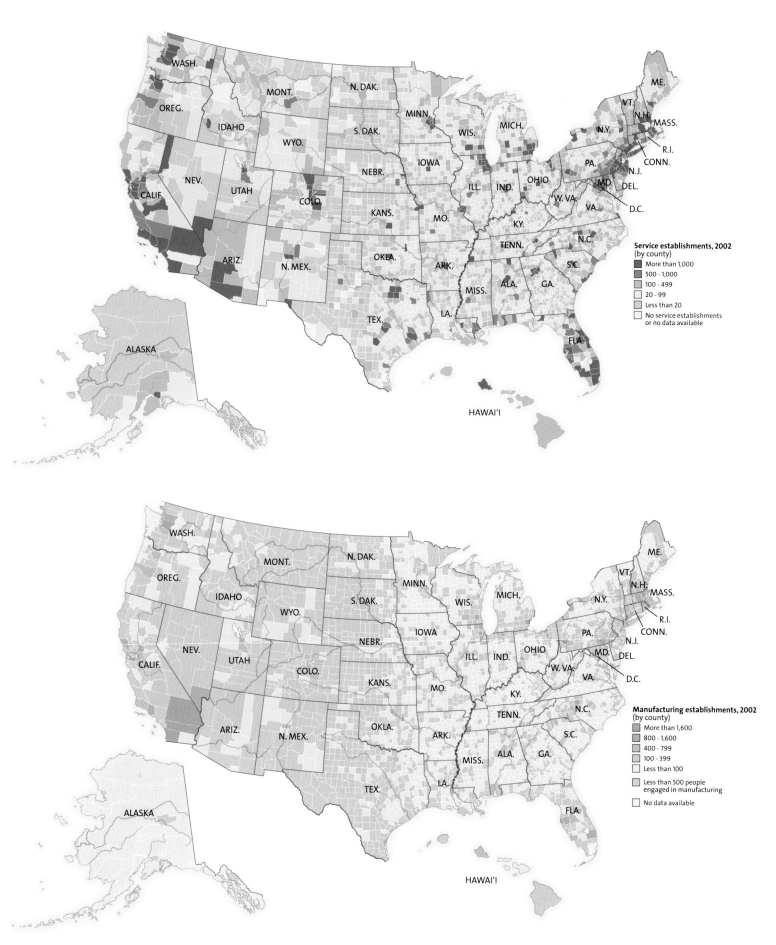

Service establishments, 2002
(by county)

More than 1,000
500 - 1,000
100 - 499
20 - 99
Less than 20
No service establishments
or no data available

Manufacturing establishments, 2002
(by county)

More than 1,600
800 - 1,600
400 - 799
100 - 399
Less than 100
Less than 500 people
engaged in manufacturing
No data available

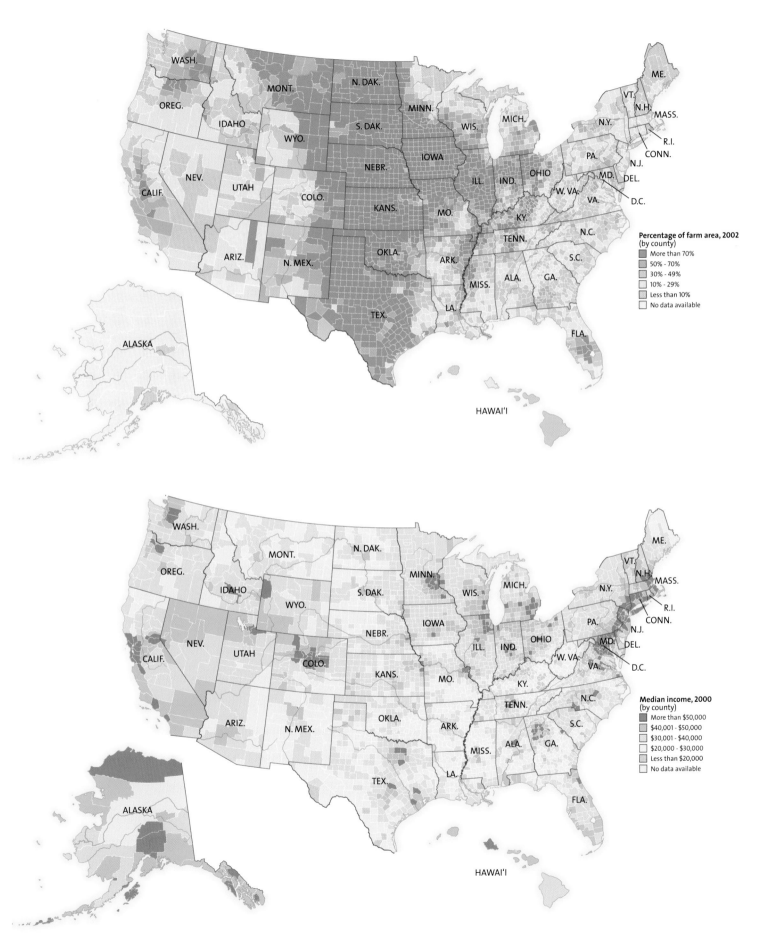

Percentage of farm area, 2002
(by county)

- More than 70%
- 50% - 70%
- 30% - 49%
- 10% - 29%
- Less than 10%
- No data available

Median income, 2000
(by county)

- More than $50,000
- $40,001 - $50,000
- $30,001 - $40,000
- $20,000 - $30,000
- Less than $20,000
- No data available

CANADA

SASKATCHEWAN

MANITOBA

ONTARIO

MONTANA

NORTH DAKOTA

MINNESOTA

SOUTH DAKOTA

WYOMING

IOWA

NEBRASKA

COLORADO

KANSAS

Saskatoon
Regina
Winnipeg

RIDING MOUNTAIN N.P.

GRASSLANDS N.P.

Old Wives Lake

Fife Lake

Lake Diefenbaker

UPPER MISSOURI RIVER BREAKS N.M.

Bears Paw Mountains 2103

Fort Peck Lake
Fort Peck Dam

THEODORE ROOSEVELT NAT. PARK

Killdeer Mountains

Lake Sakakawea

Bismarck

Big Snowy Mountains 2661

Judith Basin

Crazy Pk. 3423

Big Timber

Yellowstone

Miles City

Medicine Rocks

Devils Lake

Lake Oahe

Pierre

BADLANDS N.P.

WIND CAVE N.P.

Black Hills
Harney Pk. 2207
Rapid City

BIGHORN CANYON N.R.A.

Bighorn Mountains
Cloud Pk. 4013

Powder River Pass

Sand Hills

GRAND TETON N.P.

Gannett Pk. 4207
Fremont Pk. 4189

Wind River Range

Great Divide Basin

FLAMING GORGE N.R.A.

Medicine Bow Pk. 3662

Cheyenne

Laramie Mountains

Sierra Madre

Omaha

Lincoln

North Platte

Platte

DINOSAUR N.M.

ROCKY MOUNTAIN N.P.
Longs Pk. 4345

Fort Collins

Denver
Lakewood
Arvada
Westminster

Pikes Pk. 4301
Colorado Springs

Pueblo

Mt. Elbert 4399

Sawatch Range

BLACK CANYON OF THE GUNNISON N.M.

Grand Junction
Grand Mesa

ARCHES N.P.

CANYONLANDS N.P.

GLEN CANYON N.R.A.

Wichita

Arkansas

Smoky Hill

WYOMING
COLORADO
NEBRASKA
KANSAS
OKLAHOMA
NEW MEXICO
TEXAS
MEXICO
CHIHUAHUA
COAHUILA
NUEVO LEÓN
TAMAULIPAS
ROCKY MOUNTAINS
Great Divide Basin
HIGH PLAINS
LLANO ESTACADO
EDWARDS PLATEAU
CAPROCK ESCARPMENT
SIERRA MADRE OCCIDENTAL
SIERRA MADRE ORIENTAL
Sangre de Cristo Mountains
Sacramento Mountains
Guadalupe Mts.
Denver
Colorado Springs
Pueblo
Albuquerque
Santa Fe
El Paso
Ciudad Juárez
Chihuahua
Lubbock
Amarillo
Oklahoma City
Wichita
Lincoln
Fort Worth
Arlington
Austin
San Antonio
Laredo
Abilene
Waco
Wichita Falls
DINOSAUR NAT. MON.
ROCKY MOUNTAIN N.P.
MESA VERDE N.P.
CHACO CULTURE N.H.P.
BANDELIER N.M.
WHITE SANDS NAT. MON.
CARLSBAD CAVERNS N.P.
GUADALUPE MOUNTAINS N.P.
BIG BEND N.P.
PETRIFIED FOREST N.P.
CANYONLANDS N.P.
ARCHES N.P.
CANYON DE CHELLY NAT. MON.
RIO GRANDE WILD & SCENIC RIVER
AMISTAD N.R.A.
LAKE MEREDITH N.R.A.
108°
105°
102°
99°
39°
36°
33°
30°

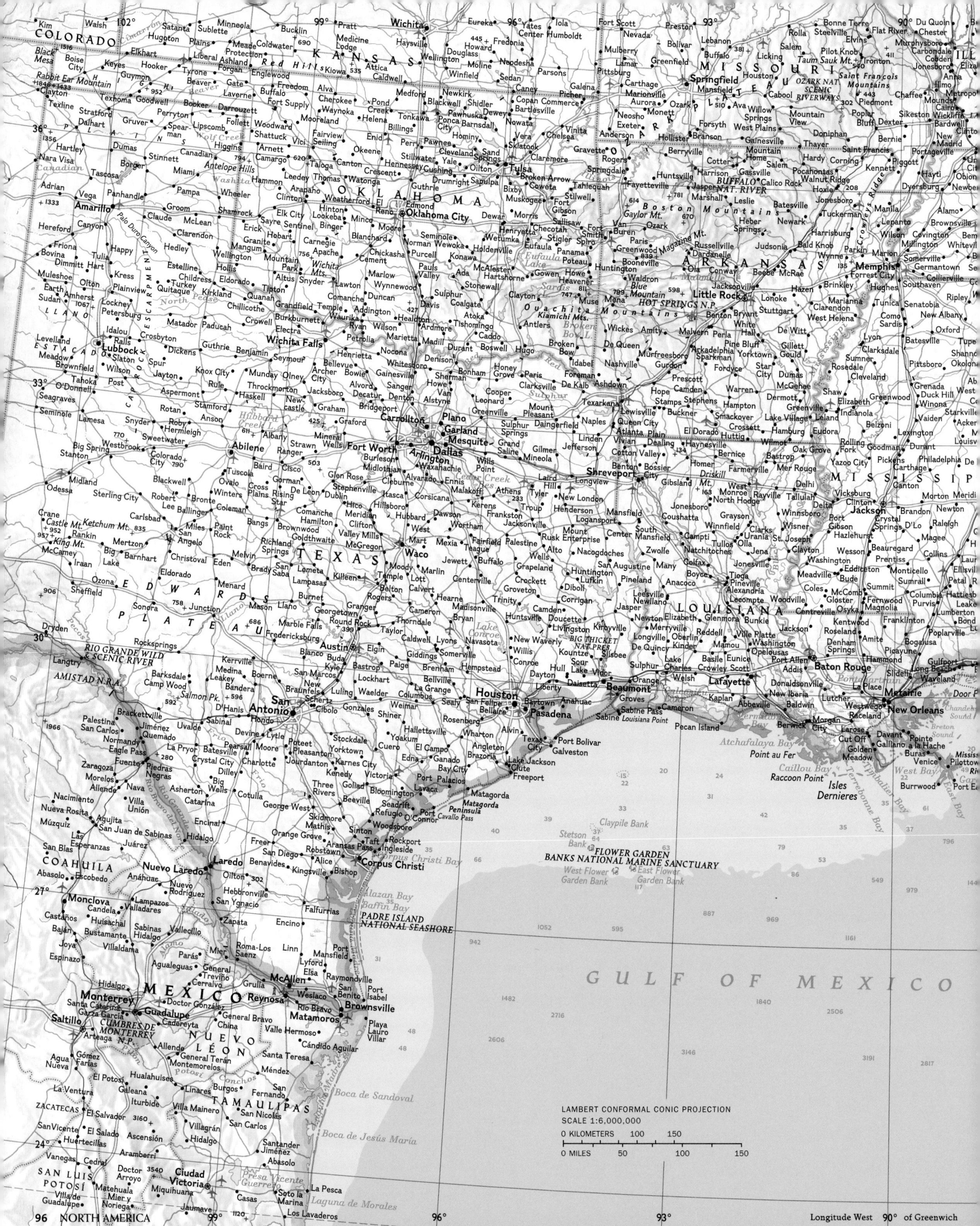
COLORADO
KANSAS
MISSOURI
OKLAHOMA
ARKANSAS
TEXAS
LOUISIANA
MISSISSIPPI
MEXICO
COAHUILA
NUEVO LEÓN
TAMAULIPAS
SAN LUIS POTOSÍ
ZACATECAS
GULF OF MEXICO
EDWARDS PLATEAU
LLANO ESTACADO
OZARK PLATEAU
Boston Mountains
Ouachita Mountains
Wichita
Tulsa
Oklahoma City
Amarillo
Lubbock
Wichita Falls
Abilene
Fort Worth
Dallas
Arlington
Garland
Plano
Mesquite
Carrollton
Waco
Austin
San Antonio
Houston
Pasadena
Beaumont
Corpus Christi
Laredo
Nuevo Laredo
Brownsville
Matamoros
Reynosa
McAllen
Monterrey
Guadalupe
Saltillo
Ciudad Victoria
Shreveport
Little Rock
Memphis
Jackson
Baton Rouge
Lafayette
Metairie
New Orleans
Springfield
PADRE ISLAND NATIONAL SEASHORE
FLOWER GARDEN BANKS NATIONAL MARINE SANCTUARY
RIO GRANDE WILD & SCENIC RIVER
AMISTAD N.R.A.
HOT SPRINGS N.P.
BUFFALO NAT. RIVER
BIG THICKET NAT. PRES.
CUMBRES DE MONTERREY N.P.
LAMBERT CONFORMAL CONIC PROJECTION
SCALE 1:6,000,000
0 KILOMETERS 100 150
0 MILES 50 100 150
Longitude West 90° of Greenwich

WEST VIRGINIA

KENTUCKY

VIRGINIA

TENNESSEE

NORTH CAROLINA

SOUTH CAROLINA

GEORGIA

ALABAMA

FLORIDA

ATLANTIC OCEAN

Nashville · Knoxville · Chattanooga · Huntsville · Birmingham · Montgomery · Columbus · Atlanta · Augusta · Columbia · Charlotte · Greensboro · Raleigh · Durham · Winston-Salem · Fayetteville · Wilmington · Myrtle Beach · Charleston · Savannah · Hilton Head Island · Jacksonville · Tallahassee · Orlando · Tampa · St. Petersburg · Clearwater · Cape Coral · Ft. Lauderdale · Hollywood · Miami

GREAT SMOKY MTS. N.P. · CAPE HATTERAS N.S. · CAPE LOOKOUT N.S. · CONGAREE SWAMP N.P. · INTRACOASTAL WATERWAY · CUMBERLAND ISLAND NATIONAL SEASHORE · CANAVERAL NATIONAL SEASHORE · JOHN F. KENNEDY SPACE CENTER · GULF ISLANDS NAT. SEASHORE · Walt Disney World · BIG CYPRESS NAT. PRESERVE · BISCAYNE N.P. · EVERGLADES N.P.

Florida Keys · Key West · Dry Tortugas · Marquesas Keys

BAHAMAS · Grand Bahama Island · Abaco Island · New Providence Island · Nassau · Andros Island · Eleuthera Island · Cat Island · Great Exuma

Straits of Florida · TROPIC OF CANCER

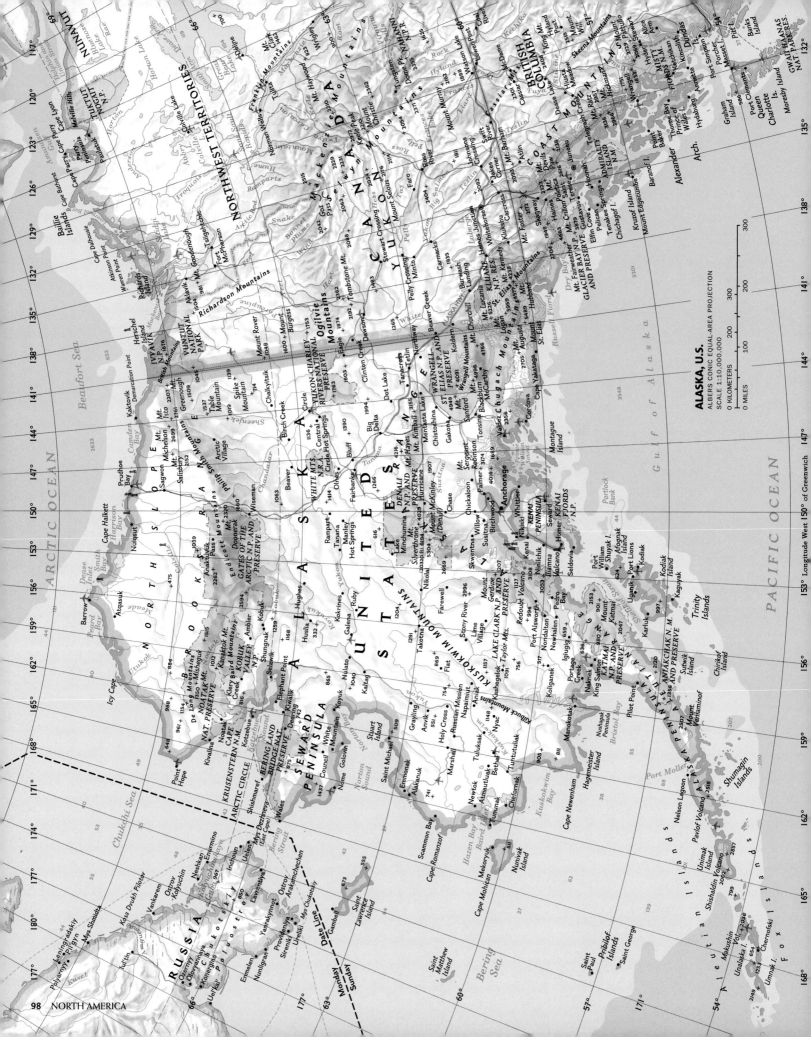

ALASKA, U.S.
ALBERS CONIC EQUAL-AREA PROJECTION
SCALE 1:10,000,000

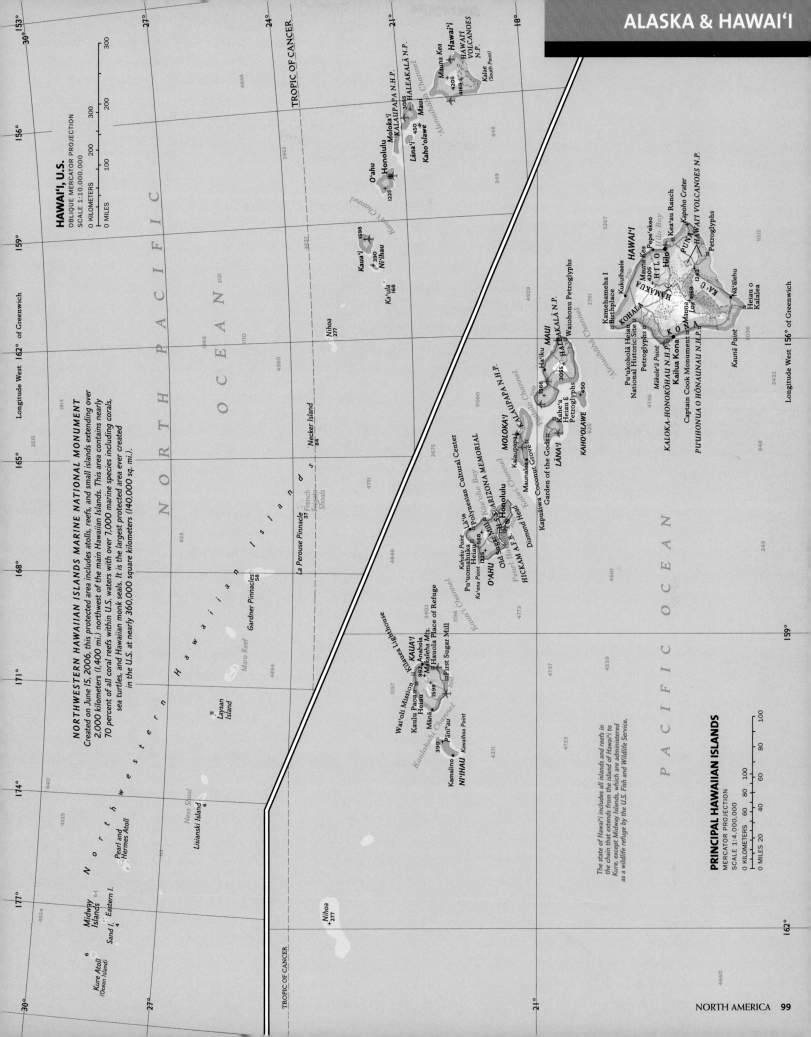

HAWAI‘I, U.S.
OBLIQUE MERCATOR PROJECTION
SCALE 1:10,000,000

NORTHWESTERN HAWAIIAN ISLANDS MARINE NATIONAL MONUMENT
Created on June 15, 2006, this protected area includes atolls, reefs, and small islands extending over 2,000 kilometers (1,400 mi.) northwest of the main Hawaiian Islands. This area contains nearly 70 percent of all coral reefs within U.S. waters with over 7,000 marine species including corals, sea turtles, and Hawaiian monk seals. It is the largest protected area ever created in the U.S. at nearly 360,000 square kilometers (140,000 sq. mi.).

NORTH PACIFIC OCEAN

PACIFIC OCEAN

PRINCIPAL HAWAIIAN ISLANDS
MERCATOR PROJECTION
SCALE 1:4,000,000

The state of Hawai‘i includes all islands and reefs in the chain that extends from the island of Hawai‘i to Kure, except Midway Islands, which are administered as a wildlife refuge by the U.S. Fish and Wildlife Service.

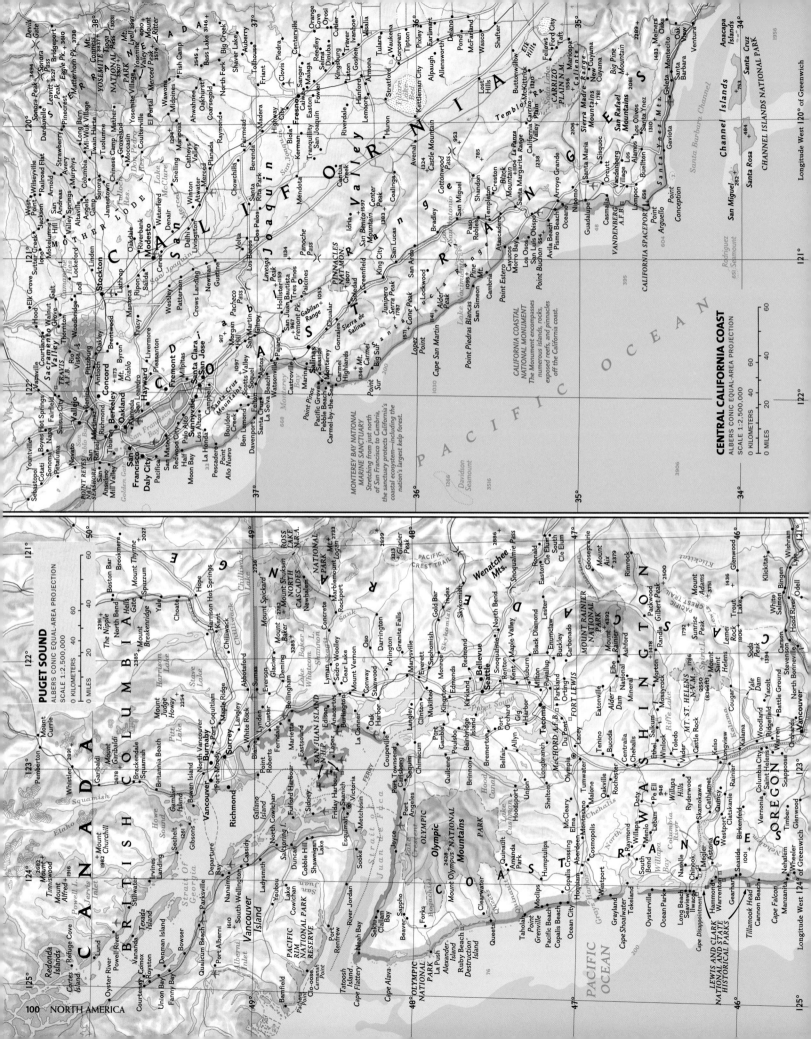

PUGET SOUND
ALBERS CONIC EQUAL-AREA PROJECTION
SCALE 1:2,500,000

CENTRAL CALIFORNIA COAST
ALBERS CONIC EQUAL-AREA PROJECTION
SCALE 1:2,500,000

MONTEREY BAY NATIONAL MARINE SANCTUARY
Stretching from just north of San Francisco to Cambria, the sanctuary protects California's coastal ecosystem—including the nation's largest kelp forest.

CALIFORNIA COASTAL NATIONAL MONUMENT
The Monument encompasses numerous islands, rocks, exposed reefs, and pinnacles off the California coast.

SOUTHERN CALIFORNIA
ALBERS CONIC EQUAL-AREA PROJECTION
SCALE 1:2,500,000

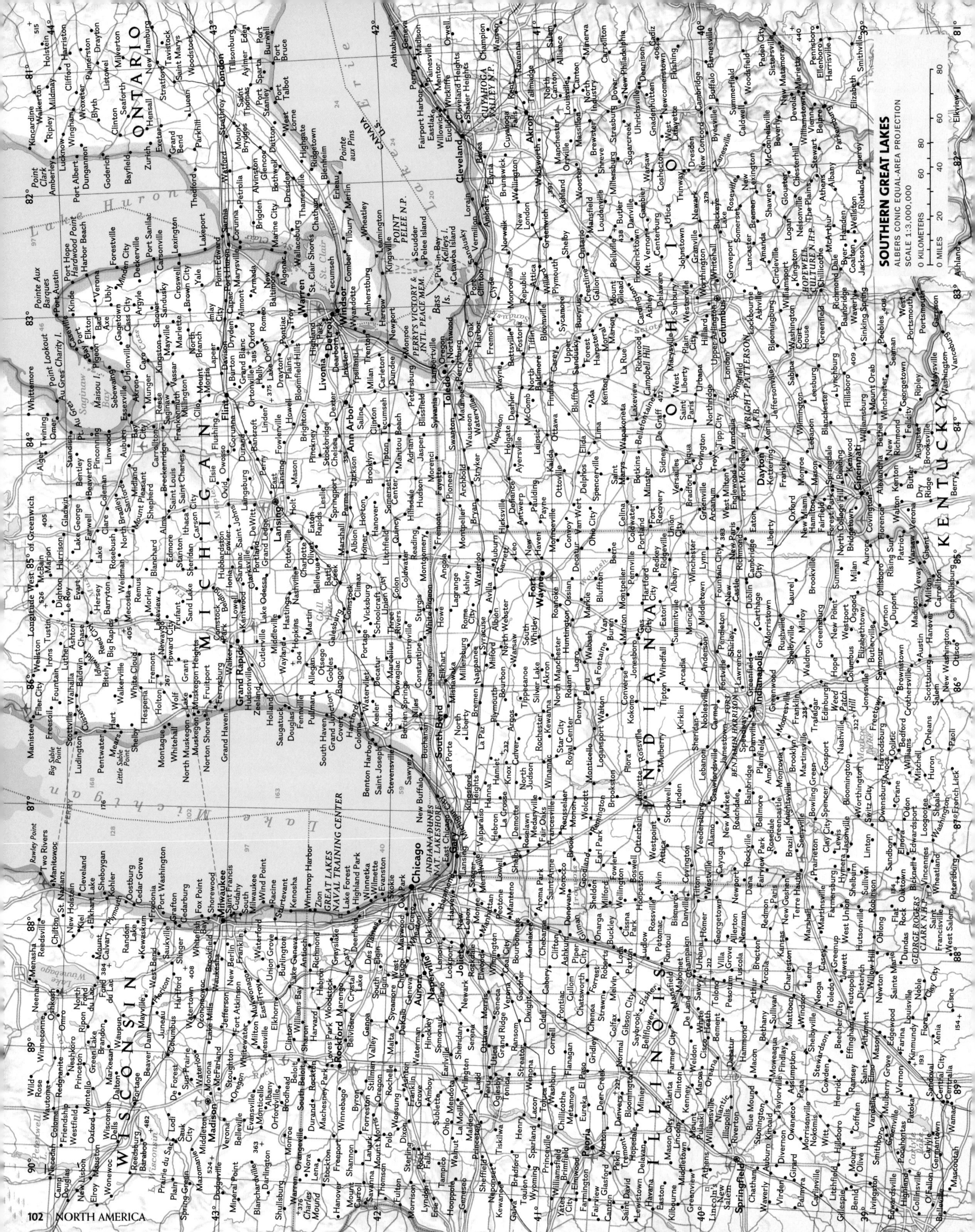

SOUTHERN GREAT LAKES
ALBERS CONIC EQUAL-AREA PROJECTION
SCALE 1:3,000,000

0 KILOMETERS 20 40 60 80

0 MILES 20 40 60 80

ONTARIO

MICHIGAN

WISCONSIN

ILLINOIS

INDIANA

OHIO

KENTUCKY

Lake Huron

Lake Erie

Lake Michigan

Lake St. Clair

Saginaw Bay

Chicago

Milwaukee

Madison

Detroit

Windsor

Toledo

Cleveland

Akron

Columbus

Dayton

Cincinnati

Indianapolis

Fort Wayne

South Bend

Grand Rapids

Lansing

Flint

Ann Arbor

Springfield

Peoria

Rockford

CUYAHOGA VALLEY N.P.

INDIANA DUNES NAT. LAKESHORE

GREAT LAKES NAVAL TRAINING CENTER

PERRY'S VICTORY & INTL. PEACE MEM.

POINT PELEE N.P.

HOPEWELL CULTURE N.H.P.

GEORGE ROGERS CLARK N.H.P.

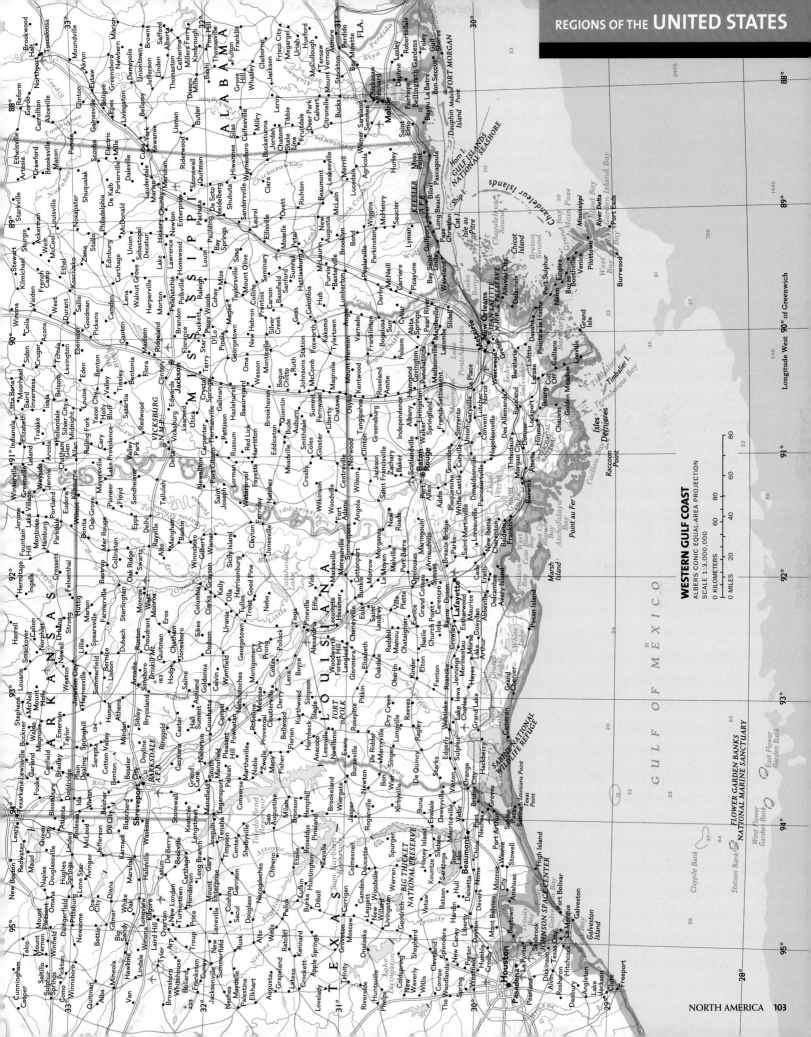

SOUTHERN NEW ENGLAND

ALBERS CONIC EQUAL-AREA PROJECTION

SCALE 1:1,750,000

0 KILOMETERS   30 40 50

0 MILES   10   20   30   40   50

83° 82° 81°

Dekle Beach
Piney Point
Salem
Steinhatchee
Jena
Horseshoe Beach
Piney Point
Horseshoe Cove
Suwannee
Cedar Key
Turtle Creek Pt.
Yankeetown
Inglis
Waccasassa Bay

Fort White
High Springs
Alachua
Waldo
Newberry
Gainesville
Trenton
Archer
Chiefland
Bronson
Williston
McIntosh
Reddick
Fairfield
Gulf Hammock
Anthony
Rainbow Springs
Silver Springs
Ocala
Dunnellon
Belleview
Beverly Hills
Crystal River
Crystal Bay
Homosassa Springs
Homosassa
Chassahowitzka
Floral City
Inverness
Coleman
Wildwood

Brooker
Hampton
Keystone Heights
Melrose
Hawthorne
Island Grove
Citra
Welaka
Georgetown
Seville
Pierson
Barberville
De Leon Springs
Oklawaha
Weirsdale
Eustis
Tavares
Leesburg
Mount Dora
Zellwood
Apopka
Bushnell
Center Hill
Webster
Groveland

CASTILLO DE SAN MARCOS N.M.
Anastasia Island
Saint Augustine
Red Snapper Sink
FORT MATANZAS N.M.
Elkton
Hastings
East Palatka
Palatka
Pomona Park
Crescent City
Bunnell
Flagler Beach
Palm Coast
Ormond by the Sea
Ormond Beach
Holly Hill
Daytona Beach
South Daytona
Port Orange
New Smyrna Beach
Edgewater
Oak Hill
Mims
Titusville
Christmas
Mosquito Lagoon
CANAVERAL N.S.

ATLANTIC OCEAN

29°

FLORIDA

Marineland

De Land
Lake Helen
Orange City
DeBary
Deltona
Sanford
Lake Monroe
Casselberry
Winter Park
Pine Hills
Ocoee
Orlando
Clermont
Walt Disney World
Lake Buena Vista
Kissimmee
Saint Cloud
Davenport
Haines City
Auburndale
Winter Haven
Singing Tower

JOHN F. KENNEDY SPACE CENTER
Cape Canaveral (Cape Kennedy)
Cape Canaveral
Merritt Island
Cocoa
Rockledge
Cocoa Beach
PATRICK A.F.B.
Satellite Beach
Indialantic
Melbourne
Melbourne Beach
Palm Bay

Weeki Wachee
Weeki Wachee Spring
Spring Hill
Hudson
Bayonet Point
New Port Richey
Elfers
Tarpon Springs
Palm Harbor
Dunedin
Clearwater
Largo
Pinellas Park
St. Petersburg
Gulfport
Mullet Key

Brooksville
Triby
Lacoochee
Dade City
Saint Leo
Land O'Lakes
Zephyrhills
Thonotosassa
Plant City
Lakeland
Eagle Lake
Mulberry
Homeland
Bradley Junction
Wimauma
Bowling Green
Wauchula
Zolfo Springs

Lake Wales
Babson Park
Frostproof
Avon Park
Sebring
Lake Placid
Venus

FLORIDA'S TURNPIKE
Kenansville
Felixmere
Sebastian
Wabasso
Gifford
Vero Beach
Florida Ridge
Saint Lucie
Fort Pierce
White City
Port Saint Lucie
Hutchinson Island
Jensen Beach
Rio
Stuart
Port Salerno
Hobe Sound

28°

Tampa
Brandon
Dover
Gibsonton
MACDILL A.F.B.
Tampa Bay

O R L A N D
R I D A
F L O

Arcadia
Nocatee
Fort Ogden
Lake Istokpoga
Lake Placid
Kissimmee
Basinger
Okeechobee
Indiantown
SAINT LUCIE CANAL
Jupiter
Juno Beach
Palm Beach Gardens
Canal Point
Bryant
Pahokee
Riviera Beach
West Palm Beach
Palm Beach
Lake Worth
Palm Springs
Lantana
Boynton Beach
Delray Beach

Palmetto
Ellenton
Bradenton
Bradenton Beach
Oneco
Longboat Key
Fruitville
Bee Ridge
Sarasota
Siesta Key
Osprey
North Port
Venice
Englewood
Port Charlotte
Placida
Gasparilla Island
Boca Grande
Pine Island
Saint James City
Captiva Island
Sanibel Island

Myakka City
Manatee
Peace
Parrish
Palmdale
Moore Haven
Clewiston
La Belle
Lake Harbor
Belle Glade
South Bay
Caloosahatchee
North Fort Myers
Fort Myers
Lehigh Acres
Cape Coral
Immokalee
Corkscrew Swamp Sanctuary
Sunniland
Okaloacoochee Slough

Lake Okeechobee

27°

GULF OF MEXICO

Fort Myers Beach
Bonita Springs
North Naples
Naples
East Naples
Marco
Goodland
Cape Romano
Ochopee
Everglades City
Chokoloskee
Ten Thousand Is.

Big Cypress Swamp
BIG CYPRESS NATIONAL PRESERVE

Boca Raton
Deerfield Beach
Pompano Beach
Lighthouse Point
Coral Springs
Lauderdale Lakes
Oakland Park
Plantation
Fort Lauderdale
Davie
Hollywood
Miramar
Hallandale
Carol City
North Miami
Hialeah
Miami
Miami Beach
Coral Gables
Key Biscayne
Kendall
Perrine
BISCAYNE N.P.
Biscayne Bay

26°

BAHAMAS

Mangrove Cay
Crishy Swash
West End Point
West End
Grand Bahama Island
Eight Mile Rock
Freeport
Lucaya
Pinders Point

Great Isaac
Little Isaac
East Isaac
North Bimini
Alice Town
Bimini Islands
South Bimini
Gun Cay
North Cat Cay
South Cat Cay
Ocean Cay
Brown's Cay

EVERGLADES N.P.
Cutler Ridge
Homestead
Florida City
Old Rhodes Key
Everglades

Ponce de Leon Bay
Whitewater Bay
Cape Sable
Flamingo
Plantation Key
Key Largo
Florida Bay
Tavernier
Islamorada
Lower Matecumbe Key
Sugarloaf Key
Snipe Keys
Long Key
Key Colony Beach
Florida Keys
INTRACOASTAL WATERWAY

DRY TORTUGAS N.P.
Dry Tortugas
Marquesas Keys
Key West
Perky
Summerland Key
Big Pine Key
Marathon

25°

Straits of Florida

PENINSULAR FLORIDA
ALBERS CONIC EQUAL-AREA PROJECTION
SCALE 1:2,500,000

0 KILOMETERS 40 60

0 MILES 20 40 60

Longitude West 81° of Greenwich

80°

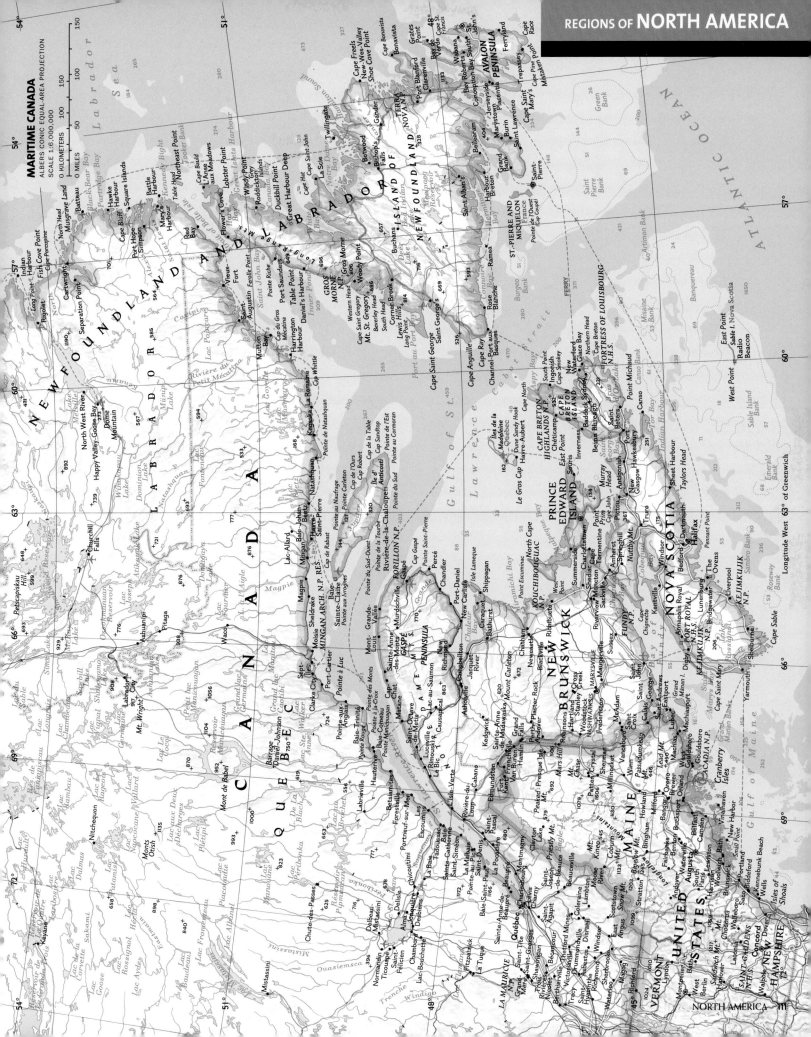

MARITIME CANADA

ALBERS CONIC EQUAL-AREA PROJECTION

SCALE 1:6,000,000

ALBERS CONIC EQUAL-AREA PROJECTION
SCALE 1:10,000,000

0 KILOMETERS   200   300

0 MILES   100   200   300

National Parks of Mexico
(National parks are numbered in blue on the map.)

1 Cañón de Río Blanco
2 Cañón del Sumidero
3 Cumbres de Monterrey
4 El Gogorrón
5 Iztaccíhuatl–Popocatépetl
6 Lago de Camécuaro
7 Lagunas de Chacahua
8 La Malinche
9 Los Mármoles
10 Nevado de Toluca
11 Palenque
12 Pico de Orizaba
13 Pico de Tancítaro
14 Sierra de San Pedro Mártir
15 Volcán Nevado de Colima

Longitude West 117° of Greenwich

GULF OF MEXICO

UNITED STATES

TEXAS · OKLAHOMA · ARKANSAS · LOUISIANA · MISSISSIPPI · ALABAMA · GEORGIA · FLORIDA

MEXICO

TAMAULIPAS · NUEVO LEÓN · SAN LUIS POTOSÍ · GUANAJUATO · HIDALGO · MÉXICO · TLAXCALA · PUEBLA · MORELOS · GUERRERO · OAXACA · VERACRUZ · TABASCO · CHIAPAS · CAMPECHE · YUCATÁN · QUINTANA ROO

CUBA · BELIZE · GUATEMALA · HONDURAS · EL SALVADOR · NICARAGUA

ATLANTIC OCEAN

Caribbean Sea

CAMPECHE BANK

YUCATÁN PENINSULA

TROPIC OF CANCER

NORTH AMERICA

National Parks and Biotopes of Guatemala
(Protected areas are numbered in blue on the map.)

16	Sierra del Lacandón	20	Dos Lagunas
17	Laguna del Tigre–Río Escondido	21	Río Azul
18	Laguna del Tigre	22	Tikal
19	Mirador		

113

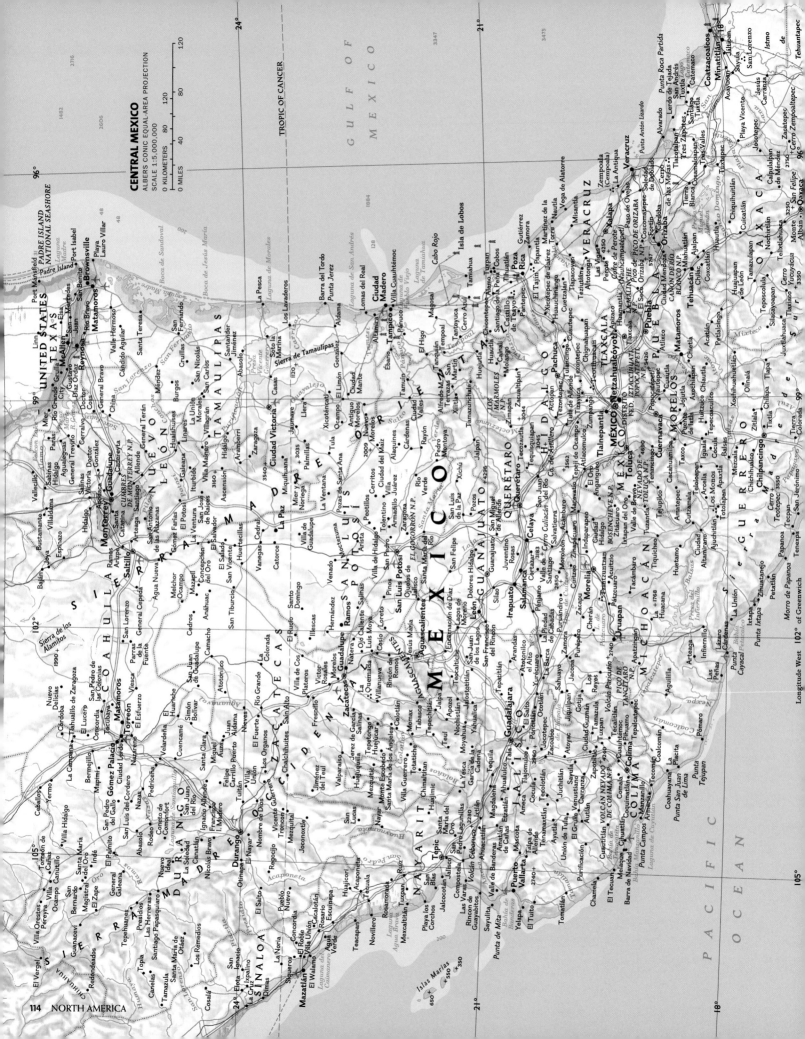

ALBERS CONIC EQUAL-AREA PROJECTION
SCALE 1:5,000,000

TROPIC OF CANCER

GULF OF MEXICO

UNITED STATES

TEXAS

Padre Island
PADRE ISLAND
NATIONAL SEASHORE

Brownsville
Matamoros
Reynosa
McAllen

T A M A U L I P A S

N U E V O   L E Ó N

Monterrey
Guadalupe
Saltillo

C O A H U I L A

Ciudad Victoria

Ciudad Madero
Tampico
Altamira

S I E R R A   M A D R E   O R I E N T A L

S A N   L U I S   P O T O S Í

San Luis Potosí

D U R A N G O

Durango

Z A C A T E C A S

Zacatecas

Gómez Palacio
Torreón

S I E R R A   M A D R E   O C C I D E N T A L

A G U A S C A L I E N T E S
Aguascalientes

G U A N A J U A T O

Q U E R É T A R O
Querétaro

H I D A L G O

Pachuca

M É X I C O
MÉXICO
Toluca

TLAXCALA

P U E B L A
Puebla

V E R A C R U Z
Veracruz

Xalapa

Orizaba

Coatzacoalcos
Minatitlán

O A X A C A
Oaxaca

MORELOS
Cuernavaca

DISTRITO
FED.

N A Y A R I T
Tepic

J A L I S C O
Guadalajara

COLIMA
Colima

M I C H O A C Á N
Morelia

G U E R R E R O
Chilpancingo

Mazatlán

S I N A L O A

Puerto
Vallarta

PACIFIC OCEAN

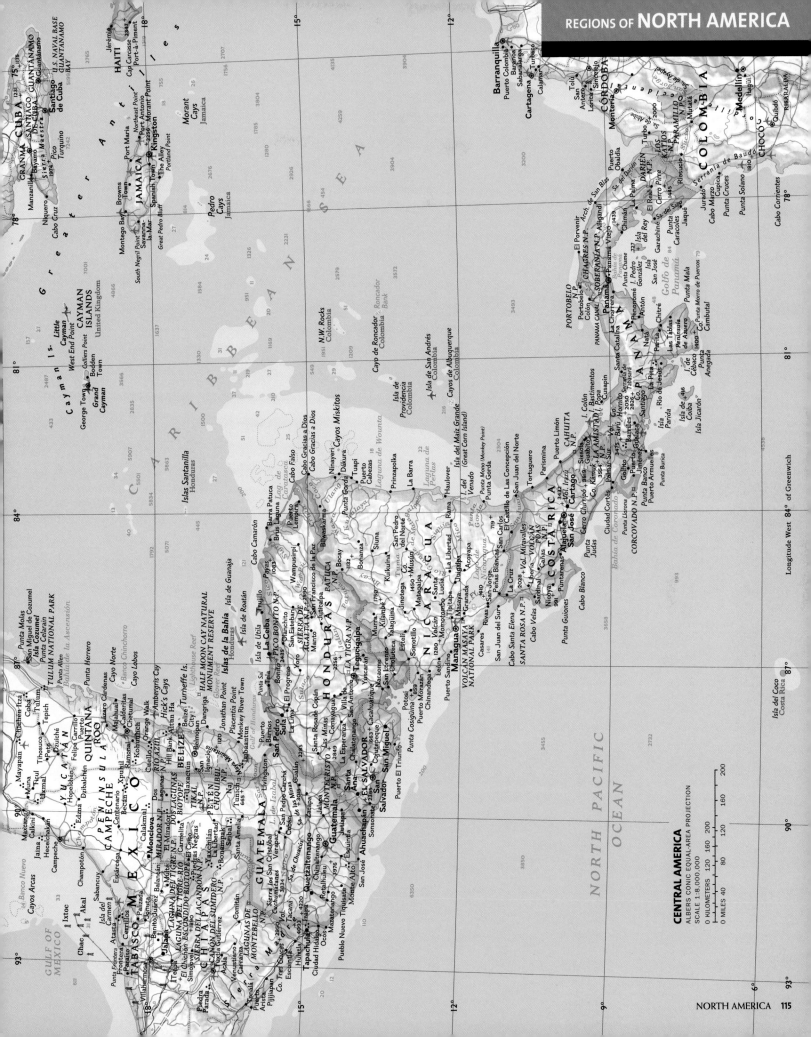

CENTRAL AMERICA
ALBERS CONIC EQUAL-AREA PROJECTION
SCALE 1:8,000,000

0 KILOMETERS 40 80 120 160 200
0 MILES 40 80 120 160 200

Longitude West 84° of Greenwich

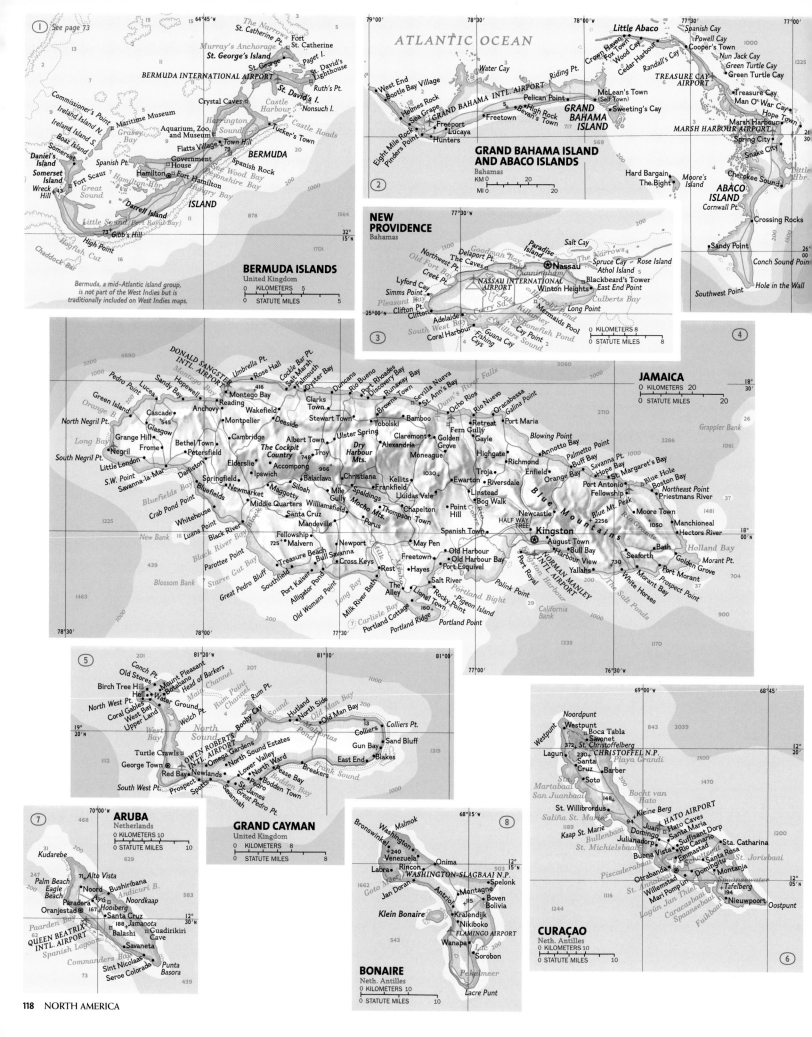

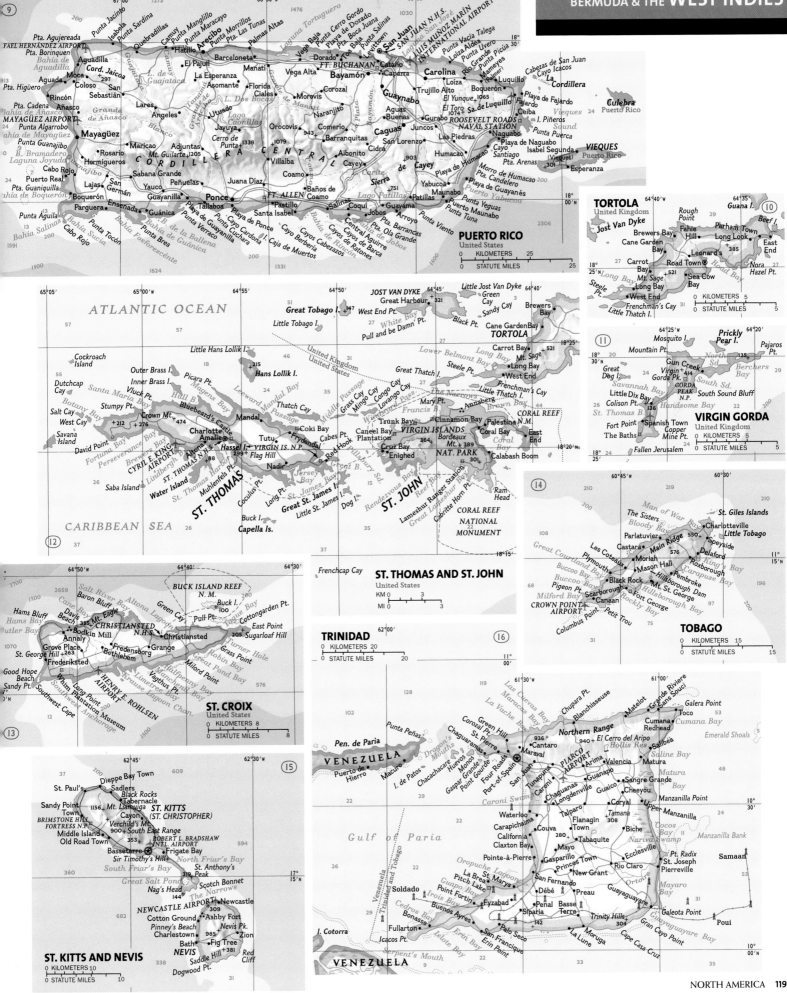

Two features dominate South America: the Andes, extending 7,242 kilometers (4,500 miles), is the world's longest and second highest mountain range; the Amazon—the world's largest river by volume and, at 6,437 kilometers (4,000 miles), the second longest—flows through the largest, most biologically rich rain forest on Earth. Some of the people in the Amazon Basin are among the least touched by the modern world, although the press of logging, agriculture, and settlement has devastated much of the forest and its scattered inhabitants. Other South American features also stand out. The Pantanal, spanning parts of Brazil, Paraguay, and Bolivia with flooded grasslands and savannas, is 17 times the size of the Florida Everglades and home to a kaleidoscopic diversity of plant and animal life. The vast grassy plains of the Argentine Pampas nourish livestock, but the Atacama Desert of Chile supports little life. Its dry, clear, thin air, however, makes it ideal for astronomical observatories. In the Andes, the Inca empire expanded between 1438 and 1527, stretching from modern Colombia to western Argentina. Weakened by internal dissension, the Inca succumbed to Francisco Pizarro's forces in 1533. Spaniards looted its golden treasures and forced native slave labor to work gold and silver mines; Portuguese overlords imported millions of slaves from Africa to work Brazilian plantations. Not until the early 19th century under Simon Bolivar, the Liberator of the Americas, did the desire for independence coalesce and rebellion spread rapidly. Yet even after the colonial period, strife continued during the 20th century with coups, civil wars, and cross-border disputes. Today mining of industrial mineral ores, fishing, forestry, petroleum extraction, and commercial agriculture support the continent's economies, but prosperity does not reach all its people. Populist leaders in countries such as Venezuela and Bolivia are raising their voices, while indigenous peoples' activists are gaining new influence.

IMAGE BY ROBERT STACEY, WORLDSAT INTERNATIONAL INC.

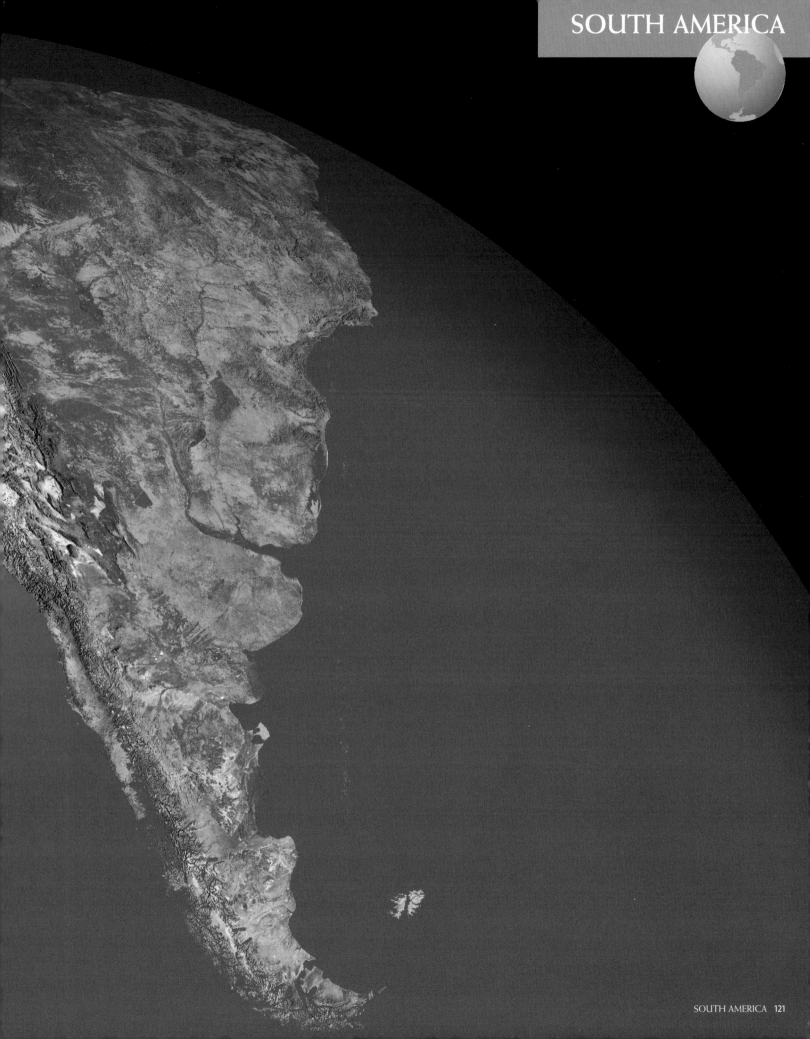

GUATEMALA HONDURAS
EL SALVADOR
Tegucigalpa
NICARAGUA
León Granada Bluefields
Managua
San José
COSTA RICA 3819
Puerto Armuelles PANAMA Panamá
David

Caribbean Sea

Puerto Cabezas

Aruba Neth.
Amuay Bonaire
Curaçao
Neth. Antilles
La Guaira
Puerto Cabello Cumaná

ST. LUCIA
ST. VINCENT &
THE GRENADINES
BARBADOS
GRENADA
Port-of-Spain
TRINIDAD AND TOBAGO

Santa Marta
Barranquilla
Cartagena +5775
Maracaibo
Montería
Mérida
Cúcuta
Bucaramanga

Caracas Maturín

Ciudad Bolívar
Ciudad Guayana
Morawhanna

VENEZUELA

Bello
Medellín
Manizales
Ibagué
BOGOTÁ
Villavicencio
Buenaventura
Cali

COLOMBIA

Puerto Ayacucho

Angel Falls
Luepa
Mt. 2772 Roraima +
+2579
Boa Vista

Georgetown
Nieuw Amsterdam
GUYANA
Paramaribo
St-Laurent du Maroni
Cayenne
SURINAME
FRENCH GUIANA
France
+5007
Cottica
Oiapoque
Calcoene
Amapá

Tumaco
Popayán
Pasto
San Lorenzo
Esmeraldas
Güeppí

Calamar
Mitú

San Carlos
Caracaraí
Pico de Neblina
3014

Barcelos

Cabo Norte
Bailique
Macapá
Chaves
ILHA DE MARAJÓ
Bragança
Belém
Abaetetuba
São Luís
Camocim

EQUATOR

Quito Ibarra
ECUADOR
Chimborazo +
Manta
Portoviejo
Cuenca
Guayaquil
Machala
Tumbes Loja

Puerto Baquerizo Moreno

Galápagos Islands
(Archipiélago de Colón)
Ecuador

La Pedrera

Japurá
Fonte Boa
São Paulo de Olivença
Tefé
Leticia
Iquitos

Monte Alegre
Óbidos
Curralinho
Parintins
Itacoatiara
Santarém

Gurupá

Brejo
Parnaíba
Sobral
Bacabal
Caxias Ipu
Teresina
Crateús Iguatu

Bragança
Fortaleza
Aracati
Mossoró
Natal

Punta Pariñas
Paita
Punta Negra
Piura
Talara

Jutaí

Manaus
Coari
Borba

Jurua

Marabá
Imperatriz
Carolina
Conceição do Araguaia

Juazeiro do Norte
Campina Grande
João Pessoa
Recife
Caruaru
Maceió

Chiclayo
Pacasmayo
Salaverry
Trujillo
Chimbote

Cajamarca
Tarapoto

Canutama
Eirunepé
Cruzeiro do Sul
Pucallpa

Lábrea
Prainha
Humaitá
Calama

Manicoré

Jacareacanga

Barra do São Manuel
Cachimbo

Pedro Afonso
Porto Nacional

Petrolina
Juazeiro
Barra
Xique Xique

Garanhuns
Arapiraca
Propriá
Penedo
Estância
Alagoinhas

PERU

Huaraz
Huánuco
Cerro de Pasco

Río Branco
Guajará-Mirim
Cobija
Riberalta
Príncipe da Beira
Ji-Paraná
Vilhena

Porto Velho

Itaúba
Sinop
Parecis

BRAZIL

Barreiras
Sítio do Mato

Feira de Santana
Salvador (Bahia)
Ilhéus

LIMA
Callao
Huancavelica
Pisco
Ica
Nasca

Huancayo
Ayacucho
Machu Picchu
Cusco
Abancay

Puerto Maldonado

Trinidad

PLANALTO DO MATO GROSSO

Porangatu
Peixe

Carinhanha
Jequié Itabuna

Vitória da Conquista
Januária

Canavieiras
Caravelas

Arequipa
Matarani
Moquegua
Tacna
Arica

Nev. Coropuna + 6425
Juliaca
L. Titicaca
La Paz
BOLIVIA
Cochabamba

Mato Grosso
Cáceres
Cuiabá

Rio Verde
Coxim

Mato Grosso

Anápolis
Goiânia
Uberlândia
Uberaba

Araguari
Curvelo

Brasília
Pirapora
Montes Claros
Diamantina
Governador Valadares

Belo Horizonte
Bandeira + 2890
Juiz de Fora
Vitória

Oruro
Potosí
Sucre
Camiri
Tarija

Santa Cruz
San José de Chiquitos
Corumbá

Campo Grande

São José do Rio Preto
Araçatuba
Bauru

Ribeirão Preto

Araraquara

Volta Redonda
Nova Friburgo
Campos

Tocopilla
Calama

Mariscal Estigarribia
Aguaray

Gran Chaco

Concepción

PARAGUAY
Asunción
Formosa

Villarrica

Campinas
Sorocaba
SÃO PAULO
Curitiba
Londrina
Iguape
Santos
RIO DE JANEIRO
Paranaguá

TROPIC OF CAPRICORN

Mejillones
Antofagasta
Taltal

Volcán Llullaillaco
Cerro Ojos del Salado
6723 +
6880

San Salvador de Jujuy
San Miguel de Tucumán
Resistencia

Iguazú Falls
Corrientes
Posadas
Passo Fundo

Joinville
Florianópolis
Imbituba
Tubarão

Isla San Félix
Isla San Ambrosio
Chile

Diego de Almagro
Chañaral
Caldera

Belén
Catamarca
La Rioja

Mercedes
Goya
Uruguaiana

Caxias do Sul
Porto Alegre

PACIFIC OCEAN

Huasco
Sarco
La Serena

Cerro del Toro
6880
Cerro del Toro

Santiago del Estero

Salto
Paraná
Rosario

Bagé
Pelotas

CHILE

Ovalle
Los Vilos
Cerro Aconcagua 6960 +
Valparaíso
Santiago
Rancagua
Curicó
Talca

San Juan
Mendoza

San Luis
Córdoba
Río Cuarto

Paysandú
URUGUAY
Treinta-y-Tres
Río Grande
Rocha

Montevideo

Islas Juan Fernández
Chile

ARGENTINA
San Rafael
Pehuajó
Buenos Aires
Santa Rosa
Olavarría
Tandil

Chillán
4709 +
Concepción
Los Ángeles
Temuco
Zapala
Valdivia

Neuquén
Río Negro
Río Colorado

Tres Arroyos
Necochea
Bahía Blanca
Mar del Plata

Osorno
Puerto Montt
Ancud

San Carlos de Bariloche

Viedma

ATLANTIC OCEAN

Isla Grande de Chiloé

Esquel

Golfo San Matías
PENÍNSULA VALDÉS
Puerto Madryn
Rawson

Archipiélago de los Chonos

Puerto Aisén
Balmaceda
4035 +
Monte San Valentín

Camarones
Golfo San Jorge
Comodoro Rivadavia
Cabo Tres Puntas
Puerto Deseado

Las Heras

6251

El Calafate
Yacimiento Río Turbio
Puerto Natales
Punta Arenas

Puerto San Julián
+105
Puerto Santa Cruz
Puerto Coig
Manantiales
Río Grande
ISLA GRANDE DE TIERRA DEL FUEGO
Ushuaia

Administered by United Kingdom
(claimed by Argentina)

Stanley
Falkland Islands
(Islas Malvinas)
U.K.

Scotia Sea

South Georgia I.
U.K.

Cabo de Hornos
(Cape Horn)
4896

AZIMUTHAL EQUIDISTANT PROJECTION
SCALE 1:31,000,000
0 KILOMETERS 600 800
0 MILES 200 400 600 800

Longitude West of Greenwich
SOUTH AMERICA 123

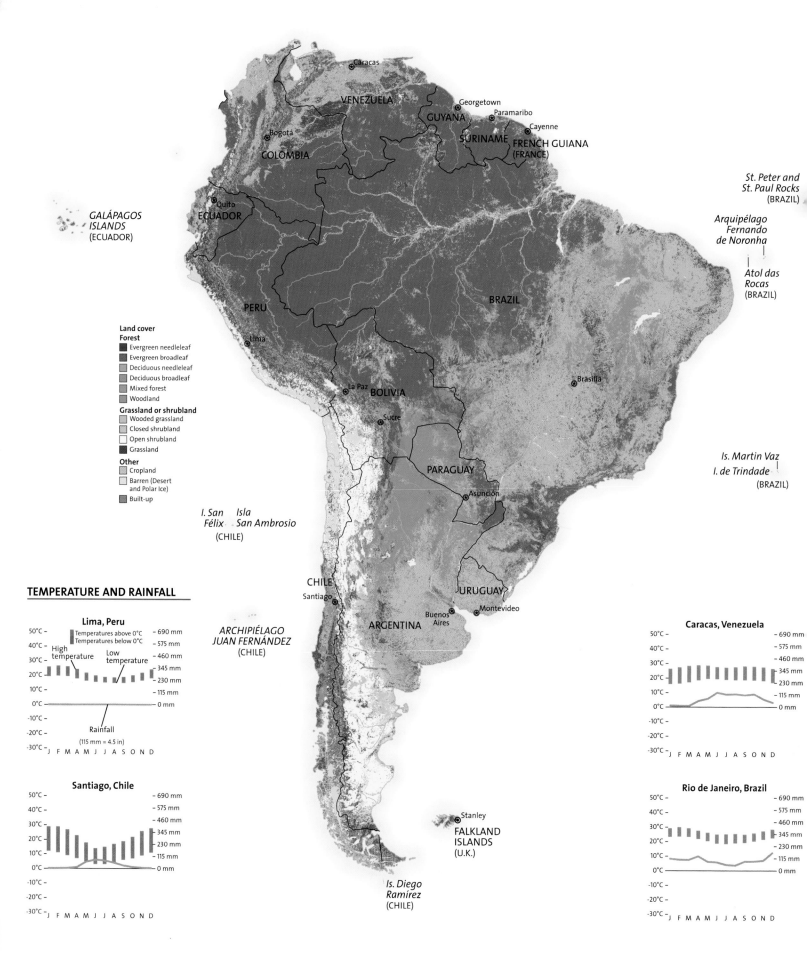

Caracas
VENEZUELA
GUYANA
Georgetown
Paramaribo
Bogotá
SURINAME
Cayenne
COLOMBIA
FRENCH GUIANA
(FRANCE)

GALÁPAGOS
ISLANDS
(ECUADOR)

Quito
ECUADOR

PERU

Lima

St. Peter and
St. Paul Rocks
(BRAZIL)

Arquipélago
Fernando
de Noronha
(BRAZIL)

Atol das
Rocas
(BRAZIL)

BRAZIL

Brasília

La Paz
BOLIVIA
Sucre

Land cover
Forest
- Evergreen needleleaf
- Evergreen broadleaf
- Deciduous needleleaf
- Deciduous broadleaf
- Mixed forest
- Woodland

Grassland or shrubland
- Wooded grassland
- Closed shrubland
- Open shrubland
- Grassland

Other
- Cropland
- Barren (Desert and Polar Ice)
- Built-up

PARAGUAY

Is. Martin Vaz
I. de Trindade
(BRAZIL)

I. San
Félix
(CHILE)

Isla
San Ambrosio

Asunción

URUGUAY

ARCHIPIÉLAGO
JUAN FERNÁNDEZ
(CHILE)

CHILE
Santiago

ARGENTINA

Buenos
Aires
Montevideo

Stanley
FALKLAND
ISLANDS
(U.K.)

Is. Diego
Ramírez
(CHILE)

TEMPERATURE AND RAINFALL

Lima, Peru

50°C – 690 mm
40°C – ■ Temperatures above 0°C – 575 mm
30°C – ■ Temperatures below 0°C – 460 mm
High
temperature   Low
temperature
20°C – – 345 mm
– 230 mm
10°C – – 115 mm
0°C – – 0 mm
-10°C –
-20°C – Rainfall
(115 mm = 4.5 in)
-30°C – J F M A M J J A S O N D

Santiago, Chile

50°C – 690 mm
40°C – 575 mm
30°C – 460 mm
20°C – 345 mm
– 230 mm
10°C – – 115 mm
0°C – – 0 mm
-10°C –
-20°C –
-30°C – J F M A M J J A S O N D

Caracas, Venezuela

50°C – 690 mm
40°C – 575 mm
30°C – 460 mm
20°C – 345 mm
– 230 mm
10°C – – 115 mm
0°C – – 0 mm
-10°C –
-20°C –
-30°C – J F M A M J J A S O N D

Rio de Janeiro, Brazil

50°C – 690 mm
40°C – 575 mm
30°C – 460 mm
20°C – 345 mm
– 230 mm
10°C – – 115 mm
0°C – – 0 mm
-10°C –
-20°C –
-30°C – J F M A M J J A S O N D

Climatic zones
(based on modified Köppen system)

Humid equatorial climate (A)
- No dry season (Af)
- Short dry season (Am)
- Dry winter (Aw)

Dry climate (B)
- Semiarid (BS)   } h = hot
- Arid (BW)   } k = cold

Humid temperate climate (C)
- No dry season (Cf)
- Dry winter (Cw)   } a = hot summer
- Dry summer (Cs)   } b = cool summer

Cold climate (E)
- Tundra and ice

Highland climate (H)
- Unclassified highlands

Population density, 2005

People per square km	People per square mi
More than 1,000	More than 2,500
100 - 1,000	250 - 2,500
Less than 100	Less than 250

Fire intensity
(from gas burn-off, slash-and-burn agriculture, or natural causes)

High

Low

Recorded natural event

Earthquake
Richter scale magnitude
- More than 7.0
- 6.0 - 7.0
- Less than 6.0

Volcano

Tsunami
Run-up height

Meters	Feet
More than 10	More than 32
5 - 10	16 - 32
Less than 5	Less than 16

Water availability
(in millimeters per-person per-year)
- More than 750
- 251 - 750
- 26 - 250
- Less than 26

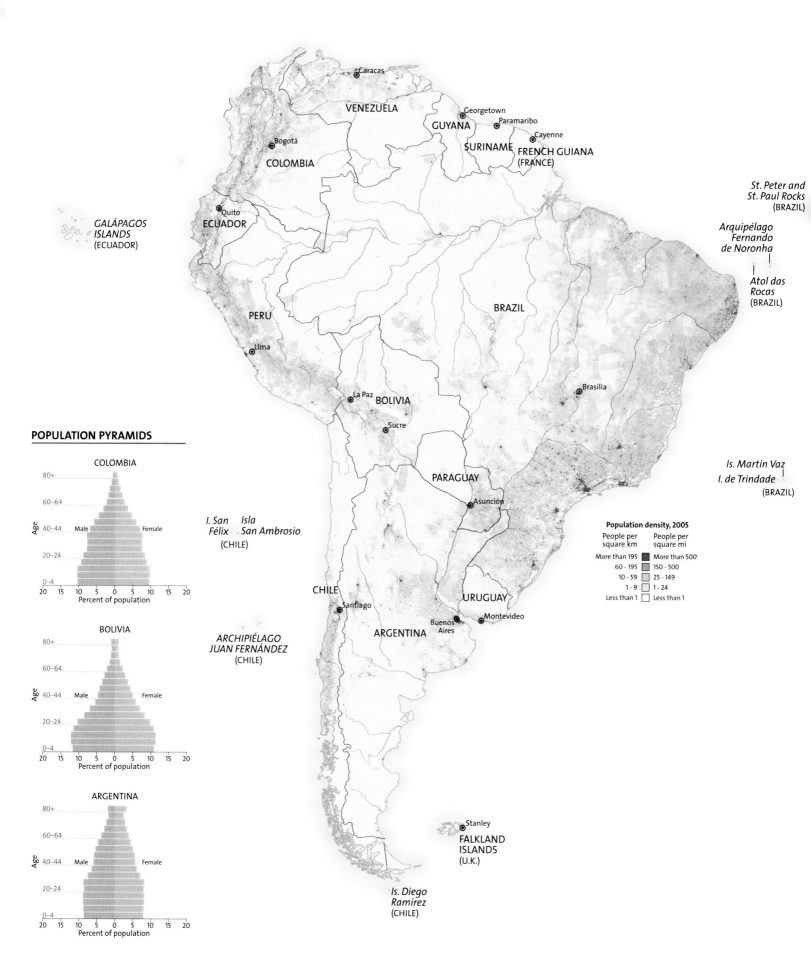

POPULATION PYRAMIDS

COLOMBIA

Age

80+

60–64

40–44   Male   Female

20–24

0–4

20 15 10   5   0   5   10 15 20
Percent of population

BOLIVIA

Age

80+

60–64

40–44   Male   Female

20–24

0–4

20 15 10   5   0   5   10 15 20
Percent of population

ARGENTINA

Age

80+

60–64

40–44   Male   Female

20–24

0–4

20 15 10   5   0   5   10 15 20
Percent of population

Caracas

VENEZUELA

Georgetown
GUYANA Paramaribo
Cayenne
Bogotá SURINAME FRENCH GUIANA
COLOMBIA (FRANCE)

*St. Peter and
St. Paul Rocks*
(BRAZIL)

Quito
ECUADOR

*Arquipélago
Fernando
de Noronha*

PERU

*Atol das
Rocas*
(BRAZIL)

BRAZIL

Lima

La Paz BOLIVIA

Brasília

Sucre

*GALÁPAGOS
ISLANDS*
(ECUADOR)

PARAGUAY

Is. Martin Vaz
I. de Trindade
(BRAZIL)

Asunción

*I. San   Isla
Félix   San Ambrosio*
(CHILE)

Population density, 2005

People per   People per
square km   square mi

More than 195   More than 500
60 - 195   150 - 500
10 - 59   25 - 149
1 - 9   1 - 24
Less than 1   Less than 1

*ARCHIPIÉLAGO
JUAN FERNÁNDEZ*
(CHILE)

CHILE Santiago

URUGUAY

Buenos Montevideo
Aires

ARGENTINA

*Is. Diego
Ramírez*
(CHILE)

Stanley

FALKLAND
ISLANDS
(U.K.)

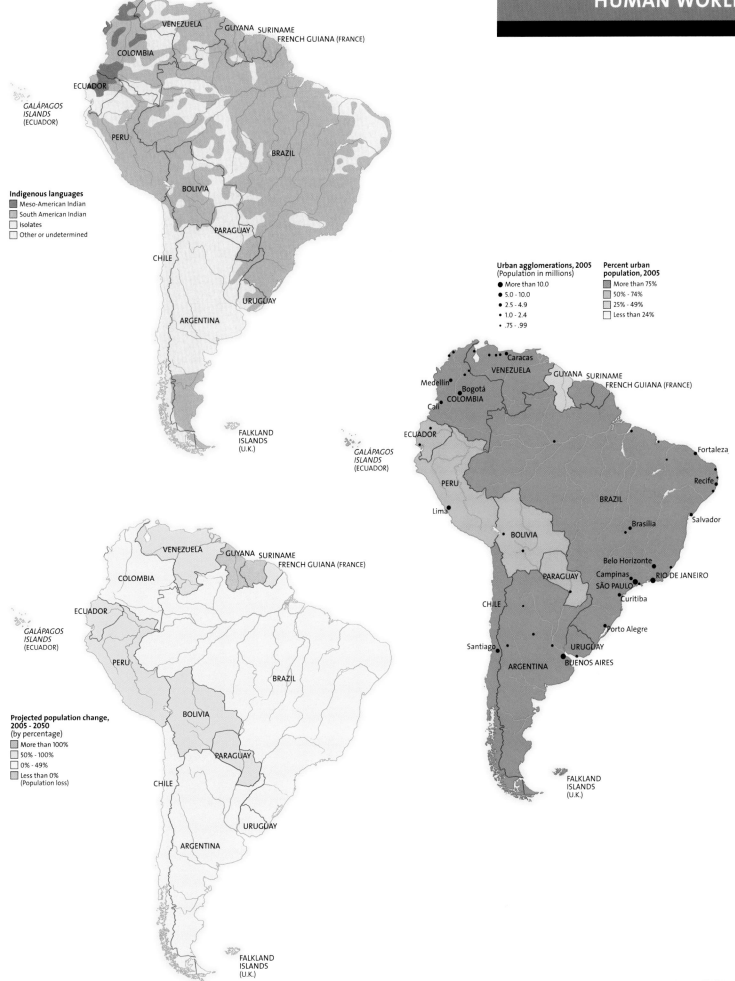

Indigenous languages
- Meso-American Indian
- South American Indian
- Isolates
- Other or undetermined

GALÁPAGOS
ISLANDS
(ECUADOR)

VENEZUELA
GUYANA SURINAME
FRENCH GUIANA (FRANCE)
COLOMBIA
ECUADOR
PERU
BRAZIL
BOLIVIA
PARAGUAY
CHILE
URUGUAY
ARGENTINA
FALKLAND
ISLANDS
(U.K.)

Urban agglomerations, 2005
(Population in millions)
- More than 10.0
- 5.0 - 10.0
- 2.5 - 4.9
- 1.0 - 2.4
- .75 - .99

**Percent urban
population, 2005**
- More than 75%
- 50% - 74%
- 25% - 49%
- Less than 24%

Caracas
VENEZUELA
Medellín
Bogotá
COLOMBIA
Cali
ECUADOR
GUYANA SURINAME
FRENCH GUIANA (FRANCE)
PERU
Lima
BOLIVIA
BRAZIL
Fortaleza
Recife
Salvador
Brasília
Belo Horizonte
Campinas
SÃO PAULO
RIO DE JANEIRO
Curitiba
Porto Alegre
PARAGUAY
CHILE
URUGUAY
Santiago
BUENOS AIRES
ARGENTINA
FALKLAND
ISLANDS
(U.K.)
GALÁPAGOS
ISLANDS
(ECUADOR)

**Projected population change,
2005 - 2050**
(by percentage)
- More than 100%
- 50% - 100%
- 0% - 49%
- Less than 0%
  (Population loss)

VENEZUELA
GUYANA SURINAME
FRENCH GUIANA (FRANCE)
COLOMBIA
ECUADOR
GALÁPAGOS
ISLANDS
(ECUADOR)
PERU
BRAZIL
BOLIVIA
PARAGUAY
CHILE
URUGUAY
ARGENTINA
FALKLAND
ISLANDS
(U.K.)

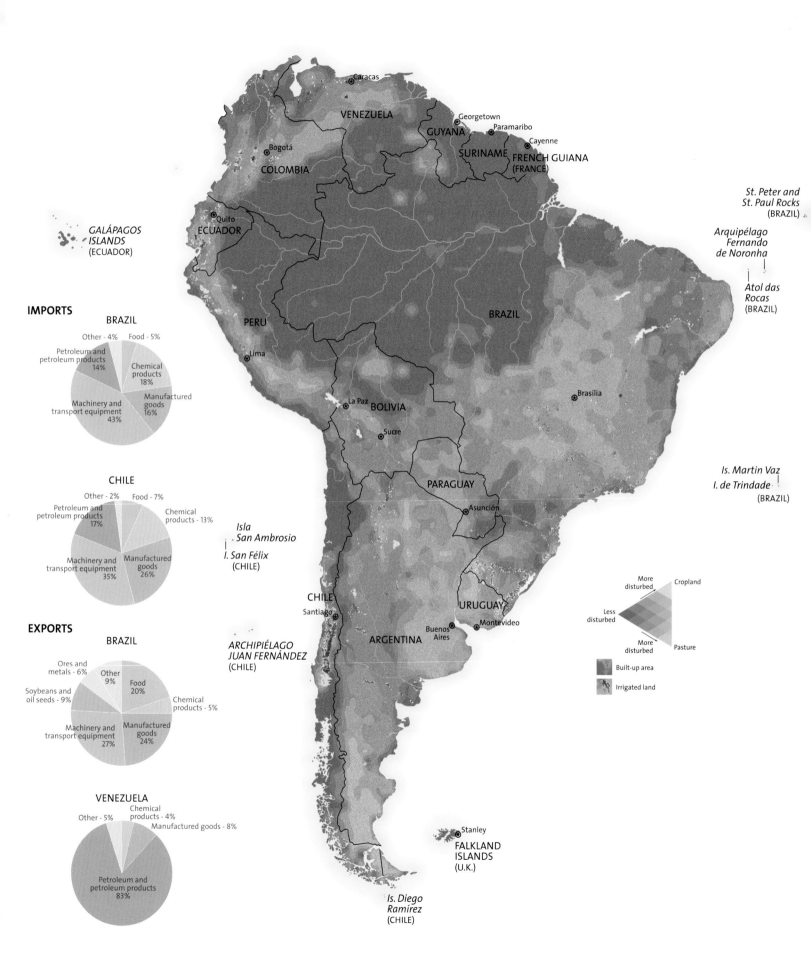

IMPORTS

BRAZIL

Other - 4% Food - 5%
Petroleum and petroleum products 14%
Chemical products 18%
Machinery and transport equipment 43%
Manufactured goods 16%

CHILE

Other - 2% Food - 7%
Petroleum and petroleum products 17%
Chemical products - 13%
Machinery and transport equipment 35%
Manufactured goods 26%

EXPORTS

BRAZIL

Ores and metals - 6%
Other 9%
Soybeans and oil seeds - 9%
Food 20%
Chemical products - 5%
Machinery and transport equipment 27%
Manufactured goods 24%

VENEZUELA

Other - 5%
Chemical products - 4%
Manufactured goods - 8%
Petroleum and petroleum products 83%

Caracas
VENEZUELA
Georgetown
GUYANA
Paramaribo
Bogotá
SURINAME
Cayenne
COLOMBIA
FRENCH GUIANA
(FRANCE)

St. Peter and St. Paul Rocks
(BRAZIL)

Quito
ECUADOR

Arquipélago Fernando de Noronha

GALÁPAGOS ISLANDS
(ECUADOR)

Atol das Rocas
(BRAZIL)

PERU
Lima

BRAZIL

Brasilia

La Paz
BOLIVIA
Sucre

Is. Martin Vaz
I. de Trindade
(BRAZIL)

PARAGUAY

Isla San Ambrosio
I. San Félix
(CHILE)

Asunción

More disturbed Cropland
Less disturbed
More disturbed Pasture

CHILE
Santiago

URUGUAY
Montevideo

Built-up area

Irrigated land

ARCHIPIÉLAGO JUAN FERNÁNDEZ
(CHILE)

Buenos Aires

ARGENTINA

Stanley
FALKLAND ISLANDS
(U.K.)

Is. Diego Ramírez
(CHILE)

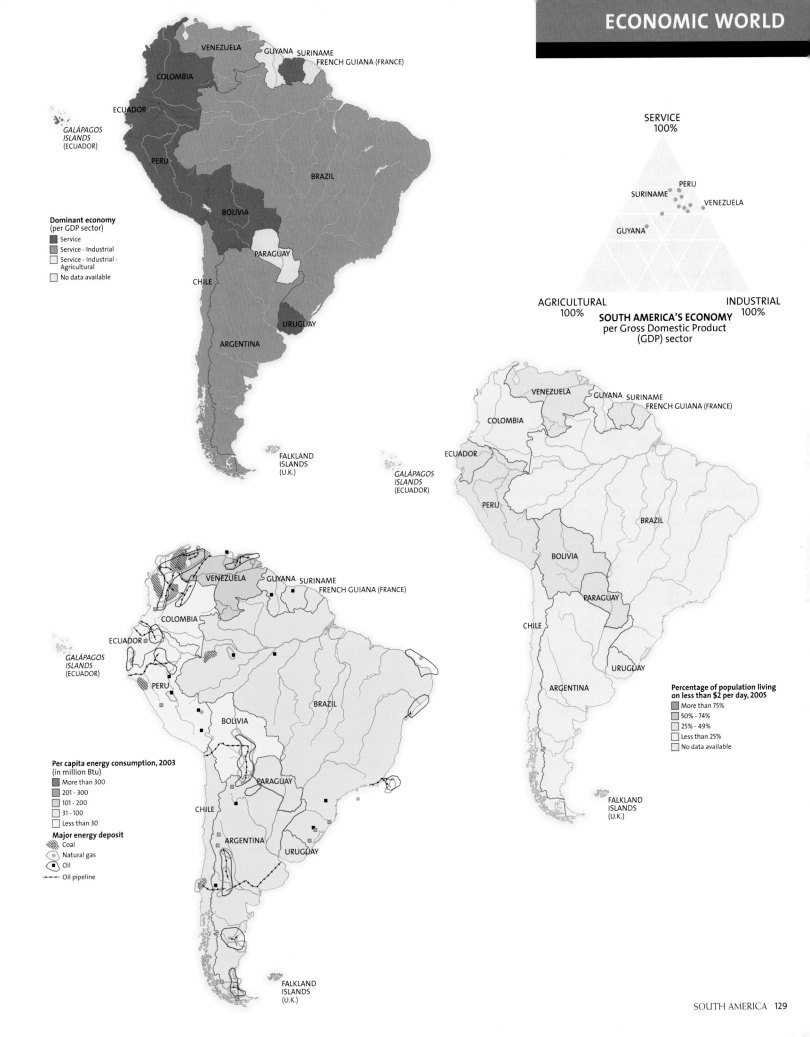

Dominant economy
(per GDP sector)

- Service
- Service - Industrial
- Service - Industrial - Agricultural
- No data available

VENEZUELA

GUYANA SURINAME
FRENCH GUIANA (FRANCE)

COLOMBIA

ECUADOR

GALÁPAGOS
ISLANDS
(ECUADOR)

PERU

BRAZIL

BOLIVIA

PARAGUAY

CHILE

URUGUAY

ARGENTINA

FALKLAND
ISLANDS
(U.K.)

GALÁPAGOS
ISLANDS
(ECUADOR)

SERVICE
100%

PERU
SURINAME
VENEZUELA

GUYANA

AGRICULTURAL
100%

SOUTH AMERICA'S ECONOMY
per Gross Domestic Product
(GDP) sector

INDUSTRIAL
100%

VENEZUELA
GUYANA SURINAME
FRENCH GUIANA (FRANCE)

COLOMBIA

ECUADOR

PERU

BRAZIL

BOLIVIA

PARAGUAY

CHILE

URUGUAY

ARGENTINA

**Percentage of population living
on less than $2 per day, 2005**

- More than 75%
- 50% - 74%
- 25% - 49%
- Less than 25%
- No data available

FALKLAND
ISLANDS
(U.K.)

VENEZUELA

GUYANA SURINAME
FRENCH GUIANA (FRANCE)

COLOMBIA

ECUADOR

GALÁPAGOS
ISLANDS
(ECUADOR)

PERU

BRAZIL

BOLIVIA

PARAGUAY

CHILE

ARGENTINA

URUGUAY

Per capita energy consumption, 2003
(in million Btu)

- More than 300
- 201 - 300
- 101 - 200
- 31 - 100
- Less than 30

Major energy deposit

- Coal
- Natural gas
- Oil
- Oil pipeline

FALKLAND
ISLANDS
(U.K.)

ADMINISTRATIVE AREAS OF
VENEZUELA AND THEIR CAPITALS
(Numbered in blue where not labeled on map)

1 **Aragua** (Maracay)
2 **Capital District** (Caracas)
3 **Miranda** (Los Teques)
4 **Vargas** (La Guaira)

GALÁPAGOS ISLANDS
(Archipiélago de Colón)
Ecuador

PACIFIC
OCEAN

AZIMUTHAL EQUIDISTANT PROJECTION
SCALE 1:12,000,000

0 KILOMETERS   200   300

0 MILES   100   200   300

SEA

ATLANTIC
OCEAN

St. Lucia
Castries
ST. LUCIA
Kingstown
ST. VINCENT
AND THE
GRENADINES
Bridgetown
BARBADOS
Tobago
GRENADA
St.
George's
Charlottetown Tobago
TRINIDAD AND TOBAGO
Port-of-Spain
Trinidad
Galera
Point
San Fernando

Is. de
Aves
Venez.
Is. Los
Roques
Bonaire
LOS ROQUES N.P.
Isla
Blanquilla
Venez.
Isla La
Tortuga
NUEVA
ESPARTA
I. de Margarita
La Asunción
Isla Coche
ARCHIPIÉLAGO
LOS ROQUES N.P.
MORROCOY N.P.
Chichiriviche
Tucacas
La Guaira
Pedernales
Punta Araguapiche

Caracas
Maracay
Petare
Los Teques
Rio
Chico
Barcelona
Puerto La Cruz
Cumaná
Gulf of
Paria
MARIUSA
N.P.

CARABOBO
El Calvario
San Juan de los Morros
San Mateo
Maturín
MONAGAS
Tucupita

GUÁRICO
AGUARO-
GUARIQUITO
N.P.
Valle de la
Pascua
Zaraza
Leona
Nipa
DELTA
AMACURO

ANZOÁTEGUI
Santa Cruz
Ciudad
Bolívar
Curiapo
San José
de Amacuro
Morawhanna
Shell Beach
Mabaruma

NEZUELA
BOLÍVAR
Ciudad Guayana
El Pao
Guri Dam
Matthew's
Ridge
Port Kaituma

Aripao Co. Bolívar
Ciudad Piar
Guasipati
El Callao
Tumeremo
Charity
Suddie
Parika
Georgetown
Buxton

El Dorado
Paima
Falls
Venamo
Issano
Bartica
Rosignol
New Amsterdam

CANAIMA
N.P.
La Gran
Sabana
Pakaraima
Mountains
Linden
Mara
Corriverton
Totness
Nieuw
Amsterdam
Paramaribo

Auyán
Tepui 2957
Uairén
Roraima
MONTE
RORAIMA
N.P.
Ayanganna
Mt.
Kurupukari
Matapi
Skeldon
Brokopondo
Brownsweg
Meerzorg
Albina
Saint-
Jean
Saint-Laurent du Maroni
Sinnamary
GUYANAIS SPACE CENTER
Kourou

SURINAME
FRENCH
GUIANA
Cayenne
Rémire
Pointe Béhague

Santa Elena
Conceição
do Maú
Annai
Apoteri
Kumaka
Wilhelmina Geb.
1230+
Granbori
Benzdorp
Grand Santi
Saint-Georges
Oiapoque
CABO ORANGE N.P.

ATLANTIC
OCEAN

AZIMUTHAL EQUIDISTANT PROJECTION
SCALE 1:12,000,000

0 KILOMETERS   200   300

0 MILES   100   200   300

TROPIC OF CAPRICORN

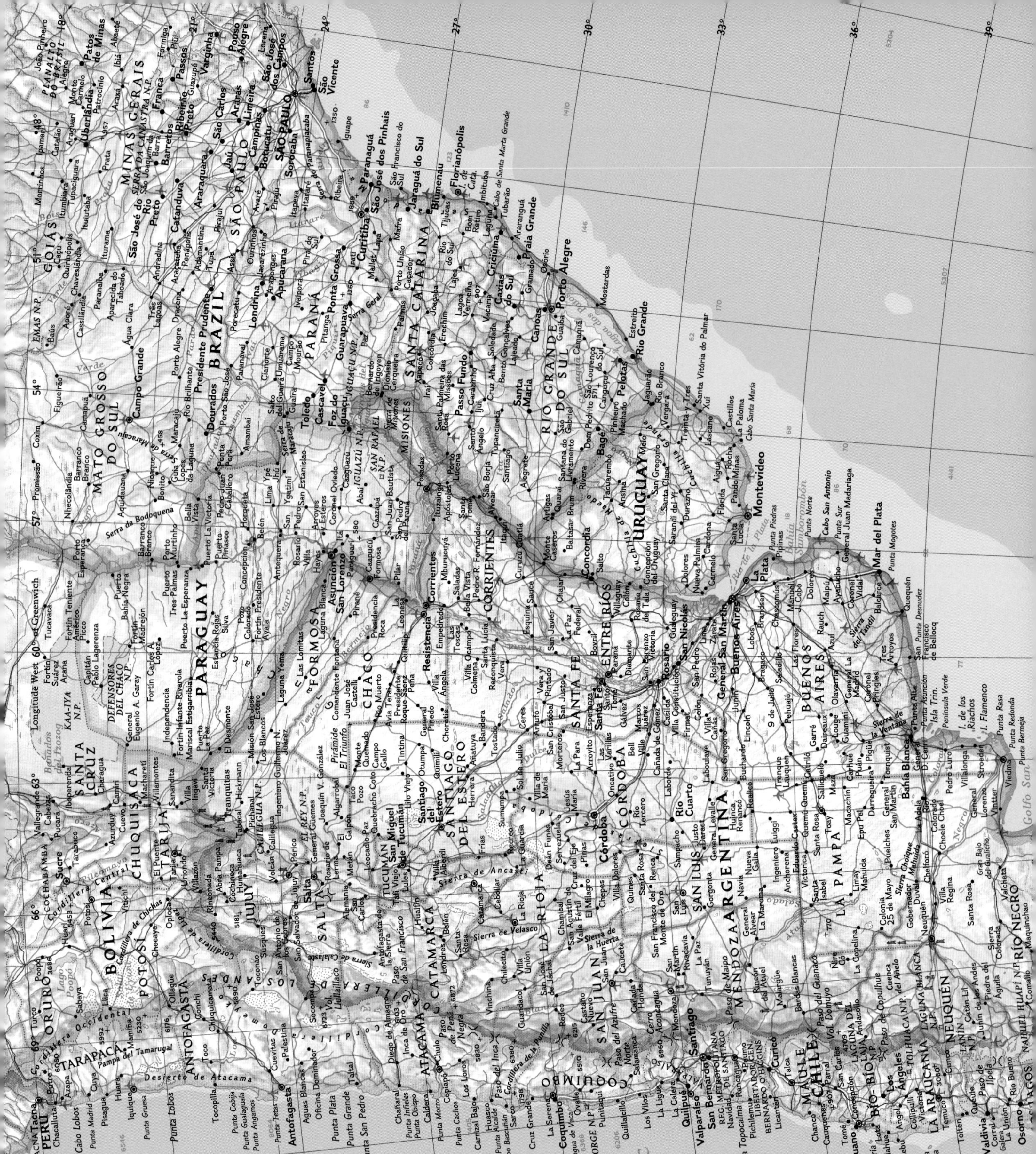

BRAZIL

MINAS GERAIS

GOIÁS

MATO GROSSO DO SUL

SÃO PAULO

PARANÁ

SANTA CATARINA

RIO GRANDE DO SUL

PARAGUAY

URUGUAY

Montevideo

BOLIVIA

SANTA CRUZ

CHUQUISACA

POTOSÍ

TARIJA

JUJUY

SALTA

FORMOSA

CHACO

CORRIENTES

MISIONES

ENTRE RÍOS

SANTIAGO DEL ESTERO

TUCUMÁN

CATAMARCA

LA RIOJA

CÓRDOBA

SANTA FE

SAN LUIS

SAN JUAN

MENDOZA

LA PAMPA

BUENOS AIRES

ARGENTINA

NEUQUÉN

RÍO NEGRO

CHILE

MAULE

BÍO-BÍO

LA ARAUCANÍA

COQUIMBO

ANTOFAGASTA

TARAPACÁ

ATACAMA

PERU

CORDILLERA DE LOS ANDES

PACIFIC OCEAN

TROPIC OF CAPRICORN

Buenos Aires

Mar del Plata

Asunción

Santiago

Valparaíso

São Paulo

Curitiba

Porto Alegre

Córdoba

Rosario

Sucre

Oruro

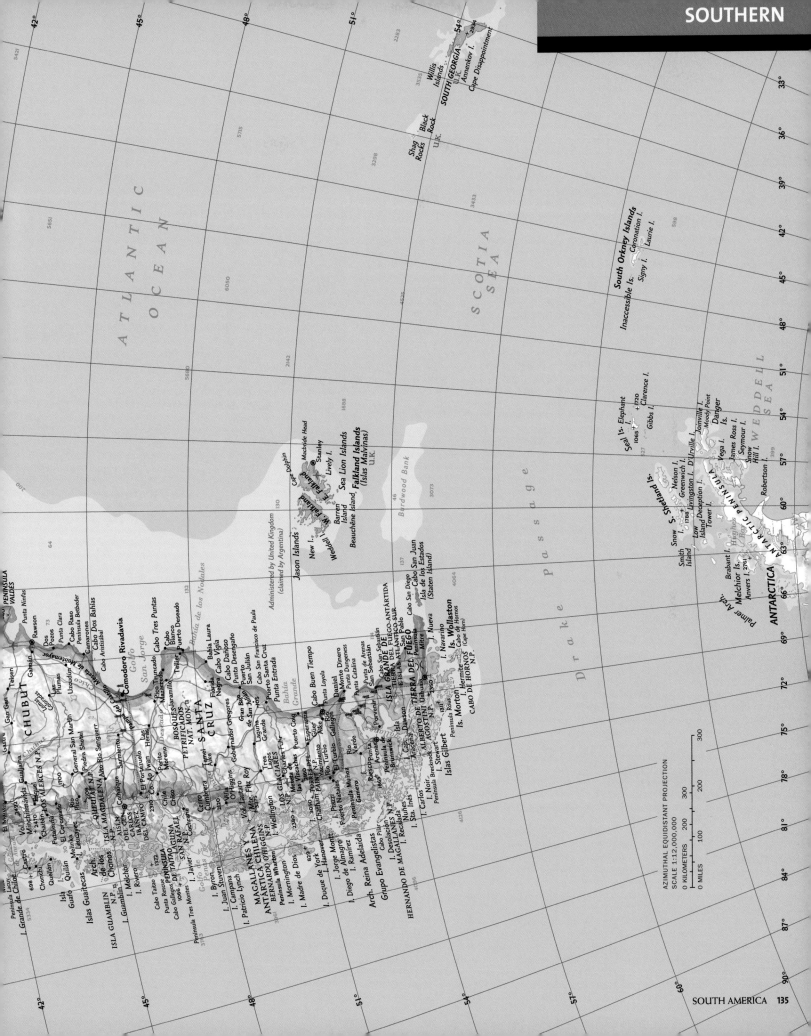

RIVER PLATE REGION
AZIMUTHAL EQUIDISTANT PROJECTION
SCALE 1:6,000,000

0 KILOMETERS   100   150

0 MILES   50   100   150

The second smallest continent with the exception of Australia, Europe has a population density second only to Asia. Its name comes from Europa, a Phoenician woman who, according to Greek myth, was seduced by the god Zeus and carried off to Crete. From the Ural Mountains in the east to peninsulas and islands in the west, Europe has had an influence in the world that far outweighs its size: From the continent's seaports in Portugal, Spain, Italy, England, France, and Holland, Europeans set out in the last 600 years and left their imprint throughout the world. The Minoan, Greek, and Roman societies that gave rise to Western civilization were Mediterranean kin and sometimes antagonists to, among others, Phoenicia, Tyre, Judea, Egypt, and Carthage. The welter of peoples, nations, philosophies, religions, arts, and customs that make up Europe and, in the 19th and 20th centuries, the various "isms"—national-, imperial-, Marx-, Nazi-, and others—kept Europe in flux throughout its history, from the fall of Rome to the jittery cold peace that followed World War II. While numerous rivers and plains gave passage for commerce and conquest, the mountain fastnesses of the Pyrenees and Alps and hard passages of the North Sea and English Channel stood as barriers against invaders. The tendency of Europe to fracture has been mended by cooperative enterprises such as the economic Common Market, followed by the European Union. The EU now has 25 members, including eight former Soviet Bloc countries, and five applicants. While members maintain open borders to each other, and 12 countries use a common currency, the Euro, the adoption of a common constitution has been rejected by voters in France and the Netherlands. Difficulties in assimilating, employing, and acculturating immigrants from former colonial states and Muslim countries challenge European societies, long steeped in democratic ideas of equality and free expression.

IMAGE BY ROBERT STACEY, WORLDSAT INTERNATIONAL INC.

AZIMUTHAL EQUIDISTANT PROJECTION
SCALE 1:23,000,000

A commonly accepted division between Asia and
Europe - here marked by a green line - is formed
by the Ural Mountains, Ural River, Caspian Sea,
Caucasus Mountains, and the Black Sea with its
outlets, the Bosporus and Dardanelles.

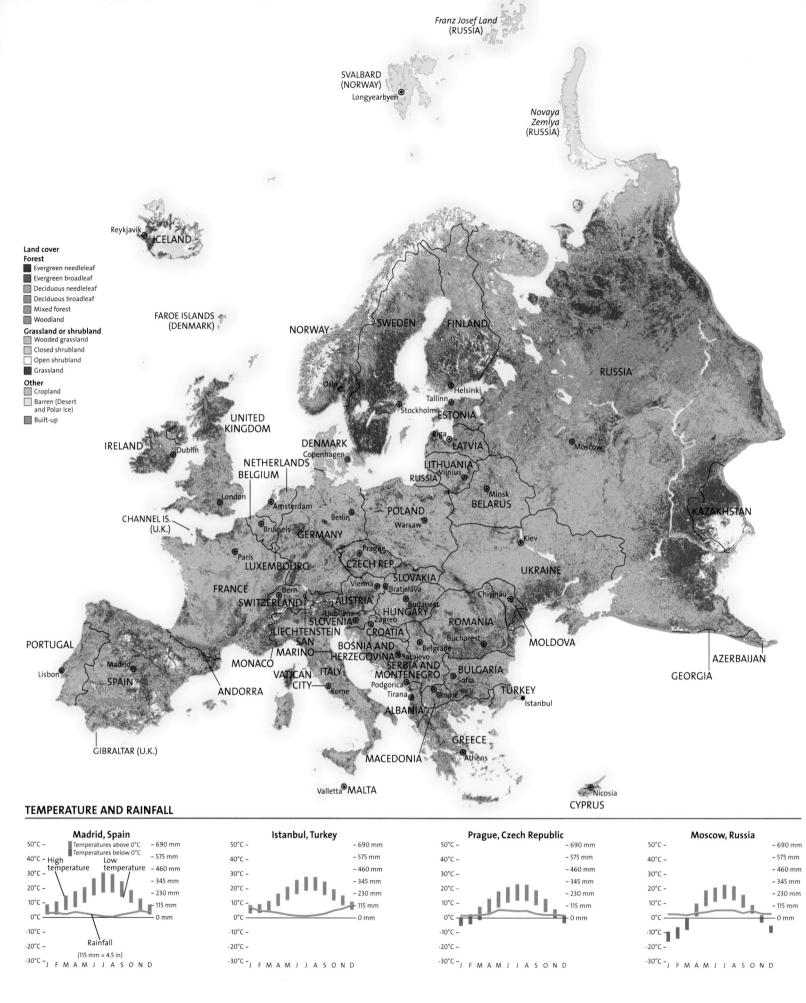

Land cover
Forest
- Evergreen needleleaf
- Evergreen broadleaf
- Deciduous needleleaf
- Deciduous broadleaf
- Mixed forest
- Woodland

Grassland or shrubland
- Wooded grassland
- Closed shrubland
- Open shrubland
- Grassland

Other
- Cropland
- Barren (Desert and Polar Ice)
- Built-up

Franz Josef Land
(RUSSIA)

SVALBARD
(NORWAY)
Longyearbyen

Novaya
Zemlya
(RUSSIA)

Reykjavík ICELAND

FAROE ISLANDS
(DENMARK)

NORWAY SWEDEN FINLAND

Oslo Helsinki

RUSSIA

Tallinn
Stockholm ESTONIA

UNITED
KINGDOM

IRELAND
Dublin

DENMARK
Copenhagen

NETHERLANDS
BELGIUM

Riga
LATVIA

LITHUANIA
Vilnius
RUSSIA

Moscow

London

CHANNEL IS.
(U.K.)

Amsterdam

Brussels
GERMANY

Berlin

POLAND
Warsaw

Minsk
BELARUS

Paris

LUXEMBOURG

Prague

CZECH REP.
SLOVAKIA

Kiev

UKRAINE

FRANCE

Bern
SWITZERLAND

AUSTRIA
Vienna
Bratislava

Ljubljana
LIECHTENSTEIN
SLOVENIA

Budapest
HUNGARY
Zagreb

Chişinău

MOLDOVA

PORTUGAL

Madrid

SAN
MARINO

MONACO

VATICAN
CITY

CROATIA
BOSNIA AND
HERZEGOVINA
Sarajevo

ROMANIA
Bucharest

ROMANIA

Lisbon
SPAIN

ANDORRA

ITALY
Rome

SERBIA AND
MONTENEGRO
Podgorica
Tirana

Belgrade

BULGARIA
Sofia

AZERBAIJAN

GEORGIA

Skopje

TURKEY

KAZAKHSTAN

ALBANIA

GIBRALTAR (U.K.)

MACEDONIA

GREECE
Athens

Istanbul

Valletta MALTA

Nicosia
CYPRUS

TEMPERATURE AND RAINFALL

Madrid, Spain
- Temperatures above 0°C
- Temperatures below 0°C

High temperature

Low temperature

Rainfall
(115 mm = 4.5 in)

J F M A M J J A S O N D

Istanbul, Turkey
J F M A M J J A S O N D

Prague, Czech Republic
J F M A M J J A S O N D

Moscow, Russia
J F M A M J J A S O N D

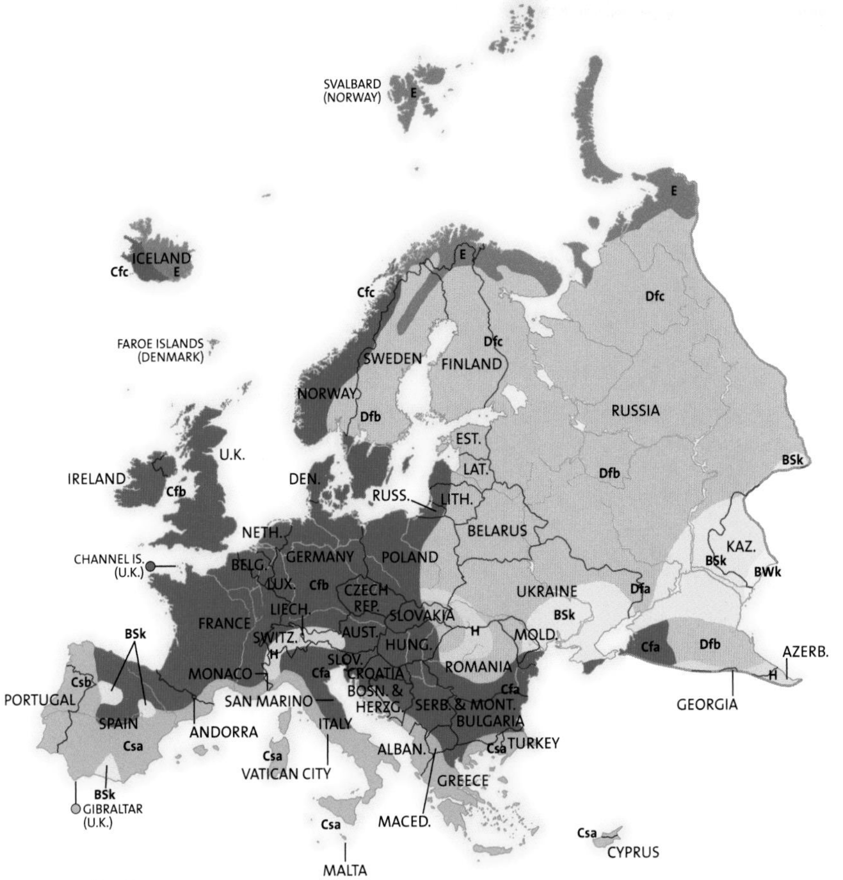
SVALBARD (NORWAY)
E
ICELAND
Cfc
E
Cfc
Dfc
FAROE ISLANDS (DENMARK)
SWEDEN
FINLAND
Dfc
NORWAY
Dfb
RUSSIA
EST.
U.K.
IRELAND
Cfb
DEN.
LAT.
Dfb
BSk
RUSS.
LITH.
BELARUS
NETH.
KAZ.
CHANNEL IS. (U.K.)
GERMANY
POLAND
BSk
BWk
BELG.
LUX.
Cfb
CZECH REP.
UKRAINE
Dfa
LIECH.
SLOVAKIA
FRANCE
BSk
AUST.
BSk
SWITZ.
HUNG.
H
MOLD.
Cfa
Dfb
AZERB.
H
SLOV.
ROMANIA
Csb
MONACO
Cfa
CROATIA
H
PORTUGAL
SAN MARINO
BOSN. & HERZG.
SERB. & MONT.
Cfa
GEORGIA
SPAIN
ANDORRA
ITALY
BULGARIA
Csa
Csa
TURKEY
ALBAN.
Csa
VATICAN CITY
GREECE
BSk
GIBRALTAR (U.K.)
Csa
MACED.
Csa
CYPRUS
MALTA

Climatic zones
(based on modified Köppen system)

Dry climate (B)
- Semiarid (BS)
- Arid (BW)

k = cold

Humid temperate climate (C)
- No dry season (Cf)
- Dry summer (Cs)

Humid cold climate (D)
- No dry season (Df)

a = hot summer
b = cool summer
c = short, cool summer

Cold climate (E)
- Tundra and ice

Highland climate (H)
- Unclassified highlands

Population density, 2005

People per square km	People per square mi
More than 1,000	More than 2,500
100 - 1,000	250 - 2,500
Less than 100	Less than 250

Fire intensity
(from gas burn-off, slash-and-burn agriculture, or natural causes)
High
Low

Recorded natural event

Earthquake
Richter scale magnitude
- More than 7.0
- 6.0 - 7.0
- Less than 6.0

Volcano

Tsunami
Run-up height

Meters	Feet
More than 10	More than 32
5 - 10	16 - 32
Less than 5	Less than 16

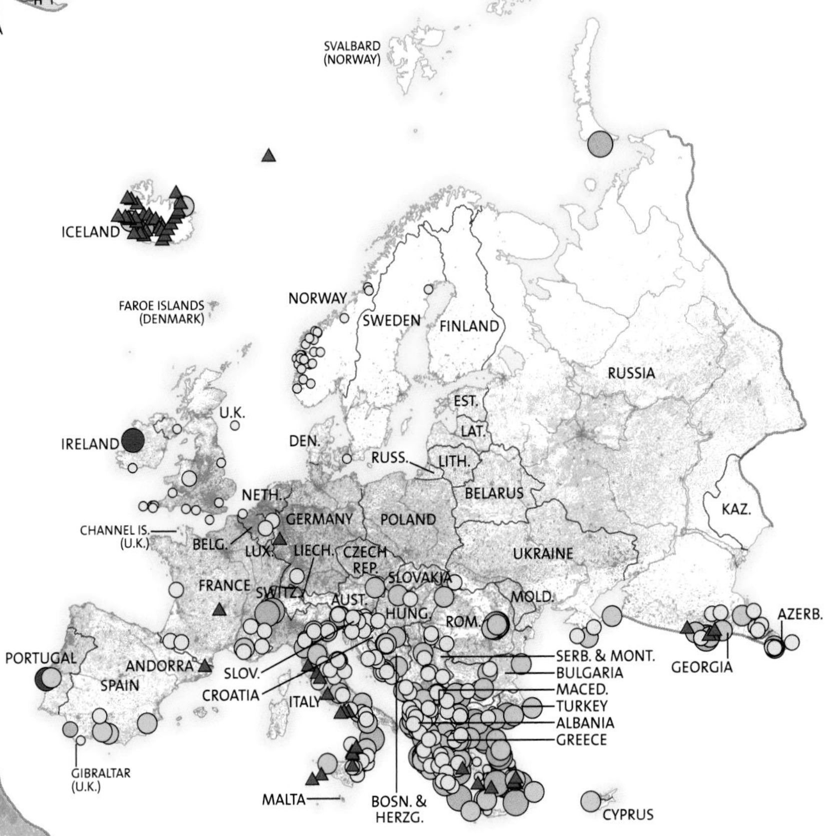
SVALBARD (NORWAY)
ICELAND
FAROE ISLANDS (DENMARK)
NORWAY
SWEDEN
FINLAND
RUSSIA
U.K.
EST.
IRELAND
LAT.
DEN.
RUSS.
LITH.
NETH.
BELARUS
KAZ.
GERMANY
POLAND
CHANNEL IS. (U.K.)
BELG.
LUX.
LIECH.
CZECH REP.
UKRAINE
SLOVAKIA
FRANCE
SWITZ.
AUST.
MOLD.
HUNG.
ROM.
AZERB.
PORTUGAL
ANDORRA
SERB. & MONT.
SLOV.
BULGARIA
GEORGIA
SPAIN
CROATIA
MACED.
ITALY
TURKEY
ALBANIA
GREECE
GIBRALTAR (U.K.)
MALTA
BOSN. & HERZG.
CYPRUS

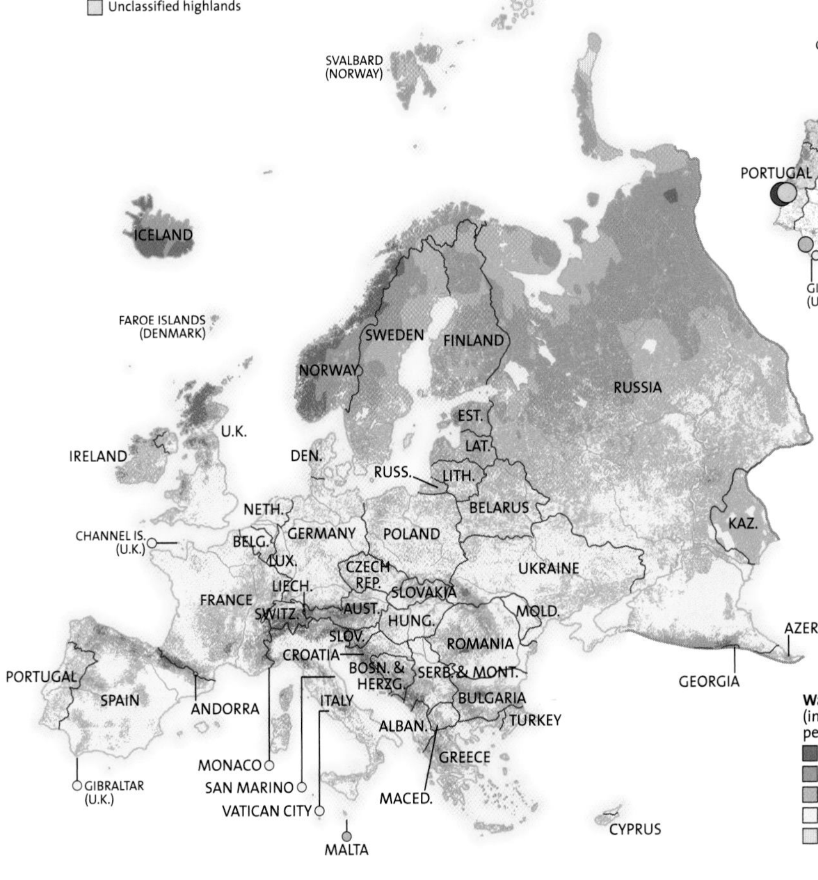
SVALBARD (NORWAY)
ICELAND
FAROE ISLANDS (DENMARK)
SWEDEN
FINLAND
NORWAY
RUSSIA
EST.
U.K.
LAT.
IRELAND
DEN.
RUSS.
LITH.
BELARUS
NETH.
KAZ.
CHANNEL IS. (U.K.)
GERMANY
POLAND
BELG.
LUX.
CZECH REP.
UKRAINE
LIECH.
SLOVAKIA
FRANCE
SWITZ.
AUST.
MOLD.
HUNG.
SLOV.
ROMANIA
AZERB.
CROATIA
PORTUGAL
BOSN. & HERZG.
SERB. & MONT.
GEORGIA
SPAIN
ANDORRA
ITALY
BULGARIA
TURKEY
ALBAN.
GREECE
MONACO
GIBRALTAR (U.K.)
SAN MARINO
MACED.
VATICAN CITY
CYPRUS
MALTA

Water availability
(in millimeters per-person per-year)
- More than 750
- 251 - 750
- 26 - 250
- Less than 26
- No data available

Franz Josef Land
(RUSSIA)

SVALBARD
(NORWAY)
Longyearbyen

Novaya
Zemlya
(RUSSIA)

ICELAND
Reykjavík

FAROE ISLANDS
(DENMARK)

NORWAY
Oslo

SWEDEN

FINLAND
Helsinki

RUSSIA
Moscow

UNITED
KINGDOM

IRELAND
Dublin

DENMARK
Copenhagen

Stockholm

Tallinn
ESTONIA

Riga
LATVIA

LITHUANIA
Vilnius
RUSSIA

Minsk
BELARUS

KAZAKHSTAN

NETHERLANDS
BELGIUM

London

Amsterdam

Berlin

POLAND
Warsaw

CHANNEL IS.
(U.K.)

Brussels
GERMANY

Paris
LUXEMBOURG

Prague
CZECH REP.

Kiev

UKRAINE

FRANCE

SWITZERLAND

Bern

SLOVAKIA
Bratislava
Vienna
AUSTRIA
Budapest
HUNGARY
Ljubljana
SLOVENIA
Zagreb
CROATIA

Chişinău

MOLDOVA

AZERBAIJAN

GEORGIA

LIECHTENSTEIN
SAN
MARINO

PORTUGAL

Lisbon

MONACO

VATICAN
CITY
ITALY
Rome

Madrid
SPAIN

ANDORRA

BOSNIA AND
HERZEGOVINA
Sarajevo
SERBIA AND
MONTENEGRO
Podgorica
Tirana

Belgrade

ROMANIA

Bucharest

BULGARIA
Sofia

Skopje

TURKEY
Istanbul

ALBANIA

MACEDONIA

GIBRALTAR (U.K.)

GREECE
Athens

Valletta MALTA

Nicosia

CYPRUS

Population density, 2005

People per square km	People per square mi
More than 195	More than 500
60 - 195	150 - 500
10 - 59	25 - 149
1 - 9	1 - 24
Less than 1	Less than 1

POPULATION PYRAMIDS

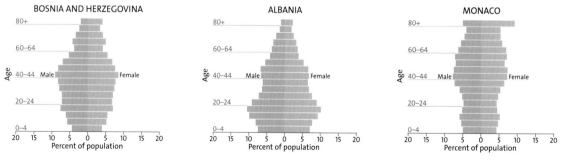

BOSNIA AND HERZEGOVINA

ALBANIA

MONACO

80+

60–64

Age   40–44 Male   Female

20–24

0–4

20 15 10   5   0   5   10 15 20
Percent of population

Urban agglomerations, 2005
(Population in millions)
● More than 10.0
● 5.0 - 10.0
● 2.5 - 4.9
· 1.0 - 2.4
· .75 - .99

Percent urban population, 2005
More than 75%
50% - 74%
25% - 49%
Less than 24%

ICELAND

FAROE ISLANDS ○⊷
(DENMARK)

SWEDEN
NORWAY
FINLAND
RUSSIA

U.K.
DEN.
EST.
LAT.
IRELAND
RUSS.
LITH.
CHANNEL IS. ○→
(U.K.)
NETH.
BELARUS
BELG.
GERMANY
POLAND
LUX.
LIECH.
CZECH
REP.
UKRAINE
KAZ.
FRANCE
SWITZ.
AUST.
SLOVAKIA
HUNG.
MOLD.
SLOV.
ROMANIA
CROATIA
AZERB.
PORTUGAL
SPAIN
BOSN. &
HERZG.
SERB. & MONT.
BULGARIA
GEORGIA
ANDORRA
ITALY
ALBAN.
TURKEY
GIBRALTAR
(U.K.)
MONACO
GREECE
SAN MARINO
MACED.
VATICAN CITY
CYPRUS
MALTA

SVALBARD
(NORWAY)

Indigenous languages
Altaic
Caucasian
Indo-European
Uralic
Isolates
Uninhabited

ICELAND

FAROE ISLANDS ○⊷
(DENMARK)

SWEDEN
NORWAY
FINLAND
St. Petersburg
RUSSIA
EST.
MOSCOW
LAT.
U.K.
DEN.
RUSS.
LITH.
IRELAND
NETH.
Hamburg
BELG.
Berlin
BELARUS
London
POLAND
CHANNEL IS. ○→
(U.K.)
3-1
GER.
Kiev
LUX.
2
CZECH REP.
Katowice
UKRAINE
Paris
4
SLOVAKIA
FRANCE
Stuttgart
KAZ.
LIECH.
AUST.
HUNG.
MOLD.
SWITZ.
Milan
SLOV.
ROMANIA
ANDORRA
CROATIA
Madrid
BOSN. &
HERZG.
SERB. & MONT.
AZERB.
PORTUGAL
Barcelona
ITALY
BULGARIA
SPAIN
Rome
ALBAN.
MACED.
Istanbul
GEORGIA
GIBRALTAR
(U.K.)
Naples
TURKEY
MONACO
GREECE
SAN MARINO
Athens
VATICAN CITY
CYPRUS
MALTA

SVALBARD
(NORWAY)

Urban agglomerations, 2005
● GERMANY

1 Rhein-Ruhr North - 6.6 million
(Duisburg, Essen, Krefeld, Mülheim, Oberhausen,
Bottrop, Gelsenkirchen, Bochum, Dortmund, Hagen,
Hamm, and Herne)

2 Rhein-Main - 3.7 million
(Darmstadt, Frankfurt, Offenbach, and Wiesbaden)

3 Rhein-Ruhr Middle - 3.3 million
(Düsseldorf, Mönchengladbach, Remscheid, Solingen,
and Wuppertal)

4 Rhein-Ruhr South - 3.1 million
(Bonn, Cologne, and Leverkusen)

ICELAND

FAROE ISLANDS ○⊷
(DENMARK)

SWEDEN
NORWAY
FINLAND
RUSSIA
U.K.
DEN.
EST.
LAT.
IRELAND
RUSS.
LITH.
CHANNEL IS. ○→
(U.K.)
NETH.
BELARUS
BELG.
GERMANY
POLAND
LUX.
LIECH.
CZECH
REP.
UKRAINE
FRANCE
SWITZ.
SLOVAKIA
AUST.
HUNG.
MOLD.
KAZ.
SLOV.
ROMANIA
CROATIA
AZERB.
PORTUGAL
SPAIN
BOSN. &
HERZG.
SERB. & MONT.
BULGARIA
GEORGIA
ANDORRA
ITALY
ALBAN.
TURKEY
GIBRALTAR
(U.K.)
MONACO
GREECE
SAN MARINO
MACED.
VATICAN CITY
CYPRUS
MALTA

Projected population change, 2005 - 2050
(by percentage)
More than 100%
50% - 100%
0% - 49%
No change
Less than 0%
(Population loss)

Franz Josef Land
(RUSSIA)

SVALBARD
(NORWAY)
Longyearbyen

Novaya
Zemlya
(RUSSIA)

Reykjavik
ICELAND

FAROE ISLANDS
(DENMARK)

SWEDEN

NORWAY

FINLAND

RUSSIA

Helsinki

Oslo

UNITED
KINGDOM

Tallinn
Stockholm
ESTONIA

Riga
LATVIA

Moscow

IRELAND   Dublin

DENMARK
Copenhagen

LITHUANIA

NETHERLANDS
BELGIUM

Vilnius
RUSSIA

London

Amsterdam

Berlin

POLAND

Minsk
BELARUS

CHANNEL IS.
(U.K.)

Brussels

GERMANY

Warsaw

Kiev

KAZAKHSTAN

Paris

Prague
CZECH REP.

LUXEMBOURG

SLOVAKIA

UKRAINE

FRANCE

Vienna
Bratislava
AUSTRIA
Budapest

Chisinau

GEORGIA

AZERBAIJAN

Bern
SWITZERLAND

Ljubljana
SLOVENIA
LIECHTENSTEIN
SAN
MARINO

Zagreb
CROATIA
HUNGARY

ROMANIA

Bucharest

MOLDOVA

PORTUGAL

MONACO
VATICAN
CITY

BOSNIA AND
HERZEGOVINA
ITALY
Rome

Sarajevo
Belgrade
SERBIA AND
MONTENEGRO
Podgorica

BULGARIA
Sofia

ANDORRA

Lisbon

Madrid

Tirana
ALBANIA

Skopje
TURKEY
Istanbul

SPAIN

MACEDONIA

GREECE
Athens

GIBRALTAR (U.K.)

More
disturbed   Cropland

Less
disturbed

More
disturbed   Pasture

Built-up area

Irrigated land

Valletta MALTA

Nicosia

CYPRUS

IMPORTS

GERMANY

Petroleum and
petroleum products - 8%   Other Food   Chemical
8% 6%   products - 10%

Machinery
and transport
equipment
38%

Manufactured
goods
30%

UNITED KINGDOM

Petroleum and   Other
petroleum products - 4%   6%   Food - 6%

Chemical
products - 10%

Machinery
and transport
equipment
46%

Manufactured
goods
28%

EXPORTS

FRANCE

Other - 6%
Beverages - 3%

Food
8%

Chemical
products
14%

Machinery
and transport
equipment
45%

Manufactured
goods
24%

GERMANY

Medical and
pharmaceutical
products - 2%   Food - 3%

Other
8%

Chemical
products - 12%

Machinery
and transport
equipment
52%

Manufactured
goods
23%

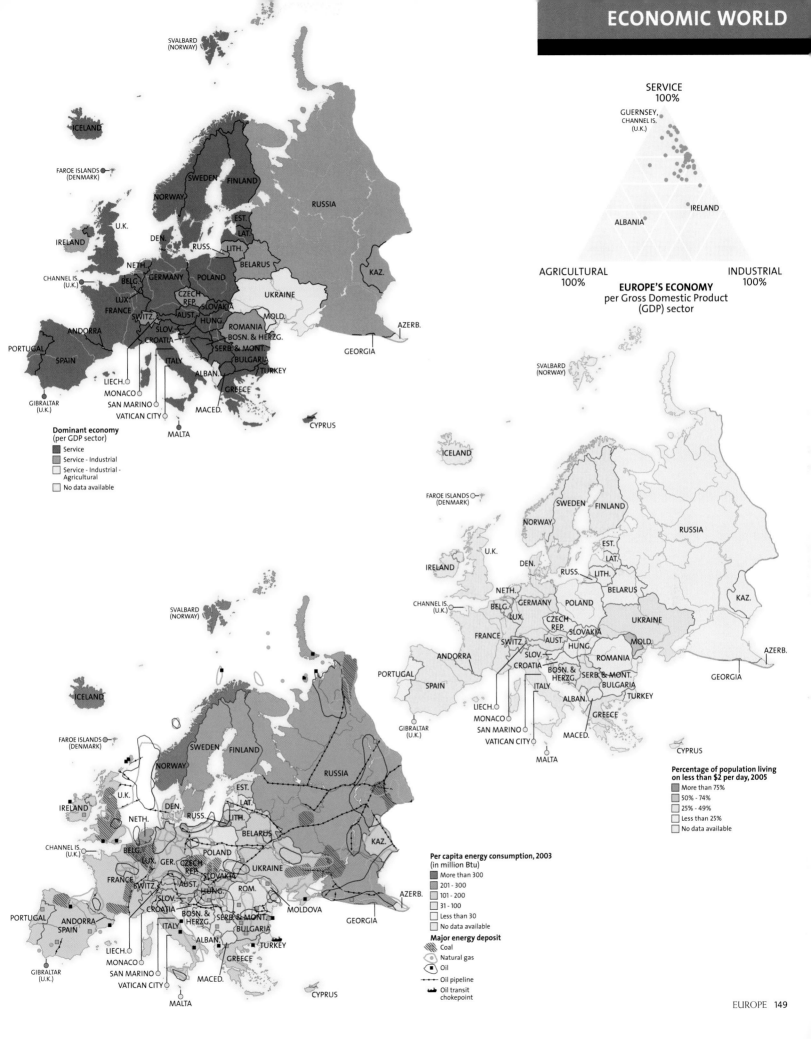

Dominant economy
(per GDP sector)

- Service
- Service - Industrial
- Service - Industrial - Agricultural
- No data available

SERVICE
100%

GUERNSEY,
CHANNEL IS.
(U.K.)

IRELAND

ALBANIA

AGRICULTURAL
100%

INDUSTRIAL
100%

EUROPE'S ECONOMY
per Gross Domestic Product
(GDP) sector

Percentage of population living on less than $2 per day, 2005

- More than 75%
- 50% - 74%
- 25% - 49%
- Less than 25%
- No data available

Per capita energy consumption, 2003
(in million Btu)

- More than 300
- 201 - 300
- 101 - 200
- 31 - 100
- Less than 30
- No data available

Major energy deposit

- Coal
- Natural gas
- Oil
- Oil pipeline
- Oil transit chokepoint

ESTONIA
LATVIA
LITHUANIA
BELARUS
UKRAINE
POLAND
GERMANY
DENMARK
CZECH REPUBLIC
SLOVAKIA
AUSTRIA
HUNGARY
ROMANIA
NETHERLANDS
NORTH SEA
SKAGERRAK
KATTEGAT
BALTIC SEA
Gulf of Riga
Stockholm
Warszawa (Warsaw)
Berlin
København (Copenhagen)
Praha (Prague)
Wien (Vienna)
Riga
Vilnius
Minsk
Hamburg
Kaliningrad

UKRAINE

Kirovohrad
Kryvyy Rih
Mykolayiv
Kherson
Odesa

MOLDOVA
TRANSDNIESTRIA
Chişinău
Bender
Tiraspol

ROMANIA
IAŞI
BACĂU
GALAŢI
Galaţi
BRĂILA
Brăila
Bucureşti (Bucharest)
Ploieşti
Braşov
Piteşti
Craiova
TULCEA
CONSTANŢA
Constanţa
DOBRICH

SEA OF AZOV
Mariupol
Berdyans'k
Melitopol
Kerch
RUSSIA
KRASNODAR
Krasnodar
Novorossiysk
CRIMEA
Simferopol'
Sevastopol'
Yalta

TRANSDNIESTRIA
Since the break-up of the
Soviet Union, Ukrainian and Russian
minorities have been struggling
for independence from Moldova.

BLACK SEA

BULGARIA
Sofiya (Sofia)
Pleven
Varna
BURGAS
Burgas
Stara Zagora
PLOVDIV
Plovdiv (Philippopolis)
Edirne (Adrianople)

MAKEDONIA
Thessaloníki (Salonica)
KAI THRÁKI

Zonguldak
Karabük
Samsun (Amisus)
Ordu
İSTANBUL (CONSTANTINOPLE)
Kocaeli (İzmit)
Adapazarı
Bursa
Ankara (Angora)
Kırıkkale
Çorum
Sivas
Eskişehir
Kütahya
Afyon
Kayseri
Aksaray
Kahramanmaraş

TURKEY

İzmir (Smyrna)
Manisa
Aydın
Denizli
Isparta
Konya (Iconium)
Karaman
Adana
Tarsus
İskenderun
HALAB (Aleppo)
Antalya

VÓREIO EGÉO

STEREÁ ELÁDA
Athína (Athens)
Pireás (Piraeus)
ATIKÍ

Kilkádes (Cyclades)

SEA OF CRETE
DODEKANISSA (DODECANESE)
Ródos (Rhodes)

KRÍTI
Iráklio (Candia)
CRETE

N. CYPRUS
Lefkosía (Nicosia, Lefkoşa)
Lemesos (Limassol)
CYPRUS

SYRIA
Al Lādhiqīyah (Latakia)
Hamāh (Hamath)
Himş (Homs)
Trâblous (Tripoli)
LEBANON

IZHNIY NOVGOROD · 45° · Ardatov · Alatyr' · Bol'shiye Tarkhany · TATARSTAN · 51° · Bugul'me · Oktyabr'skiy · 54°

Temnikov · Pervomaysk · Kemlya · Surskoye · Isheyevka · Nurlat · Koshki · Klyavlino · Bavly · Belebey · Davlekanovo · Rayevskiy

Kadom · Romodanovo · Yazykovo · Ul'yanovsk · Novomalykla · Sterlitamak

MORDOVIYA · Vindrey · Saransk · Karsun · Dimitrovgrad · Surgut · Abdulino · Ponomarevka · Salavat · 479 · Ishimbay · BASHKORTOSTAN · Bakr Uzyak · CHELYABINSK

Bednodem'yanovsk · Ruzayevka · 329 · Ignatovka · Sengiley · Novyy Buyan · Yelkhovka · Pokhvistnevo · Matveyevka · Fedorovka · Voskresenskoye · Meleuz · Yumaguzino · Mrakovo · Tubinskiy · Sibay · Kizil'skoye · Bredy · Prigorodnyy · Zhetiqara

Shiringushi · Insar · Inza · Barysh · Togliatti · 375 · Zhigulevsk · Timashevo · Otradnyy · Bugurusian · Sharlyk · Kumertau · Baymak · Buribay · Energetik · Adamovka

Nizhniy Lomov · Lunino · Nikol'sk · Syzran' · Novokuybyshevsk · Kinel' · Pavlovka · Derzhavino · Grachevka · 660 · Yuldybayevo · Kvarkeno · Aydyrlinskiy · Krasnoyarskiy · Muktikol

Pachelma · 292 · Gorodishche · Chaadayevka · Samara · SAMARA · Buzuluk · Pogromnoye · Yashkino · Aleksandrovka · Oktyabr'skoye · Tyul'gan · Troitskoye · Gay · Novoorsk · Anikhovka

PENZA · Penza · Sursk · Kuznetsk · Privolzh'ye · Chapayevsk · 273 · Sorochinsk · Novosergiyevka · Nikol'skoye · ORENBURG · Chernyy Otrog · Saraktash · Iriklinskiy · Orsk · 51° · Kumak · Ozernyy

Belinskiy · Zolotarevka · Verkhozim · Radishchevo · Khvorostyanka · Bol'shaya Glushitsa · Andreyevka · Bogdanovka · 297 · Perevolotskiy · Orenburg · Dubenskiy · Kuvandyk · Khalilovo · Mednogorsk · Novotroitsk · Dombarovskiy

Kirsanov · Kondol · Lopatino · 332 · Pavlovka · Pestravka · Bol'shaya Chernigovka · Sobolev · Tashla · Mustayevo · Krasnyy Kholm · Pervomayskiy · Belyayevka · Akbulak

Tamala · Serdobsk · Petrovsk · Bazarnyy Karabulak · Alekseyevka · Ivanteyevka · Ilek · Sol'Iletsk · Börili

R S I A · Turki · Arkadak · Atkarsk · 316 · Vol'sk · Balakovo · Pugachev · Perelyub · Krasnoye · Aqsay · Shynggyrlau · Buranooye · Mortyq · Lenīnskoe · Araltobe · Komsomol'skoe

Muchkapskiy · Rtishchevo · Yekaterinovka · Podlesnoye · Klintsovka · Solyanka · Fedorovka · Aqsay · Rodnikovka · Khromtaū

Peski · Samoylovka · Krasnyy Tekstil'shchik · SARATOV · Engels · Marx · Pervomayskoye · Yershov · Ozinki · Peremetnoe · Oral · Zashaghan · Burannoye · Shkunovka · Qarghali · Aqtöbe · Qarabutaq

Balashov · Saratov · Engels · Pushkino · Mokrous · Dergachi · Kamenka · Aqzhayyq · Alghabas · Lūbenka · Almaznoe · Qobda · Il'inka · Starvyy Karabutak · Qarabutak

Kazachka · Kalininsk · Krasnyy Kut · Novorepnoye · Oyan · Shalqar · Zhympity · Begaly · Alga · AQTÖBE

Zhirnovsk · Krasnoarmeysk · Komsomol'skoye · Aralsor · Kaztalovka · Mergenevo · Qaratöbe · Kemer · QAZAQSTAN · Qaratöbe · Temir · Rodniki · Aktogay

Yelan' · Podchinnyy · Kamenskiy · Rovnoye · Kurilovka · Kaztalovka · Zhalpaqtal · Pyatimarskoe · Bazartöbe · Aqtasay · Aqshataū · Oyyl · Kengzhaly · Embi · Birshoghyr

Novoanninskiy · 179 · Mokraya Ol'khovka · Staraya Poltavka · Gmelinka · Zhanga Qazan · Lenīnskoe · Taypaq · Bazarsholan · Qarabey · Miyaly · Shubarqudyq · Bayghanin · Shubarshi · Mugodzharskaya · 657 · Mugalzhar Taūy

Mikhaylovka · Berezovskaya · 358 · Pallasovka · Saralzhyn · Zhanga Qazan · Zhangaqala · Qarabey · Zhanbīke · Kozhasay · Qaraoba · 48°

Kalach na Donu · Frolovo · Solodcha · Balykley · Gornyy · El'ton · Sayqyn · Inderbor · Muqyr · Qarazhar

VOLGOGRAD · Log · Ilovlya · Dubovka · Zhänibek · Zelenoe · Kūlagīno · Ebeyti · Zharkamys

Perelazovskiy · Novonikol'skoye · 250 · Akhtubinsk · Verkhniy Baskunchak · Makhambet · Maqat · Komsomol · ATYRAŪ · Zhanbīke · Qaraoba

Kletskiy · Volgograd · Volzhskiy · Leninsk · Nizhniy Baskunchak · -20 · Dossor · Eskene · Bayshonas

Surovikino · Kalach · Krasnoslobodsk · Kapustin Yar · Chernyy Yar · Novobogatīnskoe · Atyraū · Qorsaq · Qulsary

Oktyabr'skiy · Aksay · Krasnoarmeysk · Akhtubinsk · Aqqystaū · Zhangaly · Zhumysker · Balyqshy · Qosshaghyl · Bīīkzhal

Malyye Derbety · Nikol'skoye · Tsagan Aman · Sasykoli · Kharabali · Agköl · Zaburūn · Qaraton · Dongyztaū · Sorqudyq

Sadovoye · Obil'noye · Nikol'skoye · Seroglazovka · Krasnyy · Ganyushkino · Prorva · Saryqamys · Tengiz · Opornyy · Dgüqara

ASTRAKHAN' · Khosheutovo · Yar · Marfino · Dongytzaū Shyngy

Sovetskoye · Zavetnoye · Yusta · Selitrennoye · Zam'yany · Oporny · Oly Qoltyq Sory

KALMYKIYA · Liman Beren · Valuyevka · Sarpa · Caspian · Beyneu · Nogayty · ARAL SEA · 68 · 45°

Glubokiy · Remontnoye · 221 · Ozero Sarpa · Ulan Erge · Utta · Khulkhuta · Astrakhan' · Iktyanoye · Oranzherei · Kirovskiy · Turysh · Matay · Qaraqalpakstan

Troitskoye · Elista · Yashkul' · Trudfront · Kamyzyak · Kamennoe

Divnoye · Priyutnoye · Naryn Khuduk · Ulan Khol · Mumra · Liman · Bozashchy · Qyzan · Qaraqalpakstan

Kalaus · Yuzhnyy · Kaspiyskiy · Tübegi · Mangqystaū Shyghanaghy

Letnyaya Stavka · Arzgir · Priozerskoye · Termita · S E A · UZBEKISTAN · Zhaslyk

Svetlograd · Blagodarnyy · Staryy Biryuzyak · Bautino · Shetpe · Zharmysh · Sayötesh · USTYURT

ropol' · Budennovsk · Levokumskoye · Neftekumsk · Fort Shevchenko · Taūshyq · 556 · MANGGHYSTAŪ

TAVROPOL' · Arkhangel'skoye · Achikulak · Kayasula · Stepnoye · Kochubey · Bryansk · Mys Sagyndyk · Syghyndy · Zhetibay · PLATEAU

rkessk · Zelenokumsk · Mineral'nyye Vody · Georgiyevsk · Suyutkino · Mangghystaū · Ozen · Zhaslyk

vka · Terekli Mekteb · Kizlyarskiy Zaliv · Lopatin · Mys · Aqtaū · Zhangaözen · Tengge · Karynzharyk (Deserti)

ovodsk · Pyatigorsk · Prokhladnyy · Naurskaya · Kizlyar · Agrakhanskiy Poluostrov · Peschannyy · Quryq · Aksu · 369 · Sarygamysh Köli · 42°

KABARDINO-BALKARIYA · Nal'chik · Nartkala · Malgobek · Babayurt · Khasavyurt · Sulak · Qazaq Shyghanaghy

5642 · 1850 ft · Tyrnyauz · Beslan · Groznyy · Shali · Achisu · Izberbash · Chink Kaplankyr

Mestia · Magas · Vladikavkaz · Vedeno · Mekhel'ta · Buynaksk · Kaspiysk · MAKHACHKALA

SEVERNAYA OSETIYA-ALANIYA · INGUSH · CHECHNYA · Khunzakh · DAGESTAN · Mys Syngyrli

Lentekhi · Ts'ageri Oni · 4638 · 5033 · Kazbek · Tebulosmta · Kakhib · Gunib · Kubachi · Dagestanskiye Ogni

Ambrolauri · Qemult'a · Uilpata · Qazbegi · 4492 · Kumukh · Berikei · Derbent · 721

ski · Chiat'aisi · 3578 · Shavildge · Kurakh · Kasumkent · Mys Sue · Garabogaz

K'ut'aisi · SOUTH OSETIYA · P'asanauri · 2206 · Kakhi · Qusar · Khuchni · Belidzhi · Mukhtadir · Garabogazköl · Garabogaz Aylagy · Mys Omchali · -19

Zestap'oni · Ts'khinvali · Gori · Telavi · 4127 · Zaqatali · Xaçmaz · 200 · Chagyl

2850 · Khashuri · GEORGIA · T'bilisi (Tiflis) · Lagodekhi · Balakän · Kusur · Quba · Däväçi · Gyzylgaya

Adigeni · Tsagveri · 2757 · Sighnaghi · Tsnori · Qax · Xudat · Siyäzän · TURKMENISTAN

Posof · Akhalts'ikhe · 2850 · Rust'avi · Mirzaani · Shaumyani · Muganly · Dashkuduk

Çildir · Bogdanovka · 3196 · 2543 · Alaverdi · Patara Shiraki · Babadag · 3629 · Siyäzän · 104

3054 · Greenwich · ARMENIA · 45° · Ijevan · Tovuz · AZERBAIJAN · Nidzh · 48° · Lahic · Altiagac · Khızı · Shuraabad · 54° · Koshoba

Date Line

TWO-POINT EQUIDISTANT PROJECTION
SCALE 1:20,000,000

0 KILOMETERS 300 400 500

0 MILES 200 300 400 500

Sunday
Monday

Administrative subdivisions of Russia are
outlined on the map; where they are not
labeled, they bear the same name as their
capitals. Subdivisions in the Caucasus
are on plate 195.

ARCTIC OCEAN

SEVERNAYA ZEMLYA
(NORTH LAND)

NOVOSIBIRSKIYE OSTROVA
(NEW SIBERIAN ISLANDS)
OSTROVA ANZHU

LAPTEV SEA

EAST SIBERIAN SEA
NORTHERN SEA ROUTE

CHUKCHI SEA

BERING STRAIT

Ostrov Vrangelya
(Wrangel I.)

BERING SEA

ALEUTIAN ISLANDS
United States
Near Islands
Rat Islands

ANADYRSKIY ZALIV

CHUKOTSKIY

KORYAKSKIY

Komandorskiye Ostrova
(Commander Is.)

KAMCHATKA

Taymyr

Ozero
Taymyr

SIBERIA

SAKHA
(YAKUTIYA)

Verkhoyanskiy Khrebet

Khrebet Cherskogo

MAGADAN

Yakutsk

ARCTIC CIRCLE

SEA OF OKHOTSK

OSTROV SAKHALIN

SAKHALIN

KURIL ISLANDS
(KURIL'SKIYE OSTROVA)

Shantarskiye Ostrova

Stanovoy Khrebet

AMUR

KHABAROVSK

BURYATIYA

CHITA

Sikhote Alin

Khrebet

MARITIME TERR.

AGIN BURYAT

HEILONGJIANG

Harbin

Hailar

Hulun Nur

Qiqihar

C H I N A

NEI
MONGOL

Ulaanbaatar
(Ulan Bator)

M O N G O L I A

G O B I

Irkutsk

Ulan Ude

Chita

Vladivostok

NORTH
KOREA

P'yongyang

SOUTH
KOREA

SEOUL

JILIN

LIAONING

SHENYANG

HEBEI

HOKKAIDO

Sapporo

Hakodate

J A P A N

SEA OF JAPAN
(EAST SEA)

HONSHU

TOKYO
Yokohama

Osaka
Kyoto
Kobe

NAMPO
SHOTO

PACIFIC OCEAN

Longitude East 102° of Greenwich

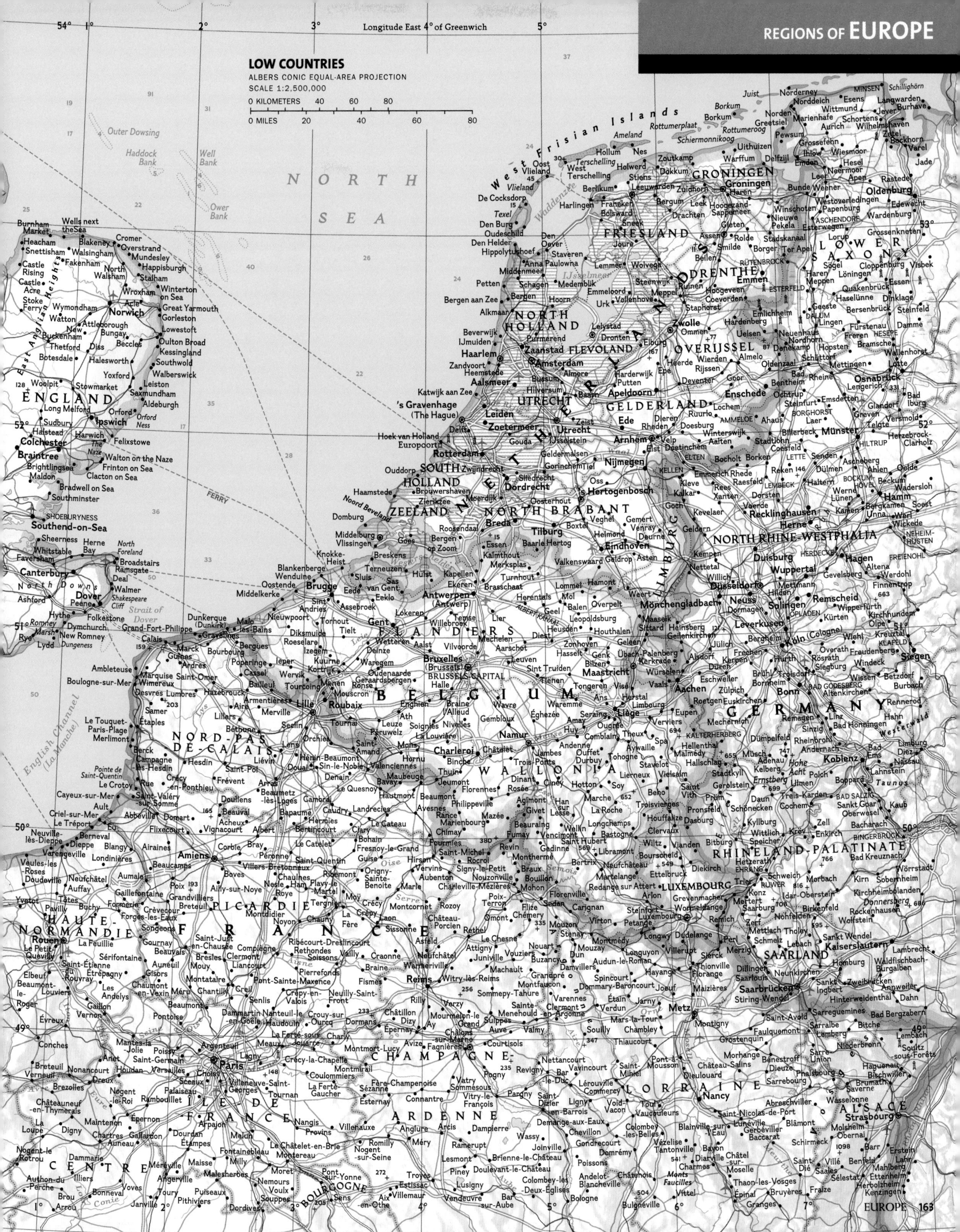

LOW COUNTRIES
ALBERS CONIC EQUAL-AREA PROJECTION
SCALE 1:2,500,000

0 KILOMETERS   40   60   80

0 MILES   20   40   60   80

Longitude East 4° of Greenwich

NORTH SEA

West Frisian Islands

NETHERLANDS

BELGIUM

GERMANY

FRANCE

ENGLAND

English Channel (La Manche)

Strait of Dover

NORTH HOLLAND · SOUTH HOLLAND · ZEELAND · NORTH BRABANT · LIMBURG · UTRECHT · GELDERLAND · OVERIJSSEL · DRENTHE · FRIESLAND · GRONINGEN · FLEVOLAND

LOWER SAXONY · NORTH RHINE-WESTPHALIA · RHINELAND-PALATINATE · SAARLAND

FLANDERS · WALLONIA · BRUSSELS CAPITAL · LUXEMBOURG

NORD-PAS-DE-CALAIS · PICARDIE · HAUTE-NORMANDIE · ÎLE-DE-FRANCE · CHAMPAGNE-ARDENNE · LORRAINE · ALSACE · CENTRE · BOURGOGNE

Amsterdam · Rotterdam · 's Gravenhage (The Hague) · Utrecht · Antwerpen (Antwerp) · Bruxelles (Brussels) · Köln (Cologne) · Paris · Reims · Lille

EUROPE 165

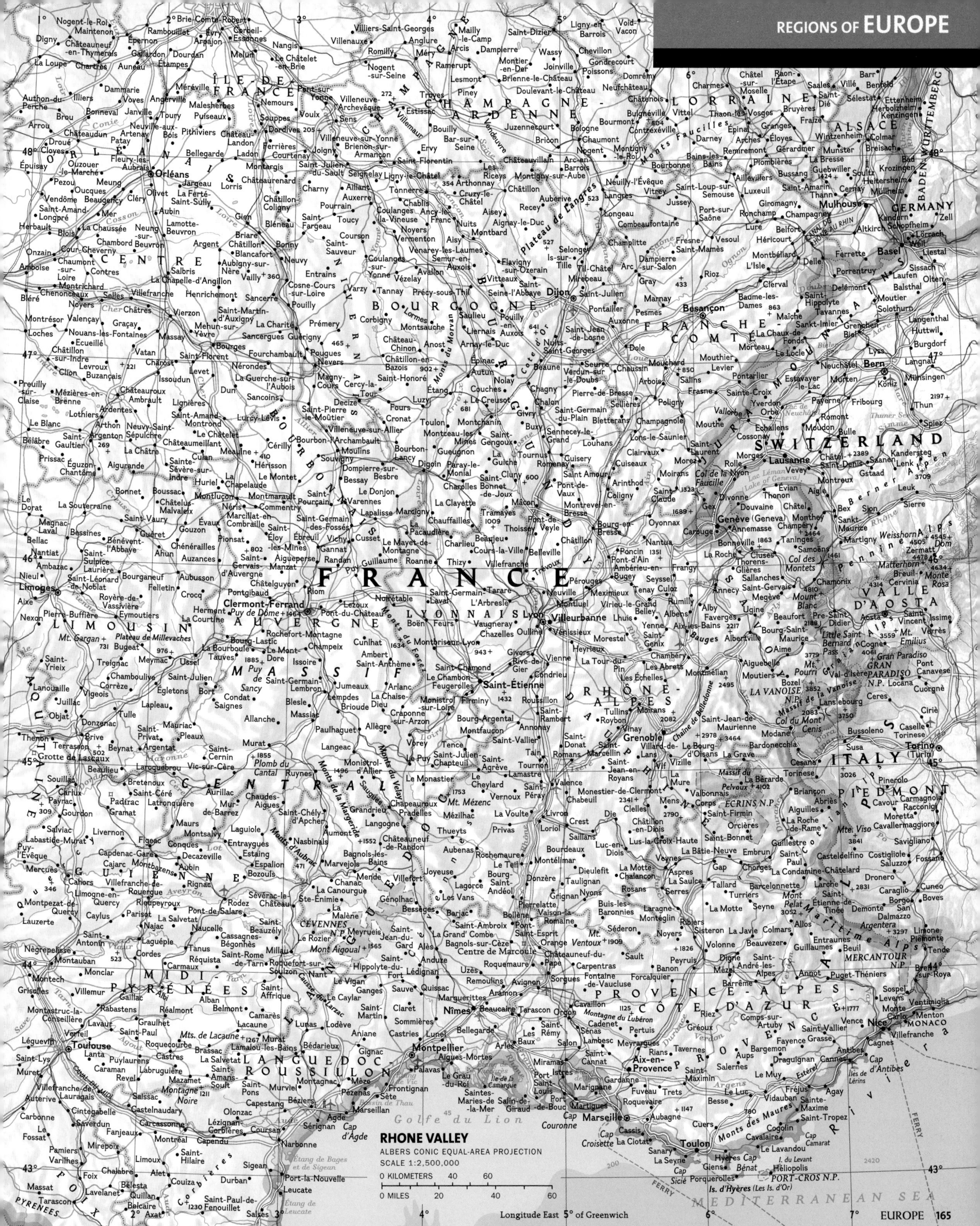

RHONE VALLEY

ALBERS CONIC EQUAL-AREA PROJECTION

SCALE 1:2,500,000

0 KILOMETERS 40 60

0 MILES 20 40 60

Longitude East 5° of Greenwich

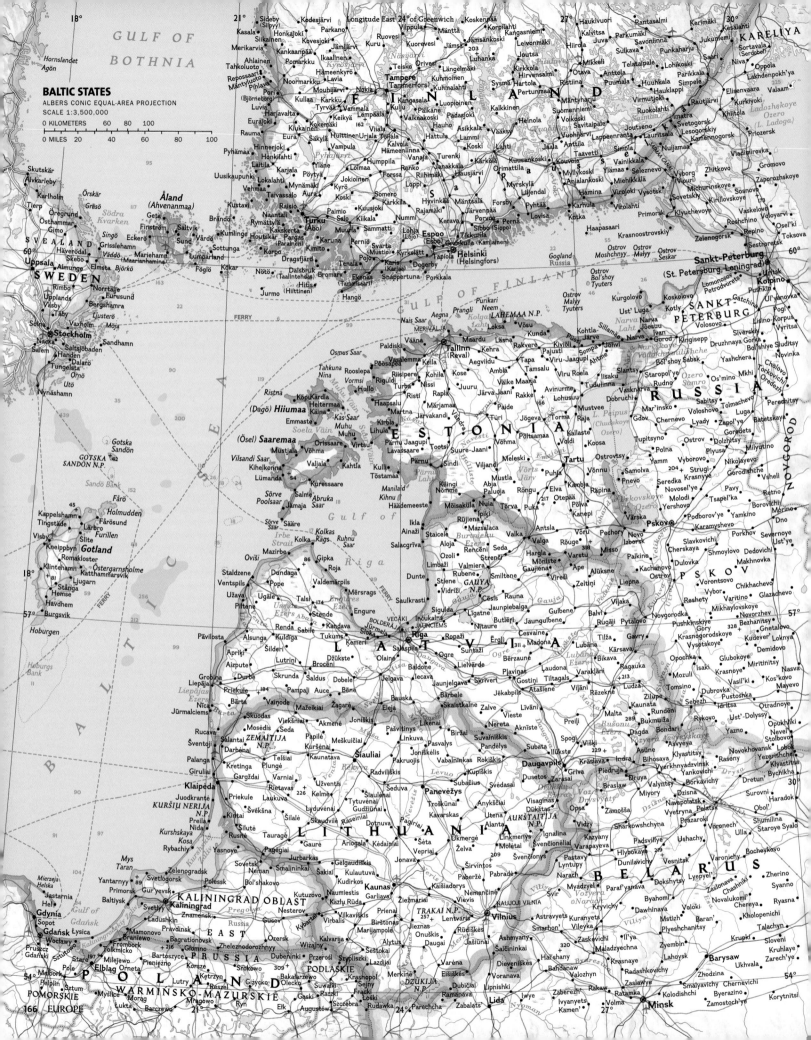

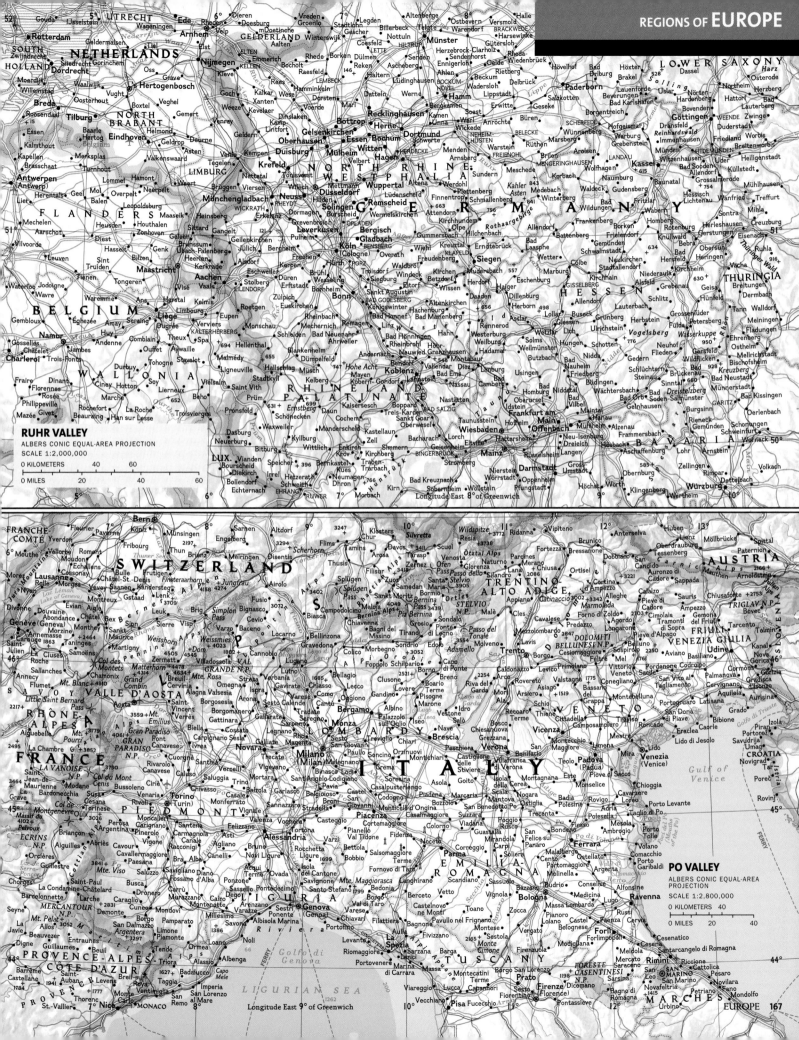

RUHR VALLEY
ALBERS CONIC EQUAL-AREA PROJECTION
SCALE 1:2,000,000
0 KILOMETERS 40 60
0 MILES 20 40 60

PO VALLEY
ALBERS CONIC EQUAL-AREA PROJECTION
SCALE 1:2,800,000
0 KILOMETERS 40
0 MILES 20 40

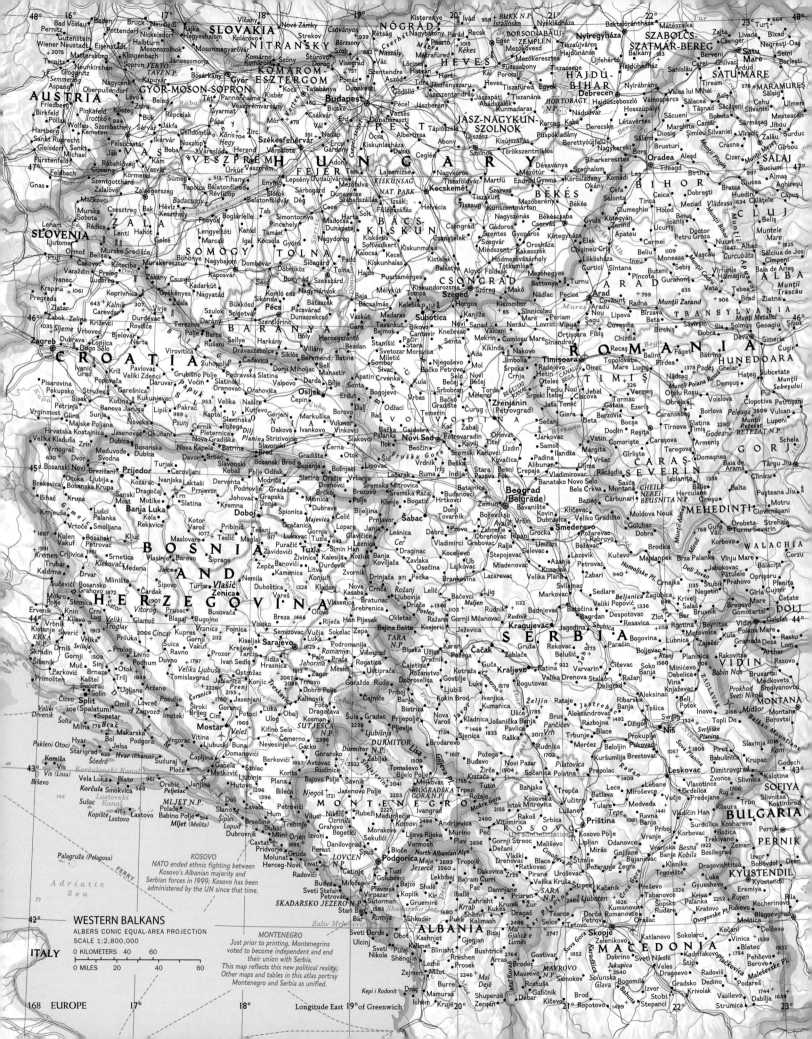

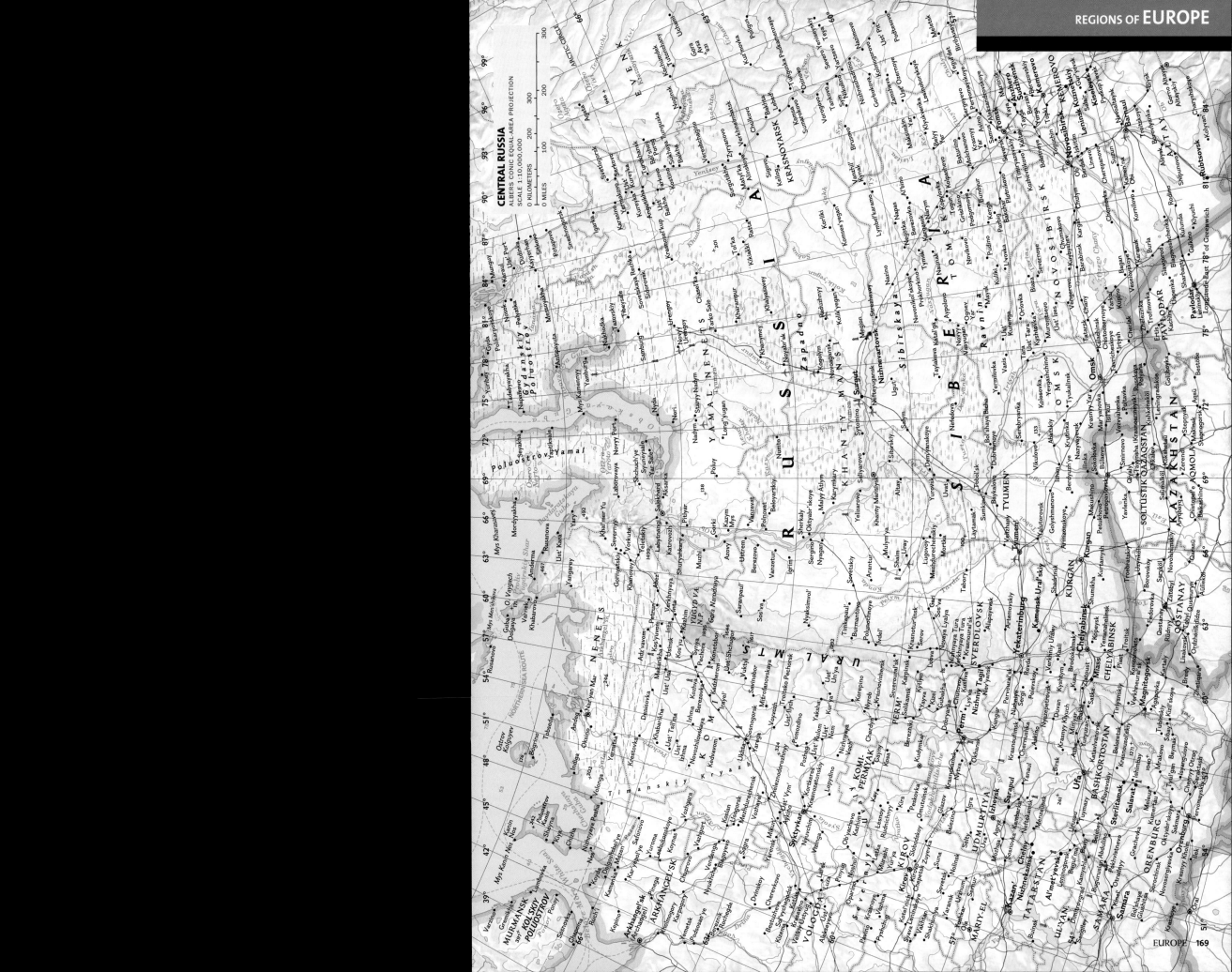

CENTRAL RUSSIA
ALBERS CONIC EQUAL-AREA PROJECTION
SCALE 1:10,000,000

0 KILOMETERS   100   200   300
0 MILES   100   200   300

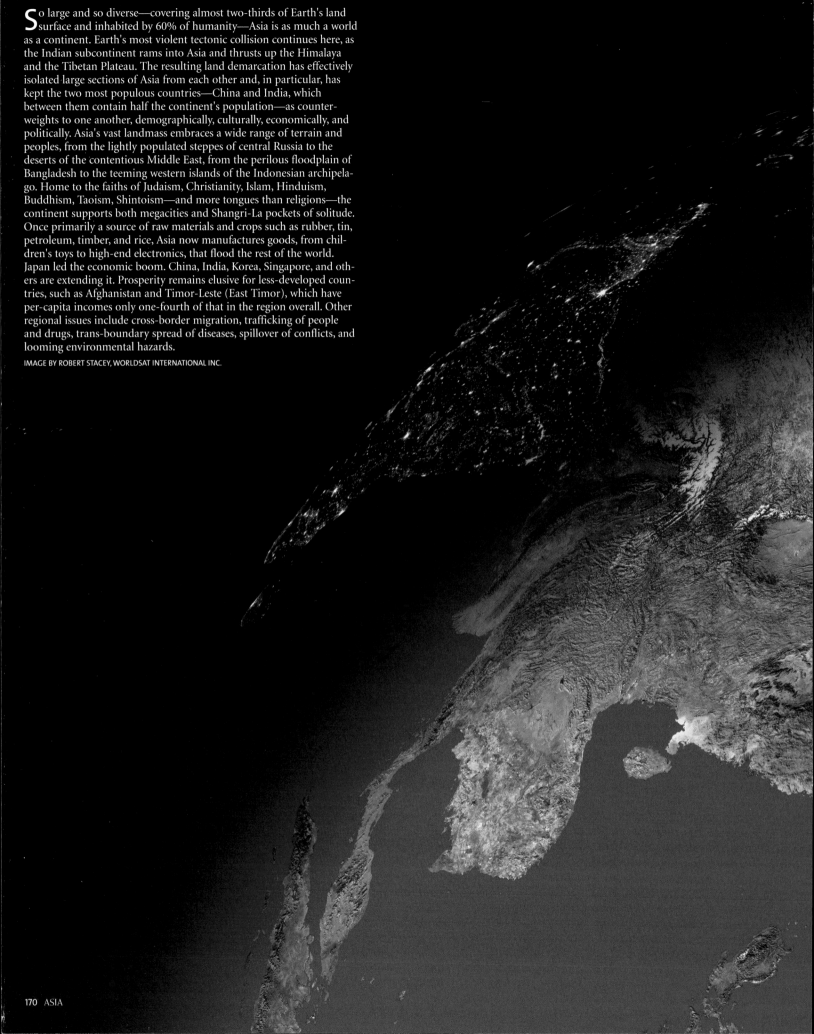

So large and so diverse—covering almost two-thirds of Earth's land surface and inhabited by 60% of humanity—Asia is as much a world as a continent. Earth's most violent tectonic collision continues here, as the Indian subcontinent rams into Asia and thrusts up the Himalaya and the Tibetan Plateau. The resulting land demarcation has effectively isolated large sections of Asia from each other and, in particular, has kept the two most populous countries—China and India, which between them contain half the continent's population—as counter-weights to one another, demographically, culturally, economically, and politically. Asia's vast landmass embraces a wide range of terrain and peoples, from the lightly populated steppes of central Russia to the deserts of the contentious Middle East, from the perilous floodplain of Bangladesh to the teeming western islands of the Indonesian archipelago. Home to the faiths of Judaism, Christianity, Islam, Hinduism, Buddhism, Taoism, Shintoism—and more tongues than religions—the continent supports both megacities and Shangri-La pockets of solitude. Once primarily a source of raw materials and crops such as rubber, tin, petroleum, timber, and rice, Asia now manufactures goods, from children's toys to high-end electronics, that flood the rest of the world. Japan led the economic boom. China, India, Korea, Singapore, and others are extending it. Prosperity remains elusive for less-developed countries, such as Afghanistan and Timor-Leste (East Timor), which have per-capita incomes only one-fourth of that in the region overall. Other regional issues include cross-border migration, trafficking of people and drugs, trans-boundary spread of diseases, spillover of conflicts, and looming environmental hazards.

IMAGE BY ROBERT STACEY, WORLDSAT INTERNATIONAL INC.

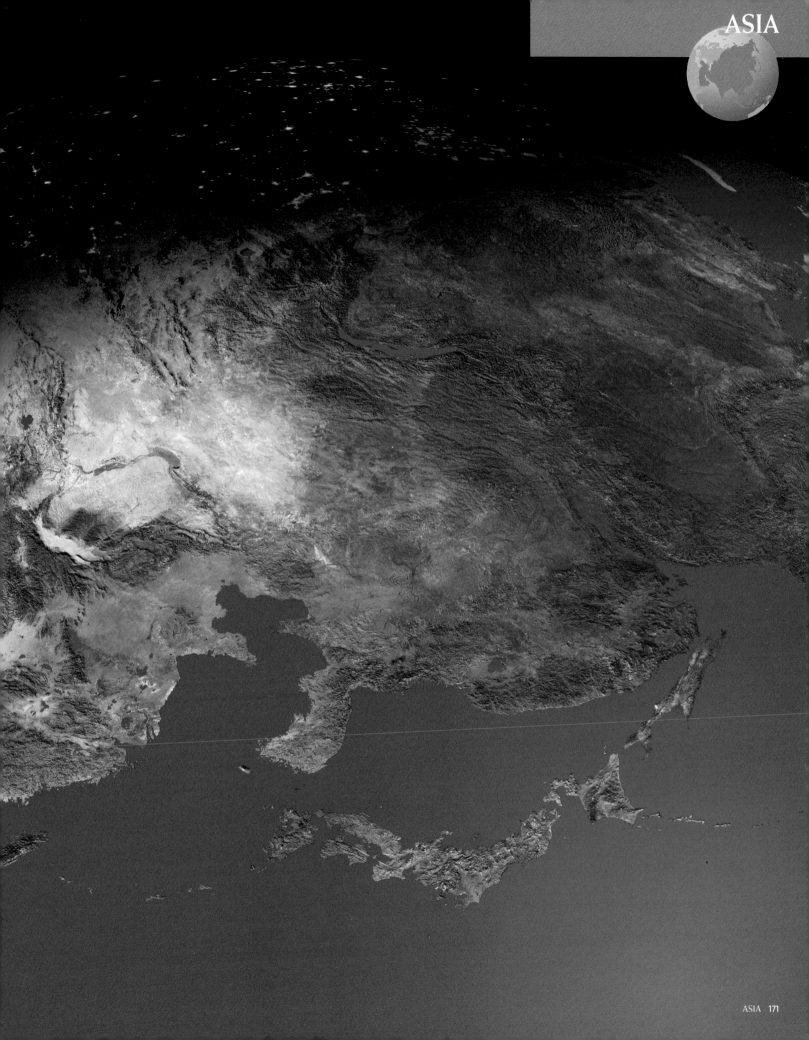

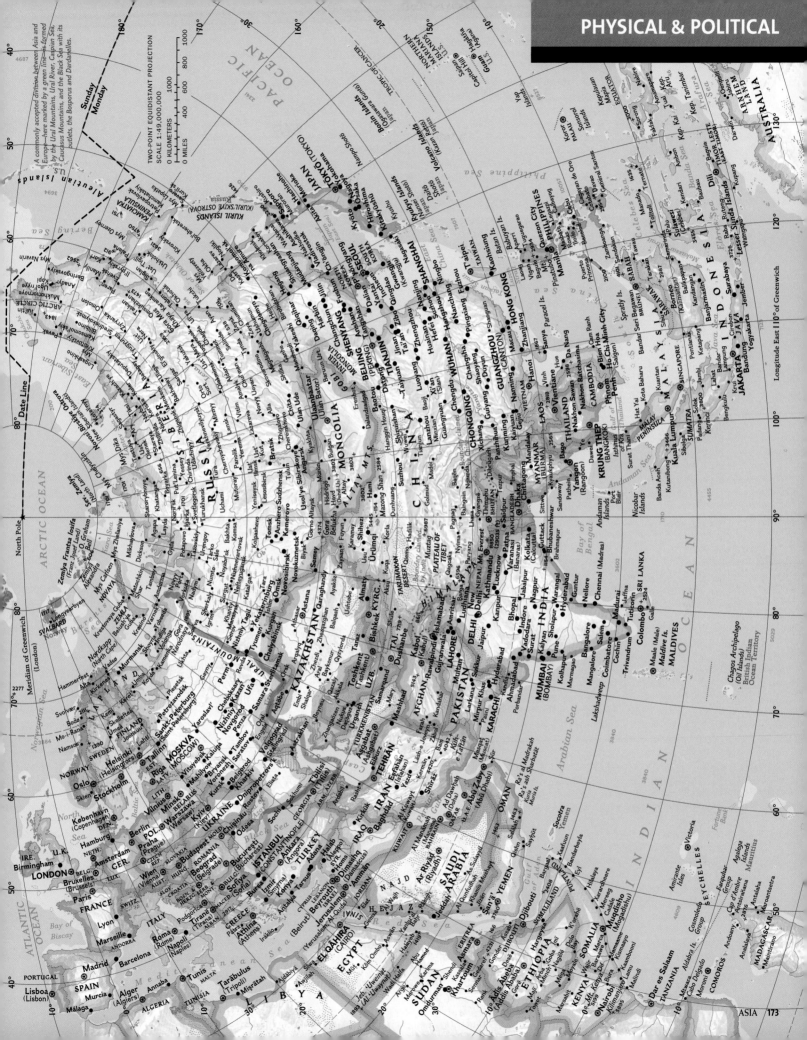

A commonly accepted division between Asia and Europe—here marked by a green line—is formed by the Ural Mountains, Ural River, Caspian Sea, Caucasus Mountains, and the Black Sea with its outlets, the Bosporus and Dardanelles.

TWO-POINT EQUIDISTANT PROJECTION
SCALE 1:49,000,000

PACIFIC OCEAN

ARCTIC OCEAN

North Pole

Aleutian Islands

Bering Sea

KAMCHATKA PENINSULA

KURIL ISLANDS (KURIL'SKIYE OSTROVA)

JAPAN

TOKYO (TŌKYŌ)

SIBERIA

RUSSIA

ALTAY MTS.

MONGOLIA

Ulaanbaatar (Ulan Bator)

BEIJING (PEKING)

SHENYANG

SHANGHAI

WUHAN

CHINA

CHONGQING

GUANGZHOU (CANTON)

HONG KONG

TAIWAN

T'aipei

PLATEAU OF TIBET

TAKLIMAKAN DESERT

KAZAKHSTAN

Astana

URAL MOUNTAINS

KYRG.

TAJ.

MYANMAR (BURMA)

LAOS

THAILAND

KRUNG THEP (BANGKOK)

CAMBODIA

VIETNAM

Ho Chi Minh City (Saigon)

PHILIPPINES

Manila

Quezon City

SABAH

BRUNEI

MALAYSIA

Kuala Lumpur

SINGAPORE

BORNEO (KALIMANTAN)

SUMATRA

INDONESIA

JAVA

JAKARTA

TIMOR LESTE (EAST TIMOR)

AUSTRALIA

ARNHEM LAND

PALAU

NORTHERN MARIANA ISLANDS

Guam (U.S.)

Philippine Sea

Banda Sea

Arafura Sea

Celebes Sea

Java Sea

SULAWESI (CELEBES)

Andaman Islands

Nicobar Islands

Bay of Bengal

SRI LANKA

Colombo

Chennai (Madras)

INDIA

MUMBAI (BOMBAY)

Bangalore

Hyderabad

Kolkata (Calcutta)

New Delhi

DELHI

BANGLADESH

Dhaka

NEPAL

Kathmandu

BHUTAN

Thimphu

HIMALAYA

Mt. Everest 8850

PAKISTAN

KARACHI

LAHORE

Islamabad

AFGHAN.

Kabul (Kābol)

TURKMENISTAN

UZB.

Toshkent (Tashkent)

Samarqand

IRAN

TEHRĀN

Eşfahān

MALDIVES

Maldive Is.

British Indian Territory

Chagos Archipelago (Oil Islands)

INDIAN OCEAN

Arabian Sea

OMAN

U.A.E. Abū Zaby (Abu Dhabi)

QATAR

Ar Riyāḍ (Riyadh)

SAUDI ARABIA

NAJD

HEJAZ

YEMEN

Şan'ā'

Aden

Socotra

Gulf of Aden

SOMALIA

Muqdisho (Mogadishu)

SOMALILAND

DJIBOUTI

ETHIOPIA

Ādīs Ābeba (Addis Ababa)

ERITREA

Asmara

SUDAN

Khartoum

KENYA

Nairobi

Mt. Kenya

Mt. Kilimanjaro 5895

TANZANIA

Dar es Salaam

COMOROS

MADAGASCAR

Antananarivo

SEYCHELLES

Victoria

Mauritius

Red Sea

EGYPT

EL QAHIRA (CAIRO)

LIBYA

Ţarābulus (Tripoli)

TUNISIA

Tunis

ALGERIA

Alger (Algiers)

SPAIN

Madrid

Barcelona

PORTUGAL

Lisboa (Lisbon)

Málaga

Murcia

ANDORRA

FRANCE

Lyon

Marseille

Paris

Bay of Biscay

Atlantic Ocean

IRE.

U.K.

LONDON

Birmingham

NETH.

Amsterdam

BELG.

Bruxelles (Brussels)

LUX.

GER.

Berlin

Hamburg

POL.

Warszawa (Warsaw)

CZECH REP.

Praha (Prague)

Wien (Vienna)

AUST.

SLOVAKIA

Budapest

HUNG.

ROMANIA

Bucureşti (Bucharest)

BULG.

Sofiya (Sofia)

SLOV.

CROATIA

BOSN. & HERZEG.

SERB. & MONT.

Beograd (Belgrade)

ITALY

Roma (Rome)

Napoli (Naples)

MALTA

GREECE

Athina (Athens)

ALB.

Tiranë (Tirana)

MACED.

MOLD.

Chişinău

UKRAINE

Kyiv (Kiev)

BELARUS

Minsk

LITH.

Vilnius

LATV.

Riga

EST.

Tallinn

FINLAND

Helsinki (Helsingfors)

SWEDEN

Stockholm

NORWAY

Oslo

DEN.

København (Copenhagen)

Mediterranean Sea

Black Sea

TURKEY

ISTANBUL (CONSTANTINOPLE)

Ankara

İzmir (Smyrna)

CYPRUS

SYRIA (S.R.)

Dimashq (Damascus)

Ḥalab (Aleppo)

LEBANON

Beyrouth (Beirut)

ISRAEL

JORDAN

'Ammān

Jerusalem (Yerushalayim) Al-Quds

IRAQ

Baghdād

KUWAIT

BAHRAIN

Al Manāmah

GEORGIA

Tbilisi (Tiflis)

ARM.

AZERB.

Baku

Caspian Sea

MOSKVA (MOSCOW)

Sankt-Peterburg

Caucasus Mts.

Mashhad

RUSSIA

NORTH KOREA

P'yongyang

SOUTH KOREA

SEOUL

TIAN JIN

Baltic Sea

North Sea

Norwegian Sea

Barents Sea

Kara Sea

SVALBARD (Norway)

ARCTIC CIRCLE

TROPIC OF CANCER

EQUATOR

Date Line

Sunday Monday

Meridian of Greenwich (London)

Longitude East 110° of Greenwich

Land cover

Forest
- Evergreen needleleaf
- Evergreen broadleaf
- Deciduous needleleaf
- Deciduous broadleaf
- Mixed forest
- Woodland

Grassland or shrubland
- Wooded grassland
- Closed shrubland
- Open shrubland
- Grassland

Other
- Cropland
- Barren (Desert and Polar Ice)
- Built-up

TEMPERATURE AND RAINFALL

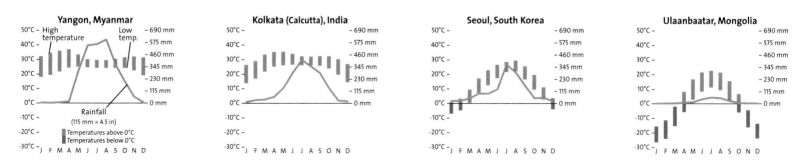

Yangon, Myanmar

High temperature
Low temp.

Rainfall
(115 mm = 4.5 in)

Temperatures above 0°C
Temperatures below 0°C

Kolkata (Calcutta), India

Seoul, South Korea

Ulaanbaatar, Mongolia

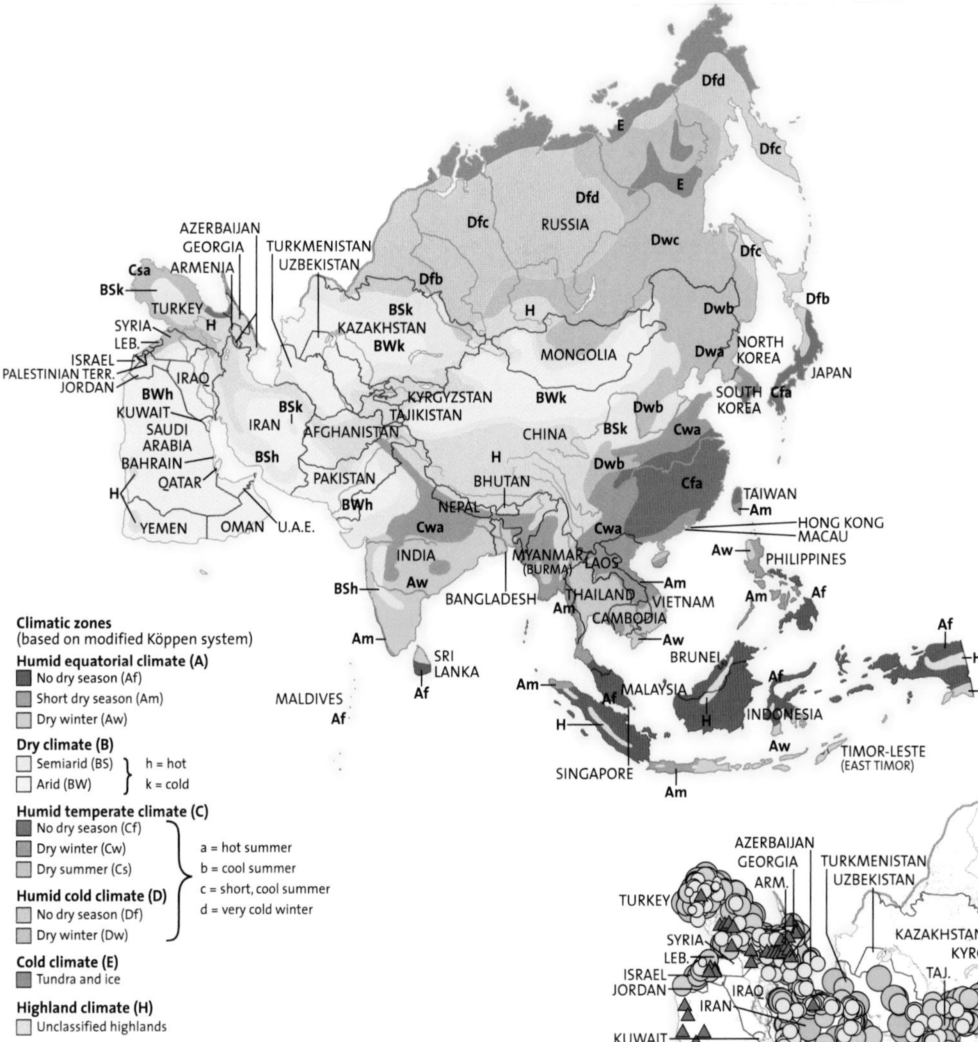
Dfd
E
Dfc
Dfd
E
Dfc
RUSSIA
Dwc
Dfc
Dfb
Dfb
AZERBAIJAN
GEORGIA
ARMENIA
TURKMENISTAN
UZBEKISTAN
Csa
BSk
TURKEY
H
SYRIA
LEB.
ISRAEL
PALESTINIAN TERR.
JORDAN
IRAQ
BSk
KAZAKHSTAN
BWk
H
MONGOLIA
Dwb
Dwa
NORTH KOREA
JAPAN
SOUTH KOREA
Cfa
BWh
KUWAIT
SAUDI ARABIA
BAHRAIN
QATAR
H
YEMEN
OMAN
U.A.E.
IRAN
BSk
BSh
KYRGYZSTAN
TAJIKISTAN
AFGHANISTAN
BWk
Dwb
BSk
CHINA
Cwa
Cfa
Dwb
H
BHUTAN
PAKISTAN
BWh
NEPAL
Cwa
INDIA
Aw
BSh
Am
TAIWAN
Am
HONG KONG
MACAU
Cwa
MYANMAR (BURMA)
LAOS
Aw
PHILIPPINES
Am
BANGLADESH
THAILAND
Am
VIETNAM
Am
Af
CAMBODIA
Aw
SRI LANKA
Af
BRUNEI
Af
H
Aw
MALDIVES
Af
Am
MALAYSIA
Af
H
INDONESIA
H
Aw
TIMOR-LESTE (EAST TIMOR)
SINGAPORE
Am
Climatic zones
(based on modified Köppen system)
Humid equatorial climate (A)
No dry season (Af)
Short dry season (Am)
Dry winter (Aw)
Dry climate (B)
Semiarid (BS)
Arid (BW)
h = hot
k = cold
Humid temperate climate (C)
No dry season (Cf)
Dry winter (Cw)
Dry summer (Cs)
a = hot summer
b = cool summer
c = short, cool summer
d = very cold winter
Humid cold climate (D)
No dry season (Df)
Dry winter (Dw)
Cold climate (E)
Tundra and ice
Highland climate (H)
Unclassified highlands

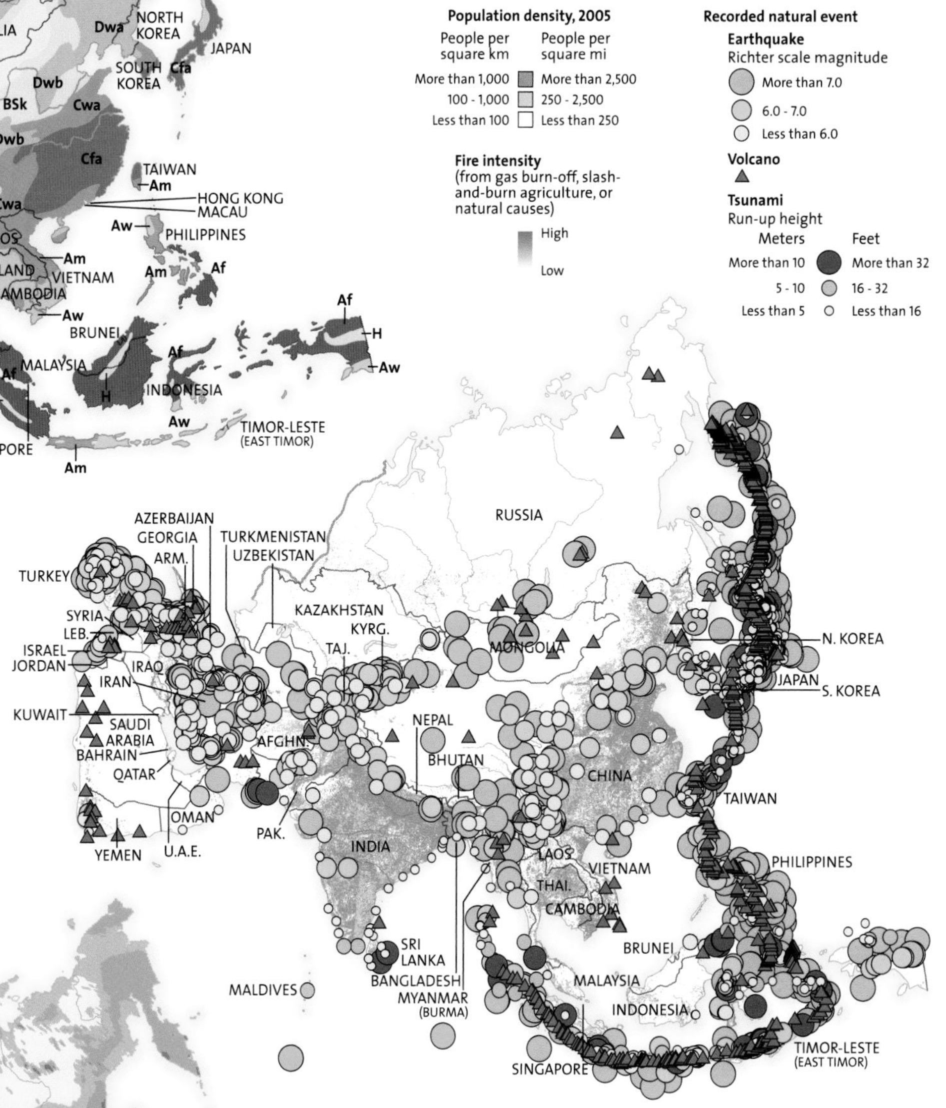
Population density, 2005
People per square km
People per square mi
More than 1,000
More than 2,500
100 - 1,000
250 - 2,500
Less than 100
Less than 250
Fire intensity
(from gas burn-off, slash-and-burn agriculture, or natural causes)
High
Low
Recorded natural event
Earthquake
Richter scale magnitude
More than 7.0
6.0 - 7.0
Less than 6.0
Volcano
Tsunami
Run-up height
Meters
Feet
More than 10
More than 32
5 - 10
16 - 32
Less than 5
Less than 16
RUSSIA
AZERBAIJAN
GEORGIA
ARM.
TURKMENISTAN
UZBEKISTAN
TURKEY
KAZAKHSTAN
KYRG.
SYRIA
LEB.
ISRAEL
JORDAN
TAJ.
MONGOLIA
N. KOREA
IRAQ
IRAN
JAPAN
S. KOREA
KUWAIT
SAUDI ARABIA
BAHRAIN
QATAR
AFGHN.
NEPAL
BHUTAN
CHINA
TAIWAN
OMAN
PAK.
YEMEN
U.A.E.
INDIA
LAOS
VIETNAM
PHILIPPINES
THAI.
CAMBODIA
SRI LANKA
BRUNEI
BANGLADESH
MALAYSIA
MYANMAR (BURMA)
MALDIVES
INDONESIA
TIMOR-LESTE (EAST TIMOR)
SINGAPORE

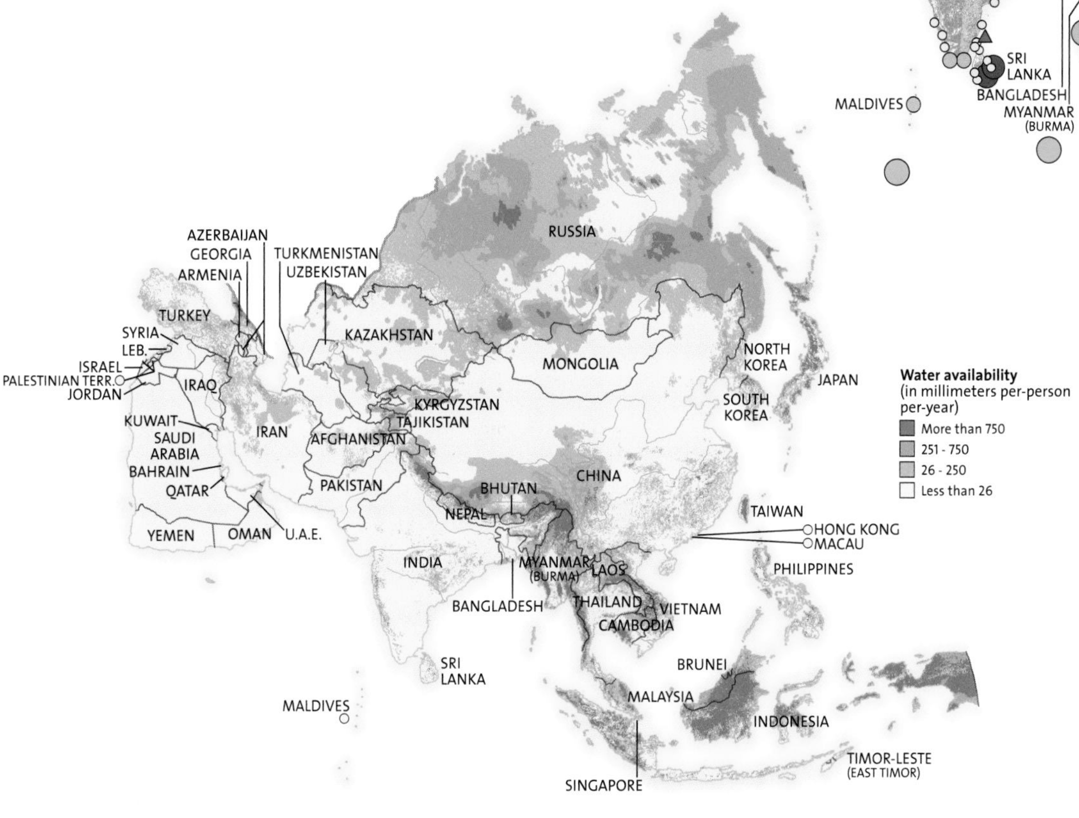
RUSSIA
AZERBAIJAN
GEORGIA
ARMENIA
TURKMENISTAN
UZBEKISTAN
TURKEY
KAZAKHSTAN
SYRIA
LEB.
ISRAEL
PALESTINIAN TERR.
JORDAN
IRAQ
MONGOLIA
NORTH KOREA
JAPAN
SOUTH KOREA
KYRGYZSTAN
TAJIKISTAN
KUWAIT
SAUDI ARABIA
BAHRAIN
QATAR
IRAN
AFGHANISTAN
PAKISTAN
BHUTAN
CHINA
NEPAL
TAIWAN
YEMEN
OMAN
U.A.E.
HONG KONG
MACAU
INDIA
MYANMAR (BURMA)
LAOS
PHILIPPINES
BANGLADESH
THAILAND
VIETNAM
CAMBODIA
SRI LANKA
BRUNEI
MALAYSIA
MALDIVES
INDONESIA
TIMOR-LESTE (EAST TIMOR)
SINGAPORE
Water availability
(in millimeters per-person per-year)
More than 750
251 - 750
26 - 250
Less than 26

Population density, 2005

People per square km	People per square mi
More than 195	More than 500
60 - 195	150 - 500
10 - 59	25 - 149
1 - 9	1 - 24
Less than 1	Less than 1

POPULATION PYRAMIDS

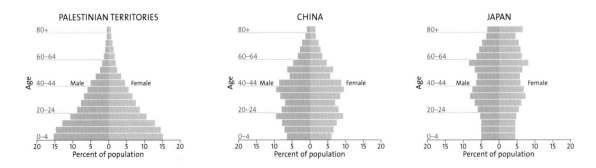

PALESTINIAN TERRITORIES

CHINA

JAPAN

Indigenous languages
- Afro-Asiatic
- Altaic
- Austro-Asiatic
- Austronesian
- Caucasian Families
- Dravidian
- Eskimo-Aleut
- Hmong-Mien
- Indo-European
- Japanese/Korean
- Kam-Tai
- Papuan Familes
- Sino-Tibetan
- Uralic
- Isolates
- Uninhabited

Urban agglomerations, 2005
(Population in millions)
- ● More than 10.0
- ● 5.0 - 10.0
- ● 2.5 - 4.9
- ● 1.0 - 2.4
- · .75 - .99

Percent urban population, 2005
- More than 75%
- 50% - 74%
- 25% - 49%
- Less than 24%

Urban agglomerations, 2005
- ● SOUTH KOREA
1 Seoul - 9.6 million
2 Busan (Pusan) - 3.5 million
3 Incheon - 2.6 million
4 Daegu - 2.5 million

- ● SYRIA
1 Ḥalab (Aleppo) - 2.5 million
2 Dimashq (Damascus) - 2.3 million

Projected population change, 2005 - 2050
(by percentage)
- More than 100%
- 50% - 100%
- 0% - 49%
- Less than 0% (Population loss)

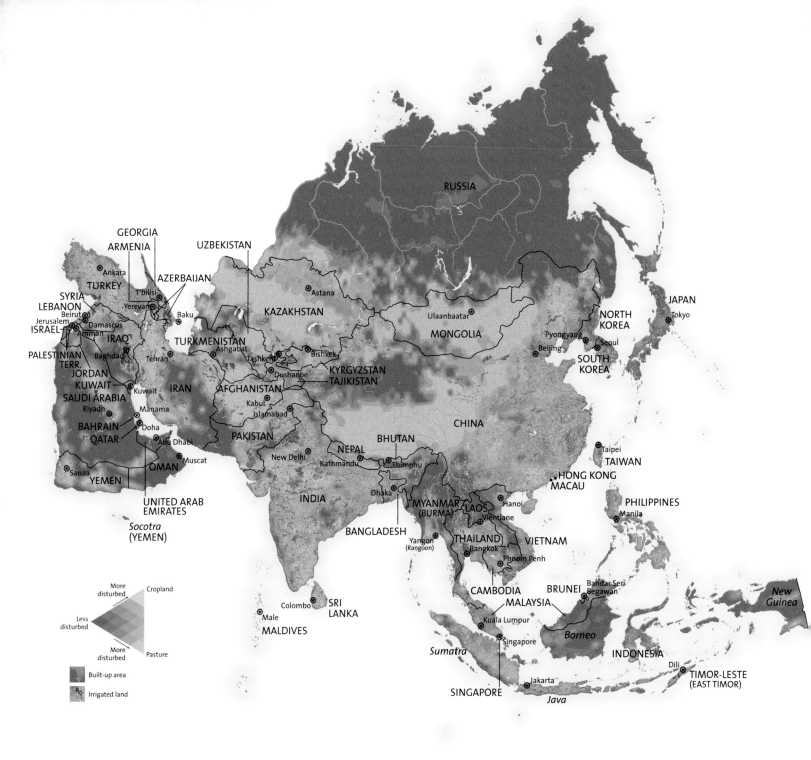

GEORGIA
ARMENIA
AZERBAIJAN
UZBEKISTAN
RUSSIA

Ankara
TURKEY
T'bilisi
Yerevan
Baku
Astana
KAZAKHSTAN
JAPAN
Tokyo

SYRIA
LEBANON
Beirut
Jerusalem
ISRAEL
Damascus
Amman
IRAQ
Baghdad
TURKMENISTAN
Ashgabat
Tashkent
Dushanbe
Bishkek
KYRGYZSTAN
TAJIKISTAN
Ulaanbaatar
MONGOLIA
Pyongyang
Beijing
NORTH
KOREA
Seoul
SOUTH
KOREA

PALESTINIAN
TERR.
JORDAN
KUWAIT
Kuwait
Tehran
IRAN
AFGHANISTAN
Kabul
Islamabad
CHINA

SAUDI ARABIA
Riyadh
Manama
BAHRAIN
Doha
QATAR
Abu Dhabi
Muscat
PAKISTAN
New Delhi
NEPAL
Kathmandu
BHUTAN
Thimphu
Taipei
TAIWAN
HONG KONG
MACAU

Sanaa
YEMEN
OMAN
UNITED ARAB
EMIRATES
INDIA
Dhaka
MYANMAR
(BURMA)
LAOS
Vientiane
Hanoi
PHILIPPINES
Manila

Socotra
(YEMEN)
BANGLADESH
Yangon
(Rangoon)
THAILAND
Bangkok
Phnom Penh
VIETNAM

Colombo
SRI
LANKA
Male
MALDIVES
CAMBODIA
MALAYSIA
BRUNEI
Bandar Seri
Begawan
New
Guinea

Kuala Lumpur
Borneo

Sumatra
Singapore
INDONESIA
Dili
TIMOR-LESTE
(EAST TIMOR)

SINGAPORE
Jakarta
Java

More
disturbed
Cropland
Less
disturbed
More
disturbed
Pasture
Built-up area
Irrigated land

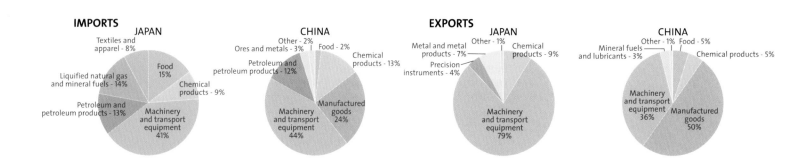

IMPORTS

JAPAN

Textiles and apparel - 8%
Liquified natural gas and mineral fuels - 14%
Petroleum and petroleum products - 13%
Machinery and transport equipment 41%
Food 15%
Chemical products - 9%

CHINA

Other - 2%
Ores and metals - 3%
Food - 2%
Petroleum and petroleum products - 12%
Chemical products - 13%
Machinery and transport equipment 44%
Manufactured goods 24%

EXPORTS

JAPAN

Metal and metal products - 7%
Precision instruments - 4%
Other - 1%
Chemical products - 9%
Machinery and transport equipment 79%

CHINA

Mineral fuels and lubricants - 3%
Other - 1%
Food - 5%
Chemical products - 5%
Machinery and transport equipment 36%
Manufactured goods 50%

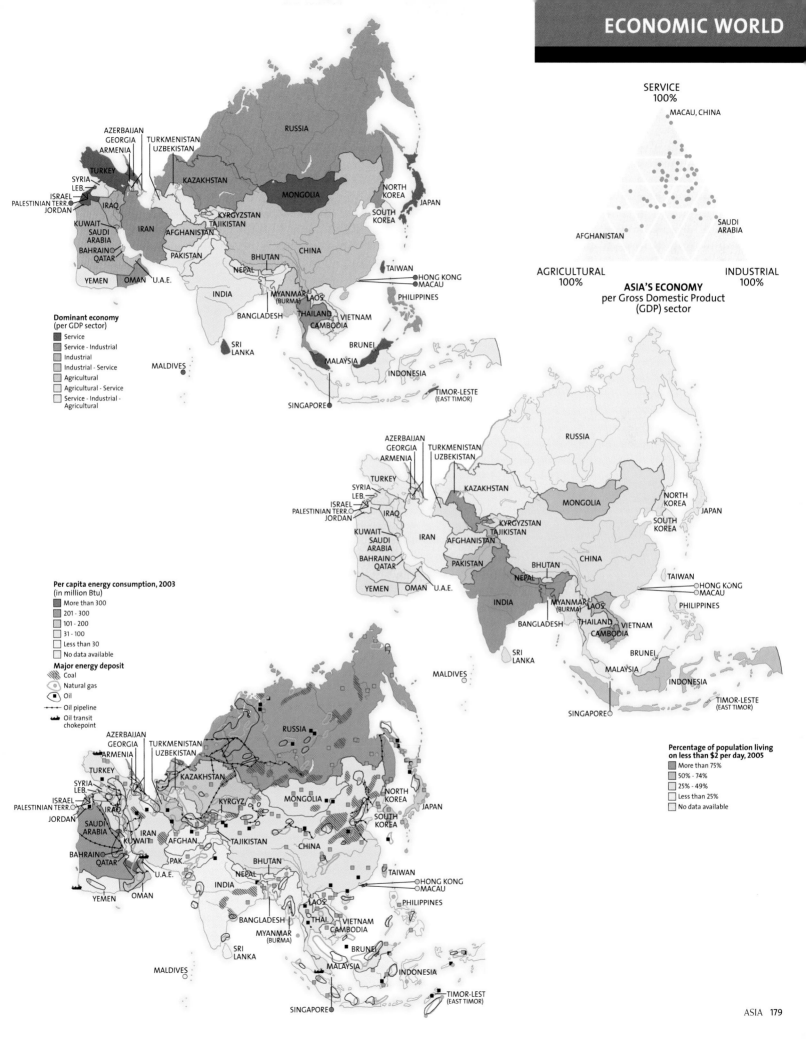

SERVICE 100%

MACAU, CHINA

SAUDI ARABIA

AFGHANISTAN

AGRICULTURAL 100%

ASIA'S ECONOMY
per Gross Domestic Product (GDP) sector

INDUSTRIAL 100%

Dominant economy
(per GDP sector)
- Service
- Service - Industrial
- Industrial
- Industrial - Service
- Agricultural
- Agricultural - Service
- Service - Industrial - Agricultural

Per capita energy consumption, 2003
(in million Btu)
- More than 300
- 201 - 300
- 101 - 200
- 31 - 100
- Less than 30
- No data available

Major energy deposit
- Coal
- Natural gas
- Oil
- Oil pipeline
- Oil transit chokepoint

Percentage of population living on less than $2 per day, 2005
- More than 75%
- 50% - 74%
- 25% - 49%
- Less than 25%
- No data available

IRAN

PAKISTAN

BALUCHISTAN

Zagros Mountains

PERSIAN GULF

Gulf of Bahrain

Strait of Hormuz

GULF OF OMAN

TROPIC OF CANCER

BAHRAIN
Al Manāmah (Manama)

QATAR
Ad Dawḥah (Doha)

UNITED ARAB EMIRATES

Sharjah
Dubayy (Dubai)
Abū Ẓaby (Abu Dhabi)

BOUNDARY UNDEFINED

O M A N

Rub' al Khālī
(Empty Quarter)

Umm as Samīm

As Sanām

Khalīj Maṣīrah

Jazīrat Maṣīrah (Masira)

Ghubbat Ṣawqirah

ZUFĀR

Kuria Muria Is.

Ghubbat al Qamar

ARABIAN SEA

ADEN

Socotra (Suquṭrá)
Yemen

'Abd al Kūrī
Yemen

Al Ikhwān (The Brothers)

SOMALIA

Cape Gwardafuy

LAMBERT CONFORMAL CONIC PROJECTION
SCALE 1:8,000,000

0 KILOMETERS 120 160 200
0 MILES 40 80 120 160 200

Garagum
TURKMENISTAN
UZBEKISTAN
Nurota   Gizilchia   Do'stlik   Guliston   Buston
Zafarobod   Langar   Yangiqishloq   Jizzax   Yangiyer   Bekobod   Korgon   Isfara
Darganata   Karmana   Navoiy   Chelak   ZAAMIN   Istaravshan   Tajikistan
Darvaza   Gazli   Buxoro   Qizltepa   Oqtosh   N.P.   Turkestan Range   Dekhisor
(Bukhara)   Nurobod   Urgut   Panjakent   Zarafshon Range   Gharm   Jirgatol   Qullai Ismoili Somoni   +7495   Uzbel
Yerbent   Qorakŭl   Qorovulbozor   Samarqand   Zarafshon   (Communism Peak)   Darxoh   Shankou
Bokurdak   Seydi   Muborak   Shahrisabz   Qarshi   Obigarm   TAJIKISTAN   Murgab   Rangkŭl   Muztagata
TURKMENISTAN   Türkmenabat   G'uzor   Dushanbe   Kofarnihon   Kalaikhum   Vanj   Kudara   Kulma Pass   Tokhtamysh   CHINA
(Chärjew)   Yangi-   Dehqonobod   Tursunzoda   Norak   Rushan   Vir   Baza'i Gonbad   Jaman Pass   Shayman   Yashichu
Asgabat   Nishon   Denow   Shar'gun   Qal'eh-ye Bar   Panj   Khorugh   Roshtkala   Khudabad   Mingteke Pass   Aijiekebey
(Ashgabat)   Babadaykhan   Sayat   Boyson   Sho'rchi   Qŭrghonteppa   Feyzabad   Baharak   Vrang   Sarhadd   Uprang
B024ymex Ing   Kerkiçi   Atamyrat   Garavuti   Moskovskij   Chah-e Ab   Eshkashem   Tirich   Wasam   Khunjerab Pass
Büzmeyin   Mary   GARAGUM CANAL   Mukry   Sherobod   Hazareh Toghay   Farkhor   Kondoz   Taloqan   Mir   Ishkuman   Gupis   778b   Karakoram Range   36°
Bäjgiran   Dargaz   Duşak   Yolöten   Termiz   Ayvaj   Panj   Zibak   7690   Chitral   Mastuj   Teru Gakuch   Rakaposhi
Shirvän Mts.   Kaka   Tejen   Andkhvoy   Aqchan   Balkh   Kholm   Khanabad   Eshkamesh   Shahr-e   Baze'i   Dir   Kalam   Skardu   NORTHERN
Quchän   Sarakhs   Sarahs   Sheberghan   Dowlatabad   Sar-e Pol   Aq Kopruk   Dahaneh-ye Ghowri   Monjan   Jabal os Saraj   Asmar   Tal   Jalkot   Chilas   Nanga   Parbat   Burzil   AREAS

ARABIAN
SEA

ASIA 187

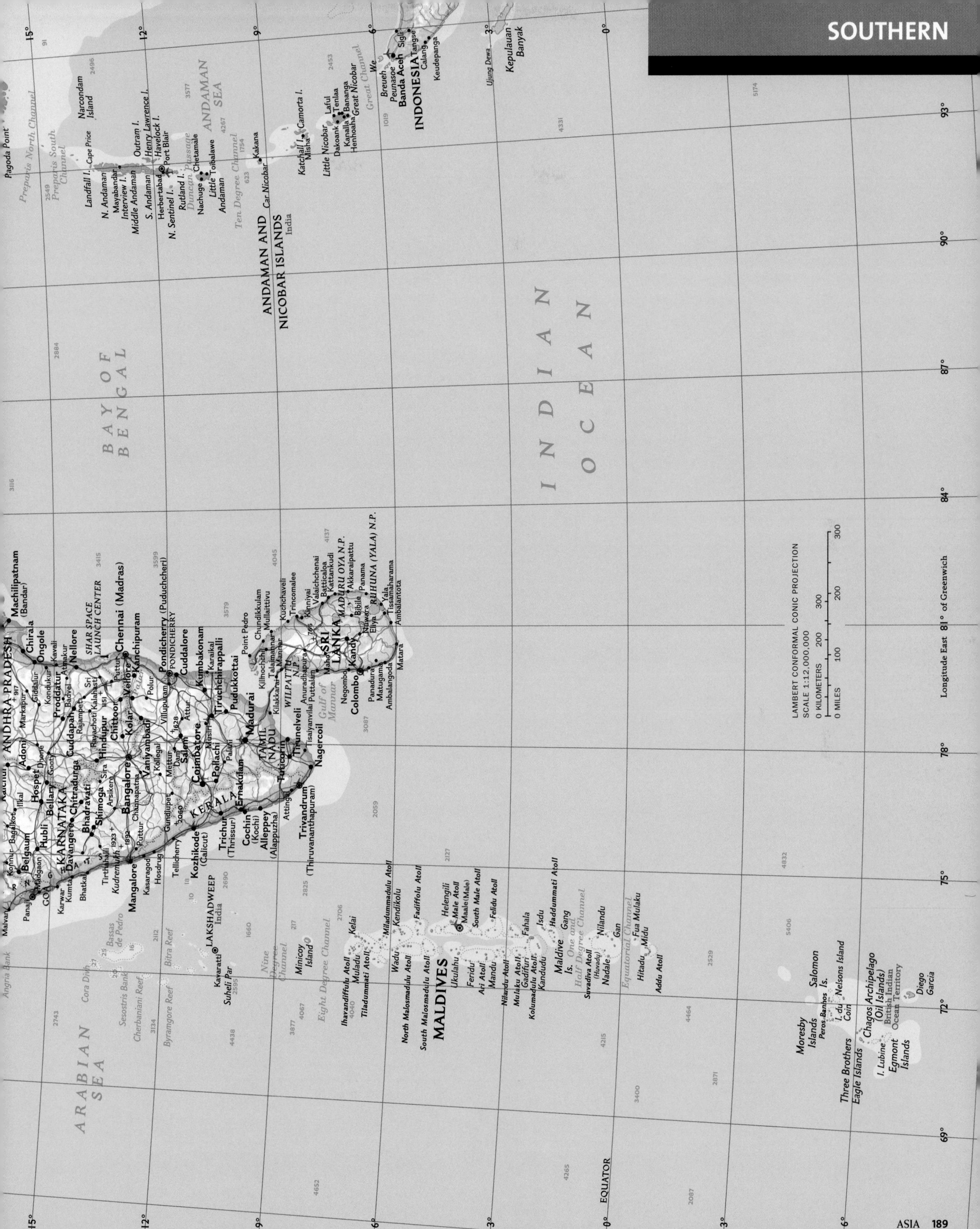

ASIA

Pagoda Point

Preparis North Channel
Preparis South Channel

Narcondam Island
2496

Landfall I.
Cape Price
N. Andaman
Mayabandar
Interview I.
Middle Andaman
Outram I.
Henry Lawrence I.
Havelock I.
3517
Herbertabad
Port Blair
S. Andaman
Rutland I.
N. Sentinel I.
Duncan Passage
Nachuge
Chetamale
Little Andaman
Todhalawe
4267
623
1754
Kakana

Katchall I.
Camorta I.
Misha
Little Nicobar
Laful
Tenlaa
Dakoank
Kanalla
Bananga
Henhoaha
2453
Great Channel
We
Breueh
Peunasoe
Banda Aceh
Sigli
Tangse
Calang
Keudepanga
INDONESIA

Kepulauan
Banyak
Ujung Dewa

ANDAMAN SEA

Ten Degree Channel
Car Nicobar

**ANDAMAN AND
NICOBAR ISLANDS**
India

B A Y   O F
B E N G A L

I N D I A N
O C E A N

A R A B I A N
S E A

Machilipatnam (Bandar)
ANDHRA PRADESH
Chirala
Ongole
Kavali
Kandukur
Nellore
Atmakur
*SHAR SPACE
LAUNCH CENTER*
Sri Harikota
Chennai (Madras)
Kanchipuram
Pondicherry (Puducheri)
PONDICHERRY
Cuddalore
Karaikal
Kumbakonam
Tiruchirappalli
Pudukkottai

Point Pedro
Chundikkulam
Kilinochchi
Kuchchaveli
Trincomalee
WILPATTU N.P.
Anuradhapura
Kinniya
Valaichchenai
Batticaloa
Kattankudi
MADURU OYA N.P.
Akkarapattu
Kandy
4137
Nuwara Eliya
Bibile
Panama
RUHUNA (YALA) N.P.
Panadura
Yala
**SRI
LANKA**
Matugama
Ambalangoda
Ambalantota
Matara

KARNATAKA
Bangalore
Mangalore
Kasaragod
Kozhikode (Galicut)
Tellicherry
KERALA
Trichur (Thrissur)
Cochin (Kochi)
Alleppey (Alappuzha)
Trivandrum (Thiruvananthapuram)
Nagercoil
Tuticorin
Thunelveli
Madurai
**TAMIL
NADU**

LAKSHADWEEP
India
Kavaratti
Suheli Par
Minicoy Island

Nine Degree Channel
Eight Degree Channel

Ihavandiffulu Atoll
Miladummadulu Atoll
Fadiffolu Atoll
Kendikolu
Helengili
Male (Male)
South Male Atoll
Felidu Atoll
Haddummati Atoll
MALDIVES
North Malosmadulu Atoll
South Malosmadulu Atoll
Gan
Half Degree Channel
Equatorial Channel
Hitadu
Fua Mulaku
Midu
Addu Atoll

Moresby Islands
Peros Banhos
Salomon Is.
Nelsons Island
Three Brothers
Eagle Islands
I. Lubine
Egmont Islands
**Chagos Archipelago
(Oil Islands)
British Indian
Ocean Territory**
Diego Garcia

LAMBERT CONFORMAL CONIC PROJECTION
SCALE 1:12,000,000
0 KILOMETERS 100 200 300
0 MILES 100 200 300

Longitude East 81° of Greenwich

EQUATOR

ASIA **189**

TAIWAN
The People's Republic of China claims Taiwan as
its 23rd province. Taiwan's government (Republic
of China) maintains that there are two political entities.
The Islands of Matsu, Pescadores, Pratas,
and Quemoy are administered by Taiwan.

LAMBERT CONFORMAL CONIC PROJECTION
SCALE 1:16,000,000

0 KILOMETERS   300   400

0 MILES   100   200   300   400

BANGLADESH
Dhaka
Khulna
Chittagong

INDIA
Sylhet
Imphal
Naga Hills +3826
Myitkyina
Tengchong
Katha
Mawlaik
Kalemyo
Shwebo
Monywa
Mandalay
Myingyan

Mizo Hills

Mt. Victoria +3053
ALAUNGDAW
KATHAPA N.P.

MYANMAR
(BURMA)

Sittwe
Kyaukpyu
Cheduba I.

Arakan Yoma

Pyinmana
Taungoo
Pyay

Yangon
(Rangoon)
Insein
Pathein

Mawlamyine

Gulf of
Martaban

Dawna Ra.

BAY OF
BENGAL

Preparis North Channel

North Andaman

Middle Andaman

ANDAMAN IS.
India

South Andaman

Little
Andaman

Ten Degree Channel

NICOBAR ISLANDS
India

Camorta I.

Little Nicobar

Great Nicobar

Great Channel

Sabang

Banda Aceh
Sigli
Julu
Rayeu
Idi
Calang
Meulaboh

GUNUNG
LEUSER N.P.

Simeulue

Kep. Banyak
SIBERUT N.P.
NIAS

Tanahmasa
Pini

Kep. Batu
Tanahbala

SIBERUT N.P.
Siberut

KEPULAUAN

Sipura

MENTAWAI

Enggano

INDIAN

OCEAN

Dali
Baoshan
Luxi
Kunming
Yuxi
Lincang
Jinggu
Simao
Pu'er
Gejiu
Mengzi

YUNNAN

Muang
Sing

Doi Luang
N.P.
Pai
Chiang
Mai +2565
Lampang
Phrae

MAE PING N.P.

Uttaradit

Tak

Phitsanulok

NAM NAO
N.P.

CHINA
Zhanyi
GUIZHOU
Dushan

Yiliang
Xingyi

Wenshan

Bose

Lao Cai

Chongzuo
Litang

Ningming

GUANGXI
ZHUANGZU

Nanning

Liuzhou
Lianxian

Dinghan

HUNAN
Shangyou
Lianxian

JIANGXI
Ganzhou

Wuyi Shan
Changting

Shaoguan

Dongguan

GUANGDONG

GUANGZHOU
(CANTON)
Macau
S.A.R.
HONG KONG, S.A.R.

SHENZHEN

Fuzhou

FUJIAN
Quanzhou
Xiamen

Haitan
Dao

Changhua

T'aipei

T'ainan

Kaohsiung

Bashi Channel

LAOS

Louangphrabang

Vientiane

Udon
Thani

Dien
Bien

Xam Nua

Hoa Binh

VIETNAM
Hanoi

Haiphong

Nam Dinh

Zhanjiang

Haikou

Dongfang

HAINAN +1867

Sanya

Mui Ron

Gulf of
Tonkin

Xuwen
Maoming

Beihai

Lang Son

Xiangkhoang +2818

Vinh

THAILAND
Nakhon Ratchasima

Ayutthaya

KHAO YAI N.P.

KRUNG THEP
(BANGKOK)
Chachoengsao

Ubon
Ratchathani

THAP LAN N.P.
Dangrek Range

Mukdahan

Ban Xéno

Saravan

Attapu

VIRACHEY N.P.

+2598
Kon Tum

Play Ku

An Khe

Qui Nhon

Quang
Tri

Hue

Da Nang

BACH MA
N.P.

Paracel Is.
Administered by China
(Claimed by Vietnam)

SOUTH CHINA SEA

Battambang

Siem
Reap

Angkor

CAMBODIA

KENG KRACHAN N.P.

+1744

Kratie

+2405

YOK DON
N.P.

Tuy Hoa

Nha Trang

Cam Ranh

Phan Rang

SPRATLY ISLANDS
The scattered islands and reefs called
the Spratly Islands are claimed by Brunei,
China, Malaysia, the Philippines, Taiwan,
and Vietnam. The Spratlys possess rich
fishing grounds and potential oil.

PHNOM
BOKOR N.P.

Phnom Penh

CAT TIEN N.P.

Di Linh

Ho Chi Minh City
(Saigon)

Kompong Som
Ream

Long
Xuyen

Go Cong

Can Tho

Soc Trang

Dao Phu
Quoc

Ca Mau

Mui Bai Bung

Con Son

Indochina refers historically to French Indochina,
which comprised Vietnam, Laos, and Cambodia.
Physical geographers extend the region
to include Thailand, Myanmar (Burma),
and peninsular Malaysia.

Mali Kyun
Kadan Kyun

Myeik

Isthmus of Kra

Kra

+1244

Ranong

Takua Pa

Ko Phuket
Phuket

Kantang

MERGUI ARCHIPELAGO

GULF OF THAILAND

ANDAMAN

SEA

Surat Thani

Ko Samui

Songkhla

Pattani

SPRATLY ISLANDS

Alor Setar

Kota
Baharu

George Town
Pinang
Butterworth

Tanah Merah

Kuala Terengganu

Taiping
Ipoh

Tahan

TAMAN NEGARA N.P.

Kuala Dungun

Chukai

Banda Aceh

Langsa
Panjang

Binjai
Medan

Kuala Lumpur
Putrajaya
Seremban
Malacca

MALAY
PENINSULA

Kuantan

Kep. Natuna Besar

Binjai
Natuna
Besar

Kep. Natuna
Selatan
Indonesia

MALAYSIA
Malaysia includes peninsular
Malaysia, Sarawak, and Sabah;
the capital is Kuala Lumpur.

North Luconia Shoals

El Nido

Puerto Princesa

PALAWAN +2100

Balabac

Kudat

Banggi

KINABALU PARK
Kota Kinabalu +4101
CROCKER RANGE N.P.

Kinabalu

SABAH

Sandakan

Balabac Strait

Cagayan Sulu I.

Zamboanga

SULU
SEA

Sulu Archipelago

Jolo

Isabela

Pematangsiantar

Tanjungbalai

Sibolga

Muar

Johor Bahru

SINGAPORE

Dumai
Bengkalis

Sebanga

Pekanbaru

Lirik

Kep. Anambas

Kep. RIAU

Bintan
Tanjungpinang

Singapore

+2912

Kep. Batu

Bukittinggi
Padang

Sawahlunto

Taluk
Jambi

BUKIT TIGAH
PULUH N.P.

Lingga

Kotadabok

Kep. LINGGA

BERBAK N.P.

Muntok
Bangka

Pangkalpinang

Kep. Karimata

Maya

BUKIT BAKA-
BUKIT RAYA N.P.

Pontianak

Sambas
Singkawang

+1701

Mempawah

Serian
Putussibau

Sintang

Nangapinoh

GUNUNG
PALUNG N.P.

Ketapang

BORNEO
(KALIMANTAN)

Samarinda

Tanahgrogot

Balikpapan

KUTAI N.P.

Bontang

KERINCI
SEBLAT N.P.

Kerinci +3800

Inderapura

Sipura

Lais

Bengkulu

Lahat

Muaraenim

Lubuklinggau

Manna

Baturaja

+3159

+5777

+5664

WAY KAMBAS N.P.

Tanjungkarang-
Telukbetung

Serang

JAKARTA
Sukabumi

Bandung

UJUNG
KULON N.P.

JAVA

Palembang

Toboali

Tanjungpandan

Belitung
(Billiton)

Selat Gelasa

BUKIT BARISAN
SELATAN N.P.

Cirebon

Pekalongan
Semarang

Kudus
Tuban

Madura
Pamekasan

Surabaya

Cilacap
Surakarta

Kediri

Malang
Semeru +3676

Denpasar

BALI

ALAS PURWO
NATIONAL PARK

Banyuwangi

LOMBOK

Mataram

SUMBAWA

GREATER

SUNDA ISLANDS

JAVA SEA

Kep. Masalumbu

Kep. Laut
Kecil

Ujungpandang
(Makassar)

Bulukumba

Bantaeng

Selayar

Moyo +3726

Raba

Reo

FLORES

LESSER SUNDA IS

Waikabubak

SUMBA

Waingapu

Sawu

MAKASSAR STRAIT

Tg. Mangkalihat

Donggala

Toli-toli
Buol

Teluk
Tomini

SULAWESI
(CELEBES)

Mamuju

Majene

Parepare

Maros

Palopo

Teluk
Bone

Kolaka

LORE
LINDU
N.P.

BOGANI NANI WARTABONE

CELEBES SEA

Tarakan

Tanjungredep

Maratua

Sebatik

BRUNEI
Bandar Seri
Begawan
Bandar Labuan (Victoria)

Seria

SARAWAK

GUNUNG
MULU N.P.

Miri

Niut

Bintulu

Sibu
Sarikei
Kapit

Kuching

Saratok

GUNUNG
BENTUANG N.P.

KAYAN-
MENTARANG
N.P.

Malinau

Tanahmerah

Tanjungselor

Kong
Kemul +2987 +2053

Menyapa +2000

Sangkulirang

LUZON

San Fernando
Vigan

Laoag
Aparri

Cape Bojeador

Fuga

Calayan

Itbayat

Basco

Baguio
Dagupan
Tarlac

Quezon City

Manila
Cavite

Batangas
Calapan

MINDORO

Calamian Group

Dumaran

PANAY

Iloilo

Cagayan Is.

NEGROS

Tawi
Tawi

Lahad
Datu

Darvel Bay

Beaufort

Tawau

LAMBERT CONFORMAL CONIC PROJECTION
SCALE 1:16,000,000

0 KILOMETERS   300   400

0 MILES   100   200   300   400

Christmas
Island
Australia

CAUCASUS REGION

ALBERS CONIC EQUAL-AREA PROJECTION

SCALE 1:4,000,000

0 KILOMETERS 20 40 60 80 100

0 MILES 20 40 60 80 100

SOUTH OSSETIA
A 1992 cease-fire ended
fighting between Ossetians
and Georgians, but with
no political settlement.

NAGORNO-KARABAKH
Since a cease-fire in 1994
Azerbaijan's ethnic Armenians have
exercised autonomous control
over the region. International
mediation to resolve the
conflict continues.

ABKHAZIA
Separatists defeated Georgian
troops to gain control of this region
in 1993—negotiations continue
on resolving the conflict.

KAZAKHSTAN

CASPIAN SEA

RUSSIA

CAUCASUS MOUNTAINS

DAGESTAN

CHECHNYA

KABARDINO-BALKARIYA

KARACHAYEVO-CHERKESIYA

KRASNODAR

NORTH OSSETIA

SOUTH OSSETIA

INGUSHETIYA

ABKHAZIA

BLACK SEA

GEORGIA

ARMENIA

AZERBAIJAN

NAGORNO-KARABAKH

NAXCIVAN
Azerbaijan

TURKEY

IRAN

IRAQ

SYRIA

Baku (Bakı)

Tbilisi

Yerevan

Sumqayıt

Gäncä

Rust'avi

Vanadzor

Gyumri

Tabrız

Erzurum

Van

Diyarbakır

Mardin

Batman

Trabzon

Elâzığ

Al Mawşil (Mosul)

Al Qāmishlī

Al Ḥasakah

Rasht

Ardabıl

Sochi

Makhachkala

Groznyy

Vladikavkaz

Mount Ararat 5137

Elbrus 5642

KOREAN PENINSULA

ALBERS CONIC EQUAL-AREA PROJECTION
SCALE 1:4,000,000

The Democratic People's Republic of Korea is
referred to as North Korea. The Republic of Korea
is known as South Korea.

PROVINCES OF KOREA
WITH THEIR CAPITALS

NORTH

1 Chagang (Kanggye)
2 Hamgyŏng, North (Ch'ŏngjin)
3 Hamgyŏng, South (Hamhŭng)
4 Hwanghae, North (Sariwŏn)
5 Hwanghae, South (Haeju)
6 Kaesŏng City
7 Kangwŏn (Wŏnsan)
8 Namp'o City
9 P'yŏngan, North (Sinŭiju)
10 P'yŏngan, South (Pyŏng-sŏng)
11 P'yŏngyang City
12 Yanggang (Hyesan)

SOUTH

13 Busan City
14 Chungcheong, North (Cheongju)
15 Chungcheong, South (Daejeon)
16 Daegu City
17 Daejeon City
18 Gangwon (Chuncheon)
19 Gwangju City
20 Gyeonggi (Suwon)
21 Gyeongsan, North (Daegu)
22 Gyeongsan, South (Changwon)
23 Incheon City
24 Jeju (Jeju) off map
25 Jeolla, North (Jeonju)
26 Jeolla, South (Gwangju)
27 Seoul City
28 Ulsan City

The above political subdivisions
are numbered in blue on the map.

200 ASIA

Longitude East 129° of Greenwich

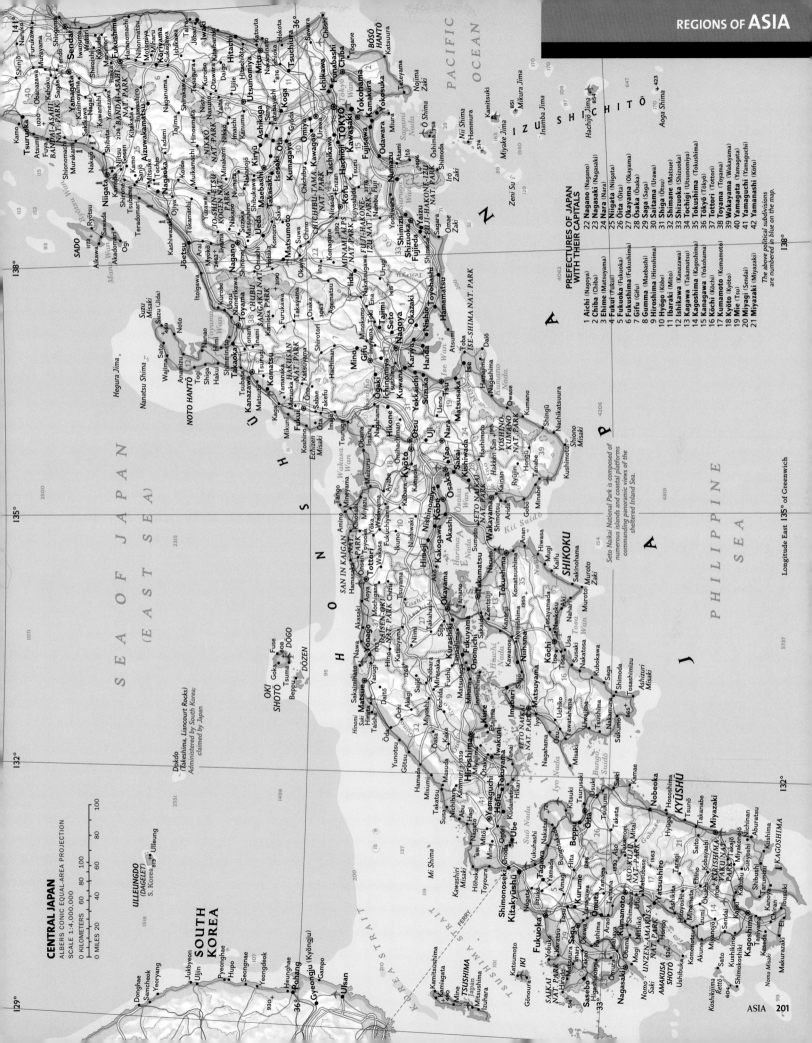

PHILIPPINES
ALBERS CONIC EQUAL-AREA PROJECTION
SCALE 1:7,000,000

0 KILOMETERS 100   150   200

0 MILES   50   100   150   200

SPRATLY ISLANDS
The scattered islands and reefs called the Spratly Islands are claimed by Brunei, China, Malaysia, the Philippines, Taiwan, and Vietnam. The Spratlys possess rich fishing grounds and potential oil.

Vereker Banks
Tungsha Tao (Pratas I.)

Stewart Seamount

Macclesfield Banks

Scarborough Shoal

Dreyer Banks

S O U T H   C H I N A   S E A

Reed Tablemount

Lys Shoal
Loaita Bank
Tizard Bank
Union Reefs

Brown Bank
Seahorse Shoal
Carnatic Reef
Sabina Shoal

Commodore Reef
Investigator Shoal

S P R A T L Y   I S L A N D S

P H I L I P P I N E   S E A

Benham Seamount

Luzon Strait
Batan Islands
Basco

Balintang Channel

Babuyan Islands
Babuyan Channel

Mayraira Point
Cape Bojeador
Bangui   Claveria   Santa Ana
Bacarra   Abulug   Aparri   Buguey
Laoag   Kabugao
San Nicolas   Batac
Espiritu   2361   Mount Sicapoo
Cabugao
Bangued
Vigan   Tuguegarao
Narvacan   Lubuagan   Bontoc   Ilagan
Candon   Roxas
Santa Cruz   Bayombong
Bangar
Bacnotan   Mount Pulog   2934
San Fernando
Baguio
Cape Bolinao   Bayombong
Lingayen   **Dagupan**   San Jose   Casiguran
Santa Cruz   **San Carlos**   Cuyapo   Baler
Masinloc   2037   Victoria   Cape Encanto
Palauig   **Tarlac**   Gapan
San Narciso   **Angeles**   San Fernando
Olongapo   Malolos   **Cabanatuan**
    Quezon City
Bataan Peninsula   **Manila**
Corregidor   **Cavite**
    San Pablo   Santa Cruz   **Lucena**
Lubang Island   **Batangas**   **Lipa**

Iligan Point
Valley Head
Baguio Point
Divilacan Bay
Aubarede Point
Palanan
NORTHERN SIERRA MADRE NATIONAL PARK
Cape San Ildefonso
LUZON

Polillo Islands
Lamon Bay
Jose Panganiban   Paracale
Santa Cruz   Daet   Pandan   Yog Point
Boac   **Naga**   Mt. Isarog   Panganiban (Payo)
Mulanay   Iriga   Mayon Volcano   Virac
Pola   Ligao   **Legazpi**   *Catanduanes*
Marinduque   Sorsogon
Burias   Magallanes   Gubat
Bulan

Lag. de Bay
Tayabas Bay
Ragay Gulf
San Miguel Bay
Manila Bay

Paluan
Mount Halcon   Calapan
Mamburao   2505
Santa Cruz
Sablayan
MINDORO   Mount Baco
2488   Roxas
Bintuan   San Jose
Busuanga
Culion
Calamian Group
El Nido   659
Taytay
703
Roxas
1603
Cleopatra Needle
Puerto Princesa   **PALAWAN**
Aborlan   Inagauan
Birong
Quezon   1709
Malabuñgan   Aboabo
Bonobono   2100
Canipaan   Brooke's Point
Cape Bulilayan   Rio Tuba
Balabac
Balabac

Mindoro Strait
Tablas Strait
Sibuyan Sea
Sulu Sea
Malampaya Sound
Imuruan Bay
Ulugan Bay

Tablas
Santa Fe
Romblon   2050   Sibuyan
Masbate
Cataingan   Ticao   Allen
Masbate
Nabas   Pandan
Cuyo Islands   Kalibo
Cuyo   Culasi   2117   **Roxas**
Mount Nangtud   Ajuy
PANAY
Cagayan Islands   Alimodian
San Jose   **Iloilo**
Dao   **Bacolod**
La Carlota
Isabela   908
NEGROS   **Cebu**
Sipalay   **San Carlos**
Hinoba-an   La Carlota   *CEBU*
Cauayan   Tanjay   870
Bayawan   Oslob
1903   Dumaguete
Siaton   Siquijor
Zamboanguita

Visayan Sea
Panay Gulf
Bohol Sea
L. Mainit

Catbalogan   Wright   Sulat
Carigara   Basey   General MacArthur
1350   **Tacloban**   Guiuan
Bogo   Borbon   Ormoc   *LEYTE*
Baybay   Sogod   Loreto
Saint Bernard   Dinagat
BOHOL   Siargao   Dapa
Tagbilaran   **Surigao**   Placer
Guindulman   Lanuza
Mambajao   Mt. Hilonghilong   2012
1713   Buenavista
Salay   **Butuan**
Gingoog   Lianga
Cagayan de Oro   Hinatuan
Malaybalay   Bislig
Iligan   *MINDANAO*   Lingig
Marawi   2896   Cateel
Kibawe   Compostela
Baganga
2316   Tagum   2810
Kibawe   Carmen   Maco   Manay
Malabang   **Davao**   Babak
Cotabato   Mount Apo   2954   Lupon   Mati
Datu Piang   Digos   1633
Buluan   Padada
Isulan   Koronadal
Lebak   Palimbang   2083   Tupi
Kiamba   **General Santos**   Jose Abad Santos
Glan   Tinaca Point   886   Sarangani Islands

San Bernardino Strait
SAMAR
Oras
Palapag
Catarman
7955
Calbayog
Calbiga
10057
Leyte Gulf
Bohol Sea
Iligan Bay
Macajalar Bay
Lake Lanao
Illana Bay
Moro Gulf
Davao Gulf
Sarangani Bay

5102
5638
4151
5004
5377
2277
5207
4517
4530
4413
4170
3932
3557
200
272

Cape San Agustin
9546

Miangas (Palmas)

INDONESIA   Kepulauan Karakaralong   Kepulauan Nanusa

Dipolog
Manukan
Oroquieta
Sindangan
Liloy
Ozamis   Tubod
1224
Siocon   **Pagadian**
Kabasalan
Alicia   2316
Sibuco   Malabang
Margosatubig
Zamboanga
Isabela   1011   Lamitan
Basilan
Basilan Strait
Sibuguey Bay

Pangutaran   Jolo   Jolo
Pangutaran Group   Parang   Luuk
Tapul   Siasi
Sulu Archipelago
Tawi Tawi
533   Bongao
Sibutu Passage

Celebes Sea
5761

Sikuati   Kudat
Bandau   Senaja
Kota   Tandik
Belud
Tuaran   4101   Kinabalu
KINABALU PARK
1219
Kota Kinabalu   Ranau
Tambunan
MALAYSIA
CROCKER RANGE N.P.
Beaufort   Bingkor
Melalap
Weston   Pinangah
Brunei Bay   **BRUNEI**   Bandar Seri Begawan
S A B A H

Banggi
Tanjong Sugut
Labuk Bay
Sukau
Lamag
Lintang   Lahad Datu
Sandakan
Cagayan Sulu I.
Pintasan

Darvel Bay

Longitude East 123° of Greenwich   126°

ASIA **203**

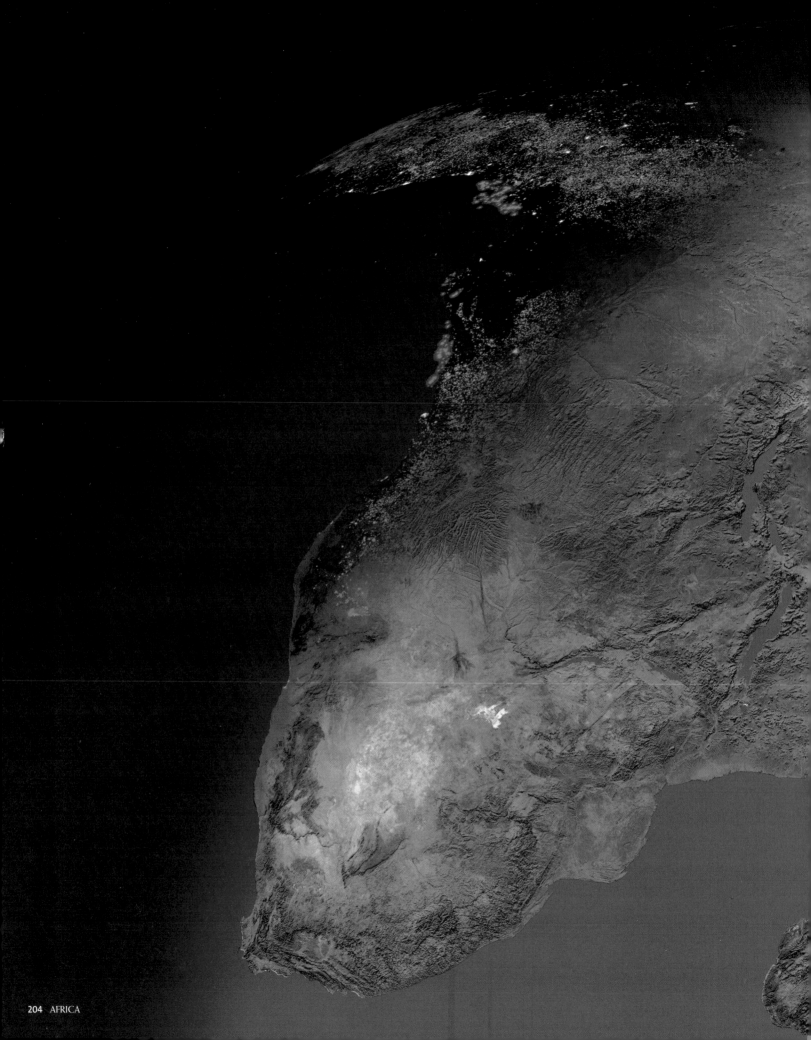

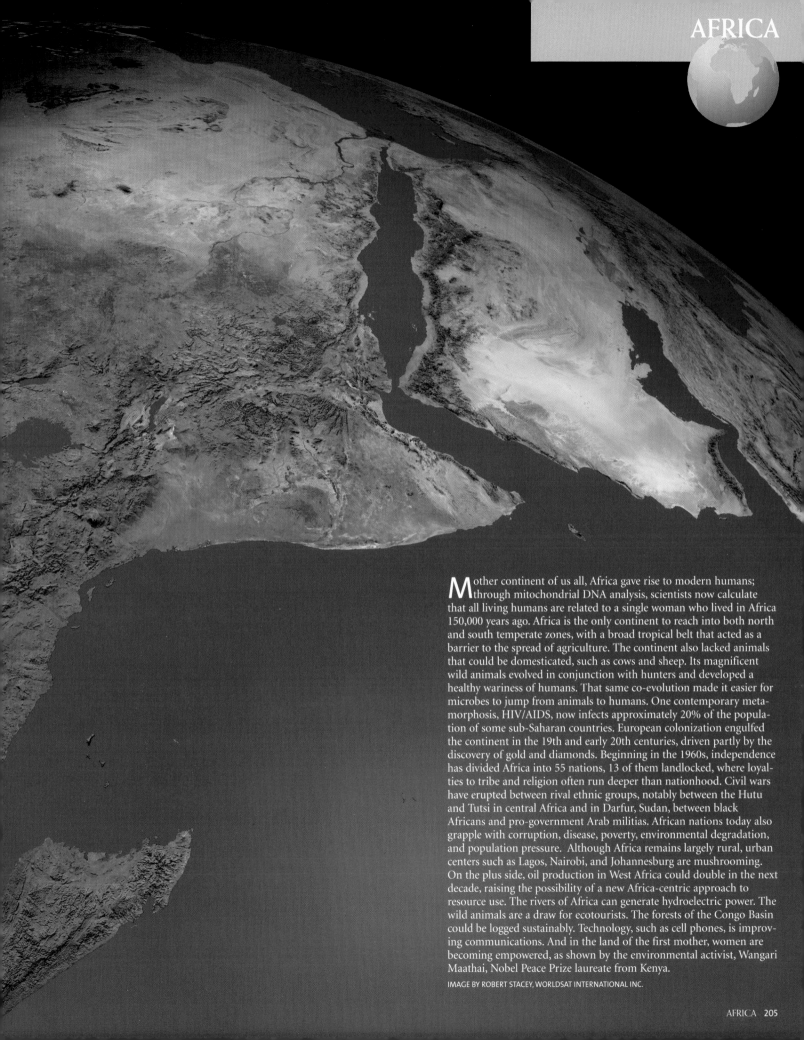

M other continent of us all, Africa gave rise to modern humans; through mitochondrial DNA analysis, scientists now calculate that all living humans are related to a single woman who lived in Africa 150,000 years ago. Africa is the only continent to reach into both north and south temperate zones, with a broad tropical belt that acted as a barrier to the spread of agriculture. The continent also lacked animals that could be domesticated, such as cows and sheep. Its magnificent wild animals evolved in conjunction with hunters and developed a healthy wariness of humans. That same co-evolution made it easier for microbes to jump from animals to humans. One contemporary metamorphosis, HIV/AIDS, now infects approximately 20% of the population of some sub-Saharan countries. European colonization engulfed the continent in the 19th and early 20th centuries, driven partly by the discovery of gold and diamonds. Beginning in the 1960s, independence has divided Africa into 55 nations, 13 of them landlocked, where loyalties to tribe and religion often run deeper than nationhood. Civil wars have erupted between rival ethnic groups, notably between the Hutu and Tutsi in central Africa and in Darfur, Sudan, between black Africans and pro-government Arab militias. African nations today also grapple with corruption, disease, poverty, environmental degradation, and population pressure. Although Africa remains largely rural, urban centers such as Lagos, Nairobi, and Johannesburg are mushrooming. On the plus side, oil production in West Africa could double in the next decade, raising the possibility of a new Africa-centric approach to resource use. The rivers of Africa can generate hydroelectric power. The wild animals are a draw for ecotourists. The forests of the Congo Basin could be logged sustainably. Technology, such as cell phones, is improving communications. And in the land of the first mother, women are becoming empowered, as shown by the environmental activist, Wangari Maathai, Nobel Peace Prize laureate from Kenya.

MADEIRA IS.
(PORTUGAL)

CANARY IS.
(SPAIN)

Algiers • Tunis
Rabat
MOROCCO   TUNISIA
                        • Tripoli
                                                        ⊗ Cairo
WESTERN
SAHARA   ALGERIA   LIBYA   EGYPT
(MOROCCO)

Nouakchott ⊗
CAPE   MAURITANIA   NIGER   CHAD   ERITREA
VERDE   MALI   Khartoum • ⊗ Asmara
• Praia
Dakar   DJIBOUTI
SENEGAL   • Niamey   SUDAN   ⊗ Djibouti
GAMBIA Banjul   Bamako BURKINA   • N'Djamena
GUINEA-BISSAU ⊗ Bissau Ouagadougou FASO   ETHIOPIA   SOMALIA
          GUINEA   CÔTE   BENIN   NIGERIA   • Addis Ababa
Conakry •   D'IVOIRE TOGO   Abuja ⊗
Freetown   (IVORY COAST)   ⊗   CENTRAL
SIERRA LEONE   GHANA Lomé Porto-Novo   AFRICAN   ⊗ Mogadishu
Monrovia   Yamoussoukro Accra Cotonou   REPUBLIC
LIBERIA   Abidjan   CAMEROON Bangui •
                              Malabo ⊗ Yaoundé •   UGANDA   KENYA
EQUATORIAL GUINEA   ⊗   Kampala ⊗   Victoria
          RIO MUNI   Kigali   Nairobi ⊗
SAO TOME   Libreville ⊗   DEMOCRATIC   RWANDA   SEYCHELLE
AND PRINCIPE   São   CONGO REPUBLIC OF   Bujumbura
          Tomé   GABON   THE CONGO   BURUNDI
          Brazzaville ⊗   Dodoma •
CABINDA   ⊗ Kinshasa   TANZANIA   • Dar es Salaam
(ANGOLA)
          Luanda ⊗   Lilongwe ⊗   COMOROS ⊗ Moroni
                                        ZAMBIA MALAWI
          ANGOLA   Lusaka ⊗   MOZAMBIQUE
                                                        Antananarivo ⊗
                         Harare •   MADAGASCAR   MAURITIUS
                    ZIMBABWE   Port
          NAMIBIA   RÉUNION   Louis
          Windhoek •   BOTSWANA   (FRANCE)
                    Gaborone ⊗   Maputo
                    Pretoria ⊗ ⊗
                    (Tshwane) Mbabane SWAZILAND
                    Bloemfontein • Lobamba
                         Maseru ⊗
                    SOUTH LESOTHO
                    AFRICA
          Cape Town ⊗

Land cover
Forest
- Evergreen needleleaf
- Evergreen broadleaf
- Deciduous needleleaf
- Deciduous broadleaf
- Mixed forest
- Woodland

Grassland or shrubland
- Wooded grassland
- Closed shrubland
- Open shrubland
- Grassland

Other
- Cropland
- Barren (Desert and Polar Ice)
- Built-up

TEMPERATURE AND RAINFALL

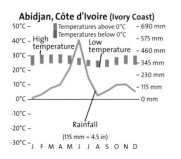

Abidjan, Côte d'Ivoire (Ivory Coast)
Temperatures above 0°C
Temperatures below 0°C
High temperature   Low temperature
Rainfall
(115 mm = 4.5 in)
J F M A M J J A S O N D

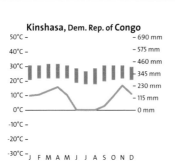

Kinshasa, Dem. Rep. of Congo
J F M A M J J A S O N D

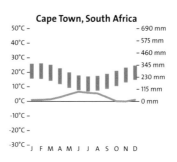

Cape Town, South Africa
J F M A M J J A S O N D

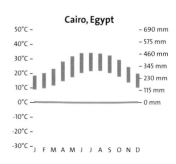

Cairo, Egypt
J F M A M J J A S O N D

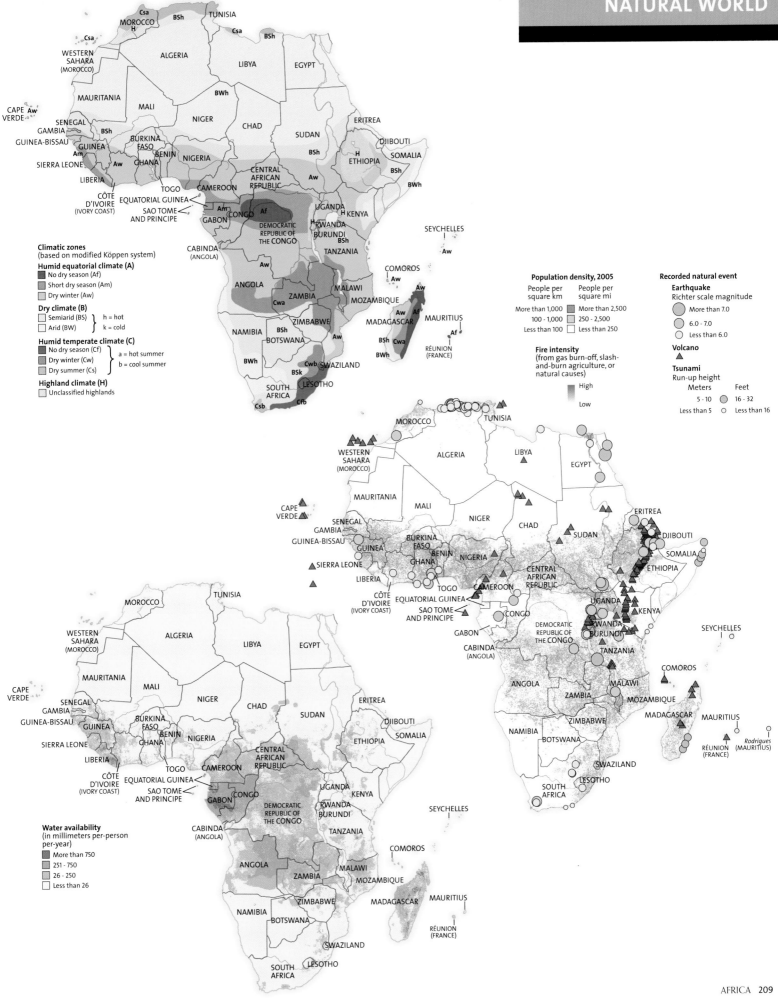

Climatic zones
(based on modified Köppen system)

Humid equatorial climate (A)
- No dry season (Af)
- Short dry season (Am)
- Dry winter (Aw)

Dry climate (B)
- Semiarid (BS) } h = hot
- Arid (BW) } k = cold

Humid temperate climate (C)
- No dry season (Cf)
- Dry winter (Cw) } a = hot summer
- Dry summer (Cs) } b = cool summer

Highland climate (H)
- Unclassified highlands

Population density, 2005

People per square km	People per square mi
More than 1,000	More than 2,500
100 - 1,000	250 - 2,500
Less than 100	Less than 250

Fire intensity
(from gas burn-off, slash-and-burn agriculture, or natural causes)

High

Low

Recorded natural event

Earthquake
Richter scale magnitude
- More than 7.0
- 6.0 - 7.0
- Less than 6.0

Volcano

Tsunami
Run-up height

Meters	Feet
5 - 10	16 - 32
Less than 5	Less than 16

Water availability
(in millimeters per-person per-year)
- More than 750
- 251 - 750
- 26 - 250
- Less than 26

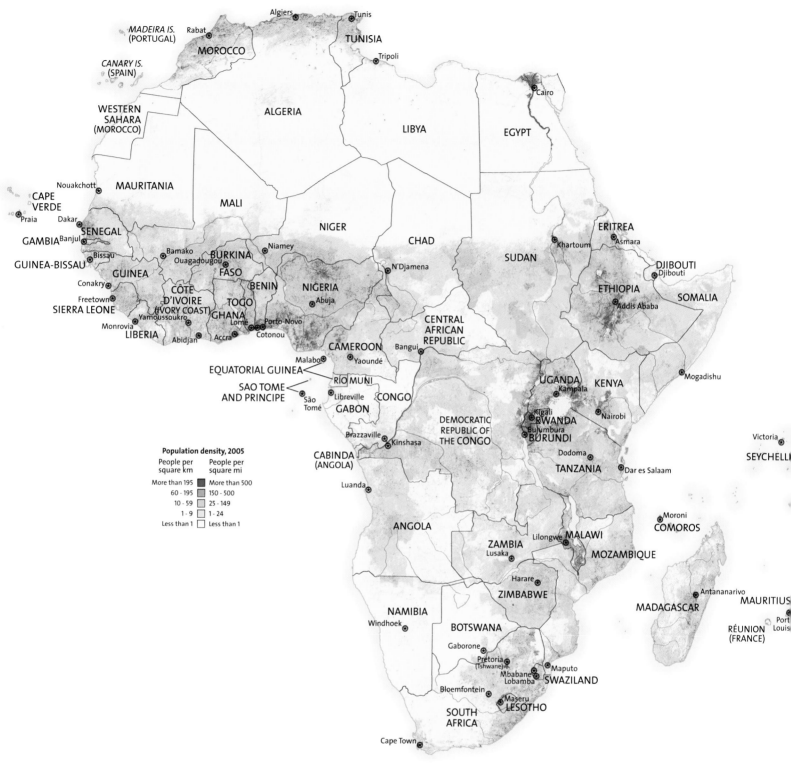

Population density, 2005

People per square km	People per square mi
More than 195	More than 500
60 - 195	150 - 500
10 - 59	25 - 149
1 - 9	1 - 24
Less than 1	Less than 1

POPULATION PYRAMIDS

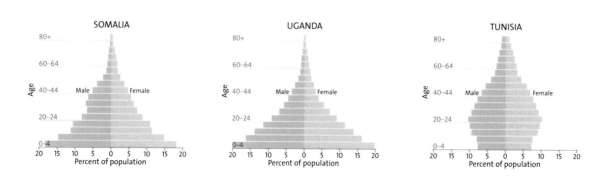

SOMALIA

UGANDA

TUNISIA

Indigenous languages
- Afro-Asiatic
- Nilo-Saharan
- Niger-Congo
- Khoisan
- Austronesian
- Indo-European
- Uninhabited

MOROCCO
TUNISIA
WESTERN SAHARA (MOROCCO)
ALGERIA
LIBYA
EGYPT
MAURITANIA
MALI
NIGER
CHAD
SUDAN
ERITREA
DJIBOUTI
CAPE VERDE
SENEGAL
GAMBIA
GUINEA-BISSAU
GUINEA
BURKINA FASO
BENIN
GHANA
NIGERIA
CENTRAL AFRICAN REPUBLIC
ETHIOPIA
SOMALIA
SIERRA LEONE
LIBERIA
CÔTE D'IVOIRE (IVORY COAST)
TOGO
EQUATORIAL GUINEA
SAO TOME AND PRINCIPE
CAMEROON
GABON
CONGO
UGANDA
RWANDA
BURUNDI
KENYA
SEYCHELLES
DEMOCRATIC REPUBLIC OF THE CONGO
CABINDA (ANGOLA)
TANZANIA
COMOROS
ANGOLA
ZAMBIA
MALAWI
MOZAMBIQUE
MADAGASCAR
MAURITIUS
RÉUNION (FRANCE)
NAMIBIA
ZIMBABWE
BOTSWANA
SWAZILAND
LESOTHO
SOUTH AFRICA

Urban agglomerations, 2005
(Population in millions)
- More than 10.0
- 5.0 - 10.0
- 2.5 - 4.9
- 1.0 - 2.4
- .75 - .99

Percent urban population, 2005
- More than 75%
- 50% - 74%
- 25% - 49%
- Less than 24%

Casablanca
Algiers
MOROCCO
TUNISIA
WESTERN SAHARA (MOROCCO)
ALGERIA
LIBYA
Alexandria
CAIRO
EGYPT
MAURITANIA
MALI
NIGER
CHAD
Khartoum
SUDAN
ERITREA
CAPE VERDE
SENEGAL
GAMBIA
GUINEA-BISSAU
GUINEA
BURKINA FASO
BENIN
Kano
NIGERIA
DJIBOUTI
ETHIOPIA
Addis Ababa
SOMALIA
SIERRA LEONE
GHANA
LIBERIA
Abidjan
CÔTE D'IVOIRE (IVORY COAST)
TOGO
LAGOS
CAMEROON
CENTRAL AFRICAN REPUBLIC
EQUATORIAL GUINEA
SAO TOME AND PRINCIPE
CONGO
Libreville
GABON
Kinshasa
CABINDA (ANGOLA)
DEMOCRATIC REPUBLIC OF THE CONGO
UGANDA
RWANDA
BURUNDI
KENYA
Nairobi
SEYCHELLES
TANZANIA
Dar es Salaam
COMOROS
Luanda
ANGOLA
ZAMBIA
MALAWI
MOZAMBIQUE
MADAGASCAR
MAURITIUS
RÉUNION (FRANCE)
NAMIBIA
ZIMBABWE
BOTSWANA
Ekurhuleni
Johannesburg
SWAZILAND
LESOTHO
Durban
SOUTH AFRICA
Cape Town

Projected population change, 2005 - 2050
(by percentage)
- More than 100%
- 50% - 100%
- 0% - 49%
- Less than 0% (Population loss)

MOROCCO
TUNISIA
WESTERN SAHARA (MOROCCO)
ALGERIA
LIBYA
EGYPT
MAURITANIA
MALI
NIGER
CHAD
SUDAN
ERITREA
CAPE VERDE
SENEGAL
GAMBIA
GUINEA-BISSAU
GUINEA
BURKINA FASO
BENIN
GHANA
NIGERIA
DJIBOUTI
ETHIOPIA
SOMALIA
SIERRA LEONE
LIBERIA
CÔTE D'IVOIRE (IVORY COAST)
TOGO
EQUATORIAL GUINEA
SAO TOME AND PRINCIPE
CAMEROON
CENTRAL AFRICAN REPUBLIC
GABON
CONGO
UGANDA
RWANDA
BURUNDI
KENYA
SEYCHELLES
DEMOCRATIC REPUBLIC OF THE CONGO
CABINDA (ANGOLA)
TANZANIA
COMOROS
ANGOLA
ZAMBIA
MALAWI
MOZAMBIQUE
MADAGASCAR
MAURITIUS
RÉUNION (FRANCE)
NAMIBIA
ZIMBABWE
BOTSWANA
SWAZILAND
LESOTHO
SOUTH AFRICA

MADEIRA IS.
(PORTUGAL)

CANARY IS.
(SPAIN)

Rabat

Algiers

Tunis
TUNISIA

MOROCCO

Tripoli

WESTERN
SAHARA
(MOROCCO)

ALGERIA

LIBYA

EGYPT

Cairo

Nouakchott

MAURITANIA

CAPE
VERDE

Praia

Dakar

MALI

NIGER

CHAD

SUDAN

Khartoum

ERITREA

Asmara

DJIBOUTI

Djibouti

SENEGAL

GAMBIA Banjul

GUINEA-BISSAU Bissau

Bamako

Niamey

N'Djamena

ETHIOPIA

SOMALIA

BURKINA
FASO

Ouagadougou

Addis Ababa

GUINEA

Conakry

CÔTE
D'IVOIRE
(IVORY COAST)

BENIN

NIGERIA

Abuja

CENTRAL
AFRICAN
REPUBLIC

Mogadishu

Freetown

SIERRA LEONE

TOGO

GHANA

Yamoussoukro

Lomé

Porto-Novo

Bangui

Monrovia

LIBERIA

Abidjan

Accra

Cotonou

CAMEROON

Yaoundé

UGANDA

Kampala

KENYA

EQUATORIAL GUINEA

Malabo

RÍO MUNI

Nairobi

SAO TOME
AND PRINCIPE

São
Tomé

Libreville

CONGO

GABON

Kigali RWANDA

Bujumbura BURUNDI

DEMOCRATIC
REPUBLIC
OF THE CONGO

CABINDA
(ANGOLA)

Brazzaville

Kinshasa

Dodoma

TANZANIA

Dar es Salaam

Victoria

SEYCHELL

Luanda

More
disturbed Cropland

Less
disturbed

More
disturbed Pasture

Built-up area

Irrigated land

ANGOLA

ZAMBIA

Lusaka

Lilongwe MALAWI

MOZAMBIQUE

Moroni

COMOROS

Harare

ZIMBABWE

Antananarivo

MADAGASCAR

MAURITIU

NAMIBIA

Windhoek

BOTSWANA

Gaborone

Pretoria
(Tshwane)

Maputo

Mbabane
Lobamba SWAZILAND

RÉUNION
(FRANCE)

Por
Lou

Bloemfontein

Maseru LESOTHO

SOUTH
AFRICA

Cape Town

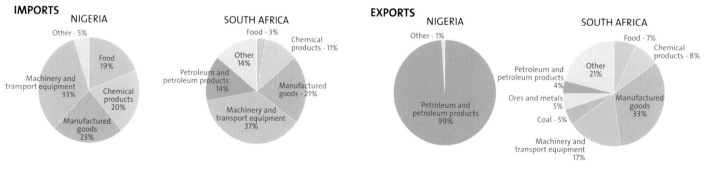

IMPORTS

NIGERIA

Other - 5%
Food 19%
Machinery and transport equipment 33%
Chemical products 20%
Manufactured goods 23%

SOUTH AFRICA

Food - 3%
Chemical products - 11%
Other 14%
Petroleum and petroleum products 14%
Manufactured goods - 21%
Machinery and transport equipment 37%

EXPORTS

NIGERIA

Other - 1%
Petroleum and petroleum products 99%

SOUTH AFRICA

Food - 7%
Chemical products - 8%
Other 21%
Petroleum and petroleum products 4%
Ores and metals 5%
Coal - 5%
Machinery and transport equipment 17%
Manufactured goods 33%

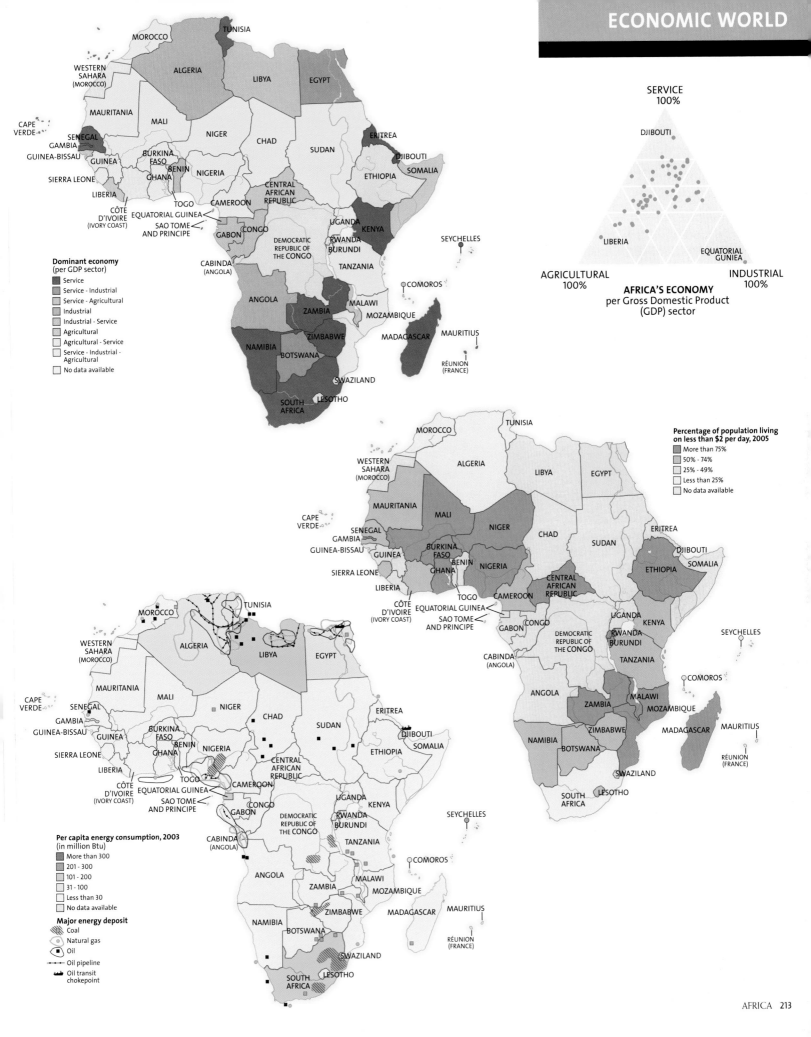

Dominant economy
(per GDP sector)
- Service
- Service - Industrial
- Service - Agricultural
- Industrial
- Industrial - Service
- Agricultural
- Agricultural - Service
- Service - Industrial - Agricultural
- No data available

SERVICE
100%

DJIBOUTI

LIBERIA

EQUATORIAL GUINEA

AGRICULTURAL
100%

INDUSTRIAL
100%

AFRICA'S ECONOMY
per Gross Domestic Product
(GDP) sector

Percentage of population living on less than $2 per day, 2005
- More than 75%
- 50% - 74%
- 25% - 49%
- Less than 25%
- No data available

Per capita energy consumption, 2003
(in million Btu)
- More than 300
- 201 - 300
- 101 - 200
- 31 - 100
- Less than 30
- No data available

Major energy deposit
- Coal
- Natural gas
- Oil
- Oil pipeline
- Oil transit chokepoint

AFRICA 213

SAO TOME
AND PRINCIPE

São Tomé

Annobón
Eq. Guinea

GULF OF GUINEA

Meridian of Greenwich
(London)

Bight of
Benin

Longitude East 3° of Greenwich

Longitude West 3° of Greenwich

LAMBERT CONFORMAL CONIC PROJECTION
SCALE 1:12,000,000

0 KILOMETERS 100 200 300
0 MILES 100 200 300

O C E A N

EQUATOR

TANZANIA

Irungu, Moba, Karema, KATAVI N.P., Itende, Kidete, Morogoro, Ruvu, Zanzibar I.
Kipili, Namanyere, Rungwa, Uluguru Mts., Dar es Salaam, Latham I.
Mbogo, Igula, Migole, Migoro, DAR ES SALAAM
Kala, Sumbawanga, Manda, Igoma, RUAHA N.P., Ruaha, Kisaki, Kisangire, Ras Mkumbi
Molino, Mkunde, Kipembawe, Dabaga, Kiberege, Utete, Mafia Island
Kasaba Bay, MBEYA, Makongolosi, Kibau, Mgeta, Madaba
Mpui, Kimamba, Mohoro, Samanga
Mpulungu, Mbala, Mbozi, Vawa, Rungwe Mt. 2961, Taveta, SELOUS, Kazimoto, Monga, Kilwa Kivinje
Kapatu, Rosa, Nakonde, IRINGA, Kilombero, GAME RES., Kilwa Masoko
Isoka, 2606, Nyia, Liuli, LINDI, Kiswere
Chinsali, Chiwanda, Nambinda, Nguruka, Lindi
Old Mkushi, Nkhata Bay, 474, Nachingwea, Masasi, Palma, Nangade
Metangula, Maniamba, Mavago, Mecula, Quiterajo
Nkhotakota, Muembe, Marrupa, Nungo, Namuno, Metuge, Pemba
Salima, Mchinji, Catur, Napa, Mecúfi
Lilongwe, Chipoka, Monkey Bay, Lichinga, Maúa, Muite, Napala, Memba
Dedza, Mangochi, Mandimba, Cuamba, Mecanhelas, Meconta, Monapo, Mossuril
Balaka, Liwonde, Lioma, Entre Rios, Ribáuè, Nampula, Nacala
Casula, Kasupe, Zomba, Namuli 2419, Corrane, Moçambique
Cahora Bassa, Moatize, Milange, Mugeba, Larde, Angoche

MOZAMBIQUE

Harare, Mutare, Beira, Quelimane, Nova Sofala

ZIMBABWE

MADAGASCAR

Antsiranana, MONTAGNE D'AMBRE N.P., Ambilobe
Mahajanga, Antananarivo, Antsirabe, Toamasina
Fianarantsoa, Toliara, Tôlanaro

COMOROS
Moroni, Njazidja

SEYCHELLES
Aldabra Islands, Cosmoledo Group, Saint Pierre Island, Providence Island
Assumption Island, Astove Island, Cerf Island, Farquhar Group

INDIAN OCEAN

MOZAMBIQUE CHANNEL

LAMBERT CONFORMAL CONIC PROJECTION
SCALE 1:12,000,000

0 KILOMETERS 200 300
0 MILES 100 200 300

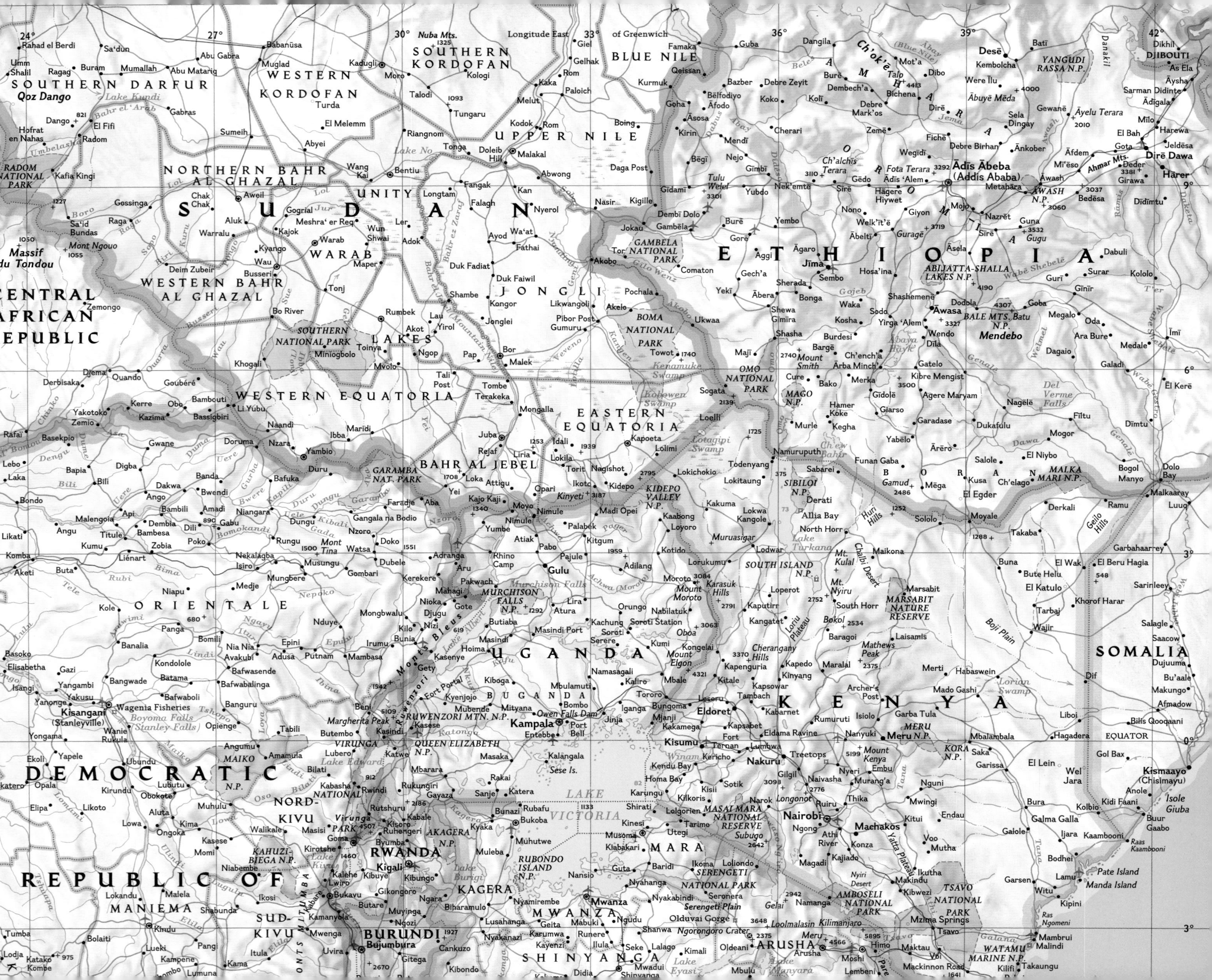
SUDAN
ETHIOPIA
CENTRAL AFRICAN REPUBLIC
DEMOCRATIC REPUBLIC OF
UGANDA
KENYA
SOMALIA
DJIBOUTI
RWANDA
BURUNDI
SOUTHERN DARFUR
WESTERN KORDOFAN
SOUTHERN KORDOFAN
BLUE NILE
UPPER NILE
NORTHERN BAHR AL GHAZAL
WESTERN BAHR AL GHAZAL
UNITY
WARAB
JONGLI
LAKES
WESTERN EQUATORIA
EASTERN EQUATORIA
BAHR AL JEBEL
AMHARA
OROMIYA
ORIENTALE
NORD-KIVU
SUD-KIVU
MANIEMA
BUGANDA
KAGERA
MARA
MWANZA
SHINYANGA
ARUSHA
Longitude East of Greenwich
EQUATOR
RADOM NATIONAL PARK
SOUTHERN NATIONAL PARK
GAMBELA NATIONAL PARK
BOMA NATIONAL PARK
OMO NATIONAL PARK
MAGO N.P.
KIDEPO VALLEY N.P.
SIBILOI N.P.
SOUTH ISLAND N.P.
MURCHISON FALLS N.P.
RUWENZORI MTN. N.P.
QUEEN ELIZABETH N.P.
VIRUNGA NATIONAL PARK
KAHUZI-BIEGA N.P.
MAIKO N.P.
AKAGERA N.P.
RUBONDO ISLAND N.P.
SERENGETI NATIONAL PARK
MASAI MARA NATIONAL RESERVE
AMBOSELI NATIONAL PARK
TSAVO NATIONAL PARK
MERU N.P.
KORA N.P.
MARSABIT NATURE RESERVE
WATAMU MARINE N.P.
AWASH N.P.
YANGUDI RASSA N.P.
ABIJATTA-SHALLA LAKES N.P.
BALE MTS. N.P.
MALKA MARI N.P.
GARAMBA NAT. PARK
Ādīs Ābeba (Addis Ababa)
Nairobi
Kampala
Kigali
Bujumbura
Kisangani (Stanleyville)
Juba
Malakal
Dirē Dawa
Harer
Kismaayo (Chisimayu)
LAKE VICTORIA
Lake Turkana
Lake Albert
Lake Edward
Lake Kivu
Chalbi Desert
Massif du Tondou
Nuba Mts.
Ch'ok'e
Mendebo
Kilimanjaro
Mount Kenya
Mount Elgon
Monts Bleus
Monts Mitumba

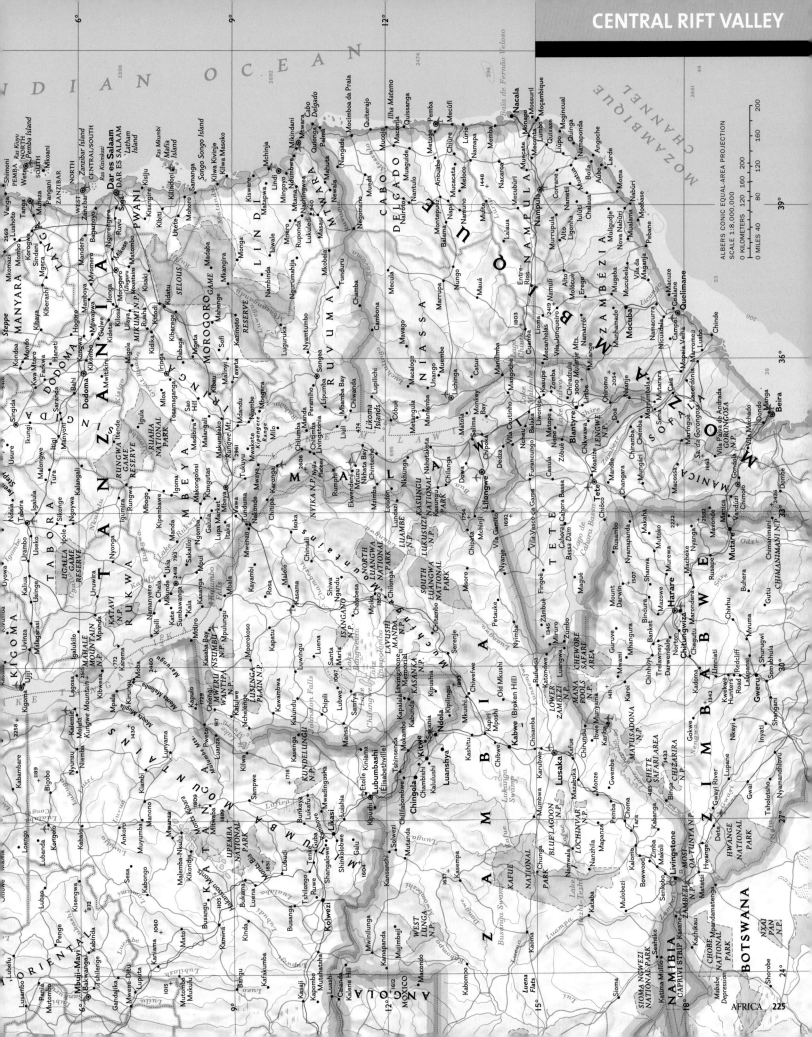

SOUTH AFRICA

ALBERS CONIC EQUAL-AREA PROJECTION

SCALE 1:8,000,000

0 KILOMETERS 40 80 120 160 200

0 MILES 40 80 120 160 200

island nation and smallest, flattest continent, with a territory about the size of the United States, Australia has gone on a planetary walkabout since it broke away from the supercontinent of Gondwana about 55 million years ago. Isolated, dry, and scoured by erosion, Australia developed unique animals, notably marsupials such as kangaroos, and plants, such as more than 600 eucalyptus species. The land surface has been stable enough to preserve some of the world's oldest rocks and mineral deposits, dating to the original formation of Earth's crust. Precambrian fossils include stromatolites—photosynthetic bacteria that generated oxygen in the early atmosphere and whose descendants still grow mounded in shallow lagoons, such as in Shark Bay in western Australia. In contrast, New Zealand's two principal islands, about the size of Colorado, are younger and tell of a more violent geology that raised high volcanic mountains above deep fjords, leaving landscapes reminiscent of Europe's Alps, Norway's coast, and Scotland's moors. Both nations were first inhabited by seafarers, Australia as long as 50,000 years ago, New Zealand little more than a thousand. From the late 18th century to the early 20th, both were British colonies. Both have transformed themselves from commerce based on exports of beef and hides, lamb and wool, to fully integrated industrialized and service-oriented economies. Both have striven with varying success to accommodate aboriginal peoples, as well as recent immigrants—many from Vietnam and China and many of the Muslim faith—as part of a diverse, modern society. Oceania, roughly those islands of the southwest Pacific that include Polynesia, Micronesia, and Melanesia, was settled by indigenous expeditions sailing in multihulled vessels. These adventurers settled nearly every inhabitable Pacific island and perhaps made landfall as far distant as South America before Europeans appeared over the horizon in the 17th century. Today these islands are in various states of nationhood or dependency, prosperity or poverty, and often ignored if not outright exploited.

IMAGE BY ROBERT STACEY, WORLDSAT INTERNATIONAL INC.

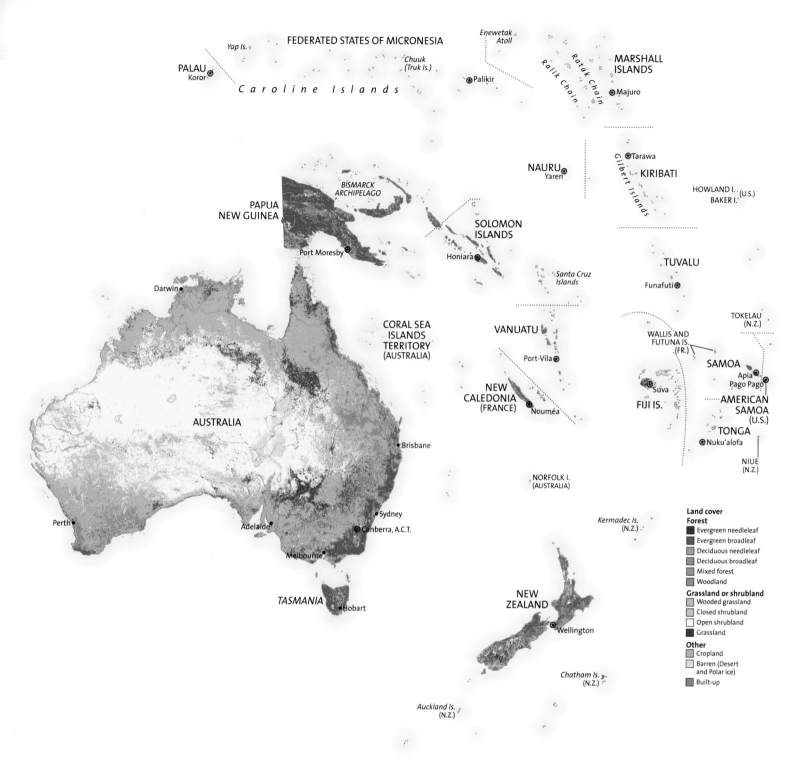

TEMPERATURE AND RAINFALL

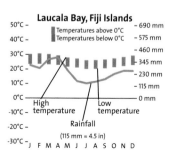

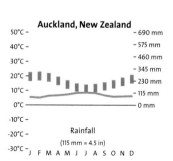

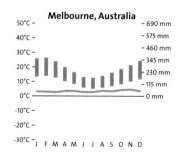

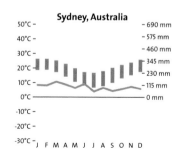

The entire extent of Oceania encompasses the islands of the Central and South Pacific, including Hawai'i, New Zealand, and Australia.

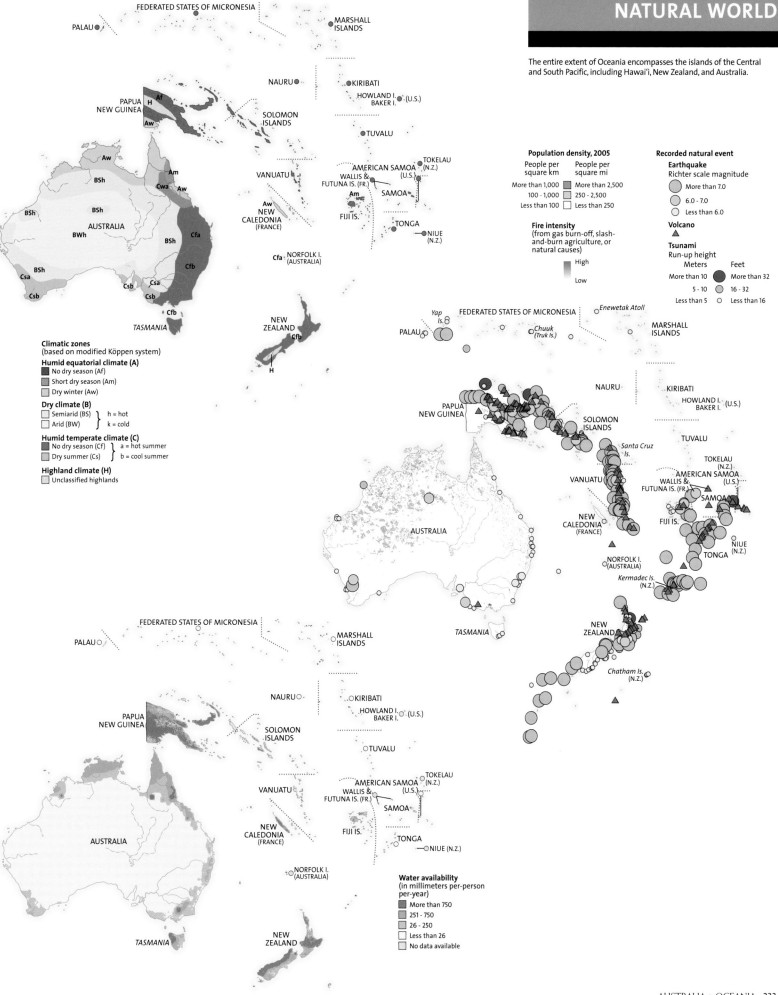

Map 1 (Climatic zones)

FEDERATED STATES OF MICRONESIA
PALAU
MARSHALL ISLANDS
NAURU
KIRIBATI
HOWLAND I.
BAKER I. (U.S.)
PAPUA NEW GUINEA
SOLOMON ISLANDS
TUVALU
TOKELAU (N.Z.)
VANUATU
AMERICAN SAMOA (U.S.)
WALLIS & FUTUNA IS. (FR.)
SAMOA
Af
H
Aw
Am
Cwa
Aw
Aw
BSh
BSh
BSh
AUSTRALIA
BWh
BSh
Csa
Cfa
BSh
Csb
Csa
Csb
Cfb
Csb
Cfb
TASMANIA
Am
FIJI IS.
TONGA
NIUE (N.Z.)
NEW CALEDONIA (FRANCE)
Aw
Cfa
NORFOLK I. (AUSTRALIA)
NEW ZEALAND
Cfb
H

Climatic zones
(based on modified Köppen system)

Humid equatorial climate (A)
- No dry season (Af)
- Short dry season (Am)
- Dry winter (Aw)

Dry climate (B)
- Semiarid (BS)   h = hot
- Arid (BW)   k = cold

Humid temperate climate (C)
- No dry season (Cf)   } a = hot summer
- Dry summer (Cs)   } b = cool summer

Highland climate (H)
- Unclassified highlands

Legends (center)

Population density, 2005

People per square km	People per square mi
More than 1,000	More than 2,500
100 - 1,000	250 - 2,500
Less than 100	Less than 250

Fire intensity
(from gas burn-off, slash-and-burn agriculture, or natural causes)
- High
- Low

Recorded natural event

Earthquake
Richter scale magnitude
- More than 7.0
- 6.0 - 7.0
- Less than 6.0

Volcano ▲

Tsunami
Run-up height

Meters	Feet
More than 10	More than 32
5 - 10	16 - 32
Less than 5	Less than 16

Map 2 (Natural events / population)

Yap Is.
FEDERATED STATES OF MICRONESIA
Enewetak Atoll
PALAU
Chuuk (Truk Is.)
MARSHALL ISLANDS
NAURU
KIRIBATI
HOWLAND I.
BAKER I. (U.S.)
PAPUA NEW GUINEA
SOLOMON ISLANDS
Santa Cruz Is.
TUVALU
TOKELAU (N.Z.)
VANUATU
AMERICAN SAMOA (U.S.)
WALLIS & FUTUNA IS. (FR.)
SAMOA
AUSTRALIA
FIJI IS.
NIUE (N.Z.)
NEW CALEDONIA (FRANCE)
TONGA
NORFOLK I. (AUSTRALIA)
Kermadec Is. (N.Z.)
TASMANIA
NEW ZEALAND
Chatham Is. (N.Z.)

Map 3 (Water availability)

FEDERATED STATES OF MICRONESIA
PALAU
MARSHALL ISLANDS
NAURU
KIRIBATI
HOWLAND I.
BAKER I. (U.S.)
PAPUA NEW GUINEA
SOLOMON ISLANDS
TUVALU
TOKELAU (N.Z.)
VANUATU
AMERICAN SAMOA (U.S.)
WALLIS & FUTUNA IS. (FR.)
SAMOA
AUSTRALIA
FIJI IS.
TONGA
NIUE (N.Z.)
NEW CALEDONIA (FRANCE)
NORFOLK I. (AUSTRALIA)
TASMANIA
NEW ZEALAND

Water availability
(in millimeters per-person per-year)
- More than 750
- 251 - 750
- 26 - 250
- Less than 26
- No data available

FEDERATED STATES OF MICRONESIA

Enewetak Atoll

PALAU
Koror ⊛

Yap Is.

Chuuk
(Truk Is.)

Caroline Islands

⊛ Palikir

MARSHALL
ISLANDS

Ralik Chain

Ratak Chain

⊛ Majuro

NAURU ⊛
Yaren

⊛ Tarawa

Gilbert Islands

KIRIBATI

HOWLAND I. (U.S.)
BAKER I.

PAPUA
NEW GUINEA

*BISMARCK
ARCHIPELAGO*

SOLOMON
ISLANDS

Port Moresby ⊛

Honiara ⊛

*Santa Cruz
Islands*

TUVALU

Funafuti ⊛

TOKELAU
(N.Z.)

Darwin •

CORAL SEA
ISLANDS
TERRITORY
(AUSTRALIA)

VANUATU

Port-Vila ⊛

WALLIS AND
FUTUNA IS.
(FR.)

SAMOA

Apia ⊛
Pago Pago ⊛

AMERICAN
SAMOA
(U.S.)

AUSTRALIA

NEW
CALEDONIA
(FRANCE)

Nouméa ⊛

Suva ⊛

FIJI IS.

TONGA
⊛ Nuku'alofa

NIUE
(N.Z.)

Brisbane •

NORFOLK I.
(AUSTRALIA)

Perth •

Adelaide •

Sydney •

⊛ Canberra, A.C.T.

*Kermadec Is.
(N.Z.)*

Melbourne •

TASMANIA

• Hobart

NEW
ZEALAND

Wellington ⊛

Population density, 2005

People per square km		People per square mi
More than 195	⬛	More than 500
60 - 195	⬛	150 - 500
10 - 59	⬜	25 - 149
1 - 9	⬜	1 - 24
Less than 1	⬜	Less than 1

*Chatham Is.
(N.Z.)*

*Auckland Is.
(N.Z.)*

POPULATION PYRAMIDS

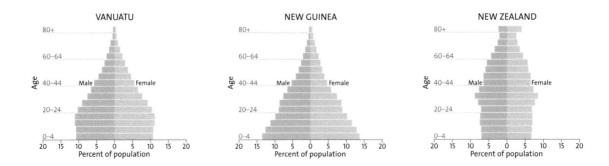

VANUATU

NEW GUINEA

NEW ZEALAND

FEDERATED STATES OF MICRONESIA

PALAU

MICRONESIA

MARSHALL ISLANDS

MELANESIA

NAURU

KIRIBATI

PAPUA NEW GUINEA

HOWLAND I.
BAKER I. (U.S.)

SOLOMON ISLANDS

TUVALU

TOKELAU (N.Z.)

AMERICAN SAMOA (U.S.)

VANUATU

WALLIS & FUTUNA IS. (FR.)

SAMOA

NEW CALEDONIA (FRANCE)

FIJI IS.

TONGA

NIUE (N.Z.)

AUSTRALIA

NORFOLK I. (AUSTRALIA)

POLYNESIA

MICRONESIA

TASMANIA

NEW ZEALAND

P

Population of capitals and urban agglomerations, 2005
(in thousands)
- More than 4,000
- 1,260 - 3,999
- 420 - 1,259
- 140 - 419
- 7 - 139

Percent urban population, 2005
- More than 75%
- 50% - 74%
- 25% - 49%
- Less than 24%
- Uninhabited

Indigenous languages
Australian
- Aboriginal
- Undetermined

- Austronesian
- Papuan
- Uninhabited

FEDERATED STATES OF MICRONESIA

PALAU

Palikir

MARSHALL ISLANDS

NAURU

KIRIBATI

HOWLAND I.
BAKER I. (U.S.)

PAPUA NEW GUINEA

Port Moresby

SOLOMON ISLANDS

Honiara

TUVALU

TOKELAU (N.Z.)

Cairns

Townsville

VANUATU

AMERICAN SAMOA (U.S.)

WALLIS & FUTUNA IS. (FR.)

Port-Vila

SAMOA
Apia

NEW CALEDONIA (FRANCE)

Nouméa

FIJI IS.
Suva

TONGA

NIUE (N.Z.)

AUSTRALIA

Brisbane

Nuku'alofa

NORFOLK I. (AUSTRALIA)

Newcastle

Perth

Canberra, A.C.T.

SYDNEY
Wollongong

Adelaide

Geelong
Melbourne

Auckland
Tauranga

Hamilton

Napier-Hastings

NEW ZEALAND
Wellington

TASMANIA

Hobart

Christchurch

Dunedin

FEDERATED STATES OF MICRONESIA

PALAU

MARSHALL ISLANDS

NAURU

KIRIBATI

HOWLAND I.
BAKER I. (U.S.)

SOLOMON ISLANDS

TUVALU

TOKELAU (N.Z.)

VANUATU

AMERICAN SAMOA (U.S.)

WALLIS & FUTUNA IS. (FR.)

SAMOA

NEW CALEDONIA (FRANCE)

PAPUA NEW GUINEA

FIJI IS.

TONGA

NIUE (N.Z.)

AUSTRALIA

NORFOLK I. (AUSTRALIA)

Projected population change, 2005 - 2050
(by percentage)
- More than 100%
- 50% - 100%
- 0% - 49%
- Less than 0% (Population loss)

TASMANIA

NEW ZEALAND

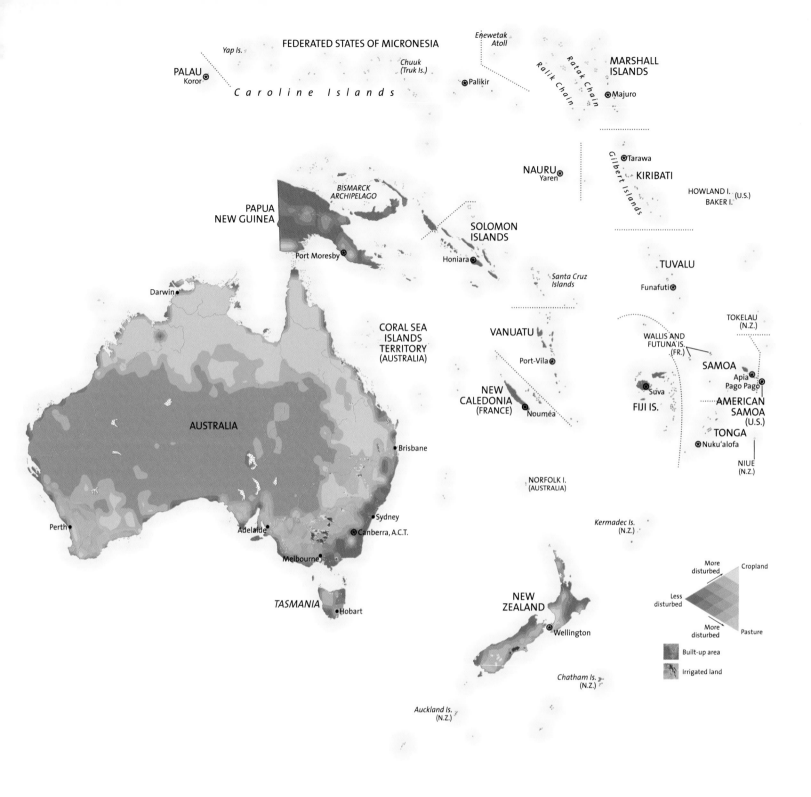

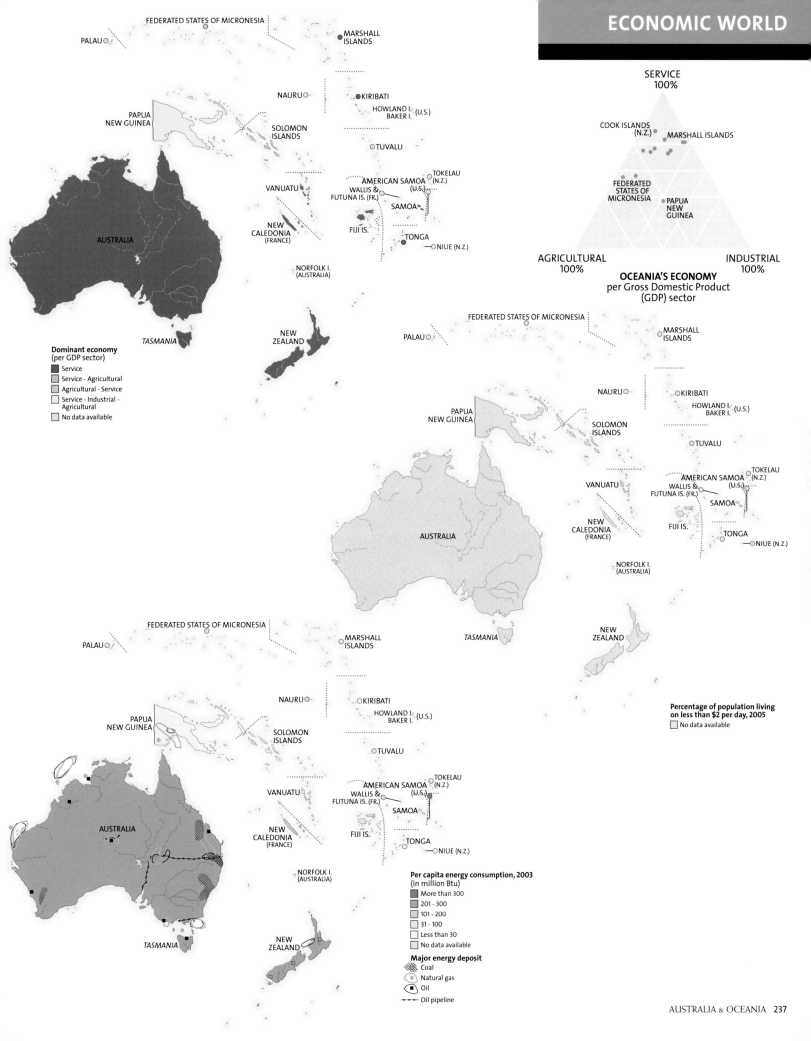

FEDERATED STATES OF MICRONESIA

PALAU

MARSHALL
ISLANDS

NAURU

KIRIBATI

HOWLAND I. (U.S.)
BAKER I.

PAPUA
NEW GUINEA

SOLOMON
ISLANDS

TUVALU

VANUATU

TOKELAU
(N.Z.)

AMERICAN SAMOA
(U.S.)

WALLIS &
FUTUNA IS. (FR.)

SAMOA

NEW
CALEDONIA
(FRANCE)

FIJI IS.

TONGA

NIUE (N.Z.)

AUSTRALIA

NORFOLK I.
(AUSTRALIA)

TASMANIA

NEW
ZEALAND

Dominant economy
(per GDP sector)
- Service
- Service - Agricultural
- Agricultural - Service
- Service - Industrial -
  Agricultural
- No data available

SERVICE 100%

COOK ISLANDS
(N.Z.)

MARSHALL ISLANDS

FEDERATED
STATES OF
MICRONESIA

PAPUA
NEW
GUINEA

AGRICULTURAL
100%

INDUSTRIAL
100%

OCEANIA'S ECONOMY
per Gross Domestic Product
(GDP) sector

FEDERATED STATES OF MICRONESIA

PALAU

MARSHALL
ISLANDS

NAURU

KIRIBATI

HOWLAND I. (U.S.)
BAKER I.

PAPUA
NEW GUINEA

SOLOMON
ISLANDS

TUVALU

VANUATU

TOKELAU
(N.Z.)

AMERICAN SAMOA
(U.S.)

WALLIS &
FUTUNA IS. (FR.)

SAMOA

NEW
CALEDONIA
(FRANCE)

FIJI IS.

TONGA

NIUE (N.Z.)

AUSTRALIA

NORFOLK I.
(AUSTRALIA)

TASMANIA

NEW
ZEALAND

**Percentage of population living
on less than $2 per day, 2005**
- No data available

FEDERATED STATES OF MICRONESIA

PALAU

MARSHALL
ISLANDS

NAURU

KIRIBATI

HOWLAND I. (U.S.)
BAKER I.

PAPUA
NEW GUINEA

SOLOMON
ISLANDS

TUVALU

VANUATU

TOKELAU
(N.Z.)

AMERICAN SAMOA
(U.S.)

WALLIS &
FUTUNA IS. (FR.)

SAMOA

NEW
CALEDONIA
(FRANCE)

FIJI IS.

TONGA

NIUE (N.Z.)

AUSTRALIA

NORFOLK I.
(AUSTRALIA)

TASMANIA

NEW
ZEALAND

Per capita energy consumption, 2003
(in million Btu)
- More than 300
- 201 - 300
- 101 - 200
- 31 - 100
- Less than 30
- No data available

Major energy deposit
- Coal
- Natural gas
- Oil
- Oil pipeline

This is a map of Australia & Oceania region showing East Asia, Southeast Asia, and the western Pacific.

110° 120° 130° 140° 150° 160° 170°

RUSSIA

Ust' Barguzin Mogocha Skovorodino Ushumun Okha Petropavlovsk Kamchatskiy Near Islands Attu
Ozero Baykal Romanovka Shimanovsk Nikolayevsk na Amure OSTROV Bol'sheretsk POLUOSTROV
Chita Shilka Sretensk Ganhe Svobodnyy Lazarev SEA OF POLUOSTROV KAMCHATKA A L
Ulan Ude Khilok Aginskoye Olovyannaya Yitulihe Blagoveshchensk Chegdomyn De Kastri OKHOTSK KAMCHATKA
Baley Borzya Heihe Komsomol'sk na Amure Poronaysk
Manzhouli Yakeshi Hailar Nehe Sovetskaya Vanino Mys Lopatka
Ulaanbaatar Choybalsan Zalantun Yichun Birobidzhan Gavan 1426
Öndörhaan Hulun Nur Nenjiang Khabarovsk Kholmsk Yuzhno Sakhalinsk HOKKAIDO KURIL ISLANDS
Saynshand (Buyant-Uhaa) Baruun Urt Arxan Jiamusi Vyazemskiy Korsakov Wakkanai (KURIL'SKIYE OSTROVA)
MONGOLIA Baicheng Qiqihar Shuangyashan Vladivostok Asahikawa 2290
Erenhot 3802 Ulanhot Daqing Qitaihe Ozero Khanka Dal'negorsk Sapporo Chitose
Xilinhot Tongliao Harbin Jixi Nakhodka Muroran Kushiro
GOBI Taibus Changchun Mudanjiang Hakodate Aomori
Hanggin Houqi Duolun Jilin Ch'ŏngjin Hirosaki Hachinohe
Baotou Zhangjiakou SHENYANG Liaoyuan NORTH KOREA Akita Morioka
Datong Anshan Fushun Hamhŭng HONSHŪ
Wuda Jining Dandong Hamatan Wŏnsan Niigata
Shizuishan Taiyuan Tangshan Anju P'yŏngyang JAPAN
BEIJING (PEKING) Shijiazhuang TIANJIN Dalian Incheon SEOUL Kanazawa
Hanggin Handan Jinan Yantai Qingdao Daejeon Daegu Kyōto 3776 Yokohama
Taiyuan Hebi Zibo SOUTH KOREA Busan TŌKYŌ
Baoji Zhengzhou Tai'an Heze Zaozhuang Gwangju Hiroshima Kōbe Nagoya
Xi'an (Sian) Luoyang Xuchang Kaifeng Xuzhou Nagasaki Fukuoka Osaka
Huainan Bengbu Kitakyūshū KYŪSHŪ
Xiangfan Hefei Nanjing Suzhou Kumamoto
WUHAN Anqing Wuxi SHANGHAI
Wanxian Shashi Hangzhou Shaoxing
CHONGQING Jiujiang Jinhua Ningbo Tokara Rettō
Zunyi Changsha Nanchang Quzhou EAST CHINA SEA
Shaoyang Zhuzhou Pingxiang Nanping Wenzhou Ryukyu Islands (Nansei Shotō)
Guiyang Hengyang Fuzhou Bonin Islands (Ogasawara Guntō)
Duyun Ganzhou
Guilin Naha Okinawa Daitō Shotō Iwo Jima Volcano Islands (Kazan Rettō) Minami Tori Shima (Marcus)
GUANGZHOU (CANTON) T'aipei (Taibei) 7507 Japan Japan
Foshan Shantou Kaohsiung Sakishima Shotō TAIWAN
Nanning HONG KONG T'ainan Batan Islands
Zhanjiang Babuyan Islands
Haikou Luzon Strait
Dongfang 1867 Aparri NORTHERN MARIANA ISLANDS Wake Island U.S.
Sanya Hainan Laoag Babuyan Islands U.S.
Quang Tri Vigan Tuguegarao PHILIPPINE Capitol Hill
Da Nang Paracel Islands Baguio 2934 LUZON SEA Tinian Saipan (11)
VIETNAM Mount Pinatubo Quezon City Rota
2598 2934 Manila PHILIPPINES U.S. Guam (12) Hagåtña (Agana)
Qui Nhon Naga Legazpi
Buon Me Thuot SOUTH CHINA SEA Masbate MICRONESIA
Nha Trang Spratly Islands Roxas Iloilo Calbayog Yap Islands
Cam Ranh Bacolod Cebu 10057 Hall Islands
Bien Hoa Puerto Princesa Ngulu Atoll 8527
Ho Chi Minh City (Saigon) Palawan 2100 Cagayan de Oro MINDANAO Koror 13 Chuuk (Truk) Islands Senyavin Is. Bikini Atoll
Con Son Sulu Sea Cotabato Davao Sonsorol Islands PALAU 18 Palikir 17 Ratak Chain MARSHALL ISLANDS
North Luconia Shoals Zamboanga 2954 General Santos Pohnpei (Ponape) Majuro 14
Kinabalu 4101 Sandakan CAROLINE ISLANDS Kosrae (Kusaie) 19 Jaluit Atoll
Bandar Seri Begawan Tawau FEDERATED STATES Mortlock Islands 15
BRUNEI Tarakan OF MICRONESIA 4261
MALAYSIA Sibu Celebes Sea Kapingamarangi Atoll Tarawa (Bairiki) 16 GILBERT ISLANDS
2987 Tolitoli MELANESIA
BORNEO Sangkulirang 1635 Ternate
Pontianak Gorontalo EQUATOR Ninigo Group NAURU 20
Ketapang Samarinda Palu 3000 Sorong Admiralty Islands Mussau Islands
Tanjungpandan Kandangan SULAWESI Sarmi Jayapura BISMARCK ARCHIPELAGO Kavieng
Balikpapan 3455 Aitape Wewak Namatanai New Ireland Green Islands
Banjarmasin Parepare Kendari NEW GUINEA Madang Rabaul Nukumanu Islands
JAKARTA Ujungpandang Ambon Amamapare Nabire Bismarck Sea 4509 New Britain 2438 Bougainville Ontong Java Atoll
Bandung Baubau Kep. Kai Tual Kepulauan Aru 46 Lae Arawa SOLOMON ISLANDS 21
INDONESIA Kepi Muting Huon Gulf Trobriand Is. Solomon Sea 2438 Stewart Islands
Tasikmalaya Surabaya Merauke D'Entrecasteaux Honiara Guadalcanal Duff Islands
Yogyakarta JAVA Jember Banda Sea PAPUA NEW GUINEA Daru Port Moresby 2438 Santa Cruz Islands
Bali 3726 Flores Ruteng Dili Baguia Gulf of Papua Louisiade Archipelago Vanikolo Is.
Sumbawa Sumba Waingapu TIMOR-LESTE (EAST TIMOR) Samarai Is. Rotuma Fiji
7125 Lesser Sunda Islands Kupang Arafura Sea Torres Strait Cape York TUVALU
INDIAN OCEAN Timor Sea Wessel Islands Samarai I. Banks Islands
Heywood Shoal Holothuria Banks Oenpelli Weipa Vanua
Seringapatam Reef Joseph Bonaparte Gulf Jabiru Nhulunbuy Coral Sea Espiritu Santo 1879 22 Levu
Scott Reef Darwin Aurukun VANUATU
Mermaid Reef Lynher Bank Ngukurr Gulf of Coen Willis Islets Éfaté Port-Vila FIJI ISLANDS
Wyndham Kununurra Borroloola Carpentaria Cooktown Flora Reef Îles Chesterfield Vitu Levu
Broome Mt. Ord Lake Halls Creek Newcastle Waters Burketown 1611 Cairns 4716 23 Ceva-i-Ra
Derby 937 Argyle Normanton Innisfail Lihou Reefs NEW CALEDONIA
Lagrange Fitzroy Crossing Georgetown Townsville France 1628 Mount Panié Loyalty Islands
Glomar Eighty Mile Beach AUSTRALIA Tennant Creek Ayr Bowen Great Barrier Reef Nouméa
Rankin Bank Great Sandy Desert Camooweal Charters Towers Mackay
Onslow Dampier Marble Bar Mount Isa Cloncurry Frederick Reef
North West Cape Roebourne Barrow Creek Winton Dajarra Swain Reefs

PHILIPPINE SEA

NORTH

Tartar Strait SAKHALIN Aleksandrovsk Sakhalinskiy Noglik Noglikskiy Korsakov La Perouse Strait
SEA OF JAPAN (EAST SEA)
YELLOW SEA
Yellow
Taiwan Strait
2341 2259 3622

TASMAN

SEA

NORTH
ISLAND

Cape
Reinga   North
Te Hapua   Cape
Te Kao   Cape
Karikari
Ninety
Mile
Beach   Mangonui
Ahipara   Kaeo   Cape
Brett
Pawarenga   Mangamuka   Paihia
Panguru   Moerewai   Opua
Waimamaku   Rawene   Kawakawa
Donnellys Crossing   Pakotai   Whakapara
Kaihu   770   Hikurangi
Te Kopuru   Waiotira   Kamo
Whangarei
Ruawai   Paparoa   Marsden Point
Maungaturoto   Waipu
Wellsford   Port
Fitzroy
Leigh   621   Great Barrier I.
Matakana   East   358   Tryphena
Head North   Coast   Cape
Bays   Colville
Helensville   Colville
Waitemata   Howick   Coromandel
Auckland   Whitianga
Manukau   Pukekohe   COROMANDEL
PEN.
Papakura   Tairua
Pokeno   688   Thames
Tuakau   Waitakaruru
Te Kauwhata   Paeroa   Waihi
Huntly   Te Aroha
Pukemiro   Waitoa   Mount
Maunganui
Ngaruawahia   Bay
of
Plenty   Cape
Runaway   Hicks
Bay
Raglan   Hamilton   Te Puke   Maketu   Te Araroa   East Cape
Kawhia   959   Cambridge   Whakatane   Matata   Te Kaha   Tikitiki
Otorohanga   Tauranga   Torere   1754   Ruatoria
Waitomo Caves   Rotorua   Te Teko   Opotiki   1440   Te Puia Springs
Te Kuiti   Mt.   Tarawera   Motu   Arowhana   Tokomaru Bay
Hangatiki   1111   Moutohora
Atiamuri   TE UREWERA   Matawai   Tolaga Bay
Benneydale   Ruatahuna   N.P.   Te Karaka   Ormond
Awakino   Ongarue   Minginui   Te Karaka
Mokau   Okahukura   Taupo   1403   Patutahi   Whangara
Taringamotu   Kakahi   Ruakituri   Gisborne
Uruti   Taumarunui   Turangi   Waitahanui   962   Whakapunake
Waitara   Lepperton   Waitahanui   1820
New Plymouth   National   Tai   Raupunga   Wairoa
Oakura   Urenui   Park   Tarawera   Putorino   Mahia Pen.
EGMONT N.P.   2518   Mt. Ngauruhoe   Tutira
Rahotu   Mt. Taranaki   WHANGANUI   1724   Eskdale
(Mt. Egmont)   Toko   N.P.   2797   Taradale   Napier
Opunake   Manaia   Eltham   TONGARIRO   229   Mt. Ruapehu   Waiouru   Kaweka   Pakipaki   Hawke
Alton   Hawera   N.P.   Raetihi   Taihape   Cape
Kakaramea   Kakatahi   Mangaweka   Pakipaki   Kidnappers   Bay
Waverley   Utiku   Waimarama
Waitotara   Mangaweka   1733   Waipawa   Pukehou
Kai Iwi   Marton   Rata   Takapau   Omakere
Castlecliff   Wanganui   Feilding   Palmerston   Waipukurau
Bulls   305   Porangahau
Foxton   North   Taumatawhakatangihangakoauauotamateaturipukakapikimaungahoronukupokaiwhenuakitanatahu
Levin   Shannon   Cape Turnagain
Cape   Ohau   Pongaroa   1820
Farewell   Pakawau   Otaki   Akitio
Collingwood   Rockville   D'Urville I.   Waikanae   Alfredton
Takaka   729   Mauriceville
KAHURANGI   ABEL   Mt.   Mitre   Tinui
NATIONAL   TASMAN   Stokes   Carterton   Castlepoint
PARK   N.P. French   Greytown
Karamea   Riwaka   Pass   1203   Porirua   Lower   Martinborough
Tasman   Picton   Hutt   NEW
Tapawera   Stoke   Havelock   Wellington   983   Mount Ross
Seddonville   Mt. Owen   Tadmor   Blenheim
Granity   1875   Valley Seddon   Wairau   Cape
Waimangaroa   Hector   Owen River   Campbell
Cape Foulwind   Charleston   Westport   Murchison   Tapuaenuku   Ward
Mt. Uriah   1532   Cronadun   Molesworth   2885   Cape
PAPAROA N.P.   Reefton   Palliser
Barrytown   Maruia   NELSON   Manakau
Rapahoe   Ikamatua   LAKES   2160   Clarence
Greymouth   Ngahere   N.P.   Hanmer   Kaikoura
Dobson   Lewis   Springs
Arahura   Moana   Pass   1875   Waiau   Oaro
Hokitika   Kumara   Rotherham   Parnassus
Kowhitirangi   Otira   ARTHUR'S   Culverden   Cheviot
Ross   2400   PASS N.P.   Hawarden   Domett
Arthur's   Omihi   Scargill
Harihari   Pass   Waipara   Amberley
Springfield   Oxford   Rangiora
Franz Josef   Whataroa   Lake   Belfast   Christchurch
WESTLAND   Glacier   2795   Coleridge   Hororata   Lyttelton
(TAI POUTINI) N.P.   Methven   Rolleston   919   BANKS PEN.
Fox Glacier   3754   Rakaia   Lincoln   Akaroa
(Mt. Cook) Aoraki   AORAKI (MT. COOK)   Mayfield   Ashburton
(Mt. Cook) Aoraki   N.P.   Lake   Hinds
2871   Tekapo   Geraldine
Jackson Head   Haast   Lake   Fairlie   Orari   Canterbury
Jackson Bay   Pukaki   Twizel   Pleasant Point   Temuka   Bight
MT. ASPIRING   Lake Pukaki   Cave   Timaru
N.P.   Omarama   1910   Saint Andrews
Awarua Bay   3027   Mt.   Otematata   Waimate   Makikihi
Lake McKerrow   2746   Aspiring   Hakataramea   Studholme Junction
Mount Tutoko   Tarras   Kurow   Moeraki   Glenavy
Milford Sound   2131   Coronet   Arrowtown   Duntroon   Oamaru
George Sound   Glenorchy   Pk.   Cromwell   Enfield   Totara   Maheno
1646   Omakau   Herbert
FIORDLAND   Queenstown   Clyde   Ranfurly   Hyde   Kakanui
The Remarkables   2324   Ranfurly   Palmerston   Hampden
NATIONAL   1853   Kingston   Clyde   Naseby
Te Anau   Athol   Roxburgh   Karitane
L. Manapouri   Coal   Ettrick   Seacliff   Waikouaiti
PARK   Mossburn   Creek   1450   Waitati   Port Chalmers
Dusky Sound   Dipton   Edievale   Allanton   Mosgiel   Dunedin
Riversdale   Tapanui   Lawrence   Waihola   Green Island
Orawia   Winton   Waipahi   Milton
1189   Otautau   Gore   Balclutha
24   Thornbury   Browns   Kaitangata
Puysegur   Waikiwi   Owaka
Point   Otatara   Invercargill   Tahakopa
73   Bluff   Tiwai   Waikawa
FOVEAUX   Point
STEWART   Mt.
ISLAND   Anglem   080
1495   Oban   RAKIURA
Mason Bay   NATIONAL
Mt. Allen   750   PARK

SOUTH
ISLAND

ZEALAND

NEW

Pegasus
Bay

Pegasus
Bay

Mernoo
Bank
.33

PACIFIC OCEAN

COOK STRAIT

Hauraki
Gulf

Tasman Bay

Polynesia

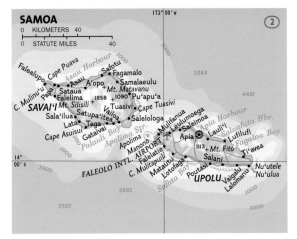

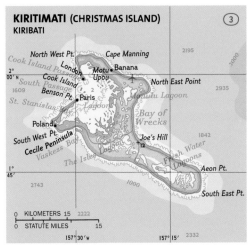

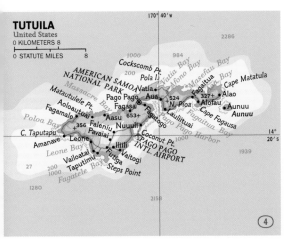

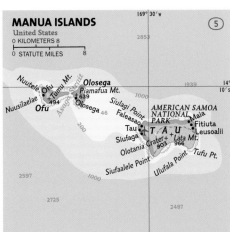

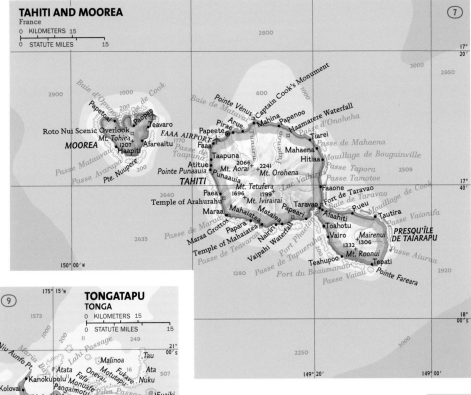

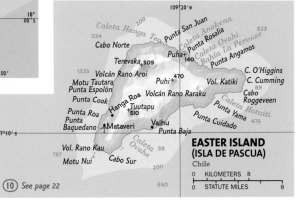

Micronesia

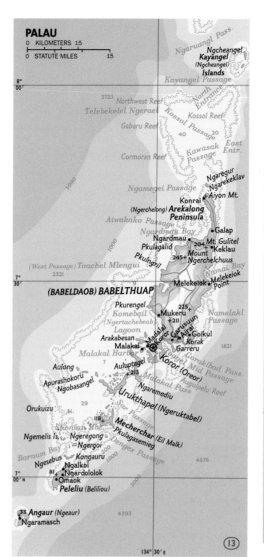
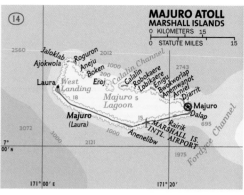

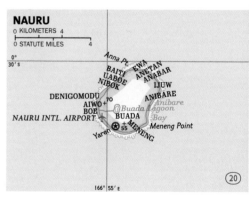

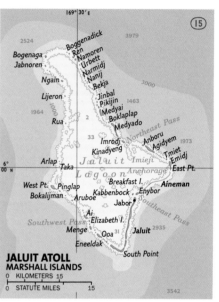
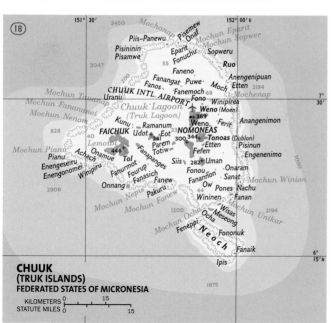
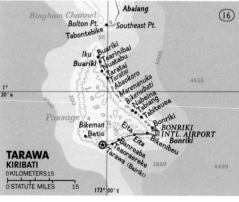

Melanesia

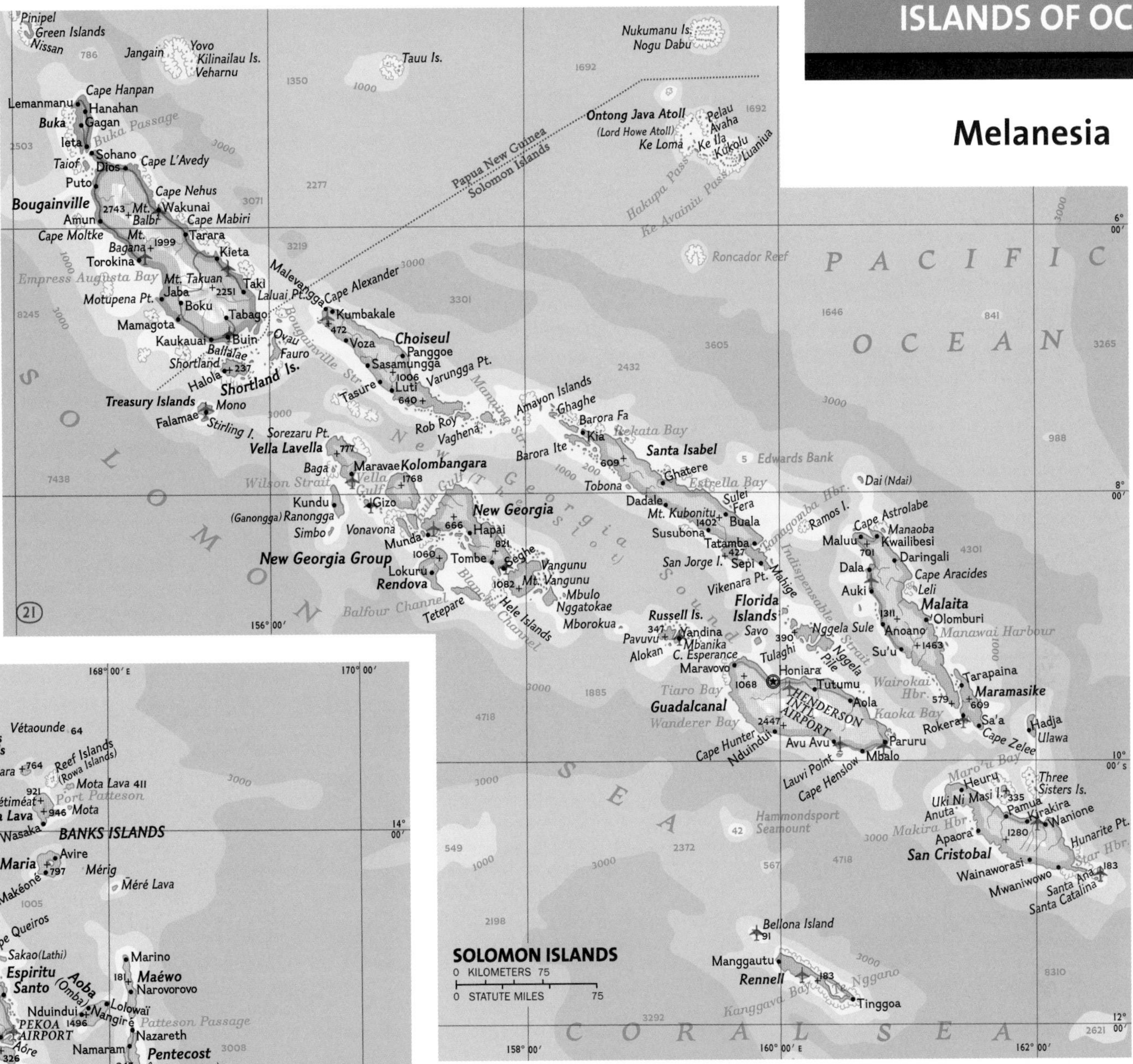

Map 21 (Solomon Islands area)

Pinipel, Green Islands, Nissan, Jangain, Yovo, Kilinailau Is., Veharnu, Tauu Is., Nukumanu Is., Nogu Dabu

Cape Hanpan, Lemanmanu, Hanahan, Buka, Gagan, Ieta, Sohano, Dios, Taiof, Puto, Cape L'Avedy

Ontong Java Atoll (Lord Howe Atoll), Ke Lomá, Pelau, Avaha, Ke Ila, Kukolu, Juaniua

Bougainville, Amun, Mt. Balbi 2743, Cape Nehus, Cape Wakunai, Cape Mabiri, Cape Moltke, Mt. Bagana 1999, Torokina, Tarara, Kieta, Empress Augusta Bay, Mt. Takuan 2251, Taki, Motupena Pt., Jaba, Boku, Tabago, Mamagota, Kaukauai, Buin, Ballalae, Shortland, Halola +237, **Shortland Is.**, Treasury Islands, Mono, Falamae, Stirling I., Sorezaru Pt.

Papua New Guinea, Solomon Islands

Roncador Reef

PACIFIC OCEAN

Malevanga, Cape Alexander, Laluai Pt., Kumbakale +472, Voza, **Choiseul**, Panggoe, Sasamungga, Luti, Varungga Pt., Tasure 640+, Rob Roy, Vaghena, Amayon Islands, Barora Fa, Kia, Ghaghe, Barora Ite, Iekata Bay

Vella Lavella +777, Baga, Maravae, **Kolombangara** +1768, Vella Gulf, Kundu, (Ganongga) Ranongga, Simbo, Gizo, Vonavona, Munda +666, Hapai, **New Georgia**, Ghatere, Tobona, 609+, **Santa Isabel**, Edwards Bank, Dai (Ndai)

New Georgia Group, Lokuru, Tombe, Seghe, **Rendova**, Tetepare, Mt. Vangunu 1082, Vangunu, Hele Islands, Mbulo, Nggatokae, Mborokua, Dadale, Mt. Kubonitu 1402, Fera, Buala, Susubona, Tatamba, Sepi, San Jorge I., Vikenara Pt., Maluu, Kwailibesi, Dala, Daringali, Cape Aracides, Leli, **Malaita**, Olomburi, Anoano +1463

Florida Islands, Russell Is., Yandina, Mbanika, Pavuvu, Alokan, C. Esperance, Maravovo, Tulaghi, Savo, Nggela Sule, Nggela Pile, Su'u, Ramos I., Cape Astrolabe, Manaoba, Kwailibesi

Honiara, Tutumu, Aola, **Guadalcanal**, HENDERSON INTL AIRPORT, Wanderer Bay, Cape Hunter, Nduindui, Avu Avu, Paruru, Mbalo, Lauvi Point, Cape Henslow, Rokera, Sa'a, **Maramasike**, Cape Zelee, Ulawa, Hadja

Tarapaina, Heuru, Uki Ni Masi I., Anuta, Pamua, Three Sisters Is., Kirakira, Wanione, Apaora, +1280, **San Cristobal**, Wainaworasi, Mwaniwiowo, Santa Ana, Santa Catalina, Hunarite Pt., Star Hbr.

Bellona Island, Manggautu, **Rennell**, Tinggoa

SOLOMON ISLANDS
0 KILOMETERS 75
0 STATUTE MILES 75

CORAL SEA

Map 22 (Vanuatu)

Hiu, Métoma, Vétaounde, Téguá, Loh, Torres Islands, Toga, Uréparapara +764, Reef Islands (Rowa Islands), Mota Lava 411, Mt. Surétiméat +921, **Vanua Lava** +946, Mota, Port Patteson, Wasaka, **BANKS ISLANDS**

Santa Maria, Avire +797, Makéoné, Mérig, Méré Lava, Cape Cumberland, Cape Queiros, Olpoi +1444, Nokuku, Sakao (Lathi), Marino, Malao, **Espiritu Santo**, Kolé, Aoba (Omba), Nangiré, **Maéwo**, Narovorovo, Wusi, +1879, Nduindui, Lolowaï, Luganville, PEKOA AIRPORT +1496, Namaram, Nazareth, Patteson Passage, Malo +326, Cape Mataabé, Bougainville Strait, Espiègle Bay, Ranwas, **Pentecost** (Île Pentecôte) +947, Homo Bay

Norsup, Port Stanley, Selwyn Strait, Lakatoro, Mégham, Marum Volcano +1270, Mt. Pénot +879, **Malakula**, Paama, **Ambrym**, Lopévi (Ulvéah) 1413, Lamap, Moriu, 84 Tomman, Maskelynes Is., **Épi** +833, Votlo, Laïka 87, Tongoa (Kuwaé) 487, **Shepherd Islands**, Émaé 644, Tongariki 521, 494 (Matah) Mataso, Makura Monument (Étarik) 155, 593 Nguna, 115 Moso, 202 Lélépa +647, **Éfaté** (Île Vaté) 448, Émao, Devil's Pt., BAUERFIELD AIRPORT, Port-Vila, Mélé Bay

Mt. Santop +886, Potnarvin, Cook Bay, Dillon's Bay +802, **Erromango**, Pilbarra Point

Tanna, Lowital, Aniwa 42, Futuna, Waïsisi Bay, Isangel, Yasur Volcano, Mt. Tukosméra +1084, 643

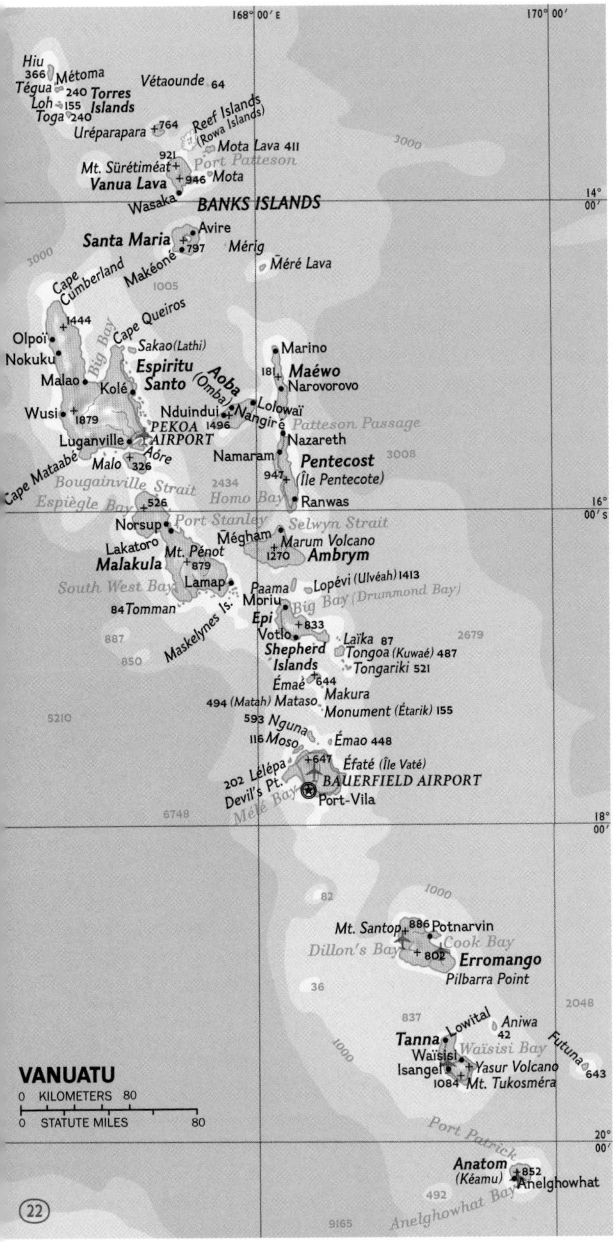

VANUATU
0 KILOMETERS 80
0 STATUTE MILES 80

Anatom (Kéamu) +852, Anelghowhat, Anelghowhat Bay

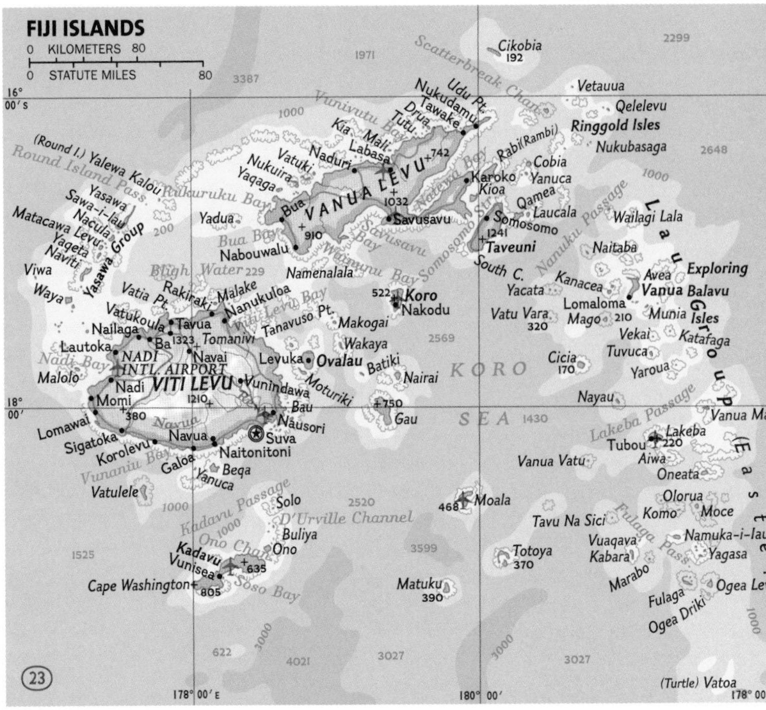

Map 23 (Fiji Islands)

FIJI ISLANDS
0 KILOMETERS 80
0 STATUTE MILES 80

Cikobia 192, Scatterbreak Chan., Vetauua, Qelelevu, Udu Pt., Nukudamu, Tawake, Drua, Tutu, Kia, Mali, Labasa, Rabi (Rambi), Ringgold Isles, Nukubasaga, (Round I.) Yalewa Kalou, Yasawa, Naduri, Vatuki, Naukura, Yagaga, **VANUA LEVU** +1032, Karoko, Yanuca, Cobia, Nukubati, Nabouwalu, Savusavu, Somosomo, Laucala, Wailagi Lala, Sawa-i-lau, Nacula, Matacawa Levu, Yageta, Naviti, Yadua, Bua Bay, Savusavu Bay, +1241, **Taveuni**, Qamea, Viwa, Waya, Vatia Pt., Rakiraki, Malake, Nanukuloa, Namenalala, Makogai, Wakaya, Gau, Nailaga, Tavua, Ba, Tomanivi +1323, Navai, Tanavuso Pt., Leyuka, **Ovalau**, Batiki, Vatu Vara 320, Mago 210, Munia, Vekai, Cicia 170, Tuvuca, Yaroua, Nayau, Vanua Masi, Lautoka, **VITI LEVU** +1210, Vunindawa, Bau, Moturiki, Nairai, Lomaloma, **Vanua Balavu**, Avea, Exploring Isles, Yacata, Kanacea, Katafaga, Lakeba, Malolo, **Nadi** NADI INTL AIRPORT, Nausori, +750, Lomawai, Momi, +380, Navua, Naitonitoni, Suva, Beqa, Vunaniu, Tubou, Aiwa, Oneata, Sigatoka, Korolevu, Galoa, Vatulele, Solo, Buliya, Ono, D'Urville Channel, Kadavu +635, Vunisea, Cape Washington +805, Ono Chan., Moala 467, Vanua Vatu, Moce, Komo, Namuka-i-lau, Vuaqava, Kabara, Tavu Na Sici, Totoya 370, Yagasa, Marabo, Fulaga, Ogea Levu, Ogea Driki, Matuku 390, (Turtle) Vatoa, KORO SEA, Lakeba Passage, Fulaga Pass, Lau Group (Eastern)

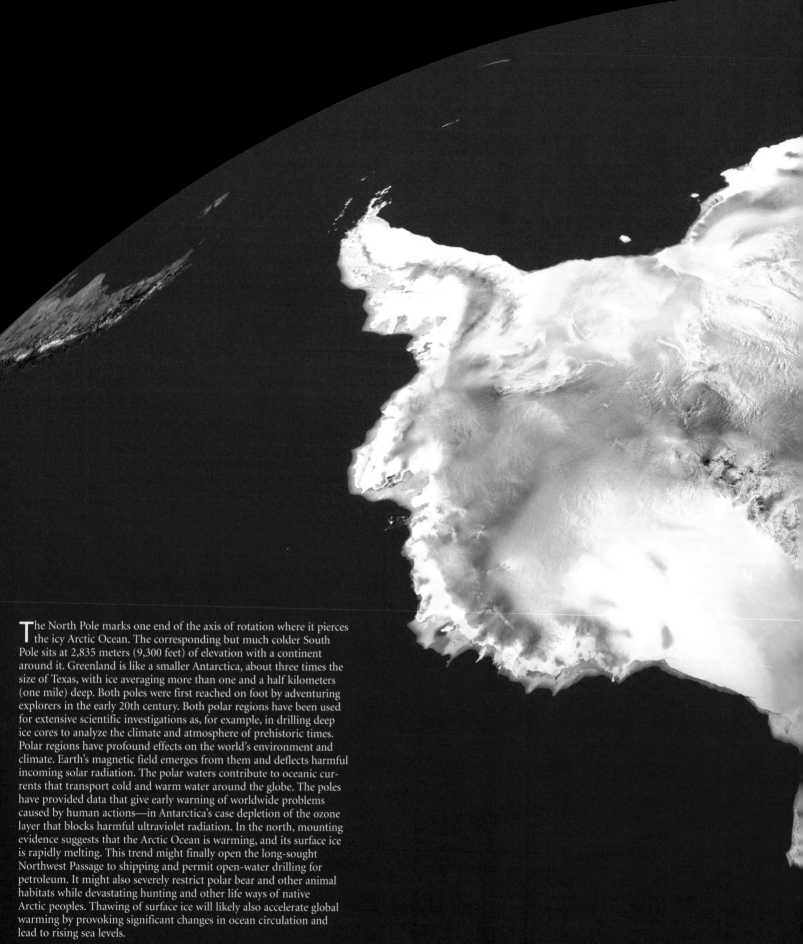

The North Pole marks one end of the axis of rotation where it pierces the icy Arctic Ocean. The corresponding but much colder South Pole sits at 2,835 meters (9,300 feet) of elevation with a continent around it. Greenland is like a smaller Antarctica, about three times the size of Texas, with ice averaging more than one and a half kilometers (one mile) deep. Both poles were first reached on foot by adventuring explorers in the early 20th century. Both polar regions have been used for extensive scientific investigations as, for example, in drilling deep ice cores to analyze the climate and atmosphere of prehistoric times. Polar regions have profound effects on the world's environment and climate. Earth's magnetic field emerges from them and deflects harmful incoming solar radiation. The polar waters contribute to oceanic currents that transport cold and warm water around the globe. The poles have provided data that give early warning of worldwide problems caused by human actions—in Antarctica's case depletion of the ozone layer that blocks harmful ultraviolet radiation. In the north, mounting evidence suggests that the Arctic Ocean is warming, and its surface ice is rapidly melting. This trend might finally open the long-sought Northwest Passage to shipping and permit open-water drilling for petroleum. It might also severely restrict polar bear and other animal habitats while devastating hunting and other life ways of native Arctic peoples. Thawing of surface ice will likely also accelerate global warming by provoking significant changes in ocean circulation and lead to rising sea levels.

IMAGE BY ROBERT STACEY, WORLDSAT INTERNATIONAL INC.

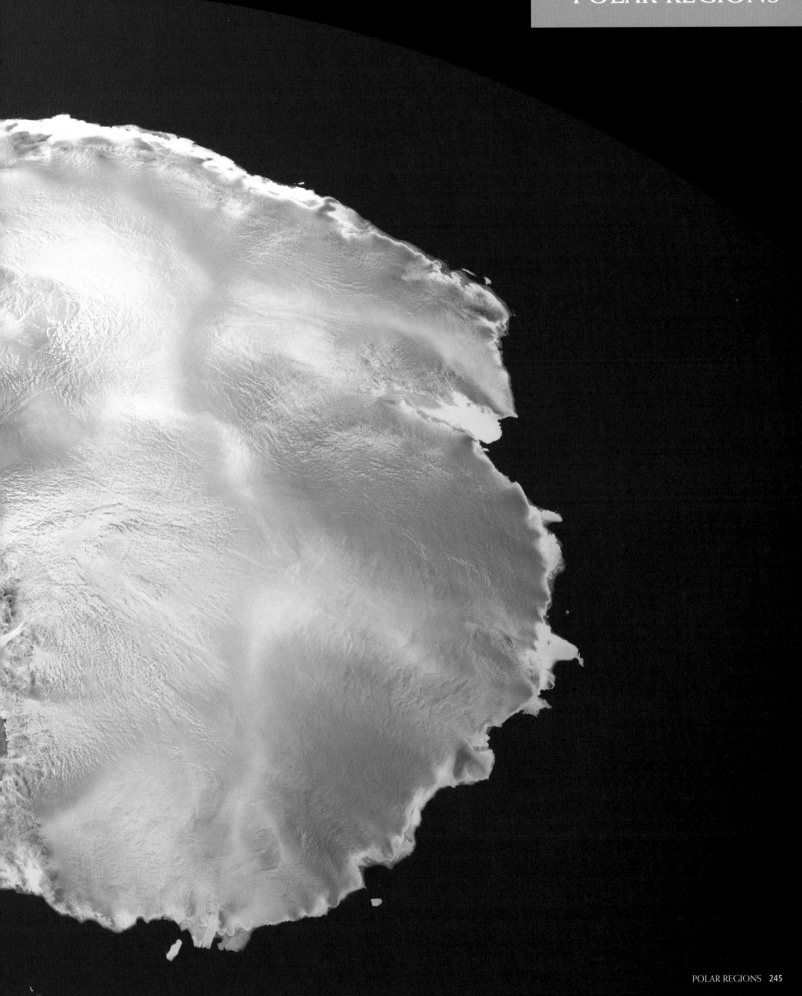

ICE

Pack ice responds to prevailing winds and ocean currents. Tabular icebergs up to 700 sq km in area sometimes break away from the northern edge of small ice shelves. These ice islands float slowly in erratic clockwise patterns around the North American side of the Arctic Ocean, completing full circuits in five to ten years, until they disintegrate or move into the Atlantic. Each year hundreds of much smaller bergs break off – calve – from the Greenland ice sheet and Canada's glaciers and move southward into the North Atlantic shipping lanes. After the sinking of the Titanic in 1912, leading maritime nations formed the International Ice Patrol to monitor icebergs and to study polar currents and iceberg dynamics.

*North Magnetic Pole

AZIMUTHAL EQUIDISTANT PROJECTION
SCALE 1:20,000,000

0 KILOMETERS   300 400 500

0 MILES   200   300   400   500

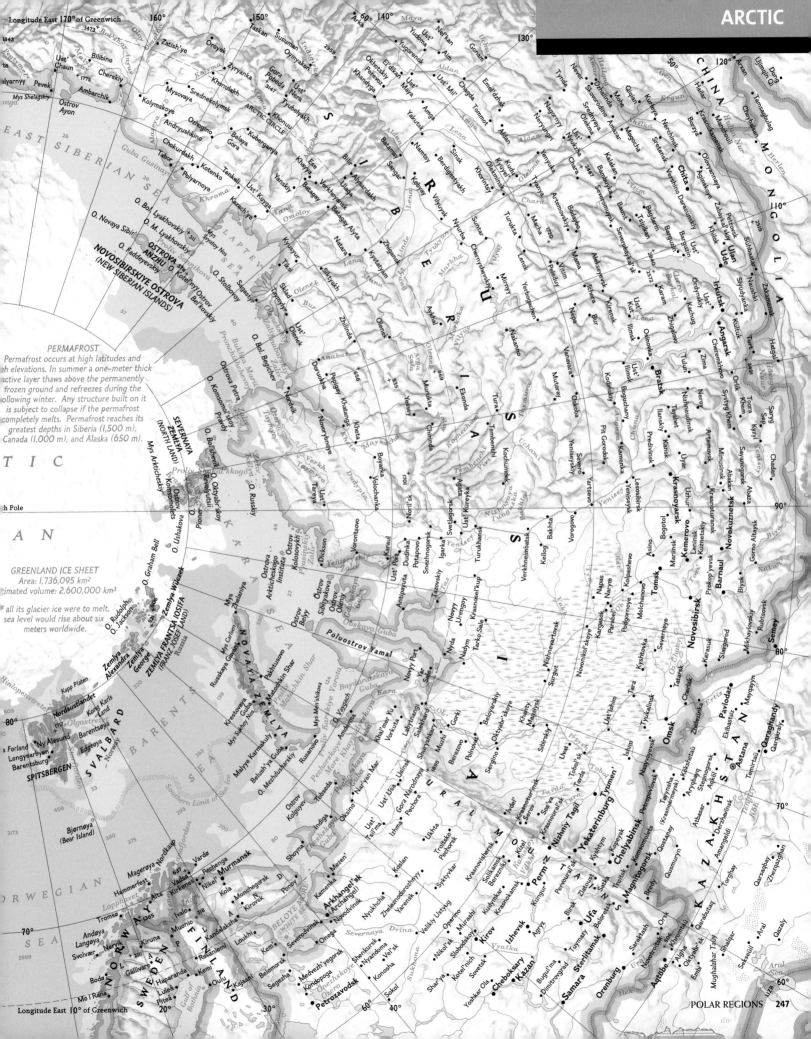

PERMAFROST

Permafrost occurs at high latitudes and high elevations. In summer a one-meter thick active layer thaws above the permanently frozen ground and refreezes during the following winter. Any structure built on it is subject to collapse if the permafrost completely melts. Permafrost reaches its greatest depths in Siberia (1,500 m), Canada (1,000 m), and Alaska (650 m).

GREENLAND ICE SHEET

Area: 1,736,095 km²
Estimated volume: 2,600,000 km³

If all its glacier ice were to melt, sea level would rise about six meters worldwide.

SOUTH ATLANTIC OCEAN

ANTARCTIC PENINSULA AREA STATIONS

Argentina
1 Jubany
Brazil
2 Comandante Ferraz
Chile
3 Escudero
4 General Bernardo O'Higgins
5 Presidente Eduardo Frei
China
6 Great Wall

Korea, South
7 King Sejong
Poland
8 Arctowski
Russia
9 Bellingshausen
Uruguay
10 Artigas

Research Stations: ● Year-round ○ Other

ICE SHELVES
Large areas of floating glacier ice fringe the coast of Antarctica. The two largest ice shelves are the Ross Ice Shelf and the Ronne Ice Shelf, both separated by glacier ice that is grounded below sea level. Large tabular icebergs periodically calve from ice shelves.

A SEA OF ICE
When winter comes, the ocean surface around Antarctica begins to freeze. Spreading over an average of 77,700 square kilometers (30,000 sq. miles) a day, the ring of sea ice eventually covers more than 18 million square kilometers (7 million sq. miles), an area larger than the continent itself. Reducing the ocean's absorption of atmospheric carbon dioxide and blocking ocean-atmosphere heat exchange, sea ice plays a role in shaping regional climate that in turn has impacts over much of the globe.

ANTARCTIC CONVERGENCE
About 1,600 km (990 mi) off-shore is the Antarctic Convergence, where cold waters meet warmer waters from the north, enclosing a distinct ecosystem sometimes called the Southern Ocean.

Longitude West of Greenwich

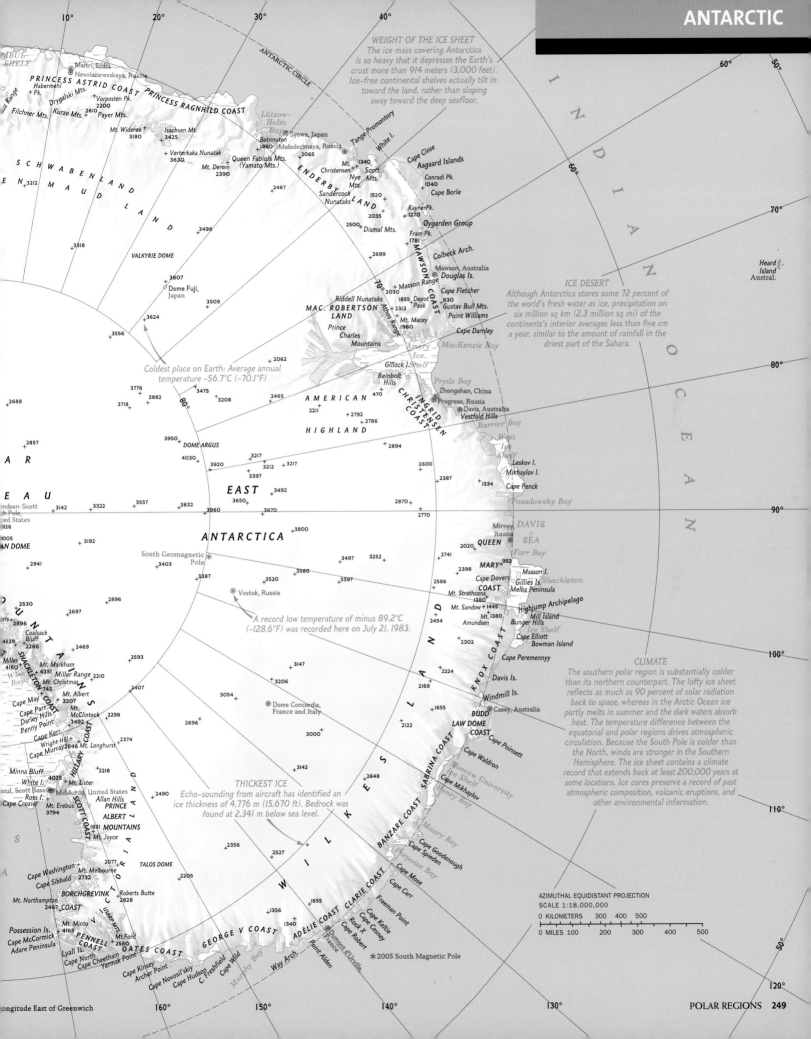

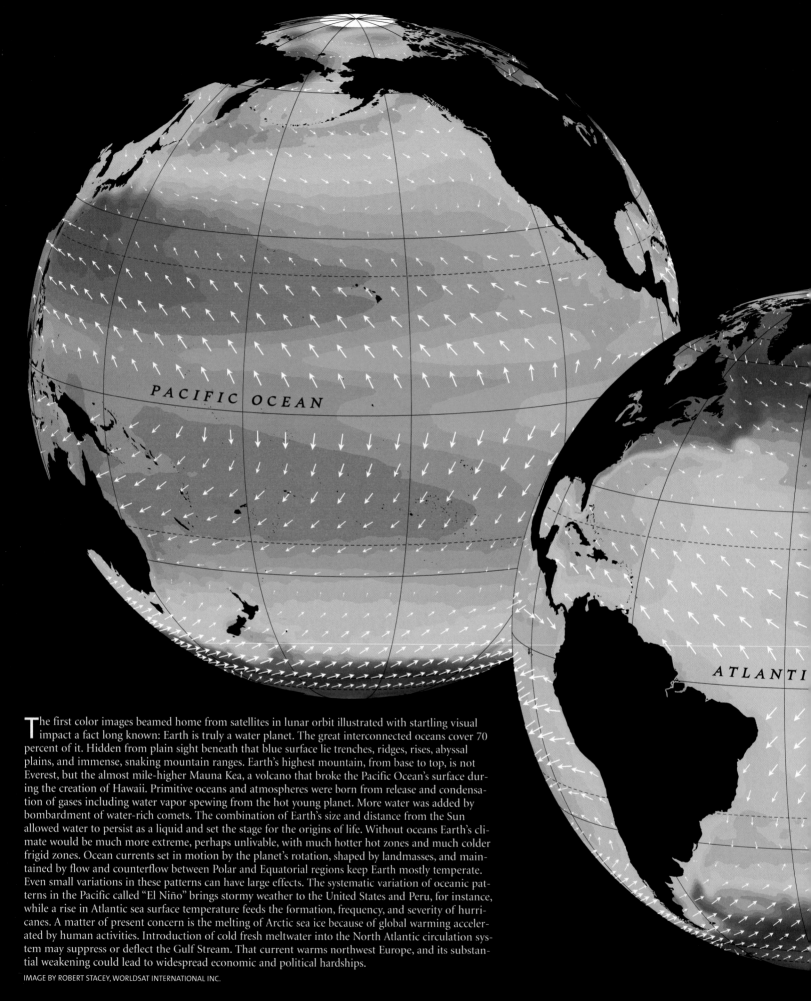

PACIFIC OCEAN

ATLANTI

The first color images beamed home from satellites in lunar orbit illustrated with startling visual impact a fact long known: Earth is truly a water planet. The great interconnected oceans cover 70 percent of it. Hidden from plain sight beneath that blue surface lie trenches, ridges, rises, abyssal plains, and immense, snaking mountain ranges. Earth's highest mountain, from base to top, is not Everest, but the almost mile-higher Mauna Kea, a volcano that broke the Pacific Ocean's surface during the creation of Hawaii. Primitive oceans and atmospheres were born from release and condensation of gases including water vapor spewing from the hot young planet. More water was added by bombardment of water-rich comets. The combination of Earth's size and distance from the Sun allowed water to persist as a liquid and set the stage for the origins of life. Without oceans Earth's climate would be much more extreme, perhaps unlivable, with much hotter hot zones and much colder frigid zones. Ocean currents set in motion by the planet's rotation, shaped by landmasses, and maintained by flow and counterflow between Polar and Equatorial regions keep Earth mostly temperate. Even small variations in these patterns can have large effects. The systematic variation of oceanic patterns in the Pacific called "El Niño" brings stormy weather to the United States and Peru, for instance, while a rise in Atlantic sea surface temperature feeds the formation, frequency, and severity of hurricanes. A matter of present concern is the melting of Arctic sea ice because of global warming accelerated by human activities. Introduction of cold fresh meltwater into the North Atlantic circulation system may suppress or deflect the Gulf Stream. That current warms northwest Europe, and its substantial weakening could lead to widespread economic and political hardships.

IMAGE BY ROBERT STACEY, WORLDSAT INTERNATIONAL INC.

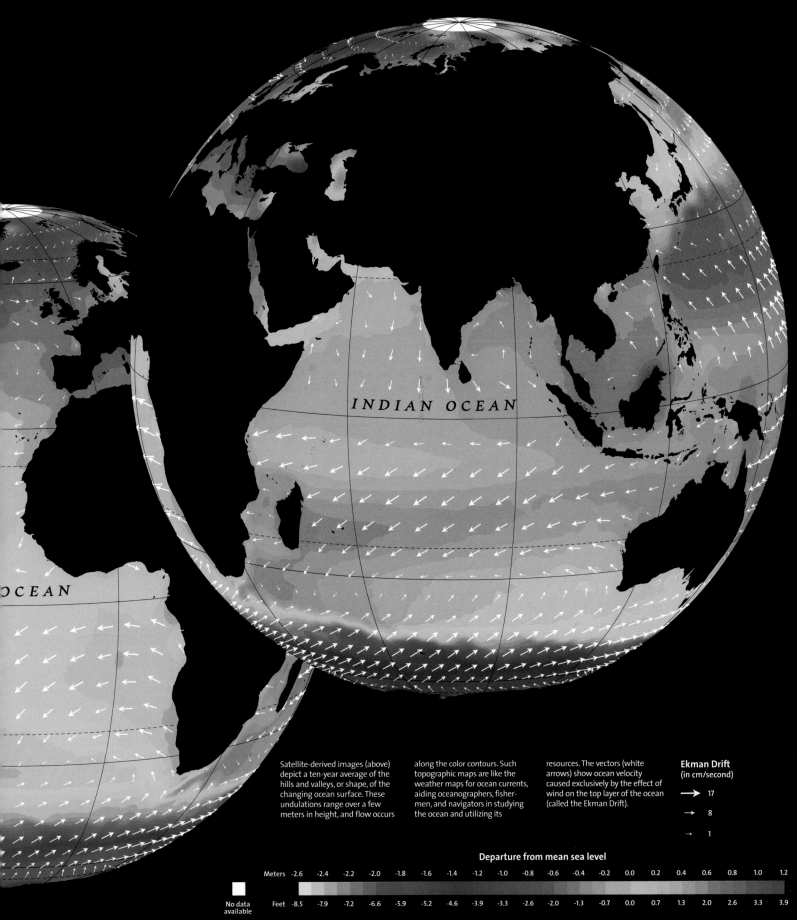

INDIAN OCEAN

OCEAN

Satellite-derived images (above) depict a ten-year average of the hills and valleys, or shape, of the changing ocean surface. These undulations range over a few meters in height, and flow occurs along the color contours. Such topographic maps are like the weather maps for ocean currents, aiding oceanographers, fishermen, and navigators in studying the ocean and utilizing its resources. The vectors (white arrows) show ocean velocity caused exclusively by the effect of wind on the top layer of the ocean (called the Ekman Drift).

Ekman Drift
(in cm/second)

→ 17

→ 8

→ 1

Departure from mean sea level

| Meters | -2.6 | -2.4 | -2.2 | -2.0 | -1.8 | -1.6 | -1.4 | -1.2 | -1.0 | -0.8 | -0.6 | -0.4 | -0.2 | 0.0 | 0.2 | 0.4 | 0.6 | 0.8 | 1.0 | 1.2 |

No data available

| Feet | -8.5 | -7.9 | -7.2 | -6.6 | -5.9 | -5.2 | -4.6 | -3.9 | -3.3 | -2.6 | -2.0 | -1.3 | -0.7 | 0.0 | 0.7 | 1.3 | 2.0 | 2.6 | 3.3 | 3.9 |

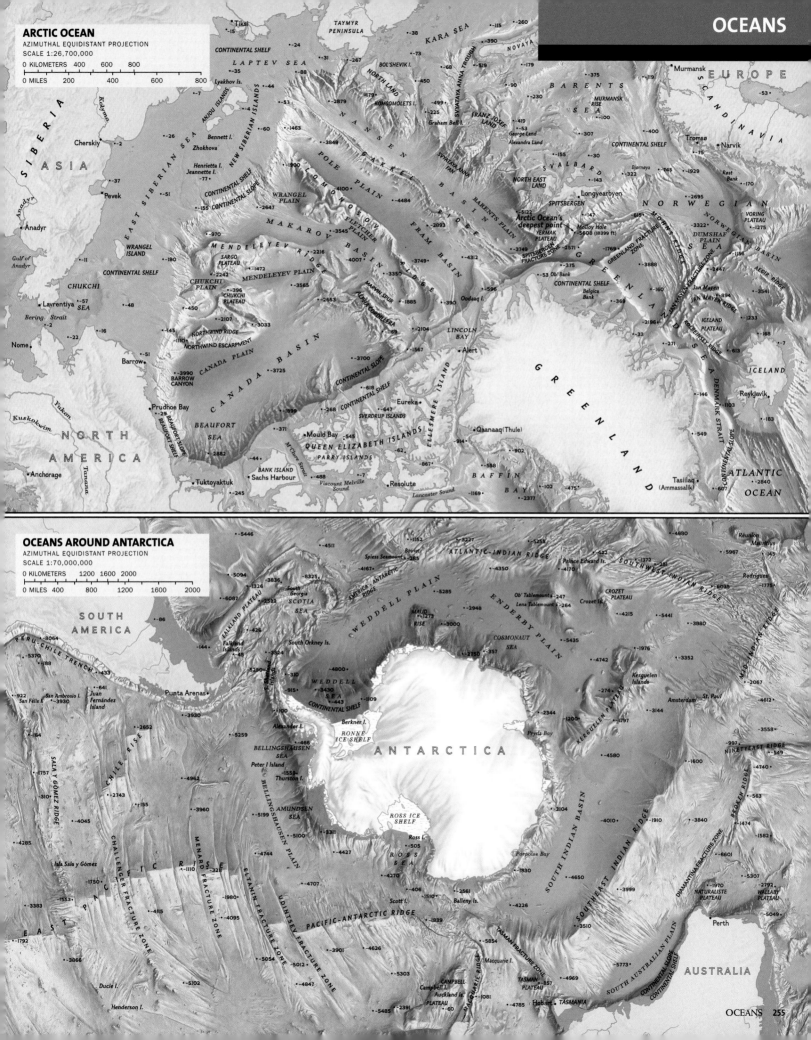

NATIONAL GEOGRAPHIC SOCIETY'S PLACE-NAMES POLICY

In keeping with the National Geographic Society's 118-year chartered purpose as a not-for-profit scientific and educational organization, the Society's cartographic policy is one of portraying de facto situations; that is, to portray to the best of our judgment a current reality. National Geographic strives to be apolitical, to consult multiple authoritative sources, and to make independent decisions based on extensive research. When there are conflicting or variant names, National Geographic does not purport to be the arbiter or determiner of a single name, but simply tries to provide the reader of the map sufficient information in which the reality of conflicting naming claims can be presented.

The Society's policy for naming geographic features is governed by a representative council of Society cartographers. This council meets frequently to assess available information about naming issues and, based on the best information and research available, seeks to make an independent judgment about future changes or clarifications on its maps, as well as to correct any errors. It is the policy of the Society to correct any errors as quickly as possible on the next published version of a particular map or Atlas.

Depending on the type of map (whether physical or political), the Society uses either conventional (English) or native spellings, or, where space permits, a combination of both. For example, when a commonly recognized form of a well-known place-name, such as Bombay, differs from the official national form – Mumbai—the conventional form is listed in parenthesis: Mumbai (Bombay). The Society does not follow any single source in making its naming determinations. Decisions regarding the naming assigned to geographic places, locations, bodies of water, and the like are checked against a number of external entities, including: the Board on Geographic Names; recognized reference books such as encyclopedias, dictionaries, geographical dictionaries, other atlases, independent academic texts and other similar sources; international bodies such as the United Nations, the European Community, and the like; as well as the policies of individual governmental entities. Names commonly recognized as alternatives or variants by such sources are often used on our maps. In such instances, the primary name is determined by using the form recognized by the de facto controlling country of the area, or by using the generally held conventional form of the name. On occasion where warranted and where space permits, explanatory notes stating the basis or context of a recognized variant naming are provided. Current examples of the application of this variant naming policy are: Falkland Islands (Islas Malvinas); Sea of Japan (East Sea).

National Geographic Maps frequently applies a secondary place-name in parenthesis ( ) after a recognized primary form of a place-name. This treatment is used even when the primary name is more widely recognized, provided that the variant name is used widely enough that National Geographic considers the inclusion of both to have real reference and educational value for the users of its products. Some instances of this use and examples are listed below.

Conventional Names
Used when the commonly recognized form (conventional) of a well-known place name differs from the official national form. The conventional form is listed in parenthesis. Conventional names are recognized as an official variant form for a place-name by multiple reference sources. On physical maps only the conventional form is generally used.

= Roma (Rome)
= Mumbai (Bombay)
= Ghazzah (Gaza)

If a feature crosses over multiple countries (usually a river), the official national form is labeled within that specific country with the conventional in parenthesis. As the feature moves into another country, then that country's official form is used as the primary name.

= Donau (Danube)
= Duna (Danube)
= Dunaj (Danube)
= Dunărea (Danube)
= Dunav (Danube)
= Dunay (Danube)

Historic Names
Given same treatment as conventional names.

= İstanbul (Constantinople)
= Guangzhou (Canton)
= Ho Chi Minh City (Saigon)

Variant Names: Similar to conventional names, but are not necessarily officially recognized as an official variant. Often used by the media.

= Al Fallūjah (Fallujah)

Names with shared possession
When a name (usually a border mountain) is jointly controlled by more then one country and has multiple official names, the general rule is to list the conventional name first and then list the official names together in parentheses. Order of the secondary names can vary. The country that is the main subject of the map would be first. If both countries are the subject of the map, the names are listed in order of the country.

• Mount Everest (Sagarmāthā, Qomolangma): for a map of South Asia when Nepal is the map subject.
• Mount Everest (Qomolangma, Sagarmāthā): for a map of China or when both countries are the map subject.

Disputed Names
When a name has differing forms recognized by different countries. The primary name is determined by using the form recognized by the de facto controlling country of the area, or using the generally held conventional form of the name.

Cyprus
= Lefkosia (Nicosia, Lefkoşa)
= Ammochostos (Famagusta, Gazimagusa)
= Keryneia (Kyrenia, Girne)
Dokdo
= Dokdo (Takeshima, Liancourt Rocks)
Southern Kuril Islands
= Iturup (Etorofu)
= Kunashir (Kunashiri)
Other Features
= English Channel (La Manche)
= Falkland Islands (Islas Malvinas)
= Sea of Japan (East Sea)

Possession Labels
National Geographic Maps applies possession labels in red type to non-contiguous territorial areas (generally islands), identifying the country that has political control of it. Where an area is controlled by one country but is also claimed by another, a longer red note identifying the controlling country and the party claiming ownership is given in red type.

= Falkland Islands (Islas Malvinas)-United Kingdom
   Administered by United Kingdom (claimed by Argentina)
= Paracel Islands-China
   Administered by China (claimed by Vietnam)
= Senkaku Shotō (Diaoyu Islands)-Japan
   Administered by Japan (claimed by China and Taiwan)

Map Notes
Where scale permits, explanatory notes, as those listed below, are added to our maps to explain the current political situation of disputed possessions or territories.

Abkhazia:
ABKHAZIA
Separatists defeated Georgian troops to gain control of this region in 1993-negotiations continue on resolving the conflict.

Cyprus:
DIVIDED CYPRUS
Cyprus was partitioned in 1974 following a coup backed by Greece and an invasion by Turkey. The island is composed of a Greek Cypriot south with an internationally recognized government and a Turkish Cypriot north (gray) with a government recognized only by Turkey. The UN patrols the dividing line and works toward reunification of the island.

Kashmir:
KASHMIR India and Pakistan both claim Kashmir-a disputed region of some 10 million people. India administers only the area south of the line of control; Pakistan controls northwestern Kashmir. China took eastern Kashmir from India in a 1962 war.

Kosovo:
KOSOVO
NATO ended ethnic fighting between Kosovo's Albanian majority and Serbian forces in 1999; Kosovo has been administered by the UN since that time.

Kuril Islands:
KURIL ISLANDS
The southern Kuril Islands of Iturup (Etorofu), Kunashir (Kunashiri), Shikotan, and the Habomai group were lost by Japan to the Soviet Union in 1945. Japan continues to claim these Russian-administered islands.

Nagorno-Karabakh:
NAGORNO-KARABAKH
Since a cease-fire in 1994 ethnic Armenians in Azerbaijan's Nagorno-Karabakh region have exercised autonomous control over the region. International mediation to resolve the conflict continues.

Somaliland:
SOMALILAND
In 1991 the Somali National Movement declared Somaliland an independent republic (in gray) with Hargeysa as the capital. It is not internationally recognized.

South Ossetia:
SOUTH OSSETIA
A 1992 cease-fire ended fighting between Ossetians and Georgians, but with no political settlement.

Taiwan:
TAIWAN (long form)
The People's Republic of China claims Taiwan as its 23rd province. Taiwan's government (Republic of China) maintains that there are two political entities. The Islands of Matsu, Pescadores, Pratas, and Quemoy are administered by Taiwan.

TAIWAN (short form)
The People's Republic of China claims Taiwan as its 23rd province. Taiwan's government (Republic of China) maintains that there are two political entities.

Transdniestria:
TRANSDNIESTRIA
Since the break-up of the Soviet Union, Ukrainian and Russian minorities have been struggling for independence from Moldova.

West Bank and Gaza:
WEST BANK & GAZA STRIP
Captured by Israel in the 1967 Six Day War, a 1993 peace agreement gives areas of the West Bank and Gaza limited Palestinian autonomy. The future for these autonomous areas and 3 million Palestinians is subject to Israeli-Palestinian negotiations.

Western Sahara:
WESTERN SAHARA
Western Sahara, formerly Spanish Sahara, was divided by Morocco and Mauritania in 1976. Morocco has administered the territory since Mauritania's withdrawal in August 1979. The United Nations does not recognize this annexation, and Western Sahara remains in dispute.

CONTINENT/Country	Capital	Language	Religion	Area sq km
NORTH AMERICA				
Antigua and Barbuda	Saint John's	English, local dialects	Anglican, other Protestant, Roman Catholic	442
Bahamas	Nassau	English, Creole	Baptist, Anglican, Roman Catholic	13,939
Barbados	Bridgetown	English	Protestant, Roman Catholic	430
Belize	Belmopan	English, Spanish, Mayan, Garífuna, Creole	Roman Catholic, Protestant	22,965
Canada	Ottawa	English, French	Roman Catholic, Protestant	9,984,670
Costa Rica	San José	Spanish, English	Roman Catholic, Evangelical	51,100
Cuba	La Habana (Havana)	Spanish	Roman Catholic, Protestant, Jehovah's Witness, Jewish, Santeria	110,860
Dominica	Roseau	English, French patios	Roman Catholic, Protestant	751
Dominican Republic	Santo Domingo	Spanish	Roman Catholic	48,442
El Salvador	San Salvador	Spanish, Nahua	Roman Catholic, Evangelical	21,041
Grenada	Saint George's	English, French patios	Roman Catholic, Anglican, other Protestant	344
Guatemala	Guatemala (Guatemala City)	Spanish, Amerindian languages	Roman Catholic, Protestant, indigenous Mayan beliefs	108,889
Haiti	Port-au-Prince	French, Creole	Roman Catholic, Protestant, Voodoo	27,750
Honduras	Tegucigalpa	Spanish, Amerindian dialects	Roman Catholic	112,492
Jamaica	Kingston	English, patois English	Protestant, Roman Catholic, other spiritual beliefs	10,991
Mexico	México (Mexico City)	Spanish, various Mayan, Nahuatl, and other indigenous languages	Roman Catholic, Protestant	1,964,375
Nicaragua	Managua	Spanish, English, indigenous languages	Roman Catholic, Protestant	130,000
Panama	Panamá (Panama City)	Spanish, English	Roman Catholic, Protestant	75,517
Saint Kitts and Nevis	Basseterre	English	Anglican, other Protestant	269
Saint Lucia	Castries	English, French patios	Roman Catholic, Protestant	616
Saint Vincent and the Grenadines	Kingstown	English, French patios	Anglican, Methodist, Roman Catholic, other Protestant	389
Trinidad and Tobago	Port-of-Spain	English, Hindi, French, Spanish	Roman Catholic, Hindu, Anglican, Muslim, Presbyterian	5,128
United States	Washington, D.C.	English, Spanish	Protestant, Roman Catholic, Jewish	9,826,630
NORTH AMERICA: TERRITORIES AND AREAS OF SPECIAL STATUS				
Denmark				
Greenland	Nuuk (Godthåb)	Greenlandic (East Inuit), Danish, English	Evangelical Lutheran	2,166,086
France				
Guadeloupe	Basse-Terre	French, Creole patios	Roman Catholic, Hindu, pagan African	1,706
Martinique	Fort-de-France	French, Creole patios	Roman Catholic, Protestant	1,101
Saint-Pierre and Miquelon	St.-Pierre	French	Roman Catholic	241
Netherlands				
Aruba	Oranjestad	Dutch, Papiamento, English, Spanish	Roman Catholic, Protestant	193
Netherlands Antilles	Willemstad, Curaçao	Dutch, Papiamento, English, Spanish	Roman Catholic, Protestant	809
United Kingdom				
Anguilla	The Valley	English	Anglican, Methodist	96
Bermuda	Hamilton	English, Portuguese	Protestant, Anglican, Roman Catholic	53
British Virgin Islands	Road Town	English	Methodist, Anglican	153
Cayman Islands	George Town	English	Protestant, Roman Catholic	262
Montserrat	Plymouth (abandoned)	English	Anglican, Methodist, Roman Catholic	102
Turks and Caicos Islands	Cockburn Town	English	Baptist, Anglican, Methodist	430
United States				
Navassa Island	Administered from Washington, D.C.	- - -	- - -	5
Puerto Rico	San Juan	Spanish, English	Roman Catholic, Protestant	9,084
Virgin Islands	Charlotte Amalie	English, Spanish, Creole	Protestant, Roman Catholic	386
SOUTH AMERICA				
Argentina	Buenos Aires	Spanish, English, Italian, German, French	Roman Catholic	2,780,400
Bolivia	La Paz (Administrative) Sucre (Constitutional)	Spanish, Quechua, Aymara	Roman Catholic	1,098,581
Brazil	Brasília	Portuguese, Spanish, English, French	Roman Catholic	8,547,403
Chile	Santiago	Spanish	Roman Catholic, Protestant	756,096
Colombia	Bogotá	Spanish	Roman Catholic	1,141,748
Ecuador	Quito	Spanish, Quechua	Roman Catholic	283,560
Guyana	Georgetown	English, Amerindian dialects, Creole, Hindi, Urdu	Christian, Hindu, Muslim	214,969
Paraguay	Asunción	Spanish, Guaraní	Roman Catholic	406,752
Peru	Lima	Spanish, Quechua, Aymara	Roman Catholic	1,285,216
Suriname	Paramaribo	Dutch, English, Sranang Tongo (Taki-Taki), Hindustani, Javanese	Hindu, Protestant (Moravian), Roman Catholic, Muslim	163,265
Uruguay	Montevideo	Spanish, Portunol, Brazilero	Roman Catholic	176,215
Venezuela	Caracas	Spanish, indigenous dialects	Roman Catholic	912,050
SOUTH AMERICA: TERRITORIES AND AREAS OF SPECIAL STATUS				
France				
French Guiana	Cayenne	French	Roman Catholic	86,504
United Kingdom				
Falkland Islands	Stanley	English	Anglican, Roman Catholic	12,173
EUROPE				
Albania	Tiranë (Tirana)	Albanian, Greek	Muslim, Albanian Orthodox, Roman Catholic	28,748
Andorra	Andorra la Vella	Catalan, French, Castilian (Spanish)	Roman Catholic	468
Austria	Wien (Vienna)	German	Roman Catholic, Protestant	83,858
Belarus	Minsk	Belarusian, Russian	Eastern Othodox, Roman Catholic, Protestant, Jewish, Muslim	207,595
Belgium	Bruxelles (Brussels)	Dutch, French, German	Roman Catholic, Protestant	30,528
Bosnia and Herzegovina	Sarajevo	Croatian, Serbian, Bosnian	Muslim, Orthodox, Roman Catholic	51,129
Bulgaria	Sofiya (Sofia)	Bulgarian	Bulgarian Orthodox, Muslim	110,994
Croatia	Zagreb	Croatian	Roman Catholic, Orthodox	56,542
Cyprus	Lefkosia (Lefkosa, Nicosia)	Greek, Turkish, English	Greek Orthodox, Muslim	9,251
Czech Republic	Praha (Prague)	Czech	Roman Catholic, Protestant, atheist	78,866
Denmark	København (Copenhagen)	Danish, Faroese, Greenlandic	Evangelical Lutheran	43,098
Estonia	Tallinn	Estonian, Russian, Ukrainian	Evangelical Lutheran, Russian Orthodox, Eastern Orthodox	45,227
Finland	Helsinki (Helsingfors)	Finnish, Swedish	Evangelical Lutheran	338,145
France	Paris	French	Roman Catholic	543,965
Germany	Berlin	German	Protestant, Roman Catholic	357,022
Greece	Athína (Athens)	Greek	Greek Orthodox	131,957
Hungary	Budapest	Hungarian	Roman Catholic, Calvinist, Lutheran	93,030
Iceland	Reykjavik	Icelandic, English, Nordic languages, German	Evangelical Lutheran	103,000
Ireland	Baile Átha Cliath (Dublin)	English, Irish	Roman Catholic	70,273
Italy	Roma (Rome)	Italian, German, French, Slovene	Roman Catholic	301,333
Latvia	Riga	Latvian, Lithuanian, Russian	Lutheran, Roman Catholic, Russian Orthodox	64,589
Liechtenstein	Vaduz	German, Alemannic dialect	Roman Catholic, Protestant	160
Lithuania	Vilnius	Lithuanian, Polish, Russian	Roman Catholic, Lutheran, Russian Orthodox, Protestant	65,300
Luxembourg	Luxembourg	Luxembourgish, German, French	Roman Catholic	2,586
Macedonia	Skopje	Macedonian, Albanian, Turkish	Macedonian Orthodox, Muslim	25,713
Malta	Valletta	Maltese, English	Roman Catholic	316
Moldova	Chisinau	Moldovan, Russian, Gagauz	Eastern Orthodox	33,800
Monaco	Monaco	French, English, Italian, Monegasque	Roman Catholic	2
Netherlands	Amsterdam	Dutch, Frisian	Roman Catholic, Protestant, Muslim	41,528

Area (sq mi)	Population Mid-2005 (in 1,000s)	Projected pop. change 2005-2050	Pop density sq km (sq mi)	Urban pop.	Natural increase	Total fertility / infant mortality rate	Pop. <15 / >65	Life expectancy: Male/Female	HIV/AIDS Pop. 15-49 2003-04	CONTINENT / Country Formal Name
										NORTH AMERICA
(171)	80	0%	181 (468)	37%	1.39%	2.30 / 20.90	26.40% / 7.80%	69.00 / 73.80	- - -	Antigua and Barbuda
(5,382)	319	46%	23 (59)	89%	1.17%	2.20 / 12.70	29.60% / 5.20%	66.60 / 72.73	3.00%	Commonwealth of The Bahamas
(166)	258	-2%	600 (1,554)	50%	0.63%	1.80 / 13.20	21.80% / 11.80%	70.00 / 74.10	1.50%	Barbados
(8,867)	292	64%	13 (33)	49%	2.25%	3.30 / 31.00	36.30% / 4.10%	66.70 / 73.50	2.40%	Belize
(3,855,101)	32,225	14%	3 (8)	79%	0.30%	1.50 / 5.40	17.90% / 13.10%	77.20 / 82.10	0.30%	Canada
(19,730)	4,331	46%	85 (220)	59%	1.33%	2.00 / 9.25	30.00% / 5.60%	76.30 / 81.10	0.60%	Republic of Costa Rica
(42,803)	11,275	-2%	102 (263)	76%	0.44%	1.50 / 5.80	20.90% / 10.30%	75.29 / 79.09	0.10%	Republic of Cuba
(290)	70	17%	93 (241)	71%	0.80%	1.90 / 22.20	27.80% / 7.90%	71.20 / 77.20	- - -	Commonwealth of Dominica
(18,704)	8,862	50%	183 (474)	64%	1.70%	2.90 / 31.00	33.60% / 5.20%	66.40 / 69.30	1.70%	Dominican Republic
(8,124)	6,881	57%	327 (847)	59%	2.03%	3.00 / 24.60	32.90% / 5.00%	67.10 / 73.00	0.70%	Republic of El Salvador
(133)	101	-14%	294 (759)	39%	1.16%	2.10 / 17.40	35.00% / 7.80%	- - - / - - -	- - -	Grenada
(42,042)	12,701	120%	117 (302)	39%	2.79%	4.40 / 39.00	41.90% / 4.00%	63.01 / 68.87	1.10%	Republic of Guatemala
(10,714)	8,288	127%	299 (774)	36%	1.87%	4.70 / 80.30	41.80% / 3.40%	51.00 / 53.70	5.60%	Republic of Haiti
(43,433)	7,212	104%	64 (166)	47%	2.79%	4.10 / 32.00	41.40% / 3.80%	67.40 / 74.30	1.80%	Republic of Honduras
(4,244)	2,666	28%	243 (628)	52%	1.29%	2.30 / 24.40	30.70% / 7.20%	71.80 / 75.20	1.20%	Jamaica
(758,449)	107,029	30%	54 (141)	75%	1.85%	2.60 / 24.90	30.60% / 4.80%	73.10 / 77.60	0.30%	United Mexican States
(50,193)	5,774	88%	44 (115)	59%	2.70%	3.80 / 35.50	41.90% / 3.10%	65.65 / 70.36	0.20%	Republic of Nicaragua
(29,157)	3,232	55%	43 (111)	62%	1.76%	2.70 / 20.64	29.30% / 5.60%	72.25 / 77.36	0.90%	Republic of Panama
(104)	48	33%	178 (462)	33%	0.98%	2.30 / 16.70	28.00% / 8.30%	67.58 / 71.65	- - -	Federation of Saint Kitts and Nevis
(238)	163	44%	265 (685)	30%	0.99%	2.20 / 14.20	30.40% / 7.40%	72.00 / 76.70	- - -	Saint Lucia
(150)	111	-12%	285 (740)	55%	1.13%	2.10 / 18.10	30.40% / 6.30%	70.30 / 73.70	- - -	Saint Vincent and the Grenadines
(1,980)	1,305	-6%	254 (659)	74%	0.65%	1.60 / 18.60	21.20% / 6.60%	67.31 / 73.73	3.20%	Republic of Trinidad and Tobago
(3,794,083)	296,483	42%	30 (78)	79%	0.58%	2.00 / 6.60	20.90% / 12.40%	74.80 / 80.10	0.60%	United States of America
										NORTH AMERICA: TERRITORIES AND AREAS OF SPECIAL STATUS
(836,086)	57	0%	0.03 (0.07)	83%	0.85%	2.40 / 8.90	25.90% / 5.40%	64.10 / 69.50	- - -	Overseas Region of Denmark
(658)	450*	5%	264 (684)	100%	1.04%	2.20 / 6.40	23.10% / 8.90%	74.50 / 81.10	- - -	French Overseas Department
(425)	397	10%	361 (934)	95%	0.66%	2.00 / 7.50	23.10% / 10.10%	75.20 / 81.70	- - -	French Overseas Department
(93)	7	-14%	29 (75)	89%	0.25%	- - - / 0	19.90% / 11.48%	- - - / - - -	- - -	French Overseas Territorial Collectivity
(75)	97	13%	503 (1,293)	47%	0.70%	2.00 / 2.60	21.00% / 10.60%	75.30 / 82.20	- - -	Overseas Region of the Netherlands
(312)	187	35%	231 (605)	69%	0.78%	2.20 / 8.80	23.40% / 9.60%	72.10 / 78.70	- - -	Overseas Region of the Netherlands
(37)	13	23%	135 (351)	100%	0.61%	1.70 / 14.40	28.00% / 8.00%	77.90 / 78.02	- - -	British Overseas Territory
(21)	62	2%	1,170 (2,952)	100%	0.67%	2.10 / 0	19.40% / 11.30%	75.20 / 79.30	- - -	British Overseas Territory
(59)	22	55%	144 (373)	61%	1.05%	2.00 / 17.86	25.61% / 4.91%	70.20 / 78.60	- - -	British Overseas Territory
(101)	44	105%	168 (436)	100%	1.18%	2.20 / 8.00	22.00% / 7.10%	76.70 / 81.80	- - -	British Overseas Territory
(39)	5	0%	49 (128)	13%	-0.30%	- - - / - - -	22.70% / 16.43%	- - - / - - -	- - -	British Overseas Territory
(166)	21	100%	49 (127)	45%	1.98%	3.20 / 16.90	32.50% / 3.70%	72.30 / 76.80	- - -	British Overseas Territory
(2)	0	- - -	- - - / - - -	- - -	- - -	- - - / - - -	- - - / - - -	- - - / - - -	- - -	Territory of the United States
(3,507)	3,912	-4%	431 (1,115)	94%	0.65%	1.80 / 9.80	22.20% / 12.20%	72.90 / 80.70	- - -	Self-Governing Commonwealth in Association with the United States
(149)	109	-6%	282 (732)	93%	0.93%	2.30 / 3.10	24.40% / 9.70%	74.90 / 82.70	- - -	Territory of the United States
										SOUTH AMERICA
(1,073,518)	38,592	39%	14 (36)	89%	1.06%	2.40 / 16.80	27.20% / 9.90%	70.60 / 78.10	0.70%	Argentine Republic
(424,164)	8,922	62%	8 (21)	63%	2.11%	3.85 / 54.00	37.10% / 4.30%	61.80 / 65.99	0.10%	Republic of Bolivia
(3,300,169)	184,184	41%	22 (56)	81%	1.41%	2.40 / 27.00	28.90% / 5.80%	67.60 / 75.20	0.70%	Federative Republic of Brazil
(291,930)	16,136	27%	21 (55)	87%	1.03%	2.05 / 7.80	24.20% / 7.20%	72.99 / 79.04	0.30%	Republic of Chile
(440,831)	46,039	44%	40 (104)	75%	1.68%	2.60 / 25.60	31.70% / 4.90%	69.17 / 75.32	0.70%	Republic of Colombia
(109,483)	13,032	56%	46 (119)	61%	2.12%	3.30 / 29.00	33.23% / 6.69%	71.30 / 77.00	0.30%	Republic of Ecuador
(83,000)	751	-35%	3 (9)	36%	1.28%	2.30 / 49.00	28.40% / 4.80%	59.81 / 65.86	2.50%	Co-operative Republic of Guyana
(157,048)	6,158	67%	15 (39)	54%	1.73%	2.90 / 37.00	32.30% / 4.40%	68.60 / 73.12	0.50%	Republic of Paraguay
(496,224)	27,947	53%	22 (56)	73%	1.61%	2.70 / 33.00	32.20% / 5.20%	67.34 / 72.42	0.50%	Republic of Peru
(63,037)	447	-4%	3 (7)	74%	1.42%	2.60 / 26.00	29.10% / 5.80%	65.75 / 72.51	1.70%	Republic of Suriname
(68,037)	3,419	23%	19 (50)	93%	0.59%	2.20 / 15.00	23.80% / 13.30%	71.29 / 79.20	0.30%	Oriental Republic of Uruguay
(352,144)	26,749	57%	29 (76)	87%	1.80%	2.70 / 19.58	30.70% / 4.60%	69.90 / 75.81	0.70%	Bolivarian Republic of Venezuela
										SOUTH AMERICA: TERRITORIES AND AREAS OF SPECIAL STATUS
(33,400)	195	91%	2 (6)	75%	2.63%	3.90 / 12.40	35.00% / 3.80%	71.70 / 79.20	- - -	French Overseas Department
(4,700)	3	3%	0.25 (0.64)	79%	0.55%	- - - / - - -	- - - / - - -	- - - / - - -	- - -	British Overseas Territory
										EUROPE
(11,100)	3,170	13%	110 (286)	42%	0.93%	2.00 / 8.40	27.29% / 8.10%	71.70 / 76.40	- - -	Republic of Albania
(181)	74	-3%	158 (409)	92%	0.71%	1.30 / 3.86	14.90% / 12.60%	- - - / - - -	- - -	Principality of Andorra
(32,378)	8,151	0%	97 (252)	54%	0.05%	1.40 / 4.50	16.30% / 15.49%	75.90 / 81.60	0.30%	Republic of Austria
(80,153)	9,776	-13%	47 (122)	72%	-0.55%	1.20 / 7.70	16.20% / 14.30%	62.70 / 74.70	- - -	Republic of Belarus
(11,787)	10,458	5%	343 (887)	97%	0.05%	1.60 / 4.40	17.40% / 17.02%	75.58 / 81.69	0.20%	Kingdom of Belgium
(19,741)	3,840	-19%	75 (195)	43%	0.09%	1.20 / 7.60	18.30% / 12.20%	71.30 / 76.50	< 0.05%	Bosnia and Herzegovina
(42,855)	7,741	-34%	70 (181)	70%	-0.52%	1.30 / 11.60	14.20% / 17.10%	68.70 / 75.60	< 0.05%	Republic of Bulgaria
(21,831)	4,438	-14%	78 (203)	56%	-0.29%	1.30 / 6.30	16.60% / 16.30%	71.20 / 78.30	< 0.05%	Republic of Croatia
(3,572)	965	12%	104 (270)	65%	0.40%	1.60 / 6.20	20.49% / 10.90%	74.80 / 79.10	- - -	Republic of Cyprus
(30,450)	10,212	-8%	129 (335)	77%	-0.09%	1.20 / 3.70	15.20% / 13.90%	72.03 / 78.51	0.10%	Czech Republic
(16,640)	5,418	1%	126 (326)	72%	0.16%	1.80 / 4.39	18.90% / 14.90%	74.89 / 79.48	0.20%	Kingdom of Denmark
(17,462)	1,345	-23%	30 (77)	69%	-0.28%	1.50 / 7.00	15.97% / 16.18%	66.04 / 76.90	1.10%	Republic of Estonia
(130,558)	5,246	1%	16 (40)	62%	0.19%	1.80 / 3.10	17.50% / 15.90%	75.30 / 82.30	0.10%	Republic of Finland
(210,026)	60,742	5%	112 (289)	76%	0.43%	1.90 / 3.90	18.57% / 16.40%	76.70 / 83.80	0.40%	French Republic
(137,847)	82,490	-9%	231 (598)	88%	-0.14%	1.30 / 4.32	14.70% / 18.00%	75.59 / 81.34	0.10%	Federal Republic of Germany
(50,949)	11,100	-4%	84 (218)	60%	0.01%	1.30 / 5.10	14.60% / 17.50%	76.40 / 81.10	0.20%	Hellenic Republic
(35,919)	10,086	-12%	108 (281)	65%	-0.37%	1.30 / 6.60	15.60% / 15.50%	68.29 / 76.53	0.10%	Republic of Hungary
(39,769)	295	21%	3 (7)	94%	0.83%	2.00 / 2.40	22.60% / 11.80%	78.70 / 82.50	0.20%	Republic of Iceland
(27,133)	4,125	14%	59 (152)	60%	0.83%	2.00 / 4.78	20.85% / 11.15%	75.10 / 80.30	0.10%	Republic of Ireland
(116,345)	58,742	-11%	195 (505)	90%	0.04%	1.30 / 4.80	14.20% / 19.20%	76.80 / 82.50	0.50%	Italian Republic
(24,938)	2,300	-23%	36 (92)	68%	-0.50%	1.30 / 9.40	15.40% / 16.20%	65.90 / 76.90	0.60%	Republic of Latvia
(62)	35	26%	219 (565)	21%	0.39%	1.30 / 2.90	18.00% / 10.80%	78.70 / 82.10	- - -	Principality of Liechtenstein
(25,212)	3,415	-16%	52 (135)	67%	-0.31%	1.30 / 7.90	17.70% / 15.00%	66.48 / 77.85	0.10%	Republic of Lithuania
(998)	457	41%	177 (458)	91%	0.41%	1.60 / 3.85	18.80% / 14.10%	74.90 / 81.50	0.20%	Grand Duchy of Luxembourg
(9,928)	2,039	-2%	79 (205)	59%	0.44%	1.50 / 11.30	20.40% / 10.80%	70.80 / 75.70	< 0.05%	Republic of Macedonia
(122)	405	-10%	1,282 (3,320)	91%	0.21%	1.50 / 7.20	18.20% / 13.00%	75.78 / 80.48	0.20%	Republic of Malta
(13,050)	4,206	-21%	124 (322)	45%	-0.18%	1.20 / 14.40	19.80% / 9.90%	64.50 / 71.60	0.20%	Republic of Moldova
(1)	33	67%	16,500 (33,000)	100%	0.64%	- - - / - - -	13.23% / 22.43%	- - - / - - -	- - -	Principality of Monaco
(16,034)	16,296	4%	392 (1,016)	62%	0.35%	1.70 / 4.14	18.55% / 13.80%	76.20 / 80.80	0.20%	Kingdom of the Netherlands

CONTINENT/Country	Capital	Language	Religion	Area sq km
Norway	Oslo	Norwegian	Evangelical Lutheran	323,758
Poland	Warszawa (Warsaw)	Polish	Roman Catholic	312,685
Portugal	Lisboa (Lisbon)	Portuguese, Mirandese	Roman Catholic	92,345
Romania	Bucuresti (Bucharest)	Romanian, Hungarian, German	Eastern Orthodox, Protestant, Catholic	238,391
Russia	Moskva (Moscow)	Russian	Russian Orthodox, Muslim, other	17,075,400
San Marino	San Marino	Italian	Roman Catholic	61
Serbia and Montenegro	Belgrade (Administrative) Podgorica (Judicial)	Serbian, Albanian	Orthodox, Muslim, Roman Catholic	102,173
Slovakia	Bratislava (Pressburg)	Slovak, Hungarian	Roman Catholic, atheist, Protestant	49,035
Slovenia	Ljubljana	Slovenian, Serbo-Croatian	Roman Catholic, other	20,273
Spain	Madrid	Castilian Spanish, Catalan, Galician, Basque	Roman Catholic	505,988
Sweden	Stockholm	Swedish	Lutheran, Roman Catholic	449,964
Switzerland	Bern	German, French, Romanisch	Roman Catholic, Protestant	41,284
Ukraine	Kyiv (Kiev)	Ukrainian, Russian, Romanian, Polish, Hungarian	Ukrainian Orthodox, Ukrainian Catholic (Uniate), Protestant, Jewish	603,700
United Kingdom	London	English, Welsh, Scottish form of Gaelic	Anglican, Roman Catholic, other Protestant, Muslim	242,910
Vatican City	Vatican City	Italian, Latin, French	Roman Catholic	0.4
EUROPE: TERRITORIES AND AREAS OF SPECIAL STATUS				
Denmark				
Faroe Islands	Tórshavn	Faroese, Danish	Evangelical Lutheran	1,399
Norway				
Jan Mayen	Administered from Svalbard	- - -	- - -	373
Svalbard	Longyearbyen	Norwegian, Russian	Evangelical Lutheran, Russian Orthodox	62,049
United Kingdom				
Channel Islands (Guernsey and Jersey)	Saint Peter Port, Guernsey Saint Helier, Jersey	English, French, Norman French dialect	Anglican, Roman Catholic, Baptist	194
Gibraltar	Gibraltar	English, Spanish, Italian, Portuguese	Roman Catholic, Church of England	7
Isle of Man	Douglas	English, Manx Gaelic	Anglican, Roman Catholic, Methodist, Baptist	572
ASIA				
Afghanistan	Kabol (Kabul)	Pashtu, Afghan Persian (Dari), Uzbek, Turkmen, 30 minor languages	Sunni and Shiite Muslim	652,090
Armenia	Yerevan	Armenian, Russian	Armenian Apostolic	29,743
Azerbaijan	Baku	Azerbaijani, Russian, Armenian	Muslim, Russian Orthodox, Armenian Orthodox	86,600
Bahrain	Al Manamah (Manama)	Arabic, English, Farsi, Urdu	Shiite and Sunni Muslim	717
Bangladesh	Dhaka	Bangla (Bengali), English	Muslim, Hindu	147,570
Bhutan	Thimphu	Dzonkha, Tibetan and Nepali dialects	Lamaistic Buddhist, Hindu	46,500
Brunei	Bandar Seri Begawan	Malay, English, Chinese	Muslim, Buddhist, Christian, indigenous beliefs	5,765
Cambodia	Phnom Penh	Khmer, French, English	Theravada Buddhist	181,035
China	Beijing (Peking)	Chinese (Mandarin), Cantonese, other dialects and minority languages	Toist, Buddhist, Muslim	9,596,960
Georgia	T'bilisi (Tiflis)	Georgian, Russian, Armenian, Azeri	Georgian Orthodox, Muslim, Russian Orthodox	69,700
India	New Delhi	Hindi, English, 14 other official languages	Hindu, Muslim, Christian, Sikh, Buddhist, Jain, Parsi	3,287,270
Indonesia	Jakarta	Bahasa Indonesia, English, Dutch, Javanese, and other local dialects	Muslim, Protestant, Roman Catholic, Hindu, Buddhist	1,922,570
Iran	Tehran	Persian, Turkic, Kurdish, various local dialects	Shiite and Sunni Muslim	1,648,000
Iraq	Baghdad	Arabic, Kurdish, Assyrian, Armenian	Shiite and Sunni Muslim	437,072
Israel	Jerusalem (Yerushalayim, Al-Quds)	Hebrew, Arabic, English	Jewish, Muslim, Christian	22,145
Japan	Tokyo	Japanese	Shinto, Buddhist	377,887
Jordan	Amman	Arabic, English	Sunni Muslim, Christian	89,342
Kazakhstan	Astana	Kazakh (Qazaq), Russian	Muslim, Russian Orthodox	2,717,300
Korea, North	Pyongyang	Korean	Buddhist, Confucianist	120,538
Korea, South	Seoul	Korean, English widely taught	Christian, Buddhist	99,250
Kuwait	Kuwait City	Arabic, English	Sunni and Shiite Muslim, Christian, Hindu, Parsi	17,818
Kyrgyzstan	Bishkek	Kyrgyz, Russian	Muslim, Russian Orthodox	199,900
Laos	Viangchan (Vientiane)	Lao, French, English, varous ethnic languages	Buddhist, Animist, other	236,800
Lebanon	Beyrouth (Beirut)	Arabic, French, English, Armenian	Muslim, Christian	10,452
Malaysia	Kuala Lumpur	Bahasa Melayu, English, Chinese /regional dialects, indigenous languages	Muslim, Buddhist, Daoist, Hindu, Christian, Sikh, Shamanist	329,847
Maldives	Maale (Male)	Maldivian Dhivehi, (dialect of Sinhala), English	Sunni Muslim	298
Mongolia	Ulaanbaatar (Ulan Bator)	Khalkha Mongol, Turkic, Russian	Tibetan Buddhist, Lamaism	1,564,116
Myanmar (Burma)	Yangon (Rangoon)	Burmese, minor languages	Buddhist, Christian, Muslim	676,552
Nepal	Kathmandu	Nepali, English, many other languages and dialects	Hindu, Buddhist, Muslim	147,181
Oman	Masqat (Muscat)	Arabic, English, Baluchi, Urdu, Indian dialects	Ibadhi Muslim, Sunni Muslim, Shiite Muslim, Hindu	309,500
Pakistan	Islamabad	Punjabi, Sindhi, Siraiki, Pashtu, Urdu, English	Sunni and Shiite Muslim, Christian, Hindu	796,095
Philippines	Manila	Filipino (based on Tagalog), English, and 8 major dialects	Roman Catholic, Protestant, Muslim, Buddhist	300,000
Qatar	Ad Dawhah (Doha)	Arabic, English	Muslim	11,521
Saudi Arabia	Ar Riyad (Riyadh)	Arabic	Muslim	1,960,582
Singapore	Singapore	Chinese, Malay, Tamil, English	Buddhist, Muslim, Christian, Hindu, Sikh, Taoist, Confucianist	660
Sri Lanka	Colombo	Sinhala, Tamil, English	Buddhist, Hindu, Christian, Muslim	65,525
Syria	Dimashq (Damascus)	Arabic, Kurdish, Armenian, Aramaic, Circassian, French, English	Sunni, Alawite, Druze and other Muslim sects, Christian	185,180
Tajikistan	Dushanbe	Tajik, Russian	Sunni and Shiite Muslim	143,100
Thailand	Krung Thep (Bangkok)	Thai, English, ethnic and regional dialects	Buddhist, Muslim	513,115
Timor-Leste (East Timor)	Dili	Tetum, Portuguese, Bahasa, Indonesian, English	Christian (mostly Roman Catholic)	14,609
Turkey	Ankara (Angora)	Turkish, Kurdish, Arabic, Armenian, Greek	Muslim (mostly Sunni)	779,452
Turkmenistan	Asgabat (Ashgabat)	Turkmen, Russian, Uzbek	Muslim, Eastern Orthodox	488,100
United Arab Emirates	Abu Zaby (Abu Dhabi)	Arabic, Persian, English, Hindi, Urdu	Sunni and Shiite Muslim, Christian, Hindu,	77,700
Uzbekistan	Toshkent (Tashkent)	Uzbek, Russian, Tajik	Muslim, Eastern Orthodox	447,400
Vietnam	Hanoi	Vietnamese, English, French, Chinese, Khmer, local languages	Buddhist, Hoa Hao, Cao Dai, Christian, indigenous beliefs, Muslim	331,114
Yemen	Sana (Sanaa)	Arabic	Sunni and Shiite Muslim	536,869
ASIA: TERRITORIES AND AREAS OF SPECIAL STATUS				
China				
Hong Kong	- - -	Chinese (Cantonese), English	Local religions, Christian	1092
Macau	- - -	Portuguese, Chinese (Cantonese)	Buddhist, Roman Catholic	25
Taiwan	Taipei (Taipei)	Mandarin Chinese, Taiwanese	Mixture of Buddhist, Confucian, and Taoist; Christian	35,980
Israel - Palestinian Areas	- - -	Arabic, Hebrew, English	Muslim (mostly Sunni), Jewish, Christian	- - -
Gaza Strip	- - -	Arabic, Hebrew, English	Muslim (mostly Sunni), Jewish	365
West Bank	- - -	Arabic, Hebrew, English	Muslim (mostly Sunni), Jewish, Christian	5,655
United Kingdom				
British Indian Ocean Territory	Administered from London	English	- - -	44
AFRICA				
Algeria	Alger (Algiers)	Arabic, French, Berber dialects	Sunni Muslim	2,381,741
Angola	Luanda	Portuguese, Bantu	Indigenous beliefs, Roman Catholic, Protestant	1,246,700
Benin	Cotonou (Administrative) Porto-Novo (Constitutional)	French, Fon, Yoruba, tribal languages	Indigenous beliefs, Christian, Muslim	112,622
Botswana	Gaborone	English, Setswana	Indigenous beliefs, Christian	581,730
Burkina Faso	Ouagadougou	French, native African languages	Muslim, indigenous beliefs, Christian	274,200
Burundi	Bujumbura	Kirundi, French, Swahili	Roman Catholic, indigenous beliefs, Muslim, Protestant	27,834
Cameroon	Yaoundé	French, English, 24 major African language groups	Indigenous beliefs, Christian, Muslim	475,442
Cape Verde	Praia	Portuguese, Crioulo (Kriolu)	Roman Catholic, Protestant	4,036
Central African Republic	Bangui	French, Sangho, Arabic, tribal languages	Indigenous beliefs, Protestant, Roman Catholic, Muslim	622,984
Chad	N'Djamena	French, Arabic, Sara, Sango, more than 120 different languages and dialects	Muslim, Christian, animist	1,284,000

Area (sq mi)	Population Mid-2005 (in 1,000s)	Projected pop. change 2005-2050	Pop density sq km (sq mi)	Urban pop.	Natural increase	Total fertility / infant mortality rate	Pop. <15 / >65	Life expectancy: Male / Female	HIV/AIDS Pop. 15-49 2003-04	CONTINENT / Country Formal Name
(125,004)	4,620	21%	14 (37)	78%	0.34%	1.80 / 3.20	19.70% / 14.70%	77.50 / 82.33	0.10%	Kingdom of Norway
(120,728)	38,163	-15%	122 (316)	62%	0.02%	1.20 / 6.75	17.20% / 12.96%	70.52 / 78.90	0.10%	Republic of Poland
(35,655)	10,576	-12%	115 (297)	53%	0.04%	1.40 / 4.10	15.70% / 16.80%	74.00 / 80.57	0.40%	Portuguese Republic
(92,043)	21,612	-29%	91 (235)	53%	-0.19%	1.30 / 16.70	16.40% / 14.40%	67.50 / 74.80		Romania
(6,592,850)	143,025	-23%	8 (22)	73%	-0.55%	1.40 / 12.40	15.70% / 13.40%	58.80 / 72.00	1.10%	Russian Federation
(24)	30	0%	492 (1,250)	84%	0.33%	1.20 / 6.70	15.00% / 16.00%	77.80 / 84.20	- - -	Republic of San Marino
(39,450)	10,722	-10%	105 (272)	52%	0.16%	1.70 / 10.20	19.47% / 14.10%	70.70 / 75.60	0.20%	Serbia and Montenegro
(18,932)	5,382	-12%	110 (284)	56%	0.01%	1.20 / 7.80	17.60% / 11.60%	69.80 / 77.80	< 0.05%	Slovak Republic
(7,827)	1,998	-5%	99 (255)	51%	-0.10%	1.20 / 4.00	14.47% / 15.20%	73.20 / 80.70	< 0.05%	Republic of Slovenia
(195,363)	43,484	1%	86 (223)	76%	0.13%	1.30 / 3.57	14.50% / 16.80%	76.90 / 83.60	0.70%	Kingdom of Spain
(173,732)	9,029	18%	20 (52)	84%	0.11%	1.70 / 3.10	17.57% / 17.25%	78.35 / 82.68	0.10%	Kingdom of Sweden
(15,940)	7,446	-4%	180 (467)	68%	0.17%	1.40 / 4.30	16.20% / 15.80%	77.90 / 83.00	0.40%	Swiss Confederation
(233,090)	47,110	-29%	78 (202)	68%	-0.70%	1.20 / 9.50	15.27% / 15.53%	62.64 / 74.06	1.40%	Ukraine
(93,788)	60,068	12%	247 (640)	89%	0.17%	1.70 / 5.20	18.34% / 15.97%	75.90 / 80.50	0.20%	United Kingdom of Great Britain and Northern Ireland
(0.2)	0.798	25%	1,995 (3,990)	100%	-0.90%	- - - / - - -	- - - / - - -	- - - / - - -	- - -	State of the Vatican City (The Holy See)
										EUROPE: TERRITORIES AND AREAS OF SPECIAL STATUS
(540)	50	16%	36 (93)	38%	0.70%	2.50 / 2.80	23.60% / 13.20%	77.00 / 81.00	- - -	Overseas Region of Denmark
(144)	0	- - -	- - - - - -	- - -	- - -	- - - / - - -	- - - / - - -	- - - / - - -	- - -	Norwegian Dependency
(23,957)	3	-0.02%	.05 (.13)	- - -	-1.99%	- - - / - - -	- - - / - - -	- - - / - - -	0.00%	Norwegian Dependency
(75)	149	15%	768 (1,987)	31%	0.23%	1.40 / 3.40	14.70% / 12.60%	75.54 / 80.33	- - -	British Crown Dependencies
(3)	29	-7%	4,143 (9,667)	100%	0.48%	- - - / 5.50	- - - / - - -	- - - / - - -	- - -	British Overseas Territory
(221)	78	6%	136 (353)	52%	0.01%	1.60 / 3.30	17.80% / 16.70%	- - - / - - -	- - -	British Crown Dependency
										ASIA
(251,773)	29,929	174%	46 (119)	22%	2.56%	6.80 / 171.90	44.90% / 2.40%	41.40 / 41.80	- - -	Transitional Islamic State of Afghanistan
(11,484)	3,033	8%	102 (264)	65%	0.25%	1.40 / 36.10	22.31% / 10.78%	67.49 / 74.97	0.10%	Republic of Armenia
(33,436)	8,388	38%	97 (251)	51%	0.99%	2.00 / 9.80	26.40% / 6.80%	69.60 / 75.20	< 0.05%	Republic of Azerbaijan
(277)	731	58%	1,020 (2,639)	87%	1.81%	2.80 / 8.00	27.90% / 2.52%	73.10 / 74.80	0.20%	Kingdom of Bahrain
(56,977)	144,233	60%	977 (2,531)	23%	1.88%	3.00 / 65.00	34.66% / 3.38%	61.00 / 61.80	- - -	People's Republic of Bangladesh
(17,954)	970	108%	21 (54)	21%	2.55%	4.70 / 60.50	40.00% / 4.30%	61.65 / 64.74	- - -	Kingdom of Bhutan
(2,226)	363	62%	63 (163)	74%	1.88%	2.60 / 8.30	31.80% / 2.60%	71.70 / 76.60	< 0.05%	Negara Brunei Darussalam
(69,898)	13,329	85%	74 (191)	15%	2.18%	4.50 / 95.10	37.10% / 3.20%	52.13 / 59.62	2.60%	Kingdom of Cambodia
(3,705,405)	1,303,701	10%	136 (352)	37%	0.59%	1.60 / 27.20	21.50% / 7.60%	70.40 / 73.70	0.10%	People's Republic of China
(26,911)	4,501	-19%	65 (167)	52%	0.01%	1.40 / 24.80	18.60% / 13.30%	68.00 / 74.80	0.10%	Republic of Georgia
(1,269,221)	1,103,596	48%	336 (870)	28%	1.68%	3.00 / 60.00	35.90% / 4.43%	60.80 / 62.50	0.90%	Republic of India
(742,308)	221,932	39%	115 (299)	42%	1.56%	2.60 / 45.70	29.71% / 4.72%	66.44 / 70.44	0.10%	Republic of Indonesia
(636,296)	69,515	47%	42 (109)	67%	1.20%	2.10 / 32.10	29.70% / 4.30%	68.83 / 71.74	0.10%	Islamic Republic of Iran
(168,754)	28,807	121%	66 (171)	68%	2.72%	5.10 / 94.00	42.00% / 2.80%	57.30 / 60.40	< 0.05%	Republic of Iraq
(8,550)	7,105	55%	321 (831)	92%	1.55%	2.90 / 5.10	28.35% / 9.90%	77.50 / 81.50	0.10%	State of Israel
(145,902)	127,728	-21%	338 (875)	79%	0.08%	1.30 / 2.80	13.80% / 19.80%	78.36 / 85.33	< 0.05%	Japan
(34,495)	5,795	79%	65 (168)	79%	2.40%	3.70 / 22.10	36.90% / 3.00%	70.60 / 72.40	< 0.05%	Hashemite Kingdom of Jordan
(1,049,155)	15,079	-1%	6 (14)	57%	0.58%	2.00 / 61.00	27.20% / 7.50%	60.50 / 71.50	0.20%	Republic of Kazakhstan
(46,540)	22,912	15%	190 (492)	60%	0.92%	2.00 / 21.00	27.00% / 7.90%	68.70 / 74.20	- - -	Democratic People's Republic of Korea
(38,321)	48,294	-12%	487 (1,260)	80%	0.51%	1.20 / 5.10	19.10% / 9.10%	73.38 / 80.44	< 0.05%	Republic of Korea
(6,880)	2,589	172%	145 (376)	96%	1.73%	4.00 / 9.60	25.60% / 1.60%	76.70 / 78.50	- - -	State of Kuwait
(77,182)	5,172	60%	26 (67)	35%	1.34%	2.60 / 55.00	33.00% / 6.00%	64.50 / 72.20	0.10%	Kyrgyz Republic
(91,429)	5,924	96%	25 (65)	19%	2.33%	4.80 / 88.00	40.20% / 3.50%	53.25 / 55.75	0.10%	Lao People's Democratic Republic
(4,036)	3,779	31%	362 (936)	87%	1.58%	2.20 / 17.20	28.10% / 6.20%	71.90 / 75.10	0.10%	Lebanese Republic
(127,355)	26,121	80%	79 (205)	62%	2.09%	3.30 / 10.00	33.00% / 4.60%	70.40 / 76.20	0.40%	Malaysia
(115)	294	83%	987 (2,557)	27%	1.40%	2.80 / 18.00	36.10% / 4.20%	71.30 / 72.30	- - -	Republic of Maldives
(603,909)	2,646	46%	2 (4)	57%	1.55%	2.50 / 58.00	31.00% / 3.60%	61.90 / 65.90	< 0.05%	Mongolia
(261,218)	50,519	26%	75 (193)	29%	1.22%	2.70 / 75.00	29.30% / 4.60%	57.35 / 62.93	1.20%	Union of Myanmar
(56,827)	25,371	89%	172 (446)	14%	2.21%	3.70 / 64.40	38.50% / 3.50%	61.76 / 62.50	0.50%	Kingdom of Nepal
(119,500)	2,436	50%	8 (20)	76%	1.83%	3.40 / 16.20	32.82% / 2.78%	72.22 / 75.43	0.10%	Sultanate of Oman
(307,374)	162,420	82%	204 (528)	34%	2.41%	4.80 / 85.10	41.80% / 4.00%	60.90 / 62.60	0.10%	Islamic Republic of Pakistan
(115,831)	84,765	68%	283 (732)	48%	2.26%	3.50 / 29.00	35.49% / 3.94%	66.93 / 72.18	< 0.05%	Republic of the Philippines
(4,448)	768	44%	67 (173)	92%	1.79%	3.30 / 11.20	25.40% / 2.20%	69.40 / 72.10	- - -	State of Qatar
(756,985)	24,573	101%	13 (32)	86%	2.73%	4.50 / 23.00	37.20% / 2.70%	69.93 / 73.76	- - -	Kingdom of Saudi Arabia
(255)	4,296	21%	6,509 (16,847)	100%	0.53%	1.30 / 1.90	20.10% / 7.99%	77.40 / 81.30	0.20%	Republic of Singapore
(25,299)	19,722	14%	301 (780)	30%	1.30%	2.00 / 11.20	26.70% / 6.40%	70.70 / 75.40	< 0.05%	Democratic Socialist Republic of Sri Lanka
(71,498)	18,389	91%	99 (257)	50%	2.67%	3.70 / 22.30	37.10% / 3.20%	70.60 / 73.10	< 0.05%	Syrian Arab Republic
(55,251)	6,813	60%	48 (123)	27%	2.32%	4.10 / 89.00	40.00% / 4.00%	60.85 / 66.13	< 0.05%	Republic of Tajikistan
(198,115)	65,002	13%	127 (328)	31%	0.72%	1.70 / 20.00	22.80% / 7.30%	67.90 / 75.00	1.50%	Kingdom of Thailand
(5,640)	947	245%	65 (168)	8%	2.70%	6.40 / 94.00	41.30% / 2.80%	54.14 / 56.25	- - -	Democratic Republic of Timor-Leste
(300,948)	72,907	38%	94 (242)	65%	1.39%	2.40 / 38.30	29.30% / 5.60%	66.40 / 71.00	- - -	Republic of Turkey
(188,456)	5,240	40%	11 (28)	47%	1.56%	2.90 / 73.90	32.10% / 4.40%	58.24 / 66.74	< 0.05%	Turkmenistan
(30,000)	4,618	101%	59 (154)	78%	1.36%	2.50 / 7.90	25.30% / 0.97%	75.50 / 79.76	- - -	United Arab Emirates
(172,742)	26,444	45%	59 (153)	37%	1.59%	2.70 / 61.70	34.70% / 4.70%	63.32 / 69.72	0.10%	Republic of Uzbekistan
(127,844)	83,305	38%	252 (652)	26%	1.29%	2.20 / 18.00	29.20% / 6.50%	70.00 / 73.00	0.40%	Socialist Republic of Vietnam
(207,286)	20,727	243%	39 (100)	26%	3.30%	6.20 / 74.80	45.70% / 3.90%	58.80 / 62.50	0.10%	Republic of Yemen
										ASIA: TERRITORIES AND AREAS OF SPECIAL STATUS
(422)	6,921	27%	6,338 (16,400)	100%	0.17%	1.00 / 2.50	14.90% / 12.00%	78.60 / 84.60	0.10%	Special Administrative Region of China
(10)	474	13%	18,960 (47,400)	99%	0.39%	0.80 / 3.47	17.10% / 8.10%	- - - / - - -	- - -	Special Administrative Region of China
(13,891)	22,731	-13%	632 (1,636)	78%	0.36%	1.20 / 5.35	19.34% / 9.48%	73.35 / 79.05	- - -	
- - -	3,762	197%	625 (1,619)	57%	3.40%	5.60 / 20.70	45.50% / 3.10%	70.70 / 73.80	- - -	Areas of Special Status
(141)	- - -	- - -	- - - - - -	- - -	- - -	- - - / - - -	- - - / - - -	- - - / - - -	- - -	Area of Special Status
(2,183)	- - -	- - -	- - - - - -	- - -	- - -	- - - / - - -	- - - / - - -	- - - / - - -	- - -	Area of Special Status
(17)	- - -	- - -	- - - - - -	- - -	- - -	- - - / - - -	- - - / - - -	- - - / - - -	- - -	British Overseas Territory
										AFRICA
(919,595)	32,814	35%	14 (36)	49%	1.53%	2.40 / 31.60	30.70% / 5.20%	72.50 / 74.40	0.10%	People's Democratic Republic of Algeria
(481,354)	15,375	173%	12 (32)	33%	2.56%	6.80 / 139.00	45.60% / 2.40%	38.85 / 41.99	3.90%	Republic of Angola
(43,484)	8,439	162%	75 (194)	40%	2.92%	5.90 / 105.00	43.60% / 2.60%	52.97 / 54.52	1.90%	Republic of Benin
(224,607)	1,640	-14%	3 (7)	54%	-0.34%	3.10 / 56.80	39.40% / 3.80%	34.20 / 35.30	37.30%	Republic of Botswana
(105,869)	13,925	184%	51 (132)	17%	2.53%	6.20 / 81.00	46.00% / 2.90%	42.19 / 44.70	1.80%	Burkina Faso
(10,747)	7,795	193%	280 (725)	9%	2.84%	6.80 / 66.90	46.60% / 2.60%	48.70 / 49.80	6.00%	Republic of Burundi
(183,569)	16,380	88%	34 (89)	48%	2.26%	5.00 / 74.00	43.60% / 3.00%	47.10 / 49.00	5.50%	Republic of Cameroon
(1,558)	476	94%	118 (306)	53%	2.26%	4.00 / 31.00	41.90% / 6.20%	66.16 / 72.16	- - -	Republic of Cape Verde
(240,535)	4,238	53%	7 (18)	41%	1.74%	4.90 / 94.10	43.20% / 4.20%	43.20 / 44.40	13.50%	Central African Republic
(495,755)	9,657	206%	8 (19)	24%	2.72%	6.30 / 101.00	48.00% / 2.80%	45.00 / 48.40	4.80%	Republic of Chad

CONTINENT/Country	Capital	Language	Religion	Area sq km
Comoros	Moroni	Arabic, French, Shikomoro	Sunni Muslim, Roman Catholic	1,862
Congo	Brazzaville	French, Lingala, Monokutuba	Christian, animist, Muslim	342,000
Congo, Dem. Rep. of the	Kinshasa (Léopoldville)	French, Lingala, Kingwana, Kikongo, Tshiluba	Roman Catholic, Protestant, Kimbanguist, Muslim, traditional	2,344,885
Côte d'Ivoire (Ivory Coast)	Abidjan (Administrative) Yamoussoukro (Legislative)	French, Dioula, 60 native dialects	Christian, Muslim, indigenous beliefs	322,462
Djibouti	Djibouti	French, Arabic, Somali, Afar	Muslim, Christian	23,200
Egypt	El Qâhira (Cairo)	Arabic, English, French	Sunni Muslim, Coptic Christian	1,002,000
Equatorial Guinea	Malabo	Spanish, French, pidgin English, Fang Bubi, Ibo	Roman Catholic, pagan practices	28,051
Eritrea	Asmara	Afar, Arabic, Tigre, Kunama, Tigrinya	Muslim, Coptic Christian, Roman Catholic, Protestant	121,144
Ethiopia	Adis Abeba (Addis Ababa)	Amharic, Tigrinya, Orominga, Guaraginga, Somali, Arabic	Muslin, Ethiopian Orthodox, animist	1,133,380
Gabon	Libreville	French, Fang, Myene, Nzebi, Bapounou/Eschira, Bandjabi	Christian, indigenous beliefs	267,667
Gambia	Banjul	English, Mandinka, Wolof, Fula	Muslim, Christian	11,295
Ghana	Accra	English, Akan, Moshi-Dagomba, Ewe, Ga	Christian, indigenous beliefs, Muslim	238,537
Guinea	Conakry	French, local languages	Muslim, Christian, indigenous beliefs	245,857
Guinea-Bissau	Bissau	Portuguese, Crioulo, African languages	Indigenous beliefs, Muslim, Christian	36,125
Kenya	Nairobi	English, Kiswahili, numerous indigenous languages	Protestant, Roman Catholic, indigenous beliefs, Muslim	580,367
Lesotho	Maseru	English, Sesotho, Zulu, Xhosa	Christian, indigenous beliefs	30,355
Liberia	Monrovia	English, 20 ethnic languages	Indigenous beliefs, Christian, Muslim	111,370
Libya	Tarabulus (Tripoli)	Arabic, Italian, English	Sunni Muslim	1,759,540
Madagascar	Antananarivo	French, Malagasy	Indigenous beliefs, Christian, Muslim	587,041
Malawi	Lilongwe	English, Chichewa	Protestant, Roman Catholic, Muslim	118,484
Mali	Bamako	French, Bambara, numerous African languages	Muslim, indigenous beliefs	1,240,192
Mauritania	Nouakchott	Hassaniya Arabic, Wolof, Pulaar, Soninke, French	Muslim	1,030,700
Mauritius	Port Louis	English, French, Creole, Hindi, Urdu, Hakka, Bhojpuri	Hindu, Christian, Muslim, Protestant	2,040
Morocco	Rabat	Arabic, Berber dialects, French	Muslim	710,850
Mozambique	Maputo	Portuguese, indigenous dialects	Indigenous beliefs, Christian, Muslim	799,380
Namibia	Windhoek	English, Afrikaans, German, indigenous languages	Christian, indigenous beliefs	824,292
Niger	Niamey	French, Hausa, Djerma	Muslim, indigenous beliefs, Christian	1,267,000
Nigeria	Abuja	English, Hausa, Yoruba, Igbo, Fulani	Muslim, Christian, indigenous beliefs	923,768
Rwanda	Kigali	Kinyarwanda, French, English, Kiswahili	Roman Catholic, Protestant, Adventist, Muslim	26,338
Sao Tome and Principe	SãoTomé	Portuguese	Roman Catholic, Evangelical, Protestant, Seventh-Day Adventist	1,001
Senegal	Dakar	French, Wolof, Pulaar Diola, Jola, Mandinka	Muslim, Christian	196,722
Seychelles	Victoria	English, French, Creole	Roman Catholic, Anglican	455
Sierra Leone	Freetown	English, Mende, Temne, Krio	Muslim, indigenous beliefs, Christian	71,740
Somalia	Muqdisho (Mogadishu)	Somali, Arabic, Italian, English	Sunni Muslim	637,657
South Africa	Pretoria(Tshwane)(Admin.) Bloenfontein (Judicial) Cape Town (Legislative)	Afrikaans, English, Ndebele, Pedi, Sotho, Swazi, Tsonga, Tswana, Venda, Xhosa,	Christian, indigenous beliefs, Muslim, Hindu	1,219,090
Sudan	Khartoum	Arabic, Nubian, Ta Bedawie, many local dialects	Sunni Muslim, indigenous beliefs, Christian	2,505,813
Swaziland	Mbabane (Administrative) Lobamba (Legislative and Royal)	English, siSwati	Indigenous beliefs, Roman Catholic, Muslim	17,363
Tanzania	Dar es Salaam (Administrative) Dodoma (Legislative)	Kiswahili, Kiungujo, English, Arabic, many local languages	Christian, Muslim, indigenous beliefs	945,087
Togo	Lomé	French, Ewe, Mina, Kabye, Dagomba	Indigenous beliefs, Christian, Muslim	56,785
Tunisia	Tunis	Arabic, French	Muslim	163,610
Uganda	Kampala	English, Ganda, Luganda, many local languages	Roman Catholic, Protestant, indigenous beliefs, Muslim	241,139
Zambia	Lusaka	English, indigenous languages	Christian, Muslim, Hindu	752,614
Zimbabwe	Harare	English, Shona, Sindebele	Syncretic (part Christian, part indigenous beliefs), Christian,	390,757

AFRICA: TERRITORIES AND AREAS OF SPECIAL STATUS

France				
Mayotte	Mamoudzou	Mahorian, French	Muslim, Christian	374
Réunion	St.-Denis	French, Creole	Roman Catholic, Hindu, Muslim, Buddhist	2,507
Morocco				
Western Sahara	- - -	Hassaniya Arabic, Moroccan Arabic	Muslim	252,120
Norway				
Bouvet Island	Administered from Oslo	- - -	- - -	59
South Africa				
Prince Edward Islands	Administered from Bisho, Eastern Cape Province	- - -	- - -	335
United Kingdom				
Saint Helena	Jamestown	English	Anglican (majority)	411

AUSTRALIA & OCEANIA

Australia	Canberra, A.T.C.	English, native languages	Protestant, Roman Catholic	7,692,024
Fiji Islands	Suva	English, Fijian, Hindustani	Christian, Hindu, Muslim	18,376
Kiribati	Tarawa	English, I-Kiribati	Roman Catholic, Protestant	811
Marshall Islands	Majuro	English, Marshallese, Japanese	Christian (mostly Protestant)	181
Micronesia	Palikir	English, Turkese, Pohnpeian, Yapese, Kosraean, Ulithian	Roman Catholic, Protestant	702
Nauru	Yaren	Nauruan, English	Protestant, Roman Catholic	21
New Zealand	Wellington	English, Maori	Protestant, Roman Catholic	270,534
Palau	Koror	English, Palauan, Japanese, 3 additional local languages	Roman Catholic, Protestant, Modekngei (indigenous)	489
Papua New Guinea	Port Moresby	715 indigenous languages	Protestant, indigenous beliefs, Roman Catholic	462,840
Samoa	Apia	Samoan, English	Christian	2,831
Solomon Islands	Honiara	Melanesian pidgin, 120 indigenous languages, English	Protestant, Roman Catholic, indigenous beliefs	28,304
Tonga	Nuku'alofa	Tongan, English	Christian	748
Tuvalu	Funafuti	Tuvaluan, English, Samoan	Church of Tuvalu (Congregationalist), Seventh-Day Adventist, Baha'i	26
Vanuatu	Port-Vila	English, French, more than 100 local languages	Protestant, Catholic, indigenous beliefs	12,190

AUSTRALIA & OCEANIA: TERRITORIES AND AREAS OF SPECIAL STATUS

Australia				
Ashmore and Cartier Islands	Administered from Canberra, A.T.C.	- - -	- - -	5
Christmas Island	The Settlement	English, Chinese, Malay	Buddhist, Muslim, Christian	135
Cocos (Keeling) Islands	West Island	Malay (Cocos dialect), English	Sunni Muslim	14
Coral Sea Islands Territory	Administered from Canberra, A.T.C.	- - -	- - -	3
Norfolk Island	Kingston	English, Norfolk	Protestant, Roman Catholic	35
France				
Clipperton Island	- - -	- - -	- - -	7
French Polynesia	Papeete, Tahiti	French, Tahitian	Protestant, Roman Catholic	4,167
New Caledonia	Nouméa	French, 33 Melanesia-Polynesian dialects	Roman Catholic, Protestant	19,060
Wallis and Futuna	Matā'utu	French, Wallisian (indigenous Polynesian language)	Roman Catholic	161
New Zealand				
Cook Islands	Avarua	English, Maori	Christian	240
Niue	Alofi	Niuean, English	Ekalesia Niue (a Protestant Church)	263
Tokelau	Administered from Wellington	Tokelauan, English	Congregational Christian Church	12
United Kingdom				
Pitcairn Islands	Adamstown	English, Pitcairnese	Seventh-Day Adventist	47
United States				
American Samoa	Pago Pago	Samoan, English	Christian Congregationalist	233
Baker Island	Administered from Washington, D.C.	- - -	- - -	2
Guam	Hagâtña (Agana)	English, Chamorro, Japanese	Roman Catholic	561
Northern Mariana Islands	Saipan	English, Chamorro, Carolinian	Christian, traditional beliefs	464

Area (sq mi)	Population Mid-2005 (in 1,000s)	Projected pop. change 2005-2050	Pop density sq km (sq mi)	Urban pop.	Natural increase	Total fertility / infant mortality rate	Pop. <15 / >65	Life expectancy: Male / Female	HIV/AIDS Pop. 15-49 2003-04	CONTINENT / Country Formal Name
(719)	671	173%	360 (933)	33%	3.04%	5.40 / 96.30	42.70% / 2.90%	57.90 / 62.30	- - -	Union of the Comoros
(132,047)	3,999	243%	12 (30)	52%	3.09%	6.30 / 72.00	45.60% / 2.90%	50.62 / 53.09	4.90%	Republic of the Congo
(905,365)	60,764	201%	26 (67)	30%	3.06%	6.70 / 94.70	47.70% / 2.50%	49.00 / 51.80	4.20%	Democratic Republic of the Congo
(124,503)	18,154	87%	56 (146)	46%	2.23%	5.20 / 118.00	41.10% / 3.10%	45.80 / 47.80	7.00%	Republic of Côte d'Ivoire
(8,958)	793	95%	34 (89)	82%	1.85%	4.20 / 99.80	41.00% / 2.70%	51.08 / 53.84	2.90%	Republic of Djibouti
(386,874)	74,033	70%	74 (191)	43%	2.01%	3.20 / 37.00	36.30% / 4.50%	67.49 / 71.83	< 0.05%	Arab Republic of Egypt
(10,831)	504	127%	18 (47)	45%	2.29%	5.90 / 102.00	42.50% / 3.80%	43.45 / 45.55	- - -	Republic of Equatorial Guinea
(46,774)	4,670	118%	39 (100)	19%	2.62%	5.40 / 49.70	44.80% / 3.40%	56.10 / 59.00	2.70%	State of Eritrea
(437,600)	77,431	120%	68 (177)	15%	2.50%	5.90 / 100.00	43.78% / 2.98%	46.51 / 48.61	4.40%	Federal Democratic Republic of Ethiopia
(103,347)	1,384	65%	5 (13)	81%	2.11%	4.30 / 57.30	40.00% / 4.30%	55.29 / 57.57	8.10%	Gabonese Republic
(4,361)	1,595	155%	141 (366)	26%	2.79%	5.50 / 76.00	44.80% / 2.70%	51.30 / 55.00	1.20%	Republic of The Gambia
(92,100)	22,019	115%	92 (239)	44%	2.25%	4.50 / 64.00	40.20% / 3.30%	56.50 / 59.30	2.20%	Republic of Ghana
(94,926)	9,453	204%	38 (100)	33%	2.66%	5.90 / 94.20	44.40% / 3.10%	47.90 / 50.40	3.20%	Republic of Guinea
(13,948)	1,586	235%	44 (114)	32%	2.96%	7.10 / 120.00	45.80% / 3.00%	42.83 / 46.08	- - -	Republic of Guinea-Bissau
(224,081)	33,830	92%	58 (151)	36%	2.23%	4.90 / 77.00	42.60% / 2.30%	48.09 / 46.30	6.70%	Republic of Kenya
(11,720)	1,804	-29%	59 (154)	13%	-0.13%	3.50 / 92.10	37.80% / 4.90%	35.80 / 34.80	28.90%	Kingdom of Lesotho
(43,000)	3,283	224%	29 (76)	45%	2.90%	6.80 / 142.00	45.90% / 2.20%	40.97 / 43.46	5.90%	Republic of Liberia
(679,362)	5,766	88%	3 (8)	86%	2.39%	3.50 / 26.80	34.50% / 4.10%	73.90 / 78.30	0.30%	Great Socialist People's Libyan Arab Jamahiriya
(226,658)	17,308	141%	29 (76)	26%	2.74%	5.20 / 87.70	44.79% / 2.83%	52.50 / 56.80	1.70%	Republic of Madagascar
(45,747)	12,341	260%	104 (270)	14%	3.16%	6.50 / 99.60	46.40% / 2.90%	43.41 / 46.03	14.20%	Republic of Malawi
(478,841)	13,518	211%	11 (28)	30%	3.24%	7.10 / 133.00	47.00% / 2.70%	46.83 / 48.28	1.90%	Republic of Mali
(397,955)	3,069	144%	3 (8)	40%	2.73%	5.90 / 97.00	43.30% / 3.40%	49.90 / 53.10	0.60%	Islamic Republic of Mauritania
(788)	1,243	21%	609 (1,577)	42%	0.87%	1.90 / 14.40	24.90% / 6.50%	68.57 / 75.29	- - -	Republic of Mauritius
(274,461)	30,704	47%	43 (112)	57%	1.55%	2.50 / 40.40	30.40% / 4.85%	68.00 / 72.10	0.10%	Kingdom of Morocco
(308,642)	19,420	94%	24 (63)	32%	2.15%	5.50 / 119.00	44.20% / 2.70%	41.01 / 42.78	12.20%	Republic of Mozambique
(318,261)	2,031	-12%	2 (6)	33%	1.07%	4.20 / 50.70	39.50% / 3.50%	46.00 / 46.10	21.3%	Republic of Namibia
(489,191)	13,957	259%	11 (29)	21%	3.41%	8.00 / 153.00	48.10% / 1.90%	43.37 / 43.53	1.20%	Republic of Niger
(356,669)	131,530	96%	142 (369)	44%	2.38%	5.90 / 100.00	43.40% / 2.90%	43.39 / 44.44	5.40%	Federal Republic of Nigeria
(10,169)	8,722	101%	331 (858)	17%	2.27%	5.70 / 107.00	43.80% / 2.30%	41.87 / 45.26	5.10%	Republic of Rwanda
(386)	153	93%	153 (396)	38%	2.54%	4.10 / 82.00	38.40% / 4.20%	61.87 / 63.83	- - -	Democratic Republic of Sao Tome and Principe
(75,955)	11,658	98%	59 (153)	43%	2.57%	5.10 / 83.00	42.10% / 3.00%	54.35 / 56.76	0.80%	Republic of Senegal
(176)	81	11%	178 (460)	50%	1.00%	2.10 / 16.00	25.50% / 7.80%	66.17 / 76.10	- - -	Republic of Seychelles
(27,699)	5,525	150%	77 (199)	37%	2.27%	6.50 / 165.00	41.40% / 3.20%	38.72 / 41.58	- - -	Republic of Sierra Leone
(246,201)	8,592	197%	13 (35)	33%	2.88%	7.00 / 120.00	44.80% / 2.70%	45.70 / 49.00	- - -	Somalia
(470,693)	46,923	3%	38 (100)	53%	0.72%	2.80 / 43.00	32.90% / 4.00%	50.00 / 53.00	21.50%	Republic of South Africa
(967,500)	40,187	110%	16 (42)	36%	2.74%	5.20 / 67.14	44.20% / 2.20%	56.20 / 58.50	2.30%	Republic of the Sudan
(6,704)	1,138	-34%	66 (170)	25%	0.34%	3.90 / 74.80	42.70% / 3.20%	33.90 / 36.80	38.80%	Kingdom of Swaziland
(364,900)	36,481	96%	39 (100)	32%	2.44%	5.70 / 68.00	44.90% / 2.60%	43.20 / 45.00	7.00%	United Republic of Tanzania
(21,925)	6,145	120%	108 (280)	33%	2.72%	5.40 / 93.00	42.60% / 3.00%	52.26 / 56.20	4.10%	Togolese Republic
(63,170)	10,043	21%	61 (159)	65%	1.10%	2.10 / 21.10	26.70% / 6.80%	71.10 / 75.10	< 0.05%	Tunisian Republic
(93,104)	26,907	387%	112 (289)	12%	3.24%	6.90 / 88.40	50.50% / 2.30%	47.60 / 48.30	7.10%	Republic of Uganda
(290,586)	11,227	95%	15 (39)	35%	1.85%	5.70 / 95.00	44.80% / 2.90%	37.88 / 36.92	16.50%	Republic of Zambia
(150,872)	13,010	21%	33 (86)	34%	1.11%	3.80 / 62.00	39.60% / 3.40%	39.90 / 41.10	24.60%	Republic of Zimbabwe
										AFRICA: TERRITORIES AND AREAS OF SPECIAL STATUS
(144)	181	207%	484 (1,257)	28%	3.07%	5.60 / - - -	42.10% / 1.70%	57.80 / 62.00	- - -	French Overseas Territorial Collectivity
(968)	782	36%	312 (808)	89%	1.44%	2.50 / 6.10	27.30% / 7.20%	71.20 / 79.60	- - -	French Overseas Department
(97,344)	341	163%	1 (4)	93%	1.98%	3.90 / 53.00	34.30% / 3.30%	62.23 / 65.71	- - -	Area of Special Status
(23)	0	- - -	- - - - - -	- - -	- - -	- - - / - - -	- - - / - - -	- - - / - - -	- - -	Territory of Norway
(129)	0	- - -	- - - - - -	- - -	- - -	- - - / - - -	- - - / - - -	- - - / - - -	- - -	Territory of South Africa
(159)	6	- - -	15 (38)	35%	-0.10%	1.50 / 0	19.10% / 9.20%	74.10 / 80.00	- - -	British Overseas Territory
										AUSTRALIA & OCEANIA
(2,969,906)	20,351	29%	3 (7)	91%	0.61%	1.80 / 4.50	19.80% / 13.00%	77.80 / 82.80	0.10%	Commonwealth of Australia
(7,095)	842	11%	46 (119)	46%	1.47%	2.70 / 15.60	29.80% / 4.20%	65.65 / 70.04	0.10%	Republic of the Fiji Islands
(313)	92	128%	113 (294)	43%	1.80%	4.30 / 43.00	40.10% / 3.30%	58.20 / 67.30	- - -	Republic of Kiribati
(70)	59	75%	326 (843)	68%	3.01%	4.40 / 35.00	41.60% / 2.70%	66.60 / 70.40	- - -	Republic of the Marshall Islands
(271)	108	-10%	154 (399)	22%	2.14%	4.40 / 40	40.30% / 3.70%	66.50 / 67.00	- - -	Federated States of Micronesia
(8)	13	77%	619 (1,625)	100%	1.78%	3.70 / 12.10	41.00% / 1.60%	57.30 / 64.50	- - -	Republic of Nauru
(104,454)	4,107	23%	15 (39)	86%	0.73%	2.00 / 5.58	21.60% / 12.04%	76.30 / 81.10	0.10%	New Zealand
(189)	21	24%	43 (111)	70%	0.87%	2.10 / 15.40	23.90% / 5.40%	66.64 / 74.54	- - -	Republic of Palau
(178,703)	5,887	80%	13 (33)	13%	2.10%	4.10 / 71.00	40.10% / 2.30%	54.67 / 55.79	0.60%	Independent State of Papua New Guinea
(1,093)	188	-15%	66 (172)	22%	2.40%	4.30 / 17.80	40.70% / 4.47%	71.80 / 73.80	- - -	Independent State of Samoa
(10,954)	472	93%	17 (43)	16%	2.60%	4.50 / 66.00	40.10% / 3.20%	61.90 / 63.10	- - -	Solomon Islands
(289)	102	68%	136 (353)	33%	1.81%	3.10 / 19.00	39.49% / 5.20%	69.80 / 71.70	- - -	Kingdom of Tonga
(10)	10	80%	385 (1,000)	47%	1.72%	3.70 / 35.00	36.20% / 5.70%	61.70 / 65.10	- - -	Tuvalu
(4,707)	218	78%	18 (46)	21%	2.57%	4.20 / 34.00	41.70% / 3.30%	65.60 / 69.00	- - -	Republic of Vanuatu
										AUSTRALIA & OCEANIA: TERRITORIES AND AREAS OF SPECIAL STATUS
(2)	0	- - -	- - - - - -	- - -	- - -	- - - / - - -	- - - / - - -	- - - / - - -	- - -	Australian External Territory
(52)	0.474	111%	4 (9)	- - -	- - -	- - - / - - -	- - - / - - -	- - - / - - -	- - -	Australian External Territory
(5)	0.632	58%	45 (126)	- - -	- - -	- - - / - - -	- - - / - - -	- - - / - - -	- - -	Australian External Territory
(1)	0	- - -								Australian External Territory
(14)	2	0%	57 (143)	80%	0.15%	- - - / 0	- - - / - - -	- - - / - - -	- - -	Australian External Territory
(3)	0	- - -	- - - - - -	- - -	- - -	- - - / - - -	- - - / - - -	- - - / - - -	- - -	French Possession
(1,608)	255	40%	61 (159)	53%	1.32%	2.50 / 5.20	30.80% / 4.30%	66.90 / 68.16	- - -	French Overseas Territory
(7,359)	227	61%	12 (31)	71%	1.35%	2.40 / 8.60	29.40% / 6.30%	69.80 / 75.80	- - -	French Overseas Territory
(62)	15	33%	93 (242)	0%	1.35%	2.70 / 5.50	- - - / - - -	- - - / - - -	- - -	French Overseas Territory
(93)	13	23%	54 (140)	63%	1.52%	3.70 / 16.90	30.00% / 5.90%	68.40 / 71.50	- - -	Self-Governing in Free Association with New Zealand
(102)	1.617	24%	6 (16)	34%	1.07%	3.00 / 29.40	29.60% / 9.30%	69.80 / 71.20	- - -	Self-Governing in Free Association with New Zealand
(5)	1.538	30%	128 (308)	0%	2.40%	4.90 / 33.00	- - - / - - -	67.80 / 70.40	- - -	Territory of New Zealand
(18)	0.045	0%	1 (3)	- - -	- - -	- - - / - - -	26.40% / 15.00%	- - - / - - -	- - -	British Overseas Territory
(90)	63	-33%	270 (700)	89%	2.31%	3.90 / 15.40	38.70% / 3.30%	70.70 / 79.80	- - -	Territory of the United States
(1)	0	- - -	- - - - - -	- - -	- - -	- - - / - - -	- - - / - - -	- - - / - - -	- - -	Territory of the United States
(217)	169	45%	301 (779)	93%	1.59%	2.60 / 6.20	30.46% / 5.30%	75.50 / 80.40	- - -	Territory of the United States
(179)	80	79%	172 (447)	90%	1.52%	1.70 / 7.00	22.50% / 1.50%	70.70 / 79.80	- - -	Commonwealth in Political Union with the United States

CONTINENT/Country	GDP per capita in U.S. dollars Mid-2005 estimate	Services as % of GDP Sector 2003	Industry as % of GDP Sector 2003	Agriculture as % of GDP Sector 2003	Total estimated value of imports in million U.S. dollars 2005	Total estimated value of exports in million U.S. dollars 2005	% of population with access to electricity 2003
NORTH AMERICA							
Antigua and Barbuda	$11,000	76.8%	18.0%	4.0%	$735	$214	- - -
Bahamas	$20,200	90.0%	7.0%	3.0%	$5,806	$1,507	- - -
Barbados	$17,000	78.0%	16.0%	6.0%	$1,476	$209	- - -
Belize	$6,800	67.3%	15.0%	17.7%	$622	$350	- - -
Canada	$34,000	71.3%	26.4%	2.3%	$317,700	$364,800	- - -
Costa Rica	$11,100	62.5%	28.7%	8.8%	$9,690	$7,005	95.7%
Cuba	$3,500	67.9%	25.5%	6.6%	$6,916	$2,388	97.0%
Dominica	$5,500	58.0%	24.0%	18.0%	$234	$74	- - -
Dominican Republic	$7,000	58.1%	30.6%	11.2%	$9,747	$5,818	66.8%
El Salvador	$4,700	59.4%	32.1%	8.5%	$6,678	$3,586	70.8%
Grenada	$5,000	68.4%	23.9%	7.7%	$276	$40	- - -
Guatemala	$4,700	58.5%	19.3%	22.3%	$7,744	$3,940	66.7%
Haiti	$1,700	50.0&	20.0%	30.0%	$1,471	$391	34.0%
Honduras	$2,900	55.8%	30.7%	13.5%	$4,161	$1,726	54.5%
Jamaica	$4,400	65.0%	29.8%	5.2%	$4,144	$1,593	90.0%
Mexico	$10,000	69.6%	26.4%	4.0%	$223,700	$213,700	- - -
Nicaragua	$2,900	56.3%	25.7%	17.9%	$2,952	$1,550	48.0%
Panama	$7,200	76.2%	16.3%	7.5%	$8,734	$7,481	76.1%
Saint Kitts and Nevis	$8,800	68.7%	28.3%	3.0%	$405	$70	- - -
Saint Lucia	$5,400	76.6%	18.0%	5.4%	$410	$82	- - -
Saint Vincent and the Grenadines	$2,900	66.9%	24.4%	8.7%	$225	$37	- - -
Trinidad and Tobago	$16,700	50.0%	48.8%	1.2%	$6,011	$9,161	99.0%
United States	$41,800	79.4%	19.7%	0.9%	$1,727,000	$927,500	- - -
NORTH AMERICA: TERRITORIES AND AREAS OF SPECIAL STATUS							
Denmark							
Greenland	$20,000	- - -	- - -	- - -	$601	$480	- - -
France							
Guadeloupe	$7,900	68.0%	17.0%	15.0%	$1,700	$140	- - -
Martinique	$14,400	83.0%	11.0%	6.0%	$2,000	$250	- - -
Saint-Pierre and Miquelon	$7,000	- - -	- - -	- - -	$70	$7	- - -
Netherlands							
Aruba	$21,800	- - -	- - -	- - -	$875	$80	- - -
Netherlands Antilles	$16,000	84.0%	15.0%	1.0%	$4,383	$2,076	- - -
United Kingdom							
Anguilla	$7,500	78.0%	18.0%	4.0%	$81	$2.6	- - -
Bermuda	$69,900	89.0%	10.0%	1.0%	$8,078	$1,469	- - -
British Virgin Islands	$38,500	92.0%	6.2%	1.8%	$187	$25.3	- - -
Cayman Islands	$32,300	95.4%	3.2%	1.4%	$457	$1.2	- - -
Montserrat	$3,400	- - -	- - -	- - -	$17	$0.7	- - -
Turks and Caicos Islands	$11,500	- - -	- - -	- - -	$176	$169	- - -
United States							
Navassa Island	- - -	- - -	- - -	- - -	- - -	- - -	- - -
Puerto Rico	$18,600	56.0%	43.0%	1.0%	$29,100	$46,900	- - -
Virgin Islands	$14,500	80.0%	19.0%	1.0%	- - -	- - -	- - -
SOUTH AMERICA							
Argentina	$13,100	54.1%	34.8%	11.1%	$28,800	$40,000	94.6%
Bolivia	$2,900	55.1%	30.1%	14.9%	$1,845	$2,371	60.4%
Brazil	$8,400	75.1%	19.1%	5.8%	$78,020	$115,100	94.9%
Chile	$11,300	56.9%	34.3%	8.8%	$30,090	$38,030	99.0%
Colombia	$7,900	58.3%	29.4%	12.3%	$20,420	$23,060	81.0%
Ecuador	$4,300	63.6%	28.7%	7.7%	$8,436	$9,224	80.0%
Guyana	$4,600	41.8%	19.9%	38.3%	$682	$587.2	- - -
Paraguay	$4,900	48.5%	24.2%	27.2%	$3,832	$3,130	74.7%
Peru	$5,900	60.4%	29.3%	10.3%	$12,150	$15,950	73.0%
Suriname	$4,100	65.0%	22.0%	13.0%	$750	$881	- - -
Uruguay	$9,600	59.9%	27.3%	12.8%	$3,540	$3,550	98.0%
Venezuela	$6,100	54.4%	41.1%	4.5%	$24,630	$52,730	94.0%
SOUTH AMERICA: TERRITORIES AND AREAS OF SPECIAL STATUS							
France							
French Guiana	$8,300	- - -	- - -	- - -	$625	$155	- - -
United Kingdom							
Falkland Islands	$25,000	- - -	- - -	- - -	$90	$125	- - -
EUROPE							
Albania	$4,900	56.1%	19.2%	24.7%	$2,473	$708.8	- - -
Andorra	$24,000	- - -	- - -	- - -	$1,077	$58	- - -
Austria	$32,700	65.9%	31.7%	2.3%	$118,800	$122,500	- - -
Belarus	$6,900	60.1%	30.1%	9.8%	$16,940	$16,140	- - -
Belgium	$31,400	72.2%	26.5%	1.3%	$264,500	$269,600	- - -
Bosnia and Herzegovina	$6,800	53.0%	32.1%	14.9%	$6,800	$2,700	- - -
Bulgaria	$9,600	57.5%	30.7%	11.7%	$15,900	$11,670	- - -
Croatia	$11,600	61.5%	30.1%	8.4%	$18,930	$10,300	- - -
Cyprus	$21,600	76.0%	19.9%	4.1%	$5,552	$1,237	- - -
Czech Republic	$19,500	57.1%	39.4%	3.5%	$76,590	$78,370	- - -
Denmark	$34,600	71.5%	26.4%	2.1%	$74,690	$84,950	- - -
Estonia	$16,700	67.0%	28.5%	4.5%	$9,189	$7,439	- - -
Finland	$30,900	66.0%	30.5%	3.5%	$56,450	$67,880	- - -
France	$29,900	72.8%	24.5%	2.7%	$473,300	$443,400	- - -
Germany	$30,400	69.4%	29.4%	1.1%	$801,000	$1,016,000	- - -
Greece	$22,200	69.3%	23.8%	6.9%	$48,200	$18,540	- - -
Hungary	$16,300	65.3%	31.4%	3.3%	$64,830	$61,750	- - -
Iceland	$35,600	79.2%	9.6%	11.2%	$4,582	$3,215	- - -
Ireland	$41,000	49.0%	46.0%	5.0%	$65,470	$102,000	- - -
Italy	$29,200	69.5%	27.8%	2.6%	$369,200	$371,900	- - -
Latvia	$13,200	71.0%	24.4%	4.5%	$8,559	$5,749	- - -
Liechtenstein	$25,000	- - -	- - -	- - -	$917	$2,470	- - -
Lithuania	$13,700	59.0%	33.8%	7.3%	$13,330	$10,950	- - -
Luxembourg	$55,600	78.9%	20.5%	0.6%	$18,740	$13,390	- - -
Macedonia	$7,800	57.3%	30.4%	12.2%	$3,196	$2,047	- - -
Malta	$19,900	74.0%	23.0%	3.0%	$3,859	$2,744	- - -
Moldova	$1,800	52.8%	24.7%	22.5%	$2,230	$1,040	- - -
Monaco	$27,000	- - -	- - -	- - -	- - -	- - -	- - -
Netherlands	$30,500	73.1%	24.5%	2.4%	$326,600	$365,100	- - -

Telephone mainlines per 1,000 people 2003	Arable & permanent cropland area 2003 sq km (sq mi)	Forested area as % of total land area 2000	Protected areas as % of total land area 2003	Average annual deforestation: % change 1990 - 2000 (Negative number indicates an increase in forest area.)	Carbon dioxide emissions : metric tonnes per capita 2000	CONTINENT / Country Formal Name
						NORTH AMERICA
- - -	100 (39)	21.4%	- - -	- - -	4.9	Antigua and Barbuda
415	120 (46)	51.5%	- - -	- - -	5.9	Commonwealth of The Bahamas
497	170 (66)	4.0%	- - -	- - -	4.4	Barbados
113	1,020 (394)	72.5%	- - -	- - -	3.1	Belize
629	521,150 (201,217)	33.6%	11.1%	0.0%	14.2	Canada
251	5,250 (2,027)	46.8%	23.0%	0.8%	1.4	Republic of Costa Rica
51	37,880 (14,626)	24.7%	69.1%	-1.3%	2.8	Republic of Cuba
304	210 (81)	61.3%	- - -	- - -	1.4	Commonwealth of Dominica
115	15,960 (6,162)	28.4%	51.9%	0.0%	3.0	Dominican Republic
116	9,100 (3,514)	14.4%	0.4%	4.6%	1.1	Republic of El Salvador
290	120 (46)	12.2%	- - -	- - -	2.1	Grenada
71	20,500 (7,915)	36.3%	20.0%	1.7%	0.9	Republic of Guatemala
17	11,000 (4,247)	3.8%	0.4%	5.7%	0.2	Republic of Haiti
48	14,280 (5,514)	41.5%	6.4%	1.0%	0.7	Republic of Honduras
170	2,840 (1,097)	31.3%	- - -	1.5%	4.2	Jamaica
158	273,000 (105,406)	33.7%	10.2%	1.1%	4.3	United Mexican States
37	21,610 (8,344)	42.7%	17.8%	3.0%	0.7	Republic of Nicaragua
122	6,950 (2,683)	57.7%	21.7%	1.6%	2.2	Republic of Panama
500	80 (31)	14.7%	- - -	- - -	- - -	Federation of Saint Kitts and Nevis
320	180 (69)	27.9%	- - -	- - -	- - -	Saint Lucia
234	140 (54)	27.4%	- - -	- - -	- - -	Saint Vincent and the Grenadines
250	1,220 (471)	44.1%	6.0%	0.8%	20.5	Republic of Trinidad and Tobago
621	1,755,000 (677,609)	33.1%	25.9%	-0.2%	19.8	United States of America
						NORTH AMERICA: TERRITORIES AND AREAS OF SPECIAL STATUS
- - -	- - - - - -	- - -	- - -	- - -	- - -	Overseas Region of Denmark
- - -	250 (97)	47.2%	- - -	- - -	- - -	French Overseas Department
- - -	210 (81)	43.9%		- - -	- - -	French Overseas Department
- - -	30 (12)	13.0%	- - -	- - -	- - -	French Overseas Territorial Collectivity
- - -	20 (8)	2.2%		- - -	- - -	Overseas Region of the Netherlands
- - -	80 (31)	1.5%		- - -	- - -	Overseas Region of the Netherlands
- - -	- - - - - -	71.4%	- - -	- - -	- - -	British Overseas Territory
- - -	10 (4)	20.0%	- - -	- - -	- - -	British Overseas Territory
- - -	40 (15)	24.4%	- - -	- - -	- - -	British Overseas Territory
- - -	10 (4)	48.4%	- - -	- - -	- - -	British Overseas Territory
- - -	20 (8)	35.0%	- - -	- - -	- - -	British Overseas Territory
- - -	10 (4)	80.0%	- - -	- - -	- - -	British Overseas Territory
- - -	- - - - - -			- - -	- - -	Territory of the United States
346	830 (320)	46.0%	3.5%	0.2%	2.3	Self-Governing Commonwealth in Association with the United States
- - -	30 (12)	27.9%		- - -	- - -	Territory of the United States
						SOUTH AMERICA
219	289,000 (111,584)	12.1%	6.6%	0.8%	3.9	Argentine Republic
72	32,560 (12,571)	54.2%	13.4%	0.3%	1.3	Republic of Bolivia
223	666,000 (257,144)	57.2%	6.7%	0.4%	1.8	Federative Republic of Brazil
221	23,070 (8,907)	21.5%	18.9%	0.1%	3.9	Republic of Chile
179	38,500 (14,865)	58.5%	10.2%	0.4%	1.4	Republic of Colombia
122	29,850 (11,525)	39.2%	18.3%	1.2%	2.0	Republic of Ecuador
- - -	5,100 (1,969)	76.7%	- - -	- - -	2.1	Co-operative Republic of Guyana
46	31,360 (12,108)	46.5%	3.5%	0.5%	0.7	Republic of Paraguay
67	43,100 (16,641)	53.7%	6.1%	0.4%	1.1	Republic of Peru
152	680 (263)	94.7%	- - -	- - -	5.0	Republic of Suriname
- - -	14,120 (5,452)	8.6%	0.3%	-5.0%	1.6	Oriental Republic of Uruguay
111	34,000 (13,127)	54.1%	63.8%	0.4%	6.5	Bolivarian Republic of Venezuela
						SOUTH AMERICA: TERRITORIES AND AREAS OF SPECIAL STATUS
- - -	160 (62)	91.8%	- - -	- - -	- - -	French Overseas Department
- - -	- - - - - -	0.0%	- - -	- - -	- - -	British Overseas Territory
						EUROPE
83	6,990 (2,699)	29.0%	3.8%	0.8%	0.9	Republic of Albania
438	10 (4)	35.6%	- - -	- - -	- - -	Principality of Andorra
481	14,620 (5,645)	46.7%	33.0%	-0.2%	7.6	Republic of Austria
311	56,810 (21,934)	38.0%	6.3%	-3.2%	5.9	Republic of Belarus
489	8,580 (3,313)	22.0%	2.6%	-0.2%	10.0	Kingdom of Belgium
245	11,010 (4,251)	43.1%	0.5%	0.0%	4.8	Bosnia and Herzegovina
380	35,340 (13,645)	32.8%	4.5%	-0.6%	5.3	Republic of Bulgaria
417	15,840 (6,116)	38.2%	7.5%	-0.1%	4.5	Republic of Croatia
572	1,400 (541)	18.9%	- - -	- - -	8.5	Republic of Cyprus
360	32,990 (12,738)	34.3%	16.1%	-0.0%	11.6	Czech Republic
669	22,740 (8,780)	11.8%	34.0%	-0.2%	8.4	Kingdom of Denmark
341	5,610 (2,166)	53.9%	11.8%	-0.6%	11.7	Republic of Estonia
492	22,180 (8,564)	73.9%	9.3%	-0.0%	10.3	Republic of Finland
566	195,730 (75,572)	28.3%	13.3%	-0.4%	6.2	French Republic
657	120,400 (46,487)	31.7%	31.9%	0.0%	9.6	Federal Republic of Germany
454	38,310 (14,792)	29.1%	3.6%	-0.9%	8.2	Hellenic Republic
349	48,040 (18,548)	21.5%	7.0%	-0.4%	5.4	Republic of Hungary
660	70 (27)	0.5%	- - -	- - -	7.7	Republic of Iceland
491	11,840 (4,571)	9.7%	1.7%	-3.0%	11.1	Republic of Ireland
484	106,970 (41,301)	33.9%	7.9%	-0.3%	7.4	Italian Republic
285	18,500 (7,143)	47.4%	13.4%	-0.4%	2.5	Republic of Latvia
583	40 (15)	43.1%	- - -	- - -	- - -	Principality of Liechtenstein
239	29,850 (11,525)	33.5%	10.3%	-0.2%	3.4	Republic of Lithuania
798	630 (243)	33.5%	- - -	- - -	19.4	Grand Duchy of Luxembourg
271	6,120 (2,363)	35.8%	7.1%	0.0%	5.5	Republic of Macedonia
521	110 (42)	1.1%	- - -	- - -	7.2	Republic of Malta
219	21,430 (8,274)	10.0%	1.4%	-0.2%	1.5	Republic of Moldova
1040	- - - - - -	0.0%	- - -	- - -	- - -	Principality of Monaco
614	9,440 (3,645)	10.8%	14.2%	-0.3%	8.7	Kingdom of the Netherlands

CONTINENT/Country	GDP per capita in U.S. dollars Mid-2005 estimate	Services as % of GDP Sector 2003	Industry as % of GDP Sector 2003	Agriculture as % of GDP Sector 2003	Total estimated value of imports in million U.S. dollars 2005	Total estimated value of exports in million U.S. dollars 2005	% of population with access to electricity 2003
Norway	$42,300	61.0%	37.5%	1.5%	$58,120	$111,200	- - -
Poland	$13,300	66.1%	30.7%	3.1%	$95,670	$92,720	- - -
Portugal	$19,300	63.9%	30.2%	5.9%	$60,350	$38,800	- - -
Romania	$8,200	52.0%	36.1%	11.9%	$38,150	$27,720	- - -
Russia	$11,100	60.7%	34.2%	5.2%	$125,000	$245,000	- - -
San Marino	$34,600	- - -	- - -	- - -	- - -	- - -	- - -
Serbia and Montenegro	$5,000	56.8%	27.6%	15.6%	$11,940	$5,485	- - -
Slovakia	$16,100	66.6%	29.7%	3.7%	$34,480	$32,390	- - -
Slovenia	$21,600	60.3%	36.9%	2.8%	$19,620	$18,530	- - -
Spain	$25,500	67.1%	29.6%	3.3%	$271,800	$194,300	- - -
Sweden	$29,800	70.3%	27.9%	1.8%	$104,400	$126,600	- - -
Switzerland	$32,300	64.5%	34.0%	1.5%	$135,000	$148,600	- - -
Ukraine	$7,200	45.6%	40.3%	14.1%	$37,180	$38,220	- - -
United Kingdom	$30,300	72.4%	26.6%	1.0%	$483,700	$372,700	- - -
Vatican City	- - -	- - -	- - -	- - -	- - -	- - -	- - -
EUROPE: TERRITORIES AND AREAS OF SPECIAL STATUS							
Denmark							
Faroe Islands	$22,000	62.0%	11.0%	27.0%	$639	$533	- - -
Norway							
Jan Mayen	- - -	- - -	- - -	- - -	- - -	- - -	- - -
Svalbard	- - -	- - -	- - -	- - -	- - -	- - -	- - -
United Kingdom							
Channel Islands	- - -	- - -	- - -	- - -	- - -	- - -	- - -
Gibraltar	$27,900	86.0%	13.0%	1.0%	$2,967	$271	- - -
Isle of Man	$28,500	- - -	- - -	- - -	- - -	- - -	- - -
ASIA							
Afghanistan	$800	20.0%	20.0%	60.0%	$3,870	$471	2.0%
Armenia	$4,500	37.3%	39.2%	23.5%	$1,500	$800	- - -
Azerbaijan	$4,800	31.1%	54.5%	14.3%	$4,656	$6,117	- - -
Bahrain	$23,000	58.3%	41.0%	0.7%	$7,830	$11,170	- - -
Bangladesh	$2,100	52.0%	26.3%	21.8%	$12,970	$9,372	20.4%
Bhutan	$1,400	27.3%	39.5%	33.2%	$196	$154	- - -
Brunei	$23,600	50.0%	45.0%	5.0%	$1,641	$4,514	- - -
Cambodia	$2,200	35.9%	29.7%	34.5%	$3,538	$2,663	15.8%
China	$6,800	33.1%	52.3%	14.6%	$631,800	$752,200	98.6%
Georgia	$3,300	54.1%	25.5%	20.5%	$2,500	$1,400	- - -
India	$3,300	51.2%	26.6%	22.2%	$113,100	$76,230	43.0%
Indonesia	$3,600	39.9%	43.6%	16.6%	$62,020	$83,640	53.4%
Iran	$8,300	47.6%	41.2%	11.3%	$42,500	$55,420	97.9%
Iraq	$3,400	27.8%	58.6%	13.6%	$19,570	$17,780	95.0%
Israel	$24,600	59.5%	37.7%	2.8%	$43,190	$40,140	100.0%
Japan	$31,500	74.0%	24.7%	1.3%	$451,100	$550,500	- - -
Jordan	$4,700	71.8%	26.0%	2.2%	$8,681	$4,226	95.0%
Kazakhstan	$8,200	53.9%	38.3%	7.8%	$17,510	$30,090	- - -
Korea, North	$1,700	56.3%	40.4%	3.3%	$2,819	$1,275	20.0%
Korea, South	$20,400	62.2%	34.6%	3.2%	$248,400	$277,600	- - -
Kuwait	$19,200	39.1%	60.5%	0.4%	$12,230	$44,430	100.0%
Kyrgyzstan	$2,100	38.4%	22.9%	38.7%	$937	$759	- - -
Laos	$1,900	25.5%	25.9%	48.6%	$541	$379	- - -
Lebanon	$6,200	67.7%	20.0%	12.2%	$8,855	$1,782	95.0%
Malaysia	$12,100	41.8%	48.5%	9.7%	$118,700	$147,100	96.9%
Maldives	$3,900	62.0%	18.0%	20.0%	$645	$123	- - -
Mongolia	$1,900	57.0%	14.9%	28.1%	$1,011	$852	90.0%
Myanmar (Burma)	$1,700	34.5%	8.9%	56.6%	$2,183	$2,514	5.0%
Nepal	$1,400	37.8%	21.6%	40.6%	$1,696	$626	15.4%
Oman	$13,200	3.1%	55.8%	41.1%	$8,709	$19,010	94.0%
Pakistan	$2,400	53.2%	23.5%	23.3%	$21,260	$14,850	52.9%
Philippines	$5,100	53.2%	32.3%	14.5%	$42,660	$41,250	87.4%
Qatar	$27,400	41.5%	58.2%	0.3%	$6,706	$24,900	- - -
Saudi Arabia	$12,800	40.3%	55.2%	4.5%	$44,930	$165,000	97.7%
Singapore	$28,100	65.0%	34.9%	0.1%	$187,500	$212,400	100.0%
Sri Lanka	$4,300	54.7%	26.3%	19.0%	$8,370	$6,442	62.0%
Syria	$3,900	48.0%	28.6%	23.5%	$5,973	$6,344	85.9%
Tajikistan	$1,200	56.4%	20.2%	23.4%	$1,250	$950	- - -
Thailand	$8,300	46.3%	44.0%	9.8%	$107,000	$105,800	82.1%
Timor-Leste (East Timor)	$400	57.4%	17.2%	25.4%	$202	$10	- - -
Turkey	$8,200	64.7%	21.9%	13.4%	$101,200	$72,490	- - -
Turkmenistan	$8,000	28.8%	42.7%	28.5%	$4,175	$4,700	- - -
United Arab Emirates	$43,400	37.5%	58.5%	4.0%	$60,150	4103,100	96.0%
Uzbekistan	$1,800	43.1%	21.7%	35.2%	$4,140	$5,360	- - -
Vietnam	$2,800	38.2%	40.0%	21.8%	$34,440	$31,340	75.8%
Yemen	$900	45.0%	40.0%	15.0%	$4,190	$6,387	50.0%
ASIA: TERRITORIES AND AREAS OF SPECIAL STATUS							
China							
Hong Kong	$32,900	88.0%	12.0%	0.0%	$291,600	$286,300	- - -
Macau	$22,000	92.7%	7.2%	0.1%	$3,478	$3,465	- - -
Taiwan	$27,600	67.4%	30.9%	1.7%	$172,900	$185,100	- - -
Israel - Palestinian Areas					$1,952	$270	- - -
Gaza Strip	$600	63.0%	28.0%	9.0%	- - -	- - -	- - -
West Bank	$1,100	63.0%	28.0%	9.0%	- - -	- - -	- - -
United Kingdom							
British Indian Ocean Territory	- - -	93.0%	2.0%	5.0%	- - -	- - -	- - -
AFRICA							
Algeria	$7,200	34.7%	55.1%	10.2%	$22,530	$49,590	98.0%
Angola	$3,200	26.6%	64.6%	8.8%	$8,165	$26,800	12.0%
Benin	$1,100	50%	14.4%	35.7%	$1,043	$827	22.0%
Botswana	$10,500	52.5%	45.2%	2.4%	$3,370	$3,680	22.0%
Burkina Faso	$1,300	50.1%	18.9%	31.0%	$992	$395	13.0%
Burundi	$700	32.0%	19.0%	49.0%	$200	$52	- - -
Cameroon	$2,400	39.1%	16.7%	44.2%	$2,514	$3,236	20.0%
Cape Verde	$6,200	73.4%	19.7%	6.8%	$500	$73	- - -
Central African Republic	$1,100	14.3%	24.9%	60.8%	$203	$131	- - -
Chad	$1,500	40.9%	13.5%	45.6%	$749,100	$3,016	- - -

Telephone mainlines per 1,000 people 2003	Arable & permanent cropland area 2003 sq km (sq mi)	Forested area as % of total land area 2000	Protected areas as % of total land area 2003	Average annual deforestation: % change 1990 - 2000 (Negative number indicates an increase in forest area.)	Carbon dioxide emissions : metric tonnes per capita 2000	CONTINENT / Country Formal Name
713	8,730 (3,371)	30.7%	6.8%	-0.4%	11.1	Kingdom of Norway
319	129,010 (49,811)	30.0%	12.4%	-0.1%	7.8	Republic of Poland
411	23,110 (8,923)	41.3%	6.6%	-1.7%	5.8	Portuguese Republic
199	98,720 (38,116)	27.7%	4.7%	-0.2%	3.8	Romania
242	1,243,730 (480,207)	47.9%	7.8%	-0.0%	9.9	Russian Federation
763	10 (4)	1.6%	- - -	- - -	- - -	Republic of San Marino
243	37,170 (14,351)	26.4%	3.3%	0.0%	- - -	Serbia and Montenegro
241	15,640 (6,039)	40.1%	22.8%	-0.3%	6.6	Slovak Republic
407	2,020 (780)	62.8%	6.0%	-0.2%	7.3	Republic of Slovenia
434	187,150 (72,259)	35.9%	8.5%	-0.6%	7.0	Kingdom of Spain
736	26,720 (10,317)	66.9%	9.1%	-0.0%	5.3	Kingdom of Sweden
744	4,330 (1,672)	30.9%	30.0%	-0.4%	5.4	Swiss Confederation
216	333,870 (128,908)	16.5%	3.9%	-0.3%	6.9	Ukraine
591	57,080 (22,039)	11.8%	20.9%	-0.8%	9.6	United Kingdom of Great Britain and Northern Ireland
- - -	- - - - - -	0.0%	- - -	- - -	- - -	State of the Vatican City (The Holy See)
						EUROPE: TERRITORIES AND AREAS OF SPECIAL STATUS
- - -	30 (12)	0.1%	- - -	- - -	- - -	Overseas Region of Denmark
- - -	- - - - - -	- - -	- - -	- - -	- - -	Norwegian Dependency
- - -	- - - - - -	- - -	- - -	- - -	- - -	Norwegian Dependency
- - -	- - - - - -	4.1%	- - -	- - -	- - -	British Crown Dependencies
- - -	- - - - - -	0.0%	- - -	- - -	- - -	British Overseas Territory
- - -	- - - - - -	6.1%	- - -	- - -	- - -	British Crown Dependency
						ASIA
2	80,480 (31,074)	1.3%	0.3%	- - -	0.0	Transitional Islamic State of Afghanistan
148	5,600 (2,162)	10.0%	7.6%	-1.3%	1.1	Republic of Armenia
114	20,120 (7,768)	11.3%	6.1%	-1.3%	3.6	Republic of Azerbaijan
268	60 (23)	0.6%	- - -	- - -	29.1	Kingdom of Bahrain
5	84,190 (32,506)	6.7%	0.8%	-1.3%	0.2	People's Republic of Bangladesh
34	1,280 (494)	68.0%	- - -	- - -	0.5	Kingdom of Bhutan
256	170 (66)	52.8%	- - -	- - -	- - -	Negara Brunei Darussalam
3	38,070 (14,699)	59.2%	18.5%	0.6%	0.0	Kingdom of Cambodia
209	1,548,500 (597,879)	21.2%	7.8%	-0.9%	2.2	People's Republic of China
133	10,660 (4,116)	39.7%	2.3%	0.0%	1.2	Republic of Georgia
46	1,697,390 (655,366)	22.8%	5.2%	-0.1%	1.1	Republic of India
39	344,000 (132,819)	48.8%	20.6%	1.2%	1.3	Republic of Indonesia
220	182,480 (70,456)	6.8%	4.8%	0.0%	4.9	Islamic Republic of Iran
28	60,190 (23,239)	1.9%	0.0%	0.0%	3.3	Republic of Iraq
458	4,280 (1,653)	8.3%	15.8%	-4.9%	10.0	State of Israel
472	47,360 (18,286)	68.2%	6.8%	0.0%	9.3	Japan
114	4,000 (1,544)	0.9%	3.4%	0.0%	3.2	Hashemite Kingdom of Jordan
130	226,860 (87,591)	1.2%	2.7%	-2.2%	8.1	Republic of Kazakhstan
41	29,000 (11,197)	51.4%	2.6%	0.0%	8.5	Democratic People's Republic of Korea
538	18,460 (7,127)	63.5%	6.9%	0.1%	9.1	Republic of Korea
198	180 (69)	0.3%	1.5%	-5.2%	21.9	State of Kuwait
76	13,650 (5,270)	4.5%	12.5%	-2.6%	0.9	Kyrgyz Republic
12	10,310 (3,981)	69.9%	3.6%	0.4%	0.1	Lao People's Democratic Republic
199	3,130 (1,208)	13.3%	0.5%	0.3%	3.5	Lebanese Republic
182	75,850 (29,286)	63.6%	5.7%	1.2%	6.2	Malaysia
102	130 (50)	3.0%	- - -	- - -	1.8	Republic of Maldives
56	12,000 (4,633)	6.5%	11.5%	0.5%	3.1	Mongolia
7	109,810 (42,398)	49.0%	0.3%	1.4%	0.2	Union of Myanmar
16	24,900 (9,614)	25.4%	8.9%	1.8%	0.1	Kingdom of Nepal
84	800 (309)	3.1%	14.0%	0.0%	8.2	Sultanate of Oman
27	201,300 (77,722)	2.5%	4.9%	1.1%	0.8	Islamic Republic of Pakistan
41	107,000 (41,313)	24.0%	5.7%	1.4%	1.0	Republic of the Philippines
261	210 (81)	- - -	- - -	- - -	69.6	State of Qatar
155	37,980 (14,664)	1.3%	38.3%	0.0%	18.1	Kingdom of Saudi Arabia
450	20 (8)	3.4%	4.9%	0.0%	14.7	Republic of Singapore
49	19,160 (7,398)	29.9%	13.5%	1.6%	0.6	Democratic Socialist Republic of Sri Lanka
123	54,210 (20,931)	2.5%	- - -	0.0%	3.3	Syrian Arab Republic
37	10,570 (4,081)	2.9%	4.2%	-0.5%	0.6	Republic of Tajikistan
105	176,870 (68,290)	28.4%	13.9%	0.7%	3.3	Kingdom of Thailand
- - -	1,900 (734)	53.7%	- - -	- - -	- - -	Democratic Republic of Timor-Leste
268	260,130 (100,437)	13.2%	1.6%	-0.2%	3.3	Republic of Turkey
77	22,660 (8,749)	8.8%	4.2%	0.0%	7.5	Turkmenistan
281	2,540 (981)	3.7%	0.0%	-2.8%	18.1	United Arab Emirates
67	50,400 (19,460)	8.0%	2.0%	-0.2%	4.8	Republic of Uzbekistan
54	89,800 (34,672)	39.7%	3.7%	-0.5%	0.7	Socialist Republic of Vietnam
28	16,690 (6,444)	1.0%	- - -	1.8%	0.5	Republic of Yemen
						ASIA: TERRITORIES AND AREAS OF SPECIAL STATUS
559	- - - - - -	- - -	- - -	- - -	5.0	Special Administrative Region of China
- - -	- - - - - -	- - -	- - -	- - -	- - -	Special Administrative Region of China
- - -	- - - - - -	- - -	- - -	- - -	- - -	
- - -	1,950 (753)	1.5%	- - -	- - -	- - -	Areas of Special Status
- - -	- - - - - -	- - -	- - -	- - -	- - -	Area of Special Status
- - -	- - - - - -	- - -	- - -	- - -	- - -	Area of Special Status
- - -	- - - - - -	- - -	- - -	- - -	- - -	British Overseas Territory
						AFRICA
69	82,150 (31,718)	1.0%	5.0%	-1.3%	2.9	People's Democratic Republic of Algeria
7	35,900 (13,861)	47.4%	6.6%	0.2%	0.5	Republic of Angola
9	29,170 (11,263)	21.3%	11.4%	2.3%	0.3	Republic of Benin
75	3,800 (1,467)	21.1%	18.5%	0.9%	2.3	Republic of Botswana
5	49,000 (18,919)	29.0%	11.5%	0.2%	0.1	Burkina Faso
3	13,550 (5,232)	5.9%	5.7%	9.0%	0.0	Republic of Burundi
7	71,600 (27,645)	45.6%	4.5%	0.9%	0.4	Republic of Cameroon
156	490 (189)	20.7%	- - -	- - -	0.3	Republic of Cape Verde
2	20,240 (7,815)	36.5%	8.7%	0.1%	0.1	Central African Republic
2	36,300 (14,016)	9.5%	9.1%	0.6%	0.0	Republic of Chad

CONTINENT/Country	GDP per capita in U.S. dollars Mid-2005 estimate	Services as % of GDP Sector 2003	Industry as % of GDP Sector 2003	Agriculture as % of GDP Sector 2003	Total estimated value of imports in million U.S. dollars 2005	Total estimated value of exports in million U.S. dollars 2005	% of population with access to electricity 2003
Comoros	$600	47.2%	11.9%	40.9%	$115	$34	- - -
Congo	$1,300	33.8%	60.1%	6.2%	$807	$2,209	20.9%
Congo, Dem. Rep. of the	$700	34.0%	11.0%	55.0%	$1,319	$1,108	6.7%
Côte d'Ivoire (Ivory Coast)	$1,600	55.2%	18.6%	26.2%	$4,759	$6,490	50.0%
Djibouti	$1,300	80.7%	15.8%	3.5%	$987	$250	- - -
Egypt	$3,900	49.8%	34%	16.1%	$24,100	$14,330	93.8%
Equatorial Guinea	$50,200	4.3%	88.9%	6.8%	$1,864	$6,727	- - -
Eritrea	$1,000	61.4%	24.7%	13.9%	$677	$33.6	17.0%
Ethiopia	$900	47.4%	10.7%	41.8%	$2,722	$612	4.7%
Gabon	$6,800	29.8%	62.1%	8.1%	$1,533	$5,813	31.0%
Gambia	$1,900	55.2%	14.6%	30.1%	$197	$140.3	- - -
Ghana	$2,500	39.3%	24.9%	35.8%	$4,273	$2,911	45.0%
Guinea	$2,000	39.0%	36.4%	24.6%	$680	$612	- - -
Guinea-Bissau	$800	17.9%	13.3%	68.7%	$176	$116	- - -
Kenya	$1,100	64.7%	19.6%	15.8%	$5,126	$3,173	7.9%
Lesotho	$2,500	39.8%	43.5%	16.6%	$1,166	$603	5.0%
Liberia	$1,000	17.7%	5.4%	76.9%	$4,839	$910	- - -
Libya	$11,400	45.6%	45.7%	8.7%	$10,820	$30,790	99.8%
Madagascar	$900	55.4%	15.4%	29.2%	$1,400	$951	8.0%
Malawi	$600	46.7%	14.9%	38.4%	$645	$364	5.0%
Mali	$1,200	35.5%	26.1%	38.4%	$1,858	$323	- - -
Mauritania	$2,200	50.8%	30.0%	19.3%	$1,124	$784	- - -
Mauritius	$13,100	63.3%	30.6%	6.1%	$2,507	$1,949	100.0%
Morocco	$4,200	53.6%	29.6%	16.8%	$18,150	$9,472	71.1%
Mozambique	$1,300	42.8%	31.2%	26.1%	$2,041	$1,690	7.2%
Namibia	$7,000	63.6%	25.6%	10.8%	$2,350	$2,040	34.0%
Niger	$900	43.4%	16.8%	39.9%	$588	$222	- - -
Nigeria	$1,400	24.2%	49.5%	26.4%	$25,950	$52,160	40.0%
Rwanda	$1,500	36.5%	21.9%	41.6%	$243	$98	- - -
Sao Tome and Principe	$1,200	68.4%	14.6%	17.0%	$38	$8	
Senegal	$1,800	62%	21.2%	16.8%	$2,405	$1,526	30.1%
Seychelles	$7,800	61.7%	35.1%	3.3%	$460	$312	- - -
Sierra Leone	$800	16.5%	30.8%	52.7%	$531	$185	- - -
Somalia	$600	25.0%	10.0%	65.0%	$576	$241	- - -
South Africa	$12,000	65.2%	31.0%	3.8%	$52,970	$50,910	66.1%
Sudan	$2,100	41.0%	20.3%	38.7%	$5,028	$6,989	30.0%
Swaziland	$5,000	36.2%	51.5%	12.2%	$2,149	$1,991	- - -
Tanzania	$700	38.6%	16.4%	45.0%	$2,391	$1,581	10.5%
Togo	$1,700	37.1%	22.2%	40.8%	$1,047	$768	9.0%
Tunisia	$8,300	59.8%	28.1%	12.1%	$12,860	$10,300	94.6%
Uganda	$1,800	46.4%	21.2%	32.4%	$1,608	$768	3.7%
Zambia	$900	50.2%	27%	22.8%	$1,934	$1,947	12.0%
Zimbabwe	$2,300	57.6%	24.3%	18.1%	$2,059	$1,644	39.7%
AFRICA: TERRITORIES AND AREAS OF SPECIAL STATUS							
France							
Mayotte	$2,600	- - -	- - -	- - -	$141	$3.44	- - -
Réunion	$6,200	73.0%	19.0%	8.0%	$2,500	$214	- - -
Morocco							
Western Sahara	- - -	- - -	- - -	- - -	- - -	- - -	- - -
Norway							
Bouvet Island	- - -	- - -	- - -	- - -	- - -	- - -	- - -
South Africa							
Prince Edward Islands	- - -	- - -	- - -	- - -	- - -	- - -	- - -
United Kingdom							
Saint Helena	$2,500	87.0%	10.0%	3.0%	$45	$19	- - -
AUSTRALIA & OCEANIA							
Australia	$31,900	71.2%	25.9%	2.9%	$119,600	$103,000	- - -
Fiji Islands	$6,000	56.8%	27.0%	16.2%	$1,235	$862	- - -
Kiribati	$800	74.9%	10.9%	14.2%	$62	$17	- - -
Marshall Islands	$2,300	70.0%	16.0%	14.0%	$54	$9	- - -
Micronesia	$3,900	46.0%	4.00%	50.0%	$149	$22	- - -
Nauru	$5,000	- - -	- - -	- - -	$20	$17	- - -
New Zealand	$25,200	68.0%	27.4%	4.6%	$24,570	$22,210	- - -
Palau	$5,800	- - -	- - -	- - -	$99	$18	- - -
Papua New Guinea	$2,600	35.2%	39.4%	25.7%	$1,651	$2,833	- - -
Samoa	$5,600	63.0%	23.0%	14.0%	$285	$94	- - -
Solomon Islands	$1,700	47.0%	11.0%	42.0%	$159	$171	- - -
Tonga	$2,300	56.4%	15.1%	28.5%	$122	$34	- - -
Tuvalu	$1,100	- - -	- - -	- - -	$31	$1	- - -
Vanuatu	$2,900	62.0%	12.0%	26.0%	$233	$205	- - -
AUSTRALIA & OCEANIA: TERRITORIES AND AREAS OF SPECIAL STATUS							
Australia							
Ashmore and Cartier Islands	- - -	- - -	- - -	- - -	- - -	- - -	- - -
Christmas Island	- - -	- - -	- - -	- - -	- - -	- - -	- - -
Cocos (Keeling) Islands	- - -	- - -	- - -	- - -	- - -	- - -	- - -
Coral Sea Islands Territory	- - -	- - -	- - -	- - -	- - -	- - -	- - -
Norfolk Island	- - -	- - -	- - -	- - -	$18	$1.5	- - -
France							
Clipperton Island	- - -	- - -	- - -	- - -			- - -
French Polynesia	$17,500	78.0%	18.0%	4.0%	$1,437	$385	- - -
New Caledonia	$15,000	65.0%	30.0%	5.0%	$1,636	$999	- - -
Wallis and Futuna	$3,800	- - -	- - -	- - -	$0.3	$0.25	- - -
New Zealand							
Cook Islands	$5,000	75.2%	7.8%	17.0%	$51	$9.1	- - -
Niue	$3,600	- - -	- - -	- - -	$2	$0.137	- - -
Tokelau	$1,000	- - -	- - -	- - -	$0.3	$0.098	- - -
United Kingdom							
Pitcairn Islands	- - -	81.0%	13.6%	5.4%	- - -	- - -	- - -
United States							
American Samoa	$5,800	- - -	- - -	- - -	$105	$10	- - -
Baker Island	- - -	- - -	- - -	- - -	- - -	- - -	- - -
Guam	$15,000	78.0%	15.0%	7.0%	$701	$45	- - -
Northern Mariana Islands	$12,500	- - -	- - -	- - -	- - -	- - -	- - -

Telephone mainlines per 1,000 people 2003	Arable & permanent cropland area 2003 sq km (sq mi)	Forested area as % of total land area 2000	Protected areas as % of total land area 2003	Average annual deforestation: % change 1990 - 2000 (Negative number indicates an increase in forest area.)	Carbon dioxide emissions : metric tonnes per capita 2000	CONTINENT / Country Formal Name
17	1,320 (510)	2.9%	- - -	- - -	0.1	Union of the Comoros
2	5,470 (2,112)	65.8%	6.5%	0.1%	0.5	Republic of the Congo
0	78,000 (30,116)	58.9%	5.0%	0.4%	0.1	Democratic Republic of the Congo
14	69,000 (26,641)	32.7%	6.0%	3.1%	0.7	Republic of Côte d'Ivoire
15	10 (4)	0.2%	- - -	- - -	0.6	Republic of Djibouti
127	34,240 (13,220)	0.1%	9.7%	-3.4%	2.2	Arab Republic of Egypt
18	2,300 (888)	58.2%	- - -	- - -	0.4	Republic of Equatorial Guinea
9	5,650 (2,181)	15.4%	4.3%	0.3%	0.1	State of Eritrea
6	117,690 (45,440)	11.9%	16.9%	0.8%	0.1	Federal Democratic Republic of Ethiopia
29	4,950 (1,911)	84.5%	0.7%	0.0%	2.8	Gabonese Republic
28	3,200 (1,236)	41.7%	2.3%	-1.0%	0.2	Republic of The Gambia
13	63,850 (24,653)	24.2%	5.6%	1.7%	0.3	Republic of Ghana
3	17,500 (6,757)	27.4%	0.7%	0.5%	0.2	Republic of Guinea
8	5,500 (2,124)	73.7%	- - -	0.9%	0.2	Republic of Guinea-Bissau
10	52,120 (20,124)	6.2%	8.0%	0.5%	0.3	Republic of Kenya
13	3,340 (1,290)	0.3%	0.2%	0.0%	- - -	Kingdom of Lesotho
- - -	6,020 (2,324)	32.7%	1.7%	2.0%	0.1	Republic of Liberia
136	21,500 (8,301)	0.1%	0.1%	-1.4%	10.9	Great Socialist People's Libyan Arab Jamahiriya
4	35,500 (13,707)	22.1%	4.3%	0.9%	0.1	Republic of Madagascar
8	25,900 (10,000)	36.2%	11.2%	2.4%	0.1	Republic of Malawi
5	47,000 (18,147)	10.3%	3.7%	0.7%	0.1	Republic of Mali
14	5,000 (1,931)	0.3%	1.7%	2.7%	1.2	Islamic Republic of Mauritania
285	1,060 (409)	18.2%	7.8%	0.6%	2.4	Republic of Mauritius
40	93,760 (36,201)	9.8%	0.7%	0.0%	1.3	Kingdom of Morocco
5	45,800 (17,683)	24.6%	8.4%	0.2%	0.1	Republic of Mozambique
66	8,200 (3,166)	9.3%	13.6%	0.9%	1.0	Republic of Namibia
2	145,000 (55,985)	1.0%	7.7%	3.7%	0.1	Republic of Niger
7	334,000 (128,958)	12.2%	3.3%	2.6%	0.3	Federal Republic of Nigeria
3	14,700 (5,676)	19.5%	6.2%	3.9%	0.1	Republic of Rwanda
46	550 (212)	28.4%	- - -	- - -	0.6	Democratic Republic of Sao Tome and Principe
22	25,070 (9,680)	45.0%	11.6%	0.7%	0.4	Republic of Senegal
256	70 (27)	88.9%	- - -	- - -	2.8	Republic of Seychelles
5	6,450 (2,490)	38.5%	2.1%	2.9%	0.1	Republic of Sierra Leone
10	10,710 (4,135)	11.4%	0.8%	1.0%	- - -	Somalia
107	157,120 (60,664)	7.6%	5.5%	0.1%	7.4	Republic of South Africa
27	174,200 (67,259)	28.4%	5.2%	1.4%	0.2	Republic of the Sudan
44	1,920 (741)	31.5%	3.5%	-1.2%	0.4	Kingdom of Swaziland
4	51,000 (19,691)	39.9%	29.8%	0.2%	0.1	United Republic of Tanzania
12	26,300 (10,154)	7.1%	7.9%	3.4%	0.4	Togolese Republic
118	49,300 (19,035)	6.8%	0.3%	-0.2%	1.9	Tunisian Republic
2	73,500 (28,379)	18.4%	24.6%	2.0%	0.1	Republic of Uganda
8	52,890 (20,421)	57.1%	31.9%	2.4%	0.2	Republic of Zambia
26	33,500 (12,934)	45.3%	12.1%	1.5%	1.2	Republic of Zimbabwe
						AFRICA: TERRITORIES AND AREAS OF SPECIAL STATUS
	- - - - - -	14.7%	- - -	- - -	- - -	French Overseas Territorial Collectivity
- - -	390 (151)	33.6%	- - -	- - -	- - -	French Overseas Department
- - -	50 (19)	3.8%	- - -	- - -	- - -	Area of Special Status
- - -	- - - - - -	- - -	- - -	- - -	- - -	Territory of Norway
- - -	- - - - - -	- - -	- - -	- - -	- - -	Territory of South Africa
- - -	40 (15)	6.5%	- - -	- - -	- - -	British Overseas Territory
						AUSTRALIA & OCEANIA
542	479,350 (185,078)	21.3%	13.4%	0.0%	18.0	Commonwealth of Australia
124	2,850 (1,100)	54.7%	- - -	- - -	0.9	Republic of the Fiji Islands
51	370 (143)	3.0%	- - -	- - -	0.3	Republic of Kiribati
83	100 (39)	- - -	- - -	- - -	- - -	Republic
103	360 (139)	90.6%	- - -	- - -	- - -	Federated
- - -	- - - - - -	0.0%	- - -	- - -	- - -	Republic of Nauru
448	33,720 (13,019)	31.0%	29.6%	-0.5%	8.3	New Zealand
- - -	60 (23)	87.6%	- - -	- - -	- - -	Republic of Palau
12	8,750 (3,378)	65.0%	2.3%	0.4%	0.5	Independent State
73	1,290 (498)	60.4%	- - -	- - -	0.8	Independent State of Samoa
13	770 (297)	77.6%	- - -	- - -	0.4	Solomon Islands
113	260 (100)	5.0%	- - -	- - -	1.2	Kingdom of Tonga
	20 (8)	33.3%	- - -	- - -	- - -	Tuvalu
31	1,050 (405)	36.1%	- - -	- - -	0.4	Republic of Vanuatu
						AUSTRALIA & OCEANIA: TERRITORIES AND AREAS OF SPECIAL STATUS
- - -	- - - - - -	- - -	- - -	- - -	- - -	Australian External Territory
- - -	- - - - - -	- - -	- - -	- - -	- - -	Australian External Territory
- - -	- - - - - -	- - -	- - -	- - -	- - -	Australian External Territory
- - -		- - -	- - -	- - -	- - -	Australian External Territory
- - -	- - - - - -	- - -	- - -	- - -	- - -	Australian External Territory
- - -	- - - - - -	- - -	- - -	- - -	- - -	French Possession
- - -	250 (97)	28.7%	- - -	- - -	- - -	French Overseas Territory
- - -	10 (4)	39.2%	- - -	- - -	- - -	French Overseas Territory
- - -	60 (23)	35.3%	- - -	- - -	- - -	French Overseas Territory
- - -	60 (23)	66.5%	- - -	- - -	- - -	Self-Governing in Free Association with New Zealand
- - -	70 (27)	54.2%	- - -	- - -	- - -	Self-Governing in Free Association with New Zealand
- - -	- - - - - -	0.0%	- - -	- - -	- - -	Territory of New Zealand
- - -	- - - - - -	83.3%	- - -	- - -	- - -	British Overseas Territory
- - -	50 (19)	89.4%	- - -	- - -	- - -	Territory of the United States
- - -	- - - - - -	- - -	- - -	- - -	- - -	Territory of the United States
- - -	120 (46)	47.1%	- - -	- - -	- - -	Territory of the United States
- - -	80 (31)	72.4%	- - -	- - -	- - -	Commonwealth in Political Union with the United States

GEOGRAPHIC COMPARISONS

THE EARTH

MASS: 5,974,000,000,000,000,000,000 metric tonnes
AREA: 510,066,000 sq km
LAND: 148,647,000 sq km (29.1%)
WATER: 361,419,000 sq km (70.9%)
POPULATION Mid-2005: 6,477,000,000

THE CONTINENTS

	AREA (SQ KM)	PERCENT OF EARTH'S LAND
Asia	44,579,000	30.0
Africa	30,065,000	20.2
North America	24,474,000	16.5
South America	17,819,000	12.0
Antarctica	13,209,000	8.9
Europe	9,938,000	6.7
Australia	7,687,000	5.2

HIGHEST POINT ON EACH CONTINENT

		METERS
1	Everest, Asia	8,850
2	Aconcagua, South America	6,960
3	McKinley (Denali), North America	6,194
4	Kilimanjaro, Africa	5,895
5	El'brus, Europe	5,642
6	Vinson Massif, Antarctica	4,897
7	Kosciuszko, Australia	2,228

LOWEST SURFACE POINT ON EACH CONTINENT

		METERS
1	Dead Sea, Asia	-416
2	Lake Assal, Africa	-156
3	Laguna del Carbón, South America	-105
4	Death Valley, North America	-86
5	Caspian Sea, Europe	-28
6	Lake Eyre, Australia	-16
7	Antarctica (ice covered)	-2,555

POPULATION OF EACH CONTINENT, Mid-2005

	POPULATION	PERCENT OF WORLD TOTAL
Asia	3,921,000,000	60.5
Africa	906,000,000	14.0
Europe	730,000,000	11.3
North America	515,000,000	7.9
South America	373,000,000	5.8
Australia	20,400,000	0.3
Islands of the Pacific	13,000,000	0.2

THE OCEANS

	AREA (SQ KM)	PERCENT OF EARTH'S WATER AREA
Pacific	169,479,000	46.8
Atlantic	91,526,400	25.3
Indian	74,694,800	20.6
Arctic	13,960,100	3.9

DEEPEST POINT IN EACH OCEAN

		METERS
1	Challenger Deep, Mariana Trench, Pacific	10,920
2	Puerto Rico Trench, Atlantic	8,605
3	Java Trench, Indian	7,125
4	Molloy Hole, Arctic	5,669

MAJOR SEAS

		AREA (SQ KM)	AVERAGE DEPTH (METERS)
1	Coral	4,183,510	2,471
2	South China	3,596,390	1,180
3	Caribbean	2,834,290	2,596
4	Bering	2,519,580	1,832
5	Mediterranean	2,469,100	1,572
6	Sea of Okhotsk	1,625,190	814
7	Gulf of Mexico	1,531,810	1,544
8	Norwegian	1,425,280	1,768
9	Greenland	1,157,850	1,443
10	Sea of Japan (East Sea)	1,008,260	1,647
11	Hudson Bay	1,005,510	119
12	East China Sea	785,986	374

LONGEST RIVERS

		LENGTH (KM)
1	Nile, Africa	6,825
2	Amazon, South America	6,437
3	Chang Jiang (Yangtze), Asia	6,380
4	Mississippi-Missouri, North America	5,971
5	Yenisey-Angara, Asia	5,536
6	Huang (Yellow), Asia	5,464
7	Ob-Irtysh, Asia	5,410
8	Amur, Asia	4,416
9	Lena, Asia	4,400
10	Congo, Africa	4,370
11	Mackenzie-Peace, North America	4,241
12	Mekong, Asia	4,184
13	Niger, Africa	4,170

METRIC CONVERSION TABLES

CONVERSION FROM METRIC MEASURES

SYMBOL	WHEN YOU KNOW	MULTIPLY BY	TO FIND	SYMBOL
LENGTH				
cm	centimeters	0.393701	inches	in
m	meters	3.280840	feet	ft
m	meters	1.093613	yards	yd
km	kilometers	0.621371	miles	mi
AREA				
cm²	square centimeters	0.155000	square inches	in²
m²	square meters	10.76391	square feet	ft²
m²	square meters	1.195990	square yards	yd²
km²	square kilometers	0.386102	square miles	mi²
ha	hectares	2.471054	acres	—
MASS				
g	grams	0.035274	ounces	oz
kg	kilograms	2.204623	pounds	lb
t	metric tonnes	1.102311	short tons	—
VOLUME				
mL	milliliters	0.061024	cubic inches	in³
mL	milliliters	0.033814	liquid ounces	liq oz
L	liters	2.113376	pints	pt
L	liters	1.056688	quarts	qt
L	liters	0.264172	gallons	gal
m³	cubic meters	35.31467	cubic feet	ft³
m³	cubic meters	1.307951	cubic yards	yd³
TEMPERATURE				
°C	degrees Celsius (centigrade)	9/5 & add 32	degrees Fahrenheit	°F

CONVERSION TO METRIC MEASURES

SYMBOL	WHEN YOU KNOW	MULTIPLY BY	TO FIND	SYMBOL
LENGTH				
in	inches	2.54	centimeters	cm
ft	feet	0.3048	meters	m
yd	yards	0.9144	meters	m
mi	miles	1.609344	kilometers	km
AREA				
in²	square inches	6.4516	square centimeters	cm²
ft²	square feet	0.092903	square meters	m²
yd²	square yards	0.836127	square meters	m²
mi²	square miles	2.589988	square kilometers	km²
—	acres	0.404686	hectares	ha
MASS				
oz	ounces	28.349523	grams	g
lb	pounds	0.453592	kilograms	kg
—	short tons	0.907185	metric tonnes	t
VOLUME				
in³	cubic inches	16.387064	milliliters	mL
liq oz	liquid ounces	29.57353	milliliters	mL
pt	pints	0.473176	liters	L
qt	quarts	0.946353	liters	L
gal	gallons	3.785412	liters	L
ft³	cubic feet	0.028317	cubic meters	m³
yd³	cubic yards	0.764555	cubic meters	m³
TEMPERATURE				
°F	degrees Fahrenheit	5/9 after subtracting 32	degrees Celsius (centigrade)	°C

URBAN AGGLOMERATIONS, 2005
(Population in thousands)

City	Country	Population
Tokyo	Japan	35,327
Mexico City	Mexico	19,013
New York-Newark	United States	18,498
Mumbai (Bombay)	India	18,336
São Paulo	Brazil	18,333
Delhi	India	15,334
Kolkata (Calcutta)	India	14,299
Buenos Aires	Argentina	13,349
Jakarta	Indonesia	13,194
Shanghai	China	12,665
Dhaka	Bangladesh	12,560
Los Angeles-Long Beach-Santa Ana,	United States	12,146
Karachi	Pakistan	11,819
Rio de Janeiro	Brazil	11,469
Osaka-Kōbe	Japan	11,286
Cairo	Egypt	11,146
Lagos	Nigeria	11,135
Beijing	China	10,849
Metro Manila	Philippines	10,677
Moscow	Russia	10,672
Paris	France	9,854
Istanbul	Turkey	9,760
Seoul	South Korea	9,592
Tianjin	China	9,346
Chicago	United States	8,711
Lima	Peru	8,180
London	United Kingdom	7,615
Bogotá	Colombia	7,594
Tehran	Iran	7,352
Hong Kong	China,	7,182
Chennai (Madras)	India	6,915
Bangkok	Thailand	6,604
Rhein-Ruhr North	Germany	6,566
(Duisburg, Essen, Krefeld, Mülheim, Oberhausen, Bottrop, Gelsenkirchen, Bochum, Dortmund, Hagen, Hamm and Herne)		
Bangalore	India	6,532
Lahore	Pakistan	6,373
Hyderabad	India	6,145
Wuhan	China	6,003
Baghdad	Iraq	5,910
Kinshasa	Dem. Rep. Congo	5,717
Santiago	Chile	5,623
Riyadh	Saudi Arabia	5,514
Miami	United States	5,380
Brasília	Brazil	5,341
Philadelphia	United States	5,325
Saint Petersburg	Russia	5,315
Belo Horizonte	Brazil	5,304
Ahmadabad	India	5,171
Madrid	Spain	5,145
Toronto	Canada	5,060
Ho Chi Minh City	Vietnam	5,030
Chongqing	China	4,975
Shenyang	China	4,916
Dallas-Fort Worth	United States	4,612
Khartoum	Sudan	4,495
Pune (Poona)	India	4,485
Barcelona	Spain	4,424
Sydney	Australia	4,388
Singapore	Singapore	4,372
Boston	United States	4,313
Atlanta	United States	4,284
Houston	United States	4,283
Washington, D.C.	United States	4,190
Chittagong	Bangladesh	4,171
Hanoi	Vietnam	4,147
Yangon (Rangoon)	Myanmar (Burma)	4,082
Bandung	Indonesia	4,020
Milan	Italy	4,007
Detroit	United States	3,980
Guadalajara	Mexico	3,881
Jeddah	Saudi Arabia	3,807
Porto Alegre	Brazil	3,795
Alexandria	Egypt	3,760
Casablanca	Morocco	3,743
Rhein-Main	Germany	3,721
(Darmstadt, Frankfurt, Offenbach and Wiesbaden)		
Surat	India	3,671
Melbourne	Australia	3,663
Ankara	Turkey	3,593
Recife	Brazil	3,527
Busan (Pusan)	South Korea	3,527
Monterrey	Mexico	3,517
Abidjan	Côte d'Ivoire (Ivory Coast)	3,516
Montréal	Canada	3,511
Chengdu	China	3,478
Phoenix-Mesa	United States	3,393
San Francisco-Oakland	United States	3,342
Salvador	Brazil	3,331
Berlin	Germany	3,328
Rhein-Ruhr Middle	Germany	3,325
(Düsseldorf, Mönchengladbach, Remscheid, Solingen and Wuppertal)		
Kabul	Afghanistan	3,288
Johannesburg	South Africa	3,288
Pyongyang	North Korea	3,284

Abbreviations

A.	Arroio, Arroyo
A. Buryat	Agin Buryat
A.C.T.	Australian Capital Territory
A.F.B.	Air Force Base
A.F.S.	Air Force Station
A.R.B.	Air Reserve Base
Adm.	Administrative
Af.	Africa
Afghan.	Afghanistan
Ala.	Alabama
Alas.	Alaska
Alban.	Albania
Alg.	Algeria
Alta.	Alberta
Amer.	America-n
Amzns.	Amazonas
Anch.	Anchorage
And. & Nic.	Andaman and Nicobar Islands
And. Prad.	Andhra Pradesh
Antil.	Antilles
Arch.	Archipelago, Archipiélago
Arg.	Argentina
Ariz.	Arizona
Ark.	Arkansas
Arkh.	Arkhangel'sk
Arm.	Armenia
Arun. Prad.	Arunachal Pradesh
Astrak.	Astrakhan'
Atl. Oc.	Atlantic Ocean
Aust.	Austria
Austral.	Australia
Auton.	Autonomous
Azerb.	Azerbaijan
B.	Baai, Baía, Baie, Bahía, Bay, Buḩayrat
B. Aires	Buenos Aires
B.C.	British Columbia
B. Qazaq.	Batys Qazaqstan
Bashk.	Bashkortostan
Bayq.	Bayqongyr
Belg.	Belgium
Bol.	Bolivia
Bol.	Bol'sh-oy, -aya, -oye
Bosn. & Herzg.	Bosnia and Herzegovina
Br.	Branch
Braz.	Brazil
Bulg.	Bulgaria
Burya.	Buryatiya
C.	Cabo, Cap, Cape, Capo
C.H.	Court House
C.P.	Conservation Park
C.R.	Costa Rica
C.S.I. Terr.	Coral Sea Islands Territory
Cach.	Cachoeira
Calif.	California
Can.	Canada
Cap.	Capitán
Catam.	Catamarca
Cd.	Ciudad
Cen. Af. Rep.	Central African Republic
Cga.	Ciénaga
Chan.	Channel
Chand.	Chandigarh
Chap.	Chapada
Chech.	Chechnya
Chely.	Chelyabinsk
Chhat.	Chhattīsgarh
Chongq.	Chongqing Shi
Chuk.	Chukotskiy
Chuv.	Chuvashiya
Chyrv.	Chyrvony, -aya, -aye
Cmte.	Comandante
Cnel.	Coronel
Co.-s.	Cerro-s
Col.	Colombia
Colo.	Colorado
Conn.	Connecticut
Cord.	Cordillera
Corr.	Corrientes
Cr.	Creek, Crique
D.	Danau
D. & Diu	Daman and Diu
D. & Nagar	Dadra and Nagar Haveli
D.C.	District of Columbia
D.F.	Distrito Federal
Del.	Delaware
Dem.	Democratic
Den.	Denmark
Dist.	District, Distrito
Dom. Rep.	Dominican Republic
Dr.	Doctor
Dz.	Dzong
E.	East-ern
E. Ríos	Entre Ríos
E. Santo	Espírito Santo
Ea.	Estancia
Ecua.	Ecuador
El Salv.	El Salvador
Emb.	Embalse
Eng.	England
Ens.	Ensenada
Entr.	Entrance
Eq.	Equatorial
Est.	Estación
Est.	Estonia
Ét.	Étang
Eth.	Ethiopia
Eur.	Europe
Ez.	Ezers
F.	Fiume
F.S.M.	Federated States of Micronesia
Falk. Is.	Falkland Islands
Fd.	Fiord, Fiordo, Fjord
Fed.	Federal, Federation
Fin.	Finland
Fk.	Fork
Fla.	Florida
Fn.	Fortín
Fr.	France, French
Ft.	Fort
Fy.	Ferry
G.	Golfe, Golfo, Gulf
G. Altay	Gorno-Altay
G.R.	Game Reserve
Ga.	Georgia
Geb.	Gebergte, Gebirge
Gen.	General
Ger.	Germany
Gez.	Gezîra-t, Gezîret
Gezr.	Gezâir
Gl.	Glacier
Gob.	Gobernador
Gr.	Greece,
Gr.	Gross-er
Gral.	General
Gt.	Great-er
Guang.	Guangdong
H.K.	Hong Kong
Hbr.	Harbor, Harbour
Hdqrs.	Headquarters
Heilong.	Heilongjiang
Hi. Prad.	Himachal Pradesh
Hist.	Historic, -al
Hond.	Honduras
Hts.	Heights
Hung.	Hungary
Hwy.	Highway
I.H.S.	International Historic Site
I.-s.	Île-s, Ilha-s, Isla-s, Island-s, Isle, Isol-a, -e
Ice.	Iceland
Ig.	Igarapé
Igr.	Ingeniero
Ill.	Illinois
Ind.	Indiana
Ind. Oc.	Indian Ocean
Ingush.	Ingushetiya
Intl.	International
Ire.	Ireland
It.	Italy
J.	Järvi, Joki
J. & Kash.	Jammu and Kashmir
J.A.R.	Jewish Autonomous Region
Jab., Jeb.	Jabal, Jebel
Jam.	Jamaica
Jct.	Jonction, Junction
Jez.	Jezero, Jezioro
Jhark.	Jharkhand
K.	Kanal
K. Balka.	Kabardino-Balkariya
K. Cherk.	Karachayevo-Cherkesiya
K. Mansi	Khanty-Mansi
K. Permy.	Komi-Permyak
Kalin.	Kaliningrad
Kalmy.	Kalmykiya
Kamchat.	Kamchatka
Kans.	Kansas
Karna.	Karnataka
Kaz.	Kazakhstan
Kemer.	Kemerovo
Kep.	Kepulauan
Kh.	Khor
Khabar.	Khabarovsk
Khak.	Khakasiya
Khr.	Khrebet
Km.	Kilómetro
Kól.	Kólpos
Kör.	Körfez,-i
Koryak.	Koryakskiy
Kr.	Krasn-yy, -aya, -oye
Krasnod.	Krasnodar
Krasnoy.	Krasnoyarsk
Ky.	Kentucky
Kyrg.	Kyrgyzstan
L.	Lac, Lago, Lake, Límni, Loch, Lough
La.	Louisiana
Lag.	Laguna
Lakshad.	Lakshadweep
Latv.	Latvia
Ldg.	Landing
Leb.	Lebanon
Lib.	Libya
Liech.	Liechtenstein
Lith.	Lithuania
Lux.	Luxembourg
M.	Mal-yy, -aya, -oye
M.C.A.S.	Marine Corps Air Station
M. Gerais	Minas Gerais
M. Grosso	Mato Grosso
M. Grosso S.	Mato Grosso do Sul
M. Prad.	Madhya Pradesh
Maced.	Macedonia
Mahar.	Maharashtra
Mal.	Mal-y-y, -aya, -aye
Man.	Manitoba
Mangg.	Mangghystaū
Maran.	Maranhão
Mass.	Massachusetts
Md.	Maryland
Me.	Maine
Medit. Sea	Mediterranean Sea
Meghal.	Meghalaya
Mex.	Mexico
Mgne.	Montagne
Mich.	Michigan
Minn.	Minnesota
Miss.	Mississippi
Mo.	Missouri
Mold.	Moldova
Mon.	Monument
Mont.	Montana
Mor.	Morocco
Mord.	Mordoviya
Mt.-s.	Mont-s, Mount-ain-s
Mte.-s.	Monte-s
Mti., Mtii.	Munţi-i
Mun.	Municipal
Murm.	Murmansk
N.	North-ern
N.A.S.	Naval Air Station
N.B.	National Battlefield
N.B.	New Brunswick
N.B.P.	National Battlefield Park
N.B.S.	National Battlefield Site
N.C.	National Cemetery
N.C.	North Carolina
N.C.A.	National Conservation Area
N. Dak.	North Dakota
N.E.	North East
N.H.	New Hampshire
N.H.P.	National Historic, -al Park
N.H.S.	National Historic Site
N. Ire.	Northern Ireland
N.J.	New Jersey
N.L.	National Lakeshore
N.M.	National Monument
N.M.P.	National Military Park
N. Mem.	National Memorial
N. Mem. P.	National Memorial Park
N. Mex.	New Mexico
N. Mongol	Nei Mongol
N.P.	National Park
N.R.	Nature Reserve
N.R.A.	National Recreation Area
N.S.	Nova Scotia, National Seashore
N.S.R.	National Scenic Riverway
N.S.R.A.	National Seashore Recreational Area
N.S.T.	National Scenic Trail
N.S.W.	New South Wales
N.T.	Northern Territory
N.T.C.	Naval Training Center
N.T.S.	Naval Training Station
N.V.M.	National Volcanic Monument
N.W.T.	Northwest Territories
N.Y.	New York
N.Z.	New Zealand
Nat. Mem.	National Memorial
Nat. Mon.	National Monument
Nat. Park	National Park
Nebr.	Nebraska
Neth.	Netherlands
Nev.	Nevada, Nevado
Nfld. & Lab.	Newfoundland and Labrador
Nicar.	Nicaragua
Niz. Nov.	Nizhniy Novogorod
Nizh.	Nizhn-iy, -yaya, -eye
Nor.	Norway
Nov.	Nov-yy, -aya, -aye, -oye
Novg.	Novgorod
Novo.	Novosibirsk
Nr.	Nørre
O.	Ostrov, Oued
Oc.	Ocean
Of.	Oficina
Okla.	Oklahoma
Ong. Qazaq.	Ongtüstik Qazaqstan
Ont.	Ontario
Ør.	Øster
Oreg.	Oregon
Orenb.	Orenburg
Oz.	Ozero
P.	Paso, Pass, Passo
P.E.I.	Prince Edward Island
P.N.G.	Papua New Guinea
P.R.	Puerto Rico
Pa.	Pennsylvania
Pac. Oc.	Pacific Ocean
Pak.	Pakistan
Pan.	Panama
Pant.	Pantano
Parag.	Paraguay
Parq. Nac.	Parque Nacional
Pass.	Passage
Peg.	Pegunungan
Pen.	Peninsula, Péninsule
Per.	Pereval
Pern.	Pernambuco
Pivd.	Pivdennyy
Pk.	Peak
Pl.	Planina
Plat.	Plateau
Pol.	Poland
Pol.	Poluostrov
Pondi.	Pondicherry
Por.	Porog
Port.	Portugal
Pres.	Presidente
Prov.	Province, Provincial
Pt.-e.	Point-e
Pta.	Ponta, Punta
Pto.	Puerto
Q.	Quebrada
Qarag.	Qaraghandy
Qnsld.	Queensland
Que.	Quebec
Qyzyl.	Qyzylorda
R.	Río, River, Rivière
R. Gr. Norte	Rio Grande do Norte
R. Gr. Sul	Rio Grande do Sul
R.I.	Rhode Island
R. Jan.	Rio de Janeiro
R. Negro	Río Negro
Ra.-s.	Range-s
Raja.	Rajasthan
Reg.	Region
Rep.	Republic
Res.	Reservoir, Reserve, Reservatório
Rk.	Rock
Rom.	Romania
Russ.	Russia
S.	South-ern
S.A.R.	Special Administrative Region
S. Aust.	South Australia
S.C.	South Carolina
S. Dak.	South Dakota
S. Estero	Santiago del Estero
S. Paulo	São Paulo
S.W.	Southwest
Sa.-s.	Serra, Sierra-s
Sal.	Salar, Salina
Sask.	Saskatchewan
Scot.	Scotland
Sd.	Sound
Sel.	Selat
Ser.	Serranía
Serb. & Mont.	Serbia and Montenegro
Sev.	Severn-yy, -aya, -oye
Sev. Oset.	Severnaya Osetiya-Alaniya
Sgt.	Sargento
Shand.	Shandong
Shy. Qazaq.	Shyghys Qazaqstan
Sk.	Shankou
Slov.	Slovenia
Solt. Qazaq.	Soltüstik Qazaqstan
Sp.	Spain, Spanish
Spr.-s.	Spring-s
Sq.	Square
Sr.	Sønder
St.-e.	Saint-e, Sankt, Sint
St. Peter.	Saint Petersburg
Sta., Sto.	Santa, Station, Santo
Sta. Cata.	Santa Catarina
Sta. Cruz.	Santa Cruz
Stavr.	Stavropol'
Str.-s.	Strait, Strait-s
Sv.	Svyat-oy, -aya, -oye
Sverd.	Sverdlovsk
Sw.	Sweden
Switz.	Switzerland
Syr.	Syria
T. Fuego	Tierra del Fuego
T. Nadu	Tamil Nadu
Taj.	Tajikistan
Tartar.	Tartarstan
Tas.	Tasmania
Tel.	Teluk
Tenn.	Tennessee
Terr.	Territory
Tex.	Texas
Tg.	Tanjung
Thai.	Thailand
Tocant.	Tocantins
Trin.	Trinidad
Tun.	Tunisia
Turk.	Turkey
Turkm.	Turkmenistan
U.A.E.	United Arab Emirates
U.K.	United Kingdom
U. O. Buryat	Ust' Ordynskiy Buryat
U. Prad.	Uttar Pradesh
U.S.	United States
Udmur.	Udmurtiya
Uj.	Ujung
Ukr.	Ukraine
Ulyan.	Ul'yanovsk
Uru.	Uruguay
Uttar.	Uttaranchal
Uzb.	Uzbekistan
Va.	Virginia
Val.	Valle
Vdkhr.	Vodokhranilishche
Vdskh.	Vodoskhovyshche
Venez.	Venezuela
Verkh.	Verkhn-iy, -yaya, -eye
Vic.	Victoria
Vol.	Volcán, Volcano
Volg.	Volgograd
Voz.	Vozyera, -yero, -yera
Vozv.	Vozvyshennost'
Vr.	Vester
Vt.	Vermont
Vyal.	Vyaliki, -ikaya, -ikaye
W.	Wadi, Wādī, Webi
W.	West-ern
W. Aust.	Western Australia
W. Bengal	West Bengal
W.H.	Water Hole
W. Va.	West Virginia
Wash.	Washington
Wis.	Wisconsin
Wyo.	Wyoming
Y. Nenets	Yemal-Nenets
Yar.	Yarymadasy
Yaro.	Yaroslavl'
Yu.	Yuzhn-yy, -aya, -oye
Zakh.	Zakhod-ni, -nyaya, -nye
Zal.	Zaliv
Zap.	Zapadn-yy, -aya, -oye
Zimb.	Zimbabwe

Foreign Terms

Aaglet	well
Aain	spring
Aauinat	spring
Āb	river, water
Ache	stream
Açude	reservoir
Ada,-si	island
Adrar	mountain-s, plateau
Aguada	dry lake bed
Aguelt	water hole, well
'Ain, Aïn	spring, well
Aïoun-et	spring-s, well
Aivi	mountain
Akra, Akrotírio	cape, promontory
Alb	mountain, ridge
Alföld	plain
Alin'	mountain range
Alpe-n	mountain-s
Altiplanicie	high-plain, plateau
Alto	hill-s, mountain-s, ridge
Älv-en	river
Āmba	hill, mountain
Anou	well
Anse	bay, inlet
Ao	bay, cove, estuary
Ap	cape, point
Archipel, Archipiélago	archipelago
Arcipelago, Arkhipelag	archipelago
Arquipélago	archipelago
Arrecife-s	reef-s
Arroio, Arroyo	brook, gully, rivulet, stream
Ås	ridge
Ava	channel
Aylagy	gulf
'Ayn	spring, well
Ba	intermittent stream,river
Baai	bay, cove, lagoon
Bāb	gate, strait
Badia	bay
Bælt	strait
Bagh	bay
Bahar	drainage basin
Bahía	bay
Bahr, Baḩr	bay, lake, river, sea, wadi
Baía, Baie	bay
Bajo-s	shoal-s
Ban	village
Bañado-s	flooded area, swamp-s
Banc, Banco-s	bank-s, sandbank-s, shoal-s
Bandao	peninsula
Baño-s	hot spring-s, spa
Baraj-ı	dam, reservoir
Barra	bar, sandbank
Barrage, Barragem	dam, lake, reservoir
Barranca	gorge, ravine
Bazar	marketplace
Ben, Benin	mountain
Belt	strait
Bereg	bank, coast, shore
Berg-e	mountain-s
Bil	lake
Biq'at	plain, valley
Bir, Bîr, Bi'r	spring, well
Birket	lake, pool, swamp
Bjerg-e	mountain-s, range
Boca, Bocca	channel, river, mouth
Bocht	bay
Bodden	bay
Boğaz, -ı	strait
Bögeni	reservoir
Boka	gulf, mouth
Bol'sh-oy, -aya, -oye	big
Bolsón	inland basin
Boubairet	lagoon, lake
Bras	arm, branch of a stream
Braţ, -ul	arm, branch of a stream
Bre, -en	glacier, ice cap
Bredning	bay, broad water
Bruch	marsh
Bucht	bay
Bugt-en	bay
Buḩayrat, Buheirat	lagoon, lake,marsh
Bukhta, Bukta, Bukt-en	bay
Bulak, Bulaq	spring
Bum	hill, mountain
Burnu, Burun	cape, point
Busen	gulf
Buuraha	hill-s, mountain-s
Buyuk	big, large
Cabeza-s	head-s, summit-s
Cabo	cape
Cachoeira	rapids, waterfall
Cal	hill, peak
Caleta	cove, inlet
Campo-s	field-s, flat country
Canal	canal, channel, strait
Caño	channel, stream
Cao Nguyen	mountain, plateau
Cap, Capo	cape
Capitán	captain
Càrn	mountain
Castillo	castle, fort
Catarata-s	cataract-s, waterfall-s
Causse	upland
Çay	brook, stream
Cay-s, Cayo-s	island-s, key-s, shoal-s
Cerro-s	hill-s, peak-s
Chaîne, Chaînons	mountain chain, range
Chapada-s	plateau, upland-s
Chedo	archipelago
Chenal	river channel
Chersónisos	peninsula
Chhung	bay
Chi	lake
Chiang	bay
Chiao	cape, point, rock
Ch'ih	lake
Chink	escarpment
Chott	intermittent salt lake, salt marsh
Chou	island
Ch'ü	canal
Ch'üntao	archipelago, islands
Chute-s	cataract-s, waterfall-s
Chyrvony	red
Cima	mountain, peak, summit
Ciudad	city
Co	lake
Col	pass
Collina, Colline	hill, mountains
Con	island
Cordillera	mountain chain
Corno	mountain, peak
Coronel	colonel
Corredeira	cascade, rapids
Costa	coast
Côte	coast, slope
Coxilha, Cuchilla	range of low hills
Crique	creek, stream
Csatorna	canal, channel
Cul de Sac	bay, inlet
Da	great, greater
Daban	pass
Dağ, -ı, Dāgh	mountain
Dağlar, -ı	mountains
Dahr	cliff, mesa
Dake	mountain, peak
Dal-en	valley
Dala	steppe
Dan	cape, point
Danau	lake
Dao	island
Dar'ya	lake, river
Daryācheh	lake, marshy lake
Dasht	desert, plain
Dawan	pass
Dawḩat	bay, cove, inlet
Deniz, -i	sea
Dent-s	peak-s
Deo	pass
Desēt	hummock, island, land-tied island
Desierto	desert
Détroit	channel, strait
Dhar	hills, ridge, tableland
Ding	mountain
Distrito	district
Djebel	mountain, range
Do	island-s, rock-s
Doi	hill, mountain
Dome	ice dome
Dong	village
Dooxo	floodplain
Dzong	castle, fortress
Eiland-en	island-s
Eilean	island
Ejland	island
Elv	river
Embalse	lake, reservoir
Emi	mountain, rock
Enseada, Ensenada	bay, cove
Ér	rivulet, stream
Erg	sand dune region
Est,e	east
Estación	railroad station
Estany	lagoon, lake
Estero	estuary, inlet, lagoon, marsh
Estrecho	strait
Étang	lake, pond
Eylandt	island
Ežeras	lake
Ezers	lake

- Falaise *cliff, escarpment*
- Farvand-et *channel, sound*
- Fell *mountain*
- Feng *mount, peak*
- Fiord-o *inlet, sound*
- Fiume *river*
- Fjäll-et *mountain*
- Fjällen *mountains*
- Fjärd-en *fjord*
- Fjarđar, Fjörđur *fjord*
- Fjeld *mountain*
- Fjell-ene *mountain-s*
- Fjöll *mountain-s*
- Fjord-en *inlet, fjord*
- Fleuve *river*
- Fljót *large river*
- Flói *bay, marshland*
- Foci *river mouths*
- Főcsatorna *principal canal*
- Förde *fjord, gulf, inlet*
- Forsen *rapids, waterfall*
- Fortaleza *fort, fortress*
- Fortín *fortified post*
- Foss-en *waterfall*
- Foum *pass, passage*
- Foz *mouth of a river*
- Fuerte *fort, fortress*
- Fwafwate *waterfalls*

- Gacan-ka *hill, peak*
- Gal *pond, spring, waterhole, well*
- Gang *harbor*
- Gangri *peak, range*
- Gaoyuan *plateau*
- Garaet, Gara'et *lake, lake bed, salt lake*
- Gardaneh *pass*
- Garet *hill, mountain*
- Gat *channel*
- Gata *bay, inlet, lake*
- Gattet *channel, strait*
- Gaud *depression, saline tract*
- Gave *mountain stream*
- Gebel *mountain-s, range*
- Gebergte *mountain range*
- Gebirge *mountains, range*
- Geçidi *mountain pass, passage*
- Geçit *mountain pass, passage*
- Gezâir *islands*
- Gezîra-t, Gezîret *island, peninsula*
- Ghats *mountain range*
- Ghubb-at, -et *bay, gulf*
- Giri *mountain*
- Gjiri *bay*
- Gletscher *glacier*
- Gobernador *governor*
- Gobi *desert*
- Gol *river, stream*
- Göl, -ü *lake*
- Golets *mountain, peak*
- Golf, -e, -o *gulf*
- Gor-a, -y, Gór-a, -y *mountain,-s*
- Got *point*
- Gowd *depression*
- Goz *sand ridge*
- Gran, -de *great, large*
- Gryada *mountains, ridge*
- Guan *pass*
- Guba *bay, gulf*
- Guelta *well*
- Guntō *archipelago*
- Gunung *mountain*
- Gura *mouth, passage*
- Guyot *table mount*

- Ḩadabat *plateau*
- Haehyŏp *strait*
- Haff *lagoon*
- Hai *lake, sea*
- Haihsia *strait*
- Haixia *channel, strait*
- Hakau *reef, rock*
- Hakuchi *anchorage*
- Halvø, Halvøy-a *peninsula*
- Hama *beach*
- Hamada, Ḩammādah *rocky desert*
- Hamn *harbor, port*
- Hāmūn, Hamun *depression, lake*
- Hana *cape, point*
- Hantō *peninsula*
- Har *hill, mound, mountain*
- Ḩarrat *lava field*
- Hasi, Hassi *spring, well*
- Hauteur *elevation, height*
- Hav-et *sea*
- Havn, Havre *harbor, port*
- Hawr *lake, marsh*
- Hāyk' *lake, reservoir*
- Hegy, -ség *mountain, -s, range*
- Heiau *temple*
- Ho *canal, lake, river*
- Hoek *hook, point*
- Hög-en *high, hill*
- Höhe, -n *height, high*
- Høj *height, hill*
- Holm, -e, Holmene *island-s, islet -s*
- Ḩolot *dunes*
- Hon *island-s*
- Hor-a, -y *mountain, -s*
- Horn *horn, peak*
- Houma *point*
- Hoved *headland, peninsula, point*
- Hraun *lava field*
- Hsü *island*
- Hu *lake, reservoir*
- Huk *cape, point*
- Hüyük *hill, mound*

- Idehan *sand dunes*
- Île-s, Ilha-s, Illa-s, Îlot-s *island-s, islet-s*
- Îlet, Ilhéu-s *islet, -s*
- Irhil *mountain-s*
- 'Irq *sand dune-s*
- Isblink *glacier, ice field*
- Is-en *glacier*
- Isla-s, Islote *island-s, islet*
- Isol-a, -e *island, -s*
- Istmo *isthmus*
- Iwa *island, islet, rock*

- Jabal, Jebel *mountain-s, range*
- Järv, -i, Jaure, Javrre *lake*
- Jazā'ir, Jazīrat, Jazīreh *island-s*
- Jehīl *lake*
- Jezero, Jezioro *lake*
- Jiang *river, stream*
- Jiao *cape*
- Jībal *hill, mountain, ridge*
- Jima *island-s, rock-s*
- Jøkel, Jökull *glacier, ice cap*
- Joki, Jokka *river*
- Jökulsá *river from a glacier*
- Jūn *bay*

- Kaap *cape*
- Kafr *village*
- Kaikyō *channel, strait*
- Kaise *mountain*
- Kaiwan *bay, gulf, sea*
- Kanal *canal, channel*
- Kangri *mountain, peak*
- Kap, Kapp *cape*
- Kavīr *salt desert*
- Kefar *village*
- Kënet' *lagoon, lake*
- Kep *cape, point*
- Kepulauan *archipelago, islands*
- Khalîg, Khalīj *bay, gulf*
- Khirb-at, -et *ancient site, ruins*
- Khrebet *mountain range*
- Kinh *canal*
- Klint *bluff, cliff*
- Kō *bay, cove, harbor*
- Ko *island, lake*
- Koh *island, mountain, range*
- Köl-i *lake*
- Kólpos *gulf*
- Kong *mountain*
- Körfez, -i *bay, gulf*
- Kosa *spit of land*
- Kou *estuary, river mouth*
- Kowtal-e *pass*
- Krasn-yy, -aya, -oye *red*
- Kryazh *mountain range, ridge*
- Kuala *estuary, river mouth*
- Kuan *mountain pass*
- Kūh, Kūhhā *mountain-s, range*
- Kul', Kuli *lake*
- Kum *sandy desert*
- Kundo *archipelago*
- Kuppe *hill-s, mountain-s*
- Kust *coast, shore*
- Kyst *coast*
- Kyun *island*

- La *pass*
- Lac, Lac-ul, -us *lake*
- Lae *cape, point*
- Lago, -a *lagoon, lake*
- Lagoen, Lagune *lagoon*
- Laguna-s *lagoon-s, lake-s*
- Laht *bay, gulf, harbor*
- Laje *reef, rock ledge*
- Laut *sea*
- Lednik *glacier*
- Leida *channel*
- Lhari *mountain*
- Li *village*
- Liedao *archipelago, islands*
- Liehtao *archipelago, islands*
- Liman-ı *bay, estuary*
- Límni *lake*
- Ling *mountain-s, range*
- Linn *pool, waterfall*
- Lintasan *passage*
- Liqen *lake*
- Llano-s *plain-s*
- Loch, Lough *lake, arm of the sea*
- Loma-s *hill-s, knoll-s*

- Mal *mountain, range*
- Mal-yy, -aya, -oye *little, small*
- Mamarr *pass, path*
- Man *bay*
- Mar, Mare *large lake, sea*
- Marsa, Marsá *bay, inlet*
- Masabb *mouth of river*
- Massif *massif, mountain-s*
- Mauna *mountain*
- Mēda *plain*
- Meer *lake, sea*
- Melkosopochnik *undulating plain*
- Mesa, Meseta *plateau, tableland*
- Mierzeja *sandspit*
- Minami *south*
- Mios *island*
- Misaki *cape, peninsula, point*
- Mochun *passage*
- Mong *town, village*
- Mont-e, -i, -s *mount, -ain, -s*
- Montagne, -s *mount, -ain, -s*
- Montaña, -s *mountain, -s*
- More *sea*
- Morne *hill, peak*
- Morro *bluff, headland, hill*
- Motu, -s *islands*
- Mouïet *well*
- Mouillage *anchorage*
- Muang *town, village*
- Mui *cape, point*
- Mull *headland, promontory*
- Munkhafad *depression*
- Munte *mountain*
- Munţi-i *mountains*
- Muong *town, village*
- Mynydd *mountain*
- Mys *cape*

- Nacional *national*
- Nada *gulf, sea*
- Næs, Näs *cape, point*
- Nafūd *area of dunes, desert*
- Nagor'ye *mountain range, plateau*
- Nahar, Nahr *river, stream*
- Nakhon *town*
- Namakzār *salt waste*
- Ne *island, reef, rock-s*
- Neem *cape, point, promontory*
- Nes, Ness *peninsula, point*
- Nevado-s *snow-capped mountain-s*
- Nez *cape, promontory*
- Ni *village*
- Nísi, Nísia, Nisís, Nísoi *island-s, islet-s*
- Nisídhes *islets*
- Nizhn-iy, -yaya, -eye *lower*
- Nizmennost' *low country*
- Noord *north*
- Nord-re *north-ern*
- Nørre *north-ern*
- Nos *cape, nose, point*
- Nosy *island, reef, rock*
- Nov-yy, -aya, -oye *new*
- Nudo *mountain*
- Numa *lake*
- Nunatak, -s, -ker *peak-s surrounded by ice cap*
- Nur *lake, salt lake*
- Nuruu *mountain range, ridge*
- Nut-en *peak*
- Nuur *lake*

- O-n, Ø-er *island-s*
- Oblast' *administrative division, province, region*
- Oceanus *ocean*
- Odde-n *cape, point*
- Øer-ne *islands*
- Oficina *nitrate plant (local usage in Chile)*
- Oglat *group of wells*
- Oguilet *well*
- Óros, -i *mountain, -s*
- Órmos *bay, port*
- Ort *place, point*
- Øst-er *east*
- Ostrov, -a, Ostrv-o, -a *island, -s*
- Otoci, Otok *islands, island*
- Ouadi, Oued *river, watercourse*
- Øy-a *island*
- Øyane *islands*
- Ozer-o, -a *lake, -s*

- Pää *mountain, point*
- Palus *marsh*
- Pampa-s *grassy plain-s*
- Pantà *lake, reservoir*
- Pantanal *marsh, swamp*
- Pao, P'ao *lake*
- Parbat *mountain*
- Parque *park*
- Pas, -ul *pass*
- Paso, Passo *pass*
- Passe *channel, pass*
- Pasul *pass*
- Pedra *rock*
- Pegunungan *mountain range*
- Pellg *bay, bight*
- Peña *cliff, rock*
- Pendi *basin*
- Penedo-s *rock-s*
- Péninsule *peninsula*
- Peñón *point, rock*
- Pereval *mountain pass*
- Pertuis *strait*
- Peski *sands, sandy region*
- Phnom *hill, mountain, range*
- Phou *mountain range*
- Phu *mountain*
- Piana-o *plain*
- Pic, Pik, Piz *peak*
- Picacho *mountain, peak*
- Pico-s *peak-s*
- Pistyll *waterfall*
- Piton-s *peak-s*
- Pivdennyy *southern*
- Plaja, Playa *beach, inlet, shore*
- Planalto, Plato *plateau*
- Planina *mountain, plateau*
- Plassen *lake*
- Ploskogor'ye *plateau, upland*
- Pointe *point*
- Polder *reclaimed land*
- Poluostrov *peninsula*
- Pongo *water gap*
- Ponta, -l *cape, point*
- Ponte *bridge*
- Poolsaar *peninsula*
- Portezuelo *pass*
- Porto *port*
- Poulo *island*
- Praia *beach, seashore*
- Presa *reservoir*
- Presidente *president*
- Presqu'île *peninsula*
- Prokhod *pass*
- Proliv *strait*
- Promontorio *promontory*
- Průsmyk *mountain pass*
- Przylądek *cape*
- Puerto *bay, pass, port*
- Pulao *island-s*
- Pulau, Pulo *island*
- Puncak *peak, summit, top*
- Punt, Punta, -n *point, -s*
- Pun *peak*
- Pu'u *hill, mountain*
- Puy *peak*

- Qā' *depression, marsh, mud flat*
- Qal'at *fort*
- Qal'eh *castle, fort*
- Qanâ *canal*
- Qārat *hill-s, mountain-s*
- Qaşr *castle, fort, hill*
- Qila *fort*
- Qiryat *settlement, suburb*
- Qolleh *peak*
- Qooriga *anchorage, bay*
- Qoz *dunes, sand ridge*
- Qu *canal*
- Quebrada *ravine, stream*
- Qullai *peak, summit*
- Qum-y *desert, sand*
- Qundao *archipelago, islands*
- Qurayyāt *hills*

- Raas *cape, point*
- Rabt *hill*
- Rada *roadstead*
- Rade *anchorage, roadstead*
- Rags *point*
- Ramat *hill, mountain*
- Rand *ridge of hills*
- Rann *swamp*
- Raqaba *wadi, watercourse*
- Ras, Râs, Ra's *cape*
- Ravnina *plain*
- Récif-s *reef-s*
- Regreg *marsh*
- Represa *reservoir*
- Reservatório *reservoir*
- Reshten *hill, mountain*
- Restinga *barrier, sand area*
- Rettō *chain of islands*
- Ri *mountain range, village*
- Ría *estuary*
- Ribeirão *stream*
- Río, Rio *river*
- Rivière *river*
- Roca-s *cliff, rock-s*
- Roche-r, -s *rock-s*
- Rosh *mountain, point*
- Rt *cape, point*
- Rubha *headland*
- Rupes *scarp*

- Saar *island*
- Saari, Sari *island*
- Sabkha-t, Sabkhet *lagoon, marsh, salt lake*
- Sagar *lake, sea*
- Sahara, Şaḩrā' *desert*
- Sahl *plain*
- Saki *cape, point*
- Salar *salt flat*
- Salina *salt pan*
- Salin-as, -es *salt flat-s, salt marsh-es*
- Salto *waterfall*
- Sammyaku *mountain range*
- San *hill, mountain*
- San, -ta, -to *saint*
- Sandur *sandy area*
- Sankt *saint*
- Sanmaek *mountain range*
- São *saint*
- Sarīr *gravel desert*
- Sasso *mountain, stone*
- Savane *savanna*
- Scoglio *reef, rock*
- Se *reef, rock-s, shoal-s*
- Sebjet *salt lake, salt marsh*
- Sebkha *salt lake, salt marsh*
- Sebkhet *lagoon, salt lake*
- See *lake, sea*
- Selat *strait*
- Selkä *lake, ridge*
- Semenanjung *peninsula*
- Sen *mountain*
- Seno *bay, gulf*
- Serra, Serranía *range of hills or mountains*
- Severn-yy, -aya, -oye *northern*
- Sgùrr *peak*
- Sha *island, shoal*
- Sha'īb *ravine, watercourse*
- Shamo *desert*
- Shan *island-s, mountain-s, range*
- Shankou *mountain pass*
- Shanmo *mountain range*
- Sharm *cove, creek, harbor*
- Shatt, Shaţţ *large river*
- Shi *administrative division, municipality*
- Shima *island-s, rock-s*
- Shō *island, reef, rock*
- Shotō *archipelago*
- Shott *intermittent salt lake*
- Shuiku *reservoir*
- Shuitao *channel*
- Shyghanaghy *bay, gulf*
- Sierra *mountain range*
- Silsilesi *mountain chain, ridge*
- Sint *saint*
- Sinus *bay, sea*
- Sjö-n *lake*
- Skarv-et *barren mountain*
- Skerry *rock*
- Slieve *mountain*
- Sø *lake*
- Sønder, Søndre *south-ern*
- Sopka *conical mountain, volcano*
- Sor *lake, salt lake*
- Sør, Sör *south-ern*
- Sory *salt lake, salt marsh*
- Spitz-e *peak, point, top*
- Sredn-iy, -yaya, -eye *central, middle*
- Stagno *lake, pond*
- Stantsiya *station*
- Stausee *reservoir*
- Stenón *channel, strait*
- Step'-i *steppe-s*
- Štít *summit, top*
- Stor-e *big, great*
- Straat *strait*
- Straum-en *current-s*
- Strelka *spit of land*
- Stretet, Stretto *strait*
- Su *reef, river, rock, stream*
- Sudo *channel, strait*
- Suidō *channel, strait*
- Şummān *rocky desert*
- Sund *sound, strait*
- Sunden *channel, inlet, sound*
- Svyat-oy, -aya, -oye *holy, saint*
- Sziget *island*

- Tagh *mountain-s*
- Tall *hill, mound*
- T'an *lake*
- Tanezrouft *desert*
- Tang *plain, steppe*
- Tangi *peninsula, point*
- Tanjong, Tanjung *cape, point*
- Tao *island-s*
- Tarso *hill-s, mountain-s*
- Tassili *plateau, upland*
- Tau *mountain-s, range*
- Taūy *hills, mountains*
- Tchabal *mountain-s*
- Tel-l *hill, mound*
- Telok, Teluk *bay*
- Tepe, -si *hill, peak*
- Tepuí *mesa, mountain*
- Terara *hill, mountain, peak*
- Testa *bluff, head*
- Thale *lake*
- Thang *plain, steppe*
- Tien *lake*
- Tierra *land, region*
- Ting *hill, mountain*
- Tir'at *canal*
- Tō *lake, pool*
- To, Tō *island-s, rock-s*
- Tonle *lake*
- Tope *hill, mountain, peak*
- Top-pen *peak-s*
- Träsk *bog, lake*
- Tso *lake*
- Tsui *cape, point*
- Tübegi *peninsula*
- Tulu *hill, mountain*
- Tunturi-t *hill-s, mountain-s*

- Uad *wadi, watercourse*
- Udde-m *point*
- Ujong, Ujung *cape, point*
- Umi *bay, lagoon, lake*
- Ura *bay, inlet, lake*
- 'Urūq *dune area*
- Uul, Uula *mountain, range*
- 'Uyûn *springs*

- Vaara *mountain*
- Vaart *canal*
- Vær *fishing station*
- Vaïn *channel, strait*
- Valle, Vallée *valley, wadi*
- Vallen *waterfall*
- Valli *lagoon, lake*
- Vallis *valley*
- Vanua *land*
- Varre *mountain*
- Vatn, Vatten, Vatnet *lake, water*
- Veld *grassland, plain*
- Verkhn-iy, -yaya, -eye *higher, upper*
- Vesi *lake, water*
- Vest-er *west*
- Via *road*
- Vidda *plateau*
- Vig, Vík, Vik, -en *bay, cove*
- Vinh *bay, gulf*
- Vodokhranilishche *reservoir*
- Vodoskhovyshche *reservoir*
- Volcan, Volcán *volcano*
- Vostochn-yy, -aya, -oye *eastern*
- Vötn *stream*
- Vozvyshennost' *plateau, upland*
- Vozyera *lake-s*
- Vrchovina *mountains*
- Vrch-y *mountain-s*
- Vrh *hill, mountain*
- Vrŭkh *mountain*
- Vyaliki *big, large*
- Vysočina *highland*

- Wabē *stream*
- Wadi, Wâdi, Wādī *valley, watercourse*
- Wâhât, Wāḩat *oasis*
- Wald *forest, wood*
- Wan *bay, gulf*
- Water *harbor*
- Webi *stream*
- Wiek *cove, inlet*

- Xia *gorge, strait*
- Xiao *lesser, little*

- Yanchi *salt lake*
- Yang *ocean*
- Yarımadası *peninsula*
- Yazovir *reservoir*
- Yŏlto *island group*
- Yoma *mountain range*
- Yü *island*
- Yumco *lake*
- Yunhe *canal*
- Yuzhn-yy, -aya, -oye *southern*

- Zaki *cape, point*
- Zaliv *bay, gulf*
- Zan *mountain, ridge*
- Zangbo *river, stream*
- Zapadn-yy, -aya, -oye *western*
- Zatoka *bay, gulf*
- Zee *bay, sea*
- Zemlya *land*
- Zhotasy *mountains*

A

150 Mile House, Can. 52°7′ N, 121°57′ W 108
19 de Abril, Uru. 34°23′ S, 54°5′ W 139
23 August, Rom. 43°55′ N, 28°35′ E 156
25 de Mayo, Arg. 35°26′ S, 60°12′ W 139
26 Baky Komissary, Azerb. 39°18′ N, 49°10′ E 195
2nd Cataract, fall(s), Sudan 21°54′ N, 30°50′ E 226
31 de Janeiro, Angola 6°53′ S, 15°18′ E 218
31 de Março, Pico, peak, Braz. 0°48′ N, 65°60′ W 136
3rd Cataract, fall(s), Sudan 19°55′ N, 29°47′ E 226
6th Cataract, fall(s), Sudan 16°29′ N, 32°36′ E 182
9 de Julio, Arg. 35°26′ S, 60°54′ W 139
A Coruña, Sp. 43°21′ N, 8°27′ W 150
Aa, river, Ger. 52°26′ N, 7°28′ E 163
Aachen, Ger. 50°46′ N, 6°5′ E 167
Aagaard Islands, Indian Ocean 65°36′ S, 52°31′ E 248
Aalsmeer, Neth. 52°15′ N, 4°45′ E 163
Aalst, Belg. 50°56′ N, 4°2′ E 163
Aalten, Neth. 51°55′ N, 6°34′ E 167
Äänekoski, Fin. 62°36′ N, 25°41′ E 152
Aansluit, S. Af. 26°46′ S, 22°30′ E 227
Aapajärvi, Fin. 67°13′ N, 27°16′ E 152
Aarau, Switz. 47°22′ N, 8°1′ E 156
Aare, river, Switz. 47°6′ N, 7°20′ E 165
Aarschot, Belg. 50°58′ N, 4°49′ E 167
Aasiaat (Egedesminde), Den. 68°45′ N, 52°53′ W 106
Aavasaksa, Fin. 66°23′ N, 23°42′ E 152
Aba, Dem. Rep. of the Congo 3°51′ N, 30°17′ E 224
Aba, Nig. 5°9′ N, 7°23′ E 222
Abā as Sa'ūd, Saudi Arabia 17°27′ N, 44°8′ E 182
Abacaxis, river, Braz. 5°29′ S, 58°39′ W 130
Abaclia, Mold. 46°22′ N, 28°55′ E 156
Abaco Island, Bahamas 26°0′ N, 77°0′ W 118
Abaco Islands, North Atlantic Ocean 27°0′ N, 77°0′ W 118
Abadab, Jebel, peak, Sudan 18°52′ N, 35°52′ E 182
Ābādān, Iran 30°20′ N, 48°21′ E 180
Ābādeh, Iran 31°6′ N, 52°39′ E 180
Abádszalók, Hung. 47°29′ N, 20°35′ E 168
Abaeté, Braz. 19°9′ S, 45°25′ W 138
Abaetetuba, Braz. 1°45′ S, 48°54′ W 130
Abag Qi (Xin Hot), China 44°1′ N, 114°56′ E 198
Abaí, Parag. 26°1′ S, 55°53′ W 139
Abaji, Nig. 8°28′ N, 6°55′ E 222
Abajo Mountains, Utah, U.S. 37°57′ N, 109°50′ W 90
Abajo Peak, Utah, U.S. 37°49′ N, 109°31′ W 92
Abak, Nig. 4°57′ N, 7°47′ E 222
Abakaliki, Nig. 6°17′ N, 8°5′ E 222
Abakan, Russ. 53°42′ N, 91°25′ E 184
Abakan, river, Russ. 52°22′ N, 89°24′ E 184
Abala, Congo 1°19′ S, 15°34′ E 218
Abala, spring, Niger 14°56′ N, 3°27′ E 222
Abalak, Niger 15°19′ N, 6°11′ E 222
Abalemma, spring, Alg. 20°57′ N, 5°55′ E 222
Abalemma, spring, Niger 16°18′ N, 7°49′ E 222
Abalessa, Alg. 22°55′ N, 4°49′ E 214
Abancay, Peru 13°40′ S, 72°52′ W 137
Abapó, Bol. 18°52′ S, 63°30′ W 137
Ābār al Hazīm, spring, Jordan 31°35′ N, 37°13′ E 194
Abār el Kanāyis, spring, Egypt 31°0′ N, 26°47′ E 180
Abarán, Sp. 38°12′ N, 1°24′ W 164
Abarqū, Iran 31°6′ N, 53°19′ E 180
Abasān, Gaza Strip 31°18′ N, 34°21′ E 194
Abashiri, Japan 43°53′ N, 144°8′ E 190
Abasolo, Mex. 27°10′ N, 101°26′ W 96
Abasolo, Mex. 25°18′ N, 104°41′ W 114
Abasolo, Mex. 24°2′ N, 98°23′ W 114
Abast'umani, Ga. 41°45′ N, 42°48′ E 195
Abatskiy, Russ. 56°15′ N, 70°27′ E 184
Abau, P.N.G. 10°10′ S, 148°43′ E 192
Abava, river, Latv. 57°6′ N, 22°18′ E 166
Abay, Kaz. 41°18′ N, 68°51′ E 197
Ābay (Blue Nile), river, Eth. 11°15′ N, 38°15′ E 224
Ābaya Hāyk', lake, Eth. 6°24′ N, 37°45′ E 224
Abaza, Russ. 52°42′ N, 90°7′ E 184
Abba, Cen. Af. Rep. 5°18′ N, 15°9′ E 218
Abbaye, Point, Mich., U.S. 46°59′ N, 88°13′ W 94
Abbeville, Ala., U.S. 31°33′ N, 85°15′ W 96
Abbeville, Fr. 50°5′ N, 1°49′ E 163
Abbeville, La., U.S. 29°57′ N, 92°8′ W 103
Abbey, Can. 50°43′ N, 108°46′ W 90
Abbotsford, Can. 49°2′ N, 122°17′ W 100
Abbotsford, Wis., U.S. 44°57′ N, 90°19′ W 110
Abbotsford, site, U.K. 55°34′ N, 2°51′ W 150
Abbottabad, Pak. 34°7′ N, 73°14′ E 186
'Abda (Eboda), ruin(s), Israel 30°47′ N, 34°43′ E 194
Abdelmalek Ramdan, Alg. 36°6′ N, 0°15′ E 150
Abdera, ruin(s), Gr. 40°55′ N, 24°52′ E 156
Abdi, Chad 12°40′ N, 21°18′ E 216
Abdulino, Russ. 53°38′ N, 53°43′ E 154
Ab-e Istadeh-ye Moqor, lake, Afghan. 32°25′ N, 66°51′ E 186
Ab-e Vakhan (Oxus), river, Afghan. 37°8′ N, 72°26′ E 186
Abéché, Chad 13°48′ N, 20°49′ E 216
Ābeltī, Eth. 8°9′ N, 37°32′ E 224
Abelvær, Nor. 64°44′ N, 11°14′ E 152
Abenab, Namibia 19°19′ S, 18°7′ E 220
Abengourou, Côte d'Ivoire 6°41′ N, 3°30′ W 222
Abenójar, Sp. 38°52′ N, 4°22′ W 164
Abeokuta, Nig. 7°12′ N, 3°22′ E 222
Ābera, Eth. 7°12′ N, 35°57′ E 224
Aberaeron, U.K. 52°13′ N, 4°15′ W 162
Abercorn see Mbala, Zambia 8°53′ S, 31°23′ E 224
Aberdare, U.K. 51°42′ N, 3°26′ W 162
Aberdeen, Idaho, U.S. 42°57′ N, 112°50′ W 90
Aberdeen, Md., U.S. 39°30′ N, 76°11′ W 94
Aberdeen, Miss., U.S. 33°49′ N, 88°33′ W 96
Aberdeen, N.C., U.S. 35°7′ N, 79°26′ W 96
Aberdeen, Ohio, U.S. 38°39′ N, 83°45′ W 102
Aberdeen, S. Af. 32°29′ S, 24°4′ E 227
Aberdeen, S. Dak., U.S. 45°26′ N, 98°30′ W 90
Aberdeen, U.K. 57°8′ N, 2°8′ W 150
Aberdeen, Wash., U.S. 46°58′ N, 123°50′ W 100
Aberdeen Lake, lake, Can. 64°17′ N, 101°1′ W 106
Aberdyfi, U.K. 52°32′ N, 4°2′ W 162
Aberedw, U.K. 52°6′ N, 3°20′ W 162
Abergavenny, U.K. 51°49′ N, 3°1′ W 162
Abergele, U.K. 53°17′ N, 3°35′ W 162
Abersychan, U.K. 51°44′ N, 3°3′ W 162
Abert, Lake, Oreg., U.S. 42°42′ N, 120°35′ W 82
Abertawe see Swansea, U.K. 51°37′ N, 3°57′ W 162
Abertillery, U.K. 51°43′ N, 3°8′ W 162
Aberystwyth, U.K. 52°25′ N, 4°4′ W 162
Abez', Russ. 66°28′ N, 61°49′ E 169
Abhā, Saudi Arabia 18°11′ N, 42°30′ E 182
Ābhē Bid Hāyk', lake, Eth. 11°2′ N, 40°54′ E 216
Abibe, Serranía de, Col. 7°44′ N, 76°42′ W 136
'Abidiya, Sudan 18°12′ N, 33°59′ E 182
Abidjan, Côte d'Ivoire 5°20′ N, 4°12′ W 222
Abijatta-Shalla Lakes National Park, Eth. 7°16′ N, 37°53′ E 224
Abilene, Kans., U.S. 38°53′ N, 97°12′ W 90
Abilene, Tex., U.S. 32°26′ N, 99°44′ W 92
Abingdon, Mo., U.S. 40°47′ N, 90°24′ W 94
Abingdon, U.K. 51°40′ N, 1°18′ W 162
Abingdon, Va., U.S. 36°42′ N, 81°59′ W 96
Abington, Conn., U.S. 41°51′ N, 72°1′ W 104
Abiquiu, N. Mex., U.S. 36°11′ N, 106°19′ W 92
Abisko, Nor. 68°20′ N, 18°47′ E 152
Abita Springs, La., U.S. 30°28′ N, 90°2′ W 103
Abitau, river, Can. 60°23′ N, 108°5′ W 108
Abitibi, Lake, Can. 48°36′ N, 80°21′ W 110
Ābīy Ādī, Eth. 13°34′ N, 38°59′ E 182
Abja Paluoja, Est. 58°6′ N, 25°20′ E 166
Abkhazia, special sovereignty, Ga. 42°59′ N, 41°14′ E 195
Abnûb, Egypt 27°18′ N, 31°8′ E 180
Åbo see Turku, Fin. 60°27′ N, 22°15′ E 166
Aboa, station, Antarctica 73°4′ S, 13°21′ W 248
Aboabo, Philippines 9°9′ N, 118°7′ E 203
Abohar, India 30°9′ N, 74°11′ E 186
Aboisso, Côte d'Ivoire 5°25′ N, 3°15′ W 222
Abomey, Benin 7°13′ N, 1°57′ E 222
Abondance, Fr. 46°16′ N, 6°44′ E 167
Abong Mbang, Cameroon 3°59′ N, 13°12′ E 218
Abongabong, peak, Indonesia 4°14′ N, 96°41′ E 196
Abony, Hung. 47°11′ N, 20°1′ E 168
Aborlan, Philippines 9°27′ N, 118°33′ E 203
Abou Deïa, Chad 11°27′ N, 19°18′ E 216
Abou Goulem, Chad 13°35′ N, 21°39′ E 216
Abra Pampa, Arg. 22°42′ S, 65°44′ W 137
Abrantes, Port. 39°29′ N, 8°16′ W 214
Abreojos, Punta, Mex. 26°44′ N, 114°58′ W 112
Abreschviller, Fr. 48°38′ N, 7°5′ E 163
Abreú, Dom. Rep. 19°41′ N, 69°59′ W 116
Abreuvoir Timg'aouine, spring, Alg. 21°40′ N, 4°29′ E 222
Abriès, Fr. 44°48′ N, 6°54′ E 167
Abrolhos, Arquipélago dos, South Atlantic Ocean 18°35′ S, 39°25′ W 132
Abruka Saar, island, Est. 58°0′ N, 22°32′ E 166
Abruzzi, adm. division, It. 41°59′ N, 13°13′ E 156
Abruzzi, Mount, Can. 50°26′ N, 115°13′ W 90
Absalom, Mount, Antarctica 80°26′ S, 26°24′ W 248
Absaroka Range, Wyo., U.S. 44°17′ N, 110°13′ W 90
Absarokee, Mont., U.S. 45°29′ N, 109°26′ W 90
Abu, Japan 34°28′ N, 131°28′ E 200
Abū al Abyaḍ, island, U.A.E. 24°17′ N, 53°46′ E 182
Abū 'Alī, island, Saudi Arabia 27°21′ N, 49°32′ E 180
Abu 'Aweigîla, Egypt 30°50′ N, 34°6′ E 194
Abu Ballâs, peak, Egypt 24°27′ N, 27°33′ E 226
Abū Dālī, Syr. 34°40′ N, 36°53′ E 194
Abu Deleiq, Sudan 15°50′ N, 33°45′ E 182
Abu Dhabi see Abū Ẓaby, U.A.E. 24°25′ N, 54°14′ E 196
Abu Dis, Sudan 19°5′ N, 33°38′ E 182
Abu Dulu, Qoz, Sudan 15°50′ N, 31°47′ E 182
Abu Gabra, Sudan 11°4′ N, 26°43′ E 224
Abu Gamal, Sudan 15°6′ N, 36°24′ E 182
Abu Gubeiha, Sudan 11°26′ N, 31°17′ E 218
Abu Hamed, Sudan 19°31′ N, 33°19′ E 182
Abu Hashim, Sudan 12°59′ N, 34°21′ E 182
Abū Kamāl, Syr. 34°27′ N, 40°54′ E 180
Abu Matariq, Sudan 10°56′ N, 26°14′ E 224
Abū Mūsá, island, Iran 25°55′ N, 54°49′ E 180
Abū Nā'im, spring, Lib. 28°57′ N, 18°46′ E 216
Abu Qurqâs, Egypt 27°58′ N, 30°47′ E 180
Abu Road, India 24°28′ N, 72°47′ E 186
Abu Safah, oil field, Saudi Arabia 27°5′ N, 50°39′ E 196
Abu Saiyal, spring, Sudan 17°16′ N, 31°12′ E 182
Abu Shagara, Ras, Sudan 21°6′ N, 37°15′ E 182
Abu Shanab, Sudan 13°55′ N, 27°43′ E 226
Abu Simbel, Egypt 24°25′ N, 33°0′ E 182
Abu Simbel, site, Egypt 22°19′ N, 31°29′ E 182
Abu Sôma, Râs, Egypt 26°31′ N, 34°1′ E 180
Abu Sufyan, Sudan 11°55′ N, 26°21′ E 216
Abu Ṣuweir, Egypt 30°32′ N, 32°4′ E 194
Abu Tabari, spring, Sudan 17°30′ N, 28°29′ E 226
Abu Tîg, Egypt 27°3′ N, 31°14′ E 180
Abu 'Uruq, Sudan 15°53′ N, 30°25′ E 226
Abu Zabad, Sudan 12°20′ N, 29°13′ E 216
Abū Ẓaby (Abu Dhabi), U.A.E. 24°25′ N, 54°14′ E 196
Abu Zenîma, Egypt 29°2′ N, 33°6′ E 180
Abuja, Nig. 9°4′ N, 7°2′ E 222
Abulug, Philippines 18°25′ N, 121°26′ E 203
Abumombazi, Dem. Rep. of the Congo 3°32′ N, 22°2′ E 218
Abunã, Braz. 9°42′ S, 65°22′ W 137
Abunã, river, South America 10°24′ S, 67°6′ W 137
Ābūr, Jordan 30°48′ N, 35°42′ E 194
Aburatsu, Japan 31°34′ N, 131°23′ E 201
Ābuyē Mēda, peak, Eth. 10°30′ N, 39°43′ E 224
Abwong, Sudan 9°5′ N, 32°9′ E 224
Abyad, Sudan 13°44′ N, 26°29′ E 226
Abyad Plateau, Jebel, Sudan 19°0′ N, 26°57′ E 226
Abyār al Ḥakīm, spring, Lib. 31°35′ N, 23°27′ E 180
Åbybro, Den. 57°8′ N, 9°43′ E 150
Abyei, Sudan 9°34′ N, 28°26′ E 224
Abyek, Iran 36°1′ N, 50°36′ E 180
Açailândia, Braz. 4°57′ S, 47°42′ W 130
Acala, Mex. 16°34′ N, 92°49′ W 115
Acámbaro, Mex. 20°0′ N, 100°43′ W 114
Acancéh, Mex. 20°47′ N, 89°27′ W 116
Acandí, Col. 8°31′ N, 77°19′ W 136
Acaponeta, Mex. 22°29′ N, 105°22′ W 114
Acaponeta, river, Mex. 23°39′ N, 105°17′ W 114
Acapulco, Mex. 16°51′ N, 99°55′ W 112
Acaraí, Serra, Guyana 1°50′ N, 57°38′ W 130
Acaraú, Braz. 2°55′ S, 40°7′ W 132
Acarí, Peru 15°28′ S, 74°35′ W 137
Acari, river, Braz. 5°32′ S, 60°5′ W 130
Acari, river, Peru 15°19′ S, 74°37′ W 137
Acaricuara, Col. 0°36′ N, 70°22′ W 136
Acarigua, Venez. 9°34′ N, 69°13′ W 136
Acatenango, Volcán de, Guatemala 14°28′ N, 90°58′ W 115
Acatlán, Mex. 18°11′ N, 98°5′ W 114
Acayucan, Mex. 17°56′ N, 94°55′ W 114
Accomac, Va., U.S. 37°42′ N, 75°41′ W 94
Accous, Fr. 42°58′ N, 0°35′ E 164
Accra, Ghana 5°34′ N, 0°22′ E 222
Accrington, U.K. 53°45′ N, 2°23′ W 162
Aceguá, Braz. 31°52′ S, 54°12′ W 139
Achacachi, Bol. 16°8′ S, 68°43′ W 137
Achaguas, Venez. 7°47′ N, 68°16′ W 136
Achahoish, U.K. 55°56′ N, 5°34′ W 150
Achalpur, India 21°17′ N, 77°30′ E 188
Achar, Uru. 32°25′ S, 56°10′ W 139
Achegour, spring, Niger 19°4′ N, 11°45′ E 222
Acheng, China 45°32′ N, 126°55′ E 198
Achénouma, Niger 19°14′ N, 12°57′ E 216
Acheux, Fr. 50°4′ N, 2°33′ E 163
Achikulak, Russ. 44°31′ N, 44°47′ E 158
Achinsk, Russ. 56°16′ N, 90°41′ E 169
Achisu, Russ. 42°37′ N, 47°45′ E 195
Achit, Russ. 56°48′ N, 57°56′ E 154
Achna, Northern Cyprus 35°2′ N, 33°46′ E 194
Acht, Hohe, peak, Ger. 50°22′ N, 6°58′ E 167
Achuyevo, Russ. 45°44′ N, 37°43′ E 156
Achwa (Moroto), river, Uganda 2°14′ N, 32°58′ E 224
Achwa, river, Uganda 3°31′ N, 32°12′ E 224
Acıgöl, lake, Turk. 37°49′ N, 29°43′ E 156
Acıpayam, Turk. 37°25′ N, 29°20′ E 156
Acîş, Rom. 47°30′ N, 22°48′ E 168
Ackerman, Miss., U.S. 33°17′ N, 89°11′ W 103
Ackley, Iowa, U.S. 42°32′ N, 93°3′ W 94
Acklins and Crooked Islands, adm. division, Bahamas 22°52′ N, 74°50′ W 116
Acklins Island, Bahamas 22°22′ N, 75°3′ W 116
Acle, U.K. 52°38′ N, 1°32′ E 163
Acobamba, Peru 12°53′ S, 74°33′ W 137
Acoma Pueblo, site, N. Mex., U.S. 34°54′ N, 107°40′ W 92
Acomayo, Peru 13°56′ S, 71°41′ W 137
Acona, Miss., U.S. 33°15′ N, 90°2′ W 103
Aconchi, Mex. 29°49′ N, 110°14′ W 92
Aconi, Point, Can. 46°21′ N, 60°50′ W 111
Acora, Peru 16°1′ S, 69°46′ W 137
Açores see Azores, islands, North Atlantic Ocean 39°29′ N, 27°35′ W 207
Acoyapa, Nicar. 11°55′ N, 85°9′ W 115
Acqui Terme, It. 44°41′ N, 8°28′ E 167
Acrae, ruin(s), It. 37°1′ N, 14°47′ E 156
Acre, adm. division, Braz. 9°34′ S, 70°21′ W 137
Acre, river, Braz. 10°24′ S, 68°2′ W 137
Acre see 'Akko, Israel 32°55′ N, 35°4′ E 194
Ács, Hung. 47°41′ N, 18°2′ E 156
Actéon, Groupe, islands, South Pacific Ocean 21°2′ S, 137°14′ W 238
Actium, ruin(s), Gr. 38°55′ N, 20°39′ E 156
Acton, Calif., U.S. 34°28′ N, 118°13′ W 101
Acton, Me., U.S. 43°31′ N, 70°55′ W 104
Actopan, Mex. 20°15′ N, 98°56′ W 114
Açuã, river, Braz. 7°39′ S, 64°12′ W 130
Acuitzio, Mex. 19°29′ N, 101°21′ W 114
Acuruaúa, river, Braz. 8°44′ S, 71°25′ W 130
Açurizal, Braz. 15°11′ S, 56°25′ W 132
Acworth, N.H., U.S. 43°12′ N, 72°18′ W 104
Ad Dahnā', Saudi Arabia 26°39′ N, 46°15′ E 196
Ad Dakhla, Western Sahara 23°42′ N, 15°58′ W 214
Aḍ Ḍāli', Yemen 13°41′ N, 44°44′ E 182
Ad Dammām, Saudi Arabia 26°23′ N, 50°5′ E 196
Ad Dār al Ḥamrā', Saudi Arabia 27°21′ N, 37°41′ E 180
Ad Dawādimī, Saudi Arabia 24°29′ N, 44°23′ E 182
Ad Dawḥah (Doha), Qatar 25°13′ N, 51°25′ E 196
Ad Dibdibah, region, Asia 28°10′ N, 46°32′ E 180
Ad Dilam, Saudi Arabia 23°57′ N, 47°13′ E 196
Ad Dīwānīyah, Iraq 31°59′ N, 44°51′ E 180
Ad Durūz, Jabal, peak, Syr. 32°39′ N, 36°41′ E 194
Ada, Ghana 5°46′ N, 0°34′ E 222
Ada, Minn., U.S. 47°16′ N, 96°32′ W 90
Ada, Ohio, U.S. 40°45′ N, 83°50′ W 102
Ada, Okla., U.S. 34°45′ N, 96°40′ W 92
Ada, Serb. and Mont. 45°48′ N, 20°7′ E 168
Adâfer el Abiod, region, Africa 18°47′ N, 10°37′ W 222
Adailo, Eritrea 14°26′ N, 40°50′ E 182
Adair, Bahía de 31°22′ N, 114°33′ W 80
Adair, Cape, Can. 71°24′ N, 71°5′ W 106
Adak, Nor. 65°20′ N, 18°34′ E 152
Adak, island, Alas., U.S. 51°18′ N, 176°44′ W 160
Adaleh, spring, Eth. 7°27′ N, 46°22′ E 218
Adam, Oman 22°23′ N, 57°30′ E 182
Adam, Mount, U.K. 51°37′ S, 60°5′ W 134
Adam Peak, Nev., U.S. 41°9′ N, 117°24′ W 90
Adamantina, Braz. 21°41′ S, 51°5′ W 138
Adamello, peak, It. 46°9′ N, 10°27′ E 167
Adamovka, Russ. 51°32′ N, 59°53′ E 154
Adams, Mass., U.S. 42°36′ N, 73°8′ W 104
Adams, Minn., U.S. 43°33′ N, 92°43′ W 94
Adams, Wis., U.S. 43°56′ N, 89°49′ W 94
Adams, Cape, Antarctica 75°10′ S, 61°57′ W 248
Adams Lake, Can. 51°15′ N, 120°1′ W 90
Adams, Mount, Wash., U.S. 46°11′ N, 121°33′ W 100
Adams Mountain, Mass., U.S. 42°40′ N, 72°55′ W 104
Adam's Peak, Sri Lanka 6°46′ N, 80°24′ E 188
Adams Point, Mich., U.S. 45°24′ N, 83°41′ W 94
Adamstown, Pitcairn Is., U.K. 25°0′ S, 130°0′ W 241
Adamsville, Tenn., U.S. 35°13′ N, 88°23′ W 96
Adamuz, Sp. 38°1′ N, 4°32′ W 164
'Adan (Aden), Yemen 12°46′ N, 44°59′ E 182
'Adan aş Şughrá, Yemen 12°35′ N, 44°1′ E 182
Adana, Turk. 36°59′ N, 35°18′ E 156
Adapazarı, Turk. 40°46′ N, 30°25′ E 156
Adar Doutchi, region, Africa 14°33′ N, 5°50′ E 222
Adarama, Sudan 17°3′ N, 34°54′ E 182
Adare Peninsula, Antarctica 71°10′ S, 175°59′ E 248
Addington, Okla., U.S. 34°13′ N, 97°58′ W 92
Addis, La., U.S. 30°19′ N, 91°17′ W 103
Addis Ababa see Ādīs Ābeba, Eth. 8°58′ N, 38°34′ E 224
Addison, Vt., U.S. 44°5′ N, 73°19′ W 104
Addo, S. Af. 33°34′ S, 25°42′ E 227
Addo Elephant National Park, S. Af. 33°31′ S, 25°41′ E 227
Addu Atoll, Maldives 0°54′ N, 72°39′ E 188
Addy, Wash., U.S. 48°20′ N, 117°50′ W 90
Adel, Ga., U.S. 31°7′ N, 83°26′ W 96
Adel, Oreg., U.S. 42°11′ N, 119°54′ W 90
Adelaide, Austral. 34°59′ S, 138°14′ E 230
Adelaide Island, Antarctica 66°56′ S, 72°20′ W 248
Adelaide Peninsula, Can. 67°53′ N, 97°8′ W 106
Adelanto, Calif., U.S. 34°35′ N, 117°26′ W 101
Adélfi, islands, Aegean Sea 36°26′ N, 26°40′ E 156
Adelia María, Arg. 33°39′ S, 64°2′ W 139
Adélie Coast, Antarctica 66°59′ S, 145°40′ E 248
Adelunga Toghi, peak, Uzb. 42°7′ N, 70°59′ E 197
Ademuz, Sp. 40°3′ N, 1°18′ W 164
Aden, Gulf of 12°29′ N, 45°45′ E 173
Aden see 'Adan, Yemen 12°46′ N, 44°59′ E 182
Adenau, Ger. 50°23′ N, 6°57′ E 163
Aderbissinat, Niger 15°39′ N, 7°53′ E 222
Aderg, peak, Mauritania 21°24′ N, 11°58′ W 222
Adh Dhayd, U.A.E. 25°16′ N, 55°48′ E 196
Adhoi, India 23°23′ N, 70°29′ E 186
Ādī Ārk'ay, Eth. 13°29′ N, 37°55′ E 182
Adi Kaie, Eritrea 14°47′ N, 39°22′ E 182
Adi Quala, Eritrea 14°38′ N, 38°49′ E 182
Ādī Ramets', Eth. 13°49′ N, 37°22′ E 182
Adi Ugri, Eritrea 14°52′ N, 38°50′ E 182
Adiaké, Côte d'Ivoire 5°12′ N, 3°20′ W 214
Adie Inlet 66°40′ S, 63°15′ W 248
Ādīgala, Eth. 10°23′ N, 42°17′ E 224
Adige, river, It. 45°11′ N, 11°20′ E 167
Adigeni, Ga. 41°41′ N, 42°42′ E 195
Ādīgrat, Eth. 14°16′ N, 39°26′ E 182
Adilabad, India 19°40′ N, 78°33′ E 188
Adilang, Uganda 2°42′ N, 33°28′ E 224
Adin, Calif., U.S. 41°11′ N, 120°58′ W 90
Adīrī, Lib. 27°32′ N, 13°13′ E 216
Adirondack Mountains, N.Y., U.S. 43°57′ N, 76°16′ W 106
Ādīs Ābeba (Addis Ababa), Eth. 8°58′ N, 38°34′ E 224
Ādīs 'Alem, Eth. 9°2′ N, 38°21′ E 224
Adıyaman, Turk. 37°45′ N, 38°16′ E 180
Adjud, Rom. 46°5′ N, 27°10′ E 156
Adlavik Islands, North Atlantic Ocean 54°39′ N, 62°27′ W 106
Adler, Russ. 43°28′ N, 40°0′ E 195
Admiralty Island, Alas., U.S. 57°30′ N, 133°39′ W 106
Admiralty Islands, Bismarck Sea 3°32′ S, 145°14′ E 192
Ado, Nig. 6°37′ N, 2°55′ E 222
Ado Ekiti, Nig. 7°38′ N, 5°13′ E 222
Adobe Flat, Nev., U.S. 40°2′ N, 119°8′ W 90
Adok, Sudan 8°7′ N, 30°17′ E 224
Adolfo López Mateos, Mex. 28°26′ N, 107°23′ W 92
Adolfo López Mateos, Presa, lake, Mex. 25°10′ N, 108°53′ W 81
Adoni, India 15°38′ N, 77°16′ E 188
Adony, Hung. 47°6′ N, 18°51′ E 168
Adorf, Ger. 50°19′ N, 12°15′ E 152
Adour, river, Fr. 43°24′ N, 1°10′ W 214
Adra, Sp. 36°44′ N, 3°1′ W 164
Adranga, Dem. Rep. of the Congo 2°53′ N, 30°25′ E 224
Adrar, Alg. 27°55′ N, 0°18′ E 214
Adrar, region, Mauritania 20°22′ N, 14°7′ W 222
Adraskan, Afghan. 33°38′ N, 62°18′ E 186
Adré, Chad 13°26′ N, 22°12′ E 216
Adria, It. 45°4′ N, 12°1′ E 167
Adrian, Mich., U.S. 41°52′ N, 84°2′ W 102
Adrian, Minn., U.S. 43°36′ N, 95°56′ W 90
Adrian, Tex., U.S. 35°15′ N, 102°40′ W 92
Adrianople see Edirne, Turk. 41°39′ N, 26°34′ E 156
Adriatic Sea 41°51′ N, 17°3′ E 156
Adun Gol, China 42°4′ N, 107°56′ E 198
Adusa, Dem. Rep. of the Congo 1°24′ N, 28°4′ E 224
Ādwa, Eth. 14°9′ N, 38°52′ E 182
Adwick le Street, U.K. 53°33′ N, 1°12′ W 162
Adycha, river, Russ. 66°53′ N, 135°23′ E 160
Adygeya, adm. division, Russ. 44°59′ N, 40°1′ E 158
Adzopé, Côte d'Ivoire 6°3′ N, 3°52′ W 222
Adz'vavom, Russ. 66°36′ N, 59°17′ E 169
Aegae, ruin(s), Gr. 38°8′ N, 22°13′ E 156
Aegean Sea 36°34′ N, 23°7′ E 156
Aegir Ridge, Norwegian Sea 65°42′ N, 4°7′ W 255
Aegna, island, Est. 59°37′ N, 24°35′ E 166
Aegviidu, Est. 59°15′ N, 25°35′ E 166
Afadé, Cameroon 12°15′ N, 14°39′ E 216
Afam, Nig. 4°45′ N, 7°23′ E 222
Afándou, Gr. 36°17′ N, 28°10′ E 156
Afar, region, Africa 12°59′ N, 40°4′ E 182
Āfdem, Eth. 9°27′ N, 41°0′ E 224
Affollé, Mauritania 16°21′ N, 11°11′ W 222
Afghanistan 34°0′ N, 66°0′ E 186
Afgooye, Somalia 2°5′ N, 45°8′ E 218
Afgooye Caddo, Somalia 3°12′ N, 45°33′ E 218
'Afīf, Saudi Arabia 23°53′ N, 42°56′ E 182
Afikpo, Nig. 5°55′ N, 7°55′ E 222
Afiq, Israel 32°46′ N, 35°42′ E 194
Åfjord, Nor. 63°57′ N, 10°14′ E 152
Aflou, Alg. 34°6′ N, 2°5′ E 214
Afmadow, Somalia 0°28′ N, 42°4′ E 224
Āfodo, Eth. 10°13′ N, 34°47′ E 224
Afognak Island, Alas., U.S. 57°51′ N, 151°54′ W 98
Afonso Cláudio, Braz. 20°6′ S, 41°10′ W 138
Afqā, Leb. 34°4′ N, 35°53′ E 194
Africa 1°0′ N, 17°0′ E 207
Afşin, Turk. 38°14′ N, 36°53′ E 156
Afton, Okla., U.S. 36°41′ N, 94°58′ W 94
Afton, Wyo., U.S. 42°42′ N, 110°55′ W 82
Afuá, Braz. 0°10′ N, 50°23′ W 130
'Afula, Israel 32°36′ N, 35°17′ E 194
Afyon, Turk. 38°44′ N, 30°31′ E 156
Agadem, Niger 16°49′ N, 13°17′ E 216
Agadez, Niger 16°59′ N, 7°58′ E 222
Agadir, Mor. 30°25′ N, 9°37′ W 214
Agaie, Nig. 8°59′ N, 6°18′ E 222
Agalega Islands, Indian Ocean 12°45′ S, 55°37′ E 173
Agamenticus, Mount, Me., U.S. 43°13′ N, 70°44′ W 104
Agamor, spring, Mali 17°16′ N, 3°178′ E 222
Agana see Hagåtña, Guam, U.S. 13°0′ N, 145°0′ E 242
Agapa, Russ. 71°43′ N, 89°24′ E 173
Agapovka, Russ. 53°20′ N, 59°12′ E 154
Agar, India 23°43′ N, 76°3′ E 197
Āgaro, Eth. 7°49′ N, 36°37′ E 224
Agartala, India 23°47′ N, 91°18′ E 197
Agaruut, Mongolia 43°18′ N, 109°26′ E 198
Agassiz Fracture Zone, South Pacific Ocean 39°32′ S, 131°55′ W 252
Agata, Russ. 66°51′ N, 93°40′ E 169
Agata, Ozero, lake, Russ. 67°14′ N, 92°22′ E 169
Agate, Colo., U.S. 39°27′ N, 103°57′ W 90
Agats, Indonesia 5°34′ S, 138°4′ E 192
Agattu, island, Alas., U.S. 52°17′ N, 171°43′ E 160
Agawam, Mass., U.S. 42°3′ N, 72°37′ W 104
Agbaja, Nig. 7°58′ N, 6°38′ E 222
Agboville, Côte d'Ivoire 5°51′ N, 4°12′ W 222
Ağdam, Azerb. 39°59′ N, 46°54′ E 195
Agde, Fr. 43°19′ N, 3°27′ E 164
Agde, Cap d', Fr. 43°11′ N, 3°30′ E 165
Agdz, Mor. 30°41′ N, 6°29′ W 214
Agematsu, Japan 35°47′ N, 137°43′ E 201
Agen, Fr. 44°14′ N, 0°36′ E 214
Àger, Sp. 41°59′ N, 0°46′ E 164
Agere Maryam, Eth. 5°37′ N, 38°16′ E 224
Agger, river, Ger. 50°55′ N, 7°20′ E 167
Aggi, Eth. 7°55′ N, 35°38′ E 224
Āghā Jārī, Iran 30°43′ N, 49°53′ E 180
Aghaylas, Western Sahara 22°28′ N, 14°23′ W 214
Aghdash, Azerb. 40°39′ N, 47°28′ E 195
Aghireşu, Rom. 46°51′ N, 23°14′ E 168
Aghjabädi, Azerb. 40°2′ N, 47°28′ E 195
Aghsu, Azerb. 40°34′ N, 48°25′ E 195
Aghwinit, Western Sahara 22°11′ N, 13°10′ W 214
Agia Napa, Cyprus 34°59′ N, 33°59′ E 194
Agiabampo, Estero de 26°15′ N, 110°30′ W 80
Agimont, Belg. 50°9′ N, 4°45′ E 163
Agin Buryat, adm. division, Russ. 51°4′ N, 114°22′ E 190
Aginskoye, Russ. 51°6′ N, 114°30′ E 190
Ágio Óros (Mount Athos), region, Europe 40°14′ N, 23°2′ E 156
Agióros, Europe 40°8′ N, 24°3′ E 156
Ágios Nikólaos, Gr. 35°12′ N, 25°40′ E 180
Agios Sergios, Northern Cyprus 35°11′ N, 33°52′ E 194
Aglat Jrayfiya, spring, Western Sahara 25°1′ N, 14°18′ W 214
Agliano, It. 44°47′ N, 8°13′ E 167
Agmar, Mauritania 25°18′ N, 10°48′ W 214
Agnes, Mount, Austral. 26°55′ S, 128°44′ E 230
Agnibilékrou, Côte d'Ivoire 7°5′ N, 3°12′ W 222
Agnières, Fr. 44°41′ N, 5°53′ E 150
Agno, river, Philippines 16°6′ N, 120°49′ E 203
Agön, island, Sw. 61°29′ N, 17°17′ E 166
Agoncillo, Sp. 42°25′ N, 2°18′ W 164
Agordat, Eritrea 15°32′ N, 37°53′ E 182
Agordo, It. 46°17′ N, 12°2′ E 167
Agostinho, Braz. 9°58′ S, 68°33′ W 137
Agoua, Benin 8°17′ N, 1°57′ E 222
Agouénit, Mauritania 16°41′ N, 7°34′ W 222
Agouma, Gabon 1°35′ S, 10°11′ E 218
Agous-n-Ehsel, spring, Mali 16°20′ N, 1°44′ E 222
Agout, river, Fr. 43°44′ N, 1°47′ E 165
Agra, India 27°9′ N, 77°59′ E 197
Agrakhanskiy Poluostrov, Russ. 43°41′ N, 47°7′ E 195
Agramunt, Sp. 41°46′ N, 1°6′ E 164
Agraouri, spring, Niger 18°16′ N, 14°14′ E 222
Agreda, Sp. 41°50′ N, 1°55′ W 164

Ağrı Dağı (Ararat, Mount), *Turk.* 39°42′ N, 44°15′ E **195**
Ağrı (Karaköse), *Turk.* 39°43′ N, 43°3′ E **195**
Agrichay, river, *Azerb.* 41°18′ N, 46°42′ E **195**
Agricola, *Miss., U.S.* 30°47′ N, 88°30′ W **103**
Agrigento, *It.* 37°18′ N, 13°34′ E **216**
Agrihan, island, *U.S.* 18°37′ N, 144°36′ E **192**
Agrínio, *Gr.* 38°35′ N, 21°22′ E **143**
Agryz, *Russ.* 56°30′ N, 53°2′ E **154**
Ağstafa, *Azerb.* 41°6′ N, 45°26′ E **195**
Agua Brava, Laguna, lake, *Mex.* 22°8′ N, 105°49′ W **114**
Água Clara, *Braz.* 20°25′ S, 52°56′ W **138**
Agua Nueva, *Mex.* 25°5′ N, 101°7′ W **114**
Água Preta, river, *Braz.* 1°58′ S, 64°53′ W **130**
Agua Prieta, *Mex.* 31°18′ N, 109°34′ W **92**
Agua Tibia Mountain, *Calif., U.S.* 33°24′ N, 117°1′ W **101**
Agua Verde, *Mex.* 22°55′ N, 105°58′ W **114**
Aguachica, *Col.* 8°19′ N, 73°38′ W **136**
Aguaclara, *Col.* 4°43′ N, 73°2′ W **136**
Aguadas, *Col.* 5°35′ N, 75°26′ W **136**
Agualeguas, *Mex.* 26°18′ N, 99°33′ W **114**
Aguanga, *Calif., U.S.* 33°26′ N, 116°52′ W **101**
Aguapeí, *Braz.* 16°12′ S, 59°41′ W **132**
Aguapeí, Serra do, peak, *Braz.* 16°5′ S, 59°29′ W **132**
Aguarey, *Arg.* 22°13′ S, 63°51′ W **137**
Aguarico, river, *Ecua.* 0°18′ N, 76°27′ W **136**
Aguaro-Guariquito National Park, *Venez.* 8°21′ N, 66°34′ W **136**
Aguas Blancas, *Chile* 24°11′ S, 69°54′ W **132**
Aguas Dulces, *Uru.* 34°20′ S, 53°50′ W **139**
Águas Formosas, *Braz.* 17°5′ S, 40°59′ W **138**
Aguas Negras, *Peru* 0°27′ N, 75°23′ W **136**
Aguascalientes, *Mex.* 21°50′ N, 102°23′ W **114**
Aguascalientes, adm. division, *Mex.* 21°45′ N, 102°53′ W **114**
Aguelal, spring, *Niger* 18°44′ N, 8°6′ E **222**
Aguelhok, *Mali* 19°27′ N, 0°50′ E **222**
Agueraktem, spring, *Mauritania* 23°11′ N, 6°24′ W **214**
Aguié, *Niger* 13°28′ N, 7°33′ E **222**
Aguilâl Faye, spring, *Mauritania* 18°27′ N, 14°47′ W **222**
Aguilar, *Colo., U.S.* 37°24′ N, 104°40′ W **92**
Aguilar de Campoo, *Sp.* 42°46′ N, 4°16′ W **150**
Águilas, *Sp.* 37°24′ N, 1°36′ W **164**
Aguililla, *Mex.* 18°44′ N, 102°45′ W **114**
Aguja, Cabo de la, *Col.* 11°20′ N, 75°3′ W **116**
Aguja, Punta, *Peru* 5°43′ S, 82°17′ W **130**
Agujita, *Mex.* 27°52′ N, 101°10′ W **92**
Āgula'i, *Eth.* 13°40′ N, 39°36′ E **182**
Agulhas Basin, *Indian Ocean* 46°55′ S, 24°17′ E **254**
Agulhas, Cape, *S. Af.* 35°7′ S, 20°3′ E **227**
Agulhas Plateau, *Indian Ocean* 39°48′ S, 26°43′ E **254**
Agustín Codazzi, *Col.* 10°2′ N, 73°16′ W **136**
Aha Hills, *Botswana* 19°49′ S, 20°57′ E **220**
Ahaggar (Hoggar), *Alg.* 21°56′ N, 4°32′ E **222**
Ahaggar National Park, *Alg.* 23°5′ N, 4°38′ E **214**
Ahar, *Iran* 38°30′ N, 47°3′ E **195**
Ahaus, *Ger.* 52°4′ N, 7°0′ E **163**
Ahelleguen, spring, *Alg.* 25°36′ N, 7°2′ E **214**
Ahipara, *N.Z.* 35°11′ S, 173°10′ E **240**
Ahlainen, *Fin.* 61°40′ N, 21°36′ E **166**
Ahlat, *Turk.* 38°43′ N, 42°26′ E **195**
Ahlatlıbel, ruin(s), *Turk.* 39°48′ N, 32°38′ E **156**
Ahlen, *Ger.* 51°46′ N, 7°54′ E **167**
Ahmadabad, *India* 22°59′ N, 72°36′ E **186**
Ahmadi, oil field, *Kuwait* 29°2′ N, 48°1′ E **196**
Ahmadpur East, *Pak.* 29°9′ N, 71°16′ E **186**
Ahmar Mountains, *Eth.* 9°9′ N, 40°49′ E **224**
Ahmeyine, spring, *Mauritania* 20°53′ N, 14°28′ W **222**
Ahnet, region, *Africa* 25°8′ N, 2°58′ E **214**
Ahoada, *Nig.* 5°6′ N, 6°37′ E **222**
Ahome, *Mex.* 25°53′ N, 109°10′ W **112**
Ahoskie, *N.C., U.S.* 36°17′ N, 77°1′ W **96**
Ahram, *Iran* 28°51′ N, 51°20′ E **196**
Ahrensburg, *Ger.* 53°40′ N, 10°13′ E **152**
Ähtäri, *Fin.* 62°32′ N, 24°4′ E **152**
Ahtme, *Est.* 59°17′ N, 27°27′ E **166**
Ahua 'Umi Heiau, site, *Hawai'i, U.S.* 19°37′ N, 155°50′ W **99**
Ahuacatlán, *Mex.* 21°2′ N, 104°30′ W **114**
Ahuachapán, *El Salv.* 13°56′ N, 89°52′ W **115**
Ahualulco, *Mex.* 20°41′ N, 103°59′ W **114**
Ahvāz (Ahwāz), *Iran* 31°19′ N, 48°41′ E **180**
Ahvenanmaa see Åland, island, *Fin.* 60°26′ N, 19°33′ E **166**
Ahwahnee, *Calif., U.S.* 37°22′ N, 119°44′ W **100**
Aḩwar, *Yemen* 13°32′ N, 46°42′ E **182**
Ahwāz see Ahvāz, *Iran* 31°19′ N, 48°41′ E **180**
Ai Qurayyāt, *Saudi Arabia* 31°19′ N, 37°20′ E **180**
Aiari, river, *Braz.* 1°15′ N, 69°5′ W **136**
Aichi, adm. division, *Japan* 35°3′ N, 136°54′ E **201**
Aigialousa, *Northern Cyprus* 35°32′ N, 34°11′ E **194**
Aigle, *Switz.* 46°20′ N, 6°58′ E **167**
Aigle, Lac à l', lake, *Can.* 51°12′ N, 65°54′ W **111**
Aigoual, Mont, peak, *Fr.* 44°7′ N, 3°32′ E **165**
Aiguá, *Uru.* 34°14′ S, 54°44′ W **139**
Aiguebelle, *Fr.* 45°32′ N, 6°18′ E **167**
Aigües, *Sp.* 38°29′ N, 0°22′ E **164**
Aiguilles, *Fr.* 44°47′ N, 6°51′ E **167**
Aijiekebey, *China* 37°11′ N, 75°22′ E **184**
Aikawa, *Japan* 38°2′ N, 138°15′ E **201**
Aiken, *S.C., U.S.* 33°33′ N, 81°44′ W **96**
Aileach, Grianan of, peak, *Ire.* 55°0′ N, 7°33′ W **150**
Ailet Jridani, *Tun.* 35°6′ N, 10°1′ E **156**
Ailigandí, *Pan.* 9°13′ N, 78°2′ W **115**
Ailigas, peak, *Fin.* 69°25′ N, 25°49′ E **152**
Ailly-sur-Noye, *Fr.* 49°45′ N, 2°20′ E **163**
Aim, *Russ.* 58°49′ N, 134°4′ E **160**
Aimorés, *Braz.* 19°29′ S, 41°5′ W **138**
Aimorés, Serra dos, *Braz.* 18°14′ S, 41°22′ W **132**
'Aïn Azaz, spring, *Alg.* 27°5′ N, 3°30′ E **214**
Aïn Ben Tili, *Mauritania* 25°57′ N, 9°34′ W **214**
Aïn Cheikr, spring, *Alg.* 22°9′ N, 9°535′ E **222**
'Ain Dalla, spring, *Egypt* 27°18′ N, 27°19′ E **180**
Aïn Deheb, *Alg.* 34°51′ N, 1°31′ E **214**
Aïn Djasser, *Alg.* 35°53′ N, 6°17′ E **150**
'Aïn el Berd, *Alg.* 35°20′ N, 0°31′ E **150**
'Ain el Ghazāl, spring, *Egypt* 25°47′ N, 30°31′ E **180**
'Aïn el Hadjel, *Alg.* 35°36′ N, 3°55′ E **214**
'Ain el Qideirât (Kadesh-Barnea), spring, *Egypt* 30°39′ N, 34°25′ E **194**
'Ain el Wâdi, spring, *Egypt* 27°22′ N, 28°12′ E **180**
'Ain Khaleifa, spring, *Egypt* 26°44′ N, 27°46′ E **180**
'Aïn M'lila, *Alg.* 36°0′ N, 6°34′ E **150**
'Aïn Oussera, *Alg.* 35°26′ N, 2°55′ E **150**
'Ain Qeiqab, spring, *Egypt* 29°35′ N, 24°56′ E **180**
Ain, river, *Fr.* 45°52′ N, 5°17′ E **165**
'Aïn Sefra, *Alg.* 32°50′ N, 0°39′ E **143**
'Aïn Sefra, *Alg.* 32°47′ N, 0°32′ E **214**
'Aïn Souf, spring, *Alg.* 28°6′ N, 2°14′ E **214**
'Aïn Taïba, spring, *Alg.* 30°18′ N, 5°49′ E **214**
'Aïn Temouchent, *Alg.* 35°17′ N, 1°9′ W **150**
'Ain Tibaghbagh, spring, *Egypt* 29°6′ N, 26°24′ E **180**
'Aïn Tidjoubar, spring, *Alg.* 27°46′ N, 1°22′ E **214**
'Aïn Tiguift, spring, *Alg.* 26°12′ N, 3°38′ E **214**
Ain Zalah, oil field, *Iraq* 36°44′ N, 42°24′ E **195**
Aïna, river, *Congo* 1°30′ N, 13°14′ E **218**
Ainaži, *Latv.* 57°51′ N, 24°20′ E **166**
Aínos National Park, *Gr.* 38°8′ N, 20°34′ E **156**
Aínsa, *Sp.* 42°25′ N, 0°7′ E **164**
Ainsworth, *Nebr., U.S.* 42°31′ N, 99°53′ W **90**
Aipe, *Col.* 3°13′ N, 75°18′ W **136**
Aiquile, *Bol.* 18°12′ S, 65°13′ W **137**
Aïr (Aïr Massif), region, *Africa* 17°26′ N, 6°28′ E **222**
Air Force Island, *Can.* 67°34′ N, 76°15′ W **106**
Aïr Massif see Aïr, region, *Africa* 17°26′ N, 6°28′ E **222**
Airaines, *Fr.* 49°57′ N, 1°55′ E **163**
Airbangis, *Indonesia* 0°14′ N, 99°22′ E **196**
Airdrie, *Can.* 51°18′ N, 114°2′ W **90**
Aire, *Fr.* 50°38′ N, 2°24′ E **163**
Aire, river, *Fr.* 49°3′ N, 5°9′ E **163**
Airiselkä, *Fin.* 66°16′ N, 23°56′ E **152**
Airolo, *Switz.* 46°32′ N, 8°36′ E **167**
Aisén del General Carlos Ibáñez del Campo, adm. division, *Chile* 48°43′ S, 77°8′ W **134**
Aishalton, *Guyana* 2°28′ N, 59°9′ W **130**
Aisne, river, *Fr.* 49°22′ N, 2°54′ E **163**
Aïssa, Djebel, peak, *Alg.* 32°52′ N, 0°38′ E **214**
Aït Baha, *Mor.* 30°3′ N, 9°10′ W **214**
Aït Ourir, *Mor.* 31°36′ N, 7°43′ W **214**
Aitape, *P.N.G.* 3°14′ S, 142°19′ E **238**
Aitkin, *Minn., U.S.* 46°30′ N, 93°43′ W **94**
Aitona, *Sp.* 41°29′ N, 0°27′ E **164**
Aiviekste, river, *Latv.* 56°47′ N, 26°29′ E **166**
Aix, Mount, *Wash., U.S.* 46°46′ N, 121°17′ W **100**
Aix-en-Othe, *Fr.* 48°13′ N, 3°45′ E **163**
Aix-en-Provence, *Fr.* 43°31′ N, 5°26′ E **150**
Aizawl, *India* 23°39′ N, 92°42′ E **197**
Aizpute, *Latv.* 56°42′ N, 21°36′ E **166**
Aizuwakamatsu, *Japan* 37°29′ N, 139°54′ E **201**
Ajaccio, *Fr.* 41°55′ N, 8°41′ E **156**
Ajajú, river, *Col.* 0°59′ N, 73°20′ W **136**
Ajalpan, *Mex.* 18°21′ N, 97°16′ W **114**
Ajax Peak, *Mont., U.S.* 45°18′ N, 113°49′ W **90**
Ajdābiyā, *Lib.* 30°44′ N, 20°15′ E **216**
Ajir, region, *Africa* 18°0′ N, 6°22′ E **222**
Ajka, *Hung.* 47°5′ N, 17°34′ E **168**
'Ajlūn, *Jordan* 32°20′ N, 35°44′ E **194**
'Ajmān, *U.A.E.* 25°26′ N, 55°28′ E **196**
Ajmer, *India* 26°27′ N, 74°38′ E **186**
Ajo, *Ariz., U.S.* 32°22′ N, 112°51′ W **92**
Ajo, Mount, *Ariz., U.S.* 32°0′ N, 112°45′ W **92**
Ajuana, river, *Braz.* 1°1′ S, 65°40′ W **136**
Ajuchitlán, *Mex.* 18°7′ N, 100°31′ W **114**
Ajuy, *Philippines* 11°11′ N, 122°59′ E **203**
Ak Dağlar, peak, *Turk.* 36°30′ N, 29°29′ E **156**
Ak Dovurak, *Russ.* 51°7′ N, 90°31′ E **184**
Aka, *Mali* 15°25′ N, 4°12′ W **222**
Aka, river, *Dem. Rep. of the Congo* 4°3′ N, 29°25′ E **224**
Akadomari, *Japan* 37°53′ N, 138°25′ E **201**
Akagera National Park, *Rwanda* 1°48′ S, 30°38′ E **224**
Akagi, *Japan* 34°59′ N, 132°43′ E **201**
Akaki, *Cyprus* 35°7′ N, 33°7′ E **194**
Akal, oil field, *Mex.* 19°26′ N, 92°7′ W **115**
Akalkot, *India* 17°31′ N, 76°11′ E **188**
Akanthou, *Northern Cyprus* 35°21′ N, 33°44′ E **194**
Akaroa, *N.Z.* 43°50′ S, 172°58′ E **240**
Akasaki, *Japan* 35°28′ N, 133°40′ E **201**
Akashi, *Japan* 34°40′ N, 134°59′ E **201**
Akaska, *S. Dak., U.S.* 45°19′ N, 100°8′ W **90**
Akbulak, *Russ.* 51°1′ N, 55°38′ E **158**
Akçaabat, *Turk.* 41°1′ N, 39°31′ E **195**
Akçadağ, *Turk.* 38°17′ N, 37°57′ E **180**
Akçakışla, *Turk.* 39°31′ N, 36°19′ E **156**
Akçakoca, *Turk.* 41°4′ N, 31°8′ E **156**
Akçay, *Turk.* 39°35′ N, 26°50′ E **156**
Akçay, *Turk.* 36°35′ N, 29°43′ E **156**
Akchâr, region, *Africa* 20°12′ N, 15°6′ W **222**
Akdağ, peak, *Turk.* 38°29′ N, 26°25′ E **156**
Akdağ, peak, *Turk.* 36°47′ N, 32°8′ E **156**
Akdağmadeni, *Turk.* 39°39′ N, 35°54′ E **156**
Akdepe, *Turkm.* 42°3′ N, 59°23′ E **180**
Akelo, *Sudan* 6°55′ N, 33°38′ E **224**
Akera, river, *Azerb.* 39°28′ N, 46°37′ E **195**
Åkernes, *Nor.* 58°44′ N, 7°29′ E **152**
Akespe, *Kaz.* 46°48′ N, 60°32′ E **184**
Aketi, *Dem. Rep. of the Congo* 2°45′ N, 23°46′ E **224**
Akhalts'ikhe, *Ga.* 41°39′ N, 42°57′ E **195**
Akhisar, *Turk.* 38°54′ N, 27°50′ E **156**
Akhmeta, *Ga.* 42°1′ N, 45°17′ E **195**
Akhmîm, *Egypt* 26°38′ N, 31°42′ E **180**
Akhta, *Arm.* 40°28′ N, 44°45′ E **195**
Akhtopol, *Bulg.* 42°7′ N, 27°54′ E **156**
Akhtuba, river, *Russ.* 47°55′ N, 46°29′ E **158**
Akhtubinsk, *Russ.* 48°17′ N, 46°10′ E **158**
Aki, *Japan* 33°30′ N, 133°54′ E **201**
Akie, river, *Can.* 57°15′ N, 124°59′ W **108**
Akimiski Island, *Can.* 53°8′ N, 84°10′ W **106**
Akita, *Japan* 39°48′ N, 140°10′ E **190**
Akitio, *N.Z.* 40°37′ S, 176°23′ E **240**
Akjoujt, *Mauritania* 19°43′ N, 14°24′ W **222**
Akka, *Mor.* 29°24′ N, 8°15′ W **214**
Akkala, *Uzb.* 43°40′ N, 59°32′ E **207**
Akkaraipattu, *Sri Lanka* 7°14′ N, 81°52′ E **188**
Akkarvik, *Nor.* 70°3′ N, 20°30′ E **152**
'Akko (Acre), *Israel* 32°55′ N, 35°4′ E **194**
Akkuş, *Turk.* 40°48′ N, 36°59′ E **156**
Aklavik, *Can.* 68°13′ N, 135°6′ W **98**
Aklera, *India* 24°24′ N, 76°34′ E **197**
Akmenė, *Lith.* 56°15′ N, 22°41′ E **166**
Akmeqit, *China* 37°7′ N, 77°0′ E **184**
Aknīste, *Latv.* 56°8′ N, 25°46′ E **166**
Akō, *Japan* 34°45′ N, 134°22′ E **201**
Akobo, *Sudan* 7°45′ N, 33°0′ E **224**
Akobo, river, *Africa* 7°0′ N, 34°13′ E **224**
Akokane, *Niger* 18°43′ N, 7°9′ E **222**
Akola, *India* 20°41′ N, 77°1′ E **188**
Akom, *Cameroon* 2°50′ N, 10°34′ E **218**
Akonolinga, *Cameroon* 3°50′ N, 12°15′ E **218**
Akor, *Mali* 14°52′ N, 6°59′ W **222**
Akosombo, *Ghana* 6°20′ N, 2°119′ E **222**
Akosombo Dam, *Ghana* 6°1′ N, 0°14′ E **222**
Akot, *India* 21°6′ N, 77°5′ E **188**
Akot, *Sudan* 6°31′ N, 30°4′ E **224**
Akpatok Island, *Can.* 60°24′ N, 72°3′ W **106**
Akqi, *China* 40°56′ N, 78°33′ E **184**
Akrabat, *Turkm.* 35°29′ N, 61°45′ E **186**
'Akramah, ruin(s), *Lib.* 31°59′ N, 23°31′ E **180**
Akranes, *Ice.* 64°21′ N, 21°60′ W **143**
Akreidil, spring, *Mauritania* 18°29′ N, 15°39′ W **222**
Akron, *Ala., U.S.* 32°52′ N, 87°44′ W **103**
Akron, *Colo., U.S.* 40°9′ N, 103°13′ W **90**
Akron, *Ind., U.S.* 41°1′ N, 86°1′ W **102**
Akron, *Iowa, U.S.* 42°48′ N, 96°34′ W **90**
Akron, *Mich., U.S.* 43°33′ N, 83°31′ W **102**
Akron, *Ohio, U.S.* 41°5′ N, 81°31′ W **102**
Akrotiri, *Cyprus* 34°35′ N, 32°56′ E **194**
Akrotírio Apolitáres, *Gr.* 35°50′ N, 23°21′ E **156**
Akrotírio Dafnoúdi, *Gr.* 38°28′ N, 19°38′ E **156**
Akrotírio Doukáto, *Gr.* 38°35′ N, 19°40′ E **156**
Akrotírio Gérakas, *Gr.* 36°46′ N, 23°7′ E **156**
Akrotírio Ginas, *Gr.* 36°4′ N, 28°5′ E **156**
Akrotírio Griá, *Gr.* 37°49′ N, 24°58′ E **156**
Akrotírio Hélatros, *Gr.* 35°12′ N, 27°2′ E **156**
Akrotírio Kafiéas, *Gr.* 38°9′ N, 24°37′ E **156**
Akrotírio Kapélo, *Gr.* 36°4′ N, 23°4′ E **156**
Akrotírio Katomfi, *Gr.* 36°50′ N, 24°36′ E **156**
Akrotírio Keáli, *Gr.* 35°49′ N, 22°34′ E **156**
Akrotírio Kilopas, *Gr.* 37°3′ N, 23°37′ E **156**
Akrotírio Korakas, *Gr.* 39°23′ N, 25°29′ E **156**
Akrotírio Maléas, *Gr.* 36°22′ N, 23°13′ E **156**
Akrotírio Mestá, *Gr.* 38°15′ N, 25°6′ E **156**
Akrotírio Moúnda, *Gr.* 37°59′ N, 19°56′ E **156**
Akrotírio Pláka, *Gr.* 35°4′ N, 26°19′ E **156**
Akrotírio Spánda, *Gr.* 35°41′ N, 23°46′ E **156**
Akrotírio Spathí, *Gr.* 36°16′ N, 22°58′ E **156**
Akrotírio Stavrí, *Gr.* 37°13′ N, 24°54′ E **156**
Akrotírio Stenó, *Gr.* 37°42′ N, 24°58′ E **156**
Akrotírio Ténaro (Matapás, Taenarum), *Gr.* 36°13′ N, 21°38′ E **156**
Aksaray, *Turk.* 38°21′ N, 34°1′ E **156**
Aksarka, *Russ.* 66°29′ N, 67°47′ E **169**
Aksay, *China* 39°25′ N, 94°14′ E **188**
Aksay, *Russ.* 47°56′ N, 43°59′ E **158**
Aksayqin Hu, lake, *China* 35°8′ N, 78°55′ E **188**
Akşehir, *Turk.* 38°20′ N, 31°25′ E **156**
Akşehir Gölü, lake, *Turk.* 38°32′ N, 31°9′ E **156**
Akseki, *Turk.* 37°2′ N, 31°47′ E **156**
'Aksha, ruin(s), *Egypt* 22°4′ N, 31°12′ E **182**
Ak-Shyyrak, *Kyrg.* 41°54′ N, 78°43′ E **184**
Aksu, *China* 41°9′ N, 80°15′ E **184**
Aksu, *Kaz.* 42°34′ N, 52°43′ E **158**
Aksu, river, *China* 40°58′ N, 80°24′ E **184**
Aksū, river, *Kaz.* 45°44′ N, 79°0′ E **184**
Āksum, *Eth.* 14°7′ N, 38°41′ E **182**
Aktag, peak, *China* 36°43′ N, 84°36′ E **184**
Aktash, *Russ.* 50°21′ N, 87°48′ E **184**
Ak-Tektir, *Kyrg.* 42°6′ N, 72°26′ E **197**
Akto, *China* 39°8′ N, 75°54′ E **184**
Aktogay, *Kaz.* 48°51′ N, 60°6′ E **158**
Aktsyabrski, *Belarus* 52°36′ N, 28°58′ E **152**
Akujärvi, *Fin.* 68°40′ N, 27°42′ E **152**
Akula, *Dem. Rep. of the Congo* 2°20′ N, 20°15′ E **218**
Akune, *Japan* 32°1′ N, 130°13′ E **201**
Akure, *Nig.* 7°18′ N, 5°11′ E **222**
Akureyri, *Ice.* 65°41′ N, 18°16′ W **246**
Akuse, *Ghana* 6°4′ N, 9°535′ E **222**
Akwatia, *Ghana* 6°0′ N, 0°48′ E **214**
Akyaka, *Turk.* 40°45′ N, 43°32′ E **195**
Āl 'Ābis, *Saudi Arabia* 18°1′ N, 43°9′ E **182**
Al 'Adam, *Lib.* 31°53′ N, 23°57′ E **180**
Al Aḩmadī, *Kuwait* 29°3′ N, 48°4′ E **180**
Al Akhḑar, *Saudi Arabia* 28°3′ N, 37°7′ E **180**
Al' Amādīyah, *Iraq* 37°7′ N, 43°29′ E **180**
Al' Amārah, *Iraq* 31°53′ N, 47°9′ E **180**
Al 'Ammārīyah, *Iraq* 37°6′ N, 43°22′ E **195**
Al 'Ānāt, *Syr.* 32°20′ N, 36°48′ E **194**
Al 'Aqabah, *Jordan* 29°34′ N, 35°4′ E **180**
Al 'Aqīq, *Saudi Arabia* 20°40′ N, 41°22′ E **182**
Al 'Arīḑah, *Leb.* 34°38′ N, 35°59′ E **194**
Al Arţāwīyah, *Saudi Arabia* 26°29′ N, 45°23′ E **180**
Al As'ad, *Saudi Arabia* 27°50′ N, 37°22′ E **180**
Al Ashkharah, *Oman* 21°52′ N, 59°32′ E **182**
Al 'Athāmīn, peak, *Iraq* 30°20′ N, 43°33′ E **180**
Al 'Ayn, *U.A.E.* 24°10′ N, 55°38′ E **196**
Al 'Ayzarīyah, *Israel* 31°45′ N, 35°15′ E **194**
Al Bad', *Saudi Arabia* 28°26′ N, 35°4′ E **180**
Al Badī', *Saudi Arabia* 22°5′ N, 46°30′ E **207**
Al Bāḩah, *Saudi Arabia* 20°3′ N, 41°33′ E **182**
Al Baḩrah, spring, *Kuwait* 29°35′ N, 47°59′ E **196**
Al Bardī, *Lib.* 31°46′ N, 25°3′ E **180**
Al Basīt, Ra's, *Syr.* 35°50′ N, 35°50′ E **156**
Al Başrah, *Iraq* 30°29′ N, 47°49′ E **180**
Al Bayād, *Saudi Arabia* 23°42′ N, 47°48′ E **196**
Al Biqā' (Bekaa Valley), region, *Asia* 33°43′ N, 35°51′ E **194**
Al Bi'r, *Saudi Arabia* 28°51′ N, 36°15′ E **180**
Al Bir Lahlou, *Western Sahara* 26°23′ N, 9°32′ W **214**
Al Bīrah, *West Bank* 31°53′ N, 35°12′ E **194**
Al Birk, *Saudi Arabia* 18°8′ N, 41°36′ E **182**
Al Birkah, *Lib.* 24°50′ N, 10°8′ E **216**
Al Bunduq, oil field, *U.A.E.* 25°2′ N, 52°25′ E **196**
Al Burayj, *Gaza Strip* 31°25′ N, 34°24′ E **194**
Al Buraymī, *Oman* 24°11′ N, 55°49′ E **196**
Al Burjayn, *Tun.* 35°40′ N, 10°35′ E **156**
Al Dafyānah, *Jordan* 32°18′ N, 36°38′ E **194**
Al Fallūjah (Fallujah), *Iraq* 33°19′ N, 43°46′ E **180**
Al Farciya, *Western Sahara* 27°8′ N, 9°52′ W **214**
Al Fāw, *Iraq* 29°59′ N, 48°28′ E **196**
Al Fayḑah, *Saudi Arabia* 25°15′ N, 44°25′ E **182**
Al Fujayrah, *U.A.E.* 25°10′ N, 56°18′ E **196**
Al Fuqahā', *Lib.* 27°50′ N, 16°20′ E **216**
Al Furāt (Euphrates), river, *Syr.* 35°43′ N, 39°21′ E **180**
Al Furāt, river, *Iraq* 32°7′ N, 44°56′ E **180**
Al Ghāriyah, *Syr.* 32°23′ N, 36°39′ E **194**
Al Ghayḑah, *Yemen* 16°12′ N, 52°14′ E **182**
Al Ghayḑah, *Yemen* 14°55′ N, 49°58′ E **182**
Al Ghayl, *Saudi Arabia* 22°33′ N, 46°18′ E **182**
Al Ghayl, *Yemen* 16°3′ N, 44°48′ E **182**
Al Ghazālah, *Saudi Arabia* 26°42′ N, 41°22′ E **180**
Al Ghuwayr, *Jordan* 31°8′ N, 35°45′ E **194**
Al Ḩaddār, *Saudi Arabia* 21°56′ N, 45°58′ E **182**
Al Ḩadīdah, *Saudi Arabia* 21°32′ N, 50°30′ E **182**
Al Ḩadīthah, *Iraq* 34°8′ N, 42°27′ E **180**
Al Haggounia, *Western Sahara* 27°25′ N, 12°26′ W **214**
Al Ḩallānīyah, island, *Oman* 17°35′ N, 55°22′ E **182**
Al Ḩamād, *Saudi Arabia* 31°17′ N, 37°38′ E **180**
Al Ḩamīdīyah, *Syr.* 34°42′ N, 35°56′ E **194**
Al Ḩammār, Hawr, lake, *Iraq* 30°49′ N, 46°38′ E **180**
Al Ḩamrā', *Lib.* 29°39′ N, 12°0′ E **216**
Al Ḩamrā', *Saudi Arabia* 23°55′ N, 38°51′ E **182**
Al Ḩamūd, *Jordan* 31°17′ N, 35°47′ E **194**
Al Ḩanākīyah, *Saudi Arabia* 24°50′ N, 40°29′ E **182**
Al Ḩaqw, *Saudi Arabia* 17°33′ N, 42°40′ E **182**
Al Ḩarīq, *Saudi Arabia* 23°35′ N, 46°33′ E **196**
Al Harūj al Aswad, *Lib.* 28°27′ N, 17°15′ E **216**
Al Ḩasakah, *Syr.* 36°31′ N, 40°46′ E **195**
Al Ḩasānī, island, *Saudi Arabia* 25°1′ N, 36°30′ E **182**
Al Ḩawīyah, *Saudi Arabia* 21°26′ N, 40°31′ E **182**
Al Ḩawrah, *Yemen* 13°51′ N, 47°33′ E **182**
Al Ḩayy, *Iraq* 32°9′ N, 46°5′ E **180**
Al Ḩījānah, *Syr.* 33°21′ N, 36°32′ E **194**
Al Ḩijāz (Hejaz), region, *Asia* 26°54′ N, 36°41′ E **180**
Al Ḩillah, *Iraq* 32°27′ N, 44°26′ E **180**
Al Ḩillah (Hauta), *Saudi Arabia* 23°28′ N, 46°52′ E **196**
Al Ḩimá, spring, *Saudi Arabia* 18°13′ N, 44°30′ E **182**
Al Ḩişn, *Jordan* 32°28′ N, 35°53′ E **194**
Al Hoceima, *Mor.* 35°14′ N, 3°57′ W **150**
Al Ḩudaydah, *Yemen* 14°48′ N, 42°56′ E **182**
Al Hufūf (Hofuf), *Saudi Arabia* 25°21′ N, 49°34′ E **196**
Al Ḩulwah, *Saudi Arabia* 23°23′ N, 46°49′ E **182**
Al Ḩunayy, *Saudi Arabia* 24°58′ N, 48°46′ E **196**
Al Hūwah, *Saudi Arabia* 23°0′ N, 45°48′ E **182**
Al Ikhwān (The Brothers), islands, *Persian Gulf* 11°24′ N, 52°52′ E **182**
Al 'Irqah, *Yemen* 13°40′ N, 47°19′ E **182**
Al 'Īsāwīyah, *Saudi Arabia* 30°41′ N, 38°1′ E **180**
Al Jabalash Sharqī (Anti-Lebanon), *Leb.* 34°5′ N, 36°21′ E **194**
Al Jaghbūb, *Lib.* 29°45′ N, 24°30′ E **180**
Al Jawf, *Lib.* 24°10′ N, 23°16′ E **216**
Al Jawf, *Saudi Arabia* 29°54′ N, 39°51′ E **143**
Al Jazīrah, spring, *Lib.* 25°43′ N, 21°7′ E **216**
Al Jehrā, *Kuwait* 29°21′ N, 47°40′ E **196**
Al Jīb, *West Bank* 31°50′ N, 35°10′ E **194**
Al Jifāra, *Tun.* 32°1′ N, 11°10′ E **214**
Al Jīzah, *Jordan* 31°41′ N, 35°57′ E **194**
Al Jubayl, *Saudi Arabia* 26°59′ N, 49°39′ E **196**
Al Jubaylah, *Saudi Arabia* 24°52′ N, 46°28′ E **196**
Al Jumaylīyah, *Qatar* 25°36′ N, 51°7′ E **196**
Al Jumaymah, spring, *Saudi Arabia* 29°41′ N, 43°37′ E **180**
Al Junaynah, *Saudi Arabia* 20°15′ N, 42°50′ E **182**
Al Kahfah, *Saudi Arabia* 27°2′ N, 43°3′ E **180**
Al Karak, *Jordan* 31°10′ N, 35°42′ E **194**
Al Kawm, *Syr.* 35°12′ N, 38°51′ E **180**
Al Khābūrah, *Oman* 23°54′ N, 57°7′ E **196**
Al Khalīl (Hebron), *West Bank* 31°31′ N, 35°6′ E **194**
Al Kharfah, *Saudi Arabia* 22°11′ N, 46°41′ E **182**
Al Kharj, *Saudi Arabia* 24°10′ N, 47°20′ E **196**
Al Khāşirah, *Saudi Arabia* 23°29′ N, 43°44′ E **182**
Al Khawr, *Qatar* 25°41′ N, 51°30′ E **196**
Al Khīrān, *Kuwait* 28°36′ N, 48°21′ E **196**
Al Khiyam, *Leb.* 33°19′ N, 35°36′ E **194**
Al Khubar, *Saudi Arabia* 26°13′ N, 50°8′ E **196**
Al Khufayfīyah, *Saudi Arabia* 24°54′ N, 44°44′ E **182**
Al Khums, *Lib.* 32°42′ N, 14°16′ E **216**
Al Khunn, *Saudi Arabia* 23°16′ N, 49°15′ E **182**
Al Khuraybah, *Yemen* 15°7′ N, 48°20′ E **182**
Al Khurmah, *Saudi Arabia* 21°51′ N, 42°3′ E **182**
Al Kifl, *Iraq* 32°16′ N, 44°24′ E **180**
Al Kūfah (Kufah), *Iraq* 32°5′ N, 44°27′ E **186**
Al Kufrah (Kufra Oasis), *Lib.* 24°20′ N, 23°44′ E **226**
Al Kūt, *Iraq* 32°34′ N, 45°49′ E **180**
Al Kuwayt (Kuwait), *Kuwait* 29°20′ N, 47°52′ E **196**
Al La'bān, *Jordan* 30°54′ N, 35°42′ E **194**
Al Labwah, *Leb.* 34°11′ N, 36°21′ E **194**
Al Lādhiqīyah (Latakia), *Syr.* 35°31′ N, 35°47′ E **194**
Al Lajā, *Syr.* 32°53′ N, 36°19′ E **194**
Al Lawz, Jabal, peak, *Saudi Arabia* 28°38′ N, 35°13′ E **180**
Al Lidām, *Saudi Arabia* 20°27′ N, 44°48′ E **182**
Al Līth, *Saudi Arabia* 20°8′ N, 40°18′ E **182**
Al Luḩayyah, *Yemen* 15°41′ N, 42°42′ E **182**
Al Luwaymī, *Saudi Arabia* 27°54′ N, 42°12′ E **180**
Al Ma'ānīyah, spring, *Iraq* 30°42′ N, 42°57′ E **180**
Al Madīnah (Medina), *Saudi Arabia* 24°26′ N, 39°34′ E **182**
Al Madwar, *Jordan* 32°17′ N, 35°59′ E **194**
Al Mafraq, *Jordan* 32°20′ N, 36°12′ E **194**
Al Mahbas, *Western Sahara* 27°27′ N, 9°2′ W **214**
Al Maḩrūqah, *Lib.* 27°29′ N, 14°0′ E **216**
Al Majma'ah, *Saudi Arabia* 25°52′ N, 45°23′ E **182**
Al Malāqī, spring, *Lib.* 26°53′ N, 16°49′ E **216**
Al Mālikīyah, *Syr.* 37°11′ N, 42°4′ E **195**
Al Manāmah (Manama), *Bahrain* 26°10′ N, 50°27′ E **196**
Al Manzil, *Jordan* 31°3′ N, 36°0′ E **194**
Al Marj (Barce), *Lib.* 32°30′ N, 20°53′ E **216**
Al Mashrafah, *Syr.* 34°50′ N, 36°52′ E **194**
Al Mawşil (Mosul), *Iraq* 36°20′ N, 43°0′ E **195**
Al Mayādīn, *Syr.* 35°0′ N, 40°24′ E **180**
Al Mayyāh, *Saudi Arabia* 27°50′ N, 42°49′ E **180**
Al Mazra'ah, *Jordan* 31°17′ N, 35°32′ E **194**
Al Mazzah, *Syr.* 33°30′ N, 36°14′ E **194**
Al Mintirib, *Oman* 22°24′ N, 58°49′ E **182**
Al Minyah, *Leb.* 34°28′ N, 35°56′ E **194**
Al Mismīyah, *Syr.* 33°7′ N, 36°23′ E **194**
Al Mubarraz, *Saudi Arabia* 25°27′ N, 49°35′ E **196**
Al Mudawwarah, *Jordan* 29°23′ N, 36°2′ E **180**
Al Mughayrā', *U.A.E.* 24°3′ N, 53°31′ E **196**
Al Mukallā, *Yemen* 14°33′ N, 49°6′ E **182**
Al Mukhā, *Yemen* 13°20′ N, 43°14′ E **182**
Al Musayyib, *Iraq* 32°47′ N, 44°21′ E **180**
Al Mushannaf, *Syr.* 32°44′ N, 36°46′ E **194**
Al Muwaqqar, ruin(s), *Jordan* 31°48′ N, 36°2′ E **194**
Al Muwayh, *Saudi Arabia* 22°43′ N, 41°37′ E **182**
Al Muwayliḩ, *Saudi Arabia* 27°41′ N, 35°28′ E **180**
Al Qābil, *Oman* 23°52′ N, 55°51′ E **196**
Al Qaḑimah, *Saudi Arabia* 22°19′ N, 39°8′ E **182**
Al Qadmūs, *Syr.* 35°5′ N, 36°9′ E **194**
Al Qā'im, *Iraq* 34°17′ N, 41°11′ E **180**
Al Qa'īyah, *Saudi Arabia* 24°19′ N, 43°32′ E **182**
Al Qā'īyah, spring, *Saudi Arabia* 26°28′ N, 45°33′ E **196**
Al Qāmishlī, *Syr.* 37°2′ N, 41°16′ E **195**
Al Qārah, *Yemen* 13°41′ N, 45°15′ E **182**
Al Qaryah ash Sharqīyah, *Lib.* 30°23′ N, 13°33′ E **216**
Al Qaryatayn, *Syr.* 34°10′ N, 37°17′ E **180**
Al Qaşr, *Jordan* 31°18′ N, 35°44′ E **194**
Al Qaţīf, *Saudi Arabia* 26°32′ N, 49°59′ E **196**
Al Qaţrānah, *Jordan* 31°14′ N, 36°1′ E **194**
Al Qaţrūn, *Lib.* 24°53′ N, 14°29′ E **216**
Al Qawārishah, *Lib.* 32°1′ N, 20°5′ E **216**
Al Qaws, site, *Lib.* 30°26′ N, 18°21′ E **216**
Al Qayşūmah, *Saudi Arabia* 28°18′ N, 46°9′ E **196**
Al Qunayţirah (Quneitra), *Syr.* 33°7′ N, 35°49′ E **194**
Al Qunfudhah, *Saudi Arabia* 19°6′ N, 41°7′ E **182**
Al Qurayni, spring, *Saudi Arabia* 21°51′ N, 53°48′ E **182**
Al Qurayyah, *Syr.* 32°32′ N, 36°35′ E **194**
Al Qurnah, *Iraq* 30°55′ N, 47°22′ E **180**
Al Quşayr, *Syr.* 34°30′ N, 36°34′ E **194**
Al Quşūrīyah, *Saudi Arabia* 23°43′ N, 44°37′ E **182**
Al Quţayfah, *Syr.* 33°43′ N, 36°35′ E **194**
Al Quway'īyah, *Saudi Arabia* 24°2′ N, 45°15′ E **182**
Al 'Ubaylah, *Saudi Arabia* 21°58′ N, 50°56′ E **182**
Al 'Udaysah, *Leb.* 33°15′ N, 35°32′ E **194**
Al 'Ulá, *Saudi Arabia* 26°36′ N, 37°51′ E **180**
Al 'Uqaylah, *Lib.* 30°13′ N, 19°11′ E **216**
Al 'Uqayr, *Saudi Arabia* 25°38′ N, 50°8′ E **196**
Al 'Uwaynāt see 'Uweinat, Jebel, peak, *Sudan* 21°51′ N, 24°58′ E **226**
Al 'Uwaynāt (Serdeles), *Lib.* 25°47′ N, 10°33′ E **216**
Al 'Uwaynid, *Saudi Arabia* 24°54′ N, 45°48′ E **182**
Al 'Uwayqīlah, *Saudi Arabia* 30°18′ N, 42°12′ E **180**
Al 'Uyūn, *Saudi Arabia* 26°30′ N, 43°40′ E **180**
Al 'Uyūn, *Saudi Arabia* 24°33′ N, 39°33′ E **182**
Al 'Uzayr, *Iraq* 31°19′ N, 47°23′ E **180**
Al Wābirīyah, spring, *Lib.* 27°24′ N, 18°5′ E **216**
Al Wafra, *Kuwait* 28°35′ N, 47°57′ E **196**
Al Wajh, *Saudi Arabia* 26°15′ N, 36°27′ E **180**
Al Wakrah, *Qatar* 25°6′ N, 51°35′ E **196**
Al Wannān, *Saudi Arabia* 26°53′ N, 48°26′ E **196**
Al Waqbah, spring, *Saudi Arabia* 28°52′ N, 45°26′ E **196**
Al Warī'ah, *Saudi Arabia* 27°47′ N, 47°32′ E **196**
Al Yādūdah, *Jordan* 31°50′ N, 35°54′ E **194**
Ala, *It.* 45°45′ N, 11°0′ E **167**
Alà, Monti di, *It.* 40°33′ N, 8°47′ E **156**
Ala-Archa National Park, site, *Kyrg.* 42°35′ N, 74°19′ E **197**
Alabama, adm. division, *Ala., U.S.* 31°51′ N, 88°21′ W **96**
Alabama, river, *Ala., U.S.* 31°12′ N, 87°54′ W **103**
Alabaster, *Ala., U.S.* 33°14′ N, 86°49′ W **96**
Alaca, *Turk.* 40°8′ N, 34°50′ E **156**
Alaca Dağ, peak, *Turk.* 37°28′ N, 32°4′ E **156**
Alacahöyük, ruin(s), *Turk.* 40°13′ N, 34°37′ E **156**
Alaçam, *Turk.* 41°35′ N, 35°36′ E **156**
Alachua, *Fla., U.S.* 29°47′ N, 82°30′ W **105**
Alacón, *Sp.* 41°1′ N, 0°43′ E **164**
Aladağ, peak, *Turk.* 37°42′ N, 35°5′ E **156**
Aladağ, peak, *Turk.* 37°56′ N, 32°0′ E **156**
Alage, Āmba, peak, *Eth.* 12°57′ N, 39°23′ E **182**
Alagir, *Russ.* 43°3′ N, 44°14′ E **180**
Alagna Valsesia, *It.* 45°51′ N, 7°56′ E **167**
Alagoas, adm. division, *Braz.* 9°35′ S, 37°52′ W **132**
Alagoinhas, *Braz.* 12°10′ S, 38°24′ W **132**
Alagón, *Sp.* 41°45′ N, 1°8′ W **164**
Alaior, *Sp.* 39°55′ N, 4°8′ E **164**

ALY-ANO

Alyangula, *Austral.* 13°52′ S, 136°30′ E **173**
Alysardakh, *Russ.* 65°53′ N, 131°29′ E **160**
Alytus, *Lith.* 54°23′ N, 24°1′ E **166**
Alyzia, ruin(s), *Gr.* 38°40′ N, 20°49′ E **156**
Alzada, *Mont., U.S.* 45°0′ N, 104°24′ W **90**
Alzenau, *Ger.* 50°5′ N, 9°3′ E **167**
Alzira, *Sp.* 39°7′ N, 0°29′ E **214**
Am Dam, *Chad* 12°45′ N, 20°28′ E **216**
Am Djéména, *Chad* 13°6′ N, 17°19′ E **216**
Am Djeress, spring, *Chad* 16°7′ N, 22°54′ E **226**
Am Khoumi, *Chad* 12°48′ N, 19°43′ E **216**
Am Léiouna, *Chad* 12°47′ N, 21°49′ E **216**
Am Timan, *Chad* 11°0′ N, 20°18′ E **216**
Am Zoer, *Chad* 14°11′ N, 21°22′ E **216**
Amacayacu National Park, *Col.* 3°48′ S, 70°34′ W **136**
Amada Gaza, *Cen. Af. Rep.* 4°45′ N, 15°10′ E **218**
Amada, ruin(s), *Egypt* 22°41′ N, 32°11′ E **182**
Amadi, *Dem. Rep. of the Congo* 3°37′ N, 26°45′ E **224**
Amadi, *Sudan* 5°30′ N, 30°21′ E **218**
Amadjuak Lake, *Can.* 64°49′ N, 73°51′ W **106**
Amadora, *Port.* 38°45′ N, 9°15′ W **150**
Amagansett, *N.Y., U.S.* 40°58′ N, 72°10′ W **104**
Amagi, *Japan* 33°24′ N, 130°39′ E **201**
Amaiur-Maia, *Sp.* 43°11′ N, 1°28′ W **164**
Åmål, *Nor.* 59°2′ N, 12°38′ E **152**
Amal, oil field, *Lib.* 29°23′ N, 21°3′ E **216**
Amalfi, *Col.* 6°57′ N, 75°5′ W **136**
Amalyk, *Russ.* 57°31′ N, 116°39′ E **173**
Amamapare, *Indonesia* 4°47′ S, 136°38′ E **238**
Amambaí, *Braz.* 23°6′ S, 55°16′ W **134**
Amambaí, river, *Braz.* 22°48′ S, 54°50′ W **132**
Amambaí, Serra de, *Braz.* 23°18′ S, 55°51′ W **132**
Amami Ō Shima, island, *Japan* 28°23′ N, 129°46′ E **190**
Amamula, *Dem. Rep. of the Congo* 0°19′ N, 27°46′ E **224**
Amanda, *Ohio, U.S.* 39°38′ N, 82°45′ W **102**
Amanda Park, *Wash., U.S.* 47°25′ N, 123°53′ W **100**
Amangeldi, *Kaz.* 50°11′ N, 65°13′ E **184**
Amaniú, river, *Braz.* 1°19′ S, 67°42′ W **136**
Amanos Dağları, *Turk.* 36°14′ N, 36°0′ E **156**
Amantea, *It.* 39°9′ N, 16°4′ E **156**
Amapá, *Braz.* 10°19′ S, 69°28′ W **137**
Amapá, *Braz.* 2°2′ N, 50°50′ W **130**
Amapá, adm. division, *Braz.* 1°12′ N, 53°2′ W **130**
Amarante, *Braz.* 6°17′ S, 42°51′ W **132**
Amardalay, *Mongolia* 46°7′ N, 106°22′ E **198**
Amargosa, *Braz.* 13°1′ S, 39°38′ W **138**
Amargosa Desert, *Nev., U.S.* 36°47′ N, 116°46′ W **101**
Amargosa Range, *Calif., U.S.* 36°17′ N, 116°48′ W **101**
Amargosa Valley, *Nev., U.S.* 36°38′ N, 116°25′ W **101**
Amarillo, *Tex., U.S.* 35°10′ N, 101°51′ W **92**
Amarkantak, *India* 22°40′ N, 81°46′ E **197**
Amaro, Monte, peak, *It.* 42°4′ N, 14°1′ E **156**
Amarpur, *India* 23°30′ N, 91°37′ E **197**
Amarwara, *India* 22°19′ N, 79°10′ E **197**
Amasa, *Mich., U.S.* 46°14′ N, 88°27′ W **94**
Amasia see Amasya, *Turk.* 40°40′ N, 35°50′ E **156**
Amasine, *Western Sahara* 25°48′ N, 13°20′ W **214**
Amasra, *Turk.* 41°44′ N, 32°24′ E **156**
Amasya (Amasia), *Turk.* 40°40′ N, 35°50′ E **156**
Amatari, *Braz.* 3°16′ S, 58°55′ W **130**
Amataurá, *Braz.* 3°32′ S, 68°4′ W **136**
Amatepec, *Mex.* 18°38′ N, 100°9′ W **114**
Amathous, ruin(s), *Cyprus* 34°42′ N, 33°5′ E **194**
Amatlán de Cañas, *Mex.* 20°49′ N, 104°27′ W **114**
Amavon Islands, *Solomon Sea* 7°0′ S, 158°0′ E **242**
Amay, *Belg.* 50°33′ N, 5°18′ E **167**
Amazar, *Russ.* 53°50′ N, 120°55′ E **190**
Amazon Fan, *North Atlantic Ocean* 5°17′ N, 46°22′ W **253**
Amazon see Amazonas, river, *Braz.* 3°8′ S, 55°59′ W **123**
Amazonas, adm. division, *Braz.* 9°10′ S, 67°35′ W **137**
Amazonas (Amazon), river, *Braz.* 3°8′ S, 55°59′ W **123**
Amazonas see Solimões, river, *Braz.* 2°50′ S, 66°35′ W **123**
Amazônia National Park, *Braz.* 4°19′ S, 57°15′ W **130**
Amb, *Pak.* 34°14′ N, 72°48′ E **186**
Āmba Gīyorgīs, *Eth.* 12°41′ N, 37°37′ E **218**
Āmba Maryam, *Eth.* 11°23′ N, 39°16′ E **182**
Ambala, *India* 30°21′ N, 76°50′ E **197**
Ambalangoda, *Sri Lanka* 6°16′ N, 80°4′ E **188**
Ambalantota, *Sri Lanka* 6°7′ N, 81°4′ E **188**
Ambarchik, *Russ.* 69°33′ N, 162°14′ E **160**
Ambato, *Ecua.* 1°21′ S, 78°48′ W **130**
Ambato Boeny, *Madagascar* 16°27′ S, 46°44′ E **220**
Ambatolampy, *Madagascar* 19°24′ S, 47°27′ E **220**
Ambatondrazaka, *Madagascar* 17°60′ S, 48°24′ E **207**
Ambazac, *Fr.* 45°57′ N, 1°23′ E **150**
Ambelau, island, *Indonesia* 4°17′ S, 127°15′ E **192**
Ambergris Cay, island, *Belize* 17°58′ N, 87°52′ W **115**
Ambergris Cays, islands, *North Atlantic Ocean* 21°19′ N, 72°57′ W **116**
Amberley, *Can.* 44°1′ N, 81°42′ W **102**
Amberley, *N.Z.* 43°10′ S, 172°44′ E **240**
Amberley, *U.K.* 50°54′ N, 0°32′ E **162**
Ambidédi, *Mali* 14°34′ N, 11°50′ W **222**
Ambikapur, *India* 23°7′ N, 83°12′ E **197**
Ambilobe, *Madagascar* 13°13′ S, 49°2′ E **220**
Ambla, *Est.* 59°10′ N, 25°48′ E **166**
Ambler, *Alas., U.S.* 67°5′ N, 157°52′ W **98**
Ambleside, *U.K.* 54°25′ N, 2°58′ W **162**
Ambleteuse, *Fr.* 50°48′ N, 1°36′ E **163**
Ambo, *Peru* 10°11′ S, 76°10′ W **130**
Amboasary, *Madagascar* 25°4′ S, 46°26′ E **220**
Ambodifotatra, *Madagascar* 16°58′ S, 49°51′ E **220**
Ambohimahasoa, *Madagascar* 21°6′ S, 47°13′ E **220**
Ambohimanga Atsimo, *Madagascar* 20°53′ S, 47°36′ E **220**
Amboise, *Fr.* 47°24′ N, 0°58′ E **150**
Amboiva, *Angola* 11°34′ S, 14°44′ E **220**
Ambolauri, *Ga.* 42°28′ N, 43°9′ E **195**
Ambon, *Indonesia* 3°41′ S, 128°3′ E **192**
Amboró National Park, *Bol.* 17°42′ S, 64°48′ W **137**
Amborompotsy, *Madagascar* 20°35′ S, 46°14′ E **220**
Amboseli National Park, *Kenya* 2°50′ S, 37°15′ E **224**
Amboy, *Ill., U.S.* 41°42′ N, 89°20′ W **102**
Amboy Crater, *Calif., U.S.* 34°31′ N, 115°48′ W **101**
Ambre, Cap d′, *Madagascar* 12°1′ S, 49°15′ E **220**
Ambre, Montagne d′, peak, *Madagascar* 12°41′ S, 48°58′ E **220**
Ambriz, *Angola* 7°51′ S, 13°6′ E **218**
Ambrogio, *It.* 44°55′ N, 11°55′ E **167**
Ambrósio, *Braz.* 2°53′ S, 68°19′ W **136**
Amburan Burnu, *Azerb.* 40°36′ N, 49°49′ E **195**
Amchitka, island, *Alas., U.S.* 51°7′ N, 177°20′ E **160**
Amderma, *Russ.* 69°42′ N, 61°41′ E **169**
Amdillis, spring, *Mali* 18°24′ N, 0°17′ E **222**
Ameca, *Mex.* 20°33′ N, 104°3′ W **114**
Ameca, river, *Mex.* 20°55′ N, 105°12′ W **114**
Ameghino, *Arg.* 34°51′ S, 62°28′ W **139**
Ameland, island, *Neth.* 53°28′ N, 5°37′ E **163**
Amelia, *La., U.S.* 29°40′ N, 91°7′ W **103**
Amenia, *N.Y., U.S.* 41°50′ N, 73°34′ W **104**
America-Antarctic Ridge, *South Atlantic Ocean* 59°11′ S, 12°30′ W **255**
American Highland, *Antarctica* 74°55′ S, 76°3′ E **248**
American, river, *Wash., U.S.* 46°53′ N, 121°26′ W **100**
American Samoa, *United States* 14°0′ S, 171°0′ W **238**
Americus, *Ga., U.S.* 32°3′ N, 84°15′ W **112**
Amersfoort, *S. Af.* 27°2′ S, 29°51′ E **227**
Amery, *Wis., U.S.* 45°18′ N, 92°23′ W **94**
Amery Ice Shelf, *Antarctica* 71°16′ S, 69°44′ E **248**
Ames, *Iowa, U.S.* 42°0′ N, 93°37′ W **94**
Amesbury, *Mass., U.S.* 42°50′ N, 70°57′ W **104**
Amesbury, *U.K.* 51°10′ N, 1°47′ W **162**
Amga, *Russ.* 61°1′ N, 131°52′ E **160**
Amga, river, *Russ.* 59°34′ N, 126°34′ E **160**
Amgu, *Russ.* 45°56′ N, 137°30′ E **190**
Amguema, river, *Russ.* 67°26′ N, 178°38′ W **98**
Amguid, *Alg.* 26°26′ N, 5°23′ E **214**
Amhara, region, *Africa* 12°12′ N, 36°11′ E **182**
Amherst, *Can.* 45°49′ N, 64°13′ W **111**
Amherst, *N.H., U.S.* 42°51′ N, 71°38′ W **104**
Amherst, *N.Y., U.S.* 42°58′ N, 78°50′ W **94**
Amherst, *Ohio, U.S.* 41°23′ N, 82°14′ W **102**
Amherst, *Tex., U.S.* 33°59′ N, 102°23′ W **92**
Amherst, *Va., U.S.* 37°34′ N, 79°4′ W **96**
Amherstburg, *Can.* 42°5′ N, 83°6′ W **102**
Amhovichy, *Belarus* 53°6′ N, 27°50′ E **158**
Amiata, Monte, peak, *It.* 42°53′ N, 11°32′ E **156**
Amidon, *N. Dak., U.S.* 46°27′ N, 103°19′ W **90**
Amiens, *Fr.* 49°52′ N, 2°18′ E **163**
Amili, *India* 28°23′ N, 95°50′ E **188**
Amino, *Japan* 35°39′ N, 135°1′ E **201**
Aminuis, *Namibia* 23°43′ S, 19°18′ E **227**
Amiot Islands, *South Pacific Ocean* 67°26′ S, 74°9′ W **248**
Amioun, *Leb.* 34°17′ N, 35°48′ E **194**
Amirante Isles, *Indian Ocean* 4°41′ S, 51°23′ E **173**
Amirante Trench, *Indian Ocean* 9°12′ S, 53°16′ E **254**
Amisk Lake, lake, *Can.* 54°33′ N, 102°35′ W **108**
Amisk, river, *Can.* 54°40′ N, 112°29′ W **108**
Amistad National Recreation Area, *Tex., U.S.* 29°32′ N, 101°42′ W **96**
Amistad Reservoir, lake, *Tex., U.S.* 29°33′ N, 101°44′ W **92**
Amisus see Samsun, *Turk.* 41°17′ N, 36°20′ E **158**
Amite, *La., U.S.* 30°42′ N, 90°31′ W **103**
Amity, *Ark., U.S.* 34°14′ N, 93°28′ W **96**
Amla, *India* 21°56′ N, 78°9′ E **197**
Åmli, *Nor.* 58°45′ N, 8°29′ E **152**
Amlia, island, *Alas., U.S.* 52°10′ N, 173°59′ W **160**
ʻAmm Adam, *Sudan* 16°21′ N, 36°4′ E **182**
ʻAmmān (Philadelphia), *Jordan* 31°56′ N, 35°53′ E **194**
Ammanford, *U.K.* 51°47′ N, 3°60′ W **162**
Ammänsaari, *Fin.* 64°50′ N, 28°52′ E **152**
Ammarfjället, peak, *Nor.* 66°4′ N, 15°30′ E **152**
Ammarnäs, *Nor.* 65°57′ N, 16°10′ E **152**
Ammeloe, *Ger.* 52°4′ N, 6°47′ E **167**
Ammochostos (Famagusta, Gazimagusa), *Northern Cyprus* 35°7′ N, 33°56′ E **194**
Amo, *Ind., U.S.* 39°41′ N, 86°37′ W **102**
ʻĀmol, *Iran* 36°36′ N, 52°17′ E **180**
Amolar, *Braz.* 18°1′ S, 57°31′ W **132**
Amos, *Can.* 48°34′ N, 78°8′ W **94**
Amot, *Mor.* 27°57′ N, 10°6′ W **214**
Åmot, *Nor.* 59°36′ N, 7°57′ E **152**
Åmotfors, *Nor.* 59°47′ N, 12°24′ E **152**
Amoúdia, peak, *Gr.* 37°31′ N, 25°56′ E **156**
Amoy see Xiamen, *China* 24°25′ N, 118°6′ E **198**
Ampani, *India* 19°34′ N, 82°36′ E **188**
Ampanihy, *Madagascar* 24°39′ S, 44°42′ E **220**
Amparafaravola, *Madagascar* 17°36′ S, 48°13′ E **220**
Amparihy Est, *Madagascar* 23°58′ S, 47°22′ E **220**
Amparo, *Braz.* 22°42′ S, 46°47′ W **138**
Ampato, Nevado, peak, *Peru* 15°52′ S, 71°55′ W **137**
Ampere, *Braz.* 25°57′ S, 53°30′ W **139**
Ampezzo, *It.* 46°23′ N, 12°47′ E **167**
Amphiareion, ruin(s), *Gr.* 38°17′ N, 23°43′ E **156**
Amphitrite Point, *Can.* 48°43′ N, 125°48′ W **90**
Amposta, *Sp.* 40°42′ N, 0°34′ E **164**
Ampthill, *U.K.* 52°1′ N, 0°30′ E **162**
Amqui, *Can.* 48°27′ N, 67°27′ W **94**
ʻAmrān, *Yemen* 15°40′ N, 43°57′ E **182**
Amravati, *India* 20°56′ N, 77°46′ E **188**
Amreli, *India* 21°36′ N, 71°12′ E **186**
ʻAmrīt (Marathus), ruin(s), *Syr.* 34°50′ N, 35°52′ E **194**
ʻAmrīt, ruin(s), *Syr.* 34°48′ N, 35°49′ E **156**
Amritsar, *India* 31°39′ N, 74°52′ E **186**
Amroha, *India* 28°54′ N, 78°28′ E **188**
Amsāʻad, *Lib.* 31°37′ N, 25°2′ E **180**
ʻAmshīt, *Leb.* 34°9′ N, 35°38′ E **194**
Amsterdam, *Neth.* 52°22′ N, 4°50′ E **163**
Amsterdam, *N.Y., U.S.* 42°56′ N, 74°12′ W **104**
Amsterdam, island, *Fr.* 37°45′ S, 78°0′ E **254**
Amstetten, *Aust.* 48°7′ N, 14°51′ E **152**
Amston, *Conn., U.S.* 41°37′ N, 72°21′ W **104**
Amu Darya, river, *Uzb.* 41°1′ N, 61°42′ E **184**
Amuay, *Venez.* 11°51′ N, 70°4′ W **123**
ʻĀmūdah, *Syr.* 37°6′ N, 40°57′ E **195**
Amukta, island, *Alas., U.S.* 52°4′ N, 171°7′ W **160**
Amuku Mountains, *Guyana* 2°4′ N, 58°12′ W **130**
Amundsen Gulf 70°20′ N, 123°56′ W **98**
Amundsen, Mount, *Antarctica* 67°13′ S, 101°28′ E **248**
Amundsen Sea 73°41′ S, 105°21′ W **248**
Amundsen-Scott South Pole, station, *Antarctica* 89°59′ S, 164°21′ W **248**
Amur, adm. division, *Russ.* 53°36′ N, 124°46′ E **190**
Amur, river, *Russ.* 51°18′ N, 138°37′ E **190**
Amurang, *Indonesia* 1°13′ N, 124°28′ E **192**
Amurrio, *Sp.* 43°2′ N, 3°1′ W **164**
Amusco, *Sp.* 42°10′ N, 4°28′ W **150**
Amvrosiyivka, *Ukr.* 47°44′ N, 38°26′ E **158**
Amydery′a, *Turkm.* 37°56′ N, 65°18′ E **197**
An, *Myanmar* 19°46′ N, 94°7′ E **202**
An Khe, *Vietnam* 13°58′ N, 108°40′ E **202**
An Nabī Shīt, *Leb.* 33°52′ N, 36°6′ E **194**
An Nabk, *Syr.* 34°1′ N, 36°44′ E **194**
An Nabk Abū Qaṣr, spring, *Saudi Arabia* 30°18′ N, 38°41′ E **180**
An Nafūd, *Saudi Arabia* 28°35′ N, 39°18′ E **180**
An Najaf (Najaf), *Iraq* 31°58′ N, 44°19′ E **180**
An Namatah, *Jordan* 30°48′ N, 35°32′ E **194**
An Nashshāsh, *U.A.E.* 23°1′ N, 54°3′ E **182**
An Nāṣirīyah, *Syr.* 33°52′ N, 36°48′ E **194**
An Nāṣirīyah (Nasiriyah), *Iraq* 31°5′ N, 46°11′ E **180**
An Nawfalīyah, *Lib.* 30°41′ N, 17°49′ E **143**
An Nimāṣ, *Saudi Arabia* 19°2′ N, 42°9′ E **182**
An Nuʻayrīyah, *Saudi Arabia* 27°28′ N, 48°27′ E **196**
An Pass, *Myanmar* 19°59′ N, 94°17′ E **202**
An Phuoc, *Vietnam* 11°36′ N, 108°54′ E **202**
An Uaimh see Navan, *Ire.* 53°38′ N, 6°42′ W **150**
Ana María, Cayos, islands, *Caribbean Sea* 21°11′ N, 79°29′ W **116**
Anabar, river, *Russ.* 70°31′ N, 114°9′ E **160**
Anabarskiy Zaliv 73°25′ N, 108°6′ E **160**
Anacapa Islands, *North Pacific Ocean* 34°4′ N, 119°29′ W **100**
Anaco, *Venez.* 9°26′ N, 64°30′ W **116**
Anacoco, *La., U.S.* 31°14′ N, 93°21′ W **103**
Anaconda, *Mont., U.S.* 46°7′ N, 112°58′ W **90**
Anaconda Range, *Mont., U.S.* 45°49′ N, 113°46′ W **90**
Anacortes, *Wash., U.S.* 48°28′ N, 122°38′ W **100**
Anactorium, ruin(s), *Gr.* 38°55′ N, 20°45′ E **156**
Anadyr′, *Russ.* 64°38′ N, 177°6′ E **160**
Anadyr, Gulf of see Anadyrskiy Zaliv 66°48′ N, 179°18′ W **160**
Anadyr′, river, *Russ.* 66°42′ N, 169°30′ E **160**
Anadyrskiy Zaliv (Anadyr, Gulf of) 66°48′ N, 179°18′ W **160**
Anáfi, *Gr.* 36°20′ N, 25°46′ E **156**
Anáfi, island, *Gr.* 36°24′ N, 25°52′ E **180**
Anagé, *Braz.* 14°45′ S, 41°10′ W **138**
Anaghit, *Eritrea* 16°20′ N, 38°35′ E **182**
ʻĀnah, *Iraq* 34°25′ N, 41°58′ E **180**
Anaheim, *Calif., U.S.* 33°50′ N, 117°56′ W **101**
Anahim Lake, *Can.* 52°28′ N, 125°20′ W **108**
Anahola, *Hawaiʻi, U.S.* 22°8′ N, 159°19′ W **99**
Anáhuac, *Mex.* 27°13′ N, 100°9′ W **96**
Anáhuac, *Mex.* 24°27′ N, 101°31′ W **114**
Anahuac, *Tex., U.S.* 29°45′ N, 94°41′ W **103**
Anai Mudi, peak, *India* 10°8′ N, 76°55′ E **188**
Anaï, spring, *Alg.* 24°9′ N, 11°27′ E **214**
Anajás, *Braz.* 0°60′ N, 49°58′ W **130**
Anak, *N. Korea* 38°29′ N, 125°29′ E **200**
Anaktuvuk Pass, *Alas., U.S.* 68°11′ N, 151°54′ W **98**
Analalava, *Madagascar* 14°38′ S, 47°47′ E **220**
Analavelona, peak, *Madagascar* 22°36′ S, 44°2′ E **220**
Anamã, *Braz.* 3°33′ S, 61°30′ W **130**
Anambas, Kepulauan, islands, *South China Sea* 2°41′ N, 105°43′ E **196**
Anamizu, *Japan* 37°13′ N, 136°54′ E **201**
Anamoose, *N. Dak., U.S.* 47°51′ N, 100°15′ W **90**
Anamosa, *Iowa, U.S.* 42°6′ N, 91°17′ W **94**
Anamu, river, *Braz.* 0°42′ N, 56°51′ W **130**
Anamur, *Turk.* 36°5′ N, 32°51′ E **156**
Anamur Burnu, *Azerb.* 36°2′ N, 32°4′ E **156**
Anan, *Japan* 33°52′ N, 134°37′ E **201**
Ananchichi, *Belarus* 52°31′ N, 27°39′ E **152**
Anand, *India* 22°33′ N, 73°0′ E **186**
Anan′yiv, *Ukr.* 47°43′ N, 29°58′ E **156**
Anapa, *Russ.* 44°54′ N, 37°23′ E **156**
Anápolis, *Braz.* 16°21′ S, 48°59′ W **138**
Anār, *Iran* 30°51′ N, 55°18′ E **180**
Anārak, *Iran* 33°20′ N, 53°43′ E **180**
Ånäset, *Nor.* 64°14′ N, 21°2′ E **152**
Anastasia Island, *Fla., U.S.* 29°52′ N, 81°16′ W **105**
Anatahan, island, *U.S.* 16°12′ N, 144°27′ E **192**
Anatolia (Asia Minor), region, *Asia* 38°39′ N, 30°18′ E **180**
Anatone, *Wash., U.S.* 46°7′ N, 117°9′ W **90**
Añatuya, *Arg.* 28°28′ S, 62°49′ W **139**
Anauá, river, *Braz.* 0°57′ N, 60°9′ W **130**
Anaurilândia, *Braz.* 22°2′ S, 52°48′ W **138**
Añavieja, *Sp.* 41°51′ N, 1°56′ W **164**
Anavilhanas, Arquipélago das, *South America* 3°13′ S, 62°22′ W **130**
Anbyŏn, *N. Korea* 39°2′ N, 127°31′ E **200**
Ancares, Sierra de, *Sp.* 42°54′ N, 7°7′ W **150**
Ancash, adm. division, *Peru* 9°4′ S, 78°36′ W **130**
Ancasti, Sierra de, *Arg.* 28°4′ S, 65°55′ W **132**
Anchieta, *Braz.* 20°51′ S, 40°44′ W **138**
Anchorage, *Alas., U.S.* 61°5′ N, 149°53′ W **98**
Anchorena, *Arg.* 35°40′ S, 65°23′ W **134**
Anclitas, Cayo, island, *Cuba* 20°30′ N, 79°14′ W **116**
Ancona, *It.* 43°36′ N, 13°30′ E **167**
Ancram, *N.Y., U.S.* 42°2′ N, 73°40′ W **104**
Ancuabe, *Mozambique* 13°2′ S, 39°54′ E **224**
Ancud, *Chile* 41°59′ S, 73°55′ W **123**
Ancud, Golfo de 42°13′ S, 73°45′ W **134**
Ancy-le-Franc, *Fr.* 47°46′ N, 4°9′ E **150**
Anda, *China* 46°22′ N, 125°24′ E **198**
Andacollo, *Arg.* 37°13′ S, 70°40′ W **134**
Andahuaylas, *Peru* 13°41′ S, 73°24′ W **137**
Andalgalá, *Arg.* 27°36′ S, 66°19′ W **132**
Åndalsnes, *Nor.* 62°33′ N, 7°42′ E **152**
Andalusia, *Ala., U.S.* 31°18′ N, 86°28′ W **96**
Andalusia, adm. division, *Sp.* 37°27′ N, 4°53′ W **164**
Andaman and Nicobar Islands, *India* 11°25′ N, 92°50′ E **192**
Andaman Basin, *Andaman Sea* 9°56′ N, 95°4′ E **254**
Andaman Islands, *Andaman Sea* 12°47′ N, 94°43′ E **202**
Andaman Sea 15°15′ N, 94°7′ E **188**
Andapa, *Madagascar* 14°39′ S, 49°40′ E **220**
Andara, *Namibia* 18°3′ S, 21°32′ E **220**
Andaraí, *Braz.* 12°49′ S, 41°21′ W **138**
Andavaka, Cap, *Madagascar* 25°40′ S, 46°43′ E **220**
Andeg, *Russ.* 67°55′ N, 53°10′ E **169**
Andelot-Blancheville, *Fr.* 48°14′ N, 5°17′ E **163**
Andenne, *Belg.* 50°29′ N, 5°5′ E **167**
Andéranboukane, *Mali* 15°27′ N, 3°2′ E **222**
Andermatt, *Switz.* 46°38′ N, 8°36′ E **167**
Andernach, *Ger.* 50°26′ N, 7°23′ E **167**
Anderson, *Calif., U.S.* 40°26′ N, 122°19′ W **90**
Anderson, *Ind., U.S.* 40°5′ N, 85°41′ W **102**
Anderson, *Mo., U.S.* 36°38′ N, 94°27′ W **96**
Anderson, *S.C., U.S.* 34°29′ N, 82°40′ W **96**
Anderson Dome, *Antarctica* 72°28′ S, 87°2′ W **248**
Anderson Massif, *Antarctica* 78°56′ S, 82°12′ W **248**
Anderson Ranch Dam, *Idaho, U.S.* 43°28′ N, 115°37′ W **90**
Anderson, river, *Can.* 68°35′ N, 127°50′ W **98**
Andersson Island, *Antarctica* 63°39′ S, 59°14′ W **134**
Andes, Cordillera de Los, mountain, *South America* 9°47′ S, 74°52′ W **137**
Andhra Pradesh, adm. division, *India* 16°8′ N, 77°38′ E **188**
Andijon, *Uzb.* 40°46′ N, 72°21′ E **197**
Andikira, *Gr.* 38°22′ N, 22°36′ E **156**
Andikíthira, island, *Gr.* 35°48′ N, 22°23′ E **180**
Andilálou, ruin(s), *Gr.* 41°29′ N, 24°9′ E **156**
Andilamena, *Madagascar* 17°2′ S, 48°33′ E **220**
Andir, river, *China* 36°34′ N, 84°8′ E **184**
Andirá, *Braz.* 3°45′ S, 66°17′ W **136**
Andırın, *Turk.* 37°34′ N, 36°21′ E **156**
Andirlangar, *China* 37°37′ N, 83°47′ E **184**
Andkhvoy, *Afghan.* 36°55′ N, 65°8′ E **186**
Andoany (Hell-Ville), *Madagascar* 13°24′ S, 48°17′ E **207**
Andoas, *Peru* 2°57′ S, 76°25′ W **136**
Andomskiy Pogost, *Russ.* 61°14′ N, 36°39′ E **154**
Andong, *S. Korea* 36°33′ N, 128°43′ E **200**
Andorra La Vella, *Andorra* 42°29′ N, 1°26′ E **164**
Andover, *Me., U.S.* 44°37′ N, 70°46′ W **94**
Andover, *N.H., U.S.* 43°26′ N, 71°50′ W **104**
Andover, *U.K.* 51°12′ N, 1°30′ W **162**
Andovoranto, *Madagascar* 18°57′ S, 49°5′ E **220**
Andøya, island, *Nor.* 69°24′ N, 14°6′ E **160**
Andradina, *Braz.* 20°56′ S, 51°24′ W **138**
Andreapol′, *Russ.* 56°39′ N, 32°18′ E **154**
Andreba, *Madagascar* 17°40′ S, 48°33′ E **220**
Andrew, *Can.* 53°52′ N, 112°20′ W **108**
Andrews, *Ind., U.S.* 40°50′ N, 85°37′ W **102**
Andrews, *S.C., U.S.* 33°26′ N, 79°34′ W **96**
Andrews, *Tex., U.S.* 32°18′ N, 102°33′ W **92**
Andreyevka, *Russ.* 52°20′ N, 51°50′ E **158**
Andrijevica, *Serb. and Mont.* 42°43′ N, 19°47′ E **168**
Androka, *Madagascar* 25°1′ S, 44°7′ E **220**
Ándros, island, *Gr.* 37°54′ N, 24°57′ E **180**
Androscoggin, river, *Me., U.S.* 44°23′ N, 71°6′ W **104**
Andryushino, *Russ.* 59°17′ N, 62°59′ E **154**
Andryushkino, *Russ.* 69°9′ N, 154°31′ E **160**
Andújar, *Sp.* 38°2′ N, 4°3′ W **164**
Andulo, *Angola* 11°31′ S, 16°41′ E **220**
Aneby, *Nor.* 57°49′ N, 14°46′ E **152**
Anefis I-n-Darane, *Mali* 18°2′ N, 0°37′ E **222**
Anegada, island, *U.K.* 18°43′ N, 65°1′ W **116**
Anegada, Punta, *Pan.* 7°14′ N, 81°48′ W **115**
Añelo, Cuenca del, *Arg.* 37°56′ S, 69°57′ W **134**
Anenii Noi, *Mold.* 46°52′ N, 29°13′ E **156**
Aneroid, *Can.* 49°42′ N, 107°18′ W **90**
Anet, *Fr.* 48°51′ N, 1°26′ E **163**
Aneta, *N. Dak., U.S.* 47°39′ N, 97°60′ W **90**
Aneto, peak, *Sp.* 42°37′ N, 0°36′ E **164**
Aney, *Niger* 19°27′ N, 12°54′ E **216**
Anfah, *Leb.* 34°21′ N, 35°44′ E **194**
Angamos, Punta, *Chile* 23°1′ S, 71°22′ W **132**
An′gang, *S. Korea* 35°58′ N, 129°15′ E **200**
Angangueo, *Mex.* 19°36′ N, 100°17′ W **114**
Ang′angxi, *China* 47°7′ N, 123°48′ E **198**
Angara, river, *Russ.* 58°38′ N, 98°21′ E **246**
Angarsk, *Russ.* 52°43′ N, 103°32′ E **190**
Angaur (Ngeaur), island, *Palau* 7°0′ N, 134°0′ E **242**
Ånge, *Nor.* 62°31′ N, 15°37′ E **152**
Ángel de la Guarda, Isla, island, *Mex.* 29°35′ N, 113°31′ W **112**
Angel Falls, *Venez.* 4°34′ N, 63°39′ W **123**
Angeles, *Philippines* 15°8′ N, 120°35′ E **203**
Angélica, *Arg.* 31°33′ S, 61°32′ W **139**
Angelina, river, *Tex., U.S.* 31°30′ N, 94°50′ W **103**
Angels Camp, *Calif., U.S.* 38°4′ N, 120°33′ W **100**
Angermünde, *Ger.* 53°1′ N, 14°0′ E **152**
Angers, *Fr.* 47°28′ N, 0°33′ E **150**
Angerville, *Fr.* 48°18′ N, 1°59′ E **163**
Angical, *Braz.* 11°60′ S, 44°40′ W **132**
Angie, *La., U.S.* 30°57′ N, 89°49′ W **103**
Angkor, ruin(s), *Cambodia* 13°28′ N, 103°45′ E **202**
Angle Inlet, *Minn., U.S.* 49°18′ N, 95°7′ W **90**
Anglem, Mount, *N.Z.* 46°46′ S, 167°48′ E **240**
Anglès, *Sp.* 41°56′ N, 2°38′ E **164**
Angleton, *Tex., U.S.* 29°9′ N, 95°26′ W **103**
Anglure, *Fr.* 48°35′ N, 3°48′ E **163**
Ango, *Dem. Rep. of the Congo* 3°58′ N, 25°52′ E **224**
Angoche, *Mozambique* 16°12′ S, 39°57′ E **224**
Angohrān, *Iran* 26°33′ N, 57°50′ E **196**
Angol, *Chile* 37°49′ S, 72°43′ W **134**
Angola 12°18′ S, 17°4′ E **220**
Angola, *Ind., U.S.* 41°38′ N, 84°60′ W **102**
Angola, *La., U.S.* 30°56′ N, 91°34′ W **103**
Angola, *N.Y., U.S.* 42°38′ N, 79°3′ W **94**
Angola Plain, *South Atlantic Ocean* 15°4′ S, 3°22′ E **253**
Angora see Ankara, *Turk.* 39°55′ N, 32°43′ E **156**
Angostura, *Col.* 0°28′ N, 72°30′ W **136**
Angostura, *Mex.* 25°21′ N, 108°10′ W **112**
Angostura, Presa de la, *Mex.* 30°32′ N, 109°47′ W **92**
Angoulême, *Fr.* 45°39′ N, 0°10′ E **150**
Angouma, *Gabon* 1°11′ N, 12°19′ E **218**
Angoumois, region, *Europe* 45°50′ N, 0°49′ E **165**
Angra dos Reis, *Braz.* 23°2′ S, 44°20′ W **138**
Angren, *Uzb.* 41°1′ N, 70°14′ E **197**
Angtassom, *Cambodia* 11°1′ N, 104°39′ E **202**
Angu, *Dem. Rep. of the Congo* 3°27′ N, 24°26′ E **224**
Angüés, *Sp.* 42°6′ N, 0°9′ E **164**
Anguil, *Arg.* 36°31′ S, 64°2′ W **139**
Anguilla Cays, *North Atlantic Ocean* 23°19′ N, 79°28′ W **116**
Anguille, Cape, *Can.* 47°49′ N, 60°20′ W **111**
Angumu, *Dem. Rep. of the Congo* 0°7′ N, 27°39′ E **224**
Anguo, *China* 38°26′ N, 115°21′ E **198**
Angutikha, *Russ.* 65°58′ N, 87°24′ E **169**
Angvik, *Nor.* 62°53′ N, 8°3′ E **152**
Anhua, *China* 28°23′ N, 111°3′ E **198**
Anhui, adm. division, *China* 29°56′ N, 116°53′ E **198**
Aniak, *Alas., U.S.* 61°24′ N, 159°45′ W **98**
Anicuns, *Braz.* 16°32′ S, 49°58′ W **138**
Anie, Pic d′, peak, *Fr.* 42°55′ N, 0°45′ E **164**
Anikhovka, *Russ.* 51°29′ N, 60°15′ E **154**
Animas, *N. Mex., U.S.* 31°57′ N, 108°47′ W **92**
Animas Peak, *N. Mex., U.S.* 31°33′ N, 108°50′ W **92**
Ánimas, Punta de las, *Mex.* 28°44′ N, 114°7′ W **112**
Anin, *Myanmar* 15°41′ N, 97°46′ E **202**
Aniñón, *Sp.* 41°26′ N, 1°43′ W **164**
Anipemza, *Arm.* 40°26′ N, 43°36′ E **195**
Anishinabi Lake, lake, *Can.* 50°26′ N, 94°1′ W **90**
Anita, *Chile* 20°29′ S, 69°51′ W **137**
Anita, *Pa., U.S.* 40°59′ N, 78°59′ W **94**
Aniva, Mys, *Russ.* 45°46′ N, 142°25′ E **190**
Anivorano, *Madagascar* 18°47′ S, 48°58′ E **220**
Anixab, *Namibia* 20°58′ S, 14°46′ E **220**
Anjalankoski, *Fin.* 60°41′ N, 26°51′ E **166**
Anjosvarden, peak, *Nor.* 61°24′ N, 14°7′ E **152**
Anjou Islands, *East Siberian Sea* 74°45′ N, 144°8′ E **255**
Anjou, region, *Europe* 47°39′ N, 1°10′ W **150**
Anju, *N. Korea* 39°35′ N, 125°44′ E **198**
Anka, spring, *Sudan* 14°37′ N, 24°51′ E **226**
Ankang, *China* 32°36′ N, 109°3′ E **198**
Ankara (Angora), *Turk.* 39°55′ N, 32°43′ E **156**
Ankaramena, *Madagascar* 21°58′ S, 46°39′ E **220**
Ankarede, *Nor.* 64°49′ N, 14°12′ E **152**
Ankasakasa, *Madagascar* 16°22′ S, 44°50′ E **220**
Ankazoabo, *Madagascar* 22°15′ S, 44°28′ E **220**
Ankazobe, *Madagascar* 18°20′ S, 47°8′ E **220**
Anklam, *Ger.* 53°51′ N, 13°41′ E **152**
Ānkober, *Eth.* 9°31′ N, 39°42′ E **224**
Ankofa, peak, *Madagascar* 16°23′ S, 48°27′ E **220**
Ankoro, *Dem. Rep. of the Congo* 6°48′ S, 26°52′ E **224**
Ankpa, *Nig.* 7°21′ N, 7°36′ E **222**
Anlong, *China* 25°0′ N, 105°26′ E **198**
Anlu, *China* 31°14′ N, 113°42′ E **198**
Ann Arbor, *Mich., U.S.* 42°15′ N, 83°46′ W **102**
Ann, Cape, *Mass., U.S.* 42°36′ N, 70°36′ W **104**
Anna, *Mo., U.S.* 37°27′ N, 89°14′ W **96**
Anna Paulowna, *Neth.* 52°52′ N, 4°50′ E **163**
Annaba (Bône), *Alg.* 36°53′ N, 7°45′ E **156**
Annai, *Guyana* 3°55′ N, 59°7′ W **130**
Annan, *U.K.* 54°59′ N, 3°16′ W **150**
Annapolis, *Md., U.S.* 38°58′ N, 76°37′ W **94**
Annapolis Royal, *Can.* 44°43′ N, 65°31′ W **111**
Annecy, *Fr.* 45°54′ N, 6°7′ E **167**
Annecy, Lac d′, lake, *Fr.* 45°52′ N, 6°0′ E **165**
Annemasse, *Fr.* 46°11′ N, 6°14′ E **167**
Annenkov Island, *U.K.* 54°35′ S, 38°57′ W **134**
Annenskiy Most, *Russ.* 60°44′ N, 37°6′ E **154**
Annette, *Alas., U.S.* 55°2′ N, 131°38′ W **108**
Anniston, *Ala., U.S.* 33°38′ N, 85°50′ W **96**
Annobón, island, *Equatorial Guinea* 1°32′ S, 4°43′ E **214**
Annweiler, *Ger.* 49°11′ N, 7°56′ E **163**
Año Nuevo, Point, *Calif., U.S.* 37°10′ N, 122°33′ W **100**
Anoka, *Minn., U.S.* 45°10′ N, 93°22′ W **94**
Anole, *Somalia* 0°54′ N, 41°57′ E **224**
Anori, *Braz.* 3°49′ S, 61°42′ W **130**
Anotaie, river, *Braz.* 3°23′ N, 52°15′ W **130**
Ânou Mellene, spring, *Mali* 17°27′ N, 0°32′ E **222**

Ânou Mellene, spring, *Mali* 18°0' N, 3°58' E **222**
Anou Meniet, spring, *Alg.* 24°59' N, 4°19' E **214**
Anou-I-n-Ouzzal, spring, *Alg.* 20°40' N, 2°27' E **222**
Anoumaba, *Côte d'Ivoire* 6°14' N, 4°32' W **222**
Anping, *China* 41°9' N, 123°28' E **200**
Anpu, *China* 21°25' N, 110°2' E **198**
Anqing, *China* 30°36' N, 116°59' E **198**
Anren, *China* 26°42' N, 113°17' E **198**
Anröchte, *Ger.* 51°33' N, 8°19' E **167**
Ans, *Belg.* 50°40' N, 5°29' E **167**
Ansai, *China* 36°53' N, 109°21' E **198**
Ansan, *S. Korea* 37°18' N, 126°52' E **198**
Ansbach, *Ger.* 49°18' N, 10°33' E **152**
Anse-à-Foleur, *Haiti* 19°53' N, 72°38' W **116**
Anse-à-Galets, *Haiti* 18°50' N, 72°53' W **116**
Anselmo, *Nebr., U.S.* 41°36' N, 99°53' W **90**
Anseong, *S. Korea* 37°0' N, 127°16' E **200**
Anse-Rouge, *Haiti* 19°39' N, 73°3' W **116**
Anshan, *China* 41°7' N, 122°59' E **200**
Anshun, *China* 26°16' N, 105°54' E **198**
Ansina, *Uru.* 31°54' S, 55°29' W **139**
Ansley, *Nebr., U.S.* 41°16' N, 99°23' W **92**
Anson, *Me., U.S.* 44°47' N, 69°55' W **94**
Anson, *Tex., U.S.* 32°44' N, 99°54' W **92**
Ansongo, *Mali* 15°39' N, 0°28' E **222**
Ansonia, *Conn., U.S.* 41°20' N, 73°5' W **104**
Ansonia, *Ohio, U.S.* 40°12' N, 84°39' W **102**
Ansonville, *Can.* 48°45' N, 80°42' W **94**
Anta, *Peru* 13°29' S, 72°9' W **137**
Antabamba, *Peru* 14°24' S, 72°53' W **137**
Antakya, *Turk.* 36°10' N, 36°6' E **143**
Antalaha, *Madagascar* 15°1' S, 50°13' E **207**
Antalya, *Turk.* 36°52' N, 30°43' E **156**
Antalya Körfezi 36°30' N, 30°36' E **180**
Antanambe, *Madagascar* 16°27' S, 49°48' E **220**
Antananarivo, *Madagascar* 18°59' S, 47°21' E **220**
Antanifotsy, *Madagascar* 19°40' S, 47°20' E **220**
Antarctic Sound 62°24' S, 58°49' W **248**
Antarctica 81°0' S, 0°0' E **248**
Antarctica 71°33' S, 29°36' E **248**
Antas, river, *Braz.* 28°48' S, 51°2' W **139**
Anteloe, *Oreg., U.S.* 44°53' N, 120°44' W **90**
Antelope Lake, lake, *Can.* 50°13' N, 108°54' W **90**
Antelope Peak, *Nev., U.S.* 39°23' N, 116°33' W **90**
Antelope Point, peak, *Mont., U.S.* 45°45' N, 109°11' W **90**
Antelope Range, *Nev., U.S.* 39°3' N, 116°34' W **90**
Antelope Valley, *Calif., U.S.* 34°47' N, 118°27' W **101**
Antequera, *Parag.* 24°5' S, 57°12' W **132**
Antequera, *Sp.* 37°1' N, 4°34' W **164**
Anterselva, *It.* 46°52' N, 12°5' E **167**
Anthony, *Fla., U.S.* 29°17' N, 82°7' W **105**
Anthony, *Kans., U.S.* 37°8' N, 98°2' W **92**
Anthony, *N. Mex., U.S.* 32°1' N, 106°38' W **112**
Anti Atlas, mountains, *Mor.* 30°17' N, 8°12' W **214**
Antibes, Cap d', *Fr.* 43°28' N, 7°8' E **165**
Anticosti, Île d', island, *Can.* 48°50' N, 63°33' W **81**
Antifer, Cap d', *Fr.* 49°39' N, 0°14' E **150**
Antigo, *Wis., U.S.* 45°8' N, 89°9' W **94**
Antigonish, *Can.* 45°36' N, 61°60' W **111**
Antigua and Barbuda 17°0' N, 62°0' W **116**
Antigua, island, *Antigua and Barbuda* 17°5' N, 61°41' W **116**
Antiguo Morelos, *Mex.* 22°32' N, 99°6' W **114**
Anti-Lebanon see Al Jabalash Sharqī, *Leb.* 34°5' N, 36°21' E **194**
Antilla, *Cuba* 20°51' N, 75°44' W **116**
Anti-m-Misaou, spring, *Alg.* 21°57' N, 3°4' E **222**
Antimony, *Utah, U.S.* 38°6' N, 111°59' W **92**
Antioch, *Calif., U.S.* 38°0' N, 121°50' W **100**
Antioch, *Ill., U.S.* 42°28' N, 88°6' W **102**
Antioch see Hatay, *Turk.* 36°12' N, 36°8' E **156**
Antioquia, *Col.* 6°34' N, 75°51' W **136**
Antioquia, adm. division, *Col.* 6°56' N, 76°39' W **136**
Antipatris, ruin(s), *Israel* 32°5' N, 34°54' E **194**
Antipayuta, *Russ.* 69°4' N, 76°54' E **169**
Antisana, peak, *Ecua.* 0°31' N, 78°23' W **136**
Antler Peak, *Nev., U.S.* 40°35' N, 117°13' W **90**
Antlers, *Okla., U.S.* 34°12' N, 95°37' W **96**
Antofagasta, *Chile* 23°40' S, 70°25' W **132**
Antofagasta, adm. division, *Chile* 22°1' S, 70°14' W **137**
Antofagasta de la Sierra, *Arg.* 26°5' S, 67°22' W **132**
Antón, *Pan.* 8°24' N, 80°16' W **115**
Anton, *Tex., U.S.* 33°48' N, 102°11' W **92**
Anton Chico, *N. Mex., U.S.* 35°11' N, 105°10' W **92**
Antón Lizardo, Punta, *Mex.* 18°49' N, 95°58' W **114**
Antonibe, *Madagascar* 15°8' S, 47°25' E **220**
Antonina, *Braz.* 25°27' S, 48°43' W **138**
Antoniny, *Ukr.* 49°48' N, 26°53' E **152**
Antonio Prado, *Braz.* 28°53' S, 51°16' W **139**
Antonito, *Colo., U.S.* 37°3' N, 106°1' W **92**
Antonovo, *Kaz.* 49°21' N, 51°45' E **158**
Antons, Lac des, lake, *Can.* 52°49' N, 74°20' W **111**
Antopal', *Belarus* 52°12' N, 24°45' E **152**
Antrim Mountains, *U.K.* 54°52' N, 6°38' W **150**
Antropovo, *Russ.* 58°24' N, 43°6' E **154**
Antsirabe, *Madagascar* 19°53' S, 47°7' E **207**
Antsirabe, *Madagascar* 13°60' S, 49°58' E **220**
Antsiranana, *Madagascar* 12°26' S, 49°16' E **220**
Antsla, *Est.* 57°48' N, 26°31' E **166**
Antsohihy, *Madagascar* 14°53' S, 47°59' E **220**
Anttila, *Fin.* 65°7' N, 29°48' E **154**
Anttila, *Fin.* 61°2' N, 26°49' E **166**
Anttis, *Nor.* 67°16' N, 22°48' E **152**
Anttola, *Fin.* 61°34' N, 27°35' E **166**
Antu, *China* 42°32' N, 128°18' E **200**
Antubia, *Ghana* 6°18' N, 2°51' W **222**
Antufash, Jazīrat, island, *Yemen* 15°45' N, 42°7' E **182**
Antwerp, *Ohio, U.S.* 41°9' N, 84°44' W **102**
Antwerpen (Antwerp), *Belg.* 51°13' N, 4°24' E **167**
Anuppur, *India* 23°7' N, 81°42' E **197**
Anupshahr, *India* 28°20' N, 78°15' E **197**
Anuradhapura, *Sri Lanka* 8°22' N, 80°22' E **188**
Anvers Island, *Antarctica* 64°36' S, 66°3' W **134**
Anvik, *Alas., U.S.* 62°30' N, 160°23' W **98**
Anxi, *China* 25°5' N, 118°13' E **198**
Anxi, *China* 40°31' N, 95°47' E **188**
Anxiang, *China* 29°24' N, 112°12' E **198**
Anxin, *China* 38°57' N, 115°54' E **198**
Anyang, *China* 36°5' N, 114°19' E **198**
Anyang, *S. Korea* 37°22' N, 126°54' E **200**
Anyi, *China* 28°49' N, 115°28' E **198**
Anyi, *China* 35°5' N, 111°4' E **198**
Anykščiai, *Lith.* 55°32' N, 25°8' E **166**
Anyou, *China* 18°11' N, 109°34' E **198**
Anyuan, *China* 25°6' N, 115°24' E **198**
Anyue, *China* 30°5' N, 105°22' E **198**
Anza, *Calif., U.S.* 33°33' N, 116°42' W **101**
Anzá, *Col.* 6°18' N, 75°54' W **136**
Anze, *China* 36°8' N, 112°10' E **198**
Anzhero Sudzhensk, *Russ.* 56°3' N, 86°8' E **169**
Anzhu, Ostrova, islands, *Ostrov Kotel'nyy;Ostrov Faddeyevskiy* 75°26' N, 135°19' E **160**
Anzio, *It.* 41°26' N, 12°37' E **156**
Anzoátegui, adm. division, *Venez.* 8°48' N, 64°48' W **116**
Aohan Qi, *China* 42°17' N, 119°55' E **198**
Aoiz, *Sp.* 42°47' N, 1°21' W **164**
Aokas, *Alg.* 36°38' N, 5°14' E **150**
Aomori, *Japan* 40°51' N, 140°48' E **190**
Aoraki (Cook, Mount), *N.Z.* 43°45' S, 170°4' E **240**
Aosta, *It.* 45°44' N, 7°19' E **167**
Aouchich, spring, *Mauritania* 22°4' N, 12°4' W **222**
Aouderas, *Niger* 17°38' N, 8°25' E **222**
Aougoundou, Lac, lake, *Mali* 15°47' N, 5°12' W **222**
'Aouinet Bel Egrâ, spring, *Alg.* 26°52' N, 6°53' W **214**
Aoukâr, plain, *Mali* 23°48' N, 5°5' W **214**
Aoukâr, region, *Africa* 17°48' N, 10°56' W **222**
Aoulef, *Alg.* 26°59' N, 1°5' E **214**
Aoya, *Japan* 35°29' N, 133°58' E **201**
Aozi, *Chad* 21°3' N, 18°40' E **216**
Aozou, *Chad* 21°49' N, 17°26' E **216**
Ap Iwan, Cerro, peak, *Chile* 46°13' S, 71°59' W **134**
Apa, river, *South America* 22°10' S, 57°17' W **132**
Apache, *Okla., U.S.* 34°52' N, 98°22' W **96**
Apache Mountain, *N. Mex., U.S.* 33°55' N, 108°41' W **92**
Apache Mountains, *Tex., U.S.* 31°9' N, 104°30' W **92**
Apahida, *Rom.* 46°48' N, 23°46' E **156**
Apalachicola, *Fla., U.S.* 29°43' N, 84°60' W **96**
Apam, *Ghana* 5°19' N, 0°47' E **222**
Apamea, ruin(s), *Syr.* 35°24' N, 36°21' E **194**
Apaporis, river, *Col.* 0°17' N, 71°46' W **136**
Aparecida do Taboado, *Braz.* 20°5' S, 51°8' W **138**
Aparri, *Philippines* 18°18' N, 121°40' E **203**
Apateu, *Rom.* 46°37' N, 21°46' E **168**
Apatin, *Serb. and Mont.* 45°39' N, 18°58' E **168**
Apatity, *Russ.* 67°34' N, 33°19' E **152**
Apatzingán, *Mex.* 19°5' N, 102°22' W **114**
Apaxtla, *Mex.* 18°8' N, 99°53' W **114**
Ape, *Latv.* 57°31' N, 26°43' E **166**
Apeldoorn, *Neth.* 52°13' N, 5°57' E **163**
Apen, *Ger.* 53°13' N, 7°50' E **163**
Apere, *Bol.* 12°7' S, 66°17' W **137**
Apere, river, *Bol.* 15°6' S, 66°7' W **137**
Aphaea, ruin(s), *Gr.* 37°44' N, 23°26' E **156**
Api, *Dem. Rep. of the Congo* 3°41' N, 25°28' E **224**
Apia, *Samoa* 14°0' S, 172°0' W **241**
Apiacá, river, *Braz.* 9°19' S, 57°6' W **130**
Apiacás, Serra dos, *Braz.* 9°38' S, 57°21' W **130**
Apiaí, *Braz.* 24°38' S, 48°58' W **138**
Apiaú, Serra do, *Braz.* 2°53' N, 61°48' W **130**
Apidiá, river, *Braz.* 12°33' S, 61°11' W **130**
Apizaco, *Mex.* 19°23' N, 98°11' W **114**
Aplao, *Peru* 16°6' S, 72°31' W **137**
Apo, Mount, *Philippines* 6°59' N, 125°11' E **203**
Apodaca, *Mex.* 25°46' N, 100°12' W **114**
Apodi, Chapada do, *Braz.* 5°8' S, 38°11' W **132**
Apollonia, ruin(s), *Alban.* 40°41' N, 19°21' E **156**
Apollonia see Sozopol, *Bulg.* 42°25' N, 27°42' E **156**
Apollonia see Sūsah, *Lib.* 32°52' N, 21°59' E **143**
Apolo, *Bol.* 14°41' S, 68°31' W **137**
Apopka, *Fla., U.S.* 28°40' N, 81°31' W **105**
Apopka, Lake, *Fla., U.S.* 28°38' N, 81°44' W **105**
Aporé, *Braz.* 18°57' S, 52°3' W **138**
Aporé, river, *Braz.* 19°9' S, 51°35' W **138**
Apostle Islands, *Lake Superior* 47°6' N, 90°53' W **94**
Apóstoles, *Arg.* 27°55' S, 55°44' W **139**
Apostolos Andreas, Cape, *Northern Cyprus* 35°34' N, 34°34' E **194**
Apostolos Andreas Monastery, site, *Northern Cyprus* 35°40' N, 34°32' E **194**
Apoteri, *Guyana* 4°0' N, 58°34' W **130**
Apozol, *Mex.* 21°28' N, 103°7' W **114**
Appalachian Mountains, *North America* 47°54' N, 68°40' W **82**
Appennini, mountains, *Europe* 44°37' N, 8°30' E **167**
Appiano, *It.* 46°27' N, 11°15' E **167**
Apple Springs, *Tex., U.S.* 31°12' N, 94°59' W **103**
Apple Valley, *Calif., U.S.* 34°30' N, 117°12' W **101**
Appleby, *U.K.* 54°34' N, 2°29' W **162**
Appleton, *Wis., U.S.* 44°16' N, 88°25' W **94**
Appleton City, *Mo., U.S.* 38°10' N, 94°2' W **94**
Apriķi, *Latv.* 56°49' N, 21°31' E **166**
Apsheron Yarymadasy, *Azerb.* 40°21' N, 49°19' E **180**
Apsheronsk, *Russ.* 44°26' N, 39°48' E **180**
Aptera, ruin(s), *Gr.* 35°26' N, 24°1' E **156**
Aptos, *Calif., U.S.* 36°59' N, 121°53' W **100**
Apuane, Alpi, *It.* 43°57' N, 10°17' E **167**
Apucarana, *Braz.* 23°36' S, 51°31' W **138**
Apuí, *Braz.* 1°11' N, 69°14' W **136**
Apuka, *Russ.* 60°35' N, 169°28' E **160**
Apure, adm. division, *Venez.* 7°4' N, 70°6' W **136**
Apurímac, adm. division, *Peru* 13°58' S, 73°41' W **137**
Apurímac, river, *Peru* 13°27' S, 73°16' W **137**
Apurito, *Venez.* 7°55' N, 68°28' W **136**
Apuseni, Munţii, *Rom.* 46°38' N, 22°39' E **168**
Aq Kopruk, *Afghan.* 36°4' N, 66°54' E **186**
Aqaba, Gulf of 28°52' N, 34°11' E **180**
Aqadyr, *Kaz.* 48°13' N, 72°52' E **184**
Aqcheh, *Afghan.* 36°57' N, 66°14' E **186**
Aqiq, *Sudan* 18°9' N, 38°7' E **182**
Aqköl, *Kaz.* 46°40' N, 49°6' E **158**
Aqköl, *Kaz.* 43°24' N, 70°46' E **184**
Aqköl, *Kaz.* 45°0' N, 75°39' E **184**
Aqköl, *Kaz.* 52°0' N, 70°59' E **184**
Aqmola, adm. division, *Kaz.* 51°31' N, 68°23' E **184**
Aqqikkol Hu, lake, *China* 37°10' N, 87°39' E **188**
Aqqystaū, *Kaz.* 47°14' N, 51°4' E **158**
'Aqrah, *Iraq* 36°45' N, 43°47' E **195**
Aqsay, *Kaz.* 51°10' N, 52°58' E **158**
Aqshataū, *Kaz.* 49°25' N, 54°45' E **158**
Aqshataū, *Kaz.* 47°58' N, 73°59' E **184**
Aqsū, *Kaz.* 52°27' N, 71°58' E **184**
Aqsū, *Kaz.* 42°25' N, 69°50' E **197**
Aqsūat, *Kaz.* 47°47' N, 82°49' E **184**
Aqsū-Ayuly, *Kaz.* 48°45' N, 73°42' E **184**
Aqsūgek, *Kaz.* 44°37' N, 74°28' E **184**
Aqtaū, *Kaz.* 43°38' N, 51°14' E **195**
Aqtaysay, *Kaz.* 49°40' N, 54°1' E **158**
Aqtöbe, *Kaz.* 50°15' N, 57°12' E **158**
Aqtöbe, adm. division, *Kaz.* 48°43' N, 56°0' E **158**
Aqtoghay, *Kaz.* 48°12' N, 75°2' E **184**
Aqtoghay, *Kaz.* 46°55' N, 79°39' E **184**
Aquarius Mountains, *Ariz., U.S.* 35°1' N, 113°36' W **101**
Aquidauana, *Braz.* 20°29' S, 55°48' W **134**
Aquileia, *It.* 45°46' N, 13°21' E **167**
Aquiles Serdán, *Mex.* 28°35' N, 105°55' W **92**
Aquitaine, adm. division, *Fr.* 44°10' N, 1°18' W **150**
Aqyrab, *Kaz.* 50°35' N, 55°8' E **158**
Aqzhal, *Kaz.* 49°13' N, 81°23' E **184**
Aqzhar, *Kaz.* 47°35' N, 83°45' E **184**
Aqzhayyq, *Kaz.* 50°50' N, 51°17' E **158**
Ar Horqin Qi (Tianshan), *China* 43°55' N, 120°7' E **198**
Ar Rabbah, *Jordan* 31°16' N, 35°44' E **194**
Ar Rafīd, *Syr.* 32°57' N, 35°53' E **194**
Ar Ramādī, *Iraq* 33°23' N, 43°14' E **180**
Ar Ramthā, *Jordan* 32°33' N, 36°0' E **194**
Ar Raqqah, *Syr.* 35°54' N, 39°2' E **180**
Ar Rashādīyah, *Jordan* 30°42' N, 35°37' E **194**
Ar Rass, *Saudi Arabia* 25°50' N, 43°28' E **182**
Ar Rastan (Arethusa), *Syr.* 34°55' N, 36°44' E **194**
Ar Rawḑah, *Saudi Arabia* 21°12' N, 42°47' E **182**
Ar Riyāḑ (Riyadh), *Saudi Arabia* 24°35' N, 46°35' E **186**
Ar Riyān, *Yemen* 14°40' N, 49°21' E **182**
Ar Rubʻ al Khālī (Empty Quarter), *Saudi Arabia* 24°33' N, 54°53' E **196**
Ar Rummān, *Jordan* 32°9' N, 35°49' E **194**
Ar Ruşayfah, *Jordan* 32°1' N, 36°2' E **194**
Ar Rustāq, *Oman* 23°32' N, 57°24' E **182**
Ar Ruţbah, *Iraq* 33°3' N, 40°14' E **180**
Ara, *India* 25°32' N, 84°37' E **197**
Ara Bure, *Eth.* 6°31' N, 41°17' E **224**
'Arab al Mulk, *Syr.* 35°16' N, 35°55' E **194**
'Arabah, Wādī al, *Israel-Jordan* 30°23' N, 35°1' E **194**
Arabian Basin, *Arabian Sea* 10°36' N, 65°57' E **254**
Arabian Sea 13°38' N, 58°38' E **173**
Araç, *Turk.* 41°15' N, 33°19' E **156**
Araç, river, *Turk.* 41°9' N, 32°58' E **156**
Aracaju, *Braz.* 10°54' S, 37°5' W **132**
Aracati, *Braz.* 4°35' S, 37°43' W **132**
Aracatu, *Braz.* 14°27' S, 41°29' W **138**
Araçatuba, *Braz.* 21°11' S, 50°27' W **138**
Aracena, *Sp.* 37°53' N, 6°35' W **164**
Aracena, Sierra de, *Sp.* 37°58' N, 6°51' W **164**
Aracruz, *Braz.* 19°51' S, 40°19' W **132**
Araçuaí, *Braz.* 16°52' S, 42°4' W **138**
Araçuaí, river, *Braz.* 17°50' S, 42°60' W **138**
'Arad, *Israel* 31°14' N, 35°12' E **194**
Arad, *Rom.* 46°11' N, 21°19' E **168**
Arad, adm. division, *Rom.* 46°9' N, 21°5' E **156**
Arada, *Chad* 15°1' N, 20°39' E **216**
Araden, ruin(s), *Gr.* 35°12' N, 23°57' E **156**
Aradu Nou, *Rom.* 46°9' N, 21°20' E **168**
Arafali, *Eritrea* 15°1' N, 39°42' E **182**
Arafura Sea 9°12' S, 134°22' E **192**
Araga, spring, *Niger* 17°25' N, 11°36' E **222**
Aragarças, *Braz.* 15°58' S, 52°14' W **138**
Aragats, peak, *Arm.* 40°30' N, 44°8' E **195**
Arago, Cape, *Oreg., U.S.* 43°20' N, 124°41' W **90**
Aragon, adm. division, *Sp.* 41°26' N, 1°15' W **164**
Aragua, adm. division, *Venez.* 10°3' N, 67°40' W **136**
Aragua de Barcelona, *Venez.* 9°29' N, 64°52' W **116**
Araguacema, *Braz.* 8°50' S, 49°37' W **130**
Araguaçu, *Braz.* 12°52' S, 49°56' W **138**
Araguaia National Park, *Braz.* 11°14' S, 50°56' W **130**
Araguaia, river, *Braz.* 15°22' S, 51°48' W **132**
Araguaína, *Braz.* 7°12' S, 48°16' W **130**
Araguao, Boca 9°11' N, 61°20' W **116**
Araguapiche, Punta, *Venez.* 9°21' N, 60°53' W **116**
Araguari, *Braz.* 18°40' S, 48°15' W **138**
Araguari, river, *Braz.* 18°56' S, 48°13' W **138**
Araguatins, *Braz.* 5°39' S, 48°8' W **130**
Arahal, *Sp.* 37°15' N, 5°34' W **164**
Arahura, *N.Z.* 42°42' S, 171°4' E **240**
Arai, *Japan* 37°0' N, 138°14' E **201**
Araia, *Sp.* 42°52' N, 2°19' W **164**
Arak, *Alg.* 25°18' N, 3°44' E **214**
Arāk, *Iran* 34°6' N, 49°42' E **180**
Araka, spring, *Niger* 18°54' N, 15°24' E **216**
Arakamchechen, Ostrov, island, *Russ.* 64°44' N, 172°1' W **98**
Arakan Yoma, *Myanmar* 19°6' N, 94°18' E **202**
Aral, *China* 38°8' N, 80°43' E **188**
Aral, *China* 40°40' N, 81°28' E **184**
Aral, *Kaz.* 46°54' N, 61°36' E **184**
Aral Mangy Qaraqumy, *Kaz.* 47°11' N, 61°51' E **184**
Aral Sea, lake 45°32' N, 58°10' E **160**
Aralqi, *China* 39°27' N, 87°44' E **188**
Aralqum, *Kaz.* 44°8' N, 58°11' E **180**
Aralsor Köli, lake, *Kaz.* 49°0' N, 48°1' E **158**
Araltobe, *Kaz.* 50°31' N, 60°6' E **158**
Aramac, *Austral.* 22°60' S, 145°16' E **231**
Aramberri, *Mex.* 24°4' N, 99°50' W **114**
Aramits, *Fr.* 43°6' N, 0°44' E **164**
Arampampa, *Bol.* 17°60' S, 65°58' W **137**
Ārān, *Iran* 34°9' N, 51°30' E **180**
Aran Islands, *Celtic Sea* 53°12' N, 10°30' W **150**
Aranda de Duero, *Sp.* 41°40' N, 3°44' W **164**
Arandas, *Mex.* 20°41' N, 102°22' W **114**
Arani, *Bol.* 17°38' S, 65°41' W **137**
Aranjuez, *Sp.* 40°1' N, 3°36' W **164**
Aranos, *Namibia* 24°5' S, 19°7' E **227**
Aransas Pass, *Tex., U.S.* 27°53' N, 97°9' W **96**
Arantes, river, *Braz.* 19°25' S, 50°20' W **138**
Arantur, *Russ.* 60°59' N, 63°37' E **169**
Aranyaprathet, *Thai.* 13°44' N, 102°31' E **202**
Arao, *Japan* 32°57' N, 130°26' E **201**
Araouane, *Mali* 18°53' N, 3°34' W **222**
Arapa, Laguna, lake, *Peru* 15°11' S, 70°11' W **137**
Arapaho, *Okla., U.S.* 35°33' N, 98°58' W **96**
Arapey, *Uru.* 30°57' S, 57°33' W **139**
Arapiraca, *Braz.* 9°45' S, 36°42' W **132**
Arapkir, *Turk.* 39°1' N, 38°31' E **180**
Arapongas, *Braz.* 23°26' S, 51°28' W **138**
Araracuara, *Col.* 0°29' N, 72°17' W **136**
Araranguá, *Braz.* 28°58' S, 49°29' W **138**
Araraquara, *Braz.* 21°48' S, 48°12' W **138**
Araras, *Braz.* 9°5' S, 68°6' W **137**
Araras, *Braz.* 6°13' S, 54°34' W **130**
Araras, *Braz.* 22°22' S, 47°23' W **138**
Ararat, *Arm.* 39°50' N, 44°40' E **195**
Ararat, Mount see Ağrı Dağı, *Turk.* 39°39' N, 44°12' E **180**
Ararat, Mount see Ağrı Dağı, peak, *Turk.* 39°42' N, 44°15' E **195**
Arari, *Braz.* 3°28' S, 44°46' W **132**
Araria, *India* 26°7' N, 87°26' E **197**
Araripe, Chapada do, *Braz.* 7°34' S, 40°28' W **132**
Araruama, *Braz.* 22°52' S, 42°22' W **138**
Aras (Araxes), river, *Asia* 40°0' N, 42°18' E **195**
Arataca, *Braz.* 15°18' S, 39°24' W **138**
Aratane, spring, *Mauritania* 18°24' N, 8°33' W **222**
Arataú, river, *Braz.* 3°14' S, 50°37' W **130**
Arauá, river, *Braz.* 4°14' S, 64°51' W **130**
Arauca, *Col.* 7°0' N, 70°47' W **136**
Arauca, adm. division, *Col.* 6°39' N, 71°44' W **136**
Arauca, river, *Venez.* 7°27' N, 67°58' W **136**
Araucanía, La, adm. division, *Chile* 38°38' S, 73°35' W **134**
Araucária, *Braz.* 25°36' S, 49°24' W **138**
Arauquita, *Col.* 6°58' N, 71°22' W **136**
Arawa, *P.N.G.* 6°14' S, 155°31' E **238**
Araxá, *Braz.* 19°36' S, 46°56' W **138**
Araxes see Aras, river, *Turk.* 40°0' N, 42°18' E **195**
Arayit Dağı, peak, *Turk.* 39°17' N, 31°39' E **156**
Ārba Minch', *Eth.* 5°59' N, 37°37' E **224**
Arbaʻat, *Sudan* 19°46' N, 36°57' E **182**
Arbazh, *Russ.* 57°41' N, 48°24' E **154**
Arbela see Irbid, *Jordan* 32°32' N, 35°51' E **194**
Arbīl, *Iraq* 36°10' N, 43°59' E **180**
Arboledas, *Arg.* 36°51' S, 61°28' W **139**
Arborea, *It.* 39°46' N, 8°34' E **156**
Arborfield, *Can.* 53°6' N, 103°40' W **108**
Arborg, *Can.* 50°53' N, 97°13' W **90**
Arbrå, *Nor.* 61°29' N, 16°19' E **152**
Arbre du Ténéré, site, *Niger* 17°44' N, 10°5' E **222**
Arbroath, *U.K.* 56°33' N, 2°38' W **150**
Arc, *Fr.* 47°27' N, 5°33' E **150**
Arc Dome, peak, *Nev., U.S.* 38°49' N, 117°26' W **90**
Arc, river, *Fr.* 45°23' N, 6°17' E **165**
Arcachon, *Fr.* 44°36' N, 1°15' W **214**
Arcadia, *Fla., U.S.* 27°13' N, 81°52' W **105**
Arcadia, *Ind., U.S.* 40°10' N, 86°1' W **102**
Arcadia, *La., U.S.* 32°31' N, 92°56' W **103**
Arcadia, *Mich., U.S.* 44°29' N, 86°14' W **94**
Arcadia, *Peru* 1°3' S, 75°18' W **136**
Arcadia, *Wis., U.S.* 44°15' N, 91°29' W **94**
Arcanum, *Ohio, U.S.* 39°59' N, 84°32' W **102**
Arcas, Cayos, islands, *Gulf of Mexico* 20°19' N, 92°6' W **115**
Arcata, *Calif., U.S.* 40°52' N, 124°6' W **90**
Arcelia, *Mex.* 18°16' N, 100°16' W **114**
Archangel see Arkhangel'sk, *Russ.* 64°35' N, 40°37' E **154**
Archar, *Bulg.* 43°48' N, 22°54' E **168**
Archbold, *Ohio, U.S.* 41°30' N, 84°18' W **102**
Archeï, spring, *Chad* 16°53' N, 21°44' E **216**
Archena, *Sp.* 38°6' N, 1°19' W **164**
Archer, *Fla., U.S.* 29°32' N, 82°32' W **105**
Archer Bay 13°40' S, 141°24' E **230**
Archer Bend National Park, *Austral.* 13°35' S, 141°56' E **238**
Archer City, *Tex., U.S.* 33°34' N, 98°38' W **92**
Archer Point, *Antarctica* 68°54' S, 161°17' E **248**
Archer, river, *Austral.* 13°39' S, 141°16' E **231**
Archer's Post, *Kenya* 0°36' N, 37°40' E **224**
Archerwill, *Can.* 52°25' N, 103°52' W **108**
Archidona, *Sp.* 37°5' N, 4°24' W **164**
Archipiélago de Colón see Galápagos Islands, *South Pacific Ocean* 0°13' N, 92°2' W **130**
Archipiélago Los Roques National Park, *Caribbean Sea* 11°50' N, 67°27' W **136**
Archman, *Turkm.* 38°33' N, 57°9' E **180**
Arci, Monte, peak, *It.* 39°46' N, 8°41' E **156**
Arcis, *Fr.* 48°32' N, 4°8' E **163**
Arco, *Idaho, U.S.* 43°38' N, 113°18' W **90**
Arco, *It.* 45°55' N, 10°52' E **167**
Arco, Paso del, pass, *Arg.* 38°47' S, 71°6' W **134**
Arcola, *Ill., U.S.* 39°41' N, 88°19' W **102**
Arcola, *Miss., U.S.* 33°14' N, 90°53' W **103**
Arcos, *Braz.* 20°17' S, 45°34' W **138**
Arcos de Jalón, *Sp.* 41°12' N, 2°17' W **150**
Arcoverde, *Braz.* 8°24' S, 37°1' W **132**
Arctic Bay, *Can.* 73°3' N, 85°6' W **73**
Arctic Ocean 79°19' N, 170°44' W **246**
Arctic Red, river, *Can.* 66°40' N, 132°38' W **98**
Arctic Village, *Alas., U.S.* 68°6' N, 145°32' W **98**
Arctowski, station, *Antarctica* 62°12' S, 58°12' W **134**
Arda, river, *Bulg.* 41°30' N, 25°42' E **156**
Ardabīl, *Iran* 38°15' N, 48°18' E **195**
Ardahan, *Turk.* 41°5' N, 42°40' E **195**
Ardakān, *Iran* 32°14' N, 54°3' E **180**
Ardakān, *Iran* 30°14' N, 51°59' E **196**
Årdal, *Nor.* 61°14' N, 7°43' E **152**
Årdal, *Nor.* 59°8' N, 6°11' E **152**
Ardales, *Sp.* 36°51' N, 4°51' W **164**
Ardanuç, *Turk.* 41°9' N, 42°2' E **195**
Ardaşşawwān, *Jordan* 30°58' N, 36°46' E **194**
Ardatov, *Russ.* 54°47' N, 46°19' E **154**
Ardencaple Fjord 74°46' N, 25°23' W **246**
Ardestān, *Iran* 33°20' N, 52°25' E **180**
Ardmore, *Okla., U.S.* 34°9' N, 97°7' W **92**
Ardmore, *S. Dak., U.S.* 43°1' N, 103°40' W **90**
Ardres, *Fr.* 50°51' N, 1°58' E **163**
Ards Peninsula, *U.K.* 54°21' N, 6°3' W **150**
Ardud, *Rom.* 47°38' N, 22°53' E **168**
Ardvrach Castle, site, *U.K.* 58°9' N, 5°6' W **150**
Ardvule, Rubha, *U.K.* 57°15' N, 8°1' W **150**
Åre, *Nor.* 63°24' N, 13°3' E **152**
Arena, Point, *U.S.* 38°47' N, 124°3' W **90**
Arenápolis, *Braz.* 14°28' S, 56°53' W **132**
Arenas, Punta de, *Arg.* 53°3' S, 68°13' W **134**
Arendal, *Nor.* 58°27' N, 8°43' E **152**
Arendsee, *Ger.* 52°53' N, 11°30' E **152**
Arenys de Mar, *Sp.* 41°34' N, 2°33' E **164**
Arenzano, *It.* 44°23' N, 8°41' E **167**
Arequipa, *Peru* 16°24' S, 71°35' W **137**
Arequipa, adm. division, *Peru* 15°51' S, 73°39' W **137**
Ārēro, *Eth.* 4°43' N, 38°48' E **224**
Arês, *Braz.* 6°14' S, 35°8' W **132**
Åreskutan, peak, *Nor.* 63°26' N, 12°55' E **152**
Arethusa see Ar Rastan, *Syr.* 34°55' N, 36°44' E **194**
Arévalo, *Sp.* 41°3' N, 4°44' W **150**
Arezzaf, spring, *Mali* 18°5' N, 1°47' W **222**
Arezzo, *It.* 43°27' N, 11°52' E **156**
Arga Sala, river, *Russ.* 67°51' N, 107°46' E **160**
Argaman, *West Bank* 32°8' N, 35°30' E **194**
Argamasilla de Alba, *Sp.* 39°7' N, 3°7' W **164**
Argamasilla de Calatrava, *Sp.* 38°44' N, 4°5' W **164**
Argan, *China* 40°6' N, 88°17' E **188**
Argatay, *Mongolia* 45°33' N, 108°4' E **198**
Argelès, *Fr.* 42°32' N, 3°0' E **164**
Argens, river, *Fr.* 43°25' N, 6°3' E **165**
Argenta, *It.* 44°36' N, 11°49' E **167**
Argentario, Monte, peak, *It.* 42°23' N, 11°5' E **156**
Argentera, peak, *It.* 44°10' N, 7°17' E **165**
Argenteuil, *Fr.* 48°55' N, 2°13' E **163**
Argentina 35°22' S, 67°13' W **134**
Argentine Plain, *South Atlantic Ocean* 46°42' S, 48°15' W **253**
Argentré, *Fr.* 48°3' N, 0°34' E **150**
Argeş, adm. division, *Rom.* 44°57' N, 24°28' E **156**
Arghandab Dam, *Afghan.* 32°2' N, 65°50' E **186**
Argo, *Sudan* 19°30' N, 30°27' E **226**
Argolas, *Braz.* 20°26' S, 40°25' W **138**
Argonaut Mountain, *Can.* 51°49' N, 118°25' W **90**
Argonne, *Fr.* 49°43' N, 4°51' E **167**
Árgos, *Gr.* 37°35' N, 22°41' E **180**
Argos, *Ind., U.S.* 41°13' N, 86°14' W **102**
Argoub, *Western Sahara* 23°35' N, 15°51' W **214**
Arguello, Point, *Calif., U.S.* 34°30' N, 120°49' W **100**
Arguin, Cap d', *Mauritania* 20°25' N, 16°42' W **214**
Argungu, *Nig.* 12°43' N, 4°31' E **222**
Argus, *Calif., U.S.* 35°44' N, 117°25' W **101**
Argus, Dome, *Antarctica* 79°52' S, 74°47' E **248**
Argus Range, *Calif., U.S.* 36°0' N, 117°34' W **101**
Arguut, *Mongolia* 45°28' N, 102°18' E **190**
Argyle, *Mich., U.S.* 43°33' N, 82°56' W **102**
Argyle, *Minn., U.S.* 48°18' N, 96°51' W **90**
Argyle, *N.Y., U.S.* 43°14' N, 73°31' W **104**
Argyle, Lake, *Austral.* 16°12' S, 128°11' E **230**
Arhebeb, spring, *Mali* 21°5' N, 0°8' E **222**
Arhrîjît, *Mauritania* 18°21' N, 9°15' W **222**
Århus, *Den.* 56°9' N, 10°11' E **150**
Ari Atoll, *Maldives* 3°33' N, 72°22' E **188**
Ariamsvlei, *Namibia* 28°7' S, 19°50' E **227**
Ariana, *Tun.* 36°51' N, 10°11' E **156**
Arias, *Arg.* 33°39' S, 62°23' W **139**
Aribinda, *Burkina Faso* 14°17' N, 0°52' E **222**
Arica, *Chile* 18°34' S, 70°20' W **137**
Arica, *Col.* 2°9' S, 71°46' W **136**
Arica, *Peru* 1°39' S, 75°12' W **136**
Arid, Mount, *Austral.* 34°1' S, 122°58' E **230**
Arida, *Japan* 34°4' N, 135°7' E **201**
Aridal, *Western Sahara* 25°59' N, 13°48' W **214**
Arīḩā, *Syr.* 35°48' N, 36°35' E **156**
Arīḩā (Jericho), *West Bank* 31°51' N, 35°27' E **194**
Arija, *Sp.* 42°57' N, 3°59' W **164**
Arikaree, river, *Colo., U.S.* 39°48' N, 102°40' W **90**
Arimã, *Braz.* 5°47' S, 63°42' W **130**
Arinos, *Braz.* 15°54' S, 46°4' W **138**
Arinos, river, *Braz.* 10°28' S, 58°34' W **132**
Ariogala, *Lith.* 55°15' N, 23°29' E **166**
Aripao, *Venez.* 7°19' N, 65°4' W **130**
Ariporo, river, *Col.* 5°57' N, 71°13' W **136**
Aripuanã, *Braz.* 9°59' S, 59°28' W **130**
Aripuanã, river, *Braz.* 7°52' S, 60°35' W **130**
Aripuanã, river, *Braz.* 11°15' S, 59°41' W **130**
Ariquemes, *Braz.* 9°57' S, 63°6' W **130**
Arismendi, *Venez.* 8°29' N, 68°22' W **136**
Arista, *Mex.* 22°37' N, 100°51' W **114**
Aristizábal, Cabo, *Arg.* 45°23' S, 66°29' W **134**
Arivechi, *Mex.* 28°54' N, 109°10' W **92**

Ariza, *Sp.* 41°18′ N, 2°4′ W **164**
Arizona, adm. division, *Ariz., U.S.* 34°22′ N, 112°38′ W **92**
Arizpe, *Mex.* 30°19′ N, 110°12′ W **92**
Arjona, *Col.* 10°16′ N, 75°22′ W **136**
Ark, The, peak, *Antarctica* 80°43′ S, 26°3′ W **248**
Arka, *Russ.* 60°10′ N, 142°13′ E **160**
Arkadak, *Russ.* 51°53′ N, 43°35′ E **158**
Arkadelphia, *Ark., U.S.* 34°6′ N, 93°5′ W **96**
Arkansas, adm. division, *Ark., U.S.* 35°4′ N, 93°21′ W **96**
Arkansas City, *Kans., U.S.* 37°2′ N, 97°3′ W **92**
Arkansas, river, *Okla., U.S.* 35°13′ N, 95°34′ W **80**
Arkanū, Jabal, peak, *Lib.* 22°16′ N, 24°40′ E **226**
Arkhangel'sk, *Russ.* 64°32′ N, 40°54′ E **160**
Arkhangel'sk, adm. division, *Russ.* 63°2′ N, 38°58′ E **154**
Arkhangel'sk (Archangel), *Russ.* 64°35′ N, 40°37′ E **154**
Arkhangel'skoye, *Russ.* 44°34′ N, 44°3′ E **158**
Arkhangel'skoye, *Russ.* 51°28′ N, 40°52′ E **158**
Arklow, *Ire.* 52°47′ N, 6°10′ W **150**
Arkona, Kap, *Ger.* 54°42′ N, 13°34′ E **152**
Arkösund, *Nor.* 58°28′ N, 16°53′ E **152**
Arkticheskiy, Mys, *Russ.* 81°1′ N, 79°59′ E **160**
Arkticheskogo Instituta, Ostrova, island, *Russ.* 75°29′ N, 77°0′ E **160**
Arkul', *Russ.* 57°19′ N, 50°9′ E **154**
Arlanzón, *Sp.* 42°18′ N, 3°27′ W **164**
Arles, *Fr.* 43°41′ N, 4°40′ E **214**
Arlington, *Ga., U.S.* 31°25′ N, 84°43′ W **96**
Arlington, *Ill., U.S.* 41°28′ N, 89°15′ W **102**
Arlington, *Mass., U.S.* 42°24′ N, 71°10′ W **104**
Arlington, *N.Y., U.S.* 41°41′ N, 73°54′ W **104**
Arlington, *Oreg., U.S.* 45°42′ N, 120°12′ W **90**
Arlington, *S. Dak., U.S.* 44°20′ N, 97°9′ W **94**
Arlington, *Tex., U.S.* 32°43′ N, 97°7′ W **92**
Arlington, *Vt., U.S.* 43°4′ N, 73°10′ W **104**
Arlington, *Wash., U.S.* 48°10′ N, 122°7′ W **100**
Arlit, *Niger* 18°50′ N, 7°14′ E **222**
Arlon, *Belg.* 49°40′ N, 5°48′ E **163**
Arly, river, *Fr.* 45°44′ N, 6°31′ E **165**
Arma, *Kans., U.S.* 37°31′ N, 94°42′ W **94**
Armada, *Mich., U.S.* 42°50′ N, 82°53′ W **102**
Armadale Castle, site, *U.K.* 57°2′ N, 6°1′ W **150**
Armadillo, *Mex.* 22°13′ N, 100°40′ W **114**
Armant, *Egypt* 25°36′ N, 32°27′ E **182**
Armavir, *Arm.* 40°9′ N, 44°2′ E **195**
Armavir, *Russ.* 44°59′ N, 41°6′ E **158**
Armenia 40°14′ N, 44°43′ E **195**
Armenia, *Col.* 4°28′ N, 75°45′ W **136**
Armenia Mountain, *Pa., U.S.* 41°44′ N, 76°60′ W **94**
Armeniş, *Rom.* 45°13′ N, 22°18′ E **168**
Armentières, *Fr.* 50°40′ N, 2°53′ E **163**
Armeria, *Mex.* 18°55′ N, 103°60′ W **114**
Armero, *Col.* 4°57′ N, 74°55′ W **136**
Armijo, *N. Mex., U.S.* 35°2′ N, 106°41′ W **92**
Armilla, *Sp.* 37°8′ N, 3°38′ W **164**
Armit, *Can.* 52°49′ N, 101°47′ W **108**
Armizonskoye, *Russ.* 55°56′ N, 67°39′ E **184**
Armona, *Calif., U.S.* 36°19′ N, 119°43′ W **100**
Armour, *S. Dak., U.S.* 43°18′ N, 98°21′ W **90**
Armstrong, *Arg.* 32°49′ S, 61°35′ W **139**
Armstrong, *Can.* 50°18′ N, 89°2′ W **110**
Armstrong, *Can.* 50°26′ N, 119°12′ W **90**
Armutcuk, *Turk.* 41°20′ N, 31°31′ E **156**
Armyans'k, *Ukr.* 46°5′ N, 33°41′ E **156**
Arnaoutis, Cape, *Cyprus* 35°5′ N, 32°4′ E **194**
Arnaud, *Can.* 49°14′ N, 97°6′ W **90**
Arnaudville, *La., U.S.* 30°23′ N, 91°57′ W **103**
Arnbach, *Aust.* 46°44′ N, 12°23′ E **167**
Årnes, *Nor.* 60°7′ N, 11°28′ E **152**
Arnett, *Okla., U.S.* 36°7′ N, 99°46′ W **92**
Arnhem, *Neth.* 51°59′ N, 5°54′ E **167**
Arnhem Land, region, *Australia* 11°54′ S, 131°40′ E **192**
Arnold, *Calif., U.S.* 38°15′ N, 120°22′ W **100**
Arnold, *Nebr., U.S.* 41°25′ N, 100°12′ W **90**
Arnold, river, *Austral.* 14°50′ S, 133°57′ E **230**
Arnolds Park, *Iowa, U.S.* 43°21′ N, 95°8′ W **90**
Arnoldstein, *Aust.* 46°33′ N, 13°42′ E **167**
Arnot, *Can.* 55°45′ N, 96°45′ W **108**
Arnsberg, *Ger.* 51°23′ N, 8°4′ E **167**
Arnstein, *Ger.* 49°58′ N, 9°58′ E **167**
Aroa, *Venez.* 10°25′ N, 68°54′ W **136**
Aroab, *Namibia* 26°50′ S, 19°43′ E **227**
Aroánia, Óri, peak, *Gr.* 37°57′ N, 22°8′ E **156**
Arock, *Oreg., U.S.* 42°55′ N, 117°31′ W **90**
Arolsen, *Ger.* 51°23′ N, 9°1′ E **167**
Aroma, *Sudan* 15°46′ N, 36°8′ E **182**
Aroma Park, *Ill., U.S.* 41°4′ N, 87°48′ W **102**
Aron, *India* 25°57′ N, 77°54′ E **197**
Arona, *It.* 45°45′ N, 8°32′ E **167**
Arosa, *Switz.* 46°46′ N, 9°38′ E **167**
Ærøskøbing, *Den.* 54°53′ N, 10°24′ E **150**
Arowhana, peak, *N.Z.* 38°8′ S, 177°45′ E **240**
Arp, *Tex., U.S.* 32°13′ N, 95°4′ W **103**
Arpa, river, *Asia* 40°28′ N, 43°31′ E **195**
Arpaçay, *Turk.* 40°52′ N, 43°19′ E **195**
Arpajon, *Fr.* 48°35′ N, 2°14′ E **163**
Arqalyq, *Kaz.* 50°13′ N, 66°54′ E **184**
Arque, *Bol.* 17°51′ S, 66°22′ W **137**
Arques, *Fr.* 50°44′ N, 2°18′ E **150**
Arquia, *Col.* 7°58′ N, 77°7′ W **136**
'Arrābah, *West Bank* 32°24′ N, 35°11′ E **194**
Arraias, *Braz.* 12°56′ S, 46°58′ W **130**
Arraias, river, *Braz.* 12°5′ S, 54°14′ W **130**
Arraias, river, *Braz.* 8°37′ S, 49°54′ W **130**
Arras, *Alban.* 41°45′ N, 20°18′ E **168**
Arras, *Fr.* 50°17′ N, 2°47′ E **163**
Arreau, *Fr.* 42°54′ N, 0°22′ E **164**
Arrecifes, *Arg.* 34°4′ S, 60°7′ W **139**
Arrée, Montagnes d', *Fr.* 48°29′ N, 4°12′ W **150**
Arriate, *Sp.* 36°47′ N, 5°9′ W **164**
Arris, *Alg.* 35°12′ N, 6°17′ E **150**
Arroio dos Ratos, *Braz.* 30°6′ S, 51°44′ W **139**
Arroio Grande, *Braz.* 32°12′ S, 53°7′ W **139**
Arrojado, river, *Braz.* 13°40′ S, 45°16′ W **138**
Arrou, *Fr.* 48°6′ N, 1°7′ E **163**
Arroux, river, *Fr.* 46°45′ N, 4°8′ E **165**
Arrowhead, river, *Can.* 60°18′ N, 123°11′ W **108**
Arrowsmith, *Ill., U.S.* 40°26′ N, 88°38′ W **102**
Arrowtown, *N.Z.* 44°57′ S, 168°51′ E **240**
Arrowwood, *Can.* 50°44′ N, 113°10′ W **90**
Arroyito, *Arg.* 31°27′ S, 63°4′ W **139**
Arroyo de la Luz, *Sp.* 39°28′ N, 6°36′ W **164**
Arroyo Grande, *Calif., U.S.* 35°8′ N, 120°35′ W **100**
Arroyo Hondo, *N. Mex., U.S.* 36°31′ N, 105°40′ W **92**
Arroyo Verde see Puerto Lobos, *Arg.* 42°2′ S, 65°5′ W **134**
Arroyos y Esteros, *Parag.* 25°5′ S, 57°7′ W **132**
Arrufó, *Arg.* 30°13′ S, 61°44′ W **139**
Ars-en-Ré, *Fr.* 46°12′ N, 1°33′ W **150**
Arshaly, *Kaz.* 50°49′ N, 72°11′ E **184**
Arshaty, *Kaz.* 49°17′ N, 86°36′ E **184**
Arsiero, *It.* 45°48′ N, 11°20′ E **167**
Arsikere, *India* 13°20′ N, 76°14′ E **188**
Arsk, *Russ.* 56°7′ N, 49°54′ E **154**
Arsuk, *Den.* 61°13′ N, 48°8′ W **106**
Artashat, *Arm.* 39°58′ N, 44°32′ E **195**
Arteaga, *Mex.* 25°25′ N, 100°52′ W **114**
Arteaga, *Mex.* 18°24′ N, 102°16′ W **114**
Artem, *Russ.* 43°26′ N, 132°21′ E **190**
Artemisa, *Cuba* 22°49′ N, 82°46′ W **116**
Artemivs'k, *Ukr.* 48°35′ N, 37°57′ E **158**
Artemovsk, *Russ.* 54°24′ N, 93°22′ E **190**
Artemovskiy, *Russ.* 58°19′ N, 114°40′ E **160**
Artemovskiy, *Russ.* 57°22′ N, 61°47′ E **154**
Artenay, *Fr.* 48°4′ N, 1°51′ E **150**
Artesa de Segre, *Sp.* 41°53′ N, 1°3′ E **164**
Artesia, *Miss., U.S.* 33°23′ N, 88°38′ W **103**
Artesia, *N. Mex., U.S.* 32°50′ N, 104°25′ W **92**
Artesian, *S. Dak., U.S.* 43°59′ N, 97°57′ W **90**
Arthez, *Fr.* 43°28′ N, 0°37′ E **150**
Arthog, *U.K.* 52°42′ N, 4°1′ W **162**
Arthonnay, *Fr.* 47°55′ N, 4°13′ E **150**
Arthur, *Ill., U.S.* 39°42′ N, 88°28′ W **102**
Arthur, *Nebr., U.S.* 41°33′ N, 101°42′ W **90**
Arthur, Lac, lake, *Can.* 51°6′ N, 62°48′ W **111**
Arthur's Pass, *N.Z.* 42°57′ S, 171°33′ E **240**
Arti, *Russ.* 56°25′ N, 58°37′ E **154**
Artigas, *Uru.* 30°24′ S, 56°31′ W **139**
Artigas, station, *Antarctica* 61°59′ S, 58°38′ W **134**
Art'ik, *Arm.* 40°37′ N, 43°57′ E **195**
Artix, *Fr.* 43°24′ N, 0°33′ E **150**
Artois, region, *Europe* 50°17′ N, 1°58′ E **163**
Artova, *Turk.* 40°2′ N, 36°16′ E **156**
Artrutx, Cabo d', *Sp.* 39°56′ N, 3°27′ E **150**
Artux, *China* 39°45′ N, 76°6′ E **184**
Artvin, *Turk.* 41°11′ N, 41°49′ E **195**
Artyom, *Azerb.* 40°28′ N, 50°19′ E **195**
Aru, *Dem. Rep. of the Congo* 2°48′ N, 30°50′ E **224**
Aru, Kepulauan, islands, *Arafura Sea* 6°8′ S, 133°44′ E **192**
Arua, *Dem. Rep. of the Congo* 3°4′ N, 30°56′ E **207**
Aruajá, *Braz.* 4°60′ S, 66°51′ W **130**
Aruanã, *Braz.* 14°58′ S, 51°8′ W **138**
Aruba, island, *Netherlands* 13°0′ N, 70°0′ W **118**
Arun Qi, *China* 48°8′ N, 123°34′ E **198**
Arunachal Pradesh, adm. division, *India* 28°39′ N, 94°2′ E **188**
Arundel, *U.K.* 50°51′ N, 0°34′ E **162**
Arusha, *Tanzania* 3°22′ S, 36°42′ E **224**
Arusha, adm. division, *Tanzania* 4°7′ S, 35°4′ E **218**
Aruwimi, river, *Dem. Rep. of the Congo* 1°37′ N, 25°21′ E **224**
Arvada, *Colo., U.S.* 39°47′ N, 105°6′ W **90**
Arvayheer, *Mongolia* 46°12′ N, 102°50′ E **198**
Arve, river, *Fr.* 46°3′ N, 6°36′ E **167**
Arvi, *India* 20°59′ N, 78°13′ E **188**
Arviat, *Can.* 61°5′ N, 94°10′ W **106**
Arvika, *Nor.* 59°39′ N, 12°36′ E **152**
Arvin, *Calif., U.S.* 35°12′ N, 118°50′ W **101**
Arvon, Mount, *Mich., U.S.* 46°44′ N, 88°14′ W **94**
Arxan, *China* 47°12′ N, 119°55′ E **198**
Ary, *Russ.* 72°50′ N, 122°37′ E **173**
Arya Köli, lake, *Kaz.* 45°55′ N, 66°3′ E **184**
Aryqbayq, *Kaz.* 52°55′ N, 68°12′ E **184**
Arys, *Kaz.* 42°25′ N, 68°47′ E **197**
Arys, river, *Kaz.* 42°32′ N, 69°1′ E **197**
Arzamas, *Russ.* 55°21′ N, 43°55′ E **154**
Aržano, *Croatia* 43°35′ N, 16°58′ E **168**
Arzew, *Alg.* 35°50′ N, 0°19′ E **150**
Arzgir, *Russ.* 45°21′ N, 44°10′ E **158**
Arzni, *Arm.* 40°19′ N, 44°36′ E **195**
As Ela, *Djibouti* 10°59′ N, 42°12′ E **224**
As Sabkhah, *Syr.* 35°46′ N, 39°19′ E **180**
Aş Şāfī, *Jordan* 31°1′ N, 35°27′ E **194**
As Salmān, *Iraq* 30°30′ N, 44°32′ E **180**
As Salţ, *Jordan* 32°2′ N, 35°43′ E **194**
As Salwá, *Saudi Arabia* 24°41′ N, 50°48′ E **196**
As Samāwah (Samawah), *Iraq* 31°15′ N, 45°15′ E **180**
As Sanām, *Saudi Arabia* 23°34′ N, 51°7′ E **196**
Aş Şanamayn, *Syr.* 33°4′ N, 36°11′ E **194**
Aş Şaqlabīyah, *Syr.* 35°21′ N, 36°22′ E **194**
Aş Şarafand, *Leb.* 33°27′ N, 35°17′ E **194**
As Sarfaia, spring, *Lib.* 23°38′ N, 17°11′ E **216**
Aş Şawrah, *Saudi Arabia* 27°52′ N, 35°22′ E **180**
As Sīb, *Oman* 23°41′ N, 58°11′ E **196**
As Sidr, *Lib.* 30°39′ N, 18°18′ E **216**
As Sidr, *Saudi Arabia* 23°24′ N, 39°44′ E **182**
As Sikr, spring, *Iraq* 30°44′ N, 43°44′ E **180**
As Sirḩān, Wādī, *Jordan* 31°9′ N, 36°42′ E **180**
Aş Şufuq, spring, *U.A.E.* 23°43′ N, 51°48′ E **196**
As Sulaymānīyah, *Iraq* 35°33′ N, 45°25′ E **180**
As Sulaymānīyah, *Saudi Arabia* 24°6′ N, 47°16′ E **196**
As Sulaymī, *Saudi Arabia* 26°15′ N, 41°23′ E **182**
As Sulayyil, *Saudi Arabia* 20°27′ N, 45°34′ E **182**
As Sulţān, *Lib.* 31°6′ N, 17°7′ E **216**
Aş Şurrah, *Yemen* 13°56′ N, 46°11′ E **182**
As Suwāqah, *Jordan* 31°21′ N, 36°6′ E **194**
Aş Şuwār, *Syr.* 35°31′ N, 40°38′ E **180**
As Suwaydā', *Syr.* 32°42′ N, 36°34′ E **194**
As Suwayḩ, *Oman* 22°6′ N, 59°41′ E **182**
Asa, river, *Dem. Rep. of the Congo* 4°55′ N, 25°15′ E **224**
Asab, *Namibia* 25°27′ S, 17°54′ E **227**
Asab, oil field, *U.A.E.* 23°12′ N, 54°8′ E **182**
Asadābād, Gardaneh-ye, pass, *Iran* 34°48′ N, 48°10′ E **180**
Asahi, river, *Japan* 35°0′ N, 133°47′ E **201**
Asahikawa, *Japan* 43°50′ N, 142°36′ E **190**
Āsalē, *Eth.* 14°12′ N, 40°18′ E **182**
Asansol, *India* 23°40′ N, 86°59′ E **197**
Āsarna, *Nor.* 62°39′ N, 14°20′ E **152**
Āsayita, *Eth.* 11°31′ N, 41°25′ E **182**
Asbest, *Russ.* 57°2′ N, 61°28′ E **154**
Asbestos, *Can.* 45°45′ N, 71°57′ W **94**
Ascención, *Bol.* 15°43′ S, 63°8′ W **132**
Ascensión, *Mex.* 24°18′ N, 99°55′ W **114**
Ascensión, *Mex.* 31°5′ N, 107°60′ W **92**
Ascensión, Bahía de la 19°30′ N, 88°2′ W **115**
Ascension Fracture Zone, *South Atlantic Ocean* 6°36′ S, 11°59′ W **253**
Aschaffenburg, *Ger.* 49°58′ N, 9°9′ E **167**
Ascheberg, *Ger.* 51°48′ N, 7°36′ E **167**
Aschendorf, *Ger.* 53°3′ N, 7°19′ E **163**
Ascira, *Somalia* 10°19′ N, 50°56′ E **216**
Ascó, *Sp.* 41°10′ N, 0°33′ E **164**
Ascot, *U.K.* 51°24′ N, 0°40′ E **162**
Ascotán, *Chile* 21°45′ S, 68°19′ W **137**
Ascutney, *Vt., U.S.* 43°24′ N, 72°25′ W **104**
Åseda, *Nor.* 57°10′ N, 15°20′ E **152**
Asedjrad, *Alg.* 24°55′ N, 1°0′ E **214**
Āsela, *Eth.* 7°51′ N, 39°2′ E **224**
Åsele, *Nor.* 64°9′ N, 17°19′ E **152**
Åseral, *Nor.* 58°36′ N, 7°25′ E **152**
Asfeld, *Fr.* 49°27′ N, 4°7′ E **163**
Asfûn el Maţā'na, *Egypt* 25°25′ N, 32°28′ E **226**
Aşgabat (Ashgabat), *Turkm.* 37°54′ N, 58°14′ E **180**
Ash Fork, *Ariz., U.S.* 35°11′ N, 112°29′ W **82**
Ash Grove, *Mo., U.S.* 37°18′ N, 93°34′ W **94**
Ash Mountain, *Can.* 59°16′ N, 130°38′ W **108**
Ash, river, *Can.* 50°27′ N, 84°56′ W **94**
Ash Shabakah, *Iraq* 30°48′ N, 43°36′ E **180**
Ash Sha'rā', *Saudi Arabia* 24°15′ N, 44°11′ E **182**
Ash Sharawrah, *Saudi Arabia* 17°54′ N, 47°26′ E **182**
Ash Sharqāţ, *Iraq* 35°26′ N, 43°15′ E **180**
Ash Shaţrah, *Iraq* 31°25′ N, 46°6′ E **180**
Ash Shawbak, *Jordan* 30°31′ N, 35°33′ E **194**
Ash Shaykh Badr, *Syr.* 34°59′ N, 36°4′ E **194**
Ash Shiḩr, *Yemen* 14°45′ N, 49°33′ E **182**
Ash Shināfīyah, *Iraq* 31°37′ N, 44°39′ E **180**
Ash Shişar, *Oman* 18°15′ N, 53°39′ E **182**
Ash Shumlūl, *Saudi Arabia* 26°29′ N, 47°22′ E **196**
Ash Shuqayq, *Saudi Arabia* 17°42′ N, 42°4′ E **182**
Ash Shurayf, *Saudi Arabia* 25°42′ N, 39°12′ E **182**
Ash Shuwayfāt, *Leb.* 33°48′ N, 35°30′ E **194**
Ash Shuwayrif, *Lib.* 29°58′ N, 14°12′ E **216**
Asha, *Russ.* 55°3′ N, 57°18′ E **154**
Ashbourne, *U.K.* 53°0′ N, 1°45′ W **162**
Ashburn, *Ga., U.S.* 31°42′ N, 83°39′ W **96**
Ashburnham, *Mass., U.S.* 42°37′ N, 71°55′ W **104**
Ashburton, *N.Z.* 43°55′ S, 171°47′ E **240**
Ashby, *Mass., U.S.* 42°40′ N, 71°50′ W **104**
Ashby de la Zouch, *U.K.* 52°44′ N, 1°29′ W **162**
Ashchy Köl, lake, *Kaz.* 45°11′ N, 67°38′ E **184**
Ashcroft, *Can.* 50°43′ N, 121°15′ W **90**
Ashdod, *Israel* 31°47′ N, 34°39′ E **194**
Ashdown, *Ark., U.S.* 33°40′ N, 94°8′ W **96**
Ashdown Forest, region, *Europe* 50°57′ N, 0°12′ E **162**
Ashern, *Can.* 51°11′ N, 98°21′ W **90**
Asherton, *Tex., U.S.* 28°26′ N, 99°45′ W **92**
Ashfield, *Mass., U.S.* 42°31′ N, 72°48′ W **104**
Ashford, *U.K.* 51°9′ N, 0°52′ E **162**
Ashford, *Wash., U.S.* 46°44′ N, 122°2′ W **100**
Ashgabat see Aşgabat, *Turkm.* 37°54′ N, 58°14′ E **180**
Ashikaga, *Japan* 36°20′ N, 139°27′ E **201**
Ashitaka, *Japan* 32°18′ N, 130°30′ E **201**
Ashizuri Misaki, *Japan* 32°36′ N, 133°0′ E **201**
Ashkadar, river, *Russ.* 53°2′ N, 55°16′ E **154**
Ashkelon, ruin(s), *Israel* 31°39′ N, 34°30′ E **194**
Ashkum, *Ill., U.S.* 40°51′ N, 87°57′ W **102**
Ashland, *Kans., U.S.* 37°11′ N, 99°47′ W **92**
Ashland, *Ky., U.S.* 38°27′ N, 82°39′ W **102**
Ashland, *La., U.S.* 32°7′ N, 93°6′ W **103**
Ashland, *Me., U.S.* 46°37′ N, 68°25′ W **94**
Ashland, *Mont., U.S.* 45°34′ N, 106°16′ W **90**
Ashland, *N.C., U.S.* 41°1′ N, 96°21′ W **94**
Ashland, *N.H., U.S.* 43°41′ N, 71°38′ W **104**
Ashland, *Ohio, U.S.* 40°52′ N, 82°18′ W **102**
Ashland, *Pa., U.S.* 40°46′ N, 76°22′ W **110**
Ashland, *Va., U.S.* 37°45′ N, 77°29′ W **94**
Ashland, *Wis., U.S.* 46°35′ N, 90°53′ W **94**
Ashland, Mount, *Oreg., U.S.* 42°5′ N, 122°48′ W **90**
Ashley, *Ind., U.S.* 41°30′ N, 85°5′ W **102**
Ashley, *N. Dak., U.S.* 46°0′ N, 99°24′ W **94**
Ashley, *Ohio, U.S.* 40°23′ N, 82°57′ W **102**
Ashmont, *Can.* 54°7′ N, 111°35′ W **108**
Ashmore Islands, *Indian Ocean* 12°34′ S, 122°16′ E **231**
Ashmyany, *Belarus* 54°26′ N, 25°55′ E **166**
Ashoknagar, *India* 24°32′ N, 77°44′ E **197**
Ashqelon, *Israel* 31°40′ N, 34°34′ E **194**
Ashtabula, *Ohio, U.S.* 41°51′ N, 80°48′ W **102**
Ashtabula, Lake, *N. Dak., U.S.* 47°10′ N, 98°38′ W **90**
Ashton, *Idaho, U.S.* 44°4′ N, 111°27′ W **90**
Ashton, *Ill., U.S.* 41°51′ N, 89°14′ W **102**
Ashton, *Mich., U.S.* 43°58′ N, 85°30′ W **102**
Ashton, *R.I., U.S.* 41°56′ N, 71°26′ W **104**
Ashton under Lyne, *U.K.* 53°29′ N, 2°6′ W **162**
Ashuanipi, *Can.* 52°45′ N, 66°6′ W **111**
Ashuanipi Lake, *Can.* 52°31′ N, 66°34′ W **111**
Ashuapmushuan, Lac, lake, *Can.* 49°10′ N, 74°40′ W **94**
Ashville, *Can.* 51°10′ N, 100°18′ W **90**
Ashville, *Ohio, U.S.* 39°43′ N, 82°57′ W **102**
Ashyrymy, Bichānāk, *Arm.* 39°33′ N, 45°7′ E **195**
'Āşī (Orontes), river, *Syr.* 35°40′ N, 36°21′ E **194**
Asia 3°0′ N, 103°0′ E **173**
Asia, Kepulauan, islands, *North Pacific Ocean* 1°12′ N, 129°17′ E **192**
Asia Minor see Anatolia, region, *Asia* 38°39′ N, 30°18′ E **180**
Asiago, *It.* 45°52′ N, 11°30′ E **167**
Asika, *India* 19°38′ N, 84°38′ E **188**
Asikkala, *Fin.* 61°11′ N, 25°28′ E **166**
Asilah, *Mor.* 35°28′ N, 6°2′ W **150**
Asillo, *Peru* 14°50′ S, 70°21′ W **137**
Asinara, Isola, island, *It.* 41°4′ N, 7°5′ E **214**
Asino, *Russ.* 56°59′ N, 86°9′ E **169**
Asipovichy, *Belarus* 53°17′ N, 28°45′ E **152**
Asis, Ras, *Sudan* 18°17′ N, 37°36′ E **182**
Ask, *Nor.* 60°28′ N, 5°10′ E **152**
Aşkale, *Turk.* 39°56′ N, 40°41′ E **195**
Askaniya Nova, *Ukr.* 46°27′ N, 33°53′ E **156**
Asker, *Nor.* 59°50′ N, 10°26′ E **152**
Askham, *S. Af.* 27°2′ S, 20°51′ E **227**
Askī Mawşil, *Iraq* 36°31′ N, 42°37′ E **195**
Askilje, *Nor.* 64°53′ N, 17°51′ E **152**
Askino, *Russ.* 56°6′ N, 56°35′ E **154**
Askiz, *Russ.* 53°10′ N, 90°33′ E **184**
Askole, *Pak.* 35°40′ N, 75°50′ E **188**
Askrigg, *U.K.* 54°18′ N, 2°5′ W **162**
Askvoll, *Nor.* 61°21′ N, 5°4′ E **152**
Asler, spring, *Mali* 18°53′ N, 0°9′ E **222**
Asmar, *Afghan.* 35°2′ N, 71°27′ E **186**
Asmara, *Eritrea* 15°16′ N, 38°48′ E **182**
Åsnes, *Nor.* 60°36′ N, 11°57′ E **152**
Asni, *Mor.* 31°14′ N, 8°1′ W **214**
Aso, peak, *Japan* 32°51′ N, 131°3′ E **201**
Asola, *It.* 45°13′ N, 10°25′ E **167**
Asopus, ruin(s), *Gr.* 36°41′ N, 22°45′ E **156**
Āsosa, *Eth.* 10°2′ N, 34°29′ E **224**
Asoteriba, *Sudan* 19°31′ N, 37°5′ E **182**
Asoteriba, Jebel, peak, *Sudan* 21°49′ N, 36°24′ E **182**
Aspang, *Aust.* 47°33′ N, 16°3′ E **168**
Aspatria, *U.K.* 54°46′ N, 3°20′ W **162**
Aspeå, *Nor.* 63°22′ N, 17°36′ E **152**
Aspen, *Colo., U.S.* 39°11′ N, 106°50′ W **92**
Aspen Butte, peak, *Oreg., U.S.* 42°18′ N, 122°11′ W **90**
Aspen Range, *Idaho, U.S.* 42°42′ N, 111°34′ W **90**
Aspermont, *Tex., U.S.* 33°6′ N, 100°14′ W **92**
Aspiring, Mount, *N.Z.* 44°25′ S, 168°39′ E **240**
Asprókavos, Ákra, *Gr.* 39°21′ N, 19°35′ E **156**
Aspromonte, *It.* 38°1′ N, 15°50′ E **156**
Aspy Bay 46°53′ N, 60°50′ W **111**
Asquith, *Can.* 52°8′ N, 107°13′ W **90**
Assa, *Mor.* 28°37′ N, 9°24′ W **214**
Assab, *Eritrea* 12°59′ N, 42°41′ E **182**
'Assâba, *Mauritania* 16°36′ N, 12°26′ W **222**
Aşşafā, *Syr.* 33°13′ N, 36°48′ E **194**
Assaikio, *Nig.* 8°34′ N, 8°53′ E **222**
Assala, *Congo* 2°18′ S, 14°28′ E **218**
Assam, adm. division, *India* 26°28′ N, 90°56′ E **188**
Assaouas, spring, *Niger* 16°53′ N, 7°24′ E **222**
Assateague Island National Seashore, *Va., U.S.* 38°4′ N, 75°9′ W **94**
Assean Lake, lake, *Can.* 56°7′ N, 97°7′ W **108**
Assebroek, *Belg.* 51°10′ N, 3°16′ E **163**
Assen, *Neth.* 52°59′ N, 6°33′ E **163**
Assiniboia, *Can.* 49°37′ N, 105°60′ W **90**
Assiniboine, Mount, *Can.* 50°51′ N, 115°44′ W **90**
Assiniboine, river, *Can.* 49°21′ N, 99°32′ W **80**
Assinica, Lac, lake, *Can.* 50°30′ N, 75°45′ W **110**
Assiou (Azéo), spring, *Alg.* 21°6′ N, 7°35′ E **222**
Assis, *Braz.* 22°40′ S, 50°28′ W **138**
Asslar, *Ger.* 50°35′ N, 8°26′ E **167**
Assodé, *Niger* 18°29′ N, 8°35′ E **222**
Assok-Ngoum, *Gabon* 1°45′ N, 11°35′ E **218**
Assos, ruin(s), *Turk.* 39°29′ N, 26°15′ E **156**
Assoul, *Mor.* 32°2′ N, 5°17′ W **214**
Assumption, *Ill., U.S.* 39°30′ N, 89°2′ W **102**
Assumption Island, *Seychelles* 9°51′ S, 46°7′ E **218**
Astana, *Kaz.* 51°7′ N, 71°14′ E **184**
Astara, *Azerb.* 38°28′ N, 48°50′ E **195**
Āstārā, *Iran* 38°25′ N, 48°48′ E **195**
Asten, *Neth.* 51°24′ N, 5°44′ E **167**
Asti, *It.* 44°54′ N, 8°12′ E **167**
Astillero, *Peru* 13°24′ S, 69°38′ W **137**
Astillero, Cerro del, peak, *Mex.* 20°16′ N, 99°39′ W **114**
Asto, Mont, peak, *Fr.* 42°34′ N, 9°8′ E **156**
Astola Island, *Pak.* 24°57′ N, 63°54′ E **182**
Astorga, *Sp.* 42°26′ N, 6°4′ W **150**
Astoria, *Oreg., U.S.* 46°10′ N, 123°48′ W **100**
Astove Island, *Seychelles* 10°29′ S, 47°53′ E **220**
Astrakhan', *Russ.* 46°19′ N, 48°4′ E **158**
Astrakhan', adm. division, *Russ.* 47°9′ N, 46°39′ E **158**
Åsträsk, *Nor.* 64°35′ N, 19°57′ E **152**
Astravyets, *Belarus* 54°36′ N, 25°57′ E **166**
Astryna, *Belarus* 53°44′ N, 24°34′ E **154**
Asturias, adm. division, *Sp.* 43°24′ N, 7°1′ W **150**
Asunción, *Bol.* 11°49′ S, 67°52′ W **137**
Asunción, *Parag.* 25°19′ S, 57°49′ W **132**
Asunción, Punta, *Arg.* 39°7′ S, 60°30′ W **139**
Åsunden, lake, *Nor.* 57°53′ N, 15°25′ E **152**
Asūne, *Latv.* 56°0′ N, 27°37′ E **166**
Åsvær, island, *Nor.* 66°16′ N, 11°14′ E **152**
Asvyeya, *Belarus* 56°1′ N, 28°5′ E **166**
Asvyeyskaye, Vozyera, lake, *Belarus* 56°1′ N, 27°32′ E **166**
Aswân, *Egypt* 24°4′ N, 32°54′ E **182**
Asyûţ, *Egypt* 27°8′ N, 31°5′ E **180**
Aszód, *Hung.* 47°39′ N, 19°28′ E **168**
Aţ Ţafīlah, *Jordan* 30°50′ N, 35°36′ E **194**
Aţ Ţā'if, *Saudi Arabia* 21°15′ N, 40°24′ E **182**
At Tāj, *Lib.* 24°17′ N, 23°15′ E **216**
At Tall, *Syr.* 33°35′ N, 36°18′ E **194**
Aţ Ţayyibah, *Jordan* 31°3′ N, 35°36′ E **194**
At Turbah, *Yemen* 12°45′ N, 43°29′ E **182**
Aţ Ţuwayyah, spring, *Saudi Arabia* 27°41′ N, 40°50′ E **180**
Ataa, *Den.* 69°46′ N, 51°1′ W **106**
Atacama, adm. division, *Chile* 27°6′ S, 70°45′ W **132**
Atacama, Desierto de, *Chile* 25°53′ S, 70°11′ W **132**
Atacuari, river, *Peru* 3°25′ S, 71°16′ W **136**
Atafu, island, *N.Z.* 8°29′ S, 172°40′ W **252**
Atakora, Chaîne de l', *Benin* 10°7′ N, 1°12′ E **222**
Atakpamé, *Togo* 7°33′ N, 1°8′ E **222**
Atalaia do Norte, *Braz.* 4°19′ S, 70°7′ W **130**
Atalaya, *Peru* 10°44′ S, 73°48′ W **137**
Ataléia, *Braz.* 18°4′ S, 41°7′ W **138**
Atami, *Japan* 35°4′ N, 139°3′ E **201**
Atammik, *Den.* 64°51′ N, 52°9′ W **106**
Atamyrat, *Turkm.* 37°52′ N, 65°11′ E **160**
Atamyrat (Kerki), *Turkm.* 37°49′ N, 65°10′ E **197**
Atar, *Mauritania* 20°31′ N, 13°3′ W **222**
Atarfe, *Sp.* 37°13′ N, 3°41′ W **164**
Atascadero, *Calif., U.S.* 35°29′ N, 120°41′ W **100**
Atašiene, *Latv.* 56°32′ N, 26°21′ E **166**
Atasta, ruin(s), *Mex.* 18°37′ N, 92°14′ W **115**
Atasū, *Kaz.* 48°40′ N, 71°39′ E **184**
Atauro, island, *Indonesia* 8°31′ S, 125°42′ E **192**
Atáviros, peak, *Gr.* 36°11′ N, 27°47′ E **156**
Atbara, *Sudan* 17°42′ N, 34°3′ E **182**
Atbara, river, *Sudan* 14°10′ N, 35°57′ E **226**
Atbasar, *Kaz.* 51°48′ N, 68°22′ E **184**
At-Bashy, *Kyrg.* 41°7′ N, 75°47′ E **184**
Atchafalaya Bay 29°27′ N, 91°38′ W **103**
Atchison, *Kans., U.S.* 39°32′ N, 95°8′ W **94**
Atea, *Sp.* 41°9′ N, 1°33′ W **164**
Ateca, *Sp.* 41°19′ N, 1°49′ W **164**
Ath, *Belg.* 50°37′ N, 3°47′ E **163**
Ath Thumāmah, spring, *Saudi Arabia* 27°41′ N, 45°0′ E **180**
Athabasca, *Can.* 54°41′ N, 113°15′ W **108**
Athabasca, Lake, *Can.* 59°8′ N, 109°58′ W **108**
Athabasca, Mount, *Can.* 52°10′ N, 117°17′ W **108**
Athabasca, oil field, *Can.* 56°54′ N, 111°38′ W **108**
Athabasca, river, *Can.* 53°26′ N, 117°6′ W **106**
Athamánon, peak, *Gr.* 39°31′ N, 21°7′ E **156**
Athenry, *Ire.* 53°17′ N, 8°46′ W **150**
Athens, *Ala., U.S.* 34°48′ N, 86°58′ W **96**
Athens, *Ga., U.S.* 33°57′ N, 83°24′ W **96**
Athens, *Ill., U.S.* 39°57′ N, 89°44′ W **102**
Athens, *La., U.S.* 32°38′ N, 93°2′ W **103**
Athens, *N.Y., U.S.* 42°15′ N, 73°50′ W **104**
Athens, *Ohio, U.S.* 39°19′ N, 82°6′ W **102**
Athens, *Pa., U.S.* 41°57′ N, 76°32′ W **110**
Athens, *Tenn., U.S.* 35°26′ N, 84°36′ W **96**
Athens, *Tex., U.S.* 32°11′ N, 95°51′ W **96**
Athens see Athína, *Gr.* 37°58′ N, 23°36′ E **156**
Atherley, *Can.* 44°35′ N, 79°21′ W **110**
Athi River, *Kenya* 1°28′ S, 36°59′ E **224**
Athi, river, *Kenya* 2°31′ S, 38°21′ E **224**
Athienou, *Northern Cyprus* 35°4′ N, 33°32′ E **194**
Athína (Athens), *Gr.* 37°58′ N, 23°36′ E **156**
Athlone, *Ire.* 53°25′ N, 7°58′ W **150**
Athna, *Cyprus* 35°2′ N, 33°47′ E **156**
Athol, *Mass., U.S.* 42°35′ N, 72°14′ W **104**
Athol, *N.Z.* 45°30′ S, 168°35′ E **240**
Atholl, Kap, *Den.* 76°6′ N, 73°24′ W **106**
Atholville, *Can.* 47°58′ N, 66°44′ W **94**
Áthos, Mount see Ágio Óros, peak, *Gr.* 40°8′ N, 24°15′ E **156**
Athos, Mount see Ágio Óros, region, *Gr.* 40°14′ N, 23°2′ E **156**
Athos Range, *Antarctica* 70°15′ S, 61°18′ E **248**
Ati, *Chad* 13°15′ N, 18°22′ E **216**
Ati Ardébé, *Chad* 12°45′ N, 17°41′ E **216**
Atiak, *Uganda* 3°14′ N, 32°7′ E **224**
Atiamuri, *N.Z.* 38°26′ S, 176°1′ E **240**
Atico, *Peru* 16°12′ S, 73°38′ W **137**
Atienza, *Sp.* 41°11′ N, 2°52′ W **164**
Atik Lake, *Can.* 55°16′ N, 96°19′ W **108**
Atikameg, *Can.* 55°54′ N, 115°41′ W **108**
Atikameg Lake, *Can.* 53°57′ N, 100°58′ W **108**
Atikameg, river, *Can.* 51°45′ N, 83°34′ W **110**
Atiki, adm. division, *Gr.* 37°26′ N, 23°14′ E **156**
Atikokan, *Can.* 48°44′ N, 91°37′ W **94**
Atikonak Lake, *Can.* 52°30′ N, 65°11′ W **111**
Atikwa Lake, lake, *Can.* 49°27′ N, 93°56′ W **90**
Atiquipa, *Peru* 15°50′ S, 74°22′ W **137**
Atka, *Alas., U.S.* 52°10′ N, 174°12′ W **160**
Atka, *Russ.* 60°51′ N, 151°50′ E **160**
Atka, island, *Alas., U.S.* 51°38′ N, 175°35′ W **160**
Atkarsk, *Russ.* 51°53′ N, 45°2′ E **158**
Atkinson, *Nebr., U.S.* 42°30′ N, 98°59′ W **90**
Atkinson, *N.H., U.S.* 42°50′ N, 71°10′ W **104**
Atkinson Lake, *Can.* 55°57′ N, 95°34′ W **108**
Atkinson Point, *Can.* 69°54′ N, 134°2′ W **98**
Atlacomulco, *Mex.* 19°47′ N, 99°55′ W **114**
Atlanta, *Ga., U.S.* 33°44′ N, 84°29′ W **96**
Atlanta, *Ill., U.S.* 40°15′ N, 89°14′ W **102**
Atlanta, *Mich., U.S.* 45°0′ N, 84°9′ W **94**
Atlanta, *Tex., U.S.* 33°6′ N, 94°10′ W **103**
Atlantic, *Iowa, U.S.* 41°22′ N, 95°1′ W **94**
Atlantic Beach, *Fla., U.S.* 30°19′ N, 81°25′ W **96**
Atlantic Beach, *N.C., U.S.* 34°42′ N, 76°46′ W **96**
Atlantic Ocean 38°49′ N, 72°7′ W **253**
Atlantic-Indian Ridge, *Indian Ocean* 53°30′ S, 21°10′ E **255**
Atlántico, adm. division, *Col.* 10°25′ N, 75°5′ W **136**
Atlántida, *Uru.* 34°46′ S, 55°43′ W **139**
Atlantis Fracture Zone, *North Atlantic Ocean* 29°7′ N, 40°8′ W **253**
Atlantis Ii Fracture Zone, *Indian Ocean* 34°58′ S, 57°3′ E **254**
Atlas Mountains, *Africa* 35°53′ N, 0°28′ E **164**
Atlas Saharien, mountains, *Alg.* 35°5′ N, 3°42′ E **150**
Atlin, *Can.* 59°35′ N, 133°44′ W **108**
'Atlit, *Israel* 32°41′ N, 34°56′ E **194**
Atlixco, *Mex.* 18°51′ N, 98°27′ W **114**
Atmakur, *India* 14°39′ N, 79°38′ E **188**
Atmakur, *India* 18°44′ N, 78°35′ E **188**
Atmautluak, *Alas., U.S.* 60°49′ N, 162°33′ W **98**
Atmore, *Ala., U.S.* 31°0′ N, 87°30′ W **103**
Atna Peak, *Can.* 53°55′ N, 128°10′ W **108**
Atocha, *Bol.* 20°60′ S, 66°20′ W **137**
Atoka, *N. Mex., U.S.* 32°46′ N, 104°24′ W **92**

B

Baena, *Sp.* 37°37′ N, 4°21′ W **164**
Baengnyeongdo, island, *S. Korea* 37°50′ N, 123°23′ E **198**
Baeza, *Sp.* 37°59′ N, 3°28′ W **164**
Bafang, *Cameroon* 5°8′ N, 10°10′ E **222**
Bafarara, *Mali* 15°23′ N, 11°29′ W **222**
Baffin Bay 73°51′ N, 73°33′ W **106**
Bafia, *Cameroon* 4°42′ N, 11°14′ E **222**
Bafing, river, *Guinea* 12°23′ N, 10°13′ W **222**
Bafoulabé, *Mali* 13°49′ N, 10°52′ W **222**
Bafousam, *Cameroon* 5°27′ N, 10°23′ E **222**
Bāfq, *Iran* 31°32′ N, 55°22′ E **180**
Bafra, *Turk.* 41°33′ N, 35°54′ E **156**
Bafra Burnu, *Turk.* 41°45′ N, 35°24′ E **156**
Bāft, *Iran* 29°16′ N, 56°39′ E **196**
Bafuka, *Dem. Rep. of the Congo* 4°9′ N, 27°52′ E **224**
Bafwabalinga, *Dem. Rep. of the Congo* 0°54′ N, 27°1′ E **224**
Bafwaboli, *Dem. Rep. of the Congo* 0°42′ N, 26°7′ E **224**
Bafwasende, *Dem. Rep. of the Congo* 1°8′ N, 27°11′ E **224**
Bagabag, island, *P.N.G.* 4°48′ S, 146°17′ E **192**
Bagadó, *Col.* 5°22′ N, 76°28′ W **136**
Bagalkot, *India* 16°10′ N, 75°42′ E **188**
Bagam, spring, *Niger* 15°40′ N, 6°34′ E **222**
Bagamoyo, *Tanzania* 6°23′ S, 38°55′ E **224**
Bagan, *Russ.* 54°3′ N, 77°45′ E **184**
Bagan Datoh, *Malaysia* 3°58′ N, 100°47′ E **196**
Bagan Serai, *Malaysia* 5°1′ N, 100°31′ E **196**
Bagana, *Nig.* 7°58′ N, 7°34′ E **222**
Baganga, *Philippines* 7°37′ N, 126°33′ E **203**
Bagansiapiapi, *Indonesia* 2°12′ N, 100°49′ E **196**
Bagan'yuvom, *Russ.* 66°5′ N, 58°2′ E **154**
Bagaroua, *Niger* 14°30′ N, 4°25′ E **222**
Bagata, *Dem. Rep. of the Congo* 3°49′ S, 17°56′ E **218**
Bagatogo, *Côte d'Ivoire* 8°42′ N, 6°42′ W **222**
Bagdad, *Ariz., U.S.* 34°34′ N, 113°12′ W **92**
Bagdad, *Fla., U.S.* 30°35′ N, 87°2′ W **96**
Bagdarin, *Russ.* 54°28′ N, 113°39′ E **190**
Bagé, *Braz.* 31°21′ S, 54°8′ W **139**
Bågede, *Nor.* 64°21′ N, 14°48′ E **152**
Baggs, *Wyo., U.S.* 41°2′ N, 107°40′ W **90**
Baghdād, *Iraq* 33°21′ N, 44°23′ E **180**
Bagheria, *It.* 38°4′ N, 13°30′ E **156**
Bāghīn, *Iran* 30°9′ N, 56°51′ E **196**
Baghlan, *Afghan.* 36°11′ N, 68°48′ E **186**
Baghran Khowleh, *Afghan.* 32°57′ N, 64°58′ E **186**
Bağırpaşa Dağı, peak, *Turk.* 39°28′ N, 40°2′ E **195**
Bağışlı, *Turk.* 37°51′ N, 44°0′ E **195**
Bagley, *Minn., U.S.* 47°30′ N, 95°25′ W **90**
Bagni del Masino, *It.* 46°15′ N, 9°35′ E **167**
Bagno di Romagna, *It.* 43°50′ N, 11°56′ E **167**
Bagnols-les-Bains, *Fr.* 44°31′ N, 3°40′ E **150**
Bagnone, *It.* 44°19′ N, 9°59′ E **167**
Bago, *Myanmar* 17°20′ N, 96°29′ E **202**
Bagodar, *India* 24°4′ N, 85°49′ E **197**
Bagoé, river, *Mali* 11°44′ N, 6°22′ W **222**
Bagot, Mount, *Can.* 59°20′ N, 135°8′ W **108**
Bagrationovsk, *Russ.* 54°22′ N, 20°31′ E **166**
Bagrax see Bohu, *China* 41°56′ N, 86°40′ E **184**
Bagrdan, *Serb. and Mont.* 44°4′ N, 21°9′ E **168**
Baguia, *Timor-Leste* 8°33′ S, 126°39′ E **238**
Baguio, *Philippines* 16°23′ N, 120°34′ E **203**
Baguio Point, *Philippines* 17°31′ N, 122°11′ E **203**
Bagzane, Monts, *Niger* 17°49′ N, 8°37′ E **222**
Bahabón de Esgueva, *Sp.* 41°51′ N, 3°44′ W **164**
Bahama Islands, *North Atlantic Ocean* 23°51′ N, 76°7′ W **253**
Bahamas 26°0′ N, 77°0′ W **118**
Baharak, *Afghan.* 37°0′ N, 70°52′ E **186**
Baharampur, *India* 24°3′ N, 88°16′ E **188**
Baḥarîya, El Wâḥât el, *Egypt* 27°49′ N, 28°21′ E **180**
Bahau, *Malaysia* 2°50′ N, 102°24′ E **196**
Bahawalnagar, *Pak.* 30°2′ N, 73°16′ E **186**
Bahawalpur, *Pak.* 29°24′ N, 71°40′ E **186**
Bahçe, *Turk.* 37°14′ N, 36°35′ E **156**
Bahçesaray, *Turk.* 38°4′ N, 42°47′ E **195**
Bahdanaw, *Belarus* 54°10′ N, 26°8′ E **166**
Bahdur Island, *Sudan* 17°59′ N, 37°52′ E **182**
Bäherden, *Turkm.* 38°22′ N, 57°10′ E **160**
Bahi, *Tanzania* 5°57′ S, 35°19′ E **224**
Bahia, adm. division, *Braz.* 14°7′ S, 43°29′ W **138**
Bahía Blanca, *Arg.* 38°43′ S, 62°17′ W **139**
Bahía de Caráquez, *Ecua.* 0°42′ N, 80°19′ W **130**
Bahía de Loreto National Park, *Mex.* 25°52′ N, 111°32′ W **238**
Bahía de los Ángeles, *Mex.* 28°56′ N, 113°37′ W **92**
Bahía, Islas de la, islands, *Isla de Roatán* 16°27′ N, 87°19′ W **115**
Bahía Kino, *Mex.* 28°49′ N, 111°55′ W **92**
Bahía Laura, *Arg.* 48°22′ S, 66°30′ W **134**
Bahia see Salvador, *Braz.* 12°59′ S, 38°28′ W **132**
Bahía Solano (Puerto Mutis), *Col.* 6°12′ N, 77°25′ W **136**
Bahía Tortugas, *Mex.* 27°41′ N, 114°52′ W **112**
Bahir Dar, *Eth.* 11°31′ N, 37°21′ E **182**
Bahlah, *Oman* 22°57′ N, 57°15′ E **182**
Bahr el 'Arab, river, *Sudan* 10°4′ N, 25°6′ E **224**
Bahr ez Zaraf, river, *Sudan* 7°42′ N, 30°43′ E **224**
Bahr Kéita (Doka), river, *Chad* 9°8′ N, 18°38′ E **218**
Bahr Salamat, river, *Chad* 10°17′ N, 19°27′ E **216**
Bahrah, oil field, *Kuwait* 29°39′ N, 47°49′ E **196**
Bahraich, *India* 27°32′ N, 81°36′ E **197**
Bahrain 26°0′ N, 51°0′ E **196**
Bahrain, Gulf of 25°31′ N, 50°13′ E **196**
Bāhū Kalāt, *Iran* 25°44′ N, 61°25′ E **182**
Bahuaja-Sonene National Park, *Peru* 13°28′ S, 69°24′ W **137**
Bai Bung, Mui, *Vietnam* 8°15′ N, 104°19′ E **202**
Baia, *Rom.* 44°43′ N, 28°40′ E **156**
Baia de Aramă, *Rom.* 44°59′ N, 22°49′ E **168**
Baia de Arieş, *Rom.* 46°21′ N, 23°16′ E **168**
Baía dos Tigres, *Angola* 16°38′ S, 11°40′ E **220**
Baia Mare, *Rom.* 47°39′ N, 23°36′ E **168**
Baibokoum, *Chad* 7°40′ N, 15°42′ E **218**
Baicheng, *China* 45°35′ N, 122°50′ E **198**
Baicheng, *China* 41°46′ N, 81°51′ E **184**
Baidoa see Baydhabo, *Somalia* 3°5′ N, 43°41′ E **218**
Baie-Comeau, *Can.* 49°13′ N, 68°10′ W **111**
Baie-du-Poste see Mistassini, *Can.* 50°24′ N, 73°50′ W **110**
Baie-Johan-Beetz, *Can.* 50°17′ N, 62°49′ W **111**
Baie-Sainte-Catherine, *Can.* 48°6′ N, 69°44′ W **94**
Baie-Sainte-Claire, site, *Can.* 49°52′ N, 64°35′ W **111**
Baie-Saint-Paul, *Can.* 47°26′ N, 70°31′ W **94**
Baihar, *India* 22°7′ N, 80°33′ E **197**
Baihe, *China* 42°22′ N, 128°7′ E **198**
Ba'ījī, *Iraq* 34°54′ N, 43°27′ E **180**
Baijnath, *India* 29°57′ N, 79°37′ E **188**
Baikal, Lake, *Russ.* 52°49′ N, 106°59′ E **238**
Baikha, *Russ.* 64°54′ N, 88°0′ E **169**
Baikonur Cosmodrome, spaceport, *Kaz.* 46°6′ N, 63°9′ E **184**
Baile Átha Cliath see Dublin, *Ire.* 53°18′ N, 6°26′ W **150**
Băile Herculane, *Rom.* 44°54′ N, 22°26′ E **168**
Bailén, *Sp.* 38°5′ N, 3°46′ W **164**
Bailey Island, *Me., U.S.* 43°43′ N, 69°60′ W **104**
Bailingmiao see Darhan Muminggan Lianheqi, *China* 41°41′ N, 110°23′ E **198**
Bailique, *Braz.* 1°0′ N, 50°3′ W **130**
Bailique, Ilha, island, *Braz.* 1°4′ N, 49°56′ W **130**
Bailleul, *Fr.* 50°43′ N, 2°44′ E **163**
Baillie Islands, *Beaufort Sea* 70°39′ N, 129°39′ W **98**
Baillieu Peak, *Antarctica* 67°57′ S, 60°27′ E **248**
Bailong, river, *China* 33°26′ N, 104°17′ E **198**
Bailundo, *Angola* 12°13′ S, 15°51′ E **220**
Bainang, *China* 29°13′ N, 89°15′ E **197**
Bainbridge, *Ga., U.S.* 30°53′ N, 84°34′ W **96**
Bainbridge, *Ind., U.S.* 39°45′ N, 86°49′ W **102**
Bainbridge, *Ohio, U.S.* 39°13′ N, 83°16′ W **102**
Bainbridge Island, *Wash., U.S.* 47°37′ N, 122°32′ W **100**
Baingoin, *China* 31°37′ N, 89°51′ E **188**
Bainville, *Mont., U.S.* 48°7′ N, 104°15′ W **90**
Baiona, *Sp.* 42°6′ N, 8°53′ W **150**
Baiquan, *China* 47°37′ N, 126°4′ E **198**
Bā'ir, *Jordan* 30°45′ N, 36°40′ E **194**
Bairab Co, lake, *China* 34°55′ N, 82°29′ E **188**
Baird, *Miss., U.S.* 33°23′ N, 90°36′ W **103**
Baird, *Tex., U.S.* 32°23′ N, 99°24′ W **92**
Baird Inlet 60°44′ N, 164°34′ W **98**
Baird, Mount, *Idaho, U.S.* 43°21′ N, 111°11′ W **90**
Baird Mountains, *Alas., U.S.* 67°24′ N, 161°29′ W **98**
Bairiki see Tarawa, *Kiribati* 1°15′ N, 169°58′ E **242**
Bairin Youqi, *China* 43°30′ N, 118°40′ E **198**
Bairin Zuoqi, *China* 43°59′ N, 119°24′ E **198**
Bairoil, *Wyo., U.S.* 42°15′ N, 107°33′ W **90**
Baisha, *China* 29°31′ N, 119°15′ E **198**
Baishan, *China* 42°38′ N, 127°12′ E **200**
Baiso, *It.* 44°29′ N, 10°37′ E **167**
Baitadi, *Nepal* 29°34′ N, 80°26′ E **197**
Baixo Guandu, *Braz.* 19°32′ S, 40°59′ W **138**
Baiyin, *China* 36°34′ N, 104°15′ E **198**
Baiyuda, spring, *Sudan* 17°29′ N, 32°8′ E **182**
Baja, *Hung.* 46°10′ N, 18°57′ E **168**
Baja California, region, *North America* 31°27′ N, 115°59′ W **92**
Baja California Sur, adm. division, *Mex.* 27°30′ N, 113°42′ W **112**
Baja, Punta, *Mex.* 28°17′ N, 111°59′ W **92**
Baja, Punta, *Mex.* 29°59′ N, 115°58′ W **92**
Bajag, *India* 22°42′ N, 81°21′ E **197**
Baján, *Mex.* 26°32′ N, 101°15′ W **114**
Bājgīrān, *Iran* 37°37′ N, 58°24′ E **180**
Bajiazi, *China* 42°41′ N, 129°9′ E **200**
Bājil, *Yemen* 14°58′ N, 43°15′ E **182**
Bajina Bašta, *Serb. and Mont.* 43°58′ N, 19°35′ E **168**
Bajitpur, *Bangladesh* 24°9′ N, 90°54′ E **197**
Bajmok, *Serb. and Mont.* 45°57′ N, 19°24′ E **168**
Bajo Baudó, *Col.* 4°57′ N, 77°22′ W **136**
Bajoga, *Nig.* 10°51′ N, 11°17′ E **222**
Bajovo Polje, *Serb. and Mont.* 43°0′ N, 18°53′ E **168**
Bajram Curri, *Alban.* 42°21′ N, 20°3′ E **168**
Bajzë, *Alban.* 42°16′ N, 19°26′ E **168**
Bak, *Hung.* 46°43′ N, 16°51′ E **168**
Bakaba, *Chad* 7°43′ N, 16°54′ E **218**
Bakal, *Russ.* 54°59′ N, 58°51′ E **154**
Bakala, *Cen. Af. Rep.* 6°9′ N, 20°21′ E **218**
Bakałarzewo, *Pol.* 54°5′ N, 22°38′ E **166**
Bakaly, *Russ.* 55°11′ N, 53°50′ E **154**
Bakanas, *Kaz.* 44°49′ N, 76°17′ E **184**
Bakaoré, *Chad* 15°17′ N, 21°47′ E **216**
Bakchar, *Russ.* 56°59′ N, 82°4′ E **169**
Bakel, *Senegal* 14°53′ N, 12°31′ W **222**
Baker, *Calif., U.S.* 35°16′ N, 116°5′ W **101**
Baker, *La., U.S.* 30°35′ N, 91°10′ W **103**
Baker, *Mont., U.S.* 46°20′ N, 104°18′ W **90**
Baker, *Nev., U.S.* 39°0′ N, 114°8′ W **92**
Baker, *Oreg., U.S.* 44°46′ N, 117°52′ W **90**
Baker Foreland, *Can.* 62°46′ N, 90°36′ W **106**
Baker Island, *U.S.* 0°18′ N, 176°37′ W **238**
Baker Lake, *Can.* 62°18′ N, 99°20′ W **106**
Baker Lake, *Can.* 64°19′ N, 96°7′ W **73**
Baker Lake, *Wash., U.S.* 48°42′ N, 121°52′ W **100**
Baker, Mount, *Wash., U.S.* 48°46′ N, 121°51′ W **100**
Bakersfield, *Calif., U.S.* 35°22′ N, 119°1′ W **101**
Bakewell, *U.K.* 53°12′ N, 1°41′ W **162**
Bakhanay, *Russ.* 66°16′ N, 123°37′ E **173**
Bakhchysaray, *Ukr.* 44°45′ N, 33°51′ E **156**
Bakhma Dam, *Iraq* 36°31′ N, 44°10′ E **195**
Bakhmach, *Ukr.* 51°11′ N, 32°48′ E **158**
Bakhta, *Russ.* 62°19′ N, 89°10′ E **160**
Bakhta, river, *Russ.* 63°49′ N, 91°20′ E **169**
Bakhtegān, Daryācheh-ye, lake, *Iran* 29°21′ N, 53°32′ E **196**
Bakı (Baku), *Azerb.* 40°23′ N, 49°44′ E **195**
Baki, spring, *Chad* 16°58′ N, 21°10′ E **216**
Bakin Birji, *Niger* 14°10′ N, 8°52′ E **222**
Bakırdağı, *Turk.* 38°12′ N, 35°47′ E **156**
Bako, *Côte d'Ivoire* 9°7′ N, 7°36′ W **222**
Bako, *Eth.* 5°50′ N, 36°37′ E **224**
Bakony, *Hung.* 47°17′ N, 17°23′ E **168**
Bakouma, *Cen. Af. Rep.* 5°42′ N, 22°50′ E **218**
Bakoye, river, *Africa* 12°50′ N, 9°26′ W **222**
Bakr Uzyak, *Russ.* 52°59′ N, 58°36′ E **154**
Baktalórántháza, *Hung.* 48°0′ N, 22°3′ E **168**
Baku see Bakı, *Azerb.* 40°23′ N, 49°44′ E **195**
Bakundi, *Nig.* 8°1′ N, 10°45′ E **222**
Bakungan, *Indonesia* 2°58′ N, 97°29′ E **196**
Bakuriani, *Ga.* 41°44′ N, 43°31′ E **195**
Bakutis Coast, *Antarctica* 74°60′ S, 115°49′ W **248**
Bakwanga see Mbuji-Mayi, *Dem. Rep. of the Congo* 6°10′ S, 23°36′ E **224**
Bala, *Senegal* 14°1′ N, 13°11′ W **222**
Bâlâ, *Turk.* 39°32′ N, 33°7′ E **156**
Bala, *U.K.* 52°54′ N, 3°37′ W **162**
Balabac, *Philippines* 8°1′ N, 117°2′ E **203**
Balabac, island, *Philippines* 7°49′ N, 115°56′ E **192**
Balabac Strait 7°38′ N, 116°33′ E **203**
Bălăciţa, *Rom.* 44°23′ N, 23°7′ E **168**
Balaena Islands, *Indian Ocean* 65°59′ S, 112°14′ E **248**
Balaghat, *India* 21°49′ N, 80°13′ E **197**
Balaguer, *Sp.* 41°47′ N, 0°46′ E **164**
Balaka, *Malawi* 14°54′ S, 34°56′ E **224**
Balakän, *Azerb.* 41°43′ N, 46°25′ E **195**
Balakété, *Cen. Af. Rep.* 6°54′ N, 19°57′ E **218**
Balakhna, *Russ.* 56°25′ N, 43°37′ E **154**
Balaki, *Guinea* 12°12′ N, 11°52′ W **222**
Balaklava, *Ukr.* 44°30′ N, 33°34′ E **158**
Balakliya, *Ukr.* 49°29′ N, 36°52′ E **158**
Balakovo, *Russ.* 52°0′ N, 47°50′ E **158**
Balama, *Mozambique* 13°15′ S, 38°38′ E **224**
Balancán, *Mex.* 17°47′ N, 91°34′ W **115**
Balangir, *India* 20°42′ N, 83°28′ E **188**
Balanikha, *Russ.* 65°56′ N, 43°19′ E **154**
Balao, *Ecua.* 3°2′ S, 79°48′ W **130**
Balashivka, *Ukr.* 50°59′ N, 26°57′ E **152**
Balashov, *Russ.* 51°29′ N, 43°10′ E **158**
Balástya, *Hung.* 46°25′ N, 20°1′ E **168**
Balâţ, *Egypt* 25°33′ N, 29°14′ E **226**
Balatina, *Mold.* 47°41′ N, 27°20′ E **158**
Balatonföldvár, *Hung.* 46°50′ N, 17°51′ E **168**
Balatonfüred, *Hung.* 46°57′ N, 17°53′ E **168**
Balavé, *Burkina Faso* 12°23′ N, 4°11′ W **222**
Balazote, *Sp.* 38°53′ N, 2°9′ W **164**
Balbina, Represa da, dam, *Braz.* 1°25′ S, 60°25′ W **130**
Balcad, *Somalia* 2°18′ N, 45°26′ E **218**
Balcarce, *Arg.* 37°51′ S, 58°17′ W **139**
Balcarres, *Can.* 50°47′ N, 103°33′ W **90**
Balchik, *Bulg.* 43°26′ N, 28°11′ E **156**
Balclutha, *N.Z.* 46°15′ S, 169°42′ E **240**
Bald Butte, peak, *Oreg., U.S.* 43°40′ N, 119°27′ W **90**
Bald Eagle Mountain, *Pa., U.S.* 40°59′ N, 77°48′ W **94**
Bald Knob, *Ark., U.S.* 35°17′ N, 91°35′ W **96**
Bald Mountain, peak, *Calif., U.S.* 40°54′ N, 121°11′ W **90**
Bald Mountain, peak, *Can.* 54°5′ N, 61°29′ W **111**
Bald Mountain, peak, *Idaho, U.S.* 44°20′ N, 114°26′ W **90**
Bald Mountain, peak, *Nev., U.S.* 38°34′ N, 117°8′ W **90**
Bald Mountain, peak, *Oreg., U.S.* 44°33′ N, 117°60′ W **90**
Bald Mountain, peak, *Vt., U.S.* 44°45′ N, 72°5′ W **94**
Baldhill Dam, *N. Dak., U.S.* 47°19′ N, 98°45′ W **82**
Baldock Lake, *Can.* 56°32′ N, 98°25′ W **108**
Baldone, *Latv.* 56°44′ N, 24°23′ E **166**
Baldwin, *La., U.S.* 29°49′ N, 91°33′ W **103**
Baldwin, *Mich., U.S.* 43°53′ N, 85°52′ W **102**
Baldwinville, *Mass., U.S.* 42°36′ N, 72°5′ W **104**
Baldwyn, *Miss., U.S.* 34°30′ N, 88°38′ W **96**
Baldy Mountain, peak, *Can.* 51°28′ N, 120°6′ W **90**
Baldy Mountain, peak, *Can.* 51°27′ N, 100°49′ W **90**
Baldy Mountain, peak, *Can.* 49°8′ N, 119°20′ W **90**
Baldy Mountain, peak, *Mont., U.S.* 45°20′ N, 113°7′ W **90**
Baldy Peak, *Ariz., U.S.* 33°53′ N, 109°37′ W **92**
Bale Mountains National Park, *Eth.* 6°33′ N, 38°57′ E **224**
Balearic Islands, *Sp.* 40°4′ N, 3°1′ E **164**
Balearic Sea 40°47′ N, 1°23′ E **150**
Baleia, Ponta da, *Braz.* 17°40′ S, 39°9′ W **132**
Baleine, Rivière à la, river, *Can.* 57°24′ N, 67°59′ W **106**
Balen, *Belg.* 51°9′ N, 5°9′ E **167**
Baler, *Philippines* 15°46′ N, 121°32′ E **203**
Balerma, *Sp.* 36°43′ N, 2°54′ W **164**
Baleshwar, *India* 21°29′ N, 86°53′ E **188**
Baley, *Russ.* 51°36′ N, 116°35′ E **238**
Baléya, *Mali* 12°16′ N, 9°58′ W **222**
Baleyara, *Niger* 13°56′ N, 2°50′ E **222**
Balezino, *Russ.* 57°57′ N, 53°5′ E **154**
Balguntay, *China* 42°46′ N, 86°18′ E **184**
Balḥāf, *Yemen* 14°1′ N, 48°10′ E **182**
Balḥo, *Djibouti* 12°2′ N, 42°12′ E **182**
Bali, *India* 25°13′ N, 73°16′ E **186**
Bali, island, *Indonesia* 9°21′ S, 114°38′ E **192**
Bali Sea 7°47′ S, 114°55′ E **192**
Baliangao, *Philippines* 8°40′ N, 123°37′ E **203**
Balige, *Indonesia* 2°21′ N, 99°3′ E **196**
Balık Göl, lake, *Turk.* 41°34′ N, 35°44′ E **156**
Balıkesir, *Turk.* 39°38′ N, 27°51′ E **156**
Balikpapan, *Indonesia* 1°12′ S, 116°46′ E **192**
Baling, *Malaysia* 5°40′ N, 100°54′ E **196**
Balinţ, *Rom.* 45°49′ N, 21°51′ E **168**
Balintang Channel 19°44′ N, 121°25′ E **203**
Balipara, *India* 26°48′ N, 92°43′ E **188**
Baliza, *Braz.* 16°14′ S, 52°25′ W **138**
Balkan Mountians, *Bulg.* 43°16′ N, 22°39′ E **168**
Balkanabat (Nebitdag), *Turkm.* 39°31′ N, 54°21′ E **180**
Balkány, *Hung.* 47°46′ N, 21°49′ E **168**
Balkany, *Russ.* 53°29′ N, 59°34′ E **154**
Balkashīno, *Kaz.* 52°27′ N, 68°40′ E **184**
Balkh, *Afghan.* 36°46′ N, 66°58′ E **186**
Balkhash, Lake, *Kaz.* 46°0′ N, 69°44′ E **173**
Ball Lake, lake, *Can.* 50°13′ N, 94°17′ W **90**
Ballâna, *Egypt* 24°17′ N, 32°58′ E **182**
Ballantine, *Mont., U.S.* 45°55′ N, 108°9′ W **90**
Ballarat, *Austral.* 37°34′ S, 143°55′ E **231**
Ballé, *Mali* 15°21′ N, 8°36′ W **222**
Ballenas, Canal de 29°14′ N, 113°60′ W **92**
Balleny Islands, *South Pacific Ocean* 66°21′ S, 162°20′ E **255**
Balleza, *Mex.* 26°57′ N, 106°22′ W **112**
Ballinger, *Tex., U.S.* 31°43′ N, 99°57′ W **92**
Ballobar, *Sp.* 41°36′ N, 0°11′ E **164**
Ball's Pyramid, island, *Austral.* 32°15′ S, 157°57′ E **230**
Ballstad, *Nor.* 68°4′ N, 13°28′ E **152**
Ballston Spa, *N.Y., U.S.* 43°0′ N, 73°52′ W **104**
Balmaceda, *Chile* 45°59′ S, 71°48′ W **123**
Balmertown, *Can.* 51°3′ N, 93°45′ W **90**
Balmoral Castle, site, *U.K.* 57°0′ N, 3°20′ W **150**
Balmorhea, *Tex., U.S.* 30°57′ N, 103°45′ W **92**
Balnearia, *Arg.* 30°60′ S, 62°40′ W **139**
Balneario de los Novillos see I, *Mex.* 29°22′ N, 101°19′ W **112**
Balod, *India* 20°44′ N, 81°12′ E **188**
Balombo, *Angola* 12°22′ S, 14°47′ E **220**
Balonne, river, *Austral.* 28°41′ S, 147°59′ E **230**
Balotra, *India* 25°51′ N, 72°14′ E **186**
Balqash, *Kaz.* 46°52′ N, 74°58′ E **184**
Balqash Köli, lake, *Kaz.* 45°35′ N, 73°9′ E **190**
Balş, *Rom.* 44°22′ N, 24°4′ E **156**
Balsas, *Braz.* 7°32′ S, 46°3′ W **130**
Balsas, *Mex.* 17°59′ N, 99°46′ W **114**
Balsas, river, *Braz.* 8°24′ S, 46°19′ W **130**
Balsas, river, *Braz.* 10°47′ S, 47°39′ W **130**
Balsas, river, *Mex.* 18°29′ N, 100°56′ W **114**
Balta, *N. Dak., U.S.* 48°9′ N, 100°3′ W **90**
Balta, *Rom.* 44°52′ N, 22°39′ E **168**
Balta, *Ukr.* 47°55′ N, 29°38′ E **156**
Balta Albă, *Rom.* 45°18′ N, 27°16′ E **156**
Baltasar Brum, *Uru.* 30°43′ S, 57°20′ W **139**
Bălţi, *Mold.* 47°45′ N, 27°57′ E **152**
Baltic Sea 59°13′ N, 17°48′ E **152**
Balṭîm, *Egypt* 31°34′ N, 31°4′ E **180**
Baltimore, *Md., U.S.* 39°17′ N, 76°38′ W **94**
Baltimore, *Ohio, U.S.* 39°50′ N, 82°36′ W **102**
Baltit, *Pak.* 36°19′ N, 74°41′ E **186**
Baltiysk, *Russ.* 54°39′ N, 19°54′ E **166**
Baltrum, island, *Ger.* 53°41′ N, 7°26′ E **163**
Balumbal, *Eth.* 8°33′ N, 45°10′ E **218**
Balurghat, *India* 25°12′ N, 88°47′ E **197**
Balvi, *Latv.* 57°6′ N, 27°14′ E **166**
Balya, *Turk.* 39°43′ N, 27°34′ E **156**
Balykcha, *Russ.* 51°18′ N, 87°43′ E **184**
Balykchy, *Kyrg.* 42°26′ N, 76°10′ E **184**
Balyksa, *Russ.* 53°23′ N, 89°8′ E **184**
Balyqshy, *Kaz.* 47°2′ N, 51°52′ E **158**
Balzola, *It.* 45°11′ N, 8°24′ E **167**
Bam, *Iran* 29°2′ N, 58°23′ E **196**
Bam Co, lake, *China* 31°29′ N, 90°37′ E **188**
Bama, *Nig.* 11°32′ N, 13°41′ E **216**
Bamako, *Mali* 12°37′ N, 8°10′ W **222**
Bamba, *Mali* 17°2′ N, 1°26′ W **222**
Bambafouga, *Guinea* 10°11′ N, 11°53′ W **222**
Bambamarca, *Peru* 6°35′ S, 78°34′ W **130**
Bambara, *Chad* 8°54′ N, 18°34′ E **218**
Bambara, *Mali* 13°25′ N, 4°11′ W **222**
Bambari, *Cen. Af. Rep.* 5°45′ N, 20°39′ E **218**
Bambesa, *Dem. Rep. of the Congo* 3°24′ N, 25°43′ E **224**
Bambey, *Senegal* 14°44′ N, 16°19′ W **222**
Bambili, *Dem. Rep. of the Congo* 3°36′ N, 26°7′ E **224**
Bambinga, *Dem. Rep. of the Congo* 3°45′ S, 18°51′ E **218**
Bambio, *Cen. Af. Rep.* 3°59′ N, 16°58′ E **218**
Bambouti, *Cen. Af. Rep.* 5°23′ N, 27°11′ E **224**
Bambuí, *Braz.* 20°2′ S, 45°57′ W **138**
Bambuyka, *Russ.* 55°46′ N, 115°33′ E **190**
Bamenda, *Cameroon* 5°53′ N, 10°9′ E **222**
Bamfield, *Can.* 48°47′ N, 125°8′ W **100**
Bamian, *Afghan.* 34°51′ N, 67°51′ E **186**
Bamingui, *Cen. Af. Rep.* 7°30′ N, 20°12′ E **218**
Bampton, *U.K.* 51°44′ N, 1°33′ W **162**
Bampton, *U.K.* 50°59′ N, 3°29′ W **162**
Bamy, *Turkm.* 38°43′ N, 56°49′ E **180**
Ban Bang Hin, *Thai.* 9°32′ N, 98°35′ E **202**
Ban Don, *Vietnam* 12°54′ N, 107°47′ E **202**
Ban Don, Ao 9°17′ N, 99°0′ E **202**
Ban Don see Surat Thani, *Thai.* 9°7′ N, 99°20′ E **202**
Ban Dong, *Thai.* 19°33′ N, 100°57′ E **202**
Ban Hinboun, *Laos* 17°37′ N, 104°37′ E **202**
Ban Khai, *Thai.* 12°47′ N, 101°20′ E **202**
Ban Nam-Om, *Laos* 20°43′ N, 101°4′ E **202**
Ban Napè, *Laos* 18°19′ N, 105°6′ E **202**
Ban Phai, *Thai.* 16°6′ N, 102°41′ E **202**
Ban Sanam Chai, *Thai.* 7°34′ N, 100°25′ E **196**
Ban Taphan, *Laos* 15°56′ N, 105°25′ E **202**
Ban Xénô, *Laos* 16°41′ N, 105°0′ E **202**
Bañados de Otuquis, marsh, *Bol.* 20°54′ S, 60°29′ W **132**
Bañados del Izozog, marsh, *Bol.* 18°55′ S, 62°31′ W **132**
Banak, *Nor.* 70°2′ N, 25°1′ E **152**
Banalia, *Dem. Rep. of the Congo* 1°33′ N, 25°25′ E **224**
Banam, *Cambodia* 11°19′ N, 105°16′ E **202**
Banamba, *Mali* 13°34′ N, 7°26′ W **222**
Banana Islands, *North Atlantic Ocean* 7°56′ N, 13°50′ W **222**
Bananfara, *Guinea* 11°19′ N, 8°56′ W **222**
Bananga, *India* 6°56′ N, 93°58′ E **188**
Banankoro, *Guinea* 9°10′ N, 9°18′ W **222**
Banaras see Varanasi, *India* 25°18′ N, 82°57′ E **197**
Banâs, Râs, *Egypt* 23°52′ N, 35°49′ E **182**
Banas, river, *India* 25°5′ N, 74°2′ E **186**
Banatsko Novo Selo, *Serb. and Mont.* 44°59′ N, 20°46′ E **168**
Banaz, *Turk.* 38°44′ N, 29°45′ E **156**
Banbalah, *Tun.* 35°42′ N, 10°48′ E **156**
Banbān, *Saudi Arabia* 24°58′ N, 46°36′ E **196**
Banbar, *China* 31°4′ N, 94°46′ E **188**
Banbury, *U.K.* 52°3′ N, 1°21′ W **162**
Banco, Punta, *C.R.* 8°17′ N, 83°54′ W **115**
Bancroft, *Can.* 45°3′ N, 77°52′ W **94**
Bancroft, *Iowa, U.S.* 43°17′ N, 94°14′ W **94**
Bancroft, *Mich., U.S.* 42°51′ N, 84°4′ W **102**
Banda, *Dem. Rep. of the Congo* 4°8′ N, 27°4′ E **224**
Banda, *India* 24°3′ N, 78°57′ E **197**
Banda, *India* 25°27′ N, 80°19′ E **197**
Banda Aceh, *Indonesia* 5°30′ N, 95°20′ E **196**
Banda, Kepulauan, islands, *Banda Sea* 5°1′ S, 129°26′ E **192**
Banda Nkwanta, *Ghana* 8°22′ N, 2°8′ W **222**
Banda, Pointe, *Gabon* 3°46′ S, 10°57′ E **218**
Banda Sea 5°42′ S, 127°27′ E **254**
Banda Sea 5°13′ S, 123°58′ E **173**
Bandai-Asahi National Park, *Japan* 38°17′ N, 139°38′ E **201**
Bandajuma, *Sierra Leone* 7°35′ N, 11°39′ W **222**
Bandān, *Iran* 31°23′ N, 60°42′ E **180**
Bandar Lampung, *Indonesia* 5°28′ S, 105°7′ E **192**
Bandar Murcaayo, *Somalia* 11°36′ N, 50°26′ E **182**
Bandar see Machilipatnam, *India* 16°11′ N, 81°10′ E **188**
Bandar Seri Begawan, *Brunei* 4°52′ N, 114°50′ E **203**
Bandarban, *Bangladesh* 22°12′ N, 92°11′ E **188**
Bandarbeyla, *Somalia* 9°25′ N, 50°48′ E **216**
Bandar-e 'Abbās, *Iran* 27°11′ N, 56°13′ E **196**
Bandar-e Anzalī, *Iran* 37°30′ N, 49°20′ E **195**
Bandar-e Būshehr, *Iran* 28°54′ N, 50°52′ E **196**
Bandar-e Chārak, *Iran* 26°46′ N, 54°17′ E **196**
Bandar-e Deylam, *Iran* 30°2′ N, 50°13′ E **196**
Bandar-e Khoemir, *Iran* 26°57′ N, 55°34′ E **196**
Bandar-e Khomeynī, *Iran* 30°27′ N, 49°3′ E **180**
Bandar-e Lengeh, *Iran* 26°37′ N, 54°54′ E **196**
Bandar-e Māh Shahr, *Iran* 30°38′ N, 49°12′ E **180**
Bandar-e Maqām, *Iran* 26°58′ N, 53°29′ E **196**
Bandar-e Rīg, *Iran* 29°29′ N, 50°39′ E **196**
Bandar-e Torkaman, *Iran* 36°54′ N, 54°3′ E **180**
Bandau, *Malaysia* 6°33′ N, 116°46′ E **203**
Bandeira, peak, *Braz.* 20°30′ S, 41°53′ W **138**
Bandeirante, *Braz.* 13°43′ S, 50°51′ W **138**
Bandéko, *Congo* 1°56′ N, 17°27′ E **218**
Bandelierkop, *S. Af.* 23°21′ S, 29°49′ E **227**
Bandera, *Arg.* 28°52′ S, 62°17′ W **139**
Bandera, *Tex., U.S.* 29°43′ N, 99°5′ W **92**
Bandiagara, *Mali* 14°20′ N, 3°38′ W **222**
Bandikui, *India* 27°2′ N, 76°35′ E **197**
Bandırma, *Turk.* 40°19′ N, 27°57′ E **156**
Bandon, *Oreg., U.S.* 43°6′ N, 124°24′ W **90**
Bändovan Burnu, *Azerb.* 39°34′ N, 49°20′ E **195**
Bandundu, *Dem. Rep. of the Congo* 3°24′ S, 17°23′ E **218**
Bandundu, adm. division, *Dem. Rep. of the Congo* 4°38′ S, 16°30′ E **218**
Bandung, *Indonesia* 7°1′ S, 107°32′ E **192**
Băneasa, *Rom.* 45°57′ N, 27°55′ E **156**
Bañeres, *Sp.* 38°43′ N, 0°40′ E **164**
Banes, *Cuba* 20°58′ N, 75°44′ W **116**
Banff, *Can.* 51°11′ N, 115°33′ W **108**
Banff National Park, *Can.* 51°29′ N, 116°37′ W **238**
Banfora, *Burkina Faso* 10°38′ N, 4°47′ W **222**
Bang Mun Nak, *Thai.* 16°1′ N, 100°21′ E **202**
Bang Saphan, *Thai.* 11°14′ N, 99°31′ E **202**
Bangalore, *India* 12°59′ N, 77°35′ E **188**
Bangar, *Philippines* 16°54′ N, 120°25′ E **203**
Bangassou, *Cen. Af. Rep.* 4°38′ N, 22°48′ E **207**
Banggai, Kepulauan, islands, *Banda Sea* 2°42′ S, 123°39′ E **192**
Banggi, island, *Malaysia* 7°2′ N, 117°21′ E **192**
Banghāzī (Benghazi), *Lib.* 32°6′ N, 20°4′ E **216**
Banghiang, river, *Laos* 16°17′ N, 105°14′ E **202**
Bangka, island, *Indonesia* 2°24′ S, 106°18′ E **192**
Bangkaru, island, *Indonesia* 1°52′ N, 97°4′ E **196**
Bangkinang, *Indonesia* 0°21′ N, 101°1′ E **196**
Bangkok see Krung Thep, *Thai.* 13°44′ N, 100°24′ E **202**
Bangladesh 24°0′ N, 90°0′ E **188**
Bangor, *Me., U.S.* 44°48′ N, 68°47′ W **111**
Bangor, *Mich., U.S.* 42°18′ N, 86°7′ W **102**
Bangor, *U.K.* 53°13′ N, 4°7′ W **162**
Bangs, *Tex., U.S.* 31°41′ N, 99°8′ W **92**
Bangs, Mount, *Ariz., U.S.* 36°46′ N, 113°54′ W **101**
Bangu, *Dem. Rep. of the Congo* 9°5′ S, 23°43′ E **224**
Bangué, *Cameroon* 3°12′ N, 15°9′ E **218**
Bangued, *Philippines* 17°37′ N, 120°38′ E **203**
Bangui, *Cen. Af. Rep.* 4°21′ N, 18°22′ E **218**
Bangui, *Congo* 2°28′ N, 17°16′ E **218**
Bangui, *Philippines* 18°32′ N, 120°46′ E **203**
Banguru, *Dem. Rep. of the Congo* 0°28′ N, 27°6′ E **224**
Bangwade, *Dem. Rep. of the Congo* 1°0′ N, 25°14′ E **224**
Banh, *Burkina Faso* 14°4′ N, 2°27′ W **222**
Banhine National Park, *Mozambique* 22°54′ S, 32°6′ E **227**
Bani, *Cen. Af. Rep.* 7°7′ N, 22°54′ E **218**
Baní, *Dom. Rep.* 18°16′ N, 70°20′ W **116**
Bani, Jebel, *Mor.* 29°44′ N, 7°57′ W **214**
Bani, river, *Mali* 13°31′ N, 4°52′ W **222**
Banī Sharfā, *Saudi Arabia* 19°38′ N, 41°30′ E **182**
Banī Walīd, *Lib.* 31°46′ N, 14°0′ E **216**
Bania, *Cen. Af. Rep.* 4°6′ N, 16°6′ E **218**
Bania, *Côte d'Ivoire* 9°0′ N, 3°10′ W **222**
Banihal Pass, *India* 33°30′ N, 75°12′ E **186**
Banikoara, *Benin* 11°19′ N, 2°27′ E **222**
Baniou, *Alg.* 35°24′ N, 4°20′ E **150**
Bāniyās, *Syr.* 35°11′ N, 35°57′ E **194**
Banja, *Serb. and Mont.* 43°33′ N, 19°33′ E **168**

Bayfield, *Wis., U.S.* 46°49′ N, 90°50′ W **94**
Bayghanīn, *Kaz.* 48°42′ N, 55°53′ E **158**
Bayḩān al Qişāb, *Yemen* 14°49′ N, 45°46′ E **182**
Baykal, Ozero, lake, *Russ.* 53°48′ N, 103°44′ E **190**
Baykalovo, *Russ.* 57°26′ N, 63°42′ E **154**
Baykalovo, *Russ.* 57°45′ N, 67°40′ E **169**
Baykan, *Turk.* 38°8′ N, 41°47′ E **195**
Baykurt, *China* 39°56′ N, 75°32′ E **184**
Bayliss, Mount, *Antarctica* 73°30′ S, 62°4′ E **248**
Baymak, *Russ.* 52°38′ N, 58°11′ E **154**
Baynū, *Leb.* 34°32′ N, 36°10′ E **194**
Bayombong, *Philippines* 16°29′ N, 121°8′ E **203**
Bayon, *Fr.* 48°28′ N, 6°19′ E **163**
Bayonet Point, *Fla., U.S.* 28°19′ N, 82°43′ W **105**
Bayonne, *Fr.* 43°29′ N, 1°30′ W **164**
Bayonne, *N.J., U.S.* 40°40′ N, 74°8′ W **104**
Bayou La Batre, *Ala., U.S.* 30°23′ N, 88°16′ W **103**
Bayou Macon, river, *La., U.S.* 32°6′ N, 91°32′ W **103**
Bayovar, *Peru* 5°47′ S, 81°4′ W **130**
Bayport, *Minn., U.S.* 45°0′ N, 92°48′ W **94**
Bayqongyr, *Kaz.* 47°47′ N, 66°0′ E **184**
Bayqongyr, adm. division, *Kaz.* 46°3′ N, 62°27′ E **184**
Bayramaly, *Turkm.* 37°36′ N, 62°10′ E **184**
Bayramiç, *Turk.* 39°48′ N, 26°35′ E **156**
Bayreuth, *Ger.* 49°56′ N, 11°34′ E **152**
Bays, Lake of, *Can.* 45°15′ N, 79°35′ W **94**
Bayshint, *Mongolia* 49°40′ N, 90°20′ E **184**
Bayshonas, *Kaz.* 47°18′ N, 53°0′ E **158**
Bayt al Faqīh, *Yemen* 14°29′ N, 43°16′ E **182**
Bayt Lahiyah, *Gaza Strip* 31°33′ N, 34°30′ E **194**
Bayt Laḩm (Bethlehem), *West Bank* 31°41′ N, 35°12′ E **194**
Baytīn, *West Bank* 31°55′ N, 35°14′ E **194**
Baytown, *Tex., U.S.* 29°43′ N, 94°58′ W **103**
Bayville, *N.Y., U.S.* 40°54′ N, 73°34′ W **104**
Bayyrqum, *Kaz.* 41°54′ N, 68°5′ E **184**
Bayzo, *Niger* 13°52′ N, 4°52′ E **222**
Baza, *Sp.* 37°29′ N, 2°48′ W **164**
Baza'i Gonbad, *Afghan.* 37°13′ N, 74°5′ E **186**
Bazar-Kurgan, *Kyrg.* 41°1′ N, 72°46′ E **197**
Bazarnyy Karabulak, *Russ.* 52°15′ N, 46°27′ E **158**
Bazarsholan, *Kaz.* 48°58′ N, 51°55′ E **158**
Bazartöbe, *Kaz.* 49°23′ N, 51°53′ E **158**
Bazaruto, Ilha do, island, *Mozambique* 21°44′ S, 34°29′ E **227**
Bazber, *Eth.* 10°36′ N, 35°7′ E **224**
Bazhong, *China* 31°53′ N, 106°39′ E **198**
Baziaş, *Rom.* 44°48′ N, 21°22′ E **168**
Bazin, river, *Can.* 47°29′ N, 74°60′ W **94**
Bazkovskaya, *Russ.* 49°33′ N, 41°35′ E **158**
Bazmān, Kūh-e, peak, *Iran* 27°51′ N, 60°2′ E **182**
Bazzano, *It.* 44°30′ N, 11°4′ E **167**
Bcharre, *Leb.* 34°14′ N, 36°0′ E **194**
Be, Nosy, island, *Madagascar* 13°24′ S, 47°23′ E **220**
Beach, *N. Dak., U.S.* 46°53′ N, 104°1′ W **90**
Beach Haven, *N.J., U.S.* 39°33′ N, 74°16′ W **94**
Beacon, *N.Y., U.S.* 41°29′ N, 73°59′ W **104**
Beaconsfield, *U.K.* 51°36′ N, 0°39′ E **162**
Beade, *Sp.* 42°19′ N, 8°10′ W **150**
Beale Air Force Base, *Calif., U.S.* 39°8′ N, 121°30′ W **90**
Beale, Cape, *Can.* 48°37′ N, 125°31′ W **90**
Beaminster, *U.K.* 50°48′ N, 2°44′ W **162**
Beampingaratra, peak, *Madagascar* 24°36′ S, 46°39′ E **220**
Bear Bay 75°23′ N, 88°10′ W **106**
Bear Creek, river, *Colo., U.S.* 37°26′ N, 102°48′ W **80**
Bear Island see Bjørnøya, *Nor.* 73°46′ N, 15°27′ E **160**
Bear Islands see Medvezh'i Ostrova, islands, *East Siberian Sea* 71°5′ N, 151°1′ E **160**
Bear Lake, *Can.* 55°2′ N, 96°49′ W **108**
Bear Lake, *Can.* 56°6′ N, 127°4′ W **108**
Bear Lake, *Mich., U.S.* 44°24′ N, 86°9′ W **94**
Bear Lodge Mountains, *Wyo., U.S.* 44°39′ N, 104°42′ W **90**
Bear Peninsula, *Antarctica* 74°18′ S, 106°40′ W **248**
Bear River, *Utah, U.S.* 41°37′ N, 112°8′ W **90**
Bear, river, *Idaho, U.S.* 42°27′ N, 111°48′ W **90**
Bear River Range, *Utah, U.S.* 41°18′ N, 111°34′ W **90**
Beardmore, *Can.* 49°37′ N, 87°57′ W **94**
Beardstown, *Mo., U.S.* 40°0′ N, 90°25′ W **94**
Béarn, region, *Europe* 42°57′ N, 0°52′ E **164**
Bears Paw Mountains, *Mont., U.S.* 48°18′ N, 109°52′ W **90**
Beas, *Sp.* 37°25′ N, 6°48′ W **164**
Beas de Segura, *Sp.* 38°14′ N, 2°52′ W **164**
Beasain, *Sp.* 43°2′ N, 2°13′ W **164**
Beata, Cabo, *Dom. Rep.* 17°30′ N, 71°22′ W **116**
Beata, Isla, island, *Dom. Rep.* 17°16′ N, 71°33′ W **116**
Beatrice, *Nebr., U.S.* 40°15′ N, 96°45′ W **90**
Beatton River, *Can.* 57°22′ N, 121°27′ W **108**
Beatton, river, *Can.* 57°18′ N, 121°27′ W **108**
Beatty, *Nev., U.S.* 36°54′ N, 116°47′ W **101**
Beattyville, *Can.* 48°51′ N, 77°10′ W **94**
Beatys Butte, peak, *Oreg., U.S.* 42°23′ N, 119°25′ W **90**
Beaucamps, *Fr.* 49°49′ N, 1°47′ E **163**
Beauceville, *Can.* 46°13′ N, 70°46′ W **111**
Beauchêne Island, *U.K.* 52°56′ S, 61°53′ W **134**
Beaufort, *Malaysia* 5°22′ N, 115°46′ E **203**
Beaufort, *S.C., U.S.* 32°24′ N, 80°53′ W **112**
Beaufort Marine Corps Air Station, *S.C., U.S.* 32°29′ N, 80°48′ W **96**
Beaufort Sea 69°54′ N, 141°54′ W **106**
Beaufort Sea 72°45′ N, 137°20′ W **255**
Beaufort see Belfort, ruin(s), *Leb.* 33°19′ N, 35°30′ E **194**
Beaufort Shelf, *Beaufort Sea* 70°4′ N, 142°6′ W **255**
Beaufort Slope, *Beaufort Sea* 70°37′ N, 141°34′ W **255**
Beaufort West, *S. Af.* 32°21′ S, 22°35′ E **227**
Beaugency, *Fr.* 47°47′ N, 1°37′ E **150**
Beaumaris, *U.K.* 53°15′ N, 4°5′ W **162**
Beaumetz-lès-Loges, *Fr.* 50°13′ N, 2°38′ E **163**
Beaumont, *Belg.* 50°14′ N, 4°14′ E **163**
Beaumont, *Calif., U.S.* 33°56′ N, 116°59′ W **101**
Beaumont, *Fr.* 49°8′ N, 2°16′ E **163**
Beaumont, *Miss., U.S.* 31°8′ N, 88°54′ W **103**
Beaumont, *Tex., U.S.* 30°4′ N, 94°7′ W **103**
Beaumont-le-Roger, *Fr.* 49°5′ N, 0°47′ E **163**
Beaupré, *Can.* 47°2′ N, 70°54′ W **94**
Beauraing, *Belg.* 50°6′ N, 4°56′ E **167**
Beauregard, *Miss., U.S.* 31°43′ N, 90°24′ W **103**
Beausejour, *Can.* 50°3′ N, 96°31′ W **108**
Beauvais, *Fr.* 49°26′ N, 2°5′ E **163**
Beauval, *Can.* 55°9′ N, 107°39′ W **108**
Beauval, *Fr.* 50°5′ N, 2°20′ E **163**
Beauvezer, *Fr.* 44°8′ N, 6°34′ E **167**
Beaver, *Alas., U.S.* 66°14′ N, 147°28′ W **98**
Beaver, *Ohio, U.S.* 39°1′ N, 82°49′ W **102**
Beaver, *Okla., U.S.* 36°47′ N, 100°32′ W **96**
Beaver, *Oreg., U.S.* 45°16′ N, 123°50′ W **90**
Beaver, *Pa., U.S.* 40°41′ N, 80°19′ W **94**
Beaver, *Utah, U.S.* 38°16′ N, 112°38′ W **90**
Beaver, *Wash., U.S.* 48°2′ N, 124°20′ W **100**
Beaver Bay, *Minn., U.S.* 47°14′ N, 91°20′ W **94**
Beaver City, *Nebr., U.S.* 40°7′ N, 99°50′ W **90**
Beaver Creek, *Can.* 62°24′ N, 140°52′ W **98**
Beaver Dam, *Ky., U.S.* 37°24′ N, 86°53′ W **96**
Beaver Dam, *Wis., U.S.* 43°27′ N, 88°50′ W **102**
Beaver Falls, *Pa., U.S.* 40°44′ N, 80°20′ W **94**
Beaver Hill Lake, *Can.* 54°14′ N, 95°24′ W **108**
Beaver Island, *Mich., U.S.* 45°20′ N, 85°49′ W **81**
Beaver Lake, *N. Dak., U.S.* 46°20′ N, 100°7′ W **90**
Beaver, river, *Can.* 60°29′ N, 126°29′ W **108**
Beaver, river, *Can.* 54°40′ N, 112°3′ W **108**
Beaver, river, *Can.* 53°43′ N, 61°38′ W **111**
Beaverdell, *Can.* 49°25′ N, 119°4′ W **90**
Beaverhead Mountains, *Mont., U.S.* 45°36′ N, 113°50′ W **90**
Beaverlodge, *Can.* 55°12′ N, 119°27′ W **108**
Beaverton, *Can.* 44°25′ N, 79°9′ W **94**
Beaverton, *Mich., U.S.* 43°51′ N, 84°30′ W **102**
Beawar, *India* 26°4′ N, 74°18′ E **186**
Bebedouro, *Braz.* 20°57′ S, 48°30′ W **138**
Bebeji, *Nig.* 11°39′ N, 8°16′ E **222**
Bebington, *U.K.* 53°22′ N, 2°60′ W **162**
Béboto, *Chad* 8°17′ N, 16°55′ E **218**
Bebra, *Ger.* 50°58′ N, 9°46′ E **167**
Becán, ruin(s), *Mex.* 18°33′ N, 89°39′ W **115**
Bécancour, *Can.* 46°21′ N, 72°25′ W **94**
Beccles, *U.K.* 52°26′ N, 1°33′ E **163**
Bečej, *Serb. and Mont.* 45°37′ N, 20°2′ E **168**
Béchar, *Alg.* 31°39′ N, 2°13′ W **214**
Becharof Lake, *Alas., U.S.* 58°4′ N, 159°33′ W **106**
Bechater, *Tun.* 37°18′ N, 9°45′ E **156**
Bechem, *Ghana* 7°7′ N, 2°3′ W **222**
Bechetu, *Rom.* 43°46′ N, 23°57′ E **156**
Becker, Mount, *Antarctica* 75°9′ S, 72°53′ W **248**
Becket, *Mass., U.S.* 42°19′ N, 73°6′ W **104**
Beckley, *W. Va., U.S.* 37°46′ N, 81°12′ W **94**
Beckum, *Ger.* 51°45′ N, 8°1′ E **167**
Beckville, *Tex., U.S.* 32°14′ N, 94°28′ W **103**
Beckwourth Pass, *Calif., U.S.* 39°47′ N, 120°8′ W **90**
Beda, oil field, *Lib.* 28°14′ N, 18°44′ E **216**
Bedale, *U.K.* 54°17′ N, 1°36′ W **162**
Beddgelert, *U.K.* 53°0′ N, 4°6′ W **162**
Beddouza, Cap, *Mor.* 32°37′ N, 10°38′ W **214**
Bedēsa, *Eth.* 8°51′ N, 40°45′ E **224**
Bedford, *Can.* 44°43′ N, 63°41′ W **111**
Bedford, *Ind., U.S.* 38°52′ N, 86°29′ W **102**
Bedford, *Iowa, U.S.* 40°39′ N, 94°43′ W **94**
Bedford, *N.H., U.S.* 42°56′ N, 71°32′ W **104**
Bedford, *Pa., U.S.* 40°0′ N, 78°31′ W **94**
Bedford, *S. Af.* 32°41′ S, 26°4′ E **227**
Bedford, *U.K.* 52°8′ N, 0°28′ E **162**
Bedi, *India* 22°32′ N, 70°0′ E **186**
Bednesti, *Can.* 53°51′ N, 123°8′ W **108**
Bednodem'yanovsk, *Russ.* 53°53′ N, 43°10′ E **154**
Bedonia, *It.* 44°30′ N, 9°38′ E **167**
Bédouaram, *Niger* 15°44′ N, 13°8′ E **216**
Bedous, *Fr.* 43°0′ N, 0°36′ E **164**
Bee Ridge, *Fla., U.S.* 27°18′ N, 82°27′ W **105**
Beebe, *Ark., U.S.* 35°3′ N, 91°53′ W **96**
Beebe River, *N.H., U.S.* 43°49′ N, 71°40′ W **104**
Beech Grove, *Ind., U.S.* 39°43′ N, 86°5′ W **102**
Beecher City, *Ill., U.S.* 39°10′ N, 88°47′ W **102**
Beechy, *Can.* 50°53′ N, 107°25′ W **90**
Beer, *Somalia* 9°21′ N, 45°48′ E **216**
Be'ér 'ada, spring, *Israel* 30°19′ N, 34°54′ E **194**
Be'ér Hafir, spring, *Israel* 30°43′ N, 34°35′ E **194**
Be'ér Sheva', *Israel* 31°13′ N, 34°50′ E **180**
Be'ér Sheva' (Beersheba), *Israel* 31°14′ N, 34°47′ E **194**
Beerberg, Grosser, peak, *Ger.* 50°38′ N, 10°38′ E **152**
Beersheba see Be'ér Sheva', *Israel* 31°14′ N, 34°47′ E **194**
Beestekraal, *S. Af.* 25°24′ S, 27°35′ E **227**
Beeston, *U.K.* 52°55′ N, 1°14′ W **162**
Beetz, Lac, lake, *Can.* 50°30′ N, 63°11′ W **111**
Beeville, *Tex., U.S.* 28°23′ N, 97°45′ W **92**
Befale, *Dem. Rep. of the Congo* 0°26′ N, 20°58′ E **218**
Befandriana, *Madagascar* 15°15′ S, 48°35′ E **220**
Befandriana Atsimo, *Madagascar* 22°7′ S, 43°51′ E **220**
Befori, *Dem. Rep. of the Congo* 0°9′ N, 22°17′ E **218**
Befotaka, *Madagascar* 23°48′ S, 47°1′ E **220**
Bega, river, *Rom.* 45°51′ N, 21°56′ E **168**
Begaly, *Kaz.* 49°55′ N, 55°17′ E **158**
Begejski Kanal, canal, *Serb. and Mont.* 45°31′ N, 20°28′ E **168**
Bēgī, *Eth.* 9°20′ N, 34°32′ E **224**
Begonte, *Sp.* 43°8′ N, 7°42′ W **150**
Béguégué, *Chad* 8°53′ N, 18°52′ E **218**
Begunitsy, *Russ.* 59°33′ N, 29°16′ E **152**
Behagle see Laï, *Chad* 9°23′ N, 16°20′ E **216**
Béhague, Pointe, *Fr.* 4°43′ N, 51°56′ W **130**
Behan, *Can.* 55°14′ N, 111°28′ W **108**
Behara, *Madagascar* 24°57′ S, 46°25′ E **220**
Behbehān, *Iran* 30°34′ N, 50°15′ E **180**
Behm Canal 55°45′ N, 132°3′ W **108**
Beho, *Belg.* 50°14′ N, 5°58′ E **167**
Behring Point, *Bahamas* 24°30′ N, 77°46′ W **96**
Behshahr, *Iran* 36°43′ N, 53°33′ E **180**
Bei'an, *China* 48°16′ N, 126°32′ E **198**
Beiarn, *Nor.* 67°0′ N, 14°35′ E **152**
Beida, river, *China* 39°9′ N, 97°39′ E **188**
Beigang, *China* 42°23′ N, 127°28′ E **200**
Beihai, *China* 21°26′ N, 109°8′ E **198**
Beijing, adm. division, *China* 40°32′ N, 116°8′ E **198**
Beijing (Peking), *China* 39°52′ N, 116°9′ E **198**
Beila, Jebel, peak, *Sudan* 13°41′ N, 34°46′ E **182**
Beilen, *Neth.* 52°51′ N, 6°31′ E **163**
Beiliu, *China* 22°42′ N, 110°19′ E **198**
Beilrode, *Ger.* 51°33′ N, 13°4′ E **152**
Beilu, river, *China* 34°47′ N, 93°23′ E **188**
Beilul, *Eritrea* 13°9′ N, 42°22′ E **182**
Beinn Bhreagh, site, *Can.* 46°4′ N, 60°48′ W **111**
Beipiao, *China* 41°52′ N, 120°47′ E **198**
Beira, *Mozambique* 19°50′ S, 34°53′ E **224**
Beirut see Beyrouth, *Leb.* 33°53′ N, 35°26′ E **194**
Beitbridge, *Zimb.* 22°10′ S, 29°58′ E **227**
Beitun, *China* 47°19′ N, 87°48′ E **184**
Beiuş, *Rom.* 46°40′ N, 22°23′ E **168**
Beizhen, *China* 41°37′ N, 121°50′ E **198**
Beja, *Port.* 38°1′ N, 7°52′ W **150**
Beja, *Tun.* 36°43′ N, 9°11′ E **156**
Beja, adm. division, *Port.* 37°41′ N, 8°36′ W **150**
Bejaïa (Bougie), *Alg.* 36°46′ N, 5°2′ E **150**
Béjar, *Sp.* 40°23′ N, 5°47′ W **150**
Bek, river, *Cameroon* 3°1′ N, 14°23′ E **218**
Bekaa Valley see Al Biqā', region, *Asia* 33°43′ N, 35°51′ E **194**
Bekaie, *Dem. Rep. of the Congo* 2°29′ S, 18°17′ E **218**
Bekdash see Karabogaz, *Turkm.* 41°32′ N, 52°35′ E **158**
Békés, *Hung.* 46°46′ N, 21°8′ E **168**
Békés, adm. division, *Hung.* 46°50′ N, 20°45′ E **156**
Békéscsaba, *Hung.* 46°40′ N, 21°5′ E **168**
Bekily, *Madagascar* 24°11′ S, 45°17′ E **220**
Bekobod, *Uzb.* 40°12′ N, 69°15′ E **197**
Bekodoka, *Madagascar* 17°1′ S, 45°7′ E **220**
Bekoropoka-Antongo, *Madagascar* 21°27′ S, 43°32′ E **220**
Bekwai, *Ghana* 6°29′ N, 1°34′ W **222**
Bela, *India* 25°53′ N, 81°58′ E **197**
Bela, *Pak.* 26°14′ N, 66°20′ E **186**
Bela Crkva, *Serb. and Mont.* 44°53′ N, 21°26′ E **168**
Bela Vista, *Mozambique* 26°18′ S, 32°40′ E **227**
Bela Vista de Goiás, *Braz.* 17°1′ S, 48°59′ W **138**
Bela-Bela (Warmbaths), *S. Af.* 24°55′ S, 28°16′ E **227**
Bélabo, *Cameroon* 4°49′ N, 13°16′ E **218**
Belalcázar, *Sp.* 38°34′ N, 5°10′ W **164**
Bélanger, river, *Can.* 53°14′ N, 97°28′ W **108**
Belarus 53°57′ N, 27°35′ E **154**
Belasica, *Gr.* 41°23′ N, 23°1′ E **168**
Belawan, *Indonesia* 3°46′ N, 98°42′ E **196**
Belaya Glina, *Russ.* 46°5′ N, 40°52′ E **158**
Belaya Gora, *Russ.* 68°8′ N, 146°6′ E **160**
Belaya Kalitva, *Russ.* 48°10′ N, 40°50′ E **158**
Belaya Kholunitsa, *Russ.* 58°50′ N, 50°52′ E **154**
Belaya, peak, *Eth.* 11°23′ N, 36°4′ E **182**
Belaya, river, *Russ.* 52°52′ N, 56°57′ E **154**
Belcaire, *Fr.* 42°48′ N, 1°56′ E **164**
Belcher, *La., U.S.* 32°44′ N, 93°51′ W **103**
Belcher Channel 76°55′ N, 100°16′ W **106**
Belcher Islands, *Hudson Bay* 56°1′ N, 80°5′ W **106**
Belcheragh, *Afghan.* 35°46′ N, 65°13′ E **186**
Belchertown, *Mass., U.S.* 42°16′ N, 72°25′ W **104**
Belchite, *Sp.* 41°17′ N, 0°46′ E **164**
Belding, *Mich., U.S.* 43°6′ N, 85°14′ W **102**
Belebey, *Russ.* 54°6′ N, 54°12′ E **154**
Belecke, *Ger.* 51°28′ N, 8°20′ E **167**
Beled, *Hung.* 47°27′ N, 17°5′ E **168**
Beledweyne, *Somalia* 4°43′ N, 45°10′ E **218**
Belej, *Croatia* 44°47′ N, 14°24′ E **156**
Belém, *Braz.* 1°24′ S, 48°28′ W **130**
Belén, *Arg.* 27°39′ S, 67°3′ W **134**
Belén, *Chile* 18°30′ S, 69°34′ W **137**
Belén, *Col.* 1°25′ N, 75°57′ W **136**
Belen, *N. Mex., U.S.* 34°39′ N, 106°46′ W **92**
Belén, *Parag.* 23°29′ S, 57°18′ W **132**
Belén, *Uru.* 30°49′ S, 57°45′ W **139**
Beles, river, *Eth.* 11°1′ N, 36°15′ E **182**
Bélesta, *Fr.* 42°54′ N, 1°54′ E **164**
Belev, *Russ.* 53°47′ N, 36°5′ E **154**
Beleza, river, *Braz.* 10°11′ S, 51°13′ W **132**
Belfair, *Wash., U.S.* 47°26′ N, 122°49′ W **100**
Belfast, *Me., U.S.* 44°25′ N, 69°2′ W **94**
Belfast, *N.Z.* 43°28′ S, 172°36′ E **240**
Belfast, *S. Af.* 25°42′ S, 30°2′ E **227**
Belfast, *U.K.* 54°34′ N, 6°5′ W **150**
Belfield, *N. Dak., U.S.* 46°52′ N, 103°13′ W **90**
Bēlfodiyo, *Eth.* 10°29′ N, 34°48′ E **224**
Belford, *U.K.* 55°35′ N, 1°50′ W **150**
Belfort, *Fr.* 47°38′ N, 6°50′ E **150**
Belfort (Beaufort), ruin(s), *Leb.* 33°19′ N, 35°30′ E **194**
Belgaum, *India* 15°49′ N, 74°31′ E **188**
Belgica Bank, *Greenland Sea* 78°11′ N, 13°45′ W **255**
Belgioioso, *It.* 45°9′ N, 9°19′ E **167**
Belgium 50°41′ N, 4°16′ E **163**
Belgorod, *Russ.* 50°36′ N, 36°32′ E **158**
Belgorod, adm. division, *Russ.* 50°59′ N, 36°52′ E **158**
Belgrade, *Me., U.S.* 44°26′ N, 69°51′ W **104**
Belgrade, *Mont., U.S.* 45°45′ N, 111°11′ W **90**
Belgrade see Beograd, *Serb. and Mont.* 44°47′ N, 20°24′ E **168**
Belgrano II, station, *Antarctica* 77°55′ S, 34°4′ W **248**
Belhaven, *N.C., U.S.* 35°33′ N, 76°38′ W **96**
Belhedan, oil field, *Lib.* 27°53′ N, 19°10′ E **216**
Beli, *Nig.* 7°49′ N, 10°58′ E **222**
Beli Manastir, *Croatia* 45°44′ N, 18°36′ E **168**
Beli Potok, *Serb. and Mont.* 43°30′ N, 22°4′ E **168**
Belica, *Alban.* 41°14′ N, 20°23′ E **156**
Belica, *Croatia* 46°25′ N, 16°31′ E **168**
Belidzhi, *Russ.* 41°50′ N, 48°28′ E **195**
Beliliou see Paleliu, island, *Palau* 7°0′ N, 134°15′ E **242**
Belinskiy, *Russ.* 52°57′ N, 43°23′ E **154**
Beliş, *Rom.* 46°39′ N, 23°2′ E **168**
Belitung (Billiton), island, *Indonesia* 3°41′ S, 107°3′ E **192**
Beliu, *Rom.* 46°29′ N, 21°59′ E **168**
Belize 16°58′ N, 89°1′ W **115**
Belize City, *Belize* 17°30′ N, 88°13′ W **115**
Beljanica, *Serb. and Mont.* 44°10′ N, 21°30′ E **168**
Bel'kovskiy, Ostrov, island, *Russ.* 75°28′ N, 126°33′ E **160**
Bell Lake, lake, *Can.* 49°47′ N, 91°13′ W **94**
Bell Peninsula, *Can.* 63°28′ N, 84°36′ W **106**
Bell, river, *Can.* 49°40′ N, 77°37′ W **94**
Bell Rock, *Can.* 60°0′ N, 112°5′ W **108**
Bell Ville, *Arg.* 32°40′ S, 62°38′ W **139**
Bella Bella, *Can.* 52°8′ N, 128°3′ W **108**
Bella Flor, *Bol.* 11°8′ S, 67°49′ W **137**
Bella Unión, *Uru.* 30°17′ S, 57°37′ W **139**
Bella Vista, *Arg.* 28°31′ S, 59°2′ W **132**
Bella Vista, *Braz.* 22°8′ S, 56°24′ W **132**
Bellac, *Fr.* 46°6′ N, 1°3′ E **150**
Bellagio, *It.* 45°58′ N, 9°14′ E **167**
Bellaire, *Mich., U.S.* 44°58′ N, 85°12′ W **94**
Bellaire, *Tex., U.S.* 29°41′ N, 95°29′ W **96**
Bellamy, *Ala., U.S.* 32°26′ N, 88°9′ W **103**
Bellary, *India* 15°8′ N, 76°53′ E **188**
Bellavista, *Peru* 5°33′ S, 78°43′ W **130**
Bellavista, *Peru* 1°35′ S, 75°33′ W **136**
Belle Fourche, *S. Dak., U.S.* 44°38′ N, 103°52′ W **82**
Belle Fourche, river, *Wyo., U.S.* 43°45′ N, 105°45′ W **80**
Belle Glade, *Fla., U.S.* 26°40′ N, 80°41′ W **105**
Belle Isle, island, *Can.* 52°4′ N, 55°26′ W **106**
Belle Isle, Strait of 51°28′ N, 56°49′ W **111**
Belle Plaine, *Iowa, U.S.* 41°53′ N, 92°17′ W **94**
Belle Plaine, *Minn., U.S.* 44°36′ N, 93°46′ W **94**
Belle Yella, *Liberia* 7°13′ N, 10°2′ W **222**
Belledonne, Chaîne de, *Fr.* 45°10′ N, 5°50′ E **165**
Bellefontaine, *Ohio, U.S.* 40°21′ N, 83°45′ W **102**
Bellefonte, *Pa., U.S.* 40°53′ N, 77°47′ W **94**
Bellenden Ker National Park, *Austral.* 17°25′ S, 145°31′ E **238**
Belleoram, *Can.* 47°30′ N, 55°25′ W **111**
Belleview, *Fla., U.S.* 29°3′ N, 82°3′ W **105**
Belleville, *Can.* 44°9′ N, 77°22′ W **94**
Belleville, *Fr.* 46°5′ N, 4°43′ E **150**
Belleville, *Ill., U.S.* 38°30′ N, 89°58′ W **102**
Belleville, *Kans., U.S.* 39°48′ N, 97°38′ W **90**
Belleville, *Mo., U.S.* 38°30′ N, 89°58′ W **94**
Belleville, *Wis., U.S.* 42°50′ N, 89°32′ W **102**
Bellevue, *Congo* 2°5′ N, 13°51′ E **218**
Bellevue, *Idaho, U.S.* 43°28′ N, 114°16′ W **90**
Bellevue, *Iowa, U.S.* 42°15′ N, 90°26′ W **94**
Bellevue, *Mich., U.S.* 42°27′ N, 85°1′ W **102**
Bellevue, *Nebr., U.S.* 41°8′ N, 95°54′ W **90**
Bellevue, *Ohio, U.S.* 41°16′ N, 82°50′ W **102**
Bellevue, *Tex., U.S.* 33°36′ N, 98°1′ W **96**
Bellevue, *Wash., U.S.* 47°35′ N, 122°13′ W **100**
Bellflower, *Ill., U.S.* 40°19′ N, 88°32′ W **102**
Bellinger, Lac, lake, *Can.* 51°10′ N, 74°60′ W **110**
Bellingham, *Wash., U.S.* 48°46′ N, 122°29′ W **100**
Bellingrath Gardens, site, *Ala., U.S.* 30°24′ N, 88°11′ W **103**
Bellingshausen Plain, *South Pacific Ocean* 65°21′ S, 112°43′ W **255**
Bellingshausen Sea 70°32′ S, 88°38′ W **248**
Bellingshausen, station, *Antarctica* 62°17′ S, 58°44′ W **248**
Bellinzona, *Switz.* 46°11′ N, 9°1′ E **167**
Bellmore, *Ind., U.S.* 39°45′ N, 87°6′ W **102**
Bello, *Col.* 6°20′ N, 75°35′ W **136**
Bello Islands, Monte, *Indian Ocean* 20°10′ S, 113°11′ E **230**
Bellona Island, *Solomon Islands* 11°0′ S, 160°0′ E **242**
Bellows Falls, *Vt., U.S.* 43°7′ N, 72°28′ W **104**
Bellpat, *Pak.* 29°1′ N, 68°5′ E **186**
Belluno, *It.* 46°8′ N, 12°12′ E **167**
Bellville, *Ohio, U.S.* 40°36′ N, 82°31′ W **102**
Bellville, *Tex., U.S.* 29°55′ N, 96°16′ W **96**
Bellvís, *Sp.* 41°39′ N, 0°49′ E **164**
Bellwood, *La., U.S.* 31°29′ N, 93°12′ W **103**
Belmar, *N.J., U.S.* 40°10′ N, 74°2′ W **94**
Bélmez, *Sp.* 38°15′ N, 5°12′ W **164**
Belmond, *Iowa, U.S.* 42°49′ N, 93°36′ W **94**
Belmont, *N.H., U.S.* 43°26′ N, 71°29′ W **104**
Belmont, *S. Af.* 29°27′ S, 24°20′ E **227**
Belmont, *Vt., U.S.* 43°24′ N, 72°50′ W **104**
Belmonte, *Braz.* 15°56′ S, 38°56′ W **132**
Belmonte, *Sp.* 39°33′ N, 2°43′ W **150**
Belmopan, *Belize* 17°10′ N, 88°56′ W **115**
Belo, *Madagascar* 20°48′ S, 44°1′ E **220**
Belo Horizonte, *Braz.* 19°55′ S, 43°55′ W **138**
Belo Horizonte, *Braz.* 5°18′ S, 52°56′ W **130**
Beloci, *Mold.* 47°52′ N, 28°56′ E **156**
Belogorsk, *Russ.* 51°2′ N, 128°27′ E **190**
Belogorsk, *Russ.* 54°59′ N, 88°33′ E **169**
Belogorskīy, *Kaz.* 49°26′ N, 83°9′ E **184**
Beloha, *Madagascar* 25°9′ S, 45°2′ E **220**
Beloit, *Kans., U.S.* 39°27′ N, 98°7′ W **90**
Beloit, *Wis., U.S.* 42°31′ N, 89°2′ W **102**
Beloljin, *Serb. and Mont.* 43°13′ N, 21°23′ E **168**
Belomorsk, *Russ.* 64°28′ N, 34°38′ E **154**
Belonia, *India* 23°12′ N, 91°28′ E **197**
Belorado, *Sp.* 42°24′ N, 3°12′ W **164**
Belorechensk, *Russ.* 44°46′ N, 39°52′ E **158**
Beloretsk, *Russ.* 53°58′ N, 58°23′ E **154**
Beloshchel'ye, *Russ.* 64°56′ N, 46°48′ E **154**
Belot'i, *Ga.* 42°17′ N, 44°7′ E **195**
Belo-Tsiribihina, *Madagascar* 19°41′ S, 44°31′ E **220**
Belovo, *Russ.* 54°22′ N, 86°22′ E **184**
Beloyarskiy, *Russ.* 63°42′ N, 66°58′ E **169**
Beloye More (White Sea) 63°17′ N, 35°24′ E **160**
Beloye Ozero, lake, *Russ.* 59°33′ N, 37°43′ E **154**
Belozersk, *Russ.* 59°57′ N, 37°50′ E **154**
Belpre, *Ohio, U.S.* 39°16′ N, 81°35′ W **102**
Belt, *Mont., U.S.* 47°22′ N, 110°56′ W **90**
Belterra, *Braz.* 2°38′ S, 54°59′ W **130**
Belton, *S.C., U.S.* 34°30′ N, 82°31′ W **96**
Belton, *Tex., U.S.* 31°2′ N, 97°27′ W **92**
Belukha, Gora, peak, *Russ.* 49°46′ N, 86°31′ E **184**
Belush'ya Guba, *Russ.* 71°28′ N, 52°29′ E **160**
Belush'ye, *Russ.* 66°52′ N, 47°37′ E **154**
Belušić, *Serb. and Mont.* 43°47′ N, 21°8′ E **168**
Belvidere, *Ill., U.S.* 42°14′ N, 88°51′ W **102**
Belvidere, *S. Dak., U.S.* 43°49′ N, 101°17′ W **90**
Belvidere Mountain, *Vt., U.S.* 44°45′ N, 72°39′ W **94**
Belvoir, *U.K.* 52°53′ N, 0°48′ E **162**
Belyayevka, *Russ.* 51°23′ N, 56°23′ E **158**
Belyy, *Russ.* 55°48′ N, 33°1′ E **154**
Belyy, Ostrov, island, *Russ.* 73°28′ N, 65°53′ E **160**
Belyy, Ostrov, island, *Russ.* 73°26′ N, 70°30′ E **160**
Belyy Yar, *Russ.* 58°25′ N, 85°8′ E **169**
Belz, *Ukr.* 50°23′ N, 24°1′ E **152**
Belzoni, *Miss., U.S.* 33°9′ N, 90°31′ W **103**
Bemaraha, *Madagascar* 20°44′ S, 44°42′ E **220**
Bembe, *Angola* 7°2′ S, 14°18′ E **218**
Bembéréké, *Benin* 10°12′ N, 2°40′ E **222**
Bement, *Ill., U.S.* 39°54′ N, 88°34′ W **102**
Bemetara, *India* 21°44′ N, 81°31′ E **188**
Bemidji, *Minn., U.S.* 47°28′ N, 94°55′ W **90**
Bemis, *Tenn., U.S.* 35°33′ N, 88°49′ W **96**
Ben Gardane, *Tun.* 33°9′ N, 11°12′ E **214**
Ben Lomond, *Calif., U.S.* 37°5′ N, 122°6′ W **100**
Ben S'Rour, *Alg.* 35°3′ N, 4°34′ E **150**
Ben Zohra, spring, *Alg.* 28°37′ N, 3°50′ W **214**
Bena Dibele, *Dem. Rep. of the Congo* 4°8′ S, 22°48′ E **218**
Bena Makima, *Dem. Rep. of the Congo* 5°2′ S, 21°7′ E **218**
Benabarre, *Sp.* 42°6′ N, 0°28′ E **164**
Benalup, *Sp.* 36°21′ N, 5°50′ W **164**
Benamaurel, *Sp.* 37°35′ N, 2°41′ W **164**
Benamejí, *Sp.* 37°16′ N, 4°33′ W **164**
Benasque, *Sp.* 42°35′ N, 0°32′ E **164**
Bénat, Cap, *Fr.* 43°1′ N, 6°11′ E **165**
Benavente, *Sp.* 42°0′ N, 5°43′ W **150**
Benavides, *Tex., U.S.* 27°35′ N, 98°24′ W **92**
Benbow, *Calif., U.S.* 40°3′ N, 123°47′ W **90**
Benbulbin, peak, *Ire.* 54°20′ N, 8°36′ W **150**
Bende, *Nig.* 5°35′ N, 7°38′ E **222**
Bender, *Mold.* 46°48′ N, 29°28′ E **156**
Bendorf, *Ger.* 50°25′ N, 7°34′ E **167**
Bēne, *Latv.* 56°28′ N, 23°1′ E **166**
Bené Beraq, *Israel* 32°5′ N, 34°50′ E **194**
Benedito Leite, *Braz.* 7°13′ S, 44°36′ W **132**
Bénéna, *Mali* 13°7′ N, 4°24′ W **222**
Benenitra, *Madagascar* 23°24′ S, 45°3′ E **220**
Beneraird, peak, *U.K.* 55°3′ N, 5°2′ W **150**
Bénestroff, *Fr.* 48°54′ N, 6°45′ E **163**
Benfeld, *Fr.* 48°22′ N, 7°34′ E **163**
Bengal, adm. division, *India* 21°51′ N, 88°25′ E **197**
Bengal, Bay of 13°12′ N, 85°28′ E **188**
Bengbu, *China* 32°53′ N, 117°21′ E **198**
Benghazi see Banghāzī, *Lib.* 32°6′ N, 20°4′ E **216**
Bengkalis, *Indonesia* 1°30′ N, 102°7′ E **196**
Bengkalis, island, *Indonesia* 1°38′ N, 102°5′ E **196**
Bengkayang, *Indonesia* 0°51′ N, 109°27′ E **196**
Bengkulu, *Indonesia* 3°49′ S, 102°18′ E **192**
Bengo, adm. division, *Angola* 8°8′ S, 13°15′ E **220**
Bengough, *Can.* 49°23′ N, 105°8′ W **90**
Benguela, *Angola* 12°38′ S, 13°23′ E **220**
Benguela, adm. division, *Angola* 13°17′ S, 12°57′ E **220**
Benguérua, Ilha, island, *Mozambique* 22°11′ S, 34°56′ E **227**
Benha, *Egypt* 30°25′ N, 31°12′ E **180**
Beni, *Dem. Rep. of the Congo* 0°24′ N, 29°26′ E **224**
Beni Abbes, *Alg.* 30°8′ N, 2°10′ W **214**
Beni, adm. division, *Bol.* 13°40′ S, 65°45′ W **137**
Beni Mazâr, *Egypt* 28°27′ N, 30°46′ E **180**
Beni Mellal, *Mor.* 32°22′ N, 6°22′ W **214**
Beni, river, *Bol.* 12°25′ S, 66°55′ W **137**
Beni Saf, *Alg.* 35°17′ N, 1°23′ W **150**
Beni Suef, *Egypt* 29°4′ N, 31°3′ E **180**
Beni Tajit, *Mor.* 32°21′ N, 3°28′ W **214**
Benicarló, *Sp.* 40°24′ N, 0°25′ E **164**
Benicasim, *Sp.* 40°3′ N, 7°416′ E **164**
Benicia, *Calif., U.S.* 38°3′ N, 122°10′ W **100**
Benidorm, *Sp.* 38°31′ N, 0°8′ E **164**
Benifaió, *Sp.* 39°16′ N, 0°26′ E **164**
Benin 10°4′ N, 1°52′ E **214**
Benin, Bight of 4°25′ N, 1°49′ E **222**
Benin City, *Nig.* 6°23′ N, 5°38′ E **222**
Benissa, *Sp.* 38°42′ N, 5°297′ E **164**
Benito, *Can.* 51°54′ N, 101°33′ W **108**
Benito Juárez, *Mex.* 17°49′ N, 92°33′ W **115**
Benito Juárez National Park see 2, *Mex.* 17°15′ N, 96°46′ W **112**
Benjamin, *Tex., U.S.* 33°34′ N, 99°48′ W **92**
Benjamin Constant, *Braz.* 4°25′ S, 70°4′ W **132**
Benjamin Hill, *Mex.* 30°11′ N, 111°8′ W **92**
Benkelman, *Nebr., U.S.* 40°3′ N, 101°33′ W **90**
Benld, *Ill., U.S.* 39°5′ N, 89°49′ W **102**
Bennane Head, *U.K.* 55°10′ N, 5°15′ W **150**
Bennett, *Can.* 59°51′ N, 134°56′ W **108**
Bennett Island, *Russ.* 77°0′ N, 149°0′ E **255**
Bennett Lake, lake, *Can.* 53°23′ N, 96°35′ W **108**
Benneydale, *N.Z.* 38°31′ S, 175°20′ E **240**
Bennington, *N.H., U.S.* 43°0′ N, 71°56′ W **104**
Bennington, *Vt., U.S.* 42°52′ N, 73°12′ W **104**
Bénnsané, *Guinea* 11°26′ N, 14°1′ W **222**
Benom, peak, *Malaysia* 3°50′ N, 102°0′ E **196**
Benoud, *Alg.* 32°20′ N, 0°15′ E **214**
Benoy, *Chad* 8°57′ N, 16°20′ E **216**
Bensberg, *Ger.* 50°58′ N, 7°8′ E **167**
Benson, *Ariz., U.S.* 31°57′ N, 110°20′ W **112**

Benson, Minn., U.S. 45°18′ N, 95°37′ W 90
Benson, N.C., U.S. 35°22′ N, 78°34′ W 96
Benson, Vt., U.S. 43°42′ N, 73°19′ W 104
Bent Jbail, Leb. 33°7′ N, 35°25′ E 194
Benta, Malaysia 4°1′ N, 101°58′ E 196
Bentiaba, Angola 14°18′ S, 12°22′ E 220
Bentinck Island, Austral. 17°25′ S, 137°54′ E 230
Bentinck, island, Myanmar 11°30′ N, 97°26′ E 202
Bentinck Point, Can. 46°26′ N, 61°17′ W 111
Bentiu, Sudan 9°9′ N, 29°47′ E 224
Bentley, Mich., U.S. 43°56′ N, 84°9′ W 102
Bento Gonçalves, Braz. 29°10′ S, 51°30′ W 139
Benton, Ark., U.S. 34°32′ N, 92°36′ W 96
Benton, Ky., U.S. 36°51′ N, 88°21′ W 94
Benton, La., U.S. 32°40′ N, 93°45′ W 103
Benton, Me., U.S. 44°34′ N, 69°34′ W 94
Benton, Miss., U.S. 32°48′ N, 90°16′ W 103
Benton, N.H., U.S. 44°5′ N, 71°55′ W 104
Benton Harbor, Mich., U.S. 42°6′ N, 86°27′ W 102
Bentong, Malaysia 3°34′ N, 101°55′ E 196
Bentonia, Miss., U.S. 32°37′ N, 90°23′ W 103
Bentonville, Ark., U.S. 36°21′ N, 94°13′ W 94
Benty, Guinea 9°8′ N, 13°13′ W 222
Benue, river, Nig. 8°0′ N, 7°50′ E 222
Benwee Head, Ire. 54°21′ N, 10°10′ W 150
Benxi, China 41°16′ N, 123°47′ E 200
Benzdorp, Suriname 3°42′ N, 54°7′ W 130
Benzú, Mor. 35°54′ N, 5°23′ W 150
Beo, Indonesia 4°15′ N, 126°52′ E 192
Beočin, Serb. and Mont. 45°11′ N, 19°44′ E 168
Beograd (Belgrade), Serb. and Mont. 44°47′ N, 20°24′ E 168
Beohari, India 24°2′ N, 81°22′ E 197
Beolgyo, S. Korea 34°48′ N, 127°21′ E 200
Beowawe, Nev., U.S. 40°35′ N, 116°30′ W 90
Beppu, Japan 36°7′ N, 133°4′ E 201
Beppu, Japan 33°16′ N, 131°29′ E 201
Bequia, island, Saint Vincent and The Grenadines 13°0′ N, 61°11′ W 116
Bera Ndjoko, Congo 3°15′ N, 16°58′ E 218
Berau, Teluk 2°35′ S, 131°10′ E 192
Berber, Sudan 18°0′ N, 34°2′ E 182
Berbérati, Cen. Af. Rep. 4°18′ N, 15°47′ E 218
Bercedo, Sp. 43°4′ N, 3°27′ W 164
Berceto, It. 44°30′ N, 9°59′ E 167
Berck, Fr. 50°25′ N, 1°35′ E 163
Berdigestyakh, Russ. 62°8′ N, 127°5′ E 160
Berdoba, Chad 16°0′ N, 22°53′ E 216
Berdsk, Russ. 54°46′ N, 83°11′ E 184
Berdún, Sp. 42°36′ N, 0°52′ E 164
Berdyans'k, Ukr. 46°46′ N, 36°46′ E 156
Berdyaush, Russ. 55°11′ N, 59°12′ E 154
Berdychiv, Ukr. 49°53′ N, 28°41′ E 152
Berdyuzh'ye, Russ. 55°48′ N, 68°20′ E 184
Berea, Ky., U.S. 37°33′ N, 84°18′ W 96
Berea, Ohio, U.S. 41°21′ N, 81°51′ W 102
Bérébi, Côte d'Ivoire 4°40′ N, 7°2′ W 222
Bereeda, Somalia 11°44′ N, 51°3′ E 182
Bereku, Tanzania 4°27′ S, 35°46′ E 224
Berekum, Ghana 7°29′ N, 2°35′ W 222
Beremend, Hung. 45°46′ N, 18°25′ E 168
Beren, Liman, lake, Russ. 46°52′ N, 44°37′ E 158
Berenda, Calif., U.S. 37°2′ N, 120°10′ W 100
Berenice, Egypt 23°54′ N, 35°25′ E 182
Berens River, Can. 52°21′ N, 96°59′ W 82
Berens, river, Can. 51°49′ N, 93°43′ W 110
Berens, river, Can. 52°5′ N, 96°53′ W 80
Berestechko, Ukr. 50°20′ N, 25°6′ E 158
Bereşti, Rom. 46°5′ N, 27°51′ E 156
Berettyó, river, Rom. 47°15′ N, 21°39′ E 168
Berettyóújfalu, Hung. 47°14′ N, 21°32′ E 168
Berevo, Madagascar 19°46′ S, 44°58′ E 220
Berezivka, Ukr. 47°16′ N, 30°54′ E 156
Bereznik, Russ. 62°49′ N, 42°49′ E 154
Berezniki, Russ. 59°24′ N, 56°48′ E 154
Berezovka, Russ. 57°38′ N, 57°22′ E 154
Berezovka, Russ. 59°20′ N, 82°47′ E 169
Berezovka, Russ. 65°0′ N, 56°38′ E 154
Berezovo, Russ. 63°58′ N, 65°5′ E 169
Berezovskaya, Russ. 50°14′ N, 43°59′ E 158
Berezovskiy, Russ. 55°34′ N, 86°18′ E 169
Berga, Nor. 57°14′ N, 16°0′ E 152
Berga, Sp. 42°6′ N, 1°50′ E 164
Bergama, Turk. 39°4′ N, 27°11′ E 180
Bergamo, It. 45°42′ N, 9°39′ E 167
Bergedorf, Ger. 53°29′ N, 10°12′ E 150
Bergen, Ger. 54°25′ N, 13°26′ E 152
Bergen, Nor. 60°23′ N, 5°19′ E 152
Bergen aan Zee, Neth. 52°40′ N, 4°38′ E 163
Bergen op Zoom, Neth. 51°29′ N, 4°17′ E 163
Bergerac, Fr. 44°51′ N, 0°28′ E 150
Bergersen, Mount, Antarctica 72°6′ S, 25°32′ E 248
Bergheim, Ger. 50°57′ N, 6°39′ E 167
Bergisch Gladbach, Ger. 50°59′ N, 7°7′ E 167
Bergkamen, Ger. 51°37′ N, 7°39′ E 167
Bergland, Namibia 22°60′ S, 17°5′ E 227
Bergö, Fin. 62°56′ N, 21°9′ E 152
Bergsfjord, Nor. 70°15′ N, 21°49′ E 152
Bergshamra, Sw. 59°37′ N, 18°35′ E 166
Bergsjö, Nor. 61°58′ N, 17°1′ E 152
Berguent, Mor. 34°1′ N, 1°60′ W 214
Bergues, Fr. 50°57′ N, 2°26′ E 163
Bergum, Neth. 53°11′ N, 5°58′ E 163
Bergville, S. Af. 28°44′ S, 29°20′ E 227
Berh, Mongolia 47°44′ N, 111°8′ E 198
Berhala, Selat 0°50′ N, 103°54′ E 196
Berikei, oil field, Russ. 42°20′ N, 47°58′ E 195
Bering Sea 65°53′ N, 166°10′ W 246
Bering Strait 65°53′ N, 168°36′ W 255
Beringil, Sudan 12°8′ N, 25°43′ E 216
Beringovskiy, Russ. 63°8′ N, 179°6′ E 160
Berja, Sp. 36°50′ N, 2°57′ W 164
Berkåk, Nor. 62°49′ N, 10°1′ E 152
Berkeley, Calif., U.S. 37°52′ N, 122°16′ W 100
Berkner Island, Antarctica 78°9′ S, 43°53′ W 248
Berkovići, Bosn. and Herzg. 43°4′ N, 18°10′ E 168
Berkshire, Mass., U.S. 42°30′ N, 73°12′ W 104
Berkshires, The, Mass., U.S. 42°27′ N, 73°8′ W 104
Berland, river, Can. 53°40′ N, 118°10′ W 108
Berlikum, Neth. 53°14′ N, 5°38′ E 163
Berlin, Ger. 52°29′ N, 13°14′ E 152
Berlin, Md., U.S. 38°19′ N, 75°14′ W 94
Berlin, N.H., U.S. 44°28′ N, 71°12′ W 104
Berlin, N.Y., U.S. 42°41′ N, 73°23′ W 104
Berlin, Wis., U.S. 43°57′ N, 88°56′ W 94
Berlin, Mount, Antarctica 75°56′ S, 135°13′ W 248
Bermeja, Punta, Arg. 41°21′ S, 63°11′ W 134
Bermeja, Sierra, Sp. 36°33′ N, 5°16′ W 164
Bermejillo, Mex. 25°52′ N, 103°39′ W 114
Bermejo, river, Arg. 25°37′ S, 60°8′ W 134
Bermeo, Sp. 43°23′ N, 2°45′ W 164
Bermuda Islands, U.K. 32°0′ N, 65°0′ W 118
Bermuda Rise, North Atlantic Ocean 32°2′ N, 64°35′ W 253
Bern, Switz. 46°55′ N, 7°21′ E 165
Bernalillo, N. Mex., U.S. 35°17′ N, 106°34′ W 82
Bernard Lake, lake, Can. 45°41′ N, 79°50′ W 110
Bernardo de Irigoyen, Arg. 32°11′ S, 61°8′ W 139
Bernardo de Irigoyen, Arg. 26°15′ S, 53°41′ W 139
Bernardston, Mass., U.S. 42°40′ N, 72°34′ W 104
Bernasconi, Arg. 37°57′ S, 63°42′ W 139
Bernay, Fr. 49°5′ N, 0°35′ E 150
Berne, Ind., U.S. 40°38′ N, 84°57′ W 102
Berner Alpen, Switz. 46°20′ N, 6°59′ E 165
Berneval, Fr. 49°57′ N, 1°10′ E 163
Bernice, La., U.S. 32°48′ N, 92°40′ W 103
Bernie, Mo., U.S. 36°40′ N, 89°58′ W 96
Bernier Bay 70°59′ N, 90°44′ W 106
Bernier Island, Austral. 24°41′ S, 111°44′ E 230
Bernina Pass, Switz. 46°26′ N, 10°0′ E 167
Bernina, Piz, peak, Switz. 46°23′ N, 9°52′ E 167
Bernkastel-Kues, Ger. 49°55′ N, 7°5′ E 167
Bernterode, Ger. 51°24′ N, 10°29′ E 167
Bero, river, Angola 15°3′ S, 12°9′ E 220
Berón de Astrada, Arg. 27°33′ S, 57°32′ W 139
Beroroha, Madagascar 21°37′ S, 45°9′ E 220
Béroubouay, Benin 10°32′ N, 2°41′ E 222
Beroun, Czech Rep. 49°58′ N, 14°4′ E 152
Berovo, Maced. 41°43′ N, 22°52′ E 168
Berri, oil field, Saudi Arabia 27°5′ N, 49°29′ E 196
Berriane, Alg. 32°51′ N, 3°45′ E 214
Berrien Springs, Mich., U.S. 41°56′ N, 86°21′ W 102
Berrouaghia, Alg. 36°7′ N, 2°54′ E 150
Berry, Ky., U.S. 38°30′ N, 84°23′ W 102
Berry Creek, river, Can. 51°34′ N, 111°39′ W 90
Berry Islands, Atlantic Ocean 25°23′ N, 77°42′ W 96
Berry, region, Europe 46°51′ N, 1°18′ E 165
Berryville, Ark., U.S. 36°21′ N, 93°35′ W 96
Berseba, Namibia 25°60′ S, 17°46′ E 227
Bersenbrück, Ger. 52°33′ N, 7°57′ E 163
Bershad', Ukr. 48°24′ N, 29°38′ E 156
Bertam, Malaysia 5°11′ N, 102°1′ E 196
Berthierville, Can. 46°5′ N, 73°11′ W 110
Berthold, N. Dak., U.S. 48°18′ N, 101°45′ W 90
Berthoud, Colo., U.S. 40°18′ N, 105°6′ W 90
Berthoud Pass, Colo., U.S. 39°47′ N, 105°47′ W 90
Bertincourt, Fr. 50°4′ N, 2°56′ E 163
Bertoua, Cameroon 4°32′ N, 13°40′ E 218
Bertrab Nunatak, peak, Antarctica 78°26′ S, 36°22′ W 248
Bertrand, Nebr., U.S. 40°31′ N, 99°39′ W 92
Bertwell, Can. 52°35′ N, 102°36′ W 108
Beru, island, Kiribati 1°12′ S, 175°57′ E 252
Beruniy, Uzb. 41°43′ N, 60°43′ E 180
Beruri, Braz. 3°53′ S, 61°23′ W 130
Berutti, Arg. 35°50′ S, 62°29′ W 139
Berveni, Rom. 47°45′ N, 22°28′ E 168
Berwick, La., U.S. 29°41′ N, 91°15′ W 103
Berwick, Me., U.S. 43°16′ N, 70°52′ W 104
Berwick upon Tweed, U.K. 55°45′ N, 2°1′ W 150
Berwyn, Can. 56°9′ N, 117°44′ W 108
Berwyn, U.K. 52°51′ N, 3°26′ W 162
Beryslav, Ukr. 46°53′ N, 33°19′ E 156
Bērzaune, Latv. 56°48′ N, 26°2′ E 166
Bērze, river, Latv. 56°37′ N, 23°18′ E 166
Berzosilla, Sp. 42°46′ N, 4°3′ W 164
Berzovia, Rom. 45°25′ N, 21°36′ E 168
Besançon, Fr. 47°14′ N, 6°1′ E 150
Beserah, Malaysia 3°54′ N, 103°20′ E 196
Beshanq, Uzb. 40°25′ N, 70°33′ E 197
Beshkent, Uzb. 38°47′ N, 65°37′ E 197
Beşiri, Turk. 37°54′ N, 41°20′ E 195
Beška, Serb. and Mont. 45°7′ N, 20°4′ E 168
Besko, Pol. 49°34′ N, 21°56′ E 152
Beskól, Kaz. 54°45′ N, 69°4′ E 184
Beslan, Russ. 43°9′ N, 44°32′ E 195
Beslet, peak, Bulg. 41°47′ N, 23°48′ E 156
Besna Kobila, peak, Serb. and Mont. 42°31′ N, 22°11′ E 168
Besnard Lake, lake, Can. 55°25′ N, 106°33′ W 108
Besni Fok, Serb. and Mont. 44°58′ N, 20°24′ E 168
Beşparmak Dağı, peak, Turk. 37°29′ N, 27°30′ E 156
Bessaker, Nor. 64°14′ N, 10°20′ E 152
Bessemer, Ala., U.S. 33°23′ N, 86°56′ W 96
Bestöbe, Kaz. 52°29′ N, 73°8′ E 184
Bestuzhevo, Russ. 61°37′ N, 44°1′ E 154
Bet Guvrin, Israel 31°36′ N, 34°53′ E 194
Bét ha Shitta, Israel 32°33′ N, 35°26′ E 194
Bét She'an (Beth-shan), Israel 32°29′ N, 35°30′ E 194
Bét She'arim, ruin(s), Israel 32°41′ N, 35°5′ E 194
Bét Shemesh, Israel 31°44′ N, 34°59′ E 194
Betafo, Madagascar 19°52′ S, 46°51′ E 220
Betamba, Dem. Rep. of the Congo 2°16′ S, 21°25′ E 218
Betanty (Faux Cap), Madagascar 25°34′ S, 45°31′ E 220
Betanzos, Bol. 19°33′ S, 65°23′ W 137
Betanzos, Sp. 43°15′ N, 8°14′ W 150
Bétaré Oya, Cameroon 5°31′ N, 14°5′ E 218
Betbeder, Península, Arg. 44°43′ S, 65°19′ W 134
Bete Hor, Eth. 11°33′ N, 38°58′ E 182
Bétera, Sp. 39°35′ N, 0°28′ E 164
Bétérou, Benin 9°12′ N, 2°13′ E 222
Bethal, S. Af. 26°26′ S, 29°25′ E 227
Bethanie, Namibia 26°31′ S, 17°9′ E 227
Bethany, Ill., U.S. 39°38′ N, 88°45′ W 102
Bethany, Mo., U.S. 40°15′ N, 94°1′ W 94
Bethany Beach, Del., U.S. 38°31′ N, 75°4′ W 94
Bethel, Alas., U.S. 60°45′ N, 161°52′ W 98
Bethel, Conn., U.S. 41°22′ N, 73°25′ W 104
Bethel, Ohio, U.S. 38°57′ N, 84°5′ W 102
Bethel, Vt., U.S. 43°49′ N, 72°38′ W 104
Bethesda, U.K. 53°11′ N, 4°3′ W 162
Bethlehem, N.H., U.S. 44°16′ N, 71°42′ W 104
Bethlehem, S. Af. 28°16′ S, 28°15′ E 227
Bethlehem see Bayt Laḩm, West Bank 31°41′ N, 35°12′ E 194
Bethpage, N.Y., U.S. 40°44′ N, 73°30′ W 104
Beth-shan see Bét She'an, Israel 32°29′ N, 35°30′ E 194
Bethulie, S. Af. 30°27′ S, 25°59′ E 227
Béthune, Fr. 50°31′ N, 2°38′ E 163
Betijoque, Venez. 9°22′ N, 70°44′ W 136
Betioky, Madagascar 23°43′ S, 44°19′ E 220
Betong, Thai. 5°47′ N, 101°4′ E 196
Bétou, Congo 3°5′ N, 18°30′ E 218
Betpaqdala, Asia 45°34′ N, 64°32′ E 184
Betroka, Madagascar 23°13′ S, 46°8′ E 220
Betsiamites, Can. 48°56′ N, 68°39′ W 94
Betsiamites, river, Can. 49°24′ N, 69°51′ W 94
Bettendorf, Iowa, U.S. 41°33′ N, 90°30′ W 94
Bettie, Tex., U.S. 32°48′ N, 94°58′ W 103
Bettioua, Alg. 35°47′ N, 0°16′ E 150
Bettola, It. 44°46′ N, 9°36′ E 167
Bettsville, Ohio, U.S. 41°14′ N, 83°13′ W 102
Betul, India 21°55′ N, 77°54′ E 197
Betws-y-Coed, U.K. 53°5′ N, 3°48′ W 162
Betzdorf, Ger. 50°47′ N, 7°52′ E 167
Béu, Angola 6°14′ S, 15°27′ E 218
Beuil, Fr. 44°5′ N, 6°57′ E 167
Beulah, Colo., U.S. 38°5′ N, 104°60′ W 90
Beulah, N. Dak., U.S. 47°15′ N, 101°48′ W 90
Beurfou, spring, Chad 15°54′ N, 14°58′ E 216
Beverley, U.K. 53°50′ N, 0°26′ E 162
Beverley Head, Can. 49°11′ N, 59°4′ W 111
Beverly, Mass., U.S. 42°32′ N, 70°53′ W 104
Beverly, Ohio, U.S. 39°32′ N, 81°38′ W 102
Beverly Hills, Fla., U.S. 28°56′ N, 82°27′ W 105
Beverungen, Ger. 51°40′ N, 9°22′ E 167
Beverwijk, Neth. 52°30′ N, 4°37′ E 163
Bewdley, U.K. 52°21′ N, 2°20′ W 162
Bex, Switz. 46°15′ N, 7°0′ E 167
Bexhill, U.K. 50°50′ N, 0°28′ E 162
Bey da ğları, Turk. 36°36′ N, 29°46′ E 156
Bey Dağı, peak, Turk. 39°41′ N, 37°47′ E 156
Bey Dağı, peak, Turk. 38°16′ N, 35°59′ E 156
Beycesultan, ruin(s), Turk. 38°14′ N, 29°33′ E 156
Beyla, Guinea 8°39′ N, 8°39′ W 222
Beyneu, Kaz. 45°18′ N, 55°13′ E 158
Beypazarı, Turk. 40°9′ N, 31°54′ E 156
Beyra, Somalia 6°55′ N, 47°25′ E 218
Beyrouth (Beirut), Leb. 33°53′ N, 35°26′ E 194
Beyşehir, Turk. 37°41′ N, 31°44′ E 156
Beyşehir Gölü, lake, Turk. 37°43′ N, 31°9′ E 180
Beysug, river, Russ. 45°53′ N, 39°3′ E 156
Beytüşşebap, Turk. 37°33′ N, 43°3′ E 195
Bezdan, Serb. and Mont. 45°50′ N, 18°55′ E 168
Bezerra, river, Braz. 13°14′ S, 47°29′ W 138
Bezhanitsy, Russ. 56°57′ N, 29°52′ E 166
Bezhetsk, Russ. 57°44′ N, 36°44′ E 154
Béziers, Fr. 43°20′ N, 3°13′ E 164
Bhadarwah, India 32°57′ N, 75°45′ E 186
Bhadra, India 29°7′ N, 75°10′ E 186
Bhadrakh, India 21°5′ N, 86°31′ E 188
Bhadravati, India 13°52′ N, 75°44′ E 188
Bhagalpur, India 25°13′ N, 87°0′ E 197
Bhairahawa, Nepal 27°32′ N, 83°23′ E 197
Bhakkar, Pak. 31°37′ N, 71°7′ E 186
Bhaktapur, Nepal 27°41′ N, 85°26′ E 197
Bhamo, Myanmar 24°17′ N, 97°16′ E 190
Bhandara, India 21°2′ N, 79°38′ E 190
Bhanpura, India 24°31′ N, 75°46′ E 197
Bharatpur, India 27°13′ N, 77°28′ E 197
Bharatpur, India 23°46′ N, 81°47′ E 197
Bharthana, India 26°43′ N, 79°14′ E 197
Bharuch, India 21°42′ N, 72°57′ E 186
Bhatapara, India 21°44′ N, 81°56′ E 188
Bhatinda, India 30°13′ N, 74°57′ E 186
Bhatkal, India 14°0′ N, 74°32′ E 188
Bhatpara, India 22°51′ N, 88°25′ E 197
Bhavnagar, India 21°46′ N, 72°7′ E 186
Bheigeir, Beinn, peak, U.K. 55°43′ N, 6°12′ W 150
Bhera, Pak. 32°27′ N, 72°58′ E 186
Bhikangaon, India 21°53′ N, 75°58′ E 197
Bhilai, India 21°13′ N, 81°21′ E 188
Bhilsa see Vidisha, India 23°32′ N, 77°51′ E 197
Bhind, India 26°32′ N, 78°46′ E 197
Bhinmal, India 24°59′ N, 72°16′ E 186
Bhiwani, India 28°46′ N, 76°9′ E 197
Bhojpur, Nepal 27°9′ N, 87°4′ E 197
Bhopal, India 23°16′ N, 77°25′ E 197
Bhubaneshwar, India 20°17′ N, 85°48′ E 188
Bhumibol Dam, Thai. 17°9′ N, 98°57′ E 202
Bhusawal, India 21°2′ N, 75°46′ E 188
Bhutan 27°24′ N, 89°54′ E 188
Bia, Monts, Dem. Rep. of the Congo 9°32′ S, 26°9′ E 224
Biá, river, Braz. 3°24′ S, 67°24′ W 136
Bia, river, Ghana 6°27′ N, 2°49′ W 222
Biak, Indonesia 1°4′ S, 136°1′ E 192
Biak, island, Indonesia 0°45′ N, 135°57′ E 192
Biała Góra, peak, Pol. 50°15′ N, 23°16′ E 152
Biała Podlaska, Pol. 52°2′ N, 23°6′ E 158
Białogard, Pol. 54°0′ N, 15°59′ E 152
Białowieża, Pol. 52°41′ N, 23°6′ E 152
Biały Bór, Pol. 53°54′ N, 16°49′ E 152
Białystok, Pol. 53°8′ N, 23°9′ E 152
Bianco, It. 38°6′ N, 16°8′ E 156
Biankouma, Côte d'Ivoire 7°38′ N, 7°36′ W 222
Biaora, India 23°56′ N, 76°55′ E 197
Biar, Sp. 38°37′ N, 0°46′ E 164
Biar Zahr, spring, Tun. 31°29′ N, 10°6′ E 214
Biārjomand, Iran 36°2′ N, 55°57′ E 180
Biarritz, Fr. 43°25′ N, 1°39′ W 214
Bias, Fr. 44°8′ N, 1°15′ W 150
Biasca, Switz. 46°21′ N, 8°58′ E 167
Biaza, Russ. 56°34′ N, 78°18′ E 169
Biba, Burkina Faso 12°49′ N, 2°59′ W 222
Biba, Egypt 28°55′ N, 30°57′ E 180
Bibai, Japan 43°18′ N, 141°52′ E 190
Bibala, Angola 14°44′ S, 13°18′ E 220
Bibémi, Cameroon 9°18′ N, 13°52′ E 216
Bibiani, Ghana 6°28′ N, 2°18′ W 222
Bibile, Sri Lanka 7°9′ N, 81°15′ E 188
Bibione, It. 45°38′ N, 13°1′ E 167
Bibury, U.K. 51°45′ N, 1°50′ W 162
Bicaj, Alban. 41°59′ N, 20°25′ E 168
Bicas, Braz. 21°43′ S, 43°6′ W 138
Bicaz, Rom. 46°54′ N, 26°4′ E 156
Bicester, U.K. 51°53′ N, 1°9′ W 162
Biche, Lac la, lake, Can. 54°53′ N, 112°30′ W 108
Bichena, Eth. 10°23′ N, 38°14′ E 224
Bichi, Nig. 12°12′ N, 8°13′ E 222
Bichvint'a, Ga. 43°9′ N, 40°20′ E 195
Bickerdike, Can. 53°32′ N, 116°39′ W 108
Bickerton Island, Austral. 13°39′ S, 134°25′ E 230
Bicknell, Ind., U.S. 38°46′ N, 87°18′ W 102
Bicknell, Utah, U.S. 38°20′ N, 111°33′ W 90
Bicske, Hung. 47°28′ N, 18°39′ E 168
Bida, Nig. 9°3′ N, 5°59′ E 222
Bidar, India 17°54′ N, 77°32′ E 188
Bidarray, Fr. 43°16′ N, 1°21′ W 164
Biddeford, Me., U.S. 43°29′ N, 70°28′ W 104
Bidwell, Mount, Calif., U.S. 41°57′ N, 120°15′ W 90
Bié, adm. division, Angola 12°56′ S, 16°44′ E 220
Bié Plateau, Angola 11°41′ S, 15°45′ E 220
Biele Karpaty, Czech Rep. 49°5′ N, 17°49′ E 152
Bieler See, lake, Switz. 47°5′ N, 7°4′ E 165
Biella, It. 45°34′ N, 8°2′ E 167
Bielsa, Sp. 42°37′ N, 0°13′ E 164
Bielsk, Pol. 52°39′ N, 19°48′ E 152
Bielsk Podlaski, Pol. 52°46′ N, 23°10′ E 152
Bielsko-Biała, Pol. 49°49′ N, 19°2′ E 152
Bien Hoa, Vietnam 10°58′ N, 106°49′ E 202
Bienvenida, Sp. 38°18′ N, 6°13′ W 164
Bienville, Lac, lake, Can. 54°59′ N, 74°39′ W 106
Biescas, Sp. 42°37′ N, 0°19′ E 164
Bieżuń, Pol. 52°57′ N, 19°52′ E 152
Bifoum, Gabon 0°20′ N, 10°24′ E 218
Big Baldy Mountain, Mont., U.S. 46°56′ N, 110°41′ W 90
Big Baldy, peak, Idaho, U.S. 44°45′ N, 115°18′ W 90
Big Bay, Mich., U.S. 46°48′ N, 87°44′ W 94
Big Bear Lake, Calif., U.S. 34°14′ N, 116°57′ W 101
Big Beaver House, Can. 52°55′ N, 89°52′ W 82
Big Belt Mountains, Mont., U.S. 46°58′ N, 111°39′ W 90
Big Bend National Park, Tex., U.S. 29°9′ N, 103°44′ W 72
Big Black, river, Miss., U.S. 32°43′ N, 90°14′ W 103
Big Blue, river, Nebr., U.S. 41°1′ N, 97°55′ W 80
Big Bog, marsh, Minn., U.S. 48°18′ N, 94°29′ W 90
Big Creek, Calif., U.S. 37°12′ N, 119°15′ W 100
Big Cypress National Preserve, Fla., U.S. 26°5′ N, 81°11′ W 105
Big Cypress Swamp, marsh, Fla., U.S. 26°1′ N, 81°12′ W 105
Big Delta, Alas., U.S. 64°1′ N, 145°49′ W 98
Big Elk Mountain, Idaho, U.S. 43°12′ N, 111°21′ W 90
Big Falls, Minn., U.S. 48°9′ N, 93°50′ W 90
Big Fork, river, Minn., U.S. 48°4′ N, 93°60′ W 90
Big Horn Peak, Ariz., U.S. 33°36′ N, 113°13′ W 92
Big Interior Mountain, Can. 49°27′ N, 125°36′ W 90
Big Lake, Minn., U.S. 45°18′ N, 93°45′ W 94
Big Lake, Tex., U.S. 31°11′ N, 101°28′ W 92
Big Lake Ranch, Can. 52°23′ N, 121°52′ W 108
Big Lookout Mountain, Oreg., U.S. 44°35′ N, 117°23′ W 90
Big Maria Mountains, Calif., U.S. 33°54′ N, 114°56′ W 101
Big Mountain, Nev., U.S. 41°16′ N, 119°9′ W 90
Big Pine, Calif., U.S. 37°10′ N, 118°19′ W 101
Big Pine Key, Fla., U.S. 24°39′ N, 81°22′ W 105
Big Pine Mountain, Calif., U.S. 34°41′ N, 119°42′ W 100
Big Piney, Wyo., U.S. 42°32′ N, 110°6′ W 90
Big Piskwanish Point, Can. 51°44′ N, 80°27′ W 110
Big Port Walter, Alas., U.S. 56°23′ N, 134°45′ W 108
Big Rapids, Mich., U.S. 43°42′ N, 85°30′ W 102
Big River, Can. 53°50′ N, 107°1′ W 108
Big, river, Mo., U.S. 38°16′ N, 90°40′ W 80
Big Sable Point, Mich., U.S. 44°2′ N, 86°40′ W 102
Big Salmon, river, Can. 61°46′ N, 134°30′ W 98
Big Sand Lake, Can. 57°33′ N, 100°35′ W 108
Big Sandy, Mont., U.S. 48°9′ N, 110°6′ W 90
Big Sandy, Tex., U.S. 32°34′ N, 95°7′ W 103
Big Sandy Lake, lake, Can. 54°22′ N, 104°45′ W 108
Big Sandy Reservoir, Wyo., U.S. 42°17′ N, 109°49′ W 90
Big Sioux, river, S. Dak., U.S. 45°17′ N, 97°38′ W 80
Big Smoky Valley, Nev., U.S. 38°13′ N, 117°46′ W 90
Big Snowy Mountains, Mont., U.S. 46°51′ N, 109°39′ W 90
Big Southern Butte, Idaho, U.S. 43°23′ N, 113°6′ W 90
Big Spring, Tex., U.S. 32°13′ N, 101°28′ W 92
Big Springs, Nebr., U.S. 41°3′ N, 102°6′ W 90
Big Squaw Mountain, Me., U.S. 45°28′ N, 69°48′ W 94
Big Stone City, S. Dak., U.S. 45°16′ N, 96°30′ W 90
Big Sur, Calif., U.S. 36°16′ N, 121°49′ W 100
Big Thicket National Preserve, Tex., U.S. 30°26′ N, 94°41′ W 103
Big Timber, Mont., U.S. 45°48′ N, 109°58′ W 90
Big Trout Lake, Can. 53°51′ N, 92°1′ W 106
Big Trout Lake, Can. 53°43′ N, 89°55′ W 106
Big Valley, Can. 52°2′ N, 112°46′ W 90
Big Valley Mountains, Calif., U.S. 41°10′ N, 121°33′ W 90
Big Wells, Tex., U.S. 28°33′ N, 99°35′ W 92
Big White Mountain, Can. 49°43′ N, 119°2′ W 90
Big Wood Cay, island, Bahamas 24°25′ N, 77°40′ W 116
Biga, Turk. 40°13′ N, 27°12′ E 156
Bigadiç, Turk. 39°23′ N, 28°7′ E 156
Bigelow Mountain, Me., U.S. 45°8′ N, 70°22′ W 94
Bigfork, Minn., U.S. 47°42′ N, 93°40′ W 90
Bigfork, Mont., U.S. 48°2′ N, 114°7′ W 90
Biggar, Can. 52°3′ N, 107°59′ W 90
Bigge Island, Austral. 14°23′ S, 124°2′ E 230
Biggeluobbal, Nor. 69°22′ N, 23°22′ E 152
Biggleswade, U.K. 52°4′ N, 0°16′ E 162
Biggs, Calif., U.S. 39°24′ N, 121°43′ W 90
Bighorn Mountains, Wyo., U.S. 43°48′ N, 107°26′ W 90
Bignasco, Switz. 46°21′ N, 8°36′ E 167
Bigniba, river, Can. 49°2′ N, 77°43′ W 94
Bignona, Senegal 12°48′ N, 16°10′ W 222
Bigobo, Dem. Rep. of the Congo 5°27′ S, 27°34′ E 224
Bigstick Lake, Can. 50°16′ N, 109°40′ W 90
Bigstone Lake, lake, Can. 53°36′ N, 96°20′ W 108
Bigstone, river, Can. 55°28′ N, 95°12′ W 108
Bihać, Bosn. and Herzg. 44°49′ N, 15°53′ E 168
Bihar, adm. division, India 25°9′ N, 84°25′ E 188
Bihar Sharif, India 25°10′ N, 85°30′ E 197
Biharamulo, Tanzania 2°40′ S, 31°21′ E 224
Biharkeresztes, Hung. 47°7′ N, 21°42′ E 168
Bihor, adm. division, Rom. 46°51′ N, 21°40′ E 156
Bihor, Munţii, Rom. 46°42′ N, 22°25′ E 168
Bihosava, Belarus 55°50′ N, 27°42′ E 166
Biïkzhal, Kaz. 46°51′ N, 54°48′ E 158
Bijagós, Arquipélago dos, North Atlantic Ocean 10°37′ N, 16°42′ W 222
Bijapur, India 18°46′ N, 80°49′ E 188
Bijapur, India 16°49′ N, 75°42′ E 188
Bījār, Iran 35°50′ N, 47°32′ E 180
Bijauri, Nepal 28°5′ N, 82°28′ E 197
Bijawar, India 24°37′ N, 79°30′ E 197
Bijeljina, Bosn. and Herzg. 44°45′ N, 19°14′ E 168
Bijelo Polje, Serb. and Mont. 43°1′ N, 19°44′ E 168
Bijie, China 27°18′ N, 105°19′ E 198
Bikaner, India 28°1′ N, 73°20′ E 186
Bikava, Latv. 56°44′ N, 27°2′ E 166
Bikin, Russ. 46°53′ N, 134°22′ E 190
Bikita, Zimb. 20°6′ S, 31°37′ E 227
Bīkkū Bīttī, peak, Lib. 22°8′ N, 19°11′ E 216
Bikoro, Dem. Rep. of the Congo 0°45′ N, 18°6′ E 218
Bikovo, Serb. and Mont. 46°0′ N, 19°45′ E 168
Bila, river, China 49°9′ N, 122°19′ E 198
Bila, Tanjung, Indonesia 1°8′ N, 108°39′ E 196
Bila Tserkva, Ukr. 49°47′ N, 30°14′ E 158
Biläcäri, Azerb. 40°27′ N, 49°47′ E 195
Bilād Banī Bū 'Alī, Oman 22°4′ N, 59°18′ E 182
Bilanga, Burkina Faso 12°32′ N, 5°296′ W 222
Bilaspur, India 22°4′ N, 82°8′ E 197
Biläsuvar, Azerb. 39°26′ N, 48°31′ E 195
Bilati, Dem. Rep. of the Congo 0°36′ N, 28°47′ E 224
Bilati, river, Dem. Rep. of the Congo 0°53′ N, 28°12′ E 224
Bilbao, Sp. 43°14′ N, 2°58′ W 150
Bile, Ukr. 51°38′ N, 26°4′ E 152
Bileća, Bosn. and Herzg. 42°52′ N, 18°24′ E 168
Bilecik, Turk. 40°9′ N, 29°58′ E 156
Bilhorod-Dnistrovs'kyy, Ukr. 46°11′ N, 30°17′ E 156
Bili, Dem. Rep. of the Congo 4°7′ N, 25°3′ E 224
Bili, river, Dem. Rep. of the Congo 4°4′ N, 24°28′ E 224
Bilibino, Russ. 67°54′ N, 166°13′ E 160
Bilican Dağları, peak, Turk. 38°56′ N, 42°6′ E 195
Bilimora, India 20°46′ N, 72°56′ E 188
Bilin, Myanmar 17°14′ N, 97°12′ E 202
Bilir, Russ. 65°29′ N, 131°52′ E 160
Bilis Qooqaani, Somalia 0°15′ N, 41°36′ E 224
Bilje, Croatia 45°35′ N, 18°45′ E 168
Bill, Wyo., U.S. 43°12′ N, 105°16′ W 90
Bill Williams, river, Ariz., U.S. 34°18′ N, 113°54′ W 101
Billerbeck, Ger. 51°58′ N, 7°17′ E 167
Billerica, Mass., U.S. 42°33′ N, 71°17′ W 104
Billingham, U.K. 54°35′ N, 1°17′ W 162
Billings, Mont., U.S. 45°46′ N, 108°31′ W 90
Billings, Okla., U.S. 36°30′ N, 97°25′ W 92
Billiton see Belitung, island, Indonesia 3°41′ S, 107°3′ E 192
Bilma, Niger 18°42′ N, 12°54′ E 216
Bilma, Grand Erg de, Niger 18°42′ N, 13°31′ E 216
Bilo Gora, Croatia 45°48′ N, 16°57′ E 168
Bilohirs'k, Ukr. 45°5′ N, 34°31′ E 156
Bilohir'ya, Ukr. 50°0′ N, 26°24′ E 152
Bilohorodka, Ukr. 49°59′ N, 26°38′ E 158
Biloli, India 18°45′ N, 77°44′ E 188
Bilopillya, Ukr. 51°7′ N, 34°20′ E 158
Biloxi, Miss., U.S. 30°23′ N, 88°55′ W 103
Bilqâs, Egypt 31°13′ N, 31°21′ E 180
Bil'shivtsi, Ukr. 49°9′ N, 24°46′ E 152
Biltine, Chad 14°30′ N, 20°55′ E 216
Bilto, Nor. 69°28′ N, 21°36′ E 152
Bilüü, Mongolia 48°58′ N, 89°21′ E 184
Bilwaskarma, Nicar. 14°45′ N, 83°52′ W 115
Bilzen, Belg. 50°52′ N, 5°30′ E 167
Bima, river, Dem. Rep. of the Congo 3°3′ N, 25°44′ E 224
Bimbila, Ghana 8°49′ N, 5°297′ E 222
Bimini, adm. division, Bahamas 25°43′ N, 79°27′ W 96
Bimini Islands, North Atlantic Ocean 25°45′ N, 79°5′ W 116

Bin Ghunaymah, Jabal, *Lib.* 24°45′ N, 15°21′ E **216**
Bina, *India* 24°10′ N, 78°12′ E **197**
Binaced, *Sp.* 41°49′ N, 0°12′ E **164**
Binasco, *It.* 45°19′ N, 9°5′ E **167**
Binche, *Belg.* 50°24′ N, 4°9′ E **163**
Bindura, *Zimb.* 17°20′ S, 31°19′ E **224**
Binford, *N. Dak., U.S.* 47°32′ N, 98°23′ W **90**
Binga, *Zimb.* 17°40′ S, 27°20′ E **224**
Bingen, *Wash., U.S.* 45°42′ N, 121°28′ W **100**
Binger, *Okla., U.S.* 35°17′ N, 98°22′ W **92**
BingerbrÜck, *Ger.* 49°57′ N, 7°52′ E **167**
Bingham, *Me., U.S.* 45°2′ N, 69°53′ W **111**
Binghamton, *N.Y., U.S.* 42°6′ N, 75°54′ W **110**
Bingkor, *Malaysia* 5°25′ N, 116°11′ E **203**
Bingley, *U.K.* 53°51′ N, 1°50′ W **162**
Bingöl, *Turk.* 38°52′ N, 40°29′ E **195**
Bingöl Dağları, peak, *Turk.* 39°19′ N, 41°24′ E **195**
Binh Khe, *Vietnam* 13°59′ N, 108°48′ E **202**
Binh Son, *Vietnam* 15°19′ N, 108°44′ E **202**
Binhai, *China* 34°2′ N, 119°51′ E **198**
Binham, *U.K.* 52°55′ N, 0°57′ E **162**
Bini Erdi, spring, *Chad* 20°9′ N, 18°1′ E **216**
Binjai, *Indonesia* 3°51′ N, 108°13′ E **196**
Binjai, *Indonesia* 3°38′ N, 98°29′ E **196**
Binna, Raas, *Somalia* 11°10′ N, 51°10′ E **216**
Binongko, island, *Indonesia* 6°16′ S, 122°51′ E **192**
Bintan, island, *Indonesia* 1°16′ N, 104°33′ E **196**
Bintuan, *Philippines* 12°2′ N, 120°2′ E **203**
Bintulu, *Malaysia* 3°11′ N, 113°2′ E **192**
Binxian, *China* 45°44′ N, 127°29′ E **198**
Binxian, *China* 35°2′ N, 108°3′ E **198**
Binyamina, *Israel* 32°30′ N, 34°56′ E **194**
Binyang, *China* 23°9′ N, 108°46′ E **198**
Binza, *Dem. Rep. of the Congo* 4°30′ S, 15°10′ E **218**
Binzhou, *China* 37°23′ N, 118°4′ E **198**
Bio Addo, *Somalia* 8°10′ N, 49°47′ E **216**
Bío-Bío, adm. division, *Chile* 37°12′ S, 73°8′ W **134**
Bioč, peak, *Serb. and Mont.* 43°12′ N, 18°43′ E **168**
Bioče, *Serb. and Mont.* 42°30′ N, 19°20′ E **168**
Bioko, island, *Equatorial Guinea* 3°20′ N, 8°35′ E **253**
Bioko, region, *Africa* 3°13′ N, 8°14′ E **218**
Biokovo, peak, *Croatia* 43°18′ N, 17°0′ E **168**
Biola, *Calif., U.S.* 36°48′ N, 120°2′ W **100**
Biópio, *Angola* 12°26′ S, 13°45′ E **220**
Bioska, *Serb. and Mont.* 43°52′ N, 19°39′ E **168**
Biota, *Sp.* 42°16′ N, 1°12′ W **164**
Bipindi, *Cameroon* 3°14′ N, 10°24′ E **218**
Bir, *India* 18°59′ N, 75°46′ E **188**
Bîr Abu el Ḥuṣein, spring, *Egypt* 22°52′ N, 29°54′ E **182**
Bîr Abu Gharâdiq, spring, *Egypt* 30°5′ N, 28°2′ E **180**
Bîr Abu Hashîm, spring, *Egypt* 23°41′ N, 34°3′ E **182**
Bîr Abu Minqâr, spring, *Egypt* 26°29′ N, 27°35′ E **180**
Bîr Abu Sa'fa, spring, *Egypt* 23°14′ N, 34°48′ E **182**
Bi'r adh Dhakar, spring, *Lib.* 25°42′ N, 22°42′ E **226**
Bi'r al Ma'rūf, spring, *Lib.* 25°6′ N, 18°31′ E **216**
Bi'r al Qāf, spring, *Lib.* 28°16′ N, 15°22′ E **216**
Bi'r al Qarḑī, spring, *Yemen* 15°35′ N, 47°18′ E **182**
Bi'r 'Allāq, spring, *Lib.* 31°7′ N, 11°54′ E **214**
Bir Anzarane, *Western Sahara* 23°51′ N, 14°33′ W **214**
Bir Bel Guerdâne, spring, *Mauritania* 25°23′ N, 10°31′ W **214**
Bir Beressof, spring, *Alg.* 32°33′ N, 7°56′ E **214**
Bi'r Bin Ghanīyah, spring, *Lib.* 31°10′ N, 21°52′ E **226**
Bi'r Bū Ḩawsh, spring, *Lib.* 25°29′ N, 22°4′ E **216**
Bi'r Bū Zurayyiq, spring, *Lib.* 25°34′ N, 22°15′ E **226**
Bir Chali, spring, *Mali* 22°58′ N, 4°60′ W **214**
Bîr Dibis, spring, *Egypt* 22°11′ N, 29°29′ E **226**
Bir ed Deheb, spring, *Alg.* 25°8′ N, 1°58′ W **214**
Bîr el 'Abd, *Egypt* 31°0′ N, 32°59′ E **194**
Bir el Hadjaj, spring, *Alg.* 26°26′ N, 1°26′ W **214**
Bîr el Ḥamma, *Egypt* 30°37′ N, 33°32′ E **194**
Bîr el Kaseiba, spring, *Egypt* 30°59′ N, 33°17′ E **194**
Bir el Khzaïm, spring, *Mauritania* 24°28′ N, 7°50′ W **214**
Bir el Ksaïb, spring, *Mali* 21°16′ N, 5°38′ W **222**
Bîr el Maqeibra, spring, *Egypt* 30°52′ N, 32°50′ E **194**
Bîr el Qanâdîl, spring, *Egypt* 30°58′ N, 33°7′ E **194**
Bîr el Roghwi, spring, *Egypt* 30°46′ N, 33°26′ E **194**
Bi'r Fardān, spring, *Saudi Arabia* 22°4′ N, 48°38′ E **182**
Bîr Fuâd, spring, *Egypt* 30°25′ N, 26°27′ E **180**
Bi'r Ghawdah, spring, *Saudi Arabia* 23°0′ N, 44°17′ E **182**
Bîr Gifgâfa, *Egypt* 30°26′ N, 33°11′ E **194**
Bîr Ḥasana, *Egypt* 30°27′ N, 33°47′ E **194**
Bîr Ḥibeiṭa, spring, *Egypt* 30°27′ N, 32°25′ E **194**
Bir Igueni, spring, *Mauritania* 20°27′ N, 14°55′ W **222**
Bi'r Juraybī'āt, spring, *Iraq* 29°10′ N, 45°30′ E **196**
Bîr Khâlda, spring, *Egypt* 30°48′ N, 27°14′ E **180**
Bîr Kiseiba, spring, *Egypt* 22°40′ N, 29°55′ E **182**
Bîr Lahfân, *Egypt* 31°0′ N, 33°51′ E **194**
Bir Lahmar, *Western Sahara* 26°4′ N, 11°4′ W **214**
Bir Larache, spring, *Alg.* 32°0′ N, 8°13′ E **214**
Bir Lemouissat, spring, *Mauritania* 25°3′ N, 10°33′ W **214**
Bîr Madkûr, spring, *Egypt* 30°42′ N, 32°31′ E **194**
Bîr Misâḥa, spring, *Egypt* 22°11′ N, 27°56′ E **226**
Bir Mogreïn (Fort Trinquet), *Mauritania* 25°13′ N, 11°37′ W **214**
Bîr Murr, spring, *Egypt* 23°21′ N, 30°4′ E **182**
Bîr Nâhid, spring, *Egypt* 30°14′ N, 28°53′ E **180**
Bîr Nakheila, spring, *Egypt* 23°59′ N, 30°51′ E **182**
Bi'r Nāṣirah, spring, *Lib.* 30°18′ N, 11°23′ E **214**
Bir Ould Brini, spring, *Alg.* 25°24′ N, 1°50′ W **214**
Bir Ounâne, spring, *Mali* 21°26′ N, 3°55′ W **222**
Bîr Qaṭia, spring, *Egypt* 30°57′ N, 32°44′ E **194**
Bir Rhorrafa, spring, *Alg.* 32°20′ N, 8°4′ E **214**
Bir Romane, spring, *Tun.* 32°32′ N, 8°21′ E **214**
Bîr Ṣahara, spring, *Egypt* 22°50′ N, 28°34′ E **226**
Bîr Salala, spring, *Sudan* 19°24′ N, 35°38′ E **182**
Bîr Seiyâla, spring, *Egypt* 26°7′ N, 33°54′ E **180**
Bîr Shalatein, spring, *Egypt* 23°3′ N, 35°35′ E **182**
Bîr Takhlîs, spring, *Egypt* 22°24′ N, 30°7′ E **182**
Bîr Ṭarfâwi, spring, *Egypt* 22°56′ N, 28°51′ E **226**
Bi'r Tārsīn, spring, *Lib.* 31°41′ N, 13°23′ E **216**
Bir Tinkardad, spring, *Western Sahara* 23°57′ N, 12°58′ W **214**
B'ir Tlakshin, oil field, *Lib.* 30°55′ N, 11°53′ E **143**
Bîr Ungât, spring, *Egypt* 22°6′ N, 33°44′ E **182**
Bi'r Uoigh, spring, *Lib.* 23°7′ N, 17°20′ E **216**
Bi'r Zalṭan, spring, *Lib.* 28°27′ N, 19°44′ E **216**
Bîr Zeidûn, spring, *Egypt* 25°42′ N, 33°42′ E **180**
Bir Zīrī, spring, *Mauritania* 21°32′ N, 10°47′ W **222**
Bir Zreïgat, spring, *Mauritania* 22°28′ N, 8°54′ W **222**
Birāk, *Lib.* 27°34′ N, 14°14′ E **216**
Birao, *Cen. Af. Rep.* 10°16′ N, 22°47′ E **218**
Biratnagar, *Nepal* 26°28′ N, 87°16′ E **197**
Birch Creek, *Alas., U.S.* 66°16′ N, 145°51′ W **98**
Birch Hills, *Can.* 52°59′ N, 105°27′ W **108**
Birch Lake, *Can.* 51°21′ N, 92°57′ W **110**
Birch Mountains, *Can.* 57°34′ N, 113°37′ W **108**
Birch River, *Can.* 52°23′ N, 101°8′ W **108**
Birch, river, *Can.* 58°17′ N, 113°56′ W **108**
Birchiş, *Rom.* 45°58′ N, 22°10′ E **168**
Birchwood, *Alas., U.S.* 61°25′ N, 149°25′ W **98**
Bird, *Can.* 56°29′ N, 94°15′ W **108**
Bird City, *Kans., U.S.* 39°45′ N, 101°31′ W **90**
Bird Island, *Minn., U.S.* 44°45′ N, 94°55′ W **94**
Bird, river, *Can.* 50°34′ N, 95°11′ W **90**
Bireun, *Indonesia* 5°11′ N, 96°41′ E **196**
Birganj, *Nepal* 27°1′ N, 84°54′ E **197**
Biri, river, *Sudan* 7°40′ N, 26°4′ E **224**
Biria, river, *Venez.* 1°14′ N, 66°34′ W **136**
Birigui, *Braz.* 21°16′ S, 50°20′ W **138**
Biriliyussy, *Russ.* 57°9′ N, 90°39′ E **169**
Birīn, *Syr.* 35°0′ N, 36°39′ E **194**
Birine, *Alg.* 35°38′ N, 3°13′ E **150**
Birini, *Cen. Af. Rep.* 7°50′ N, 22°26′ E **218**
Bīrjand, *Iran* 32°55′ N, 59°17′ E **180**
Birkenfeld, *Ger.* 49°38′ N, 7°10′ E **163**
Birkenfeld, *Oreg., U.S.* 45°58′ N, 123°19′ W **100**
Birkenhead, *U.K.* 53°24′ N, 3°2′ W **162**
Birkfeld, *Aust.* 47°20′ N, 15°41′ E **168**
Bîrlad, *Rom.* 46°13′ N, 27°40′ E **156**
Birlik, *Kaz.* 44°3′ N, 73°33′ E **184**
Birmingham, *Ala., U.S.* 33°30′ N, 86°49′ W **96**
Birmingham, *U.K.* 52°28′ N, 1°53′ W **162**
Birmitrapur, *India* 22°22′ N, 84°43′ E **197**
Birni, *Benin* 10°1′ N, 1°30′ E **222**
Birni Ngaouré, *Niger* 13°6′ N, 2°55′ E **222**
Birni Nkonni, *Niger* 13°47′ N, 5°15′ E **222**
Birnie, *Can.* 50°27′ N, 99°27′ W **90**
Birnin Gwari, *Nig.* 10°59′ N, 6°47′ E **222**
Birnin Kebbi, *Nig.* 12°26′ N, 4°12′ E **222**
Birniwa, *Nig.* 12°48′ N, 10°15′ E **222**
Birobidzhan, *Russ.* 48°54′ N, 133°0′ E **190**
Birong, *Philippines* 9°24′ N, 118°9′ E **203**
Birou, *Mali* 15°4′ N, 9°56′ W **222**
Birougou, Monts, peak, *Gabon* 1°55′ S, 12°9′ E **218**
Birrie, river, *Austral.* 29°22′ S, 146°48′ E **230**
Birshoghyr, *Kaz.* 48°24′ N, 58°43′ E **158**
Birsk, *Russ.* 55°26′ N, 55°36′ E **154**
Birštonas, *Lith.* 54°36′ N, 24°0′ E **166**
Birtin, *Rom.* 46°58′ N, 22°32′ E **168**
Birtle, *Can.* 50°26′ N, 101°4′ W **90**
Biru, *China* 31°32′ N, 93°47′ E **188**
Biryakovo, *Russ.* 59°33′ N, 41°29′ E **154**
Biržai, *Lith.* 56°11′ N, 24°44′ E **166**
Bîrzava, *Rom.* 46°6′ N, 21°59′ E **168**
Bîrzava, river, *Rom.* 45°16′ N, 20°56′ E **168**
Bisaccia, *It.* 41°1′ N, 15°22′ E **156**
Bisbee, *Ariz., U.S.* 31°27′ N, 109°54′ W **92**
Bisbee, *N. Dak., U.S.* 48°36′ N, 99°24′ W **90**
Biscarrués, *Sp.* 42°13′ N, 0°45′ E **164**
Biscay, Bay of 43°48′ N, 7°35′ W **143**
Biscay Plain, *North Atlantic Ocean* 45°12′ N, 8°17′ W **253**
Biscayne Bay 25°34′ N, 80°28′ W **105**
Biscayne, Key, island, *Fla., U.S.* 25°42′ N, 80°10′ W **105**
Biscayne National Park, *Atlantic Ocean* 25°34′ N, 80°7′ W **105**
Bischleben, *Ger.* 50°56′ N, 10°58′ E **152**
Bischofsheim, *Ger.* 50°24′ N, 10°0′ E **167**
Bischwiller, *Fr.* 48°46′ N, 7°50′ E **163**
Biscotasing, *Can.* 47°18′ N, 82°7′ W **94**
Biser, *Bulg.* 41°53′ N, 25°57′ E **156**
Biserovo, *Russ.* 59°4′ N, 53°24′ E **154**
Bisert', *Russ.* 56°52′ N, 59°4′ E **154**
Biševo, island, *Croatia* 42°53′ N, 15°57′ E **168**
Bishkek, *Kyrg.* 42°50′ N, 74°26′ E **184**
Bisho, *S. Af.* 32°49′ S, 27°31′ E **227**
Bishop, *Tex., U.S.* 27°34′ N, 97°48′ W **96**
Bishop Auckland, *U.K.* 54°40′ N, 1°42′ W **162**
Bishop Creek Reservoir, lake, *Nev., U.S.* 41°13′ N, 115°34′ W **90**
Bishops and Clerks, islands, *St George's Channel* 51°42′ N, 6°54′ W **150**
Bishop's Castle, *U.K.* 52°28′ N, 2°59′ W **162**
Bishop's Falls, *Can.* 49°1′ N, 55°31′ W **111**
Bishop's Stortford, *U.K.* 51°51′ N, 0°8′ E **162**
Biskia, *Eritrea* 15°28′ N, 37°30′ E **182**
Biskintā, *Leb.* 33°56′ N, 35°48′ E **194**
Biskra, *Alg.* 34°50′ N, 5°44′ E **214**
Bislig, *Philippines* 8°13′ N, 126°16′ E **203**
Bismarck, *Ill., U.S.* 40°15′ N, 87°36′ W **102**
Bismarck, *N. Dak., U.S.* 46°46′ N, 100°54′ W **90**
Bismarck Archipelago, *Bismarck Sea* 1°32′ S, 145°44′ E **192**
Bismarck Range, *P.N.G.* 5°1′ S, 144°9′ E **192**
Bismarck Sea 4°3′ S, 145°12′ E **192**
Bismil, *Turk.* 37°52′ N, 40°42′ E **195**
Bison, *S. Dak., U.S.* 45°31′ N, 102°28′ W **90**
Bison Lake, *Can.* 57°13′ N, 116°28′ W **108**
Bison Peak, *Colo., U.S.* 39°13′ N, 105°34′ W **90**
Bissameuttack, *India* 19°30′ N, 83°30′ E **188**
Bissau, *Guinea-Bissau* 11°49′ N, 15°45′ W **222**
Bissett, *Can.* 51°0′ N, 95°41′ W **90**
Bissiga, *Burkina Faso* 12°41′ N, 1°14′ W **222**
Bissikrima, *Guinea* 10°53′ N, 10°59′ W **222**
Bistcho Lake, *Can.* 59°49′ N, 119°18′ W **108**
Bistrica, *Serb. and Mont.* 43°28′ N, 19°41′ E **168**
Bistriḩa-Năsăud, adm. division, *Rom.* 47°20′ N, 24°9′ E **156**
Bistriṭa, *Rom.* 47°9′ N, 24°29′ E **156**
Bistriţei, Munţii, *Rom.* 47°14′ N, 25°3′ E **156**
Biswan, *India* 27°29′ N, 81°0′ E **197**
Bita, river, *Col.* 5°39′ N, 69°8′ W **136**
Bitburg, *Ger.* 49°58′ N, 6°31′ E **167**
Bitche, *Fr.* 49°3′ N, 7°26′ E **163**
Bitely, *Mich., U.S.* 43°44′ N, 85°52′ W **102**
Bitkin, *Chad* 11°58′ N, 18°18′ E **216**
Bitlis, *Turk.* 38°21′ N, 42°3′ E **195**
Bitola, *Maced.* 41°1′ N, 21°23′ E **180**
Bitter Root Range, *North America* 47°31′ N, 116°18′ W **90**
Bitterfeld, *Ger.* 51°37′ N, 12°18′ E **152**
Bitterfontein, *S. Af.* 31°3′ S, 18°14′ E **227**
Bitterroot Range, *Idaho, U.S.* 47°46′ N, 116°27′ W **80**
Bitumount, *Can.* 57°22′ N, 111°36′ W **108**
Biu, *Nig.* 10°36′ N, 12°12′ E **216**
Bivolu, peak, *Rom.* 47°13′ N, 25°51′ E **156**
Bixad, *Rom.* 47°55′ N, 23°22′ E **168**
Bixby, *Okla., U.S.* 35°54′ N, 95°54′ W **96**
Biya, river, *Russ.* 51°16′ N, 87°47′ E **190**
Biyang, *China* 32°44′ N, 113°23′ E **198**
Biysk, *Russ.* 52°35′ N, 85°13′ E **184**
Bizana, *S. Af.* 30°53′ S, 29°52′ E **227**
Bizerte, *Tun.* 37°17′ N, 9°51′ E **156**
Bjärnum, *Nor.* 56°18′ N, 13°42′ E **152**
Bjelasica, peak, *Croatia* 45°15′ N, 14°53′ E **156**
Bjelovar, *Croatia* 45°53′ N, 16°49′ E **168**
Björbo, *Nor.* 60°24′ N, 14°44′ E **152**
Björkholmen, *Nor.* 66°47′ N, 19°6′ E **152**
Björkö, island, *Sw.* 59°54′ N, 19°3′ E **166**
Björköby, *Fin.* 63°19′ N, 21°20′ E **152**
Björksele, *Nor.* 64°59′ N, 18°33′ E **152**
Björna, *Nor.* 63°32′ N, 18°35′ E **152**
Björneborg see Pori, *Fin.* 61°26′ N, 21°44′ E **166**
Bjørnøya (Bear Island), *Nor.* 73°46′ N, 15°27′ E **160**
Bjørnskinn, *Nor.* 68°59′ N, 15°41′ E **152**
Bjuröklubb, *Nor.* 64°28′ N, 21°35′ E **152**
Bjuv, *Nor.* 56°6′ N, 12°52′ E **152**
Bla, *Mali* 13°0′ N, 5°49′ W **222**
Blace, *Serb. and Mont.* 43°17′ N, 21°17′ E **168**
Blache, Lac de La, lake, *Can.* 50°5′ N, 69°53′ W **111**
Black Bay 48°37′ N, 89°19′ W **80**
Black Bay Peninsula, *Can.* 48°34′ N, 88°43′ W **94**
Black Bear Bay 53°15′ N, 56°36′ W **111**
Black Birch Lake, *Can.* 56°48′ N, 108°45′ W **108**
Black Butte, peak, *Calif., U.S.* 39°42′ N, 122°57′ W **90**
Black Butte, peak, *Mont., U.S.* 44°52′ N, 111°55′ W **90**
Black Creek, *Can.* 52°18′ N, 121°8′ W **108**
Black Creek, river, *Miss., U.S.* 31°0′ N, 88°58′ W **103**
Black Diamond, *Can.* 50°41′ N, 114°14′ W **90**
Black Diamond, *Wash., U.S.* 47°17′ N, 121°60′ W **100**
Black Fox Mountain, *Calif., U.S.* 41°20′ N, 121°59′ W **90**
Black Hills, *S. Dak., U.S.* 43°30′ N, 103°50′ W **90**
Black Island, *Antarctica* 78°21′ S, 166°54′ E **248**
Black Lake, *Can.* 59°5′ N, 105°42′ W **108**
Black Lake, lake, *Can.* 59°13′ N, 105°39′ W **108**
Black Lassic, peak, *Calif., U.S.* 40°19′ N, 123°39′ W **90**
Black Mesa, *Ariz., U.S.* 35°57′ N, 111°8′ W **80**
Black Mountain, *Colo., U.S.* 40°46′ N, 107°27′ W **90**
Black Mountain, *Ky., U.S.* 36°53′ N, 82°58′ W **96**
Black Mountain, *Va., U.S.* 36°52′ N, 83°2′ W **80**
Black Mountains, *Ariz., U.S.* 34°56′ N, 114°28′ W **101**
Black Mountains, *Calif., U.S.* 36°10′ N, 116°46′ W **101**
Black Mountains, *U.K.* 52°4′ N, 3°9′ W **162**
Black Peak, *Ariz., U.S.* 34°6′ N, 114°15′ W **101**
Black Peak, *N. Mex., U.S.* 32°54′ N, 108°14′ W **92**
Black Pine Peak, *Idaho, U.S.* 42°8′ N, 113°12′ W **90**
Black Range, *N. Mex., U.S.* 33°29′ N, 108°42′ W **112**
Black, river, *Ark., U.S.* 35°51′ N, 91°15′ W **80**
Black River Falls, *Wis., U.S.* 44°17′ N, 90°52′ W **94**
Black, river, *La., U.S.* 31°35′ N, 91°54′ W **103**
Black, river, *Minn., U.S.* 48°25′ N, 94°20′ W **90**
Black, river, *N.Y., U.S.* 44°3′ N, 75°54′ W **80**
Black Rock Desert, *Nev., U.S.* 40°50′ N, 119°26′ W **90**
Black Rock Range, *Nev., U.S.* 41°25′ N, 119°9′ W **90**
Black Sea 43°19′ N, 33°22′ E **158**
Black see Da, river, *Vietnam* 21°11′ N, 104°8′ E **202**
Black Volta, river, *Ghana* 8°33′ N, 2°3′ W **222**
Black Volta see Mouhoun, river, *Burkina Faso* 11°43′ N, 4°30′ W **222**
Black Warrior, river, *Ala., U.S.* 34°6′ N, 88°13′ W **80**
Blackall, *Austral.* 24°26′ S, 145°31′ E **231**
Blackburn, *U.K.* 53°45′ N, 2°30′ W **162**
Blackburn, Mount, *Alas., U.S.* 61°36′ N, 143°37′ W **98**
Blackdown Hills, *U.K.* 50°56′ N, 3°7′ W **162**
Blackduck, *Minn., U.S.* 47°42′ N, 94°33′ W **90**
Blackfoot, *Idaho, U.S.* 43°11′ N, 112°20′ W **90**
Blackfoot Mountains, *Idaho, U.S.* 42°58′ N, 111°45′ W **90**
Blackie, *Can.* 50°37′ N, 113°37′ W **108**
Blackmoor Vale, *U.K.* 50°57′ N, 2°24′ W **162**
Blackpool, *U.K.* 53°49′ N, 3°3′ W **162**
Blacksburg, *Va., U.S.* 37°13′ N, 80°26′ W **96**
Blackstone, *Mass., U.S.* 42°0′ N, 71°33′ W **104**
Blackstone, river, *Can.* 61°10′ N, 123°2′ W **108**
Blackville, *Can.* 46°44′ N, 65°51′ W **94**
Blackwell, *Okla., U.S.* 36°46′ N, 97°17′ W **92**
Blackwell, *Tex., U.S.* 32°3′ N, 100°19′ W **92**
Blaenau Ffestiniog, *U.K.* 52°59′ N, 3°55′ W **162**
Blåfjellhatten, peak, *Nor.* 64°6′ N, 13°15′ E **152**
Blagaj, *Bosn. and Herzg.* 44°3′ N, 17°11′ E **168**
Blagodarnyy, *Russ.* 45°3′ N, 43°20′ E **158**
Blagoevgrad, *Bulg.* 42°1′ N, 23°6′ E **168**
Blagoevgrad, adm. division, *Bulg.* 41°27′ N, 23°5′ E **168**
Blagopoluchiya, Zaliv 75°8′ N, 58°41′ E **160**
Blagoveshchenka, *Russ.* 52°49′ N, 79°55′ E **184**
Blagoveshchensk, *Russ.* 50°22′ N, 127°32′ E **198**
Blagoveshchenskoye, *Russ.* 61°28′ N, 42°36′ E **154**
Blagoyevo, *Russ.* 63°25′ N, 47°57′ E **154**
Blaiken, *Nor.* 65°15′ N, 16°49′ E **152**
Blaine, *Wash., U.S.* 48°58′ N, 122°44′ W **100**
Blainville-sur-l'Eau, *Fr.* 48°32′ N, 6°24′ E **163**
Blair, *Nebr., U.S.* 41°31′ N, 96°8′ W **90**
Blaj, *Rom.* 46°10′ N, 23°57′ E **156**
Blake Plateau, *North Atlantic Ocean* 29°56′ N, 78°19′ W **253**
Blake Point, *Mich., U.S.* 47°58′ N, 88°28′ W **110**
Blake-Bahama Ridge, *North Atlantic Ocean* 29°6′ N, 73°10′ W **253**
Blakeney, *U.K.* 52°57′ N, 1°1′ E **162**
Blakeney, *U.K.* 51°45′ N, 2°29′ W **162**
Blakiston, Mount, *Can.* 49°4′ N, 114°8′ W **90**
Blâmont, *Fr.* 48°34′ N, 6°50′ E **163**
Blanc, Cap, *Sp.* 39°9′ N, 2°28′ E **150**
Blanc, Cap, *Western Sahara* 20°59′ N, 17°36′ W **222**
Blanc, Mont, peak, *Fr.-It.* 45°50′ N, 6°49′ E **150**
Blanc, Réservoir, lake, *Can.* 47°46′ N, 73°19′ W **94**
Blanca, Bahía 39°3′ S, 62°43′ W **139**
Blanca Peak, Sierra, *N. Mex., U.S.* 33°21′ N, 105°52′ W **92**
Blanca, Sierra, peak, *Tex., U.S.* 31°13′ N, 105°30′ W **92**
Blanchard, *La., U.S.* 32°34′ N, 93°55′ W **103**
Blanchard, *Mich., U.S.* 43°30′ N, 85°5′ W **102**
Blanchard, *Okla., U.S.* 35°7′ N, 97°40′ W **92**
Blanchardville, *Wis., U.S.* 42°47′ N, 89°52′ W **102**
Blanchester, *Ohio, U.S.* 39°17′ N, 83°59′ W **102**
Blanchland, *U.K.* 54°51′ N, 2°4′ W **162**
Blanco, *Tex., U.S.* 30°5′ N, 98°25′ W **92**
Blanco, Bahía 29°0′ N, 115°4′ W **92**
Blanco, Cabo, *C.R.* 9°31′ N, 85°55′ W **115**
Blanco, Cape, *Oreg., U.S.* 42°39′ N, 124°56′ W **90**
Blanco, Lago, lake, *Arg.* 45°56′ S, 71°8′ W **134**
Blanco, Punta, *Mex.* 29°6′ N, 115°5′ W **92**
Blanco, river, *Arg.* 29°28′ S, 69°10′ W **134**
Blanco, river, *Bol.* 14°47′ S, 63°37′ W **137**
Blandford Forum, *U.K.* 50°51′ N, 2°10′ W **162**
Blanding, *Utah, U.S.* 37°37′ N, 109°29′ W **92**
Blanes, *Sp.* 41°41′ N, 2°48′ E **164**
Blangy, *Fr.* 49°54′ N, 1°37′ E **163**
Blankenberge, *Belg.* 51°18′ N, 3°7′ E **163**
Blankenheim, *Ger.* 50°26′ N, 6°39′ E **167**
Blanquilla, La, island, *Venez.* 11°59′ N, 64°58′ W **116**
Blantyre, *Malawi* 15°52′ S, 35°2′ E **224**
Blasket Islands, *Atlantic Ocean* 51°59′ N, 11°30′ W **150**
Blatec, *Maced.* 41°49′ N, 22°35′ E **168**
Blato, *Croatia* 42°55′ N, 16°46′ E **168**
Blattnicksele, *Nor.* 65°18′ N, 17°38′ E **152**
Bléneau, *Fr.* 47°42′ N, 2°56′ E **150**
Blenheim, *Can.* 42°20′ N, 81°60′ W **102**
Blenheim, *N.Z.* 41°32′ S, 173°55′ E **240**
Blenheim Palace, site, *U.K.* 51°49′ N, 1°23′ W **162**
Bletchley, *U.K.* 51°59′ N, 0°45′ E **162**
Bleue, *Indonesia* 5°0′ N, 96°13′ E **196**
Bleus, Monts, *Dem. Rep. of the Congo* 1°8′ N, 29°35′ E **224**
Blexen, *Ger.* 53°31′ N, 8°33′ E **163**
Blida, *Alg.* 36°27′ N, 2°49′ E **150**
Blind River, *Can.* 46°11′ N, 82°58′ W **94**
Blinisht, *Alban.* 41°52′ N, 19°59′ E **168**
Blissfield, *Mich., U.S.* 41°49′ N, 83°51′ W **102**
Blitta, *Togo* 8°20′ N, 0°58′ E **222**
Błaszki, *Pol.* 51°39′ N, 18°27′ E **152**
Block Island, *R.I., U.S.* 41°12′ N, 71°43′ W **104**
Bloedrivier, *S. Af.* 27°56′ S, 30°32′ E **227**
Bloemfontein, *S. Af.* 29°9′ S, 26°3′ E **227**
Bloemhof, *S. Af.* 27°40′ S, 25°34′ E **227**
Blois, *Fr.* 47°35′ N, 1°20′ E **150**
Blönduós, *Ice.* 65°39′ N, 20°21′ W **246**
Bloodvein, river, *Can.* 51°25′ N, 96°32′ W **108**
Bloody Mountain, *Calif., U.S.* 37°32′ N, 118°60′ W **92**
Bloody Run Hills, *Nev., U.S.* 41°6′ N, 117°59′ W **90**
Bloomburg, *Tex., U.S.* 33°8′ N, 94°4′ W **103**
Bloomer, *Wis., U.S.* 45°6′ N, 91°29′ W **94**
Bloomfield, *Conn., U.S.* 41°49′ N, 72°44′ W **104**
Bloomfield, *Iowa, U.S.* 40°44′ N, 92°25′ W **94**
Bloomfield, *Nebr., U.S.* 42°33′ N, 97°39′ W **90**
Bloomfield, *N. Mex., U.S.* 36°42′ N, 107°59′ W **92**
Bloomfield Hills, *Mich., U.S.* 42°35′ N, 83°16′ W **102**
Bloomingburg, *Ohio, U.S.* 39°35′ N, 83°24′ W **102**
Bloomingdale, *N.Y., U.S.* 44°24′ N, 74°6′ W **104**
Bloomington, *Ill., U.S.* 40°28′ N, 88°59′ W **102**
Bloomington, *Ind., U.S.* 39°10′ N, 86°32′ W **102**
Bloomington, *Tex., U.S.* 28°38′ N, 96°54′ W **96**
Bloomsburg, *Pa., U.S.* 40°59′ N, 76°28′ W **94**
Bloomville, *Ohio, U.S.* 41°2′ N, 83°1′ W **102**
Blouberg, peak, *S. Af.* 23°5′ S, 28°52′ E **227**
Blount Nunatak, peak, *Antarctica* 83°20′ S, 52°56′ W **248**
Blue Bell Knoll, peak, *Utah, U.S.* 38°8′ N, 111°34′ W **90**
Blue Diamond, *Nev., U.S.* 36°2′ N, 115°25′ W **101**
Blue Hill, *Nebr., U.S.* 40°18′ N, 98°27′ W **90**
Blue Hill Bay 44°6′ N, 68°45′ W **111**
Blue Lagoon National Park, *Zambia* 15°36′ S, 26°55′ E **224**
Blue Lake, *Calif., U.S.* 40°53′ N, 123°60′ W **90**
Blue Mound, *Ill., U.S.* 39°41′ N, 89°8′ W **102**
Blue Mountain, *Pa., U.S.* 40°30′ N, 76°43′ W **94**
Blue Mountain Pass, *Oreg., U.S.* 42°18′ N, 117°50′ W **90**
Blue Mountain, peak, *Ark., U.S.* 34°38′ N, 94°8′ W **96**
Blue Mountain, peak, *Calif., U.S.* 41°49′ N, 120°57′ W **90**
Blue Mountain, peak, *Nev., U.S.* 40°58′ N, 118°10′ W **90**
Blue Mountain, peak, *Oreg., U.S.* 42°19′ N, 117°58′ W **90**
Blue Mountains, *Oreg., U.S.* 45°14′ N, 118°33′ W **90**
Blue Nile, adm. division, *Sudan* 11°18′ N, 33°10′ E **182**
Blue Nile see Ābay, river, *Eth.* 11°15′ N, 38°15′ E **224**
Blue Rapids, *Kans., U.S.* 39°40′ N, 96°40′ W **94**
Blue Ridge, *Can.* 54°8′ N, 115°24′ W **108**
Blue Ridge, *Ga., U.S.* 34°50′ N, 84°19′ W **96**
Blue Ridge, mountains, *North America* 36°39′ N, 80°30′ W **96**
Blue River, *Can.* 52°6′ N, 119°19′ W **108**
Blue, river, *Can.* 59°23′ N, 129°53′ W **108**
Blue Springs, *Nebr., U.S.* 40°7′ N, 96°41′ W **92**
Blue Stack Mountains, *Ire.* 54°44′ N, 8°11′ W **150**
Bluefields, *Nicar.* 12°1′ N, 83°47′ W **116**
Bluenose Lake, *Can.* 68°21′ N, 120°48′ W **98**
Bluff, *Alas., U.S.* 64°43′ N, 147°13′ W **98**
Bluff, *N.Z.* 46°37′ S, 168°20′ E **240**
Bluff, *Utah, U.S.* 37°16′ N, 109°33′ W **92**
Bluff, Cape, *Can.* 52°49′ N, 56°38′ W **111**
Bluff Knoll, peak, *Austral.* 34°26′ S, 118°1′ E **230**
Bluffton, *Ind., U.S.* 40°44′ N, 85°10′ W **102**
Bluffton, *Ohio, U.S.* 40°53′ N, 83°53′ W **102**
Bluffy Lake, lake, *Can.* 50°46′ N, 93°23′ W **90**
Blumenau, *Braz.* 26°57′ S, 49°3′ W **138**
Blumenthal, *Ger.* 53°11′ N, 8°34′ E **163**
Blunt, *S. Dak., U.S.* 44°30′ N, 99°59′ W **90**
Blustry Mountain, *Can.* 50°36′ N, 121°48′ W **90**
Bly, *Oreg., U.S.* 42°24′ N, 121°3′ W **90**
Blyth, *Can.* 43°44′ N, 81°25′ W **102**
Blyth, *U.K.* 53°22′ N, 1°4′ W **162**
Blyth Range, *Austral.* 26°54′ S, 129°8′ E **230**
Blythe, *Calif., U.S.* 33°36′ N, 114°36′ W **101**
Blytheville, *Ark., U.S.* 35°55′ N, 89°56′ W **82**
Bø, *Nor.* 59°24′ N, 9°1′ E **152**
Bø, *Nor.* 61°8′ N, 5°18′ E **152**
Bø, *Nor.* 68°36′ N, 14°34′ E **152**
Bo, *Sierra Leone* 7°58′ N, 11°44′ W **222**
Bo Duc, *Vietnam* 11°59′ N, 106°48′ E **202**
Bo River, *Sudan* 6°50′ N, 27°54′ E **224**
Boa Nova, *Braz.* 14°25′ S, 40°11′ W **138**
Boa Vista, *Braz.* 2°50′ N, 60°43′ W **130**
Boac, *Philippines* 13°28′ N, 121°52′ E **203**
Boali, *Cen. Af. Rep.* 4°47′ N, 18°6′ E **218**
Boane, *Mozambique* 25°58′ S, 32°19′ E **227**
Boang, island, *P.N.G.* 3°20′ S, 153°22′ E **192**
Boario Terme, *It.* 45°54′ N, 10°9′ E **167**
Boatswain, Baie 51°47′ N, 79°34′ W **110**
Boaz, *Ala., U.S.* 34°11′ N, 86°10′ W **96**
Boba, *Hung.* 47°10′ N, 17°11′ E **168**
Bobai, *China* 22°16′ N, 110°1′ E **198**
Bobbio, *It.* 44°45′ N, 9°22′ E **167**
Böblingen, *Ger.* 48°40′ N, 9°0′ E **152**
Bobo Dioulasso, *Burkina Faso* 11°11′ N, 4°18′ W **222**
Bobonaza, river, *Ecua.* 2°7′ S, 76°57′ W **136**
Bobonong, *Botswana* 21°60′ S, 28°25′ E **227**
Bobota, *Rom.* 47°22′ N, 22°48′ E **168**
Bobovdol, *Bulg.* 42°22′ N, 23°0′ E **168**
Boboye, *Niger* 13°0′ N, 2°47′ E **222**
Bobrov, *Russ.* 51°7′ N, 40°1′ E **158**
Bobures, *Venez.* 9°14′ N, 71°11′ W **136**
Boby, peak, *Madagascar* 22°13′ S, 46°48′ E **220**
Boca del Río, *Mex.* 25°18′ N, 108°32′ W **112**
Boca do Acre, *Braz.* 8°48′ S, 67°24′ W **130**
Boca do Curuquetê, *Braz.* 8°23′ S, 65°43′ W **130**
Boca do Jari, *Braz.* 1°7′ S, 51°58′ W **130**
Boca Grande, *Fla., U.S.* 26°45′ N, 82°15′ W **105**
Boca Mavaca, *Venez.* 2°30′ N, 65°15′ W **136**
Boca Raton, *Fla., U.S.* 26°22′ N, 80°7′ W **105**
Bocaiúva, *Braz.* 17°9′ S, 43°47′ W **138**
Bocay, *Nicar.* 14°19′ N, 85°8′ W **115**
Bocay, river, *Nicar.* 13°34′ N, 85°23′ W **115**
Boceguillas, *Sp.* 41°20′ N, 3°38′ W **164**
Bocheykovo, *Belarus* 55°1′ N, 29°9′ E **166**
Bocholt, *Ger.* 51°50′ N, 6°37′ E **167**
Bochum, *Ger.* 51°29′ N, 7°12′ E **167**
Bockhorn, *Ger.* 53°23′ N, 8°1′ E **163**
Bockum-Hövel, *Ger.* 51°41′ N, 7°44′ E **167**
Bocón, river, *Col.* 3°4′ N, 68°58′ W **136**
Boçoroca, *Braz.* 28°42′ S, 54°57′ W **139**
Bocşa, *Rom.* 45°22′ N, 21°43′ E **168**
Boda, *Cen. Af. Rep.* 4°21′ N, 17°26′ E **218**
Böda, *Sw.* 57°15′ N, 17°1′ E **152**
Bodaybo, *Russ.* 57°59′ N, 114°13′ E **160**
Boddam, *U.K.* 57°27′ N, 1°48′ W **150**
Bodden Town, *U.K.* 19°18′ N, 81°15′ W **115**
Bode, river, *Ger.* 51°55′ N, 11°15′ E **152**
Bode Sadu, *Nig.* 8°54′ N, 4°47′ E **222**
Bodega Head, *Calif., U.S.* 38°17′ N, 123°21′ W **90**
Boden, *Nor.* 65°49′ N, 21°40′ E **152**
Bodfish, *Calif., U.S.* 35°35′ N, 118°30′ W **101**
Bodhei, *Kenya* 1°51′ S, 40°46′ E **224**
Bodiam, *U.K.* 51°0′ N, 0°33′ E **162**
Bodle, *Eth.* 5°3′ N, 42°51′ E **218**
Bodmin Moor, *U.K.* 50°30′ N, 5°4′ W **150**
Bodø, *Nor.* 67°16′ N, 14°41′ E **160**
Bodocó, *Braz.* 7°48′ S, 39°56′ W **132**
Bodoquena, Serra da, *Braz.* 20°23′ S, 56°53′ W **132**
Bodrum, *Turk.* 37°2′ N, 27°24′ E **156**
Boeae, ruin(s), *Gr.* 36°30′ N, 22°58′ E **156**

Boende, *Dem. Rep. of the Congo* 0°15' N, 20°50' E 218
Boerne, *Tex., U.S.* 29°47' N, 98°45' W 92
Boeuf, river, *La., U.S.* 32°15' N, 92°17' W 80
Boffa, *Guinea* 10°11' N, 14°6' W 222
Bofosso, *Guinea* 8°38' N, 9°43' W 222
Bogachiel, river, *Wash., U.S.* 47°52' N, 124°20' W 100
Bogalusa, *La., U.S.* 30°45' N, 89°52' W 103
Bogan, river, *Austral.* 30°31' S, 147°4' E 230
Bogandé, *Burkina Faso* 12°56' N, 0°9' E 222
Bogangolo, *Cen. Af. Rep.* 5°34' N, 18°18' E 218
Bogani Nani Wartabone National Park, *Indonesia* 0°23' N, 123°11' E 238
Bogarra, *Sp.* 38°34' N, 2°13' W 164
Bogart, Mount, *Can.* 50°55' N, 115°02' W 90
Bogatić, *Serb. and Mont.* 44°50' N, 19°29' E 168
Bogatka, Russ. 63°16' N, 44°13' E 154
Bogazi, *Northern Cyprus* 35°19' N, 33°57' E 194
Boğazkale, *Turk.* 40°1' N, 34°35' E 156
Boğazliyan, *Turk.* 39°10' N, 35°15' E 156
Bogcang, river, *China* 31°38' N, 85°48' E 188
Bogda Feng, peak, *China* 43°51' N, 88°12' E 184
Bogdan, peak, *Bulg.* 42°35' N, 24°23' E 156
Bogdanovich, Russ. 56°47' N, 62°2' E 154
Bogdanovka, *Ga.* 41°16' N, 43°34' E 195
Bogdanovka, Russ. 52°10' N, 52°33' E 158
Bögen, *Kaz.* 46°12' N, 61°16' E 184
Bogetići, *Serb. and Mont.* 42°40' N, 18°58' E 168
Boggeragh Mountains, *Ire.* 52°0' N, 9°3' W 150
Boggola, Mount, *Austral.* 23°49' S, 117°26' E 230
Boggs, *Cape, Antarctica* 70°39' S, 63°52' W 248
Boghar, *Alg.* 35°54' N, 2°43' E 150
Boglárlelle, *Hung.* 46°45' N, 17°40' E 168
Bognor Regis, *U.K.* 50°47' N, 0°40' E 162
Bogo, *Philippines* 11°3' N, 124°0' E 203
Bogogobo, *Botswana* 26°37' S, 21°54' E 227
Bogojevo, *Serb. and Mont.* 45°31' N, 19°8' E 168
Bogol Manyo, *Eth.* 4°29' N, 41°37' E 224
Bogomila, *Maced.* 41°35' N, 21°27' E 168
Bogorditsa, Russ. 53°45' N, 38°7' E 154
Bogorodsk, Russ. 62°16' N, 52°36' E 154
Bogorodskoye, Russ. 52°24' N, 140°35' E 190
Bogorodskoye, Russ. 57°48' N, 50°50' E 154
Bogotá, *Col.* 4°36' N, 74°13' W 136
Bogotol, Russ. 56°13' N, 89°39' E 169
Bogou, *Togo* 10°38' N, 0°9' E 222
Bogovina, *Serb. and Mont.* 43°53' N, 21°55' E 168
Bogra, *Bangladesh* 24°49' N, 89°21' E 197
Boguchany, Russ. 58°17' N, 97°27' E 169
Boguchar, Russ. 49°59' N, 40°33' E 158
Bogué, *Mauritania* 16°35' N, 14°19' W 222
Bogue Chitto, *Miss., U.S.* 31°26' N, 90°27' W 103
Bogue Chitto, river, *La., U.S.* 30°48' N, 90°14' W 103
Bogushevsk, *Belarus* 54°51' N, 30°17' E 152
Bogutovac, *Serb. and Mont.* 43°38' N, 20°32' E 168
Bohain, *Fr.* 49°59' N, 3°26' E 163
Bohe, *China* 21°31' N, 111°9' E 198
Bohicon, *Benin* 7°13' N, 2°3' E 222
Böhmer Wald, *Ger.* 49°28' N, 12°14' E 152
Bohodukhiv, *Ukr.* 50°11' N, 35°32' E 158
Bohol, island, *Philippines* 9°7' N, 123°42' E 192
Bohol Sea 8°50' N, 123°36' E 192
Böhönye, *Hung.* 46°24' N, 17°23' E 168
Böhöt, *Mongolia* 45°8' N, 108°10' E 198
Bohu (Bagrax), *China* 41°56' N, 86°40' E 184
Boi, *Nig.* 9°34' N, 9°29' E 222
Boiaçu, *Braz.* 0°28' N, 61°48' W 130
Boila, *Mozambique* 16°10' S, 39°50' E 224
Boim, *Braz.* 3°4' S, 55°16' W 130
Boing, *Sudan* 9°55' N, 33°45' E 224
Boinso, *Ghana* 5°31' N, 2°44' W 222
Boipeba, Ilha de, island, *Braz.* 14°3' S, 39°38' W 132
Bois Blanc Island, *Mich., U.S.* 45°25' N, 84°20' W 81
Bois, river, *Braz.* 18°11' S, 50°8' W 138
Boise, *Idaho, U.S.* 43°36' N, 116°20' W 90
Boise City, *Okla., U.S.* 36°42' N, 102°31' W 92
Boissevain, *Can.* 49°14' N, 100°4' W 90
Bojeador, Cape, *Philippines* 18°30' N, 120°11' E 203
Boji Plain, *Kenya* 1°41' N, 39°35' E 224
Bojnūrd, *Iran* 37°28' N, 57°18' E 180
Bojo, island, *Indonesia* 0°36' N, 98°30' E 196
Bojuru, *Braz.* 31°38' S, 51°31' W 139
Boka, *Serb. and Mont.* 45°21' N, 20°50' E 168
Bo'ka, *Uzb.* 40°49' N, 69°12' E 197
Bokada, *Dem. Rep. of the Congo* 4°8' N, 19°21' E 218
Bokalia, spring, *Chad* 17°24' N, 19°14' E 216
Bokani, *Nig.* 9°28' N, 5°12' E 222
Bokatola, *Dem. Rep. of the Congo* 0°36' N, 18°44' E 218
Boké, *Guinea* 10°55' N, 14°18' W 222
Bokito, *Cameroon* 4°37' N, 11°18' E 222
Bokol, peak, *Kenya* 1°46' N, 36°58' E 224
Bökönbaev, *Kyrg.* 42°7' N, 77°7' E 184
Bokongo, *Dem. Rep. of the Congo* 3°21' N, 20°56' E 218
Bokoro, *Chad* 12°21' N, 17°3' E 216
Bokote, *Dem. Rep. of the Congo* 0°7' N, 20°5' E 218
Bokovskaya, Russ. 49°14' N, 41°45' E 158
Bokpyinn, *Myanmar* 11°15' N, 98°47' E 202
Boksitogorsk, Russ. 59°28' N, 33°51' E 154
Bokungu, *Dem. Rep. of the Congo* 0°45' N, 22°27' E 218
Bokurdak, *Turkm.* 38°47' N, 58°29' E 180
Bol, *Chad* 13°33' N, 14°44' E 216
Bol, *Croatia* 43°15' N, 16°39' E 168
Bolaiti, *Dem. Rep. of the Congo* 1°25' N, 24°51' E 224
Bolama, *Guinea-Bissau* 11°35' N, 15°31' W 222
Bolan Pass, *Pak.* 29°43' N, 67°33' E 186
Bolaños, river, *Mex.* 21°18' N, 103°53' W 114
Bolderāja, *Latv.* 57°1' N, 24°1' E 166
Boldeşti, oil field, *Rom.* 45°2' N, 25°57' E 156
Bole, *China* 44°49' N, 82°9' E 184
Bole, *Ghana* 9°2' N, 2°32' W 222

Boleko, *Dem. Rep. of the Congo* 1°31' S, 19°50' E 218
Bolesławiec, *Pol.* 51°15' N, 15°35' E 152
Boleszkowice, *Pol.* 52°42' N, 14°33' E 152
Bolgatanga, *Ghana* 10°45' N, 0°53' E 222
Bolhrad, *Ukr.* 45°41' N, 28°38' E 156
Bolinao, Cape, *Philippines* 16°20' N, 119°24' E 203
Bolivar, *Col.* 1°48' N, 76°60' W 136
Bolivar, *Mo., U.S.* 37°36' N, 93°24' W 96
Bolivar, *Peru* 7°16' S, 77°50' W 130
Bolivar, *Tenn., U.S.* 35°14' N, 88°59' W 96
Bolivar, adm. division, *Col.* 9°45' N, 75°9' W 115
Bolivar, adm. division, *Venez.* 6°32' N, 66°57' W 136
Bolivar, Cerro, peak, *Venez.* 7°20' N, 63°34' W 130
Bolivar, Mount, *Oreg., U.S.* 42°46' N, 123°55' W 90
Bolivar, Pico, peak, *Venez.* 8°33' N, 71°7' W 136
Bolivia 16°4' S, 66°43' W 132
Bolivia, *Cuba* 22°4' N, 78°18' W 116
Boljevac, *Serb. and Mont.* 43°50' N, 21°58' E 168
Boljevci, *Serb. and Mont.* 44°43' N, 20°12' E 168
Bolkhov, Russ. 53°26' N, 36°1' E 154
Bollendorf, *Ger.* 49°51' N, 6°21' E 167
Bollnäs, *Nor.* 61°21' N, 16°25' E 152
Bollstabruk, *Nor.* 62°59' N, 17°39' E 152
Bolluk Gölü, lake, *Turk.* 38°27' N, 32°29' E 156
Bollullos Par del Condado, *Sp.* 37°20' N, 6°33' W 164
Bolnisi, *Ga.* 41°25' N, 44°32' E 195
Bolobo, *Dem. Rep. of the Congo* 2°12' S, 16°16' E 218
Bologna, *It.* 44°29' N, 11°20' E 167
Bologne, *Fr.* 48°11' N, 5°8' E 163
Bolognesi, *Peru* 10°3' S, 73°60' W 137
Bologoye, Russ. 57°52' N, 34°4' E 154
Bolomba, *Dem. Rep. of the Congo* 0°30' N, 19°9' E 218
Bolona, *Côte d'Ivoire* 10°18' N, 6°26' W 222
Bolong, *Chad* 12°3' N, 17°46' E 216
Bolotnoye, Russ. 55°38' N, 84°26' E 169
Bolotovskoye, Russ. 58°31' N, 62°26' E 154
Bolpebra, *Bol.* 10°59' S, 69°34' W 137
Bol'shakovo, Russ. 54°51' N, 21°38' E 166
Bol'shaya Bicha, Russ. 57°56' N, 70°36' E 169
Bol'shaya Chernigovka, Russ. 52°7' N, 50°52' E 158
Bol'shaya Glushitsa, Russ. 52°24' N, 50°28' E 158
Bol'shaya Kheta, river, Russ. 68°22' N, 82°43' E 169
Bol'shaya Pyssa, Russ. 64°11' N, 48°44' E 154
Bol'shaya Tovra, Russ. 64°5' N, 41°41' E 154
Bol'shaya Ucha, Russ. 56°36' N, 52°7' E 154
Bol'shaya Vladīmīrovka, *Kaz.* 50°53' N, 79°29' E 184
Bol'sheretsk, Russ. 52°20' N, 156°22' E 228
Bol'shevik Island, Russ. 79°0' N, 102°0' E 255
Bol'shezemel'skaya Tundra, region, *Europe* 66°30' N, 52°39' E 154
Bol'shiye Kozly, Russ. 65°18' N, 39°45' E 154
Bol'shiye Sludītsy, Russ. 59°16' N, 30°28' E 166
Bol'shiye Tarkhany, Russ. 54°42' N, 48°34' E 154
Bol'shoy Anyuy, river, Russ. 68°20' N, 161°41' E 160
Bol'shoy Begichev, Ostrov, island, Russ. 73°50' N, 113°22' E 160
Bol'shoy Begichev, Ostrov, island, Russ. 74°38' N, 106°27' E 160
Bol'shoy Chirk, Russ. 63°54' N, 47°7' E 154
Bol'shoy Entai, Russ. 60°54' N, 49°40' E 154
Bol'shoy Lyakhovskiy, Ostrov, island, Russ. 72°34' N, 143°33' E 160
Bol'shoy Porog, Russ. 65°35' N, 90°11' E 169
Bol'shoy Sabsk, Russ. 59°8' N, 29°2' E 166
Bol'shoy Shantar, Ostrov, island, Russ. 55°15' N, 136°51' E 160
Bol'shoy Tyuters, Russ. 59°48' N, 27°15' E 166
Bolsover, *U.K.* 53°13' N, 1°18' W 162
Bolsward, *Neth.* 53°4' N, 5°30' E 163
Bolt Head, *U.K.* 50°14' N, 3°49' W 150
Boltaña, *Sp.* 42°26' N, 6°356' E 164
Bolton, *U.K.* 53°34' N, 2°27' W 162
Bolton, *Vt., U.S.* 44°22' N, 72°53' W 104
Bolton Abbey, site, *U.K.* 53°59' N, 1°57' W 162
Bolton Lake, lake, *Can.* 54°10' N, 96°19' W 108
Bolton Landing, *N.Y., U.S.* 43°33' N, 73°41' W 104
Bolu, *Turk.* 40°31' N, 31°36' E 156
Boluo, *China* 23°7' N, 114°16' E 198
Bolvadin, *Turk.* 38°43' N, 31°2' E 156
Bóly, *Hung.* 45°57' N, 18°31' E 168
Bom Comércio, *Braz.* 9°46' S, 65°56' W 137
Bom Despacho, *Braz.* 19°44' S, 45°16' W 138
Bom Destino, *Braz.* 9°46' S, 67°32' W 137
Bom Jesus, *Braz.* 28°39' S, 50°24' W 138
Bom Jesus, *Braz.* 9°4' S, 44°23' W 132
Bom Jesus da Gurguéia, Serra, *Braz.* 8°41' S, 43°40' W 132
Bom Jesus da Lapa, *Braz.* 13°18' S, 43°25' W 138
Bom Jesus do Itabapoana, *Braz.* 21°11' S, 41°41' W 138
Bom Retiro, *Braz.* 27°49' S, 49°30' W 138
Boma, *Angola* 5°58' S, 13°6' E 207
Boma National Park, *Sudan* 6°33' N, 33°45' E 224
Bomana, *Dem. Rep. of the Congo* 1°25' N, 18°52' E 218
Bomassa, *Congo* 2°23' N, 16°10' E 218
Bombay see Mumbai, *India* 18°57' N, 72°49' E 188
Bombo, *Uganda* 0°32' N, 32°32' E 224
Bomdila, *India* 27°18' N, 92°25' E 188
Bomi (Bowo) *China* 29°53' N, 95°40' E 188
Bomili, *Dem. Rep. of the Congo* 1°42' N, 27°5' E 224

Bomokandi, river, *Dem. Rep. of the Congo* 3°15' N, 27°9' E 224
Bomongo, *Dem. Rep. of the Congo* 1°26' N, 18°19' E 218
Bomotu, *Dem. Rep. of the Congo* 3°46' N, 19°1' E 218
Bomu, oil field, *Nig.* 4°37' N, 7°14' E 222
Bomu, river, *Africa* 5°3' N, 23°57' E 206
Bon Secour, *Ala., U.S.* 30°18' N, 87°44' W 103
Bon Wier, *Tex., U.S.* 30°44' N, 93°39' W 103
Bonāb, *Iran* 37°19' N, 46°10' E 195
Bonaire, island, *Netherlands* 12°0' N, 68°0' W 118
Bonampak, ruin(s), *Mex.* 16°39' N, 91°8' W 115
Bonandolok, *Indonesia* 1°51' N, 98°49' E 196
Bonanza, *Nicar.* 14°0' N, 84°35' W 115
Bonanza, *Oreg., U.S.* 42°13' N, 121°26' W 90
Bonanza, *Sp.* 36°48' N, 6°21' W 164
Bonanza, *Utah, U.S.* 40°0' N, 109°10' W 90
Bonaparte Archipelago, *Indian Ocean* 13°15' S, 122°48' E 230
Bonaparte Lake, *Can.* 51°17' N, 121°3' W 90
Bonaparte, Mount, *Wash., U.S.* 48°45' N, 119°13' W 90
Boñar, *Sp.* 42°50' N, 5°20' W 150
Bonaventure, *Can.* 48°9' N, 65°35' W 82
Bonavista, *Can.* 48°38' N, 53°7' W 111
Bonavista, Cape, *Can.* 48°43' N, 53°16' W 111
Bond, *Miss., U.S.* 30°53' N, 89°9' W 103
Bondari, Russ. 56°9' N, 28°20' E 166
Bondary, Russ. 52°58' N, 41°53' E 154
Bondeno, *It.* 44°54' N, 11°23' E 167
Bondo, *Dem. Rep. of the Congo* 3°49' N, 23°48' E 224
Bondoukou, *Côte d'Ivoire* 8°3' N, 2°49' W 222
Bondyug, Russ. 60°30' N, 55°58' E 154
Bone Creek, river, *U.S.* 49°50' N, 109°24' W 90
Bône see Annaba, *Alg.* 36°53' N, 7°45' E 156
Bone, Teluk 4°59' S, 120°30' E 192
Bonesteel, *S. Dak., U.S.* 43°4' N, 98°58' W 90
Bonete, *S.* 38°52' N, 1°21' W 164
Bonete, Cerro, peak, *Arg.* 27°54' S, 68°55' W 132
Bonfinópolis de Minas, *Braz.* 16°33' S, 45°60' W 138
Bong Son, *Vietnam* 14°27' N, 109°0' E 202
Bonga, *Eth.* 7°12' N, 36°14' E 224
Bongandanga, *Dem. Rep. of the Congo* 1°29' N, 21°1' E 218
Bongao, *Philippines* 5°3' N, 119°44' E 203
Bongo, *Dem. Rep. of the Congo* 2°59' N, 20°1' E 218
Bongo, *Dem. Rep. of the Congo* 1°48' S, 17°39' E 218
Bongo, *Gabon* 2°9' S, 10°15' E 218
Bongolava, *Madagascar* 18°35' S, 45°27' E 220
Bongor, *Chad* 10°18' N, 15°23' E 216
Bongouanou, *Côte d'Ivoire* 6°35' N, 4°14' W 222
Bongoul, river, *Cen. Af. Rep.* 9°2' N, 21°9' E 218
Bonham, *Tex., U.S.* 33°34' N, 96°11' W 96
Bonifacio, *Fr.* 41°23' N, 9°11' E 167
Bonin Islands (Ogasawara Guntō), *North Pacific Ocean* 27°46' N, 140°27' E 190
Bonin Trench, *North Pacific Ocean* 23°46' N, 143°57' E 252
Bonita, *Ill., U.S.* 32°54' N, 91°41' W 103
Bonita Springs, *Fla., U.S.* 26°20' N, 81°47' W 105
Bonito, *Braz.* 21°8' S, 56°28' W 132
Bonito, peak, *Hond.* 15°35' N, 86°58' W 115
Bonkoukou, *Niger* 14°2' N, 3°10' E 222
Bonn, *Ger.* 50°44' N, 7°5' E 167
Bonne Terre, *Mo., U.S.* 37°55' N, 90°34' W 103
Bonner, *Mont., U.S.* 46°51' N, 113°48' W 90
Bonners Ferry, *Idaho, U.S.* 48°40' N, 116°21' W 90
Bonnet, *Fr.* 46°19' N, 1°54' E 150
Bonnet Plume, river, *Can.* 65°34' N, 134°14' W 98
Bonneval, *Fr.* 48°10' N, 1°24' E 163
Bonneville Salt Flats, *Utah, U.S.* 40°39' N, 114°12' W 90
Bonnie Rock, *Austral.* 30°34' S, 118°22' E 231
Bonny, *Fr.* 47°33' N, 2°50' E 150
Bonny, *Nig.* 4°26' N, 7°10' E 222
Bonny Reservoir, lake, *Colo., U.S.* 39°34' N, 102°37' W 90
Bonnyville, *Can.* 54°15' N, 110°43' W 108
Bonobono, *Philippines* 8°43' N, 117°36' E 203
Bonokoski Lake, lake, *Can.* 59°39' N, 104°7' W 108
Bonpland, *Arg.* 29°49' S, 57°27' W 139
Bonsall, *Calif., U.S.* 33°17' N, 117°15' W 101
Bonsecours, Baie 49°26' N, 64°20' W 111
Bontang, *Indonesia* 0°11' N, 117°21' E 192
Bontebok National Park, *S. Af.* 34°5' S, 20°21' E 227
Bonthe, *Sierra Leone* 7°32' N, 12°33' W 222
Bontoc, *Philippines* 17°6' N, 120°57' E 203
Bonvouloir Islands, *Solomon Sea* 10°6' S, 151°55' E 228
Bonyhád, *Hung.* 46°16' N, 18°31' E 168
Booker, *Tex., U.S.* 36°26' N, 100°33' W 96
Booker T. Washington National Monument, *Va., U.S.* 37°5' N, 79°48' W 96
Boola, *Guinea* 8°18' N, 8°43' W 222
Boomer, *W. Va., U.S.* 38°9' N, 81°18' W 94
Boone, *Colo., U.S.* 38°14' N, 104°16' W 90
Boone, *Iowa, U.S.* 42°3' N, 93°54' W 94
Boone, *N.C., U.S.* 36°13' N, 81°41' W 96
Booneville, *Ark., U.S.* 35°7' N, 93°56' W 96
Booneville, *Ind., U.S.* 37°57' N, 87°16' W 81
Boonville, *N.Y., U.S.* 43°28' N, 75°21' W 94
Boorama, *Somalia* 9°54' N, 43°6' E 216
Booroondara, Mount, *Austral.* 31°6' S, 145°3' E 230
Boothbay Harbor, *Me., U.S.* 43°51' N, 69°38' W 104
Boothia, Gulf of 70°9' N, 92°10' W 106
Boothia Peninsula, *Can.* 70°5' N, 95°32' W 106
Boothville, *La., U.S.* 29°19' N, 89°25' W 103
Booué, *Gabon* 4°237' S, 11°52' E 218
Bopolu, *Liberia* 6°58' N, 10°30' W 222
Boppard, *Ger.* 50°13' N, 7°37' E 167
Boquerão, Serra do, *Braz.* 11°10' S, 43°60' W 132

Boquerón, *Cuba* 19°58' N, 75°7' W 116
Boquilla, Presa de la, lake, *Mex.* 27°34' N, 106°8' W 81
Boquillas del Carmen, *Mex.* 29°8' N, 102°60' W 92
Bor, Russ. 56°21' N, 44°9' E 154
Bor, *Serb. and Mont.* 44°5' N, 22°6' E 168
Bor, *Sudan* 6°17' N, 31°39' E 207
Bor, *Turk.* 37°53' N, 34°31' E 156
Borah Peak, *Idaho, U.S.* 44°7' N, 113°51' W 90
Boraldway, *Kaz.* 43°20' N, 76°51' E 184
Boran, *Kaz.* 48°9' N, 85°14' E 184
Boran, region, *Africa* 3°11' N, 38°18' E 224
Borås, *Nor.* 57°43' N, 12°56' E 152
Borau, *Sp.* 42°39' N, 0°36' E 150
Borāzjān, *Iran* 29°14' N, 51°12' E 196
Borba, *Braz.* 4°24' S, 59°36' W 130
Borbon, *Philippines* 10°49' N, 124°1' E 203
Borborema, Planalto da, *Braz.* 7°28' S, 38°3' W 132
Borchgrevink Coast, *Antarctica* 73°11' S, 178°45' W 248
Borçka, *Turk.* 41°22' N, 41°40' E 195
Bordeaux, *Fr.* 44°50' N, 0°36' E 150
Borden Island, *Can.* 79°8' N, 110°41' W 246
Borden Peninsula, *Can.* 73°4' N, 89°38' W 106
Bordertown, *Austral.* 36°18' S, 140°47' E 231
Bordj bou Arreridj, *Alg.* 36°3' N, 4°45' E 150
Bordj Bou Rerhda, *Alg.* 36°8' N, 5°22' E 150
Bordj Flye Sainte Marie, *Alg.* 27°16' N, 2°59' W 214
Bordj le Prieur, *Alg.* 21°20' N, 0°53' E 222
Bordj Messouda, *Alg.* 30°13' N, 9°24' E 216
Bordj Omar Driss, *Alg.* 28°6' N, 6°49' E 214
Bordj Welvert, *Alg.* 35°39' N, 3°52' E 150
Boré, *Mali* 15°7' N, 3°30' W 222
Boreas Nunatak, peak, *Antarctica* 71°27' S, 4°34' E 248
Borga see Porvoo, *Fin.* 60°23' N, 25°40' E 166
Borgå (see Porvoo), *Fin.* 60°23' N, 25°40' E 166
Borgarfjäll, *Nor.* 64°48' N, 15°1' E 152
Børgefjell, *Nor.* 65°12' N, 13°51' E 152
Børgefjell National Park, *Nor.* 65°12' N, 14°27' E 152
Borgentreich, *Ger.* 51°34' N, 9°15' E 167
Borger, *Neth.* 52°55' N, 6°47' E 163
Borger, *Tex., U.S.* 35°38' N, 101°24' W 92
Borgholm, *Sw.* 56°51' N, 16°37' E 152
Borghorst, *Ger.* 52°7' N, 7°24' E 167
Borgne, Lake 30°1' N, 89°42' W 103
Borgo, *It.* 46°3' N, 11°27' E 167
Borgo San Dalmazzo, *It.* 44°19' N, 7°29' E 167
Borgo San Lorenzo, *It.* 43°57' N, 11°22' E 167
Borgo Val di Taro, *It.* 44°29' N, 9°46' E 167
Borgomanero, *It.* 45°42' N, 8°29' E 167
Borgosesia, *It.* 45°43' N, 8°16' E 167
Borgou, region, *Africa* 10°9' N, 2°49' E 222
Borgsjö, *Nor.* 64°11' N, 17°48' E 152
Borgvattnet, *Nor.* 63°25' N, 15°49' E 154
Borhoyn Tal, *Mongolia* 43°44' N, 111°47' E 198
Bori, *Benin* 9°2' N, 2°25' E 222
Borikhan, *Laos* 18°36' N, 103°42' E 202
Börili, *Kaz.* 52°9' N, 52°44' E 158
Borisoglebsk, Russ. 51°21' N, 42°3' E 158
Borisovo Sudskoye, Russ. 59°52' N, 36°1' E 154
Boriziny (Port-Bergé) *Madagascar* 15°35' S, 47°43' E 220
Borj el Kessira, *Tun.* 32°14' N, 10°2' E 214
Borja, *Peru* 4°32' S, 77°36' W 130
Borja, *Sp.* 41°48' N, 1°34' W 164
Borjomi, *Ga.* 41°50' N, 43°22' E 180
Borkavichy, *Belarus* 55°39' N, 28°18' E 166
Borken, *Ger.* 51°50' N, 6°52' E 167
Borken, *Ger.* 51°3' N, 9°17' E 167
Borkou, region, *Africa* 19°13' N, 15°50' E 216
Borkovskaya, Russ. 65°10' N, 49°27' E 154
Borkum, *Ger.* 53°35' N, 6°40' E 163
Borkum, island, *Ger.* 53°36' N, 6°25' E 163
Borland, Mount, *Antarctica* 74°20' S, 67°18' E 248
Borlänge, *Nor.* 60°28' N, 15°28' E 152
Borle, Cape, *Antarctica* 65°54' S, 55°17' E 248
Borleşti, *Rom.* 47°40' N, 23°19' E 168
Borlova, *Rom.* 45°22' N, 22°23' E 168
Bormio, *It.* 46°28' N, 10°21' E 167
Borneo (Kalimantan), island, *Indonesia* 4°28' S, 111°26' E 192
Bornheim, *Ger.* 50°46' N, 6°59' E 167
Bornholm, island, *Den.* 55°18' N, 14°51' E 143
Borno, *It.* 45°57' N, 10°11' E 167
Bornos, *Sp.* 36°48' N, 5°45' W 164
Boro, *Mali* 12°54' N, 9°24' W 222
Boro, river, *Sudan* 8°28' N, 24°43' E 224
Borodūlikha, *Kaz.* 50°44' N, 80°49' E 184
Borokoro, *Guinea* 9°30' N, 10°23' W 222
Boromo, *Burkina Faso* 11°45' N, 2°57' W 222
Boron, *Calif., U.S.* 35°0' N, 117°40' W 101
Borotou, *Côte d'Ivoire* 8°41' N, 7°29' W 222
Boroughbridge, *U.K.* 54°6' N, 1°24' W 162
Borove, *Ukr.* 51°38' N, 25°51' E 152
Borovichi, Russ. 58°22' N, 33°57' E 154
Borovlyanka, Russ. 52°38' N, 84°33' E 184
Borovo, *Croatia* 45°24' N, 18°57' E 168
Borovsk, Russ. 55°9' N, 36°31' E 154
Borovskoy, *Kaz.* 53°47' N, 64°10' E 184
Borovtsoi, *Bulg.* 43°18' N, 23°9' E 168
Borrego Springs, *Calif., U.S.* 33°15' N, 116°23' W 101
Borroloola, *Austral.* 16°7' S, 136°17' E 238
Borşa, *Rom.* 47°6' N, 21°48' E 168
Borzna, *Ukr.* 51°15' N, 32°25' E 158
Börzsöny, *Hung.* 47°52' N, 18°43' E 168
Borzya, Russ. 50°25' N, 116°39' E 190
Bosanska Dubica, *Bosn. and Herzg.* 45°10' N, 16°48' E 168

Bosanska Krupa, *Bosn. and Herzg.* 44°52' N, 16°9' E 168
Bosanski Brod, *Bosn. and Herzg.* 45°7' N, 18°1' E 168
Bosanski Novi, *Bosn. and Herzg.* 45°2' N, 16°22' E 168
Bosanski Petrovac, *Bosn. and Herzg.* 44°32' N, 16°21' E 168
Bosansko Grahovo, *Bosn. and Herzg.* 44°9' N, 16°20' E 168
B osárkány, *Hung.* 47°41' N, 17°17' E 168
Bosbury, *U.K.* 52°4' N, 2°27' W 162
Bosco Chiesanuova, *It.* 45°36' N, 11°1' E 167
Bose, *China* 23°54' N, 106°32' E 198
Boseong, *S. Korea* 34°43' N, 127°6' E 200
Boshof, *S. Af.* 28°33' S, 25°13' E 227
Boshrūyeh, *Iran* 33°52' N, 57°28' E 180
Bosilegrad, *Serb. and Mont.* 42°30' N, 22°29' E 168
Bosnia and Herzegovina 44°0' N, 18°0' E 156
Bošnjaci, *Croatia* 45°1' N, 18°45' E 168
Bosobele, *Dem. Rep. of the Congo* 1°11' N, 18°12' E 218
Bosobolo, *Dem. Rep. of the Congo* 4°13' N, 19°54' E 218
Bosques Petrificados Natural Monument, *Arg.* 47°43' S, 68°17' W 132
Bossangoa, *Cen. Af. Rep.* 6°28' N, 17°25' E 218
Bossé Bangou, *Niger* 13°21' N, 1°16' E 222
Bossembélé, *Cen. Af. Rep.* 5°13' N, 17°37' E 218
Bossier City, *La., U.S.* 32°30' N, 93°43' W 103
Bosso, *Niger* 13°41' N, 13°17' E 216
Bossôst, *Sp.* 42°46' N, 0°40' E 164
Bost see Lashkar Gāh, *Afghan.* 31°35' N, 64°22' E 186
Bosten Hu, lake, *China* 41°57' N, 86°51' E 184
Boston, *Mass., U.S.* 42°20' N, 71°6' W 104
Boston, *U.K.* 52°59' N, 0°1' E 162
Boston Bar, *Can.* 49°51' N, 121°25' W 100
Boston Mountains, *Ark., U.S.* 35°44' N, 94°18' W 96
Bostonnais, Grand lac, lake, *Can.* 47°51' N, 73°8' W 94
Bosut, river, *Croatia* 45°12' N, 18°57' E 168
Boswell, *Ind., U.S.* 40°30' N, 87°23' W 102
Boswell, *Okla., U.S.* 34°0' N, 95°52' W 96
Bosworth, battle, *U.K.* 52°35' N, 1°27' W 162
Bot, *Sp.* 41°0' N, 0°22' E 164
Botesdale, *U.K.* 52°20' N, 1°0' E 162
Botev, peak, *Bulg.* 42°42' N, 24°50' E 156
Botevgrad, *Bulg.* 42°51' N, 23°44' E 180
Bothaville, *S. Af.* 27°22' S, 26°36' E 227
Bothnia, Gulf of 61°26' N, 17°58' E 152
Bothwell, *Can.* 42°37' N, 81°51' W 102
Botkins, *Ohio, U.S.* 40°27' N, 84°11' W 102
Botnnuten, peak, *Antarctica* 70°22' S, 37°37' E 248
BotoŞani, adm. division, *Rom.* 47°54' N, 26°10' E 156
Botoşani, *Rom.* 47°43' N, 26°38' E 152
Botsford, *Conn., U.S.* 41°22' N, 73°16' W 104
Botsmark, *Nor.* 64°15' N, 20°14' E 152
Botswana 22°36' S, 24°16' E 220
Bottineau, *N. Dak., U.S.* 48°48' N, 100°29' W 90
Bottrop, *Ger.* 51°31' N, 6°56' E 167
Botucatu, *Braz.* 22°54' S, 48°28' W 138
Botum Sakor National Park, *Cambodia* 10°53' N, 102°54' E 202
Botwood, *Can.* 49°8' N, 55°23' W 111
Bou Akba, spring, *Alg.* 28°48' N, 7°45' W 214
Bou Ali, *Alg.* 27°11' N, 0°12' E 214
Bou Arfa, *Mor.* 32°31' N, 1°56' W 214
Boû Djébéha, *Mali* 18°31' N, 2°46' W 222
Bou Hadjar, *Alg.* 36°30' N, 8°6' E 156
Bou Izakarn, *Mor.* 29°11' N, 9°44' W 214
Bou Naga, spring, *Mauritania* 19°0' N, 13°13' W 222
Boû Rjeïmât, *Mauritania* 19°3' N, 15°8' W 222
Bou Saâda, *Alg.* 35°11' N, 4°10' E 214
Bou Thadi, *Tun.* 35°5' N, 10°14' E 214
Boû Zérîbé, spring, *Mauritania* 16°13' N, 5°25' W 222
Bouaflé, *Côte d'Ivoire* 6°56' N, 5°43' W 222
Bouaké, *Côte d'Ivoire* 5°3' N, 5°3' W 222
Bouala, *Cen. Af. Rep.* 6°18' N, 15°35' E 218
Bouali, *Gabon* 3°7' S, 11°30' E 218
Bouar, *Cen. Af. Rep.* 5°53' N, 15°34' E 218
Boubout, spring, *Alg.* 27°30' N, 4°34' W 214
Bouca, *Cen. Af. Rep.* 6°29' N, 18°18' E 218
Boucau, *Fr.* 43°31' N, 1°30' W 150
Bouchier, Lac, lake, *Can.* 50°2' N, 78°23' W 111
Boucle Du Baoulé National Park, *Mali* 13°39' N, 9°25' W 222
Boudenib, *Mor.* 32°1' N, 3°36' W 214
Boudjellil, *Alg.* 36°4' N, 4°20' E 150
Bouga, *Chad* 8°8' N, 15°34' E 218
Bougainville, Cape, *Austral.* 13°49' S, 126°3' E 231
Bougainville, island, *P.N.G.* 5°54' S, 153°10' E 192
Bougar'oûn, Cap, *Alg.* 37°7' N, 6°26' E 150
Boughzoul, *Alg.* 35°44' N, 2°50' E 150
Bougie see Bejaïa, *Alg.* 36°46' N, 5°2' E 150
Bougouni, *Mali* 11°26' N, 7°30' W 222
Bouilly, *Fr.* 48°10' N, 4°0' E 163
Bouira, *Alg.* 36°25' N, 3°53' E 150
Boujad, *Mor.* 32°50' N, 6°25' W 214
Boujdour, *Western Sahara* 26°4' N, 14°29' W 214
Boujdour, Cap, *Western Sahara* 26°7' N, 16°1' W 214
Boukombé, *Benin* 10°11' N, 1°6' E 222
Boukoula, *Cameroon* 10°9' N, 13°29' E 216
Boukra, *Western Sahara* 26°22' N, 12°53' W 214
Boula, *Mali* 15°4' N, 8°27' W 222
Boulder, *Colo., U.S.* 40°2' N, 105°17' W 90
Boulder, *Mont., U.S.* 46°13' N, 112°7' W 90
Boulder City, *Nev., U.S.* 35°55' N, 114°50' W 82
Boulder Creek, *Calif., U.S.* 37°7' N, 122°9' W 100
Boulder Peak, *Calif., U.S.* 41°34' N, 123°11' W 90
Boulogne, *Fr.* 43°17' N, 0°37' E 164
Boulogne-sur-Mer, *Fr.* 50°44' N, 1°36' E 163
Boulouli, *Mali* 15°36' N, 9°20' W 222
Boulsa, *Burkina Faso* 12°39' N, 0°37' E 222

Boultoum, *Niger* 14°41′ N, 10°18′ E **222**
Boumdeït, spring, *Mauritania* 17°27′ N, 11°22′ W **222**
Boumerdas, *Alg.* 36°45′ N, 3°29′ E **150**
Boun Nua, *Laos* 21°40′ N, 101°54′ E **202**
Boun Tai, *Laos* 21°25′ N, 101°58′ E **202**
Bouna, *Côte d'Ivoire* 9°16′ N, 2°60′ W **222**
Boundary, *Can.* 49°0′ N, 109°22′ W **90**
Boundary Bald Mountain, *Me., U.S.* 45°45′ N, 70°18′ W **94**
Boundary Peak, *Nev., U.S.* 37°50′ N, 118°26′ W **90**
Boundiali, *Côte d'Ivoire* 9°31′ N, 6°29′ W **222**
Boundji, *Congo* 1°2′ S, 15°22′ E **218**
Bountiful Islands, *Gulf of Carpentaria* 17°3′ S, 140°1′ E **230**
Bounty Trough, *South Pacific Ocean* 47°2′ S, 178°29′ W **252**
Bourbon, *Ind., U.S.* 41°17′ N, 86°7′ W **102**
Bourbonnais, *Ill., U.S.* 41°9′ N, 87°54′ W **102**
Bourbonnais, region, *Europe* 46°45′ N, 2°23′ E **165**
Bourbourg, *Fr.* 50°56′ N, 2°12′ E **163**
Bouré Siké, spring, *Mali* 15°50′ N, 5°18′ W **222**
Bourem, *Mali* 16°58′ N, 0°20′ E **222**
Bouressa, *Mali* 19°58′ N, 2°13′ E **222**
Bourg, *La., U.S.* 29°33′ N, 90°38′ W **103**
Bourges, *Fr.* 47°4′ N, 2°24′ E **150**
Bourg-Madame, *Fr.* 42°25′ N, 1°56′ E **164**
Bourgneuf, *Fr.* 47°2′ N, 1°57′ W **150**
Bourgogne, adm. division, *Fr.* 47°19′ N, 2°55′ E **150**
Bourke, *Austral.* 30°8′ S, 145°56′ E **231**
Bourlier, *Alg.* 35°23′ N, 1°38′ E **150**
Bourne, *U.K.* 52°46′ N, 0°22′ E **162**
Bournemouth, *U.K.* 50°43′ N, 1°54′ W **162**
Bouroum, *Burkina Faso* 13°38′ N, 0°39′ E **222**
Bourscheid, *Lux.* 49°53′ N, 6°4′ E **167**
Bourtoutou, *Chad* 11°14′ N, 22°50′ E **218**
Bouse, *Ariz., U.S.* 33°56′ N, 114°1′ W **101**
Boussens, *Fr.* 43°10′ N, 0°57′ E **164**
Bousso, *Chad* 10°32′ N, 16°43′ E **216**
Bouszibé Aneyda, spring, *Mali* 16°14′ N, 5°16′ W **222**
Boutilimit, *Mauritania* 17°32′ N, 14°44′ W **222**
Bouvet Island, *Norway* 54°28′ S, 3°23′ E **255**
Bouza, *Niger* 14°22′ N, 5°55′ E **222**
Bovec, *Slov.* 46°20′ N, 13°34′ E **167**
Bovenden, *Ger.* 51°35′ N, 9°56′ E **167**
Boves, *Fr.* 49°49′ N, 2°22′ E **163**
Bovill, *Idaho, U.S.* 46°50′ N, 116°24′ W **90**
Bovina, *Tex., U.S.* 34°30′ N, 102°53′ W **92**
Bovril, *Arg.* 31°19′ S, 59°25′ W **139**
Bow, *N.H., U.S.* 43°9′ N, 71°33′ W **104**
Bow Island, *Can.* 49°51′ N, 111°23′ W **90**
Bow, river, *Can.* 51°6′ N, 114°34′ W **90**
Bowbells, *N. Dak., U.S.* 48°48′ N, 102°15′ W **90**
Bowdle, *S. Dak., U.S.* 45°26′ N, 99°41′ W **90**
Bowdoin Canyon, *Can.* 53°34′ N, 65°28′ W **111**
Bowen, *Austral.* 19°60′ S, 148°15′ E **231**
Bowen Island, *Can.* 49°22′ N, 123°21′ W **100**
Bowes, *U.K.* 54°31′ N, 2°1′ W **162**
Bowie, *Ariz., U.S.* 32°19′ N, 109°28′ W **92**
Bowie, *Tex., U.S.* 33°32′ N, 97°51′ W **92**
Bowling Green, *Fla., U.S.* 27°38′ N, 81°49′ W **105**
Bowling Green, *Ind., U.S.* 39°22′ N, 87°1′ W **102**
Bowling Green, *Ky., U.S.* 36°59′ N, 86°27′ W **96**
Bowling Green, *Ohio, U.S.* 41°22′ N, 83°39′ W **102**
Bowling Green, *Va., U.S.* 38°2′ N, 77°21′ W **94**
Bowling Green Bay National Park, *Austral.* 19°34′ S, 146°39′ E **238**
Bowman, *N. Dak., U.S.* 46°10′ N, 103°26′ W **90**
Bowman Bay 65°33′ N, 77°12′ W **106**
Bowman Island, *Antarctica* 64°34′ S, 104°9′ E **248**
Bowman, Mount, *Can.* 51°11′ N, 121°52′ W **90**
Bowness, *U.K.* 54°21′ N, 2°55′ W **162**
Bowo see Bomi, *China* 29°53′ N, 95°40′ E **188**
Bowser, *Can.* 49°25′ N, 124°41′ W **100**
Bowser Lake, *Can.* 56°24′ N, 129°52′ W **108**
Bowsman, *Can.* 52°14′ N, 101°13′ W **108**
Bowwood, *Zambia* 17°7′ S, 26°16′ E **224**
Boxing, *China* 37°9′ N, 118°7′ E **198**
Boxtel, *Neth.* 51°35′ N, 5°19′ E **167**
Boyabat, *Turk.* 41°27′ N, 34°45′ E **156**
Boyacá, adm. division, *Col.* 5°17′ N, 73°33′ W **136**
Boyang, *China* 29°0′ N, 116°38′ E **198**
Boyarka, *Russ.* 70°43′ N, 97°24′ E **160**
Boyce, *La., U.S.* 31°22′ N, 92°40′ W **103**
Boyd, *Can.* 55°53′ N, 96°27′ W **108**
Boyd Lake, *Can.* 61°22′ N, 104°4′ W **108**
Boyer, river, *Can.* 57°54′ N, 117°43′ W **108**
Boyes Hot Springs, *Calif., U.S.* 38°19′ N, 122°29′ W **100**
Boykétté, *Cen. Af. Rep.* 5°24′ N, 20°49′ E **218**
Boyle, *Can.* 54°35′ N, 112°48′ W **108**
Boyle, *Ire.* 53°58′ N, 8°20′ W **150**
Boyne City, *Mich., U.S.* 45°12′ N, 85°1′ W **94**
Boynitsa, *Bulg.* 43°57′ N, 22°31′ E **168**
Boynton Beach, *Fla., U.S.* 26°32′ N, 80°5′ W **105**
Boyoma Falls, *Dem. Rep. of the Congo* 1°23′ N, 21°41′ E **206**
Boyoma Falls (Stanley Falls), *Dem. Rep. of the Congo* 0°14′ N, 25°9′ E **224**
Boyson, *Uzb.* 38°12′ N, 67°12′ E **197**
Boyuibe, *Bol.* 20°28′ S, 63°16′ W **137**
Boz Burun, *Turk.* 40°32′ N, 28°50′ E **156**
Boz Dağ, peak, *Turk.* 37°18′ N, 29°7′ E **156**
Bozalan Burun, *Turk.* 38°12′ N, 26°27′ E **156**
Bozashchy Tübegi, *Kaz.* 45°9′ N, 51°36′ E **158**
Bozburun, *Turk.* 36°41′ N, 28°4′ E **156**
Bozburun Dağı, peak, *Turk.* 37°16′ N, 31°0′ E **156**
Bozdoğan, *Turk.* 37°39′ N, 28°18′ E **156**
Bozeman, *Mont., U.S.* 45°38′ N, 111°3′ W **90**
Bozene, *Dem. Rep. of the Congo* 2°58′ N, 19°13′ E **218**
Boževac, *Serb. and Mont.* 44°32′ N, 21°23′ E **168**
Bozhou, *China* 33°49′ N, 115°44′ E **198**
Božica, *Serb. and Mont.* 42°36′ N, 22°24′ E **168**
Bozkır, *Turk.* 37°11′ N, 32°13′ E **156**
Bozkurt, *Turk.* 41°58′ N, 34°1′ E **158**
Bozoum, *Cen. Af. Rep.* 6°15′ N, 16°23′ E **218**
Bozoy, *Kaz.* 46°10′ N, 58°45′ E **158**
Bozüyük, *Turk.* 39°55′ N, 30°1′ E **156**
Bozzolo, *It.* 45°5′ N, 10°28′ E **167**
Bra, *It.* 44°41′ N, 7°51′ E **167**
Brabant Island, *Antarctica* 64°4′ S, 64°38′ W **134**
Brabant Lake, lake, *Can.* 56°0′ N, 104°18′ W **108**
Brač, island, *Croatia* 43°15′ N, 16°54′ E **168**
Bracebridge, *Can.* 45°2′ N, 79°20′ W **94**
Bräcke, *Nor.* 62°45′ N, 15°26′ E **152**
Bracken Lake, lake, *Can.* 53°35′ N, 100°14′ W **108**
Brackendale, *Can.* 49°45′ N, 123°8′ W **100**
Brackettville, *Tex., U.S.* 29°18′ N, 100°25′ W **92**
Brackley, *U.K.* 52°2′ N, 1°9′ W **162**
Bracknell, *U.K.* 51°22′ N, 0°46′ E **162**
Brackwede, *Ger.* 51°59′ N, 8°29′ E **167**
Brad, *Rom.* 46°7′ N, 22°49′ E **168**
Bradenton, *Fla., U.S.* 27°29′ N, 82°35′ W **105**
Bradenton Beach, *Fla., U.S.* 27°28′ N, 82°41′ W **105**
Bradford, *Ill., U.S.* 41°10′ N, 89°41′ W **102**
Bradford, *Ohio, U.S.* 40°7′ N, 84°26′ W **102**
Bradford, *Pa., U.S.* 41°57′ N, 78°40′ W **94**
Bradford, *U.K.* 53°47′ N, 1°46′ W **162**
Bradford, *Vt., U.S.* 43°59′ N, 72°9′ W **104**
Bradford on Avon, *U.K.* 51°21′ N, 2°15′ W **162**
Bradley, *Ark., U.S.* 33°5′ N, 93°41′ W **103**
Bradley, *Calif., U.S.* 35°52′ N, 120°49′ W **100**
Bradley, *Ill., U.S.* 41°9′ N, 87°51′ W **102**
Bradley, *S. Dak., U.S.* 45°4′ N, 97°40′ W **90**
Bradley Junction, *Fla., U.S.* 27°47′ N, 81°59′ W **105**
Bradninch, *U.K.* 50°49′ N, 3°26′ W **162**
Brador, Collines de, peak, *Can.* 51°33′ N, 57°18′ W **111**
Bradwell on Sea, *U.K.* 51°43′ N, 0°54′ E **162**
Brady, *Nebr., U.S.* 41°2′ N, 100°21′ W **90**
Brady, *Tex., U.S.* 31°7′ N, 99°20′ W **92**
BraĔov, adm. division, *Rom.* 45°42′ N, 24°42′ E **156**
Braeside, *Can.* 45°27′ N, 76°26′ W **94**
Braga, *Port.* 41°32′ N, 8°27′ W **150**
Braga, adm. division, *Port.* 41°24′ N, 8°40′ W **150**
Bragado, *Arg.* 35°7′ S, 60°30′ W **139**
Bragança, *Braz.* 1°4′ S, 46°48′ W **130**
Bragança, *Port.* 41°46′ N, 6°48′ W **214**
Bragança, *Port.* 41°49′ N, 6°47′ W **150**
Bragança, adm. division, *Port.* 41°28′ N, 7°16′ W **150**
Braham, *Minn., U.S.* 45°42′ N, 93°10′ W **94**
Brahestad see Raahe, *Fin.* 64°41′ N, 24°27′ E **152**
Brahmapur, *India* 19°19′ N, 84°47′ E **188**
Brahmaputra, river, *India* 26°18′ N, 92°11′ E **190**
Brăila, *Rom.* 45°16′ N, 27°57′ E **156**
Brăila, adm. division, *Rom.* 44°57′ N, 27°19′ E **156**
Braine, *Fr.* 49°20′ N, 3°30′ E **163**
Braine l'Alleud, *Belg.* 50°41′ N, 4°21′ E **163**
Brainerd, *Minn., U.S.* 46°20′ N, 94°11′ W **90**
Braintree, *Mass., U.S.* 42°12′ N, 71°1′ W **104**
Braintree, *U.K.* 51°53′ N, 0°32′ E **162**
Brakel, *Ger.* 51°43′ N, 9°11′ E **167**
Bräkne-Hoby, *Nor.* 56°14′ N, 15°8′ E **152**
Bralorne, *Can.* 50°47′ N, 122°48′ W **90**
Bramber, *U.K.* 50°51′ N, 0°18′ E **162**
Brampton, *Can.* 43°41′ N, 79°46′ W **94**
Bramsche, *Ger.* 52°24′ N, 7°58′ E **163**
Branchville, *S.C., U.S.* 33°14′ N, 80°49′ W **96**
Branco, river, *Braz.* 13°41′ S, 60°24′ W **130**
Brandberg, peak, *Namibia* 21°10′ S, 14°27′ E **220**
Brandbu, *Nor.* 60°24′ N, 10°31′ E **152**
Brandenburg, adm. division, *Ger.* 52°36′ N, 12°16′ E **152**
Brandfort, *S. Af.* 28°43′ S, 26°25′ E **227**
Brändö, *Fin.* 60°24′ N, 21°2′ E **166**
Brandon, *Can.* 49°49′ N, 99°57′ W **90**
Brandon, *Fla., U.S.* 27°57′ N, 82°16′ W **105**
Brandon, *Miss., U.S.* 32°15′ N, 89°60′ W **103**
Brandon, *U.K.* 52°26′ N, 0°37′ E **162**
Brandon, *Vt., U.S.* 43°47′ N, 73°7′ W **104**
Brandon, *Wis., U.S.* 43°43′ N, 88°47′ W **102**
Brandon Mountain, *Ire.* 52°13′ N, 10°20′ W **150**
Brandsen, *Arg.* 35°9′ S, 58°16′ W **139**
Brandvlei, *S. Af.* 30°26′ S, 20°26′ E **227**
Brandy Peak, *Oreg., U.S.* 42°35′ N, 123°58′ W **90**
Branford, *Conn., U.S.* 41°16′ N, 72°50′ W **104**
Branford, *Fla., U.S.* 29°58′ N, 82°56′ W **96**
Braniewo, *Pol.* 54°21′ N, 19°48′ E **166**
Brankovina, *Serb. and Mont.* 44°21′ N, 19°52′ E **168**
Bransfield Island, *Antarctica* 63°28′ S, 58°57′ W **134**
Branson, *Mo., U.S.* 36°38′ N, 93°14′ W **96**
Brant, *N.Y., U.S.* 42°34′ N, 79°2′ W **110**
Brant Lake, *N.Y., U.S.* 43°40′ N, 73°45′ W **104**
Brantford, *Can.* 43°7′ N, 80°16′ W **110**
Bras Coupé, Lac du, lake, *Can.* 49°33′ N, 75°43′ W **94**
Bras d'Or Lake, *Can.* 45°55′ N, 61°18′ W **111**
Brasil, Planalto Do, *South America* 17°41′ S, 44°49′ W **138**
Brasiléia, *Braz.* 10°57′ S, 68°44′ W **137**
Brasília, *Braz.* 15°49′ S, 47°60′ W **138**
Brasília de Minas, *Braz.* 16°13′ S, 44°28′ W **138**
Brasília Legal, *Braz.* 3°52′ S, 55°39′ W **130**
Braslaw, *Belarus* 55°38′ N, 27°3′ E **166**
Braşov, *Rom.* 45°38′ N, 25°35′ E **156**
Brass, *Nig.* 4°17′ N, 6°15′ E **222**
Brasschaat, *Belg.* 51°17′ N, 4°28′ E **167**
Brasstown Bald, peak, *Ga., U.S.* 34°51′ N, 83°53′ W **96**
Bratan, peak, *Bulg.* 42°29′ N, 25°4′ E **156**
Bratca, *Rom.* 46°54′ N, 22°39′ E **168**
Bratislava (Pressburg), *Slovakia* 48°7′ N, 16°57′ E **152**
Bratiya, peak, *Bulg.* 42°34′ N, 24°5′ E **156**
Bratsk, *Russ.* 56°24′ N, 101°23′ E **160**
Brattleboro, *Vt., U.S.* 42°50′ N, 72°34′ W **104**
Bratunac, *Bosn. and Herzg.* 44°12′ N, 19°20′ E **168**
Brauron, ruin(s), *Gr.* 37°54′ N, 23°52′ E **156**
Braux, *Fr.* 49°50′ N, 4°45′ E **163**
Brawley, *Calif., U.S.* 32°59′ N, 115°33′ W **101**
Bray, *Fr.* 49°56′ N, 2°42′ E **163**
Brazeau, Mount, *Can.* 52°31′ N, 117°27′ W **108**
Brazeau, river, *Can.* 52°46′ N, 116°22′ W **108**
Brazeau see Nordegg, *Can.* 52°28′ N, 116°7′ W **108**
Brazil 10°11′ S, 55°28′ W **132**
Brazil, *Ind., U.S.* 39°31′ N, 87°7′ W **102**
Brazoria, *Tex., U.S.* 29°2′ N, 95°34′ W **96**
Brazos Peak, *N. Mex., U.S.* 36°48′ N, 106°30′ W **92**
Brazzaville, *Congo* 4°13′ S, 15°0′ E **218**
Brčko, *Bosn. and Herzg.* 44°52′ N, 18°47′ E **168**
Brea, *Calif., U.S.* 33°55′ N, 117°55′ W **101**
Brea, Cerros de la, *Peru* 4°32′ S, 80°56′ W **130**
Breakenridge, Mount, *Can.* 49°42′ N, 121°58′ W **100**
Breaux Bridge, *La., U.S.* 30°15′ N, 91°55′ W **103**
Breaza, *Rom.* 45°11′ N, 25°38′ E **158**
Breckenridge, *Mich., U.S.* 43°23′ N, 84°29′ W **102**
Breckenridge, *Minn., U.S.* 46°14′ N, 96°35′ W **90**
Breckenridge, *Tex., U.S.* 32°45′ N, 98°55′ W **112**
Brecknock, Peninsula, *Chile* 54°36′ S, 74°29′ W **134**
Břeclav, *Czech Rep.* 48°45′ N, 16°53′ E **152**
Brecon, *U.K.* 51°56′ N, 3°23′ W **162**
Brecon Beacons, peak, *U.K.* 51°53′ N, 3°28′ W **162**
Breda, *Neth.* 51°34′ N, 4°45′ E **167**
Bredasdorp, *S. Af.* 34°32′ S, 20°2′ E **227**
Bredbyn, *Nor.* 63°26′ N, 18°6′ E **152**
Bredene, *Belg.* 51°13′ N, 2°57′ E **150**
Bredon Hill, *U.K.* 52°3′ N, 2°5′ W **162**
Bredy, *Russ.* 52°25′ N, 60°17′ E **154**
Breezewood, *Pa., U.S.* 39°59′ N, 78°15′ W **94**
Bregovo, *Bulg.* 44°9′ N, 22°38′ E **168**
Breil-sur-Roya, *Fr.* 43°56′ N, 7°29′ E **167**
Breitenworbis, *Ger.* 51°25′ N, 10°25′ E **167**
Breitungen, *Ger.* 50°45′ N, 10°18′ E **167**
Brejo, *Braz.* 3°41′ S, 42°50′ W **132**
Brejolândia, *Braz.* 12°30′ S, 43°58′ W **132**
Brekovica, *Bosn. and Herzg.* 44°51′ N, 15°51′ E **168**
Breloh, *Ger.* 53°1′ N, 10°5′ E **150**
Bremangerpollen, *Nor.* 61°51′ N, 4°58′ E **152**
Bremen, *Ga., U.S.* 33°41′ N, 85°8′ W **96**
Bremen, *Ger.* 53°5′ N, 8°47′ E **163**
Bremen, *Ind., U.S.* 41°26′ N, 86°9′ W **102**
Bremen, *Ohio, U.S.* 39°41′ N, 82°26′ W **102**
Bremen, adm. division, *Ger.* 53°4′ N, 8°27′ E **150**
Bremer Bay 34°47′ S, 119°6′ E **230**
Bremerhaven, *Ger.* 53°32′ N, 8°36′ E **150**
Bremerton, *Wash., U.S.* 47°32′ N, 122°40′ W **100**
Bremnes, *Nor.* 59°46′ N, 5°9′ E **152**
Bremsnes, *Nor.* 63°4′ N, 7°39′ E **152**
Brenes, *Sp.* 37°32′ N, 5°53′ W **164**
Brenham, *Tex., U.S.* 30°9′ N, 96°24′ W **96**
Brenner Pass, *It.* 47°0′ N, 11°30′ E **167**
Breno, *It.* 45°57′ N, 10°18′ E **167**
Brenton Bay 11°34′ S, 130°45′ E **230**
Brentwood, *Calif., U.S.* 37°55′ N, 121°43′ W **100**
Brentwood, *N.Y., U.S.* 40°47′ N, 73°14′ W **104**
Brentwood, *U.K.* 51°37′ N, 0°17′ E **162**
Brescia, *It.* 45°32′ N, 10°13′ E **167**
Breskens, *Neth.* 51°23′ N, 3°33′ E **163**
Bresles, *Fr.* 49°24′ N, 2°15′ E **163**
Bressanone, *It.* 46°44′ N, 11°38′ E **167**
Brest, *Belarus* 52°5′ N, 23°41′ E **152**
Brest, *Fr.* 48°23′ N, 4°30′ W **150**
Brest, *Pol.* 52°4′ N, 23°42′ E **160**
Brestovac, *Serb. and Mont.* 43°9′ N, 21°52′ E **168**
Bretagne, adm. division, *Fr.* 48°10′ N, 4°8′ W **150**
Breteuil, *Fr.* 49°37′ N, 2°17′ E **163**
Breteuil, *Fr.* 48°49′ N, 0°54′ E **163**
Breton, *Can.* 53°5′ N, 114°29′ W **108**
Breton, Cape, *Can.* 45°56′ N, 59°46′ W **111**
Bretón, Cayo, island, *Cuba* 21°7′ N, 80°16′ W **116**
Breton Island, Cape, *Can.* 45°19′ N, 63°50′ W **81**
Breton Sound 29°28′ N, 89°22′ W **103**
Brett, Cape, *N.Z.* 35°11′ S, 174°16′ E **240**
Breu, river, *Braz.* 3°45′ S, 66°39′ W **136**
Breu, river, *South America* 9°25′ S, 72°31′ W **137**
Breueh, island, *Indonesia* 5°47′ N, 94°35′ E **196**
Breuil-Cervinia, *It.* 45°56′ N, 7°38′ E **167**
Breves, *Braz.* 1°39′ S, 50°31′ W **130**
Brevik, *Nor.* 59°3′ N, 9°41′ E **152**
Brevoort Island, *Can.* 63°4′ N, 63°59′ W **106**
Brevoort Lake, lake, *Mich., U.S.* 45°58′ N, 85°25′ W **110**
Brew, Mount, *Can.* 50°34′ N, 122°2′ W **90**
Brewer, *Me., U.S.* 44°47′ N, 68°46′ W **94**
Brewerville, *Liberia* 6°20′ N, 10°47′ W **222**
Brewster, *Kans., U.S.* 39°22′ N, 101°24′ W **90**
Brewster, *Mass., U.S.* 41°45′ N, 70°5′ W **104**
Brewster, *Nebr., U.S.* 41°54′ N, 99°52′ W **90**
Brewster, *N.Y., U.S.* 41°23′ N, 73°39′ W **104**
Brewster, *Ohio, U.S.* 40°42′ N, 81°36′ W **102**
Brewster, *Wash., U.S.* 48°5′ N, 119°49′ W **90**
Brewster, Mount, *Antarctica* 72°54′ S, 169°59′ E **248**
Brewton, *Ala., U.S.* 31°6′ N, 87°4′ W **96**
Breza, *Bosn. and Herzg.* 44°1′ N, 18°15′ E **168**
Brezičani, *Bosn. and Herzg.* 45°0′ N, 16°40′ E **168**
Brezina, *Alg.* 33°7′ N, 1°14′ E **214**
Brezno, *Slovakia* 48°48′ N, 19°39′ E **156**
Brezolles, *Fr.* 48°41′ N, 1°4′ E **163**
Brezovo Polje, *Bosn. and Herzg.* 44°50′ N, 18°57′ E **168**
Bria, *Cen. Af. Rep.* 6°29′ N, 22°2′ E **218**
Brian Head, peak, *Utah, U.S.* 37°40′ N, 112°54′ W **92**
Briançon, *Fr.* 44°53′ N, 6°38′ E **167**
Briare, *Fr.* 47°38′ N, 2°43′ E **150**
Bribie Island, *Austral.* 27°17′ S, 151°4′ E **230**
Bridge City, *Tex., U.S.* 30°0′ N, 93°52′ W **103**
Bridgehampton, *N.Y., U.S.* 40°56′ N, 72°19′ W **104**
Bridgend, *U.K.* 51°30′ N, 3°34′ W **162**
Bridgeport, *Ala., U.S.* 34°56′ N, 85°43′ W **96**
Bridgeport, *Calif., U.S.* 38°15′ N, 119°16′ W **100**
Bridgeport, *Conn., U.S.* 41°10′ N, 73°12′ W **104**
Bridgeport, *Nebr., U.S.* 41°39′ N, 103°8′ W **90**
Bridgeport, *Tex., U.S.* 33°11′ N, 97°45′ W **92**
Bridgeport, Lake, *Tex., U.S.* 33°17′ N, 98°40′ W **81**
Bridger Peak, *Wyo., U.S.* 41°10′ N, 107°7′ W **90**
Bridgeton, *N.C., U.S.* 35°7′ N, 77°2′ W **96**
Bridgetown, *Barbados* 13°3′ N, 59°43′ W **116**
Bridgetown, *Ohio, U.S.* 39°8′ N, 84°39′ W **102**
Bridgewater, *Can.* 44°22′ N, 64°33′ W **111**
Bridgewater, *Mass., U.S.* 41°59′ N, 70°58′ W **104**
Bridgnorth, *U.K.* 52°31′ N, 2°26′ W **162**
Bridgton, *Me., U.S.* 44°3′ N, 70°43′ W **104**
Bridgwater, *U.K.* 51°7′ N, 3°1′ W **162**
Bridlington, *U.K.* 54°4′ N, 0°14′ E **162**
Bridport, *Vt., U.S.* 43°58′ N, 73°20′ W **104**
Brienne-le-Château, *Fr.* 48°23′ N, 4°31′ E **163**
Brienz, *Switz.* 46°45′ N, 8°0′ E **167**
Brienzer See, lake, *Switz.* 46°41′ N, 7°42′ E **167**
Brig, *Switz.* 46°20′ N, 8°0′ E **167**
Brigantine, *N.J., U.S.* 39°23′ N, 74°24′ W **94**
Brigden, *Can.* 42°48′ N, 82°18′ W **102**
Brigg, *U.K.* 53°32′ N, 0°29′ E **162**
Brigham City, *Utah, U.S.* 41°30′ N, 111°60′ W **90**
Brighouse, *U.K.* 53°42′ N, 1°47′ W **162**
Brightlingsea, *U.K.* 51°48′ N, 1°1′ E **162**
Brighton, *Can.* 44°1′ N, 77°43′ W **110**
Brighton, *Colo., U.S.* 39°58′ N, 104°49′ W **90**
Brighton, *Mich., U.S.* 42°30′ N, 83°47′ W **102**
Brighton, *U.K.* 50°50′ N, 0°9′ E **162**
Brijuni Otoci (Brioni Islands), *Gulf of Venice* 44°51′ N, 13°23′ E **167**
Brikama, *Gambia* 13°17′ N, 16°33′ W **222**
Brilon, *Ger.* 51°24′ N, 8°32′ E **167**
Brimfield, *Ill., U.S.* 40°49′ N, 89°54′ W **102**
Brinkburn Priory, site, *U.K.* 55°16′ N, 1°55′ W **150**
Brinkley, *Ark., U.S.* 34°51′ N, 91°12′ W **96**
Brinnon, *Wash., U.S.* 47°39′ N, 122°55′ W **100**
Brion, Île, island, *Can.* 47°28′ N, 61°18′ W **81**
Brioni Islands see Brijuni Otoci, *Gulf of Venice* 44°51′ N, 13°23′ E **167**
Brioude, *Fr.* 45°17′ N, 3°21′ E **150**
Briouze, *Fr.* 48°41′ N, 0°23′ E **150**
Brisbane, *Austral.* 27°28′ S, 152°53′ E **230**
Bristol, *Conn., U.S.* 41°40′ N, 72°56′ W **104**
Bristol, *Ind., U.S.* 41°42′ N, 85°50′ W **102**
Bristol, *N.H., U.S.* 43°35′ N, 71°45′ W **104**
Bristol, *R.I., U.S.* 41°40′ N, 71°17′ W **104**
Bristol, *S. Dak., U.S.* 45°19′ N, 97°47′ W **90**
Bristol, *Tenn., U.S.* 36°35′ N, 82°12′ W **96**
Bristol, *U.K.* 51°26′ N, 2°35′ W **162**
Bristol, *Vt., U.S.* 44°8′ N, 73°5′ W **104**
Bristol Bay 56°13′ N, 160°33′ W **106**
Bristol Channel 51°25′ N, 4°42′ W **150**
Bristol Mountains, *Calif., U.S.* 34°58′ N, 116°1′ W **101**
Bristow, *Okla., U.S.* 35°47′ N, 96°23′ W **94**
Britannia Beach, *Can.* 49°36′ N, 123°12′ W **100**
British Channel 80°37′ N, 47°37′ E **160**
British Columbia, adm. division, *Can.* 55°32′ N, 128°9′ W **106**
British Indian Ocean Territory, *United Kingdom* 7°0′ S, 72°0′ E **188**
British Mountains, *Can.* 69°15′ N, 141°7′ W **98**
British Virgin Islands, *Caribbean Sea* 19°0′ N, 65°0′ W **118**
British Virgin Islands, *United Kingdom* 18°31′ N, 64°41′ W **116**
Brits, *S. Af.* 25°40′ S, 27°46′ E **227**
Britstown, *S. Af.* 30°36′ S, 23°31′ E **227**
Britt, *Can.* 45°47′ N, 80°32′ W **94**
Britt, *Iowa, U.S.* 43°4′ N, 93°47′ W **94**
Britton, *S. Dak., U.S.* 45°46′ N, 97°46′ W **94**
Brive, *Fr.* 45°8′ N, 1°31′ E **150**
Briviesca, *Sp.* 42°32′ N, 3°21′ W **150**
Brnaze, *Croatia* 43°40′ N, 16°39′ E **168**
Brno, *Czech Rep.* 49°11′ N, 16°37′ E **152**
Broadback, river, *Can.* 51°13′ N, 78°42′ W **110**
Broaddus, *Tex., U.S.* 31°17′ N, 94°17′ W **103**
Broadstairs, *U.K.* 51°21′ N, 1°25′ E **163**
Broadus, *Mont., U.S.* 45°25′ N, 105°26′ W **90**
Broadview, *Can.* 50°22′ N, 102°35′ W **108**
Broadwater, *Nebr., U.S.* 41°36′ N, 102°52′ W **90**
Brocēni, *Latv.* 56°41′ N, 22°33′ E **166**
Brochet, *Can.* 57°54′ N, 101°39′ W **108**
Brochet, Lac au, lake, *Can.* 49°40′ N, 70°15′ W **94**
Brochet, Lac, lake, *Can.* 58°38′ N, 101°52′ W **108**
Brock Island, *Can.* 78°23′ N, 115°4′ W **246**
Brock, river, *Can.* 50°5′ N, 75°5′ W **110**
Brocken, peak, *Ger.* 51°47′ N, 10°30′ E **152**
Brockport, *N.Y., U.S.* 43°12′ N, 77°58′ W **94**
Brockport, *Pa., U.S.* 41°15′ N, 78°45′ W **94**
Brockton, *Mass., U.S.* 42°4′ N, 71°2′ W **104**
Brockville, *Can.* 44°36′ N, 75°42′ W **110**
Brockway, *Mont., U.S.* 47°16′ N, 105°46′ W **90**
Brockway, *Pa., U.S.* 41°14′ N, 78°48′ W **94**
Brocton, *Ill., U.S.* 39°43′ N, 87°56′ W **102**
Brod, *Maced.* 41°31′ N, 21°12′ E **168**
Brodarevo, *Serb. and Mont.* 43°13′ N, 19°42′ E **168**
Brodec, *Maced.* 41°46′ N, 20°41′ E **168**
Brodeur Peninsula, *Can.* 71°43′ N, 89°33′ W **106**
Brodhead, *Wis., U.S.* 42°37′ N, 89°23′ W **102**
Brodica, *Serb. and Mont.* 44°29′ N, 21°49′ E **168**
Brodick, *U.K.* 55°34′ N, 5°9′ W **150**
Brodilovo, *Bulg.* 42°5′ N, 27°51′ E **156**
Brodnytsya, *Ukr.* 51°45′ N, 26°16′ E **152**
Brodokalmak, *Russ.* 55°33′ N, 61°59′ E **154**
Brody, *Ukr.* 50°4′ N, 25°8′ E **152**
Brogan, *Oreg., U.S.* 44°14′ N, 117°32′ W **90**
Broken Arrow, *Okla., U.S.* 36°2′ N, 95°47′ W **96**
Broken Bow, *Nebr., U.S.* 41°24′ N, 99°39′ W **90**
Broken Bow, *Okla., U.S.* 34°1′ N, 94°45′ W **96**
Broken Bow Lake, lake, *Okla., U.S.* 34°10′ N, 94°57′ W **96**
Broken Hill see Kabwe, *Zambia* 14°29′ S, 28°25′ E **224**
Broken Ridge, *Indian Ocean* 31°50′ S, 95°31′ E **254**
Brokind, *Nor.* 58°12′ N, 15°40′ E **152**
Brokopondo, *Suriname* 5°4′ N, 55°2′ W **130**
Bromarv, *Fin.* 59°58′ N, 23°0′ E **166**
Bromley Mountain, *Vt., U.S.* 43°13′ N, 72°58′ W **104**
Bromyard, *U.K.* 52°10′ N, 2°31′ W **162**
Brønderslev, *Den.* 57°15′ N, 9°56′ E **150**
Broni, *It.* 45°4′ N, 9°15′ E **167**
Brønnøysund, *Nor.* 65°26′ N, 12°12′ E **152**
Bronson, *Fla., U.S.* 29°26′ N, 82°40′ W **105**
Bronson, *Tex., U.S.* 31°19′ N, 94°1′ W **103**
Bronte, *Tex., U.S.* 31°52′ N, 100°18′ W **92**
Bronyts'ka Huta, *Ukr.* 50°54′ N, 27°18′ E **152**
Brook, *Ind., U.S.* 40°51′ N, 87°22′ W **102**
Brookeland, *Tex., U.S.* 31°7′ N, 93°59′ W **103**
Brooker, *Fla., U.S.* 29°53′ N, 82°21′ W **105**
Brooke's Point, *Philippines* 8°48′ N, 117°50′ E **203**
Brookfield, *Conn., U.S.* 41°28′ N, 73°25′ W **104**
Brookfield, *Mo., U.S.* 39°46′ N, 93°3′ W **94**
Brookfield, *Wis., U.S.* 43°4′ N, 88°7′ W **102**
Brookhaven, *Miss., U.S.* 31°34′ N, 90°26′ W **103**
Brookhaven National Laboratory, *N.Y., U.S.* 40°52′ N, 72°54′ W **104**
Brookings, *Oreg., U.S.* 42°3′ N, 124°16′ W **82**
Brookline, *Mass., U.S.* 42°19′ N, 71°8′ W **104**
Brooklyn, *Conn., U.S.* 41°47′ N, 71°58′ W **104**
Brooklyn, *Ind., U.S.* 39°32′ N, 86°24′ W **102**
Brooklyn, *Mich., U.S.* 42°5′ N, 84°15′ W **102**
Brooklyn, *Miss., U.S.* 31°2′ N, 89°10′ W **103**
Brookmere, *Can.* 49°48′ N, 120°51′ W **100**
Brookport, *Mo., U.S.* 37°7′ N, 88°37′ W **96**
Brooks, *Can.* 50°33′ N, 111°55′ W **90**
Brooks Bay 50°11′ N, 128°1′ W **108**
Brooks Brook, *Can.* 60°25′ N, 133°10′ W **108**
Brooks, Cape, *Antarctica* 73°53′ S, 60°24′ W **248**
Brooks Range, *Alas., U.S.* 67°30′ N, 153°45′ W **106**
Brookston, *Ind., U.S.* 40°35′ N, 86°52′ W **102**
Brooksville, *Fla., U.S.* 28°34′ N, 82°24′ W **105**
Brooksville, *Ky., U.S.* 38°39′ N, 84°5′ W **102**
Brooksville, *Miss., U.S.* 33°12′ N, 88°35′ W **103**
Brookville, *Ind., U.S.* 39°25′ N, 85°1′ W **102**
Brookville, *Pa., U.S.* 41°9′ N, 79°5′ W **94**
Brookville Lake, *Ind., U.S.* 39°31′ N, 85°11′ W **102**
Brookwood, *Ala., U.S.* 33°16′ N, 87°19′ W **103**
Broome, *Austral.* 17°58′ S, 122°20′ E **238**
Broqueles, Punta, *Col.* 9°13′ N, 76°36′ W **136**
Brøstrud, *Nor.* 60°18′ N, 8°30′ E **152**
Brothers, The, islands, *North Atlantic Ocean* 21°50′ N, 75°43′ W **116**
Brothers, The, islands, *Red Sea* 26°35′ N, 34°31′ E **180**
Brou, *Fr.* 48°12′ N, 1°10′ E **163**
Brough, *U.K.* 54°31′ N, 2°19′ W **162**
Broughton in Furness, *U.K.* 54°17′ N, 3°13′ W **162**
Broughton Island see Qikiqtarjuaq, *Can.* 67°30′ N, 63°52′ W **73**
Broulkou, spring, *Chad* 16°39′ N, 18°11′ E **216**
Brouwershaven, *Neth.* 51°43′ N, 3°53′ E **163**
Brovary, *Ukr.* 50°30′ N, 30°52′ E **158**
Browerville, *Minn., U.S.* 46°4′ N, 94°53′ W **90**
Brown City, *Mich., U.S.* 43°13′ N, 82°59′ W **102**
Brown Willy, peak, *U.K.* 50°34′ N, 4°41′ W **150**
Browne Bay 72°57′ N, 100°30′ W **106**
Brownfield, *Me., U.S.* 43°56′ N, 70°56′ W **104**
Brownfield, *Tex., U.S.* 33°9′ N, 102°17′ W **92**
Brownhills, *U.K.* 52°39′ N, 1°56′ W **162**
Browning, *Mont., U.S.* 48°31′ N, 113°2′ W **90**
Browns, *Ala., U.S.* 32°26′ N, 87°22′ W **103**
Browns, *N.Z.* 46°10′ S, 168°25′ E **240**
Brown's Cay, island, *Bahamas* 25°19′ N, 79°26′ W **105**
Browns Town, *Jam.* 18°23′ N, 77°23′ W **115**
Browns Valley, *Minn., U.S.* 45°35′ N, 96°50′ W **90**
Brownsboro, *Tex., U.S.* 32°17′ N, 95°37′ W **103**
Brownson Islands, *Amundsen Sea* 73°56′ S, 104°11′ W **248**
Brownstown, *Ind., U.S.* 38°53′ N, 86°3′ W **102**
Brownsville, *Tenn., U.S.* 35°34′ N, 89°16′ W **96**
Brownsville, *Tex., U.S.* 25°57′ N, 97°28′ W **114**
Brownsville, *Vt., U.S.* 43°28′ N, 72°29′ W **104**
Brownsweg, *Suriname* 4°59′ N, 55°11′ W **130**
Brownwood, *Tex., U.S.* 31°41′ N, 98°58′ W **92**
Brownwood, Lake, *Tex., U.S.* 31°52′ N, 99°50′ W **81**
Bršečine, *Croatia* 42°43′ N, 17°57′ E **168**
Bru, *Nor.* 61°32′ N, 5°12′ E **152**
Bruce Mines, *Can.* 46°18′ N, 83°48′ W **94**
Bruce, Mount, *Austral.* 22°39′ S, 117°57′ E **230**
Bruce Peninsula, *North America* 44°50′ N, 81°23′ W **110**
Bruck, *Aust.* 48°1′ N, 16°47′ E **168**
Brugg, *Switz.* 47°28′ N, 8°13′ E **156**
Brugge, *Belg.* 51°12′ N, 3°13′ E **163**
Brüggen, *Ger.* 51°14′ N, 6°10′ E **167**
Brühl, *Ger.* 50°49′ N, 6°53′ E **167**
Bruini, *India* 29°10′ N, 96°8′ E **188**
Brûlé, Lac, lake, *Can.* 46°54′ N, 77°32′ W **94**
Brumado, *Braz.* 14°15′ S, 41°38′ W **138**
Brumath, *Fr.* 48°44′ N, 7°41′ E **163**
Brundidge, *Ala., U.S.* 31°42′ N, 85°49′ W **96**
Bruneau, *Idaho, U.S.* 42°53′ N, 115°48′ W **90**
Bruneau, river, *Idaho, U.S.* 42°57′ N, 115°48′ W **90**
Brunei 5°0′ N, 115°0′ E **192**
Brunico, *It.* 46°47′ N, 11°56′ E **167**
Bruno, *Can.* 52°15′ N, 105°32′ W **108**
Bruno, *It.* 44°46′ N, 8°26′ E **167**
Brunson, *S.C., U.S.* 32°55′ N, 81°12′ W **96**
Brunssum, *Neth.* 50°57′ N, 5°58′ E **167**
Brunswick, *Ga., U.S.* 31°8′ N, 81°30′ W **96**
Brunswick, *Me., U.S.* 43°54′ N, 69°59′ W **104**
Brunswick, *Ohio, U.S.* 41°13′ N, 81°51′ W **102**
Brunswick Lake, lake, *Can.* 48°56′ N, 83°57′ W **94**
Brunswick Naval Air Station, *Me., U.S.* 43°53′ N, 69°58′ W **104**
Brunswick, Península de, *Chile* 53°26′ S, 73°18′ W **134**
Brunt Ice Shelf, *Antarctica* 76°2′ S, 31°32′ W **248**
Brus, *Serb. and Mont.* 43°22′ N, 21°1′ E **168**
Brus Laguna, *Hond.* 15°44′ N, 84°32′ W **115**
Brusartsi, *Bulg.* 43°39′ N, 23°4′ E **168**
Brush, *Colo., U.S.* 40°15′ N, 103°38′ W **90**
Brusnik, *Serb. and Mont.* 44°6′ N, 22°27′ E **168**

C

Ca Mau, Vietnam 9°12′ N, 105°7′ E 202
Ca Na, Vietnam 11°22′ N, 108°51′ E 202
Ca Na, Mui, Vietnam 10°56′ N, 109°0′ E 202
Ca, river, Vietnam 19°12′ N, 104°44′ E 202
C.A. Rosetti, Rom. 45°17′ N, 29°33′ E 156
Caaguazú, Parag. 25°27′ S, 56°1′ W 132
Caamaño Sound 52°48′ N, 129°56′ W 108
Caapucú, Parag. 26°15′ S, 57°11′ W 139
Caatinga, Braz. 17°8′ S, 45°58′ W 138
Caazapá, Parag. 26°9′ S, 56°23′ W 139
Cabaiguán, Cuba 22°5′ N, 79°31′ W 116
Caballococha, Peru 3°58′ S, 70°30′ W 130
Caballos Mesteños, Llano de los, Mex. 28°36′ N, 104°37′ W 112
Cabana, Peru 8°25′ S, 78°1′ W 130
Cabanaconde, Peru 15°40′ S, 71°58′ W 137
Cabanatuan, Philippines 15°28′ N, 120°58′ E 203
Cabañeros National Park, Sp. 39°14′ N, 4°33′ W 164
Cabanes, Sp. 40°9′ N, 4°238′ E 164
Cabano, Can. 47°39′ N, 68°55′ W 94
Cabedelo, Braz. 7°4′ S, 34°52′ W 132
Cabery, Ill., U.S. 40°59′ N, 88°13′ W 102
Cabeza de Lagarto, Punta, Peru 10°15′ S, 80°8′ W 130
Cabeza de Pava, Col. 2°47′ N, 69°13′ W 136
Cabeza del Buey, Sp. 38°43′ N, 5°14′ W 164
Cabezas, Bol. 18°49′ S, 63°26′ W 137
Cabildo, Arg. 38°30′ S, 61°57′ W 139
Cabimas, Venez. 10°24′ N, 71°29′ W 136
Cabinda, Angola 5°35′ S, 12°10′ E 218
Cabinet Mountains, Mont., U.S. 48°20′ N, 116°13′ W 90
Cabiri, Angola 8°53′ S, 13°40′ E 220
Cable, Wis., U.S. 46°12′ N, 91°17′ W 94
Cabo Blanco, Arg. 47°12′ S, 65°47′ W 134
Cabo Delgado, adm. division, Mozambique 12°22′ S, 38°34′ E 220
Cabo Frio, Braz. 22°51′ S, 42°1′ W 138
Cabo Gracias a Dios, Nicar. 14°58′ N, 83°14′ W 115
Cabo Raso, Arg. 44°21′ S, 65°17′ W 134
Cabo San Lucas, Mex. 22°51′ N, 109°56′ W 112
Cabonga, Réservoir, lake, Can. 47°6′ N, 78°13′ W 81
Cabonga, Réservoir, lake, Can. 47°14′ N, 78°10′ W 106
Cabool, Mo., U.S. 37°6′ N, 92°6′ W 96
Caborca, Mex. 30°42′ N, 112°11′ W 92
Cabot, Vt., U.S. 44°23′ N, 72°20′ W 104
Cabot Head, Can. 45°15′ N, 81°17′ W 94
Cabot, Mount, N.H., U.S. 44°29′ N, 71°26′ W 104
Cabra de Santo Cristo, Sp. 37°42′ N, 3°16′ W 164
Cabral, Dom. Rep. 18°14′ N, 71°12′ W 116
Cabrera Baja, Sierra de la, Sp. 42°3′ N, 7°8′ W 150
Cabrera, island, Sp. 38°52′ N, 2°54′ E 214
Cabri, Can. 50°37′ N, 108°28′ W 90
Cabri Lake, lake, Can. 51°4′ N, 110°5′ W 90
Cabriel, river, Sp. 39°23′ N, 1°27′ W 164
Cabrillo National Monument, Calif., U.S. 32°40′ N, 117°17′ W 101
Cabrobó, Braz. 8°31′ S, 39°21′ W 132
Cabrón, Cabo, Dom. Rep. 19°22′ N, 69°11′ W 116
Cabruta, Venez. 7°40′ N, 66°16′ W 136
Cabugao, Philippines 17°49′ N, 120°27′ E 203
Cabure, Venez. 11°9′ N, 69°38′ W 136
Cabuyaro, Col. 4°16′ N, 72°48′ W 136
Caçador, Braz. 26°47′ S, 50°60′ W 139
Cacahuamilpa, Mex. 18°40′ N, 99°33′ W 114
Cacahuatepec, Mex. 16°34′ N, 98°11′ W 112
Cacahuatique, peak, El Salv. 13°45′ N, 88°20′ W 115
Čačak, Serb. and Mont. 43°52′ N, 20°20′ E 168
Cacalotán, Mex. 23°4′ N, 105°50′ W 114
Cacaoui, Lac, lake, Can. 50°52′ N, 67°26′ W 111
Caçapava do Sul, Braz. 30°30′ S, 53°30′ W 139
Caccia, Capo, It. 40°34′ N, 7°24′ E 156
Cacequi, Braz. 29°55′ S, 54°51′ W 139
Cáceres, Braz. 16°7′ S, 57°39′ W 132
Cáceres, Col. 7°35′ N, 75°19′ W 136
Cáceres, Sp. 39°28′ N, 6°23′ W 164
Cacharí, Arg. 36°23′ S, 59°31′ W 139
Cache Bay, Can. 46°22′ N, 79°59′ W 94
Cache Peak, Idaho, U.S. 42°11′ N, 113°43′ W 90
Cacheu, Guinea-Bissau 12°14′ N, 16°7′ W 222
Cachimbo, Braz. 9°19′ S, 54°51′ W 130
Cachimbo, Serra do, Braz. 7°52′ S, 56°39′ W 130
Cachingues, Angola 13°7′ S, 16°43′ E 220
Cachisca, Lac, lake, Can. 50°24′ N, 75°36′ W 110
Cachoeira, Braz. 14°23′ S, 55°34′ W 132
Cachoeira Alta, Braz. 18°51′ S, 50°56′ W 138
Cachoeira do Sul, Braz. 30°2′ S, 52°56′ W 139
Cachoeira Ipadu, fall(s), Braz. 0°15′ N, 67°20′ W 136
Cachoeira Ipanoré, fall(s), Braz. 0°13′ N, 68°29′ W 136
Cachoeiro do Itapemirim, Braz. 20°54′ S, 41°9′ W 138
Cachos, Punta, Chile 27°41′ S, 72°17′ W 134
Cachuela Esperanza, Bol. 10°36′ S, 65°34′ W 137
Cacine, Guinea-Bissau 11°6′ N, 15°2′ W 222
Cacolo, Angola 10°11′ S, 19°13′ E 207
Caconda, Angola 13°44′ S, 15°4′ E 220
Cacongo, Angola 5°15′ S, 12°7′ E 218
Cactus, Tex., U.S. 36°0′ N, 101°59′ W 92
Cactus Flat, Nev., U.S. 37°52′ N, 116°55′ W 90
Cactus Range, Nev., U.S. 37°54′ N, 117°6′ W 90
Caçu, Braz. 18°35′ S, 51°12′ W 138
Caculé, Braz. 14°34′ S, 42°12′ W 138
Cacuri, Venez. 4°48′ N, 65°20′ W 136
Cacuso, Angola 9°27′ S, 15°44′ E 218
Cadaadley, Somalia 9°44′ N, 44°40′ E 218
Cadair Idris, peak, U.K. 52°41′ N, 3°57′ W 162
Cadale, Somalia 2°44′ N, 46°27′ E 218
Cadaqués, Sp. 42°16′ N, 3°16′ E 164
Čadavica, Croatia 45°45′ N, 17°50′ E 168
Caddo, Okla., U.S. 34°6′ N, 96°16′ W 96
Caddo Lake, Tex., U.S. 32°44′ N, 94°30′ W 81
Cade, La., U.S. 30°2′ N, 91°54′ W 103
Cadereyta, Mex. 25°34′ N, 99°59′ W 114
Cadí, Serra del, Sp. 42°16′ N, 1°28′ E 164
Cadillac, Can. 49°43′ N, 107°45′ W 90
Cadillac Mountain, Me., U.S. 44°20′ N, 68°19′ W 94
Çadır Dağı, peak, Turk. 38°12′ N, 43°3′ E 195
Cadiz, Ky., U.S. 36°52′ N, 87°50′ W 96
Cadiz, Ohio, U.S. 40°15′ N, 80°60′ W 102
Cadiz, Philippines 10°56′ N, 123°16′ E 203
Cádiz, Sp. 36°31′ N, 6°18′ W 164
Cadomin, Can. 53°0′ N, 117°20′ W 108
Cady Mountains, Calif., U.S. 34°57′ N, 116°20′ W 101
Caen, Fr. 49°11′ N, 0°22′ E 150
Caerdydd see Cardiff, U.K. 51°28′ N, 3°12′ W 162
Caerlaverock Castle, site, U.K. 54°58′ N, 3°38′ W 150
Caerleon, U.K. 51°36′ N, 2°57′ W 162
Caernarfon, U.K. 53°9′ N, 4°14′ W 162
Caerphilly, U.K. 51°35′ N, 3°13′ W 162
Caesarea, ruin(s), Israel 32°29′ N, 34°51′ E 194
Caeté, Braz. 19°54′ S, 43°35′ W 138
Caeté, river, Braz. 9°29′ S, 69°35′ W 130
Caetité, Braz. 14°5′ S, 42°31′ W 138
Cafayate, Arg. 26°4′ S, 65°58′ W 132
Cafuini, river, Braz. 1°12′ N, 58°27′ W 130
Cagayan de Oro, Philippines 8°31′ N, 124°36′ E 203
Cagayan Islands, Sulu Sea 9°6′ N, 121°20′ E 203
Cagayan, river, Philippines 18°5′ N, 121°37′ E 203
Cagayan Sulu Island, Philippines 6°52′ N, 118°36′ E 203
Cagliari, It. 39°13′ N, 9°6′ E 156
Cagnano Varano, It. 41°49′ N, 15°46′ E 156
Caguán, river, Col. 1°9′ N, 74°44′ W 136
Cahama, Angola 16°15′ S, 14°12′ E 220
Cahora Bassa, Mozambique 15°38′ S, 32°46′ E 224
Cahora Bassa Dam, Mozambique 15°46′ S, 32°3′ E 224
Cahore Point, Ire. 52°34′ N, 6°9′ W 150
Cahors, Fr. 44°31′ N, 1°18′ E 214
Cahuinari National Park, Col. 1°18′ S, 71°54′ W 136
Cahuinari, river, Col. 1°22′ S, 71°29′ W 136
Cahuita National Park, C.R. 9°42′ N, 82°55′ W 115
Cahul, Mold. 45°54′ N, 28°10′ E 156
Cai Bau, Vietnam 21°8′ N, 107°28′ E 198
Caia, Mozambique 17°49′ S, 35°18′ E 224
Caiabis, Serra dos, Braz. 12°29′ S, 56°51′ W 130
Caianda, Angola 11°4′ S, 23°30′ E 224
Caiapó, river, Braz. 16°33′ S, 51°17′ W 138
Caiapó, Serra do, Braz. 17°38′ S, 53°25′ W 132
Caiaponia, Braz. 16°59′ S, 51°49′ W 138
Caibarién, Cuba 22°29′ N, 79°28′ W 116
Caicara, Venez. 7°36′ N, 66°10′ W 136
Caicó, Braz. 6°30′ S, 37°7′ W 132
Caicos Islands, North Atlantic Ocean 21°25′ N, 71°58′ W 116
Caijiapo, China 34°19′ N, 107°33′ E 198
Cailloma, Peru 15°13′ S, 71°45′ W 137
Caimito, Col. 8°49′ N, 75°8′ W 136
Cainde, Angola 15°34′ S, 13°20′ E 220
Cains, river, Can. 46°20′ N, 66°23′ W 94
Cainsville, Mo., U.S. 40°25′ N, 93°46′ W 94
Caird Coast, Antarctica 76°29′ S, 32°29′ W 248
Cairngorm Mountains, U.K. 57°3′ N, 4°35′ W 150
Cairns, Austral. 16°56′ S, 145°45′ E 231
Cairnwell Pass, U.K. 56°52′ N, 3°25′ W 150
Cairo, Ga., U.S. 30°52′ N, 84°13′ W 96
Cairo, Mo., U.S. 37°0′ N, 89°10′ W 96
Cairo, N.Y., U.S. 42°17′ N, 74°1′ W 104
Cairo Montenotte, It. 44°23′ N, 8°16′ E 167
Cairo see El Qâhira, Egypt 30°3′ N, 31°8′ E 180
Caister, U.K. 53°29′ N, 0°19′ E 162
Caithness, Ord of, peak, U.K. 58°8′ N, 3°41′ W 150
Caitou, Angola 14°31′ S, 13°4′ E 220
Caiundo, Angola 15°44′ S, 17°26′ E 220
Caiza, Bol. 20°4′ S, 65°45′ W 137
Caiza see Villa Ingavi, Bol. 21°47′ S, 63°33′ W 137
Cajamarca, Peru 7°8′ S, 78°32′ W 130
Cajamarca, adm. division, Peru 4°58′ S, 79°20′ W 130
Cajatambo, Peru 10°30′ S, 77°1′ W 130
Cajàzeiras, Braz. 6°54′ S, 38°32′ W 132
Cajniče, Bosn. and Herzg. 43°33′ N, 19°4′ E 168
Cajon Pass, Calif., U.S. 34°20′ N, 117°27′ W 101
Caju, Ilha do, island, Braz. 2°56′ S, 42°35′ W 132
Çakırgöl Dağı, peak, Turk. 40°33′ N, 39°38′ E 195
Çakmak, Turk. 39°10′ N, 31°52′ E 156
Çakmak Dağı, peak, Turk. 39°45′ N, 42°9′ E 195
Çal, Turk. 38°4′ N, 29°23′ E 156
Cal Madow, Buuraha, peak, Somalia 10°56′ N, 48°7′ E 218
Cala, Sp. 37°57′ N, 6°19′ W 164
Cala Rajada, Sp. 39°41′ N, 3°27′ E 150
Cala see Doğruyol, Turk. 41°3′ N, 43°20′ E 195
Calabar, Nig. 4°57′ N, 8°20′ E 222
Calabozo, Venez. 8°55′ N, 67°28′ W 136
Calabria, adm. division, It. 39°5′ N, 16°5′ E 156
Calaburras, Punta de, Sp. 36°20′ N, 4°39′ W 164
Calacoto, Bol. 17°22′ S, 68°43′ W 137
Calaf, Sp. 41°43′ N, 1°30′ E 164
Calafat, Rom. 43°59′ N, 22°56′ E 168
Calahorra, Sp. 42°18′ N, 1°58′ W 164
Calais, Fr. 50°57′ N, 1°51′ E 163
Calais, Me., U.S. 45°10′ N, 67°17′ W 94
Calakmul, ruin(s), Mex. 18°4′ N, 89°57′ W 115
Calalaste, Sierra de, Arg. 25°16′ S, 67°50′ W 132
Calalzo, It. 46°27′ N, 12°21′ E 167
Calama, Braz. 8°3′ S, 62°51′ W 130
Calama, Chile 22°28′ S, 68°58′ W 137
Calamar, Col. 10°13′ N, 74°58′ W 136
Calamar, Col. 1°57′ N, 72°34′ W 136
Calamarca, Bol. 16°59′ S, 68°8′ W 137
Calamian Group, islands, Sulu Sea 11°37′ N, 119°18′ E 203
Calamocha, Sp. 40°54′ N, 1°18′ W 164
Calamonte, Sp. 38°53′ N, 6°23′ W 164
Calamus, river, Nebr., U.S. 42°18′ N, 100°3′ W 90
Calañas, Sp. 37°39′ N, 6°54′ W 150
Calanda, Sp. 40°55′ N, 0°15′ E 164
Calandula, Angola 9°6′ S, 15°58′ E 218
Calang, Indonesia 4°39′ N, 95°35′ E 196
Calanscio, oil field, Lib. 28°1′ N, 21°18′ E 216
Calapan, Philippines 13°24′ N, 121°10′ E 203
Călăraşi, adm. division, Rom. 44°23′ N, 26°25′ E 156
Călăraşi, Mold. 47°16′ N, 28°18′ E 156
Călăraşi, Rom. 44°11′ N, 27°19′ E 156
Calasparra, Sp. 38°13′ N, 1°43′ W 164
Calatayud, Sp. 41°21′ N, 1°40′ W 164
Călăţele, Rom. 46°45′ N, 23°1′ E 168
Calatorao, Sp. 41°31′ N, 1°21′ W 164
Calavà, Capo, It. 38°12′ N, 14°19′ E 156
Calayan, island, Philippines 19°26′ N, 120°55′ E 198
Calbayog, Philippines 12°4′ N, 124°35′ E 203
Calbiga, Philippines 11°37′ N, 125°1′ E 203
Calca, Peru 13°19′ S, 71°59′ W 137
Calcanhar, Ponta do, Braz. 5°8′ S, 35°29′ W 132
Calcasieu Lake, La., U.S. 29°52′ N, 93°33′ W 103
Calcasieu, river, La., U.S. 30°22′ N, 93°8′ W 103
Calceta, Venez. 7°4′ N, 62°30′ W 130
Calchaquí, Arg. 29°50′ S, 60°18′ W 139
Calcutta see Kolkata, India 22°33′ N, 88°21′ E 197
Caldas, adm. division, Col. 5°10′ N, 75°51′ W 136
Caldas da Rainha, Port. 39°23′ N, 9°9′ W 150
Caldas Novas, Braz. 17°48′ S, 48°40′ W 138
Caldbeck, U.K. 54°45′ N, 3°3′ W 162
Caldera, Chile 27°6′ S, 70°52′ W 132
Calderitas, Mex. 18°34′ N, 88°17′ W 115
Caldes de Malavella, Sp. 41°50′ N, 2°49′ E 164
Çaldıran, Turk. 39°6′ N, 43°50′ E 195
Caldonazzo, It. 45°59′ N, 11°14′ E 167
Caldron Snout, lake, U.K. 54°40′ N, 2°32′ W 162
Caldwell, Idaho, U.S. 43°39′ N, 116°40′ W 82
Caldwell, Kans., U.S. 37°0′ N, 97°37′ W 92
Caldwell, Ohio, U.S. 39°44′ N, 81°31′ W 102
Caldwell, Tex., U.S. 30°31′ N, 96°42′ W 96
Caledon, S. Af. 34°13′ S, 19°26′ E 227
Caledonia, Minn., U.S. 43°38′ N, 91°29′ W 94
Calella, Sp. 41°36′ N, 2°39′ E 164
Caleta Buena, Chile 19°53′ S, 70°10′ W 137
Caleta Pabellón de Pica, Chile 20°56′ S, 70°10′ W 137
Calexico, Calif., U.S. 32°40′ N, 115°30′ W 101
Calf, The, peak, U.K. 54°22′ N, 2°33′ W 162
Calgary, Can. 51°3′ N, 114°5′ W 90
Calhoun Falls, S.C., U.S. 34°5′ N, 82°36′ W 96
Cali, Col. 3°24′ N, 76°33′ W 136
Calico Peak, Nev., U.S. 41°49′ N, 117°22′ W 90
Calico Rock, Ark., U.S. 36°6′ N, 92°10′ W 96
Caliente, Calif., U.S. 35°18′ N, 118°38′ W 101
Caliente, Nev., U.S. 37°35′ N, 114°30′ W 82
Caliente Range, Calif., U.S. 35°0′ N, 119°45′ W 100
California, Mo., U.S. 38°37′ N, 92°33′ W 94
California, adm. division, Calif., U.S. 36°52′ N, 120°58′ W 92
California City, Calif., U.S. 35°7′ N, 117°59′ W 101
California Coastal National Monument, Pacific Ocean 37°19′ N, 122°49′ W 100
California, Golfo de 30°47′ N, 114°31′ W 112
California, Gulf of 31°12′ N, 114°47′ W 73
California Hot Springs, Calif., U.S. 35°53′ N, 118°41′ W 101
California Spaceport, Calif., U.S. 34°35′ N, 120°39′ W 100
California Valley, Calif., U.S. 35°19′ N, 120°1′ W 100
Cálig, Sp. 40°26′ N, 0°20′ E 164
Calilegua, Arg. 23°45′ S, 64°46′ W 132
Cälilibad, Azerb. 39°12′ N, 48°28′ E 195
Călimani, Munţii, Rom. 47°0′ N, 24°32′ E 156
Calion, Ark., U.S. 33°18′ N, 92°33′ W 103
Calipatria, Calif., U.S. 33°7′ N, 115°31′ W 101
Calispell Peak, Wash., U.S. 48°24′ N, 117°36′ W 90
Calkini, Mex. 20°23′ N, 90°4′ W 115
Callaghan, Mount, Nev., U.S. 39°42′ N, 117°2′ W 90
Callamura, spring, Austral. 27°39′ S, 140°53′ E 230
Callander, Can. 46°13′ N, 79°22′ W 94
Callao, Peru 12°4′ S, 77°9′ W 130
Callaway, Nebr., U.S. 41°15′ N, 99°55′ W 90
Calling Lake, Can. 55°8′ N, 113°47′ W 108
Calling Lake, Can. 55°15′ N, 113°12′ W 108
Callirhoe, ruin(s), Jordan 31°35′ N, 35°32′ E 194
Calmar, Can. 53°15′ N, 113°49′ W 108
Calnali, Mex. 20°52′ N, 98°35′ W 114
Calne, U.K. 51°25′ N, 2°1′ W 162
Calonga, Angola 16°1′ S, 15°13′ E 220
Caloosahatchee, canal, Fla., U.S. 26°45′ N, 81°29′ W 105
Calotmul, Mex. 21°0′ N, 88°12′ W 112
Caloto, Col. 3°3′ N, 76°24′ W 136
Calpe, Sp. 38°38′ N, 4°238′ E 164
Calpulalpan de Méndez, Mex. 17°19′ N, 96°25′ W 114
Çaltı Burnu, Turk. 41°17′ N, 37°0′ E 156
Caluango, Angola 8°21′ S, 19°36′ E 218
Calulo, Angola 9°60′ S, 14°54′ E 220
Calunda, Angola 12°8′ S, 23°33′ E 220
Caluso, It. 45°18′ N, 7°52′ E 167
Caluula, Somalia 11°52′ N, 50°43′ E 182
Calvados Chain, islands, Solomon Sea 11°41′ S, 150°22′ E 192
Calvert, Ala., U.S. 31°9′ N, 87°60′ W 103
Calvert, Tex., U.S. 30°57′ N, 96°40′ W 96
Calvin, La., U.S. 31°56′ N, 92°47′ W 103
Calvinia, S. Af. 31°28′ S, 19°46′ E 227
Calwa, Calif., U.S. 36°42′ N, 119°45′ W 100
Calydon, ruin(s), Gr. 38°21′ N, 21°25′ E 156
Çam Burnu, Turk. 41°9′ N, 37°45′ E 156
Cam Pha, Vietnam 21°2′ N, 107°18′ E 198
Cam Ranh, Vietnam 11°53′ N, 109°14′ E 202
Cam Ranh, Vung 11°37′ N, 109°3′ E 202
Cam Xuyen, Vietnam 18°15′ N, 106°2′ E 198
Camabatela, Angola 8°11′ S, 15°22′ E 218
Camacan, Braz. 15°26′ S, 39°29′ W 138
Camachigama, Lac, lake, Can. 47°48′ N, 77°5′ W 94
Camacho, Mex. 24°25′ N, 102°22′ W 114
Camacupa, Angola 12°2′ S, 17°28′ E 220
Camaguán, Venez. 8°6′ N, 67°34′ W 136
Camagüey, Cuba 21°23′ N, 77°54′ W 116
Camagüey, adm. division, Cuba 21°27′ N, 78°32′ W 116
Camagüey, Archipiélago de, North Atlantic Ocean 22°40′ N, 78°24′ W 116
Camaleão, Ilha, island, Braz. 0°8′ N, 48°50′ W 130
Camaná, Peru 16°38′ S, 72°43′ W 137
Camanche Reservoir, lake, Calif., U.S. 38°13′ N, 121°8′ W 100
Camanongue, Angola 11°26′ S, 20°11′ E 220
Camapuã, Braz. 19°32′ S, 54°6′ W 132
Camaquã, Braz. 30°52′ S, 51°51′ W 139
Camaquã, river, Braz. 31°3′ S, 53°4′ W 139
Çamar, Rom. 47°17′ N, 22°38′ E 168
Camarat, Cap, Fr. 43°7′ N, 6°40′ E 165
Çamardı, Turk. 37°50′ N, 34°58′ E 156
Camargo, Bol. 20°40′ S, 65°16′ W 137
Camargo, Okla., U.S. 36°0′ N, 99°18′ W 92
Camargue, Île de la, islands, Golfe Dulion 43°28′ N, 4°23′ E 165
Camarón, Cabo, Hond. 15°59′ N, 84°60′ W 115
Camarones, Arg. 44°46′ S, 65°45′ W 134
Camarones, Chile 19°3′ S, 69°56′ W 137
Camas, Sp. 37°24′ N, 6°3′ W 164
Camas, Wash., U.S. 45°34′ N, 122°26′ W 90
Camas Valley, Oreg., U.S. 43°1′ N, 123°41′ W 90
Camatindi, Bol. 20°60′ S, 63°31′ W 137
Cambeak, point, U.K. 50°45′ N, 5°11′ W 150
Camblaya, river, Bol. 20°57′ S, 65°16′ W 137
Cambodia 12°37′ N, 103°48′ E 192
Cambona, Mozambique 11°47′ S, 36°33′ E 224
Camborne, U.K. 50°13′ N, 5°19′ W 150
Cambrai, Fr. 50°9′ N, 3°15′ E 163
Cambria, Calif., U.S. 35°34′ N, 121°7′ W 100
Cambria Icefield, Can. 55°51′ N, 129°25′ W 108
Cambrian Mountains, U.K. 52°2′ N, 3°33′ W 162
Cambridge, Idaho, U.S. 44°34′ N, 116°41′ W 90
Cambridge, Nebr., U.S. 40°16′ N, 100°11′ W 90
Cambridge, N.Z. 37°54′ S, 175°29′ E 240
Cambridge, Ohio, U.S. 40°1′ N, 81°35′ W 102
Cambridge, U.K. 52°12′ N, 0°9′ E 162
Cambridge Bay, Can. 69°6′ N, 105°2′ W 106
Cambridge City, Ind., U.S. 39°48′ N, 85°11′ W 102
Cambridge Gulf 15°11′ S, 127°52′ E 230
Cambrils de Mar, Sp. 41°4′ N, 1°3′ E 164
Cambulo, Angola 7°44′ S, 21°14′ E 218
Cambundi-Catembo, Angola 10°4′ S, 17°31′ E 220
Cambutal, Cerro, peak, Pan. 7°18′ N, 80°38′ W 115
Camden, Ala., U.S. 31°59′ N, 87°17′ W 96
Camden, Ark., U.S. 33°33′ N, 92°51′ W 96
Camden, Ind., U.S. 40°36′ N, 86°32′ W 102
Camden, Me., U.S. 44°13′ N, 69°4′ W 94
Camden, Miss., U.S. 32°46′ N, 89°51′ W 103
Camden, N.J., U.S. 39°56′ N, 75°8′ W 94
Camden, N.Y., U.S. 43°20′ N, 75°46′ W 94
Camden, N.C., U.S. 36°19′ N, 76°11′ W 96
Camden, Tex., U.S. 30°53′ N, 94°45′ W 103
Camden Bay 69°56′ N, 147°43′ W 98
Camdenton, Mo., U.S. 37°59′ N, 92°44′ W 94
Camelgooda Hill, Austral. 18°31′ S, 123°43′ E 230
Çameli, Turk. 37°4′ N, 29°19′ E 156
Camels Hump, peak, Austral. 23°51′ S, 131°27′ E 230
Camels Hump, peak, Vt., U.S. 44°18′ N, 72°55′ W 104
Camenca, Mold. 48°2′ N, 28°44′ E 156
Cameron, Ariz., U.S. 35°51′ N, 111°25′ W 92
Cameron, La., U.S. 29°47′ N, 93°20′ W 103
Cameron, Tex., U.S. 30°50′ N, 96°58′ W 96
Cameron Falls, Can. 49°8′ N, 88°19′ W 94
Cameron Lake, lake, Can. 48°59′ N, 84°45′ W 110
Cameroon 4°33′ N, 11°3′ E 218
Cameroon Mountain, Cameroon 4°15′ N, 9°4′ E 222
Cametá, Braz. 2°14′ S, 49°31′ W 130
Camiguin, island, Philippines 18°49′ N, 122°1′ E 198
Camilla, Ga., U.S. 31°13′ N, 84°13′ W 96
Camiña, Chile 19°18′ S, 69°27′ W 137
Caminha, Port. 41°52′ N, 8°51′ W 150
Camiranga, Braz. 1°51′ S, 46°18′ W 130
Camiri, Bol. 20°7′ S, 63°34′ W 137
Camirus, ruin(s), Gr. 36°18′ N, 27°48′ E 156
Camisea, Peru 11°43′ S, 73°2′ W 137
Camisea, river, Peru 11°57′ S, 72°59′ W 137
Camissombo, Angola 8°11′ S, 20°40′ E 218
Camocim, Braz. 2°57′ S, 40°52′ W 132
Camooweal, Austral. 19°56′ S, 138°8′ E 231
Camopi, Fr. 3°11′ N, 52°20′ W 130
Camopi, river, Braz. 2°28′ N, 53°20′ W 130
Camorta Island, India 7°38′ N, 93°39′ E 188
Camoruco, Col. 6°27′ N, 70°31′ W 136
Camousitchouane, Lac, lake, Can. 51°2′ N, 76°24′ W 110
Camp Crook, S. Dak., U.S. 45°32′ N, 103°60′ W 90
Camp David, site, Md., U.S. 39°39′ N, 77°32′ W 94
Camp Douglas, Wis., U.S. 43°54′ N, 90°16′ W 102
Camp Nelson, Calif., U.S. 36°9′ N, 118°38′ W 101
Camp Pendleton Marine Corps Base, Calif., U.S. 33°20′ N, 117°29′ W 101
Camp Point, Mo., U.S. 40°1′ N, 91°4′ W 94
Camp Wood, Tex., U.S. 29°39′ N, 100°1′ W 92
Campagne-lès-Hesdin, Fr. 50°23′ N, 1°52′ E 163
Campamento, Col. 4°30′ N, 70°24′ W 136
Campana, Arg. 34°11′ S, 58°56′ W 139
Campana, Isla, island, Chile 48°13′ S, 77°9′ W 134
Campanario, Sp. 38°51′ N, 5°37′ W 164
Campania, adm. division, It. 41°12′ N, 13°54′ E 156
Campbell, Calif., U.S. 37°17′ N, 121°57′ W 100
Campbell, Cape, N.Z. 41°44′ S, 174°12′ E 240
Campbell Hill, Ohio, U.S. 40°21′ N, 83°45′ W 102
Campbell Island, N.Z. 52°37′ S, 169°0′ E 252
Campbell Plateau, South Pacific Ocean 50°28′ S, 171°45′ E 252
Campbell River, Can. 50°1′ N, 125°15′ W 90
Campbell's Bay, Can. 45°43′ N, 76°36′ W 94
Campbellsburg, Ind., U.S. 38°38′ N, 86°16′ W 102
Campbellsburg, Ky., U.S. 38°30′ N, 85°13′ W 102
Campbellsville, Ky., U.S. 37°19′ N, 85°21′ W 96
Campbellton, Can. 47°58′ N, 66°41′ W 94
Campeche, Mex. 19°48′ N, 90°40′ W 115
Campeche, adm. division, Mex. 18°56′ N, 91°2′ W 112
Campeche Bank, Gulf of Mexico 21°58′ N, 90°5′ W 253
Camperville, Can. 52°1′ N, 100°12′ W 108
Campidano, It. 39°44′ N, 8°33′ E 156
Campina Grande, Braz. 7°11′ S, 35°53′ W 123
Campina Verde, Braz. 19°33′ S, 49°29′ W 138
Campinas, Braz. 22°56′ S, 47°5′ W 138
Campo, Calif., U.S. 32°36′ N, 116°29′ W 101
Campo, Colo., U.S. 37°6′ N, 102°35′ W 92
Campo, Mozambique 17°46′ S, 36°22′ E 224
Campo, Sp. 42°24′ N, 0°24′ E 164
Campo Belo, Braz. 20°53′ S, 45°15′ W 138
Campo Corral, Col. 5°3′ N, 70°43′ W 136
Campo de Criptana, Sp. 39°24′ N, 3°7′ W 164
Campo Durán, oil field, Arg. 22°15′ S, 63°46′ W 137
Campo Erê, Braz. 26°24′ S, 53°1′ W 139
Campo Esperanza, Parag. 22°19′ S, 59°38′ W 132
Campo Florido, Braz. 19°48′ S, 48°36′ W 138
Campo Gallo, Arg. 26°35′ S, 62°50′ W 139
Campo Grande, Braz. 20°28′ S, 54°36′ W 132
Campo Largo, Arg. 26°47′ S, 60°51′ W 139
Campo Largo, Braz. 25°30′ S, 49°34′ W 138
Campo Maior, Braz. 4°52′ S, 42°13′ W 132
Campo Mourão, Braz. 24°4′ S, 52°24′ W 138
Campo, Punta, Equatorial Guinea 2°18′ N, 9°14′ E 218
Campo Troco, Col. 4°52′ N, 68°9′ W 136
Campoalegre, Col. 2°41′ N, 75°21′ W 136
Campobasso, It. 41°34′ N, 14°39′ E 156
Campobello, S.C., U.S. 35°6′ N, 82°10′ W 96
Campodolcino, It. 46°24′ N, 9°20′ E 167
Campos, Braz. 21°48′ S, 41°23′ W 138
Campos Altos, Braz. 19°43′ S, 46°12′ W 138
Campos Belos, Braz. 13°4′ S, 46°55′ W 138
Campos Novos, Braz. 27°25′ S, 51°14′ W 139
Campos, Puntas, Mex. 18°53′ N, 104°40′ W 114
Camposampiero, It. 45°34′ N, 11°55′ E 167
Camprodon, Sp. 42°17′ N, 2°22′ E 164
Campti, La., U.S. 31°52′ N, 93°7′ W 103
Campton, N.H., U.S. 43°51′ N, 71°39′ W 104
Campuya, Peru 1°46′ S, 73°31′ W 136
Camrose, Can. 53°0′ N, 112°51′ W 108
Camsell Portage, Can. 59°37′ N, 109°14′ W 108
Camucuio, Angola 14°8′ S, 13°17′ E 220
Çan, Turk. 40°1′ N, 27°1′ E 156
Can Tho, Vietnam 10°2′ N, 105°44′ E 202
Cana Brava, Braz. 17°22′ S, 45°52′ W 138
Canaan, Conn., U.S. 42°1′ N, 73°20′ W 104
Canaan, N.H., U.S. 43°39′ N, 72°1′ W 104
Canaan, Trinidad and Tobago 11°8′ N, 60°49′ W 116
Canada 58°59′ N, 99°52′ W 106
Canada Basin, Arctic Ocean 77°38′ N, 139°23′ W 255
Canada Bay 50°40′ N, 56°41′ W 111
Cañada de Gómez, Arg. 32°50′ S, 61°21′ W 139
Cañada Honda, Arg. 31°59′ S, 68°33′ W 134
Cañada Ombú, Arg. 28°19′ S, 60°2′ W 139
Canada Plain, Arctic Ocean 76°14′ N, 148°23′ W 255
Cañada Seca, Arg. 34°25′ S, 62°57′ W 139
Canadian, Tex., U.S. 35°53′ N, 100°24′ W 92
Canadian, river, Oklahoma-Texas, U.S. 35°22′ N, 103°1′ W 92
Çanakkale, Turk. 40°9′ N, 26°23′ E 156
Canal du Midi, Fr. 43°31′ N, 1°32′ E 165
Canal du Rhône au Rhin, Fr. 47°35′ N, 6°53′ E 165
Canal Flats, Can. 50°9′ N, 115°48′ W 90
Canal Point, Fla., U.S. 26°51′ N, 80°38′ W 105
Canale, It. 44°48′ N, 7°59′ E 167
Canals, Arg. 33°35′ S, 62°50′ W 139
Canals, Sp. 38°57′ N, 0°35′ E 150
Canalul Bega, Rom. 45°39′ N, 21°1′ E 168
Canamari, Braz. 10°10′ S, 69°16′ W 137
Cañamero, Sp. 39°22′ N, 5°23′ W 164
Cananea, Mex. 30°57′ N, 110°19′ W 92
Cananéia, Braz. 25°1′ S, 47°58′ W 138
Canapiare, Cerro, peak, Col. 2°38′ N, 68°32′ W 136
Canárias, Ilha das, island, Braz. 2°42′ S, 41°53′ W 132
Canarias, Islas see Canary Islands, North Atlantic Ocean 28°47′ N, 16°41′ W 214
Canarreos, Archipiélago de los, Caribbean Sea 21°39′ N, 82°40′ W 116
Canary Islands (Canarias, Islas), North Atlantic Ocean 28°47′ N, 16°41′ W 214
Cañas, C.R. 10°26′ N, 85°7′ W 115
Canastota, N.Y., U.S. 43°4′ N, 75°46′ W 94
Canatiba, Braz. 13°6′ S, 42°51′ W 138
Canatlán, Mex. 24°30′ N, 104°46′ W 114
Cañaveral, Sp. 39°47′ N, 6°24′ W 150
Canaveral, Cape (Kennedy, Cape), Fla., U.S. 28°24′ N, 80°34′ W 105
Canaveral National Seashore, Fla., U.S. 28°37′ N, 80°47′ W 105
Cañaveras, Sp. 40°20′ N, 2°25′ W 164
Canavieiras, Braz. 15°41′ S, 38°58′ W 132
Canberra, Austral. 35°22′ S, 148°43′ E 230
Canby, Calif., U.S. 41°26′ N, 120°54′ W 90
Canby, Minn., U.S. 44°42′ N, 96°18′ W 90
Cancún, Mex. 21°6′ N, 86°52′ W 116

Castelnovo ne' Monti, *It.* 44°25′ N, 10°23′ E **167**
Castelo Branco, *Port.* 39°49′ N, 7°31′ W **150**
Castelo Branco, adm. division, *Port.* 39°50′ N, 7°58′ W **150**
Casterton, *U.K.* 54°12′ N, 2°34′ W **162**
Castets, *Fr.* 43°53′ N, 1°10′ W **150**
Castiglione delle Stiviere, *It.* 45°22′ N, 10°29′ E **167**
Castile and Leon, adm. division, *Sp.* 41°56′ N, 3°33′ W **164**
Castile La Mancha, adm. division, *Sp.* 40°28′ N, 2°58′ W **164**
Castilla, Playa de, *Sp.* 37°3′ N, 6°45′ W **164**
Castillo de San Marcos National Monument, *Fla., U.S.* 29°53′ N, 81°22′ W **105**
Castillo de Teayo, ruin(s), *Mex.* 20°39′ N, 97°45′ W **114**
Castillo, Pampa del, *Arg.* 46°18′ S, 68°44′ W **134**
Castillos, *Uru.* 34°14′ S, 53°53′ W **139**
Castle Acre, *U.K.* 52°42′ N, 0°41′ E **162**
Castle Dale, *Utah, U.S.* 39°12′ N, 111°1′ W **90**
Castle Hedingham, *U.K.* 51°59′ N, 0°36′ E **162**
Castle Mountain, peak, *Alas., U.S.* 56°51′ N, 132°16′ W **108**
Castle Mountain, peak, *Calif., U.S.* 35°56′ N, 120°23′ W **100**
Castle Mountain, peak, *Can.* 51°19′ N, 115°60′ W **90**
Castle Mountain, peak, *Tex., U.S.* 31°15′ N, 102°22′ W **92**
Castle Peak, *Colo., U.S.* 38°59′ N, 106°57′ W **90**
Castle Peak, *Idaho, U.S.* 44°1′ N, 114°40′ W **90**
Castle Rising, *U.K.* 52°47′ N, 0°29′ E **162**
Castle Rock, *Colo., U.S.* 39°22′ N, 104°52′ W **90**
Castle Rock, *Wash., U.S.* 46°16′ N, 122°54′ W **100**
Castle Rock, peak, *Oreg., U.S.* 44°0′ N, 118°16′ W **90**
Castle Sinclair, site, *U.K.* 58°26′ N, 3°12′ W **150**
Castlebar, *Ire.* 53°51′ N, 9°19′ W **150**
Castlebay, *U.K.* 56°57′ N, 7°29′ W **150**
Castlecliff, *N.Z.* 39°57′ S, 174°58′ E **240**
Castleford, *U.K.* 53°43′ N, 1°21′ W **162**
Castlegar, *Can.* 49°18′ N, 117°41′ W **90**
Castlepoint, *N.Z.* 40°55′ S, 176°12′ E **240**
Castleton, *U.K.* 54°27′ N, 0°57′ E **162**
Castleton, *Vt., U.S.* 43°36′ N, 73°11′ W **104**
Castleton-on-Hudson, *N.Y., U.S.* 42°31′ N, 73°46′ W **104**
Castlewood, *S. Dak., U.S.* 44°42′ N, 97°3′ W **90**
Castor, *Can.* 52°12′ N, 111°55′ W **90**
Castor, *La., U.S.* 32°14′ N, 93°10′ W **103**
Castries, *Saint Lucia* 13°59′ N, 61°8′ W **116**
Castril, *Sp.* 37°47′ N, 2°46′ W **164**
Castro, *Braz.* 24°46′ S, 50°1′ W **138**
Castro, *Chile* 42°27′ S, 73°51′ W **134**
Castronuño, *Sp.* 41°22′ N, 5°17′ W **150**
Castropol, *Sp.* 43°30′ N, 7°2′ W **150**
Castroville, *Calif., U.S.* 36°46′ N, 121°45′ W **100**
Castuera, *Sp.* 38°43′ N, 5°34′ W **164**
Casula, *Mozambique* 15°23′ S, 33°37′ E **224**
Casummit Lake, *Can.* 51°28′ N, 92°22′ W **110**
Çat, *Turk.* 39°37′ N, 41°1′ E **195**
Cat Island, *Bahamas* 24°30′ N, 75°28′ W **116**
Cat Island, *Miss., U.S.* 30°7′ N, 89°7′ W **103**
Cat Lake, *Can.* 51°43′ N, 91°48′ W **110**
Cat Tien National Park, *Vietnam* 11°20′ N, 106°58′ E **202**
Catacaos, *Peru* 5°11′ S, 80°44′ W **130**
Cataguases, *Braz.* 21°23′ S, 42°40′ W **138**
Catahoula Lake, *La., U.S.* 31°25′ N, 92°27′ W **103**
Cataingan, *Philippines* 12°1′ N, 123°58′ E **203**
Çatak, *Turk.* 38°0′ N, 43°2′ E **195**
Catalão, *Braz.* 18°12′ S, 47°57′ W **138**
Catalina, *Chile* 25°14′ S, 69°47′ W **132**
Catalina, Punta, *Chile* 52°44′ S, 68°43′ W **134**
Catalonia, adm. division, *Sp.* 41°46′ N, 1°7′ E **164**
Catamarca, *Arg.* 28°30′ S, 65°47′ W **132**
Catamarca, adm. division, *Arg.* 27°39′ S, 68°56′ W **134**
Catán Lil, *Arg.* 39°43′ S, 70°37′ W **134**
Catandica, *Mozambique* 18°4′ S, 33°10′ E **220**
Catanduanes, island, *Philippines* 13°52′ N, 124°26′ E **192**
Catanduva, *Braz.* 21°6′ S, 48°58′ W **138**
Catania, *It.* 37°30′ N, 15°4′ E **156**
Catania, Piana di, *It.* 37°17′ N, 14°26′ E **156**
Catanzaro, *It.* 38°53′ N, 16°35′ E **156**
Catarina, *Tex., U.S.* 28°20′ N, 99°37′ W **92**
Catarman, *Philippines* 12°29′ N, 124°38′ E **203**
Catarroja, *Sp.* 39°24′ N, 0°24′ E **164**
Catatumbo-Barí National Park, *Col.* 9°0′ N, 73°30′ W **136**
Catauara, *Braz.* 3°19′ S, 56°26′ W **130**
Cataviña, *Mex.* 29°45′ N, 114°49′ W **92**
Catawba Island, *Ohio, U.S.* 41°34′ N, 82°50′ W **102**
Catbalogan, *Philippines* 11°46′ N, 124°55′ E **203**
Cateel, *Philippines* 7°51′ N, 126°25′ E **203**
Catemaco, *Mex.* 18°25′ N, 95°7′ W **114**
Catete, *Angola* 9°8′ S, 13°40′ E **218**
Catete, river, *Braz.* 6°22′ S, 54°14′ W **130**
Cathedral Mountain, *Tex., U.S.* 30°8′ N, 103°43′ W **92**
Catherine, *Ala., U.S.* 32°10′ N, 87°29′ W **103**
Catheys Valley, *Calif., U.S.* 37°25′ N, 120°8′ W **100**
Cathlamet, *Wash., U.S.* 46°11′ N, 123°22′ W **100**
Catinaccio, peak, *It.* 46°28′ N, 11°36′ E **167**
Catió, *Guinea-Bissau* 11°16′ N, 15°15′ W **222**
Catirina, Punta, peak, *It.* 40°28′ N, 9°27′ E **156**
Catlow Valley, *Oreg., U.S.* 42°45′ N, 119°7′ W **90**
Catnip Mountain, *Nev., U.S.* 41°50′ N, 119°28′ W **90**
Catoche, Cabo, *Mex.* 21°28′ N, 87°10′ W **116**
Catoctin Mountain, *Md., U.S.* 39°50′ N, 77°35′ W **94**
Catoctin Mountain Park, *Md., U.S.* 39°37′ N, 77°33′ W **94**
Catorce, *Mex.* 23°39′ N, 100°53′ W **114**
Catota, *Angola* 14°2′ S, 17°23′ E **220**
Catria, Monte, peak, *It.* 43°26′ N, 12°37′ E **156**
Catriló, *Arg.* 36°25′ S, 63°27′ W **139**
Catskill, *N.Y., U.S.* 42°13′ N, 73°53′ W **104**
Catskill Mountains, *N.Y., U.S.* 42°26′ N, 74°10′ W **104**
Catterick, *U.K.* 54°22′ N, 1°38′ W **162**
Cattolica, *It.* 43°58′ N, 12°44′ E **167**
Catuane, *Mozambique* 26°44′ S, 32°15′ E **227**
Catur, *Mozambique* 13°45′ S, 35°37′ E **224**
Cau Giat, *Vietnam* 19°9′ N, 105°38′ E **202**
Cauaburi, river, *Braz.* 4°238′ N, 66°19′ W **136**
Cauayan, *Philippines* 9°58′ N, 122°36′ E **203**
Cauca, adm. division, *Col.* 2°29′ N, 77°31′ W **136**
Cauca, river, *Col.* 6°18′ N, 75°46′ W **136**
Caucaia, *Braz.* 3°44′ S, 38°40′ W **132**
Caucasia, *Col.* 7°57′ N, 75°14′ W **136**
Caucasus Mountains, *Asia-Europe* 42°3′ N, 44°7′ E **158**
Caucete, *Arg.* 31°40′ S, 68°18′ W **134**
Cauchon Lake, *Can.* 55°28′ N, 97°4′ W **108**
Caudéran, *Fr.* 44°51′ N, 0°38′ E **150**
Caudete, *Sp.* 38°42′ N, 0°59′ E **164**
Caudry, *Fr.* 50°7′ N, 3°23′ E **163**
Caungula, *Angola* 8°27′ S, 18°38′ E **218**
Cauquenes, *Chile* 35°59′ S, 72°21′ W **134**
Caura, river, *Venez.* 6°56′ N, 64°51′ W **130**
Caurés, river, *Braz.* 1°16′ S, 63°17′ W **130**
Cauro, *Fr.* 41°54′ N, 8°54′ E **156**
Causapscal, *Can.* 48°20′ N, 67°13′ W **94**
Căuseni, *Mold.* 46°37′ N, 29°23′ E **156**
Cautário, river, *Braz.* 11°47′ S, 63°55′ W **137**
Caution, Cape, *Can.* 50°58′ N, 128°14′ W **108**
Cauto, river, *Cuba* 20°39′ N, 76°41′ W **116**
Cavalaire, *Fr.* 43°10′ N, 6°30′ E **150**
Cavalcante, *Braz.* 13°48′ S, 47°31′ W **138**
Cavalese, *It.* 46°17′ N, 11°27′ E **167**
Cavalier, *N. Dak., U.S.* 48°45′ N, 97°39′ W **90**
Cavalla, river, *Africa* 6°18′ N, 7°56′ W **222**
Cavalleria, Cap de, *Sp.* 40°3′ N, 3°48′ E **164**
Cavallermaggiore, *It.* 44°42′ N, 7°41′ E **167**
Cavallo Pass, *U.S.* 28°17′ N, 96°20′ W **96**
Cavally, river, *Côte d'Ivoire* 6°19′ N, 8°14′ W **222**
Cavan, *Ire.* 53°58′ N, 7°22′ W **150**
Cavarzere, *It.* 45°7′ N, 12°4′ E **167**
Cave, *N.Z.* 44°19′ S, 170°59′ E **240**
Cave Creek, *Ariz., U.S.* 33°49′ N, 111°56′ W **92**
Cave Mountain, *Calif., U.S.* 35°3′ N, 116°22′ W **101**
Cave Point, *U.S.* 44°45′ N, 87°9′ W **94**
Cavendish, *Vt., U.S.* 43°23′ N, 72°37′ W **104**
Caviana, Ilha, island, *Braz.* 0°22′ N, 49°54′ W **130**
Cavignac, *Fr.* 45°5′ N, 0°24′ E **150**
Cavinas, *Bol.* 12°34′ S, 66°50′ W **137**
Cavite, *Philippines* 14°29′ N, 120°53′ E **203**
Cavo, Monte, peak, *It.* 41°44′ N, 12°37′ E **156**
Cavour, *It.* 44°46′ N, 7°23′ E **167**
Cavtat (Epidaurum), *Croatia* 42°34′ N, 18°13′ E **168**
Çavuş Burnu, *Turk.* 36°19′ N, 30°32′ E **156**
Çavuşçu Gölü, lake, *Turk.* 38°25′ N, 31°35′ E **156**
Cawker City, *Kans., U.S.* 39°29′ N, 98°27′ W **92**
Cawood, *U.K.* 53°50′ N, 1°8′ W **162**
Cawston, *U.K.* 52°45′ N, 1°9′ E **162**
Caxambu, *Braz.* 21°60′ S, 44°56′ W **138**
Caxias, *Braz.* 4°29′ S, 71°26′ W **130**
Caxias, *Braz.* 4°47′ S, 43°19′ W **132**
Caxias do Sul, *Braz.* 29°11′ S, 51°10′ W **139**
Caxito, *Angola* 8°35′ S, 13°41′ E **218**
Çay, *Turk.* 38°35′ N, 31°1′ E **156**
Cayacal, Punta, *Mex.* 17°44′ N, 102°12′ W **114**
Çaycuma, *Turk.* 41°25′ N, 32°2′ E **156**
Çayeli, *Turk.* 41°5′ N, 40°43′ E **195**
Cayenne, *Fr. Guiana, Fr.* 4°58′ N, 52°19′ W **130**
Cayeux-sur-Mer, *Fr.* 50°10′ N, 1°30′ E **163**
Cayey, *U.S.* 18°7′ N, 66°11′ W **116**
Çayıralan, *Turk.* 39°18′ N, 35°38′ E **156**
Cayman Trench, *Caribbean Sea* 17°52′ N, 80°50′ W **253**
Caynaba, *Somalia* 8°56′ N, 46°25′ E **216**
Cayo Agua, Isla, island, *Pan.* 9°2′ N, 81°60′ W **115**
Cayucos, *Calif., U.S.* 35°27′ N, 120°55′ W **100**
Cayuga, *Ind., U.S.* 39°56′ N, 87°28′ W **102**
Cayuga Lake, *N.Y., U.S.* 42°41′ N, 77°13′ W **94**
Cazage, *Angola* 11°3′ S, 20°44′ E **220**
Cazalla de la Sierra, *Sp.* 37°55′ N, 5°47′ W **164**
Cazères, *Fr.* 43°12′ N, 1°3′ E **164**
Cazombo, *Angola* 11°55′ S, 22°58′ E **220**
Cazones, river, *Mex.* 20°14′ N, 98°10′ W **114**
Cazorla, *Sp.* 37°54′ N, 3°2′ W **164**
Cazorla, *Venez.* 8°0′ N, 66°60′ W **136**
Ceadîr-Lunga, *Mold.* 46°2′ N, 28°50′ E **156**
Ceará, adm. division, *Braz.* 5°20′ S, 40°29′ W **132**
Ceará Mirim, *Braz.* 5°38′ S, 35°26′ W **132**
Ceara Plain, *South Atlantic Ocean* 0°23′ N, 37°43′ W **253**
Cébaco, Isla de, island, *Pan.* 7°22′ N, 81°30′ W **115**
Ceballos, *Mex.* 26°31′ N, 104°9′ W **114**
Cebollar, *Arg.* 29°6′ S, 66°32′ W **134**
Cebollatí, *Uru.* 33°17′ S, 53°51′ W **139**
Céboruco, Volcán, *Mex.* 21°7′ N, 104°32′ W **114**
Cebu, *Philippines* 10°20′ N, 123°54′ E **203**
Cebu, island, *Philippines* 11°11′ N, 123°27′ E **192**
Cece, *Hung.* 46°45′ N, 18°38′ E **168**
Cecil Lake, *Can.* 56°17′ N, 120°35′ W **108**
Cecil Rhodes, Mount, *Austral.* 25°28′ S, 121°15′ E **230**
Cecina, *It.* 43°18′ N, 10°31′ E **156**
Cedar Creek Peak, *Idaho, U.S.* 42°26′ N, 113°8′ W **90**
Cedar Creek Reservoir, lake, *Tex., U.S.* 32°20′ N, 96°47′ W **96**
Cedar Falls, *Iowa, U.S.* 42°30′ N, 92°28′ W **94**
Cedar Grove, *Calif., U.S.* 36°48′ N, 118°41′ W **101**
Cedar Grove, *Wis., U.S.* 43°34′ N, 87°49′ W **102**
Cedar Key, *Fla., U.S.* 29°8′ N, 83°3′ W **105**
Cedar Lake, *Can.* 53°1′ N, 101°7′ W **81**
Cedar Lake, *Can.* 50°7′ N, 93°38′ W **90**
Cedar Lake, *Ind., U.S.* 41°20′ N, 87°28′ W **102**
Cedar Lake, lake, *Can.* 45°58′ N, 78°50′ W **94**
Cedar Mountains, *Utah, U.S.* 40°35′ N, 113°9′ W **90**
Cedar Pass, *Calif., U.S.* 41°33′ N, 120°17′ W **90**
Cedar Pass, *S. Dak., U.S.* 43°45′ N, 101°56′ W **90**
Cedar Rapids, *Iowa, U.S.* 41°57′ N, 91°39′ W **94**
Cedar Ridge, *Calif., U.S.* 39°11′ N, 121°2′ W **90**
Cedar, river, *Iowa, U.S.* 42°9′ N, 92°21′ W **80**
Cedar Vale, *Kans., U.S.* 37°4′ N, 96°30′ W **92**
Cedarburg, *Wis., U.S.* 43°17′ N, 87°59′ W **102**
Cedars of Lebanon, site, *Leb.* 34°14′ N, 36°2′ E **194**
Cedarvale, *Can.* 55°0′ N, 128°19′ W **108**
Cedarville, *Calif., U.S.* 41°31′ N, 120°11′ W **90**
Cedral, *Mex.* 23°47′ N, 100°43′ W **114**
Cedros, *Mex.* 24°39′ N, 101°48′ W **114**
Cedros, Isla, island, *Mex.* 27°56′ N, 115°10′ W **112**
Cedros Trench, *North Pacific Ocean* 24°2′ N, 112°32′ W **252**
Ceek, *Somalia* 8°55′ N, 45°19′ E **216**
Ceel Afweyn, *Somalia* 9°52′ N, 47°15′ E **216**
Ceel Buur, *Somalia* 4°44′ N, 46°35′ E **218**
Ceel Dhaab, *Somalia* 8°49′ N, 46°34′ E **216**
Ceel Huur, *Somalia* 5°0′ N, 48°20′ E **218**
Ceeldheere, *Somalia* 3°52′ N, 47°13′ E **218**
Ceepeecee, *Can.* 49°53′ N, 126°44′ W **90**
Ceerigaabo (Erigavo), *Somalia* 10°34′ N, 47°24′ E **218**
Cefa, *Rom.* 46°54′ N, 21°42′ E **168**
Cegléd, *Hung.* 47°10′ N, 19°49′ E **168**
Cehegín, *Sp.* 38°5′ N, 1°48′ W **164**
Ceheng, *China* 24°58′ N, 105°49′ E **198**
Cehotina, river, *Europe* 43°30′ N, 18°48′ E **168**
Cehu Silvaniei, *Rom.* 47°24′ N, 23°12′ E **168**
Ceiba Grande, ruin(s), *Mex.* 17°22′ N, 93°51′ W **115**
Ceica, *Rom.* 46°51′ N, 22°10′ E **168**
Cejal, *Col.* 2°42′ N, 67°55′ W **136**
Cejolao, *Arg.* 27°28′ S, 62°20′ W **139**
Çekerek, *Turk.* 40°5′ N, 35°29′ E **156**
Çekerek, river, *Turk.* 40°25′ N, 35°18′ E **156**
Celarain, Punta, *Mex.* 20°10′ N, 86°59′ W **115**
Celaya, *Mex.* 20°30′ N, 100°49′ W **114**
Celebes Basin, *Celebes Sea* 3°27′ N, 121°47′ E **254**
Celebes Sea 3°49′ N, 119°35′ E **192**
Celebes (Sulawesi), island, *Indonesia* 0°39′ N, 123°14′ E **192**
Çeleken, *Turkm.* 39°26′ N, 53°8′ E **180**
Čelić, *Bosn. and Herzg.* 44°43′ N, 18°47′ E **168**
Celina, *Ohio, U.S.* 40°32′ N, 84°35′ W **102**
Celje, *Slov.* 46°14′ N, 15°14′ E **156**
Cella, *Sp.* 40°27′ N, 1°18′ W **164**
Cellar Head, *U.K.* 58°25′ N, 6°8′ W **150**
Celldömölk, *Hung.* 47°15′ N, 17°10′ E **168**
Celle, *Ger.* 52°36′ N, 10°5′ E **150**
Celtic Sea 50°32′ N, 8°3′ W **150**
Cement, *Okla., U.S.* 34°54′ N, 98°8′ W **92**
Cemerno, *Serb. and Mont.* 43°38′ N, 20°13′ E **168**
Çemişgezek, *Turk.* 39°4′ N, 38°54′ E **195**
Cempoala see Zempoala, ruin(s), *Mex.* 19°23′ N, 96°28′ W **114**
Cenchreae, ruin(s), *Gr.* 37°53′ N, 22°55′ E **156**
Cencia see Ch'ench'a, *Eth.* 6°15′ N, 37°38′ E **224**
Cenderawasih, Teluk 2°60′ S, 133°34′ E **192**
Cenicero, *Sp.* 42°28′ N, 2°39′ W **164**
Centenario, *Mex.* 18°39′ N, 90°17′ W **115**
Centennial Mountains, *Idaho, U.S.* 44°29′ N, 112°28′ W **90**
Center, *Colo., U.S.* 37°44′ N, 106°6′ W **92**
Center, *N. Dak., U.S.* 47°5′ N, 101°17′ W **90**
Center, *Tex., U.S.* 31°46′ N, 94°11′ W **103**
Center Barnstead, *N.H., U.S.* 43°20′ N, 71°17′ W **104**
Center Conway, *N.H., U.S.* 43°59′ N, 71°4′ W **104**
Center Harbor, *N.H., U.S.* 43°42′ N, 71°28′ W **104**
Center Hill, *Fla., U.S.* 28°38′ N, 81°60′ W **105**
Center Lovell, *Me., U.S.* 44°10′ N, 70°54′ W **104**
Center Moriches, *N.Y., U.S.* 40°48′ N, 72°48′ W **104**
Center Ossipee, *N.H., U.S.* 43°45′ N, 71°10′ W **104**
Center Peak, *Calif., U.S.* 36°12′ N, 120°40′ W **100**
Center Point, *Tex., U.S.* 29°54′ N, 99°2′ W **92**
Centerburg, *Ohio, U.S.* 40°17′ N, 82°41′ W **102**
Centerfield, *Utah, U.S.* 39°7′ N, 111°48′ W **92**
Centerville, *Calif., U.S.* 36°43′ N, 119°30′ W **100**
Centerville, *Iowa, U.S.* 40°43′ N, 92°53′ W **94**
Centerville, *Mass., U.S.* 41°38′ N, 70°22′ W **104**
Centerville, *S. Dak., U.S.* 43°5′ N, 96°58′ W **94**
Centerville, *Tex., U.S.* 31°14′ N, 95°58′ W **96**
Centerville, *Utah, U.S.* 40°55′ N, 111°52′ W **90**
Centinela, Picacho del, peak, *Mex.* 29°3′ N, 102°42′ W **92**
Cento, *It.* 44°43′ N, 11°17′ E **167**
Central, *Alas., U.S.* 65°33′ N, 144°52′ W **98**
Central, *Ariz., U.S.* 32°52′ N, 109°47′ W **92**
Central, adm. division, *Mongolia* 46°58′ N, 105°11′ E **198**
Central African Republic 7°1′ N, 21°10′ E **218**
Central Butte, *Can.* 50°48′ N, 106°32′ W **90**
Central City, *Ill., U.S.* 38°32′ N, 89°8′ W **102**
Central City, *Ky., U.S.* 37°17′ N, 87°7′ W **96**
Central City, *Nebr., U.S.* 41°6′ N, 98°1′ W **92**
Central City, *S. Dak., U.S.* 44°22′ N, 103°46′ W **90**
Central, Cordillera, *Dom. Rep.* 19°16′ N, 71°38′ W **116**
Central, Cordillera, *Peru* 6°52′ S, 77°30′ W **130**
Central Islip, *N.Y., U.S.* 40°47′ N, 73°12′ W **104**
Central Kalahari Game Reserve, *Botswana* 22°34′ S, 23°16′ E **227**
Central, Massif, *Europe* 44°5′ N, 1°58′ E **214**
Central Mount Wedge, peak, *Austral.* 22°57′ S, 131°37′ E **230**
Central Pacific Basin, *North Pacific Ocean* 7°5′ N, 176°34′ W **252**
Central Range, *P.N.G.* 5°6′ S, 141°26′ E **192**
Centralia, *Ill., U.S.* 38°31′ N, 89°8′ W **102**
Centralia, *Mo., U.S.* 39°11′ N, 92°8′ W **94**
Centralia, *Wash., U.S.* 46°41′ N, 122°58′ W **100**
Centre, *Ala., U.S.* 34°8′ N, 85°41′ W **96**
Centre, adm. division, *Fr.* 47°39′ N, 0°50′ E **150**
Centre de Marcoule, site, *Fr.* 44°8′ N, 4°40′ E **165**
Centre Island, *Austral.* 16°25′ S, 136°48′ E **230**
Centreville, *Mich., U.S.* 41°54′ N, 85°31′ W **102**
Centreville, *Miss., U.S.* 31°4′ N, 91°4′ W **103**
Cenxi, *China* 22°56′ N, 111°1′ E **198**
Çepan, *Alban.* 40°25′ N, 20°15′ E **156**
Cephalonia see Kefaloniá, adm. division, *Gr.* 38°22′ N, 20°3′ E **156**
Cepin, *Croatia* 45°30′ N, 18°32′ E **168**
Ceprano, *It.* 41°32′ N, 13°31′ E **156**
Cer, peak, *Serb. and Mont.* 44°35′ N, 19°27′ E **168**
Ceram, island, *Indonesia* 3°48′ S, 129°2′ E **192**
Ceram Sea 2°26′ S, 128°3′ E **192**
Cerbat Mountains, *Ariz., U.S.* 35°29′ N, 114°7′ W **101**
Cerbatana, Serranía de la, *Venez.* 6°31′ N, 66°45′ W **130**
Cerbère, *Fr.* 42°26′ N, 3°8′ E **164**
Cerbicales, Îles, islands, *Tyrrhenian Sea* 41°24′ N, 9°24′ E **156**
Cère, river, *Fr.* 44°50′ N, 2°21′ E **165**
Cerea, *It.* 45°12′ N, 11°12′ E **167**
Cereal, *Can.* 51°26′ N, 110°48′ W **90**
Cereales, *Arg.* 36°52′ S, 63°51′ W **139**
Ceres, *Arg.* 29°53′ S, 61°57′ W **139**
Ceres, *Braz.* 15°21′ S, 49°37′ W **138**
Ceres, *Calif., U.S.* 37°35′ N, 120°58′ W **100**
Ceres, *S. Af.* 33°21′ S, 19°18′ E **227**
Cerf Island, *Seychelles* 9°36′ S, 49°54′ E **218**
Cerigo see Kíthira, island, *Gr.* 36°17′ N, 23°3′ E **180**
Cermei, *Rom.* 46°33′ N, 21°50′ E **168**
Çermik, *Turk.* 38°8′ N, 39°27′ E **195**
Cerna, *Croatia* 45°11′ N, 18°41′ E **168**
Cerne Abbas, *U.K.* 50°48′ N, 2°29′ W **162**
Cernik, *Croatia* 45°17′ N, 17°23′ E **168**
Cerovljani, *Bosn. and Herzg.* 45°3′ N, 17°14′ E **168**
Cerralvo, *Mex.* 26°5′ N, 99°37′ W **114**
Cerralvo, Isla, island, *Mex.* 23°58′ N, 109°49′ W **112**
Cerrillos, ruin(s), *Mex.* 18°33′ N, 92°10′ W **115**
Cerritos, *Mex.* 22°24′ N, 100°16′ W **114**
Cerro Azul, *Mex.* 21°12′ N, 97°44′ W **114**
Cerro Azul, *Peru* 13°2′ S, 76°31′ W **130**
Cerro Chato, *Uru.* 33°5′ S, 55°10′ W **139**
Cerro de Garnica National Park, *Mex.* 19°39′ N, 101°5′ W **112**
Cerro de la Estrella National Park (8), *Mex.* 19°11′ N, 99°10′ W **112**
Cerro de las Mesas, ruin(s), *Mex.* 18°41′ N, 96°7′ W **114**
Cerro de Pasco, *Peru* 10°42′ S, 76°16′ W **130**
Cerro Gordo, *Ill., U.S.* 39°52′ N, 88°44′ W **102**
Cerro Jáua, Meseta del, *Venez.* 5°36′ N, 65°51′ W **136**
Cerrón, peak, *Venez.* 10°17′ N, 70°44′ W **136**
Cervales, peak, *Sp.* 39°32′ N, 5°21′ W **164**
Cervera, *Sp.* 41°39′ N, 1°16′ E **164**
Cervia, *It.* 44°15′ N, 12°19′ E **167**
Cervià, *Sp.* 41°26′ N, 0°51′ E **164**
Cervignano, *It.* 45°49′ N, 13°19′ E **167**
Cervo, *Sp.* 43°39′ N, 7°26′ W **150**
Cesana Torinese, *It.* 44°57′ N, 6°49′ E **167**
César, adm. division, *Col.* 9°23′ N, 73°54′ W **136**
Cesena, *It.* 44°8′ N, 12°14′ E **167**
Cesenatico, *It.* 44°11′ N, 12°24′ E **167**
Cesiomaggiore, *It.* 46°5′ N, 11°58′ E **167**
Cēsis, *Latv.* 57°17′ N, 25°15′ E **166**
Ceské Budějovice, *Czech Rep.* 48°59′ N, 14°27′ E **152**
Ceský Les, *Czech Rep.* 49°28′ N, 12°41′ E **152**
Çeşme, *Turk.* 38°16′ N, 26°18′ E **156**
Cesney, Cape, *Antarctica* 66°10′ S, 136°15′ E **248**
Cess, river, *Liberia* 5°40′ N, 8°58′ W **222**
Cessnock, *Austral.* 32°48′ S, 151°22′ E **231**
Cesvaine, *Latv.* 56°57′ N, 26°18′ E **166**
Cetate, *Rom.* 44°6′ N, 23°4′ E **168**
Cetina, *Sp.* 41°16′ N, 1°59′ W **164**
Cetinje, *Serb. and Mont.* 42°23′ N, 18°54′ E **168**
Ceuta, *Sp.* 35°53′ N, 5°20′ W **150**
Cévennes, region, *Europe* 45°7′ N, 4°13′ E **165**
Cevio, *Switz.* 46°19′ N, 8°35′ E **167**
Ceyhan, *Turk.* 37°1′ N, 35°49′ E **156**
Ceyhan, river, *Turk.* 37°21′ N, 36°16′ E **180**
Ceylanpınar, *Turk.* 36°50′ N, 40°5′ E **195**
Ceylon, *Can.* 49°27′ N, 104°36′ W **90**
Chaadayevka, *Russ.* 53°8′ N, 45°58′ E **154**
Chābahār, *Iran* 25°18′ N, 60°39′ E **182**
Chaboullié, Lac, lake, *Can.* 50°52′ N, 78°32′ W **110**
Chac, oil field, *Mex.* 19°14′ N, 92°33′ W **115**
Chacabuco, *Arg.* 34°40′ S, 60°28′ W **139**
Chacalluta, *Chile* 18°25′ S, 70°20′ W **137**
Chacarilla, *Chile* 20°39′ S, 69°8′ W **137**
Chachani, Nevado, peak, *Peru* 16°14′ S, 71°35′ W **137**
Chachapoyas, *Peru* 6°9′ S, 77°51′ W **130**
Chachersk, *Belarus* 52°50′ N, 30°57′ E **154**
Chachoengsao, *Thai.* 13°43′ N, 101°4′ E **202**
Chachora, *India* 24°10′ N, 77°0′ E **197**
Chachro, *Pak.* 25°7′ N, 70°17′ E **186**
Chaco, adm. division, *Arg.* 27°11′ S, 60°49′ W **139**
Chaco Culture National Historic Park, *N. Mex., U.S.* 36°6′ N, 108°26′ W **92**
Chaco National Park, *Arg.* 26°54′ S, 59°45′ W **139**
Chacon, Cape, *Alas., U.S.* 54°29′ N, 132°5′ W **108**
Chad 15°25′ N, 17°21′ E **216**
Chad Basain National Park, *Nig.* 12°10′ N, 13°45′ E **218**
Chad, Lake, *Chad* 13°48′ N, 13°22′ E **216**
Chadan, *Russ.* 51°19′ N, 91°41′ E **184**
Chadron, *Nebr., U.S.* 42°49′ N, 102°60′ W **90**
Chadwick, *Mo., U.S.* 36°55′ N, 93°3′ W **96**
Chaedong, *N. Korea* 39°28′ N, 126°12′ E **200**
Chaeronea, ruin(s), *Gr.* 38°28′ N, 22°43′ E **156**
Chaeryŏng, *N. Korea* 38°24′ N, 125°38′ E **200**
Chafarinas, Islas, islands, *Alboran Sea* 35°13′ N, 2°52′ W **150**
Chafe, *Nig.* 11°54′ N, 6°55′ E **222**
Chaffee, *Mo., U.S.* 37°10′ N, 89°40′ W **96**
Chafurray, *Col.* 3°9′ N, 73°16′ W **136**
Chagai, *Pak.* 29°19′ N, 64°39′ E **182**
Chagda, *Russ.* 58°44′ N, 130°49′ E **160**
Chagdo Kangri, peak, *China* 34°10′ N, 84°4′ E **188**
Chaghcharan, *Afghan.* 34°28′ N, 65°13′ E **186**
Chagoda, *Russ.* 59°7′ N, 35°18′ E **154**
Chagos Archipelago (Oil Islands), *Indian Ocean* 6°42′ S, 71°25′ E **188**
Chagos Trench, *Indian Ocean* 10°25′ S, 72°50′ E **254**
Chagos-Laccadive Plateau, *Arabian Sea* 2°17′ N, 72°13′ E **254**
Chaguaramas, *Venez.* 9°20′ N, 66°17′ W **136**
Chagyl, *Turkm.* 40°49′ N, 55°17′ E **158**
Chahar Borj, *Afghan.* 34°20′ N, 62°12′ E **186**
Chahbounia, *Alg.* 35°31′ N, 2°36′ E **150**
Chah-e Ab, *Afghan.* 37°25′ N, 69°50′ E **186**
Ch'aho, *N. Korea* 40°12′ N, 128°41′ E **200**
Chaibasa, *India* 22°32′ N, 85°49′ E **197**
Chaïmane, spring, *Mauritania* 21°4′ N, 13°6′ W **222**
Chain Fracture Zone, *South Atlantic Ocean* 1°56′ S, 16°17′ W **253**
Chai-Nat, *Thai.* 15°14′ N, 100°10′ E **202**
Chaira, Laguna, lake, *Col.* 1°13′ N, 75°21′ W **136**
Chaitén, *Chile* 42°54′ S, 72°45′ W **134**
Chaiya, *Thai.* 9°23′ N, 99°10′ E **202**
Chajarí, *Arg.* 30°44′ S, 57°57′ W **139**
Chak Chak, *Sudan* 8°36′ N, 26°57′ E **224**
Chakar, river, *Pak.* 29°24′ N, 68°7′ E **186**
Chakaran, *Afghan.* 36°54′ N, 71°9′ E **186**
Chakaria, *Bangladesh* 21°47′ N, 92°4′ E **188**
Chake Chake, *Tanzania* 5°12′ S, 39°46′ E **218**
Chakhansur, *Afghan.* 31°10′ N, 62°6′ E **186**
Chakia, *India* 25°2′ N, 83°11′ E **188**
Chakkarat, *Thai.* 15°2′ N, 102°25′ E **202**
Chakmak-Suu, *Kyrg.* 41°59′ N, 71°26′ E **197**
Chakola, *Russ.* 64°17′ N, 44°14′ E **154**
Chakradharpur, *India* 22°41′ N, 85°38′ E **197**
Chakrata, *India* 30°42′ N, 77°53′ E **197**
Chakwal, *Pak.* 32°55′ N, 72°53′ E **186**
Chala, *Peru* 15°54′ S, 74°16′ W **137**
Chala, *Tanzania* 7°37′ S, 31°17′ E **224**
Chalabesa, *Zambia* 11°23′ S, 30°59′ E **224**
Chalatenango, *El Salv.* 14°1′ N, 88°55′ W **115**
Chalaua, *Mozambique* 16°5′ S, 39°13′ E **224**
Chalbi Desert, *Kenya* 3°33′ N, 36°48′ E **224**
Chalchihuites, *Mex.* 23°27′ N, 103°54′ W **114**
Ch'alchīs Terara, peak, *Eth.* 9°6′ N, 36°37′ E **224**
Chalengkou, *China* 38°1′ N, 93°55′ E **188**
Chaleur Bay 47°51′ N, 65°60′ W **111**
Chalhuanca, *Peru* 14°19′ S, 73°15′ W **137**
Chaling, *China* 26°51′ N, 113°31′ E **198**
Chalkyitsik, *Alas., U.S.* 66°38′ N, 143°44′ W **98**
Challacollo, *Chile* 20°59′ S, 69°24′ W **137**
Challans, *Fr.* 46°51′ N, 1°54′ W **150**
Challapata, *Bol.* 18°55′ S, 66°45′ W **137**
Challenger Deep, *North Pacific Ocean* 10°16′ N, 142°13′ E **252**
Challenger Fracture Zone, *South Pacific Ocean* 33°32′ S, 105°50′ W **252**
Challenger Point, peak, *Colo., U.S.* 37°57′ N, 105°40′ W **90**
Challis, *Idaho, U.S.* 44°30′ N, 114°14′ W **90**
Chālmeh, *Iran* 39°29′ N, 48°3′ E **195**
Chalon, *Fr.* 46°47′ N, 4°50′ E **150**
Châlons-sur-Marne, *Fr.* 48°57′ N, 4°22′ E **163**
Chaloyuk, *Turkm.* 37°26′ N, 54°13′ E **180**
Chālūs, *Iran* 36°41′ N, 51°19′ E **180**
Cham, *Ger.* 49°12′ N, 12°40′ E **152**
Chama, *Ghana* 8°49′ N, 0°58′ E **222**
Chama, *N. Mex., U.S.* 36°53′ N, 106°36′ W **92**
Chamah, peak, *Malaysia* 5°12′ N, 101°29′ E **196**
Chaman, *Pak.* 30°53′ N, 66°33′ E **186**
Chaman Bid, *Iran* 37°28′ N, 56°39′ E **180**
Chamba, *Nepal* 32°34′ N, 76°9′ E **188**
Chamba, *Tanzania* 11°32′ S, 37°1′ E **224**
Chambak, *Cambodia* 11°14′ N, 104°47′ E **202**
Chambeaux, Lac, lake, *Can.* 53°39′ N, 69°17′ W **111**
Chamberlain, *S. Dak., U.S.* 43°47′ N, 99°19′ W **90**
Chamberlain Lake, *Me., U.S.* 46°8′ N, 70°3′ W **94**
Chambers, *Ariz., U.S.* 35°12′ N, 109°26′ W **92**
Chambeshi, river, *Zambia* 11°2′ S, 31°11′ E **224**
Chambira, river, *Peru* 3°58′ S, 75°57′ W **130**
Chambishi, *Zambia* 12°40′ S, 28°4′ E **224**
Chambless, *Calif., U.S.* 34°33′ N, 115°33′ W **101**
Chambley, *Fr.* 49°3′ N, 5°53′ E **163**
Chambord, *Can.* 48°24′ N, 72°4′ W **94**
Chame, Punta, *Pan.* 8°32′ N, 79°41′ W **115**
Chamela, *Mex.* 19°32′ N, 105°5′ W **114**
Chamical, *Arg.* 30°23′ S, 66°19′ W **134**
Chamiss Bay, *Can.* 50°5′ N, 127°20′ W **90**
Chamizal National Memorial, *Tex., U.S.* 31°44′ N, 106°30′ W **92**
Chamonix, *Fr.* 45°55′ N, 6°51′ E **167**
Champa, *India* 22°2′ N, 82°40′ E **197**
Champagne, region, *Europe* 49°46′ N, 4°21′ E **167**
Champagne-Ardenne, adm. division, *Fr.* 48°18′ N, 3°36′ E **150**
Champaign, *Ill., U.S.* 40°6′ N, 88°15′ W **102**
Champasak, *Laos* 14°56′ N, 105°50′ E **202**
Champion, *Can.* 50°14′ N, 113°10′ W **90**
Champion, *Ohio, U.S.* 41°18′ N, 80°51′ W **102**
Champlain, *N.Y., U.S.* 44°59′ N, 73°28′ W **94**
Champotón, *Mex.* 19°21′ N, 90°44′ W **115**
Champotón, river, *Mex.* 19°29′ N, 90°38′ W **115**
Chamzinka, *Russ.* 54°25′ N, 45°48′ E **154**
Chanac, *Fr.* 44°27′ N, 3°20′ E **150**
Chañaral, *Chile* 26°23′ S, 70°39′ W **132**
Chanārān, *Iran* 36°39′ N, 59°5′ E **180**
Chanaro, Cerro, peak, *Venez.* 5°28′ N, 63°60′ W **130**
Chancamayo, *Peru* 12°36′ S, 72°26′ W **137**
Chancay, *Peru* 11°34′ S, 77°17′ W **130**
Chanco, *Chile* 35°44′ S, 72°34′ W **134**
Chandalar, river, *Alas., U.S.* 66°56′ N, 149°16′ W **98**
Chandausi, *India* 28°26′ N, 78°46′ E **197**
Chandeleur Islands, *Gulf of Mexico* 29°39′ N, 88°48′ W **103**
Chandeleur Sound 29°48′ N, 89°15′ W **103**
Chandigarh, *India* 30°43′ N, 76°51′ E **197**
Chandigarh, adm. division, *India* 30°45′ N, 76°18′ E **188**

Cha-Chi

Chandler, *Ariz., U.S.* 33°18′ N, 111°50′ W **92**
Chandler, *Can.* 48°20′ N, 64°40′ W **111**
Chandler, *Okla., U.S.* 35°40′ N, 96°52′ W **92**
Chandler, Mount, *Antarctica* 75°19′ S, 73°25′ W **248**
Chandless, river, *Braz.* 10°2′ S, 70°12′ W **137**
Chandpur, *Bangladesh* 23°13′ N, 90°41′ E **197**
Chandpur, *India* 29°7′ N, 78°15′ E **197**
Chandrapur, *India* 20°3′ N, 79°17′ E **190**
Chang, Ko, island, *Thai.* 11°52′ N, 101°42′ E **202**
Chang La, pass, *India* 34°2′ N, 77°55′ E **188**
Changalane, *Mozambique* 26°14′ S, 32°14′ E **227**
Changane, river, *Mozambique* 24°3′ S, 34°3′ E **227**
Changara, *Mozambique* 16°50′ S, 33°16′ E **224**
Changbai, *China* 41°27′ N, 128°12′ E **200**
Changchun, *China* 43°52′ N, 125°16′ E **198**
Changde, *China* 29°5′ N, 111°43′ E **198**
Ch'angdo, *N. Korea* 38°31′ N, 127°40′ E **200**
Changhua, *Taiwan* 23°59′ N, 120°31′ E **198**
Changhŭng, *N. Korea* 40°24′ N, 128°20′ E **200**
Changji, *China* 44°3′ N, 87°19′ E **184**
Changjiang (Shiliu), *China* 19°13′ N, 109°2′ E **198**
Changjin, *N. Korea* 40°21′ N, 127°15′ E **200**
Changjin Reservoir, lake, *N. Korea* 40°29′ N, 126°46′ E **200**
Changjin, river, *N. Korea* 40°55′ N, 127°15′ E **200**
Changle, *China* 25°58′ N, 119°33′ E **198**
Changli, *China* 39°43′ N, 119°11′ E **198**
Changling, *China* 44°16′ N, 124°1′ E **198**
Changma, *China* 39°52′ N, 96°43′ E **188**
Changmar, *China* 34°27′ N, 79°57′ E **188**
Changni, *S. Korea* 37°19′ N, 128°31′ E **200**
Changning, *China* 26°23′ N, 112°24′ E **198**
Changping, *China* 40°12′ N, 116°13′ E **198**
Changsha, *China* 28°13′ N, 113°1′ E **198**
Changshou, *China* 29°51′ N, 107°4′ E **198**
Changshu, *China* 31°36′ N, 120°40′ E **198**
Changting, *China* 25°50′ N, 116°16′ E **198**
Changtu, *China* 42°43′ N, 124°8′ E **200**
Changwon, *S. Korea* 35°16′ N, 128°45′ E **200**
Changxi, *China* 31°48′ N, 105°59′ E **198**
Changxing Dao, island, *China* 39°29′ N, 120°1′ E **198**
Changyŏn, *N. Korea* 38°14′ N, 125°5′ E **200**
Changzheng, *China* 36°41′ N, 105°2′ E **198**
Changzhi, *China* 36°10′ N, 113°6′ E **198**
Changzhou, *China* 31°50′ N, 120°0′ E **198**
Channapatna, *India* 12°40′ N, 77°11′ E **188**
Channel Country, *Austral.* 25°32′ S, 138°35′ E **230**
Channel Islands, adm. division, *U.K.* 49°26′ N, 2°48′ W **150**
Channel Islands National Park, *Calif., U.S.* 34°5′ N, 120°34′ W **101**
Channel-Port aux Basques, *Can.* 47°34′ N, 59°9′ W **111**
Chanthaburi, *Thai.* 12°36′ N, 102°9′ E **202**
Chantilly, *Fr.* 49°11′ N, 2°28′ E **163**
Chantrey Inlet 67°23′ N, 98°31′ W **106**
Chanute, *Kans., U.S.* 37°39′ N, 95°28′ W **94**
Chany, *Russ.* 55°16′ N, 76°54′ E **184**
Chany, Ozero, lake, *Russ.* 54°57′ N, 76°49′ E **184**
Chany, Ozero, lake, *Russ.* 54°39′ N, 75°46′ E **160**
Chaor, river, *China* 47°14′ N, 121°38′ E **198**
Chaoyang, *China* 41°35′ N, 120°24′ E **198**
Chaoyang, *China* 23°13′ N, 116°33′ E **198**
Chaoyang see Huinan, *China* 42°42′ N, 126°4′ E **200**
Chaoyangchuan, *China* 42°51′ N, 129°19′ E **200**
Chaozhou, *China* 23°37′ N, 116°33′ E **198**
Chapada dos Guimarães, *Braz.* 15°25′ S, 55°47′ W **132**
Chapada Dos Veadeiros National Park, *Braz.* 14°10′ S, 47°50′ W **138**
Chapadinha, *Braz.* 3°46′ S, 43°20′ W **132**
Chapaev, *Kaz.* 50°11′ N, 51°8′ E **158**
Chapais, *Can.* 49°48′ N, 74°54′ W **94**
Chapala, *Mex.* 20°18′ N, 103°12′ W **112**
Chapala, Lago de, lake, *Mex.* 20°2′ N, 103°30′ W **114**
Chapare, river, *Bol.* 16°21′ S, 65°2′ W **137**
Chaparral, *Col.* 3°41′ N, 75°26′ W **136**
Chapayevsk, *Russ.* 52°58′ N, 49°48′ E **154**
Chapeau, *Can.* 45°55′ N, 77°4′ W **94**
Chapeauroux, *Fr.* 44°49′ N, 3°44′ E **150**
Chapimarca, *Peru* 13°59′ S, 73°3′ W **137**
Chapleau, *Can.* 47°49′ N, 83°24′ W **94**
Chaplin Lake, *Can.* 50°13′ N, 107°8′ W **108**
Chapman, *Ala., U.S.* 31°40′ N, 86°43′ W **96**
Chapman, *Kans., U.S.* 38°57′ N, 97°2′ W **90**
Chapman, Mount, *Antarctica* 82°25′ S, 104°25′ W **248**
Chapman, Mount, *Can.* 51°56′ N, 118°24′ W **90**
Chapoma, *Russ.* 66°8′ N, 38°44′ E **154**
Chappaquiddick Island, *Mass., U.S.* 41°23′ N, 70°27′ W **104**
Chappell, *Nebr., U.S.* 41°4′ N, 102°28′ W **90**
Chaput Hughes, *Can.* 48°8′ N, 80°4′ W **94**
Chaqui, *Bol.* 19°35′ S, 65°28′ W **137**
Char, *Mauritania* 21°32′ N, 12°50′ W **222**
Chara, *Russ.* 56°48′ N, 118°10′ E **160**
Chara, river, *Russ.* 59°0′ N, 118°31′ E **160**
Charadai, *Arg.* 27°37′ S, 59°54′ W **139**
Charagua, *Bol.* 19°48′ S, 63°18′ W **137**
Charalá, *Col.* 6°15′ N, 73°7′ W **136**
Charambirá, Punta, *Col.* 4°8′ N, 78°10′ W **136**
Charaña, *Bol.* 17°40′ S, 69°27′ W **137**
Charanwala, *India* 27°51′ N, 72°11′ E **186**
Charata, *Arg.* 27°13′ S, 61°12′ W **139**
Charay, *Mex.* 26°0′ N, 108°50′ W **112**
Charcoal Lake, *Can.* 58°44′ N, 103°14′ W **108**
Charcot Bay 63°49′ S, 61°4′ W **134**
Charcot Island, *Antarctica* 70°11′ S, 79°50′ W **248**
Chard, *Can.* 55°50′ N, 110°54′ W **108**
Chard, *U.K.* 50°52′ N, 2°58′ W **162**
Charenton, *La., U.S.* 29°52′ N, 91°32′ W **103**
Chari, river, *Africa* 13°9′ N, 14°33′ E **216**
Charikar, *Afghan.* 35°1′ N, 69°10′ E **186**
Chariton, *Iowa, U.S.* 41°1′ N, 93°19′ W **94**
Chariton, river, *Mo., U.S.* 40°44′ N, 93°9′ W **80**
Charity, *Guyana* 7°21′ N, 58°37′ W **130**
Charity Island, *Mich., U.S.* 43°59′ N, 83°25′ W **102**
Chärjew see Türkmenabat, *Turkm.* 39°4′ N, 63°35′ E **184**
Charkayuvom, *Russ.* 65°48′ N, 54°51′ E **154**
Charlemont, *Mass., U.S.* 42°37′ N, 72°53′ W **104**
Charleroi, *Belg.* 50°25′ N, 4°26′ E **167**
Charles, Cape, *Va., U.S.* 37°1′ N, 75°57′ W **96**
Charles Fuhr, *Arg.* 50°13′ S, 71°53′ W **134**
Charles Island, *Can.* 62°36′ N, 77°12′ W **106**
Charles Lake, lake, *Can.* 59°45′ N, 111°12′ W **108**
Charles Mound, *Ill., U.S.* 42°28′ N, 90°17′ W **102**
Charles, Mount, *Austral.* 27°46′ S, 117°13′ E **230**
Charlesbourg, *Can.* 46°51′ N, 71°17′ W **94**
Charleston, *Ill., U.S.* 39°29′ N, 88°11′ W **102**
Charleston, *N.Z.* 41°56′ S, 171°27′ E **240**
Charleston, *S.C., U.S.* 32°47′ N, 79°57′ W **96**
Charleston, *W. Va., U.S.* 38°19′ N, 81°43′ W **94**
Charleston Peak, *Nev., U.S.* 36°15′ N, 115°45′ W **101**
Charlestown, *N.H., U.S.* 43°13′ N, 72°26′ W **104**
Charleville-Mézières, *Fr.* 49°46′ N, 4°43′ E **163**
Charlevoix, *Mich., U.S.* 45°18′ N, 85°16′ W **94**
Charlie Lake, *Can.* 56°15′ N, 120°59′ W **108**
Charlie-Gibbs Fracture Zone, *North Atlantic Ocean* 51°53′ N, 33°3′ W **253**
Charlotte, *Mich., U.S.* 42°33′ N, 84°51′ W **102**
Charlotte, *N.C., U.S.* 35°12′ N, 80°51′ W **96**
Charlotte, *Tex., U.S.* 28°51′ N, 98°43′ W **96**
Charlotte, *Vt., U.S.* 44°18′ N, 73°16′ W **104**
Charlotte Amalie, *Virgin Islands, U.S.* 18°0′ N, 65°0′ W **118**
Charlotte Harbor 26°42′ N, 83°11′ W **80**
Charlotte Harbor, *Fla., U.S.* 26°58′ N, 82°4′ W **105**
Charlotte Lake, lake, *Can.* 52°6′ N, 125°48′ W **108**
Charlottetown, *Can.* 46°13′ N, 63°16′ W **111**
Charlotteville, *Trinidad and Tobago* 11°16′ N, 60°33′ W **116**
Charlton City, *Mass., U.S.* 42°8′ N, 71°60′ W **104**
Charlton Island, *Can.* 52°5′ N, 80°29′ W **81**
Charly, *Fr.* 48°58′ N, 3°16′ E **163**
Charmes, *Fr.* 48°21′ N, 6°17′ E **163**
Charny, *Can.* 46°43′ N, 71°16′ W **94**
Charouine, *Alg.* 29°2′ N, 0°15′ E **214**
Charron Lake, lake, *Can.* 52°39′ N, 95°47′ W **108**
Charters Towers, *Austral.* 20°7′ S, 146°17′ E **231**
Chartres, *Fr.* 48°27′ N, 1°27′ E **163**
Charyshskoye, *Russ.* 51°26′ N, 83°43′ E **184**
Chascomús, *Arg.* 35°34′ S, 58°1′ W **139**
Chase, *Alas., U.S.* 62°27′ N, 150°6′ W **98**
Chase, *Can.* 50°49′ N, 119°40′ W **90**
Chase, *Mich., U.S.* 43°53′ N, 85°38′ W **102**
Chase City, *Va., U.S.* 36°47′ N, 78°28′ W **96**
Chase, Mount, *Me., U.S.* 46°5′ N, 68°34′ W **94**
Chase Mountain, *Can.* 56°32′ N, 125°22′ W **108**
Chasel'ka, *Russ.* 65°7′ N, 81°26′ E **169**
Chashniki, *Belarus* 54°51′ N, 29°13′ E **166**
Chaska, *Minn., U.S.* 44°46′ N, 93°38′ W **94**
Chasŏng, *N. Korea* 41°26′ N, 126°38′ E **200**
Chasovo, *Russ.* 62°2′ N, 50°40′ E **154**
Chassahowitzka, *Fla., U.S.* 28°41′ N, 82°35′ W **105**
Chastyye, *Russ.* 57°16′ N, 55°4′ E **154**
Chataignier, *La., U.S.* 30°32′ N, 92°20′ W **103**
Chatawa, *Miss., U.S.* 31°2′ N, 90°29′ W **103**
Châteaumeillant, *Fr.* 46°34′ N, 2°11′ E **150**
Châteauneuf-en-Thymerais, *Fr.* 48°34′ N, 1°14′ E **163**
Château-Porcien, *Fr.* 49°32′ N, 4°14′ E **163**
Châteauroux, *Fr.* 46°49′ N, 1°41′ E **150**
Château-Salins, *Fr.* 48°49′ N, 6°30′ E **163**
Châteauvert, Lac, lake, *Can.* 47°34′ N, 74°36′ W **110**
Chateh, *Can.* 58°41′ N, 118°48′ W **108**
Châtel, *Fr.* 46°16′ N, 6°49′ E **167**
Châtelet, *Belg.* 50°24′ N, 4°32′ E **167**
Châtellerault, *Fr.* 46°48′ N, 0°31′ E **150**
Châtel-Saint-Denis, *Switz.* 46°33′ N, 6°55′ E **167**
Châtel-sur-Moselle, *Fr.* 48°18′ N, 6°24′ E **163**
Châtenois, *Fr.* 48°17′ N, 5°49′ E **163**
Chatfield, *Minn., U.S.* 43°50′ N, 92°12′ W **110**
Chatham, *Can.* 47°1′ N, 65°28′ W **94**
Chatham, *Can.* 42°23′ N, 82°11′ W **102**
Chatham, *Ill., U.S.* 39°39′ N, 89°42′ W **102**
Chatham, *La., U.S.* 32°18′ N, 92°29′ W **103**
Chatham, *Mass., U.S.* 41°40′ N, 69°58′ W **104**
Chatham, *Miss., U.S.* 33°4′ N, 91°7′ W **103**
Chatham, *Mo., U.S.* 39°39′ N, 89°42′ W **94**
Chatham, *N.H., U.S.* 44°9′ N, 71°1′ W **104**
Chatham, *N.Y., U.S.* 42°21′ N, 73°37′ W **104**
Chatham, *U.K.* 51°21′ N, 0°30′ E **162**
Chatham, *Va., U.S.* 36°48′ N, 79°25′ W **96**
Chatham, Isla, island, *Chile* 51°9′ S, 74°8′ W **134**
Chatham Rise, *South Pacific Ocean* 43°29′ S, 178°25′ W **252**
Châtillon, *Fr.* 49°6′ N, 3°46′ E **163**
Chatom, *Ala., U.S.* 31°27′ N, 88°15′ W **103**
Chatra, *India* 24°11′ N, 84°51′ E **197**
Chatsu, *India* 26°35′ N, 75°57′ E **197**
Chatsworth, *Ill., U.S.* 40°45′ N, 88°19′ W **102**
Chattahoochee, *Fla., U.S.* 30°40′ N, 84°54′ W **112**
Chattahoochee, river, *U.S.* 32°4′ N, 85°8′ W **80**
Chattanooga, *Tenn., U.S.* 35°1′ N, 85°19′ W **96**
Chattaroy, *W. Va., U.S.* 37°42′ N, 82°18′ W **96**
Chatteris, *U.K.* 52°27′ N, 5°297′ E **162**
Chatyr-Tash, *Kyrg.* 40°54′ N, 76°26′ E **184**
Chau Doc, *Vietnam* 10°41′ N, 105°7′ E **202**
Chauk, *Myanmar* 20°53′ N, 94°50′ E **202**
Chaullay, *Peru* 13°1′ S, 72°39′ W **137**
Chaulnes, *Fr.* 49°48′ N, 2°47′ E **163**
Chaumont, *Fr.* 48°6′ N, 5°8′ E **150**
Chaumont-en-Vexin, *Fr.* 49°16′ N, 1°53′ E **163**
Chaumu, *India* 27°10′ N, 75°42′ E **197**
Chauncey, *Ohio, U.S.* 39°24′ N, 82°8′ W **102**
Chaunskaya Guba 69°10′ N, 165°0′ E **160**
Chauny, *Fr.* 49°37′ N, 3°14′ E **163**
Chauvin, *Can.* 52°41′ N, 110°9′ W **108**
Chauvin, *La., U.S.* 29°26′ N, 90°36′ W **103**
Chavan'ga, *Russ.* 66°8′ N, 37°40′ E **154**
Chaves, *Braz.* 0°24′ N, 49°48′ W **123**
Chaves, *Port.* 41°44′ N, 7°30′ W **150**
Chaveslândia, *Braz.* 18°58′ S, 50°36′ W **138**
Cháviva, *Col.* 4°18′ N, 72°18′ W **136**
Chavuma, *Zambia* 13°5′ S, 22°43′ E **220**
Chavusy, *Belarus* 53°46′ N, 31°0′ E **154**
Chawang, *Thai.* 8°26′ N, 99°31′ E **202**
Chayanta, *Bol.* 18°28′ S, 66°28′ W **137**
Chaykovskiy, *Russ.* 56°48′ N, 54°9′ E **154**
Cheadle, *U.K.* 52°59′ N, 1°60′ W **162**
Cheaha Mountain, *Ala., U.S.* 33°27′ N, 85°53′ W **96**
Cheapside, *Va., U.S.* 37°12′ N, 75°59′ W **96**
Cheb, *Czech Rep.* 50°4′ N, 12°22′ E **152**
Chebanse, *Ill., U.S.* 41°0′ N, 87°55′ W **102**
Chebarkul', *Russ.* 55°0′ N, 60°19′ E **154**
Chebeague Island, *Me., U.S.* 43°44′ N, 70°8′ W **104**
Cheboksary, *Russ.* 56°5′ N, 47°11′ E **154**
Cheboygan, *Mich., U.S.* 45°38′ N, 84°30′ W **94**
Chebsara, *Russ.* 59°10′ N, 38°49′ E **154**
Checa, *Sp.* 40°34′ N, 1°47′ W **164**
Chech, Erg, *Alg.* 23°26′ N, 4°20′ W **206**
Chechnya, adm. division, *Russ.* 43°33′ N, 44°59′ E **158**
Checotah, *Okla., U.S.* 35°27′ N, 95°32′ W **96**
Cheddar, *U.K.* 51°16′ N, 2°47′ W **162**
Cheduba Island, *Myanmar* 18°29′ N, 92°36′ E **188**
Chedworth, *U.K.* 51°48′ N, 1°55′ W **162**
Cheecham, *Can.* 56°16′ N, 110°53′ W **108**
Cheepash, river, *Can.* 50°42′ N, 82°33′ W **110**
Cheepay, river, *Can.* 51°7′ N, 83°35′ W **110**
Cheetham, Cape, *Antarctica* 69°54′ S, 167°30′ E **248**
Chefornak, *Alas., U.S.* 60°12′ N, 164°14′ W **98**
Chegdomyn, *Russ.* 51°6′ N, 133°12′ E **238**
Chegga, spring, *Mauritania* 25°22′ N, 5°47′ W **214**
Chegutu, *Zimb.* 18°9′ S, 30°10′ E **224**
Chehalis, *Wash., U.S.* 46°39′ N, 122°58′ W **100**
Chehalis, river, *Wash., U.S.* 46°59′ N, 123°25′ W **100**
Chehar Borjak, *Afghan.* 30°17′ N, 62°7′ E **186**
Cheïkria, spring, *Alg.* 25°29′ N, 5°28′ W **214**
Cheju see Jeju, *S. Korea* 33°29′ N, 126°32′ E **200**
Chela, Serra da, *Angola* 16°7′ S, 12°39′ E **220**
Ch'elago, *Eth.* 4°9′ N, 40°3′ E **224**
Chelak, *Uzb.* 39°58′ N, 66°51′ E **197**
Chelan, *Wash., U.S.* 47°50′ N, 120°1′ W **90**
Chelan Falls, *Wash., U.S.* 47°47′ N, 119°59′ W **108**
Chelem, *Mex.* 21°15′ N, 89°44′ W **116**
Chelforó, *Arg.* 39°6′ S, 66°31′ W **134**
Chellal, *Alg.* 35°30′ N, 4°23′ E **150**
Chełm, *Pol.* 51°7′ N, 23°27′ E **152**
Chełmża, *Pol.* 53°21′ N, 18°26′ E **152**
Chelmsford, *Mass., U.S.* 42°35′ N, 71°22′ W **104**
Chelmsford, *U.K.* 51°44′ N, 0°29′ E **162**
Chelmuzhi, *Russ.* 62°32′ N, 35°43′ E **154**
Chelsea, *Mich., U.S.* 42°18′ N, 84°2′ W **102**
Chelsea, *Okla., U.S.* 36°31′ N, 95°26′ W **96**
Chelsea, *Vt., U.S.* 43°59′ N, 72°27′ W **104**
Cheltenham, *U.K.* 51°53′ N, 2°5′ W **162**
Chelva, *Sp.* 39°44′ N, 0°60′ E **150**
Chelyabinsk, *Russ.* 55°9′ N, 61°25′ E **154**
Chelyabinsk, adm. division, *Russ.* 53°58′ N, 59°14′ E **154**
Chelyuskin, Mys, *Russ.* 76°44′ N, 103°34′ E **172**
Chemaïa, *Mor.* 32°5′ N, 8°40′ W **214**
Chemba, *Mozambique* 17°11′ S, 34°50′ E **224**
Chemehuevi Peak, *Calif., U.S.* 34°32′ N, 114°36′ W **101**
Chémery, *Fr.* 49°35′ N, 4°50′ E **163**
Chemnitz, *Ger.* 50°48′ N, 12°55′ E **160**
Chemtou, ruin(s), *Tun.* 36°28′ N, 8°29′ E **156**
Chemult, *Oreg., U.S.* 43°13′ N, 121°48′ W **90**
Chen Barag Qi, *China* 49°17′ N, 119°24′ E **198**
Chenab, river, *Pak.* 31°18′ N, 72°22′ E **186**
Chenachane, *Alg.* 26°3′ N, 4°14′ W **214**
Chenango Bridge, *N.Y., U.S.* 42°10′ N, 75°53′ W **94**
Ch'ench'a (Cencia), *Eth.* 6°15′ N, 37°38′ E **224**
Chénérailles, *Fr.* 46°7′ N, 2°10′ E **150**
Cheney, *Wash., U.S.* 47°28′ N, 117°36′ W **90**
Cheneyville, *La., U.S.* 30°59′ N, 92°18′ W **103**
Chengbu, *China* 26°22′ N, 110°19′ E **198**
Chengchow see Zhengzhou, *China* 34°46′ N, 113°36′ E **198**
Chengde, *China* 41°0′ N, 117°55′ E **198**
Chengdu, *China* 30°43′ N, 104°2′ E **198**
Chengele, *India* 28°47′ N, 96°17′ E **188**
Chenggu, *China* 33°8′ N, 107°19′ E **198**
Chenghai, *China* 23°29′ N, 116°48′ E **198**
Chengkou, *China* 31°54′ N, 108°39′ E **198**
Ch'engkung, *Taiwan* 23°8′ N, 121°24′ E **198**
Chengshan Jiao, *China* 37°24′ N, 122°45′ E **198**
Chengxian, *China* 33°44′ N, 105°40′ E **198**
Chennai (Madras), *India* 13°5′ N, 80°16′ E **188**
Chenoa, *Ill., U.S.* 40°44′ N, 88°43′ W **102**
Chenxi, *China* 28°2′ N, 110°12′ E **198**
Chenxiangtun, *China* 41°33′ N, 123°29′ E **200**
Chenzhou, *China* 25°48′ N, 113°2′ E **198**
Cheo Reo, *Vietnam* 13°23′ N, 108°25′ E **202**
Cheom Ksan, *Cambodia* 14°16′ N, 104°56′ E **202**
Cheonan, *S. Korea* 36°47′ N, 127°8′ E **200**
Cheongeong, *S. Korea* 36°26′ N, 129°6′ E **200**
Cheongju, *S. Korea* 36°37′ N, 127°30′ E **200**
Cheongyang, *S. Korea* 36°26′ N, 126°48′ E **200**
Cheorwon, *S. Korea* 38°14′ N, 127°13′ E **200**
Chepachet, *R.I., U.S.* 41°54′ N, 71°41′ W **104**
Chepes, *Arg.* 31°20′ S, 66°35′ W **134**
Chepstow, *U.K.* 51°38′ N, 2°41′ W **162**
Cheptsa, river, *Russ.* 58°8′ N, 52°54′ E **154**
Cher, river, *Fr.* 46°54′ N, 2°17′ E **165**
Cherán, *Mex.* 19°40′ N, 101°57′ W **114**
Cherangany Hills, *Kenya* 1°32′ N, 35°1′ E **224**
Cherari, *Eth.* 9°55′ N, 35°52′ E **224**
Cheraw, *S.C., U.S.* 34°40′ N, 79°55′ W **96**
Cherchell, *Alg.* 36°35′ N, 2°12′ E **150**
Cherdyn', *Russ.* 60°24′ N, 56°25′ E **154**
Cheremkhovo, *Russ.* 53°16′ N, 102°55′ E **190**
Cheremukhovo, *Russ.* 60°21′ N, 59°59′ E **154**
Cherepanovo, *Russ.* 54°14′ N, 83°29′ E **184**
Chereponi, *Ghana* 10°7′ N, 0°17′ E **222**
Cherepovets, *Russ.* 59°7′ N, 37°55′ E **154**
Cherevkovo, *Russ.* 61°46′ N, 45°17′ E **154**
Chereya, *Belarus* 54°36′ N, 29°20′ E **166**
Chéri, *Niger* 13°25′ N, 11°21′ E **222**
Cheriton, *Va., U.S.* 37°17′ N, 75°58′ W **96**
Cherkasy, *Ukr.* 49°26′ N, 32°3′ E **158**
Cherkessk, *Russ.* 44°14′ N, 42°3′ E **158**
Cherla, *India* 18°4′ N, 80°50′ E **188**
Cherlak, *Russ.* 54°9′ N, 74°53′ E **184**
Chermenino, *Russ.* 59°2′ N, 43°59′ E **154**
Chermoz, *Russ.* 58°46′ N, 56°5′ E **154**
Chern', *Russ.* 53°25′ N, 36°57′ E **154**
Chernaya Kholunitsa, *Russ.* 58°52′ N, 51°46′ E **154**
Chernevichi, *Belarus* 54°1′ N, 28°49′ E **166**
Chernevo, *Russ.* 58°39′ N, 28°12′ E **166**
Cherni Vrŭkh, peak, *Bulg.* 42°32′ N, 23°12′ E **156**
Chernihiv, *Ukr.* 51°27′ N, 31°20′ E **158**
Chernivtsi, *Ukr.* 48°17′ N, 25°57′ E **152**
Chernoborskaya, *Russ.* 65°8′ N, 53°38′ E **154**
Chernofski, *Alas., U.S.* 53°22′ N, 167°34′ W **98**
Chernogorsk, *Russ.* 53°49′ N, 91°16′ E **184**
Chernorechenskiy, *Russ.* 60°42′ N, 52°15′ E **154**
Chernovka, *Russ.* 54°12′ N, 80°5′ E **184**
Chernushka, *Russ.* 56°30′ N, 56°1′ E **154**
Chernyakhovsk, *Russ.* 54°36′ N, 21°49′ E **152**
Chernyanka, *Russ.* 50°55′ N, 37°48′ E **158**
Chernyshevskiy, *Russ.* 62°52′ N, 112°40′ E **160**
Chernyy Otrog, *Russ.* 51°51′ N, 56°0′ E **158**
Chernyy Yar, *Russ.* 48°2′ N, 46°4′ E **158**
Cherokee, *Okla., U.S.* 36°44′ N, 98°21′ W **92**
Cherokee Sound, *Bahamas* 26°16′ N, 77°3′ W **96**
Cherokees, Lake O' The, *Okla., U.S.* 36°42′ N, 95°40′ W **80**
Cherrapunji, *India* 25°15′ N, 91°42′ E **197**
Cherry Creek Range, *Nev., U.S.* 39°59′ N, 115°6′ W **90**
Cherry Creek, river, *S. Dak., U.S.* 44°42′ N, 102°31′ W **90**
Cherskaya, *Russ.* 57°39′ N, 28°17′ E **166**
Cherskiy, *Russ.* 68°39′ N, 161°29′ E **160**
Cherskogo, Khrebet, *Russ.* 66°20′ N, 138°20′ E **160**
Chersonesus, ruin(s), *Gr.* 35°18′ N, 25°17′ E **156**
Chertkovo, *Russ.* 49°27′ N, 40°8′ E **158**
Cherva, *Russ.* 62°16′ N, 48°41′ E **154**
Chervonohrad, *Ukr.* 50°22′ N, 24°15′ E **152**
Chervyanka, *Russ.* 57°39′ N, 99°28′ E **160**
Cherykaw, *Belarus* 53°32′ N, 31°23′ E **154**
Chesaning, *Mich., U.S.* 43°10′ N, 84°7′ W **102**
Chesapeake, *Va., U.S.* 36°49′ N, 76°17′ W **96**
Chesapeake, *W. Va., U.S.* 38°12′ N, 81°34′ W **94**
Chesham, *U.K.* 51°42′ N, 0°38′ E **162**
Cheshire, *Conn., U.S.* 41°29′ N, 72°54′ W **104**
Cheshire, *Mass., U.S.* 42°33′ N, 73°10′ W **104**
Cheshskaya Guba 67°9′ N, 44°32′ E **169**
Cheshunt, *U.K.* 51°41′ N, 0°3′ E **162**
Cheslatta Lake, lake, *Can.* 53°38′ N, 125°40′ W **108**
Chesley, *Can.* 44°17′ N, 81°6′ W **110**
Chesma, *Russ.* 53°51′ N, 60°32′ E **154**
Cheste, *Sp.* 39°29′ N, 0°42′ E **164**
Chester, *Mo., U.S.* 37°54′ N, 89°49′ W **96**
Chester, *Mont., U.S.* 48°28′ N, 110°59′ W **90**
Chester, *N.H., U.S.* 42°57′ N, 71°16′ W **104**
Chester, *S.C., U.S.* 34°42′ N, 81°13′ W **96**
Chester, *U.K.* 53°12′ N, 2°51′ W **162**
Chester, *Vt., U.S.* 43°15′ N, 72°36′ W **104**
Chester le Street, *U.K.* 54°51′ N, 1°36′ W **162**
Chesterfield, *Ind., U.S.* 40°6′ N, 85°36′ W **102**
Chesterfield, *U.K.* 53°14′ N, 1°27′ W **162**
Chesterfield, Îles, islands, *Coral Sea* 18°54′ S, 154°49′ E **238**
Chesterfield Inlet, *Can.* 63°19′ N, 90°50′ W **106**
Chesterhill, *Ohio, U.S.* 39°28′ N, 81°51′ W **102**
Chesterton Range, *Austral.* 26°17′ S, 147°27′ E **230**
Chestertown, *N.Y., U.S.* 43°38′ N, 73°49′ W **104**
Chestnut Ridge, *Pa., U.S.* 40°29′ N, 79°22′ W **94**
Chetamale, *India* 10°44′ N, 92°41′ E **188**
Chete Safari Area, *Zimb.* 17°30′ S, 27°12′ E **224**
Chetek, *Wis., U.S.* 45°18′ N, 91°40′ W **94**
Chéticamp, *Can.* 46°36′ N, 61°1′ W **111**
Chetumal, *Mex.* 18°30′ N, 88°27′ W **115**
Chetwynd, *Can.* 55°41′ N, 121°39′ W **108**
Chevillon, *Fr.* 48°31′ N, 5°7′ E **163**
Cheviot, *N.Z.* 42°50′ S, 173°16′ E **240**
Cheviot Hills, *U.K.* 55°10′ N, 2°47′ W **150**
Cheviot, The, peak, *U.K.* 55°27′ N, 2°16′ W **150**
Ch'ew Bahir, lake, *Eth.* 4°40′ N, 36°40′ E **224**
Chewelah, *Wash., U.S.* 48°15′ N, 117°45′ W **90**
Chewore Safari Area, *Zimb.* 15°58′ S, 29°52′ E **224**
Cheyenne, *Okla., U.S.* 35°35′ N, 99°40′ W **92**
Cheyenne, *Wyo., U.S.* 41°6′ N, 104°55′ W **90**
Cheyenne, river, *S. Dak., U.S.* 44°24′ N, 102°2′ W **90**
Cheyenne, river, *Wyo., U.S.* 42°53′ N, 104°36′ W **80**
Cheyenne Wells, *Colo., U.S.* 38°48′ N, 102°21′ W **90**
Chezacut, *Can.* 52°25′ N, 124°2′ W **108**
Chhad Bet, site, *Pak.* 24°13′ N, 69°54′ E **186**
Chhapra, *India* 25°46′ N, 84°43′ E **197**
Chhatarpur, *India* 24°54′ N, 79°35′ E **197**
Chhattīsgarh, adm. division, *India* 18°18′ N, 81°16′ E **188**
Chhep, *Cambodia* 13°46′ N, 105°27′ E **202**
Chhindwara, *India* 22°4′ N, 78°56′ E **197**
Chhlong, *Cambodia* 12°14′ N, 105°57′ E **202**
Chhukha, *Bhutan* 27°10′ N, 89°30′ E **197**
Chi, river, *Thai.* 15°56′ N, 102°18′ E **202**
Chía, *Sp.* 42°31′ N, 0°27′ E **164**
Chiai, *Taiwan* 23°28′ N, 120°25′ E **198**
Chiang Dao, *Thai.* 19°23′ N, 98°57′ E **202**
Chiang Khan, *Thai.* 17°53′ N, 101°37′ E **202**
Chiang Mai, *Thai.* 18°48′ N, 98°58′ E **202**
Chiang Rai, *Thai.* 19°55′ N, 99°48′ E **202**
Chiang Saen, *Laos* 20°18′ N, 100°3′ E **202**
Chiange, *Angola* 15°43′ S, 13°54′ E **220**
Chiapa, *Chile* 19°33′ S, 69°14′ W **137**
Chiapas, adm. division, *Mex.* 16°25′ N, 93°33′ W **112**
Chiari, *It.* 45°32′ N, 9°54′ E **167**
Chiasso, *Switz.* 45°51′ N, 9°1′ E **167**
Chiat'aisi, *Ga.* 42°14′ N, 43°17′ E **195**
Chiautla, *Mex.* 18°15′ N, 98°36′ W **114**
Chiavari, *It.* 44°19′ N, 9°20′ E **167**
Chiavenna, *It.* 46°19′ N, 9°23′ E **167**
Chiba, *Japan* 35°34′ N, 140°9′ E **201**
Chiba, adm. division, *Japan* 35°44′ N, 139°54′ E **201**
Chibabava, *Mozambique* 20°17′ S, 33°41′ E **227**
Chibi, *Zimb.* 20°19′ S, 30°29′ E **227**
Chibia, *Angola* 15°14′ S, 13°40′ E **220**
Chibougamau, *Can.* 49°54′ N, 74°22′ W **94**
Chibougamau, Lac, lake, *Can.* 49°49′ N, 75°44′ W **81**
Chibuto, *Mozambique* 24°42′ S, 33°34′ E **227**
Chibwe, *Zambia* 14°12′ S, 28°29′ E **224**
Chic Chocs Mountains, *Can.* 48°42′ N, 67°1′ W **94**
Chicago, *Ill., U.S.* 41°51′ N, 87°37′ W **102**
Chicamba, *Angola* 4°59′ S, 12°2′ E **218**
Chichagof, *Alas., U.S.* 57°41′ N, 136°8′ W **108**
Chichagof Island, *Alas., U.S.* 58°3′ N, 138°7′ W **98**
Chichaoua, *Mor.* 31°31′ N, 8°47′ W **214**
Chichas, Cordillera de, *Bol.* 20°47′ S, 66°25′ W **132**
Chiché, river, *Braz.* 8°54′ S, 54°6′ W **130**
Chichén Itzá, ruin(s), *Mex.* 20°40′ N, 88°42′ W **115**
Chichester, *N.H., U.S.* 43°14′ N, 71°25′ W **104**
Chichester, *U.K.* 50°50′ N, 0°47′ E **162**
Chichi Jima Rettō, islands, *Philippine Sea* 26°41′ N, 142°19′ E **190**
Chichibu, *Japan* 35°58′ N, 139°6′ E **201**
Chichibu-Tama National Park, *Japan* 35°50′ N, 138°11′ E **201**
Chichihualco, *Mex.* 17°40′ N, 99°41′ W **114**
Chichiriviche, *Venez.* 10°56′ N, 68°17′ W **136**
Chickaloon, *Alas., U.S.* 61°48′ N, 148°28′ W **98**
Chickasaw, *Ala., U.S.* 30°45′ N, 88°3′ W **103**
Chickasha, *Okla., U.S.* 35°2′ N, 97°57′ W **92**
Chiclana de la Frontera, *Sp.* 36°25′ N, 6°9′ W **164**
Chiclayo, *Peru* 6°44′ S, 79°51′ W **130**
Chico, *Calif., U.S.* 39°43′ N, 121°51′ W **90**
Chico, river, *Arg.* 48°23′ S, 71°58′ W **134**
Chico, river, *Arg.* 45°2′ S, 67°5′ W **134**
Chicomo, *Mozambique* 24°31′ S, 34°9′ E **227**
Chicontepec, *Mex.* 20°57′ N, 98°10′ W **114**
Chicopee, *Ga., U.S.* 34°14′ N, 83°51′ W **96**
Chicopee, *Mass., U.S.* 42°8′ N, 72°37′ W **104**
Chicot Island, *La., U.S.* 29°39′ N, 89°22′ W **103**
Chicoutai, Point, *Can.* 50°5′ N, 61°8′ W **111**
Chicoutimi, *Can.* 48°14′ N, 70°58′ W **106**
Chicoutimi-Nord, *Can.* 48°26′ N, 71°6′ W **94**
Chicualacuala, *Mozambique* 22°4′ S, 31°43′ E **227**
Chicuma, *Angola* 13°26′ S, 14°49′ E **220**
Chidenguele, *Mozambique* 24°54′ S, 34°10′ E **227**
Chiefland, *Fla., U.S.* 29°28′ N, 82°51′ W **105**
Chiengi, *Zambia* 8°41′ S, 29°10′ E **224**
Chietla, *Mex.* 18°29′ N, 98°34′ W **114**
Chifeng, *China* 42°15′ N, 118°59′ E **198**
Chifre, Serra do, *Braz.* 17°46′ S, 42°41′ W **132**
Chifungwe, Lake, *Zambia* 11°37′ S, 29°6′ E **224**
Chignahuapan, *Mex.* 19°48′ N, 98°2′ W **114**
Chignecto Bay 45°35′ N, 64°44′ W **111**
Chignecto, Cape, *Can.* 45°15′ N, 65°39′ W **111**
Chignik, *Alas., U.S.* 56°8′ N, 158°13′ W **106**
Chiguana, *Bol.* 21°7′ S, 67°58′ W **137**
Chiguaza, *Ecua.* 2°2′ S, 77°52′ W **136**
Chigubo, *Mozambique* 22°49′ S, 33°30′ E **227**
Chihertey, *Mongolia* 48°15′ N, 89°30′ E **184**
Chihuahua, *Mex.* 28°35′ N, 106°9′ W **92**
Chihuahua, adm. division, *Mex.* 29°41′ N, 107°45′ W **92**
Chikalda, *India* 21°24′ N, 77°19′ E **188**
Chikhachevo, *Russ.* 57°17′ N, 29°55′ E **166**
Chikhli, *India* 20°21′ N, 76°16′ E **188**
Chikwawa, *Malawi* 16°6′ S, 34°45′ E **224**
Chilac, *Mex.* 18°18′ N, 97°22′ W **114**
Chilako, river, *Can.* 53°31′ N, 124°10′ W **108**
Chilanga, *Malawi* 13°14′ S, 33°31′ E **224**
Chilapa, *Mex.* 17°34′ N, 99°10′ W **114**
Chilas, *Pak.* 35°23′ N, 74°7′ E **186**
Chilcotin, river, *Can.* 52°52′ N, 124°49′ W **108**
Childersburg, *Ala., U.S.* 33°16′ N, 86°22′ W **96**
Childress, *Tex., U.S.* 34°24′ N, 100°13′ W **92**
Chile 36°9′ S, 71°58′ W **134**
Chile Chico, *Chile* 46°31′ S, 71°48′ W **134**
Chile Rise, *South Pacific Ocean* 40°45′ S, 87°42′ W **253**
Chilecito, *Arg.* 29°11′ S, 67°30′ W **134**
Chililabombwe, *Zambia* 12°23′ S, 27°49′ E **224**
Chilko, river, *Can.* 51°45′ N, 124°9′ W **108**
Chilkoot Pass, *Can.* 59°40′ N, 135°15′ W **108**
Chillán, *Chile* 36°36′ S, 72°7′ W **123**
Chillar, *Arg.* 37°20′ S, 59°58′ W **139**
Chillicothe, *Ill., U.S.* 40°54′ N, 89°31′ W **102**
Chillicothe, *Mo., U.S.* 39°47′ N, 93°33′ W **94**
Chillicothe, *Ohio, U.S.* 39°19′ N, 82°59′ W **102**
Chillicothe, *Tex., U.S.* 34°14′ N, 99°30′ W **92**
Chilliwack, *Can.* 49°9′ N, 121°57′ W **100**
Chilliwack Lake, *Can.* 49°2′ N, 121°43′ W **100**
Chilliwack, river, *Can.* 49°5′ N, 121°53′ W **100**
Chilmark, *Mass., U.S.* 41°20′ N, 70°45′ W **104**
Chilo, *India* 27°26′ N, 73°32′ E **186**
Chiloé, Isla Grande de, island, *Chile* 42°1′ S, 76°28′ W **134**
Chilonga, *Zambia* 12°2′ S, 31°20′ E **224**
Chiloquin, *Oreg., U.S.* 42°35′ N, 121°52′ W **90**
Chilpancingo, *Mex.* 17°31′ N, 99°34′ W **114**
Chil'tal'd, Gora, peak, *Russ.* 68°17′ N, 30°50′ E **152**
Chiltern Hills, *U.K.* 51°46′ N, 0°55′ E **162**
Chilton, *Wis., U.S.* 44°1′ N, 88°11′ W **102**
Chiluage, *Angola* 9°30′ S, 21°46′ E **218**
Chilumba (Deep Bay), *Malawi* 10°24′ S, 34°13′ E **224**
Chilung (Keelung), *Taiwan* 25°6′ N, 121°45′ E **198**
Chilwa, Lake, *Malawi* 15°22′ S, 35°26′ E **224**
Chim Berkaouane, *Niger* 15°8′ N, 3°37′ E **222**

Chimacum, Wash., U.S. 48°0' N, 122°46' W 100
Chimaltenango, Guatemala 14°39' N, 90°49' W 115
Chimaltitan, Mex. 21°48' N, 103°46' W 114
Chimán, Pan. 8°42' N, 78°37' W 115
Chimanimani, Zimb. 19°50' S, 32°51' E 224
Chimanimani National Park, Zimb. 19°55' S, 33°12' E 224
Chimay, Belg. 50°2' N, 4°19' E 163
Chimbote, Peru 9°5' S, 78°35' W 130
Chimboy, Uzb. 42°55' N, 59°47' E 180
Chimney Reservoir, Nev., U.S. 41°42' N, 116°53' W 90
Chimney Rock, site, N.C., U.S. 35°24' N, 82°22' W 96
Chimoio, Mozambique 19°8' S, 33°31' E 224
China 33°31' N, 97°47' E 190
China, Mex. 25°41' N, 99°13' W 114
China, Tex., U.S. 30°2' N, 94°21' W 103
China Lake, Calif., U.S. 35°39' N, 117°40' W 101
China Mountain, peak, Calif., U.S. 41°21' N, 122°40' W 90
Chinandega, Nicar. 12°36' N, 87°7' W 115
Chinati Mountains, Tex., U.S. 29°46' N, 104°36' W 92
Chinati Peak, Tex., U.S. 29°54' N, 104°32' W 92
Chinchaga, river, Can. 57°11' N, 119°35' W 108
Chincheros, Peru 13°34' S, 73°44' W 137
Chinchilla de Monte Aragón, Sp. 38°54' N, 1°45' W 164
Chinchón, Sp. 40°8' N, 3°26' W 164
Chincoteague, Va., U.S. 37°55' N, 75°22' W 94
Chincoteague Bay 37°58' N, 76°35' W 80
Chinde, Mozambique 18°36' S, 36°26' E 224
Chindu, China 33°21' N, 97°4' E 188
Chindwin, river, Myanmar 23°37' N, 95°16' E 190
Chinese Camp, Calif., U.S. 37°51' N, 120°27' W 100
Chingola, Zambia 12°36' S, 27°49' E 224
Chingpu, Taiwan 23°28' N, 121°28' E 198
Chinguetti, Mauritania 20°27' N, 12°23' W 222
Chinhoyi, Zimb. 17°23' S, 30°11' E 224
Chiniot, Pak. 31°41' N, 72°57' E 186
Chinipas, Mex. 27°23' N, 108°32' W 112
Chinko, river, Cen. Af. Rep. 5°4' N, 24°12' E 224
Chinle, Ariz., U.S. 36°8' N, 109°33' W 92
Chino, Japan 35°58' N, 138°11' E 201
Chino Valley, Ariz., U.S. 34°44' N, 112°27' W 92
Chinobampo, Mex. 26°18' N, 108°29' W 112
Chinon, Fr. 47°10' N, 0°14' E 150
Chinook, Mont., U.S. 48°17' N, 109°14' W 90
Chinook, Wash., U.S. 46°16' N, 123°56' W 100
Chinsali, Zambia 10°35' S, 32°2' E 224
Chinsong, N. Korea 41°24' N, 126°50' E 200
Chinteche, Malawi 11°52' S, 34°8' E 224
Chiôco, Mozambique 16°26' S, 32°50' E 224
Chioggia, It. 45°12' N, 12°14' E 167
Chipata, Zambia 13°39' S, 32°38' E 224
Chipchase Castle, site, U.K. 55°4' N, 2°18' W 150
Chiperceni, Mold. 47°30' N, 28°50' E 156
Chipewyan Lake, Can. 56°54' N, 113°30' W 108
Chipili, Zambia 10°46' S, 29°3' E 224
Chipinge, Zimb. 20°11' S, 32°36' E 227
Chipiona, Sp. 36°43' N, 6°26' W 164
Chipley, Fla., U.S. 30°46' N, 85°33' W 96
Chipman Lake, lake, Can. 49°58' N, 86°42' W 94
Chipoka, Malawi 13°57' S, 34°30' E 224
Chippenham, U.K. 51°28' N, 2°8' W 162
Chippewa, river, Mich., U.S. 43°37' N, 85°6' W 102
Chipping Campden, U.K. 52°2' N, 1°48' W 162
Chipping Norton, U.K. 51°56' N, 1°33' W 162
Chipping Sodbury, U.K. 51°32' N, 2°24' W 162
Chiquihuitlán, Mex. 17°56' N, 96°50' W 114
Chiquilá, Mex. 21°26' N, 87°18' W 116
Chiquimula, Guatemala 14°49' N, 89°35' W 116
Chiquimulilla, Guatemala 14°5' N, 90°25' W 116
Chiquinquirá, Col. 5°37' N, 73°50' W 136
Chiradzulu, Malawi 15°41' S, 35°13' E 224
Chirala, India 15°49' N, 80°21' E 188
Chiramba, Mozambique 16°58' S, 34°39' E 224
Chiran, Japan 31°20' N, 130°27' E 201
Chirchiq, Uzb. 41°29' N, 69°34' E 197
Chirchirri, Somalia 4°43' N, 44°43' E 218
Chiredzi, Zimb. 21°8' S, 31°48' E 227
Chireno, Tex., U.S. 31°29' N, 94°21' W 103
Chirfa, Niger 20°55' N, 12°19' E 222
Chiribiquete National Park, Col. 0°11' N, 72°51' W 136
Chiribiquete, Sierra de, Col. 1°3' N, 73°33' W 136
Chiricahua Peak, Ariz., U.S. 31°50' N, 109°20' W 92
Chiriguaná, Col. 9°20' N, 73°38' W 136
Chirikof Island, Alas., U.S. 55°35' N, 157°15' W 98
Chirinda, Russ. 67°23' N, 100°23' E 169
Chirk, U.K. 52°56' N, 3°2' W 162
Chirnogeni, Rom. 43°54' N, 28°13' E 158
Chiromo, Malawi 16°33' S, 35°7' E 224
Chiroqchi, Uzb. 39°3' N, 66°36' E 197
Chirpan, Bulg. 42°12' N, 25°19' E 156
Chirripó, Cerro, peak, C.R. 9°29' N, 83°34' W 115
Chirripó, river, C.R. 10°13' N, 83°45' W 116
Chirundu, Zambia 16°2' S, 28°48' E 224
Chisamba, Zambia 14°60' S, 28°22' E 224
Chisasibi, Can. 53°45' N, 79°1' W 106
Ch'ishan, Taiwan 22°56' N, 120°29' E 198
Chishmy, Russ. 54°35' N, 55°21' E 154
Chisholm, Can. 54°54' N, 114°8' W 108
Chisholm, Me., U.S. 44°29' N, 70°13' W 104
Chishui, China 28°34' N, 105°41' E 198
Chisimayu see Kismaayo, Somalia 0°27' N, 42°35' E 224
Chişinău, Mold. 46°56' N, 28°22' E 156
Chişineu Criş, Rom. 46°32' N, 21°32' E 168
Chişinău, Mold. 47°0' N, 28°41' E 156
Chisos Mountains, Tex., U.S. 29°10' N, 103°26' W 92
Chistochina, Alas., U.S. 62°35' N, 144°40' W 98
Chistoozernoye, Russ. 54°40' N, 76°39' E 184
Chistopel'e, Kaz. 52°32' N, 67°15' E 184
Chistopol', Russ. 55°19' N, 50°31' E 154
Chita, Col. 6°11' N, 72°30' W 136
Chita, Russ. 52°8' N, 113°31' E 190
Chitado, Angola 17°18' S, 13°55' E 220
Chitambo, Zambia 12°57' S, 30°38' E 224
Chitato, Angola 7°20' S, 20°47' E 218
Chitek Lake, lake, Can. 52°23' N, 99°49' W 108
Chitembo, Angola 13°33' S, 16°43' E 220
Chitimba, Malawi 10°33' S, 34°10' E 224
Chitipa (Fort Hill), Malawi 9°43' S, 33°14' E 224
Chitokoloki, Zambia 13°50' S, 23°14' E 220
Chitose, Japan 42°47' N, 141°49' E 238
Chitradurga, India 14°13' N, 76°24' E 188
Chitral, Pak. 35°50' N, 71°47' E 186
Chitré, Pan. 7°59' N, 80°26' W 115
Chittagong, Bangladesh 22°19' N, 91°50' E 197
Chittoor, India 13°13' N, 79°6' E 188
Chitungwiza, Zimb. 17°58' S, 31°3' E 224
Chiúchíu, Chile 22°21' S, 68°42' W 137
Chiumbe, river, Angola 8°47' S, 21°10' E 220
Chiume, Angola 15°3' S, 21°12' E 220
Chiúre, Mozambique 13°24' S, 39°58' E 224
Chiusa, It. 46°38' N, 11°32' E 167
Chiusaforte, It. 46°24' N, 13°18' E 167
Chiuta, Lago, lake, Mozambique 14°50' S, 35°36' E 224
Chiva, Sp. 39°28' N, 0°43' E 150
Chivapuri, river, Venez. 6°28' N, 66°48' W 136
Chivasso, It. 45°12' N, 7°52' E 167
Chivay, Peru 15°40' S, 71°35' W 137
Chive, Bol. 12°23' S, 68°37' W 137
Chivhu, Zimb. 19°2' S, 30°52' E 224
Chivilcoy, Arg. 34°56' S, 60°3' W 139
Chiwanda, Tanzania 11°21' S, 34°58' E 224
Chiwefwe, Zambia 13°40' S, 29°27' E 224
Chizdia, Rom. 45°56' N, 21°45' E 168
Chizha, Russ. 67°8' N, 44°18' E 169
Chizu, Japan 35°14' N, 134°12' E 201
Chkalov, Kaz. 53°37' N, 70°25' E 184
Chlef, Alg. 36°9' N, 1°19' E 150
Chloride, Ariz., U.S. 35°24' N, 114°12' W 101
Cho La, pass, China 31°55' N, 98°43' E 188
Choate, Can. 49°27' N, 121°26' W 100
Chocaya, Bol. 20°57' S, 66°23' W 137
Chocó, adm. division, Col. 5°37' N, 77°21' W 136
Chocontá, Col. 5°7' N, 73°39' W 136
Chocorua, N.H., U.S. 43°52' N, 71°14' W 104
Chocorua, Mount, N.H., U.S. 43°57' N, 71°18' W 104
Choctawhatchee Bay 30°15' N, 86°29' W 80
Chodzież, Pol. 52°59' N, 16°55' E 152
Choele Choel, Arg. 39°17' S, 65°40' W 134
Choggar, spring, Mauritania 17°20' N, 13°47' W 222
Chogyuryong Sanmaek, N. Korea 40°18' N, 126°6' E 200
Choique Mahuida, Sierra, Arg. 38°24' S, 67°41' W 134
Choirokoitia, Cyprus 34°47' N, 33°20' E 194
Choiseul, island, Solomon Islands 7°0' S, 157°0' E 242
Choisy, Fr. 48°46' N, 2°24' E 163
Choix, Mex. 26°42' N, 108°22' W 112
Chojna, Pol. 52°57' N, 14°26' E 152
Chojnice, Pol. 53°41' N, 17°33' E 152
Ch'ok'ē, Eth. 11°7' N, 36°46' E 182
Chokoloskee, Fla., U.S. 25°48' N, 81°22' W 105
Chokoyan, Chad 13°20' N, 21°13' E 216
Chókwè, Mozambique 24°31' S, 32°58' E 227
Chokurdakh, Russ. 70°36' N, 148°1' E 160
Cholovo, Russ. 58°57' N, 30°26' E 166
Cholpon-Ata, Kyrg. 42°37' N, 76°59' E 184
Ch'ŏlsan, N. Korea 39°45' N, 124°38' E 200
Choluteca, Hond. 13°17' N, 87°11' W 115
Choma, Zambia 16°49' S, 26°57' E 224
Chon Buri, Thai. 13°25' N, 101°1' E 202
Chonchi, Chile 42°38' S, 73°49' W 134
Chŏnch'ŏn, N. Korea 40°39' N, 126°28' E 200
Chone, Ecua. 0°48' N, 80°4' W 130
Chong Kal, Cambodia 13°58' N, 103°34' E 202
Chong'an, China 27°43' N, 118°2' E 198
Ch'ongch'ŏn, river, N. Korea 39°45' N, 125°51' E 200
Ch'ŏngdan, N. Korea 37°57' N, 125°54' E 200
Ch'ŏngjin, N. Korea 41°45' N, 129°44' E 200
Ch'ŏngjŏng, N. Korea 39°40' N, 125°22' E 200
Chŏngju, N. Korea 39°40' N, 125°12' E 200
Chongming, China 31°39' N, 121°27' E 198
Chongming Dao, island, China 31°22' N, 121°54' E 198
Chongoene, Mozambique 24°60' S, 33°48' E 227
Chongoroi, Angola 13°36' S, 13°58' E 220
Chŏngp'yŏng, N. Korea 39°46' N, 127°23' E 200
Chongqing, China 29°32' N, 106°28' E 198
Chongqing Shi, adm. division, China 31°28' N, 108°25' E 198
Ch'ŏngsŏng, N. Korea 40°21' N, 124°51' E 200
Chongsŏng, N. Korea 42°45' N, 129°49' E 200
Chongxin, China 35°20' N, 107°2' E 198
Chongyi, China 25°40' N, 114°17' E 198
Chongzuo, China 22°22' N, 107°24' E 190
Ch'ŏnnae, N. Korea 39°22' N, 127°11' E 200
Chonogol, Mongolia 45°52' N, 115°23' E 198
Chonos, Archipiélago de los, South Pacific Ocean 44°53' S, 74°46' W 134
Chop, Ukr. 48°25' N, 22°10' E 152
Chopim, river, Braz. 26°16' S, 52°11' W 139
Chorges, Fr. 44°32' N, 6°16' E 167
Chorley, U.K. 53°39' N, 2°38' W 162
Chornobyl', Ukr. 51°16' N, 30°15' E 158
Chornomors'ke, Ukr. 45°29' N, 32°43' E 156
Chornyy Ostriv, Ukr. 49°28' N, 26°46' E 152
Chorotis, Arg. 27°53' S, 61°24' W 139
Ch'osan, N. Korea 40°48' N, 125°46' E 200
Chōshi, Japan 35°44' N, 140°49' E 201
Chosica, Peru 11°54' S, 76°45' W 130
Choszczno, Pol. 53°10' N, 15°25' E 152
Choteau, Mont., U.S. 47°47' N, 112°10' W 90
Choudrant, La., U.S. 32°29' N, 92°32' W 103
Chouikhia, spring, Alg. 27°52' N, 4°16' W 214
Chouzé, Fr. 47°14' N, 0°7' E 150
Chowchilla, Calif., U.S. 37°6' N, 120°17' W 100
Choybalsan, Mongolia 48°4' N, 114°31' E 198
Choyr, Mongolia 46°14' N, 108°44' E 198
Chrea National Park, Alg. 36°39' N, 3°55' E 150
Christchurch, N.Z. 43°33' S, 172°37' E 240
Christensen, Mount, Antarctica 68°2' S, 47°46' E 248
Christiana, S. Af. 27°55' S, 25°9' E 227
Christianshåb see Qasigiannguit, Den. 68°47' N, 51°7' W 106
Christiansted, U.S. 17°45' N, 64°43' W 116
Christie Lake, lake, Can. 56°52' N, 97°30' W 108
Christie, Mount, Can. 62°56' N, 129°59' W 98
Christina Falls, Can. 56°38' N, 123°27' W 108
Christmas, Fla., U.S. 28°32' N, 81°1' W 105
Christmas Lake Valley, Oreg., U.S. 43°19' N, 120°39' W 90
Christmas, Mount, Antarctica 81°50' S, 163°14' E 248
Christopher Lake, Can. 53°33' N, 105°45' W 108
Christoval, Tex., U.S. 31°11' N, 100°29' W 92
Chu, river, Laos 20°3' N, 104°38' E 202
Chuacús, Sierra de, Guatemala 15°13' N, 91°12' W 115
Chualar, Calif., U.S. 36°34' N, 121°32' W 100
Chubb Crater see Cratère du Nouveau-Québec, Can. 61°19' N, 73°41' W 106
Chubu Sangaku National Park, Japan 36°22' N, 137°26' E 201
Chubut, adm. division, Arg. 43°44' S, 70°18' W 134
Chubut, river, Arg. 42°36' S, 69°41' W 134
Chuchi Lake, Can. 55°5' N, 124°57' W 108
Chuckwalla Mountains, Calif., U.S. 33°37' N, 115°29' W 101
Chudovo, Russ. 59°6' N, 31°44' E 152
Chudz'yavr, Russ. 68°17' N, 34°19' E 152
Chugach Mountains, Alas., U.S. 60°40' N, 144°17' W 98
Chuginadak, island, Alas., U.S. 52°52' N, 172°34' W 160
Chugwater, Wyo., U.S. 41°46' N, 104°49' W 90
Chuhuyiv, Ukr. 49°52' N, 36°43' E 158
Chukai, Malaysia 4°15' N, 103°25' E 196
Chukchi Plain, Arctic Ocean 76°29' N, 169°2' W 255
Chukchi Plateau, Arctic Ocean 78°6' N, 163°16' W 255
Chukchi Sea 70°53' N, 178°53' W 173
Chukhloma, Russ. 58°45' N, 42°46' E 154
Chukotskiy, adm. division, Russ. 66°24' N, 160°12' E 160
Chukotskiy, Mys, Russ. 64°15' N, 173°3' W 98
Chukotskiy Poluostrov, Russ. 66°33' N, 176°46' W 98
Chukotskoye Nagor'ye, Russ. 64°32' N, 176°36' E 73
Chula Vista, Calif., U.S. 32°38' N, 117°6' W 101
Chulkovo, Russ. 62°44' N, 88°22' E 169
Chul'man, Russ. 56°53' N, 124°50' E 173
Chulmleigh, U.K. 50°55' N, 3°52' W 162
Chulo, Chile 27°19' S, 70°13' W 132
Chulumani, Bol. 16°23' S, 67°30' W 137
Chulym, Russ. 55°7' N, 80°52' E 184
Chulym, river, Russ. 57°26' N, 88°13' E 169
Chuma, Bol. 15°23' S, 68°56' W 137
Chumakovo, Russ. 55°39' N, 79°10' E 184
Chumerna, peak, Bulg. 42°46' N, 25°53' E 156
Chumikan, Russ. 54°35' N, 135°12' E 190
Chumphon, Thai. 10°29' N, 99°11' E 202
Chumphon Buri, Thai. 15°21' N, 103°14' E 202
Chumpi, Peru 15°7' S, 73°45' W 137
Chuna, river, Russ. 57°48' N, 95°37' E 160
Chun'an, China 29°37' N, 119°9' E 198
Chuncheon, S. Korea 37°52' N, 127°44' E 200
Chundikkulam, Sri Lanka 9°27' N, 80°36' E 188
Chunga, Zambia 15°3' S, 26°58' E 224
Chunghwa, N. Korea 38°52' N, 125°48' E 200
Chungju, S. Korea 36°57' N, 127°56' E 200
Chungli, Taiwan 24°51' N, 121°8' E 198
Chŭngsan, N. Korea 39°5' N, 125°22' E 200
Chunhua, China 34°48' N, 108°36' E 198
Chunian, Pak. 30°57' N, 73°57' E 186
Chunky, Miss., U.S. 32°18' N, 88°55' W 103
Chupa, Russ. 66°16' N, 33°2' E 152
Chuprovo, Russ. 64°14' N, 46°32' E 154
Chuquibamba, Peru 15°53' S, 72°48' W 137
Chuquibambilla, Peru 14°8' S, 72°43' W 137
Chuquicamata, Chile 22°19' S, 68°58' W 137
Chuquisaca, adm. division, Bol. 19°60' S, 65°2' W 137
Chuquito, Peru 15°56' S, 69°54' W 137
Chur, Switz. 46°51' N, 9°31' E 167
Church Point, La., U.S. 30°22' N, 92°14' W 103
Church Stretton, U.K. 52°32' N, 2°49' W 162
Churchill, Can. 58°45' N, 94°9' W 73
Churchill, Cape, Can. 58°48' N, 93°13' W 108
Churchill Falls, Can. 53°31' N, 64°1' W 111
Churchill, Mount, Alas., U.S. 61°24' N, 141°56' W 98
Churchill, Mount, Can. 49°58' N, 123°52' W 100
Churchill Peak, Can. 58°12' N, 125°20' W 108
Churchill Peninsula, Antarctica 66°54' S, 60°58' W 248
Churchill, river, Can. 57°44' N, 95°11' W 108
Churchill, river, Can. 55°7' N, 105°1' W 72
Churchill Rocket Research Range, Can. 58°39' N, 94°6' W 108
Churki, India 23°50' N, 83°10' E 197
Churkino, Russ. 64°3' N, 44°17' E 154
Churuguara, Venez. 10°49' N, 69°33' W 136
Chushul, India 33°34' N, 78°38' E 188
Chuska Mountains, N. Mex., U.S. 36°20' N, 109°6' W 92
Chusovoy, Russ. 58°17' N, 57°51' E 154
Chusovskoy, Russ. 61°10' N, 56°31' E 154
Chust, Uzb. 41°0' N, 71°13' E 197
Chute Island, fall(s), Can. 52°5' N, 78°59' W 110
Chute-des-Passes, Can. 49°52' N, 71°17' W 94
Chutine, river, Can. 57°57' N, 132°47' W 108
Chuuk (Truk Islands), North Pacific Ocean 7°44' N, 152°5' E 242
Chuvashiya, adm. division, Russ. 55°39' N, 46°9' E 154
Chyrvonaya Slabada, Belarus 52°49' N, 27°10' E 154
Ciacova, Rom. 45°30' N, 21°7' E 168
Cianorte, Braz. 23°41' S, 52°42' W 138
Ciasna, Pol. 50°45' N, 18°36' E 152
Cibecue, Ariz., U.S. 34°2' N, 110°28' W 92
Cibinului, Munţii, Rom. 45°33' N, 23°16' E 156
Cibola, Ariz., U.S. 33°18' N, 114°40' W 101
Cibolo, Tex., U.S. 29°32' N, 98°14' W 96
Çiçekdağı, Turk. 39°36' N, 34°24' E 156
Cicero, Ill., U.S. 41°49' N, 87°46' W 102
Ćićevac, Serb. and Mont. 43°42' N, 21°27' E 168
Cicuco, oil field, Col. 9°13' N, 74°36' W 136
Cide, Turk. 41°53' N, 33°0' E 156
Ciechanów, Pol. 52°52' N, 20°37' E 152
Ciego de Ávila, Cuba 21°51' N, 78°46' W 116
Ciego de Ávila, adm. division, Cuba 21°59' N, 78°60' W 116
Ciempozuelos, Sp. 40°9' N, 3°38' W 164
Ciénaga, Col. 10°59' N, 74°14' W 136
Ciénaga de Oro, Col. 8°52' N, 75°38' W 136
Cienagas de Catatumbo National Park, Venez. 9°19' N, 72°17' W 136
Cienfuegos, Cuba 22°10' N, 80°27' W 116
Cienfuegos, adm. division, Cuba 22°17' N, 80°54' W 116
ierp-Gaud, Fr. 42°54' N, 0°38' E 164
Cíes, Illas, islands, North Atlantic Ocean 42°5' N, 9°35' W 150
Cieza, Sp. 38°14' N, 1°25' W 164
Cifuentes, Sp. 40°46' N, 2°37' W 164
Cihanbeyli, Turk. 38°39' N, 32°54' E 156
Cihuatlán, Mex. 19°13' N, 104°36' W 114
Ciiradhame, Somalia 10°25' N, 49°23' E 216
Çikës, Maja e, peak, Alban. 40°11' N, 19°33' E 156
Cilacap, Indonesia 7°39' S, 108°54' E 192
Çıldır, Turk. 41°7' N, 43°7' E 195
Cilibia, Rom. 45°3' N, 27°2' E 156
Cilician Gates, pass, Turk. 37°16' N, 34°47' E 156
Cilnicu, Rom. 44°57' N, 23°5' E 168
Cim, Bosn. and Herzg. 43°22' N, 17°45' E 168
Cima, Calif., U.S. 35°14' N, 115°31' W 101
Cimadle, spring, Somalia 5°14' N, 47°1' E 218
Cimarron, Kans., U.S. 37°48' N, 100°21' W 90
Cimişlia, Mold. 46°31' N, 28°48' E 158
Cimolais, It. 46°17' N, 12°26' E 167
Cimone, Monte, peak, It. 44°11' N, 10°40' E 167
Cîmpeni, Rom. 46°22' N, 23°4' E 168
Çınar, Turk. 37°43' N, 40°27' E 195
Cinaruco, river, Venez. 6°31' N, 68°40' W 136
Cinaruco-Capanaparo National Park, Venez. 6°35' N, 67°42' W 136
Cincar, peak, Bosn. and Herzg. 43°53' N, 17°0' E 168
Cincinnati, Ohio, U.S. 39°6' N, 84°32' W 102
Cinco Balas, Cayos, islands, Caribbean Sea 20°49' N, 80°20' W 116
Cîndrelu, peak, Rom. 45°34' N, 23°44' E 156
Çine, Turk. 37°36' N, 28°1' E 156
Cinema, Can. 53°10' N, 122°31' W 108
Ciney, Belg. 50°18' N, 5°5' E 167
Cinnabar Mountain, Idaho, U.S. 42°58' N, 116°45' W 90
Cintegabelle, Fr. 43°17' N, 1°31' E 164
Cinto, Monte, peak, Fr. 42°22' N, 8°52' E 156
Cintruénigo, Sp. 42°4' N, 1°47' W 164
Ciovîrnăşani, Rom. 44°45' N, 22°52' E 168
ipoal, Braz. 1°40' S, 55°29' W 130
Circeo, Monte, peak, It. 41°13' N, 12°59' E 156
Çirçir, Turk. 40°1' N, 36°49' E 156
Circle, Alas., U.S. 65°43' N, 144°18' W 98
Circle, Mont., U.S. 47°23' N, 105°37' W 90
Circle Hot Springs, Alas., U.S. 65°29' N, 144°39' W 98
Circleville, Ohio, U.S. 39°35' N, 82°56' W 102
Cirebon, Indonesia 6°47' S, 108°25' E 192
Cirencester, U.K. 51°42' N, 1°58' W 162
Cireşu, Rom. 44°49' N, 22°33' E 168
Ciria, Sp. 41°36' N, 1°58' W 164
Ciriè, It. 45°13' N, 7°36' E 167
Ciriquiri, river, Braz. 7°52' S, 65°33' W 132
Cisco, Ill., U.S. 40°0' N, 88°43' W 102
Cisco, Tex., U.S. 32°22' N, 98°59' W 92
Cisco, Utah, U.S. 38°58' N, 109°19' W 90
Cislău, Rom. 45°14' N, 26°22' E 156
Cisne, Ill., U.S. 38°30' N, 88°26' W 102
Cisneros, Col. 6°33' N, 75°5' W 136
Cissna Park, Ill., U.S. 40°33' N, 87°54' W 102
Cistern Point, Bahamas 23°39' N, 77°37' W 96
Citaré, river, Braz. 1°40' N, 55°32' W 130
Citra, Fla., U.S. 29°24' N, 82°8' W 105
Citronelle, Ala., U.S. 31°4' N, 88°14' W 103
Citrusdal, S. Af. 32°32' S, 19°1' E 227
Cittadella, It. 45°39' N, 11°46' E 167
City of Refuge National Historical Park see Pu'uhonua O Hōnaunau National Historical Park, Hawai'i, U.S. 19°24' N, 155°57' W 99
City Trenton, Mo., U.S. 40°3' N, 93°37' W 94
Ciuc, Munţii, Rom. 46°20' N, 25°49' E 156
Ciucaş, peak, Rom. 45°30' N, 25°53' E 156
Ciucea, Rom. 46°57' N, 22°51' E 168
Ciudad Acuña, Mex. 29°17' N, 100°57' W 92
Ciudad Altamirano, Mex. 18°20' N, 100°41' W 114
Ciudad Bolívar, Venez. 8°4' N, 63°34' W 116
Ciudad Bolivia, Venez. 8°19' N, 70°36' W 136
Ciudad Camargo, Mex. 27°40' N, 105°11' W 112
Ciudad Constitución, Mex. 25°0' N, 111°43' W 112
Ciudad Cortés, C.R. 8°58' N, 83°33' W 115
Ciudad de La Habana, adm. division, Cuba 23°6' N, 82°47' W 116
Ciudad del Maíz, Mex. 22°22' N, 99°37' W 114
Ciudad Guayana, Venez. 8°23' N, 62°36' W 130
Ciudad Guerrero, Mex. 28°31' N, 107°31' W 92
Ciudad Guzmán, Mex. 19°41' N, 103°29' W 114
Ciudad Hidalgo, Mex. 14°41' N, 92°11' W 115
Ciudad Hidalgo, Mex. 19°41' N, 100°33' W 114
Ciudad Juárez, Mex. 31°41' N, 106°30' W 92
Ciudad Lerdo, Mex. 25°31' N, 103°30' W 114
Ciudad Madero, Mex. 22°15' N, 97°49' W 114
Ciudad Mante, Mex. 22°44' N, 98°58' W 114
Ciudad Mendoza, Mex. 18°46' N, 97°12' W 114
Ciudad Obregón, Mex. 27°28' N, 109°57' W 112
Ciudad Ojeda, Venez. 10°12' N, 71°21' W 136
Ciudad Piar, Venez. 7°24' N, 63°19' W 130
Ciudad Real, Sp. 38°58' N, 3°56' W 164
Ciudad Sandino, Cuba 22°5' N, 84°10' W 116
Ciudad Valles, Mex. 21°58' N, 98°60' W 114
Ciudad Victoria, Mex. 23°42' N, 99°12' W 114
Ciumeghiu, Rom. 46°44' N, 21°36' E 168
Ciutadella de Menorca, Sp. 39°59' N, 3°50' E 164
Civa Burnu, Turk. 41°23' N, 36°28' E 156
Civitanova Marche, It. 43°18' N, 13°43' E 156
Civitavecchia, It. 42°5' N, 11°47' E 156
Çivril, Turk. 38°18' N, 29°43' E 156
Cixian, China 36°22' N, 114°24' E 198
Cizer, Rom. 47°4' N, 22°53' E 168
Cizre, Turk. 37°19' N, 42°8' E 195
Clach Leathad, peak, U.K. 56°35' N, 4°58' W 150
Clacton on Sea, U.K. 51°47' N, 1°8' E 162
Claiborne, Ala., U.S. 31°32' N, 87°31' W 103
Clairmont, Can. 55°15' N, 118°48' W 108
Claise, river, Fr. 46°47' N, 0°46' E 150
Clallam Bay, Wash., U.S. 48°13' N, 124°16' W 100
Clam Lake, Wis., U.S. 46°10' N, 90°55' W 94
Clan Alpine Mountains, Nev., U.S. 39°27' N, 118°20' W 90
Clanton, Ala., U.S. 32°50' N, 86°38' W 96
Clanwilliam, S. Af. 32°10' S, 18°54' E 227
Clapham, U.K. 54°7' N, 2°24' W 162
Clara, Miss., U.S. 31°35' N, 88°42' W 103
Clara, island, Myanmar 10°45' N, 97°39' E 202
Clara, Punta, Arg. 44°11' S, 65°11' W 134
Claraz, Arg. 37°53' S, 59°18' W 139
Clare, Mich., U.S. 43°48' N, 84°46' W 102
Claremont, N.H., U.S. 43°22' N, 72°21' W 104
Claremore, Okla., U.S. 36°17' N, 95°37' W 96
Clarence, N.Z. 42°9' S, 173°54' E 240
Clarence Island, Antarctica 61°30' S, 54°3' W 134
Clarendon, Ark., U.S. 34°40' N, 91°19' W 96
Clarendon, Tex., U.S. 34°56' N, 100°54' W 92
Clarendon, Vt., U.S. 43°31' N, 72°59' W 104
Clarenville, Can. 48°9' N, 53°59' W 111
Claresholm, Can. 50°1' N, 113°35' W 90
Clarie Coast, Antarctica 67°48' S, 136°42' E 248
Clarinda, Iowa, U.S. 40°43' N, 95°3' W 94
Clarines, Venez. 10°0' N, 65°10' W 136
Clarion, Iowa, U.S. 42°42' N, 93°44' W 94
Clarion, Pa., U.S. 41°12' N, 79°23' W 94
Clarion Fracture Zone, North Pacific Ocean 17°0' N, 130°47' W 252
Clarión, Isla, island, Mex. 18°27' N, 115°40' W 112
Clark, S. Dak., U.S. 44°52' N, 97°45' W 90
Clark Fork, Idaho, U.S. 48°8' N, 116°11' W 108
Clark, Mount, peak, Can. 64°21' N, 124°7' W 98
Clark Mountain, Calif., U.S. 35°31' N, 115°37' W 101
Clark Peak, Colo., U.S. 40°35' N, 105°60' W 90
Clark, Point, Can. 44°4' N, 81°54' W 102
Clarkdale, Ariz., U.S. 34°46' N, 112°3' W 92
Clarke City, Can. 50°10' N, 66°37' W 111
Clarke Island, Austral. 41°8' S, 147°50' E 230
Clarke Range, Austral. 20°29' S, 147°39' E 230
Clarks, La., U.S. 32°0' N, 92°9' W 103
Clark's Harbour, Can. 43°22' N, 65°36' W 82
Clarks Hill Lake, Ga., U.S. 33°51' N, 82°55' W 112
Clarksburg, W. Va., U.S. 39°16' N, 80°22' W 94
Clarksdale, Miss., U.S. 34°11' N, 90°34' W 96
Clarkson, Nebr., U.S. 41°41' N, 97°8' W 90
Clarksville, Mich., U.S. 42°49' N, 85°15' W 102
Clarksville, Tenn., U.S. 36°31' N, 87°21' W 96
Clarksville, Tex., U.S. 33°36' N, 95°4' W 96
Claro, river, Braz. 15°56' S, 51°12' W 138
Claro, river, Braz. 18°8' S, 51°41' W 138
Clary, Fr. 50°4' N, 3°24' E 163
Clatskanie, Oreg., U.S. 46°5' N, 123°13' W 100
Claude, Tex., U.S. 35°6' N, 101°22' W 92
Claveria, Philippines 18°36' N, 121°5' E 203
Clavering Ø, island, Den. 73°50' N, 19°47' W 246
Clawson, Utah, U.S. 39°8' N, 111°6' W 90
Claxton, Ga., U.S. 32°9' N, 81°55' W 96
Clay, Ky., U.S. 37°28' N, 87°50' W 96
Clay Center, Kans., U.S. 39°21' N, 97°8' W 90
Clay City, Ill., U.S. 38°40' N, 88°22' W 102
Clay City, Ind., U.S. 39°16' N, 87°7' W 102
Claymore, oil field, U.K. 58°26' N, 0°26' E 150
Clayoquot Sound 49°13' N, 126°37' W 90
Clayton, Ala., U.S. 31°52' N, 85°27' W 96
Clayton, Ind., U.S. 39°40' N, 86°32' W 102
Clayton, La., U.S. 31°42' N, 91°34' W 103
Clayton, N. Mex., U.S. 36°26' N, 103°11' W 92
Clayton, N.Y., U.S. 44°13' N, 76°5' W 94
Clayton, Okla., U.S. 34°33' N, 95°21' W 96
Clayton Lake, Me., U.S. 46°36' N, 69°34' W 94
Cle Elum, Wash., U.S. 47°11' N, 120°58' W 100
Clear, Alas., U.S. 64°26' N, 148°30' W 73
Clear, Cape, Ire. 51°14' N, 9°28' W 150
Clear Hills, Can. 56°29' N, 119°50' W 108
Clear Lake, S. Dak., U.S. 44°44' N, 96°42' W 90
Clear Lake, Wash., U.S. 48°27' N, 122°14' W 100
Clear Lake, Wis., U.S. 45°14' N, 92°17' W 110
Clear Lake Reservoir, Calif., U.S. 41°45' N, 122°46' W 81
Clearfield, Utah, U.S. 41°6' N, 112°2' W 90
Clearmont, Wyo., U.S. 44°36' N, 106°23' W 90
Clearwater, Fla., U.S. 27°57' N, 82°47' W 105
Clearwater, Wash., U.S. 47°34' N, 124°16' W 100
Clearwater Lake, lake, Can. 52°15' N, 120°43' W 108
Clearwater Lake, lake, Can. 54°4' N, 101°37' W 108
Clearwater Mountains, Idaho, U.S. 45°47' N, 116°18' W 90
Clearwater, river, Can. 51°58' N, 115°52' W 90
Clearwater, river, Can. 56°41' N, 111°1' W 108
Cleburne, Tex., U.S. 32°20' N, 97°23' W 92
Clee Hills, U.K. 52°27' N, 2°39' W 162
Cleethorpes, U.K. 53°32' N, 4°237' W 162
Clemence Massif, Antarctica 72°14' S, 68°11' E 248
Clendenin, W. Va., U.S. 38°28' N, 81°21' W 102
Cleopatra Needle, peak, Philippines 10°8' N, 118°55' E 203
Clermont, Fla., U.S. 28°32' N, 81°46' W 105
Clermont, Fr. 49°22' N, 2°24' E 163

Crow, river, Can. 60°16' N, 125°47' W 108
Crowell, Tex., U.S. 33°57' N, 99°44' W 92
Crowland, U.K. 52°40' N, 0°9' E 162
Crowle, U.K. 53°36' N, 0°51' E 162
Crowley, La., U.S. 30°11' N, 92°23' W 103
Crowleys Ridge, Ark., U.S. 36°2' N, 90°38' W 96
Crown City, Ohio, U.S. 38°35' N, 82°18' W 102
Crown Point, Ind., U.S. 41°24' N, 87°21' W 102
Crown Point, N.Y., U.S. 43°56' N, 73°27' W 104
Crownpoint, N. Mex., U.S. 35°40' N, 108°9' W 92
Crows Landing, Calif., U.S. 37°23' N, 121°6' W 100
Crowsnest Mountain, Can. 49°41' N, 114°40' W 90
Crowsnest Pass, Can. 49°36' N, 114°26' W 90
Croydon, Austral. 18°12' S, 142°14' E 231
Croydon, U.K. 51°22' N, 9°534' W 162
Crozet Basin, Indian Ocean 40°18' S, 59°51' E 254
Crozet Islands, Indian Ocean 46°18' S, 51°8' E 254
Crozet Plateau, Indian Ocean 45°27' S, 50°24' E 254
Crozier, Cape, Antarctica 77°1' S, 179°30' E 248
Crucero, Peru 14°22' S, 70°1' W 137
Cruces, Cuba 22°20' N, 80°16' W 116
Cruces, Punta, Col. 6°28' N, 77°32' W 136
Cruger, Miss., U.S. 33°17' N, 90°14' W 103
Cruillas, Mex. 24°44' N, 98°31' W 114
Cruta, river, Hond. 14°52' N, 83°45' W 115
Cruz Alta, Arg. 33°1' S, 61°48' W 139
Cruz Alta, Braz. 28°40' S, 53°36' W 139
Cruz, Cabo, Cuba 19°51' N, 78°25' W 115
Cruz del Eje, Arg. 30°46' S, 64°48' W 134
Cruz Grande, Chile 29°27' S, 71°19' W 134
Cruzeiro, Braz. 22°38' S, 44°58' W 138
Cruzeiro do Oeste, Braz. 23°45' S, 53°3' W 138
Cruzeiro do Sul, Braz. 7°40' S, 72°42' W 132
Crvenka, Serb. and Mont. 45°37' N, 19°27' E 168
Cry Lake, Can. 58°47' N, 129°13' W 108
Crysdale, Mount, Can. 55°53' N, 123°33' W 108
Crystal, Me., U.S. 46°0' N, 68°23' W 111
Crystal Bay 28°51' N, 82°49' W 105
Crystal City, Can. 49°8' N, 98°58' W 90
Crystal City, Tex., U.S. 28°41' N, 99°50' W 92
Crystal Falls, Mich., U.S. 46°5' N, 88°20' W 94
Crystal Lake, Ill., U.S. 42°14' N, 88°19' W 102
Crystal River, Fla., U.S. 28°54' N, 82°36' W 105
Crystal Springs, Miss., U.S. 31°59' N, 90°21' W 103
Csákvár, Hung. 47°24' N, 18°28' E 168
Csanytelek, Hung. 46°36' N, 20°7' E 168
Csenger, Hung. 47°51' N, 22°41' E 168
Csepel-sziget, Hung. 47°7' N, 18°57' E 168
Cserhát, Hung. 47°51' N, 19°8' E 168
Csesztreg, Hung. 46°42' N, 16°31' E 168
Csongrád, Hung. 46°42' N, 20°8' E 168
Csongrád, adm. division, Hung. 46°12' N, 19°42' E 156
Csorna, Hung. 47°35' N, 17°16' E 156
Csorvás, Hung. 46°38' N, 20°49' E 168
Csóványos, peak, Hung. 47°55' N, 18°56' E 168
Csurgó, Hung. 46°15' N, 17°6' E 168
Cuale, Angola 8°24' S, 16°10' E 220
Cuamba, Mozambique 14°50' S, 36°33' E 224
Cuando Cubango, adm. division, Angola 15°46' S, 17°58' E 220
Cuando, river, Angola 15°31' S, 21°12' E 220
Cuangar, Angola 17°35' S, 18°39' E 220
Cuango, Angola 6°17' S, 16°39' E 218
Cuango, Angola 9°10' S, 18°2' E 218
Cuanza Norte, adm. division, Angola 8°42' S, 14°20' E 218
Cuanza Sul, adm. division, Angola 10°29' S, 13°38' E 220
Cuaró, Uru. 31°55' S, 55°11' W 139
Cuaró, Uru. 30°37' S, 56°55' W 139
Cuatir, river, Angola 17°10' S, 18°18' E 220
Cuatro Ciénegas, Mex. 26°59' N, 102°6' W 82
Cuatro Ojos, Bol. 16°52' S, 63°38' W 137
Cuauhtémoc, Mex. 19°19' N, 103°36' W 114
Cuauhtémoc, Mex. 28°24' N, 106°52' W 112
Cuautepec, Mex. 20°1' N, 98°17' W 114
Cuautitlán, Mex. 19°26' N, 104°24' W 114
Cuautla, Mex. 18°47' N, 98°56' W 114
Cub Hills, peak, Can. 54°13' N, 104°49' W 108
Cuba 21°4' N, 77°43' W 116
Cuba, Ala., U.S. 32°26' N, 88°23' W 103
Cuba, Port. 38°9' N, 7°55' W 150
Cubabi, Cerro, peak, Mex. 31°42' N, 112°54' W 92
Cubagua, Isla, island, Venez. 10°41' N, 64°50' W 116
Çubuk, Turk. 40°14' N, 33°2' E 156
Cuchi, Angola 14°41' S, 16°54' E 220
Cuchillo Parado, Mex. 29°27' N, 104°52' W 92
Cuchivero, river, Venez. 6°28' N, 65°56' W 136
Cuchumatanes, Sierra los, Guatemala 15°39' N, 91°48' W 115
Cucui, Braz. 1°7' N, 66°49' W 136
Cucumbi, Angola 10°17' S, 19°3' E 220
Cucurpé, Mex. 30°20' N, 110°43' W 92
Cúcuta, Col. 7°54' N, 72°30' W 136
Cudahy, Wis., U.S. 42°57' N, 87°52' W 102
Cuddalore, India 11°44' N, 79°45' E 188
Cuddapah, India 14°27' N, 78°51' E 188
Cuduyari, river, Col. 1°24' N, 70°41' W 136
Cudworth, Can. 52°29' N, 105°45' W 108
Cuéllar, Sp. 41°23' N, 4°19' W 150
Cuello, ruin(s), Belize 18°3' N, 88°45' W 115
Cuenca, Ecua. 2°58' S, 79°3' W 130
Cuenca, Sp. 40°4' N, 2°8' W 164
Cuenca, Serranía de, Sp. 39°38' N, 1°55' W 164
Cuencamé, Mex. 24°51' N, 103°43' W 114
Cuernavaca, Mex. 18°52' N, 99°18' W 114
Cuero, Tex., U.S. 29°4' N, 97°18' W 96
Cuervo, N. Mex., U.S. 35°2' N, 104°24' W 92
Cuervos, Mex. 32°37' N, 114°52' W 101
Cuetzalan, Mex. 20°2' N, 97°31' W 114
Cuevas, Cerro, peak, Mex. 29°10' N, 111°29' W 92
Cuevas de Altamira, site, Sp. 43°22' N, 4°10' W 164
Cuevas de Vinromà, Sp. 40°18' N, 0°6' E 164
Cuevita, Col. 5°28' N, 77°27' W 136
Cuevitas, Chile 23°26' S, 69°60' W 134
Cuevo, Bol. 20°27' S, 63°33' W 137
Cugir, Rom. 45°49' N, 23°21' E 168
Cuiabá, Braz. 15°33' S, 56°7' W 132
Cuiabá, river, Braz. 17°6' S, 56°39' W 132
Cuiari, Braz. 1°28' N, 68°11' W 136
Cuicatlán, Mex. 17°47' N, 96°58' W 114
Cuilcagh, peak, U.K. 54°11' N, 7°55' W 150
Cuillin Hills, U.K. 57°14' N, 6°18' W 150
Cuilo, Angola 7°42' S, 19°23' E 218
Cuiluan, China 47°42' N, 128°42' E 198
Cuima, Angola 13°18' S, 15°38' E 220
Cuio, Angola 12°60' S, 12°58' E 220
Cuito Cuanavale, Angola 15°9' S, 19°8' E 220
Cuito, river, Angola 14°7' S, 18°39' E 220
Cuitzeo, Mex. 19°57' N, 101°8' W 114
Cuiuni, river, Braz. 1°19' S, 64°10' W 130
Cuizăuca, Mold. 47°36' N, 28°49' E 156
Cujmir, Rom. 44°13' N, 22°56' E 168
Çukurca, Turk. 37°14' N, 43°30' E 195
Cùl Mór, peak, U.K. 58°2' N, 5°13' W 150
Culasi, Philippines 11°25' N, 122°5' E 203
Culbertson, Nebr., U.S. 40°13' N, 100°51' W 90
Culebra, Col. 6°6' N, 69°25' W 136
Culebra, island, P.R., U.S. 18°0' N, 65°0' W 118
Culebra, Sierra de la, Sp. 41°47' N, 6°49' W 150
Culfa, Azerb. 38°58' N, 45°38' E 195
Culgoa, river, Austral. 29°14' S, 147°34' E 230
Culiacán, Mex. 24°44' N, 107°34' W 112
Culiacán, Cerro, peak, Mex. 20°18' N, 101°3' W 114
Culion, Philippines 11°53' N, 119°59' E 203
Culiseu, river, Braz. 13°23' S, 53°44' W 130
Cúllar-Baza, Sp. 37°34' N, 2°34' W 164
Cullera, Sp. 39°9' N, 0°16' E 164
Cullman, Ala., U.S. 34°12' N, 86°54' W 112
Culloden Moor, battle, U.K. 57°26' N, 4°17' W 150
Cullom, Ill., U.S. 40°52' N, 88°16' W 102
Cullompton, U.K. 50°51' N, 3°24' W 162
Culuene, river, Braz. 15°7' S, 54°17' W 132
Culver, Ind., U.S. 41°12' N, 86°26' W 102
Culverden, N.Z. 42°48' S, 172°50' E 240
Cumaná, Venez. 10°26' N, 64°11' W 116
Cumari, Braz. 18°18' S, 48°11' W 138
Cumaría, Peru 9°54' S, 73°56' W 137
Cumberland, Md., U.S. 39°39' N, 78°46' W 94
Cumberland, Wis., U.S. 45°31' N, 92°1' W 110
Cumberland House, Can. 53°56' N, 102°17' W 108
Cumberland Island, Ga., U.S. 30°47' N, 81°23' W 112
Cumberland Island National Seashore, Ga., U.S. 30°38' N, 81°26' W 96
Cumberland Islands, Coral Sea 20°47' S, 149°43' E 230
Cumberland, Lake, Ky., U.S. 36°52' N, 85°35' W 94
Cumberland Peninsula, Can. 66°44' N, 73°46' W 106
Cumberland Plateau, North America 34°11' N, 87°21' W 96
Cumberland Point, Mich., U.S. 47°38' N, 89°17' W 110
Cumberland Sound 64°31' N, 72°15' W 73
Cumbrera, Cerro, peak, Chile 48°6' S, 72°55' W 134
Cumbres de Majalca National Park see 11, Mex. 28°57' N, 106°43' W 112
Cumbres del Ajusco National Park see 10, Mex. 19°12' N, 99°24' W 112
Cumbrian Mountains, U.K. 54°43' N, 3°25' W 162
Cumming, Mount, Antarctica 76°35' S, 125°8' W 248
Cummins Peak, Oreg., U.S. 44°12' N, 124°4' W 90
Cúmpas, Mex. 29°58' N, 109°47' W 92
Çumra, Turk. 37°33' N, 32°47' E 156
Cumshewa Head, Can. 53°4' N, 131°42' W 108
Cumuruxatiba, Braz. 17°6' S, 39°12' W 132
Cunani, Braz. 2°53' N, 51°8' W 130
Cunãré, Col. 0°51' N, 72°35' W 136
Cunaviche, Venez. 7°19' N, 67°27' W 136
Cunco, Chile 38°55' S, 72°1' W 134
Cundinamarca, adm. division, Col. 4°8' N, 74°27' W 136
Cunene, adm. division, Angola 16°40' S, 13°52' E 220
Cunene, river, Angola 14°3' S, 15°29' E 220
Cuneo, It. 44°22' N, 7°32' E 167
Cuney, Tex., U.S. 32°1' N, 95°25' W 103
Cunhinga, Angola 12°15' S, 16°46' E 220
Cunjamba, Angola 15°23' S, 20°4' E 220
Cunningham, Tex., U.S. 33°24' N, 95°22' W 103
Cunningham Landing, Can. 60°4' N, 112°8' W 108
Cunningham Mountain, Ariz., U.S. 33°33' N, 114°23' W 101
Cuokkarassa, peak, Nor. 69°57' N, 24°22' E 152
Cuorgnè, It. 45°23' N, 7°38' E 167
Cupar, U.K. 56°19' N, 3°1' W 150
Cupcini, Mold. 48°4' N, 27°21' E 152
Cupica, Col. 6°44' N, 77°32' W 136
Cúpula, Pico, peak, Mex. 24°45' N, 110°50' W 112
Curaçá, Braz. 9°1' S, 39°52' W 132
Curaçao, island, Netherlands 12°0' N, 69°0' W 118
Curaguara de Carangas, Bol. 17°57' S, 68°23' W 137
Curale, Eth. 7°38' N, 44°21' E 218
Curanilahue, Chile 37°28' S, 73°25' W 134
Curanja, river, Peru 10°6' S, 71°39' W 137
Curaray, river, Ecua.-Peru 1°24' S, 77°1' W 136
Curare, Venez. 2°13' N, 66°29' W 136
Curcubăta, peak, Rom. 46°27' N, 22°37' E 168
Cure, Eth. 5°47' N, 36°28' E 224
Curiapo, Venez. 8°33' N, 61°2' W 116
Curichi, Bol. 18°43' S, 63°17' W 137
Curicó, Chile 34°57' S, 71°15' W 134
Curicuriari, river, Braz. 0°32' N, 68°34' W 136
Curicuriari, Serra, peak, Braz. 0°22' N, 66°57' W 136
Curiplaya, Col. 0°16' N, 74°52' W 136
Curitiba, Braz. 25°25' S, 49°18' W 138
Curium, ruin(s), Cyprus 34°40' N, 32°50' E 194
Curley Cut Cays, North Atlantic Ocean 23°20' N, 78°3' W 116
Currais Novos, Braz. 6°17' S, 36°32' W 132
Curralinho, Braz. 1°47' S, 49°50' W 130
Currant Mountain, Nev., U.S. 38°53' N, 115°30' W 90
Currant, pass, Colo., U.S. 38°51' N, 105°39' W 90
Curraun Peninsula, Ire. 53°50' N, 10°32' W 150
Currie Lake, lake, Can. 57°45' N, 98°3' W 108
Curtici, Rom. 46°21' N, 21°18' E 168
Curtis, Nebr., U.S. 40°38' N, 100°31' W 90
Curtis Group, islands, Bass Strait 39°55' S, 144°45' E 231
Curtis Island, Austral. 24°5' S, 150°2' E 230
Curuá, Braz. 2°25' S, 54°4' W 130
Curuá, Ilha, island, Braz. 0°52' N, 50°57' W 130
Curuá, river, Braz. 0°27' N, 54°52' W 130
Curuaés, river, Braz. 7°58' S, 54°33' W 130
Curuçá, river, South America 5°12' S, 71°29' W 132
Curug, Serb. and Mont. 45°28' N, 20°3' E 168
Curupaiti, Braz. 3°25' S, 68°53' W 136
Curupira, Serra, Braz. 1°36' N, 64°19' W 130
Cururu, river, Braz. 8°4' S, 57°21' W 130
Cururupu, Braz. 1°47' S, 44°54' W 132
Curutú, Cerro, peak, Venez. 4°16' N, 63°45' W 130
Curuzú Cuatiá, Arg. 29°46' S, 58°3' W 139
Curvelo, Braz. 18°45' S, 44°27' W 138
Cusapín, Pan. 9°10' N, 81°53' W 115
Cusárare, Mex. 27°33' N, 107°33' W 82
Cusco, Peru 13°33' S, 71°57' W 137
Cusco, adm. division, Peru 13°5' S, 72°47' W 137
Cushing, Okla., U.S. 35°57' N, 96°45' W 96
Cushing, Tex., U.S. 31°48' N, 94°50' W 103
Cushing, Mount, Can. 57°36' N, 126°57' W 108
Cushman, Lake, Wash., U.S. 47°29' N, 123°26' W 100
Cusiana, river, Col. 4°44' N, 72°25' W 136
Cusihuiriachic, Mex. 28°14' N, 106°51' W 92
Cusset, Fr. 46°8' N, 3°27' E 150
Cusson, Pointe, Can. 60°11' N, 77°35' W 106
Custer, Mich., U.S. 43°56' N, 86°13' W 102
Custer, Mont., U.S. 46°7' N, 107°33' W 90
Custer, Wash., U.S. 48°54' N, 122°39' W 100
Cut Bank, Mont., U.S. 48°37' N, 112°20' W 90
Cut Beaver Lake, Can. 53°47' N, 103°9' W 108
Cut Knife, Can. 52°45' N, 109°1' W 108
Cut Off, La., U.S. 29°32' N, 90°22' W 103
Cutbank, river, Can. 54°21' N, 119°20' W 108
Cutchogue, N.Y., U.S. 41°0' N, 72°30' W 104
Cutler, Calif., U.S. 36°31' N, 119°18' W 100
Cutler Ridge, Fla., U.S. 25°33' N, 80°22' W 105
Cutlerville, Mich., U.S. 42°49' N, 85°40' W 102
Cuttack, India 20°25' N, 85°52' E 188
Cuttingsville, Vt., U.S. 43°29' N, 72°53' W 104
Cuttyhunk, Mass., U.S. 41°25' N, 70°57' W 104
Cuttyhunk Island, Mass., U.S. 41°25' N, 71°15' W 104
Cutzamala, Mex. 18°26' N, 100°36' W 114
Cuveşdia, Rom. 45°57' N, 21°42' E 168
Cuvier Plateau, Indian Ocean 24°32' S, 108°34' E 254
Cuxhaven, Ger. 53°51' N, 8°42' E 150
Cuya, Chile 19°12' S, 70°12' W 137
Cuyahoga Falls, Ohio, U.S. 41°9' N, 81°29' W 102
Cuyama, Calif., U.S. 34°56' N, 119°38' W 100
Cuyapo, Philippines 15°47' N, 120°39' E 203
Cuyuna Range, Minn., U.S. 46°24' N, 93°60' W 90
Cuyuni, river, Guyana 6°50' N, 60°6' W 130
Cvrsnica, Bosn. and Herzg. 43°31' N, 17°25' E 168
Cwmbran, U.K. 51°38' N, 3°1' W 162
Cybur, Miss., U.S. 30°36' N, 89°46' W 103
Cyclades see Kikládes, islands, Mediterranean Sea 36°31' N, 24°28' E 156
Cygnet Lake, lake, Can. 56°45' N, 95°21' W 108
Cynthiana, Ky., U.S. 38°23' N, 84°17' W 94
Cypress Hills, Can. 49°34' N, 110°46' W 80
Cypress Lake, Can. 49°29' N, 109°47' W 90
Cyprus 35°2' N, 33°17' E 194
Cyrenaica, region, Africa 26°14' N, 24°46' E 180
Cyrene see Shaḥḥāt, Lib. 32°50' N, 21°50' E 216
Cyrus Field Bay 62°29' N, 66°6' W 106
Czech Republic 49°41' N, 14°5' E 152
Czempiń, Pol. 52°8' N, 16°46' E 152
Czeremcha, Pol. 52°31' N, 23°18' E 154
Czersk, Pol. 53°47' N, 17°58' E 152
Czerwin, Pol. 52°55' N, 21°44' E 152
Częstochowa, Pol. 50°48' N, 19°6' E 152
Czyżewo, Pol. 52°48' N, 22°17' E 152

D

Da (Black), river, Vietnam 21°11' N, 104°8' E 202
Da Lat, Vietnam 11°56' N, 108°26' E 202
Da Nang, Vietnam 16°2' N, 108°12' E 202
Da Qaidam, China 37°52' N, 95°25' E 188
Daaden, Ger. 50°43' N, 7°58' E 167
Da'an, China 45°28' N, 124°20' E 198
Dabaga, Tanzania 8°5' S, 35°55' E 224
Ḑab'ah, Jordan 31°35' N, 36°2' E 194
Dabajuro, Venez. 11°2' N, 70°42' W 136
Dabakala, Côte d'Ivoire 8°21' N, 4°27' W 222
Dabas, Hung. 47°10' N, 19°20' E 168
Dabat, Eth. 12°58' N, 37°42' E 182
Dabatou, Guinea 11°49' N, 10°41' W 222
Dabeiba, Col. 7°2' N, 76°17' W 136
Dabhoi, India 22°5' N, 73°27' E 186
Dabilja, Maced. 41°27' N, 22°42' E 168
Daboji, China 42°57' N, 126°51' E 200
Dabola, Guinea 10°44' N, 11°9' W 222
Daborow, Somalia 6°21' N, 48°43' E 218
Dabou, Côte d'Ivoire 5°19' N, 4°23' W 222
Daboya, Ghana 9°31' N, 1°26' W 222
Dabqig see Uxin Qi, China 38°24' N, 108°59' E 198
Dabsan Hu, lake, China 37°11' N, 94°22' E 188
Dâbûd, Egypt 24°34' N, 32°55' E 182
Dabuli, Eth. 7°48' N, 41°8' E 224
Dabus, river, Eth. 9°44' N, 34°54' E 224
Dabwali, India 29°57' N, 74°45' E 186
Dac To, Vietnam 14°43' N, 107°47' E 202
Dachang, China 24°50' N, 107°31' E 198
Dachigam National Park, India 34°9' N, 74°57' E 186
Daday, Turk. 41°30' N, 33°26' E 156
Ḑaḑḑa'to, Djibouti 12°20' N, 42°46' E 182
Dade City, Fla., U.S. 28°21' N, 82°12' W 105
Dadhar, Pak. 29°30' N, 67°41' E 186
Dadianzi, China 42°52' N, 128°17' E 200
Dadiya, Nig. 9°36' N, 11°26' E 222
Ḑadnah, U.A.E. 25°32' N, 56°16' E 196
Dadu, Pak. 26°43' N, 67°50' E 186
Daegu (Taegu), S. Korea 35°51' N, 128°37' E 200
Daejeon (Taejŏn), S. Korea 36°18' N, 127°27' E 200
Dăeni, Rom. 44°50' N, 28°6' E 156
Daet, Philippines 14°7' N, 122°56' E 203
Dafang, China 27°8' N, 105°33' E 198
Dafeng, China 33°15' N, 120°29' E 198
Dafoe, Can. 51°44' N, 104°31' W 90
Dafoe Lake, lake, Can. 55°38' N, 96°50' W 108
Dafoe, river, Can. 55°44' N, 95°16' W 108
Daga Medo, Eth. 7°57' N, 42°59' E 218
Daga Post, Sudan 9°11' N, 33°57' E 224
Dagaio, Eth. 6°10' N, 40°42' E 224
Dagana, Senegal 16°30' N, 15°33' W 222
Dagda, Latv. 56°5' N, 27°30' E 166
Dagestan, adm. division, Russ. 42°34' N, 46°10' E 195
Dagestanskiye Ogni, Russ. 42°4' N, 48°17' E 195
Daggett, Calif., U.S. 34°51' N, 116°54' W 101
Daggett, Mich., U.S. 45°27' N, 87°36' W 94
Dagö see Hiiumaa, island, Est. 58°49' N, 21°20' E 166
Dagongcha, China 39°44' N, 96°6' E 188
Daguijiazi, China 42°18' N, 123°24' E 200
Dagupan, Philippines 16°2' N, 120°19' E 203
Dagzê, China 29°40' N, 91°19' E 197
Dahaneh-ye Ghowri, Afghan. 35°54' N, 68°33' E 186
Dahlak Archipelago, Red Sea 16°13' N, 39°29' E 182
Dahlak Kebir, island, Eritrea 15°28' N, 39°33' E 182
Dahmouni, Alg. 35°24' N, 1°28' E 150
Dahn, Ger. 49°8' N, 7°46' E 163
Dahod, India 22°48' N, 74°15' E 188
Dahongliutan, China 36°0' N, 79°19' E 188
Dahra, Senegal 15°22' N, 15°29' W 222
Dahra, oil field, Lib. 29°27' N, 17°37' E 216
Dahuofang Shuiku, lake, China 41°55' N, 123°58' E 200
Daḥy, Nafūd ad, Saudi Arabia 21°51' N, 45°20' E 182
Daïet Abeidi, spring, Mali 21°42' N, 5°43' W 222
Daigo, Japan 36°45' N, 140°20' E 201
Dailekh, Nepal 28°50' N, 81°44' E 197
Daimiel, Sp. 39°3' N, 3°38' W 164
Daingerfield, Tex., U.S. 33°1' N, 94°44' W 103
Dainkog, China 32°30' N, 97°52' E 188
Daintree River National Park, Austral. 16°21' S, 144°50' E 238
Daiō, Japan 34°17' N, 136°53' E 201
Dair, Jebel ed, peak, Sudan 12°27' N, 30°36' E 218
Daireaux, Arg. 36°37' S, 61°42' W 139
Dairen see Dalian, China 38°56' N, 121°33' E 198
Dairûţ, Egypt 27°35' N, 30°47' E 180
Daisen-Oki National Park, Japan 35°16' N, 133°3' E 201
Daisetta, Tex., U.S. 30°6' N, 94°39' W 103
Daitō, Japan 35°18' N, 132°58' E 201
Daitō Islands, Philippine Sea 24°48' N, 129°27' E 190
Daixian, China 39°3' N, 112°55' E 198
Dajarra, Austral. 21°41' S, 139°34' E 231
Dajt, Mal, peak, Alban. 41°21' N, 19°50' E 156
Dajt National Park, Alban. 41°20' N, 19°52' E 156
Dakar, Senegal 14°39' N, 17°13' W 222
Daketa, river, Eth. 8°52' N, 42°24' E 224
Dakhfili, Sudan 19°15' N, 32°32' E 182
Dakhla, El Wâhât el, Egypt 25°35' N, 28°10' E 180
Dakingari, Nig. 11°38' N, 4°4' E 222
Dakoank, India 7°4' N, 93°45' E 188
Dakoro, Niger 14°35' N, 6°48' E 222
Đakovica, Serb. and Mont. 42°23' N, 20°26' E 168
Đakovo, Croatia 45°18' N, 18°24' E 168
Dákura, Nicar. 14°22' N, 83°14' W 115
Dakwa, Dem. Rep. of the Congo 3°59' N, 26°29' E 224
Dala, Angola 11°5' S, 20°14' E 220
Dalaba, Guinea 10°41' N, 12°18' W 222
Dalai Nur, lake, China 43°13' N, 116°7' E 198
Dalandzadgad, Mongolia 43°33' N, 104°23' E 198
Dalane, region, Europe 58°31' N, 6°0' E 150
Dalarö, Sw. 59°8' N, 18°23' E 166
Dalbandin, Pak. 28°55' N, 64°27' E 182
Dalbosjön, lake, Nor. 58°41' N, 12°30' E 152
Dale, Nor. 60°35' N, 5°47' E 152
Dale, Nor. 61°27' N, 7°25' E 152
Dale Country, region, Europe 53°35' N, 1°46' W 162
Dale Hollow Lake, U.S. 36°33' N, 86°33' W 82
Dalen, Nor. 59°27' N, 7°58' E 152
Dalet, Myanmar 19°59' N, 93°57' E 188
Daleville, Miss., U.S. 32°33' N, 88°41' W 103
Dalfors, Nor. 61°12' N, 15°24' E 152
Dalgaranga Hill, Austral. 27°54' S, 116°54' E 230
Dalhart, Tex., U.S. 36°3' N, 102°32' W 92
Dalhousie, Cape, Can. 70°7' N, 132°37' W 98
Dali, China 34°50' N, 109°57' E 198
Dali, China 25°40' N, 99°58' E 190
Dali, Cyprus 35°1' N, 33°25' E 194
Dalian (Dairen), China 38°56' N, 121°33' E 198
Dalías, Sp. 36°49' N, 2°52' W 164
Dalidag, peak, Azerb. 39°54' N, 46°0' E 195
Dalizi, China 41°44' N, 126°48' E 200
Dalj, Croatia 45°29' N, 18°57' E 168
Dall Island, Alas., U.S. 54°35' N, 135°26' W 106
Dall, river, Can. 58°41' N, 127°56' W 108
Dallas, Oreg., U.S. 44°54' N, 123°21' W 82
Dallas, Tex., U.S. 32°46' N, 96°48' W 92
Dallas Naval Air Station, Tex., U.S. 32°41' N, 96°60' W 92
Dalmā, island, U.A.E. 24°34' N, 51°58' E 182
Dalmas, Lac, lake, Can. 53°27' N, 72°16' W 111
Dalmatia, region, Adriatic Sea 42°51' N, 17°2' E 168
Dal'negorsk, Russ. 44°34' N, 135°35' E 238
Dal'nerechensk, Russ. 45°53' N, 133°51' E 190
Daloa, Côte d'Ivoire 6°48' N, 6°27' W 222
Dalol, Eth. 14°8' N, 40°15' E 182
Dalqān, spring, Saudi Arabia 24°17' N, 45°32' E 182
Dalsbruk (Taalintehdas), Fin. 60°1' N, 22°31' E 166
Daltenganj, India 24°1' N, 84°8' E 197
Dalton, Ga., U.S. 34°45' N, 84°57' W 96
Dalton, Mass., U.S. 42°28' N, 73°10' W 104
Dalton, Nebr., U.S. 41°24' N, 102°59' W 90
Dalton, Wis., U.S. 43°38' N, 89°12' W 102
Dalton in Furness, U.K. 54°9' N, 3°11' W 162
Dalton, Kap, Den. 69°11' N, 24°2' W 246
Dalum, Ger. 52°35' N, 7°13' E 163
Dalupiri, island, Philippines 19°10' N, 120°43' E 198
Dalwallinu, Austral. 30°16' S, 116°41' E 231
Daly City, Calif., U.S. 37°42' N, 122°29' W 100
Daly Lake, lake, Can. 56°26' N, 106°4' W 108
Daly, river, Austral. 13°35' S, 130°35' E 231
Daly River Wildlife Sanctuary, Austral. 13°42' S, 129°44' E 238
Daly Waters, Austral. 16°15' S, 133°20' E 231
Dam Doi, Vietnam 9°2' N, 105°10' E 202
Dam Gamad, Sudan 13°14' N, 27°26' E 226
Damagarim, region, Africa 14°13' N, 7°35' E 222
Daman and Diu, adm. division, India 20°18' N, 71°51' E 188
Daman (Damão), India 20°25' N, 72°52' E 186
Damanava, Belarus 52°49' N, 25°30' E 152
Damane, spring, Mauritania 19°20' N, 14°33' W 222
Damanhûr, Egypt 31°1' N, 30°22' E 180
Damão see Daman, India 20°25' N, 72°52' E 186
Damar, island, Indonesia 7°28' S, 127°44' E 192
Damara, Cen. Af. Rep. 4°57' N, 18°43' E 218
Damaraland, region, Africa 21°4' S, 15°26' E 227
Damas Cays, North Atlantic Ocean 23°23' N, 80°1' W 116
Damasak, Nig. 13°8' N, 12°33' E 216
Damascus see Dimashq, Syr. 33°30' N, 36°14' E 194
Damaturu, Nig. 11°44' N, 11°55' E 222
Damāvand, Qolleh-ye, peak, Iran 35°58' N, 52°0' E 180
Damba, Angola 6°41' S, 15°7' E 218
Dambarta, Nig. 12°26' N, 8°31' E 222
Damboa, Nig. 11°10' N, 12°49' E 216
Damergou, region, Africa 14°49' N, 9°0' E 222
Dāmghān, Iran 36°11' N, 54°19' E 180
Damietta see Dumyât, Egypt 31°25' N, 31°49' E 180
Daming, China 36°15' N, 115°8' E 198
Damingzhen, China 42°32' N, 123°40' E 200
Damīr Qābū, Syr. 36°57' N, 41°52' E 195
Dāmiyā, Jordan 32°6' N, 35°33' E 194
Dammarie, Fr. 48°20' N, 1°29' E 163
Dammartin-en-Goële, Fr. 49°2' N, 2°40' E 163
Damme, Ger. 52°31' N, 8°12' E 163
Damnjane, Serb. and Mont. 42°17' N, 20°31' E 168
Damongo, Ghana 9°4' N, 1°49' W 222
Damour, Leb. 33°43' N, 35°27' E 194
Damous, Alg. 36°32' N, 1°43' E 150
Dampier, Austral. 20°40' S, 116°43' E 231
Dampier Archipelago, Indian Ocean 20°18' S, 117°11' E 230
Dampier Land, Austral. 17°35' S, 122°12' E 230
Dampierre, Fr. 48°32' N, 4°21' E 163
Damqawt, Yemen 16°35' N, 52°49' E 182
Damsarkhū, Syr. 35°32' N, 35°46' E 194
Damvillers, Fr. 49°20' N, 5°23' E 163
Damxung, China 30°35' N, 91°9' E 197
Damyang, S. Korea 35°18' N, 126°59' E 200
Dan, Israel 33°13' N, 35°38' E 194
Dan Gulbi, Nig. 11°35' N, 6°16' E 222
Dan, river, N.C., U.S. 36°35' N, 79°20' W 80
Dana, Ind., U.S. 39°48' N, 87°30' W 102
Ḑānā, Jordan 30°40' N, 35°36' E 194
Dana, Mount, Calif., U.S. 37°53' N, 119°16' W 100
Dana Point, Calif., U.S. 33°28' N, 117°43' W 101
Danané, Côte d'Ivoire 7°8' N, 8°9' W 222
Danbury, Conn., U.S. 41°23' N, 73°28' W 104
Danbury, Iowa, U.S. 42°13' N, 95°44' W 90
Danbury, N.H., U.S. 43°31' N, 71°53' W 104
Danbury, Tex., U.S. 29°13' N, 95°21' W 103
Danby, Vt., U.S. 43°20' N, 72°60' W 104
Dancheng, China 33°37' N, 115°14' E 198
Danco Coast, Antarctica 64°5' S, 61°55' W 134
Dandéla, Guinea 10°55' N, 8°24' W 222
Dandeldhura, Nepal 29°16' N, 80°34' E 197
Dandong, China 40°10' N, 124°24' E 200
Dandurand, Lac, lake, Can. 47°48' N, 75°9' W 94
Dane, Can. 48°5' N, 80°1' W 94
Danfa, Mali 14°9' N, 7°30' W 222
Danfeng, China 33°42' N, 110°24' E 198
Danfina, Mali 11°2' N, 7°9' W 222
Danfort Hills, Colo., U.S. 40°20' N, 108°25' W 90
Danforth, Me., U.S. 45°39' N, 67°52' W 94
Dangara, Taj. 38°15' N, 69°16' E 197

Danger Point, S. Af. 34°53′ S, 19°1′ E 227
Dangé-Saint-Romain, Fr. 46°56′ N, 0°37′ E 150
Dangila, Eth. 11°15′ N, 36°52′ E 182
Dangjin Shankou, pass, China 39°17′ N, 94°15′ E 188
Dango, Sudan 9°58′ N, 24°43′ E 224
Dango, Qoz, Sudan 10°29′ N, 24°11′ E 224
Dangrek Range, Thai. 14°34′ N, 103°21′ E 202
Dangriga, Belize 16°57′ N, 88°15′ W 115
Dangshan, China 34°27′ N, 116°21′ E 198
Dangtu, China 31°34′ N, 118°28′ E 198
Danguya, Cen. Af. Rep. 6°27′ N, 22°41′ E 218
Daniel, Wyo., U.S. 42°52′ N, 110°4′ W 90
Daniel, oil field, Arg. 52°17′ S, 68°54′ W 134
Daniel's Harbour, Can. 50°14′ N, 57°35′ W 111
Danilov, Russ. 58°11′ N, 40°8′ E 154
Danilovgrad, Serb. and Mont. 42°32′ N, 19°7′ E 168
Danilovka, Russ. 64°42′ N, 57°47′ E 154
Danjiangkou, China 32°34′ N, 111°31′ E 198
Ḍank, Oman 23°32′ N, 56°17′ E 196
Dankov, Russ. 53°14′ N, 39°1′ E 154
Danlí, Hond. 14°1′ N, 86°31′ W 112
Danmark Havn, Den. 76°46′ N, 18°35′ W 246
Dannemora, N.Y., U.S. 44°42′ N, 73°44′ W 94
Dañoso, Cabo, Arg. 49°2′ S, 67°13′ W 134
Dansheha, Eth. 13°30′ N, 36°54′ E 182
Dansville, N.Y., U.S. 42°33′ N, 77°43′ W 94
Danu, Mold. 47°51′ N, 27°30′ E 152
Danube, river, Europe 44°29′ N, 21°15′ E 143
Danvers, Ill., U.S. 40°30′ N, 89°11′ W 102
Danvers, Mass., U.S. 42°33′ N, 70°57′ W 104
Danville, Ill., U.S. 40°9′ N, 87°37′ W 102
Danville, Ind., U.S. 39°45′ N, 86°32′ W 102
Danville, Ky., U.S. 37°38′ N, 84°46′ W 94
Danville, N.H., U.S. 42°54′ N, 71°8′ W 104
Danville, Ohio, U.S. 40°26′ N, 82°16′ W 102
Danville, Va., U.S. 36°34′ N, 79°25′ W 96
Danxian (Nada), China 19°28′ N, 109°34′ E 198
Danzhai, China 26°11′ N, 107°47′ E 198
Dao, Philippines 10°30′ N, 121°57′ E 203
Dao Timmi, Niger 20°33′ N, 13°31′ E 216
Daoxian, China 25°32′ N, 111°34′ E 198
Daozhen, China 28°52′ N, 107°40′ E 198
Dapa, Philippines 9°47′ N, 126°3′ E 203
Dapaong, Togo 10°50′ N, 0°11′ E 222
Dapchi, Nig. 12°29′ N, 11°31′ E 222
Daphne, Ala., U.S. 30°35′ N, 87°54′ W 103
Dapp, Can. 54°20′ N, 113°56′ W 108
Dapuchaihe, China 42°50′ N, 128°1′ E 200
Daqing, China 46°33′ N, 125°6′ E 198
Daqqaq, Sudan 12°57′ N, 26°53′ E 216
Dār B'ishtār, Leb. 34°15′ N, 35°47′ E 194
Dar es Salaam, Tanzania 6°49′ S, 39°6′ E 224
Dar et Touibia, Tun. 35°19′ N, 10°12′ E 156
Dar Rounga, region, Africa 10°24′ N, 23°37′ E 224
Dar'ā (Edrei), Syr. 32°37′ N, 36°6′ E 194
Dārāb, Iran 28°45′ N, 54°33′ E 196
Daraban, Pak. 31°42′ N, 70°22′ E 186
Daraina, Madagascar 13°17′ S, 49°38′ E 220
Darakhiv, Ukr. 49°17′ N, 25°33′ E 152
Darakht-e Yahya, Pak. 31°48′ N, 68°10′ E 186
Darány, Hung. 45°59′ N, 17°34′ E 168
Đaravica, peak, Serb. and Mont. 42°31′ N, 20°5′ E 168
Darâw, Egypt 24°22′ N, 32°54′ E 182
Darazo, Nig. 10°58′ N, 10°25′ E 222
Darbandi Khan Dam, Iraq 34°44′ N, 45°3′ E 180
Darbėnai, Lith. 56°1′ N, 21°12′ E 166
Darbhanga, India 26°10′ N, 85°53′ E 197
D'Arcole Islands, Indian Ocean 14°60′ S, 122°41′ E 230
Darda, Croatia 45°37′ N, 18°40′ E 168
Dardanelle, Ark., U.S. 35°12′ N, 93°10′ W 96
Dardanelle, Calif., U.S. 38°20′ N, 119°52′ W 100
Dardanelles 40°9′ N, 24°58′ E 143
Darende, Turk. 38°33′ N, 37°28′ E 156
Darero, river, Somalia 9°15′ N, 47°47′ E 218
Darfur, region, Africa 11°6′ N, 23°28′ E 224
Darganata, Turkm. 40°27′ N, 62°9′ E 180
Dargeçit, Turk. 37°33′ N, 41°46′ E 195
Dargol, Niger 13°54′ N, 1°12′ E 222
Darhan, Mongolia 46°43′ N, 109°15′ E 198
Darhan, Mongolia 49°31′ N, 105°58′ E 198
Darhan Muminggan Lianheqi (Bailingmiao), China 41°41′ N, 110°23′ E 198
Darien, Conn., U.S. 41°4′ N, 73°28′ W 104
Darien, Ga., U.S. 31°21′ N, 81°27′ W 96
Darien National Park, Pan. 7°23′ N, 77°60′ W 136
Darién, Serranía del, Pan. 8°31′ N, 77°58′ W 136
Darjiling, India 26°58′ N, 88°14′ E 197
Dark Canyon, Utah, U.S. 37°48′ N, 109°60′ W 92
Darley Hills, Antarctica 80°41′ S, 172°40′ E 248
Darling, S. Af. 33°22′ S, 18°19′ E 227
Darling Downs, Austral. 27°20′ S, 149°55′ E 230
Darling, river, Austral. 31°16′ S, 144°40′ E 230
Darlington, U.K. 54°31′ N, 1°34′ W 162
Darlington, Wis., U.S. 42°40′ N, 90°6′ W 102
Darmstadt, Ger. 49°52′ N, 8°38′ E 167
Darnah (Derna), Lib. 32°44′ N, 22°38′ E 216
Darney, Fr. 48°5′ N, 6°1′ E 150
Darnley Bay 69°23′ N, 124°25′ W 106
Daroca, Sp. 41°6′ N, 1°25′ W 164
Daroot-Korgon, Kyrg. 39°32′ N, 72°3′ E 197
Daror, Eth. 8°12′ N, 44°30′ E 218
Darou Khoudos, Senegal 15°7′ N, 16°40′ W 222
Darovskoy, Russ. 58°43′ N, 47°56′ E 154
Darregueira, Arg. 37°45′ S, 63°9′ W 139
Darreh Gaz, Iran 37°26′ N, 59°4′ E 180
Darrington, Wash., U.S. 48°13′ N, 121°38′ W 100
Darrouzett, Tex., U.S. 36°25′ N, 100°21′ W 92
Darss, Europe 54°18′ N, 12°27′ E 152
Dartmoor, region, Europe 50°45′ N, 4°7′ W 162
Dartmouth, Can. 44°40′ N, 63°35′ W 111
Dartmouth, Mass., U.S. 41°34′ N, 71°1′ W 104
Daru, P.N.G. 9°9′ S, 143°11′ E 192
Daruvar, Croatia 45°35′ N, 17°12′ E 168
Darvaza, Turkm. 40°5′ N, 58°30′ E 180
Darvel Bay 4°50′ N, 117°51′ E 203
Darwen, U.K. 53°42′ N, 2°28′ W 162
Darwendale, Zimb. 17°45′ S, 30°32′ E 224
Darwin, Austral. 12°30′ S, 130°37′ E 230
Darwin, Calif., U.S. 36°15′ N, 117°37′ W 101
Darwin, Isla, island, Ecua. 1°8′ N, 92°28′ W 130
Darwin, Mount, Calif., U.S. 37°10′ N, 118°43′ W 101
Darya Khan, Pak. 31°47′ N, 71°11′ E 186
Dārzīn, Iran 29°6′ N, 58°8′ E 196
Das, Pak. 35°6′ N, 75°5′ E 186
D'Asagny National Park, Côte d'Ivoire 5°11′ N, 4°56′ W 222
Dasburg, Ger. 50°2′ N, 6°8′ E 167
Dashbalbar, Mongolia 49°31′ N, 114°22′ E 198
Dashkäsän, Azerb. 40°30′ N, 46°3′ E 195
Dashkuduk, Turkm. 40°37′ N, 52°53′ E 158
Dasht, river, Pak. 25°37′ N, 61°59′ E 182
Dasht-e Navar, marsh, Afghan. 33°40′ N, 67°7′ E 186
Daşköpri, Turkm. 36°18′ N, 62°36′ E 186
Daşoguz, Turkm. 41°51′ N, 59°58′ E 180
Dassel, Ger. 51°47′ N, 9°40′ E 167
Datça, Turk. 36°44′ N, 27°39′ E 156
Dateland, Ariz., U.S. 32°47′ N, 113°32′ W 101
Datia, India 25°38′ N, 78°26′ E 197
Datian, China 25°40′ N, 117°51′ E 198
Datong, China 40°7′ N, 113°14′ E 198
Datteln, Ger. 51°39′ N, 7°20′ E 167
Datu Piang, Philippines 7°2′ N, 124°28′ E 203
Datu, Tanjong, Malaysia 2°8′ N, 109°23′ E 196
Datuk, island, Indonesia 0°12′ N, 108°14′ E 196
Daud Khel, Pak. 32°52′ N, 71°40′ E 186
Daudnagar, India 25°0′ N, 84°23′ E 197
Daugaard-Jensen Land, Den. 80°8′ N, 63°33′ W 246
Daugai, Lith. 54°22′ N, 24°20′ E 166
Daugava, river, Latv. 56°17′ N, 26°13′ E 166
Daugava, river, Latv. 56°46′ N, 24°10′ E 166
Daugavpils, Latv. 55°51′ N, 26°30′ E 166
Dauli, Somalia 8°48′ N, 50°26′ E 216
Daun, Ger. 50°11′ N, 6°49′ E 167
D'Aunay Bugt 68°49′ N, 28°49′ W 246
Daung Kyun, island, Myanmar 12°6′ N, 98°7′ E 202
Dauphin, Can. 51°8′ N, 100°3′ W 90
Dauphin Island, Ala., U.S. 30°6′ N, 88°18′ W 103
Dauphin Lake, Can. 51°16′ N, 100°32′ W 81
Dauphin, Péninsule du, Can. 51°18′ N, 72°54′ W 110
Dauphiné, region, Europe 44°22′ N, 4°50′ E 165
Däväçi, Azerb. 41°11′ N, 48°59′ E 195
Davangere, India 14°27′ N, 75°55′ E 188
Davant, La., U.S. 29°36′ N, 89°53′ W 103
Davao, Philippines 7°7′ N, 125°36′ E 203
Dāvar Panāh, Iran 27°18′ N, 62°21′ E 182
Davegoriale, Somalia 8°43′ N, 44°52′ E 218
Davenport, Calif., U.S. 37°0′ N, 122°12′ W 100
Davenport, Fla., U.S. 28°9′ N, 81°37′ W 105
Davenport, Iowa, U.S. 41°32′ N, 90°37′ W 110
Davenport, Mount, Austral. 22°28′ S, 130°38′ E 230
Daventry, U.K. 52°15′ N, 1°10′ W 162
David, Pan. 8°22′ N, 82°19′ W 123
Davidson, Can. 51°16′ N, 105°60′ W 90
Davie, Fla., U.S. 26°3′ N, 80°15′ W 105
Davies, Cape, Antarctica 71°35′ S, 100°20′ W 248
Davis, Calif., U.S. 38°32′ N, 121°46′ W 90
Davis, Okla., U.S. 34°29′ N, 97°7′ W 92
Davis Dam, Ariz., U.S. 35°10′ N, 114°34′ W 101
Davis Dam, Nev., U.S. 35°12′ N, 114°37′ W 101
Davis Inlet, Can. 55°53′ N, 60°48′ W 106
Davis Islands, Indian Ocean 66°35′ S, 108°0′ E 248
Davis, Mount, Pa., U.S. 39°46′ N, 79°16′ W 94
Davis Mountains, Tex., U.S. 30°44′ N, 104°13′ W 92
Davis Sea 66°31′ S, 89°40′ E 248
Davis, station, Antarctica 68°30′ S, 78°25′ E 248
Davis Strait 70°31′ N, 60°40′ W 73
Davison, Mich., U.S. 43°1′ N, 83°30′ W 102
Davlekanovo, Russ. 54°14′ N, 54°58′ E 154
Davlos, Northern Cyprus 35°24′ N, 33°54′ E 194
Davor, Croatia 45°7′ N, 17°29′ E 168
Davos, Switz. 46°47′ N, 9°47′ E 167
Davy Lake, Can. 58°51′ N, 108°49′ W 108
Dawa, river, Eth. 4°42′ N, 39°44′ E 224
Dawadawa, Ghana 8°21′ N, 1°35′ W 222
Dawei, Myanmar 14°5′ N, 98°13′ E 202
Dawhinava, Belarus 54°39′ N, 27°26′ E 166
Dawkah, Oman 18°41′ N, 53°58′ E 182
Dawmat al Jandal, Saudi Arabia 29°47′ N, 39°53′ E 180
Dawna Range, Myanmar 16°49′ N, 98°1′ E 202
Dawqah, Saudi Arabia 19°35′ N, 40°55′ E 182
Dawra, Western Sahara 27°27′ N, 12°60′ W 214
Dawros Head, Ire. 54°48′ N, 8°57′ W 150
Dawson, Can. 64°5′ N, 139°18′ W 98
Dawson, Ga., U.S. 31°45′ N, 84°27′ W 96
Dawson, Minn., U.S. 44°55′ N, 96°4′ W 90
Dawson, N. Dak., U.S. 46°51′ N, 99°46′ W 90
Dawson, Tex., U.S. 31°52′ N, 96°41′ W 96
Dawson Bay 52°50′ N, 101°22′ W 108
Dawson Creek, Can. 55°44′ N, 120°16′ W 108
Dawson, Isla, island, Chile 54°10′ S, 70°9′ W 134
Dawson, Mount, Can. 51°8′ N, 117°32′ W 90
Dawson Springs, Ky., U.S. 37°9′ N, 87°41′ W 96
Dawu, China 31°30′ N, 114°4′ E 198
Dawukou see Shizuishan, China 39°4′ N, 106°25′ E 198
Dawwah, Oman 20°39′ N, 58°53′ E 182
Dax, Fr. 43°42′ N, 1°3′ W 150
Daxian, China 31°15′ N, 107°24′ E 198
Daxing, China 39°44′ N, 116°19′ E 198
Dayang, river, China 40°15′ N, 123°18′ E 200
Dayet el Khadra, spring, Alg. 27°25′ N, 8°30′ W 214
Daying, China 42°8′ N, 127°17′ E 200
Daylight Pass, Calif., U.S. 36°46′ N, 116°57′ W 101
Daymán, river, Uru. 31°34′ S, 57°40′ W 139
Dayong, China 29°8′ N, 110°35′ E 198
Dayr Abū Sa'īd, Jordan 32°29′ N, 35°41′ E 194
Dayr al Aḥmar, Leb. 34°7′ N, 36°7′ E 194
Dayr al Balaḥ, Gaza Strip 31°25′ N, 34°21′ E 194
Dayr 'Aṭīyah, Syr. 34°5′ N, 36°46′ E 194
Dayr az Zawr, Syr. 35°19′ N, 40°5′ E 180
Daysland, Can. 52°51′ N, 112°17′ W 108
Dayton, Nev., U.S. 39°15′ N, 119°37′ W 90
Dayton, Ohio, U.S. 39°44′ N, 84°11′ W 102
Dayton, Tenn., U.S. 35°29′ N, 85°1′ W 96
Dayton, Tex., U.S. 30°1′ N, 94°54′ W 103
Dayton, Wash., U.S. 46°18′ N, 117°58′ W 82
Dayton, Wyo., U.S. 44°50′ N, 107°16′ W 90
Daytona Beach, Fla., U.S. 29°13′ N, 81°3′ W 105
Dayu, China 25°24′ N, 114°19′ E 198
Dayville, Conn., U.S. 41°50′ N, 71°54′ W 104
Dazhu, China 30°46′ N, 107°15′ E 198
Dazkırı, Turk. 37°54′ N, 29°51′ E 156
Dazu, China 29°46′ N, 105°44′ E 198
Dchira, Western Sahara 27°1′ N, 13°3′ W 214
De Aar, S. Af. 30°39′ S, 23°59′ E 227
De Beque, Colo., U.S. 39°20′ N, 108°13′ W 90
De Berry, Tex., U.S. 32°17′ N, 94°11′ W 103
De Cocksdorp, Neth. 53°9′ N, 4°51′ E 163
De Forest, Wis., U.S. 43°15′ N, 89°21′ W 102
De Graff, Ohio, U.S. 40°18′ N, 83°55′ W 102
De Kalb, Miss., U.S. 32°44′ N, 88°39′ W 103
De Kalb, Tex., U.S. 33°30′ N, 94°38′ W 96
De Kastri, Russ. 51°38′ N, 140°35′ E 190
De la Garma, Arg. 37°58′ S, 60°25′ W 139
De Land, Fla., U.S. 29°1′ N, 81°19′ W 105
De Land, Ill., U.S. 40°6′ N, 88°39′ W 102
De Leon Springs, Fla., U.S. 29°6′ N, 81°22′ W 105
De Long Mountains, Alas., U.S. 68°7′ N, 164°15′ W 98
De Long, Ostrova, islands, East Siberian Sea 75°48′ N, 158°9′ E 160
De Queen, Ark., U.S. 34°0′ N, 94°21′ W 96
De Quincy, La., U.S. 30°26′ N, 93°27′ W 103
De Ridder, La., U.S. 30°49′ N, 93°18′ W 103
De Smet, S. Dak., U.S. 44°22′ N, 97°35′ W 90
De Soto, Miss., U.S. 31°58′ N, 88°43′ W 103
De Soto, Mo., U.S. 38°7′ N, 90°34′ W 94
De Soto, Wis., U.S. 43°25′ N, 91°12′ W 94
De Tour Village, Mich., U.S. 45°59′ N, 83°55′ W 94
De Witt, Ark., U.S. 34°16′ N, 91°21′ W 96
De Witt, Iowa, U.S. 41°49′ N, 90°32′ W 94
Dead Horse Point, site, Utah, U.S. 38°30′ N, 109°47′ W 90
Dead Indian Peak, Wyo., U.S. 44°35′ N, 109°42′ W 90
Dead Mountains, Calif., U.S. 35°6′ N, 114°50′ W 101
Dead Sea, lake, Jordan 31°28′ N, 35°24′ E 194
Deadmans Cay, Bahamas 23°7′ N, 75°4′ W 116
Deadman's Cays, North Atlantic Ocean 24°6′ N, 80°37′ W 116
Deadmen Valley, Can. 61°2′ N, 124°23′ W 108
Deadwood, Can. 56°44′ N, 117°30′ W 108
Deadwood, S. Dak., U.S. 44°22′ N, 103°42′ W 82
Deadwood Lake, Can. 59°0′ N, 129°12′ W 108
Deadwood Reservoir, Idaho, U.S. 44°19′ N, 116°4′ W 90
Deakin, Austral. 30°46′ S, 128°57′ E 231
Deal, U.K. 51°13′ N, 1°23′ E 163
De'an, China 29°18′ N, 115°45′ E 198
Dean Channel 52°33′ N, 127°44′ W 108
Deán Funes, Arg. 30°25′ S, 64°21′ W 134
Dean Island, Antarctica 74°22′ S, 126°8′ W 248
Dean, river, Can. 52°53′ N, 126°11′ W 108
Dearborn, Mich., U.S. 42°18′ N, 83°13′ W 102
Dearg, Beinn, peak, U.K. 56°51′ N, 3°60′ W 150
Dearg, Beinn, peak, U.K. 57°45′ N, 5°3′ W 150
Dease Arm 66°42′ N, 120°16′ W 98
Dease Inlet 70°56′ N, 156°54′ W 98
Dease Lake, Can. 58°27′ N, 130°4′ W 108
Dease, river, Can. 58°54′ N, 130°11′ W 108
Dease Strait 69°0′ N, 106°42′ W 246
Death Valley, Calif., U.S. 36°27′ N, 116°53′ W 101
Death Valley Junction, Calif., U.S. 36°17′ N, 116°26′ W 101
Death Valley National Park (Devils Hole), Nev., U.S. 36°25′ N, 116°19′ W 101
Deatley Island, Antarctica 73°45′ S, 73°41′ W 248
Debao, China 23°16′ N, 106°34′ E 198
Debar, Maced. 41°31′ N, 20°32′ E 168
Debark', Eth. 13°12′ N, 37°51′ E 182
Debary, Fla., U.S. 28°53′ N, 81°19′ W 105
Debden, Can. 53°31′ N, 106°52′ W 108
Debdou, Mor. 33°60′ N, 3°2′ W 214
Dębek, Pol. 54°48′ N, 18°5′ E 152
Debelica, Serb. and Mont. 43°39′ N, 22°15′ E 168
Debenham, U.K. 52°13′ N, 1°10′ E 162
Débéré, Mali 15°5′ N, 3°1′ W 222
Debikut, India 25°21′ N, 88°32′ E 197
Debin, Russ. 62°18′ N, 150°29′ E 160
Debir, ruin(s), Israel 31°27′ N, 34°51′ E 194
Dęblin, Pol. 51°33′ N, 21°50′ E 152
Débo, Lake, Mali 15°13′ N, 4°26′ W 222
Debrc, Serb. and Mont. 44°36′ N, 19°53′ E 168
Debre Birhan, Eth. 9°39′ N, 39°31′ E 224
Debre Mark'os, Eth. 10°19′ N, 37°42′ E 224
Debre Tabor, Eth. 11°50′ N, 38°0′ E 182
Debre Zebīt, Eth. 11°48′ N, 38°35′ E 182
Debre Zeyit, Eth. 10°36′ N, 35°42′ E 224
Debrecen, Hung. 47°31′ N, 21°38′ E 168
Debrzno, Pol. 53°32′ N, 17°14′ E 152
Decamere, Eritrea 15°4′ N, 39°4′ E 182
Dečani, Serb. and Mont. 42°31′ N, 20°18′ E 168
Decatur, Ill., U.S. 39°50′ N, 88°57′ W 102
Decatur, Ind., U.S. 40°49′ N, 84°56′ W 102
Decatur, Mich., U.S. 42°6′ N, 85°58′ W 102
Decatur, Miss., U.S. 32°25′ N, 89°7′ W 103
Decatur, Mo., U.S. 39°50′ N, 88°57′ W 94
Decatur, Tex., U.S. 33°13′ N, 97°35′ W 92
Deception Island, Antarctica 63°16′ S, 60°43′ W 134
Dechu, India 26°47′ N, 72°19′ E 186
Deckerville, Mich., U.S. 43°31′ N, 82°44′ W 102
Decorah, Iowa, U.S. 43°17′ N, 91°48′ W 94
Deddington, U.K. 51°58′ N, 1°20′ W 162
Dededo, Guam, U.S. 14°0′ N, 147°0′ E 242
Dedegöl Dağı, peak, Turk. 37°37′ N, 31°12′ E 156
Deder, Eth. 9°17′ N, 41°26′ E 224
Dedham, Mass., U.S. 42°14′ N, 71°11′ W 104
Dedino, Maced. 41°34′ N, 22°25′ E 168
Dédougou, Burkina Faso 12°27′ N, 3°28′ W 222
Dedovichi, Russ. 57°32′ N, 30°0′ E 166
Dedu, China 48°30′ N, 126°9′ E 198
Dedza, Malawi 14°23′ S, 34°16′ E 224
Dee, river, Ire. 53°51′ N, 6°42′ W 150
Dee, river, U.K. 53°5′ N, 2°53′ W 162
Deep Bay 61°13′ N, 117°11′ W 108
Deep Bay see Chilumba, Malawi 10°24′ S, 34°13′ E 224
Deep Crater, Calif., U.S. 41°26′ N, 121°38′ W 90
Deep Creek, Bahamas 24°49′ N, 76°17′ W 96
Deep Creek Peak, Idaho, U.S. 42°28′ N, 112°43′ W 90
Deep Creek Range, Utah, U.S. 39°36′ N, 114°20′ W 90
Deep River, Can. 46°6′ N, 77°31′ W 94
Deep River, Conn., U.S. 41°23′ N, 72°27′ W 104
Deer Creek, Ill., U.S. 40°37′ N, 89°20′ W 102
Deer Lake, Can. 52°40′ N, 94°59′ W 81
Deer Lake, Can. 49°1′ N, 58°2′ W 111
Deer Lodge, Mont., U.S. 46°23′ N, 112°44′ W 90
Deer Park, Ala., U.S. 31°12′ N, 88°19′ W 103
Deer River, Minn., U.S. 47°19′ N, 93°49′ W 94
Deer, river, Can. 57°36′ N, 94°32′ W 108
Deer Trail, Colo., U.S. 39°36′ N, 104°3′ W 90
Deerfield, Ill., U.S. 42°10′ N, 87°52′ W 102
Deerfield, Mass., U.S. 42°31′ N, 72°37′ W 104
Deerfield, N.H., U.S. 43°8′ N, 71°14′ W 104
Deerfield Beach, Fla., U.S. 26°18′ N, 80°7′ W 105
Deerhurst, U.K. 51°57′ N, 2°11′ W 162
Deering, Alas., U.S. 65°54′ N, 162°50′ W 98
Deeth, Nev., U.S. 41°4′ N, 115°17′ W 90
Defa, oil field, Lib. 27°45′ N, 19°46′ E 216
Defensores del Chaco National Park, Parag. 20°12′ S, 62°1′ W 132
Defiance, Ohio, U.S. 41°15′ N, 84°23′ W 102
Défirou, spring, Niger 20°33′ N, 15°3′ E 216
Dég, Hung. 46°51′ N, 18°27′ E 168
Degana, India 26°53′ N, 74°19′ E 186
Deganya, Israel 32°41′ N, 35°34′ E 194
Dêgê, China 31°51′ N, 98°37′ E 190
Degeh Bur, Eth. 8°13′ N, 43°30′ E 218
Degelen, peak, Kaz. 49°52′ N, 77°51′ E 184
Degerby, Fin. 60°4′ N, 24°9′ E 166
Degerfors, Nor. 59°14′ N, 14°22′ E 152
Degerhamn, Sw. 56°21′ N, 16°23′ E 152
Dego, It. 44°26′ N, 8°19′ E 167
Deh Bīd, Iran 30°36′ N, 53°11′ E 180
Deh Khavak, Afghan. 35°39′ N, 69°55′ E 186
Deh Mollā, Iran 30°33′ N, 49°38′ E 186
Deh Shu, Afghan. 30°23′ N, 63°19′ E 186
Dehgam, India 23°9′ N, 72°48′ E 186
Dehibat, Tun. 32°2′ N, 10°41′ E 214
Dehqonobod, Uzb. 38°21′ N, 66°30′ E 197
Dehra Dun, India 30°20′ N, 78°2′ E 197
Dehui, China 44°30′ N, 125°40′ E 198
Deim Zubeir, Sudan 7°42′ N, 26°13′ E 224
Deinze, Belg. 50°58′ N, 3°31′ E 163
Deir Mawâs, Egypt 27°40′ N, 30°46′ E 180
Dej, Rom. 47°8′ N, 23°55′ E 156
Dejë, Mal, peak, Alban. 41°41′ N, 20°7′ E 168
Dejen, Ras, peak, Eth. 13°11′ N, 38°19′ E 182
Dejiang, China 28°16′ N, 108°6′ E 198
Dekalb, Ill., U.S. 41°55′ N, 88°44′ W 102
Dekese, Dem. Rep. of the Congo 3°29′ S, 21°24′ E 218
Dekhisor, Taj. 39°27′ N, 69°32′ E 197
Dekina, Nig. 7°38′ N, 7°0′ E 222
Dekle Beach, Fla., U.S. 29°51′ N, 83°37′ W 105
Dekoa, Cen. Af. Rep. 6°14′ N, 19°3′ E 218
Del Rio, Tex., U.S. 29°21′ N, 100°55′ W 112
Del Verme Falls, Eth. 5°9′ N, 40°15′ E 224
Delacroix, La., U.S. 29°45′ N, 89°48′ W 103
Delamar Mountains, Nev., U.S. 37°8′ N, 114°58′ W 101
Delami, Sudan 11°50′ N, 30°28′ E 218
Delano, Calif., U.S. 35°46′ N, 119°14′ W 100
Delano Peak, Utah, U.S. 38°21′ N, 112°26′ W 90
Delanson, N.Y., U.S. 42°44′ N, 74°12′ W 104
Delaram, Afghan. 32°14′ N, 63°26′ E 186
Delareyville, S. Af. 26°42′ S, 25°25′ E 220
Delavan, Ill., U.S. 40°21′ N, 89°33′ W 102
Delaware, Ohio, U.S. 40°17′ N, 83°5′ W 102
Delaware, adm. division, Del., U.S. 39°36′ N, 75°46′ W 94
Delaware Bay 38°16′ N, 76°18′ W 94
Delaware Mountains, Tex., U.S. 31°54′ N, 104°55′ W 92
Delbrück, Ger. 51°45′ N, 8°32′ E 167
Delcambre, La., U.S. 29°56′ N, 91°60′ W 103
Delčevo, Maced. 41°57′ N, 22°46′ E 168
Delémont, Switz. 47°22′ N, 7°19′ E 156
Delesseps Lake, lake, Can. 50°41′ N, 91°15′ W 110
Delft, Neth. 52°1′ N, 4°21′ E 163
Delfzijl, Neth. 53°20′ N, 6°55′ E 163
Delgada, Point, Calif., U.S. 39°51′ N, 124°30′ W 90
Delgado, Cabo, Mozambique 10°43′ S, 40°42′ E 224
Delgerhet, Mongolia 45°50′ N, 110°29′ E 198
Delgo, Sudan 20°6′ N, 30°36′ E 226
Delhi, Calif., U.S. 37°25′ N, 120°47′ W 100
Delhi, India 28°41′ N, 77°10′ E 197
Delhi, La., U.S. 32°26′ N, 91°30′ W 103
Delhi, N.Y., U.S. 42°16′ N, 74°56′ W 94
Delhi, adm. division, India 28°37′ N, 76°44′ E 188
Deli Jovan, Serb. and Mont. 44°21′ N, 22°12′ E 168
Delia, Can. 51°39′ N, 112°23′ W 90
Délices, Fr. 4°43′ N, 53°47′ W 130
Delicias, Mex. 28°9′ N, 105°29′ W 92
Deligrad, Serb. and Mont. 43°36′ N, 21°35′ E 168
Delījān, Iran 34°0′ N, 50°40′ E 180
Deliktaş, Turk. 39°19′ N, 37°12′ E 156
Déline, Can. 65°13′ N, 123°26′ W 98
Delingha, China 37°22′ N, 97°29′ E 188
Delisle, Can. 51°55′ N, 107°8′ W 90
Delisle, Can. 48°37′ N, 71°42′ W 94
Delium, battle, Gr. 38°19′ N, 23°32′ E 156
Dell, U.K. 58°28′ N, 6°20′ W 150
Dell Rapids, S. Dak., U.S. 43°48′ N, 96°43′ W 90
Delle, Fr. 47°30′ N, 6°59′ E 150
Dellenbaugh, Mount, Ariz., U.S. 36°6′ N, 113°34′ W 101
Dellys, Alg. 36°54′ N, 3°54′ E 150
Delmar, Md., U.S. 38°27′ N, 75°35′ W 94
Delmar, N.Y., U.S. 42°37′ N, 73°51′ W 104
Deloraine, Can. 49°11′ N, 100°30′ W 90
Delos, ruin(s), Gr. 37°22′ N, 25°10′ E 156
Delphi, ruin(s), Gr. 38°28′ N, 22°24′ E 156
Delphos, Ohio, U.S. 40°50′ N, 84°21′ W 102
Delray Beach, Fla., U.S. 26°28′ N, 80°6′ W 105
Delta, Colo., U.S. 38°44′ N, 108°4′ W 90
Delta, La., U.S. 32°18′ N, 90°56′ W 103
Delta, Utah, U.S. 39°20′ N, 112°34′ W 90
Delta Amacuro, adm. division, Venez. 8°57′ N, 61°48′ W 130
Delta du Saloum National Park, Senegal 13°39′ N, 16°27′ W 222
Deltona, Fla., U.S. 28°53′ N, 81°15′ W 105
Dema, river, Russ. 54°28′ N, 55°29′ E 154
Demanda, Sierra de la, Sp. 42°19′ N, 3°14′ W 164
Demange-aux-Eaux, Fr. 48°34′ N, 5°27′ E 163
Demarcation Point, Can. 69°34′ N, 143°59′ W 98
Demba, Dem. Rep. of the Congo 5°30′ S, 22°13′ E 218
Dembech'a, Eth. 10°31′ N, 37°28′ E 224
Dembī Dolo, Eth. 8°31′ N, 34°47′ E 224
Dembia, Dem. Rep. of the Congo 3°29′ N, 25°51′ E 224
Demerara Plain, North Atlantic Ocean 9°25′ N, 48°41′ W 253
Demetrias, ruin(s), Gr. 39°20′ N, 22°52′ E 156
Demidov, Russ. 55°14′ N, 31°31′ E 154
Demidovo, Russ. 56°45′ N, 29°33′ E 166
Deming, N. Mex., U.S. 32°15′ N, 107°45′ W 92
Deming, Wash., U.S. 48°49′ N, 122°13′ W 100
Demini, river, Braz. 1°24′ N, 63°13′ W 130
Demirci, Turk. 39°3′ N, 28°38′ E 156
Demirköprü Barajı, dam, Turk. 38°48′ N, 28°0′ E 156
Demirtaş, Turk. 36°25′ N, 32°10′ E 156
Demiti, river, Braz. 0°51′ N, 67°4′ W 136
Demmitt, Can. 55°25′ N, 119°55′ W 108
Democratic Republic of the Congo 1°57′ S, 17°24′ E 218
Demon, Ghana 9°29′ N, 0°11′ E 222
Demonte, It. 44°18′ N, 7°17′ E 167
Demopolis, Ala., U.S. 32°32′ N, 87°50′ W 103
Demotte, Ind., U.S. 41°11′ N, 87°13′ W 102
Demşuş, Rom. 45°34′ N, 22°48′ E 168
Demta, Indonesia 2°23′ S, 140°10′ E 192
Dem'yanka, river, Russ. 58°52′ N, 71°21′ E 169
Demyansk, Russ. 57°37′ N, 32°28′ E 154
Dem'yanskoye, Russ. 59°32′ N, 69°25′ E 169
Demydivka, Ukr. 50°24′ N, 25°20′ E 152
Den Burg, Neth. 53°3′ N, 4°46′ E 163
Den Chai, Thai. 17°59′ N, 100°3′ E 202
Den Helder, Neth. 52°57′ N, 4°45′ E 163
Den Oever, Neth. 52°55′ N, 5°1′ E 163
Denain, Fr. 50°19′ N, 3°23′ E 163
Denair, Calif., U.S. 37°31′ N, 120°49′ W 100
Denakil, region, Africa 12°35′ N, 40°8′ E 182
Denali see Mckinley, Mount, Alas., U.S. 62°54′ N, 151°17′ W 98
Denan, Eth. 6°27′ N, 43°29′ E 218
Denare Beach, Can. 54°40′ N, 102°4′ W 108
Denbigh, U.K. 53°11′ N, 3°24′ W 162
Dendtler Island, Antarctica 72°46′ S, 90°30′ W 248
Denekamp, Neth. 52°23′ N, 7°0′ E 163
Deng Deng, Cameroon 5°8′ N, 13°28′ E 218
Dengkou, China 40°18′ N, 106°54′ E 198
Dêngqên, China 31°33′ N, 95°35′ E 188
Dengu, river, Dem. Rep. of the Congo 4°30′ N, 24°14′ E 224
Dengzhou, China 32°39′ N, 112°5′ E 198
Denham Springs, La., U.S. 30°28′ N, 90°58′ W 96
Denholm, Can. 52°39′ N, 108°2′ W 108
Dénia, Sp. 38°49′ N, 9°535′ E 164
Deniliquin, Austral. 35°31′ S, 144°55′ E 231
Denio, Nev., U.S. 41°59′ N, 118°39′ W 90
Denis, Gabon 0°17′ N, 9°22′ E 218
Denison, Iowa, U.S. 41°59′ N, 95°21′ W 90
Denison, Tex., U.S. 33°44′ N, 96°32′ W 96
Denisovka, Russ. 66°14′ N, 55°19′ E 154
Denisovskaya, Russ. 60°18′ N, 41°34′ E 154
Denizli, Turk. 37°45′ N, 29°5′ E 156
Denman Island, Can. 49°32′ N, 124°49′ W 100
Denmark 56°12′ N, 8°45′ E 152
Denmark, Me., U.S. 43°58′ N, 70°49′ W 104
Denmark, S.C., U.S. 33°18′ N, 81°9′ W 96
Denmark Strait 64°13′ N, 38°12′ W 246
Dennis, Mass., U.S. 41°44′ N, 70°12′ W 104
Dennison, Ohio, U.S. 40°23′ N, 81°20′ W 102
Denow, Uzb. 38°17′ N, 67°54′ E 197
Denpasar, Indonesia 8°44′ S, 115°1′ E 192
Denso, Mali 10°27′ N, 8°5′ W 222
Denton, Md., U.S. 38°52′ N, 75°50′ W 94
Denton, Tex., U.S. 33°12′ N, 97°8′ W 92
D'Entrecasteaux Islands, Solomon Sea 9°50′ S, 151°24′ E 231
Denver, Colo., U.S. 39°43′ N, 105°6′ W 90
Denver, Ind., U.S. 40°51′ N, 86°5′ W 102
Denver City, Tex., U.S. 32°56′ N, 102°50′ W 92
Denzil, Can. 52°13′ N, 109°38′ W 108
Deoband, India 29°40′ N, 77°41′ E 197
Deobhog, India 19°56′ N, 82°39′ E 188
Deoghar, India 24°27′ N, 86°42′ E 197
Deoria, India 26°29′ N, 83°47′ E 197
Departure Bay, Can. 49°11′ N, 123°58′ W 100
Deposit, N.Y., U.S. 42°3′ N, 75°26′ W 110
Depot Harbour, Can. 45°18′ N, 80°5′ W 94
Depot Peak, Antarctica 69°6′ S, 64°14′ E 248
Deputatskiy, Russ. 69°16′ N, 139°52′ E 173
Deqing, China 30°33′ N, 120°4′ E 198
Deqing, China 23°10′ N, 111°46′ E 198
Dera Ghazi Khan, Pak. 30°3′ N, 70°41′ E 186
Dera Ismail Khan, Pak. 31°47′ N, 70°55′ E 186
Deraheib, Sudan 21°55′ N, 35°8′ E 182
Derati, spring, Kenya 3°47′ N, 36°23′ E 224
Derbent, Russ. 42°0′ N, 48°20′ E 195
Derbisaka, Cen. Af. Rep. 5°43′ N, 24°52′ E 224

Dodola, Eth. 6°57′ N, 39°9′ E 224
Dodoma, Tanzania 6°10′ S, 35°35′ E 224
Dodoma, adm. division, Tanzania 6°43′ S, 35°14′ E 218
Dodona, ruin(s), Gr. 39°31′ N, 20°39′ E 156
Dodsland, Can. 51°49′ N, 108°50′ W 90
Dodson, La., U.S. 32°3′ N, 92°40′ W 103
Dodson, Mont., U.S. 48°23′ N, 108°15′ W 90
Doe Castle, site, Ire. 55°6′ N, 7°60′ W 150
Doe River, Can. 55°59′ N, 120°7′ W 108
Doerun, Ga., U.S. 31°18′ N, 83°55′ W 96
Doesburg, Neth. 52°0′ N, 6°10′ E 167
Doetinchem, Neth. 51°57′ N, 6°18′ E 167
Dog Creek, Can. 51°37′ N, 122°14′ W 90
Dog Lake, Can. 48°48′ N, 89°57′ W 94
Dog Lake, Can. 48°15′ N, 84°26′ W 94
Dog Lake, lake, Can. 50°58′ N, 98°49′ W 90
Dog Rocks, islands, North Atlantic Ocean 24°5′ N, 79°48′ W 116
Dogai Coring, lake, China 34°25′ N, 88°11′ E 188
Dogface Lake, Can. 60°17′ N, 119°34′ W 108
Dogondoutchi, Niger 13°38′ N, 4°0′ E 222
Doğruyol (Cala), Turk. 41°3′ N, 43°20′ E 195
Doğubayazıt, Turk. 39°30′ N, 44°8′ E 195
Dogwaya, Sudan 17°48′ N, 34°33′ E 182
Doha see Ad Dawḩah, Qatar 25°13′ N, 51°25′ E 196
Dohoukota, Cen. Af. Rep. 6°1′ N, 17°27′ E 218
Doig, river, Can. 56°50′ N, 120°6′ W 108
Doilungdêqên, China 29°49′ N, 90°44′ E 197
Dois Irmãos, Serra, Braz. 8°27′ S, 41°26′ W 132
Doka, Sudan 13°27′ N, 35°45′ E 182
Doka see Bahr Kéita, river, Chad 9°8′ N, 18°38′ E 218
Dokan Dam, Iraq 36°1′ N, 44°37′ E 180
Dokka, Nor. 60°49′ N, 10°3′ E 152
Dokkara, Alg. 35°49′ N, 4°25′ E 150
Dokkum, Neth. 53°19′ N, 6°0′ E 163
Doko, Dem. Rep. of the Congo 3°6′ N, 29°34′ E 224
Dokshytsy, Belarus 54°53′ N, 27°45′ E 166
Doküchaev, Kaz. 51°40′ N, 64°13′ E 184
Dokuchayevs'k, Ukr. 47°42′ N, 37°37′ E 156
Dolak, island, Indonesia 8°43′ S, 136°42′ E 192
Dolan Springs, Ariz., U.S. 35°35′ N, 114°16′ W 101
Doland, S. Dak., U.S. 44°52′ N, 98°7′ W 90
Dolbeau, Can. 48°49′ N, 72°18′ W 82
Dolbeau-Mistassini, Can. 48°53′ N, 72°11′ W 94
Doldrums Fracture Zone, North Atlantic Ocean 8°41′ N, 33°42′ W 253
Dole, Fr. 47°5′ N, 5°28′ E 150
Doleib Hill, Sudan 9°20′ N, 31°38′ E 224
Dolgoshchel'ye, Russ. 66°3′ N, 43°29′ E 154
Dolhasca, Rom. 47°24′ N, 26°36′ E 156
Doli, Croatia 42°48′ N, 17°48′ E 168
Dolina, Ukr. 48°56′ N, 24°1′ E 152
Dolinsk, Russ. 47°19′ N, 142°44′ E 190
Dolj, adm. division, Rom. 44°2′ N, 23°6′ E 156
Dollard 53°15′ N, 7°1′ E 163
Dolleman Island, Antarctica 70°41′ S, 60°17′ W 248
Dolly Cays, North Atlantic Ocean 23°28′ N, 77°16′ W 116
Dolní Dvořiště, Czech Rep. 48°39′ N, 14°27′ E 152
Dolnośląskie, adm. division, Pol. 51°10′ N, 15°2′ E 152
Dolo, It. 45°25′ N, 12°3′ E 156
Dolo Bay, Eth. 4°10′ N, 42°6′ E 224
Dolomites, It. 46°44′ N, 11°41′ E 167
Doloon, Mongolia 44°25′ N, 105°18′ E 198
Dolores, Arg. 36°17′ S, 57°41′ W 139
Dolores, Colo., U.S. 37°28′ N, 108°30′ W 92
Dolores, Uru. 33°33′ S, 58°9′ W 139
Dolores Hidalgo, Mex. 21°8′ N, 100°57′ W 114
Dolphin and Union Strait 69°9′ N, 118°43′ W 98
Dolphin, Cape, U.K. 51°11′ S, 60°16′ W 134
Dolsan, S. Korea 34°37′ N, 127°45′ E 200
Dolzhanskaya, Russ. 46°38′ N, 37°45′ E 156
Dolzhitsy, Russ. 58°29′ N, 29°5′ E 166
Dolzhok, Ukr. 48°39′ N, 26°30′ E 156
Dom Joaquim, Braz. 18°58′ S, 43°19′ W 138
Dom, peak, Switz. 46°6′ N, 7°49′ E 165
Dom Pedrito, Braz. 30°60′ S, 54°41′ W 139
Dom Pedro, Braz. 4°60′ S, 44°28′ W 132
Domagaya Lake, Can. 51°53′ N, 65°17′ W 111
Domaniç, Turk. 39°47′ N, 29°35′ E 156
Domanovići, Bosn. and Herzg. 43°7′ N, 17°46′ E 168
Domar, China 33°49′ N, 80°14′ E 188
Domart, Fr. 50°4′ N, 2°7′ E 163
Domașnea, Rom. 45°5′ N, 22°19′ E 168
Dombarovskiy, Russ. 50°45′ N, 59°31′ E 158
Dombe, Mozambique 19°60′ S, 33°23′ E 224
Dombóvár, Hung. 46°22′ N, 18°7′ E 168
Domburg, Neth. 51°33′ N, 3°29′ E 163
Dome, Ariz., U.S. 32°44′ N, 114°22′ W 101
Dome Circe, region, Antarctica 72°58′ S, 129°17′ E 248
Dome Creek, Can. 53°41′ N, 121°2′ W 108
Dome Fuji, station, Antarctica 77°27′ S, 39°56′ E 248
Dome Mountain, peak, Can. 53°16′ N, 60°38′ W 111
Dome Peak, Can. 61°28′ N, 127°6′ W 98
Dome Peak, Wyo., U.S. 44°33′ N, 107°29′ W 90
Dome Peak, Castle, Ariz., U.S. 33°4′ N, 114°11′ W 101
Dôme, Puy de, peak, Fr. 45°45′ N, 2°55′ E 165
Dome Rock Mountains, Ariz., U.S. 33°37′ N, 114°31′ W 101
Domett, N.Z. 42°53′ S, 173°14′ E 240
Domingo M. Irala, Parag. 25°56′ S, 54°36′ W 139
Dominican Republic 18°55′ N, 70°60′ W 116
Dominion, Cape, Can. 66°9′ N, 77°33′ W 106
Dominion Lake, Can. 52°40′ N, 62°18′ W 111
Dömitz, Ger. 53°8′ N, 11°15′ E 152
Dommary-Baroncourt, Fr. 49°17′ N, 5°41′ E 163
Domo, Eth. 7°49′ N, 46°55′ E 218
Domodossola, It. 46°7′ N, 8°16′ E 167
Dompago see Badjoudé, Benin 9°42′ N, 1°23′ E 222
Domrémy, Fr. 48°26′ N, 5°40′ E 163
Dömsöd, Hung. 47°5′ N, 19°1′ E 168
Domuyo, Volcán, Arg. 36°38′ S, 70°34′ W 134
Don Benito, Sp. 38°57′ N, 5°52′ W 164
Don Pedro Reservoir, lake, Calif., U.S. 37°43′ N, 120°34′ W 100
Don Peninsula, Can. 52°27′ N, 128°10′ W 108
Dôn, river, Laos 15°43′ N, 105°56′ E 202
Don, river, Russ. 52°0′ N, 39°2′ E 160
Donadeu, Arg. 26°41′ S, 62°42′ W 139
Donald Landing, Can. 54°29′ N, 125°41′ W 108
Donalda, Can. 52°35′ N, 112°34′ W 108
Donaldson, Minn., U.S. 48°33′ N, 96°55′ W 90
Donaldsonville, La., U.S. 30°4′ N, 90°60′ W 103
Donau, river, Ger. 47°48′ N, 8°25′ E 150
Donauwörth, Ger. 48°43′ N, 10°46′ E 152
Doncaster, U.K. 53°31′ N, 1°9′ W 162
Dondo, Angola 9°41′ S, 14°26′ E 218
Dondo, Mozambique 19°39′ S, 34°43′ E 224
Donets' Kryazh, Ukr. 47°29′ N, 36°35′ E 156
Donets'k, Ukr. 47°57′ N, 37°47′ E 156
Dong Hoi, Vietnam 17°29′ N, 106°36′ E 202
Dong Taijnar Hu, lake, China 37°27′ N, 92°46′ E 188
Dong Ujimqin Qi, China 45°31′ N, 116°57′ E 198
Donga, Nig. 7°41′ N, 10°6′ E 222
Döng-Alysh, Kyrg. 42°17′ N, 74°46′ E 184
Dong'an, China 26°24′ N, 111°13′ E 198
Dongara, Austral. 29°14′ S, 114°57′ E 231
Dongbei (Manchuria), region, Asia 40°34′ N, 122°39′ E 200
Dongfang (Basuo), China 19°3′ N, 108°38′ E 198
Dongfeng, China 42°41′ N, 125°25′ E 200
Donggala, Indonesia 0°37′ N, 119°45′ E 192
Donggou, China 39°53′ N, 124°8′ E 200
Dongguan, China 23°2′ N, 113°44′ E 190
Dongguang, China 37°53′ N, 116°32′ E 198
Donghae, S. Korea 37°33′ N, 129°7′ E 200
Dônghén, Laos 16°43′ N, 105°16′ E 202
Donglan, China 24°28′ N, 107°20′ E 198
Dongo, Angola 14°38′ S, 15°39′ E 220
Dongo, Dem. Rep. of the Congo 2°40′ N, 18°27′ E 218
Dongola, Sudan 19°9′ N, 30°28′ E 182
Dongou, Congo 2°2′ N, 18°3′ E 218
Dongping, China 35°49′ N, 116°22′ E 198
Dongping, China 21°42′ N, 112°15′ E 198
Dongqiao, China 31°58′ N, 90°38′ E 188
Dongshan, China 23°37′ N, 117°23′ E 198
Dongsheng, China 39°51′ N, 109°59′ E 198
Dongtai, China 32°52′ N, 120°17′ E 198
Dongting Hu, lake, China 28°54′ N, 111°45′ E 198
Dongwe, river, Zambia 13°52′ S, 24°59′ E 224
Dongxiang, China 28°12′ N, 116°33′ E 198
Dongxing, China 21°33′ N, 107°59′ E 198
Dongyztaū, Kaz. 46°38′ N, 57°37′ E 158
Dongzhen, China 38°59′ N, 103°40′ E 198
Donington, U.K. 52°54′ N, 0°12′ E 162
Doniphan, Mo., U.S. 36°36′ N, 90°49′ W 96
Donji Kamengrad, Bosn. and Herzg. 44°47′ N, 16°33′ E 168
Donji Miholjac, Croatia 45°44′ N, 18°9′ E 168
Donji Tovarnik, Serb. and Mont. 44°48′ N, 19°56′ E 168
Donji Vakuf, Bosn. and Herzg. 44°9′ N, 17°24′ E 168
Donkese, Dem. Rep. of the Congo 1°33′ S, 18°28′ E 218
Donnacona, Can. 46°40′ N, 71°45′ W 94
Donnelly, Can. 55°43′ N, 117°8′ W 108
Donnelly Peak, Nev., U.S. 41°5′ N, 119°21′ W 90
Donnellys Crossing, N.Z. 35°43′ S, 173°36′ E 240
Donner, La., U.S. 29°41′ N, 90°57′ W 103
Donner Pass, Calif., U.S. 39°18′ N, 120°20′ W 90
Donnersberg, peak, Ger. 49°36′ N, 7°52′ E 163
Donostia-San Sebastián, Sp. 43°17′ N, 2°1′ W 164
Donovan, Ill., U.S. 40°52′ N, 87°37′ W 102
Donzère, Fr. 44°26′ N, 4°43′ E 150
Doon, river, U.K. 55°23′ N, 4°51′ W 150
Doone Valley, site, U.K. 51°11′ N, 3°47′ W 162
Doonerak, Mount, Alas., U.S. 67°55′ N, 150°54′ W 98
Door Peninsula, Wis., U.S. 44°29′ N, 87°41′ W 94
Door Point, La., U.S. 30°2′ N, 88°52′ W 103
Dora, Ala., U.S. 33°43′ N, 87°6′ W 96
Dora, N. Mex., U.S. 33°55′ N, 103°20′ W 92
Dora Riparia, river, It. 45°6′ N, 6°50′ E 165
Doran Lake, Can. 61°13′ N, 108°32′ W 108
Dorbod, China 46°54′ N, 124°27′ E 198
Dorče Petrov, Maced. 42°1′ N, 21°21′ E 168
Dorchester, U.K. 50°42′ N, 2°27′ W 162
Dorchester, U.K. 51°38′ N, 1°10′ W 162
Dorchester, Cape, Can. 65°29′ N, 81°58′ W 246
Dordabis, Namibia 22°52′ S, 17°34′ E 227
Dordives, Fr. 48°8′ N, 2°45′ E 163
Dordogne, river, Fr. 44°52′ N, 1°31′ E 165
Dordrecht, Neth. 51°47′ N, 4°40′ E 167
Dordrecht, S. Af. 31°24′ S, 27°0′ E 227
Doré Lake, Can. 54°36′ N, 107°21′ W 108
Dores do Indaiá, Braz. 19°27′ S, 45°37′ W 138
Dorfen, Ger. 48°16′ N, 12°9′ E 152
Dorfmark, Ger. 52°54′ N, 9°47′ E 150
Dori, Burkina Faso 14°1′ N, 0°3′ E 222
Dorintosh, Can. 54°21′ N, 108°38′ W 108
Dorking, U.K. 51°14′ N, 0°20′ E 162
Dormaa Ahenkro, Ghana 7°17′ N, 2°53′ W 222
Dormagen, Ger. 51°5′ N, 6°49′ E 167
Dormans, Fr. 49°4′ N, 3°39′ E 163
Dorneşti, Rom. 47°52′ N, 26°0′ E 152
Dorno Djoutougé, Chad 12°29′ N, 22°15′ E 216
Doro, Mali 16°1′ N, 1°5′ W 222
Dorog, Hung. 47°42′ N, 18°43′ E 168
Dorogobuzh, Russ. 54°52′ N, 33°22′ E 154
Dorogorskoye, Russ. 65°39′ N, 44°27′ E 154
Dorohoi, Rom. 47°56′ N, 26°22′ E 152
Dorora, spring, Chad 17°57′ N, 18°41′ E 216
Dorotea, Nor. 64°16′ N, 16°22′ E 152
Dorris, Calif., U.S. 41°57′ N, 121°56′ W 90
Dorset, Vt., U.S. 43°15′ N, 73°7′ W 104
Dorsten, Ger. 51°39′ N, 6°57′ E 167
Dortmund, Ger. 51°30′ N, 7°27′ E 167
Dörtyol, Turk. 36°50′ N, 36°12′ E 156
Doruma, Dem. Rep. of the Congo 4°42′ N, 27°39′ E 224
Doruokha, Russ. 72°6′ N, 113°30′ E 160
Dörverden, Ger. 52°50′ N, 9°14′ E 152
Dos Bahías, Cabo, Arg. 45°7′ S, 65°30′ W 134
Dos Hermanas, Sp. 37°17′ N, 5°56′ W 164
Dos Lagunas, Guatemala 17°43′ N, 89°38′ W 115
Dos Lagunas Biotope, Guatemala 17°35′ N, 90°14′ W 115
Dos Palos, Calif., U.S. 36°58′ N, 120°38′ W 100
Dos Pozos, Arg. 43°53′ S, 65°25′ W 134
Doso, Côte d'Ivoire 4°45′ N, 6°50′ W 222
Dosso, Niger 13°2′ N, 3°11′ E 222
Dossor, Kaz. 47°31′ N, 52°59′ E 158
Do'stlik, Uzb. 40°33′ N, 68°1′ E 197
Dostlux, Turkm. 37°43′ N, 65°22′ E 197
Dostyq, Kaz. 45°14′ N, 82°29′ E 184
Dot Lake, Alas., U.S. 63°41′ N, 144°9′ W 98
Dothan, Ala., U.S. 31°13′ N, 85°23′ W 96
Dothan, ruin(s), West Bank 32°23′ N, 35°12′ E 194
Dotnuva, Lith. 55°22′ N, 23°51′ E 166
Doty, Wash., U.S. 46°36′ N, 123°17′ W 100
Douai, Fr. 50°21′ N, 3°4′ E 163
Douako, Guinea 9°43′ N, 10°11′ W 222
Douala, Cameroon 4°5′ N, 9°42′ E 222
Douaouir, Mali 20°8′ N, 2°59′ W 222
Douar Sadok, Tun. 35°56′ N, 9°43′ E 156
Douara, spring, Mauritania 17°36′ N, 12°47′ W 222
Douarnenez, Fr. 48°4′ N, 4°20′ W 150
Double Mountain, Calif., U.S. 35°1′ N, 118°32′ W 101
Doubs, river, Switz. 47°19′ N, 6°48′ E 165
Doucette, Tex., U.S. 30°48′ N, 94°26′ W 103
Doudeville, Fr. 49°42′ N, 0°46′ E 163
Doué, Côte d'Ivoire 7°42′ N, 7°39′ W 222
Douentza, Mali 14°58′ N, 2°59′ W 222
Douglas, Ariz., U.S. 31°21′ N, 109°35′ W 112
Douglas, Ga., U.S. 31°29′ N, 82°52′ W 96
Douglas, Mich., U.S. 42°37′ N, 86°12′ W 102
Douglas, S. Af. 29°5′ S, 23°46′ E 227
Douglas, U.K. 54°9′ N, 4°29′ W 162
Douglas, Wyo., U.S. 42°45′ N, 105°23′ W 82
Douglas Islands, Indian Ocean 67°21′ S, 63°31′ E 248
Douglas Lake, Tenn., U.S. 35°59′ N, 84°3′ W 81
Douglas Pass, Colo., U.S. 39°36′ N, 108°49′ W 90
Douglass, Kans., U.S. 37°29′ N, 97°1′ W 92
Douglass, Tex., U.S. 31°39′ N, 94°53′ W 103
Douglassville, Tex., U.S. 33°11′ N, 94°21′ W 103
Doukoula, Cameroon 10°7′ N, 14°56′ E 218
Doulevant-le-Château, Fr. 48°22′ N, 4°55′ E 163
Doullens, Fr. 50°9′ N, 2°20′ E 163
Doulus Head, Ire. 51°58′ N, 10°38′ W 150
Douma, Leb. 34°12′ N, 35°50′ E 194
Doumé, Cameroon 4°15′ N, 13°27′ E 218
Douna, Mali 14°44′ N, 1°43′ W 222
Doura, Mali 13°16′ N, 5°58′ W 222
Dourada, Serra, Braz. 12°47′ S, 48°59′ W 130
Dourados, Braz. 22°15′ S, 54°50′ W 132
Dourados, river, Braz. 22°5′ S, 55°26′ W 132
Dourbali, Chad 11°48′ N, 15°52′ E 218
Dourdan, Fr. 48°31′ N, 2°1′ E 163
Douro, river, Port. 40°43′ N, 8°23′ W 143
Douvaine, Fr. 46°18′ N, 6°18′ E 167
Douz, Tun. 33°28′ N, 9°0′ E 216
Dove Bugt 76°15′ N, 26°60′ W 73
Dove, river, U.K. 53°8′ N, 1°52′ W 162
Dover, Del., U.S. 39°7′ N, 75°38′ W 94
Dover, Fla., U.S. 27°59′ N, 82°12′ W 105
Dover, N.H., U.S. 43°12′ N, 70°53′ W 104
Dover, Ohio, U.S. 40°31′ N, 81°28′ W 102
Dover, U.K. 51°7′ N, 1°17′ E 163
Dover Air Force Base, Del., U.S. 39°7′ N, 75°33′ W 94
Dover, Strait of 50°52′ N, 0°56′ E 162
Dover-Foxcroft, Me., U.S. 45°11′ N, 69°14′ W 94
Dovers, Cape, Antarctica 67°10′ S, 97°16′ E 248
Dovrefjell, Nor. 62°5′ N, 9°20′ E 152
Dow Gonbadān, Iran 30°20′ N, 50°46′ E 196
Dow Polān, Iran 31°54′ N, 50°43′ E 180
Dow Rūd, Iran 33°29′ N, 49°8′ E 180
Dowa, Malawi 13°38′ S, 33°56′ E 224
Dowagiac, Mich., U.S. 41°59′ N, 86°7′ W 102
Dowi, Tanjung, Indonesia 1°30′ N, 97°0′ E 196
Dowlat Yar, Afghan. 34°31′ N, 65°49′ E 186
Dowlatabad, Afghan. 36°25′ N, 64°56′ E 186
Dowlatābād, Iran 28°17′ N, 56°41′ E 196
Dowling Lake, Can. 51°42′ N, 112°39′ W 108
Downes, S. Af. 31°30′ S, 19°56′ E 227
Downey, Calif., U.S. 33°56′ N, 118°9′ W 101
Downham Market, U.K. 52°36′ N, 0°22′ E 162
Downs, Kans., U.S. 39°29′ N, 98°34′ W 90
Downs Mountain, Wyo., U.S. 43°17′ N, 109°45′ W 90
Dowshi, Afghan. 35°36′ N, 68°44′ E 186
Doyang, S. Korea 34°32′ N, 127°10′ E 200
Doyline, La., U.S. 32°31′ N, 93°25′ W 103
Dozois, Réservoir, lake, Can. 47°19′ N, 77°56′ W 94
Drâa, Cap, Mor. 28°47′ N, 11°53′ W 214
Drâa, Hamada du, Alg. 28°59′ N, 7°8′ W 214
Draç, Alban. 41°33′ N, 19°30′ E 168
Dracena, Braz. 21°29′ S, 51°30′ W 138
Drachten, Neth. 53°6′ N, 6°6′ E 163
Dracut, Mass., U.S. 42°40′ N, 71°19′ W 104
Dragaš, Serb. and Mont. 42°3′ N, 20°38′ E 168
Draginac, Serb. and Mont. 44°31′ N, 19°25′ E 168
Dragočaj, Bosn. and Herzg. 44°51′ N, 17°8′ E 168
Dragočava, Bosn. and Herzg. 43°28′ N, 18°49′ E 168
Dragoevo, Maced. 41°40′ N, 22°7′ E 168
Dragovishtitsa, Bulg. 42°21′ N, 22°39′ E 168
Dragsfjärd, Fin. 60°4′ N, 22°30′ E 166
Drake, N. Dak., U.S. 47°53′ N, 100°24′ W 90
Drake Peak, Oreg., U.S. 42°17′ N, 120°14′ W 90
Drakensberg, Africa 24°47′ S, 30°24′ E 227
Dráma, Gr. 41°10′ N, 24°17′ E 180
Drammen, Nor. 59°43′ N, 10°11′ E 152
Dran, Vietnam 11°52′ N, 108°37′ E 202
Drangedal, Nor. 59°6′ N, 9°1′ E 152
Dranov, Lacul, lake, Rom. 44°50′ N, 28°48′ E 156
Dransfeld, Ger. 51°29′ N, 9°45′ E 167
Dras, India 34°26′ N, 75°46′ E 186
Drava, river, Croatia 46°19′ N, 16°42′ E 168
Drávaszabolcs, Hung. 45°48′ N, 18°12′ E 168
Drawsko, Pol. 52°51′ N, 16°3′ E 152
Drayton, Can. 43°44′ N, 80°41′ W 102
Drayton, N. Dak., U.S. 48°32′ N, 97°12′ W 94
Drayton Plains, Mich., U.S. 42°40′ N, 83°22′ W 102
Drayton Valley, Can. 53°12′ N, 114°60′ W 108
Drebkau, Ger. 51°39′ N, 14°12′ E 152
Dreieich, Ger. 50°1′ N, 8°40′ E 167
Dreistelzberg, peak, Ger. 50°16′ N, 9°44′ E 167
Dren, Bulg. 42°25′ N, 23°9′ E 168
Drenovci, Croatia 44°54′ N, 18°54′ E 168
Dresden, Can. 42°34′ N, 82°10′ W 102
Dresden, Ger. 51°2′ N, 13°44′ E 152
Dresden, Ohio, U.S. 40°6′ N, 82°1′ W 102
Dretun', Belarus 55°41′ N, 29°10′ E 166
Dreux, Fr. 48°44′ N, 1°21′ E 163
Drevsjø, Nor. 61°52′ N, 12°2′ E 152
Drezdenko, Pol. 52°50′ N, 15°50′ E 152
Drežnik, Serb. and Mont. 43°46′ N, 19°53′ E 168
Driftwood, river, Can. 55°55′ N, 126°59′ W 108
Drin, river, Alban. 42°11′ N, 19°51′ E 168
Drinjača, Bosn. and Herzg. 44°18′ N, 19°9′ E 168
Drinkwater Pass, Oreg., U.S. 43°46′ N, 118°17′ W 90
Driscoll Island, Antarctica 75°59′ S, 145°33′ W 248
Driskill Mountain, La., U.S. 32°24′ N, 92°56′ W 103
Drlače, Serb. and Mont. 44°8′ N, 19°29′ E 168
Drniš, Croatia 43°51′ N, 16°8′ E 168
Drobeta-Turnu Severin, Rom. 44°37′ N, 22°38′ E 168
Drochia, Mold. 48°2′ N, 27°48′ E 156
Droitwich, U.K. 52°15′ N, 2°9′ W 162
Dronero, It. 44°28′ N, 7°22′ E 167
Dronten, Neth. 52°30′ N, 5°43′ E 163
Droué, Fr. 48°2′ N, 1°5′ E 150
Drowning, river, Can. 50°31′ N, 86°4′ W 110
Droyssig, Ger. 51°2′ N, 12°1′ E 152
Drozdyn', Ukr. 51°38′ N, 27°14′ E 152
Drūkšių Ežeras, lake, Lith. 55°37′ N, 26°8′ E 166
Drum Castle, site, U.K. 57°4′ N, 2°27′ W 150
Drumheller, Can. 51°28′ N, 112°43′ W 90
Drumlanrig Castle, site, U.K. 55°16′ N, 3°55′ W 150
Drummond, Mont., U.S. 46°38′ N, 113°9′ W 90
Drummond Island, Mich., U.S. 45°53′ N, 85°45′ W 81
Drummond Range, Austral. 23°59′ S, 146°26′ E 230
Drummondville, Can. 45°51′ N, 72°31′ W 94
Drumochter Pass, U.K. 56°51′ N, 4°14′ W 150
Drumright, Okla., U.S. 35°57′ N, 96°36′ W 92
Druya, Belarus 55°45′ N, 27°26′ E 166
Druzhba, Ukr. 52°2′ N, 34°3′ E 158
Druzhnaya Gorka, Russ. 59°16′ N, 30°6′ E 166
Drvar, Bosn. and Herzg. 44°21′ N, 16°22′ E 168
Dry Bay 59°1′ N, 138°60′ W 98
Dry Creek, La., U.S. 30°39′ N, 93°4′ W 103
Dry Falls, site, Wash., U.S. 47°33′ N, 119°27′ W 90
Dry Lake, Nev., U.S. 36°27′ N, 114°51′ W 101
Dry Mills, Me., U.S. 43°55′ N, 70°22′ W 104
Dry Prong, La., U.S. 31°33′ N, 92°32′ W 103
Dry Ridge, Ky., U.S. 38°40′ N, 84°36′ W 102
Dry Tortugas, islands, Gulf of Mexico 24°40′ N, 83°1′ W 105
Dry Tortugas National Park, Fla., U.S. 24°38′ N, 82°54′ W 105
Dryanovo, Bulg. 42°58′ N, 25°28′ E 156
Dryberry Lake, Can. 49°34′ N, 94°22′ W 90
Drybrough, Can. 56°32′ N, 101°15′ W 108
Dryden, Can. 49°47′ N, 92°50′ W 94
Dryden, Mich., U.S. 42°55′ N, 83°8′ W 102
Dryden, Tex., U.S. 30°2′ N, 102°7′ W 92
Dryden Flight Research Center, Calif., U.S. 34°59′ N, 117°56′ W 101
Drygalski Island, Antarctica 64°59′ S, 92°17′ E 248
Drygalski Mountains, Antarctica 71°37′ S, 10°5′ E 248
Drysa, river, Belarus 55°44′ N, 28°54′ E 166
Drysdale River National Park, Austral. 15°7′ S, 126°34′ E 238
Drysvyaty, Vozyera, lake, Belarus 55°34′ N, 26°38′ E 166
Dschang, Cameroon 5°24′ N, 10°4′ E 222
Du Bois, Pa., U.S. 41°7′ N, 78°46′ W 94
Du Pont, Wash., U.S. 47°5′ N, 122°34′ W 100
Du Quoin, Mo., U.S. 38°0′ N, 89°14′ W 96
Dua, river, Dem. Rep. of the Congo 2°54′ N, 21°59′ E 218
Duart Castle, site, U.K. 56°25′ N, 5°45′ W 150
Duarte, Pico, peak, Dom. Rep. 19°0′ N, 71°3′ W 116
Dub, Pol. 50°39′ N, 23°34′ E 158
Ḑubā, Saudi Arabia 27°21′ N, 35°43′ E 180
Dubac, Croatia 42°37′ N, 18°9′ E 168
Dubach, La., U.S. 32°40′ N, 92°40′ W 103
Dubai see Dubayy, U.A.E. 25°13′ N, 55°17′ E 196
Dubăsari, Mold. 47°15′ N, 29°10′ E 158
Dubawnt Lake, Can. 63°2′ N, 103°52′ W 106
Dubawnt, river, Can. 60°44′ N, 106°19′ W 108
Dubayy (Dubai), U.A.E. 25°13′ N, 55°17′ E 196
Dubele, Dem. Rep. of the Congo 2°52′ N, 29°33′ E 224
Dubeninki, Pol. 54°17′ N, 22°32′ E 166
Dubenskiy, Russ. 51°28′ N, 56°35′ E 158
Dubica, Croatia 45°11′ N, 16°48′ E 168
Dubičiai, Lith. 54°1′ N, 24°44′ E 166
Dubïnskaya, Kaz. 43°43′ N, 80°12′ E 184
Dubivtsi, Ukr. 49°4′ N, 24°46′ E 152
Dublán, Mex. 30°27′ N, 107°55′ W 92
Dublin, Ga., U.S. 32°31′ N, 82°55′ W 96
Dublin, Ind., U.S. 39°48′ N, 85°13′ W 102
Dublin, N.H., U.S. 42°54′ N, 72°5′ W 104
Dublin, Tex., U.S. 32°5′ N, 98°21′ W 92
Dublin (Baile Átha Cliath), Ire. 53°18′ N, 6°26′ W 150
Dubna, Russ. 56°43′ N, 37°12′ E 154
Dubois, Idaho, U.S. 44°9′ N, 112°13′ W 90
Dubois, Wyo., U.S. 43°32′ N, 109°37′ W 90
Dubose, Can. 54°16′ N, 128°40′ W 108
Duboštica, Bosn. and Herzg. 44°14′ N, 18°20′ E 168
Dubove, Ukr. 51°14′ N, 24°40′ E 152
Dubovka, Russ. 49°2′ N, 44°42′ E 158
Dubrava, Croatia 45°49′ N, 16°3′ E 168
Dubrave, Bosn. and Herzg. 44°48′ N, 18°33′ E 168
Dubravica, Serb. and Mont. 44°41′ N, 21°5′ E 168
Dubréka, Guinea 9°47′ N, 13°34′ W 222
Dubrovka, Russ. 56°22′ N, 28°39′ E 166
Dubrovnik (Ragusa), Croatia 42°38′ N, 18°5′ E 156
Dubrovnoye, Russ. 57°54′ N, 69°29′ E 169
Dubrovytsya, Ukr. 51°33′ N, 26°32′ E 152
Dubrowna, Belarus 54°36′ N, 30°49′ E 154
Dubuque, Iowa, U.S. 42°30′ N, 90°40′ W 94
Duc Tho, Vietnam 18°30′ N, 105°35′ E 202
Duchesne, Utah, U.S. 40°10′ N, 110°24′ W 90
Ducie Island, U.K. 24°38′ S, 124°48′ W 255
Duck Bay, Can. 52°8′ N, 100°10′ W 108
Duck Hill, Miss., U.S. 33°35′ N, 89°43′ W 96
Duck Lake, Can. 52°48′ N, 106°13′ W 108
Duck, river, Tenn., U.S. 35°41′ N, 86°60′ W 80
Duckbill Point, Can. 50°30′ N, 56°13′ W 111
Ducktown, Tenn., U.S. 35°2′ N, 84°23′ W 96
Ducor, Calif., U.S. 35°53′ N, 119°3′ W 101
Duda, river, Col. 2°58′ N, 74°15′ W 136
Dudelange, Lux. 49°28′ N, 6°4′ E 163
Duderstadt, Ger. 51°31′ N, 10°14′ E 167
Dudhi, India 24°12′ N, 83°13′ E 197
Dudhnai, India 25°58′ N, 90°45′ E 197
Dudinka, Russ. 69°25′ N, 86°24′ E 169
Dudley, Mass., U.S. 42°2′ N, 71°56′ W 104
Dudley, U.K. 52°30′ N, 2°6′ W 162
Dudleyville, Ariz., U.S. 32°56′ N, 110°44′ W 92
Dudo, Somalia 9°16′ N, 50°11′ E 216
Dudub, Eth. 6°54′ N, 46°44′ E 218
Dudypta, river, Russ. 71°10′ N, 91°51′ E 160
Duékoué, Côte d'Ivoire 6°39′ N, 7°20′ W 222
Dueodde, Den. 54°53′ N, 14°30′ E 152
Duero, river, Sp. 41°17′ N, 2°56′ W 214
Dufek Coast, Antarctica 84°41′ S, 154°15′ W 248
Dufek Massif, peak, Antarctica 82°41′ S, 54°13′ W 248
Duff Islands, South Pacific Ocean 9°30′ S, 167°28′ E 238
Dugo Selo, Croatia 45°48′ N, 16°13′ E 168
Dugulle, spring, Somalia 2°14′ N, 44°30′ E 218
Dugway, Utah, U.S. 40°13′ N, 112°45′ W 90
Duida-Marahuaca National Park, Venez. 3°36′ N, 65°58′ W 136
Duisburg, Ger. 51°25′ N, 6°45′ E 167
Duitama, Col. 5°49′ N, 73°3′ W 136
Duiwelskloof, S. Af. 23°42′ S, 30°9′ E 227
Dujuuma, Somalia 1°10′ N, 42°34′ E 224
Duk Fadiat, Sudan 7°42′ N, 31°25′ E 224
Duk Faiwil, Sudan 7°30′ N, 31°26′ E 224
Dukafulu, Eth. 5°7′ N, 39°7′ E 224
Dukambia, Eritrea 14°44′ N, 37°29′ E 182
Dukhān, Qatar 25°20′ N, 50°47′ E 196
Dukku, Nig. 10°47′ N, 10°46′ E 222
Dūkštas, Lith. 55°31′ N, 26°18′ E 166
Dula, Dem. Rep. of the Congo 4°41′ N, 20°17′ E 218
Dulan, China 36°19′ N, 98°8′ E 188
Dulce, river, Arg. 29°58′ S, 62°44′ W 139
Dulion, Golfe 43°2′ N, 3°49′ E 150
Dülmen, Ger. 51°50′ N, 7°16′ E 167
Dulovka, Russ. 57°30′ N, 28°20′ E 166
Duluth, Minn., U.S. 46°47′ N, 92°8′ W 94
Dulverton, U.K. 51°2′ N, 3°33′ W 162
Dūmā, Syr. 33°34′ N, 36°24′ E 194
Duma, river, Dem. Rep. of the Congo 4°32′ N, 26°35′ E 224
Dumaguete, Philippines 9°18′ N, 123°14′ E 203
Dumai, Indonesia 1°41′ N, 101°27′ E 196
Dumaran, island, Philippines 10°19′ N, 119°57′ E 192
Dumas, Ark., U.S. 33°52′ N, 91°30′ W 96
Dumas, Tex., U.S. 35°50′ N, 101°59′ W 92
Dumas, Peninsula, Chile 55°4′ S, 68°22′ W 134
Ḑumayr, Syr. 33°38′ N, 36°41′ E 194
Dume, river, Dem. Rep. of the Congo 5°3′ N, 24°48′ E 224
Dumfries, U.K. 55°4′ N, 3°36′ W 150
Dumka, India 24°14′ N, 87°15′ E 197
Dummett, Mount, Antarctica 73°16′ S, 63°25′ E 248
Dumoine, Lac, lake, Can. 46°51′ N, 78°28′ W 94
Dumont d'Urville, station, Antarctica 66°39′ S, 139°39′ E 248
Dümpelfeld, Ger. 50°26′ N, 6°57′ E 167
Dumra, India 26°33′ N, 85°30′ E 197
Dumshaf Plain, Norwegian Sea 69°58′ N, 1°51′ E 255
Dumyāṭ (Damietta), Egypt 31°25′ N, 31°49′ E 180
Dun, Fr. 49°23′ N, 5°12′ E 163
Dun Aengus, ruin(s), Ire. 53°7′ N, 9°55′ W 150
Dún Dealgan see Dundalk, Ire. 53°59′ N, 6°24′ W 150
Duna, river, Europe 47°44′ N, 17°37′ E 168
Dunaff Head, Ire. 55°17′ N, 7°53′ W 150
Dunaharaszti, Hung. 47°21′ N, 19°6′ E 168
Dunakeszi, Hung. 47°37′ N, 19°9′ E 168
Dunapataj, Hung. 46°38′ N, 19°0′ E 168
Dunărea, river, Europe 43°42′ N, 22°49′ E 180
Dunaszekcső, Hung. 46°4′ N, 18°44′ E 168
Dunaújváros, Hung. 46°58′ N, 18°55′ E 168
Dunavecse, Hung. 46°54′ N, 18°58′ E 168
Dunay, Russ. 42°53′ N, 132°20′ E 200
Dunayivtsi, Ukr. 48°52′ N, 26°51′ E 152
Dunbar, W. Va., U.S. 38°21′ N, 81°45′ W 94
Dunblane, Can. 51°12′ N, 106°55′ W 90
Duncan, Ariz., U.S. 32°42′ N, 109°6′ W 92
Duncan, Can. 48°46′ N, 123°41′ W 100
Duncan, Okla., U.S. 34°28′ N, 97°58′ W 96

Egersund, *Nor.* 58°26′ N, 6°0′ E **150**
Egerton, Mount, *Austral.* 24°50′ S, 117°30′ E **230**
Egg Lake, *Can.* 54°58′ N, 106°50′ W **108**
Egg, river, *Can.* 59°58′ N, 95°33′ W **108**
Eggan, *Nig.* 8°39′ N, 6°13′ E **222**
Eggebek, *Ger.* 54°38′ N, 9°22′ E **150**
Eggenburg, *Aust.* 48°38′ N, 15°49′ E **152**
Eghezée, *Belg.* 50°35′ N, 4°53′ E **167**
Eğil, *Turk.* 38°15′ N, 40°5′ E **195**
Egindibulaq, *Kaz.* 49°49′ N, 76°26′ E **184**
Egindiköl, *Kaz.* 51°3′ N, 69°31′ E **184**
Egio, *Gr.* 38°12′ N, 22°6′ E **180**
Eglinton Island, *Can.* 75°24′ N, 126°46′ W **106**
Eglon, ruin(s), *Israel* 31°31′ N, 34°41′ E **194**
Egmont Islands, *Indian Ocean* 7°21′ S, 70°31′ E **188**
Egmont, Mount see Taranaki, Mount, peak, *N.Z.* 39°20′ S, 173°58′ E **240**
Egremont, *U.K.* 54°28′ N, 3°32′ W **162**
Eğridir, *Turk.* 37°50′ N, 30°49′ E **156**
Eğridir Gölü, lake, *Turk.* 38°5′ N, 30°11′ E **180**
Eğrigöz Dağı, peak, *Turk.* 39°23′ N, 29°2′ E **156**
Éguas (Correntina), river, *Braz.* 13°42′ S, 45°43′ W **138**
Egvekinot, *Russ.* 66°17′ N, 179°1′ W **160**
Egyek, *Hung.* 47°38′ N, 20°52′ E **168**
Egypt 26°46′ N, 27°58′ E **216**
Ehime, adm. division, *Japan* 33°37′ N, 132°38′ E **201**
Ehingen, *Ger.* 48°16′ N, 9°44′ E **152**
Ehrang, *Ger.* 49°48′ N, 6°41′ E **167**
Ehrenberg, *Ger.* 50°30′ N, 9°59′ E **167**
Ei, *Japan* 31°12′ N, 130°30′ E **201**
Eide, *Nor.* 62°53′ N, 7°26′ E **152**
Eiderdamm, *Ger.* 54°14′ N, 7°58′ E **150**
Eidsbugarden, *Nor.* 61°22′ N, 8°15′ E **152**
Eidskog, *Nor.* 60°1′ N, 12°6′ E **152**
Eidsvoll, *Nor.* 60°19′ N, 11°12′ E **152**
Eifel, region, *Europe* 50°38′ N, 7°3′ E **167**
Eige, Càrn, peak, *U.K.* 57°16′ N, 5°13′ W **150**
Eigerøy, region, *North Sea* 58°25′ N, 5°35′ E **150**
Eight Degree Channel 7°30′ N, 71°39′ E **188**
Eight Mile Rock, *Bahamas* 26°31′ N, 78°47′ W **105**
Eighty Mile Beach, *Austral.* 20°6′ S, 119°49′ E **231**
Eil Malk see Mecherchar, island, *Palau* 7°7′ N, 134°22′ E **242**
Eilendorf, *Ger.* 50°46′ N, 6°10′ E **167**
Eiler Rasmussen, Cape, *Den.* 81°2′ N, 11°2′ W **246**
Eiler Rasmussen, Kap, *Den.* 82°38′ N, 19°35′ W **246**
Eilerts de Haan Gebergte, *Suriname* 2°50′ N, 56°17′ W **130**
Eina, *Nor.* 60°38′ N, 10°35′ E **152**
Eindhoven, *Neth.* 51°26′ N, 5°28′ E **167**
Eion, ruin(s), *Gr.* 40°46′ N, 23°46′ E **156**
Eirik Ridge, *North Atlantic Ocean* 57°47′ N, 44°35′ W **253**
Eirunepé, *Braz.* 6°40′ S, 69°55′ W **130**
Eisenach, *Ger.* 50°58′ N, 10°19′ E **167**
Eisenstadt, *Aust.* 47°50′ N, 16°31′ E **168**
Eišiškės, *Lith.* 54°10′ N, 24°58′ E **166**
Eitorf, *Ger.* 50°45′ N, 7°27′ E **167**
Eivissa, *Sp.* 38°53′ N, 1°25′ E **150**
Eixe, Sierra do, *Sp.* 42°16′ N, 7°23′ W **150**
Ejea de los Caballeros, *Sp.* 42°7′ N, 1°10′ W **164**
Ejeda, *Madagascar* 24°20′ S, 44°30′ E **220**
Ejin Horo Qi (Altan Xiret), *China* 39°33′ N, 109°44′ E **198**
Ejin Qi, *China* 42°1′ N, 101°30′ E **190**
Ejouj, spring, *Mauritania* 17°1′ N, 9°23′ W **222**
Ejura, *Ghana* 7°25′ N, 1°24′ W **222**
Ekalaka, *Mont., U.S.* 45°52′ N, 104°34′ W **90**
Ekenäs (Tammisaari), *Fin.* 59°58′ N, 23°26′ E **166**
Ekerem, *Turkm.* 38°5′ N, 53°50′ E **180**
Ekeren, *Belg.* 51°16′ N, 4°25′ E **163**
Eket, *Nig.* 4°39′ N, 7°56′ E **222**
Ekibastuz, *Kaz.* 51°44′ N, 75°19′ E **184**
Ekkerøy, *Nor.* 70°4′ N, 30°8′ E **152**
Eklund Islands, *Bellingshausen Sea* 73°25′ S, 70°57′ W **248**
Ekoli, *Dem. Rep. of the Congo* 0°25′ N, 24°16′ E **224**
Ekombe, *Dem. Rep. of the Congo* 1°8′ N, 21°32′ E **218**
Ekonda, *Russ.* 66°5′ N, 103°55′ E **160**
Ekrafane, *Niger* 15°21′ N, 3°43′ E **222**
Ekukola, *Dem. Rep. of the Congo* 0°30′ N, 18°53′ E **218**
Ekwan, river, *Can.* 53°36′ N, 84°16′ W **106**
Ekwendeni, *Malawi* 11°23′ S, 33°48′ E **224**
El Abiadh, Ras, *Tun.* 37°16′ N, 9°8′ E **156**
Ël Äbrēd, *Eth.* 5°30′ N, 45°14′ E **218**
El Adeb Larache, oil field, *Alg.* 27°23′ N, 8°44′ E **214**
El Agreb, oil field, *Alg.* 30°37′ N, 5°30′ E **214**
El Aïoun, *Mor.* 34°35′ N, 2°29′ W **214**
El 'Aiyat, *Egypt* 29°37′ N, 31°12′ E **180**
El 'Alamein, *Egypt* 30°49′ N, 28°52′ E **180**
El Álamo, *Mex.* 31°32′ N, 116°1′ W **92**
El 'Âmirîya, *Egypt* 31°1′ N, 29°48′ E **180**
El Angel, *Ecua.* 0°36′ N, 78°7′ W **136**
El 'Arag, spring, *Egypt* 28°53′ N, 26°27′ E **180**
El Aricha, *Alg.* 34°13′ N, 1°16′ W **214**
El 'Arîsh (Rhinocolura), *Egypt* 31°6′ N, 33°46′ E **194**
El Arneb, spring, *Mali* 16°19′ N, 4°55′ W **222**
El Atimine, spring, *Alg.* 28°51′ N, 3°9′ W **214**
El Badâri, *Egypt* 27°1′ N, 31°23′ E **180**
El Bagre, *Col.* 7°36′ N, 74°47′ W **136**
El Bah, *Eth.* 9°44′ N, 41°47′ E **224**
El Baḥrein, spring, *Egypt* 28°41′ N, 26°30′ E **180**
El Ballâh, *Egypt* 30°45′ N, 32°17′ E **194**
El Ballestero, *Sp.* 38°50′ N, 2°28′ W **164**
El Balyana, *Egypt* 26°14′ N, 31°55′ E **180**
El Banco, *Col.* 9°1′ N, 73°58′ W **136**
El Bauga, *Sudan* 18°13′ N, 33°52′ E **182**
El Baúl, *Venez.* 8°56′ N, 68°20′ W **136**
El Bayadh, *Alg.* 33°42′ N, 1°0′ E **214**
El Béoua, spring, *Mali* 15°6′ N, 6°25′ W **222**
El Berié, spring, *Mauritania* 16°11′ N, 9°57′ W **222**
El Beru Hagia, *Somalia* 2°47′ N, 41°3′ E **224**
El Beyed, spring, *Mauritania* 16°55′ N, 10°3′ W **222**
El Bher, spring, *Mauritania* 15°59′ N, 8°42′ W **222**
El Biar, *Alg.* 36°44′ N, 3°1′ E **150**
El Bonillo, *Sp.* 38°57′ N, 2°33′ W **164**
El Borma, oil field, *Tun.* 31°36′ N, 9°9′ E **214**
El Bosque, *Sp.* 36°45′ N, 5°31′ W **164**
El Burgo de Osma, *Sp.* 41°35′ N, 3°4′ W **164**
El Cabo de Gata, *Sp.* 36°46′ N, 2°15′ W **164**
El Caburé, *Arg.* 26°2′ S, 62°21′ W **139**
El Caín, *Arg.* 41°37′ S, 68°16′ W **134**
El Calafate (Lago Argentino), *Arg.* 50°26′ S, 72°13′ W **123**
El Callao, *Venez.* 7°22′ N, 61°49′ W **130**
El Calvario, *Venez.* 9°0′ N, 66°59′ W **136**
El Campello, *Sp.* 38°25′ N, 0°24′ E **164**
El Campillo de la Jara, *Sp.* 39°35′ N, 5°3′ W **164**
El Campo, *Tex., U.S.* 29°11′ N, 96°17′ W **96**
El Cap, *Egypt* 30°56′ N, 32°17′ E **194**
El Capitan, peak, *Mont., U.S.* 45°59′ N, 114°29′ W **90**
El Carmen, *Arg.* 24°24′ S, 65°18′ W **132**
El Carmen, *Bol.* 18°49′ S, 58°35′ W **132**
El Carmen, *Bol.* 13°60′ S, 63°41′ W **137**
El Carmen, *Col.* 5°55′ N, 76°14′ W **136**
El Carmen, *Venez.* 1°15′ N, 66°50′ W **136**
El Carpio, *Sp.* 37°56′ N, 4°31′ W **164**
El Castillo de Las Concepción, *Nicar.* 10°58′ N, 84°24′ W **115**
El Ceibo, *Guatemala* 17°16′ N, 90°55′ W **115**
El Centro, *Calif., U.S.* 32°47′ N, 115°34′ W **101**
El Chichón, peak, *Mex.* 17°21′ N, 93°23′ W **115**
El Chico, *Mex.* 20°8′ N, 98°54′ W **112**
El Choro, *Bol.* 18°24′ S, 67°9′ W **137**
El Cimaterio, *Mex.* 20°29′ N, 100°27′ W **112**
El Claro, *Mex.* 30°28′ N, 111°11′ W **92**
El Cocuy, *Col.* 6°24′ N, 72°28′ W **136**
El Cocuy National Park, *Col.* 6°35′ N, 72°43′ W **136**
El Cogoi, *Arg.* 24°48′ S, 59°12′ W **132**
El Colorado, *Arg.* 26°18′ S, 59°23′ W **139**
El Corcovado, *Arg.* 43°30′ S, 71°32′ W **134**
El Cuyo, *Mex.* 21°32′ N, 87°42′ W **116**
El 'Dab'a, *Egypt* 31°1′ N, 28°23′ E **180**
El Dakka, ruin(s), *Egypt* 23°4′ N, 32°32′ E **182**
El Deir, *Egypt* 25°19′ N, 32°33′ E **182**
El Descanso, *Mex.* 32°12′ N, 116°54′ W **92**
El Desemboque, *Mex.* 29°33′ N, 112°26′ W **92**
El Desmonte, *Arg.* 22°42′ S, 62°17′ W **132**
El Djouf, *Mauritania* 19°53′ N, 10°5′ W **222**
El Dorado, *Ark., U.S.* 33°11′ N, 92°41′ W **103**
El Dorado, *Kans., U.S.* 37°47′ N, 96°52′ W **92**
El Dorado, *Venez.* 6°43′ N, 61°36′ W **130**
El Dorado Springs, *Mo., U.S.* 37°51′ N, 94°2′ W **94**
El Egder, spring, *Eth.* 3°51′ N, 38°54′ E **224**
El Eglab, region, *Africa* 25°45′ N, 5°58′ W **214**
El Encanto, *Col.* 1°38′ S, 73°14′ W **136**
El Esfuerzo, *Mex.* 25°23′ N, 103°15′ W **114**
El Faiyûm, *Egypt* 29°16′ N, 30°48′ E **180**
El Farâid, Gebel, peak, *Egypt* 23°31′ N, 35°19′ E **182**
El Fasher, *Sudan* 13°37′ N, 25°19′ E **226**
El Fashn, *Egypt* 28°48′ N, 30°50′ E **180**
El Fifi, *Sudan* 10°3′ N, 25°1′ E **224**
El Fuerte, *Mex.* 23°49′ N, 103°8′ W **114**
El Fula, *Sudan* 11°46′ N, 28°20′ E **216**
El Gâga, *Egypt* 24°48′ N, 30°30′ E **226**
El Gallego, *Mex.* 29°48′ N, 106°23′ W **92**
El Galpón, *Arg.* 25°24′ S, 64°39′ W **134**
El Gassi, oil field, *Alg.* 30°53′ N, 5°37′ E **214**
El Geili, *Sudan* 16°0′ N, 32°37′ E **182**
El Gezira, region, *Africa* 14°22′ N, 32°15′ E **182**
El Ghobena, *Tun.* 35°29′ N, 9°38′ E **156**
El Gîza, *Egypt* 30°1′ N, 31°8′ E **180**
El Golea, *Alg.* 30°33′ N, 2°43′ E **207**
El Goled Bahri, *Sudan* 18°27′ N, 30°40′ E **226**
El Golfo de Santa Clara, *Mex.* 31°41′ N, 114°32′ W **92**
El Grau, *Sp.* 38°59′ N, 0°10′ E **164**
El Grau de Castelló, *Sp.* 39°58′ N, 1°60′ E **164**
El Grullo, *Mex.* 19°48′ N, 104°14′ W **114**
El Guapo, *Venez.* 10°8′ N, 66°2′ W **136**
El Hadjira, *Alg.* 32°37′ N, 5°31′ E **214**
El Hajeb, *Mor.* 33°41′ N, 5°25′ W **214**
El Hamma, *Tun.* 33°55′ N, 9°48′ E **216**
El Ḥammâm, *Egypt* 30°51′ N, 29°19′ E **180**
El Hank, region, *Africa* 24°58′ N, 6°26′ W **214**
El Haouaria, *Tun.* 37°3′ N, 11°0′ E **156**
El Haraïg, *Tun.* 35°47′ N, 9°13′ E **156**
El Harrach, *Alg.* 36°48′ N, 3°9′ E **214**
El Hasaheisa, *Sudan* 14°41′ N, 33°17′ E **182**
El Hawata, *Sudan* 13°24′ N, 34°36′ E **182**
El Ḥeiz, *Egypt* 28°2′ N, 28°37′ E **180**
El Hiaïda, *Mor.* 35°5′ N, 6°11′ W **150**
El Higo, *Mex.* 21°45′ N, 98°27′ W **114**
El Hilla, *Sudan* 13°24′ N, 27°5′ E **226**
El Hobra, *Alg.* 32°10′ N, 4°43′ E **214**
El Homeur, *Alg.* 29°52′ N, 1°36′ E **214**
El Huariche, *Mex.* 24°49′ N, 103°9′ W **114**
El Iskandarîya (Alexandria), *Egypt* 31°10′ N, 29°55′ E **180**
El Jabha (Puerto Capaz), *Mor.* 35°12′ N, 4°40′ W **150**
El Jadida (Mazagan), *Mor.* 33°15′ N, 8°33′ W **214**
El Jardín, *Sp.* 38°48′ N, 2°19′ W **164**
El Jebelein, *Sudan* 12°34′ N, 32°52′ E **182**
El Jemm, *Tun.* 35°18′ N, 10°43′ E **156**
El Kanâyis, spring, *Egypt* 25°0′ N, 33°16′ E **182**
El Karaba, *Sudan* 18°29′ N, 33°44′ E **182**
El Karnak, ruin(s), *Egypt* 25°44′ N, 32°37′ E **182**
El Katulo, spring, *Kenya* 2°26′ N, 40°35′ E **224**
El Kawa, *Sudan* 13°42′ N, 32°31′ E **182**
El Kef, *Tun.* 36°11′ N, 8°42′ E **156**
El Kelaa des Srarhna, *Mor.* 32°5′ N, 7°25′ W **214**
Ël Kerē, *Eth.* 5°48′ N, 42°9′ E **224**
El Khandaq, *Sudan* 18°36′ N, 30°34′ E **226**
El Khârga, *Egypt* 25°28′ N, 30°29′ E **182**
El Kharrouba, *Tun.* 35°23′ N, 9°59′ E **156**
El Khnâchîch, *Mali* 21°6′ N, 5°26′ W **222**
El Kodab, *Sudan* 16°12′ N, 32°30′ E **182**
El Koin, *Sudan* 19°18′ N, 30°33′ E **216**
El Kseïbat, *Alg.* 27°58′ N, 0°30′ E **214**
El Kseur, *Alg.* 36°40′ N, 4°51′ E **150**
El Ksiba, *Mor.* 32°38′ N, 6°3′ W **214**
El Kuntilla, *Egypt* 29°58′ N, 34°41′ E **180**
El Lagowa, *Sudan* 11°25′ N, 29°8′ E **216**
El Lein, spring, *Kenya* 0°26′ N, 40°30′ E **224**
El Leiya, *Sudan* 16°15′ N, 35°26′ E **182**
El Limón, *Mex.* 22°48′ N, 99°1′ W **114**
El Lucero, *Mex.* 25°56′ N, 103°26′ W **114**
El Macao, *Dom. Rep.* 18°45′ N, 68°31′ W **116**
El Mahalla el Kubra, *Egypt* 30°59′ N, 31°8′ E **226**
El Maḥârîq, *Egypt* 25°39′ N, 30°36′ E **226**
El Mahfoura, spring, *Alg.* 32°34′ N, 2°12′ E **214**
El Maitén, *Arg.* 42°3′ S, 71°11′ W **134**
El Maïz, *Alg.* 28°25′ N, 0°15′ E **214**
El Malpais National Monument, *N. Mex., U.S.* 34°36′ N, 110°21′ W **92**
El Manaqil, *Sudan* 14°12′ N, 33°0′ E **182**
El Mango, *Venez.* 1°54′ N, 66°33′ W **136**
El Manshâh, *Egypt* 26°29′ N, 31°42′ E **180**
El Mansour, *Alg.* 27°38′ N, 0°19′ E **214**
El Manṣûra, *Egypt* 30°58′ N, 31°24′ E **180**
El Maqdaba, spring, *Egypt* 30°53′ N, 34°0′ E **194**
El Mazâr, *Egypt* 31°1′ N, 33°23′ E **194**
El Medda, *Mauritania* 19°56′ N, 13°20′ W **222**
El Meghaïer, *Alg.* 33°56′ N, 5°54′ E **214**
El Melemm, *Sudan* 9°55′ N, 28°43′ E **224**
El Messir, spring, *Chad* 15°43′ N, 16°59′ E **216**
El Mhabes, spring, *Mauritania* 23°43′ N, 8°53′ W **214**
El Milagro, *Arg.* 31°1′ S, 65°59′ W **134**
El Milhas, spring, *Mauritania* 25°25′ N, 6°55′ W **214**
El Milia, *Alg.* 36°48′ N, 6°16′ E **150**
El Mina, *Leb.* 34°27′ N, 35°49′ E **194**
El Mîna, *Leb.* 34°27′ N, 35°49′ E **156**
El Minya, *Egypt* 28°7′ N, 30°41′ E **180**
El Mirador, ruin(s), *Guatemala* 17°43′ N, 90°3′ W **115**
El Mirage, *Ariz., U.S.* 33°37′ N, 112°19′ W **92**
El Moale, spring, *Sudan* 10°20′ N, 23°46′ E **224**
El Moïnane, spring, *Mauritania* 19°10′ N, 11°29′ W **222**
El Morro National Monument, *N. Mex., U.S.* 35°1′ N, 108°26′ W **92**
El Moueïla, *Mauritania* 21°38′ N, 10°36′ W **222**
El Mouilha, spring, *Mali* 16°40′ N, 5°6′ W **222**
El Mraïti, spring, *Mali* 19°12′ N, 2°19′ W **222**
El Mrâyer, spring, *Mauritania* 21°28′ N, 8°12′ W **222**
El Mreïti, spring, *Mauritania* 23°29′ N, 7°56′ W **214**
El Mreyyé, region, *Africa* 18°48′ N, 8°16′ W **222**
El Mughāzī, *Gaza Strip* 31°23′ N, 34°22′ E **194**
El Mulato, *Mex.* 29°22′ N, 104°11′ W **92**
El Mzereb, spring, *Mali* 24°46′ N, 6°23′ W **214**
El Nasser, *Egypt* 24°34′ N, 33°2′ E **182**
El Nayar, *Mex.* 23°55′ N, 104°41′ W **114**
El Nido, *Philippines* 11°10′ N, 119°24′ E **203**
El Niybo, *Eth.* 4°31′ N, 39°54′ E **224**
El Obeid, *Sudan* 13°8′ N, 30°11′ E **226**
El Oro, *Mex.* 19°46′ N, 100°8′ W **114**
El Oualadji, *Mali* 16°13′ N, 3°28′ W **214**
El Palmito, *Mex.* 25°35′ N, 104°59′ W **114**
El Pao, *Venez.* 8°1′ N, 62°38′ W **130**
El Pao, *Venez.* 8°46′ N, 64°39′ W **116**
El Paso, *Ill., U.S.* 40°43′ N, 89°1′ W **102**
El Paso, *Tex., U.S.* 31°45′ N, 106°29′ W **92**
El Paso Mountains, *Calif., U.S.* 35°23′ N, 117°59′ W **101**
El Payo, *Sp.* 40°18′ N, 6°45′ W **150**
El Perelló, *Sp.* 40°52′ N, 0°43′ E **164**
El Perú, *Venez.* 7°18′ N, 61°50′ W **130**
El Pescadero, *Mex.* 23°20′ N, 110°11′ W **112**
El Picazo, *Sp.* 39°26′ N, 2°7′ W **164**
El Piñal, *Venez.* 7°26′ N, 68°41′ W **136**
El Plomo, *Mex.* 31°14′ N, 112°4′ W **92**
El Pobo de Dueñas, *Sp.* 40°45′ N, 1°39′ W **164**
El Portal, *Calif., U.S.* 37°41′ N, 119°48′ W **100**
El Portezuelo, *Arg.* 46°2′ S, 71°38′ W **134**
El Porvenir, *Col.* 4°42′ N, 71°23′ W **136**
El Porvenir, *Pan.* 9°34′ N, 78°59′ W **115**
El Porvenir, *Venez.* 6°56′ N, 68°43′ W **136**
El Potosi, *Mex.* 24°50′ N, 100°20′ W **114**
El Potosi National Park, *Mex.* 21°58′ N, 100°4′ W **112**
El Pozo, *Mex.* 30°55′ N, 109°16′ W **92**
El Pozo, *Mex.* 24°54′ N, 107°15′ W **112**
El Progreso, *Hond.* 15°21′ N, 87°48′ W **115**
El Pueblito, *Mex.* 29°5′ N, 105°8′ W **92**
El Puente, *Bol.* 21°14′ S, 65°19′ W **137**
El Qâhira (Cairo), *Egypt* 30°3′ N, 31°8′ E **180**
El Qanṭara, *Egypt* 30°51′ N, 32°19′ E **194**
El Qaṣr, *Egypt* 25°42′ N, 28°50′ E **180**
El Quseima, *Egypt* 30°39′ N, 34°22′ E **194**
El Râshda, *Egypt* 25°33′ N, 28°54′ E **226**
El Real, *Pan.* 8°6′ N, 77°45′ W **115**
El Reno, *Okla., U.S.* 35°30′ N, 97°57′ W **92**
El Rhaïllassiya Oumm Amoura, spring, *Mauritania* 16°26′ N, 9°24′ W **222**
El Rio, *Calif., U.S.* 34°14′ N, 119°11′ W **101**
El Rito, *N. Mex., U.S.* 36°21′ N, 106°12′ W **92**
El Roble, *Mex.* 23°13′ N, 106°14′ W **114**
El Ronquillo, *Sp.* 37°43′ N, 6°11′ W **164**
El Rosario, *Mex.* 30°4′ N, 115°46′ W **92**
El Ruâfa, spring, *Egypt* 30°49′ N, 34°7′ E **194**
El Rubio, *Sp.* 37°21′ N, 4°60′ W **164**
El Rucio, *Mex.* 23°23′ N, 102°4′ W **114**
El Rusbayo, *Mex.* 31°1′ N, 109°15′ W **92**
El Sabinal National Park, *Mex.* 26°3′ N, 99°47′ W **112**
El Salado, *Mex.* 24°15′ N, 100°51′ W **114**
El Salto, *Mex.* 20°31′ N, 103°11′ W **114**
El Salto, *Mex.* 23°44′ N, 105°22′ W **114**
El Salvador 14°0′ N, 89°0′ W **115**
El Salvador, *Mex.* 24°28′ N, 100°53′ W **114**
El Samán de Apure, *Venez.* 7°52′ N, 68°43′ W **136**
El Sauz, *Mex.* 29°0′ N, 106°15′ W **92**
El Sauzal, *Mex.* 31°53′ N, 116°41′ W **92**
El Seco, *Mex.* 19°6′ N, 97°39′ W **114**
El Shab, spring, *Egypt* 22°18′ N, 29°45′ E **226**
El Sibû', ruin(s), *Egypt* 22°44′ N, 32°22′ E **182**
El Soberbio, *Arg.* 27°21′ S, 54°15′ W **139**
El Socorro, *Venez.* 8°59′ N, 65°45′ W **136**
El Sombrero, *Venez.* 9°23′ N, 67°4′ W **136**
El Sueco, *Mex.* 29°51′ N, 106°23′ W **92**
El Suweis (Suez), *Egypt* 30°1′ N, 32°26′ E **180**
El Tajín, ruin(s), *Mex.* 20°24′ N, 97°28′ W **114**
El Tama National Park, *Venez.* 7°10′ N, 72°14′ W **136**
El Tecuan, *Mex.* 19°21′ N, 104°58′ W **114**
El Teleno, peak, *Sp.* 42°19′ N, 6°28′ W **150**
El Tell el Ahmar, *Egypt* 30°53′ N, 32°24′ E **194**
El Tigre, *Col.* 6°45′ N, 71°46′ W **136**
El Tîna, *Egypt* 31°2′ N, 32°17′ E **194**
El Toboso, *Sp.* 39°31′ N, 3°2′ W **164**
El Tocuyo, *Venez.* 9°45′ N, 69°49′ W **136**
El Tomatal, *Mex.* 28°26′ N, 114°6′ W **92**
El Toro, peak, *Sp.* 39°58′ N, 4°5′ E **164**
El Trébol, *Arg.* 32°13′ S, 61°42′ W **139**
El Triunfo, Pirámide, peak, *Arg.* 25°45′ S, 61°51′ W **132**
El Tuito, *Mex.* 20°19′ N, 105°25′ W **114**
El Tuparro National Park, *Col.* 5°10′ N, 68°60′ W **136**
El Ṭûr, *Egypt* 28°14′ N, 33°37′ E **180**
El Turbio, *Arg.* 51°42′ S, 72°8′ W **134**
El Valle, *Col.* 6°5′ N, 77°26′ W **136**
El Veladero National Park, *Mex.* 16°53′ N, 99°60′ W **112**
El Vendrell, *Sp.* 41°13′ N, 1°32′ E **164**
El Vergel, *Mex.* 26°26′ N, 106°24′ W **114**
El Wak, *Kenya* 2°44′ N, 40°53′ E **224**
El Walamo, *Mex.* 23°6′ N, 106°13′ W **114**
El Wasifîya, *Egypt* 30°33′ N, 32°8′ E **194**
El Wâsta, *Egypt* 29°20′ N, 31°10′ E **180**
El Wuz, *Sudan* 15°1′ N, 30°12′ E **226**
El Yagual, *Venez.* 7°29′ N, 68°26′ W **136**
El Zape, *Mex.* 25°46′ N, 105°45′ W **114**
Elaho, river, *Can.* 50°14′ N, 123°38′ W **100**
Elaia, Cape, *Northern Cyprus* 35°16′ N, 34°4′ E **194**
Elan', *Russ.* 57°38′ N, 63°38′ E **154**
Elat, *Israel* 29°35′ N, 34°59′ E **180**
Elato Atoll, *F.S.M.* 6°59′ N, 145°34′ E **192**
El'Atrun, spring, *Sudan* 18°6′ N, 26°36′ E **226**
El'Auja see Nizzana, *Israel* 30°52′ N, 34°25′ E **194**
Elâzığ, *Turk.* 38°39′ N, 39°12′ E **195**
Elba, *Ala., U.S.* 31°24′ N, 86°4′ W **96**
Elba, Cape see Hadarba, Ras, *Egypt* 21°49′ N, 36°55′ E **182**
Elba, island, *It.* 42°54′ N, 9°57′ E **214**
Elbe, *Wash., U.S.* 46°45′ N, 122°12′ W **100**
Elbe, river, *Ger.* 53°7′ N, 10°4′ E **143**
Elbert, Mount, *Colo., U.S.* 39°6′ N, 106°31′ W **90**
Elberta, *Mich., U.S.* 44°35′ N, 86°13′ W **94**
Elbeuf, *Fr.* 49°17′ N, 1°0′ E **163**
Elbistan, *Turk.* 38°11′ N, 37°10′ E **156**
Elbląg, *Pol.* 54°9′ N, 19°25′ E **166**
Elbow, *Can.* 51°8′ N, 106°38′ W **90**
Elbow Cays, *North Atlantic Ocean* 23°56′ N, 81°24′ W **116**
Elbow Lake, *Minn., U.S.* 45°59′ N, 95°59′ W **90**
El'brus, peak, *Russ.* 43°18′ N, 42°24′ E **195**
Elburg, *Neth.* 52°26′ N, 5°49′ E **163**
Elburz, *Iran* 36°26′ N, 52°39′ E **207**
Elburz Mountains see Alborz, Reshteh-ye, *Iran* 36°43′ N, 49°25′ E **195**
Elche de la Sierra, *Sp.* 38°26′ N, 2°3′ W **164**
Elche (Elx), *Sp.* 38°15′ N, 0°42′ E **164**
Elcho Island, *Austral.* 11°51′ S, 135°35′ E **192**
Elda, *Sp.* 38°28′ N, 0°49′ E **150**
Eldama Ravine, *Kenya* 4°238′ N, 35°43′ E **224**
El'dikan, *Russ.* 60°48′ N, 135°14′ E **160**
Eldon, *Iowa, U.S.* 40°55′ N, 92°13′ W **94**
Eldon, *Mo., U.S.* 38°19′ N, 92°35′ W **94**
Eldorado, *Arg.* 26°29′ S, 54°42′ W **139**
Eldorado, *Mex.* 24°18′ N, 107°23′ W **112**
Eldorado, *Mo., U.S.* 37°47′ N, 88°26′ W **96**
Eldorado, *Okla., U.S.* 34°26′ N, 99°39′ W **96**
Eldorado, *Tex., U.S.* 30°51′ N, 100°36′ W **92**
Eldorado Mountains, *Nev., U.S.* 35°49′ N, 114°58′ W **101**
Eldorado Pass, *Oreg., U.S.* 44°20′ N, 118°7′ W **90**
Eldorado Paulista, *Braz.* 24°35′ S, 48°9′ W **138**
Eldoret, *Kenya* 0°28′ N, 35°18′ E **224**
Electra, *Tex., U.S.* 34°0′ N, 98°55′ W **92**
Electric Mills, *Miss., U.S.* 32°44′ N, 88°28′ W **103**
Electric Peak, *Mont., U.S.* 44°59′ N, 110°56′ W **90**
El'Ein, spring, *Sudan* 16°34′ N, 29°17′ E **226**
Eleja, *Latv.* 56°24′ N, 23°41′ E **166**
Elek, *Hung.* 46°32′ N, 21°14′ E **168**
Elektrostal', *Russ.* 55°45′ N, 38°30′ E **154**
Elephant Island, *Antarctica* 61°4′ S, 55°14′ W **134**
Elephant Mountain, *Tex., U.S.* 29°59′ N, 103°36′ W **92**
Elephant Point, *U.S.* 66°15′ N, 161°24′ W **98**
Eleşkirt, *Turk.* 39°47′ N, 42°39′ E **195**
Eleuthera Island, *Bahamas* 25°12′ N, 76°7′ W **116**
Eleutherae, ruin(s), *Gr.* 38°10′ N, 23°17′ E **156**
Eleutherna, ruin(s), *Gr.* 35°18′ N, 24°34′ E **156**
Elfers, *Fla., U.S.* 28°13′ N, 82°42′ W **105**
Elfin Cove, *U.S.* 58°11′ N, 136°20′ W **98**
Elfrida, *Ariz., U.S.* 31°41′ N, 109°40′ W **92**
Elgå, *Nor.* 62°9′ N, 11°56′ E **152**
Elgin, *Ill., U.S.* 42°2′ N, 88°16′ W **102**
Elgin, *Nebr., U.S.* 41°57′ N, 98°6′ W **90**
Elgin, *N. Dak., U.S.* 46°23′ N, 101°52′ W **90**
Elgin, *Oreg., U.S.* 45°33′ N, 117°56′ W **90**
Elgin, *Tex., U.S.* 30°20′ N, 97°22′ W **92**
El'ginskiy, *Russ.* 64°42′ N, 142°12′ E **173**
Elgon, Mount, *Uganda* 1°4′ N, 34°29′ E **224**
Elgoras, Gora, peak, *Russ.* 68°5′ N, 31°24′ E **152**
Elias Garcia, *Angola* 9°3′ S, 20°14′ E **218**
Elida, *N. Mex., U.S.* 33°56′ N, 103°40′ W **92**
Elida, *Ohio, U.S.* 40°46′ N, 84°12′ W **102**
Eliki Gounda, *Niger* 15°3′ N, 8°36′ E **222**
Elikónas (Helicon), peak, *Gr.* 38°17′ N, 22°47′ E **156**
Elila, river, *Dem. Rep. of the Congo* 3°26′ S, 27°52′ E **224**
Elila, river, *Dem. Rep. of the Congo* 2°55′ S, 26°23′ E **224**
Eliot, *Me., U.S.* 43°9′ N, 70°48′ W **104**
Elipa, *Dem. Rep. of the Congo* 1°4′ S, 24°19′ E **224**
Elis, ruin(s), *Gr.* 37°52′ N, 21°18′ E **156**
Elisabetha, *Dem. Rep. of the Congo* 1°5′ N, 23°36′ E **224**
Élisabethville see Lubumbashi, *Dem. Rep. of the Congo* 11°43′ S, 27°26′ E **224**
Elisenvaara, *Russ.* 61°23′ N, 29°45′ E **166**
Eliseu Martins, *Braz.* 8°11′ S, 43°43′ W **132**
Elista, *Russ.* 46°16′ N, 44°9′ E **158**
Elizabeth, *La., U.S.* 30°51′ N, 92°48′ W **103**
Elizabeth, *Miss., U.S.* 33°24′ N, 90°53′ W **103**
Elizabeth, *N.J., U.S.* 40°39′ N, 74°14′ W **94**
Elizabeth, *W. Va., U.S.* 39°3′ N, 81°25′ W **102**
Elizabeth City, *N.C., U.S.* 36°18′ N, 76°16′ W **96**
Elizabeth Falls, *Can.* 59°20′ N, 105°49′ W **108**
Elizabeth Islands, *Atlantic Ocean* 41°21′ N, 71°2′ W **104**
Elizabeth Mountain, *Utah, U.S.* 40°57′ N, 110°48′ W **90**
Elizabethton, *Tenn., U.S.* 36°20′ N, 82°14′ W **96**
Elizabethtown, *Ind., U.S.* 39°7′ N, 85°49′ W **102**
Elizabethtown, *Ky., U.S.* 37°40′ N, 85°52′ W **96**
Elizabethtown, *Mo., U.S.* 37°27′ N, 88°18′ W **96**
Elizabethtown, *N.Y., U.S.* 44°13′ N, 73°37′ W **104**
Elizondo, *Sp.* 43°8′ N, 1°31′ W **150**
Elk, *Calif., U.S.* 39°8′ N, 123°43′ W **90**
Elk City, *Okla., U.S.* 35°23′ N, 99°26′ W **92**
Elk Creek, river, *S. Dak., U.S.* 44°13′ N, 102°53′ W **90**
Elk Grove, *Calif., U.S.* 38°24′ N, 121°23′ W **100**
Elk Hills, *Calif., U.S.* 35°20′ N, 119°31′ W **100**
Elk Island National Park, *Can.* 53°32′ N, 113°12′ W **238**
Elk Lake, *Can.* 47°43′ N, 80°21′ W **94**
Elk Lake, *Mich., U.S.* 44°47′ N, 85°37′ W **94**
Elk Mountain, *Wyo., U.S.* 41°37′ N, 106°36′ W **90**
Elk Peak, *Mont., U.S.* 46°25′ N, 110°50′ W **90**
Elk Point, *Can.* 53°53′ N, 110°55′ W **108**
Elk Point, *S. Dak., U.S.* 42°39′ N, 96°41′ W **90**
Elk River, *Idaho, U.S.* 46°45′ N, 116°13′ W **90**
Elk River, *Minn., U.S.* 45°17′ N, 93°34′ W **94**
Elk, river, *Can.* 49°23′ N, 114°53′ W **108**
Elk, river, *Colo., U.S.* 40°34′ N, 106°58′ W **90**
Elk, river, *W. Va., U.S.* 38°25′ N, 80°55′ W **80**
Elkhart, *Ind., U.S.* 41°40′ N, 85°59′ W **82**
Elkhart, *Kans., U.S.* 37°0′ N, 101°54′ W **92**
Elkhart, *Tex., U.S.* 31°36′ N, 95°35′ W **103**
Elkhart Lake, *Wis., U.S.* 43°49′ N, 88°1′ W **102**
Elkhead Mountains, *Colo., U.S.* 40°40′ N, 107°46′ W **90**
Elkhorn, *Can.* 49°59′ N, 101°15′ W **90**
Elkhorn, *Wis., U.S.* 42°40′ N, 88°33′ W **102**
Elkhorn City, *Ky., U.S.* 37°18′ N, 82°22′ W **94**
Elkhorn Mountain, *Can.* 49°47′ N, 125°55′ W **90**
Elkhorn, river, *Nebr., U.S.* 42°21′ N, 99°26′ W **80**
Elkhovo, *Bulg.* 42°10′ N, 26°34′ E **158**
Elkin, *N.C., U.S.* 36°14′ N, 80°53′ W **96**
Elkins, *N. Mex., U.S.* 33°41′ N, 104°4′ W **92**
Elkins, *W. Va., U.S.* 38°55′ N, 79°51′ W **94**
Elkland, *Pa., U.S.* 41°59′ N, 77°20′ W **94**
Elko, *Can.* 49°18′ N, 115°7′ W **90**
Elko, *Nev., U.S.* 40°53′ N, 115°51′ W **106**
Elkton, *Fla., U.S.* 29°46′ N, 81°27′ W **105**
Elkton, *Ky., U.S.* 36°48′ N, 87°10′ W **96**
Elkton, *Md., U.S.* 39°36′ N, 75°51′ W **94**
Elkton, *Mich., U.S.* 43°48′ N, 83°11′ W **102**
Elkview, *W. Va., U.S.* 38°26′ N, 81°30′ W **102**
Ellef Ringnes Island, *Can.* 77°11′ N, 103°31′ W **106**
Elleh Creek, river, *Can.* 58°32′ N, 122°26′ W **108**
Ellen, Mount, *Utah, U.S.* 38°5′ N, 110°53′ W **90**
Ellenboro, *W. Va., U.S.* 39°16′ N, 81°4′ W **102**
Ellendale, *N. Dak., U.S.* 46°0′ N, 98°32′ W **90**
Ellensburg, *Wash., U.S.* 46°58′ N, 120°35′ W **90**
Ellenton, *Fla., U.S.* 27°32′ N, 82°30′ W **105**
Ellesmere Island, *Can.* 76°28′ N, 77°40′ W **106**
Ellesmere Port, *U.K.* 53°17′ N, 2°54′ W **162**
Ellettsville, *Ind., U.S.* 39°13′ N, 86°38′ W **102**
Ellila, spring, *Chad* 16°48′ N, 20°20′ E **216**
Ellington, *Conn., U.S.* 41°53′ N, 72°29′ W **104**
Ellinwood, *Kans., U.S.* 38°20′ N, 98°35′ W **82**
Elliot, *S. Af.* 31°21′ S, 27°49′ E **227**
Elliot Lake, *Can.* 46°23′ N, 82°40′ W **110**
Elliott, Cape, *Antarctica* 65°39′ S, 106°26′ E **248**
Elliott Lake, *Can.* 61°1′ N, 100°2′ W **108**
Ellis, *Idaho, U.S.* 44°41′ N, 114°2′ W **90**
Ellis, *Kans., U.S.* 38°55′ N, 99°34′ W **90**
Ellis, Mount, *Mont., U.S.* 45°32′ N, 111°1′ W **90**
Ellisburg, *N.Y., U.S.* 43°43′ N, 76°9′ W **110**
Ellisland, site, *U.K.* 55°6′ N, 3°46′ W **150**
Ellisras see Lephalale, *S. Af.* 23°40′ S, 27°42′ E **227**
Elliston, *Austral.* 33°40′ S, 134°54′ E **231**
Ellisville, *Miss., U.S.* 31°35′ N, 89°13′ W **103**
Ełk, *Pol.* 53°50′ N, 22°20′ E **152**
Ellore see Eluru, *India* 16°46′ N, 81°7′ E **188**
Ells, river, *Can.* 56°59′ N, 112°21′ W **108**
Ellsworth, *Kans., U.S.* 38°43′ N, 98°14′ W **90**
Ellsworth, *Me., U.S.* 44°31′ N, 68°24′ W **82**
Ellsworth Land, region, *Antarctica* 73°44′ S, 96°14′ W **248**
Ellsworth, Mount, *Utah, U.S.* 37°44′ N, 110°42′ W **92**
Ellsworth Mountains, *Antarctica* 76°23′ S, 90°19′ W **248**
Elm Creek, *Nebr., U.S.* 40°42′ N, 99°23′ W **90**
Elma, *Wash., U.S.* 47°0′ N, 123°24′ W **100**
Elmadağı, *Turk.* 39°55′ N, 33°14′ E **156**
Elmalı, *Turk.* 36°43′ N, 29°55′ E **156**
Elmer City, *Wash., U.S.* 47°59′ N, 118°56′ W **90**
Elmira, *N.Y., U.S.* 42°5′ N, 76°50′ W **94**
Elmo, *Wyo., U.S.* 41°53′ N, 106°31′ W **90**
Elmsta, *Sw.* 59°58′ N, 18°42′ E **166**
Elmwood, *Ill., U.S.* 40°45′ N, 89°58′ W **102**
Elnora, *Ind., U.S.* 38°52′ N, 87°5′ W **102**
Elortondo, *Arg.* 33°43′ S, 61°38′ W **139**
Elorza, *Venez.* 7°1′ N, 69°31′ W **136**
Elos, ruin(s), *Gr.* 36°47′ N, 22°40′ E **156**

Elota, *Mex.* 23°56′ N, 106°42′ W 114
Eloy, *Ariz., U.S.* 32°44′ N, 111°34′ W 112
Eloy Alfaro, *Ecua.* 2°16′ S, 79°51′ W 130
Elrose, *Can.* 51°12′ N, 108°4′ W 90
Elroy, *Wis., U.S.* 43°44′ N, 90°17′ W 102
Elsa, *Tex., U.S.* 26°17′ N, 97°59′ W 114
Elsas, *Can.* 48°32′ N, 82°55′ W 94
Elsberry, *Mo., U.S.* 39°9′ N, 90°47′ W 94
Elsdorf, *Ger.* 53°14′ N, 9°22′ E 152
Elsen Nur, lake, *China* 35°14′ N, 91°46′ E 188
Elsie, *Mich., U.S.* 43°4′ N, 84°24′ W 102
Elst, *Neth.* 51°55′ N, 5°50′ E 167
Elstow, *U.K.* 52°7′ N, 0°28′ E 162
Eltanin Fracture Zone, *South Pacific Ocean* 52°39′ S, 138°6′ W 252
Elten, *Ger.* 51°51′ N, 6°10′ E 167
Eltham, *N.Z.* 39°27′ S, 174°18′ E 240
Elton, *La., U.S.* 30°28′ N, 92°42′ W 103
El'ton, *Russ.* 49°9′ N, 46°47′ E 158
Eltopia, *Wash., U.S.* 46°26′ N, 119°1′ W 90
Eltville, *Ger.* 50°1′ N, 8°6′ E 167
Eluru (Ellore), *India* 16°46′ N, 81°7′ E 188
Elva, *Est.* 58°10′ N, 26°22′ E 166
Elvas, *Port.* 38°52′ N, 7°10′ W 150
Elvenes, *Nor.* 69°40′ N, 30°8′ E 152
Elvins, *Mo., U.S.* 37°49′ N, 90°33′ W 96
Elwell, Lake, *Mont., U.S.* 48°20′ N, 111°36′ W 90
Elwood, *Ill., U.S.* 41°24′ N, 88°7′ W 102
Elwood, *Ind., U.S.* 40°16′ N, 85°50′ W 102
Elwood, *Kans., U.S.* 39°43′ N, 94°53′ W 94
Elwood, *Nebr., U.S.* 40°34′ N, 99°52′ W 90
Elx see Elche, *Sp.* 38°15′ N, 0°42′ E 164
Ely, *Minn., U.S.* 47°53′ N, 91°53′ W 94
Ely, *Nev., U.S.* 39°17′ N, 114°48′ W 238
Ely, *U.K.* 52°23′ N, 0°15′ E 162
Ely, Isle of, *U.K.* 52°24′ N, 0°11′ E 162
Elyria, *Ohio, U.S.* 41°21′ N, 82°5′ W 102
Elyrus, ruin(s), *Gr.* 35°15′ N, 23°42′ E 156
Emådalen, *Nor.* 61°19′ N, 14°42′ E 152
Emajõgi, river, *Est.* 58°24′ N, 26°7′ E 166
Emām Taqī, *Iran* 35°59′ N, 59°23′ E 180
Emas National Park, *Braz.* 18°19′ S, 53°5′ W 138
Embari, river, *Braz.* 0°48′ N, 66°60′ W 136
Embarras Portage, *Can.* 58°24′ N, 111°26′ W 108
Embi, *Kaz.* 48°50′ N, 58°6′ E 158
Embira, river, *Braz.* 9°17′ S, 70°51′ W 137
Embu, *Kenya* 0°33′ N, 37°27′ E 224
Emden, *Ger.* 53°21′ N, 7°12′ E 163
Emel'dzhak, *Russ.* 58°19′ N, 126°40′ E 160
Emerald Island, *Can.* 76°42′ N, 113°8′ W 106
Emero, river, *Bol.* 13°38′ S, 68°3′ W 137
Emerson, *Ark., U.S.* 33°5′ N, 93°12′ W 103
Emerson, *Can.* 49°0′ N, 97°11′ W 90
Emerson Peak, *Calif., U.S.* 41°13′ N, 120°15′ W 90
Emery, *Utah, U.S.* 38°55′ N, 111°14′ W 90
Emery Mills, *Me., U.S.* 43°30′ N, 70°51′ W 104
Emet, *Turk.* 39°21′ N, 29°14′ E 156
Emgayet, oil field, *Lib.* 28°57′ N, 12°45′ E 143
Emigrant Pass, *Nev., U.S.* 40°40′ N, 116°14′ W 90
Emigrant Peak, *Mont., U.S.* 45°14′ N, 110°47′ W 90
Emilia-Romagna, adm. division, *It.* 44°40′ N, 10°18′ E 167
Emilius, Mount, *It.* 45°39′ N, 7°24′ E 165
Emily, *Minn., U.S.* 46°43′ N, 93°58′ W 94
Emily, Mount, *Oreg., U.S.* 45°24′ N, 118°11′ W 90
Emin, *China* 46°29′ N, 83°38′ E 184
Emin, river, *China* 46°24′ N, 83°0′ E 184
Emin, river, *Kaz.* 46°16′ N, 81°53′ E 184
Emir Dağları, peak, *Turk.* 38°50′ N, 31°9′ E 156
Emirdağ, *Turk.* 39°0′ N, 31°6′ E 156
Emisou, Tarso, peak, *Chad* 21°23′ N, 18°32′ E 216
Emlichheim, *Ger.* 52°36′ N, 6°51′ E 163
Emma, Mount, *Ariz., U.S.* 36°15′ N, 113°14′ W 92
Emmaboda, *Nor.* 56°37′ N, 15°31′ E 152
Emmaste, *Est.* 58°43′ N, 22°33′ E 166
Emmaus, *Pa., U.S.* 40°31′ N, 75°30′ W 94
Emmeloord, *Neth.* 52°42′ N, 5°44′ E 163
Emmen, *Neth.* 52°47′ N, 6°53′ E 163
Emmen, *Switz.* 47°3′ N, 8°18′ E 150
Emmerich, *Ger.* 51°49′ N, 6°15′ E 167
Emmetsburg, *Iowa, U.S.* 43°5′ N, 94°41′ W 90
Emmett, *Idaho, U.S.* 43°51′ N, 116°30′ W 90
Emmonak, *Alas., U.S.* 62°42′ N, 164°42′ W 98
Emmons, Mount, *Utah, U.S.* 40°41′ N, 110°23′ W 90
Emo, *Can.* 48°38′ N, 93°50′ W 90
Emory Peak, *Tex., U.S.* 29°12′ N, 103°21′ W 92
Empangeni, *S. Af.* 28°44′ S, 31°51′ E 227
Empedrado, *Arg.* 27°55′ S, 58°48′ W 139
Emperor Seamounts, *North Pacific Ocean* 43°13′ N, 170°0′ E 252
Emperor Trough, *North Pacific Ocean* 44°20′ N, 174°43′ E 252
Empire, *La., U.S.* 29°22′ N, 89°36′ W 103
Empire, *Mich., U.S.* 44°48′ N, 86°3′ W 94
Empoli, *It.* 43°43′ N, 10°57′ E 156
Emporia, *Kans., U.S.* 38°23′ N, 96°11′ W 90
Emporia, *Va., U.S.* 36°41′ N, 77°32′ W 96
Emporio, ruin(s), *Gr.* 38°11′ N, 25°55′ E 156
Emporium, *Pa., U.S.* 41°30′ N, 78°15′ W 94
Empress, *Can.* 50°57′ N, 110°1′ W 90
Empty Quarter see Ar Rub' al Khālī, *Saudi Arabia* 18°28′ N, 46°3′ E 182
Ems, river, *Ger.* 52°1′ N, 7°43′ E 167
Emsdetten, *Ger.* 52°10′ N, 7°32′ E 163
En Amakane, spring, *Mali* 16°35′ N, 0°59′ E 222
'En Boqeq, *Israel* 31°11′ N, 35°21′ E 194
'En Gedi, *Israel* 31°27′ N, 35°22′ E 194
'En Gev, *Israel* 32°46′ N, 35°38′ E 194
En Nahud, *Sudan* 12°40′ N, 28°26′ E 226
'En Yahav, *Israel* 30°37′ N, 35°11′ E 194
Ena, *Japan* 35°25′ N, 137°24′ E 201
Ena Lake, *Can.* 59°57′ N, 108°27′ W 108
Enånger, *Nor.* 61°32′ N, 16°58′ E 152
Encantadas, Serra das, *Braz.* 30°51′ S, 53°28′ W 139
Encantado, Cerro, peak, *Mex.* 27°2′ N, 112°38′ W 112
Encanto, Cape, *Philippines* 15°29′ N, 121°37′ E 203
Encarnación, *Parag.* 27°20′ S, 55°50′ W 139
Encarnación de Díaz, *Mex.* 21°30′ N, 102°15′ W 114
Enchi, *Ghana* 5°49′ N, 2°50′ W 222
Encinal, *Tex., U.S.* 28°2′ N, 99°21′ W 92
Encinillas, *Mex.* 29°13′ N, 106°17′ W 92
Encinillas, Laguna de, lake, *Mex.* 29°24′ N, 107°45′ W 81
Encinitas, *Calif., U.S.* 33°2′ N, 117°18′ W 101
Encino, *Tex., U.S.* 26°56′ N, 98°8′ W 96
Encontrados, *Venez.* 9°2′ N, 72°15′ W 136
Encruzilhada, *Braz.* 15°33′ S, 40°55′ W 138
Encruzilhada do Sul, *Braz.* 30°33′ S, 52°34′ W 139
Endako, *Can.* 54°5′ N, 125°1′ W 108
Endau, *Kenya* 1°19′ S, 38°34′ E 224
Endeavour, *Can.* 52°10′ N, 102°40′ W 108
Enderby, *Can.* 50°33′ N, 119°9′ W 90
Enderby Land, region, *Antarctica* 69°55′ S, 39°37′ E 248
Enderby Plain, *Indian Ocean* 58°55′ S, 44°16′ E 255
Enderlin, *N. Dak., U.S.* 46°36′ N, 97°37′ W 90
Endicott Mountains, *Alas., U.S.* 67°34′ N, 155°1′ W 98
Endr od, *Hung.* 46°56′ N, 20°46′ E 168
Endwell, *N.Y., U.S.* 42°6′ N, 76°1′ W 94
Energetik, *Russ.* 51°44′ N, 58°56′ E 154
Enez, *Turk.* 40°42′ N, 26°3′ E 156
Enfer, Pointe d', *Fr.* 14°17′ N, 61°38′ W 116
Enfida, *Tun.* 36°7′ N, 10°23′ E 156
Enfield, *Conn., U.S.* 41°57′ N, 72°36′ W 104
Enfield, *N.Z.* 45°3′ S, 170°50′ E 240
Enfield, *U.K.* 51°39′ N, 7°415′ W 162
Enfield Center, *N.H., U.S.* 43°35′ N, 72°7′ W 104
Engaño, Cabo, *Dom. Rep.* 18°35′ N, 68°15′ W 116
'En-Gedi, ruin(s), *Israel* 31°27′ N, 35°21′ E 194
Engelberg, *Switz.* 46°48′ N, 8°24′ E 167
Engelhard, *N.C., U.S.* 35°31′ N, 76°1′ W 96
Engels, *Russ.* 51°25′ N, 46°9′ E 158
Engemann Lake, *Can.* 57°49′ N, 107°49′ W 108
Engen, *Can.* 54°1′ N, 124°17′ W 108
Engerdal, *Nor.* 61°45′ N, 11°56′ E 152
Engershand, *Mongolia* 47°44′ N, 107°21′ E 198
Enggano, island, *Indonesia* 5°46′ S, 101°5′ E 192
Enghien, *Belg.* 50°41′ N, 4°2′ E 163
Engizek Dağı, *Turk.* 37°46′ N, 36°29′ E 156
England, adm. division, *U.K.* 50°14′ N, 2°22′ W 143
Englehart, *Can.* 47°50′ N, 79°52′ W 94
Englewood, *Fla., U.S.* 26°58′ N, 82°21′ W 105
Englewood, *Kans., U.S.* 37°1′ N, 99°60′ W 92
Englewood, *Ohio, U.S.* 39°52′ N, 84°19′ W 102
English Channel (La Manche) 49°57′ N, 3°16′ W 150
English River, *Can.* 49°13′ N, 90°58′ W 94
English, river, *Can.* 50°30′ N, 95°13′ W 80
English, river, *Can.* 49°50′ N, 92°1′ W 94
Engure, *Latv.* 57°8′ N, 23°12′ E 166
Engures Ezers, lake, *Latv.* 57°14′ N, 22°50′ E 166
Enid, *Okla., U.S.* 36°22′ N, 97°52′ W 92
Enid, Mount, *Austral.* 21°46′ S, 116°12′ E 230
Enilda, *Can.* 55°24′ N, 116°18′ W 108
Enken, Mys, *Russ.* 56°57′ N, 139°57′ E 172
Enkirch, *Ger.* 49°58′ N, 7°8′ E 167
Enköping, *Nor.* 59°37′ N, 17°3′ E 152
Enmelen, *Russ.* 65°1′ N, 175°51′ W 98
Enna, *It.* 37°34′ N, 14°16′ E 156
Ennadai, *Can.* 61°7′ N, 100°52′ W 108
Ennadai Lake, *Can.* 60°42′ N, 102°23′ W 108
Ennigerloh, *Ger.* 51°49′ N, 8°0′ E 167
Enning, *S. Dak., U.S.* 44°33′ N, 102°34′ W 90
Ennis, *Ire.* 52°50′ N, 8°60′ W 150
Ennis, *Tex., U.S.* 32°18′ N, 96°38′ W 96
Enniskillen, *U.K.* 54°20′ N, 7°38′ W 150
Enns, *Aust.* 48°13′ N, 14°28′ E 156
Eno, *Fin.* 62°45′ N, 30°8′ E 154
Eno, river, *Japan* 34°33′ N, 132°40′ E 201
Enonkoski, *Fin.* 62°4′ N, 28°55′ E 152
Enontekiö, *Fin.* 68°23′ N, 23°35′ E 152
Énos, Óros, peak, *Gr.* 38°7′ N, 20°35′ E 156
Enrique Urien, *Arg.* 27°33′ S, 60°37′ W 139
Enschede, *Neth.* 52°13′ N, 6°53′ E 163
Ensenada, *Mex.* 31°51′ N, 116°38′ W 92
Enshi, *China* 30°14′ N, 109°24′ E 198
Entebbe, *Uganda* 6°357′ N, 32°27′ E 224
Enterprise, *Ala., U.S.* 31°18′ N, 85°51′ W 96
Enterprise, *Can.* 60°40′ N, 116°4′ W 108
Enterprise, *Miss., U.S.* 32°10′ N, 88°48′ W 103
Enterprise, *Utah, U.S.* 37°34′ N, 113°43′ W 92
Entinas, Punta, *Sp.* 36°31′ N, 2°44′ W 150
Entrada, Punta, *Arg.* 50°22′ S, 68°28′ W 134
Entrance, *Can.* 53°21′ N, 117°42′ W 108
Entraunes, *Fr.* 44°10′ N, 6°45′ E 167
Entre Ríos, *Bol.* 21°33′ S, 64°13′ W 137
Entre Ríos, adm. division, *Arg.* 31°43′ S, 59°58′ W 139
Entre-Rios, *Mozambique* 14°58′ S, 37°24′ E 224
Entwistle, *Can.* 53°33′ N, 114°56′ W 108
Enugu, *Nig.* 6°26′ N, 7°29′ E 222
Enumclaw, *Wash., U.S.* 47°10′ N, 121°59′ W 100
Enurmino, *Russ.* 66°55′ N, 171°46′ W 98
Envigado, *Col.* 6°8′ N, 75°37′ W 130
Envira, *Braz.* 7°23′ S, 70°14′ W 130
Enyellé, *Congo* 2°51′ N, 18°4′ E 218
Enying, *Hung.* 46°56′ N, 18°15′ E 168
Enzan, *Japan* 35°41′ N, 138°44′ E 201
Eola, *La., U.S.* 30°53′ N, 92°14′ W 103
Eolie see Lipari, Isole, islands, *Mediterranean Sea* 38°39′ N, 13°46′ E 156
Eonyang, *S. Korea* 35°33′ N, 129°10′ E 200
Epe, *Neth.* 52°21′ N, 5°58′ E 163
Epembe, spring, *Namibia* 17°35′ S, 13°34′ E 220
Epéna, *Congo* 1°23′ N, 17°27′ E 218
Épernay, *Fr.* 49°2′ N, 3°56′ E 163
Épernon, *Fr.* 48°35′ N, 1°40′ E 163
Epes, *Ala., U.S.* 32°41′ N, 88°8′ W 103
Ephesus, ruin(s), *Turk.* 37°55′ N, 27°12′ E 156
Ephraim, *Utah, U.S.* 39°21′ N, 111°35′ W 90
Ephrata, *Wash., U.S.* 47°18′ N, 119°34′ W 90
Epidaurum see Cavtat, *Croatia* 42°34′ N, 18°13′ E 168
Epidaurus Limerás, ruin(s), *Gr.* 36°43′ N, 22°56′ E 156
Épilá, *Sp.* 41°37′ N, 1°17′ W 164
Épinal, *Fr.* 48°10′ N, 6°26′ E 163
Epini, *Dem. Rep. of the Congo* 1°26′ N, 28°21′ E 224
Epirus, region, *Europe* 40°27′ N, 19°28′ E 156
Episkopi, *Cyprus* 34°40′ N, 32°54′ E 194
Epping, *U.K.* 51°38′ N, 2°119′ E 162
Epps, *La., U.S.* 32°35′ N, 91°29′ W 103
Epsom, *U.K.* 51°20′ N, 0°17′ E 162
Epu Pel, *Arg.* 37°36′ S, 64°16′ W 139
Epukiro, *Namibia* 21°45′ S, 19°8′ E 227
Epulu, river, *Dem. Rep. of the Congo* 1°29′ N, 28°42′ E 224
Equator, adm. division, *Dem. Rep. of the Congo* 9°535′ N, 18°55′ E 218
Equatorial Channel 0°14′ N, 72°8′ E 188
Equatorial Guinea 1°38′ N, 10°28′ E 218
Er Rachidia, *Mor.* 31°58′ N, 4°21′ W 143
Er Rahad, *Sudan* 12°43′ N, 30°36′ E 216
Er Rif, *Mor.* 35°15′ N, 5°28′ W 150
Er Roseires, *Sudan* 11°52′ N, 34°24′ E 182
Er Rout Sanihida, spring, *Niger* 21°53′ N, 11°52′ E 222
Eraclea, *It.* 45°34′ N, 12°40′ E 167
Erath, *La., U.S.* 29°56′ N, 92°2′ W 103
Erbaa, *Turk.* 40°40′ N, 36°34′ E 156
Erbab, Jebel, peak, *Sudan* 18°40′ N, 36°59′ E 182
Erçek, *Turk.* 38°37′ N, 43°34′ E 195
Erçek Gölü, lake, *Turk.* 38°39′ N, 43°23′ E 195
Erciş, *Turk.* 38°59′ N, 43°18′ E 195
Erciyeş Dağı, peak, *Turk.* 38°30′ N, 35°22′ E 156
Ercsi, *Hung.* 47°14′ N, 18°53′ E 168
Érd, *Hung.* 47°22′ N, 18°55′ E 168
Erdao, river, *China* 42°44′ N, 127°38′ E 200
Erdaobaihe, *China* 42°26′ N, 128°7′ E 200
Erdébé, Plateau d', *Chad* 17°17′ N, 21°23′ E 216
Erdek, *Turk.* 40°24′ N, 27°45′ E 156
Erdemli, *Turk.* 36°36′ N, 34°18′ E 156
Erdenet, *Mongolia* 48°57′ N, 104°17′ E 198
Erdut, *Croatia* 45°31′ N, 19°2′ E 168
Erebus, Mount, *Antarctica* 77°26′ S, 167°55′ E 248
Erechim, *Braz.* 27°39′ S, 52°18′ W 139
Ereğli, *Turk.* 41°17′ N, 31°25′ E 156
Ereğli, *Turk.* 37°29′ N, 34°2′ E 156
Erego, *Mozambique* 16°3′ S, 37°11′ E 224
Erei, Monti, *It.* 37°23′ N, 14°3′ E 156
Eremiya, *Bulg.* 42°12′ N, 22°50′ E 168
Erenhot, *China* 43°39′ N, 111°57′ E 198
Eresus, ruin(s), *Gr.* 39°7′ N, 25°50′ E 156
Erétria, ruin(s), *Gr.* 38°23′ N, 23°42′ E 156
Ereymentaū, *Kaz.* 51°41′ N, 73°22′ E 184
Erfoud, *Mor.* 31°29′ N, 4°15′ W 214
Erft, river, *Ger.* 51°2′ N, 6°29′ E 167
Erftstadt, *Ger.* 50°47′ N, 6°44′ E 167
Erfurt, *Ger.* 50°59′ N, 11°2′ E 152
'Erg Chech, *Alg.* 25°13′ N, 3°16′ W 214
'Erg el Ahmar, *Mali* 24°14′ N, 4°55′ W 214
'Erg Iguidi, *Alg.* 24°15′ N, 8°24′ W 214
'Erg I-n-Sâkâne, *Mali* 20°43′ N, 0°54′ E 222
Ergani, *Turk.* 38°17′ N, 39°45′ E 195
Ergel, *Mongolia* 43°13′ N, 109°8′ E 198
Ērgļi, *Latv.* 56°53′ N, 25°39′ E 166
Erg-n-Ataram, *Alg.* 23°45′ N, 1°6′ E 214
Ergun, river, *Asia* 50°18′ N, 119°1′ E 190
Eriba, *Sudan* 16°37′ N, 36°3′ E 182
Éric, Lac, lake, *Can.* 51°50′ N, 65°59′ W 111
Erice, *It.* 38°2′ N, 12°35′ E 156
Erick, *Okla., U.S.* 35°11′ N, 99°53′ W 92
Erickson, *Can.* 50°30′ N, 99°54′ W 90
Erie, *Ill., U.S.* 41°38′ N, 90°5′ W 102
Erie, *Pa., U.S.* 42°6′ N, 80°5′ W 94
Erie, Lake 42°11′ N, 83°6′ W 73
Erieau, *Can.* 42°15′ N, 81°56′ W 102
Erigavo see Ceerigaabo, *Somalia* 10°34′ N, 47°24′ E 218
Eriksdale, *Can.* 50°51′ N, 98°6′ W 90
Erimanthos, Óros, peak, *Gr.* 37°58′ N, 21°45′ E 156
Erimi, *Cyprus* 34°40′ N, 32°55′ E 194
Eritrea 15°32′ N, 37°35′ E 218
Erits, river, *Kaz.* 51°34′ N, 77°33′ E 184
Erkelenz, *Ger.* 51°4′ N, 6°19′ E 167
Erkilet, *Turk.* 38°48′ N, 35°27′ E 156
Erkner, *Ger.* 52°24′ N, 13°45′ E 152
Erkowit, *Sudan* 18°45′ N, 37°3′ E 182
Erla, *Sp.* 42°6′ N, 0°57′ E 164
Erlangen, *Ger.* 49°35′ N, 11°0′ E 152
Ermelo, *S. Af.* 26°32′ S, 29°58′ E 227
Ermenek, *Turk.* 36°36′ N, 32°55′ E 156
Ermidas-Sado, *Port.* 37°59′ N, 8°25′ W 150
Ermil, *Sudan* 13°33′ N, 27°38′ E 226
Ermoúpoli, *Gr.* 37°26′ N, 24°56′ E 156
Ernakulam, *India* 9°59′ N, 76°17′ E 188
Erndtebrück, *Ger.* 50°59′ N, 8°15′ E 167
Ernstberg, peak, *Ger.* 50°13′ N, 6°44′ E 167
Eromanga, *Austral.* 26°39′ S, 143°17′ E 231
Erongo Mountains, *Namibia* 21°44′ S, 15°27′ E 227
Eros, *La., U.S.* 32°22′ N, 92°25′ W 103
Eroug, spring, *Mali* 18°20′ N, 2°4′ W 222
Erpengdianzi, *China* 41°10′ N, 125°33′ E 200
Er-Remla, *Tun.* 34°46′ N, 11°14′ E 156
Errigal Mountain, *Ire.* 55°0′ N, 8°13′ W 150
Error Tablemount, *Arabian Sea* 9°58′ N, 56°3′ E 254
Erskine, *Minn., U.S.* 47°38′ N, 96°2′ W 90
Erstein, *Fr.* 48°25′ N, 7°39′ E 163
Ertai, *China* 46°8′ N, 90°7′ E 190
Ertis, *Kaz.* 53°19′ N, 75°27′ E 184
Ertis, river, *Kaz.* 54°12′ N, 74°56′ E 160
Ertix, river, *China* 48°2′ N, 85°34′ E 184
Eruh, *Turk.* 37°44′ N, 42°9′ E 195
Erundu, *Namibia* 20°41′ S, 16°23′ E 227
Erval, *Braz.* 32°2′ S, 53°27′ W 139
Ervenik, *Croatia* 44°5′ N, 15°55′ E 168
Erwin, *N.C., U.S.* 35°19′ N, 78°42′ W 96
Erwitte, *Ger.* 51°36′ N, 8°21′ E 167
Erzgebirge, *Czech Rep.* 50°18′ N, 12°34′ E 152
Erzin, *Russ.* 50°14′ N, 95°18′ E 190
Erzincan, *Turk.* 39°44′ N, 39°28′ E 195
Erzurum, *Turk.* 39°54′ N, 41°17′ E 195
Es Bordes, *Sp.* 42°43′ N, 0°42′ E 164
Es Mercadal, *Sp.* 39°59′ N, 4°4′ E 150
Es Safiya, *Sudan* 15°31′ N, 30°6′ E 226
Es Salam, *Sudan* 18°5′ N, 33°53′ E 182
Es Sufeiya, *Sudan* 15°27′ N, 34°40′ E 182
Esa, river, *Belarus* 54°43′ N, 28°30′ E 166
Esbjerg, *Den.* 55°27′ N, 8°36′ E 160
Esbo see Espoo, *Fin.* 60°11′ N, 24°34′ E 166
Escalante, *Utah, U.S.* 37°46′ N, 111°37′ W 92
Escanaba, *Mich., U.S.* 45°48′ N, 87°7′ W 106
Escárcega, *Mex.* 18°36′ N, 90°46′ W 115
Escatawpa, river, *Ala., U.S.* 30°27′ N, 88°27′ W 103
Escatrón, *Sp.* 41°16′ N, 0°20′ E 164
Eschenburg, *Ger.* 50°48′ N, 8°20′ E 167
Eschweiler, *Ger.* 50°48′ N, 6°15′ E 167
Escobedo, *Mex.* 27°11′ N, 101°22′ W 96
Escondido, *Calif., U.S.* 33°7′ N, 117°6′ W 101
Escudero, station, *Antarctica* 62°5′ S, 58°48′ W 134
Escudilla Mountain, *Ariz., U.S.* 33°56′ N, 109°11′ W 92
Escuela de Caza de Morón, *Sp.* 37°9′ N, 5°37′ W 164
Escuinapa, *Mex.* 22°50′ N, 105°47′ W 114
Escuintla, *Guatemala* 14°16′ N, 90°47′ W 115
Escuintla, *Mex.* 15°18′ N, 92°40′ W 115
Escuminac, Point, *Can.* 47°6′ N, 64°49′ W 111
Ese Khayya, *Russ.* 67°28′ N, 134°38′ E 160
Eséka, *Cameroon* 3°41′ N, 10°47′ E 222
Esenguly, *Turkm.* 37°27′ N, 53°57′ E 180
Esens, *Ger.* 53°39′ N, 7°36′ E 163
Eşfahān (Isfahan), *Iran* 32°40′ N, 51°38′ E 180
Esfandak, *Iran* 27°5′ N, 62°51′ E 182
Eshkamesh, *Afghan.* 36°27′ N, 69°16′ E 186
Eshkashem, *Taj.* 36°44′ N, 71°34′ E 186
Eshowe, *S. Af.* 28°54′ S, 31°24′ E 227
Esiama, *Ghana* 4°58′ N, 2°21′ W 222
Esik, *Kaz.* 43°21′ N, 77°25′ E 184
Esil, *Kaz.* 51°57′ N, 66°27′ E 184
Esil, river, *Kaz.* 53°18′ N, 66°55′ E 184
Esimi, *Gr.* 41°1′ N, 25°57′ E 156
Esira, *Madagascar* 24°21′ S, 46°47′ E 220
Esk, river, *U.K.* 55°14′ N, 3°17′ W 150
Esk, river, *U.K.* 54°28′ N, 0°54′ E 162
Eskdale, *N.Z.* 39°25′ S, 176°49′ E 240
Eskene, *Kaz.* 47°20′ N, 52°52′ E 158
Esker, *Can.* 54°0′ N, 66°33′ W 106
Eskimo Point, *Can.* 58°49′ N, 94°20′ W 108
Eskipazar, *Turk.* 40°58′ N, 32°32′ E 156
Eskişehir, *Turk.* 39°46′ N, 30°31′ E 156
Eslāmābād, *Iran* 34°9′ N, 46°32′ E 180
Eşler Dağı, peak, *Turk.* 37°39′ N, 29°12′ E 156
Eşme, *Turk.* 38°24′ N, 28°57′ E 156
Esmeralda, river, *Bol.* 13°28′ S, 67°59′ W 137
Esmeraldas, *Ecua.* 0°55′ N, 79°48′ W 130
Esmoraca, *Bol.* 21°41′ S, 66°19′ W 137
Esnagi Lake, *Can.* 48°40′ N, 84°49′ W 94
Espa, *Nor.* 60°34′ N, 11°16′ E 152
Espada, Punta, *Col.* 12°4′ N, 71°8′ W 136
Espakeh, *Iran* 26°46′ N, 60°12′ E 182
Espanola, *Can.* 46°15′ N, 81°46′ W 94
Espanola, *N. Mex., U.S.* 35°59′ N, 106°6′ W 92
Esparza, *C.R.* 9°58′ N, 84°40′ W 116
Esperanza, *Arg.* 31°27′ S, 60°54′ W 139
Esperanza, *Arg.* 51°5′ S, 70°38′ W 134
Esperanza, *Peru* 9°49′ S, 70°44′ W 137
Esperanza Inlet 49°45′ N, 127°40′ W 90
Esperanza, station, *Antarctica* 63°34′ S, 57°4′ W 248
Espichel, Cabo, *Port.* 38°11′ N, 9°37′ W 150
Espiel, *Sp.* 38°11′ N, 5°1′ W 164
Espigão Mestre, *Braz.* 14°41′ S, 46°14′ W 138
Espinal, *Bol.* 17°13′ S, 58°28′ W 132
Espinar see Yauri, *Peru* 14°51′ S, 71°24′ W 137
Espinazo, *Mex.* 26°16′ N, 101°6′ W 114
Espino, *Venez.* 8°32′ N, 66°1′ W 136
Espinosa, *Braz.* 14°59′ S, 42°50′ W 138
Espírito Santo, adm. division, *Braz.* 19°55′ S, 41°11′ W 138
Espírito Santo see Vila Velha, *Braz.* 20°25′ S, 40°21′ W 138
Espiritu, *Philippines* 17°59′ N, 120°39′ E 203
Espita, *Mex.* 21°0′ N, 88°20′ W 116
Espoo (Esbo), *Fin.* 60°11′ N, 24°34′ E 166
Esposende, *Port.* 41°31′ N, 8°48′ W 150
Espuña, peak, *Sp.* 37°51′ N, 1°37′ W 164
Espungabera, *Mozambique* 20°30′ S, 32°47′ E 227
Espy, *Pa., U.S.* 41°0′ N, 76°25′ W 110
Esqueda, *Mex.* 30°41′ N, 109°35′ W 92
Esquel, *Arg.* 42°58′ S, 71°19′ W 123
Esquimalt, *Can.* 48°25′ N, 123°24′ W 100
Esquina, *Arg.* 29°60′ S, 59°33′ W 139
Essaouira, *Mor.* 31°35′ N, 9°39′ W 143
Essé, *Cameroon* 4°6′ N, 11°50′ E 218
Essen, *Belg.* 51°27′ N, 4°29′ E 167
Essen, *Ger.* 51°27′ N, 7°0′ E 167
Essen, *Ger.* 52°44′ N, 7°56′ E 163
Essendon, Mount, *Austral.* 25°2′ S, 120°18′ E 230
Essex, *Calif., U.S.* 34°44′ N, 115°15′ W 101
Essex, *Conn., U.S.* 41°21′ N, 72°24′ W 104
Essex, *Mass., U.S.* 42°37′ N, 70°48′ W 104
Essex, *N.Y., U.S.* 44°18′ N, 73°23′ W 104
Essex Junction, *Vt., U.S.* 44°29′ N, 73°7′ W 104
Essexville, *Mich., U.S.* 43°36′ N, 83°50′ W 102
Esson, *Gabon* 1°14′ N, 11°34′ E 218
Essoûk, *Mali* 18°46′ N, 1°5′ E 222
Est, Cap, *Madagascar* 15°13′ S, 50°28′ E 220
Est, Pointe de l', *Can.* 49°5′ N, 61°39′ W 111
Estacado, Llano, *North America* 34°53′ N, 103°50′ W 92
Estados, Isla de los (Staten Island), *Arg.* 55°28′ S, 64°48′ W 134
Eşţahbānāt, *Iran* 29°5′ N, 54°3′ E 196
Estância, *Braz.* 11°15′ S, 37°28′ W 132
Estancia Rojas Silva, *Parag.* 22°33′ S, 59°5′ W 132
Estancias, peak, *Sp.* 37°34′ N, 2°6′ W 164
Estavayer-le-Lac, *Switz.* 46°50′ N, 6°51′ E 167
Estcourt, *S. Af.* 29°2′ S, 29°51′ E 220
Este, *It.* 45°14′ N, 11°39′ E 167
Esteli, *Nicar.* 13°5′ N, 86°21′ W 115
Estella (Lizarra), *Sp.* 42°39′ N, 2°2′ W 164
Estelline, *S. Dak., U.S.* 44°33′ N, 96°55′ W 90
Estelline, *Tex., U.S.* 34°31′ N, 100°27′ W 92
Estepa, *Sp.* 37°17′ N, 4°54′ W 164
Estepona, *Sp.* 36°25′ N, 5°9′ W 164
Estérel, *Fr.* 43°28′ N, 6°35′ E 165
Esterfeld, *Ger.* 52°41′ N, 7°15′ E 163
Esterhazy, *Can.* 50°38′ N, 102°8′ W 90
Esternay, *Fr.* 48°43′ N, 3°32′ E 163
Estero, Point, *Calif., U.S.* 35°23′ N, 121°7′ W 100
Esteros del Iberá, marsh, *Arg.* 28°15′ S, 58°7′ W 139
Esterwegen, *Ger.* 52°59′ N, 7°37′ E 163
Estes Park, *Colo., U.S.* 40°22′ N, 105°32′ W 90
Estevan, *Can.* 49°7′ N, 103°2′ W 90
Estherville, *Iowa, U.S.* 43°23′ N, 94°49′ W 94
Estherwood, *La., U.S.* 30°10′ N, 92°28′ W 103
Estill, *S.C., U.S.* 32°45′ N, 81°15′ W 96
Estissac, *Fr.* 48°15′ N, 3°48′ E 163
Eston, *Can.* 51°9′ N, 108°45′ W 90
Estonia 58°38′ N, 25°30′ E 166
Estreito, *Braz.* 31°49′ S, 51°45′ W 139
Estreito, Serra do, *Braz.* 10°32′ S, 43°49′ W 132
Estrêla do Norte, *Braz.* 13°52′ S, 49°6′ W 138
Estrela, Serra da, *Port.* 39°59′ N, 8°2′ W 150
Estrella, peak, *Sp.* 38°23′ N, 3°39′ W 164
Estrella, Punta, *Mex.* 30°55′ N, 114°43′ W 92
Estrondo, Serra do, *Braz.* 9°16′ S, 49°36′ W 130
Etah, site, *Den.* 78°18′ N, 73°12′ W 246
Étain, *Fr.* 49°12′ N, 5°38′ E 163
Etajima, *Japan* 34°13′ N, 132°29′ E 201
Etal Atoll, *F.S.M.* 5°46′ N, 154°5′ E 192
Étampes, *Fr.* 48°25′ N, 2°9′ E 163
Étaples, *Fr.* 50°31′ N, 1°38′ E 163
Etawah, *India* 26°45′ N, 79°0′ E 197
Etawney Lake, *Can.* 57°50′ N, 97°31′ W 108
Etéké, *Gabon* 1°30′ S, 11°33′ E 218
Eternity Range, *Antarctica* 69°10′ S, 68°24′ W 248
Ethel, *Miss., U.S.* 33°6′ N, 89°28′ W 103
Ethel, *Wash., U.S.* 46°30′ N, 122°45′ W 100
Ethel, *W. Va., U.S.* 37°51′ N, 81°55′ W 94
Ethelbert, *Can.* 51°31′ N, 100°25′ W 90
Ethelsville, *Ala., U.S.* 33°23′ N, 88°12′ W 103
Ethiopia 8°36′ N, 37°8′ E 218
Etna, *Wyo., U.S.* 43°2′ N, 110°60′ W 90
Etna, peak, *It.* 37°44′ N, 14°54′ E 156
Etne, *Nor.* 59°39′ N, 5°55′ E 152
Etoile, *Dem. Rep. of the Congo* 11°38′ S, 27°31′ E 218
Etoile, *Tex., U.S.* 31°21′ N, 94°27′ W 103
Etoka, *Dem. Rep. of the Congo* 0°8′ N, 23°17′ E 218
Etosha National Park, *Namibia* 18°57′ S, 14°47′ E 220
Etoumbi, *Congo* 4°237′ S, 14°54′ E 218
Etowah, *Tenn., U.S.* 35°19′ N, 84°32′ W 96
Étrépagny, *Fr.* 49°18′ N, 1°37′ E 163
Ettenheim, *Ger.* 48°14′ N, 7°47′ E 163
Ettersberg, Grosser, peak, *Ger.* 51°0′ N, 11°10′ E 152
Ettrick, *N.Z.* 45°39′ S, 169°21′ E 240
Etulia, *Mold.* 45°32′ N, 28°27′ E 156
Etxarri-Aranatz, *Sp.* 42°55′ N, 2°3′ W 164
Etzatlán, *Mex.* 20°46′ N, 104°7′ W 114
Eu, *Fr.* 50°2′ N, 1°24′ E 163
Euca, *Braz.* 2°38′ N, 50°54′ W 130
Eucla Motel, *Austral.* 31°39′ S, 128°51′ E 231
Euclid, *Ohio, U.S.* 41°34′ N, 81°31′ W 102
Eudora, *Ark., U.S.* 33°5′ N, 91°16′ W 103
Eufaula, *Ala., U.S.* 31°53′ N, 85°9′ W 96
Eufaula, *Okla., U.S.* 35°15′ N, 95°34′ W 96
Eufaula Lake, *Okla., U.S.* 34°58′ N, 96°6′ W 96
Eugene, *Oreg., U.S.* 44°2′ N, 123°7′ W 90
Eugenia, Punta, *Mex.* 27°43′ N, 116°17′ W 112
Eumseong, *S. Korea* 36°55′ N, 127°42′ E 200
Eungella National Park, *Austral.* 21°4′ S, 148°14′ E 238
Eunice, *La., U.S.* 30°28′ N, 92°25′ W 103
Eunice, *N. Mex., U.S.* 32°26′ N, 103°9′ W 92
Eupen, *Belg.* 50°37′ N, 6°2′ E 167
Euphrates, river, *Syr.* 35°33′ N, 40°3′ E 207
Euphrates see Al Furāt, river, *Syr.* 35°43′ N, 39°21′ E 180
Eura, *Fin.* 61°6′ N, 22°9′ E 166
Eurajoki, *Fin.* 61°12′ N, 21°42′ E 166
Eure, river, *Fr.* 49°1′ N, 1°24′ E 163
Eureka, *Calif., U.S.* 40°46′ N, 124°10′ W 90
Eureka, *Can.* 80°2′ N, 85°43′ W 246
Eureka, *Ill., U.S.* 40°42′ N, 89°17′ W 102
Eureka, *Kans., U.S.* 37°48′ N, 96°18′ W 90
Eureka, *Mont., U.S.* 48°52′ N, 115°3′ W 90
Eureka, *Nev., U.S.* 39°31′ N, 115°59′ W 90
Eureka, *S. Dak., U.S.* 45°46′ N, 99°39′ W 90
Eureka, *Utah, U.S.* 39°56′ N, 112°6′ W 90
Eureka Springs, *Ark., U.S.* 36°23′ N, 93°45′ W 94
Eureka Valley, *Calif., U.S.* 37°12′ N, 117°54′ W 101
Europa, Île, *Fr.* 22°44′ S, 39°43′ E 220
Europa, Picos de, peak, *Sp.* 43°10′ N, 4°55′ W 150
Europa Point, *U.K.* 35°58′ N, 5°14′ W 164
Europe 41°0′ N, 28°0′ E 143
Euskirchen, *Ger.* 50°39′ N, 6°47′ E 167
Eustis, *Fla., U.S.* 28°51′ N, 81°41′ W 105
Eutaw, *Ala., U.S.* 32°49′ N, 87°54′ W 103
Eutin, *Ger.* 54°8′ N, 10°37′ E 152
Eutsuk Lake, *Can.* 53°11′ N, 127°16′ W 108
Evadale, *Tex., U.S.* 30°20′ N, 94°4′ W 103
Evangelistas, Grupo, islands, *South Pacific Ocean* 52°34′ S, 78°23′ W 134
Evans, *Colo., U.S.* 40°23′ N, 104°43′ W 90
Evans, *La., U.S.* 30°58′ N, 93°31′ W 103
Evans, Lac, lake, *Can.* 50°46′ N, 77°28′ W 110
Evans, Mount, *Can.* 49°32′ N, 116°23′ W 90
Evans, Mount, *Colo., U.S.* 39°34′ N, 105°42′ W 90
Evans, Mount, *Mont., U.S.* 46°2′ N, 113°18′ W 90
Evans Notch, pass, *Me., U.S.* 44°18′ N, 70°60′ W 104

Evart, Mich., U.S. 43°54' N, 85°17' W 102
Evelyn, Can. 54°53' N, 127°19' W 108
Even Yehuda, Israel 32°15' N, 34°52' E 194
Evenk, adm. division, Russ. 65°19' N, 91°42' E 169
Evensk, Russ. 61°57' N, 159°17' E 173
Everest, Mount (Qomolangma, Sagarmāthā), China-Nepal 28°0' N, 86°53' E 197
Everett, Wash., U.S. 47°58' N, 122°11' W 100
Everglades City, Fla., U.S. 25°51' N, 81°24' W 105
Everglades National Park, Fla., U.S. 25°24' N, 80°54' W 105
Evergreen, Ala., U.S. 31°26' N, 86°57' W 96
Everson, Wash., U.S. 48°54' N, 122°20' W 100
Evesham, U.K. 52°6' N, 1°57' W 162
Évia, island, Gr. 38°45' N, 23°36' E 180
Évian, Fr. 46°23' N, 6°35' E 167
Evje, Nor. 58°34' N, 7°49' E 152
Évora, Port. 38°33' N, 7°55' W 150
Évora, adm. division, Port. 38°40' N, 8°25' W 150
Évreux, Fr. 49°1' N, 1°9' E 163
Évron, Fr. 48°9' N, 0°25' E 150
Evrychou, Cyprus 35°2' N, 32°55' E 194
Ewaso Ng'iro, river, Kenya 1°16' S, 35°51' E 224
Ewenkizu Zizhiqi, China 49°4' N, 119°40' E 198
Ewing, Nebr., U.S. 42°14' N, 98°21' W 90
Ewing Island, Antarctica 69°46' S, 60°60' W 248
Ewo, Congo 0°51' N, 14°48' E 218
Exaltación, Bol. 13°18' S, 65°18' W 137
Excelsior Mountains, Nev., U.S. 38°17' N, 118°39' W 90
Exeter, Calif., U.S. 36°18' N, 119°9' W 101
Exeter, Can. 43°21' N, 81°29' W 102
Exeter, Mo., U.S. 36°40' N, 93°56' W 96
Exeter, N.H., U.S. 42°58' N, 70°58' W 104
Exeter, R.I., U.S. 41°34' N, 71°33' W 104
Exeter, U.K. 50°43' N, 3°31' W 162
Exeter Sound 66°3' N, 64°29' W 106
Exford, U.K. 51°7' N, 3°48' W 162
Exmoor, region, Europe 51°8' N, 3°55' W 162
Exmouth, Austral. 22°5' S, 114°3' E 238
Exmouth Gulf 22°8' S, 113°3' E 230
Exmouth, Peninsula, Chile 49°22' S, 75°30' W 134
Exmouth Plateau, Indian Ocean 19°26' S, 112°55' E 254
Expedition Range, Austral. 24°34' S, 148°33' E 230
Experiment, Ga., U.S. 33°15' N, 84°17' W 96
Extremadura, adm. division, Sp. 38°59' N, 6°46' W 164
Exuma, adm. division, Bahamas 23°39' N, 76°4' W 96
Exuma Sound 24°7' N, 76°20' W 96
Eyasi, Lake, Tanzania 3°38' S, 34°46' E 224
Eye, U.K. 52°19' N, 1°8' E 162
Eye Peninsula, U.K. 58°12' N, 6°42' W 150
Eyl, Somalia 7°56' N, 49°49' E 218
Eyrarbakki, Ice. 63°54' N, 21°6' W 143
Eyre Peninsula, Austral. 33°21' S, 135°33' E 230
Eyumojok, Cameroon 5°46' N, 8°56' E 222
Ezeriş, Rom. 45°24' N, 21°52' E 168
Ezeru, peak, Rom. 45°27' N, 24°51' E 156
Ezine, Turk. 39°46' N, 26°19' E 156

F

Fabala, Guinea 9°43' N, 9°6' W 222
Fabara, Sp. 41°9' N, 0°10' E 164
Faber Lake, Can. 63°42' N, 116°6' W 246
Facatativá, Col. 4°48' N, 74°22' W 130
Facha, oil field, Lib. 29°21' N, 17°3' E 216
Fachi, Niger 18°5' N, 11°33' E 222
Facho, Pico do, peak, Port. 32°55' N, 16°30' W 214
Facinas, Sp. 36°8' N, 5°43' W 164
Facture, Fr. 44°38' N, 0°59' E 150
Fada, Chad 17°11' N, 21°34' E 216
Fada N'Gourma, Burkina Faso 12°3' N, 0°19' E 222
Fadd, Hung. 46°27' N, 18°49' E 168
Faddeya, Zaliv 76°57' N, 110°31' E 246
Faddeyevskiy, Ostrov, island, Russ. 76°12' N, 127°53' E 160
Fadhili, oil field, Saudi Arabia 26°54' N, 49°6' E 196
Fadiffolu Atoll, Maldives 5°18' N, 72°47' E 188
Faenza, It. 44°17' N, 11°51' E 167
Fafa, Mali 15°17' N, 0°42' E 222
Făgăraş, Munţii, Rom. 45°29' N, 24°10' E 156
Fågelsjö, Nor. 61°47' N, 14°39' E 152
Fagersta, Nor. 59°59' N, 15°45' E 152
Făget, Rom. 45°50' N, 22°11' E 168
Făget, Munţii, Rom. 47°36' N, 23°0' E 168
Faggo, Nig. 11°25' N, 9°57' E 222
Fagnières, Fr. 48°57' N, 4°20' E 163
Fahala, island, Maldives 2°24' N, 73°19' E 188
Fahraj, Iran 28°56' N, 58°50' E 196
Fahud, oil field, Oman 22°11' N, 56°26' E 182
Faichuk, island, Federated States of Micronesia 7°0' N, 152°0' E 242
Fair Haven, Vt., U.S. 43°35' N, 73°17' W 104
Fair Oaks, Ind., U.S. 41°4' N, 87°16' W 102
Fairbanks, Alas., U.S. 64°49' N, 147°39' W 106
Fairbanks, Me., U.S. 44°42' N, 70°11' W 111
Fairbury, Mo., U.S. 40°44' N, 88°31' W 94
Fairbury, Nebr., U.S. 40°7' N, 97°11' W 92
Fairfax, Okla., U.S. 36°33' N, 96°43' W 94
Fairfax, S.C., U.S. 32°57' N, 81°15' W 96
Fairfield, Ala., U.S. 33°29' N, 86°53' W 96
Fairfield, Calif., U.S. 38°14' N, 122°3' W 100
Fairfield, Conn., U.S. 41°8' N, 73°16' W 104
Fairfield, Fla., U.S. 29°21' N, 82°16' W 105
Fairfield, Idaho, U.S. 43°21' N, 114°48' W 90
Fairfield, Mo., U.S. 38°22' N, 88°22' W 94
Fairfield, Mont., U.S. 47°36' N, 111°59' W 90
Fairfield, Ohio, U.S. 39°19' N, 84°35' W 102
Fairfield, Tex., U.S. 31°42' N, 96°9' W 96
Fairhaven, Mass., U.S. 41°38' N, 70°55' W 104
Fairhope, Ala., U.S. 30°30' N, 87°54' W 103
Fairlawn, Va., U.S. 37°8' N, 80°36' W 94
Fairlee, Vt., U.S. 43°54' N, 72°10' W 104
Fairlie, N.Z. 44°7' S, 170°49' E 240
Fairlight, Can. 49°53' N, 101°40' W 90
Fairmead, Calif., U.S. 37°4' N, 120°12' W 100
Fairmont, Minn., U.S. 43°38' N, 94°27' W 94
Fairmont, W. Va., U.S. 39°29' N, 80°11' W 94
Fairmount, Ind., U.S. 40°24' N, 85°39' W 102
Fairport, Mich., U.S. 45°37' N, 86°39' W 94
Fairport Harbor, Ohio, U.S. 41°43' N, 81°16' W 102
Fairview, Can. 56°4' N, 118°25' W 108
Fairview, Ill., U.S. 40°37' N, 90°10' W 102
Fairview, Okla., U.S. 36°15' N, 98°29' W 92
Fairview, Pa., U.S. 42°1' N, 80°16' W 94
Fairview, Tenn., U.S. 35°58' N, 87°7' W 96
Fairview Park, Ind., U.S. 39°40' N, 87°25' W 102
Fairview Peak, Oreg., U.S. 43°34' N, 122°44' W 90
Fairweather, Cape, Antarctica 64°57' S, 60°47' W 134
Fairweather, Mount, Alas., U.S. 58°54' N, 137°43' W 98
Faisalabad, Pak. 31°24' N, 73°0' E 186
Faith, S. Dak., U.S. 45°0' N, 102°4' W 90
Faizabad, India 26°46' N, 82°6' E 197
Fakel, Russ. 57°36' N, 53°6' E 154
Fakenham, U.K. 52°49' N, 0°51' E 162
Fakfak, Indonesia 2°54' S, 132°11' E 192
Fakiya, Bulg. 42°11' N, 27°4' E 156
Fakse Bugt 55°4' N, 11°41' E 152
Faku, China 42°31' N, 123°27' E 200
Falagh, Sudan 8°35' N, 31°5' E 224
Falakró, Óros, Gr. 41°12' N, 23°39' E 156
Falam, Myanmar 22°50' N, 93°39' E 188
Falces, Sp. 42°23' N, 1°49' W 164
Fălciu, Rom. 46°17' N, 28°7' E 156
Falcón, adm. division, Venez. 10°54' N, 70°36' W 136
Falcon, Cape, Oreg., U.S. 45°45' N, 123°58' W 100
Falcon Lake, Mex. 26°52' N, 99°39' W 112
Falcone, Capo del, It. 40°57' N, 7°19' E 156
Falconer, N.Y., U.S. 42°7' N, 79°14' W 110
Faléa, Mali 12°17' N, 11°18' W 222
Falémé, river, Africa 13°52' N, 12°10' W 222
Falenki, Russ. 58°22' N, 51°45' E 154
Făleşti, Mold. 47°34' N, 27°42' E 156
Falfurrias, Tex., U.S. 27°11' N, 98°8' W 96
Falher, Can. 55°44' N, 117°14' W 108
Falkenberg, Nor. 56°54' N, 12°29' E 152
Falkirk, U.K. 55°59' N, 3°48' W 150
Falkland Islands (Islas Malvinas), Falk. Is., U.K. 52°18' S, 62°14' W 134
Falkland Plateau, South Atlantic Ocean 51°7' S, 49°25' W 255
Falköping, Nor. 58°9' N, 13°33' E 152
Fallbrook, Calif., U.S. 33°23' N, 117°16' W 101
Fallon, Nev., U.S. 39°28' N, 118°48' W 90
Falls City, Nebr., U.S. 40°2' N, 95°36' W 90
Fallujah see Al Fallūjah, Iraq 33°19' N, 43°46' E 180
Falmey, Niger 12°40' N, 2°47' E 222
Falmouth, Ky., U.S. 38°39' N, 84°20' W 102
Falmouth, Mass., U.S. 41°33' N, 70°38' W 104
Falmouth, Va., U.S. 38°19' N, 77°29' W 94
Falou, Mali 14°36' N, 7°56' W 222
Falsa, Bahía 39°20' S, 62°29' W 139
False Point, India 20°17' N, 86°50' E 188
Falset, Sp. 41°8' N, 0°48' E 164
Falso, Cabo, Hond. 15°15' N, 83°23' W 115
Falso, Cabo, Mex. 22°43' N, 110°51' W 112
Falun, Nor. 60°34' N, 15°35' E 152
Famagusta see Ammochostos, Northern Cyprus 35°7' N, 33°56' E 194
Famaka, Sudan 11°18' N, 34°43' E 182
Famana, Mali 11°51' N, 7°51' W 222
Fan, river, Alban. 41°47' N, 19°44' E 168
Fana, Mali 12°47' N, 6°60' W 222
Fana, Nor. 60°13' N, 5°23' E 152
Fanchang, China 31°6' N, 118°12' E 198
Fandriana, Madagascar 20°14' S, 47°22' E 220
Fang, Thai. 19°57' N, 99°11' E 202
Fangak, Sudan 9°2' N, 30°55' E 224
Fangcheng, China 21°48' N, 108°21' E 198
Fangcheng, China 33°17' N, 113°4' E 198
Fangshan, China 37°50' N, 111°16' E 198
Fanjeaux, Fr. 43°11' N, 2°1' E 164
Fanny Bay, Can. 49°31' N, 124°51' W 100
Fano, It. 43°49' N, 13°1' E 167
Fanshan, China 27°22' N, 120°27' E 198
Fanshi, China 39°13' N, 113°18' E 198
Fanūdah, Saudi Arabia 25°25' N, 40°36' E 182
Fanxian, China 35°53' N, 115°25' E 198
Far Mountain, Can. 52°45' N, 125°25' W 108
Farabana, Guinea 9°53' N, 9°8' W 222
Faradje, Dem. Rep. of the Congo 3°43' N, 29°42' E 224
Farafangana, Madagascar 22°50' S, 47°50' E 220
Farâfra, El Wâhât el, Egypt 27°18' N, 28°17' E 180
Farah, Afghan. 32°25' N, 62°10' E 186
Farah, river, Afghan. 31°54' N, 61°33' E 186
Farallon Islands, Pacific Ocean 37°28' N, 123°10' W 90
Farallones de Cali National Park, Col. 2°54' N, 76°60' W 136
Faranah, Guinea 10°2' N, 10°45' W 222
Faraulep Atoll, F.S.M. 8°56' N, 141°38' E 192
Fareham, U.K. 50°51' N, 1°11' W 162
Farewell, Alas., U.S. 62°22' N, 153°57' W 98
Farewell, Cape, N.Z. 40°31' S, 172°44' E 240
Fargo, N. Dak., U.S. 46°49' N, 97°1' W 73
Farg'ona, Uzb. 40°23' N, 71°47' E 197
Fari, Mali 12°10' N, 10°41' W 222
Faribault, Minn., U.S. 44°16' N, 93°17' W 94
Faridpur, Bangladesh 23°33' N, 89°51' E 197
Farim, Guinea-Bissau 12°30' N, 15°13' W 222
Farīmān, Iran 35°44' N, 59°53' E 180
Farina, Ill., U.S. 38°49' N, 88°47' W 102
Færingehavn see Kangerluarsoruseq, Den. 63°43' N, 51°21' W 106
Farinha, river, Braz. 6°52' S, 47°29' W 130
Farkhar, Afghan. 36°40' N, 69°50' E 186
Farkhor, Taj. 37°29' N, 69°22' E 184
Farkovo, Russ. 65°36' N, 86°58' E 169
Farkwa, Tanzania 5°23' S, 35°35' E 224
Farmer City, Ill., U.S. 40°14' N, 88°39' W 102
Farmersburg, Ind., U.S. 39°15' N, 87°22' W 102
Farmersville, Calif., U.S. 36°18' N, 119°13' W 101
Farmerville, La., U.S. 32°45' N, 92°25' W 103
Farmingdale, Me., U.S. 44°14' N, 69°47' W 104
Farmington, Ill., U.S. 40°41' N, 90°1' W 102
Farmington, N.H., U.S. 43°23' N, 71°4' W 104
Farmington, N. Mex., U.S. 36°44' N, 108°10' W 92
Farmington, Utah, U.S. 40°58' N, 111°52' W 90
Farmville, Va., U.S. 37°17' N, 78°25' W 94
Farnborough, U.K. 51°16' N, 0°45' E 162
Farne Islands, North Sea 55°40' N, 1°35' W 150
Farnham, U.K. 51°12' N, 0°48' E 162
Farnham, Mount, Can. 50°28' N, 116°35' W 90
Faro, Braz. 2°10' S, 56°45' W 130
Faro, Can. 62°15' N, 133°24' W 98
Faro, Port. 37°2' N, 7°60' W 214
Faro, Port. 37°1' N, 7°57' W 150
Faro, adm. division, Port. 37°6' N, 8°50' W 150
Fårö, island, Sw. 57°59' N, 19°16' E 166
Faro, Punta, Col. 11°7' N, 75°4' W 136
Faro, river, Cameroon 8°17' N, 12°55' E 218
Faro, Sierra do, Sp. 42°18' N, 8°5' W 150
Faroe Islands (Føroyar), North Atlantic Ocean 62°34' N, 11°40' W 143
Faroe-Iceland Ridge, North Atlantic Ocean 63°30' N, 10°2' W 253
Fårösund, Sw. 57°50' N, 19°2' E 166
Farquhar Group, islands, Indian Ocean 9°52' S, 50°31' E 218
Farr Bay 66°23' S, 96°0' E 248
Farrāshband, Iran 28°49' N, 52°5' E 196
Farrel, Isla, island, Chile 51°2' S, 75°51' W 134
Farsi, Afghan. 33°44' N, 63°15' E 186
Farsø, Den. 56°46' N, 9°20' E 152
Farsund, Nor. 58°5' N, 6°46' E 150
Fartura, Braz. 23°23' S, 49°32' W 138
Farwell, Mich., U.S. 43°50' N, 84°51' W 102
Farwell, Tex., U.S. 34°22' N, 103°2' W 92
Farwell Island, Antarctica 72°15' S, 88°28' W 248
Fasā, Iran 28°53' N, 53°44' E 196
Fashven, peak, U.K. 58°32' N, 5°1' W 150
Fastiv, Ukr. 50°3' N, 29°59' E 158
Fatala, river, Guinea 10°42' N, 13°45' W 222
Fatehabad, India 29°30' N, 75°28' E 197
Fatehgarh, India 27°22' N, 79°33' E 197
Fatehpur, India 27°59' N, 74°59' E 186
Fatehpur, India 25°54' N, 80°49' E 197
Fatehpur Sikri, India 27°5' N, 77°40' E 197
Fatezh, Russ. 52°3' N, 35°49' E 158
Fathai, Sudan 8°2' N, 31°45' E 224
Father, Lac, lake, Can. 49°20' N, 75°52' W 94
Fátima, Port. 39°36' N, 8°40' W 150
Fatsa, Turk. 41°0' N, 37°29' E 158
Faucille, Col de la, pass, Fr. 46°21' N, 6°0' E 167
Faucilles, Monts, Fr. 48°17' N, 5°51' E 163
Faulkton, S. Dak., U.S. 45°0' N, 99°9' W 90
Faulquemont, Fr. 49°2' N, 6°36' E 163
Fauresmith, S. Af. 29°44' S, 25°17' E 227
Fauro, island, Solomon Islands 7°0' S, 156°0' E 242
Fauske, Nor. 67°15' N, 15°22' E 152
Faust, Can. 55°18' N, 115°40' W 108
Faux Cap see Betanty, Madagascar 25°34' S, 45°31' E 220
Fåvang, Nor. 61°25' N, 10°13' E 152
Faverges, Fr. 45°44' N, 6°17' E 150
Faversham, U.K. 51°18' N, 0°53' E 162
Fawcett, Can. 54°32' N, 114°6' W 108
Faya-Largeau, Chad 17°54' N, 19°6' E 216
Fayd, Saudi Arabia 27°8' N, 42°38' E 180
Fayette, Ala., U.S. 33°41' N, 87°50' W 96
Fayette, Me., U.S. 44°24' N, 70°3' W 104
Fayette, Miss., U.S. 31°41' N, 91°3' W 103
Fayette, Mo., U.S. 39°8' N, 92°41' W 94
Fayette, Ohio, U.S. 41°39' N, 84°20' W 102
Fayette, Utah, U.S. 39°13' N, 111°50' W 90
Fayetteville, Ark., U.S. 36°3' N, 94°10' W 94
Faynān, ruin(s), Jordan 30°37' N, 35°27' E 194
Fayón, Sp. 41°14' N, 0°19' E 164
Faysh Khābūr, Iraq 37°4' N, 42°17' E 195
Fazao-Malfakassa National Park, Togo 8°39' N, 0°14' E 222
Fazilka, India 30°24' N, 74°3' E 186
Fazran, oil field, Saudi Arabia 26°2' N, 49°0' E 196
Fdérik (Fort Gouraud), Mauritania 22°41' N, 12°43' W 214
Fear, Cape, N.C., U.S. 33°45' N, 77°57' W 96
Fear, Cape, N.C., U.S. 34°47' N, 78°50' W 80
Feather River Canyon, Calif., U.S. 39°50' N, 121°36' W 90
Fedala see Mohammedia, Mor. 33°43' N, 7°22' W 214
Federación, Arg. 30°59' S, 57°54' W 139
Federal, Arg. 30°55' S, 58°45' W 139
Federally Administered Tribal Areas, adm. division, Pak. 32°7' N, 69°33' E 186
Fedje, Nor. 60°46' N, 4°41' E 152
Fedorovka, Kaz. 53°38' N, 62°42' E 184
Fedorovka, Kaz. 51°10' N, 51°59' E 158
Fedorovka, Russ. 53°10' N, 55°12' E 154
Feeding Hills, Mass., U.S. 42°3' N, 72°41' W 104
Fegen, lake, Nor. 57°10' N, 12°51' E 152
Feia, Lagoa, lake, Braz. 22°1' S, 41°34' W 138
Feijó, Braz. 8°10' S, 70°23' W 130
Feilding, N.Z. 40°13' S, 175°33' E 240
Feira de Santana, Braz. 12°16' S, 38°59' W 132
Feixi, China 31°42' N, 117°8' E 198
Fejér, adm. division, Hung. 46°57' N, 18°15' E 156
Feke, Turk. 37°51' N, 35°56' E 156
Feklistova, Ostrov, island, Russ. 55°7' N, 134°15' E 160
Felanitx, Sp. 39°27' N, 3°9' E 150
Felchville, Vt., U.S. 43°27' N, 72°33' W 104
Feldbach, Aust. 46°56' N, 15°53' E 168
Feldberg, peak, Ger. 47°51' N, 7°57' E 165
Felicity, Ohio, U.S. 38°50' N, 84°6' W 102
Felidu Atoll, Maldives 3°10' N, 73°1' E 188
Felipe Carrillo Puerto, Mex. 24°17' N, 104°1' W 114
Felipe Carrillo Puerto, Mex. 19°34' N, 88°4' W 115
Felixlândia, Braz. 18°46' S, 44°54' W 138
Felixstowe, U.K. 51°57' N, 1°20' E 163
Felizzano, It. 44°54' N, 8°26' E 167
Fellit, Eritrea 16°39' N, 38°0' E 182
Fellows, Calif., U.S. 35°10' N, 119°34' W 100
Fellsmere, Fla., U.S. 27°46' N, 80°36' W 105
Felsenthal, Ark., U.S. 33°2' N, 92°10' W 103
Fels ocsatár, Hung. 47°12' N, 16°27' E 168
Felton, Calif., U.S. 37°3' N, 122°6' W 100
Feltre, It. 46°0' N, 11°53' E 167
Femund, lake, Nor. 62°4' N, 11°19' E 152
Fen, river, China 36°45' N, 111°35' E 198
Fenelon Falls, Can. 44°31' N, 78°43' W 94
Fengari, peak, Gr. 40°27' N, 25°29' E 156
Fengcheng, China 28°10' N, 115°43' E 198
Fengcheng, China 40°26' N, 124°3' E 200
Fengdu, China 29°47' N, 107°44' E 198
Fenggang, China 27°58' N, 107°44' E 198
Fenghuang, China 27°54' N, 109°37' E 198
Fengjie, China 31°5' N, 109°34' E 198
Fengkai, China 23°27' N, 111°33' E 198
Fenglin, Taiwan 23°43' N, 121°24' E 198
Fengning, China 41°9' N, 116°35' E 198
Fengshan, China 24°30' N, 107°1' E 198
Fengxian, China 33°52' N, 106°37' E 198
Fengzhen, China 40°26' N, 113°7' E 198
Fennville, Mich., U.S. 42°34' N, 86°6' W 102
Feno, Cap de, Fr. 41°19' N, 8°29' E 156
Feno, Capo di, Fr. 41°58' N, 7°55' E 156
Fenoarivo, Madagascar 18°27' S, 46°32' E 220
Fenoarivo Atsinanana, Madagascar 17°25' S, 49°23' E 220
Fenton, La., U.S. 30°21' N, 92°57' W 103
Fenxi, China 36°38' N, 111°31' E 198
Fenyang, China 37°15' N, 111°46' E 198
Feodosiya, Ukr. 45°2' N, 35°18' E 156
Ferdows, Iran 33°58' N, 58°10' E 180
Fère-Champenoise, Fr. 48°45' N, 3°59' E 163
Féres, Gr. 40°53' N, 26°10' E 156
Fērfēr, Eth. 5°4' N, 45°10' E 218
Fergana Valley, Asia 40°38' N, 70°26' E 197
Fergus Falls, Minn., U.S. 46°16' N, 96°5' W 90
Ferguson, Ky., U.S. 37°3' N, 84°36' W 96
Ferguson Lake, Ariz., U.S. 33°2' N, 114°39' W 101
Ferguson, Mount, Nev., U.S. 38°38' N, 118°15' W 90
Ferguson Seamount, North Pacific Ocean 30°46' N, 172°25' E 252
Fergusson Island, P.N.G. 9°19' S, 150°40' E 192
Feria, Sp. 38°30' N, 6°34' W 164
Feriana, Tun. 34°56' N, 8°34' E 156
Feridu, island, Maldives 3°46' N, 72°0' E 188
Ferkéssédougou, Côte d'Ivoire 9°34' N, 5°13' W 222
Fern Grotto, site, Hawai'i, U.S. 22°1' N, 159°24' W 99
Fernández Leal, Mex. 30°49' N, 108°16' W 92
Fernandina Beach, Fla., U.S. 30°39' N, 81°28' W 96
Fernandina, Isla, island, Ecua. 0°39' N, 92°41' W 130
Fernando de Noronha, Arquipélago de, South Atlantic Ocean 3°19' S, 33°15' W 132
Fernandópolis, Braz. 20°17' S, 50°15' W 138
Fernán-Núñez, Sp. 37°40' N, 4°45' W 164
Fernão Dias, Braz. 16°23' S, 44°30' W 138
Fernão Veloso, Baía de 14°30' S, 39°50' E 224
Ferndale, Calif., U.S. 40°34' N, 124°17' W 92
Ferndale, Wash., U.S. 48°50' N, 122°36' W 100
Fernie, Can. 49°30' N, 115°3' W 90
Fernley, Nev., U.S. 39°36' N, 119°17' W 90
Ferns, Ire. 52°35' N, 6°30' W 150
Fernwood, Miss., U.S. 31°10' N, 90°28' W 103
Ferolle Point, Can. 51°0' N, 57°53' W 111
Ferrara, It. 44°50' N, 11°37' E 167
Ferrara, Mount, Antarctica 82°18' S, 42°54' W 248
Ferrat, Cap, Alg. 35°54' N, 0°22' E 164
Ferreira Gomes, Braz. 0°49' N, 51°7' W 130
Ferrelo, Cape, Oreg., U.S. 41°56' N, 124°44' W 90
Ferret, Cap, Fr. 44°38' N, 1°35' W 150
Ferriday, La., U.S. 31°37' N, 91°34' W 103
Ferris Mountains, Wyo., U.S. 42°21' N, 107°23' W 90
Ferrisburg, Vt., U.S. 44°12' N, 73°15' W 104
Ferro, river, Braz. 12°60' S, 55°5' W 130
Ferro see Hierro, island, Sp. 27°25' N, 17°55' W 214
Ferrol, Sp. 43°30' N, 8°17' W 214
Ferron, Utah, U.S. 39°5' N, 111°7' W 90
Ferros, Braz. 19°16' S, 43°3' W 138
Ferryland, Can. 47°1' N, 52°54' W 111
Ferrysburg, Mich., U.S. 43°5' N, 86°12' W 102
Ferryville see Menzel Bourguiba, Tun. 37°9' N, 9°47' E 156
Fertile, Minn., U.S. 47°31' N, 96°18' W 90
Fès (Fez), Mor. 34°6' N, 4°60' W 214
Feshi, Dem. Rep. of the Congo 6°8' S, 18°6' E 218
Fessenden, N. Dak., U.S. 47°37' N, 99°38' W 90
Fet, Nor. 59°55' N, 11°10' E 152
Fété Bowé, Senegal 14°55' N, 13°33' W 222
Feteşti, Rom. 44°22' N, 27°49' E 156
Fethiye, Turk. 36°34' N, 29°9' E 180
Feuet, spring, Lib. 24°57' N, 10°2' E 214
Feuilles, Rivière aux, river, Can. 58°19' N, 73°4' W 106
Feurs, Fr. 45°44' N, 4°13' E 150
Fevral'sk, Russ. 52°30' N, 131°24' E 190
Feyzabad, Afghan. 37°8' N, 70°35' E 186
Fez see Fès, Mor. 34°6' N, 4°60' W 214
Fezzan, region, Africa 29°39' N, 9°56' E 214
Fezzane, spring, Niger 21°53' N, 14°29' E 222
Ffestiniog, U.K. 52°57' N, 3°55' W 162
Fhada, Beinn, peak, U.K. 57°12' N, 5°23' W 150
Fian, Ghana 10°22' N, 2°30' W 222
Fianarantsoa, Madagascar 21°34' S, 47°3' E 207
Fianga, Chad 9°54' N, 15°6' E 216
Fibiş, Rom. 45°58' N, 21°25' E 168
Fichē, Eth. 9°48' N, 38°42' E 224
Fichtelgebirge, Ger. 50°3' N, 11°20' E 152
Ficksburg, S. Af. 28°52' S, 27°51' E 227
Fidenza, It. 44°51' N, 10°4' E 167
Fidler Lake, Can. 57°10' N, 97°26' W 108
Field Island, Austral. 12°15' S, 131°20' E 230
Field Naval Air Station, Fla., U.S. 30°43' N, 87°5' W 96
Fields Peak, Oreg., U.S. 44°18' N, 119°20' W 90
Fier, Alban. 40°43' N, 19°32' E 156
Fier, river, Fr. 45°54' N, 5°55' E 165
Fiesole, It. 43°48' N, 11°17' E 156
Fiesso, It. 44°58' N, 11°36' E 167
Fife Lake, Can. 49°11' N, 106°19' W 90
Fife Lake, Mich., U.S. 44°34' N, 85°21' W 94
Fife Ness, U.K. 56°17' N, 2°34' W 150
Fifield, Wis., U.S. 45°52' N, 90°26' W 94
Figari, Capo, It. 41°1' N, 9°38' E 156
Figeac, Fr. 44°36' N, 2°2' E 150
Figols, Sp. 42°10' N, 1°49' E 150
Figueira da Foz, Port. 40°8' N, 8°53' W 150
Figueirão, Braz. 18°44' S, 53°41' W 132
Figueres, Sp. 42°15' N, 2°57' E 164
Figuig, Mor. 32°7' N, 1°13' W 214
Figuil, Cameroon 9°44' N, 13°56' E 216
Fihaonana, Madagascar 18°36' S, 47°13' E 220
Fiji Islands 18°0' N, 178°0' E 242
Fiji Plateau, South Pacific Ocean 17°4' S, 179°39' E 252
Fika, Nig. 11°17' N, 11°17' E 222
Filabres, Sierra de los, Sp. 37°12' N, 2°32' W 164
Filabusi, Zimb. 20°31' S, 29°17' E 227
Filadelfia, Bol. 11°24' S, 68°49' W 137
Filadélfia, Braz. 7°22' S, 47°32' W 130
Filadelfia, Parag. 22°19' S, 60°4' W 132
Fil'akovo, Slovakia 48°15' N, 19°50' E 152
Filattiera, It. 44°19' N, 9°56' E 167
Filchner Mountains, Antarctica 72°42' S, 4°23' E 248
File Axe, Lac, lake, Can. 50°15' N, 74°7' W 110
File Lake, Can. 54°50' N, 100°42' W 108
Filer, Idaho, U.S. 42°34' N, 114°37' W 90
Filer City, Mich., U.S. 44°12' N, 86°18' W 102
Filey, U.K. 54°12' N, 0°18' E 162
Filia, Gr. 39°15' N, 26°8' E 156
Filiaşi, Rom. 44°33' N, 23°31' E 156
Filimon Sîrbu, Rom. 45°5' N, 27°15' E 156
Filingué, Niger 14°23' N, 3°17' E 222
Filipów, Pol. 54°10' N, 22°36' E 152
Filisur, Switz. 46°40' N, 9°40' E 167
Fillmore, Calif., U.S. 34°24' N, 118°55' W 101
Fillmore, Utah, U.S. 38°57' N, 112°19' W 90
Fils, Lac du, lake, Can. 46°38' N, 78°36' W 94
Filton, U.K. 51°30' N, 2°35' W 162
Fītu, Eth. 5°8' N, 40°39' E 224
Filyos, river, Turk. 41°28' N, 31°53' E 180
Fimbul Ice Shelf, Antarctica 70°45' S, 0°21' E 248
Finale Emilia, It. 44°50' N, 11°17' E 167
Fiñana, Sp. 37°9' N, 2°51' W 164
Finarwa, Eth. 13°4' N, 38°59' E 182
Fındıklı, Turk. 41°16' N, 41°7' E 195
Findlay, Ill., U.S. 39°31' N, 88°45' W 102
Findlay, Ohio, U.S. 41°1' N, 83°38' W 102
Findlay, Mount, Can. 50°4' N, 116°35' W 90
Fingoè, Mozambique 15°12' S, 31°51' E 224
Finike, Turk. 36°17' N, 30°7' E 156
Finiq, Alban. 39°54' N, 20°3' E 156
Finke, Austral. 25°37' S, 134°36' E 231
Finland 63°28' N, 25°46' E 152
Finland, Minn., U.S. 47°24' N, 91°16' W 94
Finland, Gulf of 60°11' N, 25°58' E 152
Finlay, river, Can. 57°38' N, 126°26' W 108
Finley, Calif., U.S. 39°0' N, 122°53' W 90
Finley, N. Dak., U.S. 47°29' N, 97°51' W 90
Finmoore, Can. 53°56' N, 123°37' W 108
Finne, region, Europe 51°7' N, 11°16' E 152
Finnentrop, Ger. 51°11' N, 7°58' E 167
Finnmarks-vidda, Nor. 69°2' N, 22°6' E 152
Finnskog, Nor. 60°42' N, 12°22' E 152
Finnsnes, Nor. 69°14' N, 18°0' E 152
Finse, Nor. 60°36' N, 7°23' E 152
Finspång, Nor. 58°41' N, 15°44' E 152
Finsteraarhorn, peak, Switz. 46°32' N, 8°5' E 167
Finström, Fin. 60°15' N, 19°54' E 166
Fiordland National Park, N.Z. 44°60' S, 165°54' E 240
Fîrdea, Rom. 45°45' N, 22°10' E 168
Fire Island National Seashore, Atlantic Ocean 40°35' N, 73°26' W 104
Firebag, river, Can. 57°27' N, 110°59' W 108
Firedrake Lake, Can. 61°15' N, 105°31' W 108
Firenze (Florence), It. 43°47' N, 11°14' E 167
Firenzuola, It. 44°7' N, 11°22' E 167
Firmat, Arg. 33°28' S, 61°30' W 139
Firozabad, India 27°7' N, 78°22' E 197
Firozpur, India 30°57' N, 74°38' E 186
First Sugar Mill, site, Hawai'i, U.S. 21°53' N, 159°30' W 99
Fīrūzābād, Iran 28°48' N, 52°38' E 196
Fīrūzkūh, Iran 35°46' N, 52°44' E 180
Fish Camp, Calif., U.S. 37°28' N, 119°39' W 100
Fish Cove Point, Can. 54°4' N, 57°19' W 111
Fish Haven, Idaho, U.S. 42°3' N, 111°24' W 92
Fish River Canyon Nature Reserve, Namibia 28°4' S, 17°32' E 227
Fisher, Ill., U.S. 40°18' N, 88°21' W 102
Fisher, La., U.S. 31°28' N, 93°29' W 103
Fisher Branch, Can. 51°5' N, 97°38' W 90
Fisher Strait 62°55' N, 84°37' W 106
Fishers Island, N.Y., U.S. 41°15' N, 72°12' W 104
Fishers Peak, Colo., U.S. 37°4' N, 104°33' W 92
Fishing Lake, Can. 52°8' N, 95°50' W 108
Fiskdale, Mass., U.S. 42°6' N, 72°8' W 104

Franklinton, *La., U.S.* 30°50′ N, 90°10′ W 103
Franklinville, *N.Y., U.S.* 42°20′ N, 78°28′ W 94
Frankston, *Tex., U.S.* 32°2′ N, 95°31′ W 103
Fransfontein, *Namibia* 20°14′ S, 14°59′ E 220
Franske Øer, islands, *Greenland Sea* 78°16′ N, 17°28′ W 246
Fränsta, *Nor.* 62°29′ N, 16°11′ E 152
Franz, *Can.* 48°28′ N, 84°24′ W 94
Franz Josef Glacier, *N.Z.* 43°24′ S, 170°12′ E 240
Franz Josef Land, *Barents Sea* 80°39′ N, 63°19′ E 255
Frasca, Capo della, *It.* 39°41′ N, 7°36′ E 156
Fraser Island, *Austral.* 25°59′ S, 153°16′ E 230
Fraser, river, *Can.* 53°23′ N, 122°46′ W 108
Fraser, river, *Can.* 51°30′ N, 122°24′ W 90
Fraser, river, *Can.* 49°20′ N, 121°40′ W 100
Fraser, river, *Can.* 53°51′ N, 121°49′ W 108
Fraserburg, *S. Af.* 31°55′ S, 21°31′ E 227
Fraserburg Road, *S. Af.* 32°48′ S, 21°57′ E 227
Fraserdale, *Can.* 49°51′ N, 81°38′ W 94
Frasertown, *N.Z.* 38°59′ S, 177°26′ E 240
Fray Bentos, *Uru.* 33°10′ S, 58°15′ W 139
Fray Jorge National Park, *Chile* 30°42′ S, 71°48′ W 134
Frazee, *Minn., U.S.* 46°42′ N, 95°43′ W 90
Frazer Lake, *Can.* 49°13′ N, 88°56′ W 94
Frazier, Mount, *Antarctica* 77°45′ S, 154°7′ W 248
Frazier Mountain, *Calif., U.S.* 34°46′ N, 119°1′ W 101
Frazier Park, *Calif., U.S.* 34°50′ N, 118°58′ W 101
Frechen, *Ger.* 50°54′ N, 6°48′ E 167
Fredericia, *Den.* 55°33′ N, 9°43′ E 150
Frederick, *Md., U.S.* 39°23′ N, 77°25′ W 82
Frederick, *Okla., U.S.* 34°21′ N, 99°1′ W 92
Frederick, *S. Dak., U.S.* 45°49′ N, 98°33′ W 90
Frederick Sound 56°54′ N, 133°26′ W 108
Fredericksburg, *Tex., U.S.* 30°15′ N, 98°52′ W 92
Fredericksburg and Spotsylvania National Military Park, *Va., U.S.* 38°14′ N, 77°34′ W 94
Fredericktown, *Ohio, U.S.* 40°28′ N, 82°32′ W 102
Fredericton, *Can.* 45°55′ N, 66°48′ W 94
Frederikshåb see Paamiut, *Den.* 62°4′ N, 49°33′ W 106
Frederikshavn, *Den.* 57°25′ N, 10°29′ E 150
Fredonia, *Ariz., U.S.* 36°56′ N, 112°31′ W 92
Fredonia, *Kans., U.S.* 37°30′ N, 95°50′ W 96
Fredonia, *N.Y., U.S.* 42°26′ N, 79°21′ W 94
Fredonia, *Wis., U.S.* 43°27′ N, 87°57′ W 102
Fredonyer Pass, *Calif., U.S.* 40°22′ N, 120°52′ W 90
Fredonyer Peak, *Calif., U.S.* 40°40′ N, 120°42′ W 90
Fredrikstad, *Nor.* 59°13′ N, 10°56′ E 152
Free State, adm. division, *S. Af.* 28°8′ S, 25°15′ E 220
Freedom, *N.H., U.S.* 43°48′ N, 71°3′ W 104
Freedom, *Okla., U.S.* 36°45′ N, 99°7′ W 92
Freels, Cape, *Can.* 49°9′ N, 53°27′ W 111
Freeman Point, *Antarctica* 65°49′ S, 132°15′ E 248
Freeport, *Bahamas* 26°31′ N, 78°41′ W 105
Freeport, *Ill., U.S.* 42°17′ N, 89°37′ W 102
Freeport, *Me., U.S.* 43°51′ N, 70°7′ W 94
Freeport, *Mo., U.S.* 42°17′ N, 89°37′ W 94
Freeport, *N.Y., U.S.* 40°39′ N, 73°35′ W 104
Freeport, *Tex., U.S.* 28°55′ N, 95°22′ W 103
Freer, *Tex., U.S.* 27°51′ N, 98°38′ W 92
Freesoil, *Mich., U.S.* 44°6′ N, 86°13′ W 102
Freetown, *Ind., U.S.* 38°58′ N, 86°7′ W 102
Freetown, *Sierra Leone* 8°24′ N, 13°21′ W 222
Freezeout Mountain, *Oreg., U.S.* 43°36′ N, 117°40′ W 90
Fregenal de la Sierra, *Sp.* 38°10′ N, 6°40′ W 164
Freguesia do Andirá, *Braz.* 2°55′ S, 56°60′ W 130
Fréhel, Cap, *Fr.* 48°29′ N, 2°40′ W 150
Freiburg, *Ger.* 48°0′ N, 7°51′ E 152
Freienohl, *Ger.* 51°22′ N, 8°9′ E 167
Freila, *Sp.* 37°31′ N, 2°54′ W 164
Freising, *Ger.* 48°24′ N, 11°44′ E 156
Freistadt, *Aust.* 48°30′ N, 14°29′ E 152
Fremont, *Calif., U.S.* 37°33′ N, 121°59′ W 100
Fremont, *Ind., U.S.* 41°43′ N, 84°56′ W 102
Fremont, *Mich., U.S.* 43°26′ N, 85°57′ W 102
Fremont, *Nebr., U.S.* 41°24′ N, 96°30′ W 90
Fremont, *Ohio, U.S.* 41°20′ N, 83°8′ W 102
Fremont Mountains, *Oreg., U.S.* 42°49′ N, 121°27′ W 90
Fremont Peak, *Calif., U.S.* 36°46′ N, 121°35′ W 100
Fremont Peak, *Wyo., U.S.* 43°6′ N, 109°42′ W 90
Fremont, river, *Utah, U.S.* 38°17′ N, 111°42′ W 80
French Camp, *Miss., U.S.* 33°16′ N, 89°24′ W 103
French Cays see Plana Cays, *North Atlantic Ocean* 22°41′ N, 73°33′ W 116
French Guiana, *Fr.* 3°47′ N, 53°56′ W 130
French Lick, *Ind., U.S.* 38°32′ N, 86°37′ W 102
French Pass, *N.Z.* 40°59′ S, 173°50′ E 240
French River, *Can.* 46°1′ N, 80°35′ W 94
French Settlement, *La., U.S.* 30°17′ N, 90°49′ W 103
Frenchman Butte, *Can.* 53°35′ N, 109°38′ W 108
Frenchman Flat, *Nev., U.S.* 36°47′ N, 115°59′ W 101
Frenchman, river, *Can.* 49°30′ N, 108°41′ W 90
Frenchville, *Me., U.S.* 47°16′ N, 68°23′ W 94
Freren, *Ger.* 52°29′ N, 7°33′ E 163
Fresco, *Côte d'Ivoire* 5°5′ N, 5°32′ W 222
Freshfield, Cape, *Antarctica* 68°29′ S, 150°37′ E 248
Freshfield Icefield, *Can.* 51°43′ N, 117°41′ W 90
Fresnillo, *Mex.* 23°9′ N, 102°53′ W 114
Fresno, *Calif., U.S.* 36°44′ N, 119°48′ W 100
Fresno Reservoir, lake, *Mont., U.S.* 48°43′ N, 110°51′ W 90
Fresno Slough, river, *Calif., U.S.* 36°28′ N, 120°4′ W 101
Fresnoy-le-Grand, *Fr.* 49°56′ N, 3°25′ E 163
Freudenberg, *Ger.* 50°53′ N, 7°53′ E 167
Frévent, *Fr.* 50°16′ N, 2°17′ E 163
Freyre, *Arg.* 31°10′ S, 62°6′ W 139
Fria, *Guinea* 10°22′ N, 13°36′ W 222
Fria, Cape, *Namibia* 18°27′ S, 12°4′ E 220
Friant, *Calif., U.S.* 36°59′ N, 119°43′ W 100
Frías, *Arg.* 28°39′ S, 65°7′ W 132
Fribourg, *Switz.* 46°48′ N, 7°8′ E 167
Friday Creek, river, *Can.* 49°44′ N, 82°59′ W 94
Friday Harbour, *Wash., U.S.* 48°31′ N, 123°2′ W 100
Fridtjof Nansen, Mount, *Antarctica* 85°17′ S, 165°5′ W 248
Friedberg, *Aust.* 47°26′ N, 16°3′ E 168
Friedberg, *Ger.* 50°19′ N, 8°45′ E 167
Friedland, *Ger.* 51°25′ N, 9°55′ E 167
Frielendorf, *Ger.* 50°58′ N, 9°20′ E 167
Friend, *Nebr., U.S.* 40°38′ N, 97°18′ W 90
Friendship, *Wis., U.S.* 43°58′ N, 89°49′ W 102
Friguiagbé, *Guinea* 9°57′ N, 12°58′ W 222
Frinton on Sea, *U.K.* 51°50′ N, 1°15′ E 162
Friona, *Tex., U.S.* 34°37′ N, 102°43′ W 92
Frisco, *Colo., U.S.* 39°33′ N, 106°6′ W 90
Frisco City, *Ala., U.S.* 31°25′ N, 87°24′ W 103
Frisco Peak, *Utah, U.S.* 38°30′ N, 113°21′ W 90
Frissell, Mount, *Conn., U.S.* 42°2′ N, 73°30′ W 104
Fritzlar, *Ger.* 51°8′ N, 9°17′ E 167
Friuli-Venezia Giulia, adm. division, *It.* 46°11′ N, 12°48′ E 167
Froan, islands, *Norwegian Sea* 64°11′ N, 8°31′ E 152
Frobisher Bay 62°26′ N, 67°19′ W 246
Frobisher Lake, *Can.* 56°36′ N, 109°20′ W 108
Frog Lake, *Can.* 53°50′ N, 110°42′ W 108
Frog, river, *Can.* 58°16′ N, 127°1′ W 108
Frohavet 63°59′ N, 8°38′ E 152
Frolovo, *Russ.* 49°45′ N, 43°41′ E 158
Fromberg, *Mont., U.S.* 45°22′ N, 108°55′ W 90
Frombork, *Pol.* 54°20′ N, 19°40′ E 166
Frome, *U.K.* 51°13′ N, 2°20′ W 162
Fromenteau, Lac, lake, *Can.* 51°24′ N, 74°5′ W 111
Front Range, *North America* 39°3′ N, 105°43′ W 90
Front Royal, *Va., U.S.* 38°55′ N, 78°13′ W 94
Fronteiras, *Braz.* 7°6′ S, 40°37′ W 132
Frontenac, *Kans., U.S.* 37°26′ N, 94°41′ W 94
Frontera, *Arg.* 31°31′ S, 62°1′ W 139
Frontera, *Mex.* 18°31′ N, 92°39′ W 115
Frontera, *Mex.* 26°56′ N, 101°28′ W 112
Frontera, Punta, *Mex.* 18°38′ N, 93°30′ W 115
Fronteras, *Mex.* 30°56′ N, 109°33′ W 92
Frontier, *Wyo., U.S.* 41°50′ N, 110°33′ W 90
Frontignan, *Fr.* 43°27′ N, 3°44′ E 164
Frostburg, *Md., U.S.* 39°39′ N, 78°56′ W 94
Frostproof, *Fla., U.S.* 27°44′ N, 81°32′ W 105
Frotet, Lac, lake, *Can.* 50°38′ N, 75°16′ W 110
Frövi, *Nor.* 59°27′ N, 15°20′ E 152
Fruita, *Colo., U.S.* 39°9′ N, 108°44′ W 90
Fruitdale, *Ala., U.S.* 31°19′ N, 88°24′ W 103
Fruitport, *Mich., U.S.* 43°7′ N, 86°10′ W 102
Fruitville, *Fla., U.S.* 27°21′ N, 82°27′ W 105
Fruška Gora, *Serb. and Mont.* 45°10′ N, 19°19′ E 168
Frutal, *Braz.* 20°3′ S, 48°55′ W 138
Frutigen, *Switz.* 46°36′ N, 7°38′ E 167
Fryeburg, *Me., U.S.* 44°0′ N, 70°59′ W 104
Fu, river, *China* 28°10′ N, 116°2′ E 198
Fua Mulaku, island, *Maldives* 0°27′ N, 73°24′ E 188
Fu'an, *China* 27°11′ N, 119°40′ E 198
Fubo, *Angola* 5°28′ S, 12°23′ E 218
Fucecchio, *It.* 43°44′ N, 10°48′ E 167
Fuchs Dome, peak, *Antarctica* 80°38′ S, 29°4′ W 248
Fuchū, *Japan* 34°35′ N, 133°14′ E 201
Fudong, *China* 42°34′ N, 129°12′ E 200
Fuego Mountain, *Oreg., U.S.* 42°37′ N, 121°32′ W 90
Fuente, *Mex.* 28°38′ N, 100°33′ W 92
Fuente de Cantos, *Sp.* 38°14′ N, 6°19′ W 164
Fuente el Fresno, *Sp.* 39°13′ N, 3°47′ W 164
Fuente Obejuna, *Sp.* 38°15′ N, 5°26′ W 164
Fuente-Álamo, *Sp.* 38°41′ N, 1°26′ W 164
Fuenterrebollo, *Sp.* 41°17′ N, 3°56′ W 164
Fuentes de Andalucía, *Sp.* 37°28′ N, 5°22′ W 164
Fuentes de Ebro, *Sp.* 41°30′ N, 0°40′ E 164
Fuentes-Claras, *Sp.* 40°51′ N, 1°19′ W 164
Fuerteventura, island, *Sp.* 28°46′ N, 15°30′ W 214
Fuga, island, *Philippines* 18°56′ N, 121°27′ E 198
Fugou, *China* 34°1′ N, 114°24′ E 198
Fugu, *China* 39°3′ N, 111°2′ E 198
Fuhai, *China* 47°8′ N, 87°28′ E 184
Fuji, peak, *Japan* 35°20′ N, 138°41′ E 201
Fujian, adm. division, *China* 25°27′ N, 116°57′ E 198
Fujieda, *Japan* 34°52′ N, 138°15′ E 201
Fuji-Hakone-Izu National Park, *Japan* 34°42′ N, 138°36′ E 201
Fujisawa, *Japan* 35°19′ N, 139°30′ E 201
Fujiyoshida, *Japan* 35°27′ N, 138°48′ E 201
Fûka, *Egypt* 31°3′ N, 27°55′ E 180
Fukang, *China* 44°8′ N, 87°55′ E 184
Fukuchiyama, *Japan* 35°15′ N, 135°6′ E 201
Fukui, *Japan* 36°3′ N, 136°14′ E 201
Fukui, adm. division, *Japan* 35°49′ N, 136°3′ E 201
Fukuoka, *Japan* 33°35′ N, 130°24′ E 200
Fukuoka, adm. division, *Japan* 33°29′ N, 130°11′ E 201
Fukushima, *Japan* 37°45′ N, 140°26′ E 201
Fukushima, adm. division, *Japan* 37°20′ N, 139°16′ E 201
Fukushima, Mount, *Antarctica* 71°18′ S, 35°0′ E 248
Fukuyama, *Japan* 34°29′ N, 133°22′ E 201
Fulacunda, *Guinea-Bissau* 11°46′ N, 15°11′ W 222
Fulbourn, *U.K.* 52°10′ N, 0°13′ E 162
Fulda, *Ger.* 50°33′ N, 9°41′ E 167
Fulda, *Minn., U.S.* 43°51′ N, 95°36′ W 90
Fulda, river, *Ger.* 51°12′ N, 9°28′ E 167
Fulford Harbour, *Can.* 48°45′ N, 123°27′ W 100
Fuling, *China* 29°40′ N, 107°19′ E 198
Fullerton, *Calif., U.S.* 33°52′ N, 117°56′ W 101
Fullerton, *Nebr., U.S.* 41°21′ N, 97°59′ W 90
Fülöpszállás, *Hung.* 46°49′ N, 19°14′ E 168
Fulton, *Ala., U.S.* 31°47′ N, 87°43′ W 103
Fulton, *Ill., U.S.* 41°51′ N, 90°9′ W 102
Fulton, *Ky., U.S.* 36°31′ N, 88°52′ W 96
Fulton, *Miss., U.S.* 34°15′ N, 88°24′ W 96
Fulton, *Mo., U.S.* 38°50′ N, 91°58′ W 94
Fulton, *N.Y., U.S.* 43°19′ N, 76°25′ W 110
Fulufjället, peak, *Nor.* 61°34′ N, 12°29′ E 152
Fūman, *Iran* 37°14′ N, 49°18′ E 195
Fumane, *Mozambique* 24°27′ S, 33°58′ E 227
Fumel, *Fr.* 44°28′ N, 0°56′ E 150
Funabashi, *Japan* 35°41′ N, 140°0′ E 201
Funafuti, *Tuvalu* 8°42′ S, 178°24′ E 238
Funafuti (Fongafale), *Tuvalu* 9°0′ S, 179°0′ E 241
Funafuti, island, *Tuvalu* 9°0′ S, 179°0′ E 241
Funan, *China* 32°38′ N, 115°35′ E 198
Funan Gaba, *Eth.* 4°22′ N, 37°59′ E 224
Funan see Fushun, *China* 41°44′ N, 123°53′ E 200
Funan see Fusui, *China* 22°37′ N, 107°54′ E 198
Funäsdalen, *Nor.* 62°32′ N, 12°29′ E 152
Funauke, *Japan* 24°14′ N, 123°43′ E 198
Funchal, *Port.* 32°34′ N, 17°9′ W 207
Fundación, *Col.* 10°32′ N, 74°12′ W 136
Fundão, *Port.* 40°8′ N, 7°31′ W 150
Fundong, *Cameroon* 6°14′ N, 10°10′ E 222
Fundy, Bay of 45°6′ N, 66°10′ W 111
Fundy National Park, *Can.* 45°26′ N, 65°42′ W 111
Funeral Mountains, *Calif., U.S.* 36°44′ N, 116°53′ W 101
Funeral Peak, *Calif., U.S.* 36°5′ N, 116°40′ W 101
Funhalouro, *Mozambique* 23°2′ S, 34°24′ E 227
Funing, *China* 23°35′ N, 105°37′ E 198
Funtua, *Nig.* 11°29′ N, 7°19′ E 222
Fuping, *China* 34°47′ N, 109°9′ E 198
Fuqing, *China* 25°43′ N, 119°23′ E 198
Fuquan, *China* 26°44′ N, 107°30′ E 198
Furancungo, *Mozambique* 14°55′ S, 33°37′ E 224
Furawiya, spring, *Sudan* 15°20′ N, 23°41′ E 226
Furillen, island, *Sw.* 57°41′ N, 19°2′ E 166
Furmanov, *Russ.* 57°16′ N, 41°5′ E 154
Furnas Dam, *Braz.* 20°50′ S, 46°15′ W 132
Furneaux Group, islands, *Flinders Island* 39°48′ S, 148°30′ E 230
Furnes see Veurne, *Belg.* 51°4′ N, 2°40′ E 150
Furqlus, *Syr.* 34°36′ N, 37°4′ E 194
Fürstenau, *Ger.* 52°31′ N, 7°41′ E 163
Fürstenfeld, *Aust.* 47°3′ N, 16°5′ E 168
Fürth, *Ger.* 49°27′ N, 10°59′ E 152
Furudal, *Nor.* 61°10′ N, 15°8′ E 152
Furukawa, *Japan* 38°35′ N, 140°57′ E 201
Furukawa, *Japan* 36°14′ N, 137°11′ E 201
Furusund, *Sw.* 59°40′ N, 18°52′ E 166
Furuvik, *Nor.* 60°38′ N, 17°17′ E 152
Fuscaldo, *It.* 39°25′ N, 16°2′ E 156
Fuse, *Japan* 36°19′ N, 133°21′ E 201
Fushan, *China* 37°30′ N, 121°13′ E 198
Fushimi Lake, *Can.* 49°47′ N, 84°21′ W 94
Fushun, *China* 29°13′ N, 104°56′ E 198
Fushun (Funan), *China* 41°44′ N, 123°53′ E 200
Fusio, *Switz.* 46°27′ N, 8°38′ E 167
Fusong, *China* 42°16′ N, 127°18′ E 200
Fusui (Funan), *China* 22°37′ N, 107°54′ E 198
Futaleufú, *Chile* 43°12′ S, 71°55′ W 134
Fuveau, *Fr.* 43°26′ N, 5°33′ E 150
Fuwa, *Egypt* 31°12′ N, 30°32′ E 180
Fuxian, *China* 36°0′ N, 109°20′ E 198
Fuxin, *China* 42°4′ N, 121°39′ E 198
Fuya, *Japan* 38°30′ N, 139°32′ E 201
Fuyang, *China* 32°52′ N, 115°46′ E 198
Fuyang, river, *China* 37°46′ N, 115°57′ E 198
Fuyu, *China* 45°12′ N, 124°53′ E 198
Fuyu, *China* 47°46′ N, 124°28′ E 198
Fuyun, *China* 47°3′ N, 89°25′ E 184
Füzesabony, *Hung.* 47°45′ N, 20°26′ E 168
Fuzhou, *China* 26°8′ N, 119°20′ E 198
Füzuli, *Azerb.* 39°34′ N, 47°6′ E 195
Fylingdales Moor, site, *U.K.* 54°21′ N, 0°38′ E 162

G

Ga, *Ghana* 9°47′ N, 2°30′ W 222
Gaal Goble, *Somalia* 9°50′ N, 49°50′ E 216
Gaalkacyo (Galcaio), *Somalia* 6°44′ N, 47°29′ E 218
Gabakly, *Turkm.* 39°48′ N, 62°31′ E 180
Gabarus, Cape, *Can.* 45°41′ N, 60°43′ W 111
Gabasawa, *Nig.* 12°9′ N, 8°54′ E 222
Gabatit, spring, *Sudan* 20°28′ N, 35°49′ E 182
Gabbac, Raas, *Somalia* 7°37′ N, 50°3′ E 218
Gabbs, *Nev., U.S.* 38°52′ N, 117°57′ W 90
Gabbs Valley, *Nev., U.S.* 38°54′ N, 118°18′ W 90
Gabbs Valley Range, *Nev., U.S.* 38°37′ N, 118°15′ W 90
Gabela, *Angola* 10°50′ S, 14°21′ E 220
Gabela, *Bosn. and Herzg.* 43°3′ N, 17°39′ E 168
Gabes, *Tun.* 33°53′ N, 10°4′ E 214
Gabes, Gulf of 34°9′ N, 9°36′ E 156
Gabilan Range, *Calif., U.S.* 36°41′ N, 121°36′ W 100
Gabon 0°41′ N, 11°20′ E 218
Gaborone, *Botswana* 24°42′ S, 25°45′ E 227
Gabras, *Sudan* 10°16′ N, 26°15′ E 224
Gabriel, Lac, lake, *Can.* 49°15′ N, 74°57′ W 94
Gabriel Vera, *Bol.* 19°15′ S, 65°54′ W 137
Gabriels, *N.Y., U.S.* 44°25′ N, 74°12′ W 104
Gabro, *Eth.* 6°16′ N, 43°14′ E 218
Gabrovo, *Bulg.* 42°52′ N, 25°17′ E 156
Gabrovo, adm. division, *Bulg.* 42°54′ N, 24°51′ E 156
Gabu, *Dem. Rep. of the Congo* 3°22′ N, 27°2′ E 224
Gach Sārān, oil field, *Iran* 30°12′ N, 50°51′ E 196
Gackle, *N. Dak., U.S.* 46°35′ N, 99°9′ W 90
Gacko, *Bosn. and Herzg.* 43°10′ N, 18°31′ E 168
Gada, river, *Dem. Rep. of the Congo* 3°21′ N, 28°30′ E 224
Gädäbäy, *Azerb.* 40°34′ N, 45°48′ E 195
Gadamai, *Sudan* 17°5′ N, 36°4′ E 182
Gadarwara, *India* 22°53′ N, 78°46′ E 197
Gadifuri, island, *Maldives* 2°25′ N, 72°1′ E 188
Gádor, Sierra de, *Sp.* 36°55′ N, 3°1′ W 164
Gádoros, *Hung.* 46°40′ N, 20°36′ E 168
Gadra Road, *India* 25°44′ N, 70°38′ E 186
Gadrut, *Azerb.* 39°30′ N, 47°0′ E 195
Gadsden, *Ariz., U.S.* 32°32′ N, 114°46′ W 101
Gadzi, *Cen. Af. Rep.* 4°46′ N, 16°41′ E 218
Găeşti, *Rom.* 44°44′ N, 25°18′ E 156
Gafatîn, Gezâir, islands, *Red Sea* 26°59′ N, 34°2′ E 180
Gaferut, island, *F.S.M.* 9°22′ N, 144°22′ E 192
Gafsa, *Tun.* 34°24′ N, 8°48′ E 156
Gagal, *Chad* 9°1′ N, 15°9′ E 216
Gagarin, *Russ.* 55°32′ N, 35°1′ E 154
Gagetown, *Mich., U.S.* 43°38′ N, 83°15′ W 102
Gagino, *Russ.* 55°13′ N, 45°6′ E 154
Gagliano del Capo, *It.* 39°50′ N, 18°21′ E 156
Gagnoa, *Côte d'Ivoire* 6°2′ N, 5°56′ W 222
Gagra, *Ga.* 43°21′ N, 40°15′ E 195
Gagshor, *Russ.* 60°47′ N, 50°11′ E 154
Gahnpa, *Liberia* 7°5′ N, 8°60′ W 222
Gaibandha, *Bangladesh* 25°18′ N, 89°29′ E 197
Gaillefontaine, *Fr.* 49°39′ N, 1°35′ E 163
Gaillimh see Galway, *Ire.* 53°16′ N, 9°3′ W 150
Gaillon, *Fr.* 49°9′ N, 1°18′ E 163
Gaimán, *Arg.* 43°15′ S, 65°30′ W 134
Gainesville, *Ala., U.S.* 32°47′ N, 88°10′ W 103
Gainesville, *Fla., U.S.* 29°38′ N, 82°20′ W 105
Gainesville, *Ga., U.S.* 34°17′ N, 83°50′ W 96
Gainesville, *Mo., U.S.* 36°35′ N, 92°26′ W 96
Gainesville, *Tex., U.S.* 33°35′ N, 97°8′ W 92
Gainsborough, *Can.* 49°10′ N, 101°27′ W 90
Gainsborough, *U.K.* 53°24′ N, 0°47′ E 162
Gaissane, region, *Europe* 69°47′ N, 26°1′ E 152
Gaixian, *China* 40°24′ N, 122°24′ E 198
Gajdobra, *Serb. and Mont.* 45°20′ N, 19°27′ E 168
Gajiram, *Nig.* 12°32′ N, 13°12′ E 216
Gakdul, spring, *Sudan* 17°36′ N, 32°51′ E 182
Gakkel Ridge, *Arctic Ocean* 86°39′ N, 68°19′ E 255
Gakona, *Alas., U.S.* 62°16′ N, 145°16′ W 98
Gakuch, *Pak.* 36°9′ N, 73°45′ E 186
Gal Tardo, *Somalia* 3°34′ N, 46°0′ E 218
Galadi, *Eth.* 5°57′ N, 41°34′ E 224
Galadi, *Nig.* 13°0′ N, 6°24′ E 222
Galahad, *Can.* 52°31′ N, 111°57′ W 108
Galaḥi, adm. division, *Rom.* 45°48′ N, 27°19′ E 156
Galâla el Qiblîya, Gebel el, peak, *Egypt* 28°46′ N, 32°22′ E 180
Galán, Cerro, peak, *Arg.* 25°57′ S, 66°60′ W 132
Galana, river, *Kenya* 3°12′ S, 39°14′ E 224
Galaosiyo, *Uzb.* 39°52′ N, 64°29′ E 197
Galápagos Fracture Zone, *South Pacific Ocean* 3°38′ S, 139°34′ W 252
Galápagos Islands (Archipiélago de Colón), *South Pacific Ocean* 0°13′ N, 92°2′ W 130
Galápagos Rift, *North Pacific Ocean* 1°22′ N, 94°53′ W 252
Galápagos Rise, *South Pacific Ocean* 15°51′ S, 94°41′ W 252
Galateia, *Northern Cyprus* 35°25′ N, 34°4′ E 194
Galaţi, *Rom.* 45°27′ N, 28°3′ E 156
Galatxo, Punta del, *Sp.* 40°24′ N, 0°32′ E 164
Galax, *Va., U.S.* 36°40′ N, 80°56′ W 96
Galcaio see Gaalkacyo, *Somalia* 6°44′ N, 47°29′ E 218
Galdhøpiggen, peak, *Nor.* 61°37′ N, 8°9′ E 152
Galé, *Mali* 12°37′ N, 9°30′ W 222
Galeana, *Mex.* 30°6′ N, 107°38′ W 92
Galeana, *Mex.* 24°49′ N, 100°4′ W 114
Galegu, *Sudan* 12°33′ N, 35°1′ E 182
Galena, *Alas., U.S.* 64°37′ N, 156°56′ W 98
Galena, *Kans., U.S.* 37°3′ N, 94°39′ W 96
Galena, *Mo., U.S.* 42°24′ N, 90°26′ W 94
Galena Peak, *Idaho, U.S.* 43°52′ N, 114°40′ W 90
Galera, *Sp.* 37°43′ N, 2°33′ W 164
Galera Point, *Trinidad and Tobago* 10°50′ N, 61°24′ W 116
Galera, Punta, *Chile* 40°4′ S, 75°3′ W 134
Galera, Punta, *Ecua.* 0°48′ N, 81°14′ W 130
Galera, river, *Braz.* 14°22′ S, 60°3′ W 132
Galesburg, *Mich., U.S.* 42°17′ N, 85°25′ W 102
Galesburg, *Mo., U.S.* 40°57′ N, 90°22′ W 94
Galeton, *Can.* 51°8′ N, 80°56′ W 110
Galeton, *Pa., U.S.* 41°44′ N, 77°39′ W 94
Galgate, *U.K.* 53°59′ N, 2°48′ W 162
Gali, *Ga.* 42°36′ N, 41°43′ E 195
Galiano Island, *Can.* 48°56′ N, 123°26′ W 100
Galich, *Russ.* 58°20′ N, 42°24′ E 154
Galicia, adm. division, *Sp.* 42°36′ N, 8°44′ W 150
Galičnik, *Maced.* 41°35′ N, 20°39′ E 168
Galim, *Cameroon* 7°3′ N, 12°27′ E 218
Galinoporni, *Northern Cyprus* 35°31′ N, 34°18′ E 194
Galio, *Liberia* 5°42′ N, 7°34′ W 222
Galion, *Ohio, U.S.* 40°42′ N, 82°48′ W 102
Galkino, *Kaz.* 52°20′ N, 78°13′ E 184
Galla, Mount, *Antarctica* 75°49′ S, 125°18′ W 248
Gallanito, *Nor.* 68°53′ N, 22°50′ E 152
G'allaorol, *Uzb.* 40°0′ N, 67°34′ E 197
Gallarate, *It.* 45°39′ N, 8°47′ E 167
Gallardon, *Fr.* 48°31′ N, 1°41′ E 163
Gallatin, *Mo., U.S.* 39°54′ N, 93°58′ W 94
Gallatin, *Tenn., U.S.* 36°23′ N, 86°27′ W 96
Gallatin Peak, *Mont., U.S.* 45°20′ N, 111°26′ W 90
Gallatin Range, *Mont., U.S.* 45°24′ N, 111°13′ W 90
Galle, *Sri Lanka* 6°8′ N, 80°11′ E 173
Gallegos, Cabo, *Chile* 46°30′ S, 77°9′ W 134
Gallegos, river, *Arg.* 51°60′ S, 72°10′ W 134
Galliano, *La., U.S.* 29°26′ N, 90°18′ W 103
Galliate, *It.* 45°28′ N, 8°40′ E 167
Gallinas, Punta, *Col.* 12°27′ N, 71°42′ W 136
Gallipoli, *It.* 40°3′ N, 17°59′ E 156
Gallipoli see Gelibolu, *Turk.* 40°25′ N, 26°38′ E 156
Gällivare, *Nor.* 67°8′ N, 20°39′ E 152
Gallman, *Miss., U.S.* 31°55′ N, 90°24′ W 103
Gällö, *Nor.* 62°55′ N, 15°11′ E 152
Gallo, Capo, *It.* 38°15′ N, 12°42′ E 156
Gallo Mountains, *N. Mex., U.S.* 34°1′ N, 108°39′ W 92
Gallo, river, *Sp.* 40°43′ N, 2°3′ W 150
Gallup, *N. Mex., U.S.* 35°30′ N, 108°44′ W 92
Gallur, *Sp.* 41°51′ N, 1°19′ W 164
Galma Galla, spring, *Kenya* 1°14′ S, 40°49′ E 224
Galole, *Kenya* 1°27′ S, 40°0′ E 224
Galt, *Calif., U.S.* 38°14′ N, 121°19′ W 100
Galtat Zemmour, *Western Sahara* 25°9′ N, 12°24′ W 214
Galten, *Nor.* 70°42′ N, 22°44′ E 152
Galtymore, peak, *Ire.* 52°21′ N, 8°19′ W 150
Galu, *Dem. Rep. of the Congo* 11°22′ S, 26°37′ E 224
Galula, *Tanzania* 8°38′ S, 33°2′ E 224
Galva, *Ill., U.S.* 41°9′ N, 90°3′ W 102
Galveston, *Tex., U.S.* 29°16′ N, 94°49′ W 103
Galveston Bay 29°22′ N, 95°48′ W 80
Galveston Island, *Tex., U.S.* 29°4′ N, 94°58′ W 103
Gálvez, *Arg.* 32°3′ S, 61°13′ W 139
Galwa, *Nepal* 29°39′ N, 81°53′ E 197
Galway (Gaillimh), *Ire.* 53°16′ N, 9°3′ W 150
Gam, river, *Vietnam* 22°5′ N, 105°11′ E 202
Gamba, *China* 28°16′ N, 88°31′ E 197
Gamba, *Gabon* 2°43′ S, 10°0′ E 218
Gambaga, *Ghana* 10°32′ N, 0°27′ E 222
Gambēla, *Eth.* 8°14′ N, 34°35′ E 224
Gambela National Park, *Eth.* 7°42′ N, 33°59′ E 224
Gambell, *Alas., U.S.* 63°40′ N, 171°50′ W 98
Gambia 13°23′ N, 16°0′ W 214
Gambia Plain, *North Atlantic Ocean* 12°33′ N, 27°53′ W 253
Gambie, river, *Senegal* 12°54′ N, 13°7′ W 222
Gambier, *Ohio, U.S.* 40°22′ N, 82°23′ W 102
Gambier, Îles, islands, *South Pacific Ocean* 22°42′ S, 138°12′ W 238
Gambier Island, *Can.* 49°32′ N, 123°36′ W 100
Gambier Islands, *Great Australian Bight* 35°21′ S, 136°39′ E 230
Gamboma, *Congo* 1°54′ S, 15°51′ E 218
Gamboula, *Cen. Af. Rep.* 4°10′ N, 15°12′ E 218
Gamdou, *Niger* 13°27′ N, 10°3′ E 222
Gamlakarleby see Kokkola, *Fin.* 63°49′ N, 23°5′ E 152
Gamleby, *Nor.* 57°54′ N, 16°23′ E 152
Gamma, oil field, *Azerb.* 39°43′ N, 49°19′ E 195
Gammelstad, *Nor.* 65°37′ N, 22°1′ E 152
Gamoep, *S. Af.* 29°55′ S, 18°23′ E 227
Gamova, Mys, *Russ.* 42°24′ N, 131°12′ E 200
Gamph, Slieve (Ox Mountains, The), *Ire.* 54°2′ N, 9°28′ W 150
Gampo, *S. Korea* 35°47′ N, 129°32′ E 200
Gamsby, river, *Can.* 53°5′ N, 127°21′ W 108
Gamud, peak, *Eth.* 4°1′ N, 38°3′ E 224
Gamyshlyja, *Turkm.* 38°21′ N, 54°0′ E 180
Gan, *Fr.* 43°14′ N, 0°23′ E 164
Gan Gan, *Arg.* 42°29′ S, 68°11′ W 134
Gan, island, *Maldives* 0°2′ N, 73°22′ E 188
Gan, river, *China* 26°29′ N, 114°32′ E 198
Gan, river, *China* 49°20′ N, 124°41′ E 198
Ganado, *Ariz., U.S.* 35°42′ N, 109°32′ W 92
Ganado, *Tex., U.S.* 29°2′ N, 96°31′ W 96
Ganāveh, *Iran* 29°36′ N, 50°29′ E 196
Gäncä, *Azerb.* 40°41′ N, 46°21′ E 195
Gandajika, *Dem. Rep. of the Congo* 6°46′ S, 23°58′ E 224
Gander, *Can.* 48°56′ N, 54°29′ W 106
Gander, river, *Can.* 48°55′ N, 54°53′ W 111
Gandhidham, *India* 23°5′ N, 70°8′ E 186
Gandhinagar, *India* 23°19′ N, 72°38′ E 186
Gandi, *Nig.* 12°55′ N, 5°48′ E 222
Gandía, *Sp.* 38°57′ N, 0°11′ E 164
Gandino, *It.* 45°49′ N, 9°54′ E 167
Gandole, *Nig.* 8°24′ N, 11°37′ E 222
Gandu, *Braz.* 13°46′ S, 39°30′ W 138
Gang, island, *Maldives* 1°34′ N, 73°29′ E 188
Ganga (Ganges), river, *India* 26°9′ N, 81°17′ E 190
Gangala na Bodio, *Dem. Rep. of the Congo* 3°38′ N, 29°9′ E 224
Ganganagar, *India* 29°56′ N, 73°54′ E 186
Gangdaba, Tchabal, *Cameroon* 7°23′ N, 11°49′ E 218
Gangdisê Shan, *China* 30°58′ N, 83°13′ E 197
Gangelt, *Ger.* 50°59′ N, 5°59′ E 167
Ganges Fan, *Bay of Bengal* 14°34′ N, 84°35′ E 254
Ganges, river, *India* 25°40′ N, 81°12′ E 197
Ganges see Ganga, river, *India* 26°9′ N, 81°17′ E 190
Gangneung, *S. Korea* 36°9′ N, 127°3′ E 200
Ganghwa, *S. Korea* 37°44′ N, 126°29′ E 200
Gangi, *It.* 37°47′ N, 14°12′ E 156
Gangjin, *S. Korea* 34°37′ N, 126°47′ E 200
Gangneung, *S. Korea* 37°45′ N, 128°53′ E 200
Gangtok, *India* 27°23′ N, 88°35′ E 197
Gangu, *China* 34°43′ N, 105°18′ E 198
Ganhe, *China* 50°43′ N, 123°14′ E 238
Gania, *Guinea* 11°1′ N, 10°21′ W 222
Ganjam, *India* 19°25′ N, 85°3′ E 188
Gannan, *China* 47°53′ N, 123°31′ E 198
Gannat, *Fr.* 46°5′ N, 3°12′ E 150
Gannett Peak, *Wyo., U.S.* 43°10′ N, 109°45′ W 90
Ganongga see Ranongga, island, *Solomon Islands* 8°5′ S, 156°30′ E 242
Ganquan, *China* 36°19′ N, 109°25′ E 198
Ganseong, *S. Korea* 38°22′ N, 128°27′ E 200
Gansu, adm. division, *China* 40°14′ N, 94°53′ E 188
Gantgaw, *Myanmar* 22°12′ N, 94°9′ E 188
Ganwo, *Nig.* 11°11′ N, 4°37′ E 222
Ganyushkino, *Kaz.* 46°36′ N, 49°16′ E 158
Ganzhou, *China* 25°56′ N, 114°57′ E 198
Gao, *Mali* 16°16′ N, 1°59′ W 222

Gillett, *Ark., U.S.* 34°5' N, 91°23' W **96**
Gillette, *Wyo., U.S.* 44°16' N, 105°30' W **90**
Gilliam, *Mo., U.S.* 39°14' N, 92°60' W **94**
Gillies Islands, *Davis Sea* 66°37' S, 98°44' E **248**
Gillingham, *U.K.* 51°22' N, 0°32' E **162**
Gillis Range, *Nev., U.S.* 38°43' N, 118°40' W **90**
Gillock Island, *Antarctica* 70°22' S, 72°12' E **248**
Gills Rock, *Wis., U.S.* 45°16' N, 87°1' W **94**
Gilman, *Ill., U.S.* 40°45' N, 87°60' W **102**
Gilman, *Vt., U.S.* 44°24' N, 71°44' W **104**
Gilmer, *Tex., U.S.* 32°43' N, 94°58' W **103**
Gīlo Wenz, river, *Eth.* 7°40' N, 33°38' E **224**
Gilroy, *Calif., U.S.* 37°0' N, 121°35' W **100**
Gīmbī, *Eth.* 9°8' N, 35°49' E **224**
Gimcheon, *S. Korea* 36°5' N, 128°8' E **200**
Gimhae, *S. Korea* 35°12' N, 128°54' E **200**
Gimhwa, *S. Korea* 38°17' N, 127°28' E **200**
Gimje, *S. Korea* 35°48' N, 126°54' E **200**
Gimli, *Can.* 50°37' N, 97°2' W **90**
Gimo, *Sw.* 60°10' N, 18°8' E **166**
Ginâh, *Egypt* 25°21' N, 30°28' E **226**
Gingdindlovu, *S. Af.* 29°2' S, 31°32' E **227**
Gingoog, *Philippines* 8°48' N, 125°7' E **203**
Gīnīr, *Eth.* 7°12' N, 40°43' E **224**
Ginostra, *It.* 38°47' N, 15°11' E **156**
Giohar see Jawhar, *Somalia* 2°47' N, 45°34' E **218**
Gióna, Óros, peak, *Gr.* 38°38' N, 22°10' E **156**
Giovinazzo, *It.* 41°11' N, 16°40' E **156**
Ģipka, *Latv.* 57°34' N, 22°36' E **166**
Gir National Park, *India* 21°15' N, 70°30' E **186**
Girard, *Ill., U.S.* 39°26' N, 89°47' W **102**
Girard, *Kans., U.S.* 37°28' N, 94°50' W **94**
Girard, *Ohio, U.S.* 41°9' N, 80°42' W **94**
Girardot, *Col.* 4°19' N, 74°48' W **136**
Girawa, *Eth.* 9°7' N, 41°51' E **224**
Girbanat, *Sudan* 12°0' N, 33°9' E **182**
Gîrbou, *Rom.* 47°10' N, 23°24' E **168**
Gîrbovi, *Rom.* 44°48' N, 26°45' E **156**
Giresun, *Turk.* 40°55' N, 38°22' E **158**
Girga, *Egypt* 26°19' N, 31°49' E **180**
Giridih, *India* 24°9' N, 86°19' E **197**
Gîrla Mare, *Rom.* 44°12' N, 22°46' E **168**
Gîrlişte, *Rom.* 45°10' N, 21°48' E **168**
Girne see Keryneia, *Northern Cyprus* 35°20' N, 33°18' E **194**
Giroc, *Rom.* 45°42' N, 21°15' E **168**
Girolata, *Fr.* 42°21' N, 8°37' E **156**
Girona, *Sp.* 41°58' N, 2°50' E **164**
Giruliai, *Lith.* 55°46' N, 21°6' E **166**
Girvas, *Russ.* 62°28' N, 33°44' E **154**
Gisborne, *N.Z.* 38°40' S, 178°0' E **240**
Giscome, *Can.* 54°3' N, 122°23' W **108**
Gisors, *Fr.* 49°16' N, 1°45' E **163**
Gisselberg, *Ger.* 50°45' N, 8°44' E **167**
Gitega, *Burundi* 3°27' S, 29°55' E **224**
Giuba, Isole, islands, *Indian Ocean* 0°45' N, 41°29' E **224**
Giulianova, *It.* 42°44' N, 13°56' E **156**
Giuncarico, *It.* 42°55' N, 10°58' E **156**
Giurgeni, *Rom.* 44°44' N, 27°51' E **158**
Giurgiu, *Rom.* 43°53' N, 25°56' E **156**
Giurgiu, adm. division, *Rom.* 44°8' N, 25°43' E **156**
Give, *Den.* 55°49' N, 9°13' E **150**
Givet, *Fr.* 50°7' N, 4°48' E **167**
Giyani, *S. Af.* 23°17' S, 30°44' E **227**
Giyon, *Eth.* 8°34' N, 38°1' E **224**
Gizab, *Afghan.* 33°27' N, 66°0' E **186**
Gizhiga, *Russ.* 62°2' N, 160°11' E **160**
Gizhduvan, *Uzb.* 40°6' N, 64°42' E **197**
Giżycko, *Pol.* 54°1' N, 21°45' E **166**
Gjalicë e Lumës, Mal, peak, *Alban.* 42°0' N, 20°25' E **168**
Gjegjan, *Alban.* 41°56' N, 20°0' E **168**
Gjelsvik Mountains, *Antarctica* 72°8' S, 4°59' W **248**
Gjerstad, *Nor.* 58°52' N, 9°0' E **152**
Gjinar, *Alban.* 41°2' N, 20°12' E **156**
Gjoa Haven, *Can.* 68°36' N, 95°60' W **106**
Gjøvdal, *Nor.* 58°51' N, 8°17' E **152**
Gjuhëzës, Kepi i, *Alban.* 40°27' N, 18°34' E **156**
Gjuvikfjell, peak, *Nor.* 59°57' N, 7°55' E **152**
Gkreko, Cape, *Cyprus* 34°53' N, 33°55' E **194**
Gla, ruin(s), *Gr.* 38°23' N, 23°10' E **156**
Glace Bay, *Can.* 46°11' N, 59°58' W **111**
Glacier, *Wash., U.S.* 48°52' N, 121°58' W **100**
Glacier Bay *Can.* 58°40' N, 136°50' W **108**
Glacier Bay National Park and Preserve, *Alas., U.S.* 58°40' N, 137°23' W **73**
Glacier Peak, *Wash., U.S.* 48°5' N, 121°10' W **100**
Glacier Strait 75°57' N, 80°39' W **106**
Gladstone, *Can.* 50°13' N, 98°58' W **90**
Gladstone, *Mich., U.S.* 45°50' N, 87°2' W **94**
Gladstone, *Oreg., U.S.* 45°23' N, 122°37' W **90**
Gladwin, *Mich., U.S.* 43°58' N, 84°29' W **102**
Gladys Lake, *Can.* 59°52' N, 133°39' W **108**
Glamoč, *Bosn. and Herzg.* 44°2' N, 16°50' E **168**
Glan, *Philippines* 5°50' N, 125°11' E **203**
Glandore, *Ire.* 51°34' N, 9°7' W **150**
Glandorf, *Ger.* 52°4' N, 8°0' E **163**
Glarus, *Switz.* 47°2' N, 9°2' E **156**
Glas, Lac du, lake, *Can.* 51°49' N, 75°47' W **110**
Glasco, *Kans., U.S.* 39°20' N, 97°51' W **90**
Glasco, *N.Y., U.S.* 42°1' N, 73°58' W **104**
Glasford, *Ill., U.S.* 40°33' N, 89°48' W **102**
Glasgow, *Ky., U.S.* 37°0' N, 85°55' W **96**
Glasgow, *Mont., U.S.* 48°11' N, 106°39' W **90**
Glasgow, *U.K.* 55°51' N, 4°27' W **143**
Glaslyn, *Can.* 53°21' N, 108°22' W **108**
Glass Buttes, peak, *Oreg., U.S.* 43°32' N, 120°10' W **90**
Glass Mountain, *Calif., U.S.* 37°45' N, 118°47' W **90**
Glass Mountain, *Calif., U.S.* 41°35' N, 121°35' W **90**
Glass Mountains, *Tex., U.S.* 30°30' N, 103°11' W **92**
Glastonbury, *Conn., U.S.* 41°42' N, 72°37' W **104**
Glastonbury, *U.K.* 51°8' N, 2°43' W **162**
Glavičice, *Bosn. and Herzg.* 44°35' N, 19°12' E **168**
Glazachevo, *Russ.* 57°12' N, 30°13' E **166**
Glazov, *Russ.* 58°6' N, 52°43' E **154**
Gleichberg, Grosser, peak, *Ger.* 50°22' N, 10°29' E **152**
Gleichen, *Can.* 50°52' N, 113°4' W **90**
Gleisdorf, *Aust.* 47°6' N, 15°42' E **168**
Glen, *N.H., U.S.* 44°6' N, 71°11' W **104**
Glen Allan, *Miss., U.S.* 33°0' N, 91°2' W **103**
Glen Arbor, *Mich., U.S.* 44°53' N, 85°59' W **94**
Glen Cove, *N.Y., U.S.* 40°52' N, 73°38' W **104**
Glen Park, *N.Y., U.S.* 44°0' N, 75°58' W **94**
Glen, river, *U.K.* 52°47' N, 0°34' E **162**
Glen Rose, *Tex., U.S.* 32°14' N, 97°45' W **92**
Glen Ullin, *N. Dak., U.S.* 46°47' N, 101°51' W **90**
Glenada, *Oreg., U.S.* 43°56' N, 124°6' W **90**
Glenavy, *N.Z.* 44°54' S, 171°5' E **240**
Glenboro, *Can.* 49°32' N, 99°18' W **90**
Glencliff, *N.H., U.S.* 43°58' N, 71°54' W **104**
Glencoe, *Can.* 42°44' N, 81°42' W **102**
Glencoe, *Minn., U.S.* 44°45' N, 94°10' W **94**
Glendale, *Ariz., U.S.* 33°32' N, 112°10' W **92**
Glendale, *Calif., U.S.* 34°8' N, 118°16' W **101**
Glendive, *Mont., U.S.* 47°4' N, 104°44' W **90**
Glendo, *Wyo., U.S.* 42°29' N, 105°1' W **90**
Glendon, *Can.* 54°14' N, 111°10' W **108**
Glenfield, *U.K.* 52°38' N, 1°14' W **162**
Glenmora, *La., U.S.* 30°57' N, 92°36' W **103**
Glenn, Mount, *Ariz., U.S.* 31°56' N, 110°3' W **92**
Glenns Ferry, *Idaho, U.S.* 42°58' N, 115°19' W **90**
Glennville, *Calif., U.S.* 35°44' N, 118°43' W **101**
Glennville, *Ga., U.S.* 31°55' N, 81°56' W **96**
Glenora, *Can.* 57°52' N, 131°36' W **108**
Glenorchy, *N.Z.* 44°52' S, 168°26' E **240**
Glenrock, *Wyo., U.S.* 42°51' N, 105°53' W **90**
Glens Falls, *N.Y., U.S.* 43°18' N, 73°39' W **104**
Glenwood, *Minn., U.S.* 45°38' N, 95°24' W **94**
Glenwood, *N. Mex., U.S.* 33°18' N, 108°52' W **92**
Glenwood, *Oreg., U.S.* 45°38' N, 123°16' W **100**
Glenwood, *Va., U.S.* 36°35' N, 79°23' W **96**
Glenwood, *Wash., U.S.* 46°0' N, 121°18' W **100**
Glenwood, *W. Va., U.S.* 38°34' N, 82°12' W **102**
Glidden, *Wis., U.S.* 46°8' N, 90°36' W **94**
Glina, *Croatia* 45°20' N, 16°6' E **168**
Glíthion, *Gr.* 36°43' N, 22°32' E **216**
Glittertind, peak, *Nor.* 61°38' N, 8°24' E **152**
Gliwice, *Pol.* 50°17' N, 18°38' E **152**
Głogów, *Pol.* 51°39' N, 16°5' E **152**
Glomno, *Pol.* 54°18' N, 20°44' E **152**
Globe, *Ariz., U.S.* 33°24' N, 110°47' W **92**
Gloggnitz, *Aust.* 47°40' N, 15°56' E **168**
Glommersträsk, *Nor.* 65°14' N, 19°40' E **152**
Glorenza, *It.* 46°40' N, 10°33' E **167**
Glória, *Braz.* 9°13' S, 38°20' W **132**
Gloria Ridge, *North Atlantic Ocean* 54°34' N, 45°3' W **253**
Glorieuses, Îles, islands, *Indian Ocean* 11°10' S, 47°2' E **220**
Glorioso Islands, *Indian Ocean* 11°19' S, 44°49' E **207**
Gloster, *Miss., U.S.* 31°11' N, 91°2' W **103**
Gloucester, *Can.* 45°24' N, 75°35' W **94**
Gloucester, *Mass., U.S.* 42°36' N, 70°40' W **104**
Gloucester, *U.K.* 51°51' N, 2°14' W **162**
Glouster, *Ohio, U.S.* 39°29' N, 82°4' W **102**
Glubokiy, *Russ.* 46°58' N, 42°38' E **158**
Glubokiy, *Russ.* 48°32' N, 40°20' E **158**
Glūbokoe, *Kaz.* 50°8' N, 82°18' E **184**
Glubokoye, *Russ.* 56°38' N, 28°59' E **166**
Glusk, *Belarus* 52°52' N, 28°47' E **152**
Glyncorrwg, *U.K.* 51°41' N, 3°37' W **162**
Glyndon, *Minn., U.S.* 46°52' N, 96°37' W **94**
Gmelinka, *Russ.* 50°21' N, 46°52' E **158**
Gmünd, *Aust.* 48°45' N, 14°58' E **152**
Gmunden, *Aust.* 47°55' N, 13°47' E **156**
Gnadenhutten, *Ohio, U.S.* 40°20' N, 81°25' W **102**
Gnarp, *Nor.* 62°4' N, 17°12' E **152**
Gnas, *Aust.* 46°52' N, 15°51' E **168**
Gnesta, *Nor.* 59°2' N, 17°18' E **152**
Gnetalovo, *Russ.* 56°52' N, 29°37' E **166**
Gnjilane, *Serb. and Mont.* 42°27' N, 21°27' E **168**
Go Cong, *Vietnam* 10°22' N, 106°41' E **202**
Goa, adm. division, *India* 14°59' N, 74°13' E **188**
Goageb, *Namibia* 26°45' S, 17°12' E **227**
Goalpara, *India* 26°7' N, 90°34' E **197**
Goaso, *Ghana* 6°49' N, 2°32' W **222**
Goat Mountain, *Mont., U.S.* 47°17' N, 113°26' W **90**
Goat, river, *Can.* 49°10' N, 116°12' W **90**
Goathland, *U.K.* 54°24' N, 0°44' E **162**
Goba, *Eth.* 6°58' N, 39°55' E **224**
Gobabis, *Namibia* 22°27' S, 18°58' E **227**
Gobernador Crespo, *Arg.* 30°21' S, 60°24' W **139**
Gobernador Duval, *Arg.* 38°42' S, 66°26' W **134**
Gobernador Gregores, *Arg.* 48°45' S, 70°16' W **134**
Gobernador Ingeniero Valentín Virasoro, *Arg.* 28°3' S, 56°3' W **139**
Gobi, *Asia* 41°49' N, 103°50' E **198**
Gobles, *Mich., U.S.* 42°20' N, 85°52' W **102**
Gobō, *Japan* 33°53' N, 135°9' E **201**
Goch, *Ger.* 51°40' N, 6°10' E **167**
Gochang, *S. Korea* 35°26' N, 126°42' E **200**
Gochas, *Namibia* 24°51' S, 18°44' E **227**
Godalming, *U.K.* 51°11' N, 0°37' E **162**
Godbout, *Can.* 49°19' N, 67°38' W **82**
Godda, *India* 24°49' N, 87°13' E **197**
Goddard, *Can.* 56°50' N, 135°19' W **108**
Godeanu, peak, *Rom.* 45°16' N, 22°38' E **168**
Godech, *Bulg.* 43°0' N, 23°4' E **168**
Godere, *Eth.* 5°2' N, 43°59' E **218**
Goderich, *Can.* 43°43' N, 81°42' W **102**
Godfrey, *Mo., U.S.* 38°57' N, 90°12' W **94**
Godfrey Tank, spring, *Austral.* 20°15' S, 126°34' E **230**
Godhavn see Qeqertarsuaq, *Den.* 69°15' N, 53°30' W **106**
Godhra, *India* 22°46' N, 73°35' E **186**
Gödöll o, *Hung.* 47°35' N, 19°21' E **168**
Gods Lake, *Can.* 54°38' N, 94°12' W **108**
Gods, river, *Can.* 55°18' N, 93°23' W **108**
Godthåb see Nuuk, *Den.* 64°14' N, 51°38' W **106**
Godwin Austen see K2, peak, *Pak.* 35°51' N, 76°25' E **186**
Godzikowice, *Pol.* 50°54' N, 17°19' E **152**
Goéland, Lac au, lake, *Can.* 49°36' N, 78°10' W **81**
Goélands, Lac aux, lake, *Can.* 55°13' N, 66°38' W **106**
Goes, *Neth.* 51°30' N, 3°52' E **163**
Goffstown, *N.H., U.S.* 43°1' N, 71°37' W **104**
Gog Magog Hills, *U.K.* 52°4' N, 0°10' E **162**
Gogama, *Can.* 47°40' N, 81°43' W **94**
Gogebic Range, *Mich., U.S.* 46°32' N, 90°10' W **94**
Göggingen, *Ger.* 48°20' N, 10°52' E **152**
Gogland, island, *Russ.* 60°6' N, 26°43' E **166**
Gogói, *Mozambique* 20°19' S, 33°8' E **227**
Gogounou, *Benin* 10°46' N, 2°47' E **222**
Gogrial, *Sudan* 8°29' N, 28°7' E **224**
Goha, *Eth.* 10°19' N, 34°33' E **224**
Gohad, *India* 26°24' N, 78°26' E **197**
Goheung, *S. Korea* 34°35' N, 127°18' E **200**
Goiandira, *Braz.* 18°10' S, 48°7' W **138**
Goianésia, *Braz.* 15°22' S, 49°9' W **138**
Goiânia, *Braz.* 16°43' S, 49°17' W **138**
Goianinha, *Braz.* 6°17' S, 35°11' W **132**
Goiás, *Braz.* 15°55' S, 50°6' W **138**
Goiás, adm. division, *Braz.* 16°18' S, 50°32' W **138**
Goiatuba, *Braz.* 18°5' S, 49°24' W **138**
Goio Erê, *Braz.* 24°12' S, 53°3' W **138**
Goioxim, *Braz.* 25°13' S, 52°2' W **138**
Goito, *It.* 45°15' N, 10°40' E **167**
Gojeb, river, *Eth.* 7°10' N, 36°58' E **224**
Gök, river, *Turk.* 41°38' N, 34°30' E **156**
Goka, *Japan* 36°18' N, 133°14' E **201**
Gokase, river, *Japan* 32°38' N, 131°16' E **201**
Gökçeada, island, *Turk.* 39°55' N, 25°30' E **180**
Gökdepe, *Turkm.* 38°9' N, 57°58' E **180**
Göksu, river, *Turk.* 37°3' N, 32°40' E **156**
Göksu, river, *Turk.* 37°56' N, 36°21' E **156**
Göksun, *Turk.* 38°2' N, 36°29' E **156**
Gokwe, *Zimb.* 18°13' S, 28°57' E **224**
Gol, *Nor.* 60°42' N, 8°53' E **152**
Gol Bax, *Somalia* 0°19' N, 41°36' E **224**
Golaghat, *India* 26°34' N, 93°55' E **188**
Golan Heights, region, *Asia* 32°56' N, 35°38' E **194**
Gölbaşı, *Turk.* 39°47' N, 32°48' E **156**
Golconda, *Nev., U.S.* 40°57' N, 117°30' W **90**
Gölcük, *Turk.* 40°43' N, 29°48' E **158**
Gold Bar, *Wash., U.S.* 47°50' N, 121°41' W **100**
Gold Beach, *Oreg., U.S.* 42°24' N, 124°26' W **82**
Gold Coast, *Austral.* 27°58' S, 153°23' E **231**
Gold Coast, region, *Africa* 5°10' N, 2°17' W **222**
Gold Hill, *Nev., U.S.* 39°17' N, 119°40' W **92**
Gold Mines, site, *Egypt* 22°37' N, 33°13' E **182**
Gold Rock, *Can.* 49°27' N, 92°42' W **90**
Golden, *Can.* 51°18' N, 116°58' W **108**
Golden Hinde, peak, *Can.* 49°38' N, 125°50' W **90**
Golden Meadow, *La., U.S.* 29°22' N, 90°17' W **103**
Goldendale, *Wash., U.S.* 45°48' N, 120°49' W **90**
Goldfield, *Iowa, U.S.* 42°43' N, 93°55' W **94**
Goldfield, *Nev., U.S.* 37°40' N, 117°14' W **82**
Goldonna, *La., U.S.* 32°0' N, 92°55' W **103**
Goldpines, *Can.* 50°39' N, 93°11' W **90**
Goldsboro, *N.C., U.S.* 35°23' N, 78°1' W **96**
Goldsmith, *Tex., U.S.* 31°57' N, 102°37' W **92**
Goldsmith Channel 73°5' N, 111°1' W **106**
Goldthwaite, *Tex., U.S.* 31°26' N, 98°34' W **92**
Göle, *Turk.* 40°47' N, 42°35' E **195**
Golela, *Swaziland* 27°16' S, 31°55' E **227**
Goleta, *Calif., U.S.* 34°26' N, 119°51' W **100**
Golfito, *C.R.* 8°39' N, 83°11' W **115**
Goliad, *Tex., U.S.* 28°39' N, 97°23' W **96**
Gölköy, *Turk.* 40°42' N, 37°37' E **156**
Goldap, *Pol.* 54°17' N, 22°17' E **154**
Golmud, *China* 36°19' N, 94°52' E **190**
Golmud, river, *China* 35°44' N, 95°6' E **188**
Golondrina, *Arg.* 28°32' S, 60°4' W **139**
Gölören, *Turk.* 37°52' N, 33°51' E **156**
Golovin, *Alas., U.S.* 64°27' N, 162°59' W **98**
Golpāyegān, *Iran* 33°28' N, 50°14' E **180**
Gölpazarı, *Turk.* 40°16' N, 30°18' E **156**
Golran, *Afghan.* 35°7' N, 61°41' E **186**
Golubac, *Serb. and Mont.* 44°38' N, 21°37' E **168**
Golubovci, *Serb. and Mont.* 42°21' N, 19°13' E **168**
Golūboyka, *Kaz.* 53°7' N, 74°12' E **184**
Golyam Perelik, peak, *Bulg.* 41°35' N, 24°29' E **156**
Golyshmanovo, *Russ.* 56°22' N, 68°24' E **184**
Goma, *Dem. Rep. of the Congo* 1°41' S, 29°11' E **224**
Gómara, *Sp.* 41°36' N, 2°14' W **164**
Gombari, *Dem. Rep. of the Congo* 2°43' N, 29°5' E **224**
Gombe, *Nig.* 10°15' N, 11°7' E **222**
Gombe National Park, *Tanzania* 4°47' S, 29°34' E **224**
Gomera, island, *Sp.* 28°6' N, 18°13' W **214**
Gómez Farías, *Mex.* 24°56' N, 101°2' W **114**
Gómez Palacio, *Mex.* 25°34' N, 103°31' W **114**
Gomīshān, *Iran* 37°4' N, 53°59' E **180**
Gomo, *China* 33°37' N, 85°19' E **188**
Gomo Co, lake, *China* 34°1' N, 84°47' E **188**
Gomoh, *India* 23°51' N, 86°9' E **197**
Gomotartsi, *Bulg.* 44°4' N, 22°58' E **168**
Gomphi, ruin(s), *Gr.* 39°24' N, 21°30' E **156**
Gonam, *Russ.* 57°15' N, 130°53' E **160**
Gonarezhou National Park, *Zimb.* 21°50' S, 31°35' E **227**
Gonâve, Île de la, island, *Haiti* 19°1' N, 74°5' W **116**
Gonbad-e Kāvūs, *Iran* 37°22' N, 55°8' E **180**
Gonda, *India* 27°7' N, 81°58' E **197**
Gondal, *India* 21°57' N, 70°47' E **186**
Gonder, *Eth.* 12°34' N, 37°25' E **182**
Gondey, *Chad* 9°4' N, 19°21' E **218**
Gondia, *India* 21°27' N, 80°10' E **188**
Gondola, *Mozambique* 19°10' S, 33°38' E **224**
Gondrecourt, *Fr.* 48°30' N, 5°31' E **163**
Gönen, *Turk.* 40°6' N, 27°38' E **156**
Gong'an, *China* 30°1' N, 112°11' E **198**
Gongbo'gyamda, *China* 29°55' N, 93°0' E **190**
Gongcheng, *China* 24°52' N, 110°45' E **198**
Gongga Shan, peak, *China* 29°38' N, 101°36' E **190**
Gonggar, *China* 29°17' N, 90°48' E **197**
Gongju, *S. Korea* 36°25' N, 127°9' E **200**
Gonglee, *Liberia* 5°43' N, 9°27' W **222**
Gongliu, *China* 43°25' N, 82°18' E **184**
Gongola, river, *Nig.* 11°5' N, 11°29' E **222**
Gongoúe, *Gabon* 0°33' N, 9°15' E **218**
Gongxi, *China* 27°38' N, 115°51' E **198**
Gongzhuling, *China* 43°30' N, 124°52' E **198**
Goniądz, *Pol.* 53°28' N, 22°43' E **158**
Gonja, *Tanzania* 4°21' S, 38°5' E **224**
Gonjo, *China* 30°52' N, 98°16' E **188**
Gōno, river, *Japan* 34°53' N, 132°27' E **201**
Gōnoura, *Japan* 33°44' N, 129°41' E **201**
Gonzales, *Calif., U.S.* 36°30' N, 121°28' W **100**
Gonzales, *La., U.S.* 30°13' N, 90°56' W **103**
Gonzales, *Tex., U.S.* 29°29' N, 97°27' W **96**
González, *Mex.* 22°48' N, 98°26' W **114**
González Chaves, *Arg.* 38°4' S, 60°6' W **139**
González Moreno, *Arg.* 35°32' S, 63°20' W **139**
Good Hope, Cape of, *S. Af.* 34°13' S, 18°30' E **253**
Good Hope, Cape of, *S. Af.* 34°33' S, 12°22' E **206**
Good Hope Mountain, *Can.* 51°9' N, 124°15' W **90**
Good Pine, *La., U.S.* 31°40' N, 92°11' W **103**
Goodenough, Cape, *Antarctica* 65°58' S, 126°13' E **248**
Goodenough Island, *P.N.G.* 9°15' S, 149°59' E **192**
Goodenough, Mount, *Can.* 67°56' N, 135°41' W **98**
Goodhouse, *S. Af.* 28°57' S, 18°14' E **227**
Gooding, *Idaho, U.S.* 42°55' N, 114°43' W **90**
Goodland, *Fla., U.S.* 25°55' N, 81°41' W **105**
Goodland, *Ind., U.S.* 40°45' N, 87°18' W **102**
Goodland, *Kans., U.S.* 39°20' N, 101°42' W **82**
Goodman, *Miss., U.S.* 32°56' N, 89°56' W **103**
Goodman, *Wis., U.S.* 45°37' N, 88°22' W **94**
Goodnews Bay, *Alas., U.S.* 59°8' N, 161°31' W **106**
Goodrich, *Tex., U.S.* 30°35' N, 94°57' W **103**
Goodridge, *Minn., U.S.* 48°8' N, 95°50' W **90**
Goodsir, Mount, *Can.* 51°11' N, 116°28' W **90**
Goodsoil, *Can.* 54°22' N, 109°15' W **108**
Goodsprings, *Nev., U.S.* 35°49' N, 115°27' W **101**
Goodwell, *Okla., U.S.* 36°34' N, 101°39' W **92**
Goole, *U.K.* 53°42' N, 0°54' E **162**
Goondiwindi, *Austral.* 28°30' S, 150°21' E **231**
Goonhilly Downs, site, *U.K.* 50°0' N, 5°18' W **150**
Goor, *Neth.* 52°14' N, 6°35' E **163**
Goose, Lac, lake, *Can.* 53°3' N, 74°38' W **111**
Goose Lake, *Calif., U.S.* 41°58' N, 121°18' W **81**
Goose Lake, *Can.* 51°43' N, 107°47' W **90**
Goose, river, *Can.* 54°54' N, 117°3' W **108**
Goose Rocks Beach, *Me., U.S.* 43°24' N, 70°25' W **104**
Goosenest, peak, *Calif., U.S.* 41°42' N, 122°19' W **90**
Gooseprairie, *Wash., U.S.* 46°53' N, 121°17' W **100**
Gooty, *India* 15°6' N, 77°40' E **188**
Gop, *India* 22°3' N, 69°54' E **186**
Gor, *Sp.* 37°21' N, 2°58' W **164**
Gorakhpur, *India* 26°43' N, 83°21' E **197**
Goranci, *Bosn. and Herzg.* 43°25' N, 17°43' E **168**
Goransko, *Serb. and Mont.* 43°7' N, 18°50' E **168**
Goražde, *Bosn. and Herzg.* 43°40' N, 18°58' E **168**
Gorbukova, *Russ.* 59°31' N, 89°33' E **169**
Gorda, Punta, *Calif., U.S.* 40°5' N, 124°41' W **90**
Gorda, Punta, *Nicar.* 14°13' N, 84°2' W **115**
Gördalen, *Nor.* 61°35' N, 12°28' E **152**
Gordion, ruin(s), *Turk.* 39°35' N, 31°52' E **156**
Gordo, *Ala., U.S.* 33°17' N, 87°54' W **103**
Gordon, *Nebr., U.S.* 42°47' N, 102°13' W **90**
Gordon, *Wis., U.S.* 46°13' N, 91°49' W **94**
Gordon Horne Peak, *Can.* 51°47' N, 118°55' W **90**
Gordon Lake, *Can.* 56°23' N, 111°4' W **108**
Gordondale, *Can.* 55°50' N, 119°34' W **108**
Gordon's, *Bahamas* 22°52' N, 74°52' W **116**
Goré, *Chad* 7°54' N, 16°38' E **218**
Gorē, *Eth.* 8°10' N, 35°31' E **224**
Gore, *N.Z.* 46°7' S, 168°56' E **240**
Gore Bay, *Can.* 45°55' N, 82°29' W **94**
Gore Mountain, *Vt., U.S.* 44°54' N, 71°53' W **94**
Gore Range, *Colo., U.S.* 40°5' N, 106°44' W **90**
Gorecki, Mount, *Antarctica* 83°23' S, 59°14' W **248**
Goree, *Tex., U.S.* 33°27' N, 99°32' W **92**
Görele, *Turk.* 41°2' N, 38°59' E **158**
Gorey, *Ire.* 49°11' N, 2°3' W **150**
Gorgān, *Iran* 36°50' N, 54°25' E **180**
Gorgonta, *Arg.* 33°48' S, 66°45' W **134**
Gorgora, *Eth.* 12°13' N, 37°17' E **182**
Gorgova, *Rom.* 45°10' N, 29°10' E **156**
Gorguz, *Mex.* 28°53' N, 111°10' W **92**
Gorham, *Me., U.S.* 43°40' N, 70°27' W **104**
Gori, *Ga.* 41°57' N, 44°8' E **195**
Gori Rit, *Somalia* 8°0' N, 48°8' E **218**
Gorinchem, *Neth.* 51°49' N, 4°59' E **167**
Goris, *Arm.* 39°30' N, 46°20' E **195**
Gorizia, *It.* 45°56' N, 13°36' E **167**
Gorj, adm. division, *Rom.* 44°42' N, 23°8' E **156**
Gorjani, *Croatia* 45°23' N, 18°21' E **168**
Gorkha, *Nepal* 28°2' N, 84°40' E **197**
Gorki, *Russ.* 65°4' N, 65°29' E **169**
Gorleston, *U.K.* 52°34' N, 1°42' E **163**
Görlitz, *Ger.* 51°8' N, 14°58' E **152**
Gorman, *Calif., U.S.* 34°45' N, 118°49' W **101**
Gorman, *Tex., U.S.* 32°12' N, 98°41' W **92**
Gornja Tuzla, *Bosn. and Herzg.* 44°34' N, 18°44' E **168**
Gornji Muć, *Croatia* 43°41' N, 16°25' E **168**
Gornji Streoc, *Serb. and Mont.* 42°35' N, 20°18' E **168**
Gornji Vakuf (Uskoplje), *Bosn. and Herzg.* 43°55' N, 17°33' E **168**
Gorno Altaysk, *Russ.* 51°57' N, 86°2' E **184**
Gorno-Altay, adm. division, *Russ.* 50°43' N, 85°39' E **184**
Gornozavodsk, *Russ.* 46°32' N, 141°52' E **190**
Gornyak, *Russ.* 51°0' N, 81°30' E **184**
Gornyatskiy, *Russ.* 67°31' N, 64°13' E **169**
Gornyy, *Russ.* 51°43' N, 48°36' E **158**
Gornyy Balykley, *Russ.* 49°35' N, 45°0' E **158**
Goro, river, *Cen. Af. Rep.* 9°13' N, 21°36' E **218**
Gorodets, *Russ.* 58°30' N, 29°47' E **166**
Gorodets, *Russ.* 56°37' N, 43°35' E **154**
Gorodishche, *Russ.* 53°16' N, 45°45' E **154**
Gorodishche, *Russ.* 58°14' N, 29°53' E **166**
Gorodovikovsk, *Russ.* 46°4' N, 41°48' E **158**
Gorom Gorom, *Burkina Faso* 14°27' N, 0°15' E **222**
Gorong, Kepulauan, islands, *Banda Sea* 4°39' S, 130°39' E **192**
Gorongosa National Park, *Mozambique* 19°13' S, 34°35' E **224**
Gorongosa, Serra da, peak, *Mozambique* 18°27' S, 34°0' E **224**
Gorontalo, *Indonesia* 0°38' N, 123°2' E **192**
Gortyn, ruin(s), *Gr.* 35°3' N, 24°50' E **156**
Gorutuba, river, *Braz.* 15°10' S, 43°32' W **138**
Goryachiy Klyuch, *Russ.* 44°37' N, 39°6' E **156**
Gorzów Wielkopolski, *Pol.* 52°44' N, 15°15' E **152**
Górzyca, *Pol.* 52°29' N, 14°40' E **152**
Goschen Strait 10°40' S, 150°46' E **192**
Gosen, *Japan* 37°43' N, 139°10' E **201**
Goseong, *S. Korea* 34°58' N, 128°19' E **200**
Gosford, *Austral.* 33°23' S, 151°20' E **231**
Gosforth, *U.K.* 54°25' N, 3°26' W **162**
Goshen, *Calif., U.S.* 36°21' N, 119°26' W **100**
Goshen, *N.H., U.S.* 43°18' N, 72°9' W **104**
Goshen, *Utah, U.S.* 39°56' N, 111°54' W **90**
Goshute Mountains, *Nev., U.S.* 40°27' N, 114°29' W **90**
Gospić, *Croatia* 44°32' N, 15°21' E **156**
Gosport, *Ind., U.S.* 39°20' N, 86°40' W **102**
Goss, *Miss., U.S.* 31°20' N, 89°54' W **103**
Gosselies, *Belg.* 50°28' N, 4°26' E **167**
Gossinga, *Sudan* 8°38' N, 25°57' E **224**
Gostilje, *Serb. and Mont.* 43°39' N, 19°50' E **168**
Gostiņi, *Latv.* 56°36' N, 25°46' E **166**
Gostivar, *Maced.* 41°47' N, 20°54' E **168**
Gota, *Eth.* 9°31' N, 41°21' E **224**
Götaland, region, *Europe* 58°8' N, 10°51' E **150**
Gote, *Dem. Rep. of the Congo* 2°12' N, 30°48' E **224**
Göteborg, *Nor.* 57°41' N, 11°57' E **152**
Gotha, *Ger.* 50°57' N, 10°42' E **152**
Gothenburg, *Nebr., U.S.* 40°56' N, 100°11' W **92**
Gothèye, *Niger* 13°49' N, 1°31' E **222**
Gotland, island, *Sw.* 57°33' N, 18°49' E **166**
Gotska Sandön, island, *Sw.* 58°24' N, 19°12' E **166**
Gotska Sandön National Park, *Sw.* 58°12' N, 19°28' E **166**
Gōtsu, *Japan* 35°0' N, 132°13' E **200**
Göttingen, *Ger.* 51°32' N, 9°55' E **167**
Goubéré, *Cen. Af. Rep.* 5°50' N, 26°43' E **224**
Gouda, *Neth.* 52°0' N, 4°42' E **167**
Goudiry, *Senegal* 14°10' N, 12°45' W **222**
Goudoumaria, *Niger* 13°43' N, 11°8' E **222**
Gouéké, *Guinea* 7°57' N, 8°43' W **222**
Gouin, Réservoir, lake, *Can.* 48°18' N, 76°31' W **106**
Gouin, Réservoir, lake, *Can.* 48°18' N, 76°42' W **81**
Goulais, river, *Can.* 46°44' N, 84°41' W **110**
Goulburn, *Austral.* 34°46' S, 149°45' E **231**
Goulburn Islands, *Arafura Sea* 11°36' S, 133°38' E **192**
Gould, *Ark., U.S.* 33°58' N, 91°35' W **96**
Gould Bay 77°46' S, 49°17' W **248**
Gould Coast, *Antarctica* 84°15' S, 127°3' W **248**
Gouldsboro, *Me., U.S.* 44°28' N, 68°3' W **111**
Goulimine, *Mor.* 28°57' N, 10°5' W **143**
Goulmima, *Mor.* 31°43' N, 4°57' W **214**
Goumbou, *Mali* 14°58' N, 7°27' W **222**
Gouméré, *Côte d'Ivoire* 7°55' N, 2°60' W **222**
Gounarou, *Benin* 10°51' N, 2°49' E **222**
Goundam, *Mali* 16°24' N, 3°41' W **222**
Goundi, *Chad* 9°20' N, 17°21' E **216**
Gounou Gaya, *Chad* 9°39' N, 15°28' E **216**
Gouradi, spring, *Chad* 16°24' N, 17°11' E **216**
Gouré, *Niger* 14°0' N, 10°15' E **222**
Gouring, spring, *Chad* 18°44' N, 19°8' E **216**
Gourlay Lake, *Can.* 48°51' N, 85°29' W **94**
Gourma, region, *Africa* 12°15' N, 2°118' W **222**
Gourma Rharous, *Mali* 16°52' N, 1°55' W **222**
Gournay, *Fr.* 49°28' N, 1°43' E **163**
Gournia, ruin(s), *Gr.* 35°5' N, 25°42' E **156**
Gouro, *Chad* 19°32' N, 19°33' E **216**
Gove, *Kans., U.S.* 38°58' N, 100°29' W **90**
Govena, Mys, *Russ.* 59°34' N, 165°28' E **160**
Govenlock, *Can.* 49°12' N, 109°47' W **90**
Governador Valadares, *Braz.* 18°51' S, 41°55' W **138**
Governor's Harbour, adm. division, *Bahamas* 25°18' N, 77°33' W **116**
Gowanda, *N.Y., U.S.* 42°27' N, 78°57' W **94**
Gowen, *Okla., U.S.* 34°51' N, 95°29' W **96**
Gower Peninsula, *U.K.* 51°36' N, 4°6' W **162**
Gowganda, *Can.* 47°38' N, 80°45' W **110**
Gowmal Kalay, *Afghan.* 32°28' N, 69°0' E **186**
Goya, *Arg.* 29°10' S, 59°16' W **139**
Göyçay, *Azerb.* 40°38' N, 47°44' E **195**
Goyeau, Pointe, *Can.* 51°37' N, 78°58' W **110**
Goyelle, Lac, lake, *Can.* 50°43' N, 61°15' W **111**
Göynük, *Turk.* 40°24' N, 30°48' E **156**
Goz Beïda, *Chad* 12°13' N, 21°25' E **216**
Goz Pass, *Can.* 64°31' N, 132°24' W **98**
Goz Regeb, *Sudan* 16°1' N, 35°34' E **182**
Gozo, island, *Malta* 36°4' N, 13°38' E **216**
Graaff-Reinet, *S. Af.* 32°17' S, 24°27' E **227**
Graafwater, *S. Af.* 32°9' S, 18°34' E **227**
Grabo, *Côte d'Ivoire* 4°55' N, 7°30' W **214**
Grabovac, *Serb. and Mont.* 44°35' N, 20°5' E **168**
Gračanica, *Bosn. and Herzg.* 44°42' N, 18°17' E **168**
Grace, Mount, *Mass., U.S.* 42°41' N, 72°23' W **104**
Gracefield, *Can.* 46°6' N, 76°3' W **94**
Graceville, *Minn., U.S.* 45°33' N, 96°28' W **90**
Grachevka, *Russ.* 52°54' N, 52°54' E **158**
Gracias a Dios, Cabo, *Nicar.* 14°51' N, 83°10' W **115**
Gradac, *Serb. and Mont.* 43°22' N, 19°9' E **168**

Gradačac, *Bosn. and Herzg.* 44°53′ N, 18°25′ E **168**
Gradaús, *Braz.* 7°41′ S, 51°11′ W **130**
Gradaús, Serra dos, *Braz.* 8°20′ S, 50°60′ W **130**
Gradisca d'Isonzo, *It.* 45°54′ N, 13°30′ E **167**
Gradište, *Croatia* 45°8′ N, 18°42′ E **168**
Grado, *It.* 45°41′ N, 13°23′ E **167**
Gradsko, *Maced.* 41°34′ N, 21°57′ E **168**
Gräfenhainichen, *Ger.* 51°44′ N, 12°27′ E **152**
Grafing, *Ger.* 48°2′ N, 11°58′ E **152**
Graford, *Tex., U.S.* 32°55′ N, 98°15′ W **92**
Grafton, *N. Dak., U.S.* 48°23′ N, 97°27′ W **90**
Grafton, *Vt., U.S.* 43°10′ N, 72°37′ W **104**
Grafton, *W. Va., U.S.* 39°20′ N, 80°2′ W **94**
Grafton, *Wis., U.S.* 43°18′ N, 87°58′ W **102**
Grafton, Mount, *Nev., U.S.* 38°40′ N, 114°50′ W **90**
Grafton Notch, pass, *Me., U.S.* 44°35′ N, 70°56′ W **104**
Graham, *Can.* 49°15′ N, 90°34′ W **94**
Graham, *Tex., U.S.* 33°5′ N, 98°34′ W **92**
Graham Bell, Ostrov, island, *Russ.* 81°26′ N, 63°57′ E **160**
Graham Island, *Can.* 54°11′ N, 133°54′ W **98**
Graham Lake, *Can.* 56°30′ N, 115°16′ W **108**
Graham, Mount, *Ariz., U.S.* 32°41′ N, 109°56′ W **92**
Graham, river, *Can.* 56°23′ N, 123°5′ W **108**
Grahamstown, *S. Af.* 33°18′ S, 26°29′ E **227**
Grahovo, *Serb. and Mont.* 42°38′ N, 18°40′ E **168**
Graian Alps, *It.* 45°31′ N, 6°43′ E **165**
Grain Coast, region, *Africa* 5°23′ N, 9°22′ W **222**
Grajal de Campos, *Sp.* 42°18′ N, 5°3′ W **150**
Grajaú, *Braz.* 5°50′ S, 46°11′ W **130**
Grajaú, river, *Braz.* 5°19′ S, 46°2′ W **130**
Gramada, *Bulg.* 43°50′ N, 22°39′ E **168**
Gramado, *Braz.* 29°20′ S, 50°50′ W **139**
Gramercy, *La., U.S.* 30°3′ N, 90°42′ W **103**
Grámos, Óros, *Gr.* 40°11′ N, 20°38′ E **156**
Grampian Mountains, *U.K.* 56°38′ N, 5°6′ W **150**
Gran, *Nor.* 60°21′ N, 10°34′ E **152**
Gran Bajo de San Julián, *Arg.* 49°23′ S, 70°59′ W **134**
Gran Canaria, island, *Sp.* 27°21′ N, 15°22′ W **214**
Gran Chaco, region, *Parag.* 21°5′ S, 61°33′ W **134**
Gran Morelos, *Mex.* 28°14′ N, 106°33′ W **92**
Gran Pajonal, region, *South America* 10°40′ S, 74°28′ W **130**
Gran Paradiso, peak, *It.* 45°31′ N, 7°13′ E **165**
Gran Sabana, La, *Venez.* 5°4′ N, 62°25′ W **130**
Gran Sasso d'Italia, *It.* 42°24′ N, 13°13′ E **156**
Gran Tarajal, *Sp.* 28°14′ N, 14°3′ W **214**
Granada, *Col.* 3°31′ N, 73°44′ W **136**
Granada, *Colo., U.S.* 38°3′ N, 102°19′ W **90**
Granada, *Nicar.* 11°55′ N, 85°59′ W **115**
Granada, *Sp.* 37°13′ N, 3°39′ W **143**
Granada, *Sp.* 37°11′ N, 3°36′ W **164**
Granadero Gatica, *Arg.* 26°52′ S, 62°42′ W **139**
Granados, *Mex.* 29°51′ N, 109°21′ W **92**
Granbori, *Suriname* 3°48′ N, 54°54′ W **130**
Granbury, *Tex., U.S.* 32°26′ N, 97°46′ W **92**
Granby, *Colo., U.S.* 40°4′ N, 105°56′ W **90**
Granby, *Mass., U.S.* 42°15′ N, 72°31′ W **104**
Granby, *Vt., U.S.* 44°34′ N, 71°46′ W **104**
Grand Bahama, island, *Bahamas* 27°0′ N, 78°0′ W **118**
Grand Bank, *Can.* 47°4′ N, 55°48′ W **111**
Grand Banks of Newfoundland, *North Atlantic Ocean* 45°14′ N, 52°41′ W **253**
Grand Bend, *Can.* 43°18′ N, 81°44′ W **102**
Grand Blanc, *Mich., U.S.* 42°55′ N, 83°37′ W **102**
Grand Cane, *La., U.S.* 32°4′ N, 93°49′ W **103**
Grand Canyon, *Ariz., U.S.* 35°46′ N, 113°37′ W **101**
Grand Canyon National Park, *Ariz., U.S.* 35°50′ N, 114°11′ W **101**
Grand Cayman, island, *U.K.* 19°0′ N, 81°0′ W **118**
Grand Centre, *Can.* 54°23′ N, 110°14′ W **108**
Grand Cess, *Liberia* 4°40′ N, 8°11′ W **214**
Grand Chenier, *La., U.S.* 29°45′ N, 92°58′ W **103**
Grand Coteau, *La., U.S.* 30°24′ N, 92°2′ W **103**
Grand Coulee, *Wash., U.S.* 47°48′ N, 119°24′ W **90**
Grand Coulee, *Wash., U.S.* 47°55′ N, 119°1′ W **90**
Grand Falls, *Can.* 47°1′ N, 67°47′ W **94**
Grand Falls-Windsor, *Can.* 48°53′ N, 55°42′ W **106**
Grand Forks, *Can.* 49°1′ N, 118°28′ W **108**
Grand Forks, *N. Dak., U.S.* 47°53′ N, 97°3′ W **90**
Grand Forks Air Force Base, *N. Dak., U.S.* 47°56′ N, 97°31′ W **90**
Grand Haven, *Mich., U.S.* 43°2′ N, 86°14′ W **102**
Grand Island, *Nebr., U.S.* 40°54′ N, 98°22′ W **90**
Grand Isle, *La., U.S.* 29°15′ N, 89°60′ W **103**
Grand Junction, *Colo., U.S.* 39°4′ N, 108°34′ W **90**
Grand Junction, *Mich., U.S.* 42°23′ N, 86°4′ W **102**
Grand Lake, *Can.* 46°3′ N, 66°25′ W **94**
Grand Lake, *La., U.S.* 29°46′ N, 91°28′ W **103**
Grand Lake, *La., U.S.* 30°0′ N, 93°16′ W **103**
Grand Ledge, *Mich., U.S.* 42°44′ N, 84°46′ W **102**
Grand Marais, *Can.* 50°31′ N, 96°34′ W **90**
Grand Marais, *Mich., U.S.* 46°39′ N, 85°60′ W **94**
Grand Marais, *Minn., U.S.* 47°45′ N, 90°23′ W **94**
Grand Mesa, *Colo., U.S.* 38°57′ N, 108°22′ W **90**
Grand Popo, *Benin* 6°17′ N, 1°51′ E **222**
Grand Portage, *Minn., U.S.* 47°57′ N, 89°45′ W **82**
Grand Portal Point, *Mich., U.S.* 46°14′ N, 86°30′ W **94**
Grand Prairie, *Tex., U.S.* 32°43′ N, 96°58′ W **92**
Grand Rapids, *Can.* 53°10′ N, 99°20′ W **108**
Grand Rapids, *Mich., U.S.* 42°56′ N, 85°40′ W **102**
Grand Rapids, *Minn., U.S.* 47°13′ N, 93°32′ W **90**
Grand Ridge, *Ill., U.S.* 41°14′ N, 88°50′ W **102**
Grand, river, *Mich., U.S.* 42°57′ N, 85°46′ W **80**
Grand, river, *Mo., U.S.* 40°15′ N, 94°24′ W **80**
Grand, river, *S. Dak., U.S.* 45°40′ N, 101°46′ W **90**
Grand Saline, *Tex., U.S.* 32°39′ N, 95°43′ W **96**
Grand Santi, *Fr.* 4°20′ N, 54°23′ W **130**
Grand Teton, peak, *Wyo., U.S.* 43°42′ N, 110°53′ W **90**
Grand Traverse Bay 44°59′ N, 85°60′ W **110**
Grandas, *Sp.* 43°12′ N, 6°54′ W **150**
Grand-Bassam, *Côte d'Ivoire* 5°13′ N, 3°46′ W **222**
Grande, Bahía 51°3′ S, 70°13′ W **134**
Grande, Baía, lake, *Bol.* 15°28′ S, 60°41′ W **132**
Grande Cache, *Can.* 53°53′ N, 119°10′ W **108**
Grande Cayemite, island, *Haiti* 18°33′ N, 73°42′ W **116**
Grande, Cayo, island, *Cuba* 20°40′ N, 79°37′ W **116**
Grande, Cayo, island, *Venez.* 11°32′ N, 66°37′ W **116**
Grande, Corno, peak, *It.* 42°27′ N, 13°29′ E **156**
Grande, Cuchilla, *Uru.* 33°58′ S, 56°15′ W **139**
Grande de Lípez, river, *Bol.* 21°60′ S, 67°21′ W **137**
Grande Prairie, *Can.* 55°10′ N, 118°49′ W **108**
Grande, Punta, *Chile* 25°7′ S, 70°31′ W **132**
Grande, river, *Braz.* 20°30′ S, 48°51′ W **138**
Grande, river, *Braz.* 13°5′ S, 45°35′ W **138**
Grande, river, *Can.* 48°40′ N, 65°15′ W **111**
Grande, Serra, *Braz.* 10°11′ S, 61°36′ W **130**
Grande, Serra (Carauna), peak, *Braz.* 2°34′ N, 60°46′ W **130**
Grande Sertão Veredas National Park, *Braz.* 15°32′ S, 46°6′ W **138**
Grande, Sierra, *Mex.* 29°42′ N, 105°8′ W **112**
Grande-Terre, island, *Fr.* 16°32′ N, 61°28′ W **116**
Grandfalls, *Tex., U.S.* 31°19′ N, 102°51′ W **92**
Grandfather Mountain, *N.C., U.S.* 36°5′ N, 81°54′ W **96**
Grandfield, *Okla., U.S.* 34°12′ N, 98°41′ W **92**
Grand-Fort-Philippe, *Fr.* 50°59′ N, 2°5′ E **163**
Grand-Lahou, *Côte d'Ivoire* 5°8′ N, 5°2′ W **222**
Grand-Mère, *Can.* 46°36′ N, 72°43′ W **94**
Grandpré, *Fr.* 49°20′ N, 4°51′ E **163**
Grandview, *Can.* 51°9′ N, 100°43′ W **90**
Grandview, *Wash., U.S.* 46°14′ N, 119°55′ W **90**
Grandvilliers, *Fr.* 49°39′ N, 1°56′ E **163**
Grañén, *Sp.* 41°56′ N, 0°22′ E **164**
Grange, *U.K.* 54°10′ N, 2°56′ W **162**
Granger, *Ind., U.S.* 41°44′ N, 86°7′ W **102**
Granger, *Tex., U.S.* 30°41′ N, 97°27′ W **92**
Granger, *Wyo., U.S.* 41°36′ N, 109°58′ W **90**
Granges, *Fr.* 48°8′ N, 6°47′ E **163**
Grangeville, *Idaho, U.S.* 45°53′ N, 116°7′ W **82**
Granisle, *Can.* 54°54′ N, 126°18′ W **108**
Granite, *Okla., U.S.* 34°56′ N, 99°24′ W **92**
Granite Falls, *Minn., U.S.* 44°46′ N, 95°34′ W **90**
Granite Falls, *Wash., U.S.* 48°4′ N, 121°58′ W **100**
Granite Mountain, *Nev., U.S.* 40°16′ N, 117°54′ W **90**
Granite Mountains, *Wyo., U.S.* 42°44′ N, 108°1′ W **90**
Granite Pass, *Calif., U.S.* 35°25′ N, 116°35′ W **101**
Granite Peak, *Mont., U.S.* 45°8′ N, 109°53′ W **90**
Granite Peak, *Nev., U.S.* 41°38′ N, 117°41′ W **90**
Granite Peak, *Nev., U.S.* 40°46′ N, 119°31′ W **90**
Granite Peak, *Utah, U.S.* 40°6′ N, 113°20′ W **90**
Granite Peak, *Wyo., U.S.* 42°32′ N, 108°57′ W **90**
Granity, *N.Z.* 41°40′ S, 171°51′ E **240**
Granja, *Braz.* 3°9′ S, 40°51′ W **132**
Granja de Torrehermosa, *Sp.* 38°18′ N, 5°37′ W **164**
Grankulla (Kauniainen), *Fin.* 60°11′ N, 24°43′ E **152**
Granma, *Cuba* 19°51′ N, 77°33′ W **116**
Gränna, *Nor.* 58°1′ N, 14°28′ E **152**
Grannd Erg Oriental, *Alg.* 33°50′ N, 7°52′ E **156**
Gransee, *Ger.* 53°1′ N, 13°8′ E **152**
Grant, *Mich., U.S.* 43°19′ N, 85°49′ W **102**
Grant, *Nebr., U.S.* 40°50′ N, 101°44′ W **90**
Grant City, *Mo., U.S.* 40°27′ N, 94°25′ W **94**
Grant Island, *Antarctica* 73°36′ S, 131°2′ W **248**
Grant, Mount, *Nev., U.S.* 38°33′ N, 118°53′ W **90**
Grant Range, *Nev., U.S.* 38°35′ N, 115°34′ W **90**
Grantham, *N.H., U.S.* 43°29′ N, 72°8′ W **104**
Grantham, *U.K.* 52°54′ N, 0°39′ E **162**
Grant-Kohrs Ranch National Historic Site, *Mont., U.S.* 46°22′ N, 112°52′ W **90**
Grants, *N. Mex., U.S.* 35°8′ N, 107°51′ W **112**
Grants Pass, *Oreg., U.S.* 42°26′ N, 123°21′ W **90**
Grantsburg, *Wis., U.S.* 45°45′ N, 92°41′ W **110**
Grantsville, *W. Va., U.S.* 38°55′ N, 81°6′ W **102**
Grantville, *Ga., U.S.* 33°13′ N, 84°51′ W **96**
Granum, *Can.* 49°52′ N, 113°31′ W **90**
Granville, *Fr.* 48°50′ N, 1°36′ W **150**
Granville, *N. Dak., U.S.* 48°14′ N, 100°51′ W **90**
Granville, *Vt., U.S.* 43°58′ N, 72°51′ W **104**
Granville, *W. Va., U.S.* 39°38′ N, 79°60′ W **94**
Granville Lake, *Can.* 56°16′ N, 101°37′ W **108**
Granvin, *Nor.* 60°34′ N, 6°41′ E **152**
Grão Mogol, *Braz.* 16°35′ S, 42°57′ W **138**
Grapeland, *Tex., U.S.* 31°28′ N, 95°29′ W **103**
Grapevine Mountains, *Calif., U.S.* 36°56′ N, 117°13′ W **101**
Grapevine Peak, *Nev., U.S.* 36°57′ N, 117°11′ W **101**
Graphite Peak, *Antarctica* 85°15′ S, 167°50′ E **248**
Grapska Donja, *Bosn. and Herzg.* 44°47′ N, 18°4′ E **168**
Graskop, *S. Af.* 24°58′ S, 30°50′ E **227**
Grasmere, *U.K.* 54°27′ N, 3°1′ W **162**
Gräsö, island, *Sw.* 60°26′ N, 18°25′ E **166**
Grass, river, *Can.* 55°6′ N, 98°33′ W **108**
Grass Valley, *Calif., U.S.* 39°12′ N, 121°5′ W **90**
Grasset, Lac, lake, *Can.* 49°55′ N, 78°40′ W **94**
Grassington, *U.K.* 54°4′ N, 1°59′ W **162**
Grassland, *Can.* 54°48′ N, 112°42′ W **108**
Grasslands National Park, *Can.* 48°54′ N, 107°60′ W **90**
Grassrange, *Mont., U.S.* 47°0′ N, 108°48′ W **90**
Grassy Butte, *N. Dak., U.S.* 47°22′ N, 103°17′ W **90**
Grassy Island Lake, *Can.* 51°51′ N, 110°51′ W **90**
Grassy Key, island, *Fla., U.S.* 24°43′ N, 80°55′ W **105**
Grassy Mountain, *Oreg., U.S.* 42°37′ N, 117°25′ W **90**
Grästorp, *Nor.* 58°19′ N, 12°39′ E **152**
Grates Point, *Can.* 48°11′ N, 53°9′ W **111**
Graton, *Calif., U.S.* 38°26′ N, 122°53′ W **92**
Gråträsk, *Nor.* 65°28′ N, 19°45′ E **152**
Graus, *Sp.* 42°10′ N, 0°19′ E **164**
Grave, *Neth.* 51°45′ N, 5°43′ E **167**
Grave Peak, *Idaho, U.S.* 46°22′ N, 114°49′ W **90**
Gravedona, *It.* 46°9′ N, 9°17′ E **167**
Gravelbourg, *Can.* 49°52′ N, 106°34′ W **90**
Gravelines, *Fr.* 50°59′ N, 2°8′ E **163**
Gravelotte, *S. Af.* 23°56′ S, 30°36′ E **227**
Gravenhurst, *Can.* 44°54′ N, 79°22′ W **94**
Gravesend, *U.K.* 51°25′ N, 0°21′ E **162**
Gravette, *Ark., U.S.* 36°23′ N, 94°28′ W **96**
Gravvik, *Nor.* 64°59′ N, 11°48′ E **152**
Gray, *Me., U.S.* 43°53′ N, 70°20′ W **104**
Gray, Mount, *Antarctica* 74°53′ S, 136°11′ W **248**
Grayland, *Wash., U.S.* 46°47′ N, 124°6′ W **100**
Grayling, *Alas., U.S.* 62°57′ N, 160°9′ W **98**
Grayling, *Mich., U.S.* 44°40′ N, 84°43′ W **94**
Grays, *U.K.* 51°29′ N, 0°20′ E **162**
Grays Harbor 46°49′ N, 125°15′ W **80**
Grays Peak, *Colo., U.S.* 39°36′ N, 105°54′ W **90**
Grayslake, *Ill., U.S.* 42°20′ N, 88°3′ W **102**
Grayson, *Ky., U.S.* 38°19′ N, 82°57′ W **94**
Grayson, *La., U.S.* 32°2′ N, 92°7′ W **103**
Grayville, *Mo., U.S.* 38°14′ N, 87°60′ W **94**
Grayvoron, *Russ.* 50°28′ N, 35°39′ E **158**
Graz, *Aust.* 47°4′ N, 15°26′ E **156**
Grazie, Monte le, peak, *It.* 42°10′ N, 11°50′ E **156**
Grdelica, *Serb. and Mont.* 42°53′ N, 22°4′ E **168**
Grea de Albarracín, *Sp.* 40°24′ N, 1°22′ W **164**
Great Artesian Basin, *Australia* 22°45′ S, 142°18′ E **230**
Great Australian Bight 37°7′ S, 130°17′ E **231**
Great Badminton, *U.K.* 51°32′ N, 2°17′ W **162**
Great Barrier Reef, *Coral Sea* 16°34′ S, 147°16′ E **252**
Great Barrier Reef Marine Park, *Coral Sea* 19°12′ S, 147°53′ E **238**
Great Barrington, *Mass., U.S.* 42°11′ N, 73°23′ W **104**
Great Basalt Wall National Park, *Austral.* 20°7′ S, 144°57′ E **238**
Great Basin, *North America* 36°22′ N, 114°27′ W **101**
Great Basin National Park, *Nev., U.S.* 38°36′ N, 114°29′ W **90**
Great Bear Lake, *Can.* 65°31′ N, 121°54′ W **106**
Great Britain, island, *U.K.* 52°5′ N, 1°42′ W **143**
Great Channel 6°12′ N, 93°33′ E **188**
Great Corn Island see Maíz Grande, Isla del, *Nicar.* 11°44′ N, 83°2′ W **115**
Great Crater, *Israel* 30°55′ N, 34°59′ E **194**
Great Divide Basin, *Wyo., U.S.* 41°58′ N, 108°11′ W **90**
Great Dividing Range, *Australia* 11°52′ S, 142°8′ E **192**
Great Driffield, *U.K.* 54°0′ N, 0°26′ E **162**
Great Exuma, island, *Bahamas* 23°23′ N, 76°30′ W **116**
Great Falls, *Can.* 50°23′ N, 96°4′ W **90**
Great Falls, *Mont., U.S.* 47°28′ N, 111°18′ W **90**
Great Falls, *S.C., U.S.* 34°33′ N, 80°54′ W **96**
Great Fish, river, *S. Af.* 33°1′ S, 25°53′ E **227**
Great Guana Cay, island, *Bahamas* 23°53′ N, 76°37′ W **116**
Great Harbour Cay, island, *Bahamas* 25°39′ N, 77°45′ W **81**
Great Harbour Deep, *Can.* 50°22′ N, 56°33′ W **111**
Great Inagua Island, *Bahamas* 21°14′ N, 73°53′ W **116**
Great Indian Desert, *India* 26°55′ N, 68°30′ E **186**
Great Isaac, island, *Bahamas* 26°0′ N, 79°20′ W **105**
Great Island, peak, *Can.* 58°59′ N, 96°42′ W **108**
Great Islets Harbour 51°7′ N, 56°40′ W **111**
Great Kei, river, *S. Af.* 32°20′ S, 27°54′ E **227**
Great Lakes Naval Training Center, *Ill., U.S.* 42°17′ N, 87°54′ W **102**
Great Namaland, region, *Africa* 26°5′ S, 14°59′ E **227**
Great Nicobar, island, *India* 6°29′ N, 93°53′ E **188**
Great Orme's Head, *U.K.* 53°20′ N, 3°60′ W **162**
Great Ouse, river, *U.K.* 52°36′ N, 0°17′ E **162**
Great Pedro Bluff, *Jam.* 17°45′ N, 78°41′ W **115**
Great Point, *Mass., U.S.* 41°23′ N, 70°8′ W **104**
Great Pond, lake, *Me., U.S.* 44°29′ N, 70°3′ W **104**
Great Ruaha, river, *Tanzania* 7°21′ S, 35°14′ E **224**
Great Sacandaga Lake, *N.Y., U.S.* 43°17′ N, 74°11′ W **104**
Great Salt Lake, *Utah, U.S.* 41°16′ N, 113°26′ W **106**
Great Salt Lake Desert, *Utah, U.S.* 40°26′ N, 113°47′ W **90**
Great Salt Plains Lake, *Okla., U.S.* 36°45′ N, 99°5′ W **81**
Great Sandy Desert, *Australia* 20°22′ S, 122°54′ E **230**
Great Sitkin, island, *Alas., U.S.* 52°12′ N, 177°22′ W **160**
Great Slave Lake, *Can.* 61°13′ N, 117°25′ W **73**
Great Smoky Mountains, *N.C., U.S.* 35°44′ N, 83°34′ W **96**
Great Snow Mountain, *Can.* 57°25′ N, 124°12′ W **108**
Great Victoria Desert, *Austral.* 28°18′ S, 126°42′ E **230**
Great Wall, *China* 39°15′ N, 110°33′ E **198**
Great Wall, station, *Antarctica* 62°21′ S, 58°57′ W **134**
Great Yarmouth, *U.K.* 52°36′ N, 1°42′ E **163**
Great Zab, river, *Turk.* 37°27′ N, 43°41′ E **195**
Great Zab see Zāb al Kabīr, river, *Iraq* 36°32′ N, 43°40′ E **195**
Great Zimbabwe, ruin(s), *Zimb.* 20°24′ S, 30°58′ E **227**
Greater Antilles, *Caribbean Sea* 17°49′ N, 73°28′ W **116**
Greater Khingan Range, *China* 52°0′ N, 122°48′ E **172**
Grebbestad, *Nor.* 58°41′ N, 11°15′ E **152**
Grebenau, *Ger.* 50°44′ N, 9°27′ E **167**
Grebenstein, *Ger.* 51°27′ N, 9°25′ E **167**
Gréboun, peak, *Niger* 19°55′ N, 8°29′ E **222**
Greco, Monte, peak, *It.* 41°47′ N, 13°54′ E **156**
Gredos, Sierra de, *Sp.* 40°16′ N, 5°43′ W **150**
Greece 39°6′ N, 21°44′ E **156**
Greeley, *Colo., U.S.* 40°25′ N, 104°43′ W **90**
Greeley, *Nebr., U.S.* 41°32′ N, 98°33′ W **90**
Green Bay 44°38′ N, 87°59′ W **94**
Green Island, *N.Z.* 45°53′ S, 170°24′ E **240**
Green Islands, *South Pacific Ocean* 3°45′ S, 153°35′ E **192**
Green Islands, *South Pacific Ocean* 4°1′ S, 154°11′ E **238**
Green Lake, *Can.* 54°18′ N, 107°47′ W **108**
Green Lake, *Wis., U.S.* 43°49′ N, 88°57′ W **102**
Green Mountains, *Vt., U.S.* 44°2′ N, 72°60′ W **104**
Green Mountains, *Wyo., U.S.* 42°27′ N, 107°57′ W **90**
Green River, *Utah, U.S.* 38°59′ N, 110°10′ W **92**
Green River, *Wyo., U.S.* 41°32′ N, 109°28′ W **90**
Green, river, *Ky., U.S.* 37°37′ N, 87°33′ W **94**
Green, river, *U.S.* 39°51′ N, 109°57′ W **90**
Greenacres, *Calif., U.S.* 35°23′ N, 119°8′ W **101**
Greenbush, *Minn., U.S.* 48°40′ N, 96°13′ W **90**
Greenbush Lake, *Can.* 50°55′ N, 90°38′ W **110**
Greencastle, *Ind., U.S.* 39°38′ N, 86°52′ W **102**
Greene, *Me., U.S.* 44°11′ N, 70°8′ W **104**
Greeneville, *Tenn., U.S.* 36°9′ N, 82°51′ W **96**
Greenfield, *Calif., U.S.* 36°19′ N, 121°15′ W **100**
Greenfield, *Ind., U.S.* 39°47′ N, 85°46′ W **102**
Greenfield, *Iowa, U.S.* 41°18′ N, 94°27′ W **94**
Greenfield, *Mo., U.S.* 37°24′ N, 93°51′ W **96**
Greenfield, *N.H., U.S.* 42°56′ N, 71°53′ W **104**
Greenfield, *N. Mex., U.S.* 33°9′ N, 104°21′ W **92**
Greenfield, *Ohio, U.S.* 39°21′ N, 83°24′ W **102**
Greenhorn Mountain, *Colo., U.S.* 37°52′ N, 105°6′ W **90**
Greenhorn Mountains, *Calif., U.S.* 35°41′ N, 118°54′ W **92**
Greenland (Kalaallit Nunaat), *Den.* 67°11′ N, 50°25′ W **106**
Greenland, *N.H., U.S.* 43°1′ N, 70°51′ W **104**
Greenland Fracture Zone, *Greenland Sea* 74°53′ N, 2°12′ E **255**
Greenland Sea 74°52′ N, 4°29′ E **160**
Greenland Sea 68°26′ N, 25°49′ W **246**
Greenland Sea 73°24′ N, 12°53′ W **255**
Greenough, Mount, *Alas., U.S.* 69°6′ N, 141°54′ W **98**
Greenport, *N.Y., U.S.* 41°6′ N, 72°23′ W **104**
Greensboro, *Ala., U.S.* 32°42′ N, 87°36′ W **103**
Greensboro, *Ga., U.S.* 33°33′ N, 83°11′ W **96**
Greensboro, *N.C., U.S.* 36°3′ N, 79°49′ W **96**
Greensboro Bend, *Vt., U.S.* 44°32′ N, 72°16′ W **104**
Greensburg, *Ind., U.S.* 39°19′ N, 85°29′ W **102**
Greensburg, *Kans., U.S.* 37°35′ N, 99°18′ W **92**
Greensburg, *La., U.S.* 30°49′ N, 90°41′ W **103**
Greensburg, *Pa., U.S.* 40°17′ N, 79°34′ W **94**
Greentown, *Ind., U.S.* 40°28′ N, 85°58′ W **102**
Greenup, *Ill., U.S.* 39°13′ N, 88°10′ W **102**
Greenup, *Ky., U.S.* 38°33′ N, 82°50′ W **102**
Greenview, *Ill., U.S.* 40°4′ N, 89°45′ W **102**
Greenville, *Ala., U.S.* 31°49′ N, 86°37′ W **96**
Greenville, *Can.* 55°3′ N, 129°36′ W **108**
Greenville, *Fla., U.S.* 30°26′ N, 83°38′ W **96**
Greenville, *Ill., U.S.* 38°53′ N, 89°24′ W **102**
Greenville, *Ky., U.S.* 37°12′ N, 87°11′ W **94**
Greenville, *Liberia* 5°0′ N, 9°3′ W **222**
Greenville, *Me., U.S.* 45°27′ N, 69°36′ W **94**
Greenville, *Mich., U.S.* 43°10′ N, 85°16′ W **102**
Greenville, *Miss., U.S.* 33°23′ N, 91°4′ W **103**
Greenville, *N.H., U.S.* 42°46′ N, 71°50′ W **104**
Greenville, *Ohio, U.S.* 40°5′ N, 84°38′ W **102**
Greenville, *Pa., U.S.* 41°24′ N, 80°23′ W **94**
Greenville, *S.C., U.S.* 34°50′ N, 82°25′ W **96**
Greenville, *Tex., U.S.* 33°6′ N, 96°6′ W **96**
Greenwich, *Conn., U.S.* 41°1′ N, 73°38′ W **104**
Greenwich, *N.Y., U.S.* 43°5′ N, 73°31′ W **104**
Greenwich, *Ohio, U.S.* 41°1′ N, 82°31′ W **102**
Greenwich, *U.K.* 51°27′ N, 3°180′ E **162**
Greenwich Island, *Antarctica* 62°45′ S, 59°27′ W **134**
Greenwood, *Ark., U.S.* 35°11′ N, 94°16′ W **96**
Greenwood, *Can.* 49°5′ N, 118°41′ W **90**
Greenwood, *Ind., U.S.* 39°37′ N, 86°6′ W **102**
Greenwood, *Me., U.S.* 44°18′ N, 70°39′ W **104**
Greenwood, *Miss., U.S.* 33°29′ N, 90°11′ W **96**
Greenwood, *S.C., U.S.* 34°11′ N, 82°11′ W **112**
Greenwood, Mount, *Austral.* 13°47′ S, 129°52′ E **230**
Greer, *Ariz., U.S.* 34°1′ N, 109°27′ W **92**
Greetsiel, *Ger.* 53°30′ N, 7°5′ E **163**
Gregoire Lake, *Can.* 56°27′ N, 111°36′ W **108**
Gregório, river, *Braz.* 7°39′ S, 71°13′ W **130**
Gregory, *S. Dak., U.S.* 43°12′ N, 99°27′ W **90**
Gregory National Park, *Austral.* 16°23′ S, 129°58′ E **238**
Gregory Range, *Austral.* 18°43′ S, 142°20′ E **230**
Greiffenberg, *Ger.* 53°5′ N, 13°56′ E **152**
Greifswald, *Ger.* 54°6′ N, 13°22′ E **152**
Gremikha, *Russ.* 68°0′ N, 39°23′ E **169**
Gremyachinsk, *Russ.* 58°35′ N, 57°52′ E **154**
Grenå, *Den.* 56°25′ N, 10°51′ E **150**
Grenada 12°0′ N, 62°0′ W **116**
Grenada, *Calif., U.S.* 41°39′ N, 122°32′ W **92**
Grenada, *Miss., U.S.* 33°43′ N, 89°49′ W **96**
Grenchen, *Switz.* 47°11′ N, 7°22′ E **150**
Grenfell, *Can.* 50°24′ N, 102°56′ W **90**
Grenoble, *Fr.* 45°11′ N, 5°43′ E **150**
Grenora, *N. Dak., U.S.* 48°36′ N, 103°57′ W **90**
Grenville, *Can.* 45°37′ N, 74°37′ W **94**
Grenville Channel 53°42′ N, 130°45′ W **108**
Grenville, Mount, *Can.* 50°58′ N, 124°36′ W **90**
Grenville, Point, *Wash., U.S.* 47°13′ N, 124°31′ W **100**
Gresford, *U.K.* 53°5′ N, 2°59′ W **162**
Gressåmoen National Park, *Nor.* 64°18′ N, 12°52′ E **152**
Gretna, *La., U.S.* 29°54′ N, 90°4′ W **103**
Greven, *Ger.* 52°5′ N, 7°37′ E **163**
Grevenbroich, *Ger.* 51°5′ N, 6°35′ E **167**
Grevenmacher, *Lux.* 49°40′ N, 6°25′ E **163**
Grevesmühlen, *Ger.* 53°51′ N, 11°12′ E **152**
Grey Islands, *Labrador Sea* 50°26′ N, 55°8′ W **106**
Grey Range, *Austral.* 28°39′ S, 142°4′ E **230**
Greybull, *Wyo., U.S.* 44°28′ N, 108°4′ W **90**
Greylock, Mount, *Mass., U.S.* 42°37′ N, 73°12′ W **104**
Greymouth, *N.Z.* 42°30′ S, 171°13′ E **240**
Greytown, *N.Z.* 41°6′ S, 175°29′ E **240**
Grezzana, *It.* 45°30′ N, 11°0′ E **167**
Griam More, Ben, peak, *U.K.* 58°18′ N, 4°9′ W **150**
Gribanovskiy, *Russ.* 51°27′ N, 41°53′ E **158**
Gribe, Mal, *Alban.* 40°15′ N, 19°29′ E **156**
Grico, oil field, *Venez.* 8°55′ N, 66°40′ W **136**
Gridino, *Russ.* 65°53′ N, 34°28′ E **152**
Gridley, *Ill., U.S.* 40°44′ N, 88°53′ W **102**
Grieskirchen, *Aust.* 48°13′ N, 13°50′ E **152**
Griffin, *Ga., U.S.* 33°13′ N, 84°16′ W **96**
Grigorevka, *Kyrg.* 42°44′ N, 77°48′ E **184**
Grigoriopol, *Mold.* 47°9′ N, 29°17′ E **158**
Grimari, *Cen. Af. Rep.* 5°43′ N, 20°5′ E **218**
Grimsby, *Can.* 43°10′ N, 79°34′ W **94**
Grimsby, *U.K.* 53°34′ N, 0°5′ E **162**
Grimshaw, *Can.* 56°11′ N, 117°37′ W **108**
Grimstad, *Nor.* 58°20′ N, 8°34′ E **150**
Grindelwald, *Switz.* 46°37′ N, 8°2′ E **167**
Grinnell, *Iowa, U.S.* 41°44′ N, 92°43′ W **94**
Grinnell Peninsula, *Can.* 76°38′ N, 95°22′ W **106**
Griñón, *Sp.* 40°12′ N, 3°51′ W **164**
Grintavec, peak, *Slov.* 46°21′ N, 14°28′ E **156**
Gripsholm, site, *Nor.* 59°14′ N, 17°5′ E **152**
Griquatown, *S. Af.* 28°51′ S, 23°15′ E **227**
Grise Fiord, *Can.* 76°21′ N, 82°51′ W **106**
Grishkino, *Russ.* 57°57′ N, 82°44′ E **169**
Grisslehamn, *Sw.* 60°4′ N, 18°44′ E **166**
Griswoldville, *Mass., U.S.* 42°39′ N, 72°43′ W **104**
Griva, *Latv.* 55°49′ N, 26°31′ E **166**
Griva, *Russ.* 60°34′ N, 50°55′ E **154**
Grizim, spring, *Alg.* 25°25′ N, 3°4′ W **214**
Grizzly Bear Hills, *Can.* 55°35′ N, 109°42′ W **108**
Grizzly Mountain, *Can.* 51°42′ N, 120°20′ W **90**
Grmeic, *Bosn. and Herzg.* 44°21′ N, 16°29′ E **168**
Grobiņa, *Latv.* 56°32′ N, 21°9′ E **166**
Grocka, *Serb. and Mont.* 44°39′ N, 20°42′ E **168**
Groenlo, *Neth.* 52°2′ N, 6°36′ E **167**
Grombalia, *Tun.* 36°35′ N, 10°31′ E **214**
Gromovo, *Russ.* 60°41′ N, 30°16′ E **166**
Grong, *Nor.* 64°27′ N, 12°20′ E **152**
Groningen, *Neth.* 53°12′ N, 6°33′ E **163**
Gronlid, *Can.* 53°5′ N, 104°28′ W **108**
Grønøy, *Nor.* 66°47′ N, 13°25′ E **152**
Groom, *Tex., U.S.* 35°13′ N, 101°5′ W **92**
Groot Karasberge, peak, *Namibia* 27°12′ S, 18°37′ E **227**
Groote Eylandt, island, *Austral.* 14°27′ S, 137°3′ E **230**
Grootfontein, *Namibia* 19°32′ S, 18°7′ E **220**
Gros Mécatina, Cap du, *Can.* 50°38′ N, 59°8′ W **111**
Gros Morne National Park, *Can.* 49°46′ N, 58°30′ W **111**
Gros Morne, peak, *Can.* 49°34′ N, 57°52′ W **111**
Gros Ventre, *Wyo., U.S.* 43°24′ N, 111°16′ W **80**
Gros Ventre Range, *Wyo., U.S.* 43°28′ N, 110°52′ W **90**
Grosio, *It.* 46°17′ N, 10°14′ E **167**
Grosne, river, *Fr.* 46°32′ N, 4°38′ E **165**
Grossa, Ponta, *Braz.* 1°14′ N, 49°54′ W **130**
Grossa, Punta, *Sp.* 39°5′ N, 1°16′ E **150**
Grossalmerode, *Ger.* 51°15′ N, 9°46′ E **167**
Grossefehn, *Ger.* 53°24′ N, 7°36′ E **163**
Grossenkneten, *Ger.* 52°56′ N, 8°16′ E **163**
Grossenlüder, *Ger.* 50°36′ N, 9°32′ E **167**
Grosseto, *It.* 42°45′ N, 11°5′ E **156**
Grossglockner, peak, *Aust.* 47°4′ N, 12°37′ E **156**
Gross-Umstadt, *Ger.* 49°52′ N, 8°54′ E **167**
Grostenquin, *Fr.* 48°57′ N, 6°43′ E **163**
Grosvenor Seamount, *North Pacific Ocean* 28°4′ N, 166°46′ E **252**
Groton, *Mass., U.S.* 42°36′ N, 71°35′ W **104**
Groton, *S. Dak., U.S.* 45°26′ N, 98°7′ W **90**
Groton, *Vt., U.S.* 44°12′ N, 72°12′ W **104**
Grøtøy, *Nor.* 67°49′ N, 14°42′ E **152**
Grottammare, *It.* 42°59′ N, 13°51′ E **156**
Grotte de Lascaux, site, *Fr.* 45°2′ N, 1°9′ E **165**
Grouard, *Can.* 55°31′ N, 116°8′ W **108**
Groundhog, river, *Can.* 49°22′ N, 82°15′ W **94**
Grouse Creek, *Utah, U.S.* 41°42′ N, 113°54′ W **92**
Grouse Creek Mountain, *Idaho, U.S.* 44°21′ N, 113°59′ W **90**
Grouse Creek Mountains, *Utah, U.S.* 41°29′ N, 114°8′ W **90**
Grovane, *Nor.* 58°17′ N, 7°58′ E **152**
Grove Hill, *Ala., U.S.* 31°42′ N, 87°46′ W **103**
Groveland, *Calif., U.S.* 37°49′ N, 120°15′ W **100**
Groveland, *Fla., U.S.* 28°33′ N, 81°51′ W **105**
Groveport, *Ohio, U.S.* 39°51′ N, 82°53′ W **102**
Grover, *Colo., U.S.* 40°52′ N, 104°15′ W **90**
Grover, *Pa., U.S.* 41°36′ N, 76°53′ W **94**
Grover Beach, *Calif., U.S.* 35°7′ N, 120°38′ W **92**
Groves, *Tex., U.S.* 29°55′ N, 93°56′ W **103**
Groveton, *N.H., U.S.* 44°36′ N, 71°32′ W **94**
Groveton, *Tex., U.S.* 31°2′ N, 95°7′ W **103**
Growler Pass, *Ariz., U.S.* 32°10′ N, 112°55′ W **92**
Groznyy, *Russ.* 43°18′ N, 45°39′ E **195**
Grubišno Polje, *Croatia* 45°41′ N, 17°10′ E **168**
Gruda, *Croatia* 42°30′ N, 18°22′ E **168**
Grudopole, *Belarus* 52°53′ N, 25°42′ E **152**
Grudovo, *Bulg.* 42°20′ N, 27°10′ E **156**
Grue, *Nor.* 60°26′ N, 12°2′ E **152**

Hillsville, Va., U.S. 36°45′ N, 80°45′ W 94
Hilo, Hawai'i, U.S. 19°43′ N, 155°6′ W 99
Hilo, region, Oceania 19°48′ N, 155°25′ W 99
Hilonghilong, Mount, Philippines 9°5′ N, 125°37′ E 203
Hilton Head Island, S.C., U.S. 32°12′ N, 80°46′ W 96
Hiltrup, Ger. 51°54′ N, 7°38′ E 167
Hilversum, Neth. 52°12′ N, 5°10′ E 163
Hima, Ky., U.S. 37°6′ N, 83°48′ W 96
Himachal Pradesh, adm. division, India 32°20′ N, 75°58′ E 188
Himalaya, Asia 32°53′ N, 74°1′ E 186
Himanka, Fin. 64°3′ N, 23°38′ E 152
Himatnagar, India 23°36′ N, 72°58′ E 186
Himeji, Japan 34°50′ N, 134°41′ E 201
Himi, Japan 36°51′ N, 136°58′ E 201
Himo, Tanzania 3°25′ S, 37°33′ E 224
Himora, Eth. 14°12′ N, 36°36′ E 182
Ḥimş, Syr. 34°43′ N, 36°42′ E 143
Ḥimş, Baḩrat, lake, Syr. 34°39′ N, 36°29′ E 194
Ḥimş (Homs), Syr. 34°43′ N, 36°42′ E 194
Hinatuan, Philippines 8°24′ N, 126°16′ E 203
Hinche, Haiti 19°8′ N, 72°2′ W 116
Hinchinbrook Island, Austral. 18°47′ S, 143°13′ E 231
Hinchinbrook Island National Park, Coral Sea 18°32′ S, 145°55′ E 238
Hinckley, Ill., U.S. 41°45′ N, 88°39′ W 102
Hinckley, Minn., U.S. 46°0′ N, 92°58′ W 94
Hinckley, U.K. 52°32′ N, 1°23′ W 162
Hinckley, Utah, U.S. 39°19′ N, 112°40′ W 90
Hindon, U.K. 51°5′ N, 2°8′ W 162
Hinds, N.Z. 44°1′ S, 171°33′ E 240
Hindubagh, Pak. 30°51′ N, 67°45′ E 186
Hindupur, India 13°50′ N, 77°29′ E 188
Hines, Oreg., U.S. 43°33′ N, 119°5′ W 90
Hines Creek, Can. 56°14′ N, 118°36′ W 108
Hinesburg, Vt., U.S. 44°19′ N, 73°7′ W 104
Hinesville, Ga., U.S. 31°50′ N, 81°37′ W 96
Hinganghat, India 20°31′ N, 78°51′ E 188
Hinggan Ling, Da, China 44°15′ N, 118°1′ E 198
Hingham, Mass., U.S. 42°14′ N, 70°54′ W 104
Hingol, river, Pak. 25°50′ N, 65°26′ E 182
Hınıs, Turk. 39°22′ N, 41°43′ E 195
Hinkley, Calif., U.S. 34°56′ N, 117°13′ W 101
Hinkley Point, site, U.K. 51°11′ N, 3°4′ W 162
Hinks, Mount, Antarctica 67°54′ S, 65°45′ E 248
Hinlopenstretet 79°46′ N, 9°22′ E 160
Hinnerjoki, Fin. 60°59′ N, 21°57′ E 166
Hinnøya, Norwegian Sea 68°37′ N, 15°28′ E 152
Hino, Japan 35°12′ N, 133°25′ E 201
Hinoba-an, Philippines 9°37′ N, 122°29′ E 203
Hinoemata, Japan 37°1′ N, 139°22′ E 201
Hinojosa del Duque, Sp. 38°29′ N, 5°9′ W 164
Hinomi Saki, Japan 35°25′ N, 132°28′ E 201
Hinsdale, N.H., U.S. 42°47′ N, 72°30′ W 104
Hinterweidenthal, Ger. 49°11′ N, 7°44′ E 163
Hinthada, Myanmar 17°38′ N, 95°26′ E 202
Hinton, Can. 53°24′ N, 117°35′ W 108
Hinton, Okla., U.S. 35°26′ N, 98°22′ W 96
Hinton, W. Va., U.S. 37°39′ N, 80°54′ W 96
Hınzır Burnu, Turk. 36°18′ N, 35°2′ E 156
Híos, Gr. 38°22′ N, 26°6′ E 180
Híos, island, Gr. 38°9′ N, 25°31′ E 180
Hippolytushoef, Neth. 52°54′ N, 4°57′ E 163
Hirado, Japan 33°22′ N, 129°32′ E 201
Hiram, Me., U.S. 43°52′ N, 70°49′ W 104
Hirata, Japan 35°23′ N, 132°47′ E 201
Hirfanlı Barajı, dam, Turk. 39°4′ N, 33°36′ E 156
Hirky, Ukr. 51°53′ N, 25°16′ E 152
Hirnyky, Ukr. 51°42′ N, 24°27′ E 152
Hirosaki, Japan 40°33′ N, 140°25′ E 190
Hiroshima, Japan 34°23′ N, 132°27′ E 200
Hiroshima, adm. division, Japan 34°32′ N, 132°9′ E 201
Hirson, Fr. 49°54′ N, 4°4′ E 163
Hîrşova, Rom. 44°41′ N, 27°57′ E 156
Hirtshals, Den. 57°34′ N, 9°57′ E 150
Hirvasvaara, Fin. 66°32′ N, 28°34′ E 152
Hirvensalmi, Fin. 61°37′ N, 26°46′ E 166
Hisar, India 29°7′ N, 75°44′ E 197
Hisarönü, Turk. 41°34′ N, 32°2′ E 156
Ḩişn al 'Abr, Yemen 16°8′ N, 47°18′ E 182
Ḩişn Tāqrifat, Lib. 29°12′ N, 17°20′ E 216
Hisor, Taj. 38°33′ N, 68°33′ E 197
Hispaniola, island, Caribbean Sea 18°54′ N, 71°8′ W 253
Hispaniola, island, Dom. Rep. 19°57′ N, 70°50′ W 116
Ḩisyah, Syr. 34°24′ N, 36°45′ E 194
Hīt, Iraq 33°37′ N, 42°44′ E 180
Hita, Japan 33°19′ N, 130°56′ E 201
Hitachi, Japan 36°35′ N, 140°38′ E 201
Hitachiōta, Japan 36°31′ N, 140°32′ E 201
Hitadu, island, Maldives 0°36′ N, 72°17′ E 188
Hitchcock, Tex., U.S. 29°20′ N, 95°2′ W 103
Hitchin, U.K. 51°57′ N, 0°17′ E 162
Hitis (Hiittinen), Fin. 59°51′ N, 22°29′ E 166
Hitoyoshi, Japan 32°13′ N, 130°45′ E 201
Hitra, Nor. 63°35′ N, 8°42′ E 152
Hitterdal, Minn., U.S. 46°56′ N, 96°17′ W 90
Hiuchi Nada 34°5′ N, 133°12′ E 201
Hiusta Meadow, Can. 58°4′ N, 130°59′ W 98
Hiver, Lac de l', lake, Can. 53°55′ N, 72°38′ W 111
Hiwannee, Miss., U.S. 31°47′ N, 88°40′ W 103
Hiwasa, Japan 33°44′ N, 134°31′ E 201
Hixon, Can. 53°26′ N, 122°37′ W 108
Hizan, Turk. 38°9′ N, 42°24′ E 195
Hjallerup, Den. 57°10′ N, 10°8′ E 152
Hjalmar Lake, Can. 61°30′ N, 110°6′ W 108
Hjartdal, Nor. 59°35′ N, 8°42′ E 152
Hjerkinn, Nor. 62°13′ N, 9°35′ E 152
Hjørring, Den. 57°26′ N, 9°58′ E 150
Hlaingbwe, Myanmar 17°8′ N, 97°50′ E 202
Hlohovec, Slovakia 48°25′ N, 17°47′ E 152
Hluhluwe, S. Af. 28°1′ S, 32°16′ E 227
Hlukhiv, Ukr. 51°38′ N, 33°57′ E 158
Hlyboka, Ukr. 48°4′ N, 25°55′ E 152
Hlybokaye, Belarus 55°9′ N, 27°41′ E 166
Ho, Ghana 6°36′ N, 0°28′ E 222
Ho Chi Minh City (Saigon), Vietnam 10°48′ N, 106°40′ E 202
Ho Xa, Vietnam 17°4′ N, 107°2′ E 202
Hoa Binh, Vietnam 20°52′ N, 105°17′ E 202
Hoachanas, Namibia 23°57′ S, 18°4′ E 220
Hoai An, Vietnam 14°23′ N, 108°58′ E 202
Hoare Bay 65°23′ N, 64°55′ W 106
Hoback Peak, Wyo., U.S. 43°4′ N, 110°39′ W 90
Hobart, Austral. 42°53′ S, 146°56′ E 230
Hobart, Okla., U.S. 35°0′ N, 99°6′ W 92
Hobbs, N. Mex., U.S. 32°41′ N, 103°8′ W 92
Hobbs Coast, Antarctica 75°18′ S, 127°36′ W 248
Hobe Sound, Fla., U.S. 27°3′ N, 80°9′ W 105
Hobo, Col. 2°33′ N, 75°29′ W 136
Hoboksar, China 46°47′ N, 85°47′ E 184
Hobot Xar see Xianghuang Qi, China 42°11′ N, 113°53′ E 198
Hobro, Den. 56°38′ N, 9°46′ E 150
Hobucken, N.C., U.S. 35°15′ N, 76°35′ W 96
Hoburgen, Sw. 56°52′ N, 18°10′ E 166
Hobyo, Somalia 5°22′ N, 48°36′ E 218
Hŏch'ŏn, N. Korea 40°38′ N, 128°35′ E 200
Hochschwab, Aust. 47°35′ N, 14°46′ E 156
Höchst, Ger. 49°48′ N, 8°59′ E 167
Hochstetter Forland, Den. 75°16′ N, 18°24′ W 246
Hodda, peak, Somalia 11°30′ N, 50°32′ E 182
Hoddesdon, U.K. 51°45′ N, 2°118′ W 162
Hodge, Calif., U.S. 34°49′ N, 117°12′ W 101
Hodge, La., U.S. 32°16′ N, 92°44′ W 103
Hodges Hill, peak, Can. 49°3′ N, 55°59′ W 111
Hodgeville, Can. 50°6′ N, 106°58′ W 90
Hodgson, Can. 51°12′ N, 97°35′ W 90
Hodh, region, Africa 16°35′ N, 8°36′ W 222
Hódmez ovásárhely, Hung. 46°25′ N, 20°20′ E 168
Hodonín, Czech Rep. 48°51′ N, 17°8′ E 152
Hödrögö, Mongolia 48°54′ N, 96°51′ E 173
Hoek van Holland, Neth. 51°58′ N, 4°7′ E 163
Hoeryŏng, N. Korea 42°28′ N, 129°46′ E 200
Hoeyang, N. Korea 38°41′ N, 127°37′ E 200
Hof, Ger. 50°18′ N, 11°55′ E 152
Hoffman, Minn., U.S. 45°48′ N, 95°50′ W 90
Hofgeismar, Ger. 51°30′ N, 9°22′ E 167
Hofheim, Ger. 50°5′ N, 8°26′ E 167
Höfn, Ice. 64°20′ N, 15°13′ W 143
Hofors, Nor. 60°32′ N, 16°18′ E 152
Hofra, oil field, Lib. 29°18′ N, 17°43′ E 216
Hofrat en Nahas, Sudan 9°41′ N, 24°16′ E 224
Hofstad, Nor. 64°12′ N, 10°24′ E 152
Hōfu, Japan 34°2′ N, 131°34′ E 200
Hofuf see Al Hufūf, Saudi Arabia 25°21′ N, 49°34′ E 196
Hogback Mountain, Mont., U.S. 44°52′ N, 112°12′ W 90
Hogback Mountain, Va., U.S. 38°45′ N, 78°20′ W 94
Högby, Sw. 57°10′ N, 16°59′ E 152
Högen, Nor. 58°54′ N, 11°41′ E 152
Hoggar see Ahaggar, Alg. 21°56′ N, 4°32′ E 222
Hogoro, Tanzania 5°54′ S, 36°28′ E 224
Högsby, Nor. 57°10′ N, 16°1′ E 152
Høgstegia, peak, Nor. 62°22′ N, 10°0′ E 152
Hogtinden, peak, Nor. 66°57′ N, 14°24′ E 152
Hogup Mountains, Utah, U.S. 41°26′ N, 113°12′ W 90
Hoh Xil Hu, lake, China 35°37′ N, 90°47′ E 188
Hohenau, Parag. 27°6′ S, 55°42′ W 139
Hohenlimburg, Ger. 51°20′ N, 7°33′ E 167
Hoher Dachstein, peak, Aust. 47°27′ N, 13°30′ E 156
Hohhot, China 40°51′ N, 111°42′ E 198
Hohoe, Ghana 7°10′ N, 0°26′ E 222
Hōhoku, Japan 34°19′ N, 130°55′ E 200
Höhr-Grenzhausen, Ger. 50°25′ N, 7°40′ E 167
Hoi An, Vietnam 15°54′ N, 108°20′ E 202
Hoima, Uganda 1°23′ N, 31°21′ E 224
Hoisington, Kans., U.S. 38°29′ N, 98°47′ W 92
Hok, Nor. 57°30′ N, 14°15′ E 152
Hokitika, N.Z. 42°44′ S, 171°0′ E 240
Hokkaidō, island, Japan 44°1′ N, 139°29′ E 190
Hokksund, Nor. 59°47′ N, 9°54′ E 152
Hokota, Japan 36°9′ N, 140°30′ E 201
Hōkūkano Heiau, site, Hawai'i, U.S. 21°3′ N, 156°54′ W 99
Hol, Nor. 60°34′ N, 8°21′ E 152
Hola Prystan', Ukr. 46°30′ N, 32°30′ E 156
Holanda, Bol. 11°50′ S, 68°38′ W 137
Holandsfjord, Nor. 66°43′ N, 13°39′ E 152
Holbeach, U.K. 52°47′ N, 1°59′ E 162
Holberg, Can. 50°39′ N, 127°60′ W 90
Holbox, Isla, island, Mex. 21°39′ N, 87°14′ W 116
Holbrook, Ariz., U.S. 34°54′ N, 110°10′ W 92
Holbrook, Idaho, U.S. 42°11′ N, 112°39′ W 92
Holbrook, Mass., U.S. 42°9′ N, 71°1′ W 104
Holcombe, Wis., U.S. 45°12′ N, 91°7′ W 94
Hold with Hope, Den. 73°19′ N, 20°18′ W 246
Holden, Can. 53°13′ N, 112°13′ W 108
Holden, Mass., U.S. 42°20′ N, 71°52′ W 104
Holden, Mo., U.S. 38°41′ N, 93°59′ W 94
Holden, Utah, U.S. 39°5′ N, 112°16′ W 90
Holdenville, Okla., U.S. 35°3′ N, 96°24′ W 96
Holdfast, Can. 50°57′ N, 105°26′ W 90
Holdrege, Nebr., U.S. 40°25′ N, 99°23′ W 90
Hole in the Ground, site, Oreg., U.S. 43°22′ N, 121°16′ W 90
Hole in the Mountain Peak, Nev., U.S. 40°56′ N, 115°12′ W 90
Holgate, Ohio, U.S. 41°13′ N, 84°8′ W 102
Holguín, Cuba 20°53′ N, 76°15′ W 115
Holguín, adm. division, Cuba 20°31′ N, 75°55′ W 116
Holinshead Lake, lake, Can. 49°38′ N, 90°16′ W 94
Holladay, Utah, U.S. 40°40′ N, 111°48′ W 90
Holland, Mich., U.S. 42°46′ N, 86°6′ W 102
Hollandale, Miss., U.S. 33°8′ N, 90°54′ W 103
Hollick-Kenyon Peninsula, Antarctica 69°3′ S, 60°55′ W 248
Hollick-Kenyon Plateau, Antarctica 78°34′ S, 104°13′ W 248
Hollis, Alas., U.S. 55°28′ N, 132°45′ W 108
Hollis, N.H., U.S. 42°44′ N, 71°36′ W 104
Hollis, Okla., U.S. 34°39′ N, 99°55′ W 92
Hollis Center, Me., U.S. 43°36′ N, 70°36′ W 104
Hollister, Calif., U.S. 36°50′ N, 121°25′ W 100
Hollister, Mo., U.S. 36°36′ N, 93°13′ W 96
Holliston, Mass., U.S. 42°12′ N, 71°26′ W 104
Holloman Air Force Base, N. Mex., U.S. 32°51′ N, 106°9′ W 92
Hollum, Neth. 53°26′ N, 5°37′ E 163
Holly, Colo., U.S. 38°2′ N, 102°7′ W 90
Holly, Mich., U.S. 42°46′ N, 83°37′ W 102
Holly Bluff, Miss., U.S. 32°48′ N, 90°43′ W 103
Holly Hill, Fla., U.S. 29°14′ N, 81°3′ W 105
Holly Ridge, N.C., U.S. 34°29′ N, 77°34′ W 96
Holly Springs, Miss., U.S. 34°42′ N, 89°27′ W 112
Hollywood, Calif., U.S. 34°6′ N, 118°22′ W 101
Hollywood, Fla., U.S. 26°1′ N, 80°10′ W 105
Holm Land, Den. 80°13′ N, 19°10′ W 246
Holman, Can. 70°42′ N, 117°39′ W 106
Holman, N. Mex., U.S. 36°2′ N, 105°24′ W 92
Hólmavík, Ice. 65°35′ N, 21°53′ W 73
Holmer, Lac, lake, Can. 54°2′ N, 72°13′ W 111
Holmes Lake, Can. 57°3′ N, 97°17′ W 108
Holmes, Mount, Wyo., U.S. 44°47′ N, 110°55′ W 90
Holmestrand, Nor. 59°29′ N, 10°18′ E 152
Holmfors, Nor. 65°13′ N, 18°9′ E 152
Holmudden, Sw. 57°52′ N, 19°12′ E 166
Holoby, Ukr. 51°5′ N, 25°0′ E 152
Holod, Rom. 46°47′ N, 22°8′ E 168
Holohit, Punta, Mex. 21°42′ N, 89°4′ W 116
Holoog, Namibia 27°23′ S, 17°54′ E 227
Holopaw, Fla., U.S. 28°8′ N, 81°5′ W 105
Holstebro, Den. 56°21′ N, 8°36′ E 150
Holstein, Can. 44°3′ N, 80°46′ W 102
Holstein, Iowa, U.S. 42°28′ N, 95°33′ W 94
Holsteinsborg see Sisimiut, Den. 66°56′ N, 53°43′ W 106
Holt, Ala., U.S. 33°13′ N, 87°29′ W 103
Holt, Mich., U.S. 42°37′ N, 84°31′ W 102
Holt, U.K. 52°54′ N, 1°5′ E 162
Holton, Kans., U.S. 39°26′ N, 95°45′ W 90
Holton, Mich., U.S. 43°24′ N, 86°5′ W 102
Holtorf, Ger. 52°41′ N, 9°15′ E 150
Holtville, Calif., U.S. 32°48′ N, 115°23′ W 101
Holtyre, Can. 48°28′ N, 80°17′ W 110
Holwerd, Neth. 53°21′ N, 5°53′ E 163
Holy Cross, Alas., U.S. 62°3′ N, 159°60′ W 98
Holyoke, Colo., U.S. 40°34′ N, 102°18′ W 90
Holyoke, Mass., U.S. 42°12′ N, 72°37′ W 104
Holywell, U.K. 53°16′ N, 3°13′ W 162
Holzminden, Ger. 51°48′ N, 9°27′ E 167
Homa Bay, Kenya 0°35′ N, 34°29′ E 224
Homberg, Ger. 51°2′ N, 9°24′ E 167
Hombori, Mali 15°16′ N, 1°43′ W 222
Homburg, Ger. 49°18′ N, 7°19′ E 163
Home Bay 68°36′ N, 67°37′ W 106
Homedale, Idaho, U.S. 43°37′ N, 116°57′ W 90
Homeland, Fla., U.S. 27°49′ N, 81°49′ W 105
Homeland, Ga., U.S. 30°50′ N, 82°2′ W 96
Homer, Alas., U.S. 59°37′ N, 151°36′ W 98
Homer, Ill., U.S. 40°2′ N, 87°58′ W 102
Homer, La., U.S. 32°46′ N, 93°4′ W 103
Homer, Mich., U.S. 42°8′ N, 84°49′ W 102
Homer, N.Y., U.S. 42°38′ N, 76°12′ W 94
Homerville, Ga., U.S. 31°1′ N, 82°46′ W 96
Homestead, Fla., U.S. 25°28′ N, 80°30′ W 105
Homewood, Miss., U.S. 32°14′ N, 89°30′ W 103
Hominy, Okla., U.S. 36°23′ N, 96°24′ W 92
Hommalinn, Myanmar 24°51′ N, 94°54′ E 188
Hommura, Japan 34°22′ N, 139°16′ E 201
Homnabad, India 17°45′ N, 77°8′ E 188
Homodji, spring, Niger 16°34′ N, 13°40′ E 222
Homoíne, Mozambique 23°50′ S, 35°9′ E 227
Homoljske Planina, Serb. and Mont. 44°18′ N, 21°36′ E 168
Homosassa, Fla., U.S. 28°46′ N, 82°36′ W 105
Homosassa Springs, Fla., U.S. 28°48′ N, 82°35′ W 105
Homs, Syr. 34°32′ N, 36°57′ E 173
Homs see Ḩimş, Syr. 34°43′ N, 36°42′ E 194
Homyel', Belarus 52°25′ N, 31°4′ E 154
Hon Chong, Vietnam 10°10′ N, 104°37′ E 202
Hon Quan, Vietnam 11°41′ N, 106°37′ E 202
Honaz, Turk. 37°44′ N, 29°15′ E 156
Honda, Col. 5°10′ N, 74°46′ W 136
Honda, Bahía 12°19′ N, 72°15′ W 136
Hondeklipbaai, S. Af. 30°20′ S, 17°16′ E 227
Hondo, Can. 55°3′ N, 114°3′ W 108
Hondo, Japan 32°27′ N, 130°10′ E 201
Hondo, N. Mex., U.S. 33°23′ N, 105°16′ W 92
Hondo, Tex., U.S. 29°20′ N, 99°8′ W 96
Honduras 14°39′ N, 87°51′ W 115
Hønefoss, Nor. 60°9′ N, 10°15′ E 152
Honey Grove, Tex., U.S. 33°34′ N, 95°55′ W 96
Honey Island, Tex., U.S. 30°23′ N, 94°27′ W 103
Hong Gai, Vietnam 20°58′ N, 107°5′ E 198
Hong Kong, China 22°15′ N, 114°10′ E 198
Hong Kong (Xianggang), island, China 21°55′ N, 114°15′ E 198
Hong'an, China 31°17′ N, 114°35′ E 198
Hongcheon, S. Korea 37°42′ N, 127°53′ E 200
Honghe, China 23°18′ N, 102°22′ E 202
Honghu, China 29°51′ N, 113°28′ E 198
Hongjiang, China 27°3′ N, 109°55′ E 198
Hongliuyuan, China 41°3′ N, 95°26′ E 188
Hongnong, S. Korea 35°24′ N, 126°34′ E 200
Hongor, Mongolia 45°47′ N, 112°43′ E 198
Hongqiling, China 42°56′ N, 126°24′ E 200
Hongseong, S. Korea 36°35′ N, 126°40′ E 200
Hongshi, China 42°58′ N, 127°7′ E 200
Hongtong, China 36°16′ N, 111°42′ E 198
Hongū, Japan 33°50′ N, 135°44′ E 201
Hongwŏn, N. Korea 40°1′ N, 127°58′ E 200
Hongze Hu, lake, China 32°58′ N, 117°53′ E 198
Honiara, Solomon Islands 9°29′ S, 159°10′ E 238
Honiara, Solomon Islands 9°0′ S, 160°0′ E 242
Honiton, U.K. 50°47′ N, 3°11′ W 162
Honkajoki, Fin. 61°58′ N, 22°13′ E 166
Honkilahti, Fin. 60°56′ N, 22°5′ E 166
Hönö, Sw. 57°41′ N, 11°39′ E 152
Honokōhau, Hawai'i, U.S. 19°39′ N, 156°2′ W 99
Honolulu, Hawai'i, U.S. 21°17′ N, 157°55′ W 99
Honshū, island, Japan 35°3′ N, 130°44′ E 190
Hontoria del Pinar, Sp. 41°51′ N, 3°10′ W 164
Hood, Calif., U.S. 38°21′ N, 121°32′ W 100
Hood Bay, Alas., U.S. 57°23′ N, 134°26′ W 108
Hood Canal 48°6′ N, 122°38′ W 100
Hood, Mount, Oreg., U.S. 45°20′ N, 121°48′ W 90
Hood Point, P.N.G. 10°21′ S, 146°34′ E 192
Hood River, Oreg., U.S. 45°41′ N, 121°33′ W 100
Hoodsport, Wash., U.S. 47°22′ N, 123°9′ W 100
Hoogeveen, Neth. 52°44′ N, 6°28′ E 163
Hoogezand-Sappemeer, Neth. 53°9′ N, 6°47′ E 163
Hook Head, Ire. 51°55′ N, 6°59′ W 150
Hooker, Okla., U.S. 36°50′ N, 101°14′ W 92
Hooksett, N.H., U.S. 43°5′ N, 71°28′ W 104
Hoonah, Alas., U.S. 58°1′ N, 135°23′ W 98
Hooper Bay, Alas., U.S. 61°39′ N, 166°2′ W 73
Hooper, Cape, Can. 68°22′ N, 66°48′ W 106
Hoopeston, Ill., U.S. 40°28′ N, 87°40′ W 102
Hooppole, Ill., U.S. 41°31′ N, 89°55′ W 102
Hoopstad, S. Af. 27°50′ S, 25°54′ E 227
Höör, Nor. 55°56′ N, 13°32′ E 152
Hoorn, Neth. 52°38′ N, 5°4′ E 163
Hoosick Falls, N.Y., U.S. 42°54′ N, 73°22′ W 104
Hoover, Ala., U.S. 33°24′ N, 86°50′ W 96
Hoover Dam, Nev., U.S. 35°55′ N, 114°54′ W 101
Höövör, Mongolia 48°27′ N, 113°23′ E 198
Hopa, Turk. 41°25′ N, 41°25′ E 195
Hope, Ariz., U.S. 33°42′ N, 113°43′ W 101
Hope, Ark., U.S. 33°38′ N, 93°36′ W 96
Hope, Can. 49°21′ N, 121°26′ W 100
Hope, Ind., U.S. 39°17′ N, 85°46′ W 102
Hope, N. Dak., U.S. 47°18′ N, 97°44′ W 90
Hope, Ben, peak, U.K. 58°23′ N, 4°43′ W 150
Hope, Cape, Can. 68°55′ N, 118°27′ W 98
Hope Mills, N.C., U.S. 34°58′ N, 78°58′ W 96
Hope Point, Myanmar 15°5′ N, 97°20′ E 202
Hope Town, Bahamas 26°31′ N, 76°58′ W 96
Hope Valley, R.I., U.S. 41°30′ N, 71°44′ W 104
Hopedale, Can. 55°24′ N, 60°19′ W 106
Hopedale, Ill., U.S. 40°24′ N, 89°25′ W 102
Hopelchén, Mex. 19°44′ N, 89°51′ W 115
Hopeless, Mount, Austral. 29°41′ S, 139°27′ E 230
Hopen, Nor. 63°26′ N, 8°0′ E 152
Hopetoun, Austral. 33°55′ S, 120°8′ E 231
Hopetown, S. Af. 29°41′ S, 24°4′ E 227
Hopewell, Va., U.S. 37°17′ N, 77°18′ W 96
Hopewell Culture National Historic Park, Ohio, U.S. 39°21′ N, 83°4′ W 102
Hopewell Furnace National Historic Site, Pa., U.S. 40°10′ N, 75°52′ W 94
Hopewell Islands, Hudson Bay 58°28′ N, 82°13′ W 106
Hopi Buttes, Ariz., U.S. 35°29′ N, 110°23′ W 92
Hopkins, Mich., U.S. 42°36′ N, 85°45′ W 102
Hopkins, Mount, Ariz., U.S. 31°39′ N, 110°57′ W 92
Hopkinsville, Ky., U.S. 36°51′ N, 87°29′ W 96
Hopkinton, N.H., U.S. 43°11′ N, 71°41′ W 104
Hopseidet, Nor. 70°46′ N, 27°42′ E 152
Hopsten, Ger. 52°23′ N, 7°36′ E 163
Hoque, Angola 14°41′ S, 13°49′ E 220
Hoquiam, Wash., U.S. 46°58′ N, 123°54′ W 100
Hora, Polonyna Runa, peak, Ukr. 48°46′ N, 22°44′ E 152
Horace, Kans., U.S. 38°29′ N, 101°49′ W 90
Horasan, Turk. 40°5′ N, 42°14′ E 195
Horcajo de Santiago, Sp. 39°50′ N, 2°60′ W 164
Horche, Sp. 40°33′ N, 3°4′ W 164
Horgos, Serb. and Mont. 46°8′ N, 19°58′ E 168
Hörh Uul, peak, Mongolia 42°38′ N, 105°16′ E 198
Horicon, Wis., U.S. 43°26′ N, 88°37′ W 102
Horinger, China 40°22′ N, 111°48′ E 198
Horizonte, Braz. 9°41′ S, 68°27′ W 137
Horki, Belarus 54°17′ N, 30°59′ E 154
Horlivka, Ukr. 48°18′ N, 38°1′ E 158
Ḩormak, Iran 29°57′ N, 60°55′ E 182
Hormoz, island, Iran 26°53′ N, 56°25′ E 180
Hormuz, Strait of 26°20′ N, 55°54′ E 196
Horn, Ben, peak, U.K. 58°1′ N, 4°9′ W 150
Horn, Cape see Hornos, Cabo de, Chile 55°49′ S, 66°59′ W 134
Horn Island, Austral. 10°30′ S, 141°38′ E 230
Horn Island, Miss., U.S. 30°9′ N, 88°44′ W 103
Horn (North Cape), Ice. 66°30′ N, 26°3′ W 246
Horn, river, Can. 61°33′ N, 117°58′ W 108
Horn, The, peak, Austral. 36°53′ S, 146°34′ E 230
Hornachos, Sp. 38°33′ N, 6°5′ W 164
Hornachuelos, Sp. 37°50′ N, 5°15′ W 164
Hornavan, lake, Nor. 65°37′ N, 17°40′ E 152
Hornbeck, La., U.S. 31°19′ N, 93°24′ W 103
Hornbrook, Calif., U.S. 41°54′ N, 122°34′ W 90
Horncastle, U.K. 53°12′ N, 0°7′ E 162
Hornell, N.Y., U.S. 42°18′ N, 77°41′ W 94
Hornepayne, Can. 49°14′ N, 84°47′ W 94
Hornito, Cerro, peak, Pan. 8°41′ N, 82°10′ W 115
Hornos, Cabo de (Horn, Cape), Chile 55°49′ S, 66°59′ W 134
Hornsea, U.K. 53°54′ N, 0°11′ E 162
Hörnsjö, Nor. 63°48′ N, 19°30′ E 154
Hornslandet, Sw. 61°35′ N, 17°29′ E 166
Hornsund 76°46′ N, 11°11′ E 160
Hornu, Belg. 50°25′ N, 3°48′ E 163
Horodnya, Ukr. 51°51′ N, 31°39′ E 158
Horodnytsya, Ukr. 50°49′ N, 27°18′ E 158
Horodok, Ukr. 50°40′ N, 26°7′ E 152
Horodok, Ukr. 49°8′ N, 26°32′ E 152
Horodyshche, Ukr. 49°21′ N, 31°31′ E 158
Horokhiv, Ukr. 50°29′ N, 24°45′ E 152
Hororata, N.Z. 43°33′ S, 171°58′ E 240
Horqin Youyi Zhongqi (Bayan Huxu), China 45°5′ N, 121°25′ E 198
Horqin Zuoyi Houqi, China 42°58′ N, 122°22′ E 198
Horqin Zuoyi Zhongqi, China 44°7′ N, 123°20′ E 198
Horqueta, Parag. 23°19′ S, 57°4′ W 132
Horse Lake, Can. 51°35′ N, 121°40′ W 90
Horse, river, Can. 56°23′ N, 112°4′ W 108
Horsehead Lake, N. Dak., U.S. 46°58′ N, 100°21′ W 90
Horsens, Den. 55°51′ N, 9°49′ E 150
Horseshoe Beach, Fla., U.S. 29°27′ N, 83°18′ W 105
Horseshoe Bend, Idaho, U.S. 43°55′ N, 116°11′ W 90
Horseshoe Cove 29°23′ N, 83°26′ W 105
Horsham, Austral. 36°40′ S, 142°10′ E 231
Horsham, U.K. 51°3′ N, 0°21′ E 162
Horsvær, islands, Norwegian Sea 65°24′ N, 10°32′ E 152
Hort, Hung. 47°41′ N, 19°48′ E 168
Horten, Nor. 59°25′ N, 10°28′ E 152
Horton, Mich., U.S. 42°8′ N, 84°31′ W 102
Horton Lake, Can. 67°30′ N, 124°4′ W 98
Horton, river, Can. 69°0′ N, 125°15′ W 98
Horwood Lake, Can. 47°58′ N, 82°55′ W 94
Hosa'ina, Eth. 7°29′ N, 37°51′ E 224
Hösbach, Ger. 50°0′ N, 9°12′ E 167
Hosdrug, India 12°15′ N, 75°8′ E 188
Hosenofu, spring, Lib. 23°39′ N, 20°58′ E 216
Hoshab, Pak. 26°0′ N, 63°56′ E 182
Hoshiarpur, India 31°32′ N, 75°58′ E 188
Höshööt, Mongolia 48°5′ N, 102°26′ E 198
Hosmer, S. Dak., U.S. 45°34′ N, 99°29′ W 90
Hosororo, Guyana 8°11′ N, 59°46′ W 130
Hososhima, Japan 32°25′ N, 131°39′ E 201
Hospet, India 15°17′ N, 76°23′ E 188
Hossa, Fin. 65°26′ N, 29°33′ E 152
Hosszúpályi, Hung. 47°23′ N, 21°43′ E 168
Hoste, Isla, island, Chile 55°53′ S, 70°2′ W 248
Hot, Thai. 18°7′ N, 98°33′ E 202
Hot Creek Range, Nev., U.S. 38°10′ N, 116°28′ W 90
Hot Springs, Ark., U.S. 34°29′ N, 93°5′ W 112
Hot Springs, S. Dak., U.S. 43°26′ N, 103°29′ W 90
Hot Springs National Park, Ark., U.S. 34°29′ N, 93°9′ W 96
Hot Springs Peak, Calif., U.S. 40°20′ N, 120°12′ W 90
Hot Springs Peak, Nev., U.S. 41°21′ N, 117°31′ W 90
Hotaka, Japan 36°20′ N, 137°53′ E 201
Hotan, China 37°7′ N, 79°51′ E 184
Hotan, river, China 38°20′ N, 80°51′ E 184
Hotchkiss, Can. 57°4′ N, 117°34′ W 108
Hotchkiss, Colo., U.S. 38°48′ N, 107°44′ W 90
Hotchkiss, river, Can. 57°19′ N, 118°33′ W 108
Hotevilla, Ariz., U.S. 35°54′ N, 110°41′ W 92
Hottah Lake, Can. 65°19′ N, 119°32′ W 106
Hotte, Massif de la, Haiti 18°34′ N, 74°30′ W 115
Hottentot Bay 26°20′ S, 14°43′ E 220
Hotton, Belg. 50°15′ N, 5°26′ E 167
Houayxay, Laos 20°18′ N, 100°27′ E 202
Houdan, Fr. 48°47′ N, 1°35′ E 163
Houghton Lake, Mich., U.S. 44°15′ N, 85°60′ W 81
Houghton, Point, Mich., U.S. 47°41′ N, 89°29′ W 94
Houlton, Me., U.S. 46°7′ N, 67°49′ W 82
Houma, China 35°37′ N, 111°21′ E 198
Houma, La., U.S. 29°34′ N, 90°44′ W 103
Houndé, Burkina Faso 11°30′ N, 3°33′ W 222
Housatonic, Mass., U.S. 42°15′ N, 73°23′ W 104
House Range, Utah, U.S. 39°16′ N, 113°32′ W 90
House, river, Can. 55°51′ N, 112°25′ W 108
Houston, Can. 54°24′ N, 126°40′ W 108
Houston, Minn., U.S. 43°44′ N, 91°35′ W 94
Houston, Mo., U.S. 37°19′ N, 91°56′ W 96
Houston, Tex., U.S. 29°44′ N, 95°22′ W 103
Houthalen, Belg. 51°2′ N, 5°22′ E 167
Houtman Abrolhos, islands, Indian Ocean 28°8′ S, 110°9′ E 230
Houtskär, Fin. 60°12′ N, 21°20′ E 166
Hovd (Dund-Us), Mongolia 48°2′ N, 91°40′ E 190
Hovden, Nor. 59°31′ N, 7°21′ E 152
Hövelhof, Ger. 51°49′ N, 8°38′ E 167
Hoven, S. Dak., U.S. 45°13′ N, 99°48′ W 90
Hovenweep National Monument, Utah, U.S. 37°17′ N, 109°15′ W 92
Hoverla, Hora, peak, Ukr. 48°7′ N, 24°24′ E 152
Hoveyzeh, Iran 31°26′ N, 48°5′ E 180
Hövsgöl, Mongolia 43°38′ N, 109°37′ E 198
Hövsgöl Nuur, lake, Mongolia 50°48′ N, 98°47′ E 190
Howard, Kans., U.S. 37°27′ N, 96°17′ W 90
Howard, S. Dak., U.S. 43°59′ N, 97°34′ W 90
Howard City, Mich., U.S. 43°23′ N, 85°28′ W 102
Howard Island, Austral. 12°4′ S, 135°3′ E 230
Howard Lake, Can. 62°45′ N, 107°53′ W 106
Howe, Ind., U.S. 41°43′ N, 85°25′ W 102
Howe, Okla., U.S. 34°55′ N, 94°39′ W 96
Howe, Tex., U.S. 33°29′ N, 96°36′ W 96
Howe, Cape, Austral. 38°13′ S, 149°59′ E 230
Howe, Mount, Antarctica 87°17′ S, 145°9′ W 248
Howe Sound 49°26′ N, 123°24′ W 100
Howell, Mich., U.S. 42°35′ N, 83°56′ W 102
Howells, Nebr., U.S. 41°42′ N, 97°1′ W 90
Howick, N.Z. 36°55′ S, 174°56′ E 240
Howland Island, United States 1°0′ N, 177°0′ W 238
Howland, Me., U.S. 45°13′ N, 68°40′ W 94
Howth, Ire. 53°22′ N, 6°4′ W 150
Hoxie, Ark., U.S. 36°2′ N, 90°59′ W 96
Hoxie, Kans., U.S. 39°20′ N, 100°27′ W 90
Höxter, Ger. 51°46′ N, 9°23′ E 167
Hoxud, China 42°13′ N, 86°58′ E 184
Høyanger, Nor. 61°13′ N, 6°4′ E 152
Hoyt Peak, Utah, U.S. 40°40′ N, 111°16′ W 90
Hozat, Turk. 39°5′ N, 39°11′ E 195
Hpa-an, Myanmar 16°54′ N, 97°39′ E 202
Hradec Králové, Czech Rep. 50°13′ N, 15°51′ E 152
Hrasnica, Bosn. and Herzg. 43°46′ N, 18°18′ E 168
Hrastnik, Slov. 46°8′ N, 15°5′ E 156
Hrazdan, Arm. 40°4′ N, 44°35′ E 195
Hrazdan, river, Arm. 40°16′ N, 44°31′ E 195

I

Ise Wan 34°39′ N, 136°34′ E 201
Iseo, It. 45°39′ N, 10°2′ E 167
Isère, Pointe, Fr. 5°48′ N, 53°50′ W 130
Isère, river, Fr. 44°59′ N, 5°2′ E 165
Isesaki, Japan 36°18′ N, 139°13′ E 201
Ise-Shima National Park, Japan 34°19′ N, 136°29′ E 201
Iset′, river, Russ. 56°7′ N, 64°54′ E 184
Iseyin, Nig. 8°1′ N, 3°37′ E 222
Isfahan see Eşfahān, Iran 32°40′ N, 51°38′ E 180
Isfara, Taj. 40°8′ N, 70°36′ E 197
Ishëm, Alban. 41°32′ N, 19°34′ E 168
Isheyevka, Russ. 54°25′ N, 48°23′ E 154
Ishigaki, Japan 24°16′ N, 124°9′ E 198
Ishigaki Shima, island, Japan 24°35′ N, 123°54′ E 198
Ishikawa, Japan 37°8′ N, 140°27′ E 201
Ishikawa, adm. division, Japan 36°16′ N, 136°18′ E 201
Ishim, Russ. 56°8′ N, 69°36′ E 184
Ishim, river, Russ. 56°1′ N, 70°27′ E 184
Ishimbay, Russ. 53°28′ N, 56°4′ E 154
Ishinomaki, Japan 38°33′ N, 141°5′ E 190
Ishioka, Japan 36°10′ N, 140°17′ E 201
Ishkuman, Pak. 36°30′ N, 73°47′ E 186
Ishpatina Ridge, Can. 47°20′ N, 80°48′ W 94
Ishpeming, Mich., U.S. 46°29′ N, 87°40′ W 110
Ishtixon, Uzb. 40°0′ N, 66°33′ E 197
Isiboro, river, Bol. 16°16′ S, 65°15′ W 137
Isiboro Sécure National Park, Bol. 16°2′ S, 66°19′ W 137
Isidora, Col. 6°7′ N, 68°31′ W 136
Işık Dağı, peak, Turk. 40°40′ N, 32°40′ E 156
Iskilveren, Turk. 37°23′ N, 42°58′ E 195
Isil′kul′, Russ. 54°52′ N, 71°18′ E 184
Isiolo, Kenya 0°18′ N, 37°36′ E 224
Isiro (Paulis), Dem. Rep. of the Congo 2°43′ N, 27°39′ E 224
İskenderun, Turk. 36°33′ N, 36°13′ E 180
İskilip, Turk. 40°44′ N, 34°28′ E 156
Iskitim, Russ. 54°39′ N, 83°17′ E 184
Iskrets, Bulg. 42°59′ N, 23°14′ E 168
Iskŭr, river, Bulg. 43°21′ N, 24°5′ E 156
Iskushuban, Somalia 10°11′ N, 50°15′ E 216
Iskut, river, Can. 57°9′ N, 130°24′ W 108
Isla de Lobos, oil field, Mex. 21°20′ N, 97°12′ W 114
Isla Guamblin National Park, site, Chile 44°51′ S, 75°19′ W 134
Isla Isabel National Park, Mex. 21°51′ N, 106°1′ W 112
Isla Mujeres, Mex. 21°17′ N, 86°50′ W 116
Isla Verde, Arg. 33°15′ S, 62°24′ W 139
Islamabad, Pak. 33°37′ N, 73°2′ E 186
Islamkot, Pak. 24°43′ N, 70°11′ E 186
Islamorada, Fla., U.S. 24°55′ N, 80°38′ W 105
Island Falls, Me., U.S. 46°0′ N, 68°16′ W 94
Island Grove, Fla., U.S. 29°27′ N, 82°8′ W 105
Island Lake, Can. 53°51′ N, 94°42′ W 108
Island Lake, Can. 53°58′ N, 95°7′ W 108
Island Lake, Minn., U.S. 47°48′ N, 94°31′ W 90
Island Park, Idaho, U.S. 44°25′ N, 111°22′ W 90
Isle of Hope, Ga., U.S. 31°58′ N, 81°4′ W 96
Isle Pierre, Can. 53°56′ N, 123°16′ W 108
Isle, river, Fr. 45°30′ N, 1°3′ E 165
Isleton, Calif., U.S. 38°9′ N, 121°37′ W 100
Ismâ′ilîya, Egypt 30°35′ N, 32°15′ E 194
Ismoili Somoni, Qullai (Communism Peak), Taj. 39°3′ N, 72°1′ E 197
Isna, Egypt 25°16′ N, 32°29′ E 182
Isoanala, Madagascar 23°48′ S, 45°46′ E 220
Isojoki, Fin. 62°6′ N, 21°55′ E 152
Isoka, Zambia 10°11′ S, 32°36′ E 224
Isola, Miss., U.S. 33°14′ N, 90°36′ W 103
Isola del Cantone, It. 44°39′ N, 8°57′ E 167
Isola della Scala, It. 45°16′ N, 11°0′ E 167
Isola delle Correnti, Capo, It. 36°32′ N, 15°5′ E 156
Isola Peak, Can. 50°6′ N, 114°37′ W 90
Isparta, Turk. 37°44′ N, 30°32′ E 156
Ispica, It. 36°46′ N, 14°53′ E 156
Ispir, Turk. 40°29′ N, 41°0′ E 195
Ispra, It. 45°49′ N, 8°36′ E 167
Israel 31°0′ N, 34°41′ E 194
Israelite Bay 33°48′ S, 122°33′ E 230
Isratu, island, Eritrea 16°21′ N, 39°48′ E 182
Issa, river, Russ. 56°18′ N, 28°20′ E 166
Issano, Guyana 5°46′ N, 59°30′ W 130
Issel, river, Ger. 51°47′ N, 6°29′ E 167
Issia, Côte d′Ivoire 6°23′ N, 6°35′ W 222
Issoudun, Fr. 46°56′ N, 1°59′ E 150
Issus, battle, Turk. 36°53′ N, 36°4′ E 156
Istállósko, peak, Hung. 48°2′ N, 20°22′ E 168
İstanbul (Constantinople), Turk. 41°1′ N, 28°55′ E 156
Istaravshan (Üroteppa), Taj. 39°53′ N, 69°0′ E 197
Istmina, Col. 5°10′ N, 76°42′ W 136
Isto, Mount, Alas., U.S. 69°5′ N, 144°8′ W 98
Istok, Serb. and Mont. 42°46′ N, 20°29′ E 168
Istokpoga, Lake, Fla., U.S. 27°24′ N, 81°25′ W 105
Istres, Fr. 43°29′ N, 4°58′ E 150
Istria, Croatia 45°16′ N, 13°33′ E 167
Isulan, Philippines 6°37′ N, 124°37′ E 203
Isyangulovo, Russ. 52°12′ N, 56°27′ E 154
Itá, Parag. 25°31′ S, 57°21′ W 132
Itabaiana, Braz. 10°37′ S, 37°22′ W 132
Itabaianinha, Braz. 11°17′ S, 37°47′ W 132
Itabapoana, Braz. 21°20′ S, 41°1′ W 138
Itaberaba, Braz. 12°33′ S, 40°21′ W 132
Itaberaí, Braz. 16°6′ S, 49°49′ W 138
Itabira, Braz. 19°39′ S, 43°13′ W 138
Itabirito, Braz. 20°21′ S, 43°48′ W 138
Itabuna, Braz. 14°27′ S, 39°36′ W 123
Itacaiúnas, river, Braz. 5°58′ S, 50°40′ W 130
Itacajá, Braz. 8°22′ S, 47°46′ W 130
Itacarambi, Braz. 15°8′ S, 44°9′ W 138
Itacoatiara, Braz. 3°9′ S, 58°33′ W 130
Itaeté, Braz. 13°1′ S, 41°1′ W 138
Itaguari, river, Braz. 14°36′ S, 45°16′ W 138
Itagüí, Col. 6°11′ N, 75°41′ W 136
Itahuania, Peru 12°38′ S, 71°9′ W 137
Itaí, Braz. 23°25′ S, 49°8′ W 138
Itaituba, Braz. 4°15′ S, 56°1′ W 130
Itajaí, Braz. 26°56′ S, 48°40′ W 138
Itajimirim, Braz. 16°5′ S, 39°36′ W 138
Itajubá, Braz. 22°24′ S, 45°30′ W 138
Itaka, Tanzania 8°54′ S, 32°48′ E 224
Italia, Monte, peak, Chile 54°48′ S, 69°21′ W 134
Italy 42°58′ N, 11°46′ E 156
Itamaraju, Braz. 17°11′ S, 39°33′ W 138
Itamarandiba, Braz. 17°53′ S, 42°55′ W 138
Itambacuri, Braz. 18°3′ S, 41°42′ W 138
Itambé, Braz. 15°18′ S, 40°40′ W 138
Itambé, Pico de, peak, Braz. 18°27′ S, 43°24′ W 138
Itanagar, India 27°7′ N, 93°46′ E 188
Itanhaém, Braz. 24°11′ S, 46°47′ W 138
Itanhauã, river, Braz. 5°2′ S, 64°50′ W 130
Itanhém, Braz. 17°9′ S, 40°20′ W 138
Itany, river, Suriname 2°48′ N, 54°14′ W 130
Itapaci, Braz. 14°60′ S, 49°37′ W 138
Itapagipe, Braz. 19°56′ S, 49°22′ W 138
Itapaiuna, river, Braz. 7°28′ S, 63°50′ W 130
Itaparica, Ilha de, island, Braz. 13°16′ S, 40°1′ W 132
Itapebi, Braz. 15°58′ S, 39°33′ W 138
Itapecerica, Braz. 20°31′ S, 45°8′ W 138
Itapecuru Mirim, Braz. 3°25′ S, 44°22′ W 132
Itapemirim, Braz. 21°5′ S, 40°52′ W 138
Itaperina, Pointe, Madagascar 25°18′ S, 47°14′ E 220
Itaperuna, Braz. 21°13′ S, 41°53′ W 138
Itapetinga, Braz. 15°18′ S, 40°18′ W 138
Itapetininga, Braz. 23°35′ S, 48°5′ W 138
Itapeva, Braz. 23°58′ S, 48°53′ W 138
Itapiranga, Braz. 27°9′ S, 53°44′ W 139
Itápolis, Braz. 21°34′ S, 48°49′ W 138
Itaporanga, Braz. 23°43′ S, 49°31′ W 138
Itapuranga, Braz. 15°35′ S, 49°58′ W 138
Itaqui, Braz. 29°11′ S, 56°36′ W 139
Itararé, Braz. 24°7′ S, 49°19′ W 138
Itararé, river, Braz. 24°16′ S, 49°13′ W 138
Itarsi, India 22°37′ N, 77°46′ E 197
Itarumã, Braz. 18°44′ S, 51°29′ W 138
Itasca, Tex., U.S. 32°8′ N, 97°9′ W 92
Itasca, Lake, Minn., U.S. 47°9′ N, 96°14′ W 82
Itatá, river, Braz. 4°13′ S, 52°7′ W 132
Itatí, Arg. 27°17′ S, 58°13′ W 139
Itatupã, Braz. 0°36′ N, 51°14′ W 130
Itaú, Bol. 21°41′ S, 63°55′ W 137
Itaúba, Braz. 10°55′ S, 55°8′ W 123
Itaúna, Braz. 20°5′ S, 44°34′ W 138
Itaúna, Braz. 2°59′ S, 66°5′ W 136
Itaúnas, Braz. 18°24′ S, 39°44′ W 138
Itbayat, island, Philippines 20°44′ N, 121°21′ E 198
Itende, Tanzania 6°44′ S, 34°23′ E 224
Itezhi-Tezhi, Lake, Zambia 15°55′ S, 25°14′ E 224
Ithaca, Mich., U.S. 43°16′ N, 84°37′ W 102
Ithaca, N.Y., U.S. 42°26′ N, 76°31′ W 94
Itigi, Tanzania 5°39′ S, 34°29′ E 224
Itimbiri, river, Dem. Rep. of the Congo 2°20′ N, 23°1′ E 218
Itinga, Braz. 16°36′ S, 41°50′ W 138
Itiquines, Col. 0°38′ N, 73°15′ W 136
Itiquira, Braz. 17°12′ S, 54°9′ W 132
Itiquira, river, Braz. 17°15′ S, 56°29′ W 132
Itiruçu, Braz. 13°30′ S, 40°10′ W 138
Itiúba, Serra de, Braz. 10°6′ S, 40°31′ W 132
Itō, Japan 34°57′ N, 139°5′ E 201
Itobo, Tanzania 4°12′ S, 33°1′ E 224
Itoigawa, Japan 37°2′ N, 137°51′ E 201
Itoko, Dem. Rep. of the Congo 0°60′ N, 21°46′ E 218
Iton, river, Fr. 49°7′ N, 1°7′ E 163
Itonamas, river, Bol. 12°30′ S, 64°25′ W 137
Itta Bena, Miss., U.S. 33°28′ N, 90°20′ W 103
Ittoqqortoormiit (Scoresbysund), Den. 70°26′ N, 21°53′ W 246
Itu, Braz. 23°17′ S, 47°21′ W 138
Itu, river, Braz. 29°20′ S, 55°23′ W 139
Ituaçu, Braz. 13°51′ S, 41°19′ W 138
Ituí, river, Braz. 4°59′ S, 70°47′ W 130
Ituiutaba, Braz. 19°1′ S, 49°31′ W 138
Itula, Dem. Rep. of the Congo 3°32′ S, 27°49′ E 224
Itumbiara, Braz. 18°28′ S, 49°15′ W 138
Ituna, Can. 51°9′ N, 103°31′ W 90
Ituni, Guyana 5°24′ N, 58°18′ W 130
Itupiranga, Braz. 5°12′ S, 49°19′ W 130
Iturama, Braz. 19°43′ S, 50°14′ W 138
Iturbe, Arg. 22°60′ S, 65°21′ W 137
Iturbe, Parag. 26°2′ S, 56°28′ W 139
Iturbide, Mex. 24°42′ N, 99°54′ W 114
Ituri, river, Dem. Rep. of the Congo 1°41′ N, 27°21′ E 224
Iturup, island, Russ. 44°16′ N, 147°11′ E 190
Ituverava, Braz. 20°21′ S, 47°50′ W 138
Ituxi, river, Braz. 7°58′ S, 65°3′ W 130
Ituzaingó, Arg. 27°37′ S, 56°40′ W 139
Itzehoe, Ger. 53°55′ N, 9°31′ E 150
Iuka, Miss., U.S. 34°47′ N, 88°12′ W 96
Iul′tin, Russ. 67°49′ N, 178°46′ W 98
Iulúti, Mozambique 15°53′ S, 39°2′ E 224
Iúna, Braz. 20°22′ S, 41°35′ W 138
Iutica, Braz. 1°4′ N, 69°31′ W 136
Ivád, Hung. 48°1′ N, 20°4′ E 168
Ivaí, river, Braz. 23°19′ S, 53°24′ W 138
Ivaipora, Braz. 24°16′ S, 51°43′ W 138
Ivalo, Fin. 68°37′ N, 27°33′ E 160
Ivan Gorod, Russ. 59°21′ N, 28°12′ E 166
Ivan Sedlo, Bosn. and Herzg. 43°46′ N, 18°2′ E 168
Ivanava, Belarus 52°8′ N, 25°32′ E 152
Ivanchina, Russ. 60°3′ N, 54°17′ E 154
Ivanec, Croatia 46°13′ N, 16°8′ E 168
Ivangrad, Serb. and Mont. 42°50′ N, 19°50′ E 168
Ivanhoe, Austral. 32°53′ S, 144°17′ E 231
Ivanhoe, Calif., U.S. 36°23′ N, 119°14′ W 100
Ivanhoe Lake, Can. 60°23′ N, 107°8′ W 108
Ivanhoe, river, Can. 48°19′ N, 82°29′ W 110
Ivanić Grad, Croatia 45°41′ N, 16°24′ E 168
Ivanjica, Serb. and Mont. 43°34′ N, 20°13′ E 168
Ivanjska, Bosn. and Herzg. 44°55′ N, 17°4′ E 168
Ivankovo, Croatia 45°16′ N, 18°39′ E 168
Ivano-Frankivs′k, Ukr. 48°53′ N, 24°41′ E 152
Ivanovo, Russ. 57°0′ N, 40°58′ E 154
Ivanovo, adm. division, Russ. 56°50′ N, 40°5′ E 154
Ivanpah, Calif., U.S. 35°19′ N, 115°20′ W 101
Ivanteyevka, Russ. 52°15′ N, 49°8′ E 158
Ivatsevichy, Belarus 52°43′ N, 25°22′ E 152
Ivaylovgrad, Bulg. 41°31′ N, 26°6′ E 156
Ivdel′, Russ. 60°40′ N, 60°23′ E 154
Ivi, Cap, Alg. 36°6′ N, 0°8′ E 164
Ivinheima, Braz. 22°12′ S, 53°33′ W 138
Iviza see Ibiza, island, Sp. 39°1′ N, 6°356′ W 214
Ivo, Bol. 20°29′ S, 63°28′ W 137
Ivohibe, Madagascar 22°29′ S, 46°53′ E 220
Ivón, Bol. 11°10′ S, 66°9′ W 137
Ivory Coast, region, Africa 5°58′ N, 5°7′ W 222
Ivory Coast see Côte d′Ivoire 7°16′ N, 7°29′ W 214
Ivoryton, Conn., U.S. 41°20′ N, 72°27′ W 104
Ivrea, It. 45°29′ N, 7°52′ E 167
Ivrognes, Pointe aux, Can. 49°42′ N, 65°31′ W 111
Ivujivik, Can. 62°22′ N, 78°2′ W 106
Ivyanyets, Belarus 53°52′ N, 26°44′ E 166
Ivydale, W. Va., U.S. 38°32′ N, 81°3′ W 102
Iwaki, Japan 36°58′ N, 140°52′ E 201
Iwanuma, Japan 38°7′ N, 140°51′ E 201
Iwembere Steppe, Tanzania 4°26′ S, 33°20′ E 224
Iwo, Nig. 7°42′ N, 4°11′ E 222
Iwŏn, N. Korea 40°20′ N, 128°39′ E 200
Iwye, Belarus 53°55′ N, 25°45′ E 166
Ixhuatán, Mex. 16°21′ N, 94°30′ W 112
Ixiamas, Bol. 13°47′ S, 68°8′ W 137
Ixopo, S. Af. 30°11′ S, 30°3′ E 227
Ixpalino, Mex. 23°52′ N, 106°39′ W 114
Ixtapa, Mex. 17°39′ N, 101°36′ W 114
Ixtapa, Punta, Mex. 17°29′ N, 101°52′ W 114
Ixtapan del Oro, Mex. 19°14′ N, 100°16′ W 114
Ixtlán, Mex. 21°1′ N, 104°22′ W 114
Ixtoc, oil field, Mex. 19°36′ N, 92°21′ W 115
′Iyal Bakhit, Sudan 13°25′ N, 28°43′ E 226
Iyo, Japan 33°44′ N, 132°42′ E 201
Iyo Nada 33°29′ N, 131°49′ E 201
Iyomishima, Japan 33°57′ N, 133°31′ E 201
Izabal, Lago de, lake, Guatemala 15°22′ N, 89°53′ W 115
Izad Khvāst, Iran 31°31′ N, 52°5′ E 180
Izamal, Mex. 20°55′ N, 89°2′ W 116
Izapa, ruin(s), Mex. 14°53′ N, 92°17′ W 115
Izberbash, Russ. 42°31′ N, 47°52′ E 195
Izbica, Pol. 50°53′ N, 23°9′ E 152
Izdeshkovo, Russ. 55°7′ N, 33°41′ E 154
Izegem, Belg. 50°54′ N, 3°12′ E 163
Izhevsk, Russ. 56°48′ N, 53°15′ E 154
Izhma, Russ. 64°59′ N, 53°53′ E 154
Izhma, river, Russ. 64°25′ N, 53°38′ E 154
Izmayil, Ukr. 45°21′ N, 28°51′ E 156
İzmir (Smyrna), Turk. 38°24′ N, 27°8′ E 156
İzmit see Kocaeli, Turk. 40°47′ N, 29°46′ E 180
Iznalloz, Sp. 37°24′ N, 3°32′ W 164
İznik, Turk. 40°25′ N, 29°43′ E 156
Izobil′nyy, Russ. 45°22′ N, 41°37′ E 158
Izola, Slov. 45°32′ N, 13°39′ E 167
Izra′, Syr. 32°52′ N, 36°15′ E 194
Izsák, Hung. 46°48′ N, 19°22′ E 168
Izu Trench, North Pacific Ocean 30°26′ N, 142°40′ E 252
Izuhara, Japan 34°12′ N, 129°17′ E 201
Izumi, Japan 32°4′ N, 130°22′ E 201
Izvor, Bulg. 42°26′ N, 22°53′ E 168
Izvor, Maced. 41°33′ N, 21°41′ E 168
Izvori, Serb. and Mont. 42°36′ N, 18°45′ E 168
Izyaslav, Ukr. 50°5′ N, 26°49′ E 152
Izyum, Ukr. 49°14′ N, 37°20′ E 158

J

Jaab Lake, Can. 51°6′ N, 83°27′ W 110
Jaala, Fin. 61°3′ N, 26°29′ E 166
Jaalanka, Fin. 64°33′ N, 27°7′ E 152
Jabal os Saraj, Afghan. 35°7′ N, 69°16′ E 186
Jabal Zuqar, Jazīrat, island, Yemen 14°5′ N, 42°31′ E 182
Jabalan Nuşayrīyah, Syr. 35°39′ N, 36°8′ E 194
Jabalar Ruwāq, Syr. 33°42′ N, 36°57′ E 194
Jabalón, river, Sp. 38°46′ N, 3°44′ W 164
Jabalpur, India 23°8′ N, 79°57′ E 197
Jābir, Jordan 32°30′ N, 36°12′ E 194
Jabiru, Austral. 12°38′ S, 132°52′ E 238
Jablah, Syr. 35°21′ N, 35°55′ E 194
Jablanica, Bosn. and Herzg. 43°39′ N, 17°43′ E 168
Jablanica, Maced. 41°26′ N, 20°21′ E 168
Jabłonowo, Pol. 53°23′ N, 19°10′ E 152
Jablunkovský Průsmyk, pass, Slovakia 49°29′ N, 18°46′ E 152
Jaboticabal, Braz. 21°13′ S, 48°21′ W 138
Jäbrayyl, Azerb. 39°24′ N, 47°1′ E 195
Jabukovac, Serb. and Mont. 44°20′ N, 22°23′ E 168
Jabung, Tanjung, Indonesia 1°15′ S, 104°23′ E 196
Jaca, Sp. 42°33′ N, 0°34′ E 164
Jacareacanga, Braz. 6°13′ S, 57°40′ W 123
Jacareí, Braz. 23°17′ S, 45°55′ W 138
Jacarèzinho, Braz. 23°10′ S, 49°58′ W 138
Jacinto, Braz. 16°10′ S, 40°20′ W 138
Jaciparaná, Braz. 9°19′ S, 64°25′ W 137
Jackfish, river, Can. 59°31′ N, 113°37′ W 108
Jackhead Harbour, Can. 51°51′ N, 97°19′ W 108
Jackman, Me., U.S. 45°38′ N, 70°14′ W 82
Jackpot, Nev., U.S. 41°59′ N, 114°40′ W 90
Jacks Mountain, Pa., U.S. 40°46′ N, 77°40′ W 94
Jacks Peak, Utah, U.S. 38°58′ N, 112°11′ W 90
Jacksboro, Tex., U.S. 33°11′ N, 98°10′ W 92
Jackson, Ala., U.S. 31°30′ N, 87°54′ W 103
Jackson, Calif., U.S. 38°21′ N, 120°47′ W 100
Jackson, Ga., U.S. 33°16′ N, 83°58′ W 96
Jackson, La., U.S. 30°49′ N, 91°13′ W 103
Jackson, Mich., U.S. 42°14′ N, 84°26′ W 102
Jackson, Minn., U.S. 43°35′ N, 95°1′ W 94
Jackson, Miss., U.S. 32°16′ N, 90°15′ W 103
Jackson, Mo., U.S. 37°23′ N, 89°40′ W 94
Jackson, N.H., U.S. 44°8′ N, 71°12′ W 104
Jackson, Ohio, U.S. 39°2′ N, 82°38′ W 102
Jackson, S.C., U.S. 33°18′ N, 81°48′ W 96
Jackson, Tenn., U.S. 35°36′ N, 88°48′ W 96
Jackson Bay, N.Z. 44°1′ S, 168°37′ E 240
Jackson Field, oil field, Austral. 27°37′ S, 142°0′ E 230
Jackson Head, N.Z. 43°58′ S, 168°36′ E 240
Jackson, Mount, Antarctica 71°28′ S, 63°49′ W 248
Jackson Mountains, Nev., U.S. 41°28′ N, 118°41′ W 90
Jackson, Ostrov, island, Russ. 81°23′ N, 53°33′ E 160
Jacksonville, Ark., U.S. 34°51′ N, 92°8′ W 96
Jacksonville, Fla., U.S. 30°20′ N, 81°40′ W 96
Jacksonville, N.C., U.S. 34°45′ N, 77°26′ W 96
Jacksonville, Oreg., U.S. 42°18′ N, 122°59′ W 90
Jacksonville, Tex., U.S. 31°56′ N, 95°16′ W 103
Jacksonville Beach, Fla., U.S. 30°16′ N, 81°24′ W 96
Jäckvik, Nor. 66°22′ N, 16°56′ E 152
Jacmel, Haiti 18°15′ N, 72°31′ W 116
Jacob Lake, Ariz., U.S. 36°42′ N, 112°12′ W 92
Jacobabad, Pak. 28°17′ N, 68°29′ E 186
Jacobina, Braz. 11°11′ S, 40°32′ W 132
Jacona, Mex. 19°57′ N, 102°18′ W 114
Jacques-Cartier, Mont, peak, Can. 48°57′ N, 66°2′ W 94
Jacquet River, Can. 47°54′ N, 66°2′ W 94
Jacuí, Braz. 21°2′ S, 46°45′ W 138
Jacumba, Calif., U.S. 32°37′ N, 116°11′ W 101
Jacupiranga, Braz. 24°42′ S, 48°2′ W 138
J.A.D. Jensen Nunatakker, peak, Den. 62°50′ N, 49°7′ W 106
Jada, Nig. 8°45′ N, 12°8′ E 218
Jaddi, Ras, Pak. 25°2′ N, 63°0′ E 182
Jade, Ger. 53°20′ N, 8°15′ E 163
Jadraque, Sp. 40°55′ N, 2°56′ W 164
Jādū, Lib. 31°59′ N, 12°1′ E 216
Jaén, Sp. 37°46′ N, 3°48′ W 164
Jaffna, Sri Lanka 9°33′ N, 80°8′ E 173
Jagadhri, India 30°12′ N, 77°20′ E 197
Jagdalpur, India 19°5′ N, 82°1′ E 188
Jagersfontein, S. Af. 29°47′ S, 25°26′ E 227
Jāghir Bāzār, Syr. 36°52′ N, 40°56′ E 195
Jaghjagh, river, Syr. 36°35′ N, 41°11′ E 195
Jagodina, Serb. and Mont. 43°58′ N, 21°14′ E 168
Jaguaquara, Braz. 13°33′ S, 39°59′ W 138
Jaguarão, Braz. 32°31′ S, 53°24′ W 139
Jaguari, river, Braz. 29°45′ S, 54°40′ W 134
Jaguariaíva, Braz. 24°18′ S, 49°43′ W 138
Jahanabad, India 25°11′ N, 84°59′ E 197
Jahorina, peak, Bosn. and Herzg. 43°42′ N, 18°30′ E 168
Jahrom, Iran 28°33′ N, 53°34′ E 196
Jaicós, Braz. 7°22′ S, 41°8′ W 132
Jaigarh, India 17°17′ N, 73°13′ E 188
Jailolo, Indonesia 1°4′ N, 127°25′ E 192
Jaina, ruin(s), Mex. 20°11′ N, 90°39′ W 115
Jaipur, India 26°54′ N, 75°49′ E 186
Jaisalmer, India 26°55′ N, 70°58′ E 186
Jajarkot, Nepal 28°41′ N, 82°11′ E 197
Jājarm, Iran 36°56′ N, 56°24′ E 180
Jajce, Bosn. and Herzg. 44°21′ N, 17°15′ E 168
Jajiri, Niger 13°38′ N, 11°26′ E 222
Jajpur Road, India 20°56′ N, 86°6′ E 188
Ják, Hung. 47°8′ N, 16°34′ E 168
Jakar, Bhutan 27°31′ N, 90°42′ E 197
Jakarta, Indonesia 6°22′ S, 106°14′ E 238
Jakes Corner, Can. 60°21′ N, 134°1′ W 98
Jákfa, Hung. 47°18′ N, 16°58′ E 168
Jakhal, India 29°47′ N, 75°49′ E 197
Jakhau, India 23°13′ N, 68°43′ E 186
Jakobshavn see Ilulissat, Den. 69°11′ N, 50°60′ W 106
Jakobstad (Pietarsaari), Fin. 63°39′ N, 22°39′ E 152
Jakupica, Maced. 41°43′ N, 21°22′ E 168
Jal, N. Mex., U.S. 32°6′ N, 103°12′ W 92
Jalaaqsi, Somalia 3°23′ N, 45°36′ E 218
Jalaid Qi (Inder), China 46°41′ N, 122°53′ E 198
Jalālābād, Afghan. 34°26′ N, 70°30′ E 186
Jalal-Abad, Kyrg. 40°55′ N, 72°59′ E 197
Jalán, river, Hond. 14°17′ N, 86°43′ W 115
Jalapa, Guatemala 14°38′ N, 89°60′ W 115
Jalapa, Mex. 17°43′ N, 92°49′ W 115
Jalasjärvi, Fin. 62°29′ N, 22°45′ E 152
Jalcocotán, Mex. 21°29′ N, 105°8′ W 114
Jales, Braz. 20°12′ S, 50°36′ W 138
Jalesar, India 27°25′ N, 78°19′ E 197
Jaleswar, India 21°49′ N, 87°13′ E 197
Jalgaon, India 21°1′ N, 75°33′ E 188
Jalingo, Nig. 8°51′ N, 11°20′ E 222
Jalisco, Mex. 21°26′ N, 104°53′ W 114
Jalisco, adm. division, Mex. 20°33′ N, 104°13′ W 114
Jalitah Island, Tun. 37°31′ N, 7°53′ E 214
Jalkot, Pak. 35°17′ N, 73°23′ E 186
Jałowka, Pol. 53°1′ N, 23°54′ E 154
Jalna, India 19°50′ N, 75°52′ E 188
Jalor, India 25°19′ N, 72°38′ E 186
Jalostotitlán, Mex. 21°10′ N, 102°29′ W 114
Jalpa, Mex. 18°10′ N, 93°5′ W 112
Jalpa, Mex. 21°37′ N, 102°60′ W 114
Jalpaiguri, India 26°26′ N, 88°40′ E 197
Jalpan, Mex. 21°10′ N, 99°33′ W 114
Jáltipan, Mex. 17°57′ N, 94°44′ W 114
Jālū, Lib. 29°1′ N, 21°30′ E 216
Jaluit Atoll, Marshall Islands 6°0′ N, 170°0′ E 242
Jam, Iran 27°50′ N, 52°22′ E 196
Jamaame, Somalia 2°119′ N, 42°46′ E 218
Jamaica 18°0′ N, 78°0′ W 118
Jämaja, Est. 58°0′ N, 22°3′ E 166
Jamalpur, Bangladesh 24°53′ N, 89°54′ E 197
Jaman Pass, Taj. 37°25′ N, 74°41′ E 197
Jamanari, river, Braz. 2°26′ S, 69°13′ W 136
Jamari, river, Braz. 8°52′ S, 63°30′ W 130
Jambes, Belg. 50°27′ N, 4°53′ E 167
Jambi, Indonesia 1°41′ S, 103°33′ E 192
Jambur, oil field, Iraq 35°1′ N, 44°31′ E 180
Jambusar, India 22°3′ N, 72°48′ E 186
James Bay 52°12′ N, 81°23′ W 110
James City, Pa., U.S. 41°36′ N, 78°50′ W 94
James Lake, Can. 57°15′ N, 100°15′ W 108
James, river, Can. 51°47′ N, 115°9′ W 90
James, river, N. Dak., U.S. 46°39′ N, 98°34′ W 90
James, river, S. Dak., U.S. 45°3′ N, 98°16′ W 94
James, river, Va., U.S. 37°54′ N, 78°33′ W 94
James Ross Island, Antarctica 64°13′ S, 57°4′ W 134
Jameson Land, Den. 70°56′ N, 23°8′ W 246
Jamesport, N.Y., U.S. 40°56′ N, 72°35′ W 104
Jamestown, Calif., U.S. 37°56′ N, 120°26′ W 100
Jamestown, Ind., U.S. 39°55′ N, 86°38′ W 102
Jamestown, N.Y., U.S. 42°6′ N, 79°15′ W 94
Jamestown, N.C., U.S. 35°59′ N, 79°57′ W 96
Jamestown, R.I., U.S. 41°29′ N, 71°23′ W 104
Jamestown, S. Af. 31°7′ S, 26°47′ E 227
Jämijärvi, Fin. 61°48′ N, 22°40′ E 166
Jamkhandi, India 16°30′ N, 75°16′ E 188
Jammu, India 32°44′ N, 74°51′ E 186
Jammu and Kashmir, adm. division, India 33°37′ N, 74°7′ E 188
Jamnagar, India 22°26′ N, 70°4′ E 186
Jamno, Pol. 54°14′ N, 16°11′ E 152
Jampur, Pak. 29°33′ N, 70°35′ E 186
Jämsä, Fin. 61°51′ N, 25°10′ E 166
Jämsänkoski, Fin. 61°54′ N, 25°8′ E 166
Jamshedpur, India 22°46′ N, 86°13′ E 197
Jämtlands Sikås, Nor. 63°37′ N, 15°13′ E 152
Jamui, India 24°54′ N, 86°12′ E 197
Jan Mayen, Nor. 71°0′ N, 8°0′ W 246
Jan Mayen Fracture Zone, Norwegian Sea 70°55′ N, 6°54′ W 255
Jan Mayen Ridge, Norwegian Sea 69°26′ N, 8°15′ W 255
Jana, oil field, Saudi Arabia 27°23′ N, 49°48′ E 196
Janakkala, Fin. 60°53′ N, 24°33′ E 166
Janakpur, Nepal 26°40′ N, 85°55′ E 197
Janaúba, Braz. 15°47′ S, 43°20′ W 138
Janaucu, Ilha, island, Braz. 0°27′ N, 51°15′ W 130
Jandaq, Iran 34°2′ N, 54°28′ E 180
Janesville, Wis., U.S. 42°42′ N, 88°60′ W 102
Jangamo, Mozambique 24°4′ S, 35°18′ E 227
Janghang, S. Korea 36°1′ N, 126°44′ E 200
Jangheung, S. Korea 34°38′ N, 126°54′ E 200
Janghowon, S. Korea 37°6′ N, 127°37′ E 200
Jangpyeong, S. Korea 37°35′ N, 128°24′ E 200
Jangseong, S. Korea 35°17′ N, 126°51′ E 200
Janikowo, Pol. 52°45′ N, 18°7′ E 152
Janīn, West Bank 32°27′ N, 35°18′ E 194
Janja, Bosn. and Herzg. 44°40′ N, 19°16′ E 168
Janjina, Croatia 42°54′ N, 17°25′ E 168
Jannaale, Somalia 1°45′ N, 44°41′ E 218
Janos, Mex. 30°51′ N, 108°10′ W 92
Jánossomorja, Hung. 47°46′ N, 17°8′ E 168
Jansen, Colo., U.S. 37°10′ N, 104°33′ W 92
Jansenville, S. Af. 32°54′ S, 24°44′ E 227
Januária, Braz. 15°27′ S, 44°26′ W 138
Janville, Fr. 48°11′ N, 1°52′ E 163
Jaora, India 23°37′ N, 75°9′ E 188
Japan 36°0′ N, 137°35′ E 190
Japan, Sea of (East Sea) 39°9′ N, 128°12′ E 200
Japan Trench, North Pacific Ocean 35°43′ N, 143°30′ E 252
Japurá, Braz. 1°52′ S, 66°41′ W 136
Jaqué, Pan. 7°30′ N, 78°9′ W 136
Jaquí, Peru 15°31′ S, 74°27′ W 137
Jarābulus, Syr. 36°47′ N, 37°58′ E 180
Jarafuel, Sp. 39°8′ N, 1°5′ W 164
Jaraguá, Braz. 15°49′ S, 49°23′ W 138
Jaraguá do Sul, Braz. 26°29′ S, 49°3′ W 138
Jaraicejo, Sp. 39°39′ N, 5°49′ W 150
Jarales, N. Mex., U.S. 34°36′ N, 106°46′ W 92
Jaramillo, Arg. 47°9′ S, 67°8′ W 134
Jarash (Gerasa), Jordan 32°17′ N, 35°53′ E 194
Jarauçu, river, Braz. 2°47′ S, 53°6′ W 130
Jaray, Sp. 41°41′ N, 2°8′ W 164
Jarbidge, Nev., U.S. 41°53′ N, 115°25′ W 90
Jarbidge, river, Idaho, U.S. 42°24′ N, 115°39′ W 90
Järbo, Nor. 60°41′ N, 16°35′ E 152
Jardim, Braz. 21°30′ S, 56°5′ W 132
Jardim do Seridó, Braz. 6°38′ S, 36°47′ W 132
Jardine River National Park, Austral. 11°20′ S, 142°18′ E 238
Jardinésia, Braz. 19°17′ S, 48°44′ W 138
Jæren, region, Europe 58°33′ N, 5°32′ E 150
Jargalant, Mongolia 46°57′ N, 115°15′ E 198
Jari, river, Braz. 1°49′ N, 54°28′ W 130
Jari, river, Braz. 0°15′ N, 53°7′ W 130
Jarkovac, Serb. and Mont. 45°16′ N, 20°46′ E 168
Jarny, Fr. 49°10′ N, 5°53′ E 163
Jarocin, Pol. 51°57′ N, 17°30′ E 152
Järpen, Nor. 63°21′ N, 13°28′ E 152
Jars, Plain of, Laos 19°24′ N, 103°2′ E 202
Jartai, China 39°45′ N, 105°47′ E 198
Jaru, Braz. 10°25′ S, 62°30′ W 130
Jaru, river, Braz. 10°38′ S, 62°25′ W 132
Jarud Qi, China 44°35′ N, 120°55′ E 198
Järva Jaani, Est. 59°0′ N, 25°51′ E 166
Järvakandi, Est. 58°46′ N, 24°47′ E 166
Järvenpää, Fin. 69°27′ N, 28°47′ E 152
Järvenpää, Fin. 60°27′ N, 25°4′ E 166
Jarvie, Can. 54°26′ N, 113°59′ W 108
Järvsö, Nor. 61°42′ N, 16°6′ E 152
Jarwa, India 27°38′ N, 82°30′ E 197
Jaša Tomić, Serb. and Mont. 45°27′ N, 20°50′ E 168
Jasdan, India 22°1′ N, 71°12′ E 186
Jasenjani, Bosn. and Herzg. 43°29′ N, 17°49′ E 168
Jasenovac, Croatia 45°16′ N, 16°54′ E 168

Jungfrau, peak, *Switz.* 46°32′ N, 7°56′ E **167**
Junggar Pendi, *China* 45°57′ N, 84°44′ E **184**
Junín, *Arg.* 34°37′ S, 60°55′ W **139**
Junín, *Col.* 1°19′ N, 78°17′ W **136**
Junín, adm. division, *Peru* 11°26′ S, 74°42′ W **137**
Junín de los Andes, *Arg.* 39°55′ S, 71°6′ W **134**
Juniper Mountain, peak, *Oreg., U.S.* 42°55′ N, 120°1′ W **90**
Juniper Peak, *Nev., U.S.* 39°46′ N, 119°17′ W **90**
Junipero Serra Peak, *Calif., U.S.* 36°8′ N, 121°28′ W **100**
Juniville, *Fr.* 49°23′ N, 4°22′ E **163**
Junnar, *India* 19°12′ N, 73°53′ E **188**
Juno Beach, *Fla., U.S.* 26°52′ N, 80°4′ W **105**
Junosuando, *Nor.* 67°25′ N, 22°28′ E **152**
Junsele, *Nor.* 63°41′ N, 16°56′ E **152**
Juntura, *Oreg., U.S.* 43°44′ N, 118°5′ W **90**
Juntusranta, *Fin.* 65°12′ N, 29°27′ E **152**
Juodkrantė, *Russ.* 55°34′ N, 21°6′ E **166**
Jupaguá, *Braz.* 11°50′ S, 44°20′ W **132**
Jupiter, *Fla., U.S.* 26°56′ N, 80°6′ W **105**
Jupiter, river, *Can.* 49°40′ N, 63°36′ W **111**
Jupiter Well, spring, *Austral.* 22°59′ S, 126°42′ E **230**
Juquiá, *Braz.* 24°19′ S, 47°37′ W **138**
Jur, river, *Sudan* 8°34′ N, 28°35′ E **224**
Jura Mountains, *Switz.* 46°58′ N, 6°23′ E **165**
Jura, Paps of, mountain, *U.K.* 55°53′ N, 6°7′ W **150**
Juradó, *Col.* 7°7′ N, 77°47′ W **136**
Juramento, *Braz.* 16°50′ S, 43°36′ W **138**
Juramento see Pasaje, river, *Arg.* 28°44′ S, 62°58′ W **139**
Jurbarkas, *Lith.* 55°4′ N, 22°45′ E **166**
Jurf ad Darāwīsh, *Jordan* 30°41′ N, 35°51′ E **194**
Jurien Bay 30°46′ S, 114°35′ E **230**
Jūrmala, *Latv.* 56°57′ N, 23°48′ E **166**
Jūrmalciems, *Latv.* 56°18′ N, 21°0′ E **166**
Jurmo, *Fin.* 59°49′ N, 21°34′ E **166**
Juruá, *Braz.* 3°28′ S, 66°9′ W **136**
Juruá, river, *Braz.* 3°1′ S, 66°9′ W **132**
Jurumirim Dam, *Braz.* 23°24′ S, 49°18′ W **138**
Juruti, *Braz.* 2°10′ S, 56°8′ W **130**
Jussey, *Fr.* 47°49′ N, 5°53′ E **150**
Justo Daract, *Arg.* 33°53′ S, 65°10′ W **134**
Jutaí, *Braz.* 5°11′ S, 68°52′ W **130**
Jutai, Ilha Grande de, islands, *South America* 3°21′ S, 49°31′ W **130**
Jutaí, river, *Braz.* 3°21′ S, 67°32′ W **136**
Jutiapa, *Guatemala* 14°17′ N, 89°52′ W **115**
Juticalpa, *Hond.* 14°43′ N, 86°12′ W **115**
Jutland, *Europe* 55°35′ N, 8°29′ E **150**
Juuru, *Est.* 59°2′ N, 24°56′ E **166**
Juva, *Fin.* 61°53′ N, 27°47′ E **166**
Juventino Rosas, *Mex.* 20°37′ N, 100°60′ W **114**
Juventud, Isla de La, adm. division, *Cuba* 21°24′ N, 83°32′ W **116**
Juxian, *China* 35°36′ N, 118°50′ E **198**
Juxtlahuaca, *Mex.* 17°19′ N, 98°2′ W **114**
Juye, *China* 35°22′ N, 116°6′ E **198**
Jūymand, *Iran* 34°20′ N, 58°41′ E **180**
Jūyom, *Iran* 28°5′ N, 53°49′ E **196**
Juzennecourt, *Fr.* 48°10′ N, 4°58′ E **163**
Jwaneng, *Botswana* 24°34′ S, 24°35′ E **227**
Jyderup, *Den.* 55°39′ N, 11°24′ E **152**
Jyrgalang, *Kyrg.* 42°38′ N, 78°58′ E **184**
Jyväskylä, *Fin.* 62°12′ N, 25°42′ E **152**

K

K2 (Qoghir, Godwin Austen), peak, *Pak.* 35°51′ N, 76°25′ E **186**
Ka, river, *Nig.* 11°38′ N, 5°19′ E **222**
Ka' Ū, region, *Oceania* 19°15′ N, 155°39′ W **99**
Kaabong, *Uganda* 3°30′ N, 34°6′ E **224**
Kaa-Iya National Park, *Bol.* 19°25′ S, 61°49′ W **132**
Kaamanen, *Fin.* 69°6′ N, 27°12′ E **152**
Kaambooni, *Somalia* 1°38′ S, 41°36′ E **224**
Kaambooni, Raas, *Somalia* 1°36′ S, 40°53′ E **224**
Kaaresuvanto, *Fin.* 68°27′ N, 22°27′ E **152**
Kaba, *Hung.* 47°22′ N, 21°16′ E **168**
Kaba see Habahe, *China* 48°4′ N, 86°21′ E **184**
Kabaena, island, *Indonesia* 5°48′ S, 121°7′ E **192**
Kabala, *Sierra Leone* 9°34′ N, 11°34′ W **222**
Kabale, *Uganda* 1°19′ S, 29°59′ E **224**
Kabalo, *Dem. Rep. of the Congo* 6°4′ S, 26°55′ E **224**
Kabambare, *Dem. Rep. of the Congo* 4°44′ S, 27°38′ E **224**
Kabanga, *Zambia* 17°30′ S, 26°47′ E **224**
Kabangoué, *Côte d'Ivoire* 10°10′ N, 7°33′ W **222**
Kabanjahe, *Indonesia* 3°8′ N, 98°29′ E **196**
Kabara, *Mali* 16°40′ N, 2°60′ W **222**
Kabardino-Balkariya, adm. division, *Russ.* 43°33′ N, 42°31′ E **195**
Kabare, *Dem. Rep. of the Congo* 2°32′ S, 28°42′ E **224**
Kabarnet, *Kenya* 0°28′ N, 35°45′ E **224**
Kabasalan, *Philippines* 7°50′ N, 122°45′ E **203**
Kabasha, *Dem. Rep. of the Congo* 0°43′ N, 29°12′ E **224**
Kabba, *Nig.* 7°52′ N, 6°3′ E **222**
Kåbdalis, *Nor.* 66°8′ N, 19°56′ E **152**
Kabenung Lake, *Can.* 48°15′ N, 85°30′ W **94**
Kabinakagami Lake, *Can.* 48°47′ N, 86°7′ W **81**
Kabinda, *Dem. Rep. of the Congo* 6°11′ S, 24°27′ E **224**
Kabīr, river, *Asia* 34°35′ N, 36°7′ E **194**
Kabo, *Cen. Af. Rep.* 7°36′ N, 18°36′ E **218**
Kabol (Kabul), *Afghan.* 34°34′ N, 69°2′ E **186**
Kabompo, *Zambia* 13°37′ S, 24°10′ E **224**
Kabompo, river, *Zambia* 13°34′ S, 24°16′ E **224**
Kabongo, *Dem. Rep. of the Congo* 7°21′ S, 25°34′ E **224**
Kabore-Tambi National Park, *Burkina Faso* 11°10′ N, 1°50′ W **222**
Kabosa Island, *Myanmar* 12°51′ N, 97°24′ E **202**
Kaboudia, Ras, *Tun.* 35°10′ N, 11°9′ E **156**
Kabūd Gombad, *Iran* 37°1′ N, 59°48′ E **180**
Kabugao, *Philippines* 18°3′ N, 121°8′ E **203**
Kabul see Kabol, *Afghan.* 34°34′ N, 69°2′ E **186**
Kabunda, *Dem. Rep. of the Congo* 12°29′ S, 29°20′ E **224**
Kabushiya, *Sudan* 16°51′ N, 33°42′ E **182**
Kabwe (Broken Hill), *Zambia* 14°29′ S, 28°25′ E **224**
Kabylie, region, *Africa* 36°31′ N, 4°4′ E **150**
Kać, *Serb. and Mont.* 45°18′ N, 19°56′ E **168**
Kačanik, *Serb. and Mont.* 42°14′ N, 21°15′ E **168**
Kachanovo, *Russ.* 57°27′ N, 27°46′ E **166**
Kachia, *Nig.* 9°52′ N, 7°57′ E **222**
Kachikau, *Botswana* 18°10′ S, 24°28′ E **224**
Kachīry, *Kaz.* 53°4′ N, 76°7′ E **184**
Kachkanar, *Russ.* 58°44′ N, 59°30′ E **154**
Kachreti, *Ga.* 41°39′ N, 45°40′ E **195**
Kachug, *Russ.* 54°3′ N, 105°59′ E **190**
Kachung, *Uganda* 1°54′ N, 32°56′ E **224**
Kaçkar Dağı, peak, *Turk.* 40°50′ N, 41°6′ E **195**
Kada, spring, *Chad* 19°21′ N, 19°36′ E **216**
Kadaingti, *Myanmar* 17°37′ N, 97°30′ E **202**
Kadan Kyun, island, *Myanmar* 12°33′ N, 98°29′ E **202**
Kadarkút, *Hung.* 46°14′ N, 17°37′ E **168**
Kade, *Ghana* 6°6′ N, 0°52′ E **222**
Kadé, *Guinea* 12°10′ N, 13°53′ W **222**
Kadéï, river, *Cen. Af. Rep.* 3°48′ N, 15°32′ E **218**
Kadesh, battle, *Syr.* 34°34′ N, 36°25′ E **194**
Kadesh-Barnea see 'Ain el Qideirât, spring, *Egypt* 30°39′ N, 34°25′ E **194**
Kadiana, *Mali* 10°44′ N, 6°31′ W **222**
Kadıköy, *Turk.* 40°39′ N, 26°52′ E **158**
Kadiköy, *Turk.* 40°58′ N, 29°2′ E **158**
Kading, river, *Laos* 18°19′ N, 104°10′ E **202**
Kadınhanı, *Turk.* 38°13′ N, 32°13′ E **156**
Kadiolo, *Mali* 10°33′ N, 5°46′ W **222**
Kadiria, *Alg.* 36°31′ N, 3°41′ E **150**
Kadirli, *Turk.* 37°21′ N, 36°5′ E **156**
Kadivka, *Ukr.* 48°31′ N, 38°36′ E **158**
Kadnikov, *Russ.* 59°30′ N, 40°21′ E **154**
Kado, *Nig.* 7°37′ N, 9°40′ E **222**
Kadom, *Russ.* 54°32′ N, 42°30′ E **154**
Kadoma, *Zimb.* 18°21′ S, 29°56′ E **224**
Kadrifakovo, *Maced.* 41°48′ N, 22°3′ E **168**
Kadugli, *Sudan* 10°57′ N, 29°40′ E **224**
Kaduna, *Nig.* 10°30′ N, 7°24′ E **222**
Kaduy, *Russ.* 59°10′ N, 37°12′ E **154**
Kadyy, *Russ.* 57°47′ N, 43°10′ E **154**
Kadzherom, *Russ.* 64°40′ N, 55°48′ E **154**
Kaech'ŏn, *N. Korea* 39°42′ N, 125°52′ E **200**
Kaédi, *Mauritania* 16°8′ N, 13°36′ W **222**
Kaélé, *Cameroon* 10°6′ N, 14°26′ E **216**
Ka'ena Point, *Hawai'i, U.S.* 21°34′ N, 158°40′ W **99**
Kaeng Krachan National Park, *Thai.* 12°44′ N, 98°58′ E **202**
Kaeo, *N.Z.* 35°6′ S, 173°47′ E **240**
Ka'eo, peak, *Hawai'i, U.S.* 21°53′ N, 160°12′ W **99**
Kaesŏng, *N. Korea* 37°58′ N, 126°32′ E **200**
Kafakumba, *Dem. Rep. of the Congo* 9°41′ S, 23°45′ E **224**
Kafanchan, *Nig.* 9°36′ N, 8°18′ E **222**
Kaffrine, *Senegal* 14°6′ N, 15°32′ W **222**
Kafia Kingi, *Sudan* 9°15′ N, 24°24′ E **224**
Kafin, *Nig.* 9°29′ N, 7°5′ E **222**
Kåfjord, *Nor.* 69°56′ N, 23°0′ E **152**
Kåfjord, *Nor.* 69°31′ N, 20°51′ E **152**
Kafr Buhum, *Syr.* 35°3′ N, 36°41′ E **194**
Kafu, river, *Uganda* 1°8′ N, 31°26′ E **224**
Kafue, *Zambia* 15°47′ S, 28°10′ E **224**
Kafue National Park, *Zambia* 14°52′ S, 25°40′ E **224**
Kafue, river, *Zambia* 14°31′ S, 26°26′ E **224**
Kafue, river, *Zambia* 15°41′ S, 26°27′ E **224**
Kafufu, river, *Tanzania* 7°5′ S, 31°31′ E **224**
Kafulwe, *Zambia* 8°60′ S, 29°1′ E **224**
Kaga, *Japan* 36°18′ N, 136°17′ E **201**
Kaga Bandoro, *Cen. Af. Rep.* 6°54′ N, 19°11′ E **218**
Kagan, *Pak.* 34°45′ N, 73°34′ E **186**
Kagawa, adm. division, *Japan* 34°11′ N, 133°41′ E **201**
Kåge, *Nor.* 64°49′ N, 20°56′ E **152**
Kagera, adm. division, *Tanzania* 2°38′ S, 30°33′ E **218**
Kagera, river, *Africa* 1°8′ S, 30°42′ E **224**
Kagianagami Lake, *Can.* 50°58′ N, 88°38′ W **110**
Kağızman, *Turk.* 40°8′ N, 43°6′ E **195**
Kagmar, *Sudan* 14°25′ N, 30°23′ E **226**
Kagopal, *Chad* 8°15′ N, 16°26′ E **218**
Kagoshima, *Japan* 31°34′ N, 130°32′ E **201**
Kagoshima, adm. division, *Japan* 31°15′ N, 130°34′ E **201**
Kagoshima Space Center, *Japan* 31°16′ N, 131°0′ E **201**
Kaguyak, *Alas., U.S.* 56°51′ N, 153°51′ W **98**
Kahama, *Tanzania* 3°49′ S, 32°35′ E **224**
Kahan, *Pak.* 29°18′ N, 68°57′ E **186**
Kahemba, *Dem. Rep. of the Congo* 7°20′ S, 18°59′ E **218**
Kāhili, peak, *Hawai'i, U.S.* 21°58′ N, 159°33′ W **99**
Kahler Asten, peak, *Ger.* 51°10′ N, 8°26′ E **167**
Kahlotus, *Wash., U.S.* 46°37′ N, 118°33′ W **90**
Kahntah, *Can.* 58°19′ N, 120°55′ W **108**
Kahntah, river, *Can.* 57°50′ N, 120°51′ W **108**
Kahnūj, *Iran* 27°54′ N, 57°45′ E **196**
Kahoku, *Japan* 38°26′ N, 140°18′ E **201**
Kaho'olawe, island, *Hawai'i, U.S.* 20°21′ N, 157°18′ W **99**
Kahperusvaara, peak, *Fin.* 69°8′ N, 21°1′ E **152**
Kahramanmaraş, *Turk.* 37°35′ N, 36°55′ E **156**
Kahtla, *Est.* 58°24′ N, 22°59′ E **166**
Kahuku Point, *Hawai'i, U.S.* 21°44′ N, 158°21′ W **99**
Kahurangi National Park, *N.Z.* 41°11′ S, 171°19′ E **240**
Kahuzi-Biega National Park, *Dem. Rep. of the Congo* 1°60′ S, 27°14′ E **224**
Kai Iwi, *N.Z.* 39°53′ S, 174°54′ E **240**
Kai, Kepulauan, islands, *Banda Sea* 5°58′ S, 130°47′ E **192**
Kaiama, *Nig.* 9°35′ N, 4°0′ E **222**
Kaibara, *Japan* 35°7′ N, 135°3′ E **201**
Kā'id, spring, *Iraq* 32°2′ N, 40°57′ E **180**
Kaifeng, *China* 34°48′ N, 114°19′ E **198**
Kaifu, *Japan* 33°36′ N, 134°20′ E **201**
Kaiholena, peak, *Hawai'i, U.S.* 19°10′ N, 155°38′ W **99**
Kaihu, *N.Z.* 35°45′ S, 173°42′ E **240**
Kaikoura, *N.Z.* 42°25′ S, 173°39′ E **240**
Kailahun, *Sierra Leone* 8°14′ N, 10°35′ W **222**
Kaili, *China* 26°34′ N, 107°59′ E **198**
Kailu, *China* 43°39′ N, 121°16′ E **198**
Kaimana, *Indonesia* 3°39′ S, 133°45′ E **192**
Käina, *Est.* 58°49′ N, 22°46′ E **166**
Kainan, *Japan* 34°9′ N, 135°13′ E **201**
Kainji Dam, *Nig.* 9°40′ N, 4°19′ E **222**
Kainji Lake National Park, *Nig.* 9°45′ N, 5°4′ E **222**
Kainuunkylä, *Fin.* 66°13′ N, 23°47′ E **152**
Kairala, *Fin.* 67°10′ N, 27°23′ E **152**
Kaisersesch, *Ger.* 50°13′ N, 7°8′ E **167**
Kaiserslautern, *Ger.* 49°26′ N, 7°45′ E **163**
Kaishantun, *China* 42°42′ N, 129°44′ E **200**
Kaišiadorys, *Lith.* 54°52′ N, 24°26′ E **166**
Kaitangata, *N.Z.* 46°17′ S, 169°50′ E **240**
Kaithal, *India* 29°47′ N, 76°25′ E **197**
Ka'iwaloa Heiau and Olowalu Petroglyphs, site, *Hawai'i, U.S.* 20°49′ N, 156°40′ W **99**
Kaixian, *China* 31°11′ N, 108°20′ E **198**
Kaiyang, *China* 27°4′ N, 107°0′ E **198**
Kaiyuan, *China* 42°32′ N, 124°3′ E **200**
Kaiyuan, *China* 23°40′ N, 103°9′ E **202**
Kajaani, *Fin.* 64°12′ N, 27°39′ E **152**
Kajaki, *Afghan.* 32°12′ N, 65°5′ E **186**
Kajaki Dam, *Afghan.* 32°1′ N, 64°29′ E **186**
Kajang, *Malaysia* 3°0′ N, 101°45′ E **196**
Kajiado, *Kenya* 1°52′ S, 36°48′ E **224**
Kajiki, *Japan* 31°43′ N, 130°40′ E **201**
Kajo Kaji, *Sudan* 3°48′ N, 31°36′ E **224**
Kajok, *Sudan* 8°16′ N, 27°58′ E **224**
Kajuru, *Nig.* 10°19′ N, 7°38′ E **222**
Kaka, *Sudan* 10°37′ N, 32°7′ E **224**
Kaka, *Turkm.* 37°21′ N, 59°36′ E **180**
Kakada, spring, *Chad* 16°8′ N, 15°29′ E **216**
Kakadu National Park, *Austral.* 13°22′ S, 132°5′ E **238**
Kakahi, *N.Z.* 38°59′ S, 175°21′ E **240**
Kakamas, *S. Af.* 28°47′ S, 20°35′ E **227**
Kakamega, *Kenya* 0°15′ N, 34°46′ E **224**
Kakana, *India* 9°9′ N, 92°55′ E **188**
Kakanj, *Bosn. and Herzg.* 44°9′ N, 18°5′ E **168**
Kakanui, *N.Z.* 45°12′ S, 170°53′ E **240**
Kakaramea, *N.Z.* 39°43′ S, 174°25′ E **240**
Kakasszék, *Hung.* 46°32′ N, 20°36′ E **168**
Kakata, *Liberia* 6°25′ N, 10°21′ W **222**
Kakatahi, *N.Z.* 39°41′ S, 175°21′ E **240**
Kake, *Alas., U.S.* 56°58′ N, 133°57′ W **108**
Kake, *Japan* 34°36′ N, 132°20′ E **201**
Kaketsa Mountain, *Can.* 58°10′ N, 131°59′ W **108**
Kakhib, *Russ.* 42°23′ N, 46°36′ E **195**
Kākhk, *Iran* 34°7′ N, 58°38′ E **180**
Kakhovka, *Ukr.* 46°48′ N, 33°29′ E **156**
Kakhovs'ke Vodoskhovyshche, lake, *Ukr.* 46°59′ N, 32°23′ E **156**
Kakinada (Cocanada), *India* 16°59′ N, 82°15′ E **188**
Kakisa, *Can.* 60°54′ N, 117°21′ W **108**
Kakisa Lake, *Can.* 60°57′ N, 118°37′ W **108**
Kakisa, river, *Can.* 60°44′ N, 119°16′ W **108**
Kakogawa, *Japan* 34°46′ N, 134°51′ E **201**
Kakshaal Range see Kök Shal Tau, *Kyrg.* 41°22′ N, 77°33′ E **184**
Kakskerta, *Fin.* 60°20′ N, 22°13′ E **166**
Kaktovik, *Alas., U.S.* 69°59′ N, 143°40′ W **98**
Kakuda, *Japan* 37°58′ N, 140°45′ E **201**
Kakuma, *Kenya* 3°40′ N, 34°50′ E **224**
Kakwa, river, *Can.* 54°13′ N, 118°43′ W **108**
Kál, *Hung.* 47°43′ N, 20°17′ E **168**
Kala, *Azerb.* 40°27′ N, 50°10′ E **195**
Kala, *Tanzania* 8°8′ S, 31°0′ E **224**
Kalabagh, *Pak.* 32°59′ N, 71°35′ E **186**
Kalabo, *Zambia* 14°59′ S, 22°40′ E **220**
Kalâbsha and Beit el Wâli, ruin(s), *Egypt* 23°32′ N, 32°42′ E **182**
Kalach, *Russ.* 50°25′ N, 40°58′ E **158**
Kalach na Donu, *Russ.* 48°43′ N, 43°32′ E **158**
Kalachinsk, *Russ.* 54°59′ N, 74°36′ E **184**
Kalae (South Point), *Hawai'i, U.S.* 18°40′ N, 155°43′ W **99**
Kalahari Desert, *Africa* 19°27′ S, 24°2′ E **224**
Kalahari Gemsbok National Park, *S. Af.* 26°6′ S, 19°47′ E **227**
Kalaikhum, *Taj.* 38°28′ N, 70°47′ E **197**
Kalajoki, *Fin.* 64°12′ N, 23°55′ E **152**
Kalakamate, *Botswana* 20°39′ S, 27°18′ E **227**
Kalakan, *Russ.* 55°11′ N, 116°45′ E **190**
Kalakepen, *Indonesia* 2°47′ N, 97°48′ E **196**
Kalalua, peak, *Hawai'i, U.S.* 19°23′ N, 155°7′ W **99**
Kalam, *Pak.* 35°31′ N, 72°36′ E **186**
Kalama, *Wash., U.S.* 46°0′ N, 122°50′ W **100**
Kalama, river, *Wash., U.S.* 46°1′ N, 122°45′ W **100**
Kalamalka Lake, *Can.* 50°5′ N, 119°57′ W **108**
Kalamáta, *Gr.* 37°2′ N, 22°7′ E **216**
Kalamazoo, *Mich., U.S.* 42°17′ N, 85°36′ W **102**
Kalambo Falls, *Zambia* 8°51′ S, 31°17′ E **224**
Kalana, *Mali* 10°47′ N, 8°13′ W **222**
Kalangala, *Uganda* 0°23′ N, 32°16′ E **224**
Kalangali, *Tanzania* 6°6′ S, 33°55′ E **224**
Kalanshiyū ar Ramlī al Kabīr, Sarīr (Sand Sea of Calanscio), *Lib.* 28°52′ N, 23°25′ E **180**
Kalanshiyū, Sarīr, *Lib.* 26°35′ N, 20°7′ E **216**
Kalao, island, *Indonesia* 7°27′ S, 119°55′ E **192**
Kalaotoa, island, *Indonesia* 7°28′ S, 121°50′ E **192**
Kälarne, *Nor.* 62°59′ N, 16°4′ E **152**
Kalasin, *Thai.* 16°28′ N, 103°31′ E **202**
Kalat, *Pak.* 29°2′ N, 66°33′ E **186**
Kalaupapa National Historic Park, *Hawai'i, U.S.* 20°42′ N, 157°60′ W **99**
Kalaus, river, *Russ.* 45°50′ N, 43°15′ E **158**
Kalawao, site, *Hawai'i, U.S.* 21°10′ N, 156°60′ W **99**
Kalay'mor, *Turkm.* 35°41′ N, 62°33′ E **186**
Kalay-wa, *Myanmar* 23°10′ N, 94°13′ E **202**
Kalbā, *U.A.E.* 25°4′ N, 56°17′ E **196**
Kälbäjär, *Azerb.* 40°8′ N, 46°1′ E **195**
Kalbān, *Oman* 20°17′ N, 58°41′ E **182**
Kaldrma, *Bosn. and Herzg.* 44°18′ N, 16°11′ E **168**
Kale Burnu, *Turk.* 41°4′ N, 38°54′ E **195**
Kale (Myra), *Turk.* 36°13′ N, 29°57′ E **156**
Kalecik, *Turk.* 40°6′ N, 33°25′ E **156**
Kalehe, *Dem. Rep. of the Congo* 2°7′ S, 28°50′ E **224**
Kalemie, *Dem. Rep. of the Congo* 5°57′ S, 29°11′ E **224**
Kalemyo, *Myanmar* 23°10′ N, 94°1′ E **202**
Kalene Hill, *Zambia* 11°13′ S, 24°10′ E **224**
Kalenyy, *Kaz.* 49°32′ N, 51°35′ E **158**
Kalesija, *Bosn. and Herzg.* 44°27′ N, 18°55′ E **168**
Kaletnik, *Pol.* 54°10′ N, 23°5′ E **152**
Kalevala, *Russ.* 65°12′ N, 31°12′ E **152**
Kaleybar, *Iran* 38°56′ N, 47°3′ E **195**
Kalgachikha, *Russ.* 63°20′ N, 36°48′ E **154**
Kalí Límni, peak, *Gr.* 35°34′ N, 27°4′ E **156**
Kali Sindh, river, *India* 24°28′ N, 76°7′ E **197**
Kaliakoúda, peak, *Gr.* 38°47′ N, 21°40′ E **156**
Kaliakra, Nos, *Bulg.* 43°17′ N, 28°17′ E **156**
Kalibo, *Philippines* 11°40′ N, 122°22′ E **203**
Kalida, *Ohio, U.S.* 40°58′ N, 84°12′ W **102**
Kalima, *Dem. Rep. of the Congo* 2°39′ S, 26°35′ E **218**
Kalimantan see Borneo, island, *Indonesia* 4°28′ S, 111°26′ E **192**
Kalimash, *Alban.* 42°5′ N, 20°18′ E **168**
Kálimnos, *Gr.* 36°57′ N, 26°59′ E **156**
Kalimpang, *India* 27°4′ N, 88°26′ E **197**
Kaliningrad, *Russ.* 54°42′ N, 20°27′ E **166**
Kaliningrad Oblast, adm. division, *Russ.* 54°47′ N, 20°9′ E **166**
Kalinino, *Arm.* 41°7′ N, 44°15′ E **195**
Kalinino, *Russ.* 45°9′ N, 39°1′ E **156**
Kalinino, *Russ.* 57°18′ N, 56°23′ E **154**
Kalininsk, *Russ.* 51°29′ N, 44°28′ E **158**
Kalinivka, *Ukr.* 49°28′ N, 28°42′ E **152**
Kalinkavichy, *Belarus* 52°5′ N, 29°26′ E **152**
Kalino, *Russ.* 58°14′ N, 57°38′ E **154**
Kalinovik, *Bosn. and Herzg.* 43°30′ N, 18°26′ E **168**
Kaliro, *Uganda* 0°52′ N, 33°29′ E **224**
Kalis, *Somalia* 8°23′ N, 49°3′ E **216**
Kalispell, *Mont., U.S.* 48°12′ N, 114°21′ W **106**
Kalisz, *Pol.* 51°45′ N, 18°5′ E **152**
Kaliua, *Tanzania* 5°4′ S, 31°46′ E **224**
Kalix, *Nor.* 65°51′ N, 23°7′ E **154**
Kalixälven, river, *Nor.* 67°41′ N, 19°45′ E **152**
Kalkan, *Turk.* 36°15′ N, 29°25′ E **156**
Kalkar, *Ger.* 51°42′ N, 6°17′ E **167**
Kalkaska, *Mich., U.S.* 44°43′ N, 85°11′ W **94**
Kalkfeld, *Namibia* 20°55′ S, 16°12′ E **227**
Kalkkinen, *Fin.* 61°17′ N, 25°41′ E **166**
Kalkrand, *Namibia* 24°5′ S, 17°35′ E **227**
Kallam, *India* 18°32′ N, 76°1′ E **188**
Kallaste, *Est.* 58°38′ N, 27°7′ E **166**
Kallithéa, *Gr.* 37°57′ N, 23°42′ E **156**
Kałuszyn, *Pol.* 52°12′ N, 21°47′ E **152**
Kallmet, *Alban.* 41°50′ N, 19°41′ E **168**
Kallo, *Fin.* 67°25′ N, 24°27′ E **152**
Kallunki, *Fin.* 66°38′ N, 28°54′ E **152**
Kalmar, *Nor.* 56°39′ N, 16°20′ E **152**
Kalmthout, *Belg.* 51°23′ N, 4°28′ E **167**
Kalmykiya, adm. division, *Russ.* 46°7′ N, 43°37′ E **158**
Kalnai, *India* 22°47′ N, 83°29′ E **197**
Kalnik, peak, *Croatia* 46°7′ N, 16°26′ E **168**
Kalo Chorio, *Cyprus* 34°50′ N, 33°2′ E **194**
Kalocsa, *Hung.* 46°31′ N, 18°58′ E **168**
Kaloko-Honokōhau National Historical Park, *Hawai'i, U.S.* 19°40′ N, 156°5′ W **99**
Kaloli Point, *U.S.* 19°34′ N, 154°56′ W **99**
Kalomo, *Zambia* 17°3′ S, 26°28′ E **224**
Kalotina, *Bulg.* 42°59′ N, 22°51′ E **168**
Kalpi, *India* 26°6′ N, 79°43′ E **197**
Kalpin, *China* 40°34′ N, 78°54′ E **184**
Kalsubai, peak, *India* 19°34′ N, 73°34′ E **188**
Kaltag, *Alas., U.S.* 64°11′ N, 158°53′ W **98**
Kaltay, *Russ.* 56°14′ N, 84°54′ E **169**
Kalterherberg, *Ger.* 50°31′ N, 6°12′ E **167**
Kaltungo, *Nig.* 9°48′ N, 11°18′ E **222**
Kaluga, *Russ.* 54°34′ N, 36°20′ E **154**
Kaluga, adm. division, *Russ.* 54°14′ N, 34°5′ E **154**
Kalulushi, *Zambia* 12°52′ S, 28°5′ E **224**
Kalundu, *Zambia* 10°17′ S, 29°22′ E **224**
Kalungwishi, river, *Zambia* 9°40′ S, 29°0′ E **220**
Kalush, *Ukr.* 49°0′ N, 24°21′ E **158**
Kalvåg, *Nor.* 61°46′ N, 4°51′ E **152**
Kalvarija, *Lith.* 54°26′ N, 23°11′ E **166**
Kälviä, *Fin.* 63°51′ N, 23°24′ E **152**
Kalvitsa, *Fin.* 61°53′ N, 27°15′ E **166**
Kalvola, *Fin.* 61°5′ N, 24°7′ E **166**
Kalwang, *Aust.* 47°26′ N, 14°46′ E **156**
Kalweyn, Ghubbet, *Somalia* 11°7′ N, 46°28′ E **216**
Kal'ya, *Russ.* 60°17′ N, 59°54′ E **154**
Kalyan, *India* 19°14′ N, 73°8′ E **188**
Kalyazin, *Russ.* 57°12′ N, 37°50′ E **154**
Kám, *Hung.* 47°5′ N, 16°53′ E **168**
Kam, river, *Nig.* 8°10′ N, 11°4′ E **222**
Kama, *Dem. Rep. of the Congo* 3°38′ S, 27°7′ E **224**
Kama, *Myanmar* 19°3′ N, 95°4′ E **202**
Kama, *Russ.* 60°8′ N, 62°1′ E **154**
Kama, river, *Dem. Rep. of the Congo* 3°30′ S, 26°55′ E **218**
Kama, river, *Russ.* 60°10′ N, 55°25′ E **154**
Kamae, *Japan* 32°47′ N, 131°55′ E **201**
Kamaing, *Myanmar* 25°29′ N, 96°40′ E **188**
Kamaishi, *Japan* 39°17′ N, 141°42′ E **190**
Kamakou, peak, *Hawai'i, U.S.* 21°6′ N, 156°55′ W **99**
Kamakura, *Japan* 35°18′ N, 139°34′ E **201**
Kamalia, *Pak.* 30°45′ N, 72°38′ E **186**
Kamalino, *Hawai'i, U.S.* 21°50′ N, 160°15′ W **99**
Kamalu, *Sierra Leone* 9°22′ N, 12°17′ W **222**
Kaman, *India* 27°38′ N, 77°14′ E **197**
Kaman, *Turk.* 39°21′ N, 33°43′ E **156**
Kamanjab, *Namibia* 19°40′ S, 14°49′ E **220**
Kamanyola, *Dem. Rep. of the Congo* 2°47′ S, 28°57′ E **224**
Kamapanda, *Zambia* 12°1′ S, 24°6′ E **224**
Kamarān, island, *Yemen* 15°16′ N, 41°57′ E **182**
Kamarod, *Pak.* 27°28′ N, 63°36′ E **186**
Kamba, *Nig.* 11°51′ N, 3°40′ E **222**
Kambarka, *Russ.* 56°16′ N, 54°17′ E **154**
Kambaya, *Guinea* 10°40′ N, 13°1′ W **222**
Kambia, *Sierra Leone* 9°5′ N, 12°56′ W **222**
Kambja, *Est.* 58°12′ N, 26°41′ E **166**
Kambove, *Dem. Rep. of the Congo* 10°51′ S, 26°36′ E **224**
Kamchatka, adm. division, *Russ.* 43°39′ N, 145°30′ E **160**
Kamchatka, Poluostrov, *Asia* 58°47′ N, 161°17′ E **160**
Kamchatskiy Zaliv 55°17′ N, 159°46′ E **160**
Kameda, *Japan* 37°52′ N, 139°7′ E **201**
Kamehameha I Birthplace, site, *Hawai'i, U.S.* 20°14′ N, 155°56′ W **99**
Kamen', *Belarus* 53°51′ N, 26°40′ E **166**
Kamen, *Ger.* 51°35′ N, 7°39′ E **167**
Kamen, Gora, peak, *Russ.* 69°6′ N, 95°4′ E **169**
Kamenica, *Bosn. and Herzg.* 44°20′ N, 18°12′ E **168**
Kamenka, *Kaz.* 51°5′ N, 50°16′ E **158**
Kamenka, *Russ.* 65°53′ N, 44°0′ E **154**
Kamenka, *Russ.* 58°29′ N, 95°34′ E **160**
Kamenka, *Russ.* 53°9′ N, 44°5′ E **154**
Kamenka, *Russ.* 65°52′ N, 43°51′ E **173**
Kamen'na Obi, *Russ.* 53°44′ N, 81°27′ E **184**
Kamennoe, *Kaz.* 44°55′ N, 54°47′ E **158**
Kamennogorsk, *Russ.* 60°57′ N, 29°6′ E **166**
Kamensk Shakhtinskiy, *Russ.* 48°16′ N, 40°16′ E **158**
Kamensk Ural'skiy, *Russ.* 56°27′ N, 61°47′ E **154**
Kamenskiy, *Russ.* 50°50′ N, 45°29′ E **158**
Kamenskoye, *Russ.* 62°31′ N, 165°59′ E **160**
Kameoka, *Japan* 35°0′ N, 135°34′ E **201**
Kameur, river, *Cen. Af. Rep.* 9°42′ N, 21°14′ E **218**
Kamiagata, *Japan* 34°38′ N, 129°24′ E **200**
Kamieskroon, *S. Af.* 30°12′ S, 17°54′ E **227**
Kamiji, *Dem. Rep. of the Congo* 6°37′ S, 23°16′ E **218**
Kâmil, Gebel, peak, *Egypt* 22°15′ N, 26°33′ E **226**
Kamina, *Dem. Rep. of the Congo* 8°45′ S, 24°58′ E **224**
Kaministiquia, *Can.* 48°32′ N, 89°34′ W **94**
Kaminoyama, *Japan* 38°9′ N, 140°15′ E **201**
Kaminuriak Lake, *Can.* 63°4′ N, 97°47′ W **106**
Kamioka, *Japan* 36°20′ N, 137°19′ E **201**
Kamitsuki, *Japan* 34°6′ N, 139°32′ E **201**
Kamitsushima, *Japan* 34°39′ N, 129°28′ E **200**
Kamkhat Muḩaywir, peak, *Jordan* 31°7′ N, 36°28′ E **194**
Kamloops, *Can.* 50°39′ N, 120°20′ W **82**
Kammuri, peak, *Japan* 34°28′ N, 132°2′ E **200**
Kamo, *Arm.* 40°22′ N, 45°5′ E **195**
Kamo, *Japan* 37°39′ N, 139°3′ E **201**
Kamo, *Japan* 38°46′ N, 139°44′ E **201**
Kamo, *N.Z.* 35°42′ S, 174°18′ E **240**
Kamoa Mountains, *Guyana* 1°32′ N, 60°5′ W **130**
Kampala, *Uganda* 0°14′ N, 32°22′ E **224**
Kampar, *Malaysia* 4°18′ N, 101°9′ E **196**
Kampene, *Dem. Rep. of the Congo* 3°37′ S, 26°39′ E **224**
Kamphaeng Phet, *Thai.* 16°28′ N, 99°28′ E **202**
Kamp-Lintfort, *Ger.* 51°29′ N, 6°33′ E **167**
Kampolombo, Lake, *Zambia* 11°49′ S, 28°59′ E **224**
Kâmpóng Cham, *Cambodia* 11°59′ N, 105°25′ E **202**
Kampong Kuala Besut, *Malaysia* 5°48′ N, 102°35′ E **196**
Kampos, *Cyprus* 35°1′ N, 32°43′ E **194**
Kampot, *Cambodia* 10°37′ N, 104°12′ E **202**
Kampti, *Burkina Faso* 10°8′ N, 3°28′ W **222**
Kamsack, *Can.* 51°34′ N, 101°56′ W **90**
Kamsar, *Guinea* 10°39′ N, 14°35′ W **222**
Kamskoye Vdkhr., lake, *Russ.* 58°48′ N, 56°38′ E **246**
Kamskoye Vodokhranilishche, lake, *Russ.* 58°35′ N, 54°17′ E **154**
Kamsuuma, *Somalia* 0°14′ N, 42°48′ E **218**
Kámuk, Cerro, peak, *C.R.* 9°15′ N, 83°6′ W **115**
Kam'yanka-Dniprovs'ka, *Ukr.* 47°28′ N, 34°24′ E **156**
Kamyshin, *Russ.* 50°6′ N, 45°22′ E **158**
Kamyshla, *Russ.* 54°7′ N, 52°9′ E **154**
Kamyzyak, *Russ.* 46°5′ N, 48°6′ E **158**
Kan, *Sudan* 8°57′ N, 31°47′ E **224**
Kanab, *Utah, U.S.* 37°2′ N, 112°32′ W **82**
Kanagawa, adm. division, *Japan* 35°20′ N, 139°2′ E **201**
Kanak, river, *Turk.* 39°33′ N, 34°58′ E **156**
Kanākir, *Syr.* 33°15′ N, 36°5′ E **194**
Kanaktok Mountain, *Alas., U.S.* 67°48′ N, 160°12′ W **98**
Kanal, *Slov.* 46°5′ N, 13°38′ E **167**
Kanalla, *India* 6°53′ N, 93°52′ E **188**
Kananga, *Dem. Rep. of the Congo* 5°54′ S, 22°25′ E **218**
Kanash, *Russ.* 55°28′ N, 47°29′ E **154**
Kanata, *Can.* 45°16′ N, 75°51′ W **82**
Kanava, *Russ.* 61°5′ N, 55°4′ E **154**
Kanâyis, Râs el, *Egypt* 31°16′ N, 27°50′ E **180**
Kanazawa, *Japan* 36°33′ N, 136°40′ E **201**
Kanbalu, *Myanmar* 23°11′ N, 95°31′ E **202**
Kanchipuram, *India* 12°51′ N, 79°43′ E **188**
Kanda Kanda, *Dem. Rep. of the Congo* 6°55′ S, 23°32′ E **218**
Kandahar, *Afghan.* 31°36′ N, 65°43′ E **186**
Kandalaksha, *Russ.* 67°9′ N, 32°24′ E **152**
Kandalakshskiy Zaliv 66°18′ N, 29°7′ E **160**
Kandale, *Dem. Rep. of the Congo* 6°2′ S, 19°23′ E **218**

KAN-KAY

Kandang, Indonesia 3°6′ N, 97°18′ E 196
Kandangan, Indonesia 2°43′ S, 115°13′ E 192
Kandava, Latv. 57°2′ N, 22°44′ E 166
Kandel, Ger. 49°5′ N, 8°10′ E 152
Kandersteg, Switz. 46°29′ N, 7°40′ E 167
Kandhkot, Pak. 28°13′ N, 69°12′ E 186
Kandi, Benin 11°7′ N, 2°56′ E 222
Kandiaro, Pak. 27°6′ N, 68°15′ E 186
Kandıra, Turk. 41°4′ N, 30°8′ E 156
Kandla, India 23°12′ N, 70°25′ E 173
Kandrach, Pak. 25°29′ N, 65°27′ E 182
Kandreho, Madagascar 17°31′ S, 46°6′ E 220
Kandudu, island, Maldives 2°2′ N, 72°0′ E 188
Kandy, Sri Lanka 7°16′ N, 80°40′ E 188
Kane, Pa., U.S. 41°39′ N, 78°49′ W 94
Kāneʻākī Heiau, site, Hawaiʻi, U.S. 21°29′ N, 158°14′ W 99
Kāneiolouma Heiau, site, Hawaiʻi, U.S. 21°52′ N, 159°30′ W 99
Kanel, Senegal 15°29′ N, 13°14′ W 222
Kanepi, Est. 57°58′ N, 26°45′ E 166
Kanevskaya, Russ. 46°6′ N, 38°55′ E 156
Kang, Afghan. 31°7′ N, 61°55′ E 186
Kang, Botswana 23°41′ S, 22°48′ E 227
Kangaamiut, Den. 65°50′ N, 53°21′ W 106
Kangaatsiaq, Den. 68°18′ N, 53°25′ W 106
Kangaba, Mali 11°57′ N, 8°26′ W 222
Kangal, Turk. 39°13′ N, 37°22′ E 156
Kangān, Iran 25°49′ N, 57°28′ E 196
Kangān, Iran 27°51′ N, 52°7′ E 196
Kangar, Malaysia 6°25′ N, 100°12′ E 202
Kangaroo Island, Austral. 36°51′ S, 137°17′ E 230
Kangasala, Fin. 61°26′ N, 24°2′ E 166
Kangasniemi, Fin. 61°58′ N, 26°34′ E 166
Kangatet, Kenya 1°55′ N, 36°6′ E 224
Kangāvar, Iran 34°26′ N, 47°48′ E 180
Kangbao, China 41°51′ N, 114°36′ E 198
Kangdong, N. Korea 39°8′ N, 126°5′ E 200
Kangean, Kepulauan, islands, Java Sea 6°17′ S, 113°56′ E 192
Kangeeak Point, Can. 67°47′ N, 64°28′ W 106
Kangen, river, Sudan 6°35′ N, 33°17′ E 224
Kangerluarsoruseq (Færingehavn), Den. 63°43′ N, 51°21′ W 106
Kangerlussuaq 67°49′ N, 35°25′ W 246
Kangerlussuaq, Den. 67°4′ N, 50°50′ W 106
Kangersuatsiaq, Den. 72°16′ N, 55°39′ W 106
Kanggye, N. Korea 40°58′ N, 126°35′ E 200
Kangikajiip Agpalia, Den. 69°48′ N, 22°11′ W 246
Kangiqsualujjuaq, Can. 58°30′ N, 65°54′ W 106
Kangiqsujuaq, Can. 61°35′ N, 72°2′ W 106
Kangmar, China 28°36′ N, 89°41′ E 197
Kangmar, China 30°48′ N, 85°39′ E 197
Kangnyŏng, N. Korea 37°53′ N, 125°31′ E 200
Kango, Gabon 0°11′ N, 10°8′ E 218
Kangping, China 42°45′ N, 123°24′ E 200
Kangrinboqê Feng, peak, China 31°4′ N, 81°18′ E 197
Kangsang, N. Korea 40°6′ N, 128°23′ E 200
Kangsŏ, N. Korea 38°56′ N, 125°30′ E 200
Kangto, peak, China 27°40′ N, 92°10′ E 190
Kaniama, Dem. Rep. of the Congo 7°33′ S, 24°10′ E 224
Kaniet Islands, South Pacific Ocean 0°47′ N, 145°35′ E 192
Kanin Nos, Russ. 68°34′ N, 43°22′ E 169
Kanin Nos, Mys, Russ. 68°10′ N, 42°25′ E 169
Kanin, Poluostrov, Russ. 68°1′ N, 39°53′ E 160
Kanin, Poluostrov, Russ. 67°0′ N, 44°14′ E 160
Kanirom, Chad 14°26′ N, 13°45′ E 216
Kanish, ruin(s), Turk. 38°51′ N, 35°29′ E 156
Kaniv, Ukr. 49°43′ N, 31°30′ E 158
Kanjarkot, site, Pak. 24°15′ N, 69°5′ E 186
Kanjiža, Serb. and Mont. 46°4′ N, 20°3′ E 168
Kankaanpää, Fin. 61°47′ N, 22°23′ E 166
Kankakee, Ill., U.S. 41°7′ N, 87°52′ W 102
Kankan, Guinea 10°25′ N, 9°19′ W 222
Kankossa, Mauritania 15°54′ N, 11°32′ W 222
Kanmaw Kyun, island, Myanmar 11°33′ N, 98°32′ E 202
Kanmen, China 28°5′ N, 121°16′ E 198
Kannapolis, N.C., U.S. 35°29′ N, 80°38′ W 96
Kannauj, India 27°1′ N, 79°54′ E 197
Kannod, India 22°40′ N, 76°46′ E 197
Kannusuo, Russ. 65°8′ N, 31°54′ E 152
Kano, Nig. 11°59′ N, 8°30′ E 222
Kanonji, Japan 34°7′ N, 133°38′ E 201
Kanopolis, Kans., U.S. 38°41′ N, 98°10′ W 90
Kanorado, Kans., U.S. 39°20′ N, 102°2′ W 90
Kanosh, Utah, U.S. 38°48′ N, 112°26′ W 90
Kanoya, Japan 31°21′ N, 130°51′ E 201
Kanpur, India 26°25′ N, 80°19′ E 197
Kansanshi, Zambia 12°5′ S, 26°22′ E 224
Kansas, Ill., U.S. 39°32′ N, 87°56′ W 102
Kansas, adm. division, Kans., U.S. 38°7′ N, 100°3′ W 82
Kansas City, Mo., U.S. 39°4′ N, 94°33′ W 82
Kansas, river, Kans., U.S. 39°18′ N, 96°32′ W 80
Kansk, Russ. 56°6′ N, 95°41′ E 160
Kant, Kyrg. 42°52′ N, 74°55′ E 184
Kantang, Thai. 7°24′ N, 99°31′ E 196
Kantankufri, Ghana 7°49′ N, 2°118′ W 222
Kantara Castle, site, Northern Cyprus 35°23′ N, 33°53′ E 194
Kantchari, Burkina Faso 12°32′ N, 1°33′ E 222
Kanté, Togo 9°56′ N, 1°1′ E 222
Kantemirovka, Russ. 49°43′ N, 39°53′ E 158
Kanuma, Japan 36°33′ N, 139°45′ E 201
Kanyato, Tanzania 4°28′ S, 30°15′ E 224
Kanye, Botswana 24°60′ S, 25°19′ E 227
Kaohsiung, Taiwan 22°41′ N, 120°20′ E 198
Kaokoveld, Namibia 19°17′ S, 13°48′ E 220
Kaolack, Senegal 14°11′ N, 16°3′ W 222
Kaoma, Zambia 14°49′ S, 24°47′ E 224
Kaongeshi, river, Dem. Rep. of the Congo 7°48′ S, 22°22′ E 218
Kaouar, Niger 19°41′ N, 12°17′ E 222
Kap Farvel see Nunap Isua, Den. 59°20′ N, 43°43′ W 106
Kapa Moračka, peak, Serb. and Mont. 42°48′ N, 19°13′ E 168
Kapalala, Zambia 12°24′ S, 29°22′ E 224
Kapan, Arm. 39°11′ N, 46°23′ E 195
Kapanga, Dem. Rep. of the Congo 8°23′ S, 22°35′ E 218
Kapatu, Zambia 9°45′ S, 30°45′ E 224
Kapedo, Kenya 1°9′ N, 36°3′ E 224
Kapela, Croatia 44°50′ N, 15°10′ E 156
Kapellen, Belg. 51°20′ N, 4°25′ E 167
Kapenguria, Kenya 1°15′ N, 35°6′ E 224
Kapıdağı, peak, Turk. 40°26′ N, 27°43′ E 156
Kapikik Lake, Can. 51°30′ N, 92°24′ W 110
Kapili, river, Dem. Rep. of the Congo 3°45′ N, 27°51′ E 224
Kapingamarangi Atoll, North Pacific Ocean 0°43′ N, 152°44′ E 238
Kapiri Mposhi, Zambia 13°60′ S, 28°40′ E 224
Kapisillit, Den. 64°23′ N, 50°19′ W 106
Kapiskau, river, Can. 52°0′ N, 84°33′ W 110
Kapit, Malaysia 1°55′ N, 112°57′ E 192
Kaplan, La., U.S. 29°59′ N, 92°18′ W 96
Kaplice, Czech Rep. 48°44′ N, 14°28′ E 152
Kapoeta, Sudan 4°45′ N, 33°35′ E 224
Kapoho Crater, Hawaiʻi, U.S. 19°29′ N, 154°53′ W 99
Kapombo, Dem. Rep. of the Congo 10°39′ S, 23°27′ E 224
Kaposvár, Hung. 46°22′ N, 17°47′ E 168
Kappeln, Ger. 54°40′ N, 9°56′ E 150
Kappelshamn, Sw. 57°50′ N, 18°45′ E 166
Kapsabet, Kenya 0°10′ N, 35°8′ E 224
Kapsan, N. Korea 41°4′ N, 128°19′ E 200
Kapsowar, Kenya 0°57′ N, 35°35′ E 224
Kapterko, spring, Chad 16°50′ N, 23°12′ E 226
Kaptol, Croatia 45°25′ N, 17°42′ E 168
Kapuāiwa Coconut Grove, site, Hawaiʻi, U.S. 21°5′ N, 157°6′ W 99
Kapuas, river, Indonesia 0°28′ N, 110°18′ E 192
Kapulo, Dem. Rep. of the Congo 8°18′ S, 29°11′ E 224
Kapuskasing, Can. 49°24′ N, 82°24′ W 82
Kapustin Yar, Russ. 48°35′ N, 45°45′ E 158
Kaputir, Kenya 2°3′ N, 35°27′ E 224
Kapuvár, Hung. 47°35′ N, 17°2′ E 168
Kapydzhik, peak, Arm. 39°9′ N, 45°59′ E 195
Kara Balta, Kyrg. 42°48′ N, 73°52′ E 184
Kara Burun, Turk. 36°40′ N, 31°40′ E 156
Kara Burun, Turk. 38°41′ N, 26°21′ E 156
Kara Dağ, peak, Turk. 37°40′ N, 43°33′ E 195
Kara Dağ, peak, Turk. 37°22′ N, 33°5′ E 156
Kara, river, Russ. 69°10′ N, 65°11′ E 246
Kara Sea 78°26′ N, 78°5′ E 160
Karabash, Russ. 55°27′ N, 60°19′ E 154
Karabekaul, Turkm. 38°25′ N, 64°13′ E 197
Karabiga, Turk. 40°24′ N, 27°16′ E 158
Karabogaz (Bekdash), Turkm. 41°32′ N, 52°35′ E 158
Karabudakhkent, Russ. 42°42′ N, 47°37′ E 195
Karabük, Turk. 41°12′ N, 32°36′ E 156
Karaburun, Alban. 40°21′ N, 19°4′ E 156
Karaca Dağ, peak, Turk. 37°40′ N, 39°50′ E 195
Karacabey, Turk. 40°12′ N, 28°20′ E 156
Karacadağ, Turk. 37°43′ N, 39°39′ E 195
Karacaköy, Turk. 41°24′ N, 28°21′ E 156
Karacasu, Turk. 37°43′ N, 28°35′ E 156
Karachala, Azerb. 39°48′ N, 48°56′ E 195
Karachayevo-Cherkesiya, adm. division, Russ. 43°42′ N, 40°40′ E 195
Karachayevsk, Russ. 43°46′ N, 41°55′ E 195
Karachev, Russ. 53°3′ N, 35°0′ E 154
Karachi, Pak. 24°49′ N, 67°2′ E 186
Karád, Hung. 46°40′ N, 17°50′ E 168
Karadag, Azerb. 40°17′ N, 49°34′ E 195
Karadžica, Maced. 41°54′ N, 21°14′ E 168
Karaga, Ghana 9°54′ N, 0°29′ E 222
Karaginskiy, Ostrov, island, Russ. 57°53′ N, 163°44′ E 160
Karagosh, Gora, peak, Russ. 51°41′ N, 89°17′ E 184
Karahallı, Turk. 38°19′ N, 29°31′ E 156
Karahüyük, Turk. 37°47′ N, 32°25′ E 156
Karaidel′, Russ. 55°50′ N, 56°35′ E 154
Karaidel′skiy, Russ. 55°50′ N, 57°2′ E 154
Karaikal, India 10°56′ N, 79°48′ E 188
Karaisalı, Turk. 37°15′ N, 35°2′ E 156
Karaj, Iran 35°51′ N, 50°57′ E 186
Karakaralong, Kepulauan, islands, Philippine Sea 4°51′ N, 125°34′ E 203
Karakax, river, China 36°39′ N, 78°58′ E 184
Karakeçi, Turk. 37°26′ N, 39°27′ E 195
Karakoçan, Turk. 38°56′ N, 40°2′ E 195
Kara-Köl, Kyrg. 41°35′ N, 72°38′ E 197
Karakol, Kyrg. 42°27′ N, 78°17′ E 190
Kara-Koo, Kyrg. 42°13′ N, 76°36′ E 184
Karakoram Pass, China 35°32′ N, 77°52′ E 188
Karakoro, river, Mauritania 15°22′ N, 11°47′ W 222
Karakorum see Har Horin, ruin(s), Mongolia 47°14′ N, 102°43′ E 198
Karaköse see Ağrı, Turk. 39°43′ N, 43°3′ E 195
Karakul′, Taj. 39°0′ N, 73°34′ E 197
Karakulino, Russ. 56°2′ N, 53°43′ E 154
Karakuwisa, Namibia 18°54′ S, 19°40′ E 220
Karam, Russ. 55°14′ N, 107°37′ E 190
Karaman, Turk. 37°10′ N, 33°12′ E 156
Karamay, China 45°30′ N, 84°51′ E 184
Karamea, N.Z. 41°16′ S, 172°8′ E 240
Karamiran, river, China 37°12′ N, 85°3′ E 188
Karamiran Shankou, pass, China 36°18′ N, 87°4′ E 188
Karamken, Russ. 60°25′ N, 151°27′ E 173
Karamyshevo, Russ. 57°45′ N, 28°41′ E 166
Karan, Serb. and Mont. 43°54′ N, 19°53′ E 168
Karan, oil field, Saudi Arabia 27°41′ N, 49°45′ E 196
Karapınar, Turk. 37°41′ N, 33°33′ E 156
Kara-Say, Kyrg. 41°34′ N, 77°57′ E 184
Karasburg, Namibia 28°1′ S, 18°42′ E 227
Karašica, river, Croatia 45°44′ N, 17°41′ E 156
Karasino, Russ. 66°46′ N, 86°56′ E 169
Karasu, Taj. 37°57′ N, 73°57′ E 197
Karasu, Turk. 41°6′ N, 30°39′ E 156
Karasu, river, Turk. 39°54′ N, 40°4′ E 195
Karasu, river, Turk. 38°46′ N, 43°37′ E 195
Karasuk, Russ. 53°42′ N, 78°4′ E 184
Karasuk Hills, Kenya 2°16′ N, 34°57′ E 224
Kara-Suu, Kyrg. 41°5′ N, 75°34′ E 184
Karataş, Turk. 36°34′ N, 35°22′ E 156
Karathuri, Myanmar 10°56′ N, 98°46′ E 202
Karatsu, Japan 33°26′ N, 129°57′ E 201
Karaul, Russ. 70°5′ N, 83°22′ E 169
Karauli, India 26°31′ N, 76°58′ E 197
Kara-Ünkür, Kyrg. 41°43′ N, 75°45′ E 184
Karavás, Gr. 36°20′ N, 22°57′ E 156
Karavónissia, islands, Aegean Sea 35°54′ N, 25°36′ E 156
Karavostasi, Northern Cyprus 35°8′ N, 32°49′ E 194
Karawa, Dem. Rep. of the Congo 3°14′ N, 20°17′ E 218
Karawanken, Aust. 46°31′ N, 13°54′ E 156
Karayazı, Turk. 39°40′ N, 42°8′ E 195
Karayün, Turk. 39°38′ N, 37°19′ E 156
Karbalāʼ, Iraq 32°36′ N, 44°2′ E 180
Kårböle, Nor. 61°58′ N, 15°17′ E 152
Karcag, Hung. 47°18′ N, 20°54′ E 168
Kardašova Řečice, Czech Rep. 49°10′ N, 14°52′ E 152
Kardítsa, Gr. 39°20′ N, 21°56′ E 180
Kardiva Channel 4°49′ N, 72°13′ E 188
Kärdla, Est. 58°59′ N, 22°42′ E 166
Kareliya, adm. division, Russ. 61°46′ N, 30°7′ E 166
Karel′skaya, Russ. 62°11′ N, 39°27′ E 154
Karem Shalom, Israel 31°13′ N, 34°16′ E 194
Karema, Tanzania 6°48′ S, 30°24′ E 224
Karera, India 25°28′ N, 78°10′ E 197
Karesuando, Nor. 68°26′ N, 22°26′ E 152
Karêt, region, Africa 23°35′ N, 9°38′ W 214
Kargānrūd, Iran 37°52′ N, 48°56′ E 195
Kargasok, Russ. 58°58′ N, 80°50′ E 169
Kargat, Russ. 55°10′ N, 80°21′ E 184
Kargı, Turk. 41°8′ N, 34°29′ E 156
Kargil, India 34°32′ N, 76°7′ E 186
Kargilik see Yecheng, China 37°52′ N, 77°31′ E 184
Kargopol′, Russ. 61°30′ N, 38°53′ E 154
Karhula, Fin. 60°30′ N, 26°55′ E 166
Kari, Nig. 11°12′ N, 10°35′ E 222
Kariá, Gr. 39°59′ N, 22°23′ E 156
Karia, Gr. 38°45′ N, 20°38′ E 156
Kariba, Zimb. 16°28′ S, 28°51′ E 224
Kariba, Lake, Zimb. 17°27′ S, 25°50′ E 207
Karibib, Namibia 21°56′ S, 15°52′ E 227
Karijini National Park, Austral. 22°48′ S, 117°59′ E 238
Karikari, Cape, N.Z. 34°49′ S, 173°25′ E 240
Karima, Sudan 18°30′ N, 31°50′ E 182
Karimata, Kepulauan, islands, Indian Ocean 1°31′ S, 106°26′ E 192
Karimganj, India 24°44′ N, 92°22′ E 188
Karimnagar, India 18°25′ N, 79°7′ E 188
Kariniemi, Fin. 65°36′ N, 27°56′ E 152
Karis (Karjaa), Fin. 60°4′ N, 23°39′ E 166
Karitane, N.Z. 45°39′ S, 170°38′ E 240
Kariya, Japan 34°57′ N, 137°0′ E 201
Karizak, Afghan. 32°26′ N, 61°28′ E 186
Karjaa see Karis, Fin. 60°4′ N, 23°39′ E 166
Karjala, Fin. 60°46′ N, 22°4′ E 166
Karkaar, Somalia 9°42′ N, 48°36′ E 216
Karkar, island, P.N.G. 4°49′ S, 145°4′ E 192
Karkas, Kūh-e, peak, Iran 33°26′ N, 51°41′ E 180
Karkkila, Fin. 60°31′ N, 24°7′ E 166
Karkku, Fin. 61°23′ N, 22°57′ E 166
Karkoj, Sudan 12°57′ N, 34°2′ E 182
Kärkölä, Fin. 60°54′ N, 25°14′ E 166
Karlholm, Sw. 60°30′ N, 17°34′ E 166
Karlino, Pol. 54°2′ N, 15°53′ E 152
Karlıova, Turk. 39°16′ N, 41°0′ E 195
Karlovac, Croatia 45°28′ N, 15°33′ E 156
Karlovarský, adm. division, Czech Rep. 49°55′ N, 12°2′ E 152
Karlovka, Ukr. 49°29′ N, 35°9′ E 158
Karlovy Vary, Czech Rep. 50°13′ N, 12°52′ E 152
Karlsborg, Nor. 65°48′ N, 23°16′ E 152
Karlsborg, Nor. 58°31′ N, 14°29′ E 152
Karlskrona, Nor. 56°9′ N, 15°33′ E 152
Karlsøy, Nor. 70°0′ N, 19°54′ E 152
Karlsøyvær, islands, Norwegian Sea 67°35′ N, 12°59′ E 152
Karlsruhe, Ger. 49°0′ N, 8°24′ E 150
Karlstad, Minn., U.S. 48°33′ N, 96°33′ W 90
Karluk, Alas., U.S. 57°25′ N, 154°33′ W 98
Karma, Belarus 53°5′ N, 30°51′ E 154
Karmana, Uzb. 40°9′ N, 65°20′ E 197
Karmir Blur, ruin(s), Arm. 40°7′ N, 44°22′ E 195
Karnack, Tex., U.S. 32°39′ N, 94°10′ W 103
Karnal, India 29°41′ N, 77°1′ E 197
Karnataka, adm. division, India 13°56′ N, 74°36′ E 188
Karnes City, Tex., U.S. 28°52′ N, 97°54′ W 96
Karoi, Zimb. 16°50′ S, 29°39′ E 224
Karokh, Afghan. 34°33′ N, 62°30′ E 186
Kārokh, peak, Iraq 36°28′ N, 44°36′ E 195
Karonga, Malawi 9°55′ S, 33°54′ E 224
Karoo National Park, S. Af. 32°30′ S, 21°51′ E 227
Karor, Pak. 31°14′ N, 71°0′ E 186
Karora, Sudan 17°41′ N, 38°17′ E 182
Karou, Mali 15°6′ N, 0°37′ E 222
Karpasia Peninsula, Northern Cyprus 35°21′ N, 33°59′ E 194
Kárpathos, island, Gr. 35°15′ N, 27°9′ E 180
Karpinsk, Russ. 59°45′ N, 60°0′ E 154
Karpogory, Russ. 64°1′ N, 44°33′ E 154
Kärrgruvan, Nor. 60°4′ N, 15°56′ E 152
Kars, Turk. 40°34′ N, 43°10′ E 180
Kärsämäki, Fin. 63°58′ N, 25°44′ E 152
Kārsava, Latv. 56°47′ N, 27°40′ E 166
Karsiyang, India 26°49′ N, 88°17′ E 197
Karskiye Vorota, Proliv 70°38′ N, 59°23′ E 246
Karsun, Russ. 54°10′ N, 47°1′ E 154
Kartal, Turk. 40°54′ N, 29°10′ E 156
Kartaly, Russ. 53°5′ N, 60°35′ E 154
Kartayel′, Russ. 64°29′ N, 53°12′ E 154
Karttula, Fin. 62°50′ N, 27°7′ E 152
Kartung, Senegal 13°6′ N, 16°39′ W 222
Karubwe, Zambia 15°8′ S, 28°22′ E 224
Karufa, Indonesia 3°47′ S, 133°17′ E 192
Karumwa, Tanzania 3°12′ S, 32°37′ E 224
Kārūn, river, Iran 30°44′ N, 48°16′ E 180
Karuna, Fin. 60°15′ N, 22°31′ E 166
Karungu, Kenya 0°51′ N, 34°12′ E 224
Karvio, Fin. 62°30′ N, 28°38′ E 152
Karwar, India 14°47′ N, 74°8′ E 188
Karwi, India 25°12′ N, 80°55′ E 197
Karyaí, Gr. 40°15′ N, 24°15′ E 156
Kar′yepol′ye, Russ. 65°34′ N, 43°42′ E 154
Karymkary, Russ. 62°4′ N, 67°38′ E 169
Kas, Sudan 12°30′ N, 24°19′ E 216
Kaş, Turk. 36°11′ N, 29°37′ E 156
Kas, river, Russ. 59°33′ N, 90°5′ E 169
Kas Saar, Est. 58°41′ N, 22°52′ E 166
Kasaan, Alas., U.S. 55°33′ N, 132°25′ W 108
Kasaba, Turk. 36°17′ N, 29°44′ E 156
Kasaba Bay, Zambia 8°35′ S, 30°43′ E 224
Kasai, river, Dem. Rep. of the Congo 6°48′ S, 20°59′ E 218
Kasai-Occidental, adm. division, Dem. Rep. of the Congo 5°59′ S, 20°39′ E 218
Kasai-Oriental, adm. division, Dem. Rep. of the Congo 4°17′ S, 23°24′ E 218
Kasaji, Dem. Rep. of the Congo 10°22′ S, 23°28′ E 224
Kasala, Fin. 61°57′ N, 21°21′ E 166
Kasama, Zambia 10°13′ S, 31°10′ E 224
Kasane, Botswana 17°51′ S, 25°5′ E 224
Kasanga, Tanzania 8°27′ S, 31°10′ E 224
Kasanka National Park, Zambia 12°48′ S, 29°40′ E 224
Kasar, Ras, Eritrea 17°50′ N, 38°34′ E 182
Kasaragod, India 12°31′ N, 75°1′ E 188
Kasari, river, Est. 58°44′ N, 23°54′ E 166
Kasba Lake, Can. 60°2′ N, 103°43′ W 106
Kaseda, Japan 31°23′ N, 130°20′ E 201
Kasempa, Zambia 13°29′ S, 25°48′ E 224
Kasenga, Dem. Rep. of the Congo 10°18′ S, 28°40′ E 224
Kasenye, Dem. Rep. of the Congo 1°23′ N, 30°26′ E 224
Kasese, Dem. Rep. of the Congo 1°37′ S, 27°13′ E 224
Kasese, Uganda 0°10′ N, 30°7′ E 224
Kasganj, India 27°48′ N, 78°39′ E 197
Kāshān, Iran 34°1′ N, 51°27′ E 180
Kashegelok, Alas., U.S. 60°50′ N, 157°48′ W 98
Kashi, China 39°31′ N, 75°59′ E 184
Kashima, Japan 33°6′ N, 130°5′ E 201
Kashin, Russ. 57°18′ N, 37°31′ E 154
Kashipur, India 29°11′ N, 78°57′ E 197
Kashira, Russ. 54°48′ N, 38°10′ E 154
Kashishibog Lake, Can. 49°47′ N, 90°36′ W 94
Kashitu, Zambia 13°44′ S, 28°38′ E 224
Kashiwazaki, Japan 37°21′ N, 138°33′ E 201
Kashkadar′ya, Uzb. 38°55′ N, 65°45′ E 197
Kashkarantsy, Russ. 66°21′ N, 35°55′ E 154
Kāshmar, Iran 35°13′ N, 58°28′ E 180
Kashmor, Pak. 28°29′ N, 69°34′ E 186
Kashnjet, Alban. 41°54′ N, 19°48′ E 168
Kasimov, Russ. 54°55′ N, 41°26′ E 154
Kasindi, Dem. Rep. of the Congo 2°119′ N, 29°40′ E 224
Kaskaskia, river, Ill., U.S. 38°42′ N, 89°26′ W 80
Kaskö (Kaskinen), Fin. 62°22′ N, 21°12′ E 152
Kasli, Russ. 55°52′ N, 60°45′ E 154
Kaslo, Can. 49°54′ N, 116°56′ W 90
Kasmere Lake, Can. 59°35′ N, 101°38′ W 108
Kasongo, Dem. Rep. of the Congo 4°29′ S, 26°36′ E 224
Kasongo-Lunda, Dem. Rep. of the Congo 6°30′ S, 16°49′ E 220
Kaspiysk, Russ. 42°51′ N, 47°41′ E 195
Kaspiyskiy, Russ. 45°21′ N, 47°21′ E 158
Kasrik see Kırkgeçit, Turk. 38°7′ N, 43°27′ E 195
Kassala, Sudan 15°25′ N, 36°22′ E 182
Kassala, adm. division, Sudan 15°49′ N, 34°29′ E 182
Kassándra, Gr. 40°1′ N, 23°7′ E 156
Kassari, spring, Mauritania 15°50′ N, 7°54′ W 222
Kassaro, Mali 13°0′ N, 8°54′ W 222
Kassel, Ger. 51°19′ N, 9°29′ E 167
Kasserine see Qasserine, Tun. 35°9′ N, 8°51′ E 156
Kasson, Minn., U.S. 44°0′ N, 92°47′ W 94
Kássos, island, Gr. 35°11′ N, 26°48′ E 180
Kassouloua, spring, Niger 14°29′ N, 11°23′ E 222
Kastamonu, Turk. 41°23′ N, 33°45′ E 156
Kaštel Sućurac, Croatia 43°32′ N, 16°25′ E 168
Kastellaun, Ger. 50°3′ N, 7°25′ E 167
Kastornoye, Russ. 51°48′ N, 38°5′ E 158
Kastrossikiá, Gr. 39°6′ N, 20°38′ E 156
Kastsyukovichy, Belarus 53°19′ N, 32°5′ E 154
Kasulu, Tanzania 4°36′ S, 30°6′ E 224
Kasumkent, Russ. 41°40′ N, 48°11′ E 195
Kasungu, Malawi 13°4′ S, 33°28′ E 224
Kasungu National Park, Malawi 12°58′ S, 32°56′ E 224
Kasupe, Malawi 15°12′ S, 35°16′ E 224
Kasur, Pak. 31°9′ N, 74°26′ E 186
Kata Tjuta (Mount Olga), Austral. 25°21′ S, 130°31′ E 230
Kataba, Zambia 16°5′ S, 25°6′ E 224
Kataeregi, Nig. 9°20′ N, 6°18′ E 222
Katagum, Nig. 12°17′ N, 10°21′ E 222
Katahdin, Mount, Me., U.S. 45°53′ N, 69°1′ W 94
Katako Kombe, Dem. Rep. of the Congo 3°28′ S, 24°21′ E 224
Katal′ga, Russ. 59°8′ N, 76°50′ E 169
Katanda, Russ. 50°11′ N, 86°14′ E 184
Katanga, adm. division, Dem. Rep. of the Congo 8°40′ S, 23°51′ E 220
Katanning, Austral. 33°41′ S, 117°33′ E 231
Katav Ivanovsk, Russ. 54°45′ N, 58°10′ E 154
Katavi National Park, Tanzania 7°21′ S, 30°38′ E 224
Katavía, Gr. 35°57′ N, 27°46′ E 156
Katavivanovsk, Russ. 54°44′ N, 58°13′ E 184
Katchall Island, India 7°40′ N, 92°29′ E 188
Kate, Tanzania 7°50′ S, 31°8′ E 224
Katera, Uganda 0°55′ S, 31°37′ E 224
Katerini, Gr. 40°15′ N, 22°33′ E 180
Kates Needle, peak, Can. 57°2′ N, 132°14′ W 108
Katha, Myanmar 24°8′ N, 96°19′ E 188
Katherine, Austral. 14°29′ S, 132°20′ E 231
Kathleen, Mount, Austral. 23°56′ S, 135°13′ E 230
Kathmandu, Nepal 27°46′ N, 85°11′ E 197
Kati, Mali 12°44′ N, 8°4′ W 222
Katihar, India 25°30′ N, 87°33′ E 197
Katima Mulilo, Namibia 17°33′ S, 24°16′ E 224
Katimik Lake, Can. 52°51′ N, 99°52′ W 108
Katiola, Côte d'Ivoire 8°6′ N, 5°5′ W 222
Kätkäsuvanto, Fin. 68°7′ N, 23°20′ E 152
Katlanovo, Maced. 41°53′ N, 21°40′ E 168
Katmai, Mount, Alas., U.S. 58°10′ N, 155°14′ W 98
Katonah, N.Y., U.S. 41°14′ N, 73°42′ W 104
Katondwe, Zambia 15°15′ S, 30°12′ E 224
Katonga, river, Uganda 3°179′ N, 30°33′ E 224
Katowice, Pol. 50°15′ N, 19°1′ E 152
Katrancık Dağı, peak, Turk. 37°26′ N, 30°15′ E 156
Katrineholm, Nor. 59°0′ N, 16°8′ E 152
Katrovozh, Russ. 66°22′ N, 66°9′ E 169
Katsina, Nig. 13°0′ N, 7°38′ E 222
Katsina Ala, river, Nig. 7°51′ N, 8°33′ E 222
Katsumoto, Japan 33°50′ N, 129°42′ E 200
Katsuta, Japan 36°23′ N, 140°32′ E 201
Katsuura, Japan 35°9′ N, 140°18′ E 201
Katsuyama, Japan 35°5′ N, 133°40′ E 201
Katsuyama, Japan 36°4′ N, 136°31′ E 201
Kattankudi, Sri Lanka 7°34′ N, 81°48′ E 188
Kattaqo′rg′on, Uzb. 39°54′ N, 66°16′ E 197
Kattegat 55°53′ N, 10°43′ E 150
Katthammarsvik, Sw. 57°25′ N, 18°49′ E 166
Kattisavan, Nor. 64°46′ N, 18°8′ E 152
Kattskill Bay, N.Y., U.S. 43°28′ N, 73°38′ W 104
Katul, Jebel, peak, Sudan 14°13′ N, 29°19′ E 226
Katumbi, Zambia 10°49′ S, 33°30′ E 220
Katun′, river, Russ. 51°28′ N, 86°4′ E 184
Katwa, India 23°34′ N, 88°6′ E 197
Katwe, Uganda 0°10′ N, 29°51′ E 224
Katwijk aan Zee, Neth. 52°12′ N, 4°25′ E 163
Kauaʻi, island, Hawaiʻi, U.S. 22°7′ N, 160°15′ W 99
Kauakaiakaola Heiau, site, Hawaiʻi, U.S. 19°37′ N, 156°1′ W 99
Kaub, Ger. 50°5′ N, 7°46′ E 163
Kaugama, Nig. 12°28′ N, 9°46′ E 222
Kauhajoki, Fin. 62°24′ N, 22°8′ E 154
Kauhako Crater, peak, Hawaiʻi, U.S. 21°11′ N, 157°1′ W 99
Kauhava, Fin. 63°5′ N, 23°2′ E 152
Kaukau Veld, Namibia 20°24′ S, 18°49′ E 227
Kaukonen, Fin. 67°29′ N, 24°52′ E 152
Kaʻula, island, Hawaiʻi, U.S. 21°27′ N, 160°43′ W 99
Kauliranta, Fin. 66°27′ N, 23°40′ E 152
Kaulu Paoa Heiau, site, Hawaiʻi, U.S. 22°12′ N, 159°38′ W 99
Kaunā Point, Hawaiʻi, U.S. 18°59′ N, 156°18′ W 99
Kaunas, Lith. 54°53′ N, 23°54′ E 166
Kaunata, Latv. 56°19′ N, 27°33′ E 166
Kaunatava, Lith. 55°58′ N, 22°32′ E 166
Kauniainen see Grankulla, Fin. 60°11′ N, 24°43′ E 152
Kaunolū, site, Hawaiʻi, U.S. 20°43′ N, 156°60′ W 99
Kaʻūpūlehu, site, Hawaiʻi, U.S. 19°49′ N, 156°2′ W 99
Kaura-Namoda, Nig. 12°36′ N, 6°35′ E 222
Kauru, Nig. 10°33′ N, 8°11′ E 222
Kavacha, Russ. 60°22′ N, 169°55′ E 160
Kavak, Turk. 41°4′ N, 36°2′ E 156
Kavála, Gr. 40°57′ N, 24°24′ E 180
Kavali, India 14°55′ N, 79°59′ E 188
Kavaratti, India 10°34′ N, 72°38′ E 188
Kavarna, Bulg. 43°26′ N, 28°19′ E 158
Kavarskas, Lith. 55°26′ N, 24°55′ E 166
Kavieng, P.N.G. 2°41′ S, 150°59′ E 238
Kavkaz, Russ. 45°22′ N, 36°39′ E 156
Kavungo, Angola 11°32′ S, 23°2′ E 220
Kawagoe, Japan 35°54′ N, 139°29′ E 201
Kawaihoa Point, Hawaiʻi, U.S. 21°42′ N, 160°13′ W 99
Kawakawa, N.Z. 35°25′ S, 174°5′ E 240
Kawambwa, Zambia 9°49′ S, 29°5′ E 224
Kawanishi, Japan 38°0′ N, 140°3′ E 201
Kawanoe, Japan 34°0′ N, 133°35′ E 201
Kawardha, India 22°1′ N, 81°14′ E 197
Kawasaki, Japan 35°30′ N, 139°43′ E 201
Kawashiri Misaki, Japan 34°23′ N, 130°41′ E 200
Kawaweogama Lake, Can. 50°9′ N, 91°3′ W 110
Kaweah, Mount, Calif., U.S. 36°31′ N, 118°32′ W 101
Kaweka, peak, N.Z. 39°20′ S, 176°18′ E 240
Kawela Place of Refuge, site, Hawaiʻi, U.S. 21°4′ N, 157°1′ W 99
Kawhia, N.Z. 38°4′ S, 174°48′ E 240
Kawich Peak, Nev., U.S. 37°58′ N, 116°33′ W 90
Kawich Range, Nev., U.S. 37°53′ N, 116°38′ W 90
Kawlinn, Myanmar 23°46′ N, 95°41′ E 202
Kawnipi Lake, Can. 48°27′ N, 91°30′ W 94
Kawthoung, Myanmar 9°59′ N, 98°32′ E 202
Kax, river, China 43°44′ N, 84°4′ E 184
Kay, Russ. 59°57′ N, 53°1′ E 154
Kaya, Burkina Faso 13°5′ N, 1°6′ W 222
Kayambi, Zambia 9°28′ S, 31°59′ E 224
Kayan-Mentarang National Park, Indonesia 2°38′ N, 115°12′ E 238
Kayapınar, Turk. 37°32′ N, 41°12′ E 195
Kayar, Senegal 14°55′ N, 16°52′ W 222
Kayasula, Russ. 44°17′ N, 45°0′ E 158
Kaycee, Wyo., U.S. 43°42′ N, 106°39′ W 90
Kayenzi, Tanzania 3°16′ S, 32°37′ E 224
Kayes, Congo 4°12′ S, 13°10′ E 218
Kayes, Congo 4°25′ S, 11°39′ E 218
Kayes, Mali 14°26′ N, 11°28′ W 222
Kaymaz, Turk. 39°31′ N, 31°10′ E 156
Kaynar, Turk. 38°53′ N, 36°25′ E 156
Käyrämo, Fin. 66°57′ N, 26°17′ E 152
Kaysatskoye, Russ. 49°43′ N, 46°46′ E 158
Kayser Gebergte, Suriname 3°5′ N, 56°60′ W 130
Kayseri, Turk. 38°41′ N, 35°30′ E 156

Kayyerhan, *Russ.* 69°12′ N, 83°53′ E **169**
Kaz Dağı, peak, *Turk.* 39°41′ N, 26°47′ E **156**
Kazachka, *Russ.* 51°27′ N, 43°57′ E **158**
Kazach'ye, *Russ.* 70°40′ N, 136°18′ E **160**
Kazakh Uplands, *Asia* 47°30′ N, 69°46′ E **184**
Kazakhstan 48°18′ N, 63°42′ E **184**
Kazan', *Russ.* 55°45′ N, 49°9′ E **154**
Kazan Rettō see Volcano Islands, *Philippine Sea* 23°11′ N, 139°38′ E **190**
Kazan, river, *Can.* 63°10′ N, 98°16′ W **72**
Kazanlŭk, *Bulg.* 42°35′ N, 25°24′ E **180**
Kazanskaya, *Russ.* 49°50′ N, 41°9′ E **158**
Kazanskoye, *Russ.* 57°9′ N, 49°9′ E **154**
Kazarman, *Kyrg.* 41°22′ N, 74°3′ E **197**
Kazbek, peak, *Ga.* 42°40′ N, 44°29′ E **195**
Kāzerūn, *Iran* 29°35′ N, 51°37′ E **196**
Kazhim, *Russ.* 60°20′ N, 51°36′ E **154**
Kazima, *Cen. Af. Rep.* 5°14′ N, 26°13′ E **224**
Kazimoto, *Tanzania* 9°6′ S, 36°50′ E **224**
Kazlų Rūda, *Lith.* 54°44′ N, 23°26′ E **166**
Kaztalovka, *Kaz.* 49°45′ N, 48°41′ E **158**
Kazumba, *Dem. Rep. of the Congo* 6°26′ S, 21°59′ E **218**
Kazyany, *Belarus* 55°18′ N, 26°51′ E **166**
Kazym Mys, *Russ.* 64°45′ N, 65°52′ E **169**
Kazym, river, *Russ.* 63°54′ N, 67°41′ E **169**
Ké Macina, *Mali* 14°1′ N, 5°22′ W **222**
Kéa, *Gr.* 37°38′ N, 24°20′ E **156**
Kéa, island, *Gr.* 37°28′ N, 24°23′ E **180**
Kea, Mauna, peak, *Hawai'i, U.S.* 19°49′ N, 155°31′ W **99**
Kea'au Ranch, site, *Hawai'i, U.S.* 19°37′ N, 155°2′ W **99**
Keams Canyon, *Ariz., U.S.* 35°48′ N, 110°12′ W **92**
Kearney, *Can.* 45°32′ N, 79°13′ W **94**
Kearney, *Nebr., U.S.* 40°41′ N, 99°5′ W **90**
Kearny, *Ariz., U.S.* 33°3′ N, 110°54′ W **92**
Kearsarge, *Mich., U.S.* 47°16′ N, 88°26′ W **94**
Keatchie, *La., U.S.* 32°9′ N, 93°55′ W **103**
Keauhou Landing, site, *Hawai'i, U.S.* 19°16′ N, 155°17′ W **99**
Kebbe, *Nig.* 12°4′ N, 4°46′ E **222**
Kébémer, *Senegal* 15°24′ N, 16°27′ W **222**
Kebili, *Tun.* 33°42′ N, 8°59′ E **214**
Kebkabiya, *Sudan* 13°35′ N, 24°5′ E **216**
Keble, peak, *Nor.* 67°12′ N, 20°10′ E **152**
Kebnekaise, peak, *Nor.* 67°52′ N, 18°23′ E **152**
K'ebrī Dehar, *Eth.* 6°46′ N, 44°10′ E **218**
Kecel, *Hung.* 46°30′ N, 19°16′ E **168**
Kechika, river, *Can.* 59°5′ N, 127°25′ W **108**
Keçiborlu, *Turk.* 37°56′ N, 30°18′ E **156**
Kecskemét, *Hung.* 46°54′ N, 19°42′ E **168**
Kėdainiai, *Lith.* 55°17′ N, 23°56′ E **166**
Kedarnath, *India* 30°44′ N, 79°4′ E **197**
Kédédésé, *Chad* 11°8′ N, 16°44′ E **216**
Kedgwick, river, *Can.* 48°2′ N, 68°7′ W **94**
Kedia Hill, *Botswana* 21°25′ S, 24°28′ E **227**
Kediri, *Indonesia* 7°50′ S, 111°54′ E **192**
Kédougou, *Senegal* 12°35′ N, 12°13′ W **222**
Kedvavom, *Russ.* 64°13′ N, 53°27′ E **154**
Keele Peak, *Can.* 63°23′ N, 130°26′ W **98**
Keele, river, *Can.* 64°3′ N, 127°57′ W **98**
Keeler, *Calif., U.S.* 36°29′ N, 117°53′ W **101**
Keeler, *Mich., U.S.* 42°6′ N, 86°9′ W **102**
Keeley Lake, *Can.* 54°51′ N, 108°44′ W **108**
Keelung see Chilung, *Taiwan* 25°6′ N, 121°45′ E **198**
Keen, Mount, *U.K.* 56°56′ N, 3°5′ W **150**
Keene, *Calif., U.S.* 35°13′ N, 118°35′ W **101**
Keene, *N.H., U.S.* 42°55′ N, 72°17′ W **104**
Keene, *N.Y., U.S.* 44°15′ N, 73°48′ W **104**
Keep R. National Park, *Austral.* 15°55′ S, 128°49′ E **238**
Keeper Hill, *Ire.* 52°44′ N, 8°21′ W **150**
Keeseville, *N.Y., U.S.* 44°30′ N, 73°30′ W **104**
Keesler Air Force Base, *Miss., U.S.* 30°22′ N, 88°60′ W **103**
Keetmanshoop, *Namibia* 26°35′ S, 18°7′ E **227**
Keewatin, *Can.* 49°45′ N, 94°32′ W **90**
Keezhik Lake, *Can.* 51°40′ N, 89°8′ W **110**
Kefaloniá (Cephalonia), adm. division, *Gr.* 38°22′ N, 20°3′ E **156**
Kefar 'Ezyon, *West Bank* 31°37′ N, 35°5′ E **194**
Kefar Rosh ha Niqra, *Israel* 33°4′ N, 35°6′ E **194**
Kefar Sava, *Israel* 32°10′ N, 34°53′ E **194**
Kefar Yona, *Israel* 32°19′ N, 34°56′ E **194**
Keffi, *Nig.* 8°51′ N, 7°49′ E **222**
Keflavík, *Ice.* 63°58′ N, 22°41′ W **143**
Keg River, *Can.* 57°43′ N, 117°35′ W **108**
Kegaska, Lac, lake, *Can.* 50°17′ N, 61°56′ W **111**
Kegen, *Kaz.* 43°1′ N, 79°13′ E **184**
Kegha, *Eth.* 5°5′ N, 36°48′ E **224**
Keheili, *Sudan* 19°24′ N, 32°49′ E **182**
Kehlstein, peak, *Ger.* 47°35′ N, 12°57′ E **156**
Kehra, *Est.* 59°19′ N, 25°18′ E **166**
Keighley, *U.K.* 53°51′ N, 1°55′ W **162**
Keikyä, *Fin.* 61°15′ N, 22°42′ E **166**
Keila, *Est.* 59°17′ N, 24°23′ E **166**
Keila, river, *Est.* 59°18′ N, 24°28′ E **166**
Keimoes, *S. Af.* 28°40′ S, 20°55′ E **227**
Keïta, *Niger* 14°40′ N, 5°44′ E **222**
Keitele, lake, *Fin.* 62°56′ N, 25°33′ E **152**
Keithley Creek, *Can.* 52°44′ N, 121°26′ W **108**
Keithsburg, *Mo., U.S.* 41°5′ N, 90°56′ W **94**
Keizer, *Oreg., U.S.* 44°59′ N, 123°2′ W **90**
Kejimkujik National Park, *Can.* 43°42′ N, 64°46′ W **111**
Kekerengu, *N.Z.* 41°60′ S, 174°0′ E **240**
Kékes, peak, *Hung.* 47°51′ N, 19°59′ E **168**
Kekurskiy, Mys, *Russ.* 69°55′ N, 32°9′ E **152**
K'elafo, *Eth.* 5°35′ N, 44°11′ E **218**
Kelai, island, *Maldives* 6°43′ N, 73°12′ E **188**
Kélakam, *Niger* 13°32′ N, 11°48′ E **222**
Kelamet, *Eritrea* 16°4′ N, 38°41′ E **182**
Kelang, *Malaysia* 3°3′ N, 101°26′ E **196**
Kelberg, *Ger.* 50°17′ N, 6°55′ E **167**
Keld, *U.K.* 54°24′ N, 2°11′ W **162**
Kelebia, *Hung.* 46°10′ N, 19°37′ E **168**
Keleft, *Afghan.* 37°18′ N, 66°15′ E **186**
Kelkit, *Turk.* 40°7′ N, 39°26′ E **195**
Kelkit, river, *Turk.* 40°0′ N, 38°38′ E **180**
Kellé, *Congo* 0°8′ N, 14°31′ E **218**
Kéllé, *Niger* 14°15′ N, 10°9′ E **222**
Kellen, *Ger.* 51°47′ N, 6°9′ E **167**
Keller Lake, *Can.* 63°22′ N, 119°60′ W **246**
Kellet, Cape, *Can.* 71°57′ N, 130°22′ W **106**
Kellett Strait 75°40′ N, 120°58′ W **106**
Kelleys Island, *Ohio, U.S.* 41°37′ N, 82°40′ W **102**
Kelliher, *Can.* 51°15′ N, 103°46′ W **90**
Kello, *Fin.* 65°6′ N, 25°23′ E **152**
Kellog, *Russ.* 62°27′ N, 86°21′ E **169**
Kellogora, *Russ.* 64°19′ N, 32°14′ E **152**
Kellojärvi, lake, *Fin.* 64°13′ N, 28°24′ E **152**
Kelly, *La., U.S.* 31°58′ N, 92°11′ W **103**
Kelly Air Force Base, *Tex., U.S.* 29°19′ N, 98°38′ W **92**
Kelmė, *Lith.* 55°38′ N, 22°55′ E **166**
Kelmis, *Belg.* 50°42′ N, 6°0′ E **167**
Kélo, *Chad* 9°18′ N, 15°47′ E **216**
Kelottijärvi, *Fin.* 68°31′ N, 22°1′ E **152**
Kelowna, *Can.* 49°51′ N, 119°28′ W **106**
Kelsall, Mount, *Can.* 59°48′ N, 136°28′ W **108**
Kelsey, *Can.* 56°2′ N, 96°31′ W **108**
Kelsey Creek, river, *Can.* 57°47′ N, 94°17′ W **108**
Kelso, *Calif., U.S.* 35°1′ N, 115°39′ W **101**
Kelso, *N.Z.* 45°55′ S, 169°16′ E **240**
Kelso, *Wash., U.S.* 46°8′ N, 122°54′ W **100**
Keltie, Cape, *Antarctica* 65°44′ S, 135°58′ E **248**
Keluang, *Malaysia* 2°3′ N, 103°20′ E **196**
Kelvä, *Fin.* 63°3′ N, 30°6′ E **152**
Kelvington, *Can.* 52°10′ N, 103°31′ W **108**
Kelyexed, *Somalia* 8°45′ N, 49°11′ E **216**
Kem', *Russ.* 64°59′ N, 34°31′ E **152**
Kemah, *Turk.* 39°35′ N, 39°2′ E **195**
Kemano, *Can.* 53°33′ N, 127°56′ W **108**
Kemasik, *Malaysia* 4°26′ N, 103°26′ E **196**
Kembé, *Cen. Af. Rep.* 4°35′ N, 21°52′ E **218**
Kembolcha, *Eth.* 11°1′ N, 39°46′ E **224**
Kemboma, *Gabon* 0°40′ N, 13°31′ E **218**
Kemer, *Kaz.* 49°32′ N, 54°58′ E **158**
Kemer, *Turk.* 40°24′ N, 27°2′ E **156**
Kemer, *Turk.* 36°37′ N, 29°19′ E **156**
Kemer, *Turk.* 36°34′ N, 30°34′ E **156**
Ķemeri, *Latv.* 56°56′ N, 23°28′ E **166**
Kemerovo, *Russ.* 55°17′ N, 86°11′ E **184**
Kemetern, *Aust.* 47°14′ N, 16°9′ E **168**
Kemi, *Fin.* 65°43′ N, 24°49′ E **160**
Kemijärvi, *Fin.* 66°42′ N, 27°23′ E **152**
Kemin, *Kyrg.* 42°47′ N, 75°40′ E **184**
Kemlya, *Russ.* 54°39′ N, 45°17′ E **154**
Kemmerer, *Wyo., U.S.* 41°48′ N, 110°33′ W **90**
Kemp, Lake, *Tex., U.S.* 33°45′ N, 99°23′ W **92**
Kemp Peninsula, *Antarctica* 73°32′ S, 59°37′ W **248**
Kemparana, *Mali* 12°51′ N, 4°57′ W **222**
Kempen, *Ger.* 51°22′ N, 6°25′ E **167**
Kemps Bay, *Bahamas* 24°2′ N, 77°34′ W **96**
Kemps Bay, adm. division, *Bahamas* 24°34′ N, 78°20′ W **116**
Kenadsa, *Alg.* 31°34′ N, 2°25′ W **214**
Kenai, *Alas., U.S.* 60°27′ N, 151°19′ W **98**
Kenai Peninsula, *North America* 60°23′ N, 150°43′ W **98**
Kenamu, river, *Can.* 52°45′ N, 60°4′ W **111**
Kenamuke Swamp, marsh, *Sudan* 5°52′ N, 33°30′ E **224**
Kenansville, *Fla., U.S.* 27°52′ N, 80°60′ W **105**
Kenaston, *Can.* 51°31′ N, 106°18′ W **90**
Kendal, *U.K.* 54°20′ N, 2°43′ W **162**
Kendall, *Fla., U.S.* 25°41′ N, 80°20′ W **105**
Kendall, Cape, *Can.* 63°48′ N, 88°54′ W **106**
Kendallville, *Ind., U.S.* 41°26′ N, 85°17′ W **102**
Kendari, *Indonesia* 3°55′ S, 122°27′ E **192**
Kendikolu, island, *Maldives* 5°45′ N, 73°26′ E **188**
Këndrevicës, Maja e, peak, *Alban.* 40°16′ N, 19°45′ E **156**
Kendrick, *Idaho, U.S.* 46°36′ N, 116°41′ W **90**
Kendu Bay, *Kenya* 0°25′ N, 34°40′ E **224**
Kenedy, *Tex., U.S.* 28°48′ N, 97°51′ W **92**
Kenema, *Sierra Leone* 7°49′ N, 11°12′ W **222**
Kenga, *Russ.* 57°24′ N, 81°5′ E **169**
Kenge, *Dem. Rep. of the Congo* 4°59′ S, 17°2′ E **218**
Kèngkok, *Laos* 16°26′ N, 105°11′ E **202**
Kengtung, *Myanmar* 21°18′ N, 99°38′ E **202**
Kengyel, *Hung.* 47°5′ N, 20°20′ E **168**
Kengzhaly, *Kaz.* 48°57′ N, 56°13′ E **158**
Kenhardt, *S. Af.* 29°20′ S, 21°9′ E **227**
Kéniéba, *Mali* 12°50′ N, 11°15′ W **222**
Kenilworth, *U.K.* 52°20′ N, 1°35′ W **162**
Kenitra (Port Lyautey), *Mor.* 34°17′ N, 6°37′ W **214**
Kenli, *China* 37°36′ N, 118°35′ E **198**
Kenmare, *N. Dak., U.S.* 48°39′ N, 102°4′ W **90**
Kenna, *N. Mex., U.S.* 33°50′ N, 103°47′ W **92**
Kennard, *Tex., U.S.* 31°20′ N, 95°11′ W **103**
Kennebec, *S. Dak., U.S.* 43°53′ N, 99°53′ W **90**
Kennebunk, *Me., U.S.* 43°23′ N, 70°33′ W **104**
Kennebunk Beach, *Me., U.S.* 43°20′ N, 70°31′ W **104**
Kennebunkport, *Me., U.S.* 43°21′ N, 70°29′ W **104**
Kennedy, *Can.* 50°0′ N, 102°22′ W **90**
Kennedy Bight 52°5′ N, 56°24′ W **111**
Kennedy, Cape see Canaveral, Cape, *Fla., U.S.* 28°24′ N, 80°34′ W **105**
Kennedy Channel 78°17′ N, 71°33′ W **246**
Kennedy, Mount, *Can.* 60°18′ N, 139°5′ W **98**
Kennett, *Mo., U.S.* 36°14′ N, 90°3′ W **96**
Kenney, *Ill., U.S.* 40°5′ N, 89°5′ W **102**
Kenney Dam, *Can.* 53°27′ N, 125°23′ W **108**
Kenny, Mount, *Can.* 56°54′ N, 123°58′ W **108**
Keno Hill, *Can.* 63°53′ N, 135°25′ W **106**
Kenogami, river, *Can.* 50°5′ N, 85°54′ W **94**
Kenogamissi Lake, *Can.* 48°13′ N, 82°18′ W **94**
Kenora, *Can.* 49°47′ N, 94°28′ W **90**
Kenosha, *Wis., U.S.* 42°36′ N, 87°50′ W **102**
Kenova, *W. Va., U.S.* 38°23′ N, 82°36′ W **94**
Kent, *Can.* 49°13′ N, 121°46′ W **100**
Kent, *Conn., U.S.* 41°42′ N, 73°29′ W **104**
Kent, *Ohio, U.S.* 41°8′ N, 81°21′ W **102**
Kent, *Oreg., U.S.* 45°9′ N, 120°42′ W **90**
Kent, *Tex., U.S.* 31°2′ N, 104°13′ W **92**
Kent, *Wash., U.S.* 47°22′ N, 122°15′ W **100**
Kent Group, islands, *Bass Strait* 39°20′ S, 147°14′ E **230**
Kent Peninsula, *Can.* 68°39′ N, 107°16′ W **106**
Kentaū, *Kaz.* 43°28′ N, 68°26′ E **184**
Kentland, *Ind., U.S.* 40°45′ N, 87°27′ W **102**
Kenton, *Ky., U.S.* 38°51′ N, 84°28′ W **102**
Kenton, *Ohio, U.S.* 40°38′ N, 83°36′ W **102**
Kentozero, *Russ.* 64°51′ N, 31°8′ E **152**
Kentrikí Macedonia, adm. division, *Gr.* 40°52′ N, 21°59′ E **156**
Kents Hill, *Me., U.S.* 44°23′ N, 70°1′ W **104**
Kentuck, *W. Va., U.S.* 38°38′ N, 81°37′ W **102**
Kentucky, adm. division, *Ky., U.S.* 37°37′ N, 86°20′ W **94**
Kentville, *Can.* 45°4′ N, 64°31′ W **111**
Kentwood, *La., U.S.* 30°56′ N, 90°31′ W **103**
Kentwood, *Mich., U.S.* 42°54′ N, 85°35′ W **102**
Kenville, *Can.* 51°59′ N, 101°20′ W **108**
Kenwood, *Ohio, U.S.* 39°11′ N, 84°23′ W **102**
Kenya 0°37′ N, 37°25′ E **224**
Kenya, Mount, *Kenya* 0°10′ N, 37°14′ E **224**
Kenzingen, *Ger.* 48°11′ N, 7°45′ E **163**
Keokuk, *Iowa, U.S.* 40°24′ N, 91°28′ W **82**
Kep, *Cambodia* 10°30′ N, 104°18′ E **202**
Kepa, *Russ.* 65°9′ N, 32°9′ E **152**
Kepi, *Indonesia* 6°26′ S, 139°11′ E **192**
Kepino, *Russ.* 65°24′ N, 41°41′ E **154**
Kępno, *Pol.* 51°16′ N, 17°59′ E **152**
Keppel Bay 23°35′ S, 149°50′ E **230**
Kepsut, *Turk.* 39°40′ N, 28°8′ E **156**
Kerälä, *Fin.* 64°45′ N, 28°46′ E **152**
Kerala, adm. division, *India* 11°32′ N, 75°48′ E **188**
Keran, *India* 34°39′ N, 73°59′ E **186**
Kéran National Park, *Togo* 9°51′ N, 0°8′ E **222**
Kerava, *Fin.* 60°23′ N, 25°3′ E **166**
Kerby, *Oreg., U.S.* 42°12′ N, 123°38′ W **90**
Kerch, *Ukr.* 45°24′ N, 36°29′ E **156**
Kerchel', *Russ.* 59°19′ N, 64°43′ E **154**
Kerchem'ya, *Russ.* 61°26′ N, 53°59′ E **154**
Kerchenskiy Proliv 45°5′ N, 35°45′ E **156**
Kerchevskiy, *Russ.* 59°56′ N, 56°16′ E **154**
Kerchouel, *Mali* 17°10′ N, 0°15′ E **222**
Kerekere, *Dem. Rep. of the Congo* 2°37′ N, 30°33′ E **224**
Kerempe Burnu, *Turk.* 42°2′ N, 33°13′ E **156**
Keren, *Eritrea* 15°44′ N, 38°27′ E **182**
Kerend-e Gharb, *Iran* 34°15′ N, 46°14′ E **180**
Kerens, *Tex., U.S.* 32°6′ N, 96°13′ W **96**
Keret', *Russ.* 66°17′ N, 33°38′ E **152**
Kericho, *Kenya* 0°22′ N, 35°16′ E **224**
Kerimäki, *Fin.* 61°54′ N, 29°16′ E **166**
Kerinci, peak, *Indonesia* 1°45′ S, 100°55′ E **192**
Keriske, *Russ.* 69°56′ N, 132°21′ E **173**
Keriya, river, *China* 36°46′ N, 81°26′ E **184**
Keriya see Yutian, *China* 36°55′ N, 81°36′ E **184**
Keriya Shankou, pass, *China* 35°9′ N, 81°33′ E **188**
Kerki, *Russ.* 63°43′ N, 54°13′ E **154**
Kerki see Atamyrat, *Turkm.* 37°49′ N, 65°10′ E **197**
Kerkiçi, *Turkm.* 37°52′ N, 65°15′ E **197**
Kérkira, *Gr.* 39°37′ N, 19°54′ E **156**
Kérkira (Corfu), island, *Gr.* 39°10′ N, 16°33′ E **143**
Kerkour Nourene, Massif du, *Chad* 15°41′ N, 21°0′ E **216**
Kerkrade, *Neth.* 50°52′ N, 6°3′ E **167**
Kerma, *Sudan* 19°38′ N, 30°28′ E **226**
Kerman, *Calif., U.S.* 36°43′ N, 120°5′ W **100**
Kermānshāh, *Iran* 34°15′ N, 47°0′ E **180**
Kermānshāh, *Iran* 31°16′ N, 54°56′ E **180**
Kermit, *Tex., U.S.* 31°50′ N, 103°5′ W **92**
Kermode, Mount, *Can.* 52°56′ N, 131°58′ W **108**
Kern Canyon, *Calif., U.S.* 36°20′ N, 118°26′ W **101**
Kern, river, *Calif., U.S.* 36°22′ N, 118°28′ W **101**
Kernville, *Calif., U.S.* 35°45′ N, 118°27′ W **101**
Keroh, *Malaysia* 5°41′ N, 101°1′ E **196**
Kérouané, *Guinea* 9°17′ N, 8°60′ W **222**
Kerpen, *Ger.* 50°51′ N, 6°41′ E **167**
Kerr, Cape, *Antarctica* 80°4′ S, 170°43′ E **248**
Kerre, *Cen. Af. Rep.* 5°21′ N, 25°35′ E **224**
Kerrobert, *Can.* 51°56′ N, 109°9′ W **90**
Kerrville, *Tex., U.S.* 30°1′ N, 99°8′ W **92**
Kershaw, *S.C., U.S.* 34°32′ N, 80°35′ W **96**
Kersilö, *Fin.* 67°34′ N, 26°41′ E **152**
Kersley, *Can.* 52°47′ N, 122°25′ W **108**
Kertamulia, *Indonesia* 0°20′ N, 109°7′ E **196**
Kerulen, river, *Mongolia* 47°22′ N, 111°2′ E **198**
Keryneia (Girne, Kyrenia), *Northern Cyprus* 35°20′ N, 33°18′ E **194**
Keryneia Range, *Northern Cyprus* 35°16′ N, 33°25′ E **194**
Kerzaz, *Alg.* 29°30′ N, 1°24′ W **214**
Kesagami Lake, *Can.* 50°23′ N, 80°52′ W **94**
Kesagami, river, *Can.* 50°27′ N, 80°10′ W **110**
Kesälahti, *Fin.* 61°52′ N, 29°48′ E **166**
Keşan, *Turk.* 40°49′ N, 26°40′ E **180**
Keşap, *Turk.* 40°55′ N, 38°29′ E **158**
Keshan, *China* 48°2′ N, 125°50′ E **198**
Keşiş Dağı, peak, *Turk.* 39°47′ N, 39°37′ E **195**
Keskal, *India* 20°3′ N, 81°36′ E **188**
Kes'ma, *Russ.* 58°22′ N, 37°7′ E **154**
Kessingland, *U.K.* 52°25′ N, 1°42′ E **163**
Kesten'ga, *Russ.* 65°54′ N, 31°51′ E **152**
Kestilä, *Fin.* 64°21′ N, 26°14′ E **152**
Keswick, *U.K.* 54°35′ N, 3°8′ W **162**
Keszthely, *Hung.* 46°45′ N, 17°14′ E **168**
Ket', river, *Russ.* 58°33′ N, 85°20′ E **169**
Keta, *Ghana* 5°54′ N, 0°57′ E **222**
Ketapang, *Indonesia* 1°57′ S, 109°59′ E **192**
Ketchikan, *Alas., U.S.* 55°22′ N, 131°41′ W **108**
Ketchum Mountain, *Tex., U.S.* 31°19′ N, 101°7′ W **92**
Kétegyháza, *Hung.* 46°33′ N, 21°11′ E **168**
Keti Bandar, *Pak.* 24°4′ N, 67°30′ E **186**
Kętrzyn, *Pol.* 54°4′ N, 21°23′ E **166**
Kettering, *Ohio, U.S.* 39°40′ N, 84°10′ W **102**
Kettering, *U.K.* 52°23′ N, 0°43′ W **162**
Kettle Lake, *Can.* 47°0′ N, 82°54′ W **110**
Kettle Rapids, fall(s), *Can.* 56°23′ N, 94°37′ W **108**
Kettle River Range, *Wash., U.S.* 48°10′ N, 118°29′ W **90**
Kettleman City, *Calif., U.S.* 36°0′ N, 119°58′ W **100**
Keudepanga, *Indonesia* 4°33′ N, 95°41′ E **196**
Keur Momar Sarr, *Senegal* 15°58′ N, 16°1′ W **222**
Keuru, *Fin.* 62°14′ N, 24°38′ E **152**
Keuruunselkä, lake, *Fin.* 61°53′ N, 23°10′ E **152**
Kevelaer, *Ger.* 51°34′ N, 6°14′ E **167**
Kewanee, *Ala., U.S.* 32°25′ N, 88°25′ W **103**
Kewanee, *Ill., U.S.* 41°14′ N, 89°56′ W **102**
Kewanna, *Ind., U.S.* 41°0′ N, 86°25′ W **102**
Kewaskum, *Wis., U.S.* 43°30′ N, 88°15′ W **102**
Keweenaw Peninsula, *U.S.* 47°1′ N, 88°60′ W **94**
Keweenaw Point, *Mich., U.S.* 47°26′ N, 87°44′ W **94**
Key Colony Beach, *Fla., U.S.* 24°45′ N, 80°58′ W **105**
Key Harbour, *Can.* 45°53′ N, 80°43′ W **94**
Key Largo, *Fla., U.S.* 25°6′ N, 80°27′ W **105**
Key West, *Fla., U.S.* 24°33′ N, 81°48′ W **105**
Keya Paha, river, *S. Dak., U.S.* 43°11′ N, 100°19′ W **90**
Keyano, *Can.* 53°50′ N, 73°26′ W **111**
Keyes, *Okla., U.S.* 36°48′ N, 102°15′ W **92**
Keyi, *China* 42°8′ N, 82°40′ E **184**
Keynsham, *U.K.* 51°24′ N, 2°30′ W **162**
Keys View, peak, *Calif., U.S.* 33°55′ N, 116°15′ W **101**
Keyser, *W. Va., U.S.* 39°26′ N, 78°59′ W **94**
Keystone, *W. Va., U.S.* 37°24′ N, 81°27′ W **94**
Keystone Heights, *Fla., U.S.* 29°46′ N, 82°3′ W **105**
Keystone Peak, *Ariz., U.S.* 31°52′ N, 111°16′ W **92**
Kez, *Russ.* 57°53′ N, 53°46′ E **154**
Kezar Falls, *Me., U.S.* 43°48′ N, 70°54′ W **104**
Khabab, *Syr.* 33°1′ N, 36°16′ E **194**
Khabarikha, *Russ.* 65°49′ N, 52°20′ E **154**
Khabarovo, *Russ.* 69°35′ N, 60°21′ E **169**
Khabarovsk, *Russ.* 48°30′ N, 135°8′ E **190**
Khabarovsk, adm. division, *Russ.* 51°56′ N, 133°28′ E **160**
Khabrat Umm al Ḩīrān, spring, *Kuwait* 29°25′ N, 47°14′ E **196**
Khābūr, river, *Syr.* 36°11′ N, 40°54′ E **195**
Khadyzhensk, *Russ.* 44°24′ N, 39°31′ E **158**
Khagaria, *India* 25°30′ N, 86°25′ E **197**
Khairpur, *Pak.* 27°30′ N, 68°47′ E **186**
Khaishi, *Ga.* 42°58′ N, 42°16′ E **195**
Khakasiya, adm. division, *Russ.* 54°37′ N, 88°39′ E **169**
Khakhea, *Botswana* 24°44′ S, 23°30′ E **227**
Khalasa, ruin(s), *Israel* 31°5′ N, 34°35′ E **194**
Khalatse, *India* 34°21′ N, 76°54′ E **188**
Khālid Ibn al Walīd, dam, *Asia* 32°36′ N, 35°19′ E **194**
Khalilovo, *Russ.* 51°20′ N, 58°4′ E **158**
Khalkhāl, *Iran* 37°39′ N, 48°33′ E **195**
Khal'mer Yu, *Russ.* 67°56′ N, 64°55′ E **169**
Khalturin, *Russ.* 58°32′ N, 48°52′ E **154**
Khalūf, *Oman* 20°30′ N, 58°2′ E **182**
Khalyasavey, *Russ.* 63°22′ N, 78°26′ E **169**
Khambhaliya, *India* 22°12′ N, 69°40′ E **186**
Khamīs Mushayţ, *Saudi Arabia* 18°17′ N, 42°44′ E **182**
Khammam, *India* 17°14′ N, 80°10′ E **188**
Khammouan, *Laos* 17°24′ N, 104°49′ E **202**
Khamr, *Yemen* 15°59′ N, 43°56′ E **182**
Khamsa, *Egypt* 30°26′ N, 32°22′ E **194**
Khān Abū Shāmāt, *Syr.* 33°39′ N, 36°53′ E **194**
Khān az Zābīb, *Jordan* 31°28′ N, 36°5′ E **194**
Khān Shaykhūn, *Syr.* 35°26′ N, 36°38′ E **194**
Khan Tängiri (Khan Tengri), peak, *Kyrg.* 42°11′ N, 80°5′ E **184**
Khan Tengri see Khan Tängiri, peak, *Kyrg.* 42°11′ N, 80°5′ E **184**
Khān Yūnis, *Gaza Strip* 31°20′ N, 34°18′ E **194**
Khanabad, *Afghan.* 36°39′ N, 69°9′ E **186**
Khanai, *Pak.* 30°29′ N, 67°15′ E **186**
Khānaqīn, *Iraq* 34°21′ N, 45°22′ E **180**
Khandwa, *India* 21°49′ N, 76°21′ E **197**
Khandyga, *Russ.* 62°32′ N, 135°34′ E **160**
Khanewal, *Pak.* 30°19′ N, 71°57′ E **186**
Khangarh, *Pak.* 28°21′ N, 71°43′ E **186**
Khanka, Ozero, lake, *Russ.* 45°12′ N, 129°53′ E **173**
Khanlar, *Azerb.* 40°35′ N, 46°20′ E **195**
Khanovey, *Russ.* 67°15′ N, 63°36′ E **169**
Khanpur, *Pak.* 28°38′ N, 70°39′ E **186**
Khansiir, Raas, *Somalia* 10°50′ N, 44°43′ E **216**
Khantaū, *Kaz.* 44°12′ N, 73°48′ E **184**
Khantayskoye, Ozero, lake, *Russ.* 68°13′ N, 88°18′ E **169**
Khanty Mansiysk, *Russ.* 61°2′ N, 69°10′ E **169**
Khanty-Mansi, adm. division, *Russ.* 62°2′ N, 69°26′ E **169**
Khanymey, *Russ.* 63°47′ N, 75°58′ E **169**
Khao Yai National Park, *Thai.* 14°17′ N, 101°43′ E **202**
Khapalu, *Pak.* 35°8′ N, 76°21′ E **186**
Khapcheranga, *Russ.* 49°41′ N, 112°26′ E **198**
Kharabali, *Russ.* 47°23′ N, 47°10′ E **158**
Kharagauli, *Ga.* 42°0′ N, 43°7′ E **195**
Kharagpur, *India* 22°19′ N, 87°19′ E **197**
Kharampur, *Russ.* 64°18′ N, 78°12′ E **169**
Kharan, *Pak.* 28°36′ N, 65°25′ E **182**
Kharānaq, *Iran* 32°20′ N, 54°41′ E **180**
Kharasavey, Mys, *Russ.* 70°41′ N, 64°10′ E **169**
Khârga, El Wâhât el, *Egypt* 25°41′ N, 29°48′ E **180**
Khargon, *India* 21°47′ N, 75°38′ E **197**
Khārk, island, *Iran* 29°4′ N, 50°10′ E **180**
Kharkiv, *Ukr.* 49°59′ N, 36°15′ E **158**
Kharlovka, *Russ.* 68°44′ N, 37°15′ E **152**
Kharlu, *Russ.* 61°47′ N, 30°53′ E **152**
Kharsān, *Syr.* 35°17′ N, 37°2′ E **194**
Khartoum, *Sudan* 15°27′ N, 32°23′ E **182**
Khartoum, adm. division, *Sudan* 15°48′ N, 31°44′ E **216**
Khartoum North, *Sudan* 15°37′ N, 32°34′ E **226**
Khaşab, *Oman* 26°10′ N, 56°12′ E **196**
Khasan, *Russ.* 42°24′ N, 130°41′ E **200**
Khasavyurt, *Russ.* 43°12′ N, 46°34′ E **195**
Khash, *Afghan.* 31°31′ N, 62°54′ E **186**
Khāsh, *Iran* 28°10′ N, 61°11′ E **182**
Khash, river, *Afghan.* 32°42′ N, 64°13′ E **186**
Khashm el Qirba, *Sudan* 14°55′ N, 35°55′ E **182**
Khashm el Qirba Dam, *Sudan* 14°25′ N, 34°49′ E **182**
Khashri, *Ga.* 41°57′ N, 43°33′ E **195**
Khaskovo, *Bulg.* 41°56′ N, 25°32′ E **156**
Khaskovo, adm. division, *Bulg.* 41°52′ N, 25°17′ E **156**
Khatanga, *Russ.* 71°57′ N, 102°45′ E **160**
Khātūnīyah, *Syr.* 36°23′ N, 41°14′ E **195**
Khatyrka, *Russ.* 62°1′ N, 174°56′ E **160**
Khaur, *Pak.* 33°16′ N, 72°33′ E **186**
Khavda, *India* 23°51′ N, 69°45′ E **186**
Khaydarkan, *Kyrg.* 39°56′ N, 71°26′ E **197**
Khaypudyrskaya Guba 68°30′ N, 59°0′ E **160**
Khayryuzovo, *Russ.* 56°58′ N, 157°7′ E **160**
Khed Brahma, *India* 24°3′ N, 73°2′ E **186**
Khemmarat, *Thai.* 16°2′ N, 105°12′ E **202**
Kherson, *Ukr.* 46°40′ N, 32°35′ E **156**
Kheta, *Russ.* 71°31′ N, 99°56′ E **160**
Kheta, river, *Russ.* 71°30′ N, 99°5′ E **160**
Khewra, *Pak.* 32°37′ N, 73°4′ E **186**
Khibiny, *Russ.* 67°49′ N, 33°16′ E **152**
Khiitola, *Russ.* 61°13′ N, 29°40′ E **166**
Khilchipur, *India* 24°2′ N, 76°34′ E **197**
Khilok, *Russ.* 51°30′ N, 110°29′ E **190**
Khimki, *Russ.* 55°53′ N, 37°26′ E **154**
Khirbat Ad Dayr, ruin(s), *Jordan* 31°32′ N, 35°35′ E **194**
Khirbat al Ghazālah, *Syr.* 32°43′ N, 36°12′ E **194**
Khirbat aş Şafrā', ruin(s), *Jordan* 31°37′ N, 35°36′ E **194**
Khirbat as Samrā', ruin(s), *Jordan* 32°10′ N, 36°8′ E **194**
Khirbat Qumrān, ruin(s), *West Bank* 31°43′ N, 35°25′ E **194**
Khirbat Umm al Jimāl, ruin(s), *Jordan* 32°19′ N, 36°20′ E **194**
Khiri Ratthanikhom, *Thai.* 9°2′ N, 98°53′ E **202**
Khislavichi, *Russ.* 54°12′ N, 32°10′ E **154**
Khiwa, *Uzb.* 41°23′ N, 60°22′ E **180**
Khizy, *Azerb.* 40°54′ N, 49°4′ E **195**
Khlevnoye, *Russ.* 52°12′ N, 39°0′ E **158**
Khmel'nyts'kyy, *Ukr.* 49°24′ N, 26°58′ E **158**
Khoai, Hon, island, *Vietnam* 8°9′ N, 104°40′ E **202**
Khodoriv, *Ukr.* 49°23′ N, 24°19′ E **152**
Khodzhatau, *Taj.* 39°11′ N, 71°41′ E **197**
Khogali, *Sudan* 6°9′ N, 27°46′ E **224**
Khok Kloi, *Thai.* 8°17′ N, 98°17′ E **202**
Khokhol'skiy, *Russ.* 51°29′ N, 38°42′ E **158**
Khokhropar, *Pak.* 25°42′ N, 70°14′ E **186**
Kholm, *Afghan.* 36°42′ N, 67°41′ E **186**
Kholm, *Russ.* 57°8′ N, 31°12′ E **154**
Kholmogorskaya, *Russ.* 63°49′ N, 40°40′ E **154**
Kholmogory, *Russ.* 64°13′ N, 41°37′ E **154**
Kholmsk, *Russ.* 47°1′ N, 142°5′ E **190**
Kholopenichi, *Belarus* 54°30′ N, 29°1′ E **166**
Khomeyn, *Iran* 33°42′ N, 50°6′ E **180**
Khomeynīshahr, *Iran* 32°44′ N, 51°32′ E **180**
Khon Kaen, *Thai.* 16°29′ N, 102°40′ E **202**
Không, *Laos* 14°9′ N, 105°49′ E **202**
Khôngxédôn, *Laos* 15°37′ N, 105°47′ E **202**
Khonsa, *India* 27°37′ N, 93°50′ E **188**
Khonulakh, *Russ.* 66°20′ N, 151°26′ E **160**
Khonuu, *Russ.* 66°30′ N, 143°15′ E **160**
Khoper, river, *Russ.* 52°5′ N, 43°18′ E **158**
Khoper, river, *Russ.* 50°14′ N, 41°53′ E **184**
Khor, *Russ.* 48°0′ N, 135°3′ E **190**
Khorāsān, region, *Asia* 34°30′ N, 53°1′ E **180**
Khorat see Nakhon Ratchasima, *Thai.* 14°58′ N, 102°7′ E **202**
Khorb el Ethel, spring, *Alg.* 28°34′ N, 6°19′ W **214**
Khorintsy, *Russ.* 60°41′ N, 121°20′ E **160**
Khorixas, *Namibia* 20°24′ S, 14°55′ E **220**
Khorof Harar, *Kenya* 2°7′ N, 40°42′ E **224**
Khorol, *Ukr.* 49°48′ N, 33°12′ E **158**
Khoroûfa, spring, *Mauritania* 17°21′ N, 15°49′ W **222**
Khorramābād, *Iran* 33°29′ N, 48°19′ E **180**
Khorramshahr, *Iran* 30°29′ N, 48°9′ E **180**
Khorugh, *Taj.* 37°29′ N, 71°35′ E **184**
Khosheutovo, *Russ.* 47°0′ N, 47°50′ E **158**
Khost, *Afghan.* 33°22′ N, 69°58′ E **186**
Khost, *Pak.* 30°14′ N, 67°38′ E **186**
Khotyn, *Ukr.* 48°30′ N, 26°30′ E **152**
Khouribga, *Mor.* 32°56′ N, 6°57′ W **214**
Khoyniki, *Belarus* 51°51′ N, 30°4′ E **158**
Khrami, river, *Ga.* 41°31′ N, 44°3′ E **195**
Khrenovoye, *Russ.* 51°8′ N, 40°15′ E **158**
Khroma, river, *Russ.* 71°50′ N, 144°2′ E **160**
Khromtaū, *Kaz.* 50°16′ N, 58°27′ E **158**
Khuchni, *Russ.* 41°53′ N, 47°55′ E **195**
Khudabad, *Pak.* 36°42′ N, 74°53′ E **186**
Khudosey, river, *Russ.* 65°23′ N, 82°18′ E **169**
Khudumelapye, *Botswana* 23°53′ S, 24°53′ E **227**
Khuff, oil field, *Lib.* 28°8′ N, 18°17′ E **216**
Khuis, *Botswana* 26°37′ S, 21°49′ E **227**
Khujand, *Taj.* 40°15′ N, 69°41′ E **197**
Khŭjayli, *Uzb.* 42°24′ N, 59°27′ E **180**
Khulkhuta, *Russ.* 46°16′ N, 46°21′ E **158**
Khulna, *Bangladesh* 22°48′ N, 89°28′ E **197**
Khun Yuam, *Thai.* 18°53′ N, 97°52′ E **202**
Khunjerab Pass, *China* 36°50′ N, 75°26′ E **184**
Khunsar, *Iran* 33°14′ N, 50°17′ E **180**
Khunti, *India* 23°6′ N, 85°16′ E **197**
Khunzakh, *Russ.* 42°29′ N, 46°42′ E **195**
Khurais, oil field, *Saudi Arabia* 25°10′ N, 48°1′ E **196**
Khushab, *Pak.* 32°18′ N, 72°24′ E **186**
Khutse Game Reserve, *Botswana* 23°43′ S, 23°52′ E **227**
Khuwei, *Sudan* 13°3′ N, 29°14′ E **216**
Khuzdar, *Pak.* 27°43′ N, 66°34′ E **186**
Khvāf, *Iran* 34°36′ N, 60°9′ E **180**
Khvalynsk, *Russ.* 52°28′ N, 48°6′ E **158**
Khvor, *Iran* 33°49′ N, 55°5′ E **180**
Khvormūj, *Iran* 28°35′ N, 51°24′ E **196**
Khvorostyanka, *Russ.* 52°37′ N, 49°0′ E **158**
Khvosh Asia, *Afghan.* 32°53′ N, 62°14′ E **186**
Khvoy, *Iran* 38°34′ N, 44°55′ E **195**

Kovd Ozero, lake, *Russ.* 66°27′ N, 31°8′ E **154**
Kovdor, *Russ.* 67°33′ N, 30°24′ E **152**
Kovel′, *Ukr.* 51°11′ N, 24°42′ E **152**
Kovero, *Fin.* 62°31′ N, 30°30′ E **152**
Kovesjoki, *Fin.* 61°54′ N, 22°43′ E **166**
Kovic, Baie 61°15′ N, 78°53′ W **106**
Kovilj, *Serb. and Mont.* 45°12′ N, 20°1′ E **168**
Kovin, *Serb. and Mont.* 44°44′ N, 20°57′ E **168**
Kovrov, *Russ.* 56°21′ N, 41°24′ E **154**
Kowalów, *Pol.* 52°24′ N, 14°46′ E **152**
Kowhitirangi, *N.Z.* 42°53′ S, 171°1′ E **240**
Kowkcheh, river, *Afghan.* 37°3′ N, 69°44′ E **186**
Kowŏn, *N. Korea* 39°26′ N, 127°14′ E **200**
Köyceğiz, *Turk.* 36°57′ N, 28°40′ E **156**
Koyda, *Russ.* 66°21′ N, 42°33′ E **154**
Koygorodok, *Russ.* 60°28′ N, 51°9′ E **154**
Koynas, *Russ.* 64°46′ N, 47°26′ E **154**
Koyuk, *Alas., U.S.* 64°48′ N, 161°14′ W **98**
Koyukuk, river, *Alas., U.S.* 65°51′ N, 155°8′ W **106**
Koyukuk, river, *Alas., U.S.* 65°2′ N, 156°36′ W **98**
Koyulhisar, *Turk.* 40°18′ N, 37°49′ E **156**
Kozan, *Turk.* 37°26′ N, 35°48′ E **156**
Kozáni, *Gr.* 40°18′ N, 21°47′ E **156**
Kozarac, *Bosn. and Herzg.* 44°57′ N, 16°51′ E **168**
Kozel′shchyna, *Ukr.* 49°16′ N, 33°45′ E **158**
Kozel′sk, *Russ.* 54°0′ N, 35°46′ E **154**
Kozhasay, *Kaz.* 48°15′ N, 57°11′ E **158**
Kozhevnikovo, *Russ.* 56°14′ N, 83°59′ E **169**
Kozhim, *Russ.* 65°44′ N, 59°31′ E **154**
Kozhva, *Russ.* 65°4′ N, 56°59′ E **154**
Kozhva, river, *Russ.* 64°32′ N, 54°57′ E **154**
Kozjak, peak, *Maced.* 41°22′ N, 21°37′ E **156**
Kozlu, *Turk.* 41°25′ N, 31°44′ E **156**
Kozluk, *Bosn. and Herzg.* 44°30′ N, 19°7′ E **168**
Kozluk, *Turk.* 38°11′ N, 41°31′ E **195**
Koz′modem′yansk, *Russ.* 56°13′ N, 46°43′ E **154**
Kozova, *Ukr.* 49°25′ N, 25°9′ E **152**
Kožuf, *Maced.* 41°8′ N, 22°4′ E **156**
Kozyatyn, *Ukr.* 49°45′ N, 29°0′ E **158**
Kpalimé, *Togo* 6°55′ N, 0°36′ E **222**
Kpandae, *Ghana* 8°26′ N, 2°118′ W **222**
Kpandu, *Ghana* 6°59′ N, 0°17′ E **222**
Kra, Isthmus of, *Thai.* 10°18′ N, 98°8′ E **192**
Krabi, *Thai.* 8°4′ N, 98°55′ E **202**
Kragerø, *Nor.* 58°52′ N, 9°22′ E **152**
Kragujevac, *Serb. and Mont.* 44°0′ N, 20°54′ E **168**
Krak des Chevaliers, site, *Syr.* 34°45′ N, 36°17′ E **194**
Krakor, *Cambodia* 12°31′ N, 104°10′ E **202**
Kraków, *Pol.* 50°3′ N, 19°58′ E **152**
Kralanh, *Cambodia* 13°36′ N, 103°24′ E **202**
Kraljevo, *Serb. and Mont.* 43°43′ N, 20°41′ E **168**
Kramators′k, *Ukr.* 48°43′ N, 37°27′ E **158**
Kramfors, *Nor.* 62°55′ N, 17°47′ E **152**
Kramis, Cap, *Alg.* 36°19′ N, 0°28′ E **164**
Kranzberg, *Namibia* 21°56′ S, 15°43′ E **227**
Krapina, *Croatia* 46°9′ N, 15°53′ E **168**
Krasavino, *Russ.* 60°57′ N, 46°30′ E **154**
Krasino, *Russ.* 70°47′ N, 54°21′ E **173**
Kraskino, *Russ.* 42°42′ N, 130°46′ E **200**
Krāslava, *Latv.* 55°53′ N, 27°10′ E **166**
Krasnaya Polyana, *Russ.* 43°41′ N, 40°10′ E **195**
Krasnaye, *Belarus* 54°14′ N, 27°3′ E **166**
Krasneno, *Russ.* 64°38′ N, 174°49′ E **160**
Krasnoarmeysk, *Russ.* 48°30′ N, 44°29′ E **158**
Krasnoarmeysk, *Russ.* 50°58′ N, 45°40′ E **158**
Krasnoarmeyskaya, *Russ.* 45°22′ N, 38°5′ E **158**
Krasnodar, *Russ.* 45°4′ N, 39°0′ E **156**
Krasnodar, adm. division, *Russ.* 45°40′ N, 38°18′ E **160**
Krasnodon, *Ukr.* 48°16′ N, 39°40′ E **158**
Krasnogorodskoye, *Russ.* 56°51′ N, 28°19′ E **166**
Krasnogorskoye, *Russ.* 52°17′ N, 86°16′ E **184**
Krasnohrad, *Ukr.* 49°24′ N, 35°25′ E **158**
Krasnokamensk, *Russ.* 50°8′ N, 118°0′ E **190**
Krasnokamsk, *Russ.* 58°5′ N, 55°45′ E **154**
Krasnolesnyy, *Russ.* 51°51′ N, 39°30′ E **158**
Krasnoostrovskiy, *Russ.* 60°16′ N, 28°39′ E **166**
Krasnoperekops′k, *Ukr.* 45°57′ N, 33°47′ E **156**
Krasnopillya, *Ukr.* 50°43′ N, 35°16′ E **158**
Krasnopol, *Pol.* 54°6′ N, 23°12′ E **166**
Krasnosel′kup, *Russ.* 65°41′ N, 82°35′ E **169**
Krasnosel′sk, *Arm.* 40°36′ N, 45°19′ E **195**
Krasnoslobodsk, *Russ.* 48°40′ N, 44°30′ E **158**
Krasnoturansk, *Russ.* 54°19′ N, 91°31′ E **190**
Krasnotur′insk, *Russ.* 59°46′ N, 60°15′ E **154**
Krasnoufimsk, *Russ.* 56°37′ N, 57°47′ E **154**
Krasnoural′sk, *Russ.* 58°21′ N, 60°6′ E **154**
Krasnousol′skiy, *Russ.* 53°56′ N, 56°23′ E **154**
Krasnovishersk, *Russ.* 60°25′ N, 57°9′ E **154**
Krasnoy Armii, Proliv 79°41′ N, 91°44′ E **160**
Krasnoyarsk, *Russ.* 56°10′ N, 92°39′ E **160**
Krasnoyarsk, adm. division, *Russ.* 62°17′ N, 84°57′ E **169**
Krasnoyarskiy, *Russ.* 51°57′ N, 59°52′ E **154**
Krasnoye, *Belarus* 52°42′ N, 24°24′ E **154**
Krasnoye, *Russ.* 59°12′ N, 47°51′ E **154**
Krasnoye, *Russ.* 51°37′ N, 51°30′ E **158**
Krasnoye, *Russ.* 56°35′ N, 29°21′ E **166**
Krasnozatonskiy, *Russ.* 61°42′ N, 51°9′ E **169**
Krasnyy, *Russ.* 54°37′ N, 31°30′ E **154**
Krasnyy Kholm, *Russ.* 58°2′ N, 37°5′ E **154**
Krasnyy Kholm, *Russ.* 51°35′ N, 54°10′ E **158**
Krasnyy Klyuch, *Russ.* 55°24′ N, 56°43′ E **154**
Krasnyy Kut, *Russ.* 50°56′ N, 46°54′ E **158**
Krasnyy Luch, *Ukr.* 48°8′ N, 39°0′ E **158**
Krasnyy Lyman, *Ukr.* 49°1′ N, 37°46′ E **158**
Krasnyy Steklovar, *Russ.* 56°15′ N, 48°47′ E **154**
Krasnyy Sulin, *Russ.* 47°53′ N, 40°5′ E **158**
Krasnyy Tekstil′shchik, *Russ.* 51°18′ N, 45°45′ E **158**
Krasnyy Yar, *Russ.* 50°39′ N, 44°43′ E **158**
Krasnyy Yar, *Russ.* 46°30′ N, 48°22′ E **158**
Krasnyy Yar, *Russ.* 55°14′ N, 72°51′ E **184**
Krasnyy Yar, *Russ.* 57°4′ N, 84°38′ E **169**
Krasnyye Baki, *Russ.* 57°5′ N, 45°12′ E **154**
Kratie, *Cambodia* 12°30′ N, 106°3′ E **202**
Kratovo, *Maced.* 42°4′ N, 22°11′ E **168**
Kraulshavn see Nuussuaq, *Den.* 74°9′ N, 57°1′ W **106**
Krefeld, *Ger.* 51°19′ N, 6°34′ E **167**
Kreïjé, spring, *Mauritania* 16°4′ N, 8°32′ W **222**
Kremen, peak, *Croatia* 44°26′ N, 15°51′ E **168**
Kremenchuk, *Ukr.* 49°7′ N, 33°19′ E **158**
Kremenchuts′ke Vdskh., lake, *Ukr.* 49°32′ N, 30°53′ E **158**
Kremenets′, *Ukr.* 50°5′ N, 25°45′ E **152**
Kremna, *Bosn. and Herzg.* 44°48′ N, 17°39′ E **168**
Kremnica, *Slovakia* 48°41′ N, 18°55′ E **152**
Krems, *Aust.* 48°24′ N, 15°36′ E **156**
Kreševo, *Bosn. and Herzg.* 43°51′ N, 18°3′ E **168**
Kress, *Tex., U.S.* 34°21′ N, 101°46′ W **92**
Kresta, Zaliv 65°38′ N, 178°8′ E **160**
Krestovaya Guba, *Russ.* 74°2′ N, 55°18′ E **246**
Krestovka, *Russ.* 66°23′ N, 52°29′ E **154**
Krestovskiy, Mys, *Russ.* 69°24′ N, 143°33′ E **172**
Kresttsy, *Russ.* 58°13′ N, 32°32′ E **154**
Kretinga, *Lith.* 55°52′ N, 21°15′ E **166**
Kreuzberg, peak, *Ger.* 50°22′ N, 9°57′ E **167**
Kreuztal, *Ger.* 50°57′ N, 7°59′ E **167**
Krieglach, *Aust.* 47°32′ N, 15°33′ E **156**
Krim, peak, *Slov.* 45°55′ N, 14°23′ E **156**
Krims′ke Hory, *Ukr.* 44°50′ N, 33°47′ E **156**
Kristiansand, *Nor.* 58°10′ N, 7°47′ E **160**
Kristiansund, *Nor.* 63°5′ N, 7°45′ E **160**
Kristiinankaupunki see Kristinestad, *Fin.* 62°15′ N, 21°20′ E **152**
Kristineberg, *Nor.* 65°3′ N, 18°34′ E **152**
Kristinehamn, *Nor.* 59°18′ N, 14°4′ E **152**
Kristinestad (Kristiinankaupunki), *Fin.* 62°15′ N, 21°20′ E **152**
Kríti see Crete, island, *Gr.* 35°36′ N, 24°6′ E **180**
Kriva Palanka, *Maced.* 42°11′ N, 22°20′ E **168**
Krivaja, river, *Bosn. and Herzg.* 44°15′ N, 18°20′ E **168**
Krivelj, *Serb. and Mont.* 44°8′ N, 22°6′ E **168**
Krivolak, *Maced.* 41°31′ N, 22°5′ E **168**
Krivoy Porog, *Russ.* 65°2′ N, 33°38′ E **152**
Križ, *Croatia* 45°39′ N, 16°31′ E **168**
Križevci, *Croatia* 46°2′ N, 16°32′ E **168**
Krnalovnehradeckny, adm. division, *Czech Rep.* 50°32′ N, 14°58′ E **152**
Krnjeuša, *Bosn. and Herzg.* 44°41′ N, 16°12′ E **168**
Krnov, *Czech Rep.* 50°5′ N, 17°42′ E **152**
Krognes, *Nor.* 70°24′ N, 30°46′ E **152**
Krokom, *Nor.* 63°19′ N, 14°26′ E **152**
Krokstrand, *Nor.* 66°27′ N, 15°5′ E **152**
Krolevets′, *Ukr.* 51°29′ N, 33°28′ E **158**
Kromy, *Russ.* 52°39′ N, 35°45′ E **158**
Kronoby (Kruunupyy), *Fin.* 63°43′ N, 23°1′ E **152**
Kronprins Christian Land, *Den.* 80°7′ N, 38°45′ W **246**
Kronprins Frederik Bjerge, *Den.* 67°31′ N, 34°33′ W **246**
Kronshtadt, *Russ.* 59°59′ N, 29°45′ E **152**
Kroonstad, *S. Af.* 27°40′ S, 27°15′ E **227**
Kropotkin, *Russ.* 45°26′ N, 40°29′ E **158**
Kroshin, *Belarus* 53°10′ N, 26°10′ E **152**
Krosno, *Pol.* 49°39′ N, 21°46′ E **152**
Kröv, *Ger.* 49°58′ N, 7°4′ E **167**
Krrab, peak, *Alban.* 42°6′ N, 19°56′ E **168**
Krrabë, peak, *Alban.* 41°12′ N, 19°56′ E **156**
Krš, *Serb. and Mont.* 44°5′ N, 21°59′ E **168**
Krško, *Slov.* 45°58′ N, 15°27′ E **156**
Krstača, peak, *Serb. and Mont.* 42°57′ N, 20°4′ E **168**
Kruger National Park, *S. Af.* 23°37′ S, 31°8′ E **227**
Kruhlaye, *Belarus* 54°14′ N, 29°51′ E **166**
Krui, *Indonesia* 5°13′ S, 103°53′ E **192**
Krujë, *Alban.* 41°30′ N, 19°47′ E **168**
Krumë, *Alban.* 42°11′ N, 20°25′ E **168**
Krung Thep (Bangkok), *Thai.* 13°44′ N, 100°24′ E **202**
Krupa, *Bosn. and Herzg.* 44°50′ N, 16°10′ E **168**
Krupac, *Serb. and Mont.* 43°6′ N, 22°41′ E **168**
Krupanj, *Serb. and Mont.* 44°22′ N, 19°23′ E **156**
Krupište, *Maced.* 41°51′ N, 22°14′ E **168**
Krupki, *Belarus* 54°20′ N, 29°12′ E **166**
Krutaya, *Russ.* 63°2′ N, 54°46′ E **154**
Krutets, *Russ.* 60°18′ N, 39°24′ E **154**
Krutinka, *Russ.* 55°58′ N, 71°35′ E **184**
Kruunupyy see Kronoby, *Fin.* 63°43′ N, 23°1′ E **152**
Kruzof Island, *Alas., U.S.* 57°3′ N, 137°39′ W **98**
Krychaw, *Belarus* 53°38′ N, 31°44′ E **154**
Krylovskaya, *Russ.* 46°18′ N, 39°57′ E **158**
Krymsk, *Russ.* 44°56′ N, 37°55′ E **156**
Krynki, *Pol.* 53°16′ N, 23°45′ E **152**
Krychivy, *Belarus* 54°42′ N, 27°16′ E **166**
Kryvyy Rih, *Ukr.* 47°56′ N, 33°22′ E **156**
Ksabi, *Alg.* 29°6′ N, 0°56′ E **214**
Ksabi, *Mor.* 32°55′ N, 4°24′ W **214**
Ksar Chellala (Reïbell), *Alg.* 35°12′ N, 2°19′ E **150**
Ksar el Barka, *Mauritania* 18°23′ N, 12°16′ W **222**
Ksar el Boukhari, *Alg.* 35°54′ N, 2°46′ E **216**
Ksar el Hirane, *Alg.* 33°47′ N, 3°14′ E **214**
Ksar el Kebir, *Mor.* 35°1′ N, 5°54′ W **214**
Ksar Torchane, *Mauritania* 20°41′ N, 12°60′ W **222**
Kshwan Mountain, *Can.* 55°40′ N, 129°51′ W **108**
Ktima, *Cyprus* 34°46′ N, 32°24′ E **194**
Kuah, *Malaysia* 6°19′ N, 99°51′ E **196**
Kuaidamao see Tonghua, *China* 41°41′ N, 125°45′ E **200**
Kuala, *Indonesia* 2°58′ N, 105°47′ E **196**
Kuala, *Indonesia* 3°35′ N, 98°24′ E **196**
Kuala Berang, *Malaysia* 5°5′ N, 103°1′ E **196**
Kuala Dungun, *Malaysia* 4°46′ N, 103°24′ E **196**
Kuala Kelawang, *Malaysia* 2°58′ N, 102°4′ E **196**
Kuala Kerai, *Malaysia* 5°32′ N, 102°12′ E **196**
Kuala Kubu Baharu, *Malaysia* 3°34′ N, 101°38′ E **196**
Kuala Lipis, *Malaysia* 4°12′ N, 102°1′ E **196**
Kuala Lumpur, *Malaysia* 3°8′ N, 101°32′ E **196**
Kuala Nerang, *Malaysia* 6°14′ N, 100°36′ E **196**
Kuala Rompin, *Malaysia* 2°48′ N, 103°27′ E **196**
Kuala Selangor, *Malaysia* 3°20′ N, 101°16′ E **196**
Kuala Terengganu, *Malaysia* 5°18′ N, 103°7′ E **196**
Kualakapuas, *Indonesia* 2°55′ S, 114°14′ E **192**
Kualalangsa, *Indonesia* 4°32′ N, 98°1′ E **196**
Kualatungkal, *Indonesia* 0°49′ N, 103°29′ E **196**
Kuancheng, *China* 40°35′ N, 118°31′ E **198**
Kuandian, *China* 40°43′ N, 124°46′ E **200**
Kuanshan, *Taiwan* 23°1′ N, 121°7′ E **198**
Kuantan, *Malaysia* 3°50′ N, 103°19′ E **196**
Kubachi, *Russ.* 42°6′ N, 47°40′ E **195**
Kuban′, river, *Russ.* 45°4′ N, 38°18′ E **156**
Kubaybāt, *Syr.* 35°11′ N, 37°9′ E **194**
Kubbum, *Sudan* 11°47′ N, 23°44′ E **216**
Kubenskoye, *Russ.* 59°24′ N, 39°38′ E **154**
Kubenskoye, Ozero, lake, *Russ.* 59°41′ N, 38°13′ E **154**
Kuberganya, *Russ.* 67°41′ N, 144°18′ E **160**
Kubokawa, *Japan* 33°11′ N, 133°7′ E **201**
Kučevo, *Serb. and Mont.* 44°29′ N, 21°40′ E **168**
Kuchaman, *India* 27°8′ N, 74°52′ E **186**
Kuchchaveli, *Sri Lanka* 8°48′ N, 81°6′ E **188**
Kuchin Tundra, Gora, peak, *Russ.* 69°3′ N, 30°57′ E **152**
Kuching, *Malaysia* 1°27′ N, 110°24′ E **192**
Kuchva, river, *Russ.* 57°7′ N, 27°57′ E **166**
Küçüksu, *Turk.* 38°25′ N, 42°16′ E **195**
Kudamatsu, *Japan* 34°0′ N, 131°53′ E **201**
Kudara, *Taj.* 38°28′ N, 72°41′ E **197**
Kudat, *Malaysia* 6°56′ N, 116°49′ E **203**
Kudever′, *Russ.* 56°47′ N, 29°26′ E **166**
Kudeyevskiy, *Russ.* 54°54′ N, 56°45′ E **154**
Kūdī, Qārat, peak, *Lib.* 23°22′ N, 23°45′ E **226**
Kudirkos Naumiestis, *Lith.* 54°47′ N, 22°52′ E **166**
Kudremukh, peak, *India* 13°5′ N, 75°8′ E **188**
Kudu Kyuyel′, *Russ.* 59°23′ N, 121°3′ E **160**
Kudus, *Indonesia* 6°51′ S, 110°46′ E **192**
Kudymkar, *Russ.* 59°0′ N, 54°43′ E **154**
Kufah see Al Kūfah, *Iraq* 32°5′ N, 44°27′ E **186**
Kufra Oasis see Al Kufrah, *Lib.* 24°20′ N, 23°30′ N, 23°40′ E **226**
Kugluktuk, *Can.* 67°48′ N, 115°16′ W **106**
Kugul′ta, *Russ.* 45°21′ N, 42°18′ E **158**
Kūhak, *Iran* 27°6′ N, 63°14′ E **182**
Kuh-e Sangan, peak, *Afghan.* 33°30′ N, 64°46′ E **186**
Kūhestak, *Iran* 26°49′ N, 57°6′ E **196**
Kühlung, peak, *Ger.* 54°5′ N, 11°40′ E **152**
Kuhmalahti, *Fin.* 61°29′ N, 24°32′ E **166**
Kuhmo, *Fin.* 64°5′ N, 29°28′ E **152**
Kuhmoinen, *Fin.* 61°33′ N, 25°9′ E **166**
Kuhn Ø, island, *Den.* 74°29′ N, 24°60′ W **246**
Kūhpāyeh, *Iran* 32°41′ N, 52°28′ E **180**
Kui Buri, *Thai.* 12°4′ N, 99°52′ E **202**
Kuibis, *Namibia* 26°42′ S, 16°49′ E **227**
Kuikuina, *Nicar.* 13°28′ N, 84°48′ W **115**
Kūʻīlioloa Heiau, site, *Hawaiʻi, U.S.* 21°25′ N, 158°14′ W **99**
Kuitan, *China* 23°4′ N, 115°57′ E **198**
Kuito, *Angola* 12°25′ S, 16°56′ E **220**
Kuivaniemi, *Fin.* 65°34′ N, 25°11′ E **152**
Kuizhuang, *China* 40°3′ N, 118°46′ E **198**
Kujang, *N. Korea* 39°52′ N, 126°2′ E **200**
Kujawsko-Pomorskie, adm. division, *Pol.* 52°58′ N, 17°33′ E **152**
Kukalaya, river, *Nicar.* 14°14′ N, 84°13′ W **115**
Kūkaniloko, site, *Hawaiʻi, U.S.* 21°30′ N, 158°6′ W **99**
Kukas, *Russ.* 66°25′ N, 31°20′ E **152**
Kukës, *Alban.* 42°5′ N, 20°24′ E **168**
Kukisvumchorr, *Russ.* 67°39′ N, 33°43′ E **152**
Kukmor, *Russ.* 56°11′ N, 50°58′ E **154**
Kukuihaele, *Hawaiʻi, U.S.* 20°7′ N, 155°35′ W **99**
Kukukus Lake, *Can.* 49°47′ N, 92°11′ W **110**
Kukunjevac, *Croatia* 45°28′ N, 17°6′ E **168**
Kula, *Bulg.* 43°53′ N, 22°31′ E **168**
Kula, *Serb. and Mont.* 45°36′ N, 19°33′ E **168**
Kula, *Turk.* 38°32′ N, 28°38′ E **156**
Kūlagīno, *Kaz.* 48°15′ N, 51°31′ E **158**
Kulal, Mount, *Kenya* 2°40′ N, 36°51′ E **224**
Kūlani, peak, *Hawaiʻi, U.S.* 19°30′ N, 155°21′ W **99**
Kular, *Russ.* 70°37′ N, 134°19′ E **173**
Kulata, *Bulg.* 41°23′ N, 23°21′ E **156**
Kulautuva, *Lith.* 54°58′ N, 23°38′ E **166**
Kuldīga, *Latv.* 56°57′ N, 21°57′ E **166**
Kuldo, *Can.* 55°51′ N, 127°54′ W **108**
Kule, *Botswana* 22°56′ S, 20°6′ E **227**
Kulebaki, *Russ.* 55°24′ N, 42°33′ E **154**
Kulen Vakuf, *Bosn. and Herzg.* 44°34′ N, 16°5′ E **168**
Kuliki, *Russ.* 57°21′ N, 79°0′ E **169**
Kulju, *Fin.* 61°22′ N, 23°44′ E **166**
Kulkuduk, *Uzb.* 42°33′ N, 63°17′ E **197**
Kullaa, *Fin.* 61°27′ N, 22°8′ E **166**
Kullen, *Sw.* 56°21′ N, 11°57′ E **152**
Kulli, *Est.* 58°21′ N, 23°46′ E **166**
Kullorsuaq, *Den.* 74°37′ N, 56°57′ W **106**
Küllstedt, *Ger.* 51°17′ N, 10°16′ E **167**
Kulm, *N. Dak., U.S.* 46°17′ N, 98°58′ W **90**
Kulma Pass, *China* 38°3′ N, 74°50′ E **197**
Kŭlob, *Taj.* 37°53′ N, 69°46′ E **197**
Kuloy, *Russ.* 60°59′ N, 42°35′ E **154**
Kuloy, *Russ.* 65°1′ N, 43°31′ E **154**
Kulp, *Turk.* 38°29′ N, 41°2′ E **195**
Kultuk, *Russ.* 51°48′ N, 103°53′ E **190**
Kulu, *Turk.* 39°4′ N, 33°5′ E **156**
Kululli, *Eritrea* 14°22′ N, 40°21′ E **182**
Kulunda, *Russ.* 52°32′ N, 79°0′ E **184**
Kum, river, *S. Korea* 35°34′ N, 127°29′ E **200**
Kumylzhenskaya, *Russ.* 44°53′ N, 45°59′ E **158**
Kumagaya, *Japan* 36°9′ N, 139°23′ E **201**
Kumak, *Russ.* 51°10′ N, 60°10′ E **158**
Kumak, river, *Russ.* 51°16′ N, 59°10′ E **158**
Kumaka, *Guyana* 3°53′ N, 58°26′ W **130**
Kumamoto, *Japan* 32°48′ N, 130°42′ E **201**
Kumamoto, adm. division, *Japan* 32°57′ N, 130°25′ E **201**
Kumanica, *Serb. and Mont.* 43°27′ N, 20°13′ E **168**
Kumano, *Japan* 33°53′ N, 136°6′ E **201**
Kumano Nada 34°2′ N, 136°23′ E **201**
Kumanovo, *Maced.* 42°7′ N, 21°41′ E **168**
Kumara, *N.Z.* 42°40′ S, 171°11′ E **240**
Kumasi, *Ghana* 6°44′ N, 1°38′ W **222**
Kumba, *Cameroon* 4°37′ N, 9°24′ E **222**
Kumbakonam, *India* 11°0′ N, 79°21′ E **188**
Kumbher, *Nepal* 28°15′ N, 81°25′ E **197**
Kumbo, *Cameroon* 6°9′ N, 10°38′ E **222**
Kŭmch′ŏn, *N. Korea* 38°9′ N, 126°28′ E **200**
Kumeny, *Russ.* 58°6′ N, 49°55′ E **154**
Kumertau, *Russ.* 52°46′ N, 55°46′ E **154**
Kŭmgang, *N. Korea* 38°36′ N, 127°58′ E **200**
Kumi, *Uganda* 1°27′ N, 33°54′ E **224**
Kumiva Peak, *Nev., U.S.* 40°23′ N, 119°21′ W **90**
Kumkol, oil field, *Kaz.* 46°17′ N, 65°22′ E **184**
Kumla, *Nor.* 59°7′ N, 15°7′ E **152**
Kumlinge, *Fin.* 60°15′ N, 20°47′ E **166**
Kumma, ruin(s), *Sudan* 21°30′ N, 30°58′ E **182**
Kumo, *Nig.* 10°2′ N, 11°8′ E **222**
Kumphawapi, *Thai.* 17°13′ N, 102°54′ E **202**
Kumputunturi, peak, *Fin.* 67°41′ N, 25°23′ E **152**
Kŭmsŏng see Kimhwa, *N. Korea* 38°26′ N, 127°36′ E **200**
Kumta, *India* 14°24′ N, 74°24′ E **188**
Kumu, *Dem. Rep. of the Congo* 3°2′ N, 25°14′ E **224**
Kumukh, *Russ.* 42°6′ N, 47°4′ E **195**
Kumzār, *Oman* 26°19′ N, 56°23′ E **196**
Kunanaggi Well, spring, *Austral.* 23°24′ S, 122°31′ E **230**
Künas Linchang, *China* 43°12′ N, 84°40′ E **184**
Kunashak, *Russ.* 55°41′ N, 61°27′ E **154**
Kunashir, island, *Russ.* 44°21′ N, 144°17′ E **190**
Kunchha, *Nepal* 28°9′ N, 84°21′ E **197**
Kunda, *Est.* 59°28′ N, 26°29′ E **166**
Kundelungu National Park, *Dem. Rep. of the Congo* 10°41′ S, 27°43′ E **224**
Kundi, Lake, *Sudan* 10°24′ N, 24°45′ E **224**
Kundian, *Pak.* 32°28′ N, 71°33′ E **186**
Kundozero, *Russ.* 66°19′ N, 31°10′ E **152**
Kundur, island, *Indonesia* 0°30′ N, 103°27′ E **196**
Kunene, river, *Africa* 17°33′ S, 11°31′ E **220**
Künes, river, *China* 43°30′ N, 82°59′ E **184**
Kungsbacka, *Nor.* 57°29′ N, 12°6′ E **152**
Kungu, *Dem. Rep. of the Congo* 2°47′ N, 19°10′ E **218**
Kungur, *Russ.* 57°26′ N, 57°3′ E **154**
Kungutas, *Tanzania* 8°29′ S, 33°16′ E **224**
Kungwe Mountain, *Tanzania* 6°12′ S, 29°44′ E **224**
Kunlon, *Myanmar* 23°22′ N, 98°36′ E **202**
Kunlun Mountains, *Asia* 33°11′ N, 97°38′ E **172**
Kunlun Shankou, pass, *China* 35°37′ N, 94°5′ E **188**
Kunlunshan, *Asia* 37°6′ N, 84°45′ E **184**
Kunmadaras, *Hung.* 47°25′ N, 20°48′ E **168**
Kunming, *China* 25°3′ N, 102°41′ E **190**
Kunszentmárton, *Hung.* 46°49′ N, 20°18′ E **168**
Kuntaur, *Gambia* 13°40′ N, 14°52′ W **222**
Kununurra, *Austral.* 15°45′ S, 128°45′ E **238**
Kunya, *Nig.* 12°13′ N, 8°32′ E **222**
Kuoliovaara, *Fin.* 65°50′ N, 28°49′ E **152**
Kuolismaa, *Russ.* 62°41′ N, 31°36′ E **154**
Kuopio, *Fin.* 62°53′ N, 27°38′ E **154**
Kuorboaivi, peak, *Fin.* 69°40′ N, 27°34′ E **152**
Kuorevesi, *Fin.* 61°55′ N, 24°38′ E **166**
Kuormakka, peak, *Nor.* 68°9′ N, 21°42′ E **152**
Kuortane, *Fin.* 62°47′ N, 23°30′ E **152**
Kuoutatjärro, peak, *Nor.* 68°36′ N, 20°10′ E **152**
Kupa, river, *Croatia* 45°30′ N, 15°48′ E **168**
Kupang, *Indonesia* 10°21′ S, 123°32′ E **192**
Kupino, *Russ.* 54°21′ N, 77°18′ E **184**
Kupiškis, *Lith.* 55°48′ N, 24°59′ E **166**
Kupopolo Heiau, site, *Hawaiʻi, U.S.* 21°38′ N, 158°7′ W **99**
Kupreanof, *Alas., U.S.* 56°50′ N, 133°3′ W **108**
Kupres, *Bosn. and Herzg.* 43°58′ N, 17°16′ E **168**
Kup″yans′k, *Ukr.* 49°43′ N, 37°33′ E **158**
Kuqa, *China* 41°43′ N, 83°3′ E **184**
Kur Dili, *Azerb.* 38°51′ N, 49°9′ E **195**
Kür, river, *Azerb.* 40°12′ N, 47°24′ E **195**
Kurakh, *Russ.* 41°33′ N, 47°47′ E **195**
Kūrān Dap, *Iran* 26°4′ N, 59°40′ E **182**
Kuranyets, *Belarus* 54°33′ N, 26°58′ E **166**
Kurashiki, *Japan* 34°35′ N, 133°46′ E **201**
Kŭrchatov, *Kaz.* 50°46′ N, 78°28′ E **184**
Kürdämir, *Azerb.* 40°20′ N, 48°10′ E **195**
Kurdoğlu Burnu, *Turk.* 36°31′ N, 28°11′ E **156**
Kŭrdzhali, *Bulg.* 41°38′ N, 25°21′ E **156**
Kŭrdzhali, adm. division, *Bulg.* 41°24′ N, 25°11′ E **156**
Kure, *Japan* 34°14′ N, 132°33′ E **201**
Küre, *Turk.* 41°48′ N, 33°42′ E **156**
Kurenala, *Fin.* 65°21′ N, 26°57′ E **152**
Kuressaare, *Est.* 58°15′ N, 22°28′ E **166**
Kureyka, *Russ.* 66°16′ N, 87°17′ E **169**
Kureyka, river, *Russ.* 67°53′ N, 96°35′ E **169**
Kurgan, *Russ.* 55°30′ N, 65°19′ E **184**
Kurgan, adm. division, *Russ.* 55°27′ N, 63°22′ E **169**
Kurganinsk, *Russ.* 44°54′ N, 40°30′ E **158**
Kurgolovo, *Russ.* 59°45′ N, 28°5′ E **166**
Kuria Muria Islands, *Persian Gulf* 17°13′ N, 55°40′ E **182**
Kurikka, *Fin.* 62°36′ N, 22°20′ E **152**
Kuril Islands (Kuril′skiye Ostrova), *Sea of Okhotsk* 47°9′ N, 148°32′ E **190**
Kurilovka, *Russ.* 50°42′ N, 48°0′ E **158**
Kuril′skiye Ostrova see Kuril Islands, *Sea of Okhotsk* 47°9′ N, 148°32′ E **190**
Kurkiyoki, *Russ.* 61°18′ N, 29°54′ E **166**
Kurleya, *Russ.* 52°6′ N, 119°8′ E **190**
Kurmuk, *Sudan* 10°35′ N, 34°15′ E **224**
Kurobe, *Japan* 36°52′ N, 137°26′ E **201**
Kuroiso, *Japan* 36°56′ N, 140°3′ E **201**
Kuropta, *Russ.* 67°29′ N, 30°50′ E **152**
Kuror, Jebel, peak, *Sudan* 20°29′ N, 31°30′ E **182**
Kurow, *N.Z.* 44°45′ S, 170°25′ E **240**
Kurów, *Pol.* 51°23′ N, 22°10′ E **152**
Kursavka, *Russ.* 44°28′ N, 42°32′ E **158**
Kuršėnai, *Lith.* 56°0′ N, 22°56′ E **166**
Kurshim, *Kaz.* 48°46′ N, 83°30′ E **184**
Kurshskaya Kosa, *Russ.* 55°11′ N, 20°37′ E **166**
Kuršių Nerija National Park, *Russ.* 55°29′ N, 20°37′ E **166**
Kursk, *Russ.* 51°43′ N, 36°12′ E **158**
Kursk, adm. division, *Russ.* 51°39′ N, 34°47′ E **160**
Kurskaya Kosa, *Russ.* 55°4′ N, 20°28′ E **166**
Kursu, *Fin.* 66°45′ N, 28°7′ E **152**
Kuršumlija, *Serb. and Mont.* 43°7′ N, 21°16′ E **168**
Kurşunlu, *Turk.* 40°51′ N, 33°15′ E **156**
Kurtalan, *Turk.* 37°55′ N, 41°43′ E **195**
Kurtamysh, *Russ.* 54°53′ N, 64°31′ E **184**
Kürten, *Ger.* 51°3′ N, 7°16′ E **163**
Kurthwood, *La., U.S.* 31°18′ N, 93°10′ W **103**
Kürti, *Kaz.* 43°56′ N, 76°19′ E **184**
Kurtti, *Fin.* 65°28′ N, 28°8′ E **152**
Kuru, *Fin.* 61°51′ N, 23°39′ E **166**
Kuru, river, *Sudan* 7°58′ N, 26°31′ E **224**
Kurulush, *Kyrg.* 41°39′ N, 70°53′ E **197**
Kuruman, *S. Af.* 27°29′ S, 23°25′ E **227**
Kurume, *Japan* 33°17′ N, 130°31′ E **201**
Kurupukari, *Guyana* 4°40′ N, 58°40′ W **130**
Kur′ya, *Russ.* 61°38′ N, 57°13′ E **154**
Kur′ya, *Russ.* 51°36′ N, 82°17′ E **184**
Kurze Mountains, *Antarctica* 72°38′ S, 10°13′ E **248**
Kurzheksa, *Russ.* 61°25′ N, 36°45′ E **154**
Kus Gölü, lake, *Turk.* 40°9′ N, 27°46′ E **156**
Kusa, *Eth.* 4°11′ N, 38°58′ E **224**
Kusa, *Russ.* 55°21′ N, 59°30′ E **154**
Kusadak, *Serb. and Mont.* 44°24′ N, 20°47′ E **168**
Kuşadası, *Turk.* 37°50′ N, 27°14′ E **156**
Kushereka, *Russ.* 63°49′ N, 37°9′ E **154**
Kusheriki, *Nig.* 10°32′ N, 6°26′ E **222**
Kushikino, *Japan* 31°41′ N, 130°18′ E **201**
Kushima, *Japan* 31°26′ N, 131°14′ E **201**
Kushimoto, *Japan* 33°28′ N, 135°46′ E **201**
Kushiro, *Japan* 43°6′ N, 144°14′ E **190**
Kushkushara, *Russ.* 65°0′ N, 40°19′ E **154**
Kushnarenkovo, *Russ.* 55°7′ N, 55°24′ E **154**
Kushnīya, *Israel* 33°0′ N, 35°48′ E **194**
Kushva, *Russ.* 58°18′ N, 59°47′ E **154**
Kuskokwim Bay 59°21′ N, 163°25′ W **98**
Kuskokwim Mountains, *North America* 61°20′ N, 157°59′ W **98**
Kuskokwim, river, *Alas., U.S.* 60°24′ N, 161°42′ W **98**
Kusŏng, *N. Korea* 39°58′ N, 125°14′ E **200**
Kustavi, *Fin.* 60°33′ N, 21°20′ E **166**
Kusur, *Russ.* 41°44′ N, 46°57′ E **195**
Kūt Barrage, dam, *Iraq* 32°23′ N, 44°49′ E **216**
Kut, Ko, island, *Thai.* 11°30′ N, 102°5′ E **202**
Kuta, *Nig.* 9°50′ N, 6°44′ E **222**
Kutabuloh, *Indonesia* 3°28′ N, 97°3′ E **196**
Kutacane, *Indonesia* 3°31′ N, 97°47′ E **196**
Kütahya, *Turk.* 39°26′ N, 29°58′ E **156**
Kutai National Park, *Indonesia* 0°15′ N, 116°57′ E **238**
K′ut′aisi, *Ga.* 42°13′ N, 42°40′ E **195**
Kutanibong, *Indonesia* 3°56′ N, 96°20′ E **173**
Kutcho Creek, river, *Can.* 58°35′ N, 128°59′ W **108**
Kutina, *Croatia* 45°27′ N, 16°46′ E **168**
Kutjevo, *Croatia* 45°24′ N, 17°52′ E **168**
Kutno, *Pol.* 52°14′ N, 19°22′ E **152**
Kutu, *Dem. Rep. of the Congo* 2°43′ S, 18°6′ E **218**
Kutum, *Sudan* 14°9′ N, 24°40′ E **226**
Kutuzovo, *Russ.* 54°46′ N, 22°48′ E **166**
Kúty, *Slovakia* 48°37′ N, 17°1′ E **156**
Kuujjuaq, *Can.* 58°5′ N, 68°38′ W **106**
Kuujjuarapik, *Can.* 55°17′ N, 77°47′ W **106**
Kuurne, *Belg.* 50°51′ N, 3°19′ E **163**
Kuusamo, *Fin.* 65°58′ N, 29°8′ E **152**
Kuusankoski, *Fin.* 60°53′ N, 26°36′ E **166**
Kuusivaara, *Fin.* 66°39′ N, 27°0′ E **152**
Kuusjärvi, *Fin.* 62°41′ N, 28°54′ E **154**
Kuusjoki, *Fin.* 60°30′ N, 23°11′ E **166**
Kuvandyk, *Russ.* 51°27′ N, 57°20′ E **158**
Kuvango, *Angola* 14°32′ S, 16°15′ E **220**
Kuvet, river, *Russ.* 69°3′ N, 176°7′ E **98**
Kuvshinovo, *Russ.* 57°0′ N, 34°13′ E **154**
Kuwait 29°39′ N, 47°15′ E **196**
Kuwait see Al Kuwayt, *Kuwait* 29°20′ N, 47°52′ E **196**
Kuwana, *Japan* 35°3′ N, 136°41′ E **201**
Kuybishevskiy, *Taj.* 37°56′ N, 68°46′ E **197**
Kuybyshev, *Russ.* 55°30′ N, 78°21′ E **184**
Kuyeda, *Russ.* 56°27′ N, 55°31′ E **154**
Kuytun, *China* 44°29′ N, 84°56′ E **184**
Kuyuwini, river, *Guyana* 1°55′ N, 59°25′ W **130**
Kuzey Anadolu Dağlarx, *Turk.* 40°38′ N, 36°33′ E **180**
Kuz′movka, *Russ.* 62°21′ N, 92°9′ E **169**
Kuznetsk, *Russ.* 53°5′ N, 46°37′ E **154**
Kuźnica, *Pol.* 53°30′ N, 23°38′ E **152**
Kuzomen′, *Russ.* 66°17′ N, 36°44′ E **154**
Kuzomen′, *Russ.* 64°19′ N, 43°4′ E **154**
Kvalsund, *Nor.* 70°29′ N, 23°58′ E **152**
Kvænangsbotn, *Nor.* 69°43′ N, 22°4′ E **152**
Kvarkeno, *Russ.* 52°5′ N, 59°41′ E **154**
K′vemo Azhara, *Turk.* 43°8′ N, 41°49′ E **158**
Kvernes, *Nor.* 62°59′ N, 7°42′ E **152**
Kvikkjokk, *Nor.* 66°56′ N, 17°44′ E **152**
Kvikne, *Nor.* 62°34′ N, 10°19′ E **152**
Kvisvik, *Nor.* 63°3′ N, 7°58′ E **152**
Kwa Mtoro, *Tanzania* 5°12′ S, 35°26′ E **224**
Kwadacha, river, *Can.* 57°28′ N, 125°37′ W **108**
Kwail (P′ungch′ŏn), *N. Korea* 38°25′ N, 125°1′ E **200**
Kwajaffa Babur, *Nig.* 10°27′ N, 12°24′ E **218**
Kwaksan, *N. Korea* 39°40′ N, 125°4′ E **200**
Kwale, *Kenya* 4°12′ S, 39°27′ E **224**
Kwale Station, *Nig.* 5°48′ N, 6°21′ E **222**
Kwali, *Nig.* 8°51′ N, 7°0′ E **222**
Kwamouth, *Dem. Rep. of the Congo* 3°16′ S, 16°14′ E **218**
Kwangju see Gwangju, *S. Korea* 35°8′ N, 126°56′ E **200**
Kwania, Lake, *Uganda* 0°52′ N, 32°45′ E **224**
Kwazulu-Natal, adm. division, *S. Af.* 29°6′ S, 29°21′ E **227**
Kwekwe, *Zimb.* 18°56′ S, 29°47′ E **224**
Kwenge, river, *Dem. Rep. of the Congo* 6°16′ S, 18°20′ E **218**
Kwiambana, *Nig.* 11°5′ N, 6°33′ E **222**
Kwikila, *P.N.G.* 9°48′ S, 147°39′ E **192**
Kwilu, river, *Dem. Rep. of the Congo* 3°35′ S, 17°14′ E **218**
Kwokullie Lake, *Can.* 59°14′ N, 121°43′ W **108**
Ky Son, *Vietnam* 19°24′ N, 104°8′ E **202**

Lalibela, Eth. 12° 1′ N, 39° 2′ E 182
Lalinde, Fr. 44° 50′ N, 0° 44′ E 150
Lalitpur, India 24° 42′ N, 78° 24′ E 197
Lalitpur (Patan), Nepal 27° 36′ N, 85° 22′ E 197
Laloche, river, Can. 61° 36′ N, 112° 26′ W 108
Lal'sk, Russ. 60° 45′ N, 47° 36′ E 154
Lalsot, India 26° 32′ N, 76° 21′ E 197
Lama, Ozero, lake, Russ. 69° 34′ N, 89° 20′ E 169
Lamag, Malaysia 5° 30′ N, 117° 48′ E 203
Lamaing, Myanmar 15° 29′ N, 97° 50′ E 202
Lama-Kara, Togo 9° 36′ N, 1° 11′ E 222
Lamar, Colo., U.S. 38° 4′ N, 102° 37′ W 90
Lamar, Mo., U.S. 37° 28′ N, 94° 16′ W 96
Lamas, Peru 6° 26′ S, 76° 35′ W 130
Lamas, Turk. 36° 34′ N, 34° 14′ E 156
Lambach, Aust. 48° 5′ N, 13° 52′ E 156
Lambaréné, Gabon 0° 44′ N, 10° 11′ E 218
Lambasa, Fiji Islands 16° 18′ S, 179° 25′ E 238
Lambayeque, Peru 6° 39′ S, 79° 56′ W 130
Lambayeque, adm. division, Peru 5° 30′ S, 80° 27′ W 130
Lamberhurst, U.K. 51° 5′ N, 0° 23′ E 162
Lambert Land, Norske Øer 78° 56′ N, 27° 17′ W 246
Lambert's Bay, S. Af. 32° 5′ S, 18° 18′ E 227
Lambertville, Mich., U.S. 41° 45′ N, 83° 38′ W 102
Lambourn, U.K. 51° 30′ N, 1° 33′ W 162
Lambrecht, Ger. 49° 22′ N, 8° 4′ E 163
Lambton, Can. 45° 49′ N, 71° 6′ W 111
Lambton, Cape, Can. 70° 53′ N, 127° 37′ W 106
Lamé, Chad 9° 15′ N, 14° 33′ E 216
Lame Deer, Mont., U.S. 45° 35′ N, 106° 41′ W 90
Lamesa, Tex., U.S. 32° 43′ N, 101° 57′ W 92
L'Ametlla de Mar, Sp. 40° 53′ N, 0° 47′ E 164
Lamía, Gr. 38° 54′ N, 22° 26′ E 156
Lamitan, Philippines 6° 40′ N, 122° 7′ E 203
Lamjaybir, Africa 25° 21′ N, 14° 48′ W 214
Lammeulo, Indonesia 5° 15′ N, 95° 53′ E 196
Lammhult, Nor. 57° 9′ N, 14° 34′ E 152
Lammi, Fin. 61° 4′ N, 25° 0′ E 166
Lamoille, Nev., U.S. 40° 44′ N, 115° 28′ W 90
Lamoille, river, Vt., U.S. 44° 41′ N, 73° 18′ W 110
Lamon Bay 14° 26′ N, 122° 0′ E 203
Lamoni, Iowa, U.S. 40° 37′ N, 93° 56′ W 94
Lamont, Calif., U.S. 35° 16′ N, 118° 56′ W 101
Lamont, Can. 53° 45′ N, 112° 47′ W 108
Lamont, Wyo., U.S. 42° 12′ N, 107° 29′ W 90
Lamotrek Atoll 6° 36′ N, 147° 0′ E 192
Lamoure, N. Dak., U.S. 46° 20′ N, 98° 18′ W 90
Lampa, Peru 15° 24′ S, 70° 21′ W 137
Lampang, Thai. 18° 17′ N, 99° 31′ E 202
Lampasas, Tex., U.S. 31° 3′ N, 98° 11′ W 92
Lampaul, Fr. 48° 27′ N, 5° 6′ W 150
Lampazos, Mex. 27° 1′ N, 100° 31′ W 96
Lampedusa, island, It. 35° 22′ N, 11° 14′ E 216
Lampeter, U.K. 52° 6′ N, 4° 4′ W 162
Lamphun, Thai. 18° 36′ N, 99° 3′ E 202
L'Ampolla, Sp. 40° 48′ N, 0° 40′ E 164
Lampozhnya, Russ. 65° 42′ N, 44° 20′ E 154
Lamskoye, Russ. 52° 55′ N, 38° 2′ E 154
Lamu, Kenya 2° 16′ S, 40° 50′ E 224
Lămu, Myanmar 19° 12′ N, 94° 12′ E 202
Lan', river, Belarus 52° 45′ N, 27° 4′ E 154
Lan Yü, island, Taiwan 22° 6′ N, 121° 35′ E 198
Lana, It. 46° 36′ N, 11° 8′ E 167
Lana, river, Mex. 17° 27′ N, 95° 38′ W 114
Lāna'i, island, Hawai'i, U.S. 20° 35′ N, 157° 29′ W 99
Lanaja, Sp. 41° 45′ N, 0° 19′ E 164
Lanao, Lake, Philippines 7° 53′ N, 123° 54′ E 203
Lanark, Ill., U.S. 42° 6′ N, 89° 50′ W 102
Lanbi Kyun, island, Myanmar 10° 38′ N, 98° 18′ E 202
Lancang, China 22° 33′ N, 99° 56′ E 202
Lancang (Mekong), river, China 32° 3′ N, 97° 14′ E 190
Lancaster, Calif., U.S. 34° 41′ N, 118° 9′ W 101
Lancaster, Mo., U.S. 40° 31′ N, 92° 31′ W 94
Lancaster, N.H., U.S. 44° 29′ N, 71° 35′ W 104
Lancaster, N.Y., U.S. 42° 53′ N, 78° 40′ W 94
Lancaster, Ohio, U.S. 39° 43′ N, 82° 36′ W 102
Lancaster, S.C., U.S. 34° 42′ N, 80° 47′ W 96
Lancaster, U.K. 54° 2′ N, 2° 48′ W 162
Lancaster, Wis., U.S. 42° 50′ N, 90° 42′ W 110
Lancaster Sound 73° 38′ N, 94° 47′ W 72
Lance Creek, Wyo., U.S. 43° 1′ N, 104° 38′ W 90
Land Between the Lakes, Ky., U.S. 37° 1′ N, 87° 60′ W 80
Land O'Lakes, Fla., U.S. 28° 12′ N, 82° 28′ W 105
Landau, Ger. 51° 21′ N, 9° 5′ E 167
Landay, Afghan. 30° 29′ N, 63° 47′ E 186
Landeck, Aust. 47° 8′ N, 10° 34′ E 156
Lander, Wyo., U.S. 42° 50′ N, 108° 44′ W 90
Landers, Calif., U.S. 34° 16′ N, 116° 25′ W 101
Landeryd, Nor. 57° 5′ N, 13° 15′ E 152
Landeta, Arg. 32° 1′ S, 62° 2′ W 139
Landete, Sp. 39° 54′ N, 1° 23′ W 164
Landfall Island, India 13° 40′ N, 92° 0′ E 188
Landis, Can. 52° 12′ N, 108° 28′ W 108
Landis, N.C., U.S. 35° 32′ N, 80° 37′ W 96
Landrecies, Fr. 50° 7′ N, 3° 42′ E 163
Landrum, S.C., U.S. 35° 10′ N, 82° 12′ W 96
Lands End, Can. 76° 47′ N, 123° 5′ W 246
Land's End, U.K. 50° 0′ N, 6° 1′ W 150
Lane Mountain, peak, Calif., U.S. 35° 4′ N, 116° 59′ W 101
Lanercost Priory, site, U.K. 54° 57′ N, 2° 49′ W 150
Lanesboro, Pa., U.S. 41° 57′ N, 75° 35′ W 110
Lanesborough, Mass., U.S. 42° 30′ N, 73° 14′ W 104
Lanett, Ala., U.S. 32° 51′ N, 85° 12′ W 96
Laneville, Tex., U.S. 31° 57′ N, 94° 48′ W 103
Lang Son, Vietnam 21° 51′ N, 106° 44′ E 198
Lang Suan, Thai. 9° 55′ N, 99° 5′ E 202
Langå, Den. 56° 24′ N, 9° 51′ E 150
La'nga Co, lake, China 30° 37′ N, 80° 48′ E 197
Langa de Duero, Sp. 41° 36′ N, 3° 24′ W 164
Langanes, Ice. 66° 23′ N, 14° 29′ W 246
Langao, China 32° 16′ N, 108° 55′ E 198
Langar, Uzb. 40° 26′ N, 65° 59′ E 197
Langarūd, Iran 37° 10′ N, 50° 9′ E 195
Långban, Nor. 59° 51′ N, 14° 15′ E 152
Langdon, N. Dak., U.S. 48° 44′ N, 98° 24′ W 90
Längelmäki, Fin. 61° 41′ N, 24° 41′ E 166
Langen, Ger. 49° 59′ N, 8° 40′ E 167
Langenau, Ger. 48° 29′ N, 10° 6′ E 152
Langenburg, Can. 50° 50′ N, 101° 43′ W 90
Langfang, China 39° 33′ N, 116° 38′ E 198
Langfjordnes, Nor. 70° 42′ N, 28° 4′ E 152
Långflon, Nor. 61° 2′ N, 12° 32′ E 152
Langford, S. Dak., U.S. 45° 35′ N, 97° 51′ W 90
Langham, Can. 52° 21′ N, 106° 56′ W 108
Langhirano, It. 44° 36′ N, 10° 14′ E 167
Langjökull, glacier, Ice. 64° 48′ N, 29° 24′ W 72
Langkawi, island, Malaysia 6° 14′ N, 99° 5′ E 196
Langley, Can. 49° 5′ N, 122° 39′ W 100
Langley, Wash., U.S. 48° 1′ N, 122° 26′ W 100
Langley Air Force Base, Va., U.S. 37° 4′ N, 76° 26′ W 94
Langley, Mount, peak, Calif., U.S. 36° 31′ N, 118° 17′ W 101
Langlois, Oreg., U.S. 42° 55′ N, 124° 27′ W 90
Langøya, island, Nor. 68° 55′ N, 11° 48′ E 246
Langport, U.K. 51° 2′ N, 2° 49′ W 162
Langres, Plateau de, Fr. 47° 41′ N, 4° 44′ E 165
Langsa, Indonesia 4° 29′ N, 97° 57′ E 196
Långsele, Nor. 64° 33′ N, 15° 51′ E 154
Långsele, Nor. 63° 9′ N, 17° 2′ E 152
Langtou, China 40° 1′ N, 124° 19′ E 200
Långträsk, Nor. 65° 21′ N, 20° 17′ E 152
Langtry, Tex., U.S. 29° 47′ N, 101° 35′ W 92
Langu, Thai. 6° 52′ N, 99° 46′ E 196
Languedoc-Roussillon, adm. division, Fr. 42° 36′ N, 2° 13′ E 150
Languedog, region, Fr. 44° 39′ N, 3° 3′ E 165
Langwarden, Ger. 53° 36′ N, 8° 19′ E 163
Langzhong, China 31° 40′ N, 105° 51′ E 190
Laniel, Can. 47° 3′ N, 79° 15′ W 94
Lanigan, Can. 51° 51′ N, 105° 3′ W 90
Lanín National Park, Arg. 40° 54′ S, 71° 5′ W 134
Lanjarón, Sp. 36° 55′ N, 3° 29′ W 164
Länkäran, Azerb. 38° 44′ N, 48° 49′ E 195
Lankio, Côte d'Ivoire 9° 51′ N, 3° 26′ W 222
Lankoveri, Nig. 9° 1′ N, 11° 22′ E 222
Lanlacuni Bajo, Peru 13° 33′ S, 70° 25′ W 137
Lannemezan, Fr. 43° 7′ N, 0° 22′ E 164
Lansdale, Pa., U.S. 40° 13′ N, 75° 18′ W 94
Lansdowne House, Can. 52° 11′ N, 87° 55′ W 82
L'Anse, Mich., U.S. 46° 45′ N, 88° 27′ W 94
L'Anse aux Meadows, Can. 51° 36′ N, 55° 32′ W 111
Lansing, Ill., U.S. 41° 33′ N, 87° 32′ W 102
Lansing, Iowa, U.S. 43° 21′ N, 91° 14′ W 94
Lansing, Mich., U.S. 42° 42′ N, 84° 36′ W 102
Lanta Yai, Ko, island, Thai. 7° 20′ N, 98° 23′ E 196
Lantana, Fla., U.S. 26° 34′ N, 80° 5′ W 105
Lantewa, Nig. 12° 15′ N, 11° 46′ E 222
Lantz, Sp. 42° 59′ N, 1° 38′ W 164
Lanús, Arg. 34° 46′ S, 58° 24′ W 139
Lanuza, Philippines 9° 15′ N, 126° 3′ E 203
Lanxian, China 38° 16′ N, 111° 36′ E 198
Lanz Peak, Antarctica 77° 18′ S, 87° 11′ W 248
Lanzai, Nig. 11° 20′ N, 10° 49′ E 222
Lanzarote, island, Sp. 29° 6′ N, 14° 51′ W 214
Lanzhou, China 36° 3′ N, 103° 44′ E 198
Lao Cai, China 22° 29′ N, 104° 1′ E 202
Laoag, Philippines 18° 12′ N, 120° 38′ E 198
Laocheng, China 42° 37′ N, 124° 5′ E 200
Laohekou, China 32° 22′ N, 111° 40′ E 198
Laon, Fr. 49° 33′ N, 3° 37′ E 163
Laona, Wis., U.S. 45° 34′ N, 88° 40′ W 94
Laos 19° 46′ N, 102° 26′ E 202
Laoshan, China 36° 13′ N, 120° 25′ E 198
Laotougou, China 42° 55′ N, 129° 8′ E 200
Laouni, spring, Alg. 20° 30′ N, 5° 44′ E 222
Lapa, Braz. 25° 46′ S, 49° 43′ W 138
Lapai, Nig. 9° 0′ N, 6° 43′ E 222
Lapeer, Mich., U.S. 43° 2′ N, 83° 18′ W 102
Lapinlahti, Fin. 63° 21′ N, 27° 22′ E 152
Lapithos 35° 20′ N, 33° 9′ E 194
Lapovo, Serb. and Mont. 44° 10′ N, 21° 3′ E 156
Lappa, ruin(s), Gr. 35° 16′ N, 24° 15′ E 156
Lappfjärd (Lapväärtti), Fin. 62° 13′ N, 21° 29′ E 152
Laprida, Arg. 37° 35′ S, 60° 48′ W 139
Lâpseki, Turk. 40° 20′ N, 26° 39′ E 156
Laptev Sea 72° 2′ N, 139° 4′ E 246
Lapua, Fin. 62° 57′ N, 22° 59′ E 152
Lăpuş, Munţii, Rom. 47° 26′ N, 23° 26′ E 168
Lăpuşna, Mold. 46° 52′ N, 28° 25′ E 156
Lapväärtti see Lappfjärd, Fin. 62° 13′ N, 21° 29′ E 152
Łapy, Pol. 52° 59′ N, 22° 51′ E 152
Laqiya Arba'in, Sudan 20° 2′ N, 28° 2′ E 226
Laqiya 'Umran, spring, Sudan 19° 52′ N, 28° 10′ E 226
L'Aquila, It. 42° 21′ N, 13° 23′ E 156
Lār, Iran 27° 38′ N, 54° 16′ E 196
Lara, Gabon 0° 19′ N, 11° 22′ E 218
Lara, adm. division, Venez. 9° 56′ N, 70° 10′ W 136
Larabanga, Ghana 9° 13′ N, 1° 52′ W 222
Laracha, Sp. 43° 15′ N, 8° 35′ W 150
Larache, Mor. 35° 11′ N, 6° 10′ W 150
Lārak, island, Iran 26° 43′ N, 56° 24′ E 180
Laramate, Peru 14° 18′ S, 74° 51′ W 137
Laramie, Wyo., U.S. 41° 19′ N, 105° 34′ W 90
Laramie Mountains, Wyo., U.S. 42° 32′ N, 106° 11′ W 90
Laramie Peak, Wyo., U.S. 42° 15′ N, 105° 31′ W 90
Laranjeiras do Sul, Braz. 25° 27′ S, 52° 27′ W 138
Larat, Indonesia 7° 15′ S, 131° 43′ E 192
Larb Creek, river, Mont., U.S. 48° 15′ N, 107° 43′ W 90
Lärbro, Sw. 57° 47′ N, 18° 47′ E 166
Larche, Fr. 44° 27′ N, 6° 50′ E 167
Larde, Mozambique 16° 27′ S, 39° 42′ E 224
Larder Lake, Can. 48° 6′ N, 79° 43′ W 94
Laredo, Sp. 43° 23′ N, 3° 27′ W 150
Laredo, Tex., U.S. 27° 31′ N, 99° 28′ W 73
Laredo Sound 52° 24′ N, 129° 26′ W 108
Largepike Lake, Can. 60° 5′ N, 111° 15′ W 108
Largo, Fla., U.S. 27° 55′ N, 82° 46′ W 105
Largo, Cayo, island, Cuba 21° 45′ N, 81° 42′ W 116
Laribosière, Lac, lake, Can. 53° 38′ N, 72° 24′ W 111
Larimore, N. Dak., U.S. 47° 52′ N, 97° 39′ W 90
Larioja, adm. division, Sp. 42° 11′ N, 3° 3′ W 164
Lárissa, Gr. 39° 38′ N, 22° 24′ E 156
Lark Pass 15° 11′ S, 144° 46′ E 230
Larkana, Pak. 27° 32′ N, 68° 13′ E 186
Larnaka, Cyprus 34° 55′ N, 33° 38′ E 194
Larned, Kans., U.S. 38° 10′ N, 99° 6′ W 92
Laro, Burkina Faso 11° 17′ N, 2° 51′ W 222
Laro, Cameroon 8° 15′ N, 12° 16′ E 218
Larose, La., U.S. 29° 34′ N, 90° 23′ W 103
Lars Christensen Peak, Antarctica 68° 47′ S, 90° 5′ W 248
Larsen Inlet 64° 52′ S, 60° 11′ W 248
Larsen, Mount, peak, Antarctica 74° 44′ S, 162° 27′ E 248
Larsen Sound 70° 15′ N, 101° 52′ W 106
Larsmont, Minn., U.S. 46° 58′ N, 91° 46′ W 94
Larvik, Nor. 59° 3′ N, 10° 2′ E 152
Larzac, Causse du, Fr. 43° 53′ N, 3° 1′ E 165
Las Alpujarras, Sp. 36° 44′ N, 3° 26′ W 164
Las Animas, Colo., U.S. 38° 3′ N, 103° 14′ W 90
Las Arrias, Arg. 30° 22′ S, 63° 38′ W 139
Las Avispas, Arg. 29° 51′ S, 61° 18′ W 139
Las Bonitas, Venez. 7° 48′ N, 65° 42′ W 136
Las Breñas, Arg. 27° 5′ S, 61° 6′ W 139
Las Cabezas de San Juan, Sp. 36° 58′ N, 5° 57′ W 164
Las Cruces, Mex. 29° 25′ N, 107° 23′ W 92
Las Cruces, N. Mex., U.S. 32° 17′ N, 106° 48′ W 112
Las Esperanzas, Mex. 27° 44′ N, 101° 21′ W 92
Las Flores, Arg. 36° 2′ S, 59° 9′ W 139
Las Garzas, Arg. 28° 49′ S, 59° 32′ W 139
Las Heras, Arg. 46° 31′ S, 68° 55′ W 134
Las Herreras, Mex. 25° 7′ N, 105° 30′ W 114
Las Juntas, Col. 2° 4′ N, 72° 14′ W 136
Las Lajitas, Venez. 6° 54′ N, 65° 42′ W 136
Las Lomitas, Arg. 24° 43′ S, 60° 36′ W 132
Las Mercedes, Venez. 9° 6′ N, 66° 24′ W 136
Las Minas, peak, Hond. 14° 32′ N, 88° 44′ W 115
Las Palmas, Sp. 28° 4′ N, 15° 29′ W 214
Las Palmeras, Arg. 30° 35′ S, 61° 39′ W 139
Las Peñas, Mex. 18° 3′ N, 102° 30′ W 114
Las Piedras, Bol. 11° 2′ S, 66° 12′ W 130
Las Piedras, Uru. 34° 42′ S, 56° 12′ W 139
Las Plumas, Arg. 43° 39′ S, 67° 16′ W 134
Las Tablas, Pan. 7° 47′ N, 80° 17′ W 115
Las Tinajas, Arg. 27° 30′ S, 62° 51′ W 139
Las Toscas, Arg. 28° 20′ S, 59° 16′ W 139
Las Tres Virgenes, Volcán, peak, Mex. 27° 26′ N, 112° 43′ W 112
Las Trincheras, Mex. 30° 21′ N, 111° 33′ W 92
Las Tunas, Cuba 20° 57′ N, 76° 59′ W 115
Las Tunas, island, Cuba 20° 23′ N, 77° 42′ W 116
Las Varas, Mex. 28° 7′ N, 105° 21′ W 92
Las Varas, Mex. 29° 28′ N, 108° 2′ W 92
Las Varas, Mex. 21° 11′ N, 105° 10′ W 114
Las Varillas, Arg. 31° 54′ S, 62° 43′ W 139
Las Vegas, Nev., U.S. 36° 9′ N, 115° 10′ W 101
Las Vegas, N. Mex., U.S. 35° 35′ N, 105° 13′ W 92
Las Vegas Valley, Nev., U.S. 36° 21′ N, 115° 27′ W 101
Las Vigas, Mex. 19° 36′ N, 97° 6′ W 114
Las Yaras, Peru 17° 54′ S, 70° 33′ W 137
Las Zorras, Punta, Peru 10° 32′ S, 79° 30′ W 130
Lasalle, Can. 45° 25′ N, 73° 39′ W 94
Lascano, Uru. 33° 42′ S, 54° 13′ W 139
Lasengmiao, China 39° 19′ N, 106° 54′ E 198
Lashburn, Can. 53° 7′ N, 109° 36′ W 108
Lāsh-e Joveyn, Afghan. 31° 40′ N, 61° 42′ E 186
Lashio, Myanmar 22° 51′ N, 97° 42′ E 190
Lashkar, India 26° 10′ N, 78° 7′ E 197
Lashkar Gah (Bost), Afghan. 31° 35′ N, 64° 22′ E 186
Lasia, island, Indonesia 2° 12′ N, 96° 36′ E 196
Lāsjerd, Iran 35° 22′ N, 53° 0′ E 180
Łaskarzew, Pol. 51° 46′ N, 21° 38′ E 152
Laško, Slov. 46° 9′ N, 15° 14′ E 156
Laskowice, Pol. 53° 29′ N, 18° 26′ E 152
Läsna, Est. 59° 25′ N, 25° 53′ E 166
Lassen Peak, Calif., U.S. 40° 28′ N, 121° 36′ W 90
L'Assomption, Can. 45° 49′ N, 73° 27′ W 94
Last Chance Range, Calif., U.S. 37° 9′ N, 117° 46′ W 101
Last Mountain Lake, Can. 51° 17′ N, 107° 2′ W 80
Last Mountain, peak, Can. 60° 45′ N, 126° 47′ W 108
Lastoursville, Gabon 0° 52′ N, 12° 39′ E 218
Lastovo, Croatia 42° 45′ N, 16° 53′ E 168
Lastovski Kanal 42° 45′ N, 16° 39′ E 168
Latady Island, Antarctica 70° 55′ S, 81° 57′ W 248
Latakia see Al Lādhiqīyah, Syr. 35° 31′ N, 35° 47′ E 194
Latehar, India 23° 45′ N, 84° 31′ E 197
Latexo, Tex., U.S. 31° 22′ N, 95° 29′ W 103
Latham Island, Tanzania 7° 9′ S, 40° 1′ E 224
Lathrop, Calif., U.S. 37° 49′ N, 121° 17′ W 100
Latina, It. 41° 28′ N, 12° 52′ E 156
Latisana, It. 45° 46′ N, 12° 59′ E 167
Lato, ruin(s), Gr. 35° 9′ N, 25° 32′ E 156
Laton, Calif., U.S. 36° 26′ N, 119° 43′ W 100
Latouma, spring, Niger 22° 12′ N, 14° 47′ E 216
Latrobe, Mount, peak, Austral. 39° 2′ S, 146° 10′ E 230
Latta, S.C., U.S. 34° 19′ N, 79° 27′ W 96
Latur, India 18° 23′ N, 76° 33′ E 188
Latvia 56° 59′ N, 25° 20′ E 166
Latvozero, Russ. 64° 49′ N, 29° 54′ E 152
Lau, Nig. 9° 10′ N, 11° 18′ E 222
Lau, Sudan 6° 44′ N, 30° 25′ E 224
Lau Group, islands, South Pacific Ocean 16° 60′ S, 178° 20′ W 238
Lau Ridge, South Pacific Ocean 27° 20′ S, 178° 35′ W 252
Lauca National Park, Chile 18° 11′ S, 69° 43′ W 137
Lauca, river, Bol. 18° 29′ S, 68° 50′ W 137
Laudal, Nor. 58° 14′ N, 7° 28′ E 152
Lauderdale, Miss., U.S. 32° 28′ N, 88° 32′ W 103
Lauderdale Lakes, Fla., U.S. 26° 10′ N, 80° 12′ W 105
Ļaudona, Latv. 56° 43′ N, 26° 10′ E 166
Lauenburg, Ger. 53° 22′ N, 10° 34′ E 152
Lauenförde, Ger. 51° 39′ N, 9° 24′ E 167
Laufen, Switz. 47° 25′ N, 7° 29′ E 150
Laughlan Islands, Solomon Sea 9° 41′ S, 152° 47′ E 192
Laughlin, Nev., U.S. 35° 11′ N, 114° 36′ W 101
Laughlin Peak, N. Mex., U.S. 36° 36′ N, 104° 17′ W 92
Laujar de Andarax, Sp. 36° 59′ N, 2° 54′ W 164
Laukuva, Lith. 55° 37′ N, 22° 15′ E 166
Laurel, Del., U.S. 38° 32′ N, 75° 35′ W 94
Laurel, Ind., U.S. 39° 30′ N, 85° 11′ W 102
Laurel, Miss., U.S. 31° 41′ N, 89° 7′ W 103
Laurel, Mont., U.S. 45° 39′ N, 108° 46′ W 90
Laurel, Nebr., U.S. 42° 24′ N, 97° 6′ W 90
Laurel Hill, Pa., U.S. 39° 57′ N, 79° 23′ W 94
Laurens, Iowa, U.S. 42° 50′ N, 94° 53′ W 90
Laurens, S.C., U.S. 34° 29′ N, 82° 2′ W 96
Laurentian Fan, North Atlantic Ocean 41° 51′ N, 56° 17′ W 253
Laurentian Valley, Can. 46° 1′ N, 77° 28′ W 110
Lauria, It. 40° 2′ N, 15° 49′ E 156
Laurie Island, Antarctica 61° 15′ S, 44° 38′ W 134
Laurie River, Can. 56° 14′ N, 101° 1′ W 108
Laurinburg, N.C., U.S. 34° 45′ N, 79° 29′ W 96
Lauritsala, Fin. 61° 2′ N, 28° 14′ E 166
Lausanne, Switz. 46° 32′ N, 6° 39′ E 150
Laut, island, Indonesia 4° 49′ N, 107° 51′ E 196
Laut, island, Indonesia 4° 6′ S, 116° 19′ E 192
Laut Kecil, Kepulauan, islands, Java Sea 4° 59′ S, 116° 1′ E 192
Lautaro, Volcán, peak, Chile 49° 3′ S, 73° 43′ W 134
Lautem, Timor-Leste 8° 30′ S, 126° 56′ E 192
Lauterbach, Ger. 50° 38′ N, 9° 24′ E 167
Lava Beds National Monument, Calif., U.S. 41° 28′ N, 122° 46′ W 80
Lava Cast Forest, site, Oreg., U.S. 43° 47′ N, 121° 22′ W 90
Lava River Cave, site, Oreg., U.S. 43° 52′ N, 121° 27′ W 90
Laval, Can. 45° 36′ N, 73° 46′ W 94
Laval, Fr. 48° 2′ N, 0° 54′ E 143
Lavalle, Arg. 29° 2′ S, 59° 12′ W 139
Lavalleja, Uru. 31° 5′ S, 57° 2′ W 139
Lavangen, Nor. 68° 46′ N, 17° 48′ E 152
Lavassaare, Est. 58° 30′ N, 24° 20′ E 166
Laveaga Peak, Calif., U.S. 36° 52′ N, 121° 14′ W 100
Lavelanet, Fr. 42° 55′ N, 1° 49′ E 164
Lavenham, U.K. 52° 6′ N, 0° 47′ E 162
Laverne, Okla., U.S. 36° 41′ N, 99° 54′ W 92
Lavia, Fin. 61° 34′ N, 22° 35′ E 166
Lavina, Mont., U.S. 46° 17′ N, 108° 57′ W 90
Lavis, It. 46° 9′ N, 11° 6′ E 167
Lavoisier Island, Antarctica 66° 11′ S, 67° 28′ W 248
Lavos, Port. 40° 5′ N, 8° 51′ W 150
Lavras, Braz. 21° 15′ S, 44° 60′ W 138
Lavras da Mangabeira, Braz. 6° 44′ S, 38° 59′ W 132
Lavras do Sul, Braz. 30° 51′ S, 53° 55′ W 139
Lavrentiya, Russ. 65° 37′ N, 171° 9′ W 98
Lavushi Manda National Park, Zambia 12° 46′ S, 30° 57′ E 224
Law Dome, Antarctica 67° 27′ S, 114° 17′ E 248
Lawabiskau, river, Can. 51° 21′ N, 81° 25′ W 110
Lawagamau Lake, Can. 49° 47′ N, 80° 49′ W 94
Lawers, Ben, peak, U.K. 56° 32′ N, 4° 19′ W 150
Lawford Lake, Can. 54° 25′ N, 97° 14′ W 108
Lawnhill, Can. 53° 25′ N, 131° 60′ W 108
Lawqah, Saudi Arabia 29° 46′ N, 42° 47′ E 180
Lawra, Ghana 10° 38′ N, 2° 54′ W 222
Lawrence, Ind., U.S. 39° 49′ N, 86° 1′ W 102
Lawrence, Kans., U.S. 38° 56′ N, 95° 14′ W 94
Lawrence, Mass., U.S. 42° 42′ N, 71° 11′ W 104
Lawrence, Miss., U.S. 32° 18′ N, 89° 13′ W 103
Lawrence, N.Z. 45° 55′ S, 169° 39′ E 240
Lawrenceburg, Ind., U.S. 39° 5′ N, 84° 52′ W 94
Lawrenceburg, Tenn., U.S. 35° 14′ N, 87° 19′ W 96
Lawrenceville, Ill., U.S. 38° 43′ N, 87° 41′ W 102
Lawyet el Lagâma, spring, Egypt 30° 47′ N, 33° 26′ E 194
Laxå, Nor. 58° 58′ N, 14° 36′ E 152
Laxong Co, lake, China 34° 18′ N, 84° 18′ E 188
Layda, Russ. 71° 30′ N, 83° 1′ E 173
Laydasalma, Russ. 65° 57′ N, 30° 55′ E 152
Laysan Island, Hawai'i, U.S. 25° 26′ N, 171° 52′ W 99
Layshi, Myanmar 25° 27′ N, 94° 54′ E 188
Laytamak, Russ. 58° 26′ N, 67° 26′ E 169
Layton, Utah, U.S. 41° 3′ N, 111° 57′ W 90
Lazarev, Russ. 52° 13′ N, 141° 17′ E 238
Lazareva, Russ. 57° 36′ N, 107° 47′ E 173
Lazarevac, Serb. and Mont. 44° 23′ N, 20° 15′ E 168
Lazarevskoye, Russ. 43° 56′ N, 39° 18′ E 158
Lázaro Cárdenas, Mex. 18° 55′ N, 88° 16′ W 115
Lázaro Cárdenas, Mex. 17° 59′ N, 102° 13′ W 114
Lázaro Cardenas, Presa, lake, Mex. 25° 31′ N, 106° 28′ W 80
Lazdijai, Lith. 54° 14′ N, 23° 30′ E 166
Lazio, adm. division, It. 41° 57′ N, 12° 5′ E 156
Lbera, Serra de l', Sp. 42° 23′ N, 2° 32′ E 164
Le Barcarès, Fr. 42° 47′ N, 3° 0′ E 164
Le Bic, Can. 48° 21′ N, 68° 42′ W 94
Le Bugue, Fr. 44° 55′ N, 0° 55′ E 150
Le Cateau, Fr. 50° 5′ N, 3° 33′ E 163
Le Catelet, Fr. 49° 59′ N, 3° 15′ E 163
Le Châtelet-en-Brie, Fr. 48° 29′ N, 2° 47′ E 163
Le Chesne, Fr. 49° 31′ N, 4° 46′ E 163
Le Cocq, Lac, lake, Can. 52° 16′ N, 68° 32′ W 111
Le Conquet, Fr. 48° 21′ N, 4° 47′ W 150
Le Crotoy, Fr. 50° 13′ N, 1° 39′ E 163
Le Gros Cap, Can. 47° 8′ N, 62° 50′ W 111
Le Guelta, Alg. 36° 20′ N, 0° 52′ E 164
Le Havre, Fr. 49° 29′ N, 0° 6′ E 150
Le Madonie, It. 37° 46′ N, 13° 33′ E 156
Le Mans, Fr. 48° 0′ N, 0° 11′ E 150
Le Mars, Iowa, U.S. 42° 46′ N, 96° 11′ W 94
Le Mont-Saint-Michel, Fr. 48° 37′ N, 1° 31′ W 150
Le Moyen, La., U.S. 30° 46′ N, 92° 3′ W 103
Le Perthus, Fr. 42° 28′ N, 2° 51′ E 164
Le Petit-Quevilly, Fr. 49° 24′ N, 1° 2′ E 163
Le Puy, Fr. 45° 2′ N, 3° 53′ E 150
Le Quesnoy, Fr. 50° 14′ N, 3° 38′ E 163
Le Rageois, Lac, lake, Can. 53° 16′ N, 69° 31′ W 111
Le Roy, Ill., U.S. 40° 20′ N, 88° 46′ W 102
Le Roy, Mich., U.S. 44° 2′ N, 85° 27′ W 102
Le Roy, N.Y., U.S. 42° 58′ N, 77° 60′ W 94
Le Thuy, Vietnam 17° 14′ N, 106° 52′ E 202
Le Touquet-Paris-Plage, Fr. 50° 31′ N, 1° 35′ E 163
Le Tréport, Fr. 50° 3′ N, 1° 21′ E 163
Le Veneur, Île, Can. 51° 36′ N, 74° 11′ W 110
Le Verdon-sur-Mer, Fr. 45° 32′ N, 1° 6′ W 150
Le Vigan, Fr. 43° 59′ N, 3° 34′ E 150
Leach, Cambodia 12° 20′ N, 103° 44′ E 202
Leach Lake Mountain, peak, Calif., U.S. 39° 54′ N, 123° 10′ W 90
Lead, S. Dak., U.S. 44° 20′ N, 103° 47′ W 82
Lead Mountain, peak, Me., U.S. 44° 51′ N, 68° 12′ W 94
Leadenham, U.K. 53° 3′ N, 0° 36′ E 162
Leader, Can. 50° 53′ N, 109° 32′ W 90
Leadore, Idaho, U.S. 44° 39′ N, 113° 22′ W 90
Leadville, Colo., U.S. 39° 14′ N, 106° 17′ W 90
Leaf Rapids, Can. 56° 28′ N, 100° 3′ W 108
Leaf, river, Miss., U.S. 31° 17′ N, 89° 14′ W 103
League, Slieve, peak, Ire. 54° 38′ N, 8° 49′ W 150
Leakesville, Miss., U.S. 31° 7′ N, 88° 33′ W 103
Leakey, Tex., U.S. 29° 42′ N, 99° 46′ W 92
Lealui, Zambia 15° 13′ S, 23° 2′ E 220
Leamington, Can. 42° 3′ N, 82° 36′ W 102
Leamington, U.K. 52° 17′ N, 1° 33′ W 162
Leandro N. Alem, Arg. 27° 36′ S, 55° 20′ W 139
Leaota, peak, Rom. 45° 18′ N, 25° 13′ E 156
Learned, Miss., U.S. 32° 10′ N, 90° 34′ W 103
Leatherman Peak, Idaho, U.S. 44° 4′ N, 113° 48′ W 90
Leavenworth, Kans., U.S. 39° 17′ N, 94° 56′ W 94
Leavitt Bay 57° 10′ N, 107° 38′ W 108
Leavitt Peak, Calif., U.S. 38° 16′ N, 119° 42′ W 100
Łeba, Pol. 54° 45′ N, 17° 34′ E 152
Lebach, Ger. 49° 25′ N, 6° 54′ E 163
Lebak, Philippines 6° 33′ N, 124° 3′ E 203
Lebam, Wash., U.S. 46° 33′ N, 123° 33′ W 100
Lebane, Serb. and Mont. 42° 55′ N, 21° 44′ E 168
Lebango, Congo 0° 15′ N, 14° 51′ E 218
Lebanon, Ind., U.S. 40° 2′ N, 86° 28′ W 102
Lebanon, Kans., U.S. 39° 48′ N, 98° 33′ W 90
Lebanon, Ky., U.S. 37° 34′ N, 85° 15′ W 96
Lebanon, Leb. 34° 27′ N, 36° 5′ E 194
Lebanon 34° 0′ N, 35° 51′ E 194
Lebanon, Mo., U.S. 37° 40′ N, 92° 40′ W 96
Lebanon, N.H., U.S. 43° 38′ N, 72° 15′ W 104
Lebanon, Ohio, U.S. 39° 25′ N, 84° 12′ W 102
Lebanon, Oreg., U.S. 44° 31′ N, 122° 55′ W 90
Lebanon, Tenn., U.S. 36° 11′ N, 86° 18′ W 82
Lebec, Calif., U.S. 34° 50′ N, 118° 53′ W 101
Lebed', Russ. 62° 1′ N, 89° 15′ E 169
Lebedyan', Russ. 52° 59′ N, 39° 2′ E 154
Lebedyn, Ukr. 50° 34′ N, 34° 26′ E 158
Leben, ruin(s), Gr. 34° 55′ N, 24° 49′ E 156
Lebo, Dem. Rep. of the Congo 4° 28′ N, 23° 55′ E 224
Lebombo Mountains, S. Af. 24° 10′ S, 31° 21′ E 227
Lebon Régis, Braz. 26° 56′ S, 50° 45′ W 139
Lębork, Pol. 54° 31′ N, 17° 45′ E 152
Lebowakgomo, S. Af. 24° 12′ S, 29° 31′ E 227
Lebrija, Sp. 36° 55′ N, 6° 5′ W 164
Lebu, Chile 37° 39′ S, 73° 40′ W 134
Lecce, It. 40° 20′ N, 18° 10′ E 156
Lecco, It. 45° 51′ N, 9° 23′ E 167
Lece, Serb. and Mont. 42° 53′ N, 21° 32′ E 168
Lechang, China 25° 8′ N, 113° 23′ E 198
Lecompte, La., U.S. 31° 4′ N, 92° 25′ W 103
Léconi, Gabon 1° 37′ S, 14° 15′ E 218
Léconi, river, Gabon 1° 5′ S, 13° 17′ E 218
Ledaña, Sp. 39° 21′ N, 1° 43′ W 164
Ledbury, U.K. 52° 2′ N, 2° 26′ W 162
Ledo, India 27° 19′ N, 95° 48′ E 188
Ledo, Indonesia 1° 3′ N, 109° 34′ E 196
Ledo, Cabo, Angola 9° 46′ S, 12° 47′ E 218
Ledong, China 18° 41′ N, 109° 6′ E 198
Leduc, Can. 53° 15′ N, 113° 33′ W 108
Lee, Mass., U.S. 42° 18′ N, 73° 15′ W 104
Lee, Nev., U.S. 40° 34′ N, 115° 36′ W 90
Leech Lake, Minn., U.S. 47° 9′ N, 94° 56′ W 90
Leedey, Okla., U.S. 35° 50′ N, 99° 21′ W 92
Leeds, Ala., U.S. 33° 32′ N, 86° 33′ W 96
Leeds, N. Dak., U.S. 48° 16′ N, 99° 28′ W 90
Leeds, U.K. 53° 48′ N, 1° 33′ W 162
Leeds, Utah, U.S. 37° 13′ N, 113° 21′ W 92
Leek, Neth. 53° 10′ N, 6° 23′ E 163
Leek, U.K. 53° 6′ N, 2° 2′ W 162
Leek Spring Hill, peak, Calif., U.S. 38° 36′ N, 120° 22′ W 90
Leer, Ger. 53° 13′ N, 7° 27′ E 163
Leesburg, Fla., U.S. 28° 48′ N, 81° 54′ W 105
Leesburg, Ohio, U.S. 39° 20′ N, 83° 33′ W 102
Leesburg, Va., U.S. 39° 6′ N, 77° 34′ W 94
Leeste, Ger. 52° 59′ N, 8° 48′ E 163
Leesville, La., U.S. 31° 7′ N, 93° 17′ W 103
Leesville, S.C., U.S. 33° 54′ N, 81° 31′ W 96
Leeuwarden, Neth. 53° 11′ N, 5° 46′ E 163
Leeuwin, Cape, Austral. 34° 5′ S, 113° 51′ E 230
Leeville, La., U.S. 29° 15′ N, 90° 13′ W 103
Leeward Islands, Caribbean Sea 15° 40′ N, 61° 42′ W 116
Léfini Faunal Reserve, Congo 2° 51′ S, 15° 5′ E 206
Lefka 35° 6′ N, 32° 51′ E 194
Lefká Óri, Gr. 35° 15′ N, 23° 47′ E 156
Lefkoniko 35° 15′ N, 33° 43′ E 194
Lefkoşa see Lefkosia, Cyprus 35° 9′ N, 33° 18′ E 194
Lefkosia (Nicosia, Lefkoşa), Cyprus 35° 9′ N, 33° 18′ E 194
Leftrook Lake, Can. 56° 2′ N, 99° 9′ W 108
Legal, Can. 53° 56′ N, 113° 35′ W 108
Légaré, Lac, lake, Can. 46° 56′ N, 74° 25′ W 110
Legat, Mauritania 16° 45′ N, 14° 52′ W 222
Legazpi, Philippines 13° 8′ N, 123° 43′ E 203
Legden, Ger. 52° 1′ N, 7° 6′ E 167
Legges Tor, peak, Austral. 41° 34′ S, 147° 31′ E 230
Leggett, Tex., U.S. 30° 48′ N, 94° 52′ W 103

Leghorn see Livorno, *It.* 43°33′ N, 10°19′ E **156**
Legnano, *It.* 45°35′ N, 8°53′ E **167**
Legnica, *Pol.* 51°12′ N, 16°9′ E **152**
Leh, *India* 34°9′ N, 77°33′ E **190**
Lehi, *Utah, U.S.* 40°23′ N, 111°51′ W **90**
Lehigh Acres, *Fla., U.S.* 26°36′ N, 81°38′ W **105**
Lehliu, *Rom.* 44°29′ N, 26°48′ E **158**
Lehman Caves, site, *Nev., U.S.* 39°0′ N, 114°18′ W **90**
Lehr, *N. Dak., U.S.* 46°16′ N, 99°23′ W **90**
Lehtimäki, *Fin.* 62°45′ N, 23°51′ E **154**
Lehututu, *Botswana* 23°57′ S, 21°52′ E **227**
Leiah, *Pak.* 30°54′ N, 70°59′ E **186**
Leicester, *Mass., U.S.* 42°14′ N, 71°55′ W **104**
Leicester, *U.K.* 52°37′ N, 1°8′ W **162**
Leiden, *Neth.* 52°9′ N, 4°29′ E **163**
Leie, river, *Belg.* 50°57′ N, 3°24′ E **163**
Leigh, *N.Z.* 36°19′ S, 174°47′ E **240**
Leigh, *U.K.* 53°30′ N, 2°31′ W **162**
Leighton Buzzard, *U.K.* 51°55′ N, 0°39′ E **162**
Leikanger, *Nor.* 61°11′ N, 6°46′ E **152**
Leiktho, *Myanmar* 19°14′ N, 96°33′ E **202**
Leippe, *Ger.* 51°24′ N, 14°4′ E **152**
Leipsic, *Ohio, U.S.* 41°5′ N, 83°59′ W **102**
Leipzig, *Ger.* 51°19′ N, 12°22′ E **152**
Leirbotn, *Nor.* 70°6′ N, 23°23′ E **152**
Leiria, *Port.* 39°44′ N, 8°50′ W **150**
Leiria, adm. division, *Port.* 39°53′ N, 8°54′ W **150**
Leirpollen, *Nor.* 70°25′ N, 28°28′ E **152**
Leishan, *China* 26°24′ N, 108°0′ E **198**
Leisler, Mount, peak, *Austral.* 23°21′ S, 129°4′ E **230**
Leismer, *Can.* 55°44′ N, 111°3′ W **108**
Leiston, *U.K.* 52°12′ N, 1°34′ E **163**
Leitchfield, *Ky., U.S.* 37°28′ N, 86°18′ W **96**
Leitza, *Sp.* 43°4′ N, 1°55′ W **164**
Leivonmäki, *Fin.* 61°54′ N, 26°4′ E **166**
Leiway, *Myanmar* 19°38′ N, 96°4′ E **202**
Leiyang, *China* 26°28′ N, 112°51′ E **198**
Leizhou Wan 20°35′ N, 110°18′ E **198**
Leka, *Nor.* 65°4′ N, 11°42′ E **152**
Lekatero, *Dem. Rep. of the Congo* 0°41′ N, 23°57′ E **224**
Lekbibaj, *Alban.* 42°18′ N, 19°55′ E **168**
Lekemt see Nek'emtē, *Eth.* 9°2′ N, 36°33′ E **224**
Lekhovskoye, *Russ.* 62°43′ N, 42°50′ E **154**
Lekhwair, oil field, *Oman* 22°41′ N, 55°26′ E **182**
Lekmartovskaya, *Russ.* 60°49′ N, 56°9′ E **154**
Léko, *Mali* 13°36′ N, 9°3′ W **222**
Lekshmozero, *Russ.* 61°46′ N, 38°5′ E **154**
Leksula, *Indonesia* 3°46′ S, 126°30′ E **192**
Lekunberri, *Sp.* 43°0′ N, 1°54′ W **164**
Leland, *Miss., U.S.* 33°23′ N, 90°55′ W **103**
Lel'chytsy, *Belarus* 51°45′ N, 28°22′ E **152**
Lelić, *Serb. and Mont.* 44°13′ N, 19°49′ E **168**
Lely Gebergte, *Suriname* 4°17′ N, 55°41′ W **130**
Lelystad, *Neth.* 52°30′ N, 5°24′ E **163**
Lema, *Nig.* 12°56′ N, 4°14′ E **222**
Lembach, *Fr.* 48°59′ N, 7°47′ E **163**
Lembé, *Cameroon* 4°16′ N, 12°19′ E **218**
Lembeck, *Ger.* 51°45′ N, 6°59′ E **167**
Lembeni, *Tanzania* 3°46′ S, 37°37′ E **224**
Lemberg, *Fr.* 49°0′ N, 7°22′ E **163**
Leme, *Braz.* 22°10′ S, 47°25′ W **138**
Lemei Rock, peak, *Wash., U.S.* 46°0′ N, 121°49′ W **100**
Lemesos (Limassol), *Cyprus* 34°40′ N, 33°1′ E **194**
Lemhi Range, *Idaho, U.S.* 44°45′ N, 113°59′ W **90**
Lemieux Islands, *Davis Strait* 63°50′ N, 63°57′ W **106**
Lemitar, *N. Mex., U.S.* 34°10′ N, 106°55′ W **92**
Lemmer, *Neth.* 52°51′ N, 5°42′ E **163**
Lemmon, *S. Dak., U.S.* 45°54′ N, 102°9′ W **90**
Lemmon, Mount, peak, *Ariz., U.S.* 32°25′ N, 110°51′ W **92**
Lemoïlé, *Mauritania* 16°10′ N, 7°12′ W **222**
Lemon Grove, *Calif., U.S.* 32°44′ N, 117°3′ W **101**
Lemoncove, *Calif., U.S.* 36°23′ N, 119°2′ W **101**
Lemont, *Ill., U.S.* 41°38′ N, 88°1′ W **102**
Lemoore, *Calif., U.S.* 36°18′ N, 119°48′ W **100**
Lempäälä, *Fin.* 61°18′ N, 23°44′ E **166**
Lempster, *N.H., U.S.* 43°14′ N, 72°13′ W **104**
Lemsid, *Africa* 26°31′ N, 13°49′ W **214**
Lemtybozh, *Russ.* 63°51′ N, 57°2′ E **154**
Lemva, river, *Russ.* 65°28′ N, 61°4′ E **154**
Lemvig, *Den.* 56°32′ N, 8°17′ E **150**
Lem'yu, *Russ.* 64°17′ N, 54°59′ E **154**
Lem'yu, river, *Russ.* 64°15′ N, 55°12′ E **154**
Lena, *Ill., U.S.* 42°22′ N, 89°49′ W **102**
Lena, *La., U.S.* 31°26′ N, 92°47′ W **103**
Lena, *Miss., U.S.* 32°34′ N, 89°37′ W **103**
Lena, Mount, peak, *Utah, U.S.* 40°45′ N, 109°29′ W **90**
Lena, river, *Russ.* 69°16′ N, 124°52′ E **172**
Lena Tablemount, *Indian Ocean* 53°10′ S, 44°34′ E **255**
Lenart, *Slov.* 46°35′ N, 15°50′ E **168**
Lençóis, *Braz.* 12°34′ S, 41°24′ W **132**
Lençóis Maranhenses National Park, *Braz.* 2°37′ S, 43°24′ W **122**
Lendery, *Russ.* 63°24′ N, 31°12′ E **152**
Lenger, *Kaz.* 42°10′ N, 69°50′ E **197**
Lengerich, *Ger.* 52°11′ N, 7°52′ E **163**
Lenghu, *China* 38°48′ N, 93°23′ E **188**
Lengua de Vaca, Punta, *Chile* 30°20′ S, 73°37′ W **134**
Lengwe National Park, *Malawi* 16°30′ S, 33°58′ E **224**
Lengyeltóti, *Hung.* 46°39′ N, 17°38′ E **168**
Lenhovda, *Nor.* 56°59′ N, 15°14′ E **152**
Lenin Peak, *Kyrg.* 39°21′ N, 72°46′ E **197**
Leningrad see Sankt-Peterburg, *Russ.* 59°55′ N, 30°17′ E **166**
Leningradskaya, *Russ.* 46°21′ N, 39°23′ E **156**
Leningradskiy, *Russ.* 69°19′ N, 178°23′ E **98**
Leninogradskoe, *Kaz.* 53°33′ N, 71°31′ E **184**
Lenino, *Belarus* 53°2′ N, 27°13′ E **152**
Leninogorsk, *Russ.* 54°37′ N, 52°32′ E **154**
Leninogorsk see Ridder, *Kaz.* 50°21′ N, 83°32′ E **184**
Leninpol', *Kyrg.* 42°28′ N, 71°58′ E **197**
Leninsk, *Russ.* 48°42′ N, 45°12′ E **158**
Leninsk Kuznetskiy, *Russ.* 54°39′ N, 86°18′ E **184**
Leninsk see Baykonur, *Kaz.* 45°50′ N, 63°18′ E **173**
Leninskiy, *Kaz.* 52°14′ N, 76°46′ E **184**
Leninskiy, *Russ.* 56°32′ N, 46°3′ E **154**
Lenïnskoe, *Kaz.* 49°5′ N, 49°59′ E **158**
Lenïnskoe, *Kaz.* 50°45′ N, 57°53′ E **158**
Leninskoye, *Russ.* 58°18′ N, 47°7′ E **154**
Lenk, *Switz.* 46°27′ N, 7°28′ E **167**
Lennox, *S. Dak., U.S.* 43°19′ N, 96°54′ W **94**
Lenoir, *N.C., U.S.* 35°54′ N, 81°33′ W **96**
Lenoir City, *Tenn., U.S.* 35°48′ N, 84°16′ W **96**
Lenora, *Kans., U.S.* 39°37′ N, 99°60′ W **90**
Lenox, *Mass., U.S.* 42°21′ N, 73°18′ W **104**
Lenox Dale, *Mass., U.S.* 42°19′ N, 73°16′ W **104**
Lens, *Fr.* 50°25′ N, 2°49′ E **163**
Lensk, *Russ.* 60°44′ N, 114°42′ E **160**
Lenskoye, *Russ.* 58°10′ N, 63°7′ E **154**
Lentekhi, *Ga.* 42°46′ N, 42°43′ E **195**
Lenti, *Hung.* 46°37′ N, 16°32′ E **168**
Lentiira, *Fin.* 64°22′ N, 29°47′ E **152**
Lentini, *It.* 37°16′ N, 15°3′ E **216**
Lentvaris, *Lith.* 54°38′ N, 25°3′ E **166**
Lenwood, *Calif., U.S.* 34°52′ N, 117°8′ W **101**
Léo, *Burkina Faso* 11°5′ N, 2°7′ W **222**
Leo, *Ind., U.S.* 41°13′ N, 85°1′ W **102**
Leoben, *Aust.* 47°22′ N, 15°6′ E **156**
Leocadio Paz, *Arg.* 26°9′ S, 65°19′ W **132**
Leola, *S. Dak., U.S.* 45°42′ N, 98°58′ W **90**
Leominster, *Mass., U.S.* 42°31′ N, 71°46′ W **104**
Leominster, *U.K.* 52°13′ N, 2°44′ W **162**
Leon, *Iowa, U.S.* 40°43′ N, 93°45′ W **94**
León, *Mex.* 21°5′ N, 101°43′ W **112**
León, *Nicar.* 12°25′ N, 86°53′ W **115**
León, *Sp.* 42°36′ N, 5°35′ W **150**
León, *Sp.* 42°34′ N, 5°37′ W **214**
León, Cerro, peak, *Parag.* 20°21′ S, 60°29′ W **132**
León, Montes de, *Sp.* 42°22′ N, 6°30′ W **150**
León, Punta, *Arg.* 50°36′ S, 68°56′ W **134**
Leon, river, *Tex., U.S.* 31°36′ N, 97°52′ W **112**
Leona, oil field, *Venez.* 8°57′ N, 63°57′ W **116**
Leonard, *Tex., U.S.* 33°22′ N, 96°15′ W **96**
Leonardville, *Namibia* 23°31′ S, 18°43′ E **227**
Leonarisso 35°28′ N, 34°8′ E **194**
Leonding, *Aust.* 48°16′ N, 14°14′ E **152**
Leones, Isla, island, *Pan.* 7°38′ N, 81°35′ W **115**
Leopoldina, *Braz.* 21°33′ S, 42°40′ W **138**
Leopoldo de Bulhões, *Braz.* 16°39′ S, 48°47′ W **138**
Leopoldsburg, *Belg.* 51°7′ N, 5°16′ E **167**
Léopoldville see Kinshasa, *Dem. Rep. of the Congo* 4°24′ S, 15°6′ E **218**
Leoti, *Kans., U.S.* 38°29′ N, 101°22′ W **90**
Leoville, *Can.* 53°38′ N, 107°31′ W **108**
Lepanto, *Ark., U.S.* 35°36′ N, 90°21′ W **96**
Lephalale (Ellisras), *S. Af.* 23°40′ S, 27°42′ E **227**
Lephepe, *Botswana* 23°19′ S, 25°47′ E **227**
Leping, *China* 28°58′ N, 117°3′ E **198**
L'Épiphanie, *Can.* 45°51′ N, 73°29′ W **94**
Lepontine Alps, *Switz.* 46°17′ N, 8°24′ E **167**
Lepperton, *N.Z.* 39°6′ S, 174°13′ E **240**
Lepsény, *Hung.* 46°59′ N, 18°14′ E **168**
Lepsi, *Kaz.* 46°14′ N, 78°54′ E **184**
Lepsi, river, *Kaz.* 45°59′ N, 79°47′ E **184**
Ler, *Sudan* 8°18′ N, 30°5′ E **224**
Léraba, *Côte d'Ivoire* 10°7′ N, 5°6′ W **222**
Léraba, river, *Africa* 9°55′ N, 5°6′ W **222**
Lerdo de Tejada, *Mex.* 18°37′ N, 95°30′ W **114**
Léré, *Chad* 9°38′ N, 14°14′ E **216**
Léré, *Mali* 15°42′ N, 4°57′ W **222**
Lerici, *It.* 44°4′ N, 9°55′ E **167**
Lérida, *Col.* 0°8′ N, 70°44′ W **136**
Lerik, *Azerb.* 38°45′ N, 48°23′ E **195**
Lerín, *Sp.* 42°28′ N, 1°58′ W **164**
Lérins, Îles de, islands, *Mediterranean Sea* 43°21′ N, 7°0′ E **165**
Lerma, *Sp.* 42°0′ N, 3°45′ W **164**
Lerma, river, *Mex.* 20°23′ N, 102°10′ W **114**
Lerna, *Ill., U.S.* 39°24′ N, 88°17′ W **102**
Lerna, ruin(s), *Gr.* 37°33′ N, 22°36′ E **156**
Lérouville, *Fr.* 48°47′ N, 5°31′ E **163**
Leroy, *Ala., U.S.* 31°30′ N, 87°59′ W **103**
Leroy, *Can.* 52°1′ N, 104°45′ W **90**
Leroy, *Kans., U.S.* 38°3′ N, 95°38′ W **94**
Lerwick, *U.K.* 60°11′ N, 1°17′ W **143**
Leş, *Rom.* 46°57′ N, 21°51′ E **168**
Les, *Sp.* 42°48′ N, 0°41′ E **164**
Les Andelys, *Fr.* 49°14′ N, 1°25′ E **163**
Les Borges Blanques, *Sp.* 41°31′ N, 0°50′ E **164**
Les Cabannes, *Fr.* 42°47′ N, 1°40′ E **164**
Les Cayes, *Haiti* 18°14′ N, 73°46′ W **116**
Les Escoumins, *Can.* 48°20′ N, 69°26′ W **94**
Les Essarts, *Fr.* 46°46′ N, 1°15′ W **150**
Les Landes, region, *Fr.* 43°32′ N, 1°26′ W **164**
Les Sables-d'Olonne, *Fr.* 46°29′ N, 1°47′ W **150**
Les Salines, *Tun.* 36°4′ N, 8°57′ E **156**
L'Escala, *Sp.* 42°7′ N, 3°6′ E **164**
Lescar, *Fr.* 43°19′ N, 0°26′ E **164**
Leseru, *Kenya* 0°34′ N, 35°10′ E **224**
Leshan, *China* 29°22′ N, 103°49′ E **190**
Leshukonskoye, *Russ.* 64°53′ N, 45°37′ E **154**
Lesja, *Nor.* 62°7′ N, 8°49′ E **152**
Leskov Island, *Antarctica* 66°30′ S, 82°12′ E **248**
Leskovac, *Serb. and Mont.* 42°59′ N, 21°58′ E **168**
Leslie, *Ark., U.S.* 35°48′ N, 92°34′ W **96**
Leslie, *Mich., U.S.* 42°26′ N, 84°26′ W **102**
Leslie, *S. Af.* 26°25′ S, 28°54′ E **227**
Lesmont, *Fr.* 48°25′ N, 4°24′ E **163**
Leśnica, *Serb. and Mont.* 44°39′ N, 19°18′ E **168**
Lesnoy, *Russ.* 59°50′ N, 52°8′ E **154**
Lesnoye, *Russ.* 58°16′ N, 35°32′ E **154**
Lesogorskiy, *Russ.* 61°1′ N, 28°56′ E **166**
Lesosibirsk, *Russ.* 58°2′ N, 92°33′ E **160**
Lesotho 29°27′ S, 28°14′ E **227**
Lesovo, *Bulg.* 41°59′ N, 26°35′ E **158**
Lesozavodsk, *Russ.* 45°27′ N, 133°20′ E **190**
Lesozavodskiy, *Russ.* 66°43′ N, 32°52′ E **152**
L'Espluga de Francolí, *Sp.* 41°23′ N, 1°3′ E **164**
Lessebo, *Nor.* 56°45′ N, 15°15′ E **152**
Lesser Antilles, *North Atlantic Ocean* 11°25′ N, 62°26′ W **116**
Lesser Caucasus, *Arm.* 40°7′ N, 45°47′ E **180**
Lesser Slave Lake, *Can.* 55°12′ N, 117°10′ W **106**
Lesser Sunda Islands, *Indian Ocean* 10°13′ S, 121°5′ E **238**
Lester, *Wash., U.S.* 47°12′ N, 121°30′ W **100**
Lestijärvi, *Fin.* 63°30′ N, 24°36′ E **152**
Lésvos, island, *Gr.* 38°50′ N, 26°5′ E **180**
Leszno, *Pol.* 51°49′ N, 16°35′ E **152**
Letaba, site, *S. Af.* 23°52′ S, 31°30′ E **227**
Létavértes, *Hung.* 47°23′ N, 21°53′ E **168**
Letchworth, *U.K.* 51°58′ N, 0°14′ E **162**
Letea, *Rom.* 45°18′ N, 29°30′ E **156**
Lethbridge, *Can.* 49°40′ N, 112°49′ W **82**
Lethem, *Guyana* 3°19′ N, 59°48′ W **130**
Leticia, *Col.* 4°8′ S, 69°59′ W **136**
Leting, *China* 39°24′ N, 118°57′ E **198**
Letka, *Russ.* 59°35′ N, 49°24′ E **154**
Letlhakane, *Botswana* 21°25′ S, 25°34′ E **227**
Letlhakeng, *Botswana* 24°6′ S, 25°2′ E **227**
Letnerechenskiy, *Russ.* 64°19′ N, 34°12′ E **152**
Letniy Navolok, *Russ.* 65°8′ N, 36°57′ E **154**
Letnyaya Stavka, *Russ.* 45°22′ N, 43°16′ E **158**
Letnyaya Zolotitsa, *Russ.* 64°58′ N, 36°42′ E **154**
Letsôk-aw Kyun, island, *Myanmar* 11°20′ N, 98°15′ E **202**
Lette, *Ger.* 51°54′ N, 7°11′ E **167**
Letur, *Sp.* 38°22′ N, 2°5′ W **164**
Léua, *Angola* 11°39′ S, 20°24′ E **220**
Leucadia, *Calif., U.S.* 33°4′ N, 117°19′ W **101**
Leucate, *Fr.* 42°54′ N, 3°0′ E **164**
Leucayec, Isla, island, *Chile* 43°55′ S, 73°41′ W **134**
Leuk, *Switz.* 46°20′ N, 7°37′ E **167**
Leuna, *Ger.* 51°19′ N, 12°1′ E **152**
Leuser, peak, *Indonesia* 3°45′ N, 97°5′ E **196**
Leuven, *Belg.* 50°52′ N, 4°41′ E **167**
Leuze, *Belg.* 50°35′ N, 3°37′ E **163**
Lev Tolstoy, *Russ.* 53°11′ N, 39°23′ E **154**
Levajok, *Nor.* 69°54′ N, 26°24′ E **152**
Levanger, *Nor.* 63°44′ N, 11°17′ E **152**
Levant, *Kans., U.S.* 39°23′ N, 101°13′ W **90**
Levant, Île du, island, *Fr.* 43°3′ N, 6°30′ E **165**
Levanto, *It.* 44°10′ N, 9°37′ E **167**
Levaya Khetta, river, *Russ.* 64°9′ N, 71°21′ E **169**
Levelland, *Tex., U.S.* 33°34′ N, 102°23′ W **92**
Levens, *Fr.* 43°51′ N, 7°12′ E **167**
Leveque, Cape, *Austral.* 16°19′ S, 121°59′ E **230**
Lever, river, *Braz.* 11°3′ S, 50°17′ W **130**
Leverkusen, *Ger.* 51°0′ N, 6°59′ E **167**
Levico, *It.* 46°1′ N, 11°18′ E **167**
Levidi, *Gr.* 37°41′ N, 22°17′ E **156**
Levikha, *Russ.* 57°36′ N, 59°52′ E **154**
Levin, *N.Z.* 40°39′ S, 175°17′ E **240**
Lévis, *Can.* 46°47′ N, 71°11′ W **94**
Levittown, *Pa., U.S.* 40°8′ N, 74°51′ W **94**
Levokumskoye, *Russ.* 44°48′ N, 44°38′ E **158**
Lévrier, Baie du 20°6′ N, 16°46′ W **222**
Lévuo, river, *Lith.* 55°49′ N, 24°28′ E **166**
Lewellen, *Nebr., U.S.* 41°19′ N, 102°10′ W **90**
Lewes, *U.K.* 50°52′ N, 2°120′ E **162**
Lewis, *Ind., U.S.* 39°15′ N, 87°16′ W **102**
Lewis, *Kans., U.S.* 37°56′ N, 99°16′ W **92**
Lewis, *N.Y., U.S.* 44°16′ N, 73°35′ W **104**
Lewis and Clark Range, *Mont., U.S.* 48°1′ N, 113°19′ W **90**
Lewis Chain 80°2′ S, 29°5′ W **248**
Lewis Hills, peak, *Can.* 48°48′ N, 58°35′ W **111**
Lewis, Isle of, island, *U.K.* 58°31′ N, 8°23′ W **142**
Lewis, Mount, peak, *Nev., U.S.* 40°23′ N, 116°57′ W **90**
Lewis Pass, *N.Z.* 42°26′ S, 172°23′ E **240**
Lewis, river, *Wash., U.S.* 46°7′ N, 121°50′ W **100**
Lewiston, *Me., U.S.* 44°6′ N, 70°13′ W **104**
Lewistown, *Ill., U.S.* 40°23′ N, 90°9′ W **102**
Lewistown, *Pa., U.S.* 40°35′ N, 77°36′ W **94**
Lewisville, *Ark., U.S.* 33°21′ N, 93°35′ W **96**
Lexington, *Ky., U.S.* 38°1′ N, 84°30′ W **94**
Lexington, *Mich., U.S.* 43°16′ N, 82°32′ W **102**
Lexington, *Miss., U.S.* 33°5′ N, 90°3′ W **103**
Lexington, *Mo., U.S.* 39°10′ N, 93°52′ W **94**
Lexington, *Nebr., U.S.* 40°45′ N, 99°45′ W **92**
Lexington, *N.C., U.S.* 35°48′ N, 80°16′ W **96**
Lexington, *Ohio, U.S.* 40°40′ N, 82°35′ W **102**
Lexington, *Oreg., U.S.* 45°26′ N, 119°41′ W **90**
Lexington Park, *Md., U.S.* 38°14′ N, 76°28′ W **82**
Leyburn, *U.K.* 54°18′ N, 1°50′ W **162**
Leye, *China* 24°47′ N, 106°25′ E **198**
Leyte, island, *Philippines* 10°16′ N, 125°21′ E **192**
Leżajsk, *Pol.* 50°14′ N, 22°25′ E **152**
Lezha, *Russ.* 58°56′ N, 40°49′ E **154**
Lezhë, *Alban.* 41°47′ N, 19°39′ E **168**
Lezhi, *China* 30°15′ N, 105°5′ E **198**
Lezuza, *Sp.* 38°56′ N, 2°21′ W **164**
L'gov, *Russ.* 51°41′ N, 35°16′ E **158**
Lhari, *China* 30°50′ N, 93°22′ E **188**
Lhasa, *China* 29°46′ N, 91°3′ E **197**
Lhasa, river, *China* 29°20′ N, 90°55′ E **197**
Lhazhong, *China* 32°2′ N, 86°46′ E **188**
L'Hillil, *Alg.* 35°43′ N, 0°22′ E **150**
Lhokseumawe, *Indonesia* 5°10′ N, 97°5′ E **196**
Lhorong, *China* 30°44′ N, 95°51′ E **188**
L'Hospitalet, *Fr.* 42°35′ N, 1°47′ E **164**
L'Hospitalet de Llobregat, *Sp.* 41°21′ N, 2°6′ E **164**
Lhozhag, *China* 28°19′ N, 90°50′ E **197**
Lhünzê, *China* 28°26′ N, 92°27′ E **197**
Lhünzhub, *China* 30°10′ N, 91°13′ E **197**
Li, river, *China* 29°23′ N, 110°55′ E **198**
Li Yubu, *Sudan* 5°23′ N, 27°17′ E **224**
Lian, river, *China* 24°28′ N, 112°44′ E **198**
Liancheng, *China* 25°40′ N, 116°44′ E **198**
Liancourt, *Fr.* 49°19′ N, 2°28′ E **163**
Lianga, *Philippines* 8°40′ N, 126°5′ E **203**
Liangcheng, *China* 40°31′ N, 112°30′ E **198**
Liangdang, *China* 33°54′ N, 106°19′ E **198**
Liangjiangkou, *China* 42°38′ N, 128°2′ E **200**
Liangping, *China* 30°37′ N, 107°47′ E **198**
Liangshui, *China* 44°58′ N, 125°51′ E **200**
Lianjiang, *China* 26°15′ N, 119°33′ E **198**
Lianjiang, *China* 21°36′ N, 110°14′ E **198**
Lianping, *China* 24°21′ N, 114°27′ E **198**
Lianshan, *China* 24°31′ N, 112°6′ E **198**
Lianxian, *China* 24°45′ N, 112°24′ E **198**
Lianyun, *China* 34°41′ N, 119°23′ E **198**
Lianyungang (Xinpu), *China* 34°38′ N, 119°14′ E **198**
Liao, river, *China* 42°7′ N, 123°29′ E **200**
Liaocheng, *China* 36°25′ N, 115°53′ E **198**
Liaodong Wan 40°21′ N, 120°30′ E **198**
Liaoning, adm. division, *China* 41°19′ N, 123°22′ E **200**
Liaoyang, *China* 41°17′ N, 123°10′ E **200**
Liaoyuan, *China* 42°54′ N, 125°8′ E **200**
Liaozhong, *China* 41°31′ N, 122°41′ E **200**
Liard Island, *Antarctica* 66°36′ S, 67°58′ W **248**
Liard River, *Can.* 59°24′ N, 126°6′ W **108**
Liard, river, *Can.* 60°45′ N, 123°3′ W **106**
Liathach, peak, *U.K.* 57°32′ N, 5°34′ W **150**
Libanga, *Dem. Rep. of the Congo* 0°21′ N, 18°43′ E **218**
Libby, *Mont., U.S.* 48°22′ N, 115°34′ W **90**
Libby Dam, *Mont., U.S.* 48°8′ N, 115°34′ W **90**
Libenge, *Dem. Rep. of the Congo* 3°35′ N, 18°41′ E **218**
Liberal, *Kans., U.S.* 37°1′ N, 100°56′ W **92**
Liberdade, river, *Braz.* 8°19′ S, 71°53′ W **130**
Liberdade, river, *Braz.* 11°14′ S, 52°11′ W **130**
Liberec, *Czech Rep.* 50°45′ N, 15°2′ E **152**
Liberia, *C.R.* 10°38′ N, 85°27′ W **115**
Liberia 6°38′ N, 10°19′ W **214**
Libertad, *Venez.* 9°18′ N, 68°35′ W **136**
Libertad, *Venez.* 8°20′ N, 69°37′ W **136**
Libertador General Bernardo O'Higgins, adm. division, *Chile* 34°44′ S, 72°20′ W **134**
Liberty, *Ind., U.S.* 39°37′ N, 84°56′ W **102**
Liberty, *Miss., U.S.* 31°8′ N, 90°48′ W **103**
Liberty, *N.Y., U.S.* 41°47′ N, 74°45′ W **94**
Liberty, *Tex., U.S.* 30°2′ N, 94°47′ W **103**
Libni, Gebel, peak, *Egypt* 30°43′ N, 33°48′ E **194**
Libo, *China* 25°24′ N, 107°50′ E **198**
Libode, *S. Af.* 31°34′ S, 29°1′ E **227**
Liboi, *Kenya* 0°17′ N, 40°49′ E **224**
Libourne, *Fr.* 44°55′ N, 0°14′ E **150**
Libral Well, spring, *Austral.* 22°8′ S, 125°29′ E **230**
Libreville, *Gabon* 0°20′ N, 9°18′ E **218**
Libya 26°52′ N, 15°56′ E **216**
Libyan Desert, *Lib.* 26°27′ N, 24°26′ E **180**
Libyan Plateau, *Egypt* 30°0′ N, 25°33′ E **180**
Licantén, *Chile* 34°58′ S, 72°1′ W **134**
Lice, *Turk.* 38°27′ N, 40°39′ E **195**
Lich, *Ger.* 50°31′ N, 8°49′ E **167**
Lichfield, *U.K.* 52°40′ N, 1°50′ W **162**
Lichinga, *Mozambique* 13°20′ S, 35°13′ E **224**
Lichtenburg, *S. Af.* 26°11′ S, 26°8′ E **227**
Lichuan, *China* 30°18′ N, 108°55′ E **198**
Lichuan, *China* 27°22′ N, 116°51′ E **198**
Licking, *Mo., U.S.* 37°29′ N, 91°51′ W **96**
Licosa, Punta, *It.* 40°8′ N, 14°25′ E **156**
Licungo, river, *Mozambique* 17°5′ S, 37°3′ E **224**
Lida, *Belarus* 53°52′ N, 25°18′ E **166**
Liddon Gulf 74°53′ N, 117°12′ W **106**
Liden, *Nor.* 62°41′ N, 16°48′ E **152**
Lidgerwood, *N. Dak., U.S.* 46°3′ N, 97°10′ W **90**
Lidhult, *Nor.* 56°50′ N, 13°25′ E **152**
Lidice, *Czech Rep.* 50°7′ N, 14°10′ E **152**
Lidingö, *Sw.* 59°21′ N, 18°9′ E **166**
Lidköping, *Nor.* 58°29′ N, 13°7′ E **152**
Lido, *It.* 45°25′ N, 12°22′ E **167**
Lido, *Niger* 12°51′ N, 3°36′ E **222**
Lido di Jesolo, *It.* 45°30′ N, 12°38′ E **167**
Liebig, Mount, peak, *Austral.* 23°21′ S, 131°16′ E **230**
Liechtenstein, *Switz.* 47°6′ N, 9°26′ E **206**
Liège, *Belg.* 50°38′ N, 5°33′ E **167**
Liège Island, *Antarctica* 64°7′ S, 61°45′ W **134**
Liége, river, *Can.* 56°55′ N, 114°1′ W **108**
Lieksa, *Fin.* 63°17′ N, 29°59′ E **152**
Lielvārde, *Latv.* 56°42′ N, 24°51′ E **166**
Liénart, *Dem. Rep. of the Congo* 3°0′ N, 25°36′ E **224**
Lienz, *Aust.* 46°49′ N, 12°44′ E **167**
Liepāja, *Latv.* 56°31′ N, 21°1′ E **166**
Liepājas Ezers, lake, *Latv.* 56°25′ N, 20°37′ E **166**
Liepna, *Latv.* 57°19′ N, 27°28′ E **166**
Lier, *Belg.* 51°8′ N, 4°33′ E **167**
Lierneux, *Belg.* 50°16′ N, 5°47′ E **167**
Lieşti, *Rom.* 45°37′ N, 27°32′ E **156**
Liétor, *Sp.* 38°32′ N, 1°57′ W **164**
Liévin, *Fr.* 50°24′ N, 2°46′ E **163**
Lifford, *Ire.* 54°49′ N, 7°31′ W **150**
Liftāyā, *Syr.* 34°39′ N, 36°27′ E **194**
Ligao, *Philippines* 13°14′ N, 123°31′ E **203**
Līgatne, *Latv.* 57°10′ N, 25°1′ E **166**
Lighthouse Point, *Fla., U.S.* 29°47′ N, 84°30′ W **96**
Lighthouse Point, *Fla., U.S.* 26°16′ N, 80°6′ W **105**
Ligneuville, *Belg.* 50°22′ N, 6°3′ E **167**
Ligny-en-Barrois, *Fr.* 48°41′ N, 5°19′ E **163**
Liguria, adm. division, *It.* 44°26′ N, 8°24′ E **167**
Ligurian Sea 43°49′ N, 8°37′ E **167**
Lihir Group, islands, *South Pacific Ocean* 2°55′ S, 152°47′ E **192**
Lihula, *Est.* 58°41′ N, 23°47′ E **166**
Lijeva Rijeka, *Europe* 42°38′ N, 19°29′ E **168**
Likasi, *Dem. Rep. of the Congo* 10°60′ S, 26°44′ E **224**
Likati, *Dem. Rep. of the Congo* 3°19′ N, 23°56′ E **224**
Likati, river, *Dem. Rep. of the Congo* 3°23′ N, 22°32′ E **218**
Likely, *Can.* 52°36′ N, 121°34′ W **108**
Likely Mountain, peak, *Calif., U.S.* 41°8′ N, 120°40′ W **90**
Likėnai, *Lith.* 56°12′ N, 24°37′ E **166**
Líkeo, Óros, peak, *Gr.* 37°26′ N, 21°53′ E **156**
Likhoslavl', *Russ.* 57°7′ N, 35°31′ E **154**
Likódimo, Óros, peak, *Gr.* 36°55′ N, 21°47′ E **156**
Likoma Islands, *Malawi* 11°51′ S, 34°22′ E **224**
Likoto, *Dem. Rep. of the Congo* 1°12′ S, 24°50′ E **224**
Likwangoli, *Sudan* 6°59′ N, 33°2′ E **224**
Lilbourn, *Mo., U.S.* 36°35′ N, 89°36′ W **94**
L'Île-Rousse, *Fr.* 42°38′ N, 8°56′ E **156**
Lilian, Point, peak, *Austral.* 27°43′ S, 125°51′ E **230**
Liling, *China* 27°41′ N, 113°27′ E **198**
Liljendal, *Fin.* 60°34′ N, 26°3′ E **166**
Lille, *Fr.* 50°37′ N, 3°4′ E **163**
Lillers, *Fr.* 50°34′ N, 2°28′ E **163**
Lillesand, *Nor.* 58°15′ N, 8°21′ E **150**
Lillhamra, *Nor.* 61°39′ N, 14°47′ E **152**
Lillhärdal, *Nor.* 61°50′ N, 14°2′ E **152**
Lillie, *La., U.S.* 32°55′ N, 92°40′ W **103**
Lillooet, *Can.* 50°42′ N, 121°57′ W **108**
Lillooet Lake, *Can.* 50°16′ N, 122°51′ W **108**
Lilo Viejo, *Arg.* 26°56′ S, 62°58′ W **139**
Lilongwe, *Malawi* 13°59′ S, 33°39′ E **224**
Liloy, *Philippines* 8°8′ N, 122°40′ E **203**
Lima, *Arg.* 34°3′ S, 59°10′ W **139**
Lima, *Mont., U.S.* 44°38′ N, 112°36′ W **90**
Lima, *Ohio, U.S.* 40°44′ N, 84°7′ W **102**
Lima, *Parag.* 23°54′ S, 56°28′ W **132**
Lima, *Peru* 12°9′ S, 77°12′ W **130**
Lima, adm. division, *Peru* 11°45′ S, 77°10′ W **130**
Lima Duarte, *Braz.* 21°52′ S, 43°51′ W **138**
Lima, river, *Port.* 41°43′ N, 8°47′ W **150**
Limal, *Bol.* 22°28′ S, 64°33′ W **137**
Liman, *Russ.* 45°44′ N, 47°10′ E **158**
Limas, *Indonesia* 0°13′ N, 104°31′ E **196**
Limassol see Lemesos, *Cyprus* 34°40′ N, 33°1′ E **194**
Limaumanis, *Indonesia* 1°37′ N, 109°19′ E **196**
Limay Mahuida, *Arg.* 37°11′ S, 66°40′ W **134**
Limbani, *Peru* 14°11′ S, 69°43′ W **137**
Limbara, Monte, peak, *It.* 40°50′ N, 9°4′ E **156**
Limbaži, *Latv.* 57°30′ N, 24°41′ E **166**
Limbe, *Cameroon* 4°4′ N, 9°10′ E **222**
Limbe, *Malawi* 15°59′ S, 35°4′ E **224**
Limbourg, *Belg.* 50°37′ N, 5°56′ E **167**
Limbung, *Indonesia* 0°13′ N, 109°48′ E **196**
Limburg, *Ger.* 50°23′ N, 8°3′ E **167**
Lime Village, *Alas., U.S.* 61°21′ N, 155°30′ W **98**
Limedsforsen, *Nor.* 60°54′ N, 13°21′ E **152**
Limeira, *Braz.* 22°34′ S, 47°26′ W **138**
Limena, *It.* 45°29′ N, 11°49′ E **167**
Limerick, *Can.* 49°38′ N, 106°16′ W **90**
Limerick, *Me., U.S.* 43°41′ N, 70°48′ W **104**
Limerick (Luimneach), *Ire.* 52°39′ N, 8°37′ W **150**
Limestone, *Me., U.S.* 46°53′ N, 67°50′ W **82**
Limestone Point, *Can.* 53°31′ N, 98°23′ W **108**
Limestone, river, *Can.* 56°38′ N, 94°48′ W **108**
Limington, *Me., U.S.* 43°43′ N, 70°43′ W **104**
Liminka, *Fin.* 64°48′ N, 25°21′ E **152**
Limmared, *Nor.* 57°32′ N, 13°21′ E **152**
Límnos, island, *Gr.* 39°42′ N, 25°22′ E **180**
Limoges, *Fr.* 45°50′ N, 1°15′ E **150**
Limon, *Colo., U.S.* 39°16′ N, 103°41′ W **90**
Limone Piemonte, *It.* 44°12′ N, 7°34′ E **167**
Limoquije, *Bol.* 15°28′ S, 64°49′ W **137**
Limousin, adm. division, *Fr.* 45°39′ N, 1°16′ E **165**
Limousin, region, *Fr.* 45°39′ N, 1°5′ E **165**
Limpias, *Sp.* 43°21′ N, 3°26′ W **164**
Limpopo, adm. division, *S. Af.* 23°30′ S, 28°24′ E **227**
Limpopo, river, *Africa* 22°10′ S, 29°16′ E **227**
Līnah, *Saudi Arabia* 28°45′ N, 43°47′ E **180**
Linakhamari, *Russ.* 69°38′ N, 31°20′ E **152**
Lin'an, *China* 30°15′ N, 119°44′ E **198**
Linares, *Mex.* 24°50′ N, 99°35′ W **114**
Linares, *Sp.* 38°5′ N, 3°42′ W **214**
Linares, *Sp.* 38°5′ N, 3°37′ W **164**
Linaro, Capo, *It.* 41°57′ N, 11°18′ E **156**
Linas, Monte, peak, *It.* 39°26′ N, 8°32′ E **156**
Lincang, *China* 23°51′ N, 99°58′ E **202**
Linchuan, *China* 27°58′ N, 116°18′ E **198**
Linck Nunataks, *Antarctica* 83°20′ S, 104°39′ W **248**
Lincoln, *Arg.* 34°53′ S, 61°30′ W **139**
Lincoln, *Calif., U.S.* 38°53′ N, 121°19′ W **90**
Lincoln, *Ill., U.S.* 40°8′ N, 89°22′ W **102**
Lincoln, *Kans., U.S.* 39°1′ N, 98°10′ W **90**
Lincoln, *Mich., U.S.* 44°40′ N, 83°26′ W **94**
Lincoln, *Mo., U.S.* 40°8′ N, 89°22′ W **94**
Lincoln, *Nebr., U.S.* 40°46′ N, 96°49′ W **90**
Lincoln, *N.H., U.S.* 44°2′ N, 71°41′ W **104**
Lincoln, *N. Mex., U.S.* 33°28′ N, 105°23′ W **92**
Lincoln, *N.Z.* 43°40′ S, 172°28′ E **240**
Lincoln, *S. Dak., U.S.* 40°39′ N, 97°21′ W **72**
Lincoln, *U.K.* 53°13′ N, 0°33′ E **162**
Lincoln, *Vt., U.S.* 44°6′ N, 72°60′ W **104**
Lincoln Bay 83°25′ N, 56°35′ W **255**
Lincoln Boyhood National Monument, *Ind., U.S.* 38°5′ N, 87°4′ W **96**
Lincoln City, *Oreg., U.S.* 44°57′ N, 124°1′ W **90**
Lincoln Heights, *U.K.* 53°24′ N, 0°40′ E **162**
Lincoln Park, *Colo., U.S.* 38°25′ N, 105°13′ W **92**
Lincoln Park, *Mich., U.S.* 42°14′ N, 83°11′ W **102**
Lincoln Sea 81°13′ N, 60°27′ W **246**
Lincoln's New Salem, site, *Ill., U.S.* 39°57′ N, 89°55′ W **102**
Lincolnton, *Ga., U.S.* 33°46′ N, 82°29′ W **96**
Lind, *Wash., U.S.* 46°58′ N, 118°37′ W **90**
Linda, *Calif., U.S.* 39°7′ N, 121°35′ W **90**
Lindale, *Tex., U.S.* 32°30′ N, 95°24′ W **103**
Linde, river, *Russ.* 66°15′ N, 120°13′ E **160**
Linden, *Ala., U.S.* 32°18′ N, 87°49′ W **103**
Linden, *Calif., U.S.* 38°1′ N, 121°6′ W **100**
Linden, *Guyana* 6°1′ N, 58°21′ W **130**
Linden, *Ind., U.S.* 40°11′ N, 86°54′ W **102**
Linden, *Mich., U.S.* 42°47′ N, 83°47′ W **102**
Linden, *Tex., U.S.* 33°0′ N, 94°23′ W **103**
Lindenhurst, *N.Y., U.S.* 40°41′ N, 73°22′ W **104**
Lindenow Fjord 60°10′ N, 43°49′ W **106**
Lindesberg, *Nor.* 59°35′ N, 15°14′ E **152**
Lindesnes, *Nor.* 57°55′ N, 6°21′ E **150**
Lindi, *Tanzania* 9°57′ S, 39°38′ E **224**
Lindi, adm. division, *Tanzania* 9°36′ S, 37°48′ E **224**
Lindi, river, *Dem. Rep. of the Congo* 0°23′ N, 28°1′ E **224**
Lindian, *China* 47°11′ N, 124°54′ E **198**
Lindley, *S. Af.* 27°56′ S, 27°52′ E **227**

Lindsay, Calif., U.S. 36°12′ N, 119°6′ W 101
Lindsay, Can. 44°21′ N, 78°43′ W 94
Lindsay, Mont., U.S. 47°12′ N, 105°10′ W 90
Lindsay, Okla., U.S. 34°48′ N, 97°36′ W 92
Lindsborg, Kans., U.S. 38°33′ N, 97°41′ W 90
Lindsey Islands, Amundsen Sea 73°24′ S, 103°46′ W 248
Linevo, Russ. 54°29′ N, 83°25′ E 184
Linfen, China 36°6′ N, 111°35′ E 198
Lingao, China 19°56′ N, 109°40′ E 198
Lingayen, Philippines 15°59′ N, 120°12′ E 203
Lingbao, China 34°32′ N, 110°50′ E 198
Lingbi, China 33°33′ N, 117°31′ E 198
Lingbo, Nor. 61°2′ N, 16°39′ E 152
Lingchuan, China 25°31′ N, 110°21′ E 198
Lingen, Ger. 52°31′ N, 7°19′ E 163
Lingga, island, Indonesia 0°41′ N, 105°0′ E 192
Lingga, Kepulauan, islands, South China Sea 0°19′ N, 105°1′ E 196
Lingig, Philippines 8°5′ N, 126°24′ E 203
Lingle, Wyo., U.S. 42°8′ N, 104°21′ W 90
Lingomo, Dem. Rep. of the Congo 0°37′ N, 22°2′ E 218
Lingshan, China 22°25′ N, 109°14′ E 198
Lingshui, China 18°27′ N, 109°59′ E 198
Lingtai, China 35°4′ N, 107°33′ E 198
Linguère, Senegal 15°25′ N, 15°8′ W 222
Lingui, China 25°11′ N, 110°11′ E 198
Lingwu, China 38°6′ N, 106°18′ E 198
Lingxian, China 26°30′ N, 113°45′ E 198
Lingyuan, China 41°18′ N, 119°26′ E 198
Lingyun, China 24°16′ N, 106°33′ E 198
Linhai, China 28°49′ N, 121°11′ E 198
Linhares, Braz. 19°24′ S, 40°3′ W 138
Linhe, China 40°44′ N, 107°22′ E 198
Linjiang, China 41°48′ N, 126°55′ E 200
Linkmenys, Lith. 55°19′ N, 25°57′ E 166
Linköping, Nor. 58°23′ N, 15°35′ E 152
Linkuva, Lith. 56°4′ N, 23°57′ E 166
Linn, Tex., U.S. 26°34′ N, 98°7′ W 114
Linova, Belarus 52°27′ N, 24°30′ E 152
Linqing, China 36°50′ N, 115°43′ E 198
Linquan, China 33°4′ N, 115°15′ E 198
Linru, China 34°10′ N, 112°53′ E 198
Lins, Braz. 21°41′ S, 49°46′ W 138
Linsell, Nor. 62°8′ N, 13°53′ E 152
Linshui, China 30°20′ N, 106°54′ E 198
Lintang, Malaysia 5°20′ N, 118°28′ E 203
Linthal, Switz. 46°55′ N, 9°0′ E 167
Linton, Ind., U.S. 39°1′ N, 87°10′ W 102
Linton, N. Dak., U.S. 46°15′ N, 100°14′ W 90
Lintong, China 34°22′ N, 109°16′ E 198
Linwood, Mich., U.S. 43°44′ N, 83°58′ W 102
Linxi, China 39°44′ N, 118°29′ E 198
Linxi, China 43°36′ N, 118°2′ E 198
Linxia, China 35°29′ N, 103°1′ E 190
Linxian, China 37°57′ N, 110°53′ E 198
Linyi, China 35°3′ N, 118°20′ E 198
Linyi, China 37°8′ N, 116°52′ E 198
Linz, Aust. 48°16′ N, 14°18′ E 152
Linz, Ger. 50°33′ N, 7°17′ E 167
Lioma, Mozambique 15°12′ S, 36°49′ E 224
Lion, Golfe du 42°17′ N, 3°17′ E 142
Lion's Head, Can. 44°58′ N, 81°13′ W 94
Liot Point, Can. 73°12′ N, 128°57′ W 106
Liouesso, Congo 1°1′ N, 15°42′ E 218
Lipa, Philippines 13°57′ N, 121°9′ E 203
Lipari, Isole (Eolie), islands, It. 38°39′ N, 13°46′ E 156
Lipcani, Mold. 48°16′ N, 26°47′ E 152
Lipce, Pol. 51°53′ N, 19°57′ E 152
Lipetsk, Russ. 52°37′ N, 39°28′ E 154
Lipetsk, adm. division, Russ. 53°14′ N, 38°42′ E 154
Lipez, Cordillera de, Bol. 21°42′ S, 66°59′ W 132
Lipiany, Pol. 53°0′ N, 14°58′ E 152
Lipik, Croatia 45°25′ N, 17°9′ E 168
Liping, China 26°13′ N, 109°7′ E 198
Lipljan, Europe 42°31′ N, 21°8′ E 168
Lipnica, Pol. 53°59′ N, 17°25′ E 152
Lipník, Czech Rep. 49°31′ N, 17°35′ E 152
Lipnishki, Belarus 54°0′ N, 25°36′ E 166
Lipova, Rom. 46°5′ N, 21°43′ E 168
Lipovac, Croatia 45°3′ N, 19°4′ E 168
Lippe, river, Ger. 51°37′ N, 8°5′ E 167
Lippstadt, Ger. 51°39′ N, 8°21′ E 167
Lipscomb, Tex., U.S. 36°12′ N, 100°16′ W 92
Lipsí, Gr. 37°18′ N, 26°46′ E 156
Lipsko, Pol. 51°9′ N, 21°39′ E 152
Lipton, Can. 50°54′ N, 103°53′ W 90
Liptovský Mikuláš, Slovakia 49°4′ N, 19°39′ E 152
Lipu, China 24°30′ N, 110°23′ E 198
Lipu Lekh Pass, China 30°14′ N, 81°2′ E 197
Lipumba, Tanzania 10°51′ S, 35°3′ E 224
Lira, Uganda 2°13′ N, 32°54′ E 224
Liranga, Congo 0°41′ N, 17°30′ E 218
Lircay, Peru 13°1′ S, 74°43′ W 137
Liria, Sudan 4°36′ N, 32°4′ E 224
Lirik, oil field, Indonesia 0°13′ N, 102°8′ E 196
Lirik Ukul, oil field, Indonesia 5°296′ S, 101°48′ E 192
Lisa, Europe 43°9′ N, 19°33′ E 168
Lisakovsk, Kaz. 52°32′ N, 62°31′ E 184
Lisala, Dem. Rep. of the Congo 2°10′ N, 21°28′ E 218
Lisboa (Lisbon), Port. 38°42′ N, 9°17′ W 150
Lisbon, Ill., U.S. 41°28′ N, 88°30′ W 102
Lisbon, La., U.S. 32°47′ N, 92°53′ W 103
Lisbon, Me., U.S. 44°1′ N, 70°7′ W 104
Lisbon, N. Dak., U.S. 46°26′ N, 97°41′ W 90
Lisboa, adm. division, Port. 38°57′ N, 9°25′ W 150
Lisbon Falls, Me., U.S. 44°0′ N, 70°4′ W 104
Lisbon see Lisboa, Port. 38°42′ N, 9°17′ W 150
Lisburne, Cape, Alas., U.S. 69°21′ N, 163°16′ W 246
Lishu, China 43°22′ N, 124°20′ E 198
Lishui, China 28°29′ N, 119°54′ E 198
Lisieux, Fr. 49°8′ N, 0°14′ E 150
Lisino-Korpus, Russ. 59°25′ N, 30°41′ E 166
Lisitsa, river, Russ. 58°59′ N, 85°2′ E 169
Liski, Rom. 46°14′ N, 26°44′ E 156
Liski, Russ. 51°1′ N, 39°30′ E 158
L'Isle-Verte, Can. 47°59′ N, 69°21′ W 94
Lisman, Ala., U.S. 32°11′ N, 88°17′ W 103
Lisok, pass, Ukr. 48°47′ N, 23°8′ E 152
Lissa see Vis, island, Croatia 42°57′ N, 16°5′ E 168
Lister, Mount, peak, Antarctica 77°58′ S, 163°35′ E 248
Listerlandet, Nor. 55°55′ N, 14°45′ E 152
Listowel, Can. 43°43′ N, 80°57′ W 102
Lit, Nor. 63°19′ N, 14°47′ E 152
Litang, China 23°9′ N, 109°7′ E 198
Līṭānī, river, Leb. 33°20′ N, 35°14′ E 194
Litani, river, Suriname 2°12′ N, 54°24′ W 130
Litberg, peak, Ger. 53°23′ N, 9°31′ E 150
Litchfield, Conn., U.S. 41°44′ N, 73°12′ W 104
Litchfield, Ill., U.S. 39°10′ N, 89°39′ W 102
Litchfield, Mich., U.S. 42°2′ N, 84°46′ W 102
Litchfield, Minn., U.S. 45°7′ N, 94°33′ W 90
Litchfield, Mo., U.S. 39°10′ N, 89°39′ W 94
Litchfield National Park, Austral. 13°22′ S, 130°32′ E 238
Liteni, Rom. 47°30′ N, 26°30′ E 156
Lithuania 55°20′ N, 23°34′ E 166
Litija, Slov. 46°3′ N, 14°49′ E 156
Little Abaco, island, Bahamas 26°52′ N, 77°44′ W 118
Little Abitibi Lake, Can. 49°21′ N, 81°12′ W 94
Little Abitibi, river, Can. 50°30′ N, 81°35′ W 94
Little America (historic), site, Antarctica 78°27′ S, 162°60′ W 248
Little Andaman, island, India 10°2′ N, 91°45′ E 188
Little Beaver, river, Can. 57°34′ N, 97°4′ W 108
Little Belt Mountains, Mont., U.S. 46°43′ N, 110°43′ W 90
Little Bighorn, river, Mont., U.S. 46°3′ N, 108°23′ W 80
Little Blue, river, Nebr., U.S. 40°31′ N, 98°31′ W 80
Little Buffalo, Can. 56°27′ N, 116°10′ W 108
Little Buffalo, river, Can. 60°48′ N, 113°36′ W 108
Little Cadotte, river, Can. 56°34′ N, 117°5′ W 108
Little Cayman, island, Little Cayman 19°23′ N, 80°33′ W 115
Little Creek Peak, Utah, U.S. 37°51′ N, 112°40′ W 92
Little Current, Can. 45°57′ N, 81°57′ W 94
Little Current, river, Can. 50°31′ N, 86°53′ W 110
Little Duck Lake, Can. 59°23′ N, 98°26′ W 108
Little Exuma, island, Bahamas 23°9′ N, 75°51′ W 116
Little Falls, Minn., U.S. 45°57′ N, 94°22′ W 90
Little Falls, N.Y., U.S. 43°2′ N, 74°53′ W 110
Little Gombi, Nig. 10°9′ N, 12°46′ E 216
Little Grand Rapids, Can. 52°2′ N, 95°27′ W 108
Little Inagua Island, Bahamas 21°36′ N, 73°21′ W 116
Little Isaac, island, Bahamas 25°56′ N, 78°59′ W 105
Little Juniper Mountain, peak, Oreg., U.S. 43°8′ N, 119°55′ W 90
Little Lake, Calif., U.S. 35°56′ N, 117°55′ W 101
Little Lake, Mich., U.S. 46°18′ N, 87°21′ W 110
Little Longlac, Can. 49°41′ N, 86°57′ W 94
Little Namaland, region, S. Af. 28°17′ S, 16°49′ E 227
Little Nicobar, island, India 7°21′ N, 92°20′ E 188
Little River, Calif., U.S. 39°16′ N, 123°47′ W 90
Little, river, La., U.S. 31°35′ N, 92°27′ W 103
Little, river, Okla., U.S. 34°9′ N, 95°7′ W 112
Little Rock, Ark., U.S. 34°40′ N, 92°24′ W 96
Little Rocky Mountains, Mont., U.S. 47°56′ N, 108°26′ W 90
Little Sable Point, Mich., U.S. 43°37′ N, 86°41′ W 102
Little Saint Bernard Pass, It. 45°41′ N, 6°54′ E 167
Little San Bernardino Mountains, Calif., U.S. 34°0′ N, 116°19′ W 101
Little San Salvador, island, Bahamas 24°26′ N, 77°1′ W 116
Little Seal, river, Can. 59°3′ N, 95°41′ W 108
Little Sioux, river, Iowa, U.S. 41°43′ N, 96°20′ W 80
Little Sitkin, island, Alas., U.S. 52°9′ N, 178°28′ E 160
Little Smoky, Can. 54°43′ N, 117°7′ W 108
Little Smoky, river, Can. 54°4′ N, 117°46′ W 108
Little Suamico, Wis., U.S. 44°42′ N, 88°1′ W 94
Little White Mountain, peak, Can. 49°40′ N, 119°26′ W 90
Littlefield, Ariz., U.S. 36°52′ N, 113°56′ W 101
Littlefield, Tex., U.S. 33°55′ N, 102°20′ W 92
Littlefork, Minn., U.S. 48°21′ N, 93°32′ W 94
Littlehampton, U.K. 50°48′ N, 0°32′ E 162
Littleton, Colo., U.S. 39°35′ N, 105°2′ W 90
Littleton, Mass., U.S. 42°32′ N, 71°32′ W 104
Littleton, N.H., U.S. 44°18′ N, 71°47′ W 104
Litva, Bosn. and Herzg. 44°24′ N, 18°31′ E 168
Lityn, Ukr. 49°18′ N, 28°13′ E 152
Liu, river, China 42°25′ N, 125°40′ E 200
Liu, river, China 42°13′ N, 122°39′ E 200
Liuba, China 33°37′ N, 106°53′ E 198
Liucheng, China 24°39′ N, 109°16′ E 198
Liudaogou, China 41°33′ N, 127°12′ E 200
Liuhe, China 42°16′ N, 125°45′ E 200
Liuli, Tanzania 11°5′ S, 34°40′ E 224
Liúpo, Mozambique 15°36′ S, 39°59′ E 224
Liuwa Plain, Zambia 14°33′ S, 22°27′ E 220
Liuwa Plain National Park, Zambia 14°41′ S, 22°14′ E 206
Liuzhou, China 24°18′ N, 109°23′ E 198
Livada, Rom. 47°52′ N, 23°6′ E 168
Līvāni, Latv. 56°20′ N, 26°10′ E 166
Live Oak, Fla., U.S. 30°16′ N, 82°59′ W 96
Live Oak Springs, Calif., U.S. 32°41′ N, 116°22′ W 101
Lively Island, Lively Island 52°14′ S, 58°23′ W 134
Livermore, Calif., U.S. 37°40′ N, 121°47′ W 100
Livermore, Ky., U.S. 37°29′ N, 87°9′ W 96
Livermore Falls, Me., U.S. 44°28′ N, 70°12′ W 104
Livermore, Mount, peak, Tex., U.S. 30°35′ N, 104°14′ W 92
Liverpool, Can. 44°1′ N, 64°44′ W 111
Liverpool, N.Y., U.S. 43°6′ N, 76°14′ W 110
Liverpool, U.K. 53°24′ N, 2°59′ W 162
Liverpool Bay 70°0′ N, 130°43′ W 98
Liverpool Land 70°41′ N, 21°27′ W 246
Livingston, Ala., U.S. 32°35′ N, 88°12′ W 103
Livingston, Calif., U.S. 37°23′ N, 120°43′ W 100
Livingston, Guatemala 15°49′ N, 88°49′ W 115
Livingston, Ill., U.S. 38°58′ N, 89°47′ W 102
Livingston, La., U.S. 30°29′ N, 90°46′ W 103
Livingston, Mont., U.S. 45°39′ N, 110°33′ W 90
Livingston, Tenn., U.S. 36°22′ N, 85°19′ W 96
Livingston, Tex., U.S. 30°41′ N, 94°56′ W 103
Livingston Island, Antarctica 62°59′ S, 60°12′ W 134
Livingstone, Zambia 17°50′ S, 25°50′ E 224
Livingstone Lake, Can. 58°33′ N, 108°4′ W 108
Livingstone Memorial, site, Zambia 12°21′ S, 30°13′ E 224
Livingstonia, Malawi 10°38′ S, 34°8′ E 224
Livno, Bosn. and Herzg. 43°49′ N, 17°1′ E 168
Livny, Russ. 52°24′ N, 37°32′ E 158
Livo, Fin. 65°32′ N, 26°56′ E 152
Livonia, Mich., U.S. 42°22′ N, 83°23′ W 102
Livorno (Leghorn), It. 43°33′ N, 10°19′ E 156
Livramento do Brumado, Braz. 13°38′ S, 41°53′ W 138
Livron, Fr. 44°46′ N, 4°50′ E 150
Liwale, Tanzania 9°46′ S, 38°0′ E 224
Liwonde, Malawi 15°7′ S, 35°13′ E 224
Lixian, China 29°40′ N, 111°44′ E 198
Lixian, China 34°13′ N, 105°6′ E 198
Lizard Head Peak, Wyo., U.S. 42°47′ N, 109°17′ W 90
Lizard Islands, Lake Superior 47°8′ N, 85°17′ W 94
Lizard Point, U.K. 49°44′ N, 5°17′ W 150
Lizarra see Estella, Sp. 42°39′ N, 2°2′ W 164
Ljig, Serb. and Mont. 44°13′ N, 20°14′ E 168
Ljubija, Bosn. and Herzg. 44°56′ N, 16°36′ E 168
Ljubinje, Bosn. and Herzg. 42°57′ N, 18°5′ E 168
Ljubiš, Serb. and Mont. 43°36′ N, 19°51′ E 168
Ljubišnja, peak, Europe 43°18′ N, 19°3′ E 168
Ljubljana, Slov. 46°2′ N, 14°21′ E 156
Ljuboten, peak, Europe 42°11′ N, 21°4′ E 168
Ljubovija, Serb. and Mont. 44°12′ N, 19°22′ E 168
Ljubuški, Bosn. and Herzg. 43°11′ N, 17°33′ E 168
Ljugarn, Sw. 57°20′ N, 18°40′ E 166
Ljungby, Nor. 56°50′ N, 13°54′ E 152
Ljusdal, Nor. 61°49′ N, 16°6′ E 152
Ljusterö, island, Sw. 59°31′ N, 18°45′ E 166
Ljutomer, Slov. 46°31′ N, 16°10′ E 168
Llaima, Volcán, peak, Chile 38°44′ S, 71°52′ W 134
Llajta Mauca, Arg. 28°11′ S, 63°6′ W 139
Llallagua, Bol. 18°25′ S, 66°42′ W 137
Llanbedr, U.K. 52°48′ N, 4°5′ W 162
Llanbister, U.K. 52°20′ N, 3°18′ W 162
Llançà, Sp. 42°21′ N, 3°9′ E 164
Llancanelo, Laguna, lake, Arg. 35°37′ S, 70°31′ W 134
Llanddewi Brefi, U.K. 52°10′ N, 3°57′ W 162
Llandeilo, U.K. 51°53′ N, 3°59′ W 162
Llandovery, U.K. 51°59′ N, 3°47′ W 162
Llandrindod Wells, U.K. 52°14′ N, 3°23′ W 162
Llanelltyd, U.K. 52°45′ N, 3°54′ W 162
Llanenddwyn, U.K. 52°47′ N, 4°5′ W 162
Llanfair Caereinion, U.K. 52°38′ N, 3°19′ W 162
Llanfyllin, U.K. 52°45′ N, 3°15′ W 162
Llangadog, U.K. 51°55′ N, 3°52′ W 162
Llanganates National Park, Ecua. 1°28′ S, 78°12′ W 136
Llangefni, U.K. 53°15′ N, 4°18′ W 162
Llangeitho, U.K. 52°12′ N, 4°1′ W 162
Llangollen, U.K. 52°57′ N, 3°10′ W 162
Llangorse, U.K. 51°56′ N, 3°15′ W 162
Llanidan, U.K. 53°13′ N, 4°13′ W 162
Llanidloes, U.K. 52°25′ N, 3°32′ W 162
Llanilar, U.K. 52°20′ N, 4°1′ W 162
Llanllugan, U.K. 52°36′ N, 3°23′ W 162
Llano, Tex., U.S. 30°44′ N, 98°40′ W 92
Llanrwst, U.K. 53°8′ N, 3°46′ W 162
Llanuwchllyn, U.K. 52°51′ N, 3°40′ W 162
Llanwrtyd Wells, U.K. 52°6′ N, 3°38′ W 162
Llavorsí, Sp. 42°29′ N, 1°10′ E 164
Lleida, Sp. 41°37′ N, 0°37′ E 164
Llera, Mex. 23°18′ N, 99°1′ W 114
Llerena, Sp. 38°14′ N, 6°2′ W 164
Lleyn Peninsula, U.K. 52°55′ N, 4°14′ W 162
Llica, Bol. 19°52′ S, 68°16′ W 137
Llimiana, Sp. 42°5′ N, 0°54′ E 164
łapy, Pol. 53°0′ N, 23°0′ E 152
łaskarzew, Pol. 52°0′ N, 22°0′ E 152
łeba, Pol. 55°0′ N, 18°0′ E 152
łochów, Pol. 52°0′ N, 22°0′ E 152
łódź, Pol. 52°0′ N, 20°0′ E 152
łódźkie, adm. division, Pol. 51°0′ N, 19°0′ E 152
łomża, Pol. 53°0′ N, 22°0′ E 152
łoniów, Pol. 52°0′ N, 22°0′ E 152
łowicz, Pol. 52°0′ N, 20°0′ E 152
łuków, Pol. 52°0′ N, 22°0′ E 152
Llodio, Sp. 43°7′ N, 2°59′ W 164
Lloret de Mar, Sp. 41°42′ N, 2°51′ E 164
Llorona, Punta, C.R. 8°41′ N, 84°26′ W 115
Lloyd, Cape 60°36′ S, 54°60′ W 248
Lloyd George, Mount, peak, Can. 57°52′ N, 125°10′ W 108
Lloyd Lake, Can. 57°20′ N, 109°27′ W 108
Lloydminster, Can. 53°16′ N, 109°59′ W 108
Llullaillaco National Park, Chile 24°58′ S, 69°4′ W 122
Llullaillaco, Volcán, peak, Chile 24°46′ S, 68°42′ W 132
Lluta, Peru 16°4′ S, 72°3′ W 137
Llyswen, U.K. 52°1′ N, 3°16′ W 162
Lo, river, China 22°54′ N, 104°33′ E 202
Loa, Utah, U.S. 38°23′ N, 111°38′ W 90
Loa, Mauna, peak, Hawai'i, U.S. 19°28′ N, 155°40′ W 99
Loa, river, Chile 22°37′ S, 69°18′ W 137
Loanda, Braz. 22°58′ S, 53°14′ W 138
Loange, river, Dem. Rep. of the Congo 4°20′ S, 20°8′ E 218
Loango, Congo 4°42′ S, 11°47′ E 218
Loano, It. 44°7′ N, 8°16′ E 167
Loarre, Sp. 42°18′ N, 0°37′ E 164
Lobamba, Swaziland 26°28′ S, 31°3′ E 227
Loban, Russ. 65°43′ N, 45°28′ E 154
Lobatse, Botswana 25°15′ S, 25°35′ E 227
Lobería, Arg. 42°7′ S, 63°48′ W 134
Lobería, Arg. 38°11′ S, 58°47′ W 139
Lobito, Angola 12°26′ S, 13°32′ E 220
Lobitos, Peru 4°21′ S, 81°17′ W 130
Lobo, river, Côte d'Ivoire 6°27′ N, 6°42′ W 222
Lobok, Belarus 55°51′ N, 30°2′ E 166
Lobos, Arg. 35°9′ S, 59°8′ W 139
Lobos, Cabo, Chile 19°1′ S, 70°43′ W 137
Lobos, Cabo, Mex. 29°43′ N, 113°4′ W 92
Lobos, Cayo 18°17′ N, 87°26′ W 115
Lobos de Afuera, Islas, islands, South Pacific Ocean 7°20′ S, 81°52′ W 130
Lobos de Tierra, Isla, island, Peru 6°23′ S, 82°43′ W 130
Lobos, Estero de 27°17′ N, 111°33′ W 80
Lobos, Isla, island, Mex. 27°26′ N, 111°21′ W 112
Lobos, Point, U.S. 36°22′ N, 122°16′ W 92
Lobos, Punta, Chile 21°13′ S, 70°29′ W 137
Lobster Point, Can. 51°13′ N, 55°36′ W 111
Lobva, Russ. 59°14′ N, 60°31′ E 154
Loc Binh, Vietnam 21°46′ N, 106°55′ E 198
Loc Ninh, Vietnam 11°50′ N, 106°36′ E 202
Locarno, Switz. 46°11′ N, 8°46′ E 167
Lochem, Neth. 52°8′ N, 6°24′ E 163
Lochinvar National Park, Zambia 16°3′ S, 26°49′ E 224
Łochów, Pol. 52°31′ N, 21°42′ E 152
Lock Haven, Pa., U.S. 41°7′ N, 77°27′ W 94
Lockbourne, Ohio, U.S. 39°47′ N, 82°58′ W 102
Locke Mills, Me., U.S. 44°24′ N, 70°43′ W 104
Lockeford, Calif., U.S. 38°9′ N, 121°10′ W 100
Lockhart, Ala., U.S. 31°1′ N, 86°21′ W 96
Lockhart, Tex., U.S. 29°51′ N, 97°40′ W 92
Lockney, Tex., U.S. 34°5′ N, 101°26′ W 92
Lockport, Ill., U.S. 41°35′ N, 88°3′ W 102
Lockport, La., U.S. 29°37′ N, 90°32′ W 103
Lockwood, Calif., U.S. 35°56′ N, 121°6′ W 100
Loco Mountain, peak, Mont., U.S. 46°11′ N, 110°24′ W 90
Locri, It. 38°15′ N, 16°15′ E 156
Locumba, Peru 17°37′ S, 70°47′ W 137
Lod (Lydda), Israel 31°56′ N, 34°53′ E 194
Loda, Ill., U.S. 40°31′ N, 88°4′ W 102
Lodalskåpa, peak, Nor. 61°46′ N, 7°4′ E 152
Lodeyka, Russ. 60°41′ N, 45°45′ E 154
Lodeynoye Pole, Russ. 60°42′ N, 33°34′ E 154
Lodge Creek, river, Can. 49°32′ N, 110°34′ W 90
Lodge Grass, Mont., U.S. 45°17′ N, 107°23′ W 90
Lodge, Mount, peak, Can. 59°3′ N, 137°34′ W 108
Lodgepole, Nebr., U.S. 41°9′ N, 102°40′ W 92
Lodhran, Pak. 29°35′ N, 71°38′ E 186
Lodi, Calif., U.S. 38°7′ N, 121°18′ W 100
Lodi, It. 45°18′ N, 9°29′ E 167
Lodi, Wis., U.S. 43°19′ N, 89°31′ W 102
Lodja, Dem. Rep. of the Congo 3°31′ S, 23°32′ E 224
Lodore, Canyon of, Colo., U.S. 40°18′ N, 109°1′ W 90
Lodosa, Sp. 42°25′ N, 2°5′ W 164
Lodwar, Kenya 3°4′ N, 35°35′ E 224
Łódź, Pol. 51°44′ N, 19°27′ E 152
Łodzkie, adm. division, Pol. 51°30′ N, 18°23′ E 152
Loei, Thai. 17°32′ N, 101°32′ E 202
Loelli, spring, Sudan 5°6′ N, 34°41′ E 224
Loen, Nor. 61°53′ N, 6°51′ E 152
Loengo, Dem. Rep. of the Congo 4°50′ S, 26°30′ E 224
Loera, river, Mex. 26°39′ N, 107°32′ W 80
Loeriesfontein, S. Af. 30°57′ S, 19°27′ E 227
Lofgren Peninsula 72°44′ S, 91°41′ W 248
Lofoten, islands, Norwegian Sea 67°57′ N, 12°59′ E 152
Lofthouse, U.K. 54°8′ N, 1°49′ W 162
Loftus, U.K. 54°33′ N, 0°53′ E 162
Log, Russ. 49°27′ N, 43°49′ E 158
Log Lane Village, Colo., U.S. 40°15′ N, 103°52′ W 90
Loga, Niger 13°33′ N, 3°21′ E 222
Logan, Iowa, U.S. 41°38′ N, 95°48′ W 90
Logan, Kans., U.S. 39°39′ N, 99°34′ W 90
Logan, N. Mex., U.S. 35°21′ N, 103°25′ W 92
Logan, Ohio, U.S. 39°32′ N, 82°24′ W 102
Logan, Utah, U.S. 41°44′ N, 111°48′ W 82
Logan, Mount, peak, Ariz., U.S. 36°20′ N, 113°16′ W 92
Logan, Mount, peak, Can. 60°37′ N, 140°32′ W 98
Logan, Mount, peak, Can. 48°52′ N, 66°44′ W 111
Logan, Mount, peak, Wash., U.S. 48°31′ N, 120°59′ W 100
Logan Pass, Mont., U.S. 48°41′ N, 113°42′ W 90
Logandale, Nev., U.S. 36°35′ N, 114°30′ W 101
Logăneşti, Mold. 46°55′ N, 28°32′ E 158
Logansport, Ind., U.S. 40°44′ N, 86°21′ W 102
Logansport, La., U.S. 31°57′ N, 94°1′ W 103
Logashkino, Russ. 70°49′ N, 153°44′ E 173
Loge, river, Angola 7°44′ S, 13°12′ E 220
Logone Birni, Cameroon 11°46′ N, 15°2′ E 216
Logoniégué, Burkina Faso 9°54′ N, 4°33′ W 222
Logoualé, Côte d'Ivoire 7°3′ N, 7°33′ W 222
Logroño, Sp. 42°26′ N, 2°27′ W 164
Logrosán, Sp. 39°20′ N, 5°30′ W 164
Løgstør, Den. 56°56′ N, 9°14′ E 150
Loharano, Madagascar 21°45′ S, 48°9′ E 220
Lohardaga, India 23°24′ N, 84°41′ E 197
Loharghat, India 25°57′ N, 91°26′ E 197
Loharu, India 28°26′ N, 75°49′ E 197
Lohatlha, S. Af. 28°3′ S, 23°2′ E 227
Lohikoski, Fin. 61°36′ N, 28°42′ E 166
Lohiniva, Fin. 67°9′ N, 24°58′ E 152
Lohja (Lojo), Fin. 60°14′ N, 24°1′ E 166
Lôho, Côte d'Ivoire 8°38′ N, 5°9′ W 222
Lohr, Ger. 49°59′ N, 9°33′ E 167
Lohusuu, Est. 58°55′ N, 27°0′ E 166
Loi Mwe, Myanmar 21°9′ N, 99°46′ E 202
Loi, Phou, peak, Laos 20°17′ N, 103°5′ E 202
Loiano, It. 44°16′ N, 11°18′ E 167
Loikaw, Myanmar 19°42′ N, 97°10′ E 202
Loile, river, Dem. Rep. of the Congo 1°11′ S, 20°17′ E 218
Loimaa, Fin. 60°49′ N, 23°1′ E 166
Loir, river, Fr. 48°13′ N, 1°17′ E 163
Loire, river, Fr. 46°26′ N, 3°56′ E 165
Loire, river, Fr. 46°48′ N, 1°52′ W 142
Loire, river, Fr. 45°9′ N, 3°58′ E 165
Loire, river, Fr. 48°16′ N, 2°37′ E 165
Loja, Ecua. 4°1′ S, 79°13′ W 130
Loja, Sp. 37°9′ N, 4°9′ W 164
Lojo see Lohja, Fin. 60°14′ N, 24°1′ E 166
Loka, Sudan 4°15′ N, 30°57′ E 224
Lokachi, Ukr. 50°44′ N, 24°38′ E 152
Lokalahti, Fin. 60°40′ N, 21°28′ E 166
Lokandu, Dem. Rep. of the Congo 2°34′ S, 25°45′ E 224
Lokchim, river, Russ. 61°36′ N, 51°43′ E 154
Lokeren, Belg. 51°5′ N, 4°0′ E 163
Lokhwabe, Botswana 24°9′ S, 21°50′ E 227
Lokichokio, Kenya 4°13′ N, 34°20′ E 224
Lokila, Sudan 4°38′ N, 32°26′ E 224
Lokitaung, Kenya 4°12′ N, 35°45′ E 224
Lokka, Fin. 67°47′ N, 27°40′ E 152
Løkken, Nor. 63°5′ N, 9°42′ E 152
Loknya, Russ. 56°50′ N, 30°10′ E 166
Lokoja, Nig. 7°45′ N, 6°41′ E 222
Lokolama, Dem. Rep. of the Congo 2°36′ S, 19°51′ E 218
Lokolenge, Dem. Rep. of the Congo 1°9′ N, 22°36′ E 218
Lokomo, Cameroon 2°52′ N, 15°17′ E 218
Lőkösháza, Hung. 46°25′ N, 21°14′ E 168
Lokossa, Benin 6°39′ N, 1°40′ E 222
Loks Land, island, Can. 62°9′ N, 64°30′ W 106
Loksa, Est. 59°33′ N, 25°45′ E 166
Lokwa Kangole, Kenya 3°26′ N, 35°50′ E 224
Lol, river, Sudan 8°56′ N, 26°15′ E 224
Lol, river, Sudan 8°48′ N, 28°36′ E 224
Loleta, Calif., U.S. 40°38′ N, 124°14′ W 90
Lolgorien, Kenya 1°14′ S, 34°48′ E 224
Lolimi, Sudan 4°34′ N, 34°2′ E 224
Loliondo, Tanzania 2°3′ S, 35°39′ E 224
Lollar, Ger. 50°38′ N, 8°43′ E 167
Lolo, Mount, peak, Can. 50°48′ N, 120°12′ W 90
Lolo Pass, Idaho, U.S. 46°37′ N, 114°36′ W 90
Lolobau, island, P.N.G. 4°51′ S, 150°14′ E 192
Lolowau, Indonesia 0°57′ N, 97°33′ E 196
Lom, Bulg. 43°49′ N, 23°13′ E 168
Lom, Nor. 61°50′ N, 8°31′ E 152
Lom Sak, Thai. 16°47′ N, 101°7′ E 202
Loma Mountains, Sierra Leone 9°5′ N, 11°27′ W 222
Lomami, river, Dem. Rep. of the Congo 0°47′ N, 24°17′ E 224
Lomami, river, Dem. Rep. of the Congo 4°35′ S, 24°49′ E 224
Lomami, river, Dem. Rep. of the Congo 7°19′ S, 25°26′ E 224
Lomas del Real, Mex. 22°30′ N, 97°55′ W 114
Lombarda, Serra, Braz. 3°17′ N, 51°55′ W 130
Lombardy, adm. division, It. 45°33′ N, 9°3′ E 167
Lombez, Fr. 43°28′ N, 0°52′ E 164
Lomblen, island, Indonesia 8°58′ S, 123°36′ E 192
Lombok, island, Indonesia 9°26′ S, 115°17′ E 192
Lomé, Togo 6°10′ N, 1°7′ E 222
Lomela, Dem. Rep. of the Congo 2°19′ S, 23°17′ E 218
Lomela, river, Dem. Rep. of the Congo 0°35′ N, 21°5′ E 218
Lometa, Tex., U.S. 31°12′ N, 98°24′ W 92
Lomié, Cameroon 3°21′ N, 13°37′ E 218
Lomira, Wis., U.S. 43°35′ N, 88°27′ W 102
Lommel, Belg. 51°13′ N, 5°18′ E 167
Lomond, Ben, peak, U.K. 56°10′ N, 4°44′ W 150
Lomonosov, Russ. 59°51′ N, 29°42′ E 166
Lomonosov Ridge, Arctic Ocean 88°59′ N, 116°17′ W 255
Lomovoye, Russ. 64°2′ N, 40°38′ E 154
Lomphat, Cambodia 13°39′ N, 106°57′ E 202
Lompoc, Calif., U.S. 34°39′ N, 120°28′ W 100
Łomża, Pol. 53°10′ N, 22°5′ E 152
Lon, Hon, island, Vietnam 12°32′ N, 109°26′ E 202
Lonauli, India 18°43′ N, 73°24′ E 188
Londinières, Fr. 49°50′ N, 1°24′ E 163
London, Can. 42°59′ N, 81°13′ W 102
London, Ohio, U.S. 39°52′ N, 83°27′ W 102
London, U.K. 51°31′ N, 0°9′ E 162
Londonderry, U.K. 54°58′ N, 7°16′ W 143
Londonderry, Vt., U.S. 43°13′ N, 72°49′ W 104
Londonderry, Isla, island, Chile 55°33′ S, 72°31′ W 248
Londres, Arg. 27°43′ S, 67°9′ W 132
Londrina, Braz. 23°18′ S, 51°11′ W 138
Lone Pine, Calif., U.S. 36°36′ N, 118°5′ W 101
Lone Star, Tex., U.S. 32°55′ N, 94°44′ W 103
Lonely Bay 61°39′ N, 115°31′ W 108
Lonepine, Mont., U.S. 47°40′ N, 114°40′ W 90
Long Barn, Calif., U.S. 38°5′ N, 120°9′ W 100
Long Bay Cays, islands, North Atlantic Ocean 23°49′ N, 76°60′ W 116
Long Beach, Calif., U.S. 33°46′ N, 118°12′ W 101
Long Beach, Miss., U.S. 30°20′ N, 89°10′ W 103
Long Beach, N.Y., U.S. 40°35′ N, 73°40′ W 104
Long Beach, Wash., U.S. 46°20′ N, 124°3′ W 100
Long Branch, N.J., U.S. 40°18′ N, 74°1′ W 94
Long Branch, Tex., U.S. 32°4′ N, 94°35′ W 103
Long Cay (Fortune Island), Bahamas 22°35′ N, 76°5′ W 116
Long Creek, Oreg., U.S. 44°41′ N, 119°7′ W 90
Long Creek, river, North America 49°3′ N, 103°40′ W 90
Long Eaton, U.K. 52°53′ N, 1°17′ W 162

ong Island, *Austral.* 22° 4' S, 148° 43' E **230**
ong Island, *Bahamas* 23° 4' N, 74° 52' W **116**
ong Island, *Can.* 54° 23' N, 81° 10' W **106**
ong Island, *Can.* 44° 20' N, 67° 13' W **80**
ong Island, *N.Y., U.S.* 40° 58' N, 73° 14' W **104**
ong Island, *P.N.G.* 5° 35' S, 146° 13' E **192**
ong Island Sound 41° 5' N, 73° 6' W **104**
ong Key, island, *Fla., U.S.* 24° 47' N, 80° 49' W **105**
ong Lake, *Can.* 49° 20' N, 87° 26' W **110**
ong Meg, ruin(s), *U.K.* 54° 43' N, 2° 42' W **162**
ong Melford, *U.K.* 52° 4' N, 0° 43' E **162**
ong Point, *Can.* 42° 30' N, 80° 6' W **94**
ong Point, *Can.* 54° 13' N, 58° 6' W **111**
ong Point, *Can.* 48° 45' N, 59° 26' W **111**
ong Point, *Can.* 53° 2' N, 98° 26' W **108**
ong Pond, lake, *Mass., U.S.* 41° 47' N, 71° 5' W **104**
ong Prairie, *Minn., U.S.* 45° 57' N, 94° 52' W **90**
ong Sutton, *U.K.* 52° 46' N, 0° 7' E **162**
ong Xuyen, *Vietnam* 10° 19' N, 105° 18' E **192**
onga, *Angola* 14° 43' S, 18° 30' E **220**
onga, Proliv 70° 18' N, 174° 28' E **160**
ong'an, *China* 23° 7' N, 107° 39' E **198**
ongares, *Sp.* 41° 23' N, 1° 10' W **164**
ongarone, *It.* 46° 16' N, 12° 17' E **167**
ongboat Key, *Fla., U.S.* 27° 26' N, 82° 40' W **105**
ongbranch, *Wash., U.S.* 47° 11' N, 122° 46' W **100**
ongchuan, *China* 24° 4' N, 115° 17' E **198**
ongde, *China* 35° 37' N, 106° 6' E **198**
ongfellow Mountains, *Me., U.S.* 44° 27' N, 71° 10' W **104**
ongford, *Ire.* 53° 43' N, 7° 49' W **150**
onghai, *China* 24° 19' N, 117° 51' E **198**
onghua, *China* 41° 21' N, 117° 47' E **198**
onghurst, *N.C., U.S.* 36° 25' N, 78° 59' W **96**
onghurst, Mount, peak, *Antarctica* 79° 19' S, 158° 10' E **248**
ongjiang, *China* 47° 23' N, 123° 13' E **198**
ongjing see Yanji, *China* 42° 46' N, 129° 24' E **200**
ongju, *India* 28° 38' N, 93° 31' E **188**
ongkou, *China* 37° 42' N, 120° 25' E **198**
onglac, *Can.* 49° 47' N, 86° 32' W **110**
ongleaf, *La., U.S.* 30° 59' N, 92° 34' W **103**
ongli, *China* 26° 30' N, 106° 57' E **198**
onglin, *China* 24° 47' N, 105° 19' E **198**
ongmeadow, *Mass., U.S.* 42° 3' N, 72° 35' W **104**
ongmen, *China* 23° 43' N, 114° 15' E **198**
ongmont, *Colo., U.S.* 40° 10' N, 105° 2' W **106**
ongnan, *China* 24° 49' N, 114° 49' E **198**
ongobucco, *It.* 39° 27' N, 16° 37' E **156**
ongonot, peak, *Kenya* 0° 54' N, 36° 22' E **224**
ongquan, *China* 28° 6' N, 119° 7' E **198**
ongrais, Lac, lake, *Can.* 54° 10' N, 68° 48' W **111**
ongs Peak, *Colo., U.S.* 40° 14' N, 105° 41' W **90**
ongshan, *China* 29° 28' N, 109° 28' E **198**
ongstreet, *La., U.S.* 32° 4' N, 93° 57' W **103**
ongtam, *Sudan* 8° 55' N, 30° 44' E **224**
ongueuil, *Can.* 45° 31' N, 73° 30' W **94**
onguyon, *Fr.* 49° 26' N, 5° 35' E **163**
ongview, *N.C., U.S.* 35° 44' N, 81° 23' W **96**
ongview, *Tex., U.S.* 32° 29' N, 94° 44' W **103**
ongview, *Wash., U.S.* 46° 7' N, 122° 57' W **100**
ongville, *La., U.S.* 30° 35' N, 93° 15' W **103**
ongwy, *Fr.* 49° 31' N, 5° 45' E **163**
ongxi, *China* 35° 1' N, 104° 36' E **198**
ongxian, *China* 34° 53' N, 106° 48' E **198**
ongyan, *China* 25° 4' N, 117° 0' E **198**
ongyearbyen, *Nor.* 78° 10' N, 15° 34' E **160**
ong"yugan, *Russ.* 64° 54' N, 71° 25' E **169**
ongzhen, *China* 48° 41' N, 126° 49' E **198**
ongzhou, *China* 22° 23' N, 106° 48' E **198**
öningen, *Ger.* 52° 44' N, 7° 45' E **163**
oniów, *Pol.* 50° 32' N, 21° 31' E **152**
onjica, *Croatia* 45° 50' N, 16° 20' E **168**
onkala, *Dem. Rep. of the Congo* 4° 38' S, 23° 15' E **218**
onquimay, *Arg.* 36° 30' S, 63° 37' W **139**
ønsdal, *Nor.* 66° 44' N, 15° 25' E **152**
ons-le-Saunier, *Fr.* 46° 40' N, 5° 32' E **150**
oogootee, *Ind., U.S.* 38° 40' N, 86° 54' W **102**
ookeba, *Okla., U.S.* 35° 20' N, 98° 22' W **92**
ookout, Cape, *Alas., U.S.* 54° 54' N, 133° 53' W **108**
ookout, Cape, *Antarctica* 62° 6' S, 55° 18' W **248**
ookout, Cape, *N.C., U.S.* 34° 30' N, 76° 32' W **96**
ookout, Cape, *U.S.* 45° 8' N, 124° 26' W **90**
ookout Mountain, peak, *Can.* 53° 35' N, 64° 13' W **111**
ookout Mountain, peak, *N. Mex., U.S.* 35° 12' N, 108° 21' W **92**
ookout Mountain, peak, *Oreg., U.S.* 45° 19' N, 121° 37' W **90**
ookout, Point, *Mich., U.S.* 44° 3' N, 83° 35' W **102**
oolmalasin, peak, *Tanzania* 3° 3' S, 35° 45' E **224**
oon Lake, *Can.* 54° 2' N, 109° 9' W **108**
oon Lake, *N.Y., U.S.* 44° 32' N, 74° 4' W **104**
oon, Pointe, *Can.* 51° 52' N, 78° 39' W **110**
oon, river, *Can.* 56° 33' N, 115° 24' W **108**
op, *China* 37° 6' N, 80° 6' E **184**
op Buri, *Thai.* 14° 49' N, 100° 36' E **202**
op Nur, lake, *China* 40° 35' N, 89° 42' E **188**
opare, *Bosn. and Herzg.* 44° 38' N, 18° 48' E **168**
opatin, *Russ.* 43° 50' N, 47° 40' E **195**
opatino, *Russ.* 52° 36' N, 45° 49' E **158**
opatka, Mys, *Russ.* 51° 8' N, 156° 37' E **160**
opatyn, *Ukr.* 50° 11' N, 24° 48' E **152**
ope Reserve, *Gabon* 0° 38' N, 11° 20' E **206**
opera, *Sp.* 37° 57' N, 4° 13' W **164**
operot, *Kenya* 2° 17' N, 35° 51' E **224**
opez, *Wash., U.S.* 48° 30' N, 122° 54' W **100**
ópez Collada, *Mex.* 31° 40' N, 113° 59' W **92**
opez Lake, *Calif., U.S.* 35° 12' N, 120° 34' W **101**
opez Point, *Calif., U.S.* 35° 57' N, 121° 42' W **100**
opi, *Congo* 2° 55' N, 16° 39' E **218**
oppa, *Nor.* 70° 19' N, 21° 26' E **152**
opphavet 70° 9' N, 18° 9' E **160**
oppi, *Fin.* 60° 41' N, 24° 24' E **166**
opshen'ga, *Russ.* 64° 59' N, 37° 25' E **154**
opud, island, *Croatia* 42° 37' N, 17° 49' E **168**
Lopydino, *Russ.* 61° 8' N, 52° 8' E **154**
Lora del Río, *Sp.* 37° 39' N, 5° 33' W **164**
Lorain, *Ohio, U.S.* 41° 26' N, 82° 11' W **102**
Loralai, *Pak.* 30° 21' N, 68° 39' E **186**
Lorca, *Sp.* 37° 40' N, 1° 42' W **164**
Lorch, *Ger.* 50° 2' N, 7° 48' E **167**
Lord Howe Island, *Austral.* 31° 31' S, 156° 53' E **230**
Lord Howe Rise, *Tasman Sea* 33° 48' S, 163° 25' E **252**
Lord Loughborough, island, *Myanmar* 10° 28' N, 96° 37' E **202**
Lord Mayor Bay 69° 41' N, 94° 10' W **106**
Lord, river, *Can.* 50° 52' N, 123° 36' W **90**
Lordsburg, *N. Mex., U.S.* 32° 21' N, 108° 42' W **92**
Lore Lindu National Park, *Indonesia* 1° 40' S, 119° 48' E **238**
Loreauville, *La., U.S.* 30° 2' N, 91° 45' W **103**
Lorena, *Braz.* 22° 46' S, 45° 6' W **138**
Lorengau, *P.N.G.* 2° 6' S, 147° 14' E **192**
Lorenzo, *Idaho, U.S.* 43° 43' N, 111° 53' W **90**
Lorenzo, *Tex., U.S.* 33° 38' N, 101° 32' W **92**
Lorenzo Geyres, *Uru.* 32° 2' S, 57° 51' W **139**
Loreo, *It.* 45° 3' N, 12° 10' E **167**
Loreto, *Bol.* 15° 16' S, 64° 39' W **137**
Loreto, *Braz.* 7° 5' S, 45° 9' W **132**
Loreto, *Ecua.* 0° 44' N, 77° 21' W **136**
Loreto, *Mex.* 22° 16' N, 101° 58' W **114**
Loreto, *Philippines* 10° 22' N, 125° 35' E **203**
Loreto, adm. division, *Peru* 3° 3' S, 74° 42' W **136**
Loretto, *Tenn., U.S.* 35° 3' N, 87° 26' W **96**
Lorian Swamp, marsh, *Kenya* 0° 52' N, 39° 6' E **224**
Lorica, *Col.* 9° 14' N, 75° 50' W **136**
L orinci, *Hung.* 47° 44' N, 19° 41' E **168**
Loriol, *Fr.* 44° 45' N, 4° 49' E **150**
Loris, *S.C., U.S.* 34° 3' N, 78° 54' W **96**
Loriu Plateau, *Kenya* 1° 51' N, 36° 13' E **224**
Lorman, *Miss., U.S.* 31° 48' N, 91° 3' W **103**
Lormi, *India* 22° 17' N, 81° 40' E **197**
Lornel, Pointe de, *Fr.* 50° 34' N, 1° 24' E **163**
Loro, *Col.* 2° 11' N, 69° 33' W **136**
Lorraine, adm. division, *Fr.* 48° 37' N, 5° 1' E **150**
Lorraine, region, *Fr.* 49° 50' N, 4° 47' E **167**
Lorukumu, *Kenya* 2° 50' N, 35° 12' E **224**
Lorup, *Ger.* 52° 55' N, 7° 38' E **163**
Los, *Nor.* 61° 43' N, 15° 8' E **152**
Los Alamos, *Calif., U.S.* 34° 44' N, 120° 18' W **100**
Los Alamos, *N. Mex., U.S.* 35° 52' N, 106° 19' W **92**
Los Alerces National Park, *Arg.* 42° 54' S, 72° 10' W **122**
Los Altos, *Calif., U.S.* 37° 21' N, 122° 9' W **100**
Los Amores, *Arg.* 28° 6' S, 59° 60' W **139**
Los Angeles, *Calif., U.S.* 34° 3' N, 118° 16' W **101**
Los Ángeles, *Chile* 37° 28' S, 72° 22' W **134**
Los Banos, *Calif., U.S.* 37° 3' N, 120° 52' W **100**
Los Barrios, *Sp.* 36° 11' N, 5° 30' W **164**
Los Blancos, *Arg.* 23° 34' S, 62° 38' W **132**
Los Dolores, *Sp.* 37° 38' N, 1° 1' W **150**
Los Frentones, *Arg.* 26° 24' S, 61° 27' W **139**
Los Glaciares National Park, *Arg.* 50° 6' S, 73° 33' W **122**
Los Hermanos, islands, *Caribbean Sea* 11° 55' N, 64° 25' W **116**
Los, Îles de, islands, *North Atlantic Ocean* 9° 5' N, 13° 56' W **222**
Los Juries, *Arg.* 28° 27' S, 62° 7' W **139**
Los Katios National Park, *Col.* 7° 35' N, 77° 6' W **136**
Los Lagos, adm. division, *Chile* 41° 7' S, 73° 59' W **134**
Los Lavaderos, *Mex.* 23° 27' N, 98° 3' W **114**
Los Loros, *Chile* 27° 51' S, 70° 10' W **132**
Los Mármoles National Park, *Mex.* 20° 47' N, 99° 35' W **72**
Los Mochis, *Mex.* 25° 45' N, 108° 60' W **112**
Los Monjes, Islas, islands, *Caribbean Sea* 12° 0' N, 71° 6' W **116**
Los Monos, ruin(s), *Mex.* 18° 9' N, 100° 30' W **114**
Los Ojos, *N. Mex., U.S.* 36° 43' N, 106° 34' W **92**
Los Olivos, *Calif., U.S.* 34° 40' N, 120° 8' W **100**
Los Organos, *Mex.* 23° 43' N, 103° 51' W **114**
Los Osos, *Calif., U.S.* 35° 18' N, 120° 51' W **100**
Los Palacios, *Cuba* 22° 35' N, 83° 15' W **116**
Los Pirpintos, *Arg.* 26° 10' S, 62° 4' W **139**
Los Remedios, *Mex.* 24° 34' N, 106° 25' W **114**
Los Remedios National Park, *Mex.* 19° 28' N, 99° 23' W **112**
Los Reyes, *Mex.* 19° 34' N, 102° 29' W **114**
Los Reyes Islands, *South Pacific Ocean* 1° 51' S, 147° 45' E **192**
Los Roques, Islas, islands, *Caribbean Sea* 12° 4' N, 66° 32' W **116**
Los Santos de Maimona, *Sp.* 38° 27' N, 6° 24' W **164**
Los Telares, *Arg.* 29° 1' S, 63° 27' W **139**
Los Teques, *Venez.* 10° 21' N, 67° 3' W **136**
Los Vilos, *Chile* 31° 55' S, 71° 31' W **134**
Los Yébenes, *Sp.* 39° 34' N, 3° 53' W **164**
Losada, river, *Col.* 2° 19' N, 74° 30' W **136**
Losap Atoll 6° 37' N, 153° 19' E **192**
Losha, *Belarus* 53° 26' N, 27° 23' E **152**
Łosice, *Pol.* 52° 11' N, 22° 43' E **152**
Losinoborskaya, *Russ.* 58° 24' N, 89° 23' E **169**
Łoski, *Pol.* 53° 55' N, 23° 24' E **166**
Lost Hills, *Calif., U.S.* 35° 36' N, 119° 42' W **100**
Lost River Range, *Idaho, U.S.* 44° 20' N, 113° 53' W **90**
Lost Springs, *Wyo., U.S.* 42° 45' N, 104° 57' W **90**
Lost Trail Pass, *Mont., U.S.* 45° 39' N, 113° 57' W **90**
Lost World Caverns, site, *W. Va., U.S.* 37° 49' N, 80° 32' W **96**
Lostmans River, *Fla., U.S.* 25° 25' N, 81° 21' W **105**
Lot, river, *Fr.* 44° 28' N, 3° 3' E **165**
Lota, *Chile* 37° 8' S, 73° 9' W **134**
Lotagipi Swamp, marsh, *Kenya* 4° 51' N, 34° 29' E **224**
Lothair, *S. Af.* 26° 24' S, 30° 25' E **227**
Lotilla, river, *Sudan* 5° 40' N, 32° 46' E **224**
Lotmozero, *Russ.* 68° 7' N, 30° 11' E **152**
Loto, *Dem. Rep. of the Congo* 2° 50' S, 22° 29' E **218**
Lott, *Tex., U.S.* 31° 11' N, 97° 2' W **96**
Lotte, *Ger.* 52° 16' N, 7° 56' E **163**
Lou, island, *P.N.G.* 2° 42' S, 146° 53' E **192**
Louangphrabang, *Laos* 19° 51' N, 102° 6' E **202**
Louann, *Ark., U.S.* 33° 22' N, 92° 48' W **103**
Loubet Coast, *Antarctica* 67° 22' S, 66° 45' W **248**
Loudon, *Malawi* 12° 9' S, 33° 27' E **224**
Loudon, *N.H., U.S.* 43° 17' N, 71° 28' W **104**
Loudonville, *Ohio, U.S.* 40° 37' N, 82° 14' W **102**
Loue, river, *Fr.* 47° 1' N, 5° 29' E **165**
Loufan, *China* 38° 3' N, 111° 46' E **198**
Louga, *Côte d'Ivoire* 5° 4' N, 6° 14' W **222**
Louga, *Senegal* 15° 37' N, 16° 14' W **222**
Louge, *Arg.* 36° 54' S, 61° 39' W **139**
Loughborough, *U.K.* 52° 46' N, 1° 13' W **162**
Lougheed Island, *Can.* 76° 50' N, 107° 36' W **106**
Louin, *Miss., U.S.* 32° 3' N, 89° 16' W **103**
Louis Trichardt see Makhado, *S. Af.* 23° 3' S, 29° 53' E **227**
Louis Ussing, Kap 67° 2' N, 33° 5' W **246**
Louisa, *Ky., U.S.* 38° 5' N, 82° 37' W **94**
Louisburg, *N.C., U.S.* 36° 6' N, 78° 18' W **96**
Louise, *Miss., U.S.* 32° 58' N, 90° 36' W **103**
Louise Falls, *Can.* 60° 15' N, 116° 34' W **108**
Louisiade Archipelago, islands, *Solomon Sea* 12° 43' S, 154° 40' E **238**
Louisiade Archipelago, islands, *Solomon Sea* 12° 7' S, 149° 11' E **192**
Louisiana, *Mo., U.S.* 39° 26' N, 91° 4' W **94**
Louisiana, adm. division, *La., U.S.* 31° 7' N, 93° 7' W **103**
Louisiana Point, *La., U.S.* 29° 43' N, 93° 52' W **103**
Louisville, *Ill., U.S.* 38° 45' N, 88° 30' W **102**
Louisville, *Ky., U.S.* 38° 14' N, 85° 46' W **94**
Louisville, *Miss., U.S.* 33° 6' N, 89° 3' W **103**
Louisville, *Ohio, U.S.* 40° 49' N, 81° 16' W **102**
Louis-Xiv, Pointe, *Can.* 54° 27' N, 79° 40' W **106**
Loukhi, *Russ.* 66° 4' N, 33° 0' E **152**
Loukouo, *Congo* 3° 37' S, 14° 39' E **218**
Loulan Yiji, ruin(s), *China* 40° 25' N, 89° 43' E **188**
Loulay, *Fr.* 46° 2' N, 0° 32' E **150**
Loulouni, *Mali* 10° 54' N, 5° 38' W **222**
Loum, *Cameroon* 4° 41' N, 9° 46' E **222**
Lount Lake, *Can.* 50° 6' N, 94° 40' W **90**
Louny, *Czech Rep.* 50° 20' N, 13° 47' E **152**
Loup City, *Nebr., U.S.* 41° 15' N, 98° 59' W **90**
Loup, river, *Nebr., U.S.* 41° 14' N, 97° 58' W **90**
Lourdes, *Fr.* 43° 6' N, 4° 237' W **164**
Lourdes-de-Blanc-Sablon, *Can.* 51° 26' N, 57° 17' W **106**
Louth, *U.K.* 53° 21' N, 3° 179' W **162**
Louviers, *Fr.* 49° 12' N, 1° 9' E **163**
Louza, *Tun.* 35° 3' N, 10° 58' E **156**
Lov Ozero, lake, *Russ.* 67° 55' N, 35° 28' E **152**
Lövånger, *Nor.* 64° 21' N, 21° 17' E **152**
Lovat', river, *Russ.* 57° 29' N, 31° 34' E **154**
Lövberga, *Nor.* 63° 57' N, 15° 49' E **152**
Lovea, *Cambodia* 13° 21' N, 102° 55' E **202**
Lovech, *Bulg.* 43° 8' N, 24° 42' E **156**
Lovech, adm. division, *Bulg.* 42° 53' N, 24° 11' E **156**
Lovelady, *Tex., U.S.* 31° 6' N, 95° 27' W **103**
Loveland Pass, *Colo., U.S.* 39° 39' N, 105° 52' W **90**
Lovell, *Me., U.S.* 44° 7' N, 70° 55' W **104**
Lovell, *Wyo., U.S.* 44° 49' N, 108° 24' W **90**
Lovelock, *Nev., U.S.* 40° 11' N, 118° 29' W **90**
Lovere, *It.* 45° 49' N, 10° 4' E **167**
Loverna, *Can.* 51° 40' N, 109° 58' W **90**
Loves Park, *Ill., U.S.* 42° 18' N, 89° 4' W **102**
Loviisa see Lovisa, *Fin.* 60° 26' N, 26° 12' E **166**
Loving, *N. Mex., U.S.* 32° 17' N, 104° 6' W **92**
Lovington, *N. Mex., U.S.* 32° 56' N, 103° 21' W **92**
Lovisa (Loviisa), *Fin.* 60° 26' N, 26° 12' E **166**
Lovlya, *Russ.* 59° 55' N, 49° 22' E **154**
Löv o, *Hung.* 47° 29' N, 16° 47' E **168**
Lovozero, *Russ.* 68° 0' N, 35° 2' E **152**
Lovran, *Croatia* 45° 17' N, 14° 15' E **156**
Lovreč, *Croatia* 43° 29' N, 16° 58' E **168**
Lovrin, *Rom.* 45° 58' N, 20° 47' E **168**
Lóvua, *Angola* 11° 38' S, 23° 41' E **220**
Lóvua, *Angola* 7° 19' S, 20° 10' E **218**
Low Bush River, *Can.* 48° 56' N, 80° 10' W **94**
Low, Cape, *Can.* 62° 51' N, 87° 4' W **106**
Low Island, *Antarctica* 63° 21' S, 61° 57' W **134**
Lowa, *Dem. Rep. of the Congo* 1° 25' S, 25° 50' E **224**
Lowa, river, *Dem. Rep. of the Congo* 1° 23' S, 26° 55' E **224**
Lowell, *Ind., U.S.* 41° 16' N, 87° 25' W **102**
Lowell, *Mass., U.S.* 42° 38' N, 71° 20' W **104**
Lowell, *Mich., U.S.* 42° 56' N, 85° 21' W **102**
Lower Arrow Lake, *Can.* 49° 29' N, 118° 56' W **90**
Lower Hutt, *N.Z.* 41° 13' S, 174° 57' E **240**
Lower Matecumbe Key, island, *Fla., U.S.* 24° 50' N, 80° 42' W **105**
Lower Post, *Can.* 59° 57' N, 128° 27' W **108**
Lower Red Lake, *Minn., U.S.* 48° 0' N, 95° 35' W **94**
Lower Saxony, adm. division, *Ger.* 51° 47' N, 9° 27' E **167**
Lower Zambezi National Park, *Zambia* 15° 25' S, 28° 48' E **224**
Lowestoft, *U.K.* 52° 28' N, 1° 43' E **163**
Łowicz, *Pol.* 52° 5' N, 19° 54' E **152**
Lowland, *N.C., U.S.* 35° 18' N, 76° 36' W **96**
Lowry, *Minn., U.S.* 45° 41' N, 95° 32' W **90**
Lowry, Îles, islands, *Indian Ocean* 12° 35' S, 49° 42' E **220**
Lowville, *N.Y., U.S.* 43° 47' N, 75° 30' W **110**
Loxley, *Ala., U.S.* 30° 36' N, 87° 45' W **103**
Loxton, *S. Af.* 31° 30' S, 22° 19' E **227**
Loya, river, *Dem. Rep. of the Congo* 8° 475' N, 27° 45' E **224**
Loyal, Ben, peak, *U.K.* 58° 23' N, 4° 33' W **150**
Loyall, *Ky., U.S.* 36° 50' N, 83° 21' W **96**
Loyalty Islands 20° 7' S, 166° 47' E **238**
Loyew, *Belarus* 51° 55' N, 30° 53' E **158**
Loyola, Punta, *Arg.* 51° 48' S, 68° 54' W **134**
Loyoro, *Uganda* 3° 19' N, 34° 13' E **224**
Lozenets, *Bulg.* 42° 12' N, 27° 48' E **156**
Loznica, *Serb. and Mont.* 44° 31' N, 19° 12' E **168**
Lozova, *Ukr.* 48° 54' N, 36° 19' E **158**
Lozovik, *Serb. and Mont.* 44° 28' N, 21° 4' E **168**
Loz'va, river, *Russ.* 61° 47' N, 59° 54' E **154**
Lü Tao, island, *Taiwan* 22° 30' N, 121° 31' E **198**
Lua Dekere, river, *Dem. Rep. of the Congo* 3° 53' N, 19° 30' E **218**
Lua, river, *Dem. Rep. of the Congo* 2° 49' N, 18° 31' E **218**
Luabo, *Mozambique* 18° 24' S, 36° 8' E **224**
Luacano, *Angola* 11° 11' S, 21° 39' E **220**
Luaha-sibuha, *Indonesia* 0° 30' N, 98° 27' E **196**
Luahiwa Petroglyphs, site, *Hawai'i, U.S.* 20° 47' N, 156° 57' W **99**
Lualaba (Congo), river, *Dem. Rep. of the Congo* 5° 35' S, 27° 7' E **224**
Luama, river, *Dem. Rep. of the Congo* 4° 41' S, 27° 17' E **224**
Luambe National Park, *Zambia* 12° 37' S, 31° 37' E **224**
Luampa, river, *Zambia* 15° 16' S, 24° 38' E **224**
Lu'an, *China* 31° 44' N, 116° 31' E **198**
Luan, river, *China* 41° 27' N, 117° 5' E **198**
Luanda, *Angola* 8° 54' S, 13° 3' E **218**
Luanda, adm. division, *Angola* 9° 17' S, 12° 39' E **218**
Luando, *Angola* 11° 43' S, 18° 33' E **220**
Luando Integral Nature Reserve, *Angola* 11° 24' S, 16° 28' E **220**
Luang, Thale, lake, *Thai.* 7° 24' N, 99° 51' E **196**
Luangundo, river, *Angola* 16° 17' S, 19° 35' E **220**
Luangwa, *Zambia* 15° 37' S, 30° 20' E **224**
Luangwa, river, *Zambia* 12° 14' S, 32° 10' E **224**
Luanping, *China* 40° 54' N, 117° 18' E **198**
Luanshya, *Zambia* 13° 8' S, 28° 22' E **224**
Luanxian, *China* 39° 46' N, 118° 41' E **198**
Luanza, *Dem. Rep. of the Congo* 8° 42' S, 28° 39' E **224**
Luarca, *Sp.* 43° 31' N, 6° 34' W **150**
Luashi, *Dem. Rep. of the Congo* 10° 56' S, 23° 34' E **224**
Luau, *Angola* 10° 44' S, 22° 14' E **220**
Lubaantun, ruin(s), *Belize* 16° 15' N, 89° 7' W **115**
Lubamiti, *Dem. Rep. of the Congo* 2° 32' S, 17° 46' E **218**
Lubāna, *Latv.* 56° 53' N, 26° 42' E **166**
Lubānas Ezers, lake, *Latv.* 56° 45' N, 26° 36' E **166**
Lubanda, *Dem. Rep. of the Congo* 5° 13' S, 26° 38' E **224**
Lubango, *Angola* 14° 57' S, 13° 28' E **220**
Lubao, *Dem. Rep. of the Congo* 5° 20' S, 25° 43' E **224**
Lubba Gerih, spring, *Somalia* 10° 21' N, 44° 38' E **216**
Lübben, *Ger.* 51° 56' N, 13° 53' E **152**
Lubbock, *Tex., U.S.* 33° 32' N, 101° 50' W **92**
Lubec, *Me., U.S.* 44° 50' N, 66° 60' W **94**
Lübeck, *Ger.* 53° 51' N, 10° 42' E **152**
Lubefu, *Dem. Rep. of the Congo* 4° 44' S, 24° 24' E **224**
Lubelskie, adm. division, *Pol.* 51° 2' N, 21° 49' E **152**
Lübenka, *Kaz.* 50° 27' N, 54° 6' E **158**
Lubero, *Dem. Rep. of the Congo* 0° 12' N, 29° 11' E **224**
Lubéron, Montagne du, *Fr.* 43° 42' N, 5° 16' E **165**
Lubi, river, *Dem. Rep. of the Congo* 5° 49' S, 23° 28' E **224**
Lubicon Lake, *Can.* 56° 22' N, 116° 23' W **108**
Lubilash, river, *Dem. Rep. of the Congo* 8° 21' S, 24° 7' E **224**
Lubine, Île, island, *U.K.* 6° 46' S, 70° 20' E **188**
Lublin, *Pol.* 51° 15' N, 22° 33' E **152**
Lubliniec, *Pol.* 50° 40' N, 18° 41' E **152**
Lubnica, *Serb. and Mont.* 43° 51' N, 22° 12' E **168**
Lubny, *Ukr.* 50° 1' N, 32° 56' E **158**
Lubongola, *Dem. Rep. of the Congo* 2° 39' S, 27° 52' E **218**
Lubosalma, *Russ.* 63° 4' N, 31° 45' E **152**
Lubuagan, *Philippines* 17° 21' N, 121° 10' E **203**
Lubudi, *Dem. Rep. of the Congo* 9° 58' S, 25° 58' E **224**
Lubudi, river, *Dem. Rep. of the Congo* 9° 52' S, 24° 52' E **224**
Lubukbertubung, *Indonesia* 5° 297' N, 102° 6' E **196**
Lubuksikaping, *Indonesia* 0° 8' N, 100° 10' E **196**
Lubumbashi (Élisabethville), *Dem. Rep. of the Congo* 11° 43' S, 27° 26' E **224**
Lubuskie, adm. division, *Pol.* 51° 47' N, 14° 40' E **152**
Lubutu, *Dem. Rep. of the Congo* 0° 45' N, 26° 32' E **224**
Lubwe, *Zambia* 11° 5' S, 29° 34' E **224**
Luc, Pointe à, *Can.* 49° 44' N, 67° 4' W **111**
Lucala, river, *Angola* 9° 26' S, 15° 21' E **220**
Lucan, *Can.* 43° 10' N, 81° 24' W **102**
Lucanas, *Peru* 14° 39' S, 74° 15' W **137**
Lucania, Mount, peak, *Can.* 60° 59' N, 140° 39' W **98**
Lucapa, *Angola* 8° 40' S, 20° 57' E **218**
Lucas, *Braz.* 13° 7' S, 55° 57' W **130**
Lucas, *Kans., U.S.* 39° 1' N, 98° 33' W **90**
Lucaya, *Bahamas* 26° 31' N, 78° 39' W **105**
Lucca, *It.* 43° 50' N, 10° 30' E **167**
Lucedale, *Miss., U.S.* 30° 53' N, 88° 36' W **103**
Lucena, *Philippines* 13° 56' N, 121° 36' E **203**
Lucena, *Sp.* 37° 24' N, 4° 30' W **164**
Lucena del Cid, *Sp.* 40° 8' N, 0° 17' E **164**
Lučenec, *Slovakia* 48° 19' N, 19° 41' E **152**
Lucerne, *Can.* 52° 51' N, 118° 33' W **108**
Lucerne Valley, *Calif., U.S.* 34° 27' N, 116° 58' W **101**
Lucero, *Mex.* 30° 48' N, 106° 31' W **92**
Luceville, *Can.* 48° 30' N, 68° 21' W **111**
Lüchow, *Ger.* 52° 58' N, 11° 9' E **152**
Luchuan, *China* 22° 22' N, 110° 15' E **198**
Luchulingo, river, *Mozambique* 12° 21' S, 35° 30' E **224**
Lüchun, *China* 23° 1' N, 102° 16' E **202**
Lučice, *Croatia* 43° 49' N, 15° 17' E **156**
Lucie, Lac, lake, *Can.* 50° 22' N, 78° 55' W **94**
Lucie, river, *Suriname* 3° 37' N, 57° 29' W **130**
Lucira, *Angola* 13° 55' S, 12° 31' E **220**
Lucknow, *Can.* 43° 57' N, 81° 31' W **102**
Lucknow, *India* 26° 47' N, 80° 53' E **197**
Lucky Boy Pass, *Nev., U.S.* 38° 26' N, 118° 47' W **90**
Luçon, *Fr.* 46° 27' N, 1° 11' W **150**
Lucunga, *Angola* 6° 51' S, 14° 35' E **218**
Lucusse, *Angola* 12° 34' S, 20° 48' E **220**
Ludborough, *U.K.* 53° 26' N, 4° 237' W **162**
Ludbreg, *Croatia* 46° 15' N, 16° 36' E **168**
Lüdenscheid, *Ger.* 51° 13' N, 7° 37' E **167**
Lüderitz, *Namibia* 26° 41' S, 15° 12' E **220**
Ludgershall, *U.K.* 51° 14' N, 1° 39' W **162**
Ludhiana, *India* 30° 53' N, 75° 53' E **186**
Lüdinghausen, *Ger.* 51° 46' N, 7° 26' E **167**
Ludington, *Mich., U.S.* 43° 56' N, 86° 26' W **102**
Ludlow, *Calif., U.S.* 34° 43' N, 116° 11' W **101**
Ludlow, *Ill., U.S.* 40° 23' N, 88° 7' W **102**
Ludlow, *Mass., U.S.* 42° 9' N, 72° 29' W **104**
Ludlow, *U.K.* 52° 21' N, 2° 44' W **162**
Ludlow, *Vt., U.S.* 43° 23' N, 72° 43' W **104**
Ludogorsko Plato, *Bulg.* 43° 26' N, 26° 11' E **156**
Ludwigsfelde, *Ger.* 52° 18' N, 13° 15' E **152**
Ludwigshafen, *Ger.* 49° 28' N, 8° 26' E **150**
Ludza, *Latv.* 56° 32' N, 27° 43' E **166**
Luebo, *Dem. Rep. of the Congo* 5° 21' S, 21° 26' E **218**
Lueki, *Dem. Rep. of the Congo* 3° 26' S, 25° 49' E **224**
Luembe, river, *Dem. Rep. of the Congo* 6° 50' S, 24° 24' E **224**
Luena, *Angola* 11° 48' S, 19° 55' E **220**
Luena, *Dem. Rep. of the Congo* 9° 27' S, 25° 44' E **224**
Luena, *Zambia* 10° 37' S, 30° 11' E **224**
Luena Flats, *Zambia* 14° 33' S, 23° 29' E **224**
Luena, river, *Angola–Zambia* 12° 19' S, 21° 31' E **220**
Lueo, river, *Dem. Rep. of the Congo* 9° 33' S, 23° 43' E **224**
Luepa, *Venez.* 5° 52' N, 61° 27' W **123**
Luesia, *Sp.* 42° 22' N, 1° 1' W **164**
Lufeng, *China* 22° 54' N, 115° 38' E **198**
Lufico, *Angola* 6° 24' S, 13° 21' E **218**
Lufira, river, *Dem. Rep. of the Congo* 9° 40' S, 27° 14' E **224**
Lufkin, *Tex., U.S.* 31° 19' N, 94° 43' W **103**
Lufu, *Dem. Rep. of the Congo* 5° 41' S, 13° 52' E **218**
Luga, *Russ.* 58° 42' N, 29° 49' E **166**
Lugano, *Switz.* 46° 0' N, 8° 57' E **167**
Lugg, river, *U.K.* 52° 16' N, 2° 57' W **162**
Lugnaquillia, peak, *Ire.* 52° 57' N, 6° 34' W **150**
Lugo, *It.* 44° 24' N, 11° 54' E **167**
Lugo, *Sp.* 43° 0' N, 7° 34' W **150**
Lugoj, *Rom.* 45° 42' N, 21° 54' E **168**
Lugones, *Arg.* 28° 21' S, 63° 19' W **139**
Lugovaya Proleyka, *Russ.* 49° 19' N, 45° 4' E **158**
Lugovoy, *Russ.* 59° 40' N, 65° 56' E **169**
Lŭgovoy see Qulan, *Kaz.* 42° 54' N, 72° 44' E **184**
Lugulu, river, *Dem. Rep. of the Congo* 2° 18' S, 26° 54' E **224**
Luguruka, *Tanzania* 9° 59' S, 36° 39' E **224**
Luhanka, *Fin.* 61° 47' N, 25° 39' E **166**
Luhans'k, *Ukr.* 48° 32' N, 39° 14' E **158**
Lui, Ben, peak, *U.K.* 56° 22' N, 4° 55' W **150**
Lui, river, *Zambia* 15° 50' S, 23° 27' E **224**
Luiana, *Angola* 17° 23' S, 23° 0' E **220**
Luiana, river, *Angola* 17° 22' S, 22° 1' E **220**
Luilu, river, *Dem. Rep. of the Congo* 7° 2' S, 23° 27' E **224**
Luimneach see Limerick, *Ire.* 52° 39' N, 8° 37' W **150**
Luino, *It.* 46° 0' N, 8° 45' E **167**
Luis Gonzaga, *Mex.* 29° 48' N, 114° 28' W **92**
Luis Moya, *Mex.* 22° 25' N, 102° 16' W **114**
Luishia, *Dem. Rep. of the Congo* 11° 12' S, 27° 1' E **224**
Luisiana, *Peru* 12° 43' S, 73° 44' W **137**
Luitpold Coast, *Antarctica* 77° 40' S, 35° 8' W **248**
Luiza, *Dem. Rep. of the Congo* 7° 13' S, 22° 25' E **218**
Luizi, river, *Dem. Rep. of the Congo* 6° 4' S, 27° 33' E **224**
Luján, *Arg.* 34° 36' S, 59° 6' W **139**
Luka, *Bosn. and Herzg.* 43° 25' N, 18° 7' E **168**
Lukafu, *Dem. Rep. of the Congo* 10° 29' S, 27° 29' E **224**
Lukanga Swamp, marsh, *Zambia* 14° 27' S, 27° 19' E **224**
Lukashi, river, *Dem. Rep. of the Congo* 6° 7' S, 24° 45' E **224**
Lukavac, *Bosn. and Herzg.* 44° 34' N, 18° 31' E **168**
Luke, *Maced.* 42° 19' N, 22° 16' E **168**
Luke, *Serb. and Mont.* 43° 36' N, 20° 16' E **168**
Luke Air Force Base, *Ariz., U.S.* 33° 32' N, 112° 26' W **92**
Luke, Mount, peak, *Austral.* 27° 16' S, 116° 39' E **230**
Lukenie, river, *Dem. Rep. of the Congo* 3° 33' S, 22° 5' E **218**
Lukeville, *Ariz., U.S.* 31° 53' N, 112° 48' W **92**
Lukolela, *Dem. Rep. of the Congo* 1° 10' S, 17° 10' E **218**
Lukovë, *Alban.* 39° 59' N, 19° 54' E **156**
Łuków, *Pol.* 51° 55' N, 22° 21' E **152**
Lukoyanov, *Russ.* 55° 1' N, 44° 33' E **154**
Łukta, *Pol.* 53° 47' N, 20° 5' E **166**
Lukuga, river, *Dem. Rep. of the Congo* 5° 59' S, 27° 21' E **224**
Lukula, *Dem. Rep. of the Congo* 5° 26' S, 12° 53' E **218**
Lukuledi, *Tanzania* 10° 35' S, 38° 48' E **224**
Lukulu, *Zambia* 14° 23' S, 23° 15' E **220**
Lukunor Atoll 5° 17' N, 153° 45' E **192**
Lukup, *Indonesia* 4° 25' N, 97° 29' E **196**
Lukusuzi National Park, *Zambia* 13° 8' S, 32° 20' E **224**
Luleå, *Nor.* 65° 35' N, 22° 9' E **152**
Lüleburgaz, *Turk.* 41° 24' N, 27° 21' E **158**
Lules, *Arg.* 26° 60' S, 65° 22' W **132**
Luling, *Tex., U.S.* 29° 39' N, 97° 39' W **92**
Lulonga, *Dem. Rep. of the Congo* 0° 32' N, 18° 24' E **218**

Lulu, river, Dem. Rep. of the Congo 1°35′ N, 23°48′ E 224
Lulua, river, Dem. Rep. of the Congo 8°22′ S, 22°45′ E 218
Lumajangdong Co, lake, China 34°0′ N, 80°21′ E 188
Lümanda, Est. 58°17′ N, 22°2′ E 166
Lumbala Kaquengue, Angola 12°41′ S, 22°38′ E 220
Lumbala N'guimbo, Angola 14°8′ S, 21°24′ E 220
Lumberton, Miss., U.S. 30°59′ N, 89°28′ W 103
Lumberton, N.C., U.S. 34°37′ N, 79°1′ W 96
Lumbo, Mozambique 15°4′ S, 40°38′ E 224
Lumbovka, Russ. 67°39′ N, 40°33′ E 169
Lumbreras, Sp. 42°5′ N, 2°37′ W 164
Lumbres, Fr. 50°42′ N, 2°7′ E 163
Lumbwa, Kenya 0°10′ N, 35°30′ E 224
Lumding, India 25°44′ N, 93°8′ E 188
Lumeje, Angola 11°35′ S, 20°48′ E 220
Lumholtz National Park, Austral. 18°27′ S, 145°30′ E 238
Lumivaara, peak, Nor. 67°32′ N, 22°51′ E 152
Lumparland, Fin. 60°5′ N, 20°15′ E 166
Lumuna, Dem. Rep. of the Congo 3°50′ S, 26°29′ E 224
Lumut, Malaysia 4°12′ N, 100°36′ E 196
Lun, Croatia 44°41′ N, 14°45′ E 156
Lün, Mongolia 47°24′ N, 102°54′ E 198
Lün, Mongolia 47°49′ N, 105°17′ E 198
Luna, N. Mex., U.S. 33°48′ N, 108°57′ W 92
Lunar Crater, Nev., U.S. 38°23′ N, 115°60′ W 90
Lunavada, India 23°7′ N, 73°36′ E 186
Lund, Can. 49°59′ N, 124°45′ W 100
Lund, Nev., U.S. 38°51′ N, 115°1′ W 90
Lunda Norte, adm. division, Angola 8°37′ S, 18°34′ E 218
Lunda Sul, adm. division, Angola 9°13′ S, 20°41′ E 218
Lundar, Can. 50°41′ N, 98°3′ W 90
Lundazi, Zambia 12°16′ S, 33°13′ E 224
Lunde, Nor. 62°51′ N, 17°47′ E 152
Lundu, Malaysia 1°42′ N, 109°51′ E 196
Lune, river, U.K. 54°13′ N, 2°37′ W 162
Lüneburger Heide, region, Ger. 53°2′ N, 9°31′ E 150
Lunel, Fr. 43°40′ N, 4°7′ E 150
Lünen, Ger. 51°37′ N, 7°32′ E 163
Lunenburg, Can. 44°21′ N, 64°20′ W 111
Lunenburg, Mass., U.S. 42°35′ N, 71°44′ W 104
Lunenburg, Vt., U.S. 44°27′ N, 71°42′ W 104
Lunéville, Fr. 48°35′ N, 6°30′ E 163
Lunga, river, Zambia 13°1′ S, 26°36′ E 224
Lungdo, China 33°54′ N, 82°10′ E 188
Lunggar, China 31°8′ N, 84°1′ E 188
Lungi, Sierra Leone 8°40′ N, 13°14′ W 222
Lunglei, India 22°52′ N, 92°42′ E 188
Luni, India 26°1′ N, 73°0′ E 186
Luni, river, India 25°31′ N, 71°49′ E 186
Lunino, Russ. 53°36′ N, 45°15′ E 154
Luninyets, Belarus 52°14′ N, 26°47′ E 152
Lunkaransar, India 28°29′ N, 73°45′ E 186
Lunsar, Sierra Leone 8°41′ N, 12°34′ W 222
Lunsemfwa, river, Zambia 15°3′ S, 29°20′ E 224
Luntai, China 41°44′ N, 84°17′ E 184
Lunyama, Dem. Rep. of the Congo 7°49′ S, 28°20′ E 224
Lunz, Aust. 47°51′ N, 15°1′ E 156
Luo, river, China 36°39′ N, 108°16′ E 198
Luo, river, China 34°16′ N, 111°45′ E 198
Luocheng, China 24°46′ N, 108°53′ E 198
Luodian, China 25°24′ N, 106°45′ E 198
Luoding, China 22°42′ N, 111°35′ E 198
Luohe, China 33°37′ N, 114°4′ E 198
Luonan, China 34°5′ N, 110°10′ E 198
Luopioinen, Fin. 61°22′ N, 24°37′ E 166
Luoshan, China 32°13′ N, 114°34′ E 198
Luoyang, China 34°41′ N, 112°25′ E 198
Luoyuan, China 26°32′ N, 119°33′ E 198
Luozi, Dem. Rep. of the Congo 4°56′ S, 14°4′ E 218
Lupa Market, Tanzania 8°42′ S, 33°16′ E 224
Lupane, Zimb. 18°56′ S, 27°45′ E 224
Lupeni, Rom. 45°20′ N, 23°15′ E 168
Lupilichi, Mozambique 11°46′ S, 35°15′ E 224
Lupin, Can. 65°41′ N, 111°19′ W 106
Lupiñén, Sp. 42°9′ N, 0°34′ E 164
Lupire, Angola 14°38′ S, 19°28′ E 220
Lupon, Philippines 6°55′ N, 126°1′ E 203
Luputa, Dem. Rep. of the Congo 7°6′ S, 23°40′ E 224
Lupweji, river, Dem. Rep. of the Congo 10°26′ S, 24°13′ E 224
Luque, Sp. 37°33′ N, 4°17′ W 164
Luråsen, peak, Nor. 62°1′ N, 16°32′ E 152
Lure, Fr. 47°41′ N, 6°29′ E 150
Luremo, Angola 8°33′ S, 17°52′ E 218
Luribay, Bol. 17°8′ S, 67°43′ W 137
Lúrio, Mozambique 13°35′ S, 40°33′ E 224
Lúrio, river, Mozambique 14°19′ S, 38°43′ E 224
Luro, Arg. 36°38′ S, 62°9′ W 139
Lurøy, Nor. 66°25′ N, 12°51′ E 152
Lusahanga, Tanzania 2°54′ S, 31°14′ E 224
Lusaka, Zambia 15°26′ S, 28°10′ E 224
Lusambo, Dem. Rep. of the Congo 4°58′ S, 23°25′ E 224
Lusanga, Dem. Rep. of the Congo 4°50′ S, 18°39′ E 218
Lušci Palanka, Bosn. and Herzg. 44°44′ N, 16°25′ E 168
Luseland, Can. 52°5′ N, 109°23′ W 90
Lusenga Plain National Park, Zambia 9°45′ S, 29°1′ E 224
Lushi, China 34°4′ N, 111°0′ E 198
Lushiko, river, Angola 6°26′ S, 19°26′ E 218
Lushoto, Tanzania 4°48′ S, 38°19′ E 224
Lüshun (Port Arthur), China 38°52′ N, 121°16′ E 198
Lusigny, Fr. 48°15′ N, 4°15′ E 163
Lusikisiki, S. Af. 31°22′ S, 29°33′ E 227
Lusk, Wyo., U.S. 42°45′ N, 104°27′ W 90
Lussanvira, Braz. 20°43′ S, 51°9′ W 138
Lustenau, Aust. 47°25′ N, 9°39′ E 156
Lüt, Dasht-e, Iran 31°50′ N, 56°19′ E 160
Lūţak, Iran 30°41′ N, 61°27′ E 186
Lutcher, La., U.S. 30°2′ N, 90°44′ W 103
Lutembo, Angola 13°29′ S, 21°17′ E 220
Luther, Mich., U.S. 44°2′ N, 85°42′ W 102
Luton, U.K. 51°52′ N, 0°26′ E 162
Lutriņi, Latv. 56°44′ N, 22°23′ E 166
Lutry, Pol. 54°0′ N, 20°53′ E 166
Lutsen, Minn., U.S. 47°39′ N, 90°42′ W 94
Lutshima, river, Dem. Rep. of the Congo 6°29′ S, 18°21′ E 218
Luts'k, Ukr. 50°44′ N, 25°18′ E 152
Lutterworth, U.K. 52°26′ N, 1°13′ W 162
Lutuai, Angola 12°42′ S, 20°7′ E 220
Lututów, Pol. 51°22′ N, 18°27′ E 152
Lützow-Holm Bay 69°52′ S, 35°52′ E 248
Lutzputs, S. Af. 28°24′ S, 20°43′ E 227
Luuk, Philippines 5°58′ N, 121°19′ E 203
Luuq, Somalia 3°48′ N, 42°34′ E 224
Luverne, Ala., U.S. 31°42′ N, 86°16′ W 96
Luverne, Minn., U.S. 43°37′ N, 96°13′ W 90
Luvia, Fin. 61°21′ N, 21°35′ E 166
Luvidjo, river, Dem. Rep. of the Congo 7°7′ S, 26°25′ E 224
Luvo, Angola 5°52′ S, 14°4′ E 218
Luvos, Nor. 66°38′ N, 18°51′ E 152
Luvozero, Russ. 64°26′ N, 30°40′ E 152
Luvua, river, Dem. Rep. of the Congo 6°44′ S, 26°58′ E 224
Luvuei, Angola 13°6′ S, 21°12′ E 220
Luwegu, river, Tanzania 9°40′ S, 36°30′ E 224
Luwingu, Zambia 10°15′ S, 29°53′ E 224
Luwuk, Indonesia 0°58′ N, 122°46′ E 192
Luxembourg, Lux. 49°46′ N, 6°1′ E 163
Luxembourg 49°43′ N, 5°50′ E 163
Luxeuil, Fr. 47°49′ N, 6°23′ E 150
Luxi, China 24°25′ N, 98°38′ E 190
Luxi, China 28°18′ N, 110°9′ E 198
Luxor, Egypt 25°40′ N, 32°38′ E 182
Luyi, China 33°52′ N, 115°26′ E 198
Luz, Braz. 19°48′ S, 45°42′ W 138
Luz Range, Antarctica 72°22′ S, 4°40′ E 248
Luza, Russ. 60°40′ N, 47°18′ E 154
Luza, river, Russ. 60°20′ N, 48°39′ E 154
Luzaga, Sp. 40°57′ N, 2°27′ W 164
Luzaide (Valcarlos), Fr. 43°5′ N, 1°19′ W 164
Lužane, Europe 42°47′ N, 21°10′ E 168
Luzhai, China 24°23′ N, 109°43′ E 198
Luzhi, China 26°19′ N, 105°16′ E 198
Luzhma, Russ. 63°29′ N, 30°33′ E 152
Luzhou, China 28°54′ N, 105°22′ E 198
Luziânia, Braz. 16°18′ S, 47°58′ W 138
Luzon, island, Philippines 17°39′ N, 122°18′ E 190
Luzon Strait 19°39′ N, 119°44′ E 238
L'viv, Ukr. 49°50′ N, 24°2′ E 152
L'vovka, Russ. 57°9′ N, 78°48′ E 169
Lwiro, Dem. Rep. of the Congo 2°17′ S, 28°43′ E 224
Lyady, Russ. 58°36′ N, 28°46′ E 166
Lyakhov Islands, East Siberian Sea 73°46′ N, 140°46′ E 255
Lyaki, Azerb. 40°33′ N, 47°24′ E 195
Lyall Islands, South Pacific Ocean 70°47′ S, 166°57′ E 248
Lyall, Mount, peak, Can. 50°4′ N, 114°47′ W 90
Lyamtsa, Russ. 64°32′ N, 36°54′ E 154
Lyasnaya, Belarus 52°59′ N, 25°50′ E 154
Lychkovo, Russ. 57°53′ N, 32°25′ E 154
Lycksele, Nor. 64°35′ N, 18°39′ E 152
Lycosura, ruin(s), Gr. 37°22′ N, 21°56′ E 156
Lydd, U.K. 50°56′ N, 0°55′ E 162
Lydda see Lod, Israel 31°56′ N, 34°53′ E 194
Lyddal, Can. 55°0′ N, 98°25′ W 108
Lyddan Island, Antarctica 73°46′ S, 25°33′ W 248
Lydenburg, S. Af. 25°6′ S, 30°25′ E 227
Lydney, U.K. 51°43′ N, 2°32′ W 162
Lyduvėnai, Lith. 55°30′ N, 23°2′ E 166
Lyell Brown, Mount, peak, Austral. 23°24′ S, 130°9′ E 230
Lyell, Mount, peak, Calif., U.S. 37°43′ N, 119°20′ W 100
Lyepyel', Belarus 54°51′ N, 28°40′ E 166
Lyford, Tex., U.S. 26°23′ N, 97°47′ W 96
Lyle, Oreg., U.S. 45°40′ N, 121°18′ W 100
Lyman, Miss., U.S. 30°29′ N, 89°7′ W 103
Lyman, Utah, U.S. 38°23′ N, 111°35′ W 92
Lyman, Wash., U.S. 48°31′ N, 122°4′ W 100
Lyman, Wyo., U.S. 41°21′ N, 110°18′ W 90
Lymbel'karamo, Russ. 60°14′ N, 83°47′ E 169
Lynch, Nebr., U.S. 42°49′ N, 98°29′ W 90
Lynch Station, Va., U.S. 37°8′ N, 79°19′ W 96
Lynchburg, Ohio, U.S. 39°14′ N, 83°47′ W 102
Lynden, Wash., U.S. 48°57′ N, 122°27′ W 100
Lyndhurst, U.K. 50°52′ N, 1°34′ W 162
Lyndon, Ill., U.S. 41°42′ N, 89°57′ W 102
Lyndon, Vt., U.S. 44°30′ N, 72°2′ W 104
Lyndonville, Vt., U.S. 44°31′ N, 72°1′ W 104
Lynn, Ind., U.S. 40°3′ N, 84°57′ W 102
Lynn, Mass., U.S. 42°27′ N, 70°58′ W 104
Lynn Canal 58°40′ N, 135°29′ W 108
Lynn Lake, Can. 56°48′ N, 101°3′ W 106
Lynton, U.K. 51°13′ N, 3°49′ W 162
Lyntupy, Belarus 55°4′ N, 26°20′ E 166
Lyon, Miss., U.S. 34°12′ N, 90°33′ W 96
Lyon, Cape, Can. 69°41′ N, 122°54′ W 98
Lyonnais, region, Fr. 45°45′ N, 3°45′ E 165
Lyons, Kans., U.S. 38°20′ N, 98°13′ W 90
Lyons, Nebr., U.S. 41°54′ N, 96°29′ W 90
Lyons, N.Y., U.S. 43°3′ N, 76°60′ W 110
Lyons, Ohio, U.S. 41°41′ N, 84°4′ W 102
Lyons, Tex., U.S. 30°22′ N, 96°34′ W 96
Lyozna, Belarus 55°3′ N, 30°53′ E 154
Lys, river, Fr. 50°34′ N, 2°9′ E 163
Lysekil, Nor. 58°17′ N, 11°26′ E 152
Lysi 35°5′ N, 33°41′ E 194
Łysica, Pol. 54°22′ N, 19°24′ E 166
Lys'va, Russ. 58°6′ N, 57°49′ E 154
Lysychans'k, Ukr. 48°51′ N, 38°27′ E 158
Lytham Saint Anne's, U.K. 53°45′ N, 2°60′ W 162
Lytle, Tex., U.S. 29°11′ N, 98°49′ W 96
Lyttelton, N.Z. 43°36′ S, 172°43′ E 240
Lytton, Can. 50°14′ N, 121°33′ W 108
Lyttus, ruin(s), Gr. 35°10′ N, 25°16′ E 156
Lyuban', Russ. 59°21′ N, 31°17′ E 152
Lyubcha, Belarus 53°44′ N, 26°4′ E 154
Lyubeshiv, Ukr. 51°46′ N, 25°30′ E 152
Lyubim, Russ. 58°21′ N, 40°44′ E 154
Lyubytino, Russ. 58°48′ N, 33°28′ E 154
Lyubytiv, Ukr. 51°7′ N, 24°50′ E 152
Lyudinovo, Russ. 53°48′ N, 34°28′ E 154
Lyushcha, Belarus 52°25′ N, 26°41′ E 152
Lyzha, river, Russ. 65°44′ N, 55°56′ E 154

M

M' Bomou, river, Africa 4°36′ N, 23°30′ E 224
Ma, Pol. 52°41′ N, 22°0′ E 152
Ma, river, Asia 20°38′ N, 104°57′ E 202
Maafer, Alg. 35°51′ N, 5°21′ E 150
Maale (Male), Maldives 4°9′ N, 73°15′ E 188
Ma'āmīr, Iraq 30°2′ N, 48°24′ E 196
Ma'ān, Jordan 30°10′ N, 35°44′ E 180
Maaninka, Fin. 66°26′ N, 28°26′ E 154
Maanĭt, Mongolia 48°16′ N, 103°27′ E 198
Maanselkä, Fin. 67°46′ N, 27°51′ E 152
Ma'anshan, China 31°41′ N, 118°32′ E 198
Maardu, Est. 59°27′ N, 25°0′ E 166
Maarestunturit, peak, Fin. 68°44′ N, 25°31′ E 152
Maarianhamina see Mariehamn, Fin. 60°5′ N, 19°55′ E 166
Ma'arrat an Nu'mān, Syr. 35°39′ N, 36°41′ E 194
Maas, river, Neth. 51°46′ N, 5°19′ E 167
Maaseik, Belg. 51°6′ N, 5°46′ E 167
Maastricht, Neth. 50°51′ N, 5°43′ E 167
Mababe Depression, Botswana 18°50′ S, 23°43′ E 224
Mabalane, Mozambique 23°48′ S, 32°39′ E 227
Ma'bar, Yemen 14°47′ N, 44°18′ E 182
Mabaruma, Guyana 8°12′ N, 59°43′ W 116
Mabel Lake, Can. 50°37′ N, 118°59′ W 90
Mabélé, Cameroon 6°0′ N, 13°58′ E 218
Mabenga, Dem. Rep. of the Congo 3°40′ S, 18°38′ E 218
Mabirou, Congo 1°8′ S, 15°45′ E 218
Mablethorpe, U.K. 53°19′ N, 0°15′ E 162
Mabote, Mozambique 22°2′ S, 34°8′ E 227
Mabroûk, spring, Mali 19°29′ N, 1°15′ W 222
Mabroûk, spring, Mauritania 17°58′ N, 12°20′ W 222
Mabrous, spring, Niger 21°17′ N, 13°34′ E 222
Mabruk, oil field, Lib. 29°45′ N, 17°7′ E 216
Mabuasehube Game Reserve, Botswana 25°21′ S, 21°41′ E 227
Mabuki, Tanzania 2°59′ S, 33°10′ E 224
Mac. Robertson Land, region, Antarctica 72°44′ S, 59°21′ E 248
Macachín, Arg. 37°10′ S, 63°41′ W 134
Macaé, Braz. 22°23′ S, 41°50′ W 138
Macaíba, Braz. 5°50′ S, 35°21′ W 132
Macaloge, Mozambique 12°29′ S, 35°26′ E 224
Macalpine Lake, Can. 66°32′ N, 105°59′ W 106
Maçambara, Braz. 29°7′ S, 56°4′ W 139
Macapá, Braz. 7°416′ N, 51°5′ W 130
Macapá, Braz. 9°31′ S, 67°30′ W 137
Macará, Ecua. 4°16′ S, 79°59′ W 130
Macaranay, Col. 0°55′ N, 72°10′ W 136
Macarani, Braz. 15°36′ S, 40°27′ W 138
Macareo, river, Venez. 9°9′ N, 61°55′ W 116
Macas, Ecua. 2°23′ S, 78°10′ W 136
Macau, Braz. 5°9′ S, 36°36′ W 132
Macau, China 22°10′ N, 113°31′ E 198
Macauã, river, Braz. 10°14′ S, 69°54′ W 137
Macaúba, Braz. 10°33′ S, 50°32′ W 130
Macaúbas, Braz. 13°1′ S, 42°42′ W 138
Macbride Head, East Falkland 51°29′ S, 57°44′ W 134
Macclenny, Fla., U.S. 30°16′ N, 82°7′ W 96
Macclesfield, U.K. 53°15′ N, 2°8′ W 162
Macdiarmid, Can. 49°27′ N, 88°6′ W 94
Macdill Air Force Base, Fla., U.S. 27°50′ N, 82°30′ W 105
Macdonnell Ranges, Austral. 23°31′ S, 131°40′ E 230
Macdui, Ben, peak, U.K. 57°3′ N, 3°46′ W 150
Macedonia 41°38′ N, 21°37′ E 168
Maceió, Braz. 9°36′ S, 35°42′ W 132
Macenta, Guinea 8°30′ N, 9°28′ W 222
Macerata, It. 43°18′ N, 13°26′ E 156
Macey, Mount, peak, Antarctica 69°58′ S, 64°49′ E 248
Macgillycuddy's Reeks, Ire. 51°43′ N, 10°50′ W 150
Macgregor, Can. 49°58′ N, 98°46′ W 90
Macha, Russ. 59°47′ N, 117°28′ E 160
Machacalis, Braz. 17°3′ S, 40°47′ W 138
Machacamarca, Bol. 18°12′ S, 67°5′ W 137
Machado, Braz. 21°40′ S, 45°54′ W 138
Machadodorp, S. Af. 25°43′ S, 30°11′ E 227
Machaerus, ruin(s), Jordan 31°33′ N, 35°36′ E 194
Machaíla, Mozambique 22°17′ S, 32°57′ E 227
Machakos, Kenya 1°32′ S, 37°15′ E 224
Machala, Ecua. 3°23′ S, 79°56′ W 130
Machalilla National Park, Ecua. 1°42′ S, 80°55′ W 122
Machaneng, Botswana 23°9′ S, 27°26′ E 227
Machanga, Mozambique 20°56′ S, 34°55′ E 227
Macharetí, Bol. 20°49′ S, 63°31′ W 137
Machault, Fr. 49°22′ N, 4°30′ E 163
Machawaian Lake, Can. 51°50′ N, 88°56′ W 110
Machaze, Mozambique 20°53′ S, 33°22′ E 227
Macheke, Zimb. 18°10′ S, 31°45′ E 224
Macheng, China 31°12′ N, 114°58′ E 198
Machero, peak, Sp. 39°19′ N, 4°22′ W 164
Machesney Park, Ill., U.S. 42°20′ N, 89°4′ W 102
Machghara, Leb. 33°31′ N, 35°38′ E 194
Machias, Me., U.S. 44°43′ N, 67°28′ W 94
Machiasport, Me., U.S. 44°41′ N, 67°25′ W 94
Machilipatnam (Bandar), India 16°11′ N, 81°10′ E 188
Machipongo, Va., U.S. 37°24′ N, 75°54′ W 94
Machiques, Venez. 10°1′ N, 72°34′ W 136
Machu Picchu, ruin(s), Peru 13°11′ S, 72°40′ W 137
Machupo, river, Bol. 13°10′ S, 64°44′ W 137
Machynlleth, U.K. 52°34′ N, 3°50′ W 162
Macia, Mozambique 25°1′ S, 33°7′ E 227
Macintyre, river, Austral. 28°52′ S, 148°46′ E 230
Macizo de la Maladeta, Sp. 42°29′ N, 0°38′ E 164
Mack, Colo., U.S. 39°13′ N, 108°53′ W 90
Mack Lake, Can. 58°1′ N, 95°56′ W 108
Maçka, Turk. 40°49′ N, 39°37′ E 195
Mackay, Austral. 21°15′ S, 149°7′ E 238
Mackay, Idaho, U.S. 43°54′ N, 113°37′ W 90
Mackay, river, Can. 56°45′ N, 112°13′ W 108
Mackenzie, Can. 55°21′ N, 123°3′ W 108
Mackenzie Bay 68°47′ N, 136°30′ W 98
Mackenzie Bay 68°37′ S, 67°9′ E 248
Mackenzie King Island, Can. 77°32′ N, 109°35′ W 106
Mackenzie Mountains, Can. 63°16′ N, 128°53′ W 108
Mackenzie, river, Can. 62°28′ N, 123°8′ W 106
Mackinaw City, Mich., U.S. 45°46′ N, 84°44′ W 94
Mackinnon, Cap, Can. 50°25′ N, 59°23′ W 111
Mackinnon Road, Kenya 3°44′ S, 39°2′ E 224
Mackintosh, Cape, Antarctica 72°59′ S, 59°28′ W 248
Macklin, Can. 52°20′ N, 109°58′ W 108
Mačkovci, Slov. 46°47′ N, 16°10′ E 168
Macksville, Kans., U.S. 37°57′ N, 98°58′ W 90
Maclear, S. Af. 31°6′ S, 28°19′ E 227
Maclovio Herrera, Mex. 28°58′ N, 105°7′ W 92
Maco, Philippines 7°24′ N, 125°49′ E 203
Macocola, Angola 6°60′ S, 16°7′ E 218
Macomb, Mo., U.S. 40°27′ N, 90°41′ W 94
Macomer, It. 40°16′ N, 8°46′ E 156
Macomia, Mozambique 12°12′ S, 40°8′ E 224
Macon, Ga., U.S. 32°48′ N, 83°38′ W 96
Macon, Ill., U.S. 39°42′ N, 88°60′ W 102
Macon, Miss., U.S. 33°5′ N, 88°33′ W 103
Macon, Mo., U.S. 39°43′ N, 92°28′ W 94
Macondo, Angola 12°38′ S, 23°46′ E 224
Macossa, Mozambique 17°55′ S, 33°55′ E 224
Macoun Lake, Can. 56°29′ N, 104°24′ W 108
Macovane, Mozambique 21°28′ S, 35°1′ E 227
Macquarie Island, Austral. 54°55′ S, 158°31′ E 255
Macquarie Ridge, South Pacific Ocean 52°33′ S, 160°15′ E 252
Macrae, Can. 60°37′ N, 134°56′ W 108
Macswyne's Gun, site, Ire. 55°10′ N, 8°7′ W 150
Macuapanim, Ilhas, islands, Braz. 3°8′ S, 66°19′ W 130
Macujer, Col. 0°23′ N, 73°7′ W 136
Macurijes, Punta, Cuba 20°56′ N, 79°8′ W 116
Macuro, Venez. 10°41′ N, 61°54′ W 116
Macururé, Braz. 9°13′ S, 39°5′ W 132
Macusani, Peru 14°4′ S, 70°27′ W 137
Macuze, Mozambique 17°44′ S, 37°13′ E 224
Ma'dabā, Jordan 31°42′ N, 35°47′ E 194
Madaba, Tanzania 8°38′ S, 37°45′ E 224
Madadi, Chad 18°29′ N, 20°43′ E 216
Madagascar 18°5′ S, 45°32′ E 220
Madagascar Basin, Indian Ocean 27°1′ S, 55°8′ E 254
Madagascar Plateau, Indian Ocean 30°16′ S, 46°6′ E 254
Madā'in Şāliḩ, Saudi Arabia 26°47′ N, 37°55′ E 180
Madaket, Mass., U.S. 41°15′ N, 70°12′ W 104
Madama, Niger 21°56′ N, 13°40′ E 216
Madang, P.N.G. 5°15′ S, 145°43′ E 238
Madaoua, Niger 14°5′ N, 5°55′ E 222
Madara, Bulg. 43°15′ N, 27°5′ E 156
Madaras, Hung. 46°2′ N, 19°16′ E 168
Madaripur, Bangladesh 23°11′ N, 90°11′ E 197
Madarounfa, Niger 13°19′ N, 7°4′ E 222
Madau, island, P.N.G. 8°54′ S, 152°10′ E 192
Madaure, ruin(s), Alg. 36°3′ N, 7°48′ E 156
Madaw, Turkm. 38°11′ N, 54°42′ E 180
Madayar, Myanmar 22°13′ N, 96°4′ E 202
Maddock, N. Dak., U.S. 47°56′ N, 99°32′ W 90
Madeira Islands, Portugal 33°23′ N, 18°12′ W 214
Madeira, river, Braz. 5°30′ S, 60°51′ W 122
Madeirinha, river, Braz. 9°56′ S, 61°3′ W 130
Madeleine, Îles de la, island, Can. 47°31′ N, 63°44′ W 106
Madelia, Minn., U.S. 44°2′ N, 94°25′ W 90
Maden, Turk. 38°22′ N, 39°40′ E 195
Madera, Calif., U.S. 36°57′ N, 120°4′ W 100
Madera, Mex. 29°11′ N, 108°10′ W 92
Madgaon, India 15°16′ N, 73°59′ E 188
Madhya Pradesh, adm. division, India 23°57′ N, 78°8′ E 197
Madi Opei, Uganda 3°35′ N, 33°4′ E 224
Madibira, Tanzania 8°16′ S, 34°47′ E 224
Madida, China 42°57′ N, 130°47′ E 200
Madidi, Bol. 13°21′ S, 68°37′ W 137
Madidi National Park, Bol. 14°46′ S, 68°6′ W 137
Madidi, river, Bol. 12°38′ S, 67°26′ W 137
Madill, Okla., U.S. 34°4′ N, 96°45′ W 92
Madimba, Dem. Rep. of the Congo 5°1′ S, 15°8′ E 218
Madina, Mali 13°24′ N, 8°52′ W 222
Madina do Boé, Guinea-Bissau 11°46′ N, 14°14′ W 222
Madīnat ash Sha'b, Yemen 12°52′ N, 44°52′ E 182
Madingo, Congo 4°6′ S, 11°21′ E 218
Madingou, Congo 4°12′ S, 13°31′ E 218
Madira, Nig. 12°38′ N, 6°29′ E 222
Madirovalo, Madagascar 16°26′ S, 46°31′ E 220
Madison, Fla., U.S. 30°26′ N, 83°25′ W 96
Madison, Ga., U.S. 33°34′ N, 83°28′ W 96
Madison, Ind., U.S. 38°44′ N, 85°23′ W 102
Madison, Kans., U.S. 38°6′ N, 96°9′ W 90
Madison, Me., U.S. 44°47′ N, 69°53′ W 94
Madison, Miss., U.S. 32°27′ N, 90°8′ W 103
Madison, Nebr., U.S. 41°48′ N, 97°28′ W 90
Madison, N.H., U.S. 43°53′ N, 71°10′ W 104
Madison, Ohio, U.S. 41°45′ N, 81°3′ W 102
Madison, S. Dak., U.S. 43°59′ N, 97°8′ W 90
Madison, W. Va., U.S. 38°3′ N, 81°50′ W 94
Madison, Wis., U.S. 43°4′ N, 89°27′ W 102
Madison Heights, Va., U.S. 37°25′ N, 79°8′ W 94
Madison Range, Mont., U.S. 45°12′ N, 111°48′ W 90
Madisonville, Ky., U.S. 37°19′ N, 87°31′ W 94
Madisonville, La., U.S. 30°23′ N, 90°10′ W 103
Madisonville, Tex., U.S. 30°55′ N, 95°55′ W 96
Madjori, Burkina Faso 11°27′ N, 1°12′ E 222
Madley, U.K. 52°2′ N, 2°52′ W 162
Madley, Mount, peak, Austral. 24°37′ S, 123°41′ E 230
Mado Gashi, Kenya 0°41′ N, 39°11′ E 224
Madoc, Can. 44°29′ N, 77°29′ W 94
Madocsa, Hung. 46°41′ N, 18°56′ E 168
Madoi, China 34°54′ N, 98°10′ E 188
Madona, Latv. 56°50′ N, 26°12′ E 166
Madras, Oreg., U.S. 44°37′ N, 121°8′ W 90
Madras see Chennai, India 13°5′ N, 80°16′ E 188
Madrasat Lukk, Lib. 32°0′ N, 24°43′ E 180
Madre de Dios, Peru 12°39′ S, 70°8′ W 137
Madre de Dios, adm. division, Peru 12°9′ S, 71°9′ W 137
Madre de Dios, Isla, island, Chile 50°5′ S, 77°46′ W 134
Madre de Dios, river, Bol. 11°52′ S, 68°3′ W 137
Madre de Dios, river, Peru 12°32′ S, 70°34′ W 137
Madre del Sur, Sierra, Mex. 18°15′ N, 101°45′ W 114
Madre, Laguna 25°6′ N, 97°56′ W 114
Madre Mountain, peak, N. Mex., U.S. 34°17′ N, 107°58′ W 92
Madre, Sierra, Guatemala 15°44′ N, 93°15′ W 115
Madre, Sierra, Philippines 16°12′ N, 121°14′ E 203
Madre, Sierra, Wyo., U.S. 41°4′ N, 106°60′ W 90
Madrid, Sp. 40°24′ N, 3°47′ W 164
Madrid, adm. division, Sp. 40°20′ N, 3°58′ W 164
Madrid, Punta, Chile 19°2′ S, 70°21′ W 137
Madridejos, Sp. 39°28′ N, 3°34′ W 164
Madrigalejo, Sp. 39°7′ N, 5°38′ W 164
Madrona, Sierra, Sp. 38°28′ N, 4°17′ W 164
Madsen, Can. 50°57′ N, 93°55′ W 90
Madura, island, Indonesia 6°59′ S, 113°19′ E 192
Madurai, India 9°54′ N, 78°4′ E 188
Maduru Oya National Park, Sri Lanka 7°25′ N, 80°46′ E 172
Madzha, Russ. 61°53′ N, 51°32′ E 154
Mae Chaem, Thai. 18°29′ N, 98°22′ E 202
Mae Hong Son, Thai. 19°18′ N, 97°56′ E 202
Mae Ping National Park, Thai. 17°23′ N, 98°20′ E 202
Mae Rim, Thai. 18°55′ N, 98°56′ E 202
Mae Sariang, Thai. 18°10′ N, 97°55′ E 202
Mae Sot, Thai. 16°42′ N, 98°31′ E 202
Mae Suai, Thai. 19°48′ N, 99°32′ E 202
Maebashi, Japan 36°23′ N, 139°4′ E 201
Maella, Sp. 41°7′ N, 0°7′ E 164
Maentwrog, U.K. 52°56′ N, 3°59′ W 162
Maeruş, Rom. 45°54′ N, 25°32′ E 156
Maesteg, U.K. 51°36′ N, 3°39′ W 162
Maestra, Sierra, Cuba 20°12′ N, 76°53′ W 115
Maevatanana, Madagascar 16°60′ S, 46°51′ E 220
Mafaza, Sudan 13°35′ N, 34°32′ E 182
Mafeking, Can. 52°41′ N, 101°9′ W 108
Mafeteng, Lesotho 29°50′ S, 27°14′ E 227
Mafia Island, Tanzania 8°11′ S, 39°52′ E 224
Mafikeng, S. Af. 25°51′ S, 25°36′ E 227
Mafra, Braz. 26°9′ S, 49°50′ W 138
Magadan, Russ. 59°36′ N, 150°33′ E 160
Magadan, adm. division, Russ. 61°8′ N, 149°18′ E 160
Magadi, Kenya 1°53′ S, 36°21′ E 224
Magal Umm Rûs, spring, Egypt 25°28′ N, 34°35′ E 180
Magallanes, Philippines 12°49′ N, 123°51′ E 203
Magallanes Y Antártica Chilena, adm. division, Chile 49°4′ S, 76°47′ W 134
Magangué, Col. 9°13′ N, 74°47′ W 130
Magaria, Niger 12°57′ N, 8°54′ E 222
Magazine Mountain, peak, Ark., U.S. 35°7′ N, 93°43′ W 96
Magdagachi, Russ. 53°29′ N, 125°48′ E 190
Magdalena, Arg. 35°4′ S, 57°33′ W 139
Magdalena, Bol. 13°21′ S, 64°11′ W 137
Magdalena, Mex. 20°54′ N, 103°58′ W 114
Magdalena, Mex. 30°37′ N, 110°59′ W 92
Magdalena, N. Mex., U.S. 34°6′ N, 107°15′ W 92
Magdalena, adm. division, Col. 10°33′ N, 74°45′ W 136
Magdalena, Bahía 24°32′ N, 112°50′ W 112
Magdalena, Isla, island, Mex. 25°20′ N, 113°13′ W 112
Magdalena, Llano de la, Mex. 24°13′ N, 111°25′ W 112
Magdalena, river, Mex. 30°32′ N, 112°42′ W 92
Magdeburg, Ger. 52°7′ N, 11°37′ E 152
Magdelaine Cays, islands, Coral Sea 17°5′ S, 150°25′ E 230
Magee, Miss., U.S. 31°52′ N, 89°42′ W 103
Magee Island, U.K. 54°45′ N, 6°12′ W 150
Magellan Seamounts, North Pacific Ocean 15°24′ N, 154°39′ E 252
Magellan, Straits of 52°41′ S, 72°44′ W 122
Magenta, It. 45°27′ N, 8°53′ E 167
Magerøya, island, Nor. 71°11′ N, 21°17′ E 160
Maggie Mountain, peak, Calif., U.S. 36°16′ N, 118°39′ W 101
Maggiorasca, Monte, peak, It. 44°32′ N, 9°27′ E 167
Maghâgha, Egypt 28°38′ N, 30°48′ E 182
Maghama, Mauritania 15°30′ N, 12°55′ W 222
Magid, oil field, Lib. 28°15′ N, 22°8′ E 216

Magilligan Point, U.K. 54°58' N, 6°57' W 150
Magina, peak, Sp. 37°43' N, 3°29' W 164
Magione, It. 43°8' N, 12°12' E 156
Magistral, Mex. 25°57' N, 105°21' W 114
Maglaj, Bosn. and Herzg. 44°33' N, 18°5' E 168
Maglie, It. 40°7' N, 18°17' E 156
Magnetic Island National Park, Austral. 19°14' S, 146°30' E 238
Magnitka, Russ. 55°20' N, 59°44' E 154
Magnitogorsk, Russ. 53°26' N, 59°8' E 154
Magnolia, Ark., U.S. 33°15' N, 93°15' W 103
Magnolia, Ill., U.S. 41°6' N, 89°12' W 102
Magnolia, Miss., U.S. 31°7' N, 90°29' W 103
Magnor, Nor. 59°57' N, 12°11' E 152
Mago National Park, Eth. 5°21' N, 35°30' E 224
Magog, Can. 45°15' N, 72°9' W 111
Magosal, Mex. 21°37' N, 97°59' W 114
Magpie, Can. 50°19' N, 64°30' W 111
Magpie, river, Can. 50°54' N, 64°47' W 111
Magrath, Can. 49°25' N, 112°52' W 90
Magruder Mountain, peak, Nev., U.S. 37°24' N, 117°38' W 92
Maguan, China 22°59' N, 104°23' E 202
Maguari, Cabo, Braz. 0°28' N, 49°15' W 130
Maguarichic, Mex. 27°51' N, 107°58' W 112
Magude, Mozambique 24°60' S, 32°37' E 227
Magué, Mozambique 15°50' S, 31°43' E 224
Maguire, Mount, peak, Antarctica 74°5' S, 66°32' E 248
Magumeri, Nig. 12°6' N, 12°50' E 216
Magwa Falls, S. Af. 31°14' S, 28°52' E 227
Magwa, oil field, Kuwait 29°3' N, 47°52' E 196
Magway, Myanmar 20°9' N, 94°57' E 202
Mahābād, Iran 36°45' N, 45°41' E 195
Mahabo, Madagascar 20°21' S, 44°38' E 220
Mahagi, Dem. Rep. of the Congo 2°15' N, 30°59' E 224
Mahajanga, Madagascar 15°42' S, 46°20' E 220
Mahalapye, Botswana 23°4' S, 26°46' E 227
Mahale Mountain National Park, Tanzania 6°26' S, 29°29' E 224
Maḩallāt, Iran 33°56' N, 50°24' E 180
Mahanadi, river, India 20°55' N, 84°19' E 190
Mahanoro, Madagascar 19°52' S, 48°46' E 220
Mahanoy City, Pa., U.S. 40°48' N, 76°9' W 94
Mahao, China 43°11' N, 128°2' E 200
Maharajganj, India 27°7' N, 83°32' E 197
Maharashtra, adm. division, India 19°35' N, 73°17' E 188
Mahasthan, ruin(s), Bangladesh 24°54' N, 89°13' E 197
Mahavelona, Madagascar 17°40' S, 49°28' E 220
Mahbubnagar, India 16°43' N, 77°57' E 188
Mahd adh Dhahab, Saudi Arabia 23°26' N, 40°53' E 182
Mahdere Maryam, Eth. 11°41' N, 37°53' E 182
Mahdia, Guyana 5°14' N, 59°16' W 130
Mahdia, Tun. 35°31' N, 11°1' E 156
Mahendra Giri, peak, India 18°58' N, 84°11' E 188
Mahenge, Tanzania 8°39' S, 36°42' E 224
Maheno, N.Z. 45°12' S, 170°49' E 240
Mahesana, India 23°33' N, 72°24' E 186
Maheshwar, India 22°11' N, 75°34' E 197
Mahewa, India 24°23' N, 80°10' E 197
Mahi, river, India 23°6' N, 73°41' E 186
Mahia Peninsula, N.Z. 39°7' S, 177°45' E 240
Mahilyow, Belarus 53°57' N, 30°21' E 154
Mahim, India 19°39' N, 72°45' E 188
Mahin, Nig. 6°16' N, 4°45' E 222
Mahires, Tun. 34°34' N, 10°31' E 156
Mahlberg, Ger. 48°17' N, 7°48' E 163
Mahmudiye, Turk. 39°30' N, 30°58' E 156
Mahnomen, Minn., U.S. 47°18' N, 95°58' W 90
Maho, Sri Lanka 7°50' N, 80°17' E 188
Mahoba, India 25°17' N, 79°51' E 197
Mahogany Hills, Nev., U.S. 39°26' N, 116°21' W 90
Mahogany Mountain, peak, Oreg., U.S. 43°13' N, 117°21' W 90
Mahomet, Ill., U.S. 40°10' N, 88°24' W 102
Mahón, Sp. 39°54' N, 4°14' E 143
Mahopac, N.Y., U.S. 41°22' N, 73°44' W 104
Mahora, Sp. 39°12' N, 1°44' W 164
Mahuta, Tanzania 10°53' S, 39°25' E 224
Mahuva, India 21°4' N, 71°45' E 188
Maials, Sp. 41°22' N, 0°30' E 164
Maicao, Col. 11°21' N, 72°15' W 136
Maicasagi, Lac, lake, Can. 49°53' N, 77°19' W 94
Maicasagi, river, Can. 49°59' N, 76°54' W 110
Maiden Castle, ruin(s), U.K. 50°40' N, 2°37' W 150
Maidenhead, U.K. 51°31' N, 0°44' E 162
Maidstone, Can. 53°5' N, 109°17' W 108
Maidstone, U.K. 51°16' N, 0°31' E 162
Maiduguri, Nig. 11°51' N, 13°9' E 216
Maigualida, Sierra, Venez. 5°34' N, 65°28' W 130
Maihar, India 24°15' N, 80°44' E 197
Maiko National Park, Dem. Rep. of the Congo 0°35' N, 27°15' E 224
Maiko, river, Dem. Rep. of the Congo 0°20' N, 26°51' E 224
Maikona, Kenya 2°53' N, 37°30' E 224
Mailsi, Pak. 29°48' N, 72°11' E 186
Main Centre, Can. 50°35' N, 107°22' W 90
Main Channel 45°19' N, 82°17' W 110
Main Pass 29°20' N, 89°20' W 103
Main, river, Ger. 49°59' N, 10°12' E 167
Maine, adm. division, Me., U.S. 45°16' N, 69°59' W 94
Maine, Gulf of 43°8' N, 67°56' W 253
Maine, Gulf of 44°10' N, 69°15' W 94
Maine, region, Fr. 48°25' N, 0°48' E 163
Maïné Soroa, Niger 13°14' N, 12°3' E 222
Maingkwan, Myanmar 26°20' N, 96°35' E 188
Mainit, Lake, Philippines 9°25' N, 125°15' E 203
Mainland, island, U.K. 59°44' N, 0°54' E 142
Mainling, China 29°12' N, 94°6' E 188
Mainpuri, India 27°12' N, 79°1' E 197
Maintal, Ger. 50°9' N, 8°49' E 167
Maintenon, Fr. 48°34' N, 1°34' E 163
Maintirano, Madagascar 18°4' S, 44°1' E 220
Mainz, Ger. 49°59' N, 8°15' E 167
Maipo, Paso de, pass, Chile 34°15' S, 69°52' W 134
Maipú, Arg. 36°52' S, 57°53' W 139
Maipures, Col. 5°8' N, 67°51' W 136
Maisí, Punta de, Cuba 20°14' N, 74°6' W 116
Maiskhal, island, Bangladesh 21°23' N, 90°54' E 188
Maisou Island, Mich., U.S. 43°46' N, 83°45' W 102
Maisse, Fr. 48°23' N, 2°22' E 163
Maitengwe, Botswana 20°8' S, 27°10' E 227
Maitri, India, station, Antarctica 70°37' S, 11°36' E 248
Maíz Grande, Isla del (Great Corn Island), Nicar. 11°44' N, 83°2' W 115
Maizhokunggar, China 29°52' N, 91°45' E 197
Maizières, Fr. 49°12' N, 6°9' E 163
Maizuru, Japan 35°24' N, 135°19' E 201
Majagual, Col. 8°33' N, 74°37' W 136
Majahual, Mex. 18°45' N, 87°45' W 115
Majdal Shams, Israel 33°16' N, 35°46' E 194
Majdanpek, Serb. and Mont. 44°24' N, 21°56' E 168
Majene, Indonesia 3°29' S, 118°54' E 192
Majevica, Bosn. and Herzg. 44°42' N, 18°31' E 168
Majī, Eth. 6°12' N, 35°37' E 224
Majorca see Mallorca, island, Sp. 39°38' N, 2°37' E 150
Majske Poljane, Croatia 45°19' N, 16°8' E 168
Majuro, Marshall Islands 7°5' N, 171°22' E 242
Majuro Atoll, Marshall Islands 7°7' N, 171°10' E 242
Mak, Ko, island, Thai. 11°40' N, 101°58' E 202
Maka, Senegal 13°40' N, 14°20' W 222
Makabana, Congo 3°30' S, 12°36' E 218
Makaha, Zimb. 17°20' S, 32°34' E 224
Makalamabedi, Botswana 20°20' S, 23°48' E 227
Makaleha Mountains, peak, Hawai'i, U.S. 22°6' N, 159°28' W 99
Makalu, peak, Nepal 27°52' N, 87°2' E 197
Makalu-Barun National Park, Nepal 27°29' N, 86°21' E 197
Makandja, Dem. Rep. of the Congo 0°46' N, 23°14' E 218
Makanya, Tanzania 4°22' S, 37°49' E 224
Makanza, Dem. Rep. of the Congo 1°35' N, 19°4' E 218
Makarfi, Nig. 11°19' N, 7°53' E 222
Makari, Cameroon 12°36' N, 14°29' E 216
Makarikha, Russ. 66°13' N, 58°23' E 169
Makarov, Russ. 48°34' N, 142°40' E 190
Makarov Basin, Arctic Ocean 87°7' N, 170°10' W 255
Makarska, Croatia 43°17' N, 17°1' E 168
Makar'yev, Russ. 57°53' N, 43°46' E 154
Makassar see Ujungpandang, Indonesia 5°11' S, 119°25' E 192
Makassar Strait 1°31' S, 117°0' E 192
Makeni, Sierra Leone 8°54' N, 12°4' W 222
Maketu, N.Z. 37°48' S, 176°26' E 240
Makgadikgadi Pans Game Reserve, Botswana 20°54' S, 24°49' E 227
Makhachkala, Russ. 42°55' N, 47°35' E 195
Makhad, Pak. 33°8' N, 71°46' E 186
Makhado (Louis Trichardt), S. Af. 23°3' S, 29°53' E 227
Makhambet, Kaz. 47°40' N, 51°33' E 158
Makhana, Senegal 16°8' N, 16°26' W 222
Makhfar al Buşayyah, Iraq 30°6' N, 46°5' E 196
Makhnovka, Russ. 57°25' N, 29°20' E 166
Makikihi, N.Z. 44°39' S, 171°8' E 240
Makindu, Kenya 2°19' S, 37°49' E 224
Makinsk, Kaz. 52°39' N, 70°25' E 184
Makiyivka, Ukr. 48°2' N, 37°59' E 158
Makkah (Mecca), Saudi Arabia 21°24' N, 39°49' E 182
Makkovik, Can. 54°59' N, 59°10' W 106
Makó, Hung. 46°13' N, 20°29' E 168
Mako, Senegal 12°53' N, 12°24' W 222
Makoino, Madagascar 16°21' S, 48°11' E 220
Makok, Gabon 1°59' S, 9°36' E 218
Makokibatan Lake, Can. 51°14' N, 88°52' W 80
Makokou, Gabon 0°31' N, 12°48' E 218
Mākole'ā Point, Hawai'i, U.S. 19°47' N, 156°31' W 99
Makoli, Zambia 17°28' S, 26°3' E 224
Makongolosi, Tanzania 8°25' S, 33°10' E 224
Makrai, India 22°6' N, 77°6' E 197
Makrana, India 27°1' N, 74°43' E 186
Maksatikha, Russ. 57°44' N, 35°52' E 154
Maksimkin Yar, Russ. 58°42' N, 86°50' E 169
Maktau, Kenya 3°27' S, 38°6' E 224
Mākū, Iran 39°20' N, 44°31' E 195
Makumbako, Tanzania 8°50' S, 34°49' E 224
Makung, Taiwan 23°31' N, 119°34' E 198
Makungo, Somalia 0°48' N, 42°33' E 224
Makunudu Atoll, Maldives 5°26' N, 67°51' E 172
Makurazaki, Japan 31°15' N, 130°18' E 201
Makurdi, Nig. 7°41' N, 8°33' E 222
Makushin Volcano, peak, Alas., U.S. 53°51' N, 167°3' W 98
Makushino, Russ. 55°12' N, 67°14' E 184
Mal, Mauritania 16°59' N, 13°25' W 222
Malá, Sp. 37°6' N, 3°43' W 164
Mala, Punta, Pan. 7°24' N, 79°59' W 115
Mala Vyska, Ukr. 48°39' N, 31°39' E 158
Malabang, Philippines 7°39' N, 124°6' E 203
Malabo, Equatorial Guinea 3°45' N, 8°40' E 222
Malabuñgan, Philippines 9°2' N, 117°40' E 203
Malacca, Malaysia 2°13' N, 102°16' E 196
Malacca, Strait of 6°12' N, 97°6' E 196
Malad City, Idaho, U.S. 42°11' N, 112°14' W 82
Maladzyechna, Belarus 54°18' N, 26°50' E 166
Malaga, Calif., U.S. 36°40' N, 119°45' W 100
Málaga, Col. 6°41' N, 72°45' W 136
Malaga, N. Mex., U.S. 32°13' N, 104°4' W 92
Málaga, Sp. 36°42' N, 4°27' W 164
Málaga, Sp. 36°45' N, 4°28' W 214
Malagarasi, Tanzania 5°6' S, 30°51' E 224
Malagón, Sp. 39°10' N, 3°51' W 164
Malaita, island, Solomon Islands 9°0' S, 161°0' E 242
Malakal, Sudan 9°32' N, 31°45' E 224
Malakoff, Tex., U.S. 32°9' N, 96°1' W 96
Malalbergo, It. 44°44' N, 11°32' E 167
Malampaya Sound 10°55' N, 118°41' E 203
Malang, Indonesia 8°2' S, 112°27' E 192
Malangali, Tanzania 8°35' S, 34°52' E 224
Malangen, Nor. 69°23' N, 18°37' E 152
Malanje, Angola 9°34' S, 16°13' E 218
Malanje, adm. division, Angola 8°41' S, 15°42' E 218
Malanville, Benin 11°51' N, 3°23' E 222
Malargüe, Arg. 35°27' S, 69°36' W 134
Malartic, Can. 48°8' N, 78°9' W 94
Malaryta, Belarus 51°46' N, 24°2' E 154
Malaspina Glacier, Alas., U.S. 59°14' N, 143°10' W 106
Malatya, Turk. 38°20' N, 38°17' E 180
Malavate, South America 3°16' N, 54°6' W 130
Malawi 13°0' S, 34°0' E 224
Malawiya, Sudan 15°13' N, 36°12' E 182
Malay Peninsula, Malaysia 7°4' N, 99°57' E 196
Malaya Vishera, Russ. 58°48' N, 32°20' E 154
Malayagiri, peak, India 21°21' N, 85°8' E 188
Malaybalay, Philippines 8°12' N, 125°8' E 203
Malāyer, Iran 34°17' N, 48°51' E 180
Malaysia 2°20' N, 112°47' E 192
Malazgirt, Turk. 39°8' N, 42°30' E 195
Malbaza, Niger 13°58' N, 5°39' E 222
Malbork, Pol. 54°1' N, 19°2' E 166
Malbrán, Arg. 29°21' S, 62°27' W 139
Mal'chevskaya, Russ. 49°2' N, 40°21' E 158
Malden, Ill., U.S. 41°25' N, 89°22' W 102
Malden, Mo., U.S. 36°33' N, 89°58' W 94
Maldive Islands, Arabian Sea 1°14' N, 72°26' E 188
Maldives, Maldives 2°12' N, 74°34' E 188
Maldon, U.K. 51°43' N, 0°40' E 162
Maldonado, Uru. 34°53' S, 54°59' W 139
Maldonado, Punta, Mex. 15°32' N, 103°13' W 72
Malè, It. 46°20' N, 10°55' E 167
Male Atoll, Maldives 4°29' N, 73°0' E 188
Malé Karpaty, Slovakia 48°25' N, 17°3' E 152
Male see Maale, Maldives 4°9' N, 73°15' E 188
Malegaon, India 20°33' N, 74°33' E 188
Maléha, Guinea 11°50' N, 9°44' W 222
Malek, Sudan 6°2' N, 31°38' E 224
Malela, Dem. Rep. of the Congo 2°26' S, 26°7' E 224
Malela, Dem. Rep. of the Congo 4°23' S, 26°8' E 224
Malemba-Nkulu, Dem. Rep. of the Congo 8°1' S, 26°46' E 224
Malembé, Congo 3°5' S, 12°2' E 218
Malengoia, Dem. Rep. of the Congo 3°26' N, 25°24' E 224
Maler Kotla, India 30°31' N, 75°55' E 197
Maleševske Planina, Maced. 41°38' N, 22°40' E 168
Malesherbes, Fr. 48°16' N, 2°23' E 163
Maleza, Col. 4°22' N, 69°25' W 136
Malfa, It. 38°34' N, 14°49' E 156
Malgobek, Russ. 43°30' N, 44°33' E 195
Malgrat de Mar, Sp. 41°38' N, 2°44' E 164
Malha, spring, Sudan 15°4' N, 26°9' E 226
Malhada, Braz. 14°20' S, 43°48' W 138
Malhão, Serra do, Port. 37°24' N, 8°28' W 150
Malheur Cave, site, Oreg., U.S. 43°13' N, 118°28' W 90
Mali, Guinea 12°6' N, 12°20' W 222
Mali 18°26' N, 1°60' W 214
Mali Drvenik, island, Croatia 43°20' N, 15°55' E 168
Mali Kyun, island, Myanmar 13°17' N, 98°7' E 202
Mali Lošinj, Croatia 44°32' N, 14°27' E 156
Mali, river, Myanmar 25°18' N, 97°11' E 188
Malibu, Calif., U.S. 34°2' N, 118°43' W 101
Målilla, Nor. 57°22' N, 15°48' E 152
Malimba, Monts, Dem. Rep. of the Congo 7°41' S, 29°8' E 224
Malinau, Indonesia 3°41' N, 116°30' E 192
Malindi, Kenya 3°13' S, 40°6' E 224
Malinyi, Tanzania 8°57' S, 35°59' E 224
Malipo, China 23°5' N, 104°42' E 202
Mališevo, Europe 42°32' N, 20°43' E 168
Maljen, Serb. and Mont. 44°9' N, 19°56' E 168
Malka Mari National Park, Kenya 3°54' N, 40°5' E 224
Malkaaray, Somalia 3°54' N, 41°53' E 224
Malkara, Turk. 40°53' N, 26°53' E 156
Malki, Russ. 53°31' N, 157°39' E 160
Malko Tŭrnovo, Bulg. 41°59' N, 27°31' E 156
Mal'kovichi, Belarus 52°31' N, 26°35' E 152
Mallāḩ, Syr. 32°30' N, 36°50' E 194
Mallaoua, Niger 13°2' N, 9°36' E 222
Mallawi, Egypt 27°46' N, 30°46' E 180
Mallén, Sp. 41°52' N, 1°26' W 164
Malles Venosta, It. 46°42' N, 10°33' E 167
Mallet, Braz. 25°55' S, 50°52' W 138
Malletts Bay, Vt., U.S. 44°32' N, 73°14' W 104
Małkinia Górna, Pol. 53°0' N, 22°0' E 152
Mallorca (Majorca), island, Sp. 39°38' N, 2°37' E 150
Mallory Swamp, marsh, Fla., U.S. 29°42' N, 83°17' W 105
Malm, Nor. 64°4' N, 11°12' E 152
Malmédy, Belg. 50°26' N, 6°1' E 167
Malmesbury, S. Af. 33°28' S, 18°41' E 227
Malmesbury, U.K. 51°35' N, 2°6' W 162
Malmö, Nor. 55°35' N, 12°59' E 152
Malmstrom Air Force Base, Mont., U.S. 47°28' N, 111°16' W 90
Maloarkhangel'sk, Russ. 52°21' N, 36°30' E 158
Maloca, Braz. 0°42' N, 55°58' W 130
Maloca, Braz. 10°49' S, 70°9' W 137
Maloca de Índios, Braz. 11°42' S, 58°16' W 130
Maloca Timbé, Braz. 3°3' S, 47°45' W 130
Maloja, Switz. 46°26' N, 9°42' E 167
Malole, Zambia 10°8' S, 31°33' E 224
Malo-les-Bains, Fr. 51°1' N, 2°25' E 163
Malolos, Philippines 14°49' N, 120°47' E 203
Malombe, Lake, Malawi 14°40' S, 34°54' E 224
Malone, N.Y., U.S. 44°50' N, 74°19' W 94
Malone, Wash., U.S. 46°56' N, 123°20' W 100
Malonga, Dem. Rep. of the Congo 10°26' S, 23°9' E 220
Malongwe, Tanzania 5°24' S, 33°39' E 224
Malorad, Bulg. 43°29' N, 23°40' E 156
Maloshuyka, Russ. 63°44' N, 37°28' E 154
Malouin, river, Can. 50°9' N, 79°11' W 110
Mal'ovitsa, peak, Bulg. 42°9' N, 23°16' E 156
Måløy, Nor. 61°56' N, 5°6' E 152
Maloyaz, Russ. 55°13' N, 58°11' E 154
Malpas, U.K. 53°1' N, 2°46' W 162
Malpeque Bay 46°28' N, 64°26' W 111
Malpura, India 26°16' N, 75°23' E 197
Malta, Idaho, U.S. 42°19' N, 113°23' W 90
Malta, Ill., U.S. 41°55' N, 88°52' W 102
Malta, Latv. 56°19' N, 27°8' E 166
Malta, Malta 35°56' N, 14°26' E 156
Malta, Mont., U.S. 48°20' N, 107°53' W 90
Malta, Ohio, U.S. 39°38' N, 81°53' W 102
Malta Channel 36°15' N, 14°16' E 156
Malta, island, Malta 35°56' N, 14°26' E 156
Malta, river, Latv. 56°26' N, 26°47' E 166
Maltahöhe, Namibia 24°50' S, 16°56' E 227
Maltby, U.K. 53°25' N, 1°13' W 162
Maltese Islands, Malta 35°30' N, 14°3' E 156
Malton, U.K. 54°8' N, 0°48' E 162
Ma'lūlā, Syr. 33°50' N, 36°32' E 194
Malumfashi, Nig. 11°46' N, 7°37' E 222
Malvan, India 16°4' N, 73°29' E 188
Malvern, Ark., U.S. 34°20' N, 92°50' W 96
Malvern, Iowa, U.S. 41°0' N, 95°35' W 90
Malvern, U.K. 52°6' N, 2°20' W 162
Malvinas, Islas see Falkland Islands, Falk. Is., U.K. 53°40' S, 58°56' W 134
Malybay, Kaz. 43°30' N, 78°30' E 184
Malyn, Ukr. 50°47' N, 29°23' E 158
Malyns'k, Ukr. 51°4' N, 26°32' E 152
Malyy Anyuy, river, Russ. 67°32' N, 168°13' E 246
Malyy Atlym, Russ. 62°19' N, 67°4' E 169
Malyy Lyakhovskiy, Ostrov, island, Russ. 74°11' N, 150°36' E 246
Malyy, Ostrov, island, Russ. 60°3' N, 28°0' E 166
Malyy Tyuters, Ostrov, island, Russ. 59°37' N, 26°44' E 166
Malyye Derbety, Russ. 47°56' N, 44°34' E 158
Malyye Karmakuly, Russ. 72°15' N, 52°58' E 160
Mama, Russ. 58°17' N, 112°55' E 160
Mamadysh, Russ. 55°42' N, 51°16' E 154
Maman, Sudan 16°20' N, 36°46' E 182
Mambajao, Philippines 9°15' N, 124°44' E 203
Mambali, Tanzania 4°33' S, 32°40' E 224
Mambasa, Dem. Rep. of the Congo 1°19' N, 29°3' E 224
Mamboya, Tanzania 6°15' S, 37°9' E 224
Mambrui, Kenya 3°7' S, 40°8' E 224
Mamburao, Philippines 13°15' N, 120°36' E 203
Mamfé, Cameroon 5°43' N, 9°17' E 222
Mamiña, Chile 20°3' S, 69°15' W 137
Maminas, Alban. 41°23' N, 19°36' E 156
Mammamattawa, Can. 50°27' N, 84°23' W 94
Mammoth Cave National Park, Ky., U.S. 37°17' N, 88°6' W 80
Mamonovo, Russ. 54°27' N, 19°54' E 166
Mamoré, river, Bol. 13°52' S, 65°11' W 137
Mamori, Lago, lake, Braz. 3°39' S, 60°46' W 130
Mamoriá, Braz. 7°34' S, 66°20' W 130
Mamoriá, river, Braz. 7°16' S, 67°19' W 130
Mamou, Guinea 10°23' N, 12°7' W 222
Mamou, La., U.S. 30°37' N, 92°26' W 103
Mampikony, Madagascar 16°5' S, 47°39' E 220
Mampong, Ghana 7°5' N, 1°26' W 222
Mamshit, ruin(s), Israel 31°0' N, 35°1' E 194
Mamuju, Indonesia 2°43' S, 118°47' E 192
Mamuno, Botswana 22°11' S, 20°2' E 227
Mamuras, Alban. 41°35' N, 19°40' E 168
Man, Côte d'Ivoire 7°18' N, 7°34' W 222
Man Aung, Myanmar 18°51' N, 93°46' E 188
Man, Isle of 54°17' N, 4°55' W 150
Man of War Point, Can. 54°25' N, 58°25' W 111
Man, river, China 42°10' N, 127°23' E 200
Mānā, Hawai'i, U.S. 22°2' N, 159°47' W 99
Mana, South America 5°40' N, 53°50' W 130
Mana La, pass, India 31°4' N, 79°25' E 197
Mana Pools National Park, Zimb. 16°11' S, 28°55' E 224
Manacacías, river, Col. 3°42' N, 72°26' W 136
Manacapuru, Braz. 3°19' S, 60°36' W 130
Manacor, Sp. 39°34' N, 3°11' E 214
Manado, Indonesia 1°30' N, 124°42' E 192
Managua, Nicar. 12°3' N, 86°24' W 115
Managua, Lago de, lake, Nicar. 12°14' N, 87°5' W 116
Manaia, N.Z. 39°34' S, 174°7' E 240
Manakara, Madagascar 22°15' S, 48°2' E 207
Manakau, peak, N.Z. 42°15' S, 173°32' E 240
Manākhah, Yemen 15°2' N, 43°44' E 182
Manam, island, P.N.G. 4°16' S, 145°8' E 192
Manama see Al Manāmah, Bahrain 26°10' N, 50°27' E 196
Manambolo, river, Madagascar 19°6' S, 43°47' E 220
Manankoro, Mali 10°30' N, 7°27' W 222
Manantenina, Madagascar 24°20' S, 47°20' E 220
Manantiales, Chile 52°46' S, 69°16' W 123
Manapouri, N.Z. 45°36' S, 167°39' E 240
Manapouri, Lake, N.Z. 45°31' S, 166°52' E 240
Manas, China 44°16' N, 86°16' E 184
Manas Hu, lake, China 45°38' N, 85°18' E 184
Manassa, Colo., U.S. 37°9' N, 105°57' W 92
Manassas National Battlefield Park, Va., U.S. 38°48' N, 77°37' W 94
Manatee, river, Fla., U.S. 27°25' N, 82°11' W 105
Manaus, Braz. 3°5' S, 60°1' W 130
Manavgat, Turk. 36°45' N, 31°26' E 180
Manay, Philippines 7°14' N, 126°32' E 203
Manbazar, India 23°4' N, 86°39' E 197
Mancha Real, Sp. 37°47' N, 3°37' W 164
Manchester, Conn., U.S. 41°46' N, 72°32' W 104
Manchester, Iowa, U.S. 42°29' N, 91°28' W 94
Manchester, Ky., U.S. 37°9' N, 83°47' W 96
Manchester, Me., U.S. 44°19' N, 69°52' W 104
Manchester, Mich., U.S. 42°9' N, 84°2' W 102
Manchester, N.H., U.S. 42°59' N, 71°28' W 104
Manchester, Ohio, U.S. 40°55' N, 81°34' W 102
Manchester, Tenn., U.S. 35°28' N, 86°5' W 96
Manchester, U.K. 53°28' N, 2°16' W 162
Manchester, Vt., U.S. 43°9' N, 73°5' W 104
Manchester Center, Vt., U.S. 43°10' N, 73°4' W 104
Manchester Lake, Can. 61°24' N, 108°30' W 108
Manchuria see Dongbei, region 40°34' N, 122°39' E 200
Mancos, Colo., U.S. 37°20' N, 108°18' W 92
Mand, Pak. 26°1' N, 62°7' E 182
Mand, river, Iran 28°19' N, 51°45' E 196
Manda, Tanzania 7°58' S, 32°26' E 224
Manda, Tanzania 10°29' S, 34°35' E 224
Manda Island, Kenya 2°24' S, 40°58' E 224
Manda National Park, Chad 9°9' N, 17°26' E 216
Mandab, Bāb al 12°28' N, 42°51' E 182
Mandabe, Madagascar 21°3' S, 44°54' E 220
Mandaguari, Braz. 23°31' S, 51°49' W 138
Mandal, Mongolia 48°26' N, 106°42' E 198
Mandal, Nor. 58°1' N, 7°30' E 150
Mandala, Puncak, peak, Indonesia 4°42' S, 140°2' E 192
Mandalay, Myanmar 21°58' N, 96°7' E 202
Mandalgovĭ, Mongolia 45°47' N, 106°16' E 198
Mandalī, Iraq 33°45' N, 45°31' E 180
Mandan, N. Dak., U.S. 46°49' N, 100°54' W 90
Mandara Mountains, Cameroon 9°18' N, 12°57' E 216
Mandau, river, Indonesia 1°7' N, 101°17' E 196
Mandel, Afghan. 33°19' N, 61°52' E 186
Mandera, Tanzania 6°10' S, 38°23' E 224
Manderfield, Utah, U.S. 38°21' N, 112°39' W 90
Manderscheid, Ger. 50°5' N, 6°48' E 167
Mandeville, La., U.S. 30°21' N, 90°5' W 103
Mandi, Nepal 31°41' N, 76°56' E 188
Mandiana, Guinea 10°40' N, 8°42' W 222
Mandie, Mozambique 16°30' S, 33°33' E 224
Mandimba, Mozambique 14°22' S, 35°40' E 224
Mandjafa, Chad 11°13' N, 15°26' E 216
Mandla, India 22°38' N, 80°22' E 197
Mandor, Indonesia 0°19' N, 109°18' E 196
Mandoto, Madagascar 19°38' S, 46°19' E 220
Mandráki, Gr. 36°36' N, 27°8' E 156
Mandu, island, Maldives 3°19' N, 72°0' E 188
Mandvi, India 22°50' N, 69°21' E 186
Manevichi, Ukr. 51°17' N, 25°31' E 152
Manfalūt, Egypt 27°19' N, 30°52' E 180
Manfredonia, Golfo di 41°29' N, 15°9' E 156
Manga, Braz. 14°49' S, 43°58' W 138
Manga, Burkina Faso 11°40' N, 1°6' W 222
Manga, Mozambique 19°46' S, 34°55' E 224
Manga, region, Niger 14°17' N, 11°19' E 222
Mangabeiras, Chapada das, Braz. 9°35' S, 46°50' W 130
Mangai, Dem. Rep. of the Congo 4°4' S, 19°29' E 218
Mangaia, island, N.Z. 21°52' S, 157°57' W 252
Mangaïzé, Niger 14°54' N, 2°6' E 222
Mangalia, Rom. 43°49' N, 28°32' E 156
Mangalmé, Chad 12°24' N, 19°37' E 216
Mangalore, India 12°52' N, 74°52' E 188
Mangamuka, N.Z. 35°13' S, 173°31' E 240
Mangando, Angola 8°4' S, 17°6' E 218
Mangawan, India 24°42' N, 81°31' E 197
Mangaweka, N.Z. 39°50' S, 175°46' E 240
Mangeigne, Chad 10°31' N, 21°16' E 216
Mangghystau, adm. division, Kaz. 43°56' N, 51°44' E 158
Mangghyystaū, Kaz. 43°40' N, 51°17' E 158
Mangham, La., U.S. 32°18' N, 91°47' W 103
Mangkalihat, Tanjung, Indonesia 0°49' N, 117°56' E 192
Manglares, Cabo, Col. 1°33' N, 80°27' W 130
Mangnai, China 37°50' N, 91°45' E 188
Mangnai Zhen, China 38°25' N, 90°17' E 188
Mango, Togo 10°22' N, 0°25' E 222
Mangoche, Malawi 14°29' S, 35°19' E 224
Mangoky, river, Madagascar 22°3' S, 44°28' E 220
Mangole, island, Indonesia 1°43' S, 125°43' E 192
Mangonui, N.Z. 35°2' S, 173°31' E 240
Mangqystaū Shyghanaghy 44°28' N, 50°41' E 158
Mangrol, India 21°7' N, 70°7' E 188
Mangrove Cay, island, Bahamas 26°55' N, 78°46' W 105
Mangueira, Lagoa, lake, Braz. 32°60' S, 53°19' W 139
Manguéni, Plateau de, Niger 23°9' N, 12°2' E 216
Manguinho, Ponta do, Braz. 11°5' S, 36°25' W 132
Mangum, Okla., U.S. 34°51' N, 99°31' W 92
Mangunça, Ilha, island, Braz. 1°36' S, 44°38' W 132
Mangut, Russ. 49°38' N, 112°38' E 198
Mangwe, Zimb. 20°41' S, 28°2' E 227
Manhattan, Ill., U.S. 41°24' N, 87°59' W 102
Manhattan, Kans., U.S. 39°10' N, 96°34' W 90
Manhattan, Nev., U.S. 38°32' N, 117°5' W 90
Manhiça, Mozambique 25°21' S, 32°49' E 227
Manhuaçu, Braz. 20°19' S, 41°60' W 138
Maní, Col. 4°50' N, 72°18' W 136
Mania, river, Madagascar 19°58' S, 45°19' E 220
Maniamba, Mozambique 12°47' S, 34°58' E 224
Manic Trois, Réservoir, lake, Can. 50°11' N, 70°32' W 80
Manica, Mozambique 18°57' S, 32°54' E 224
Manica, adm. division, Mozambique 18°9' S, 32°59' E 224
Maniçauá Miçu, river, Braz. 11°35' S, 55°7' W 132
Manicoré, Braz. 5°51' S, 61°16' W 130
Manicoré, river, Braz. 6°45' S, 61°2' W 130
Manicouagan, Petit lac, lake, Can. 51°49' N, 68°45' W 111
Manicouagan, Pointe, Can. 49°1' N, 68°18' W 111
Manicouagan, Réservoir, lake, Can. 51°39' N, 69°10' W 111
Manicouagan, Réservoir, lake, Can. 51°19' N, 70°56' W 106

MAN-MAR

Maniema, adm. division, Dem. Rep. of the Congo 3°18′ S, 25°0′ E 218
Manīfah, Saudi Arabia 27°28′ N, 48°59′ E 196
Manigotagan, Can. 51°6′ N, 96°16′ W 90
Manihiki Plateau, South Pacific Ocean 10°15′ S, 159°44′ W 252
Maniitsoq (Sukkertoppen) 65°26′ N, 52°60′ W 106
Manikpur, India 25°1′ N, 81°6′ E 197
Manila, Ark., U.S. 35°52′ N, 90°11′ W 96
Manila, Philippines 14°33′ N, 120°53′ E 203
Manilaid, island, Est. 58°10′ N, 24°9′ E 166
Manily, Russ. 62°34′ N, 165°18′ E 173
Manipur, adm. division, India 24°32′ N, 93°6′ E 188
Manisa, Turk. 38°34′ N, 27°24′ E 180
Manistee, Mich., U.S. 44°13′ N, 86°20′ W 102
Manistee, river, Mich., U.S. 44°1′ N, 86°6′ W 82
Manistique, Mich., U.S. 45°58′ N, 86°15′ W 94
Manitoba, adm. division, Can. 50°5′ N, 99°36′ W 90
Manitoba, Lake, Can. 50°18′ N, 98°55′ W 90
Manitou, Can. 49°14′ N, 98°32′ W 90
Manitou Beach, Mich., U.S. 41°57′ N, 84°19′ W 102
Manitou Islands, Lake Michigan 44°29′ N, 86°12′ W 80
Manitou, Lac, lake, Can. 50°47′ N, 65°38′ W 111
Manitou Lake, Can. 52°43′ N, 110°13′ W 108
Manitoulin Island, Can. 45°15′ N, 83°28′ W 80
Manitouwadge, Can. 49°8′ N, 85°47′ W 94
Manitowik Lake, Can. 48°8′ N, 84°60′ W 94
Manitowoc, Wis., U.S. 44°4′ N, 87°41′ W 102
Maniwaki, Can. 46°21′ N, 75°58′ W 94
Manizales, Col. 5°1′ N, 75°32′ W 136
Manjā, Jordan 31°44′ N, 35°51′ E 194
Manja, Madagascar 21°30′ S, 44°22′ E 207
Manjacaze, Mozambique 24°41′ S, 33°53′ E 227
Mankato, Kans., U.S. 39°46′ N, 98°14′ W 90
Mankato, Minn., U.S. 44°8′ N, 94°1′ W 94
Mankera, Pak. 31°22′ N, 71°29′ E 186
Mankim, Cameroon 5°0′ N, 12°1′ E 218
Mankono, Côte d'Ivoire 8°1′ N, 6°12′ W 222
Manley Hot Springs, Alas., U.S. 64°59′ N, 150°36′ W 98
Manlleu, Sp. 42°0′ N, 2°16′ E 164
Manly, Iowa, U.S. 43°15′ N, 93°12′ W 94
Mann Ranges, Austral. 25°59′ S, 128°46′ E 230
Manna, Indonesia 4°27′ S, 102°51′ E 192
Mannar, Sri Lanka 8°58′ N, 79°53′ E 188
Mannar, Gulf of 7°42′ N, 78°20′ E 188
Mannheim, Ger. 49°29′ N, 8°27′ E 152
Manning, Can. 56°54′ N, 117°37′ W 108
Manning, Iowa, U.S. 41°53′ N, 95°5′ W 94
Manning, N. Dak., U.S. 47°12′ N, 102°47′ W 90
Manning, S.C., U.S. 33°40′ N, 80°13′ W 96
Manningtree, U.K. 51°56′ N, 1°3′ E 162
Mannsville, N.Y., U.S. 43°42′ N, 76°4′ W 94
Mannu, Capo, It. 40°1′ N, 7°43′ E 156
Mannville, Can. 53°20′ N, 111°11′ W 108
Mano, Sierra Leone 8°2′ N, 12°4′ W 222
Mano, river, Liberia 7°14′ N, 10°57′ W 222
Manoa, Bol. 9°45′ S, 65°27′ W 137
Manoharpur, India 22°21′ N, 85°13′ E 197
Manokotak, Alas., U.S. 58°58′ N, 159°3′ W 98
Manokwari, Indonesia 0°50′ N, 133°55′ E 192
Manombo, Madagascar 22°54′ S, 43°24′ E 220
Manomet, Mass., U.S. 41°55′ N, 70°34′ W 104
Manomet Point, Mass., U.S. 41°55′ N, 70°33′ W 104
Manono, Dem. Rep. of the Congo 7°18′ S, 27°23′ E 224
Manoron, Myanmar 11°37′ N, 98°59′ E 202
Manouane, Can. 47°14′ N, 74°24′ W 94
Manouane, Lac, lake, Can. 47°33′ N, 74°43′ W 94
Manouane, Lac, lake, Can. 50°32′ N, 71°22′ W 111
Manouba, Tun. 36°47′ N, 10°5′ E 156
Manovo, river, Cen. Af. Rep. 9°7′ N, 20°15′ E 218
Manovo-Gounda-Saint Floris National Park, Cen. Af. Rep. 9°23′ N, 20°58′ E 206
Manp'o, N. Korea 41°10′ N, 126°19′ E 200
Manpur, India 23°16′ N, 83°35′ E 197
Manresa, Sp. 41°43′ N, 1°46′ E 214
Mansa, Zambia 11°12′ S, 28°53′ E 224
Mansa Konko, Gambia 13°26′ N, 15°30′ W 222
Mansabá, Guinea-Bissau 12°18′ N, 15°11′ W 222
Mansalar see Musala, island, Indonesia 1°31′ N, 97°47′ E 196
Mansehra, Pak. 34°19′ N, 73°15′ E 186
Mansel Island, Can. 61°4′ N, 80°49′ W 106
Manseriche, Pongo de, Peru 4°16′ S, 78°36′ W 130
Mansfield, Ill., U.S. 40°11′ N, 88°31′ W 102
Mansfield, La., U.S. 32°1′ N, 93°44′ W 103
Mansfield, Mass., U.S. 42°1′ N, 71°14′ W 104
Mansfield, Mo., U.S. 37°5′ N, 92°35′ W 96
Mansfield, Ohio, U.S. 40°44′ N, 82°30′ W 102
Mansfield, Pa., U.S. 41°46′ N, 77°5′ W 82
Mansfield, U.K. 53°8′ N, 1°12′ W 162
Mansfield Center, Conn., U.S. 41°45′ N, 72°12′ W 104
Mansfield, Mount, peak, Vt., U.S. 44°32′ N, 72°51′ W 104
Manso (Rio das Mortes), river, Braz. 15°20′ S, 53°1′ W 138
Manson, Iowa, U.S. 42°30′ N, 94°33′ W 94
Manson Creek, Can. 55°38′ N, 124°31′ W 108
Mansourah, Alg. 36°4′ N, 4°28′ E 150
Manta, Ecua. 1°4′ S, 80°31′ W 130
Mantakari, Niger 13°52′ N, 3°59′ E 222
Mantaro, river, Peru 11°55′ S, 74°47′ W 137
Manteca, Calif., U.S. 37°47′ N, 121°13′ W 100
Mantecal, Venez. 7°33′ N, 69°8′ W 136
Mantena, Braz. 18°51′ S, 40°59′ W 138
Manteno, Ill., U.S. 41°14′ N, 87°50′ W 102
Manteo, N.C., U.S. 35°54′ N, 75°42′ W 96
Mantes-la-Jolie, Fr. 48°59′ N, 1°42′ E 163
Manti, Utah, U.S. 39°15′ N, 111°38′ W 90
Mantinea 362 B.C., battle, Gr. 37°36′ N, 22°17′ E 156
Manto, Hond. 14°55′ N, 86°20′ W 115
Manton, Mich., U.S. 44°24′ N, 85°25′ W 94
Mantova, It. 45°8′ N, 10°47′ E 167
Mäntsälä, Fin. 60°37′ N, 25°18′ E 166
Mänttä, Fin. 62°0′ N, 24°36′ E 166
Mantua, Cuba 22°17′ N, 84°18′ W 116
Manturovo, Russ. 58°20′ N, 44°47′ E 154
Mäntyharju, Fin. 61°22′ N, 26°48′ E 166
Mäntyluoto, Fin. 61°34′ N, 21°28′ E 166
Manú, Peru 12°17′ S, 70°55′ W 137
Manu National Park, Peru 12°19′ S, 71°54′ W 137
Manu see Mapiri, river, Bol. 10°40′ S, 66°53′ W 137
Manua Islands, South Pacific Ocean 14°14′ S, 169°35′ W 241
Manuel Alves, river, Braz. 11°53′ S, 48°4′ W 130
Manuel Benavides, Mex. 29°5′ N, 103°55′ W 92
Manuel J. Cobo, Arg. 35°53′ S, 57°54′ W 139
Manuel Ribas, Braz. 24°34′ S, 51°40′ W 138
Manuel Vitorino, Braz. 14°12′ S, 40°16′ W 138
Manuelzinho, Braz. 7°24′ S, 54°54′ W 130
Manukan, Philippines 8°33′ N, 123°5′ E 203
Manukau, N.Z. 37°3′ S, 174°54′ E 240
Manupari, river, Bol. 12°36′ S, 67°42′ W 137
Manuripi, river, Bol. 11°42′ S, 68°35′ W 137
Manus, island, P.N.G. 2°27′ S, 145°40′ E 192
Manusela National Park, Indonesia 3°14′ S, 129°4′ E 238
Manvers, Port 56°47′ N, 63°21′ W 246
Manville, R.I., U.S. 41°58′ N, 71°29′ W 104
Many, La., U.S. 31°33′ N, 93°29′ W 103
Many Farms, Ariz., U.S. 36°21′ N, 109°37′ W 92
Manyara, Lake, Tanzania 3°37′ S, 35°16′ E 224
Manyberries, Can. 49°24′ N, 110°42′ W 90
Manyinga, river, Africa 12°17′ S, 24°1′ E 220
Manyoni, Tanzania 5°42′ S, 34°49′ E 224
Manzala, Buheirat el, lake, Egypt 31°12′ N, 32°3′ E 194
Manzanares, Sp. 38°59′ N, 3°27′ W 214
Manzanera, Sp. 40°3′ N, 0°50′ E 164
Manzanillo, Mex. 19°2′ N, 104°18′ W 114
Manzanita, Oreg., U.S. 45°42′ N, 123°56′ W 100
Manzano Peak, N. Mex., U.S. 34°34′ N, 106°31′ W 92
Manzanola, Colo., U.S. 38°6′ N, 103°52′ W 92
Manzhouli, China 49°34′ N, 117°26′ E 198
Manzini, Swaziland 26°31′ S, 31°20′ E 227
Mao, Chad 14°6′ N, 15°17′ E 216
Mao, Dom. Rep. 19°34′ N, 71°5′ W 116
Maoke, Pegunungan, Indonesia 4°23′ S, 135°14′ E 192
Maoming, China 21°40′ N, 110°50′ E 198
Maoudass, Mauritania 15°33′ N, 10°55′ W 222
Mapai, Mozambique 22°49′ S, 32°1′ E 227
Mapam Yumco, lake, China 30°45′ N, 80°50′ E 197
Mapanza, Zambia 16°17′ S, 26°55′ E 224
Maper, Sudan 7°42′ N, 29°38′ E 224
Mapia, Kepulauan, islands, North Pacific Ocean 0°52′ N, 134°31′ E 192
Mapimí, Mex. 25°47′ N, 103°52′ W 114
Mapimí, Bolsón de, Mex. 26°47′ N, 104°34′ W 112
Mapinhane, Mozambique 22°19′ S, 35°2′ E 227
Mapiri, Bol. 15°13′ S, 68°11′ W 137
Mapiri (Manu), river, Bol. 10°40′ S, 66°53′ W 137
Mapiripán, river, Col. 3°10′ N, 71°37′ W 136
Mapiripana, Col. 2°39′ N, 70°58′ W 136
Maple Creek, Can. 49°53′ N, 109°28′ W 90
Maple Ridge, Can. 49°13′ N, 122°36′ W 100
Maple, river, Mich., U.S. 43°3′ N, 84°41′ W 102
Maple Valley, Wash., U.S. 47°23′ N, 122°3′ W 100
Mapleton, Iowa, U.S. 42°8′ N, 95°47′ W 90
Mapleville, R.I., U.S. 41°56′ N, 71°40′ W 104
Mapmaker Seamounts, North Pacific Ocean 26°45′ N, 166°56′ E 252
Mapuera, river, Braz. 1°6′ S, 58°10′ W 130
Mapulanguene, Mozambique 24°29′ S, 32°7′ E 227
Maputo, Mozambique 25°55′ S, 32°27′ E 227
Maputo, adm. division, Mozambique 25°22′ S, 32°6′ E 227
Maqanshy, Kaz. 46°45′ N, 82°9′ E 184
Maqat, Kaz. 47°38′ N, 53°21′ E 158
Maqdam, Ras, Sudan 18°48′ N, 36°58′ E 182
Maqên Gangri, peak, China 34°24′ N, 99°22′ E 190
Maqnā, Saudi Arabia 28°22′ N, 34°45′ E 180
Maqshūsh, Saudi Arabia 23°36′ N, 38°41′ E 182
Maquela do Zombo, Angola 6°3′ S, 15°4′ E 218
Maquinchao, Arg. 41°14′ S, 68°43′ W 134
Maquoketa, Iowa, U.S. 42°3′ N, 90°41′ W 94
Mar Chiquita, Laguna, lake, Arg. 30°34′ S, 62°57′ W 139
Mar de Ajó, Arg. 36°42′ S, 56°43′ W 139
Mar del Plata, Arg. 37°59′ S, 57°36′ W 139
Mar, Serra do, Braz. 27°45′ S, 48°59′ W 132
Mara, Guyana 5°57′ N, 57°37′ W 130
Mara, India 28°10′ N, 94°6′ E 188
Mara, adm. division, Tanzania 1°45′ S, 33°47′ E 224
Mara, oil field, Venez. 10°49′ N, 71°58′ W 136
Mara Rosa, Braz. 13°57′ S, 49°10′ W 138
Maraã, Braz. 1°50′ S, 65°26′ W 136
Marabá, Braz. 5°24′ S, 49°9′ W 130
Marabitanas, Braz. 0°56′ N, 66°54′ W 136
Maracá, Ilha de, island, Braz. 2°3′ N, 50°17′ W 130
Maracaibo, Venez. 10°41′ N, 71°41′ W 136
Maracaibo, Lago de 9°20′ N, 74°22′ W 73
Maracaju, Braz. 21°39′ S, 55°9′ W 132
Maracaju, Serra de, Braz.-Parag. 19°12′ S, 55°27′ W 132
Maracanã, Braz. 0°47′ N, 47°27′ W 130
Maracás, Braz. 13°26′ S, 40°29′ W 138
Maracay, Venez. 10°12′ N, 67°38′ W 136
Marādah, Lib. 29°14′ N, 19°12′ E 216
Maradi, Niger 13°30′ N, 7°7′ E 222
Marāgheh, Iran 37°26′ N, 46°15′ E 195
Maragogipe, Braz. 12°48′ S, 38°57′ W 132
Marahoué National Park, Côte d'Ivoire 7°5′ N, 6°41′ W 222
Marahuaca, Cerro, peak, Venez. 3°32′ N, 65°30′ W 136
Marajó, Ilha de, South America 0°41′ N, 50°31′ W 123
Maralal, Kenya 1°4′ N, 36°42′ E 224
Maralaleng, Botswana 25°49′ S, 22°40′ E 227
Marali, Cen. Af. Rep. 6°0′ N, 18°23′ E 218
Maralinga, Austral. 30°7′ S, 131°24′ E 231
Maramasike, island, Solomon Islands 9°35′ S, 161°30′ E 242
Marambio, station, Antarctica 64°17′ S, 56°44′ W 134
MaramureĔ, adm. division, Rom. 47°36′ N, 23°20′ E 156
Maramureşului, Munţii, Rom. 47°57′ N, 24°19′ E 152
Maran, Malaysia 3°36′ N, 102°45′ E 196
Marana, Ariz., U.S. 32°26′ N, 111°13′ W 92
Maranchón, Sp. 41°2′ N, 2°13′ W 164
Marand, Iran 38°29′ N, 45°43′ E 195
Mărăndeni, Mold. 47°39′ N, 27°51′ E 152
Marang, Malaysia 5°12′ N, 103°12′ E 196
Maranguape, Braz. 3°53′ S, 38°41′ W 132
Maranhão, adm. division, Braz. 5°35′ S, 47°22′ W 130
Marañón, river, Peru 5°34′ S, 76°27′ W 122
Marão, Serra do, Port. 41°6′ N, 8°31′ W 150
Mararaba, Cameroon 5°37′ N, 13°47′ E 218
Marargiu, Capo, It. 40°17′ N, 7°38′ E 156
Marari, Braz. 5°45′ S, 67°45′ W 130
Mărăşeşti, Rom. 45°52′ N, 27°13′ E 156
Marathon 490 B.C., battle, Gr. 38°6′ N, 23°51′ E 156
Marathon, Can. 48°43′ N, 86°22′ W 94
Marathon, Fla., U.S. 24°42′ N, 81°5′ W 105
Marathon, Tex., U.S. 30°11′ N, 103°15′ W 92
Marathus see 'Amrīt, ruin(s), Syr. 34°50′ N, 35°52′ E 194
Maratua, island, Indonesia 2°16′ N, 118°39′ E 192
Marau, Braz. 28°32′ S, 52°13′ W 139
Marauá, Braz. 3°26′ S, 66°23′ W 136
Marauiá, river, Braz. 0°28′ N, 65°22′ W 136
Maravatío, Mex. 19°52′ N, 100°27′ W 114
Marāveh Tappeh, Iran 37°54′ N, 55°55′ E 180
Marawi, Philippines 8°5′ N, 124°19′ E 203
Maraza, Azerb. 40°33′ N, 48°55′ E 195
Marbella, Sp. 36°30′ N, 4°53′ W 164
Marble, Minn., U.S. 47°18′ N, 93°18′ W 94
Marble Bar, Austral. 21°10′ S, 119°45′ E 231
Marble Canyon, Ariz., U.S. 36°32′ N, 112°1′ W 92
Marble Falls, Tex., U.S. 30°33′ N, 98°16′ W 92
Marble Hall, S. Af. 24°59′ S, 29°16′ E 227
Marble Mountains, Calif., U.S. 34°42′ N, 115°35′ W 101
Marblehead, Mass., U.S. 42°30′ N, 70°52′ W 104
Marblemount, Wash., U.S. 48°31′ N, 121°28′ W 100
Marbleton, Wyo., U.S. 42°34′ N, 110°5′ W 90
Mårbu, Nor. 60°11′ N, 8°10′ E 152
Marburg, Ger. 50°48′ N, 8°46′ E 167
Marca, Ponta da, Angola 16°36′ S, 11°3′ E 220
Marcali, Hung. 46°34′ N, 17°24′ E 168
Marcapata, Peru 13°34′ S, 70°54′ W 137
Marcaria, It. 45°7′ N, 10°32′ E 167
Marcelin, Can. 52°56′ N, 106°47′ W 108
Marceline, Mo., U.S. 39°42′ N, 92°56′ W 94
Marcelino, Braz. 1°48′ S, 66°25′ W 136
Marcelino Ramos, Braz. 27°30′ S, 51°57′ W 139
Marcellus, Mich., U.S. 42°1′ N, 85°48′ W 102
March, U.K. 52°33′ N, 8°475′ E 162
March Air Force Base, Calif., U.S. 33°53′ N, 117°17′ W 101
Marchamalo, Sp. 40°39′ N, 3°12′ W 164
Marchand, Can. 49°26′ N, 96°22′ W 90
Marche, Belg. 50°13′ N, 5°20′ E 167
Marche, region, Fr. 46°21′ N, 1°10′ E 165
Marchena, Sp. 37°19′ N, 5°26′ W 164
Marches, adm. division, It. 43°44′ N, 12°22′ E 167
Marchinbar Island, Austral. 11°17′ S, 134°53′ E 192
Marck, Fr. 50°56′ N, 1°55′ E 163
Marco, Fla., U.S. 25°57′ N, 81°43′ W 105
Marcola, Oreg., U.S. 44°9′ N, 122°53′ W 90
Marcos Juárez, Arg. 32°42′ S, 62°5′ W 139
Marcus, Wash., U.S. 48°39′ N, 118°4′ W 90
Marcy, Mount, peak, N.Y., U.S. 44°6′ N, 73°57′ W 104
Mardan, Pak. 34°11′ N, 72°6′ E 188
Mardin, Turk. 37°19′ N, 40°46′ E 195
Mære, Nor. 63°55′ N, 11°23′ E 152
Mare, Muntele, peak, Rom. 46°29′ N, 23°11′ E 168
Marechal Taumaturgo, Braz. 8°58′ S, 72°48′ W 137
Mareer, Somalia 1°35′ N, 44°26′ E 218
Marengo, Can. 51°29′ N, 109°47′ W 90
Marengo, Ill., U.S. 42°14′ N, 88°37′ W 102
Marennes, Fr. 45°50′ N, 1°8′ W 150
Mareshah, ruin(s), Israel 31°34′ N, 34°50′ E 194
Marevo, Russ. 57°17′ N, 32°6′ E 154
Marfa, Tex., U.S. 30°17′ N, 104°2′ W 92
Marfa, Massif de, Chad 13°2′ N, 20°4′ E 216
Marfino, Russ. 46°23′ N, 48°44′ E 158
Margai Caka, lake, China 35°6′ N, 86°25′ E 188
Margaret Lake, Can. 58°53′ N, 116°9′ W 108
Margaret, Mount, peak, Austral. 22°3′ S, 117°39′ E 230
Margarita, Arg. 29°39′ S, 60°13′ W 139
Margarita, Isla de, island, Venez. 10°47′ N, 63°53′ W 116
Margat (Marghab), ruin(s), Syr. 35°9′ N, 35°55′ E 194
Margat, ruin(s), Syr. 35°7′ N, 35°52′ E 156
Margate, S. Af. 30°52′ S, 30°20′ E 227
Margento, Col. 8°2′ N, 74°56′ W 136
Margeride, Monts de la, Fr. 45°6′ N, 3°1′ E 165
Marghab see Margat, ruin(s), Syr. 35°9′ N, 35°55′ E 194
Margherita Peak, Dem. Rep. of the Congo 0°19′ N, 29°46′ E 224
Marghita, Rom. 47°20′ N, 22°21′ E 168
Margie, Can. 55°24′ N, 111°23′ W 108
Marg'ilon, Uzb. 40°27′ N, 71°44′ E 197
Mărgineni, oil field, Rom. 44°56′ N, 25°40′ E 156
Margita, Serb. and Mont. 45°12′ N, 21°12′ E 168
Margog Caka, lake, China 33°47′ N, 86°6′ E 188
Margosatubig, Philippines 7°36′ N, 123°11′ E 203
Marguerite, Can. 52°30′ N, 122°25′ W 108
Marhanets', Ukr. 47°37′ N, 34°44′ E 156
María, Sp. 37°42′ N, 2°9′ W 164
María Elena, Chile 22°20′ S, 69°43′ W 137
Maria Island, Austral. 14°45′ S, 135°43′ E 230
María Madre, Isla, island, Mex. 21°39′ N, 108°7′ W 112
María, peak, Sp. 37°40′ N, 2°15′ W 164
María Teresa, Arg. 34°3′ S, 61°55′ W 139
Mariakani, Kenya 3°54′ S, 39°28′ E 224
Mariana Lake, Can. 55°59′ N, 112°2′ W 108
Mariana Trench, North Pacific Ocean 16°4′ N, 148°3′ E 252
Marianao, Cuba 23°3′ N, 82°29′ W 116
Marianna, Ark., U.S. 34°46′ N, 90°47′ W 96
Marianna, Fla., U.S. 30°46′ N, 85°14′ W 96
Mariannelund, Nor. 57°37′ N, 15°32′ E 152
Marías, Islas, islands, North Pacific Ocean 21°3′ N, 107°18′ W 112
Marias Pass, Mont., U.S. 48°18′ N, 113°20′ W 90
Ma'rib, Yemen 15°32′ N, 45°19′ E 182
Maribo, Den. 54°47′ N, 11°29′ E 152
Maribor, Slov. 46°32′ N, 15°39′ E 156
Maricopa, Ariz., U.S. 33°3′ N, 112°3′ W 92
Maricopa, Calif., U.S. 35°3′ N, 119°25′ W 100
Maridi, Sudan 4°56′ N, 29°30′ E 224
Marie Byrd Land, region, Antarctica 76°41′ S, 109°34′ W 248
Marié, river, Braz. 0°50′ N, 67°36′ W 136
Marie-Galante, island, Marie-Galante 15°48′ N, 61°11′ W 116
Mariehamn (Maarianhamina), Fin. 60°5′ N, 19°55′ E 166
Marienbourg, Belg. 50°5′ N, 4°30′ E 163
Marienhafe, Ger. 53°31′ N, 7°17′ E 163
Mariental, Namibia 24°38′ S, 17°57′ E 227
Mariestad, Nor. 58°42′ N, 13°49′ E 152
Marietta, Ga., U.S. 33°57′ N, 84°34′ W 96
Marietta, Ohio, U.S. 39°25′ N, 81°27′ W 102
Marietta, Okla., U.S. 33°55′ N, 97°6′ W 92
Marietta, Wash., U.S. 48°47′ N, 122°34′ W 100
Marigny, Fr. 49°5′ N, 1°15′ W 150
Marii Pronchishchevoy, Bukhta 75°46′ N, 120°4′ E 246
Mariinsk, Russ. 56°13′ N, 87°45′ E 169
Marijampolė, Lith. 54°33′ N, 23°19′ E 166
Marilândia do Sul, Braz. 23°47′ S, 51°18′ W 138
Marília, Braz. 22°15′ S, 49°59′ W 138
Marilla, Can. 53°42′ N, 125°50′ W 108
Marimba, Angola 8°25′ S, 17°1′ E 218
Marina, Calif., U.S. 36°41′ N, 121°47′ W 100
Marina di Carrara, It. 44°2′ N, 10°1′ E 167
Marina di Ravenna, It. 44°28′ N, 12°15′ E 167
Marine City, Mich., U.S. 42°41′ N, 82°31′ W 102
Marineland, Fla., U.S. 29°39′ N, 81°14′ W 105
Marinette, Wis., U.S. 45°4′ N, 87°38′ W 94
Maringá, Braz. 23°25′ S, 51°60′ W 138
Maringouin, La., U.S. 30°28′ N, 91°32′ W 103
Maringuè, Mozambique 17°60′ S, 34°23′ E 224
Mar'ino, Russ. 51°12′ N, 36°43′ E 158
Mar'insko, Russ. 58°47′ N, 28°32′ E 166
Marinuma, Col. 2°15′ N, 69°22′ W 136
Marion, Ala., U.S. 32°37′ N, 87°20′ W 103
Marion, Ark., U.S. 35°12′ N, 90°13′ W 96
Marion, Ind., U.S. 40°33′ N, 85°41′ W 102
Marion, Iowa, U.S. 42°1′ N, 91°36′ W 94
Marion, Kans., U.S. 38°20′ N, 97°2′ W 90
Marion, La., U.S. 32°53′ N, 92°15′ W 103
Marion, Mass., U.S. 41°41′ N, 70°47′ W 104
Marion, Mich., U.S. 44°6′ N, 85°8′ W 102
Marion, Miss., U.S. 32°24′ N, 88°39′ W 103
Marion, Mo., U.S. 37°43′ N, 88°55′ W 94
Marion, Ohio, U.S. 40°34′ N, 83°8′ W 102
Marion, S.C., U.S. 34°10′ N, 79°24′ W 96
Marion, S. Dak., U.S. 43°24′ N, 97°16′ W 90
Marion, Va., U.S. 36°50′ N, 81°32′ W 94
Marion Nunataks 69°34′ S, 79°8′ W 248
Marionville, Mo., U.S. 36°59′ N, 93°38′ W 96
Maripa, Venez. 7°21′ N, 65°8′ W 136
Mariposa, Calif., U.S. 37°29′ N, 119°59′ W 100
Marir, Gezaîr (Mirear), islands, Egypt 23°5′ N, 35°51′ E 182
Mariscal Estigarribia, Parag. 22°2′ S, 60°37′ W 132
Maristova, Nor. 61°6′ N, 8°1′ E 152
Maritime Alps, Fr. 44°2′ N, 6°45′ E 165
Mariupol', Ukr. 47°5′ N, 37°28′ E 156
Mariusa National Park, Venez. 9°23′ N, 61°33′ W 116
Marīvān, Iran 35°31′ N, 46°11′ E 180
Mariy-El, adm. division, Russ. 56°19′ N, 46°11′ E 154
Mariyets, Russ. 56°30′ N, 49°53′ E 154
Marj 'Uyūn, Leb. 33°21′ N, 35°35′ E 194
Märjamaa, Est. 58°54′ N, 24°23′ E 166
Marjonbuloq, Uzb. 39°59′ N, 67°21′ E 197
Marka see Merca, Somalia 1°41′ N, 44°53′ E 207
Markala, Mali 13°40′ N, 6°4′ W 222
Markansu, Taj. 39°19′ N, 73°21′ E 197
Markapur, India 15°42′ N, 79°17′ E 188
Markaryd, Nor. 56°28′ N, 13°35′ E 152
Markdale, Can. 44°18′ N, 80°39′ W 110
Markelsdorfer Huk, Kattegat 54°37′ N, 10°49′ E 152
Markesan, Wis., U.S. 43°42′ N, 88°59′ W 102
Market Drayton, U.K. 52°53′ N, 2°30′ W 162
Market Harborough, U.K. 52°28′ N, 0°55′ E 162
Market Rasen, U.K. 53°22′ N, 0°21′ E 162
Market Weighton, U.K. 53°51′ N, 0°41′ E 162
Markha, river, Russ. 64°57′ N, 116°6′ E 160
Markham, Can. 43°51′ N, 79°17′ W 94
Markham Bay 63°24′ N, 74°18′ W 106
Markham, Mount, peak, Antarctica 82°47′ S, 162°59′ E 248
Markit, China 38°57′ N, 77°37′ E 184
Markkina, Fin. 68°29′ N, 22°16′ E 152
Markle, Ind., U.S. 40°49′ N, 85°20′ W 102
Markounda, Cen. Af. Rep. 7°33′ N, 16°57′ E 218
Markovac, Serb. and Mont. 44°13′ N, 21°5′ E 168
Markovo, Russ. 64°41′ N, 170°4′ E 160
Marks Butte, peak, Colo., U.S. 40°48′ N, 102°36′ W 90
Marksville, La., U.S. 31°6′ N, 92°5′ W 103
Markušica, Croatia 45°22′ N, 18°41′ E 168
Marl, Ger. 51°39′ N, 7°6′ E 167
Marlboro, Vt., U.S. 42°51′ N, 72°44′ W 104
Marlborough, N.H., U.S. 42°53′ N, 72°13′ W 104
Marlborough, U.K. 51°24′ N, 1°44′ W 162
Marle, Fr. 49°44′ N, 3°47′ E 163
Marles, Fr. 50°30′ N, 2°30′ E 163
Marlette, Mich., U.S. 43°19′ N, 83°5′ W 102
Marlin, Tex., U.S. 31°17′ N, 96°53′ W 96
Marlin, oil field, Bass Strait 38°17′ S, 148°12′ E 230
Marlow, N.H., U.S. 43°6′ N, 72°13′ W 104
Marlow, Okla., U.S. 34°38′ N, 97°58′ W 92
Marlow, U.K. 51°34′ N, 0°47′ E 162
Marmagao, India 15°23′ N, 73°48′ E 173
Marmara Denizi 40°37′ N, 27°43′ E 156
Marmaris, Turk. 36°51′ N, 28°14′ E 156
Marmarth, N. Dak., U.S. 46°16′ N, 103°54′ W 90
Marmolada, peak, It. 46°26′ N, 11°47′ E 167
Marmolejo, Sp. 38°2′ N, 4°11′ W 164
Marmul, oil field, Oman 18°10′ N, 55°23′ E 182
Marne, river, Fr. 48°49′ N, 2°37′ E 163
Maroa, Ill., U.S. 40°1′ N, 88°57′ W 102
Maroa, Venez. 2°45′ N, 67°33′ W 136
Maroantsetra, Madagascar 15°25′ S, 49°41′ E 220
Marol, Pak. 34°45′ N, 76°16′ E 188
Marolambo, Madagascar 20°4′ S, 48°8′ E 220
Maromandia, Madagascar 14°9′ S, 48°5′ E 220
Maromokotro, peak, Madagascar 14°4′ S, 48°50′ E 220
Marondera, Zimb. 18°14′ S, 31°30′ E 224
Marone, It. 45°44′ N, 10°5′ E 167
Marónia, Gr. 40°54′ N, 25°31′ E 156
Maronne, river, Fr. 45°1′ N, 1°59′ E 165
Maros, Indonesia 4°58′ S, 119°32′ E 192
Marotandrano, Madagascar 16°11′ S, 48°48′ E 220
Marotiri, island, Fr. 27°49′ S, 143°42′ W 252
Maroua, Cameroon 10°36′ N, 14°20′ E 216
Marouini, river, South America 2°10′ N, 53°57′ W 130
Marovoay, Madagascar 16°8′ S, 46°39′ E 220
Marqaköl, lake, Kaz. 48°42′ N, 85°14′ E 184
Marquard, S. Af. 28°41′ S, 27°23′ E 227
Marquesas Fracture Zone, South Pacific Ocean 10°40′ S, 131°47′ W 252
Marquesas Islands, South Pacific Ocean 11°28′ S, 141°48′ W 238
Marquesas Keys, islands, Gulf of Mexico 24°26′ N, 82°20′ W 105
Marquette, Mich., U.S. 46°32′ N, 87°24′ W 94
Marquette, Lac, lake, Can. 48°54′ N, 74°33′ W 94
Marquise, Fr. 50°49′ N, 1°42′ E 163
Marra, Jebel, peak, Sudan 12°50′ N, 23°50′ E 206
Marrakech, Mor. 31°39′ N, 8°1′ W 214
Marrasjärvi, Fin. 66°53′ N, 25°6′ E 152
Marrecas, Serra das, Braz. 9°33′ S, 41°40′ W 132
Marromeu, Mozambique 18°19′ S, 35°55′ E 224
Marrupa, Mozambique 13°12′ S, 37°30′ E 224
Mars Hill, peak, Me., U.S. 46°30′ N, 67°54′ W 94
Marsá al 'Uwayjā', Lib. 30°54′ N, 17°51′ E 216
Marsa 'Alam, spring, Egypt 25°4′ N, 34°51′ E 182
Marsa Fatma, Eritrea 14°51′ N, 40°20′ E 182
Marsa Sha'ab, Egypt 22°49′ N, 35°45′ E 182
Marsabit, Kenya 2°18′ N, 38°0′ E 224
Marsabit National Reserve, Kenya 1°54′ N, 37°47′ E 224
Marsala, It. 37°48′ N, 12°26′ E 156
Marsberg, Ger. 51°27′ N, 8°52′ E 167
Marsden Point, N.Z. 35°53′ S, 174°28′ E 240
Marseillan, Fr. 43°21′ N, 3°30′ E 164
Marseille, Fr. 43°17′ N, 5°22′ E 150
Marsfjället, peak, Nor. 65°5′ N, 15°13′ E 152
Marsh Island, La., U.S. 29°24′ N, 92°2′ W 103
Marsh Pass, Ariz., U.S. 36°38′ N, 110°25′ W 92
Marsh Peak, Utah, U.S. 40°41′ N, 109°54′ W 90
Marsh Point, Can. 57°5′ N, 92°20′ W 108
Marshall, Alas., U.S. 61°52′ N, 162°4′ W 98
Marshall, Ark., U.S. 35°53′ N, 92°39′ W 96
Marshall, Ill., U.S. 39°23′ N, 87°41′ W 102
Marshall, Liberia 6°4′ N, 10°23′ W 222
Marshall, Mich., U.S. 42°16′ N, 84°57′ W 102
Marshall, Minn., U.S. 44°26′ N, 95°48′ W 90
Marshall, Mo., U.S. 39°6′ N, 93°16′ W 82
Marshall, Tex., U.S. 32°32′ N, 94°23′ W 103
Marshall Bennett Islands, Solomon Sea 8°46′ S, 152°2′ E 230
Marshall Islands, Marshall Islands 9°2′ N, 170°3′ E 238
Marshalltown, Iowa, U.S. 42°4′ N, 92°53′ W 82
Marshfield, Mo., U.S. 37°19′ N, 92°54′ W 94
Marshfield, Vt., U.S. 44°21′ N, 72°22′ W 104
Marshfield, Wis., U.S. 44°39′ N, 90°11′ W 94
Marsland, Nebr., U.S. 42°26′ N, 103°18′ W 90
Mars-la-Tour, Fr. 49°6′ N, 5°53′ E 163
Marston Moor, battle, U.K. 53°58′ N, 1°16′ W 162
Marstrand, Sw. 57°53′ N, 11°33′ E 150
Marsyaty, Russ. 60°4′ N, 60°25′ E 154
Mart, Tex., U.S. 31°31′ N, 96°49′ W 96
Martaban, Myanmar 16°34′ N, 97°35′ E 202
Martaban, Gulf of 15°50′ N, 96°1′ E 192
Martap, Cameroon 6°50′ N, 13°3′ E 218
Martapura, Indonesia 3°30′ S, 114°45′ E 192
Marte R. Gómez, Presa, lake, Mex. 26°12′ N, 100°24′ W 80
Martem'yanovskaya, Russ. 61°58′ N, 39°11′ E 154
Marten Mountain, peak, Can. 55°28′ N, 114°50′ W 108
Martés, peak, Sp. 39°18′ N, 0°60′ E 164
Martf u, Hung. 47°0′ N, 20°17′ E 168
Martha's Vineyard, island, Mass., U.S. 41°14′ N, 70°47′ W 104
Marthaville, La., U.S. 31°43′ N, 93°25′ W 103
Martigny, Switz. 46°6′ N, 7°3′ E 167
Martigues, Fr. 43°23′ N, 5°3′ E 150

Martil, *Mor.* 35°37′ N, 5°17′ W **150**
Martin, *Mich., U.S.* 42°32′ N, 85°39′ W **102**
Martin, *S. Dak., U.S.* 43°10′ N, 101°44′ W **90**
Martin, Lake, *Ala., U.S.* 32°51′ N, 86°22′ W **80**
Martin, river, *Can.* 61°31′ N, 122°26′ W **108**
Martin Vaz Islands, *South Atlantic Ocean* 20°29′ S, 28°57′ W **253**
Martinborough, *N.Z.* 41°15′ S, 175°29′ E **240**
Martinez, *Calif., U.S.* 38°1′ N, 122°9′ W **100**
Martinez, *Ga., U.S.* 33°30′ N, 82°6′ W **96**
Martinez Lake, *Ariz., U.S.* 32°58′ N, 114°28′ W **101**
Martinique, *Fr.* 14°26′ N, 61°27′ W **116**
Martinique Passage 15°1′ N, 62°3′ W **116**
Martinsburg, *N.Y., U.S.* 43°44′ N, 75°29′ W **94**
Martinsville, *Ill., U.S.* 39°19′ N, 87°53′ W **102**
Martinsville, *Ind., U.S.* 39°25′ N, 86°26′ W **102**
Martinsville, *Va., U.S.* 36°40′ N, 79°53′ W **96**
Martna, *Est.* 58°50′ N, 23°47′ E **166**
Marton, *N.Z.* 40°6′ S, 175°24′ E **240**
Martorell, *Sp.* 41°27′ N, 1°54′ E **164**
Martos, *Sp.* 37°43′ N, 3°59′ W **164**
Martti, *Fin.* 67°28′ N, 28°21′ E **152**
Martuni, *Arm.* 40°8′ N, 45°16′ E **195**
Martuni, *Azerb.* 39°48′ N, 47°5′ E **195**
Martyn, Mount, peak, *Antarctica* 69°19′ S, 157°39′ E **248**
Ma'ruf, *Afghan.* 31°29′ N, 67°3′ E **186**
Maruia, *N.Z.* 42°12′ S, 172°14′ E **240**
Marumori, *Japan* 37°55′ N, 140°46′ E **201**
Marungu, *Dem. Rep. of the Congo* 8°10′ S, 29°36′ E **224**
Maruoka, *Japan* 36°8′ N, 136°16′ E **201**
Marv Dasht, *Iran* 29°55′ N, 52°56′ E **196**
Marvin Spur, *Arctic Ocean* 86°15′ N, 118°55′ W **255**
Marvine, Mount, peak, *Utah, U.S.* 38°39′ N, 111°42′ W **90**
Marwar, *India* 25°43′ N, 73°37′ E **186**
Marx, *Russ.* 51°36′ N, 46°42′ E **158**
Mary, *Turkm.* 37°36′ N, 61°50′ E **180**
Mary, river, *Austral.* 25°36′ S, 152°13′ E **230**
Mar'yanovka, *Russ.* 54°55′ N, 72°44′ E **184**
Marydale, *S. Af.* 29°28′ S, 22°7′ E **227**
Maryland, adm. division, *Md., U.S.* 39°33′ N, 77°50′ W **94**
Maryport, *U.K.* 54°42′ N, 3°30′ W **162**
Mary's Harbour, *Can.* 52°24′ N, 55°58′ W **73**
Marystown, *Can.* 47°10′ N, 55°9′ W **111**
Marysvale, *Utah, U.S.* 38°26′ N, 112°13′ W **90**
Marysville, *Calif., U.S.* 39°9′ N, 121°37′ W **92**
Marysville, *Can.* 45°58′ N, 66°37′ W **94**
Marysville, *Kans., U.S.* 39°49′ N, 96°39′ W **92**
Marysville, *Mich., U.S.* 42°53′ N, 82°30′ W **102**
Marysville, *Ohio, U.S.* 40°13′ N, 83°22′ W **102**
Marysville, *Wash., U.S.* 48°2′ N, 122°11′ W **100**
Maryville, *Mo., U.S.* 40°20′ N, 94°53′ W **82**
Maryville, *Tenn., U.S.* 35°45′ N, 83°58′ W **96**
Marzafal, *Mali* 17°56′ N, 0°59′ E **222**
Marzo, Cabo, *Col.* 6°41′ N, 78°6′ W **136**
Marzūq, *Lib.* 25°55′ N, 13°53′ E **216**
Mas de las Matas, *Sp.* 40°51′ N, 0°15′ E **164**
Masada, ruin(s), *Israel* 31°18′ N, 35°19′ E **194**
Masai Mara National Reserve, *Kenya* 1°27′ S, 35°5′ E **224**
Masai Steppe, *Tanzania* 5°43′ S, 37°1′ E **224**
Masaka, *Uganda* 0°22′ N, 31°43′ E **224**
Masalasef, *Chad* 11°45′ N, 17°10′ E **216**
Masallı, *Azerb.* 39°1′ N, 48°39′ E **195**
Masalembu, Kepulauan, islands, *Java Sea* 5°56′ S, 113°19′ E **192**
Masan, *S. Korea* 35°11′ N, 128°33′ E **200**
Masasi, *Tanzania* 10°43′ S, 38°47′ E **224**
Masavi, *Bol.* 19°24′ S, 63°18′ W **137**
Masaya, *Nicar.* 11°57′ N, 86°6′ W **115**
Masayama, *Sierra Leone* 8°14′ N, 10°49′ W **222**
Masbate, *Philippines* 12°20′ N, 123°36′ E **203**
Masbate, island, *Philippines* 11°55′ N, 122°11′ E **192**
Mascara, *Alg.* 35°23′ N, 0°7′ E **150**
Mascarene Basin, *Indian Ocean* 13°57′ S, 55°8′ E **254**
Mascarene Plain, *Indian Ocean* 21°15′ S, 51°32′ E **254**
Mascart, Cape, *Antarctica* 66°35′ S, 71°50′ W **248**
Mascota, *Mex.* 20°31′ N, 104°48′ W **114**
Mascoutah, *Ill., U.S.* 38°28′ N, 89°47′ W **102**
Masein, *Myanmar* 23°22′ N, 94°21′ E **202**
Maseru, *Lesotho* 29°19′ S, 27°24′ E **227**
Masfjorden, *Nor.* 60°47′ N, 5°19′ E **152**
Mash'abbé Sade, *Israel* 30°59′ N, 34°46′ E **194**
Mashābih, island, *Saudi Arabia* 25°35′ N, 35°47′ E **182**
Masham, *U.K.* 54°13′ N, 1°40′ W **162**
Mashan, *China* 23°40′ N, 108°10′ E **198**
Mashhad, *Iran* 36°19′ N, 59°35′ E **180**
Mashigina, Guba 74°4′ N, 47°51′ E **160**
Mashkai, river, *Pak.* 26°44′ N, 65°14′ E **182**
Mashuray, *Afghan.* 32°8′ N, 68°20′ E **186**
Masi, *Nor.* 69°26′ N, 23°38′ E **152**
Masindi, *Uganda* 1°38′ N, 31°42′ E **224**
Masindi Port, *Uganda* 1°39′ N, 32°4′ E **224**
Masinloc, *Philippines* 15°34′ N, 119°58′ E **203**
Maşīrah, Jazīrat (Masira), island, *Oman* 20°43′ N, 58°55′ E **182**
Masisea, *Peru* 8°40′ S, 74°21′ W **130**
Masisi, *Dem. Rep. of the Congo* 1°24′ S, 28°47′ E **224**
Maşiyah, Tall al, peak, *Syr.* 32°47′ N, 36°39′ E **194**
Masjed Soleymān, *Iran* 31°54′ N, 49°20′ E **180**
Maska, *Nig.* 11°17′ N, 7°19′ E **222**
Maskan, Raas, *Somalia* 11°9′ N, 43°34′ E **216**
Maskūtān, *Iran* 26°51′ N, 59°53′ E **182**
Maslen Nos, *Bulg.* 42°20′ N, 27°46′ E **156**
Maslovare, *Bosn. and Herzg.* 44°33′ N, 17°31′ E **168**
Maslovo, *Russ.* 60°9′ N, 60°31′ E **154**
Masoala, Presqu'île de, *Madagascar* 16°16′ S, 50°11′ E **220**
Masoller, *Uru.* 31°7′ S, 55°59′ W **139**
Masomeloka, *Madagascar* 20°17′ S, 48°37′ E **220**
Mason, *Ill., U.S.* 38°57′ N, 88°38′ W **102**
Mason, *Mich., U.S.* 42°34′ N, 84°26′ W **102**
Mason, *Ohio, U.S.* 39°21′ N, 84°19′ W **102**
Mason, *Tex., U.S.* 30°43′ N, 99°13′ W **92**
Mason Bay 47°3′ S, 167°36′ E **240**
Mason City, *Ill., U.S.* 40°12′ N, 89°42′ W **102**
Mason City, *Iowa, U.S.* 43°7′ N, 93°12′ W **94**
Masqaţ (Muscat), *Oman* 23°30′ N, 58°32′ E **196**
Massa, *Congo* 3°46′ S, 15°27′ E **218**
Massa, *It.* 44°1′ N, 10°8′ E **167**
Massa Lombarda, *It.* 44°26′ N, 11°49′ E **167**
Massachusetts, adm. division, *Mass., U.S.* 42°14′ N, 72°39′ W **104**
Massachusetts Bay 42°11′ N, 70°43′ W **104**
Massafra, *It.* 40°35′ N, 17°7′ E **156**
Massaguet, *Chad* 12°31′ N, 15°25′ E **216**
Massakory, *Chad* 13°0′ N, 15°42′ E **216**
Massangena, *Mozambique* 21°33′ S, 33°2′ E **227**
Massat, *Fr.* 42°52′ N, 1°20′ E **164**
Massava, *Russ.* 60°38′ N, 62°5′ E **154**
Massawa, *Eritrea* 15°37′ N, 39°23′ E **182**
Massenya, *Chad* 11°27′ N, 16°9′ E **216**
Masset, *Can.* 53°59′ N, 132°2′ W **98**
Masseube, *Fr.* 43°25′ N, 0°33′ E **164**
Massillon, *Ohio, U.S.* 40°47′ N, 81°31′ W **102**
Massinga, *Mozambique* 23°16′ S, 35°20′ E **227**
Massingir, *Mozambique* 23°47′ S, 32°7′ E **227**
Masson Island, *Antarctica* 66°3′ S, 96°8′ E **248**
Masson Range, *Antarctica* 68°32′ S, 59°23′ E **248**
Mastābah, *Saudi Arabia* 20°49′ N, 39°26′ E **182**
Maştağa, *Azerb.* 40°33′ N, 49°59′ E **195**
Mastic Beach, *N.Y., U.S.* 40°45′ N, 72°51′ W **104**
Mastic Point, *Bahamas* 25°4′ N, 77°60′ W **96**
Mastuj, *Pak.* 36°15′ N, 72°33′ E **186**
Mastūrah, *Saudi Arabia* 23°7′ N, 38°51′ E **182**
Masty, *Belarus* 53°25′ N, 24°33′ E **152**
Masuda, *Japan* 34°39′ N, 131°51′ E **200**
Masuria, region, *Pol.* 54°12′ N, 19°41′ E **166**
Masvingo, *Zimb.* 20°6′ S, 30°47′ E **227**
Maşyāf, *Syr.* 35°3′ N, 36°20′ E **194**
Mat, river, *Alban.* 41°38′ N, 19°38′ E **168**
Mata, *Dem. Rep. of the Congo* 7°55′ S, 21°56′ E **218**
Mata Mata, *S. Af.* 25°50′ S, 20°3′ E **227**
Mata Ortíz, *Mex.* 30°7′ N, 108°4′ W **92**
Matachewan, *Can.* 47°56′ N, 80°38′ W **94**
Matachic, *Mex.* 28°50′ N, 107°44′ W **92**
Matadi, *Dem. Rep. of the Congo* 5°49′ S, 13°27′ E **218**
Matador, *Tex., U.S.* 33°59′ N, 100°50′ W **92**
Matagalpa, *Nicar.* 12°54′ N, 85°54′ W **115**
Matagami, *Can.* 49°47′ N, 77°39′ W **94**
Matagami, Lac, lake, *Can.* 50°0′ N, 78°4′ W **94**
Matagorda, *Tex., U.S.* 28°41′ N, 95°58′ W **96**
Matagorda Bay 28°28′ N, 97°19′ W **80**
Matagorda Peninsula, *Tex., U.S.* 28°31′ N, 96°26′ W **96**
Matak, island, *Indonesia* 3°25′ N, 106°17′ E **196**
Matakana, *N.Z.* 36°23′ S, 174°42′ E **240**
Matala, *Angola* 14°47′ S, 14°59′ E **220**
Matala, ruin(s), *Gr.* 34°58′ N, 24°39′ E **156**
Matam, *Senegal* 15°39′ N, 13°21′ W **222**
Matameye, *Niger* 13°23′ N, 8°26′ E **222**
Matamoros, *Mex.* 18°34′ N, 98°29′ W **114**
Matamoros, *Mex.* 25°31′ N, 103°15′ W **114**
Matamoros, *Mex.* 25°53′ N, 97°31′ W **114**
Ma'ţan al Ḩusayyāt, spring, *Lib.* 30°21′ N, 20°33′ E **216**
Ma'ţan as Sarra, spring, *Lib.* 21°35′ N, 21°52′ E **216**
Ma'ţan Bishrah, spring, *Lib.* 23°0′ N, 22°41′ E **226**
Ma'ţan Shârib, spring, *Egypt* 30°16′ N, 28°26′ E **180**
Matandu, river, *Tanzania* 8°52′ S, 38°38′ E **224**
Matane, *Can.* 48°49′ N, 67°33′ W **94**
Matanzas, *Cuba* 23°4′ N, 81°36′ W **96**
Matanzas, adm. division, *Cuba* 22°59′ N, 81°44′ W **116**
Matanzas, island, *Cuba* 22°5′ N, 82°46′ W **116**
Matão, Serra do, *Braz.* 9°38′ S, 51°31′ W **130**
Mataojo, *Uru.* 31°11′ S, 56°23′ W **139**
Matapás see Akrotírio Ténaro, *Gr.* 36°13′ N, 21°38′ E **156**
Matapi, *Suriname* 4°59′ N, 57°21′ W **130**
Mataporquera, *Sp.* 42°52′ N, 4°11′ W **150**
Matapwa, *Tanzania* 9°42′ S, 39°24′ E **224**
Matara, *Sri Lanka* 5°58′ N, 80°32′ E **188**
Mataram, *Indonesia* 8°36′ S, 116°6′ E **192**
Matarani, *Peru* 16°60′ S, 72°7′ W **137**
Matarka, *Mor.* 33°21′ N, 2°42′ W **214**
Mataró, *Sp.* 41°32′ N, 2°26′ E **164**
Matassi, spring, *Sudan* 18°49′ N, 29°47′ E **226**
Mätäsvaara, *Fin.* 63°25′ N, 29°32′ E **152**
Matata, *N.Z.* 37°55′ S, 176°46′ E **240**
Matatiele, *S. Af.* 30°22′ S, 28°46′ E **227**
Matauná, river, *Braz.* 6°15′ S, 60°59′ W **130**
Matawai, *N.Z.* 38°22′ S, 177°33′ E **240**
Matay, *Kaz.* 45°31′ N, 57°6′ E **158**
Matay, *Kaz.* 45°52′ N, 78°41′ E **184**
Mateguá, *Bol.* 13°3′ S, 62°49′ W **130**
Matehuala, *Mex.* 23°37′ N, 100°39′ W **96**
Matemo, Ilha, island, *Mozambique* 12°11′ S, 40°39′ E **224**
Matera, *It.* 40°39′ N, 16°36′ E **156**
Matese, *It.* 41°26′ N, 14°7′ E **156**
Mátészalka, *Hung.* 47°56′ N, 22°21′ E **168**
Matetsi, *Zimb.* 18°19′ S, 25°56′ E **224**
Matfors, *Nor.* 62°20′ N, 17°0′ E **152**
Matguia, *Tun.* 34°40′ N, 10°20′ E **156**
Mather, *Calif., U.S.* 37°52′ N, 119°52′ W **100**
Mather, Mount, peak, *Antarctica* 73°32′ S, 60°30′ E **248**
Matheson, *Can.* 48°32′ N, 80°29′ W **94**
Matheson Island, *Can.* 51°43′ N, 96°57′ W **108**
Mathews, *Va., U.S.* 37°25′ N, 76°20′ W **96**
Mathews Peak, *Kenya* 1°13′ N, 37°14′ E **224**
Mathis, *Tex., U.S.* 28°5′ N, 97°49′ W **92**
Mathura, *India* 27°27′ N, 77°38′ E **197**
Mati, *Philippines* 6°59′ N, 126°12′ E **203**
Matiakoali, *Burkina Faso* 12°21′ N, 1°3′ E **222**
Matias Cardoso, *Braz.* 14°56′ S, 43°55′ W **138**
Matin, *India* 22°46′ N, 82°25′ E **197**
Matkasel'kya, *Russ.* 61°57′ N, 30°30′ E **152**
Matlabas, *S. Af.* 24°15′ S, 27°30′ E **227**
Matli, *Pak.* 25°4′ N, 68°47′ E **186**
Matlock, *U.K.* 53°8′ N, 1°33′ W **162**
Mato, *Dem. Rep. of the Congo* 8°1′ S, 24°54′ E **224**
Mato, Cerro, peak, *Venez.* 7°12′ N, 65°23′ W **136**
Mato Grosso, *Braz.* 15°1′ S, 59°57′ W **132**
Mato Grosso, adm. division, *Braz.* 14°29′ S, 52°39′ W **138**
Mato Grosso do Sul, adm. division, *Braz.* 20°12′ S, 53°26′ W **138**
Mato Grosso, Planalto do, *South America* 14°13′ S, 58°51′ W **123**
Mato Verde, *Braz.* 15°25′ S, 42°55′ W **138**
Matobo National Park, *Zimb.* 20°38′ S, 28°11′ E **206**
Matochkin Shar, *Russ.* 73°21′ N, 56°33′ E **160**
Matochkin Shar, Proliv 72°52′ N, 49°46′ E **160**
Matoio, *Angola* 7°28′ S, 14°37′ E **220**
Matola, *Malawi* 13°39′ S, 34°55′ E **224**
Matombo, *Tanzania* 7°2′ S, 37°47′ E **224**
Matope, *Malawi* 15°21′ S, 34°58′ E **224**
Matopos, *Zimb.* 20°25′ S, 28°28′ E **227**
Matos, river, *Bol.* 14°30′ S, 65°60′ W **137**
Matosinhos, *Port.* 41°10′ N, 8°43′ W **150**
Mátra, *Hung.* 47°47′ N, 19°43′ E **168**
Matraca, *Col.* 3°1′ N, 69°7′ W **136**
Mátrafüred, *Hung.* 47°48′ N, 19°58′ E **168**
Maţraḩ, *Oman* 23°36′ N, 58°32′ E **182**
Maţrûḩ, *Egypt* 31°20′ N, 27°12′ E **180**
Matsena, *Nig.* 13°8′ N, 10°3′ E **222**
Matsu Tao (Matsu), island, *China* 26°16′ N, 120°3′ E **198**
Matsubase, *Japan* 32°37′ N, 130°41′ E **201**
Matsue, *Japan* 35°27′ N, 133°3′ E **201**
Matsumoto, *Japan* 36°13′ N, 137°59′ E **201**
Matsunaga, *Japan* 34°27′ N, 133°16′ E **201**
Matsusaka, *Japan* 34°33′ N, 136°33′ E **201**
Matsushiro, *Japan* 36°34′ N, 138°13′ E **201**
Matsutō, *Japan* 36°30′ N, 136°33′ E **201**
Matsuura, *Japan* 33°20′ N, 129°42′ E **201**
Matsuyama, *Japan* 33°49′ N, 132°46′ E **201**
Mattagami Lake, lake, *Can.* 47°47′ N, 82°6′ W **110**
Mattagami, river, *Can.* 50°10′ N, 82°17′ W **110**
Mattapoisett, *Mass., U.S.* 41°39′ N, 70°50′ W **104**
Mattawa, *Can.* 46°18′ N, 78°41′ W **94**
Matterhorn Peak, *Calif., U.S.* 38°5′ N, 119°25′ W **100**
Matterhorn, peak, *Nev., U.S.* 41°48′ N, 115°28′ W **90**
Matterhorn, peak, *Switz.* 45°59′ N, 7°37′ E **165**
Mattersburg, *Aust.* 47°43′ N, 16°24′ E **168**
Matthews Peak, *Ariz., U.S.* 36°21′ N, 109°13′ W **92**
Matthew's Ridge, *Guyana* 7°27′ N, 60°6′ W **130**
Mattili, *India* 18°32′ N, 82°13′ E **188**
Mattinata, *It.* 41°42′ N, 16°2′ E **168**
Mattituck, *N.Y., U.S.* 40°59′ N, 72°32′ W **104**
Mattoon, *Ill., U.S.* 39°29′ N, 88°22′ W **102**
Matugama, *Sri Lanka* 6°30′ N, 80°7′ E **188**
Matunuck, *R.I., U.S.* 41°22′ N, 71°33′ W **104**
Maturango Peak, *Calif., U.S.* 36°6′ N, 117°35′ W **92**
Maturín, *Venez.* 9°42′ N, 63°12′ W **116**
Matusadona National Park, *Zimb.* 17°10′ S, 28°4′ E **224**
Matveyevka, *Russ.* 53°29′ N, 53°35′ E **154**
Matxitxako, Cabo, *Sp.* 43°19′ N, 2°48′ W **164**
Matyl'ka, *Russ.* 63°20′ N, 85°34′ E **169**
Matzen, oil field, *Aust.* 48°21′ N, 16°35′ E **152**
Mau, *India* 25°54′ N, 83°31′ E **197**
Mau Ranipur, *India* 25°13′ N, 79°8′ E **197**
Mauá, *Mozambique* 13°52′ S, 37°10′ E **224**
Maubeuge, *Fr.* 50°16′ N, 3°58′ E **163**
Ma-ubin, *Myanmar* 16°43′ N, 95°36′ E **202**
Maubourguet, *Fr.* 43°27′ N, 3°178′ E **164**
Maud, *Tex., U.S.* 33°19′ N, 94°22′ W **103**
Maud Rise, *South Atlantic Ocean* 65°26′ S, 4°0′ E **255**
Maude, Cape, *Antarctica* 82°34′ S, 179°24′ E **248**
Maudheim, Sweden, station, *Antarctica* 71°4′ S, 10°46′ W **248**
Maués, *Braz.* 3°23′ S, 57°43′ W **130**
Maués, river, *Braz.* 4°23′ S, 57°25′ W **130**
Maug Islands, *Maug Islands* 20°2′ N, 145°20′ E **192**
Mauganj, *India* 24°42′ N, 81°52′ E **197**
Maugerville, *Can.* 45°53′ N, 66°28′ W **94**
Maui, island, *Hawai'i, U.S.* 20°39′ N, 156°2′ W **99**
Maukme, *Myanmar* 20°13′ N, 97°42′ E **202**
Maule, adm. division, *Chile* 35°44′ S, 72°37′ W **134**
Mauléon, *Fr.* 43°12′ N, 0°53′ E **164**
Maullín, *Chile* 41°38′ S, 73°37′ W **134**
Maumakeogh, peak, *Ire.* 54°15′ N, 9°36′ W **150**
Maumee, *Ohio, U.S.* 41°33′ N, 83°40′ W **102**
Maumelle, Lake, *Ark., U.S.* 34°50′ N, 93°1′ W **96**
Maumere, *Indonesia* 8°47′ S, 122°13′ E **192**
Maun, *Botswana* 19°59′ S, 23°23′ E **220**
Mauna Kea Observatories, site, *Hawai'i, U.S.* 19°49′ N, 155°32′ W **99**
Mauna Loa Observatory, site, *Hawai'i, U.S.* 19°31′ N, 155°38′ W **99**
Maungaturoto, *N.Z.* 36°7′ S, 174°21′ E **240**
Maungdaw, *Myanmar* 20°52′ N, 92°22′ E **188**
Maungmagan Islands, *Andaman Sea* 13°58′ N, 97°13′ E **202**
Maunoir, Lac, lake, *Can.* 67°36′ N, 118°28′ W **246**
Maurepas, Lake, *La., U.S.* 30°11′ N, 90°56′ W **96**
Maurepas, Lake, *La., U.S.* 30°14′ N, 90°46′ W **103**
Maures, Monts des, *Fr.* 43°19′ N, 5°52′ E **165**
Maurice, *La., U.S.* 30°5′ N, 92°8′ W **103**
Mauriceville, *N.Z.* 40°47′ S, 175°42′ E **240**
Mauriceville, *Tex., U.S.* 30°10′ N, 93°53′ W **103**
Mauritania 20°5′ N, 14°29′ W **214**
Mauritius 20°18′ S, 57°35′ E **254**
Mauritius Trench, *Indian Ocean* 22°23′ S, 56°10′ E **254**
Maurs, *Fr.* 44°42′ N, 2°11′ E **150**
Maury Bay 66°27′ S, 127°0′ E **248**
Maury Mountains, peak, *Oreg., U.S.* 44°1′ N, 120°27′ W **90**
Maury Seachannel, *North Atlantic Ocean* 56°23′ N, 24°27′ W **253**
Mauston, *Wis., U.S.* 43°46′ N, 90°4′ W **102**
Mauthen, *Aust.* 46°39′ N, 13°0′ E **167**
Mavago, *Mozambique* 12°27′ S, 36°13′ E **224**
Maverick, *Ariz., U.S.* 33°44′ N, 109°33′ W **92**
Mavinga, *Angola* 15°47′ S, 20°11′ E **207**
Mavonde, *Mozambique* 18°33′ S, 33°3′ E **224**
Mavroli, *Cyprus* 35°3′ N, 32°27′ E **194**
Mavrovo, *Maced.* 41°40′ N, 20°45′ E **168**
Mavrovo National Park, *Maced.* 41°13′ N, 20°50′ E **180**
Mavrovouni Mine, site, *Cyprus* 35°5′ N, 32°47′ E **194**
Mavrovoúni, peak, *Gr.* 39°26′ N, 22°31′ E **156**
Mawlá Maţar, *Yemen* 14°48′ N, 48°38′ E **182**
Mawlamyine, *Myanmar* 16°24′ N, 97°41′ E **192**
Mawlite, *Myanmar* 23°36′ N, 94°19′ E **202**
Mawlu, *Myanmar* 24°26′ N, 96°13′ E **188**
Mawqaq, *Saudi Arabia* 27°25′ N, 41°9′ E **180**
Mawshij, *Yemen* 13°43′ N, 43°19′ E **182**
Mawson, Australia, station, *Antarctica* 67°38′ S, 63°5′ E **248**
Mawson, Cape, *Antarctica* 70°29′ S, 77°38′ W **248**
Mawson Coast, *Antarctica* 67°50′ S, 61°7′ E **248**
Max, *N. Dak., U.S.* 47°48′ N, 101°19′ W **90**
Maxaas, *Somalia* 4°23′ N, 46°8′ E **218**
Maxcanú, *Mex.* 20°33′ N, 89°60′ W **115**
Maxhamish Lake, *Can.* 59°48′ N, 124°19′ W **108**
Maxixe, *Mozambique* 23°45′ S, 35°18′ E **227**
Maxton, *N.C., U.S.* 34°43′ N, 79°22′ W **96**
Maxwell, *N. Mex., U.S.* 36°31′ N, 104°34′ W **92**
Maxwell Bay 74°19′ N, 89°56′ W **106**
Maxwelton House, site, *U.K.* 55°11′ N, 3°57′ W **150**
May, Cape 81°35′ S, 173°55′ E **248**
May Point, Cape, *N.J., U.S.* 38°38′ N, 75°1′ W **94**
Maya, island, *Indonesia* 1°39′ S, 109°16′ E **192**
Maya, Mesa de, *Colo., U.S.* 37°1′ N, 103°46′ W **92**
Maya Mountains, *Belize* 16°41′ N, 89°8′ W **115**
Maya, river, *Russ.* 55°23′ N, 132°42′ E **160**
Maya, river, *Russ.* 58°9′ N, 137°20′ E **160**
Mayabandar, *India* 12°52′ N, 92°59′ E **188**
Mayaguana, adm. division, *Bahamas* 22°15′ N, 73°18′ W **116**
Mayaguana Island, *Bahamas* 22°31′ N, 73°18′ W **116**
Mayagüez 18°11′ N, 67°10′ W **116**
Mayahi, *Niger* 13°52′ N, 7°31′ E **222**
Mayāmey, *Iran* 36°30′ N, 55°46′ E **180**
Mayang, *China* 27°54′ N, 109°48′ E **198**
Mayapán, ruin(s), *Mex.* 20°35′ N, 89°35′ W **115**
Mayarí, *Cuba* 20°40′ N, 75°42′ W **116**
Maybeury, *W. Va., U.S.* 37°21′ N, 81°23′ W **96**
Maych'ew, *Eth.* 12°47′ N, 39°32′ E **182**
Mayda, *Russ.* 66°20′ N, 41°53′ E **154**
Maydān Ikbiz, *Syr.* 36°48′ N, 36°39′ E **156**
Maydelle, *Tex., U.S.* 31°46′ N, 95°18′ W **103**
Maydh, *Somalia* 10°53′ N, 47°4′ E **216**
Maydh, island, *Somalia* 11°21′ N, 46°49′ E **216**
Maydī, *Yemen* 16°18′ N, 42°52′ E **182**
Mayen, *Ger.* 50°19′ N, 7°13′ E **167**
Mayersville, *Miss., U.S.* 32°52′ N, 91°3′ W **103**
Mayerthorpe, *Can.* 53°56′ N, 115°11′ W **108**
Mayevo, *Russ.* 56°22′ N, 29°51′ E **166**
Mayfa'ah, *Yemen* 14°19′ N, 47°31′ E **182**
Mayfield, *Ky., U.S.* 36°44′ N, 88°40′ W **82**
Mayfield, *N.Z.* 43°51′ S, 171°25′ E **240**
Mayfield Peak, *Idaho, U.S.* 44°29′ N, 114°50′ W **90**
Mayhill, *N. Mex., U.S.* 32°53′ N, 105°29′ W **92**
Maykop, *Russ.* 44°38′ N, 40°3′ E **156**
Maymecha, river, *Russ.* 71°36′ N, 97°42′ E **160**
Maymont, *Can.* 52°32′ N, 107°42′ W **108**
Maynooth, *Can.* 45°14′ N, 77°57′ W **94**
Mayo, *Can.* 63°32′ N, 136°2′ W **246**
Mayo, Cerro, peak, *Chile* 50°22′ S, 73°40′ W **134**
Mayo Darlé, *Cameroon* 6°25′ N, 11°32′ E **222**
Mayo Faran, *Nig.* 8°56′ N, 12°5′ E **216**
Mayo Mayo, *Bol.* 12°19′ S, 65°12′ W **137**
Mayo Ndaga, *Nig.* 6°52′ N, 11°25′ E **222**
Mayodan, *N.C., U.S.* 36°24′ N, 79°59′ W **96**
Mayon Volcano, peak, *Philippines* 13°14′ N, 123°36′ E **203**
Mayor Buratovich, *Arg.* 39°17′ S, 62°37′ W **139**
Mayotte 12°58′ S, 44°34′ E **220**
Mayotte, Île de, island, *Fr.* 12°33′ S, 45°6′ E **220**
Mayqayyn, *Kaz.* 51°28′ N, 75°47′ E **184**
Mayraira Point, *Philippines* 18°39′ N, 120°38′ E **203**
Maysk, *Russ.* 57°47′ N, 77°10′ E **169**
Maysville, *Ky., U.S.* 38°37′ N, 83°45′ W **102**
Maysville, *Mo., U.S.* 39°52′ N, 94°22′ W **94**
Maytag see Dushanzi, *China* 44°17′ N, 84°53′ E **184**
Mayum La, pass, *China* 30°34′ N, 82°31′ E **197**
Mayumba, *Gabon* 3°29′ S, 10°40′ E **218**
Mayville, *Mich., U.S.* 43°19′ N, 83°20′ W **102**
Mayville, *N. Dak., U.S.* 47°28′ N, 97°20′ W **90**
Mayville, *Wis., U.S.* 43°28′ N, 88°34′ W **102**
Maywood, *Ill., U.S.* 41°52′ N, 87°50′ W **102**
Maza, *Arg.* 36°49′ S, 63°20′ W **139**
Mazabuka, *Zambia* 15°53′ S, 27°45′ E **224**
Mazagan see El Jadida, *Mor.* 33°15′ N, 8°33′ W **214**
Mazagão, *Braz.* 0°8′ N, 51°18′ W **130**
Mazalij, oil field, *Saudi Arabia* 24°24′ N, 48°26′ E **196**
Mazamet, *Fr.* 43°28′ N, 2°22′ E **164**
Mazán, *Peru* 3°29′ S, 73°9′ W **136**
Mazán, river, *Peru* 3°10′ S, 73°49′ W **136**
Mazapil, *Mex.* 24°37′ N, 101°34′ W **114**
Mazar-e Sharif, *Afghan.* 36°42′ N, 67°9′ E **186**
Mazarredo, *Arg.* 47°5′ S, 66°41′ W **134**
Mazarrón, *Sp.* 37°35′ N, 1°19′ W **164**
Mazatenango, *Guatemala* 14°30′ N, 91°30′ W **115**
Mazatlán, *Mex.* 23°10′ N, 106°24′ W **114**
Mazatlán, *Mex.* 29°1′ N, 110°10′ W **92**
Mazatzal Mountains, *Ariz., U.S.* 34°11′ N, 111°34′ W **92**
Mazée, *Belg.* 50°6′ N, 4°40′ E **167**
Mažeikiai, *Lith.* 56°19′ N, 22°20′ E **166**
Mazgirt, *Turk.* 39°1′ N, 39°36′ E **195**
Mazıdağı, *Turk.* 37°30′ N, 40°32′ E **195**
Mazīnān, *Iran* 36°22′ N, 56°43′ E **180**
Mazirbe, *Latv.* 57°38′ N, 22°10′ E **166**
Mazo Cruz, *Peru* 16°47′ S, 69°44′ W **137**
Mazomanie, *Wis., U.S.* 43°9′ N, 89°48′ W **102**
Mazong Shan, peak, *China* 41°27′ N, 96°25′ E **172**
Mazowe, *Zimb.* 17°31′ S, 30°59′ E **224**
Mazowieckie, adm. division, *Pol.* 52°21′ N, 19°23′ E **152**
Mazrag, oil field, *Oman* 18°17′ N, 55°30′ E **182**
Mazrub, *Sudan* 13°52′ N, 29°19′ E **226**
Mazsalaca, *Latv.* 57°51′ N, 25°2′ E **166**
Mazunga, *Zimb.* 21°44′ S, 29°53′ E **227**
Mazyr, *Belarus* 52°0′ N, 29°21′ E **152**
Mbabane, *Swaziland* 26°19′ S, 30°58′ E **227**
Mbahiakro, *Côte d'Ivoire* 7°24′ N, 4°21′ W **222**
Mbaïki, *Cen. Af. Rep.* 3°55′ N, 18°2′ E **218**
Mbala, *Cen. Af. Rep.* 7°47′ N, 20°49′ E **218**
Mbala (Abercorn), *Zambia* 8°53′ S, 31°23′ E **224**
Mbalabala, *Zimb.* 20°28′ S, 29°1′ E **227**
Mbalambala, *Kenya* 4°237′ S, 39°4′ E **224**
Mbale, *Uganda* 1°1′ N, 34°7′ E **224**
Mbalmayo, *Cameroon* 3°40′ N, 11°31′ E **222**
Mbamba Bay, *Tanzania* 11°15′ S, 34°50′ E **224**
Mbandaka (Coquilhatville), *Dem. Rep. of the Congo* 2°119′ N, 18°17′ E **218**
Mbandjok, *Cameroon* 4°21′ N, 11°50′ E **218**
Mbang, Monts, *Cameroon* 7°11′ N, 13°29′ E **218**
Mbanga, *Cameroon* 4°30′ N, 9°33′ E **222**
Mbanika, island, *Solomon Islands* 9°5′ S, 159°11′ E **242**
M'banza Congo, *Angola* 6°17′ S, 14°14′ E **218**
Mbanza-Ngungu, *Dem. Rep. of the Congo* 5°18′ S, 14°49′ E **218**
Mbarangandu, river, *Tanzania* 10°4′ S, 36°47′ E **224**
Mbarara, *Uganda* 0°37′ N, 30°40′ E **224**
Mbari, river, *Cen. Af. Rep.* 4°56′ N, 22°52′ E **218**
Mbé, *Cameroon* 7°43′ N, 13°31′ E **218**
Mbé, *Congo* 3°20′ S, 15°52′ E **218**
Mbegera, *Tanzania* 9°34′ S, 34°58′ E **224**
Mbengwi, *Cameroon* 6°2′ N, 10°2′ E **222**
Mbeya, *Tanzania* 8°54′ S, 33°29′ E **224**
Mbeya, adm. division, *Tanzania* 8°32′ S, 32°46′ E **224**
M'Binda, *Congo* 2°10′ S, 12°52′ E **218**
Mbitao, *Cameroon* 7°13′ N, 15°14′ E **218**
Mbizi, *Zimb.* 21°24′ S, 31°1′ E **227**
Mbogo, *Tanzania* 7°25′ S, 33°26′ E **224**
Mboi, *Dem. Rep. of the Congo* 6°57′ S, 21°53′ E **218**
Mbomo, *Congo* 0°22′ N, 14°42′ E **218**
Mborokua, island, *Solomon Islands* 9°2′ S, 158°45′ E **242**
Mbour, *Senegal* 14°25′ N, 16°43′ W **222**
Mbout, *Mauritania* 16°1′ N, 12°38′ W **222**
Mbrés, *Cen. Af. Rep.* 6°36′ N, 19°48′ E **218**
Mbuji-Mayi (Bakwanga), *Dem. Rep. of the Congo* 6°10′ S, 23°36′ E **224**
Mbulamuti, *Uganda* 0°47′ N, 33°2′ E **224**
Mbulo, island, *Solomon Islands* 8°45′ S, 158°19′ E **242**
Mbulu, *Tanzania* 3°49′ S, 35°33′ E **224**
Mburucuyá, *Arg.* 28°2′ S, 58°13′ W **139**
Mcadam, *Can.* 45°35′ N, 67°19′ W **94**
Mcafee Peak, *Nev., U.S.* 41°30′ N, 116°4′ W **90**
Mcalester, *Okla., U.S.* 34°54′ N, 95°46′ W **96**
Mcallen, *Tex., U.S.* 26°10′ N, 98°13′ W **112**
Mcarthur, *Ohio, U.S.* 39°13′ N, 82°29′ W **102**
Mcbain, *Mich., U.S.* 44°11′ N, 85°13′ W **102**
Mcbride, *Can.* 53°17′ N, 120°12′ W **108**
Mccall, *Idaho, U.S.* 44°53′ N, 116°5′ W **90**
Mccamey, *Tex., U.S.* 31°7′ N, 102°12′ W **92**
Mccann Lake, *Can.* 61°13′ N, 107°4′ W **108**
Mccarran International Airport, *Nev., U.S.* 36°2′ N, 115°14′ W **101**
Mccarthy, *Alas., U.S.* 61°25′ N, 142°56′ W **98**
Mccarthy Inlet 78°49′ S, 51°2′ W **248**
Mcchord Air Force Base, *Wash., U.S.* 47°7′ N, 122°32′ W **100**
Mccleary, *Wash., U.S.* 47°2′ N, 123°16′ W **100**
Mcclellanville, *S.C., U.S.* 33°5′ N, 79°28′ W **96**
Mcclintock, Mount, peak, *Antarctica* 80°10′ S, 158°39′ E **248**
Mcclure, Lake, *Calif., U.S.* 37°35′ N, 120°23′ W **100**
Mccomb, *Miss., U.S.* 31°13′ N, 90°27′ W **103**
Mccomb, *Ohio, U.S.* 41°6′ N, 83°46′ W **102**
Mcconaughy, Lake, *Nebr., U.S.* 41°13′ N, 103°23′ W **80**
Mcconnell Air Force Base, *Kans., U.S.* 37°35′ N, 97°20′ W **90**
Mcconnelsville, *Ohio, U.S.* 39°38′ N, 81°51′ W **102**
Mccook, *Nebr., U.S.* 40°11′ N, 100°39′ W **90**
Mccool, *Miss., U.S.* 33°11′ N, 89°20′ W **103**
Mccormick, Cape, *Antarctica* 71°28′ S, 176°52′ E **248**
Mccoy, Mount, peak, *Antarctica* 75°46′ S, 140°8′ W **248**
Mccoy Mountains, *Calif., U.S.* 33°45′ N, 114°52′ W **101**
Mccrea Lake, *Can.* 50°49′ N, 90°44′ W **110**
Mccreary, *Can.* 50°47′ N, 99°30′ W **90**
Mccullough, *Ala., U.S.* 31°9′ N, 87°31′ W **103**
Mccullough Range, *Nev., U.S.* 35°31′ N, 115°17′ W **101**
Mccusker Lake, *Can.* 51°42′ N, 95°38′ W **108**
Mcdame, *Can.* 59°12′ N, 129°14′ W **108**
Mcdills, spring, *Austral.* 25°50′ S, 135°15′ E **230**
Mcdonald, *Kans., U.S.* 39°46′ N, 101°22′ W **90**
Mcdonald, *Miss., U.S.* 32°39′ N, 89°8′ W **103**
Mcdonald Peak, *Calif., U.S.* 40°55′ N, 120°30′ W **90**

Mcevoy, Mount, peak, Can. 56°45′ N, 128°25′ W 108
Mcfarland, Calif., U.S. 35°40′ N, 119°15′ W 100
Mcfarland, Kans., U.S. 39°2′ N, 96°15′ W 90
Mcfarland, Wis., U.S. 43°0′ N, 89°18′ W 102
Mcgehee, Ark., U.S. 33°36′ N, 91°23′ W 96
Mcgill, Nev., U.S. 39°24′ N, 114°47′ W 90
Mcgrath, Alas., U.S. 63°4′ N, 155°28′ W 73
Mcgregor, Tex., U.S. 31°25′ N, 97°24′ W 92
Mcgregor Lake, Can. 50°26′ N, 113°32′ W 90
Mcgregor, river, Can. 54°14′ N, 121°26′ W 108
Mcguire Air Force Base, N.J., U.S. 39°59′ N, 74°41′ W 94
Mcguire, Mount, peak, Idaho, U.S. 45°9′ N, 114°41′ W 90
Mchenry, Ky., U.S. 37°22′ N, 86°55′ W 96
Mchenry, Miss., U.S. 30°41′ N, 89°7′ W 103
Mcherrah, region, Alg. 26°45′ N, 5°3′ W 214
Mchinja, Tanzania 9°46′ S, 39°41′ E 224
Mchinji, Malawi 13°48′ S, 32°54′ E 224
Mcindoe Falls, Vt., U.S. 44°15′ N, 72°5′ W 104
Mcinnes Lake, Can. 52°8′ N, 95°4′ W 80
Mcintosh, Fla., U.S. 29°26′ N, 82°15′ W 105
Mcintosh, Minn., U.S. 47°36′ N, 95°55′ W 90
Mcintosh, S. Dak., U.S. 45°54′ N, 101°22′ W 90
Mcivor, river, Can. 57°53′ N, 112°1′ W 108
Mckay Lake, Can. 49°33′ N, 86°52′ W 94
Mckay Lake, Can. 53°45′ N, 65°58′ W 111
Mckay, Mount, peak, Can. 48°19′ N, 89°22′ W 94
Mckeesport, Pa., U.S. 40°20′ N, 79°49′ W 82
Mckelvey, Mount, peak, Antarctica 85°26′ S, 87°27′ W 248
Mckenzie Island, Can. 51°4′ N, 93°49′ W 82
Mckenzie Pass, Oreg., U.S. 44°14′ N, 121°48′ W 90
Mckerrow, Can. 46°16′ N, 81°45′ W 94
Mckerrow, Lake, N.Z. 44°30′ S, 167°28′ E 240
Mckinley, Mount (Denali), peak, Alas., U.S. 62°54′ N, 151°17′ W 98
Mckinley Peak, Antarctica 77°46′ S, 147°15′ W 248
Mckinney, Tex., U.S. 33°12′ N, 96°39′ W 112
Mckinnon, Wyo., U.S. 41°2′ N, 109°56′ W 90
Mckittrick, Calif., U.S. 35°18′ N, 119°38′ W 100
Mclain, Miss., U.S. 31°4′ N, 88°49′ W 103
Mclaughlin, S. Dak., U.S. 45°47′ N, 100°50′ W 90
Mclaurin, Miss., U.S. 31°9′ N, 89°12′ W 103
Mclean, Ill., U.S. 40°18′ N, 89°11′ W 102
Mclean, Tex., U.S. 35°12′ N, 100°36′ W 92
Mclean Mountain, peak, Me., U.S. 47°6′ N, 68°57′ W 94
Mcleansboro, Mo., U.S. 38°5′ N, 88°32′ W 94
Mclennan, Can. 55°41′ N, 116°55′ W 108
Mcleod, Tex., U.S. 32°55′ N, 94°6′ W 103
Mcleod Bay 62°35′ N, 110°40′ W 106
Mcleod Lake, Can. 54°59′ N, 123°2′ W 108
Mcleod Valley, Can. 53°44′ N, 116°1′ W 108
M'Clintock Channel 70°55′ N, 106°28′ W 72
Mcloughlin, Mount, peak, Oreg., U.S. 42°27′ N, 122°24′ W 90
M'Clure Strait 74°40′ N, 118°17′ W 255
Mcmechen, W. Va., U.S. 39°58′ N, 80°45′ W 94
Mcminnville, Tenn., U.S. 35°41′ N, 85°46′ W 96
Mcmurdo, U.S., station, Antarctica 77°48′ S, 166°8′ E 248
Mcnary, Ariz., U.S. 34°3′ N, 109°51′ W 92
Mcneil, Ark., U.S. 33°20′ N, 93°13′ W 103
Mcneill, Miss., U.S. 30°39′ N, 89°38′ W 103
Mcphadyen, river, Can. 53°57′ N, 67°39′ W 111
Mcpherson, Kans., U.S. 38°21′ N, 97°41′ W 90
Mcrae, Ark., U.S. 35°5′ N, 91°49′ W 96
Mcrae, Ga., U.S. 32°3′ N, 82°54′ W 96
Mctaggart Lake, Can. 58°2′ N, 108°60′ W 108
Mctavish Lake, Can. 55°54′ N, 105°52′ W 108
Mcveigh, Can. 56°42′ N, 101°15′ W 108
Mcvicar Arm 64°55′ N, 122°55′ W 106
Mcville, N. Dak., U.S. 47°44′ N, 98°12′ W 90
Mdandu, Tanzania 9°9′ S, 34°41′ E 224
Mdennah, region, Mali 24°19′ N, 6°3′ W 214
Mdiq, Mor. 35°40′ N, 5°20′ W 150
Mead, Lake, Nev., U.S. 36°26′ N, 114°32′ W 101
Meade, Kans., U.S. 37°17′ N, 100°21′ W 92
Meade Peak, Idaho, U.S. 42°29′ N, 111°19′ W 90
Meade, river, Alas., U.S. 69°34′ N, 156°47′ W 98
Meadow Lake, Can. 54°8′ N, 108°26′ W 108
Meadow Valley Wash, river, Nev., U.S. 36°53′ N, 114°44′ W 101
Meadows, Idaho, U.S. 44°56′ N, 116°15′ W 90
Meadows, N.H., U.S. 44°21′ N, 71°29′ W 104
Meadville, Miss., U.S. 31°27′ N, 90°54′ W 103
Meadville, Pa., U.S. 41°38′ N, 80°9′ W 94
Meander River, Can. 59°2′ N, 117°41′ W 108
Meares, Cape, Oreg., U.S. 45°20′ N, 124°24′ W 90
Mears, Mich., U.S. 43°40′ N, 86°25′ W 102
Meath Park, Can. 53°26′ N, 105°25′ W 108
Meaux, Fr. 48°57′ N, 2°53′ E 163
Mebane, N.C., U.S. 36°5′ N, 79°17′ W 96
Mecanhelas, Mozambique 15°11′ S, 35°53′ E 224
Mecca, Calif., U.S. 33°34′ N, 116°6′ W 101
Mecca see Makkah, Saudi Arabia 21°24′ N, 39°49′ E 182
Mechanic Falls, Me., U.S. 44°6′ N, 70°25′ W 104
Mechanicville, N.Y., U.S. 42°54′ N, 73°43′ W 104
Mechelen, Belg. 51°1′ N, 4°29′ E 167
Mechems, region, Alg. 27°0′ N, 8°15′ W 214
Mecheraa Asfa, Alg. 35°22′ N, 1°4′ E 150
Mecherchar (Eil Malk), island, Palau 7°7′ N, 134°22′ E 242
Mecheria, Alg. 33°33′ N, 0°17′ E 214
Mechernich, Ger. 50°35′ N, 6°39′ E 167
Mechetinskaya, Russ. 46°43′ N, 40°26′ E 158
Mechta Gara, Alg. 36°15′ N, 5°25′ E 150
Mechtat el Hiout, Alg. 36°33′ N, 6°40′ E 150
Mecitözü, Turk. 40°31′ N, 35°17′ E 156
Mecklenburg-West Pomerania, adm. division, Ger. 53°29′ N, 10°59′ E 152
Meconta, Mozambique 14°58′ S, 39°54′ E 224
Mecosta, Mich., U.S. 43°37′ N, 85°14′ W 102
Mecsek, Hung. 46°15′ N, 17°37′ E 168
Mecubúri, Mozambique 14°41′ S, 38°55′ E 224
Mecúfi, Mozambique 13°22′ S, 40°33′ E 224
Mecula, Mozambique 12°6′ S, 37°42′ E 224
Medak, India 18°4′ N, 78°15′ E 188
Médala, Mauritania 15°31′ N, 5°38′ W 222
Medale, Eth. 6°23′ N, 41°54′ E 224
Medan, Indonesia 3°35′ N, 98°40′ E 196
Médanos, Arg. 33°26′ S, 59°4′ W 139
Médanos, Arg. 38°51′ S, 62°42′ W 139
Médanos de Coro National Park, Venez. 11°34′ N, 70°3′ W 122
Medanosa, Punta, Arg. 48°17′ S, 65°58′ W 134
Medaryville, Ind., U.S. 41°3′ N, 86°54′ W 102
Médéa, Alg. 36°15′ N, 2°45′ E 150
Medebach, Ger. 51°11′ N, 8°42′ E 167
Medeiros Neto, Braz. 17°22′ S, 40°15′ W 138
Medellín, Col. 6°13′ N, 75°34′ W 136
Medemblik, Neth. 52°46′ N, 5°6′ E 163
Medena Selišta, Bosn. and Herzg. 44°7′ N, 16°47′ E 168
Medenine, Tun. 33°21′ N, 10°28′ E 214
Meder, Eritrea 14°41′ N, 40°42′ E 182
Mederdra, Mauritania 16°56′ N, 15°42′ W 222
Medes, Les, islands, Sp. 42°5′ N, 3°8′ E 164
Medford, Mass., U.S. 42°25′ N, 71°7′ W 104
Medford, Okla., U.S. 36°47′ N, 97°43′ W 92
Medford, Oreg., U.S. 42°21′ N, 122°50′ W 106
Medford, Wis., U.S. 45°8′ N, 90°20′ W 94
Medgidia, Rom. 44°14′ N, 28°16′ E 156
Mediaş, Rom. 46°10′ N, 24°20′ E 156
Medical Lake, Wash., U.S. 47°33′ N, 117°42′ W 90
Medicina, It. 44°29′ N, 11°36′ E 167
Medicine Bow, Wyo., U.S. 41°54′ N, 106°13′ W 92
Medicine Bow Mountains, Wyo., U.S. 41°44′ N, 106°32′ W 90
Medicine Bow Peak, Wyo., U.S. 41°21′ N, 106°23′ W 90
Medicine Hat, Can. 50°2′ N, 110°43′ W 82
Medicine Lake, Mont., U.S. 48°23′ N, 105°1′ W 90
Medicine Lodge, Kans., U.S. 37°16′ N, 98°37′ W 90
Medicine Rocks, site, Mont., U.S. 45°56′ N, 104°38′ W 90
Medina, Braz. 16°13′ S, 41°33′ W 138
Medina, Col. 4°30′ N, 73°21′ W 136
Medina, N.Y., U.S. 43°12′ N, 78°25′ W 110
Medina, N. Dak., U.S. 46°53′ N, 99°20′ W 90
Medina, Ohio, U.S. 41°7′ N, 81°52′ W 102
Medina, Tex., U.S. 29°47′ N, 99°15′ W 92
Medina de Pomar, Sp. 42°53′ N, 3°29′ W 164
Medina de Rioseco, Sp. 41°51′ N, 5°7′ W 214
Medina del Campo, Sp. 41°18′ N, 4°55′ W 150
Médina Gadaoundou, Guinea 11°51′ N, 11°36′ W 222
Medina see Al Madīnah, Saudi Arabia 24°26′ N, 39°34′ E 182
Medina Sidonia, Sp. 36°28′ N, 5°58′ W 164
Medinaceli, Sp. 41°9′ N, 2°27′ W 164
Médine, Mali 14°22′ N, 11°24′ W 222
Medinipur, India 22°27′ N, 87°20′ E 197
Mediodía, Col. 1°51′ S, 72°9′ W 136
Mediterranean Sea 34°7′ N, 16°43′ E 143
Medje, Dem. Rep. of the Congo 2°24′ N, 27°16′ E 224
Medjerda, Monts de la, Tun. 36°40′ N, 8°6′ E 156
Medkovets, Bulg. 43°37′ N, 23°10′ E 168
Medley, Can. 54°25′ N, 110°16′ W 108
Mednogorsk, Russ. 51°24′ N, 57°34′ E 158
Médoc, region, Fr. 44°43′ N, 1°16′ W 150
Mêdog, China 29°19′ N, 95°24′ E 188
Medstead, Can. 53°17′ N, 108°5′ W 108
Međurječje, Europe 42°43′ N, 19°22′ E 168
Međuvođe, Bosn. and Herzg. 45°6′ N, 16°46′ E 168
Medveđa, Serb. and Mont. 42°50′ N, 21°35′ E 168
Medveditsa, river, Russ. 49°40′ N, 43°1′ E 184
Medvezh'i Ostrova (Bear Islands), East Siberian Sea 71°5′ N, 151°1′ E 160
Medvezh'yegorsk, Russ. 62°54′ N, 34°28′ E 154
Medway, Mass., U.S. 42°8′ N, 71°25′ W 104
Medzhybizh, Ukr. 49°26′ N, 27°26′ E 152
Meehaus, Mount, peak, Can. 58°0′ N, 130°41′ W 108
Meeker, Colo., U.S. 40°2′ N, 107°56′ W 90
Meelpaeg Reservoir, lake, Can. 48°15′ N, 57°26′ W 111
Meerut, India 28°59′ N, 77°40′ E 197
Meerzorg, Suriname 5°47′ N, 55°9′ W 130
Meeteetse, Wyo., U.S. 44°8′ N, 108°51′ W 90
Mefjell Mount, peak, Antarctica 72°10′ S, 24°38′ E 248
Mēga, Eth. 4°1′ N, 38°17′ E 224
Megalo, Eth. 6°52′ N, 40°47′ E 224
Megargel, Ala., U.S. 31°22′ N, 87°25′ W 103
Meghalaya, adm. division, India 25°20′ N, 89°54′ E 197
Meghri, Arm. 38°53′ N, 46°13′ E 195
Megiddo, Israel 32°34′ N, 35°10′ E 194
Megiddo, Tel, peak, Israel 32°34′ N, 35°8′ E 194
Megion, Russ. 61°1′ N, 76°19′ E 169
Mégiscane, Lac, lake, Can. 48°37′ N, 76°28′ W 94
Megler, Wash., U.S. 46°14′ N, 123°51′ W 100
Mehar, Pak. 27°13′ N, 67°50′ E 186
Meharry, Mount, peak, Austral. 22°59′ S, 118°24′ E 230
Meharry, Mount, peak, Austral. 23°10′ S, 118°10′ E 238
Mehedinți, adm. division, Rom. 44°49′ N, 22°12′ E 156
Mehedinți, Munții, Rom. 44°51′ N, 22°25′ E 168
Mehola, West Bank 32°20′ N, 35°31′ E 194
Mehrīz, Iran 31°32′ N, 54°35′ E 180
Meia Ponte, river, Braz. 18°4′ S, 49°32′ W 138
Meiganga, Cameroon 6°28′ N, 14°17′ E 218
Meighen Island, Can. 79°58′ N, 102°32′ W 246
Meigs, Ga., U.S. 31°3′ N, 84°6′ W 96
Meihekou, China 42°31′ N, 125°37′ E 200
Meikle Says Law, peak, U.K. 55°49′ N, 2°47′ W 150
Meiners Oaks, Calif., U.S. 34°27′ N, 119°17′ W 100
Meiningen, Ger. 50°34′ N, 10°24′ E 167
Meira, Sp. 43°12′ N, 7°19′ W 150
Meiringen, Switz. 46°43′ N, 8°11′ E 167
Meister, river, Can. 60°20′ N, 131°12′ W 108
Meizhou, China 24°19′ N, 116°4′ E 198
Meja, India 25°9′ N, 82°6′ E 197
Mejillones, Chile 23°8′ S, 70°30′ W 132
Mékambo, Gabon 0°59′ N, 13°53′ E 218
Mek'elē, Eth. 13°29′ N, 39°25′ E 182
Mekhel'ta, Russ. 42°44′ N, 46°30′ E 195
Mekhtar, Pak. 30°29′ N, 69°24′ E 186
Mékinac, Lac, lake, Can. 47°1′ N, 73°13′ W 110
Meknassy, Tun. 34°32′ N, 9°36′ E 156
Meko, Nig. 7°28′ N, 2°50′ E 222
Mekong see Lancang, river, China 32°3′ N, 97°14′ E 190
Mekoryuk, Alas., U.S. 60°17′ N, 166°21′ W 98
Mel, It. 46°3′ N, 12°4′ E 167
Melalap, Malaysia 5°15′ N, 116°0′ E 203
Melanesia, islands, Coral Sea 7°19′ S, 149°12′ E 192
Melaque, Mex. 19°14′ N, 104°43′ W 114
Melba Peninsula 65°39′ S, 98°7′ E 248
Melbourne, Austral. 37°51′ S, 144°38′ E 230
Melbourne, Fla., U.S. 28°6′ N, 80°40′ W 105
Melbourne Beach, Fla., U.S. 28°4′ N, 80°35′ W 105
Melbourne, Mount, peak, Antarctica 74°22′ S, 165°18′ E 248
Melbu, Nor. 68°29′ N, 14°49′ E 152
Melchett Lake, Can. 50°42′ N, 87°36′ W 110
Melchior Islands, Weddell Sea 64°16′ S, 65°56′ W 134
Melchor, Isla, island, Chile 45°15′ S, 75°39′ W 134
Melchor Ocampo, Mex. 24°48′ N, 101°39′ W 114
Meldola, It. 44°6′ N, 12°2′ E 167
Meldorf, Ger. 54°5′ N, 9°4′ E 150
Meldrum Creek, Can. 52°6′ N, 122°22′ W 108
Mele, Capo, It. 43°53′ N, 8°10′ E 167
Melegnano, It. 45°20′ N, 9°18′ E 167
Melenci, Serb. and Mont. 45°30′ N, 20°19′ E 168
Melenki, Russ. 55°19′ N, 41°40′ E 154
Meleski, Est. 58°24′ N, 26°5′ E 166
Meletsk, Russ. 57°28′ N, 90°20′ E 169
Meleuz, Russ. 52°58′ N, 55°53′ E 154
Melfi, Chad 11°3′ N, 17°58′ E 216
Melfi, It. 40°59′ N, 15°39′ E 156
Melfort, Can. 52°51′ N, 104°37′ W 108
Melilla, Sp. 35°15′ N, 2°58′ W 214
Melinka, Chile 43°52′ S, 73°49′ W 134
Melita, Can. 49°17′ N, 100°58′ W 90
Melita see Mljet, island, Croatia 42°37′ N, 17°23′ E 168
Melito di Porto Salvo, It. 37°55′ N, 15°47′ E 156
Melitopol', Ukr. 46°50′ N, 35°19′ E 156
Melksham, U.K. 51°21′ N, 2°9′ W 162
Mellakou, Alg. 35°15′ N, 1°14′ E 150
Mellansel, Nor. 63°25′ N, 18°20′ E 152
Mellen, Wis., U.S. 46°19′ N, 90°41′ W 94
Mellerud, Nor. 58°42′ N, 12°26′ E 152
Mellifont Abbey, site, Ire. 53°43′ N, 6°32′ W 150
Mellit, Sudan 14°6′ N, 25°34′ E 226
Mellrichstadt, Ger. 50°26′ N, 10°17′ E 167
Mellum, island, Ger. 53°39′ N, 8°10′ E 163
Melmerby, U.K. 54°43′ N, 2°37′ W 162
Melo, Arg. 34°20′ S, 63°27′ W 139
Melo, Uru. 32°20′ S, 54°13′ W 139
Meloco, Mozambique 13°31′ S, 39°15′ E 224
Melos, ruin(s), Aegean Sea 36°42′ N, 24°20′ E 156
Melouprey, Cambodia 13°49′ N, 105°16′ E 202
Melrose, Fla., U.S. 29°41′ N, 82°3′ W 105
Melrose, La., U.S. 31°36′ N, 92°59′ W 103
Melrose, Mass., U.S. 42°27′ N, 71°4′ W 104
Melrose, Minn., U.S. 45°38′ N, 94°50′ W 90
Melrose, N. Mex., U.S. 34°26′ N, 103°38′ W 92
Melsungen, Ger. 51°7′ N, 9°32′ E 167
Meltaus, Fin. 66°54′ N, 25°20′ E 152
Melton Constable, U.K. 52°51′ N, 1°2′ E 162
Melton Mowbray, U.K. 52°46′ N, 0°53′ E 162
Melun, Fr. 48°31′ N, 2°39′ E 163
Melut, Sudan 10°27′ N, 32°12′ E 224
Melville, Can. 50°55′ N, 102°51′ W 90
Melville, La., U.S. 30°41′ N, 91°46′ W 103
Melville, Cape, Austral. 14°8′ S, 144°30′ E 230
Melville Hills, Can. 69°17′ N, 122°25′ W 106
Melville Island, Austral. 11°9′ S, 131°5′ E 192
Melville Island, Can. 74°39′ N, 109°22′ W 106
Melville Peninsula, Can. 67°59′ N, 85°41′ W 106
Melville Sound 68°17′ N, 103°42′ W 246
Melvin, Ill., U.S. 40°33′ N, 88°15′ W 102
Melvin, Ky., U.S. 37°21′ N, 82°42′ W 96
Melvin, Tex., U.S. 31°10′ N, 99°35′ W 92
Melvin Lake, Can. 57°7′ N, 100°46′ W 108
Melvin, river, Can. 59°0′ N, 117°27′ W 108
Melvin Village, N.H., U.S. 43°41′ N, 71°19′ W 104
Mélykút, Hung. 46°12′ N, 19°23′ E 168
Mêmar Co, lake, China 34°13′ N, 81°36′ E 188
Memba, Mozambique 14°13′ S, 40°31′ E 224
Mēmele, river, Europe 56°21′ N, 24°9′ E 166
Mempawah, Indonesia 0°24′ N, 108°57′ E 196
Memphis, Mo., U.S. 40°27′ N, 92°11′ W 94
Memphis, Tenn., U.S. 35°8′ N, 90°2′ W 96
Memphis, Tex., U.S. 34°42′ N, 100°33′ W 92
Memphis, site, Egypt 29°51′ N, 31°5′ E 180
Mena, Ark., U.S. 34°33′ N, 94°16′ W 96
Mena, Ukr. 51°29′ N, 32°13′ E 158
Menahga, Minn., U.S. 46°43′ N, 95°7′ W 90
Ménaka, Mali 15°52′ N, 2°25′ E 222
Ménalo, Óros, peak, Gr. 37°38′ N, 22°12′ E 156
Menands, N.Y., U.S. 42°41′ N, 73°45′ W 104
Menard, Tex., U.S. 30°55′ N, 99°47′ W 92
Menard Fracture Zone, South Pacific Ocean 49°46′ S, 113°56′ W 252
Menasha, Wis., U.S. 44°12′ N, 88°27′ W 102
Menawashei, Sudan 12°41′ N, 24°57′ E 216
Mende, Fr. 44°30′ N, 3°29′ E 150
Mende, ruin(s), Gr. 39°58′ N, 23°20′ E 156
Mendebo, Eth. 6°21′ N, 38°52′ E 224
Mendeleyev Plain, Arctic Ocean 81°8′ N, 167°15′ W 255
Mendeleyev Ridge, Arctic Ocean 83°35′ N, 172°10′ W 255
Mendeleyevsk, Russ. 55°54′ N, 52°24′ E 154
Mendelssohn Inlet 71°19′ S, 77°46′ W 248
Menden, Ger. 51°26′ N, 7°47′ E 167
Méndez, Ecua. 2°47′ S, 78°23′ W 136
Méndez, Mex. 25°7′ N, 98°35′ W 114
Mendī, Eth. 9°46′ N, 35°4′ E 224
Mendip Hills, U.K. 51°9′ N, 2°41′ W 162
Mendocino, Cape, Calif., U.S. 40°25′ N, 124°58′ W 90
Mendocino Fracture Zone, North Pacific Ocean 40°1′ N, 144°6′ W 252
Mendol, island, Indonesia 0°23′ N, 103°14′ E 196
Mendon, Ohio, U.S. 40°39′ N, 84°31′ W 102
Mendota, Calif., U.S. 36°45′ N, 120°24′ W 100
Mendota, Ill., U.S. 41°32′ N, 89°7′ W 102
Mendoza, Arg. 32°52′ S, 68°54′ W 134
Mendoza, adm. division, Arg. 34°30′ S, 70°3′ W 134
Mendung, Indonesia 0°33′ N, 103°11′ E 196
Mene de Mauroa, Venez. 10°43′ N, 70°58′ W 136
Mene Grande, Venez. 9°50′ N, 70°55′ W 136
Menemen, Turk. 38°32′ N, 27°2′ E 180
Menemsha, Mass., U.S. 41°21′ N, 70°46′ W 104
Menen, Belg. 50°47′ N, 3°7′ E 163
Mengcheng, China 33°15′ N, 116°32′ E 198
Mengen, Ger. 48°3′ N, 9°19′ E 152
Mengen, Turk. 40°56′ N, 32°10′ E 156
Mengene Dağı, peak, Turk. 38°13′ N, 43°56′ E 195
Mengeringhausen, Ger. 51°22′ N, 8°58′ E 167
Menghai, China 21°58′ N, 100°26′ E 202
Mengíbar, Sp. 37°58′ N, 3°48′ W 164
Mengla, China 21°29′ N, 101°30′ E 202
Menglian, China 22°21′ N, 99°32′ E 202
Mengoub, Mor. 32°20′ N, 2°20′ W 214
Mengzi, China 23°22′ N, 103°23′ E 202
Menindee, Austral. 32°19′ S, 142°28′ E 231
Menindee Lake, Austral. 32°16′ S, 141°18′ E 230
Menkere, Russ. 67°52′ N, 123°17′ E 173
Menlo, Wash., U.S. 46°35′ N, 123°40′ W 100
Menno, S. Dak., U.S. 43°12′ N, 97°35′ W 90
Menominee, river, U.S. 46°11′ N, 88°37′ W 80
Menomonie, Wis., U.S. 44°51′ N, 91°55′ W 94
Menongue, Angola 14°39′ S, 17°39′ E 220
Menorca, island, Sp. 39°29′ N, 4°14′ E 142
Menorca (Minorca), island, Sp. 39°47′ N, 3°33′ E 164
Menouarar, Alg. 31°12′ N, 2°16′ W 214
Men'shikova, Mys, Russ. 70°24′ N, 56°10′ E 169
Mentasta Lake, Alas., U.S. 62°56′ N, 143°52′ W 98
Mentawai, Kepulauan, islands, Indian Ocean 1°1′ S, 97°24′ E 196
Mentekab, Malaysia 3°29′ N, 102°20′ E 196
Mentès, spring, Niger 16°58′ N, 4°17′ E 222
Mentmore, N. Mex., U.S. 35°30′ N, 108°50′ W 92
Mentor, Ohio, U.S. 41°39′ N, 81°20′ W 102
Menyapa, peak, Indonesia 1°6′ N, 115°48′ E 192
Menza, Russ. 49°21′ N, 108°51′ E 198
Menzel Bourguiba (Ferryville), Tun. 37°9′ N, 9°47′ E 156
Menzel Chaker, Tun. 34°59′ N, 10°22′ E 156
Menzelinsk, Russ. 55°40′ N, 53°8′ E 154
Menzies, Austral. 29°42′ S, 121°0′ E 231
Menzies, Mount, peak, Antarctica 73°29′ S, 61°23′ E 248
Menzies, Mount, peak, Can. 50°12′ N, 125°35′ W 90
Me'ona, Israel 33°0′ N, 35°15′ E 194
Meota, Can. 53°2′ N, 108°28′ W 108
Meppel, Neth. 52°41′ N, 6°10′ E 163
Meppen, Ger. 52°42′ N, 7°18′ E 163
Mequens, river, Braz. 12°56′ S, 62°11′ W 132
Mequinenza, Sp. 41°21′ N, 0°17′ E 164
Mer Rouge, La., U.S. 32°45′ N, 91°48′ W 103
Meråker, Nor. 63°25′ N, 11°43′ E 152
Merakert, Asia 40°12′ N, 46°47′ E 195
Merano, It. 46°40′ N, 11°8′ E 167
Merauke, Indonesia 8°36′ S, 140°31′ E 192
Merca (Marka), Somalia 1°41′ N, 44°53′ E 207
Mercaderes, Col. 1°47′ N, 77°14′ W 136
Mercan Dağları, peak, Turk. 39°32′ N, 39°28′ E 195
Mercato Saraceno, It. 43°57′ N, 12°10′ E 167
Merced, Calif., U.S. 37°18′ N, 120°29′ W 100
Merced Peak, Calif., U.S. 37°37′ N, 119°27′ W 100
Mercedes, Arg. 34°42′ S, 59°25′ W 139
Mercedes, Arg. 29°12′ S, 58°3′ W 139
Mercedes, Tex., U.S. 26°10′ N, 97°55′ W 114
Mercedes, Uru. 33°17′ S, 57°59′ W 139
Merćez, Serb. and Mont. 43°13′ N, 21°4′ E 168
Mercoal, Can. 53°8′ N, 117°7′ W 108
Mercury, Nev., U.S. 36°39′ N, 115°60′ W 101
Mercy Bay 73°58′ N, 119°36′ W 106
Mercy, Cape, Can. 64°47′ N, 63°27′ W 106
Meredith, N.H., U.S. 43°38′ N, 71°31′ W 104
Meredith, Cape, West Falkland 52°28′ S, 63°10′ W 248
Meredith Center, N.H., U.S. 43°36′ N, 71°33′ W 104
Mereeg, Somalia 3°44′ N, 47°20′ E 218
Mereer-Gur, Somalia 5°46′ N, 46°31′ E 218
Merefa, Ukr. 49°47′ N, 36°9′ E 158
Méréville, Fr. 48°19′ N, 2°4′ E 163
Merga see Nukheila, spring, Sudan 19°3′ N, 26°20′ E 226
Mergenevo, Kaz. 49°57′ N, 51°15′ E 158
Mergui Archipelago, islands, Andaman Sea 11°3′ N, 97°30′ E 202
Méri, Cameroon 10°51′ N, 14°6′ E 218
Meriç, Turk. 41°10′ N, 26°24′ E 158
Meriç, river, Turk. 41°3′ N, 26°22′ E 180
Mérida, Mex. 20°56′ N, 89°44′ W 116
Mérida, Sp. 38°54′ N, 6°24′ W 214
Mérida, Sp. 38°54′ N, 6°20′ W 164
Mérida, Venez. 8°36′ N, 71°10′ W 136
Mérida, adm. division, Venez. 8°18′ N, 71°50′ W 136
Mérida, Cordillera de, Venez. 9°41′ N, 69°46′ W 136
Meriden, Conn., U.S. 41°32′ N, 72°48′ W 104
Meriden, N.H., U.S. 43°32′ N, 72°16′ W 104
Meridian, Miss., U.S. 32°21′ N, 88°42′ W 103
Meridian, Tex., U.S. 31°54′ N, 97°39′ W 92
Merijärvi, Fin. 64°17′ N, 24°25′ E 152
Merikarvia, Fin. 61°50′ N, 21°29′ E 166
Měřín, Czech Rep. 49°24′ N, 15°52′ E 152
Merinaghène, ruin(s), Senegal 16°1′ N, 16°6′ W 222
Merino Jarpa, Isla, island, Chile 47°44′ S, 74°20′ W 134
Merirumã, Braz. 1°7′ N, 54°37′ W 130
Merivälja, Est. 59°29′ N, 24°48′ E 166
Meriwether Lewis Monument, Tenn., U.S. 35°31′ N, 87°33′ W 96
Merka, Eth. 5°52′ N, 37°6′ E 224
Merke, Kaz. 42°51′ N, 73°9′ E 184
Merkinė, Lith. 54°10′ N, 24°12′ E 166
Merkoya, Mali 13°56′ N, 8°13′ W 222
Merksplas, Belg. 51°20′ N, 4°51′ E 167
Merkushino, Russ. 58°48′ N, 61°32′ E 154
Merkys, river, Lith. 54°21′ N, 24°46′ E 166
Merlimont, Fr. 50°27′ N, 1°36′ E 163
Merlin, Can. 42°14′ N, 82°14′ W 102
Mermentau, La., U.S. 30°10′ N, 92°36′ W 103
Meroë, ruin(s), Sudan 17°3′ N, 33°45′ E 182
Meron, Israel 32°59′ N, 35°26′ E 194
Merouana, Alg. 35°37′ N, 5°54′ E 150
Merowe, Sudan 18°23′ N, 31°49′ E 182
Merrill, Miss., U.S. 30°57′ N, 88°43′ W 103
Merrill, Wis., U.S. 45°10′ N, 89°41′ W 94
Merrillville, Ind., U.S. 41°28′ N, 87°21′ W 102
Merrimack, N.H., U.S. 42°51′ N, 71°31′ W 104
Merriman, Nebr., U.S. 42°55′ N, 101°42′ W 90
Merritt, Can. 50°5′ N, 120°46′ W 108
Merritt Island, Fla., U.S. 28°21′ N, 80°42′ W 105
Merritt Pass, Ariz., U.S. 34°5′ N, 112°59′ W 92
Merryville, La., U.S. 30°44′ N, 93°33′ W 103
Mers el Kebir, Alg. 35°43′ N, 0°43′ E 150
Mersey, river, U.K. 53°22′ N, 2°58′ W 162
Mersin see İçel, Turk. 36°48′ N, 34°36′ E 156
Mersing, Malaysia 2°25′ N, 103°49′ E 196
Mērsrags, Latv. 57°20′ N, 23°6′ E 166
Merta Road, India 26°43′ N, 73°55′ E 186
Mertert, Lux. 49°42′ N, 6°30′ E 163
Merthyr Tydfil, U.K. 51°45′ N, 3°22′ W 162
Merti, Kenya 1°1′ N, 38°40′ E 224
Mértola, Port. 37°38′ N, 7°41′ W 150
Mertzon, Tex., U.S. 31°15′ N, 100°50′ W 92
Méru, Fr. 49°14′ N, 2°8′ E 163
Meru, Kenya 1°60′ N, 37°40′ E 224
Meru National Park, Kenya 2°119′ N, 38°27′ E 224
Meru, peak, Tanzania 3°15′ S, 36°41′ E 224
Merville, Fr. 50°38′ N, 2°38′ E 163
Méry, Fr. 48°30′ N, 3°53′ E 163
Merz Peninsula 72°30′ S, 59°28′ W 248
Merzifon, Turk. 40°52′ N, 35°28′ E 156
Merzig, Ger. 49°26′ N, 6°38′ E 163
Mesa, Ariz., U.S. 33°25′ N, 111°49′ W 92
Mesa Verde National Park, Colo., U.S. 37°21′ N, 111°23′ W 80
Mesaaroole, spring, Somalia 3°20′ N, 45°2′ E 218
Mesabi Range, Minn., U.S. 47°26′ N, 93°37′ W 90
Mesach Mellet, Lib. 25°30′ N, 11°3′ E 216
Mésaconane, Pointe, Can. 51°31′ N, 79°28′ W 110
Mesagne, It. 40°33′ N, 17°50′ E 156
Mesai, river, Col. 6°357′ N, 72°43′ W 136
Mesará, Gr. 35°0′ N, 24°48′ E 156
Mescalero, N. Mex., U.S. 33°8′ N, 105°46′ W 92
Meschede, Ger. 51°20′ N, 8°16′ E 167
Mescit Dağı, peak, Turk. 40°22′ N, 41°8′ E 195
Meselefors, Nor. 64°25′ N, 16°50′ E 152
Mesemvria see Nesebŭr, Bulg. 42°39′ N, 27°44′ E 156
Meshchovsk, Russ. 54°18′ N, 35°18′ E 158
Meshkān, Iran 36°37′ N, 58°7′ E 180
Meshra' er Req, Sudan 8°24′ N, 29°15′ E 224
Mesići, Bosn. and Herzg. 43°44′ N, 18°59′ E 168
Mesier, Canal 48°31′ S, 75°10′ W 134
Mesilinka, river, Can. 56°26′ N, 126°8′ W 108
Mesilla, N. Mex., U.S. 32°16′ N, 106°49′ W 92
Meškuičiai, Lith. 56°4′ N, 23°26′ E 166
Mesola, It. 44°55′ N, 12°13′ E 167
Mesomikenda Lake, Can. 47°34′ N, 82°41′ W 110
Mesopotamia, region, Iraq 35°1′ N, 40°11′ E 180
Mesplet, Lac, lake, Can. 48°45′ N, 76°18′ W 94
Mesquite, Nev., U.S. 36°48′ N, 114°4′ W 101
Mesquite, Tex., U.S. 32°45′ N, 96°36′ W 96
Mesra, Alg. 35°50′ N, 0°10′ E 164
Messaad, Alg. 34°12′ N, 3°31′ E 214
Messalo, river, Mozambique 12°3′ S, 39°41′ E 224
Messdar, oil field, Alg. 31°1′ N, 6°35′ E 214
Messeïed, Mor. 27°57′ N, 10°51′ W 214
Messene, ruin(s), Gr. 37°9′ N, 21°49′ E 156
Messina, It. 38°11′ N, 15°31′ E 156
Messina see Musina, S. Af. 22°21′ S, 30°1′ E 227
Messoyakha, Russ. 69°12′ N, 82°44′ E 169
Mestanza, Sp. 38°34′ N, 4°4′ W 164
Mesteacăn, Rom. 47°22′ N, 23°32′ E 168
Mestia, Ga. 43°2′ N, 42°43′ E 195
Mestre, It. 45°29′ N, 12°14′ E 167
Meszah Peak, Can. 58°29′ N, 131°34′ W 108
Meta, adm. division, Col. 3°26′ N, 73°20′ W 136
Meta Incognita Peninsula, Can. 62°38′ N, 68°39′ W 106
Meta Lake, Can. 50°28′ N, 87°42′ W 110
Meta, river, Col. 5°22′ N, 70°30′ W 136
Metahāra, Eth. 8°51′ N, 39°55′ E 224
Metairie, La., U.S. 29°58′ N, 90°9′ W 103
Metalici, Munții, Rom. 46°2′ N, 22°43′ E 168
Metaline Falls, Wash., U.S. 48°51′ N, 117°21′ W 90
Metallifere, Colline, It. 43°8′ N, 10°24′ E 156
Metamora, Ill., U.S. 40°47′ N, 89°22′ W 102
Metán, Arg. 25°31′ S, 64°58′ W 134
Metangula, Mozambique 12°40′ S, 34°50′ E 224

Métascouac, Lac, lake, *Can.* 47°43′ N, 72°23′ W **94**
Metchosin, *Can.* 48°22′ N, 123°33′ W **100**
Metema, *Eth.* 12°55′ N, 36°11′ E **182**
Metemma, *Sudan* 16°43′ N, 33°20′ E **182**
Meteor Crater, *Ariz., U.S.* 35°1′ N, 111°1′ W **92**
Meteora, ruin(s), *Gr.* 39°43′ N, 21°30′ E **156**
Methánon, *Gr.* 37°34′ N, 23°5′ E **156**
Methone, ruin(s), *Gr.* 40°25′ N, 22°29′ E **156**
Methuen, *Mass., U.S.* 42°43′ N, 71°13′ W **104**
Methven, *N.Z.* 43°40′ S, 171°39′ E **240**
Metileo, *Arg.* 35°47′ S, 63°56′ W **139**
Metković, *Croatia* 43°1′ N, 17°37′ E **168**
Metlakatla, *Alas., U.S.* 55°6′ N, 131°37′ W **108**
Metlaoui, *Tun.* 34°18′ N, 8°26′ E **156**
Metlili Chaamba, *Alg.* 32°20′ N, 3°40′ E **214**
Metovnica, *Serb. and Mont.* 43°57′ N, 22°9′ E **168**
Metropolis, *Mo., U.S.* 37°9′ N, 88°43′ W **96**
Mettingen, *Ger.* 52°19′ N, 7°46′ E **163**
Mettlach, *Ger.* 49°29′ N, 6°36′ E **163**
Mettler, *Calif., U.S.* 35°3′ N, 118°58′ W **101**
Mettmann, *Ger.* 51°16′ N, 6°57′ E **167**
Mettur Dam, *India* 11°47′ N, 77°49′ E **188**
Metuge, *Mozambique* 13°1′ S, 40°24′ E **224**
Metulla, *Israel* 33°15′ N, 35°34′ E **194**
Metz, *Fr.* 49°6′ N, 6°9′ E **163**
Meuaú, river, *Braz.* 1°23′ S, 66°42′ W **136**
Meulaboh, *Indonesia* 4°12′ N, 96°5′ E **196**
Meung, *Fr.* 47°49′ N, 1°41′ E **150**
Meureudu, *Indonesia* 5°15′ N, 96°10′ E **196**
Meurthe, river, *Fr.* 48°26′ N, 6°41′ E **163**
Meuse, river, *Belg.* 50°8′ N, 4°55′ E **167**
Mexborough, *U.K.* 53°29′ N, 1°17′ W **162**
Mexcaltitán, *Mex.* 21°54′ N, 105°30′ W **114**
Mexia, *Tex., U.S.* 31°39′ N, 96°29′ W **96**
Mexiana, Ilha, island, *Braz.* 0°8′ N, 49°32′ W **130**
Mexicali, *Mex.* 32°38′ N, 115°32′ W **101**
Mexican Hat, *Utah, U.S.* 37°9′ N, 109°52′ W **92**
Mexicanos, Laguna de los, lake, *Mex.* 28°10′ N, 107°54′ W **81**
México, *Mex.* 19°23′ N, 99°13′ W **114**
Mexico 21°24′ N, 102°50′ W **112**
Mexico, *Mo., U.S.* 39°9′ N, 91°54′ W **94**
México, adm. division, *Mex.* 19°21′ N, 100°13′ W **114**
Mexico Basin, *Gulf of Mexico* 24°13′ N, 92°2′ W **253**
Mexico, Gulf of 25°10′ N, 89°8′ W **253**
Mexico, Gulf of 24°35′ N, 91°4′ W **112**
Meydan Khvolah, *Afghan.* 33°34′ N, 69°54′ E **186**
Meyers Chuck, *Alas., U.S.* 55°44′ N, 132°16′ W **108**
Meymac, *Fr.* 45°32′ N, 2°8′ E **150**
Meymaneh, *Afghan.* 35°55′ N, 64°48′ E **186**
Mezcala, *Mex.* 17°53′ N, 99°39′ W **114**
Mezdra, *Bulg.* 43°9′ N, 23°43′ E **156**
Mèze, *Fr.* 43°26′ N, 3°35′ E **164**
Mezen', *Russ.* 65°51′ N, 44°18′ E **154**
Mezen', river, *Russ.* 64°14′ N, 49°8′ E **154**
Mézenc, Mont, peak, *Fr.* 44°52′ N, 4°7′ E **165**
Mężenin, *Pol.* 53°5′ N, 22°28′ E **152**
Mezenskaya Guba 66°33′ N, 43°17′ E **154**
Mezeș, Munții, *Rom.* 47°9′ N, 22°55′ E **168**
Mezhdurechensk, *Russ.* 63°8′ N, 48°37′ E **154**
Mezhdurechenskiy, *Russ.* 59°30′ N, 66°2′ E **169**
Mezhdusharskiy, Ostrov, island, *Russ.* 70°47′ N, 53°44′ E **246**
Mezhdusharskiy, Ostrov, island, *Russ.* 70°34′ N, 47°7′ E **160**
Meziad, *Rom.* 46°44′ N, 22°25′ E **168**
Mezőberény, *Hung.* 46°49′ N, 21°1′ E **168**
Mezőfalva, *Hung.* 46°55′ N, 18°47′ E **168**
Mezőhegyes, *Hung.* 46°19′ N, 20°49′ E **168**
Mezőkeresztes, *Hung.* 47°49′ N, 20°42′ E **168**
Mezőkövesd, *Hung.* 47°47′ N, 20°34′ E **168**
Mezőtúr, *Hung.* 47°0′ N, 20°37′ E **168**
Mezquital, *Mex.* 23°26′ N, 104°21′ W **114**
Mezquitic, *Mex.* 22°22′ N, 103°44′ W **114**
Mezzolombardo, *It.* 46°12′ N, 11°5′ E **167**
Mfouati, *Congo* 4°24′ S, 13°47′ E **218**
Mgera, *Tanzania* 5°25′ S, 37°34′ E **224**
Mgeta, *Tanzania* 8°16′ S, 36°2′ E **224**
Mglin, *Russ.* 53°2′ N, 32°52′ E **158**
M'goun, Irhil, peak, *Mor.* 31°29′ N, 6°35′ W **214**
Mhangura, *Zimb.* 16°52′ S, 30°8′ E **224**
Mholach, Beinn, peak 58°14′ N, 6°37′ W **150**
Mhòr, Beinn, peak 57°14′ N, 7°33′ W **150**
Mhow, *India* 22°32′ N, 75°45′ E **197**
Miahuatlán, *Mex.* 18°31′ N, 97°25′ W **114**
Miajadas, *Sp.* 39°8′ N, 5°55′ W **164**
Miami, *Ariz., U.S.* 33°23′ N, 110°53′ W **112**
Miami, *Fla., U.S.* 25°48′ N, 80°13′ W **105**
Miami, *Okla., U.S.* 36°52′ N, 94°53′ W **82**
Miami, *Tex., U.S.* 35°40′ N, 100°38′ W **92**
Miami Beach, *Fla., U.S.* 25°47′ N, 80°10′ W **105**
Miami, river, *Ohio, U.S.* 39°16′ N, 84°50′ W **80**
Mīānābād, *Iran* 37°2′ N, 57°28′ E **180**
Mianchi, *China* 34°45′ N, 111°49′ E **198**
Mīāndoāb, *Iran* 37°1′ N, 46°2′ E **195**
Mianduhe, *China* 49°7′ N, 120°58′ E **198**
Mīāneh, *Iran* 37°26′ N, 47°42′ E **195**
Mianwali, *Pak.* 32°35′ N, 71°36′ E **186**
Mianxian, *China* 33°9′ N, 106°41′ E **198**
Mianyang, *China* 31°25′ N, 104°39′ E **198**
Miaoli, *Taiwan* 24°33′ N, 120°47′ E **198**
Miarinarivo, *Madagascar* 16°37′ S, 48°14′ E **220**
Miarinarivo, *Madagascar* 18°60′ S, 46°54′ E **220**
Miass, *Russ.* 54°59′ N, 60°7′ E **154**
Miass, river, *Russ.* 55°21′ N, 61°22′ E **154**
Miastkowo, *Pol.* 53°9′ N, 21°49′ E **152**
Mica, Cerro de la, peak, *Chile* 21°42′ S, 70°2′ W **137**
Mica Creek, *Can.* 52°2′ N, 118°34′ W **108**
Micanopy, *Fla., U.S.* 29°30′ N, 82°17′ W **105**
Micay, *Col.* 3°0′ N, 77°38′ W **136**
Michaichmon', *Russ.* 64°13′ N, 50°4′ E **154**
Michaud, Point 45°27′ N, 60°44′ W **111**
Michel, *Can.* 55°59′ N, 109°8′ W **108**
Michel Peak, *Can.* 53°32′ N, 126°35′ W **108**
Michelson, Mount, peak, *Alas., U.S.* 69°10′ N, 144°39′ W **98**
Michigamme Reservoir, *Mich., U.S.* 46°7′ N, 89°1′ W **110**
Michigan, adm. division, *Mich., U.S.* 42°56′ N, 84°53′ W **102**
Michigan Center, *Mich., U.S.* 42°13′ N, 84°19′ W **102**
Michigan City, *Ind., U.S.* 41°42′ N, 86°54′ W **102**
Michigan, Lake 42°44′ N, 87°43′ W **110**
Michipicoten, *Can.* 47°57′ N, 84°54′ W **94**
Michipicoten Island, *Can.* 47°31′ N, 87°15′ W **80**
Michipicoten River, *Can.* 47°56′ N, 84°50′ W **94**
Michoacán, adm. division, *Mex.* 19°9′ N, 102°33′ W **114**
Michurinsk, *Russ.* 52°53′ N, 40°24′ E **154**
Michurinskoye, *Russ.* 60°35′ N, 29°48′ E **166**
Mico, river, *Nicar.* 11°55′ N, 84°38′ W **115**
Miconje, *Angola* 4°28′ S, 12°50′ E **218**
Micronesia, Federated States of 8°0′ N, 147°0′ E **192**
Micronesia, islands, *North Pacific Ocean* 15°29′ N, 140°15′ E **190**
Micuí, *Braz.* 0°29′ N, 69°5′ W **136**
Midai, island, *Indonesia* 3°4′ N, 107°25′ E **196**
Mid-Atlantic Ridge, *North Atlantic Ocean* 3°49′ N, 31°17′ W **253**
Middelburg, *Neth.* 51°29′ N, 3°37′ E **163**
Middelburg, *S. Af.* 25°48′ S, 29°27′ E **227**
Middelfart, *Den.* 55°29′ N, 9°44′ E **150**
Middelkerke, *Belg.* 51°10′ N, 2°48′ E **163**
Middelwit, *S. Af.* 24°52′ S, 27°2′ E **227**
Middenmeer, *Neth.* 52°48′ N, 4°59′ E **163**
Middle America Trench, *North Pacific Ocean* 11°50′ N, 89°38′ W **253**
Middle Andaman, island, *India* 12°25′ N, 91°5′ E **188**
Middle Bight 24°6′ N, 78°41′ W **96**
Middle Butte, peak, *Idaho, U.S.* 43°28′ N, 112°49′ W **90**
Middle Foster Lake, *Can.* 56°34′ N, 106°19′ W **108**
Middle Govç, adm. division, *Mongolia* 45°3′ N, 104°54′ E **198**
Middle Loup, river, *Nebr., U.S.* 42°8′ N, 101°26′ W **80**
Middle River, *Minn., U.S.* 48°23′ N, 96°12′ W **90**
Middle, river, *Iowa, U.S.* 41°11′ N, 94°15′ W **94**
Middleboro, *Mass., U.S.* 41°53′ N, 70°55′ W **104**
Middlebourne, *W. Va., U.S.* 39°29′ N, 80°55′ W **102**
Middleburg, *S. Af.* 31°31′ S, 24°58′ E **227**
Middlebury, *Ind., U.S.* 41°39′ N, 85°43′ W **102**
Middlebury, *Vt., U.S.* 44°0′ N, 73°10′ W **104**
Middleport, *Ohio, U.S.* 38°59′ N, 82°4′ W **94**
Middlesboro, *Ky., U.S.* 36°36′ N, 83°43′ W **96**
Middlesbrough, *U.K.* 54°33′ N, 1°15′ W **162**
Middlesex, *Vt., U.S.* 44°17′ N, 72°41′ W **104**
Middleton, *Idaho, U.S.* 43°42′ N, 116°38′ W **90**
Middleton, *Mass., U.S.* 42°35′ N, 71°1′ W **104**
Middleton, *U.K.* 53°33′ N, 2°12′ W **162**
Middleton, *Wis., U.S.* 43°6′ N, 89°30′ W **102**
Middleton in Teesdale, *U.K.* 54°38′ N, 2°6′ W **162**
Middletown, *Conn., U.S.* 41°33′ N, 72°40′ W **104**
Middletown, *Ill., U.S.* 40°5′ N, 89°35′ W **102**
Middletown, *Ind., U.S.* 40°3′ N, 85°32′ W **102**
Middletown, *N.Y., U.S.* 41°26′ N, 74°26′ W **94**
Middletown, *Ohio, U.S.* 39°29′ N, 84°25′ W **82**
Middletown, *R.I., U.S.* 41°31′ N, 71°18′ W **104**
Middletown Springs, *Vt., U.S.* 43°29′ N, 73°8′ W **104**
Middleville, *Mich., U.S.* 42°41′ N, 85°28′ W **102**
Midhurst, *U.K.* 50°58′ N, 0°44′ E **162**
Mid-Indian Basin, *Indian Ocean* 8°1′ S, 79°3′ E **254**
Mid-Indian Ridge, *Indian Ocean* 13°41′ S, 66°4′ E **254**
Midi-Pyrénées, adm. division, *Fr.* 43°57′ N, 0°59′ E **150**
Midland, *Can.* 44°44′ N, 79°53′ W **94**
Midland, *Mich., U.S.* 43°36′ N, 84°14′ W **102**
Midland, *Tex., U.S.* 31°58′ N, 102°3′ W **92**
Midlothian, *Tex., U.S.* 32°29′ N, 96°60′ W **96**
Midnight, *Miss., U.S.* 33°1′ N, 90°35′ W **103**
Midongy Atsimo, *Madagascar* 23°35′ S, 47°2′ E **220**
Mid-Pacific Mountains, *North Pacific Ocean* 19°40′ N, 164°22′ E **252**
Midpines, *Calif., U.S.* 37°32′ N, 119°56′ W **100**
Midu, island, *Maldives* 0°41′ N, 73°11′ E **188**
Midway, *Utah, U.S.* 40°30′ N, 111°28′ W **92**
Midway Islands, *North Pacific Ocean* 28°27′ N, 177°29′ W **99**
Midwest, *Wyo., U.S.* 43°24′ N, 106°16′ W **90**
Midwest City, *Okla., U.S.* 35°25′ N, 97°22′ W **92**
Midyat, *Turk.* 37°24′ N, 41°26′ E **195**
Midžor, peak, *Serb. and Mont.* 43°23′ N, 22°38′ E **168**
Mie, adm. division, *Japan* 34°30′ N, 136°11′ E **201**
Miechów, *Pol.* 50°22′ N, 20°1′ E **152**
Międzyrzec Podlaski, *Pol.* 51°58′ N, 22°45′ E **152**
Międzyzdroje, *Pol.* 53°55′ N, 14°27′ E **152**
Miehikkälä, *Fin.* 60°40′ N, 27°40′ E **166**
Miélan, *Fr.* 43°26′ N, 0°18′ E **164**
Mielec, *Pol.* 50°16′ N, 21°26′ E **152**
Mier, *Mex.* 26°27′ N, 99°9′ W **114**
Mier y Noriega, *Mex.* 23°24′ N, 100°6′ W **114**
Miercurea Ciuc, *Rom.* 46°22′ N, 25°48′ E **156**
Mieres, *Sp.* 43°14′ N, 5°46′ W **150**
Mieslahti, *Fin.* 64°23′ N, 27°57′ E **152**
Mī'ēso, *Eth.* 9°12′ N, 40°47′ E **224**
Mifol, *Alban.* 40°36′ N, 19°28′ E **156**
Migang Shan, peak, *China* 35°30′ N, 106°7′ E **198**
Migdal, *Israel* 32°50′ N, 35°30′ E **194**
Migole, *Tanzania* 7°5′ S, 35°52′ E **224**
Miguel Alemán, Presa, lake, *Mex.* 18°15′ N, 96°49′ W **114**
Miguel Auza, *Mex.* 24°16′ N, 103°28′ W **114**
Miguel Calmon, *Braz.* 11°27′ S, 40°37′ W **132**
Miguelturra, *Sp.* 38°57′ N, 3°53′ W **164**
Migues, *Uru.* 34°29′ S, 55°38′ W **139**
Migyaunglaung, *Myanmar* 14°41′ N, 98°9′ E **202**
Mihai Viteazu, *Rom.* 44°37′ N, 28°39′ E **156**
Mihailovca, *Mold.* 46°32′ N, 28°56′ E **156**
Mihalţ, *Rom.* 46°9′ N, 23°44′ E **156**
Mihara, *Japan* 34°24′ N, 133°5′ E **201**
Miharu, *Japan* 37°26′ N, 140°29′ E **201**
Mihla, *Ger.* 51°4′ N, 10°19′ E **167**
Mijas, *Sp.* 36°35′ N, 4°39′ W **150**
Mijdaḩah, *Yemen* 14°2′ N, 48°27′ E **182**
Mijek, *Africa* 23°34′ N, 12°56′ W **214**
Mikashevichy, *Belarus* 52°12′ N, 27°27′ E **154**
Mikese, *Tanzania* 6°42′ S, 37°56′ E **224**
Mikhanavichy, *Belarus* 53°46′ N, 27°43′ E **152**
Mikhaylov, *Russ.* 54°13′ N, 38°59′ E **154**
Mikhaylov, Cape 67°4′ S, 118°8′ E **248**
Mikhaylov Island, *Antarctica* 67°19′ S, 86°6′ E **248**
Mikhaylova, *Russ.* 75°2′ N, 87°8′ E **173**
Mikhaylovka, *Russ.* 50°3′ N, 43°12′ E **158**
Mikhaylovskiy, *Russ.* 51°47′ N, 79°32′ E **190**
Mikhaylovskoye, *Russ.* 57°3′ N, 28°53′ E **166**
Mikindani, *Tanzania* 10°18′ S, 40°4′ E **224**
Mikkeli, *Fin.* 61°40′ N, 27°13′ E **166**
Mikkolya, *Russ.* 65°13′ N, 31°40′ E **152**
Mikkwa, river, *Can.* 57°56′ N, 115°14′ W **108**
Mikniya, *Sudan* 16°59′ N, 33°39′ E **226**
Mikumi, *Tanzania* 7°26′ S, 36°58′ E **220**
Mikumi National Park, *Tanzania* 7°14′ S, 36°41′ E **224**
Mikun', *Russ.* 62°21′ N, 50°12′ E **154**
Mikuni, *Japan* 36°12′ N, 136°10′ E **201**
Milaca, *Minn., U.S.* 45°44′ N, 93°38′ W **94**
Miladummadulu Atoll, *Maldives* 6°13′ N, 73°12′ E **188**
Milam, *Tex., U.S.* 31°24′ N, 93°51′ W **103**
Milan, *Ind., U.S.* 39°7′ N, 85°8′ W **102**
Milan, *Mich., U.S.* 42°5′ N, 83°41′ W **102**
Milan, *Mo., U.S.* 41°26′ N, 90°35′ W **94**
Milan, *Mo., U.S.* 40°11′ N, 93°6′ W **94**
Milan, *N.H., U.S.* 44°34′ N, 71°12′ W **104**
Milan see Milano, *It.* 45°27′ N, 9°10′ E **167**
Milando, *Angola* 8°51′ S, 17°32′ E **218**
Milange, *Mozambique* 16°7′ S, 35°46′ E **224**
Milano (Milan), *It.* 45°27′ N, 9°10′ E **167**
Milâs, *Turk.* 37°17′ N, 27°45′ E **156**
Milbank, *S. Dak., U.S.* 45°12′ N, 96°40′ W **90**
Milbridge, *Me., U.S.* 44°31′ N, 67°54′ W **94**
Mildenhall, *U.K.* 52°20′ N, 0°30′ E **162**
Mildmay, *Can.* 44°2′ N, 81°7′ W **102**
Milejewo, *Pol.* 54°13′ N, 19°33′ E **166**
Miles, *Tex., U.S.* 31°34′ N, 100°11′ W **92**
Miles City, *Mont., U.S.* 46°23′ N, 105°51′ W **90**
Milestone, *Can.* 49°59′ N, 104°31′ W **90**
Miletto, Monte, peak, *It.* 41°26′ N, 14°17′ E **156**
Miletus, ruin(s), *Turk.* 37°29′ N, 27°10′ E **156**
Milford, *Conn., U.S.* 41°13′ N, 73°4′ W **104**
Milford, *Ill., U.S.* 40°37′ N, 87°42′ W **102**
Milford, *Ind., U.S.* 41°24′ N, 85°51′ W **102**
Milford, *Iowa, U.S.* 43°19′ N, 95°9′ W **90**
Milford, *Me., U.S.* 44°56′ N, 68°38′ W **94**
Milford, *Nebr., U.S.* 40°45′ N, 97°5′ W **90**
Milford, *N.H., U.S.* 42°49′ N, 71°40′ W **104**
Milford, *Utah, U.S.* 38°23′ N, 113°1′ W **90**
Milford Sound, *N.Z.* 44°40′ S, 167°56′ E **240**
Miliana, *Alg.* 36°18′ N, 2°13′ E **150**
Milk River, *Can.* 49°8′ N, 112°5′ W **90**
Milk, river, *Mont., U.S.* 48°55′ N, 110°39′ W **90**
Milk River Ridge, *Can.* 48°57′ N, 112°24′ W **90**
Mil'kovo, *Russ.* 54°49′ N, 158°55′ E **160**
Mill Island, *Antarctica* 65°5′ S, 102°22′ E **248**
Mill Island, *Can.* 63°40′ N, 79°52′ W **106**
Mill Valley, *Calif., U.S.* 37°54′ N, 122°34′ W **100**
Millau, *Fr.* 44°6′ N, 3°3′ E **150**
Millbrook, *N.Y., U.S.* 41°46′ N, 73°43′ W **104**
Mille Lacs, Lac des, lake, *Can.* 48°44′ N, 91°27′ W **94**
Milledgeville, *Ga., U.S.* 33°4′ N, 83°12′ W **112**
Millen, *Ga., U.S.* 32°47′ N, 81°56′ W **96**
Miller, Mount, peak, *Antarctica* 83°18′ S, 167°27′ E **248**
Miller Peak, *Ariz., U.S.* 31°23′ N, 110°21′ W **92**
Miller Range, *Antarctica* 82°19′ S, 158°47′ E **248**
Millerovo, *Russ.* 48°54′ N, 40°25′ E **158**
Millers Ferry, *Ala., U.S.* 32°6′ N, 87°22′ W **103**
Millersburg, *Ind., U.S.* 41°31′ N, 85°42′ W **102**
Millersburg, *Ohio, U.S.* 40°32′ N, 81°54′ W **102**
Millerton, *N.Y., U.S.* 41°57′ N, 73°32′ W **104**
Millesimo, *It.* 44°22′ N, 8°14′ E **167**
Millevaches, Plateau de, *Fr.* 45°18′ N, 1°29′ E **165**
Milligan Creek, river, *Can.* 56°43′ N, 121°25′ W **108**
Millington, *Mich., U.S.* 43°16′ N, 83°31′ W **102**
Millington, *Tenn., U.S.* 35°19′ N, 89°54′ W **96**
Millinocket, *Me., U.S.* 45°39′ N, 68°43′ W **111**
Millom, *U.K.* 54°12′ N, 3°16′ W **162**
Millry, *Ala., U.S.* 31°38′ N, 88°18′ W **103**
Mills, *Wyo., U.S.* 42°50′ N, 106°22′ W **90**
Millstream-Chichester National Park, *Austral.* 21°30′ S, 117°1′ E **238**
Millville, *Mass., U.S.* 42°1′ N, 71°35′ W **104**
Millville, *N.J., U.S.* 39°23′ N, 75°3′ W **94**
Millwater, *Can.* 54°35′ N, 101°36′ W **108**
Millwood Lake, *Ark., U.S.* 33°43′ N, 94°23′ W **96**
Milly, *Fr.* 48°23′ N, 2°28′ E **163**
Milmarcos, *Sp.* 41°4′ N, 1°52′ W **164**
Milna, *Croatia* 43°19′ N, 16°26′ E **168**
Milnor, *N. Dak., U.S.* 46°14′ N, 97°28′ W **94**
Milo, *Eth.* 10°0′ N, 42°2′ E **224**
Milo, *Tanzania* 9°55′ S, 34°38′ E **224**
Milo, river, *Guinea* 10°11′ N, 9°32′ W **222**
Miločer, *Europe* 42°16′ N, 18°53′ E **168**
Mílos, island, *Gr.* 36°37′ N, 23°49′ E **180**
Milot, *Alban.* 41°40′ N, 19°43′ E **168**
Milparinka, *Austral.* 29°45′ S, 141°55′ E **231**
Milpitas, *Calif., U.S.* 37°26′ N, 121°55′ W **100**
Milroy, *Ind., U.S.* 39°29′ N, 85°28′ W **102**
Milton, *Fla., U.S.* 30°38′ N, 87°2′ W **96**
Milton, *Ky., U.S.* 38°42′ N, 85°23′ W **102**
Milton, *Mass., U.S.* 42°15′ N, 71°5′ W **104**
Milton, *N.H., U.S.* 43°24′ N, 70°60′ W **104**
Milton, *N.Z.* 46°8′ S, 169°56′ E **240**
Milton, *Pa., U.S.* 41°1′ N, 76°51′ W **94**
Milton, *Wash., U.S.* 47°13′ N, 122°19′ W **100**
Milton, *Wis., U.S.* 42°46′ N, 88°57′ W **102**
Milton Ernest, *U.K.* 52°11′ N, 0°31′ E **162**
Milton Keynes, *U.K.* 52°1′ N, 0°46′ E **162**
Milton Lake, *Can.* 59°27′ N, 104°22′ W **108**
Milton Mills, *N.H., U.S.* 43°30′ N, 70°59′ W **104**
Miltonvale, *Kans., U.S.* 39°19′ N, 97°28′ W **92**
Milverton, *Can.* 43°33′ N, 80°55′ W **102**
Milverton, *U.K.* 51°1′ N, 3°15′ W **162**
Milwaukee, *Wis., U.S.* 43°1′ N, 87°56′ W **102**
Mīlyutinka, *Kaz.* 51°58′ N, 61°3′ E **154**
Milyutino, *Russ.* 58°21′ N, 29°38′ E **166**
Mimizan-Plage, *Fr.* 44°13′ N, 1°19′ W **150**
Mimongo, *Gabon* 1°40′ S, 11°39′ E **218**
Mimot, *Cambodia* 11°49′ N, 106°11′ E **202**
Mims, *Fla., U.S.* 28°40′ N, 80°52′ W **105**
Min, river, *China* 26°20′ N, 118°32′ E **198**
Min, river, *China* 29°27′ N, 104°1′ E **190**
Mina, *Nev., U.S.* 38°23′ N, 118°8′ W **90**
Mīnā' al Faḩl, *Oman* 23°34′ N, 58°24′ E **196**
Mina Bazar, *Pak.* 31°3′ N, 69°18′ E **186**
Mīnā' Jabal 'Alī, *U.A.E.* 25°1′ N, 55°6′ E **196**
Mīnāb, *Iran* 27°5′ N, 57°4′ E **196**
Minabe, *Japan* 33°46′ N, 135°19′ E **201**
Minagish, oil field, *Kuwait* 28°59′ N, 47°28′ E **196**
Minago, river, *Can.* 54°2′ N, 99°40′ W **108**
Minakami, *Japan* 36°45′ N, 138°57′ E **201**
Minaki, *Can.* 49°58′ N, 94°41′ W **90**
Minamata, *Japan* 32°11′ N, 130°24′ E **201**
Minami Alps National Park, *Japan* 35°25′ N, 138°3′ E **201**
Minas, *Cuba* 21°28′ N, 77°37′ W **116**
Minas, *Uru.* 34°23′ S, 55°14′ W **139**
Minas de Corrales, *Uru.* 31°35′ S, 55°31′ W **139**
Minas Gerais, adm. division, *Braz.* 18°58′ S, 47°16′ W **138**
Minas Novas, *Braz.* 17°13′ S, 42°36′ W **138**
Minas, oil field, *Indonesia* 0°49′ N, 101°19′ E **196**
Minas, Sierra de las, *Guatemala* 15°10′ N, 90°16′ W **115**
Minatitlán, *Mex.* 17°58′ N, 94°33′ W **114**
Minbu, *Myanmar* 20°11′ N, 94°50′ E **202**
Minch, The, channel 58°2′ N, 6°8′ W **150**
Minchinmávida, Volcán, peak, *Chile* 42°48′ S, 72°36′ W **134**
Minco, *Okla., U.S.* 35°17′ N, 97°56′ W **92**
Mindanao, island, *Philippines* 5°26′ N, 123°17′ E **192**
Minden, *La., U.S.* 32°36′ N, 93°17′ W **103**
Minden, *Nebr., U.S.* 40°29′ N, 98°58′ W **90**
Minden City, *Mich., U.S.* 43°40′ N, 82°47′ W **102**
Mindif, *Cameroon* 10°24′ N, 14°27′ E **216**
Mindon, *Myanmar* 19°20′ N, 94°44′ E **202**
Mindoro, island, *Philippines* 12°31′ N, 119°20′ E **192**
Mindszent, *Hung.* 46°32′ N, 20°12′ E **168**
Mindyak, *Russ.* 54°3′ N, 58°47′ E **154**
Mine, *Japan* 34°27′ N, 129°20′ E **200**
Mine, *Japan* 34°8′ N, 131°13′ E **200**
Mine Centre, *Can.* 48°46′ N, 92°37′ W **94**
Minehead, *U.K.* 51°12′ N, 3°28′ W **162**
Mineiros, *Braz.* 17°36′ S, 52°34′ W **138**
Mineola, *Tex., U.S.* 32°39′ N, 95°30′ W **103**
Mineral, *Wash., U.S.* 46°41′ N, 122°12′ W **100**
Mineral King, *Calif., U.S.* 36°27′ N, 118°36′ W **101**
Mineral Point, *Wis., U.S.* 42°51′ N, 90°10′ W **102**
Mineral Wells, *Tex., U.S.* 32°47′ N, 98°7′ W **92**
Mineral'nyye Vody, *Russ.* 44°13′ N, 43°10′ E **158**
Minersville, *Utah, U.S.* 38°12′ N, 112°55′ W **92**
Minerva, *N.Y., U.S.* 43°46′ N, 73°60′ W **104**
Minerva, *Ohio, U.S.* 40°43′ N, 81°7′ W **102**
Minetto, *N.Y., U.S.* 43°23′ N, 76°30′ W **94**
Mineville, *N.Y., U.S.* 44°5′ N, 73°32′ W **104**
Mineyama, *Japan* 35°36′ N, 135°3′ E **201**
Minfeng, *China* 37°5′ N, 82°38′ E **184**
Mingäçevir, *Azerb.* 40°46′ N, 47°3′ E **195**
Mingäçevir Reservoir, *Azerb.* 41°2′ N, 46°18′ E **195**
Mingan, *Can.* 50°18′ N, 64°2′ W **111**
Mingin, *Myanmar* 22°51′ N, 94°24′ E **202**
Minginui, *N.Z.* 38°41′ S, 176°45′ E **240**
Ming-Kush, *Kyrg.* 41°38′ N, 74°18′ E **197**
Minglanilla, *Sp.* 39°31′ N, 1°37′ W **164**
Mingoyo, *Tanzania* 10°6′ S, 39°35′ E **224**
Mingteke, *China* 37°6′ N, 74°59′ E **186**
Mingteke Pass, *China* 37°2′ N, 74°44′ E **184**
Mingyuegou, *China* 43°7′ N, 128°54′ E **200**
Minhla, *Myanmar* 17°59′ N, 95°41′ E **202**
Miničevo, *Serb. and Mont.* 43°41′ N, 22°17′ E **168**
Minicoy Island, *India* 7°59′ N, 72°19′ E **188**
Minidoka, *Idaho, U.S.* 42°45′ N, 113°30′ W **90**
Minidoka Internment National Monument, *Idaho, U.S.* 42°40′ N, 114°27′ W **90**
Minier, *Ill., U.S.* 40°25′ N, 89°20′ W **102**
Minimarg, *Pak.* 34°46′ N, 75°3′ E **186**
Miñimiñi, *Chile* 19°14′ S, 69°42′ W **137**
Miniogbolo, *Sudan* 6°20′ N, 28°44′ E **224**
Minipi Lake, *Can.* 52°21′ N, 60°55′ W **111**
Ministra, peak, *Sp.* 41°6′ N, 2°32′ W **164**
Ministro João Alberto, *Braz.* 14°39′ S, 52°23′ W **138**
Minitonas, *Can.* 52°5′ N, 101°3′ W **108**
Min'kovo, *Russ.* 59°30′ N, 44°7′ E **154**
Minna, *Nig.* 9°36′ N, 6°33′ E **222**
Minna Bluff 78°41′ S, 176°42′ E **248**
Minneapolis, *Kans., U.S.* 39°6′ N, 97°43′ W **90**
Minneapolis, *Minn., U.S.* 44°56′ N, 93°17′ W **94**
Minnedosa, *Can.* 50°15′ N, 99°55′ W **82**
Minneola, *Kans., U.S.* 37°26′ N, 100°2′ W **90**
Minneota, *Minn., U.S.* 44°32′ N, 95°60′ W **90**
Minnesota, adm. division, *Minn., U.S.* 46°13′ N, 95°54′ W **94**
Minnesota, river, *Minn., U.S.* 44°56′ N, 95°41′ W **80**
Minnewaukan, *N. Dak., U.S.* 48°3′ N, 99°16′ W **90**
Minnitaki Lake, *Can.* 49°55′ N, 92°40′ W **110**
Mino, *Japan* 35°31′ N, 136°56′ E **201**
Minokamo, *Japan* 35°25′ N, 137°0′ E **201**
Minonk, *Mo., U.S.* 40°53′ N, 89°3′ W **110**
Minorca see Menorca, island, *Sp.* 39°47′ N, 3°33′ E **164**
Minot, *N. Dak., U.S.* 48°12′ N, 101°20′ W **90**
Minqin, *China* 38°46′ N, 103°4′ E **190**
Minsen, *Ger.* 53°42′ N, 7°58′ E **163**
Minsk, *Belarus* 53°52′ N, 27°26′ E **166**
Minster, *Ohio, U.S.* 40°23′ N, 84°23′ W **102**
Minta, *Cameroon* 4°33′ N, 12°48′ E **218**
Minto, *Can.* 62°37′ N, 136°47′ W **98**
Minto, *N. Dak., U.S.* 48°16′ N, 97°24′ W **90**
Minto Inlet 71°5′ N, 120°37′ W **106**
Minto, Lac, lake, *Can.* 57°22′ N, 75°53′ W **106**
Minto, Mount, peak, *Antarctica* 71°48′ S, 170°19′ E **248**
Minton, *Can.* 49°9′ N, 104°35′ W **90**
Minusinsk, *Russ.* 53°42′ N, 91°46′ E **190**
Minuteman Missle National Historic Site, *S. Dak., U.S.* 43°51′ N, 102°2′ W **90**
Minvoul, *Gabon* 2°8′ N, 12°8′ E **218**
Minwakh, *Yemen* 16°51′ N, 48°4′ E **182**
Minxian, *China* 34°22′ N, 104°0′ E **173**
Min'yar, *Russ.* 55°7′ N, 57°31′ E **154**
Mio, *Mich., U.S.* 44°38′ N, 84°8′ W **94**
Mionica, *Bosn. and Herzg.* 44°51′ N, 18°29′ E **168**
Mionica, *Serb. and Mont.* 44°14′ N, 20°5′ E **168**
Miquelon, *Can.* 49°25′ N, 76°26′ W **94**
Miquihuana, *Mex.* 23°33′ N, 99°46′ W **114**
Mir, *Niger* 14°3′ N, 11°58′ E **222**
Mira, *It.* 45°26′ N, 12°6′ E **167**
Mirabela, *Braz.* 16°18′ S, 44°12′ W **138**
Miracema, *Braz.* 21°26′ S, 42°13′ W **138**
Miracema do Norte, *Braz.* 9°34′ S, 48°28′ W **130**
Miracle Hot Springs, *Calif., U.S.* 35°34′ N, 118°33′ W **101**
Mirador, *Braz.* 6°23′ S, 44°25′ W **132**
Miraflores, *Col.* 1°16′ N, 72°5′ W **136**
Miragoâne, *Haiti* 18°26′ N, 73°7′ W **116**
Miraj, *India* 16°50′ N, 74°39′ E **188**
Miram Shah, *Pak.* 32°57′ N, 70°10′ E **186**
Miramar, *Arg.* 30°55′ S, 62°39′ W **139**
Miramar, *Arg.* 38°16′ S, 57°51′ W **139**
Miramar, *Fla., U.S.* 25°59′ N, 80°13′ W **105**
Miramar Naval Air Station, *Calif., U.S.* 32°52′ N, 117°10′ W **101**
Miramas, *Fr.* 43°34′ N, 5°0′ E **150**
Miramonte, *Calif., U.S.* 36°42′ N, 119°4′ W **101**
Miran, *China* 39°16′ N, 88°51′ E **188**
Miranda, *Braz.* 20°14′ S, 56°22′ W **132**
Miranda, adm. division, *Venez.* 10°18′ N, 66°47′ W **136**
Miranda de Ebro, *Sp.* 42°41′ N, 2°58′ W **164**
Mirande, *Fr.* 43°30′ N, 0°23′ E **164**
Mirandola, *It.* 44°52′ N, 11°3′ E **167**
Mirandópolis, *Braz.* 21°7′ S, 51°8′ W **138**
Mirapinima, *Braz.* 2°14′ S, 61°10′ W **130**
Miras, *Alban.* 40°30′ N, 20°54′ E **156**
Mirăs, *Europe* 42°28′ N, 21°12′ E **168**
Mirasaka, *Japan* 34°46′ N, 132°57′ E **201**
Mirassol, *Braz.* 20°51′ S, 49°31′ W **138**
Miravalles, Volcán, peak, *C.R.* 10°43′ N, 85°15′ W **115**
Mirbashir, *Azerb.* 40°20′ N, 46°55′ E **195**
Mirbāţ, *Oman* 16°58′ N, 54°45′ E **182**
Mirear see Marir, Gezaîr, islands, *Egypt* 23°5′ N, 35°51′ E **182**
Mirik see Timiris, Cap, *Mauritania* 19°28′ N, 16°53′ W **222**
Mirim, lake, *Braz.* 32°41′ S, 53°9′ W **139**
Mirimire, *Venez.* 11°7′ N, 68°45′ W **136**
Mírina, *Gr.* 39°52′ N, 25°4′ E **156**
Miringa, *Nig.* 10°45′ N, 12°9′ E **216**
Mirití, *Col.* 0°25′ N, 71°9′ W **136**
Mirití Paraná, river, *Col.* 9°534′ S, 71°31′ W **136**
Miritinitsy, *Russ.* 56°38′ N, 29°50′ E **166**
Mīrjāveh, *Iran* 28°57′ N, 61°24′ E **182**
Mirnyy, *Russ.* 62°27′ N, 113°27′ E **160**
Mirnyy, Russia, station, *Antarctica* 66°41′ S, 93°5′ E **248**
Miroč, *Serb. and Mont.* 44°26′ N, 22°14′ E **168**
Mirond Lake, *Can.* 55°4′ N, 103°18′ W **108**
Miros, *Pol.* 53°21′ N, 16°6′ E **152**
Miroševce, *Serb. and Mont.* 42°51′ N, 21°50′ E **168**
Mirpur, *Pak.* 33°10′ N, 73°48′ E **186**
Mirpur Batoro, *Pak.* 24°43′ N, 68°18′ E **186**
Mirpur Khas, *Pak.* 25°33′ N, 69°3′ E **186**
Mirria, *Niger* 13°42′ N, 9°6′ E **222**
Mirror, *Can.* 52°27′ N, 113°7′ W **108**
Mirror Lake, *N.H., U.S.* 43°37′ N, 71°17′ W **104**
Mirsaale, *Somalia* 5°57′ N, 47°57′ E **218**
Mirsíni, *Gr.* 37°55′ N, 21°14′ E **156**
Miruro, *Mozambique* 15°19′ S, 30°24′ E **224**
Miryang, *S. Korea* 35°29′ N, 128°45′ E **200**
Mirzaani, oil field, *Ga.* 41°21′ N, 46°7′ E **195**
Mirzapur, *India* 25°6′ N, 82°33′ E **197**
Misa, river, *Latv.* 56°38′ N, 23°50′ E **166**
Misaki, *Japan* 33°23′ N, 132°7′ E **201**
Misantla, *Mex.* 19°55′ N, 96°51′ W **114**
Misaw Lake, *Can.* 59°51′ N, 102°59′ W **108**
Misekumaw Lake, *Can.* 59°4′ N, 104°30′ W **108**
Miseno, Capo, *It.* 40°49′ N, 13°26′ E **156**
Mish Mountains, Slieve, peak, *Ire.* 52°11′ N, 9°55′ W **150**
Misha, *India* 7°59′ N, 93°28′ E **188**
Mishahua, river, *Peru* 11°24′ S, 72°40′ W **137**
Mishawaka, *Ind., U.S.* 41°38′ N, 86°11′ W **102**
Misheguk Mountain, peak, *Alas., U.S.* 68°13′ N, 161°20′ W **98**
Mishkino, *Russ.* 55°35′ N, 55°56′ E **154**
Misi, *Fin.* 66°36′ N, 26°40′ E **152**
Misima, island, *P.N.G.* 10°40′ S, 152°54′ E **192**
Misión San José Estero, *Parag.* 23°44′ S, 60°60′ W **132**
Misiones, adm. division, *Arg.* 27°5′ S, 55°22′ W **139**
Misiones, Sierra de, *Arg.* 26°48′ S, 54°11′ W **139**
Miskah, *Saudi Arabia* 24°48′ N, 42°56′ E **182**
Miski, *Sudan* 14°50′ N, 24°11′ E **226**
Miskitos, Cayos, islands, *Caribbean Sea* 14°20′ N, 82°37′ W **115**
Miskolc, *Hung.* 48°6′ N, 20°48′ E **168**
Mislea, oil field, *Rom.* 44°48′ N, 25°15′ E **156**
Misool, island, *Indonesia* 1°57′ S, 130°29′ E **192**
Misquah Hills, peak, *Minn., U.S.* 47°56′ N, 90°35′ W **94**
Mişrātah, *Lib.* 32°22′ N, 15°5′ E **216**

MON-MOU

Montejicar, Sp. 37°35′ N, 3°30′ W 164
Montelíbano, Col. 8°2′ N, 75°27′ W 136
Montélimar, Fr. 44°33′ N, 4°45′ E 150
Montello, Nev., U.S. 41°15′ N, 114°12′ W 90
Montello, Wis., U.S. 43°47′ N, 89°20′ W 102
Montemayor, Meseta de, Arg. 44°60′ S, 66°39′ W 134
Montemorelos, Mex. 25°11′ N, 99°48′ W 96
Montemuro, peak, Port. 40°57′ N, 8°4′ W 150
Montenegro 42°48′ N, 18°40′ E 168
Montepuez, Mozambique 13°8′ S, 39°8′ E 224
Monterado, Indonesia 0°47′ N, 109°7′ E 196
Montereau, Fr. 48°23′ N, 2°56′ E 163
Monterey, Calif., U.S. 36°35′ N, 121°55′ W 100
Monterey, Mass., U.S. 42°10′ N, 73°14′ W 104
Monterey, Tenn., U.S. 36°8′ N, 85°16′ W 96
Monterey Bay National Marine Sanctuary, Pacific Ocean 36°45′ N, 122°6′ W 100
Montería, Col. 8°44′ N, 75°53′ W 136
Montero, Bol. 17°23′ S, 63°17′ W 137
Monterrey, Col. 4°53′ N, 72°56′ W 136
Monterrey, Mex. 25°39′ N, 100°24′ W 114
Montes Claros, Braz. 16°45′ S, 43°52′ W 138
Montesano, Wash., U.S. 46°58′ N, 123°36′ W 100
Montese, It. 44°15′ N, 10°55′ E 167
Montets, Col des, pass, Fr. 45°59′ N, 6°54′ E 167
Montevallo, Ala., U.S. 33°5′ N, 86°53′ W 96
Montevideo, Minn., U.S. 44°56′ N, 95°43′ W 90
Montevideo, Uru. 34°55′ S, 56°19′ W 139
Montezuma, Ga., U.S. 32°17′ N, 84°2′ W 96
Montezuma, Iowa, U.S. 41°34′ N, 92°31′ W 94
Montezuma, Kans., U.S. 37°35′ N, 100°28′ W 90
Montezuma Castle National Monument, Ariz., U.S. 34°36′ N, 111°53′ W 92
Montezuma Creek, Utah, U.S. 37°16′ N, 109°20′ W 92
Montfaucon, Fr. 49°15′ N, 5°7′ E 163
Montfort, Fr. 48°8′ N, 1°58′ W 150
Montfort, ruin(s), Israel 33°1′ N, 35°10′ E 194
Montgomery, Ala., U.S. 32°20′ N, 86°24′ W 96
Montgomery, La., U.S. 31°39′ N, 92°54′ W 103
Montgomery, Mich., U.S. 41°46′ N, 84°48′ W 102
Montgomery, U.K. 52°33′ N, 3°9′ W 162
Montgomery Pass, Nev., U.S. 37°59′ N, 118°20′ W 90
Monthermé, Fr. 49°52′ N, 4°44′ E 163
Monthey, Switz. 46°15′ N, 6°56′ E 167
Monticelli d'Ongina, It. 45°5′ N, 9°56′ E 167
Monticello, Ark., U.S. 33°36′ N, 91°49′ W 112
Monticello, Fla., U.S. 30°32′ N, 83°51′ W 96
Monticello, Ind., U.S. 40°44′ N, 86°46′ W 102
Monticello, Iowa, U.S. 42°13′ N, 91°12′ W 110
Monticello, Ky., U.S. 36°50′ N, 84°52′ W 96
Monticello, Minn., U.S. 45°16′ N, 93°49′ W 94
Monticello, Miss., U.S. 31°33′ N, 90°7′ W 103
Monticello, Mo., U.S. 40°0′ N, 88°34′ W 94
Monticello, N. Mex., U.S. 33°24′ N, 107°27′ W 92
Monticello, N.Y., U.S. 41°38′ N, 74°42′ W 110
Monticello, Utah, U.S. 37°51′ N, 109°20′ W 92
Monticello, Wis., U.S. 42°44′ N, 89°35′ W 102
Monticello, site, Va., U.S. 37°59′ N, 78°32′ W 94
Montichiari, It. 45°24′ N, 10°23′ E 167
Montigny, Fr. 49°5′ N, 6°9′ E 163
Montijo, Port. 38°42′ N, 8°59′ W 150
Montijo, Sp. 38°53′ N, 6°37′ W 164
Montilla, Sp. 37°35′ N, 4°39′ W 164
Montividiu, Braz. 17°29′ S, 51°14′ W 138
Mont-Joli, Can. 48°34′ N, 68°11′ W 94
Mont-Laurier, Can. 46°31′ N, 75°34′ W 106
Mont-Laurier, Can. 46°33′ N, 75°31′ W 94
Mont-Louis, Can. 49°13′ N, 65°45′ W 111
Mont-Louis, Fr. 42°30′ N, 2°5′ E 164
Montmagny, Can. 46°57′ N, 70°36′ W 94
Montmartre, Can. 50°14′ N, 103°27′ W 90
Montmédy, Fr. 49°31′ N, 5°20′ E 163
Montmirail, Fr. 48°52′ N, 3°32′ E 163
Montmort-Lucy, Fr. 48°55′ N, 3°47′ E 163
Monto, Austral. 24°51′ S, 151°6′ E 231
Montoro, Sp. 38°0′ N, 4°23′ W 164
Montour Falls, N.Y., U.S. 42°20′ N, 76°50′ W 94
Montpelier, Idaho, U.S. 42°18′ N, 111°19′ W 82
Montpelier, Ind., U.S. 40°32′ N, 85°18′ W 102
Montpelier, Ohio, U.S. 41°34′ N, 84°36′ W 102
Montpelier, Vt., U.S. 44°14′ N, 72°37′ W 104
Montpellier, Fr. 43°36′ N, 3°52′ E 164
Montréal, Can. 45°30′ N, 73°36′ W 94
Montreal, Wis., U.S. 46°25′ N, 90°16′ W 110
Montreal Lake, Can. 54°3′ N, 105°51′ W 108
Montreal Lake, Can. 54°19′ N, 106°9′ W 108
Montreal Point, Can. 53°23′ N, 97°57′ W 108
Montreux, Switz. 46°26′ N, 6°56′ E 167
Montrichard, Fr. 47°20′ N, 1°11′ E 150
Montrose, Ark., U.S. 33°17′ N, 91°30′ W 103
Montrose, Colo., U.S. 38°28′ N, 107°53′ W 90
Montrose, Iowa, U.S. 40°31′ N, 91°25′ W 94
Montrose, Mich., U.S. 43°9′ N, 83°53′ W 102
Montrose, Miss., U.S. 32°7′ N, 89°13′ W 103
Montrose, U.K. 56°43′ N, 2°28′ W 150
Montrose, oil field, North Sea 57°22′ N, 1°19′ E 150
Monts des Nementcha, Alg. 35°7′ N, 5°41′ E 150
Monts, Pointe des, Can. 49°22′ N, 67°43′ W 94
Montsec, Serra del, Sp. 42°2′ N, 0°51′ E 164
Montserrat, U.K. 16°40′ N, 62°43′ W 116
Montserrat, island, Montserrat 16°49′ N, 62°11′ W 116
Montsûrs, Fr. 48°7′ N, 0°34′ E 150
Monturque, Sp. 37°28′ N, 4°36′ W 164
Monument Beach, Mass., U.S. 41°43′ N, 70°37′ W 104
Monument Butte, peak, Wyo., U.S. 42°12′ N, 110°2′ W 90
Monument Valley, Ariz., U.S. 37°3′ N, 110°8′ W 92
Monumental Buttes, peak, Idaho, U.S. 47°0′ N, 115°53′ W 90
Monveda, Dem. Rep. of the Congo 2°55′ N, 21°34′ E 218
Monywa, Myanmar 22°9′ N, 95°9′ E 202
Monywar, Myanmar 22°9′ N, 95°8′ E 190
Monza, It. 45°35′ N, 9°15′ E 167
Monze, Zambia 16°16′ S, 27°28′ E 224
Monzón, Sp. 41°54′ N, 0°11′ E 164
Moodus, Conn., U.S. 41°30′ N, 72°27′ W 104
Moody, Me., U.S. 43°16′ N, 70°37′ W 104
Moody, Tex., U.S. 31°18′ N, 97°21′ W 92
Moody Point, Antarctica 63°23′ S, 55°6′ W 134
Moogooloo Hill, peak, Austral. 23°39′ S, 114°31′ E 230
Mooketsi, S. Af. 23°34′ S, 30°4′ E 227
Mookgophong (Naboomspruit), S. Af. 24°31′ S, 28°44′ E 227
Moonie, oil field, Austral. 27°47′ S, 150°7′ E 230
Moorcroft, Wyo., U.S. 44°14′ N, 104°57′ W 90
Moore, Okla., U.S. 35°18′ N, 97°28′ W 92
Moore, Tex., U.S. 29°2′ N, 99°1′ W 96
Moore Haven, Fla., U.S. 26°50′ N, 81°6′ W 105
Moore, Mount, peak, Antarctica 80°18′ S, 96°46′ W 248
Moorea, island, France 17°35′ S, 149°50′ W 241
Mooreland, Okla., U.S. 36°25′ N, 99°12′ W 96
Moore's Island, Bahamas 26°8′ N, 78°13′ W 116
Mooresville, Ind., U.S. 39°36′ N, 86°22′ W 102
Mooresville, N.C., U.S. 35°35′ N, 80°49′ W 96
Moorfoot Hills, U.K. 55°42′ N, 3°33′ W 150
Moorhead, Minn., U.S. 46°52′ N, 96°45′ W 82
Moorpark, Calif., U.S. 34°17′ N, 118°54′ W 101
Moorrinya National Park, Austral. 21°27′ S, 144°33′ E 238
Moors, The, U.K. 54°56′ N, 4°58′ W 150
Moose Factory, Can. 51°15′ N, 80°37′ W 110
Moose Jaw, Can. 50°24′ N, 105°33′ W 90
Moose Jaw, river, Can. 50°10′ N, 105°12′ W 90
Moose Lake, Can. 53°39′ N, 100°21′ W 108
Moose Lake, Minn., U.S. 46°27′ N, 92°46′ W 94
Moose Mountain, peak, Can. 49°47′ N, 102°40′ W 90
Moose River, Can. 50°47′ N, 81°18′ W 110
Moose River, Me., U.S. 45°39′ N, 70°16′ W 111
Moosehead Lake, Me., U.S. 45°29′ N, 70°57′ W 80
Moosehorn, Can. 51°17′ N, 98°26′ W 90
Moosomin, Can. 50°9′ N, 101°41′ W 90
Moosonee, Can. 51°17′ N, 80°41′ W 82
Moosup, Conn., U.S. 41°43′ N, 71°53′ W 104
Mopeia Velha, Mozambique 17°59′ S, 35°43′ E 224
Mopipi, Botswana 21°11′ S, 24°52′ E 227
Mopti, Mali 14°30′ N, 4°11′ W 222
Moqatta', Sudan 14°38′ N, 35°51′ E 182
Moqor, Afghan. 32°51′ N, 67°50′ E 186
Moquegua, Peru 17°14′ S, 70°56′ W 137
Moquegua, adm. division, Peru 16°48′ S, 71°18′ W 137
Mór, Hung. 47°22′ N, 18°13′ E 168
Mor Dağı, peak, Turk. 37°45′ N, 44°12′ E 195
Mor, Glen, U.K. 56°59′ N, 4°49′ W 150
Mora, Cameroon 11°2′ N, 14°10′ E 216
Mora, Minn., U.S. 45°52′ N, 93°18′ W 94
Mora, N. Mex., U.S. 35°57′ N, 105°19′ W 92
Mora, Nor. 60°58′ N, 14°31′ E 152
Mora, Port. 38°55′ N, 8°10′ W 150
Móra d'Ebre, Sp. 41°5′ N, 0°36′ E 164
Morach, Belarus 52°50′ N, 26°50′ E 152
Moradabad, India 28°48′ N, 78°45′ E 197
Morąg, Pol. 53°54′ N, 19°56′ E 166
Moraine Point, Can. 61°20′ N, 115°40′ W 108
Morakovo, Europe 42°41′ N, 19°11′ E 168
Morales, Col. 2°44′ N, 76°41′ W 136
Morales, Laguna de 23°38′ N, 97°43′ W 114
Moramoria, Guinea 10°12′ N, 9°39′ W 222
Morane, island, Fr. 23°6′ S, 137°9′ W 252
Morant Cays, islands, Caribbean Sea 17°1′ N, 76°7′ W 115
Morant Point, Jam. 17°56′ N, 76°8′ W 115
Morata de Jiloca, Sp. 41°14′ N, 1°36′ W 164
Moratalla, Sp. 38°11′ N, 1°53′ W 164
Moravskoslezský, adm. division, Czech Rep. 49°54′ N, 16°50′ E 152
Morawhanna, Guyana 8°16′ N, 59°41′ W 116
Moray Firth 57°28′ N, 4°34′ W 142
Moraya, Bol. 21°44′ S, 65°32′ W 137
Morbach, Ger. 49°48′ N, 7°6′ E 167
Morbegno, It. 46°8′ N, 9°33′ E 167
Morbi, India 22°48′ N, 70°49′ E 186
Morcenx, Fr. 44°1′ N, 0°56′ E 150
Morden, Can. 49°10′ N, 98°7′ W 90
Mordino, Russ. 61°21′ N, 51°56′ E 154
Mordoviya, adm. division, Russ. 54°19′ N, 42°53′ E 154
Mordovo, Russ. 52°2′ N, 40°39′ E 158
Mordyyakha, Russ. 70°19′ N, 67°29′ E 169
More Assynt, Ben, peak, U.K. 58°7′ N, 4°58′ W 150
More, Ben, peak, U.K. 56°22′ N, 4°39′ W 150
More Coigach, Ben, peak, U.K. 57°58′ N, 5°20′ W 150
Moreau, river, S. Dak., U.S. 45°2′ N, 102°50′ W 90
Moreauville, La., U.S. 31°0′ N, 91°60′ W 103
Morebeng (Soekmekaar), S. Af. 23°30′ S, 29°56′ E 227
Morecambe, U.K. 54°3′ N, 2°52′ W 162
Morecambe Bay 54°4′ N, 3°11′ W 162
Morehead, Ky., U.S. 38°10′ N, 83°27′ W 94
Morehead City, N.C., U.S. 34°43′ N, 76°43′ W 82
Morehouse, Mo., U.S. 36°49′ N, 89°40′ W 94
Morelia, Col. 1°30′ N, 75°51′ W 136
Morelia, Mex. 19°39′ N, 101°15′ W 114
Morella, Sp. 40°36′ N, 9°534′ W 164
Morelos, Mex. 22°50′ N, 102°38′ W 114
Morelos, Mex. 28°23′ N, 100°53′ W 92
Morelos, adm. division, Mex. 18°38′ N, 99°28′ W 114
Moremi Game Reserve, Botswana 19°20′ S, 23°29′ E 224
Morena, India 26°29′ N, 78°0′ E 197
Morena, Sierra, Sp. 38°19′ N, 5°6′ W 164
Morenci, Ariz., U.S. 33°5′ N, 109°22′ W 92
Morenci, Mich., U.S. 41°42′ N, 84°13′ W 102
Moreni, oil field, Rom. 45°0′ N, 25°36′ E 156
Moreno, Bol. 11°7′ S, 66°13′ W 137
Moreno, Cerro, peak, Chile 23°32′ S, 70°46′ W 132
Moreno Valley, Calif., U.S. 33°55′ N, 117°11′ W 101
Moresby Island, Can. 52°51′ N, 134°23′ W 98
Moresby Islands, Indian Ocean 5°3′ S, 70°55′ E 188
Moret, Fr. 48°21′ N, 2°48′ E 163
Moreton Island, Austral. 27°10′ S, 153°32′ E 230
Morey Peak, Nev., U.S. 38°37′ N, 116°22′ W 90
Morez, Fr. 46°31′ N, 6°1′ E 167
Morfou 35°11′ N, 32°58′ E 194
Morgam Viibus, peak, Fin. 68°37′ N, 25°47′ E 152
Morgan City, La., U.S. 29°41′ N, 91°12′ W 103
Morgan Hill, Calif., U.S. 37°7′ N, 121°40′ W 100
Morganfield, Ky., U.S. 37°40′ N, 87°55′ W 96
Morganito, Venez. 5°2′ N, 67°42′ W 136
Morgantina, ruin(s), It. 37°23′ N, 14°18′ E 156
Morganza, La., U.S. 30°44′ N, 91°37′ W 103
Morges, Switz. 46°30′ N, 6°30′ E 167
Morghab, river, Afghan. 35°10′ N, 64°35′ E 186
Morhange, Fr. 48°55′ N, 6°38′ E 163
Morhiban, Lac de, lake, Can. 51°51′ N, 63°21′ W 111
Mori, It. 45°51′ N, 10°58′ E 167
Moriah, Mount, peak, Nev., U.S. 39°15′ N, 114°17′ W 90
Moriarty, N. Mex., U.S. 34°59′ N, 106°3′ W 92
Morice Lake, Can. 53°59′ N, 128°1′ W 108
Moricetown, Can. 55°1′ N, 127°24′ W 108
Moriki, Nig. 12°52′ N, 6°29′ E 222
Morin Dawa (Nirji), China 48°27′ N, 124°30′ E 198
Morino, Russ. 57°51′ N, 30°23′ E 166
Morinville, Can. 53°47′ N, 113°39′ W 108
Morioka, Japan 39°40′ N, 141°0′ E 190
Moriri, Tso, lake, India 32°55′ N, 77°53′ E 188
Morkoka, river, Russ. 65°55′ N, 109°43′ E 160
Morlaas, Fr. 43°20′ N, 0°15′ E 164
Morley, Mich., U.S. 43°29′ N, 85°27′ W 102
Morley, U.K. 53°44′ N, 1°36′ W 162
Mormon Mountain, peak, Idaho, U.S. 44°59′ N, 114°58′ W 90
Mormon Mountains, Nev., U.S. 36°54′ N, 114°34′ W 101
Mormon Peak, Nev., U.S. 36°58′ N, 114°33′ W 101
Mormon Temple, site, Hawai'i, U.S. 21°38′ N, 157°59′ W 99
Morning, Mount, peak, Antarctica 78°25′ S, 164°24′ E 248
Mornington, Isla, island, Chile 49°52′ S, 77°35′ W 134
Mornington Island, Austral. 16°11′ S, 138°32′ E 230
Moro, Pak. 26°42′ N, 68°1′ E 186
Moro, Sudan 10°48′ N, 30°5′ E 224
Moro Gulf 6°56′ N, 123°4′ E 203
Moro, Punta del, Sp. 36°31′ N, 2°60′ W 164
Moro, river, Africa 7°22′ N, 10°46′ W 222
Morobe, P.N.G. 7°48′ S, 147°41′ E 192
Morocco, Ind., U.S. 40°56′ N, 87°28′ W 102
Morocco 32°22′ N, 6°40′ W 214
Morogoro, Tanzania 6°47′ S, 37°43′ E 224
Morogoro, adm. division, Tanzania 8°10′ S, 36°22′ E 224
Morolaba, Burkina Faso 11°54′ N, 5°2′ W 222
Moroleón, Mex. 20°6′ N, 101°14′ W 114
Morombe, Madagascar 21°53′ S, 43°32′ E 207
Mörön, Mongolia 47°22′ N, 110°15′ E 198
Mörön, Mongolia 49°39′ N, 100°9′ E 190
Morón de Almazán, Sp. 41°24′ N, 2°26′ W 164
Morón de la Frontera, Sp. 37°7′ N, 5°28′ W 164
Morona, river, Peru 2°60′ S, 77°44′ W 136
Morondo, Côte d'Ivoire 8°57′ N, 6°46′ W 222
Morongo Valley, Calif., U.S. 34°2′ N, 116°36′ W 101
Moroni, Comoros 11°49′ S, 43°11′ E 220
Morotai, island, Indonesia 2°6′ N, 128°37′ E 192
Moroto, Uganda 2°29′ N, 34°39′ E 224
Moroto, Mount, peak, Uganda 2°29′ N, 34°38′ E 224
Moroto see Achwa, river, Uganda 2°14′ N, 32°58′ E 224
Morozovsk, Russ. 48°18′ N, 41°45′ E 158
Morpará, Braz. 11°36′ S, 43°16′ W 132
Morral, Ohio, U.S. 40°40′ N, 83°12′ W 102
Morrill, Nebr., U.S. 41°57′ N, 103°57′ W 90
Morrinhos, Braz. 17°46′ S, 49°8′ W 138
Morrinhos, Braz. 3°16′ S, 40°9′ W 132
Morris, Can. 49°19′ N, 97°23′ W 90
Morris, Conn., U.S. 41°40′ N, 73°12′ W 104
Morris, Ill., U.S. 41°21′ N, 88°26′ W 102
Morris, Minn., U.S. 45°34′ N, 95°56′ W 90
Morris, Mo., U.S. 41°21′ N, 88°26′ W 94
Morris, Okla., U.S. 35°35′ N, 95°51′ W 96
Morris Jesup, Kap 82°56′ N, 53°20′ W 246
Morris, Mount, peak, Austral. 26°11′ S, 130°52′ E 230
Morrisburg, Can. 44°54′ N, 75°12′ W 94
Morrison, Ill., U.S. 41°47′ N, 89°58′ W 102
Morrisonville, Ill., U.S. 39°24′ N, 89°28′ W 102
Morristown, Ind., U.S. 39°39′ N, 85°41′ W 102
Morristown, N.Y., U.S. 44°34′ N, 75°40′ W 94
Morristown, S. Dak., U.S. 45°55′ N, 101°44′ W 90
Morristown National Historical Park, N.J., U.S. 40°44′ N, 74°38′ W 94
Morrisville, Pa., U.S. 39°53′ N, 80°10′ W 94
Morrisville, Vt., U.S. 44°33′ N, 72°36′ W 104
Morro, Braz. 16°1′ S, 44°44′ W 138
Morro Agudo, Braz. 20°44′ S, 48°6′ W 138
Morro Bay, Calif., U.S. 35°22′ N, 120°52′ W 100
Morro de Puercos, Punta, Pan. 7°12′ N, 80°22′ W 115
Morro, Punta, Chile 27°6′ S, 71°35′ W 132
Morrocoy National Park, Venez. 10°52′ N, 68°23′ W 136
Morros, Braz. 2°54′ S, 44°2′ W 132
Morrow, La., U.S. 30°49′ N, 92°6′ W 103
Morrumbala, Mozambique 17°19′ S, 35°35′ E 224
Morrumbene, Mozambique 23°35′ S, 35°18′ E 227
Morse, Can. 50°25′ N, 107°4′ W 90
Morse, La., U.S. 30°6′ N, 92°31′ W 103
Morshansk, Russ. 53°25′ N, 41°42′ E 154
Morskaya Masel'ga, Russ. 63°5′ N, 34°57′ E 154
Morson, Can. 49°5′ N, 94°19′ W 90
Morsott, Alg. 35°40′ N, 8°0′ E 156
Mortara, It. 45°14′ N, 8°43′ E 167
Morteros, Arg. 30°43′ S, 61°59′ W 139
Mortka, Russ. 59°14′ N, 66°8′ E 169
Mortlach, Can. 50°26′ N, 106°5′ W 90
Mortlock Islands, North Pacific Ocean 4°53′ N, 151°50′ E 192
Morton, Ill., U.S. 40°35′ N, 89°27′ W 102
Morton, Miss., U.S. 32°19′ N, 89°39′ W 103
Morton, Tex., U.S. 33°42′ N, 102°46′ W 92
Morton, Wash., U.S. 46°31′ N, 122°17′ W 100
Morton, Islas, islands, South Pacific Ocean 55°53′ S, 69°42′ W 134
Morton Pass, Wyo., U.S. 41°40′ N, 105°31′ W 90
Mortyq, Kaz. 50°45′ N, 56°28′ E 158
Morvan, Monts du, Fr. 46°51′ N, 3°43′ E 165
Morven, N.Z. 44°51′ S, 171°6′ E 240
Morven, peak, U.K. 58°12′ N, 3°49′ W 150
Morven, peak, U.K. 57°6′ N, 3°9′ W 150
Morvern, U.K. 56°36′ N, 6°2′ W 150
Morwamosu, Botswana 24°4′ S, 23°1′ E 227
Morzine, Fr. 46°10′ N, 6°41′ E 167
Mosal'sk, Russ. 54°29′ N, 34°59′ E 154
Moscow, Idaho, U.S. 46°42′ N, 117°1′ W 90
Moscow, Tex., U.S. 30°54′ N, 94°50′ W 103
Moscow, Vt., U.S. 44°26′ N, 72°44′ W 104
Moskva, adm. division, Russ. 55°26′ N, 36°31′ E 154
Moscow Canal, Russ. 56°28′ N, 37°14′ E 154
Moscow see Moskva, Russ. 55°44′ N, 37°29′ E 154
Moscow University Ice Shelf, Antarctica 67°17′ S, 124°55′ E 248
Mose, Cape, Antarctica 66°28′ S, 130°6′ E 248
Mosėdis, Lith. 56°9′ N, 21°33′ E 166
Moselle, Miss., U.S. 31°29′ N, 89°17′ W 103
Moselle, river, Fr. 49°2′ N, 6°4′ E 163
Moses Coulee, Wash., U.S. 47°37′ N, 119°54′ W 90
Moses Lake, Wash., U.S. 47°6′ N, 119°17′ W 90
Moses, Mount, peak, Nev., U.S. 40°8′ N, 117°30′ W 90
Mosetse, Botswana 20°39′ S, 26°36′ E 227
Mosgiel, N.Z. 45°53′ S, 170°20′ E 240
Mosha, Russ. 61°44′ N, 40°51′ E 154
Mosha, river, Russ. 61°35′ N, 40°57′ E 154
Moshchnyy, Ostrov, island, Russ. 60°3′ N, 27°18′ E 166
Moshi, Tanzania 3°23′ S, 37°21′ E 224
Mosinee, Wis., U.S. 44°47′ N, 89°43′ W 94
Mosi-Oa-Tunya National Park, Zambia 17°59′ S, 25°53′ E 224
Mosjøen, Nor. 65°48′ N, 13°12′ E 160
Moskal'vo, Russ. 53°23′ N, 142°18′ E 160
Moskosel, Nor. 65°51′ N, 19°27′ E 152
Moskva, Taj. 37°36′ N, 69°37′ E 184
Moskva (Moscow), Russ. 55°44′ N, 37°29′ E 154
Moskva, river, Russ. 55°33′ N, 36°39′ E 154
Mosonmagyaróvár, Hung. 47°51′ N, 17°17′ E 168
Mosonszolhok, Hung. 47°50′ N, 17°11′ E 168
Mosquera, Col. 2°29′ N, 78°25′ W 130
Mosquero, N. Mex., U.S. 35°45′ N, 103°58′ W 82
Mosquito Lagoon, lake, Fla., U.S. 28°46′ N, 80°60′ W 105
Mosquito, Ponta do, Braz. 4°14′ N, 51°24′ W 130
Moss, Nor. 59°26′ N, 10°42′ E 152
Moss Agate Hill, peak, Wyo., U.S. 42°38′ N, 105°46′ W 90
Moss Point, Miss., U.S. 30°23′ N, 88°30′ W 103
Mossaka, Congo 1°16′ S, 16°46′ E 218
Mossbank, Can. 49°56′ N, 105°59′ W 90
Mossburn, N.Z. 45°42′ S, 168°14′ E 240
Mossel Bay see Mosselbaai, S. Af. 34°11′ S, 22°4′ E 227
Mosselbaai (Mossel Bay), S. Af. 34°11′ S, 22°4′ E 227
Mossendjo, Congo 2°56′ S, 12°41′ E 218
Mossi, region, Burkina Faso 12°5′ N, 2°36′ W 222
Mossoró, Braz. 5°12′ S, 37°22′ W 132
Mossuril, Mozambique 14°59′ S, 40°42′ E 224
Mossy, river, Can. 54°1′ N, 103°28′ W 108
Mossyrock, Wash., U.S. 46°30′ N, 122°29′ W 100
Most, Czech Rep. 50°31′ N, 13°38′ E 152
Mostaganem, Alg. 35°55′ N, 9°535′ E 150
Mostar, Bosn. and Herzg. 43°20′ N, 17°47′ E 168
Mostardas, Braz. 31°5′ S, 50°57′ W 139
Moster, Nor. 59°43′ N, 5°20′ E 152
Moštica, Maced. 42°3′ N, 22°35′ E 168
Møsting, Kap 63°52′ N, 40°54′ W 106
Mostoos Hills, Can. 54°59′ N, 109°21′ W 108
Mostrim (Edgeworthstown), Ire. 53°41′ N, 7°38′ W 150
Mosul see Al Mawşil, Iraq 36°20′ N, 43°0′ E 195
Mot'a, Eth. 11°3′ N, 37°51′ E 224
Mota del Cuervo, Sp. 39°29′ N, 2°52′ W 164
Motacucito, Bol. 17°37′ S, 61°27′ W 132
Motal', Belarus 52°18′ N, 25°37′ E 152
Mother Lode, region, Calif., U.S. 37°38′ N, 120°36′ W 100
Motihari, India 26°38′ N, 84°54′ E 197
Motike, Bosn. and Herzg. 44°48′ N, 17°7′ E 168
Motilla del Palancar, Sp. 39°33′ N, 1°56′ W 164
Motomiya, Japan 37°31′ N, 140°23′ E 201
Motril, Sp. 36°44′ N, 3°32′ W 164
Motru, Rom. 44°45′ N, 23°1′ E 168
Mott, N. Dak., U.S. 46°22′ N, 102°19′ W 90
Motu, N.Z. 38°17′ S, 177°34′ E 240
Motupe, Peru 6°5′ S, 79°45′ W 130
Mouali, Congo 0°15′ N, 15°33′ E 218
Mouchoir Passage 21°6′ N, 71°34′ W 116
Moudjéria, Mauritania 17°52′ N, 12°24′ W 222
Moudon, Switz. 46°41′ N, 6°48′ E 167
Mouhijärvi, Fin. 61°30′ N, 22°59′ E 166
Mouhoun (Black Volta), river, Burkina Faso 11°43′ N, 4°30′ W 222
Mouiat el Behima, spring, Alg. 32°55′ N, 6°48′ E 214
Mouila, Gabon 1°52′ S, 11°3′ E 218
Mouilah, spring, Alg. 26°6′ N, 0°39′ E 214
Mouit, Mauritania 16°34′ N, 13°10′ W 222
Mould Bay, Can. 76°21′ N, 119°15′ W 106
Mouling National Park, India 28°31′ N, 94°46′ E 188
Moulins, Fr. 46°34′ N, 3°19′ E 150
Moulouya, Oued, river, Mor. 32°0′ N, 3°54′ W 142
Moulton, Ala., U.S. 34°28′ N, 87°17′ W 96
Moulton, Mount, peak, Antarctica 75°58′ S, 134°21′ W 248
Moultrie, Ga., U.S. 31°10′ N, 83°48′ W 96
Moultrie, Lake, S.C., U.S. 33°17′ N, 80°40′ W 80
Mounana, Gabon 1°25′ S, 13°6′ E 218
Mound City, Mo., U.S. 37°5′ N, 89°10′ W 94
Mound City, Mo., U.S. 40°7′ N, 95°14′ W 94
Moundou, Chad 8°35′ N, 16°4′ E 218
Mounds, Mo., U.S. 37°6′ N, 89°12′ W 96
Moundville, Ala., U.S. 32°59′ N, 87°38′ W 103
Moung Tong, Vietnam 22°10′ N, 102°35′ E 202
Mounlapamôk, Laos 14°20′ N, 105°51′ E 202
Mount Airy, N.C., U.S. 36°28′ N, 80°37′ W 96
Mount Ayr, Iowa, U.S. 40°42′ N, 94°15′ W 94
Mount Baldy, Calif., U.S. 34°14′ N, 117°40′ W 101
Mount Brydges, Can. 42°53′ N, 81°29′ W 102
Mount Calvary, Wis., U.S. 43°49′ N, 88°15′ W 102
Mount Carroll, Ill., U.S. 42°5′ N, 89°59′ W 102
Mount Ch' Ilbo National Park, N. Korea 41°2′ N, 129°26′ E 200
Mount Charleston, Nev., U.S. 36°15′ N, 115°40′ W 101
Mount Clemens, Mich., U.S. 42°35′ N, 82°54′ W 94
Mount Cook, N.Z. 43°45′ S, 170°4′ E 240
Mount Cook see Aoraki, peak, N.Z. 43°37′ S, 170°7′ E 240
Mount Currie, Can. 50°20′ N, 122°42′ W 100
Mount Darwin, Zimb. 16°48′ S, 31°35′ E 224
Mount Dora, Fla., U.S. 28°47′ N, 81°38′ W 105
Mount Edgecumbe, Hecate Strait 56°59′ N, 135°21′ W 98
Mount Enterprise, Tex., U.S. 31°54′ N, 94°41′ W 103
Mount Erie, Ill., U.S. 38°30′ N, 88°14′ W 102
Mount Gilead, Ohio, U.S. 40°32′ N, 82°50′ W 102
Mount Grace Priory, site, U.K. 54°22′ N, 1°21′ W 162
Mount Hermon, La., U.S. 30°57′ N, 90°18′ W 103
Mount Holly, Ark., U.S. 33°17′ N, 92°57′ W 103
Mount Hope, W. Va., U.S. 37°53′ N, 81°11′ W 94
Mount Isa, Austral. 20°45′ S, 139°33′ E 238
Mount Kenya National Park, Kenya 0°14′ N, 36°59′ E 206
Mount Kisco, N.Y., U.S. 41°11′ N, 73°44′ W 104
Mount Kŭmgang National Park, N. Korea 38°32′ N, 128°4′ E 200
Mount Kuwol National Park, N. Korea 38°30′ N, 125°15′ E 200
Mount Laguna, Calif., U.S. 32°52′ N, 116°26′ W 101
Mount Maunganui, N.Z. 37°41′ S, 176°12′ E 240
Mount Morgan, Austral. 23°39′ S, 150°23′ E 231
Mount Morris, Ill., U.S. 42°2′ N, 89°26′ W 102
Mount Morris, Mich., U.S. 43°6′ N, 83°41′ W 102
Mount Morris, Mo., U.S. 42°2′ N, 89°26′ W 110
Mount Olive, Ill., U.S. 39°3′ N, 89°43′ W 102
Mount Olive, Miss., U.S. 31°45′ N, 89°39′ W 103
Mount Olivet, Ky., U.S. 38°31′ N, 84°2′ W 102
Mount Orab, Ohio, U.S. 39°0′ N, 83°55′ W 102
Mount Pleasant, Mich., U.S. 43°35′ N, 84°46′ W 94
Mount Pleasant, S.C., U.S. 32°47′ N, 79°53′ W 96
Mount Pleasant, Tex., U.S. 33°8′ N, 94°60′ W 103
Mount Pulaski, Ill., U.S. 40°0′ N, 89°17′ W 102
Mount Rainier National Park, Wash., U.S. 46°54′ N, 121°49′ W 100
Mount Revelstoke National Park, Can. 51°4′ N, 118°24′ W 238
Mount Robson, Can. 52°59′ N, 119°16′ W 108
Mount Saint Helens National Volcanic Monument, Wash., U.S. 46°17′ N, 122°35′ W 100
Mount Sangbe National Park, Côte d'Ivoire 7°45′ N, 8°1′ W 222
Mount Sangbe National Park, Côte d'Ivoire 7°49′ N, 7°37′ W 206
Mount Shasta, Calif., U.S. 41°18′ N, 122°20′ W 90
Mount Somers, N.Z. 43°42′ S, 171°24′ E 240
Mount Sterling, Ohio, U.S. 39°42′ N, 83°16′ W 102
Mount Stewart, site, U.K. 54°32′ N, 5°41′ W 150
Mount Sunapee, N.H., U.S. 43°20′ N, 72°5′ W 104
Mount Vernon, Ala., U.S. 31°5′ N, 87°60′ W 103
Mount Vernon, Ky., U.S. 37°20′ N, 84°21′ W 96
Mount Vernon, N.Y., U.S. 40°54′ N, 73°51′ W 104
Mount Vernon, Ohio, U.S. 40°23′ N, 82°28′ W 102
Mount Vernon, Tex., U.S. 33°10′ N, 95°14′ W 103
Mount Vernon, Wash., U.S. 48°24′ N, 122°20′ W 100
Mount Vernon, site, Va., U.S. 38°42′ N, 77°10′ W 94
Mountain Center, Calif., U.S. 33°41′ N, 116°44′ W 101
Mountain City, Nev., U.S. 41°50′ N, 115°58′ W 90
Mountain City, Tenn., U.S. 36°28′ N, 81°49′ W 94
Mountain Grove, Mo., U.S. 37°7′ N, 92°16′ W 96
Mountain Home, Ark., U.S. 36°19′ N, 92°23′ W 96
Mountain Home, Idaho, U.S. 43°9′ N, 115°43′ W 82
Mountain Home Air Force Base, Idaho, U.S. 43°2′ N, 115°59′ W 90
Mountain Lake, Minn., U.S. 43°55′ N, 94°56′ W 94
Mountain Park, Okla., U.S. 34°41′ N, 98°57′ W 92

Mountain Pass, Calif., U.S. 35°28′ N, 115°35′ W 101
Mountain Point, Alas., U.S. 55°20′ N, 131°35′ W 108
Mountain, river, Can. 65°41′ N, 129°37′ W 98
Mountain View, Mo., U.S. 36°59′ N, 91°42′ W 96
Mountain View, Wyo., U.S. 41°17′ N, 110°20′ W 92
Mountain Zebra National Park, S. Af. 32°12′ S, 25°23′ E 227
Mountainair, N. Mex., U.S. 34°31′ N, 106°14′ W 92
Mountjoy, Can. 48°29′ N, 81°23′ W 94
Moupitou, Congo 2°26′ S, 11°57′ E 218
Moura, Braz. 1°31′ S, 61°40′ W 130
Moura, Chad 13°47′ N, 21°11′ E 216
Mourão, Port. 38°22′ N, 7°21′ W 150
Mourdi, Dépression du, Chad 18°1′ N, 20°25′ E 216
Mourdiah, Mali 14°27′ N, 7°28′ W 222
Mourmelon-le-Grand, Fr. 49°8′ N, 4°21′ E 163
Mourne Mountains, U.K. 54°4′ N, 6°49′ W 150
Mouscron, Belg. 50°44′ N, 3°14′ E 163
Moussoro, Chad 13°39′ N, 16°31′ E 216
Mouthe, Fr. 46°43′ N, 6°10′ E 167
Moutier, Switz. 47°17′ N, 7°21′ E 150
Moutohora, N.Z. 38°19′ S, 177°33′ E 240
Mouy, Fr. 49°18′ N, 2°19′ E 163
Mouzarak, Chad 13°19′ N, 15°58′ E 216
Mouzay, Fr. 49°28′ N, 5°12′ E 163
Mouzon, Fr. 49°36′ N, 5°3′ E 163
Mowchadz′, Belarus 53°18′ N, 25°41′ E 152
Moweaqua, Ill., U.S. 39°36′ N, 89°1′ W 102
Moxico, adm. division, Angola 12°22′ S, 23°22′ E 220
Moÿ, Fr. 49°43′ N, 3°21′ E 163
Moyahua, Mex. 21°14′ N, 103°9′ W 114
Moyale, Kenya 3°28′ N, 39°3′ E 224
Moyamba, Sierra Leone 8°8′ N, 12°27′ W 222
Moyen Atlas, Mor. 33°3′ N, 5°20′ W 214
Moyie, river, Idaho, U.S. 49°2′ N, 116°14′ W 90
Moyo, Uganda 3°39′ N, 31°44′ E 224
Moyo, island, Indonesia 8°18′ S, 116°47′ E 192
Moyobamba, Peru 6°1′ S, 76°59′ W 130
Moyto, Chad 12°35′ N, 16°35′ E 216
Moyu, China 37°16′ N, 79°42′ E 184
Moyynqum, Kaz. 44°16′ N, 72°55′ E 184
Moyynqum, Kaz. 43°38′ N, 71°25′ E 184
Moyynty, Kaz. 47°11′ N, 73°22′ E 184
Mozambique 17°30′ S, 33°5′ E 220
Mozambique 23°32′ S, 33°38′ E 206
Mozambique Channel 17°57′ S, 38°34′ E 224
Mozambique Escarpment, Indian Ocean 35°57′ S, 35°12′ E 254
Mozambique Plateau, Indian Ocean 30°54′ S, 36°3′ E 254
Mozarlândia, Braz. 14°47′ S, 50°44′ W 138
Mozdok, Russ. 43°43′ N, 44°35′ E 195
Mozdūrān, Iran 36°10′ N, 60°30′ E 180
Mozhaysk, Russ. 55°29′ N, 36°3′ E 154
Mozhga, Russ. 56°25′ N, 52°17′ E 154
Mozuli, Russ. 56°34′ N, 28°11′ E 166
Mpala, Dem. Rep. of the Congo 6°46′ S, 29°32′ E 224
Mpanda, Tanzania 6°21′ S, 31°1′ E 224
Mpandamatenga, Botswana 18°39′ S, 25°41′ E 224
Mphoengs, Zimb. 21°11′ S, 27°51′ E 227
Mpika, Zambia 11°49′ S, 31°24′ E 224
Mpoko, river, Cen. Af. Rep. 6°1′ N, 17°30′ E 218
Mporokoso, Zambia 9°23′ S, 30°7′ E 224
Mpouya, Congo 2°37′ S, 16°8′ E 218
Mpui, Tanzania 8°20′ S, 31°50′ E 224
Mpulungu, Zambia 8°48′ S, 31°6′ E 224
Mpumalanga, adm. division, S. Af. 26°16′ S, 28°35′ E 227
Mpwapwa, Tanzania 6°19′ S, 36°28′ E 224
Mqanduli, S. Af. 31°50′ S, 28°45′ E 227
Mrągowo, Pol. 53°51′ N, 21°16′ E 166
Mrakovo, Russ. 52°43′ N, 56°29′ E 154
Mrkojević, Zaliv 42°0′ N, 18°51′ E 168
Msaken, Tun. 35°43′ N, 10°34′ E 156
M′sila, Alg. 35°41′ N, 4°33′ E 150
Msoro, Zambia 13°39′ S, 31°53′ E 224
Msta, river, Russ. 58°34′ N, 31°50′ E 154
Mstizh, Belarus 54°34′ N, 28°9′ E 166
Mstsislaw, Belarus 54°1′ N, 31°43′ E 154
Mtama, Tanzania 10°18′ S, 39°20′ E 224
Mtouf, spring, Mauritania 19°27′ N, 11°24′ W 222
Mtsensk, Russ. 53°15′ N, 36°39′ E 154
Mts′khet′a, Ga. 41°51′ N, 44°42′ E 195
Mtwara, Tanzania 10°20′ S, 40°11′ E 224
Mtwara, adm. division, Tanzania 10°52′ S, 38°25′ E 224
Mu, river, Myanmar 22°22′ N, 95°24′ E 202
Muaguide, Mozambique 12°31′ S, 40°5′ E 224
Mualama, Mozambique 16°54′ S, 38°19′ E 224
Muaná, Braz. 1°31′ S, 49°14′ W 130
Muang Bèng, Laos 20°24′ N, 101°47′ E 202
Muang Gnômmarat, Laos 17°37′ N, 105°10′ E 202
Muang Ham, Laos 20°21′ N, 103°59′ E 202
Muang Kao, Laos 14°55′ N, 106°53′ E 202
Muang Khamkeut, Laos 18°15′ N, 104°43′ E 202
Muang La, Laos 20°53′ N, 102°7′ E 202
Muang Namo, Laos 21°4′ N, 101°49′ E 202
Muang Ngoy, Laos 20°44′ N, 102°41′ E 202
Muang Paklay, Laos 18°13′ N, 101°23′ E 202
Muang Paktha, Laos 20°8′ N, 100°37′ E 202
Muang Sing, Laos 21°12′ N, 101°8′ E 202
Muang Souy, Laos 19°33′ N, 102°55′ E 202
Muang Va, Laos 21°54′ N, 102°19′ E 202
Muang Xai, Laos 20°45′ N, 101°58′ E 202
Muang Xon, Laos 20°28′ N, 103°16′ E 202
Muar, Malaysia 2°4′ N, 102°34′ E 196
Muara, Indonesia 0°39′ N, 100°58′ E 196
Muaraenim, Indonesia 3°36′ S, 103°36′ E 192
Muarakumpe, Indonesia 1°22′ S, 104°1′ E 196
Muarasabak, Indonesia 1°8′ S, 103°49′ E 196
Muarasipongi, Indonesia 0°38′ N, 99°53′ E 196
Muaratewe, Indonesia 0°54′ N, 114°42′ E 192
Muari, Ras, Pak. 24°48′ N, 66°18′ E 186
Muatua, Mozambique 15°46′ S, 39°45′ E 224
Mubarras, oil field, Persian Gulf 24°23′ N, 53°38′ E 196
Mubende, Uganda 0°32′ N, 31°23′ E 224
Mubi, Nig. 10°15′ N, 13°17′ E 216
Muborak, Uzb. 39°11′ N, 65°19′ E 197
Mubur, island, Indonesia 3°27′ N, 105°51′ E 196
Mucacata, Mozambique 13°25′ S, 39°46′ E 224
Mucajá, Braz. 3°58′ S, 57°32′ W 130
Mucajaí, river, Braz. 2°49′ N, 62°49′ W 130
Mucajaí, Serra do, Braz. 2°3′ N, 62°21′ W 130
Much Wenlock, U.K. 52°36′ N, 2°34′ W 162
Muchea, Austral. 31°35′ S, 115°59′ E 231
Muchinga Mountains, Zambia 10°53′ S, 31°40′ E 224
Muchkapskiy, Russ. 51°51′ N, 42°27′ E 158
Muckish Mountain, peak, Ire. 55°5′ N, 8°7′ W 150
Mucojo, Mozambique 12°4′ S, 40°29′ E 224
Muconda, Angola 10°37′ S, 21°19′ E 220
Mucubela, Mozambique 16°54′ S, 37°50′ E 224
Mucucuaú, river, Braz. 0°29′ N, 61°23′ W 130
Mucuim, river, Braz. 7°13′ S, 64°31′ W 130
Mucur, Turk. 39°3′ N, 34°22′ E 156
Mucuri, Braz. 18°5′ S, 39°36′ W 138
Mucuri, river, Braz. 17°26′ S, 41°23′ W 138
Mucurici, Braz. 18°5′ S, 40°37′ W 138
Mucusso, Angola 17°58′ S, 21°25′ E 220
Mud Lake, S. Dak., U.S. 45°43′ N, 98°32′ W 90
Mudanjiang, China 44°41′ N, 129°43′ E 190
Muddy Peak, Nev., U.S. 36°17′ N, 114°45′ W 101
Muddy, river, Nev., U.S. 36°39′ N, 114°32′ W 101
Mudersbach, Ger. 50°49′ N, 7°56′ E 167
Mudjatik, river, Can. 56°18′ N, 107°33′ W 108
Mudon, Myanmar 16°15′ N, 97°43′ E 202
Mudurnu, Turk. 40°28′ N, 31°12′ E 156
Mudvær, islands, Norwegian Sea 65°41′ N, 10°17′ E 152
Mud′yuga, Russ. 63°47′ N, 39°17′ E 154
Muecate, Mozambique 14°52′ S, 39°39′ E 224
Mueda, Mozambique 11°39′ S, 39°34′ E 224
Muembe, Mozambique 13°6′ S, 35°39′ E 224
Muen, peak, Nor. 61°42′ N, 10°3′ E 152
Muertos Cays, islands, North Atlantic Ocean 24°10′ N, 80°51′ W 82
Mufulira, Zambia 12°35′ S, 28°14′ E 220
Mug, river, China 34°8′ N, 93°6′ E 188
Muga, peak, Sp. 41°59′ N, 6°55′ W 150
Muganly, Azerb. 41°28′ N, 46°29′ E 195
Mugeba, Mozambique 16°35′ S, 37°14′ E 224
Mughalzhar Taūy, Kaz. 47°23′ N, 56°0′ E 184
Mugharet el Wad, ruin(s), Israel 32°38′ N, 34°56′ E 194
Mughayyir, Jordan 31°24′ N, 35°46′ E 194
Mugi, Japan 33°40′ N, 134°25′ E 201
Mugila, Monts, Dem. Rep. of the Congo 7°35′ S, 28°49′ E 224
Muğla, Turk. 37°12′ N, 28°20′ E 156
Muglad, Sudan 11°3′ N, 27°43′ E 224
Mugodzharskaya, Kaz. 48°37′ N, 58°25′ E 158
Mugu, Nepal 29°46′ N, 82°37′ E 197
Muhagiriya, Sudan 11°56′ N, 25°34′ E 216
Muhamdi, India 27°57′ N, 80°12′ E 197
Muhammad Qol, Sudan 20°52′ N, 37°6′ E 182
Muḩammad, Râs, Egypt 27°30′ N, 34°16′ E 180
Muḩayy, Jordan 30°59′ N, 35°50′ E 194
Muhembo, Botswana 18°18′ S, 21°45′ E 220
Muheza, Tanzania 5°10′ S, 38°47′ E 224
Mühlhausen, Ger. 51°12′ N, 10°27′ E 167
Mühlheim, Ger. 50°7′ N, 8°50′ E 167
Muhos, Fin. 64°46′ N, 25°58′ E 152
Muḩradah, Syr. 35°15′ N, 36°34′ E 194
Muhu, Est. 58°35′ N, 23°13′ E 166
Muhu, island, Est. 58°39′ N, 23°20′ E 166
Muhu Väin 58°55′ N, 22°51′ E 166
Muhulu, Dem. Rep. of the Congo 1°4′ S, 27°13′ E 224
Muhutwe, Tanzania 1°35′ S, 31°43′ E 224
Muié, Angola 14°26′ S, 20°35′ E 220
Muikamachi, Japan 37°3′ N, 138°52′ E 201
Muir Woods National Monument, Calif., U.S. 37°52′ N, 122°37′ W 100
Muiron Islands, Indian Ocean 21°36′ S, 111°35′ E 230
Muisne, Ecua. 0°35′ N, 80°1′ W 130
Muite, Mozambique 14°3′ S, 39°3′ E 224
Mujejärvi, Fin. 63°47′ N, 29°26′ E 152
Mujimbeji, Zambia 12°11′ S, 24°55′ E 224
Muju, S. Korea 36°0′ N, 127°40′ E 200
Mukacheve, Ukr. 48°25′ N, 22°43′ E 152
Mukawwar Island, Sudan 20°42′ N, 37°16′ E 182
Mukdahan, Thai. 16°33′ N, 104°41′ E 202
Mukhayzināt, Jibāl al, peak, Jordan 31°55′ N, 36°31′ E 194
Mukhomornoye, Russ. 66°21′ N, 173°19′ E 173
Mukhtadir, Azerb. 41°41′ N, 48°43′ E 195
Mukhtolovo, Russ. 55°25′ N, 43°14′ E 154
Mukilteo, Wash., U.S. 47°55′ N, 122°17′ W 100
Muko Jima Rettō, islands, Philippine Sea 27°36′ N, 142°16′ E 190
Mukry, Turkm. 37°36′ N, 65°45′ E 184
Muktiköl, Kaz. 51°50′ N, 60°52′ E 154
Muktinath, Nepal 28°48′ N, 83°54′ E 197
Mukutawa, river, Can. 53°3′ N, 97°29′ W 108
Mukwonago, Wis., U.S. 42°52′ N, 88°20′ W 102
Mul, India 20°3′ N, 79°40′ E 188
Mula, Sp. 38°2′ N, 1°29′ W 164
Muladu, island, Maldives 6°38′ N, 72°7′ E 188
Mulaku Atoll, Persian Gulf 2°38′ N, 72°47′ E 188
Mulan, China 45°59′ N, 128°4′ E 198
Mulanay, Philippines 13°32′ N, 122°26′ E 203
Mulanje Mountains, Malawi 15°60′ S, 35°30′ E 224
Mulatos, Col. 8°38′ N, 76°42′ W 136
Mulatos, Mex. 28°37′ N, 108°51′ W 92
Mulberry, Fla., U.S. 27°54′ N, 81°58′ W 105
Mulberry, Ind., U.S. 40°20′ N, 86°40′ W 102
Mulberry, Kans., U.S. 37°32′ N, 94°38′ W 96
Mulberry Grove, Ill., U.S. 38°55′ N, 89°16′ W 102
Muldraugh, Ky., U.S. 37°56′ N, 85°59′ W 96
Muleba, Tanzania 1°53′ S, 31°39′ E 224
Mulegé, Mex. 26°52′ N, 112°4′ W 112
Muleshoe, Tex., U.S. 34°12′ N, 102°44′ W 92
Mulhacén, peak, Sp. 37°2′ N, 3°21′ W 164
Mülheim, Ger. 51°25′ N, 6°52′ E 167
Muligudje, Mozambique 16°31′ S, 38°54′ E 224
Mulkonbar, spring, Austral. 27°45′ S, 140°45′ E 230
Mull, Ross of 56°13′ N, 6°46′ W 150
Mullaittivu, Sri Lanka 9°14′ N, 80°51′ E 188
Mullen, Nebr., U.S. 42°2′ N, 101°3′ W 90
Mullens, W. Va., U.S. 37°34′ N, 81°24′ W 96
Mullet Key, island, Fla., U.S. 27°34′ N, 82°51′ W 105
Mullet Peninsula, Atlantic Ocean 54°8′ N, 10°41′ W 150
Mullewa, Austral. 28°31′ S, 115°33′ E 231
Mullikkulam, Sri Lanka 8°36′ N, 79°57′ E 188
Mullingar, Ire. 53°31′ N, 7°21′ W 150
Mullsjö, Nor. 57°54′ N, 13°53′ E 152
Mulobezi, Zambia 16°50′ S, 25°11′ E 224
Mulondo, Angola 15°39′ S, 15°13′ E 220
Multan, Pak. 30°10′ N, 71°28′ E 186
Multé, Mex. 17°40′ N, 91°27′ W 115
Mulumbe Mountains, Dem. Rep. of the Congo 8°27′ S, 27°53′ E 224
Mulym′ya, Russ. 60°34′ N, 64°53′ E 169
Muma, Dem. Rep. of the Congo 3°28′ N, 23°17′ E 218
Mumallah, Sudan 10°49′ N, 25°30′ E 224
Mumbai (Bombay), India 18°57′ N, 72°49′ E 188
Mumbué, Angola 13°55′ S, 17°12′ E 220
Mumbwa, Zambia 14°59′ S, 27°2′ E 224
Mumra, Russ. 45°44′ N, 47°43′ E 158
Mumu, Sudan 12°7′ N, 23°42′ E 216
Mun, river, Thai. 15°9′ N, 103°28′ E 202
Muna, Mex. 20°28′ N, 89°44′ W 115
Muna, island, Indonesia 5°9′ S, 121°36′ E 192
Muna, river, Russ. 67°48′ N, 119°58′ E 160
München (Munich), Ger. 48°8′ N, 11°34′ E 152
Muncho Lake, Can. 58°55′ N, 125°47′ W 108
Munch′ŏn, N. Korea 39°17′ N, 127°16′ E 200
Munch′ŏn-ŭp, N. Korea 39°13′ N, 127°20′ E 200
Muncie, Ind., U.S. 40°10′ N, 85°23′ W 102
Muncy, Pa., U.S. 41°12′ N, 76°48′ W 94
Muncy Valley, Pa., U.S. 41°20′ N, 76°36′ W 94
Mundare, Can. 53°34′ N, 112°20′ W 108
Munday, Tex., U.S. 33°25′ N, 99°38′ W 92
Mundemba, Cameroon 4°53′ N, 8°50′ E 222
Münden, Ger. 51°24′ N, 9°40′ E 167
Mundesley, U.K. 52°52′ N, 1°25′ E 163
Mundeung-ni, S. Korea 38°19′ N, 127°58′ E 200
Mundra, India 22°50′ N, 69°44′ E 186
Mundybash, Russ. 53°13′ N, 87°24′ E 184
Munenga, Angola 10°2′ S, 14°38′ E 220
Munera, Sp. 39°2′ N, 2°29′ W 164
Mungári, Mozambique 17°12′ S, 33°32′ E 224
Mungbere, Dem. Rep. of the Congo 2°38′ N, 28°25′ E 224
Mungeli, India 22°4′ N, 81°39′ E 197
Munger, India 25°21′ N, 86°29′ E 197
Munger, Mich., U.S. 43°30′ N, 83°46′ W 102
Mungia, Sp. 43°20′ N, 2°51′ W 164
Mungret, Ire. 52°37′ N, 8°42′ W 150
Munguba, Braz. 0°58′ N, 52°25′ W 130
Munguy, Russ. 70°22′ N, 83°51′ E 169
Mungyeong, S. Korea 36°42′ N, 128°6′ E 200
Munhamade, Mozambique 16°37′ S, 36°58′ E 224
Munich see München, Ger. 48°8′ N, 11°34′ E 152
Munising, Mich., U.S. 46°24′ N, 86°41′ W 94
Muniz Freire, Braz. 20°28′ S, 41°26′ W 138
Munk, Can. 55°59′ N, 95°59′ W 108
Munkedal, Nor. 58°27′ N, 11°38′ E 152
Munkelv, Nor. 69°38′ N, 29°27′ E 152
Munkfors, Nor. 59°51′ N, 13°32′ E 152
Munksund, Nor. 65°17′ N, 21°29′ E 152
Münnerstadt, Ger. 50°15′ N, 10°10′ E 167
Muñoz Gamero, Peninsula, Chile 52°9′ S, 74°21′ W 134
Munroe Lake, Can. 59°6′ N, 99°12′ W 108
Munsan, S. Korea 37°51′ N, 126°48′ E 200
Münsingen, Switz. 46°52′ N, 7°34′ E 167
Munsonville, N.H., U.S. 43°0′ N, 72°9′ W 104
Münster, Ger. 51°57′ N, 7°38′ E 167
Munsungan Lake, Me., U.S. 46°20′ N, 69°36′ W 94
Muntok, Indonesia 2°3′ S, 105°11′ E 192
Munzur Vadisi National Park, Turk. 39°15′ N, 39°24′ E 195
Muodoslompolo, Nor. 67°56′ N, 23°19′ E 152
Muong Te, Vietnam 22°24′ N, 102°48′ E 202
Muonio, Fin. 67°54′ N, 24°4′ E 160
Mupa National Park, Angola 15°34′ S, 14°45′ E 220
Muping, China 37°24′ N, 121°37′ E 198
Muqakoori, Somalia 4°2′ N, 46°5′ E 218
Muqdisho (Mogadishu), Somalia 1°58′ N, 45°10′ E 218
Muqyr, Kaz. 48°3′ N, 54°27′ E 158
Mur, river, Europe 47°2′ N, 13°30′ E 156
Mura, river, Europe 46°39′ N, 16°2′ E 168
Muradiye, Turk. 38°59′ N, 43°44′ E 195
Murakami, Japan 38°13′ N, 139°30′ E 201
Murakeresztúr, Hung. 46°21′ N, 16°53′ E 168
Muramvya, Burundi 3°16′ S, 29°35′ E 218
Murang′a, Kenya 0°44′ N, 37°10′ E 224
Murashi, Russ. 59°22′ N, 48°59′ E 154
Murat Dağı, peak, Turk. 38°54′ N, 29°40′ E 156
Murat, river, Turk. 39°41′ N, 43°11′ E 195
Muratlı, Turk. 41°9′ N, 27°28′ E 158
Muravera, It. 39°25′ N, 9°35′ E 156
Murayama, Japan 38°29′ N, 140°23′ E 201
Murazzano, It. 44°28′ N, 8°1′ E 167
Mürcheh Khvort, Iran 33°4′ N, 51°30′ E 180
Murchison, N.Z. 41°50′ S, 172°20′ E 240
Murchison Falls, Uganda 2°25′ N, 31°41′ E 224
Murchison Falls National Park, Uganda 2°0′ N, 31°26′ E 224
Murchison, Mount, peak, Antarctica 73°22′ S, 166°55′ E 248
Murchison, Mount, peak, Austral. 26°49′ S, 116°14′ E 230
Murcia, Sp. 37°58′ N, 1°8′ W 164
Murcia, adm. division, Sp. 37°51′ N, 1°52′ W 164
Murdo, S. Dak., U.S. 43°53′ N, 100°43′ W 90
Murdochville, Can. 48°57′ N, 65°32′ W 111
MureȘ, adm. division, Rom. 46°20′ N, 24°2′ E 156
Mureş, river, Rom. 46°7′ N, 21°3′ E 168
Muret, Fr. 43°27′ N, 1°19′ E 164
Murewa, Zimb. 17°41′ S, 31°46′ E 224
Murfreesboro, Ark., U.S. 34°2′ N, 93°41′ W 96
Murfreesboro, N.C., U.S. 36°26′ N, 77°7′ W 96
Murfreesboro, Tenn., U.S. 35°50′ N, 86°23′ W 96
Murgab, Taj. 38°42′ N, 73°30′ E 197
Murgenella Wildlife Sanctuary, Austral. 11°48′ S, 132°31′ E 238
Murghob, Taj. 38°12′ N, 74°3′ E 197
Murghob, river, Taj. 38°7′ N, 73°26′ E 197
Murguz, peak, Arm. 40°43′ N, 45°12′ E 195
Muri, China 38°9′ N, 99°6′ E 188
Muri, India 23°22′ N, 85°50′ E 197
Muri, Nig. 9°12′ N, 10°52′ E 222
Muriaé, Braz. 21°8′ S, 42°22′ W 138
Muriege, Angola 9°56′ S, 21°13′ E 220
Murilo Atoll 8°38′ N, 153°0′ E 192
Murino, Europe 42°39′ N, 19°53′ E 168
Muritiba, Braz. 12°39′ S, 39°2′ W 132
Murjek, Nor. 66°28′ N, 20°50′ E 152
Murle, Eth. 5°5′ N, 36°12′ E 224
Murmansk, Russ. 68°58′ N, 33°3′ E 152
Murmansk, adm. division, Russ. 67°31′ N, 36°54′ E 169
Murmansk Rise, Barents Sea 74°41′ N, 37°39′ E 255
Murmino, Russ. 54°37′ N, 40°0′ E 154
Murnei, Sudan 12°55′ N, 22°48′ E 218
Muro, Capo di, Fr. 41°39′ N, 7°59′ E 156
Murom, Russ. 55°33′ N, 42°3′ E 154
Muromtsevo, Russ. 56°20′ N, 75°15′ E 169
Muroran, Japan 42°26′ N, 140°52′ E 190
Muroto, Japan 33°18′ N, 134°9′ E 201
Muroto Zaki, Japan 33°9′ N, 134°11′ E 201
Murphy, Idaho, U.S. 43°13′ N, 116°34′ W 90
Murphy Bay 67°28′ S, 149°3′ E 248
Murphy Inlet 71°42′ S, 96°56′ W 248
Murphy, Mount, peak, Antarctica 75°17′ S, 110°10′ W 248
Murphys, Calif., U.S. 38°7′ N, 120°29′ W 100
Murphysboro, Mo., U.S. 37°45′ N, 89°21′ W 96
Murra, Nicar. 13°42′ N, 85°60′ W 115
Murray, Ky., U.S. 36°37′ N, 88°17′ W 96
Murray, Cape 79°16′ S, 171°16′ E 248
Murray Fracture Zone, North Pacific Ocean 30°51′ N, 143°25′ W 252
Murray Head, Can. 45°53′ N, 62°30′ W 111
Murray Islands, Coral Sea 10°20′ S, 144°2′ E 192
Murray, Mount, peak, Can. 60°52′ N, 128°58′ W 108
Murray, river, Can. 54°50′ N, 121°21′ W 108
Murraysburg, S. Af. 31°58′ S, 23°44′ E 227
Murree, Pak. 33°53′ N, 73°28′ E 186
Murrells Inlet, S.C., U.S. 33°32′ N, 79°3′ W 96
Murro di Porco, Capo, It. 36°54′ N, 15°20′ E 156
Murrumbidgee, river, Austral. 34°41′ S, 143°38′ E 230
Murrupula, Mozambique 15°28′ S, 38°47′ E 224
Murska Sobota, Slov. 46°39′ N, 16°9′ E 168
Mursko Središće, Croatia 46°30′ N, 16°25′ E 168
Murtovaara, Fin. 65°40′ N, 29°20′ E 152
Muru, river, Braz. 9°9′ S, 71°27′ W 137
Muruasigar, peak, Kenya 3°6′ N, 34°51′ E 224
Murukta, Russ. 67°49′ N, 102°25′ E 160
Muruntau, Uzb. 41°27′ N, 64°41′ E 197
Murwara, India 23°49′ N, 80°23′ E 197
Murygino, Russ. 58°44′ N, 49°31′ E 154
Muş, Turk. 38°44′ N, 41°31′ E 195
Mus Khaya, Gora, peak, Russ. 62°18′ N, 140°8′ E 172
Musa, Dem. Rep. of the Congo 2°36′ N, 19°20′ E 218
Musa Ālī Terara, peak, Eth. 12°22′ N, 42°15′ E 182
Musa Dağ, peak, Turk. 36°9′ N, 35°50′ E 156
Mûsa, Gebel (Sinai, Mount), peak, Egypt 28°30′ N, 33°54′ E 226
Mūša, river, Lith. 56°18′ N, 24°7′ E 166
Musala (Mansalar), island, Indonesia 1°31′ N, 97°47′ E 196
Musala, peak, Bulg. 42°10′ N, 23°31′ E 156
Musan, N. Korea 42°15′ N, 129°15′ E 200
Musawa, Nig. 12°7′ N, 7°38′ E 222
Musaymīr, Yemen 13°25′ N, 44°36′ E 182
Muscat see Masqaţ, Oman 23°30′ N, 58°32′ E 196
Muscatine, Iowa, U.S. 41°25′ N, 91°4′ W 94
Müsch, Ger. 50°23′ N, 6°49′ E 167
Muse, Okla., U.S. 34°38′ N, 94°46′ W 96
Musgrave Land, Can. 53°36′ N, 56°12′ W 111
Musgrave, Port 12°9′ S, 141°2′ E 230
Musgrave Ranges, Austral. 25°59′ S, 131°49′ E 230
Mushandike Sanctuary, Zimb. 20°13′ S, 30°18′ E 206
Mushâsh el Sirr, spring, Egypt 30°37′ N, 33°46′ E 194
Mushenge, Dem. Rep. of the Congo 4°29′ S, 21°18′ E 218
Mushie, Dem. Rep. of the Congo 3°2′ S, 16°51′ E 218
Mushorah, oil field, Iraq 36°55′ N, 42°14′ E 195
Mushu, island, P.N.G. 3°39′ S, 142°39′ E 192
Music Mountains, peak, Ariz., U.S. 35°31′ N, 113°43′ W 101
Musina (Messina), S. Af. 22°21′ S, 30°1′ E 227
Musiri, India 10°58′ N, 78°29′ E 188
Muskeg, river, Can. 60°16′ N, 123°9′ W 108
Muskeget Channel 41°19′ N, 70°29′ W 104
Muskeget Island, Mass., U.S. 41°19′ N, 70°18′ W 104
Muskegon, Mich., U.S. 43°13′ N, 86°16′ W 102
Muskegon Heights, Mich., U.S. 43°11′ N, 86°15′ W 102
Muskegon, river, Mich., U.S. 43°50′ N, 85°18′ W 102
Muskogee, Okla., U.S. 35°44′ N, 95°22′ W 96
Muskwa, Can. 58°44′ N, 122°43′ W 108
Muskwa, river, Can. 56°8′ N, 114°38′ W 108
Musmar, Sudan 18°11′ N, 35°35′ E 182
Musoma, Tanzania 1°31′ S, 33°49′ E 224
Musquaro, Lac, lake, Can. 50°29′ N, 61°41′ W 111
Mussau, island, P.N.G. 1°31′ S, 149°47′ E 192
Mussau Islands, P.N.G. 1°17′ S, 149°36′ E 192
Musselshell, Mont., U.S. 46°28′ N, 108°6′ W 90
Musselshell, river, Mont., U.S. 46°28′ N, 109°57′ W 90
Mussende, Angola 10°33′ S, 16°2′ E 220
Mussuma, Angola 14°17′ S, 21°57′ E 220
Mustafakemalpaşa, Turk. 40°4′ N, 28°23′ E 180
Mustahīl, Eth. 5°14′ N, 44°42′ E 218
Mustang, Nepal 29°12′ N, 83°58′ E 197
Mustayevo, Russ. 51°47′ N, 53°27′ E 158
Mustio see Svarta, Fin. 60°8′ N, 23°51′ E 166
Mustjala, Est. 58°27′ N, 22°14′ E 166
Mustla, Est. 58°13′ N, 25°50′ E 166
Mustvee, Est. 58°50′ N, 26°53′ E 166
Musudan, N. Korea 40°46′ N, 129°44′ E 200
Musún, Cerro, peak, Nicar. 12°58′ N, 85°18′ W 115
Musungu, Dem. Rep. of the Congo 2°45′ N, 28°22′ E 224
Muswabik, river, Can. 51°56′ N, 85°31′ W 110
Mût, Egypt 25°28′ N, 28°57′ E 226
Mut, Turk. 36°38′ N, 33°26′ E 156
Mutá, Ponta do, Braz. 14°23′ S, 38°50′ W 132
Mu′tah, Jordan 31°5′ N, 35°41′ E 194
Mutalahti, Fin. 62°25′ N, 31°4′ E 152
Mutanda, Zambia 12°23′ S, 26°14′ E 224
Mutarara, Mozambique 17°27′ S, 35°8′ E 224
Mutare, Zimb. 18°58′ S, 32°39′ E 224
Mutatá, Col. 7°16′ N, 76°32′ W 136
Mutha, Kenya 1°49′ S, 38°24′ E 224
Muting, Indonesia 7°21′ S, 140°14′ E 192
Mutki, Turk. 38°24′ N, 41°54′ E 195
Mutnyy Materik, Russ. 65°55′ N, 55°0′ E 154
Mutoko, Zimb. 17°26′ S, 32°13′ E 224
Mutombo Mukulu, Dem. Rep. of the Congo 7°58′ S, 23°59′ E 224
Mutoray, Russ. 61°27′ N, 100°26′ E 160
Mutriba, oil field, Kuwait 29°46′ N, 47°14′ E 196
Mutshatsha, Dem. Rep. of the Congo 10°40′ S, 24°26′ E 224
Mutumbo, Angola 13°15′ S, 17°18′ E 220
Mutumparaná, Braz. 9°40′ S, 64°60′ W 137
Mutunópolis, Braz. 13°41′ S, 49°17′ W 138
Muurla, Fin. 60°20′ N, 23°14′ E 166
Muuruvesi, Fin. 63°0′ N, 28°10′ E 152
Muxía, Sp. 43°5′ N, 9°14′ W 150
Muyinga, Burundi 2°52′ S, 30°19′ E 224
Mŭynoq, Uzb. 43°49′ N, 58°56′ E 160
Muyumba, Dem. Rep. of the Congo 7°15′ S, 27°1′ E 224
Muzaffarabad, Pak. 34°23′ N, 73°33′ E 186
Muzaffargarh, Pak. 30°4′ N, 71°12′ E 186
Muzaffarnagar, India 29°29′ N, 77°40′ E 197
Muzaffarpur, India 26°5′ N, 85°23′ E 197
Muzhi, Russ. 65°21′ N, 64°36′ E 169
Muzon, Cape, Alas., U.S. 54°29′ N, 132°42′ W 108
Múzquiz, Mex. 27°52′ N, 101°31′ W 92
Muztag, peak, China 36°24′ N, 87°20′ E 188
Muztag, peak, China 35°59′ N, 80°10′ E 188
Muztagata, peak, China 38°17′ N, 75°2′ E 184
Muztagh Pass, China 35°53′ N, 76°12′ E 186
Mvadhi-Ousyé, Gabon 1°12′ N, 13°11′ E 218
Mvolo, Sudan 6°3′ N, 29°55′ E 224
Mvomero, Tanzania 6°17′ S, 37°26′ E 224
Mvouti, Congo 4°16′ S, 12°26′ E 218
Mvuma, Zimb. 19°19′ S, 30°29′ E 224
Mwadingusha, Dem. Rep. of the Congo 10°45′ S, 27°10′ E 224
Mwadui, Tanzania 3°35′ S, 33°39′ E 224
Mwakete, Tanzania 9°20′ S, 34°14′ E 224
Mwali, island, Comoros 12°34′ S, 43°15′ E 220
Mwami, Zimb. 16°41′ S, 29°46′ E 224
Mwanza, Dem. Rep. of the Congo 7°51′ S, 26°39′ E 224
Mwanza, Tanzania 2°32′ S, 32°55′ E 224
Mwanza, adm. division, Tanzania 2°57′ S, 31°56′ E 224
Mwatate, Kenya 3°32′ S, 38°21′ E 218
Mwaya, Tanzania 9°32′ S, 33°55′ E 224
Mweelrea, peak, Ire. 53°36′ N, 9°56′ W 150
Mweka, Dem. Rep. of the Congo 4°52′ S, 21°31′ E 218
Mwene-Ditu, Dem. Rep. of the Congo 7°1′ S, 23°24′ E 224
Mwenezi, Zimb. 21°25′ S, 30°45′ E 227
Mwenezi, river, Zimb. 21°45′ S, 31°8′ E 227
Mwenga, Dem. Rep. of the Congo 3°4′ S, 28°26′ E 224
Mwenzo, Zambia 9°21′ S, 32°41′ E 224
Mweru, Lake, Dem. Rep. of the Congo 9°16′ S, 26°39′ E 207
Mweru Wantipa National Park, Zambia 9°9′ S, 29°20′ E 224
Mwimba, Dem. Rep. of the Congo 9°12′ S, 22°46′ E 218
Mwingi, Kenya 0°57′ N, 38°4′ E 224
Mwinilunga, Zambia 11°44′ S, 24°25′ E 224
Mwitikira, Tanzania 6°30′ S, 35°39′ E 224
Mwombezhi, river, Zambia 12°41′ S, 25°43′ E 224
My Tho, Vietnam 10°21′ N, 106°21′ E 202
Myadzyel, Belarus 54°51′ N, 26°56′ E 166
Myakit, Russ. 61°29′ N, 151°59′ E 160
Myakka City, Fla., U.S. 27°21′ N, 82°9′ W 105
Myakka, river, Fla., U.S. 27°13′ N, 82°22′ W 105
Myaksa, Russ. 58°52′ N, 38°15′ E 154
Myanaung, Myanmar 18°20′ N, 95°13′ E 202
Myanmar (Burma) 21°5′ N, 95°9′ E 192
Myeik, Myanmar 12°35′ N, 98°38′ E 192
Myingyan, Myanmar 21°28′ N, 95°25′ E 202
Myitkyinā, Myanmar 25°29′ N, 97°20′ E 190
Myitta, Myanmar 14°10′ N, 98°30′ E 202
Myken, islands, Norwegian Sea 66°43′ N, 11°26′ E 152
Mykhaylivka, Ukr. 47°14′ N, 35°15′ E 156
Mykolayiv, Ukr. 49°31′ N, 23°57′ E 158
Mykolayiv, Ukr. 46°59′ N, 32°2′ E 156

Myla, *Russ.* 65°25′ N, 50°42′ E 154
Mylius Erichsen Land 80°43′ N, 42°2′ W 246
Myllykoski, *Fin.* 60°46′ N, 26°46′ E 166
Mymensingh, *Bangladesh* 24°53′ N, 90°40′ E 197
Mynämäki, *Fin.* 60°40′ N, 21°56′ E 166
Mynbulak, *Uzb.* 42°12′ N, 62°55′ E 180
Myohaung, *Myanmar* 20°38′ N, 93°10′ E 188
Myohyang Sanmaek, *N. Korea* 39°58′ N, 126°24′ E 200
Myōkō, *Japan* 36°55′ N, 138°12′ E 201
Myoungmya, *Myanmar* 16°34′ N, 94°55′ E 202
Myra see Kale, *Turk.* 36°13′ N, 29°57′ E 156
Mýrdalsjökull, glacier, *Ice.* 63°11′ N, 18°33′ W 142
Myrhorod, *Ukr.* 49°57′ N, 33°31′ E 158
Myrskylä, *Fin.* 60°39′ N, 25°48′ E 166
Myrtle Beach, *S.C., U.S.* 33°39′ N, 78°54′ W 82
Myrtle Creek, *Oreg., U.S.* 43°1′ N, 123°17′ W 90
Myrtle Point, *Oreg., U.S.* 43°3′ N, 124°8′ W 90
Mys Kamennyy, *Russ.* 68°29′ N, 73°26′ E 169
Mys Shmidta, *Russ.* 68°54′ N, 179°31′ W 98
Mys Zhelaniya, *Russ.* 76°50′ N, 68°29′ E 160
Mysen, *Nor.* 59°34′ N, 11°19′ E 152
Myshkino, *Russ.* 57°46′ N, 38°26′ E 154
Myślice, *Pol.* 53°54′ N, 19°30′ E 166
Mysovaya, *Russ.* 67°44′ N, 155°59′ E 160
Mystic, *Conn., U.S.* 41°21′ N, 71°58′ W 104
Mystic, *Iowa, U.S.* 40°46′ N, 92°57′ W 94
Mysy, *Russ.* 60°36′ N, 54°4′ E 154
Mytilene see Mitilíni, *Gr.* 39°6′ N, 26°33′ E 156
Myton, *Utah, U.S.* 40°11′ N, 110°3′ W 90
Myyeldino, *Russ.* 61°48′ N, 54°46′ E 154
Mzima Springs, *Kenya* 2°59′ S, 38°4′ E 224
Mzimba, *Malawi* 11°52′ S, 33°32′ E 224
Mzuzu, *Malawi* 11°27′ S, 33°54′ E 224

N

Nā'ālehu, *Hawai'i, U.S.* 19°3′ N, 155°36′ W 99
Naama, *Alg.* 33°16′ N, 0°21′ E 214
Naandi, *Sudan* 4°58′ N, 27°49′ E 224
Naantali, *Fin.* 60°28′ N, 22°2′ E 166
Naas, *Ire.* 53°12′ N, 6°40′ W 150
Nabā, Jabal (Nebo, Mount), peak, *Jordan* 31°45′ N, 35°43′ E 194
Nababiep, *S. Af.* 29°36′ S, 17°47′ E 227
Nabas, *Philippines* 11°49′ N, 122°6′ E 203
Naberera, *Tanzania* 4°12′ S, 36°56′ E 224
Naberezhnyye Chelny, *Russ.* 55°40′ N, 52°22′ E 154
Nabeul, *Tun.* 36°27′ N, 10°44′ E 156
Nabilatuk, *Uganda* 2°3′ N, 34°35′ E 224
Nabire, *Indonesia* 3°21′ S, 135°28′ E 238
Nablus see Nābulus, *West Bank* 32°12′ N, 35°17′ E 194
Naboomspruit see Mookgophong, *S. Af.* 24°31′ S, 28°44′ E 227
Nabordo, *Nig.* 10°11′ N, 9°25′ E 222
Naborton, *La., U.S.* 32°1′ N, 93°35′ W 103
Nabq, *Egypt* 28°7′ N, 34°23′ E 180
Nābulus (Nablus), *West Bank* 32°12′ N, 35°17′ E 194
Nabúri, *Mozambique* 16°57′ S, 39°0′ E 224
Nacala, *Mozambique* 14°33′ S, 40°43′ E 224
Nacaome, *Hond.* 13°31′ N, 87°29′ W 115
Nacaroa, *Mozambique* 14°18′ S, 39°49′ E 224
Nacebe, *Bol.* 10°58′ S, 67°27′ W 137
Naches, *Wash., U.S.* 46°42′ N, 120°42′ W 90
Nachikatsuura, *Japan* 33°35′ N, 135°54′ E 201
Nachingwea, *Tanzania* 10°25′ S, 38°46′ E 224
Nachna, *India* 27°31′ N, 71°44′ E 186
Náchod, *Czech Rep.* 50°24′ N, 16°10′ E 152
Nachuge, *India* 10°44′ N, 92°31′ E 188
Nacimiento, *Mex.* 28°3′ N, 101°45′ W 92
Nacimiento, Lake, *Calif., U.S.* 35°44′ N, 121°17′ W 100
Naciria, *Alg.* 36°44′ N, 3°50′ E 150
Nacka, *Sw.* 59°17′ N, 18°7′ E 166
Nackhörn 54°18′ N, 7°50′ E 152
Naco, *Mex.* 31°17′ N, 109°58′ W 92
Nacogdoches, *Tex., U.S.* 31°34′ N, 94°39′ W 103
Nácori Chico, *Mex.* 29°39′ N, 109°5′ W 92
Nacozari, river, *Mex.* 29°23′ N, 109°44′ W 80
Nacozari Viejo, *Mex.* 30°21′ N, 109°39′ W 92
Ñacunday, *Parag.* 26°4′ S, 54°35′ W 139
Nada see Danxian, *China* 19°28′ N, 109°34′ E 198
Nadale, island, *Maldives* 0°16′ N, 72°12′ E 188
Nadanbo, *China* 43°9′ N, 125°27′ E 200
Nadap, *Hung.* 47°15′ N, 18°36′ E 168
Nadiad, *India* 22°41′ N, 72°51′ E 186
Nădlac, *Rom.* 46°10′ N, 20°47′ E 168
Nădrag, *Rom.* 45°40′ N, 22°13′ E 168
Nadu, adm. division, *India* 11°19′ N, 79°30′ E 188
Nádudvar, *Hung.* 47°25′ N, 21°9′ E 168
Nadvoitsy, *Russ.* 63°53′ N, 34°13′ E 152
Nadym, *Russ.* 65°35′ N, 72°33′ E 169
Nadym, river, *Russ.* 63°43′ N, 72°30′ E 169
Naf ūsah, Jabal, *Lib.* 31°17′ N, 10°13′ E 214
Nafada, *Nig.* 11°2′ N, 11°19′ E 222
Nafana, *Côte d'Ivoire* 9°11′ N, 4°48′ W 222
Naft Khaneh Naft-e-Shāh, oil field, *Iraq* 34°6′ N, 45°18′ E 180
Naft-e Safīd, oil field, *Iran* 31°41′ N, 49°12′ E 180
Nafuce, *Nig.* 12°19′ N, 6°30′ E 222
Nag, *Pak.* 27°21′ N, 65°4′ E 186
Nag 'Hammâdi, *Egypt* 26°3′ N, 32°9′ E 180
Naga, *Philippines* 13°38′ N, 123°10′ E 203
Naga Hills, *Myanmar* 25°34′ N, 94°35′ E 188
Nagagami Lake, *Can.* 49°21′ N, 85°32′ W 94
Nagagami, river, *Can.* 49°45′ N, 84°34′ W 94
Nagagamisis Lake, *Can.* 49°27′ N, 85°16′ W 94
Nagahama, *Japan* 35°22′ N, 136°16′ E 201
Nagahama, *Japan* 33°36′ N, 132°29′ E 201
Nagai, *Japan* 38°6′ N, 140°1′ E 201
Nagano, *Japan* 36°40′ N, 138°12′ E 201
Nagano, adm. division, *Japan* 35°59′ N, 137°38′ E 201
Naganuma, *Japan* 37°17′ N, 140°12′ E 201
Nagaoka, *Japan* 37°26′ N, 138°51′ E 201
Nagar, *India* 32°5′ N, 77°13′ E 188
Nagar Parkar, *Pak.* 24°23′ N, 70°47′ E 186
Nagarzê, *China* 28°58′ N, 90°21′ E 197
Nagas Point, *Can.* 52°1′ N, 131°45′ W 108
Nagasaki, *Japan* 32°45′ N, 129°52′ E 201
Nagasaki, adm. division, *Japan* 32°47′ N, 129°50′ E 201
Nagashima, *Japan* 34°12′ N, 136°20′ E 201
Nagato, *Japan* 34°21′ N, 131°11′ E 200
Nagaur, *India* 27°10′ N, 73°45′ E 186
Nagda, *India* 23°26′ N, 75°27′ E 197
Nagēlē, *Eth.* 5°20′ N, 39°36′ E 224
Nagercoil, *India* 8°10′ N, 77°25′ E 188
Nagina, *India* 29°26′ N, 78°24′ E 197
Nagishot, *Sudan* 4°15′ N, 33°33′ E 224
Nagorno-Karabakh 39°45′ N, 46°34′ E 195
Nagornyy, *Russ.* 55°58′ N, 124°54′ E 160
Nagorsk, *Russ.* 59°19′ N, 50°49′ E 154
Nagoya, *Japan* 35°8′ N, 136°55′ E 201
Nagpur, *India* 21°8′ N, 79°5′ E 197
Nagqu, *China* 31°27′ N, 92°0′ E 188
Nagyatád, *Hung.* 46°13′ N, 17°22′ E 168
Nagybajom, *Hung.* 46°23′ N, 17°30′ E 168
Nagybátony, *Hung.* 47°58′ N, 19°49′ E 168
Nagycenk, *Hung.* 47°36′ N, 16°41′ E 168
Nagydorog, *Hung.* 46°37′ N, 18°39′ E 168
Nagykereki, *Hung.* 47°11′ N, 21°47′ E 168
Nagyk oros, *Hung.* 47°1′ N, 19°46′ E 168
Nagymányok, *Hung.* 46°16′ N, 18°28′ E 168
Nagyszénás, *Hung.* 46°41′ N, 20°40′ E 168
Naha, *Japan* 26°13′ N, 127°38′ E 190
Nahal Hever, ruin(s), *Israel* 31°25′ N, 35°17′ E 194
Naḥal 'Oz, *Israel* 31°27′ N, 34°29′ E 194
Nahanni Butte, *Can.* 61°2′ N, 123°23′ W 108
Nahanni National Park Reserve, *Can.* 61°8′ N, 125°57′ W 108
Nahant, *Mass., U.S.* 42°25′ N, 70°55′ W 104
Nahari, *Japan* 33°25′ N, 134°1′ E 201
Nahariyya, *Israel* 33°0′ N, 35°5′ E 194
Nahāvand, *Iran* 34°12′ N, 48°21′ E 180
Nahlin, river, *Can.* 58°48′ N, 131°26′ W 108
Nahrin, *Afghan.* 36°2′ N, 69°8′ E 186
Nahuel Huapí National Park, *Arg.* 41°4′ S, 71°53′ W 122
Naicam, *Can.* 52°25′ N, 104°29′ W 108
Naij Gol, river, *China* 35°52′ N, 92°56′ E 188
Nailsworth, *U.K.* 51°41′ N, 2°13′ W 162
Na'ima, *Sudan* 14°36′ N, 32°15′ E 182
Naiman Qi, *China* 42°48′ N, 120°38′ E 198
Nain, *Can.* 56°29′ N, 61°49′ W 106
Nā'īn, *Iran* 32°50′ N, 53°7′ E 180
Nainpur, *India* 22°25′ N, 80°7′ E 197
Nainwa, *India* 25°47′ N, 75°53′ E 197
Nairn, *La., U.S.* 29°25′ N, 89°37′ W 103
Nairn, *U.K.* 57°35′ N, 3°53′ W 150
Nairobi, *Kenya* 1°20′ S, 36°39′ E 224
Nairobi National Park, *Kenya* 1°28′ S, 36°31′ E 206
Nairôto, *Mozambique* 12°24′ S, 39°6′ E 224
Nais Saar, island, *Est.* 59°32′ N, 23°57′ E 166
Naivasha, *Kenya* 0°45′ N, 36°27′ E 224
Naj Tunich, site, *Guatemala* 16°18′ N, 89°22′ W 115
Najaf see An Najaf, *Iraq* 31°58′ N, 44°19′ E 180
Najafābād, *Iran* 32°38′ N, 51°25′ E 180
Najd, region, *Saudi Arabia* 26°8′ N, 42°8′ E 182
Najin (Rajin), *N. Korea* 42°15′ N, 130°19′ E 200
Najrān, *Saudi Arabia* 17°44′ N, 44°27′ E 182
Naju, *S. Korea* 35°0′ N, 126°44′ E 200
Naka, river, *Japan* 33°44′ N, 134°17′ E 201
Nakajō, *Japan* 38°3′ N, 139°24′ E 201
Nakaminato, *Japan* 36°20′ N, 140°36′ E 201
Nakamura, *Japan* 32°58′ N, 132°55′ E 201
Nakanno, *Russ.* 62°57′ N, 108°15′ E 160
Nakano, *Japan* 36°44′ N, 138°22′ E 201
Nakanojō, *Japan* 36°35′ N, 138°50′ E 201
Nakatosa, *Japan* 33°18′ N, 133°12′ E 201
Nakatsu, *Japan* 33°35′ N, 131°12′ E 201
Nakatsugawa, *Japan* 35°28′ N, 137°31′ E 201
Nakfa, *Eritrea* 16°38′ N, 38°25′ E 182
Nakhl, *Egypt* 29°52′ N, 33°47′ E 180
Nakhodka, *Russ.* 67°40′ N, 77°44′ E 169
Nakhodka, *Russ.* 42°51′ N, 132°48′ E 190
Nakhon Nayok, *Thai.* 14°13′ N, 101°12′ E 202
Nakhon Phanom, *Thai.* 17°23′ N, 104°44′ E 202
Nakhon Ratchasima (Khorat), *Thai.* 14°58′ N, 102°7′ E 202
Nakhon Sawan, *Thai.* 15°41′ N, 100°5′ E 202
Nakhon Si Thammarat, *Thai.* 8°26′ N, 99°57′ E 202
Nakina, *Can.* 50°11′ N, 86°38′ W 82
Nakina, river, *Can.* 58°51′ N, 133°3′ W 108
Näkkälä, *Fin.* 68°36′ N, 23°31′ E 152
Naknek, *Alas., U.S.* 58°41′ N, 157°5′ W 98
Nako, *Burkina Faso* 10°39′ N, 3°3′ W 222
Nakonde, *Zambia* 9°23′ S, 32°45′ E 224
Nakop, *Namibia* 28°6′ S, 19°59′ E 227
Nakovo, *Serb. and Mont.* 45°52′ N, 20°32′ E 168
Nakuru, *Kenya* 0°18′ N, 36°5′ E 224
Nakusp, *Can.* 50°14′ N, 117°49′ W 90
Nal'chik, *Russ.* 43°30′ N, 43°38′ E 195
Nallıhan, *Turk.* 40°11′ N, 31°21′ E 156
Nālūt, *Lib.* 31°54′ N, 10°58′ E 214
Nam Can, *Vietnam* 8°48′ N, 105°1′ E 202
Nam Co, lake, *China* 30°45′ N, 89°50′ E 188
Nam Dinh, *Vietnam* 20°26′ N, 106°8′ E 198
Nam Nao National Park, *Thai.* 16°25′ N, 101°24′ E 202
Nam Ngum Dam, *Laos* 18°42′ N, 102°29′ E 202
Nam Phong Dam, *Thai.* 16°34′ N, 102°8′ E 202
Nam Phung Dam, *Thai.* 16°49′ N, 102°59′ E 202
Nam, river, *S. Korea* 35°17′ N, 128°16′ E 200
Nam Tok, *Thai.* 14°23′ N, 98°57′ E 202
Namaacha, *Mozambique* 25°57′ S, 32°1′ E 227
Namacunde, *Angola* 17°19′ S, 15°49′ E 220
Namacurra, *Mozambique* 17°29′ S, 37°2′ E 224
Namanga, *Kenya* 2°33′ S, 36°49′ E 224
Namangan, *Uzb.* 40°59′ N, 71°38′ E 197
Namanyere, *Tanzania* 7°31′ S, 31°2′ E 224
Namapa, *Mozambique* 13°44′ S, 39°51′ E 224
Namaponda, *Mozambique* 15°51′ S, 39°53′ E 224
Namaqualand, region, *S. Af.* 30°11′ S, 17°12′ E 227
Namarrói, *Mozambique* 15°58′ S, 36°49′ E 224
Namasagali, *Uganda* 0°59′ N, 32°58′ E 224
Namatanai, *P.N.G.* 3°41′ S, 152°25′ E 238
Nambinda, *Tanzania* 9°37′ S, 37°37′ E 224
Nambu, *Japan* 35°16′ N, 138°26′ E 201
Namdae, river, *N. Korea* 41°8′ N, 129°4′ E 200
Namdapha National Park, *India* 27°30′ N, 96°34′ E 188
Nameigos Lake, *Can.* 48°45′ N, 85°12′ W 94
Namerikawa, *Japan* 36°45′ N, 137°19′ E 201
Nametil, *Mozambique* 15°44′ S, 39°24′ E 224
Namgia, *India* 31°46′ N, 78°41′ E 188
Namib Desert, *Angola* 15°54′ S, 12°10′ E 220
Namibe, *Angola* 15°14′ S, 12°10′ E 220
Namibe, adm. division, *Angola* 16°24′ S, 11°50′ E 220
Namibia 21°53′ S, 15°16′ E 220
Namib-Naukluft Park, *Namibia* 25°49′ S, 15°21′ E 227
Namies, *S. Af.* 29°17′ S, 19°11′ E 227
Namīn, *Iran* 38°29′ N, 48°30′ E 195
Namiquipa, *Mex.* 29°14′ N, 107°25′ W 92
Namjagbarwa Feng, peak, *China* 29°37′ N, 94°55′ E 188
Namji, *S. Korea* 35°23′ N, 128°29′ E 200
Namlea, *Indonesia* 3°16′ S, 127°1′ E 192
Namling, *China* 29°42′ N, 89°3′ E 197
Namoi, river, *Austral.* 30°32′ S, 147°10′ E 231
Nāmolokama Mountain, peak, *Hawai'i, U.S.* 22°7′ N, 159°33′ W 99
Namoluk Atoll 5°35′ N, 150°28′ E 192
Namonuito Atoll, *North Pacific Ocean* 8°43′ N, 149°21′ E 192
Nampa, *Can.* 56°3′ N, 117°9′ W 108
Nampa, *Idaho, U.S.* 43°32′ N, 116°34′ W 82
Nampala, *Mali* 15°15′ N, 5°34′ W 222
Namp'o, *N. Korea* 38°43′ N, 125°25′ E 200
Nampō Shotō, islands, *North Pacific Ocean* 30°47′ N, 138°20′ E 190
Nampula, *Mozambique* 15°8′ S, 39°17′ E 224
Nampula, adm. division, *Mozambique* 14°60′ S, 37°41′ E 224
Namsos, *Nor.* 64°29′ N, 11°41′ E 160
Namsskogan, *Nor.* 64°55′ N, 13°12′ E 152
Namtsy, *Russ.* 62°41′ N, 129°32′ E 160
Namtu, *Myanmar* 23°1′ N, 97°27′ E 202
Namu, *Can.* 51°50′ N, 127°49′ W 108
Namuli, peak, *Mozambique* 15°26′ S, 36°59′ E 224
Namuno, *Mozambique* 13°31′ S, 38°52′ E 224
Namur, *Belg.* 50°28′ N, 4°51′ E 167
Namur Lake, *Can.* 57°18′ N, 113°21′ W 108
Namuruputh, *Kenya* 4°31′ N, 35°54′ E 224
Namutoni, *Namibia* 18°51′ S, 16°57′ E 220
Namwala, *Zambia* 15°46′ S, 26°25′ E 224
Namwon, *S. Korea* 35°23′ N, 127°23′ E 200
Namyang, *N. Korea* 40°44′ N, 129°17′ E 200
Nan, *Thai.* 18°48′ N, 100°45′ E 202
Nan Hulsan Hu, lake, *China* 36°42′ N, 94°42′ E 188
Nan, river, *Thai.* 18°37′ N, 100°46′ E 202
Nana Kru, *Liberia* 4°52′ N, 8°45′ W 222
Nana, river, *Cen. Af. Rep.* 5°48′ N, 15°21′ E 218
Nanaimo, *Can.* 49°9′ N, 123°57′ W 100
Nanam, *N. Korea* 41°41′ N, 129°39′ E 200
Nan'an, *China* 24°55′ N, 118°22′ E 198
Nanao, *Japan* 37°2′ N, 136°56′ E 201
Nanbu, *China* 31°20′ N, 106°0′ E 198
Nanchang, *China* 28°41′ N, 115°54′ E 198
Nancheng, *China* 27°33′ N, 116°37′ E 198
Nanchong, *China* 30°49′ N, 106°2′ E 198
Nanchuan, *China* 29°11′ N, 107°3′ E 198
Ñancorainza, *Bol.* 20°41′ S, 63°28′ W 137
Nancy, *Fr.* 48°41′ N, 6°11′ E 163
Nanda Devi, peak, *India* 30°22′ N, 79°52′ E 197
Nandan, *China* 24°57′ N, 107°30′ E 198
Nanded, *India* 19°11′ N, 77°19′ E 188
Nanfen, *China* 41°8′ N, 123°48′ E 200
Nanfeng, *China* 27°13′ N, 116°25′ E 198
Nanga Parbat, peak, *Pak.* 35°13′ N, 74°28′ E 186
Nangade, *Mozambique* 11°6′ S, 39°43′ E 224
Nangapinoh, *Indonesia* 0°21′ N, 111°38′ E 192
Nangin, *Myanmar* 10°32′ N, 98°29′ E 202
Nangis, *Fr.* 48°33′ N, 3°0′ E 163
Nangnim, *N. Korea* 40°57′ N, 127°8′ E 200
Nangong, *China* 37°18′ N, 115°23′ E 198
Nangqên, *China* 32°15′ N, 96°28′ E 188
Nangtud, Mount, peak, *Philippines* 11°16′ N, 122°6′ E 203
Nangxian, *China* 29°5′ N, 93°6′ E 188
Nanika Lake, lake, *Can.* 53°45′ N, 128°5′ W 108
Nanjiang, *China* 32°24′ N, 106°46′ E 198
Nanjing, *China* 32°5′ N, 118°48′ E 198
Nanjing, *China* 24°22′ N, 117°16′ E 198
Nankang, *China* 25°39′ N, 114°41′ E 198
Nankoku, *Japan* 33°34′ N, 133°38′ E 201
Nanle, *China* 36°3′ N, 115°11′ E 198
Nanning, *China* 22°49′ N, 108°19′ E 198
Nanortalik 60°13′ N, 45°14′ W 106
Nanpara, *India* 27°50′ N, 81°30′ E 197
Nanping, *China* 42°18′ N, 129°12′ E 200
Nanping, *China* 26°37′ N, 118°4′ E 198
Nanri Dao, island, *China* 24°53′ N, 119°22′ E 198
Nansan Dao, island, *China* 21°1′ N, 110°37′ E 198
Nansei Shotō see Ryukyu Islands, *East China Sea* 25°0′ N, 125°56′ E 190
Nansen Basin, *Arctic Ocean* 85°0′ N, 78°46′ E 255
Nansen Land 82°0′ N, 43°58′ W 246
Nansen Sound 80°31′ N, 104°17′ W 72
Nansio, *Tanzania* 2°7′ S, 33°4′ E 224
Nantais, Lac, lake, *Can.* 61°33′ N, 76°5′ W 246
Nantes, *Fr.* 47°12′ N, 1°36′ W 150
Nanteuil-le-Haudouin, *Fr.* 49°8′ N, 2°48′ E 163
Nanticoke, *Can.* 42°46′ N, 80°11′ W 94
Nanticoke, *Pa., U.S.* 41°11′ N, 76°1′ W 110
Nanton, *Can.* 50°20′ N, 113°47′ W 108
Nantong, *China* 32°2′ N, 120°54′ E 198
Nantucket, *Mass., U.S.* 41°16′ N, 70°7′ W 104
Nantucket Inlet 74°39′ S, 66°32′ W 248
Nantucket Island, *Mass., U.S.* 41°22′ N, 70°2′ W 104
Nantucket Sound 41°26′ N, 70°19′ W 104
Nantulo, *Mozambique* 12°30′ S, 39°1′ E 224
Nantwich, *U.K.* 53°3′ N, 2°31′ W 162
Nanuque, *Braz.* 17°49′ S, 40°21′ W 138
Nanusa, Kepulauan, islands, *Philippine Sea* 4°57′ N, 126°54′ E 203
Nanxi, *China* 28°51′ N, 104°56′ E 198
Nanxian, *China* 29°23′ N, 112°23′ E 198
Nanxiong, *China* 25°6′ N, 114°15′ E 198
Nanyang, *China* 33°1′ N, 112°34′ E 198
Nanyuki, *Kenya* 1°58′ S, 37°4′ E 224
Nanzhang, *China* 31°47′ N, 111°50′ E 198
Nanzhila, *Zambia* 16°6′ S, 26°1′ E 224
Nao, Cabo de La, *Sp.* 38°30′ N, 0°10′ E 214
Naococane, Lac, lake, *Can.* 52°47′ N, 71°20′ W 111
Naozhou Dao, island, *China* 20°51′ N, 110°39′ E 198
Napa, *Calif., U.S.* 38°18′ N, 122°19′ W 100
Napá, *Mozambique* 13°17′ S, 39°3′ E 224
Napaimiut, *Alas., U.S.* 61°32′ N, 158°41′ W 98
Napaleofú, *Arg.* 37°38′ S, 58°46′ W 139
Napalkovo, *Russ.* 70°3′ N, 73°54′ E 169
Napanee, *Can.* 44°14′ N, 76°59′ W 82
Napas, *Russ.* 59°48′ N, 81°57′ E 169
Napasoq 65°4′ N, 52°21′ W 106
Napenay, *Arg.* 26°44′ S, 60°38′ W 139
Naperville, *Ill., U.S.* 41°46′ N, 88°9′ W 102
Napier, *N.Z.* 39°30′ S, 176°54′ E 240
Napier Bay 11°54′ S, 131°12′ E 231
Naples, *Fla., U.S.* 26°9′ N, 81°48′ W 105
Naples, *Me., U.S.* 43°57′ N, 70°37′ W 104
Naples, *Tex., U.S.* 33°11′ N, 94°41′ W 103
Naples see Napoli, *It.* 40°51′ N, 14°15′ E 156
Napo, *China* 23°21′ N, 105°50′ E 198
Napo, river, *Ecua.* 1°14′ S, 77°33′ W 136
Napo, river, *Peru* 2°38′ S, 74°29′ W 122
Napoleon, *N. Dak., U.S.* 46°29′ N, 99°47′ W 90
Napoleon, *Ohio, U.S.* 41°22′ N, 84°8′ W 102
Napoleonville, *La., U.S.* 29°55′ N, 91°3′ W 103
Napoli (Naples), *It.* 40°51′ N, 14°15′ E 156
Nappanee, *Ind., U.S.* 41°26′ N, 86°1′ W 102
Nāpu'ukūlua, peak, *Hawai'i, U.S.* 19°42′ N, 155°40′ W 99
Naqoura, *Leb.* 33°7′ N, 35°8′ E 194
Nara, *Japan* 34°42′ N, 135°50′ E 201
Nara, *Mali* 15°10′ N, 7°18′ W 222
Nara, adm. division, *Japan* 34°17′ N, 135°40′ E 201
Nara, river, *Pak.* 24°46′ N, 69°35′ E 186
Nara Visa, *N. Mex., U.S.* 35°36′ N, 103°6′ W 92
Narach, *Belarus* 54°55′ N, 26°41′ E 166
Narach, Vozyera, lake, *Belarus* 54°52′ N, 26°17′ E 166
Na'rān, *Israel* 33°2′ N, 35°42′ E 194
Naranbulag, *Mongolia* 49°14′ N, 113°19′ E 198
Narang, *Afghan.* 34°44′ N, 70°57′ E 186
Narasannapeta, *India* 18°24′ N, 84°5′ E 188
Narasapur, *India* 16°27′ N, 81°40′ E 188
Narathiwat, *Thai.* 6°26′ N, 101°49′ E 196
Narayanganj, *Bangladesh* 23°26′ N, 90°40′ E 197
Nærbø, *Nor.* 58°40′ N, 5°38′ E 152
Narbonne, *Fr.* 43°10′ N, 2°59′ E 164
Narcondam Island, *India* 13°28′ N, 94°19′ E 188
Nardīn, *Iran* 37°0′ N, 55°57′ E 180
Naré, *Arg.* 30°58′ S, 60°28′ W 139
Nares Land 81°45′ N, 45°60′ W 72
Nares Plain, *North Atlantic Ocean* 22°43′ N, 63°8′ W 253
Narib, *Namibia* 24°12′ S, 17°46′ E 227
Naricual, *Venez.* 10°2′ N, 64°37′ W 116
Narimanabad, *Azerb.* 38°51′ N, 48°50′ E 195
Narin, river, *China* 36°20′ N, 92°32′ E 188
Nariño, adm. division, *Col.* 1°27′ N, 78°30′ W 136
Narlı, *Turk.* 37°25′ N, 37°8′ E 156
Narmada, river, *India* 22°56′ N, 78°26′ E 197
Narodnaya, Gora, peak, *Russ.* 65°6′ N, 59°49′ E 154
Narok, *Kenya* 1°6′ S, 35°50′ E 224
Narowlya, *Belarus* 51°44′ N, 29°38′ E 158
Nærøy, *Nor.* 64°48′ N, 11°16′ E 152
Närpiö see Närpes, *Fin.* 62°27′ N, 21°18′ E 152
Narragansett Pier, *R.I., U.S.* 41°25′ N, 71°28′ W 104
Narran Lake, lake, *Austral.* 29°60′ S, 146°18′ E 230
Narrogin, *Austral.* 32°56′ S, 117°11′ E 231
Narsaq 60°59′ N, 45°60′ W 246
Narsarsuaq 61°10′ N, 45°21′ W 106
Narsimhapur, *India* 22°56′ N, 79°12′ E 197
Narsinghgarh, *India* 23°41′ N, 77°5′ E 197
Narsipatnam, *India* 17°39′ N, 82°37′ E 188
Nart, *Mongolia* 49°8′ N, 105°27′ E 198
Narta, *Croatia* 45°49′ N, 16°47′ E 168
Nartháki, Óros, peak, *Gr.* 39°12′ N, 22°20′ E 156
Nartkala, *Russ.* 43°32′ N, 43°53′ E 195
Naruko, *Japan* 38°45′ N, 140°43′ E 201
Naruto, *Japan* 34°10′ N, 134°34′ E 201
Narva, *Est.* 59°21′ N, 28°8′ E 154
Narva Jõesuu, *Est.* 59°26′ N, 28°1′ E 166
Narvacan, *Philippines* 17°26′ N, 120°28′ E 203
Narvik, *Nor.* 68°16′ N, 17°45′ E 160
Narvskoye Vodokhranilishche, lake, *Russ.* 59°17′ N, 27°33′ E 166
Narwana, *India* 29°36′ N, 76°8′ E 197
Nar'yan Mar, *Russ.* 67°43′ N, 53°6′ E 169
Narym, *Russ.* 58°57′ N, 81°41′ E 169
Naryn, *Kyrg.* 41°24′ N, 76°2′ E 184
Naryn Khuduk, *Russ.* 45°26′ N, 46°32′ E 158
Naryn Qum, *Kaz.* 48°1′ N, 47°52′ E 184
Naryn, river, *Kyrg.* 41°47′ N, 73°27′ E 197
Narynqol, *Kaz.* 42°41′ N, 80°11′ E 184
Naryshkino, *Russ.* 52°55′ N, 35°46′ E 154
Näs, *Nor.* 62°57′ N, 14°33′ E 152
Nasa, peak, *Nor.* 66°28′ N, 15°13′ E 152
Nasarawa, *Nig.* 8°29′ N, 7°41′ E 222
Nasca, *Peru* 14°53′ S, 74°58′ W 137
Nasca Ridge, *South Pacific Ocean* 20°50′ S, 79°49′ W 253
Naseby 1645, battle, *U.K.* 52°23′ N, 0°59′ E 162
Naselle, *Wash., U.S.* 46°20′ N, 123°49′ W 100
Nash, *Tex., U.S.* 33°25′ N, 94°9′ W 103
Nashua, *Iowa, U.S.* 42°56′ N, 92°33′ W 94
Nashua, *Mont., U.S.* 48°8′ N, 106°24′ W 90
Nashville, *Ark., U.S.* 33°54′ N, 93°51′ W 96
Nashville, *Ga., U.S.* 31°11′ N, 83°15′ W 96
Nashville, *Ind., U.S.* 39°12′ N, 86°15′ W 102
Nashville, *Mich., U.S.* 42°35′ N, 85°5′ W 102
Nashville, *Mo., U.S.* 38°20′ N, 89°23′ W 94
Nashville, *Tenn., U.S.* 36°7′ N, 86°54′ W 96
Nashwaaksis, *Can.* 45°58′ N, 66°42′ W 94
Našice, *Croatia* 45°29′ N, 18°5′ E 168
Näsijärvi, lake, *Fin.* 61°42′ N, 23°24′ E 166
Nasik, *India* 19°59′ N, 73°46′ E 188
Nasir, *Sudan* 8°36′ N, 33°4′ E 224
Nasirabad, *India* 26°16′ N, 74°44′ E 186
Nasiriyah see An Nāṣirīyah, *Iraq* 31°5′ N, 46°11′ E 180
Naskaupi, river, *Can.* 54°6′ N, 62°58′ W 111
Nasri, spring, *Mauritania* 19°49′ N, 15°52′ W 222
Nass, river, *Can.* 56°14′ N, 128°29′ W 108
Nassau, *Bahamas* 25°4′ N, 77°23′ W 118
Nassau, *Ger.* 50°19′ N, 7°48′ E 167
Nassau, *N.Y., U.S.* 42°30′ N, 73°37′ W 104
Nassau, island, *American Samoa, U.S.* 11°34′ S, 165°33′ W 252
Nassawadox, *Va., U.S.* 37°28′ N, 75°52′ W 96
Nasser, Lake, *Egypt* 23°18′ N, 32°21′ E 182
Nassian, *Côte d'Ivoire* 8°29′ N, 3°29′ W 222
Nässjö, *Nor.* 57°38′ N, 14°41′ E 152
Nastapoka Islands, islands, *Hudson Bay* 57°26′ N, 76°40′ W 106
Nastätten, *Ger.* 50°12′ N, 7°51′ E 167
Næstved, *Den.* 55°13′ N, 11°45′ E 152
Nasukoin Mountain, peak, *Mont., U.S.* 48°46′ N, 114°39′ W 90
Nasva, *Russ.* 56°34′ N, 30°13′ E 166
Näsviken, *Nor.* 61°43′ N, 16°49′ E 152
Naszály, peak, *Hung.* 47°50′ N, 19°8′ E 168
Nat, river, *Can.* 48°49′ N, 82°8′ W 94
Nata, *Botswana* 20°15′ S, 26°5′ E 227
Natá, *Pan.* 8°20′ N, 80°31′ W 115
Nata, river, *Botswana* 19°53′ S, 26°31′ E 224
Natal, *Braz.* 5°49′ S, 35°12′ W 132
Natal, *Braz.* 6°60′ S, 60°19′ W 130
Natal, *Indonesia* 0°36′ N, 99°7′ E 196
Natal Basin, *Indian Ocean* 29°34′ S, 40°22′ E 254
Natal'inskiy, *Russ.* 61°13′ N, 172°5′ E 160
Naṭanz, *Iran* 33°31′ N, 51°55′ E 180
Natara, *Russ.* 68°19′ N, 124°1′ E 160
Natashquan, *Can.* 50°11′ N, 61°48′ W 106
Natashquan, Pointe de, *Can.* 49°58′ N, 61°45′ W 111
Natashquan, river, *Can.* 52°21′ N, 63°26′ W 111
Natchitoches, *La., U.S.* 31°45′ N, 93°5′ W 103
Natera, *Mex.* 22°39′ N, 102°7′ W 114
Natick, *Mass., U.S.* 42°17′ N, 71°21′ W 104
Natih, oil field, *Oman* 22°26′ N, 56°41′ E 182
Nation, river, *Can.* 55°12′ N, 124°23′ W 108
National, *Wash., U.S.* 46°45′ N, 122°4′ W 100
National Bison Range, site, *Mont., U.S.* 47°18′ N, 114°20′ W 90
National City, *Calif., U.S.* 32°40′ N, 117°7′ W 101
National Park, *N.Z.* 39°13′ S, 175°23′ E 240
Natitiai, Gebel, peak, *Egypt* 23°2′ N, 34°20′ E 182
Natividade, *Braz.* 11°41′ S, 47°48′ W 130
Natkyizin, *Myanmar* 14°55′ N, 97°57′ E 202
Natogami Lake, lake, *Can.* 50°11′ N, 81°5′ W 94
Natoma, *Kans., U.S.* 39°11′ N, 99°2′ W 90
Nator, *Bangladesh* 24°20′ N, 88°54′ E 197
Nattavaara, *Nor.* 66°44′ N, 20°54′ E 152
Natuna Besar, island, *Indonesia* 3°37′ N, 108°21′ E 196
Natuna Besar, Kepulauan, islands, *Indonesia* 4°7′ N, 107°49′ E 196
Natuna Selatan, Kepulauan, islands, *South China Sea* 2°45′ N, 107°49′ E 196
Naturaliste, Cape, *Austral.* 33°25′ S, 113°28′ E 230
Naturaliste Plateau, *Indian Ocean* 34°20′ S, 112°15′ E 254
Naturita, *Colo., U.S.* 38°12′ N, 108°34′ W 90
Naturno, *It.* 46°40′ N, 10°59′ E 167
Naubinway, *Mich., U.S.* 46°5′ N, 85°28′ W 94
Nauchas, *Namibia* 23°41′ S, 16°20′ E 227
Naufrage, Pointe au, *Can.* 49°52′ N, 63°31′ W 111
Naugatuck, *Conn., U.S.* 41°29′ N, 73°4′ W 104
Nauhcampatépetl see Cofre de Perote, peak, *Mex.* 19°27′ N, 97°13′ W 114
Naujoji Vilnia, *Lith.* 54°42′ N, 25°24′ E 166
Naulila, *Angola* 17°12′ S, 14°40′ E 220
Naumburg, *Ger.* 51°8′ N, 11°48′ E 152
Naumburg, *Ger.* 51°14′ N, 9°10′ E 167
Naunak, *Russ.* 58°58′ N, 80°11′ E 169
Naungpale, *Myanmar* 19°32′ N, 97°6′ E 202
Nā'ūr, *Jordan* 31°52′ N, 35°49′ E 194
Naurskaya, *Russ.* 43°33′ N, 45°21′ E 195
Nauru 0°32′ N, 166°55′ E 242
Naushahra, *India* 33°9′ N, 74°13′ E 186
Naushki, *Russ.* 50°33′ N, 106°15′ E 190
Naushon Island, *Mass., U.S.* 41°31′ N, 70°45′ W 104
Nauta, *Peru* 4°29′ S, 73°37′ W 130
Nautla, *Mex.* 20°9′ N, 96°47′ W 114
Nautla, river, *Mex.* 20°7′ N, 97°14′ W 114
Nautsi, *Russ.* 68°58′ N, 29°0′ E 152
Nauvoo, *Mo., U.S.* 40°32′ N, 91°23′ W 94
Nava, *Mex.* 28°24′ N, 100°46′ W 92
Navabelitsa, *Belarus* 52°22′ N, 31°8′ E 158
Navadwip, *India* 23°22′ N, 88°18′ E 197
Navahrudak, *Belarus* 53°36′ N, 25°50′ E 152
Naval, *Sp.* 42°11′ N, 0°9′ E 164
Naval Submarine Base, *Conn., U.S.* 41°24′ N, 72°7′ W 104
Navalvillar de Pelea, *Sp.* 39°5′ N, 5°28′ W 164
Navan (An Uaimh), *Ire.* 53°38′ N, 6°42′ W 150
Navapolatsk, *Belarus* 55°30′ N, 28°35′ E 152
Navarin, Mys, *Russ.* 62°4′ N, 179°6′ E 160
Navarino, Isla, island, *Chile* 55°25′ S, 67°12′ W 134

Newport, *Oreg., U.S.* 44°38′ N, 124°5′ W **82**
Newport, *R.I., U.S.* 41°29′ N, 71°19′ W **104**
Newport, *Tenn., U.S.* 35°57′ N, 83°12′ W **96**
Newport, *U.K.* 50°41′ N, 1°18′ W **162**
Newport, *U.K.* 51°35′ N, 2°60′ W **162**
Newport, *U.K.* 52°45′ N, 2°23′ W **162**
Newport, *Vt., U.S.* 44°56′ N, 72°13′ W **82**
Newport, *Wash., U.S.* 48°10′ N, 117°4′ W **108**
Newport Beach, *Calif., U.S.* 33°38′ N, 117°57′ W **101**
Newport News, *Va., U.S.* 36°58′ N, 76°26′ W **94**
Newport Pagnell, *U.K.* 52°4′ N, 0°44′ E **162**
Newry, *Me., U.S.* 44°29′ N, 70°48′ W **104**
Newry, *S.C., U.S.* 34°43′ N, 82°56′ W **96**
Newsome, *Tex., U.S.* 32°57′ N, 95°8′ W **103**
Newtok, *Alas., U.S.* 60°57′ N, 164°37′ W **98**
Newton, *Ill., U.S.* 38°58′ N, 88°11′ W **102**
Newton, *Iowa, U.S.* 41°41′ N, 93°3′ W **94**
Newton, *Kans., U.S.* 38°2′ N, 97°21′ W **90**
Newton, *Mass., U.S.* 42°19′ N, 71°15′ W **104**
Newton, *Miss., U.S.* 32°18′ N, 89°9′ W **103**
Newton, *Mo., U.S.* 38°58′ N, 88°11′ W **94**
Newton, *Tex., U.S.* 30°49′ N, 93°46′ W **103**
Newton Falls, *Ohio, U.S.* 41°10′ N, 80°58′ W **102**
Newtown, *Conn., U.S.* 41°24′ N, 73°19′ W **104**
Newtown, *U.K.* 52°30′ N, 3°18′ W **162**
New-Wes-Valley, *Can.* 49°9′ N, 53°35′ W **111**
Nexpa, river, *Mex.* 18°7′ N, 102°40′ W **114**
Neya, *Russ.* 58°17′ N, 43°52′ E **154**
Neyrīz, *Iran* 29°12′ N, 54°18′ E **196**
Neyshābūr, *Iran* 36°12′ N, 58°51′ E **180**
Neyto, Ozero, lake, *Russ.* 69°51′ N, 68°36′ E **169**
Neyvo Shaytanskiy, *Russ.* 57°46′ N, 61°14′ E **154**
Nez Perce Pass, *Mont., U.S.* 45°42′ N, 114°31′ W **90**
Nezperce, *Idaho, U.S.* 46°13′ N, 116°14′ W **90**
N'Gabé, *Congo* 3°14′ S, 16°8′ E **218**
Ngahere, *N.Z.* 42°25′ S, 171°27′ E **240**
Ngambé, *Cameroon* 4°15′ N, 10°39′ E **222**
Ngamda, *China* 31°5′ N, 96°37′ E **188**
Ngamring, *China* 29°17′ N, 87°11′ E **197**
Ngangla Ringco, lake, *China* 31°40′ N, 82°35′ E **188**
Nganglong Kangri, peak, *China* 32°50′ N, 80°41′ E **188**
Ngangzê Co, lake, *China* 30°56′ N, 86°20′ E **197**
N'Gao, *Congo* 2°30′ S, 15°45′ E **218**
Ngao, *Thai.* 18°46′ N, 99°57′ E **202**
Ngaoundal, *Cameroon* 6°26′ N, 13°25′ E **218**
Ngaoundéré, *Cameroon* 7°16′ N, 13°34′ E **218**
Ngaputaw, *Myanmar* 16°31′ N, 94°42′ E **188**
Ngara, *Tanzania* 2°31′ S, 30°39′ E **224**
Ngaruawahia, *N.Z.* 37°43′ S, 175°10′ E **240**
Ngauruhoe, Mount, peak, *N.Z.* 39°12′ S, 175°32′ E **240**
Ngayu, river, *Dem. Rep. of the Congo* 1°53′ N, 27°25′ E **224**
Ngcheangel, island, *Palau* 8°4′ N, 134°43′ E **242**
Ngeaur see Angaur, island, *Palau* 7°0′ N, 134°0′ E **242**
Ngerengere, *Tanzania* 6°42′ S, 38°7′ E **224**
Ngeruktabel see Urukthapel, island, *Palau* 7°13′ N, 134°24′ E **242**
Nggatokae, island, *Solomon Islands* 8°45′ S, 158°10′ E **242**
Nghia Lo, *Vietnam* 21°37′ N, 104°28′ E **202**
Ngoïla, *Cameroon* 2°45′ N, 14°0′ E **218**
Ngoko, *Congo* 0°35′ N, 15°21′ E **218**
Ngola Shankou, pass, *China* 35°30′ N, 99°28′ E **188**
Ngomba, *Tanzania* 8°25′ S, 32°54′ E **224**
Ngomeni, Ras, *Kenya* 2°59′ S, 40°14′ E **224**
Ngong, *Kenya* 1°23′ S, 36°40′ E **224**
Ngop, *Sudan* 6°13′ N, 30°10′ E **224**
Ngoqumaima, *China* 32°30′ N, 86°51′ E **188**
Ngorno-Karabakh, special sovereignty, *Asia* 39°59′ N, 46°23′ E **195**
Ngorongoro Crater, peak, *Tanzania* 3°15′ S, 35°31′ E **224**
Ngoto, *Cen. Af. Rep.* 4°4′ N, 17°18′ E **218**
Ngouo, Mont, peak, *Cen. Af. Rep.* 7°55′ N, 24°32′ E **224**
Ngouri, *Chad* 13°39′ N, 15°23′ E **216**
Ngourti, *Niger* 15°19′ N, 13°11′ E **216**
Ngoywa, *Tanzania* 5°55′ S, 32°47′ E **224**
Ngozi, *Burundi* 2°56′ S, 29°47′ E **224**
Ngudu, *Tanzania* 2°56′ S, 33°21′ E **224**
Nguigmi, *Niger* 14°17′ N, 13°6′ E **216**
Ngukurr, *Austral.* 14°44′ S, 134°46′ E **238**
Ngulu Atoll, *F.S.M.* 8°42′ N, 134°55′ E **192**
Ngum, river, *Laos* 18°47′ N, 102°47′ E **202**
N'gungo, *Angola* 11°47′ S, 14°9′ E **220**
Nguni, *Kenya* 0°49′ N, 38°17′ E **224**
Nguru, *Nig.* 12°53′ N, 10°28′ E **222**
Ngurumahija, *Tanzania* 10°18′ S, 37°57′ E **224**
Nha Trang, *Vietnam* 12°15′ N, 109°10′ E **202**
Nhamundá, *Braz.* 2°13′ S, 56°44′ W **130**
Nhamundá, river, *Braz.* 1°33′ S, 57°60′ W **132**
Nhecolândia, *Braz.* 19°15′ S, 57°1′ W **132**
Nho Quan, *Vietnam* 20°20′ N, 105°45′ E **202**
Nhulunbuy, *Austral.* 12°18′ S, 136°48′ E **238**
Nia Nia, *Dem. Rep. of the Congo* 1°29′ N, 27°40′ E **224**
Niabembe, *Dem. Rep. of the Congo* 2°11′ S, 27°40′ E **224**
Niadi, *Dem. Rep. of the Congo* 4°25′ S, 18°50′ E **218**
Niafounké, *Mali* 15°56′ N, 4°1′ W **222**
Niagassola, *Guinea* 12°20′ N, 9°8′ W **222**
Niamey, *Niger* 13°29′ N, 2°0′ E **222**
Niandan Koro, *Guinea* 11°6′ N, 9°14′ W **222**
Niangara, *Dem. Rep. of the Congo* 3°41′ N, 27°53′ E **224**
Niangay, Lac, lake, *Mali* 15°54′ N, 3°22′ W **222**
Niangoloko, *Burkina Faso* 10°17′ N, 4°56′ W **222**
Niantic, *Conn., U.S.* 41°19′ N, 72°12′ W **104**
Niantic, *Ill., U.S.* 39°50′ N, 89°10′ W **102**
Nianzishan, *China* 47°33′ N, 122°54′ E **198**
Niapidou, *Côte d'Ivoire* 5°18′ N, 6°3′ W **222**
Niapu, *Dem. Rep. of the Congo* 2°24′ N, 26°32′ E **224**
Niari, river, *Congo* 3°33′ S, 12°45′ E **218**
Nias, island, *Indonesia* 0°26′ N, 97°33′ E **196**
Niassa, adm. division, *Mozambique* 12°52′ S, 35°24′ E **224**
Niaza, spring, *Mauritania* 18°13′ N, 10°60′ W **222**
Nīca, *Latv.* 56°21′ N, 21°1′ E **166**
Nicaragua 12°38′ N, 85°49′ W **115**
Nice, *Fr.* 43°42′ N, 7°15′ E **167**
Nichihara, *Japan* 34°31′ N, 131°51′ E **201**
Nichinan, *Japan* 31°36′ N, 131°21′ E **201**
Nicholasville, *Ky., U.S.* 37°52′ N, 84°34′ W **96**
Nicholls' Town, *Bahamas* 25°7′ N, 78°2′ W **96**
Nichollstown and Berry Islands, adm. division, *Bahamas* 25°47′ N, 78°22′ W **96**
Nicholson, *Can.* 47°58′ N, 83°46′ W **94**
Nickel Centre, *Can.* 46°33′ N, 80°52′ W **94**
Nickelsdorf, *Aust.* 47°56′ N, 17°4′ E **168**
Nickerson, *Kans., U.S.* 38°8′ N, 98°6′ W **90**
Nickol Bay 20°40′ S, 115°56′ E **230**
Nicobar Islands, *Andaman Sea* 8°59′ N, 93°39′ E **192**
Nicolás Bravo, *Mex.* 24°21′ N, 104°44′ W **114**
Nicolet, *Can.* 46°13′ N, 72°37′ W **94**
Nicopolis, ruin(s), *Gr.* 38°59′ N, 20°37′ E **156**
Nicopolis see Suşehri, *Turk.* 40°8′ N, 38°5′ E **180**
Nicosia see Lefkosia, *Cyprus* 35°9′ N, 33°18′ E **194**
Nicotera, *It.* 38°34′ N, 15°55′ E **156**
Nicoya, *C.R.* 10°8′ N, 85°26′ W **115**
Nicuadala, *Mozambique* 17°38′ S, 36°48′ E **224**
Nida, *Russ.* 55°19′ N, 21°2′ E **166**
Nidda, *Ger.* 50°24′ N, 9°1′ E **167**
Niddatal, *Ger.* 50°17′ N, 8°48′ E **167**
Nidder, river, *Ger.* 50°22′ N, 9°3′ E **167**
Nidže, *Maced.* 41°1′ N, 21°41′ E **156**
Nidzh, *Azerb.* 40°57′ N, 47°39′ E **195**
Niebla, *Sp.* 37°21′ N, 6°42′ W **164**
Niechorze, *Pol.* 54°5′ N, 15°4′ E **152**
Nied, river, *Fr.* 49°5′ N, 6°20′ E **163**
Nieddu, Monte, peak, *It.* 40°44′ N, 9°30′ E **156**
Niederaula, *Ger.* 50°48′ N, 9°35′ E **167**
Niederbronn, *Fr.* 48°57′ N, 7°38′ E **163**
Niedere Tauern, *Aust.* 47°11′ N, 13°24′ E **156**
Niedoradz, *Pol.* 51°52′ N, 15°40′ E **152**
Niéjirane, spring, *Mauritania* 17°32′ N, 9°51′ W **222**
Niem, *Cen. Af. Rep.* 6°5′ N, 15°15′ E **218**
Niemba, *Dem. Rep. of the Congo* 5°59′ S, 28°24′ E **224**
Niéna, *Mali* 11°26′ N, 6°21′ W **222**
Niers, river, *Ger.* 51°41′ N, 5°58′ E **167**
Nierstein, *Ger.* 49°52′ N, 8°20′ E **167**
Nieuw Amsterdam, *Suriname* 5°50′ N, 55°6′ W **130**
Nieuwe Pekela, *Neth.* 53°4′ N, 6°56′ E **163**
Nieuwpoort, *Belg.* 51°7′ N, 2°44′ E **163**
Nieves, *Bol.* 14°5′ S, 65°54′ W **137**
Nieves, *Mex.* 24°0′ N, 103°2′ W **114**
Nif, *Indonesia* 3°19′ S, 130°34′ E **192**
Niğde, *Turk.* 37°58′ N, 34°42′ E **180**
Niger 17°56′ N, 8°41′ E **216**
Niger Delta, *Nig.* 5°29′ N, 6°7′ E **222**
Niger, river, *Africa* 5°54′ N, 6°33′ E **222**
Nigeria 9°25′ N, 6°48′ E **216**
Nightingale Island see Bach Long Vi, Dao, *Vietnam* 19°46′ N, 107°30′ E **198**
Nihonmatsu, *Japan* 37°35′ N, 140°26′ E **201**
Niigata, *Japan* 37°55′ N, 139°5′ E **201**
Niigata, adm. division, *Japan* 37°27′ N, 138°42′ E **201**
Niihama, *Japan* 33°56′ N, 133°17′ E **201**
Ni'ihau, island, *Hawai'i, U.S.* 21°36′ N, 160°11′ W **99**
Niimi, *Japan* 35°0′ N, 133°28′ E **201**
Niitsu, *Japan* 37°47′ N, 139°8′ E **201**
Nijar, *Sp.* 36°57′ N, 2°13′ W **164**
Nijmegen, *Neth.* 51°50′ N, 5°51′ E **167**
Nīk Pey, *Iran* 36°52′ N, 48°12′ E **195**
Nikel', *Russ.* 69°24′ N, 30°10′ E **152**
Nikiniki, *Indonesia* 9°49′ S, 124°28′ E **192**
Nikiski, *Gulf of Alaska* 60°43′ N, 151°18′ W **98**
Nikitin Seamount, *Indian Ocean* 3°48′ S, 82°58′ E **254**
Nikki, *Benin* 9°56′ N, 3°9′ E **222**
Nikkō, *Japan* 36°43′ N, 139°37′ E **201**
Nikkō National Park, *Japan* 37°3′ N, 139°40′ E **201**
Nikolai, *Alas., U.S.* 63°0′ N, 154°11′ W **98**
Nikolayevo, *Russ.* 58°15′ N, 29°28′ E **166**
Nikolayevsk, *Russ.* 50°3′ N, 45°33′ E **158**
Nikolayevsk na Amure, *Russ.* 53°14′ N, 140°36′ E **190**
Nikolo Berezovka, *Russ.* 56°6′ N, 54°18′ E **154**
Nikol'sk, *Russ.* 53°41′ N, 46°7′ E **154**
Nikol'sk, *Russ.* 59°30′ N, 45°32′ E **154**
Nikol'skoye, *Russ.* 52°4′ N, 55°42′ E **154**
Nikol'skoye, *Russ.* 47°43′ N, 46°21′ E **158**
Nikol'skoye, *Russ.* 55°13′ N, 165°54′ E **160**
Nikonga, river, *Tanzania* 4°2′ S, 31°30′ E **224**
Nikopol', *Ukr.* 47°34′ N, 34°24′ E **156**
Niksar, *Turk.* 40°35′ N, 36°57′ E **156**
Nīkshahr, *Iran* 26°13′ N, 60°13′ E **182**
Nikšić, *Europe* 42°46′ N, 18°56′ E **168**
Nikulino, *Russ.* 60°21′ N, 90°1′ E **169**
Niland, *Calif., U.S.* 33°14′ N, 115°32′ W **101**
Nilandu Atoll, *Maldives* 2°56′ N, 72°16′ E **188**
Nilandu, island, *Maldives* 0°27′ N, 73°24′ E **188**
Nile, river, *Africa* 27°17′ N, 31°18′ E **206**
Niles, *Mich., U.S.* 41°48′ N, 86°15′ W **102**
Niles, *Ohio, U.S.* 41°10′ N, 80°45′ W **94**
Nili, *Alg.* 33°24′ N, 3°2′ E **214**
Nilka, *China* 43°47′ N, 82°38′ E **184**
Nilsen, Mount, peak, *Antarctica* 77°54′ S, 154°11′ W **248**
Nilsen Plateau, *Antarctica* 86°27′ S, 180°0′ E **248**
Nilsiä, *Fin.* 63°10′ N, 28°0′ E **152**
Nimach, *India* 24°27′ N, 74°51′ E **188**
Nimba Mountains, *Guinea* 8°22′ N, 9°5′ W **222**
Nimbahera, *India* 24°38′ N, 74°40′ E **188**
Nimberra Well, spring, *Austral.* 23°6′ S, 123°18′ E **230**
Nîmes, *Fr.* 43°49′ N, 4°22′ E **214**
Nīmfai, *Gr.* 39°45′ N, 19°47′ E **156**
Nimule, *Sudan* 3°34′ N, 32°5′ E **224**
Nin, *Croatia* 44°14′ N, 15°9′ E **156**
Ninayeri, *Nicar.* 14°27′ N, 83°18′ W **115**
Ninda, *Angola* 14°54′ S, 21°25′ E **220**
Nine Degree Channel 8°40′ N, 71°55′ E **188**
Ninemile Peak, *Nev., U.S.* 39°8′ N, 116°20′ W **90**
Ninety East Ridge, *Indian Ocean* 8°11′ S, 88°50′ E **254**
Ninety Mile Beach, *N.Z.* 35°3′ S, 172°43′ E **240**
Nineveh, ruin(s), *Iraq* 36°21′ N, 42°59′ E **195**
Ninfas, Punta, *Arg.* 43°10′ S, 64°20′ W **134**
Ning'an, *China* 44°20′ N, 129°32′ E **190**
Ningbo, *China* 29°54′ N, 121°29′ E **198**
Ningcheng, *China* 41°34′ N, 119°20′ E **198**
Ningde, *China* 26°40′ N, 119°31′ E **198**
Ningdu, *China* 26°26′ N, 115°55′ E **198**
Ningguo, *China* 30°34′ N, 119°1′ E **198**
Ningi, *Nig.* 11°3′ N, 9°32′ E **222**
Ningming, *China* 22°5′ N, 107°1′ E **198**
Ningshan, *China* 33°20′ N, 108°19′ E **198**
Ningwu, *China* 39°0′ N, 112°13′ E **198**
Ningxia, adm. division, *China* 36°46′ N, 105°17′ E **198**
Ningyuan, *China* 25°36′ N, 111°56′ E **198**
Ninh Binh, *Vietnam* 20°14′ N, 105°56′ E **198**
Ninh Hoa, *Vietnam* 12°30′ N, 109°8′ E **202**
Ninigo Group, islands, *South Pacific Ocean* 0°49′ N, 142°30′ E **192**
Ninigo Islands, islands, *South Pacific Ocean* 1°10′ S, 142°49′ E **192**
Ninilchik, *Gulf of Alaska* 60°3′ N, 151°39′ W **98**
Nioaque, *Braz.* 21°9′ S, 55°50′ W **132**
Niobrara, river, *Nebr., U.S.* 42°37′ N, 102°2′ W **90**
Nioka, *Dem. Rep. of the Congo* 2°8′ N, 30°39′ E **224**
Nioki, *Dem. Rep. of the Congo* 2°44′ S, 17°38′ E **218**
Niokolo-Koba National Park, *Senegal* 13°2′ N, 13°30′ W **222**
Niono, *Mali* 14°16′ N, 5°60′ W **222**
Nioro du Sahel, *Mali* 15°14′ N, 9°38′ W **222**
Niort, *Fr.* 46°19′ N, 0°28′ E **150**
Niout, spring, *Mauritania* 16°3′ N, 6°52′ W **222**
Nipa, oil field, *Venez.* 9°6′ N, 64°8′ W **116**
Nipani, *India* 16°24′ N, 74°23′ E **188**
Nipawin, *Can.* 53°21′ N, 104°1′ W **108**
Nipigon, *Can.* 49°1′ N, 88°16′ W **94**
Nipigon Bay 48°50′ N, 89°13′ W **80**
Nipigon, Lake, *Can.* 50°12′ N, 88°35′ W **94**
Nipin, river, *Can.* 55°24′ N, 109°25′ W **108**
Nipissing, Lake, *Can.* 46°21′ N, 80°13′ W **80**
Nipomo, *Calif., U.S.* 35°2′ N, 120°29′ W **100**
Nipple, The, peak, *Can.* 49°56′ N, 121°38′ W **100**
Nipton, *Calif., U.S.* 35°27′ N, 115°17′ W **101**
Niquelândia, *Braz.* 14°33′ S, 48°30′ W **138**
Niquero, *Cuba* 20°2′ N, 77°34′ W **115**
Nīr, *Iran* 38°3′ N, 47°59′ E **195**
Nir Yizhaq, *Israel* 31°14′ N, 34°21′ E **194**
Nir'am, *Israel* 31°30′ N, 34°34′ E **194**
Nirasaki, *Japan* 35°41′ N, 138°27′ E **201**
Ñire Có, *Arg.* 36°60′ S, 68°28′ W **134**
Nirji see Morin Dawa, *China* 48°27′ N, 124°30′ E **198**
Nirmal, *India* 19°6′ N, 78°20′ E **188**
Nirmali, *India* 26°18′ N, 86°34′ E **197**
Niš, *Serb. and Mont.* 43°18′ N, 21°54′ E **168**
Nişāb, *Saudi Arabia* 29°8′ N, 44°44′ E **180**
Nişāb, *Yemen* 14°31′ N, 46°33′ E **182**
Nišava, river, *Serb. and Mont.* 43°18′ N, 22°7′ E **168**
Nishi Nasuno, *Japan* 36°52′ N, 139°58′ E **201**
Nishikō, *Japan* 32°36′ N, 130°27′ E **201**
Nishinomiya, *Japan* 34°44′ N, 135°18′ E **201**
Nishio, *Japan* 34°50′ N, 137°4′ E **201**
Nishiwaki, *Japan* 34°58′ N, 134°57′ E **201**
Nishtūn, *Yemen* 15°48′ N, 52°10′ E **182**
Niska, *Fin.* 64°35′ N, 26°33′ E **152**
Niskayuna, *N.Y., U.S.* 42°45′ N, 73°51′ W **104**
Nissedal, *Nor.* 59°9′ N, 8°30′ E **152**
Nissi, *Est.* 59°4′ N, 24°17′ E **166**
Nissilä, *Fin.* 63°56′ N, 26°48′ E **152**
Nisswa, *Minn., U.S.* 46°30′ N, 94°18′ W **90**
Niţā', *Saudi Arabia* 27°10′ N, 48°23′ E **196**
Nītaure, *Latv.* 57°3′ N, 25°7′ E **166**
Nitchequon, *Can.* 53°12′ N, 70°53′ W **111**
Niterói, *Braz.* 22°56′ S, 43°3′ W **138**
Nitmiluk National Park, *Austral.* 14°16′ S, 132°7′ E **238**
Nitra, *Slovakia* 48°18′ N, 18°6′ E **168**
Nitransky, adm. division, *Slovakia* 48°10′ N, 17°51′ E **152**
Nitro, *W. Va., U.S.* 38°25′ N, 81°51′ W **94**
Nitsa, river, *Russ.* 57°45′ N, 63°3′ E **154**
Niut, peak, *Indonesia* 0°59′ N, 109°50′ E **196**
Niutou Shan, island, *China* 28°54′ N, 121°49′ E **198**
Niuxintai, *China* 41°20′ N, 123°55′ E **200**
Niva, *Fin.* 65°9′ N, 28°21′ E **152**
Niva, *Russ.* 61°36′ N, 30°14′ E **166**
Nivala, *Fin.* 63°54′ N, 24°55′ E **152**
Nivelles, *Belg.* 50°35′ N, 4°19′ E **163**
Nivernais, region, *Fr.* 47°30′ N, 3°17′ E **165**
Nivshera, *Russ.* 62°24′ N, 53°1′ E **154**
Nixon, *Tex., U.S.* 29°15′ N, 97°45′ W **92**
Nizamabad, *India* 18°40′ N, 78°5′ E **188**
Nizamghat, *India* 28°14′ N, 95°43′ E **188**
Nizao, *Dom. Rep.* 18°14′ N, 70°13′ W **116**
Nizhnekamsk, *Russ.* 55°33′ N, 51°53′ E **154**
Nizhneshadrino, *Russ.* 59°53′ N, 90°38′ E **169**
Nizhneudinsk, *Russ.* 54°53′ N, 99°14′ E **190**
Nizhnevartovsk, *Russ.* 60°54′ N, 76°35′ E **169**
Nizhniy Baskunchak, *Russ.* 48°11′ N, 46°42′ E **158**
Nizhniy Lomov, *Russ.* 53°30′ N, 43°40′ E **154**
Nizhniy Novgorod, *Russ.* 56°15′ N, 44°0′ E **154**
Nizhniy Novgorod, adm. division, *Russ.* 56°0′ N, 43°9′ E **154**
Nizhniy Tagil, *Russ.* 57°56′ N, 59°59′ E **154**
Nizhniy Ufaley, *Russ.* 55°56′ N, 60°3′ E **154**
Nizhniye Nikulyasy, *Russ.* 60°27′ N, 30°44′ E **152**
Nizhniye Sergi, *Russ.* 56°40′ N, 59°16′ E **154**
Nizhnyaya Mgla, *Russ.* 66°29′ N, 44°27′ E **154**
Nizhnyaya Omra, *Russ.* 62°46′ N, 55°51′ E **154**
Nizhnyaya Pesha, *Russ.* 66°46′ N, 47°38′ E **154**
Nizhnyaya Salda, *Russ.* 58°5′ N, 60°44′ E **154**
Nizhnyaya Tunguska, river, *Russ.* 64°30′ N, 90°34′ E **169**
Nizhnyaya Tura, *Russ.* 58°41′ N, 59°49′ E **154**
Nizhnyaya Voch', *Russ.* 61°12′ N, 54°11′ E **154**
Nizhyn, *Ukr.* 51°2′ N, 31°53′ E **158**
Nizi, *Dem. Rep. of the Congo* 1°44′ N, 30°17′ E **224**
Nizip, *Turk.* 36°58′ N, 37°50′ E **180**
Nízke Tatry, *Slovakia* 48°51′ N, 19°24′ E **152**
Nizwá, *Oman* 22°55′ N, 57°31′ E **182**
Nizza Monferrato, *It.* 44°46′ N, 8°21′ E **167**
Nizzana (El'Auja), *Israel* 30°52′ N, 34°25′ E **194**
Njazidja, island, *Comoros* 11°46′ S, 43°35′ E **220**
Njegoš, peak, *Europe* 42°54′ N, 18°43′ E **168**
Njegoševo, *Serb. and Mont.* 45°45′ N, 19°44′ E **168**
Njombe, *Tanzania* 9°22′ S, 34°45′ E **224**
Njombe, river, *Tanzania* 7°22′ S, 34°8′ E **224**
Njunnesvarre, peak, *Nor.* 68°45′ N, 19°17′ E **152**
Njurunda, *Nor.* 62°14′ N, 17°20′ E **152**
Nkambe, *Cameroon* 6°29′ N, 10°43′ E **222**
Nkawkaw, *Ghana* 6°33′ N, 0°46′ E **222**
Nkayi, *Zimb.* 19°3′ S, 28°55′ E **224**
Nkhata Bay, *Malawi* 11°35′ S, 34°17′ E **224**
Nkhotakota, *Malawi* 12°56′ S, 34°15′ E **224**
Nkhunga, *Malawi* 12°29′ S, 34°3′ E **224**
Nkongsamba, *Cameroon* 4°53′ N, 9°56′ E **222**
Nkoul, *Cameroon* 3°30′ N, 13°33′ E **218**
Nkululu, river, *Tanzania* 6°19′ S, 32°39′ E **224**
Nkurenkuru, *Namibia* 17°39′ S, 18°36′ E **220**
Nkusi, river, *Uganda* 1°8′ N, 30°56′ E **224**
No, Lake, *Sudan* 9°22′ N, 30°7′ E **224**
Noamundi, *India* 22°11′ N, 85°31′ E **197**
Noarvas, peak, *Nor.* 68°47′ N, 24°35′ E **152**
Noatak, *Alas., U.S.* 67°29′ N, 163°5′ W **98**
Noatak, river, *Alas., U.S.* 68°4′ N, 159°51′ W **98**
Nobeoka, *Japan* 32°35′ N, 131°39′ E **201**
Noble, *Ill., U.S.* 38°41′ N, 88°14′ W **102**
Noble, *La., U.S.* 31°40′ N, 93°42′ W **103**
Noblesville, *Ind., U.S.* 40°2′ N, 85°60′ W **102**
Nobska Point, *Mass., U.S.* 41°28′ N, 70°40′ W **104**
Nocatee, *Fla., U.S.* 27°10′ N, 81°53′ W **105**
Noce, river, *It.* 46°16′ N, 10°59′ E **167**
Noceto, *It.* 44°48′ N, 10°10′ E **167**
Nochistlán, *Mex.* 21°20′ N, 102°52′ W **114**
Nochixtlán, *Mex.* 17°26′ N, 97°14′ W **114**
Nocona, *Tex., U.S.* 33°46′ N, 97°42′ W **92**
Nodales, Bahía de los 48°5′ S, 67°43′ W **134**
Nodaway, river, *Iowa, U.S.* 40°1′ N, 95°9′ W **80**
Noel Kempff Mercado National Park, *Bol.* 14°31′ S, 62°11′ W **132**
Noel, Mount, peak, *Can.* 50°43′ N, 122°56′ W **90**
Noelville, *Can.* 46°7′ N, 80°26′ W **94**
Nofre, Peña, peak, *Sp.* 42°0′ N, 7°26′ W **150**
Nogales, *Ariz., U.S.* 31°21′ N, 110°57′ W **112**
Nogáles, *Mex.* 31°17′ N, 110°57′ W **92**
Nogara, *It.* 45°10′ N, 11°3′ E **167**
Nōgata, *Japan* 33°43′ N, 130°42′ E **200**
Nogayskaya Step', *Russ.* 44°29′ N, 46°3′ E **180**
Nogayty, *Kaz.* 45°17′ N, 55°55′ E **158**
Nogent-le-Roi, *Fr.* 48°38′ N, 1°32′ E **163**
Nogent-le-Rotrou, *Fr.* 48°19′ N, 0°49′ E **163**
Nogent-sur-Seine, *Fr.* 48°29′ N, 3°30′ E **163**
Noginsk, *Russ.* 64°25′ N, 91°16′ E **169**
Nogliki, *Russ.* 51°47′ N, 143°4′ E **190**
Nógrád, adm. division, *Hung.* 47°58′ N, 19°1′ E **156**
Nohar, *India* 29°11′ N, 74°47′ E **186**
Nohfelden, *Ger.* 49°34′ N, 7°8′ E **163**
Nohona o Hae, peak, *Hawai'i, U.S.* 19°54′ N, 155°44′ W **99**
Noia, *Sp.* 42°47′ N, 8°55′ W **150**
Noir, Isla, island, *Chile* 54°23′ S, 74°10′ W **134**
Noire, Montagne, peak, *Fr.* 43°25′ N, 2°25′ E **165**
Noire, river, *Can.* 46°46′ N, 77°41′ W **94**
Noires, Montagnes, *Fr.* 48°2′ N, 4°9′ W **150**
Nojima Zaki, *Japan* 34°45′ N, 139°53′ E **201**
Nok Kundi, *Pak.* 28°49′ N, 62°47′ E **182**
Nokaneng, *Botswana* 19°41′ S, 22°11′ E **220**
Nokara, *Mali* 15°10′ N, 2°24′ W **222**
Nokia, *Fin.* 61°28′ N, 23°31′ E **166**
Nokola, *Russ.* 61°10′ N, 38°51′ E **154**
Nokomis, *Can.* 51°30′ N, 105°2′ W **90**
Nokomis, *Ill., U.S.* 39°17′ N, 89°17′ W **102**
Nokou, *Chad* 14°35′ N, 14°45′ E **216**
Nola, *Cen. Af. Rep.* 3°42′ N, 16°5′ E **218**
Noli, *It.* 44°12′ N, 8°25′ E **167**
Nolinsk, *Russ.* 57°33′ N, 49°57′ E **154**
Noma Misaki, *Japan* 31°16′ N, 129°55′ E **201**
Nomans Land, island, *Mass., U.S.* 41°11′ N, 70°52′ W **104**
Nomansland Point, *Can.* 52°1′ N, 81°2′ W **110**
Nombre de Dios, *Mex.* 23°49′ N, 104°14′ W **114**
Nombre de Dios, *Mex.* 28°42′ N, 106°7′ W **92**
Nome, *Alas., U.S.* 64°25′ N, 165°28′ W **98**
Nome, *Tex., U.S.* 30°1′ N, 94°26′ W **103**
Nome Lake, *Can.* 59°38′ N, 131°35′ W **108**
Nomgon, *Mongolia* 42°52′ N, 104°53′ E **198**
Nomhon, *China* 36°22′ N, 96°26′ E **188**
Nomhon, river, *China* 36°31′ N, 96°27′ E **188**
Nomo Saki, *Japan* 32°28′ N, 129°35′ E **201**
Nomoneas, island, *F.S.M.* 7°25′ N, 151°52′ E **242**
Nomwin Atoll, *F.S.M.* 9°13′ N, 150°41′ E **192**
Nonancourt, *Fr.* 48°46′ N, 1°12′ E **163**
Nonburg, *Russ.* 65°33′ N, 50°32′ E **154**
Nondalton, *Alas., U.S.* 59°56′ N, 154°60′ W **98**
Nong Khai, *Thai.* 17°52′ N, 102°44′ E **202**
Nong'an, *China* 44°27′ N, 125°11′ E **198**
Nongoma, *S. Af.* 27°54′ S, 31°37′ E **227**
Nongpoh, *India* 25°51′ N, 91°51′ E **197**
Nono, *Eth.* 8°30′ N, 37°22′ E **224**
Nonoava, *Mex.* 27°28′ N, 106°44′ W **112**
Nonsan, *S. Korea* 36°11′ N, 127°6′ E **200**
Nonthaburi, *Thai.* 13°53′ N, 100°31′ E **202**
Noonan, *N. Dak., U.S.* 48°52′ N, 103°1′ W **108**
Noord Beveland, *Neth.* 51°33′ N, 3°42′ E **163**
Noordoewer, *Namibia* 28°44′ S, 17°37′ E **227**
Noormarkku, *Fin.* 61°35′ N, 21°51′ E **166**
Nootka, *Can.* 49°37′ N, 126°39′ W **90**
Nopah Range, *Calif., U.S.* 36°4′ N, 116°10′ W **101**
Nóqui, *Angola* 5°55′ S, 13°28′ E **218**
Nora, *Ill., U.S.* 42°26′ N, 89°57′ W **102**
Nora, *Nor.* 59°30′ N, 14°59′ E **152**
Nora, island, *Eritrea* 16°4′ N, 39°43′ E **182**
Nora, ruin(s), *It.* 38°59′ N, 8°55′ E **156**
Norak, *Taj.* 38°23′ N, 69°21′ E **197**
Norberg, *Nor.* 60°3′ N, 15°54′ E **152**
Norco, *La., U.S.* 29°59′ N, 90°25′ W **103**
Nord 81°43′ N, 17°32′ W **246**
Nord Frøya, *Nor.* 63°45′ N, 8°47′ E **152**
Nord, Petit lac du, lake, *Can.* 50°46′ N, 67°57′ W **111**
Nordaustlandet, island, *Nor.* 80°34′ N, 5°48′ E **160**
Norddalsfjord, *Nor.* 61°39′ N, 5°22′ E **152**
Norddeich, *Ger.* 53°37′ N, 7°10′ E **163**
Nordegg (Brazeau), *Can.* 52°28′ N, 116°7′ W **108**
Norden, *Ger.* 53°36′ N, 7°11′ E **163**
Norderny, island, *Ger.* 53°43′ N, 6°52′ E **163**
Nordfold, *Nor.* 67°45′ N, 15°11′ E **152**
Nordhordland, region, *North Sea* 60°50′ N, 4°39′ E **152**
Nordhorn, *Ger.* 52°26′ N, 7°3′ E **163**
Nordkapp (North Cape), *Nor.* 71°6′ N, 25°55′ E **152**
Nordkinnhalvøya, *Nor.* 70°45′ N, 26°37′ E **152**
Nord-Kivu, adm. division, *Dem. Rep. of the Congo* 0°10′ N, 28°8′ E **224**
Nordli, *Nor.* 64°28′ N, 13°36′ E **152**
Nordmaling, *Nor.* 63°33′ N, 19°30′ E **152**
Nordøstrundingen 80°22′ N, 30°36′ W **72**
Nordøyan, islands, *Norwegian Sea* 64°47′ N, 9°13′ E **152**
Nordøyane, islands, *Nor.* 62°38′ N, 4°46′ E **152**
Nordoyar, islands, *Norwegian Sea* 62°30′ N, 9°12′ W **72**
Nord-Pas-De-Calais, adm. division, *Fr.* 50°24′ N, 1°57′ E **150**
Nordreisa, *Nor.* 69°46′ N, 21°2′ E **152**
Nordvik, *Nor.* 66°7′ N, 12°31′ E **152**
Nordvik, *Russ.* 73°59′ N, 111°16′ E **160**
Norfolk, *Conn., U.S.* 41°59′ N, 73°12′ W **104**
Norfolk, *Nebr., U.S.* 42°0′ N, 97°26′ W **90**
Norfolk, *Va., U.S.* 36°51′ N, 76°17′ W **96**
Norfolk Island, *Australia* 29°0′ S, 168°0′ E
Norfolk Ridge, *South Pacific Ocean* 27°44′ S, 167°48′ E **252**
Norfork Lake, *Ark., U.S.* 36°16′ N, 93°15′ W **80**
Nori, *Russ.* 66°11′ N, 72°31′ E **169**
Noril'sk, *Russ.* 69°20′ N, 88°8′ E **169**
Normal, *Ill., U.S.* 40°30′ N, 88°59′ W **102**
Norman, *Okla., U.S.* 35°11′ N, 97°27′ W **92**
Norman Wells, *Can.* 65°18′ N, 126°44′ W **98**
Normanby Island, *P.N.G.* 9°58′ S, 151°19′ E **192**
Normandin, *Can.* 48°49′ N, 72°31′ W **94**
Normandy, *Tex., U.S.* 28°53′ N, 100°35′ W **96**
Normandy, region, *Fr.* 48°57′ N, 0°46′ E **163**
Normanton, *Austral.* 17°46′ S, 141°10′ E **238**
Normétal, *Can.* 49°0′ N, 79°23′ W **94**
Norphlet, *Ark., U.S.* 33°17′ N, 92°40′ W **103**
Ñorquincó, *Arg.* 41°50′ S, 70°51′ W **134**
Norra Storfjället, peak, *Nor.* 65°51′ N, 15°10′ E **152**
Norrby, *Nor.* 64°25′ N, 15°37′ E **152**
Nørresundby, *Den.* 57°3′ N, 9°55′ E **150**
Norrfors, *Nor.* 63°46′ N, 18°59′ E **152**
Norrhult, *Nor.* 57°7′ N, 15°9′ E **152**
Norris Lake, lake, *Tenn., U.S.* 36°18′ N, 84°3′ W **94**
Norrköping, *Nor.* 58°33′ N, 16°9′ E **152**
Norrland, region, *Sw.* 61°29′ N, 17°15′ E **166**
Norrtälje, *Sw.* 59°45′ N, 18°39′ E **166**
Norseman, *Austral.* 32°12′ S, 121°47′ E **231**
Norske Øer, islands, *Norske Øer* 78°33′ N, 16°48′ W **246**
Norte, adm. division, *Braz.* 4°51′ S, 37°14′ W **132**
Norte, Cabo, *Braz.* 1°44′ N, 49°56′ W **130**
Norte, Cayo 18°50′ N, 87°32′ W **115**
Norte de Santander, adm. division, *Col.* 8°18′ N, 73°17′ W **136**
Norte, Punta, *Arg.* 36°18′ S, 56°43′ W **139**
Norte, Punta, *Arg.* 50°51′ S, 69°6′ W **134**
Norte, Serra do, *Braz.* 10°18′ S, 59°11′ W **130**
Nortelândia, *Braz.* 14°29′ S, 56°48′ W **132**
Nörten-Hardenberg, *Ger.* 51°37′ N, 9°57′ E **167**
North Adams, *Mass., U.S.* 42°41′ N, 73°7′ W **104**
North Albanian Alps, *Alban.* 42°31′ N, 19°47′ E **168**
North America 25°0′ N, 112°0′ W **73**
North Amherst, *Mass., U.S.* 42°24′ N, 72°32′ W **104**
North Andaman, island, *India* 13°28′ N, 91°39′ E **188**
North Andover, *Mass., U.S.* 42°41′ N, 71°9′ W **104**
North Anson, *Me., U.S.* 44°51′ N, 69°55′ W **94**
North Atlantic Ocean 20°33′ N, 74°37′ W **253**
North Augusta, *S.C., U.S.* 33°30′ N, 81°59′ W **96**
North Aulatsivik Island, *Can.* 59°49′ N, 63°58′ W **106**
North Australian Basin, *Indian Ocean* 14°56′ S, 117°17′ E **254**
North Baldy, peak, *Wash., U.S.* 48°31′ N, 117°14′ W **90**
North Baltimore, *Ohio, U.S.* 41°10′ N, 83°40′ W **102**
North Barrule, peak 54°16′ N, 4°29′ W **150**
North Battleford, *Can.* 52°47′ N, 108°19′ W **108**
North Bay, *Can.* 46°18′ N, 79°27′ W **94**
North Belcher Islands, islands, *Hudson Bay* 56°39′ N, 83°25′ W **106**
North Bend, *Can.* 49°52′ N, 121°27′ W **100**
North Bend, *Wash., U.S.* 47°28′ N, 121°47′ W **100**
North Bennington, *Vt., U.S.* 42°55′ N, 73°15′ W **104**
North Berwick, *Me., U.S.* 43°18′ N, 70°44′ W **104**
North Bimini, island, *Bahamas* 25°46′ N, 79°29′ W **105**

North Bonneville, *Wash., U.S.* 45°38′ N, 121°58′ W **100**
North Boston, *N.Y., U.S.* 42°40′ N, 78°48′ W **110**
North Bradley, *Mich., U.S.* 43°41′ N, 84°29′ W **102**
North Branch, *Mich., U.S.* 43°13′ N, 83°9′ W **102**
North Branch, *Minn., U.S.* 45°30′ N, 92°59′ W **94**
North Branford, *Conn., U.S.* 41°19′ N, 72°47′ W **104**
North Bridgton, *Me., U.S.* 44°6′ N, 70°43′ W **104**
North Caicos, island, *North Caicos* 22°1′ N, 72°1′ W **80**
North Canton, *Ohio, U.S.* 40°52′ N, 81°24′ W **102**
North, Cape, *Antarctica* 70°15′ S, 169°9′ E **248**
North, Cape, *Can.* 47°2′ N, 60°54′ W **111**
North Cape, *Can.* 46°59′ N, 64°47′ W **111**
North Cape, *N.Z.* 34°24′ S, 172°51′ E **240**
North Cape May, *N.J., U.S.* 38°58′ N, 74°58′ W **94**
North Cape see Horn, *Ice.* 66°30′ N, 26°3′ W **246**
North Cape see Nordkapp, *Nor.* 71°10′ N, 25°50′ E **152**
North Carolina, adm. division, *N.C., U.S.* 35°44′ N, 80°14′ W **96**
North Carver, *Mass., U.S.* 41°55′ N, 70°49′ W **104**
North Cascades National Park, *Wash., U.S.* 48°34′ N, 121°27′ W **100**
North Cat Cay, island, *Bahamas* 25°32′ N, 79°16′ W **105**
North Channel 45°49′ N, 83°42′ W **80**
North Channel 54°35′ N, 5°17′ W **150**
North Clarendon, *Vt., U.S.* 43°34′ N, 72°59′ W **104**
North College Hill, *Ohio, U.S.* 39°12′ N, 84°34′ W **102**
North Conway, *N.H., U.S.* 44°2′ N, 71°8′ W **104**
North Cowichan, *Can.* 48°51′ N, 123°42′ W **100**
North Creek, *N.Y., U.S.* 43°41′ N, 73°60′ W **104**
North Dakota, adm. division, *N. Dak., U.S.* 47°45′ N, 101°21′ W **90**
North Dartmouth, *Mass., U.S.* 41°37′ N, 70°60′ W **104**
North Downs, region, *U.K.* 51°8′ N, 0°49′ E **162**
North Eagle Butte, *S. Dak., U.S.* 44°59′ N, 101°15′ W **90**
North East Land, island, *Nor.* 79°53′ N, 23°37′ E **255**
North Edgecomb, *Me., U.S.* 43°59′ N, 69°39′ W **104**
North Edwards, *Calif., U.S.* 35°2′ N, 117°50′ W **101**
North Egremont, *Mass., U.S.* 42°11′ N, 73°27′ W **104**
North Fiji Basin, *South Pacific Ocean* 17°30′ S, 173°1′ E **252**
North Fond du Lac, *Wis., U.S.* 43°48′ N, 88°30′ W **102**
North Foreland, *Drake Passage* 61°14′ S, 61°24′ W **248**
North Foreland, *U.K.* 51°22′ N, 1°25′ E **163**
North Fork, *Calif., U.S.* 37°13′ N, 119°32′ W **100**
North Fork, river, *Kans., U.S.* 39°29′ N, 100°4′ W **90**
North Fort Myers, *Fla., U.S.* 26°40′ N, 81°53′ W **105**
North Fryeburg, *Me., U.S.* 44°7′ N, 70°59′ W **104**
North Grosvenor Dale, *Conn., U.S.* 41°58′ N, 71°55′ W **104**
North Hampton, *N.H., U.S.* 42°58′ N, 70°51′ W **104**
North Hartland, *Vt., U.S.* 43°35′ N, 72°22′ W **104**
North Haven, *N.Y., U.S.* 41°1′ N, 72°19′ W **104**
North Head, *Can.* 53°43′ N, 56°24′ W **111**
North Head, *N.Z.* 36°36′ S, 173°49′ E **240**
North Hodge, *La., U.S.* 32°18′ N, 92°43′ W **96**
North Holland, adm. division, *Neth.* 53°6′ N, 4°6′ E **150**
North Horr, *Kenya* 3°18′ N, 37°4′ E **224**
North Hudson, *N.Y., U.S.* 43°57′ N, 73°44′ W **104**
North Industry, *Ohio, U.S.* 40°44′ N, 81°22′ W **102**
North Island, *Austral.* 15°27′ S, 136°40′ E **230**
North Jay, *Me., U.S.* 44°32′ N, 70°15′ W **104**
North Judson, *Ind., U.S.* 41°12′ N, 86°46′ W **102**
North Kingstown (Wickford), *R.I., U.S.* 41°34′ N, 71°28′ W **104**
North Knife Lake, *Can.* 58°2′ N, 97°42′ W **108**
North La Veta Pass, *Colo., U.S.* 37°36′ N, 105°13′ W **90**
North Land see Severnaya Zemlya, islands, *Russ.* 80°22′ N, 102°0′ E **160**
North Las Vegas, *Nev., U.S.* 36°11′ N, 115°9′ W **101**
North Liberty, *Ind., U.S.* 41°31′ N, 86°26′ W **102**
North Little Rock, *Ark., U.S.* 34°47′ N, 92°16′ W **82**
North Loup, river, *Nebr., U.S.* 42°25′ N, 101°5′ W **80**
North Luangwa National Park, *Zambia* 11°43′ S, 32°2′ E **224**
North Mamm Peak, *Colo., U.S.* 39°22′ N, 107°57′ W **90**
North Manchester, *Ind., U.S.* 40°59′ N, 85°46′ W **102**
North Miami, *Fla., U.S.* 25°54′ N, 80°12′ W **105**
North Montpelier, *Vt., U.S.* 44°17′ N, 72°28′ W **104**
North Moose Lake, *Can.* 54°10′ N, 100°33′ W **108**
North Muskegon, *Mich., U.S.* 43°15′ N, 86°17′ W **102**
North Myrtle Beach, *S.C., U.S.* 33°48′ N, 78°42′ W **96**
North Naples, *Fla., U.S.* 26°13′ N, 81°48′ W **105**
North Negril Point, *Jam.* 18°23′ N, 79°33′ W **116**
North Orange, *Mass., U.S.* 42°37′ N, 72°17′ W **104**
North Oxford, *Mass., U.S.* 42°9′ N, 71°53′ W **104**
North Pacific Ocean 22°12′ N, 118°57′ W **252**
North Palisade, peak, *Calif., U.S.* 37°5′ N, 118°34′ W **101**
North Palmetto Point, *Bahamas* 25°10′ N, 76°10′ W **96**
North Pass, *Colo., U.S.* 38°11′ N, 106°35′ W **90**
North Peak, *Nev., U.S.* 40°39′ N, 117°13′ W **90**
North Pine, *Can.* 56°24′ N, 120°48′ W **108**
North Platte, *Nebr., U.S.* 41°10′ N, 100°44′ W **106**
North Platte, river, *Wyo., U.S.* 42°50′ N, 105°34′ W **106**
North Point, *Mich., U.S.* 44°49′ N, 83°16′ W **94**
North Port, *Fla., U.S.* 27°4′ N, 82°15′ W **105**
North Powder, *Oreg., U.S.* 45°1′ N, 117°56′ W **90**
North Pownal, *Vt., U.S.* 42°47′ N, 73°16′ W **104**
North Rhine-Westphalia, adm. division, *Ger.* 51°18′ N, 6°44′ E **167**
North River, *Can.* 59°0′ N, 94°54′ W **73**
North, river, *Can.* 53°53′ N, 58°14′ W **111**
North, river, *Wash., U.S.* 46°48′ N, 123°42′ W **100**
North Salem, *N.H., U.S.* 42°50′ N, 71°15′ W **104**
North Saskatchewan, river, *Can.* 52°15′ N, 116°35′ W **108**
North Scituate, *Mass., U.S.* 42°13′ N, 70°48′ W **104**
North Sea 55°38′ N, 2°30′ E **150**
North Sentinel Island, *India* 11°29′ N, 91°2′ E **188**
North Shapleigh, *Me., U.S.* 43°36′ N, 70°54′ W **104**
North Shore, *Calif., U.S.* 33°31′ N, 115°56′ W **101**
North Shoshone Peak, *Nev., U.S.* 39°8′ N, 117°34′ W **90**
North Slope, *Alas., U.S.* 69°31′ N, 155°32′ W **98**
North Springfield, *Pa., U.S.* 41°59′ N, 80°27′ W **94**
North Springfield, *Vt., U.S.* 43°19′ N, 72°32′ W **104**
North Star, *Can.* 56°51′ N, 117°39′ W **108**
North Stradbroke Island, *Austral.* 28°5′ S, 150°57′ E **230**
North Tawton, *U.K.* 50°48′ N, 3°54′ W **162**
North Thetford, *Vt., U.S.* 43°50′ N, 72°12′ W **104**
North Truro, *Mass., U.S.* 42°2′ N, 70°6′ W **104**
North Turner, *Me., U.S.* 44°20′ N, 70°15′ W **104**
North Vancouver, *Can.* 49°19′ N, 123°3′ W **100**
North Vassalboro, *Me., U.S.* 44°29′ N, 69°38′ W **104**
North Vernon, *Ind., U.S.* 39°0′ N, 85°38′ W **102**
North Wabasca Lake, *Can.* 56°2′ N, 114°57′ W **108**
North Walpole, *N.H., U.S.* 43°8′ N, 72°27′ W **104**
North Walsham, *U.K.* 52°49′ N, 1°22′ E **163**
North Warren, *Pa., U.S.* 41°52′ N, 79°10′ W **110**
North Waterford, *Me., U.S.* 44°13′ N, 70°46′ W **104**
North Webster, *Ind., U.S.* 41°19′ N, 85°42′ W **102**
North West Cape, *Austral.* 21°48′ S, 114°19′ E **230**
North West Point, *Can.* 53°25′ N, 60°2′ W **111**
North West River, *Can.* 53°34′ N, 60°8′ W **111**
North West Rocks, islands, *Caribbean Sea* 14°31′ N, 80°34′ W **115**
North Wildwood, *N.J., U.S.* 39°0′ N, 74°48′ W **94**
North Yolla Bolly Mountains, peak, *Calif., U.S.* 40°11′ N, 123°4′ W **90**
North York Moors, *U.K.* 54°20′ N, 1°2′ W **162**
Northallerton, *U.K.* 54°20′ N, 1°27′ W **162**
Northam, *Austral.* 31°41′ S, 116°41′ E **231**
Northam, *S. Af.* 24°58′ S, 27°15′ E **227**
Northampton, *Mass., U.S.* 42°18′ N, 72°38′ W **104**
Northampton, *U.K.* 52°14′ N, 0°54′ E **162**
Northampton, Mount, peak, *Antarctica* 72°37′ S, 169°35′ E **248**
Northbluff Point, *Can.* 51°27′ N, 80°24′ W **110**
Northeast Cape, *Alas., U.S.* 63°5′ N, 167°44′ W **160**
Northeast Pacific Basin, *North Pacific Ocean* 26°5′ N, 145°35′ W **252**
Northeast Point, *Bahamas* 22°48′ N, 74°14′ W **80**
Northeast Point, *Can.* 51°54′ N, 55°18′ W **111**
Northeast Point, *Jam.* 18°12′ N, 76°20′ W **115**
Northeim, *Ger.* 51°42′ N, 9°59′ E **167**
Northern, adm. division, *Sudan* 20°14′ N, 31°0′ E **182**
Northern Areas, adm. division, *Pak.* 35°38′ N, 73°27′ E **186**
Northern Bahr Al Ghazal, adm. division, *Sudan* 9°11′ N, 26°10′ E **224**
Northern Cape, adm. division, *S. Af.* 30°2′ S, 19°39′ E **227**
Northern Cay, island, *Belize* 17°21′ N, 87°29′ W **116**
Northern Cyprus, special sovereignty 35°16′ N, 32°56′ E **194**
Northern Darfur, adm. division, *Sudan* 16°39′ N, 23°59′ E **226**
Northern Head, *Can.* 46°4′ N, 59°46′ W **111**
Northern Ireland, adm. division, *U.K.* 54°35′ N, 7°41′ W **150**
Northern Mariana Islands, *U.S.* 20°7′ N, 141°10′ E **192**
Northern Sierra Madre National Park, *Philippines* 16°48′ N, 121°37′ E **203**
Northern Territory, adm. division, *Austral.* 19°14′ S, 130°35′ E **231**
Northfield, *Minn., U.S.* 44°26′ N, 93°8′ W **94**
Northfield, *N.H., U.S.* 43°25′ N, 71°36′ W **104**
Northfield, *Vt., U.S.* 44°8′ N, 72°40′ W **104**
Northfield Falls, *Vt., U.S.* 44°9′ N, 72°39′ W **104**
Northford, *Conn., U.S.* 41°23′ N, 72°48′ W **104**
Northport, *Ala., U.S.* 33°13′ N, 87°35′ W **103**
Northport, *Nebr., U.S.* 41°41′ N, 103°6′ W **92**
Northport, *Wash., U.S.* 48°53′ N, 117°48′ W **90**
Northridge, *Ohio, U.S.* 39°59′ N, 83°46′ W **102**
Northumberland, *N.H., U.S.* 44°33′ N, 71°34′ W **104**
Northumberland Islands, *Coral Sea* 22°8′ S, 150°56′ E **230**
Northville, *N.Y., U.S.* 43°13′ N, 74°11′ W **104**
Northway, *Alas., U.S.* 62°51′ N, 141°59′ W **98**
North-West, adm. division, *S. Af.* 26°44′ S, 24°15′ E **227**
Northwest Angle, *Minn., U.S.* 49°4′ N, 95°20′ W **90**
Northwest Atlantic Mid-Ocean Canyon, *North Atlantic Ocean* 52°31′ N, 45°36′ W **253**
North-West Frontier, adm. division, *Pak.* 34°28′ N, 71°45′ E **186**
Northwest Hawaiian Ridge, *North Pacific Ocean* 31°13′ N, 173°59′ W **252**
Northwest Miscou Point, *Can.* 48°11′ N, 65°14′ W **94**
Northwest Pacific Basin, *North Pacific Ocean* 39°52′ N, 157°39′ E **252**
Northwest Passages 70°33′ N, 125°19′ W **72**
Northwest Territories, adm. division, *Can.* 60°25′ N, 115°14′ W **108**
Northwestern Hawaiian Islands, *North Pacific Ocean* 23°42′ N, 165°44′ W **99**
Northwich, *U.K.* 53°15′ N, 2°31′ W **162**
Northwind Escarpment, *Arctic Ocean* 75°55′ N, 153°20′ W **255**
Northwind Ridge, *Arctic Ocean* 76°13′ N, 156°12′ W **255**
Northwood, *N.H., U.S.* 43°11′ N, 71°10′ W **104**
Northwood, *N. Dak., U.S.* 47°43′ N, 97°35′ W **90**
Northwood, *Ohio, U.S.* 41°35′ N, 83°27′ W **102**
Norton, *Kans., U.S.* 39°49′ N, 99°54′ W **90**
Norton, *Va., U.S.* 36°55′ N, 82°39′ W **94**
Norton, *Zimb.* 17°56′ S, 30°40′ E **224**
Norton Bay 64°20′ N, 162°6′ W **98**
Norton Shores, *Mich., U.S.* 43°9′ N, 86°16′ W **102**
Norton Sound 63°37′ N, 165°6′ W **98**
Norvalspont, *S. Af.* 30°38′ S, 25°24′ E **227**
Norvegia, Cape, *Antarctica* 71°16′ S, 18°23′ W **248**
Norwalk, *Calif., U.S.* 33°55′ N, 118°4′ W **101**
Norwalk, *Conn., U.S.* 41°7′ N, 73°25′ W **104**
Norwalk, *Ohio, U.S.* 41°13′ N, 82°37′ W **102**
Norway, *Me., U.S.* 44°12′ N, 70°33′ W **104**
Norway, *Mich., U.S.* 45°47′ N, 87°55′ W **94**
Norway 63°25′ N, 10°58′ E **152**
Norway House, *Can.* 53°56′ N, 97°52′ W **108**
Norwegian Basin, *Norwegian Sea* 68°5′ N, 1°43′ E **255**
Norwegian Sea 68°1′ N, 5°35′ E **152**
Norwich, *Conn., U.S.* 41°31′ N, 72°5′ W **104**
Norwich, *N.Y., U.S.* 42°31′ N, 75°33′ W **94**
Norwich, *U.K.* 52°37′ N, 1°16′ E **162**
Norwich, *Vt., U.S.* 43°42′ N, 72°19′ W **104**
Norwood, *Colo., U.S.* 38°7′ N, 108°17′ W **90**
Norwood, *La., U.S.* 30°57′ N, 91°7′ W **103**
Norwood, *Mass., U.S.* 42°11′ N, 71°13′ W **104**
Norwood, *Ohio, U.S.* 39°9′ N, 84°27′ W **94**
Noshul′, *Russ.* 60°8′ N, 49°35′ E **154**
Nosivka, *Ukr.* 50°54′ N, 31°38′ E **158**
Nosok, *Russ.* 70°8′ N, 82°7′ E **169**
Nosovshchina, *Russ.* 62°57′ N, 37°3′ E **154**
Noşratābād, *Iran* 29°51′ N, 59°56′ E **180**
Nosy-Varika, *Madagascar* 20°33′ S, 48°31′ E **220**
Noszlop, *Hung.* 47°10′ N, 17°26′ E **168**
Not Ozero, lake, *Russ.* 66°26′ N, 30°49′ E **152**
Notch Peak, *Utah, U.S.* 39°7′ N, 113°29′ W **90**
Notikewin, *Can.* 56°58′ N, 117°38′ W **108**
Notikewin, river, *Can.* 56°55′ N, 119°2′ W **108**
Nötö, *Fin.* 59°57′ N, 21°45′ E **166**
Noto, *It.* 36°53′ N, 15°4′ E **156**
Noto, *Japan* 37°19′ N, 137°8′ E **201**
Notodden, *Nor.* 59°33′ N, 9°17′ E **152**
Notre Dame Bay 49°29′ N, 55°32′ W **111**
Notre Dame de Lourdes, *Can.* 49°31′ N, 98°34′ W **90**
Notre-Dame-du-Nord, *Can.* 47°36′ N, 79°29′ W **94**
Notsé, *Togo* 6°57′ N, 1°9′ E **222**
Nottaway, river, *Can.* 51°13′ N, 78°54′ W **80**
Nottingham, *N.H., U.S.* 43°6′ N, 71°7′ W **104**
Nottingham, *U.K.* 52°57′ N, 1°9′ W **162**
Nottingham Island, *Can.* 63°12′ N, 82°17′ W **106**
Nottuln, *Ger.* 51°55′ N, 7°21′ E **167**
Nouabalé-Ndoki National Park, *Congo* 2°47′ N, 16°11′ E **206**
Nouadhibou (Port Étienne), *Mauritania* 20°56′ N, 17°2′ W **222**
Nouakchott, *Mauritania* 18°6′ N, 16°11′ W **222**
Nouamrhar, *Mauritania* 19°22′ N, 16°32′ W **222**
Nouaoudar, *Mauritania* 16°46′ N, 7°18′ W **222**
Nouart, *Fr.* 49°26′ N, 5°3′ E **163**
Nouasser, *Mor.* 33°22′ N, 7°39′ W **214**
Nouméa 22°5′ S, 166°32′ E **238**
Nouna, *Burkina Faso* 12°43′ N, 3°53′ W **222**
Noupoort, *S. Af.* 31°10′ S, 24°55′ E **227**
Nourounba, *Mali* 12°31′ N, 9°8′ W **222**
Nousu, *Fin.* 67°10′ N, 28°36′ E **152**
Nouzonville, *Fr.* 49°47′ N, 4°44′ E **163**
Nova América, *Braz.* 15°3′ S, 49°60′ W **138**
Nova Andradina, *Braz.* 22°15′ S, 53°21′ W **138**
Nova Esperança, *Braz.* 23°10′ S, 52°17′ W **138**
Nova Esperança, *Braz.* 16°34′ S, 43°56′ W **138**
Nova Friburgo, *Braz.* 22°18′ S, 42°31′ W **138**
Nova Gorica, *Slov.* 45°57′ N, 13°38′ E **167**
Nova Gradiška, *Croatia* 45°15′ N, 17°22′ E **168**
Nova Granada, *Braz.* 20°32′ S, 49°21′ W **138**
Nova Iguaçu, *Braz.* 22°45′ S, 43°28′ W **138**
Nova Kakhovka, *Ukr.* 46°45′ N, 33°17′ E **156**
Nova Kapela, *Croatia* 45°12′ N, 17°36′ E **168**
Nova Kasaba, *Bosn. and Herzg.* 44°13′ N, 19°7′ E **168**
Nova Lamego, *Guinea-Bissau* 12°17′ N, 14°16′ W **222**
Nova Lima, *Braz.* 19°58′ S, 43°51′ W **138**
Nova Mambone, *Mozambique* 21°1′ S, 34°57′ E **227**
Nova Nabúri, *Mozambique* 16°50′ S, 38°55′ E **224**
Nova Odesa, *Ukr.* 47°21′ N, 31°45′ E **156**
Nova Olinda do Norte, *Braz.* 3°49′ S, 59°2′ W **130**
Nova Prata, *Braz.* 28°50′ S, 51°35′ W **139**
Nova Roma, *Braz.* 13°53′ S, 46°59′ W **138**
Nova Scotia, adm. division, *Can.* 44°50′ N, 65°14′ W **111**
Nova Sofala, *Mozambique* 20°10′ S, 34°43′ E **227**
Nova Trento, *Braz.* 27°20′ S, 48°56′ W **138**
Nova Varoš, *Serb. and Mont.* 43°27′ N, 19°48′ E **168**
Nova Venécia, *Braz.* 18°46′ S, 40°26′ W **138**
Nova Viçosa, *Braz.* 17°54′ S, 39°24′ W **138**
Novafeltria, *It.* 43°53′ N, 12°17′ E **167**
Novalukoml′, *Belarus* 54°42′ N, 29°11′ E **166**
Novara, *It.* 45°26′ N, 8°36′ E **167**
Novato, *Calif., U.S.* 38°7′ N, 122°35′ W **100**
Novaya Lyalya, *Russ.* 59°1′ N, 60°39′ E **154**
Novaya Shul′ba, *Kaz.* 50°32′ N, 81°19′ E **184**
Novaya Sibir′, Ostrov, island, *Russ.* 75°1′ N, 151°6′ E **160**
Novaya Vodolaga, *Ukr.* 49°44′ N, 35°53′ E **158**
Novaya Zemlya, island, *Russ.* 70°43′ N, 57°35′ E **169**
Nové Zámky, *Slovakia* 47°59′ N, 18°10′ E **168**
Novelda, *Sp.* 38°22′ N, 0°47′ E **164**
Novgorod, adm. division, *Russ.* 58°2′ N, 30°16′ E **166**
Novgorodka, *Russ.* 57°2′ N, 28°33′ E **166**
Novhorod-Sivers′kyy, *Ukr.* 51°58′ N, 33°18′ E **158**
Novi Bečej, *Serb. and Mont.* 45°35′ N, 20°8′ E **168**
Novi Kneževac, *Serb. and Mont.* 46°2′ N, 20°6′ E **168**
Novi Ligure, *It.* 44°45′ N, 8°47′ E **167**
Novi Pazar, *Bulg.* 43°20′ N, 27°11′ E **158**
Novi Pazar, *Serb. and Mont.* 43°11′ N, 20°33′ E **180**
Novi Pazar, *Serb. and Mont.* 43°8′ N, 20°31′ E **168**
Novi Sad, *Serb. and Mont.* 45°14′ N, 19°46′ E **168**
Novigrad, *Croatia* 45°20′ N, 13°34′ E **167**
Novikovo, *Russ.* 58°9′ N, 80°35′ E **169**
Novilara, *It.* 43°51′ N, 12°55′ E **167**
Noville Peninsula, *Antarctica* 71°26′ S, 95°25′ W **248**
Novillero, *Mex.* 22°21′ N, 105°40′ W **114**
Novinka, *Russ.* 59°10′ N, 30°20′ E **166**
Novo Acordo, *Braz.* 10°9′ S, 47°20′ W **130**
Novo Aripuanã, *Braz.* 5°9′ S, 60°21′ W **130**
Novo Cruzeiro, *Braz.* 17°29′ S, 41°53′ W **138**
Novo Hamburgo, *Braz.* 29°42′ S, 51°7′ W **139**
Novo Horizonte, *Braz.* 21°29′ S, 49°15′ W **138**
Novo Izborsk, *Russ.* 57°47′ N, 27°55′ E **166**
Novo Paraíso, *Braz.* 1°15′ N, 60°18′ W **123**
Novo, river, *Braz.* 4°47′ S, 53°49′ W **130**
Novoagansk, *Russ.* 61°57′ N, 76°26′ E **169**
Novoaleksandrovsk, *Russ.* 45°31′ N, 41°6′ E **158**
Novoaltaysk, *Russ.* 53°27′ N, 84°6′ E **184**
Novoanninskiy, *Russ.* 50°28′ N, 42°42′ E **158**
Novobogatīnskoe, *Kaz.* 47°21′ N, 51°11′ E **158**
Novocheremshansk, *Russ.* 54°21′ N, 50°5′ E **154**
Novodvinsk, *Russ.* 64°25′ N, 40°48′ E **154**
Novohrad-Volyns′kyy, *Ukr.* 50°34′ N, 27°35′ E **152**
Novoīshīmskīy, *Kaz.* 53°13′ N, 66°48′ E **184**
Novokhovansk, *Russ.* 55°55′ N, 29°43′ E **166**
Novokuybyshevsk, *Russ.* 53°6′ N, 50°0′ E **154**
Novokuznetsk, *Russ.* 53°48′ N, 87°8′ E **184**
Novolazarevskaya, Russia, station, *Antarctica* 70°47′ S, 11°39′ E **248**
Novomalykla, *Russ.* 54°10′ N, 49°50′ E **154**
Novomichurinsk, *Russ.* 53°59′ N, 39°49′ E **154**
Novomikhaylovskoye, *Russ.* 44°15′ N, 38°55′ E **156**
Novomoskovsk, *Russ.* 54°3′ N, 38°12′ E **154**
Novomoskovs′k, *Ukr.* 48°40′ N, 35°18′ E **158**
Novonikolayevskiy, *Russ.* 50°56′ N, 42°20′ E **158**
Novonikol′skoye, *Russ.* 49°5′ N, 45°4′ E **158**
Novonikol′skoye, *Russ.* 59°43′ N, 79°17′ E **169**
Novooleksiyivka, *Ukr.* 46°15′ N, 34°37′ E **156**
Novoorsk, *Russ.* 51°23′ N, 58°57′ E **158**
Novopokrovskaya, *Russ.* 45°58′ N, 40°37′ E **158**
Novopskov, *Ukr.* 49°34′ N, 39°9′ E **158**
Novorepnoye, *Russ.* 51°3′ N, 48°21′ E **158**
Novorossiysk, *Russ.* 44°46′ N, 37°41′ E **156**
Novorybnoye, *Russ.* 72°45′ N, 105°56′ E **160**
Novorzhev, *Russ.* 57°1′ N, 29°18′ E **166**
Novosel′ye, *Russ.* 58°5′ N, 28°52′ E **166**
Novosergiyevka, *Russ.* 52°3′ N, 53°36′ E **158**
Novoshakhtinsk, *Russ.* 47°43′ N, 39°57′ E **158**
Novosi Birskiye Ostrova (New Siberian Islands), *Russ.* 76°14′ N, 142°6′ E **160**
Novosibirsk, *Russ.* 55°3′ N, 83°2′ E **184**
Novosibirsk, adm. division, *Russ.* 54°25′ N, 77°40′ E **184**
Novosil′, *Russ.* 52°57′ N, 37°1′ E **154**
Novosil′skiy, Cape, *Antarctica* 68°20′ S, 159°52′ E **248**
Novosokol′niki, *Russ.* 56°20′ N, 30°13′ E **154**
Novotitarovskaya, *Russ.* 45°16′ N, 39°1′ E **156**
Novotroitsk, *Russ.* 51°13′ N, 58°16′ E **158**
Novoukrayinka, *Ukr.* 48°21′ N, 31°36′ E **156**
Novouzensk, *Russ.* 50°29′ N, 48°7′ E **158**
Novovyatsk, *Russ.* 58°28′ N, 49°41′ E **154**
Novozhilovskaya, *Russ.* 64°49′ N, 51°24′ E **154**
Novozybkov, *Russ.* 52°30′ N, 31°58′ E **154**
Novska, *Croatia* 45°19′ N, 16°59′ E **168**
Novvy Oskol, *Russ.* 50°46′ N, 37°53′ E **158**
Novyy Bor, *Russ.* 66°43′ N, 52°16′ E **154**
Novyy Buh, *Ukr.* 47°41′ N, 32°25′ E **156**
Novyy Buyan, *Russ.* 53°40′ N, 50°5′ E **154**
Novyy Port, *Russ.* 67°40′ N, 72°54′ E **169**
Novyy Uoyan, *Russ.* 56°5′ N, 111°38′ E **173**
Novyy Urengoy, *Russ.* 65°53′ N, 77°10′ E **169**
Novyy Vasyugan, *Russ.* 58°34′ N, 76°25′ E **169**
Now Zad, *Afghan.* 32°23′ N, 64°30′ E **186**
Nowa Sól, *Pol.* 51°47′ N, 15°43′ E **152**
Nowata, *Okla., U.S.* 36°41′ N, 95°39′ W **96**
Nowbarān, *Iran* 35°12′ N, 49°40′ E **180**
Nowgong, *India* 25°4′ N, 79°26′ E **197**
Nowra, *Austral.* 34°49′ S, 150°36′ E **231**
Nowshera, *Pak.* 33°57′ N, 72°0′ E **186**
Nowy Sącz, *Pol.* 49°40′ N, 20°47′ E **160**
Noxapater, *Miss., U.S.* 32°58′ N, 89°4′ W **103**
Noxon, *Mont., U.S.* 47°57′ N, 115°47′ W **90**
Noxubee, river, *Ala., U.S.* 33°11′ N, 88°47′ W **103**
Noy, river, *Laos* 17°6′ N, 105°20′ E **202**
Noyabr′sk, *Russ.* 63°12′ N, 75°24′ E **169**
Noyes, *Minn., U.S.* 48°57′ N, 97°13′ W **94**
Noyo, *Calif., U.S.* 39°25′ N, 123°49′ W **90**
Noyo, river, *Calif., U.S.* 39°20′ N, 123°46′ W **90**
Noyon, *Fr.* 49°34′ N, 3°0′ E **163**
Nsanje (Port Herald), *Malawi* 16°56′ S, 35°13′ E **224**
Nsawam, *Ghana* 5°50′ N, 0°21′ E **222**
Nsélé, *Gabon* 6°357′ N, 10°10′ E **218**
Nsoc, *Equatorial Guinea* 1°13′ N, 11°14′ E **218**
Nsontin, *Dem. Rep. of the Congo* 3°9′ S, 17°54′ E **218**
Nsukka, *Nig.* 6°51′ N, 7°23′ E **222**
Nsumbu National Park, *Zambia* 8°52′ S, 30°7′ E **206**
Ntakat, spring, *Mauritania* 16°49′ N, 11°45′ W **222**
N'Tima, *Congo* 3°47′ S, 12°3′ E **218**
Ntui, *Cameroon* 4°25′ N, 11°36′ E **222**
Nu (Salween), river, *Asia* 31°21′ N, 93°34′ E **190**
Nu'aymah, *Syr.* 32°38′ N, 36°10′ E **194**
Nuba Mountains, *Sudan* 10°45′ N, 30°5′ E **224**
Nubia, Lake, *Sudan* 21°56′ N, 30°53′ E **182**
Nubian Desert, *Sudan* 20°50′ N, 30°59′ E **182**
Nucet, *Rom.* 46°30′ N, 22°35′ E **168**
Nucla, *Colo., U.S.* 38°16′ N, 108°33′ W **90**
Nüden, *Mongolia* 43°58′ N, 110°37′ E **198**
Nueces, river, *Tex., U.S.* 28°12′ N, 98°46′ W **92**
Nueltin Lake, *Can.* 59°37′ N, 102°11′ W **106**
Nueva Esparta, adm. division, *Venez.* 10°57′ N, 64°24′ W **130**
Nueva Galia, *Arg.* 35°6′ S, 65°13′ W **134**
Nueva Gerona, *Cuba* 21°53′ N, 82°49′ W **116**
Nueva, Isla, island, *Chile* 55°13′ S, 66°24′ W **134**
Nueva Palmira, *Uru.* 33°54′ S, 58°20′ W **139**
Nueva Rosita, *Mex.* 27°55′ N, 101°12′ W **92**
Nuevo Berlín, *Uru.* 32°59′ S, 57°59′ W **139**
Nuevo Casas Grandes, *Mex.* 30°24′ N, 107°55′ W **92**
Nuevo Delicias, *Mex.* 26°16′ N, 102°48′ W **114**
Nuevo Ideal, *Mex.* 24°51′ N, 105°4′ W **114**
Nuevo Laredo, *Mex.* 27°28′ N, 99°32′ W **96**
Nuevo León, *Mex.* 32°25′ N, 115°14′ W **101**
Nuevo León, adm. division, *Mex.* 25°9′ N, 100°14′ W **114**
Nuevo Morelos, *Mex.* 22°30′ N, 99°13′ W **114**
Nuevo Rocafuerte, *Ecua.* 0°60′ N, 75°27′ W **136**
Nuevo Rodríguez, *Mex.* 27°8′ N, 100°4′ W **96**
Nugaaleed, Dooxa, *Somalia* 8°39′ N, 47°24′ E **216**
Nugruş, Gebel, peak, *Egypt* 24°47′ N, 34°29′ E **182**
Nuh, Ras, *Pak.* 24°55′ N, 62°25′ E **182**
Nuia, *Est.* 58°5′ N, 25°30′ E **166**
Nuijamaa, *Fin.* 60°58′ N, 28°34′ E **166**
Nuiqsut, *Alas., U.S.* 70°12′ N, 151°2′ W **98**
Nuits, *Fr.* 47°43′ N, 4°11′ E **150**
Nukhayb, *Iraq* 32°3′ N, 42°15′ E **180**
Nukheila (Merga), spring, *Sudan* 19°3′ N, 26°20′ E **226**
Nuku'alofa, *Tonga* 21°8′ S, 175°12′ W **241**
Nukumanu Islands, *South Pacific Ocean* 4°52′ S, 159°33′ E **238**
Nukus, *Uzb.* 42°26′ N, 59°39′ E **180**
Nulato, *Alas., U.S.* 64°36′ N, 158°12′ W **98**
Nules, *Sp.* 39°51′ N, 0°10′ E **164**
Nullarbor Plain, *Austral.* 30°43′ S, 125°29′ E **230**
Numan, *Nig.* 9°29′ N, 12°5′ E **216**
Numata, *Japan* 36°38′ N, 139°2′ E **201**
Numazu, *Japan* 35°5′ N, 138°53′ E **201**
Numedal, region, *Nor.* 60°8′ N, 8°56′ E **152**
Numfoor, island, *Indonesia* 1°23′ S, 134°21′ E **192**
Nummi, *Fin.* 60°23′ N, 23°52′ E **166**
Numto, *Russ.* 63°30′ N, 71°20′ E **169**
Nunap Isua (Kap Farvel) 59°20′ N, 43°43′ W **106**
Nunavik 71°32′ N, 56°33′ W **106**
Nunavut, adm. division, *Can.* 65°9′ N, 74°23′ W **106**
Nunchía, *Col.* 5°35′ N, 72°14′ W **136**
Nuneaton, *U.K.* 52°31′ N, 1°27′ W **162**
Nuñes, island, *Chile* 53°38′ S, 74°58′ W **134**
Nungesser Lake, *Can.* 51°31′ N, 94°27′ W **80**
Nungnain Sum, *China* 45°42′ N, 119°0′ E **198**
Nungo, *Mozambique* 13°23′ S, 37°46′ E **224**
Nunim Lake, lake, *Can.* 59°28′ N, 102°54′ W **108**
Nunivak Island, *Alas., U.S.* 59°24′ N, 166°59′ W **98**
Nunkiní, *Mex.* 20°21′ N, 90°13′ W **112**
Nunligran, *Russ.* 64°51′ N, 175°16′ W **98**
Nuñoa, *Peru* 14°31′ S, 70°37′ W **137**
Nuoro, *It.* 40°19′ N, 9°19′ E **156**
Nuqayr, spring, *Saudi Arabia* 27°50′ N, 48°17′ E **196**
Nuquí, *Col.* 5°41′ N, 77°16′ W **136**
Nura, river, *Kaz.* 50°28′ N, 71°12′ E **184**
Nurki, Mys, *Russ.* 56°29′ N, 138°30′ E **160**
Nurlat, *Russ.* 54°26′ N, 50°41′ E **154**
Nurmes, *Fin.* 63°31′ N, 29°7′ E **152**
Nurmo, *Fin.* 62°49′ N, 22°50′ E **154**
Nürnberg, *Ger.* 49°26′ N, 11°0′ E **143**
Nurobod, *Uzb.* 39°34′ N, 66°17′ E **197**
Nurota, *Uzb.* 40°33′ N, 65°41′ E **197**
Nurri, Mount, peak, *Austral.* 31°45′ S, 145°48′ E **230**
Nushagak Peninsula, *Alas., U.S.* 58°17′ N, 160°46′ W **98**
Nushki, *Pak.* 29°31′ N, 66°3′ E **182**
Nut Mountain, *Can.* 52°8′ N, 103°23′ W **108**
Nuttby Mountain, peak, *Can.* 45°32′ N, 63°18′ W **111**
Nu'uanu Pali Overlook, site, *Hawai'i, U.S.* 21°20′ N, 157°50′ W **99**
Nuugaatsiaq 71°35′ N, 53°13′ W **106**
Nuuk (Godthåb) 64°14′ N, 51°38′ W **106**
Nuupas, *Fin.* 66°0′ N, 26°19′ E **154**
Nuussuaq 70°6′ N, 51°42′ W **106**
Nuussuaq (Kraulshavn) 74°9′ N, 57°1′ W **106**
Nuwara Eliya, *Sri Lanka* 6°56′ N, 80°47′ E **188**
Nuwerus, *S. Af.* 31°8′ S, 18°20′ E **227**
Nuyno, *Ukr.* 51°31′ N, 24°53′ E **158**
Nuyts Archipelago, islands, *Great Australian Bight* 32°45′ S, 130°56′ E **230**
Nwayfadh, *Africa* 24°53′ N, 14°50′ W **214**

Nxai Pan National Park, Botswana 20°3′ S, 24°40′ E 224
Ny Ålesund, Nor. 78°50′ N, 12°1′ E 160
Nyaake, Liberia 4°50′ N, 7°36′ W 222
Nyac, Alas., U.S. 60°53′ N, 160°7′ W 98
Nyagan', Russ. 62°19′ N, 65°34′ E 169
Nyahanga, Tanzania 2°22′ S, 33°34′ E 224
Nyainqêntanglha Feng, peak, China 30°23′ N, 90°32′ E 197
Nyainrong, China 32°2′ N, 92°14′ E 188
Nyakabindi, Tanzania 2°37′ S, 33°55′ E 224
Nyakanazi, Tanzania 3°6′ S, 31°15′ E 224
Nyåker, Nor. 63°47′ N, 19°19′ E 152
Nyakrom, Ghana 5°37′ N, 0°48′ E 222
Nyaksimvol', Russ. 62°29′ N, 60°51′ E 169
Nyala, Sudan 12°2′ N, 24°55′ E 224
Nyalam, China 28°11′ N, 85°57′ E 197
Nyamandhlovu, Zimb. 19°53′ S, 28°16′ E 224
Nyamapanda, Zimb. 16°56′ S, 32°48′ E 224
Nyambiti, Tanzania 2°49′ S, 33°24′ E 218
Nyamirembe, Tanzania 2°33′ S, 31°42′ E 224
Nyamtumbo, Tanzania 10°31′ S, 36°6′ E 224
Nyanding, river, Sudan 8°8′ N, 32°18′ E 224
Nyandoma, Russ. 61°39′ N, 40°10′ E 154
Nyanga, Zimb. 18°11′ S, 32°42′ E 224
Nyanga Nature Reserve, Congo 3°2′ S, 11°27′ E 206
Nyangwe, Dem. Rep. of the Congo 4°12′ S, 26°11′ E 218
Nyanje, Zambia 14°24′ S, 31°47′ E 224
Nyanza Lac, Burundi 4°20′ S, 29°36′ E 224
Nyarling, river, Can. 60°20′ N, 114°23′ W 108
Nyashabozh, Russ. 65°28′ N, 53°52′ E 154
Nyaunglebin, Myanmar 17°58′ N, 96°42′ E 202
Nyazepetrovsk, Russ. 56°3′ N, 59°39′ E 154
Nyborg, Den. 55°17′ N, 10°47′ E 150
Nyborg, Nor. 70°10′ N, 28°36′ E 152
Nybro, Nor. 56°45′ N, 15°53′ E 152
Nyda, Russ. 66°34′ N, 73°2′ E 169
Nye Mountains, Antarctica 68°4′ S, 48°39′ E 248
Nyeboe Land 81°28′ N, 53°44′ W 246
Nyeharelaye, Belarus 53°33′ N, 27°4′ E 152
Nyékládháza, Hung. 47°59′ N, 20°48′ E 168
Nyeri, Kenya 0°26′ N, 36°57′ E 224
Nyerol, Sudan 8°40′ N, 32°2′ E 224
Nyika National Park, Malawi 11°6′ S, 34°9′ E 224
Nyika Plateau, Malawi 10°39′ S, 33°28′ E 224
Nyima, China 31°55′ N, 87°49′ E 188
Nyimba, Zambia 14°35′ S, 30°50′ E 224
Nyingchi, China 29°36′ N, 94°24′ E 188
Nyírábrány, Hung. 47°33′ N, 22°3′ E 168
Nyírbátor, Hung. 47°49′ N, 22°8′ E 168
Nyíregyháza, Hung. 47°56′ N, 21°44′ E 168
Nyiri Desert, Kenya 2°23′ S, 37°10′ E 224
Nyiru, Mount, peak, Kenya 2°16′ N, 36°42′ E 224
Nykarleby (Uusikaarlepyy), Fin. 63°31′ N, 22°32′ E 152
Nykøbing, Den. 54°46′ N, 11°53′ E 152
Nykøbing, Den. 56°47′ N, 8°49′ E 150
Nykøbing, Den. 55°55′ N, 11°39′ E 152
Nyköping, Nor. 58°44′ N, 16°59′ E 152
Nylstroom see Modimolle, S. Af. 24°44′ S, 28°24′ E 227
Nynäshamn, Sw. 58°53′ N, 17°53′ E 166
Nyoma Rap, India 33°9′ N, 78°39′ E 188
Nyoman, river, Belarus 53°52′ N, 25°34′ E 166
Nyon, Switz. 46°25′ N, 6°16′ E 167
Nyonga, Tanzania 6°42′ S, 32°3′ E 224
Nyrob, Russ. 60°44′ N, 56°43′ E 154
Nyrud, Nor. 69°9′ N, 29°12′ E 152
Nyrza, Russ. 63°27′ N, 43°37′ E 154
Nysa, Pol. 50°29′ N, 17°20′ E 152
Nyssa, Oreg., U.S. 43°52′ N, 117°1′ W 90
Nytva, Russ. 57°56′ N, 55°21′ E 154
Nyukhcha, Russ. 63°27′ N, 46°28′ E 154
Nyukka, Russ. 66°3′ N, 32°41′ E 152
Nyuksenitsa, Russ. 60°24′ N, 44°18′ E 154
Nyunzu, Dem. Rep. of the Congo 5°58′ S, 27°57′ E 224
Nyurba, Russ. 63°22′ N, 118°13′ E 160
Nyuvchim, Russ. 61°22′ N, 50°50′ E 154
Nyzhn'ohirs'kyy, Ukr. 45°26′ N, 34°41′ E 156
Nzara, Sudan 4°41′ N, 28°14′ E 224
Nzega, Tanzania 4°14′ S, 33°11′ E 224
Nzérékoré, Guinea 7°38′ N, 8°50′ W 222
N'zeto, Angola 7°19′ S, 12°52′ E 218
Nzi, river, Côte d'Ivoire 6°6′ N, 4°51′ W 222
Nzo, Guinea 7°35′ N, 8°20′ W 222
Nzo, river, Côte d'Ivoire 6°49′ N, 7°36′ W 222
Nzoro, Dem. Rep. of the Congo 3°14′ N, 29°31′ E 224
Nzoro, river, Dem. Rep. of the Congo 3°25′ N, 30°25′ E 224
Nzwani, island, Comoros 12°36′ S, 44°15′ E 220

O

Oacoma, S. Dak., U.S. 43°47′ N, 99°24′ W 90
Oahe Dam, S. Dak., U.S. 44°39′ N, 101°32′ W 82
Oahe, Lake, N. Dak., U.S. 45°33′ N, 100°54′ W 80
O'ahu, island, Hawai'i, U.S. 21°43′ N, 157°60′ W 99
Oak Bluffs, Mass., U.S. 41°27′ N, 70°35′ W 104
Oak Creek, Colo., U.S. 40°17′ N, 106°57′ W 90
Oak Grove, La., U.S. 32°50′ N, 91°23′ W 103
Oak Harbor, Ohio, U.S. 41°30′ N, 83°9′ W 102
Oak Harbor, Wash., U.S. 48°17′ N, 122°38′ W 100
Oak Hill, Fla., U.S. 28°51′ N, 80°52′ W 105
Oak Hill, W. Va., U.S. 37°58′ N, 81°9′ W 94
Oak Lake, Can. 49°45′ N, 100°39′ W 90
Oak Lawn, Ill., U.S. 41°43′ N, 87°45′ W 102
Oak Park, Ill., U.S. 41°53′ N, 87°48′ W 102
Oak Ridge, La., U.S. 32°36′ N, 91°46′ W 103
Oak Ridge, Tenn., U.S. 36°0′ N, 84°15′ W 96
Oak View, Calif., U.S. 34°24′ N, 119°19′ W 100
Oakdale, Calif., U.S. 37°45′ N, 120°52′ W 100
Oakdale, La., U.S. 30°47′ N, 92°40′ W 103
Oakdale, Mass., U.S. 42°23′ N, 71°48′ W 104
Oakengates, U.K. 52°41′ N, 2°26′ W 162
Oakes, N. Dak., U.S. 46°7′ N, 98°6′ W 90
Oakesdale, Wash., U.S. 47°7′ N, 117°15′ W 90
Oakham, U.K. 52°39′ N, 0°44′ E 162
Oakhurst, Calif., U.S. 37°20′ N, 119°40′ W 100
Oakland, Calif., U.S. 37°48′ N, 122°16′ W 100
Oakland, Ill., U.S. 39°38′ N, 88°2′ W 102
Oakland, Iowa, U.S. 41°17′ N, 95°22′ W 90
Oakland, Me., U.S. 44°32′ N, 69°44′ W 104
Oakland, Nebr., U.S. 41°48′ N, 96°28′ W 90
Oakland, Oreg., U.S. 43°24′ N, 123°18′ W 90
Oakland, Pa., U.S. 41°56′ N, 75°38′ W 94
Oakland Park, Fla., U.S. 26°10′ N, 80°9′ W 105
Oakley, Calif., U.S. 37°59′ N, 121°44′ W 100
Oakley, Kans., U.S. 39°7′ N, 100°52′ W 90
Oakridge, Oreg., U.S. 43°44′ N, 122°28′ W 90
Oaktown, Ind., U.S. 38°51′ N, 87°27′ W 102
Oakura, N.Z. 39°10′ S, 173°57′ E 240
Oakville, Conn., U.S. 41°35′ N, 73°5′ W 104
Oakville, Wash., U.S. 46°48′ N, 123°14′ W 100
Oamaru, N.Z. 45°6′ S, 170°57′ E 240
Oaro, N.Z. 42°33′ S, 173°28′ E 240
Ōasa, Japan 34°45′ N, 132°28′ E 201
Oates Coast, Antarctica 69°56′ S, 159°4′ E 248
Oatman, Ariz., U.S. 35°0′ N, 114°23′ W 101
Oaxaca, Mex. 17°2′ N, 96°46′ W 114
Oaxaca, adm. division, Mex. 17°32′ N, 97°22′ W 114
Ob', Russ. 54°59′ N, 82°50′ E 184
Ob' Bank, Greenland Sea 80°34′ N, 10°39′ W 255
Ob', river, Russ. 51°41′ N, 83°0′ E 172
Ob' Tablemount, Indian Ocean 52°22′ S, 41°12′ E 255
Oba, Can. 49°5′ N, 84°6′ W 94
Oba Lake, Can. 48°34′ N, 84°44′ W 94
Obabika Lake, lake, Can. 47°3′ N, 80°43′ W 94
Obak, spring, Sudan 18°10′ N, 34°51′ E 182
Obala, Cameroon 4°12′ N, 11°31′ E 222
Obalj, Bosn. and Herzg. 43°27′ N, 18°20′ E 168
Obama, Japan 32°44′ N, 130°13′ E 201
Obama, Japan 35°28′ N, 135°44′ E 201
Obamsca, Lac, lake, Can. 50°23′ N, 78°51′ W 110
Obamsca, river, Can. 50°51′ N, 78°50′ W 110
Oban, U.K. 56°25′ N, 5°28′ W 150
Oban (Halfmoon Bay), N.Z. 46°55′ S, 168°7′ E 240
Obanazawa, Japan 38°36′ N, 140°25′ E 201
Obando, Col. 3°48′ N, 67°51′ W 136
Obed, Can. 53°34′ N, 117°14′ W 108
Obed Wild and Scenic River, Tenn., U.S. 35°51′ N, 87°55′ W 80
Oberá, Arg. 27°29′ S, 55°10′ W 139
Oberdrauburg, Aust. 46°45′ N, 12°58′ E 167
Oberhausen, Ger. 51°28′ N, 6°51′ E 167
Oberlin, Kans., U.S. 39°49′ N, 100°33′ W 90
Oberlin, La., U.S. 30°36′ N, 92°47′ W 103
Oberlin, Ohio, U.S. 41°16′ N, 82°13′ W 102
Obernai, Fr. 48°27′ N, 7°28′ E 163
Obernburg, Ger. 49°50′ N, 9°9′ E 167
Oberpullendorf, Aust. 47°30′ N, 16°31′ E 168
Obersuhl, Ger. 50°57′ N, 10°1′ E 167
Oberursel, Ger. 50°12′ N, 8°33′ E 167
Oberwesel, Ger. 50°6′ N, 7°42′ E 167
Obi, Nig. 8°20′ N, 8°45′ E 222
Obi, island, Indonesia 1°21′ S, 127°18′ E 192
Obi, Kepulauan, islands, Indonesia 2°17′ S, 126°42′ E 192
Óbidos, Braz. 1°53′ S, 55°32′ W 130
Óbidos, Port. 39°21′ N, 9°11′ W 150
Obigarm, Taj. 38°43′ N, 69°45′ E 197
Obihiro, Japan 42°55′ N, 143°9′ E 190
Obili, Gabon 0°42′ N, 14°22′ E 218
Obil'noye, Russ. 47°29′ N, 44°20′ E 158
Obion, Tenn., U.S. 36°15′ N, 89°12′ W 96
Obispo, Punta, Chile 26°45′ S, 71°27′ W 132
Obispo Trejo, Arg. 30°47′ S, 63°26′ W 139
Obispos, Venez. 8°37′ N, 70°8′ W 136
Oblivskaya, Russ. 48°31′ N, 42°25′ E 158
Oblong, Ill., U.S. 39°0′ N, 87°54′ W 102
Obluch'ye, Russ. 49°6′ N, 131°5′ E 190
Obninsk, Russ. 55°4′ N, 36°40′ E 154
Obo, Cen. Af. Rep. 5°21′ N, 26°30′ E 224
Obo Liang, China 38°48′ N, 92°39′ E 188
Oboa, peak, Uganda 1°45′ N, 34°37′ E 224
Obock, Djibouti 11°55′ N, 43°20′ E 182
Obokote, Dem. Rep. of the Congo 0°52′ N, 26°19′ E 224
Obol', Belarus 55°23′ N, 29°22′ E 166
Obonga Lake, Can. 49°58′ N, 89°45′ W 94
Obot, Alban. 41°59′ N, 19°25′ E 168
Obouya, Congo 0°57′ N, 15°43′ E 218
Oboyan', Russ. 51°12′ N, 36°21′ E 158
Obozerskiy, Russ. 63°27′ N, 40°24′ E 154
Obra, river, Pol. 52°31′ N, 15°33′ E 152
Obre Lake, lake, Can. 60°19′ N, 103°25′ W 108
Obreja, Rom. 45°28′ N, 22°16′ E 168
Obrenovac, Serb. and Mont. 44°38′ N, 20°10′ E 168
Obrian Peak see Trident Peak, Nev., U.S. 41°53′ N, 118°30′ W 90
O'Brien, Can. 47°40′ N, 80°45′ W 110
Obruk, Turk. 38°8′ N, 33°11′ E 156
Observation Peak, Calif., U.S. 40°45′ N, 120°16′ W 90
Obskaya Guba 67°26′ N, 71°48′ E 169
Obuasi, Ghana 6°15′ N, 1°40′ W 222
Obubra, Nig. 6°2′ N, 8°19′ E 222
Ob'yachevo, Russ. 60°21′ N, 49°39′ E 154
Obzor, Bulg. 42°49′ N, 27°52′ E 158
Oca, Montes de, Sp. 42°24′ N, 3°38′ W 164
Ocala, Fla., U.S. 29°10′ N, 82°9′ W 105
Ocampo, Mex. 22°49′ N, 99°19′ W 114
Ocampo, Mex. 21°36′ N, 101°29′ W 114
Ocaña, Col. 8°12′ N, 73°20′ W 136
Ocaña, Sp. 39°57′ N, 3°30′ W 164
Occidental, Cordillera, South America 4°36′ N, 76°51′ W 122
Occidental, Grand Erg, Alg. 30°22′ N, 0°26′ E 214
Ocean Cay, island, Bahamas 25°25′ N, 79°26′ W 105
Ocean City, Md., U.S. 38°20′ N, 75°6′ W 94
Ocean City, Wash., U.S. 47°3′ N, 124°10′ W 100
Ocean Falls, Can. 52°22′ N, 127°43′ W 108
Ocean Grove, Mass., U.S. 41°43′ N, 71°13′ W 104
Ocean Island see Kure Atoll, Hawai'i, U.S. 28°6′ N, 179°12′ W 99
Ocean Lake, lake, Wyo., U.S. 43°9′ N, 108°57′ W 90
Ocean Park, Wash., U.S. 46°28′ N, 124°3′ W 100
Ocean Springs, Miss., U.S. 30°24′ N, 88°50′ W 96
Oceano, Calif., U.S. 35°6′ N, 120°37′ W 100
Oceanographer Fracture Zone, North Atlantic Ocean 34°28′ N, 33°24′ W 253
Oceanside, Calif., U.S. 33°11′ N, 117°23′ W 101
Ochakiv, Ukr. 46°41′ N, 31°29′ E 156
Och'amch'ire, Asia 42°42′ N, 41°31′ E 195
Ocher, Russ. 57°52′ N, 54°49′ E 154
Ōchi, Japan 35°4′ N, 132°36′ E 201
Ochobo, Nig. 7°10′ N, 7°59′ E 222
Ochogavía, Sp. 42°55′ N, 1°6′ W 164
Ochopee, Fla., U.S. 25°53′ N, 81°18′ W 105
Ochre River, Can. 51°4′ N, 99°48′ W 90
Ochtrup, Ger. 52°12′ N, 7°12′ E 163
Ocilla, Ga., U.S. 31°35′ N, 83°16′ W 96
Ockelbo, Nor. 60°53′ N, 16°42′ E 152
Ocmulgee, river, Ga., U.S. 32°46′ N, 83°37′ W 80
Ocnele Mari, Rom. 45°5′ N, 24°17′ E 156
Ocniţa, Mold. 48°23′ N, 27°26′ E 156
Ocoee, Fla., U.S. 28°34′ N, 81°33′ W 105
Ocoña, Peru 16°27′ S, 73°6′ W 137
Ocoña, river, Peru 16°2′ S, 73°19′ W 137
Oconee, Lake, Ga., U.S. 33°21′ N, 83°39′ W 96
Oconee, river, Ga., U.S. 32°41′ N, 83°14′ W 80
Oconomowoc, Wis., U.S. 43°6′ N, 88°30′ W 102
Oconto, Wis., U.S. 44°54′ N, 87°52′ W 94
Oconto Falls, Wis., U.S. 44°52′ N, 88°8′ W 94
Ocoruro, Peru 15°4′ S, 71°8′ W 137
Ocós, Guatemala 14°32′ N, 92°12′ W 115
Ocotillo, Calif., U.S. 32°44′ N, 116°2′ W 101
Ocotillo Wells, Calif., U.S. 33°8′ N, 116°9′ W 101
Ocotlán, Mex. 20°21′ N, 102°46′ W 114
Ocoyo, Peru 14°3′ S, 75°1′ W 137
Ocracoke, N.C., U.S. 35°6′ N, 75°60′ W 96
Ocracoke Inlet 34°49′ N, 75°39′ W 80
Ócsa, Hung. 47°17′ N, 19°14′ E 168
Octave, river, Can. 48°52′ N, 78°35′ W 94
Ocumare del Tuy, Venez. 10°5′ N, 66°47′ W 136
Ocuri, Bol. 18°55′ S, 65°52′ W 137
Oda, Eth. 6°41′ N, 41°10′ E 224
Oda, Ghana 5°55′ N, 0°60′ E 222
Ōda, Japan 35°11′ N, 132°30′ E 201
Oda, Jebel, peak, Sudan 20°17′ N, 36°32′ E 182
Ŏdaejin, N. Korea 41°21′ N, 129°47′ E 200
Odanovce, Serb. and Mont. 42°32′ N, 21°41′ E 168
Odawara, Japan 35°15′ N, 139°9′ E 201
Odda, Nor. 60°5′ N, 6°31′ E 152
Oddur see Xuddur, Somalia 4°6′ N, 43°55′ E 218
Odebolt, Iowa, U.S. 42°18′ N, 95°15′ W 90
Odei, river, Can. 56°18′ N, 98°57′ W 108
Odell, Ill., U.S. 41°0′ N, 88°31′ W 102
Odell, Oreg., U.S. 45°36′ N, 121°33′ W 100
Ödemiş, Turk. 38°13′ N, 27°56′ E 156
Odendaalsrus, S. Af. 27°53′ S, 26°39′ E 227
Odense, Den. 55°23′ N, 10°23′ E 150
Odenwald, Ger. 49°45′ N, 8°35′ E 167
Odesa, Ukr. 46°28′ N, 30°43′ E 156
Odesdino, Russ. 63°28′ N, 54°25′ E 154
Odessa, Tex., U.S. 31°49′ N, 102°22′ W 92
Odessa, Wash., U.S. 47°18′ N, 118°42′ W 90
Odiel, river, Sp. 37°34′ N, 6°47′ W 164
Odienné, Côte d'Ivoire 9°31′ N, 7°34′ W 222
Odin, Mount, peak, Can. 50°32′ N, 118°14′ W 90
Odolanów, Pol. 51°35′ N, 17°41′ E 152
Odon, Ind., U.S. 38°50′ N, 86°60′ W 102
O'Donnell, Tex., U.S. 32°57′ N, 101°49′ W 92
Odra, river, Pol. 51°37′ N, 16°16′ E 160
Odra, river, Sp. 42°29′ N, 4°3′ W 164
Odžaci, Serb. and Mont. 45°29′ N, 19°16′ E 168
Odžak, Bosn. and Herzg. 45°0′ N, 18°18′ E 168
Odzala, Congo 0°32′ N, 14°34′ E 218
Odzala National Park, Congo 0°45′ N, 14°35′ E 206
Odzi, river, Zimb. 19°11′ S, 32°22′ E 224
Oecusse see Pante Makasar, Indonesia 9°21′ S, 124°20′ E 192
Oederan, Ger. 50°51′ N, 13°10′ E 152
Oeiras, Braz. 6°60′ S, 42°10′ W 132
Oelde, Ger. 51°49′ N, 8°7′ E 167
Oelrichs, S. Dak., U.S. 43°10′ N, 103°15′ W 90
Oelwein, Iowa, U.S. 42°40′ N, 91°55′ W 94
Oeniadae, ruin(s), Gr. 38°23′ N, 21°5′ E 156
Oenpelli, Austral. 12°22′ S, 133°6′ E 238
Oerlenbach, Ger. 50°9′ N, 10°7′ E 167
Oeta, Mount see Oiti, Óros, peak, Gr. 38°47′ N, 22°10′ E 156
Of, Turk. 40°57′ N, 40°17′ E 195
O'Fallon, Ill., U.S. 38°34′ N, 89°55′ W 102
O'Fallon Creek, river, Mont., U.S. 46°49′ N, 105°31′ W 90
Ofaqim, Israel 31°19′ N, 34°37′ E 194
Ofen Pass, Switz. 46°38′ N, 10°17′ E 167
Offa, Nig. 8°12′ N, 4°43′ E 222
Offenbach, Ger. 50°5′ N, 8°46′ E 167
Offutt Air Force Base, Nebr., U.S. 41°5′ N, 95°60′ W 90
Oficina Dominador, Chile 24°23′ S, 69°34′ W 132
Oficina, oil field, Venez. 8°43′ N, 64°27′ W 116
Oficina Santa Fe, Chile 21°52′ S, 69°37′ W 137
Ofin, river, Ghana 6°26′ N, 2°2′ W 222
Ofu, island, United States 14°11′ S, 169°38′ W 241
Ogadēn, region, Eth. 6°45′ N, 42°8′ E 224
Ōgaki, Japan 35°21′ N, 136°37′ E 201
Ogallala, Nebr., U.S. 41°7′ N, 101°44′ W 92
Ogasawara Guntō see Bonin Islands, North Pacific Ocean 25°25′ N, 143°8′ E 238
Ogbomosho, Nig. 8°10′ N, 4°16′ E 222
Ogden, Iowa, U.S. 42°0′ N, 94°2′ W 94
Ogden, Utah, U.S. 41°13′ N, 111°58′ W 90
Ogden, Mount, peak, Can. 58°25′ N, 133°32′ W 108
Ogema, Can. 49°33′ N, 104°56′ W 90
Oggiono, It. 45°46′ N, 9°19′ E 167
Ogi, Japan 37°49′ N, 138°16′ E 201
Ogilvie Mountains, Can. 64°46′ N, 139°9′ W 106
Oglanly, Turkm. 39°52′ N, 54°22′ E 180
Oglat Beraber, spring, Alg. 30°24′ N, 3°34′ W 214
Oglat d'Admamlalmat, spring, Mauritania 23°25′ N, 11°48′ W 214
'Oglât ed Daoud, spring, Mauritania 23°31′ N, 6°57′ W 214
'Oglât el Fersig, spring, Mauritania 21°49′ N, 6°21′ W 222
'Oglat el Khnâchîch, spring, Mali 21°51′ N, 3°59′ W 222
Oglats de Mkhaïzira, spring, Mauritania 22°44′ N, 10°18′ W 214
Oglesby, Ill., U.S. 41°17′ N, 89°5′ W 102
Oglethorpe, Ga., U.S. 32°17′ N, 84°4′ W 96
Oglethorpe, Mount, peak, Ga., U.S. 34°28′ N, 84°24′ W 96
Ogna, Nor. 58°31′ N, 5°48′ E 150
Ognev Yar, Russ. 58°21′ N, 76°30′ E 169
Ognon, river, Fr. 47°17′ N, 5°59′ E 165
Ogoja, Nig. 6°38′ N, 8°42′ E 222
Ogoki, Can. 51°40′ N, 85°52′ W 82
Ogoki Reservoir, lake, Can. 50°50′ N, 89°14′ W 80
Ogoki, river, Can. 51°5′ N, 86°10′ W 110
Ögöömör, Mongolia 46°47′ N, 107°50′ E 198
Ogōri, Japan 34°6′ N, 131°24′ E 200
Ogou, river, Togo 8°48′ N, 1°25′ E 222
Ogr, Sudan 12°2′ N, 27°1′ E 218
Ogražden, Maced. 41°25′ N, 22°52′ E 168
Ogre, Latv. 56°49′ N, 24°33′ E 166
Ogre, river, Latv. 56°46′ N, 25°27′ E 166
'Ogueïlet en Nmâdi, spring, Mauritania 19°45′ N, 11°1′ W 222
Oguma, Nig. 7°51′ N, 7°2′ E 222
Ogunquit, Me., U.S. 43°14′ N, 70°37′ W 104
Ogwashi Uku, Nig. 6°17′ N, 6°28′ E 222
Ohanet, oil field, Alg. 28°46′ N, 8°49′ E 214
Ohangoron, Uzb. 40°56′ N, 69°35′ E 197
Ohau, N.Z. 40°41′ S, 175°15′ E 240
Óhi, Óros, peak, Gr. 38°3′ N, 24°23′ E 156
Ohio, Ill., U.S. 41°33′ N, 89°28′ W 102
Ohio, adm. division, Ohio, U.S. 40°15′ N, 83°3′ W 102
Ohio City, Ohio, U.S. 40°45′ N, 84°37′ W 102
Ohio Range, Antarctica 85°4′ S, 101°32′ W 248
Ohio, river, U.S. 37°37′ N, 87°7′ W 80
Ōi, river, Japan 35°9′ N, 138°8′ E 201
Oiapoque, Braz. 3°50′ N, 51°48′ W 130
Oijärvi, Fin. 65°38′ N, 25°48′ E 152
Oil City, La., U.S. 32°44′ N, 93°58′ W 103
Oil City, Pa., U.S. 41°24′ N, 79°43′ W 94
Oil Islands see Chagos Archipelago, Indian Ocean 6°42′ S, 71°25′ E 188
Oildale, Calif., U.S. 35°25′ N, 119°2′ W 101
Oilton, Okla., U.S. 36°3′ N, 96°35′ W 92
Oilton, Tex., U.S. 27°27′ N, 98°58′ W 92
Oise, river, Fr. 49°51′ N, 3°39′ E 163
Ōita, Japan 33°13′ N, 131°37′ E 201
Ōita, adm. division, Japan 33°42′ N, 131°34′ E 200
Oíti, Óros (Oeta, Mount), peak, Gr. 38°47′ N, 22°10′ E 156
Oiticica, South America 5°2′ S, 41°6′ W 132
Oituz, Rom. 46°6′ N, 26°23′ E 156
Ojai, Calif., U.S. 34°26′ N, 119°15′ W 101
Öje, Nor. 60°48′ N, 13°49′ E 152
Ojeda, Arg. 35°18′ S, 63°59′ W 139
Ojinaga, Mex. 29°33′ N, 104°27′ W 92
Ojiya, Japan 37°17′ N, 138°47′ E 201
Ojo Caliente, Mex. 22°33′ N, 102°16′ W 114
Ojo de Laguna, Mex. 29°26′ N, 106°25′ W 92
Ojós, Sp. 38°8′ N, 1°22′ W 164
Ojos del Salado, Cerro, peak, Chile 27°6′ S, 68°45′ W 132
Ojuelos de Jalisco, Mex. 21°51′ N, 101°35′ W 114
Oka, river, Russ. 55°43′ N, 42°12′ E 154
Oka, river, Russ. 53°14′ N, 36°17′ E 154
Okaba, Indonesia 8°7′ S, 139°37′ E 192
Okahandja, Namibia 21°59′ S, 16°53′ E 227
Okahukura, N.Z. 38°49′ S, 175°14′ E 240
Okak Islands, Can. 57°32′ N, 65°21′ W 106
Okakarara, Namibia 20°36′ S, 17°30′ E 227
Okaloacoochee Slough, marsh, Fla., U.S. 26°26′ N, 80°42′ W 105
Okanagan Lake, Can. 49°50′ N, 120°51′ W 80
Okanogan, Wash., U.S. 48°21′ N, 119°37′ W 90
Okanogan Range, Wash., U.S. 48°48′ N, 120°27′ W 90
Okány, Hung. 46°53′ N, 21°21′ E 168
Okaputa, Namibia 20°7′ S, 16°58′ E 227
Okara, Pak. 30°49′ N, 73°27′ E 186
Okatjoruu, Namibia 19°38′ S, 18°34′ E 220
Okaukuejo, Namibia 19°9′ S, 15°57′ E 220
Okavango Delta, Botswana 19°33′ S, 23°16′ E 224
Ōkawa, Japan 33°12′ N, 130°22′ E 201
Okawville, Ill., U.S. 38°25′ N, 89°33′ W 102
Okaya, Japan 36°4′ N, 138°2′ E 201
Okayama, Japan 34°38′ N, 133°53′ E 201
Okayama, adm. division, Japan 34°54′ N, 133°20′ E 201
Okazaki, Japan 34°56′ N, 137°10′ E 201
Okcheon, S. Korea 36°18′ N, 127°34′ E 200
Okeechobee, Fla., U.S. 27°15′ N, 80°50′ W 105
Okeechobee, Lake, Fla., U.S. 26°57′ N, 80°59′ W 105
Okeene, Okla., U.S. 36°6′ N, 98°20′ W 92
Okefenokee Swamp, marsh, Ga., U.S. 30°35′ N, 83°9′ W 80
Okene, Nig. 7°34′ N, 6°14′ E 222
Okha, India 22°26′ N, 69°3′ E 186
Okha, Russ. 53°33′ N, 142°43′ E 160
Okhaldhunga, Nepal 27°20′ N, 86°30′ E 197
Okhansk, Russ. 57°42′ N, 55°19′ E 154
Okhotsk, Russ. 59°26′ N, 143°20′ E 160
Okhotsk, Sea of 57°51′ N, 141°45′ E 160
Okhotskiy Perevoz, Russ. 61°52′ N, 135°38′ E 160
Okhtyrka, Ukr. 50°19′ N, 34°55′ E 158
Oki Guntō, islands, Sea of Japan 35°59′ N, 133°6′ E 201
Okiep, S. Af. 29°36′ S, 17°52′ E 227
Okinawa, island, Japan 26°22′ N, 128°16′ E 190
Okino Erabu Shima, island, Japan 27°2′ N, 128°25′ E 190
Okkang, N. Korea 40°18′ N, 124°46′ E 200
Oklahoma, adm. division, Okla., U.S. 35°37′ N, 98°23′ W 96
Oklahoma City, Okla., U.S. 35°25′ N, 97°36′ W 92
Oklawaha, Fla., U.S. 29°2′ N, 81°56′ W 105
Okletac, Serb. and Mont. 44°5′ N, 19°34′ E 168
Okmulgee, Okla., U.S. 35°36′ N, 95°58′ W 94
Okolona, Miss., U.S. 33°58′ N, 88°45′ W 96
Okotoks, Can. 50°44′ N, 113°59′ W 90
Okounfo, Benin 8°20′ N, 2°37′ E 222
Okoyo, Congo 1°27′ S, 15°1′ E 218
Okpara, river, Africa 7°44′ N, 2°37′ E 222
Okp'yŏng, N. Korea 39°16′ N, 127°20′ E 200
Oksino, Russ. 67°34′ N, 52°20′ E 169
Oksovskiy, Russ. 62°36′ N, 39°56′ E 154
Okstindan, peak, Nor. 65°59′ N, 14°11′ E 152
Oktyabr'sk, Kaz. 49°26′ N, 57°25′ E 158
Oktyabr'skīy, Kaz. 49°39′ N, 83°37′ E 184
Oktyabr'skiy, Russ. 55°5′ N, 60°10′ E 154
Oktyabr'skiy, Russ. 47°55′ N, 43°34′ E 158
Oktyabr'skiy, Russ. 54°27′ N, 53°35′ E 154
Oktyabr'skoe, Kaz. 52°8′ N, 65°40′ E 184
Oktyabr'skoye, Russ. 62°34′ N, 66°2′ E 160
Oktyabr'skoye, Russ. 52°23′ N, 55°37′ E 154
Oktyabr'skoye, Russ. 52°21′ N, 55°22′ E 184
Okučani, Croatia 45°15′ N, 17°12′ E 168
Ōkuchi, Japan 32°3′ N, 130°37′ E 201
Okulovka, Russ. 58°24′ N, 33°19′ E 154
Okunev Nos, Russ. 66°16′ N, 52°39′ E 154
Okushiri, island, Japan 41°45′ N, 138°29′ E 190
Okuta, Nig. 9°12′ N, 3°15′ E 222
Ola, Ark., U.S. 35°1′ N, 93°14′ W 96
Ola, Russ. 59°37′ N, 151°11′ E 160
Ólafsvík, Ice. 64°53′ N, 23°45′ W 246
Olaine, Latv. 56°48′ N, 23°57′ E 166
Olancha, Calif., U.S. 36°17′ N, 118°2′ W 101
Olancha Peak, Calif., U.S. 36°15′ N, 118°10′ W 101
Olanchito, Hond. 15°28′ N, 86°35′ W 115
Ölands Norra Udde, Sw. 57°23′ N, 16°58′ E 152
Ölands Södra Udde, Sw. 55°54′ N, 16°3′ E 152
Olanga, Russ. 66°9′ N, 30°35′ E 152
Olary, Austral. 32°16′ S, 140°20′ E 231
Olasan, spring, Eth. 5°17′ N, 45°4′ E 218
Olascoaga, Arg. 35°15′ S, 60°39′ W 139
Olathe, Kans., U.S. 38°51′ N, 94°49′ W 94
Olavarría, Arg. 36°55′ S, 60°17′ W 139
Olbia, It. 40°55′ N, 9°28′ E 214
Old Cove Fort, site, Utah, U.S. 38°39′ N, 112°38′ W 90
Old Crow, Can. 67°32′ N, 139°56′ W 73
Old Dongola, ruin(s), Sudan 18°12′ N, 30°42′ E 226
Old Fort, Can. 55°4′ N, 126°20′ W 108
Old Man of the Mountain, site, N.H., U.S. 44°10′ N, 71°44′ W 104
Old Mkushi, Zambia 14°22′ S, 29°20′ E 224
Old Orchard Beach, Me., U.S. 43°30′ N, 70°24′ W 104
Old Rhodes Key, island, Fla., U.S. 25°22′ N, 80°14′ W 105
Old Sarum, ruin(s), U.K. 51°5′ N, 1°50′ W 162
Old Saybrook, Conn., U.S. 41°17′ N, 72°23′ W 104
Old Slains Castle, site, U.K. 57°20′ N, 2°1′ W 150
Old Speck Mountain, peak, Me., U.S. 44°33′ N, 70°60′ W 104
Old Sturbridge, site, Mass., U.S. 42°5′ N, 72°8′ W 104
Old Sugar Mill, site, Hawai'i, U.S. 21°30′ N, 157°53′ W 99
Old Town, Fla., U.S. 29°36′ N, 82°60′ W 105
Old Wives Lake, Can. 50°3′ N, 106°39′ W 90
Old Woman Mountains, Calif., U.S. 34°26′ N, 115°25′ W 101
Oldbury, U.K. 52°29′ N, 2°1′ W 162
Oldeani, Tanzania 3°20′ S, 35°34′ E 224
Olden, Nor. 61°50′ N, 6°49′ E 152
Oldenburg, Ger. 53°8′ N, 8°13′ E 163
Oldenzaal, Neth. 52°18′ N, 6°55′ E 163
Oldham, U.K. 53°32′ N, 2°7′ W 162
Olds, Can. 51°49′ N, 114°6′ W 90
Olduvai Gorge, site, Tanzania 2°57′ S, 35°14′ E 224
Öldzeyte Suma, Mongolia 44°33′ N, 106°10′ E 198
Öldziyt, Mongolia 44°39′ N, 109°3′ E 198
Olean, N.Y., U.S. 42°4′ N, 78°27′ W 94
Olecko, Pol. 54°1′ N, 22°31′ E 166
Olekma, river, Russ. 59°23′ N, 120°19′ E 160
Olekminsk, Russ. 60°23′ N, 120°16′ E 160
Oleksandriya, Ukr. 50°44′ N, 26°20′ E 152
Olema, Russ. 64°28′ N, 46°2′ E 154
Ølen, Nor. 59°35′ N, 5°47′ E 152
Olenegorsk, Russ. 68°8′ N, 33°15′ E 152
Olenek, Russ. 68°30′ N, 112°22′ E 160
Olenek, river, Russ. 66°59′ N, 107°5′ E 160
Olenekskiy Zaliv 72°54′ N, 114°57′ E 160
Olenino, Russ. 56°12′ N, 33°37′ E 154
Olenitsa, Russ. 66°26′ N, 35°13′ E 152
Oleniy, Ostrov, island, Russ. 72°2′ N, 72°25′ E 160
Olesno, Pol. 50°52′ N, 18°25′ E 152
Olevs'k, Ukr. 51°13′ N, 27°40′ E 152
Ølfjellet, peak, Nor. 66°46′ N, 15°4′ E 152
Olga, Lac, lake, Can. 49°45′ N, 77°35′ W 94
Olga, Mount see Kata Tjuta, peak, Austral. 25°21′ S, 130°31′ E 230
Olgastretet 78°6′ N, 20°12′ E 160
Ölgiy, Mongolia 48°57′ N, 89°50′ E 184

Ølgod, Den. 55°48′ N, 8°35′ E 150
Olhava, Fin. 65°28′ N, 25°22′ E 152
Oli Qoltyq Sory, marsh, Kaz. 45°20′ N, 53°31′ E 158
Oli, river, Nig. 9°46′ N, 4°0′ E 222
Oliete, Sp. 40°59′ N, 0°41′ E 164
Olifants, river, S. Af. 24°36′ S, 30°29′ E 227
Olifantshoek, S. Af. 27°58′ S, 22°42′ E 227
Olimarao Atoll 7°48′ N, 143°3′ E 192
Ólimbos, Gr. 35°44′ N, 27°11′ E 156
Ólimbos, Óros (Olympus), peak, Gr. 40°3′ N, 22°17′ E 156
Olímpia, Braz. 20°43′ S, 48°55′ W 138
Olinalá, Mex. 17°48′ N, 98°51′ W 114
Olinda, Braz. 7°60′ S, 34°55′ W 138
Olinda Entrance 11°17′ S, 142°53′ E 192
Olite, Sp. 42°28′ N, 1°39′ W 164
Oliva, Arg. 32°3′ S, 63°33′ W 139
Oliva, Sp. 38°55′ N, 0°8′ E 164
Oliva de la Frontera, Sp. 38°16′ N, 6°56′ W 150
Oliveira, Braz. 20°40′ S, 44°51′ W 138
Oliver, Can. 49°10′ N, 119°34′ W 90
Oliver Lake, lake, Can. 56°50′ N, 103°50′ W 108
Olivet, Mich., U.S. 42°27′ N, 84°55′ W 102
Olivia, Minn., U.S. 44°46′ N, 94°60′ W 90
Ol'khovka, Russ. 49°51′ N, 44°31′ E 158
Olla, La., U.S. 31°53′ N, 92°15′ W 103
Ollachea, Peru 13°49′ S, 70°32′ W 137
Ollagüe (Oyahue), Chile 21°14′ S, 68°18′ W 137
Ollagüe, Volcan, peak, Chile 21°19′ S, 68°20′ W 137
Ollanta, Peru 9°45′ S, 74°2′ W 137
Ollerton, U.K. 53°11′ N, 1°2′ W 162
Oława, Pol. 50°57′ N, 17°17′ E 152
Olmaliq, Uzb. 40°50′ N, 69°35′ E 197
Olnes, Alas., U.S. 65°5′ N, 147°40′ W 98
Olney, Ill., U.S. 38°42′ N, 88°1′ W 82
Olney, Tex., U.S. 33°21′ N, 98°46′ W 92
Olney, U.K. 52°9′ N, 0°42′ E 162
Oloibiri, oil field, Nig. 4°39′ N, 6°16′ E 222
Olomouc, Czech Rep. 49°35′ N, 17°16′ E 152
Olonets, Russ. 60°56′ N, 33°2′ E 154
Olongapo, Philippines 14°50′ N, 120°17′ E 203
Olonzac, Fr. 43°16′ N, 2°42′ E 164
Oloron, Fr. 43°12′ N, 0°36′ E 164
Oloru, Nig. 8°39′ N, 4°35′ E 222
Olosega, island, United States 14°11′ S, 169°36′ W 241
Olot, Sp. 42°11′ N, 2°28′ E 164
Olovo, Bosn. and Herzg. 44°7′ N, 18°34′ E 168
Olovyannaya, Russ. 50°54′ N, 115°24′ E 190
Olovyannaya, Russ. 66°13′ N, 178°56′ W 98
Oloy, river, Russ. 66°12′ N, 160°20′ E 160
Olpe, Ger. 51°1′ N, 7°50′ E 167
Olshammar, Nor. 58°45′ N, 14°45′ E 152
Olsztyn, Pol. 53°46′ N, 20°28′ E 166
Olt, adm. division, Rom. 44°11′ N, 24°12′ E 156
Olt, river, Rom. 45°46′ N, 24°19′ E 156
Olten, Switz. 47°21′ N, 7°53′ E 156
Olteni, Rom. 44°11′ N, 25°18′ E 156
Oltenița, Rom. 44°6′ N, 26°39′ E 156
Olton, Tex., U.S. 34°9′ N, 102°8′ W 92
Oltu, Turk. 40°34′ N, 41°57′ E 195
Oltu, river, Turk. 40°43′ N, 41°41′ E 195
Oluan Pi, Taiwan 21°39′ N, 120°53′ E 198
Olukonda, Namibia 18°6′ S, 16°4′ E 220
Ólvega, Sp. 41°45′ N, 1°59′ W 164
Olvera, Sp. 36°55′ N, 5°17′ W 164
Olympia, Wash., U.S. 47°1′ N, 122°56′ W 100
Olympia, ruin(s), Gr. 37°38′ N, 21°32′ E 156
Olympic Mountains, Wash., U.S. 47°16′ N, 123°50′ W 100
Olympic National Park, Wash., U.S. 48°0′ N, 125°7′ W 100
Olympos, peak, Cyprus 34°55′ N, 32°50′ E 194
Olympus, Mount, peak, Wash., U.S. 47°47′ N, 123°45′ W 100
Olympus, Mount see Ulu Dağ, peak, Turk. 40°4′ N, 29°7′ E 156
Olympus see Ólimbos, Óros, peak, Gr. 40°3′ N, 22°17′ E 156
Olynthus, ruin(s), Gr. 40°16′ N, 23°17′ E 156
Olyutorskiy, Mys, Russ. 59°44′ N, 170°18′ E 160
Om', river, Russ. 55°17′ N, 77°33′ E 184
Oma, China 32°26′ N, 83°17′ E 188
Oma, Miss., U.S. 31°43′ N, 90°9′ W 103
Oma, river, Russ. 66°23′ N, 46°47′ E 154
Ōmachi, Japan 36°30′ N, 137°51′ E 201
Omae Zaki, Japan 34°29′ N, 138°14′ E 201
Omaha, Nebr., U.S. 41°15′ N, 95°58′ W 90
Omaha, Tex., U.S. 33°10′ N, 94°45′ W 103
Omaha Beach, Fr. 49°17′ N, 1°13′ W 150
Omak, Wash., U.S. 48°24′ N, 119°33′ W 90
Omakau, N.Z. 45°5′ S, 169°38′ E 240
Omakere, N.Z. 40°3′ S, 176°49′ E 240
Oman 21°52′ N, 57°32′ E 182
Oman, Gulf of 24°46′ N, 57°23′ E 172
Oman, Gulf of 24°30′ N, 58°46′ E 254
Omarama, N.Z. 44°31′ S, 169°58′ E 240
Omaruru, Namibia 21°27′ S, 15°55′ E 227
Ombabika, Can. 50°14′ N, 87°54′ W 94
Ombaïa, Congo 2°24′ S, 13°10′ E 218
Ombombo, spring, Namibia 18°44′ S, 13°55′ E 220
Ombwe, Dem. Rep. of the Congo 4°23′ S, 25°32′ E 224
Omchali, Mys, Turkm. 40°54′ N, 53°5′ E 158
Omdurman, Sudan 15°36′ N, 32°27′ E 182
Omegna, It. 45°52′ N, 8°24′ E 167
Omer, Mich., U.S. 44°3′ N, 83°51′ W 102
Ometepec, Mex. 16°30′ N, 98°28′ W 73
Ōmihachiman, Japan 35°6′ N, 136°5′ E 201
Omihi, N.Z. 43°2′ S, 172°52′ E 240
Omineca, river, Can. 55°54′ N, 126°9′ W 108
Omiš, Croatia 43°26′ N, 16°42′ E 168
Ōmiya, Japan 35°54′ N, 139°38′ E 201
Ommaney, Cape, Alas., U.S. 56°0′ N, 135°20′ W 108
Ommen, Neth. 52°31′ N, 6°24′ E 163
Omo National Park, Eth. 5°39′ N, 35°20′ E 224
Omo, river, Eth. 5°54′ N, 35°55′ E 224
Omolon, Russ. 65°10′ N, 160°34′ E 173
Omolon, river, Russ. 69°30′ N, 155°38′ E 172
Omoloy, river, Russ. 69°50′ N, 132°42′ E 160
Omont, Fr. 49°35′ N, 4°42′ E 163
Omro, Wis., U.S. 44°1′ N, 88°45′ W 102
Omsk, Russ. 54°58′ N, 73°26′ E 184
Omsk, adm. division, Russ. 54°44′ N, 72°20′ E 184
Omsukchan, Russ. 62°29′ N, 155°44′ E 173
Omu Aran, Nig. 8°9′ N, 5°6′ E 222
Omul, peak, Rom. 45°26′ N, 25°22′ E 156
Omullyakhskaya Guba 72°1′ N, 138°2′ E 160
Ōmura, Japan 32°54′ N, 129°58′ E 201
Ōmuta, Japan 33°1′ N, 130°26′ E 201
Omutninsk, Russ. 58°40′ N, 52°15′ E 154
Oña, Sp. 42°43′ N, 3°26′ W 164
Onaga, Kans., U.S. 39°28′ N, 96°10′ W 90
Onakawana, Can. 50°36′ N, 81°27′ W 110
Onalaska, Tex., U.S. 30°47′ N, 95°7′ W 103
Onaman Lake, Can. 50°0′ N, 87°59′ W 110
Onamia, Minn., U.S. 46°3′ N, 93°41′ W 94
Onaping Lake, Can. 46°56′ N, 82°3′ W 94
Onarga, Ill., U.S. 40°42′ N, 88°1′ W 102
Onatchiway, Lac, lake, Can. 48°59′ N, 71°46′ W 94
Oñati, Sp. 43°1′ N, 2°24′ W 164
Onavas, Mex. 28°27′ N, 109°32′ W 92
Onawa, Iowa, U.S. 42°0′ N, 96°6′ W 90
Oncativo, Arg. 31°55′ S, 63°41′ W 139
Onda, Sp. 39°58′ N, 0°17′ E 164
Ondangwa, Namibia 17°56′ S, 15°59′ E 220
Ondas, river, Braz. 12°42′ S, 46°4′ W 132
Ondjiva, Angola 17°6′ S, 15°39′ E 220
Ondo, Nig. 7°7′ N, 4°49′ E 222
Ondor Sum, China 42°30′ N, 112°50′ E 198
Öndörhaan, Mongolia 47°22′ N, 110°40′ E 198
Öndörhushuu, Mongolia 47°59′ N, 113°55′ E 198
One and Half Degree Channel 0°58′ N, 72°7′ E 188
Oneco, Conn., U.S. 41°41′ N, 71°49′ W 104
Oneco, Fla., U.S. 27°27′ N, 82°32′ W 105
Onega, Russ. 63°55′ N, 38°12′ E 154
Oneida, N.Y., U.S. 43°5′ N, 75°41′ W 94
Oneida, Tenn., U.S. 36°29′ N, 84°31′ W 96
Oneida Lake, N.Y., U.S. 43°14′ N, 76°34′ W 80
O'Neill, Nebr., U.S. 42°26′ N, 98°40′ W 90
Oneonta, Ala., U.S. 33°56′ N, 86°29′ W 96
Oneonta, N.Y., U.S. 42°27′ N, 75°5′ W 94
Onezhskaya Guba 64°4′ N, 36°13′ E 154
Onezhskoye Ozero, lake, Russ. 60°31′ N, 33°29′ E 160
Ongarue, N.Z. 38°43′ S, 175°17′ E 240
Ongcheon, S. Korea 36°41′ N, 128°42′ E 200
Ongi, Mongolia 45°28′ N, 103°56′ E 198
Ongjin, N. Korea 37°55′ N, 125°22′ E 200
Ongniud Qi, China 42°56′ N, 118°59′ E 198
Ongoka, Dem. Rep. of the Congo 1°24′ S, 26°2′ E 224
Ongole, India 15°30′ N, 80°4′ E 188
Ongtustik Qazaqstan, adm. division, Kaz. 42°4′ N, 67°24′ E 197
Ongwediva, Namibia 17°55′ S, 15°54′ E 220
Oni, Ga. 42°33′ N, 43°27′ E 195
Onib, Sudan 21°26′ N, 35°16′ E 182
Onitsha, Nig. 6°15′ N, 6°46′ E 222
Onizuka Center for International Astronomy, site, Hawai'i, U.S. 19°43′ N, 155°29′ W 99
Önjüül, Mongolia 46°46′ N, 105°32′ E 198
Onley, Va., U.S. 37°41′ N, 75°44′ W 94
Onnela, Fin. 69°54′ N, 26°59′ E 152
Ōno, Japan 35°58′ N, 136°29′ E 201
Onoda, Japan 33°58′ N, 131°11′ E 200
Onolimbu, Indonesia 1°3′ N, 97°51′ E 196
Onomichi, Japan 34°25′ N, 133°12′ E 201
Onon, Mongolia 49°9′ N, 112°41′ E 198
Onon, Mongolia 48°32′ N, 110°30′ E 198
Onon, river, Asia 49°19′ N, 112°28′ E 198
Onoto, Venez. 9°36′ N, 65°12′ W 136
Onoway, Can. 53°42′ N, 114°13′ W 108
Onsen, Japan 35°32′ N, 134°29′ E 201
Onslow, Austral. 21°39′ S, 115°7′ E 231
Onsŏng, N. Korea 42°57′ N, 129°59′ E 200
Onsugok, S. Korea 37°37′ N, 126°28′ E 200
Ontario, Calif., U.S. 34°3′ N, 117°40′ W 101
Ontario, Ohio, U.S. 40°44′ N, 82°38′ W 102
Ontario, Oreg., U.S. 43°58′ N, 116°58′ W 82
Ontario, adm. division, Can. 51°1′ N, 90°29′ W 106
Ontario, Lake 43°37′ N, 78°57′ W 80
Ontojärvi, lake, Fin. 64°19′ N, 26°24′ E 154
Ontong Java Atoll, islands, South Pacific Ocean 7°9′ S, 159°58′ E 238
Ontur, Sp. 38°36′ N, 1°30′ W 164
Onuškis, Lith. 54°27′ N, 24°36′ E 166
Onyx, Calif., U.S. 35°41′ N, 118°15′ W 101
Oodaaq Island, 83°32′ N, 30°53′ W 255
Oodnadatta, Austral. 27°34′ S, 135°27′ E 231
Oodweyne, Somalia 9°22′ N, 45°5′ E 216
Ooldea, Austral. 30°28′ S, 131°50′ E 231
Oolitic, Ind., U.S. 38°53′ N, 86°33′ W 102
Oona River, Can. 53°57′ N, 130°19′ W 108
Ooruk-Tam, Kyrg. 41°26′ N, 76°39′ E 184
Oost Vlieland, Neth. 53°17′ N, 5°2′ E 163
Oostburg, Wis., U.S. 43°37′ N, 87°48′ W 102
Oostende (Ostend), Belg. 51°13′ N, 2°55′ E 163
Oosterhout, Neth. 51°39′ N, 4°51′ E 167
Ootsa Lake, Can. 53°50′ N, 126°3′ W 108
Opachuanau Lake, lake, Can. 56°42′ N, 100°14′ W 108
Opal, Wyo., U.S. 41°47′ N, 110°19′ W 92
Opala, Dem. Rep. of the Congo 0°38′ N, 24°20′ E 224
Opari, Sudan 3°55′ N, 32°5′ E 224
Oparino, Russ. 59°52′ N, 48°14′ E 154
Opasatica, Lac, lake, Can. 48°1′ N, 79°53′ W 110
Opasatika Lake, lake, Can. 49°2′ N, 83°40′ W 94
Opasatika, river, Can. 49°32′ N, 82°56′ W 94
Opataca, Lac, lake, Can. 50°13′ N, 75°49′ W 94
Opataouaga, Lac, lake, Can. 50°19′ N, 77°24′ W 94
Opelika, Ala., U.S. 32°38′ N, 85°24′ W 96
Opelousas, La., U.S. 30°30′ N, 92°6′ W 103
Opheim, Mont., U.S. 48°50′ N, 106°25′ W 90
Ophir, peak, Indonesia 8°475′ N, 99°55′ E 196
Ophthalmia Range, Austral. 23°24′ S, 118°34′ E 230
Opienge, Dem. Rep. of the Congo 0°15′ N, 27°21′ E 224
Opinaca, Réservoir, lake, Can. 52°3′ N, 77°47′ W 110
Opinaca, river, Can. 52°14′ N, 78°18′ W 106
Opladen, Ger. 51°4′ N, 7°0′ E 167
Oploca, Bol. 21°22′ S, 65°48′ W 137
Opobo, Nig. 4°34′ N, 7°32′ E 222
Opochka, Russ. 56°41′ N, 28°40′ E 166
Opoczno, Pol. 51°23′ N, 20°15′ E 152
Opodepe, Mex. 29°55′ N, 110°38′ W 92
Opole, Pol. 50°39′ N, 17°57′ E 152
Opornyy, Kaz. 46°3′ N, 54°37′ E 158
Oporto see Porto, Port. 41°8′ N, 8°38′ W 150
Opotiki, N.Z. 38°2′ S, 177°19′ E 240
Opp, Ala., U.S. 31°16′ N, 86°15′ W 96
Oppenheim, Ger. 49°50′ N, 8°21′ E 167
Oppola, Russ. 61°34′ N, 30°19′ E 166
Oprişoru, Rom. 44°16′ N, 23°6′ E 168
Opsa, Belarus 55°32′ N, 26°49′ E 166
Opua, N.Z. 35°21′ S, 174°5′ E 240
Opukhliki, Russ. 56°5′ N, 30°9′ E 166
Opunake, N.Z. 39°28′ S, 173°51′ E 240
Opuwo, Namibia 18°6′ S, 13°50′ E 220
Oqtosh, Uzb. 39°55′ N, 65°55′ E 197
Or, Les Îles d' see Hyères, Îles d', islands, Mediterranean Sea 42°57′ N, 6°33′ E 165
Or, river, Asia 49°38′ N, 58°38′ E 158
Ora, oil field, Lib. 28°26′ N, 19°15′ E 216
Oradea, Rom. 47°3′ N, 21°57′ E 168
Öræfajökull, glacier, Ice. 63°52′ N, 15°30′ W 142
Orahovica, Croatia 45°32′ N, 17°54′ E 168
Oral, Kaz. 51°12′ N, 51°24′ E 158
Oran, Alg. 35°39′ N, 0°38′ E 214
Orange, Fr. 44°8′ N, 4°47′ E 214
Orange, Mass., U.S. 42°35′ N, 72°19′ W 104
Orange, Tex., U.S. 30°5′ N, 93°45′ W 103
Orange, Va., U.S. 38°14′ N, 78°7′ W 94
Orange, Cabo, Braz. 4°26′ N, 51°35′ W 130
Orange City, Fla., U.S. 28°57′ N, 81°19′ W 105
Orange City, Iowa, U.S. 42°58′ N, 96°5′ W 90
Orange Cove, Calif., U.S. 36°37′ N, 119°20′ W 100
Orange Grove, Tex., U.S. 27°56′ N, 97°56′ W 96
Orange (Oranje), river, Africa 28°40′ S, 18°39′ E 227
Orange, river, S. Af. 30°46′ S, 26°51′ E 227
Orange Walk, Belize 18°5′ N, 88°35′ W 115
Orangeburg, S.C., U.S. 33°29′ N, 80°51′ W 96
Orangeville, Can. 43°55′ N, 80°6′ W 94
Orangeville, Ill., U.S. 42°27′ N, 89°39′ W 102
Orango, island, Guinea-Bissau 11°1′ N, 16°41′ W 222
Oranienburg, Ger. 52°45′ N, 13°14′ E 152
Oranje Gebergte, Suriname 3°12′ N, 56°2′ W 130
Oranje see Orange, river, Africa 28°40′ S, 18°39′ E 227
Oranjemund, Namibia 28°31′ S, 16°25′ E 227
Oranjestad, Aruba, Neth. 12°34′ N, 70°2′ W 118
Oranzherei, Russ. 45°49′ N, 47°35′ E 158
Orapa, Botswana 21°16′ S, 25°17′ E 227
Orari, N.Z. 44°9′ S, 171°17′ E 240
Oras, Philippines 12°10′ N, 125°26′ E 203
Orašac, Maced. 42°3′ N, 21°48′ E 168
Orašje, Bosn. and Herzg. 45°1′ N, 18°40′ E 168
Oravais (Oravainen), Fin. 63°16′ N, 22°21′ E 152
Orawia, N.Z. 46°4′ S, 167°46′ E 240
Orba Co, lake, China 34°28′ N, 80°29′ E 188
Örbyhus, Nor. 60°13′ N, 17°39′ E 152
Orcadas, station, Antarctica 60°46′ S, 44°52′ W 134
Orce, Sp. 37°42′ N, 2°29′ W 164
Orcera, Sp. 38°18′ N, 2°39′ W 164
Orchard City, Colo., U.S. 38°50′ N, 107°58′ W 92
Orchards, Wash., U.S. 45°39′ N, 122°34′ W 100
Orchies, Fr. 50°28′ N, 3°14′ E 163
Orchomenus, ruin(s), Gr. 38°29′ N, 22°50′ E 156
Orcières, Fr. 44°41′ N, 6°19′ E 167
Orco, river, It. 45°23′ N, 7°25′ E 167
Orcutt, Calif., U.S. 34°51′ N, 120°28′ W 100
Ord, Nebr., U.S. 41°35′ N, 98°57′ W 90
Ord, Mount, peak, Austral. 17°22′ S, 125°22′ E 230
Ord Mountains, Calif., U.S. 34°40′ N, 116°49′ W 101
Orda, Russ. 57°11′ N, 56°56′ E 154
Orderville, Utah, U.S. 37°16′ N, 112°38′ W 92
Ordu, Turk. 40°58′ N, 37°51′ E 156
Ordubad, Asia 38°53′ N, 46°0′ E 195
Orduña, Sp. 42°58′ N, 3°2′ W 164
Orduña, peak, Sp. 37°19′ N, 3°33′ W 164
Ordway, Colo., U.S. 38°13′ N, 103°46′ W 90
Ordzhonīkīdze, Kaz. 52°27′ N, 61°41′ E 184
Ordzhonikidze, Ukr. 47°41′ N, 34°5′ E 156
Ore City, Tex., U.S. 32°48′ N, 94°44′ W 103
Orea, Sp. 40°32′ N, 1°43′ W 164
Oreana, Ill., U.S. 39°56′ N, 88°52′ W 102
Orebić, Croatia 42°58′ N, 17°9′ E 168
Örebro, Nor. 59°16′ N, 15°10′ E 152
Oredezh, Russ. 58°49′ N, 30°20′ E 166
Oregon, Ohio, U.S. 41°38′ N, 83°29′ W 102
Oregon, Wis., U.S. 42°55′ N, 89°23′ W 102
Oregon, adm. division, Oreg., U.S. 43°43′ N, 121°32′ W 90
Oregon Caves National Monument, Oreg., U.S. 42°5′ N, 123°29′ W 90
Oregon Dunes National Recreation Area, Oreg., U.S. 43°59′ N, 129°37′ W 80
Öregrund, Sw. 60°18′ N, 18°22′ E 166
Orekhovo-Zuyevo, Russ. 55°49′ N, 38°56′ E 154
Orel, Russ. 52°55′ N, 36°4′ E 154
Orel, adm. division, Russ. 52°59′ N, 35°55′ E 154
Orellana, Peru 6°56′ S, 75°14′ W 130
Orellana la Vieja, Sp. 39°0′ N, 5°32′ W 164
Orem, Utah, U.S. 40°18′ N, 111°41′ W 90
Ören, Turk. 37°1′ N, 27°57′ E 156
Orenburg, Russ. 51°47′ N, 55°9′ E 154
Orenburg, adm. division, Russ. 52°50′ N, 51°59′ E 154
Orense, Arg. 38°41′ S, 59°45′ W 139
Örenşehir, Turk. 38°59′ N, 36°40′ E 156
Orford, N.H., U.S. 43°54′ N, 72°8′ W 104
Orford, U.K. 52°5′ N, 1°31′ E 163
Orford Ness, U.K. 52°0′ N, 1°35′ E 163
Orfordville, N.H., U.S. 43°52′ N, 72°7′ W 104
Orfordville, Wis., U.S. 42°38′ N, 89°15′ W 102
Organ Peak, N. Mex., U.S. 32°20′ N, 106°43′ W 82
Organ Pipe Cactus National Monument, Ariz., U.S. 32°2′ N, 112°37′ W 80
Organt, Kaz. 44°7′ N, 66°46′ E 184
Organyà, Sp. 42°12′ N, 1°18′ E 164
Órgiva, Sp. 36°53′ N, 3°26′ W 164
Orgon, Fr. 43°47′ N, 5°1′ E 150
Orgun, Afghan. 32°52′ N, 69°11′ E 186
Orhaneli, Turk. 39°54′ N, 28°57′ E 156
Orhangazi, Turk. 40°29′ N, 29°17′ E 158
Orhei, Mold. 47°22′ N, 28°50′ E 156
Orhi, peak, Fr. 42°58′ N, 1°3′ W 164
Orhon, river, Mongolia 48°34′ N, 104°41′ E 190
Orhontuul, Mongolia 48°54′ N, 104°57′ E 198
Oria, Sp. 37°29′ N, 2°18′ W 164
Orick, Calif., U.S. 41°16′ N, 124°5′ W 92
Oricum see Orikon, ruin(s), Alban. 40°17′ N, 19°19′ E 156
Orient, N.Y., U.S. 41°8′ N, 72°18′ W 104
Orient, Wash., U.S. 48°51′ N, 118°14′ W 90
Orient Point, N.Y., U.S. 41°9′ N, 72°20′ W 104
Oriental, Cordillera, Peru 5°11′ S, 77°46′ W 130
Oriental, Grand Erg, Alg. 29°30′ N, 4°11′ E 214
Oriente, Arg. 38°44′ S, 60°37′ W 139
Oriente, Braz. 10°1′ S, 64°7′ W 137
Origny-Sainte-Benoite, Fr. 49°50′ N, 3°29′ E 163
Orihuela, Sp. 38°4′ N, 0°57′ E 164
Orikhiv, Ukr. 47°32′ N, 35°47′ E 156
Orikon (Oricum), ruin(s), Alban. 40°17′ N, 19°19′ E 156
Orillia, Can. 44°36′ N, 79°25′ W 94
Orimattila, Fin. 60°47′ N, 25°42′ E 166
Orinoca, Bol. 18°59′ S, 67°15′ W 137
Orinoco, river, Venez. 3°9′ N, 65°14′ W 130
Orissa, adm. division, India 21°55′ N, 84°41′ E 197
Orissaare, Est. 58°32′ N, 23°3′ E 166
Oristano, It. 39°54′ N, 8°35′ E 214
Orivesi, Fin. 61°40′ N, 24°18′ E 166
Oriximiná, Braz. 1°44′ S, 55°54′ W 130
Orizaba, Mex. 18°50′ N, 97°6′ W 114
Orizaba, Pico de, peak, Mex. 18°59′ N, 97°20′ W 114
Orizona, Braz. 17°4′ S, 48°19′ W 138
Orjen, peak, Europe 42°33′ N, 18°30′ E 168
Orkney, S. Af. 26°59′ S, 26°38′ E 227
Orkney Islands, North Atlantic Ocean 59°28′ N, 6°40′ W 142
Orland, Calif., U.S. 39°44′ N, 122°13′ W 90
Orland, Me., U.S. 44°34′ N, 68°45′ W 94
Orlando, Fla., U.S. 28°32′ N, 81°23′ W 105
Orlando, Capo d', It. 38°11′ N, 13°59′ E 156
Orléanais, region, Fr. 48°23′ N, 1°15′ E 163
Orléans, Fr. 47°54′ N, 1°54′ E 163
Orleans, Ind., U.S. 38°39′ N, 86°27′ W 102
Orleans, Mass., U.S. 41°46′ N, 69°60′ W 104
Orleans, Nebr., U.S. 40°6′ N, 99°27′ W 90
Orlik, Russ. 52°36′ N, 99°50′ E 190
Orlová, Czech Rep. 49°50′ N, 18°25′ E 152
Orlovat, Serb. and Mont. 45°15′ N, 20°33′ E 168
Orlovka, Russ. 56°55′ N, 76°24′ E 169
Orlovskiy, Russ. 46°49′ N, 41°56′ E 158
Orlu, Nig. 5°45′ N, 7°10′ E 222
Ormara, Pak. 25°12′ N, 64°35′ E 182
Ormara, Ras, Pak. 25°2′ N, 64°39′ E 182
Ormea, It. 44°9′ N, 7°54′ E 167
Ormoc, Philippines 11°2′ N, 124°36′ E 203
Ormond, N.Z. 38°33′ S, 177°55′ E 240
Ormond Beach, Fla., U.S. 29°16′ N, 81°4′ W 105
Ormond by the Sea, Fla., U.S. 29°19′ N, 81°4′ W 105
Ormož, Slov. 46°24′ N, 16°7′ E 168
Ormskirk, U.K. 53°34′ N, 2°53′ W 162
Orne, river, Fr. 49°7′ N, 5°44′ E 163
Orneta, Pol. 54°5′ N, 20°7′ E 166
Ornö, island, Sw. 59°0′ N, 18°32′ E 166
Orno Peak, Colo., U.S. 40°3′ N, 107°10′ W 90
Örnsköldsvik, Nor. 63°16′ N, 18°43′ E 152
Oro Blanco, Peru 3°11′ S, 73°14′ W 136
Oro Grande, Calif., U.S. 34°36′ N, 117°21′ W 101
Oro Ingenio, Bol. 21°16′ S, 66°1′ W 137
Oro, river, Mex. 25°55′ N, 105°18′ W 80
Orobie, Alpi, It. 46°18′ N, 9°48′ E 167
Orocopia Mountains, Calif., U.S. 33°38′ N, 115°55′ W 101
Orocué, Col. 4°47′ N, 71°21′ W 136
Orodara, Burkina Faso 10°57′ N, 4°56′ W 222
Orofino, Idaho, U.S. 46°29′ N, 116°15′ W 90
Orokam, Nig. 7°1′ N, 7°33′ E 222
Oromia, region, Eth. 5°54′ N, 38°39′ E 224
Oron, Israel 30°54′ N, 35°0′ E 194
Oron, Nig. 4°49′ N, 8°12′ E 222
Orono, Me., U.S. 44°52′ N, 68°41′ W 111
Oronoquekamp, Guyana 2°43′ N, 57°32′ W 130
Orontes see 'Āṣī, river, Syr. 35°40′ N, 36°21′ E 194
Oropesa, Sp. 40°5′ N, 0°7′ E 164
Oroquieta, Philippines 8°31′ N, 123°46′ E 203
Orós, Braz. 6°21′ S, 38°53′ W 132
Oros Áskio, peak, Gr. 40°23′ N, 21°28′ E 156
Orosháza, Hung. 46°33′ N, 20°40′ E 168
Orosi, Calif., U.S. 36°33′ N, 119°18′ W 100
Orotukan, Russ. 62°13′ N, 151°26′ E 160
Oroville, Calif., U.S. 39°30′ N, 121°35′ W 90
Oroyek, Russ. 64°52′ N, 153°22′ E 160
Oroz Betelu, Sp. 42°54′ N, 1°19′ W 164
Orqohan, China 49°29′ N, 121°22′ E 198
Orr, Minn., U.S. 48°2′ N, 92°50′ W 94
Orrs Island, Me., U.S. 43°45′ N, 69°59′ W 104
Orrville, Ohio, U.S. 40°49′ N, 81°45′ W 102
Orsa, Nor. 61°6′ N, 14°35′ E 152
Orsha, Belarus 54°31′ N, 30°31′ E 154
Orshanka, Russ. 56°54′ N, 47°55′ E 154
Orsk, Russ. 51°11′ N, 58°36′ E 158
Örskär, island, Sw. 60°31′ N, 18°12′ E 166
Orta, Turk. 40°37′ N, 33°6′ E 156
Ortaca, Turk. 36°50′ N, 28°45′ E 156
Ortegal, Cabo, Sp. 43°46′ N, 7°54′ W 150
Orthez, Fr. 43°29′ N, 0°46′ E 164
Orting, Wash., U.S. 47°4′ N, 122°13′ W 100
Ortisei, It. 46°36′ N, 11°39′ E 167
Orţişoara, Rom. 45°58′ N, 21°12′ E 168
Ortiz, Mex. 28°17′ N, 110°44′ W 92
Ortiz, Mex. 28°14′ N, 105°33′ W 92
Ortiz, Venez. 9°35′ N, 67°19′ W 136
Ortles, It. 46°22′ N, 10°15′ E 167
Orto Surt, Russ. 62°34′ N, 125°4′ E 173
Ortón, river, Bol. 11°2′ S, 66°58′ W 137
Ortona, It. 42°21′ N, 14°23′ E 156
Ortonville, Mich., U.S. 42°51′ N, 83°28′ W 102
Ortonville, Minn., U.S. 45°17′ N, 96°27′ W 90
Örträsk, Nor. 64°8′ N, 18°59′ E 152
Orūmīyeh, Iran 37°30′ N, 44°58′ E 143
Orūmīyeh, Daryācheh-ye (Urmia, Lake), Iran 38°7′ N, 45°16′ E 195
Orūmīyeh (Urmia), Iran 37°37′ N, 45°4′ E 195
Orungo, Uganda 2°0′ N, 33°28′ E 224
Oruro, Bol. 17°59′ S, 67°8′ W 137
Oruro, adm. division, Bol. 18°53′ S, 68°19′ W 137
Orwell, Ohio, U.S. 41°31′ N, 80°52′ W 102
Orwell, Vt., U.S. 43°48′ N, 73°19′ W 104
Orxon, river, China 48°16′ N, 117°47′ E 198
Orynyn, Ukr. 48°44′ N, 26°25′ E 152
Orzinuovi, It. 45°24′ N, 9°55′ E 167
Os, Nor. 60°11′ N, 5°27′ E 152
Osa, Russ. 57°15′ N, 55°32′ E 154
Osage, Iowa, U.S. 43°15′ N, 92°49′ W 94
Osage, Wyo., U.S. 43°57′ N, 104°25′ W 90
Osage City, Kans., U.S. 38°36′ N, 95°50′ W 90
Ōsaka, Japan 34°42′ N, 135°32′ E 190
Ōsaka, Japan 35°57′ N, 137°17′ E 201
Ōsaka, Japan 34°40′ N, 135°30′ E 201
Ōsaka, adm. division, Japan 34°20′ N, 135°21′ E 201
Osakarovka, Kaz. 50°34′ N, 72°35′ E 184
Osakis, Minn., U.S. 45°50′ N, 95°11′ W 90
Osan, S. Korea 37°8′ N, 127°4′ E 200
Osawatomie, Kans., U.S. 38°28′ N, 94°57′ W 94
Osborn Plateau, Indian Ocean 14°42′ S, 86°43′ E 254
Osborne, Kans., U.S. 39°25′ N, 98°43′ W 90
Osby, Nor. 56°23′ N, 13°57′ E 152
Oscar II Coast, Antarctica 65°25′ S, 61°36′ W 134
Osceola, Iowa, U.S. 41°2′ N, 93°45′ W 94
Osečina, Serb. and Mont. 44°22′ N, 19°35′ E 168
Ösel see Saaremaa, island, Est. 58°32′ N, 21°21′ E 166
Osel'ki, Russ. 60°14′ N, 30°26′ E 166
Osen, Nor. 64°18′ N, 10°31′ E 152
Osgood, Ind., U.S. 39°7′ N, 85°17′ W 102
Osgood Mountains, Nev., U.S. 41°3′ N, 117°37′ W 90
Osh, Kyrg. 40°31′ N, 72°49′ E 197
Oshakati, Namibia 17°54′ S, 15°48′ E 220
Oshawa, Can. 43°53′ N, 78°50′ W 94
Oshikango, Namibia 17°28′ S, 15°52′ E 220
Ōshima, Japan 34°44′ N, 139°21′ E 201
Oshkosh, Nebr., U.S. 41°24′ N, 102°22′ W 90
Oshkosh, Wis., U.S. 44°1′ N, 88°33′ W 102
Oshkur'ya, Russ. 66°0′ N, 56°40′ E 154
Oshogbo, Nig. 7°50′ N, 4°35′ E 222
Oshta, Russ. 60°49′ N, 35°33′ E 154
Oshwe, Dem. Rep. of the Congo 3°27′ S, 19°29′ E 218
Osian, India 26°41′ N, 72°55′ E 186
Osijek, Croatia 45°32′ N, 18°40′ E 168
Osilinka, river, Can. 56°4′ N, 125°26′ W 108
Osinovka, Russ. 56°33′ N, 102°11′ E 160
Osinovo, Russ. 61°18′ N, 89°49′ E 169
Oskaloosa, Iowa, U.S. 41°17′ N, 92°38′ W 94
Öskemen (Ust' Kamenogorsk), Kaz. 49°59′ N, 82°38′ E 184
Oskoba, Russ. 60°20′ N, 100°33′ E 160
Oskol, river, Russ. 50°34′ N, 37°37′ E 158
Oslo, Minn., U.S. 48°10′ N, 97°8′ W 90
Oslo, Nor. 59°53′ N, 10°33′ E 152
Oslob, Philippines 9°32′ N, 123°23′ E 203
Osma, Sp. 43°3′ N, 3°6′ W 164
Osmancık, Turk. 40°58′ N, 34°47′ E 156
Osmaniye, Turk. 37°4′ N, 36°13′ E 156
Os'mino, Russ. 59°1′ N, 29°7′ E 166
Osmus Saar, island, Est. 59°9′ N, 23°14′ E 166
Osnabrück, Ger. 52°16′ N, 8°2′ E 163
Osnaburgh House, Can. 51°8′ N, 90°17′ W 110
Oso, Wash., U.S. 48°16′ N, 121°56′ W 100
Oso, river, Dem. Rep. of the Congo 0°60′ N, 27°43′ E 224
Osogovske Planina, Maced. 42°2′ N, 22°2′ E 168
Osor, Croatia 44°42′ N, 14°23′ E 156
Osório, Braz. 29°54′ S, 50°17′ W 134
Osorno, Chile 40°34′ S, 73°9′ W 134
Osorno, Sp. 42°24′ N, 4°22′ W 150
Osoyoos, Can. 49°1′ N, 119°30′ W 108
Ospika, river, Can. 57°3′ N, 124°28′ W 108
Osprey, Fla., U.S. 27°12′ N, 82°28′ W 105
Oss, Neth. 51°45′ N, 5°31′ E 167
Ossa, Mount, peak, Austral. 41°53′ S, 145°50′ E 230
Óssa, Óros, peak, Gr. 39°47′ N, 22°36′ E 156
Ossabaw Island, Ga., U.S. 31°36′ N, 81°3′ W 112
Osse, river, Nig. 7°44′ N, 5°58′ E 222
Osselé, Congo 1°26′ S, 15°19′ E 218
Osseo, Wis., U.S. 44°33′ N, 91°13′ W 94
Ossian, Ind., U.S. 40°52′ N, 85°10′ W 102
Ossining, N.Y., U.S. 41°9′ N, 73°52′ W 104
Ossipee, N.H., U.S. 43°40′ N, 71°8′ W 104
Ossjøen, lake, Nor. 61°10′ N, 11°24′ E 152
Ossokmanuan Reservoir, lake, Can. 52°59′ N, 66°19′ W 111
Ossora, Russ. 59°14′ N, 163°0′ E 160
Ostaboningue, Lac, lake, Can. 47°7′ N, 79°36′ W 94
Ostashkov, Russ. 57°7′ N, 33°12′ E 154
Östavall, Nor. 62°25′ N, 15°29′ E 152

Ostbevern, *Ger.* 52°2′ N, 7°50′ E **167**
Ostellato, *It.* 44°44′ N, 11°56′ E **167**
Ostend see Oostende, *Belg.* 51°13′ N, 2°55′ E **163**
Østerdalen, *Nor.* 61°50′ N, 10°47′ E **152**
Östergarnsholme, island, *Sw.* 57°25′ N, 19°1′ E **166**
Osterode, *Ger.* 51°44′ N, 10°13′ E **167**
Östersund, *Nor.* 63°10′ N, 14°40′ E **152**
Osterville, *Mass., U.S.* 41°37′ N, 70°24′ W **104**
Östhammar, *Sw.* 60°14′ N, 18°18′ E **166**
Ostheim, *Ger.* 50°27′ N, 10°13′ E **167**
Ostiglia, *It.* 45°3′ N, 11°8′ E **167**
Östra Kvarken 63°31′ N, 20°16′ E **152**
Ostrava, *Czech Rep.* 49°49′ N, 18°15′ E **152**
Ostro, *Pol.* 53°4′ N, 21°33′ E **152**
Ostróda, *Pol.* 53°41′ N, 19°58′ E **152**
Ostrov, *Russ.* 57°21′ N, 28°21′ E **166**
Ostrov, *Russ.* 58°28′ N, 28°37′ E **166**
Ostrov Russkiy, island, *Russ.* 76°38′ N, 89°18′ E **160**
Ostrovtsy, *Russ.* 58°23′ N, 27°42′ E **166**
Ostrožac, *Bosn. and Herzg.* 43°40′ N, 17°50′ E **168**
Ostuni, *It.* 40°43′ N, 17°35′ E **156**
O'sullivan Lake, lake, *Can.* 50°22′ N, 87°38′ W **110**
Osuna, *Sp.* 37°14′ N, 5°7′ W **164**
Osvaldo Cruz, *Braz.* 21°47′ S, 50°52′ W **138**
Oswego, *N.Y., U.S.* 43°26′ N, 76°32′ W **110**
Oswestry, *U.K.* 52°51′ N, 3°4′ W **162**
Osyka, *Miss., U.S.* 31°0′ N, 90°30′ W **103**
Ōta, *Japan* 35°56′ N, 136°3′ E **201**
Ōta, *Japan* 36°16′ N, 139°24′ E **201**
Ōta, river, *Japan* 34°29′ N, 132°11′ E **201**
Otaci, *Mold.* 48°25′ N, 27°47′ E **152**
Ōtake, *Japan* 34°12′ N, 132°13′ E **200**
Otaki, *N.Z.* 40°46′ S, 175°8′ E **240**
Otanmäki, *Fin.* 64°4′ N, 27°4′ E **152**
Otar, *Kaz.* 43°31′ N, 75°12′ E **184**
Otare, Cerro, peak, *Col.* 1°43′ N, 72°49′ W **136**
Otaru, *Japan* 43°12′ N, 140°49′ E **190**
Otatara, *N.Z.* 46°27′ S, 168°18′ E **240**
Otautau, *N.Z.* 46°11′ S, 167°58′ E **240**
Otava, *Fin.* 61°37′ N, 27°2′ E **166**
Otavalo, *Ecua.* 0°11′ N, 78°24′ W **136**
Otavi, *Namibia* 19°39′ S, 17°19′ E **220**
Otawara, *Japan* 36°49′ N, 140°1′ E **201**
Otay, *Calif., U.S.* 32°36′ N, 117°6′ W **101**
Otchinjau, *Angola* 16°30′ S, 13°56′ E **220**
Otelec, *Rom.* 45°36′ N, 20°50′ E **168**
Oțelu Roșu, *Rom.* 45°30′ N, 22°23′ E **168**
Otematata, *N.Z.* 44°37′ S, 170°11′ E **240**
Otepää, *Est.* 58°2′ N, 26°29′ E **166**
Oteros, river, *Mex.* 27°19′ N, 108°36′ W **80**
Othello, *Wash., U.S.* 46°48′ N, 119°11′ W **90**
Otherside, river, *Can.* 59°5′ N, 107°21′ W **108**
Óthris, Óros, *Gr.* 38°57′ N, 22°19′ E **156**
Oti, river, *Ghana* 8°32′ N, 8°476′ E **222**
Otinapa, *Mex.* 24°0′ N, 105°1′ W **114**
Otira, *N.Z.* 42°50′ S, 171°33′ E **240**
Otis, *Colo., U.S.* 40°9′ N, 102°58′ W **90**
Otis, *Mass., U.S.* 42°11′ N, 73°6′ W **104**
Otisco, *Ind., U.S.* 38°32′ N, 85°39′ W **102**
Otish, Monts, peak, *Can.* 52°17′ N, 70°36′ W **111**
Otjikondo, *Namibia* 19°52′ S, 15°29′ E **220**
Otjimbingwe, *Namibia* 22°19′ S, 16°7′ E **227**
Otjivero, *Namibia* 22°16′ S, 17°51′ E **227**
Otjiwarongo, *Namibia* 20°27′ S, 16°39′ E **227**
Otley, *U.K.* 53°54′ N, 1°41′ W **162**
Otmök, *Kyrg.* 42°11′ N, 73°16′ E **197**
Otog Qi, *China* 39°6′ N, 107°58′ E **198**
Otok, *Croatia* 45°8′ N, 18°51′ E **168**
Otok, *Croatia* 43°41′ N, 16°43′ E **168**
Otoka, *Bosn. and Herzg.* 44°57′ N, 16°8′ E **168**
Otorohanga, *N.Z.* 38°11′ S, 175°13′ E **240**
Otoskwin, river, *Can.* 51°48′ N, 90°58′ W **80**
Otosquen, *Can.* 53°16′ N, 102°1′ W **108**
Otradnaya, *Russ.* 44°22′ N, 41°27′ E **158**
Otradnoye, *Russ.* 51°59′ N, 156°39′ E **160**
Otradnoye, *Russ.* 56°13′ N, 30°3′ E **166**
Otradnyy, *Russ.* 53°24′ N, 51°26′ E **154**
Otranto, Capo d', *It.* 40°2′ N, 18°31′ E **156**
Otsego, *Mich., U.S.* 42°26′ N, 85°42′ W **102**
Ōtsu, *Japan* 35°1′ N, 135°51′ E **201**
Otta, *Nig.* 6°44′ N, 3°13′ E **222**
Ottawa, *Can.* 45°22′ N, 75°50′ W **94**
Ottawa, *Ill., U.S.* 41°20′ N, 88°51′ W **102**
Ottawa, *Kans., U.S.* 38°34′ N, 95°17′ W **94**
Ottawa, *Mo., U.S.* 41°20′ N, 88°51′ W **110**
Ottawa, *Ohio, U.S.* 41°1′ N, 84°3′ W **102**
Ottawa Islands, *Hudson Bay* 59°8′ N, 83°8′ W **106**
Ottenby, *Sw.* 56°14′ N, 16°26′ E **152**
Otter Creek, *Fla., U.S.* 29°19′ N, 82°47′ W **105**
Otter Head, *Can.* 47°53′ N, 86°14′ W **94**
Otter Rapids, *Can.* 50°11′ N, 81°40′ W **94**
Otterbein, *Ind., U.S.* 40°29′ N, 87°6′ W **102**
Otterndorf, *Ger.* 53°48′ N, 8°54′ E **152**
Ottoville, *Ohio, U.S.* 40°55′ N, 84°20′ W **102**
Otú, *Col.* 6°55′ N, 74°45′ W **136**
Otukpa, *Nig.* 7°4′ N, 7°40′ E **222**
Otukpo, *Nig.* 7°12′ N, 8°9′ E **222**
Otumpa, *Arg.* 27°20′ S, 62°16′ W **139**
Otynya, *Ukr.* 48°43′ N, 24°49′ E **152**
Ötztal Alps, *Aust.* 46°46′ N, 10°36′ E **167**
Ou Nua, *Laos* 22°16′ N, 101°48′ E **202**
Ou, river, *Laos* 21°49′ N, 102°6′ E **202**
Ouachita, Lake, *Ark., U.S.* 34°41′ N, 93°59′ W **80**
Ouachita Mountains, *Ark., U.S.* 34°26′ N, 95°36′ W **96**
Ouachita, river, *La., U.S.* 32°16′ N, 92°10′ W **103**
Ouadane, *Mauritania* 20°57′ N, 11°37′ W **222**
Ouadda, *Cen. Af. Rep.* 8°4′ N, 22°24′ E **218**
Ouagadougou, *Burkina Faso* 12°19′ N, 1°43′ W **222**
Ouagama, Lac, lake, *Can.* 50°37′ N, 77°43′ W **110**
Ouahigouya, *Burkina Faso* 13°34′ N, 2°26′ W **222**
Ouaka, river, *Cen. Af. Rep.* 5°11′ N, 19°49′ E **218**
Oualâta, *Mauritania* 17°18′ N, 7°2′ W **222**
Oualâta, Dahr, *Mauritania* 17°41′ N, 8°22′ W **222**
Oualidia, *Mor.* 32°43′ N, 9°4′ W **214**
Ouallam, *Niger* 14°22′ N, 1°59′ E **222**
Ouan Taredert, oil field, *Alg.* 27°26′ N, 9°29′ E **214**
Oua-n-Ahaggar, Tassili, *Alg.* 21°14′ N, 4°57′ E **222**
Ouanda Djallé, *Cen. Af. Rep.* 8°52′ N, 22°48′ E **218**
Ouandjia, *Cen. Af. Rep.* 9°17′ N, 22°40′ E **218**
Ouando, *Cen. Af. Rep.* 5°58′ N, 25°45′ E **224**
Ouango, *Cen. Af. Rep.* 4°20′ N, 22°29′ E **218**
Ouaouizarht, *Mor.* 32°12′ N, 6°23′ W **214**
Ouarane, *Mauritania* 20°48′ N, 11°23′ W **222**
Ouargaye, *Burkina Faso* 11°31′ N, 2°119′ E **222**
Ouargla, *Alg.* 31°56′ N, 5°20′ E **214**
Ouarkoye, *Burkina Faso* 12°6′ N, 3°41′ W **222**
Ouarkziz, Jebel, *Mor.* 28°10′ N, 9°37′ W **214**
Ouarra, river, *Cen. Af. Rep.* 5°49′ N, 25°48′ E **224**
Ouarsenis, Djebel, peak, *Alg.* 35°52′ N, 1°34′ E **150**
Ouas Ouas, spring, *Mali* 16°6′ N, 1°20′ E **222**
Ouasiemsca, river, *Can.* 49°43′ N, 73°11′ W **111**
Ouassane, spring, *Mauritania* 17°56′ N, 13°13′ W **222**
Ouassou, *Guinea* 10°2′ N, 13°45′ W **222**
Ouche, river, *Fr.* 47°15′ N, 4°48′ E **165**
Ouchennane, spring, *Mali* 17°23′ N, 1°59′ E **222**
Ouddorp, *Neth.* 51°48′ N, 3°55′ E **163**
Oude Rijn, river, *Neth.* 52°12′ N, 4°26′ E **163**
Oudeïka, spring, *Mali* 17°27′ N, 1°42′ W **222**
Oudenaarde, *Belg.* 50°50′ N, 3°36′ E **163**
Oudeschild, *Neth.* 53°2′ N, 4°50′ E **163**
Oudon, *Fr.* 47°21′ N, 1°19′ W **150**
Oudtshoorn, *S. Af.* 33°35′ S, 22°11′ E **227**
Oued Laou, *Mor.* 35°26′ N, 5°6′ W **150**
Oued Lili, *Alg.* 35°30′ N, 1°16′ E **150**
Oued Rhiou, *Alg.* 35°57′ N, 0°55′ E **164**
Oued Taria, *Alg.* 35°6′ N, 9°535′ E **150**
Oued Tlelat, *Alg.* 35°32′ N, 0°28′ E **150**
Oueïba, spring, *Chad* 18°24′ N, 23°18′ E **226**
Oueïta, spring, *Chad* 17°43′ N, 20°42′ E **216**
Ouella, spring, *Niger* 14°39′ N, 3°53′ E **222**
Ouellé, *Côte d'Ivoire* 7°14′ N, 4°2′ W **222**
Ouémé, river, *Benin* 8°19′ N, 2°11′ E **222**
Ouescapis, Lac, lake, *Can.* 50°15′ N, 77°36′ W **94**
Ouessa, *Burkina Faso* 11°3′ N, 2°48′ W **222**
Ouesso, *Congo* 1°51′ N, 16°2′ E **218**
Ouest, Pointe, *Haiti* 18°51′ N, 74°1′ W **116**
Ouest, Pointe de l' (Coupé, Cap), *Fr.* 46°48′ N, 56°60′ W **111**
Ouffet, *Belg.* 50°26′ N, 5°26′ E **167**
Oufrane, *Alg.* 28°31′ N, 0°10′ E **214**
Ougarta, *Alg.* 29°40′ N, 2°16′ W **214**
Ougrée, *Belg.* 50°35′ N, 5°33′ E **167**
Ouidah, *Benin* 6°23′ N, 2°5′ E **222**
Oujaf, spring, *Mauritania* 17°50′ N, 7°54′ W **222**
Oujda, *Mor.* 34°38′ N, 1°55′ W **214**
Oujeft, *Mauritania* 20°2′ N, 13°4′ W **222**
Oulad el Abed, *Tun.* 35°59′ N, 10°17′ E **156**
Oulad Hammou, *Mor.* 35°7′ N, 6°9′ W **150**
Oulad Saïd, *Alg.* 29°27′ N, 0°15′ E **214**
Oulainen, *Fin.* 64°15′ N, 24°44′ E **152**
Ould Mouloud, spring, *Alg.* 23°46′ N, 0°9′ E **214**
Ouled Amar, *Alg.* 35°27′ N, 5°8′ E **150**
Ouled Djellal, *Alg.* 34°23′ N, 5°3′ E **214**
Oulou, river, *Cen. Af. Rep.* 10°27′ N, 22°30′ E **218**
Oulton Broad, *U.K.* 52°27′ N, 1°41′ E **163**
Oulton Lake, lake, *Can.* 60°45′ N, 111°53′ W **108**
Oulu, *Fin.* 64°59′ N, 25°47′ E **160**
Oulu (Uleåborg), *Fin.* 65°0′ N, 25°25′ E **152**
Oulx, *It.* 45°1′ N, 6°51′ E **167**
Oum Chalouba, *Chad* 15°47′ N, 20°45′ E **216**
Oum er Rbia, Oued, river, *Mor.* 32°10′ N, 8°13′ W **142**
Oum Hadjer, *Chad* 13°15′ N, 19°40′ E **216**
Oum Mesgué, *Mauritania* 16°17′ N, 7°15′ W **222**
Oumache, *Alg.* 34°40′ N, 5°42′ E **214**
Oumé, *Côte d'Ivoire* 6°17′ N, 5°25′ W **222**
Oumm el A'sel, spring, *Mali* 23°32′ N, 4°46′ W **214**
Oumm el Khez, spring, *Mauritania* 17°7′ N, 11°3′ W **222**
Ounasselkä, *Fin.* 67°32′ N, 24°23′ E **152**
Oundle, *U.K.* 52°28′ N, 0°29′ E **162**
Ounianga Kébir, *Chad* 19°4′ N, 20°31′ E **216**
Ounianga Sérir, spring, *Chad* 18°54′ N, 20°54′ E **216**
Ounissouli, spring, *Niger* 17°33′ N, 12°3′ E **222**
Ouolodo, *Mali* 13°13′ N, 7°55′ W **222**
Ourafane, *Niger* 14°2′ N, 8°8′ E **222**
Ouray, *Utah, U.S.* 40°5′ N, 109°41′ W **90**
Ouray, Mount, peak, *Colo., U.S.* 38°24′ N, 106°18′ W **90**
Ourense, *Sp.* 42°19′ N, 7°53′ W **150**
Ouri, *Chad* 21°35′ N, 19°13′ E **216**
Ourinhos, *Braz.* 22°58′ S, 49°52′ W **138**
Ouro, *Braz.* 8°13′ S, 46°14′ W **130**
Ouro Preto, *Braz.* 20°24′ S, 43°31′ W **138**
Ouro Prêto, river, *Braz.* 10°44′ S, 64°28′ W **137**
Ours, Cap de l', *Can.* 49°36′ N, 62°30′ W **111**
Oursi, *Burkina Faso* 14°40′ N, 4°238′ E **222**
Ourthe, river, *Belg.* 50°11′ N, 5°34′ E **167**
Ouse, river, *U.K.* 54°4′ N, 1°21′ W **162**
Oust, *Fr.* 42°51′ N, 1°12′ E **164**
Outardes Quatre, Réservoir, lake, *Can.* 49°34′ N, 70°50′ W **94**
Outat Oulad el Hajj, *Mor.* 33°25′ N, 3°44′ W **214**
Outeniqua Mountains, *S. Af.* 33°49′ S, 22°28′ E **227**
Outer Banks, islands, *North Atlantic Ocean* 35°28′ N, 75°25′ W **96**
Outer Santa Barbara Channel 33°9′ N, 118°41′ W **101**
Outjo, *Namibia* 20°7′ S, 16°10′ E **227**
Outlook, *Can.* 51°29′ N, 107°5′ W **90**
Outokumpu, *Fin.* 62°43′ N, 29°0′ E **152**
Outram Island, *India* 12°17′ N, 93°14′ E **188**
Outtaye, *Mali* 14°28′ N, 8°23′ W **222**
Ovacık, *Turk.* 39°21′ N, 39°12′ E **195**
Ovada, *It.* 44°38′ N, 8°39′ E **167**
Oval Peak, *Wash., U.S.* 48°15′ N, 120°31′ W **90**
Ovalle, *Chile* 30°35′ S, 71°14′ W **134**
Ovalo, *Tex., U.S.* 32°10′ N, 99°50′ W **92**
Ovamboland, region, *Namibia* 19°53′ S, 15°29′ E **227**
Ovana, Cerro, peak, *Venez.* 4°37′ N, 67°4′ W **136**
Ovar, *Port.* 40°51′ N, 8°40′ W **150**
Overath, *Ger.* 50°56′ N, 7°16′ E **167**
Øverbygd, *Nor.* 69°0′ N, 19°7′ E **152**
Overflowing River, *Can.* 53°6′ N, 101°10′ W **108**
Overland Park, *Kans., U.S.* 38°56′ N, 94°41′ W **94**
Overland Pass, *Nev., U.S.* 40°1′ N, 115°36′ W **90**
Övermark (Ylimarkku), *Fin.* 62°35′ N, 21°25′ E **152**
Overpelt, *Belg.* 51°11′ N, 5°24′ E **167**
Överstjuktan, lake, *Nor.* 65°39′ N, 15°22′ E **152**
Overstrand, *U.K.* 52°54′ N, 1°20′ E **162**
Overton, *Nev., U.S.* 36°32′ N, 114°27′ W **101**
Overton, *Tex., U.S.* 32°16′ N, 94°59′ W **103**
Overton, *U.K.* 52°57′ N, 2°55′ W **162**
Överum, *Nor.* 58°0′ N, 16°17′ E **152**
Ovett, *Miss., U.S.* 31°27′ N, 89°1′ W **103**
Ovid, *Colo., U.S.* 40°57′ N, 102°23′ W **90**
Ovid, *Mich., U.S.* 43°0′ N, 84°22′ W **102**
Oviedo, *Sp.* 43°21′ N, 5°51′ W **150**
Oviši, *Latv.* 57°29′ N, 21°33′ E **166**
Ovoot, *Mongolia* 45°20′ N, 113°38′ E **198**
Övör-Ereen, *Mongolia* 49°16′ N, 112°25′ E **198**
Ovruch, *Ukr.* 51°19′ N, 28°52′ E **152**
Owaka, *N.Z.* 46°28′ S, 169°42′ E **240**
Owando, *Congo* 0°33′ N, 15°53′ E **218**
Owaneco, *Ill., U.S.* 39°28′ N, 89°12′ W **102**
Owase, *Japan* 34°3′ N, 136°12′ E **201**
Owbeh, *Afghan.* 34°26′ N, 63°10′ E **186**
Owego, *N.Y., U.S.* 42°6′ N, 76°17′ W **94**
Owen Falls Dam, *Uganda* 0°5′ N, 33°1′ E **224**
Owen Fracture Zone, *Arabian Sea* 11°9′ N, 57°40′ E **254**
Owen, Mount, peak, *N.Z.* 41°34′ S, 172°28′ E **240**
Owen River, *N.Z.* 41°42′ S, 172°27′ E **240**
Owen Sound, *Can.* 44°34′ N, 80°56′ W **94**
Owen Stanley Range, *P.N.G.* 8°34′ S, 147°0′ E **192**
Owens Peak, *Calif., U.S.* 35°44′ N, 118°2′ W **101**
Owensboro, *Ky., U.S.* 37°45′ N, 87°7′ W **96**
Owensburg, *Ind., U.S.* 38°55′ N, 86°44′ W **102**
Owensville, *Mo., U.S.* 38°20′ N, 91°30′ W **94**
Owenton, *Ky., U.S.* 38°31′ N, 84°50′ W **102**
Owerri, *Nig.* 5°30′ N, 7°0′ E **222**
Owickeno, *Can.* 51°41′ N, 127°16′ W **108**
Owl Creek Mountains, *Wyo., U.S.* 43°36′ N, 109°5′ W **90**
Owlshead Mountains, *Calif., U.S.* 35°46′ N, 116°46′ W **101**
Owo, *Nig.* 6°28′ N, 7°43′ E **222**
Owo, *Nig.* 7°15′ N, 5°36′ E **222**
Owosso, *Mich., U.S.* 43°0′ N, 84°8′ W **102**
Owschlag, *Ger.* 54°24′ N, 9°35′ E **150**
Owyhee, *Nev., U.S.* 41°57′ N, 116°6′ W **90**
Owyhee Mountains, *Idaho, U.S.* 43°10′ N, 116°45′ W **90**
Owyhee, river, *Idaho, U.S.* 42°25′ N, 117°4′ W **106**
Ox Mountains, the see Gamph, Slieve, *Ire.* 54°2′ N, 9°28′ W **150**
Öxarfjördur 66°6′ N, 19°60′ W **142**
Oxbow Dam, *U.S.* 45°1′ N, 116°55′ W **90**
Oxford, *Kans., U.S.* 37°15′ N, 97°11′ W **90**
Oxford, *Me., U.S.* 44°7′ N, 70°30′ W **104**
Oxford, *Mich., U.S.* 42°48′ N, 83°16′ W **102**
Oxford, *Miss., U.S.* 34°20′ N, 89°31′ W **96**
Oxford, *Nebr., U.S.* 40°14′ N, 99°39′ W **90**
Oxford, *N.Z.* 43°19′ S, 172°11′ E **240**
Oxford, *Ohio, U.S.* 39°30′ N, 84°45′ W **102**
Oxford, *U.K.* 51°44′ N, 1°16′ W **162**
Oxford, *Wis., U.S.* 43°46′ N, 89°33′ W **102**
Oxford House, *Can.* 54°54′ N, 95°17′ W **108**
Oxford Peak, *Idaho, U.S.* 42°17′ N, 112°10′ W **90**
Oxnard, *Calif., U.S.* 34°11′ N, 119°12′ W **101**
Oxus see Ab-e Vakhan, river, *Afghan.* 37°8′ N, 72°26′ E **186**
Oya, *Malaysia* 2°47′ N, 111°52′ E **192**
Oyahue see Ollagüe, *Chile* 21°14′ S, 68°18′ W **137**
Oyan, *Kaz.* 50°44′ N, 50°23′ E **158**
Øye, *Nor.* 62°11′ N, 6°39′ E **152**
Oyé Yeska, spring, *Chad* 18°36′ N, 19°31′ E **216**
Oyem, *Gabon* 1°35′ N, 11°36′ E **207**
Oyen, *Can.* 51°22′ N, 110°29′ W **90**
Øygarden Group, islands, *Indian Ocean* 66°53′ S, 57°43′ E **248**
Oymyakon, *Russ.* 63°25′ N, 142°41′ E **160**
Oyo, *Congo* 1°10′ S, 15°59′ E **218**
Oyo, *Nig.* 7°54′ N, 3°57′ E **222**
Oyo, *Sudan* 21°56′ N, 36°12′ E **182**
Oyonnax, *Fr.* 46°15′ N, 5°38′ E **150**
Oyster Bay, *N.Y., U.S.* 40°52′ N, 73°32′ W **104**
Oyster River, *Can.* 49°53′ N, 125°8′ W **100**
Oysterville, *Wash., U.S.* 46°32′ N, 124°2′ W **100**
Oyyl, *Kaz.* 49°4′ N, 54°38′ E **158**
Özalp, *Turk.* 38°38′ N, 43°57′ E **195**
Ozamis, *Philippines* 8°13′ N, 123°50′ E **203**
Ozark, *Ala., U.S.* 31°27′ N, 85°39′ W **96**
Ozark, *Ark., U.S.* 35°28′ N, 93°51′ W **96**
Ozark, *Mo., U.S.* 37°0′ N, 93°11′ W **96**
Ozark National Scenic Riverways, *Mo., U.S.* 37°0′ N, 96°4′ W **80**
Ozark Plateau, *Mo., U.S.* 35°31′ N, 93°28′ W **96**
Ozen, *Kaz.* 43°27′ N, 53°3′ E **158**
Ozernovskiy, *Russ.* 51°32′ N, 156°34′ E **160**
Ozernoy, Mys, *Russ.* 57°26′ N, 163°12′ E **160**
Ozernyy, *Russ.* 55°30′ N, 32°29′ E **154**
Ozernyy, *Russ.* 51°6′ N, 60°57′ E **158**
Ozernyy, *Russ.* 66°23′ N, 179°3′ W **98**
Ozersk, *Russ.* 54°25′ N, 21°58′ E **166**
Ozery, *Russ.* 54°52′ N, 38°30′ E **154**
Ozgon, *Kyrg.* 40°45′ N, 73°18′ E **197**
Ozhiski Lake, *Can.* 51°57′ N, 89°4′ W **110**
Ozhogino, *Russ.* 68°59′ N, 147°39′ E **160**
Ozieri, *It.* 40°35′ N, 9°1′ E **156**
Ozinki, *Russ.* 51°11′ N, 49°46′ E **158**
Ozoli, *Latv.* 57°38′ N, 24°55′ E **166**
Ozona, *Tex., U.S.* 30°41′ N, 101°12′ W **92**
Ozorków, *Pol.* 51°57′ N, 19°17′ E **152**
Ozrinići, *Europe* 42°44′ N, 19°0′ E **168**
Ōzu, *Japan* 33°30′ N, 132°32′ E **201**
Ozurget'i, *Ga.* 41°54′ N, 42°0′ E **195**

P

Pa Kha, *Vietnam* 22°34′ N, 104°16′ E **202**
Pa Mong Dam, *Asia* 18°10′ N, 101°26′ E **202**
Pa Sak, river, *Thai.* 15°27′ N, 101°2′ E **202**
Paakkola, *Fin.* 66°0′ N, 24°40′ E **152**
Paamiut (Frederikshåb) 62°4′ N, 49°33′ W **106**
Paarl, *S. Af.* 33°45′ S, 18°55′ E **227**
Paavola, *Fin.* 64°35′ N, 25°9′ E **152**
Paberžė, *Lith.* 54°56′ N, 25°14′ E **166**
Pabo, *Uganda* 2°58′ N, 32°7′ E **224**
Pabradė, *Lith.* 54°59′ N, 25°43′ E **166**
Pac, *Alban.* 42°17′ N, 20°12′ E **168**
Pacaás Novos National Park, *Braz.* 11°14′ S, 63°35′ W **137**
Pacaás Novos, river, *Braz.* 11°13′ S, 65°5′ W **137**
Pacaás Novos, Serra dos, *Braz.* 10°27′ S, 64°29′ W **130**
Pacahuaras, river, *Bol.* 10°25′ S, 66°13′ W **137**
Pacajus, *Braz.* 4°14′ S, 38°30′ W **132**
Pacanów, *Pol.* 50°24′ N, 21°2′ E **152**
Pacaraima, Sierra, *Venez.* 4°3′ N, 63°19′ W **130**
Pacasmayo, *Peru* 7°23′ S, 79°35′ W **130**
Pacaya, *Peru* 10°9′ S, 74°7′ W **137**
Paceco, *It.* 37°58′ N, 12°32′ E **156**
Pacheco Pass, *Calif., U.S.* 37°4′ N, 121°14′ W **100**
Pachelma, *Russ.* 53°18′ N, 43°20′ E **154**
Pachena Point, *Can.* 48°44′ N, 125°5′ W **100**
Pachía, *Peru* 17°56′ S, 70°9′ W **137**
Pachuca, *Mex.* 20°6′ N, 98°48′ W **114**
Pachuta, *Miss., U.S.* 32°1′ N, 88°53′ W **103**
Pacific, *Can.* 54°44′ N, 128°20′ W **108**
Pacific Beach, *Wash., U.S.* 47°10′ N, 124°11′ W **100**
Pacific Crest Trail, *U.S.* 47°55′ N, 121°14′ W **100**
Pacific Grove, *Calif., U.S.* 36°36′ N, 121°56′ W **100**
Pacific Missile Test Center, *Calif., U.S.* 34°6′ N, 119°10′ W **101**
Pacific Ocean 35°4′ N, 121°60′ W **252**
Pacific Rim National Park Reserve, *Can.* 48°38′ N, 124°46′ W **100**
Pacifica, *Calif., U.S.* 37°37′ N, 122°30′ W **100**
Pacific-Antarctic Ridge, *South Pacific Ocean* 63°11′ S, 161°29′ W **255**
Pačir, *Serb. and Mont.* 45°54′ N, 19°26′ E **168**
Packwood, *Wash., U.S.* 46°35′ N, 121°41′ W **100**
Pacov, *Czech Rep.* 49°27′ N, 14°59′ E **152**
Padada, *Philippines* 6°41′ N, 125°21′ E **203**
Padang, *Indonesia* 3°2′ N, 105°42′ E **196**
Padang, *Indonesia* 0°55′ N, 100°22′ E **196**
Padang Endau, *Malaysia* 2°39′ N, 103°38′ E **196**
Padang, island, *Indonesia* 0°55′ N, 101°49′ E **196**
Padangpanjang, *Indonesia* 0°28′ N, 100°23′ E **196**
Padangsidempuan, *Indonesia* 1°23′ N, 99°17′ E **196**
Padany, *Russ.* 63°17′ N, 33°24′ E **152**
Padas, river, *Malaysia* 4°40′ N, 115°43′ E **203**
Padasjoki, *Fin.* 61°20′ N, 25°15′ E **166**
Padauiri, river, *Braz.* 0°59′ N, 64°48′ W **130**
Padcaya, *Bol.* 21°52′ S, 64°48′ W **137**
Paddle Prairie, *Can.* 57°55′ N, 117°27′ W **108**
Paden City, *W. Va., U.S.* 39°35′ N, 80°56′ W **102**
Paderborn, *Ger.* 51°43′ N, 8°45′ E **167**
Padeș, peak, *Rom.* 45°39′ N, 22°18′ E **168**
Padilla, *Bol.* 19°17′ S, 64°21′ W **137**
Padina, *Serb. and Mont.* 45°7′ N, 20°44′ E **168**
Padirac, site, *Fr.* 44°51′ N, 1°42′ E **165**
Padlei, *Can.* 61°56′ N, 96°42′ W **73**
Padloping Island, *Can.* 67°11′ N, 62°19′ W **246**
Padova (Padua), *It.* 45°24′ N, 11°52′ E **167**
Padrauna, *India* 26°52′ N, 83°58′ E **197**
Padre Island National Seashore, *Gulf of Mexico* 27°4′ N, 97°18′ W **96**
Padrela, Serra da, *Port.* 41°35′ N, 7°53′ W **150**
Padsvillye, *Belarus* 55°10′ N, 27°57′ E **166**
Padua see Padova, *It.* 45°24′ N, 11°52′ E **167**
Paducah, *Ky., U.S.* 37°4′ N, 88°37′ W **96**
Paducah, *Tex., U.S.* 34°0′ N, 100°19′ W **92**
Padul, *Sp.* 37°1′ N, 3°37′ W **164**
Padun, *Russ.* 68°37′ N, 31°48′ E **152**
Padwa, *India* 18°23′ N, 82°41′ E **188**
Paech'ŏn, *N. Korea* 37°58′ N, 126°18′ E **200**
Paektu-san, peak, *N. Korea* 41°58′ N, 128°4′ E **200**
Paeroa, *N.Z.* 37°22′ S, 175°40′ E **240**
Paesana, *It.* 44°41′ N, 7°16′ E **167**
Paestum, ruin(s), *It.* 40°24′ N, 14°54′ E **156**
Páez, *Col.* 2°37′ N, 75°59′ W **136**
Pafos, *Cyprus* 34°45′ N, 32°24′ E **194**
Pafúri, *Mozambique* 22°27′ S, 31°23′ E **227**
Paga Conta, *Braz.* 4°58′ S, 54°37′ W **130**
Pagadian, *Philippines* 7°52′ N, 123°25′ E **203**
Pagan, island, *Pagan* 18°7′ N, 144°58′ E **192**
Pagasae, ruin(s), *Gr.* 39°18′ N, 22°49′ E **156**
Pagashi, river, *Can.* 51°31′ N, 83°51′ W **110**
Pagato, river, *Can.* 56°4′ N, 102°44′ W **108**
Page, *N. Dak., U.S.* 47°9′ N, 97°35′ W **90**
Pagėgiai, *Lith.* 55°8′ N, 21°54′ E **166**
Pager, river, *Uganda* 3°18′ N, 33°13′ E **224**
Paghman, *Afghan.* 34°38′ N, 68°57′ E **186**
Pagiriai, *Lith.* 55°21′ N, 24°20′ E **166**
Pagnag, *China* 32°19′ N, 91°44′ E **188**
Pago Pago, *American Samoa, U.S.* 14°14′ S, 170°42′ W **241**
Pagoda Peak, *Colo., U.S.* 40°7′ N, 107°26′ W **90**
Pagoda Point, *Myanmar* 15°59′ N, 94°14′ E **202**
Paguchi Lake, lake, *Can.* 49°31′ N, 92°2′ W **94**
Pagwa River, *Can.* 50°1′ N, 85°12′ W **94**
Pagwachuan Lake, lake, *Can.* 49°40′ N, 86°46′ W **94**
Pah Rah Range, *Nev., U.S.* 39°42′ N, 119°42′ W **90**
Pahang, river, *Malaysia* 3°19′ N, 102°37′ E **196**
Paharpur, *Pak.* 32°5′ N, 71°1′ E **186**
Pahokee, *Fla., U.S.* 26°49′ N, 80°40′ W **105**
Pahranagat Range, *Nev., U.S.* 37°6′ N, 115°19′ W **101**
Pahranagat Valley, *Nev., U.S.* 37°11′ N, 115°11′ W **101**
Pahrock Range, *Nev., U.S.* 38°1′ N, 115°7′ W **90**
Pah-rum Peak, *Nev., U.S.* 40°22′ N, 119°40′ W **90**
Pahrump, *Nev., U.S.* 36°12′ N, 115°60′ W **101**
Pahute Mesa, *Nev., U.S.* 37°12′ N, 116°41′ W **92**
Pai, *Thai.* 19°18′ N, 98°23′ E **202**
Paiaguás, *Braz.* 18°24′ S, 57°9′ W **132**
Paicines, *Calif., U.S.* 36°43′ N, 121°17′ W **100**
Paide, *Est.* 58°53′ N, 25°33′ E **166**
Paige, *Tex., U.S.* 30°11′ N, 97°7′ W **96**
Paihia, *N.Z.* 35°20′ S, 174°4′ E **240**
Paiján, *Peru* 7°44′ S, 79°18′ W **130**
Päijänne, lake, *Fin.* 61°36′ N, 25°27′ E **166**
Pailin City, *Cambodia* 12°52′ N, 102°37′ E **202**
Paimio, *Fin.* 60°26′ N, 22°41′ E **166**
Paimpol, *Fr.* 48°47′ N, 3°4′ W **150**
Painan, *Indonesia* 1°19′ S, 100°34′ E **196**
Paincourtville, *La., U.S.* 29°58′ N, 91°4′ W **103**
Paine, Cerro, peak, *Chile* 50°60′ S, 73°13′ W **134**
Painesville, *Ohio, U.S.* 41°42′ N, 81°15′ W **102**
Paint Lake, lake, *Can.* 55°23′ N, 98°23′ W **108**
Paint Rock, *Tex., U.S.* 31°29′ N, 99°56′ W **92**
Painted Desert, *Ariz., U.S.* 36°17′ N, 110°60′ W **92**
Painter, Mount, peak, *Austral.* 30°19′ S, 139°7′ E **230**
Paintsville, *Ky., U.S.* 37°49′ N, 82°49′ W **94**
Paisley, *Oreg., U.S.* 42°41′ N, 120°33′ W **90**
Paistunturit, peak, *Fin.* 69°35′ N, 26°13′ E **152**
Paita, *Peru* 4°60′ S, 81°9′ W **130**
Pajala, *Nor.* 67°12′ N, 23°22′ E **152**
Pajares, Puerto de, pass, *Sp.* 43°0′ N, 5°47′ W **150**
Pajarito, *N. Mex., U.S.* 34°59′ N, 106°42′ W **92**
Pajaro, *Calif., U.S.* 36°52′ N, 121°45′ W **100**
Pájaro, *Col.* 11°40′ N, 72°40′ W **136**
Pajule, *Uganda* 2°56′ N, 32°54′ E **224**
Pajusti, *Est.* 59°15′ N, 26°22′ E **166**
Pak Nam Chumphon, *Thai.* 10°22′ N, 99°16′ E **202**
Pak Phanang, *Thai.* 8°22′ N, 100°13′ E **202**
Pakaraima Mountains, *Guyana* 5°59′ N, 60°35′ W **130**
Pakaur, *India* 24°36′ N, 87°50′ E **197**
Pakawau, *N.Z.* 40°38′ S, 172°40′ E **240**
Pakbèng, *Laos* 19°55′ N, 101°11′ E **202**
Pakch'ŏn, *N. Korea* 39°43′ N, 125°36′ E **200**
Pakhtusovo, *Russ.* 74°23′ N, 59°40′ E **160**
Paki, *Nig.* 11°28′ N, 8°10′ E **222**
Pakipaki, *N.Z.* 39°42′ S, 176°46′ E **240**
Pakistan 33°52′ N, 73°37′ E **186**
Pakleni Otoci, island, *Croatia* 43°10′ N, 15°56′ E **168**
Pakokku, *Myanmar* 21°24′ N, 95°5′ E **202**
Pakotai, *N.Z.* 35°43′ S, 173°54′ E **240**
Pak-Ou, *Laos* 20°5′ N, 102°13′ E **202**
Pakowki Lake, *Can.* 49°12′ N, 111°36′ W **90**
Pakpattan, *Pak.* 30°22′ N, 73°22′ E **186**
Pakrac, *Croatia* 45°26′ N, 17°12′ E **168**
Pakruojis, *Lith.* 55°58′ N, 23°51′ E **166**
Pakwach, *Uganda* 2°25′ N, 31°28′ E **224**
Pakxan, *Laos* 18°23′ N, 103°40′ E **202**
Pal Lahara, *India* 21°26′ N, 85°12′ E **188**
Pala, *Calif., U.S.* 33°22′ N, 117°6′ W **101**
Pala, *Chad* 9°23′ N, 14°55′ E **216**
Pala, *Myanmar* 12°51′ N, 98°39′ E **202**
Palabek, *Uganda* 3°27′ N, 32°34′ E **224**
Palacios, *Tex., U.S.* 28°42′ N, 96°13′ W **96**
Palaeopolis, ruin(s), *Gr.* 40°28′ N, 25°24′ E **156**
Palafrugell, *Sp.* 41°54′ N, 3°9′ E **164**
Palagruža (Pelagosa), island, *Croatia* 42°25′ N, 16°0′ E **168**
Palaichori, *Cyprus* 34°55′ N, 33°4′ E **194**
Palaiseau, *Fr.* 48°41′ N, 2°14′ E **163**
Palamau National Park, *India* 23°45′ N, 84°9′ E **197**
Palamós, *Sp.* 41°50′ N, 3°7′ E **164**
Palana, *Russ.* 59°7′ N, 160°9′ E **160**
Palanan, *Philippines* 17°4′ N, 122°25′ E **203**
Palanga, *Lith.* 55°54′ N, 21°4′ E **166**
Palani, *India* 10°27′ N, 77°30′ E **188**
Palanpur, *India* 24°10′ N, 72°26′ E **186**
Palapag, *Philippines* 12°33′ N, 125°7′ E **203**
Palapye, *Botswana* 22°30′ S, 27°5′ E **227**
Palar, river, *India* 12°46′ N, 79°11′ E **188**
Palatia, ruin(s), *Gr.* 35°51′ N, 27°9′ E **156**
Palatka, *Fla., U.S.* 29°38′ N, 81°39′ W **105**
Palatka, *Russ.* 60°13′ N, 150°51′ E **160**
Palau 5°28′ N, 132°55′ E **242**
Palau Trench, *North Pacific Ocean* 4°9′ N, 133°9′ E **254**
Palauig, *Philippines* 15°26′ N, 119°55′ E **203**
Palauk, *Myanmar* 13°16′ N, 98°38′ E **202**
Palaw, *Myanmar* 12°58′ N, 98°39′ E **202**
Palawan, island, *Philippines* 8°51′ N, 116°11′ E **192**
Palawan Trough, *South China Sea* 9°2′ N, 116°31′ E **254**
Palazzo San Gervasio, *It.* 40°56′ N, 15°59′ E **156**
Palazzolo sull'Oglio, *It.* 45°36′ N, 9°51′ E **167**
Paldiski, *Est.* 59°20′ N, 24°2′ E **166**
Pale, *Bosn. and Herzg.* 43°49′ N, 18°34′ E **168**
Pale, ruin(s), *Gr.* 38°10′ N, 20°18′ E **156**
Palel, *India* 24°27′ N, 94°3′ E **188**
Paleleh, *Indonesia* 1°2′ N, 121°53′ E **192**
Paleliu (Beliliou), island, *Palau* 7°0′ N, 134°15′ E **242**
Palembang, *Indonesia* 2°59′ S, 104°39′ E **192**
Palen Mountains, *Calif., U.S.* 33°47′ N, 115°10′ W **101**
Palencia, *Sp.* 42°0′ N, 4°33′ W **150**
Palenque National Park, *Mex.* 17°29′ N, 92°9′ W **115**
Palenque, ruin(s), *Mex.* 17°28′ N, 92°8′ W **115**
Palermo, *Col.* 0°24′ N, 73°29′ W **136**
Palermo, *It.* 38°8′ N, 13°20′ E **156**
Palestina, *Chile* 23°52′ S, 69°47′ W **132**
Palestina, *Mex.* 29°8′ N, 100°59′ W **92**
Palestine, *Ill., U.S.* 39°0′ N, 87°37′ W **102**
Palestine, *Tex., U.S.* 31°44′ N, 95°38′ W **103**
Paletwa, *Myanmar* 21°19′ N, 92°46′ E **188**
Palgrave, Mount, peak, *Austral.* 23°25′ S, 115°46′ E **230**
Palgrave Point, *Namibia* 20°47′ S, 12°44′ E **220**
Pali, *India* 25°46′ N, 73°21′ E **186**

PAL-PAT

Pali, *India* 25°46′ N, 73°21′ E **186**
Pali, river, *Sri Lanka* 9°4′ N, 79°55′ E **188**
Palian, *Thai.* 7°13′ N, 99°40′ E **196**
Palić, *Serb. and Mont.* 46°5′ N, 19°46′ E **168**
Palikir, *F.S.M.* 6°57′ N, 158°10′ E **242**
Palimbang, *Philippines* 6°15′ N, 124°12′ E **203**
Palinuro, Capo, *It.* 39°56′ N, 14°28′ E **156**
Palisade, *Colo., U.S.* 39°7′ N, 108°22′ W **90**
Palisade, *Nebr., U.S.* 40°20′ N, 101°7′ W **90**
Palisade Glacier, *Calif., U.S.* 37°3′ N, 118°46′ W **101**
Palizada, *Mex.* 18°14′ N, 92°8′ W **115**
Pälkäne, *Fin.* 61°20′ N, 24°14′ E **166**
Palkino, *Russ.* 57°32′ N, 28°0′ E **166**
Pallasovka, *Russ.* 50°2′ N, 46°51′ E **158**
Pallës, Bishti i, *Alban.* 41°20′ N, 18°42′ E **156**
Palling, *Can.* 54°21′ N, 125°55′ W **108**
Palliser, Cape, *N.Z.* 41°49′ S, 174°57′ E **240**
Palm Bay, *Fla., U.S.* 28°2′ N, 80°37′ W **105**
Palm Beach, *Fla., U.S.* 26°42′ N, 80°3′ W **105**
Palm Beach Gardens, *Fla., U.S.* 26°50′ N, 80°8′ W **105**
Palm Coast, *Fla., U.S.* 29°30′ N, 81°11′ W **105**
Palm Harbor, *Fla., U.S.* 28°3′ N, 82°45′ W **105**
Palm Islands, *Coral Sea* 18°27′ S, 146°34′ E **230**
Palm Point, *Nig.* 4°9′ N, 5°30′ E **222**
Palm Springs, *Calif., U.S.* 33°51′ N, 116°33′ W **101**
Palm Springs, *Fla., U.S.* 26°38′ N, 80°7′ W **105**
Palma, *Mozambique* 10°46′ S, 40°29′ E **224**
Palma, *Sp.* 39°40′ N, 2°37′ E **143**
Palma de Mallorca, *Sp.* 39°34′ N, 2°39′ E **150**
Palma del Río, *Sp.* 37°42′ N, 5°17′ W **164**
Palma, river, *Braz.* 12°27′ S, 47°55′ W **130**
Palma Sola, *Venez.* 10°33′ N, 68°34′ W **136**
Palmachim, spaceport, *Israel* 31°51′ N, 34°39′ E **194**
Palmaner, *India* 13°12′ N, 78°45′ E **188**
Palmanova, *It.* 45°54′ N, 13°18′ E **167**
Palmar Sur, *C.R.* 8°57′ N, 83°27′ W **115**
Palmares, *Braz.* 10°27′ S, 67°47′ W **137**
Palmares, *Braz.* 8°38′ S, 35°34′ W **132**
Palmarito, *Venez.* 7°38′ N, 70°9′ W **136**
Palmas, *Braz.* 26°28′ S, 52°1′ W **139**
Palmas, *Braz.* 10°11′ S, 48°18′ W **130**
Palmas, Cape 4°10′ N, 7°35′ W **222**
Palmas de Monte Alto, *Braz.* 14°19′ S, 43°7′ W **138**
Palmdale, *Calif., U.S.* 34°35′ N, 118°8′ W **101**
Palmdale, *Fla., U.S.* 26°56′ N, 81°19′ W **105**
Palmeira das Missões, *Braz.* 27°54′ S, 53°18′ W **139**
Palmeira dos Índios, *Braz.* 9°25′ S, 36°37′ W **132**
Palmeirante, *Braz.* 7°49′ S, 47°55′ W **130**
Palmela, *Port.* 38°33′ N, 8°55′ W **150**
Palmer, *Alas., U.S.* 61°31′ N, 149°10′ W **98**
Palmer, *Mass., U.S.* 42°9′ N, 72°20′ W **104**
Palmer Archipelago, islands, *Weddell Sea* 63°51′ S, 63°17′ W **134**
Palmer Land, region, *Antarctica* 69°25′ S, 65°11′ W **248**
Palmer, river, *Austral.* 16°10′ S, 142°53′ E **230**
Palmer, station, *Antarctica* 64°48′ S, 63°60′ W **134**
Palmerston, *Can.* 43°49′ N, 80°50′ W **102**
Palmerston, *N.Z.* 45°30′ S, 170°43′ E **240**
Palmerston North, *N.Z.* 40°23′ S, 175°36′ E **240**
Palmertown, *Conn., U.S.* 41°26′ N, 72°8′ W **104**
Palmetto, *Fla., U.S.* 27°31′ N, 82°33′ W **105**
Palmillas, *Mex.* 23°17′ N, 99°34′ W **114**
Palmira, *Col.* 3°29′ N, 76°18′ W **136**
Palmira, *Venez.* 8°49′ N, 72°24′ W **136**
Palmitas, *Uru.* 33°31′ S, 57°48′ W **139**
Palmyra, *Ill., U.S.* 39°25′ N, 89°60′ W **102**
Palmyra, *Mo., U.S.* 39°47′ N, 91°33′ W **94**
Palmyras Point, *India* 20°32′ N, 87°4′ E **188**
Palo Alto, *Calif., U.S.* 37°27′ N, 122°11′ W **100**
Palo Duro Canyon, *Tex., U.S.* 34°39′ N, 101°35′ W **92**
Palo Negro, *Arg.* 29°39′ S, 62°10′ W **139**
Palo Negro, *Col.* 1°29′ N, 72°20′ W **136**
Palo Verde, *Calif., U.S.* 33°25′ N, 114°45′ W **101**
Paloh, *Indonesia* 1°45′ N, 109°17′ E **196**
Paloich, *Sudan* 10°27′ N, 32°32′ E **224**
Palojärvi, *Fin.* 68°16′ N, 23°5′ E **152**
Palokoski, *Fin.* 66°51′ N, 25°23′ E **152**
Palomar Mountain, peak, *Calif., U.S.* 33°21′ N, 116°53′ W **101**
Palomas, *Mex.* 31°41′ N, 107°37′ W **92**
Palopo, *Indonesia* 2°60′ S, 120°10′ E **192**
Palos, Cabo de, *Sp.* 37°38′ N, 0°42′ E **164**
Palouse Hills, *Wash., U.S.* 47°11′ N, 117°57′ W **90**
Palouse, river, *Wash., U.S.* 46°37′ N, 118°22′ W **90**
Palpa, *Peru* 14°35′ S, 75°11′ W **132**
Palpa, *Peru* 11°30′ S, 77°7′ W **130**
Palpana, Cerro, peak, *Chile* 21°34′ S, 68°37′ W **137**
Paltamo, *Fin.* 64°24′ N, 27°45′ E **152**
Pältsa, peak, *Nor.* 69°0′ N, 20°2′ E **152**
Palu, *Indonesia* 0°54′ N, 119°51′ E **238**
Palu, *Turk.* 38°42′ N, 39°56′ E **195**
Paluan, *Philippines* 13°27′ N, 120°28′ E **203**
Palwal, *India* 28°8′ N, 77°19′ E **197**
Pama, *Burkina Faso* 11°14′ N, 0°42′ E **222**
Pama, river, *Cen. Af. Rep.* 4°42′ N, 17°8′ E **218**
Pamekasan, *Indonesia* 7°13′ S, 113°28′ E **192**
Pamiers, *Fr.* 43°6′ N, 1°36′ E **164**
Pamir, river, *Taj.* 37°15′ N, 72°46′ E **184**
Pamirs, *Taj.* 37°33′ N, 72°10′ E **190**
Pamoni, *Venez.* 2°49′ N, 65°54′ W **136**
Pampa, *Tex., U.S.* 35°30′ N, 100°58′ W **92**
Pampa de los Guanacos, *Arg.* 26°15′ S, 61°54′ W **139**
Pampa del Indio, *Arg.* 26°3′ S, 59°55′ W **139**
Pampa del Infierno, *Arg.* 26°30′ S, 61°12′ W **139**
Pampa Grande, *Bol.* 18°7′ S, 64°7′ W **137**
Pampaļi, *Latv.* 56°32′ N, 22°11′ E **166**
Pamparato, *It.* 44°15′ N, 7°55′ E **167**
Pampas, *Peru* 12°20′ S, 74°58′ W **137**
Pampeiro, *Braz.* 30°37′ S, 55°18′ W **139**
Pamplona, *Col.* 7°25′ N, 72°37′ W **136**
Pamplona (Iruña), *Sp.* 42°47′ N, 1°40′ W **164**
Pamzal, *India* 34°13′ N, 78°47′ E **188**
Pan de Azúcar, *Bol.* 21°56′ S, 67°28′ W **137**
Pan de Azúcar, *Uru.* 34°48′ S, 55°16′ W **139**
Pana, *Ill., U.S.* 39°23′ N, 89°5′ W **102**
Pana Tinai, island, *P.N.G.* 11°9′ S, 153°5′ E **230**
Panabá, *Mex.* 21°17′ N, 88°17′ W **112**
Panaca, *Nev., U.S.* 37°47′ N, 114°24′ W **92**
Panacea, *Fla., U.S.* 30°2′ N, 84°23′ W **96**
Panadura, *Sri Lanka* 6°41′ N, 79°56′ E **188**
Panahaïkó, Óros, peak, *Gr.* 38°10′ N, 21°47′ E **156**
Panaji, *India* 15°27′ N, 73°51′ E **188**
Panama, *Okla., U.S.* 35°8′ N, 94°41′ W **96**
Panama 8°20′ N, 81°0′ W **115**
Panamá, *Pan.* 8°58′ N, 79°39′ W **115**
Panama, *Sri Lanka* 6°45′ N, 81°48′ E **188**
Panamá, Bahía de 8°46′ N, 80°20′ W **115**
Panama Basin, *North Pacific Ocean* 2°47′ N, 83°11′ W **252**
Panama City, *Fla., U.S.* 30°9′ N, 85°40′ W **96**
Panamá, Golfo de 7°45′ N, 80°2′ W **115**
Panamá Viejo, ruin(s), *Golfo de Panamá* 8°59′ N, 79°33′ W **115**
Panambi, *Braz.* 28°20′ S, 53°29′ W **139**
Panamint Range, *Calif., U.S.* 36°18′ N, 117°20′ W **101**
Panamint Springs, *Calif., U.S.* 36°20′ N, 117°29′ W **101**
Panamint Valley, *Calif., U.S.* 36°3′ N, 117°25′ W **101**
Panay, island, *Philippines* 10°6′ N, 121°16′ E **192**
Pancake Range, *Nev., U.S.* 38°34′ N, 116°13′ W **90**
Pančevo, *Europe* 44°52′ N, 20°38′ E **156**
Pančićev Vrh, peak, *Europe* 43°15′ N, 20°47′ E **168**
Pancorbo, *Sp.* 42°37′ N, 3°6′ W **164**
Pancurbatu, *Indonesia* 3°29′ N, 98°37′ E **196**
Panda, *Mozambique* 23°60′ S, 34°42′ E **227**
Pandan, *Philippines* 14°3′ N, 124°10′ E **203**
Pandan, *Philippines* 11°41′ N, 122°6′ E **203**
Pandėlys, *Lith.* 56°0′ N, 25°12′ E **166**
Pando, *Uru.* 34°41′ S, 55°57′ W **139**
Pando, adm. division, *Bol.* 10°53′ S, 67°31′ W **137**
Pandora Entrance 11°42′ S, 143°12′ E **230**
Panetolikó, Óros, peak, *Gr.* 38°40′ N, 21°30′ E **156**
Panevėžys, *Lith.* 55°42′ N, 24°20′ E **166**
Panfilovo, *Russ.* 50°22′ N, 42°50′ E **158**
Panga, *Dem. Rep. of the Congo* 1°50′ N, 26°23′ E **224**
Pangala, *Congo* 3°20′ S, 14°34′ E **218**
Pangani, *Tanzania* 5°23′ S, 38°59′ E **224**
Panganiban (Payo), *Philippines* 13°56′ N, 124°17′ E **203**
Pangéo, Óros, *Gr.* 40°51′ N, 23°44′ E **156**
Panghyŏn, *N. Korea* 39°52′ N, 125°14′ E **200**
Pangi, *Dem. Rep. of the Congo* 3°14′ S, 26°39′ E **224**
Pangkalanbrandan, *Indonesia* 4°2′ N, 98°18′ E **196**
Pangkalanbuun, *Indonesia* 2°44′ S, 111°31′ E **192**
Pangkalankotabaru, *Indonesia* 0°7′ N, 100°43′ E **196**
Pangkalpinang, *Indonesia* 2°3′ S, 106°2′ E **192**
Pangkor, island, *Malaysia* 4°4′ N, 100°3′ E **196**
Pangnirtung, *Can.* 66°7′ N, 65°46′ W **106**
Panguitch, *Utah, U.S.* 37°49′ N, 112°26′ W **92**
Panguma, *Sierra Leone* 8°9′ N, 11°8′ W **222**
Panguru, *N.Z.* 35°24′ S, 173°22′ E **240**
Pangutaran, *Philippines* 6°20′ N, 120°33′ E **203**
Panhandle, *Tex., U.S.* 35°20′ N, 101°23′ W **92**
Pania Mutombo, *Dem. Rep. of the Congo* 5°13′ S, 23°52′ E **224**
Pāniʻau, peak, *Hawaiʻi, U.S.* 21°55′ N, 160°8′ W **99**
Panié, Mount, peak 20°39′ S, 164°24′ E **238**
Panipat, *India* 29°23′ N, 77°0′ E **197**
Panj, *Taj.* 37°14′ N, 69°6′ E **186**
Panj, river, *Asia* 37°40′ N, 71°30′ E **197**
Panjab, *Afghan.* 34°23′ N, 67°6′ E **186**
Panjakent, *Taj.* 39°28′ N, 67°32′ E **197**
Panjang, island, *Indonesia* 2°48′ N, 108°57′ E **196**
Panjang, oil field, *Strait of Malacca* 4°10′ N, 98°14′ E **196**
Panjgur, *Pak.* 26°55′ N, 64°7′ E **182**
Pankakoski, *Fin.* 63°17′ N, 30°8′ E **152**
Pankow, *Ger.* 52°35′ N, 13°25′ E **152**
Pankshin, *Nig.* 9°18′ N, 9°24′ E **222**
Panmunjom, site, *N. Korea* 37°56′ N, 126°34′ E **200**
Panna, *India* 24°42′ N, 80°12′ E **197**
Pannonhalma, *Hung.* 47°32′ N, 17°48′ E **168**
Panny, river, *Can.* 57°17′ N, 114°41′ W **108**
Pano Lefkara, *Cyprus* 34°52′ N, 33°18′ E **194**
Pano Panagia, *Cyprus* 34°55′ N, 32°37′ E **194**
Pano Platres, *Cyprus* 34°52′ N, 32°51′ E **194**
Panoche Pass, *Calif., U.S.* 36°37′ N, 121°1′ W **100**
Panola, *Ala., U.S.* 32°58′ N, 88°15′ W **103**
Panolik, *Russ.* 60°23′ N, 101°25′ E **173**
Panorama, *Braz.* 21°19′ S, 51°51′ W **138**
Panozero, *Russ.* 64°57′ N, 32°50′ E **152**
P'anp'yŏng, *N. Korea* 40°26′ N, 125°50′ E **200**
Panshi, *China* 42°55′ N, 126°3′ E **200**
Pantanal Matogrossense National Park, *Braz.* 17°45′ S, 58°17′ W **132**
Pantar, island, *Indonesia* 8°15′ S, 123°28′ E **192**
Pante Makasar (Oecusse), *Indonesia* 9°21′ S, 124°20′ E **192**
Pantelleria, island, *It.* 36°47′ N, 10°43′ E **216**
Pantepec, *Mex.* 20°35′ N, 97°55′ W **114**
Pantoja, *Peru* 0°59′ N, 75°11′ W **136**
Pantonlabu, *Indonesia* 5°7′ N, 97°26′ E **196**
Pantyy, *Russ.* 62°27′ N, 48°55′ E **154**
Pánuco, *Mex.* 22°1′ N, 98°11′ W **114**
Pánuco, river, *Mex.* 21°56′ N, 98°25′ W **114**
Panyam, *Nig.* 9°23′ N, 9°12′ E **222**
Panza Range, La, *Calif., U.S.* 35°22′ N, 120°19′ W **100**
Panzhihua, *China* 26°21′ N, 101°45′ E **190**
Panzi, *Dem. Rep. of the Congo* 7°17′ S, 18°0′ E **218**
Pao, river, *Thai.* 17°1′ N, 103°9′ E **202**
Pao, river, *Venez.* 8°23′ N, 64°24′ W **116**
Paola, *It.* 39°22′ N, 16°2′ E **156**
Paola, *Kans., U.S.* 38°33′ N, 94°52′ W **94**
Paoli, *Ind., U.S.* 38°33′ N, 86°28′ W **102**
Paonia, *Colo., U.S.* 38°51′ N, 107°35′ W **90**
Paoua, *Cen. Af. Rep.* 7°12′ N, 16°25′ E **218**
Paouignan, *Benin* 7°44′ N, 2°12′ E **222**
Paoziyan, *China* 41°19′ N, 125°24′ E **200**
Pap, *Sudan* 6°6′ N, 31°12′ E **224**
Pápa, *Hung.* 47°19′ N, 17°28′ E **168**
Pāpā Heiau, site, *Hawaiʻi, U.S.* 21°9′ N, 156°48′ W **99**
Papakura, *N.Z.* 37°4′ S, 174°58′ E **240**
Papanoa, *Mex.* 17°16′ N, 101°2′ W **114**
Papanoa, Morro de, *Mex.* 17°15′ N, 101°1′ W **114**
Papantla, *Mex.* 20°26′ N, 97°19′ W **114**
Paparoa, *N.Z.* 36°7′ S, 174°15′ E **240**
Papeete, *French Polynesia, Fr.* 17°32′ S, 149°35′ W **241**
Papenburg, *Ger.* 53°5′ N, 7°23′ E **163**
Papigochic, river, *Mex.* 29°0′ N, 108°1′ W **80**
Papíkio, peak, *Gr.* 41°12′ N, 25°13′ E **156**
Papilė, *Lith.* 56°9′ N, 22°46′ E **166**
Papua, Gulf of 8°59′ S, 144°26′ E **192**
Papua New Guinea 6°34′ S, 142°53′ E **192**
Papuk, *Croatia* 45°32′ N, 17°20′ E **168**
Papun, *Myanmar* 18°4′ N, 97°26′ E **202**
Papuri, river, *Braz.* 0°36′ N, 70°11′ W **130**
Pará, adm. division, *Braz.* 4°16′ S, 53°14′ W **130**
Paracale, *Philippines* 14°16′ N, 122°47′ E **203**
Paracari, river, *Braz.* 4°42′ S, 57°55′ W **130**
Paracas, Península, *Peru* 13°53′ S, 77°45′ W **130**
Paracatu, *Braz.* 17°16′ S, 46°52′ W **138**
Paracatu, river, *Braz.* 17°25′ S, 46°35′ W **138**
Paracel Islands, islands, *South China Sea* 16°38′ N, 111°40′ E **192**
Parachinar, *Pak.* 33°52′ N, 70°8′ E **186**
Parachute, *Colo., U.S.* 39°27′ N, 108°4′ W **90**
Paraćin, *Serb. and Mont.* 43°51′ N, 21°24′ E **168**
Paracuru, *Braz.* 3°25′ S, 39°7′ W **132**
Parád, *Hung.* 47°54′ N, 20°2′ E **168**
Parada, Punta, *Peru* 15°37′ S, 75°39′ W **132**
Paradas, *Sp.* 37°17′ N, 5°31′ W **150**
Paradis, *Can.* 48°14′ N, 76°35′ W **94**
Paradise, *Calif., U.S.* 39°45′ N, 121°39′ W **90**
Paradise, *Mich., U.S.* 46°37′ N, 85°4′ W **94**
Paradise, *Mont., U.S.* 47°22′ N, 114°49′ W **90**
Paradise, *Nev., U.S.* 36°5′ N, 115°9′ W **101**
Paradise Valley, *Nev., U.S.* 41°29′ N, 117°32′ W **90**
Paraf'yanava, *Belarus* 54°52′ N, 27°35′ E **166**
Paragon Lake, lake, *Can.* 58°16′ N, 97°49′ W **108**
Paragould, *Ark., U.S.* 36°3′ N, 90°29′ W **94**
Paraguá, river, *Bol.* 15°1′ S, 61°6′ W **132**
Paragua, river, *Venez.* 5°37′ N, 63°43′ W **130**
Paraguaçu Paulista, *Braz.* 22°26′ S, 50°39′ W **138**
Paraguaçu, river, *Braz.* 13°10′ S, 40°53′ W **138**
Paraguai, river, *South America* 20°11′ S, 58°21′ W **132**
Paraguaipoa, *Venez.* 11°21′ N, 71°60′ W **136**
Paraguaná, Península de, *Venez.* 12°6′ N, 70°25′ W **116**
Paraguaná, Península de, *Venez.* 12°3′ N, 70°14′ W **136**
Paraguarí, *Parag.* 25°38′ S, 57°9′ W **132**
Paraguay 23°21′ S, 59°9′ W **132**
Paraíba, adm. division, *Braz.* 7°3′ S, 38°22′ W **132**
Parainen see Pargas, *Fin.* 60°17′ N, 22°17′ E **166**
Paraíso, *Braz.* 19°3′ S, 53°2′ W **138**
Paraíso, *Braz.* 6°41′ S, 59°1′ W **130**
Paraíso, *Mex.* 18°24′ N, 93°14′ W **115**
Paraíso do Tocantins, *Braz.* 10°15′ S, 48°57′ W **132**
Parakhonsk, *Belarus* 52°13′ N, 26°26′ E **152**
Parakou, *Benin* 9°19′ N, 2°36′ E **222**
Paralimni, *Cyprus* 35°2′ N, 33°58′ E **194**
Paramaribo, *Suriname* 5°42′ N, 55°27′ W **130**
Paramé, *Fr.* 48°39′ N, 1°60′ W **150**
Paramera, Sierra de la, *Sp.* 40°22′ N, 5°33′ W **150**
Paramillo National Park, *Col.* 7°21′ N, 76°14′ W **136**
Paramirim, *Braz.* 13°27′ S, 42°16′ W **138**
Paraná, *Arg.* 31°46′ S, 60°31′ W **139**
Paranã, *Braz.* 12°35′ S, 47°50′ W **130**
Paraná, river, *Arg.* 29°37′ S, 58°49′ W **123**
Paranaguá, *Braz.* 25°34′ S, 48°33′ W **138**
Paranaíba, *Braz.* 19°40′ S, 51°13′ W **138**
Paranaíba, river, *Braz.* 19°34′ S, 51°11′ W **138**
Paranaiguara, *Braz.* 18°53′ S, 50°33′ W **138**
Paranaíta, river, *Braz.* 9°31′ S, 56°55′ W **130**
Paranapanema, river, *Braz.* 22°26′ S, 52°17′ W **138**
Paranapiacaba, Serra do, *Braz.* 24°13′ S, 49°11′ W **132**
Paranavaí, *Braz.* 23°4′ S, 52°37′ W **138**
Parang, *Philippines* 5°58′ N, 120°53′ E **203**
Parapetí, river, *Bol.* 20°14′ S, 63°34′ W **137**
Parás, *Mex.* 26°27′ N, 99°31′ W **114**
Parati, *Braz.* 23°13′ S, 44°45′ W **132**
Paratinga, *Braz.* 12°43′ S, 43°11′ W **138**
Parauapebas, river, *Braz.* 6°60′ S, 50°16′ W **130**
Parauaquara, Serra, peak, *Braz.* 1°34′ S, 53°13′ W **130**
Paraúna, *Braz.* 17°4′ S, 50°28′ W **138**
Parbati, river, *India* 24°46′ N, 77°3′ E **197**
Parbhani, *India* 19°15′ N, 76°45′ E **188**
Parbig, *Russ.* 57°11′ N, 81°29′ E **169**
Parcines, *It.* 46°41′ N, 11°4′ E **167**
Parczew, *Pol.* 51°38′ N, 22°53′ E **152**
Pardés Hanna-Karkur, *Israel* 32°28′ N, 34°58′ E **194**
Pardilla, *Sp.* 41°32′ N, 3°43′ W **164**
Pardo, river, *Braz.* 20°59′ S, 53°16′ W **138**
Pardo, river, *Braz.* 15°49′ S, 42°6′ W **138**
Pardo, river, *Braz.* 21°32′ S, 46°54′ W **138**
Pardo, river, *Braz.* 15°29′ S, 45°7′ W **138**
Pardubice, *Czech Rep.* 50°1′ N, 15°47′ E **152**
Pare Mountains, *Tanzania* 3°29′ S, 37°42′ E **224**
Parec, Serra dos, *Braz.* 9°47′ S, 64°10′ W **137**
Parechcha, *Belarus* 53°51′ N, 24°8′ E **166**
Parecis, *Braz.* 13°34′ S, 55°55′ W **123**
Parecis, river, *Braz.* 13°39′ S, 57°13′ W **130**
Paren', *Russ.* 62°24′ N, 162°51′ E **160**
Parent, *Can.* 47°56′ N, 74°38′ W **94**
Parent, Lac, lake, *Can.* 48°44′ N, 77°24′ W **94**
Parepare, *Indonesia* 3°60′ S, 119°37′ E **192**
Pargas (Parainen), *Fin.* 60°17′ N, 22°17′ E **166**
Pargny, *Fr.* 48°45′ N, 4°48′ E **163**
Parguaza, *Venez.* 6°24′ N, 67°5′ W **136**
Paria, *Bol.* 17°52′ S, 67°1′ W **137**
Paria, Gulf of 10°13′ N, 62°40′ W **116**
Paria, Peninsula de, *Venez.* 10°47′ N, 62°56′ W **116**
Pariacaca, Cerro, peak, *Peru* 11°58′ S, 76°5′ W **130**
Pariaman, *Indonesia* 0°36′ N, 100°8′ E **196**
Paricá, Lago, lake, *Braz.* 1°54′ S, 66°4′ W **136**
Paricutín, Volcán, peak, *Mex.* 19°28′ N, 102°21′ W **114**
Parida, Isla, island, *Pan.* 7°48′ N, 82°24′ W **115**
Parika, *Guyana* 6°47′ N, 58°27′ W **130**
Parikkala, *Fin.* 61°31′ N, 29°30′ E **166**
Parima, river, *Braz.* 2°30′ N, 63°49′ W **130**
Parima, Serra, *Braz.* 3°17′ N, 64°33′ W **130**
Parima-Tapirapecó National Park, *Venez.* 1°56′ N, 65°41′ W **136**
Pariñas, Punta, *Peru* 4°31′ S, 82°26′ W **130**
Parintins, *Braz.* 2°42′ S, 56°48′ W **130**
Paris, *Ark., U.S.* 35°16′ N, 93°45′ W **96**
Paris, *Fr.* 48°52′ N, 2°17′ E **163**
Paris, *Ill., U.S.* 39°36′ N, 87°42′ W **102**
Paris, *Ky., U.S.* 38°12′ N, 84°16′ W **94**
Paris, *Me., U.S.* 44°16′ N, 70°30′ W **104**
Paris, *Mo., U.S.* 39°28′ N, 92°1′ W **94**
Paris, *Mo., U.S.* 39°36′ N, 87°42′ W **94**
Paris, *Tenn., U.S.* 36°17′ N, 88°20′ W **96**
Paris, *Tex., U.S.* 33°38′ N, 95°32′ W **96**
Parismina, *C.R.* 10°15′ N, 83°22′ W **115**
Parit Buntar, *Malaysia* 5°6′ N, 100°29′ E **196**
Parita, *Pan.* 8°0′ N, 80°32′ W **115**
Park Falls, *Wis., U.S.* 45°55′ N, 90°28′ W **94**
Park Range, *Colo., U.S.* 40°43′ N, 106°47′ W **90**
Park Rapids, *Minn., U.S.* 46°54′ N, 95°5′ W **90**
Park River, *N. Dak., U.S.* 48°21′ N, 97°47′ W **90**
Parkajoki, *Nor.* 67°18′ N, 23°24′ E **152**
Parkal, *India* 18°11′ N, 79°42′ E **188**
Parkano, *Fin.* 62°0′ N, 22°58′ E **166**
Parkdale, *Ark., U.S.* 33°6′ N, 91°33′ W **103**
Parker, *Ariz., U.S.* 34°8′ N, 114°18′ W **101**
Parker, *S. Dak., U.S.* 43°22′ N, 97°8′ W **90**
Parker Dam, *Calif., U.S.* 34°16′ N, 114°10′ W **101**
Parker Dam, *Calif., U.S.* 34°19′ N, 114°16′ W **101**
Parkersburg, *W. Va., U.S.* 39°15′ N, 81°34′ W **102**
Parkhill, *Can.* 43°9′ N, 81°41′ W **102**
Parkin, *Ark., U.S.* 35°14′ N, 90°34′ W **96**
Parkland, *Wash., U.S.* 47°7′ N, 122°26′ W **100**
Parks, *La., U.S.* 30°11′ N, 91°51′ W **103**
Parks Lake, lake, *Can.* 49°25′ N, 87°58′ W **110**
Parksley, *Va., U.S.* 37°46′ N, 75°40′ W **94**
Parkston, *S. Dak., U.S.* 43°22′ N, 97°59′ W **90**
Parksville, *Can.* 49°18′ N, 124°19′ W **100**
Parkumäki, *Fin.* 61°56′ N, 28°27′ E **166**
Parkview Mountain, peak, *Colo., U.S.* 40°18′ N, 106°12′ W **90**
Parli, *India* 18°51′ N, 76°31′ E **188**
Parlier, *Calif., U.S.* 36°36′ N, 119°33′ W **101**
Parma, *Idaho, U.S.* 43°46′ N, 116°57′ W **90**
Parma, *It.* 44°47′ N, 10°20′ E **167**
Parma, *Mich., U.S.* 42°14′ N, 84°36′ W **102**
Parma, *Ohio, U.S.* 41°23′ N, 81°42′ W **94**
Parma, river, *It.* 44°25′ N, 10°3′ E **167**
Parnaguá, *Braz.* 10°16′ S, 44°36′ W **132**
Parnaíba, *Braz.* 2°58′ S, 41°45′ W **132**
Parnaíba, river, *Braz.* 8°21′ S, 45°45′ W **130**
Parnamirim, *Braz.* 8°8′ S, 39°35′ W **132**
Parnarama, *Braz.* 5°43′ S, 43°9′ W **132**
Parnassós National Park, *Gr.* 38°29′ N, 22°26′ E **180**
Parnassós, peak, *Gr.* 38°31′ N, 22°32′ E **156**
Parnassus, *N.Z.* 42°42′ S, 173°17′ E **240**
Párnitha National Park, *Gr.* 38°8′ N, 23°38′ E **156**
Párnitha, Óros, peak, *Gr.* 38°10′ N, 23°38′ E **156**
Párnonas, Óros, *Gr.* 37°22′ N, 22°31′ E **156**
Pärnu, *Est.* 58°23′ N, 24°29′ E **166**
Pärnu Jaagupi, *Est.* 58°36′ N, 24°27′ E **166**
Pärnu Laht 58°18′ N, 24°7′ E **166**
Pärnu, river, *Est.* 58°45′ N, 25°16′ E **166**
Paroho, lake, *S. Korea* 38°8′ N, 127°41′ E **200**
Páros, *Gr.* 37°4′ N, 25°9′ E **156**
Páros, island, *Gr.* 36°50′ N, 24°52′ E **180**
Parowan, *Utah, U.S.* 37°50′ N, 112°49′ W **92**
Parr, Cape 81°8′ S, 171°43′ E **248**
Parral, *Chile* 36°7′ S, 71°52′ W **134**
Parras de la Fuente, *Mex.* 25°25′ N, 102°12′ W **114**
Parris Island, *S.C., U.S.* 32°5′ N, 80°27′ W **112**
Parrish, *Fla., U.S.* 27°35′ N, 82°25′ W **105**
Parrs Halt, *Botswana* 23°22′ S, 27°16′ E **227**
Parry, Cape, *Can.* 69°59′ N, 124°19′ W **106**
Parry, Cape, *Can.* 70°11′ N, 126°24′ W **98**
Parry Islands, *Foxe Basin* 74°19′ N, 107°51′ W **106**
Parry, Kap 76°58′ N, 75°51′ W **106**
Parry, Kap, *Traill Ø* 72°1′ N, 21°53′ W **246**
Parry Peninsula, *Can.* 69°48′ N, 125°21′ W **98**
Parry Sound, *Can.* 45°20′ N, 80°2′ W **94**
Parshall, *N. Dak., U.S.* 47°57′ N, 102°10′ W **90**
Parsi, oil field, *Iran* 31°0′ N, 49°54′ E **180**
Parsnip Peak, *Nev., U.S.* 38°8′ N, 114°25′ W **90**
Parsnip Peak, *Oreg., U.S.* 42°50′ N, 117°11′ W **90**
Parsnip, river, *Can.* 54°34′ N, 122°18′ W **108**
Parsons, *Kans., U.S.* 37°19′ N, 95°16′ W **96**
Pårtefjället, peak, *Nor.* 67°9′ N, 17°29′ E **152**
Partridge Bay 53°8′ N, 56°28′ W **111**
Partridge, river, *Can.* 50°50′ N, 80°23′ W **110**
Parú, river, *Venez.* 4°34′ N, 66°7′ W **136**
Parucito, river, *Venez.* 5°2′ N, 66°8′ W **136**
Paruro, *Peru* 13°48′ S, 71°51′ W **137**
P'arvani, Tba, lake, *Ga.* 41°23′ N, 43°28′ E **195**
Parvatipuram, *India* 18°45′ N, 83°26′ E **188**
Paryang, *China* 30°11′ N, 83°20′ E **197**
Parychy, *Belarus* 52°46′ N, 29°29′ E **152**
Parys, *S. Af.* 26°58′ S, 27°27′ E **227**
Pasadena, *Calif., U.S.* 34°8′ N, 118°11′ W **101**
Pasadena, *Tex., U.S.* 29°41′ N, 95°12′ W **103**
Pasado, Cabo, *Ecua.* 0°22′ N, 81°24′ W **130**
Pasaje, *Ecua.* 3°28′ S, 79°49′ W **130**
Pasaje (Juramento), river, *Arg.* 28°44′ S, 62°58′ W **139**
P'asanauri, *Ga.* 42°19′ N, 44°37′ E **195**
Pascagoula, *Miss., U.S.* 30°21′ N, 88°32′ W **103**
Paşcani, *Rom.* 47°14′ N, 26°42′ E **156**
Pasco, *Wash., U.S.* 46°13′ N, 119°5′ W **90**
Pasco, adm. division, *Peru* 10°15′ S, 74°55′ W **137**
Pascoag, *R.I., U.S.* 41°57′ N, 71°43′ W **104**
Pascoal, Monte, peak, *Braz.* 16°53′ S, 39°25′ W **138**
Pascua, Isla de see Easter Island, *Chile* 27°0′ S, 109°0′ W **241**
Pasewalk, *Ger.* 53°30′ N, 13°59′ E **152**
Pasfield Lake, *Can.* 58°24′ N, 105°44′ W **108**
Pasha, river, *Russ.* 59°46′ N, 34°4′ E **154**
Pashiya, *Russ.* 58°26′ N, 58°22′ E **154**
Pashskiy Perevoz, *Russ.* 60°23′ N, 33°8′ E **154**
Pasinler, *Turk.* 39°59′ N, 41°40′ E **195**
Pasir Mas, *Malaysia* 6°3′ N, 102°7′ E **196**
Pasir Puteh, *Malaysia* 5°50′ N, 102°23′ E **196**
Paskwachi Bay 57°14′ N, 102°46′ W **108**
Pasley, Cape, *Austral.* 34°26′ S, 123°41′ E **231**
Pasni, *Pak.* 25°15′ N, 63°26′ E **182**
Paso de los Libres, *Arg.* 29°40′ S, 57°9′ W **139**
Paso de los Toros, *Uru.* 32°46′ S, 56°31′ W **139**
Paso de Ovejas, *Mex.* 19°16′ N, 96°26′ W **114**
Paso Robles, *Calif., U.S.* 35°37′ N, 120°42′ W **100**
Pasorapa, *Bol.* 18°21′ S, 64°39′ W **137**
Pasque Island, *Mass., U.S.* 41°27′ N, 70°53′ W **104**
Pass Christian, *Miss., U.S.* 30°18′ N, 89°15′ W **103**
Passadumkeag Mountain, peak, *Me., U.S.* 45°6′ N, 68°28′ W **94**
Passat Nunatak, peak, *Antarctica* 71°25′ S, 4°12′ W **248**
Passau, *Ger.* 48°33′ N, 13°28′ E **152**
Passero, Capo, *It.* 36°39′ N, 15°9′ E **216**
Passo Fundo, *Braz.* 28°16′ S, 52°27′ W **139**
Passos, *Braz.* 20°43′ S, 46°37′ W **138**
Pastavy, *Belarus* 55°7′ N, 26°50′ E **166**
Pastaza, river, *Ecua.* 2°3′ S, 77°39′ W **130**
Pastaza, river, *Peru* 4°29′ S, 76°33′ W **130**
Pasteur, *Arg.* 35°7′ S, 62°14′ W **139**
Pasto, *Col.* 1°13′ N, 77°17′ W **136**
Pastora Peak, *Ariz., U.S.* 36°46′ N, 109°14′ W **92**
Pastos Bons, *Braz.* 6°38′ S, 44°5′ W **132**
Pastrana, *Sp.* 40°24′ N, 2°56′ W **150**
Pasvalys, *Lith.* 56°3′ N, 24°22′ E **166**
Pasvik, *Nor.* 69°47′ N, 30°32′ E **152**
Pašvitinys, *Lith.* 56°9′ N, 23°47′ E **166**
Pásztó, *Hung.* 47°54′ N, 19°43′ E **168**
Pata, *Cen. Af. Rep.* 8°2′ N, 21°28′ E **218**
Patagonia, *Ariz., U.S.* 31°31′ N, 110°45′ W **92**
Patamisk, Lac, lake, *Can.* 52°52′ N, 71°43′ W **111**
Patan, *India* 23°50′ N, 72°7′ E **186**
Patan, *India* 17°24′ N, 73°55′ E **188**
Patan, *India* 23°16′ N, 79°43′ E **197**
Patan see Lalitpur, *Nepal* 27°36′ N, 85°22′ E **197**
Patani, *Indonesia* 0°15′ N, 128°46′ E **192**
Patara Shiraki, *Ga.* 41°17′ N, 46°20′ E **195**
Patchogue, *N.Y., U.S.* 40°45′ N, 73°1′ W **104**
Pate Island, *Kenya* 2°16′ S, 41°4′ E **224**
Pategi, *Nig.* 8°43′ N, 5°44′ E **222**
Pateley Bridge, *U.K.* 54°5′ N, 1°45′ W **162**
Patensie, *S. Af.* 33°46′ S, 24°48′ E **227**
Paternion, *Aust.* 46°43′ N, 13°40′ E **167**
Paterson, *N.J., U.S.* 40°53′ N, 74°11′ W **92**
Paterson Range, *Austral.* 21°46′ S, 121°56′ E **230**
Pathankot, *India* 32°16′ N, 75°42′ E **186**
Pathein, *Myanmar* 16°44′ N, 94°45′ E **202**
Pathfinder Dam, *Wyo., U.S.* 42°28′ N, 106°49′ W **90**
Pathum Thani, *Thai.* 14°1′ N, 100°31′ E **202**
Pati, river, *Braz.* 3°40′ S, 67°54′ W **136**
Patiala, *India* 30°19′ N, 76°22′ E **197**
Pativilca, *Peru* 10°42′ S, 77°47′ W **130**
Pátmos, *Gr.* 37°18′ N, 26°33′ E **156**
Patna, *India* 25°33′ N, 85°5′ E **197**
Patnos, *Turk.* 39°13′ N, 42°52′ E **195**
Pató, *Col.* 7°27′ N, 74°55′ W **136**
Patoka, *Ill., U.S.* 38°44′ N, 89°6′ W **102**
Patoka, *Ind., U.S.* 38°24′ N, 87°36′ W **94**
Patos, *Braz.* 6°60′ S, 37°15′ W **132**
Patos de Minas, *Braz.* 18°36′ S, 46°30′ W **138**
Patos, Lagoa dos, lake, *Braz.* 31°15′ S, 51°35′ W **139**
Patos, Laguna de, lake, *Mex.* 30°41′ N, 107°3′ W **92**
Patos, Ponta dos, *Braz.* 2°59′ S, 39°40′ W **132**
Pátra, *Gr.* 38°12′ N, 21°47′ E **180**
Patrae see Pátra, *Gr.* 38°14′ N, 21°43′ E **156**
Patricio Lynch, Isla, island, *Chile* 48°27′ S, 77°53′ W **134**
Patrick Air Force Base, *Fla., U.S.* 28°14′ N, 80°39′ W **105**
Patrick, Croagh, peak, *Ire.* 53°44′ N, 9°46′ W **150**
Patrick Point, peak, *Antarctica* 73°36′ S, 66°6′ E **248**
Patrimonio, *Braz.* 19°30′ S, 48°31′ W **138**
Patrington, *U.K.* 53°40′ N, 7°419′ W **162**
Patriot, *Ind., U.S.* 38°50′ N, 84°49′ W **102**
Patriot Hills, station, *Antarctica* 81°29′ S, 81°27′ W **248**
Patrocínio, *Braz.* 18°57′ S, 46°58′ W **138**
Pattani, *Thai.* 6°50′ N, 101°16′ E **196**
Patten, *Me., U.S.* 45°59′ N, 68°27′ W **94**
Patterson, *Calif., U.S.* 37°28′ N, 121°9′ W **100**
Patterson Lake, lake, *Can.* 57°37′ N, 109°54′ W **108**
Patterson, Mount, peak, *Calif., U.S.* 38°25′ N, 119°24′ W **90**
Patterson Mountain, peak, *Calif., U.S.* 36°58′ N, 119°6′ W **101**
Patti, *India* 31°16′ N, 74°53′ E **186**
Pattison, *Miss., U.S.* 31°53′ N, 90°53′ W **103**
Patton Seamounts, *North Pacific Ocean* 54°12′ N, 150°21′ W **252**
Pattullo, Mount, peak, *Can.* 56°13′ N, 129°48′ W **108**
Patu, *Braz.* 6°8′ S, 37°38′ W **132**
Patuakhali, *Bangladesh* 22°18′ N, 90°19′ E **197**
Patuanak, *Can.* 55°55′ N, 107°44′ W **108**
Patuca National Park, *Hond.* 14°27′ N, 85°53′ W **115**

345

Peto, Mex. 20°6′ N, 88°57′ W 115
Petolahti see Petalax, Fin. 62°49′ N, 21°24′ E 154
Petoskey, Mich., U.S. 45°20′ N, 84°60′ W 82
Petra, Ostrova, islands, Laptev Sea 75°41′ N, 108°52′ E 160
Petra, ruin(s), Jordan 30°17′ N, 35°23′ E 180
Petra Velikogo, Zaliv 42°40′ N, 131°45′ E 200
Petras, Mount, peak, Antarctica 75°47′ S, 127°55′ W 248
Petre, Point, Can. 43°38′ N, 77°26′ W 94
Petriano, It. 43°46′ N, 12°43′ E 167
Petrich, Bulg. 41°24′ N, 23°9′ E 180
Petrified Forest National Park, Ariz., U.S. 34°44′ N, 109°45′ W 92
Petrinja, Croatia 45°26′ N, 16°16′ E 168
Petrodvorets, Russ. 59°49′ N, 29°47′ E 166
Petroglyphs, site, Hawai'i, U.S. 19°0′ N, 155°50′ W 99
Petrolândia, Braz. 9°1′ S, 38°15′ W 132
Petrólea, Col. 8°29′ N, 72°40′ W 136
Petrolia, Calif., U.S. 40°19′ N, 124°18′ W 90
Petrolia, Can. 42°52′ N, 82°10′ W 102
Petrolia, Tex., U.S. 33°59′ N, 98°14′ W 92
Petrolina, Braz. 9°20′ S, 40°31′ W 123
Petrolina de Goiás, Braz. 16°9′ S, 49°21′ W 138
Petropavlovsk, Kaz. 54°51′ N, 69°7′ E 184
Petropavlovsk Kamchatskiy, Russ. 53°10′ N, 158°42′ E 160
Petroșani, Rom. 45°24′ N, 23°22′ E 168
Petrovac, Serb. and Mont. 42°11′ N, 18°57′ E 168
Petrovac, Serb. and Mont. 44°23′ N, 21°25′ E 168
Petrovaradin, Serb. and Mont. 45°14′ N, 19°52′ E 168
Petrovgrad see Zrenjanin, Serb. and Mont. 45°23′ N, 20°22′ E 168
Petrovići, Europe 42°46′ N, 18°29′ E 168
Petrovsk, Russ. 52°19′ N, 45°26′ E 158
Petrovsk Zabaykal'skiy, Russ. 51°25′ N, 108°56′ E 190
Petrovskoye, Russ. 57°0′ N, 39°11′ E 154
Petrozavodsk, Russ. 61°45′ N, 34°23′ E 154
Petrun', Russ. 66°27′ N, 60°54′ E 169
Petscapiskau Hill, peak, Can. 54°23′ N, 64°34′ W 111
Petten, Neth. 52°44′ N, 4°39′ E 163
Petukhovo, Russ. 55°5′ N, 67°57′ E 184
Peukankuala, Indonesia 4°6′ N, 96°12′ E 196
Peumo, Chile 34°22′ S, 71°13′ W 134
Peunasoe, island, Indonesia 5°31′ N, 94°35′ E 202
Peuplier, Pointe du, Can. 51°13′ N, 79°32′ W 110
Peurasuvanto, Fin. 67°48′ N, 26°43′ E 152
Peureulak, Indonesia 4°50′ N, 97°53′ E 196
Pevek, Russ. 69°40′ N, 170°27′ E 160
Pevensey, U.K. 50°49′ N, 0°20′ E 162
Pewsum, Ger. 53°26′ N, 7°4′ E 163
Peyia, Cyprus 34°53′ N, 32°22′ E 194
Peza, river, Russ. 65°37′ N, 46°57′ E 154
Pézenas, Fr. 43°27′ N, 3°24′ E 164
Pezmog, Russ. 61°53′ N, 51°50′ E 154
Pezu, Pak. 32°18′ N, 70°47′ E 186
Pfungstadt, Ger. 49°48′ N, 8°35′ E 167
Phaestus, ruin(s), Gr. 35°1′ N, 24°42′ E 156
Phalasarna, ruin(s), Gr. 35°29′ N, 23°29′ E 156
Phalodi, India 27°6′ N, 72°21′ E 186
Phalsbourg, Fr. 48°45′ N, 7°14′ E 163
Phan, Thai. 19°31′ N, 99°43′ E 202
Phan Ly, Vietnam 11°13′ N, 108°34′ E 202
Phan Rang, Vietnam 11°34′ N, 108°58′ E 202
Phan Thiet, Vietnam 10°56′ N, 108°4′ E 202
Phanae, ruin(s), Gr. 38°11′ N, 25°49′ E 156
Phangan, Ko, island, Thai. 9°49′ N, 99°43′ E 202
Phangnga, Thai. 8°30′ N, 98°32′ E 202
Pharus see Hvar, island, Croatia 43°3′ N, 16°47′ E 168
Phato, Thai. 9°47′ N, 98°49′ E 202
Phatthalung, Thai. 7°38′ N, 100°6′ E 196
Phayao, Thai. 19°13′ N, 99°55′ E 202
Phelps, Tex., U.S. 30°41′ N, 95°26′ W 103
Phelps Lake, lake, Can. 59°10′ N, 103°45′ W 108
Pheneus, ruin(s), Gr. 37°53′ N, 22°14′ E 156
Phenix City, Ala., U.S. 32°27′ N, 85°1′ W 96
Phetchabun, Thai. 16°25′ N, 101°8′ E 202
Phetchaburi, Thai. 13°7′ N, 99°55′ E 202
Phiafai, Laos 14°49′ N, 105°58′ E 202
Phibun Mangsahan, Thai. 15°15′ N, 105°14′ E 202
Phichai, Thai. 17°18′ N, 100°6′ E 202
Phichit, Thai. 16°25′ N, 100°19′ E 202
Philadelphia, Miss., U.S. 32°45′ N, 89°7′ W 103
Philadelphia, Pa., U.S. 39°57′ N, 75°11′ W 94
Philadelphia see 'Ammān, Jordan 31°56′ N, 35°53′ E 194
Philae, ruin(s), Egypt 23°56′ N, 32°44′ E 182
Philbin Inlet 74°5′ S, 113°45′ W 248
Philip, S. Dak., U.S. 44°2′ N, 101°41′ W 90
Philip Smith Mountains, Alas., U.S. 67°56′ N, 149°31′ W 98
Philippeville, Belg. 50°11′ N, 4°32′ E 167
Philippi, W. Va., U.S. 39°8′ N, 80°3′ W 94
Philippi, ruin(s), Gr. 41°0′ N, 24°10′ E 156
Philippine Basin, Philippine Sea 14°23′ N, 128°46′ E 254
Philippine Sea 15°8′ N, 123°42′ E 203
Philippine Trench, Philippine Sea 11°16′ N, 127°0′ E 254
Philippines 15°0′ N, 121°0′ E 203
Philippolis, S. Af. 30°16′ S, 25°16′ E 227
Philippopolis see Plovdiv, Bulg. 42°9′ N, 24°45′ E 156
Philippopolis see Shahbā', Syr. 32°51′ N, 36°37′ E 194
Philipstown, S. Af. 30°25′ S, 24°27′ E 227
Phillip Bay, Port 38°18′ S, 143°6′ E 231
Phillip Island, island, Austral. 38°56′ S, 144°23′ E 230
Phillips, Tex., U.S. 35°40′ N, 101°22′ W 92
Phillips, Wis., U.S. 45°41′ N, 90°24′ W 94
Phillips, Mount, peak, Austral. 24°29′ S, 116°18′ E 230
Phillipsburg, Kans., U.S. 39°44′ N, 99°20′ W 92
Phillipsburg, N.J., U.S. 40°41′ N, 75°12′ W 110
Philmont, N.Y., U.S. 42°14′ N, 73°39′ W 104
Philomath, Oreg., U.S. 44°31′ N, 123°22′ W 90
Philomena, Can. 55°9′ N, 111°40′ W 108
Phitsanulok, Thai. 16°52′ N, 100°12′ E 202
Phnom Bokor National Park, Cambodia 10°46′ N, 103°34′ E 172
Phnom Penh, Cambodia 11°32′ N, 104°45′ E 202
Pho, Laem, Thai. 6°54′ N, 101°24′ E 196
Phoenix, Ariz., U.S. 33°25′ N, 112°8′ W 92
Phoenix Islands, South Pacific Ocean 4°31′ S, 173°41′ W 238
Phon Phisai, Thai. 18°3′ N, 103°6′ E 202
Phong Tho, Vietnam 22°32′ N, 103°21′ E 202
Phôngsali, Laos 21°44′ N, 102°5′ E 202
Phra Thong, Ko, island, Thai. 8°47′ N, 97°49′ E 202
Phraaspa, ruin(s), Iran 36°44′ N, 47°18′ E 195
Phrae, Thai. 18°9′ N, 100°9′ E 202
Phran Kratai, Thai. 16°40′ N, 99°37′ E 202
Phrao, Thai. 18°7′ N, 100°7′ E 190
Phrao, Thai. 19°24′ N, 99°11′ E 202
Phrom Phiram, Thai. 17°3′ N, 100°12′ E 202
Phu Cat, Vietnam 14°1′ N, 109°4′ E 202
Phu Loc, Vietnam 16°17′ N, 107°53′ E 202
Phu Ly, Vietnam 20°33′ N, 105°55′ E 198
Phu My, Vietnam 14°12′ N, 109°2′ E 202
Phu Quoc, Dao, island, Vietnam 9°53′ N, 103°33′ E 202
Phu Rieng, Vietnam 11°42′ N, 106°56′ E 202
Phuket, Thai. 7°54′ N, 98°23′ E 202
Phuket, Ko, island, Thai. 7°38′ N, 97°55′ E 196
Phum Kompadou, Cambodia 13°48′ N, 107°25′ E 202
Phuntsholing, Bhutan 26°52′ N, 89°20′ E 197
Phuoc Long, Vietnam 9°27′ N, 105°25′ E 202
Phuthaditjhaba, S. Af. 28°33′ S, 28°47′ E 227
Phutthaisong, Thai. 15°28′ N, 102°56′ E 202
Phyarpon, Myanmar 16°17′ N, 95°39′ E 202
Pi, Pol. 53°8′ N, 16°44′ E 152
Piacenza, It. 45°2′ N, 9°40′ E 167
Piacouadie, Lac, lake, Can. 51°13′ N, 71°36′ W 111
Piadena, It. 45°7′ N, 10°21′ E 167
Piana, Fr. 42°14′ N, 8°38′ E 156
Pianello Val Tidone, It. 44°56′ N, 9°23′ E 167
Pianguan, China 39°27′ N, 111°29′ E 198
Pianoro, It. 44°22′ N, 11°20′ E 167
Pianosa, It. 42°35′ N, 10°5′ E 156
Piapot, Can. 49°58′ N, 109°7′ W 90
Piaseczno, Pol. 52°4′ N, 21°1′ E 152
Piatã, Braz. 13°13′ S, 41°45′ W 138
Piatra, Rom. 43°48′ N, 25°10′ E 156
Piatra Neamț, Rom. 46°56′ N, 26°22′ E 156
Piauí, adm. division, Braz. 10°24′ S, 45°55′ W 130
Piauí, Serra do, Braz. 9°52′ S, 42°4′ W 132
Piaxtla, river, Mex. 23°54′ N, 106°6′ W 114
Piazzi, Isla, island, Chile 51°36′ S, 73°59′ W 134
Pibor Post, Sudan 6°44′ N, 33°6′ E 224
Pic, river, Can. 48°51′ N, 86°10′ W 94
Pica, Chile 20°31′ S, 69°22′ W 137
Picacho, Ariz., U.S. 32°43′ N, 111°28′ W 92
Picacho Pass, Ariz., U.S. 32°37′ N, 111°24′ W 92
Picachos, Cerro dos, peak, Mex. 29°21′ N, 114°12′ W 92
Picardie, adm. division, Fr. 49°35′ N, 1°44′ E 150
Picardy, region, Fr. 49°58′ N, 1°57′ E 163
Picassent, Sp. 39°20′ N, 0°29′ E 164
Picayune, Miss., U.S. 30°31′ N, 89°40′ W 103
Picerno, It. 40°39′ N, 15°38′ E 156
Pichanal, Arg. 23°17′ S, 64°13′ W 134
Picher, Okla., U.S. 36°57′ N, 94°51′ W 96
Pichhor, India 25°56′ N, 78°23′ E 197
Pichilemu, Chile 34°25′ S, 71°60′ W 134
Pichilingue, Mex. 24°17′ N, 110°20′ W 112
Pickens, Miss., U.S. 32°53′ N, 89°59′ W 103
Pickerel Lake, Can. 48°33′ N, 91°59′ W 110
Pickering, U.K. 54°14′ N, 0°47′ E 162
Pickering Nunatak, peak, Antarctica 71°27′ S, 70°58′ E 248
Pickle Crow, Can. 51°29′ N, 90°4′ W 110
Pickle Lake, Can. 51°28′ N, 90°11′ W 110
Pickton, Tex., U.S. 33°1′ N, 95°23′ W 103
Pico da Neblina National Park, Braz. 0°7′ N, 65°34′ W 136
Pico de Orizaba National Park, Mex. 19°0′ N, 97°34′ W 72
Pico de Tancítaro National Park, Mex. 19°18′ N, 102°43′ W 72
Pico, island, Port. 38°21′ N, 28°24′ W 253
Pico Truncado, Arg. 46°45′ S, 67°57′ W 134
Picos, Braz. 7°6′ S, 41°26′ W 132
Picton, Can. 44°0′ N, 77°9′ W 94
Picton, N.Z. 41°19′ S, 174°0′ E 240
Pictou, Can. 45°41′ N, 62°43′ W 111
Picture Gorge, site, Oreg., U.S. 44°32′ N, 119°43′ W 90
Pictured Rocks, Mich., U.S. 46°30′ N, 87°10′ W 80
Pictured Rocks National Lakeshore, Mich., U.S. 46°12′ N, 92°34′ W 80
Picuris Peak, N. Mex., U.S. 36°13′ N, 105°44′ W 92
Pidurutalagala, peak, Sri Lanka 6°58′ N, 80°41′ E 188
Piedecuesta, Col. 6°58′ N, 73°4′ W 136
Piedmont, Mo., U.S. 37°9′ N, 90°42′ W 96
Piedmont, adm. division, It. 44°51′ N, 6°58′ E 165
Piedra, Calif., U.S. 36°49′ N, 119°23′ W 100
Piedra del Águila, Arg. 40°2′ S, 70°6′ W 134
Piedra Lais, Venez. 3°6′ N, 65°56′ W 136
Piedra Parada, ruin(s), Mex. 16°48′ N, 93°33′ W 115
Piedra Shotel, Arg. 44°23′ S, 70°30′ W 134
Piedra Sola, Uru. 32°4′ S, 56°19′ W 139
Piedrabuena, Sp. 39°2′ N, 4°11′ W 164
Piedras Blancas, Point, Calif., U.S. 35°41′ N, 121°29′ W 100
Piedras Negras, Mex. 28°40′ N, 100°31′ W 92
Piedras Negras, ruin(s), Guatemala 17°11′ N, 91°23′ W 115
Piedras, Punta, Arg. 35°25′ S, 57°9′ W 139
Piedras, river, Peru 11°22′ S, 70°42′ W 137
Piedritas, Arg. 34°47′ S, 62°58′ W 139
Piedruja, Latv. 55°47′ N, 27°26′ E 166
Pieksämäki, Fin. 62°16′ N, 27°7′ E 154
Piendamó, Col. 2°38′ N, 76°33′ W 136
Pieniężno, Pol. 54°13′ N, 20°8′ E 166
Pierce, Idaho, U.S. 46°28′ N, 115°47′ W 90
Pierce, Nebr., U.S. 42°11′ N, 97°32′ W 90
Piéria, Óros, Gr. 40°7′ N, 22°3′ E 156
Pierre, S. Dak., U.S. 44°21′ N, 100°26′ W 90
Pierre Lake, lake, Can. 49°28′ N, 81°6′ W 94
Pierrefonds, Fr. 49°20′ N, 2°58′ E 163
Pierrelatte, Fr. 44°22′ N, 4°41′ E 150
Pierson, Fla., U.S. 29°14′ N, 81°28′ W 105
Piet Retief, S. Af. 27°1′ S, 30°45′ E 227
Pietarsaari see Jakobstad, Fin. 63°39′ N, 22°39′ E 152
Pietermaritzburg, S. Af. 29°35′ S, 30°21′ E 227
Pietersburg see Polokwane, S. Af. 23°54′ S, 29°26′ E 227
Pietro Verri, Somalia 3°20′ N, 45°39′ E 218
Pietrosu, peak, Rom. 47°5′ N, 25°4′ E 156
Pietrosul, peak, Rom. 47°34′ N, 24°32′ E 156
Pieve d'Alpago, It. 46°9′ N, 12°20′ E 167
Pieve di Cadore, It. 46°25′ N, 12°20′ E 167
Pigailoe (West Fayu Atoll) 8°36′ N, 146°3′ E 192
Pigeon, Mich., U.S. 43°49′ N, 83°16′ W 102
Pigeon Cove, Mass., U.S. 42°40′ N, 70°38′ W 104
Pigeon Lake, Can. 53°2′ N, 114°24′ W 108
Pigeon Point, Lake Superior 47°46′ N, 89°36′ W 94
Pigeon, river, Can. 52°13′ N, 96°58′ W 108
Piggott, Ark., U.S. 36°22′ N, 90°12′ W 96
Pigüé, Arg. 37°37′ S, 62°23′ W 139
Pihlava, Fin. 61°32′ N, 21°36′ E 166
Pihtipudas, Fin. 63°21′ N, 25°32′ E 154
Pihuamo, Mex. 19°15′ N, 103°22′ W 114
P'ihyŏn, N. Korea 40°0′ N, 124°35′ E 200
Pi'ilanihale Heiau, site, Hawai'i, U.S. 20°47′ N, 156°6′ W 99
Pijijiapan, Mex. 15°40′ N, 93°15′ W 115
Pikalevo, Russ. 59°33′ N, 34°5′ E 154
Pikangikum, Can. 51°48′ N, 93°57′ W 82
Pike, river, Wis., U.S. 45°31′ N, 88°3′ W 94
Pikelot, island, F.S.M. 8°17′ N, 147°41′ E 192
Pikes Peak, Colo., U.S. 38°49′ N, 105°7′ W 90
Piketberg, S. Af. 32°54′ S, 18°43′ E 227
Piketon, Ohio, U.S. 39°3′ N, 83°1′ W 102
Pikeville, Ky., U.S. 37°29′ N, 82°32′ W 96
Pikounda, Congo 0°30′ N, 16°38′ E 218
Pikwitonei, Can. 55°35′ N, 97°12′ W 108
Pila, Arg. 36°2′ S, 58°10′ W 139
Pila, peak, Sp. 38°15′ N, 1°14′ W 164
Pilani, India 28°21′ N, 75°37′ E 197
Pilão Arcado, Braz. 9°57′ S, 42°32′ W 132
Pilar, Arg. 31°26′ S, 61°16′ W 139
Pilar, Parag. 26°51′ S, 58°16′ W 139
Pilar, Cabo, Chile 52°46′ S, 76°6′ W 134
Pilatovica, peak, Europe 43°7′ N, 20°54′ E 168
Pilaya, river, Bol. 21°13′ S, 64°29′ W 137
Pilcaniyeu, Arg. 41°9′ S, 70°41′ W 134
Pilcomayo, river, Bol. 19°19′ S, 65°2′ W 137
Pil'dozero, Russ. 65°40′ N, 33°27′ E 152
Pil'gyn, Russ. 69°19′ N, 179°3′ E 98
Pilibhit, India 28°37′ N, 79°47′ E 197
Pilio, Gr. 38°48′ N, 23°34′ E 156
Pílio, Óros, peak, Gr. 39°25′ N, 22°58′ E 156
Pillcopata, Peru 13°5′ S, 71°11′ W 137
Pilling, U.K. 53°55′ N, 2°55′ W 162
Pilón, river, Mex. 25°15′ N, 100°31′ W 114
Pilón-Lajas National Park, Bol. 14°51′ S, 66°41′ W 137
Pilos, Gr. 36°54′ N, 21°41′ E 156
Pilot Butte, peak, Oreg., U.S. 44°3′ N, 121°20′ W 90
Pilot Knob, Mo., U.S. 37°37′ N, 90°39′ W 96
Pilot Knob, peak, Ark., U.S. 35°33′ N, 93°20′ W 96
Pilot Knob, peak, Idaho, U.S. 45°52′ N, 115°47′ W 90
Pilot Mound, Can. 49°12′ N, 98°55′ W 108
Pilot Peak, Nev., U.S. 38°20′ N, 118°4′ W 90
Pilot Peak, Nev., U.S. 41°0′ N, 114°9′ W 90
Pilot Peak, Wyo., U.S. 44°57′ N, 109°59′ W 90
Pilot Point, Alas., U.S. 57°31′ N, 157°38′ W 98
Pilottown, La., U.S. 29°11′ N, 89°15′ W 103
Pilsen see Plzeň, Czech Rep. 49°44′ N, 13°23′ E 152
Pil'skaya Guba, Russ. 66°47′ N, 34°12′ E 152
Piltene, Latv. 57°13′ N, 21°40′ E 166
Pil'tun, Zaliv 52°48′ N, 141°39′ E 160
Pim, river, Russ. 62°20′ N, 71°29′ E 169
Pimenta Bueno, Braz. 11°41′ S, 61°15′ W 130
Piña, Pan. 9°16′ N, 80°2′ W 130
Pinacate, Cerro del, peak, Mex. 31°44′ N, 113°35′ W 92
Pinang, island, Malaysia 5°14′ N, 99°44′ E 196
Pinangah, Malaysia 5°15′ N, 116°48′ E 203
Pinar del Río, Cuba 22°25′ N, 83°43′ W 116
Pinar del Río, adm. division, Cuba 22°33′ N, 83°55′ W 116
Pinar del Río, island, Cuba 23°1′ N, 83°27′ W 116
Pınarbaşı, Turk. 38°42′ N, 36°24′ E 156
Pinardville, N.H., U.S. 42°59′ N, 71°31′ W 104
Pinas, Arg. 31°9′ S, 65°28′ W 134
Pinatubo, Mount, peak, Philippines 15°5′ N, 120°1′ E 238
Pinawa, Can. 50°8′ N, 95°52′ W 90
Pincehely, Hung. 46°41′ N, 18°25′ E 168
Pincén, Arg. 34°51′ S, 63°55′ W 139
Pincher, Can. 49°31′ N, 113°57′ W 90
Pincher Creek, Can. 49°28′ N, 113°56′ W 90
Pinchi Lake, lake, Can. 54°32′ N, 124°49′ W 108
Pinckney, Mich., U.S. 42°26′ N, 83°57′ W 102
Pinconning, Mich., U.S. 43°50′ N, 83°59′ W 102
Pîncota, Rom. 46°20′ N, 21°43′ E 168
Pindamonhangaba, Braz. 22°57′ S, 45°27′ W 138
Pinders Point, Bahamas 26°27′ N, 78°42′ W 105
Pindi Bhattian, Pak. 31°54′ N, 73°14′ E 186
Pindi Gheb, Pak. 33°14′ N, 72°17′ E 186
Pindos, peak, Gr. 39°18′ N, 21°28′ E 156
Pindus Mountains, Gr. 39°54′ N, 20°40′ E 156
Pine Bluff, Ark., U.S. 34°12′ N, 92°1′ W 96
Pine Bluffs, Wyo., U.S. 41°11′ N, 104°5′ W 90
Pine, Cape, Can. 46°38′ N, 54°6′ W 111
Pine City, Minn., U.S. 45°47′ N, 92°60′ W 94
Pine Creek, Austral. 13°51′ S, 131°51′ E 231
Pine Falls, Can. 50°31′ N, 96°17′ W 108
Pine Flat, Calif., U.S. 35°52′ N, 118°39′ W 101
Pine Flat Lake, Calif., U.S. 36°50′ N, 119°32′ W 101
Pine Forest Range, Nev., U.S. 41°41′ N, 119°7′ W 90
Pine Hill, Ala., U.S. 31°58′ N, 87°35′ W 103
Pine Hills, Fla., U.S. 28°34′ N, 81°28′ W 105
Pine Island, Fla., U.S. 26°37′ N, 82°25′ W 105
Pine Island Bay 74°36′ S, 97°34′ W 248
Pine Mountain, Ky., U.S. 37°17′ N, 82°36′ W 96
Pine Mountain, peak, Calif., U.S. 35°41′ N, 121°9′ W 100
Pine Mountain, peak, Calif., U.S. 35°33′ N, 118°49′ W 101
Pine Pass, Can. 55°23′ N, 122°41′ W 108
Pine Plains, N.Y., U.S. 41°58′ N, 73°40′ W 104
Pine Point, Can. 60°46′ N, 114°19′ W 73
Pine Point, Can. 60°46′ N, 114°22′ W 108
Pine Point, Me., U.S. 43°32′ N, 70°21′ W 104
Pine River, Can. 51°46′ N, 100°33′ W 90
Pine River, Can. 55°55′ N, 107°28′ W 108
Pine River, Minn., U.S. 46°42′ N, 94°25′ W 90
Pine, river, Can. 55°52′ N, 121°7′ W 108
Pine, river, Mich., U.S. 44°1′ N, 85°39′ W 102
Pine Valley, Can. 55°38′ N, 122°10′ W 108
Pinecrest, Calif., U.S. 38°11′ N, 120°1′ W 100
Pinedale, Calif., U.S. 36°50′ N, 119°48′ W 92
Pinega, Russ. 64°43′ N, 43°19′ E 154
Pinega, river, Russ. 63°44′ N, 45°11′ E 154
Pinehouse Lake, Can. 55°33′ N, 107°14′ W 108
Pinehouse Lake, lake, Can. 55°30′ N, 106°37′ W 108
Pinehurst, Ga., U.S. 32°11′ N, 83°46′ W 96
Pinehurst, N.C., U.S. 35°11′ N, 79°29′ W 96
Pineland, Tex., U.S. 31°14′ N, 93°58′ W 103
Pinellas Park, Fla., U.S. 27°51′ N, 82°42′ W 105
Pinerolo, It. 44°53′ N, 7°20′ E 167
Pinetown, S. Af. 29°49′ S, 30°46′ E 227
Pineville, Ky., U.S. 36°44′ N, 83°43′ W 96
Pineville, La., U.S. 31°18′ N, 92°26′ W 103
Piney, Fr. 48°22′ N, 4°19′ E 163
Piney Buttes, Mont., U.S. 47°27′ N, 107°14′ W 90
Piney Point, Fla., U.S. 29°46′ N, 83°35′ W 105
Piney Woods, Miss., U.S. 32°2′ N, 89°59′ W 103
Ping, river, Thai. 16°8′ N, 99°46′ E 202
Pingba, China 26°26′ N, 106°14′ E 198
Pingchang, China 31°35′ N, 107°4′ E 198
Pingdingshan, China 33°44′ N, 113°19′ E 198
Pingdu, China 36°49′ N, 119°58′ E 198
Pinggang, China 42°56′ N, 124°50′ E 200
Pingguo, China 23°18′ N, 107°34′ E 198
Pingjiang, China 28°45′ N, 113°37′ E 198
Pingle, China 24°35′ N, 110°41′ E 198
Pingli, China 32°29′ N, 109°24′ E 198
Pingliang, China 35°31′ N, 106°39′ E 198
Pinglu, China 39°31′ N, 112°17′ E 198
Pinglu, China 34°53′ N, 111°12′ E 198
Pingluo, China 38°57′ N, 106°33′ E 198
Pingnan, China 23°34′ N, 110°23′ E 198
Pingquan, China 41°2′ N, 118°39′ E 198
Pingsha, China 22°2′ N, 113°12′ E 198
Pingtan, China 25°28′ N, 119°51′ E 198
Pingtang, China 25°50′ N, 107°17′ E 198
P'ingtung, Taiwan 22°43′ N, 120°31′ E 198
Pingwu, China 32°28′ N, 104°34′ E 198
Pingxiang, China 27°41′ N, 113°48′ E 198
Pingxiang, China 22°5′ N, 106°44′ E 198
Pingyang, China 27°37′ N, 120°33′ E 198
Pingyao, China 37°15′ N, 112°9′ E 198
Pingyi, China 35°28′ N, 117°39′ E 198
Pingyin, China 36°18′ N, 116°26′ E 198
Pingyuan, China 24°32′ N, 115°52′ E 198
Pinhal, Braz. 22°13′ S, 46°47′ W 138
Pinhão, Braz. 25°42′ S, 51°38′ W 138
Pinheiro, Braz. 2°31′ S, 45°7′ W 132
Pinheiro Machado, Braz. 31°37′ S, 53°22′ W 139
Pinhuã, river, Braz. 7°4′ S, 65°60′ W 130
Pini, island, Indonesia 0°6′ N, 98°51′ E 196
Pink Mountain, Can. 57°4′ N, 122°36′ W 108
Pink, river, Can. 56°39′ N, 104°24′ W 108
Pinkafeld, Aust. 47°21′ N, 16°8′ E 168
Pinlaung, Myanmar 20°7′ N, 96°42′ E 202
Pinleibu, Myanmar 24°1′ N, 95°22′ E 188
Pinnacles National Monument, Calif., U.S. 36°27′ N, 121°20′ W 100
Pino Hachado, Paso de, pass, Chile 38°34′ S, 70°54′ W 134
Pinola, Miss., U.S. 31°52′ N, 89°58′ W 103
Pinon Hills, Calif., U.S. 34°26′ N, 117°39′ W 101
Pinos, Mex. 22°17′ N, 101°34′ W 114
Pinos, Mount, peak, Calif., U.S. 34°48′ N, 119°11′ W 101
Pinos, Point, Calif., U.S. 36°38′ N, 122°3′ W 100
Pinos-Puente, Sp. 37°15′ N, 3°46′ W 150
Pinotepa Nacional, Mex. 16°20′ N, 98°2′ W 112
Pins, Pointe aux, Can. 42°6′ N, 81°50′ W 102
Pinsk, Belarus 52°7′ N, 26°6′ E 152
Pinsk Marshes, Belarus 52°39′ N, 25°28′ E 142
Pinta, Sierra, Ariz., U.S. 32°27′ N, 113°48′ W 101
Pinta, Sierra, Mex. 31°26′ N, 115°33′ W 112
Pintados, Chile 20°37′ S, 69°38′ W 137
Pintasan, Malaysia 5°27′ N, 117°40′ E 203
Pinto, Arg. 29°9′ S, 62°40′ W 139
Pinto, Sp. 40°14′ N, 3°42′ W 164
Pinto Butte, peak, Can. 49°18′ N, 107°30′ W 90
Pinto Mountains, Calif., U.S. 34°4′ N, 115°57′ W 101
Pintoyacu, river, Peru 2°58′ S, 74°37′ W 136
Pintwater Range, Nev., U.S. 36°42′ N, 115°35′ W 101
Pinyon Pines, Calif., U.S. 33°35′ N, 116°29′ W 101
Pinyug, Russ. 60°15′ N, 47°45′ E 154
Pioche, Nev., U.S. 37°55′ N, 114°27′ W 92
Piombino, It. 42°56′ N, 10°32′ E 156
Pioneer, La., U.S. 32°43′ N, 91°26′ W 103
Pioneer, Ohio, U.S. 41°40′ N, 84°33′ W 102
Pioneer Fracture Zone, North Pacific Ocean 37°39′ N, 139°49′ W 252
Pioneer Mountains, Idaho, U.S. 43°34′ N, 114°3′ W 90
Pioneer Mountains, Mont., U.S. 45°30′ N, 113°21′ W 90
Pioneer Point, Calif., U.S. 35°47′ N, 117°23′ W 101
Pioneer Tank, spring, Austral. 31°47′ S, 123°48′ E 230
Pioner, Ostrov, island, Russ. 79°38′ N, 99°4′ E 246
Pionki, Pol. 51°29′ N, 21°25′ E 152
Piorini, Lago, lake, Braz. 3°38′ S, 63°31′ W 130
Piorini, river, Braz. 2°34′ S, 64°7′ W 130
Piotrków Trybunalski, Pol. 51°23′ N, 19°41′ E 152
Piove di Sacco, It. 45°18′ N, 12°1′ E 167
Pipar, India 26°20′ N, 73°33′ E 186
Piparia, India 21°55′ N, 77°22′ E 197
Piper City, Ill., U.S. 40°45′ N, 88°12′ W 102
Piper, oil field, North Sea 58°26′ N, 0°10′ E 150
Pipestone, Minn., U.S. 43°58′ N, 96°19′ W 94
Pipestone Lake, lake, Can. 48°59′ N, 94°9′ W 90
Pipestone, river, Can. 57°57′ N, 106°36′ W 108
Pipinas, Arg. 35°32′ S, 57°21′ W 139
Pipmuacan, Réservoir, lake, Can. 49°28′ N, 71°47′ W 94
Piqua, Ohio, U.S. 40°7′ N, 84°16′ W 102
Piquiá, Braz. 1°49′ S, 66°8′ W 136
Piquiri, river, Braz. 24°58′ S, 52°42′ W 138
Pira, Benin 8°30′ N, 1°44′ E 222
Piracanjuba, Braz. 17°21′ S, 49°2′ W 138
Piracicaba, Braz. 22°45′ S, 47°38′ W 138
Piracuruca, Braz. 3°56′ S, 41°42′ W 132
Piraeus see Pireás, Gr. 37°57′ N, 23°38′ E 156
Piraí do Sul, Braz. 24°34′ S, 49°57′ W 138
Piraju, Braz. 23°15′ S, 49°25′ W 138
Pirajuí, Braz. 22°1′ S, 49°28′ W 138
Piran, Slov. 45°31′ N, 13°35′ E 167
Pirané, Arg. 25°45′ S, 59°6′ W 132
Pirane, Europe 42°17′ N, 20°41′ E 168
Piranhas, Braz. 16°34′ S, 51°49′ W 138
Piranhas, Braz. 9°37′ S, 37°45′ W 132
Pirapora, Braz. 17°22′ S, 44°55′ W 138
Piraraja, Uru. 33°45′ S, 54°44′ W 139
Piratuba, Braz. 27°27′ S, 51°48′ W 139
Piray, river, Bol. 16°49′ S, 63°37′ W 137
Pire Goureye, Senegal 15°2′ N, 16°34′ W 222
Pireás, Gr. 37°57′ N, 23°36′ E 180
Pireás (Piraeus), Gr. 37°57′ N, 23°38′ E 156
Pirenópolis, Braz. 15°55′ S, 48°60′ W 138
Pires do Rio, Braz. 17°20′ S, 48°17′ W 138
Pirgos, Gr. 37°38′ N, 21°26′ E 216
Piriá, river, Braz. 2°10′ S, 46°28′ W 130
Piriápolis, Uru. 34°53′ S, 55°16′ W 139
Pirin, Bulg. 41°21′ N, 23°26′ E 156
Pirin National Park, Bulg. 41°37′ N, 22°39′ E 180
Piripiri, Braz. 4°17′ S, 41°49′ W 132
Piritu, Venez. 9°22′ N, 69°15′ W 136
Pirna, Ger. 50°58′ N, 13°56′ E 152
Pirojpur, Bangladesh 22°35′ N, 89°58′ E 197
Pirot, Serb. and Mont. 43°8′ N, 22°34′ E 168
Pirre, Cerro, peak, Pan. 7°47′ N, 77°49′ W 136
Pirsagat, river, Azerb. 40°28′ N, 48°40′ E 195
Pirtleville, Ariz., U.S. 31°22′ N, 109°34′ W 92
Pirttikylä see Pörtom, Fin. 62°41′ N, 21°35′ E 154
Piru, Calif., U.S. 34°25′ N, 118°48′ W 101
Piru, Indonesia 3°6′ S, 128°7′ E 192
Pisa, It. 43°44′ N, 10°24′ E 167
Pisac, Peru 13°27′ S, 71°50′ W 137
Pisagua, Chile 19°37′ S, 70°14′ W 137
Pisarovina, Croatia 45°35′ N, 15°51′ E 168
Pisco, Peru 13°45′ S, 76°12′ W 130
Pisek, Czech Rep. 49°17′ N, 14°8′ E 152
Pisgah Crater, Calif., U.S. 34°44′ N, 116°23′ W 101
Pisgah, Mount, peak, Oreg., U.S. 44°26′ N, 120°20′ W 90
Pishan (Guma), China 37°39′ N, 78°22′ E 184
Pishcha, Ukr. 51°35′ N, 23°47′ E 158
Pīshīn, Iran 26°4′ N, 61°46′ E 182
Pishin, Pak. 30°34′ N, 67°2′ E 186
Pishin Lora, river, Pak. 29°14′ N, 65°33′ E 186
Piskom, Uzb. 41°53′ N, 70°19′ E 197
Pismo Beach, Calif., U.S. 35°9′ N, 120°39′ W 100
Pis'moguba, Russ. 64°33′ N, 31°50′ E 152
Pisogne, It. 45°48′ N, 10°6′ E 167
Pissouri, Cyprus 34°39′ N, 32°42′ E 194
Pisté, Mex. 20°42′ N, 88°38′ W 116
Pistoia, It. 43°55′ N, 10°55′ E 156
Pisz, Pol. 53°37′ N, 21°46′ E 152
Piszczac, Pol. 51°58′ N, 23°22′ E 152
Pit, river, Calif., U.S. 41°25′ N, 121°5′ W 90
Pita, Guinea 11°3′ N, 12°26′ W 222
Pitaga, Can. 52°26′ N, 65°48′ W 111
Pitanga, Braz. 24°45′ S, 51°47′ W 138
Pitangui, Braz. 19°41′ S, 44°54′ W 138
Pitcairn Island, U.K. 25°5′ S, 130°6′ W 241
Piteå, Nor. 65°19′ N, 21°29′ E 152
Pitești, Rom. 44°52′ N, 24°52′ E 156
Pithiviers, Fr. 48°9′ N, 2°15′ E 163
Pithora, India 21°15′ N, 82°30′ E 188
Pithoragarh, India 29°36′ N, 80°12′ E 197
Pitkin, La., U.S. 30°54′ N, 92°57′ W 103
Pitkyaranta, Russ. 61°31′ N, 31°33′ E 152
Pitlochrie, Can. 55°0′ N, 111°45′ W 108
Pitlyar, Russ. 65°50′ N, 66°4′ E 169
Pitman, river, Can. 57°53′ N, 128°36′ W 108
Pitomača, Croatia 45°57′ N, 17°15′ E 168
Pitre, Isle au, island, La., U.S. 30°1′ N, 89°11′ W 103
Pitsligo Castle, site, U.K. 57°39′ N, 2°13′ W 150
Pitt Island, Can. 53°37′ N, 130°52′ W 98
Pitt Island, island, Can. 53°43′ N, 129°56′ W 106
Pitt Lake, Can. 49°22′ N, 122°43′ W 100
Pittsboro, Miss., U.S. 33°55′ N, 89°20′ W 96
Pittsburg, Calif., U.S. 38°1′ N, 121°54′ W 100
Pittsburg, Kans., U.S. 37°23′ N, 94°42′ W 96
Pittsburg, Tex., U.S. 32°59′ N, 94°59′ W 103
Pittsburgh, Pa., U.S. 40°26′ N, 79°59′ W 94
Pittsfield, Mass., U.S. 42°26′ N, 73°16′ W 104
Pittsfield, Mo., U.S. 39°35′ N, 90°49′ W 94
Pittsfield, N.H., U.S. 43°18′ N, 71°20′ W 104
Pittsfield, Vt., U.S. 43°46′ N, 72°49′ W 104
Pittsford, Vt., U.S. 43°42′ N, 73°2′ W 104
Pittston, Pa., U.S. 41°18′ N, 75°48′ W 94

ua Petrii, *Rom.* 44°41′ N, 27°51′ E **156**
ũí, *Braz.* 20°31′ S, 45°57′ W **138**
ura, *Peru* 5°6′ S, 80°40′ W **130**
ura, adm. division, *Peru* 4°50′ S, 81°6′ W **130**
ute Pass, *Calif., U.S.* 37°14′ N, 118°41′ W **101**
ute Peak, *Calif., U.S.* 35°26′ N, 118°26′ W **101**
ute Valley, *Calif., U.S.* 35°1′ N, 114°54′ W **101**
va, river, *Europe* 43°8′ N, 18°52′ E **168**
vabiska, river, *Can.* 49°53′ N, 83°45′ W **94**
vdennyy Buh, river, *Ukr.* 48°3′ N, 30°39′ E **158**
vka, *Slov.* 45°41′ N, 14°11′ E **156**
vot Mountain, peak, *Can.* 54°0′ N, 133°6′ W **108**
ixariá Óros, peak, *Gr.* 38°42′ N, 23°34′ E **156**
ixian, *China* 34°17′ N, 117°58′ E **198**
ixley, *Calif., U.S.* 35°58′ N, 119°18′ W **100**
izacoma, *Peru* 16°57′ S, 69°22′ W **137**
izarra, *Sp.* 36°45′ N, 4°43′ W **164**
izhma, river, *Russ.* 64°37′ N, 51°1′ E **154**
lacentia, *Can.* 47°12′ N, 53°60′ W **111**
lacentia Point, *Belize* 16°26′ N, 88°21′ W **115**
lacer, *Philippines* 9°40′ N, 125°35′ E **203**
lacerville, *Calif., U.S.* 38°44′ N, 120°47′ W **82**
lacid, Lake, *Fla., U.S.* 27°14′ N, 81°27′ W **105**
lacid Lake, *Mont., U.S.* 47°3′ N, 114°1′ W **90**
lacida, *Fla., U.S.* 26°51′ N, 82°17′ W **105**
lácido de Castro, *Braz.* 10°19′ S, 67°11′ W **137**
lačkovica, *Maced.* 41°44′ N, 22°13′ E **168**
lahn, *Liberia* 5°20′ N, 8°51′ W **222**
lain, *Wis., U.S.* 43°16′ N, 90°3′ W **102**
lain, Cape, *South Atlantic Ocean* 34°50′ S, 7°54′ E **253**
lain City, *Ohio, U.S.* 40°5′ N, 83°17′ W **102**
lain Dealing, *La., U.S.* 32°53′ N, 93°42′ W **103**
lainfield, *Conn., U.S.* 41°40′ N, 71°56′ W **104**
lainfield, *Ind., U.S.* 39°41′ N, 86°24′ W **102**
lainfield, *Mass., U.S.* 42°30′ N, 72°56′ W **104**
lainfield, *Vt., U.S.* 44°16′ N, 72°27′ W **104**
lains, *Kans., U.S.* 37°15′ N, 100°36′ W **92**
lains, *Mont., U.S.* 47°26′ N, 114°54′ W **90**
lains, *Pa., U.S.* 41°16′ N, 75°51′ W **110**
lains, *Tex., U.S.* 33°9′ N, 102°50′ W **92**
lainview, *Nebr., U.S.* 42°19′ N, 97°49′ W **90**
lainview, *Tex., U.S.* 34°10′ N, 101°43′ W **92**
lainwell, *Mich., U.S.* 42°26′ N, 85°37′ W **110**
laistow, *N.H., U.S.* 42°49′ N, 71°6′ W **104**
láka, *Gr.* 40°0′ N, 25°25′ E **156**
lakoti, Cape 35°32′ N, 34°1′ E **194**
lan, *Sp.* 42°34′ N, 0°20′ E **164**
lana, *Bosn. and Herzg.* 42°57′ N, 18°24′ E **168**
lana Cays (French Cays), islands, *North Atlantic Ocean* 22°41′ N, 73°33′ W **116**
lana o Nueva Tabarca, Isla, island, *Sp.* 38°5′ N, 0°28′ E **164**
lanada, *Calif., U.S.* 37°17′ N, 120°20′ W **100**
laneta Rica, *Col.* 8°25′ N, 75°35′ W **116**
laninica, *Serb. and Mont.* 43°49′ N, 22°7′ E **168**
lano, *Ill., U.S.* 41°39′ N, 88°33′ W **102**
lano, *Tex., U.S.* 33°0′ N, 96°42′ W **96**
lant City, *Fla., U.S.* 28°1′ N, 82°7′ W **105**
lantation, *Fla., U.S.* 26°8′ N, 80°15′ W **105**
lantation Key, island, *Fla., U.S.* 25°16′ N, 80°41′ W **105**
lantsite, *Ariz., U.S.* 33°2′ N, 109°18′ W **92**
laquemine, *La., U.S.* 30°16′ N, 91°15′ W **103**
lasencia, *Sp.* 40°2′ N, 6°5′ W **150**
laški, *Croatia* 45°4′ N, 15°20′ E **156**
lassen, *Nor.* 61°8′ N, 12°29′ E **152**
last, *Russ.* 54°22′ N, 60°43′ E **154**
laster City, *Calif., U.S.* 32°47′ N, 115°52′ W **101**
laster Rock, *Can.* 46°54′ N, 67°24′ W **111**
lata, Punta, *Chile* 25°1′ S, 71°10′ W **132**
lata, Río de la, *South America* 35°34′ S, 57°6′ W **139**
lataea 479 B.C., battle, *Gr.* 38°11′ N, 23°9′ E **156**
latanal, *Venez.* 2°22′ N, 64°58′ W **130**
látano, river, *Hond.* 15°18′ N, 85°2′ W **116**
lateau, *Can.* 48°57′ N, 108°46′ W **90**
lateau Station (closed), site, *Antarctica* 80°37′ S, 36°13′ E **248**
laten, Kapp, *Nor.* 80°28′ N, 23°58′ E **160**
lateros, *Mex.* 23°13′ N, 102°52′ W **114**
lato, *Col.* 9°46′ N, 74°47′ W **136**
latte, *S. Dak., U.S.* 43°21′ N, 98°51′ W **90**
latte, river, *Nebr., U.S.* 40°56′ N, 100°48′ W **80**
latteville, *Wis., U.S.* 42°43′ N, 90°28′ W **94**
lattsburg, *Mo., U.S.* 39°32′ N, 94°27′ W **94**
lattsmouth, *Nebr., U.S.* 40°59′ N, 95°53′ W **94**
lauen, *Ger.* 50°30′ N, 12°8′ E **152**
lav, *Europe* 42°35′ N, 19°56′ E **168**
lavča Draga, *Croatia* 45°2′ N, 15°23′ E **156**
laviņas, *Latv.* 56°36′ N, 25°42′ E **166**
lavnica, *Europe* 42°17′ N, 19°13′ E **168**
lavsk, *Russ.* 53°40′ N, 37°19′ E **154**
lay Ku, *Vietnam* 14°2′ N, 107°48′ E **192**
laya Grande, *Mex.* 31°8′ N, 114°56′ W **92**
laya Lauro Villar, *Mex.* 25°52′ N, 97°10′ W **114**
laya los Corchos, *Mex.* 21°41′ N, 105°28′ W **114**
laya Vicente, *Mex.* 17°49′ N, 95°49′ W **114**
laya Vicente, river, *Mex.* 17°50′ N, 95°40′ W **114**
layas, *Ecua.* 2°43′ S, 80°22′ W **130**
leasant Grove, *Utah, U.S.* 40°21′ N, 111°43′ W **90**
leasant Hill, *La., U.S.* 31°47′ N, 93°31′ W **103**
leasant Point, *N.Z.* 44°17′ S, 171°8′ E **240**
leasant Valley, *N.Y., U.S.* 41°44′ N, 73°51′ W **104**
leasanton, *Calif., U.S.* 37°39′ N, 121°52′ W **100**
leasanton, *Kans., U.S.* 38°10′ N, 94°42′ W **94**
leasanton, *Tex., U.S.* 28°56′ N, 98°30′ W **96**
leasantville, *N.J., U.S.* 39°23′ N, 74°33′ W **94**
leniţa, *Rom.* 44°12′ N, 23°13′ E **168**
lentywood, *Mont., U.S.* 48°45′ N, 104°34′ W **90**
lentzia, *Sp.* 43°23′ N, 2°58′ W **164**
lesetsk, *Russ.* 62°43′ N, 40°18′ E **154**
lesetsk Cosmodrome, spaceport, *Russ.* 62°17′ N, 39°54′ E **160**
lessisville, *Can.* 46°13′ N, 71°47′ W **94**
leternica, *Croatia* 45°16′ N, 17°47′ E **168**
létipi, Lac, lake, *Can.* 51°43′ N, 70°26′ W **111**
lettenberg, *Ger.* 51°13′ N, 7°52′ E **167**
Pleuron, ruin(s), *Gr.* 38°23′ N, 21°18′ E **156**
Pleven, *Bulg.* 43°25′ N, 24°37′ E **156**
Pleven, adm. division, *Bulg.* 43°34′ N, 24°18′ E **156**
Plevna, *Mont., U.S.* 46°23′ N, 104°33′ W **90**
Plibo, *Liberia* 4°38′ N, 7°42′ W **222**
Plješevica, *Croatia* 44°42′ N, 15°49′ E **168**
Pljevlja, *Europe* 43°21′ N, 19°20′ E **168**
Ploče, *Croatia* 43°2′ N, 17°26′ E **168**
Ploieşti, *Rom.* 44°57′ N, 26°1′ E **156**
Plomb du Cantal, peak, *Fr.* 45°3′ N, 2°43′ E **165**
Płonsk, *Pol.* 52°32′ N, 19°41′ E **152**
Plopiş, Munţii, *Rom.* 47°12′ N, 22°17′ E **168**
Plotnikovo, *Russ.* 56°50′ N, 83°15′ E **169**
Plougastel, *Fr.* 48°22′ N, 4°22′ W **150**
Plovdiv, *Bulg.* 42°5′ N, 24°45′ E **180**
Plovdiv, adm. division, *Bulg.* 42°0′ N, 24°30′ E **156**
Plovdiv (Philippopolis), *Bulg.* 42°9′ N, 24°45′ E **156**
Plugari, *Rom.* 47°28′ N, 27°6′ E **158**
Plum, *Pa., U.S.* 40°29′ N, 79°46′ W **94**
Plum Island, *Mass., U.S.* 42°44′ N, 70°48′ W **104**
Plum Island, *N.Y., U.S.* 41°9′ N, 72°10′ W **104**
Plummer, *Idaho, U.S.* 47°18′ N, 116°54′ W **90**
Plumtree, *Zimb.* 20°30′ S, 27°47′ E **227**
Plungė, *Lith.* 55°55′ N, 21°52′ E **166**
Pluscarden Abbey, site, *U.K.* 57°35′ N, 3°33′ W **150**
Plyeshchanitsy, *Belarus* 54°26′ N, 27°49′ E **166**
Plymouth, *Conn., U.S.* 41°40′ N, 73°3′ W **104**
Plymouth, *Ind., U.S.* 41°20′ N, 86°19′ W **102**
Plymouth, *Mass., U.S.* 41°57′ N, 70°41′ W **104**
Plymouth, *Montserrat* 16°44′ N, 62°14′ W **116**
Plymouth, *N.C., U.S.* 35°51′ N, 76°46′ W **96**
Plymouth, *Ohio, U.S.* 40°58′ N, 82°40′ W **102**
Plymouth, *U.K.* 50°29′ N, 4°11′ W **143**
Plymouth, *Wash., U.S.* 45°56′ N, 119°22′ W **90**
Plymouth, *Wis., U.S.* 43°44′ N, 87°60′ W **102**
Plympton, *Mass., U.S.* 41°57′ N, 70°50′ W **104**
Plyusa, *Russ.* 58°25′ N, 29°20′ E **166**
Plyusa, river, *Russ.* 58°47′ N, 27°53′ E **154**
Plzeň (Pilsen), *Czech Rep.* 49°44′ N, 13°23′ E **152**
Plzeňský, adm. division, *Czech Rep.* 49°46′ N, 12°31′ E **152**
Pnevo, *Russ.* 58°13′ N, 27°33′ E **166**
Pô, *Burkina Faso* 11°9′ N, 1°12′ W **222**
Po di Volano, river, *It.* 44°44′ N, 11°57′ E **167**
Po, river, *It.* 45°7′ N, 9°19′ E **167**
Pobé, *Benin* 7°2′ N, 2°39′ E **222**
Pobeda, Gora, peak, *Russ.* 65°15′ N, 145°7′ E **160**
Pobedy Peak (Jengish Chokusu, Victory Peak), *China* 42°2′ N, 80°3′ E **184**
Pocahontas, *Ark., U.S.* 36°14′ N, 90°59′ W **96**
Pocahontas, *Can.* 53°11′ N, 117°56′ W **108**
Pocahontas, *Ill., U.S.* 38°48′ N, 89°32′ W **102**
Pocahontas, *Iowa, U.S.* 42°43′ N, 94°41′ W **94**
Pocasset, *Mass., U.S.* 41°41′ N, 70°37′ W **104**
Pocatello, *Idaho, U.S.* 42°53′ N, 112°26′ W **90**
Pochala, *Sudan* 7°11′ N, 34°2′ E **224**
Pochep, *Russ.* 52°53′ N, 33°25′ E **154**
Pochinok, *Russ.* 54°24′ N, 32°30′ E **154**
Pochutla, *Mex.* 15°44′ N, 96°28′ W **112**
Pocklington, *U.K.* 53°55′ N, 0°48′ E **162**
Poções, *Braz.* 14°34′ S, 40°21′ W **138**
Pocoata, *Angola* 15°45′ S, 13°41′ E **220**
Pocoma, *Peru* 17°29′ S, 71°23′ W **137**
Poconé, *Braz.* 16°17′ S, 56°39′ W **132**
Pocono Mountains, *Pa., U.S.* 41°21′ N, 75°15′ W **94**
Poços de Caldas, *Braz.* 21°47′ S, 46°35′ W **138**
Podareš, *Maced.* 41°37′ N, 22°32′ E **168**
Podberez'ye, *Russ.* 56°57′ N, 30°40′ E **152**
Podborov'ye, *Russ.* 57°52′ N, 28°35′ E **166**
Podchinnyy, *Russ.* 50°49′ N, 45°13′ E **158**
Poddor'ye, *Russ.* 57°27′ N, 31°6′ E **152**
Podgora, *Croatia* 43°14′ N, 17°4′ E **168**
Podgorac, *Serb. and Mont.* 43°56′ N, 21°57′ E **168**
Podgorica, *Serb. & Mont.* 42°25′ N, 19°11′ E **168**
Podgornoye, *Russ.* 57°45′ N, 82°46′ E **169**
Podhum, *Bosn. and Herzg.* 43°42′ N, 16°58′ E **168**
Podil's'ka Vysochyna, *Ukr.* 48°46′ N, 25°47′ E **152**
Podkamennaya Tunguska, river, *Russ.* 61°52′ N, 89°40′ E **160**
Podkarpakie, adm. division, *Pol.* 50°9′ N, 21°13′ E **152**
Podlaskie, adm. division, *Pol.* 54°9′ N, 22°33′ E **166**
Podlesnoye, *Russ.* 51°46′ N, 47°3′ E **158**
Podnovlje, *Bosn. and Herzg.* 44°56′ N, 18°5′ E **168**
Podocarpus National Park, *Ecua.* 4°22′ S, 79°17′ W **122**
Podoleni, *Rom.* 46°47′ N, 26°37′ E **156**
Podol'sk, *Russ.* 55°23′ N, 37°31′ E **154**
Podor, *Senegal* 16°38′ N, 14°60′ W **222**
Podosinovets, *Russ.* 60°17′ N, 47°3′ E **154**
Podporozh'ye, *Russ.* 60°52′ N, 34°12′ E **154**
Podravska Slatina, *Croatia* 45°41′ N, 17°40′ E **168**
Podromanija, *Bosn. and Herzg.* 43°55′ N, 18°45′ E **168**
Podsosan'ye (Zvoz), *Russ.* 63°17′ N, 42°2′ E **154**
Podtesovo, *Russ.* 58°36′ N, 92°11′ E **169**
Podyuga, *Russ.* 61°6′ N, 40°49′ E **154**
Pofadder, *S. Af.* 29°8′ S, 19°22′ E **227**
Poggio Rusco, *It.* 44°59′ N, 11°6′ E **167**
Pogi, *Russ.* 59°31′ N, 30°35′ E **166**
Pogny, *Fr.* 48°51′ N, 4°29′ E **163**
Pogŏ, *N. Korea* 40°42′ N, 128°54′ E **200**
Pogorelets, *Russ.* 65°26′ N, 45°5′ E **154**
Pogost, *Belarus* 52°50′ N, 27°40′ E **152**
Pogromnoye, *Russ.* 52°35′ N, 52°28′ E **154**
P'oha, *N. Korea* 40°58′ N, 129°43′ E **200**
Pohang, *S. Korea* 36°2′ N, 129°22′ E **200**
Pohja see Pojo, *Fin.* 60°5′ N, 23°31′ E **166**
Pohnpei (Ponape), island, *F.S.M.* 6°55′ N, 158°15′ E **242**
Pohorje, *Slov.* 46°25′ N, 15°37′ E **168**
Poiana Mare, *Rom.* 43°55′ N, 23°4′ E **168**
Poiana Ruscă, Munţii, *Rom.* 45°36′ N, 22°18′ E **168**
Poie, *Dem. Rep. of the Congo* 2°52′ S, 23°11′ E **218**
Poim, *Russ.* 53°0′ N, 43°7′ E **154**
Poincaré, Lac, lake, *Can.* 51°43′ N, 58°54′ W **111**
Poinsett, Cape, *Antarctica* 65°27′ S, 117°42′ E **248**
Point Baker, *Alas., U.S.* 56°19′ N, 133°32′ W **108**
Point, China, *Calif., U.S.* 32°44′ N, 118°33′ W **101**
Point Coulomb National Park, *Austral.* 17°22′ S, 121°55′ E **238**
Point Edward, *Can.* 42°59′ N, 82°24′ W **102**
Point Hope, *Alas., U.S.* 68°19′ N, 166°40′ W **98**
Point Judith, *R.I., U.S.* 41°21′ N, 71°30′ W **104**
Point Lake, *Can.* 64°58′ N, 113°44′ W **106**
Point Lay, *Alas., U.S.* 69°46′ N, 163°10′ W **73**
Point Pedro, *Sri Lanka* 9°49′ N, 80°14′ E **188**
Point Pelee National Park, *Can.* 41°53′ N, 82°56′ W **102**
Point Pleasant, *W. Va., U.S.* 38°50′ N, 82°9′ W **102**
Point Reyes National Seashore, *Calif., U.S.* 38°16′ N, 127°9′ W **80**
Point Roberts, *Can.* 48°58′ N, 123°4′ W **100**
Pointe a la Hache, *La., U.S.* 29°34′ N, 89°49′ W **103**
Pointe, Lac de la, lake, *Can.* 52°42′ N, 70°54′ W **111**
Pointe-à-Gravois, *Haiti* 17°54′ N, 74°4′ W **116**
Pointe-à-Pitre, *Grande-Terre* 16°15′ N, 61°31′ W **116**
Pointe-au-Pic, *Can.* 47°36′ N, 70°10′ W **94**
Pointe-aux-Anglais, *Can.* 49°40′ N, 67°12′ W **111**
Pointe-Noire, *Congo* 4°49′ S, 11°50′ E **218**
Poipet, *Cambodia* 13°40′ N, 102°37′ E **202**
Poissons, *Fr.* 48°24′ N, 5°12′ E **163**
Poissy, *Fr.* 48°56′ N, 2°3′ E **163**
Poitiers, *Fr.* 46°34′ N, 0°19′ E **150**
Poitou, region, *Fr.* 46°19′ N, 1°0′ E **165**
Poitou-Charentes, adm. division, *Fr.* 46°13′ N, 0°37′ E **150**
Poix, *Fr.* 49°46′ N, 1°58′ E **163**
Poix-Terron, *Fr.* 49°38′ N, 4°39′ E **163**
Pojo, *Bol.* 17°47′ S, 64°53′ W **137**
Pojo (Pohja), *Fin.* 60°5′ N, 23°31′ E **166**
Pokcha, *Russ.* 62°56′ N, 56°11′ E **154**
Pokeno, *N.Z.* 37°15′ S, 175°3′ E **240**
Pokhara, *Nepal* 28°17′ N, 83°58′ E **197**
Pokhvistnevo, *Russ.* 53°38′ N, 52°4′ E **154**
Pokka, *Fin.* 68°9′ N, 25°47′ E **152**
Poko, *Dem. Rep. of the Congo* 3°7′ N, 26°53′ E **224**
Pokrashevo, *Belarus* 53°11′ N, 27°33′ E **152**
Pokrovsk Ural'skiy, *Russ.* 60°7′ N, 59°48′ E **154**
Pokshen'ga, river, *Russ.* 63°31′ N, 43°43′ E **154**
Pokupsko, *Croatia* 45°29′ N, 16°0′ E **168**
Pola, *Philippines* 13°10′ N, 121°25′ E **203**
Pola, *Russ.* 57°54′ N, 31°50′ E **154**
Polače, *Croatia* 42°46′ N, 17°22′ E **168**
Polān, *Iran* 25°32′ N, 61°11′ E **182**
Poland 51°58′ N, 18°31′ E **152**
Polar Plateau, *Antarctica* 88°4′ S, 20°29′ W **248**
Polatlı, *Turk.* 39°34′ N, 32°9′ E **156**
Polatna, *Europe* 43°2′ N, 21°7′ E **168**
Polatsk, *Belarus* 55°29′ N, 28°47′ E **166**
Polch, *Ger.* 50°17′ N, 7°18′ E **163**
Polcirkeln, *Nor.* 66°33′ N, 20°58′ E **152**
Pol-e Khomrī, *Afghan.* 35°56′ N, 68°50′ E **186**
Pole Plain, *Arctic Ocean* 83°54′ N, 131°5′ E **255**
Polesella, *It.* 44°58′ N, 11°46′ E **167**
Polessk, *Russ.* 54°50′ N, 21°2′ E **166**
Poletica, Mount, peak, *Alas., U.S.* 59°4′ N, 134°43′ W **98**
Polevskoy, *Russ.* 56°26′ N, 60°13′ E **154**
Poli, *Cameroon* 8°26′ N, 13°14′ E **218**
Poligus, *Russ.* 62°0′ N, 94°40′ E **169**
Polikarpovskoye, *Russ.* 70°41′ N, 82°13′ E **169**
Polillo Islands, *Philippine Sea* 14°33′ N, 121°54′ E **203**
Polis, *Cyprus* 35°2′ N, 32°25′ E **194**
Polje, *Bosn. and Herzg.* 44°59′ N, 17°57′ E **168**
Polkville, *Miss., U.S.* 32°10′ N, 89°42′ W **103**
Pollachi, *India* 10°40′ N, 77°1′ E **188**
Pöllau, *Aust.* 47°18′ N, 15°49′ E **168**
Pollino, Monte, peak, *It.* 39°53′ N, 16°8′ E **156**
Pollock, *La., U.S.* 31°30′ N, 92°26′ W **103**
Pollock, *S. Dak., U.S.* 45°52′ N, 100°19′ W **90**
Pollok, *Tex., U.S.* 31°26′ N, 94°52′ W **103**
Pollos, *Sp.* 41°25′ N, 5°9′ W **150**
Polna, *Russ.* 58°27′ N, 28°8′ E **166**
Polnovat, *Russ.* 63°47′ N, 66°2′ E **169**
Polo, *Ill., U.S.* 41°58′ N, 89°35′ W **102**
Polohy, *Ukr.* 47°26′ N, 36°14′ E **156**
Polokwane (Pietersburg), *S. Af.* 23°54′ S, 29°26′ E **227**
Polom, *Russ.* 59°11′ N, 50°54′ E **154**
Polonne, *Ukr.* 50°5′ N, 27°31′ E **152**
Polson, *Mont., U.S.* 47°38′ N, 114°12′ W **82**
Poltava, *Ukr.* 49°36′ N, 34°29′ E **158**
Poltavka, *Russ.* 54°19′ N, 71°47′ E **184**
Põltsamaa, *Est.* 58°38′ N, 25°55′ E **166**
Polunochnoye, *Russ.* 60°51′ N, 60°26′ E **154**
Polur, *India* 12°32′ N, 79°7′ E **188**
Poluy, *Russ.* 65°5′ N, 69°7′ E **169**
Põlva, *Est.* 58°2′ N, 27°2′ E **166**
Polvadera, *N. Mex., U.S.* 34°12′ N, 106°55′ W **92**
Polyarnyy, *Russ.* 71°1′ N, 149°0′ E **160**
Polyarnyy, *Russ.* 69°11′ N, 33°27′ E **152**
Polyarnyy, *Russ.* 69°8′ N, 178°45′ E **98**
Polyarnyy Krug, *Russ.* 66°26′ N, 32°51′ E **154**
Polyarnyye Zori, *Russ.* 67°19′ N, 32°27′ E **152**
Polynesian Cultural Center, site, *Hawai'i, U.S.* 21°37′ N, 157°58′ W **99**
Polyrrhenia, ruin(s), *Gr.* 35°25′ N, 23°35′ E **156**
Pomabamba, *Peru* 8°52′ S, 77°28′ W **130**
Pomarão, *Port.* 37°33′ N, 7°33′ W **150**
Pomarkku, *Fin.* 61°40′ N, 22°1′ E **166**
Pómaro, *Mex.* 18°17′ N, 103°18′ W **114**
Pomáz, *Hung.* 47°38′ N, 19°1′ E **168**
Pombal, *Braz.* 6°47′ S, 37°48′ W **132**
Pomene, *Mozambique* 22°53′ S, 35°29′ E **220**
Pomerania, region, *Pol.* 54°38′ N, 18°22′ E **166**
Pomeroy, *Ohio, U.S.* 39°1′ N, 82°2′ W **102**
Pomeroy, *Wash., U.S.* 46°28′ N, 117°37′ W **90**
Pomichna, *Ukr.* 48°15′ N, 31°31′ E **156**
Pomona, *Calif., U.S.* 34°3′ N, 117°46′ W **101**
Pomona Park, *Fla., U.S.* 29°29′ N, 81°36′ W **105**
Pomorskie, adm. division, *Pol.* 53°54′ N, 18°28′ E **166**
Pomos Point, *Cyprus* 35°9′ N, 32°27′ E **194**
Pomovaara, peak, *Fin.* 67°54′ N, 26°14′ E **152**
Pomozdino, *Russ.* 62°10′ N, 54°10′ E **154**
Pompano Beach, *Fla., U.S.* 26°14′ N, 80°9′ W **105**
Pompéia, *Braz.* 22°8′ S, 50°12′ W **138**
Pompeii, ruin(s), *It.* 40°45′ N, 14°24′ E **156**
Pompeiopolis, ruin(s), *Turk.* 36°43′ N, 34°26′ E **156**
Pompéu, *Braz.* 19°14′ S, 44°60′ W **138**
Pompeys Pillar, *Mont., U.S.* 45°57′ N, 107°56′ W **90**
Pompeys Pillar National Monument, *Mont., U.S.* 45°58′ N, 108°2′ W **90**
Pomuq, *Uzb.* 39°1′ N, 65°0′ E **197**
Ponape see Pohnpei, island, *F.S.M.* 6°55′ N, 158°15′ E **242**
Ponca City, *Okla., U.S.* 36°40′ N, 97°7′ W **82**
Ponce 18°1′ N, 66°37′ W **116**
Ponce de Leon Bay 25°20′ N, 81°22′ W **105**
Ponchatoula, *La., U.S.* 30°25′ N, 90°26′ W **103**
Poncheville, Lac, lake, *Can.* 50°8′ N, 77°36′ W **94**
Poncin, *Fr.* 46°5′ N, 5°24′ E **156**
Poncitlán, *Mex.* 20°22′ N, 102°57′ W **114**
Pond, *Calif., U.S.* 35°43′ N, 119°21′ W **100**
Pond Creek, *Okla., U.S.* 36°39′ N, 97°48′ W **92**
Pond Inlet, *Can.* 72°36′ N, 77°53′ W **73**
Pondicherry, adm. division, *India* 11°44′ N, 79°20′ E **188**
Pondicherry (Puduchcheri), *India* 11°56′ N, 79°47′ E **188**
Ponferrada, *Sp.* 42°33′ N, 6°37′ W **150**
Pong, *Thai.* 19°12′ N, 100°15′ E **202**
Pongaroa, *N.Z.* 40°34′ S, 176°13′ E **240**
Pongo, river, *Sudan* 7°39′ N, 27°11′ E **224**
Pon'goma, *Russ.* 65°19′ N, 34°15′ E **152**
Ponlei, *Cambodia* 12°26′ N, 104°27′ E **202**
Ponoka, *Can.* 52°40′ N, 113°40′ W **108**
Ponomarevka, *Russ.* 53°18′ N, 54°10′ E **154**
Ponoy, *Russ.* 67°4′ N, 40°59′ E **154**
Ponoy, river, *Russ.* 66°59′ N, 38°23′ E **154**
Pons, *Fr.* 45°34′ N, 0°33′ E **150**
Pont Canavese, *It.* 45°25′ N, 7°36′ E **167**
Pont de Suert, *Sp.* 42°23′ N, 0°44′ E **164**
Ponta Delgada, *Port.* 37°40′ N, 25°51′ W **207**
Ponta Grossa, *Braz.* 25°6′ S, 50°9′ W **138**
Ponta Porã, *Braz.* 22°32′ S, 55°40′ W **132**
Pontalina, *Braz.* 17°34′ S, 49°29′ W **138**
Pont-à-Mousson, *Fr.* 48°54′ N, 6°2′ E **163**
Pontarlier, *Fr.* 46°54′ N, 6°19′ E **156**
Pontassieve, *It.* 43°47′ N, 11°25′ E **167**
Pontax, river, *Can.* 51°50′ N, 77°1′ W **110**
Pontchartrain, Lake, *La., U.S.* 30°10′ N, 90°24′ W **103**
Pontchâteau, *Fr.* 47°26′ N, 2°7′ W **150**
Ponte Branca, *Braz.* 16°25′ S, 52°42′ W **138**
Ponte de Lima, *Port.* 41°45′ N, 8°37′ W **150**
Ponte di Legno, *It.* 46°16′ N, 10°29′ E **167**
Ponte Firme, *Braz.* 18°4′ S, 46°26′ W **138**
Ponte Nova, *Braz.* 20°25′ S, 42°53′ W **138**
Ponteareas, *Sp.* 42°9′ N, 8°31′ W **150**
Pontedecimo, *It.* 44°30′ N, 8°55′ E **167**
Pontedera, *It.* 43°39′ N, 10°36′ E **156**
Pontefract, *U.K.* 53°41′ N, 1°18′ W **162**
Ponteix, *Can.* 49°43′ N, 107°28′ W **90**
Pontevedra, *Sp.* 42°24′ N, 8°39′ W **150**
Pontiac, *Ill., U.S.* 40°52′ N, 88°38′ W **102**
Pontiac, *Mich., U.S.* 42°37′ N, 83°18′ W **102**
Pontiac, *Mo., U.S.* 40°52′ N, 88°38′ W **94**
Pontian Kechil, *Malaysia* 1°29′ N, 103°23′ E **196**
Pontianak, *Indonesia* 3°178′ S, 109°18′ E **196**
Pontoise, *Fr.* 49°3′ N, 2°4′ E **163**
Ponton, *Can.* 54°37′ N, 99°11′ W **108**
Ponton, river, *Can.* 58°26′ N, 116°3′ W **108**
Pontós, *Sp.* 42°10′ N, 2°54′ E **164**
Pontrieux, *Fr.* 48°41′ N, 3°10′ W **150**
Ponts, *Sp.* 41°54′ N, 1°11′ E **164**
Pont-Sainte-Maxence, *Fr.* 49°18′ N, 2°37′ E **163**
Pont-sur-Yonne, *Fr.* 48°16′ N, 3°12′ E **163**
Pontypool, *U.K.* 51°41′ N, 3°3′ W **162**
Ponyri, *Russ.* 52°17′ N, 36°17′ E **158**
Ponziane, Isole, islands, *Tyrrhenian Sea* 40°46′ N, 12°1′ E **156**
Ponzone, *It.* 44°35′ N, 8°29′ E **167**
Poole, *U.K.* 50°43′ N, 1°59′ W **162**
Poondinna, Mount, peak, *Austral.* 27°22′ S, 129°46′ E **230**
Poopó, *Bol.* 18°23′ S, 66°59′ W **137**
Poopó, Lago, lake, *Bol.* 18°59′ S, 67°12′ W **137**
Pöösapea, *Est.* 59°12′ N, 23°29′ E **166**
Popa, Isla, island, *Pan.* 8°52′ N, 82°18′ W **115**
Popayán, *Col.* 2°23′ N, 76°37′ W **136**
Pope, *Latv.* 57°23′ N, 21°50′ E **166**
Poperinge, *Belg.* 50°51′ N, 2°43′ E **163**
Popham Beach, *Me., U.S.* 43°44′ N, 69°48′ W **104**
Popigay, *Russ.* 72°1′ N, 110°58′ E **160**
Poplar, *Calif., U.S.* 36°3′ N, 119°10′ W **101**
Poplar, *Mont., U.S.* 48°5′ N, 105°11′ W **90**
Poplar Bluff, *Mo., U.S.* 36°45′ N, 90°24′ W **96**
Poplar Point, *Can.* 52°54′ N, 97°53′ W **108**
Poplar, river, *Can.* 61°22′ N, 121°44′ W **108**
Poplar, river, *Can.* 52°27′ N, 95°49′ W **108**
Poplarville, *Miss., U.S.* 30°50′ N, 89°33′ W **103**
Popocatépetl, peak, *Mex.* 19°0′ N, 98°40′ W **114**
Popokabaka, *Dem. Rep. of the Congo* 5°41′ S, 16°36′ E **218**
Popovača, *Croatia* 45°34′ N, 16°37′ E **168**
Poppi, *It.* 43°43′ N, 11°44′ E **167**
Poprad, *Slovakia* 49°3′ N, 20°18′ E **152**
Pŏptong, *N. Korea* 38°58′ N, 127°4′ E **200**
Populonia, *It.* 42°58′ N, 10°30′ E **156**
Por Chaman, *Afghan.* 33°10′ N, 63°52′ E **186**
Porangahau, *N.Z.* 40°19′ S, 176°38′ E **240**
Porangatu, *Braz.* 13°30′ S, 49°12′ W **138**
Porazava, *Belarus* 52°56′ N, 24°21′ E **152**
Porbandar, *India* 21°39′ N, 69°37′ E **186**
Porcher Island, *Can.* 54°1′ N, 130°53′ W **98**
Porco, *Bol.* 19°50′ S, 66°1′ W **137**
Porcos, river, *Braz.* 13°5′ S, 45°10′ W **138**
Porcuna, *Sp.* 37°53′ N, 4°12′ W **164**
Porcupine, Cape, *Can.* 53°57′ N, 57°8′ W **111**
Porcupine Hill, peak, *Can.* 53°42′ N, 61°5′ W **111**
Porcupine Mountains, peak, *Mich., U.S.* 46°43′ N, 89°52′ W **94**
Porcupine Plain, *Can.* 52°35′ N, 103°16′ W **108**
Porcupine Plain, *North Atlantic Ocean* 47°55′ N, 15°54′ W **253**
Porcupine, river, *Can.* 66°51′ N, 144°4′ W **106**
Pordenone, *It.* 45°57′ N, 12°39′ E **167**
Pordim, *Bulg.* 43°22′ N, 24°50′ E **156**
Poreč, *Croatia* 45°13′ N, 13°36′ E **167**
Porecatu, *Braz.* 22°47′ S, 51°28′ W **138**
Poretskoye, *Russ.* 55°11′ N, 46°19′ E **154**
Pórfido, Punta, *Arg.* 41°56′ S, 64°57′ W **134**
Porga, *Benin* 11°0′ N, 0°58′ E **222**
Porgho, *Mali* 16°34′ N, 6°356′ W **222**
Pori (Björneborg), *Fin.* 61°26′ N, 21°44′ E **166**
Porirua, *N.Z.* 41°10′ S, 174°51′ E **240**
Porjus, *Nor.* 66°56′ N, 19°50′ E **152**
Porkhov, *Russ.* 57°44′ N, 29°39′ E **166**
Porkkala, *Fin.* 59°58′ N, 24°24′ E **166**
Porlock, *U.K.* 51°12′ N, 3°35′ W **162**
Porog, *Russ.* 62°1′ N, 56°40′ E **154**
Poroma, *Bol.* 18°30′ S, 65°34′ W **137**
Poronaysk, *Russ.* 49°15′ N, 143°0′ E **190**
Poronin, *Pol.* 49°20′ N, 20°0′ E **152**
Poroslyany, *Belarus* 52°39′ N, 24°21′ E **152**
Porosozero, *Russ.* 62°43′ N, 32°44′ E **152**
Poroszló, *Hung.* 47°38′ N, 20°38′ E **168**
Porozhsk, *Russ.* 63°56′ N, 53°41′ E **154**
Porpoise Bay 66°28′ S, 128°20′ E **255**
Porsangerhalvøya, *Nor.* 70°46′ N, 23°56′ E **152**
Porsuk, river, *Turk.* 39°30′ N, 29°57′ E **156**
Port Alberni, *Can.* 49°14′ N, 124°48′ W **100**
Port Albert, *Can.* 43°52′ N, 81°42′ W **102**
Port Alexander, *Alas., U.S.* 56°15′ N, 134°41′ W **108**
Port Alfred, *S. Af.* 33°35′ S, 26°52′ E **227**
Port Alice, *Can.* 50°22′ N, 127°26′ W **90**
Port Allen, *La., U.S.* 30°27′ N, 91°14′ W **103**
Port Alsworth, *Alas., U.S.* 60°11′ N, 154°20′ W **98**
Port Angeles, *Wash., U.S.* 48°5′ N, 123°26′ W **100**
Port Antonio, *Jam.* 18°10′ N, 76°27′ W **115**
Port Arthur, *Tex., U.S.* 29°53′ N, 93°56′ W **103**
Port Arthur see Lüshun, *China* 38°52′ N, 121°16′ E **198**
Port Austin, *Mich., U.S.* 44°2′ N, 82°60′ W **102**
Port Barre, *La., U.S.* 30°32′ N, 91°58′ W **103**
Port Bay, Port au 48°38′ N, 59°28′ W **111**
Port Beaufort, *S. Af.* 34°21′ S, 20°46′ E **227**
Port Bell, *Uganda* 0°16′ N, 32°36′ E **224**
Port Blair, *India* 11°44′ N, 92°52′ E **188**
Port Blanford, *Can.* 48°21′ N, 54°11′ W **111**
Port Bolivar, *Tex., U.S.* 29°21′ N, 94°46′ W **103**
Port Bouet, *Côte d'Ivoire* 5°16′ N, 3°59′ W **222**
Port Bruce, *Can.* 42°38′ N, 81°1′ W **102**
Port Burwell, *Can.* 42°38′ N, 80°47′ W **102**
Port Burwell, *Can.* 60°19′ N, 64°39′ W **106**
Port Canning, *India* 22°18′ N, 88°38′ E **197**
Port Carling, *Can.* 45°6′ N, 79°33′ W **94**
Port Chalmers, *N.Z.* 45°48′ S, 170°36′ E **240**
Port Charlotte, *Fla., U.S.* 26°59′ N, 82°5′ W **105**
Port Clements, *Can.* 53°41′ N, 132°11′ W **108**
Port Clinton, *Ohio, U.S.* 41°29′ N, 82°57′ W **102**
Port Colborne, *Can.* 42°52′ N, 79°15′ W **110**
Port Coquitlam, *Can.* 49°15′ N, 122°46′ W **100**
Port de Sóller, *Sp.* 39°47′ N, 2°42′ E **164**
Port Dickson, *Malaysia* 2°35′ N, 101°48′ E **196**
Port Eads, *La., U.S.* 29°1′ N, 89°9′ W **103**
Port Edward, *Can.* 54°13′ N, 130°16′ W **108**
Port Edwards, *Wis., U.S.* 44°20′ N, 89°53′ W **110**
Port Elgin, *Can.* 44°25′ N, 81°23′ W **94**
Port Elizabeth, *S. Af.* 33°56′ S, 25°34′ E **227**
Port Étienne see Nouadhibou, *Mauritania* 20°56′ N, 17°2′ W **222**
Port Ewen, *N.Y., U.S.* 41°53′ N, 73°60′ W **104**
Port Fitzroy, *N.Z.* 36°11′ S, 175°22′ E **240**
Port Gamble, *Wash., U.S.* 47°49′ N, 122°37′ W **100**
Port Gibson, *Miss., U.S.* 31°57′ N, 90°60′ W **103**
Port Harcourt, *Nig.* 4°46′ N, 7°0′ E **222**
Port Hardy, *Can.* 50°43′ N, 127°32′ W **108**
Port Hawkesbury, *Can.* 45°36′ N, 61°22′ W **111**
Port Henry, *N.Y., U.S.* 44°2′ N, 73°29′ W **104**
Port Herald see Nsanje, *Malawi* 16°56′ S, 35°13′ E **224**
Port Hope, *Can.* 43°56′ N, 78°19′ W **94**
Port Hope, *Mich., U.S.* 43°56′ N, 82°44′ W **102**
Port Hueneme, *Calif., U.S.* 34°9′ N, 119°12′ W **101**
Port Huron, *Mich., U.S.* 42°57′ N, 82°28′ W **102**
Port Isabel, *Tex., U.S.* 26°5′ N, 97°13′ W **114**
Port Jefferson, *N.Y., U.S.* 40°56′ N, 73°4′ W **104**
Port Jervis, *N.Y., U.S.* 41°22′ N, 74°42′ W **110**
Port Joinville, *Fr.* 46°43′ N, 2°22′ W **150**
Port Kaituma, *Guyana* 7°47′ N, 59°55′ W **116**
Port Katon, *Russ.* 46°51′ N, 38°44′ E **156**
Port Kelang, *Malaysia* 2°58′ N, 101°26′ E **196**
Port Láirge see Waterford, *Ire.* 52°15′ N, 7°8′ W **150**
Port Laoise, *Ire.* 53°2′ N, 7°18′ W **150**
Port Lavaca, *Tex., U.S.* 28°35′ N, 96°37′ W **96**
Port Lions, *Alas., U.S.* 57°50′ N, 152°56′ W **98**
Port Loko, *Sierra Leone* 8°46′ N, 12°47′ W **222**
Port Lyautey see Kenitra, *Mor.* 34°17′ N, 6°37′ W **214**
Port Mansfield, *Tex., U.S.* 26°33′ N, 97°26′ W **114**
Port Maria, *Jam.* 18°21′ N, 76°54′ W **115**
Port Mcneill, *Can.* 50°33′ N, 127°6′ W **90**
Port Mcnicoll, *Can.* 44°44′ N, 79°48′ W **94**
Port Moody, *Can.* 49°15′ N, 122°51′ W **100**
Port Moresby, *P.N.G.* 9°30′ S, 146°47′ E **230**
Port Neches, *Tex., U.S.* 29°58′ N, 93°57′ W **103**
Port Neville, *Can.* 50°29′ N, 126°2′ W **90**
Port Nolloth, *S. Af.* 29°15′ S, 16°52′ E **227**
Port O'Connor, *Tex., U.S.* 28°26′ N, 96°26′ W **96**
Port Ontario, *N.Y., U.S.* 43°33′ N, 76°12′ W **94**
Port Orange, *Fla., U.S.* 29°7′ N, 80°60′ W **105**
Port Orchard, *Wash., U.S.* 47°30′ N, 122°39′ W **100**
Port Pirie, *Austral.* 33°12′ S, 138°0′ E **231**
Port Renfrew, *Can.* 48°32′ N, 124°25′ W **100**

uca Urco, Peru 2°22′ S, 71°54′ W **136**
ucacuro, river, Peru 2°55′ S, 75°18′ W **136**
ucallpa, Peru 8°25′ S, 74°36′ W **137**
ucará, Bol. 18°44′ S, 64°18′ W **137**
ucará, Peru 15°6′ S, 70°24′ W **137**
ucarani, Bol. 16°24′ S, 68°30′ W **137**
ucheng, China 34°56′ N, 109°34′ E **198**
ucheng, China 27°58′ N, 118°30′ E **198**
uckett, Miss., U.S. 32°3′ N, 89°46′ W **103**
udasjärvi, Fin. 65°24′ N, 26°52′ E **152**
udem, Russ. 58°18′ N, 52°15′ E **154**
udimoe, S. Af. 27°26′ S, 24°42′ E **227**
udino, Russ. 57°35′ N, 79°26′ E **169**
udozh, Russ. 61°49′ N, 36°38′ E **154**
udu, Indonesia 0°25′ N, 102°16′ E **196**
uduchcheri see Pondicherry, India 11°56′ N, 79°47′ E **188**
udukkottai, India 10°25′ N, 78°48′ E **188**
uebla, Mex. 18°59′ N, 98°16′ W **114**
uebla, adm. division, Mex. 18°51′ N, 98°31′ W **114**
uebla de Alcocer, Sp. 38°59′ N, 5°16′ W **150**
uebla de Don Rodrigo, Sp. 39°4′ N, 4°38′ W **164**
uebla, Colo., U.S. 38°17′ N, 104°39′ W **90**
uebla Bonito, site, N. Mex., U.S. 36°3′ N, 108°2′ W **92**
ueblo Mountains, Oreg., U.S. 42°14′ N, 118°57′ W **90**
ueblo Nuevo, Mex. 23°23′ N, 105°21′ W **114**
ueblo Nuevo, Peru 16°44′ S, 72°27′ W **137**
ueblo Nuevo, Venez. 11°57′ N, 69°57′ W **136**
ueblo Nuevo Tiquisate, Guatemala 14°15′ N, 91°22′ W **115**
uelches, Arg. 38°9′ S, 65°56′ W **134**
uente de Ixtla, Mex. 18°35′ N, 99°21′ W **114**
uente la Reina (Gares), Sp. 42°39′ N, 1°49′ W **164**
uente-Genil, Sp. 37°23′ N, 4°47′ W **164**
u'er, China 22°56′ N, 101°3′ E **202**
uertecitos, Mex. 30°14′ N, 114°41′ W **92**
uerto Acosta, Bol. 15°34′ S, 69°15′ W **137**
uerto Aisén, Chile 45°25′ S, 72°59′ W **123**
uerto Alegre, Peru 8°44′ S, 74°14′ W **130**
uerto Alfonso, Col. 2°13′ S, 71°2′ W **136**
uerto América, Peru 4°42′ S, 77°3′ W **130**
uerto Ángel, Mex. 15°39′ N, 96°31′ W **112**
uerto Arista, Mex. 15°58′ N, 93°50′ W **115**
uerto Armuelles, Pan. 8°18′ N, 82°51′ W **115**
uerto Asís, Col. 0°27′ N, 76°32′ W **136**
uerto Aurora, Peru 2°12′ S, 74°18′ W **136**
uerto Ayacucho, Venez. 5°37′ N, 67°32′ W **136**
uerto Ayora, Ecua. 0°45′ N, 90°20′ W **130**
uerto Bahía Negra, Parag. 20°12′ S, 58°14′ W **132**
uerto Baquerizo Moreno, Ecua. 0°57′ N, 89°27′ W **130**
uerto Barrios, Guatemala 15°42′ N, 88°36′ W **115**
uerto Belgrano, Arg. 38°53′ S, 62°6′ W **139**
uerto Bermúdez, Peru 10°19′ S, 74°54′ W **137**
uerto Berrío, Col. 6°28′ N, 74°26′ W **136**
uerto Boy, Col. 0°11′ N, 74°53′ W **136**
uerto Cabello, Venez. 10°27′ N, 68°1′ W **136**
uerto Cabezas, Nicar. 14°2′ N, 83°24′ W **115**
uerto Cahuinari, Col. 1°26′ S, 70°44′ W **136**
uerto Capaz see El Jabha, Mor. 35°12′ N, 4°40′ W **150**
uerto Carabuco, Bol. 15°44′ S, 69°5′ W **137**
uerto Carlos, Col. 1°41′ S, 71°52′ W **136**
uerto Carlos, Peru 12°57′ S, 70°15′ W **137**
uerto Carranza, Col. 2°38′ S, 70°11′ W **136**
uerto Carreño, Col. 6°9′ N, 67°25′ W **136**
uerto Chicama, Peru 7°43′ S, 79°26′ W **130**
uerto Coig, Arg. 50°54′ S, 69°13′ W **134**
uerto Colombia, Col. 10°57′ N, 74°57′ W **136**
uerto Copal, Peru 3°1′ S, 74°46′ W **136**
uerto Córdoba, Col. 1°20′ S, 69°53′ W **136**
uerto Cortés, Hond. 15°49′ N, 87°56′ W **116**
uerto Cumarebo, Venez. 11°27′ N, 69°22′ W **136**
uerto Curaray, Peru 2°26′ S, 74°7′ W **136**
uerto de Lomas, Peru 15°34′ S, 74°50′ W **137**
uerto de Luna, N. Mex., U.S. 34°49′ N, 104°37′ W **92**
uerto de Nutrias, Venez. 8°5′ N, 69°20′ W **136**
uerto de Santa Cruz, Sp. 39°18′ N, 5°51′ W **164**
uerto Deseado, Arg. 47°43′ S, 65°55′ W **134**
uerto El Triunfo, El Salv. 13°16′ N, 88°34′ W **115**
uerto Escondido, Col. 9°2′ N, 76°15′ W **136**
uerto Escondido, Mex. 15°52′ N, 97°6′ W **112**
uerto Estrella, Col. 12°19′ N, 71°20′ W **136**
uerto Francisco de Orellana, Ecua. 0°30′ N, 77°2′ W **136**
Puerto Frey, Bol. 14°44′ S, 61°10′ W **132**
Puerto General Ovando, Bol. 9°51′ S, 65°39′ W **137**
Puerto Grether, Bol. 17°14′ S, 64°23′ W **137**
Puerto Heath, Bol. 12°33′ S, 68°39′ W **137**
Puerto Huitoto, Col. 0°16′ N, 74°3′ W **136**
Puerto Inírida, Col. 3°44′ N, 67°53′ W **136**
Puerto Iradier, Equatorial Guinea 1°6′ N, 9°43′ E **218**
Puerto Jiménez, C.R. 8°32′ N, 83°19′ W **115**
Puerto La Concordia, Col. 2°38′ N, 72°49′ W **136**
Puerto La Cruz, Venez. 10°12′ N, 64°39′ W **130**
Puerto La Esperanza, Parag. 21°60′ S, 58°3′ W **132**
Puerto La Paz, Arg. 22°29′ S, 62°24′ W **132**
Puerto La Victoria, Parag. 22°17′ S, 57°58′ W **132**
Puerto Lápice, Sp. 39°19′ N, 3°29′ W **164**
Puerto Leguízamo, Col. 0°11′ N, 74°47′ W **136**
Puerto Leigue, Bol. 14°19′ S, 64°53′ W **137**
Puerto Lempira, Hond. 15°10′ N, 83°47′ W **115**
Puerto Limón, Col. 1°0′ N, 76°32′ W **136**
Puerto Limón, C.R. 9°45′ N, 83°4′ W **123**
Puerto Limón, C.R. 9°59′ N, 83°2′ W **115**
Puerto Lobos, Mex. 30°16′ N, 112°51′ W **92**
Puerto Lobos (Arroyo Verde), Arg. 42°2′ S, 65°5′ W **134**
Puerto López, Col. 4°6′ N, 72°59′ W **136**
Puerto López (Tucacas), Col. 11°56′ N, 71°18′ W **136**
Puerto Lumbreras, Sp. 37°33′ N, 1°50′ W **164**
Puerto Macaco, Col. 2°0′ N, 71°5′ W **136**
Puerto Madryn, Arg. 42°53′ S, 64°59′ W **123**
Puerto Maldonado, Peru 12°39′ S, 69°13′ W **137**
Puerto Mamoré, Bol. 16°43′ S, 64°51′ W **137**
Puerto Miraña, Col. 1°21′ S, 70°20′ W **136**
Puerto Mirando, Venez. 10°46′ N, 71°34′ W **116**
Puerto Montt, Chile 41°29′ S, 72°58′ W **134**
Puerto Morazán, Nicar. 12°50′ N, 87°10′ W **115**
Puerto Morelos, Mex. 20°50′ N, 86°56′ W **116**
Puerto Mutis see Bahía Solano, Col. 6°12′ N, 77°25′ W **136**
Puerto Napo, Ecua. 1°7′ S, 77°52′ W **136**
Puerto Naré, Col. 6°9′ N, 74°37′ W **136**
Puerto Natales, Chile 51°39′ S, 72°29′ W **134**
Puerto Nuevo, Col. 5°43′ N, 70°1′ W **136**
Puerto Obaldía, Col. 8°40′ N, 77°25′ W **115**
Puerto Olaya, Col. 6°29′ N, 74°22′ W **136**
Puerto Páez, Venez. 6°14′ N, 67°23′ W **136**
Puerto Pardo, Peru 12°33′ S, 68°48′ W **137**
Puerto Patiño, Bol. 16°36′ S, 65°50′ W **137**
Puerto Peñasco, Mex. 31°18′ N, 113°33′ W **92**
Puerto Pinasco, Parag. 22°36′ S, 57°52′ W **132**
Puerto Piracuacito, Arg. 28°11′ S, 59°10′ W **139**
Puerto Píritu, Venez. 10°3′ N, 65°3′ W **116**
Puerto Pizarro, Col. 0°16′ N, 73°28′ W **136**
Puerto Plata, Dom. Rep. 19°46′ N, 70°41′ W **116**
Puerto Portillo, Peru 9°46′ S, 72°46′ W **137**
Puerto Prado, Peru 11°11′ S, 74°20′ W **137**
Puerto Princesa, Philippines 9°44′ N, 118°45′ E **203**
Puerto Príncipe, Col. 0°27′ N, 75°9′ W **136**
Puerto Real, Sp. 36°31′ N, 6°12′ W **164**
Puerto Rico, Bol. 11°8′ S, 67°35′ W **137**
Puerto Rico, Col. 2°33′ N, 74°14′ W **136**
Puerto Rico, adm. division, U.S. 18°13′ N, 66°29′ W **118**
Puerto Rico Trench, North Atlantic Ocean 19°41′ N, 63°30′ W **253**
Puerto Rondón, Col. 6°19′ N, 71°7′ W **136**
Puerto Salgar, Col. 5°28′ N, 74°38′ W **136**
Puerto Salvatierra, Peru 3°34′ S, 76°31′ W **136**
Puerto San Augustín, Peru 2°45′ S, 71°25′ W **136**
Puerto San Julián, Arg. 49°17′ S, 67°46′ W **134**
Puerto Sandino, Nicar. 12°10′ N, 86°44′ W **115**
Puerto Santa Cruz, Arg. 49°60′ S, 68°33′ W **134**
Puerto Saucedo, Bol. 14°1′ S, 62°50′ W **130**
Puerto Siles, Bol. 12°47′ S, 65°7′ W **137**
Puerto Socorro, Col. 2°48′ S, 69°59′ W **136**
Puerto Tejada, Col. 3°14′ N, 76°25′ W **136**
Puerto Tirol, Arg. 27°22′ S, 59°6′ W **139**
Puerto Tres Palmas, Parag. 21°43′ S, 57°59′ W **132**
Puerto Umbría, Col. 0°47′ N, 76°35′ W **136**
Puerto Vallarta, Mex. 20°35′ N, 105°16′ W **114**
Puerto Velarde, Bol. 16°31′ S, 63°41′ W **137**
Puerto Velasco Ibarra, Ecua. 1°22′ S, 90°33′ W **130**
Puerto Villamil, Ecua. 0°55′ N, 90°57′ W **130**
Puerto Villarroel, Bol. 16°54′ S, 64°49′ W **137**
Puerto Villazón, Bol. 13°29′ S, 61°56′ W **130**
Puerto Wilches, Col. 7°20′ N, 73°52′ W **136**
Puertollano, Sp. 38°41′ N, 4°7′ W **164**
Pueşti, Rom. 46°24′ N, 27°30′ E **156**
Puesto Arturo, Peru 1°51′ S, 73°20′ W **136**
Pugachev, Russ. 52°1′ N, 48°48′ E **158**
Pugal, India 28°30′ N, 72°49′ E **186**
Puget Sound 47°46′ N, 123°32′ W **80**
Puget-Théniers, Fr. 43°57′ N, 6°52′ E **167**
Puglia, adm. division, It. 41°12′ N, 15°15′ E **156**
Pugŏ, N. Korea 42°2′ N, 129°58′ E **200**
Puhja, Est. 58°19′ N, 26°18′ E **166**
Pui, Rom. 45°31′ N, 23°6′ E **168**
Puig Major, peak, Sp. 39°47′ N, 2°45′ E **164**
Puigcerdà, Fr. 42°25′ N, 1°55′ E **164**
Puigmal d'Err, peak, Sp. 42°22′ N, 2°3′ E **164**
Puig-reig, Sp. 41°57′ N, 1°52′ E **164**
Puiseaux, Fr. 48°11′ N, 2°28′ E **163**
Pujehun, Sierra Leone 7°21′ N, 11°44′ W **222**
Pujiang, China 29°30′ N, 119°55′ E **198**
Pujŏn, N. Korea 40°26′ N, 127°37′ E **200**
Pujŏn, river, N. Korea 40°54′ N, 127°33′ E **200**
Puka, Est. 58°3′ N, 26°13′ E **166**
Puka see Pukë, Alban. 42°2′ N, 19°53′ E **168**
Pukaki, Lake, N.Z. 44°7′ S, 169°48′ E **240**
Pukapuka Atoll (Danger Islands), South Pacific Ocean 10°35′ S, 167°12′ W **238**
Pukapuka, island, Fr. 14°46′ S, 138°53′ W **252**
Pukari, Russ. 65°58′ N, 30°1′ E **152**
Pukaskwa National Park, Can. 48°16′ N, 88°31′ W **94**
Pukatawagan, Can. 55°45′ N, 101°17′ W **108**
Pukchin, N. Korea 40°12′ N, 125°44′ E **200**
Pukch'ŏng, N. Korea 40°14′ N, 128°21′ E **200**
Pukë (Puka), Alban. 42°2′ N, 19°53′ E **168**
Pukeashun Mountain, peak, Can. 51°12′ N, 119°19′ W **90**
Pukehou, N.Z. 39°51′ S, 176°38′ E **240**
Pukekohe, N.Z. 37°13′ S, 174°53′ E **240**
Pukemiro, N.Z. 37°38′ S, 175°0′ E **240**
Pukovac, Serb. and Mont. 43°10′ N, 21°50′ E **168**
Puksa, Russ. 62°35′ N, 40°35′ E **154**
Puksoozero, Russ. 62°36′ N, 40°34′ E **154**
Pula, Capo di, It. 38°53′ N, 8°59′ E **156**
Pulacayo, Bol. 20°28′ S, 66°40′ W **137**
Pulaj, Alban. 41°53′ N, 19°23′ E **168**
Pulap Atoll 7°29′ N, 150°1′ E **192**
Pular, Cerro, peak, Chile 24°12′ S, 68°12′ W **132**
Pulaski, N.Y., U.S. 43°34′ N, 76°8′ W **94**
Pulaski, Tenn., U.S. 35°10′ N, 87°1′ W **96**
Pulaski, Va., U.S. 37°2′ N, 80°47′ W **96**
Pulaukijang, Indonesia 0°42′ N, 103°11′ E **196**
Pulheim, Ger. 51°0′ N, 6°47′ E **167**
Puli, Taiwan 23°52′ N, 120°57′ E **198**
Pulkkila, Fin. 64°16′ N, 25°50′ E **152**
Pullen Island, island, Antarctica 73°2′ S, 63°3′ W **248**
Pullman, Mich., U.S. 42°28′ N, 86°5′ W **102**
Pullman, Wash., U.S. 46°44′ N, 117°10′ W **90**
Pullo, Peru 15°15′ S, 73°50′ W **137**
Pulog, Mount, peak, Philippines 16°35′ N, 120°49′ E **203**
Pulozero, Russ. 68°21′ N, 33°18′ E **152**
Pulpí, Sp. 37°24′ N, 1°44′ W **164**
Púlpito, Punta, Mex. 26°33′ N, 111°32′ W **112**
Pülümür, Turk. 39°29′ N, 39°53′ E **195**
Puluwat Atoll 6°50′ N, 149°57′ E **192**
Puma Yumco, lake, China 28°40′ N, 90°6′ E **197**
Pummanki, Russ. 69°46′ N, 31°53′ E **152**
Pumpsaint, U.K. 52°1′ N, 3°56′ W **162**
Puna, Arg. 27°47′ S, 62°30′ W **139**
Puná, Isla, island, Ecua. 3°11′ S, 80°46′ W **130**
Puna, region, Hawai'i, U.S. 19°32′ N, 155°23′ W **99**
Punakha, Bhutan 27°37′ N, 89°51′ E **197**
Punata, Bol. 17°35′ S, 65°47′ W **137**
Punch, India 33°46′ N, 74°6′ E **186**
Punchaw, Can. 53°27′ N, 123°15′ W **108**
Pune, India 18°30′ N, 73°53′ E **188**
Pungan, Uzb. 40°47′ N, 70°55′ E **197**
P'ungch'ŏn see Kwail, N. Korea 38°25′ N, 125°1′ E **200**
Punggi, S. Korea 36°51′ N, 128°32′ E **200**
Punilla, Cordillera de la, Chile 29°37′ S, 71°36′ W **134**
Punitaqui, Chile 30°50′ S, 71°17′ W **134**
Punjab, adm. division, India 30°2′ N, 74°58′ E **197**
Punjab, adm. division, Pak. 30°51′ N, 71°22′ E **186**
Punkaharju, Fin. 61°47′ N, 29°18′ E **166**
Puno, Peru 15°53′ S, 70°1′ W **137**
Puno, adm. division, Peru 15°4′ S, 70°39′ W **137**
Punta Abreojos, Mex. 26°44′ N, 113°38′ W **112**
Punta Alta, Arg. 38°49′ S, 62°4′ W **139**
Punta Arenas, Chile 53°6′ S, 70°56′ W **134**
Punta Cardón, Venez. 11°38′ N, 70°13′ W **136**
Punta de Bombón, Peru 17°13′ S, 71°46′ W **137**
Punta de Díaz, Chile 28°3′ S, 70°38′ W **132**
Punta del Este, Uru. 34°58′ S, 54°58′ W **139**
Punta Gorda, Fla., U.S. 26°55′ N, 82°2′ W **105**
Punta Gorda, Nicar. 11°31′ N, 83°48′ W **115**
Punta Gorda, river, Nicar. 11°45′ N, 84°16′ W **115**
Punta Indio, Arg. 35°21′ S, 57°18′ W **139**
Punta La Marmora, peak, It. 39°58′ N, 9°14′ E **156**
Punta Maldonado, Mex. 16°19′ N, 98°33′ W **112**
Punta Prieta, Mex. 28°54′ N, 114°21′ W **92**
Punta San Francisquito, Mex. 28°24′ N, 112°54′ W **92**
Punta Skala, Croatia 44°11′ N, 15°8′ E **156**
Puntarenas, C.R. 9°59′ N, 84°50′ W **115**
Punto Fijo, Venez. 11°41′ N, 70°14′ W **136**
Puntzi Lake, lake, Can. 52°10′ N, 124°26′ W **108**
Punxsutawney, Pa., U.S. 40°56′ N, 78°59′ W **94**
Puok, Cambodia 13°28′ N, 103°46′ E **202**
Puokio, Fin. 64°44′ N, 27°16′ E **152**
Puolanka, Fin. 64°50′ N, 27°36′ E **152**
Puqi, China 29°38′ N, 113°51′ E **198**
Puquina, Peru 16°40′ S, 71°11′ W **137**
Puquio, Peru 14°43′ S, 74°9′ W **137**
Puračić, Bosn. and Herzg. 44°33′ N, 18°28′ E **168**
Puranpur, India 28°31′ N, 80°7′ E **197**
Purari, river, P.N.G. 7°1′ S, 144°29′ E **192**
Purcell, Okla., U.S. 35°0′ N, 97°22′ W **92**
Purcell Mountains, Can. 48°59′ N, 116°12′ W **108**
Purchena, Sp. 37°19′ N, 2°22′ W **164**
Purdy Islands, Bismarck Sea 3°3′ S, 144°14′ E **192**
Purépero, Mex. 19°53′ N, 102°1′ W **114**
Puri, Angola 7°43′ S, 15°40′ E **218**
Puri, India 19°48′ N, 85°49′ E **188**
Purificación, Mex. 19°42′ N, 104°39′ W **114**
Purikari Neem, Est. 59°39′ N, 25°21′ E **166**
Purmerend, Neth. 52°30′ N, 4°56′ E **163**
Purnema, Russ. 64°24′ N, 37°21′ E **154**
Purnia, India 25°45′ N, 87°28′ E **197**
Purnululu National Park, Austral. 17°30′ S, 128°16′ E **238**
Pursat, Cambodia 12°35′ N, 103°48′ E **202**
Puruándiro, Mex. 20°4′ N, 101°31′ W **114**
Puruê, river, Braz. 2°12′ S, 68°30′ W **136**
Purukcahu, Indonesia 0°34′ N, 114°29′ E **192**
Purulia, India 23°20′ N, 86°21′ E **197**
Purus, river, Braz. 9°3′ S, 69°52′ W **132**
Purvis, Miss., U.S. 31°7′ N, 89°24′ W **103**
Puryŏng, N. Korea 42°3′ N, 129°41′ E **200**
Pusad, India 19°53′ N, 77°34′ E **188**
Pusan see Busan, S. Korea 35°6′ N, 129°3′ E **200**
Pushkin, Russ. 59°41′ N, 30°21′ E **152**
Pushkino, Russ. 51°12′ N, 46°55′ E **158**
Pushkinskiye Gory, Russ. 57°1′ N, 28°53′ E **166**
Pusi, Peru 15°30′ S, 69°58′ W **137**
Püspökladány, Hung. 47°18′ N, 21°7′ E **168**
Püssi, Est. 59°20′ N, 27°2′ E **166**
Pusticamica, Lac, lake, Can. 49°19′ N, 77°6′ W **110**
Pustoshka, Russ. 56°19′ N, 29°28′ E **166**
Pusztamérges, Hung. 46°19′ N, 19°41′ E **168**
Puta, Azerb. 40°19′ N, 49°38′ E **195**
Putahow Lake, lake, Can. 59°50′ N, 101°15′ W **108**
Putao, Myanmar 27°23′ N, 97°19′ E **190**
Putari, Lagoa, lake, Braz. 13°3′ S, 61°54′ W **130**
Putaruru, N.Z. 38°3′ S, 175°46′ E **240**
Putian, China 25°26′ N, 119°3′ E **198**
Putilovo, Russ. 59°22′ N, 44°35′ E **154**
Putina, Peru 14°57′ S, 69°54′ W **137**
Put-in-Bay, Ohio, U.S. 41°39′ N, 82°48′ W **102**
Putla, Mex. 17°0′ N, 97°56′ W **112**
Put'Lenina, Russ. 68°28′ N, 107°40′ E **173**
Putna, Rom. 47°52′ N, 25°37′ E **156**
Putnam, Conn., U.S. 41°54′ N, 71°55′ W **104**
Putnam, Dem. Rep. of the Congo 1°25′ N, 28°34′ E **224**
Putorana, Plato, Russ. 68°46′ N, 91°28′ E **169**
Putorino, N.Z. 39°8′ S, 177°1′ E **240**
Putre, Chile 18°14′ S, 69°37′ W **137**
Putsonderwater, S. Af. 29°12′ S, 21°50′ E **227**
Puttalam, Sri Lanka 8°2′ N, 79°51′ E **188**
Putten, Neth. 52°14′ N, 5°36′ E **163**
Puttur, India 12°44′ N, 75°12′ E **188**
Puttur, India 13°27′ N, 79°33′ E **188**
Putu Range, Liberia 5°32′ N, 7°50′ W **222**
Putumayo, Ecua. 9°535′ N, 75°53′ W **136**
Putumayo, adm. division, Col. 0°34′ N, 77°9′ W **136**
Putumayo, river, South America 2°52′ S, 73°10′ W **122**
Putussibau, Indonesia 0°52′ N, 112°51′ E **192**
Pu'u Kūlua, peak, Hawai'i, U.S. 19°31′ N, 155°29′ W **99**
Pu'u Lehua, peak, Hawai'i, U.S. 19°33′ N, 155°51′ W **99**
Pu'u Maka'ala, peak, Hawai'i, U.S. 19°31′ N, 155°17′ W **99**
Pu'u Mākanaka, peak, Hawai'i, U.S. 19°50′ N, 155°29′ W **99**
Pu'uhonua O Hōnaunau National Historical Park (City of Refuge National Historical Park), Hawai'i, U.S. 19°24′ N, 155°57′ W **99**
Pu'ukoholā Heiau National Historic Site, Hawai'i, U.S. 20°1′ N, 155°52′ W **99**
Puulavesi, lake, Fin. 61°41′ N, 26°26′ E **166**
Puumala, Fin. 61°31′ N, 28°9′ E **166**
Pu'uomahuka Heiau, site, Hawai'i, U.S. 21°38′ N, 158°6′ W **99**
Puvirnituq, Can. 60°5′ N, 77°15′ W **73**
Puxian, China 36°24′ N, 111°5′ E **198**
Puyallup, Wash., U.S. 47°9′ N, 122°18′ W **100**
Puyang, China 35°41′ N, 114°58′ E **198**
Puylaurens, Fr. 43°34′ N, 2°0′ E **150**
Puyo, Ecua. 1°36′ S, 78°4′ W **136**
Puyoô-Bellocq-Ramous, Fr. 43°32′ N, 0°55′ E **164**
Puysegur Point, N.Z. 46°21′ S, 166°20′ E **240**
Pwani, adm. division, Tanzania 7°19′ S, 38°26′ E **224**
Pweto, Zambia 8°29′ S, 28°52′ E **224**
Pwllheli, U.K. 52°53′ N, 4°25′ W **150**
Pyakupur, river, Russ. 63°23′ N, 73°59′ E **169**
Pyalitsa, Russ. 66°14′ N, 39°28′ E **154**
Pyal'ma, Russ. 62°24′ N, 35°58′ E **154**
P'yana, river, Russ. 55°26′ N, 44°27′ E **154**
Pyasina, river, Russ. 71°11′ N, 90°11′ E **160**
Pyasino, Ozero, lake, Russ. 69°58′ N, 86°36′ E **169**
Pyasinskiy Zaliv 73°39′ N, 78°4′ E **160**
Pyatigorsk, Russ. 44°4′ N, 43°6′ E **158**
Pyatīmarskoe, Kaz. 49°31′ N, 50°28′ E **158**
P'yatykhatky, Ukr. 48°24′ N, 33°40′ E **156**
Pyay, Myanmar 18°51′ N, 95°14′ E **202**
Pydna 168 B.C., battle, Gr. 40°22′ N, 22°27′ E **156**
Pyeongchang, S. Korea 37°21′ N, 128°23′ E **200**
Pyeonghae, S. Korea 36°43′ N, 129°28′ E **200**
Pyeongtaek, S. Korea 36°57′ N, 127°7′ E **200**
Pyetrikaw, Belarus 52°8′ N, 28°34′ E **152**
Pyhäjärvi, lake, Fin. 60°59′ N, 21°55′ E **166**
Pyhäjoki, Fin. 64°27′ N, 24°13′ E **152**
Pyhämaa, Fin. 60°56′ N, 21°20′ E **166**
Pyhäntä, Fin. 64°5′ N, 26°18′ E **152**
Pyhäsalmi, Fin. 63°40′ N, 25°54′ E **152**
Pyhäselkä, Fin. 62°24′ N, 29°56′ E **152**
Pyhätunturi, peak, Fin. 66°59′ N, 26°56′ E **152**
Pyhtää (Pyttis), Fin. 60°29′ N, 26°33′ E **166**
Pyinkayaing, Myanmar 15°58′ N, 94°25′ E **202**
Pyinmanaa, Myanmar 19°46′ N, 96°10′ E **202**
Pyin-U-Lwin, Myanmar 22°1′ N, 96°27′ E **202**
Pylos, ruin(s), Ionian Sea 36°56′ N, 21°34′ E **156**
P'yŏngyang, N. Korea 39°1′ N, 125°45′ E **200**
P'yŏngsan, N. Korea 38°20′ N, 126°24′ E **200**
P'yŏngsan, N. Korea 40°36′ N, 127°57′ E **200**
P'yŏng-sŏng, N. Korea 39°13′ N, 125°52′ E **200**
P'yŏngwŏn, N. Korea 39°18′ N, 125°37′ E **200**
Pyote, Tex., U.S. 31°31′ N, 103°8′ W **92**
Pyramid Lake, Nev., U.S. 39°50′ N, 120°31′ W **80**
Pyramid Mountain, peak, Can. 58°52′ N, 129°60′ W **108**
Pyramid Peak, Calif., U.S. 36°22′ N, 116°40′ W **101**
Pyrds Bay 68°45′ S, 74°19′ E **255**
Pyrenees, Sp. 43°7′ N, 1°10′ E **165**
Pyrrha, ruin(s), Gr. 39°8′ N, 26°12′ E **156**
Pyryatyn, Ukr. 50°12′ N, 32°30′ E **158**
Pyshchug, Russ. 58°52′ N, 45°43′ E **154**
Pyshma, Russ. 56°58′ N, 63°13′ E **154**
Pytalovo, Russ. 57°3′ N, 27°52′ E **166**
Pýthion, Gr. 41°22′ N, 26°36′ E **156**
Pytteggja, peak, Nor. 62°11′ N, 7°34′ E **152**
Pyttis see Pyhtää, Fin. 60°29′ N, 26°33′ E **166**
Pyu, Myanmar 18°30′ N, 96°25′ E **202**

Q

Qaa, Leb. 34°22′ N, 36°29′ E **194**
Qaanaaq (Thule) 77°32′ N, 69°13′ W **106**
Qabanbay, Kaz. 45°49′ N, 80°36′ E **184**
Qabb Ilyās, Leb. 33°47′ N, 35°49′ E **194**
Qades, Afghan. 34°48′ N, 63°26′ E **186**
Qāḑub, Yemen 12°37′ N, 53°50′ E **182**
Qā'emshahr, Iran 36°30′ N, 52°55′ E **186**
Qagan Nur, China 43°18′ N, 112°57′ E **198**
Qagan Nur, lake, China 43°18′ N, 114°17′ E **198**
Qagcaka, China 32°33′ N, 81°52′ E **188**
Qahar Youyi Houqi, China 41°28′ N, 113°11′ E **198**
Qahar Youyi Zhongqi, China 41°15′ N, 112°36′ E **198**
Qaharir, oil field, Oman 17°55′ N, 55°30′ E **182**
Qaidam Pendi, China 37°41′ N, 91°15′ E **188**
Qaidam, river, China 36°29′ N, 97°23′ E **188**
Qairouan, Tun. 35°40′ N, 10°5′ E **156**
Qaiyara, oil field, Iraq 35°43′ N, 43°6′ E **180**
Qal 'at al Ḩasā, ruin(s), Jordan 30°49′ N, 35°53′ E **194**
Qala 'en Nahl, Sudan 13°36′ N, 34°55′ E **182**
Qalaa Kebira, Tun. 35°53′ N, 10°31′ E **156**
Qalansīyah, Yemen 12°38′ N, 53°26′ E **182**
Qalat, Afghan. 32°8′ N, 66°58′ E **186**
Qal'at al Azlam, ruin(s), Saudi Arabia 27°3′ N, 35°55′ E **180**
Qal'at al Maḑīq, Syr. 35°25′ N, 36°22′ E **194**
Qal'at Bīshah, Saudi Arabia 19°59′ N, 42°37′ E **182**
Qal'at Şahyūn, ruin(s), Syr. 35°34′ N, 36°0′ E **194**
Qal'at Şāliḩ, ruin(s), Syr. 35°33′ N, 35°59′ E **156**
Qal'eh-ye Bar Panj, Afghan. 37°32′ N, 71°27′ E **184**
Qal'eh-ye Now, Afghan. 34°57′ N, 63°11′ E **186**
Qal'eh-ye Saber, Afghan. 34°3′ N, 69°4′ E **186**
Qal'eh-ye Sarkari, Afghan. 35°51′ N, 67°16′ E **186**
Qalhāt, Oman 22°40′ N, 59°20′ E **182**
Qallabat, Sudan 12°56′ N, 36°6′ E **182**
Qalqaman, Kaz. 51°57′ N, 76°4′ E **184**
Qalqīlyah, West Bank 32°11′ N, 34°58′ E **194**
Qaltat Bū as Su'ūd, spring, Lib. 27°39′ N, 18°13′ E **216**
Qalzhat, Kaz. 43°32′ N, 80°35′ E **184**
Qamar, Ghubbat al 15°45′ N, 52°17′ E **182**
Qamashi, Uzb. 38°49′ N, 66°27′ E **197**
Qamata, S. Af. 31°60′ S, 27°26′ E **227**
Qamdo, China 31°10′ N, 97°6′ E **188**
Qamīnis, Lib. 31°39′ N, 20°1′ E **216**
Qamystybas, Kaz. 46°13′ N, 61°58′ E **184**
Qanā, Saudi Arabia 27°44′ N, 41°30′ E **180**
Qanawāt, Syr. 32°45′ N, 36°36′ E **194**
Qandala, Somalia 11°23′ N, 49°50′ E **216**
Qanshenggel, Kaz. 44°18′ N, 75°30′ E **184**
Qapqal, China 43°49′ N, 81°18′ E **184**
Qapshaghay, Kaz. 43°54′ N, 77°6′ E **184**
Qaqortoq (Julianehåb) 60°47′ N, 46°7′ W **106**
Qâra, Egypt 29°38′ N, 26°32′ E **180**
Qarabey, Kaz. 48°46′ N, 53°2′ E **158**
Qarabulaq, Kaz. 44°53′ N, 78°28′ E **184**
Qarabulaq, Kaz. 42°32′ N, 69°49′ E **197**
Qarabutaq, Kaz. 49°57′ N, 60°7′ E **158**
Qaraghandy, Kaz. 49°49′ N, 73°9′ E **184**
Qaraghandy, adm. division, Kaz. 48°3′ N, 68°19′ E **184**
Qaraghayly, Kaz. 49°20′ N, 75°43′ E **184**
Qārah, Syr. 34°9′ N, 36°44′ E **194**
Qarah Bagh, Afghan. 33°9′ N, 68°10′ E **186**
Qaraoba, Kaz. 47°0′ N, 56°14′ E **158**
Qaraqalpakstan, Uzb. 44°49′ N, 56°10′ E **158**
Qarasū, Kaz. 52°39′ N, 65°30′ E **184**
Qaratal, river, Kaz. 45°59′ N, 77°1′ E **184**
Qarataū, Kaz. 43°5′ N, 70°28′ E **184**
Qarataū Zhotasy, Kaz. 42°32′ N, 70°38′ E **197**
Qaratöbe, Kaz. 49°43′ N, 53°26′ E **158**
Qaratoghay, Kaz. 48°24′ N, 84°29′ E **184**
Qaraton, Kaz. 46°20′ N, 53°35′ E **158**
Qaraūt, Kaz. 48°56′ N, 79°15′ E **184**
Qarazhal, Kaz. 48°1′ N, 70°49′ E **184**
Qarazhar, Kaz. 47°45′ N, 56°8′ E **158**
Qardho, Somalia 9°30′ N, 49°7′ E **216**
Qareh, river, Iran 38°31′ N, 47°57′ E **195**
Qarghaly, Kaz. 50°18′ N, 57°17′ E **158**
Qarn Alam, oil field, Oman 20°59′ N, 57°3′ E **182**
Qarokŭl, lake, Taj. 39°5′ N, 73°10′ E **197**
Qarqan, river, China 38°25′ N, 86°14′ E **188**
Qarqan, river, China 38°31′ N, 85°47′ E **190**
Qarqaraly, Kaz. 49°29′ N, 75°23′ E **184**
Qarsaqbay, Kaz. 47°47′ N, 66°37′ E **184**
Qarshi, Uzb. 38°51′ N, 65°48′ E **197**
Qarţabā, Leb. 34°5′ N, 35°51′ E **194**
Qaryah al 'Ulyā, Saudi Arabia 27°32′ N, 47°40′ E **196**
Qaryat abu Nujaym, Lib. 30°34′ N, 15°21′ E **216**
Qaryat al Qaddāḩīyah, Lib. 31°21′ N, 15°13′ E **216**
Qaryat az Zuwaytīnah, Lib. 30°56′ N, 20°8′ E **216**
Qaryat Shumaykh, Lib. 31°21′ N, 13°57′ E **216**
Qarynzharyq, desert, Kaz. 42°45′ N, 53°31′ E **180**
Qasigiannguit (Christianshåb) 68°47′ N, 51°7′ W **106**
Qāsim, Syr. 32°59′ N, 36°3′ E **194**
Qaskeleng, Kaz. 43°12′ N, 76°39′ E **184**
Qaşr al Azraq, ruin(s), Jordan 31°51′ N, 36°46′ E **194**
Qaşr al Ḩallābāt, ruin(s), Jordan 32°3′ N, 36°19′ E **194**
Qaşr al Ḩammām, ruin(s), Jordan 31°31′ N, 36°8′ E **194**
Qaşr al Kharānah, ruin(s), Jordan 31°43′ N, 36°26′ E **194**
Qaşr al Mushayyish, ruin(s), Jordan 30°54′ N, 36°5′ E **194**
Qaşr 'Amrah, ruin(s), Jordan 31°47′ N, 36°32′ E **194**
Qaşr ash Shaqqah, ruin(s), Lib. 30°48′ N, 24°52′ E **180**
Qaşr aţ Ţūbah, ruin(s), Jordan 31°18′ N, 36°31′ E **194**
Qaşr Bū Hādī, ruin(s), Lib. 31°3′ N, 16°20′ E **216**
Qaşr Burqu', ruin(s), Jordan 32°34′ N, 37°48′ E **180**
Qaşr Farâfra, Egypt 27°2′ N, 27°58′ E **180**
Qaşr Ḩamām, Saudi Arabia 20°47′ N, 45°51′ E **182**
Qaşr Ibrîm, ruin(s), Egypt 22°30′ N, 31°51′ E **182**
Qaşr-e Qand, Iran 26°11′ N, 60°50′ E **182**
Qaşr-e Shīrīn, Iran 34°31′ N, 45°34′ E **180**
Qasserine (Kasserine), Tun. 35°9′ N, 8°51′ E **156**
Qatar 25°0′ N, 51°0′ E **196**
Qattara Depression, Egypt 29°32′ N, 26°42′ E **180**
Qaţţâra, spring, Egypt 30°10′ N, 27°9′ E **180**
Qax, Azerb. 41°25′ N, 46°55′ E **195**
Qāyen, Iran 33°44′ N, 59°14′ E **180**
Qaynar, Kaz. 49°16′ N, 77°29′ E **184**
Qazakh, Azerb. 41°5′ N, 45°21′ E **195**
Qazaly, Kaz. 45°49′ N, 62°7′ E **184**
Qazaq Shyghanaghy 42°42′ N, 51°45′ E **158**
Qazbegi, Ga. 42°38′ N, 44°40′ E **195**
Qazimämmäd, Azerb. 40°2′ N, 48°54′ E **195**
Qazvīn, Iran 36°18′ N, 49°59′ E **195**
Qazyqurt, Kaz. 41°48′ N, 69°27′ E **197**
Qeissan, Sudan 10°47′ N, 34°48′ E **224**
Qelibia, Tun. 36°51′ N, 11°5′ E **156**
Qemult'a, Asia 42°26′ N, 43°47′ E **158**
Qena, Egypt 26°12′ N, 32°40′ E **180**
Qeqertarsuaq (Disko), island, Qeqertarsuaq 69°31′ N, 62°11′ W **106**
Qeqertarsuaq (Godhavn), Qeqertarsuaq 69°15′ N, 53°30′ W **106**

Qeqertarsuatsiaat (Fiskenæsset) 63°6′ N, 50°43′ W 106
Qeren Naftali, peak, *Israel* 33°3′ N, 35°30′ E 194
Qerqenah Islands, *Tun.* 35°1′ N, 11°13′ E 214
Qertassi see Qirţâs, ruin(s), *Egypt* 23°39′ N, 32°43′ E 182
Qeshm, *Iran* 26°55′ N, 56°12′ E 196
Qeshm, island, *Iran* 26°36′ N, 56°3′ E 180
Qeys, island, *Iran* 26°22′ N, 53°46′ E 180
Qeysar, *Afghan.* 35°42′ N, 64°14′ E 186
Qezel Owzan, river, *Iran* 37°3′ N, 48°34′ E 195
Qian Gorlos, *China* 45°3′ N, 124°48′ E 198
Qian'an, *China* 44°58′ N, 124°4′ E 198
Qianxi, *China* 27°3′ N, 106°2′ E 198
Qianxian, *China* 34°31′ N, 108°15′ E 198
Qianyang, *China* 27°16′ N, 110°11′ E 198
Qianyang, *China* 34°38′ N, 107°6′ E 198
Qiaowan, *China* 40°35′ N, 96°43′ E 188
Qibā', *Saudi Arabia* 27°22′ N, 44°23′ E 180
Qidaogou, *China* 41°32′ N, 126°21′ E 200
Qidong, *China* 31°48′ N, 121°38′ E 198
Qidong, *China* 26°44′ N, 112°8′ E 198
Qiemo, *China* 38°12′ N, 85°18′ E 190
Qijiang, *China* 28°58′ N, 106°38′ E 198
Qikiqtarjuaq (Broughton Island), *Can.* 67°30′ N, 63°52′ W 73
Qila Ladgasht, *Pak.* 27°49′ N, 63°0′ E 182
Qila Safed, *Pak.* 28°58′ N, 61°35′ E 182
Qilian Shan, *China* 39°14′ N, 96°43′ E 188
Qimen, *China* 29°51′ N, 117°40′ E 198
Qimusseriarsuaq 75°28′ N, 66°10′ W 106
Qin'an, *China* 34°51′ N, 105°40′ E 198
Qing, river, *China* 30°28′ N, 110°40′ E 198
Qing'an, *China* 46°53′ N, 127°30′ E 198
Qingchengzi, *China* 40°43′ N, 123°37′ E 200
Qingdao, *China* 36°5′ N, 120°24′ E 198
Qinggang, *China* 46°40′ N, 126°7′ E 198
Qinghai, adm. division, *China* 35°28′ N, 92°33′ E 188
Qinghai Hu, lake, *China* 36°45′ N, 99°5′ E 190
Qinghe, *China* 42°32′ N, 124°9′ E 200
Qingjian, *China* 37°8′ N, 110°11′ E 198
Qingjiang, *China* 28°1′ N, 115°30′ E 198
Qingshuihe, *China* 33°42′ N, 97°4′ E 188
Qingshuihe, *China* 39°54′ N, 111°40′ E 198
Qingtian, *China* 28°10′ N, 120°17′ E 198
Qingtongxia, *China* 38°4′ N, 106°3′ E 198
Qingxu, *China* 37°36′ N, 112°19′ E 198
Qingyang, *China* 36°2′ N, 107°54′ E 198
Qingyuan, *China* 42°6′ N, 124°52′ E 200
Qingyuan, *China* 23°40′ N, 113°2′ E 198
Qinhuangdao, *China* 39°56′ N, 119°36′ E 198
Qinxian, *China* 36°45′ N, 112°42′ E 198
Qinzhou, *China* 21°56′ N, 108°34′ E 198
Qionghai, *China* 19°14′ N, 110°31′ E 198
Qiqian, *China* 52°21′ N, 120°47′ E 190
Qiqihar, *China* 47°21′ N, 123°59′ E 198
Qira, *China* 37°2′ N, 80°54′ E 184
Qir'awn, Buḩayrat al, lake, *Leb.* 33°34′ N, 35°35′ E 194
Qirţâs (Qertassi), ruin(s), *Egypt* 23°39′ N, 32°43′ E 182
Qiryat Arba', *West Bank* 31°32′ N, 35°7′ E 194
Qiryat Ata, *Israel* 32°47′ N, 35°6′ E 194
Qiryat Gat, *Israel* 31°36′ N, 34°46′ E 194
Qiryat Mal'akhi, *Israel* 31°43′ N, 34°43′ E 194
Qiryat Motzkin, *Israel* 32°49′ N, 35°3′ E 194
Qiryat Shemona, *Israel* 33°12′ N, 35°34′ E 194
Qishn, *Yemen* 15°26′ N, 51°39′ E 182
Qitaihe, *China* 45°49′ N, 130°52′ E 238
Qixia, *China* 37°16′ N, 120°47′ E 198
Qiyaly, *Kaz.* 54°11′ N, 69°37′ E 184
Qiyang, *China* 26°38′ N, 111°48′ E 198
Qızılağac Körfäzi 39°6′ N, 48°36′ E 195
Qizilcha, *Uzb.* 40°42′ N, 66°11′ E 197
Qizilqum, *Uzb.* 41°58′ N, 64°9′ E 197
Qiziltepa, *Uzb.* 40°1′ N, 64°50′ E 197
Qobda, *Kaz.* 50°8′ N, 55°37′ E 158
Qoghaly, *Kaz.* 44°25′ N, 78°37′ E 184
Qoghir see K2, peak, *Pak.* 35°51′ N, 76°25′ E 186
Qom (Qum), *Iran* 34°39′ N, 50°50′ E 180
Qom, river, *Iran* 34°17′ N, 50°22′ E 180
Qomolangma see Everest, Mount, peak, *China-Nepal* 28°0′ N, 86°53′ E 197
Qomsheh, *Iran* 32°1′ N, 51°51′ E 180
Qonaqkänd, *Azerb.* 41°3′ N, 48°36′ E 195
Qonggyai, *China* 29°5′ N, 91°37′ E 197
Qongyrat, *Kaz.* 46°59′ N, 74°57′ E 184
Qoornoq 64°33′ N, 51°9′ W 106
Qoow, *Somalia* 11°11′ N, 48°57′ E 216
Qo'qon, *Uzb.* 40°31′ N, 70°55′ E 197
Qorakŭl, *Uzb.* 39°30′ N, 63°51′ E 197
Qorday, *Kaz.* 43°17′ N, 74°54′ E 184
Qorghalzhyn, *Kaz.* 50°36′ N, 69°50′ E 184
Qorovulbozor, *Uzb.* 39°31′ N, 64°51′ E 197
Qorsaq, *Kaz.* 47°0′ N, 53°18′ E 158
Qorveh, *Iran* 35°11′ N, 47°44′ E 180
Qoryaale, *Somalia* 7°28′ N, 49°11′ E 218
Qo'shrabot, *Uzb.* 40°15′ N, 66°39′ E 197
Qosköl, *Kaz.* 49°36′ N, 67°3′ E 184
Qosshaghyl, *Kaz.* 46°54′ N, 53°54′ E 158
Qostanay, *Kaz.* 53°13′ N, 63°35′ E 184
Qostanay, adm. division, *Kaz.* 52°2′ N, 60°25′ E 154
Qotanqaraghay, *Kaz.* 49°10′ N, 85°36′ E 184
Qoton, *Somalia* 9°30′ N, 50°27′ E 216
Qoţūr, *Iran* 38°27′ N, 44°23′ E 195
Qoubaiyat, *Leb.* 34°34′ N, 36°17′ E 194
Qsar Ghilan, *Tun.* 33°3′ N, 9°35′ E 216
Qsour Essaf, *Tun.* 35°26′ N, 10°58′ E 156
Qu' Appelle Valley Dam, *Can.* 50°47′ N, 106°26′ W 90
Quail Mountains, *Calif., U.S.* 35°39′ N, 117°1′ W 101
Quakenbrück, *Ger.* 52°40′ N, 7°58′ E 163
Qualicum Beach, *Can.* 49°20′ N, 124°26′ W 100
Quan Hoa, *Vietnam* 20°25′ N, 105°7′ E 202
Quanah, *Tex., U.S.* 34°16′ N, 99°45′ W 92
Quang Ngai, *Vietnam* 15°7′ N, 108°47′ E 202
Quang Tri, *Vietnam* 16°44′ N, 107°12′ E 202
Quannan, *China* 24°41′ N, 114°28′ E 198
Quantz Lake, *Can.* 51°7′ N, 85°56′ W 110
Quanzhou, *China* 25°59′ N, 111°4′ E 198
Quanzhou, *China* 24°58′ N, 118°36′ E 198
Qu'Appelle, *Can.* 50°32′ N, 103°54′ W 90
Qu'Appelle, river, *Can.* 50°40′ N, 103°48′ W 108
Quaraí, *Braz.* 30°25′ S, 56°24′ W 139
Quaraí, river, *South America* 30°8′ S, 57°11′ W 139
Quartz Hill, *Calif., U.S.* 34°39′ N, 118°14′ W 101
Quartzite Mountain, peak, *Nev., U.S.* 37°29′ N, 116°25′ W 92
Quartzsite, *Ariz., U.S.* 33°39′ N, 114°15′ W 101
Quatsino, *Can.* 50°32′ N, 127°38′ W 90
Quba, *Azerb.* 41°20′ N, 48°32′ E 195
Qūchān, *Iran* 37°4′ N, 58°29′ E 180
Que Son, *Vietnam* 15°40′ N, 108°13′ E 202
Québec, *Can.* 46°47′ N, 71°22′ W 94
Quebec, adm. division, *Can.* 53°50′ N, 76°4′ W 106
Quebracho, *Uru.* 31°57′ S, 57°52′ W 139
Quebracho Coto, *Arg.* 26°20′ S, 64°28′ W 132
Quedal, Cabo, *Chile* 41°11′ S, 75°34′ W 134
Queen Bess, Mount, peak, *Can.* 51°15′ N, 124°39′ W 90
Queen Charlotte Islands, *Hecate Strait* 53°6′ N, 132°30′ W 98
Queen Charlotte Sound 51°46′ N, 130°1′ W 108
Queen City, *Tex., U.S.* 33°8′ N, 94°10′ W 103
Queen Elizabeth Islands, *Northwest Passage* 76°21′ N, 116°41′ W 106
Queen Elizabeth National Park, *Uganda* 0°25′ N, 30°10′ E 224
Queen Mary Coast, *Antarctica* 69°42′ S, 97°55′ E 248
Queen Maud Gulf 67°52′ N, 102°7′ W 106
Queen Maud Land, region, *Antarctica* 76°48′ S, 8°55′ E 248
Queen Maud Mountains, *Antarctica* 86°1′ S, 141°33′ W 248
Queen Victoria's Profile, site, *Hawai'i, U.S.* 21°55′ N, 159°27′ W 99
Queens Channel 75°46′ N, 100°43′ W 106
Queens Sound 51°48′ N, 128°37′ W 108
Queensbury, *U.K.* 53°46′ N, 1°52′ W 162
Queensland, adm. division, *Austral.* 23°32′ S, 140°33′ E 231
Queenstown, *Austral.* 42°3′ S, 145°33′ E 231
Queenstown, *N.Z.* 45°1′ S, 168°39′ E 240
Queenstown, *S. Af.* 31°54′ S, 26°45′ E 207
Queenstown, *S. Af.* 31°53′ S, 26°51′ E 227
Queets, *Wash., U.S.* 47°31′ N, 124°20′ W 100
Queets, river, *Wash., U.S.* 47°28′ N, 124°16′ W 100
Queimadas, *Braz.* 11°2′ S, 39°38′ W 132
Quela, *Angola* 9°17′ S, 17°4′ E 218
Quelimane, *Mozambique* 17°55′ S, 36°52′ E 224
Quellón, *Chile* 43°6′ S, 73°39′ W 134
Quelo, *Angola* 6°28′ S, 12°48′ E 218
Quemado, *N. Mex., U.S.* 34°19′ N, 108°29′ W 92
Quemado, *Tex., U.S.* 28°56′ N, 100°37′ W 92
Quemado de Güines, *Cuba* 22°47′ N, 80°15′ W 116
Quembo, river, *Angola* 13°59′ S, 19°30′ E 220
Quemoy see Kinmen, island, *China* 24°23′ N, 118°32′ E 198
Quemú Quemú, *Arg.* 36°4′ S, 63°33′ W 139
Quentin, *Miss., U.S.* 31°29′ N, 90°45′ W 103
Quequén, *Arg.* 38°31′ S, 58°43′ W 139
Quequeña, *Peru* 16°36′ S, 71°26′ W 137
Querco, *Peru* 13°53′ S, 74°52′ W 137
Quercy, *Fr.* 44°40′ N, 1°10′ E 165
Querétaro, *Mex.* 20°34′ N, 100°27′ W 114
Querétaro, adm. division, *Mex.* 20°44′ N, 100°33′ W 114
Quesada, *Sp.* 37°51′ N, 3°5′ W 164
Queshan, *China* 32°46′ N, 114°2′ E 198
Quesnel, *Can.* 52°59′ N, 122°21′ W 106
Quesnel Lake, lake, *Can.* 52°41′ N, 121°20′ W 108
Quetico Lake, lake, *Can.* 48°32′ N, 92°24′ W 94
Quetta, *Pak.* 30°13′ N, 67°5′ E 182
Quetzaltenango, *Guatemala* 14°50′ N, 91°31′ W 115
Queulat National Park, *Chile* 44°30′ S, 72°44′ W 122
Queule, *Chile* 39°18′ S, 73°12′ W 134
Quevedo, *Ecua.* 1°8′ S, 79°37′ W 130
Quevedo, Península de, *Mex.* 23°56′ N, 108°18′ W 112
Quévillon, Lac, lake, *Can.* 49°2′ N, 77°31′ W 94
Quezon, *Philippines* 9°15′ N, 118°2′ E 203
Quezon City, *Philippines* 14°43′ N, 121°1′ E 203
Qufār, *Saudi Arabia* 27°24′ N, 41°40′ E 180
Qufu, *China* 35°34′ N, 116°54′ E 198
Qui Nhon, *Vietnam* 13°47′ N, 109°12′ E 202
Quibala, *Angola* 10°45′ S, 14°58′ E 220
Quibaxe, *Angola* 8°30′ S, 14°36′ E 220
Quibdó, *Col.* 5°40′ N, 76°38′ W 136
Quibell, *Can.* 49°57′ N, 93°26′ W 90
Quiberon, Presqu'île de, *Fr.* 47°32′ N, 3°9′ W 150
Quicabo, *Angola* 8°20′ S, 13°47′ E 220
Quick, *Can.* 54°35′ N, 126°58′ W 108
Quigley, *Can.* 56°5′ N, 110°55′ W 108
Quiĩama National Park, *Angola* 9°57′ S, 13°20′ E 206
Quiindy, *Parag.* 25°60′ S, 57°14′ W 139
Quilá, *Mex.* 24°23′ N, 107°13′ W 112
Quilán, Isla, island, *Chile* 43°34′ S, 74°35′ W 134
Quilcene, *Wash., U.S.* 47°48′ N, 122°53′ W 100
Quilengues, *Angola* 14°6′ S, 14°3′ E 220
Quill Lake, *Can.* 52°4′ N, 104°16′ W 108
Quillabamba, *Peru* 12°50′ S, 72°43′ W 137
Quillacollo, *Bol.* 17°29′ S, 66°13′ W 137
Quillagua, *Chile* 21°40′ S, 69°33′ W 137
Quillaicillo, *Chile* 31°24′ S, 71°37′ W 134
Quillan, *Fr.* 42°52′ N, 2°9′ E 164
Quilpie, *Austral.* 26°37′ S, 144°15′ E 231
Quilpué, *Chile* 33°3′ S, 71°26′ W 134
Quimbele, *Angola* 6°32′ S, 16°10′ E 218
Quime, *Bol.* 17°5′ S, 67°18′ W 137
Quimili, *Arg.* 27°38′ S, 62°25′ W 139
Quimistán, *Hond.* 15°22′ N, 88°22′ W 116
Quinault, *Wash., U.S.* 47°26′ N, 123°51′ W 100
Quinault, river, *Wash., U.S.* 47°22′ N, 124°9′ W 100
Quince Mil, *Peru* 13°15′ S, 70°44′ W 137
Quincy, *Fla., U.S.* 30°34′ N, 84°35′ W 96
Quincy, *Mass., U.S.* 42°14′ N, 71°1′ W 104
Quincy, *Mich., U.S.* 41°56′ N, 84°54′ W 102
Quincy, *Mo., U.S.* 39°55′ N, 91°25′ W 94
Quincy, *Oreg., U.S.* 46°7′ N, 123°10′ W 100
Quines, *Arg.* 32°15′ S, 65°48′ W 134
Quinga, *Mozambique* 15°49′ S, 40°17′ E 224
Quinhagak, *Alas., U.S.* 59°41′ N, 161°45′ W 106
Quinigua, Serranía, peak, *Venez.* 4°19′ N, 65°41′ W 136
Quintana Roo, adm. division, *Mex.* 19°18′ N, 88°58′ W 115
Quintanar de la Orden, *Sp.* 39°35′ N, 3°2′ W 164
Quinter, *Kans., U.S.* 39°3′ N, 100°14′ W 90
Quintette Mountain, peak, *Can.* 54°51′ N, 120°59′ W 108
Quintin, *Fr.* 48°24′ N, 2°55′ W 150
Quinto, *Sp.* 41°24′ N, 0°31′ E 164
Quinzau, *Angola* 6°50′ S, 12°43′ E 218
Quionga, *Mozambique* 10°37′ S, 40°33′ E 224
Quiquibey, river, *Bol.* 14°48′ S, 67°39′ W 137
Quiriguá, ruin(s), *Guatemala* 15°15′ N, 89°10′ W 115
Quirima, *Angola* 10°49′ S, 18°4′ E 220
Quirinópolis, *Braz.* 18°35′ S, 50°32′ W 138
Quirke Lake, *Can.* 46°27′ N, 83°4′ W 94
Quiroga, *Arg.* 35°18′ S, 61°27′ W 139
Quiroga, Punta, *Arg.* 42°23′ S, 66°1′ W 134
Quirusillas, *Bol.* 18°23′ S, 63°57′ W 137
Quisiro, *Venez.* 10°56′ N, 71°18′ W 136
Quissanga, *Mozambique* 12°24′ S, 40°30′ E 224
Quissico, *Mozambique* 24°40′ S, 34°43′ E 227
Quitapa, *Angola* 10°23′ S, 18°11′ E 220
Quitaque, *Tex., U.S.* 34°21′ N, 101°4′ W 92
Quiterajo, *Mozambique* 11°45′ S, 40°27′ E 224
Quitilipi, *Arg.* 26°53′ S, 60°13′ W 139
Quitman, *Ga., U.S.* 30°46′ N, 83°34′ W 96
Quitman, *La., U.S.* 32°20′ N, 92°44′ W 103
Quitman, *Miss., U.S.* 32°2′ N, 88°43′ W 103
Quitman, *Tex., U.S.* 32°47′ N, 95°27′ W 103
Quito, *Ecua.* 0°17′ N, 78°49′ W 130
Quitor, *Chile* 22°50′ S, 68°14′ W 137
Quitovac, *Mex.* 31°30′ N, 112°45′ W 92
Quixadá, *Braz.* 4°56′ S, 39°4′ W 132
Quixaxe, *Mozambique* 15°16′ S, 40°9′ E 224
Qujiang, *China* 24°38′ N, 113°34′ E 198
Qulan (Lügovoy), *Kaz.* 42°54′ N, 72°44′ E 184
Qulandy, *Kaz.* 46°6′ N, 59°28′ E 184
Qulbān Layyah, spring, *Iraq* 29°47′ N, 46°1′ E 196
Qullissat, *Qeqertarsuaq* 70°3′ N, 53°2′ W 106
Qulsary, *Kaz.* 46°58′ N, 54°1′ E 158
Qum see Qom, *Iran* 34°39′ N, 50°50′ E 180
Qumarlêb, *China* 34°27′ N, 95°24′ E 188
Qumsay, *Kaz.* 49°27′ N, 58°25′ E 158
Qunayyah, *Syr.* 34°30′ N, 37°1′ E 194
Quneitra see Al Qunayţirah, *Syr.* 33°7′ N, 35°49′ E 194
Qŭnghirot, *Uzb.* 43°1′ N, 58°50′ E 180
Qu'nyido, *China* 31°18′ N, 97°58′ E 188
Quogue, *N.Y., U.S.* 40°49′ N, 72°36′ W 104
Quoin Point, *S. Af.* 35°3′ S, 19°34′ E 227
Quorn, *Can.* 49°25′ N, 90°54′ W 94
Qurayyāt, *Oman* 23°16′ N, 58°54′ E 182
Qŭrghonteppa, *Taj.* 37°49′ N, 68°48′ E 197
Quryq, *Kaz.* 43°11′ N, 51°41′ E 158
Qûs, *Egypt* 25°54′ N, 32°44′ E 182
Qusar, *Azerb.* 41°24′ N, 48°27′ E 195
Quṣeir, *Egypt* 26°8′ N, 34°13′ E 180
Qusmuryn, *Kaz.* 52°27′ N, 64°37′ E 184
Qusum, *China* 29°5′ N, 92°12′ E 197
Quthing, *Lesotho* 30°25′ S, 27°41′ E 227
Quttinirpaaq National Park, *Can.* 81°58′ N, 73°8′ W 72
Quwo, *China* 35°40′ N, 111°27′ E 198
Quxian, *China* 30°51′ N, 106°52′ E 198
Qüxü, *China* 29°21′ N, 90°39′ E 197
Quy Chau, *Vietnam* 19°32′ N, 105°7′ E 202
Quzhou, *China* 36°49′ N, 114°53′ E 198
Quzhou, *China* 28°56′ N, 118°49′ E 198
Qvareli, *Ga.* 41°57′ N, 45°48′ E 195
Qyyq, *Kaz.* 43°46′ N, 70°57′ E 184
Qyzan, *Kaz.* 44°56′ N, 52°45′ E 158
Qyzylkayyn, *Kaz.* 45°47′ N, 80°14′ E 184
Qyzylorda, *Kaz.* 44°49′ N, 65°34′ E 184
Qyzylorda, adm. division, *Kaz.* 42°40′ N, 66°6′ E 197
Qyzylorda, adm. division, *Kaz.* 44°54′ N, 61°41′ E 184
Qyzylqaq Köli, lake, *Kaz.* 53°27′ N, 73°13′ E 184
Qyzylzhar, *Kaz.* 48°17′ N, 69°38′ E 184

R

Raab, river, *Aust.* 47°2′ N, 15°40′ E 168
Raahe (Brahestad), *Fin.* 64°41′ N, 24°27′ E 152
Raanujärvi, *Fin.* 66°39′ N, 24°41′ E 152
Raate, *Fin.* 64°47′ N, 29°43′ E 152
Rab, *Croatia* 44°46′ N, 14°45′ E 156
Raba, *Indonesia* 8°31′ S, 118°52′ E 192
Rába, river, *Hung.* 47°26′ N, 17°10′ E 168
Rábahidvég, *Hung.* 47°4′ N, 16°45′ E 168
Rabai, *Kenya* 3°54′ S, 39°35′ E 224
Rabak, *Sudan* 13°6′ N, 32°46′ E 182
Rabast, Cap de, *Can.* 49°59′ N, 64°15′ W 111
Rabastens, *Fr.* 43°48′ N, 1°42′ E 150
Rabastens, *Fr.* 43°23′ N, 0°8′ E 164
Rabat, *Mor.* 33°53′ N, 7°7′ W 214
Rabaul, *P.N.G.* 4°15′ S, 152°8′ E 238
Rabbit Ears Pass, *Colo., U.S.* 40°22′ N, 106°38′ W 90
Rabbit Lake, *Can.* 53°8′ N, 107°46′ W 108
Rabbit, river, *Can.* 59°25′ N, 127°17′ W 108
Rabga Pass, *China* 27°51′ N, 87°33′ E 197
Rābigh, *Saudi Arabia* 22°48′ N, 39°0′ E 182
Rabrovo, *Serb. and Mont.* 44°33′ N, 21°32′ E 168
Rabyānah, spring, *Lib.* 24°16′ N, 21°57′ E 216
Răcăşdia, *Rom.* 44°59′ N, 21°37′ E 168
Racconigi, *It.* 44°45′ N, 7°41′ E 167
Raccoon Point, *La., U.S.* 28°58′ N, 91°7′ W 103
Race, Cape, *Can.* 46°41′ N, 53°15′ W 111
Race Point, *Mass., U.S.* 42°3′ N, 70°21′ W 104
Race Point, *N.Y., U.S.* 41°11′ N, 72°2′ W 104
Race, The 41°11′ N, 72°9′ W 104
Raceland, *La., U.S.* 29°42′ N, 90°37′ W 103
Rach Gia, *Vietnam* 10°1′ N, 105°5′ E 202
Raciąż, *Pol.* 52°46′ N, 20°5′ E 152
Racine, *Wis., U.S.* 42°42′ N, 87°48′ W 102
Racing, river, *Can.* 58°36′ N, 125°4′ W 108
Raco, *Mich., U.S.* 46°22′ N, 84°44′ W 94
Raczki, *Pol.* 53°58′ N, 22°46′ E 166
Radan, *Serb. and Mont.* 43°1′ N, 21°22′ E 168
Radashkovichy, *Belarus* 54°9′ N, 27°14′ E 166
Rădăuţi, *Rom.* 47°50′ N, 25°55′ E 152
Radcliff, *Ky., U.S.* 37°50′ N, 85°57′ W 96
Radebeul, *Ger.* 51°6′ N, 13°37′ E 152
Radford, *Va., U.S.* 37°6′ N, 80°35′ W 96
Radhanpur, *India* 23°50′ N, 71°38′ E 186
Radio Beacon, site, *Can.* 43°55′ N, 60°7′ W 111
Radishchevo, *Russ.* 52°49′ N, 47°52′ E 154
Radisson, *Can.* 52°28′ N, 107°23′ W 108
Radisson, *Can.* 53°44′ N, 77°40′ W 106
Raditsa Krylovka, *Russ.* 53°17′ N, 34°23′ E 154
Radlinski, Mount, peak, *Antarctica* 82°22′ S, 102°9′ W 248
Radna, *Rom.* 46°6′ N, 21°42′ E 168
Radojevo, *Serb. and Mont.* 45°44′ N, 20°47′ E 168
Radolfzell, *Ger.* 47°44′ N, 8°57′ E 150
Radom, *Pol.* 51°23′ N, 21°9′ E 152
Radom, *Sudan* 9°49′ N, 24°50′ E 224
Radom National Park, *Sudan* 9°1′ N, 23°41′ E 224
Radomiru, *Rom.* 44°8′ N, 24°10′ E 156
Radomsko, *Pol.* 51°4′ N, 19°27′ E 152
Radomyshl', *Ukr.* 50°29′ N, 29°19′ E 158
Radovići, *Europe* 42°23′ N, 18°40′ E 168
Radoviš, *Maced.* 41°38′ N, 22°27′ E 168
Radstock, *U.K.* 51°17′ N, 2°27′ W 162
Raduzhnyy, *Russ.* 62°0′ N, 77°39′ E 169
Radviliškis, *Lith.* 55°47′ N, 23°30′ E 166
Radville, *Can.* 49°26′ N, 104°19′ W 90
Raḑwá, Jabal, peak, *Saudi Arabia* 24°32′ N, 38°11′ E 182
Radway, *Can.* 54°3′ N, 112°57′ W 108
Radziwiłłówka, *Pol.* 52°22′ N, 23°1′ E 152
Rae Bareli, *India* 26°13′ N, 81°14′ E 197
Rae Isthmus, *Can.* 66°53′ N, 90°60′ W 106
Rae, Mount, peak, *Can.* 50°36′ N, 115°4′ W 90
Rae, river, *Can.* 68°7′ N, 118°55′ W 98
Rae-Edzo, *Can.* 62°42′ N, 116°26′ W 106
Raesfeld, *Ger.* 51°46′ N, 6°51′ E 167
Raetihi, *N.Z.* 39°27′ S, 175°15′ E 240
Rāf, Jabal, peak, *Saudi Arabia* 29°12′ N, 39°47′ E 180
Rafaela, *Arg.* 31°14′ S, 61°27′ W 139
Rafah, *Gaza Strip* 31°16′ N, 34°15′ E 194
Rafaï, *Cen. Af. Rep.* 4°58′ N, 23°58′ E 224
Rafalivka, *Ukr.* 51°18′ N, 25°55′ E 152
Rafḩā', *Saudi Arabia* 29°41′ N, 43°31′ E 180
Rafsanjān, *Iran* 30°22′ N, 56°5′ E 196
Raft River Mountains, *Utah, U.S.* 41°48′ N, 113°46′ W 90
Rafter, *Can.* 55°38′ N, 101°11′ W 108
Rafz, *Switz.* 47°36′ N, 8°32′ E 150
Raga, *Sudan* 8°25′ N, 25°39′ E 224
Raga, river, *Sudan* 8°11′ N, 25°30′ E 224
Ragachow, *Belarus* 53°5′ N, 30°9′ E 154
Ragag, *Sudan* 10°56′ N, 24°45′ E 224
Ragauka, *Latv.* 56°41′ N, 27°24′ E 166
Ragay Gulf 13°35′ N, 122°30′ E 203
Ragged, Mount, peak, *Austral.* 33°29′ S, 123°13′ E 230
Raglan, *N.Z.* 37°51′ S, 174°54′ E 240
Ragley, *La., U.S.* 30°29′ N, 93°15′ W 103
Raguba, oil field, *Lib.* 29°1′ N, 18°57′ E 216
Ragunda, *Nor.* 63°3′ N, 16°23′ E 154
Ragusa, *It.* 36°54′ N, 14°42′ E 216
Ragusa see Dubrovnik, *Croatia* 42°38′ N, 18°5′ E 156
Rahad el Berdi, *Sudan* 11°16′ N, 23°52′ E 224
Raheita, *Eritrea* 12°43′ N, 43°5′ E 218
Rahib, Jebel, peak, *Sudan* 17°41′ N, 27°5′ E 226
Rahimyar Khan, *Pak.* 28°24′ N, 70°18′ E 186
Rahotu, *N.Z.* 39°20′ S, 173°49′ E 240
Rahuri, *India* 19°25′ N, 74°38′ E 188
Raíces, *Arg.* 31°53′ S, 59°14′ W 139
Raichur, *India* 16°12′ N, 77°20′ E 188
Raiganj, *India* 25°35′ N, 88°6′ E 197
Raigarh, *India* 21°54′ N, 83°22′ E 197
Rakiura National Park, *N.Z.* 47°25′ S, 168°23′ E 240
Railroad Flat, *Calif., U.S.* 38°20′ N, 120°32′ W 100
Railroad Pass, *Nev., U.S.* 39°22′ N, 117°25′ W 90
Rainbach, *Aust.* 48°33′ N, 14°28′ E 156
Rainbow, *Calif., U.S.* 33°24′ N, 117°10′ W 101
Rainbow Falls, site, *Hawai'i, U.S.* 19°42′ N, 155°10′ W 99
Rainbow Lake, *Can.* 58°28′ N, 119°29′ W 108
Rainbow Springs, site, *Fla., U.S.* 29°6′ N, 82°27′ W 105
Rainer, *Minn., U.S.* 48°35′ N, 93°21′ W 94
Rainier, *Oreg., U.S.* 46°4′ N, 122°57′ W 100
Rainier, Mount, peak, *Wash., U.S.* 46°49′ N, 121°49′ W 100
Rainy Lake, *Can.* 48°41′ N, 94°17′ W 80
Rainy River, *Can.* 48°44′ N, 94°34′ W 90
Rainy, river, *Can.* 48°31′ N, 94°41′ W 82
Raippaluoto see Replot, *Fin.* 63°13′ N, 21°24′ E 152
Raipur, *India* 21°15′ N, 81°38′ E 197
Rairakhol, *India* 21°4′ N, 84°20′ E 188
Ra's, *Saudi Arabia* 23°33′ N, 38°37′ E 182
Raisduoddarhalddde, peak, *Nor.* 69°19′ N, 21°11′ E 152
Raisin, *Calif., U.S.* 36°36′ N, 119°55′ W 101
Raisinghnagar, *India* 29°31′ N, 73°27′ E 186
Raisio, *Fin.* 60°28′ N, 22°10′ E 166
Raj Samund, *India* 25°1′ N, 73°51′ E 186
Raja, *Est.* 58°46′ N, 26°53′ E 166
Raja, Ujung, *Indonesia* 3°30′ N, 96°14′ E 196
Rajada, *Braz.* 8°46′ S, 40°50′ W 132
Rajahmundry, *India* 17°0′ N, 81°48′ E 190
Rajamäki, *Fin.* 60°30′ N, 24°44′ E 166
Rajampet, *India* 14°11′ N, 79°8′ E 188
Rajanpur, *Pak.* 29°8′ N, 70°21′ E 186
Rajasthan, adm. division, *India* 26°20′ N, 70°59′ E 186
Rajasthan Canal, *India* 28°0′ N, 72°30′ E 186
Rajbari, *Bangladesh* 23°40′ N, 89°36′ E 197
Rajgarh, *India* 28°38′ N, 75°24′ E 197
Rajin see Najin, *N. Korea* 42°15′ N, 130°19′ E 20[illegible]
Rajka, *Hung.* 47°59′ N, 17°12′ E 168
Rajkot, *India* 22°17′ N, 70°46′ E 186
Rajshahi, *Bangladesh* 24°21′ N, 88°33′ E 197
Raka, river, *China* 29°23′ N, 85°57′ E 197
Rakai, *Uganda* 0°43′ N, 31°22′ E 224
Rakaia, *N.Z.* 43°46′ S, 172°0′ E 240
Rakamaz, *Hung.* 48°6′ N, 21°27′ E 152
Rakaposhi, peak, *Pak.* 36°7′ N, 74°22′ E 186
Rakaw, *Belarus* 53°58′ N, 27°2′ E 166
Rakhshan, river, *Pak.* 26°58′ N, 63°58′ E 186
Rakhyūt, *Oman* 16°41′ N, 53°18′ E 182
Rakisvaara, peak, *Nor.* 68°13′ N, 20°6′ E 152
Rakke, *Est.* 58°58′ N, 26°13′ E 166
Rakops, *Botswana* 21°3′ S, 24°24′ E 227
Rakoš, *Europe* 42°46′ N, 20°34′ E 168
Rakovitsa, *Bulg.* 43°46′ N, 22°27′ E 168
Rakovo, *Bulg.* 42°5′ N, 22°43′ E 168
Rakow, *Ger.* 54°2′ N, 13°2′ E 152
Rakula, *Russ.* 63°42′ N, 41°36′ E 154
Rakulka, *Russ.* 61°50′ N, 45°19′ E 154
Rakvere, *Est.* 59°20′ N, 26°19′ E 166
Raleigh, *Miss., U.S.* 32°1′ N, 89°31′ W 103
Raleigh, *N.C., U.S.* 35°45′ N, 78°43′ W 96
Ralik Chain, islands, *North Pacific Ocean* 7°28′ N, 166°35′ E 238
Ralja, *Serb. and Mont.* 44°33′ N, 20°32′ E 168
Ralls, *Tex., U.S.* 33°39′ N, 101°23′ W 92
Ralston, *Can.* 50°15′ N, 111°12′ W 90
Rām Allāh, *West Bank* 31°53′ N, 35°11′ E 194
Rama, *Israel* 32°56′ N, 35°22′ E 194
Rama, *Nicar.* 12°10′ N, 84°10′ W 115
Ramādī Barrage, dam, *Iraq* 33°39′ N, 42°10′ E 180
Ramage Point 73°23′ S, 115°8′ W 248
Ramah, *Colo., U.S.* 39°6′ N, 104°11′ W 92
Ramah, *N. Mex., U.S.* 35°7′ N, 108°29′ W 92
Ramales de la Victoria, *Sp.* 43°14′ N, 3°30′ W 16[illegible]
Ramalho, Serra do, *Braz.* 13°60′ S, 44°39′ W 13[illegible]
Ramallo, *Arg.* 33°31′ S, 60°1′ W 139
Raman, *Thai.* 6°24′ N, 101°22′ E 196
Raman, oil field, *Turk.* 37°45′ N, 41°29′ E 195
Ramanava, *Belarus* 53°56′ N, 24°37′ E 166
Ramanuj Ganj, *India* 23°46′ N, 83°39′ E 197
Ramat Magshimim, *Israel* 32°51′ N, 35°49′ E 194
Ramatlabama, *Botswana* 25°38′ S, 25°31′ E 227
Rambau, Lac, lake, *Can.* 53°39′ N, 70°45′ W 111
Rambouillet, *Fr.* 48°38′ N, 1°49′ E 163
Rambutyo, island, *P.N.G.* 2°44′ S, 147°51′ E 192
Ramea, *Can.* 47°31′ N, 57°24′ W 111
Ramerupt, *Fr.* 48°30′ N, 4°17′ E 163
Rameshki, *Russ.* 57°18′ N, 36°1′ E 154
Ramgarh, *India* 23°35′ N, 85°32′ E 197
Ramgarh, *India* 27°22′ N, 70°29′ E 186
Ramírez, Isla, island, *Chile* 51°49′ S, 76°41′ W 13[illegible]
Rāmis, river, *Eth.* 8°27′ N, 41°27′ E 224
Ramla, *Israel* 31°55′ N, 34°52′ E 194
Ramlu, peak, *Eritrea* 13°22′ N, 41°38′ E 182
Ramnagar, *India* 25°14′ N, 83°3′ E 197
Ramnagar, *India* 29°24′ N, 79°6′ E 197
Ramnäs, *Nor.* 59°46′ N, 16°10′ E 152
Râmnicu Vâlcea, *Rom.* 45°7′ N, 24°21′ E 156
Ramon', *Russ.* 51°52′ N, 39°13′ E 158
Ramon, Har, peak, *Israel* 30°29′ N, 34°36′ E 19[illegible]
Ramón Santamarina, *Arg.* 38°28′ S, 59°21′ W 13[illegible]
Ramón Trigo, *Uru.* 32°21′ S, 54°39′ W 139
Ramona, *Calif., U.S.* 33°2′ N, 116°53′ W 101
Ramonal, *Mex.* 18°25′ N, 88°34′ W 115
Ramore, *Can.* 48°26′ N, 80°20′ W 94
Ramos, *Mex.* 22°48′ N, 101°56′ W 114
Ramos Arizpe, *Mex.* 25°32′ N, 100°57′ W 114
Ramos, oil field, *Arg.* 22°41′ S, 64°15′ W 137
Ramos, river, *Mex.* 25°13′ N, 105°19′ W 114
Ramotswa, *Botswana* 24°52′ S, 25°47′ E 227
Rampart, *Alas., U.S.* 65°19′ N, 150°13′ W 98
Ramparts, river, *Can.* 66°25′ N, 130°46′ W 98
Rampur, *India* 28°46′ N, 79°3′ E 197
Rampur Hat, *India* 24°9′ N, 87°48′ E 197
Ramsay, *Mich., U.S.* 46°28′ N, 90°1′ W 94
Ramsele, *Nor.* 63°31′ N, 16°29′ E 152
Ramsey, *Ill., U.S.* 39°8′ N, 89°6′ W 102
Ramsey, *N.J., U.S.* 41°3′ N, 74°9′ W 104
Ramsey Lake, *Can.* 47°9′ N, 82°46′ W 110
Ramsgate, *U.K.* 51°20′ N, 1°24′ E 163
Ramsjö, *Nor.* 62°11′ N, 15°38′ E 152
Ramu, *Kenya* 3°50′ N, 41°13′ E 224
Ramu, river, *P.N.G.* 5°7′ S, 144°53′ E 192
Ramvik, *Nor.* 62°48′ N, 17°49′ E 152
Rana, Cerro, peak, *Col.* 3°34′ N, 68°9′ W 136
Ranaghat, *India* 23°7′ N, 88°35′ E 197
Ranai, *Indonesia* 3°59′ N, 108°23′ E 196
Ranau, *Malaysia* 5°57′ N, 116°41′ E 203
Rancagua, *Chile* 34°11′ S, 70°50′ W 134
Rance, *Belg.* 50°7′ N, 4°17′ E 163
Rancharia, *Braz.* 22°14′ S, 50°56′ W 138
Rancheria, river, *Can.* 60°0′ N, 130°57′ W 108
Ranchester, *Wyo., U.S.* 44°54′ N, 107°10′ W 90
Ranchi, *India* 23°22′ N, 85°19′ E 197
Ranchita, *Calif., U.S.* 33°13′ N, 116°33′ W 101
Rancho California, *Calif., U.S.* 33°30′ N, 117°11′ W 101
Rancho Cordova, *Calif., U.S.* 38°35′ N, 121°19′ W 92
Rancho de Caça dos Tapiúnas, *Braz.* 10°50′ S, 56°2′ W 130
Rancho Mirage, *Calif., U.S.* 33°43′ N, 116°26′ W 101

Rancho Santa Fe, *Calif., U.S.* 33°1′ N, 117°13′ W **101**
Ranchos de Taos, *N. Mex., U.S.* 36°20′ N, 105°37′ W **92**
Randa, *Nig.* 9°7′ N, 8°27′ E **222**
Randers, *Den.* 56°27′ N, 10°0′ E **152**
Randers Fjord 56°32′ N, 9°59′ E **152**
Randijaur, lake, *Nor.* 66°41′ N, 18°35′ E **152**
Randle, *Wash., U.S.* 46°31′ N, 121°59′ W **100**
Randolph, *Me., U.S.* 44°14′ N, 69°46′ W **104**
Randolph, *Nebr., U.S.* 42°21′ N, 97°21′ W **90**
Randolph, *N.H., U.S.* 44°22′ N, 71°17′ W **104**
Randolph, *Utah, U.S.* 41°40′ N, 111°11′ W **90**
Randolph, *Vt., U.S.* 43°55′ N, 72°41′ W **104**
Randolph, *Wis., U.S.* 43°32′ N, 88°60′ W **102**
Randolph Air Force Base, *Tex., U.S.* 29°28′ N, 98°21′ W **92**
Randolph Center, *Vt., U.S.* 43°56′ N, 72°37′ W **104**
Random Lake, *Wis., U.S.* 43°32′ N, 87°58′ W **102**
Randsburg, *Calif., U.S.* 35°21′ N, 117°41′ W **101**
Råneå, *Nor.* 65°51′ N, 22°16′ E **152**
Ranérou, *Senegal* 15°19′ N, 13°60′ W **222**
Ranfurly, *N.Z.* 45°8′ S, 170°6′ E **240**
Rangae, *Thai.* 6°19′ N, 101°45′ E **196**
Rangamati, *Bangladesh* 22°37′ N, 92°7′ E **188**
Rangeley, *Me., U.S.* 44°57′ N, 70°40′ W **94**
Rangely, *Colo., U.S.* 40°4′ N, 108°48′ W **90**
Ranger, *Tex., U.S.* 32°27′ N, 98°41′ W **92**
Rangiora, *N.Z.* 43°20′ S, 172°34′ E **240**
Rangkŭl, *Taj.* 38°27′ N, 74°25′ E **184**
Rangoon see Yangon, *Myanmar* 16°45′ N, 96°0′ E **202**
Rangpur, *Bangladesh* 25°41′ N, 89°12′ E **197**
Rangsang, island, *Indonesia* 1°1′ N, 103°5′ E **196**
Raniganj, *India* 23°37′ N, 87°7′ E **197**
Ranikhet, *India* 29°40′ N, 79°25′ E **197**
Rāniyah, *Iraq* 36°15′ N, 44°52′ E **195**
Rankin, *Tex., U.S.* 31°12′ N, 101°57′ W **92**
Rankin Inlet, *Can.* 62°50′ N, 92°9′ W **106**
Rankūs, *Syr.* 33°45′ N, 36°22′ E **194**
Rann of Kutch 23°59′ N, 69°56′ E **186**
Rano, *Nig.* 11°32′ N, 8°34′ E **222**
Ranohira, *Madagascar* 22°36′ S, 45°22′ E **220**
Ranomafana, *Madagascar* 24°33′ S, 46°59′ E **220**
Ranomafana, *Madagascar* 21°13′ S, 47°23′ E **220**
Ranomena, *Madagascar* 23°24′ S, 47°16′ E **220**
Ranong, *Thai.* 9°54′ N, 98°38′ E **192**
Ranongga (Ganongga), island, *Solomon Islands* 8°5′ S, 156°30′ E **242**
Ranot, *Thai.* 7°48′ N, 100°20′ E **196**
Ransiki, *Indonesia* 1°27′ S, 134°2′ E **192**
Ransom, *Ill., U.S.* 41°9′ N, 88°39′ W **102**
Rantasalmi, *Fin.* 62°2′ N, 28°15′ E **166**
Rantau, oil field, *Indonesia* 4°23′ N, 98°7′ E **196**
Rantauprapat, *Indonesia* 2°6′ N, 99°50′ E **196**
Rantoul, *Ill., U.S.* 40°18′ N, 88°9′ W **102**
Rantsila, *Fin.* 64°30′ N, 25°37′ E **152**
Ranua, *Fin.* 65°53′ N, 26°30′ E **152**
Rao, *Senegal* 15°56′ N, 16°26′ W **222**
Raoui, Erg er, *Alg.* 30°3′ N, 3°41′ W **214**
Rapahoe, *N.Z.* 42°23′ S, 171°17′ E **240**
Raper, Cabo 46°54′ S, 77°3′ W **134**
Raper, Cape, *Can.* 69°39′ N, 67°9′ W **106**
Rapid City, *Can.* 50°9′ N, 100°3′ W **90**
Rapid City, *S. Dak., U.S.* 44°3′ N, 103°15′ W **90**
Rapid River, *Mich., U.S.* 45°55′ N, 86°59′ W **94**
Rapid, river, *Minn., U.S.* 48°16′ N, 95°2′ W **90**
Räpina, *Est.* 58°6′ N, 27°27′ E **166**
Rapla, *Est.* 59°0′ N, 24°47′ E **166**
Rappahannock, river, *Va., U.S.* 38°36′ N, 77°58′ W **80**
Rápulo, river, *Bol.* 14°24′ S, 66°30′ W **137**
Raqiq, ruin(s), *Israel* 31°16′ N, 34°39′ E **194**
Rara National Park, *Nepal* 29°29′ N, 81°58′ E **197**
Rarotonga, island, *N.Z.* 21°14′ S, 159°47′ W **241**
Ra's Abū Madd, *Saudi Arabia* 24°44′ N, 37°10′ E **182**
Ra's Abū Qumayyiş, *Saudi Arabia* 24°33′ N, 51°30′ E **196**
Ra's al Arḑ, *Kuwait* 29°19′ N, 48°8′ E **196**
Ra's al ʽAyn, *Syr.* 36°49′ N, 40°7′ E **195**
Ra's al Basīt 35°52′ N, 35°13′ E **156**
Ra's al Bayyāḑah, *Leb.* 33°9′ N, 35°0′ E **194**
Ra's al Ḩadd, *Oman* 22°33′ N, 59°46′ E **182**
Ra's al Hilāl, *Lib.* 33°2′ N, 22°7′ E **216**
Ra's al Kalb, *Yemen* 13°55′ N, 48°41′ E **182**
Ra's al Khaymah, *U.A.E.* 25°45′ N, 55°57′ E **196**
Ra's al Madrakah, *Oman* 18°59′ N, 56°39′ E **182**
Ra's al Milḩ, *Lib.* 32°1′ N, 24°56′ E **180**
Ra's al Mishʽāb, *Saudi Arabia* 28°9′ N, 48°36′ E **196**
Ra's al Qulayʽah, *Kuwait* 28°53′ N, 48°17′ E **196**
Ra's al Unūf, *Lib.* 30°31′ N, 18°31′ E **216**
Ra's ʽĀmir, *Lib.* 33°2′ N, 20°43′ E **216**
Ra's an Naqb, *Jordan* 29°59′ N, 35°32′ E **180**
Ra's as Saʽdīyāt, *Leb.* 33°41′ N, 35°14′ E **194**
Ra's ash Shaqq, *Leb.* 34°19′ N, 35°34′ E **194**
Ra's ash Sharbatāt, *Oman* 17°42′ N, 56°21′ E **182**
Ra's aţ Ţarfā, *Saudi Arabia* 16°55′ N, 41°35′ E **182**
Ra's at Tīn, *Lib.* 32°41′ N, 23°5′ E **180**
Ra's az Zawr, *Saudi Arabia* 27°28′ N, 49°0′ E **196**
Ra's Baʽlabakk, *Leb.* 34°15′ N, 36°24′ E **194**
Ra's Ḑarbat ʽAlī, *Oman* 16°42′ N, 52°15′ E **182**
Râs el ʽIsh, *Egypt* 31°8′ N, 32°17′ E **194**
Ras el Ma, *Alg.* 36°7′ N, 5°31′ E **150**
Ras el Ma, *Alg.* 34°29′ N, 0°48′ E **214**
Râs el Mâ, *Mali* 16°36′ N, 4°38′ W **222**
Ra's Fartak, *Yemen* 15°38′ N, 51°28′ E **182**
Râs Ghârib, *Egypt* 28°21′ N, 33°0′ E **180**
Râs Ghârib, oil field, *Egypt* 27°56′ N, 32°47′ E **143**
Ra's Ḩāţibah, *Saudi Arabia* 21°55′ N, 38°6′ E **182**
Ra's Ibn Hāniʼ, *Syr.* 35°35′ N, 35°44′ E **194**
Ra's Jibsh, *Oman* 21°28′ N, 58°38′ E **182**
Ra's Mirbāţ, *Oman* 16°48′ N, 54°46′ E **182**
Ras Muhammed National Park, *Egypt* 27°44′ N, 33°47′ E **206**
Ra's Musandam, *Oman* 26°18′ N, 56°29′ E **196**
Ra's Shamrah, site, *Mediterranean Sea* 35°35′ N, 35°41′ E **156**
Ra's Shamrah (Ugarit), site, *Syr.* 35°33′ N, 35°44′ E **194**
Ra's Sharwayn, *Yemen* 15°11′ N, 51°29′ E **182**
Ra's Shūʽab, *Yemen* 12°24′ N, 52°34′ E **182**
Ra's Tannūrah, *Saudi Arabia* 26°39′ N, 50°7′ E **196**
Rasa, Punta, *Arg.* 40°51′ S, 62°17′ W **134**
Raseiniai, *Lith.* 55°22′ N, 23°5′ E **166**
Rashaant, *Mongolia* 45°21′ N, 106°14′ E **198**
Rashad, *Sudan* 11°51′ N, 31°4′ E **216**
Rashayya, *Leb.* 33°29′ N, 35°50′ E **194**
Rashi, oil field, *Iraq* 30°9′ N, 47°1′ E **196**
Rashīd (Rosetta), *Egypt* 31°23′ N, 30°21′ E **180**
Rasht, *Iran* 37°15′ N, 49°32′ E **195**
Raška, *Serb. and Mont.* 43°17′ N, 20°36′ E **168**
Raška, river, *Serb. and Mont.* 43°7′ N, 20°35′ E **168**
Rasony, *Belarus* 55°52′ N, 28°50′ E **166**
Rasovo, *Bulg.* 43°42′ N, 23°14′ E **168**
Răspopeni, *Mold.* 47°45′ N, 28°37′ E **156**
Rasskazovo, *Russ.* 52°37′ N, 41°49′ E **158**
Rastatt, *Ger.* 48°50′ N, 8°10′ E **150**
Rastede, *Ger.* 53°14′ N, 8°11′ E **163**
Rastigaissa, peak, *Nor.* 69°58′ N, 26°5′ E **152**
Rastu, *Rom.* 43°53′ N, 23°17′ E **168**
Rasua Garhi, *Nepal* 28°18′ N, 85°24′ E **197**
Rat, island, *Alas., U.S.* 51°33′ N, 177°41′ E **160**
Rat Islands, *Bering Sea* 51°41′ N, 174°8′ E **160**
Rat Lake, lake, *Can.* 56°23′ N, 99°38′ W **108**
Rat Rapids, *Can.* 51°10′ N, 90°13′ W **110**
Rat, river, *Can.* 56°8′ N, 99°19′ W **108**
Rat, river, *Wis., U.S.* 45°33′ N, 88°38′ W **94**
Rata, *N.Z.* 39°60′ S, 175°30′ E **240**
Rataje, *Serb. and Mont.* 43°28′ N, 21°7′ E **168**
Ratak Chain, islands, *North Pacific Ocean* 9°43′ N, 169°11′ E **238**
Ratamka, *Belarus* 53°54′ N, 27°21′ E **166**
Ratangarh, *India* 28°3′ N, 74°38′ E **186**
Ratanpur, *India* 22°18′ N, 82°10′ E **197**
Ratcliff, *Tex., U.S.* 31°22′ N, 95°8′ W **103**
Rath, *India* 25°35′ N, 79°34′ E **197**
Rätikon, *Switz.* 46°55′ N, 9°41′ E **167**
Ratina, *Serb. and Mont.* 43°42′ N, 20°44′ E **168**
Ratkovac, *Europe* 42°24′ N, 20°33′ E **168**
Ratlam, *India* 23°18′ N, 75°1′ E **188**
Ratnagiri, *India* 17°0′ N, 73°19′ E **188**
Ratne, *Ukr.* 51°38′ N, 24°32′ E **152**
Raton, *N. Mex., U.S.* 36°53′ N, 104°27′ W **92**
Raton Pass, *N. Mex., U.S.* 36°58′ N, 104°29′ W **92**
Ratta, *Russ.* 63°34′ N, 83°50′ E **169**
Rattlesnake Hills, *Wash., U.S.* 46°30′ N, 120°25′ W **90**
Rattlesnake Hills, *Wyo., U.S.* 42°50′ N, 107°40′ W **90**
Rättvik, *Nor.* 60°52′ N, 15°6′ E **152**
Ratz, Mount, peak, *Can.* 57°23′ N, 132°27′ W **108**
Raub, *Malaysia* 3°47′ N, 101°50′ E **196**
Rauch, *Arg.* 36°47′ S, 59°8′ W **139**
Raudal Yupurari (Devils Cataract), fall(s), *Col.* 0°58′ N, 71°28′ W **136**
Raudhatain, oil field, *Kuwait* 29°51′ N, 47°39′ E **196**
Rauer Islands, *Indian Ocean* 68°54′ S, 74°26′ E **248**
Raufarhöfn, *Ice.* 66°28′ N, 16°5′ W **143**
Raul Soares, *Braz.* 20°7′ S, 42°29′ W **138**
Rauma, *Fin.* 61°7′ N, 21°29′ E **166**
Rauna, *Latv.* 57°19′ N, 25°37′ E **166**
Raupunga, *N.Z.* 39°3′ S, 177°8′ E **240**
Raurkela, *India* 22°14′ N, 84°57′ E **197**
Rautas, *Nor.* 67°59′ N, 19°53′ E **152**
Rautavaara, *Fin.* 63°28′ N, 28°15′ E **152**
Rautio, *Fin.* 64°4′ N, 24°10′ E **154**
Rautjärvi, *Fin.* 61°16′ N, 29°7′ E **166**
Ravānsar, *Iran* 34°43′ N, 46°41′ E **180**
Rāvar, *Iran* 31°12′ N, 56°55′ E **180**
Ravelo, *Bol.* 18°51′ S, 65°36′ W **137**
Ravena, *N.Y., U.S.* 42°28′ N, 73°50′ W **104**
Ravenglass, *U.K.* 54°21′ N, 3°24′ W **162**
Ravenna, *It.* 44°24′ N, 12°11′ E **167**
Ravenna, *Ky., U.S.* 37°40′ N, 83°57′ W **94**
Ravenna, *Nebr., U.S.* 41°1′ N, 98°55′ W **90**
Ravenna, *Ohio, U.S.* 41°8′ N, 81°14′ W **102**
Ravensthorpe, *Austral.* 33°35′ S, 120°1′ E **231**
Ravenswood, *W. Va., U.S.* 38°56′ N, 81°46′ W **94**
Ravi, river, *Pak.* 30°34′ N, 71°52′ E **186**
Ravn, Kap 68°9′ N, 28°16′ W **246**
Ravna Banja, *Serb. and Mont.* 42°45′ N, 21°40′ E **168**
Ravne, *Slov.* 46°31′ N, 14°57′ E **156**
Ravno, *Bosn. and Herzg.* 43°50′ N, 17°22′ E **168**
Rawa Aopa Watumohai National Park, *Indonesia* 4°22′ S, 121°38′ E **238**
Rāwah, *Iraq* 34°30′ N, 41°55′ E **180**
Rawalpindi, *Pak.* 33°31′ N, 73°4′ E **186**
Rawandoz, *Iraq* 36°39′ N, 44°31′ E **195**
Rawene, *N.Z.* 35°26′ S, 173°30′ E **240**
Rawḩah, *Saudi Arabia* 19°28′ N, 41°44′ E **182**
Rawhide Lake, *Can.* 46°36′ N, 83°11′ W **94**
Rawi, Ko, island, *Thai.* 6°36′ N, 98°58′ E **196**
Rawicz, *Pol.* 51°36′ N, 16°52′ E **152**
Rawley Point, *Wis., U.S.* 44°7′ N, 87°30′ W **102**
Rawlinna, *Austral.* 30°60′ S, 125°19′ E **231**
Rawlins, *Wyo., U.S.* 41°48′ N, 107°14′ W **90**
Rawlinson Range, *Austral.* 25°29′ S, 127°57′ E **230**
Rawson, *Arg.* 43°16′ S, 65°7′ W **134**
Rawtenstall, *U.K.* 53°42′ N, 2°17′ W **162**
Raxaul, *India* 26°58′ N, 84°48′ E **197**
Ray, *N. Dak., U.S.* 48°19′ N, 103°11′ W **90**
Ray, Cape, *Can.* 47°39′ N, 59°56′ W **111**
Raya, peak, *Indonesia* 0°40′ N, 112°25′ E **192**
Rayachoti, *India* 14°2′ N, 78°46′ E **188**
Rayagada, *India* 19°10′ N, 83°24′ E **188**
Rayakoski, *Russ.* 68°56′ N, 28°44′ E **152**
Raychikhinsk, *Russ.* 49°52′ N, 129°24′ E **190**
Rayevskiy, *Russ.* 54°4′ N, 54°54′ E **154**
Raymond, *Calif., U.S.* 37°13′ N, 119°56′ W **100**
Raymond, *Can.* 49°27′ N, 112°40′ W **90**
Raymond, *N.H., U.S.* 43°2′ N, 71°12′ W **104**
Raymond, *Wash., U.S.* 46°41′ N, 123°44′ W **100**
Raymondville, *Tex., U.S.* 26°28′ N, 97°47′ W **114**
Raymore, *Can.* 51°24′ N, 104°31′ W **90**
Rayna, *India* 23°2′ N, 87°52′ E **197**
Rayne, *La., U.S.* 30°13′ N, 92°17′ W **103**
Rayner Peak, *Antarctica* 67°30′ S, 55°30′ E **248**
Raynham Center, *Mass., U.S.* 41°55′ N, 71°4′ W **104**
Rayón, *Mex.* 29°42′ N, 110°34′ W **92**
Rayón, *Mex.* 21°49′ N, 99°39′ W **114**
Rayón National Park, *Mex.* 19°58′ N, 100°9′ W **112**
Rayong, *Thai.* 12°41′ N, 101°18′ E **202**
Rayside-Balfour, *Can.* 46°35′ N, 81°11′ W **94**
Rayville, *La., U.S.* 32°27′ N, 91°46′ W **103**
Raz, Pointe du, *Fr.* 47°46′ N, 4°59′ W **150**
Razan, *Iran* 35°24′ N, 49°2′ E **180**
Ražana, *Serb. and Mont.* 44°5′ N, 19°54′ E **168**
Ražanj, *Serb. and Mont.* 43°40′ N, 21°32′ E **168**
Razbojna, *Serb. and Mont.* 43°19′ N, 21°10′ E **168**
Razgrad, *Bulg.* 43°33′ N, 26°31′ E **156**
Razgrad, adm. division, *Bulg.* 43°33′ N, 26°7′ E **156**
Razhanka, *Belarus* 53°31′ N, 24°46′ E **158**
Razzaza Lake, *Iraq* 32°54′ N, 42°53′ E **180**
Re, Cu Lao, island, *Vietnam* 15°15′ N, 109°10′ E **202**
Readfield, *Me., U.S.* 44°23′ N, 69°59′ W **104**
Reading, *Mich., U.S.* 41°49′ N, 84°46′ W **102**
Reading, *Ohio, U.S.* 39°13′ N, 84°27′ W **102**
Reading, *U.K.* 51°27′ N, 0°57′ W **162**
Readsboro, *Vt., U.S.* 42°46′ N, 72°58′ W **104**
Real, Cordillera, *Bol.* 17°2′ S, 67°51′ W **132**
Real del Castillo, *Mex.* 31°55′ N, 116°20′ W **92**
Realicó, *Arg.* 35°2′ S, 64°14′ W **134**
Ream, *Cambodia* 10°30′ N, 103°39′ E **202**
Rębków, *Pol.* 51°52′ N, 21°33′ E **152**
Rebojo, Cachoeira do, fall(s), *Braz.* 9°44′ S, 59°8′ W **130**
Reboly, *Russ.* 63°49′ N, 30°47′ E **152**
Rebouças, *Braz.* 25°37′ S, 50°42′ W **138**
Rebun, island, *Japan* 45°31′ N, 139°42′ E **190**
Recalada, Isla, island, *Chile* 53°26′ S, 76°1′ W **134**
Recalde, *Arg.* 36°41′ S, 61°9′ W **139**
Recaş, *Rom.* 45°48′ N, 21°30′ E **168**
Recherche, Archipelago of the, islands, *Great Australian Bight* 34°52′ S, 120°32′ E **230**
Rechytsa, *Belarus* 52°19′ N, 30°26′ E **154**
Recife, *Braz.* 8°4′ S, 34°57′ W **132**
Recife, Cape, *S. Af.* 34°19′ S, 25°42′ E **227**
Recklinghausen, *Ger.* 51°36′ N, 7°12′ E **167**
Recoaro Terme, *It.* 45°43′ N, 11°13′ E **167**
Reconquista, *Arg.* 29°10′ S, 59°39′ W **139**
Recreo, *Arg.* 29°17′ S, 65°6′ W **134**
Recsk, *Hung.* 47°55′ N, 20°7′ E **168**
Red Bay, *Ala., U.S.* 34°26′ N, 88°8′ W **96**
Red Bay, *Can.* 51°44′ N, 56°26′ W **111**
Red Bluff, *Calif., U.S.* 40°11′ N, 122°16′ W **106**
Red Cedar Lake, lake, *Can.* 46°38′ N, 80°30′ W **94**
Red Cinder, peak, *Calif., U.S.* 40°29′ N, 121°20′ W **90**
Red Cliff, *Wis., U.S.* 46°51′ N, 90°49′ W **94**
Red Cloud, *Nebr., U.S.* 40°4′ N, 98°33′ W **90**
Red Deer, *Can.* 52°13′ N, 113°48′ W **108**
Red Deer Lake, lake, *Can.* 52°56′ N, 101°58′ W **108**
Red Deer Point, *Can.* 52°4′ N, 99°51′ W **108**
Red Deer, river, *Can.* 51°41′ N, 115°26′ W **108**
Red Devil, *Alas., U.S.* 61°48′ N, 157°13′ W **73**
Red Hill see Puʽu ʽUlaʽula, peak, *Hawaiʽi, U.S.* 20°42′ N, 156°18′ W **99**
Red Hill, site, *Va., U.S.* 37°0′ N, 78°58′ W **96**
Red Hills, *Kans., U.S.* 37°28′ N, 99°23′ W **90**
Red Hook, *N.Y., U.S.* 41°59′ N, 73°53′ W **104**
Red Indian Lake, *Can.* 48°41′ N, 57°34′ W **111**
Red Lake, *Can.* 51°0′ N, 93°50′ W **90**
Red Lake, *Can.* 50°55′ N, 95°1′ W **80**
Red Lake, *Minn., U.S.* 47°50′ N, 95°1′ W **90**
Red Lake Falls, *Minn., U.S.* 47°50′ N, 96°18′ W **90**
Red Lake Road, *Can.* 49°57′ N, 93°23′ W **90**
Red Lick, *Miss., U.S.* 31°46′ N, 90°58′ W **103**
Red Mountain, *Calif., U.S.* 35°21′ N, 117°38′ W **101**
Red Mountain, peak, *Calif., U.S.* 41°30′ N, 123°60′ W **90**
Red Mountain, peak, *Mont., U.S.* 47°4′ N, 112°49′ W **90**
Red Oak, *Iowa, U.S.* 40°59′ N, 95°12′ W **94**
Red Pass, *Can.* 52°57′ N, 119°3′ W **108**
Red, river, *Can.* 59°17′ N, 128°11′ W **108**
Red, river, *Can.* 49°16′ N, 97°12′ W **90**
Red, river, *La., U.S.* 31°11′ N, 92°26′ W **103**
Red, river, *Okla., U.S.* 33°56′ N, 97°49′ W **80**
Red, river, *Tenn., U.S.* 36°26′ N, 87°15′ W **96**
Red Rock, *Can.* 48°56′ N, 88°16′ W **94**
Red Sea 18°15′ N, 39°26′ E **182**
Red Sea, adm. division, *Sudan* 19°37′ N, 35°5′ E **182**
Red Sucker Lake, *Can.* 54°8′ N, 93°38′ W **108**
Red Wing, *Minn., U.S.* 44°32′ N, 92°32′ W **94**
Redang, island, *Malaysia* 5°44′ N, 103°4′ E **196**
Redcar, *U.K.* 54°36′ N, 1°5′ W **162**
Redcliff, *Can.* 50°4′ N, 110°46′ W **90**
Redcliff, *Zimb.* 19°3′ S, 29°47′ E **224**
Redcliffe, Mount, peak, *Austral.* 28°27′ S, 121°20′ E **230**
Reddell, *La., U.S.* 30°39′ N, 92°26′ W **103**
Reddick, *Fla., U.S.* 29°22′ N, 82°12′ W **105**
Redding, *Calif., U.S.* 40°35′ N, 122°24′ W **90**
Redding, *Conn., U.S.* 41°18′ N, 73°23′ W **104**
Redditch, *U.K.* 52°18′ N, 1°57′ W **162**
Redeyef, *Tun.* 34°21′ N, 8°7′ E **214**
Redfield, *S. Dak., U.S.* 44°51′ N, 98°33′ W **90**
Redgranite, *Wis., U.S.* 44°1′ N, 89°6′ W **102**
Rédics, *Hung.* 46°36′ N, 16°29′ E **168**
Redig, *S. Dak., U.S.* 45°15′ N, 103°33′ W **90**
Redkey, *Ind., U.S.* 40°20′ N, 85°9′ W **102**
Redknife, river, *Can.* 60°49′ N, 119°41′ W **108**
Redlands, *Calif., U.S.* 34°3′ N, 117°13′ W **101**
Redmon, *Ill., U.S.* 39°38′ N, 87°52′ W **102**
Redmond, *Oreg., U.S.* 44°16′ N, 121°9′ W **238**
Redmond, *Wash., U.S.* 47°39′ N, 122°7′ W **100**
Redon, *Fr.* 47°39′ N, 2°7′ W **150**
Redonda Islands, *Strait of Georgia* 50°12′ N, 124°55′ W **100**
Redonda, Punta, *Arg.* 41°8′ S, 62°40′ W **134**
Redondeados, *Mex.* 25°51′ N, 106°48′ W **114**
Redondo, *Port.* 38°38′ N, 7°34′ W **150**
Redondo Beach, *Calif., U.S.* 33°50′ N, 118°24′ W **101**
Redondo, Pico, peak, *Braz.* 2°29′ N, 63°33′ W **130**
Redoubt Volcano, peak, *Alas., U.S.* 60°28′ N, 152°55′ W **98**
Redvers, *Can.* 49°34′ N, 101°43′ W **90**
Redwater, *Can.* 53°57′ N, 113°7′ W **108**
Redwater, *Tex., U.S.* 33°21′ N, 94°16′ W **103**
Redwood, *Miss., U.S.* 32°29′ N, 90°48′ W **103**
Redwood City, *Calif., U.S.* 37°29′ N, 122°15′ W **100**
Redwood Empire, region, *Calif., U.S.* 39°43′ N, 123°40′ W **92**
Redwood National Park, *Calif., U.S.* 41°20′ N, 126°3′ W **92**
Reed City, *Mich., U.S.* 43°52′ N, 85°31′ W **102**
Reeder, *N. Dak., U.S.* 46°6′ N, 102°57′ W **90**
Reedley, *Calif., U.S.* 36°35′ N, 119°28′ W **100**
Reedsburg, *Wis., U.S.* 43°32′ N, 90°1′ W **102**
Reedsport, *Oreg., U.S.* 43°41′ N, 124°6′ W **90**
Reedsville, *Wis., U.S.* 44°9′ N, 87°58′ W **102**
Reefton, *N.Z.* 42°7′ S, 171°52′ E **240**
Rees, *Ger.* 51°45′ N, 6°24′ E **167**
Reese, *Mich., U.S.* 43°26′ N, 83°42′ W **102**
Reeth, *U.K.* 54°23′ N, 1°57′ W **162**
Reeves, *La., U.S.* 30°30′ N, 93°4′ W **103**
Refahiye, *Turk.* 39°53′ N, 38°47′ E **180**
Reform, *Ala., U.S.* 33°21′ N, 88°1′ W **103**
Refuge Cove, *Can.* 50°7′ N, 124°50′ W **100**
Refugio, *Tex., U.S.* 28°18′ N, 97°17′ W **96**
Regbat, region, *Alg.* 26°23′ N, 6°14′ W **214**
Regência, *Braz.* 19°40′ S, 39°54′ W **138**
Regência, Pontal de, *Braz.* 19°60′ S, 39°48′ W **138**
Regeneração, *Braz.* 6°16′ S, 42°43′ W **132**
Regensburg, *Ger.* 49°0′ N, 12°6′ E **152**
Reggane, *Alg.* 26°42′ N, 0°8′ E **214**
Reggio di Calabria, *It.* 38°13′ N, 15°40′ E **143**
Regina, *Can.* 50°26′ N, 104°46′ W **90**
Régina, *South America* 4°21′ N, 52°11′ W **130**
Registro, *Braz.* 24°30′ S, 47°48′ W **138**
Registro do Araguaia, *Braz.* 15°45′ S, 51°47′ W **138**
Regocijo, *Mex.* 23°39′ N, 105°9′ W **114**
Regozero, *Russ.* 65°30′ N, 31°17′ E **152**
Rehoboth, *Namibia* 23°18′ S, 17°3′ E **227**
Reḩovot, *Israel* 31°53′ N, 34°48′ E **194**
Reïbell see Ksar Chellala, *Alg.* 35°12′ N, 2°19′ E **150**
Reidsville, *Ga., U.S.* 32°4′ N, 82°7′ W **96**
Reidsville, *N.C., U.S.* 36°21′ N, 79°41′ W **94**
Reigate, *U.K.* 51°14′ N, 0°13′ E **162**
Reims, *Fr.* 49°15′ N, 4°2′ E **163**
Reina Adelaida, Archipiélago, islands, *Chile* 52°7′ S, 78°46′ W **134**
Reina, Jardines de la, islands, *Caribbean Sea* 20°13′ N, 79°3′ W **115**
Reinbolt Hills, *Antarctica* 71°11′ S, 72°8′ E **248**
Reindeer Lake, *Can.* 57°3′ N, 111°32′ W **72**
Reine, *Nor.* 67°55′ N, 13°4′ E **152**
Reinga, Cape, *N.Z.* 34°27′ S, 172°19′ E **240**
Reinhardswald, *Ger.* 51°28′ N, 9°23′ E **167**
Reinosa, *Sp.* 43°0′ N, 4°9′ W **150**
Reir, spring, *Sudan* 15°19′ N, 34°38′ E **182**
Reisjärvi, *Fin.* 63°36′ N, 24°52′ E **154**
Reitz, *S. Af.* 27°50′ S, 28°24′ E **227**
Rejaf, *Sudan* 4°43′ N, 31°33′ E **224**
Rekavice, *Bosn. and Herzg.* 44°40′ N, 17°7′ E **168**
Reken, *Ger.* 51°50′ N, 7°3′ E **167**
Rekinniki, *Russ.* 60°45′ N, 163°30′ E **160**
Rekovac, *Serb. and Mont.* 43°51′ N, 21°6′ E **168**
Rėkyva, lake, *Lith.* 55°51′ N, 23°5′ E **166**
Reliance, *Can.* 62°44′ N, 109°4′ W **106**
Reliance, *Wyo., U.S.* 41°40′ N, 109°11′ W **90**
Relizane, *Alg.* 35°44′ N, 0°33′ E **150**
Remada, *Tun.* 32°21′ N, 10°24′ E **216**
Remagen, *Ger.* 50°34′ N, 7°13′ E **167**
Remansão, *Braz.* 4°28′ S, 49°35′ W **130**
Remanso, *Braz.* 9°34′ S, 42°8′ W **132**
Remarkables, The, peak, *N.Z.* 45°6′ S, 168°45′ E **240**
Remate de Males, *Braz.* 4°25′ S, 70°13′ W **130**
Remecó, *Arg.* 37°39′ S, 63°37′ W **139**
Remer, *Minn., U.S.* 47°2′ N, 93°56′ W **90**
Remeshk, *Iran* 26°48′ N, 58°51′ E **196**
Remich, *Lux.* 49°33′ N, 6°21′ E **163**
Remington, *Ind., U.S.* 40°45′ N, 87°10′ W **102**
Rémire, *South America* 4°54′ N, 52°17′ W **130**
Remmel Mountain, peak, *Wash., U.S.* 48°54′ N, 120°17′ W **90**
Remontnoye, *Russ.* 46°30′ N, 43°34′ E **158**
Remscheid, *Ger.* 51°10′ N, 7°11′ E **167**
Remus, *Mich., U.S.* 43°36′ N, 85°9′ W **102**
Rena, *Nor.* 61°8′ N, 11°19′ E **152**
Renascença, *Braz.* 3°51′ S, 66°30′ W **130**
Renaud Island, *Antarctica* 65°34′ S, 68°9′ W **134**
Renca, *Arg.* 32°47′ S, 65°19′ W **134**
Rencēni, *Latv.* 57°43′ N, 25°23′ E **166**
Renda, *Latv.* 57°3′ N, 22°15′ E **166**
Rendakoma, *Eth.* 14°25′ N, 40°2′ E **182**
Rendova, island, *Solomon Islands* 8°35′ S, 157°15′ E **242**
Renfrew, *Can.* 45°28′ N, 76°43′ W **94**
Rengat, *Indonesia* 0°23′ N, 102°30′ E **196**
Renholmen, *Nor.* 65°0′ N, 21°20′ E **152**
Renhuai, *China* 27°46′ N, 106°24′ E **198**
Reni, *India* 28°40′ N, 75°4′ E **186**
Renison, *Can.* 50°58′ N, 81°9′ W **110**
Renk, *Sudan* 11°44′ N, 32°48′ E **182**
Renko, *Fin.* 60°53′ N, 24°16′ E **166**
Rennell, island, *Solomon Islands* 11°41′ S, 160°19′ E **242**
Rennell Sound 53°18′ N, 132°59′ W **108**
Rennerod, *Ger.* 50°36′ N, 8°3′ E **167**
Rennes, *Fr.* 48°6′ N, 1°42′ W **150**
Reno, *Nev., U.S.* 39°32′ N, 119°50′ W **90**
Reno, river, *It.* 44°34′ N, 11°58′ E **167**
Rensselaer, *Ind., U.S.* 40°56′ N, 87°10′ W **102**
Rensselaer, *N.Y., U.S.* 42°37′ N, 73°45′ W **104**
Rentería, *Sp.* 43°17′ N, 1°54′ W **164**
Renton, *Wash., U.S.* 47°28′ N, 122°14′ W **100**
Renville, *Minn., U.S.* 44°46′ N, 95°13′ W **90**
Reo, *Indonesia* 8°26′ S, 120°26′ E **192**
Répcelak, *Hung.* 47°25′ N, 17°1′ E **168**
Repino, *Russ.* 60°10′ N, 29°52′ E **166**
Replot (Raippaluoto), *Fin.* 63°13′ N, 21°24′ E **152**
Repossaari, *Fin.* 61°36′ N, 21°25′ E **166**
Repparfjord, *Nor.* 70°26′ N, 24°19′ E **152**
Republic, *Mich., U.S.* 46°24′ N, 87°58′ W **94**
Republic, *Ohio, U.S.* 41°6′ N, 83°1′ W **102**
Republican, river, *Nebr., U.S.* 40°17′ N, 100°48′ W **80**
Repulse Bay, *Can.* 66°39′ N, 86°29′ W **73**
Requa, *Calif., U.S.* 41°32′ N, 124°4′ W **90**
Requena, *Peru* 5°5′ S, 73°50′ W **130**
Requena, *Sp.* 39°30′ N, 1°7′ W **164**
Requeña, *Venez.* 7°58′ N, 65°33′ W **136**
Reşadiye, *Turk.* 40°23′ N, 37°19′ E **156**
Resavica, *Serb. and Mont.* 44°1′ N, 21°34′ E **168**
Rescue, Punta, *Chile* 46°16′ S, 76°41′ W **134**
Resende, *Braz.* 22°29′ S, 44°22′ W **138**
Reserva, *Braz.* 24°41′ S, 50°55′ W **138**
Reserve, *N. Mex., U.S.* 33°41′ N, 108°46′ W **92**
Reshadat, oil field, *Persian Gulf* 25°57′ N, 52°43′ E **196**
Reshety, *Russ.* 57°8′ N, 28°27′ E **166**
Resia, *It.* 46°49′ N, 10°32′ E **167**
Resistencia, *Arg.* 27°27′ S, 59°2′ W **139**
Reşiţa, *Rom.* 45°18′ N, 21°53′ E **168**
Resolute, *Can.* 74°39′ N, 94°58′ W **73**
Resolution Island, *Can.* 61°20′ N, 64°59′ W **106**
Restigouche, *Can.* 48°1′ N, 66°43′ W **94**
Reston, *Can.* 49°32′ N, 101°7′ W **90**
Restrepo, *Col.* 4°14′ N, 73°34′ W **136**
Reszel, *Pol.* 54°2′ N, 21°8′ E **166**
Retalhuleu, *Guatemala* 14°32′ N, 91°40′ W **115**
Retezat, Munţii, *Rom.* 45°19′ N, 22°47′ E **168**
Rethel, *Fr.* 49°30′ N, 4°21′ E **163**
Rethondes, *Fr.* 49°24′ N, 2°56′ E **163**
Reti, *Pak.* 28°4′ N, 69°49′ E **186**
Retno, *Russ.* 57°59′ N, 30°12′ E **166**
Rétság, *Hung.* 47°54′ N, 19°9′ E **168**
Return Point, *Antarctica* 60°50′ S, 47°56′ W **134**
Réunion, island, *Fr.* 21°9′ S, 55°35′ E **254**
Reus, *Sp.* 41°8′ N, 1°6′ E **164**
Reva, *S. Dak., U.S.* 45°32′ N, 103°6′ W **90**
Reval see Tallinn, *Est.* 59°23′ N, 24°37′ E **166**
Revda, *Russ.* 67°58′ N, 34°30′ E **152**
Revda, *Russ.* 56°47′ N, 59°56′ E **154**
Revelle Peak, *Nev., U.S.* 37°50′ N, 116°13′ W **90**
Revelle Inlet 68°43′ S, 66°23′ W **248**
Revelstoke, *Can.* 51°0′ N, 118°12′ W **90**
Révfülöp, *Hung.* 46°50′ N, 17°38′ E **168**
Revigny, *Fr.* 48°50′ N, 4°59′ E **163**
Revillagigedo, Islas, islands, *North Pacific Ocean* 18°28′ N, 113°41′ W **112**
Revin, *Fr.* 49°55′ N, 4°38′ E **163**
Revivim, *Israel* 31°1′ N, 34°43′ E **194**
Rewa, *India* 24°31′ N, 81°19′ E **197**
Rex, Mount, peak, *Antarctica* 74°52′ S, 76°39′ W **248**
Rexburg, *Idaho, U.S.* 43°49′ N, 111°48′ W **90**
Rexford, *Mont., U.S.* 48°52′ N, 115°10′ W **90**
Rexton, *Mich., U.S.* 46°9′ N, 85°15′ W **110**
Rey, *Iran* 35°34′ N, 51°30′ E **180**
Rey Bouba, *Cameroon* 8°38′ N, 14°12′ E **218**
Rey, Isla del, island, *Pan.* 8°7′ N, 79°3′ W **115**
Rey, river, *Cameroon* 8°10′ N, 14°26′ E **218**
Reyes, *Bol.* 14°22′ S, 67°25′ W **137**
Reyes, Point 38°2′ N, 123°22′ W **90**
Reyes, Punta, *Col.* 2°40′ N, 78°24′ W **136**
Reykjanes Ridge, *North Atlantic Ocean* 59°58′ N, 29°41′ W **253**
Reykjavík, *Ice.* 64°4′ N, 22°23′ W **246**
Reynoldsburg, *Ohio, U.S.* 39°56′ N, 82°49′ W **102**
Rēzekne, *Latv.* 56°29′ N, 27°19′ E **166**
Rezh, *Russ.* 57°23′ N, 61°22′ E **154**
Rezh, river, *Russ.* 57°26′ N, 60°57′ E **154**
Rezovo, *Bulg.* 41°59′ N, 28°1′ E **156**
Rgotina, *Serb. and Mont.* 44°0′ N, 22°16′ E **168**
Rhaetian Alps, *Switz.* 46°22′ N, 9°21′ E **167**
Rhafsaï, *Mor.* 34°39′ N, 4°55′ W **214**
Rhame, *N. Dak., U.S.* 46°13′ N, 103°40′ W **90**
Rhamnus, ruin(s), *Gr.* 38°12′ N, 23°56′ E **156**
Rhayader, *U.K.* 52°17′ N, 3°31′ W **162**
Rheda-Wiedenbrück, *Ger.* 51°51′ N, 8°17′ E **167**
Rhede, *Ger.* 51°50′ N, 6°42′ E **167**
Rheden, *Neth.* 52°0′ N, 6°3′ E **167**
Rhein, river, *Ger.* 51°47′ N, 6°15′ E **167**
Rheinbach, *Ger.* 50°37′ N, 6°57′ E **167**
Rheinbrohl, *Ger.* 50°29′ N, 7°21′ E **167**
Rheine, *Ger.* 52°16′ N, 7°26′ E **163**
Rheinland-Palatinate, adm. division, *Ger.* 49°50′ N, 6°34′ E **150**
Rhemilès, spring, *Alg.* 28°28′ N, 4°22′ W **214**
Rhens, *Ger.* 50°16′ N, 7°37′ E **167**
Rheydt, *Ger.* 51°9′ N, 6°26′ E **167**
Rhinebeck, *N.Y., U.S.* 41°55′ N, 73°55′ W **104**
Rhinelander, *Wis., U.S.* 45°38′ N, 89°23′ W **94**
Rhineland-Palatinate, adm. division, *Ger.* 50°15′ N, 6°36′ E **167**
Rhino Camp, *Uganda* 2°58′ N, 31°23′ E **224**
Rhinocolura see El ʽArîsh, *Egypt* 31°6′ N, 33°46′ E **194**
Rhiou, river, *Alg.* 35°59′ N, 0°58′ E **150**
Rhir, Cap, *Mor.* 30°41′ N, 10°44′ W **214**
Rho, *It.* 45°32′ N, 9°1′ E **167**
Rhode Island, adm. division, *R.I., U.S.* 41°45′ N, 71°46′ W **104**
Rhode Island Sound 41°14′ N, 71°13′ W **104**
Rhodes Peak, *Idaho, U.S.* 46°38′ N, 114°53′ W **90**
Rhodes see Ródos, *Gr.* 36°25′ N, 28°13′ E **156**
Rhodes see Ródos, adm. division, *Gr.* 35°58′ N, 27°21′ E **156**
Rhodes see Ródos, island, *Gr.* 35°44′ N, 27°53′ E **156**
Rhodope Mountains, *Bulg.* 41°50′ N, 23°44′ E **156**
Rhön, *Ger.* 50°36′ N, 9°54′ E **167**
Rhône, river, *Europe* 46°10′ N, 7°16′ E **165**

S

Sakhalinskiy Zaliv 53°48' N, 139°32' E 160
Sakhar, *Afghan.* 32°54' N, 65°32' E 186
Şäki, *Azerb.* 41°12' N, 47°9' E 195
Šakiai, *Lith.* 54°57' N, 23°1' E 166
Sakinohama, *Japan* 33°24' N, 134°11' E 201
Sakishima Shotō, islands, *East China Sea* 22°44' N, 124°24' E 238
Sakmara, *Russ.* 52°1' N, 55°21' E 158
Sa-koi, *Myanmar* 19°54' N, 97°1' E 202
Sakon Nakhon, *Thai.* 17°13' N, 103°59' E 202
Sakora, *Mali* 14°10' N, 9°21' W 222
Sakrand, *Pak.* 26°10' N, 68°16' E 186
Sakrivier, *S. Af.* 30°53' S, 20°25' E 227
Saku, *Japan* 36°13' N, 138°25' E 201
Saky, *Ukr.* 45°8' N, 33°35' E 156
Säkylä, *Fin.* 61°2' N, 22°19' E 166
Sal Mountains, La, *Utah, U.S.* 38°24' N, 109°18' W 90
Sal, Punta, *Hond.* 15°53' N, 87°37' W 115
Sal, river, *Russ.* 47°22' N, 43°19' E 184
Sal, river, *Russ.* 47°12' N, 41°50' E 158
Sala, *Eritrea* 16°56' N, 37°25' E 182
Sala, *Nor.* 59°54' N, 16°34' E 152
Šaľa, *Slovakia* 48°9' N, 17°52' E 152
Salaberry-de-Valleyfield, *Can.* 45°16' N, 74°9' W 110
Sălacea, *Rom.* 47°26' N, 22°18' E 168
Salacgrīva, *Latv.* 57°44' N, 24°20' E 166
Saladas, *Arg.* 28°16' S, 58°37' W 139
Saladillo, *Arg.* 35°39' S, 59°47' W 139
Saladillo, river, *Arg.* 28°47' S, 64°10' W 134
Salado, river, *Arg.* 29°28' S, 62°14' W 139
Salado, river, *Arg.* 35°50' S, 57°49' W 139
Salado, river, *Arg.* 36°1' S, 66°45' W 134
Salado, river, *Mex.* 26°57' N, 99°51' W 96
Salaga, *Ghana* 8°33' N, 0°32' E 222
Salagle, *Somalia* 1°48' N, 42°17' E 224
Şalah ad Dīn, *Iraq* 36°23' N, 44°8' E 195
Salahīyah, *Syr.* 35°0' N, 37°3' E 194
Salahmi, *Fin.* 63°47' N, 26°53' E 152
Salair, *Russ.* 54°11' N, 85°49' E 184
Sălaj, adm. division, *Rom.* 47°1' N, 22°45' E 156
Salal, *Chad* 14°49' N, 17°14' E 216
Salala, *Sudan* 21°15' N, 36°16' E 182
Salālah, *Oman* 17°2' N, 54°6' E 182
Salamanca, *Chile* 31°46' S, 71°1' W 134
Salamanca, *Mex.* 20°34' N, 101°12' W 114
Salamanca, *Sp.* 40°58' N, 5°38' W 214
Salamis 480 B.C., battle, *Aegean Sea* 37°56' N, 23°25' E 156
Salamis, ruin(s) 35°10' N, 33°51' E 194
Salang, Kowtal-e, pass, *Afghan.* 35°21' N, 69°5' E 186
Salangen, *Nor.* 68°51' N, 17°51' E 152
Salantai, *Lith.* 56°2' N, 21°34' E 166
Sălard, *Rom.* 47°13' N, 22°1' E 168
Salardú, *Sp.* 42°42' N, 0°55' E 164
Salaš, *Serb. and Mont.* 44°6' N, 22°19' E 168
Salas de Bureba, *Sp.* 42°41' N, 3°29' W 164
Salas de los Infantes, *Sp.* 42°0' N, 3°17' W 164
Salaspils, *Latv.* 56°52' N, 24°18' E 166
Salavat, *Russ.* 53°22' N, 55°51' E 154
Salaverry, *Peru* 8°13' S, 78°57' W 123
Salavina, *Arg.* 28°48' S, 63°26' W 139
Salawati, island, *Indonesia* 1°28' S, 129°43' E 192
Salay, *Philippines* 8°53' N, 124°50' E 203
Salay Gómez Ridge, *South Pacific Ocean* 26°4' S, 95°15' W 252
Sala-y-Gómez, Isla, island, *Chile* 26°25' S, 105°19' W 252
Salbris, *Fr.* 47°25' N, 2°2' E 150
Šalčininkai, *Lith.* 54°19' N, 25°22' E 166
Sălciua de Jos, *Rom.* 46°24' N, 23°27' E 168
Saldanha, *S. Af.* 32°59' S, 17°55' E 220
Saldé, *Senegal* 16°9' N, 13°59' W 222
Saldungaray, *Arg.* 38°13' S, 61°48' W 139
Saldus, *Latv.* 56°38' N, 22°28' E 166
Sale, *Austral.* 38°6' S, 147°3' E 231
Sale, *U.K.* 53°25' N, 2°20' W 162
Salekhard, *Russ.* 66°29' N, 66°46' E 169
Salem, *Ark., U.S.* 36°21' N, 91°49' W 96
Salem, *Conn., U.S.* 41°29' N, 72°17' W 104
Salem, *Fla., U.S.* 29°52' N, 83°26' W 105
Salem, *India* 11°37' N, 78°10' E 188
Salem, *Ind., U.S.* 38°36' N, 86°6' W 102
Salem, *Mo., U.S.* 37°37' N, 91°32' W 96
Salem, *Mo., U.S.* 38°36' N, 88°57' W 94
Salem, *N.H., U.S.* 42°47' N, 71°13' W 104
Salem, *N.Y., U.S.* 43°10' N, 73°21' W 104
Salem, *Ohio, U.S.* 40°53' N, 80°51' W 102
Salem, *Oreg., U.S.* 44°55' N, 123°8' W 90
Salem, *S. Dak., U.S.* 43°42' N, 97°24' W 90
Salem, *Sw.* 59°14' N, 17°47' E 166
Salem, *Va., U.S.* 37°17' N, 80°4' W 96
Salem, *W. Va., U.S.* 39°16' N, 80°34' W 94
Sälen, *Nor.* 61°10' N, 13°13' E 152
Salford, *U.K.* 53°28' N, 2°19' W 162
Salgótarján, *Hung.* 48°5' N, 19°49' E 168
Salgueiro, *Braz.* 8°8' S, 39°7' W 132
Salhus, *Nor.* 60°30' N, 5°16' E 152
Sali, *Alg.* 26°58' N, 2°118' W 214
Salida, *Calif., U.S.* 37°42' N, 121°6' W 100
Salida, *Colo., U.S.* 38°32' N, 106°2' W 82
Salies-du-Salat, *Fr.* 43°6' N, 0°56' E 164
Şalīf, *Yemen* 15°18' N, 42°41' E 182
Salihorsk, *Belarus* 52°47' N, 27°29' E 158
Salima, *Malawi* 13°46' S, 34°24' E 224
Salin, *Myanmar* 20°35' N, 94°39' E 202
Salina, *Kans., U.S.* 38°49' N, 97°38' W 94
Salina, *Utah, U.S.* 38°57' N, 111°52' W 90
Salinas, *Braz.* 16°11' S, 42°22' W 138
Salinas, *Calif., U.S.* 36°40' N, 121°40' W 100
Salinas, *Ecua.* 2°17' S, 80°56' W 130
Salinas, *Mex.* 22°36' N, 101°43' W 114
Salinas de Añana, *Sp.* 42°48' N, 2°59' W 164
Salinas de G. Mendoza, *Bol.* 19°39' S, 67°43' W 137
Salinas, Ponta das, *Angola* 12°55' S, 12°20' E 220
Salinas, Sierra de, *Calif., U.S.* 36°20' N, 121°30' W 100
Salinas Victoria, *Mex.* 25°57' N, 100°18' W 114
Saline, *La., U.S.* 32°9' N, 92°59' W 103
Saline, *Mich., U.S.* 42°9' N, 83°48' W 102
Saline, river, *Ark., U.S.* 33°9' N, 92°6' W 103
Saline, river, *Kans., U.S.* 39°0' N, 99°22' W 90
Saline, river, *La., U.S.* 32°20' N, 93°2' W 103
Saline Valley, *Calif., U.S.* 36°47' N, 117°55' W 101
Salines, Point, *Grenada* 11°53' N, 62°36' W 116
Salinópolis, *Braz.* 0°38' N, 47°19' W 130
Salisbury, *Conn., U.S.* 41°59' N, 73°26' W 104
Salisbury, *N.H., U.S.* 43°22' N, 71°44' W 104
Salisbury, *U.K.* 51°4' N, 1°47' W 162
Salisbury, *Vt., U.S.* 43°53' N, 73°7' W 104
Salisbury Island, *Can.* 63°31' N, 76°33' W 106
Salisbury, Mount, peak, *Alas., U.S.* 69°7' N, 146°30' W 98
Salisbury Plain, *U.K.* 51°18' N, 2°5' W 162
Salisbury Sound 57°16' N, 136°9' W 108
Salish Mountains, *Mont., U.S.* 48°30' N, 115°8' W 90
Săliște, *Rom.* 45°48' N, 23°54' E 156
Şalkhad, *Syr.* 32°29' N, 36°43' E 194
Salkum, *Wash., U.S.* 46°30' N, 122°39' W 100
Salla, *Fin.* 66°49' N, 28°39' E 152
Sallanches, *Fr.* 45°56' N, 6°37' E 167
Sallent, *Sp.* 41°50' N, 1°54' E 164
Sallent de Gállego, *Sp.* 42°46' N, 0°20' E 164
Salliqueló, *Arg.* 36°45' S, 62°57' W 139
Sallis, *Miss., U.S.* 33°0' N, 89°47' W 103
Sallisaw, *Okla., U.S.* 35°26' N, 94°47' W 96
Sallom, *Sudan* 19°23' N, 37°3' E 182
Salluit, *Can.* 62°11' N, 75°42' W 106
Salmās, *Iran* 38°17' N, 44°44' E 195
Salme, *Est.* 58°9' N, 22°14' E 166
Salmerón, *Sp.* 40°33' N, 2°30' W 164
Salmi, *Russ.* 61°21' N, 31°56' E 152
Salmo, *Can.* 49°11' N, 117°17' W 90
Salmon, *Idaho, U.S.* 45°9' N, 113°54' W 90
Salmon Arm, *Can.* 50°41' N, 119°17' W 90
Salmon Falls Creek Reservoir, lake, *Idaho, U.S.* 42°19' N, 118°19' W 80
Salmon Mountain, peak, *Idaho, U.S.* 45°34' N, 114°56' W 90
Salmon Mountains, *Calif., U.S.* 41°7' N, 123°27' W 90
Salmon, river, *Idaho, U.S.* 45°31' N, 116°2' W 106
Salmon River Mountains, *Idaho, U.S.* 45°9' N, 116°18' W 90
Salo, *Cen. Af. Rep.* 3°23' N, 16°8' E 218
Salo, *Fin.* 60°23' N, 23°5' E 166
Salò, *It.* 45°37' N, 10°31' E 167
Salobelyak, *Russ.* 57°8' N, 48°5' E 154
Salole, *Eth.* 4°27' N, 39°33' E 224
Salome, *Ariz., U.S.* 33°46' N, 113°36' W 101
Salomon Islands, *Indian Ocean* 5°16' S, 72°22' E 188
Salon, *Fr.* 43°38' N, 5°5' E 150
Salonae see Solin, *Croatia* 43°32' N, 16°28' E 168
Salonga National Park, *Dem. Rep. of the Congo* 2°60' S, 20°3' E 218
Salonga, river, *Dem. Rep. of the Congo* 1°6' S, 20°36' E 218
Salonica see Thessaloníki, *Gr.* 40°38' N, 22°57' E 156
Salonta, *Rom.* 46°48' N, 21°42' E 168
Salor, river, *Sp.* 39°19' N, 6°20' W 164
Salou, Cap de, *Sp.* 40°53' N, 1°8' E 164
Salpausselkä, *Fin.* 61°19' N, 28°51' E 166
Salsberry Pass, *Calif., U.S.* 35°55' N, 116°26' W 101
Salses, *Fr.* 42°49' N, 2°53' E 164
Sălsig, *Rom.* 47°30' N, 23°19' E 168
Sal'sk, *Russ.* 46°27' N, 41°26' E 158
Salsomaggiore Terme, *It.* 44°48' N, 9°58' E 167
Salt, *Sp.* 41°57' N, 2°47' E 164
Salt Fork Brazos, river, *Tex., U.S.* 33°9' N, 101°34' W 80
Salt Fork Red, river, *Tex., U.S.* 35°5' N, 100°57' W 112
Salt Lake, *Calif., U.S.* 36°41' N, 117°58' W 101
Salt Lake City, *Utah, U.S.* 40°43' N, 111°59' W 90
Salt River, *Can.* 60°6' N, 112°22' W 108
Salt, river, *Can.* 59°36' N, 112°15' W 108
Salt, river, *Mo., U.S.* 39°29' N, 91°35' W 94
Salt River Range, *Wyo., U.S.* 42°53' N, 111°5' W 90
Salta, *Arg.* 24°47' S, 65°25' W 132
Saltburn by the Sea, *U.K.* 54°35' N, 0°59' E 162
Saltcoats, *Can.* 51°2' N, 102°11' W 90
Saltdal, *Nor.* 67°4' N, 15°24' E 152
Saltee Islands, *Ire.* 51°49' N, 6°37' W 150
Saltfleetby Saint Peter, *U.K.* 53°23' N, 0°10' E 162
Saltillo, *Mex.* 25°23' N, 101°5' W 114
Salto, *Arg.* 34°18' S, 60°16' W 139
Salto, *Uru.* 31°22' S, 57°55' W 139
Salto Angostura I, fall(s), *Col.* 1°59' N, 73°53' W 136
Salto Angostura Ii, fall(s), *Col.* 2°11' N, 73°35' W 136
Salto Angostura Iii, fall(s), *Col.* 2°54' N, 72°16' W 136
Salto del Guairá, *Parag.* 24°3' S, 54°19' W 132
Salto Grande, *Braz.* 22°54' S, 49°60' W 138
Salto, river, *Mex.* 22°12' N, 99°19' W 114
Saltoluokta, *Nor.* 67°23' N, 18°31' E 152
Salton City, *Calif., U.S.* 33°16' N, 115°58' W 101
Salton Sea Beach, *Calif., U.S.* 33°20' N, 115°60' W 101
Salton Sea, lake, *Calif., U.S.* 33°19' N, 115°53' W 101
Saltoro Kangri, peak, *Pak.* 35°22' N, 76°45' E 188
Saltpond, *Ghana* 5°14' N, 1°5' W 222
Saltsjöbaden, *Sw.* 59°15' N, 18°15' E 166
Saltspring Island, *Can.* 48°48' N, 123°16' W 100
Saltvik, *Fin.* 60°15' N, 20°3' E 166
Saluda, *S.C., U.S.* 34°0' N, 81°47' W 96
Saluggia, *It.* 45°13' N, 8°0' E 167
Salûm, *Egypt* 31°33' N, 25°11' E 180
Salur, *India* 18°31' N, 83°12' E 188
Saluzzo, *It.* 44°38' N, 7°30' E 167
Salvacañete, *Sp.* 40°5' N, 1°31' W 164
Salvador (Bahia), *Braz.* 12°59' S, 38°28' W 132
Salvador Mazza, *Arg.* 22°5' S, 63°48' W 137
Salvage Islands see Selvagens, Ilhas, *North Atlantic Ocean* 30°18' N, 16°15' W 214
Salvaterra, *Braz.* 0°46' N, 48°33' W 130
Salvatierra, *Mex.* 20°11' N, 100°54' W 114
Salvatierra, *Sp.* 42°50' N, 2°23' W 150
Salwá, Dawḩat 24°39' N, 49°59' E 196
Salween see Nu, river, *Asia* 31°21' N, 93°34' E 190
Salween see Thanlwin, river, *Asia* 21°45' N, 98°44' E 202
Salyan, *Azerb.* 39°36' N, 48°58' E 195
Salyan, *Azerb.* 41°3' N, 49°6' E 180
Salyersville, *Ky., U.S.* 37°44' N, 83°4' W 96
Salym, *Russ.* 60°6' N, 71°26' E 169
Salzbrunn, *Namibia* 24°24' S, 17°57' E 227
Salzburg, *Aust.* 47°49' N, 13°3' E 156
Salzgitter, *Ger.* 52°2' N, 10°22' E 152
Salzkammergut, region, *Aust.* 47°39' N, 12°48' E 156
Salzkotten, *Ger.* 51°40' N, 8°36' E 167
Sam, *India* 26°47' N, 70°34' E 186
Sam Rayburn Reservoir, lake, *Tex., U.S.* 31°3' N, 94°60' W 103
Sam Son, *Vietnam* 19°45' N, 105°52' E 198
Sama, river, *Peru* 18°11' S, 70°36' W 137
Samah, oil field, *Lib.* 28°7' N, 19°0' E 216
Samāḩ, spring, *Saudi Arabia* 29°2' N, 45°26' E 196
Samaipata, *Bol.* 18°13' S, 63°52' W 137
Samâlût, *Egypt* 28°16' N, 30°39' E 180
Samaná, *Dom. Rep.* 19°12' N, 69°20' W 116
Samaná, Cabo, *Dom. Rep.* 19°12' N, 69°7' W 116
Samana Cay, island, *Bahamas* 23°10' N, 74°2' W 116
Samandaği (Seleucia), *Turk.* 36°4' N, 35°57' E 156
Samanga, *Tanzania* 8°20' S, 39°13' E 224
Samaqua, river, *Can.* 49°53' N, 72°31' W 94
Samar, *Jordan* 32°39' N, 35°48' E 194
Samar, island, *Philippines* 12°14' N, 125°25' E 192
Samara, *Russ.* 53°14' N, 50°14' E 154
Samara, adm. division, *Russ.* 53°31' N, 49°15' E 154
Samara, river, *Russ.* 52°22' N, 53°17' E 184
Samarai, *P.N.G.* 10°38' S, 150°40' E 231
Samaria Mountain, peak, *Idaho, U.S.* 42°4' N, 112°26' W 90
Samariapo, *Venez.* 5°10' N, 67°44' W 136
Samarinda, *Indonesia* 0°30' N, 117°7' E 192
Samarqand, *Uzb.* 39°39' N, 67°0' E 197
Sāmarrā', *Iraq* 34°17' N, 43°52' E 180
Samarskoe, *Kaz.* 49°1' N, 83°23' E 184
Samarskoye, *Russ.* 46°57' N, 39°38' E 156
Samastipur, *India* 25°50' N, 85°47' E 197
Samatiguila, *Côte d'Ivoire* 9°49' N, 7°35' W 222
Samaúma, *Braz.* 0°8' N, 69°16' W 136
Samaúma, *Braz.* 8°43' S, 67°22' W 130
Samawah see As Samāwah, *Iraq* 31°15' N, 45°15' E 180
Samba, *Burkina Faso* 12°40' N, 2°26' W 222
Samba, *Gabon* 1°4' S, 10°41' E 218
Samba, *India* 32°33' N, 75°9' E 188
Sambalpur, *India* 21°29' N, 83°59' E 188
Sambalpur, *India* 20°18' N, 81°2' E 188
Sambas, *Indonesia* 1°22' N, 109°17' E 196
Sambava, *Madagascar* 14°19' S, 50°8' E 220
Sambhal, *India* 28°32' N, 78°34' E 197
Sambhar, *India* 26°54' N, 75°13' E 197
Sambiase, *It.* 38°58' N, 16°15' E 156
Sambir, *Ukr.* 49°30' N, 23°11' E 152
Sambolabbo, *Cameroon* 7°3' N, 11°57' E 218
Samborombón, Bahía 34°27' S, 58°24' W 134
Samburg, *Russ.* 66°52' N, 78°20' E 169
Samburu Reserve, *Kenya* 0°29' N, 37°10' E 206
Samcheok, *S. Korea* 37°27' N, 129°9' E 200
Samdari, *India* 25°49' N, 72°34' E 186
Samdŭng, *N. Korea* 38°59' N, 126°12' E 200
Same, *Tanzania* 4°5' S, 37°44' E 224
Samedan, *Switz.* 46°33' N, 9°52' E 167
Samer, *Fr.* 50°38' N, 1°45' E 163
Samfya, *Zambia* 11°21' S, 29°30' E 224
Samgi, *N. Korea* 40°27' N, 128°20' E 200
Samho, *N. Korea* 39°55' N, 127°51' E 200
Şāmiţah, *Saudi Arabia* 16°35' N, 42°55' E 182
Sammatti, *Fin.* 60°18' N, 23°48' E 166
Samnangjin, *S. Korea* 35°24' N, 128°51' E 200
Samnū, *Lib.* 27°17' N, 14°52' E 216
Samnye, *S. Korea* 35°54' N, 127°5' E 200
Samoa, *Calif., U.S.* 40°48' N, 124°11' W 90
Samoa 13°50' S, 172°8' W 241
Samoa, islands, *South Pacific Ocean* 13°58' S, 175°18' W 238
Samoded, *Russ.* 63°37' N, 40°30' E 154
Samoëns, *Fr.* 46°5' N, 6°43' E 167
Samokov, *Maced.* 41°40' N, 21°8' E 168
Samolva, *Russ.* 58°15' N, 27°37' E 166
Samorogouan, *Burkina Faso* 11°24' N, 4°58' W 222
Samoš, *Serb. and Mont.* 45°12' N, 20°47' E 168
Sámos, island, *Gr.* 37°50' N, 26°34' E 180
Samos, ruin(s), *Gr.* 37°40' N, 26°51' E 156
Samothráki, island, *Gr.* 40°31' N, 25°17' E 180
Samoylovka, *Russ.* 51°8' N, 43°44' E 158
Sampa, *Ghana* 7°58' N, 2°43' W 222
Sampacho, *Arg.* 33°24' S, 64°43' W 134
Samparha Koura, *Mali* 14°38' N, 8°5' W 222
Samper de Calanda, *Sp.* 41°10' N, 0°23' E 164
Sampit, *Indonesia* 2°32' S, 112°46' E 192
Samp'o, *N. Korea* 41°1' N, 127°9' E 200
Sam'po, *N. Korea* 41°13' N, 129°42' E 200
Sampwe, *Dem. Rep. of the Congo* 9°20' S, 27°23' E 224
Samrē, *Eth.* 13°10' N, 39°12' E 182
Samro, Ozero, lake, *Russ.* 58°58' N, 28°36' E 166
Samrong, *Cambodia* 14°12' N, 103°34' E 202
Samsŏ, *N. Korea* 41°17' N, 127°39' E 200
Samsu, *N. Korea* 41°18' N, 128°2' E 200
Samsun, *Turk.* 41°13' N, 36°13' E 143
Samsun (Amisus), *Turk.* 41°17' N, 36°20' E 158
Samthar, *India* 25°51' N, 78°55' E 197
Samtredia, *Ga.* 42°9' N, 42°22' E 195
Samuel, Mount, peak, *Austral.* 19°42' S, 133°57' E 230
Samuhú, *Arg.* 27°30' S, 60°30' W 139
Samui, Ko, island, *Thai.* 9°15' N, 99°59' E 202
Samur, river, *Europe* 41°22' N, 48°3' E 195
Samus', *Russ.* 56°46' N, 84°47' E 169
Samut Prakan, *Thai.* 13°36' N, 100°36' E 202
Samut Songkhram, *Thai.* 13°26' N, 100°2' E 202
San, *Mali* 13°17' N, 4°56' W 222
San Adrián, Cabo, *Sp.* 43°1' N, 8°54' W 150
San Agustín, *Col.* 1°53' N, 76°18' W 136
San Agustin, Cape, *Philippines* 6°17' N, 126°14' E 203
San Agustín de Valle Fértil, *Arg.* 30°39' S, 67°35' W 134
San Ambrosio Island, *Chile* 26°14' S, 79°39' W 253
San Andreas, *Calif., U.S.* 38°11' N, 120°42' W 100
San Andrés, *Bol.* 15°2' S, 64°28' W 137
San Andrés, Isla de, island, *Col.* 12°23' N, 82°18' W 115
San Andrés, Laguna de 22°40' N, 98°25' W 114
San Andrés Tuxtla, *Mex.* 18°25' N, 95°12' W 114
San Angelo, *Tex., U.S.* 31°27' N, 100°26' W 92
San Anselmo, *Calif., U.S.* 37°58' N, 122°35' W 100
San Antero, *Col.* 9°21' N, 75°46' W 136
San Antonio, *Bol.* 14°56' S, 64°32' W 137
San Antonio, *Col.* 1°48' N, 78°19' W 136
San Antonio, *Peru* 3°45' S, 74°25' W 136
San Antonio, *Tex., U.S.* 29°25' N, 98°30' W 92
San Antonio, *Venez.* 3°29' N, 66°46' W 136
San Antonio Bay 28°9' N, 96°58' W 112
San Antonio, Cabo, *Arg.* 36°48' S, 57°6' W 139
San Antonio da Cachoeira, *Braz.* 0°39' N, 52°31' W 130
San Antonio de Areco, *Arg.* 34°15' S, 59°27' W 139
San Antonio de Bravo, *Tex., U.S.* 30°11' N, 104°42' W 92
San Antonio de Caparo, *Venez.* 7°32' N, 71°31' W 136
San Antonio de las Alazanas, *Mex.* 25°15' N, 100°35' W 114
San Antonio de los Cobres, *Arg.* 24°11' S, 66°23' W 132
San Antonio, Lake, *Calif., U.S.* 35°49' N, 121°4' W 100
San Antonio, Mount, peak, *Calif., U.S.* 34°17' N, 117°42' W 101
San Antonio Mountain, peak, *Tex., U.S.* 31°56' N, 105°38' W 92
San Antonio Mountains, *Nev., U.S.* 38°9' N, 117°34' W 90
San Antonio, Punta, *Mex.* 29°28' N, 116°4' W 92
San Antonio, river, *Tex., U.S.* 29°18' N, 99°13' W 80
San Antonio, Sierra de, *Mex.* 30°9' N, 110°53' W 112
San Ardo, *Calif., U.S.* 36°1' N, 120°55' W 100
San Asensio, *Sp.* 42°29' N, 2°45' W 164
San Augustine, *Tex., U.S.* 31°30' N, 94°7' W 103
San Bartolo, *Peru* 12°28' S, 76°48' W 130
San Benedetto Po, *It.* 45°2' N, 10°55' E 167
San Benedicto, Isla, island, *Isla San Benedicto* 19°4' N, 110°53' W 112
San Benito, *Tex., U.S.* 26°6' N, 97°37' W 114
San Benito, Islas, islands, *North Pacific Ocean* 28°23' N, 116°19' W 112
San Benito Mountain, peak, *Calif., U.S.* 36°21' N, 120°42' W 100
San Bernardino, *Calif., U.S.* 34°6' N, 117°18' W 101
San Bernardino Mountains, *Calif., U.S.* 34°12' N, 117°25' W 101
San Bernardino Strait 12°35' N, 123°0' E 192
San Bernardo, *Chile* 33°36' S, 70°45' W 134
San Bernardo, *Mex.* 25°59' N, 105°28' W 114
San Blas, *Mex.* 21°33' N, 105°17' W 114
San Blas, *Mex.* 27°26' N, 101°45' W 96
San Blas, Archipiélago de, *North America* 9°22' N, 78°6' W 115
San Blas, Cape, *Fla., U.S.* 29°33' N, 85°57' W 96
San Bonifacio, *It.* 45°23' N, 11°17' E 167
San Borja, *Bol.* 14°51' S, 66°52' W 137
San Borja, Sierra de, *Mex.* 29°34' N, 115°3' W 112
San Buenaventura, *Bol.* 14°33' S, 67°38' W 137
San Candido, *It.* 46°43' N, 12°17' E 167
San Carlos, *Arg.* 27°45' S, 55°58' W 139
San Carlos, *Arg.* 25°57' S, 65°57' W 134
San Carlos, *Chile* 36°24' S, 71°59' W 134
San Carlos, *Mex.* 29°0' N, 100°54' W 92
San Carlos, *Mex.* 24°33' N, 98°56' W 114
San Carlos, *Mex.* 27°59' N, 111°4' W 112
San Carlos, *Mex.* 24°46' N, 112°6' W 112
San Carlos, *Nicar.* 11°8' N, 84°46' W 115
San Carlos, *Philippines* 15°55' N, 120°19' E 203
San Carlos, *Philippines* 10°27' N, 123°22' E 203
San Carlos, *Uru.* 34°48' S, 54°56' W 139
San Carlos, *Venez.* 9°39' N, 68°36' W 136
San Carlos, *Venez.* 1°56' N, 66°59' W 123
San Carlos Centro, *Arg.* 31°44' S, 61°4' W 139
San Carlos de Bolívar, *Arg.* 36°13' S, 61°6' W 139
San Carlos de Río Negro, *Venez.* 1°52' N, 67°2' W 136
San Carlos, Mesa de, peak, *Mex.* 29°37' N, 115°25' W 92
San Carlos, Punta, *Mex.* 29°17' N, 115°44' W 92
San Cayetano, *Arg.* 38°21' S, 59°37' W 139
San Clemente, *Calif., U.S.* 33°25' N, 117°38' W 101
San Clemente, island, *Calif., U.S.* 32°46' N, 118°22' W 101
San Cosme, *Arg.* 27°22' S, 58°33' W 139
San Cosme y Damián, *Parag.* 27°18' S, 56°20' W 139
San Cristóbal, *Arg.* 30°17' S, 61°14' W 139
San Cristóbal, *Bol.* 21°6' S, 67°10' W 137
San Cristóbal, *Col.* 2°18' S, 73°2' W 136
San Cristóbal, *Venez.* 7°44' N, 72°14' W 136
San Cristóbal, Isla, island, *Ecua.* 0°45' N, 89°16' W 130
San Cristobal, island, *Solomon Islands* 10°35' S, 161°45' E 242
San Cristóbal Verapaz, *Guatemala* 15°23' N, 90°26' W 115
San Custodio, *Venez.* 1°35' N, 66°13' W 136
San Diego, *Calif., U.S.* 32°43' N, 117°11' W 101
San Diego, *Tex., U.S.* 27°45' N, 98°14' W 92
San Diego, Cabo, *Arg.* 54°39' S, 65°11' W 134
San Donà di Piave, *It.* 45°38' N, 12°33' E 167
San Estanislao, *Parag.* 24°39' S, 56°29' W 132
San Esteban, *Hond.* 15°17' N, 85°52' W 115
San Esteban de Gormaz, *Sp.* 41°34' N, 3°13' W 164
San Esteban de Litera, *Sp.* 41°54' N, 0°19' E 164
San Esteban, island, *Mex.* 28°29' N, 112°33' W 112
San Felice sul Panaro, *It.* 44°50' N, 11°8' E 167
San Felipe, *Col.* 1°51' N, 67°5' W 136
San Felipe, *Mex.* 21°27' N, 101°14' W 114
San Felipe, *Tex., U.S.* 29°47' N, 96°6' W 96
San Felipe, *Venez.* 10°18' N, 68°46' W 136
San Felipe, Cayos de, *Caribbean Sea* 21°35' N, 84°7' W 116
San Felipe, peak, *Mex.* 17°8' N, 96°43' W 114
San Félix, *Venez.* 8°5' N, 72°15' W 136
San Félix Island, *Chile* 26°7' S, 80°18' W 253
San Fermín, Punta, *Mex.* 30°19' N, 114°38' W 92
San Fernando, *Calif., U.S.* 34°17' N, 118°27' W 101
San Fernando, *Mex.* 24°50' N, 98°9' W 114
San Fernando, *Philippines* 15°1' N, 120°40' E 203
San Fernando, *Philippines* 16°38' N, 120°20' E 203
San Fernando, *Sp.* 36°27' N, 6°12' W 164
San Fernando, *Trinidad and Tobago* 10°16' N, 61°26' W 116
San Fernando de Apure, *Venez.* 7°51' N, 67°30' W 136
San Fernando de Atabapo, *Venez.* 3°59' N, 67°42' W 136
San Fernando, river, *Mex.* 25°12' N, 98°37' W 114
San Francisco, *Arg.* 31°27' S, 62°6' W 139
San Francisco, *Bol.* 15°18' S, 65°33' W 137
San Francisco, *Calif., U.S.* 37°46' N, 122°26' W 100
San Francisco, *Col.* 1°10' N, 76°58' W 136
San Francisco, *Mex.* 30°49' N, 112°37' W 92
San Francisco Bay 37°36' N, 122°19' W 100
San Francisco, Cabo de, *Ecua.* 0°33' N, 81°47' W 130
San Francisco de Bellocq, *Arg.* 38°42' S, 60°2' W 139
San Francisco de Conchos, *Mex.* 27°35' N, 105°18' W 112
San Francisco de la Paz, *Hond.* 14°55' N, 86°4' W 115
San Francisco de Macorís, *Dom. Rep.* 19°16' N, 70°15' W 116
San Francisco de Paula, Cabo, *Arg.* 49°56' S, 67°41' W 134
San Francisco del Monte de Oro, *Arg.* 32°36' S, 66°7' W 134
San Francisco del Oro, *Mex.* 26°51' N, 105°51' W 112
San Francisco del Rincón, *Mex.* 21°0' N, 101°52' W 114
San Francisco Javier, *Sp.* 38°41' N, 1°25' E 150
San Francisco Mountain, *Ariz., U.S.* 35°17' N, 111°58' W 92
San Francisco Mountain, peak, *Ariz., U.S.* 35°19' N, 111°47' W 112
San Francisco, Paso de, pass, *Chile* 26°53' S, 68°22' W 132
San Gabriel, *Ecua.* 0°34' N, 77°60' W 136
San Gabriel Mountains, *Calif., U.S.* 34°24' N, 118°19' W 101
San Germán 18°4' N, 67°4' W 116
San Gervàs, peak, *Sp.* 42°17' N, 0°47' E 164
San Gregorio, *Arg.* 34°21' S, 62°2' W 139
San Gregorio, *Uru.* 32°36' S, 55°50' W 139
San Guillermo, *Arg.* 30°22' S, 61°55' W 139
San Hipólito, Punta, *Mex.* 26°55' N, 115°40' W 112
San Ignacio, *Arg.* 27°15' S, 55°33' W 132
San Ignacio, *Belize* 17°9' N, 89°7' W 115
San Ignacio, *Bol.* 16°29' S, 60°60' W 132
San Ignacio, *Bol.* 14°58' S, 65°38' W 137
San Ignacio, *Mex.* 23°56' N, 106°26' W 114
San Ignacio, *Mex.* 27°18' N, 112°55' W 112
San Ignacio, *Parag.* 26°51' S, 56°58' W 139
San Ignacio, *Peru* 14°5' S, 68°58' W 137
San Ignacio, *Peru* 5°2' S, 78°60' W 130
San Ildefonso, Cape, *Philippines* 15°40' N, 122°1' E 203
San In Kaigan National Park, *Japan* 35°30' N, 134°30' E 201
San Isidro, *Peru* 4°55' S, 76°17' W 130
San Jacinto, *Calif., U.S.* 33°47' N, 116°59' W 101
San Jacinto Mountains, *Calif., U.S.* 33°47' N, 116°41' W 101
San Jaime, *Arg.* 30°17' S, 58°21' W 139
San Javier, *Arg.* 30°33' S, 59°58' W 139
San Javier, *Arg.* 27°52' S, 55°9' W 139
San Javier, *Bol.* 14°38' S, 64°42' W 137
San Javier, *Bol.* 16°28' S, 62°37' W 132
San Javier, *Mex.* 28°36' N, 109°45' W 92
San Javier, *Sp.* 37°48' N, 0°51' E 164
San Javier, *Uru.* 32°40' S, 58°5' W 139
San Jerónimo, *Mex.* 17°7' N, 100°28' W 114
San Jerónimo, *Peru* 7°52' S, 74°53' W 130
San Joaquín, *Bol.* 13°8' S, 64°51' W 137
San Joaquin, *Calif., U.S.* 36°36' N, 120°12' W 100
San Joaquin Valley, *Calif., U.S.* 35°29' N, 119°46' W 100
San Jon, *N. Mex., U.S.* 35°6' N, 103°20' W 92
San Jorge, *Arg.* 31°54' S, 61°49' W 139
San Jorge, *Nicar.* 11°26' N, 85°48' W 115
San Jorge, Bahía de 31°0' N, 113°17' W 92
San Jorge, Golfo 46°26' S, 68°15' W 134
San Jorge, Golfo 46°19' S, 69°42' W 122
San Jorge, Golfo 45°51' S, 70°25' W 123
San Jorge, Gulf of 46°6' S, 66°41' W 253
San Jorge, river, *Col.* 7°40' N, 75°55' W 115
San José, *Arg.* 27°45' S, 55°46' W 139
San Jose, *Calif., U.S.* 37°19' N, 121°54' W 100
San José, *Col.* 2°40' N, 68°3' W 136
San José, *C.R.* 9°54' N, 84°11' W 115
San José, *Guatemala* 13°56' N, 90°50' W 115

Sault Sainte Marie, *Mich., U.S.* 46°29′ N, 84°22′ W 94
Saūmalkōl, *Kaz.* 53°18′ N, 68°8′ E 184
Saumlaki, *Indonesia* 7°58′ S, 131°10′ E 192
Saundatti, *India* 15°46′ N, 75°6′ E 188
Saunders Coast, *South Pacific Ocean* 76°48′ S, 132°37′ W 248
Saunders Mount, peak, *Antarctica* 76°46′ S, 144°52′ W 248
Saunders, Mount, peak, *Antarctica* 85°40′ S, 163°7′ E 248
Saurimo, *Angola* 9°38′ S, 20°25′ E 218
Sauris, *It.* 46°27′ N, 12°42′ E 167
Sautar, *Angola* 11°6′ S, 18°27′ E 220
Sauterelles, Lac aux, lake, *Can.* 51°58′ N, 65°8′ W 111
Sava, river, *Croatia* 45°46′ N, 15°48′ E 168
Savage, *Mont., U.S.* 47°25′ N, 104°22′ W 90
Savai'i, island, *Samoa* 13°38′ S, 172°38′ W 241
Savalou, *Benin* 7°57′ N, 1°57′ E 222
Savanna, *Ill., U.S.* 42°4′ N, 90°9′ W 102
Savannah, *Ga., U.S.* 32°3′ N, 81°6′ W 96
Savannah, *Mo., U.S.* 39°55′ N, 94°50′ W 94
Savannah, river, *U.S.* 33°27′ N, 82°1′ W 80
Savannakhét, *Laos* 16°32′ N, 104°46′ E 202
Savanna-la-Mar, *Jam.* 18°14′ N, 78°8′ W 115
Savant Lake, *Can.* 50°14′ N, 90°42′ W 110
Savant Lake, *Can.* 50°14′ N, 90°42′ W 94
Savanur, *India* 14°58′ N, 75°20′ E 188
Savar Kundla, *India* 21°21′ N, 71°17′ E 186
Savaştepe, *Turk.* 39°22′ N, 27°38′ E 156
Savé, *Benin* 8°4′ N, 2°27′ E 222
Save, river, *Africa* 21°16′ S, 32°29′ E 207
Save, river, *Fr.* 43°40′ N, 1°10′ E 165
Sāveh, *Iran* 35°3′ N, 50°19′ E 180
Savelugu, *Ghana* 9°37′ N, 0°51′ E 222
Saverdun, *Fr.* 43°13′ N, 1°33′ E 164
Saverne, *Fr.* 48°44′ N, 7°21′ E 163
Savigliano, *It.* 44°37′ N, 7°39′ E 167
Savignano sul Rubicone, *It.* 44°6′ N, 12°24′ E 156
Savignone, *It.* 44°33′ N, 8°59′ E 167
Savinobor, *Russ.* 63°35′ N, 56°27′ E 154
Savio, river, *It.* 44°8′ N, 12°11′ E 167
Săvîrşin, *Rom.* 46°1′ N, 22°14′ E 168
Savissivik 75°59′ N, 64°51′ W 246
Savitaipale, *Fin.* 61°11′ N, 27°40′ E 166
Šavnik, *Europe* 42°56′ N, 19°5′ E 168
Savona, *It.* 44°18′ N, 8°28′ E 167
Savonlinna, *Fin.* 61°51′ N, 28°51′ E 166
Savonranta, *Fin.* 62°9′ N, 29°11′ E 152
Savoy, *Ill., U.S.* 40°3′ N, 88°15′ W 102
Savoy, *Mass., U.S.* 42°33′ N, 73°2′ W 104
Savoy, region, *Fr.* 45°19′ N, 6°12′ E 165
Şavşat, *Turk.* 41°15′ N, 42°20′ E 195
Savu Sea 9°59′ S, 121°35′ E 192
Savudrija, *Croatia* 45°29′ N, 13°30′ E 167
Savukoski, *Fin.* 67°18′ N, 28°6′ E 152
Savur, *Turk.* 37°32′ N, 40°56′ E 195
Saw, *Myanmar* 21°12′ N, 94°5′ E 202
Sawada, *Japan* 38°0′ N, 138°20′ E 201
Sawahlunto, *Indonesia* 0°40′ N, 100°47′ E 196
Sawai Madhopur, *India* 26°0′ N, 76°25′ E 197
Sawankhalok, *Thai.* 17°19′ N, 99°51′ E 202
Sawara, *Japan* 35°52′ N, 140°31′ E 201
Sawārah Tūkā, *Iraq* 37°0′ N, 43°6′ E 195
Sawatch Range, *Colo., U.S.* 39°21′ N, 106°52′ W 90
Sawdā', Jabal as, *Lib.* 29°0′ N, 14°26′ E 216
Sawdā', Qurnat as, peak, *Leb.* 34°18′ N, 36°5′ E 194
Sawe, *Indian Ocean* 1°31′ N, 97°23′ E 196
Sawi, *Thai.* 10°13′ N, 99°6′ E 202
Sāwinnū, ruin(s), *Lib.* 30°59′ N, 20°45′ E 216
Sawkanah, *Lib.* 29°6′ N, 15°45′ E 216
Sawla, *Ghana* 9°16′ N, 2°26′ W 222
Sawn Lake, *Can.* 56°57′ N, 116°29′ W 108
Şawqirah, *Oman* 18°5′ N, 56°29′ E 182
Şawqirah, Ghubbat 18°31′ N, 56°2′ E 182
Sawtooth Mountains, *Minn., U.S.* 47°35′ N, 91°23′ W 94
Sawtooth National Recreation Area, *Idaho, U.S.* 43°42′ N, 121°19′ W 80
Sawtooth Range, *Idaho, U.S.* 44°7′ N, 115°16′ W 90
Sawu, island, *Indonesia* 10°33′ S, 122°2′ E 192
Sawyer, *Mich., U.S.* 41°52′ N, 86°35′ W 102
Sawyer Bay 41°3′ S, 145°0′ E 230
Sax, *Sp.* 38°31′ N, 0°51′ E 164
Saxmundham, *U.K.* 52°12′ N, 1°28′ E 163
Saxnäs, *Nor.* 64°56′ N, 15°17′ E 152
Saxony, adm. division, *Ger.* 51°7′ N, 12°33′ E 152
Saxony-Anhalt, adm. division, *Ger.* 52°38′ N, 10°57′ E 152
Saxtons River, *Vt., U.S.* 43°8′ N, 72°31′ W 104
Say, *Niger* 13°5′ N, 2°18′ E 222
Sayak, *Kaz.* 47°0′ N, 77°24′ E 184
Sayanogorsk, *Russ.* 52°48′ N, 91°19′ E 190
Sayat, *Turkm.* 38°47′ N, 63°53′ E 197
Saybrook, *Ill., U.S.* 40°25′ N, 88°32′ W 102
Şaydnāyā, *Syr.* 33°41′ N, 36°22′ E 194
Sayḩūt, *Yemen* 15°15′ N, 51°15′ E 182
Saylac, *Somalia* 11°16′ N, 43°27′ E 216
Säyneinen, *Fin.* 63°10′ N, 28°24′ E 152
Saynshand (Buyant-Uhaa), *Mongolia* 44°51′ N, 110°9′ E 190
Sayōtesh, *Kaz.* 44°18′ N, 53°33′ E 158
Sayqyn, *Kaz.* 48°48′ N, 46°47′ E 158
Sayram Hu, lake, *China* 44°27′ N, 80°40′ E 184
Sayre, *Okla., U.S.* 35°16′ N, 99°39′ W 92
Sayre, *Pa., U.S.* 41°58′ N, 76°32′ W 94
Sayrob, *Uzb.* 38°2′ N, 67°0′ E 197
Sayula, *Mex.* 19°52′ N, 103°37′ W 114
Sayula, *Mex.* 17°51′ N, 94°58′ W 114
Sayulita, *Mex.* 20°51′ N, 105°28′ W 114
Sayville, *N.Y., U.S.* 40°44′ N, 73°5′ W 104
Sbaa, *Alg.* 28°14′ N, 0°11′ E 214
Sbikha, *Tun.* 35°56′ N, 10°1′ E 156
Scafell Pike, peak, *U.K.* 54°26′ N, 3°15′ W 162
Scalea, *It.* 39°49′ N, 15°47′ E 156
Scammon Bay, *Alas., U.S.* 61°50′ N, 165°35′ W 98
Scandia, *Kans., U.S.* 39°46′ N, 97°47′ W 90
Scandiano, *It.* 44°36′ N, 10°41′ E 167
Scanzano Ionico, *It.* 40°15′ N, 16°42′ E 156
Scapegoat Mountain, peak, *Mont., U.S.* 47°16′ N, 112°55′ W 90
Scappoose, *Oreg., U.S.* 45°44′ N, 122°52′ W 100
Scaraben, peak, *U.K.* 58°12′ N, 3°43′ W 150
Scarborough, *Me., U.S.* 43°34′ N, 70°19′ W 104
Scarborough, *U.K.* 54°16′ N, 0°26′ E 162
Scardona see Skradin, *Croatia* 43°49′ N, 15°54′ E 168
Scargill, *N.Z.* 42°58′ S, 172°57′ E 240
Scauri, *It.* 36°45′ N, 11°59′ E 156
Sceale Bay 33°7′ S, 132°54′ E 230
Sceaux, *Fr.* 48°46′ N, 2°18′ E 163
Šćedro, island, *Croatia* 43°2′ N, 16°29′ E 168
Schagen, *Neth.* 52°47′ N, 4°46′ E 163
Schaghticoke, *N.Y., U.S.* 42°54′ N, 73°36′ W 104
Schefferville, *Can.* 54°51′ N, 67°3′ W 106
Schela, *Rom.* 45°9′ N, 23°18′ E 168
Schell Creek Range, *Nev., U.S.* 39°34′ N, 114°51′ W 90
Schenectady, *N.Y., U.S.* 42°48′ N, 73°57′ W 104
Scherfede, *Ger.* 51°31′ N, 9°2′ E 167
Scherhorn, peak, *Switz.* 46°47′ N, 8°47′ E 167
Schertz, *Tex., U.S.* 29°31′ N, 98°16′ W 92
Schiermonnikoog, island, *Neth.* 53°25′ N, 6°1′ E 163
Schillighörn 53°39′ N, 7°51′ E 163
Schilpario, *It.* 46°1′ N, 10°9′ E 167
Schio, *It.* 45°43′ N, 11°21′ E 167
Schirmeck, *Fr.* 48°28′ N, 7°12′ E 163
Schleiden, *Ger.* 50°31′ N, 6°28′ E 167
Schleswig-Holstein, adm. division, *Ger.* 54°2′ N, 9°4′ E 150
Schlitz, *Ger.* 50°40′ N, 9°33′ E 167
Schlossbach, Cape, *Antarctica* 75°51′ S, 61°41′ W 248
Schlüchtern, *Ger.* 50°20′ N, 9°31′ E 167
Schmallenberg, *Ger.* 51°9′ N, 8°16′ E 167
Schmelz, *Ger.* 49°26′ N, 6°51′ E 163
Schmücke, peak, *Ger.* 51°13′ N, 11°12′ E 152
Schofield, *Wis., U.S.* 44°54′ N, 89°36′ W 110
Schofield Barracks, *Hawai'i, U.S.* 21°29′ N, 158°7′ W 99
Schönecken, *Ger.* 50°9′ N, 6°28′ E 167
Schonungen, *Ger.* 50°3′ N, 10°17′ E 167
Schoolcraft, *Mich., U.S.* 42°6′ N, 85°38′ W 102
Schortens, *Ger.* 53°31′ N, 7°57′ E 163
Schotten, *Ger.* 50°30′ N, 9°7′ E 167
Schouten Islands, islands, *Bismarck Sea* 3°8′ S, 142°32′ E 192
Schreiber, *Can.* 48°48′ N, 87°15′ W 110
Schreiner Peak, *Oreg., U.S.* 44°52′ N, 122°8′ W 90
Schroeder, *Minn., U.S.* 47°32′ N, 90°56′ W 110
Schroon Lake, *N.Y., U.S.* 43°50′ N, 73°47′ W 104
Schubert Inlet 71°7′ S, 72°22′ W 248
Schuler, *Can.* 50°20′ N, 110°5′ W 90
Schull, *Ire.* 51°31′ N, 9°33′ W 150
Schumacher, *Can.* 48°29′ N, 81°17′ W 94
Schüttorf, *Ger.* 52°19′ N, 7°14′ E 163
Schuyler, *Nebr., U.S.* 41°26′ N, 97°4′ W 92
Schuylerville, *N.Y., U.S.* 43°5′ N, 73°36′ W 104
Schwaben, region, *Ger.* 48°8′ N, 7°50′ E 163
Schwäbische Alb, *Ger.* 48°9′ N, 8°23′ E 150
Schwalmstadt, *Ger.* 50°55′ N, 9°12′ E 167
Schwarzwald, region, *Ger.* 48°6′ N, 7°38′ E 163
Schweich, *Ger.* 49°49′ N, 6°45′ E 167
Schweinfurt, *Ger.* 50°2′ N, 10°13′ E 167
Schweizer Reneke, *S. Af.* 27°11′ S, 25°18′ E 227
Schwerin, *Ger.* 53°38′ N, 11°25′ E 152
Schwerte, *Ger.* 51°26′ N, 7°33′ E 167
Schwob Peak, *Antarctica* 75°50′ S, 127°59′ W 248
Scicli, *It.* 36°47′ N, 14°42′ E 156
Scilly, Isles of, islands, *Celtic Sea* 49°48′ N, 6°58′ W 150
Scînteia, *Rom.* 46°55′ N, 27°34′ E 156
Scione, ruin(s), *Gr.* 39°56′ N, 23°26′ E 156
Scioto, river, *Ohio, U.S.* 40°26′ N, 83°16′ W 102
Scipio, *Utah, U.S.* 39°14′ N, 112°6′ W 90
Scituate, *Mass., U.S.* 42°11′ N, 70°44′ W 104
Scobey, *Mont., U.S.* 48°46′ N, 105°26′ W 90
Scooba, *Miss., U.S.* 32°47′ N, 88°30′ W 103
Scoresby Land 71°45′ N, 24°3′ W 246
Scoresby Sund 70°5′ N, 21°35′ W 72
Scoresbysund see Ittoqqortoormiit 70°26′ N, 21°53′ W 246
Scorpion Bight 32°38′ S, 126°15′ E 230
Scorton, *U.K.* 54°24′ N, 1°37′ W 162
Scotch Corner, *U.K.* 54°26′ N, 1°41′ W 162
Scotia, *Calif., U.S.* 40°28′ N, 124°6′ W 92
Scotia, *N.Y., U.S.* 42°49′ N, 73°59′ W 104
Scotia Sea 56°22′ S, 49°38′ W 134
Scotland, *S. Dak., U.S.* 43°6′ N, 97°43′ W 90
Scotland, adm. division, *U.K.* 56°50′ N, 5°37′ W 150
Scotland Neck, *N.C., U.S.* 36°7′ N, 77°26′ W 96
Scotlandville, *La., U.S.* 30°30′ N, 91°12′ W 103
Scotstown, *Can.* 45°31′ N, 71°17′ W 111
Scott, *Can.* 52°21′ N, 108°51′ W 108
Scott, *La., U.S.* 30°13′ N, 92°6′ W 96
Scott Air Force Base, *Ill., U.S.* 38°31′ N, 89°54′ W 102
Scott Bar Mountains, *Calif., U.S.* 41°51′ N, 122°60′ W 90
Scott Base, New Zealand, station, *Antarctica* 77°52′ S, 166°42′ E 248
Scott, Cape, *Can.* 50°35′ N, 128°45′ W 90
Scott City, *Kans., U.S.* 38°29′ N, 100°55′ W 90
Scott Coast, *Antarctica* 76°20′ S, 169°0′ E 248
Scott Island, *South Pacific Ocean* 67°24′ S, 179°50′ E 255
Scott Islands, *North Pacific Ocean* 50°18′ N, 130°51′ W 106
Scott, Mount, peak, *Oreg., U.S.* 42°54′ N, 122°7′ W 90
Scott Mountains, *Antarctica* 67°31′ S, 49°49′ E 248
Scott Mountains, *Calif., U.S.* 41°14′ N, 122°55′ W 90
Scott Nunataks, *Antarctica* 77°13′ S, 156°24′ W 248
Scott Point, *Mich., U.S.* 45°47′ N, 85°60′ W 94
Scottburgh, *S. Af.* 30°17′ S, 30°41′ E 227
Scotts Valley, *Calif., U.S.* 37°3′ N, 122°2′ W 100
Scottsbluff, *Nebr., U.S.* 41°51′ N, 103°39′ W 82
Scottsboro, *Ala., U.S.* 34°39′ N, 86°1′ W 96
Scottsburg, *Ind., U.S.* 38°41′ N, 85°46′ W 102
Scottsville, *Ky., U.S.* 36°44′ N, 86°12′ W 96
Scottville, *Mich., U.S.* 43°57′ N, 86°17′ W 102
Scourie, *U.K.* 58°21′ N, 5°9′ W 150
Scout Mountain, peak, *Idaho, U.S.* 42°40′ N, 112°24′ W 90
Scranton, *Pa., U.S.* 41°24′ N, 75°40′ W 94
Scranton, *S.C., U.S.* 33°54′ N, 79°46′ W 96
Scribner, *Nebr., U.S.* 41°38′ N, 96°41′ W 90
Scudder, *Can.* 41°48′ N, 82°38′ W 102
Scugog, Lake, *Can.* 44°7′ N, 79°16′ W 110
Scullin Monolith, peak, *Antarctica* 67°52′ S, 66°27′ E 248
Scunthorpe, *U.K.* 53°34′ N, 0°40′ E 162
Scuol, *Switz.* 46°48′ N, 10°17′ E 167
Scutari see Shkodër, *Alban.* 42°4′ N, 19°30′ E 168
Sea Gull Lake, lake, *Minn., U.S.* 48°5′ N, 91°4′ W 110
Sea Island, *Ga., U.S.* 31°10′ N, 81°22′ W 96
Sea Lion Islands, *Scotia Sea* 52°42′ S, 58°40′ W 134
Seabrook, *N.H., U.S.* 42°53′ N, 70°53′ W 104
Seabrook, *Tex., U.S.* 29°34′ N, 95°1′ W 103
Seacliff, *N.Z.* 45°41′ S, 170°37′ E 240
Seadrift, *Tex., U.S.* 28°24′ N, 96°43′ W 96
Seaford, *Del., U.S.* 38°38′ N, 75°37′ W 94
Seaford, *U.K.* 50°46′ N, 9°535′ E 162
Seaforth, *Can.* 43°33′ N, 81°24′ W 102
Seagraves, *Tex., U.S.* 32°55′ N, 102°34′ W 92
Seaham, *U.K.* 54°50′ N, 1°21′ W 162
Seal Bay 71°46′ S, 14°44′ W 248
Seal, Cape, *S. Af.* 34°21′ S, 23°27′ E 227
Seal Islands, *Scotia Sea* 60°59′ S, 56°17′ W 134
Seal Nunataks 64°59′ S, 60°8′ W 248
Seal, river, *Can.* 58°50′ N, 96°21′ W 108
Sealy, *Tex., U.S.* 29°45′ N, 96°9′ W 96
Seaman, *Ohio, U.S.* 38°55′ N, 83°34′ W 102
Seaman Range, *Nev., U.S.* 37°57′ N, 115°22′ W 90
Searchlight, *Nev., U.S.* 35°27′ N, 114°56′ W 101
Searcy, *Ark., U.S.* 35°14′ N, 91°47′ W 112
Seascale, *U.K.* 54°24′ N, 3°29′ W 162
Seaside, *Calif., U.S.* 36°36′ N, 121°52′ W 100
Seaside, *Oreg., U.S.* 45°59′ N, 123°54′ W 100
Seaside Park, *N.J., U.S.* 39°54′ N, 74°6′ W 94
Seattle, *Wash., U.S.* 47°35′ N, 122°19′ W 100
Seaview, *Wash., U.S.* 46°18′ N, 124°3′ W 100
Sebago Lake, *Me., U.S.* 43°50′ N, 70°38′ W 104
Sebago Lake, *Me., U.S.* 43°45′ N, 70°32′ W 104
Sebanga, oil field, *Indonesia* 1°16′ N, 101°10′ E 196
Sebastian, *Fla., U.S.* 27°48′ N, 80°29′ W 105
Sebastian, Cape, *Oreg., U.S.* 42°18′ N, 124°56′ W 90
Sebastián Elcano, *Arg.* 30°10′ S, 63°38′ W 139
Sebastián Vizcaíno, Bahía 28°3′ N, 115°1′ W 92
Sebastopol, *Calif., U.S.* 38°24′ N, 122°50′ W 100
Sebastopol, *Miss., U.S.* 32°33′ N, 89°21′ W 103
Sebba, *Burkina Faso* 13°26′ N, 0°30′ E 222
Sébé, river, *Gabon* 0°56′ N, 13°15′ E 218
Seben, *Turk.* 40°24′ N, 31°33′ E 156
Seberi, *Braz.* 27°43′ S, 53°19′ W 139
Seberi, Cerro, peak, *Mex.* 27°46′ N, 110°21′ W 112
Sebeşului, Munţii, *Rom.* 45°34′ N, 23°9′ E 168
Sebeta, Rabt, *Africa* 23°59′ N, 14°47′ W 214
Sebewaing, *Mich., U.S.* 43°43′ N, 83°26′ W 102
Sebezh, *Russ.* 56°17′ N, 28°29′ E 166
Sebina, *Botswana* 20°53′ S, 27°13′ E 227
Sebiş, *Rom.* 46°23′ N, 22°10′ E 168
Sebring, *Fla., U.S.* 27°30′ N, 81°26′ W 105
Sečanj, *Serb. and Mont.* 45°22′ N, 20°47′ E 168
Sechelt, *Can.* 49°28′ N, 123°46′ W 100
Sechura, *Peru* 5°30′ S, 80°51′ W 130
Sechura, Desierto de, *Peru* 6°10′ S, 82°8′ W 130
Seclin, *Fr.* 50°32′ N, 3°1′ E 163
Second Mesa, *Ariz., U.S.* 35°46′ N, 110°30′ W 92
Secret Pass, *Nev., U.S.* 40°50′ N, 115°12′ W 90
Secunderabad, *India* 17°28′ N, 78°28′ E 188
Securé, river, *Bol.* 15°44′ S, 65°44′ W 137
Seda, *Latv.* 57°39′ N, 25°44′ E 166
Seda, *Lith.* 56°9′ N, 22°4′ E 166
Sedalia, *Mo., U.S.* 38°41′ N, 93°14′ W 94
Sedan, *Fr.* 49°42′ N, 4°56′ E 163
Sedano, *Sp.* 42°42′ N, 3°44′ W 164
Sedbergh, *U.K.* 54°19′ N, 2°32′ W 162
Seddon, *N.Z.* 41°43′ S, 174°3′ E 240
Seddon, Kap 75°11′ N, 58°11′ W 106
Seddonville, *N.Z.* 41°35′ S, 171°58′ E 240
Sedé Boqér, *Israel* 30°51′ N, 34°47′ E 194
Sedeh, *Iran* 33°20′ N, 59°16′ E 180
Sederot, *Israel* 31°31′ N, 34°36′ E 194
Sedgemoor 1685, battle, *U.K.* 51°8′ N, 2°56′ W 162
Sédhiou, *Senegal* 12°43′ N, 15°33′ W 222
Sedlare, *Serb. and Mont.* 44°12′ N, 21°16′ E 168
Sedley, *Can.* 50°9′ N, 104°2′ W 90
Sedom, *Israel* 31°4′ N, 35°23′ E 194
Sedro Woolley, *Wash., U.S.* 48°30′ N, 122°15′ W 100
Šeduva, *Lith.* 55°44′ N, 23°44′ E 166
Seeheim, *Namibia* 26°50′ S, 17°46′ E 227
Seeis, *Namibia* 22°28′ S, 17°34′ E 227
Seekonk, *Mass., U.S.* 41°48′ N, 71°21′ W 104
Seeley, *Calif., U.S.* 32°47′ N, 115°42′ W 101
Seelig, Mount, peak, *Antarctica* 82°14′ S, 102°46′ W 248
Seelow, *Ger.* 52°32′ N, 14°22′ E 152
Seelyville, *Ind., U.S.* 39°29′ N, 87°16′ W 102
Seemade, *Somalia* 7°9′ N, 48°31′ E 218
Sefare, *Botswana* 22°60′ S, 27°27′ E 227
Sefophe, *Botswana* 22°16′ S, 27°59′ E 227
Sefrou, *Mor.* 33°51′ N, 4°53′ W 214
Seg Ozero, lake, *Russ.* 63°15′ N, 33°33′ E 154
Segag, *Eth.* 7°32′ N, 42°55′ E 218
Ségala, *Mali* 14°35′ N, 10°58′ W 222
Segamat, *Malaysia* 2°33′ N, 102°49′ E 196
Segbana, *Benin* 10°57′ N, 3°38′ E 222
Segesta, ruin(s), *It.* 37°54′ N, 12°43′ E 156
Segezha, *Russ.* 63°45′ N, 34°16′ E 154
Segorbe, *Sp.* 39°50′ N, 0°30′ E 164
Ségou, *Mali* 13°25′ N, 6°16′ W 222
Segovia, *Sp.* 40°55′ N, 4°8′ W 150
Séguédine, *Niger* 20°17′ N, 12°55′ E 216
Séguéla, *Côte d'Ivoire* 7°53′ N, 6°40′ W 222
Séguéla, *Mali* 14°6′ N, 6°44′ W 222
Seguin, *Tex., U.S.* 29°33′ N, 97°58′ W 92
Segura, Sierra de, *Sp.* 37°58′ N, 2°57′ W 164
Sehithwa, *Botswana* 20°26′ S, 22°39′ E 227
Sehnkwehn, *Liberia* 5°13′ N, 9°22′ W 222
Sehore, *India* 23°11′ N, 77°5′ E 197
Seibal, ruin(s), *Guatemala* 16°28′ N, 90°13′ W 115
Seida, *Nor.* 70°12′ N, 28°6′ E 152
Seiling, *Okla., U.S.* 36°8′ N, 98°56′ W 92
Seine, river, *Fr.* 48°9′ N, 4°21′ E 165
Seine, river, *Fr.* 49°4′ N, 1°35′ E 163
Seini, *Rom.* 47°44′ N, 23°16′ E 168
Seira, *Sp.* 42°28′ N, 0°26′ E 164
Sejenane, *Tun.* 37°4′ N, 9°15′ E 156
Sejny, *Pol.* 54°5′ N, 23°20′ E 166
Seke, *Tanzania* 3°19′ S, 33°30′ E 224
Seke Banza, *Dem. Rep. of the Congo* 5°20′ S, 13°15′ E 218
Seken Seyfūllīn, *Kaz.* 48°50′ N, 72°48′ E 184
Sekenke, *Tanzania* 4°17′ S, 34°9′ E 224
Sekhira, *Tun.* 34°21′ N, 10°4′ E 156
Sekikawa, *Japan* 38°5′ N, 139°33′ E 201
Sekiu, *Wash., U.S.* 48°14′ N, 124°20′ W 100
Sekondi-Takoradi, *Ghana* 4°58′ N, 1°45′ W 222
Sekseūil, *Kaz.* 47°4′ N, 61°9′ E 184
Sekulići, *Europe* 42°33′ N, 19°9′ E 168
Sela Dingay, *Eth.* 9°55′ N, 39°37′ E 224
Selama, *Malaysia* 5°12′ N, 100°43′ E 196
Selaru, island, *Indonesia* 8°39′ S, 130°27′ E 192
Selatpampang, *Indonesia* 0°13′ N, 109°8′ E 196
Selawik, *Alas., U.S.* 66°28′ N, 159°60′ W 98
Selayar, island, *Indonesia* 6°45′ S, 119°37′ E 192
Selby, *S. Dak., U.S.* 45°30′ N, 100°3′ W 90
Selby, *U.K.* 53°47′ N, 1°4′ W 162
Selce, *Maced.* 42°3′ N, 20°55′ E 168
Selden, *Kans., U.S.* 39°32′ N, 100°34′ W 90
Selden, *N.Y., U.S.* 40°52′ N, 73°3′ W 104
Seldovia, *Alas., U.S.* 59°19′ N, 151°43′ W 98
Selebi Phikwe, *Botswana* 21°59′ S, 27°52′ E 227
Selečka Planina, *Maced.* 41°14′ N, 21°7′ E 156
Selendi, *Turk.* 38°46′ N, 28°51′ E 156
Selenge, adm. division, *Mongolia* 49°12′ N, 105°4′ E 198
Selenge, river, *Mongolia* 48°15′ N, 99°37′ E 172
Selenge, river, *Mongolia* 49°25′ N, 103°10′ E 190
Sélestat, *Fr.* 48°16′ N, 7°27′ E 163
Seleucia see Samandaği, *Turk.* 36°4′ N, 35°57′ E 156
Selevac, *Serb. and Mont.* 44°29′ N, 20°52′ E 168
Seleznevo, *Russ.* 60°45′ N, 28°37′ E 166
Selfridge, *N. Dak., U.S.* 46°2′ N, 100°57′ W 90
Selib, *Russ.* 63°47′ N, 48°28′ E 154
Sélibaby, *Mauritania* 15°9′ N, 12°13′ W 222
Seliger, Ozero, lake, *Russ.* 57°16′ N, 32°32′ E 154
Seligman, *Ariz., U.S.* 35°19′ N, 112°52′ W 92
Selima Oasis, *Sudan* 21°22′ N, 29°21′ E 226
Selinde, *Russ.* 57°16′ N, 132°39′ E 173
Selinus, ruin(s), *It.* 37°34′ N, 12°43′ E 156
Selitrennoye, *Russ.* 47°9′ N, 47°23′ E 158
Seliyarovo, *Russ.* 61°17′ N, 70°16′ E 169
Selizharovo, *Russ.* 56°50′ N, 33°38′ E 154
Selje, *Nor.* 62°3′ N, 5°22′ E 152
Selkirk, *Can.* 50°8′ N, 96°54′ W 90
Selkirk Mountains, *Can.* 51°22′ N, 117°56′ W 108
Selles, *Fr.* 47°16′ N, 1°33′ E 150
Sells, *Ariz., U.S.* 31°54′ N, 111°52′ W 92
Sellye, *Hung.* 45°51′ N, 17°51′ E 168
Selma, *Ala., U.S.* 32°24′ N, 87°1′ W 96
Selma, *Calif., U.S.* 36°34′ N, 119°37′ W 100
Selma, *N.C., U.S.* 35°32′ N, 78°18′ W 96
Selmer, *Tenn., U.S.* 35°9′ N, 88°35′ W 96
Selous Game Reserve, *Tanzania* 9°29′ S, 36°6′ E 224
Selous, Mount, peak, *Can.* 62°56′ N, 132°38′ W 98
Sel'tso, *Russ.* 63°19′ N, 41°23′ E 154
Selty, *Russ.* 57°19′ N, 52°8′ E 169
Seluan, island, *Indonesia* 4°1′ N, 107°25′ E 196
Selva, *Arg.* 29°45′ S, 62°3′ W 139
Selvagens, Ilhas (Salvage Islands), *North Atlantic Ocean* 30°18′ N, 16°15′ W 214
Selwyn Mountains, *Can.* 62°26′ N, 129°39′ W 98
Selwyn Range, *Austral.* 21°1′ S, 139°47′ E 230
Selyatyn, *Ukr.* 47°51′ N, 25°11′ E 156
Semarang, *Indonesia* 7°5′ S, 110°15′ E 192
Sembé, *Congo* 1°38′ N, 14°37′ E 218
Sembo, *Eth.* 7°32′ N, 36°37′ E 224
Şemdinli, *Turk.* 37°18′ N, 44°31′ E 195
Semenov, *Russ.* 56°45′ N, 44°35′ E 154
Semepalatinsk see Semey, *Kaz.* 50°23′ N, 80°14′ E 184
Semeru, peak, *Indonesia* 8°5′ S, 112°44′ E 192
Semey (Semepalatinsk), *Kaz.* 50°23′ N, 80°14′ E 184
Semichi Islands, islands, *Alas., U.S.* 52°28′ N, 175°7′ E 160
Sémien, *Côte d'Ivoire* 7°33′ N, 7°9′ W 222
Semiluki, *Russ.* 51°40′ N, 38°58′ E 158
Seminary, *Miss., U.S.* 31°33′ N, 89°29′ W 103
Seminole, *Okla., U.S.* 35°13′ N, 96°41′ W 96
Seminole, *Tex., U.S.* 32°42′ N, 102°38′ W 92
Sémit, spring, *Mali* 16°43′ N, 0°41′ E 222
Semizovac, *Bosn. and Herzg.* 43°55′ N, 18°17′ E 168
Semmé, *Senegal* 15°11′ N, 12°60′ W 222
Semmens Lake, lake, *Can.* 54°57′ N, 94°50′ W 108
Semmering, pass, *Aust.* 47°37′ N, 15°47′ E 168
Semmes, *Ala., U.S.* 30°46′ N, 88°15′ W 103
Semna West, ruin(s), *Sudan* 21°30′ N, 30°49′ E 182
Semnān, *Iran* 35°36′ N, 53°26′ E 180
Semzha, *Russ.* 66°9′ N, 44°11′ E 154
Sen, river, *Cambodia* 13°50′ N, 104°36′ E 202
Sena, *Bol.* 11°31′ S, 67°11′ W 137
Sena, *Mozambique* 17°27′ S, 34°59′ E 224
Sena, *Sp.* 41°42′ N, 3°177′ W 164
Sena Madureira, *Braz.* 9°8′ S, 68°41′ W 137
Senador José Porfírio, *Braz.* 2°39′ S, 51°56′ W 130
Senaja, *Malaysia* 6°50′ N, 117°3′ E 203
Senanga, *Zambia* 16°8′ S, 23°16′ E 220
Senatobia, *Miss., U.S.* 34°37′ N, 89°58′ W 96
Sendai, *Japan* 31°47′ N, 130°19′ E 201
Sendai, *Japan* 38°16′ N, 140°53′ E 201
Senden, *Ger.* 51°51′ N, 7°29′ E 167
Sendenhorst, *Ger.* 51°50′ N, 7°49′ E 167
Senec, *Slovakia* 48°13′ N, 17°24′ E 152
Seneca, *Ill., U.S.* 41°19′ N, 88°38′ W 102
Seneca, *Kans., U.S.* 39°48′ N, 96°4′ W 90
Seneca, *Oreg., U.S.* 44°8′ N, 118°58′ W 90
Seneca, *Pa., U.S.* 41°23′ N, 79°42′ W 110
Seneca, *S.C., U.S.* 34°40′ N, 82°58′ W 96
Seneca Rocks, site, *W. Va., U.S.* 38°48′ N, 79°31′ W 82
Senecaville Lake, *Ohio, U.S.* 39°52′ N, 81°41′ W 102
Senegal 15°10′ N, 15°27′ W 214
Sénégal, river, *Africa* 16°36′ N, 15°57′ W 206
Seneki, *Ga.* 42°16′ N, 42°4′ E 195
Senetosa, Punta di, *Fr.* 41°29′ N, 7°54′ E 156
Senftenberg, *Ger.* 51°31′ N, 13°59′ E 152
Sengés, *Braz.* 24°7′ S, 49°29′ W 138
Sengiley, *Russ.* 53°54′ N, 48°47′ E 154
Senguerr, river, *Arg.* 45°3′ S, 71°6′ W 134
Sengwa, river, *Zimb.* 18°24′ S, 28°11′ E 224
Senhor do Bonfim, *Braz.* 10°27′ S, 40°11′ W 132
Senigallia, *It.* 43°42′ N, 13°12′ E 167
Senkobo, *Zambia* 17°38′ S, 25°54′ E 224
Senlin Shan, peak, *China* 43°10′ N, 130°35′ E 200
Senlis, *Fr.* 49°12′ N, 2°35′ E 163
Senmonorom, *Cambodia* 12°37′ N, 107°14′ E 202
Sennar, *Sudan* 13°31′ N, 33°34′ E 182
Senneterre, *Can.* 48°24′ N, 77°16′ W 94
Sénoudébou, *Senegal* 14°21′ N, 12°18′ W 222
Senozero, *Russ.* 66°9′ N, 31°44′ E 154
Sens, *Fr.* 48°11′ N, 3°17′ E 163
Sensuntepeque, *El Salv.* 13°52′ N, 88°38′ W 116
Senta, *Serb. and Mont.* 45°55′ N, 20°4′ E 168
Sentein, *Fr.* 42°52′ N, 0°55′ E 164
Sentinel, *Okla., U.S.* 35°7′ N, 99°10′ W 96
Sentinel Peak, *Can.* 54°53′ N, 122°4′ W 108
Senyavin Islands, *North Pacific Ocean* 7°29′ N, 156°35′ E 238
Seocheon, *S. Korea* 36°4′ N, 126°43′ E 200
Seogwipo, *S. Korea* 33°18′ N, 126°35′ E 198
Seokjeong, *S. Korea* 34°53′ N, 127°0′ E 200
Seomjin, river, *S. Korea* 35°11′ N, 127°28′ E 200
Seongnae, *S. Korea* 36°30′ N, 129°26′ E 200
Seoni, *India* 22°5′ N, 79°33′ E 197
Seoni Malwa, *India* 22°27′ N, 77°28′ E 197
Seonsan, *S. Korea* 36°13′ N, 128°19′ E 200
Seosan, *S. Korea* 36°45′ N, 126°26′ E 200
Seoul, *S. Korea* 37°33′ N, 126°54′ E 200
Sepahua, *Peru* 11°7′ S, 73°4′ W 137
Separation Point, *Can.* 53°36′ N, 57°26′ W 111
Sepatini, river, *Braz.* 8°4′ S, 66°6′ W 132
Sept Îles, Les, islands, *English Channel* 48°57′ N, 3°38′ W 150
Sept-Îles, *Can.* 50°11′ N, 66°22′ W 111
Sepupa, *Botswana* 18°48′ S, 22°10′ E 220
Sequim, *Wash., U.S.* 48°3′ N, 123°6′ W 100
Serafimovich, *Russ.* 49°32′ N, 42°41′ E 158
Seraing, *Belg.* 50°35′ N, 5°30′ E 167
Seram, *India* 17°11′ N, 77°18′ E 188
Serang, *Indonesia* 6°13′ S, 106°7′ E 192
Serasan, island, *Indonesia* 2°24′ N, 108°36′ E 196
Seraya, island, *Indonesia* 2°33′ N, 108°11′ E 196
Sērba, *Eth.* 13°12′ N, 40°32′ E 182
Serbia, adm. division, *Serb. and Mont.* 43°45′ N, 20°29′ E 168
Serbia and Montenegro 44°9′ N, 20°31′ E 168
Sercaia, *Rom.* 45°50′ N, 25°9′ E 158
Serdeles see Al 'Uwaynāt, *Lib.* 25°47′ N, 10°33′ E 216
Serdo, *Eth.* 11°54′ N, 41°19′ E 182
Serdobol see Sortavala, *Russ.* 61°42′ N, 30°39′ E 166
Serdobsk, *Russ.* 52°28′ N, 44°13′ E 158
Serebryanka, *Russ.* 57°6′ N, 70°43′ E 169
Serebryansk, *Kaz.* 49°42′ N, 83°21′ E 184
Seredka, *Russ.* 58°8′ N, 28°10′ E 166
Şereflikoçhisar, *Turk.* 38°54′ N, 33°32′ E 156
Seregno, *It.* 45°38′ N, 9°12′ E 167
Seremban, *Malaysia* 2°45′ N, 101°55′ E 196
Serena, *Ill., U.S.* 41°28′ N, 88°44′ W 102
Serengeti National Park, *Tanzania* 2°26′ S, 34°26′ E 224
Serengeti Plain, *Tanzania* 1°51′ S, 35°12′ E 224
Serenje, *Zambia* 13°16′ S, 30°14′ E 224
Serere, *Uganda* 1°29′ N, 33°25′ E 224
Séres, *Gr.* 41°5′ N, 23°31′ E 180
Serg Ozero, lake, *Russ.* 66°45′ N, 36°13′ E 154
Ser'ga, *Russ.* 57°47′ N, 57°1′ E 154
Sergach, *Russ.* 55°31′ N, 45°33′ E 154
Sergeant Robinson, Mount, peak, *Alas., U.S.* 61°33′ N, 148°2′ W 98
Sergeevka, *Kaz.* 53°53′ N, 67°23′ E 184
Sergeyevo, *Russ.* 57°17′ N, 86°6′ E 169
Sergino, *Russ.* 62°37′ N, 65°34′ E 169
Sergipe, adm. division, *Braz.* 9°54′ S, 37°48′ W 132
Sergiyev Posad, *Russ.* 56°19′ N, 38°7′ E 154
Seria, *Brunei* 4°35′ N, 114°25′ E 192
Serian, *Malaysia* 1°3′ N, 110°33′ E 192
Seribudolok, *Indonesia* 2°56′ N, 98°36′ E 196
Sérifontaine, *Fr.* 49°21′ N, 1°46′ E 163
Sérignan, *Fr.* 43°16′ N, 3°15′ E 164
Serik, *Turk.* 36°54′ N, 31°5′ E 156
Seringa, Serra da, *Braz.* 7°31′ S, 50°60′ W 130
Seripe, *Ghana* 8°55′ N, 2°24′ W 222
Serkovo, *Russ.* 66°35′ N, 88°25′ E 169
Sermata, island, *Indonesia* 8°38′ S, 128°59′ E 192
Sermyle, ruin(s), *Gr.* 40°13′ N, 23°27′ E 156
Sernur, *Russ.* 56°57′ N, 49°12′ E 154
Séro, *Mali* 14°49′ N, 11°4′ W 222
Seroglazovka, *Russ.* 46°56′ N, 47°27′ E 158
Serón, *Sp.* 37°19′ N, 2°31′ W 164

Seronera, *Tanzania* 2°28′ S, 34°50′ E 224
Serov, *Russ.* 59°38′ N, 60°37′ E 154
Serowe, *Botswana* 22°23′ S, 26°42′ E 227
Serpent's Mouth 9°50′ N, 62°13′ W 116
Serpukhov, *Russ.* 54°54′ N, 37°22′ E 154
Serra Bonita, *Braz.* 15°16′ S, 46°50′ W 138
Serra da Bocaina National Park, *Braz.* 23°22′ S, 44°57′ W 122
Serra da Canastra National Park, *Braz.* 20°24′ S, 46°53′ W 138
Serra da Capivara National Park, *Braz.* 8°44′ S, 42°32′ W 122
Serra das Araras, *Braz.* 15°34′ S, 45°24′ W 138
Serra Do Divisor National Park, *Braz.* 9°11′ S, 73°16′ W 137
Serra do Navio, *Braz.* 0°57′ N, 52°5′ W 130
Serra Dourada, *Braz.* 12°45′ S, 43°59′ W 138
Serrado Espinhaço, *Braz.* 17°53′ S, 43°58′ W 138
Serrado Roncador, *Braz.* 14°7′ S, 53°7′ W 138
Serranía de la Macarena National Park, *Col.* 2°33′ N, 73°56′ W 136
Serrania de La Neblina National Park, *Venez.* 1°4′ N, 66°23′ W 136
Serrano, *Arg.* 34°29′ S, 63°33′ W 139
Serre, river, *Fr.* 49°41′ N, 3°44′ E 163
Serrezuela, *Arg.* 30°39′ S, 65°23′ W 134
Serrinha, *Braz.* 11°40′ S, 39°3′ W 132
Serro, *Braz.* 18°38′ S, 43°25′ W 138
Sertã, *Port.* 39°47′ N, 8°7′ W 150
Sertânia, *Braz.* 8°5′ S, 37°16′ W 132
Sertanópolis, *Braz.* 23°5′ S, 51°6′ W 138
Serti, *Nig.* 7°30′ N, 11°20′ E 222
Serui, *Indonesia* 1°48′ S, 136°11′ E 192
Serule, *Botswana* 21°58′ S, 27°13′ E 227
Sêrxü, *China* 33°0′ N, 98°5′ E 188
Seryesik-Atyraū Qumy, *Kaz.* 46°3′ N, 75°39′ E 184
Sesa, *Dem. Rep. of the Congo* 7°2′ S, 26°7′ E 224
Sese Islands, *Uganda* 0°34′ N, 32°5′ E 224
Seseganaga Lake, *Can.* 49°54′ N, 91°13′ W 94
Sesfontein, *Namibia* 19°10′ S, 13°36′ E 220
Sesheke, *Zambia* 17°28′ S, 24°17′ E 224
Seskar, Ostrov, island, *Russ.* 60°0′ N, 28°26′ E 166
Seskarö, *Sw.* 65°43′ N, 23°43′ E 152
Sessa, *Angola* 13°57′ S, 20°37′ E 220
Séssao, spring, *Mali* 16°59′ N, 4°5′ E 222
Sestino, *It.* 43°43′ N, 12°16′ E 167
Sesto Calende, *It.* 45°44′ N, 8°37′ E 167
Sesto Fiorentino, *It.* 43°50′ N, 11°12′ E 167
Sesto San Giovanni, *It.* 45°32′ N, 9°14′ E 167
Šeštokai, *Lith.* 54°21′ N, 23°26′ E 166
Sestola, *It.* 44°13′ N, 10°45′ E 167
Sestri Ponente, *It.* 44°25′ N, 8°52′ E 167
Sestroretsk, *Russ.* 60°4′ N, 29°55′ E 166
Šeta, *Lith.* 55°16′ N, 24°13′ E 166
Sete, *Angola* 14°56′ S, 21°44′ E 220
Sète, *Fr.* 43°24′ N, 3°40′ E 164
Sete Lagoas, *Braz.* 19°27′ S, 44°16′ W 138
Sete Quedas, Cachoeira das, fall(s), *Braz.* 9°42′ S, 56°32′ W 130
Setenil, *Sp.* 36°51′ N, 5°11′ W 164
Setesdal, region, *Nor.* 58°58′ N, 7°4′ E 152
Sétif, *Alg.* 36°13′ N, 5°25′ E 150
Setit, river, *Africa* 14°20′ N, 37°5′ E 182
Seto, *Japan* 35°10′ N, 137°6′ E 201
Seto Naikai National Park, *Japan* 34°16′ N, 134°16′ E 201
Settat, *Mor.* 33°2′ N, 7°38′ W 214
Setté Cama, *Gabon* 2°32′ S, 9°46′ E 218
Settle, *U.K.* 54°4′ N, 2°16′ W 162
Setúbal, *Port.* 38°31′ N, 8°54′ W 150
Setúbal, adm. division, *Port.* 38°28′ N, 8°42′ W 150
Seul Choix Point, *Mich., U.S.* 45°39′ N, 86°8′ W 110
Seul, Lac, lake, *Can.* 50°33′ N, 93°10′ W 80
Seulimeum, *Indonesia* 5°21′ N, 95°33′ E 202
Seumanyam, *Indonesia* 3°47′ N, 96°37′ E 196
Sevan, *Arm.* 40°33′ N, 44°56′ E 195
Sevan National Park, *Arm.* 40°21′ N, 45°12′ E 195
Sevana Lich, lake, *Arm.* 40°14′ N, 45°15′ E 195
Sevar, *Bulg.* 43°50′ N, 26°36′ E 156
Sevaruyo, *Bol.* 19°26′ S, 66°53′ W 137
Sevastopol', *Ukr.* 44°34′ N, 33°28′ E 156
Seven Heads, *Ire.* 51°22′ N, 8°41′ W 150
Seven Sisters Peaks, *Can.* 54°56′ N, 128°18′ W 108
Seven Stones, islands, *Celtic Sea* 50°5′ N, 7°11′ W 150
Seven Troughs Range, *Nev., U.S.* 40°36′ N, 118°57′ W 90
Sevenoaks, *U.K.* 51°16′ N, 0°11′ E 162
Severn y ye Uvaly, *Russ.* 59°38′ N, 46°36′ E 169
Severnaya Dvina, river, *Russ.* 62°37′ N, 43°16′ E 154
Severnaya Osetiya-Alaniya, adm. division, *Russ.* 42°59′ N, 43°49′ E 195
Severnaya, river, *Russ.* 63°21′ N, 41°46′ E 154
Severnaya, river, *Russ.* 63°21′ N, 40°44′ E 246
Severnaya Zemlya (North Land), islands, *Russ.* 80°22′ N, 102°0′ E 160
Severnoye, *Russ.* 56°21′ N, 78°15′ E 169
Severnoye Ust'ye, *Russ.* 57°34′ N, 30°16′ E 166
Severnyy, *Russ.* 67°39′ N, 64°18′ E 169
Severnyy Kommunar, *Russ.* 58°21′ N, 54°4′ E 154
Severnyy Mayak, *Russ.* 65°19′ N, 43°39′ E 154
Severnyye Uvaly, *Russ.* 60°56′ N, 51°45′ E 154
Severo Kuril'sk, *Russ.* 50°35′ N, 155°59′ E 160
Severo Yeniseyskiy, *Russ.* 60°23′ N, 93°13′ E 169
Severobaykal'sk, *Russ.* 55°49′ N, 109°7′ E 190
Severodvinsk, *Russ.* 64°34′ N, 39°52′ E 154
Severomuysk, *Russ.* 56°20′ N, 113°25′ E 190
Severoural'sk, *Russ.* 60°10′ N, 59°55′ E 154
Seversk, *Russ.* 56°39′ N, 84°51′ E 169
Sevettijärvi, *Fin.* 69°32′ N, 28°35′ E 152
Sevier Desert, *Utah, U.S.* 39°38′ N, 112°60′ W 90
Sevier, river, *Utah, U.S.* 38°27′ N, 112°24′ W 80
Sevilla, *Col.* 4°14′ N, 75°57′ W 136
Sevilla, *Sp.* 37°22′ N, 5°58′ W 214
Sevilla (Seville), *Sp.* 37°23′ N, 5°60′ W 164
Seville, *Fla., U.S.* 29°18′ N, 81°29′ W 105
Seville see Sevilla, *Sp.* 37°23′ N, 5°60′ W 164
Sevnica, *Slov.* 46°0′ N, 15°18′ E 156
Sevsk, *Russ.* 52°7′ N, 34°30′ E 158
Seward, *Alas., U.S.* 60°2′ N, 149°33′ W 98
Seward, *Nebr., U.S.* 40°53′ N, 97°6′ W 90
Seward Peninsula, *Alas., U.S.* 67°2′ N, 167°43′ W 160
Seward Peninsula, *Alas., U.S.* 65°17′ N, 165°10′ W 98
Sexsmith, *Can.* 55°20′ N, 118°47′ W 108
Sexton Mountain Pass, *Oreg., U.S.* 42°34′ N, 123°25′ W 90
Seyakha, *Russ.* 70°8′ N, 72°28′ E 169
Seychelles 8°7′ S, 51°26′ E 173
Seydi, *Turkm.* 39°25′ N, 62°55′ E 184
Seydişehir, *Turk.* 37°24′ N, 31°51′ E 156
Seyitgazi, *Turk.* 39°27′ N, 30°41′ E 156
Seym, river, *Russ.* 51°24′ N, 36°36′ E 158
Seym, river, *Ukr.* 51°19′ N, 33°0′ E 158
Seymchan, *Russ.* 62°55′ N, 152°12′ E 160
Seymour, *Conn., U.S.* 41°23′ N, 73°5′ W 104
Seymour, *Ind., U.S.* 38°57′ N, 85°54′ W 102
Seymour, *Tex., U.S.* 33°34′ N, 99°16′ W 92
Seymour, *Wis., U.S.* 44°30′ N, 88°20′ W 94
Seymour Island, *Antarctica* 64°25′ S, 56°33′ W 134
Seyne, *Fr.* 44°21′ N, 6°19′ E 167
Sézanne, *Fr.* 48°43′ N, 3°44′ E 163
Sfax, *Tun.* 34°48′ N, 10°46′ E 156
Sferracavallo, Capo, *It.* 39°44′ N, 9°42′ E 156
Sfîntu Gheorghe, *Rom.* 45°52′ N, 25°47′ E 156
Sfizef, *Alg.* 35°13′ N, 0°15′ E 150
Sha, river, *China* 26°5′ N, 117°4′ E 198
Shaanxi, adm. division, *China* 37°13′ N, 107°48′ E 198
Shabasha, *Sudan* 14°7′ N, 32°11′ E 226
Shabla, *Bulg.* 43°33′ N, 28°32′ E 156
Shabla, Nos, *Bulg.* 43°34′ N, 28°38′ E 156
Shabogamo Lake, *Can.* 53°13′ N, 67°3′ W 111
Shabunda, *Dem. Rep. of the Congo* 2°41′ S, 27°19′ E 224
Shaburovo, *Russ.* 59°40′ N, 62°8′ E 154
Shabwah, *Yemen* 15°21′ N, 47°5′ E 182
Shache (Yarkant), *China* 38°27′ N, 77°17′ E 184
Shackleton Base (historic), site, *Weddell Sea* 78°21′ S, 37°47′ W 248
Shackleton Coast, *Antarctica* 82°30′ S, 179°30′ E 248
Shadehill Reservoir, lake, *S. Dak., U.S.* 45°46′ N, 102°37′ W 90
Shadrinsk, *Russ.* 56°5′ N, 63°40′ E 184
Shaduzup, *Myanmar* 25°56′ N, 96°40′ E 188
Shadyside, *Ohio, U.S.* 39°57′ N, 80°46′ W 94
Sha'f, *Syr.* 32°36′ N, 36°50′ E 194
Shafer Peak, *Antarctica* 73°56′ S, 163°9′ E 248
Shafter, *Calif., U.S.* 35°30′ N, 119°18′ W 100
Shaftesbury, *U.K.* 51°0′ N, 2°12′ W 162
Shaftsbury, *Vt., U.S.* 43°0′ N, 73°12′ W 104
Shag Rocks, islands, *Scotia Sea* 54°7′ S, 42°46′ W 134
Shagamu, *Nig.* 7°0′ N, 3°37′ E 222
Shaghan, *Kaz.* 50°34′ N, 79°13′ E 184
Shah Bandar, *Pak.* 24°10′ N, 67°58′ E 186
Shah Juy, *Afghan.* 32°31′ N, 67°28′ E 186
Shah Malan, *Afghan.* 31°11′ N, 64°5′ E 186
Shahabad, *India* 27°38′ N, 79°54′ E 197
Shahabad, *India* 25°16′ N, 77°10′ E 197
Shahbā' (Philippopolis), *Syr.* 32°51′ N, 36°37′ E 194
Shahdadkot, *Pak.* 27°51′ N, 67°55′ E 186
Shahdol, *India* 23°18′ N, 81°22′ E 197
Shahgarh, *India* 27°6′ N, 69°58′ E 186
Shaḩḩāt (Cyrene), *Lib.* 32°50′ N, 21°50′ E 216
Shahimardan, *Uzb.* 39°56′ N, 71°45′ E 197
Shahjahanpur, *India* 27°51′ N, 79°54′ E 197
Shahpur, *Pak.* 28°42′ N, 68°22′ E 186
Shahpura, *India* 23°11′ N, 80°43′ E 197
Shahrak, *Afghan.* 34°11′ N, 64°24′ E 186
Shahr-e Bābak, *Iran* 30°7′ N, 55°9′ E 196
Shahr-e Kord, *Iran* 32°19′ N, 50°51′ E 180
Shahr-e Monjan, *Afghan.* 36°2′ N, 70°58′ E 186
Shahrisabz, *Uzb.* 39°5′ N, 66°51′ E 197
Shahriston, *Taj.* 39°46′ N, 68°52′ E 197
Shahrtuz, *Taj.* 37°14′ N, 68°9′ E 186
Shāhrūd, *Iran* 36°27′ N, 54°59′ E 180
Shaim, *Russ.* 60°15′ N, 64°16′ E 169
Shajapur, *India* 23°24′ N, 76°16′ E 197
Shakawe, *Botswana* 18°25′ S, 21°48′ E 220
Shaker Heights, *Ohio, U.S.* 41°26′ N, 81°34′ W 102
Shakespeare Cliff, *U.K.* 51°6′ N, 1°21′ E 163
Shakhbuz, *Asia* 39°24′ N, 45°34′ E 195
Shakhtakhty, *Asia* 39°19′ N, 45°7′ E 195
Shakhtīnsk, *Kaz.* 49°44′ N, 72°37′ E 184
Shakhty, *Russ.* 47°40′ N, 40°9′ E 156
Shakhun'ya, *Russ.* 57°39′ N, 46°41′ E 154
Shaki, *Nig.* 8°40′ N, 3°23′ E 222
Shâkir, Gezîrat, island, *Egypt* 27°25′ N, 32°57′ E 180
Shalaamboot, *Somalia* 1°38′ N, 44°41′ E 218
Shalakusha, *Russ.* 62°11′ N, 40°18′ E 154
Shalë, *Alban.* 42°18′ N, 19°48′ E 168
Shali, *Russ.* 43°6′ N, 45°52′ E 195
Shaling, *China* 41°19′ N, 123°5′ E 200
Shalkar Yega Kara, Ozero, lake, *Russ.* 50°39′ N, 59°7′ E 158
Shallowater, *Tex., U.S.* 33°41′ N, 101°59′ W 92
Shalqar, *Kaz.* 50°29′ N, 51°49′ E 158
Shalqar, *Kaz.* 47°56′ N, 59°36′ E 160
Shalqar, *Kaz.* 47°50′ N, 59°39′ E 158
Shalqar Köli, lake, *Kaz.* 50°35′ N, 51°20′ E 158
Shalqīya, *Kaz.* 47°15′ N, 70°38′ E 184
Shal'skiy, *Russ.* 61°48′ N, 36°4′ E 154
Shām, Jabal ash, peak, *Oman* 23°10′ N, 57°11′ E 182
Shamattawa, *Can.* 55°59′ N, 91°53′ W 106
Shambe, *Sudan* 7°5′ N, 30°43′ E 224
Shamīl, *Iran* 27°28′ N, 56°53′ E 196
Shamkhor, *Azerb.* 40°49′ N, 46°0′ E 195
Shammar, Jabal, *Saudi Arabia* 27°8′ N, 40°8′ E 180
Shamokin, *Pa., U.S.* 40°47′ N, 76°34′ W 94
Shamrock, *Fla., U.S.* 29°38′ N, 83°11′ W 105
Shamrock, *Tex., U.S.* 35°12′ N, 100°15′ W 92
Shamva, *Zimb.* 17°21′ S, 31°34′ E 224
Shanchengzhen, *China* 42°22′ N, 125°27′ E 200
Shandon, *Calif., U.S.* 35°39′ N, 120°24′ W 100
Shandong, adm. division, *China* 36°25′ N, 116°37′ E 198
Shandur Pass, *Pak.* 36°3′ N, 72°31′ E 186
Shangalowe, *Dem. Rep. of the Congo* 10°50′ S, 26°30′ E 224
Shangaly, *Russ.* 61°8′ N, 43°18′ E 154
Shangani, *Zimb.* 19°48′ S, 29°21′ E 224
Shangcai, *China* 33°17′ N, 114°17′ E 198
Shangcheng, *China* 31°48′ N, 115°23′ E 198
Shangchuan Dao, island, *China* 21°31′ N, 112°51′ E 198
Shangdu, *China* 41°35′ N, 113°33′ E 198
Shanghai, *China* 31°15′ N, 121°27′ E 198
Shanghang, *China* 24°58′ N, 116°21′ E 198
Shanghekou, *China* 40°25′ N, 124°49′ E 200
Shanglin, *China* 23°29′ N, 108°35′ E 198
Shangnan, *China* 33°32′ N, 110°55′ E 198
Shangombo, *Zambia* 16°20′ S, 22°7′ E 220
Shangqiu, *China* 34°27′ N, 115°34′ E 198
Shangrao, *China* 28°27′ N, 117°56′ E 198
Shangsi, *China* 22°12′ N, 107°57′ E 198
Shangxian, *China* 33°55′ N, 109°56′ E 198
Shangyi, *China* 41°5′ N, 113°58′ E 198
Shangyou, *China* 25°50′ N, 114°30′ E 198
Shangyou Shuiku, lake, *China* 40°24′ N, 79°49′ E 184
Shangzhi, *China* 45°12′ N, 127°53′ E 198
Shani, *Nig.* 10°12′ N, 12°5′ E 218
Shanidar Cave, ruin(s), *Iraq* 36°48′ N, 44°8′ E 195
Shaniko, *Oreg., U.S.* 44°59′ N, 120°46′ W 90
Shannock, *R.I., U.S.* 41°26′ N, 71°39′ W 104
Shannon, *Ill., U.S.* 42°8′ N, 89°44′ W 102
Shannon, *Ire.* 52°52′ N, 8°49′ W 143
Shannon, *Miss., U.S.* 34°6′ N, 88°43′ W 96
Shannon, *N.Z.* 40°35′ S, 175°25′ E 240
Shannon Airport, *Ire.* 52°40′ N, 9°8′ W 150
Shannon, island, *Shannon* 75°18′ N, 17°23′ W 246
Shannon, Lake, *Wash., U.S.* 48°35′ N, 121°58′ W 100
Shantarskiye Ostrova, islands, *Russ.* 54°31′ N, 138°48′ E 160
Shantou (Swatow), *China* 23°23′ N, 116°40′ E 198
Shanwa, *Tanzania* 3°8′ S, 33°45′ E 224
Shanxi, adm. division, *China* 38°43′ N, 111°16′ E 198
Shanxian, *China* 34°49′ N, 116°5′ E 198
Shanyang, *China* 33°33′ N, 109°54′ E 198
Shanyin, *China* 39°29′ N, 112°51′ E 198
Shanyincheng, *China* 39°24′ N, 112°56′ E 198
Shaoguan, *China* 24°52′ N, 113°32′ E 198
Shaowu, *China* 27°14′ N, 117°27′ E 198
Shaoxing, *China* 29°59′ N, 120°34′ E 198
Shaoyang, *China* 27°15′ N, 111°29′ E 198
Shap, *U.K.* 54°32′ N, 2°41′ W 162
Shapa, *China* 21°32′ N, 111°28′ E 198
Shapleigh, *Me., U.S.* 43°33′ N, 70°52′ W 104
Shaqlāwah, *Iraq* 36°24′ N, 44°16′ E 195
Shaqqā, *Syr.* 32°53′ N, 36°41′ E 194
Shaqrā', *Saudi Arabia* 25°12′ N, 45°18′ E 182
Shaqrā', *Yemen* 13°24′ N, 45°41′ E 182
Shar, *Kaz.* 49°37′ N, 81°1′ E 184
Shār, Jabal, peak, *Saudi Arabia* 27°36′ N, 35°40′ E 180
Shar Space Launch Center, spaceport, *India* 13°36′ N, 80°5′ E 188
Sharafkhāneh, *Iran* 38°17′ N, 45°26′ E 195
Sharbaqty, *Kaz.* 52°30′ N, 78°11′ E 184
Sharbatāt, *Oman* 17°53′ N, 56°18′ E 182
Shardara, *Kaz.* 41°16′ N, 67°54′ E 197
Sharg'un, *Uzb.* 38°21′ N, 68°0′ E 197
Sharhulsan, *Mongolia* 44°37′ N, 104°1′ E 198
Sharjah, *U.A.E.* 25°21′ N, 55°24′ E 196
Shark Bay 25°46′ S, 113°18′ E 230
Sharkan, *Russ.* 57°15′ N, 53°54′ E 154
Sharkowshchyna, *Belarus* 55°22′ N, 27°24′ E 166
Sharlawuk, *Turkm.* 38°14′ N, 55°42′ E 180
Sharlyk, *Russ.* 52°55′ N, 54°46′ E 154
Sharon, *Conn., U.S.* 41°52′ N, 73°29′ W 104
Sharon, *Mass., U.S.* 42°7′ N, 71°11′ W 104
Sharon, *Pa., U.S.* 41°13′ N, 80°31′ W 94
Sharon, *Vt., U.S.* 43°47′ N, 72°28′ W 104
Sharon, *Wis., U.S.* 42°30′ N, 88°44′ W 102
Sharon Springs, *Kans., U.S.* 38°53′ N, 101°46′ W 90
Sharp Top, peak, *Oreg., U.S.* 42°50′ N, 120°34′ W 90
Sharpe, Lake, *S. Dak., U.S.* 43°9′ N, 99°14′ W 80
Sharuhen, ruin(s), *Israel* 31°15′ N, 34°26′ E 194
Shar'ya, *Russ.* 58°20′ N, 45°34′ E 154
Sharypovo, *Russ.* 55°34′ N, 89°15′ E 169
Shasha, *Eth.* 6°28′ N, 35°55′ E 224
Shashe, river, *Africa* 21°47′ S, 28°27′ E 227
Shashemenē, *Eth.* 7°12′ N, 38°32′ E 224
Shashi, *China* 30°22′ N, 112°18′ E 198
Shass Mountain, peak, *Can.* 54°25′ N, 124°58′ W 108
Shasta, Mount, peak, *Calif., U.S.* 41°24′ N, 122°18′ W 90
Shatsk, *Belarus* 53°25′ N, 27°42′ E 152
Shatsk, *Russ.* 54°0′ N, 41°39′ E 154
Shats'k, *Ukr.* 51°27′ N, 23°54′ E 152
Shatskiy Rise, *North Pacific Ocean* 34°16′ N, 160°36′ E 252
Shattuck, *Okla., U.S.* 36°15′ N, 99°53′ W 92
Shatura, *Russ.* 55°33′ N, 39°31′ E 154
Shaumyan, *Azerb.* 40°26′ N, 46°33′ E 195
Shaumyani, *Ga.* 41°20′ N, 44°44′ E 195
Shaunavon, *Can.* 49°37′ N, 108°26′ W 90
Shaver Lake, *Calif., U.S.* 37°6′ N, 119°20′ W 100
Shaverki, *Russ.* 63°14′ N, 31°27′ E 154
Shaviklde, peak, *Ga.* 42°14′ N, 45°35′ E 195
Shaw, *Miss., U.S.* 33°35′ N, 90°47′ W 96
Shaw Air Force Base, *S.C., U.S.* 33°57′ N, 80°33′ W 96
Shaw Island, *Austral.* 20°22′ S, 149°7′ E 230
Shawan, *China* 44°20′ N, 85°39′ E 184
Shawano, *Wis., U.S.* 44°46′ N, 88°37′ W 94
Shawinigan, *Can.* 46°33′ N, 72°46′ W 94
Shawinigan-Sud, *Can.* 46°30′ N, 72°45′ W 94
Shawnee, *Ohio, U.S.* 39°35′ N, 82°13′ W 102
Shawnee, *Wyo., U.S.* 42°44′ N, 105°1′ W 90
Shawnigan Lake, *Can.* 48°38′ N, 123°37′ W 100
Shaxian, *China* 26°24′ N, 117°44′ E 198
Shaxrixon, *Uzb.* 40°41′ N, 72°4′ E 197
Shaybah, oil field, *Saudi Arabia* 22°23′ N, 53°55′ E 182
Shaybārā, island, *Saudi Arabia* 25°25′ N, 36°3′ E 182
Shâyib el Banât, Gebel, peak, *Egypt* 26°58′ N, 33°22′ E 180
Shaykh, Jabal ash (Hermon, Mount), peak, *Leb.* 33°24′ N, 35°49′ E 194
Shaykh Miskīn, *Syr.* 32°50′ N, 36°10′ E 194
Shaykh 'Uthmān, *Yemen* 12°52′ N, 44°59′ E 182
Shayman, *Taj.* 37°29′ N, 74°51′ E 184
Shayrāt, *Syr.* 34°29′ N, 36°57′ E 194
Shaytanovka, *Russ.* 62°2′ N, 58°6′ E 154
Shchekino, *Russ.* 53°59′ N, 37°33′ E 154
Shchel'yabozh, *Russ.* 66°17′ N, 56°23′ E 154
Shchel'yayur, *Russ.* 65°18′ N, 53°26′ E 154
Shchigry, *Russ.* 51°49′ N, 36°57′ E 158
Shchuch'ye, *Russ.* 67°6′ N, 68°36′ E 169
Shchūīnsk, *Kaz.* 52°52′ N, 70°14′ E 184
Shchurovo, *Russ.* 55°1′ N, 38°49′ E 154
Shchurovychi, *Ukr.* 50°16′ N, 25°0′ E 152
Shchyrets', *Ukr.* 49°38′ N, 23°50′ E 152
Shchytkavichy, *Belarus* 53°13′ N, 27°58′ E 154
Shebar, Kowtal-e, pass, *Afghan.* 34°57′ N, 68°9′ E 186
Shebekino, *Russ.* 50°24′ N, 36°56′ E 158
Shebele, river, *Eth.* 5°47′ N, 42°0′ E 207
Sheberghan, *Afghan.* 36°40′ N, 65°46′ E 186
Sheboya, *Peru* 9°59′ S, 74°8′ W 137
Sheboygan, *Wis., U.S.* 43°45′ N, 87°44′ W 102
Shediac, *Can.* 46°12′ N, 64°32′ W 111
Shedin Peak, *Can.* 55°56′ N, 127°36′ W 108
Shedok, *Russ.* 44°12′ N, 40°44′ E 158
Sheenjek, river, *Alas., U.S.* 66°50′ N, 144°27′ W 98
Sheep Hole Mountains, *Calif., U.S.* 34°21′ N, 115°45′ W 101
Sheep Mountain, peak, *Colo., U.S.* 39°54′ N, 107°13′ W 90
Sheep Mountain, peak, *Mont., U.S.* 45°4′ N, 110°46′ W 90
Sheep Peak, *Nev., U.S.* 36°34′ N, 115°18′ W 101
Sheep Range, *Nev., U.S.* 36°44′ N, 115°13′ W 101
Sheepeater Mountain, peak, *Idaho, U.S.* 45°22′ N, 115°25′ W 90
Sheep's Head, *Ire.* 51°22′ N, 10°11′ W 150
Sheerness, *U.K.* 51°25′ N, 0°45′ E 162
Sheet Harbour, *Can.* 44°56′ N, 62°32′ W 111
Sheffield, *Ala., U.S.* 34°45′ N, 87°41′ W 96
Sheffield, *Ill., U.S.* 41°21′ N, 89°44′ W 102
Sheffield, *Mass., U.S.* 42°6′ N, 73°22′ W 104
Sheffield, *Tex., U.S.* 30°40′ N, 101°49′ W 92
Sheffield, *U.K.* 53°22′ N, 1°28′ W 162
Sheguiandah, *Can.* 45°54′ N, 81°55′ W 94
Sheikh Idris, *Sudan* 11°45′ N, 33°28′ E 182
Sheksna, *Russ.* 59°11′ N, 38°29′ E 154
Shelagskiy, Mys, *Russ.* 69°48′ N, 174°42′ E 160
Shelburn, *Ind., U.S.* 39°10′ N, 87°24′ W 102
Shelburne, *Can.* 43°44′ N, 65°20′ W 111
Shelburne, *Vt., U.S.* 44°22′ N, 73°15′ W 104
Shelburne Falls, *Vt., U.S.* 44°21′ N, 73°13′ W 104
Shelby, *Ind., U.S.* 41°11′ N, 87°21′ W 102
Shelby, *Mich., U.S.* 43°36′ N, 86°21′ W 102
Shelby, *Mont., U.S.* 48°28′ N, 111°51′ W 90
Shelby, *Ohio, U.S.* 40°51′ N, 82°39′ W 102
Shelbyville, *Ill., U.S.* 39°23′ N, 88°48′ W 102
Shelbyville, *Ind., U.S.* 39°30′ N, 85°46′ W 102
Shelbyville, *Tex., U.S.* 31°44′ N, 94°5′ W 103
Sheldon, *Ill., U.S.* 40°45′ N, 87°34′ W 102
Sheldon, *Iowa, U.S.* 43°10′ N, 95°51′ W 94
Sheldrake, *Can.* 50°16′ N, 64°54′ W 111
Shelikhova, Zaliv 61°11′ N, 158°34′ E 160
Shelikof Strait 58°3′ N, 154°5′ W 98
Shell Beach, *Guyana* 8°8′ N, 59°42′ W 116
Shell Lake, *Can.* 53°17′ N, 107°1′ W 108
Shell Lake, *Wis., U.S.* 45°44′ N, 91°57′ W 94
Shell Mountain, peak, *Calif., U.S.* 40°5′ N, 123°10′ W 90
Shellbrook, *Can.* 53°13′ N, 106°24′ W 108
Shellem, *Nig.* 9°57′ N, 12°2′ E 218
Shellman, *Ga., U.S.* 31°45′ N, 84°37′ W 96
Shellrock Peak, *Idaho, U.S.* 44°56′ N, 115°1′ W 90
Shelokhovskaya, *Russ.* 61°54′ N, 39°3′ E 154
Shelter Island, *N.Y., U.S.* 41°3′ N, 72°21′ W 104
Shelton, *Conn., U.S.* 41°18′ N, 73°6′ W 104
Shelton, *Wash., U.S.* 47°11′ N, 123°7′ W 100
Sheltozero, *Russ.* 61°20′ N, 35°25′ E 154
Shemakha, *Azerb.* 40°37′ N, 48°37′ E 195
Shemgang, *Bhutan* 27°7′ N, 90°45′ E 197
Shemonaīkha, *Kaz.* 50°38′ N, 81°55′ E 184
Shëmri, *Alban.* 42°6′ N, 20°13′ E 168
Shenandoah, *Pa., U.S.* 40°49′ N, 76°13′ W 94
Shenandoah Mountain, *Va., U.S.* 38°29′ N, 79°32′ W 94
Shenandoah National Park, *Va., U.S.* 37°29′ N, 79°36′ W 80
Shenchi, *China* 39°4′ N, 112°10′ E 198
Shendam, *Nig.* 8°53′ N, 9°29′ E 222
Shendi, *Sudan* 16°39′ N, 33°24′ E 182
Shenge, *Sierra Leone* 7°54′ N, 12°57′ W 222
Shëngjin, *Alban.* 41°49′ N, 19°34′ E 168
Shengli Daban, pass, *China* 43°6′ N, 86°48′ E 184
Shengxian, *China* 29°39′ N, 120°44′ E 198
Shenkursk, *Russ.* 62°4′ N, 42°58′ E 154
Shenmu, *China* 38°51′ N, 110°31′ E 198
Shennongjia, *China* 31°44′ N, 110°45′ E 198
Shenqiu, *China* 33°27′ N, 115°6′ E 198
Shenton, Mount, peak, *Austral.* 28°1′ S, 123°11′ E 230
Shenyang, *China* 41°49′ N, 123°28′ E 200
Shenzhen, *China* 22°34′ N, 114°7′ E 198
Sheopur, *India* 25°41′ N, 76°43′ E 197
Shepard Island, *Antarctica* 73°49′ S, 134°36′ W 248
Shepetivka, *Ukr.* 50°10′ N, 27°4′ E 152
Shepherd, *Mich., U.S.* 43°30′ N, 84°42′ W 102
Shepherd, *Tex., U.S.* 30°29′ N, 94°59′ W 103
Shepparton, *Austral.* 36°23′ S, 145°27′ E 231
Sherada, *Eth.* 7°17′ N, 36°29′ E 224
Sherborne, *U.K.* 50°56′ N, 2°31′ W 162
Sherbro Island, *Sierra Leone* 7°8′ N, 12°52′ W 222
Sherbrooke, *Can.* 45°24′ N, 71°56′ W 94
Sherburn, *Minn., U.S.* 43°38′ N, 94°44′ W 90
Sherda, spring, *Chad* 20°10′ N, 16°43′ E 216
Shereiq, *Sudan* 18°44′ N, 33°36′ E 182
Sherghati, *India* 24°33′ N, 84°49′ E 197
Shergui Island, *Tun.* 34°39′ N, 11°21′ E 216
Sheridan, *Ill., U.S.* 41°31′ N, 88°41′ W 102
Sheridan, *Ind., U.S.* 40°7′ N, 86°13′ W 102
Sheridan, *Mich., U.S.* 43°12′ N, 85°5′ W 102
Sheridan, *Wyo., U.S.* 44°47′ N, 106°56′ W 90
Sheridan, Cape, *Can.* 81°51′ N, 73°43′ W 246
Sheringham, *U.K.* 52°56′ N, 1°12′ E 162
Sherkaly, *Russ.* 62°48′ N, 65°41′ E 169
Sherman, *Me., U.S.* 45°51′ N, 68°25′ W 94
Sherman, *Tex., U.S.* 33°37′ N, 96°36′ W 96
Sherman Island, island, *Antarctica* 72°20′ S, 100°58′ W 248
Sherman Mountain, peak, *Nev., U.S.* 40°6′ N, 115°40′ W 90
Sherman Peak, *Calif., U.S.* 36°0′ N, 118°26′ W 101
Sherman Peak, *Idaho, U.S.* 42°28′ N, 111°38′ W 90
Sherman Peak, *Idaho, U.S.* 44°31′ N, 114°44′ W 90
Sherobod, *Uzb.* 37°39′ N, 67°1′ E 197
Sherridon, *Can.* 55°6′ N, 101°6′ W 108
Sherwood, *N. Dak., U.S.* 48°57′ N, 101°40′ W 108
Sherwood Forest, *U.K.* 53°14′ N, 1°13′ W 162
Sherwood Lake, *Can.* 60°48′ N, 104°14′ W 108
Sherwood Peak, *Calif., U.S.* 39°30′ N, 123°36′ W 90
Sheshea, river, *Peru* 9°26′ S, 73°51′ W 137
Sheslay, river, *Can.* 58°27′ N, 132°15′ W 108
Shestakovo, *Russ.* 58°55′ N, 50°9′ E 154
Shethanei Lake, *Can.* 58°47′ N, 98°24′ W 108
Shetland Islands, *North Atlantic Ocean* 61°2′ N, 3°52′ W 72
Shetlands Islands, *U.K.* 60°53′ N, 3°18′ W 142
Shetpe, *Kaz.* 44°9′ N, 52°6′ E 158
Shetrunja, peak, *India* 21°26′ N, 71°41′ E 186
Shewa Gīmīra, *Eth.* 6°59′ N, 35°49′ E 224
Shexian, *China* 29°52′ N, 118°26′ E 198
Sheyang, *China* 33°45′ N, 120°15′ E 198
Sheyenne, *N. Dak., U.S.* 47°48′ N, 99°8′ W 90
Sheyenne, river, *N. Dak., U.S.* 47°40′ N, 98°56′ W 90
Sheyenne, river, *N. Dak., U.S.* 46°26′ N, 97°38′ W 90
Sheykhabad, *Afghan.* 34°6′ N, 68°45′ E 186
Shhīm, *Leb.* 33°38′ N, 35°29′ E 194
Shibām, *Yemen* 15°54′ N, 48°36′ E 182
Shibata, *Japan* 37°57′ N, 139°20′ E 201
Shibîn el Kôm, *Egypt* 30°34′ N, 30°57′ E 180
Shibing, *China* 27°0′ N, 108°4′ E 198
Shibukawa, *Japan* 36°29′ N, 138°59′ E 201
Shibushi, *Japan* 31°27′ N, 131°5′ E 201
Shicheng, *China* 26°21′ N, 116°16′ E 198
Shidao, *China* 36°55′ N, 122°25′ E 198
Shiderti, *Kaz.* 51°40′ N, 74°27′ E 184
Shidler, *Okla., U.S.* 36°45′ N, 96°40′ W 92
Shiega, *Ghana* 10°42′ N, 0°44′ E 222
Shīeli, *Kaz.* 44°9′ N, 66°44′ E 184
Shi'erdaogou, *China* 41°30′ N, 127°35′ E 200
Shifnal, *U.K.* 52°39′ N, 2°22′ W 162
Shiga, *Japan* 37°1′ N, 136°46′ E 201
Shiga, adm. division, *Japan* 35°12′ N, 135°52′ E 201
Shiguaigou, *China* 40°42′ N, 110°17′ E 198
Shiḩan, *Yemen* 17°41′ N, 52°27′ E 182
Shihezi, *China* 44°17′ N, 86°1′ E 184
Shiikh, *Somalia* 9°55′ N, 45°12′ E 216
Shijiazhuang, *China* 38°5′ N, 114°30′ E 198
Shikag Lake, lake, *Can.* 49°41′ N, 91°15′ W 94
Shikarpur, *Pak.* 27°53′ N, 68°42′ E 186
Shikoku, island, *Japan* 32°22′ N, 133°0′ E 190
Shilabo, *Eth.* 6°5′ N, 44°45′ E 218
Shildon, *U.K.* 54°38′ N, 1°40′ W 162
Shīli, *Kaz.* 50°34′ N, 62°34′ E 184
Shiliguri, *India* 26°43′ N, 88°28′ E 190
Shilik, *Kaz.* 43°34′ N, 78°12′ E 184
Shiliu see Changjiang, *China* 19°13′ N, 109°2′ E 198
Shiliyn Bogd Uul, peak, *Mongolia* 45°26′ N, 114°24′ E 198
Shilka, *Russ.* 51°54′ N, 116°0′ E 238
Shilka, river, *Russ.* 52°45′ N, 119°25′ E 190
Shilla, peak, *Nepal* 32°22′ N, 78°4′ E 188
Shillong, *India* 25°32′ N, 91°52′ E 197
Shiloh, ruin(s), *West Bank* 32°2′ N, 35°15′ E 194
Shilou, *China* 37°2′ N, 110°47′ E 198
Shilovo, *Russ.* 54°17′ N, 40°50′ E 154
Shimabara, *Japan* 32°46′ N, 130°20′ E 201
Shimada, *Japan* 34°50′ N, 138°11′ E 201
Shimane, adm. division, *Japan* 34°32′ N, 131°43′ E 200
Shimanovsk, *Russ.* 52°4′ N, 127°46′ E 190
Shimen, *China* 29°36′ N, 111°24′ E 198
Shimizu, *Japan* 35°0′ N, 138°28′ E 201
Shimminato, *Japan* 36°46′ N, 137°5′ E 201
Shimoda, *Japan* 32°57′ N, 132°58′ E 201
Shimoda, *Japan* 34°41′ N, 138°58′ E 201
Shimoga, *India* 13°55′ N, 75°33′ E 188
Shimokoshiki, *Japan* 31°38′ N, 129°43′ E 201
Shimoni, *Kenya* 4°35′ S, 39°22′ E 224
Shimonoseki, *Japan* 33°58′ N, 130°56′ E 200
Shimotsu, *Japan* 34°7′ N, 135°8′ E 201
Shimozero, *Russ.* 60°29′ N, 35°37′ E 154
Shimsk, *Russ.* 58°13′ N, 30°44′ E 152
Shīn, *Syr.* 34°46′ N, 36°26′ E 194
Shināş, *Oman* 24°45′ N, 56°25′ E 196
Shindand (Sabzawar), *Afghan.* 33°17′ N, 62°11′ E 186
Shiner, *Tex., U.S.* 29°25′ N, 97°11′ W 96

Shingū, *Japan* 33°41′ N, 135°58′ E **201**
Shinjō, *Japan* 38°46′ N, 140°18′ E **201**
Shinkafi, *Nig.* 13°3′ N, 6°30′ E **222**
Shinkay, *Afghan.* 31°54′ N, 67°27′ E **186**
Shinkolobwe, *Dem. Rep. of the Congo* 11°3′ S, 26°36′ E **224**
Shinnston, *W. Va., U.S.* 39°23′ N, 80°18′ W **94**
Shinonoi, *Japan* 36°35′ N, 138°9′ E **201**
Shinshār, *Syr.* 34°36′ N, 36°43′ E **194**
Shinyanga, *Tanzania* 3°42′ S, 33°26′ E **224**
Shinyanga, adm. division, *Tanzania* 3°36′ S, 31°46′ E **224**
Shiogama, *Japan* 38°19′ N, 141°0′ E **201**
Shiono Misaki, *Japan* 33°17′ N, 135°45′ E **201**
Shionomachi, *Japan* 38°19′ N, 139°33′ E **201**
Ship Island, *Miss., U.S.* 30°9′ N, 88°55′ W **103**
Shiping, *China* 23°41′ N, 102°26′ E **202**
Shipitsino, *Russ.* 61°17′ N, 46°32′ E **154**
Shipki La, pass, *China* 31°51′ N, 78°43′ E **188**
Shipley, *U.K.* 53°49′ N, 1°47′ W **162**
Shippagan, *Can.* 47°44′ N, 64°44′ W **94**
Shiprock, *N. Mex., U.S.* 36°46′ N, 108°42′ W **82**
Shipu, *China* 29°12′ N, 121°52′ E **198**
Shipunovo, *Russ.* 52°15′ N, 82°24′ E **184**
Shiqian, *China* 27°30′ N, 108°14′ E **198**
Shiqiao, *China* 31°21′ N, 107°4′ E **198**
Shiqijie, *China* 42°56′ N, 128°29′ E **200**
Shiquan, *China* 33°4′ N, 108°15′ E **198**
Shiquanhe, *China* 32°29′ N, 79°48′ E **188**
Shir Khan, *Afghan.* 37°9′ N, 68°40′ E **186**
Shīr Kūh, peak, *Iran* 31°35′ N, 54°0′ E **180**
Shirakawa, *Japan* 37°6′ N, 140°12′ E **201**
Shirase Coast, *Antarctica* 79°5′ S, 139°50′ W **248**
Shirati, *Tanzania* 1°11′ S, 34°0′ E **224**
Shīrāz, *Iran* 29°40′ N, 52°29′ E **196**
Shirbīn, *Egypt* 31°12′ N, 31°30′ E **180**
Shire, river, *Malawi* 15°60′ S, 34°49′ E **224**
Shireet, *Mongolia* 45°42′ N, 112°21′ E **198**
Shiren, *China* 41°57′ N, 126°38′ E **200**
Shiringushi, *Russ.* 53°47′ N, 42°44′ E **154**
Shirley, *Ind., U.S.* 39°52′ N, 85°34′ W **102**
Shirley, *N.Y., U.S.* 40°48′ N, 72°53′ W **104**
Shirley, Mount, peak, *Antarctica* 75°30′ S, 141°18′ W **248**
Shirley Mountains, *Wyo., U.S.* 42°8′ N, 106°39′ W **90**
Shiroishi, *Japan* 38°0′ N, 140°37′ E **201**
Shirone, *Japan* 37°45′ N, 139°0′ E **201**
Shirotori, *Japan* 35°52′ N, 136°53′ E **201**
Shīrvān, *Iran* 37°27′ N, 57°56′ E **180**
Shiryayevo, *Russ.* 59°58′ N, 46°17′ E **154**
Shishaldin Volcano, peak, *Alas., U.S.* 54°39′ N, 164°14′ W **98**
Shishmaref, *Alas., U.S.* 66°12′ N, 166°3′ W **98**
Shishou, *China* 29°39′ N, 112°24′ E **198**
Shitai, *China* 30°12′ N, 117°26′ E **198**
Shiv, *India* 26°11′ N, 71°17′ E **186**
Shivpuri, *India* 25°26′ N, 77°39′ E **197**
Shiwa Ngandu, *Zambia* 11°10′ S, 31°44′ E **224**
Shixian, *China* 43°5′ N, 129°47′ E **200**
Shiyan, *China* 32°39′ N, 110°48′ E **198**
Shizhu, *China* 29°59′ N, 108°9′ E **198**
Shizui, *China* 43°3′ N, 126°9′ E **200**
Shizuishan, *China* 39°19′ N, 106°44′ E **198**
Shizuishan (Dawukou), *China* 39°4′ N, 106°25′ E **198**
Shizuoka, *Japan* 34°57′ N, 138°23′ E **201**
Shizuoka, adm. division, *Japan* 35°4′ N, 137°51′ E **201**
Shklow, *Belarus* 54°14′ N, 30°19′ E **154**
Shkodër (Scutari), *Alban.* 42°4′ N, 19°30′ E **168**
Shkunovka, *Russ.* 50°45′ N, 55°23′ E **158**
Shmoylovo, *Russ.* 57°35′ N, 28°52′ E **166**
Shoal Lake, *Can.* 50°27′ N, 100°36′ W **90**
Shoals, *Ind., U.S.* 38°39′ N, 86°47′ W **102**
Shoals, Isles of, islands, *Gulf of Maine* 42°56′ N, 70°34′ W **104**
Shoalwater, Cape, *Wash., U.S.* 46°38′ N, 124°24′ W **100**
Shōbara, *Japan* 34°50′ N, 133°2′ E **201**
Shocha, *Russ.* 63°9′ N, 46°50′ E **154**
Shoe Cove Point, *Can.* 48°56′ N, 53°37′ W **111**
Shoeburyness, *U.K.* 51°31′ N, 0°47′ E **162**
Shokal'skogo, Proliv 78°34′ N, 90°29′ E **160**
Sholapur, *India* 17°40′ N, 75°52′ E **188**
Shollar, *Azerb.* 41°37′ N, 48°39′ E **195**
Shombozero, *Russ.* 65°18′ N, 32°18′ E **152**
Shomvukva, *Russ.* 63°41′ N, 51°50′ E **154**
Shonga, *Nig.* 9°5′ N, 5°7′ E **222**
Shonzhy, *Kaz.* 43°31′ N, 79°28′ E **184**
Shoqpar, *Kaz.* 43°49′ N, 74°21′ E **184**
Sho'rchi, *Uzb.* 37°42′ N, 67°31′ E **197**
Shoreham, *Vt., U.S.* 43°53′ N, 73°19′ W **104**
Shoreham by Sea, *U.K.* 50°50′ N, 0°17′ E **162**
Shorewood, *Wis., U.S.* 43°4′ N, 87°53′ W **102**
Shorobe, *Botswana* 19°46′ S, 23°42′ E **224**
Shortland, island, *Solomon Islands* 7°5′ S, 155°40′ E **242**
Shortland Islands, *Solomon Sea* 7°0′ S, 155°49′ E **242**
Shoshone, *Calif., U.S.* 35°58′ N, 116°17′ W **101**
Shoshone Mountains, *Nev., U.S.* 38°54′ N, 117°37′ W **90**
Shoshone Range, *Nev., U.S.* 40°34′ N, 116°58′ W **90**
Shoshong, *Botswana* 23°1′ S, 26°27′ E **227**
Shoshoni, *Wyo., U.S.* 43°14′ N, 108°7′ W **90**
Shostka, *Ukr.* 51°49′ N, 33°33′ E **158**
Shotor Khun Kowtal, pass, *Afghan.* 34°25′ N, 64°54′ E **186**
Shoval, *Israel* 31°24′ N, 34°43′ E **194**
Showak, *Sudan* 14°22′ N, 35°46′ E **182**
Shoyna, *Russ.* 67°47′ N, 44°12′ E **169**
Shpola, *Ukr.* 49°1′ N, 31°32′ E **158**
Shreve, *Ohio, U.S.* 40°40′ N, 82°2′ W **102**
Shreveport, *La., U.S.* 32°29′ N, 93°46′ W **103**
Shrewsbury, *U.K.* 52°42′ N, 2°45′ W **162**
Shri Mohangarh, *India* 27°15′ N, 71°14′ E **186**
Shrub Oak, *N.Y., U.S.* 41°18′ N, 73°51′ W **104**
Shū, *Kaz.* 43°35′ N, 73°45′ E **190**
Shū, river, *Kaz.* 44°51′ N, 70°15′ E **190**
Shuangcheng, *China* 45°22′ N, 126°19′ E **198**
Shuangchengzi, *China* 40°18′ N, 99°45′ E **190**
Shuangjiang, *China* 23°29′ N, 99°48′ E **202**
Shuangliao, *China* 43°31′ N, 123°27′ E **198**
Shuangyang, *China* 43°32′ N, 125°42′ E **198**
Shuangyashan, *China* 46°41′ N, 131°11′ E **238**
Shubararköl, *Kaz.* 49°7′ N, 68°46′ E **184**
Shubarquduyq, *Kaz.* 49°8′ N, 56°26′ E **158**
Shubarshī, *Kaz.* 48°35′ N, 57°17′ E **158**
Shubuta, *Miss., U.S.* 31°51′ N, 88°42′ W **103**
Shucheng, *China* 31°26′ N, 116°56′ E **198**
Shudino, *Russ.* 61°41′ N, 48°9′ E **154**
Shufu, *China* 39°22′ N, 75°44′ E **184**
Shugozero, *Russ.* 59°55′ N, 34°16′ E **154**
Shukpa Kunzang, *India* 34°22′ N, 78°21′ E **188**
Shuksan, Mount, peak, *Wash., U.S.* 48°48′ N, 121°38′ W **100**
Shulan, *China* 44°25′ N, 126°58′ E **198**
Shulaps Peak, *Can.* 50°57′ N, 122°37′ W **90**
Shule, *China* 39°23′ N, 76°3′ E **184**
Shullsburg, *Wis., U.S.* 42°34′ N, 90°14′ W **102**
Shumagin Islands, *Gulf of Alaska* 54°23′ N, 161°29′ W **98**
Shumanay, *Uzb.* 42°35′ N, 58°59′ E **180**
Shumen (Kolarovgrad), *Bulg.* 43°16′ N, 26°55′ E **156**
Shumerlya, *Russ.* 55°29′ N, 46°29′ E **154**
Shumikha, *Russ.* 55°13′ N, 63°16′ E **184**
Shumilina, *Belarus* 55°21′ N, 29°41′ E **166**
Shunchang, *China* 26°50′ N, 117°47′ E **198**
Shun'ga, *Russ.* 62°34′ N, 34°59′ E **154**
Shungnak, *Alas., U.S.* 66°47′ N, 157°12′ W **98**
Shungopavi, *Ariz., U.S.* 35°48′ N, 110°31′ W **92**
Shuozhou, *China* 39°18′ N, 112°26′ E **198**
Shupenzë, *Alban.* 41°31′ N, 20°25′ E **168**
Shuqualak, *Miss., U.S.* 32°57′ N, 88°34′ W **103**
Shūr Gaz, *Iran* 29°9′ N, 59°21′ E **180**
Shuraabad, *Azerb.* 40°49′ N, 49°27′ E **195**
Shūrāb, *Iran* 33°42′ N, 56°32′ E **180**
Shurma, *Russ.* 56°56′ N, 50°24′ E **154**
Shurob, *Taj.* 40°4′ N, 70°32′ E **197**
Shurugwi, *Zimb.* 19°40′ S, 29°58′ E **224**
Shuryshkary, *Russ.* 65°56′ N, 65°25′ E **169**
Shūsf, *Iran* 31°47′ N, 60°5′ E **180**
Shushan, *N.Y., U.S.* 43°5′ N, 73°21′ W **104**
Shushenskoye, *Russ.* 53°19′ N, 92°2′ E **184**
Shūshtar, *Iran* 32°1′ N, 48°55′ E **180**
Shuya, *Russ.* 56°50′ N, 41°21′ E **154**
Shuya, *Russ.* 61°58′ N, 34°19′ E **154**
Shuyak Island, *Alas., U.S.* 58°22′ N, 152°19′ W **98**
Shuyang, *China* 34°8′ N, 118°50′ E **198**
Shuyskoye, *Russ.* 59°21′ N, 40°58′ E **154**
Shwebo, *Myanmar* 22°33′ N, 95°44′ E **202**
Shwegu, *Myanmar* 24°10′ N, 96°45′ E **188**
Shwegyin, *Myanmar* 17°56′ N, 96°52′ E **202**
Shweli, river, *Asia* 23°29′ N, 97°5′ E **202**
Shyghys Qazaqstan, adm. division, *Kaz.* 48°56′ N, 80°14′ E **184**
Shymkent, *Kaz.* 42°17′ N, 69°34′ E **197**
Shyngghyrlau, *Kaz.* 51°5′ N, 54°3′ E **158**
Shyok, river, *India* 35°1′ N, 76°45′ E **188**
Siabu, *Indonesia* 1°1′ N, 99°29′ E **196**
Sīah Chashmeh, *Iran* 39°4′ N, 44°26′ E **195**
Sialkot, *Pak.* 32°27′ N, 74°33′ E **186**
Sian see Xi'an, *China* 34°6′ N, 108°48′ E **190**
Sianów, *Pol.* 54°13′ N, 16°18′ E **152**
Siantan, island, *Indonesia* 3°6′ N, 106°18′ E **196**
Siapa, river, *Venez.* 1°57′ N, 66°5′ W **136**
Siargao, island, *Philippines* 9°56′ N, 126°9′ E **192**
Siasconset, *Mass., U.S.* 41°15′ N, 69°59′ W **104**
Siasi, *Philippines* 5°35′ N, 120°49′ E **203**
Siaton, *Philippines* 9°4′ N, 123°2′ E **203**
Šiaulėnai, *Lith.* 55°40′ N, 23°24′ E **166**
Šiauliai, *Lith.* 55°55′ N, 23°17′ E **166**
Sibā'i, Gebel el, peak, *Egypt* 25°42′ N, 34°3′ E **182**
Sibari, *It.* 39°45′ N, 16°27′ E **156**
Sibay, *Russ.* 52°44′ N, 58°37′ E **154**
Sibaya, Lake, *S. Af.* 27°21′ S, 32°5′ E **227**
Sibbald, Cape, *Antarctica* 73°46′ S, 172°14′ E **248**
Sibbo (Sipoo), *Fin.* 60°22′ N, 25°13′ E **166**
Šibenik, *Croatia* 43°44′ N, 15°53′ E **168**
Siberia, region, *Russ.* 68°9′ N, 99°54′ E **172**
Siberut, island, *Indonesia* 1°23′ S, 99°7′ E **196**
Siberut National Park, *Indonesia* 1°17′ S, 98°20′ E **172**
Siberut, Selat 0°52′ N, 98°4′ E **196**
Sibi, *Pak.* 29°37′ N, 67°53′ E **186**
Sibigo, *Indonesia* 2°49′ N, 95°53′ E **196**
Sibiloi National Park, *Kenya* 3°55′ N, 36°36′ E **224**
Sibirskiy, *Russ.* 60°36′ N, 69°51′ E **169**
Sibiryakova, Ostrov, island, *Russ.* 72°47′ N, 79°54′ E **160**
Sibiti, *Congo* 3°42′ S, 13°18′ E **218**
Sibiu, *Rom.* 45°49′ N, 24°8′ E **156**
Sibiu, adm. division, *Rom.* 45°38′ N, 23°39′ E **156**
Sibley, *La., U.S.* 32°31′ N, 93°18′ W **103**
Sibolga, *Indonesia* 1°46′ N, 98°48′ E **196**
Siborongborong, *Indonesia* 2°14′ N, 98°59′ E **196**
Şibot, *Rom.* 45°56′ N, 23°20′ E **168**
Sibsagar, *India* 27°0′ N, 94°38′ E **188**
Sibsey, *U.K.* 53°2′ N, 2°119′ E **162**
Sibu, *Malaysia* 2°18′ N, 111°51′ E **192**
Sibu, island, *Malaysia* 2°9′ N, 104°6′ E **196**
Sibuco, *Philippines* 7°20′ N, 122°4′ E **203**
Sibut, *Cen. Af. Rep.* 5°42′ N, 19°5′ E **218**
Sibuyan Sea 12°34′ N, 122°29′ E **203**
Siby, *Mali* 12°23′ N, 8°20′ W **222**
Sicapoo, Mount, peak, *Philippines* 18°1′ N, 120°51′ E **203**
Sicasica, *Bol.* 17°24′ S, 67°48′ W **137**
Sichuan, adm. division, *China* 31°1′ N, 105°8′ E **198**
Sicié, Cap, *Fr.* 42°57′ N, 5°44′ E **165**
Sicilia (Sicily), adm. division, *It.* 37°28′ N, 13°21′ E **156**
Sicily Island, *La., U.S.* 31°49′ N, 91°41′ W **103**
Sicily, island, *It.* 36°26′ N, 14°37′ E **156**
Sicilia see Sicily, adm. division, *Sicily* 38°18′ N, 12°49′ E **156**
Sico, river, *Hond.* 15°38′ N, 85°43′ W **115**
Sicuani, *Peru* 14°19′ S, 71°12′ W **137**
Sicyon, ruin(s), *Gr.* 37°58′ N, 22°38′ E **156**
Šid, *Serb. and Mont.* 45°7′ N, 19°13′ E **168**
Sidaogou, *China* 41°44′ N, 127°5′ E **200**
Sidaouet, *Niger* 18°32′ N, 8°4′ E **222**
Sidas, *Indonesia* 0°23′ N, 109°42′ E **196**
Siddhapur, *India* 23°56′ N, 72°22′ E **186**
Side, ruin(s), *Mediterranean Sea* 36°43′ N, 31°17′ E **156**
Sideby (Siipyy), *Fin.* 62°1′ N, 21°19′ E **166**
Sideia, island, *P.N.G.* 10°56′ S, 150°17′ E **192**
Sidéradougou, *Burkina Faso* 10°39′ N, 4°16′ W **222**
Sidi Aïch, *Alg.* 36°36′ N, 4°42′ E **150**
Sidi Aïssa, *Alg.* 35°52′ N, 3°46′ E **150**
Sidi Akacha, *Alg.* 36°27′ N, 1°18′ E **150**
Sidi Ali, *Alg.* 36°5′ N, 0°25′ E **150**
Sidi Amar, *Alg.* 36°32′ N, 2°18′ E **150**
Sîdi Barrâni, *Egypt* 31°39′ N, 25°57′ E **180**
Sidi Bel Abbès, *Alg.* 35°10′ N, 0°38′ E **150**
Sidi Bel Atar, *Alg.* 36°1′ N, 0°16′ E **164**
Sidi Bernous, Djebel, peak, *Alg.* 36°20′ N, 1°31′ E **150**
Sidi bou Haous, *Alg.* 32°4′ N, 2°3′ E **214**
Sidi Bouzid, *Tun.* 35°2′ N, 9°29′ E **156**
Sidi Daoud, *Alg.* 36°50′ N, 3°51′ E **150**
Sidi el Hadj bou Haous, *Alg.* 31°38′ N, 2°0′ E **214**
Sidi el Hadj Zaoui, *Alg.* 28°17′ N, 4°36′ E **214**
Sidi Hosni, *Alg.* 35°28′ N, 1°35′ E **150**
Sidi Ifni, *Mor.* 29°21′ N, 10°10′ W **214**
Sidi Kada, *Alg.* 35°19′ N, 0°19′ E **150**
Sidi Lakhdar, *Alg.* 36°9′ N, 0°26′ E **164**
Sîdi 'Omar, *Egypt* 31°24′ N, 24°55′ E **180**
Siding Spring Observatory, *Austral.* 31°21′ S, 148°51′ E **230**
Sidlaw Hills, *U.K.* 56°22′ N, 3°17′ W **150**
Sidley, Mount, peak, *Antarctica* 76°57′ S, 125°31′ W **248**
Sidney, *Can.* 48°38′ N, 123°24′ W **100**
Sidney, *Iowa, U.S.* 40°44′ N, 95°39′ W **90**
Sidney, *Mont., U.S.* 47°40′ N, 104°11′ W **90**
Sidney, *Nebr., U.S.* 41°8′ N, 102°60′ W **90**
Sidney, *N.Y., U.S.* 42°18′ N, 75°24′ W **94**
Sidney, *Ohio, U.S.* 40°17′ N, 84°9′ W **102**
Sido, *Mali* 11°41′ N, 7°36′ W **222**
Sidoktaya, *Myanmar* 20°27′ N, 94°13′ E **202**
Sidon, *Miss., U.S.* 33°23′ N, 90°13′ W **103**
Sidon see Saida, *Leb.* 33°33′ N, 35°22′ E **194**
Sidorovsk, *Russ.* 66°34′ N, 82°24′ E **169**
Sidra, Gulf of 31°40′ N, 16°22′ E **142**
Sidra see Surt, *Lib.* 31°12′ N, 16°32′ E **216**
Siedlce, *Pol.* 52°10′ N, 22°16′ E **152**
Siegal, Mount, peak, *Nev., U.S.* 38°53′ N, 119°36′ W **90**
Siegburg, *Ger.* 50°48′ N, 7°11′ E **167**
Siegen, *Ger.* 50°53′ N, 8°1′ E **167**
Siem Pang, *Cambodia* 14°9′ N, 106°19′ E **202**
Siem Reap, *Cambodia* 13°24′ N, 103°51′ E **202**
Siempurgo, *Côte d'Ivoire* 9°31′ N, 6°13′ W **222**
Siena, *It.* 43°20′ N, 11°19′ E **214**
Sieppijärvi, *Fin.* 67°8′ N, 23°56′ E **152**
Sieradz, *Pol.* 51°35′ N, 18°43′ E **152**
Sierck, *Fr.* 49°25′ N, 6°21′ E **163**
Sierra Blanca, *Tex., U.S.* 31°9′ N, 105°22′ W **92**
Sierra Colorada, *Arg.* 40°35′ S, 67°46′ W **134**
Sierra de San Pedro Mártir National Park, *Mex.* 30°58′ N, 115°45′ W **238**
Sierra Gorda, *Chile* 22°54′ S, 69°22′ W **137**
Sierra Grande, *Arg.* 41°35′ S, 65°22′ W **134**
Sierra Leone 8°30′ N, 12°17′ W **214**
Sierra Leone Rise, *North Atlantic Ocean* 5°17′ N, 20°42′ W **253**
Sierra Madre Mountains, *Calif., U.S.* 34°57′ N, 120°5′ W **100**
Sierra Madre Occidental, *Mex.* 25°42′ N, 106°57′ W **114**
Sierra Madre Oriental, *Mex.* 23°10′ N, 100°33′ W **114**
Sierra Mojada, *Mex.* 27°18′ N, 103°42′ W **112**
Sierra Nevada de Santa Marta National Park, *Col.* 11°19′ N, 74°8′ W **130**
Sierra Nevada National Park, *Venez.* 8°41′ N, 71°26′ W **136**
Sierra Vista, *Ariz., U.S.* 31°33′ N, 110°18′ W **92**
Sierre, *Switz.* 46°18′ N, 7°31′ E **167**
Sieruela, *Sp.* 38°58′ N, 5°3′ W **164**
Siesta Key, island, *Fla., U.S.* 27°10′ N, 82°37′ W **105**
Siete Aguas, *Sp.* 39°28′ N, 0°56′ E **164**
Şieu, *Rom.* 47°0′ N, 24°36′ E **156**
Sif Fatima, spring, *Alg.* 31°6′ N, 8°40′ E **214**
Sifié, *Côte d'Ivoire* 7°54′ N, 6°56′ W **222**
Sifnos, island, *Gr.* 36°51′ N, 24°9′ E **180**
Sifton, *Can.* 51°22′ N, 100°8′ W **90**
Sifton Pass, *Can.* 57°53′ N, 126°10′ W **108**
Sig, *Russ.* 65°34′ N, 34°9′ E **152**
Sigdal, *Nor.* 60°3′ N, 9°37′ E **152**
Sigean, *Fr.* 43°1′ N, 2°56′ E **164**
Sigep, *Indonesia* 0°59′ N, 98°49′ E **196**
Sighnaghi, *Ga.* 41°37′ N, 45°55′ E **195**
Siglan, *Russ.* 59°17′ N, 152°31′ E **173**
Sigli, *Indonesia* 5°23′ N, 95°55′ E **196**
Siglufjördur, *Ice.* 66°10′ N, 19°5′ W **143**
Sigmaringen, *Ger.* 48°4′ N, 9°12′ E **152**
Signai, site, *Can.* 48°18′ N, 76°55′ W **94**
Signal Hill, peak, *Austral.* 21°59′ S, 139°52′ E **230**
Signal Peak, *Ariz., U.S.* 33°21′ N, 114°8′ W **101**
Signy Island, *Antarctica* 60°60′ S, 46°55′ W **134**
Signy-le-Petit, *Fr.* 49°53′ N, 4°17′ E **163**
Sigourney, *Iowa, U.S.* 41°20′ N, 92°12′ W **94**
Sigovo, *Russ.* 62°39′ N, 87°2′ E **169**
Sigre, river, *Hond.* 15°21′ N, 84°51′ W **115**
Sigüenza, *Sp.* 41°3′ N, 2°40′ W **164**
Siguiri, *Guinea* 11°27′ N, 9°11′ W **222**
Sigulda, *Latv.* 57°8′ N, 24°51′ E **166**
Sihor, *India* 21°42′ N, 71°56′ E **186**
Sihora, *India* 23°29′ N, 80°7′ E **197**
Siikainen, *Fin.* 61°51′ N, 21°47′ E **166**
Siilinjärvi, *Fin.* 63°2′ N, 27°38′ E **152**
Siipyy see Sideby, *Fin.* 62°1′ N, 21°19′ E **166**
Siirt, *Turk.* 37°54′ N, 41°57′ E **195**
Sikanni Chief, *Can.* 57°15′ N, 122°44′ W **108**
Sikanni Chief, river, *Can.* 57°26′ N, 122°27′ W **108**
Sikar, *India* 27°36′ N, 75°10′ E **197**
Sikasso, *Mali* 11°19′ N, 5°41′ W **222**
Sikeå, *Nor.* 64°9′ N, 20°55′ E **152**
Sikes, *La., U.S.* 32°3′ N, 92°31′ W **103**
Sikeston, *Mo., U.S.* 36°51′ N, 89°35′ W **96**
Sikhote Alin', Khrebet 43°1′ N, 132°36′ E **200**
Sikinos, island, *Gr.* 36°44′ N, 24°37′ E **180**
Sikkim, adm. division, *India* 27°29′ N, 88°6′ E **197**
Siklós, *Hung.* 45°50′ N, 18°17′ E **168**
Siknäs, *Nor.* 65°50′ N, 22°40′ E **152**
Sikonda, *Hung.* 46°9′ N, 18°14′ E **168**
Sikonge, *Tanzania* 5°36′ S, 32°47′ E **224**
Siksjö, *Nor.* 64°21′ N, 17°47′ E **152**
Siktyakh, *Russ.* 69°51′ N, 124°43′ E **160**
Sikuati, *Malaysia* 6°54′ N, 116°40′ E **203**
Sila, La, *It.* 39°31′ N, 16°21′ E **156**
Silacayoapan, *Mex.* 17°29′ N, 98°9′ W **114**
Šilalė, *Lith.* 55°29′ N, 22°10′ E **166**
Silame, *Nig.* 13°2′ N, 4°51′ E **222**
Silandro, *It.* 46°37′ N, 10°47′ E **167**
Silao, *Mex.* 20°54′ N, 101°26′ W **114**
Silas, *Ala., U.S.* 31°46′ N, 88°20′ W **103**
Šilderi, *Latv.* 56°51′ N, 22°10′ E **166**
Şile, *Turk.* 41°10′ N, 29°36′ E **156**
Silesia, region, *Pol.* 49°36′ N, 17°59′ E **152**
Silet, *Alg.* 22°39′ N, 4°34′ E **214**
Siletitengi Köli, lake, *Kaz.* 53°9′ N, 72°22′ E **184**
Siliana, *Alg.* 36°32′ N, 6°17′ E **150**
Silifke, *Turk.* 36°20′ N, 33°55′ E **156**
Silil, spring, *Somalia* 10°52′ N, 43°18′ E **182**
Siling Co, lake, *China* 31°37′ N, 88°26′ E **188**
Silistra, *Bulg.* 44°5′ N, 27°15′ E **156**
Silistra, adm. division, *Bulg.* 43°56′ N, 26°22′ E **156**
Silivri, *Turk.* 41°5′ N, 28°14′ E **156**
Silkeborg, *Den.* 56°8′ N, 9°31′ E **150**
Silla, *Sp.* 39°21′ N, 0°24′ E **164**
Sillamäe, *Est.* 59°22′ N, 27°43′ E **166**
Silli, *Burkina Faso* 11°35′ N, 2°30′ W **222**
Silliman, Mount, peak, *Calif., U.S.* 36°37′ N, 118°44′ W **101**
Silloth, *U.K.* 54°52′ N, 3°23′ W **162**
Silo, peak, *Gr.* 41°9′ N, 25°51′ E **156**
Silogui, *Indonesia* 1°12′ S, 98°58′ E **196**
Silopi, *Turk.* 37°14′ N, 42°17′ E **195**
Silsbee, *Tex., U.S.* 30°19′ N, 94°11′ W **103**
Silt Lake, *Can.* 60°2′ N, 119°18′ W **108**
Siltou, spring, *Chad* 16°51′ N, 15°42′ E **216**
Siluas, *Indonesia* 1°17′ N, 109°49′ E **196**
Šilutė, *Lith.* 55°22′ N, 21°28′ E **166**
Silvan, *Turk.* 38°8′ N, 41°3′ E **195**
Silvânia, *Braz.* 16°42′ S, 48°37′ W **138**
Silvassa, *India* 20°16′ N, 73°3′ E **186**
Silver Bay, *Minn., U.S.* 47°17′ N, 91°17′ W **110**
Silver City, *Idaho, U.S.* 43°1′ N, 116°46′ W **90**
Silver City, *Miss., U.S.* 33°4′ N, 90°31′ W **103**
Silver City, *Nev., U.S.* 39°15′ N, 119°39′ W **90**
Silver City, *N. Mex., U.S.* 32°45′ N, 108°18′ W **112**
Silver Cliff, *Colo., U.S.* 38°8′ N, 105°26′ W **90**
Silver Creek, *Miss., U.S.* 31°34′ N, 89°59′ W **103**
Silver Lake, *Ind., U.S.* 41°4′ N, 85°53′ W **102**
Silver Lake, *N.H., U.S.* 43°53′ N, 71°11′ W **104**
Silver Peak, *Nev., U.S.* 37°45′ N, 117°39′ W **92**
Silver Run Peak, *Mont., U.S.* 45°5′ N, 109°37′ W **90**
Silver Springs, *Fla., U.S.* 29°12′ N, 82°4′ W **105**
Silver Star Mountain, peak, *Can.* 50°21′ N, 119°9′ W **90**
Silver Zone Pass, *Nev., U.S.* 40°56′ N, 114°21′ W **90**
Silverthrone, Mount, peak, *Alas., U.S.* 63°6′ N, 150°53′ W **98**
Silverthrone Mountain, peak, *Can.* 51°29′ N, 126°10′ W **108**
Silverton, *Colo., U.S.* 37°48′ N, 107°40′ W **82**
Silverton, *Tex., U.S.* 34°27′ N, 101°19′ W **92**
Silves, *Braz.* 2°52′ S, 58°14′ W **130**
Silvretta, *Aust.* 46°49′ N, 9°58′ E **167**
Silwa Baḥari, *Egypt* 24°42′ N, 32°55′ E **182**
Sim, *Russ.* 54°59′ N, 57°39′ E **154**
Sim, Cap, *Mor.* 31°25′ N, 10°40′ W **214**
Simaleke-hilir, *Indonesia* 1°10′ S, 98°37′ E **196**
Sim'ān, Jabal, *Syr.* 36°31′ N, 36°38′ E **156**
Simao, *China* 22°37′ N, 101°12′ E **202**
Şīmareh, river, *Iran* 33°25′ N, 46°51′ E **180**
Simav, *Turk.* 39°4′ N, 28°58′ E **156**
Simav, river, *Turk.* 39°17′ N, 28°15′ E **156**
Simba, *Dem. Rep. of the Congo* 0°36′ N, 22°56′ E **218**
Simbo, island, *Solomon Islands* 8°17′ S, 156°30′ E **242**
Simcoe, *Can.* 42°49′ N, 80°18′ W **94**
Simcoe, Lake, *Can.* 44°27′ N, 79°55′ W **80**
Simcoe Mountains, peak, *Wash., U.S.* 45°57′ N, 120°55′ W **90**
Simdega, *India* 22°35′ N, 84°30′ E **197**
Simeria, *Rom.* 45°50′ N, 23°1′ E **168**
Simeulue, island, *Indonesia* 2°43′ N, 95°5′ E **196**
Simferopol', *Ukr.* 44°57′ N, 34°1′ E **156**
Simhana, *China* 39°40′ N, 73°57′ E **197**
Simi, *Gr.* 36°36′ N, 27°49′ E **156**
Simi Valley, *Calif., U.S.* 34°16′ N, 118°46′ W **101**
Simikot, *Nepal* 29°59′ N, 81°51′ E **197**
Simin Han, *Bosn. and Herzg.* 44°32′ N, 18°44′ E **168**
Simití, *Col.* 7°57′ N, 73°59′ W **136**
Simla, *Colo., U.S.* 39°8′ N, 104°6′ W **92**
Simla, *Nepal* 31°8′ N, 77°9′ E **197**
Şimleu Silvaniei, *Rom.* 47°14′ N, 22°50′ E **168**
Simme, river, *Switz.* 46°34′ N, 7°25′ E **165**
Simmern, *Ger.* 49°58′ N, 7°30′ E **167**
Simmesport, *La., U.S.* 30°57′ N, 91°50′ W **103**
Simojärvi, *Fin.* 65°55′ N, 27°7′ E **152**
Simojovel, *Mex.* 17°9′ N, 92°44′ W **115**
Simola, *Fin.* 60°54′ N, 28°7′ E **166**
Simón Bolívar, *Mex.* 24°39′ N, 103°15′ W **114**
Simonette, river, *Can.* 54°1′ N, 118°37′ W **108**
Simonhouse, *Can.* 54°26′ N, 101°24′ W **108**
Simon's Town, *S. Af.* 34°12′ S, 18°25′ E **227**
Simontornya, *Hung.* 46°45′ N, 18°32′ E **168**
Simpang, *Indonesia* 0°9′ N, 103°16′ E **196**
Simpang, *Indonesia* 1°15′ S, 104°5′ E **196**
Simpele, *Fin.* 61°25′ N, 29°20′ E **166**
Simplício Mendes, *Braz.* 7°51′ S, 41°55′ W **132**
Simplon Pass, *Switz.* 46°15′ N, 8°1′ E **167**
Simpson, *La., U.S.* 31°14′ N, 93°1′ W **103**
Simpson, *Pa., U.S.* 41°34′ N, 75°29′ W **94**
Simpson Desert, *Austral.* 25°28′ S, 135°47′ E **230**
Simpson Hill, peak, *Austral.* 26°34′ S, 126°21′ E **230**
Simpson Lake, *Can.* 60°47′ N, 129°44′ W **108**
Simpson Park Mountains, *Nev., U.S.* 39°45′ N, 116°58′ W **90**
Simpson Peninsula, *Can.* 68°27′ N, 91°51′ W **106**
Simrishamn, *Nor.* 55°32′ N, 14°20′ E **152**
Sims Lake, *Can.* 53°59′ N, 66°28′ W **111**
Simsboro, *La., U.S.* 32°31′ N, 92°49′ W **103**
Simushir, island, *Russ.* 46°43′ N, 152°15′ E **190**
Sina, *Peru* 14°34′ S, 69°16′ W **137**
Sinabang, *Indonesia* 2°29′ N, 96°20′ E **196**
Sinabung, peak, *Indonesia* 3°11′ N, 98°17′ E **196**
Sinai, *Egypt* 30°23′ N, 33°2′ E **194**
Sinai, Mount see Mûsa, Gebel, peak, *Egypt* 28°30′ N, 33°54′ E **226**
Sinal, Morro do, *Braz.* 10°41′ S, 55°37′ W **130**
Sinaloa, adm. division, *Mex.* 23°42′ N, 106°50′ W **114**
Sinaloa, river, *Mex.* 25°46′ N, 108°25′ W **80**
Sinamaica, *Venez.* 11°6′ N, 71°53′ W **136**
Sinan, *China* 27°56′ N, 108°13′ E **198**
Sînandrei, *Rom.* 45°52′ N, 21°10′ E **168**
Sinanju, *N. Korea* 39°35′ N, 125°36′ E **200**
Sīnāwin, *Lib.* 31°4′ N, 10°37′ E **216**
Sinbang-ni, *N. Korea* 41°5′ N, 127°28′ E **200**
Sincelejo, *Col.* 9°16′ N, 75°26′ W **136**
Sincennes, Lac, lake, *Can.* 47°27′ N, 74°27′ W **94**
Sinch'ang, *N. Korea* 40°7′ N, 128°28′ E **200**
Sinch'ang, *N. Korea* 39°23′ N, 126°7′ E **200**
Sinchiyacu, *Peru* 3°11′ S, 76°44′ W **136**
Sinch'ŏn, *N. Korea* 38°21′ N, 125°29′ E **200**
Sinclair, *Wyo., U.S.* 41°46′ N, 107°6′ W **90**
Sinclair, Lake, *Ga., U.S.* 33°12′ N, 83°57′ W **112**
Sindangan, *Philippines* 8°16′ N, 123°0′ E **203**
Sindara, *Gabon* 1°4′ S, 10°37′ E **218**
Sindeni, *Tanzania* 5°18′ S, 38°15′ E **224**
Sindèr, *Niger* 14°14′ N, 1°14′ E **222**
Sindeya, *Russ.* 60°5′ N, 61°29′ E **154**
Sindh, adm. division, *Pak.* 25°54′ N, 68°3′ E **186**
Sindi, *Est.* 58°22′ N, 24°39′ E **166**
Sindi, *Sudan* 14°22′ N, 25°48′ E **226**
Sindri, *India* 23°40′ N, 86°30′ E **197**
Sinegorskiy, *Russ.* 47°56′ N, 40°49′ E **158**
Sines, *Port.* 37°57′ N, 8°52′ W **150**
Sines, Cabo de, *Port.* 37°42′ N, 9°11′ W **150**
Sinfra, *Côte d'Ivoire* 6°31′ N, 5°55′ W **222**
Sing Buri, *Thai.* 14°53′ N, 100°23′ E **202**
Singa, *Sudan* 13°8′ N, 33°56′ E **182**
Singapore, *Singapore* 1°16′ N, 103°43′ E **196**
Singer, *La., U.S.* 30°38′ N, 93°25′ W **103**
Sîngerei, *Mold.* 47°38′ N, 28°8′ E **158**
Singida, *Tanzania* 4°49′ S, 34°43′ E **224**
Singida, adm. division, *Tanzania* 5°60′ S, 34°4′ E **224**
Singing Tower, site, *Fla., U.S.* 27°55′ N, 81°36′ W **105**
Singkawang, *Indonesia* 0°55′ N, 108°58′ E **196**
Singkep, island, *Indonesia* 0°38′ N, 104°36′ E **196**
Singkil, *Indonesia* 2°19′ N, 97°46′ E **196**
Singkuang, *Indonesia* 1°6′ N, 98°57′ E **196**
Singleton, Mount, peak, *Austral.* 22°5′ S, 130°37′ E **230**
Singö, island, *Sw.* 60°10′ N, 18°46′ E **166**
Singoli, *India* 24°58′ N, 75°18′ E **188**
Singtam, *India* 27°17′ N, 88°29′ E **197**
Singu, *Myanmar* 22°34′ N, 96°0′ E **202**
Singus, ruin(s), *Gr.* 40°9′ N, 23°41′ E **156**
Sin'gye, *N. Korea* 38°30′ N, 126°32′ E **200**
Singye Dzong, *Bhutan* 28°0′ N, 91°18′ E **197**
Sinhŭng, *N. Korea* 40°11′ N, 127°36′ E **200**
Sini Vrŭkh, peak, *Bulg.* 41°49′ N, 24°56′ E **156**
Sinianka-Minia Game Reserve, *Chad* 10°5′ N, 17°4′ E **218**
Şinifḩah, *Jordan* 30°50′ N, 35°33′ E **194**
Sinj, *Croatia* 43°42′ N, 16°37′ E **168**
Sinjajevina, *Europe* 43°0′ N, 19°6′ E **168**
Sinjār, *Iraq* 36°20′ N, 41°53′ E **195**
Sinkat, *Sudan* 18°51′ N, 36°48′ E **182**
Sinkiang, region 38°43′ N, 73°57′ E **197**
Sinkiang, region, *China* 46°12′ N, 83°11′ E **184**
Sinking Spring, *Ohio, U.S.* 39°3′ N, 83°24′ W **102**
Sin-le-Noble, *Fr.* 50°20′ N, 3°7′ E **163**
Sinnamary, *South America* 5°23′ N, 52°57′ W **130**
Sinnar, adm. division, *Sudan* 12°44′ N, 33°18′ E **182**
Sinntal, *Ger.* 50°18′ N, 9°38′ E **167**
Sinnûris, *Egypt* 29°25′ N, 30°50′ E **180**
Sinop, *Braz.* 11°55′ S, 55°35′ W **130**
Sinop, *Turk.* 41°53′ N, 34°57′ E **143**
Sinop Burnu, *Turk.* 42°1′ N, 35°14′ E **156**
Sinop (Sinope), *Turk.* 42°1′ N, 35°8′ E **156**
Sinope see Sinop, *Turk.* 42°1′ N, 35°8′ E **156**
Sinp'a see Kimjŏngsuk, *N. Korea* 41°24′ N, 127°48′ E **200**
Sinp'o, *N. Korea* 40°1′ N, 128°13′ E **200**
Sinsang, *N. Korea* 39°39′ N, 127°25′ E **200**
Sinsk, *Russ.* 61°9′ N, 126°40′ E **160**
Sint Andries, *Belg.* 51°11′ N, 3°11′ E **163**
Sint Georgen, *Ger.* 48°7′ N, 8°19′ E **152**
Sint Mang, *Ger.* 47°43′ N, 10°20′ E **152**
Sint Truiden, *Belg.* 50°48′ N, 5°11′ E **167**
Sîntana, *Rom.* 46°20′ N, 21°31′ E **168**
Sintang, *Indonesia* 4°238′ N, 111°27′ E **192**
Sinton, *Tex., U.S.* 28°1′ N, 97°30′ W **96**
Sintuya, *Peru* 12°44′ S, 71°17′ W **137**
Sinú, river, *Col.* 7°52′ N, 76°16′ W **136**
Sinŭiju, *N. Korea* 40°3′ N, 124°23′ E **200**
Sinujiif, *Somalia* 8°32′ N, 48°59′ E **216**
Sinwŏn, *N. Korea* 38°12′ N, 125°43′ E **200**
Sinyaya, river, *Latv.* 56°26′ N, 28°2′ E **166**
Sinzig, *Ger.* 50°32′ N, 7°15′ E **163**
Sió, river, *Hung.* 46°48′ N, 18°13′ E **168**
Sióagárd, *Hung.* 46°23′ N, 18°39′ E **168**
Siocon, *Philippines* 7°45′ N, 122°8′ E **203**

Siófok, *Hung.* 46°54' N, 18°5' E **168**
Sioma, *Zambia* 16°41' S, 23°30' E **224**
Sioma Ngwezi National Park, *Zambia* 17°7' S, 23°42' E **224**
Sion, *Switz.* 46°14' N, 7°20' E **167**
Siorapaluk 77°50' N, 70°37' W **246**
Sioux City, *Iowa, U.S.* 42°29' N, 96°26' W **82**
Sioux Falls, *S. Dak., U.S.* 43°31' N, 96°44' W **90**
Sioux Lookout, *Can.* 50°5' N, 91°51' W **82**
Sioux Narrows, *Can.* 49°25' N, 94°7' W **90**
Sioux Rapids, *Iowa, U.S.* 42°52' N, 95°10' W **90**
Sipalay, *Philippines* 9°45' N, 122°24' E **203**
Sipan, island, *Croatia* 42°44' N, 17°54' E **168**
Sipapo, Cerro, peak, *Venez.* 4°51' N, 67°15' W **136**
Sipapo, river, *Venez.* 4°35' N, 67°40' W **136**
Siphanqeni, *S. Af.* 31°5' S, 29°29' E **227**
Siping, *China* 43°8' N, 124°22' E **200**
Sipirok, *Indonesia* 1°37' N, 99°17' E **196**
Sipiwesk, *Can.* 55°28' N, 97°25' W **108**
Siple Coast, *Antarctica* 82°60' S, 148°28' W **248**
Siple Island, *Antarctica* 72°30' S, 127°21' W **248**
Siple, Mount, peak, *Antarctica* 73°20' S, 126°3' W **248**
Šipovo, *Bosn. and Herzg.* 44°17' N, 17°4' E **168**
Sippo see Sibbo, *Fin.* 60°22' N, 25°13' E **166**
Šiprage, *Bosn. and Herzg.* 44°27' N, 17°33' E **168**
Sipsey, river, *Ala., U.S.* 33°25' N, 87°46' W **103**
Sipura, island, *Indonesia* 2°5' S, 99°22' E **192**
Siqueros, *Mex.* 23°18' N, 106°15' W **114**
Siquia, river, *Nicar.* 12°31' N, 84°32' W **115**
Siquijor, *Philippines* 9°13' N, 123°29' E **203**
Siquisique, *Venez.* 10°31' N, 69°46' W **136**
Sir Alexander, Mount, peak, *Can.* 53°55' N, 120°29' W **108**
Şīr Banī Yās, island, *U.A.E.* 24°23' N, 52°28' E **182**
Sir Douglas, Mount, peak, *Can.* 50°43' N, 115°25' W **90**
Sir Edward Pellew Group, islands, *Austral.* 15°27' S, 136°56' E **230**
Sir Francis Drake, Mount, peak, *Can.* 50°48' N, 124°54' W **90**
Sir Graham Moore Islands, *Austral.* 13°44' S, 124°3' E **230**
Sir James Macbrien, Mount, peak, *Can.* 61°57' N, 129°1' W **78**
Sir Sandford, Mount, peak, *Can.* 51°40' N, 117°58' W **90**
Sir Thomas, Mount, peak, *Austral.* 27°13' S, 129°31' E **230**
Sira, *India* 13°44' N, 76°56' E **188**
Siracusa, *It.* 37°3' N, 15°14' E **216**
Siracusa (Syracuse), *It.* 37°3' N, 15°17' E **156**
Sirajganj, *Bangladesh* 24°22' N, 89°39' E **197**
Şiran, *Turk.* 40°12' N, 39°8' E **195**
Sirba, river, *Burkina Faso* 12°25' N, 0°32' E **222**
Sirdaryo, *Uzb.* 40°50' N, 68°39' E **197**
Sīrē, *Eth.* 8°14' N, 39°27' E **224**
Sīrē, *Eth.* 9°1' N, 36°53' E **224**
Sireniki, *Russ.* 64°30' N, 173°50' W **98**
Sirghāyā, *Syr.* 33°48' N, 36°9' E **194**
Siri, Cape, *P.N.G.* 11°54' S, 153°3' E **192**
Siri, Gebel, peak, *Egypt* 22°6' N, 31°3' E **182**
Sīrīk, *Iran* 26°32' N, 57°9' E **196**
Sirino, Monte, peak, *It.* 40°7' N, 15°44' E **156**
Sīrjan see Saʿīdābād, *Iran* 29°29' N, 55°40' E **196**
Sirkka, *Fin.* 67°48' N, 24°47' E **152**
Sirma, *Nor.* 70°1' N, 27°21' E **152**
Sirmilik National Park, *Can.* 73°2' N, 83°20' W **72**
Şırnak, *Turk.* 37°30' N, 42°27' E **195**
Siro, Jebel, peak, *Sudan* 14°22' N, 24°16' E **226**
Sirohi, *India* 24°52' N, 72°52' E **186**
Široki Brijeg, *Bosn. and Herzg.* 43°22' N, 17°35' E **168**
Sirombu, *Indonesia* 1°0' N, 97°23' E **196**
Sirrī, island, *Iran* 25°47' N, 54°21' E **180**
Sirsa, *India* 29°32' N, 75°4' E **186**
Sirur, *India* 18°49' N, 74°23' E **188**
Şirvan, *Turk.* 38°1' N, 42°0' E **195**
Širvintos, *Lith.* 55°1' N, 24°56' E **166**
Sisak, *Croatia* 45°27' N, 16°22' E **168**
Sisal, *Mex.* 21°9' N, 90°6' W **116**
Sishen, *S. Af.* 27°47' S, 23°3' E **227**
Sisian, *Arm.* 39°32' N, 46°2' E **195**
Sisib Lake, lake, *Can.* 52°34' N, 99°41' W **108**
Sisimiut (Holsteinsborg) 66°56' N, 53°43' W **106**
Siskiyou Mountains, *Calif., U.S.* 41°51' N, 123°44' W **90**
Sisophon, *Cambodia* 13°37' N, 102°58' E **202**
Sisquoc, *Calif., U.S.* 34°52' N, 120°19' W **100**
Sisseton, *S. Dak., U.S.* 45°38' N, 97°5' W **90**
Sissonne, *Fr.* 49°34' N, 3°53' E **163**
Sīstān, Daryācheh-ye, lake, *Iran* 30°44' N, 60°36' E **186**
Sīstān, region, *Iran* 32°6' N, 59°49' E **180**
Sister Bay, *Wis., U.S.* 45°11' N, 87°7' W **110**
Sistersville, *W. Va., U.S.* 39°32' N, 80°60' W **102**
Sitampiky, *Madagascar* 16°41' S, 46°8' E **220**
Sitapur, *India* 27°33' N, 80°42' E **197**
Siteki, *Swaziland* 26°23' S, 31°56' E **227**
Sitges, *Sp.* 41°14' N, 1°48' E **164**
Sithonía, *Gr.* 40°12' N, 23°39' E **156**
Sitía, *Gr.* 35°9' N, 26°6' E **180**
Sitidgi Lake, *Can.* 68°28' N, 134°8' W **98**
Sítio da Abadia, *Braz.* 14°51' S, 46°15' W **138**
Sítio do Mato, *Braz.* 13°5' S, 43°30' W **138**
Sitka, *Alas., U.S.* 57°6' N, 135°14' W **73**
Sitka National Historical Park, *Alas., U.S.* 57°2' N, 135°18' W **108**
Sitkalidak Island, *Alas., U.S.* 56°43' N, 153°12' W **106**
Sitkovo, *Russ.* 69°7' N, 86°19' E **169**
Sitra, spring, *Egypt* 28°42' N, 26°53' E **180**
Sittard, *Neth.* 51°0' N, 5°50' E **167**
Sittingbourne, *U.K.* 51°19' N, 0°43' E **162**
Sittong, river, *Myanmar* 19°24' N, 96°14' E **202**
Sittwe, *Myanmar* 20°12' N, 92°52' E **188**
Siuna, *Nicar.* 13°44' N, 84°46' W **115**
Siuri, *India* 23°51' N, 87°31' E **197**
Siv. Donets, river, *Ukr.* 49°25' N, 36°31' E **158**
Sivac, *Serb. and Mont.* 45°41' N, 19°23' E **168**
Sivas, *Turk.* 39°45' N, 37°0' E **156**
Siverek, *Turk.* 37°43' N, 39°19' E **195**
Siverić, *Croatia* 43°52' N, 16°11' E **168**
Siverskiy, *Russ.* 59°20' N, 30°5' E **166**
Sivil, peak, *Sp.* 42°12' N, 6°356' W **164**
Sivrihisar, *Turk.* 39°27' N, 31°31' E **156**
Sivuchiy, Mys, *Russ.* 56°56' N, 162°44' E **160**
Sivulya, Hora, peak, *Ukr.* 48°31' N, 24°2' E **152**
Sīwa, *Egypt* 29°13' N, 25°33' E **180**
Siwan, *India* 26°11' N, 84°21' E **197**
Sixaola, *Pan.* 9°30' N, 82°37' W **115**
Sixian, *China* 33°30' N, 117°53' E **198**
Siyal Islands, *Red Sea* 22°17' N, 35°39' E **182**
Siyäzän, *Azerb.* 41°4' N, 49°5' E **195**
Siziwang Qi, *China* 41°33' N, 111°46' E **198**
Sjenica, *Serb. and Mont.* 43°15' N, 19°59' E **168**
Sjoa, *Nor.* 61°41' N, 9°34' E **152**
Sjoutnäs, *Nor.* 64°54' N, 14°54' E **152**
Sjøvegan, *Nor.* 68°53' N, 17°50' E **152**
Skadovs'k, *Ukr.* 46°8' N, 32°54' E **156**
Skaftung, *Fin.* 62°6' N, 21°18' E **152**
Skagen, *Den.* 57°42' N, 10°33' E **150**
Skagens Odde, *Den.* 57°30' N, 10°37' E **150**
Skagerrak, strait 57°52' N, 7°50' E **152**
Skaget, peak, *Nor.* 61°16' N, 9°3' E **152**
Skagit, river, *Wash., U.S.* 48°31' N, 122°3' W **100**
Skagway, *Alas., U.S.* 59°26' N, 135°19' W **108**
Skaistkalne, *Latv.* 56°23' N, 24°38' E **166**
Skala-Podil's'ka, *Ukr.* 48°50' N, 26°11' E **156**
Skamokawa, *Wash., U.S.* 46°15' N, 123°27' W **100**
Skånevik, *Nor.* 59°43' N, 5°54' E **152**
Skänninge, *Nor.* 58°22' N, 15°3' E **152**
Skærbæk, *Den.* 55°9' N, 8°44' E **150**
Skardu, *Pak.* 35°17' N, 75°39' E **186**
Skærfjorden 77°13' N, 24°16' W **246**
Skärhamn, *Sw.* 57°59' N, 11°33' E **150**
Skarnes, *Nor.* 60°14' N, 11°41' E **152**
Skarvdalsegga, peak, *Nor.* 62°4' N, 7°55' E **152**
Skattkärr, *Nor.* 59°24' N, 13°38' E **152**
Skaudvilė, *Lith.* 55°24' N, 22°34' E **166**
Skaymat, *Africa* 24°29' N, 15°7' W **214**
Skebo, *Sw.* 59°57' N, 18°35' E **152**
Skeena Crossing, *Can.* 55°4' N, 127°48' W **108**
Skeena Mountains, *Can.* 56°49' N, 129°31' W **98**
Skeena, river, *Can.* 55°21' N, 127°45' W **108**
Skegness, *U.K.* 53°8' N, 0°20' E **162**
Skeldon, *Guyana* 5°46' N, 57°12' W **130**
Skeleton Coast Park, *Namibia* 17°59' S, 10°48' E **220**
Skeleton Coast, region, *Namibia* 17°31' S, 11°47' E **220**
Skellefteå, *Nor.* 64°45' N, 20°53' E **152**
Skelleftehamn, *Nor.* 64°40' N, 21°14' E **152**
Skender Vakuf, *Bosn. and Herzg.* 44°29' N, 17°22' E **168**
Skępe, *Pol.* 52°51' N, 19°21' E **152**
Skerries, *Ire.* 53°33' N, 6°8' W **150**
Ski, *Nor.* 59°43' N, 10°51' E **152**
Skiatook, *Okla., U.S.* 36°21' N, 95°60' W **96**
Skibo Castle, site, *U.K.* 57°51' N, 4°16' W **150**
Skibotn, *Nor.* 69°23' N, 20°21' E **152**
Skidal', *Belarus* 53°35' N, 24°14' E **152**
Skiddaw, peak, *U.K.* 54°38' N, 3°11' W **162**
Skidmore, *Tex., U.S.* 28°14' N, 97°41' W **92**
Skidmore, Mount, peak, *Antarctica* 80°29' S, 29°26' W **248**
Skien, *Nor.* 59°13' N, 9°32' E **160**
Skihist Mountain, peak, *Can.* 50°10' N, 121°59' W **108**
Skillingaryd, *Nor.* 57°25' N, 14°4' E **152**
Skipskjolen, peak, *Nor.* 70°20' N, 29°32' E **152**
Skipton, *U.K.* 53°57' N, 2°1' W **162**
Skíros, island, *Gr.* 38°57' N, 24°31' E **180**
Skive, *Den.* 56°33' N, 9°0' E **150**
Skjåk, *Nor.* 61°52' N, 8°21' E **152**
Skjern, *Den.* 55°56' N, 8°27' E **150**
Skjern Å, river, *Den.* 55°50' N, 8°41' E **152**
Skjervøy, *Nor.* 70°1' N, 20°59' E **152**
Sklad, *Russ.* 71°53' N, 123°21' E **160**
Sklinna, islands, *Norwegian Sea* 65°8' N, 9°53' E **152**
Skodje, *Nor.* 62°29' N, 6°42' E **152**
Skokie, *Ill., U.S.* 42°1' N, 87°44' W **102**
Skokowa, *Pol.* 51°23' N, 16°52' E **152**
Skole, *Ukr.* 49°2' N, 23°31' E **152**
Skönvik, *Nor.* 62°26' N, 17°17' E **152**
Skopin, *Russ.* 53°50' N, 39°30' E **154**
Skopje, *Maced.* 41°58' N, 21°21' E **168**
Skotoúsa, *Gr.* 41°7' N, 23°23' E **156**
Skövde, *Nor.* 58°22' N, 13°48' E **152**
Skovorodino, *Russ.* 53°52' N, 123°53' E **190**
Skowhegan, *Me., U.S.* 44°43' N, 69°44' W **82**
Skrad, *Croatia* 45°25' N, 14°53' E **156**
Skradin (Scardona), *Croatia* 43°49' N, 15°54' E **168**
Skrīveri, *Latv.* 56°37' N, 25°7' E **166**
Skrunda, *Latv.* 56°39' N, 21°58' E **166**
Skudeneshavn, *Nor.* 59°9' N, 5°15' E **152**
Skulerud, *Nor.* 59°40' N, 11°32' E **152**
Skull Mountain, peak, *Nev., U.S.* 36°46' N, 116°13' W **101**
Skultuna, *Nor.* 59°42' N, 16°25' E **152**
Skuodas, *Lith.* 56°15' N, 21°32' E **166**
Skutskär, *Sw.* 60°38' N, 17°23' E **166**
Skvyra, *Ukr.* 49°44' N, 29°47' E **158**
Skwentna, *Alas., U.S.* 61°48' N, 151°17' W **98**
Skykomish, *Wash., U.S.* 47°41' N, 121°22' W **100**
Skykomish, river, *Wash., U.S.* 47°48' N, 121°58' W **100**
Slagelse, *Den.* 55°23' N, 11°22' E **152**
Slagle, *La., U.S.* 31°11' N, 93°9' W **103**
Slains Castle, site, *U.K.* 57°24' N, 1°57' W **150**
Slakovci, *Croatia* 45°13' N, 18°55' E **168**
Slano, *Croatia* 42°46' N, 17°52' E **168**
Slantsy, *Russ.* 59°5' N, 28°0' E **166**
Slaný, *Czech Rep.* 50°13' N, 14°4' E **152**
Śląskie, adm. division, *Pol.* 50°19' N, 18°25' E **152**
Slate Islands, *Can.* 48°29' N, 87°23' W **94**
Slate Mountain, peak, *Calif., U.S.* 40°48' N, 120°57' W **90**
Slate Range, *Calif., U.S.* 35°49' N, 117°22' W **101**
Slater, *Mo., U.S.* 39°12' N, 93°4' W **94**
Slatersville, *R.I., U.S.* 41°59' N, 71°35' W **104**
Slatina, *Bosn. and Herzg.* 44°49' N, 17°16' E **168**
Slatina, *Bosn. and Herzg.* 44°57' N, 18°26' E **168**
Slatina, *Rom.* 44°27' N, 24°21' E **156**
Slatina Timiş, *Rom.* 45°15' N, 22°16' E **168**
Slatinski Drenovac, *Croatia* 45°32' N, 17°42' E **168**
Slaton, *Tex., U.S.* 33°25' N, 101°39' W **92**
Slave Coast, region, *Nig.* 5°48' N, 5°8' E **222**
Slave Lake, *Can.* 55°17' N, 114°47' W **108**
Slave Point, *Can.* 61°1' N, 115°56' W **108**
Slave, river, *Can.* 59°1' N, 111°30' W **106**
Slavgorod, *Belarus* 53°23' N, 31°1' E **154**
Slavgorod, *Russ.* 52°59' N, 78°47' E **184**
Slavinja, *Serb. and Mont.* 43°8' N, 22°52' E **168**
Slavkovichi, *Russ.* 57°37' N, 29°4' E **166**
Slavonia, region, *Croatia* 45°20' N, 16°50' E **168**
Slavonice, *Czech Rep.* 48°59' N, 15°21' E **152**
Slavonski Kobaš, *Croatia* 45°6' N, 17°44' E **168**
Slavuta, *Ukr.* 50°18' N, 26°53' E **152**
Slavyanka, *Russ.* 42°51' N, 131°22' E **200**
Slavyansk na Kubani, *Russ.* 45°17' N, 38°3' E **156**
Slayton, *Minn., U.S.* 43°57' N, 95°45' W **94**
Sleaford, *U.K.* 52°59' N, 0°25' E **162**
Sleat, Point of 56°43' N, 6°3' W **150**
Sled Lake, lake, *Can.* 54°22' N, 107°42' W **108**
Sleeper Islands, islands, *Can.* 57°9' N, 82°37' W **106**
Sleepy Eye, *Minn., U.S.* 44°16' N, 94°44' W **94**
Ślesin, *Pol.* 53°10' N, 17°42' E **152**
Slide Mountain, peak, *N.Y., U.S.* 41°58' N, 74°29' W **94**
Slidell, *La., U.S.* 30°14' N, 89°47' W **103**
Sliedrecht, *Neth.* 51°49' N, 4°45' E **167**
Slievemore, peak, *Ire.* 53°59' N, 10°10' W **150**
Slievenamon, peak, *Ire.* 52°24' N, 7°40' W **150**
Sligo, *Ire.* 54°15' N, 8°29' W **150**
Slim Buttes, peak, *S. Dak., U.S.* 45°21' N, 103°16' W **90**
Slinger, *Wis., U.S.* 43°19' N, 88°17' W **102**
Slingerlands, *N.Y., U.S.* 42°37' N, 73°53' W **104**
Slite, *Sw.* 57°42' N, 18°47' E **166**
Sliven, *Bulg.* 42°40' N, 26°18' E **156**
Sliven, adm. division, *Bulg.* 42°40' N, 25°52' E **156**
Slivnica, *Serb. and Mont.* 42°58' N, 22°45' E **168**
Slivnitsa, *Bulg.* 42°51' N, 23°2' E **168**
Sljeme, peak, *Croatia* 45°54' N, 15°55' E **168**
Słomniki, *Pol.* 50°14' N, 20°6' E **152**
Słupca, *Pol.* 52°17' N, 17°52' E **152**
Słupsk, *Pol.* 54°21' N, 16°40' E **152**
Sloan, *Nev., U.S.* 35°56' N, 115°14' W **101**
Slobodchikovo, *Russ.* 61°45' N, 48°16' E **154**
Slobodskoy, *Russ.* 58°46' N, 50°10' E **169**
Slobozia, *Rom.* 44°34' N, 27°21' E **156**
Slocan, *Can.* 49°45' N, 117°28' W **90**
Sloka, *Latv.* 56°57' N, 23°37' E **166**
Slonim, *Belarus* 53°4' N, 25°18' E **152**
Slotten, *Nor.* 70°44' N, 24°33' E **152**
Slottsbron, *Nor.* 59°18' N, 13°3' E **152**
Slough, *U.K.* 51°31' N, 0°37' E **162**
Slovakia 48°50' N, 18°49' E **152**
Sloveni, *Belarus* 54°20' N, 29°35' E **166**
Slovenia 46°4' N, 14°46' E **156**
Slov"yans'k, *Ukr.* 48°51' N, 37°37' E **158**
Sludka, *Russ.* 61°56' N, 50°12' E **154**
Sludka, *Russ.* 59°22' N, 49°43' E **154**
Sluis, *Neth.* 51°18' N, 3°23' E **163**
Slumbering Hills, *Nev., U.S.* 41°16' N, 118°18' W **90**
Slŭnchev Bryag, *Bulg.* 42°41' N, 27°42' E **156**
Slussfors, *Nor.* 65°26' N, 16°14' E **152**
Slutsk, *Belarus* 53°0' N, 27°33' E **152**
Slyudyanka, *Russ.* 51°32' N, 103°50' E **190**
Smackover, *Ark., U.S.* 33°20' N, 92°44' W **103**
Smalininkai, *Lith.* 55°4' N, 22°35' E **166**
Small Lake, lake, *Can.* 57°40' N, 97°46' W **108**
Small Point, *Me., U.S.* 43°38' N, 69°52' W **104**
Smalltree Lake, lake, *Can.* 61°0' N, 105°43' W **108**
Smallwood Reservoir, lake, *Can.* 53°25' N, 70°28' W **106**
Smalyavichy, *Belarus* 54°1' N, 28°5' E **166**
Smara, *Africa* 26°45' N, 11°43' W **214**
Smarhon', *Belarus* 54°29' N, 26°22' E **166**
Smederevo, *Serb. and Mont.* 44°39' N, 20°55' E **168**
Smedjebacken, *Nor.* 60°6' N, 15°23' E **152**
Smeïda see Taoudenni, *Mali* 22°41' N, 3°59' W **214**
Śmigiel, *Pol.* 52°0' N, 16°31' E **152**
Smila, *Ukr.* 49°15' N, 31°48' E **160**
Smilavichy, *Belarus* 53°46' N, 28°2' E **152**
Smilde, *Neth.* 52°56' N, 6°28' E **163**
Smiltene, *Latv.* 57°25' N, 25°52' E **166**
Smirnovo, *Kaz.* 54°30' N, 69°26' E **184**
Smith, *Can.* 55°8' N, 114°3' W **108**
Smith Arm 66°9' N, 124°31' W **98**
Smith Bay 70°41' N, 155°33' W **98**
Smith Bay 76°54' N, 81°57' W **106**
Smith Canyon, *Colo., U.S.* 37°23' N, 103°35' W **92**
Smith Center, *Kans., U.S.* 39°46' N, 98°47' W **90**
Smith Island, *Antarctica* 62°54' S, 63°41' W **134**
Smith Island, *Can.* 60°21' N, 80°16' W **106**
Smith, Mount, peak, *Eth.* 6°15' N, 36°15' E **224**
Smith River, *Can.* 59°52' N, 126°26' W **108**
Smith Sound 51°10' N, 128°2' W **108**
Smith Sound 78°12' N, 79°48' W **246**
Smithboro, *Ill., U.S.* 38°53' N, 89°21' W **102**
Smithdale, *Miss., U.S.* 31°19' N, 90°41' W **103**
Smithers, *Can.* 54°44' N, 127°15' W **106**
Smithers, *W. Va., U.S.* 38°10' N, 81°19' W **94**
Smithfield, *N.C., U.S.* 35°30' N, 78°21' W **96**
Smithfield, *S. Af.* 30°12' S, 26°32' E **227**
Smiths Falls, *Can.* 44°54' N, 75°58' W **82**
Smithtown, *N.Y., U.S.* 40°51' N, 73°12' W **104**
Smithville, *W. Va., U.S.* 39°4' N, 81°6' W **102**
Smoke Creek Desert, *Nev., U.S.* 40°32' N, 120°5' W **90**
Smokey, Cape, *Can.* 46°30' N, 60°22' W **111**
Smokvica, *Croatia* 42°54' N, 16°52' E **168**
Smoky Falls, *Can.* 50°3' N, 82°11' W **94**
Smoky Hill, river, *Kans., U.S.* 38°41' N, 99°5' W **90**
Smoky Hills, *Kans., U.S.* 39°16' N, 99°19' W **90**
Smoky Lake, *Can.* 54°6' N, 112°28' W **108**
Smoky Mountains, *Idaho, U.S.* 43°40' N, 114°50' W **90**
Smoky, river, *Can.* 53°52' N, 119°16' W **108**
Smoky, river, *Can.* 55°21' N, 118°10' W **108**
Smolensk, *Russ.* 54°48' N, 32°7' E **154**
Smolensk, adm. division, *Russ.* 54°59' N, 31°37' E **154**
Smolijana, *Bosn. and Herzg.* 44°37' N, 16°25' E **168**
Smólikas, peak, *Gr.* 40°4' N, 20°51' E **156**
Smolyan, *Bulg.* 41°35' N, 24°40' E **156**
Smolyan, adm. division, *Bulg.* 41°37' N, 24°7' E **156**
Smolyanovtsi, *Bulg.* 43°31' N, 22°59' E **168**
Smooth Rock Falls, *Can.* 49°17' N, 81°38' W **94**
Smyley Island, *Antarctica* 72°41' S, 82°11' W **248**
Smyrna see İzmir, *Turk.* 38°24' N, 27°8' E **156**
Snaefell, peak 54°14' N, 4°33' W **150**
Snaght, Slieve, peak, *Ire.* 55°10' N, 7°27' W **150**
Snake Falls, *Can.* 50°50' N, 93°26' W **90**
Snake Range, *Nev., U.S.* 39°18' N, 114°25' W **90**
Snake River, *Can.* 59°5' N, 122°26' W **108**
Snake, river, *Can.* 65°50' N, 133°4' W **98**
Snake River Plain, *Idaho, U.S.* 43°24' N, 116°24' W **90**
Snake, river, *U.S.* 45°5' N, 116°27' W **90**
Snappertuna, *Fin.* 59°59' N, 23°39' E **166**
Snare Lake, *Can.* 58°25' N, 108°18' W **108**
Snare, river, *Can.* 58°23' N, 107°39' W **108**
Snåsa, *Nor.* 64°13' N, 12°20' E **152**
Sneek, *Neth.* 53°1' N, 5°40' E **163**
Snelland, *U.K.* 53°18' N, 0°24' E **162**
Snelling, *Calif., U.S.* 37°31' N, 120°28' W **100**
Snettisham, *U.K.* 52°52' N, 0°30' E **162**
Snezhnogorsk, *Russ.* 68°6' N, 87°36' E **169**
Snezhnoye, *Russ.* 65°27' N, 173°3' E **160**
Sněžka, peak, *Czech Rep.* 50°43' N, 15°37' E **152**
Snihurivka, *Ukr.* 47°5' N, 32°48' E **156**
Snilfjord, *Nor.* 63°23' N, 9°30' E **152**
Snipe Keys, islands, *Gulf of Mexico* 24°43' N, 81°46' W **105**
Snøhetta, peak, *Nor.* 62°18' N, 9°9' E **152**
Snohomish, *Wash., U.S.* 47°54' N, 122°6' W **100**
Snonuten, peak, *Nor.* 59°29' N, 6°45' E **152**
Snoqualmie, *Wash., U.S.* 47°30' N, 121°50' W **100**
Snoqualmie Pass, *Wash., U.S.* 47°24' N, 121°25' W **100**
Snov, river, *Ukr.* 51°34' N, 31°44' E **158**
Snover, *Mich., U.S.* 43°27' N, 82°58' W **102**
Snow Hill Island, *Antarctica* 64°55' S, 56°59' W **134**
Snow Island, *Antarctica* 62°42' S, 61°37' W **134**
Snow Lake, *Can.* 54°52' N, 100°3' W **108**
Snow, Mount, peak, *Vt., U.S.* 42°57' N, 72°57' W **104**
Snow Mountain, peak, *Calif., U.S.* 39°22' N, 122°51' W **90**
Snow Mountain, peak, *Me., U.S.* 45°16' N, 70°48' W **94**
Snow Peak, *Wash., U.S.* 48°33' N, 118°33' W **90**
Snowbird Lake, *Can.* 60°37' N, 103°28' W **108**
Snowden, *Can.* 53°29' N, 104°40' W **108**
Snowdon, peak, *U.K.* 53°4' N, 4°6' W **162**
Snowflake, *Ariz., U.S.* 34°30' N, 110°5' W **92**
Snowmass Mountain, peak, *Colo., U.S.* 39°7' N, 107°10' W **90**
Snowshoe Peak, *Mont., U.S.* 48°11' N, 115°46' W **90**
Snowy Mountains, *Austral.* 36°23' S, 147°16' E **230**
Snuol, *Cambodia* 12°6' N, 106°24' E **202**
Snyder, *Colo., U.S.* 40°19' N, 103°37' W **90**
Snyder, *Okla., U.S.* 34°38' N, 98°58' W **92**
Snyder, *Tex., U.S.* 32°41' N, 100°54' W **92**
Soala see Sokolo, *Mali* 14°45' N, 6°7' W **222**
Soanierana-Ivongo, *Madagascar* 16°54' S, 49°33' E **220**
Soatá, *Col.* 6°19' N, 72°42' W **136**
Soavinandriana, *Madagascar* 19°11' S, 46°44' E **220**
Soba, *Nig.* 10°57' N, 8°5' E **222**
Sobat, river, *Sudan* 8°53' N, 32°30' E **224**
Soberania National Park, *Pan.* 9°9' N, 79°51' W **115**
Sobernheim, *Ger.* 49°46' N, 7°39' E **167**
Sobinka, *Russ.* 55°58' N, 40°1' E **154**
Sobolev, *Russ.* 51°54' N, 51°41' E **158**
Sobozo, spring, *Niger* 21°10' N, 14°47' E **222**
Sobral, *Braz.* 3°41' S, 40°23' W **132**
Sobti, spring, *Mali* 22°45' N, 1°46' W **214**
Soc Trang, *Vietnam* 9°36' N, 105°57' E **202**
Sočanica, *Europe* 43°3' N, 20°50' E **168**
Socha, *Col.* 5°59' N, 72°41' W **136**
Sochaczew, *Pol.* 52°13' N, 20°14' E **152**
Sochi, *Russ.* 43°36' N, 39°46' E **195**
Society Islands, *South Pacific Ocean* 17°21' S, 152°59' W **238**
Socompa, *Chile* 24°25' S, 68°21' W **132**
Socorro, *N. Mex., U.S.* 34°2' N, 106°53' W **82**
Socorro, Isla, island, *Isla Socorro* 18°28' N, 110°60' W **112**
Socotra (Suquṭrā), island, *Yemen* 12°19' N, 54°12' E **182**
Socovos, *Sp.* 38°20' N, 1°59' W **164**
Socuéllamos, *Sp.* 39°17' N, 2°48' W **164**
Soda Creek, *Can.* 52°20' N, 122°16' W **108**
Soda Lake, *Calif., U.S.* 35°12' N, 120°2' W **100**
Soda Mountains, *Calif., U.S.* 35°16' N, 116°20' W **101**
Soda Peak, *Wash., U.S.* 45°51' N, 122°6' W **100**
Sodankylä, *Fin.* 67°25' N, 26°33' E **152**
Söderhamn, *Nor.* 61°18' N, 17°0' E **152**
Södertälje, *Nor.* 59°10' N, 17°34' E **152**
Sodiri, *Sudan* 14°23' N, 29°8' E **226**
Sodo, *Eth.* 6°49' N, 37°46' E **224**
Södra Kvarken 60°17' N, 18°40' E **166**
Södra Storfjället, peak, *Nor.* 65°36' N, 14°36' E **152**
Södra Sunderbyn, *Nor.* 65°39' N, 21°56' E **152**
Södra Vi, *Nor.* 57°44' N, 15°46' E **152**
Sodus, *Mich., U.S.* 42°1' N, 86°22' W **102**
Soekmekaar see Morebeng, *S. Af.* 23°30' S, 29°56' E **227**
Soela Väin 58°37' N, 22°8' E **166**
Soest, *Ger.* 51°34' N, 8°6' E **167**
Sofala, adm. division, *Mozambique* 18°26' S, 34°1' E **224**
Sofara, *Mali* 14°1' N, 4°15' W **222**
Sofi, *Sudan* 14°8' N, 35°51' E **226**
Sofi, *Tanzania* 8°47' S, 36°9' E **224**
Sofia see Sofiya, *Bulg.* 42°41' N, 23°12' E **156**
Sofiya, adm. division, *Bulg.* 42°51' N, 22°47' E **168**
Sofiya (Sofia), *Bulg.* 42°41' N, 23°12' E **156**
Sofiya-Grad, adm. division, *Bulg.* 42°35' N, 23°7' E **156**
Sofporog, *Russ.* 65°48' N, 31°28' E **152**
Sof'yanga, *Russ.* 65°52' N, 31°17' E **152**
Soga, *Tanzania* 6°47' S, 38°55' E **224**
Sogamoso, *Col.* 5°41' N, 72°56' W **136**
Sogata, *Eth.* 5°41' N, 35°8' E **224**
Sögel, *Ger.* 52°50' N, 7°32' E **163**
Sogod, *Philippines* 10°24' N, 125°0' E **203**
Sogolle, spring, *Chad* 15°20' N, 15°20' E **216**
Sogra, *Russ.* 62°49' N, 47°28' E **169**
Sogra, *Russ.* 62°39' N, 46°16' E **154**
Söğüt, *Turk.* 40°0' N, 30°10' E **180**
Söğüt Gölü, lake, *Turk.* 37°4' N, 29°39' E **156**
Sogxian, *China* 31°51' N, 93°40' E **188**
Sohâg, *Egypt* 26°33' N, 31°35' E **180**
Soham, *U.K.* 52°19' N, 0°20' E **162**
Soheuksando, island, *S. Korea* 34°7' N, 124°32' E **198**
Sohm Plain, *North Atlantic Ocean* 37°43' N, 53°36' W **253**
Sŏhŭng, *N. Korea* 38°28' N, 126°10' E **200**
Soignies, *Belg.* 50°35' N, 4°4' E **163**
Şoimuş, *Rom.* 45°55' N, 22°55' E **168**
Soissons, *Fr.* 49°22' N, 3°18' E **163**
Sōja, *Japan* 34°40' N, 133°45' E **201**
Sojat, *India* 25°54' N, 73°42' E **186**
Sok, river, *Russ.* 53°53' N, 51°16' E **154**
Sokcho, *S. Korea* 38°13' N, 128°34' E **200**
Söke, *Turk.* 37°44' N, 27°22' E **156**
Soko Banja, *Serb. and Mont.* 43°38' N, 21°51' E **168**
Sokodé, *Togo* 8°57' N, 1°8' E **214**
Sokol, *Russ.* 59°28' N, 40°12' E **154**
Sokolac, *Bosn. and Herzg.* 43°56' N, 18°49' E **168**
Sokolarci, *Maced.* 41°54' N, 22°17' E **168**
Sokółka, *Pol.* 53°24' N, 23°29' E **152**
Sokolo (Soala), *Mali* 14°45' N, 6°7' W **222**
Sokolovka, *Kaz.* 55°9' N, 69°11' E **184**
Sokolovo, *Russ.* 65°21' N, 57°1' E **154**
Sokol'skoye, *Russ.* 57°8' N, 43°13' E **154**
Sokoto, *Nig.* 13°1' N, 5°13' E **222**
Soksa, *N. Korea* 40°38' N, 127°17' E **200**
Sokuluk, *Kyrg.* 42°51' N, 74°23' E **184**
Sol, Costa del, *Sp.* 36°34' N, 4°40' W **164**
Sol de Julio, *Arg.* 29°33' S, 63°27' W **139**
Sol, river, *Braz.* 6°42' S, 67°47' W **130**
Solana Beach, *Calif., U.S.* 32°59' N, 117°17' W **101**
Solano, *Venez.* 1°56' N, 66°56' W **136**
Solano, Punta, *Col.* 6°16' N, 77°53' W **136**
Solberg, *Nor.* 63°47' N, 17°38' E **152**
Solberget, peak, *Nor.* 63°47' N, 17°27' E **152**
Solec, *Pol.* 51°8' N, 21°45' E **152**
Soledad, *Arg.* 30°38' S, 60°55' W **139**
Soledad, *Calif., U.S.* 36°25' N, 121°20' W **100**
Soledad, *Col.* 10°52' N, 74°48' W **136**
Soledad, *Peru* 3°32' S, 77°49' W **136**
Soledad, *Venez.* 8°11' N, 63°33' W **116**
Soledad de Doblado, *Mex.* 19°3' N, 96°25' W **114**
Soledad Pass, *Calif., U.S.* 34°30' N, 118°9' W **101**
Soledade, *Braz.* 28°50' S, 52°32' W **139**
Soledade, *Braz.* 6°38' S, 69°9' W **130**
Solhan, *Turk.* 38°57' N, 41°3' E **195**
Soliera, *It.* 44°44' N, 10°55' E **167**
Soligalich, *Russ.* 59°5' N, 42°16' E **154**
Solignano, *It.* 44°38' N, 9°58' E **156**
Solikamsk, *Russ.* 59°38' N, 56°45' E **154**
Solimões (Amazonas), river, *Braz.* 2°50' S, 66°35' W **122**
Solin (Salonae), *Croatia* 43°32' N, 16°28' E **168**
Solingen, *Ger.* 51°9' N, 7°5' E **167**
Sollefteå, *Nor.* 63°9' N, 17°15' E **152**
Solling, *Ger.* 51°43' N, 9°23' E **167**
Sol'Iletsk, *Russ.* 51°9' N, 55°2' E **158**
Solms, *Ger.* 50°31' N, 8°24' E **167**
Solna, *Sw.* 59°22' N, 17°58' E **166**
Solnechnogorsk, *Russ.* 56°9' N, 37°0' E **154**
Solobkivtsi, *Ukr.* 49°3' N, 26°54' E **152**
Solodcha, *Russ.* 49°37' N, 44°18' E **158**
Solok, *Indonesia* 0°47' N, 100°39' E **196**
Sololo, *Kenya* 3°27' N, 38°34' E **224**
Solomennoye, *Russ.* 61°50' N, 34°19' E **154**
Solomon, *Can.* 53°21' N, 117°56' W **108**
Solomon, *Kans., U.S.* 38°53' N, 97°22' W **90**
Solomon Islands 10°21' S, 162°22' E **242**
Solomon Islands, *South Pacific Ocean* 10°55' S, 162°35' E **238**
Solomon, river, *Kans., U.S.* 39°41' N, 99°17' W **90**
Solomon Sea 6°43' S, 150°46' E **238**
Solon Springs, *Wis., U.S.* 46°21' N, 91°50' W **94**
Solotcha, *Russ.* 54°47' N, 39°49' E **154**
Solothurn, *Switz.* 47°12' N, 7°31' E **150**
Solovetskiye Ostrova, islands, *Beloye More* 64°40' N, 35°18' E **154**
Solsona, *Sp.* 41°59' N, 1°31' E **164**
Solstad, *Nor.* 65°10' N, 12°8' E **152**
Solt, *Hung.* 46°47' N, 19°1' E **168**
Šolta, island, *Croatia* 43°18' N, 16°9' E **168**
Soltan Bagh, *Afghan.* 33°19' N, 68°39' E **186**
Solṭānābād, *Iran* 36°24' N, 57°56' E **180**
Solṭānābād, *Iran* 31°2' N, 49°44' E **184**
Soltan-e Bakva, *Afghan.* 32°18' N, 62°58' E **186**
Soltustik Qazaqstan, adm. division, *Kaz.* 53°58' N, 67°52' E **184**

ruce Pine, N.C., U.S. 35°55' N, 82°5' W 96
ry, Pa., U.S. 39°54' N, 76°41' W 94
ulico, Capo, It. 39°57' N, 16°40' E 156
ur, Tex., U.S. 33°27' N, 100°51' W 92
urger, Tex., U.S. 30°40' N, 94°11' W 103
urn Head, U.K. 53°30' N, 0°7' E 162
už, Europe 42°31' N, 19°13' E 168
uzzum, Can. 49°41' N, 121°26' W 100
uamish, Can. 49°42' N, 123°8' W 100
uamish, river, Can. 50°7' N, 123°20' W 100
uare Islands, Can. 52°43' N, 55°51' W 111
uires, Mount, peak, Austral. 26°15' S, 127°12' E 230
uirrel, river, Can. 50°25' N, 84°20' W 110
bac, Bosn. and Herzg. 45°5' N, 17°31' E 168
bica, Europe 42°44' N, 20°46' E 168
bobran, Serb. and Mont. 45°33' N, 19°47' E 168
e Umbell, Cambodia 11°6' N, 103°45' E 202
ebrenica, Bosn. and Herzg. 44°6' N, 19°19' E 168
edinnyy Khrebet, Russ. 57°35' N, 160°3' E 160
ednekolymsk, Russ. 67°27' N, 153°21' E 160
edneye Bugayevo, Russ. 66°0' N, 52°28' E 154
ednyaya Olekma, Russ. 55°20' N, 120°33' E 190
emska Mitrovica, Serb. and Mont. 44°58' N, 19°37' E 168
emska Rača, Serb. and Mont. 44°54' N, 19°19' E 168
emski Karlovci, Serb. and Mont. 45°11' N, 19°55' E 168
etensk, Russ. 52°17' N, 117°45' E 190
i Kalahasti, India 13°46' N, 79°40' E 188
i Lanka 7°26' N, 80°15' E 188
i Madhopur, India 27°28' N, 75°37' E 197
ikakulam, India 18°17' N, 83°55' E 188
inagar, India 34°7' N, 74°48' E 186
ivardhan, India 18°5' N, 73°0' E 188
netica, Bosn. and Herzg. 44°26' N, 16°35' E 168
okowo, Pol. 54°11' N, 21°31' E 166
pska Crnja, Serb. and Mont. 45°43' N, 20°42' E 168
pski Itebej, Serb. and Mont. 45°34' N, 20°43' E 168
sanggyo, N. Korea 37°46' N, 125°26' E 200
taaten River National Park, Austral. 16°39' S, 142°26' E 238
taberhuk, Kattegat 54°18' N, 10°48' E 152
tack, Ben, peak, U.K. 58°19' N, 5°5' W 150
tade, Ger. 53°36' N, 9°28' E 150
tädjan, peak, Nor. 61°54' N, 12°44' E 152
tadskanaal, Neth. 52°59' N, 6°57' E 163
tadtallendorf, Ger. 50°49' N, 9°0' E 167
tadtkyll, Ger. 50°20' N, 6°32' E 167
tadtlohn, Ger. 51°59' N, 6°54' E 167
tafford, Kans., U.S. 37°56' N, 98°36' W 90
tafford, U.K. 52°47' N, 2°7' W 162
tafford Springs, Conn., U.S. 41°57' N, 72°19' W 104
taffordsville, Ky., U.S. 37°49' N, 82°51' W 94
tage Road Pass, Oreg., U.S. 42°43' N, 123°22' W 90
tagira, ruin(s), Gr. 40°31' N, 23°38' E 156
tagnone, Isole dello, islands, Mediterranean Sea 37°35' N, 11°52' E 156
taicele, Latv. 57°51' N, 24°44' E 166
taigue Fort, site, Ire. 51°47' N, 10°7' W 150
taines, U.K. 51°26' N, 0°31' E 162
taithes, U.K. 54°33' N, 0°48' E 162
talać, Serb. and Mont. 43°41' N, 21°25' E 168
taldzene, Latv. 57°25' N, 21°35' E 166
talham, U.K. 52°46' N, 1°31' E 163
talingrad see Volgograd, Russ. 48°46' N, 44°28' E 158
tallo, Miss., U.S. 32°53' N, 89°6' W 103
tallworthy, Cape, Can. 81°41' N, 95°15' W 246
talowa Wola, Pol. 50°33' N, 22°2' E 152
tamford, Conn., U.S. 41°2' N, 73°33' W 104
tamford, N.Y., U.S. 42°24' N, 74°39' W 110
tamford, Tex., U.S. 32°55' N, 99°49' W 92
tamford, U.K. 52°39' N, 0°29' E 162
tamford Bridge, U.K. 53°59' N, 0°55' E 162
tamovo, Bulg. 42°26' N, 25°50' E 156
tampriet, Namibia 24°18' S, 18°23' E 227
tamps, Ark., U.S. 33°21' N, 93°31' W 103
tanberry, Mo., U.S. 40°12' N, 94°32' W 94
tanderton, S. Af. 26°57' S, 29°13' E 227
tandish, Me., U.S. 43°43' N, 70°33' W 104
tandish, Mich., U.S. 43°58' N, 83°58' W 102
tandish Ranges, Austral. 21°44' S, 138°59' E 230
tanfield, Oreg., U.S. 45°46' N, 119°14' W 90
tanford, Ky., U.S. 37°31' N, 84°40' W 94
tanford, Mont., U.S. 47°7' N, 110°14' W 90
tånga, Sw. 57°16' N, 18°27' E 166
tanger, S. Af. 29°21' S, 31°15' E 227
taniard Creek, Bahamas 24°50' N, 77°55' W 96
tanišić, Serb. and Mont. 45°55' N, 19°9' E 168
taňkov, Czech Rep. 49°33' N, 13°4' E 152
tanley, Can. 46°16' N, 66°45' W 111
tanley, Falk. Is., U.K. 51°42' S, 57°52' W 134
tanley, Idaho, U.S. 44°12' N, 114°56' W 90
tanley, N. Dak., U.S. 48°17' N, 102°24' W 90
tanley, Wis., U.S. 44°57' N, 90°56' W 94
tanley Falls see Boyoma Falls, Dem. Rep. of the Congo 0°14' N, 25°9' E 224
tanley Mission, Can. 55°25' N, 104°30' W 108
tanley, Mount, peak, Austral. 22°50' S, 130°28' E 230
tanley, Mount, peak, Austral. 40°6' S, 143°46' E 230
tanley Peak, Can. 51°11' N, 116°6' W 90
tanleyville see Kisangani, Dem. Rep. of the Congo 0°33' N, 25°16' E 224
tanovoy Khrebet, Russ. 54°46' N, 122°14' E 190
tanton, Mich., U.S. 43°17' N, 85°5' W 102
tanton, Tex., U.S. 32°7' N, 101°47' W 92
tanwick, U.K. 52°20' N, 0°33' E 162
tanwood, Wash., U.S. 48°13' N, 122°23' W 100
taphorst, Neth. 52°39' N, 6°12' E 163
taples, Minn., U.S. 46°20' N, 94°48' W 90
tapleton, Nebr., U.S. 41°28' N, 100°31' W 90
Star, Miss., U.S. 32°5' N, 90°2' W 103
Star City, Ark., U.S. 33°56' N, 91°51' W 96
Star City, Ind., U.S. 40°58' N, 86°34' W 102
Star Peak, Nev., U.S. 40°31' N, 118°16' W 90
Star Valley, Wyo., U.S. 42°38' N, 111°3' W 90
Stara Moravica, Serb. and Mont. 45°52' N, 19°28' E 168
Stara Pazova, Serb. and Mont. 44°58' N, 20°9' E 168
Stara Ushytsya, Ukr. 48°34' N, 27°5' E 152
Stara Vyzhivka, Ukr. 51°25' N, 24°25' E 152
Stara Zagora, Bulg. 42°25' N, 25°36' E 156
Stara Zagora, adm. division, Bulg. 42°39' N, 25°6' E 156
Staraya, Russ. 70°56' N, 112°20' E 173
Staraya Poltavka, Russ. 50°28' N, 46°26' E 158
Staraya Russa, Russ. 57°56' N, 31°23' E 152
Starbuck, Wash., U.S. 46°30' N, 118°8' W 90
Stare Pole, Pol. 54°3' N, 19°11' E 166
Stargard Szczeciński, Pol. 53°19' N, 15°1' E 152
Stari Bar, Europe 42°6' N, 19°8' E 168
Stari Mikanovci, Croatia 45°15' N, 18°33' E 168
Starigrad, Croatia 43°10' N, 16°35' E 168
Staritsa, Belarus 53°14' N, 27°15' E 154
Staritsa, Russ. 56°28' N, 34°56' E 154
Starke, Fla., U.S. 29°56' N, 82°8' W 96
Starks, La., U.S. 30°17' N, 93°40' W 103
Starksboro, Vt., U.S. 44°13' N, 73°4' W 104
Starkville, Colo., U.S. 37°7' N, 104°33' W 92
Starkville, Miss., U.S. 33°26' N, 88°48' W 103
Starobaltachevo, Russ. 56°1' N, 55°56' E 154
Starobil's'k, Ukr. 49°18' N, 38°53' E 158
Starobin, Belarus 52°42' N, 27°27' E 152
Starodub, Russ. 52°31' N, 32°51' E 154
Starokostyantyniv, Ukr. 49°44' N, 27°12' E 152
Starominskaya, Russ. 46°32' N, 39°1' E 156
Staropol'ye, Russ. 59°1' N, 28°34' E 166
Starorybnoye, Russ. 72°48' N, 104°49' E 173
Staroshcherbinovskaya, Russ. 46°37' N, 38°38' E 156
Staroye Syalo, Belarus 55°17' N, 29°58' E 166
Start Point, English Channel 50°2' N, 3°37' W 150
Starvyy Karabutak, Kaz. 49°49' N, 59°54' E 158
Staryy Biryuzyak, Russ. 44°45' N, 46°47' E 158
Staryy Krym, Ukr. 45°1' N, 35°0' E 156
Staryy Kryvyn, Ukr. 50°21' N, 26°42' E 152
Staryy Nadym, Russ. 65°36' N, 72°50' E 169
Staryy Oskol, Russ. 51°17' N, 37°45' E 158
Staryy Sambir, Ukr. 49°23' N, 22°55' E 152
Staszów, Pol. 50°33' N, 21°10' E 152
State Line, Miss., U.S. 31°24' N, 88°28' W 103
Staten Island, N.Y., U.S. 40°27' N, 74°6' W 104
Staten Island see de los Estados, Isla, Arg. 55°28' S, 64°48' W 134
Statesboro, Ga., U.S. 32°25' N, 81°47' W 112
Station 10, Sudan 19°41' N, 33°8' E 182
Station 5, Sudan 21°2' N, 32°19' E 182
Station 6, Sudan 20°44' N, 32°30' E 182
Staunton, Ill., U.S. 39°0' N, 89°47' W 102
Staunton, Va., U.S. 38°8' N, 79°5' W 94
Stavanger, Nor. 58°56' N, 5°43' E 152
Stave Lake, Can. 49°18' N, 122°30' W 100
Stavelot, Belg. 50°23' N, 5°56' E 167
Stavely, Can. 50°10' N, 113°39' W 90
Staveren, Neth. 52°53' N, 5°22' E 163
Stavnoye, Ukr. 48°56' N, 22°42' E 156
Stavropol', Russ. 45°3' N, 41°58' E 158
Stavropol', adm. division, Russ. 45°26' N, 41°12' E 160
Stawiski, Pol. 53°22' N, 22°8' E 154
Stayner, Can. 44°24' N, 80°6' W 110
Steamboat, Can. 58°40' N, 123°45' W 108
Steamboat Mountain, peak, Wyo., U.S. 41°57' N, 109°2' W 90
Stederdorf, Ger. 52°21' N, 10°13' E 150
Steele, N. Dak., U.S. 46°50' N, 99°56' W 108
Steele Island, island, Antarctica 71°8' S, 60°19' W 248
Steelpoort, S. Af. 24°46' S, 30°11' E 227
Steelton, Pa., U.S. 40°13' N, 76°51' W 94
Steelville, Mo., U.S. 37°57' N, 91°21' W 96
Steen River, Can. 59°39' N, 117°11' W 108
Steen, river, Can. 59°17' N, 118°21' W 108
Steens Mountain, Oreg., U.S. 43°21' N, 118°14' W 90
Steensby Inlet 69°57' N, 81°26' W 106
Steenstrup Gletscher, glacier 74°42' N, 64°7' W 106
Steenwijk, Neth. 52°46' N, 6°6' E 163
Steep Rock, Can. 51°26' N, 98°48' W 90
Steep Rock Lake, Can. 48°49' N, 91°38' W 94
Steers Head 81°45' S, 164°32' W 248
Stefansson Island, island, Can. 73°43' N, 112°11' W 106
Stege, Den. 54°59' N, 12°17' E 152
Steger, Ill., U.S. 41°27' N, 87°38' W 102
Steigen, Nor. 67°55' N, 14°58' E 152
Steigerwald, Ger. 49°45' N, 10°17' E 167
Stein Pass, Ger. 47°39' N, 12°45' E 152
Stein, river, Can. 50°10' N, 122°21' W 90
Steinau, Ger. 50°18' N, 9°27' E 167
Steinbach, Can. 49°31' N, 96°42' W 90
Steinfeld, Ger. 52°36' N, 8°13' E 163
Steinfort, Lux. 49°39' N, 5°55' E 163
Steinfurt, Ger. 52°8' N, 7°19' E 163
Steinhatchee, Fla., U.S. 29°40' N, 83°24' W 105
Steinhausen, Namibia 21°49' S, 18°15' E 227
Steinkjer, Nor. 63°57' N, 11°44' E 160
Steinkopf, S. Af. 29°15' S, 17°42' E 227
Stellaland, region, S. Af. 27°19' S, 24°2' E 227
Stelle, Ger. 53°22' N, 10°6' E 152
Stellenbosch, S. Af. 33°55' S, 18°48' E 227
Stelvio, Passo dello, It. 46°31' N, 10°26' E 167
Stenay, Fr. 49°29' N, 5°11' E 163
Stende, Latv. 57°8' N, 22°32' E 166
Stenstorp, Nor. 58°15' N, 13°41' E 152
Stenträsk, Nor. 66°19' N, 19°50' E 152
Stepanakert (Xankändi), Asia 39°48' N, 46°43' E 195
Step'anavan, Arm. 41°0' N, 44°21' E 195
Stepanci, Maced. 41°29' N, 21°38' E 168
Stephen, Minn., U.S. 48°26' N, 96°53' W 94
Stephens, Ark., U.S. 33°23' N, 93°5' W 103
Stephens Lake, lake, Can. 56°42' N, 94°17' W 108
Stephens Passage 57°46' N, 134°48' W 108
Stephens, Port 32°50' S, 150°48' E 230
Stephenson, Mich., U.S. 45°24' N, 87°36' W 94
Stephenson, Mount, peak, Antarctica 69°49' S, 70°21' W 248
Stephenville, Can. 48°31' N, 58°39' W 106
Stephenville, Tex., U.S. 32°13' N, 98°13' W 92
Stepnogorsk, Kaz. 52°23' N, 71°54' E 184
Stepnoye, Russ. 44°15' N, 44°32' E 158
Stepnyak, Kaz. 52°49' N, 70°47' E 184
Stepojevac, Serb. and Mont. 44°30' N, 20°18' E 168
Steptoe Butte, peak, Wash., U.S. 46°59' N, 117°24' W 90
Sterling, Colo., U.S. 40°37' N, 103°14' W 90
Sterling, Ill., U.S. 41°47' N, 89°42' W 102
Sterling, Kans., U.S. 38°12' N, 98°13' W 90
Sterling, Mich., U.S. 44°1' N, 84°2' W 102
Sterling, Mo., U.S. 41°47' N, 89°42' W 94
Sterling, N. Dak., U.S. 46°48' N, 100°18' W 90
Sterling City, Tex., U.S. 31°49' N, 100°60' W 92
Sterlington, La., U.S. 32°40' N, 92°5' W 103
Sterlitamak, Russ. 53°39' N, 55°53' E 154
Stettler, Can. 52°19' N, 112°42' W 108
Stevenage, U.K. 51°54' N, 0°13' E 162
Stevens Point, Wis., U.S. 44°31' N, 89°35' W 94
Stevenson, Wash., U.S. 45°41' N, 121°54' W 100
Stevenson Lake, lake, Can. 53°54' N, 96°43' W 108
Stevenson Mountain, peak, Oreg., U.S. 44°33' N, 120°32' W 90
Stevensville, Mich., U.S. 42°0' N, 86°30' W 102
Stewardson, Ill., U.S. 39°15' N, 88°39' W 102
Stewart, Can. 55°56' N, 130°1' W 108
Stewart, Miss., U.S. 33°25' N, 89°26' W 103
Stewart, Ohio, U.S. 39°18' N, 81°54' W 102
Stewart Crossing, Can. 63°27' N, 136°41' W 98
Stewart, Isla, island, Chile 54°51' S, 72°56' W 134
Stewart Islands, South Pacific Ocean 7°60' S, 163°3' E 238
Stewart River, Can. 63°21' N, 139°26' W 98
Steynsburg, S. Af. 31°18' S, 25°47' E 227
Steyr, Aust. 48°2' N, 14°24' E 152
Steytlerville, S. Af. 33°20' S, 24°18' E 227
Stia, It. 43°48' N, 11°41' E 167
Stickney, S. Dak., U.S. 43°34' N, 98°26' W 90
Stiene, Latv. 57°23' N, 24°33' E 166
Stiens, Neth. 53°15' N, 5°44' E 163
Stigler, Okla., U.S. 35°13' N, 95°9' W 96
Stih, Hora, peak, Ukr. 48°35' N, 23°12' E 152
Stikine, river, Can. 57°15' N, 131°59' W 108
Stikine, river, Can. 58°11' N, 130°31' W 98
Stikine, river, Can. 58°0' N, 129°22' W 108
Stillman Valley, Ill., U.S. 42°6' N, 89°11' W 102
Stillwater, Can. 49°46' N, 124°17' W 100
Stillwater, Minn., U.S. 45°2' N, 92°50' W 94
Stillwater, N.Y., U.S. 42°56' N, 73°40' W 104
Stillwater, Okla., U.S. 36°5' N, 97°2' W 92
Stillwater Range, Nev., U.S. 39°59' N, 118°14' W 90
Stilo, Punta, It. 38°27' N, 16°35' E 156
Stilton, U.K. 52°29' N, 0°17' E 162
Stilwell, Okla., U.S. 35°46' N, 94°38' W 96
Štimlje, Europe 42°27' N, 21°3' E 168
Stine Mountain, peak, Mont., U.S. 45°41' N, 113°11' W 90
Stinear, Mount, peak, Antarctica 73°18' S, 66°2' E 248
Stinkingwater Pass, Oreg., U.S. 43°42' N, 118°32' W 90
Stinnett, Tex., U.S. 35°47' N, 101°27' W 92
Stinson Lake, N.H., U.S. 43°51' N, 71°50' W 104
Štip, Maced. 41°44' N, 22°11' E 168
Stiring-Wendel, Fr. 49°12' N, 6°55' E 163
Stirling Island, Solomon Islands 7°20' S, 155°30' E 242
Stirling, Mount, peak, Nev., U.S. 36°26' N, 116°1' W 101
Stobi, ruin(s), Maced. 41°31' N, 21°54' E 168
Stock Route, Austral. 19°46' S, 126°40' E 231
Stockbridge, Mass., U.S. 42°16' N, 73°20' W 104
Stockbridge, Mich., U.S. 42°25' N, 84°11' W 102
Stockbridge, U.K. 51°6' N, 1°29' W 162
Stockbridge, Vt., U.S. 43°47' N, 72°46' W 104
Stockdale, Tex., U.S. 29°13' N, 97°57' W 96
Stockholm, Sw. 59°19' N, 17°55' E 166
Stockport, U.K. 53°23' N, 2°10' W 162
Stockton, Ala., U.S. 30°58' N, 87°51' W 103
Stockton, Calif., U.S. 37°57' N, 121°17' W 100
Stockton, Ill., U.S. 42°20' N, 90°1' W 102
Stockton, Kans., U.S. 39°26' N, 99°17' W 90
Stockton, Mo., U.S. 37°40' N, 93°48' W 94
Stockton on Tees, U.K. 54°34' N, 1°20' W 162
Stockwell, Ind., U.S. 40°16' N, 86°46' W 102
Stoddard, N.H., U.S. 43°4' N, 72°8' W 104
Stöde, Nor. 62°24' N, 16°33' E 152
Stogovo, Maced. 41°28' N, 20°32' E 168
Stoke, N.Z. 41°21' S, 173°14' E 240
Stoke Ferry, U.K. 52°34' N, 0°31' E 162
Stoke on Trent, U.K. 53°0' N, 2°11' W 162
Stokes, Bahia 54°9' S, 73°50' W 134
Stokes, Mount, peak, N.Z. 41°8' S, 174°2' E 240
Stokesay, U.K. 52°25' N, 2°50' W 162
Stoksund, Nor. 64°2' N, 10°4' E 152
Stolac, Bosn. and Herzg. 43°3' N, 17°57' E 168
Stolberg, Ger. 50°46' N, 6°12' E 167
Stolbovo, Russ. 55°59' N, 30°1' E 166
Stolbovoy, Ostrov, island, Russ. 73°52' N, 128°4' E 160
Stolin, Belarus 51°53' N, 26°49' E 152
Stöllet, Nor. 60°23' N, 13°16' E 152
Stolnici, Rom. 44°35' N, 24°47' E 156
Stone, U.K. 52°54' N, 2°8' W 162
Stone Lake, lake, Can. 50°34' N, 87°51' W 110
Stonehenge, site, U.K. 51°9' N, 1°51' W 162
Stoner, Can. 53°38' N, 122°40' W 108
Stonewall, Can. 50°7' N, 97°19' W 108
Stonewall, La., U.S. 32°16' N, 93°50' W 103
Stonewall, Miss., U.S. 32°7' N, 88°46' W 103
Stonglandet, Nor. 69°5' N, 17°12' E 152
Stonington, Ill., U.S. 39°37' N, 89°12' W 102
Stony Brook, N.Y., U.S. 40°55' N, 73°9' W 104
Stony Creek, N.Y., U.S. 43°25' N, 73°57' W 104
Stony Lake, Can. 58°53' N, 99°17' W 108
Stony Plain, Can. 53°31' N, 114°3' W 108
Stony Point, N.Y., U.S. 43°39' N, 76°34' W 94
Stony Point, N.Y., U.S. 41°13' N, 73°60' W 104
Stony Rapids, Can. 59°10' N, 105°60' W 106
Stony River, Alas., U.S. 61°48' N, 156°33' W 98
Stooping, river, Can. 51°19' N, 82°32' W 110
Støren, Nor. 63°0' N, 10°18' E 152
Storfjord, Nor. 69°16' N, 19°59' E 152
Storfjorden 77°20' N, 7°31' E 172
Storkerson Bay 72°55' N, 128°56' W 106
Storlien, Nor. 63°18' N, 12°7' E 152
Storm Berg, peak, S. Af. 31°22' S, 26°27' E 227
Storm King Mountain, peak, Colo., U.S. 37°55' N, 106°29' W 90
Storm Lake, Iowa, U.S. 42°38' N, 95°13' W 90
Storozhevsk, Russ. 61°56' N, 52°18' E 154
Storr, The, peak 57°29' N, 6°18' W 150
Storriten, peak, Nor. 68°6' N, 17°7' E 152
Storrs, Conn., U.S. 41°48' N, 72°16' W 104
Storsjö, Nor. 62°47' N, 13°2' E 152
Storskavlen, peak, Nor. 60°44' N, 7°10' E 152
Storuman, Nor. 65°5' N, 17°6' E 152
Storvätteshågna, peak, Nor. 62°7' N, 12°21' E 152
Storvik, Nor. 60°34' N, 16°28' E 152
Story, Wyo., U.S. 44°34' N, 106°53' W 90
Story City, Iowa, U.S. 42°11' N, 93°36' W 94
Stoughton, Can. 49°40' N, 103°4' W 90
Stoughton, Wis., U.S. 42°54' N, 89°12' W 102
Stour, river, U.K. 51°58' N, 0°47' E 162
Stourbridge, U.K. 52°27' N, 2°9' W 162
Stourport on Severn, U.K. 52°20' N, 2°16' W 162
Stovepipe Wells, Calif., U.S. 36°36' N, 117°10' W 101
Stow, Ohio, U.S. 41°8' N, 81°26' W 94
Stow on the Wold, U.K. 51°55' N, 1°44' W 162
Stowbtsy, Belarus 53°29' N, 26°45' E 154
Stowe, Vt., U.S. 44°27' N, 72°42' W 104
Stowell, Tex., U.S. 29°46' N, 94°24' W 103
Stowmarket, U.K. 52°11' N, 0°59' E 162
Stoyaniv, Ukr. 50°22' N, 24°39' E 158
Stradella, It. 45°4' N, 9°17' E 167
Strait 69°45' N, 84°55' W 106
Straldzha, Bulg. 42°36' N, 26°41' E 158
Stralsund, Ger. 54°16' N, 13°4' E 160
Strand, S. Af. 34°6' S, 18°51' E 227
Strandebarm, Nor. 60°16' N, 5°59' E 152
Strasbourg, Can. 51°3' N, 104°57' W 90
Strasbourg, Fr. 48°34' N, 7°44' E 163
Strasburg, N. Dak., U.S. 46°7' N, 100°11' W 90
Strasburg, Ohio, U.S. 40°35' N, 81°32' W 102
Strasburg, Va., U.S. 38°59' N, 78°22' W 94
Strășeni, Mold. 47°7' N, 28°38' E 156
Strata Florida, U.K. 52°16' N, 3°50' W 162
Stratford, Calif., U.S. 36°11' N, 119°50' W 100
Stratford, Can. 43°21' N, 80°58' W 102
Stratford, Conn., U.S. 41°11' N, 73°9' W 104
Stratford, Tex., U.S. 36°19' N, 102°5' W 92
Stratford upon Avon, U.K. 52°11' N, 1°44' W 162
Strathcona, Mount, peak, Antarctica 67°24' S, 99°40' E 248
Strathmore, Calif., U.S. 36°9' N, 119°5' W 101
Strathmore, Can. 51°2' N, 113°25' W 90
Strathmore, U.K. 56°24' N, 3°37' W 150
Strathnaver, Can. 53°20' N, 122°33' W 108
Strathroy, Can. 42°56' N, 81°36' W 102
Stratobowl, S. Dak., U.S. 43°58' N, 103°25' W 90
Stratonicea, ruin(s), Gr. 40°30' N, 23°42' E 156
Stratton, Colo., U.S. 39°17' N, 102°36' W 90
Stratton, Me., U.S. 45°8' N, 70°27' W 111
Stratton, Nebr., U.S. 40°8' N, 101°14' W 90
Stratus, ruin(s), Gr. 38°40' N, 21°12' E 156
Straubing, Ger. 48°52' N, 12°34' E 152
Straw Peak, Calif., U.S. 35°37' N, 117°14' W 101
Strawberry, Calif., U.S. 38°12' N, 120°2' W 100
Strawberry Mountain, peak, Oreg., U.S. 44°18' N, 118°48' W 90
Strawn, Ill., U.S. 40°38' N, 88°24' W 102
Strawn, Tex., U.S. 32°32' N, 98°31' W 92
Strážske, Slovakia 48°51' N, 21°50' E 156
Streaky Bay, Austral. 32°51' S, 134°11' E 231
Streatfield Lake, lake, Can. 52°7' N, 86°30' W 110
Streator, Ill., U.S. 41°7' N, 88°50' W 102
Středočeský, adm. division, Czech Rep. 49°52' N, 13°50' E 152
Streeter, N. Dak., U.S. 46°38' N, 99°23' W 90
Strehaia, Rom. 44°37' N, 23°12' E 168
Strekov, Slovakia 47°53' N, 18°26' E 168
Strel'na, Russ. 66°5' N, 38°28' E 154
Strel'skaya, Russ. 59°28' N, 47°40' E 154
Strenči, Latv. 57°37' N, 25°40' E 166
Stresa, It. 45°53' N, 8°32' E 167
Strezhevoy, Russ. 60°41' N, 77°27' E 169
Strickland, river, P.N.G. 7°53' S, 141°4' E 192
Strilki, Ukr. 49°18' N, 22°53' E 152
Strimasund, Nor. 66°3' N, 14°54' E 152
Strizhi, Russ. 58°23' N, 49°2' E 154
Strizivojna, Croatia 45°13' N, 18°24' E 168
Strmica, Croatia 44°8' N, 16°14' E 168
Stroeder, Arg. 40°12' S, 62°36' W 134
Strofádes, Nísoi, islands, Ionian Sea 37°9' N, 20°20' E 156
Ströhen, Ger. 52°32' N, 8°41' E 163
Stromberg, Ger. 49°57' N, 7°46' E 167
Stromsburg, Nebr., U.S. 41°6' N, 97°37' W 90
Strömsnäsbruk, Nor. 56°32' N, 13°43' E 152
Strömstad, Nor. 58°56' N, 11°12' E 152
Strömsund, Nor. 63°51' N, 15°33' E 152
Strong, Ark., U.S. 33°5' N, 92°22' W 103
Stroud, Okla., U.S. 35°42' N, 96°40' W 92
Stroud, U.K. 51°44' N, 2°13' W 162
Stroudsburg, Pa., U.S. 40°59' N, 75°13' W 94
Strpce, Europe 42°15' N, 21°2' E 168
Struer, Den. 56°28' N, 8°34' E 150
Strugi-Krasnyye, Russ. 58°16' N, 29°6' E 166
Strumica, Maced. 41°26' N, 22°37' E 168
Struthers, Ohio, U.S. 41°2' N, 80°36' W 94
Stružec, Croatia 45°30' N, 16°32' E 168
Strydenburg, S. Af. 29°58' S, 23°40' E 227
Stryker, Ohio, U.S. 41°29' N, 84°25' W 102
Stryy, Ukr. 49°14' N, 23°50' E 152
Strzelce Opolskie, Pol. 50°31' N, 18°19' E 152
Stuart, Fla., U.S. 27°11' N, 80°14' W 105
Stuart, Iowa, U.S. 41°30' N, 94°20' W 94
Stuart, Nebr., U.S. 42°34' N, 99°9' W 90
Stuart, Va., U.S. 36°38' N, 80°17' W 94
Stuart Bluff Range, Austral. 22°37' S, 131°45' E 231
Stuart Island, Alas., U.S. 63°34' N, 163°8' W 98
Stuart Lake, lake, Can. 54°8' N, 124°56' W 106
Stuart Range, Austral. 28°48' S, 134°5' E 230
Stuart, river, Can. 54°16' N, 124°4' W 108
Stubbenkammer 54°29' N, 13°54' E 152
Stubica, Serb. and Mont. 43°56' N, 21°29' E 168
Štubik, Serb. and Mont. 44°16' N, 22°21' E 168
Studholme Junction, N.Z. 44°45' S, 171°7' E 240
Stugun, Nor. 63°10' N, 15°39' E 154
Stumpy Point, N.C., U.S. 35°43' N, 75°46' W 96
Stupart, river, Can. 55°25' N, 94°34' W 108
Stupino, Russ. 54°53' N, 38°2' E 154
Sturbridge, Mass., U.S. 42°6' N, 72°5' W 104
Sturgeon Bay 51°59' N, 98°31' W 108
Sturgeon Falls, Can. 46°22' N, 79°53' W 94
Sturgeon Lake, Can. 50°1' N, 91°23' W 110
Sturgeon Landing, Can. 54°17' N, 101°52' W 108
Sturgeon Point, Mich., U.S. 44°32' N, 83°15' W 110
Sturgeon, river, Can. 50°14' N, 94°26' W 90
Sturgis, Can. 51°55' N, 102°33' W 90
Sturgis, Ky., U.S. 37°32' N, 87°59' W 96
Sturgis, Mich., U.S. 41°47' N, 85°25' W 102
Sturgis, Miss., U.S. 33°19' N, 89°3' W 103
Sturgis, S. Dak., U.S. 44°23' N, 103°31' W 90
Štúrovo, Slovakia 47°48' N, 18°42' E 168
Sturt Stony Desert, Austral. 26°37' S, 139°38' E 230
Sturtevant, Wis., U.S. 42°41' N, 87°54' W 102
Stuttgart, Ark., U.S. 34°30' N, 91°36' W 82
Stuttgart, Ger. 48°47' N, 9°11' E 150
Styx, river, Ala., U.S. 30°49' N, 87°44' W 103
Suakin, Sudan 19°5' N, 37°16' E 182
Suakin Archipelago, islands, Red Sea 18°49' N, 37°56' E 182
Suao, Taiwan 24°27' N, 121°45' E 198
Suaqui Grande, Mex. 28°24' N, 109°54' W 92
Suardi, Arg. 30°29' S, 61°56' W 139
Subačius, Lith. 55°45' N, 24°46' E 166
Subaşı Dağı, peak, Turk. 38°22' N, 41°30' E 195
Subata, Latv. 56°0' N, 25°54' E 166
Subcetate, Rom. 45°36' N, 23°0' E 168
Subei, China 39°30' N, 94°57' E 188
Subeita, ruin(s), Israel 30°53' N, 34°35' E 194
Subi, island, Indonesia 3°3' N, 108°52' E 196
Sublette, Ill., U.S. 41°38' N, 89°14' W 102
Sublette, Kans., U.S. 37°28' N, 100°51' W 92
Sublime, Point, peak, Ariz., U.S. 36°10' N, 112°18' W 92
Subotica, Serb. and Mont. 46°5' N, 19°40' E 168
Subugo, peak, Kenya 1°40' S, 35°44' E 224
Suceava, Rom. 47°38' N, 26°15' E 152
Suceava, adm. division, Rom. 47°27' N, 25°9' E 156
Sučevići, Croatia 44°16' N, 16°4' E 168
Suchdol, Czech Rep. 48°53' N, 14°52' E 152
Suchixtepec, Mex. 16°4' N, 96°28' W 112
Suchowola, Pol. 51°42' N, 22°43' E 152
Sucio, river, Col. 7°26' N, 77°3' W 136
Sucre, Bol. 19°3' S, 65°22' W 137
Sucre, Col. 8°52' N, 74°44' W 136
Sucre, Col. 1°48' N, 75°40' W 136
Sucre, adm. division, Col. 8°42' N, 75°15' W 136
Sucre, adm. division, Venez. 10°19' N, 63°47' W 116
Sucuaro, Col. 4°32' N, 68°50' W 136
Sucunduri, river, Braz. 5°30' S, 59°32' W 130
Sucunduri, river, Braz. 9°5' S, 58°59' W 132
Sućuraj, Croatia 43°6' N, 17°9' E 168
Sucuriú, river, Braz. 18°42' S, 53°20' W 138
Sud Kivu, adm. division, Dem. Rep. of the Congo 3°59' S, 28°18' E 218
Sud, Pointe du, Can. 48°58' N, 62°57' W 111
Suda, Russ. 59°7' N, 37°29' E 154
Suda, river, Russ. 59°33' N, 36°18' E 154
Sudak, Ukr. 44°51' N, 34°54' E 156
Sudan 13°26' N, 24°57' E 207
Sudan, Tex., U.S. 34°3' N, 102°32' W 92
Suday, Russ. 58°59' N, 43°9' E 154
Sudbury, Can. 46°29' N, 80°60' W 94
Sudbury, Mass., U.S. 42°22' N, 71°26' W 104
Sudbury, U.K. 52°2' N, 0°43' E 162
Suddie, Guyana 7°3' N, 58°33' W 130
Sudeten, Pol. 50°58' N, 14°40' E 152
Sud-Ouest, Pointe du, Can. 49°20' N, 64°50' W 111
Sudr, Egypt 29°38' N, 32°42' E 180
Suðuroy, island, Suðuroy 61°26' N, 10°6' W 142
Sudzha, Russ. 51°10' N, 35°18' E 158
Sue, Mys, Kaz. 41°34' N, 52°11' E 158
Sue, river, Sudan 7°1' N, 28°7' E 224
Sueca, Sp. 39°11' N, 0°19' E 150
Suehn, Liberia 6°31' N, 10°43' W 222
Sueyoshi, Japan 31°39' N, 131°1' E 201
Suez Canal, Egypt 30°19' N, 32°20' E 206
Suez see El Suweis, Egypt 30°1' N, 32°26' E 180
Sūf, Jordan 32°18' N, 35°50' E 194
Şufaynah, Saudi Arabia 23°5' N, 40°36' E 182
Suffield, Can. 50°12' N, 111°10' W 90
Suffield, Conn., U.S. 41°58' N, 72°39' W 104
Suffolk, Va., U.S. 36°43' N, 76°35' W 96
Şūfiān, Iran 38°18' N, 46°0' E 195
Sugar City, Colo., U.S. 38°14' N, 103°40' W 90
Sugar City, Idaho, U.S. 43°52' N, 111°45' W 90
Sugar Hill, N.H., U.S. 44°12' N, 71°48' W 104
Sugarbush Hill, peak, Wis., U.S. 45°31' N, 88°55' W 94
Sugarcreek, Ohio, U.S. 40°29' N, 81°37' W 102

Sugarloaf Key, island, Fla., U.S. 24°44′ N, 81°39′ W 105
Sugarloaf Mountain, peak, Me., U.S. 45°0′ N, 70°23′ W 94
Sugarloaf Mountain, peak, N.H., U.S. 44°43′ N, 71°33′ W 94
Suggi Lake, lake, Can. 54°20′ N, 103°12′ W 108
Suğla Gölü, lake, Turk. 37°18′ N, 31°44′ E 180
Sugut, river, Malaysia 6°0′ N, 117°8′ E 203
Sugut, Tanjong, Malaysia 6°25′ N, 117°46′ E 203
Suhai Hu, lake, China 38°49′ N, 93°36′ E 188
Şuḩār, Oman 24°19′ N, 56°44′ E 196
Sühbaatar, Mongolia 50°14′ N, 106°13′ E 198
Sühbaatar, adm. division, Mongolia 46°0′ N, 111°56′ E 198
Suheli Par 10°5′ N, 71°16′ E 188
Suhopolje, Croatia 45°46′ N, 17°29′ E 168
Şuhut, Turk. 38°31′ N, 30°32′ E 156
Sui, Pak. 28°38′ N, 69°18′ E 186
Šuica, Bosn. and Herzg. 43°49′ N, 17°10′ E 168
Suichang, China 28°36′ N, 119°15′ E 198
Suichuan, China 26°20′ N, 114°33′ E 198
Suide, China 37°28′ N, 110°14′ E 198
Suihua, China 46°38′ N, 127°2′ E 198
Suileng, China 47°14′ N, 127°11′ E 198
Suining, China 33°53′ N, 117°58′ E 198
Suining, China 26°38′ N, 110°11′ E 198
Suippes, Fr. 49°8′ N, 4°32′ E 163
Suisun City, Calif., U.S. 38°13′ N, 122°3′ W 100
Suixi, China 33°51′ N, 116°48′ E 198
Suixi, China 21°23′ N, 110°14′ E 202
Suiyang, China 27°57′ N, 107°10′ E 198
Suizhong, China 40°19′ N, 120°19′ E 198
Suizhou, China 31°45′ N, 113°20′ E 198
Sujangarh, India 27°42′ N, 74°29′ E 186
Sukabumi, Indonesia 6°59′ S, 106°51′ E 192
Sukagawa, Japan 37°17′ N, 140°21′ E 201
Sukau, Malaysia 5°33′ N, 118°16′ E 203
Sukch'ŏn, N. Korea 39°24′ N, 125°38′ E 200
Sukeva, Fin. 63°49′ N, 27°21′ E 152
Sŭkh, Uzb. 40°0′ N, 71°7′ E 197
Sukhaya Tunguska, Russ. 65°3′ N, 88°4′ E 169
Sukhinichi, Russ. 54°3′ N, 35°24′ E 154
Sukhona, river, Russ. 60°0′ N, 42°51′ E 160
Sukhona, river, Russ. 60°19′ N, 44°4′ E 154
Sukhothai, Thai. 17°4′ N, 99°49′ E 202
Sukhoy Nos, Mys, Russ. 73°37′ N, 46°36′ E 160
Sukkertoppen see Maniitsoq 65°26′ N, 52°60′ W 106
Sukkur, Pak. 27°45′ N, 68°55′ E 186
Sukon, Ko, island, Thai. 7°0′ N, 98°57′ E 196
Suksun, Russ. 57°9′ N, 57°26′ E 154
Sukumo, Japan 32°56′ N, 132°41′ E 201
Sukunka, river, Can. 55°9′ N, 121°33′ W 108
Šula, Europe 43°23′ N, 19°4′ E 168
Sula, Kepulauan, islands, Banda Sea 1°49′ S, 124°12′ E 192
Sula, river, Russ. 66°58′ N, 50°14′ E 169
Sula, river, Ukr. 50°48′ N, 33°36′ E 158
Sulaco, river, Hond. 15°4′ N, 87°41′ W 115
Sulak, Russ. 43°18′ N, 47°35′ E 195
Sulak, Russ. 51°50′ N, 48°23′ E 184
Sulanheer, Mongolia 42°42′ N, 109°24′ E 198
Sulat, Philippines 11°48′ N, 125°26′ E 203
Sulawesi see Celebes, island, Indonesia 0°39′ N, 123°14′ E 192
Sulb, ruin(s), Sudan 20°23′ N, 30°12′ E 226
Sulechów, Pol. 52°5′ N, 15°38′ E 152
Suleya, Russ. 55°14′ N, 58°46′ E 154
Süleymanlı, Turk. 37°52′ N, 36°49′ E 156
Sulgrave, U.K. 52°5′ N, 1°13′ W 162
Sulima, Sierra Leone 6°57′ N, 11°32′ W 222
Sulina, Rom. 45°9′ N, 29°38′ E 156
Sulitjelma, peak, Nor. 67°7′ N, 16°13′ E 152
Sulkava, Fin. 61°46′ N, 28°21′ E 166
Sull Basin, Sulu Sea 8°31′ N, 120°28′ E 254
Sullivan, Ill., U.S. 39°35′ N, 88°37′ W 102
Sullivan, Ind., U.S. 39°5′ N, 87°25′ W 102
Sullivan, Mo., U.S. 38°12′ N, 91°10′ W 94
Sullivan Bay, Can. 50°51′ N, 126°47′ W 90
Sullivan Lake, Can. 52°1′ N, 112°19′ W 90
Sulphur, La., U.S. 30°12′ N, 93°23′ W 103
Sulphur, Okla., U.S. 34°29′ N, 96°58′ W 92
Sulphur Point, Can. 60°56′ N, 114°51′ W 108
Sulphur, river, Tex., U.S. 33°23′ N, 95°13′ W 103
Sulphur Springs, Tex., U.S. 33°7′ N, 95°36′ W 103
Sultan Kheyl, Afghan. 33°50′ N, 68°42′ E 186
Sultanhanı, Turk. 38°14′ N, 33°33′ E 156
Sultanpur, India 26°14′ N, 82°3′ E 197
Sul'tsa, Russ. 63°28′ N, 46°0′ E 154
Sulu Archipelago, islands, Sulu Sea 5°31′ N, 121°16′ E 203
Sulu Sea 7°57′ N, 119°4′ E 192
Sülüklü, Turk. 38°52′ N, 32°22′ E 156
Suluova, Turk. 40°48′ N, 35°41′ E 156
Sulūq, Lib. 31°39′ N, 20°15′ E 216
Sulütöbe, Kaz. 44°39′ N, 66°1′ E 184
Sulz, Ger. 48°21′ N, 8°36′ E 150
Sumaco Napo Galeras National Park, Ecua. 0°49′ N, 78°13′ W 136
Sumampa, Arg. 29°22′ S, 63°30′ W 139
Sumapaz National Park, Col. 3°40′ N, 74°55′ W 136
Sumarokovo, Russ. 61°36′ N, 89°38′ E 169
Sumas, Wash., U.S. 48°59′ N, 122°17′ W 100
Sumatra, island, Indonesia 4°43′ S, 105°52′ E 192
Šumava, Czech Rep. 49°13′ N, 13°12′ E 152
Sumba, island, Indonesia 10°3′ S, 117°57′ E 192
Sumbar, river, Turkm. 38°12′ N, 55°30′ E 180
Sumbawa, island, Indonesia 8°13′ S, 117°31′ E 192
Sumbawanga, Tanzania 7°56′ S, 31°37′ E 224
Sumbay, Peru 15°60′ S, 71°22′ W 137
Sumbe, Angola 11°15′ S, 13°53′ E 220
Sumbuya, Sierra Leone 7°39′ N, 11°58′ W 222
Sumé, Braz. 7°39′ S, 36°53′ W 132
Sümeg, Hung. 46°57′ N, 17°17′ E 168
Sumeih, Sudan 9°47′ N, 27°34′ E 224
Sumiton, Ala., U.S. 33°44′ N, 87°3′ W 96
Sümiyn Bulag, Mongolia 49°38′ N, 114°59′ E 198
Sumkino, Russ. 58°3′ N, 68°14′ E 169
Summer Lake, Oreg., U.S. 42°45′ N, 121°49′ W 80
Summerfield, La., U.S. 32°53′ N, 92°50′ W 103
Summerfield, Ohio, U.S. 39°47′ N, 81°20′ W 102
Summerland, Calif., U.S. 34°25′ N, 119°37′ W 101
Summerland, Can. 49°36′ N, 119°40′ W 108
Summerland Key, Fla., U.S. 24°39′ N, 81°27′ W 105
Summerside, Can. 46°23′ N, 63°47′ W 111
Summersville, W. Va., U.S. 38°16′ N, 80°52′ W 94
Summerville, S.C., U.S. 33°0′ N, 80°11′ W 96
Summit, Miss., U.S. 31°16′ N, 90°28′ W 103
Summit, Sudan 18°47′ N, 36°48′ E 182
Summit Lake, Can. 58°39′ N, 124°39′ W 108
Summit Lake, Can. 54°16′ N, 122°37′ W 108
Summit Mountain, peak, Nev., U.S. 39°21′ N, 116°33′ W 90
Summitville, Ind., U.S. 40°20′ N, 85°39′ W 102
Sumner, Lake, N. Mex., U.S. 34°36′ N, 105°23′ W 80
Sumner Strait 56°10′ N, 134°28′ W 108
Sumoto, Japan 34°20′ N, 134°52′ E 201
Sumprabum, Myanmar 26°35′ N, 97°32′ E 188
Sumqayıt, Azerb. 40°36′ N, 49°36′ E 195
Sumrall, Miss., U.S. 31°24′ N, 89°33′ W 103
Sumsa, Fin. 64°14′ N, 29°50′ E 152
Sumskiy Posad, Russ. 64°14′ N, 35°22′ E 154
Sumter, S.C., U.S. 33°54′ N, 80°23′ W 82
Sumy, Ukr. 50°55′ N, 34°46′ E 158
Sun, La., U.S. 30°38′ N, 89°54′ W 103
Sun City, Calif., U.S. 33°43′ N, 117°13′ W 101
Sun City, S. Af. 25°20′ S, 27°0′ E 227
Sun Kosi, river, Nepal 27°20′ N, 85°44′ E 197
Sun Prairie, Wis., U.S. 43°11′ N, 89°14′ W 102
Sun, river, Mont., U.S. 47°24′ N, 112°20′ W 90
Sun, river, Mont., U.S. 47°55′ N, 113°15′ W 80
Suna, Russ. 57°50′ N, 50°10′ E 154
Suna, river, Russ. 62°38′ N, 32°38′ E 152
Sunan, N. Korea 39°11′ N, 125°42′ E 200
Sunapee, N.H., U.S. 43°23′ N, 72°5′ W 104
Sunburst, Mont., U.S. 48°52′ N, 111°57′ W 90
Sunbury, Ohio, U.S. 40°14′ N, 82°52′ W 102
Sunbury, Pa., U.S. 40°51′ N, 76°48′ W 94
Sunchales, Arg. 30°58′ S, 61°34′ W 139
Suncho Corral, Arg. 27°57′ S, 63°27′ W 139
Sunch'ŏn, N. Korea 39°21′ N, 126°1′ E 200
Sund, Fin. 60°14′ N, 20°5′ E 166
Sundance, Wyo., U.S. 44°22′ N, 104°23′ W 90
Sundargarh, India 22°6′ N, 84°4′ E 197
Sunderland, U.K. 54°54′ N, 1°24′ W 162
Sunderland, Vt., U.S. 43°6′ N, 73°6′ W 104
Sundern, Ger. 51°19′ N, 8°0′ E 167
Sündiken Dağ, peak, Turk. 39°57′ N, 31°2′ E 156
Sundown, Tex., U.S. 33°26′ N, 102°30′ W 92
Sundridge, Can. 45°45′ N, 79°25′ W 94
Sundsvall, Nor. 62°22′ N, 17°15′ E 152
Sunflower, Mount, peak, Kans., U.S. 39°0′ N, 102°7′ W 90
Sungai Petani, Malaysia 5°37′ N, 100°29′ E 196
Sungaidareh, Indonesia 0°57′ N, 101°31′ E 196
Sungaiguntung, Indonesia 0°19′ N, 103°37′ E 196
Sŭngam, N. Korea 41°39′ N, 129°40′ E 200
Sungikai, Sudan 12°19′ N, 29°47′ E 218
Sungurlu, Turk. 40°9′ N, 34°23′ E 156
Suni, Sudan 13°3′ N, 24°27′ E 226
Sunja, Croatia 45°21′ N, 16°33′ E 168
Sunjiapuzi, China 42°0′ N, 126°38′ E 200
Sunman, Ind., U.S. 39°13′ N, 85°6′ W 102
Sunne, Nor. 59°51′ N, 13°6′ E 152
Sunnhordland, region, North Sea 59°51′ N, 5°0′ E 152
Sunniland, Fla., U.S. 26°15′ N, 81°21′ W 105
Sunnmøre, region, Nor. 62°8′ N, 5°42′ E 152
Sunnyvale, Calif., U.S. 37°22′ N, 122°2′ W 100
Sunray, Tex., U.S. 36°0′ N, 101°50′ W 92
Sunrise, Wyo., U.S. 42°19′ N, 104°42′ W 90
Sunrise Peak, Wash., U.S. 46°18′ N, 121°48′ W 100
Sunsas, Serranía de, Bol. 18°7′ S, 59°38′ W 132
Sunset, La., U.S. 30°23′ N, 92°5′ W 103
Sunset Peak, Mont., U.S. 44°50′ N, 112°13′ W 90
Sunset Prairie, Can. 55°49′ N, 120°48′ W 108
Suntar, Russ. 62°9′ N, 117°28′ E 160
Suntaži, Latv. 56°52′ N, 24°55′ E 166
Suntsar, Pak. 25°26′ N, 62°2′ E 182
Sunwu, China 49°24′ N, 127°21′ E 198
Sunyani, Ghana 7°21′ N, 2°22′ W 222
Suō Nada 33°46′ N, 131°13′ E 200
Suolahti, Fin. 62°33′ N, 25°49′ E 152
Suomenniemi, Fin. 61°19′ N, 27°26′ E 166
Suomenselkä, Fin. 61°47′ N, 23°16′ E 166
Suomussalmi, Fin. 64°53′ N, 29°3′ E 152
Suonenjoki, Fin. 62°36′ N, 27°4′ E 152
Suorsa Pää, peak, Fin. 68°32′ N, 28°16′ E 152
Suorva, Nor. 67°32′ N, 18°15′ E 152
Suoyarvi, Russ. 62°6′ N, 32°22′ E 152
Superior, Ariz., U.S. 33°17′ N, 111°6′ W 92
Superior, Nebr., U.S. 40°0′ N, 98°5′ W 90
Superior, Wis., U.S. 46°42′ N, 92°5′ W 94
Superior, Wyo., U.S. 41°46′ N, 108°58′ W 90
Superior, Lake 47°32′ N, 89°30′ W 110
Superstition Mountains, Ariz., U.S. 33°22′ N, 111°40′ W 92
Supetar, Croatia 43°22′ N, 16°32′ E 168
Süphan Dağı, peak, Turk. 38°54′ N, 42°45′ E 195
Supiori, island, Indonesia 0°31′ N, 135°18′ E 192
Sūq Suwayq, Saudi Arabia 24°21′ N, 38°27′ E 182
Suqa el Gamal, Sudan 12°48′ N, 27°39′ E 216
Suquṭrá see Socotra, island, Yemen 12°19′ N, 54°12′ E 182
Şūr, Oman 22°31′ N, 59°32′ E 182
Sur, Point, Calif., U.S. 36°13′ N, 121°58′ W 100
Sur, Punta, Arg. 37°5′ S, 56°40′ W 134
Sura, river, Russ. 53°23′ N, 45°15′ E 154
Sura, river, Russ. 53°16′ N, 46°16′ E 154
Surab, Pak. 28°29′ N, 66°19′ E 186
Surabaya, Indonesia 7°19′ S, 112°37′ E 192
Surahammar, Nor. 59°42′ N, 16°11′ E 152
Sūrak, Iran 25°41′ N, 58°49′ E 196
Surakarta, Indonesia 7°30′ S, 110°35′ E 192
Surama, Venez. 6°57′ N, 63°19′ W 130
Şūrān, Syr. 35°17′ N, 36°44′ E 194
Surar, Eth. 7°30′ N, 40°53′ E 224
Surat, India 21°11′ N, 72°51′ E 186
Surat Thani (Ban Don), Thai. 9°7′ N, 99°20′ E 202
Suraxanı, Azerb. 40°26′ N, 50°1′ E 195
Surazh, Russ. 52°59′ N, 32°25′ E 154
Surduc, Rom. 47°15′ N, 23°22′ E 168
Surdulica, Serb. and Mont. 42°41′ N, 22°10′ E 168
Surendranagar, India 22°39′ N, 71°39′ E 186
Surfside, Mass., U.S. 41°14′ N, 70°6′ W 104
Surgidero de Batabanó, Cuba 22°42′ N, 82°16′ W 112
Surgut, Russ. 61°15′ N, 73°19′ E 169
Surgut, Russ. 53°55′ N, 51°6′ E 154
Surgutikha, Russ. 63°49′ N, 87°18′ E 169
Surianu, peak, Rom. 45°34′ N, 23°25′ E 156
Surigao, Philippines 9°47′ N, 125°30′ E 203
Surimena, Col. 3°51′ N, 73°16′ W 136
Surin, Thai. 14°53′ N, 103°28′ E 202
Surin Nua, Ko, island, Thai. 9°22′ N, 96°58′ E 202
Suriname 4°0′ N, 55°51′ W 122
Sürmene, Turk. 40°55′ N, 40°5′ E 195
Surovikino, Russ. 48°37′ N, 42°45′ E 158
Surovni, Belarus 55°31′ N, 29°38′ E 166
Surprise Lake, lake, Can. 59°37′ N, 134°3′ W 108
Surrey, Can. 49°11′ N, 122°54′ W 100
Sursee, Switz. 47°10′ N, 8°7′ E 156
Sursk, Russ. 53°2′ N, 45°45′ E 154
Surskoye, Russ. 54°29′ N, 46°44′ E 154
Surt (Sidra), Lib. 31°12′ N, 16°32′ E 216
Surtanahu, Pak. 26°22′ N, 70°3′ E 186
Surte, Nor. 57°50′ N, 12°1′ E 152
Surtsey, island, Iceland 63°16′ N, 20°29′ W 253
Surud Cad, Buuraha, peak, Somalia 10°38′ N, 47°9′ E 218
Surumu, river, Braz. 4°11′ N, 61°30′ W 130
Susa, It. 45°7′ N, 7°2′ E 167
Susa, Japan 34°36′ N, 131°36′ E 200
Sušac, island, Croatia 42°46′ N, 16°25′ E 168
Sūsah (Apollonia), Lib. 32°52′ N, 21°59′ E 143
Susaki, Japan 33°23′ N, 133°16′ E 201
Süsangerd, Iran 31°29′ N, 48°15′ E 216
Susanino, Russ. 58°8′ N, 41°38′ E 154
Suşehri (Nicopolis), Turk. 40°8′ N, 38°5′ E 180
Susitna, Alas., U.S. 61°31′ N, 150°30′ W 98
Susitna, river, Alas., U.S. 62°30′ N, 147°57′ W 98
Suslonger, Russ. 56°18′ N, 48°14′ E 154
Susoh, Indonesia 3°44′ N, 96°48′ E 196
Suspiro, Braz. 30°39′ S, 54°23′ W 139
Susques, Arg. 23°25′ S, 66°32′ W 132
Sussex, Can. 45°42′ N, 65°31′ W 94
Sustut Peak, Can. 56°33′ N, 126°42′ W 108
Sustut, river, Can. 56°15′ N, 127°9′ W 108
Susuman, Russ. 62°56′ N, 147°27′ E 160
Susurluk, Turk. 39°54′ N, 28°8′ E 156
Susz, Pol. 53°43′ N, 19°20′ E 152
Sutak, India 33°7′ N, 77°34′ E 188
Sutatenza, Col. 5°2′ N, 73°24′ W 136
Sütçüler, Turk. 37°29′ N, 30°58′ E 156
Sutherland, Nebr., U.S. 41°9′ N, 101°9′ W 90
Sutherland, S. Af. 32°23′ S, 20°38′ E 227
Sutherlin, Oreg., U.S. 43°22′ N, 123°20′ W 90
Sutjesca National Park, Bosn. and Herzg. 43°16′ N, 18°28′ E 168
Sutlej, river, Pak. 29°35′ N, 72°12′ E 186
Sutorman, Europe 42°10′ N, 19°7′ E 168
Sutter Buttes, peak, Calif., U.S. 39°11′ N, 121°55′ W 90
Sutter Creek, Calif., U.S. 38°22′ N, 120°49′ W 100
Sutton, Nebr., U.S. 40°35′ N, 97°51′ W 90
Sutton Coldfield, U.K. 52°33′ N, 1°50′ W 162
Sutton on Sea, U.K. 53°18′ N, 0°16′ E 162
Sutton, river, Can. 54°19′ N, 84°35′ W 106
Sutwik Island, Alas., U.S. 56°8′ N, 157°43′ W 98
Suure-Jaani, Est. 58°31′ N, 25°27′ E 166
Suva, Fiji Islands 18°12′ S, 178°26′ E 242
Suva Gora, Maced. 41°54′ N, 21°2′ E 168
Suva Planina, Serb. and Mont. 43°14′ N, 21°58′ E 168
Suvadiva Atoll (Huvadu), Maldives 0°39′ N, 72°35′ E 188
Suvainiškis, Lith. 56°9′ N, 25°15′ E 166
Suvorov, Russ. 54°8′ N, 36°29′ E 154
Suwa, Eritrea 14°12′ N, 41°8′ E 182
Suwa, Japan 36°3′ N, 138°8′ E 201
Suwałki, Pol. 54°6′ N, 22°57′ E 166
Suwannaphum, Thai. 15°35′ N, 103°47′ E 202
Suwannee, Fla., U.S. 29°19′ N, 83°9′ W 105
Suwannee, river, Fla., U.S. 29°20′ N, 83°1′ W 105
Suwannee Sound 29°11′ N, 83°18′ W 105
Şuwaylih, Jordan 32°1′ N, 35°50′ E 194
Suwon, S. Korea 37°16′ N, 127°1′ E 200
Suydam, Mount, peak, Antarctica 84°32′ S, 67°31′ W 248
Suyevat, Russ. 61°36′ N, 60°30′ E 154
Süyqbulaq, Kaz. 49°50′ N, 80°48′ E 184
Suyutkino, Russ. 44°10′ N, 47°12′ E 158
Suzaka, Japan 36°39′ N, 138°18′ E 201
Suzhou, China 31°22′ N, 120°38′ E 198
Suzhou, China 39°31′ N, 98°39′ E 173
Suzhou, China 33°38′ N, 116°56′ E 198
Suzu (Iida), Japan 37°26′ N, 137°15′ E 201
Suzu Misaki, Japan 37°32′ N, 137°21′ E 201
Suzuka, Japan 34°52′ N, 136°36′ E 201
Suzun, Russ. 53°47′ N, 82°27′ E 184
Suzzara, It. 44°59′ N, 10°45′ E 167
Svalbard, islands, Barents Sea 76°55′ N, 20°18′ E 246
Svalbard, islands, Barents Sea 78°21′ N, 22°28′ E 255
Svaneke, Den. 55°7′ N, 15°7′ E 152
Svanstein, Nor. 66°39′ N, 23°49′ E 152
Svarta (Mustio), Fin. 60°8′ N, 23°51′ E 166
Svatove, Ukr. 49°25′ N, 38°12′ E 158
Svatsum, Nor. 61°18′ N, 9°50′ E 152
Svay Chek, Cambodia 13°53′ N, 103°1′ E 202
Svay Rieng, Cambodia 11°5′ N, 105°46′ E 202
Svealand, region, Sw. 60°4′ N, 17°28′ E 166
Svecha, Russ. 58°16′ N, 47°30′ E 154
Svėdasai, Lith. 55°40′ N, 25°21′ E 166
Švėkšna, Lith. 55°31′ N, 21°36′ E 166
Švenčionėliai, Lith. 55°10′ N, 26°0′ E 166
Švenčionys, Lith. 55°9′ N, 26°1′ E 166
Svendborg, Den. 55°3′ N, 10°36′ E 152
Šventoji, Lith. 56°1′ N, 21°6′ E 166
Sverdlovs'k, Ukr. 48°6′ N, 39°41′ E 158
Sverdlovsk, adm. division, Russ. 58°42′ N, 60°3′ E 154
Sverdrup Islands, Foxe Basin 77°45′ N, 99°50′ W 106
Sverdrup Mountains, Antarctica 72°33′ S, 2°60′ W 248
Svēte, river, Latv. 56°22′ N, 23°26′ E 166
Sveti Đorđe, Europe 41°57′ N, 19°20′ E 168
Sveti Nikola, Europe 41°53′ N, 19°21′ E 168
Sveti Nikola, Prokhod, pass, Bulg. 43°27′ N, 22°34′ E 168
Sveti Nikole, Maced. 41°51′ N, 21°57′ E 168
Sveti Stefan, Europe 42°14′ N, 18°53′ E 168
Světlá, Czech Rep. 49°40′ N, 15°24′ E 152
Svetlaya, Russ. 46°36′ N, 138°10′ E 190
Svetlogorsk, Russ. 54°55′ N, 20°9′ E 166
Svetlogorsk, Russ. 66°47′ N, 88°30′ E 169
Svetlograd, Russ. 45°18′ N, 42°42′ E 158
Svetlyy, Russ. 54°40′ N, 20°6′ E 166
Svetogorsk, Russ. 61°6′ N, 28°51′ E 166
Svetozar Miletić, Serb. and Mont. 45°50′ N, 19°12′ E 168
Svilaja, Croatia 43°48′ N, 16°18′ E 168
Svilajnac, Serb. and Mont. 44°14′ N, 21°11′ E 168
Svilengrad, Bulg. 41°46′ N, 26°11′ E 158
Svir, Belarus 54°50′ N, 26°22′ E 166
Svir', river, Russ. 60°32′ N, 33°2′ E 154
Sviritsa, Russ. 60°28′ N, 32°51′ E 154
Svir'stroy, Russ. 60°47′ N, 33°48′ E 154
Svislach, Belarus 53°2′ N, 24°5′ E 152
Svitavy, Czech Rep. 49°45′ N, 16°29′ E 152
Svobodny Cosmodrome, spaceport, Russ. 51°43′ N, 128°9′ E 190
Svobodnyy, Russ. 51°27′ N, 128°5′ E 238
Svodna, Bosn. and Herzg. 45°3′ N, 16°31′ E 168
Svolvær, Nor. 68°16′ N, 14°14′ E 160
Svrljig, Serb. and Mont. 43°24′ N, 22°7′ E 168
Svrljiške Planina, Serb. and Mont. 43°16′ N, 22°16′ E 168
Svyataya Anna Fan, Arctic Ocean 84°7′ N, 59°47′ E 255
Svyataya Anna Trough, Kara Sea 80°7′ N, 71°25′ E 255
Svyatitsa, Belarus 52°44′ N, 26°1′ E 154
Svyatoy Nos, Mys, Russ. 72°24′ N, 133°19′ E 160
Svyetlahorsk, Belarus 52°34′ N, 29°48′ E 154
Swa Tenda, Dem. Rep. of the Congo 7°12′ S, 17°5′ E 218
Swadlincote, U.K. 52°45′ N, 1°34′ W 162
Swaffham, U.K. 52°38′ N, 0°41′ E 162
Swain Post, Can. 51°17′ N, 92°40′ W 110
Swains Island, U.S. 11°4′ S, 171°10′ W 252
Swainsboro, Ga., U.S. 32°35′ N, 82°21′ W 96
Swakopmund, Namibia 22°31′ S, 14°28′ E 207
Swale, river, U.K. 54°23′ N, 1°51′ W 162
Swampscott, Mass., U.S. 42°28′ N, 70°56′ W 104
Swan Hills, Can. 54°43′ N, 115°35′ W 108
Swan Lake, S. Dak., U.S. 45°14′ N, 100°18′ W 90
Swan Lake, lake, Can. 55°45′ N, 129°7′ W 108
Swan Range, Mont., U.S. 47°43′ N, 113°44′ W 90
Swan River, Can. 52°4′ N, 101°15′ W 108
Swan, river, Can. 52°16′ N, 102°16′ W 108
Swanquarter, N.C., U.S. 35°24′ N, 76°21′ W 96
Swansea (Abertawe), U.K. 51°37′ N, 3°57′ W 162
Swanton, Ohio, U.S. 41°35′ N, 83°53′ W 102
Swanzey, N.H., U.S. 42°51′ N, 72°18′ W 104
Swartmodder, S. Af. 28°5′ S, 20°34′ E 227
Swartruggens, S. Af. 25°41′ S, 26°41′ E 227
Swartz, La., U.S. 32°33′ N, 91°59′ W 103
Swarzędz, Pol. 52°24′ N, 17°4′ E 152
Swasey Peak, Utah, U.S. 39°22′ N, 113°23′ W 90
Swat, river, Pak. 34°46′ N, 72°20′ E 186
Swatow see Shantou, China 23°23′ N, 116°40′ E 198
Swaziland 26°31′ S, 31°28′ E 227
Sweden 63°13′ N, 16°14′ E 152
Swedru, Ghana 5°32′ N, 0°44′ E 222
Sweeney Mountains, Antarctica 74°37′ S, 74°59′ W 248
Sweet Home, Oreg., U.S. 44°22′ N, 122°44′ W 90
Sweetgrass, Mont., U.S. 48°58′ N, 111°59′ W 90
Sweetwater, Tenn., U.S. 35°35′ N, 84°28′ W 96
Sweetwater, Tex., U.S. 32°27′ N, 100°24′ W 96
Sweetwater Summit, pass, Nev., U.S. 38°30′ N, 119°14′ W 100
Świdwin, Pol. 53°45′ N, 15°47′ E 152
Świebodzin, Pol. 52°15′ N, 15°31′ E 152
Świętokrzyskie, Pol. 51°5′ N, 19°47′ E 152
Świętokrzyskie, adm. division, Pol. 50°51′ N, 19°47′ E 152
Swift Current, Can. 50°17′ N, 107°49′ W 90
Swift River, Can. 60°2′ N, 131°13′ W 108
Swift, river, Can. 59°57′ N, 131°54′ W 108
Swindon, U.K. 51°33′ N, 1°47′ W 162
Świnoujście, Pol. 53°54′ N, 14°14′ E 152
Switz City, Ind., U.S. 39°1′ N, 87°3′ W 102
Switzerland 46°48′ N, 7°57′ E 156
Syamzha, Russ. 60°3′ N, 41°9′ E 154
Syanno, Belarus 54°48′ N, 29°46′ E 166
Syas', river, Russ. 59°47′ N, 32°43′ E 154
Syas'stroy, Russ. 60°7′ N, 32°41′ E 154
Syava, Russ. 58°0′ N, 46°21′ E 154
Sycamore, Ga., U.S. 31°39′ N, 83°38′ W 96
Sycamore, Ill., U.S. 41°59′ N, 88°41′ W 102
Sycamore, Ohio, U.S. 40°56′ N, 83°10′ W 102
Sycewice, Pol. 54°25′ N, 16°51′ E 152
Sychevka, Russ. 55°49′ N, 34°21′ E 154
Sydney, Austral. 33°56′ S, 150°50′ E 230
Sydney, Can. 46°8′ N, 60°11′ W 111
Sydney Lake, Can. 50°40′ N, 94°47′ W 90
Syelishcha, Belarus 53°0′ N, 27°23′ E 154
Syghyndy, Kaz. 43°45′ N, 51°4′ E 195
Syktyvkar, Russ. 61°44′ N, 50°56′ E 154
Sylacauga, Ala., U.S. 33°9′ N, 86°20′ W 112
Sylarna, peak, Nor. 62°59′ N, 12°5′ E 152
Sylhet, Bangladesh 24°53′ N, 91°53′ E 197
Sylte, Nor. 62°30′ N, 7°15′ E 152
Sylva, Russ. 58°1′ N, 56°46′ E 154
Sylvan Lake, Can. 52°18′ N, 114°7′ W 108
Sylvan Pass, Wyo., U.S. 44°27′ N, 110°8′ W 90
Sylvania, Ga., U.S. 32°43′ N, 81°39′ W 96
Sylvania, Ohio, U.S. 41°42′ N, 83°42′ W 102
Sylvester, Tex., U.S. 32°43′ N, 100°17′ W 92
Sylvester, Mount, peak, Can. 48°9′ N, 55°11′ W 1
Sylvia, Mount, peak, Can. 58°5′ N, 124°32′ W 108
Sym, Russ. 60°19′ N, 88°25′ E 169
Sym, river, Russ. 60°42′ N, 87°3′ E 169
Synel'nykove, Ukr. 48°18′ N, 35°32′ E 158
Syngyrli, Mys, Kaz. 41°54′ N, 51°54′ E 158
Synnfjell, peak, Nor. 61°3′ N, 9°40′ E 152
Synnot, Mount, peak, Austral. 16°43′ S, 125°3′ E 230
Synya, Russ. 65°23′ N, 58°1′ E 154
Syowa, Japan, station, Antarctica 68°60′ S, 39°36′ E 248
Syr Darya, river, Kaz. 44°30′ N, 65°40′ E 184
Syracuse, Ind., U.S. 41°25′ N, 85°45′ W 102
Syracuse, Kans., U.S. 37°59′ N, 101°45′ W 90
Syracuse, Nebr., U.S. 40°38′ N, 96°11′ W 90
Syracuse, N.Y., U.S. 43°3′ N, 76°10′ W 94
Syracuse see Siracusa, It. 37°3′ N, 15°17′ E 156
Syria 34°59′ N, 38°11′ E 180
Syrian Desert, Iraq 32°22′ N, 37°50′ E 180
Syrian Gates, pass, Turk. 36°28′ N, 36°12′ E 156
Sýrna, island, Gr. 36°13′ N, 26°43′ E 180
Sysert', Russ. 56°30′ N, 60°50′ E 154
Sysmä, Fin. 61°29′ N, 25°38′ E 166
Sysola, river, Russ. 61°2′ N, 50°31′ E 154
Systyg Khem, Russ. 52°52′ N, 95°43′ E 190
Sytomino, Russ. 61°18′ N, 71°21′ E 169
Syumsi, Russ. 57°5′ N, 51°42′ E 154
Syuneysale, Russ. 66°54′ N, 71°23′ E 169
Syutkya, peak, Bulg. 41°52′ N, 23°56′ E 156
Syzran', Russ. 53°11′ N, 48°33′ E 154
Szabadszállás, Hung. 46°51′ N, 19°13′ E 168
Szabolcs-Szatmár-Bereg, adm. division, Hung. 48°6′ N, 21°43′ E 156
Szamotuły, Pol. 52°36′ N, 16°34′ E 152
Szarvas, Hung. 46°52′ N, 20°33′ E 168
Szczebra, Pol. 53°55′ N, 22°57′ E 166
Szczecin, Pol. 53°25′ N, 14°33′ E 152
Szczecinek, Pol. 53°42′ N, 16°42′ E 152
Szczuczyn, Pol. 53°33′ N, 22°14′ E 152
Szeged, Hung. 46°15′ N, 20°8′ E 168
Szeghalom, Hung. 47°1′ N, 21°9′ E 168
Szegvár, Hung. 46°35′ N, 20°14′ E 168
Székesfehérvár, Hung. 47°11′ N, 18°25′ E 168
Szekszárd, Hung. 46°20′ N, 18°42′ E 168
Szentendre, Hung. 47°39′ N, 19°6′ E 168
Szentes, Hung. 46°39′ N, 20°16′ E 168
Szentgotthárd, Hung. 46°56′ N, 16°16′ E 168
Szentl orinc, Hung. 46°2′ N, 17°59′ E 168
Szepietowo, Pol. 52°51′ N, 22°31′ E 152
Szigetvár, Hung. 46°2′ N, 17°48′ E 168
Szikszó, Hung. 48°12′ N, 20°56′ E 152
Szob, Hung. 47°48′ N, 18°54′ E 168
Szolnok, Hung. 47°11′ N, 20°11′ E 168
Szombathely, Hung. 47°14′ N, 16°39′ E 168
Sz ony, Hung. 47°44′ N, 18°10′ E 168
Sz oreg, Hung. 46°12′ N, 20°12′ E 168
Sztum, Pol. 53°54′ N, 19°0′ E 166
Sztutowo, Pol. 54°19′ N, 19°9′ E 166
Szulok, Hung. 46°3′ N, 17°32′ E 168
Szypliszki, Pol. 54°14′ N, 23°5′ E 166

T

Ta La, Vietnam 11°26′ N, 107°26′ E 202
Taalintehdas see Dalsbruk, Fin. 60°1′ N, 22°31′ E 166
Taavetti, Fin. 60°54′ N, 27°31′ E 166
Tab, Hung. 46°43′ N, 18°1′ E 168
Tabacal, Arg. 23°14′ S, 64°16′ W 132
Ţābah, Saudi Arabia 27°3′ N, 42°11′ E 180
Tabalak, Niger 15°3′ N, 6°0′ E 222
Tabane Lake, lake, Can. 60°33′ N, 102°21′ W 108
Tabankort, spring, Mali 17°49′ N, 0°15′ E 222
Tabanovce, Maced. 42°11′ N, 21°42′ E 168
Ţabaqat Faḩl, Jordan 32°26′ N, 35°36′ E 194
Tabar Islands, islands, P.N.G. 2°35′ S, 152°4′ E 19
Ţabas, Iran 33°35′ N, 56°54′ E 180
Ţabas, Iran 32°49′ N, 60°13′ E 180
Tabasará, Serranía de, Pan. 8°29′ N, 81°39′ W 115
Tabasco, Mex. 21°51′ N, 102°55′ W 114
Tabasco, adm. division, Mex. 18°12′ N, 93°42′ W 114
Tabatinga, Serra da, Braz. 10°53′ S, 45°27′ W 13
Tabelbala, Alg. 29°25′ N, 3°15′ W 143
Tabelkoza, Alg. 29°46′ N, 0°44′ E 214
Tabelot, Niger 17°34′ N, 8°55′ E 222
Taber, Can. 49°46′ N, 112°8′ W 90
Tabernas, Sp. 37°2′ N, 2°24′ W 164
Tabili, Dem. Rep. of the Congo 0°6′ N, 27°59′ E 224
Tablas Strait 12°28′ N, 121°16′ E 203
Tablat, Alg. 36°24′ N, 3°19′ E 150
Table, Cap de la, Can. 49°21′ N, 61°51′ W 111
Table Head, Can. 51°59′ N, 55°45′ W 111
Table Hill, peak, Austral. 14°33′ S, 129°35′ E 230
Table Mountain, peak, Alas., U.S. 68°12′ N, 144°2′ W 98
Table Mountain, peak, S. Dak., U.S. 45°51′ N, 103°46′ W 90
Table Point, Can. 50°23′ N, 58°21′ W 111
Table Rock, Nebr., U.S. 40°9′ N, 96°5′ W 94
Taboose Pass, Calif., U.S. 36°59′ N, 118°26′ W 10
Tábor, Czech Rep. 49°25′ N, 14°38′ E 152
Tabor, Russ. 71°9′ N, 150°45′ E 160

Tabor City, N.C., U.S. 34°8′ N, 78°54′ W 96
Tabora, Tanzania 5°2′ S, 32°49′ E 224
Tabora, adm. division, Tanzania 5°32′ S, 31°41′ E 224
Tabory, Russ. 58°31′ N, 64°28′ E 154
Taboshar, Taj. 40°35′ N, 69°37′ E 197
Tabou, Côte d'Ivoire 4°33′ N, 7°22′ W 222
Tabrīz, Iran 38°4′ N, 46°16′ E 195
Tabūk, Saudi Arabia 28°23′ N, 36°34′ E 180
Tabuleiro, Braz. 5°7′ S, 58°28′ W 130
Tabusintac Bay 47°18′ N, 65°36′ W 111
Tabusintac, river, Can. 47°18′ N, 65°51′ W 94
Tabuyung, Indonesia 0°51′ N, 98°59′ E 196
Täby, Sw. 59°29′ N, 18°2′ E 166
Tacalé, Braz. 1°37′ N, 54°46′ W 130
Tacámbaro, Mex. 19°13′ N, 101°28′ W 114
Tacaná, Volcán, peak, Mex. 15°8′ N, 92°14′ W 115
Tacheng, China 46°41′ N, 83°5′ E 184
Tachichilte, Isla de, island, Mex. 24°40′ N, 109°13′ W 112
Tachikawa, Japan 35°41′ N, 139°25′ E 201
Táchira, adm. division, Venez. 7°32′ N, 72°29′ W 136
Tacloban, Philippines 11°13′ N, 125°0′ E 203
Tacna, Ariz., U.S. 32°41′ N, 113°58′ W 101
Tacna, Col. 2°25′ S, 70°38′ W 136
Tacna, Peru 18°2′ S, 70°14′ W 137
Tacna, adm. division, Peru 17°46′ S, 70°53′ W 137
Taco Pozo, Arg. 25°38′ S, 63°16′ W 132
Tacoma, Wash., U.S. 47°13′ N, 122°26′ W 100
Tacuarembó, Uru. 31°45′ S, 55°59′ W 139
Tacubaya, Mex. 25°38′ N, 103°2′ W 114
Tacupeto, Mex. 28°47′ N, 109°9′ W 92
Tadami, Japan 37°21′ N, 139°18′ E 201
Tadcaster, U.K. 53°53′ N, 1°15′ W 162
Tadebyayakha, Russ. 70°26′ N, 74°21′ E 169
Tadélaka, spring, Niger 15°29′ N, 7°57′ E 222
Tademaït, Plateau du, Alg. 28°24′ N, 1°10′ E 214
Tadjakant, Mauritania 18°36′ N, 14°34′ W 222
Tadjetaret, spring, Alg. 22°39′ N, 7°52′ E 214
Tadjmout, Alg. 25°32′ N, 3°42′ E 214
Tadjoura, Djibouti 11°43′ N, 42°54′ E 216
Tadmor, N.Z. 41°28′ S, 172°46′ E 240
Tadmur, Syr. 34°32′ N, 38°19′ E 180
Tadoba National Park, India 20°18′ N, 79°12′ E 188
Tadoule Lake, Can. 58°32′ N, 99°4′ W 108
Tadoussac, Can. 48°8′ N, 69°43′ W 94
Taean, S. Korea 36°44′ N, 126°18′ E 200
T'aech'ŏn, N. Korea 39°55′ N, 125°29′ E 200
Taedong, N. Korea 40°37′ N, 125°27′ E 200
Taedong, river, N. Korea 39°51′ N, 126°37′ E 200
Taegu see Daegu, S. Korea 35°51′ N, 128°37′ E 200
Taegwan, N. Korea 40°11′ N, 125°10′ E 200
Taehŭng, N. Korea 40°5′ N, 126°56′ E 200
Taejŏn see Daejeon, S. Korea 36°18′ N, 127°27′ E 200
Taenarum see Akrotírio Ténaro, Gr. 36°13′ N, 21°38′ E 156
T'aet'an, N. Korea 38°2′ N, 125°18′ E 200
Tafalla, Sp. 42°31′ N, 1°41′ W 164
Tafara, Mali 15°38′ N, 11°22′ W 222
Tafarit, Cap, Mauritania 20°0′ N, 16°12′ W 222
Ţafas, Syr. 32°43′ N, 36°3′ E 194
Tafí Viejo, Arg. 26°46′ S, 65°16′ W 134
Tafiré, Côte d'Ivoire 9°4′ N, 5°10′ W 222
Tafraout, Mor. 29°43′ N, 8°59′ W 214
Taft, Calif., U.S. 35°8′ N, 119°29′ W 100
Taft, Tex., U.S. 27°57′ N, 97°23′ W 96
Taftān, Kūh-e, peak, Iran 28°37′ N, 61°7′ E 182
Tagama, region, Niger 15°46′ N, 7°16′ E 222
Taganrog, Russ. 47°14′ N, 38°51′ E 156
Taganrogskiy Zaliv 47°0′ N, 38°41′ E 158
Tagant, region, Mauritania 17°21′ N, 12°13′ W 222
Tagarma, China 38°1′ N, 75°5′ E 184
Tagawa, Japan 33°37′ N, 130°49′ E 201
Tagbilaran, Philippines 9°40′ N, 123°52′ E 203
Taggafadi, Niger 18°31′ N, 9°14′ E 222
Taggia, It. 43°51′ N, 7°50′ E 167
Taghit, Alg. 30°58′ N, 1°60′ W 214
Tagil, river, Russ. 58°14′ N, 61°20′ E 154
Tagish, Can. 60°20′ N, 134°22′ W 108
Taglio di Po, It. 45°0′ N, 12°10′ E 167
Tagnout Chagguerет, spring, Mali 21°15′ N, 0°48′ E 222
Tagounit, Mor. 29°57′ N, 5°39′ W 214
Tagtabazar, Turkm. 35°55′ N, 62°56′ E 186
Tagua, Bol. 19°54′ S, 67°44′ W 137
Taguedoufat, spring, Niger 16°8′ N, 8°24′ E 222
Tagula, island, P.N.G. 11°20′ S, 153°16′ E 192
Tagum, Philippines 7°30′ N, 125°47′ E 203
Tagus see Tajo, river, Sp. 39°56′ N, 6°57′ W 214
Tahaetkun Mountain, peak, Can. 50°15′ N, 119°49′ W 90
Tahakopa, N.Z. 46°31′ S, 169°22′ E 240
Tahala, Mor. 34°6′ N, 4°25′ W 214
Tahan, peak, Malaysia 4°37′ N, 102°8′ E 196
Tahat, Mount, peak, Alg. 23°15′ N, 5°23′ E 214
Ţāherī, Iran 27°43′ N, 52°22′ E 196
Tahiti, island, French Polynesia, Fr. 17°38′ S, 149°25′ W 241
Tahkoluoto, Fin. 61°37′ N, 21°25′ E 166
Tahkuna Nina, Est. 59°5′ N, 22°35′ E 166
Tahlequah, Okla., U.S. 35°53′ N, 94°59′ W 96
Tahltan, Can. 58°1′ N, 131°1′ W 108
Tahltan Lake, Can. 57°56′ N, 132°22′ W 108
Tahoe City, Calif., U.S. 39°10′ N, 120°10′ W 90
Tahoka, Tex., U.S. 33°8′ N, 101°49′ W 92
Taholah, Wash., U.S. 47°18′ N, 124°17′ W 100
Tahoua, Niger 14°54′ N, 5°17′ E 222
Tahquamenon, river, Mich., U.S. 46°27′ N, 86°7′ W 94
Tahsis, Can. 49°55′ N, 126°40′ W 90
Tahtalı Dağ, peak, Turk. 38°45′ N, 36°42′ E 156
Tahtalıdağı, peak, Turk. 36°30′ N, 30°22′ E 156
Tahuamanu, river, Bol. 11°13′ S, 68°47′ W 137
Tahuamanu, river, Peru 11°7′ S, 70°52′ W 137
Tahuna, Indonesia 3°41′ N, 125°26′ E 192
Taï, Côte d'Ivoire 5°49′ N, 7°28′ W 222
Tai Hu, lake, China 31°13′ N, 120°0′ E 198
Taï National Park, Côte d'Ivoire 5°49′ N, 7°11′ W 222
Tai'an, China 36°12′ N, 117°8′ E 198
Taibai, China 34°0′ N, 107°19′ E 198
Taibei see T'aipei, Taiwan 24°58′ N, 121°21′ E 198
Taibilla, Sierra de, Sp. 37°57′ N, 2°28′ W 164
Taibus Qi, China 41°52′ N, 115°15′ E 198
T'aichung, Taiwan 24°7′ N, 120°41′ E 198
Taigbe, Sierra Leone 7°25′ N, 12°23′ W 222
Taígetos, Óros, Gr. 37°10′ N, 22°10′ E 156
Taigu, China 37°26′ N, 112°30′ E 198
Taihape, N.Z. 39°42′ S, 175°46′ E 240
Taihe, China 26°47′ N, 114°50′ E 198
Taihe, China 33°12′ N, 115°36′ E 198
Taihu, China 30°26′ N, 116°15′ E 198
Taikkyee, Myanmar 17°20′ N, 95°56′ E 202
Tailai, China 46°18′ N, 123°27′ E 198
Taim, Braz. 32°30′ S, 52°38′ W 139
Taïmana, Mali 13°55′ N, 6°45′ W 222
Tain, Fr. 45°4′ N, 4°50′ E 150
T'ainan, Taiwan 22°59′ N, 120°12′ E 198
Taining, China 26°56′ N, 117°7′ E 198
Taiobeiras, Braz. 15°49′ S, 42°15′ W 138
Taipale, Fin. 62°38′ N, 29°9′ E 152
T'aipei (Taibei), Taiwan 24°58′ N, 121°21′ E 198
Taiping, Malaysia 4°51′ N, 100°44′ E 196
Taiping Ling, peak, China 47°35′ N, 120°26′ E 198
Taipingshao, China 40°53′ N, 125°12′ E 200
Taipudia, India 27°49′ N, 94°35′ E 188
Taira, Japan 37°2′ N, 140°52′ E 201
Tairua, N.Z. 36°60′ S, 175°50′ E 240
Taisha, Japan 35°22′ N, 132°41′ E 201
Taishan, China 22°16′ N, 112°43′ E 198
Taitao, Cabo, Chile 45°60′ S, 76°26′ W 134
Taitao, Península de, South America 46°27′ S, 75°28′ W 134
T'aitung, Taiwan 22°44′ N, 121°6′ E 198
Taivalkoski, Fin. 65°34′ N, 28°13′ E 152
Taivassalo, Fin. 60°33′ N, 21°36′ E 166
Taiwan 23°41′ N, 120°53′ E 198
Taiwan, island, Taiwan 24°25′ N, 121°54′ E 198
Taiwan Strait 23°49′ N, 118°3′ E 198
Taiyara, Sudan 13°8′ N, 30°45′ E 226
Taiyuan, China 37°52′ N, 112°35′ E 198
Taiyuan Space Launch Center, spaceport, China 37°33′ N, 112°32′ E 198
Taizhou, China 32°30′ N, 119°55′ E 198
Ta'izz, Yemen 13°35′ N, 44°1′ E 182
Tajarḩī, Lib. 24°21′ N, 14°12′ E 216
Tajerouine, Tun. 35°53′ N, 8°33′ E 156
Tajikistan 38°32′ N, 69°13′ E 184
Tajima, Japan 37°11′ N, 139°46′ E 201
Tajimi, Japan 35°18′ N, 137°10′ E 201
Tajo, river, Sp. 40°5′ N, 3°6′ W 164
Tajo (Tagus), river, Sp. 39°56′ N, 6°57′ W 214
Tajrīsh, Iran 35°52′ N, 51°35′ E 180
Tajumulco, Volcán, peak, Guatemala 15°0′ N, 91°60′ W 115
Tak, Thai. 16°52′ N, 99°7′ E 202
Takāb, Iran 36°27′ N, 47°5′ E 195
Takaba, Kenya 3°20′ N, 40°10′ E 224
Takahashi, Japan 34°48′ N, 133°37′ E 201
Takahe, Mount, peak, Antarctica 76°12′ S, 111°45′ W 248
Takajō, Japan 31°47′ N, 131°7′ E 201
Takaka, N.Z. 40°54′ S, 172°50′ E 240
Takamatsu, Japan 34°20′ N, 134°2′ E 201
Takamori, Japan 32°48′ N, 131°7′ E 201
Takanabe, Japan 32°7′ N, 131°29′ E 201
Takaoka, Japan 36°44′ N, 137°1′ E 201
Takapau, N.Z. 40°4′ S, 176°22′ E 240
Takasaki, Japan 36°18′ N, 139°0′ E 201
Takatsu, Japan 34°40′ N, 131°48′ E 200
Takaungu, Kenya 3°43′ S, 39°51′ E 224
Tā-kaw, Myanmar 21°15′ N, 98°39′ E 202
Takayama, Japan 36°8′ N, 137°16′ E 201
Takefu, Japan 35°53′ N, 136°10′ E 201
Takengon, Indonesia 4°38′ N, 96°49′ E 196
Takeo, Cambodia 10°58′ N, 104°47′ E 202
Takeo, Japan 33°11′ N, 130°1′ E 201
Tākestān, Iran 36°6′ N, 49°39′ E 180
Taketa, Japan 32°57′ N, 131°24′ E 201
Takhiatosh, Uzb. 42°20′ N, 59°36′ E 180
Takhini, Can. 60°51′ N, 135°25′ W 108
Takhta, Russ. 45°51′ N, 41°58′ E 158
Takiéta, Niger 13°41′ N, 8°31′ E 222
Takijuq Lake, Can. 66°22′ N, 115°33′ W 106
Takipy, Can. 55°24′ N, 100°58′ W 108
Takla Lake, Can. 55°9′ N, 126°12′ W 108
Takla Landing, Can. 55°28′ N, 125°59′ W 108
Taklimakan Shamo, China 39°27′ N, 77°39′ E 184
Takotna, Alas., U.S. 62°59′ N, 156°4′ W 98
Taksa Bor, Russ. 67°4′ N, 34°40′ E 152
Taku, river, Can. 58°39′ N, 133°35′ W 108
Taku Pa, Thai. 8°53′ N, 98°20′ E 202
Takum, India 27°48′ N, 93°37′ E 188
Takum, Nig. 7°13′ N, 9°57′ E 222
Takwa, river, Can. 51°32′ N, 72°10′ W 110
Tal, Pak. 35°28′ N, 72°14′ E 186
Tala, Mex. 20°38′ N, 103°40′ W 114
Tala, Tun. 35°32′ N, 8°38′ E 156
Talachyn, Belarus 54°24′ N, 29°42′ E 166
Talaimannar, Sri Lanka 9°6′ N, 79°42′ E 188
Talak, region, Niger 18°15′ N, 4°51′ E 222
Talara, Peru 4°37′ S, 81°13′ W 123
Talas, Kyrg. 42°27′ N, 72°33′ E 197
Talas, river, Kyrg. 42°37′ N, 71°44′ E 197
Talâta, Egypt 30°35′ N, 32°20′ E 194
Talata Mafara, Nig. 12°33′ N, 6°2′ E 222
Talaud, Kepulauan, islands, Philippine Sea 4°1′ N, 127°6′ E 192
Talavera de la Reina, Sp. 39°57′ N, 4°51′ W 150
Talavera la Real, Sp. 38°52′ N, 6°48′ W 164
Talayón, peak, Sp. 37°32′ N, 1°34′ W 164
Talayuelas, Sp. 39°51′ N, 1°17′ W 164
Talbahat, India 25°2′ N, 78°27′ E 197
Talbert, Sillon de, English Channel 48°54′ N, 3°10′ W 150
Talbot, Cape, Austral. 13°51′ S, 123°45′ E 172
Talbot, Mount, peak, Austral. 26°10′ S, 126°25′ E 230
Talca, Chile 35°25′ S, 71°41′ W 134
Talcahuano, Chile 36°45′ S, 73°7′ W 134
Talco, Tex., U.S. 33°20′ N, 95°6′ W 103
Taldyq, Kaz. 49°18′ N, 59°52′ E 158
Taldyqorghan, Kaz. 44°59′ N, 78°22′ E 184
Taleex, Somalia 9°10′ N, 48°25′ E 216
Talgarth, U.K. 51°59′ N, 3°13′ W 162
Talguharai, Sudan 18°14′ N, 35°52′ E 182
Tali Post, Sudan 5°54′ N, 30°48′ E 224
Taliabu, island, Indonesia 2°22′ S, 124°26′ E 192
Talibong, Ko, island, Thai. 7°10′ N, 98°36′ E 196
Talitsa, Russ. 61°8′ N, 60°28′ E 154
Talitsa, Russ. 58°2′ N, 51°32′ E 154
Talitsa, Russ. 56°59′ N, 63°44′ E 154
Talkot, Nepal 29°33′ N, 81°18′ E 197
Tall Abū Z̧ahir, Iraq 36°50′ N, 42°23′ E 195
Tall 'Afar, Iraq 36°22′ N, 42°19′ E 195
Tall as Sulţān, ruin(s), West Bank 31°52′ N, 35°24′ E 194
Tall Birāk, Syr. 36°39′ N, 41°6′ E 195
Tall Bīsah, Syr. 34°50′ N, 36°43′ E 194
Tall Ḩalaf, ruin(s), Syr. 36°46′ N, 40°1′ E 195
Tall Kalakh, Syr. 34°40′ N, 36°16′ E 194
Tall Kayf, Iraq 36°30′ N, 43°1′ E 195
Tall Kūjik, Syr. 36°48′ N, 42°1′ E 195
Tall Tamir, Syr. 36°38′ N, 40°25′ E 195
Tall Trees Grove, site, Calif., U.S. 41°12′ N, 124°4′ W 90
Tallahassee, Fla., U.S. 30°24′ N, 84°23′ W 96
Tallaringa Well, spring, Austral. 28°60′ S, 133°24′ E 230
Tallassee, Ala., U.S. 32°31′ N, 85°54′ W 96
Tällberg, Nor. 60°48′ N, 14°59′ E 152
Talley, U.K. 51°58′ N, 3°59′ W 162
Tallinn, Est. 59°11′ N, 23°47′ E 160
Tallinn (Reval), Est. 59°23′ N, 24°37′ E 166
Tallmadge, Ohio, U.S. 41°5′ N, 81°26′ W 102
Tallulah, La., U.S. 32°23′ N, 91°12′ W 103
Talmage, Calif., U.S. 39°8′ N, 123°10′ W 90
Talmine, Alg. 29°21′ N, 0°29′ E 214
Talnakh, Russ. 69°28′ N, 88°34′ E 169
Tal'ne, Ukr. 48°51′ N, 30°49′ E 158
Talo, peak, Eth. 10°38′ N, 37°55′ E 224
Talodi, Sudan 10°35′ N, 30°24′ E 224
Taloga, Okla., U.S. 36°1′ N, 98°58′ W 92
Talon, Russ. 59°47′ N, 148°39′ E 173
Taloqan, Afghan. 36°45′ N, 69°31′ E 186
Talorha, Mauritania 18°52′ N, 12°23′ W 222
Talos Dome, Antarctica 73°6′ S, 161°47′ E 248
Taloyoak, Can. 69°25′ N, 93°20′ W 106
Talpa de Allende, Mex. 20°26′ N, 104°50′ W 114
Talshand, Mongolia 45°20′ N, 97°55′ E 190
Talsi, Latv. 57°14′ N, 22°34′ E 166
Talsint, Mor. 32°34′ N, 3°27′ W 214
Taltal, Chile 25°25′ S, 70°30′ W 132
Taltson, river, Can. 60°34′ N, 111°59′ W 108
Talu, Indonesia 0°14′ N, 100°0′ E 196
Taluk, Indonesia 0°30′ N, 101°33′ E 196
Talvik, Nor. 70°2′ N, 22°54′ E 152
Talybont, U.K. 52°28′ N, 3°59′ W 162
Talyllyn, U.K. 52°38′ N, 3°53′ W 162
Tam Ky, Vietnam 15°34′ N, 108°29′ E 202
Tam Quan, Vietnam 14°34′ N, 109°1′ E 202
Tamada, spring, Alg. 21°37′ N, 3°10′ E 222
Tamala, Russ. 52°32′ N, 43°14′ E 158
Tamalameque, Col. 8°51′ N, 73°48′ W 136
Tamale, Ghana 9°24′ N, 0°52′ E 222
Tamale Port see Yapei, Ghana 9°10′ N, 1°11′ W 222
Taman', Russ. 45°13′ N, 36°40′ E 156
Taman Negara National Park, Malaysia 4°30′ N, 102°51′ E 196
Tamana, Japan 32°55′ N, 130°33′ E 201
Tamanar, Mor. 30°59′ N, 9°41′ W 214
Tamânco, Peru 5°48′ S, 74°18′ W 130
Tamano, Japan 34°29′ N, 133°55′ E 201
Tamanrasset, Alg. 22°48′ N, 5°18′ E 207
Tamara, Col. 5°47′ N, 72°10′ W 136
Tamarugal, Pampa del, Chile 20°34′ S, 69°24′ W 132
Tamashima, Japan 34°32′ N, 133°39′ E 201
Tamási, Hung. 46°38′ N, 18°16′ E 168
Tamaulipas, adm. division, Mex. 24°20′ N, 99°35′ W 114
Tamaulipas, Sierra de, Mex. 23°9′ N, 98°45′ W 112
Tamaya, river, Peru 8°59′ S, 74°11′ W 137
Tamayya, Africa 23°56′ N, 15°42′ W 214
Tamazula, Mex. 19°39′ N, 103°15′ W 114
Tamazula, Mex. 24°55′ N, 106°57′ W 114
Tamazulapan, Mex. 17°38′ N, 97°34′ W 114
Tamazunchale, Mex. 21°12′ N, 98°48′ W 114
Tambach, Kenya 0°35′ N, 35°33′ E 224
Tambacounda, Senegal 13°46′ N, 13°43′ W 222
Tambaga, Mali 13°0′ N, 9°53′ W 222
Tambaqui, Braz. 5°15′ S, 62°50′ W 130
Tambelan Besar, island, Indonesia 0°49′ N, 106°57′ E 196
Tambey, Russ. 71°30′ N, 71°56′ E 173
Tambo de Mora, Peru 13°32′ S, 76°12′ W 130
Tambo, river, Peru 10°48′ S, 73°53′ W 137
Tambo, river, Peru 17°4′ S, 71°21′ W 137
Tamboril, Braz. 4°50′ S, 40°22′ W 132
Tambov, Russ. 52°41′ N, 41°19′ E 154
Tambov, adm. division, Russ. 53°5′ N, 40°14′ E 154
Tambunan, Malaysia 5°41′ N, 116°20′ E 203
Tambura, Sudan 5°34′ N, 27°29′ E 218
Tamchaket, Mauritania 17°16′ N, 10°44′ W 222
Tamel Aike, Arg. 48°18′ S, 70°57′ W 134
Tamesí, river, Mex. 22°26′ N, 98°27′ W 114
Tamesna, region, Niger 18°45′ N, 4°10′ E 222
Tamgak, Adrar, peak, Niger 19°11′ N, 8°37′ E 222
Tamgrout, Mor. 30°19′ N, 5°45′ W 214
Tamgué, Guinea 12°18′ N, 12°21′ W 222
Tamiahua, Mex. 21°14′ N, 97°27′ W 114
Tamiahua, Laguna de 21°29′ N, 98°2′ W 114
Tamil Nadu, adm. division, India 9°23′ N, 77°23′ E 188
Tamīnah, Lib. 32°16′ N, 15°3′ E 216
Tamins, Switz. 46°50′ N, 9°23′ E 167
Tamitatoala (Batovi), river, Braz. 14°11′ S, 53°58′ W 132
Tamitsa, Russ. 64°10′ N, 38°5′ E 154
Tammerfors see Tampere, Fin. 61°29′ N, 23°43′ E 166
Tammisaari see Ekenäs, Fin. 59°58′ N, 23°26′ E 166
Tampa, Fla., U.S. 27°58′ N, 82°26′ W 105
Tampa Bay 27°37′ N, 83°17′ W 80
Tampere, Fin. 61°23′ N, 23°51′ E 160
Tampere (Tammerfors), Fin. 61°29′ N, 23°43′ E 166
Tampico, Ill., U.S. 41°37′ N, 89°48′ W 102
Tampico, Mex. 22°11′ N, 97°51′ W 112
Tampin, Malaysia 2°29′ N, 102°12′ E 196
Tamrida see Hadiboh, Yemen 12°37′ N, 53°49′ E 173
Tamsagbulag, Mongolia 47°13′ N, 117°15′ E 198
Tamsalu, Est. 59°7′ N, 26°5′ E 166
Tamshiyacu, Peru 4°1′ S, 73°6′ W 130
Tamu, Myanmar 24°10′ N, 94°19′ E 188
Tamuín, Mex. 21°59′ N, 98°46′ W 114
Tamuning, U.S. 13°28′ N, 144°46′ E 242
Tamur, river, Nepal 26°56′ N, 87°39′ E 197
Tamworth, N.H., U.S. 43°51′ N, 71°17′ W 104
Tamworth, U.K. 52°39′ N, 1°42′ W 162
Tan An, Vietnam 10°32′ N, 106°25′ E 202
Tan Quang, Vietnam 22°30′ N, 104°51′ E 202
Tana, Nor. 70°27′ N, 28°15′ E 152
Tana, Lake, Eth. 11°57′ N, 35°26′ E 206
Tana, river, Europe 68°26′ N, 25°33′ E 160
Tana, river, Kenya 1°37′ S, 40°7′ E 224
Tanabe, Japan 33°43′ N, 135°23′ E 201
Tanacross, Alas., U.S. 63°14′ N, 143°23′ W 98
Tanafjorden 70°37′ N, 25°20′ E 160
Tanaga, island, Alas., U.S. 51°25′ N, 178°58′ W 160
Tanagra, ruin(s), Gr. 38°19′ N, 23°26′ E 156
Tanagura, Japan 37°1′ N, 140°23′ E 201
Tanah Merah, Malaysia 5°48′ N, 102°7′ E 196
Tanahbala, island, Indonesia 0°38′ N, 97°40′ E 196
Tanahgrogot, Indonesia 1°56′ S, 116°11′ E 192
Tanahmasa, island, Indonesia 0°18′ N, 98°33′ E 196
Tanahmerah, Indonesia 3°44′ N, 117°33′ E 192
Tanahmerah, Indonesia 6°14′ S, 140°17′ E 192
Tanakpur, India 29°4′ N, 80°3′ E 197
Tanalyk, river, Russ. 52°38′ N, 58°2′ E 154
Tanama, river, Russ. 69°45′ N, 78°33′ E 169
Tanami Desert, Austral. 19°13′ S, 130°40′ E 230
Tanami, Mount, peak, Austral. 19°59′ S, 129°25′ E 230
Tanana, Alas., U.S. 65°3′ N, 152°16′ W 98
Tanana, river, Alas., U.S. 63°31′ N, 144°53′ W 98
Tancheng, China 34°36′ N, 118°23′ E 198
Tanch'ŏn, N. Korea 40°26′ N, 128°56′ E 200
Tanda, India 26°31′ N, 82°38′ E 197
Ţăndărei, Rom. 44°38′ N, 27°39′ E 156
Tandaué, river, Angola 15°55′ S, 16°59′ E 220
Tandik, Malaysia 6°37′ N, 116°52′ E 203
Tandil, Arg. 37°20′ S, 59°11′ W 139
Tandil, Sierra del, Arg. 37°52′ S, 59°49′ W 134
Tando Allahyar, Pak. 25°29′ N, 68°45′ E 186
Tando Muhammad Khan, Pak. 25°10′ N, 68°34′ E 186
Tandur, India 19°9′ N, 79°28′ E 188
Tandur, India 17°16′ N, 77°34′ E 188
Tanega Shima, island, Japan 30°14′ N, 131°3′ E 190
Tanegashima Space Center, spaceport, Japan 30°37′ N, 130°50′ E 190
Tanezrouft, region, Alg. 21°41′ N, 2°31′ W 222
Tang Paloch, Cambodia 12°3′ N, 104°21′ E 202
Tanga, Tanzania 5°6′ S, 39°4′ E 224
Tanga, adm. division, Tanzania 5°32′ S, 37°29′ E 224
Tangail, Bangladesh 24°13′ N, 89°54′ E 197
Tangaza, Nig. 13°21′ N, 4°55′ E 222
Tange Promontory, Antarctica 67°10′ S, 40°56′ E 248
Tanggu, China 39°4′ N, 117°40′ E 198
Tanggula Shan, China 32°34′ N, 90°26′ E 188
Tanggula Shankou, pass, China 32°52′ N, 91°57′ E 188
Tanggulashan (Tuotuoheyan), China 34°10′ N, 92°24′ E 188
Tanghe, China 32°38′ N, 112°53′ E 198
Tangi, India 19°53′ N, 85°23′ E 188
Tangier, Mor. 35°47′ N, 5°46′ W 143
Tangipahoa, La., U.S. 30°52′ N, 90°31′ W 103
Tanglewood, site, Mass., U.S. 42°20′ N, 73°21′ W 104
Tangmai, China 30°6′ N, 95°7′ E 188
Tango, Japan 35°42′ N, 135°6′ E 201
Tangra Yumco, lake, China 30°46′ N, 85°46′ E 197
Tangse, Indonesia 5°3′ N, 95°55′ E 196
Tangshan, China 39°34′ N, 118°10′ E 198
Tanguiéta, Benin 10°38′ N, 1°16′ E 222
Tanguro, river, Braz. 12°42′ S, 52°30′ W 138
Tanh Linh, Vietnam 11°6′ N, 107°41′ E 202
Tanimbar, Kepulauan, islands, Banda Sea 10°2′ S, 131°4′ E 238
Tanimbar, Kepulauan, islands, Indonesia 7°56′ S, 132°5′ E 192
Taninges, Fr. 46°6′ N, 6°35′ E 167
Tanintharyi, Myanmar 12°3′ N, 98°59′ E 202
Taniyama, Japan 31°29′ N, 130°30′ E 201
Tanjay, Philippines 9°31′ N, 123°7′ E 203
Tanjung Puting National Park, Indonesia 3°4′ S, 111°39′ E 238
Tanjungbalai, Indonesia 2°59′ N, 99°48′ E 196
Tanjungpandan, Indonesia 2°45′ S, 107°40′ E 192
Tanjungpinang, Indonesia 0°54′ N, 104°29′ E 196
Tanjungpura, Indonesia 3°56′ N, 98°24′ E 196
Tanjungredep, Indonesia 2°10′ N, 117°18′ E 192
Tanjungselor, Indonesia 2°53′ N, 117°16′ E 192
Tank, Pak. 32°10′ N, 70°25′ E 186
Tankābon, Iran 36°47′ N, 50°54′ E 180
Tankapirtti, Fin. 68°15′ N, 27°15′ E 152
Ta-n-Kena, Alg. 26°33′ N, 9°36′ E 214
Tankovo, Russ. 60°38′ N, 89°47′ E 169
Tann, Ger. 50°38′ N, 10°1′ E 167
Tännäs, Nor. 62°26′ N, 12°39′ E 152
Tannersville, N.Y., U.S. 42°11′ N, 74°9′ W 104
Tannila, Fin. 65°27′ N, 26°0′ E 152
Tannin, Can. 49°39′ N, 91°1′ W 94
Tannur, ruin(s), Jordan 30°57′ N, 35°40′ E 194
Tano, river, Ghana 6°13′ N, 2°45′ W 222
Tanobato, Indonesia 0°46′ N, 99°32′ E 196
Tanot, India 27°47′ N, 70°19′ E 186
Tanoûchert, spring, Mauritania 20°46′ N, 11°51′ W 222
Tanoudert, Mauritania 20°10′ N, 16°10′ W 222
Tânout, Niger 14°57′ N, 8°50′ E 222
Tanquián, Mex. 21°35′ N, 98°40′ W 114
Ţanţa, Egypt 30°46′ N, 30°58′ E 180
Tantabin, Myanmar 18°50′ N, 96°26′ E 202
Tantallon Castle, site, U.K. 56°2′ N, 2°45′ W 150
Tan-Tan, Mor. 28°25′ N, 11°9′ W 214
Tantonville, Fr. 48°27′ N, 6°8′ E 163
Tantoyuca, Mex. 21°19′ N, 98°14′ W 114
Tanus, Fr. 44°6′ N, 2°18′ E 150
Tanyang, S. Korea 36°55′ N, 128°20′ E 200
Tanzania 6°44′ S, 33°1′ E 224
Tao, Ko, island, Thai. 10°6′ N, 99°39′ E 202
Tao'er, river, China 45°25′ N, 123°5′ E 198
Taojiang, China 28°31′ N, 112°5′ E 198
Taokest, peak, Mauritania 18°6′ N, 9°32′ W 222
Taole, China 38°47′ N, 106°44′ E 198
Taonan, China 45°19′ N, 122°47′ E 198
Taos, N. Mex., U.S. 36°24′ N, 105°34′ W 92
Taoudenni (Smeïda), Mali 22°41′ N, 3°59′ W 214
Taoujafet, spring, Mauritania 18°53′ N, 11°50′ W 222
Taourirt, Alg. 26°43′ N, 0°13′ E 214
Taourirt, Mor. 34°27′ N, 2°51′ W 214
Taoussa, Mali 16°56′ N, 0°33′ E 222
Taouz, Mor. 30°57′ N, 3°58′ W 214
Taoyuan, China 28°54′ N, 111°28′ E 198
T'aoyüan, Taiwan 24°58′ N, 121°14′ E 198
Tapa, Est. 59°14′ N, 25°56′ E 166
Tapachula, Mex. 14°54′ N, 92°16′ W 115
Tapah, Malaysia 4°11′ N, 101°16′ E 196
Tapajós, river, Braz. 4°53′ S, 55°51′ W 123
Tapaktuan, Indonesia 3°17′ N, 97°11′ E 196
Tapalquén, Arg. 36°22′ S, 60°5′ W 139
Tapanui, N.Z. 45°57′ S, 169°17′ E 240
Tapauá, river, Braz. 6°25′ S, 65°55′ W 130
Tapawera, N.Z. 41°23′ S, 172°50′ E 240
Tapera, Braz. 28°37′ S, 52°55′ W 139
Tapera, river, Braz. 0°22′ N, 61°45′ W 130
Tapes, Braz. 30°40′ S, 51°27′ W 139
Tapeta, Liberia 6°20′ N, 8°54′ W 222
Taphan Hin, Thai. 16°19′ N, 100°27′ E 202
Tapi, river, India 21°17′ N, 73°33′ E 186
Tapiola, Fin. 60°9′ N, 24°48′ E 166
Tápiószele, Hung. 47°20′ N, 19°53′ E 168
Tapira, Braz. 1°20′ N, 68°3′ W 136
Tapirapecó, Sierra, Venez. 1°27′ N, 65°2′ W 130
Tapley Mountains, Antarctica 84°46′ S, 134°49′ W 248
Tapol, Chad 8°31′ N, 15°34′ E 218
Tapolca, Hung. 46°53′ N, 17°27′ E 168
Tappahannock, Va., U.S. 37°55′ N, 76°53′ W 94
Tapuaenuku, peak, N.Z. 42°2′ S, 173°35′ E 240
Tapul, Philippines 5°45′ N, 120°53′ E 203
Tapurucuará, Braz. 0°27′ N, 65°6′ W 130
Ţaqah, Oman 17°3′ N, 54°22′ E 182
Taquara, Braz. 29°39′ S, 50°48′ W 139
Taquari, Braz. 17°52′ S, 53°18′ W 138
Taquari, river, Braz. 18°45′ S, 57°2′ W 132
Tar, Croatia 45°18′ N, 13°37′ E 167
Tar, river, N.C., U.S. 36°12′ N, 78°32′ W 80
Tara, Russ. 56°50′ N, 74°26′ E 169
Tara, Zambia 16°57′ S, 26°45′ E 224
Tara, Hill of, peak, Ire. 53°33′ N, 6°44′ W 150
Tara National Park, Serb. and Mont. 43°49′ N, 19°20′ E 168
Tara, river, Russ. 56°17′ N, 76°25′ E 169
Taraba, river, Nig. 7°55′ N, 10°57′ E 222
Tarabuco, Bol. 19°8′ S, 64°58′ W 137
Ţarābulus (Tripoli), Leb. 34°22′ N, 35°53′ E 216
Ţarābulus (Tripoli), Lib. 32°37′ N, 12°35′ E 216
Taraclia, Mold. 46°33′ N, 29°7′ E 156
Taraco, Peru 15°21′ S, 69°58′ W 137
Taradale, N.Z. 39°32′ S, 176°50′ E 240
Taragi, Japan 32°15′ N, 130°56′ E 201
Taragma, Sudan 16°42′ N, 33°36′ E 182
Tarairí, Bol. 21°9′ S, 63°31′ W 137
Tarakan, Indonesia 3°22′ N, 117°29′ E 192
Taran, Mys, Russ. 54°56′ N, 19°42′ E 166
Taranaki, Mount (Egmont, Mount), peak, N.Z. 39°20′ S, 173°58′ E 240
Tarancón, Sp. 40°0′ N, 3°1′ W 164
Tarangire National Park, Tanzania 4°20′ S, 35°41′ E 224
Taranto, It. 40°27′ N, 17°13′ E 156
Tarapacá, Chile 19°56′ S, 69°35′ W 137
Tarapacá, Col. 2°56′ S, 69°44′ W 136
Tarapacá, adm. division, Chile 19°30′ S, 70°16′ W 137
Tarapoto, Peru 6°31′ S, 76°21′ W 123
Taraquá, Braz. 7°416′ N, 68°25′ W 136
Tarare, Fr. 45°53′ N, 4°25′ E 150
Tarasa Dwip, island, India 8°24′ N, 91°59′ E 188
Tarascon, Fr. 42°50′ N, 1°35′ E 150
Tarasovo, Russ. 66°16′ N, 46°43′ E 154
Tarasp, Switz. 46°45′ N, 10°13′ E 167
Tarat, Alg. 26°7′ N, 9°22′ E 214
Tarata, Bol. 17°39′ S, 65°53′ W 137
Tarata, Peru 17°33′ S, 70°3′ W 137
Taratakbuluh, Indonesia 0°25′ N, 101°26′ E 196
Tarauacá, Braz. 8°12′ S, 70°48′ W 130
Tarauacá, river, Braz. 7°43′ S, 70°59′ W 130
Tarawa (Bairiki), Kiribati 1°15′ N, 169°58′ E 242
Tarawa, island, Kiribati 1°30′ N, 173°0′ E 242
Tarawera, N.Z. 39°3′ S, 176°34′ E 240
Tarawera, Mount, peak, N.Z. 38°15′ S, 176°27′ E 240
Taraz, Kaz. 42°52′ N, 71°23′ E 197
Tarazit, Massif de, Niger 19°41′ N, 7°25′ E 222
Tarazit, spring, Niger 20°3′ N, 8°18′ E 222
Tarazona, Sp. 41°53′ N, 1°45′ W 164
Tarazona de la Mancha, Sp. 39°15′ N, 1°56′ W 164

Tarbagatay Zhotasy, *Kaz.* 47°15′ N, 81°21′ E 184
Tarbaj, *Kenya* 2°8′ N, 40°5′ E 224
Tarbes, *Fr.* 43°13′ N, 0°4′ E 164
Tarboro, *N.C., U.S.* 35°54′ N, 77°34′ W 96
Tarcău, Munţii, *Rom.* 46°42′ N, 25°42′ E 156
Tarcento, *It.* 46°12′ N, 13°14′ E 167
Tarčin, *Bosn. and Herzg.* 43°48′ N, 18°6′ E 168
Tarcoola, *Austral.* 30°44′ S, 134°34′ E 231
Tardajos, *Sp.* 42°20′ N, 3°50′ W 164
Tardienta, *Sp.* 41°58′ N, 0°32′ E 164
Tärendö, *Nor.* 67°9′ N, 22°35′ E 152
Tareraimbu, Cachoeira do, fall(s), *Braz.* 7°51′ S, 53°36′ W 130
Tarfaya (Villa Bens), *Mor.* 27°55′ N, 12°54′ W 214
Targane, spring, *Niger* 16°32′ N, 5°43′ E 222
Targhee Pass, *Mont., U.S.* 44°39′ N, 111°17′ W 90
Târgu Mureş, *Rom.* 46°33′ N, 24°33′ E 156
Tarhaouhaout (Fort Motylinski), *Alg.* 22°38′ N, 5°55′ E 214
Tarhmert, *Niger* 18°45′ N, 8°51′ E 222
Tarhūnī, Jabal at, peak, *Lib.* 22°9′ N, 22°14′ E 216
Tariana, *Braz.* 0°24′ N, 68°46′ W 136
Târié, spring, *Mauritania* 20°8′ N, 11°37′ W 222
Ţarif, *U.A.E.* 24°1′ N, 53°44′ E 196
Tarifa, *Sp.* 36°0′ N, 5°37′ W 164
Tarifa, Punta de, *Sp.* 35°51′ N, 5°36′ W 164
Tariffville, *Conn., U.S.* 41°53′ N, 72°47′ W 104
Tarija, *Bol.* 21°34′ S, 64°44′ W 137
Tarija, adm. division, *Bol.* 21°51′ S, 64°52′ W 137
Tarik Ibn Ziad, *Alg.* 35°59′ N, 2°9′ E 150
Tarīm, *Yemen* 16°5′ N, 49°1′ E 182
Tarim, river, *China* 40°9′ N, 80°48′ E 190
Tarime, *Tanzania* 1°20′ S, 34°26′ E 224
Taringamotu, *N.Z.* 38°51′ S, 175°16′ E 240
Taritatu, river, *Indonesia* 2°42′ S, 138°14′ E 192
Tarka, *Niger* 14°36′ N, 7°54′ E 222
Tarkastad, *S. Af.* 32°2′ S, 26°14′ E 227
Tarkhankut, Mys, *Ukr.* 45°24′ N, 31°29′ E 156
Tarkhoj, *Afghan.* 35°22′ N, 66°36′ E 186
Tarkio, *Mo., U.S.* 40°25′ N, 95°23′ W 90
Tarko Sale, *Russ.* 64°52′ N, 77°50′ E 169
Tarkwa, *Ghana* 5°19′ N, 1°56′ W 222
Tarlac, *Philippines* 15°30′ N, 120°35′ E 203
Tarm, *Den.* 55°53′ N, 8°29′ E 150
Tarma, *Peru* 3°23′ S, 71°45′ W 136
Tarn, *Bahía* 47°57′ S, 75°13′ W 134
Tarn, river, *Fr.* 43°47′ N, 1°35′ E 165
Tarnak, river, *Afghan.* 31°51′ N, 66°45′ E 186
Tarnogskiy Gorodok, *Russ.* 60°27′ N, 43°38′ E 154
Tarnów, *Pol.* 50°0′ N, 20°59′ E 152
Tarnya, *Russ.* 62°5′ N, 42°24′ E 154
Ţārom, *Iran* 28°8′ N, 55°43′ E 196
Tarou, spring, *Chad* 20°41′ N, 19°14′ E 216
Tarpon Springs, *Fla., U.S.* 28°8′ N, 82°44′ W 105
Tarporley, *U.K.* 53°9′ N, 2°38′ W 162
Tarragona, *Sp.* 41°7′ N, 1°15′ E 164
Tarras, *N.Z.* 44°50′ S, 169°25′ E 240
Tàrrega, *Sp.* 41°38′ N, 1°8′ E 164
Tarrekaise, peak, *Nor.* 67°1′ N, 17°14′ E 152
Tarrytown, *N.Y., U.S.* 41°3′ N, 73°52′ W 104
Tarsus, *Turk.* 36°53′ N, 34°53′ E 156
Tart, *China* 37°4′ N, 92°51′ E 188
Tartagal, *Arg.* 28°37′ S, 59°53′ W 139
Tartagal, *Arg.* 22°29′ S, 63°53′ W 137
Tartar Strait 47°18′ N, 139°16′ E 238
Tartas, river, *Russ.* 56°24′ N, 78°32′ E 169
Tartu, *Est.* 58°21′ N, 26°40′ E 166
Ţarţūs (Tortosa), *Syr.* 34°53′ N, 35°53′ E 194
Tarumizu, *Japan* 31°28′ N, 130°43′ E 201
Tarusa, *Russ.* 54°42′ N, 37°10′ E 154
Tarutao, Ko, island, *Thai.* 6°38′ N, 99°41′ E 196
Tarutung, *Indonesia* 2°0′ N, 98°56′ E 196
Tarvisio, *It.* 46°30′ N, 13°34′ E 156
Tasa, *N. Korea* 39°49′ N, 124°23′ E 200
Tasajera, Sierra de la, *Mex.* 29°34′ N, 105°52′ W 112
Tasāwah, *Lib.* 26°2′ N, 13°31′ E 216
Taschereau, *Can.* 48°40′ N, 78°43′ W 110
Tascosa, *Tex., U.S.* 35°28′ N, 102°14′ W 92
Taseko Mountain, peak, *Can.* 51°13′ N, 123°36′ W 90
Taseko, river, *Can.* 51°45′ N, 123°40′ W 108
Tashanta, *Russ.* 49°41′ N, 89°10′ E 184
Tashigang, *Bhutan* 27°16′ N, 91°33′ E 188
Tashk, Daryācheh-ye, lake, *Iran* 29°46′ N, 53°13′ E 196
Tashkent see Toshkent, *Uzb.* 41°18′ N, 69°10′ E 197
Tash-Kömür, *Kyrg.* 41°23′ N, 72°15′ E 197
Tashla, *Russ.* 51°46′ N, 52°44′ E 158
Tashota, *Can.* 50°14′ N, 87°40′ W 94
Tashtagol, *Russ.* 52°48′ N, 88°0′ E 184
Tashtyp, *Russ.* 52°49′ N, 89°56′ E 184
Tasiilaq 65°39′ N, 37°48′ W 106
Tasikmalaya, *Indonesia* 7°21′ S, 108°12′ E 238
Tasiusaq 73°22′ N, 56°3′ W 106
Tåsjö, *Nor.* 64°12′ N, 15°56′ E 152
Tåsjön, lake, *Nor.* 64°20′ N, 15°12′ E 152
Task, *Niger* 14°54′ N, 10°43′ E 222
Taskan, *Russ.* 63°14′ N, 150°29′ E 160
Tasker, *Niger* 15°12′ N, 10°46′ E 222
Taskesken, *Kaz.* 47°14′ N, 80°45′ E 184
Taskinigup Falls, *Can.* 55°24′ N, 98°60′ W 108
Taşköprü, *Turk.* 41°30′ N, 34°12′ E 156
Tasman, *N.Z.* 41°14′ S, 173°2′ E 240
Tasman Fracture Zone, *South Pacific Ocean* 52°43′ S, 147°43′ E 255
Tasman Peninsula, *Austral.* 42°49′ S, 147°14′ E 230
Tasman Plain, *Tasman Sea* 35°46′ S, 153°34′ E 252
Tasman Sea 37°36′ S, 153°44′ E 231
Tasmania, adm. division, *Austral.* 42°4′ S, 145°43′ E 231
Tăşnad, *Rom.* 47°27′ N, 22°36′ E 168
Taşova, *Turk.* 40°47′ N, 36°19′ E 156
Tass, *Hung.* 47°1′ N, 19°2′ E 168
Tassara, *Niger* 16°49′ N, 5°29′ E 222
Tassialouc, Lac, lake, *Can.* 58°58′ N, 76°3′ W 106
Tassili-n-Ajjer National Park, *Alg.* 25°43′ N, 7°49′ E 214
Tassili-n-Ajjer, region, *Alg.* 25°32′ N, 7°10′ E 214
Tasso Fragoso, *Braz.* 8°30′ S, 45°46′ W 130
Tast, Lac du, lake, *Can.* 50°58′ N, 77°53′ W 110
Tasty-Taldy, *Kaz.* 50°43′ N, 66°37′ E 184
Tata, *Mor.* 29°45′ N, 7°59′ W 214
Tatabánya, *Hung.* 47°32′ N, 18°26′ E 168
Tatalin, river, *China* 37°33′ N, 96°37′ E 188
Tatar Strait 48°40′ N, 136°53′ E 172
Tatarbunary, *Ukr.* 45°49′ N, 29°35′ E 156
Tatarsk, *Russ.* 55°10′ N, 75°59′ E 184
Tatarskiy Proliv 50°55′ N, 141°25′ E 190
Tatarstan, adm. division, *Russ.* 55°18′ N, 48°59′ E 154
Tatau, island, *P.N.G.* 2°42′ S, 151°9′ E 192
Tate, *Ga., U.S.* 34°24′ N, 84°24′ W 96
Tatebayashi, *Japan* 36°14′ N, 139°32′ E 201
Tateyama, *Japan* 34°58′ N, 139°52′ E 201
Tathlina Lake, *Can.* 60°31′ N, 118°6′ W 108
Tathlīth, *Saudi Arabia* 19°30′ N, 43°30′ E 182
Tatishchevo, *Russ.* 51°39′ N, 45°35′ E 158
Tatkon, *Myanmar* 20°8′ N, 96°14′ E 202
Tatlatui Lake, *Can.* 56°53′ N, 127°53′ W 108
Tatlayoko Lake, *Can.* 51°34′ N, 125°6′ W 108
Tatman Mountain, peak, *Wyo., U.S.* 44°16′ N, 108°33′ W 90
Tatnam, Cape, *Can.* 57°19′ N, 90°49′ W 106
Tatoosh Island, *Wash., U.S.* 48°17′ N, 124°55′ W 100
Tatrang, *China* 38°35′ N, 85°50′ E 184
Tatrart, spring, *Mauritania* 17°32′ N, 10°21′ W 222
Tatry, *Pol.* 49°7′ N, 19°22′ E 152
Tatsamenie Lake, *Can.* 58°19′ N, 133°15′ W 108
Tattershall, *U.K.* 53°4′ N, 0°12′ E 162
Tätti, *Kaz.* 43°12′ N, 73°20′ E 184
Tatuí, *Braz.* 23°22′ S, 47°50′ W 138
Tatuke, *Liberia* 5°9′ N, 8°17′ W 222
Tatum, *N. Mex., U.S.* 33°14′ N, 103°19′ W 92
Tatum, *Tex., U.S.* 32°18′ N, 94°32′ W 103
Tatvan, *Turk.* 38°30′ N, 42°14′ E 195
Tau, island, *U.S.* 14°14′ S, 169°29′ W 241
Tauá, *Braz.* 6°2′ S, 40°24′ W 132
Tauapeçaçu, *Braz.* 2°41′ S, 60°57′ W 130
Taubaté, *Braz.* 23°3′ S, 45°34′ W 138
Tauern, Hohe, *Aust.* 46°51′ N, 12°14′ E 167
Taulabé National Monument, *Hond.* 14°42′ N, 88°3′ W 115
Taum Sauk Mountain, peak, *Mo., U.S.* 37°32′ N, 90°48′ W 96
Taumarunui, *N.Z.* 38°54′ S, 175°17′ E 240
Taumatawhakatangihangakoauauotamateapokai-whenuakitanatahu, peak, *N.Z.* 40°21′ S, 176°29′ E 240
Taung, *S. Af.* 27°33′ S, 24°47′ E 227
Taunggok, *Myanmar* 18°51′ N, 94°15′ E 202
Taunggoo, *Myanmar* 18°58′ N, 96°23′ E 202
Taungup Pass, *Myanmar* 18°40′ N, 94°45′ E 202
Taunsa, *Pak.* 30°42′ N, 70°40′ E 186
Taunsa Barrage, dam, *Pak.* 30°13′ N, 70°38′ E 186
Taunton, *Mass., U.S.* 41°54′ N, 71°6′ W 104
Taunton, *U.K.* 51°0′ N, 3°7′ W 162
Taunus, *Ger.* 50°18′ N, 7°54′ E 167
Taunusstein, *Ger.* 50°8′ N, 8°11′ E 167
Taupo, *N.Z.* 38°43′ S, 176°7′ E 240
Tauragė, *Lith.* 55°15′ N, 22°17′ E 166
Tauramena, *Col.* 5°1′ N, 72°45′ W 136
Taureau, Réservoir, lake, *Can.* 46°45′ N, 74°23′ W 94
Taurus see Toros Dağlar, *Turk.* 36°29′ N, 32°7′ E 156
Taūshyq, *Kaz.* 44°17′ N, 51°18′ E 158
Tauste, *Sp.* 41°55′ N, 1°16′ W 164
Tauyskaya Guba 59°1′ N, 147°41′ E 160
Tavankut, *Serb. and Mont.* 46°2′ N, 19°29′ E 168
Tavares, *Braz.* 31°13′ S, 50°60′ W 139
Tavares, *Fla., U.S.* 28°48′ N, 81°45′ W 105
Tavas, *Turk.* 37°34′ N, 29°3′ E 156
Tavda, *Russ.* 57°58′ N, 65°19′ E 160
Tavda, river, *Russ.* 59°37′ N, 62°54′ E 154
Tavernes de la Valldigna, *Sp.* 39°4′ N, 0°16′ E 164
Tavernier, *Fla., U.S.* 25°1′ N, 80°32′ W 105
Taveta, *Kenya* 3°25′ S, 37°40′ E 218
Taveta, *Tanzania* 9°2′ S, 35°32′ E 224
Taviche, *Mex.* 16°43′ N, 96°35′ W 112
Tavistock, *Can.* 43°19′ N, 80°49′ W 102
Tavoy Point, *Myanmar* 13°31′ N, 97°43′ E 202
Tavricheskoye, *Russ.* 54°32′ N, 73°36′ E 184
Tavşanlı, *Turk.* 39°33′ N, 29°30′ E 156
Tawai, *India* 27°46′ N, 96°46′ E 188
Tawake, *Liberia* 5°10′ N, 7°38′ W 222
Tawang, *India* 27°36′ N, 91°51′ E 197
Tawau, *Malaysia* 4°19′ N, 117°53′ E 192
Taweisha, *Sudan* 12°14′ N, 26°39′ E 216
Tawi Tawi, island, *Philippines* 5°14′ N, 119°31′ E 192
Tawu, *Taiwan* 22°22′ N, 120°52′ E 198
Ţawūq, *Iraq* 35°9′ N, 44°26′ E 180
Tāwurghā', *Lib.* 32°5′ N, 15°8′ E 216
Taxco, *Mex.* 18°32′ N, 99°37′ W 114
Taxila, ruin(s), *Pak.* 33°43′ N, 72°38′ E 186
Taxkorgan, *China* 37°48′ N, 75°9′ E 184
Tay Ninh, *Vietnam* 11°18′ N, 106°4′ E 202
Tay, river, *Can.* 62°38′ N, 133°39′ W 98
Tayabas Bay 13°36′ N, 121°40′ E 203
Tayarte, spring, *Alg.* 23°6′ N, 0°20′ E 214
Tayeeglow, *Somalia* 4°1′ N, 44°31′ E 218
Tayga, *Russ.* 56°3′ N, 85°46′ E 169
Taygonos, Poluostrov, *Russ.* 62°44′ N, 159°36′ E 160
Tayildara, *Taj.* 38°40′ N, 70°31′ E 197
Taylakova, *Russ.* 59°11′ N, 74°0′ E 169
Taylor, *Ariz., U.S.* 34°28′ N, 110°5′ W 92
Taylor, *Ark., U.S.* 33°6′ N, 93°28′ W 103
Taylor, *Tex., U.S.* 30°33′ N, 97°24′ W 96
Taylor, Mount, peak, *N. Mex., U.S.* 35°14′ N, 107°42′ W 92
Taylor Mountain, peak, *Idaho, U.S.* 44°52′ N, 114°17′ W 90
Taylor Mountains, peak, *Alas., U.S.* 60°47′ N, 157°45′ W 98
Taylors Head, *Can.* 44°41′ N, 62°34′ W 111
Taylorsville, *Ind., U.S.* 39°17′ N, 85°57′ W 102
Taylorsville, *Miss., U.S.* 31°50′ N, 89°26′ W 103
Taylorville, *Ill., U.S.* 39°32′ N, 89°18′ W 102
Taymā', *Saudi Arabia* 27°36′ N, 38°28′ E 180
Taymura, river, *Russ.* 63°11′ N, 99°3′ E 160
Taymylyr, *Russ.* 72°29′ N, 122°5′ E 160
Taymyr, adm. division, *Russ.* 68°43′ N, 85°44′ E 169
Taymyr, Ozero, lake, *Russ.* 74°33′ N, 99°13′ E 160
Taymyr, Poluostrov, *Russ.* 75°28′ N, 84°4′ E 160
Taypaq, *Kaz.* 48°57′ N, 51°47′ E 158
Tayshet, *Russ.* 55°57′ N, 98°2′ E 160
Taytay, *Philippines* 10°47′ N, 119°31′ E 203
Ţayyebāt, *Iran* 34°50′ N, 60°47′ E 180
Tayynsha, *Kaz.* 53°49′ N, 69°25′ E 160
Taz, river, *Russ.* 64°55′ N, 81°39′ E 169
Taz, river, *Russ.* 63°43′ N, 84°32′ E 169
Taza, *Mor.* 34°15′ N, 4°4′ W 214
Tazadite, spring, *Mali* 24°32′ N, 4°56′ W 214
Taze, *Myanmar* 22°57′ N, 95°25′ E 202
Tazin Lake, *Can.* 59°50′ N, 110°4′ W 108
Tazin, river, *Can.* 59°41′ N, 108°48′ W 108
Tazin, river, *Can.* 60°21′ N, 110°59′ W 108
Tāzirbū, *Lib.* 25°47′ N, 21°2′ E 216
Tazolé, *Niger* 17°12′ N, 9°10′ E 222
Tazouikert, spring, *Mali* 21°32′ N, 1°19′ W 222
Tazovskaya Guba 68°46′ N, 74°22′ E 169
Tazovskiy, *Russ.* 67°21′ N, 78°43′ E 169
Tazzaït, spring, *Alg.* 26°57′ N, 5°55′ E 214
Tazzarine, *Mor.* 30°46′ N, 5°34′ W 214
T'bilisi, *Ga.* 41°42′ N, 44°42′ E 195
Tbilisskaya, *Russ.* 45°22′ N, 40°7′ E 158
Tchamba, *Togo* 8°56′ N, 1°22′ E 222
Tchaourou, *Benin* 8°54′ N, 2°35′ E 222
Tchentlo Lake, *Can.* 55°11′ N, 125°26′ W 108
Tchibanga, *Gabon* 2°58′ S, 10°56′ E 207
Tchié, spring, *Chad* 17°6′ N, 18°53′ E 216
Tchin-Tabaradène, *Niger* 15°45′ N, 5°38′ E 222
Tchula, *Miss., U.S.* 33°9′ N, 90°14′ W 103
Te Anau, *N.Z.* 45°26′ S, 167°44′ E 240
Te Anau, Lake, *N.Z.* 45°12′ S, 167°25′ E 240
Te Araroa, *N.Z.* 37°40′ S, 178°20′ E 240
Te Aroha, *N.Z.* 37°33′ S, 175°43′ E 240
Te Hapua, *N.Z.* 34°32′ S, 172°54′ E 240
Te Kaha, *N.Z.* 37°46′ S, 177°41′ E 240
Te Kao, *N.Z.* 34°40′ S, 172°57′ E 240
Te Karaka, *N.Z.* 38°29′ S, 177°51′ E 240
Te Kauwhata, *N.Z.* 37°25′ S, 175°9′ E 240
Te Kopuru, *N.Z.* 36°3′ S, 173°55′ E 240
Te Kuiti, *N.Z.* 38°23′ S, 175°8′ E 240
Te Pohue, *N.Z.* 39°16′ S, 176°42′ E 240
Te Puia Springs, *N.Z.* 38°3′ S, 178°18′ E 240
Te Puke, *N.Z.* 37°48′ S, 176°19′ E 240
Te Teko, *N.Z.* 38°3′ S, 176°47′ E 240
Tea, river, *Braz.* 0°37′ N, 65°37′ W 136
Teacapan, *Mex.* 22°33′ N, 105°44′ W 114
Teague, *Tex., U.S.* 31°36′ N, 96°17′ W 96
Teapa, *Mex.* 17°32′ N, 92°57′ W 115
Teapot Dome, peak, *Wyo., U.S.* 43°13′ N, 106°16′ W 90
Tearce, *Maced.* 42°4′ N, 21°3′ E 168
Teba, *Sp.* 36°59′ N, 4°56′ W 164
Ţebea, *Rom.* 46°10′ N, 22°45′ E 168
Teberda, *Russ.* 43°27′ N, 41°42′ E 195
Tébessa, *Alg.* 35°23′ N, 8°8′ E 156
Tebicuary, river, *Parag.* 26°29′ S, 58°1′ W 139
Tebingtinggi, *Indonesia* 3°19′ N, 99°8′ E 196
Tebingtinggi, island, *Indonesia* 0°36′ N, 102°10′ E 196
Teboursouq, *Tun.* 36°26′ N, 9°14′ E 216
Tebra, river, *Latv.* 56°53′ N, 21°20′ E 152
Tebulosmta, peak, *Russ.* 42°34′ N, 45°21′ E 195
Tecalitlán, *Mex.* 19°27′ N, 103°18′ W 114
Tecate, *Mex.* 32°34′ N, 116°39′ W 101
Techa, river, *Russ.* 55°37′ N, 61°59′ E 154
Tecolote, *Mex.* 32°34′ N, 114°60′ W 101
Tecolotlán, *Mex.* 20°12′ N, 104°3′ W 114
Tecomán, *Mex.* 18°54′ N, 103°53′ W 112
Tecopa, *Calif., U.S.* 35°50′ N, 116°14′ W 101
Tecopa Hot Springs, *Calif., U.S.* 35°52′ N, 116°14′ W 101
Tecoripa, *Mex.* 28°36′ N, 109°56′ W 92
Tecozautla, *Mex.* 20°31′ N, 99°38′ W 114
Tecpan, *Mex.* 17°11′ N, 100°38′ W 114
Tecuala, *Mex.* 22°23′ N, 105°29′ W 114
Tecumseh, *Can.* 42°17′ N, 82°53′ W 102
Tecumseh, *Mich., U.S.* 42°0′ N, 83°57′ W 102
Ted Ceidaar Dabole, *Somalia* 4°21′ N, 43°56′ E 218
Teerijärvi see Terjärv, *Fin.* 63°32′ N, 23°29′ E 154
Tefé, *Braz.* 3°29′ S, 64°46′ W 123
Tefé, river, *Braz.* 3°50′ S, 65°20′ W 130
Tefenni, *Turk.* 37°17′ N, 29°46′ E 156
Tegalhusi, *Sudan* 15°29′ N, 36°14′ E 182
Tegea, ruin(s), *Gr.* 37°27′ N, 22°19′ E 156
Tegelen, *Neth.* 51°20′ N, 6°8′ E 167
Tegina, *Nig.* 10°3′ N, 6°11′ E 222
Tégouma, spring, *Niger* 15°42′ N, 9°15′ E 222
Tegucigalpa, *Hond.* 14°3′ N, 87°21′ W 115
Teguidda-n-Tessoumt, *Niger* 17°26′ N, 6°38′ E 222
Tegul'det, *Russ.* 57°18′ N, 88°16′ E 169
Tehachapi, *Calif., U.S.* 35°8′ N, 118°28′ W 101
Tehachapi Mountains, *Calif., U.S.* 34°56′ N, 118°40′ W 101
Tehachapi Pass, *Calif., U.S.* 35°6′ N, 118°18′ W 101
Tehama, *Calif., U.S.* 40°1′ N, 122°8′ W 92
Tehamiyam, *Sudan* 18°19′ N, 36°28′ E 182
Tehek Lake, *Can.* 65°13′ N, 97°17′ W 106
Téhini, *Côte d'Ivoire* 9°36′ N, 3°41′ W 222
Tehrān, *Iran* 35°41′ N, 51°20′ E 180
Tehuacán, *Mex.* 18°25′ N, 97°25′ W 114
Tehuantepec, Istmo de, *Mex.* 17°38′ N, 95°8′ W 114
Tehuantepec, Golfo de 15°10′ N, 96°44′ W 73
Teide, Pico de, peak, *Sp.* 28°12′ N, 16°47′ W 214
Teifi, river, *U.K.* 52°6′ N, 4°40′ W 150
Teisko, *Fin.* 61°40′ N, 23°47′ E 166
Teixeiro, *Sp.* 43°5′ N, 8°4′ W 150
Tejen, *Turkm.* 37°23′ N, 60°30′ E 180
Tejo, river, *Braz.* 9°12′ S, 72°23′ W 137
Tejo, river, *Port.* 39°28′ N, 8°16′ W 150
Tejon Pass, *Calif., U.S.* 34°47′ N, 118°53′ W 101
Teju, *India* 27°54′ N, 96°11′ E 188
Tejupan, Punta, *Mex.* 18°21′ N, 103°32′ W 114
Tejupilco, *Mex.* 18°52′ N, 100°9′ W 114
Tekamah, *Nebr., U.S.* 41°45′ N, 96°13′ W 90
Tekax, *Mex.* 20°11′ N, 89°18′ W 112
Tekes, *China* 43°11′ N, 81°50′ E 184
Tekes, river, *Asia* 42°55′ N, 80°51′ E 184
Tekezē, river, *Eth.* 13°44′ N, 38°33′ E 182
Tekiliktag, peak, *China* 36°31′ N, 80°15′ E 184
Tekirdağ, *Turk.* 40°58′ N, 27°30′ E 156
Tekirova, *Turk.* 36°29′ N, 30°29′ E 156
Tekkali, *India* 18°37′ N, 84°13′ E 188
Tekman, *Turk.* 39°37′ N, 41°30′ E 195
Teknaf, *Bangladesh* 20°52′ N, 92°16′ E 188
Tekoa, *Wash., U.S.* 47°13′ N, 117°6′ W 90
Tekro, spring, *Chad* 19°29′ N, 20°56′ E 216
Tel Aviv-Yafo, *Israel* 32°2′ N, 34°45′ E 194
Tel Jemmeh, ruin(s), *Israel* 31°22′ N, 34°24′ E 194
Tela, *Hond.* 15°45′ N, 87°26′ W 115
Télabit, *Mali* 19°4′ N, 0°56′ E 222
Telaga, island, *Indonesia* 3°10′ N, 105°42′ E 196
Telataipale, *Fin.* 61°37′ N, 28°36′ E 166
T'elavi, *Ga.* 41°55′ N, 45°28′ E 195
Tele, river, *Dem. Rep. of the Congo* 2°29′ N, 24°31′ E 224
Telegraph Creek, *Can.* 57°55′ N, 131°12′ W 108
Telêmaco Borba, *Braz.* 24°25′ S, 50°38′ W 138
Telemark, region, *Nor.* 59°13′ N, 7°55′ E 152
Teleneşti, *Mold.* 47°29′ N, 28°21′ E 156
Teleorman, adm. division, *Rom.* 43°47′ N, 24°43′ E 156
Telerhteba, Djebel, peak, *Alg.* 24°11′ N, 6°46′ E 214
Teles Pires (São Manuel), river, *Braz.* 9°30′ S, 55°14′ W 122
Telescope Peak, *Calif., U.S.* 36°9′ N, 117°8′ W 101
Teletskoye Ozero, lake, *Russ.* 51°38′ N, 86°38′ E 184
Telfel, spring, *Mali* 19°9′ N, 3°39′ W 222
Telford, *U.K.* 52°40′ N, 2°29′ W 162
Telgte, *Ger.* 51°58′ N, 7°46′ E 167
Télimélé, *Guinea* 10°54′ N, 13°5′ W 222
Telixtlahuaca, *Mex.* 17°15′ N, 96°51′ W 114
Teljo, Jebel, peak, *Sudan* 14°40′ N, 25°52′ E 226
Telkwa, *Can.* 54°40′ N, 127°7′ W 108
Tell City, *Ind., U.S.* 37°56′ N, 86°45′ W 96
Tell el 'Amârna, ruin(s), *Egypt* 27°39′ N, 30°48′ E 180
Tell Tayinat, ruin(s), *Turk.* 36°14′ N, 36°16′ E 156
Tellicherry (Thalassery), *India* 11°45′ N, 75°29′ E 188
Tellier, *Arg.* 47°37′ S, 66°4′ W 134
Telluride, *Colo., U.S.* 37°56′ N, 107°50′ W 92
Telo, *Indonesia* 2°118′ S, 98°15′ E 196
Teloloapan, *Mex.* 18°20′ N, 99°53′ W 114
Telsen, *Arg.* 42°28′ S, 66°51′ W 134
Telšiai, *Lith.* 55°59′ N, 22°14′ E 166
Teluk Intan, *Malaysia* 4°1′ N, 101°1′ E 196
Telukbutun, *Indonesia* 4°14′ N, 108°13′ E 196
Telukdalem, *Indonesia* 0°37′ N, 97°48′ E 196
Tema, *Ghana* 5°41′ N, 1°60′ E 222
Temagami, Lake, *Can.* 46°59′ N, 80°43′ W 110
Tembenchi, *Russ.* 64°56′ N, 99°16′ E 246
Tembenchi, river, *Russ.* 66°3′ N, 94°53′ E 169
Témbi, *Gr.* 39°46′ N, 22°18′ E 156
Tembilahan, *Indonesia* 0°18′ N, 103°8′ E 196
Temblor Range, *Calif., U.S.* 35°28′ N, 120°5′ W 100
Teme, river, *U.K.* 52°17′ N, 2°29′ W 162
Temecula, *Calif., U.S.* 33°29′ N, 117°10′ W 101
Temerin, *Serb. and Mont.* 45°23′ N, 19°53′ E 168
Temerloh, *Malaysia* 3°28′ N, 102°23′ E 196
Temiang, island, *Indonesia* 2°57′ N, 106°9′ E 196
Temir, *Kaz.* 49°8′ N, 57°7′ E 158
Temir, *Kaz.* 42°48′ N, 68°26′ E 197
Temirgoyevskaya, *Russ.* 45°6′ N, 40°15′ E 158
Temirtaū, *Kaz.* 50°10′ N, 73°2′ E 190
Temirtaū, *Kaz.* 50°5′ N, 72°53′ E 184
Temirtau, *Russ.* 53°9′ N, 87°35′ E 184
Témiscamie, Lac, lake, *Can.* 51°6′ N, 72°55′ W 110
Témiscaming, *Can.* 46°44′ N, 79°6′ W 94
Temnikov, *Russ.* 54°38′ N, 43°16′ E 154
Temósachic, *Mex.* 28°57′ N, 107°50′ W 92
Tempe, *Ariz., U.S.* 33°24′ N, 111°58′ W 112
Tempestad, *Peru* 1°20′ S, 74°56′ W 136
Temple, *N.H., U.S.* 42°48′ N, 71°51′ W 104
Temple, *Okla., U.S.* 34°14′ N, 98°14′ W 92
Temple, *Tex., U.S.* 31°5′ N, 97°20′ W 96
Temple Bar, *Ariz., U.S.* 36°0′ N, 114°20′ W 101
Temple, Mount, peak, *Can.* 51°20′ N, 116°17′ W 90
Templeman, Mount, peak, *Can.* 50°40′ N, 117°19′ W 90
Templeton, *Calif., U.S.* 35°33′ N, 120°44′ W 100
Templeton, *Mass., U.S.* 42°33′ N, 72°5′ W 104
Tempoal, *Mex.* 21°31′ N, 98°26′ W 114
Tempué, *Angola* 13°30′ S, 18°50′ E 220
Temryuk, *Russ.* 45°18′ N, 37°24′ E 156
Temryukskiy Zaliv 45°23′ N, 37°2′ E 158
Temse, *Belg.* 51°7′ N, 4°12′ E 163
Temuco, *Chile* 38°43′ S, 72°39′ W 134
Temuka, *N.Z.* 44°15′ S, 171°18′ E 240
Ten Degree Channel 9°44′ N, 91°13′ E 188
Ten Sleep, *Wyo., U.S.* 44°1′ N, 107°26′ W 90
Ten Thousand Islands, *Gulf of Mexico* 25°48′ N, 81°41′ W 105
Tena, *Ecua.* 1°4′ S, 77°55′ W 136
Tenabo, Mount, peak, *Nev., U.S.* 40°9′ N, 116°42′ W 90
Tenaha, *Tex., U.S.* 31°55′ N, 94°15′ W 103
Tenakee Springs, *Alas., U.S.* 57°48′ N, 135°11′ W 108
Tenala, *Fin.* 60°2′ N, 23°17′ E 166
Tenamaxtlán, *Mex.* 20°11′ N, 104°10′ W 114
Tenancingo, *Mex.* 18°56′ N, 99°38′ W 114
Tenay, *Fr.* 45°55′ N, 5°30′ E 156
Tenbury, *U.K.* 52°17′ N, 2°36′ W 162
Tendaho, *Eth.* 11°39′ N, 40°56′ E 182
Tende, *Fr.* 44°5′ N, 7°34′ E 167
Tendelti, *Sudan* 13°0′ N, 31°52′ E 182
Tendō, *Japan* 38°22′ N, 140°22′ E 201
Tendoy Mountains, *Mont., U.S.* 44°49′ N, 113°6′ W 90
Tendrara, *Mor.* 33°5′ N, 1°60′ W 214
Tendürek Dağı, peak, *Turk.* 39°20′ N, 43°50′ E 195
Tenekert, spring, *Mali* 17°48′ N, 3°9′ E 222
Ténenkou, *Mali* 14°28′ N, 4°57′ W 222
Ténéré, *Niger* 19°23′ N, 9°29′ E 222
Ténéré du Tafassâsset, region, *Niger* 20°49′ N, 9°47′ E 222
Ténéré, 'Erg du, *Niger* 17°10′ N, 9°47′ E 222
Tenerife, island, *Sp.* 28°32′ N, 16°3′ W 214
Ténès, *Alg.* 36°30′ N, 1°18′ E 150
Tenexpa, *Mex.* 17°10′ N, 100°43′ W 114
Teng'aopu, *China* 41°5′ N, 122°48′ E 200
Tengchong, *China* 25°3′ N, 98°26′ E 190
Tengge, *Kaz.* 43°16′ N, 52°46′ E 158
Tengiz, oil field, *Kaz.* 46°7′ N, 53°23′ E 158
Tengizy Köli, lake, *Kaz.* 50°11′ N, 68°11′ E 184
Tengxian, *China* 35°5′ N, 117°9′ E 198
Tengxian, *China* 23°16′ N, 110°51′ E 198
Teniente Origone, *Arg.* 39°6′ S, 62°35′ W 139
Tenino, *Wash., U.S.* 46°50′ N, 122°52′ W 100
Tenke, *Dem. Rep. of the Congo* 10°36′ S, 26°10′ E 224
Tenkeli, *Russ.* 70°10′ N, 140°46′ E 160
Tenkergynpil'gyn, Laguna 68°29′ N, 178°36′ E 98
Ten'ki, *Russ.* 55°24′ N, 48°54′ E 154
Tenkodogo, *Burkina Faso* 11°46′ N, 0°22′ E 222
Tenlaa, *India* 7°1′ N, 93°58′ E 188
Tennant Creek, *Austral.* 19°38′ S, 134°13′ E 231
Tennessee, adm. division, *Tenn., U.S.* 35°41′ N, 87°31′ W 96
Tennessee Pass, *Colo., U.S.* 39°20′ N, 106°19′ W 90
Tenojoki, river, *Europe* 68°54′ N, 25°39′ E 160
Tenosique, *Mex.* 17°28′ N, 91°26′ W 116
Tenryū, river, *Japan* 35°7′ N, 137°41′ E 201
Tensas, river, *La., U.S.* 32°8′ N, 91°21′ W 103
Tensaw, *Ala., U.S.* 31°8′ N, 87°48′ W 103
Tentane, *Mauritania* 19°55′ N, 13°3′ W 222
Teocaltiche, *Mex.* 21°25′ N, 102°34′ W 114
Teodelina, *Arg.* 34°12′ S, 61°34′ W 139
Teófilo Otoni, *Braz.* 17°49′ S, 41°32′ W 138
Teofipol', *Ukr.* 49°49′ N, 26°24′ E 152
Teolo, *It.* 45°20′ N, 11°40′ E 167
Teora, *It.* 40°52′ N, 15°16′ E 156
Teotepec, Cerro, peak, *Mex.* 17°26′ N, 100°13′ W 114
Teotihuacan, ruin(s), *Mex.* 19°40′ N, 98°57′ W 114
Tepache, *Mex.* 29°31′ N, 109°31′ W 92
Tepalcatepec, *Mex.* 19°10′ N, 102°52′ W 114
Tepalcatepec, river, *Mex.* 19°0′ N, 102°44′ W 114
Tepatitlán, *Mex.* 20°48′ N, 102°47′ W 114
Tepe Gawra, ruin(s), *Iraq* 36°32′ N, 43°7′ E 195
Tepe Musyan, ruin(s), *Iran* 32°34′ N, 47°9′ E 180
Tepe, peak, *Europe* 42°43′ N, 21°31′ E 168
Tepechitlán, *Mex.* 21°38′ N, 103°19′ W 114
Tepecoacuilco, *Mex.* 18°16′ N, 99°29′ W 114
Tepehuanes, *Mex.* 25°21′ N, 105°42′ W 114
Tepeji de Ocampo, *Mex.* 19°52′ N, 99°20′ W 114
Tepetongo, *Mex.* 22°27′ N, 103°8′ W 114
Tepic, *Mex.* 21°29′ N, 104°57′ W 114
Tepich, *Mex.* 20°17′ N, 88°14′ W 115
Tepoca, Cabo, *Mex.* 30°4′ N, 113°13′ W 92
Teposcolula, *Mex.* 17°29′ N, 97°31′ W 114
Tequila, *Mex.* 20°53′ N, 103°49′ W 114
Tequisquiapan, *Mex.* 20°30′ N, 99°54′ W 114
Ter Apel, *Neth.* 52°52′ N, 7°4′ E 163
T'er, river, *Eth.* 7°14′ N, 41°49′ E 224
Téra, *Niger* 13°59′ N, 0°46′ E 222
Teradomari, *Japan* 37°37′ N, 138°47′ E 201
Terakeka, *Sudan* 5°25′ N, 31°43′ E 224
Teramo, *It.* 42°39′ N, 13°42′ E 156
Tercan, *Turk.* 39°47′ N, 40°22′ E 195
Teregova, *Rom.* 45°7′ N, 22°18′ E 168
Terek, river, *Russ.* 43°24′ N, 46°17′ E 195
Terekhovka, *Belarus* 52°10′ N, 31°30′ E 158
Terekli Mekteb, *Russ.* 44°9′ N, 45°53′ E 158
Terekty, *Kaz.* 48°22′ N, 85°39′ E 184
Terempa, *Indonesia* 3°14′ N, 106°12′ E 196
Terengözek, *Kaz.* 45°2′ N, 64°59′ E 184
Terenos, *Braz.* 20°24′ S, 54°51′ W 132
Tereressene, spring, *Mali* 16°55′ N, 2°39′ E 222
Teresa Cristina, *Braz.* 24°52′ S, 51°6′ W 138
Teresina, *Braz.* 5°3′ S, 42°48′ W 132
Teresinha, *Braz.* 0°57′ N, 52°1′ W 130
Teresita, *Peru* 12°35′ S, 73°47′ W 137
Terezino Polje, *Croatia* 45°56′ N, 17°27′ E 168
Tergnier, *Fr.* 49°39′ N, 3°17′ E 163
Terhazza, ruin(s), *Mali* 23°34′ N, 5°9′ W 214
Teriberka, *Russ.* 69°10′ N, 35°9′ E 152
Teriberskiy, Mys, *Russ.* 69°1′ N, 35°15′ E 152
Terisaqqan, river, *Kaz.* 51°22′ N, 67°25′ E 184
Terjärv (Teerijärvi), *Fin.* 63°32′ N, 23°29′ E 154
Terkezi, spring, *Chad* 18°24′ N, 21°28′ E 216
Termas de Río Hondo, *Arg.* 27°29′ S, 64°52′ W 134
Terme, *Turk.* 41°12′ N, 36°57′ E 156
Termini Imerese, *It.* 37°58′ N, 13°41′ E 156
Terminus Mountain, peak, *Can.* 58°46′ N, 127°12′ W 108
Termit, *Niger* 16°5′ N, 11°11′ E 222
Termit, Massif de, *Niger* 16°8′ N, 10°42′ E 222
Termit, spring, *Niger* 15°58′ N, 11°15′ E 206
Termita, *Russ.* 45°5′ N, 45°14′ E 158
Termit-Kaoboul, *Niger* 15°37′ N, 11°26′ E 222
Termiz, *Uzb.* 37°14′ N, 67°16′ E 186
Termoli, *It.* 41°59′ N, 14°59′ E 156
Termópilas, *Peru* 10°41′ S, 73°53′ W 137
Ternate, *Indonesia* 0°41′ N, 127°25′ E 192
Terneuzen, *Neth.* 51°19′ N, 3°50′ E 163
Terney, *Russ.* 45°6′ N, 136°31′ E 190
Terni, *It.* 42°34′ N, 12°39′ E 156
Ternitz, *Aust.* 47°43′ N, 16°0′ E 168
Ternopil', *Ukr.* 49°31′ N, 25°35′ E 152
Terpeniya, Mys, *Russ.* 48°8′ N, 144°42′ E 190
Terpeniya, Zaliv 47°55′ N, 142°48′ E 190
Terra Bella, *Calif., U.S.* 35°58′ N, 119°3′ W 101

Terra Nova Bay, Italy, station, Antarctica 74°45' S, 163°39' E 248
Terra Nova National Park, Can. 48°30' N, 54°55' W 111
Terrace, Can. 54°31' N, 128°36' W 108
Terrace Bay, Can. 48°47' N, 87°6' W 94
Terracina, It. 41°18' N, 13°14' E 156
Terralba, It. 39°42' N, 8°37' E 214
Terrassa, Sp. 41°33' N, 2°1' E 164
Terre Haute, Ind., U.S. 39°27' N, 87°25' W 102
Terrebonne Bay 29°1' N, 90°39' W 96
Terrecht, region, Mali 20°26' N, 0°35' E 222
Terrell, Tex., U.S. 32°45' N, 96°18' W 112
Terry, Miss., U.S. 32°4' N, 90°18' W 103
Terry, Mont., U.S. 46°46' N, 105°20' W 90
Terry Peak, S. Dak., U.S. 44°18' N, 103°55' W 90
Terschelling, island, Neth. 53°27' N, 5°7' E 163
Tertenia, It. 39°40' N, 9°33' E 156
Teru, Pak. 36°8' N, 72°48' E 186
Teruel, Sp. 40°19' N, 1°9' W 214
Tervo, Fin. 62°55' N, 26°41' E 152
Tešanj, Bosn. and Herzg. 44°36' N, 17°59' E 168
Teshi, Ghana 5°37' N, 7°415' W 222
Teshi, river, Nig. 9°17' N, 4°3' E 222
Tešica, Serb. and Mont. 43°25' N, 21°45' E 168
Teslić, Bosn. and Herzg. 44°36' N, 17°50' E 168
Teslin, Can. 60°13' N, 132°47' W 108
Teslin Lake, Can. 59°45' N, 132°58' W 108
Teslin, river, Can. 59°16' N, 132°5' W 108
Tesouro, Braz. 16°7' S, 53°33' W 132
Tesovo Netyl'skiy, Russ. 58°56' N, 31°8' E 152
Tessalit, Mali 20°12' N, 0°58' E 222
Tessaoua, Niger 13°47' N, 7°57' E 222
Tessenberg, Aust. 46°45' N, 12°28' E 167
Tessenei, Eritrea 15°6' N, 36°39' E 182
Tessier, Lac, lake, Can. 48°10' N, 75°44' W 94
Tessounfat, spring, Mali 20°51' N, 0°37' E 222
Tét, Hung. 47°30' N, 17°31' E 168
Tetas, Punta, Chile 23°28' S, 71°8' W 132
Tétat ed Douaïr, Alg. 35°59' N, 2°53' E 150
Tete, Mozambique 16°13' S, 33°34' E 224
Tete, adm. division, Mozambique 15°27' S, 31°58' E 224
Tête Jaune Cache, Can. 52°57' N, 119°26' W 108
Tetepare, island, Solomon Islands 8°45' S, 157°30' E 242
Tetford, U.K. 53°15' N, 2°119' E 162
Tethul, river, Can. 60°30' N, 112°25' W 108
Tetlin, Alas., U.S. 63°9' N, 142°29' W 98
Tetney, U.K. 53°29' N, 0°1' E 162
Teton Pass, Wyo., U.S. 43°30' N, 110°58' W 90
Teton Range, Wyo., U.S. 43°29' N, 110°59' W 90
Teton, river, Mont., U.S. 47°56' N, 111°43' W 90
Tétouan (Tetuán), Mor. 35°35' N, 5°23' W 150
Tetovo, Maced. 42°1' N, 20°58' E 168
Tetrino, Russ. 66°5' N, 38°6' E 154
Tetuán see Tétouan, Mor. 35°35' N, 5°23' W 150
Tetyushi, Russ. 54°56' N, 48°44' E 154
Teuco, river, Arg. 24°41' S, 61°45' W 132
Teul, Mex. 21°27' N, 103°29' W 114
Teulada, Capo, It. 38°48' N, 7°59' E 156
Teulon, Can. 50°23' N, 97°18' W 90
Teutopolis, Ill., U.S. 39°7' N, 88°29' W 102
Teutschenthal, Ger. 51°27' N, 11°48' E 152
Teuva, Fin. 62°28' N, 21°41' E 152
Teverya (Tiberias), Israel 32°47' N, 35°31' E 194
Tewantin, Austral. 26°26' S, 153°2' E 231
Tewkesbury, U.K. 51°59' N, 2°9' W 162
Texada Island, Can. 49°38' N, 124°16' W 100
Texarkana, Ark., U.S. 33°24' N, 94°3' W 103
Texas, adm. division, Tex., U.S. 31°8' N, 101°3' W 82
Texas City, Tex., U.S. 29°21' N, 94°54' W 103
Texas Point, Tex., U.S. 29°34' N, 93°54' W 103
Texcoco, Mex. 19°27' N, 99°15' W 112
Texel, island, Neth. 53°5' N, 4°33' E 163
Texhoma, Okla., U.S. 36°30' N, 101°47' W 92
Texico, Tex., U.S. 34°23' N, 103°4' W 92
Texline, Tex., U.S. 36°22' N, 103°2' W 92
Texon, Tex., U.S. 31°11' N, 101°41' W 92
Teya, Russ. 60°20' N, 92°46' E 169
Teykovo, Russ. 56°52' N, 40°27' E 154
Teylan, Afghan. 35°34' N, 64°49' E 186
Teziutlán, Mex. 19°48' N, 97°23' W 114
Tezontepec, Mex. 19°50' N, 98°48' W 114
Tezpur, India 26°43' N, 92°45' E 188
Tezzeron Lake, Can. 54°38' N, 125°6' W 108
Tfaritiy, Africa 26°11' N, 10°34' W 214
Tha Li, Thai. 17°39' N, 101°23' E 202
Tha, river, Laos 21°6' N, 101°15' E 202
Tha Sala, Thai. 8°40' N, 99°56' E 202
Thaba Nchu, S. Af. 29°14' S, 26°48' E 227
Thabaung, Myanmar 17°4' N, 94°46' E 202
Thabazimbi, S. Af. 24°38' S, 27°23' E 227
Thādiq, Saudi Arabia 25°16' N, 45°53' E 182
Thaga Pass, India 31°26' N, 79°8' E 188
Thagyettaw, Myanmar 13°46' N, 98°8' E 202
Thai Binh, Vietnam 20°27' N, 106°20' E 198
Thai Hoa, Vietnam 19°20' N, 105°26' E 202
Thai Nguyen, Vietnam 21°35' N, 105°50' E 198
Thailand 15°33' N, 101°6' E 202
Thailand, Gulf of 9°44' N, 101°14' E 202
Thal, Pak. 33°22' N, 70°38' E 186
Thalabarivat, Cambodia 13°35' N, 105°56' E 202
Thalassery see Tellicherry, India 11°45' N, 75°29' E 188
Thamad Bū Ḩashīshah, spring, Lib. 26°23' N, 18°44' E 216
Thamarīt, Oman 17°38' N, 54°1' E 182
Thames, N.Z. 37°10' S, 175°34' E 240
Thames, river, Can. 42°16' N, 82°26' W 102
Thamesville, Can. 42°32' N, 81°57' W 102
Thamūd, Yemen 17°18' N, 49°55' E 182
Thane, India 19°12' N, 72°56' E 188
Thanggu, India 27°53' N, 88°36' E 197
Thanh Hoa, Vietnam 19°48' N, 105°44' E 202
Thanh Tri, Vietnam 9°26' N, 105°43' E 202
Thanlwin (Salween), river, Asia 21°45' N, 98°44' E 202
Thann, Fr. 47°48' N, 7°5' E 150
Thaon-les-Vosges, Fr. 48°14' N, 6°25' E 163
Thap Lan National Park, Thai. 14°1' N, 102°29' E 202
Tharabwin, Myanmar 12°19' N, 99°3' E 202
Tharad, India 24°24' N, 71°41' E 186
Tharrawaddy, Myanmar 17°40' N, 95°47' E 202
Tharros, ruin(s), It. 39°52' N, 8°21' E 156
Tharthār Lake, Iraq 33°57' N, 42°50' E 180
Thássos, island, Gr. 40°26' N, 24°36' E 180
That Khe, Vietnam 22°18' N, 106°30' E 198
That Phanom, Thai. 16°58' N, 104°42' E 202
Thatcher, Ariz., U.S. 32°50' N, 109°45' W 92
Thaton, Myanmar 16°56' N, 97°21' E 202
Thatta, Pak. 24°45' N, 67°55' E 186
Thaungdut, Myanmar 24°25' N, 94°37' E 188
Thawatti, Myanmar 19°31' N, 96°12' E 202
Thaxted, U.K. 51°56' N, 0°21' E 162
Thayawthadangyi Kyun, island, Myanmar 12°20' N, 96°28' E 202
Thayer, Ill., U.S. 39°32' N, 89°45' W 102
Thayer, Mo., U.S. 36°31' N, 91°33' W 96
Thayetchaung, Myanmar 13°52' N, 98°16' E 202
The Alley, Jam. 17°47' N, 77°16' W 115
The Brothers see Al Ikhwān, islands, Persian Gulf 11°24' N, 52°52' E 182
The Caterthuns, ruin(s), U.K. 56°46' N, 2°53' W 150
The Curragh, site, Ire. 53°8' N, 6°56' W 150
The Dalles, Oreg., U.S. 45°34' N, 121°11' W 90
The English Company's Islands, Arafura Sea 11°39' S, 136°42' E 230
The Four Archers, site, Austral. 15°30' S, 135°13' E 230
The Hague see 's Gravenhage, Neth. 52°5' N, 4°18' E 167
The Mumbles, U.K. 51°34' N, 3°60' W 162
The Ovens, site, Can. 44°18' N, 64°23' W 111
The Pas, Can. 53°47' N, 101°17' W 108
The Plains, Ohio, U.S. 39°21' N, 82°8' W 102
The Rivals see Yr Eifl, peak, U.K. 52°57' N, 4°32' W 150
The Slot see New Georgia Sound 8°11' S, 158°30' E 242
The Two Rivers, Can. 55°45' N, 103°15' W 108
The Valley, Anguilla 18°13' N, 63°4' W 116
The Woodlands, Tex., U.S. 30°10' N, 95°28' W 103
Theano Point, Can. 47°10' N, 84°40' W 110
Thebes, ruin(s), Egypt 25°40' N, 32°2' E 206
Thedford, Can. 43°9' N, 81°51' W 102
Thedford, Nebr., U.S. 41°58' N, 100°35' W 90
Thekulthili Lake, Can. 61°2' N, 110°46' W 108
Thelon, river, Can. 63°20' N, 104°51' W 106
Thenon, Fr. 45°8' N, 1°4' E 150
Theo, Mount, peak, Austral. 21°23' S, 131°9' E 230
Théodat, Lac, lake, Can. 50°53' N, 76°41' W 110
Theodore Roosevelt National Park, Elkhorn Ranch Site, N. Dak., U.S. 47°12' N, 103°45' W 90
Theodore Roosevelt National Park, North Unit, N. Dak., U.S. 47°17' N, 105°57' W 80
Theodore Roosevelt, river, Braz. 11°28' S, 60°30' W 130
Thepha, Thai. 6°51' N, 100°56' E 196
Thera, ruin(s), Gr. 36°20' N, 25°23' E 156
Therien, Can. 54°13' N, 111°17' W 108
Thermal, Calif., U.S. 33°38' N, 116°9' W 101
Thermiá, ruin(s), Gr. 41°27' N, 24°20' E 156
Thermopolis, Wyo., U.S. 43°38' N, 108°13' W 90
Thermopylae 480 B.C., battle, Gr. 38°47' N, 22°27' E 156
Thermum, ruin(s), Gr. 38°33' N, 21°36' E 156
Thessalía, adm. division, Gr. 39°19' N, 21°28' E 156
Thessalon, Can. 46°16' N, 83°34' W 94
Thessaloníki (Salonica), Gr. 40°38' N, 22°57' E 156
Thetford, U.K. 52°25' N, 0°45' E 162
Thetford Mines, Can. 46°4' N, 71°18' W 111
Theux, Belg. 50°31' N, 5°48' E 167
Thiaucourt, Fr. 48°57' N, 5°50' E 163
Thibodaux, La., U.S. 29°46' N, 90°50' W 103
Thicket Portage, Can. 55°18' N, 97°42' W 108
Thief River Falls, Minn., U.S. 48°6' N, 96°13' W 90
Thielsen, Mount, peak, Oreg., U.S. 43°8' N, 122°9' W 90
Thiene, It. 45°42' N, 11°28' E 167
Thiès, Senegal 14°48' N, 16°41' W 222
Thignica, ruin(s), Tun. 36°31' N, 9°15' E 156
Thika, Kenya 1°3' S, 37°4' E 224
Thilogne, Senegal 15°57' N, 13°40' W 222
Thimphu, Bhutan 27°32' N, 89°31' E 197
Thinahtea Lake, Can. 59°40' N, 121°4' W 108
Thio, Eritrea 14°36' N, 40°54' E 182
Thionville, Fr. 49°22' N, 6°9' E 163
Thiou, Burkina Faso 13°47' N, 2°42' W 222
Thíra, island, Gr. 36°11' N, 25°9' E 180
Thirsk, U.K. 54°14' N, 1°21' W 162
Thiruvananthapuram see Trivandrum, India 8°28' N, 76°56' E 188
Thisted, Den. 56°57' N, 8°40' E 150
Thistle Island, island, Austral. 35°8' S, 134°33' E 230
Thíva, Gr. 38°20' N, 23°20' E 180
Thiviers, Fr. 45°24' N, 0°55' E 150
Thlewiaza, river, Can. 60°54' N, 99°1' W 108
Tho Chu, Dao, island, Vietnam 9°2' N, 103°21' E 202
Thoa, river, Can. 60°39' N, 108°55' W 108
Thoen, Thai. 17°37' N, 99°10' E 202
Thohoyandou, S. Af. 22°58' S, 30°25' E 227
Tholey, Ger. 49°29' N, 7°5' E 163
Thomas, Okla., U.S. 35°43' N, 98°44' W 92
Thomas Mountains, Antarctica 76°11' S, 75°43' W 248
Thomaston, Ala., U.S. 32°15' N, 87°37' W 103
Thomaston, Ga., U.S. 32°53' N, 84°19' W 96
Thomaston, Me., U.S. 44°4' N, 69°12' W 94
Thomasville, Ala., U.S. 31°55' N, 87°44' W 103
Thomasville, Ga., U.S. 30°49' N, 83°59' W 96
Thomasville, N.C., U.S. 35°52' N, 80°6' W 96
Thompson, Can. 55°44' N, 97°51' W 108
Thompson, Utah, U.S. 38°58' N, 109°43' W 90
Thompson Lake, Me., U.S. 44°1' N, 70°41' W 104
Thompson Peak, Calif., U.S. 40°59' N, 123°9' W 90
Thompson Peak, Mont., U.S. 47°43' N, 114°56' W 90
Thompson Point, Can. 58°14' N, 92°60' W 108
Thompson, river, Can. 49°56' N, 121°12' W 80
Thomson, Ill., U.S. 41°57' N, 90°6' W 102
Thomson, Mount, peak, Austral. 24°1' S, 115°37' E 230
Thon Buri, Thai. 13°39' N, 100°25' E 202
Thongwa, Myanmar 16°46' N, 96°35' E 202
Thonotosassa, Fla., U.S. 28°4' N, 82°18' W 105
Thorenc, Fr. 43°47' N, 6°49' E 167
Thorhild, Can. 54°9' N, 113°8' W 108
Thornaby on Tees, U.K. 54°33' N, 1°19' W 162
Thornapple, river, Mich., U.S. 42°40' N, 85°22' W 102
Thornbury, Can. 44°33' N, 80°27' W 94
Thornbury, N.Z. 46°18' S, 168°6' E 240
Thornbury, U.K. 51°37' N, 2°31' W 162
Thorndale, Tex., U.S. 30°35' N, 97°12' W 96
Thorne, U.K. 53°36' N, 0°59' E 162
Thorne Bay, Alas., U.S. 55°42' N, 132°35' W 98
Thornton, Calif., U.S. 38°13' N, 121°26' W 100
Thornton, W. Va., U.S. 39°20' N, 79°57' W 94
Thorp, Wash., U.S. 47°2' N, 120°42' W 90
Thorp, Wis., U.S. 44°57' N, 90°49' W 94
Thouars, Fr. 46°59' N, 0°14' E 150
Thousand Oaks, Calif., U.S. 34°11' N, 118°53' W 101
Thrapston, U.K. 52°23' N, 0°31' E 162
Three Brothers, islands, Indian Ocean 5°55' S, 69°39' E 188
Three Brothers Mountain, peak, Can. 49°8' N, 120°51' W 90
Three Cocks, U.K. 52°1' N, 3°12' W 162
Three Fingered Jack, peak, Oreg., U.S. 44°27' N, 121°56' W 90
Three Forks, Mont., U.S. 45°52' N, 111°34' W 90
Three Hills, Can. 51°43' N, 113°17' W 90
Three Lakes, Wis., U.S. 45°48' N, 89°10' W 94
Three Oaks, Mich., U.S. 41°47' N, 86°36' W 102
Three Pagodas Pass, Thai. 15°19' N, 98°24' E 202
Three Points, Calif., U.S. 34°44' N, 118°37' W 101
Three Points, Cape 4°29' N, 3°5' W 222
Three Rivers, Calif., U.S. 36°26' N, 118°55' W 101
Three Rivers, Mass., U.S. 42°10' N, 72°23' W 104
Three Rivers, Mich., U.S. 41°56' N, 85°38' W 102
Three Rivers, Tex., U.S. 28°27' N, 98°11' W 92
Three Sisters, S. Af. 31°53' S, 23°5' E 227
Three Sisters Islands, Solomon Sea 10°11' S, 161°55' E 242
Three Sisters, peak, Oreg., U.S. 44°4' N, 121°51' W 90
Thrissur see Trichur, India 10°31' N, 76°11' E 188
Throckmorton, Tex., U.S. 33°10' N, 99°11' W 92
Throssell Range, Austral. 21°43' S, 120°55' E 230
Thu, Cu Lao, island, Vietnam 10°16' N, 108°52' E 202
Thugga, ruin(s), Tun. 36°24' N, 9°7' E 156
Thuin, Belg. 50°20' N, 4°17' E 163
Thulaythiwāt, Tilāl ath, peak, Jordan 30°58' N, 36°38' E 194
Thule Air Base 76°28' N, 69°3' W 106
Thule see Qaanaaq 77°32' N, 69°13' W 106
Thuli, river, Zimb. 21°21' S, 28°59' E 227
Thun, Switz. 46°44' N, 7°36' E 167
Thunder Bay, Can. 48°24' N, 89°14' W 94
Thunder Hills, Can. 54°19' N, 106°33' W 108
Thuner See, lake, Switz. 46°42' N, 7°28' E 165
Thung Song, Thai. 8°10' N, 99°41' E 202
Thüringer Wald, Ger. 50°54' N, 10°1' E 167
Thuringia, adm. division, Ger. 50°46' N, 9°58' E 167
Thurston Island, Antarctica 72°13' S, 98°45' W 255
Thusis, Switz. 46°42' N, 9°25' E 167
Thutade Lake, Can. 56°46' N, 127°52' W 108
Thyborøn, Den. 56°41' N, 8°10' E 150
Thynne, Mount, peak, Can. 49°41' N, 120°57' W 100
Thyou, Burkina Faso 11°55' N, 2°14' W 222
Tiago, Braz. 0°59' N, 57°1' W 130
Tian Head, Can. 53°38' N, 133°34' W 108
Tian Shan 40°8' N, 71°21' E 197
Tianbaoshan, China 42°57' N, 128°56' E 200
Tiandeng, China 23°3' N, 107°6' E 198
Tiandong, China 23°33' N, 107°6' E 198
Tian'e, China 25°0' N, 107°9' E 198
Tianguá, Braz. 3°43' S, 40°60' W 132
Tianjin, China 38°52' N, 117°15' E 190
Tianjin, adm. division, China 39°47' N, 117°15' E 190
Tianjin (Tientsin), China 39°3' N, 117°9' E 198
Tianjun, China 37°18' N, 99°0' E 188
Tianlin, China 24°16' N, 106°14' E 198
Tianmen, China 30°40' N, 113°10' E 198
Tianshan see Ar Horqin Qi, China 43°55' N, 120°7' E 198
Tianshifu, China 41°14' N, 124°19' E 200
Tianshui, China 34°36' N, 105°42' E 198
Tianyang, China 23°45' N, 106°51' E 198
Tianzhu, China 26°56' N, 109°11' E 198
Tiaret, Alg. 35°21' N, 1°19' E 150
Tiaret, spring, Tun. 30°56' N, 10°6' E 214
Tiaski, Senegal 15°40' N, 14°18' W 222
Tiassalé, Côte d'Ivoire 5°49' N, 4°53' W 222
Tib, Ras el, Tun. 36°57' N, 10°31' E 156
Tibagi, Braz. 24°31' S, 50°27' W 138
Tibagi, river, Braz. 23°51' S, 50°44' W 138
Tibasti, Sarīr, Lib. 22°48' N, 15°52' E 216
Tibati, Cameroon 6°23' N, 12°36' E 218
Tibbie, Ala., U.S. 31°21' N, 88°15' W 103
Tibé, Pic de, peak, Guinea 8°49' N, 8°58' W 222
Tiber Dam, Mont., U.S. 48°8' N, 111°8' W 90
Tiberias see Teverya, Israel 32°47' N, 35°31' E 194
Tibesti, Chad 19°48' N, 17°13' E 216
Tibet, Plateau of, China 33°55' N, 81°5' E 172
Tibeysale, Russ. 67°3' N, 79°31' E 169
Tibidabo, peak, Sp. 41°24' N, 2°6' E 164
Tibiri, Niger 13°5' N, 3°55' E 222
Tibiri, Niger 13°34' N, 7°3' E 222
Ţibleş, Munţii, Rom. 47°31' N, 23°48' E 156
Ţibleş, peak, Rom. 47°30' N, 24°11' E 156
Tibnine, Leb. 33°11' N, 35°24' E 194
Tibrikot, Nepal 29°0' N, 82°50' E 197
Tibú, Col. 8°37' N, 72°42' W 136
Tiburon, Calif., U.S. 37°52' N, 122°29' W 100
Tiburón, Cabo, Col. 8°41' N, 77°31' W 136
Tiburón, Isla, island, Mex. 28°30' N, 112°28' W 80
Tichégami, river, Can. 51°50' N, 73°58' W 110
Tîchît, Mauritania 18°28' N, 9°30' W 222
Tîchît, Dahr, Mauritania 18°36' N, 10°27' W 214
Ticonderoga, N.Y., U.S. 43°50' N, 73°26' W 104
Ticouapé, Can. 48°42' N, 72°30' W 94
Ticul, Mex. 20°23' N, 89°33' W 115
Tide Lake, Can. 50°33' N, 111°32' W 108
Tidikelt, region, Alg. 26°28' N, 1°9' E 214
Tidjidit, Erg, Alg. 23°32' N, 0°8' E 214
Tidjikdja, Mauritania 18°30' N, 11°27' W 207
Tidra, Île, island, Mauritania 19°47' N, 16°46' W 222
Tiébissou, Côte d'Ivoire 7°5' N, 5°14' W 222
Tiechang, China 41°40' N, 126°13' E 200
Tiehnpo, Liberia 5°13' N, 8°6' W 222
Tiel, Neth. 51°53' N, 5°25' E 167
Tiel, Senegal 14°55' N, 15°2' W 222
Tieli, China 47°3' N, 128°3' E 198
Tieling, China 42°17' N, 123°51' E 200
Tielt, Belg. 51°0' N, 3°19' E 163
Tien Yen, Vietnam 21°20' N, 107°21' E 198
Tienen, Belg. 50°48' N, 4°55' E 167
Tiensuu, Fin. 65°35' N, 25°59' E 152
Tientsin see Tianjin, China 39°3' N, 117°9' E 198
Tiéré, Mali 11°54' N, 5°26' W 222
Tiermas, Sp. 42°37' N, 1°7' W 164
Tieroko, peak, Chad 20°46' N, 17°43' E 216
Tierp, Sw. 60°20' N, 17°29' E 166
Tierra Blanca, Mex. 18°26' N, 96°20' W 114
Tierra Colorada, Mex. 17°9' N, 99°32' W 114
Tierra del Fuego, Isla Grande de, island, Arg.-Chile 53°3' S, 68°33' W 248
Tierra del Fuego National Park, Arg. 54°39' S, 68°60' W 122
Tierra del Fuego-Antártida E Islas Atlántico Sur, adm. division, Arg. 53°44' S, 70°49' W 134
Tietê, river, Braz. 23°28' S, 46°16' W 138
Tiffany Mountain, peak, Wash., U.S. 48°38' N, 120°1' W 90
Tiffin, Ohio, U.S. 41°6' N, 83°11' W 102
Tifristós, peak, Gr. 38°56' N, 21°44' E 156
Tifton, Ga., U.S. 31°27' N, 83°31' W 96
Tigharry 57°37' N, 7°29' W 150
Tighennif, Alg. 35°24' N, 0°20' E 150
Tigil', Russ. 57°51' N, 158°45' E 160
Tignère, Cameroon 7°20' N, 12°39' E 218
Tigray, region, Eth. 13°57' N, 36°41' E 182
Tigre, river, Peru 3°28' S, 74°47' W 136
Tigre, river, Venez. 8°56' N, 63°10' W 116
Tigris (Dicle, Dijlah), river, Iraq 32°8' N, 46°36' E 180
Tiguent, Mauritania 17°17' N, 16°7' W 222
Tiguentourine, oil field, Alg. 27°44' N, 9°4' E 214
Tiguidit, Falaise de, region, Niger 16°40' N, 6°58' E 222
Tigyaing, Myanmar 23°45' N, 96°3' E 202
Tîh, Gebel el, Egypt 29°35' N, 33°0' E 180
Tihany, Hung. 46°54' N, 17°53' E 168
Tihosuco, Mex. 20°12' N, 88°26' W 115
Tihuatlán, Mex. 20°41' N, 97°33' W 114
Tijamré, spring, Mauritania 20°18' N, 11°16' W 222
Tijesno, Croatia 43°47' N, 15°38' E 156
Tijola, Sp. 37°19' N, 2°26' W 164
Tijti, spring, Mauritania 17°52' N, 7°15' W 222
Tijuana, Mex. 32°31' N, 117°4' W 101
Tijucas, Braz. 27°16' S, 48°39' W 138
Tijucas do Sul, Braz. 25°57' S, 49°12' W 138
Tikal National Park, Guatemala 17°13' N, 90°10' W 115
Tikamgarh, India 24°44' N, 78°50' E 197
Tikanlik, China 40°40' N, 87°40' E 188
Tikaré, Burkina Faso 13°16' N, 1°44' W 222
Tikattane, Mauritania 19°2' N, 16°15' W 222
Tikhmanga, Russ. 61°14' N, 38°31' E 154
Tikhoretsk, Russ. 45°52' N, 40°5' E 158
Tikhtozero, Russ. 65°33' N, 30°31' E 154
Tikhvin, Russ. 59°38' N, 33°32' E 154
Tikitiki, N.Z. 37°48' S, 178°23' E 240
Tikkurila, Fin. 60°16' N, 24°58' E 166
Tiko, Cameroon 4°5' N, 9°21' E 222
Tikshozero, Russ. 64°6' N, 31°47' E 152
Tikshozero, Russ. 66°0' N, 32°23' E 152
Tiksi, Russ. 71°22' N, 128°46' E 160
Tilaiya Dam, India 24°20' N, 85°35' E 197
Tilamuta, Indonesia 0°34' N, 122°17' E 192
Tilatou, Alg. 35°19' N, 5°47' E 150
Tilburg, Neth. 51°33' N, 5°4' E 163
Tilbury, Can. 42°15' N, 82°27' W 102
Tilbury, U.K. 51°27' N, 0°21' E 162
Til-Châtel, Fr. 47°30' N, 5°9' E 150
Tilden, Nebr., U.S. 42°1' N, 97°50' W 90
Tileagd, Rom. 47°3' N, 22°14' E 168
Tilemsoun, Mor. 28°13' N, 10°57' W 214
Tilichiki, Russ. 60°28' N, 165°53' E 160
Tillabéri, Niger 14°12' N, 1°26' E 222
Tillamook, Oreg., U.S. 45°27' N, 123°51' W 90
Tillamook Head, Oreg., U.S. 45°56' N, 124°9' W 100
Tillanchang Dwip, island, India 8°34' N, 93°43' E 188
Tillia, Niger 15°53' N, 4°35' E 222
Tilloo Cay, island, Bahamas 26°33' N, 76°56' W 116
Tillson, N.Y., U.S. 41°49' N, 74°5' W 104
Tillsonburg, Can. 42°51' N, 80°43' W 102
Tilos, island, Gr. 36°24' N, 27°25' E 180
Tilpa, Austral. 30°56' S, 144°26' E 231
Tilrhemt, Alg. 33°11' N, 3°21' E 214
Tiltagals, Latv. 56°33' N, 26°39' E 166
Tilton, Ill., U.S. 40°5' N, 87°40' W 102
Tilton, N.H., U.S. 43°26' N, 71°36' W 104
Tilža, Latv. 56°53' N, 27°21' E 166
Tim, Russ. 51°34' N, 37°9' E 158
Ţima, Egypt 26°55' N, 31°21' E 180
Timanskiy Kryazh, Russ. 65°21' N, 50°38' E 154
Timaru, N.Z. 44°24' S, 171°13' E 240
Timashevo, Russ. 53°22' N, 51°5' E 154
Timashevsk, Russ. 45°40' N, 38°58' E 156
Timbáki, Gr. 35°2' N, 24°44' E 180
Timbalier Bay 29°8' N, 90°33' W 103
Timbalier Island, La., U.S. 28°57' N, 90°34' W 103
Timbédra, Mauritania 16°16' N, 8°12' W 222
Timber, Oreg., U.S. 45°42' N, 123°19' W 100
Timber Bay, Can. 54°9' N, 105°40' W 108
Timber Lake, S. Dak., U.S. 45°25' N, 101°6' W 90
Timber Mountain, peak, Calif., U.S. 41°37' N, 121°23' W 90
Timber Mountain, peak, Nev., U.S. 37°2' N, 116°30' W 101
Timbío, Col. 2°17' N, 76°43' W 136
Timbiquí, Col. 2°41' N, 77°45' W 136
Timbo, Guinea 10°37' N, 11°52' W 222
Timbo, Liberia 5°31' N, 9°42' W 222
Timbuktu see Tombouctou, Mali 16°44' N, 3°2' W 222
Timeïaouine, spring, Alg. 20°28' N, 1°48' E 222
Timellouline, spring, Alg. 29°15' N, 8°55' E 214
Timerein, Sudan 16°58' N, 36°29' E 182
Timétrine, region, Mali 19°15' N, 1°20' W 222
Timfi, Óros, peak, Gr. 39°58' N, 20°43' E 156
Timgad, ruin(s), Alg. 35°25' N, 6°21' E 150
Tîmia, Niger 18°3' N, 8°39' E 222
Timiş, adm. division, Rom. 45°49' N, 20°44' E 156
Timimoun, Alg. 29°6' N, 0°13' E 207
Timiris, Cap (Mirik), Mauritania 19°28' N, 16°53' W 222
Timiryazevskiy, Russ. 56°28' N, 84°44' E 169
Timiskaming, Lake, Can. 47°15' N, 80°13' W 94
Timişoara, Rom. 45°46' N, 21°14' E 168
Timkapaul', Russ. 61°29' N, 62°16' E 169
Timmiarmiut 62°33' N, 42°19' W 106
Timmins, Can. 48°29' N, 81°16' W 82
Timms Hill, peak, Wis., U.S. 45°25' N, 90°16' W 94
Timon, Braz. 5°6' S, 42°53' W 132
Timor, island, Indonesia 9°36' S, 122°49' E 192
Timor Sea 11°14' S, 126°40' E 192
Timor-Leste (East Timor) 9°0' S, 125°0' E 192
Timote, Arg. 35°20' S, 62°15' W 139
Timpanogos Cave National Monument, Utah, U.S. 40°25' N, 111°46' W 90
Timpson, Tex., U.S. 31°53' N, 94°23' W 103
Timrå, Nor. 62°28' N, 17°17' E 152
Tin Férané, spring, Mali 15°6' N, 0°53' E 222
Tin Fouye, oil field, Alg. 28°31' N, 7°20' E 214
Tin Mountain, peak, Calif., U.S. 36°52' N, 117°33' W 92
Tîna, Khalîg el 31°3' N, 32°35' E 194
Tina, Mont, peak, Dem. Rep. of the Congo 2°56' N, 28°32' E 224
Tinaca Point, Philippines 5°25' N, 125°1' E 203
Tinaco, Venez. 9°41' N, 68°28' W 136
Ti-n-Assamert, spring, Mali 16°12' N, 0°30' E 222
Ti-n-Brahim, spring, Mauritania 19°31' N, 15°58' W 222
Tinca, Rom. 46°46' N, 21°58' E 168
Tinde see Jomu, Tanzania 3°53' S, 33°11' E 224
Ti-n-Deïla, spring, Mauritania 17°59' N, 15°32' W 222
Tindel, spring, Mauritania 17°0' N, 12°57' W 222
Tindouf, Alg. 27°43' N, 8°9' W 143
Tiné, Chad 14°59' N, 22°47' E 216
Ti-n-Ekkart, spring, Mali 16°14' N, 3°17' E 222
Ti-n-Essako, spring, Mali 18°25' N, 2°29' E 222
Ti-n-Ethisane, spring, Mali 19°2' N, 0°50' E 222
Tinfouchy, spring, Alg. 28°53' N, 5°49' W 214
Tinfunque National Park, Parag. 24°3' S, 60°28' W 122
Tinggi, island, Malaysia 2°21' N, 103°58' E 196
Tingo María National Park, Peru 9°13' S, 76°11' W 130
Tingréla, Côte d'Ivoire 10°30' N, 6°25' W 222
Tingri (Xêgar), China 28°40' N, 87°3' E 197
Tingsryd, Nor. 56°31' N, 14°59' E 152
Tingstäde, Sw. 57°44' N, 18°36' E 166
Tinkisso, river, Guinea 11°27' N, 10°6' W 222
Tinn, Nor. 59°58' N, 8°44' E 152
Tinniswood, Mount, peak, Can. 50°18' N, 123°52' W 100
Tinogasta, Arg. 28°5' S, 67°34' W 132
Tinombo, Indonesia 0°24' N, 120°13' E 192
Ti-n-Orfane, Mali 16°30' N, 2°15' W 222
Tiñoso, Cabo, Sp. 37°25' N, 1°15' W 164
Ti-n-Rerhoh, spring, Alg. 20°45' N, 4°1' E 222
Tinrhert, Hamada de, Lib. 28°3' N, 6°55' E 206
Tinsley, Miss., U.S. 32°42' N, 90°28' W 103
Tinsukia, India 27°29' N, 95°22' E 188
Tintagel (King Arthur's Castle), site, U.K. 50°39' N, 4°49' W 150
Tintane, spring, Mauritania 20°51' N, 16°32' W 222
Ti-n-Taourdi, spring, Alg. 22°46' N, 8°0' E 214
Tintina, Arg. 27°1' S, 62°43' W 139
Tinto Hills, peak, U.K. 55°34' N, 3°47' W 150
Ti-n-Toumma, region, Niger 16°27' N, 12°0' E 222
Tinui, N.Z. 40°54' S, 176°5' E 240
Ti-n-Zaouâtene (Fort Pierre Bordes), Alg. 19°58' N, 2°57' E 222
Tioga, La., U.S. 31°22' N, 92°26' W 103
Tioga, N. Dak., U.S. 48°23' N, 102°57' W 90
Tioga Pass, Calif., U.S. 37°54' N, 119°16' W 100
Tioman, peak, Malaysia 2°47' N, 104°4' E 196
Tionaga, Can. 48°5' N, 82°6' W 94
Tip Top Mountain, peak, Can. 48°16' N, 86°4' W 94
Tipitapa, Nicar. 12°9' N, 86°4' W 115
Tipp City, Ohio, U.S. 39°57' N, 84°10' W 102
Tippecanoe, Ind., U.S. 41°11' N, 86°7' W 102
Tipton, Calif., U.S. 36°3' N, 119°20' W 100
Tipton, Ind., U.S. 40°17' N, 86°2' W 102
Tipton, Iowa, U.S. 41°45' N, 91°8' W 110

TIP-TOY

Tipton, Mich., U.S. 42°0' N, 84°4' W 102
Tipton, Okla., U.S. 34°28' N, 99°9' W 92
Tipton, Mount, peak, Ariz., U.S. 35°31' N, 114°13' W 101
Tipuani, Bol. 15°35' S, 67°60' W 137
Tiputini, river, Ecua. 1°6' S, 77°6' W 136
Tiquicheo, Mex. 18°52' N, 100°45' W 114
Tiquié, river, Braz. 0°7' N, 69°41' W 136
Tir Pol, Afghan. 34°38' N, 61°20' E 180
Tiracambu, Serra do, Braz. 3°36' S, 46°54' W 130
Tīrān, island, Saudi Arabia 27°57' N, 34°5' E 180
Tirana see Tiranë, Alban. 41°19' N, 19°41' E 156
Tiranë (Tirana), Alban. 41°19' N, 19°41' E 156
Tirano, It. 46°12' N, 10°9' E 167
Tiraspol, Mold. 46°49' N, 29°37' E 156
Tirat Karmel, Israel 32°45' N, 34°58' E 194
Tire, Turk. 38°3' N, 27°42' E 156
Tiream, Rom. 47°37' N, 22°29' E 168
Tirebolu, Turk. 41°0' N, 38°46' E 195
Tirest, spring, Mali 20°21' N, 1°6' E 222
Tîrgovişte, Rom. 44°57' N, 25°26' E 156
Tîrgu Jiu, Rom. 45°1' N, 23°18' E 168
Tîrguşor, Rom. 44°28' N, 28°24' E 158
Tirich Mir, peak, Pak. 36°16' N, 71°46' E 186
Tiririne, spring, Alg. 23°34' N, 8°31' E 214
Tirlyanskiy, Russ. 54°14' N, 58°28' E 154
Tîrnova, Mold. 48°9' N, 27°39' E 152
Tîrnova, Rom. 45°19' N, 21°59' E 168
Tiroungoulou, Cen. Af. Rep. 9°34' N, 22°8' E 216
Tirthahalli, India 13°42' N, 75°14' E 188
Tiruchchirappalli, India 10°48' N, 78°41' E 188
Tirunelveli, India 8°44' N, 77°40' E 188
Tiruntán, Peru 7°56' S, 74°56' W 130
Tiryns, ruin(s), Gr. 37°35' N, 22°42' E 156
Tisaiyanvilai, India 8°20' N, 77°49' E 188
Tisdale, Can. 52°50' N, 104°4' W 108
Tishomingo, Okla., U.S. 34°13' N, 96°40' W 92
Tiskilwa, Ill., U.S. 41°17' N, 89°31' W 102
Tissamaharama, Sri Lanka 6°17' N, 81°18' E 188
Tissemsilt, Alg. 35°36' N, 1°49' E 150
Tissint, Mor. 29°53' N, 7°20' W 214
Tista, river, India 25°59' N, 89°9' E 197
Tisul', Russ. 55°43' N, 88°25' E 169
Tisza, river, Hung. 46°31' N, 20°4' E 156
Tiszacsege, Hung. 47°40' N, 20°58' E 168
Tiszaföldvár, Hung. 46°59' N, 20°15' E 168
Tiszafüred, Hung. 47°37' N, 20°45' E 168
Tiszakürt, Hung. 46°53' N, 20°8' E 168
Tiszanána, Hung. 47°32' N, 20°32' E 168
Tiszaug, Hung. 46°50' N, 20°2' E 168
Tiszaújváros, Hung. 47°53' N, 21°2' E 168
Tit, Alg. 26°56' N, 1°30' E 214
Titaf, Alg. 27°27' N, 0°12' E 214
Titan Dome, Antarctica 88°11' S, 165°43' W 248
Titel, Serb. and Mont. 45°12' N, 20°17' E 168
Titicaca, Lago, lake, Peru 15°34' S, 70°43' W 122
Titu, Rom. 44°40' N, 25°31' E 158
Titule, Dem. Rep. of the Congo 3°12' N, 25°32' E 224
Titusville, Fla., U.S. 28°36' N, 80°50' W 105
Titusville, Pa., U.S. 41°37' N, 79°41' W 94
Tivaouane, Senegal 14°57' N, 16°38' W 222
Tivat, Europe 42°26' N, 18°41' E 168
Tiverton, U.K. 50°54' N, 3°28' W 162
Tivissa, Sp. 41°2' N, 0°44' E 164
Tivoli, N.Y., U.S. 42°3' N, 73°55' W 104
Tiwai Point, N.Z. 46°35' S, 168°23' E 240
Tiwanacu, Bol. 16°38' S, 68°43' W 137
Tixtla, Mex. 17°32' N, 99°23' W 114
Tizayuca, Mex. 19°49' N, 98°57' W 114
Tizi Ouzou, Alg. 36°42' N, 4°3' E 150
Tizimín, Mex. 21°7' N, 88°11' W 116
Tiznit, Mor. 29°42' N, 9°45' W 214
Tjåmotis, Nor. 66°54' N, 18°39' E 152
Tlacotalpan, Mex. 18°37' N, 95°40' W 114
Tlahualilo de Zaragoza, Mex. 26°6' N, 103°27' W 114
Tlajomulco, Mex. 20°27' N, 103°28' W 114
Tlalnepantla, Mex. 19°31' N, 99°11' W 114
Tlapa, Mex. 17°31' N, 98°34' W 114
Tlapacoyan, Mex. 19°57' N, 97°13' W 114
Tlaquepaque, Mex. 20°37' N, 103°19' W 112
Tlaxcala, Mex. 19°15' N, 98°19' W 114
Tlaxcala, adm. division, Mex. 19°30' N, 98°38' W 114
Tlaxiaco, Mex. 17°15' N, 97°42' W 114
Tlell, Can. 53°36' N, 131°59' W 108
Tlemcen, Alg. 34°51' N, 1°18' W 214
Tleta, Alg. 36°47' N, 5°52' E 150
Tlīsan, spring, Lib. 28°27' N, 17°28' E 216
Tlyarata, Russ. 42°3' N, 46°22' E 195
Tmassah, Lib. 26°22' N, 15°46' E 216
Tni Haïa, spring, Alg. 24°20' N, 2°45' W 214
Toad River, Can. 58°50' N, 125°15' W 108
Toadlena, N. Mex., U.S. 36°13' N, 108°53' W 92
Toahayana, Mex. 26°8' N, 107°42' W 112
Toamasina, Madagascar 18°8' S, 49°22' E 220
Toana Range, Nev., U.S. 40°51' N, 114°29' W 90
Toano, It. 44°22' N, 10°33' E 167
Toast, N.C., U.S. 36°28' N, 80°39' W 96
Toay, Arg. 36°41' S, 64°23' W 134
Toba, Japan 34°27' N, 136°51' E 201
Toba, Danau, lake, Indonesia 2°47' N, 98°39' E 196
Toba Inlet 50°19' N, 124°52' W 90
Toba, river, Can. 50°35' N, 124°16' W 108
Tobacco Root Mountains, Mont., U.S. 45°25' N, 112°19' W 90
Tobago, island, Trinidad and Tobago 11°13' N, 60°39' W 118
Tobarra, Sp. 38°35' N, 1°42' W 164
Tobelo, Indonesia 1°41' N, 127°54' E 192
Tobermory 56°37' N, 6°5' W 150
Tobermory, Can. 45°13' N, 81°40' W 94
Tobin, Mount, peak, Nev., U.S. 40°22' N, 117°37' W 90
Tobli, Liberia 6°16' N, 8°33' W 222
Toboali, Indonesia 3°3' S, 106°26' E 192
Tobol, river, Russ. 56°41' N, 66°37' E 169
Tobol'sk, Russ. 58°14' N, 68°22' E 169
Tobruk, Lib. 31°52' N, 23°50' E 207
Tobruk see Ţubruq, Lib. 32°3' N, 23°57' E 216
Tobseda, Russ. 68°31' N, 52°47' E 160
Toby, Mount, peak, Mass., U.S. 42°28' N, 72°34' W 104
Tobyl, Kaz. 52°41' N, 62°39' E 184
Tobyl, river, Kaz. 53°48' N, 63°50' E 184
Tobysh, river, Russ. 66°21' N, 50°21' E 154
Tocantínia, Braz. 9°36' S, 48°23' W 130
Tocantinópolis, Braz. 6°19' S, 47°28' W 130
Tocantins, adm. division, Braz. 12°57' S, 48°39' W 138
Tocantins, river, Braz. 5°23' S, 56°13' W 132
Tocantins, river, Braz. 11°43' S, 48°39' W 130
Toccoa, Ga., U.S. 34°33' N, 83°20' W 96
Tochigi, adm. division, Japan 36°37' N, 139°24' E 201
Tochio, Japan 37°28' N, 138°59' E 201
Toco, Chile 22°5' S, 69°41' W 137
Toconao, Chile 23°12' S, 68°2' W 132
Tocopilla, Chile 22°8' S, 70°13' W 137
Tocuyo de la Costa, Venez. 11°1' N, 68°25' W 136
Tocuyo, river, Venez. 10°43' N, 69°31' W 136
Todal, Nor. 62°48' N, 8°44' E 152
Todd, Alas., U.S. 57°29' N, 135°5' W 108
Todenyang, Kenya 4°27' N, 35°53' E 224
Todireni, Rom. 47°36' N, 27°5' E 156
Todmorden, U.K. 53°43' N, 2°6' W 162
Todo Santos, Peru 1°16' S, 73°47' W 136
Todorovo, Bulg. 43°43' N, 26°55' E 156
Todos Santos, Bol. 16°49' S, 65°10' W 137
Todos Santos, Mex. 23°26' N, 110°13' W 112
Toe Head 57°49' N, 7°32' W 150
Tofield, Can. 53°21' N, 112°40' W 108
Tofino, Can. 49°6' N, 125°52' W 82
Tōfsingdalens National Park, Nor. 62°11' N, 12°23' E 152
Tōgane, Japan 35°30' N, 140°19' E 201
Togi, Japan 37°7' N, 136°44' E 201
Togiak, Alas., U.S. 59°3' N, 160°25' W 106
Togian, Kepulauan, islands, Indonesia 0°10' N, 122°30' E 192
Togliatti, Russ. 53°30' N, 49°34' E 154
Togni, Sudan 18°2' N, 35°9' E 182
Tognuf, Eritrea 16°8' N, 37°23' E 182
Togo, Can. 51°24' N, 101°37' W 90
Togo 8°41' N, 1°2' E 214
Togobala, Guinea 9°16' N, 7°57' W 222
Togtoh, China 40°17' N, 111°8' E 198
Togur, Russ. 58°21' N, 82°43' E 169
Togüsken, Kaz. 43°34' N, 67°24' E 184
Togwotee Pass, Wyo., U.S. 43°44' N, 110°3' W 90
Togyz, Kaz. 47°36' N, 60°30' E 184
Tohatchi, N. Mex., U.S. 35°51' N, 108°46' W 92
Tohma, river, Turk. 38°58' N, 37°29' E 156
Tohogne, Belg. 50°22' N, 5°29' E 167
Toholampi, Fin. 63°45' N, 24°11' E 152
Töhöm, Mongolia 44°26' N, 108°17' E 198
Toibalawe, India 10°35' N, 92°39' E 188
Toijala, Fin. 61°9' N, 23°52' E 166
Toinya, Sudan 6°16' N, 29°42' E 224
Toiyabe Range, Nev., U.S. 39°23' N, 117°19' W 90
Tok, river, Russ. 52°40' N, 52°27' E 154
Tōkamachi, Japan 37°6' N, 138°45' E 201
Tokar, Sudan 18°26' N, 37°41' E 182
Tokara Rettō, islands, East China Sea 29°46' N, 128°15' E 190
Tokat, Turk. 40°18' N, 36°34' E 156
Tŏkch'ŏn, N. Korea 39°44' N, 126°18' E 200
Tokeland, Wash., U.S. 46°41' N, 123°59' W 100
Tokelau, islands, South Pacific Ocean 8°1' S, 173°11' W 238
Tokewanna Peak, Utah, U.S. 40°47' N, 110°42' W 90
Tokhtamysh, Taj. 37°49' N, 74°40' E 184
Toki, Japan 35°21' N, 137°13' E 201
Tokmak, Ukr. 47°12' N, 35°45' E 156
Tokmok, Kyrg. 42°48' N, 75°17' E 184
Toko, N.Z. 39°21' S, 174°22' E 240
Tokomaru Bay, N.Z. 38°8' S, 178°17' E 240
Tokoroa, N.Z. 38°15' S, 175°52' E 240
Toksovo, Russ. 60°9' N, 30°31' E 166
Toksu see Xinhe, China 41°35' N, 82°38' E 184
Toktogul Reservoir, lake, Kyrg. 41°50' N, 72°37' E 197
Tokuno Shima, island, Japan 27°22' N, 129°2' E 190
Tokushima, Japan 34°4' N, 134°32' E 201
Tokushima, adm. division, Japan 33°53' N, 133°42' E 201
Tokuyama, Japan 34°4' N, 131°50' E 200
Tōkyō, Japan 35°39' N, 139°40' E 201
Tōkyō, adm. division, Japan 35°38' N, 139°16' E 201
Tolaga Bay, N.Z. 38°21' S, 178°17' E 240
Tôlañaro, Madagascar 24°56' S, 46°58' E 207
Tolbo, Mongolia 48°22' N, 90°16' E 184
Tolchin, Mount, peak, Antarctica 85°6' S, 67°14' W 248
Tōle Bī, Kaz. 43°36' N, 73°47' E 184
Toledo, Braz. 24°41' S, 53°46' W 132
Toledo, Braz. 5°56' S, 73°6' W 130
Toledo, Ill., U.S. 39°16' N, 88°15' W 102
Toledo, Iowa, U.S. 41°59' N, 92°35' W 94
Toledo, Ohio, U.S. 41°38' N, 83°32' W 102
Toledo, Sp. 39°52' N, 4°2' W 164
Toledo, Wash., U.S. 46°25' N, 122°52' W 100
Toledo Bend Reservoir, lake, La., U.S. 31°49' N, 93°56' W 103
Toledo, Montes de, Sp. 39°29' N, 4°52' W 164
Tolentino, It. 43°12' N, 13°16' E 156
Tolentino, Mex. 22°14' N, 100°34' W 114
Tolhuaca National Park, Chile 38°8' S, 71°55' W 134
Toli, China 45°47' N, 83°40' E 184
Toliara, Madagascar 23°18' S, 43°50' E 207
Tolima, adm. division, Col. 4°1' N, 75°40' W 136
Tolitoli, Indonesia 1°5' N, 120°45' E 192
Tol'ka, Russ. 63°57' N, 82°2' E 169
Tolkaboua, Burkina Faso 10°11' N, 2°59' W 222
Tolkmicko, Pol. 54°18' N, 19°32' E 166
Tollhouse, Calif., U.S. 37°1' N, 119°25' W 100
Tollimarjon, Uzb. 38°17' N, 65°33' E 197
Tollya, Zaliv 76°15' N, 98°2' E 160
Tolmachevo, Russ. 58°51' N, 29°52' E 166
Tolmin, Slov. 46°11' N, 13°44' E 167
Tolna, Hung. 46°25' N, 18°46' E 168
Tolna, adm. division, Hung. 46°26' N, 18°4' E 156
Tolo, Teluk 2°28' S, 121°52' E 192
Tolono, Ill., U.S. 39°58' N, 88°16' W 102
Tolosa, Sp. 43°8' N, 2°3' W 164
Tolstoi, Can. 49°5' N, 96°49' W 90
Toltén, Chile 39°12' S, 73°13' W 134
Tolti, Pak. 35°0' N, 76°6' E 186
Tolú, Col. 9°31' N, 75°34' W 136
Toluca, Ill., U.S. 41°0' N, 89°8' W 102
Toluca, Mex. 19°14' N, 99°43' W 114
Toluca, Mo., U.S. 41°0' N, 89°8' W 94
Tom Burke, S. Af. 23°5' S, 27°59' E 227
Tom, Mount, peak, Mass., U.S. 42°14' N, 72°41' W 104
Tom Price, Austral. 22°41' S, 117°49' E 238
Tom', river, Russ. 55°15' N, 85°0' E 160
Tom White, Mount, peak, Alas., U.S. 60°38' N, 143°50' W 98
Tomah, Wis., U.S. 43°58' N, 90°30' W 94
Tomahawk, Wis., U.S. 45°27' N, 89°43' W 94
Tomales Point, Calif., U.S. 38°13' N, 122°57' W 90
Tomar, Braz. 0°25' N, 63°54' W 130
Tómaros, peak, Gr. 39°28' N, 20°43' E 156
Tomás Barrón, Bol. 17°41' S, 67°29' W 137
Tomás Gomensoro, Uru. 30°24' S, 57°27' W 139
Tomaševo, Europe 43°4' N, 19°39' E 168
Tomashevka, Belarus 51°32' N, 23°35' E 152
Tomatin, U.K. 57°20' N, 3°60' W 150
Tomatlán, Mex. 19°56' N, 105°17' W 114
Tomatlán, river, Mex. 19°46' N, 105°21' W 114
Tombador, Serra do, Braz. 10°46' S, 58°16' W 130
Tombe, Sudan 5°47' N, 31°39' E 224
Tombigbee, river, Ala., U.S. 31°46' N, 88°8' W 103
Tomboco, Angola 6°51' S, 13°17' E 218
Tombos, Braz. 20°54' S, 42°3' W 138
Tombouctou (Timbuktu), Mali 16°44' N, 3°2' W 222
Tombstone, Ariz., U.S. 31°41' N, 110°4' W 112
Tombstone Mountain, peak, Can. 64°19' N, 138°47' W 98
Tombua, Angola 15°52' S, 11°50' E 220
Tomdibuloq, Uzb. 41°45' N, 64°39' E 197
Tomé, Chile 36°35' S, 72°57' W 134
Tomelloso, Sp. 39°9' N, 3°2' W 164
Tomini, Teluk 0°22' N, 120°27' E 192
Tomislavgrad, Bosn. and Herzg. 43°40' N, 17°12' E 168
Tommot, Russ. 58°59' N, 126°27' E 160
Tomo, river, Col. 5°29' N, 68°18' W 136
Tomorit, Maja e, peak, Alban. 40°41' N, 20°4' E 156
Tompa, Hung. 46°11' N, 19°32' E 168
Tompkinsville, Ky., U.S. 36°41' N, 85°42' W 96
Tomsino, Russ. 56°26' N, 28°32' E 166
Tomsk, Russ. 56°30' N, 85°3' E 169
Tomsk, adm. division, Russ. 58°34' N, 80°3' E 169
Tonalá, Mex. 16°4' N, 93°46' W 115
Tonale, Passo del, It. 46°16' N, 10°34' E 167
Tonami, Japan 36°37' N, 136°56' E 201
Tonantins, Braz. 2°45' S, 67°46' W 136
Tonantins, river, Braz. 2°26' S, 68°35' W 136
Tonasket, Wash., U.S. 48°41' N, 119°27' W 90
Tonbridge, U.K. 51°11' N, 0°16' E 162
Tondi Kiwindi, Niger 14°40' N, 1°51' E 222
Tondou, Massif du, Cen. Af. Rep. 7°50' N, 23°43' E 224
Toney Mount, peak, Antarctica 75°44' S, 115°16' W 248
Tonga, Sudan 9°30' N, 31°3' E 224
Tonga, islands, South Pacific Ocean 20°25' S, 173°41' W 238
Tonga Trench, South Pacific Ocean 21°53' S, 172°51' W 252
Tong'an, China 24°43' N, 118°9' E 198
Tongatapu Group, islands, Tonga 22°46' S, 174°39' W 238
Tongatapu, island, Tonga 21°11' S, 175°11' W 241
Tongcheng, China 31°3' N, 116°56' E 198
Tongchuan, China 35°7' N, 109°9' E 198
Tongdao, China 26°9' N, 109°45' E 198
Tongeren, Belg. 50°46' N, 5°27' E 167
Tonghe, China 46°0' N, 128°45' E 198
Tonghua, China 41°42' N, 125°54' E 200
Tonghua (Kuaidamao), China 41°41' N, 125°45' E 200
Tongjiang, China 31°59' N, 107°14' E 198
Tongjosŏn-man 39°23' N, 128°10' E 200
Tongliang, China 29°50' N, 106°4' E 198
Tongliao, China 43°35' N, 122°17' E 198
Tongling, China 30°53' N, 117°48' E 198
Tonglu, China 29°47' N, 119°37' E 198
Tongnae, S. Korea 35°11' N, 129°6' E 200
Tongobory, Madagascar 23°28' S, 44°18' E 220
Tongren, China 27°45' N, 109°13' E 198
Tongshi, China 18°43' N, 109°29' E 198
Tongtian, river, China 33°51' N, 93°30' E 190
Tongue of the Ocean 23°55' N, 77°32' W 96
Tongue, river, Mont., U.S. 45°47' N, 106°6' W 90
Tongwei, China 35°14' N, 105°12' E 198
Tongxian, China 39°52' N, 116°38' E 198
Tongxin, China 37°1' N, 105°53' E 198
Tongyeong, S. Korea 34°50' N, 128°26' E 200
Tongyu, China 44°47' N, 123°4' E 198
Tongyuanpu, China 40°47' N, 123°57' E 200
Tongzi, China 28°8' N, 106°48' E 198
Tonica, Ill., U.S. 41°12' N, 89°4' W 102
Tonichí, Mex. 28°35' N, 109°33' W 92
Tönisvorst, Ger. 51°18' N, 6°30' E 167
Tonj, Sudan 7°16' N, 28°45' E 224
Tonj see Ibba, river, Sudan 6°16' N, 28°21' E 224
Tonk, India 26°9' N, 75°48' E 197
Tonkawa, Okla., U.S. 36°39' N, 97°18' W 92
Tonkin, Gulf of 19°38' N, 107°25' E 190
Tonneins, Fr. 44°23' N, 0°17' E 150
Tonopah, Nev., U.S. 38°4' N, 117°15' W 92
Tonota, Botswana 21°30' S, 27°26' E 227
Tønsberg, Nor. 59°16' N, 10°26' E 152
Tonsina, Alas., U.S. 61°38' N, 145°11' W 98
Tonto National Monument, Ariz., U.S. 33°37' N, 111°10' W 92
Tonya, Turk. 40°52' N, 39°15' E 195
Tooele, Utah, U.S. 40°32' N, 112°14' W 106
Toora Khem, Russ. 52°29' N, 96°34' E 190
Toore, Somalia 1°21' N, 44°22' E 218
Tootsi, Est. 58°34' N, 24°47' E 166
Topaz Mountain, peak, Utah, U.S. 39°41' N, 113°11' W 90
Topeka, Kans., U.S. 38°59' N, 95°48' W 90
Topia, Mex. 25°9' N, 106°33' W 114
Topki, Russ. 55°15' N, 85°43' E 169
Topley, Can. 54°31' N, 126°20' W 108
Topley Landing, Can. 54°47' N, 126°11' W 108
Topli Do, Serb. and Mont. 43°20' N, 22°40' E 168
Topocalma, Punta, Chile 34°15' S, 73°58' W 134
Topock, Ariz., U.S. 34°42' N, 114°28' W 101
Topola, Serb. and Mont. 44°15' N, 20°40' E 168
Topolobampo, Bahía de 25°32' N, 110°21' W 80
Topolovăţu Mare, Rom. 45°47' N, 21°38' E 168
Toppenish, Wash., U.S. 46°21' N, 120°20' W 90
Topsfield, Mass., U.S. 42°38' N, 70°58' W 104
Topsham, Me., U.S. 43°55' N, 69°58' W 104
Toquepala, Peru 17°18' S, 70°35' W 137
Toquima Range, Nev., U.S. 39°28' N, 116°59' W 90
Tor, Eth. 7°48' N, 33°32' E 224
Tor Bay 45°10' N, 61°39' W 111
Torà, Sp. 41°48' N, 1°23' E 164
Toragay, oil field, Azerb. 40°9' N, 49°21' E 195
Toranou, Côte d'Ivoire 8°48' N, 7°47' W 222
Torata, Peru 17°7' S, 70°51' W 137
Torbalı, Turk. 38°10' N, 27°20' E 156
Torbat-e Heydarīyeh, Iran 35°17' N, 59°13' E 180
Torbat-e Jām, Iran 35°16' N, 60°34' E 180
Torbay, U.K. 50°27' N, 3°34' W 150
Torbert, Mount, peak, Antarctica 83°32' S, 55°58' W 248
Torch, river, Can. 53°33' N, 104°9' W 108
Torchiara, It. 40°19' N, 15°2' E 156
Torda, Serb. and Mont. 45°35' N, 20°26' E 168
Tordesillos, Sp. 40°39' N, 1°35' W 164
Töre, Nor. 65°54' N, 22°39' E 152
Töreboda, Nor. 58°41' N, 14°7' E 152
Torelló, Sp. 42°2' N, 2°15' E 164
Torere, N.Z. 37°59' S, 177°30' E 240
Torez, Ukr. 47°59' N, 38°37' E 158
Torgau, Ger. 51°34' N, 12°59' E 152
Torghay, Kaz. 49°46' N, 63°35' E 184
Torghay, river, Kaz. 48°34' N, 62°27' E 184
Torhout, Belg. 51°3' N, 3°6' E 163
Torija, Sp. 40°44' N, 3°2' W 164
Torino (Turin), It. 45°4' N, 7°40' E 167
Torit, Sudan 4°24' N, 32°33' E 224
Torixoreu, Braz. 16°13' S, 52°31' W 138
Torkovichi, Russ. 58°53' N, 30°26' E 166
Torma, Est. 58°47' N, 26°43' E 166
Tormac, Rom. 45°31' N, 21°30' E 168
Tornado Mountain, peak, Can. 49°56' N, 114°45' W 90
Torneå see Tornio, Fin. 65°51' N, 24°7' E 154
Torneträsk, lake, Nor. 67°53' N, 19°22' E 152
Torngat Mountains, Can. 59°30' N, 64°3' W 106
Tornillo, Tex., U.S. 31°26' N, 106°5' W 92
Tornio (Torneå), Fin. 65°51' N, 24°7' E 154
Tornquist, Arg. 38°6' S, 62°15' W 139
Toro, Nig. 10°2' N, 9°3' E 222
Toro, Sp. 41°31' N, 5°25' W 150
Toro Doum, spring, Chad 16°31' N, 16°37' E 216
Toro Peak, Calif., U.S. 33°31' N, 116°28' W 101
Torodi, Niger 13°18' N, 1°42' E 222
Torodo, Mali 14°33' N, 8°52' W 222
Törökszentmiklos, Hung. 47°10' N, 20°26' E 168
Torom, Russ. 54°20' N, 135°47' E 190
Torone, ruin(s), Gr. 40°0' N, 23°43' E 156
Toronto, Can. 43°39' N, 79°29' W 94
Toronto, Kans., U.S. 37°46' N, 95°57' W 94
Toropalca, Bol. 20°25' S, 65°49' W 137
Toropets, Russ. 56°29' N, 31°39' E 154
Tororo, Uganda 0°39' N, 34°12' E 224
Toros Dağlar (Taurus), Turk. 36°29' N, 32°7' E 156
Toros Dağları, Turk. 36°26' N, 32°15' E 180
Torotoro, Bol. 18°7' S, 65°50' W 137
Torquato Severo, Braz. 31°4' S, 54°14' W 139
Torra Bay, Namibia 20°17' S, 13°15' E 220
Torrance, Calif., U.S. 33°50' N, 118°21' W 101
Torre Astura, It. 41°25' N, 12°44' E 156
Torre de Moncorvo, Port. 41°9' N, 7°4' W 150
Torre Pacheco, Sp. 37°43' N, 0°58' E 164
Torreblanca, Sp. 40°12' N, 0°10' E 164
Torre-Cardela, Sp. 37°31' N, 3°21' W 164
Torrecilla en Cameros, Sp. 42°15' N, 2°38' W 164
Torredelcampo, Sp. 37°46' N, 3°54' W 164
Torredonjimeno, Sp. 37°46' N, 3°58' W 164
Torrelaguna, Sp. 40°49' N, 3°32' W 164
Torremolinos, Sp. 36°37' N, 4°31' W 164
Torrent, Arg. 28°49' S, 56°28' W 139
Torrent, Sp. 39°26' N, 0°28' E 164
Torrenueva, Sp. 38°39' N, 3°22' W 164
Torreón, Mex. 25°31' N, 103°26' W 114
Torreón de Cañas, Mex. 26°22' N, 105°16' W 114
Torres, Mex. 28°45' N, 110°46' W 92
Torres del Paine National Park, Chile 51°6' S, 73°25' W 122
Torres Islands, South Pacific Ocean 14°42' S, 164°17' E 238
Torres Strait 9°40' S, 141°19' E 231
Torrevieja, Sp. 37°58' N, 0°41' E 164
Torrijo, Sp. 41°29' N, 1°53' W 164
Torrijos, Sp. 39°59' N, 4°17' W 150
Torrington, Conn., U.S. 41°47' N, 73°8' W 104
Torrington, Wyo., U.S. 42°4' N, 104°11' W 90
Torroella de Montgri, Sp. 42°2' N, 3°7' E 164
Torrox, Sp. 36°45' N, 3°58' W 164
Torsås, Nor. 56°25' N, 15°58' E 152
Tórshavn 62°10' N, 6°53' W 143
Torsken, Nor. 69°21' N, 17°8' E 152
Tortola, island, U.K. 18°26' N, 64°38' W 118
Tortolì, It. 39°55' N, 9°36' E 214
Tortona, It. 44°53' N, 8°52' E 167
Tortosa, Sp. 40°50' N, 0°34' E 214
Tortosa, Cap, Sp. 40°33' N, 0°54' E 214
Tortosa, Cap de, Sp. 40°29' N, 0°59' E 143
Tortosa see Ţarţūs, Syr. 34°53' N, 35°53' E 194
Tortue, Île de la, island, Haiti 20°9' N, 73°9' W 116
Tortuguero, C.R. 10°33' N, 83°32' W 115
Tortum, Turk. 40°19' N, 41°34' E 195
Ţorūd, Iran 35°26' N, 55°6' E 180
Torul, Turk. 40°35' N, 39°18' E 195
Tõrva, Est. 57°59' N, 25°54' E 166
Torzhok, Russ. 57°0' N, 34°57' E 154
Tosa, Japan 33°30' N, 133°25' E 201
Tosa Wan 33°16' N, 133°37' E 201
Tosamaganga, Tanzania 7°50' S, 35°35' E 224
T'osan, N. Korea 38°17' N, 126°43' E 200
Tosanachi, Mex. 28°32' N, 108°3' W 92
Tosashimizu, Japan 32°46' N, 132°55' E 201
Tosayamada, Japan 33°37' N, 133°40' E 201
Tosca, S. Af. 26°9' S, 23°51' E 227
Tosca, Punta, Mex. 24°19' N, 112°36' W 112
Toshkent (Tashkent), Uzb. 41°18' N, 69°10' E 19[illegible]
Toson Hu, lake, China 37°3' N, 96°15' E 188
Tossa de Mar, Sp. 41°43' N, 2°55' E 164
Tostado, Arg. 29°13' S, 61°48' W 139
Tõstamaa, Est. 58°19' N, 23°56' E 166
Tostuya, Russ. 73°10' N, 113°42' E 173
Tosu, Japan 33°22' N, 130°31' E 201
Tosya, Turk. 41°1' N, 34°1' E 156
Toszek, Pol. 50°26' N, 18°31' E 152
Totana, Sp. 37°46' N, 1°31' W 164
Totara, N.Z. 45°9' S, 170°52' E 240
Totatiche, Mex. 21°55' N, 103°27' W 114
Toten, region, Nor. 60°41' N, 10°37' E 152
Toteng, Botswana 20°23' S, 22°57' E 227
Tôtes, Fr. 49°40' N, 1°2' E 163
Tótkomlós, Hung. 46°24' N, 20°45' E 168
Tot'ma, Russ. 59°58' N, 42°48' E 154
Totness (Coronie), Suriname 5°49' N, 56°18' W 130
Tôto, Angola 7°11' S, 14°18' E 218
Totogan Lake, lake, Can. 52°3' N, 89°35' W 110
Totokro, Côte d'Ivoire 7°10' N, 5°8' W 222
Totolapan, Mex. 18°7' N, 100°23' W 114
Totora, Bol. 17°47' S, 65°9' W 137
Totoras, Arg. 32°37' S, 61°9' W 139
Totskoye, Russ. 52°31' N, 52°43' E 154
Tottori, Japan 35°27' N, 134°14' E 201
Tottori, adm. division, Japan 35°19' N, 133°25' E 201
Touba, Côte d'Ivoire 8°12' N, 7°41' W 222
Touba, Senegal 14°52' N, 15°49' W 222
Toubakouta, Senegal 13°48' N, 16°22' W 222
Toubkal, Jebel, peak, Mor. 31°3' N, 8°6' W 214
Toueïla, spring, Mauritania 18°24' N, 15°46' W 222
Touerat, spring, Mali 17°57' N, 3°16' W 222
Toufourine, spring, Mali 24°38' N, 4°43' W 214
Tougan, Burkina Faso 13°4' N, 3°6' W 222
Tougourt, Alg. 32°58' N, 5°58' E 207
Tougouri, Burkina Faso 13°18' N, 0°34' E 222
Tougouya, Burkina Faso 13°27' N, 2°5' W 222
Tougué, Guinea 11°26' N, 11°42' W 222
Touila, spring, Mauritania 25°56' N, 6°22' W 214
Toukoto, Mali 13°29' N, 9°52' W 222
Toul, Fr. 48°39' N, 5°52' E 163
Touléplеu, Côte d'Ivoire 6°27' N, 8°24' W 222
Touliu, Taiwan 23°40' N, 120°31' E 198
Toulon, Fr. 43°7' N, 5°55' E 150
Toulon, Ill., U.S. 41°5' N, 89°52' W 102
Toulouse, Fr. 43°35' N, 1°27' E 164
Toumania, Guinea 10°24' N, 10°50' W 222
Toumbélaga, spring, Niger 15°52' N, 7°48' E 222
Toummo, Lib. 22°39' N, 14°11' E 216
Toumodi, Côte d'Ivoire 6°28' N, 5°2' W 222
Toungad, Mauritania 20°4' N, 13°9' W 222
Toungo, Nig. 8°3' N, 12°2' E 218
Touraine, region, Fr. 47°35' N, 0°56' E 165
Tourassine, ruin(s), Mauritania 24°40' N, 11°36' W 214
Tourba, Chad 12°53' N, 15°17' E 216
Tourbe, Pointe de la, Can. 49°14' N, 64°15' W 111
Tourcoing, Fr. 50°43' N, 3°9' E 163
Tourine, spring, Mauritania 22°31' N, 11°53' W 21[illegible]
Tournai, Belg. 50°35' N, 3°23' E 163
Tournan, Fr. 48°44' N, 2°46' E 163
Tournus, Fr. 46°34' N, 4°53' E 150
Touros, Braz. 5°14' S, 35°29' W 132
Touroua, Cameroon 9°0' N, 12°58' E 216
Tours, Fr. 47°23' N, 0°41' E 150
Toury, Fr. 48°11' N, 1°55' E 163
Touside, Pic, peak, Chad 21°1' N, 16°19' E 216
Tovar, Venez. 8°20' N, 71°48' W 136
Tovarkovskiy, Russ. 53°39' N, 38°13' E 154
Tovik, Nor. 68°40' N, 16°54' E 152
Tovste, Ukr. 48°50' N, 25°43' E 156
Tovuz, Azerb. 40°58' N, 45°35' E 195
Towanda, Pa., U.S. 41°45' N, 76°28' W 94
Towcester, U.K. 52°7' N, 0°60' E 162
Tower, Minn., U.S. 47°47' N, 92°17' W 110
Tower Hill, Ill., U.S. 39°22' N, 88°58' W 102
Tower Island, Antarctica 63°32' S, 61°29' W 134
Tower Mountain, peak, Oreg., U.S. 45°2' N, 118°40' W 90
Towne Pass, Calif., U.S. 36°23' N, 117°18' W 101
Towner, N. Dak., U.S. 48°19' N, 100°25' W 90
Townsend, Mass., U.S. 42°39' N, 71°43' W 104
Townsend, Mont., U.S. 46°17' N, 111°30' W 90
Townsend, Va., U.S. 37°10' N, 75°58' W 96
Townshend, Vt., U.S. 43°2' N, 72°41' W 104
Townshend Island, island, Austral. 22°30' S, 150°37' E 230
Towot, Sudan 6°12' N, 34°22' E 224
Towraghondi, Afghan. 35°13' N, 62°15' E 186
Towrzi, Afghan. 30°10' N, 66°2' E 186
Towuti, Danau, lake, Indonesia 2°51' S, 120°29' E 192
Toxkan, river, China 40°55' N, 76°50' E 184
Toyah, Tex., U.S. 31°17' N, 103°48' W 92
Toyahvale, Tex., U.S. 30°55' N, 103°47' W 92
Toyama, Japan 36°41' N, 137°14' E 201

Toyama, adm. division, Japan 36°32' N, 136°50' E 201
Toyama Wan 36°50' N, 137°8' E 201
Toyohashi, Japan 34°44' N, 137°23' E 201
Toyooka, Japan 35°31' N, 134°47' E 201
Toyoura, Japan 34°9' N, 130°56' E 200
To'ytepa, Uzb. 41°2' N, 69°21' E 197
Tozeur, Tun. 33°54' N, 8°1' E 143
Tozeur, spring, Chad 18°9' N, 18°22' E 216
Tpig, Russ. 41°45' N, 47°36' E 195
Tqvarch'eli, Asia 42°49' N, 41°41' E 195
Traben-Trarbach, Ger. 49°57' N, 7°7' E 167
Trablous (Tripoli), Leb. 34°26' N, 35°50' E 194
Trabzon, Turk. 40°58' N, 39°41' E 195
Trachonas 35°12' N, 33°20' E 194
Tracy, Calif., U.S. 37°44' N, 121°27' W 100
Tracy, Can. 46°0' N, 73°10' W 111
Tracy, Minn., U.S. 44°12' N, 95°38' W 90
Tracy Arm 57°52' N, 134°8' W 108
Tradate, It. 45°43' N, 8°54' E 167
Trade Lake, lake, Can. 55°19' N, 104°14' W 108
Trade Town, Liberia 5°41' N, 9°51' W 222
Trädet, Nor. 57°58' N, 13°32' E 152
Trading, river, Can. 51°33' N, 89°29' W 110
Traeger Hills, peak, Austral. 23°53' S, 124°26' E 230
Traer, Iowa, U.S. 42°10' N, 92°28' W 94
Trafalgar, Ind., U.S. 39°24' N, 86°9' W 102
Trafalgar, Cabo, Sp. 36°5' N, 6°14' W 164
Trafford, Lake, Fla., U.S. 26°25' N, 81°37' W 105
Tragacete, Sp. 40°19' N, 1°52' W 164
Traian, Rom. 45°10' N, 27°44' E 156
Tráighlí see Tralee, Ire. 52°16' N, 9°42' W 150
Trail, Can. 49°6' N, 117°44' W 108
Traill Ø, island, Traill Ø 72°17' N, 28°9' W 246
Trainor Lake, Can. 60°26' N, 120°43' W 108
Traíra Taraira, river, South America 5°296' S, 69°56' W 136
Trakai National Park, Lith. 54°37' N, 24°35' E 166
Tralake, Miss., U.S. 33°14' N, 90°48' W 103
Tralee (Tráighlí), Ire. 52°16' N, 9°42' W 150
Tramonti di Sopra, It. 46°18' N, 12°47' E 167
Træna, islands, Norwegian Sea 66°33' N, 11°1' E 152
Tranås, Nor. 58°2' N, 14°58' E 152
Tranebjerg, Den. 55°49' N, 10°34' E 150
Trang, Thai. 7°35' N, 99°38' E 196
Trangan, island, Indonesia 7°9' S, 133°3' E 192
Tranqueras, Uru. 31°13' S, 55°43' W 139
Tranquillity, Calif., U.S. 36°38' N, 120°16' W 100
Tranquitas, oil field, Arg. 22°41' S, 63°60' W 137
Transantarctic Mountains, Antarctica 81°39' S, 40°42' W 248
Transcona, Can. 49°52' N, 96°58' W 90
Transdniester, special sovereignty, Mold. 48°6' N, 27°46' E 152
Transit Hill, peak, Austral. 15°21' S, 129°21' E 230
Transylvania, region, Rom. 46°2' N, 22°9' E 168
Transylvanian Alps, Rom. 44°55' N, 22°35' E 168
Trapper Peak, Mont., U.S. 45°51' N, 114°26' W 80
Trarza, region, Mauritania 17°53' N, 15°24' W 222
Trascău, Munţii, Rom. 46°14' N, 23°13' E 168
Trasury Islands, Solomon Sea 7°20' S, 155°30' E 242
Trat, Thai. 12°15' N, 102°31' E 202
Trauira, Ilha da, island, Braz. 1°34' S, 46°34' W 130
Travemünde, Ger. 53°58' N, 10°52' E 150
Traver, Calif., U.S. 36°27' N, 119°30' W 100
Travers Reservoir, lake, Can. 50°9' N, 113°19' W 90
Travis Air Force Base, Calif., U.S. 38°14' N, 121°59' W 100
Travnik, Bosn. and Herzg. 44°14' N, 17°41' E 168
Trawsfynydd, U.K. 52°54' N, 3°54' W 162
Trbunje, Serb. and Mont. 43°15' N, 21°16' E 168
Trebinje, Bosn. and Herzg. 42°43' N, 18°19' E 168
Trebujena, Sp. 36°51' N, 6°11' W 164
Trecate, It. 45°25' N, 8°43' E 167
Trecenta, It. 45°1' N, 11°28' E 167
Treetops, site, Kenya 0°24' N, 36°41' E 224
Treffurt, Ger. 51°8' N, 10°14' E 167
Tregaron, U.K. 52°12' N, 3°55' W 162
Tregrosse Islets, islands, Coral Sea 18°3' S, 149°35' E 230
Treinta-y-Tres, Uru. 33°13' S, 54°22' W 139
Treis-Karden, Ger. 50°10' N, 7°18' E 167
Treklyano, Bulg. 42°32' N, 22°36' E 168
Trelawney, Zimb. 17°31' S, 30°28' E 224
Trelleborg, Nor. 55°22' N, 13°8' E 152
Tremblant, Mount, peak, Can. 46°13' N, 74°40' W 94
Tremiti, Isole, islands, Adriatic Sea 42°11' N, 15°36' E 156
Tremont, Ill., U.S. 40°30' N, 89°30' W 102
Tremp, Sp. 42°9' N, 0°52' E 164
Trenary, Mich., U.S. 46°11' N, 86°58' W 94
Trenche, river, Can. 48°43' N, 73°43' W 94
Trenčín, Slovakia 48°52' N, 18°3' E 152
Trenque Lauquen, Arg. 35°57' S, 62°42' W 139
Trent, river, U.K. 53°33' N, 0°46' E 162
Trent, river, U.K. 53°1' N, 2°10' W 162
Trentino-Alto Adige, adm. division, It. 46°32' N, 10°41' E 167
Trento, It. 46°4' N, 11°8' E 167
Trenton, Can. 44°6' N, 77°35' W 110
Trenton, Fla., U.S. 29°36' N, 82°50' W 105
Trenton, Mich., U.S. 42°8' N, 83°12' W 102
Trenton, Nebr., U.S. 40°10' N, 101°1' W 90
Trenton, N.J., U.S. 40°11' N, 74°53' W 94
Trepassey, Can. 46°43' N, 53°22' W 111
Trepča, Europe 42°56' N, 20°55' E 168
Tres Arboles, Uru. 32°26' S, 56°43' W 139
Tres Arroyos, Arg. 38°23' S, 60°14' W 139
Três Corações, Braz. 21°42' S, 45°14' W 138
Tres Cruces, Cerro, peak, Mex. 15°26' N, 92°32' W 115
Tres Esquinas, Col. 0°43' N, 75°14' W 136
Tres Isletas, Arg. 26°20' S, 60°25' W 139
Três Lagoas, Braz. 20°47' S, 51°44' W 138
Tres Lagos, Arg. 49°36' S, 71°30' W 134
Tres Lomas, Arg. 36°28' S, 62°51' W 139
Três Marias Dam, Braz. 18°6' S, 45°17' W 138
Tres Montes, Península, Chile 47°7' S, 77°36' W 134
Três Passos, Braz. 27°28' S, 53°58' W 139
Tres Picos, Arg. 38°18' S, 62°14' W 139
Tres Pinos, Calif., U.S. 36°47' N, 121°20' W 100
Três Pontas, Braz. 21°24' S, 45°29' W 138
Tres Pozos, Arg. 28°23' S, 62°15' W 139
Tres Puntas, Cabo, Arg. 47°1' S, 65°54' W 134
Tres Puntas, Cabo de, Guatemala 15°59' N, 88°44' W 115
Três Rios, Braz. 22°5' S, 43°14' W 138
Tres Valles, Mex. 18°14' N, 96°8' W 114
Tres Zapotes, ruin(s), Mex. 18°26' N, 95°32' W 114
Treskavica, Bosn. and Herzg. 43°39' N, 18°12' E 168
Trespaderne, Sp. 42°47' N, 3°25' W 164
Tretower, U.K. 51°52' N, 3°11' W 162
Treungen, Nor. 58°50' N, 8°29' E 152
Trêve, Lac la, lake, Can. 49°55' N, 76°5' W 94
Treviglio, It. 45°30' N, 9°35' E 167
Treviño, Sp. 42°43' N, 2°45' W 164
Treviso, It. 45°39' N, 12°13' E 167
Trgovište, Serb. and Mont. 42°22' N, 22°6' E 168
Tría, islands, Aegean Sea 36°9' N, 26°46' E 156
Triánda (Ialysus), Gr. 36°24' N, 28°10' E 156
Triangle, Zimb. 21°3' S, 31°33' E 227
Triángulo Oeste, islands, Gulf of Mexico 21°5' N, 93°24' W 112
Triángulo Sur, islands, Gulf of Mexico 20°49' N, 92°7' W 112
Triberg, Ger. 48°7' N, 8°14' E 152
Tribune, Kans., U.S. 38°28' N, 101°46' W 90
Tricase, It. 39°55' N, 18°21' E 156
Trichur (Thrissur), India 10°31' N, 76°11' E 188
Trident Peak (Obrian Peak), Nev., U.S. 41°53' N, 118°30' W 90
Trie, Fr. 43°19' N, 0°21' E 164
Trier, Ger. 49°45' N, 6°39' E 163
Trieste, It. 45°38' N, 13°45' E 167
Trigal, Bol. 18°18' S, 64°14' W 137
Triglav, peak, Slov. 46°22' N, 13°46' E 156
Trigo Mountains, Ariz., U.S. 33°7' N, 114°37' W 101
Trijebovo, Bosn. and Herzg. 44°30' N, 17°4' E 168
Tríkala, Gr. 39°32' N, 21°46' E 180
Trikomo 35°17' N, 33°53' E 194
Trikora, Puncak, peak, Indonesia 4°10' S, 138°25' E 192
Trilby, Fla., U.S. 28°26' N, 82°14' W 105
Trilj, Croatia 43°37' N, 16°42' E 168
Trillo, Sp. 40°42' N, 2°36' W 164
Trilsbeck Lake, lake, Can. 50°46' N, 84°38' W 110
Trincomalee, Sri Lanka 8°34' N, 81°14' E 188
Trindade, Braz. 16°41' S, 49°30' W 138
Trindade, island, Braz. 20°45' S, 30°23' W 132
Trinidad, Bol. 14°49' S, 64°48' W 137
Trinidad, Colo., U.S. 37°10' N, 104°29' W 92
Trinidad, Uru. 33°32' S, 56°54' W 139
Trinidad and Tobago 10°41' N, 61°3' W 118
Trinidad Head, Calif., U.S. 40°52' N, 124°27' W 90
Trinidad, Isla, island, Arg. 39°21' S, 61°52' W 134
Trinidad, island, Trinidad and Tobago 10°8' N, 60°56' W 116
Trinidad, island, Trinidad and Tobago 10°25' N, 61°14' W 118
Trinity, Tex., U.S. 30°55' N, 95°23' W 103
Trinity Bay 47°57' N, 54°30' W 106
Trinity Island, island, Antarctica 64°12' S, 61°28' W 248
Trinity Islands, Alas., U.S. 55°55' N, 155°52' W 98
Trinity Mountains, Calif., U.S. 40°56' N, 122°47' W 90
Trinity Range, Nev., U.S. 40°23' N, 118°49' W 90
Trinity, river, Calif., U.S. 40°38' N, 123°37' W 80
Trinity, river, Tex., U.S. 30°26' N, 94°56' W 103
Trinkitat, Sudan 18°37' N, 37°41' E 182
Trino, It. 45°12' N, 8°17' E 167
Trinway, Ohio, U.S. 40°8' N, 82°1' W 102
Trion, Ga., U.S. 34°31' N, 85°19' W 96
Triora, It. 43°59' N, 7°46' E 167
Trípoli, Gr. 37°31' N, 22°22' E 156
Tripoli see Ţarābulus, Lib. 32°37' N, 12°35' E 216
Tripoli see Trablous, Leb. 34°26' N, 35°50' E 194
Tripolitania, region, Lib. 30°23' N, 11°4' E 214
Tripp, S. Dak., U.S. 43°11' N, 97°58' W 90
Tripura, adm. division, India 23°47' N, 91°18' E 197
Tristan da Cunha Group, islands, South Atlantic Ocean 36°47' S, 14°34' W 206
Tristao, Îles, islands, North Atlantic Ocean 10°23' N, 15°45' W 222
Triunfo, river, Braz. 6°38' S, 53°18' W 130
Trivandrum (Thiruvananthapuram), India 8°28' N, 76°56' E 188
Trivento, It. 41°46' N, 14°32' E 156
Trn, Bosn. and Herzg. 44°50' N, 17°13' E 168
Trnava, Slovakia 48°22' N, 17°35' E 152
Trnavský, adm. division, Slovakia 48°34' N, 16°56' E 152
Trnovo, Bosn. and Herzg. 43°39' N, 18°27' E 168
Trobriand Islands, P.N.G. 8°14' S, 150°59' E 238
Trobriand Islands, Solomon Sea 7°51' S, 149°6' E 192
Trochu, Can. 51°51' N, 113°14' W 90
Troebratskiy, Kaz. 54°19' N, 66°7' E 184
Troezen, ruin(s), Gr. 37°29' N, 23°16' E 156
Trofimovka, Kaz. 53°27' N, 76°59' E 184
Trofors, Nor. 65°32' N, 13°19' E 152
Troilus, Lac, lake, Can. 50°53' N, 75°5' W 110
Troisdorf, Ger. 50°49' N, 7°8' E 167
Trois-Pistoles, Can. 48°6' N, 69°9' W 94
Trois-Ponts, Belg. 50°24' N, 4°42' E 167
Trois-Rivières, Can. 46°20' N, 72°34' W 94
Troisvierges, Lux. 50°7' N, 6°0' E 167
Troitsk, Russ. 54°9' N, 61°32' E 154
Troitskiy, Russ. 57°5' N, 63°42' E 154
Troitsko Pechorsk, Russ. 62°42' N, 56°7' E 154
Troitskoye, Russ. 46°22' N, 44°11' E 158
Troitskoye, Russ. 52°19' N, 56°1' E 154
Troitskoye, Russ. 53°1' N, 84°43' E 184
Troll, Norway, station, Antarctica 71°50' S, 2°56' E 248
Trolla, spring, Chad 15°26' N, 14°48' E 216
Troll-heimen, Nor. 62°57' N, 8°39' E 152
Trombas, Braz. 13°29' S, 48°47' W 138
Tromelin Island, Fr. 15°58' S, 54°27' E 254
Tromsø, Nor. 69°38' N, 18°53' E 152
Tron, peak, Nor. 62°9' N, 10°34' E 152
Trona, Calif., U.S. 35°45' N, 117°24' W 101
Troncon, Mex. 23°29' N, 104°20' W 114
Trondheim, Nor. 63°23' N, 10°27' E 152
Trondheimsfjorden 63°25' N, 5°22' E 142
Trones, Nor. 64°45' N, 12°50' E 152
Trönninge, Nor. 56°38' N, 12°57' E 152
Troodos Mountains, Cyprus 34°58' N, 32°24' E 194
Tropea, It. 38°41' N, 15°53' E 156
Tropic, Utah, U.S. 37°37' N, 112°4' W 92
Tropojë, Alban. 42°24' N, 20°9' E 168
Trosa, Nor. 58°54' N, 17°29' E 152
Trosh, Russ. 66°22' N, 55°59' E 154
Troškūnai, Lith. 55°35' N, 24°52' E 166
Trostan, peak, U.K. 55°1' N, 6°16' W 150
Trostyanets', Ukr. 50°28' N, 34°57' E 158
Trotternish, region 57°35' N, 6°46' W 150
Trotwood, Ohio, U.S. 39°47' N, 84°19' W 102
Troup, Tex., U.S. 32°8' N, 95°8' W 103
Troup Head 57°42' N, 2°42' W 150
Trout, La., U.S. 31°41' N, 92°12' W 103
Trout Creek, Can. 45°59' N, 79°21' W 94
Trout Lake, Can. 50°39' N, 117°33' W 90
Trout Lake, Can. 51°10' N, 93°47' W 110
Trout Lake, Can. 60°25' N, 121°11' W 108
Trout Lake, Minn., U.S. 47°55' N, 92°47' W 94
Trout Lake, Wash., U.S. 45°58' N, 121°32' W 100
Trout Lake, lake, Can. 51°6' N, 94°18' W 106
Trout Peak, Wyo., U.S. 44°34' N, 109°37' W 90
Trout, river, Can. 60°58' N, 120°45' W 108
Trout, river, Can. 56°18' N, 114°30' W 108
Troutdale, Oreg., U.S. 45°32' N, 122°25' W 90
Trouville, Fr. 49°21' N, 8°475' E 150
Trowbridge, U.K. 51°18' N, 2°12' W 162
Troy, Ala., U.S. 31°48' N, 85°59' W 96
Troy, Mich., U.S. 42°34' N, 83°9' W 102
Troy, Mo., U.S. 38°58' N, 90°59' W 94
Troy, Mont., U.S. 48°26' N, 115°54' W 90
Troy, N.H., U.S. 42°49' N, 72°12' W 104
Troy, N.Y., U.S. 42°43' N, 73°42' W 104
Troy, N.C., U.S. 35°21' N, 79°55' W 96
Troy, Ohio, U.S. 40°1' N, 84°13' W 102
Troy Peak, Nev., U.S. 38°18' N, 115°35' W 90
Troy, ruin(s), Turk. 39°56' N, 26°7' E 156
Troyes, Fr. 48°17' N, 4°4' E 163
Trozadero, Peru 2°60' S, 76°47' W 136
Trpezi, Europe 42°53' N, 20°0' E 168
Trubar, Bosn. and Herzg. 44°21' N, 16°13' E 168
Trubchevsk, Russ. 52°33' N, 33°49' E 158
Truckee, Calif., U.S. 39°19' N, 120°12' W 90
Trudfront, Russ. 45°53' N, 47°40' E 158
Trufant, Mich., U.S. 43°17' N, 85°21' W 102
Trujillo, Hond. 15°54' N, 85°59' W 115
Trujillo, Peru 8°8' S, 79°2' W 130
Trujillo, Sp. 39°27' N, 5°53' W 164
Trujillo, Venez. 9°20' N, 70°27' W 136
Trujillo, adm. division, Venez. 9°26' N, 71°6' W 136
Trujillo Alto, U.S. 18°21' N, 66°0' W 118
Truk Islands see Chuuk, islands, North Pacific Ocean 7°44' N, 152°5' E 192
Trumbull, Conn., U.S. 41°14' N, 73°12' W 104
Trumbull, Mount, peak, Ariz., U.S. 36°23' N, 113°12' W 92
Trumon, Indonesia 2°51' N, 97°36' E 196
Trŭn, Bulg. 42°49' N, 22°37' E 168
Truro, Can. 45°21' N, 63°17' W 111
Truro, Mass., U.S. 41°59' N, 70°4' W 104
Truşeşti, Rom. 47°45' N, 27°1' E 152
Trutch, Can. 57°44' N, 122°57' W 108
Truth or Consequences, N. Mex., U.S. 33°8' N, 107°15' W 92
Trutnov, Czech Rep. 50°33' N, 15°54' E 152
Truxton, Ariz., U.S. 35°29' N, 113°33' W 101
Trwyn Cilan, U.K. 52°36' N, 4°52' W 150
Tryphena, N.Z. 36°19' S, 175°27' E 240
Trysil, Nor. 61°19' N, 12°15' E 152
Trzcianka, Pol. 53°1' N, 16°27' E 152
Trzebież, Pol. 53°39' N, 14°31' E 152
Trzemeszno, Pol. 52°33' N, 17°49' E 152
Tsacha Lake, Can. 52°59' N, 125°26' W 108
Tsada, Cyprus 34°50' N, 32°28' E 194
Tsagaanders, Mongolia 48°5' N, 114°21' E 198
Tsagaangol, Mongolia 49°1' N, 89°3' E 184
Tsagaannuur, Mongolia 49°28' N, 89°39' E 184
Tsagan Aman, Russ. 47°30' N, 46°37' E 158
Ts'ageri, Ga. 42°36' N, 42°42' E 195
Tsagveri, Ga. 41°48' N, 43°27' E 195
Tsaka La, pass, India 33°20' N, 78°50' E 188
Tsalka, Ga. 41°34' N, 44°3' E 195
Tsao see Tsau, Botswana 20°13' S, 22°23' E 227
Tsapel'ka, Russ. 58°2' N, 28°57' E 166
Tsaratanana, Massif du, Madagascar 14°17' S, 48°37' E 220
Tsarevo, Bulg. 42°10' N, 27°51' E 158
Tsau (Tsao), Botswana 20°13' S, 22°23' E 227
Tsavo, Kenya 3°3' S, 38°29' E 224
Tsavo National Park, Kenya 2°59' S, 39°7' E 218
Tsavo, river, Kenya 3°15' S, 37°42' E 224
Tsawisis, Namibia 26°16' S, 18°8' E 227
Tsayta Lake, lake, Can. 55°31' N, 125°57' W 108
Tschaukaib, Namibia 26°37' S, 15°36' E 227
Tschida, Lake, N. Dak., U.S. 46°33' N, 102°24' W 90
Tselina, Russ. 46°33' N, 40°59' E 158
Tsenogora, Russ. 64°55' N, 46°34' E 154
Tserovo, Bulg. 42°21' N, 24°3' E 156
Tses, Namibia 25°53' S, 18°3' E 227
Tsetsegnuur, Mongolia 46°32' N, 93°6' E 190
Tsetseng, Botswana 23°32' S, 23°6' E 227
Tsetserleg, Mongolia 47°28' N, 101°24' E 198
Tsévié, Togo 6°28' N, 1°12' E 222
Tshabong, Botswana 26°4' S, 22°27' E 227
Tshane, Botswana 24°3' S, 21°53' E 227
Tshela, Dem. Rep. of the Congo 5°1' S, 12°52' E 218
Tshibamba, Dem. Rep. of the Congo 9°7' S, 22°31' E 218
Tshikapa, Dem. Rep. of the Congo 6°25' S, 20°50' E 218
Tshilenge, Dem. Rep. of the Congo 6°17' S, 23°45' E 224
Tshilongo, Dem. Rep. of the Congo 10°31' S, 26°0' E 224
Tshinota, Dem. Rep. of the Congo 7°2' S, 20°55' E 218
Tshinsenda, Dem. Rep. of the Congo 12°18' S, 27°56' E 224
Tshisenga, Dem. Rep. of the Congo 7°17' S, 22°0' E 218
Tsholotsho, Zimb. 19°47' S, 27°45' E 224
Tshootsha, Botswana 22°5' S, 20°54' E 227
Tshopo, river, Dem. Rep. of the Congo 0°26' N, 26°42' E 224
Tshuapa, river, Dem. Rep. of the Congo 2°15' S, 24°11' E 224
Tshumbe, Dem. Rep. of the Congo 4°10' S, 24°21' E 218
Tshwane see Pretoria, S. Af. 25°48' S, 28°3' E 227
Tsiigehtchic, Can. 67°25' N, 133°35' W 98
Tsil'ma, river, Russ. 65°29' N, 51°1' E 154
Tsimanampetsotsa, Lac, lake, Madagascar 24°15' S, 42°16' E 220
Tsimkavichy, Belarus 53°4' N, 27°0' E 152
Tsimlyansk, Russ. 47°37' N, 41°58' E 158
Tsinjomitondraka, Madagascar 15°40' S, 47°9' E 220
Tsintsabis, Namibia 18°43' S, 17°58' E 220
Tsiombe, Madagascar 25°17' S, 45°32' E 220
Tsipikan, Russ. 54°57' N, 113°20' E 190
Tsiteli Tskaro, Ga. 41°24' N, 46°8' E 180
Tsitondroina, Madagascar 21°16' S, 46°0' E 220
Tsitsikamma Forest and Coastal National Park, Indian Ocean 34°5' S, 23°29' E 206
Tsivory, Madagascar 24°3' S, 46°6' E 220
Ts'khinvali, Asia 42°11' N, 43°53' E 195
Tsna, river, Russ. 53°52' N, 41°47' E 154
Tsnori, Ga. 41°36' N, 45°57' E 195
Tsomog, Mongolia 45°53' N, 109°8' E 198
Tsoohor, Mongolia 43°16' N, 104°5' E 198
Tsu, Japan 34°42' N, 136°31' E 201
Tsu Lake, lake, Can. 60°38' N, 112°18' W 108
Tsubame, Japan 37°39' N, 138°56' E 201
Tsubata, Japan 36°40' N, 136°43' E 201
Tsuchiura, Japan 36°5' N, 140°12' E 201
Tsugaru Kaikyō 41°4' N, 138°25' E 190
Tsukumi, Japan 33°3' N, 131°51' E 201
Tsuma, Japan 36°12' N, 133°14' E 201
Tsumeb, Namibia 19°16' S, 17°41' E 220
Tsumis Park, Namibia 23°42' S, 17°25' E 227
Tsumkwe, Namibia 19°38' S, 20°35' E 220
Tsunō, Japan 32°14' N, 131°33' E 201
Tsuru, Japan 35°32' N, 138°54' E 201
Tsuruga, Japan 35°37' N, 136°4' E 201
Tsurugi, Japan 36°27' N, 136°37' E 201
Tsuruoka, Japan 38°43' N, 139°50' E 201
Tsurusaki, Japan 33°14' N, 131°41' E 201
Tsushima, Japan 35°9' N, 136°44' E 201
Tsushima, Japan 33°6' N, 132°31' E 201
Tsushima Strait 33°56' N, 125°37' E 198
Tsutsu, Japan 34°7' N, 129°11' E 200
Tsuyama, Japan 35°4' N, 134°0' E 201
Tsyp Navolok, Russ. 69°42' N, 33°5' E 152
Tsyurupyns'k, Ukr. 46°37' N, 32°43' E 156
Tua, Dem. Rep. of the Congo 3°42' S, 16°36' E 218
Tuai, N.Z. 38°51' S, 177°9' E 240
Tuakau, N.Z. 37°17' S, 174°58' E 240
Tual, Indonesia 5°46' S, 132°37' E 192
Tuan Giao, Vietnam 21°45' N, 103°19' E 202
Tuangku, island, Indonesia 2°9' N, 97°18' E 196
Tuapí, Nicar. 14°8' N, 83°19' W 115
Tuapse, Russ. 44°6' N, 39°4' E 156
Tuaran, Malaysia 6°12' N, 116°14' E 203
Tuba City, Ariz., U.S. 36°8' N, 111°15' W 92
Tuban, Indonesia 7°3' S, 111°53' E 192
Tubarão, Braz. 28°32' S, 48°60' W 138
Ţūbās, West Bank 32°19' N, 35°21' E 194
Tubinskiy, Russ. 52°54' N, 58°10' E 154
Tubmanburg, Liberia 6°47' N, 10°53' W 222
Tubod, Philippines 8°3' N, 123°48' E 203
Ţubruq (Tobruk), Lib. 32°3' N, 23°57' E 216
Tubuai Islands see Austral Islands, South Pacific Ocean 21°30' S, 152°33' W 238
Tubutama, Mex. 30°53' N, 111°29' W 92
Tucacas, Venez. 10°47' N, 68°21' W 136
Tucacas see Puerto López, Col. 11°56' N, 71°18' W 136
Tucano, Braz. 10°58' S, 38°49' W 132
Tucavaca, Bol. 18°39' S, 58°58' W 132
Tuchomie, Pol. 54°7' N, 17°21' E 152
Tuckerman, Ark., U.S. 35°43' N, 91°13' W 96
Tuckernuck Island, Mass., U.S. 41°16' N, 70°36' W 104
Tuckerton, N.J., U.S. 39°35' N, 74°21' W 94
Tucki Mountain, peak, Calif., U.S. 36°29' N, 117°13' W 92
Tucson, Ariz., U.S. 32°14' N, 110°58' W 92
Tucumán, adm. division, Arg. 26°30' S, 66°11' W 132
Tucumcari, N. Mex., U.S. 35°10' N, 103°44' W 92
Tucupita, Venez. 9°5' N, 62°5' W 116
Tucuruí, Braz. 3°44' S, 49°46' W 130
Tuczno, Pol. 53°11' N, 16°9' E 152
Tudela, Sp. 42°3' N, 1°37' W 164
Tudulinna, Est. 59°1' N, 27°1' E 166
Ţufayḩ, Saudi Arabia 26°49' N, 49°39' E 196
Tuffé, Fr. 48°6' N, 0°30' E 150
Tufts Plain, North Pacific Ocean 44°55' N, 143°12' W 252
Tughyl, Kaz. 47°42' N, 84°11' E 184
Tuguegarao, Philippines 17°38' N, 121°42' E 203
Tugur, Russ. 53°46' N, 136°38' E 190
Tui, Sp. 42°2' N, 8°41' W 214
Tuichi, river, Bol. 14°14' S, 68°23' W 137
Tuitán, Mex. 23°59' N, 104°15' W 114
Tukan, Russ. 53°52' N, 57°26' E 154
Tukayyid, spring, Iraq 29°45' N, 45°38' E 196
Tukchi, Russ. 57°28' N, 139°21' E 173
Tukhkala, Russ. 65°41' N, 30°41' E 152
Tukhlya, Ukr. 48°52' N, 23°30' E 152
Tukita, Can. 64°53' N, 125°16' W 106
Tūkrah, Lib. 32°32' N, 20°34' E 216
Tuktoyaktuk, Can. 69°24' N, 133°11' W 73
Tuktut Nogait National Park, Can. 68°46' N, 123°49' W 98
Tukums, Latv. 56°58' N, 23°7' E 166
Tukuyu, Tanzania 9°17' S, 33°39' E 224
Tula, Mex. 22°58' N, 99°43' W 114
Tula, Mex. 20°1' N, 99°27' W 112
Tula, Russ. 54°10' N, 37°36' E 154
Tula, adm. division, Russ. 53°58' N, 36°48' E 154
Tula de Allende, Mex. 20°0' N, 99°21' W 114
Tulak, Afghan. 33°56' N, 63°38' E 186
Tulameen, Can. 49°32' N, 120°47' W 90
Tulancingo, Mex. 20°2' N, 98°22' W 114
Tulare, Calif., U.S. 36°13' N, 119°21' W 100
Tulare, Serb. and Mont. 42°48' N, 21°27' E 168
Tularosa Valley, N. Mex., U.S. 33°7' N, 106°27' W 92
Tulcán, Ecua. 0°44' N, 77°57' W 136
Tulcea, Rom. 45°10' N, 28°47' E 156
Tulcea, adm. division, Rom. 44°58' N, 28°9' E 156
Tul'chyn, Ukr. 48°40' N, 28°57' E 156
Tülen Araldary, islands, Caspian Sea 44°43' N, 49°2' E 180
Tuli, Zimb. 21°55' S, 29°14' E 227
Tulia, Tex., U.S. 34°30' N, 101°47' W 92
Tulita, Can. 64°56' N, 125°23' W 98
Tulivaara, Russ. 63°37' N, 30°26' E 154
Ţulkarm, West Bank 32°18' N, 35°1' E 194
Tülkibas, Kaz. 42°28' N, 70°19' E 197
Tullahoma, Tenn., U.S. 35°21' N, 86°13' W 96
Tullamore, Ire. 53°15' N, 7°30' W 150
Tulloch Reservoir, lake, Calif., U.S. 37°52' N, 120°46' W 100
Tullos, La., U.S. 31°48' N, 92°20' W 103
Tully Lake, Mass., U.S. 42°38' N, 72°21' W 104
Tulpan, Russ. 61°23' N, 57°22' E 154
Tulsa, Okla., U.S. 36°8' N, 95°59' W 96
Tulsequah, Can. 58°36' N, 133°36' W 108
Tuluá, Col. 4°4' N, 76°13' W 136
Tuluksak, Alas., U.S. 61°4' N, 160°59' W 98
Tulum National Park, Mex. 20°8' N, 87°35' W 115
Tulum, ruin(s), Mex. 20°11' N, 87°36' W 115
Tulun, Russ. 54°40' N, 100°27' E 160
Tuma, Russ. 55°8' N, 40°34' E 154
Tuma, river, Nicar. 13°20' N, 85°36' W 115
Tumaco, Col. 1°39' N, 78°37' W 123
Tumanskaya, Russ. 64°3' N, 178°9' E 73
Tumany, Russ. 60°57' N, 155°46' E 160
Tumba, Dem. Rep. of the Congo 3°10' S, 23°35' E 224
Tumbes, Peru 3°39' S, 80°25' W 130
Tumble Mountain, peak, Mont., U.S. 45°17' N, 110°6' W 90
Tumbledown Mountain, peak, Me., U.S. 45°26' N, 70°33' W 94
Tumbler Ridge, Can. 55°3' N, 120°60' W 108
Tumcha, Russ. 66°34' N, 30°46' E 152
Tumd Youqi, China 40°31' N, 110°31' E 198
Tumd Zuoqi, China 40°44' N, 111°8' E 198
Tumeka Lake, Can. 57°11' N, 130°21' W 108
Tumen, China 42°57' N, 129°49' E 200
Tumen, river, Asia 42°21' N, 128°35' E 200
Tumeremo, Venez. 7°18' N, 61°30' W 130
Tumiã, river, Braz. 8°15' S, 66°37' W 132
Tumiritinga, Braz. 18°60' S, 41°39' W 138
Tumpat, Malaysia 6°11' N, 102°8' E 196
Tumu, Ghana 10°51' N, 1°60' W 222
Tumucumaque National Park, Braz. 1°51' N, 56°1' W 130
Tumucumaque, Serra de, Braz. 0°45' N, 55°55' W 130
Tumupasa, Bol. 14°11' S, 67°55' W 137
Tumusla, Bol. 20°32' S, 65°41' W 137
Tumwater, Wash., U.S. 46°59' N, 122°55' W 100
Tuna, Ghana 9°29' N, 2°27' W 222
Tunapuna, Trinidad and Tobago 10°37' N, 61°24' W 118
Tunas, Braz. 25°1' S, 49°6' W 138
Tunas, Sierra de las, Mex. 30°5' N, 107°50' W 112
Tunbridge, Vt., U.S. 43°53' N, 72°30' W 104
Tunbridge Wells, U.K. 51°7' N, 0°15' E 162
Tunceli, Turk. 39°5' N, 39°31' E 195
Tunchang, China 19°21' N, 110°4' E 202
Tünchel, Mongolia 48°50' N, 106°42' E 198
Tundubai, Sudan 14°47' N, 22°42' E 216
Tundubai, spring, Sudan 18°25' N, 28°30' E 226
Tunduma, Tanzania 9°19' S, 32°46' E 224
Tunduru, Tanzania 11°7' S, 37°22' E 224
Tunel, Pol. 50°25' N, 19°58' E 152
Tunga, Nig. 8°2' N, 9°21' E 222
Tŭngam, N. Korea 37°44' N, 125°26' E 200
Tungaru, Sudan 10°12' N, 30°45' E 224
Tungelsta, Sw. 59°6' N, 18°2' E 166
Tungkang, Taiwan 22°29' N, 120°30' E 198
Tungsten, Can. 62°1' N, 128°21' W 98
Tunguska Podkamennaya, Russ. 61°35' N, 90°11' E 169
Tuni, India 17°21' N, 82°32' E 188
Tunica, Miss., U.S. 34°39' N, 90°24' W 96
Tunis, Tun. 36°46' N, 10°3' E 156
Tunisia 34°0' N, 9°0' E 214
Tunja, Col. 5°32' N, 73°23' W 136
Tunkinsky National Park, Russ. 51°26' N, 101°42' E 172
Tŭnkovo, Bulg. 41°42' N, 25°45' E 156
Tuntutuliak, Alas., U.S. 60°20' N, 162°38' W 98
Tununak, Alas., U.S. 60°29' N, 165°20' W 98
Tunuyán, Arg. 33°35' S, 69°3' W 134
Tuolumne, Calif., U.S. 37°57' N, 120°15' W 100
Tuong Duong, Vietnam 19°15' N, 104°23' E 202
Tuotuo, river, China 34°3' N, 91°7' E 188

Tuotuoheyan see Tanggulashan, *China* 34°10′ N, 92°24′ E **188**
Tup, *Kyrg.* 42°43′ N, 78°21′ E **184**
Tupã, *Braz.* 21°56′ S, 50°29′ W **138**
Tupaciguara, *Braz.* 18°36′ S, 48°45′ W **138**
Tupanciretã, *Braz.* 29°6′ S, 53°50′ W **139**
Tuparro, river, *Col.* 4°42′ N, 69°28′ W **136**
Tupelo, *Miss., U.S.* 34°15′ N, 88°44′ W **112**
Tupi, *Philippines* 6°13′ N, 125°1′ E **203**
Tupinambarama, Ilha, *Braz.* 3°24′ S, 58°32′ W **130**
Tupiraçaba, *Braz.* 14°34′ S, 48°36′ W **138**
Tupitsyno, *Russ.* 58°34′ N, 28°21′ E **166**
Tupiza, *Bol.* 21°29′ S, 65°46′ W **137**
Tupper, *Can.* 55°31′ N, 120°4′ W **108**
Tupper Lake, *N.Y., U.S.* 44°13′ N, 74°29′ W **94**
Tüpqaraghan Tübegi, *Kaz.* 44°24′ N, 50°30′ E **180**
Tuquan, *China* 45°23′ N, 121°32′ E **198**
Túquerres, *Col.* 1°6′ N, 77°39′ W **136**
Túr, river, *Hung.* 48°0′ N, 22°23′ E **168**
Tura, *Hung.* 47°35′ N, 19°36′ E **168**
Tura, *India* 25°26′ N, 90°11′ E **188**
Tura, *Russ.* 64°22′ N, 100°29′ E **173**
Tura, *Russ.* 64°22′ N, 100°29′ E **160**
Tura, *Tanzania* 5°28′ S, 33°50′ E **224**
Tura, river, *Russ.* 58°20′ N, 62°52′ E **154**
Turabah, *Saudi Arabia* 21°12′ N, 41°40′ E **182**
Turabah, spring, *Saudi Arabia* 28°12′ N, 42°53′ E **180**
Turan Lowland, *Uzb.* 40°50′ N, 57°48′ E **180**
Turangi, *N.Z.* 39°1′ S, 175°47′ E **240**
Turar Ryskulov, *Kaz.* 42°30′ N, 70°20′ E **197**
Turaw, *Belarus* 52°4′ N, 27°44′ E **152**
Ţurayf, *Saudi Arabia* 31°39′ N, 38°38′ E **180**
Turba, *Est.* 59°3′ N, 24°11′ E **166**
Turbaco, *Col.* 10°19′ N, 75°25′ W **136**
Turbacz, peak, *Pol.* 49°31′ N, 20°1′ E **152**
Turbat, *Pak.* 25°56′ N, 63°6′ E **182**
Turbe, *Bosn. and Herzg.* 44°15′ N, 17°35′ E **168**
Turbo, *Col.* 8°7′ N, 76°43′ W **136**
Turco, *Bol.* 18°14′ S, 68°13′ W **137**
Turda, spring, *Sudan* 10°22′ N, 28°33′ E **224**
Turégano, *Sp.* 41°9′ N, 4°1′ W **164**
Turenki, *Fin.* 60°54′ N, 24°38′ E **166**
Tureta, *Nig.* 12°35′ N, 5°35′ E **222**
Turgeon, river, *Can.* 49°32′ N, 79°47′ W **94**
Türgovishte, *Bulg.* 43°14′ N, 26°34′ E **156**
Turgovishte, adm. division, *Bulg.* 43°1′ N, 25°52′ E **156**
Turgut, *Turk.* 38°37′ N, 31°47′ E **156**
Turhal, *Turk.* 40°23′ N, 36°6′ E **156**
Türi, *Est.* 58°47′ N, 25°25′ E **166**
Turiaçu, *Braz.* 1°40′ S, 45°25′ W **130**
Turin, *Can.* 49°57′ N, 112°33′ W **90**
Turin see Torino, *It.* 45°4′ N, 7°40′ E **167**
Turinsk, *Russ.* 58°2′ N, 63°35′ E **154**
Turinskaya Sloboda, *Russ.* 57°36′ N, 64°21′ E **154**
Turjak, *Bosn. and Herzg.* 45°0′ N, 17°10′ E **168**
Turkana, Lake, *Kenya* 2°32′ N, 34°10′ E **207**
Turkestan Range, *Uzb.* 39°30′ N, 68°9′ E **184**
Túrkeve, *Hung.* 47°6′ N, 20°45′ E **168**
Turkey, *Tex., U.S.* 34°22′ N, 100°55′ W **96**
Turkey 38°54′ N, 33°55′ E **180**
Turki, *Russ.* 51°57′ N, 43°17′ E **158**
Türkistan, *Kaz.* 43°17′ N, 68°13′ E **184**
Türkmenabat (Chärjew), *Turkm.* 39°4′ N, 63°35′ E **184**
Türkmenbaşy, *Turkm.* 40°0′ N, 52°58′ E **180**
Turkmenistan 39°37′ N, 57°48′ E **184**
Turks and Caicos Islands, *U.K.* 21°58′ N, 72°29′ W **116**
Turks Islands, *North Atlantic Ocean* 21°27′ N, 70°58′ W **116**
Turku, *Fin.* 60°27′ N, 22°0′ E **160**
Turku (Åbo), *Fin.* 60°27′ N, 22°15′ E **166**
Turmalina, *Braz.* 17°16′ S, 42°46′ W **138**
Turnagain, Cape, *N.Z.* 40°43′ S, 176°35′ E **240**
Turnberry, *Can.* 53°26′ N, 101°42′ W **108**
Turneffe Islands, *Caribbean Sea* 17°35′ N, 87°42′ W **115**
Turner, *Me., U.S.* 44°15′ N, 70°16′ W **104**
Turner, *Mont., U.S.* 48°49′ N, 108°25′ W **90**
Turner Mountain, peak, *Calif., U.S.* 40°17′ N, 121°43′ W **90**
Turners Falls, *Mass., U.S.* 42°35′ N, 72°34′ W **104**
Turnertown, *Tex., U.S.* 32°11′ N, 94°58′ W **103**
Turnhout, *Belg.* 51°19′ N, 4°56′ E **167**
Turnu, *Rom.* 46°16′ N, 21°6′ E **168**
Turnu Roşu, Pasul, pass, *Rom.* 45°34′ N, 24°14′ E **156**
Turobin, *Pol.* 50°48′ N, 22°44′ E **152**
Turpan, *China* 43°3′ N, 89°14′ E **190**
Turpan Depression, *China* 42°8′ N, 91°23′ E **190**
Turquino, Pico, peak, *Cuba* 19°58′ N, 76°56′ W **115**
Turre, *Sp.* 37°8′ N, 1°54′ W **164**
Tursunzoda, *Taj.* 38°31′ N, 68°19′ E **197**
Turt, *Mongolia* 51°22′ N, 100°56′ E **190**
Turţ, *Rom.* 47°59′ N, 23°13′ E **168**
Turtas, river, *Russ.* 58°37′ N, 69°48′ E **169**
Türtkŭl, *Uzb.* 41°32′ N, 61°0′ E **180**
Turtle Creek Point, *Fla., U.S.* 29°2′ N, 83°11′ W **105**
Turtle Islands, *North Atlantic Ocean* 7°30′ N, 13°42′ W **222**
Turtle Mountain, peak, *N. Dak., U.S.* 48°59′ N, 100°31′ W **90**
Turtle Mountains, *Calif., U.S.* 34°14′ N, 114°53′ W **101**
Turtle, river, *Can.* 49°6′ N, 92°32′ W **110**
Turtleford, *Can.* 53°23′ N, 108°58′ W **108**
Turugart Pass, *Kyrg.* 40°33′ N, 75°23′ E **184**
Turugart, pass, *China* 40°31′ N, 75°21′ E **184**
Turukhansk, *Russ.* 65°45′ N, 88°6′ E **169**
Turukta, *Russ.* 60°39′ N, 116°3′ E **160**
Turvo, *Braz.* 28°59′ S, 49°43′ W **138**
Turvo, river, *Braz.* 16°24′ S, 50°11′ W **138**
Tur'ya, *Russ.* 62°50′ N, 50°41′ E **154**
Turysh, *Kaz.* 45°27′ N, 56°5′ E **158**
Turza Wielka, *Pol.* 53°18′ N, 20°4′ E **152**
Tuscaloosa, *Ala., U.S.* 33°11′ N, 87°34′ W **103**
Tuscany, adm. division, *It.* 44°2′ N, 10°22′ E **167**
Tuscarora, *Nev., U.S.* 41°19′ N, 116°14′ W **90**
Tuscarora Mountains, *Nev., U.S.* 40°44′ N, 116°22′ W **90**
Tuscola, *Ill., U.S.* 39°48′ N, 88°17′ W **102**
Tuscola, *Tex., U.S.* 32°12′ N, 99°48′ W **92**
Tuscumbia, *Ala., U.S.* 34°43′ N, 87°42′ W **96**
Tuskegee, *Ala., U.S.* 32°24′ N, 85°41′ W **96**
Tustin, *Mich., U.S.* 44°6′ N, 85°28′ W **102**
Tustna, *Nor.* 63°12′ N, 8°7′ E **152**
Tutak, *Turk.* 39°30′ N, 42°41′ E **195**
Tutayev, *Russ.* 57°52′ N, 39°30′ E **154**
Tuticorin, *India* 8°47′ N, 78°6′ E **188**
Tutin, *Serb. and Mont.* 42°59′ N, 20°20′ E **168**
Tutira, *N.Z.* 39°13′ S, 176°53′ E **240**
Tutoko, Mount, peak, *N.Z.* 44°38′ S, 167°56′ E **240**
Tutonchany, *Russ.* 64°14′ N, 93°42′ E **169**
Tutshi Lake, lake, *Can.* 59°53′ N, 135°14′ W **108**
Tutuaca, river, *Mex.* 29°32′ N, 108°48′ W **80**
Tutuala, *Timor-Leste* 8°31′ S, 127°6′ E **192**
Tutubu, *Tanzania* 5°29′ S, 32°41′ E **218**
Tutuila, *American Samoa, U.S.* 14°20′ S, 170°45′ W **241**
Tututepec, *Mex.* 16°6′ N, 97°37′ W **112**
Tuul, river, *Mongolia* 47°17′ N, 105°0′ E **198**
Tuupovaara, *Fin.* 62°28′ N, 30°37′ E **152**
Tuusniemi, *Fin.* 62°48′ N, 28°26′ E **152**
Tuve, Mount, peak, *Antarctica* 73°50′ S, 80°43′ W **248**
Ţuwayq, Jabal, *Saudi Arabia* 24°12′ N, 46°21′ E **196**
Tuxford, *U.K.* 53°13′ N, 0°54′ E **162**
Tuxpan, *Mex.* 20°56′ N, 97°24′ W **114**
Tuxpan, *Mex.* 19°32′ N, 103°23′ W **114**
Tuxpan, *Mex.* 21°55′ N, 105°19′ W **114**
Tuxtepec, *Mex.* 18°5′ N, 96°7′ W **114**
Tuxtla Gutiérrez, *Mex.* 16°42′ N, 93°14′ W **115**
Tuy An, *Vietnam* 13°17′ N, 109°12′ E **202**
Tuy Hoa, *Vietnam* 13°4′ N, 109°18′ E **202**
Tuya Lake, *Can.* 59°3′ N, 131°11′ W **108**
Tuya, river, *Can.* 58°24′ N, 130°35′ W **108**
Tuyen Hoa, *Vietnam* 17°51′ N, 106°12′ E **198**
Tuyen Quang, *Vietnam* 21°49′ N, 105°11′ E **202**
Tuymazy, *Russ.* 54°34′ N, 53°45′ E **154**
Tüysarkān, *Iran* 34°30′ N, 48°23′ E **180**
Tuz Gölü, lake, *Turk.* 38°40′ N, 33°18′ E **156**
Tuzantla, *Mex.* 19°2′ N, 100°23′ W **114**
Tuzi, *Europe* 42°21′ N, 19°19′ E **168**
Tuzigoot National Monument, *Ariz., U.S.* 34°46′ N, 112°5′ W **92**
Tuzla, *Bosn. and Herzg.* 44°32′ N, 18°39′ E **168**
Tuzla Gölü, lake, *Turk.* 38°59′ N, 35°27′ E **156**
Tuzluca, *Turk.* 40°3′ N, 43°39′ E **195**
Tvedestrand, *Nor.* 58°37′ N, 8°53′ E **152**
Tver', *Russ.* 56°50′ N, 35°54′ E **154**
Tver', adm. division, *Russ.* 56°49′ N, 33°43′ E **154**
Tverrvik, *Nor.* 67°2′ N, 14°31′ E **152**
Twain Harte, *Calif., U.S.* 38°1′ N, 120°15′ W **100**
Twee Rivieren, *S. Af.* 26°28′ S, 20°31′ E **227**
Tweedy Mountain, peak, *Mont., U.S.* 45°27′ N, 113°2′ W **90**
Twelve Bens, The, peak, *Ire.* 53°30′ N, 9°56′ W **150**
Twentynine Palms, *Calif., U.S.* 34°8′ N, 116°3′ W **101**
Twifu Praso, *Ghana* 5°37′ N, 1°32′ W **222**
Twillingate, *Can.* 49°38′ N, 54°46′ W **111**
Twin Falls, *Idaho, U.S.* 42°34′ N, 114°28′ W **90**
Twin Lakes, *Can.* 57°25′ N, 117°31′ W **108**
Twin Lakes, *Nebr., U.S.* 42°17′ N, 102°55′ W **90**
Twin Lakes Mountain, peak, *Oreg., U.S.* 43°12′ N, 122°42′ W **90**
Twin Mountain, *N.H., U.S.* 44°16′ N, 71°33′ W **104**
Twin Mountain, peak, *Oreg., U.S.* 44°54′ N, 118°5′ W **90**
Twin Peaks, *Idaho, U.S.* 44°35′ N, 114°33′ W **90**
Twin Valley, *Minn., U.S.* 47°14′ N, 96°17′ W **90**
Twining, *Mich., U.S.* 44°6′ N, 83°49′ W **102**
Twisp, *Wash., U.S.* 48°20′ N, 120°9′ W **90**
Twitya, river, *Can.* 63°42′ N, 129°33′ W **98**
Twizel, *N.Z.* 44°16′ S, 170°6′ E **240**
Two Buttes, *Colo., U.S.* 37°33′ N, 102°24′ W **92**
Two Buttes, peak, *Colo., U.S.* 37°38′ N, 102°38′ W **90**
Two Creeks, *Can.* 54°17′ N, 116°21′ W **108**
Two Harbors, *Minn., U.S.* 47°1′ N, 91°41′ W **94**
Two Hills, *Can.* 53°42′ N, 111°45′ W **108**
Two Ocean Pass, *Wyo., U.S.* 44°1′ N, 110°10′ W **90**
Two Rivers, *Wis., U.S.* 44°9′ N, 87°35′ W **102**
Two Top Peak, *S. Dak., U.S.* 44°57′ N, 103°41′ W **90**
Twofold Bay 37°24′ S, 149°35′ E **230**
Tyab, *Iran* 26°58′ N, 57°1′ E **196**
Tyanya, *Russ.* 59°0′ N, 119°43′ E **160**
Tydal, *Nor.* 63°3′ N, 11°34′ E **152**
Tyee, *Queen Charlotte Sound* 57°2′ N, 134°32′ W **108**
Tygda, *Russ.* 53°9′ N, 126°19′ E **190**
Tyin, *Nor.* 61°13′ N, 8°12′ E **152**
Tyler, *Minn., U.S.* 44°15′ N, 96°10′ W **90**
Tyler, *Tex., U.S.* 32°20′ N, 95°18′ W **103**
Tylertown, *Miss., U.S.* 31°6′ N, 90°9′ W **103**
Tym, river, *Russ.* 60°2′ N, 83°35′ E **169**
Tymsk, *Russ.* 59°19′ N, 80°23′ E **169**
Tynda, *Russ.* 55°10′ N, 124°44′ E **190**
Tyndall, *S. Dak., U.S.* 42°58′ N, 97°53′ W **90**
Tyndaris, ruin(s), *It.* 38°7′ N, 14°55′ E **156**
Tynset, *Nor.* 62°17′ N, 10°45′ E **152**
Tyre see Soûr, *Leb.* 33°16′ N, 35°12′ E **194**
Tyree, Mount, peak, *Antarctica* 78°25′ S, 87°7′ W **248**
Tyrnyauz, *Russ.* 43°24′ N, 42°56′ E **195**
Tyrol, region, *It.* 46°1′ N, 10°30′ E **167**
Tyrone, *N. Mex., U.S.* 32°43′ N, 108°17′ W **92**
Tyrone, *Okla., U.S.* 36°56′ N, 101°6′ W **92**
Tyrrhenian Sea 40°7′ N, 11°28′ E **156**
Tyrvää, *Fin.* 61°21′ N, 22°51′ E **166**
Tysvær, *Nor.* 59°18′ N, 5°28′ E **152**
Tytuvėnai, *Lith.* 55°36′ N, 23°9′ E **166**
Tyubelyakh, *Russ.* 65°18′ N, 142°53′ E **160**
Tyugyuren, *Russ.* 67°12′ N, 142°36′ E **173**
Tyukalinsk, *Russ.* 55°52′ N, 72°13′ E **184**
Tyukyun, river, *Russ.* 65°42′ N, 118°13′ E **160**
Tyulenovo, *Bulg.* 43°31′ N, 28°35′ E **156**
Tyul'gan, *Russ.* 52°22′ N, 56°2′ E **154**
Tyul'kino, *Russ.* 59°47′ N, 56°30′ E **154**
Tyumen', *Russ.* 57°7′ N, 65°32′ E **184**
Tyumen', adm. division, *Russ.* 55°59′ N, 66°44′ E **184**
Tyung, river, *Russ.* 66°37′ N, 116°51′ E **160**
Tyungur, *Russ.* 50°12′ N, 86°38′ E **184**
Tyva, adm. division, *Russ.* 50°56′ N, 89°32′ E **184**
Tyvoll, *Nor.* 62°43′ N, 11°21′ E **152**
Tywyn, *U.K.* 52°34′ N, 4°5′ W **162**
Tzintzuntzan, ruin(s), *Mex.* 19°34′ N, 101°37′ W **114**

U

U. P. Mammoth Kill Site, *Wyo., U.S.* 41°30′ N, 107°43′ W **90**
Uacari, *Braz.* 1°12′ N, 69°26′ W **136**
Üälīkhanov, *Kaz.* 52°47′ N, 71°52′ E **184**
Uamba, *Angola* 7°21′ S, 16°9′ E **218**
Uarandab, *Eth.* 7°8′ N, 44°6′ E **218**
Uarirambá, *Braz.* 1°40′ N, 69°26′ W **136**
Uatumã, river, *Braz.* 0°2′ N, 59°58′ W **130**
Uauá, *Braz.* 9°50′ S, 39°32′ W **132**
Uaupés, river, *Braz.* 0°7′ N, 67°56′ W **136**
Uaxactún, ruin(s), *Guatemala* 17°20′ N, 89°46′ W **115**
Ub, *Serb. and Mont.* 44°26′ N, 20°4′ E **168**
Ubá, *Braz.* 21°7′ S, 42°55′ W **138**
Uba, *Nig.* 10°29′ N, 13°12′ E **216**
Übach-Palenberg, *Ger.* 50°55′ N, 6°7′ E **167**
Ubaitaba, *Braz.* 14°20′ S, 39°18′ W **132**
Ubangi, river, *Africa* 4°24′ N, 19°9′ E **206**
Ubari see Awbārī, *Lib.* 26°37′ N, 12°45′ E **216**
Ubatã, *Braz.* 14°15′ S, 39°28′ W **138**
Úbeda, *Sp.* 38°0′ N, 3°22′ W **164**
Ubehebe Crater, *Calif., U.S.* 37°1′ N, 117°27′ W **101**
Uberaba, *Braz.* 19°44′ S, 47°56′ W **138**
Uberlândia, *Braz.* 18°55′ S, 48°20′ W **138**
Ubiaja, *Nig.* 6°41′ N, 6°22′ E **222**
Ubiatã, *Braz.* 24°33′ S, 53°1′ W **138**
Ubierna, *Sp.* 42°28′ N, 3°43′ W **164**
Ubinas, *Peru* 16°25′ S, 70°52′ W **137**
Ubly, *Mich., U.S.* 43°42′ N, 82°55′ W **102**
Ubombo, *S. Af.* 27°32′ S, 32°9′ E **227**
Ubon Ratchathani, *Thai.* 15°14′ N, 104°53′ E **202**
Ubrique, *Sp.* 36°40′ N, 5°27′ W **164**
Ubundu, *Dem. Rep. of the Congo* 0°24′ N, 25°30′ E **224**
Ucacha, *Arg.* 33°3′ S, 63°30′ W **139**
Üçajy, *Turkm.* 38°4′ N, 62°45′ E **184**
Ucar, *Azerb.* 40°31′ N, 47°38′ E **195**
Ucayali, adm. division, *Peru* 10°3′ S, 73°40′ W **137**
Ucayali, river, *Peru* 6°29′ S, 75°37′ W **122**
Uchab, *Namibia* 19°44′ S, 17°47′ E **220**
Uchaly, *Russ.* 54°22′ N, 59°24′ E **154**
Uchami, *Russ.* 63°49′ N, 96°31′ E **169**
Uchami, river, *Russ.* 62°30′ N, 94°55′ E **160**
Uchami, river, *Russ.* 62°38′ N, 93°54′ E **169**
Uchi Lake, *Can.* 51°4′ N, 92°34′ W **110**
Uchiko, *Japan* 33°33′ N, 132°38′ E **201**
Uchiza, *Peru* 8°26′ S, 76°24′ W **130**
Uchqo'rg'on, *Uzb.* 41°12′ N, 71°59′ E **197**
Uchquduq, *Uzb.* 42°6′ N, 63°37′ E **197**
Uchsay, *Uzb.* 43°48′ N, 58°56′ E **180**
Uchur, river, *Russ.* 56°55′ N, 130°38′ E **160**
Ucluelet, *Can.* 48°56′ N, 125°34′ W **90**
Ucuriş, *Rom.* 46°37′ N, 21°57′ E **168**
Uda, river, *Russ.* 53°59′ N, 133°25′ E **190**
Udachnoye, *Russ.* 47°45′ N, 46°51′ E **184**
Udachnyy, *Russ.* 66°22′ N, 112°38′ E **173**
Udainagar, *India* 22°31′ N, 76°13′ E **197**
Udaipur, *India* 24°33′ N, 73°41′ E **186**
Udala, *India* 21°35′ N, 86°33′ E **188**
Uddevalla, *Nor.* 58°20′ N, 11°56′ E **152**
Uder, *Ger.* 51°21′ N, 10°3′ E **167**
Udhampur, *India* 32°54′ N, 75°10′ E **186**
Udi, *Nig.* 6°19′ N, 7°23′ E **222**
Udine, *It.* 46°4′ N, 13°15′ E **167**
Udintsev Fracture Zone, *South Pacific Ocean* 52°14′ S, 155°38′ W **252**
Udmurtiya, adm. division, *Russ.* 57°3′ N, 51°20′ E **154**
Udobnaya, *Russ.* 44°11′ N, 41°30′ E **158**
Udomlya, *Russ.* 57°51′ N, 35°5′ E **154**
Udorn see Udon Thani, *Thai.* 17°26′ N, 102°46′ E **202**
Udovo, *Maced.* 41°21′ N, 22°26′ E **156**
Udzungwa Mountain National Park, *Tanzania* 7°50′ S, 36°22′ E **206**
Uebonti, *Indonesia* 0°59′ N, 121°35′ E **192**
Ueda, *Japan* 36°24′ N, 138°17′ E **201**
Uele, river, *Dem. Rep. of the Congo* 3°32′ N, 28°10′ E **224**
Uelen, *Russ.* 66°7′ N, 169°51′ W **98**
Uel'kal', *Russ.* 65°34′ N, 179°24′ W **98**
Uelsen, *Ger.* 52°29′ N, 6°53′ E **163**
Ueno, *Japan* 34°44′ N, 136°7′ E **201**
Uere, river, *Dem. Rep. of the Congo* 3°44′ N, 25°23′ E **224**
Ufa, *Russ.* 54°45′ N, 56°0′ E **154**
Ufa, river, *Russ.* 56°29′ N, 58°7′ E **154**
Uftyuga, river, *Russ.* 61°36′ N, 46°15′ E **154**
Ugāle, *Latv.* 57°15′ N, 22°1′ E **166**
Ugalla Game Reserve, *Tanzania* 6°5′ S, 31°39′ E **224**
Ugalla, river, *Tanzania* 5°55′ S, 31°20′ E **224**
Ugam-Chatkal National Park, *Uzb.* 41°38′ N, 70°0′ E **197**
Uganda 1°13′ N, 32°13′ E **224**
Uganik, *Gulf of Alaska* 57°45′ N, 153°38′ W **98**
Ugarit see Ra's Shamrah, site, *Syr.* 35°33′ N, 35°44′ E **194**
Ugleural'skiy, *Russ.* 58°57′ N, 57°36′ E **154**
Uglich, *Russ.* 57°27′ N, 38°20′ E **154**
Ugljane, *Croatia* 43°33′ N, 16°44′ E **168**
Uglovka, *Russ.* 58°15′ N, 33°34′ E **154**
Ugol'nyye Kopi, *Russ.* 64°47′ N, 177°47′ E **73**
Ugoma, *Dem. Rep. of the Congo* 4°28′ S, 28°25′ E **224**
Ugra, river, *Russ.* 54°44′ N, 35°45′ E **154**
Ugut, *Russ.* 60°27′ N, 74°6′ E **169**
Uhlenhorst, *Namibia* 23°42′ S, 17°53′ E **227**
Uhrichsville, *Ohio, U.S.* 40°23′ N, 81°22′ W **102**
Uig 58°11′ N, 7°1′ W **150**
Uíge, *Angola* 7°37′ S, 15°4′ E **218**
Uíge, adm. division, *Angola* 7°15′ S, 14°43′ E **218**
Uijeongbu, *S. Korea* 37°43′ N, 127°2′ E **200**
Uilpata, peak, *Russ.* 42°42′ N, 43°48′ E **195**
Uimaharju, *Fin.* 62°53′ N, 30°13′ E **152**
Uinta Mountains, *Utah, U.S.* 40°23′ N, 110°42′ W **90**
Uiseong, *S. Korea* 36°19′ N, 128°42′ E **200**
Uitenhage, *S. Af.* 33°46′ S, 25°25′ E **220**
Uithuizen, *Neth.* 53°24′ N, 6°40′ E **163**
Újfehértó, *Hung.* 47°47′ N, 21°41′ E **168**
Uji, *Japan* 34°51′ N, 135°51′ E **201**
Ujiie, *Japan* 36°40′ N, 139°58′ E **201**
Ujiji, *Tanzania* 4°57′ S, 29°40′ E **224**
Ujjain, *India* 23°10′ N, 75°47′ E **197**
Újszász, *Hung.* 47°17′ N, 20°5′ E **168**
Ujung Kulon National Park, *Indian Ocean* 7°5′ S, 104°54′ E **172**
Ujungpandang (Makassar), *Indonesia* 5°11′ S, 119°25′ E **192**
Uka, *Russ.* 57°50′ N, 161°48′ E **160**
Ukhiya, *Bangladesh* 21°16′ N, 92°7′ E **188**
Ukhrul, *India* 25°9′ N, 94°22′ E **188**
Ukhta, *Russ.* 63°31′ N, 53°44′ E **169**
Ukhvala, *Belarus* 54°5′ N, 29°16′ E **166**
Ukia, *Tanzania* 7°43′ S, 31°46′ E **224**
Ukiah, *Calif., U.S.* 39°8′ N, 123°14′ W **90**
Ukmergė, *Lith.* 55°15′ N, 24°43′ E **166**
Ukraine 49°12′ N, 31°23′ E **158**
Uktym, *Russ.* 62°38′ N, 49°0′ E **154**
Uku, *Angola* 11°27′ S, 14°19′ E **220**
Ukulahu, island, *Maldives* 4°11′ N, 71°57′ E **188**
Ukuma, *Angola* 12°53′ S, 15°2′ E **220**
Ukwaa, *Sudan* 6°41′ N, 34°37′ E **224**
Ula, *Turk.* 37°5′ N, 28°24′ E **156**
Ulaanbaatar (Ulan Bator), *Mongolia* 47°56′ N, 106°41′ E **198**
Ulaangom, *Mongolia* 49°57′ N, 92°3′ E **184**
Ulaanjirem, *Mongolia* 45°5′ N, 105°45′ E **190**
Ulaan-Uul, *Mongolia* 44°8′ N, 111°15′ E **198**
Ulaga, *Russ.* 66°15′ N, 131°36′ E **160**
Ulan, *China* 36°55′ N, 98°27′ E **188**
Ulan Bator see Ulaanbaatar, *Mongolia* 47°56′ N, 106°41′ E **198**
Ulan Erge, *Russ.* 46°15′ N, 44°51′ E **158**
Ulan Khol, *Russ.* 45°25′ N, 46°48′ E **158**
Ulan Ude, *Russ.* 51°54′ N, 107°30′ E **190**
Ulan Ul Hu, lake, *China* 34°51′ N, 89°56′ E **188**
Ulanbel, *Kaz.* 44°45′ N, 71°9′ E **184**
Ulang, river, *Nicar.* 14°37′ N, 83°51′ W **115**
Ulanhot, *China* 46°5′ N, 122°5′ E **198**
Ulaş, *Turk.* 39°25′ N, 37°2′ E **156**
Ulaya, *Tanzania* 7°3′ S, 36°55′ E **224**
Ülbi, *Kaz.* 50°16′ N, 83°23′ E **184**
Ulbio, *Braz.* 10°20′ S, 70°24′ W **137**
Ulcinj, *Europe* 41°55′ N, 19°12′ E **168**
Uldz, *Mongolia* 48°38′ N, 112°2′ E **198**
Uldz, river, *Mongolia* 49°24′ N, 113°23′ E **198**
Uleåborg see Oulu, *Fin.* 65°0′ N, 25°25′ E **152**
Ulen, *Minn., U.S.* 47°3′ N, 96°17′ W **90**
Ulfborg, *Den.* 56°16′ N, 8°17′ E **150**
Uliastay, *Mongolia* 47°48′ N, 96°47′ E **190**
Ulindi, river, *Dem. Rep. of the Congo* 1°43′ S, 26°5′ E **224**
Ulithi Atoll, *F.S.M.* 9°6′ N, 138°40′ E **192**
Uljin, *S. Korea* 36°59′ N, 129°24′ E **200**
Uljma, *Serb. and Mont.* 45°2′ N, 21°10′ E **168**
Ülken, *Kaz.* 45°12′ N, 73°57′ E **184**
Ülken Borsyq Qumy, *Kaz.* 46°18′ N, 58°51′ E **184**
Ülkennaryn, *Kaz.* 49°13′ N, 84°31′ E **184**
Ulla, *Belarus* 55°12′ N, 29°15′ E **166**
Ullared, *Nor.* 57°9′ N, 12°42′ E **152**
Ulldecona, *Sp.* 40°35′ N, 0°26′ E **164**
Ulleung, *S. Korea* 37°31′ N, 130°55′ E **200**
Ulloma, *Bol.* 17°37′ S, 68°29′ W **137**
Ullswater, lake, *U.K.* 54°34′ N, 2°59′ W **162**
Ulm, *Ger.* 48°24′ N, 9°59′ E **152**
Ulmen, *Ger.* 50°12′ N, 6°59′ E **163**
Ulmeni, *Rom.* 47°27′ N, 23°19′ E **168**
Ulmer, Mount, peak, *Antarctica* 77°32′ S, 87°5′ W **248**
Ulog, *Bosn. and Herzg.* 43°24′ N, 18°17′ E **168**
Ulrichstein, *Ger.* 50°34′ N, 9°12′ E **167**
Ulsan, *S. Korea* 35°33′ N, 129°21′ E **200**
Ulsteinvik, *Nor.* 62°20′ N, 5°52′ E **152**
Ulu Dağ (Olympus, Mount), peak, *Turk.* 40°4′ N, 29°7′ E **156**
Ulubat Gölü, lake, *Turk.* 40°4′ N, 28°7′ E **156**
Uluborlu, *Turk.* 38°5′ N, 30°28′ E **156**
Ulugan Bay 10°1′ N, 118°25′ E **203**
Ulugqat, *China* 39°49′ N, 74°21′ E **197**
Uluguru Mountains, *Tanzania* 7°28′ S, 37°2′ E **224**
Ulukışla, *Turk.* 37°32′ N, 34°28′ E **156**
Ulul, island, *F.S.M.* 8°19′ N, 149°8′ E **192**
Ulundi, *S. Af.* 28°17′ S, 31°33′ E **227**
Ulungur Hu, lake, *China* 47°14′ N, 86°46′ E **184**
Ulungur, river, *China* 46°35′ N, 87°38′ E **184**
Ulupō Heiau, site, *Hawai'i, U.S.* 21°22′ N, 157°47′ W **99**
Uluru (Ayers Rock), peak, *Austral.* 25°23′ S, 130°52′ E **230**
Ulus, *Turk.* 41°36′ N, 32°38′ E **158**
Uluyul, river, *Russ.* 57°34′ N, 85°49′ E **169**
Ulverston, *U.K.* 54°12′ N, 3°6′ W **162**
Ulvöhamn, *Sw.* 63°1′ N, 18°38′ E **152**
Ulvvik, *Nor.* 62°40′ N, 17°50′ E **152**
Uly Balkan Gershi, *Turkm.* 39°30′ N, 54°0′ E **180**
Ul'ya, *Russ.* 58°57′ N, 141°46′ E **160**
Ul'yanovka, *Russ.* 59°38′ N, 30°46′ E **166**
Ul'yanovsk, *Russ.* 54°19′ N, 48°24′ E **154**
Ul'Yanovsk, adm. division, *Russ.* 53°58′ N, 46°12′ E **154**
Ül'yanovskīy, *Kaz.* 50°4′ N, 73°47′ E **184**
Ulysses, *Kans., U.S.* 37°34′ N, 101°22′ W **90**
Ūlytaū, *Kaz.* 48°25′ N, 66°48′ E **184**
Ulyzhylanshyq, river, *Kaz.* 49°32′ N, 64°32′ E **184**
Umag, *Croatia* 45°25′ N, 13°32′ E **167**
Umala, *Bol.* 17°22′ S, 67°59′ W **137**
Umán, *Mex.* 20°51′ N, 89°46′ W **116**
Uman', *Ukr.* 48°44′ N, 30°23′ E **158**
Umaria, *India* 23°30′ N, 80°50′ E **197**
Umarkot, *Pak.* 25°22′ N, 69°44′ E **186**
Umasi La, pass, *India* 33°26′ N, 76°36′ E **186**
Umatilla, *Oreg., U.S.* 45°53′ N, 119°22′ W **90**
Umb Ozero, lake, *Russ.* 67°35′ N, 34°0′ E **152**
Umba, *Russ.* 66°40′ N, 34°16′ E **152**
Umbelasha, river, *Sudan* 9°29′ N, 24°3′ E **224**
Umberto Primo, *Arg.* 30°54′ S, 61°21′ W **139**
Umboi, island, *P.N.G.* 5°59′ S, 147°5′ E **192**
Umbria, adm. division, *It.* 42°41′ N, 11°58′ E **156**
Umbukta, *Nor.* 66°9′ N, 14°35′ E **152**
Umčari, *Serb. and Mont.* 44°34′ N, 20°44′ E **168**
Umeå, *Nor.* 63°49′ N, 20°15′ E **152**
Umfors, *Nor.* 65°57′ N, 15°2′ E **152**
Umm al 'Abīd, *Lib.* 27°30′ N, 15°1′ E **216**
Umm al Arānib, *Lib.* 26°9′ N, 14°45′ E **216**
Umm al Qaywayn, *U.A.E.* 25°33′ N, 55°33′ E **196**
Umm az Zumūl, spring, *Saudi Arabia* 22°36′ N, 55°20′ E **182**
Umm Badr, spring, *Sudan* 14°10′ N, 27°56′ E **226**
Umm Bel, *Sudan* 13°31′ N, 28°3′ E **226**
Umm Buru, spring, *Sudan* 15°1′ N, 23°45′ E **226**
Umm Busha, *Sudan* 13°25′ N, 30°35′ E **226**
Umm Dam, *Sudan* 13°46′ N, 30°58′ E **226**
Umm Gudair, oil field, *Kuwait* 28°49′ N, 47°39′ E **196**
Umm Hagar, *Eritrea* 14°16′ N, 36°37′ E **182**
Umm Haraz, *Sudan* 11°57′ N, 23°10′ E **216**
Umm Keddada, *Sudan* 13°35′ N, 26°39′ E **226**
Umm Lahai, spring, *Sudan* 15°38′ N, 25°50′ E **226**
Umm Lajj, *Saudi Arabia* 25°4′ N, 37°15′ E **182**
Umm Qaşr, *Iraq* 30°2′ N, 47°55′ E **196**
Umm Qays, *Jordan* 32°39′ N, 35°40′ E **194**
Umm Qozein, spring, *Sudan* 14°15′ N, 27°16′ E **226**
Umm Rahau, *Sudan* 18°53′ N, 32°0′ E **182**
Umm Ruwaba, *Sudan* 12°52′ N, 31°11′ E **216**
Umm Sa'īd, *Qatar* 24°58′ N, 51°33′ E **196**
Umm Saiyala, *Sudan* 14°24′ N, 31°9′ E **226**
Umm Shalil, *Sudan* 10°50′ N, 23°41′ E **224**
Umm Shanqa, *Sudan* 13°12′ N, 27°11′ E **226**
Umm Urūmah, island, *Saudi Arabia* 25°48′ N, 35°31′ E **182**
Umniati, *Zimb.* 18°41′ S, 29°46′ E **224**
Umpulo, *Angola* 12°43′ S, 17°39′ E **220**
Umreth, *India* 22°38′ N, 73°5′ E **186**
Umtanum Ridge, *Wash., U.S.* 46°50′ N, 120°53′ W **90**
Umtata, *S. Af.* 31°35′ S, 28°41′ E **227**
Umuahia, *Nig.* 5°33′ N, 7°30′ E **222**
Umuarama, *Braz.* 23°47′ S, 53°27′ W **138**
Umzimkulu, *S. Af.* 30°16′ S, 29°58′ E **227**
Umzimvubu, *S. Af.* 31°31′ S, 29°24′ E **207**
Umzinto, *S. Af.* 30°19′ S, 30°36′ E **227**
Una, *Russ.* 64°36′ N, 38°5′ E **154**
Una, river, *Bosn. and Herzg.* 44°39′ N, 16°0′ E **168**
Unac, river, *Bosn. and Herzg.* 44°22′ N, 16°24′ E **168**
Unadilla, *Ga., U.S.* 32°15′ N, 83°45′ W **96**
Unaí, *Braz.* 16°24′ S, 46°54′ W **138**
Unalakleet, *Alas., U.S.* 63°50′ N, 160°39′ W **106**
Unalaska, *Alas., U.S.* 53°51′ N, 166°33′ W **238**
Unalaska Island, *Alas., U.S.* 53°58′ N, 168°29′ W **98**
Unango, *Mozambique* 12°52′ S, 35°25′ E **224**
Unari, *Fin.* 67°8′ N, 25°42′ E **152**
'Unayzah, *Jordan* 30°28′ N, 35°47′ E **194**
'Unayzah, *Saudi Arabia* 26°5′ N, 43°59′ E **182**
'Unayzah, Jabal, peak, *Iraq* 32°9′ N, 39°13′ E **180**
Uncastillo, *Sp.* 42°21′ N, 1°8′ W **164**
Uncasville, *Conn., U.S.* 41°25′ N, 72°7′ W **104**
Uncía, *Bol.* 18°29′ S, 66°39′ W **137**
Uncompahgre Peak, *Colo., U.S.* 38°3′ N, 107°32′ W **90**
Underberg, *S. Af.* 29°49′ S, 29°30′ E **227**
Underhill, *Vt., U.S.* 44°31′ N, 72°57′ W **104**
Underwood, *N. Dak., U.S.* 47°26′ N, 101°9′ W **90**
Ŭndŏk, *N. Korea* 42°32′ N, 130°19′ E **200**
Unduksa, *Russ.* 65°39′ N, 34°4′ E **152**
Unecha, *Russ.* 52°49′ N, 32°44′ E **154**
Uneiuxi, river, *Braz.* 1°8′ S, 66°18′ W **136**
Ungava Bay 59°10′ N, 68°2′ W **106**
Unggi, *N. Korea* 42°29′ N, 130°25′ E **190**
Unggok, *S. Korea* 34°36′ N, 126°2′ E **200**
Unhŭng, *N. Korea* 41°17′ N, 128°31′ E **200**
União, *Braz.* 4°36′ S, 42°52′ W **132**
União, *Braz.* 9°18′ S, 70°58′ W **137**
União da Vitória, *Braz.* 26°15′ S, 51°8′ W **139**
Unicoi, *Tenn., U.S.* 36°11′ N, 82°21′ W **96**
Unimak Island, *Alas., U.S.* 55°1′ N, 164°53′ W **98**
Union, *La., U.S.* 30°4′ N, 90°54′ W **103**
Union, *Miss., U.S.* 32°34′ N, 89°7′ W **103**
Union, *N.H., U.S.* 43°29′ N, 71°3′ W **104**
Union, *Oreg., U.S.* 45°12′ N, 117°52′ W **90**
Union, *S.C., U.S.* 34°42′ N, 81°38′ W **96**
Union, *Wash., U.S.* 47°19′ N, 123°6′ W **100**
Union Bay, *Can.* 49°34′ N, 124°54′ W **100**
Union City, *Ind., U.S.* 40°11′ N, 84°49′ W **102**
Union City, *Mich., U.S.* 42°4′ N, 85°8′ W **102**
Union City, *Tenn., U.S.* 36°24′ N, 89°3′ W **96**
Unión de Tula, *Mex.* 19°56′ N, 104°17′ W **114**
Union Grove, *Wis., U.S.* 42°41′ N, 88°4′ W **102**

Union, islands, *Caribbean Sea* 12°47' N, 61°42' W **116**
Union Pass, *Wyo., U.S.* 43°28' N, 109°51' W **90**
Union Springs, *Ala., U.S.* 32°8' N, 85°43' W **96**
Uniondale, *S. Af.* 33°40' S, 23°6' E **227**
Uniontown, *Ala., U.S.* 32°27' N, 87°32' W **103**
Uniontown, *Pa., U.S.* 39°54' N, 79°45' W **94**
Unionville, *Mich., U.S.* 43°38' N, 83°28' W **102**
United Arab Emirates 24°7' N, 54°35' E **196**
United Kingdom 51°54' N, 2°36' W **150**
United States 39°40' N, 101°22' W **82**
United States Naval Base Guantánamo Bay, *Cuba* 19°53' N, 75°14' W **115**
Unity, *Can.* 52°26' N, 109°10' W **108**
Unity, adm. division, *Sudan* 8°46' N, 29°13' E **224**
Universales, Montes, *Sp.* 40°18' N, 1°37' W **164**
University Park, *Iowa, U.S.* 41°16' N, 92°36' W **94**
Unknown Lake, *Can.* 58°19' N, 105°10' W **108**
Unna, *Ger.* 51°32' N, 7°41' E **167**
Unnao, *India* 26°32' N, 80°29' E **197**
Ŭnnyul, *N. Korea* 38°29' N, 125°12' E **200**
Unsan, *N. Korea* 40°5' N, 125°52' E **200**
Unuk, river, *Can.* 56°12' N, 131°1' W **108**
Ünye, *Turk.* 41°7' N, 37°16' E **156**
Unzen-Amakusa National Park, *Japan* 32°27' N, 130°11' E **201**
Unzha, *Russ.* 58°0' N, 44°2' E **154**
Uozu, *Japan* 36°49' N, 137°24' E **201**
Upemba National Park, *Dem. Rep. of the Congo* 9°6' S, 25°37' E **224**
Upernavik 72°49' N, 56°14' W **106**
Upernavik Kujalleq 72°9' N, 55°36' W **106**
Upham, *N. Dak., U.S.* 48°34' N, 100°45' W **90**
Upía, river, *Col.* 4°38' N, 73°10' W **136**
Upington, *S. Af.* 28°25' S, 21°13' E **227**
Upland, *Calif., U.S.* 34°5' N, 117°40' W **101**
Upoloksha, *Russ.* 67°32' N, 31°56' E **152**
Upolu, island, *Samoa* 13°56' S, 171°50' W **241**
Upper Arlington, *Ohio, U.S.* 40°0' N, 83°3' W **102**
Upper Delaware Scenic and Recreational River, *N.Y., U.S.* 41°45' N, 82°49' W **80**
Upper Foster Lake, lake, *Can.* 56°48' N, 105°45' W **108**
Upper Goose Lake, lake, *Can.* 51°42' N, 93°24' W **110**
Upper Laberge, *Can.* 60°57' N, 135°7' W **98**
Upper Lake, *Calif., U.S.* 41°45' N, 120°35' W **90**
Upper Liard, *Can.* 60°3' N, 128°59' W **108**
Upper Missouri River Breaks National Monument, *Mont., U.S.* 47°43' N, 110°27' W **90**
Upper Nile, adm. division, *Sudan* 11°36' N, 32°24' E **182**
Upper Roslyn Lake, lake, *Can.* 49°14' N, 88°9' W **94**
Upper Sandusky, *Ohio, U.S.* 40°48' N, 83°18' W **102**
Uppingham, *U.K.* 52°35' N, 0°44' E **162**
Upplands Väsby, *Sw.* 59°31' N, 17°52' E **166**
Uppsala, *Sw.* 59°51' N, 17°38' E **166**
Uprang, *China* 36°36' N, 75°56' E **186**
Upstart Bay 19°49' S, 146°34' E **230**
Upton, *Wyo., U.S.* 44°5' N, 104°37' W **90**
Uqturpan see Wushi, *China* 41°9' N, 79°17' E **184**
Urabá, Golfo de 8°18' N, 77°25' W **136**
Urad Houqi, *China* 41°30' N, 107°3' E **198**
Urad Qianqi, *China* 40°41' N, 108°38' E **198**
Urad Zhongqi, *China* 41°33' N, 108°33' E **198**
Ural Mountains, *Russ.* 63°37' N, 58°26' E **154**
Ural, river, *Kaz.-Russ.* 52°59' N, 58°53' E **154**
Urambo, *Tanzania* 5°3' S, 32°4' E **224**
Urandi, *Braz.* 14°48' S, 42°40' W **138**
Urania, *La., U.S.* 31°51' N, 92°18' W **103**
Uranium City, *Can.* 59°33' N, 108°42' W **106**
Uraricoera, *Braz.* 3°27' N, 61°1' W **130**
Uravan, *Colo., U.S.* 38°23' N, 108°44' W **90**
Urawa, *Japan* 35°51' N, 139°39' E **201**
Uray, *Russ.* 60°6' N, 65°2' E **169**
'Uray'irah, *Saudi Arabia* 25°56' N, 48°53' E **182**
Urbana, *Ark., U.S.* 33°8' N, 92°27' W **103**
Urbana, *Ill., U.S.* 40°5' N, 88°13' W **102**
Urbana, *Ohio, U.S.* 40°6' N, 83°45' W **102**
Urbandale, *Iowa, U.S.* 41°37' N, 93°43' W **94**
Urbania, *It.* 43°40' N, 12°32' E **156**
Urbano Santos, *Braz.* 3°13' S, 43°25' W **132**
Urbel, river, *Sp.* 42°40' N, 3°57' W **164**
Urbino, *It.* 43°43' N, 12°38' E **167**
Urbión, Picos de, *Sp.* 42°5' N, 2°58' W **164**
Urcos, *Peru* 13°45' S, 71°40' W **137**
Urda, *Sp.* 39°24' N, 3°43' W **164**
Urdos, *Fr.* 42°52' N, 0°33' E **164**
Ure, river, *U.K.* 54°16' N, 1°49' W **162**
Urechcha, *Belarus* 52°56' N, 27°51' E **152**
Ureliki, *Russ.* 64°24' N, 173°17' W **98**
Uren', *Russ.* 57°27' N, 45°51' E **154**
Urengoy, *Russ.* 65°54' N, 78°30' E **169**
Urenui, *N.Z.* 39°1' S, 174°26' E **240**
Ures, *Mex.* 29°25' N, 110°24' W **92**
Urgut, *Uzb.* 39°22' N, 67°18' E **197**
Uri, *India* 34°3' N, 74°4' E **188**
Uriah, *Ala., U.S.* 31°17' N, 87°30' W **103**
Uriah, Mount, peak, *N.Z.* 42°3' S, 171°33' E **240**
Uribe, *Col.* 3°13' N, 74°25' W **136**
Uribia, *Col.* 11°41' N, 72°17' W **136**
Urimán, *Venez.* 5°23' N, 62°43' W **130**
Uriondo, *Bol.* 21°42' S, 64°46' W **137**
Urique, river, *Mex.* 27°18' N, 107°56' W **80**
Uritsk, *Russ.* 59°49' N, 30°8' E **166**
Urjala, *Fin.* 61°4' N, 23°31' E **166**
Urk, *Neth.* 52°40' N, 5°35' E **163**
Úrkút, *Hung.* 47°4' N, 17°38' E **168**
Urkut, *Somalia* 3°29' N, 42°44' E **218**
Urla, *Turk.* 38°18' N, 26°44' E **156**
Urman, *Russ.* 54°53' N, 56°56' E **154**
Urmia, Lake see Orūmīyeh, Daryācheh-ye, *Iran* 38°7' N, 45°16' E **195**
Urmia see Orūmīyeh, *Iran* 37°37' N, 45°4' E **195**
Uroševac, *Europe* 42°22' N, 21°9' E **168**
Üroteppa see Istaravshan, *Taj.* 39°53' N, 69°0' E **197**
Urroz, *Sp.* 42°46' N, 1°29' W **164**
Ursus, *Pol.* 52°11' N, 20°50' E **152**
Urszulin, *Pol.* 51°23' N, 23°11' E **152**
Urt Moron, river, *China* 37°3' N, 93°7' E **188**
Uruaçu, *Braz.* 14°33' S, 49°12' W **138**
Uruana, *Braz.* 15°33' S, 49°41' W **138**
Uruapan, *Mex.* 19°24' N, 102°4' W **114**
Urubamba, *Peru* 13°19' S, 72°8' W **130**
Urubamba, river, *Peru* 10°42' S, 73°24' W **137**
Urubaxi, river, *Braz.* 1°30' S, 64°53' W **130**
Urubuquara, Serra, peak, *Braz.* 3°34' S, 52°27' W **130**
Uruçanga, *Braz.* 28°32' S, 49°19' W **138**
Urucará, *Braz.* 2°31' S, 57°46' W **130**
Urucu, river, *Braz.* 4°18' S, 64°15' W **130**
Uruçuí, *Braz.* 7°17' S, 44°34' W **132**
Uruçuí, Serra do, *Braz.* 9°25' S, 45°41' W **130**
Urucuia, *Braz.* 16°8' S, 45°45' W **138**
Urucuia, river, *Braz.* 15°33' S, 46°47' W **138**
Urucurituba, *Braz.* 2°40' S, 57°39' W **130**
Urugi, *Japan* 35°17' N, 137°44' E **201**
Uruguai, river, *Braz.* 27°14' S, 54°6' W **139**
Uruguaiana, *Braz.* 29°48' S, 57°5' W **139**
Uruguay 32°54' S, 55°57' W **139**
Uruguay, river, *South America* 27°36' S, 55°4' W **134**
Urukthapel (Ngeruktabel), island, *Palau* 7°13' N, 134°24' E **242**
Ürümqi, *China* 43°46' N, 87°37' E **184**
Urung, *Indonesia* 2°39' N, 96°4' E **196**
Urup, island, *Russ.* 45°21' N, 148°49' E **190**
Urupá, river, *Braz.* 11°13' S, 62°43' W **130**
Urussu, *Russ.* 54°37' N, 53°25' E **154**
Urutaí, *Braz.* 17°29' S, 48°11' W **138**
Uruti, *N.Z.* 38°59' S, 174°32' E **240**
Uruwira, *Tanzania* 6°24' S, 31°22' E **224**
Urville, Tanjung d', *Indonesia* 1°31' S, 137°53' E **192**
Uryupinsk, *Russ.* 50°47' N, 41°57' E **158**
Ürzhar, *Kaz.* 47°4' N, 81°35' E **184**
Urzhum, *Russ.* 57°8' N, 50°1' E **154**
Us Nuur, Har, lake, *Mongolia* 48°7' N, 91°1' E **190**
Usa, *Japan* 33°28' N, 133°26' E **201**
Usa, river, *Russ.* 66°8' N, 58°13' E **160**
Uşak, *Turk.* 38°40' N, 29°24' E **156**
Usakos, *Namibia* 22°2' S, 15°36' E **227**
Usambara Mountains, peak, *Tanzania* 4°33' S, 38°15' E **224**
Usarp Mountains, *Antarctica* 71°32' S, 161°30' E **248**
Ušće, *Serb. and Mont.* 43°27' N, 20°37' E **168**
Used, *Sp.* 41°3' N, 1°33' W **164**
Useko, *Tanzania* 5°6' S, 32°33' E **224**
Ushachy, *Belarus* 55°10' N, 28°33' E **166**
Ushakova, Ostrov, island, *Russ.* 80°20' N, 74°7' E **160**
Üsharal, *Kaz.* 46°11' N, 80°54' E **184**
'Ushayrah, *Saudi Arabia* 21°43' N, 40°39' E **182**
Ushetu, *Tanzania* 4°10' S, 32°16' E **224**
Ushibuka, *Japan* 32°12' N, 130°1' E **201**
Üshtöbe, *Kaz.* 45°14' N, 77°58' E **184**
Ushtobe, *Kaz.* 45°18' N, 78°3' E **173**
Ushuaia, *Arg.* 54°43' S, 68°18' W **134**
Ushumun, *Russ.* 52°45' N, 126°37' E **190**
Usinge, *Tanzania* 5°6' S, 31°16' E **224**
Usingen, *Ger.* 50°19' N, 8°32' E **167**
Usinsk, *Russ.* 65°58' N, 57°27' E **154**
Usk, *Can.* 54°38' N, 128°27' W **108**
Usk, river, *U.K.* 51°54' N, 3°17' W **162**
Uska, *India* 27°11' N, 83°5' E **197**
Uskoplje see Gornji Vakuf, *Bosn. and Herzg.* 43°55' N, 17°33' E **168**
Üsküdar, *Turk.* 41°1' N, 29°1' E **156**
Uslar, *Ger.* 51°39' N, 9°38' E **167**
Usman', *Russ.* 52°0' N, 39°36' E **158**
Usmas Ezers, lake, *Latv.* 57°10' N, 21°57' E **166**
Usogorsk, *Russ.* 63°25' N, 48°43' E **154**
Usol'ye, *Russ.* 59°25' N, 56°35' E **154**
Usol'ye Sibirskoye, *Russ.* 52°47' N, 103°33' E **173**
Usove, *Ukr.* 51°20' N, 28°5' E **152**
Üspenka, *Kaz.* 52°54' N, 77°22' E **184**
Uspenovka, *Kaz.* 43°12' N, 74°29' E **184**
U.S.S. Arizona Memorial, *Pacific Ocean* 21°21' N, 157°60' W **99**
Usson, *Fr.* 42°44' N, 2°5' E **164**
Ussuriysk, *Russ.* 43°53' N, 132°4' E **190**
Ust' Alekseyevo, *Russ.* 60°28' N, 46°31' E **154**
Ust' Baikha, *Russ.* 65°48' N, 86°14' E **169**
Ust' Barguzin, *Russ.* 53°29' N, 109°8' E **190**
Ust' Bol'sheretsk, *Russ.* 52°58' N, 156°14' E **160**
Ust' Buzulukskaya, *Russ.* 50°7' N, 42°5' E **158**
Ust' Chaun, *Russ.* 68°42' N, 170°21' E **160**
Ust' Chernaya, *Russ.* 60°27' N, 52°41' E **154**
Ust' Ilimsk, *Russ.* 57°46' N, 102°17' E **160**
Ust' Ilych, *Russ.* 62°31' N, 56°48' E **154**
Ust' Ishim, *Russ.* 57°35' N, 71°1' E **160**
Ust' Izes, *Russ.* 55°57' N, 76°55' E **184**
Ust' Izhma, *Russ.* 65°17' N, 52°58' E **154**
Ust' Kalmanka, *Russ.* 52°7' N, 83°28' E **184**
Ust' Kamchatsk, *Russ.* 56°18' N, 162°17' E **160**
Ust' Kamenogorsk see Öskemen, *Kaz.* 49°59' N, 82°38' E **184**
Ust' Kan, *Russ.* 51°2' N, 84°50' E **184**
Ust' Kara, *Russ.* 69°11' N, 65°7' E **169**
Ust' Katav, *Russ.* 54°56' N, 58°14' E **154**
Ust' Khayryuzovo, *Russ.* 57°10' N, 156°50' E **160**
Ust' Kosa, *Russ.* 60°12' N, 55°15' E **154**
Ust' Kozha, *Russ.* 63°37' N, 38°43' E **154**
Ust' Kulom, *Russ.* 61°41' N, 53°46' E **154**
Ust' Kurenga, *Russ.* 57°26' N, 75°32' E **169**
Ust' Kureyka, *Russ.* 66°25' N, 87°23' E **169**
Ust' Kut, *Russ.* 56°55' N, 105°58' E **160**
Ust' Kuyga, *Russ.* 70°5' N, 135°32' E **160**
Ust' Labinsk, *Russ.* 45°15' N, 39°39' E **158**
Ust' Luga, *Russ.* 59°38' N, 28°14' E **166**
Ust' Lyzha, *Russ.* 65°42' N, 56°38' E **154**
Ust' Maya, *Russ.* 60°29' N, 134°29' E **160**
Ust' Mil', *Russ.* 59°45' N, 132°55' E **160**
Ust' Nem, *Russ.* 61°38' N, 54°48' E **154**
Ust' Nera, *Russ.* 64°31' N, 143°13' E **160**
Ust' Nyukzha, *Russ.* 56°25' N, 121°35' E **160**
Ust' Olenek, *Russ.* 72°53' N, 119°39' E **160**
Ust' Ordynskiy, *Russ.* 52°51' N, 104°47' E **190**
Ust' Ordynskiy Buryat, adm. division, *Russ.* 53°23' N, 102°46' E **160**
Ust' Ozernoye, *Russ.* 58°53' N, 87°48' E **169**
Ust' Paden'ga, *Russ.* 61°51' N, 42°37' E **154**
Ust' Pinega, *Russ.* 64°10' N, 42°2' E **154**
Ust' Pit, *Russ.* 58°59' N, 91°53' E **169**
Ust' Port, *Russ.* 69°44' N, 84°25' E **169**
Ust' Shchugor, *Russ.* 64°18' N, 57°30' E **154**
Ust' Shonosha, *Russ.* 61°11' N, 41°16' E **154**
Ust' Tara, *Russ.* 56°40' N, 74°46' E **169**
Ust' Tareya, *Russ.* 73°22' N, 90°50' E **160**
Ust' Tigil', *Russ.* 57°56' N, 158°12' E **173**
Ust' Tsil'ma, *Russ.* 65°26' N, 52°11' E **154**
Ust' Ulagan, *Russ.* 50°41' N, 87°57' E **184**
Ust' Uls, *Russ.* 60°35' N, 58°28' E **154**
Ust' Un'ya, *Russ.* 61°49' N, 57°51' E **154**
Ust' Ura, *Russ.* 63°7' N, 44°48' E **154**
Ust' Usa, *Russ.* 65°59' N, 56°59' E **154**
Ust' Vayen'ga, *Russ.* 63°0' N, 42°44' E **154**
Ust' Voya, *Russ.* 64°28' N, 57°37' E **154**
Ust' Voyampolka, *Russ.* 58°30' N, 159°20' E **160**
Ust' Vym', *Russ.* 62°15' N, 50°25' E **154**
Ust' Yegralyaga, *Russ.* 62°27' N, 59°4' E **154**
Ust' Yudoma, *Russ.* 59°14' N, 135°9' E **160**
Ustaoset, *Nor.* 60°30' N, 8°0' E **152**
Ust'-Dolyssy, *Russ.* 56°9' N, 29°42' E **166**
Ústí nad Labem, *Czech Rep.* 50°39' N, 14°2' E **152**
Ustica, *It.* 38°42' N, 13°11' E **156**
Ustiprača, *Bosn. and Herzg.* 43°42' N, 19°6' E **168**
Ustrem, *Russ.* 64°18' N, 65°28' E **169**
Ust'ye, *Russ.* 59°38' N, 39°40' E **154**
Ustyluh, *Ukr.* 50°51' N, 24°9' E **158**
Ustyurt Plateau, *Uzb.* 42°38' N, 55°45' E **158**
Ustyuzhna, *Russ.* 58°49' N, 36°29' E **154**
Usu, *China* 44°27' N, 84°41' E **184**
Usuki, *Japan* 33°7' N, 131°47' E **201**
Usure, *Tanzania* 4°39' S, 34°19' E **224**
Us'va, *Russ.* 58°41' N, 57°39' E **154**
Usvyaty, *Russ.* 55°44' N, 30°49' E **154**
Utah, adm. division, *Utah, U.S.* 39°29' N, 112°5' W **92**
Utah Beach, *Fr.* 49°24' N, 1°36' W **150**
Utajärvi, *Fin.* 64°44' N, 26°23' E **152**
'Utaybah, *Syr.* 33°29' N, 36°36' E **194**
Utegi, *Tanzania* 1°23' S, 34°13' E **224**
Utembo, river, *Angola* 16°30' S, 21°27' E **220**
Utena, *Lith.* 55°29' N, 25°35' E **166**
Utete, *Tanzania* 7°60' S, 38°46' E **224**
Uthai Thani, *Thai.* 15°21' N, 100°2' E **202**
Uthal, *Pak.* 25°45' N, 66°38' E **186**
Uthina, ruin(s), *Tun.* 36°36' N, 10°5' E **156**
Utiariti, *Braz.* 13°3' S, 58°21' W **130**
Utica, *Ill., U.S.* 41°20' N, 89°1' W **102**
Utica, *Miss., U.S.* 32°6' N, 90°38' W **103**
Utica, *Mo., U.S.* 41°20' N, 89°1' W **110**
Utica, *N.Y., U.S.* 43°6' N, 75°14' W **94**
Utica, *Ohio, U.S.* 40°13' N, 82°26' W **102**
Utica, ruin(s), *Tun.* 37°3' N, 9°57' E **156**
Utiel, *Sp.* 39°34' N, 1°13' W **164**
Utiku, *N.Z.* 39°47' S, 175°50' E **240**
Utikuma, river, *Can.* 56°5' N, 115°18' W **108**
Utila, Isla de, island, *Hond.* 16°8' N, 87°17' W **115**
Utkholok, *Russ.* 57°35' N, 157°8' E **173**
Uto, *Japan* 32°41' N, 130°41' E **201**
Utö, island, *Sw.* 58°54' N, 18°19' E **166**
Utonkon, *Nig.* 6°55' N, 8°3' E **222**
Utraula, *India* 27°17' N, 82°23' E **197**
Utrecht, *Neth.* 52°4' N, 5°6' E **167**
Utrecht, *S. Af.* 27°40' S, 30°18' E **227**
Utrera, *Sp.* 37°11' N, 5°48' W **164**
Utroya, river, *Russ.* 57°8' N, 28°15' E **166**
Utsunomiya, *Japan* 36°33' N, 139°52' E **201**
Utta, *Russ.* 46°20' N, 45°55' E **158**
Uttar Pradesh, adm. division, *India* 27°12' N, 79°59' E **197**
Uttaradit, *Thai.* 17°39' N, 100°5' E **202**
Uttaranchal, adm. division, *India* 29°54' N, 78°19' E **197**
Uttoxeter, *U.K.* 52°53' N, 1°53' W **162**
Utuado 18°15' N, 66°44' W **116**
Utubulak, *China* 46°51' N, 86°26' E **184**
Utukok, river, *Alas., U.S.* 69°53' N, 161°22' W **98**
Uubulan, *Mongolia* 48°36' N, 101°54' E **198**
Uummannaq 70°36' N, 52°9' W **106**
Uummannaq, island, *Uummannaq* 62°51' N, 41°19' W **106**
Uummannaq Kangerlua 70°45' N, 56°41' W **106**
Uurainen, *Fin.* 62°29' N, 25°25' E **152**
Uusikaarlepyy see Nykarleby, *Fin.* 63°31' N, 22°32' E **152**
Uusikaupunki, *Fin.* 60°47' N, 21°24' E **166**
Uva, *Russ.* 56°57' N, 52°15' E **154**
Uvá, river, *Col.* 3°38' N, 70°3' W **136**
Uvac, river, *Serb. and Mont.* 43°33' N, 19°38' E **168**
Uvalde, *Tex., U.S.* 29°11' N, 99°47' W **92**
Uvarovo, *Russ.* 51°57' N, 42°9' E **158**
Uvat, *Russ.* 59°4' N, 68°52' E **169**
Uvel'skiy, *Russ.* 54°29' N, 61°19' E **154**
Uvinza, *Tanzania* 5°4' S, 30°20' E **224**
Uvira, *Dem. Rep. of the Congo* 3°27' S, 29°4' E **224**
Uvs, adm. division, *Mongolia* 49°54' N, 90°12' E **184**
Uvs Nuur, lake, *Mongolia* 50°29' N, 90°48' E **172**
Uwajima, *Japan* 33°12' N, 132°33' E **201**
'Uweinat, Jebel (Al 'Uwaynāt), peak, *Sudan* 21°51' N, 24°58' E **226**
Uwi, island, *Indonesia* 1°5' N, 107°5' E **196**
Uxbridge, *Mass., U.S.* 42°4' N, 71°39' W **104**
Uxin Qi (Dabqig), *China* 38°24' N, 108°59' E **198**
Uxmal, ruin(s), *Mex.* 20°17' N, 89°54' W **115**
Uy, river, *Russ.* 54°11' N, 60°11' E **154**
Uyar, *Russ.* 55°40' N, 94°17' E **160**
Üydzin, *Mongolia* 44°7' N, 107°1' E **198**
Uyo, *Nig.* 5°3' N, 7°56' E **222**
Uyowa, *Tanzania* 4°33' S, 32°1' E **224**
Uyuni, *Bol.* 20°33' S, 66°55' W **137**
Uza, river, *Russ.* 52°48' N, 45°39' E **158**
Užava, *Latv.* 57°14' N, 21°27' E **166**
Užava, river, *Latv.* 57°8' N, 21°24' E **166**
Uzbekistan 41°0' N, 63°0' E **184**
Uzbel Shankou, pass, *China* 38°39' N, 73°48' E **197**
Uzcudún, *Arg.* 44°13' S, 66°7' W **134**
Uzdin, *Serb. and Mont.* 45°12' N, 20°37' E **168**
Uzhur, *Russ.* 55°21' N, 89°52' E **169**
Užice, *Serb. and Mont.* 43°51' N, 19°50' E **168**
Uzlovaya, *Russ.* 53°57' N, 38°8' E **154**
Üzümlü, *Turk.* 36°44' N, 29°13' E **156**
Uzunköprü, *Turk.* 41°14' N, 26°39' E **156**
Užventis, *Lith.* 55°46' N, 22°39' E **166**
Uzynaghash, *Kaz.* 43°14' N, 76°16' E **184**
Uzynköl, *Kaz.* 53°57' N, 64°52' E **184**

V

Vääksy, *Fin.* 61°9' N, 25°32' E **166**
Vaal, river, *S. Af.* 26°51' S, 29°39' E **227**
Vaala, *Fin.* 64°33' N, 26°48' E **152**
Vaals, *Neth.* 50°46' N, 6°0' E **167**
Vääna, *Est.* 59°22' N, 24°23' E **166**
Vaasa, *Fin.* 63°4' N, 21°42' E **160**
Vaasa (Vasa), *Fin.* 63°5' N, 21°37' E **152**
Vabalninkas, *Lith.* 55°58' N, 24°43' E **166**
Vác, *Hung.* 47°45' N, 19°10' E **168**
Vacaria, *Braz.* 28°31' S, 50°55' W **139**
Vacaville, *Calif., U.S.* 38°21' N, 121°60' W **100**
Vacha, *Ger.* 50°49' N, 10°1' E **167**
Väddö, *Sw.* 60°0' N, 18°49' E **166**
Vader, *Wash., U.S.* 46°23' N, 122°58' W **100**
Vadheim, *Nor.* 61°12' N, 5°49' E **152**
Vadodara, *India* 22°17' N, 73°13' E **186**
Vadsø, *Nor.* 70°10' N, 29°50' E **160**
Vaduz, *Liech.* 47°6' N, 9°22' E **156**
Vaga, river, *Russ.* 61°42' N, 42°48' E **154**
Vagan, *Bosn. and Herzg.* 44°10' N, 17°9' E **168**
Vagay, river, *Russ.* 56°29' N, 68°53' E **169**
Vågen, *Nor.* 64°39' N, 13°43' E **152**
Vaiden, *Miss., U.S.* 33°17' N, 89°45' W **103**
Väike Maarja, *Est.* 59°5' N, 26°15' E **166**
Vailly, *Fr.* 49°24' N, 3°30' E **163**
Vainikkala, *Fin.* 60°51' N, 28°18' E **166**
Vaiņode, *Latv.* 56°25' N, 21°50' E **166**
Vakh, river, *Russ.* 60°45' N, 79°42' E **160**
Vakh, river, *Russ.* 61°22' N, 83°43' E **169**
Vakhsh, river, *Taj.* 37°50' N, 68°58' E **197**
Vakhtan, *Russ.* 57°56' N, 46°45' E **154**
Vál, *Hung.* 47°20' N, 18°39' E **168**
Val Grande National Park, *It.* 45°57' N, 8°7' E **167**
Val Marie, *Can.* 49°13' N, 107°45' W **90**
Val Verde Park, *Calif., U.S.* 34°27' N, 118°41' W **101**
Vala, river, *Russ.* 56°41' N, 52°16' E **154**
Valaam, *Russ.* 61°21' N, 30°58' E **166**
Valaichchenai, *Sri Lanka* 7°54' N, 81°34' E **188**
Valamaz, *Russ.* 57°32' N, 52°8' E **154**
Valatie, *N.Y., U.S.* 42°24' N, 73°41' W **104**
Valberg, *Nor.* 68°11' N, 13°56' E **152**
Vălcani, *Rom.* 46°0' N, 20°23' E **168**
Valcarlos see Luzaide, *Fr.* 43°5' N, 1°19' W **164**
Valcheta, *Arg.* 40°39' S, 66°11' W **134**
Valday, *Russ.* 57°57' N, 33°15' E **154**
Valdayskaya Vozvyshennost', *Russ.* 56°12' N, 30°12' E **152**
Valdemārpils, *Latv.* 57°21' N, 22°34' E **166**
Valdepeñas, *Sp.* 38°45' N, 3°23' W **164**
Valderrobres, *Sp.* 40°51' N, 0°8' E **164**
Valders, *Wis., U.S.* 44°3' N, 87°53' W **102**
Valdés, Península, *Arg.* 42°42' S, 64°40' W **134**
Valdez, *Ecua.* 1°10' N, 79°11' W **130**
Valdivia, *Chile* 39°47' S, 73°17' W **134**
Valdivia, *Col.* 7°4' N, 75°28' W **136**
Valdivia, *Sp.* 39°1' N, 5°42' W **164**
Val-d'Or, *Can.* 48°7' N, 77°48' W **94**
Valdosta, *Ga., U.S.* 30°49' N, 83°17' W **96**
Valdres, region, *Nor.* 60°44' N, 8°54' E **152**
Vale, *Oreg., U.S.* 43°59' N, 117°16' W **90**
Valea lui Mihai, *Rom.* 47°31' N, 22°8' E **168**
Valea Vişeului, *Rom.* 47°54' N, 24°10' E **156**
Valemount, *Can.* 52°49' N, 119°16' W **108**
Valença, *Braz.* 13°23' S, 39°9' W **132**
Valença, *Port.* 41°56' N, 8°40' W **214**
Valence, *Fr.* 44°56' N, 4°55' E **143**
Valencia, *Calif., U.S.* 34°23' N, 118°34' W **101**
Valencia, *Sp.* 39°28' N, 0°23' E **164**
Valencia, *Venez.* 10°9' N, 67°59' W **136**
Valencia, adm. division, *Sp.* 40°10' N, 0°26' E **164**
Valencia, Golfo de 39°40' N, 0°51' E **150**
Valenciennes, *Fr.* 50°20' N, 3°32' E **163**
Valentine, *Ariz., U.S.* 35°24' N, 113°40' W **101**
Valentine, *Nebr., U.S.* 42°50' N, 100°34' W **90**
Valentine, *Tex., U.S.* 30°33' N, 104°29' W **92**
Valentine, Cape, *Antarctica* 61°6' S, 54°60' W **134**
Valenza, *It.* 45°0' N, 8°38' E **167**
Våler, *Nor.* 60°40' N, 11°49' E **152**
Valera, *Venez.* 9°17' N, 70°39' W **136**
Valestrand, *Nor.* 59°40' N, 5°26' E **152**
Valets, Lac, lake, *Can.* 48°30' N, 76°55' W **94**
Valga, *Est.* 57°45' N, 26°3' E **166**
Valier, *Mo., U.S.* 38°0' N, 89°3' W **94**
Valier, *Mont., U.S.* 48°17' N, 112°16' W **90**
Valjala, *Est.* 58°24' N, 22°46' E **166**
Valjevo, *Serb. and Mont.* 44°16' N, 19°52' E **168**
Valjok, *Nor.* 69°41' N, 25°54' E **152**
Valka, *Latv.* 57°45' N, 25°59' E **166**
Valkeakoski, *Fin.* 61°16' N, 23°59' E **166**
Valkenswaard, *Neth.* 51°20' N, 5°26' E **167**
Valkyrie Dome, *Antarctica* 76°20' S, 28°43' E **248**
Valla, *Nor.* 59°1' N, 16°20' E **152**
Valladares, *Mex.* 26°54' N, 100°39' W **96**
Valladolid, *Mex.* 20°41' N, 88°13' W **116**
Valladolid, *Sp.* 41°38' N, 4°44' W **150**
Valladolid de los Bimviles, *Equatorial Guinea* 1°50' N, 10°42' E **218**
Vallard, Lac, lake, *Can.* 52°49' N, 69°26' W **111**
Valle, *Nor.* 59°11' N, 7°32' E **152**
Valle Crucis Abbey, site, *U.K.* 52°59' N, 3°13' W **162**
Valle D'Aosta, adm. division, *It.* 45°49' N, 7°2' E **165**
Valle de Banderas, *Mex.* 20°47' N, 105°17' W **114**
Valle de Bravo, *Mex.* 19°9' N, 100°8' W **114**
Valle de la Pascua, *Venez.* 9°12' N, 66°2' W **136**
Valle de Santiago, *Mex.* 20°22' N, 101°11' W **114**
Valle de Zaragoza, *Mex.* 27°26' N, 105°49' W **112**
Valle del Cauca, adm. division, *Col.* 3°59' N, 78°23' W **130**
Valle del Cauca, adm. division, *Col.* 3°38' N, 76°58' W **136**
Valle Fértil, Sierra del, *Arg.* 30°20' S, 68°17' W **134**
Valle Hermoso, *Mex.* 25°40' N, 97°48' W **114**
Vallecillo, *Mex.* 26°39' N, 99°58' W **114**
Vallecito Mountains, *Calif., U.S.* 33°5' N, 116°22' W **101**
Valledupar, *Col.* 10°26' N, 73°15' W **136**
Vallegrande, *Bol.* 18°32' S, 64°12' W **137**
Vallejo, *Calif., U.S.* 38°5' N, 122°15' W **100**
Vallendar, *Ger.* 50°24' N, 7°37' E **167**
Valletta, *Malta* 35°52' N, 14°23' E **156**
Valley, *Miss., U.S.* 32°45' N, 90°30' W **103**
Valley City, *N. Dak., U.S.* 46°54' N, 98°2' W **90**
Valley Falls, *R.I., U.S.* 41°54' N, 71°24' W **104**
Valley Head, *Philippines* 17°53' N, 122°13' E **203**
Valley Mills, *Tex., U.S.* 31°38' N, 97°28' W **92**
Valley Park, *Miss., U.S.* 32°38' N, 90°53' W **103**
Valley Pass, *Nev., U.S.* 41°8' N, 114°26' W **90**
Valley Springs, *Calif., U.S.* 38°11' N, 120°51' W **100**
Valleyview, *Can.* 55°3' N, 117°19' W **108**
Vallibona, *Sp.* 40°35' N, 6°357' E **164**
Vallo della Lucania, *It.* 40°14' N, 15°16' E **156**
Vallorbe, *Switz.* 46°42' N, 6°23' E **167**
Valls, *Sp.* 41°17' N, 1°15' E **164**
Valmeyer, *Mo., U.S.* 38°16' N, 90°19' W **94**
Valmiera, *Latv.* 57°31' N, 25°23' E **166**
Valmy, *Fr.* 49°5' N, 4°48' E **163**
Valozhyn, *Belarus* 54°4' N, 26°31' E **166**
Valparaíso, *Braz.* 21°16' S, 50°55' W **138**
Valparaíso, *Chile* 33°5' S, 71°40' W **134**
Valparaíso, *Col.* 1°10' N, 75°44' W **136**
Valparaiso, *Ind., U.S.* 41°27' N, 87°3' W **102**
Valparaíso, *Mex.* 22°46' N, 103°35' W **114**
Valparaíso, adm. division, *Chile* 33°23' S, 71°33' W **134**
Valpovo, *Croatia* 45°38' N, 18°24' E **168**
Vals, *Fr.* 44°40' N, 4°21' E **150**
Vals, Tanjung, *Indonesia* 8°24' S, 136°6' E **192**
Valsad, *India* 20°35' N, 72°56' E **188**
Valsjöbyn, *Nor.* 64°4' N, 14°5' E **152**
Valstagna, *It.* 45°52' N, 11°41' E **167**
Valtimo, *Fin.* 63°39' N, 28°48' E **152**
Valuyevka, *Russ.* 46°39' N, 43°40' E **158**
Valuyki, *Russ.* 50°13' N, 38°4' E **158**
Valvær, islands, *Norwegian Sea* 66°51' N, 11°54' E **152**
Valverde del Camino, *Sp.* 37°34' N, 6°46' W **164**
Valyntsy, *Belarus* 55°42' N, 28°10' E **166**
Vammala, *Fin.* 61°19' N, 22°53' E **166**
Vámospércs, *Hung.* 47°31' N, 21°54' E **168**
Vampula, *Fin.* 60°59' N, 22°41' E **166**
Van, *Tex., U.S.* 32°30' N, 95°37' W **103**
Van, *Turk.* 38°27' N, 43°18' E **195**
Van Alstyne, *Tex., U.S.* 33°25' N, 96°35' W **96**
Van Blommestein Meer, lake, *Suriname* 4°38' N, 56°23' W **130**
Van Buren, *Ark., U.S.* 35°24' N, 94°21' W **96**
Van Buren, *Ind., U.S.* 40°36' N, 85°30' W **102**
Van Buren, *Me., U.S.* 47°8' N, 67°57' W **94**
Van Gölü, lake, *Turk.* 38°34' N, 42°36' E **195**
Van Hoa, *Vietnam* 21°11' N, 107°33' E **198**
Van Horn, *Tex., U.S.* 31°1' N, 104°51' W **82**
Van, Lake, *Turk.* 38°10' N, 41°15' E **206**
Van Ninh, *Vietnam* 12°42' N, 109°12' E **202**
Van Tassell, *Wyo., U.S.* 42°40' N, 104°5' W **90**
Van Wert, *Ohio, U.S.* 40°51' N, 84°36' W **102**
Van Yen, *Vietnam* 21°6' N, 104°41' E **202**
Vanadzor, *Arm.* 40°47' N, 44°28' E **195**
Vanaja, *Fin.* 60°58' N, 24°29' E **166**
Vananda, *Can.* 49°44' N, 124°32' W **100**
Vanavara, *Russ.* 60°22' N, 102°12' E **160**
Vanceboro, *Me., U.S.* 45°33' N, 67°28' W **94**
Vanceburg, *Ky., U.S.* 38°34' N, 83°19' W **102**
Vancorum, *Colo., U.S.* 38°14' N, 108°37' W **90**
Vancouver, *Can.* 49°16' N, 123°7' W **100**
Vancouver, *Wash., U.S.* 45°37' N, 122°41' W **100**
Vancouver Island, *Can.* 49°11' N, 123°48' W **100**
Vandalia, *Ill., U.S.* 38°57' N, 89°6' W **102**
Vandalia, *Ohio, U.S.* 39°52' N, 84°12' W **102**
Vandenberg Air Force Base, *Calif., U.S.* 34°43' N, 120°38' W **100**
Vandenberg Village, *Calif., U.S.* 34°42' N, 120°29' W **100**
Vanderlin Island, *Austral.* 15°49' S, 137°10' E **230**
Vändra, *Est.* 58°38' N, 25°1' E **166**
Vandúzi, *Mozambique* 18°60' S, 33°17' E **224**
Vandysh, *Russ.* 61°20' N, 40°12' E **154**
Vanegas, *Mex.* 23°49' N, 100°53' W **114**
Vänern, lake, *Sw.* 58°24' N, 11°45' E **160**
Vanern, lake, *Sw.* 57°33' N, 12°11' E **172**
Vang, Mount, peak, *Antarctica* 73°58' S, 69°22' W **248**
Vanga, *Kenya* 4°38' S, 39°12' E **224**
Vangaindrano, *Madagascar* 23°22' S, 47°35' E **220**
Vangozero, *Russ.* 65°34' N, 33°18' E **152**
Vanguard, *Can.* 49°54' N, 107°18' W **90**
Vangunu, island, *Solomon Islands* 8°41' S, 158°0' E **242**
Vangviang, *Laos* 18°56' N, 102°27' E **202**
Vanikolo Islands, *Solomon Islands* 12°49' S, 164°8' E **238**
Vanino, *Russ.* 49°4' N, 140°3' E **190**
Vaniyambadi, *India* 12°40' N, 78°37' E **188**

Vilafranca del Penedès, Sp. 41°20′ N, 1°41′ E 164
Viļaka, Latv. 57°10′ N, 27°37′ E 166
Vilaller, Sp. 42°26′ N, 0°42′ E 164
Vilán, Cabo, Sp. 43°10′ N, 9°27′ W 150
Viļāni, Latv. 56°32′ N, 26°56′ E 166
Vilanova i la Geltrú, Sp. 41°12′ N, 1°43′ E 164
Vilar Formoso, Port. 40°36′ N, 6°52′ W 150
Vilcabamba, Cordillera, Peru 12°60′ S, 73°16′ W 130
Vilcabamba, ruin(s), Peru 13°7′ S, 73°25′ W 137
Vilcea, adm. division, Rom. 44°57′ N, 23°47′ E 156
Vileyka, Belarus 54°30′ N, 26°54′ E 166
Vil'gort, Russ. 60°35′ N, 56°25′ E 154
Vil'gort, Russ. 61°37′ N, 50°49′ E 154
Vilhelmina, Nor. 64°37′ N, 16°38′ E 152
Vilhena, Braz. 12°42′ S, 60°9′ W 130
Viliya, Ukr. 50°11′ N, 26°17′ E 152
Viliya, river, Belarus 54°49′ N, 25°58′ E 166
Viljandi, Est. 58°20′ N, 25°33′ E 166
Vilkaviškis, Lith. 54°40′ N, 23°1′ E 166
Vil'kitskogo, Proliv 76°58′ N, 84°44′ E 172
Villa Abecia, Bol. 20°60′ S, 65°24′ W 137
Villa Ahumada, Mex. 30°36′ N, 106°32′ W 92
Villa Alberdi, Arg. 27°35′ S, 65°37′ W 134
Villa Ana, Arg. 28°28′ S, 59°37′ W 139
Villa Ángela, Arg. 27°34′ S, 60°43′ W 139
Villa Bella, Bol. 10°29′ S, 65°24′ W 137
Villa Bens see Tarfaya, Mor. 27°55′ N, 12°54′ W 214
Villa Berthet, Arg. 27°16′ S, 60°25′ W 139
Villa Cañás, Arg. 34°1′ S, 61°37′ W 139
Villa Clara, adm. division, Cuba 22°39′ N, 80°15′ W 116
Villa Clara, island, Cuba 23°7′ N, 80°39′ W 116
Villa Constitución, Arg. 33°16′ S, 60°19′ W 139
Villa Cuauhtémoc, Mex. 22°9′ N, 97°49′ W 114
Villa de Cos, Mex. 23°17′ N, 102°21′ W 114
Villa de Guadalupe, Mex. 23°20′ N, 100°46′ W 114
Villa de Hidalgo, Mex. 22°24′ N, 100°41′ W 114
Villa de María, Arg. 29°54′ S, 63°42′ W 139
Villa de San Antonio, Hond. 14°20′ N, 87°36′ W 115
Villa del Río, Sp. 37°59′ N, 4°19′ W 164
Villa del Rosario, Arg. 31°37′ S, 63°32′ W 139
Villa Dolores, Arg. 31°56′ S, 65°9′ W 134
Villa Elisa, Arg. 32°9′ S, 58°23′ W 139
Villa Escobedo, Mex. 27°1′ N, 105°47′ W 112
Villa Florida, Parag. 26°26′ S, 57°6′ W 139
Villa Grove, Ill., U.S. 39°52′ N, 88°11′ W 102
Villa Guerrero, Mex. 21°57′ N, 103°35′ W 114
Villa Guillermina, Arg. 28°13′ S, 59°29′ W 139
Villa Hayes, Parag. 25°5′ S, 57°33′ W 132
Villa Hernandarias, Arg. 31°15′ S, 59°58′ W 139
Villa Hidalgo, Mex. 26°14′ N, 104°54′ W 114
Villa Ingavi (Caiza), Bol. 21°47′ S, 63°33′ W 137
Villa Iris, Arg. 38°12′ S, 63°13′ W 139
Villa Jesus Maria, Mex. 28°11′ N, 114°3′ W 92
Villa Juan José Pérez, Bol. 15°16′ S, 69°4′ W 137
Villa Juárez, Mex. 22°18′ N, 100°16′ W 114
Villa Mainero, Mex. 24°33′ N, 99°38′ W 114
Villa María, Arg. 32°25′ S, 63°14′ W 139
Villa Martín, Bol. 20°47′ S, 67°41′ W 137
Villa Minetti, Arg. 28°37′ S, 61°39′ W 139
Villa Nueva, Arg. 32°29′ S, 63°15′ W 139
Villa Ocampo, Arg. 28°28′ S, 59°22′ W 139
Villa Ocampo, Mex. 26°26′ N, 105°30′ W 114
Villa O'Higgins, Chile 48°28′ S, 72°38′ W 134
Villa Ojo de Agua, Arg. 29°27′ S, 63°45′ W 139
Villa Oliva, Parag. 25°60′ S, 57°50′ W 139
Villa Opicina, It. 45°41′ N, 13°46′ E 156
Villa Orestes Pereyra, Mex. 26°28′ N, 105°40′ W 114
Villa Pesqueira, Mex. 29°6′ N, 109°57′ W 92
Villa Ramírez, Arg. 32°10′ S, 60°12′ W 139
Villa Regina, Arg. 39°7′ S, 67°7′ W 134
Villa San José, Arg. 32°12′ S, 58°12′ W 139
Villa Serrano, Bol. 19°5′ S, 64°25′ W 137
Villa Talavera, Bol. 19°48′ S, 65°23′ W 137
Villa Tunari, Bol. 16°60′ S, 65°28′ W 137
Villa Unión, Arg. 29°25′ S, 62°47′ W 139
Villa Unión, Arg. 29°18′ S, 68°12′ W 134
Villa Unión, Mex. 23°10′ N, 106°14′ W 114
Villa Unión, Mex. 23°58′ N, 104°3′ W 114
Villa Unión, Mex. 28°12′ N, 100°45′ W 92
Villa Vaca Guzmán, Bol. 19°57′ S, 63°48′ W 137
Villacañas, Sp. 39°37′ N, 3°20′ W 164
Villacarrillo, Sp. 38°6′ N, 3°5′ W 164
Villach, Aust. 46°36′ N, 13°50′ E 156
Villada, Sp. 42°14′ N, 4°58′ W 150
Villadossola, It. 46°3′ N, 8°14′ E 167
Villafeliche, Sp. 41°12′ N, 1°30′ W 164
Villafranca, Sp. 42°16′ N, 1°45′ W 164
Villafranca de los Barros, Sp. 38°34′ N, 6°20′ W 164
Villafranca del Cid, Sp. 40°25′ N, 0°17′ E 164
Villafranca di Verona, It. 45°21′ N, 10°51′ E 167
Villagrán, Mex. 24°28′ N, 99°30′ W 114
Villaguay, Arg. 31°51′ S, 59°1′ W 139
Villaharta, Sp. 38°7′ N, 4°55′ W 164
Villahermosa, Mex. 17°56′ N, 93°2′ W 115
Villahermosa, Sp. 38°45′ N, 2°52′ W 164
Villajoyosa (La Villa Joiosa), Sp. 38°29′ N, 0°14′ E 164
Villaldama, Mex. 26°29′ N, 100°27′ W 114
Villalonga, Arg. 39°54′ S, 62°36′ W 139
Villamartín, Sp. 36°52′ N, 5°39′ W 164
Villamontes, Bol. 21°15′ S, 63°33′ W 137
Villanueva, Mex. 22°21′ N, 102°54′ W 114
Villanueva, N. Mex., U.S. 35°16′ N, 105°22′ W 92
Villanueva de Castellón, Sp. 39°4′ N, 0°31′ E 164
Villanueva de la Concepción, Sp. 36°55′ N, 4°33′ W 164
Villanueva de la Jara, Sp. 39°26′ N, 1°58′ W 164
Villanueva de la Serena, Sp. 38°58′ N, 5°48′ W 164
Villanueva de los Infantes, Sp. 38°44′ N, 3°2′ W 164
Villanueva del Arzobispo, Sp. 38°10′ N, 2°60′ W 164
Villanueva del Duque, Sp. 38°23′ N, 5°1′ W 164
Villanueva del Río y Minas, Sp. 37°39′ N, 5°43′ W 164
Villány, Hung. 45°52′ N, 18°27′ E 168
Villapalacios, Sp. 38°34′ N, 2°38′ W 164
Villaputzu, It. 39°27′ N, 9°35′ E 156
Villaquejida, Sp. 42°8′ N, 5°36′ W 150
Villar del Rey, Sp. 39°8′ N, 6°51′ W 164
Villarcayo, Sp. 42°55′ N, 3°34′ W 164
Villarino, Punta, Arg. 40°60′ S, 64°58′ W 134
Villarrica, Parag. 25°45′ S, 56°27′ W 132
Villarrica National Park, Chile 39°24′ S, 72°10′ W 134
Villarrobledo, Sp. 39°15′ N, 2°37′ W 164
Villarroya de la Sierra, Sp. 41°28′ N, 1°48′ W 164
Villasayas, Sp. 41°20′ N, 2°37′ W 164
Villavicencio, Col. 4°8′ N, 73°40′ W 136
Villaviciosa de Córdoba, Sp. 38°4′ N, 5°1′ W 164
Villavieja, Col. 3°13′ N, 75°13′ W 136
Villazón, Bol. 22°7′ S, 65°39′ W 137
Villé, Fr. 48°19′ N, 7°17′ E 163
Ville Platte, La., U.S. 30°40′ N, 92°17′ W 103
Villebon, Lac, lake, Can. 47°54′ N, 77°50′ W 94
Villefranche, Fr. 45°59′ N, 4°43′ E 150
Villefranche, Fr. 47°17′ N, 1°46′ E 150
Villefranche-de-Lauragais, Fr. 43°23′ N, 1°43′ E 164
Villel, Sp. 40°13′ N, 1°13′ W 164
Villemaur, Fr. 48°15′ N, 3°45′ E 163
Villena, Sp. 38°37′ N, 0°53′ E 164
Villenauxe, Fr. 48°35′ N, 3°32′ E 163
Villeneuve-Saint-Georges, Fr. 48°43′ N, 2°26′ E 163
Villers-Bretonneux, Fr. 49°52′ N, 2°30′ E 163
Villerupt, Fr. 49°27′ N, 5°55′ E 163
Villiers, S. Af. 27°7′ S, 28°36′ E 227
Villisca, Iowa, U.S. 40°56′ N, 94°59′ W 94
Villupuram, India 11°56′ N, 79°30′ E 188
Vilna, Can. 54°6′ N, 111°56′ W 108
Vilnius, Lith. 54°38′ N, 25°12′ E 166
Vilppula, Fin. 62°1′ N, 24°25′ E 166
Vilsandi Saar, island, Est. 58°23′ N, 21°35′ E 166
Vilshofen, Ger. 48°37′ N, 13°11′ E 152
Vilusi, Europe 42°42′ N, 18°35′ E 168
Vilvoorde, Belg. 50°55′ N, 4°26′ E 167
Vilyuy, river, Russ. 62°48′ N, 120°41′ E 172
Vilyuy, river, Russ. 64°45′ N, 108°36′ E 160
Vilyuy, river, Russ. 63°0′ N, 115°4′ E 160
Vilyuysk, Russ. 63°38′ N, 121°30′ E 160
Vilyuyskoye Plato, Russ. 66°22′ N, 99°40′ E 172
Vilyuyskoye Vodokhranilishche, lake, Russ. 63°5′ N, 101°50′ E 172
Vimioso, Port. 41°34′ N, 6°32′ W 150
Vimpeli, Fin. 63°9′ N, 23°46′ E 152
Vina, Calif., U.S. 39°56′ N, 122°4′ W 90
Vina, Serb. and Mont. 43°37′ N, 22°8′ E 168
Vinalhaven, Me., U.S. 44°2′ N, 68°50′ W 94
Vinaròs, Sp. 40°27′ N, 0°27′ E 150
Vinça, Fr. 42°39′ N, 2°29′ E 164
Vincennes, Ind., U.S. 38°40′ N, 87°31′ W 102
Vincent Lake, lake, Can. 50°34′ N, 91°27′ W 110
Vinchina, Arg. 28°46′ S, 68°14′ W 134
Vindeln, Nor. 64°11′ N, 19°43′ E 152
Vindrey, Russ. 54°15′ N, 43°0′ E 154
Vinegar Hill, peak, Oreg., U.S. 44°41′ N, 118°39′ W 90
Vineta, Namibia 22°34′ S, 14°30′ E 220
Vineyard Sound 41°24′ N, 70°48′ W 104
Vinga, Rom. 46°1′ N, 21°12′ E 168
Vinh, Vietnam 18°42′ N, 105°38′ E 202
Vinh Chau, Vietnam 9°21′ N, 105°59′ E 202
Vinh Long, Vietnam 10°13′ N, 105°57′ E 202
Vinica, Maced. 41°53′ N, 22°30′ E 168
Vinita, Okla., U.S. 36°37′ N, 95°10′ W 96
Vinje, Nor. 59°38′ N, 7°51′ E 152
Vinjeøra, Nor. 63°12′ N, 8°58′ E 152
Vînju Mare, Rom. 44°25′ N, 22°53′ E 168
Vinkovci, Croatia 45°16′ N, 18°46′ E 168
Vinnytsya, Ukr. 49°12′ N, 28°37′ E 152
Vinson Massif, peak, Antarctica 78°33′ S, 86°54′ W 248
Vinton, Iowa, U.S. 42°9′ N, 92°2′ W 110
Vinton, La., U.S. 30°11′ N, 93°36′ W 103
Violet Grove, Can. 53°8′ N, 115°4′ W 108
Vipiteno, It. 46°54′ N, 11°25′ E 167
Vir, Taj. 37°42′ N, 72°11′ E 197
Virac, Philippines 13°33′ N, 124°13′ E 203
Virachei, Cambodia 14°0′ N, 106°46′ E 202
Virachey National Park, Cambodia 14°12′ N, 106°23′ E 202
Viramgam, India 23°5′ N, 72°3′ E 186
Virandozero, Russ. 64°1′ N, 36°7′ E 154
Viranşehir, Turk. 37°12′ N, 39°46′ E 195
Virbalis, Lith. 54°38′ N, 22°48′ E 166
Virden, Can. 49°51′ N, 100°57′ W 90
Virden, Ill., U.S. 39°29′ N, 89°46′ W 102
Virden, Mo., U.S. 39°29′ N, 89°46′ W 94
Vire, Fr. 48°50′ N, 0°54′ E 150
Vireši, Latv. 57°27′ N, 26°21′ E 166
Vîrfurile, Rom. 46°18′ N, 22°33′ E 168
Virgem da Lapa, Braz. 16°48′ S, 42°23′ W 138
Virgin Gorda, island, U.K. 18°28′ N, 64°26′ W 118
Virgin Islands, Caribbean Sea 18°4′ N, 64°50′ W 118
Virgin Mountains, Nev., U.S. 36°39′ N, 114°12′ W 101
Virgin, river, Can. 57°0′ N, 108°9′ W 108
Virgin, river, Nev., U.S. 36°39′ N, 114°20′ W 101
Virginia, Minn., U.S. 47°31′ N, 92°35′ W 82
Virginia, S. Af. 28°11′ S, 26°51′ E 227
Virginia, adm. division, Va., U.S. 37°56′ N, 79°15′ W 94
Virginia Beach, Va., U.S. 36°50′ N, 75°60′ W 96
Virginia Falls, Can. 61°52′ N, 128°14′ W 98
Virgolândia, Braz. 18°29′ S, 42°18′ W 138
Virje, Croatia 46°3′ N, 16°58′ E 168
Virmutjoki, Fin. 61°20′ N, 28°44′ E 166
Virojoki, Fin. 60°34′ N, 27°40′ E 166
Virolahti, Fin. 60°30′ N, 27°40′ E 166
Virovitica, Croatia 45°49′ N, 17°24′ E 168
Virpazar, Europe 42°15′ N, 19°5′ E 168
Virrat, Fin. 62°12′ N, 23°43′ E 154
Vîrşolţ, Rom. 47°12′ N, 22°55′ E 168
Virtaniemi, Russ. 68°53′ N, 28°27′ E 152
Virton, Belg. 49°34′ N, 5°32′ E 163
Virtsu, Est. 58°33′ N, 23°30′ E 166
Virú, Peru 8°28′ S, 78°46′ W 130
Viru Roela, Est. 59°9′ N, 26°35′ E 166
Viru-Jaagupl, Est. 59°14′ N, 26°27′ E 166
Virunga, Dem. Rep. of the Congo 1°1′ S, 29°0′ E 224
Virunga National Park, Dem. Rep. of the Congo 0°40′ N, 29°47′ E 224
Vis, Croatia 43°2′ N, 16°10′ E 168
Vis (Lissa), island, Croatia 42°57′ N, 16°5′ E 168
Visaginas, Lith. 55°34′ N, 26°23′ E 166
Visalia, Calif., U.S. 36°20′ N, 119°18′ W 100
Visayan Sea 11°27′ N, 123°36′ E 203
Visbek, Ger. 52°50′ N, 8°19′ E 163
Visby, Sw. 57°37′ N, 18°17′ E 166
Visconde do Rio Branco, Braz. 2°54′ S, 69°39′ W 136
Viscount Melville Sound 74°17′ N, 105°54′ W 255
Visé, Belg. 50°44′ N, 5°42′ E 167
Višegrad, Bosn. and Herzg. 43°47′ N, 19°18′ E 168
Visegrád, Hung. 47°46′ N, 18°59′ E 168
Viseu, Braz. 1°13′ S, 46°10′ W 130
Viseu, Port. 40°39′ N, 7°56′ W 150
Viseu, adm. division, Port. 40°41′ N, 8°16′ W 150
Vishakhapatnam, India 17°44′ N, 83°18′ E 188
Vishera, river, Russ. 61°4′ N, 58°44′ E 154
Višķi, Latv. 56°1′ N, 26°46′ E 166
Vislanda, Nor. 56°46′ N, 14°25′ E 152
Viso del Marqués, Sp. 38°30′ N, 3°34′ W 164
Viso, Monte, peak, It. 44°39′ N, 7°4′ E 165
Visoko, Bosn. and Herzg. 43°58′ N, 18°9′ E 168
Visp, Switz. 46°17′ N, 7°53′ E 167
Vista, Calif., U.S. 33°12′ N, 117°16′ W 101
Vista Alegre, Braz. 4°21′ S, 56°17′ W 130
Vista Alegre, Braz. 6°18′ S, 68°10′ W 130
Vista Alegre, Braz. 1°27′ N, 68°14′ W 136
Vista, Cerro, peak, N. Mex., U.S. 36°13′ N, 105°29′ W 92
Vital Lake, lake, Can. 61°31′ N, 108°33′ W 108
Vitån, river, Nor. 66°17′ N, 21°49′ E 152
Viterbo, It. 42°25′ N, 12°5′ E 214
Viti Levu, island, Fiji Islands 17°50′ S, 178°0′ E 242
Vitichi, Bol. 20°16′ S, 65°29′ W 137
Vitim, Russ. 59°27′ N, 112°22′ E 160
Vitim, river, Russ. 53°53′ N, 114°38′ E 190
Vitina, Bosn. and Herzg. 43°13′ N, 17°29′ E 168
Vitomirica, Europe 42°41′ N, 20°20′ E 168
Vitor, Chile 18°48′ S, 70°22′ W 137
Vítor, Peru 16°29′ S, 71°48′ W 137
Vitória, Braz. 20°17′ S, 40°18′ W 138
Vitória, Braz. 2°56′ S, 52°3′ W 130
Vitória da Conquista, Braz. 14°52′ S, 40°52′ W 138
Vitória Seamount, South Atlantic Ocean 20°20′ S, 36°60′ W 253
Vitoria-Gasteiz, Sp. 42°50′ N, 2°41′ W 164
Vitorog, peak, Bosn. and Herzg. 44°6′ N, 17°2′ E 168
Vitry-le-François, Fr. 48°43′ N, 4°35′ E 163
Vitsyebsk, Belarus 55°12′ N, 30°20′ E 152
Vittangi, Nor. 67°40′ N, 21°37′ E 152
Vittel, Fr. 48°12′ N, 5°58′ E 163
Vittoria, It. 36°57′ N, 14°31′ E 156
Vittorio Veneto, It. 45°58′ N, 12°16′ E 167
Vitvattnet, Nor. 66°3′ N, 23°9′ E 152
Vityaz Trench, South Pacific Ocean 11°20′ S, 174°17′ E 252
Viveiro, Sp. 43°36′ N, 7°38′ W 214
Viver, Sp. 39°55′ N, 0°36′ E 164
Vivi, Ozero, lake, Russ. 66°19′ N, 92°55′ E 169
Vivi, river, Russ. 65°5′ N, 96°4′ E 169
Vivian, La., U.S. 32°51′ N, 93°59′ W 103
Vivoratá, Arg. 37°41′ S, 57°42′ W 139
Vizcachas, Meseta de las, Arg. 50°35′ S, 73°58′ W 134
Vizcaino, Cape, Calif., U.S. 39°45′ N, 124°16′ W 90
Vizcaíno, Desierto de, Mex. 27°41′ N, 113°54′ W 112
Vizcaíno, Sierra, Mex. 27°31′ N, 114°24′ W 112
Vize, Turk. 41°34′ N, 27°45′ E 156
Vizhas, Russ. 66°38′ N, 45°50′ E 154
Vizhay, Russ. 61°14′ N, 60°13′ E 154
Vizhevo, Russ. 64°41′ N, 43°55′ E 154
Vizianagaram, India 18°5′ N, 83°24′ E 188
Vizinga, Russ. 61°6′ N, 50°6′ E 154
Vlădeasa, peak, Rom. 46°44′ N, 22°46′ E 168
Vladičin Han, Serb. and Mont. 42°42′ N, 22°3′ E 168
Vladikavkaz, Russ. 43°0′ N, 44°44′ E 195
Vladimir, Russ. 56°9′ N, 40°19′ E 154
Vladimir, adm. division, Russ. 56°2′ N, 39°15′ E 154
Vladimirci, Serb. and Mont. 44°35′ N, 19°46′ E 168
Vladimirovac, Serb. and Mont. 45°1′ N, 20°52′ E 168
Vladimirovka, Russ. 60°48′ N, 30°28′ E 166
Vladimirskiy Tupik, Russ. 55°40′ N, 33°25′ E 154
Vladivostok, Russ. 43°8′ N, 131°54′ E 200
Vlasenica, Bosn. and Herzg. 44°11′ N, 18°55′ E 168
Vlašić, Bosn. and Herzg. 44°18′ N, 17°21′ E 168
Vlasinje, Bosn. and Herzg. 44°26′ N, 17°12′ E 168
Vlaški Drenovac, Europe 42°27′ N, 20°38′ E 168
Vlasotince, Serb. and Mont. 42°57′ N, 22°7′ E 168
Vlčany, Slovakia 48°0′ N, 17°57′ E 168
Vlieland, island, Neth. 53°18′ N, 4°49′ E 163
Vlissingen (Flushing), Neth. 51°27′ N, 3°34′ E 163
Vltava, river, Czech Rep. 49°29′ N, 14°4′ E 152
Vobkent, Uzb. 40°1′ N, 64°33′ E 197
Voćin, Croatia 45°37′ N, 17°31′ E 168
Voden, Bulg. 42°4′ N, 26°54′ E 156
Vodil, Uzb. 40°9′ N, 71°44′ E 197
Vodl Ozero, lake, Russ. 62°16′ N, 36°18′ E 154
Vodnyy, Russ. 63°31′ N, 53°28′ E 154
Voerde, Ger. 51°36′ N, 6°40′ E 167
Vogan, Togo 6°21′ N, 1°30′ E 222
Vogelsberg, Ger. 50°40′ N, 8°44′ E 167
Voghera, It. 44°58′ N, 9°0′ E 167
Võhandu, river, Est. 57°46′ N, 27°7′ E 166
Vohipeno, Madagascar 22°21′ S, 47°53′ E 220
Võhma, Est. 58°36′ N, 25°32′ E 166
Võhma, Est. 58°31′ N, 22°20′ E 166
Vöhringen, Ger. 48°16′ N, 10°4′ E 152
Voi, Kenya 3°23′ S, 38°35′ E 224
Void-Vacon, Fr. 48°41′ N, 5°36′ E 163
Voikoski, Fin. 61°14′ N, 26°47′ E 166
Vóïo, Óros, peak, Gr. 40°16′ N, 20°59′ E 156
Voislova, Rom. 45°31′ N, 22°27′ E 168
Voiteg, Rom. 45°28′ N, 21°14′ E 156
Vojmån, Nor. 64°47′ N, 16°48′ E 152
Vojmsjön, lake, Nor. 64°51′ N, 16°2′ E 152
Vojvodina, region, Serb. and Mont. 45°21′ N, 19°4′ E 168
Voknavolok, Russ. 64°56′ N, 30°33′ E 152
Voláda, Gr. 35°32′ N, 27°11′ E 156
Volán Domuyo, peak, Arg. 36°44′ S, 70°47′ W 122
Volborg, Mont., U.S. 45°49′ N, 105°40′ W 90
Volcán, Arg. 23°54′ S, 65°29′ W 132
Volcán Isluga National Park, Chile 19°20′ S, 69°19′ W 122
Volcán Masaya National Park, Nicar. 11°56′ N, 86°13′ W 115
Volcán Nevado de Colima National Park, Mex. 19°27′ N, 103°57′ W 72
Volcán Poás National Park, C.R. 10°11′ N, 84°19′ W 115
Volcano Islands (Kazan Rettō), islands, Philippine Sea 23°11′ N, 139°38′ E 190
Volcano Peak, Calif., U.S. 35°57′ N, 117°53′ W 101
Volchansk, Russ. 59°57′ N, 60°3′ E 154
Voldi, Est. 58°32′ N, 26°35′ E 166
Vol'dino, Russ. 62°15′ N, 54°8′ E 154
Volga, Russ. 57°57′ N, 38°22′ E 154
Volga, S. Dak., U.S. 44°17′ N, 96°57′ W 90
Volga, river, Russ. 55°48′ N, 44°12′ E 160
Volga-Don Canal, Russ. 48°33′ N, 43°47′ E 158
Volgodonsk, Russ. 47°30′ N, 42°2′ E 158
Volgograd, adm. division, Russ. 49°28′ N, 42°54′ E 158
Volgograd (Stalingrad), Russ. 48°46′ N, 44°28′ E 158
Volgogradskoye Vodokhranilishche, lake, Russ. 50°16′ N, 45°9′ E 158
Volgorechensk, Russ. 57°27′ N, 41°16′ E 154
Volímes, Gr. 37°52′ N, 20°39′ E 156
Volintiri, Mold. 46°26′ N, 29°35′ E 156
Volkach, Ger. 49°51′ N, 10°13′ E 167
Volkhov, Russ. 59°55′ N, 32°25′ E 154
Volkhov, river, Russ. 58°34′ N, 31°39′ E 154
Volksrust, S. Af. 27°22′ S, 29°50′ E 227
Vollenhove, Neth. 52°40′ N, 5°58′ E 163
Volma, Belarus 53°52′ N, 26°57′ E 166
Volnovakha, Ukr. 47°36′ N, 37°29′ E 156
Volochanka, Russ. 71°2′ N, 94°36′ E 160
Volochys'k, Ukr. 49°30′ N, 26°11′ E 152
Volodarsk, Russ. 56°13′ N, 43°11′ E 154
Volodskaya, Russ. 62°22′ N, 41°56′ E 154
Vologda, Russ. 59°10′ N, 39°48′ E 154
Vologda, adm. division, Russ. 59°52′ N, 39°27′ E 154
Voloki, Belarus 54°35′ N, 28°11′ E 166
Volokonovka, Russ. 50°29′ N, 37°51′ E 158
Volonga, Russ. 67°3′ N, 47°52′ E 169
Vólos, Gr. 39°24′ N, 22°55′ E 180
Voloshka, Russ. 61°19′ N, 40°2′ E 154
Voloshovo, Russ. 58°42′ N, 29°17′ E 166
Volosovo, Russ. 59°26′ N, 29°28′ E 166
Volovo, Russ. 53°32′ N, 38°0′ E 154
Voloyarvi, Russ. 60°17′ N, 30°46′ E 166
Vol'sk, Russ. 52°5′ N, 47°22′ E 158
Volta, Calif., U.S. 37°5′ N, 120°56′ W 100
Volta, Lake, Ghana 8°15′ N, 1°21′ W 214
Volta Redonda, Braz. 22°27′ S, 44°6′ W 138
Volterra, It. 43°24′ N, 10°50′ E 156
Volubilis, ruin(s), Mor. 34°6′ N, 5°46′ W 214
Voluntown, Conn., U.S. 41°34′ N, 71°52′ W 104
Volzhsk, Russ. 55°52′ N, 48°25′ E 154
Volzhskiy, Russ. 48°49′ N, 44°50′ E 184
Vonavona, island, Solomon Islands 8°17′ S, 157°0′ E 242
Vonda, Can. 52°19′ N, 106°5′ W 108
Vondrozo, Madagascar 22°49′ S, 47°19′ E 220
Võnnu, Est. 58°16′ N, 27°3′ E 166
Voo, Kenya 1°41′ S, 38°20′ E 224
Voranava, Belarus 54°8′ N, 25°18′ E 166
Vorder-rhein, river, Switz. 46°40′ N, 8°52′ E 167
Vordingborg, Den. 55°0′ N, 11°55′ E 152
Vorga, Russ. 53°42′ N, 32°45′ E 154
Vóries Sporádes, islands, Aegean Sea 39°8′ N, 23°37′ E 180
Voring Plateau, Norwegian Sea 67°13′ N, 4°23′ E 255
Vorkuta, Russ. 67°25′ N, 64°4′ E 169
Vorlich, Ben, peak, U.K. 56°20′ N, 4°20′ W 150
Vormsi, island, Est. 59°3′ N, 23°1′ E 166
Vorogovo, Russ. 60°57′ N, 89°25′ E 169
Vorona, river, Russ. 52°8′ N, 42°26′ E 158
Voronech', Belarus 55°18′ N, 28°35′ E 166
Voronezh, Russ. 51°38′ N, 39°11′ E 158
Voronezh, adm. division, Russ. 50°50′ N, 38°58′ E 158
Voronezh, river, Russ. 52°21′ N, 39°31′ E 158
Vorontsovka, Russ. 59°37′ N, 60°12′ E 154
Vorontsovo, Russ. 57°18′ N, 28°42′ E 166
Vorontsovo, Russ. 71°40′ N, 83°35′ E 160
Voron'ye, Russ. 68°28′ N, 35°20′ E 152
Vorposten Peak, Antarctica 71°31′ S, 14°56′ E 248
Vorskla, river, Ukr. 49°36′ N, 34°40′ E 158
Vørterkaka Nunatak, peak, Antarctica 72°42′ S, 27°23′ E 248
Võrts Järv, lake, Est. 58°19′ N, 25°43′ E 166
Võru, Est. 57°49′ N, 27°0′ E 166
Vorukh, Taj. 39°50′ N, 70°34′ E 197
Vosburg, S. Af. 30°35′ S, 22°49′ E 227
Vose, Taj. 37°46′ N, 69°41′ E 197
Vosges, Fr. 48°57′ N, 6°56′ E 163
Voskresensk, Russ. 55°19′ N, 38°43′ E 154
Voskresenskoye, Russ. 56°48′ N, 45°28′ E 154
Voskresenskoye, Russ. 59°25′ N, 37°56′ E 154
Voskresenskoye, Russ. 53°8′ N, 56°4′ E 154
Voss, Nor. 60°37′ N, 6°22′ E 152
Vostochnaya Guba, Russ. 67°24′ N, 32°38′ E 152
Vostok, Russia, station, Antarctica 78°31′ S, 107°1′ E 248
Võsu, Est. 59°33′ N, 25°56′ E 166
Votaw, Tex., U.S. 30°24′ N, 94°41′ W 103
Votice, Czech Rep. 49°38′ N, 14°37′ E 152
Votkinsk, Russ. 57°0′ N, 53°55′ E 154
Votuporanga, Braz. 20°25′ S, 49°59′ W 138
Voulgára, peak, Gr. 39°5′ N, 21°50′ E 156
Voulx, Fr. 48°14′ N, 2°59′ E 163
Vounása, peak, Gr. 39°56′ N, 21°41′ E 156
Voúrnios, Óros, Gr. 40°3′ N, 21°16′ E 156
Vouziers, Fr. 49°23′ N, 4°43′ E 163
Vovchans'k, Ukr. 50°16′ N, 36°57′ E 158
Voves, Fr. 48°15′ N, 1°38′ E 163
Vovodo, river, Cen. Af. Rep. 5°59′ N, 24°33′ E 218
Vowchyn, Belarus 52°17′ N, 23°17′ E 152
Voyageurs National Park, Minn., U.S. 48°14′ N, 94°58′ W 94
Voynitsa, Russ. 65°9′ N, 30°18′ E 152
Voyvozh, Russ. 62°54′ N, 55°5′ E 154
Vozhayel', Russ. 62°50′ N, 51°22′ E 154
Vozhe, Ozero, lake, Russ. 60°35′ N, 38°36′ E 154
Vozhega, Russ. 60°27′ N, 40°10′ E 154
Vozhgora, Russ. 64°34′ N, 48°21′ E 154
Vozhma, Russ. 58°55′ N, 46°47′ E 154
Vozh'yel', Russ. 63°14′ N, 49°37′ E 154
Voznesens'k, Ukr. 47°36′ N, 31°21′ E 156
Voznesen'ye, Russ. 61°1′ N, 35°30′ E 154
Vozvyahenka, Kaz. 54°28′ N, 70°52′ E 184
Vrachíonas, peak, Gr. 37°49′ N, 20°39′ E 156
Vrancea, adm. division, Rom. 45°41′ N, 26°29′ E 156
Vrancei, Munţii, Rom. 45°49′ N, 25°55′ E 156
Vrang, Taj. 37°1′ N, 72°22′ E 186
Vrangelya, Ostrov (Wrangel Island), island, Russ. 71°29′ N, 175°23′ E 160
Vranica, peak, Bosn. and Herzg. 43°56′ N, 17°40′ E 168
Vranje, Serb. and Mont. 42°33′ N, 21°54′ E 168
Vranjska Banja, Serb. and Mont. 42°32′ N, 22°1′ E 168
Vratsa, Bulg. 43°12′ N, 23°33′ E 156
Vratsa, adm. division, Bulg. 43°18′ N, 23°27′ E 156
Vrbanja, Croatia 44°58′ N, 18°55′ E 168
Vrbas, Serb. and Mont. 45°33′ N, 19°38′ E 168
Vrbnik, Croatia 44°0′ N, 16°9′ E 168
Vrbnik, Croatia 45°4′ N, 14°39′ E 156
Vrboska, Croatia 43°9′ N, 16°40′ E 156
Vrbovec, Croatia 45°53′ N, 16°25′ E 168
Vrčin, Serb. and Mont. 44°40′ N, 20°33′ E 168
Vrdnik, Serb. and Mont. 45°7′ N, 19°47′ E 168
Vrede, S. Af. 27°27′ S, 29°8′ E 227
Vreden, Ger. 52°2′ N, 6°49′ E 167
Vredenburg, S. Af. 32°55′ S, 17°58′ E 227
Vrginmost, Croatia 45°20′ N, 15°52′ E 168
Vrgorac, Croatia 43°11′ N, 17°22′ E 168
Vrlika, Croatia 43°55′ N, 16°24′ E 168
Vrnograč, Bosn. and Herzg. 45°9′ N, 15°57′ E 168
Vršac, Serb. and Mont. 45°7′ N, 21°18′ E 168
Vrtoče, Bosn. and Herzg. 44°38′ N, 16°10′ E 168
Vryburg, S. Af. 26°59′ S, 24°42′ E 227
Vryheid, S. Af. 27°48′ S, 30°45′ E 227
Vsevolodo Blagodatskiy, Russ. 60°28′ N, 59°59′ E 154
Vsheli, Russ. 58°10′ N, 29°50′ E 166
Vu Liet, Vietnam 18°42′ N, 105°22′ E 202
Vučitrn, Europe 42°49′ N, 20°58′ E 168
Vučja Luka, Bosn. and Herzg. 43°55′ N, 18°31′ E 168
Vučje, Serb. and Mont. 42°51′ N, 21°54′ E 168
Vught, Neth. 51°38′ N, 5°17′ E 167
Vuka, river, Croatia 45°27′ N, 18°32′ E 168
Vuktyl, Russ. 63°54′ N, 57°28′ E 154
Vulcan, Can. 50°24′ N, 113°16′ W 90
Vulcan, Rom. 45°22′ N, 23°18′ E 168
Vulci, ruin(s), It. 42°23′ N, 11°31′ E 156
Vung Tau, Vietnam 10°21′ N, 107°4′ E 202
Vuntut National Park, Can. 68°11′ N, 139°49′ W 98
Vuoggatjålme, Nor. 66°33′ N, 16°21′ E 152
Vuohijärvi, Fin. 61°4′ N, 26°47′ E 166
Vuohijärvi, lake, Fin. 61°7′ N, 26°20′ E 166
Vuokatti, Fin. 64°7′ N, 28°13′ E 152
Vuollerim, Nor. 66°25′ N, 20°36′ E 152
Vuonislahti, Fin. 63°8′ N, 29°59′ E 152
Vuotso, Fin. 68°5′ N, 27°6′ E 152
Vurnary, Russ. 55°28′ N, 47°1′ E 154
Vyartsilya, Russ. 62°10′ N, 30°41′ E 152
Vyatka, river, Russ. 59°20′ N, 52°0′ E 154
Vyatskiye Polyany, Russ. 56°11′ N, 51°11′ E 154
Vyazemskiy, Russ. 47°31′ N, 134°46′ E 190
Vyaz'ma, Russ. 55°13′ N, 34°21′ E 154
Vyazniki, Russ. 56°14′ N, 42°9′ E 154
Vybor, Russ. 57°13′ N, 29°7′ E 166
Vyborg (Viipuri), Russ. 60°41′ N, 28°45′ E 166
Vyborovo, Russ. 58°19′ N, 29°0′ E 166
Vychegda, river, Russ. 61°31′ N, 48°11′ E 154
Vyderta, Ukr. 51°43′ N, 25°1′ E 152
Vyerkhnyadzvinsk, Belarus 55°46′ N, 27°56′ E 166
Vyetryna, Belarus 55°24′ N, 28°26′ E 166
Vyg Ozero, lake, Russ. 63°48′ N, 33°40′ E 152
Vyksa, Russ. 55°18′ N, 42°12′ E 154
Vylkove, Ukr. 45°26′ N, 29°35′ E 156
Vylok, Ukr. 48°6′ N, 22°50′ E 156
Vym', river, Russ. 62°41′ N, 50°53′ E 154
Vym', river, Russ. 63°22′ N, 51°36′ E 154
Vymsk, Russ. 60°24′ N, 48°19′ E 154
Vyritsa, Russ. 59°24′ N, 30°17′ E 166
Vyshhorod, Ukr. 50°32′ N, 30°35′ E 158
Vyshniy Volochek, Russ. 57°34′ N, 34°38′ E 154
Vysočina, adm. division, Czech Rep. 49°10′ N, 15°21′ E 152
Vysokaye, Belarus 52°21′ N, 23°20′ E 152
Vysokovsk, Russ. 56°17′ N, 36°31′ E 154
Vysotsk, Russ. 60°36′ N, 28°34′ E 166
Vysotskoye, Russ. 56°49′ N, 29°1′ E 166

Vytegra, Russ. 61°1' N, 36°30' E 154

W

"w" National Park, Benin 11°49' N, 2°27' E 222
Wa, Ghana 10°2' N, 2°30' W 222
Wa, Pol. 50°45' N, 16°16' E 152
Waajid, Somalia 3°47' N, 43°16' E 218
Waal, river, Neth. 51°54' N, 5°35' E 167
Waalwijk, Neth. 51°41' N, 5°5' E 167
Waas, Mount, peak, Utah, U.S. 38°31' N, 109°19' W 90
Wa'at, Sudan 8°8' N, 32°7' E 224
Wababimiga Lake, Can. 50°18' N, 87°9' W 94
Wabakimi Lake, Can. 50°34' N, 90°20' W 110
Wabana, Can. 47°38' N, 52°56' W 111
Wabasca, river, Can. 56°15' N, 113°42' W 108
Wabasca-Desmarais, Can. 55°59' N, 113°52' W 108
Wabash, Ind., U.S. 40°48' N, 85°50' W 102
Wabash, river, Ind., U.S. 40°48' N, 85°14' W 102
Wabasha, Minn., U.S. 44°21' N, 92°3' W 110
Wabassi, river, Can. 51°46' N, 87°39' W 110
Wabasso, Fla., U.S. 27°44' N, 80°27' W 105
Wabē Gestro, river, Eth. 5°53' N, 41°38' E 224
Wabē Shebelē, river, Eth. 7°25' N, 39°36' E 224
Wabern, Ger. 51°6' N, 9°21' E 167
Wabimeig Lake, Can. 51°26' N, 86°15' W 110
Waboose Dam, Can. 50°51' N, 87°60' W 110
Wabowden, Can. 54°54' N, 98°38' W 108
Wabuk Point, Can. 55°18' N, 87°23' W 106
W.A.C. Bennett Dam, Can. 55°51' N, 123°2' W 108
Waccasassa Bay 29°6' N, 82°54' W 105
Wächtersbach, Ger. 50°15' N, 9°17' E 167
Waco, Can. 51°26' N, 65°36' W 111
Waco, Tex., U.S. 31°31' N, 97°8' W 96
Waconichi, Lac, lake, Can. 50°5' N, 74°39' W 94
Wad Abu Nahl, Sudan 13°6' N, 34°53' E 182
Wad Banda, Sudan 13°4' N, 27°56' E 216
Wad el Haddad, Sudan 13°48' N, 33°30' E 182
Wad Hamid, Sudan 16°27' N, 32°45' E 182
Wad Medani, Sudan 14°23' N, 33°29' E 182
Wadamago, Somalia 8°52' N, 46°15' E 216
Wadayama, Japan 35°19' N, 134°48' E 201
Waddān, Lib. 29°10' N, 16°6' E 216
Waddenzee 53°5' N, 4°54' E 163
Waddington, N.Y., U.S. 44°51' N, 75°13' W 94
Waddington, Mount, peak, Can. 51°22' N, 125°21' W 90
Wadena, Can. 51°56' N, 103°48' W 90
Wadena, Minn., U.S. 46°25' N, 95°9' W 94
Wadersloh, Ger. 51°44' N, 8°14' E 167
Wādī al Masīlah, river, Yemen 16°12' N, 49°33' E 182
Wādī as Sīr, Jordan 31°56' N, 35°48' E 194
Wâdi Gimâl, Gezîrat, island, Egypt 24°30' N, 33°51' E 182
Wadi Halfa, Sudan 21°46' N, 31°20' E 182
Wādīas Sir ḩān, Saudi Arabia 31°38' N, 37°3' E 194
Wadsworth, Nev., U.S. 39°38' N, 119°19' W 90
Wadsworth, Ohio, U.S. 41°0' N, 81°44' W 102
Wadu, island, Maldives 5°44' N, 72°17' E 188
Waelder, Tex., U.S. 29°40' N, 97°18' W 96
Waesche, Mount, peak, Antarctica 77°3' S, 126°15' W 248
Wafangdian, China 39°39' N, 121°59' E 198
Wafania, Dem. Rep. of the Congo 1°23' S, 20°19' E 218
Wafra, oil field, Kuwait 28°34' N, 47°52' E 196
Wagenia Fisheries, site, Dem. Rep. of the Congo 0°25' N, 25°17' E 224
Wageningen, Neth. 51°58' N, 5°39' E 167
Wager Bay 65°25' N, 90°48' W 106
Wager, Isla, island, Chile 47°34' S, 75°43' W 134
Waglisla, Can. 52°10' N, 128°10' W 108
Wagner, S. Dak., U.S. 43°3' N, 98°19' W 90
Wagner Nunatak, peak, Antarctica 83°59' S, 68°23' W 248
Wagon Mound, N. Mex., U.S. 36°0' N, 104°43' W 92
Wagontire Mountain, peak, Oreg., U.S. 43°20' N, 119°58' W 90
Wah Wah Range, Utah, U.S. 38°29' N, 113°52' W 90
Waha, oil field, Lib. 28°2' N, 19°46' E 216
Waha'ula Heiau, site, Hawai'i, U.S. 19°19' N, 155°5' W 99
Wahoo, Nebr., U.S. 41°12' N, 96°38' W 90
Wahpeton, N. Dak., U.S. 46°15' N, 96°38' W 90
Wai, India 17°58' N, 73°55' E 188
Wai'ale'ale, peak, Hawai'i, U.S. 22°4' N, 159°33' W 99
Wāīas Sir'ān, Jordan 31°26' N, 36°56' E 194
Waiau, N.Z. 42°40' S, 173°3' E 240
Waiau, river, N.Z. 45°42' S, 167°34' E 240
Waigeo, island, Indonesia 7°416' N, 130°3' E 192
Waihi, N.Z. 37°23' S, 175°50' E 240
Waihola, N.Z. 46°3' S, 170°7' E 240
Waikabubak, Indonesia 9°39' S, 119°20' E 192
Waikanae, N.Z. 40°54' S, 175°6' E 240
Waikawa, N.Z. 46°38' S, 169°6' E 240
Waikiwi, N.Z. 46°24' S, 168°20' E 240
Waikouaiti, N.Z. 45°35' S, 170°40' E 240
Waimamaku, N.Z. 35°34' S, 173°28' E 240
Waimangaroa, N.Z. 41°45' S, 171°45' E 240
Waimarama, N.Z. 39°49' S, 176°58' E 240
Waimate, N.Z. 44°45' S, 171°2' E 240
Wainfleet All Saints, U.K. 53°7' N, 0°14' E 162
Waingapu, Indonesia 9°41' S, 120°4' E 192
Waini Point, Guyana 8°25' N, 59°51' W 116
Wainwright, Alas., U.S. 70°37' N, 160°3' W 246
Wainwright, Can. 52°50' N, 110°51' W 108
Waiohonu Petroglyphs, site, Hawai'i, U.S. 20°42' N, 156°3' W 99
Wai'oli Mission, site, Hawai'i, U.S. 22°11' N, 159°33' W 99
Waiotira, N.Z. 35°57' S, 174°12' E 240
Waiouru, N.Z. 39°30' S, 175°40' E 240
Waipahi, N.Z. 46°9' S, 169°14' E 240
Waipara, N.Z. 43°4' S, 172°45' E 240
Waipawa, N.Z. 39°58' S, 176°35' E 240
Waipu, N.Z. 35°60' S, 174°26' E 240
Waipukurau, N.Z. 40°1' S, 176°35' E 240
Wairau Valley, N.Z. 41°36' S, 173°31' E 240
Wairoa, N.Z. 39°4' S, 177°23' E 240
Waitahanui, N.Z. 38°48' S, 176°5' E 240
Waitakaruru, N.Z. 37°16' S, 175°24' E 240
Waitara, N.Z. 39°2' S, 174°13' E 240
Waitati, N.Z. 45°46' S, 170°34' E 240
Waite, Cape, Antarctica 72°42' S, 103°44' W 248
Waitemata, N.Z. 36°52' S, 174°37' E 240
Waitoa, N.Z. 37°36' S, 175°39' E 240
Waitomo Caves, site, N.Z. 38°18' S, 175°2' E 240
Waitotara, N.Z. 39°49' S, 174°43' E 240
Wajima, Japan 37°23' N, 136°53' E 201
Wajir, Kenya 1°42' N, 40°2' E 224
Waka, Dem. Rep. of the Congo 0°50' N, 20°3' E 218
Waka, Dem. Rep. of the Congo 0°58' N, 20°13' E 218
Waka, Eth. 7°5' N, 37°18' E 224
Wakami Lake, Can. 47°27' N, 83°25' W 94
Wakasa, Japan 35°18' N, 134°22' E 201
Wakasa Wan 35°32' N, 135°31' E 201
Wakaw, Can. 52°39' N, 105°45' W 108
Wakayama, Japan 34°12' N, 135°10' E 201
Wakayama, adm. division, Japan 34°13' N, 135°16' E 201
Wake Forest, N.C., U.S. 35°58' N, 78°31' W 96
Wake Island, U.S. 19°19' N, 166°31' E 252
Wakeeney, Kans., U.S. 39°0' N, 99°54' W 90
Wakefield, Kans., U.S. 39°11' N, 97°2' W 90
Wakefield, Mich., U.S. 46°28' N, 89°57' W 94
Wakefield, Nebr., U.S. 42°15' N, 96°52' W 94
Wakefield, R.I., U.S. 41°26' N, 71°30' W 104
Wakefield, U.K. 53°41' N, 1°30' W 162
Wakema, Myanmar 16°36' N, 95°9' E 202
Wakenaam Island, Guyana 6°59' N, 58°35' W 130
Wakkanai, Japan 45°18' N, 141°48' E 190
Wakkerstroom, S. Af. 27°20' S, 30°7' E 227
Wakuach, Lac, lake, Can. 55°34' N, 69°29' W 106
Wakulla Springs, site, Fla., U.S. 30°12' N, 84°23' W 96
Walachia, region, Rom. 44°28' N, 22°46' E 168
Walberswick, U.K. 52°18' N, 1°39' E 163
Walcott, Can. 54°30' N, 126°54' W 108
Walcott Inlet 16°45' S, 123°56' E 230
Waldbröl, Ger. 50°52' N, 7°36' E 167
Waldeck, Ger. 51°12' N, 9°4' E 167
Walden, Vt., U.S. 44°26' N, 72°14' W 104
Waldfischbach-Burgalben, Ger. 49°16' N, 7°38' E 163
Waldheim, Can. 52°37' N, 106°39' W 108
Waldo, Ark., U.S. 33°20' N, 93°18' W 103
Waldo, Fla., U.S. 29°47' N, 82°11' W 105
Waldport, Oreg., U.S. 44°23' N, 124°3' W 90
Waldron, Ark., U.S. 34°52' N, 94°6' W 96
Waldron, Ind., U.S. 39°27' N, 85°40' W 102
Waldron, Cape, Antarctica 66°15' S, 119°43' E 248
Wales, Alas., U.S. 65°31' N, 168°7' W 98
Wales, Mass., U.S. 42°3' N, 72°11' W 104
Wales, adm. division, U.K. 52°21' N, 3°52' W 162
Wales Island, island, Can. 67°38' N, 89°20' W 106
Walewale, Ghana 10°21' N, 0°49' E 222
Walgreen Coast, Antarctica 75°29' S, 102°49' W 248
Walhalla, Mich., U.S. 43°56' N, 86°7' W 102
Walhalla, N. Dak., U.S. 48°54' N, 97°56' W 90
Walhalla, S.C., U.S. 34°45' N, 83°5' W 96
Walikale, Dem. Rep. of the Congo 1°30' S, 28°5' E 224
Walker, La., U.S. 30°29' N, 90°52' W 103
Walker, Mich., U.S. 42°59' N, 85°43' W 102
Walker, Minn., U.S. 47°4' N, 94°37' W 90
Walker, Lac, lake, Can. 50°24' N, 67°30' W 111
Walker Lake, Nev., U.S. 38°38' N, 119°38' W 80
Walker Lake, lake, Can. 54°36' N, 97°31' W 108
Walker Pass, Calif., U.S. 35°39' N, 118°3' W 101
Walkerton, Can. 44°7' N, 81°9' W 102
Walkerton, Ind., U.S. 41°28' N, 86°29' W 102
Walkerville, Mich., U.S. 43°42' N, 86°7' W 102
Wall, S. Dak., U.S. 43°59' N, 102°16' W 90
Wall, Mount, peak, Austral. 22°50' S, 116°37' E 230
Walla Walla, Wash., U.S. 46°4' N, 118°22' W 106
Wallabi Group, islands, Indian Ocean 28°15' S, 113°42' E 230
Wallaby Plateau, Indian Ocean 22°32' S, 104°34' E 254
Wallace, Idaho, U.S. 47°26' N, 115°54' W 82
Wallace, Nebr., U.S. 40°50' N, 101°11' W 90
Wallace, N.C., U.S. 34°44' N, 77°60' W 96
Wallace Mountain, peak, Can. 54°55' N, 115°56' W 108
Wallaceburg, Can. 42°34' N, 82°22' W 102
Wallaroo, Austral. 33°55' S, 137°39' E 231
Wallasey, U.K. 53°25' N, 3°2' W 162
Walldorf, Ger. 50°36' N, 10°23' E 167
Wallenhorst, Ger. 52°20' N, 7°59' E 163
Wallingford, Conn., U.S. 41°27' N, 72°50' W 104
Wallingford, Vt., U.S. 43°28' N, 72°59' W 104
Wallis, Îles, islands, South Pacific Ocean 14°55' S, 177°49' W 238
Wallops Island, Va., U.S. 37°25' N, 75°20' W 80
Wallowa Mountains, Oreg., U.S. 45°28' N, 117°49' W 90
Walmer, U.K. 51°12' N, 1°23' E 163
Walnum, Mount, peak, Antarctica 72°8' S, 23°50' E 248
Walnut, Ill., U.S. 41°33' N, 89°36' W 102
Walnut Cove, N.C., U.S. 36°18' N, 80°10' W 94
Walnut Grove, Calif., U.S. 38°13' N, 121°32' W 100
Walnut Grove, Miss., U.S. 32°34' N, 89°28' W 103
Walnut Ridge, Ark., U.S. 36°3' N, 90°58' W 96
Walong, India 28°10' N, 97°0' E 188
Walpi, Ariz., U.S. 35°49' N, 110°24' W 92
Walpole, Mass., U.S. 42°5' N, 71°16' W 104
Walpole, N.H., U.S. 43°4' N, 72°26' W 104
Walsall, U.K. 52°35' N, 1°60' W 162
Walsenburg, Colo., U.S. 37°37' N, 104°48' W 92
Walsh, Colo., U.S. 37°22' N, 102°17' W 92
Walsingham, U.K. 52°53' N, 0°52' E 163
Walt Disney World, Fla., U.S. 28°23' N, 81°34' W 105
Walterboro, S.C., U.S. 32°54' N, 80°41' W 96
Walters Shoal, Indian Ocean 33°25' S, 43°32' E 254
Waltham, Mass., U.S. 42°22' N, 71°15' W 104
Walton, Ind., U.S. 40°39' N, 86°14' W 102
Walton, Ky., U.S. 38°51' N, 84°36' W 102
Walton, N.Y., U.S. 42°10' N, 75°9' W 94
Walton on the Naze, U.K. 51°50' N, 1°15' E 163
Walvis Bay, Namibia 22°60' S, 14°33' E 207
Walvis Ridge, South Atlantic Ocean 26°7' S, 5°31' E 253
Walyahmoning Rock, peak, Austral. 30°41' S, 118°32' E 230
Wamac, Ill., U.S. 38°29' N, 89°8' W 102
Wamba, Dem. Rep. of the Congo 1°37' S, 22°28' E 218
Wamba, Dem. Rep. of the Congo 2°9' N, 27°57' E 218
Wamba, Nig. 8°55' N, 8°35' E 222
Wampú, river, Hond. 15°0' N, 85°36' W 115
Wampusirpi, Hond. 15°11' N, 84°38' W 115
Wamsutter, Wyo., U.S. 41°40' N, 107°58' W 90
Wana, Pak. 32°19' N, 69°40' E 188
Wan'an, China 26°28' N, 114°46' E 198
Wandel Sea 82°11' N, 24°59' W 246
Wandering River, Can. 55°9' N, 112°27' W 108
Wando, S. Korea 34°17' N, 126°47' E 200
Wanfried, Ger. 51°11' N, 10°10' E 167
Wang Kai, Sudan 9°3' N, 29°29' E 224
Wang, river, Thai. 17°37' N, 99°18' E 202
Wanganui, N.Z. 39°57' S, 175°2' E 240
Wangcang, China 32°17' N, 106°21' E 198
Wangda see Zogang, China 29°42' N, 97°53' E 188
Wangdiphodrang, Bhutan 27°30' N, 89°54' E 197
Wangdu, China 38°40' N, 115°6' E 198
Wangkui, China 46°50' N, 126°30' E 198
Wangmo, China 25°10' N, 106°6' E 198
Wangou, China 42°4' N, 126°56' E 200
Wangpan Yang 30°22' N, 120°37' E 198
Wanham, Can. 55°43' N, 118°22' W 108
Wani, India 20°2' N, 78°57' E 188
Wanie Rukula, Dem. Rep. of the Congo 0°12' N, 25°35' E 224
Wankaner, India 22°35' N, 70°56' E 186
Wanning, China 18°48' N, 110°19' E 198
Wanow, Afghan. 32°37' N, 65°55' E 186
Wantage, U.K. 51°35' N, 1°26' W 162
Wantagh, N.Y., U.S. 40°40' N, 73°30' W 104
Wanxian, China 30°47' N, 108°17' E 198
Wanyuan, China 32°5' N, 108°7' E 198
Wanzai, China 28°5' N, 114°27' E 198
Wapakoneta, Ohio, U.S. 40°33' N, 84°11' W 102
Wapata Lake, lake, Can. 58°46' N, 106°16' W 108
Wapawekka Lake, lake, Can. 54°49' N, 105°23' W 108
Wapella, Can. 50°17' N, 101°60' W 90
Wapello, Iowa, U.S. 41°10' N, 91°12' W 110
Wapesi, river, Can. 50°25' N, 92°17' W 110
Wapiti, river, Can. 54°43' N, 119°50' W 108
Wapou, Côte d'Ivoire 4°38' N, 7°12' W 222
Wappingers Falls, N.Y., U.S. 41°35' N, 73°56' W 104
Wapta Icefield, glacier, Can. 51°44' N, 116°60' W 108
Wapusk National Park, Can. 57°35' N, 93°37' W 108
War, W. Va., U.S. 37°18' N, 81°42' W 96
War Galoh, Somalia 6°15' N, 47°36' E 218
Warab, Sudan 8°2' N, 28°35' E 224
Warab, adm. division, Sudan 7°50' N, 28°24' E 224
Warangal, India 17°59' N, 79°33' E 188
Warburg, Ger. 51°29' N, 9°8' E 167
Ward, N.Z. 41°51' S, 174°7' E 240
Ward Cove, Alas., U.S. 55°26' N, 131°46' W 108
Ward Hill, peak 58°52' N, 3°28' W 150
Ward, Mount, peak, Antarctica 71°45' S, 66°36' W 248
Ward Mountain, peak, Nev., U.S. 39°5' N, 114°60' W 90
Warden, S. Af. 27°53' S, 28°55' E 227
Warden, Wash., U.S. 46°56' N, 119°3' W 90
Wardenburg, Ger. 53°4' N, 8°12' E 163
Wardha, India 20°43' N, 78°36' E 188
Ward's Stone, peak, U.K. 54°1' N, 2°40' W 162
Wardsboro, Vt., U.S. 43°2' N, 72°48' W 104
Ware, Can. 57°26' N, 125°37' W 108
Ware, Mass., U.S. 42°15' N, 72°15' W 104
Ware Shoals, S.C., U.S. 34°23' N, 82°16' W 96
Waregem, Belg. 50°53' N, 3°26' E 163
Wareham, Mass., U.S. 41°45' N, 70°45' W 104
Warehouse Point, Conn., U.S. 41°55' N, 72°37' W 104
Waremme, Belg. 50°41' N, 5°14' E 167
Waren, Indonesia 2°27' S, 136°18' E 192
Warendorf, Ger. 51°57' N, 7°59' E 167
Warffum, Neth. 53°23' N, 6°34' E 163
Warka, Pol. 51°47' N, 21°11' E 152
Warkworth, U.K. 55°20' N, 1°37' W 150
Warlubie, Pol. 53°35' N, 18°37' E 152
Warm Springs, Ga., U.S. 32°53' N, 84°41' W 96
Warman, Can. 52°17' N, 106°34' W 108
Warmbad, Namibia 28°28' S, 18°45' E 227
Warmbaths see Bela-Bela, S. Af. 24°55' S, 28°16' E 227
Warmeriville, Fr. 49°21' N, 4°13' E 163
Warmińsko-Mazurskie, adm. division, Pol. 53°57' N, 19°25' E 152
Warminster, U.K. 51°12' N, 2°12' W 162
Warner, Can. 49°16' N, 112°12' W 90
Warner, N.H., U.S. 43°16' N, 71°49' W 104
Warner, Mount, peak, Can. 51°4' N, 123°17' W 90
Warner Mountains, Calif., U.S. 41°1' N, 120°16' W 90
Warner Robins, Ga., U.S. 32°32' N, 83°36' W 112
Warner Valley, Oreg., U.S. 42°48' N, 119°59' W 90
Warnes, Arg. 34°54' S, 60°30' W 139
Warora, India 20°13' N, 79°0' E 188
Warralu, Sudan 8°10' N, 27°17' E 224
Warrego Range, Austral. 25°4' S, 145°24' E 230
Warren, Ark., U.S. 33°35' N, 92°5' W 96
Warren, Ill., U.S. 42°29' N, 89°59' W 102
Warren, Ind., U.S. 40°40' N, 85°25' W 102
Warren, Mich., U.S. 42°30' N, 83°3' W 102
Warren, Minn., U.S. 48°9' N, 96°47' W 90
Warren, Ohio, U.S. 41°13' N, 80°48' W 102
Warren, Oreg., U.S. 45°48' N, 122°52' W 100
Warren, Pa., U.S. 41°51' N, 79°10' W 94
Warren, R.I., U.S. 41°43' N, 71°17' W 104
Warren, Tex., U.S. 30°36' N, 94°24' W 103
Warren, Vt., U.S. 44°6' N, 72°52' W 104
Warren Landing, Can. 53°41' N, 97°56' W 108
Warren Peak, Calif., U.S. 41°21' N, 120°19' W 90
Warren Point, Can. 69°43' N, 134°16' W 98
Warrender, Cape, Can. 74°24' N, 80°17' W 106
Warrensburg, N.Y., U.S. 43°29' N, 73°47' W 104
Warrenton, Ga., U.S. 33°23' N, 82°40' W 96
Warrenton, Oreg., U.S. 46°9' N, 123°55' W 100
Warrenton, S. Af. 28°11' S, 24°50' E 227
Warri, Nig. 5°32' N, 5°42' E 222
Warrington, U.K. 53°23' N, 2°36' W 162
Warrnambool, Austral. 38°21' S, 142°29' E 231
Warroad, Minn., U.S. 48°53' N, 95°22' W 90
Warsaw, Ind., U.S. 41°13' N, 85°51' W 102
Warsaw, Ky., U.S. 38°45' N, 84°54' W 102
Warsaw, N.C., U.S. 34°59' N, 78°6' W 96
Warsaw, Ohio, U.S. 40°20' N, 82°1' W 102
Warsaw see Warszawa, Pol. 52°12' N, 20°50' E 152
Warshiikh, Somalia 2°15' N, 45°53' E 218
Warsop, U.K. 53°12' N, 1°9' W 162
Warstein, Ger. 51°26' N, 8°20' E 167
Warszawa (Warsaw), Pol. 52°12' N, 20°50' E 152
Warton, U.K. 53°44' N, 2°54' W 162
Warwick, Austral. 28°12' S, 152°3' E 231
Warwick, R.I., U.S. 41°41' N, 71°23' W 104
Warwick, U.K. 52°16' N, 1°36' W 162
Wasagu, Nig. 11°20' N, 5°51' E 222
Wasam, Pak. 36°32' N, 72°53' E 186
Wasatch Range, Utah, U.S. 39°56' N, 111°51' W 90
Wasco, Calif., U.S. 35°36' N, 119°21' W 100
Wasco, Oreg., U.S. 45°34' N, 120°43' W 90
Wase, Nig. 9°5' N, 9°58' E 222
Wase, river, Nig. 9°8' N, 9°47' E 222
Waseca, Minn., U.S. 44°3' N, 93°33' W 82
Wash, The 52°55' N, 0°9' E 162
Washakie Needles, peak, Wyo., U.S. 43°44' N, 109°17' W 90
Washburn, Ill., U.S. 40°54' N, 89°18' W 102
Washburn, N. Dak., U.S. 47°17' N, 101°4' W 108
Washburn, Mount, peak, Wyo., U.S. 44°46' N, 110°31' W 90
Washington, D.C., U.S. 38°52' N, 77°9' W 94
Washington, Ga., U.S. 33°43' N, 82°45' W 96
Washington, Ill., U.S. 40°41' N, 89°25' W 102
Washington, Ind., U.S. 38°39' N, 87°10' W 102
Washington, Kans., U.S. 39°48' N, 97°3' W 90
Washington, Ky., U.S. 38°36' N, 83°49' W 102
Washington, Md., U.S. 38°38' N, 77°41' W 72
Washington, Miss., U.S. 31°34' N, 91°18' W 96
Washington, Mo., U.S. 38°32' N, 90°60' W 94
Washington, N.H., U.S. 43°10' N, 72°7' W 104
Washington, N.C., U.S. 35°33' N, 77°4' W 96
Washington, Pa., U.S. 40°8' N, 80°15' W 82
Washington, R.I., U.S. 41°40' N, 71°35' W 104
Washington, Utah, U.S. 37°7' N, 113°31' W 101
Washington, Wis., U.S. 45°23' N, 86°55' W 94
Washington, adm. division, Wash., U.S. 47°10' N, 122°22' W 90
Washington, Cape, Antarctica 74°14' S, 172°22' E 248
Washington Court House, Ohio, U.S. 39°32' N, 83°26' W 102
Washington Depot, Conn., U.S. 41°38' N, 73°20' W 104
Washington Land 80°27' N, 66°2' W 246
Washington, Mount, peak, N.H., U.S. 44°15' N, 71°20' W 104
Washington, Mount, peak, Oreg., U.S. 44°18' N, 121°56' W 90
Washita, river, Okla., U.S. 35°38' N, 99°16' W 80
Washita, river, Tex., U.S. 35°36' N, 100°25' W 96
Washtucna, Wash., U.S. 46°44' N, 118°20' W 90
Wasior, Indonesia 2°39' S, 134°28' E 192
Wasipe, Ghana 8°33' N, 2°14' W 222
Waskaganish, Can. 51°27' N, 78°42' W 82
Waskaiowaka Lake, Can. 56°28' N, 97°29' W 108
Waskesiu Lake, Can. 53°55' N, 106°2' W 108
Waskom, Tex., U.S. 32°29' N, 94°5' W 103
Wasselonne, Fr. 48°37' N, 7°26' E 163
Wasserkuppe, peak, Ger. 50°29' N, 9°54' E 167
Wassuk Range, Nev., U.S. 38°57' N, 118°59' W 90
Wassy, Fr. 48°30' N, 4°56' E 163
Waswanipi, Lac, lake, Can. 49°22' N, 77°51' W 80
Waţā al Khān, Syr. 35°40' N, 36°3' E 194
Watamu Marine National Park, Kenya 3°20' S, 39°58' E 224
Watapi Lake, lake, Can. 55°18' N, 110°3' W 108
Watari, Japan 38°2' N, 140°51' E 201
Watch Hill, R.I., U.S. 41°18' N, 71°52' W 104
Watchet, U.K. 51°10' N, 3°19' W 162
Water Cays, islands, North Atlantic Ocean 23°36' N, 79°7' W 80
Waterboro, Me., U.S. 43°32' N, 70°43' W 104
Waterbury, Conn., U.S. 41°33' N, 73°3' W 104
Waterbury, Vt., U.S. 44°19' N, 72°46' W 104
Waterbury Center, Vt., U.S. 44°22' N, 72°44' W 104
Waterbury Lake, lake, Can. 58°2' N, 105°7' W 108
Wateree Lake, S.C., U.S. 34°20' N, 81°49' W 80
Waterford, Calif., U.S. 37°38' N, 120°47' W 100
Waterford, Conn., U.S. 41°20' N, 72°9' W 104
Waterford, Wis., U.S. 42°46' N, 88°14' W 102
Waterford (Port Láirge), Ire. 52°15' N, 7°8' W 150
Waterfound, river, Can. 58°27' N, 104°45' W 108
Waterloo, Can. 45°20' N, 72°33' W 94
Waterloo, Can. 43°27' N, 80°32' W 94
Waterloo, Ind., U.S. 41°25' N, 85°2' W 102
Waterloo, Iowa, U.S. 42°28' N, 92°22' W 94
Waterloo, Mo., U.S. 38°19' N, 90°9' W 94
Waterloo, Sierra Leone 8°20' N, 13°4' W 222
Waterloo, Wis., U.S. 43°10' N, 88°60' W 102
Waterman, Ill., U.S. 41°45' N, 88°48' W 102
Waterman, Isla, island, Chile 55°22' S, 71°46' W 134
Waterproof, La., U.S. 31°47' N, 91°24' W 103
Watersmeet, Mich., U.S. 46°16' N, 89°11' W 94
Waterton Lakes National Park, Can. 49°4' N, 113°35' W 80
Watertown, Conn., U.S. 41°36' N, 73°7' W 104
Watertown, N.Y., U.S. 43°58' N, 75°55' W 94
Watertown, S. Dak., U.S. 44°52' N, 97°7' W 90
Watertown, Wis., U.S. 43°10' N, 88°43' W 102
Waterval Bo, S. Af. 25°40' S, 30°17' E 227
Waterville, Kans., U.S. 39°40' N, 96°45' W 90
Waterville, Me., U.S. 44°32' N, 69°39' W 104
Waterville, Minn., U.S. 44°11' N, 93°35' W 94
Waterville, Ohio, U.S. 41°29' N, 83°44' W 102
Waterville, Wash., U.S. 47°38' N, 120°5' W 90
Waterville Valley, N.H., U.S. 43°57' N, 71°31' W 104
Watervliet, Mich., U.S. 42°10' N, 86°15' W 102
Watervliet, N.Y., U.S. 42°43' N, 73°44' W 104
Watford, Can. 42°56' N, 81°52' W 102
Watford, U.K. 51°39' N, 0°25' E 162
Watford City, N. Dak., U.S. 47°47' N, 103°18' W 90
Wathaman Lake, lake, Can. 56°56' N, 104°28' W 108
Wathena, Kans., U.S. 39°44' N, 94°57' W 94
Watino, Can. 55°41' N, 117°41' W 108
Watling see San Salvador, island, Bahamas 23°41' N, 74°29' W 116
Watonga, Okla., U.S. 35°49' N, 98°24' W 92
Watrous, Can. 51°41' N, 105°29' W 90
Watrous, N. Mex., U.S. 35°46' N, 104°59' W 92
Watsa, Dem. Rep. of the Congo 2°59' N, 29°31' E 224
Watseka, Ill., U.S. 40°45' N, 87°44' W 102
Watsi Kengo, Dem. Rep. of the Congo 0°47' N, 20°31' E 218
Watson, Can. 52°7' N, 104°32' W 108
Watson Lake, Can. 60°6' N, 128°46' W 98
Watsonville, Calif., U.S. 36°54' N, 121°46' W 100
Watton, U.K. 52°33' N, 0°51' E 162
Wattwil, Switz. 47°19' N, 9°5' E 156
Wau, P.N.G. 7°22' S, 146°41' E 192
Wau, Sudan 7°39' N, 27°58' E 224
Wau, river, Sudan 6°8' N, 27°1' E 224
Waubay, S. Dak., U.S. 45°18' N, 97°19' W 90
Wauchula, Fla., U.S. 27°33' N, 81°49' W 105
Waucoba Mountain, peak, Calif., U.S. 37°1' N, 118°3' W 101
Waugh, Can. 49°37' N, 95°13' W 90
Waukena, Calif., U.S. 36°8' N, 119°31' W 100
Waukesha, Wis., U.S. 43°1' N, 88°14' W 102
Waupaca, Wis., U.S. 44°20' N, 89°6' W 94
Waupun, Wis., U.S. 43°37' N, 88°44' W 102
Wauregan, Conn., U.S. 41°44' N, 71°55' W 104
Waurika, Okla., U.S. 34°8' N, 97°59' W 96
Wausa, Nebr., U.S. 42°29' N, 97°33' W 90
Wausau, Wis., U.S. 44°56' N, 89°37' W 94
Wauseon, Ohio, U.S. 41°32' N, 84°9' W 102
Wautoma, Wis., U.S. 44°4' N, 89°18' W 102
Wauwinet, Mass., U.S. 41°19' N, 69°60' W 104
Waveland, Miss., U.S. 30°16' N, 89°23' W 103
Waverley, N.Z. 39°47' S, 174°37' E 240
Waverly, Ill., U.S. 39°34' N, 89°58' W 102
Waverly, Iowa, U.S. 42°42' N, 92°29' W 94
Waverly, Nebr., U.S. 40°54' N, 96°33' W 90
Waverly, N.Y., U.S. 42°0' N, 76°33' W 110
Waverly, Ohio, U.S. 39°6' N, 82°60' W 102
Waverly, Va., U.S. 37°2' N, 77°6' W 96
Wavre, Belg. 50°42' N, 4°36' E 167
Wāw al Kabīr, Lib. 25°20' N, 16°43' E 216
Wāw an Nāmūs, spring, Lib. 24°58' N, 17°46' E 216
Wawa, Can. 47°59' N, 84°47' W 94
Wawa, Nig. 9°54' N, 4°24' E 222
Wawa, river, Nicar. 14°1' N, 84°24' W 115
Wawagosic, river, Can. 50°6' N, 79°5' W 94
Wawona, Calif., U.S. 37°32' N, 119°40' W 100
Waxahachie, Tex., U.S. 32°23' N, 96°51' W 96
Waxweiler, Ger. 50°5' N, 6°22' E 167
Waxxari, China 38°46' N, 87°29' E 188
Way Archipelago, islands, Antarctica 66°37' S, 147°19' E 248
Way Kambas National Park, Indonesia 5°4' S, 105°20' E 172
Wayagamac, Lac, lake, Can. 47°20' N, 73°14' W 94
Waycross, Ga., U.S. 31°11' N, 82°23' W 112
Wayland, Mich., U.S. 42°39' N, 85°39' W 102
Wayne, Can. 51°24' N, 112°42' W 90
Wayne, Me., U.S. 44°20' N, 70°4' W 104
Wayne, Nebr., U.S. 42°12' N, 97°1' W 90
Wayne, Ohio, U.S. 41°17' N, 83°29' W 102
Waynesboro, Ga., U.S. 33°4' N, 82°2' W 96
Waynesboro, Miss., U.S. 31°40' N, 88°38' W 103
Waynesboro, Tenn., U.S. 35°19' N, 87°45' W 96
Waynesboro, Va., U.S. 38°4' N, 78°54' W 94
Waynoka, Okla., U.S. 36°34' N, 98°54' W 92
Wayside, Miss., U.S. 33°14' N, 91°2' W 103
Waza, Cameroon 11°24' N, 14°35' E 216

Whitney, Mount, peak, *Calif., U.S.* 36°34′ N, 118°20′ W **101**
Whitstable, *U.K.* 51°21′ N, 1°2′ E **162**
Whitsunday Island National Park, *Austral.* 20°21′ S, 148°39′ E **238**
Whittemore, *Mich., U.S.* 44°13′ N, 83°48′ W **102**
Whittier, *Alas., U.S.* 60°40′ N, 148°51′ W **98**
Whittier, *Calif., U.S.* 33°58′ N, 118°3′ W **101**
Whittle, Cap, *Can.* 50°6′ N, 60°13′ W **111**
Whittlesey, *U.K.* 52°32′ N, 0°8′ E **162**
Wholdaia Lake, *Can.* 60°42′ N, 105°15′ W **108**
Whyalla, *Austral.* 32°60′ S, 137°33′ E **231**
Wiarton, *Can.* 44°43′ N, 81°9′ W **94**
Wibaux, *Mont., U.S.* 46°57′ N, 104°13′ W **90**
Wichita, *Kans., U.S.* 37°39′ N, 97°20′ W **90**
Wichita Falls, *Tex., U.S.* 33°52′ N, 98°30′ W **92**
Wichita, river, *Tex., U.S.* 33°47′ N, 99°19′ W **80**
Wick, *U.K.* 58°27′ N, 3°9′ W **143**
Wickede, *Ger.* 51°30′ N, 7°52′ E **167**
Wickenburg, *Ariz., U.S.* 33°58′ N, 112°47′ W **112**
Wickford see North Kingstown, *R.I., U.S.* 41°34′ N, 71°28′ W **104**
Wickliffe, *Ky., U.S.* 36°58′ N, 89°4′ W **96**
Wickliffe, *Ohio, U.S.* 41°35′ N, 81°28′ W **102**
Wicklow, *Ire.* 52°58′ N, 6°4′ W **150**
Wicklow Mountains, *Ire.* 53°1′ N, 6°59′ W **150**
Wickrath, *Ger.* 51°7′ N, 6°24′ E **167**
Widerøe, Mount, peak, *Antarctica* 72°7′ S, 22°53′ E **248**
Widnes, *U.K.* 53°21′ N, 2°44′ W **162**
Wiehl, *Ger.* 50°56′ N, 7°32′ E **167**
Wielbark, *Pol.* 53°23′ N, 20°55′ E **152**
Wielkopolskie, adm. division, *Pol.* 52°11′ N, 15°54′ E **152**
Wien (Vienna), *Aust.* 48°10′ N, 16°14′ E **152**
Wiener Neustadt, *Aust.* 47°48′ N, 16°14′ E **168**
Wierden, *Neth.* 52°21′ N, 6°35′ E **163**
Wiergate, *Tex., U.S.* 30°59′ N, 93°43′ W **103**
Wiesbaden, *Ger.* 50°4′ N, 8°13′ E **167**
Wiesmoor, *Ger.* 53°24′ N, 7°44′ E **163**
Wieżyca, peak, *Pol.* 54°13′ N, 18°2′ E **152**
Wigan, *U.K.* 53°32′ N, 2°38′ W **162**
Wiggins, *Miss., U.S.* 30°50′ N, 89°6′ W **103**
Wignes Lake, *Can.* 60°11′ N, 106°37′ W **108**
Wigton, *U.K.* 54°49′ N, 3°10′ W **162**
Wikieup, *Ariz., U.S.* 34°43′ N, 113°37′ W **101**
Wil, *Switz.* 47°27′ N, 9°2′ E **156**
Wilberforce, Cape, *Austral.* 11°50′ S, 136°37′ E **192**
Wilbur, *Wash., U.S.* 47°44′ N, 118°42′ W **90**
Wilcox, *Can.* 50°5′ N, 104°45′ W **90**
Wilczek, Zemlya, islands, *Russ.* 79°47′ N, 64°40′ E **160**
Wild, Cape, *Antarctica* 67°58′ S, 152°38′ E **248**
Wild Rice, river, *Minn., U.S.* 46°57′ N, 96°45′ W **94**
Wild Rose, *Wis., U.S.* 44°10′ N, 89°16′ W **102**
Wildcat Peak, *Nev., U.S.* 39°0′ N, 116°55′ W **90**
Wilder, *Vt., U.S.* 43°40′ N, 72°19′ W **104**
Wildflicken, *Ger.* 50°23′ N, 9°55′ E **167**
Wildomar, *Calif., U.S.* 33°36′ N, 117°17′ W **101**
Wildon, *Aust.* 46°52′ N, 15°28′ E **156**
Wildrose, *N. Dak., U.S.* 48°37′ N, 103°12′ W **90**
Wildspitze, peak, *Aust.* 46°53′ N, 10°48′ E **167**
Wildwood, *Can.* 53°35′ N, 115°16′ W **108**
Wildwood, *Fla., U.S.* 28°51′ N, 82°3′ W **105**
Wildwood, *N.J., U.S.* 38°59′ N, 74°50′ W **94**
Wiley, *Colo., U.S.* 38°9′ N, 102°43′ W **90**
Wilhelm, Mount, peak, *P.N.G.* 5°48′ S, 144°54′ E **192**
Wilhelmina Gebergte, *Suriname* 3°44′ N, 56°34′ W **130**
Wilhelmshaven, *Ger.* 53°31′ N, 8°8′ E **163**
Wilhelmstal, *Namibia* 21°53′ S, 16°31′ E **227**
Wilkes, U.S., station, *Antarctica* 66°5′ S, 110°43′ E **248**
Wilkesboro, *N.C., U.S.* 36°8′ N, 81°10′ W **96**
Wilkesland, region, *Antarctica* 69°56′ S, 132°51′ E **248**
Wilkie, *Can.* 52°25′ N, 108°43′ W **108**
Wilkinson, *Miss., U.S.* 31°13′ N, 91°14′ W **103**
Will, Mount, peak, *Can.* 57°31′ N, 128°55′ W **108**
Willacoochee, *Ga., U.S.* 31°20′ N, 83°3′ W **96**
Willapa, *Wash., U.S.* 46°40′ N, 123°40′ W **100**
Willapa Bay 46°32′ N, 125°1′ W **80**
Willapa Bay, *Wash., U.S.* 46°40′ N, 124°4′ W **100**
Willapa Hills, *Wash., U.S.* 46°20′ N, 123°12′ W **100**
Willard, *N. Mex., U.S.* 34°35′ N, 106°2′ W **92**
Willard, *Ohio, U.S.* 41°2′ N, 82°44′ W **102**
Willaumez Peninsula, *P.N.G.* 5°15′ S, 149°24′ E **192**
Willcox, *Ariz., U.S.* 32°14′ N, 109°51′ W **112**
Willebroek, *Belg.* 51°2′ N, 4°21′ E **163**
Willemstad, *Neth. Antilles, Neth.* 51°41′ N, 4°25′ E **167**
William Lake, lake, *Can.* 53°49′ N, 99°46′ W **108**
William Point, *Can.* 58°55′ N, 109°47′ W **108**
William, river, *Can.* 58°9′ N, 108°60′ W **108**
Williams, *Ariz., U.S.* 35°13′ N, 112°11′ W **82**
Williams, *Calif., U.S.* 39°9′ N, 122°10′ W **90**
Williams, *Ind., U.S.* 38°48′ N, 86°39′ W **102**
Williams, *Minn., U.S.* 48°44′ N, 94°58′ W **90**
Williams Bay, *Wis., U.S.* 42°34′ N, 88°33′ W **102**
Williams Island, *Bahamas* 24°33′ N, 78°35′ W **105**
Williams Lake, *Can.* 51°46′ N, 91°23′ W **110**
Williams Lake, *Can.* 52°6′ N, 122°5′ W **106**
Williams Lake, *Can.* 52°8′ N, 122°7′ W **108**
Williams, Point, *Antarctica* 67°54′ S, 68°26′ E **248**
Williamsburg, *Ky., U.S.* 36°44′ N, 84°10′ W **96**
Williamsburg, *Mass., U.S.* 42°23′ N, 72°43′ W **104**
Williamsburg, *Ohio, U.S.* 39°3′ N, 84°4′ W **102**
Williamsburg, *Va., U.S.* 37°16′ N, 76°43′ W **94**
Williamsfield, *Ill., U.S.* 40°54′ N, 90°2′ W **102**
Williamson, *W. Va., U.S.* 37°40′ N, 82°17′ W **96**
Williamson, Mount, peak, *Calif., U.S.* 36°39′ N, 118°21′ W **101**
Williamsport, *Ind., U.S.* 40°16′ N, 87°18′ W **102**
Williamsport, *Ohio, U.S.* 39°34′ N, 83°7′ W **102**
Williamsport, *Pa., U.S.* 41°14′ N, 77°1′ W **94**
Williamstown, *Ky., U.S.* 38°37′ N, 84°34′ W **102**
Williamstown, *Vt., U.S.* 44°7′ N, 72°33′ W **104**
Williamstown, *W. Va., U.S.* 39°23′ N, 81°28′ W **102**
Williamsville, *Ill., U.S.* 39°56′ N, 89°33′ W **102**
Willich, *Ger.* 51°15′ N, 6°33′ E **167**
Willimantic, *Conn., U.S.* 41°42′ N, 72°13′ W **104**
Willingdon, Mount, peak, *Can.* 51°46′ N, 116°20′ W **90**
Willis, *Tex., U.S.* 30°24′ N, 95°28′ W **103**
Willis Islands, *Scotia Sea* 53°50′ S, 39°43′ W **134**
Willis Islets, islands, *Coral Sea* 15°9′ S, 149°13′ E **230**
Williston, *Fla., U.S.* 29°22′ N, 82°28′ W **105**
Williston, *N. Dak., U.S.* 48°7′ N, 103°39′ W **90**
Williston, *S. Af.* 31°19′ S, 20°53′ E **227**
Williston Lake, *Can.* 55°59′ N, 124°26′ W **108**
Willits, *Calif., U.S.* 39°24′ N, 123°22′ W **90**
Willmar, *Minn., U.S.* 45°6′ N, 95°3′ W **90**
Willoughby, *U.K.* 53°13′ N, 0°12′ E **162**
Willow, *Alas., U.S.* 61°44′ N, 150°4′ W **98**
Willow Bunch, *Can.* 49°22′ N, 105°38′ W **90**
Willow City, *N. Dak., U.S.* 48°34′ N, 100°19′ W **94**
Willow Hill, *Ill., U.S.* 38°58′ N, 88°1′ W **102**
Willow Island, *Nebr., U.S.* 40°53′ N, 100°5′ W **90**
Willow Reservoir, lake, *Wis., U.S.* 45°42′ N, 90°22′ W **94**
Willow River, *Can.* 54°2′ N, 122°31′ W **108**
Willow Springs, *Mo., U.S.* 36°58′ N, 91°59′ W **96**
Willowick, *Ohio, U.S.* 41°37′ N, 81°28′ W **102**
Willowmore, *S. Af.* 33°17′ S, 23°29′ E **227**
Willows, *Calif., U.S.* 39°31′ N, 122°13′ W **92**
Wills Point, *Tex., U.S.* 32°41′ N, 96°1′ W **96**
Willsboro, *N.Y., U.S.* 44°21′ N, 73°25′ W **104**
Wilmer, *Ala., U.S.* 30°49′ N, 88°21′ W **103**
Wilmer, *Can.* 50°32′ N, 116°4′ W **108**
Wilmette, *Ill., U.S.* 42°4′ N, 87°42′ W **102**
Wilmington, *Del., U.S.* 39°43′ N, 75°33′ W **94**
Wilmington, *Ill., U.S.* 41°18′ N, 88°8′ W **102**
Wilmington, *N.Y., U.S.* 44°23′ N, 73°50′ W **104**
Wilmington, *N.C., U.S.* 34°14′ N, 77°55′ W **73**
Wilmington, *Ohio, U.S.* 39°26′ N, 83°49′ W **102**
Wilmington, *Vt., U.S.* 42°51′ N, 72°52′ W **104**
Wilmot, *Ark., U.S.* 33°2′ N, 91°35′ W **103**
Wilmot, *S. Dak., U.S.* 45°23′ N, 96°53′ W **90**
Wilmot Flat, *N.H., U.S.* 43°25′ N, 71°54′ W **104**
Wilmslow, *U.K.* 53°19′ N, 2°14′ W **162**
Wilpattu National Park, *Sri Lanka* 8°19′ N, 79°37′ E **172**
Wilsall, *Mont., U.S.* 45°58′ N, 110°40′ W **90**
Wilseyville, *Calif., U.S.* 38°22′ N, 120°32′ W **100**
Wilson, *Ark., U.S.* 35°33′ N, 90°3′ W **96**
Wilson, *Kans., U.S.* 38°48′ N, 98°29′ W **92**
Wilson, *La., U.S.* 30°54′ N, 91°7′ W **103**
Wilson, *N.C., U.S.* 35°42′ N, 77°56′ W **96**
Wilson, *Okla., U.S.* 34°8′ N, 97°25′ W **92**
Wilson, *Tex., U.S.* 33°18′ N, 101°44′ W **92**
Wilson Creek, *Wash., U.S.* 47°25′ N, 119°8′ W **90**
Wilson Creek Range, *Nev., U.S.* 38°23′ N, 114°38′ W **90**
Wilson Inlet 35°22′ S, 116°46′ E **230**
Wilson, Mount, peak, *Colo., U.S.* 37°49′ N, 108°4′ W **92**
Wilson, Mount, peak, *Nev., U.S.* 38°13′ N, 114°28′ W **90**
Wilson, Mount, peak, *Oreg., U.S.* 45°2′ N, 121°45′ W **90**
Wilsonville, *Ill., U.S.* 39°3′ N, 89°51′ W **102**
Wilton, *Conn., U.S.* 41°11′ N, 73°27′ W **104**
Wilton, *N.H., U.S.* 42°50′ N, 71°45′ W **104**
Wilton, *N. Dak., U.S.* 47°8′ N, 100°49′ W **90**
Wilton, *U.K.* 51°5′ N, 1°53′ W **162**
Wilton, river, *Austral.* 13°31′ S, 133°56′ E **231**
Wiluna, *Austral.* 26°36′ S, 120°13′ E **231**
Wimauma, *Fla., U.S.* 27°43′ N, 82°17′ W **105**
Wimbledon, *U.K.* 51°25′ N, 0°13′ E **162**
Wimereux, *Fr.* 50°46′ N, 1°37′ E **163**
Winam 0°21′ N, 34°13′ E **224**
Winamac, *Ind., U.S.* 41°2′ N, 86°37′ W **102**
Winburg, *S. Af.* 28°33′ S, 26°58′ E **227**
Wincanton, *U.K.* 51°3′ N, 2°25′ W **162**
Winchelsea, *U.K.* 50°55′ N, 0°43′ E **162**
Winchelsea Island, *Austral.* 13°36′ S, 136°22′ E **230**
Winchendon, *Mass., U.S.* 42°40′ N, 72°4′ W **104**
Winchester, *Calif., U.S.* 33°42′ N, 117°6′ W **101**
Winchester, *Ind., U.S.* 40°10′ N, 84°59′ W **102**
Winchester, *N.H., U.S.* 42°45′ N, 72°23′ W **104**
Winchester, *Ohio, U.S.* 38°55′ N, 83°38′ W **102**
Winchester, *U.K.* 51°3′ N, 1°19′ W **162**
Winchester, *Va., U.S.* 39°10′ N, 78°10′ W **94**
Winchester Bay 43°35′ N, 125°25′ W **80**
Wind Cave National Park, *S. Dak., U.S.* 43°29′ N, 103°16′ W **80**
Wind Point, *Wis., U.S.* 42°46′ N, 87°46′ W **102**
Wind, river, *Can.* 65°23′ N, 135°18′ W **98**
Wind River Peak, *Wyo., U.S.* 42°42′ N, 109°13′ W **90**
Wind River Range, *Wyo., U.S.* 42°39′ N, 109°21′ W **90**
Wind, river, *Wyo., U.S.* 43°22′ N, 109°9′ W **80**
Windeck, *Ger.* 50°48′ N, 7°36′ E **167**
Winder, *Ga., U.S.* 33°58′ N, 83°44′ W **96**
Windermere, *U.K.* 54°22′ N, 2°54′ W **162**
Windfall, *Can.* 54°9′ N, 116°18′ W **108**
Windfall, *Ind., U.S.* 40°21′ N, 85°58′ W **102**
Windham, *Conn., U.S.* 41°41′ N, 72°10′ W **104**
Windhoek, *Namibia* 22°34′ S, 16°56′ E **227**
Windigo, river, *Can.* 48°22′ N, 73°33′ W **94**
Windmill Islands, *Indian Ocean* 66°40′ S, 114°44′ E **248**
Windom, *Minn., U.S.* 43°51′ N, 95°7′ W **90**
Windom Peak, *Colo., U.S.* 37°36′ N, 107°41′ W **92**
Window Rock, *Ariz., U.S.* 35°41′ N, 109°3′ W **92**
Winds, Bay of 66°11′ S, 99°28′ E **248**
Windsor, *Can.* 45°34′ N, 72°1′ W **94**
Windsor, *Can.* 42°18′ N, 83°1′ W **102**
Windsor, *Can.* 44°59′ N, 64°8′ W **111**
Windsor, *Colo., U.S.* 40°28′ N, 104°55′ W **90**
Windsor, *Conn., U.S.* 41°50′ N, 72°39′ W **104**
Windsor, *Ill., U.S.* 39°25′ N, 88°36′ W **102**
Windsor, *Mo., U.S.* 38°31′ N, 93°31′ W **94**
Windsor, *N.C., U.S.* 35°59′ N, 76°60′ W **96**
Windsor, *U.K.* 51°28′ N, 0°37′ E **162**
Windsor, *Vt., U.S.* 43°28′ N, 72°24′ W **104**
Windsorton, *S. Af.* 28°21′ S, 24°39′ E **227**
Windward Islands, *Caribbean Sea* 13°41′ N, 61°20′ W **116**
Windy Lake, *Can.* 60°18′ N, 100°44′ W **108**
Windy Peak, *Wash., U.S.* 48°54′ N, 120°3′ W **90**
Windy Point, *Can.* 50°56′ N, 55°48′ W **111**
Winefred Lake, *Can.* 55°25′ N, 111°16′ W **108**
Winfall, *N.C., U.S.* 36°13′ N, 76°29′ W **96**
Winfield, *Can.* 52°56′ N, 114°27′ W **108**
Winfield, *Tex., U.S.* 33°9′ N, 95°7′ W **103**
Wingham, *Can.* 43°53′ N, 81°19′ W **102**
Winifred, *Mont., U.S.* 47°31′ N, 109°23′ W **90**
Winifreda, *Arg.* 36°15′ S, 64°15′ W **139**
Winisk Lake, *Can.* 52°49′ N, 88°29′ W **80**
Winisk, river, *Can.* 54°27′ N, 86°26′ W **106**
Wink, *Tex., U.S.* 31°43′ N, 103°9′ W **92**
Winkleigh, *U.K.* 50°51′ N, 3°57′ W **162**
Winkler, *Can.* 49°10′ N, 97°56′ W **94**
Winlock, *Wash., U.S.* 46°28′ N, 122°56′ W **100**
Winn, *Me., U.S.* 45°28′ N, 68°23′ W **94**
Winneba, *Ghana* 5°22′ N, 0°40′ E **222**
Winnebago, *Ill., U.S.* 42°15′ N, 89°15′ W **102**
Winnebago, *Minn., U.S.* 43°45′ N, 94°10′ W **94**
Winnebago, Lake, *Wis., U.S.* 43°50′ N, 88°27′ W **102**
Winneconne, *Wis., U.S.* 44°6′ N, 88°45′ W **102**
Winner, *S. Dak., U.S.* 43°21′ N, 99°52′ W **90**
Winnetka, *Ill., U.S.* 42°6′ N, 87°44′ W **102**
Winnfield, *La., U.S.* 31°54′ N, 92°39′ W **103**
Winnibigoshish, Lake, *Minn., U.S.* 47°21′ N, 96°1′ W **80**
Winnie, *Tex., U.S.* 29°48′ N, 94°23′ W **103**
Winnipeg, *Can.* 49°53′ N, 97°19′ W **90**
Winnipeg Beach, *Can.* 50°29′ N, 97°2′ W **90**
Winnipeg, Lake, *Can.* 53°1′ N, 98°32′ W **80**
Winnipegosis, *Can.* 51°39′ N, 99°57′ W **90**
Winnipegosis, Lake, *Can.* 52°3′ N, 99°36′ W **80**
Winnisquam, *N.H., U.S.* 43°30′ N, 71°32′ W **104**
Winnsboro, *La., U.S.* 32°9′ N, 91°44′ W **103**
Winnsboro, *S.C., U.S.* 34°21′ N, 81°5′ W **96**
Winnsboro, *Tex., U.S.* 32°57′ N, 95°17′ W **103**
Winokapau Lake, *Can.* 53°13′ N, 63°41′ W **111**
Winona, *Kans., U.S.* 39°3′ N, 101°15′ W **90**
Winona, *Minn., U.S.* 44°2′ N, 91°38′ W **94**
Winona, *Miss., U.S.* 33°27′ N, 89°44′ W **103**
Winona, *Tex., U.S.* 32°29′ N, 95°10′ W **103**
Winona Lake, *Ind., U.S.* 41°12′ N, 85°49′ W **94**
Winschoten, *Neth.* 53°8′ N, 7°1′ E **163**
Winsen, *Ger.* 53°22′ N, 10°12′ E **150**
Winsford, *U.K.* 53°11′ N, 2°32′ W **162**
Winslow, *Ariz., U.S.* 35°1′ N, 110°41′ W **92**
Winslow, *Me., U.S.* 44°32′ N, 69°38′ W **94**
Winstead, *S. Af.* 28°51′ S, 22°8′ E **227**
Winsted, *Conn., U.S.* 41°55′ N, 73°4′ W **104**
Winter Harbour, *Can.* 50°30′ N, 128°4′ W **90**
Winter Haven, *Fla., U.S.* 28°1′ N, 81°44′ W **105**
Winter Park, *Fla., U.S.* 28°35′ N, 81°22′ W **105**
Winterberg, *Ger.* 51°11′ N, 8°32′ E **167**
Winterhaven, *Calif., U.S.* 32°44′ N, 114°40′ W **101**
Wintering Lake, lake, *Can.* 49°23′ N, 87°51′ W **94**
Winters, *Tex., U.S.* 31°56′ N, 99°58′ W **96**
Winterswijk, *Neth.* 51°58′ N, 6°43′ E **167**
Winterton on Sea, *U.K.* 52°43′ N, 1°41′ E **163**
Winterville, *Miss., U.S.* 33°29′ N, 91°3′ W **103**
Winthrop, *Mass., U.S.* 42°22′ N, 70°60′ W **104**
Winthrop, *Minn., U.S.* 44°32′ N, 94°23′ W **90**
Winthrop, *Wash., U.S.* 48°27′ N, 120°10′ W **108**
Winthrop Harbor, *Ill., U.S.* 42°28′ N, 87°50′ W **102**
Winton, *Austral.* 22°25′ S, 143°2′ E **238**
Winton, *Calif., U.S.* 37°23′ N, 120°38′ W **100**
Winton, *Minn., U.S.* 47°54′ N, 91°49′ W **94**
Winton, *N.Z.* 46°9′ S, 168°18′ E **240**
Wipperfürth, *Ger.* 51°7′ N, 7°23′ E **163**
Wis, river, *Pol.* 53°7′ N, 18°11′ E **142**
Wis, river, *Pol.* 50°1′ N, 20°37′ E **152**
Wisbech, *U.K.* 52°39′ N, 0°9′ E **162**
Wiscasset, *Me., U.S.* 44°0′ N, 69°41′ W **94**
Wisconsin, adm. division, *Wis., U.S.* 44°20′ N, 91°11′ W **94**
Wisconsin Dells, *Wis., U.S.* 43°37′ N, 89°46′ W **102**
Wisconsin, Lake, *Wis., U.S.* 43°21′ N, 89°53′ W **102**
Wisconsin Range, *Antarctica* 84°42′ S, 105°9′ W **248**
Wisconsin Rapids, *Wis., U.S.* 44°23′ N, 89°50′ W **110**
Wisconsin, river, *Wis., U.S.* 42°45′ N, 91°14′ W **80**
Wise Bay 82°34′ S, 170°4′ E **248**
Wiseman, *Alas., U.S.* 67°18′ N, 150°16′ W **98**
Wishek, *N. Dak., U.S.* 46°14′ N, 99°35′ W **90**
Wishram, *Wash., U.S.* 45°39′ N, 120°58′ W **100**
Wisner, *La., U.S.* 31°58′ N, 91°39′ W **103**
Wissen, *Ger.* 50°46′ N, 7°43′ E **167**
Wistaria, *Can.* 53°51′ N, 126°18′ W **108**
Witbank, *S. Af.* 25°53′ S, 29°11′ E **227**
Witdraai, *S. Af.* 27°1′ S, 20°41′ E **227**
Witham, *U.K.* 51°48′ N, 0°38′ E **162**
Witherbee, *N.Y., U.S.* 44°5′ N, 73°33′ W **104**
Withernsea, *U.K.* 53°43′ N, 3°179′ E **162**
Witney, *U.K.* 51°47′ N, 1°29′ W **162**
Witry-lès-Reims, *Fr.* 49°17′ N, 4°7′ E **163**
Witt, *Ill., U.S.* 39°14′ N, 89°21′ W **102**
Wittdün, *Ger.* 54°37′ N, 8°23′ E **150**
Witten, *Ger.* 51°25′ N, 7°19′ E **167**
Witten, *S. Dak., U.S.* 43°25′ N, 100°6′ W **90**
Wittenberge, *Ger.* 53°3′ N, 11°43′ E **160**
Wittlich, *Ger.* 49°59′ N, 6°54′ E **167**
Wittmund, *Ger.* 53°34′ N, 7°47′ E **163**
Wittow, *Ger.* 54°38′ N, 13°6′ E **152**
Witu, *Kenya* 2°23′ S, 40°26′ E **224**
Witu Islands, islands, *Bismarck Sea* 4°24′ S, 148°22′ E **192**
Witvlei, *Namibia* 22°24′ S, 18°32′ E **227**
Witzenhausen, *Ger.* 51°20′ N, 9°51′ E **167**
Wivenhoe, *Can.* 56°11′ N, 95°11′ W **108**
Wiwŏn, *N. Korea* 40°53′ N, 126°2′ E **200**
Wiżajny, *Pol.* 54°21′ N, 22°52′ E **166**
Włocławek, *Pol.* 52°38′ N, 19°4′ E **152**
Włodawa, *Pol.* 51°32′ N, 23°31′ E **152**
Woburn, *Mass., U.S.* 42°28′ N, 71°10′ W **104**
Woc, *Pol.* 54°16′ N, 18°45′ E **162**
Wofford Heights, *Calif., U.S.* 35°43′ N, 118°28′ W **101**
Wokam, island, *Indonesia* 5°44′ S, 134°34′ E **192**
Woking, *Can.* 55°34′ N, 118°47′ W **108**
Woking, *U.K.* 51°18′ N, 0°35′ E **162**
Wokingham, *U.K.* 51°22′ N, 0°52′ E **162**
Wolcott, *Ind., U.S.* 40°45′ N, 87°3′ W **102**
Wolds, The, *U.K.* 53°56′ N, 0°40′ E **162**
Woleai Atoll, *F.M.S.* 7°26′ N, 141°37′ E **192**
Wolf Creek, *Mont., U.S.* 46°58′ N, 112°3′ W **90**
Wolf Creek Pass, *Colo., U.S.* 37°29′ N, 106°49′ W **90**
Wolf Lake, *Can.* 60°38′ N, 132°17′ W **108**
Wolf Lake, *Mich., U.S.* 43°14′ N, 86°7′ W **102**
Wolf Mountains, *Mont., U.S.* 45°9′ N, 107°18′ W **90**
Wolf, river, *Miss., U.S.* 30°33′ N, 89°23′ W **103**
Wolf, river, *Wis., U.S.* 45°17′ N, 88°60′ W **94**
Wolfau, *Aust.* 47°15′ N, 16°5′ E **168**
Wolfeboro, *N.H., U.S.* 43°34′ N, 71°13′ W **104**
Wolfeboro Falls, *N.H., U.S.* 43°35′ N, 71°13′ W **104**
Wolfen, *Ger.* 51°40′ N, 12°16′ E **152**
Wolfforth, *Tex., U.S.* 33°29′ N, 102°1′ W **92**
Wolfhagen, *Ger.* 51°19′ N, 9°10′ E **167**
Wolfsburg, *Ger.* 52°25′ N, 10°47′ E **152**
Wolfstein, *Ger.* 49°34′ N, 7°36′ E **163**
Wolin, *Pol.* 53°51′ N, 14°36′ E **152**
Wollaston Forland 74°31′ N, 18°52′ W **246**
Wollaston, Islas, islands, *Chile* 56°6′ S, 67°3′ W **134**
Wollaston Lake, *Can.* 57°56′ N, 103°5′ W **73**
Wollaston Peninsula, *Can.* 69°41′ N, 121°29′ W **106**
Wollongong, *Austral.* 34°24′ S, 150°50′ E **231**
Wöllstein, *Ger.* 49°48′ N, 7°57′ E **167**
Wolmaransstad, *S. Af.* 27°13′ S, 25°58′ E **227**
Wolseley, *Can.* 50°25′ N, 103°17′ W **90**
Wolsingham, *U.K.* 54°44′ N, 1°54′ W **162**
Wolsztyn, *Pol.* 52°7′ N, 16°7′ E **152**
Wolvega, *Neth.* 52°52′ N, 6°0′ E **163**
Wolverhampton, *U.K.* 52°35′ N, 2°9′ W **162**
Wolverine, river, *Can.* 57°46′ N, 116°59′ W **108**
Wolverton, *U.K.* 52°3′ N, 0°49′ E **162**
Wondong, *S. Korea* 34°21′ N, 126°42′ E **200**
Wonewoc, *Wis., U.S.* 43°38′ N, 90°12′ W **102**
Wonga Wongué National Park, *Gabon* 0°29′ N, 9°13′ E **206**
Wonju, *S. Korea* 37°19′ N, 127°57′ E **200**
Wonotobo Vallen, fall(s), *Suriname* 4°22′ N, 58°6′ W **130**
Wonowon, *Can.* 56°43′ N, 121°48′ W **108**
Wŏnsan, *N. Korea* 39°8′ N, 127°24′ E **200**
Wonyulgunna Hill, peak, *Austral.* 24°53′ S, 119°34′ E **230**
Wood Buffalo National Park, *Can.* 59°16′ N, 114°1′ W **73**
Wood Lake, *Nebr., U.S.* 42°37′ N, 100°15′ W **90**
Wood Lake, lake, *Can.* 55°13′ N, 103°45′ W **108**
Wood, Mount, peak, *Mont., U.S.* 45°14′ N, 109°53′ W **90**
Wood River, *Nebr., U.S.* 40°48′ N, 98°37′ W **90**
Wood, river, *Can.* 49°22′ N, 107°21′ W **80**
Woodah, Isle, island, *Austral.* 13°20′ S, 134°37′ E **230**
Woodall Mountain, peak, *Miss., U.S.* 34°43′ N, 88°18′ W **96**
Woodbine, *Ky., U.S.* 36°53′ N, 84°6′ W **96**
Woodbridge, *Calif., U.S.* 38°8′ N, 121°19′ W **100**
Woodbridge, *U.K.* 52°5′ N, 1°17′ E **162**
Woodburn, *Ind., U.S.* 41°6′ N, 84°51′ W **102**
Woodburn, *Oreg., U.S.* 45°7′ N, 122°51′ W **90**
Woodbury, *Conn., U.S.* 41°32′ N, 73°13′ W **104**
Woodbury, *N.J., U.S.* 39°50′ N, 75°11′ W **94**
Woodcock, Mount, peak, *Austral.* 19°17′ S, 133°51′ E **230**
Woodhall Spa, *U.K.* 53°9′ N, 0°13′ E **162**
Woodlake, *Calif., U.S.* 36°25′ N, 119°7′ W **101**
Woodland, *Calif., U.S.* 38°40′ N, 121°47′ W **90**
Woodland, *Wash., U.S.* 45°53′ N, 122°46′ W **100**
Woodlark, island, *P.N.G.* 9°5′ S, 153°2′ E **192**
Woodmont, *Conn., U.S.* 41°13′ N, 72°60′ W **104**
Woodpecker, *Can.* 53°30′ N, 122°39′ W **108**
Woodridge, *Can.* 49°15′ N, 96°9′ W **90**
Woodroffe, Mount, peak, *Austral.* 26°23′ S, 131°32′ E **230**
Woodruff, *Utah, U.S.* 41°31′ N, 111°10′ W **90**
Woods, Lake of the, *Can.* 49°4′ N, 96°1′ W **106**
Woodsboro, *Tex., U.S.* 28°13′ N, 97°19′ W **96**
Woodsfield, *Ohio, U.S.* 39°44′ N, 81°7′ W **102**
Woodstock, *Can.* 43°7′ N, 80°44′ W **102**
Woodstock, *Can.* 46°9′ N, 67°36′ W **94**
Woodstock, *Ill., U.S.* 42°18′ N, 88°26′ W **102**
Woodstock, *N.Y., U.S.* 42°2′ N, 74°8′ W **104**
Woodstock, *U.K.* 51°50′ N, 1°22′ W **162**
Woodstock, *Vt., U.S.* 43°37′ N, 72°31′ W **104**
Woodsville, *N.H., U.S.* 44°8′ N, 72°3′ W **104**
Woodville, *Calif., U.S.* 36°5′ N, 119°13′ W **101**
Woodville, *Ga., U.S.* 33°39′ N, 83°7′ W **96**
Woodville, *Miss., U.S.* 31°4′ N, 91°18′ W **103**
Woodville, *Tex., U.S.* 30°45′ N, 94°26′ W **103**
Woodward, *Okla., U.S.* 36°24′ N, 99°23′ W **96**
Woodworth, *La., U.S.* 31°8′ N, 92°31′ W **103**
Woody, *Calif., U.S.* 35°42′ N, 118°51′ W **101**
Woody Point, *Can.* 49°30′ N, 57°56′ W **111**
Woollard, Mount, peak, *Antarctica* 80°27′ S, 95°39′ W **248**
Woollett, Lac, lake, *Can.* 51°22′ N, 74°22′ W **110**
Woolpit, *U.K.* 52°13′ N, 0°53′ E **162**
Woolwich, *Me., U.S.* 43°55′ N, 69°49′ W **104**
Woolwich, *U.K.* 51°29′ N, 6°357′ E **162**
Woomera, *Austral.* 31°13′ S, 136°55′ E **231**
Woonsocket, *S. Dak., U.S.* 44°2′ N, 98°18′ W **90**
Wooster, *Ohio, U.S.* 40°47′ N, 81°56′ W **102**
Woosung, *Ill., U.S.* 41°53′ N, 89°33′ W **102**
Worbis, *Ger.* 51°25′ N, 10°21′ E **167**
Worcester, *Mass., U.S.* 42°16′ N, 71°48′ W **104**
Worcester, *S. Af.* 33°38′ S, 19°23′ E **227**
Worcester, *U.K.* 52°11′ N, 2°12′ W **162**
Worden, *Mont., U.S.* 45°57′ N, 108°10′ W **90**
Wordie Nunatak, peak, *Antarctica* 66°19′ S, 51°16′ E **248**
Workington, *U.K.* 54°38′ N, 3°33′ W **162**
Worksop, *U.K.* 53°17′ N, 1°8′ W **162**
Worland, *Wyo., U.S.* 44°0′ N, 107°56′ W **90**
World's View Hill, site, *Zimb.* 20°31′ S, 28°29′ E **227**
Wormeldange, *Lux.* 49°37′ N, 6°24′ E **163**
Woronoco, *Mass., U.S.* 42°9′ N, 72°51′ W **104**
Wörrstadt, *Ger.* 49°49′ N, 8°6′ E **167**
Worsley, *Can.* 56°33′ N, 119°8′ W **108**
Wörth, *Ger.* 49°47′ N, 9°10′ E **167**
Wortham, *Tex., U.S.* 31°45′ N, 96°28′ W **96**
Worthing, *U.K.* 50°49′ N, 0°23′ E **162**
Worthington, *Ind., U.S.* 39°6′ N, 86°59′ W **102**
Worthington, *Minn., U.S.* 43°35′ N, 95°37′ W **90**
Worthington, *Ohio, U.S.* 40°5′ N, 82°60′ W **102**
Worthington Peak, *Nev., U.S.* 37°54′ N, 115°42′ W **90**
Worthville, *Ky., U.S.* 38°36′ N, 85°4′ W **102**
Wosi, *Indonesia* 0°10′ N, 127°46′ E **192**
Woumbou, *Cameroon* 5°15′ N, 14°14′ E **218**
Wounta, Laguna de, lake, *Nicar.* 13°34′ N, 84°18′ W **115**
Wour, *Chad* 21°21′ N, 15°57′ E **216**
Wowoni, island, *Indonesia* 4°20′ S, 123°14′ E **192**
Woyla, river, *Indonesia* 4°21′ N, 96°4′ E **196**
Wragby, *U.K.* 53°16′ N, 0°19′ E **162**
Wrangel Island see Vrangelya, Ostrov, island, *Russ.* 71°29′ N, 175°23′ E **160**
Wrangel Plain, *Arctic Ocean* 81°41′ N, 157°4′ E **255**
Wrangell, *Alas., U.S.* 56°28′ N, 132°25′ W **108**
Wrangell Mountains, *Alas., U.S.* 61°51′ N, 144°32′ W **98**
Wrangell-Saint Elias National Park and Preserve, *Alas., U.S.* 62°15′ N, 143°49′ W **98**
Wray, *Colo., U.S.* 40°3′ N, 102°14′ W **90**
Wreck Point, *S. Af.* 29°7′ S, 16°12′ E **227**
Wrekin, The, peak, *U.K.* 52°39′ N, 2°36′ W **162**
Wren, *Ala., U.S.* 34°25′ N, 87°17′ W **96**
Wrens, *Ga., U.S.* 33°11′ N, 82°24′ W **96**
Wrexham, *U.K.* 53°2′ N, 2°59′ W **162**
Wright, *Philippines* 11°47′ N, 125°1′ E **203**
Wright, *Wyo., U.S.* 43°42′ N, 105°32′ W **90**
Wright Hill, peak, *Antarctica* 79°36′ S, 159°27′ E **248**
Wright, Mont, peak, *Can.* 52°43′ N, 67°27′ W **111**
Wright Patman Lake, *Ark., U.S.* 33°1′ N, 94°59′ W **80**
Wright-Patterson Air Force Base, *Ohio, U.S.* 39°48′ N, 84°6′ W **102**
Wrightsville Beach, *N.C., U.S.* 34°12′ N, 77°49′ W **96**
Wrightwood, *Calif., U.S.* 34°21′ N, 117°39′ W **101**
Wrigley, *Can.* 63°19′ N, 123°21′ W **98**
Wrigley Gulf 73°35′ S, 126°58′ W **248**
Wrington, *U.K.* 51°21′ N, 2°46′ W **162**
Wroc, *Pol.* 51°6′ N, 17°0′ E **152**
Wrong Lake, lake, *Can.* 52°34′ N, 96°38′ W **108**
Wronki, *Pol.* 52°42′ N, 16°23′ E **152**
Wroxeter, *Can.* 43°51′ N, 81°11′ W **102**
Wroxham, *U.K.* 52°43′ N, 1°24′ E **163**
Wroxton, *Can.* 51°12′ N, 101°54′ W **90**
Wroxton, *U.K.* 52°4′ N, 1°25′ W **162**
Wu, river, *China* 28°38′ N, 108°25′ E **198**
Wu, river, *China* 27°14′ N, 108°4′ E **190**
Wu'an, *China* 36°42′ N, 114°13′ E **198**
Wubu, *China* 37°27′ N, 110°40′ E **198**
Wuchang, *China* 44°55′ N, 127°8′ E **198**
Wuchuan, *China* 41°7′ N, 111°33′ E **198**
Wuchuan, *China* 28°26′ N, 108°1′ E **198**
Wuchuan, *China* 21°24′ N, 110°47′ E **198**
Wuda, *China* 39°33′ N, 106°44′ E **198**
Wudalianchi, *China* 48°38′ N, 126°10′ E **198**
Wudaogou, *China* 42°5′ N, 125°51′ E **200**
Wudaoliang, *China* 35°13′ N, 93°2′ E **188**
Wudi, *China* 37°45′ N, 117°35′ E **198**
Wudu, *China* 33°25′ N, 104°54′ E **198**
Wufeng, *China* 30°14′ N, 110°40′ E **198**
Wugang, *China* 26°44′ N, 110°34′ E **198**
Wugong, *China* 34°17′ N, 108°11′ E **198**
Wuhai, *China* 39°39′ N, 106°50′ E **198**
Wuhan, *China* 30°30′ N, 114°21′ E **198**
Wuhe, *China* 33°9′ N, 117°55′ E **198**
Wuhu, *China* 31°23′ N, 118°26′ E **198**
Wüjang, *China* 33°36′ N, 79°54′ E **188**
Wukari, *Nig.* 7°49′ N, 9°48′ E **222**
Wulff Land 81°57′ N, 58°19′ W **246**
Wuli, *China* 34°22′ N, 92°45′ E **188**
Wulian, *China* 35°44′ N, 119°13′ E **198**
Wulongbei, *China* 40°15′ N, 124°15′ E **200**
Wum, *Cameroon* 6°19′ N, 10°3′ E **222**
Wuming, *China* 23°8′ N, 108°18′ E **198**
Wun Shwai, *Sudan* 8°1′ N, 29°24′ E **224**
Wuning, *China* 29°18′ N, 115°1′ E **198**
Wünnenberg, *Ger.* 51°30′ N, 8°43′ E **167**
Wunstorf, *Ger.* 52°25′ N, 9°26′ E **152**
Wuping, *China* 25°4′ N, 116°4′ E **198**
Wuppertal, *Ger.* 51°16′ N, 7°10′ E **167**
Wuqi, *China* 36°57′ N, 108°14′ E **198**
Wuqia, *China* 39°45′ N, 75°6′ E **184**
Wuqing, *China* 39°25′ N, 117°0′ E **198**
Wurno, *Nig.* 13°14′ N, 5°27′ E **222**
Würselen, *Ger.* 50°49′ N, 6°7′ E **163**
Würzburg, *Ger.* 49°47′ N, 9°56′ E **167**
Wusa'a, *Sudan* 13°0′ N, 32°31′ E **182**
Wushan, *China* 31°6′ N, 109°51′ E **198**
Wushi (Uqturpan), *China* 41°9′ N, 79°17′ E **184**
Wutai, *China* 38°41′ N, 113°11′ E **198**
Wuvulu Island, *P.N.G.* 2°23′ S, 142°45′ E **192**
Wuwei, *China* 38°0′ N, 102°55′ E **190**
Wuwei, *China* 31°17′ N, 117°47′ E **198**
Wuxi, *China* 31°23′ N, 109°36′ E **198**
Wuxi, *China* 31°37′ N, 120°18′ E **198**
Wuxue, *China* 29°54′ N, 115°33′ E **198**
Wuyi Shan, *China* 26°4′ N, 116°25′ E **198**
Wuyiling, *China* 48°37′ N, 129°21′ E **198**

Wuyuan, *China* 41° 4′ N, 108° 19′ E **198**
Wuzhai, *China* 38° 54′ N, 111° 49′ E **198**
Wuzhong, *China* 38° 1′ N, 106° 12′ E **198**
Wuzhou, *China* 23° 34′ N, 111° 21′ E **198**
Wyandotte, *Mich., U.S.* 42° 11′ N, 83° 11′ W **102**
Wyanet, *Ill., U.S.* 41° 22′ N, 89° 34′ W **102**
Wye, river, *U.K.* 52° 15′ N, 3° 30′ W **162**
Wyemandoo, peak, *Austral.* 28° 36′ S, 118° 19′ E **230**
Wylatowo, *Pol.* 52° 36′ N, 17° 55′ E **152**
Wymondham, *U.K.* 52° 34′ N, 1° 6′ E **163**
Wymore, *Nebr., U.S.* 40° 5′ N, 96° 40′ W **90**
Wyndham, *Austral.* 15° 29′ S, 128° 14′ E **238**
Wyndmere, *N. Dak., U.S.* 46° 15′ N, 97° 10′ W **90**
Wynne, *Ark., U.S.* 35° 12′ N, 90° 49′ W **96**
Wynnewood, *Okla., U.S.* 34° 37′ N, 97° 9′ W **96**
Wynyard, *Can.* 51° 45′ N, 104° 11′ W **90**
Wyoming, *Can.* 42° 56′ N, 82° 7′ W **102**
Wyoming, *Ill., U.S.* 41° 3′ N, 89° 47′ W **102**
Wyoming, adm. division, *Wyo., U.S.* 42° 49′ N, 108° 38′ W **90**
Wyoming Peak, *Wyo., U.S.* 42° 36′ N, 110° 43′ W **90**
Wyoming Range, *Wyo., U.S.* 42° 46′ N, 110° 47′ W **90**
Wysox, *Pa., U.S.* 41° 46′ N, 76° 25′ W **110**
Wytheville, *Va., U.S.* 36° 56′ N, 81° 6′ W **96**
Wyville Thomson Ridge, *North Atlantic Ocean* 59° 30′ N, 10° 10′ W **253**
Wyvis, Ben, peak, *U.K.* 57° 39′ N, 4° 41′ W **150**

X

X, Rock, *Antarctica* 66° 2′ S, 138° 54′ E **248**
Xá Muteba, *Angola* 9° 33′ S, 17° 49′ E **218**
Xaafuun, *Somalia* 10° 21′ N, 51° 18′ E **216**
Xaafuun, Raas, *Somalia* 10° 26′ N, 51° 28′ E **216**
Xàbia see Jávea, *Sp.* 38° 47′ N, 0° 9′ E **164**
Xaçmaz, *Azerb.* 41° 27′ N, 48° 49′ E **195**
Xaignabouri, *Laos* 19° 16′ N, 101° 43′ E **202**
Xainza, *China* 30° 57′ N, 88° 37′ E **197**
Xaitongmoin, *China* 29° 27′ N, 88° 9′ E **188**
Xai-Xai, *Mozambique* 25° 3′ S, 33° 39′ E **227**
Xalapa, *Mex.* 19° 28′ N, 96° 59′ W **114**
Xalin, *Somalia* 9° 5′ N, 48° 37′ E **216**
Xam Nua, *Laos* 20° 27′ N, 104° 0′ E **202**
Xamure, *Somalia* 7° 11′ N, 48° 56′ E **218**
Xamure, spring, *Somalia* 7° 12′ N, 48° 55′ E **216**
Xangongo, *Angola* 16° 45′ S, 15° 0′ E **220**
Xankändi see Stepanakert, *Asia* 39° 48′ N, 46° 43′ E **195**
Xanten, *Ger.* 51° 39′ N, 6° 27′ E **167**
Xánthi, *Gr.* 41° 8′ N, 24° 54′ E **180**
Xanthus, ruin(s), *Turk.* 36° 19′ N, 29° 12′ E **156**
Xanxerê, *Braz.* 26° 52′ S, 52° 25′ W **138**
Xapecó, *Braz.* 27° 4′ S, 52° 36′ W **139**
Xapecó, river, *Braz.* 26° 39′ S, 52° 30′ W **139**
Xapuri, *Braz.* 10° 42′ S, 68° 32′ W **137**
Xapuri, river, *Braz.* 10° 43′ S, 69° 13′ W **137**
Xar Moron, river, *China* 43° 17′ N, 119° 27′ E **198**
Xarardheere, *Somalia* 4° 38′ N, 47° 53′ E **218**
Xassengue, *Angola* 10° 26′ S, 18° 33′ E **220**
Xàtiva, *Sp.* 38° 58′ N, 0° 31′ E **164**
Xavantina, *Braz.* 21° 15′ S, 52° 50′ W **138**
Xayar, *China* 41° 14′ N, 82° 51′ E **184**
Xcalak National Park, *Mex.* 18° 20′ N, 88° 6′ W **72**
Xêgar see Tingri, *China* 28° 40′ N, 87° 3′ E **197**
Xèng, river, *Laos* 20° 10′ N, 102° 44′ E **202**
Xenia, *Ill., U.S.* 38° 37′ N, 88° 38′ W **102**
Xenia, *Ohio, U.S.* 39° 41′ N, 83° 56′ W **102**
Xépôn, *Laos* 16° 41′ N, 106° 15′ E **202**
Xeriuini, river, *Braz.* 0° 50′ N, 62° 15′ W **130**
Xhora, *S. Af.* 31° 59′ S, 28° 39′ E **227**
Xi Ujimqin Qi, *China* 44° 36′ N, 117° 36′ E **198**
Xiachuan Dao, island, *China* 21° 17′ N, 112° 22′ E **198**
Xiajiang, *China* 27° 35′ N, 115° 3′ E **198**
Xiamen (Amoy), *China* 24° 25′ N, 118° 6′ E **198**
Xi'an, *China* 34° 17′ N, 108° 57′ E **198**
Xianfeng, *China* 29° 41′ N, 109° 8′ E **198**
Xiang, river, *China* 26° 33′ N, 112° 13′ E **198**
Xiangfan, *China* 32° 6′ N, 112° 2′ E **198**
Xianggang see Hong Kong, island, *China* 21° 55′ N, 114° 15′ E **198**
Xianghuang Qi (Hobot Xar), *China* 42° 11′ N, 113° 53′ E **198**
Xiangkhoang, *Laos* 19° 20′ N, 103° 23′ E **202**
Xiangning, *China* 35° 57′ N, 110° 48′ E **198**
Xiangshan, *China* 29° 26′ N, 121° 52′ E **198**
Xiangtan, *China* 27° 54′ N, 112° 51′ E **198**
Xiangyin, *China* 28° 42′ N, 112° 50′ E **198**
Xianju, *China* 28° 53′ N, 120° 43′ E **198**
Xiantao, *China* 30° 19′ N, 113° 26′ E **198**
Xianyou, *China* 25° 22′ N, 118° 42′ E **198**
Xiaogan, *China* 30° 55′ N, 113° 55′ E **198**
Xiaojiang, *China* 27° 33′ N, 120° 28′ E **198**
Xiaoshan, *China* 30° 8′ N, 120° 18′ E **198**
Xiaoyi, *China* 37° 7′ N, 111° 46′ E **198**
Xiapu, *China* 26° 53′ N, 119° 59′ E **198**
Xichang, *China* 27° 53′ N, 102° 16′ E **190**
Xichang Space Launch Center, spaceport, *China* 28° 13′ N, 101° 49′ E **190**
Xichú, *Mex.* 21° 23′ N, 100° 5′ W **114**
Xichuan, *China* 33° 10′ N, 111° 31′ E **198**
Xicoténcatl, *Mex.* 22° 58′ N, 98° 56′ W **114**
Xicotepec de Juárez, *Mex.* 20° 16′ N, 97° 57′ W **114**
Xié, river, *Braz.* 1° 12′ N, 67° 15′ W **136**
Xiejia, *China* 42° 23′ N, 125° 43′ E **200**
Xifeng, *China* 42° 45′ N, 124° 39′ E **200**
Xifeng, *China* 35° 47′ N, 107° 39′ E **198**
Xigazê, *China* 29° 13′ N, 88° 53′ E **190**
Xihe, *China* 33° 59′ N, 105° 16′ E **198**
Xiis, *Somalia* 10° 47′ N, 46° 52′ E **216**
Xiji, *China* 36° 0′ N, 105° 43′ E **198**
Xijir Ulan Hu, lake, *China* 35° 9′ N, 89° 12′ E **188**
Xiliao, river, *China* 43° 45′ N, 122° 32′ E **198**
Xilinhot, *China* 43° 56′ N, 116° 8′ E **198**
Xilitla, *Mex.* 21° 23′ N, 98° 58′ W **114**
Ximeng, *China* 22° 43′ N, 99° 25′ E **202**
Xin Barag Youqi, *China* 48° 39′ N, 116° 47′ E **198**
Xin Barag Zuoqi, *China* 48° 10′ N, 118° 13′ E **198**
Xin Hot see Abag Qi, *China* 44° 1′ N, 114° 56′ E **198**
Xinavane, *Mozambique* 25° 2′ S, 32° 47′ E **227**
Xinbin, *China* 41° 43′ N, 125° 4′ E **200**
Xincai, *China* 32° 46′ N, 114° 53′ E **198**
Xincheng, *China* 38° 32′ N, 106° 11′ E **198**
Xinchengzi, *China* 42° 4′ N, 123° 33′ E **200**
Xinfeng, *China* 25° 24′ N, 114° 54′ E **198**
Xinfeng, *China* 24° 1′ N, 114° 10′ E **198**
Xing'an, *China* 25° 33′ N, 110° 37′ E **198**
Xingcheng, *China* 40° 39′ N, 120° 46′ E **198**
Xingdi, *China* 41° 17′ N, 87° 58′ E **188**
Xinge, *Angola* 9° 47′ S, 19° 11′ E **220**
Xinghe, *China* 40° 51′ N, 113° 54′ E **198**
Xinghua, *China* 32° 56′ N, 119° 53′ E **198**
Xingning, *China* 24° 6′ N, 115° 43′ E **198**
Xingshan, *China* 31° 22′ N, 110° 44′ E **198**
Xingtai, *China* 37° 1′ N, 114° 31′ E **198**
Xingu, river, *Braz.* 5° 8′ S, 54° 18′ W **122**
Xingxian, *China* 38° 28′ N, 111° 3′ E **198**
Xingyi, *China* 25° 1′ N, 105° 8′ E **190**
Xingzi, *China* 29° 27′ N, 115° 59′ E **198**
Xinhe, *China* 37° 31′ N, 115° 13′ E **198**
Xinhe (Toksu), *China* 41° 35′ N, 82° 38′ E **184**
Xinhuang, *China* 27° 20′ N, 109° 17′ E **198**
Xinhui, *China* 22° 26′ N, 113° 1′ E **198**
Xining, *China* 36° 30′ N, 101° 51′ E **190**
Xinji, *China* 37° 56′ N, 115° 15′ E **198**
Xinjiang, *China* 35° 38′ N, 111° 12′ E **198**
Xinjiang, adm. division, *China* 41° 27′ N, 81° 29′ E **184**
Xinjin, *China* 39° 25′ N, 122° 2′ E **198**
Xinmin, *China* 41° 59′ N, 122° 49′ E **200**
Xinning, *China* 26° 28′ N, 110° 48′ E **198**
Xinpu see Lianyungang, *China* 34° 38′ N, 119° 14′ E **198**
Xinshao, *China* 27° 21′ N, 111° 28′ E **198**
Xinwen, *China* 35° 53′ N, 117° 43′ E **198**
Xinxiang, *China* 35° 12′ N, 113° 48′ E **198**
Xinxing, *China* 22° 43′ N, 112° 9′ E **198**
Xinyang, *China* 32° 9′ N, 114° 6′ E **198**
Xinye, *China* 32° 31′ N, 112° 26′ E **198**
Xinyi, *China* 34° 19′ N, 118° 20′ E **198**
Xinyu, *China* 27° 46′ N, 114° 52′ E **198**
Xinyuan, *China* 43° 25′ N, 83° 25′ E **184**
Xinzhou, *China* 38° 24′ N, 112° 45′ E **198**
Xique Xique, *Braz.* 10° 51′ S, 42° 43′ W **132**
Xiruá, river, *Braz.* 7° 19′ S, 68° 34′ W **130**
Xishui, *China* 30° 27′ N, 115° 13′ E **198**
Xishui, *China* 28° 20′ N, 106° 11′ E **198**
Xiushan, *China* 28° 25′ N, 108° 59′ E **198**
Xiushui, *China* 29° 4′ N, 114° 30′ E **198**
Xiuyan, *China* 40° 16′ N, 123° 15′ E **200**
Xiuying, *China* 19° 59′ N, 110° 12′ E **198**
Xixia, *China* 33° 21′ N, 111° 30′ E **198**
Xixian, *China* 32° 22′ N, 114° 41′ E **198**
Xixiang, *China* 33° 4′ N, 107° 44′ E **198**
Xizang, adm. division, *China* 29° 28′ N, 87° 1′ E **197**
Xizhong Dao, island, *China* 39° 8′ N, 121° 11′ E **198**
Xochihuehuetlán, *Mex.* 17° 54′ N, 98° 28′ W **114**
Xorkol, *China* 38° 52′ N, 91° 10′ E **188**
Xpuhil, ruin(s), *Mex.* 18° 31′ N, 89° 33′ W **115**
Xuan Loc, *Vietnam* 10° 56′ N, 107° 14′ E **202**
Xuan'en, *China* 30° 1′ N, 109° 28′ E **198**
Xuanhan, *China* 31° 21′ N, 107° 36′ E **198**
Xuanhua, *China* 40° 38′ N, 115° 5′ E **198**
Xuanzhou, *China* 30° 54′ N, 118° 46′ E **198**
Xuchang, *China* 34° 3′ N, 113° 49′ E **198**
Xudat, *Azerb.* 41° 37′ N, 48° 41′ E **195**
Xuddur (Oddur), *Somalia* 4° 6′ N, 43° 55′ E **218**
Xudun, *Somalia* 9° 31′ N, 47° 29′ E **216**
Xui, *Uru.* 33° 40′ S, 53° 29′ W **139**
Xulun Hoh see Zhenglan Qi, *China* 42° 13′ N, 116° 2′ E **198**
Xümatang, *China* 33° 52′ N, 97° 21′ E **188**
Xunwu, *China* 24° 52′ N, 115° 37′ E **198**
Xunyang, *China* 32° 53′ N, 109° 22′ E **198**
Xunyi, *China* 35° 10′ N, 108° 18′ E **198**
Xupu, *China* 27° 56′ N, 110° 35′ E **198**
Xuwen, *China* 20° 18′ N, 110° 9′ E **198**
Xuyong, *China* 28° 9′ N, 105° 28′ E **198**
Xuzhou, *China* 34° 16′ N, 117° 7′ E **198**
Xylofagou, *Cyprus* 34° 58′ N, 33° 50′ E **194**

Y

Yaak, *Mont., U.S.* 48° 49′ N, 115° 43′ W **90**
Yaak, river, *Can.* 48° 43′ N, 116° 2′ W **90**
Ya'an, *China* 30° 2′ N, 103° 1′ E **190**
Yabassi, *Cameroon* 4° 25′ N, 9° 58′ E **222**
Yabēlo, *Eth.* 4° 51′ N, 38° 8′ E **224**
Yablunyts'kyy, Pereval, pass, *Ukr.* 48° 17′ N, 24° 27′ E **152**
Yabrīn, spring, *Saudi Arabia* 23° 11′ N, 48° 57′ E **182**
Yabrūd, *Syr.* 33° 58′ N, 36° 38′ E **194**
Yachi, river, *China* 26° 59′ N, 106° 14′ E **198**
Yacimiento Río Turbio, *Arg.* 51° 35′ S, 72° 21′ W **134**
Yaco, *Bol.* 17° 13′ S, 67° 34′ W **137**
Yaco, river, *Peru* 10° 47′ S, 70° 49′ W **137**
Yacolt, *Wash., U.S.* 45° 51′ N, 122° 25′ W **100**
Yacuma, river, *Bol.* 14° 6′ S, 66° 36′ W **137**
Yadgir, *India* 16° 46′ N, 77° 8′ E **188**
Yaenengu, *Dem. Rep. of the Congo* 2° 27′ N, 23° 11′ E **218**
Yag, river, *China* 34° 0′ N, 93° 55′ E **188**
Yağca, *Turk.* 37° 1′ N, 30° 32′ E **156**
Yagodnoye, *Russ.* 62° 34′ N, 149° 33′ E **160**
Yagoua, *Cameroon* 10° 22′ N, 15° 14′ E **216**
Yagradagzê Shan, peak, *China* 35° 8′ N, 95° 34′ E **188**
Yaguarón, river, *South America* 31° 60′ S, 54° 1′ W **139**
Yaguas, river, *Peru* 3° 11′ S, 71° 2′ W **136**
Yahia Lehouas, *Alg.* 35° 36′ N, 4° 55′ E **150**
Yahk, *Can.* 49° 5′ N, 116° 7′ W **90**
Yahualica, *Mex.* 21° 9′ N, 102° 54′ W **114**
Yahuma, *Dem. Rep. of the Congo* 1° 5′ N, 23° 5′ E **218**
Yahyalı, *Turk.* 38° 5′ N, 35° 21′ E **156**
Yainax Butte, peak, *Oreg., U.S.* 42° 19′ N, 121° 20′ W **90**
Yaita, *Japan* 36° 47′ N, 139° 56′ E **201**
Yaizu, *Japan* 34° 51′ N, 138° 18′ E **201**
Yakeshi, *China* 49° 15′ N, 120° 43′ E **198**
Yakima, *Wash., U.S.* 46° 35′ N, 120° 30′ W **90**
Yakkabog', *Uzb.* 39° 1′ N, 66° 41′ E **197**
Yakmach, *Pak.* 28° 43′ N, 63° 48′ E **182**
Yakoma, *Dem. Rep. of the Congo* 4° 2′ N, 22° 21′ E **218**
Yakossi, *Cen. Af. Rep.* 5° 37′ N, 23° 22′ E **218**
Yakotoko, *Cen. Af. Rep.* 5° 20′ N, 25° 16′ E **224**
Yaksha, *Russ.* 61° 49′ N, 56° 50′ E **154**
Yaku Shima, island, *Japan* 29° 39′ N, 130° 35′ E **190**
Yakusu, *Dem. Rep. of the Congo* 0° 35′ N, 25° 1′ E **224**
Yakutsk, *Russ.* 62° 2′ N, 129° 36′ E **160**
Yala, *Ghana* 10° 7′ N, 1° 52′ W **222**
Yala, *Sri Lanka* 6° 22′ N, 81° 31′ E **188**
Yala, *Thai.* 6° 30′ N, 101° 16′ E **196**
Yalagüina, *Nicar.* 13° 28′ N, 86° 28′ W **115**
Yale, *Can.* 49° 34′ N, 121° 26′ W **100**
Yale, *Mich., U.S.* 43° 8′ N, 82° 47′ W **102**
Yale, *Okla., U.S.* 36° 5′ N, 96° 41′ W **92**
Yale Dam, *Wash., U.S.* 45° 59′ N, 122° 25′ W **100**
Yali, *Dem. Rep. of the Congo* 1° 59′ N, 21° 5′ E **218**
Yaligimba, *Dem. Rep. of the Congo* 2° 11′ N, 22° 54′ E **218**
Yalinga, *Cen. Af. Rep.* 6° 30′ N, 23° 19′ E **218**
Yalkubul, Punta, *Mex.* 21° 34′ N, 89° 27′ W **116**
Yalova, *Turk.* 40° 38′ N, 29° 15′ E **156**
Yalta, *Ukr.* 44° 30′ N, 34° 5′ E **156**
Yalu, river, *Asia* 41° 46′ N, 128° 2′ E **200**
Yalutorovsk, *Russ.* 56° 40′ N, 66° 11′ E **169**
Yalvaç, *Turk.* 38° 17′ N, 31° 9′ E **156**
Yamada, *Japan* 33° 33′ N, 130° 45′ E **201**
Yamaga, *Japan* 33° 0′ N, 130° 41′ E **201**
Yamagata, *Japan* 38° 15′ N, 140° 20′ E **201**
Yamagata, adm. division, *Japan* 38° 22′ N, 139° 45′ E **201**
Yamaguchi, *Japan* 34° 11′ N, 131° 29′ E **200**
Yamaguchi, adm. division, *Japan* 34° 6′ N, 131° 0′ E **200**
Yamal, Poluostrov, *Russ.* 70° 23′ N, 70° 9′ E **169**
Yamanaka, *Japan* 36° 14′ N, 136° 22′ E **201**
Yamanashi, adm. division, *Japan* 35° 30′ N, 138° 17′ E **201**
Yamato Mountains, *Antarctica* 71° 23′ S, 36° 56′ E **248**
Yambio, *Sudan* 4° 32′ N, 28° 24′ E **224**
Yambol, *Bulg.* 42° 29′ N, 26° 30′ E **156**
Yambol, adm. division, *Bulg.* 42° 12′ N, 26° 17′ E **156**
Yamburg, *Russ.* 68° 18′ N, 77° 12′ E **169**
Yamdena, island, *Indonesia* 7° 13′ S, 131° 2′ E **192**
Yamethinn, *Myanmar* 20° 26′ N, 96° 7′ E **202**
Yamkino, *Russ.* 57° 53′ N, 29° 17′ E **166**
Yamm, *Russ.* 58° 24′ N, 28° 4′ E **166**
Yammaw, *Myanmar* 26° 15′ N, 97° 42′ E **188**
Yamoussoukro, *Côte d'Ivoire* 6° 44′ N, 5° 24′ W **222**
Yampa, river, *Colo., U.S.* 40° 33′ N, 108° 7′ W **92**
Yampil', *Ukr.* 48° 14′ N, 28° 20′ E **156**
Yampol', *Ukr.* 49° 57′ N, 26° 16′ E **152**
Yamsay Mountain, peak, *Oreg., U.S.* 42° 55′ N, 121° 27′ W **90**
Yamsk, *Russ.* 59° 35′ N, 153° 56′ E **160**
Yamuna, river, *India* 29° 23′ N, 77° 4′ E **190**
Yamzho Yumco, lake, *China* 28° 59′ N, 90° 26′ E **197**
Yana, *Sierra Leone* 9° 43′ N, 12° 22′ W **222**
Yana, river, *Russ.* 69° 54′ N, 135° 39′ E **160**
Yanachaga Chemillén National Park, *Peru* 10° 31′ S, 75° 37′ W **122**
Yanagawa, *Japan* 33° 9′ N, 130° 24′ E **201**
Yanai, *Japan* 33° 58′ N, 132° 7′ E **201**
Yanam, *India* 16° 45′ N, 82° 5′ E **190**
Yan'an, *China* 36° 33′ N, 109° 28′ E **198**
Yanaoca, *Peru* 14° 15′ S, 71° 25′ W **137**
Yanaul, *Russ.* 56° 16′ N, 55° 4′ E **154**
Yanbu'al Baḩr, *Saudi Arabia* 24° 5′ N, 38° 4′ E **182**
Yanchang, *China* 36° 36′ N, 110° 3′ E **198**
Yancheng, *China* 33° 21′ N, 120° 6′ E **198**
Yanchi, *China* 37° 46′ N, 107° 20′ E **198**
Yanchuan, *China* 36° 50′ N, 110° 10′ E **198**
Yandoon, *Myanmar* 17° 3′ N, 95° 37′ E **202**
Yanfolila, *Mali* 11° 11′ N, 8° 10′ W **222**
Yangambi, *Dem. Rep. of the Congo* 0° 47′ N, 24° 25′ E **224**
Yangarey, *Russ.* 68° 43′ N, 61° 29′ E **169**
Yangasso, *Mali* 13° 4′ N, 5° 20′ W **222**
Yangbajain, *China* 30° 11′ N, 90° 29′ E **197**
Yangchun, *China* 22° 8′ N, 111° 47′ E **198**
Yangdŏk, *N. Korea* 39° 12′ N, 126° 40′ E **200**
Yanggu, *S. Korea* 38° 7′ N, 127° 59′ E **200**
Yanghe, *China* 40° 4′ N, 123° 25′ E **200**
Yangi-Nishon, *Uzb.* 38° 37′ N, 65° 40′ E **197**
Yangiqishloq, *Uzb.* 40° 25′ N, 67° 13′ E **197**
Yangiyer, *Uzb.* 40° 12′ N, 68° 51′ E **197**
Yangiyŭl, *Uzb.* 41° 9′ N, 69° 4′ E **197**
Yangjiang, *China* 21° 50′ N, 111° 59′ E **198**
Yangon (Rangoon), *Myanmar* 16° 45′ N, 96° 0′ E **202**
Yangory, *Russ.* 62° 46′ N, 37° 48′ E **154**
Yangou Gala, *Cen. Af. Rep.* 7° 21′ N, 20° 11′ E **218**
Yangquan, *China* 37° 52′ N, 113° 36′ E **198**
Yangsan, *S. Korea* 35° 20′ N, 129° 3′ E **200**
Yangshan, *China* 24° 29′ N, 112° 39′ E **198**
Yangshuo, *China* 24° 45′ N, 110° 26′ E **198**
Yangtze, lake, *China* 30° 23′ N, 106° 28′ E **172**
Yangtze, river, *China* 27° 59′ N, 104° 57′ E **172**
Yangtze see Jinsha, river, *China* 25° 47′ N, 103° 15′ E **190**
Yangtze, Source of the, *China* 33° 16′ N, 90° 53′ E **188**
Yangudi Rassa National Park, *Eth.* 10° 46′ N, 41° 7′ E **224**
Yangxian, *China* 33° 13′ N, 107° 31′ E **198**
Yangxin, *China* 29° 51′ N, 115° 6′ E **198**
Yangyang, *S. Korea* 38° 5′ N, 128° 37′ E **200**
Yangyuan, *China* 40° 7′ N, 114° 8′ E **198**
Yangzhou, *China* 32° 25′ N, 119° 27′ E **198**
Yangzishao, *China* 42° 25′ N, 126° 7′ E **200**
Yanhe, *China* 28° 32′ N, 108° 25′ E **198**
Yanis'yarvi, Ozero, lake, *Russ.* 61° 52′ N, 29° 54′ E **152**
Yanji, *China* 42° 55′ N, 129° 27′ E **200**
Yanji (Longjing), *China* 42° 46′ N, 129° 24′ E **200**
Yankari National Park, *Nig.* 9° 47′ N, 9° 50′ E **222**
Yankeetown, *Fla., U.S.* 29° 2′ N, 82° 44′ W **105**
Yankovichi, *Belarus* 55° 47′ N, 28° 48′ E **166**
Yankton, *S. Dak., U.S.* 42° 51′ N, 97° 24′ W **90**
Yanonge, *Dem. Rep. of the Congo* 0° 33′ N, 24° 39′ E **224**
Yanqi, *China* 42° 8′ N, 86° 39′ E **184**
Yanrakynnot, *Russ.* 64° 59′ N, 172° 39′ W **98**
Yanshan, *China* 38° 4′ N, 117° 13′ E **198**
Yanshan, *China* 23° 32′ N, 104° 20′ E **202**
Yanshan, *China* 28° 16′ N, 117° 38′ E **198**
Yanshou, *China* 45° 30′ N, 128° 21′ E **198**
Yanskiy, *Russ.* 68° 22′ N, 135° 8′ E **160**
Yantai, *China* 37° 32′ N, 121° 21′ E **198**
Yantarnyy, *Russ.* 54° 51′ N, 19° 56′ E **166**
Yao, *Japan* 34° 38′ N, 135° 35′ E **201**
Yaoundé, *Cameroon* 3° 55′ N, 11° 24′ E **222**
Yaoxian, *China* 34° 59′ N, 109° 0′ E **198**
Yap Islands, *Philippine Sea* 9° 43′ N, 136° 10′ E **192**
Yap Trench, *North Pacific Ocean* 7° 20′ N, 137° 57′ E **254**
Yapacana National Park, *Venez.* 3° 44′ N, 66° 47′ W **136**
Yapacani, river, *Bol.* 15° 52′ S, 64° 33′ W **137**
Yapei (Tamale Port), *Ghana* 9° 10′ N, 1° 11′ W **222**
Yapele, *Dem. Rep. of the Congo* 0° 12′ N, 24° 25′ E **224**
Yapen, island, *Indonesia* 1° 32′ S, 135° 43′ E **192**
Yapeyú, *Arg.* 29° 26′ S, 56° 53′ W **139**
Yaptiksale, *Russ.* 69° 20′ N, 72° 36′ E **169**
Yaqui, river, *Mex.* 28° 10′ N, 110° 3′ W **112**
Yaquina Head, *Oreg., U.S.* 44° 29′ N, 124° 22′ W **90**
Yar, *Russ.* 58° 13′ N, 52° 9′ E **154**
Yar Sale, *Russ.* 66° 49′ N, 70° 48′ E **169**
Yaracuy, adm. division, *Venez.* 10° 25′ N, 69° 4′ W **136**
Yaraka, *Austral.* 24° 54′ S, 144° 4′ E **231**
Yaralıgöz, peak, *Turk.* 41° 45′ N, 34° 1′ E **156**
Yaransk, *Russ.* 57° 18′ N, 47° 57′ E **154**
Yarda, spring, *Chad* 18° 31′ N, 18° 58′ E **216**
Yardımcı Burnu, *Turk.* 36° 6′ N, 30° 26′ E **156**
Yardymly, *Azerb.* 38° 54′ N, 48° 14′ E **195**
Yarega, *Russ.* 63° 26′ N, 53° 35′ E **154**
Yaren, *Nauru* 0° 33′ N, 166° 55′ E **242**
Yarenga, *Russ.* 62° 43′ N, 49° 33′ E **154**
Yarensk, *Russ.* 62° 10′ N, 49° 11′ E **154**
Yarí, river, *Col.* 0° 20′ N, 72° 50′ W **136**
Yarīm, *Yemen* 14° 17′ N, 44° 24′ E **182**
Yarkant, river, *China* 37° 58′ N, 76° 14′ E **184**
Yarkant see Shache, *China* 38° 27′ N, 77° 17′ E **184**
Yarkul', *Russ.* 54° 36′ N, 77° 17′ E **184**
Yarma, *Turk.* 37° 49′ N, 32° 53′ E **156**
Yarmouth, *Can.* 43° 48′ N, 66° 8′ W **94**
Yarmouth, *Me., U.S.* 43° 47′ N, 70° 12′ W **104**
Yarnema, *Russ.* 62° 59′ N, 39° 23′ E **154**
Yaroslavl', *Russ.* 57° 34′ N, 39° 48′ E **154**
Yaroslavl', adm. division, *Russ.* 57° 40′ N, 37° 38′ E **154**
Yaroto, Ozera, lake, *Russ.* 67° 59′ N, 70° 25′ E **169**
Yarozero, *Russ.* 60° 27′ N, 38° 35′ E **154**
Yartsevo, *Russ.* 60° 9′ N, 90° 14′ E **169**
Yarumal, *Col.* 6° 58′ N, 75° 26′ W **136**
Yary, *Russ.* 68° 50′ N, 66° 41′ E **169**
Yashalta, *Russ.* 46° 18′ N, 42° 6′ E **158**
Yashchera, *Russ.* 59° 8′ N, 29° 54′ E **166**
Yashi, *Nig.* 12° 21′ N, 7° 55′ E **222**
Yashichu, *China* 37° 25′ N, 75° 22′ E **184**
Yashikera, *Nig.* 9° 44′ N, 3° 29′ E **222**
Yashkino, *Russ.* 52° 41′ N, 53° 30′ E **154**
Yashkul', *Russ.* 46° 8′ N, 45° 18′ E **158**
Yasnoye, *Russ.* 55° 11′ N, 21° 31′ E **166**
Yasnyy, *Russ.* 51° 5′ N, 59° 53′ E **158**
Yasothon, *Thai.* 15° 48′ N, 104° 9′ E **202**
Yasugi, *Japan* 35° 24′ N, 133° 15′ E **201**
Yāsūj, *Iran* 30° 39′ N, 51° 35′ E **180**
Yasun Burnu, *Turk.* 41° 10′ N, 37° 6′ E **156**
Yasuní National Park, *Ecua.* 0° 57′ N, 76° 27′ W **136**
Yata, *Bol.* 13° 20′ S, 66° 48′ W **137**
Yata, *Braz.* 10° 40′ S, 65° 21′ W **137**
Yata, river, *Bol.* 11° 14′ S, 65° 43′ W **137**
Yata, river, *Cen. Af. Rep.* 10° 13′ N, 23° 2′ E **218**
Yatakala, *Niger* 14° 47′ N, 0° 22′ E **222**
Yates Center, *Kans., U.S.* 37° 51′ N, 95° 44′ W **96**
Yates City, *Ill., U.S.* 40° 45′ N, 90° 1′ W **102**
Yates, river, *Can.* 59° 31′ N, 116° 31′ W **108**
Yatina, *Bol.* 20° 46′ S, 64° 45′ W **137**
Yatou see Rongcheng, *China* 37° 10′ N, 122° 26′ E **198**
Yatsushiro, *Japan* 32° 30′ N, 130° 36′ E **201**
Yatta Plateau, *Kenya* 1° 52′ S, 37° 52′ E **224**
Yauca, *Peru* 15° 42′ S, 74° 31′ W **137**
Yauca, river, *Peru* 15° 13′ S, 74° 7′ W **137**
Yauna Moloca, *Col.* 0° 55′ N, 70° 9′ W **136**
Yaupi, *Ecua.* 2° 55′ S, 77° 53′ W **136**
Yauri (Espinar), *Peru* 14° 51′ S, 71° 24′ W **137**
Yautepec, *Mex.* 18° 51′ N, 99° 2′ W **114**
Yavarate, *Col.* 0° 38′ N, 69° 13′ W **136**
Yavarí Mirim, river, *Peru* 5° 10′ S, 73° 8′ W **130**
Yavaros, *Mex.* 26° 42′ N, 109° 33′ W **112**
Yavatmal, *India* 20° 23′ N, 78° 7′ E **188**
Yavero, river, *Peru* 12° 25′ S, 72° 51′ W **137**
Yavi, *Arg.* 22° 10′ S, 65° 30′ W **137**
Yavita, *Venez.* 2° 53′ N, 67° 28′ W **136**
Yavlenka, *Kaz.* 54° 17′ N, 68° 22′ E **184**
Yavne, *Israel* 31° 51′ N, 34° 44′ E **194**
Yavoriv, *Ukr.* 49° 56′ N, 23° 22′ E **152**
Yavr, river, *Russ.* 68° 14′ N, 29° 36′ E **152**
Yawatahama, *Japan* 33° 26′ N, 132° 25′ E **201**
Yawnghwe, *Myanmar* 20° 40′ N, 96° 57′ E **202**
Yawri Bay 8° 3′ N, 13° 19′ W **222**
Yaxchilán, ruin(s), *Mex.* 16° 50′ N, 91° 7′ W **115**
Yaya, *Russ.* 56° 11′ N, 86° 22′ E **169**
Yaynangyoung, *Myanmar* 20° 28′ N, 94° 54′ E **202**
Yayuan, *China* 41° 42′ N, 126° 9′ E **200**
Yayva, *Russ.* 59° 19′ N, 57° 21′ E **154**
Yazd, *Iran* 31° 53′ N, 54° 26′ E **180**
Yazdān, *Iran* 33° 34′ N, 60° 53′ E **180**
Yazevets, *Russ.* 65° 44′ N, 46° 27′ E **154**
Yazhma, *Russ.* 66° 57′ N, 44° 43′ E **154**
Yazılıkaya, *Turk.* 39° 11′ N, 30° 42′ E **156**
Yazlıca Dağı, peak, *Turk.* 37° 45′ N, 42° 27′ E **195**
Yazno, *Russ.* 56° 2′ N, 29° 18′ E **166**
Yazoo City, *Miss., U.S.* 32° 50′ N, 90° 26′ W **103**
Yazoo, river, *Miss., U.S.* 32° 33′ N, 90° 50′ W **103**
Yazykovo, *Russ.* 54° 16′ N, 47° 27′ E **154**
Ybakoura, spring, *Chad* 22° 6′ N, 15° 44′ E **216**
Ye, *Myanmar* 15° 15′ N, 97° 50′ E **202**
Yebbi Bou, *Chad* 21° 0′ N, 18° 8′ E **216**
Yebyu, *Myanmar* 14° 16′ N, 98° 8′ E **202**
Yecheng (Kargilik), *China* 37° 52′ N, 77° 31′ E **184**
Yecheon, *S. Korea* 36° 38′ N, 128° 26′ E **200**
Yecla, *Sp.* 38° 36′ N, 1° 7′ W **164**
Yécora, *Mex.* 28° 22′ N, 108° 58′ W **92**
Yédri, spring, *Chad* 22° 11′ N, 17° 25′ E **216**
Yeed, *Somalia* 4° 28′ N, 43° 5′ E **218**
Yefremov, *Russ.* 53° 8′ N, 38° 4′ E **154**
Yeggueba, spring, *Niger* 19° 52′ N, 12° 53′ E **222**
Yegorovskaya, *Russ.* 65° 43′ N, 52° 3′ E **154**
Yegor'yevsk, *Russ.* 55° 22′ N, 39° 1′ E **154**
Yegozero, *Russ.* 62° 44′ N, 36° 38′ E **154**
Yegros, *Parag.* 26° 23′ S, 56° 24′ W **139**
Yeguas, Sierra de, *Sp.* 37° 8′ N, 4° 58′ W **164**
Yei, *Sudan* 4° 3′ N, 30° 40′ E **224**
Yei, river, *Sudan* 5° 11′ N, 30° 17′ E **224**
Yeji, *Ghana* 8° 11′ N, 0° 43′ E **222**
Yekaterinburg, *Russ.* 56° 49′ N, 60° 35′ E **154**
Yekaterinovka, *Russ.* 52° 1′ N, 44° 23′ E **158**
Yekepa, *Liberia* 7° 26′ N, 8° 34′ W **222**
Yekhrimyanvara, *Russ.* 64° 32′ N, 30° 9′ E **152**
Yekī, *Eth.* 7° 10′ N, 35° 17′ E **224**
Yekia Sahal, spring, *Chad* 16° 14′ N, 17° 38′ E **216**
Yelabuga, *Russ.* 55° 46′ N, 52° 6′ E **154**
Yelan', *Russ.* 50° 56′ N, 43° 46′ E **158**
Yelan Kolenovskiy, *Russ.* 51° 8′ N, 41° 14′ E **158**
Yelapa, *Mex.* 20° 28′ N, 105° 29′ W **114**
Yelat'ma, *Russ.* 54° 56′ N, 41° 44′ E **154**
Yelets, *Russ.* 52° 37′ N, 38° 27′ E **158**
Yeletskiy, *Russ.* 67° 3′ N, 64° 0′ E **169**
Yelizarovo, *Russ.* 61° 22′ N, 68° 18′ E **169**
Yelizavety, Mys, *Russ.* 54° 19′ N, 142° 29′ E **160**
Yelkhovka, *Russ.* 53° 50′ N, 50° 16′ E **154**
Yellandu, *India* 17° 34′ N, 80° 18′ E **188**
Yellow Butte, peak, *Oreg., U.S.* 43° 31′ N, 123° 29′ W **90**
Yellow Grass, *Can.* 49° 47′ N, 104° 10′ W **90**
Yellow Sea 36° 17′ N, 121° 47′ E **190**
Yellow see Huang, river, *China* 37° 14′ N, 104° 6′ E **198**
Yellowknife, *Can.* 62° 27′ N, 114° 50′ W **106**
Yellowstone, river, *Mont., U.S.* 47° 11′ N, 104° 31′ W **90**
Yelm, *Wash., U.S.* 46° 55′ N, 122° 37′ W **90**
Yel'nya, *Russ.* 54° 36′ N, 33° 14′ E **154**
Yeloguy, river, *Russ.* 61° 32′ N, 85° 41′ E **169**
Yel'sk, *Belarus* 51° 47′ N, 29° 14′ E **152**
Yelva, river, *Russ.* 63° 26′ N, 50° 49′ E **154**
Yelverton Bay 81° 31′ N, 98° 43′ W **72**
Yelwa, *Nig.* 10° 52′ N, 4° 45′ E **222**
Yemal-Nenets, adm. division, *Russ.* 65° 24′ N, 62° 21′ E **160**
Yemanzhelinsk, *Russ.* 54° 45′ N, 61° 21′ E **154**
Yemaotai, *China* 42° 20′ N, 122° 54′ E **200**
Yemassee, *S.C., U.S.* 32° 41′ N, 80° 51′ W **96**
Yembo, *Eth.* 8° 17′ N, 35° 56′ E **224**
Yemel'yanovka, *Russ.* 63° 54′ N, 30° 56′ E **152**
Yemen 15° 57′ N, 48° 3′ E **182**
Yemetsk, *Russ.* 63° 29′ N, 41° 48′ E **154**
Yemtsa, *Russ.* 63° 4′ N, 40° 22′ E **154**
Yen, *Cameroon* 2° 28′ N, 12° 42′ E **218**
Yen Bai, *Vietnam* 21° 44′ N, 104° 52′ E **202**
Yena, *Russ.* 67° 36′ N, 31° 9′ E **152**
Yenakiyeve, *Ukr.* 48° 12′ N, 38° 12′ E **158**
Yenanma, *Myanmar* 19° 46′ N, 94° 49′ E **202**
Yendéré, *Burkina Faso* 10° 12′ N, 4° 59′ W **222**
Yendi, *Ghana* 9° 24′ N, 4° 237′ W **222**
Yenge, river, *Dem. Rep. of the Congo* 1° 46′ S, 21° 21′ E **218**
Yengisar, *China* 38° 55′ N, 76° 9′ E **184**
Yéni, *Niger* 13° 27′ N, 3° 0′ E **222**
Yeniçağa, *Turk.* 40° 47′ N, 32° 0′ E **156**
Yenice, *Turk.* 39° 18′ N, 32° 41′ E **156**
Yeniceoba, *Turk.* 38° 51′ N, 32° 46′ E **156**
Yenisey, river, *Russ.* 51° 38′ N, 92° 28′ E **190**
Yeniseysk, *Russ.* 58° 21′ N, 92° 10′ E **160**
Yeniseyskiy Zaliv 72° 20′ N, 75° 5′ E **160**
Yenyuka, *Russ.* 57° 53′ N, 121° 44′ E **160**
Yeo, river, *U.K.* 51° 0′ N, 2° 45′ W **162**
Yeoju, *S. Korea* 37° 17′ N, 127° 38′ E **200**
Yeola, *India* 20° 1′ N, 74° 29′ E **188**
Yeoncheon, *S. Korea* 38° 5′ N, 127° 5′ E **200**
Yeongam, *S. Korea* 34° 46′ N, 126° 41′ E **200**
Yeongdeok, *S. Korea* 36° 24′ N, 129° 25′ E **200**
Yeongdong, *S. Korea* 36° 9′ N, 127° 47′ E **200**
Yeonggwang, *S. Korea* 35° 14′ N, 126° 30′ E **200**
Yeongju, *S. Korea* 36° 48′ N, 128° 38′ E **200**
Yeongwol, *S. Korea* 37° 11′ N, 128° 28′ E **200**
Yeoryang, *S. Korea* 37° 22′ N, 129° 15′ E **200**
Yeosu, *S. Korea* 34° 45′ N, 127° 45′ E **200**
Yeovil, *U.K.* 50° 56′ N, 2° 38′ W **162**
Yepes, *Sp.* 39° 54′ N, 3° 38′ W **164**
Yepómera, *Mex.* 29° 2′ N, 107° 51′ W **92**
Yerakhtur, *Russ.* 54° 40′ N, 41° 5′ E **154**
Yerbent, *Turkm.* 39° 16′ N, 58° 35′ E **180**
Yerbogachen, *Russ.* 61° 19′ N, 108° 10′ E **160**

CONSULTANTS

PHYSICAL and POLITICAL MAPS and EDITORIAL CONTENT

United States Government

Central Intelligence Agency
Departments of economic development in each state
Library of Congress, *Geography and Map Division*
National Aeronautics and Space Administration (NASA)
Earth Observatory System (EOS)
Goddard Space Flight Center (GSFC)
Marshall Space Flight Center (MSFC)
National Geospatial-Intelligence Agency (NGA)
Hydrographic and Topographic Center
Naval Research Laboratory
U.S. Board on Geographic Names (BGN)
U.S. Department of Agriculture (USDA)
U.S. Department of Commerce
Bureau of Census
Bureau of Economic Affairs
National Oceanic and Atmospheric Administration (NOAA)
National Marine Fisheries Service (NMFS)
National Environmental Satellite, Data, and Information Service (NESDIS)
National Climatic Data Center (NCDC)
National Geophysical Data Center (NGDC)
National Ocean Service (NOS)
U.S. Department of Defense
Air Force Space and Missile systems Center (SMC)
Defense Meteorological Satellite Program (DMSP)
U.S. Department of Interior
Bureau of Land Management (BLM)
Geological Survey (USGS)
National Biological Survey
EROS Data Center
National Park Service
National Wetlands Research Center
Office of Territories
U.S. Department of State
U.S. Naval Oceanographic Office
U.S. Navy/NOAA Joint Ice Center

Government of Canada

Department of Energy, Mines and Resource
Canadian Permanent Committee on Geographic Names
Government du Québec
Commission de toponymie
Offices of provincial premiers and of commissioners of the territories
Statistics Canada

Other

Embassies and statistical agencies of foreign nations
International Astronomical Union
Working Group for Planetary System Nomenclature
International Telecommunication Union (ITU)
Norwegian Polar Institute
Population Reference Bureau (PRB)
Scripps Institution of Oceanography
State Economic Agencies
United Nations (UN)
Cartography Unit, Map Library, Department of Technical Cooperation, Documentation, Reference and Terminology Section
Department of Economic and Social Affairs, Statistics Division
Environmental Program (UNEP), World Conservation Monitoring Centre (WCMC), Protected Areas Program
Food and Agriculture Organization (FAO)
Global Resources Information Database (GRID)
United Nations High Commission on Refugees (UNHCR)
University of Cambridge, *Scott Polar Research Institute*
Wildlife Conservation Society (WCS), *Human Footprint Project*
World Bank
Map Library, Statistical Office
World Development Indicators
World Health Organization (WHO)
World Resources Institute (WRI), *Global Forest Watch*
World Wildlife Fund (WWF)

WORLD THEMATIC MAPS and EDITORIAL CONTENT

OVERALL CONSULTANTS

HARM J. DE BLIJ, *John A. Hannah Professor of Geography, Michigan State University*
ROGER DOWNS, *Pennsylvania State University*

THEMATIC CONSULTANTS

World From Above
ROBERT STACEY, *WorldSat International Inc.*

Geospatial Concepts
STEVEN STEINBERG, *Humboldt State University*

Tectonics
SETH STEIN, *Northwestern University*

Geomorphology
STEPHEN CUNHA, *Humboldt State University*

Earth's Surface
PETER SLOSS, *NOAA*

JONATHAN T. OVERPECK, *Department of Geosciences, The University of Arizona*

JEREMY L. WEISS, *Department of Geosciences, The University of Arizona*

Climate and Weather
JOHN OLIVER, *Indiana State University*

Biosphere
GENE CARL FELDMAN, *SeaWIFs, NASA/Goddard Space Flight Center*

Water
AARON WOLF, *Oregon State University*

Land Cover
PAUL DAVIS, *University of Maryland, Global Land Cover Facility*

Biodiversity
JOHN KUPTER, *University of South Carolina*

Land Use
NAVIN RAMANKUTTY, *University of Wisconsin, Madison*

Human Population and Population Trends
CARL HAUB, *Population Reference Bureau*

Cultures
BERNARD COMRIE, *Max Planck Institute for Revolutionary Anthropology*
DENNIS COSGROVE, *University of California, Los Angeles*

Health & Literacy
MICHAEL REICH, *Harvard University*

Economy
AMY GLASMEIER, *Pennsylvania State University*

Food
GIL LATZ, *Portland State University*

Trade & Globalization
AMY GLASMEIER, *Pennsylvania State University*

Transportation
JEAN-PAUL RODRIGUE, *Hofstra University*

Communication
GREG DOWNEY, *University of Wisconsin, Madison*

Energy
BARRY D. SOLOMON, *Michigan Technological University*

Defense & Conflict
ALEXANDER MURPHY, *University of Oregon*

Environment
TANIA DEL MAR LÓPEZ MARRERO, *Pennsylvania State University*

Protected Lands
PHILIP DEARDEN, *University of Victoria*
ERIC SANDERSON, *Wildlife Conservation Society*

Geographic Comparisons
DAVID DIVINS, *NOAA/NGDC*
ROBERT FISHER, *Scripps Institute of Oceanography*
CARL HAUB, *Population Reference Bureau*
MARTIN JAKOBSSON, *University of New Hampshire*
CHARLES O'REILLY, *Canadian Hydrographic Service*
RON SALVASON, *Canadian Hydrographic Service*
HANS WERNER SCHENKE, *Alfred Wegener Institute for Polar and Marine Research*

CREDITS and SOURCES

Abbreviations: Advanced Very High Resolution Radiometer (AVHRR); Digital Elevation Model (DEM); Moderate Resolution Imaging Spectroradiometer (MODIS); Shuttle Radar Topography Mission (SRTM).

Cover and Dust Jacket: Globes *Left to Right* (Topography and Bathymetry) Land relief: SRTM30 DEMs with Natural Earth vegetation drape; Ocean relief: ETOPO2 data; Tibor G. Tóth, *Tóth Graphix*; (True-Color Land Surface) *NASA, Blue Marble: Next Generation, Terra, Earth Observatory System (EOS)*, February 2004; (Terrestrial Ecoregions) *WWF*; (Lights at Night) *NASA; DMSP*; Tibor G. Tóth, *Tóth Graphix*; (Average Sea Surface Temperature) MODIS data, *NASA/GSFC*; (True-Color Land and Bathymetry) Land data: *NASA, Blue Marble: Next Generation, Terra, Earth Observatory System (EOS)*, May 2004; Ocean bathymetry data: ETOPO2, *NGDC*; (Human Footprint) Human Footprint Project, *WCS* and *Center for International Earth Science Information Network (CIESIN), Columbia University*; (Biosphere) Gene Carl Feldman, *SeaWIFs, NASA/GSFC; ORBIMAGE*; (Land Cover) AVHRR data, *Global Land Cover Facility, University of Maryland Institute for Advanced Computer Studies*; (Land Cover and Bathymetry) AVHRR and ETOPO2 data processed by Robert Stacey, *WorldSat International Inc.*; (Population Density) Gridded Population of the World (GPWv3), *Center for International Earth Science Information Network (CIESIN), Columbia University; Centro Internacional de Agricultura Tropical (CIAT)*; (Political Boundaries) © *National Geographic Society.*

Title Page: (Map: World) MODIS, ETOPO-2, Lights at Night data; *NOAA/NGDC; DMSP.*

CHAPTER OPENERS

The World, pages 18-19: (Map: World) Human Footprint Project © *Wildlife Conservation Society (WCS) and Center for International Earth Science Information Network (CIESIN)* 2006; Project leads: Eric Sanderson, Kent Redford, *WCS;* Marc Levy, *CIESIN;* Funding: *Center for Environmental Research and Conservation (CERC) at Columbia University, ESRI Conservation Program, Prospect Hill Foundation.*

The Human Footprint Project illustrates the application of geographic information systems (GIS) as a way to combine diverse geographic data to reveal new patterns on the land. The authors of the study from the Wildlife Conservation Society and Columbia University combined nine global data layers to create this "human footprint" map. The layers covered the following themes: human population density, human land use and infrastructure, and human access. They concluded that 83% of the earth's land surface is influenced directly by human beings, whether through human land uses, human access from roads, railways, or major rivers, electrical infrastructure (indicated by lights detected at night), or direct occupancy by human populations at densities above one person per square kilometer. The researchers scored each of the variables on a one to ten scale, summed the numbers, and mapped the results. The lower the score, the lesser the degree of human influence. Antarctica was not mapped in the original study, but human influence there is known to be quite low, so it is shown in a uniform green color.

Continental Images: North America, pages 70-71; South America, pages 120-121; Europe, pages 140-141; Asia, pages 170-171; Africa, pages 204-205; Australia & Oceania, pages 228-229; Polar Regions, pages 244-245: (All Imagery) Landsat, AVHRR, Lights at Night data rendered by Robert Stacey, *WorldSat International Inc.; NOAA/NGDC; DMSP.*

To "paint" the images of continents, polar regions, and oceans which open the chapters, data from multiple passes of numerous satellites, Space Shuttle, and sonar soundings—recorded at varying scales and levels of resolution—were combined digitally to form mosaics. This level of detail, rendered cloud free, captured nighttime lights of populated areas, flares from natural gas burning above oil wells, and lights from fishing fleets. The images were further enhanced and blended to approximate true color. Shaded relief, as if the sun were shining from the northwest, was added for realism, and elevation was exaggerated twenty times to make variations in elevation easily visible. The images were then reproduced as if viewed from space.

Oceans, pages 250-251: (All Globes) Gregory W. Shirah, *NASA/GSFC Scientific Visualization Studio;* David W. Pierce, *Scripps Institution of Oceanography.*

The speed and direction of ocean currents can be computed from small variations in the height of the sea surface just as the speed and direction of the wind is computed from surface air pressure differences. Satellite-derived images depict a ten-year average of the hills and valleys, or shape, of the changing ocean surface. These undulations range over a few meters in height, and flow occurs along the color contours. The vectors (white arrows) show ocean velocity caused exclusively by the effect of wind on the top layer of the ocean (called the Ekman Drift). Estimates of the Ekman Drift are used by ocean researchers to determine the shape of the sea surface and as a component of the overall surface current (which also includes thermal, saline, tidal, and wave-driven components).

WORLD THEMATIC SECTION

World From Above, pages 14-15: (Aerial Photographs: Washington, D.C.) National Capital Planning Commission and District of Columbia, processed by *Photo Science, Gaithersburg, Maryland*; (Radar Imagery, Rio de Janeiro) Radar data by *Canadian Space Agency*, processed by *Radarsat International;* (Imagery: Rio de Janeiro) Landsat/Thermal, Near Infrared, Visible data from *Brazilian Ministry of Science and Technology's National Institute for Space Research*, processed by Stephen W. Stetson, *Systems for World Surveillance*; (Globes) Nimbus satellite data processed by *Laboratory for Oceans and Ice, NASA/GSFC*; (Map: North America) Landsat, AVHRR, and Lights at Night data rendered by Robert Stacey, *WorldSat International Inc.; NOAA/NGDC; DMSP*; (Imagery: Beaufort Sea) Landsat, SPOT, and RADARSAT data processed by *Canada Centre for Remote Sensing;* (Imagery: North Carolina Flooding in 1999) RADARSAT ScanSAR data processed by *Canada Centre for Remote Sensing;* (Imagery: Southern California Wildfire) Landsat-5 data courtesy of *USGS*; (Imagery: Ancient Footpaths, Arenal, Costa Rica) *NASA/MSFC.*

Geospatial Concepts, pages 16-17: (Map series: California) © *National Geographic Society;* (GIS Application: Urban Planning) *Community Cartography*; (GIS Application Sample: TransCAD Transportation Planning) *Caliper Corporation*; (GIS Application: Emergency Management) CalMAST and the San Bernadino County Sheriff used *ESRI's* ArcGIS technology to visualize a 3-D flyover of the Old and Grand Prix Fire perimeters (data provided courtesy of CalMAST and *USGS*); (GIS Application: Demographic/Census) Courtesy of *CBS News* and *ESRI*; (GIS Application: Health) Copyright © 2001-2005 *ESRI.* All rights reserved. Used by permission; (GIS Application: Conservation) *National Zoological Park, Smithsonian Institution.*

Tectonics, pages 24-25: (Map series: Paleogeography) Christopher R. Scotese, *PALEOMAP project*; (Map: Earth Tectonics) Seth Stein, *Northwestern University; USGS Earthquake Hazard Program; Global Volcanism Program, Smithsonian Institution;* (Artwork: *"Tectonic Block Diagrams"*) Susan Sanford.

Geomorphology, pages 26-27: (Artwork: *"Eolian Landforms"*) Chris Orr; (Map: World Landforms) © *National Geographic Society*; (Photo: Crater Lake, Oregon) James Balog; (Photo: Misti Volcano, Peru) Stefano Scata, *Getty Images;* (Photo: Mount Fuji, Japan) George Mobley; (Photo: Isle of Skye, Scotland) Wilfried Krecicwost, *Getty Images;* (Photo: Southern China) James Blair; (Photo: Namibia) *Natphotos/Getty Images;* (Photo: Blyde River Canyon, South Africa) *Natphotos/Getty Images*; (Photo: Victoria, Australia) Rob Brander; (Photo:, Kejimkujik Lake, Nova Scotia) Douglas Grant, *Parks Canada*; (Photo: Mississippi River Delta, Louisiana) *SPOT Image/Photo Researchers; (CNES)*; (Photo: Meteor Crater, Arizona) Adriel Heisey; (Artwork: *"Fluvial Landforms" and "Glacial Landforms"*) Steven Fick; (Maps: Eolian Landforms, Watersheds, Ice Age) © *National Geographic Society.*

Earth's Surface, pages 28-29: (Map series: Sea level changes) © *National Geographic Society*; Jonathan T. Overpeck, Jeremy L. Weiss, *Department of Geosciences, The University of Arizona*; (Map: Surface Elevation and Cross-section) ETOPO2 data rendered by Peter W. Sloss, Ph.D., *NOAA, NGDC.*

Climate, pages 30-31: (Artwork: *"Hadley Cells"*) Don Foley; (Artwork: *"The Seasons"*) Shusei Nagaoka; (Map: Modified Köppen Classification) © H. J. de Blij, P. O. Muller, and *John Wiley & Sons, Inc.*; (Map series: Seasonal Temperature) Barbara Summey, *NASA/GSFC Visualization Analysis Laboratory;* (Map: Mean Annual Precipitation) Data from *NOAA/NESDIS/NCDC/Satellite Data Services Division (SDSD)* compiled by *UNEP-GRID.*

Weather, pages 32-33: (Maps: Air pressure and Winds) *NOAA/Cooperative Institute for Research in Environmental Sciences (CIRES) Climate Diagnostic Center; National Centers for Environmental Prediction (NCEP)/National Center for Atmospheric Research (NCAR)* Reanalysis Project Data; (Map: Oceans and Cyclones) *NASA; NOAA;* (Globes: El Niño/La Niña) TOPEX/Poseidon satellite data from *NASA, Jet Propulsion Laboratory (JPL), California Institute of Technology;* (Artwork: *"Cyclonic Activity"*) Don Foley; (Artwork: *"How Weather Happens"*) Robert Hynes.

Biosphere, pages 34-35: (Map: Biosphere) Gene Carl Feldman, *SeaWIFs, NASA/Goddard Space Flight Center;* (Map: Ocean Circulation) Don Foley; (Artwork: *"Our Layered Ocean"*) Don Foley; (Artwork: *"Water and Carbon Cycle"*) Edward S. Gazsi.

Water, pages 36-37: (Graph: Water by Volume) Peter Gleick, *The Pacific Institute*; (Map: Primary Watersheds) *World Resources Institute*; Peter Gleick, *The Pacific Institute*; (Artwork: *"Hydrologic Cycle"*) Don Foley; (Map: Access to Fresh Water) *World Health Organization*; (Graph: Water Withdrawals) *AQUASTAT-FAO.*

Land Cover, pages 38-39: (Graph and Map: Global Land Cover) Paul Davis, *The Global Land Cover Facility, University of Maryland Institute for Advanced Computer Studies*, *see description below; (Photo: Evergreen Needleleaf Forest) Tom and Pat Leeson, *Photo Researchers*; (Photo: Evergreen Broadleaf Forest) Michael Nichols, *National Geographic Society Image Collection*; (Photo: Deciduous Needleleaf Forest) Stephen Krasemann, *PhotoResearchers*; (Photo: Deciduous Broadleaf Forest) Rod Planck, *Photo Researchers*; (Photo: Mixed Forest) Jim Steinberg, *Photo Researchers*; (Photo: Woodland) Matthew Hansen; (Photo: Wooded Grassland) Gregory Dimijian, *Photo Researchers*; (Photo: Closed Shrubland) Sharon G. Johnson; (Photo: Open Shrubland) Georg Gerster, *Photo Researchers*; (Photo: Grassland) Rod Planck, *Photo Researchers;* (Photo: Cropland) Jim Richardson; (Photo: Barren/Desert) George Steinmetz; (Photo: Built-up) Steve McCurry; (Photo: Barren/Polar Ice) B.&C. Alexander, *Photo Researchers.*

**This land cover classification was created using imagery from the NOAA AVHRR satellites and the NASA Landsat satellites. Using remote sensing, the imagery measures radiation occurring on the planet surface. Data from these measurements are grouped by scientists into classes representing particular land cover types. For example a type of forest will have values in a discrete range, and grasslands will have different values in a different range. Interpretation of values from single images can be very subjective, so scientists analyzed values from a series of global images collected over several years, resulting in an objective classification. It is important to note that this land cover classification explains what the Earth's land cover was when the imagery was collected. Land cover change occurs from natural and human causes.*

Biodiversity, pages 40-41: (Maps: Terrestrial and Aquatic Ecoregions) *Conservation Science Program, World Wildlife Fund—U.S.*; (Graph: Threatened Mammals and Birds) *IUCN Red List*; (Map: Biodiversity Hotspots and Status of Biodiversity) *Conservation International*; (Photo: The Bering Sea) Stephen Krasemann, *Getty Images*; (Photo: Southeastern United States Rivers and Streams) *Kevin Schafer Photography*; (Photo: The Amazon River and Flooded Forests) Flip Nicklin, *Minden Pictures*; (Photo: Rift Valley Lakes) John Ginstina, *Getty Images;* (Photo: Eastern Himalayan Broadleaf and Conifer Forests) ZSSD, *Minden Pictures;* (Photo: Sulu-Sulawesi Seas) Fred Bavendam, *Minden Pictures.*

Land Use, pages 42-43: (Map: Land Use) Jonathan Foley, Navin Ramankutty, Billie Leff, *Center for Sustainability and the Global Environment, University of Wisconsin, Madison;* (Imagery *Left to Right*) Bolivia Deforestation; Black Hills, South Dakota Fire Damage; Saudi Arabia Agricultural Development; Aral Sea Shoreline Changes) Landsat-5 satellite data courtesy of *USGS.*

Human Population, pages 44-45: (Photo: Philippines) Karen Kasmauski, *National Geographic Society Image Collection*; (Map: Population Density) *LandScan, Oak Ridge National Laboratory, Department of Energy;* (Cartogram: World Population) *CIA, The World Factbook; PRB;* (Graph: Regional Population Growth) © *National Geographic Society*; (Graphs: Population Pyramids), International Data Base (IDB), *U.S. Census Bureau.*

Population Trends, pages 46-47: (Maps: Fertility, Infant Mortality, Life Expectancy) *PRB*; (Maps and Charts: Migrant Population, Urban Population Growth, Most Populated Places) *United Nations Department of Economic & Social Affairs: Population Division.* Used by permission.

Cultures, pages 48-49: (Maps and Graphs: World Language, World Religion, Indigenous Languages) © *National Geographic Society;* (Graph: Regional Religion Adherence) *Encyclopedia Britannica*; (Graph: Religious Adherence) © *Adherents.com*; (Imagery *left to right*: Jerusalem, Israel; Mecca, Saudi Arabia; Allahabad, India) IKONOS satellite data courtesy of *Space Imaging.*

Health & Literacy, pages 50-51: (Maps and Graph: Causes of Death, Cardiovascular Deaths, Physicians) *WHO*; (Map: HIV/AIDS) *The Joint United Nations Programme on HIV/AIDS;* (Map: Malaria endemicity*) Robert Snow, *Malaria Atlas Project; Funded by the Wellcome Trust UK;* (Maps: Calorie Supply and Undernourished) *SOFI, UN; WHO*; *The Joint United Nations Programme on HIV/AIDS;* (Map and Graph: Literacy Rate) *CIA, The World Factbook.*

**Endemicity defines the intensity of Plasmodium falciparum transmission and is measured by the percentage of children infected with the parasite at any moment in time.*

Economy, pages 52-53: (Cartogram, Map, Graphs: GDP, GNI, Industry Sector) *CIA, The World Factbook, World Bank*; (Map: Labor Migration, GDP) *World Bank, Institute for the Study of International Migration, Georgetown University.*

Food, pages 54-55: (Maps: Cereals, Roots and Tubers, Sugar-bearing Crops, Pulses, Oil-bearing Crops) Jonathan Foley, Navin Ramankutty, Billie Leff, *Center for Sustainability and the Global Environment, Nelson Institute for Environmental Studies, University of Wisconsin-Madison; FAO;* (Map: Livestock) *Global Livestock Production Health Atlas (GLiPHA), FAO*; (Photo: Corn) Richard Olsenius, *National Geographic Society Image Collection*; (Photo: Wheat) Jim Richardson; (Photo: Rice) Steven L. Raymer, *National Geographic Society Image Collection*; (Graph: World Diets and Chart of World Crop Production by Region) FAOSTAT-FAO; (Map: Fisheries and Aquaculture) Reg Watson and Daniel Pauly, *Fisheries Centre, University of British Columbia; SOFIA, FAO;* (Map: Biotech Cropland) Clive James, Ph.D., *International Service for the Acquisition of Agri-Biotech Applications (ISAAA).*

Trade & Globalization, pages 56-57: (Maps and Graphs: Regional Trade Blocs, World Debt, Imports, Exports) *CIA, The World Factbook;* (Map: Trade Flow) *World Bank, CIA, The World Factbook; World Trade Organization; USGS Minerals Yearbook; United Nations Conference on Trade and Development; FAO;* (Graph: Trade) *World Trade Organization.*

Transportation, pages 58-59: (Map: Airline Passenger Volume) *International Civil Aviation Organization*; (Map: Transportation Routes) © *National Geographic Society; American Association of Port Authorities; Bureau of Transportation Statistics, U.S. Department of Transportation;* (Chart: World's Largest Airports) *Airports Council International;* (Chart: World's Largest Ports) *American Association of Port Authorities.*

Communication, pages 60-61: (Map: Satellite Capacity) *Telegeography Research Group, PriMetrica, Inc*. 2004; (Map of the Internet) Hal Burch and Bill Cheswick, *Lumeta Corporation* Patent(s) Pending & Copyright © *Lumeta Corporation* 2006. All Rights Reserved; (Map: Internet Explosion) Reproduced with the kind permission of *ITU;* (Map: Computer Virus/Code Red Worm) David Moore, *Cooperative Association for Internet Data Analysis (CAIDA)*, Copyright © 2001 *The Regents of the University of California*; (Map: Connecting the Planet) Reproduced with the kind permission of *ITU; Telegeography Research Group, PriMetrica, Inc*. 2004, *www.primetrica.com;* Buckminster Fuller Projection courtesy of the *Buckminster Fuller Institute.*

Energy, pages 62-63: (Photo: Hydropower) Jim Richardson; (Photo: Nuclear) Mark Burnett, *Photo Researchers*; (Photo: Solar) Courtesy *National Renewable Energy Lab*; (Photo: Wind) John Mead, *Science Photo Library/Photo Researchers*; (Photo: Geothermal) *Science Photo Library/Photo Researchers;* (Map: Annual Energy consumption) Energy Infrastructure data courtesy of the *Petroleum Economist Ltd, London; BP Statistical Review of World Energy; Energy Information Administration, U.S. Department of Energy; USGS Mineral Resources Program; International Iron and Steel Institute; FAO*; (Map: Geothermal and Photovoltaic/Solar Electric Power Plants) *The Geothermal Energy Association*; Barry Soloman, *Michigan Technological University; Sandia National Laboratories; Windpower Monthly News Magazine*; © Denis Lenardic, *pvresources.com-photovoltaic technologies and applications*; (Map, Chart: Flow of Oil) *BP Statistical Review of World Energy.*

Defense & Conflict, pages 64-65: (Photo: Srebrenica Refugees) Chris Rainier, *Corbis;* (Map: Regime Type and Active Military) Monty G. Marshall, *Center for Systemic Peace; International Institute of Strategic Studies*; (Graph: Refugees and Uprooted People by Country) *United Nations High Commission on Refugees*; (Map: Defense Spending and Military Services) *CIA, The World Factbook; International Institute of Strategic Studies*; (Maps: Biological, Nuclear, and Chemical Weapons) © *National Geographic Society; Center for Nonproliferation Studies, Monterey Institute of International Studies; Carnegie Endowment for International Peace; Henry Stimson Center; U.S. Department of Energy;* Ken Alibeck.

Environment, pages 66-67: (Graph: Atmospheric Carbon Dioxide) Gene Carl Feldman, *SeaWIFs, NASA/GSFC*; (Map: Habitat Loss) Lara Hansen, Adam Markham, *WWF*; Jay Malcom, University of Toronto; (Photo: Logging) *Photodisc/Getty Images;* (Map: Vanishing Forests) *Global Forest Watch, WRI*; (Photo: Coral) Bruce Fouke and Michael Fortwengler; (Map: Threatened Oceans) *NOAA/NMFS; UNEP-WCMC*; (Photo: Desertification) Bruce Dale, *National Geographic Society Image Collection;* (Map: Risk of Desertification) *USDA Global Desertification Vulnerability Map;* (Map: Polar Ice Cap) *National/Naval Ice Center*; © *National Geographic Society*; (Map: Environmental Stress Factors) © *National Geographic Society*, (Globes: Atmospheric Ozone) *NASA.*

Protected Lands, pages 68-69: (Graph: Protected Areas Worldwide) © *National Geographic Society; UNEP-WCMC*; (Map: Wildest Biomes) © *Wildlife Conservation Society (WCS) and Center for International Earth Science Information Network (CIESIN)*; (Photo: Hawai'i Volcanoes N.P., U.S.) Bryan Lowry, *Seapics.com*; (Photo: Galápagos, N.P., Ecuador) Cristina G. Mittermeier; (Photo: Arches N.P., Western U.S.) Art Wolfe; (Photo: Madidi N.P., Bolivia) Joel Sartore; (Photo: Amazon Basin, Brazil) Michael Nichols; (Photo: Arctic Regions) Flip Nicklin; (Photo: Sareks N.P., Sweden) Jan-Peter Lahall; (Photo: African Reserves) Beverly Joubert, *National Geographic Television and Film*; (Photo: Wolong Nature Reserve, China) Daniel J. Cox, *Natural Exposures*; (Photo: Kamchatka Peninsula, Russia) Sarah Leen; (Photo: Gunung Palung N.P., Indonesia) Tim Laman; (Photo: Australia and New Zealand) Art Wolfe; (Map: Protected Areas Worldwide) *WDPA Consortium,* World Database on Protected Areas. Copyright © *World Conservation Union (IUCN); UNEP-WCMC.*

CONTINENTAL THEMATIC

Natural World: North America, pages 74-75; United States, pages 84-85; South America, pages 124-125; Europe, pages 144-145; Asia, pages 174-175; Africa, pages 208-209; Australia & Oceania, pages 232-233: (Map: Land Cover) Paul Davis, *The Global Land Cover Facility, University of Maryland Institute for Advanced Computer Studies*; (Map: Climate Modified Köppen) © H. J. de Blij, P. O. Muller, and *John Wiley & Sons, Inc.*; (Map: Natural Hazards) © *National Geographic Society; USGS Earthquake Hazard Program; Global Volcanism Program, Smithsonian Institution;* Lights at Night data, *DMSP*; (Map: Watershed Basins) Aaron Wolf, *Oregon State University; (*Climagraphs*) National Climatic Data Center, NOAA;* (Map: U.S. Federal Lands*) National Park Service, Bureau of Land Management; USDA Forest Service; U.S. Fish and Wildlife Service; Bureau of Indian Affairs; Department of Defense; Department of Energy; NOAA.*

Human World: North America, pages 76-77; United States, pages 86-87; South America, pages 126-127; Europe, pages 146-147; Asia, pages 176-177; Africa, pages 210-211; Australia & Oceania, pages 234-235: (Map: Population Density) *LandScan, Oak Ridge National Laboratory, Department of Energy;* (Map: Percent Population Change 2000-2030) *PRB;* (Map: Percent Urban Population) *United Nations Department of Economic & Social Affairs: Population Division.* Used by permission; (Map: Language) © *National Geographic Society;* (Age/Sex Pyramids) International Data Base (IDB), *U.S. Census Bureau*; (Map: Percent Change in U.S. Population 2000-2005; U.S. Population Density by County; Ancestry by County) *U. S. Census Bureau*; (Map: Reported Church Membership in the U.S. by County) Data for Major Religious Families by Counties of the United States, 2000 from "Religious Congregations and Membership in the United States 2000," Dale E. Jones, et. al. Nashville, TN: *Glenmary Research Center*. © 2002 *Association of Statisticians of American Religious Bodies.* All rights reserved.

Economic World: North America, pages 78-79; United States, pages 88-89; South America, pages 128-129; Europe, pages 148-149; Asia, pages 178-179; Africa, pages 212-213; Australia & Oceania, pages 236-237: (Map: Land Use) Jonathan Foley, Navin Ramankutty, Billie Leff, *Center for Sustainability and the Global Environment, University of Wisconsin, Madison*; (Map: Per Capita Energy Consumption) *PRB;* (Maps: GDP Per Sector) *CIA, The World Factbook* (Map: People Living on Less than $2 per day) *World Bank, World Development Indicators*; (Graph: Imports/Exports) *The Europa World Year Book;* (Map: U.S. Manufacturing by County, Agricultural Land by County, Service Employment by County, Income by County, Employment by Region) *U.S. Census Bureau.*

Demographic and Socioeconomic Information, pages 258-269: (Capital, Language, Religion, Area sq. km/sq. mi) © *National Geographic Society;* (Population Mid-2005, Projected Pop. Change 2005-2050, Pop. Density, Urban Pop., Natural Increase, Total Fertility/Infant Mortality Rate, Percent of Pop. Age <15/ >65, Life Expectancy, HIV/AIDS Pop. Age 15-49) *PRB*; (GDP Mid-2005) *CIA, The World Factbook*; (Services/Industry/Agriculture as % of GDP Sector, Total Estimated Value of Imports/Exports, Percent of Pop. with Access to Electricity, Telephone Mainlines) *World Bank, World Development Indicators;* (Arable and Permanent Cropland Area, Forested Area as % of Land Area) *FAO;* (Protected Areas as % of Land Area) *UNEP-WCMC;* (Average Annual Deforestation, Carbon Dioxide Emissions) *World Bank, World Development Indicators.*

Geographic Information: Comparisons & Conversions, pages 270-271: (Statistical Information) *PRB; National Park Service; Grand Canyon Information*; Helen Brachmanski, *Great Barrier Reef Marine Park Authority; Atlas of Canada; International Hydrographic Organization*; Ronald Mair, *New Zealand Statistical Office; The Columbia Gazetteer of the World; Encyclopedia Britannica; The World Almanac and Book of Facts; Geodata: The World Geographical Encyclopedia;* (Urban Population) *United Nations Department of Economic & Social Affairs: Population Division.* Used by permission.

ADDITIONAL SOURCES

BP Statistical Review of World Energy. London: BP p.l.c., 2005. Available online at www.bp.com.

Busby, Rebecca L., ed. *International Petroleum Encyclopedia.* Tulsa, Oklahoma: Penwell Corporation, 2005.

Central Intelligence Agency. *The World Factbook.* Washington, D.C.: GPO, 2006. Available online at www.cia.gov/cia/publications/factbook/index.html.

Cohen, Saul. *The Columbia Gazetteer of the World.* New York: Columbia University Press, 1998.

Comrie, Bernard. *The World's Major Languages.* London: Croom Helm, 1997.

Crystal, David. *The Cambridge Encyclopedia of Language.* New York: Cambridge University Press, 1977.

de Blij, H. J. and Peter O. Muller. *Geography: Realms, Regions, and Concepts,* 12th ed. New York: John Wiley & Sons, Inc., 2006.

de Blij, H. J., Peter O. Muller, and Richard S. Williams, Jr. *Physical Geography: The Global Environment.* 3rd ref. ed. New York: Oxford University Press, 2004.

Encyclopedia Britannica. Chicago, Illinois: Encyclopedia Britannica, Inc., 2006. Available online at www.britannica.com.

Energy Information Administration. *International Energy Annual (IEA).* Washington, D.C.: Department of Energy, 2003. Available online at www.eia.doe.gov/iea.

FAO. *Review of Water Resources by Country.* Rome: FAO, 2003. Available online at www.fao.org/ag/agl/aglw/aquastat/water_res.

" " *Statistical Yearbook: 2004.* Rome: FAO, 2005. Available online at www.fao.org/WAICENT/FAOINFO/ ECONOMIC/ESS/yearbook. Data from FAOSTAT available online at faostat.fao.org.

" " *The State of Food Insecurity in the World (SOFI): Eradicating World Hunger-Key to achieving the Millennium Development Goals.* Rome: FAO, 2004. Available online at www.fao.org/SOF/sofi.

" " *The State of World Fisheries and Aquaculture (SOFIA).* Rome: FAO, 2004. Available online at www.fao.org/sof/sofia/index_en.htm.

" " *The State of the World's Forests, 2005.* Rome: FAO, 2005. Available online at www.fao.org/forestry/fo/sofo/sofo-e.st.

Foley, J. A., R. DeFries, G. P. Asner, C. Barford, G. Bonan, S. R. Carpenter, F. S. Chapin, M. T. Coe, G. C. Daily, H. K. Gibbs, J. H. Helkowski, T. Holloway, E. A. Howard, C. J. Kucharik, C. Monfreda, J. A. Patz, I. C. Prentice, N. Ramankutty, and P. K. Snyder. "Global Consequences of Land Use," *Science* (22 July 2005), 570-574.

Gleick, Peter. *The World's Water, 2006-2007: The Biennial Report on Freshwater Resources.* Washington, D.C.: Island Press, 2006.

Goddard, Ives, Vol. ed. *Handbook of North American Indians.* Vol. 17, *Languages.* Washington, D.C.: Smithsonian Institution, 1996.

Hansen, M., R. DeFries, J. R. G. Townshend and R. Sohlberg. *1-Km Land Cover Classification Derived from AVHRR.* College Park, Maryland: The Global Land Cover Facility, 1998. Description available online at glcf.umiacs.umd.edu.

James, Clive. "Global Status of Commercialized Biotech/GM Crops: 2005," *ISAAA Briefs, no. 34* (2005). Available online at www.isaaa.org.

Jones, Dale E., Sherri Doty, Clifford Grammich, James E. Horsch, Richard Houseal, Mac Lynn, John P. Marcum, Kenneth M. Sanchagrin, and Richard H. Taylor. *Religious Congregations and Membership in the United States 2000: An Enumeration by Region, State and County Based on Data Reported by 149 Religious Bodies.* Nashville, TN: Glenmary Research Center, 2002.

Langton, Christopher, ed. *The Military Balance, 2005-06.* Washington, D.C.: International Institute for Strategic Studies, 2005.

Leff, B., N. Ramankutty, and J. A. Foley. "Geographic distribution of major crops across the world," *Global Biogeochemical Cycles* (16 January 2004), GB1009. Available online at www.agu.org/pubs/back/gb/2004/index.php?month=January.

Mackay, J, and G. Mensah, eds. *Atlas of Heart Disease and Stroke.* Geneva, Switzerland: World Health Organization, 2004. Available online at www.who.int/cardiovascular_diseases/resources/atlas/en.

Maher, Joanne and Philip McIntyre, eds. *The Europa World Year Book.* London: Europa Publications, 2004.

McCoy, John, ed. *Geo-Data: The World Geographical Encyclopedia.* Farmington Hills, MI: Thomson Gale, 2003.

Morrell, Virginia. "California's Wild Crusade," *National Geographic* (February 2006), 2-35.

Moseley, Christopher and R. E. Asher, eds. *Atlas of the World's Languages.* London: Routledge, 1994.

National Geographic. "Humans and Habitats: Cultural Extinctions Loom," *National Geographic* (September 2001), *EarthPulse* feature.

National Geographic Maps. "Challenges for Humanity: A Thirsty Planet." Supplement map, *National Geographic* (September 2002).

" " "Danger Zones: Earthquake Risk-A Global View." Supplement map, *National Geographic* (April 2006).

" " "Earth At Night." Supplement map, *National Geographic* (November 2004).

" " "Millennium in Maps: Biodiversity." Supplement map, *National Geographic* (February 1999).

" " "Millennium in Maps: Cultures." Supplement map, *National Geographic* (June 1999).

" " "State of the Planet: A World Transformed." Supplement map, *National Geographic* (September 2002).

Olson, D. M. and E. Dinerstein.1998. "The Global 200: A representation approach to conserving the earth's most biologically valuable ecoregions," *Conservation Biology* (1998), 502-515.

Olson, D. M., E. Dinerstein, E. D. Wikramanayake, N. D. Burgess, G. V. N. Powell, E. C. Underwood, J. A. D'Amico, I. Itoua, H. E. Strand, J. C. Morrison, C. J. Loucks, T. F. Allnutt, T. H. Ricketts, Y. Kura, J. F. Lamoreux, W. W. Wettengel, P. Hedao, and K. R. Kassem. "Terrestrial Ecoregions of the World: A New Map of Life on Earth," *BioScience* (2001), 933-938.

Overpeck J. T., B. L. Otto-Bliesner, G. H. Miller, D. R. Muhs, R. B. Alley, and J. T. Kiehl. "Paleoclimatic evidence for future ice-sheet instability and rapid sea-level rise," *Science* (24 March 2006), 1747-50.

Population Reference Bureau. *2005 World Population Data Sheet.* Washington, D.C.: PRB, 2006. Available online at www.prb.org.

Ramankutty, N. and J. A. Foley. "Characterizing patterns of global land use: An analysis of global croplands data," *Global Biogeochemical Cycles* (1998), 667-685.

Sarmiento, Jorge L. and Nicolas Gruber. "Sinks for Anthropogenic Carbon," *Physics Today* (August 2002), 30-36.

Scotese, C.R. *Atlas of Earth History, Volume 1, Paleogeography.* Arlington, Texas: PALEOMAP Project, 2001.

Simons, Lewis M. "Weapons of Mass Destruction," *National Geographic* (February 2006), 2-35.

Snow, R. W., C. A. Guerra, A. M. Noor, H. Y. Myint, and S. I. Hay. "The global distribution of clinical episodes of *Plasmodium falciparum* malaria," *Nature* (March 10, 2005), 214-217.

The World Almanac and Book of Facts. New York: World Almanac Education Group, 2006.

UNEP. *One Planet Many People: Atlas of Our Changing Environment.* UNEP/DEWAL/GRID, 2005. Available online at grid2.cr.usgs.gov/OnePlanetManyPeople/index.php.

UNEP. *World Atlas of Desertification.* London: Edward Arnold, 1992.

United Nations, Department of Economic and Social Affairs, Population Division. *International Migration, 2002.* New York, NY: October 2002. Available online at www.un.org/esa/population/publications.

United Nations, Department of Economic and Social Affairs, Population Division. *World Population Prospects: The 2004 Revision.* New York, NY: United Nations, 2005. Available online at esa.un.org/unpp.

United Nations. *World Urbanization Prospects: The 2003 Revision.* New York, NY: United Nations, 2004. Available online at www.un.org/esa/population/unpop.htm.

United States Geological Survey. *Minerals Yearbook, Vol. III, International.* Washington, D.C.: U.S. Department of the Interior, 2003. Available online at minerals.usgs.gov.minerals/pubs.

Watson, R, J. Alder, A. Kitchingman, and D. Pauly. "Catching some needed attention," *Marine Policy* (2005) 281-284.

Watson, R., A. Kitchingman, A. Gelchu, and D. Pauly. "Mapping fisheries: sharpening our focus," *Fish and Fisheries* (2004), 168-

WDPA Consortium. *World Database on Protected Areas.* Cambridge, U.K.: World Conservation Union (IUCN) and UNEP-World Conservation Monitoring Centre (UNEP-WCMC), 2004. Available online at www.wcmc.org.uk/data/database.un_combo.html.

Wilford, John Noble. "Revolutions in Mapping," *National Geographic* (February 1998), 6-39.

World Bank. *World Development Indicators.* Washington, D.C.: The World Bank Group, 2005. Available online at www.worldbank.org/data.

World Health Organization (WHO), UNICEF, and Roll Back Malaria (RBM). *World Malaria Report, 2005.* WHO: Geneva, Switzerland, 2005. Available online at www.rbm.who.int/wmr2005.

World Trade Organization. *International Trade Statistics.* Geneva, Switzerland: World Trade Organization, 2005. Available online at www.wto.org.

ONLINE SOURCES

Central Intelligence Agency
www.cia.gov

Conservation International
www.conservation.org

Energy Information Agency
www.eia.doe.gov

Food and Agriculture Organization of the UN (FAO)
www.fao.org

International Telecommunication Union (ITU)
www.itu.int

National Aeronautics and Space Administration
www.nasa.gov

National Atmospheric and Oceanic Administration
www.noaa.gov

National Climatic Data Center
www.ncdc.noaa.gov

National Park Service
www.nps.gov

Ozone hole
www.gsfc.nasa.gov

Pacific Institute-The World's Water
www.worldwater.org

Population Reference Bureau
www.prb.org

United Nations
www.un.org

UNEP Global Resources Information Database (GRID)
www.grid.unep.ch/data/index

UNEP-World Conservation Monitoring Centre
www.unep-wcmc.org

UNESCO
www.unesco.org

U.S. Geological Survey
www.usgs.gov

World Bank
www.worldbank.org

World Conservation Union
www.iucn.org

World Health Organization
www.who.int

World Resources Institute
www.wri.org

World Wildlife Fund
www.worldwildlife.org

Library of Congress Cataloging in Publication data is available upon request.
Regular
ISBN-10: 0-7922-3662-9
ISBN-13: 978-0-7922-3662-7
Deluxe
ISBN-10: 0-7922-7976-X
ISBN-13: 978-0-7922-7976-1

NATIONAL GEOGRAPHIC
COLLEGIATE
ATLAS OF THE WORLD

NATIONAL GEOGRAPHIC SOCIETY

John M. Fahey, Jr.	*President and Chief Executive Officer*
Gilbert M. Grosvenor	*Chairman of the Board*
Nina D. Hoffman	*Executive Vice President, and President, Book Publishing Group*

Prepared by NATIONAL GEOGRAPHIC MAPS

Frances A. Marshall	*President, National Geographic Maps*
Allen Carroll	*Chief Cartographer*
Daniel J. Ortiz	*Vice President, Consumer Products*
Kevin P. Allen	*Director of Map Services*
Kris Viesselman	*Director of Design*

Published by NATIONAL GEOGRAPHIC BOOK DIVISION

Kevin Mulroy	*Senior Vice President and Publisher*

NATIONAL GEOGRAPHIC MAPS ATLAS STAFF

Richard W. Bullington	*Project Manager, NGMaps Atlas Development*
Michael J. Horner	*Supervisor, NGMaps Database Editorial*
Juan José Valdés	*Project Manager, Editorial*
Billie Leff	*Project Manager, GIS*
Sally Suominen-Summerall	*Art Director*
Dierdre Bevington-Attardi	*Project Manager, Research*
Kaitlin M. Yarnall	*Supervisor of Map Research*
Glenn C. Caillouet	*Supervisor of Map Production*
Maureen J. Flynn, Eric A. Lindstrom, David Byers Miller, Jr.	*Map Editors*
Kristine L. French, Katherine R. Krezel, Linda R. Kriete	*Research Cartographers*
Jess D. Elder, Michael E. Jones, Windy A. Robertson, Andrew L. Wunderlich	*GIS Analysts*
Geoffrey W. Hatchard, Dianne C. Hunt, Micki Anne Laws, Stephen P. Wells	*Production Cartographers*
Robert E. Pratt	*Designer*
Debbie J. Gibbons	*Project Manager, Large Format Mapping*
Eric A. Lindstrom	*Map Librarian*
Denise Shaffer	*Executive Assistant*
William C. Gordon, Raya Guruswamy, Jennifer A. Hogue	*Interns*

ADDITIONAL STAFF

TEXT

Cynthia Barry	*Text Editor*
Cynthia Barry, David Jeffery, David Byers Miller, Jr., Priit J. Vesilind, Amy Jo Woodruff	*Contributing Writers*

COVER DESIGN

Carl Mehler	*Director of Maps*
Marianne R. Koszorus	*Design Director*

PRODUCTION SERVICES

Christopher A. Liedel	*Executive Vice President and Chief Financial Officer*
Phillip L. Schlosser	*Vice President, Manufacturing and Quality Management*
Edward J. Holland	*Manager of Print Quality Control*
Gary Colbert	*Production Director*

Printed and bound by RR Donnelley & Sons Company
Willard, Ohio

Printed in the U.S.A.